Philosophic Classics, Sixth Edition

From Plato to Derrida

Forrest E. Baird, Editor
Whitworth University

LONDON AND NEW YORK

First published 2011, 2008, 2003 by Pearson Education, Inc.

Published 2016 by Routledge
2 Park Square, Milton Park, Abingdon, Oxon OX14 4RN
711 Third Avenue, New York, NY 10017, USA

Routledge is an imprint of the Taylor & Francis Group, an informa business

Cover Designer: Bruce Kenselaar

ISBN-13: 9780205783861 (pbk)

Library of Congress Cataloging-in-Publication Data

From Plato to Derrida/Forrest E. Baird, editor.—6th ed.
p. cm.
Rev. ed. of: Philosophic classics. c2008.
Includes bibliographical references.
ISBN-13: 978-0-205-78386-1 (alk. paper)
1. Philosophy. I. Baird, Forrest E. II. Philosophic classics.
B72.P45 2010
100—dc22

2009048537

Contents

Preface

There is no better introduction to philosophy than to read some of the great philosophers. But few books are more difficult to read than Aristotle's *Metaphysics* or Spinoza's *Ethics*. Even works that are less puzzling are sometimes like snippets of a conversation that you overhear on entering a room: What is said is clear, only you cannot be sure you have got the point because you do not know just what has gone before. A slight point may be crucial to refute some earlier suggestion, and a seemingly pointless remark may contain a barbed allusion. As a result of this difficulty, some students of philosophy cry out for a simple summary of the "central doctrines" of the great philosophers. Yet carving up great books to excerpt essential doctrines is one of the greatest sins against the spirit of philosophy. If the reading of a whole Platonic dialogue leaves one more doubtful and less sure of oneself than the perusal of a brief summary, so much the better. It is part of the point of philosophy to make us a little less sure about things. After all, Socrates himself insisted that what distinguished him from other persons was not that he knew all, or even most, answers but rather that he realized his ignorance.

Still, one need not despair of joining this ongoing conversation. In the first place, you can get in near the beginning of this conversation by starting with Plato and moving on from there. Given that they are over two thousand years old, his early dialogues are surprisingly easy to follow. The later Platonic dialogues, Aristotle, and much which follows will be more difficult, but by that point you will have some idea of what the conversation is about.

Secondly, the structure of this book is designed to make this conversation accessible. There are section introductions and introductions to the individual philoso-phers. These latter introductions are divided into three sections: (1) biographical (a glimpse of the life), (2) philosophical (a resume of the philosopher's thought), and (3) bibliographical (suggestions for further reading). To give a sense of the development of ideas, there are short representative passages from some of the less important, but transitional, thinkers. To make all the works more readable, most footnotes treating textual matters (variant readings, etc.) have been omitted and all Greek words have been transliterated and put in angle brackets. My goal throughout this volume is to be unobtrusive and allow you to hear, and perhaps join in, the ongoing conversation that is Western philosophy.

WHAT'S NEW IN THIS EDITION?

- New translations of Plato's *Republic*, Aristotle's *Physics*, *Metaphysics*, and *On the Soul* by Joe Sachs.
- New translation of Spinoza's *Ethics* by Samuel Shirley.
- New section on Pyrrho using a reading from Sextus Empiricus, *Outlines of Pyrrhonism*.
- New section on Charles Sanders Peirce with the reading "The Fixation of Belief."
- New section on William James with the reading "What Pragmatism Means" from *Pragmatism*.
- New section on W.E.B. Du Bois with the reading "Of Our Spiritual Strivings" from *The Souls of Black Folks*.
- Jean-Paul Sartre's *Existentialism is a Humanism* is now given complete.
- New reading by Jacques Derrida, "The Written Being/The Being Written" from *Of Grammatology*.
- Updated bibliographies reflecting the most recent scholarship on each thinker and philosophical school.

Throughout the editing of this edition, I have tried to follow the editorial principles established by Walter Kaufmann in his 2 volume *Philosophic Classics* (1961) on which this current series is based: (1) to use complete works or, where more appropriate, complete sections of works (2) in clear translations (3) of texts central to the thinker's philosophy or widely accepted as part of the "canon." While little remains of Professor Kaufmann's introductions or editing—and the series has now grown to 7 volumes—his spirit of inclusion and respect for ideas continues. Those who use this volume in a one-term introduction to philosophy, history of philosophy, or history of intellectual thought course will find more material here than can easily fit a normal semester. But this embarrassment of riches gives teachers some choice and, for those who offer the same course year after year, an opportunity to change the menu.

* * *

I would like to thank the many people who assisted me in this volume, including the library staff of Whitworth College, especially Hans Bynagle, Gail Fielding, and Jeanette Langston; my colleagues, F. Dale Bruner, who made helpful suggestions on all the introductions, Barbara Filo, who helped make selections for the artwork, and

Corliss Slack and John Yoder, who provided historical context; Stephen Davis, Claremont McKenna College; Jerry H. Gill, The College of St. Rose; Rex Hollowell, Spokane Falls Community College; Arthur F. Holmes, Wheaton College; Stanley Obitts, Westmont College; Wayne Pomerleau, Gonzaga University; Timothy A. Robinson, The College of St. Benedict; Glenn Ross, Franklin & Marshall College; and Charles Young, The Claremont Graduate School, who each read some of the introductions and gave helpful advice; Edward Beach, University of Wisconsin, Eau Claire, and John Justice, Randolph-Macon Women's College who graciously called my attention to errors in previous editions; my former secretary, Michelle Seefried; my production editor, Shiny Rajesh of Integra, my project managers, Sarah Holle and Cheryl Keenan of Prentice Hall; and my former acquisitions editors, Mical Moser, Ross Miller, Karita France, Angela Stone and Ted Bolen. I would also like to acknowledge the following reviewers who made helpful suggestions: Marianina Alcott, San Jose State University; James W. Allard, Montana State University; David Apolloni, Augsburg College; Robert C. Bennett, El Centro College; Sarah Borden, Wheaton College; Herbert L. Carson, Ferris State University; Mary T. Clark, Manhattanville College; Stuart Dalton, Monmouth College; Sandra S. Edwards, University of Arkansas; Steven M. Emmanuel, Virginia Wesleyan College; David Griesedieck, University of Missouri, Saint Louis; John Hurley, Central Connecticut Sate University; Stephen E. Lahey, LaMoyne College; Helen S. Lang, Trinity College; R. James Long, Fairfield University; Scott MacDonald, University of Iowa; Angel Medina, Georgia State University; Nick More, Westminster College; Paul Newberry, California State University–Bakersfield; Eric Palmer, Allegheny College; David F. T. Rodier, American University; Katherine Rogers, University of Delaware; Gregory Schultz, Wisconsin Lutheran College; Stephen Scott, Eastern Washington University; Daniel C. Shartin, Worcester State College; Walter G. Scott, Oklahoma State University; Howard N. Tuttle, University of New Mexico; Richard J. Van Iten, Iowa State University; Donald Phillip Verene, Emory University; Tamara Welsh, Univeristy of Tennessee–Chattanooga; Sarah Worth, Allegheny College; and Wilhelm S. Wurzer, Duquesne University.

I am especially thankful to my wife, Joy Lynn Fulton Baird, and to our children, Whitney, Sydney, and Soren, who have supported me throughout this enterprise.

Forrest E. Baird
Professor of Philosophy
Whitworth University
Spokane, WA 99251
email: fbaird@whitworth.edu

Philosophers in this Volume

400 B.C. | 200 B.C. | 0 | A.D. 200 | 400 | 600 | 800 | 1000

Plato
Aristotle
Pyrrho
Epicurus
Epictetus
Sextus Empiricus
Plotinus
Augustine
Boethius
Anselm

Other Important Figures

Socrates
Alexander the Great
Porphyry
Zeno of Citium
Pseudo-Dionysius Areopagite
Cleanthes
Mohammed
Julius Caesar
Charlemagne
Lucretius
Avicenna
Philo of Alexandria
Jesus
Paul
Justin Martyr
Marcus Aurelius
Ptolemy (astronomer)
Clement of Alexandria
Tertullian
Origen

A Sampling of Major Events

Death of Socrates
Punic Wars and rise of Roman Empire
Wall of China built
Jerusalem Temple destroyed
Furthest extent of the Roman Empire
Council of Nicea
Roman Empire divided
Fall of Rome
Schools of philosophy in Athens closed by Justinian
Muslim conquest of Northern Africa and Spain
Peak of Mayan civilization in Central America

400 B.C. | 200 B.C. | 0 | A.D. 200 | 400 | 600 | 800 | 1000

1200	1400	1600	1800	2000

Hildegard of Bingen
Moses Maimonides
Thomas Aquinas
William of Ockham
Pico della Mirandola
Thomas Hobbes
René Descartes
Princess Elizabeth of Bohemia
Blaise Pascal
Baruch Spinoza
John Locke
Gottfried Leibniz
George Berkeley
David Hume
Jean-Jacques Rousseau
Immanuel Kant
G.W.F. Hegel
Mary Wollstonecraft
John Stuart Mill
Søren Kierkegaard
Karl Marx
Friedrich Nietzsche
Edmund Husserl
Bertrand Russell
Martin Heidegger
Ludwig Wittgenstein
Jean-Paul Sartre
Simone de Beauvoir
Willard Van Orman Quine
Jacques Derrida

Peter Abelard
Averroës
Zhu Xi (Chu Hsi)
Genghis Khan
Francis of Assisi
Bonaventure
Dante Alighieri
Catherine of Siena
Leonardo da Vinci
Martin Luther
John Calvin
Galileo
Shakespeare
Rembrandt
Louis XIV
Isaac Newton
J. S. Bach
Voltaire
Thomas Reid
J. W. Goethe
Mozart
Napoleon Bonaparte
Beethoven
Simon Bolivar
Queen Victoria
John Dewey
Henri Bergson
George Santayana
Mahatma Gandhi
G. E. Moore
Martin Buber
Jacques Martin
Adolf Hitler
Gilbert Ryle
A. J. Ayer
Michel Foucault

Paris University founded
Magna Carta
Bubonic Plague
Ming Dynasty in China
Gutenberg invents moveable-type printing
Columbus sails to America
Luther begins Protestant Reformation
English defeat Spanish Armada
Charles I executed
English "Glorious Revolution"
Declaration of Independence
French Revolution
Chaka founds Zulu Empire
American Civil War
Wright brothers invent airplane
World War I
Russian Revolution
World War II
Korean War
Vietnam War
First men on the moon

1200	1400	1600	1800	2000

ANCIENT GREEK PHILOSOPHY

Something unusual happened in Greece and in the Greek colonies of the Aegean Sea some twenty-five hundred years ago. Whereas the previous great cultures of the Mediterranean had used mythological stories of the gods to explain the operations of the world and of the self, some of the Greeks began to discover new ways of explaining these phenomena. Instead of reading their ideas into, or out of, ancient scriptures or poems, they began to use reason, contemplation, and sensory observation to make sense of reality.

The story as we know it began with the Greeks living on the coast of Asia Minor (present-day Turkey). Colonists there, such as Thales, tried to find the one common element in the diversity of nature. Subsequent thinkers, such as Anaximenes, sought not only to find this one common element, but also to find the process by which one form changes into another. Other thinkers, such as Pythagoras, turned to the nature of form itself rather than the basic stuff that takes on a particular form.

With Socrates, the pursuit of knowledge turned inward as he sought not to understand the world, but himself. His call to "know thyself," together with his uncompromising search for truth, inspired generations of thinkers. With the writings of Plato and Aristotle, ancient Greek thought reached its zenith. These giants of human thought developed all-embracing systems that explained both the nature of the universe and the humans who inhabit it.

All these lovers of wisdom, or *philosophers,* came to different conclusions and often spoke disrespectfully of one another. Some held the universe to be one single entity, whereas others insisted that it must be made of many parts. Some believed that human knowledge was capable of understanding virtually everything about the world and the self, whereas others thought that it was not possible to have any knowledge at all. But despite all their differences, there is a thread of continuity, a continuing focus among them: the *human* attempt to understand the world and the self, using *human* reason. This fact distinguishes these philosophers from the great minds that preceded them.

The philosophers of ancient Greece have fascinated thinking persons for centuries, and their writings have been one of the key influences on the development of Western civilization. The works of Plato and Aristotle, especially, have defined the questions and suggested many of the answers for subsequent generations. As the great Greek statesman Pericles sagely predicted, "Future ages will wonder at us, as the present age wonders at us now."

* * *

For a comprehensive, yet readable, work on Greek philosophy, see W.K.C. Guthrie's authoritative *The History of Greek Philosophy,* six volumes. (Cambridge: Cambridge University Press, 1962–1981). W.T. Jones, *The Classical Mind* (New York: Harcourt, Brace & World, 1969); Frederick Copleston, *A History of Philosophy: Volume I, Greece & Rome* (Garden City, NY: Doubleday, 1962); Friedo Ricken, *Philosophy of the Ancients,* translated by Eric Watkins (Notre Dame, IN: University of Notre Dame Press, 1991); J.V. Luce, *An Introduction to Greek Philosophy* (New York: Thames and Hudson, 1992); C.C.W. Taylor, ed., *Routledge History of Philosophy, Volume 1: From the Beginning to Plato* (London: Routledge, 1997); David Furley, ed., *Routledge History of Philosophy, Volume 2: Aristotle to Augustine* (London: Routledge, 1997); Julia Annas, *Ancient Philosophy: A Very Short Introduction* (Oxford: Oxford University Press, 2000); James A. Arieti, *Philosophy in the Ancient World* (Lanham, MD: Rowman & Littlefield, 2005); Anthony Kenny, *Ancient Philosophy: A New History of Western Philosophy* (Oxford University Press, 2004); and Stephanie Lynn Budin, *The Ancient Greeks: An Introduction* (Oxford: Oxford University Press, 2009) provide basic introductions. Julie K. Ward, ed., *Feminism and Ancient Philosophy* (London: Routledge, 1996) provides a feminist critique while Robert S. Brumbaugh, *The Philosophers of Greece* (Albany, NY: SUNY Press, 1981) is an accessible introduction with pictures, charts, and maps.

Socrates
470–399 B.C.
Plato
428/7–348/7 B.C.

Socrates has fascinated and inspired men and women for over two thousand years. All five of the major "schools" of ancient Greece (Academics, Peripatetics, Epicureans, Stoics, and Cynics) were influenced by his thought. Some of the early Christian thinkers, such as Justin Martyr, considered him a "proto-Christian," while others, such as St. Augustine (who rejected this view) still expressed deep admiration for Socrates' ethical life. More recently, existentialists have found in Socrates' admonition "know thyself" an encapsulation of their thought, and opponents of unjust laws have seen in Socrates' trial a blueprint for civil disobedience. In short, Socrates is one of the most admired men who ever lived.

The Athens into which Socrates was born in 470 B.C. was a city still living in the flush of its epic victory over the Persians, and it was bursting with new ideas. The playwrights Euripides and Sophocles were young boys, and Pericles, the great Athenian democrat, was still a young man. The Parthenon's foundation was laid when Socrates was twenty-two, and its construction was completed fifteen years later.

Socrates was the son of Sophroniscus, a sculptor, and of Phaenarete, a midwife. As a boy, Socrates received a classical Greek education in music, gymnastics, and grammar (or the study of language), and he decided early on to become a sculptor like his father. Tradition says he was a gifted artist who fashioned impressively simple statues of the Graces. He married a woman named Xanthippe, and together they had three children. He took an early interest in the developing science of the Milesians, and then he served for a time in the army.

When he was a middle-aged man, Socrates' friend, Chaerephon, asked the oracle at Delphi "if there was anyone who was wiser than Socrates." For once the mysterious oracle gave an unambiguous answer: "No one." When Socrates heard of the incident, he was confused. He knew that he was not a wise man. So he set out to find a wiser man to prove the answer wrong. Socrates later described the method and results of his mission:

> So I examined the man—I need not tell you his name, he was a politician—but this was the result. Athenians. When I conversed with him I came to see that, though a great many persons, and most of all he himself, thought that he was wise, yet he was not wise. Then I tried to prove to him that he was not wise, though he fancied that he was. By so doing I made him indignant, and many of the bystanders. So when I went away, I thought to myself, "I am wiser than this man: neither of us knows anything that is really worth knowing, but he thinks that he has knowledge when he has not, while I, having no knowledge, do not think that I have. I seem, at any rate, to be a little wiser than he is on this point: I do not think that I know what I do not know." Next I went to another man who was reputed to be still wiser than the last, with exactly the same result. And there again I made him, and many other men, indignant. (*Apology* 21c)

As Socrates continued his mission by interviewing the politicians, poets, and artisans of Athens, young men followed along. They enjoyed seeing the authority figures humiliated by Socrates' intense questioning. Those in authority, however, were not amused. Athens was no longer the powerful, self-confident city of 470 B.C., the year of Socrates' birth. An exhausting succession of wars with Sparta (the Peloponnesian Wars) and an enervating series of political debacles had left the city narrow in vision and suspicious of new ideas and of dissent. In 399 B.C., Meletus and Anytus brought an indictment of impiety and corrupting the youth against Socrates. As recorded in the *Apology,* the Athenian assembly found him guilty by a vote of 281 to 220 and sentenced him to death. His noble death is described incomparably in the closing pages of the *Phaedo* by Plato.

Socrates wrote nothing, and our knowledge of his thought comes exclusively from the report of others. The playwright Aristophanes (455–375 B.C.) satirized Socrates in his comedy *The Clouds.* His caricature of Socrates as a cheat and charlatan was apparently so damaging that Socrates felt compelled to offer a rebuttal before the Athenian assembly (see the *Apology,* following). The military general Xenophon (ca. 430–350 B.C.) honored his friend Socrates in his *Apology of Socrates,* his *Symposium,* and, later, in his *Memorabilia* ("Recollections of Socrates"). In an effort to defend his dead friend's memory, Xenophon's writings illumine Socrates' life and character. Though born fifteen years after the death of Socrates, Aristotle (384–322 B.C.) left many fascinating allusions to Socrates in his philosophic works, as did several later Greek philosophers. But the primary source of our knowledge of Socrates comes from one of those young men who followed him: Plato.

* * *

Plato was probably born in 428/7 B.C. He had two older brothers, Adeimantus and Glaucon, who appear in Plato's *Republic,* and a sister, Potone. Though he may have known Socrates since childhood, Plato was probably nearer twenty when he came under the intellectual spell of Socrates. The death of Socrates made an enormous impression on Plato and contributed to his call to bear witness to posterity of "the best, . . . the wisest and most just" person that he knew (*Phaedo,* 118). Though Plato was from a distinguished family and might have followed his relatives into politics, he chose philosophy.

Following Socrates' execution, the twenty-eight-year-old Plato left Athens and traveled for a time. He is reported to have visited Egypt and Cyrene—though some scholars doubt this. During this time he wrote his early dialogues on Socrates' life and teachings. He also visited Italy and Sicily, where he became the friend of Dion, a relative of Dionysius, the tyrant of Syracuse, Sicily.

On returning to Athens from Sicily, Plato founded a school, which came to be called the Academy. One might say it was the world's first university, and it endured as a center of higher learning for nearly one thousand years, until the Roman emperor Justinian closed it in A.D. 529. Except for two later trips to Sicily, where he unsuccessfully sought to institute his political theories, Plato spent the rest of his life at the Athenian Academy. Among his students was Aristotle. Plato died at eighty in 348/7 B.C.

Plato's influence was best described by the twentieth-century philosopher Alfred North Whitehead when he said, "The safest general characterization of the European philosophical tradition is that it consists of a series of footnotes to Plato."

* * *

It is difficult to separate the ideas of Plato from those of his teacher, Socrates. In virtually all of Plato's dialogues, Socrates is the main character, and it is possible that in the early dialogues Plato is recording his teacher's actual words. But in the later dialogues, "Socrates" gives Plato's views—views that, in some cases, in fact, the historical Socrates denied.

The first four dialogues presented in this text describe the trial and death of Socrates and are arranged in narrative order. The first, the *Euthyphro,* takes place as Socrates has just learned of the indictment against him. He strikes up a conversation with a "theologian" so sure of his piety that he is prosecuting his own father for murder. The dialogue moves on, unsuccessfully, to define piety. Along the way, Socrates asks a question that has vexed philosophers and theologians for centuries: Is something good because the gods say it is, or do the gods say it is good because it is?

The next dialogue, the *Apology,* is generally regarded as one of Plato's first, and as eminently faithful to what Socrates said at his trial on charges of impiety and corruption of youth. The speech was delivered in public and heard by a large audience; Plato has Socrates mention that Plato was present; and there is no need to doubt the historical veracity of the speech, at least in essentials. There are two breaks in the narrative: one after Socrates' defense (during which the Athenians vote "guilty") and one after Socrates proposes an alternative to the death penalty (during which the Athenians decide on death). This dialogue includes Socrates' famous characterization of his mission and purpose in life.

In the *Crito,* Plato has Crito visit Socrates in prison to assure him that his escape from Athens has been well prepared and to persuade him to consent to leave. Socrates argues that one has an obligation to obey the state even when it orders one to suffer wrong. That Socrates, in fact, refused to leave is certain; that he used the arguments Plato ascribes to him is less certain. In any case, anyone who has read the *Apology* will agree that after his speech Socrates could not well escape.

The moving account of Socrates' death is given at the end of the *Phaedo,* the last of our group of dialogues. There is common agreement that this dialogue was written much later than the other three and that the earlier part of the dialogue, with its Platonic doctrine of Forms and immortality, uses "Socrates" as a vehicle for Plato's own ideas. These first four dialogues are given in the F.J. Church translation.

There are few books in Western civilization that have had the impact of Plato's *Republic*—aside from the Bible, perhaps none. Like the Bible, there are also few books whose interpretation and evaluation have differed so widely. Apparently it is a description of Plato's ideal society: a utopian vision of the just state, possible only if philosophers were kings. But some (see the following suggested readings) claim that its purpose is not to give a model of the ideal state, but to show the impossibility of such a state and to convince aspiring philosophers to shun politics. Evaluations of the *Republic* have also varied widely: from the criticisms of Karl Popper, who denounced the *Republic* as totalitarian, to the admiration of more traditional interpreters, such as Francis MacDonald Cornford and Gregory Vlastos.

Given the importance of this work and the diversity of opinions concerning its point and value, it was extremely difficult to decide which sections of the *Republic* to include in this series. I chose to include the discussion of justice from Books I and II, the descriptions of the guardians and of the "noble lie" from Book III, the discussions of the virtues and the soul in Book IV, the presentations of the guardians' qualities and lifestyles in Book V, and the key sections on knowledge (including the analogy of the line and the myth of the cave) from the end of Book VI and the beginning of Book VII. I admit that space constraints have forced me to exclude important sections. Ideally, the selections chosen will whet the student's appetite to read the rest of this classic. I am pleased to offer the *Republic* in the outstanding new translation by Joe Sachs.

The marginal page numbers are those of all scholarly editions, Greek, English, German, or French.

* * *

For studies of Socrates, see the classic A.E. Taylor, *Socrates: The Man and His Thought* (London: Methuen, 1933); the second half of Volume III of W.K.C. Guthrie, *The History of Greek Philosophy* (Cambridge: Cambridge University Press, 1969); Hugh H. Benson, *Essays on the Philosophy of Socrates* (Oxford: Oxford University Press, 1992); Anthony Gottlieb, *Socrates* (London: Routledge, 1999); Christopher Taylor's pair of introductions, *Socrates* and *Socrates: A Very Short Introduction* (both Oxford: Oxford University Press, 1999 and 2000); Nalin Ranasingle, *The Soul of Socrates* (Ithaca, NY: Cornell University Press, 2000); Thomas C. Brickhouse and Nicholas D. Smith, *The Philosophy of Socrates* (Boulder, CO: Westview, 2000); and James Colaiazo, *Socrates Against Athens* (London: Routledge, 2001). For collections of essays, see Gregory Vlastos, ed., *The Philosophy of Socrates* (Garden City, NY: Doubleday, 1971); Hugh H. Benson, ed., *Essays on the Philosophy of Socrates* (Oxford: Oxford University Press, 1992); Terence Irwin, ed., *Socrates and His Contemporaries* (Hamden, CT: Garland Publishing, 1995); and the multivolume William J. Prior, ed., *Socrates* (Oxford: Routledge, 1996); and Lindsay Judson and Vassilis Karasmanis, eds., *Remembering Socrates: Philosophical Essays* (Oxford: Oxford University Press, 2006). For discussions of the similarities and differences between the historical Socrates and the "Socrates" of the Platonic dialogues, see Gregory Vlastos, *Socrates: Ironist and Moral Philosopher* (Ithaca, NY: Cornell University Press, 1991), especially Chapters 2 and 3.

Books about Plato are legion. Once again the work of W.K.C. Guthrie is sensible, comprehensive, yet readable. See Volumes IV and V of his *The History of Greek Philosophy* (Cambridge: Cambridge University Press, 1975 and 1978). Paul Shorey, *What Plato Said* (Chicago: Chicago University Press, 1933); and G.M.A. Grube, *Plato's Thought* (London: Methuen, 1935) are classic treatments of Plato, while Robert

Brumbaugh, *Plato for a Modern Age* (New York: Macmillan, 1964); I.M. Crombie, *An Examination of Plato's Doctrines,* two volumes (New York: Humanities Press, 1963–1969), R.M. Hare, *Plato* (Oxford: Oxford University Press, 1982); David J. Melling, *Understanding Plato* (Oxford: Oxford University Press, 1987); Bernard Williams, *Plato* (London: Routledge, 1999); Julius Moravcsik, *Plato and Platonism* (Oxford: Basil Blackwell, 2000); and Gail Fine, *The Oxford Handbook of Plato* (Oxford: Oxford University Press, 2008) are more recent studies. For collections of essays, see Gregory Vlastos, ed., *Plato: A Collection of Critical Essays,* two volumes (Garden City, NY: Doubleday, 1971); Richard Kraut, ed., *The Cambridge Companion to Plato* (Cambridge: Cambridge University Press, 1991); Nancy Tuana, ed., *Feminist Interpretations of Plato* (College Park, PA: Pennsylvania State University Press, 1994); Terence Irwin, ed., *Plato's Ethics* and *Plato's Metaphysics and Epistemology* (both Hamden, CT: Garland Publishing, 1995); Gregory Vlastos, ed., *Studies in Greek Philosophy, Volume II: Socrates, Plato, and Their Tradition* (Princeton, NJ: Princeton University Press, 1995); Nicholas D. Smith, ed., *Plato: Critical Assessments* (London: Routledge, 1998); Gail Fine, ed., *Plato* (Oxford: Oxford University Press, 2000); and Gerald A. Press, ed., *Who Speaks for Plato?* (Lanham, MD: Rownan and Littlefield, 2000). C.D.C. Reeve, *Socrates in the Apology* (Indianapolis, IN: Hackett, 1989) provides insights on this key dialogue. For further reading on the *Republic,* see Nicholas P. White, *A Companion to Plato's* Republic (Indianapolis, IN: Hackett, 1979); Julia Annas, *An Introduction to Plato's* Republic (Oxford: Clarendon Press, 1981); Nickolas Pappas, *Routledge Guidebook to Plato and the* Republic (Oxford: Routledge, 1995); Daryl Rice, *A Guide to Plato's* Republic (Oxford: Oxford University Press, 1997); Richard Kraut, ed., *Plato's* Republic: *Critical Essays* (Lanham, MD: Rowan & Littlefield, 1997); Sean Sayers, *Plato's* Republic: *An Introduction* (Edinburgh: Edinburgh University Press, 1999); Stanley Rosen, *Plato's* Republic (New Haven, CT: Yale University Press, 2005); Luke Purshouse, *Plato's* Republic: *A Reader's Guide* (London: Continuum, 2006); and C.R.F. Ferrari, ed., *The Cambridge Companion to Plato's* Republic (Cambridge: Cambridge University Press, 2007). Terence Irwin, *Plato's Ethics* (Oxford: Oxford University Press, 1995) and Gabriela Roxanna Carone, *Plato's Cosmology and Its Ethical Dimensions* (Cambridge: Cambridge University Press, 2005) examine several dialogues while thoroughly exploring Plato's ethical thought. Finally, for unusual interpretations of Plato and his work, see Werner Jaeger, *Paideia,* Vols. II and III, translated by Gilbert Highet (New York: Oxford University Press, 1939–1943); Karl R. Popper, *The Open Society and Its Enemies; Volume I: The Spell of Plato* (Princeton, NJ: Princeton University Press, 1962); and Allan Bloom's interpretive essay in Plato, *Republic,* translated by Allan Bloom (New York: Basic Books, 1968).

EUTHYPHRO

Characters
Socrates
Euthyphro
Scene—The Hall of the King*

2 Euthyphro: What in the world are you doing here in the king's hall, Socrates?
Why have you left your haunts in the Lyceum? You surely cannot have a suit before
him, as I have.

Socrates: The Athenians, Euthyphro, call it an indictment, not a suit.

b Euthyphro: What? Do you mean that someone is prosecuting you? I cannot
believe that you are prosecuting anyone yourself.

Socrates: Certainly I am not.

Euthyphro: Then is someone prosecuting you?

Socrates: Yes.

Euthyphro: Who is he?

Socrates: I scarcely know him myself, Euthyphro; I think he must be some unknown young man. His name, however, is Meletus, and his district Pitthis, if you can call to mind any Meletus of that district—a hook-nosed man with lanky hair and rather a scanty beard.

Euthyphro: I don't know him, Socrates. But tell me, what is he prosecuting you for?

c Socrates: What for? Not on trivial grounds, I think. It is no small thing for so
young a man to have formed an opinion on such an important matter. For he, he says,
knows how the young are corrupted, and who are their corrupters. He must be a wise
d man who, observing my ignorance, is going to accuse me to the state, as his mother, of
corrupting his friends. I think that he is the only one who begins at the right point in his
political reforms; for his first care is to make the young men as good as possible, just as
a good farmer will take care of his young plants first, and, after he has done that, of the
3 others. And so Meletus, I suppose, is first clearing us away who, as he says, corrupt the
young men growing up; and then, when he has done that, of course he will turn his
attention to the older men, and so become a very great public benefactor. Indeed, that is
only what you would expect when he goes to work in this way.

Euthyphro: I hope it may be so, Socrates, but I fear the opposite. It seems to me that in trying to injure you, he is really setting to work by striking a blow at the foundation of the state. But how, tell me, does he say that you corrupt the youth?

b Socrates: In a way which sounds absurd at first, my friend. He says that I am a
maker of gods; and so he is prosecuting me, he says, for inventing new gods and for not
believing in the old ones.

Euthyphro: I understand, Socrates. It is because you say that you always have a divine guide. So he is prosecuting you for introducing religious reforms; and he is going into court to arouse prejudice against you, knowing that the multitude are easily prejudiced

*The anachronistic title "king" was retained by the magistrate who had jurisdiction over crimes affecting the state religion.

Plato: *Euthyphro,* Apology, Crito, translated by F.J. Church (Pearson/Library of the Liberal Arts, 1987).

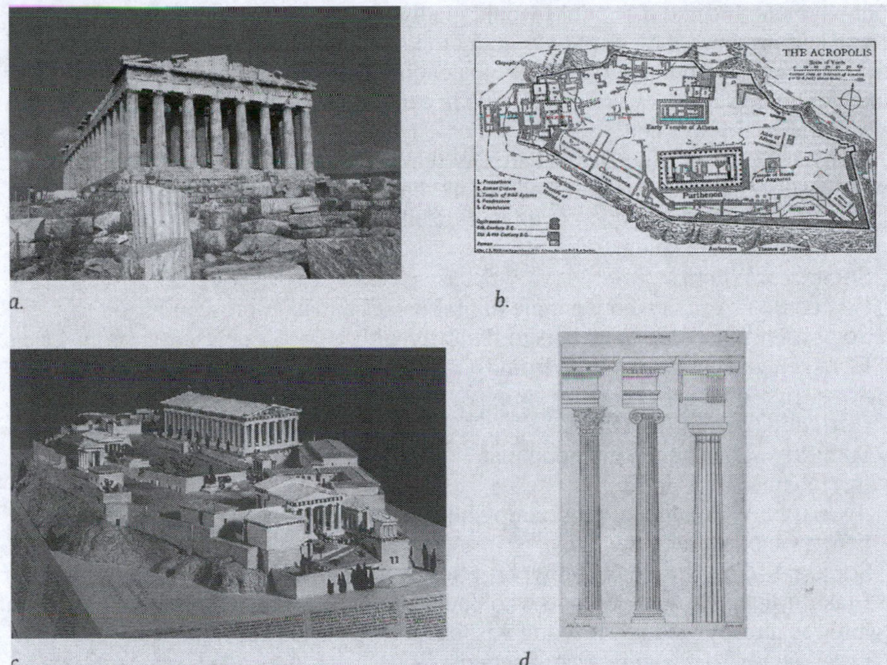

The Acropolis and the Parthenon

a. The *Parthenon*, Athens, built 477–438 B.C. The Parthenon, dedicated to Athena, patron deity of Athens, was at one period rededicated to the Christian Virgin Mary and then later became a Turkish mosque. In 1687 a gunpowder explosion created the ruin we see today. The Doric shell remains as a monument to ancient architectural engineering expertise and to a sense of classical beauty and order. (©*James Davis/Eye Ubiquitous/*Corbis)

b. Restored plan of the Acropolis, 400 B.C. The history of the Acropolis is as varied as the style and size of the temples and buildings constructed atop the ancient site. (*Public Domain*)

c. This model of the Acropolis of Athens recreates the complexity of fifth century B.C. public space, which included centers for worship, public forum, and entertainment. (With permission of the *Royal Ontario Museum* © *ROM*)

d. Doric, Ionic, and Corinthian columns with their characteristic capitals. (©*AS400 DB/Corbis*)

about such matters. Why, they laugh even at me, as if I were out of my mind, when I talk
about divine things in the assembly and tell them what is going to happen; and yet I have c
never foretold anything which has not come true. But they are resentful of all people like us. We must not worry about them; we must meet them boldly.

SOCRATES: My dear Euthyphro, their ridicule is not a very serious matter. The Athenians, it seems to me, may think a man to be clever without paying him much attention, so long as they do not think that he teaches his wisdom to others. But as soon
as they think that he makes other people clever, they get angry, whether it be from d
resentment, as you say, or for some other reason.

EUTHYPHRO: I am not very anxious to test their attitude toward me in this matter.

SOCRATES: No, perhaps they think that you are reserved, and that you are not anxious to teach your wisdom to others. But I fear that they may think that I am; for my love of men makes me talk to everyone whom I meet quite freely and unreservedly, and without payment. Indeed, if I could I would gladly pay people myself to listen to me. If then, as I said just now, they were only going to laugh at me, as you say they do at you, it would not be at all an unpleasant way of spending the day—to spend it in court, joking and laughing. But if they are going to be in earnest, then only prophets like you can tell where the matter will end.

EUTHYPHRO: Well, Socrates, I dare say that nothing will come of it. Very likely you will be successful in your trial, and I think that I shall be in mine.

SOCRATES: And what is this suit of yours, Euthyphro? Are you suing, or being sued?

EUTHYPHRO: I am suing.

SOCRATES: Whom?

4 EUTHYPHRO: A man whom people think I must be mad to prosecute.

SOCRATES: What? Has he wings to fly away with?

EUTHYPHRO: He is far enough from flying; he is a very old man.

SOCRATES: Who is he?

EUTHYPHRO: He is my father.

SOCRATES: Your father, my good man?

EUTHYPHRO: He is indeed.

SOCRATES: What are you prosecuting him for? What is the accusation?

EUTHYPHRO: Murder, Socrates.

b SOCRATES: Good heavens, Euthyphro! Surely the multitude are ignorant of what is right. I take it that it is not everyone who could rightly do what you are doing; only a man who was already well advanced in wisdom.

EUTHYPHRO: That is quite true, Socrates.

SOCRATES: Was the man whom your father killed a relative of yours? But, of course, he was. You would never have prosecuted your father for the murder of a stranger?

EUTHYPHRO: You amuse me, Socrates. What difference does it make whether
the murdered man were a relative or a stranger? The only question that you have to
ask is, did the murderer kill justly or not? If justly, you must let him alone; if unjustly,
c you must indict him for murder, even though he share your hearth and sit at your
table. The pollution is the same if you associate with such a man, knowing what he
has done, without purifying yourself, and him too, by bringing him to justice. In the
present case the murdered man was a poor laborer of mine, who worked for us on our
farm in Naxos. While drunk he got angry with one of our slaves and killed him. My
father therefore bound the man hand and foot and threw him into a ditch, while he
sent to Athens to ask the priest what he should do. While the messenger was gone, he
entirely neglected the man, thinking that he was a murderer, and that it would be no
d great matter, even if he were to die. And that was exactly what happened; hunger and
cold and his bonds killed him before the messenger returned. And now my father and
the rest of my family are indignant with me because I am prosecuting my father for
the murder of this murderer. They assert that he did not kill the man at all; and they
say that, even if he had killed him over and over again, the man himself was a mur-
e derer, and that I ought not to concern myself about such a person because it is impious for a son to prosecute his father for murder. So little, Socrates, do they know the
divine law of piety and impiety.

SOCRATES: And do you mean to say, Euthyphro, that you think that you understand divine things and piety and impiety so accurately that, in such a case as you have stated, you can bring your father to justice without fear that you yourself may be doing something impious?

EUTHYPHRO: If I did not understand all these matters accurately, Socrates, I should
not be worth much—Euthyphro would not be any better than other men. 5

SOCRATES: Then, my dear Euthyphro, I cannot do better than become your pupil
and challenge Meletus on this very point before the trial begins. I should say that I had
always thought it very important to have knowledge about divine things; and that now,
when he says that I offend by speaking carelessly about them, and by introducing
reforms, I have become your pupil. And I should say, "Meletus, if you acknowledge b
Euthyphro to be wise in these matters and to hold the correct belief, then think the same
of me and do not put me on trial; but if you do not, then bring a suit, not against me, but
against my master, for corrupting his elders—namely, myself whom he corrupts by his
teaching, and his own father whom he corrupts by admonishing and punishing him."
And if I did not succeed in persuading him to release me from the suit or to indict you
in my place, then I could repeat my challenge in court.

EUTHYPHRO: Yes, by Zeus! Socrates, I think I should find out his weak points if he
were to try to indict me. I should have a good deal to say about him in court long before c
I spoke about myself.

SOCRATES: Yes, my dear friend, and knowing this I am anxious to become your
pupil. I see that Meletus here, and others too, seem not to notice you at all, but he sees
through me without difficulty and at once prosecutes me for impiety. Now, therefore,
please explain to me what you were so confident just now that you knew. Tell me what d
are righteousness and sacrilege with respect to murder and everything else. I suppose
that piety is the same in all actions, and that impiety is always the opposite of piety, and
retains its identity, and that, as impiety, it always has the same character, which will be
found in whatever is impious.

EUTHYPHRO: Certainly, Socrates, I suppose so.

SOCRATES: Tell me, then, what is piety and what is impiety?

EUTHYPHRO: Well, then, I say that piety means prosecuting the unjust individual
who has committed murder or sacrilege, or any other such crime, as I am doing now,
whether he is your father or your mother or whoever he is; and I say that impiety means e
not prosecuting him. And observe, Socrates, I will give you a clear proof, which I have
already given to others, that it is so, and that doing right means not letting off unpunished the sacrilegious man, whosoever he may be. Men hold Zeus to be the best and the
most just of the gods; and they admit that Zeus bound his own father, Cronos, for 6
wrongfully devouring his children; and that Cronos, in his turn, castrated his father for
similar reasons. And yet these same men are incensed with me because I proceed
against my father for doing wrong. So, you see, they say one thing in the case of the
gods and quite another in mine.

SOCRATES: Is not that why I am being prosecuted, Euthyphro? I mean, because
I find it hard to accept such stories people tell about the gods? I expect that I shall be
found at fault because I doubt those stories. Now if you who understand all these matters so well agree in holding all those tales true, then I suppose that I must yield to your b
authority. What could I say when I admit myself that I know nothing about them? But
tell me, in the name of friendship, do you really believe that these things have actually
happened?

EUTHYPHRO: Yes, and more amazing things, too, Socrates, which the multitude do
not know of.

SOCRATES: Then you really believe that there is war among the gods, and bitter
hatreds, and battles, such as the poets tell of, and which the great painters have depicted c
in our temples, notably in the pictures which cover the robe that is carried up to the

Acropolis at the great Panathenaic festival? Are we to say that these things are true, Euthyphro?

EUTHYPHRO: Yes, Socrates, and more besides. As I was saying, I will report to you many other stories about divine matters, if you like, which I am sure will astonish you when you hear them.

SOCRATES: I dare say. You shall report them to me at your leisure another time. At
present please try to give a more definite answer to the question which I asked you just
d now. What I asked you, my friend, was, What is piety? and you have not explained it to
me to my satisfaction. You only tell me that what you are doing now, namely, prosecuting your father for murder, is a pious act.

EUTHYPHRO: Well, that is true, Socrates.

SOCRATES: Very likely. But many other actions are pious, are they not, Euthyphro?

EUTHYPHRO: Certainly.

SOCRATES: Remember, then, I did not ask you to tell me one or two of all the many
e pious actions that there are; I want to know what is characteristic of piety which makes
all pious actions pious. You said, I think, that there is one characteristic which makes all
pious actions pious, and another characteristic which makes all impious actions impious. Do you not remember?

EUTHYPHRO: I do.

SOCRATES: Well, then, explain to me what is this characteristic, that I may have it to turn to, and to use as a standard whereby to judge your actions and those of other men, and be able to say that whatever action resembles it is pious, and whatever does not, is not pious.

EUTHYPHRO: Yes, I will tell you that if you wish, Socrates.

SOCRATES: Certainly I do.

7 EUTHYPHRO: Well, then, what is pleasing to the gods is pious, and what is not
pleasing to them is impious.

SOCRATES: Fine, Euthyphro. Now you have given me the answer that I wanted. Whether what you say is true, I do not know yet. But, of course, you will go on to prove that it is true.

EUTHYPHRO: Certainly.

SOCRATES: Come, then, let us examine our statement. The things and the men that are pleasing to the gods are pious, and the things and the men that are displeasing to the gods are impious. But piety and impiety are not the same; they are as opposite as possible—was not that what we said?

EUTHYPHRO: Certainly.

SOCRATES: And it seems the appropriate statement?

b EUTHYPHRO: Yes, Socrates, certainly.

SOCRATES: Have we not also said, Euthyphro, that there are quarrels and disagreements and hatreds among the gods?

EUTHYPHRO: We have.

SOCRATES: But what kind of disagreement, my friend, causes hatred and anger?
Let us look at the matter thus. If you and I were to disagree as to whether one number
c were more than another, would that make us angry and enemies? Should we not settle
such a dispute at once by counting?

EUTHYPHRO: Of course.

SOCRATES: And if we were to disagree as to the relative size of two things, we should measure them and put an end to the disagreement at once, should we not?

EUTHYPHRO: Yes.

SOCRATES: And should we not settle a question about the relative weight of two things by weighing them?

EUTHYPHRO: Of course.

SOCRATES: Then what is the question which would make us angry and enemies if
we disagreed about it, and could not come to a settlement? Perhaps you have not an d
answer ready; but listen to mine. Is it not the question of the just and unjust, of the honorable and the dishonorable, of the good and the bad? Is it not questions about these matters which make you and me and everyone else quarrel, when we do quarrel, if we differ about them and can reach no satisfactory agreement?

EUTHYPHRO: Yes, Socrates, it is disagreements about these matters.

SOCRATES: Well, Euthyphro, the gods will quarrel over these things if they quarrel at all, will they not?

EUTHYPHRO: Necessarily.

SOCRATES: Then, my good Euthyphro, you say that some of the gods think one e
thing just, the others another; and that what some of them hold to be honorable or good, others hold to be dishonorable or evil. For there would not have been quarrels among them if they had not disagreed on these points, would there?

EUTHYPHRO: You are right.

SOCRATES: And each of them loves what he thinks honorable, and good, and just; and hates the opposite, does he not?

EUTHYPHRO: Certainly.

SOCRATES: But you say that the same action is held by some of them to be just,
and by others to be unjust; and that then they dispute about it, and so quarrel and fight 8
among themselves. Is it not so?

EUTHYPHRO: Yes.

SOCRATES: Then the same thing is hated by the gods and loved by them; and the same thing will be displeasing and pleasing to them.

EUTHYPHRO: Apparently.

SOCRATES: Then, according to your account, the same thing will be pious and impious.

EUTHYPHRO: So it seems.

SOCRATES: Then, my good friend, you have not answered my question. I did not ask you to tell me what action is both pious and impious; but it seems that whatever is
pleasing to the gods is also displeasing to them. And so, Euthyphro, I should not be sur- b
prised if what you are doing now in punishing your father is an action well pleasing to Zeus, but hateful to Cronos and Uranus, and acceptable to Hephaestus, but hateful to Hera; and if any of the other gods disagree about it, pleasing to some of them and displeasing to others.

EUTHYPHRO: But on this point, Socrates, I think that there is no difference of opinion among the gods: they all hold that if one man kills another unjustly, he must be punished.

SOCRATES: What, Euthyphro? Among mankind, have you never heard disputes c
whether a man ought to be punished for killing another man unjustly, or for doing some other unjust deed?

EUTHYPHRO: Indeed, they never cease from these disputes, especially in courts of justice. They do all manner of unjust things; and then there is nothing which they will not do and say to avoid punishment.

SOCRATES: Do they admit that they have done something unjust, and at the same time deny that they ought to be punished, Euthyphro?

EUTHYPHRO: No, indeed, that they do not.

SOCRATES: Then it is not the case that there is nothing which they will not do and say. I take it, they do not dare to say or argue that they must not be punished if they have
d done something unjust. What they say is that they have not done anything unjust, is it not so?

EUTHYPHRO: That is true.

SOCRATES: Then they do not disagree over the question that the unjust individual must be punished. They disagree over the question, who is unjust, and what was done and when, do they not?

EUTHYPHRO: That is true.

SOCRATES: Well, is not exactly the same thing true of the gods if they quarrel about justice and injustice, as you say they do? Do not some of them say that the others are doing something unjust, while the others deny it? No one, I suppose, my dear friend,
e whether god or man, dares to say that a person who has done something unjust must not be punished.

EUTHYPHRO: No, Socrates, that is true, by and large.

SOCRATES: I take it, Euthyphro, that the disputants, whether men or gods, if the gods do disagree, disagree over each separate act. When they quarrel about any act, some of them say that it was just, and others that it was unjust. Is it not so?

EUTHYPHRO: Yes.

9 SOCRATES: Come, then, my dear Euthyphro, please enlighten me on this point. What proof have you that all the gods think that a laborer who has been imprisoned for murder by the master of the man whom he has murdered, and who dies from his imprisonment before the master has had time to learn from the religious authorities what he should do, dies unjustly? How do you know that it is just for a son to indict his father and to prosecute him for the murder of such a man? Come, see if you can make it clear
b to me that the gods necessarily agree in thinking that this action of yours is just; and if you satisfy me, I will never cease singing your praises for wisdom.

EUTHYPHRO: I could make that clear enough to you, Socrates; but I am afraid that it would be a long business.

SOCRATES: I see you think that I am duller than the judges. To them, of course, you will make it clear that your father has committed an unjust action, and that all the gods agree in hating such actions.

EUTHYPHRO: I will indeed, Socrates, if they will only listen to me.

c SOCRATES: They will listen if they think that you are a good speaker. But while you were talking, it occurred to me to ask myself this question: suppose that Euthyphro were to prove to me as clearly as possible that all the gods think such a death unjust, how has he brought me any nearer to understanding what piety and impiety are? This particular act, perhaps, may be displeasing to the gods, but then we have just seen that piety and impiety cannot be defined in that way; for we have seen that what is displeas-
d ing to the gods is also pleasing to them. So I will let you off on this point, Euthyphro; and all the gods shall agree in thinking your father's action wrong and in hating it, if you like. But shall we correct our definition and say that whatever all the gods hate is impious, and whatever they all love is pious; while whatever some of them love, and others hate, is either both or neither? Do you wish us now to define piety and impiety in this manner?

EUTHYPHRO: Why not, Socrates?

SOCRATES: There is no reason why I should not, Euthyphro. It is for you to consider whether that definition will help you to teach me what you promised.

EUTHYPHRO: Well, I should say that piety is what all the gods love, and that impi- e
ety is what they all hate.

SOCRATES: Are we to examine this definition, Euthyphro, and see if it is a good one? Or are we to be content to accept the bare statements of other men or of ourselves without asking any questions? Or must we examine the statements?

EUTHYPHRO: We must examine them. But for my part I think that the definition is right this time.

SOCRATES: We shall know that better in a little while, my good friend. Now consider this question. Do the gods love piety because it is pious, or is it pious because they love it?

EUTHYPHRO: I do not understand you, Socrates.

SOCRATES: I will try to explain myself: we speak of a thing being carried and carrying, and being led and leading, and being seen and seeing; and you understand that all such expressions mean different things, and what the difference is.

EUTHYPHRO: Yes, I think I understand.

SOCRATES: And we talk of a thing being loved, of a thing loving, and the two are different?

EUTHYPHRO: Of course.

SOCRATES: Now tell me, is a thing which is being carried in a state of being carried b
because it is carried, or for some other reason?

EUTHYPHRO: No, because it is carried.

SOCRATES: And a thing is in a state of being led because it is led, and of being seen because it is seen?

EUTHYPHRO: Certainly.

SOCRATES: Then a thing is not seen because it is in a state of being seen: it is in a state of being seen because it is seen; and a thing is not led because it is in a state of being led: it is in a state of being led because it is led; and a thing is not carried because it is in a state of being carried: it is in a state of being carried because it is carried. Is my meaning clear now, Euthyphro? I mean this: if anything becomes or is affected, it does
not become because it is in a state of becoming: it is in a state of becoming because it c
becomes; and it is not affected because it is in a state of being affected: it is in a state of being affected because it is affected. Do you not agree?

EUTHYPHRO: I do.

SOCRATES: Is not that which is being loved in a state either of becoming or of being affected in some way by something?

EUTHYPHRO: Certainly.

SOCRATES: Then the same is true here as in the former cases. A thing is not loved by those who love it because it is in a state of being loved; it is in a state of being loved because they love it.

EUTHYPHRO: Necessarily.

SOCRATES: Well, then, Euthyphro, what do we say about piety? Is it not loved by d
all the gods, according to your definition?

EUTHYPHRO: Yes.

SOCRATES: Because it is pious, or for some other reason?

EUTHYPHRO: No, because it is pious.

SOCRATES: Then it is loved by the gods because it is pious; it is not pious because it is loved by them?

EUTHYPHRO: It seems so.

SOCRATES: But, then, what is pleasing to the gods is pleasing to them, and is in a state of being loved by them, because they love it?

Euthyphro: Of course.

Socrates: Then piety is not what is pleasing to the gods, and what is pleasing to the gods is not pious, as you say, Euthyphro. They are different things.

e Euthyphro: And why, Socrates?

Socrates: Because we are agreed that the gods love piety because it is pious, and that it is not pious because they love it. Is not this so?

Euthyphro: Yes.

Socrates: And that what is pleasing to the gods because they love it, is pleasing to them by reason of this same love, and that they do not love it because it is pleasing to them.

Euthyphro: True.

Socrates: Then, my dear Euthyphro, piety and what is pleasing to the gods are
11 different things. If the gods had loved piety because it is pious, they would also have loved what is pleasing to them because it is pleasing to them; but if what is pleasing to them had been pleasing to them because they loved it, then piety, too, would have been piety because they loved it. But now you see that they are opposite things, and wholly different from each other. For the one is of a sort to be loved because it is loved, while the other is loved because it is of a sort to be loved. My question, Euthyphro, was, What is piety? But it turns out that you have not explained to me the essential character of piety; you have been content to mention an effect which belongs to it—namely, that all
b the gods love it. You have not yet told me what its essential character is. Do not, if you please, keep from me what piety is; begin again and tell me that. Never mind whether the gods love it, or whether it has other effects: we shall not differ on that point. Do your best to make clear to me what is piety and what is impiety.

Euthyphro: But, Socrates, I really don't know how to explain to you what is in my mind. Whatever statement we put forward always somehow moves round in a circle, and will not stay where we put it.

Socrates: I think that your statements, Euthyphro, are worthy of my ancestor
c Daedalus.* If they had been mine and I had set them down, I dare say you would have made fun of me, and said that it was the consequence of my descent from Daedalus that the statements which I construct run away, as his statues used to, and will not stay where they are put. But, as it is, the statements are yours, and the joke would have no point. You yourself see that they will not stay still.

Euthyphro: Nay, Socrates, I think that the joke is very much in point. It is not my
d fault that the statement moves round in a circle and will not stay still. But you are the Daedalus, I think; as far as I am concerned, my statements would have stayed put.

Socrates: Then, my friend, I must be a more skillful artist than Daedalus; he only used to make his own works move, while I, you see, can make other people's works move, too. And the beauty of it is that I am wise against my will. I would rather that our statements had remained firm and immovable than have all the wisdom of Daedalus and
e all the riches of Tantalus to boot. But enough of this. I will do my best to help you to explain to me what piety is, for I think that you are lazy. Don't give in yet. Tell me, do you not think that all piety must be just?

Euthyphro: I do.

12 Socrates: Well, then, is all justice pious, too? Or, while all piety is just, is a part only of justice pious, and the rest of it something else?

Euthyphro: I do not follow you, Socrates.

*Daedalus' statues were reputed to have been so lifelike that they came alive.

SOCRATES: Yet you have the advantage over me in your youth no less than your wisdom. But, as I say, the wealth of your wisdom makes you complacent. Exert yourself, my good friend: I am not asking you a difficult question. I mean the opposite of what the poet [Stasinus] said, when he wrote:

> "You shall not name Zeus the creator, who made all things: for where there is fear b
> there also is reverence."

Now I disagree with the poet. Shall I tell you why?

EUTHYPHRO: Yes.

SOCRATES: I do not think it true to say that where there is fear, there also is reverence. Many people who fear sickness and poverty and other such evils seem to me to have fear, but no reverence for what they fear. Do you not think so?

EUTHYPHRO: I do.

SOCRATES: But I think that where there is reverence there also is fear. Does any
man feel reverence and a sense of shame about anything, without at the same time c
dreading and fearing the reputation of wickedness?

EUTHYPHRO: No, certainly not.

SOCRATES: Then, though there is fear wherever there is reverence, it is not correct to say that where there is fear there also is reverence. Reverence does not always accompany fear; for fear, I take it, is wider than reverence. It is a part of fear, just as the odd is a part of number, so that where you have the odd you must also have number, though where you have number you do not necessarily have the odd. Now I think you follow me?

EUTHYPHRO: I do.

SOCRATES: Well, then, this is what I meant by the question which I asked you. Is
there always piety where there is justice? Or, though there is always justice where there
is piety, yet there is not always piety where there is justice, because piety is only a part d
of justice? Shall we say this, or do you differ?

EUTHYPHRO: No, I agree. I think that you are right.

SOCRATES: Now observe the next point. If piety is a part of justice, we must find out, I suppose, what part of justice it is? Now, if you had asked me just now, for instance, what part of number is the odd, and what number is an odd number, I should have said that whatever number is not even is an odd number. Is it not so?

EUTHYPHRO: Yes.

SOCRATES: Then see if you can explain to me what part of justice is piety, that I e
may tell Meletus that now that I have been adequately instructed by you as to what
actions are righteous and pious, and what are not, he must give up prosecuting me
unjustly for impiety.

EUTHYPHRO: Well, then, Socrates, I should say that righteousness and piety are that part of justice which has to do with the careful attention which ought to be paid to the gods; and that what has to do with the careful attention which ought to be paid to men is the remaining part of justice.

SOCRATES: And I think that your answer is a good one, Euthyphro. But there is
one little point about which I still want to hear more. I do not yet understand what the 13
careful attention is to which you refer. I suppose you do not mean that the attention
which we pay to the gods is like the attention which we pay to other things. We say, for
instance, do we not, that not everyone knows how to take care of horses, but only the
trainer of horses?

EUTHYPHRO: Certainly.

SOCRATES: For I suppose that the skill that is concerned with horses is the art of taking care of horses.

EUTHYPHRO: Yes.

SOCRATES: And not everyone understands the care of dogs, but only the huntsman.

EUTHYPHRO: True.

b SOCRATES: For I suppose that the huntsman's skill is the art of taking care of dogs.

EUTHYPHRO: Yes.

SOCRATES: And the herdsman's skill is the art of taking care of cattle.

EUTHYPHRO: Certainly.

SOCRATES: And you say that piety and righteousness are taking care of the gods, Euthyphro?

EUTHYPHRO: I do.

SOCRATES: Well, then, has not all care the same object? Is it not for the good and benefit of that on which it is bestowed? For instance, you see that horses are benefited and improved when they are cared for by the art which is concerned with them. Is it not so?

EUTHYPHRO: Yes, I think so.

c SOCRATES: And dogs are benefited and improved by the huntsman's art, and cattle by the herdsman's, are they not? And the same is always true. Or do you think care is ever meant to harm that which is cared for?

EUTHYPHRO: No, indeed; certainly not.

SOCRATES: But to benefit it?

EUTHYPHRO: Of course.

SOCRATES: Then is piety, which is our care for the gods, intended to benefit the gods, or to improve them? Should you allow that you make any of the gods better when you do a pious action?

EUTHYPHRO: No indeed; certainly not.

SOCRATES: No, I am quite sure that that is not your meaning, Euthyphro. It was for
d that reason that I asked you what you meant by the careful attention which ought to be paid to the gods. I thought that you did not mean that.

EUTHYPHRO: You were right, Socrates. I do not mean that.

SOCRATES: Good. Then what sort of attention to the gods will piety be?

EUTHYPHRO: The sort of attention, Socrates, slaves pay to their masters.

SOCRATES: I understand; then it is a kind of service to the gods?

EUTHYPHRO: Certainly.

SOCRATES: Can you tell me what result the art which serves a doctor serves to produce? Is it not health?

EUTHYPHRO: Yes.

e SOCRATES: And what result does the art which serves a ship-wright serve to produce?

EUTHYPHRO: A ship, of course, Socrates.

SOCRATES: The result of the art which serves a builder is a house, is it not?

EUTHYPHRO: Yes.

SOCRATES: Then tell me, my good friend: What result will the art which serves the gods serve to produce? You must know, seeing that you say that you know more about divine things than any other man.

EUTHYPHRO: Well, that is true, Socrates.

SOCRATES: Then tell me, I beg you, what is that grand result which the gods use our services to produce?

EUTHYPHRO: There are many notable results, Socrates.

SOCRATES: So are those, my friend, which a general produces. Yet it is easy to see 14
that the crowning result of them all is victory in war, is it not?

EUTHYPHRO: Of course.

SOCRATES: And, I take it, the farmer produces many notable results; yet the principal result of them all is that he makes the earth produce food.

EUTHYPHRO: Certainly.

SOCRATES: Well, then, what is the principal result of the many notable results which the gods produce?

EUTHYPHRO: I told you just now, Socrates, that accurate knowledge of all these
matters is not easily obtained. However, broadly I say this: if any man knows that his b
words and actions in prayer and sacrifice are acceptable to the gods, that is what is
pious; and it preserves the state, as it does private families. But the opposite of what
is acceptable to the gods is sacrilegious, and this it is that undermines and destroys
everything.

SOCRATES: Certainly, Euthyphro, if you had wished, you could have answered my
main question in far fewer words. But you are evidently not anxious to teach me. Just c
now, when you were on the very point of telling me what I want to know, you stopped
short. If you had gone on then, I should have learned from you clearly enough by this
time what piety is. But now I am asking you questions, and must follow wherever you
lead me; so tell me, what is it that you mean by piety and impiety? Do you not mean a
science of prayer and sacrifice?

EUTHYPHRO: I do.

SOCRATES: To sacrifice is to give to the gods, and to pray is to ask of them, is it not?

EUTHYPHRO: It is, Socrates.

SOCRATES: Then you say that piety is the science of asking of the gods and giving d
to them?

EUTHYPHRO: You understand my meaning exactly, Socrates.

SOCRATES: Yes, for I am eager to share your wisdom, Euthyphro, and so I am all attention; nothing that you say will fall to the ground. But tell me, what is this service of the gods? You say it is to ask of them, and to give to them?

EUTHYPHRO: I do.

SOCRATES: Then, to ask rightly will be to ask of them what we stand in need of e
from them, will it not?

EUTHYPHRO: Naturally.

SOCRATES: And to give rightly will be to give back to them what they stand in need of from us? It would not be very skillful to make a present to a man of something that he has no need of.

EUTHYPHRO: True, Socrates.

SOCRATES: Then piety, Euthyphro, will be the art of carrying on business between gods and men?

EUTHYPHRO: Yes, if you like to call it so.

SOCRATES: But I like nothing except what is true. But tell me, how are the gods
benefited by the gifts which they receive from us? What they give is plain enough. Every
good thing that we have is their gift. But how are they benefited by what we give them? 15
Have we the advantage over them in these business transactions to such an extent that we
receive from them all the good things we possess, and give them nothing in return?

EUTHYPHRO: But do you suppose, Socrates, that the gods are benefited by the gifts which they receive from us?

SOCRATES: But what *are* these gifts, Euthyphro, that we give the gods?

EUTHYPHRO: What do you think but honor and praise, and, as I have said, what is acceptable to them.

b SOCRATES: Then piety, Euthyphro, is acceptable to the gods, but it is not profitable to them nor loved by them?

EUTHYPHRO: I think that nothing is more loved by them.

SOCRATES: Then I see that piety means that which is loved by the gods.

EUTHYPHRO: Most certainly.

SOCRATES: After that, shall you be surprised to find that your statements move about instead of staying where you put them? Shall you accuse me of being the Daedalus that makes them move, when you yourself are far more skillful than Daedalus was, and make them go round in a circle? Do you not see that our statement has come
c round to where it was before? Surely you remember that we have already seen that piety and what is pleasing to the gods are quite different things. Do you not remember?

EUTHYPHRO: I do.

SOCRATES: And now do you not see that you say that what the gods love is pious? But does not what the gods love come to the same thing as what is pleasing to the gods?

EUTHYPHRO: Certainly.

SOCRATES: Then either our former conclusion was wrong or, if it was right, we are wrong now.

EUTHYPHRO: So it seems.

SOCRATES: Then we must begin again and inquire what piety is. I do not mean to
d give in until I have found out. Do not regard me as unworthy; give your whole mind to the question, and this time tell me the truth. For if anyone knows it, it is you; and you are a Proteus whom I must not let go until you have told me. It cannot be that you would ever have undertaken to prosecute your aged father for the murder of a laboring man unless you had known exactly what piety and impiety are. You would have feared to risk the anger of the gods, in case you should be doing wrong, and you would have been
e afraid of what men would say. But now I am sure that you think that you know exactly what is pious and what is not; so tell me, my good Euthyphro, and do not conceal from me what you think.

EUTHYPHRO: Another time, then, Socrates. I am in a hurry now, and it is time for me to be off.

SOCRATES: What are you doing, my friend! Will you go away and destroy all my hopes of learning from you what is pious and what is not, and so of escaping Meletus?
16 I meant to explain to him that now Euthyphro has made me wise about divine things, and that I no longer in my ignorance speak carelessly about them or introduce reforms. And then I was going to promise him to live a better life for the future.

APOLOGY

Characters
Socrates
Meletus
Scene—The Court of Justice

SOCRATES: I do not know what impression my accusers have made upon you, 17
Athenians. But I do know that they nearly made me forget who I was, so persuasive were
they. And yet they have scarcely spoken one single word of truth. Of all their many falsehoods, the one which astonished me most was their saying that I was a clever speaker,
and that you must be careful not to let me deceive you. I thought that it was most shame- b
less of them not to be ashamed to talk in that way. For as soon as I open my mouth they
will be refuted, and I shall prove that I am not a clever speaker in any way at all—unless,
indeed, by a clever speaker they mean someone who speaks the truth. If that is their
meaning, I agree with them that I am an orator not to be compared with them. My
accusers, I repeat, have said little or nothing that is true, but from me you shall hear the
whole truth. Certainly you will not hear a speech, Athenians, dressed up, like theirs, with
fancy words and phrases. I will say to you what I have to say, without artifice, and I shall c
use the first words which come to mind, for I believe that what I have to say is just; so let
none of you expect anything else. Indeed, my friends, it would hardly be right for me, at
my age, to come before you like a schoolboy with his concocted phrases. But there is one
thing, Athenians, which I do most earnestly beg and entreat of you. Do not be surprised
and do not interrupt with shouts if in my defense I speak in the same way that I am accus- d
tomed to speak in the market place, at the tables of the money-changers, where many of
you have heard me, and elsewhere. The truth is this: I am more than seventy, and this is
the first time that I have ever come before a law court; thus your manner of speech here
is quite strange to me. If I had really been a stranger, you would have forgiven me for 18
speaking in the language and the manner of my native country. And so now I ask you to
grant me what I think I have a right to claim. Never mind the manner of my speech—it
may be superior or it may be inferior to the usual manner. Give your whole attention to
the question, whether what I say is just or not? That is what is required of a good judge,
as speaking the truth is required of a good orator.

I have to defend myself, Athenians, first against the older false accusations of my
old accusers, and then against the more recent ones of my present accusers. For many men b
have been accusing me to you, and for very many years, who have not spoken a word of
truth; and I fear them more than I fear Anytus* and his associates, formidable as they are.
But, my friends, the others are still more formidable, since they got hold of most of you
when you were children and have been more persistent in accusing me untruthfully,
persuading you that there is a certain Socrates, a wise man, who speculates about the
heavens, who investigates things that are beneath the earth, and who can make the worse
argument appear the stronger. These men, Athenians, who spread abroad this report are c

*Anytus is singled out as politically the most influential member of the prosecution. He had played a prominent part in the restoration of the democratic regime at Athens.

Plato: *Euthyphro,* Apology, Crito, translated by F.J. Church (Pearson/Library of the Liberal Arts, 1987).

the accusers whom I fear; for their hearers think that persons who pursue such inquiries
never believe in the gods. Besides they are many, their attacks have been going on for a
long time, and they spoke to you when you were most ready to believe them, since you
were all young, and some of you were children. And there was no one to answer them
when they attacked me. The most preposterous thing of all is that I do not even know their
d names: I cannot tell you who they are except when one happens to be a comic poet. But all
the rest who have persuaded you, from motives of resentment and prejudice, and sometimes, it may be, from conviction, are hardest to cope with. For I cannot call any one of
them forward in court to cross-examine him. I have, as it were, simply to spar with shadows in my defense, and to put questions which there is no one to answer. I ask you, therefore, to believe that, as I say, I have been attacked by two kinds of accusers—first, by
e Meletus* and his associates, and, then, by those older ones of whom I have spoken. And,
with your leave, I will defend myself first against my old accusers, since you heard their
accusations first, and they were much more compelling than my present accusers are.

19 Well, I must make my defense, Athenians, and try in the short time allowed me to
remove the prejudice which you have been so long a time acquiring. I hope that I may
manage to do this, if it be best for you and for me, and that my defense may be successful;
but I am quite aware of the nature of my task, and I know that it is a difficult one. Be the
outcome, however, as is pleasing to god, I must obey the law and make my defense.

Let us begin from the beginning, then, and ask what is the accusation that has
b given rise to the prejudice against me, on which Meletus relied when he brought his
indictment. What is the prejudice which my enemies have been spreading about me?
I must assume that they are formally accusing me, and read their indictment. It would
run somewhat in this fashion: "Socrates is guilty of engaging in inquiries into things
beneath the earth and in the heavens, of making the weaker argument appear the
c stronger, and of teaching others these same things." That is what they say. And in the
comedy of Aristophanes** you yourselves saw a man called Socrates swinging around
in a basket and saying that he walked on air, and sputtering a great deal of nonsense
about matters of which I understand nothing at all. I do not mean to disparage that kind
of knowledge if there is anyone who is wise about these matters. I trust Meletus may
never be able to prosecute me for that. But the truth is, Athenians, I have nothing to do
d with these matters, and almost all of you are yourselves my witnesses of this. I beg all
of you who have ever heard me discussing, and they are many, to inform your neighbors
and tell them if any of you have ever heard me discussing such matters at all. That will
e show you that the other common statements about me are as false as this one.

But the fact is that not one of these is true. And if you have heard that I undertake
20 to educate men, and make money by so doing, that is not true either, though I think that
it would be a fine thing to be able to educate men, as Gorgias of Leontini, and Prodicus
of Ceos, and Hippias of Elis do. For each of them, my friends, can go into any city, and
persuade the young men to leave the society of their fellow citizens, with any of whom
they might associate for nothing, and to be only too glad to be allowed to pay money for
the privilege of associating with themselves. And I believe that there is another wise
man from Paros residing in Athens at this moment. I happened to meet Callias, the son

*Apparently, in order to obscure the political implications of the trial, the role of chief prosecutor was assigned to Meletus, a minor poet with fervent religious convictions. Anytus was evidently ready to make political use of Meletus' convictions without entirely sharing his fervor, for in the same year as this trial Meletus also prosecuted Andocides for impiety, but Anytus came to Andocides' defense.

***The Clouds*. The basket was satirically assumed to facilitate Socrates' inquiries into things in the heavens.

of Hipponicus, a man who has spent more money on sophists than everyone else put together. So I said to him (he has two sons), "Callias, if your two sons had been foals or
calves, we could have hired a trainer for them who would have trained them to excel in b
doing what they are naturally capable of. He would have been either a groom or a farmer. But whom do you intend to take to train them, seeing that they are men? Who understands the excellence which a man and citizen is capable of attaining? I suppose that you must have thought of this, because you have sons. Is there such a person or not?" "Certainly there is," he replied. "Who is he," said I, "and where does he come from, and what is his fee?" "Evenus, Socrates," he replied, "from Paros, five minae."
Then I thought that Evenus was a fortunate person if he really understood this art and c
could teach so cleverly. If I had possessed knowledge of that kind, I should have been conceited and disdainful. But, Athenians, the truth is that I do not possess it.

Perhaps some of you may reply: "But, Socrates, what is the trouble with you? What has given rise to these prejudices against you? You must have been doing something out of the ordinary. All these rumors and reports of you would never have arisen if you had not been doing something different from other men. So tell us what it is, that
we may not give our verdict arbitrarily." I think that that is a fair question, and I will try d
to explain to you what it is that has raised these prejudices against me and given me this reputation. Listen, then. Some of you, perhaps, will think that I am joking, but I assure you that I will tell you the whole truth. I have gained this reputation, Athenians, simply

The *Thólos* at Delphi with the *Sanctuary of Apollo* in the background. Socrates' friend, Chaerophon, went to the famous oracle at Delphi to ask if there was anyone wiser than Socrates. The oracle, who usually gave very cryptic answers, responded with a simple "no." This led Socrates on a quest to find someone wiser than himself—a quest which resulted in Socrates making a number of influential enemies. (*Forrest E. Baird*)

by reason of a certain wisdom. But by what kind of wisdom? It is by Just that wisdom
which is perhaps human wisdom. In that, it may be, I am really wise. But the men of
e whom I was speaking just now must be wise in a wisdom which is greater than human
wisdom, or else I cannot describe it, for certainly I know nothing of it myself, and if any
man says that I do, he lies and speaks to arouse prejudice against me. Do not interrupt
me with shouts, Athenians, even if you think that I am boasting. What I am going to say
is not my own statement. I will tell you who says it, and he is worthy of your respect.
I will bring the god of Delphi to be the witness of my wisdom, if it is wisdom at all, and
21 of its nature. You remember Chaerephon. From youth upwards he was my comrade; and
also a partisan of your democracy, sharing your recent exile* and returning with you.
You remember, too, Chaerephon's character–how impulsive he was in carrying through
whatever he took in hand. Once he went to Delphi and ventured to put this question to
the oracle—I entreat you again, my friends, not to interrupt me with your shouts—he
asked if there was anyone who was wiser than I. The priestess answered that there was
no one. Chaerephon himself is dead, but his brother here will witness to what I say.

b Now see why I tell you this. I am going to explain to you how the prejudice against
me has arisen. When I heard of the oracle I began to reflect: What can the god mean by
this riddle? I know very well that I am not wise, even in the smallest degree. Then what
can he mean by saying that I am the wisest of men? It cannot be that he is speaking falsely,
for he is a god and cannot lie. For a long time I was at a loss to understand his meaning.
Then, very reluctantly, I turned to investigate it in this manner: I went to a man who was
reputed to be wise, thinking that there, if anywhere, I should prove the answer wrong, and
c meaning to point out to the oracle its mistake, and to say, "You said that I was the wisest
of men, but this man is wiser than I am." So I examined the man—I need not tell you his
name, he was a politician—but this was the result, Athenians. When I conversed with him
I came to see that, though a great many persons, and most of all he himself, thought that
he was wise, yet he was not wise. Then I tried to prove to him that he was not wise, though
d he fancied that he was. By so doing I made him indignant, and many of the bystanders. So
when I went away, I thought to myself, "I am wiser than this man: neither of us knows
anything that is really worth knowing, but he thinks that he has knowledge when he has
not, while I, having no knowledge, do not think that I have. I seem, at any rate, to be a little wiser than he is on this point: I do not think that I know what I do not know." Next
I went to another man who was reputed to be still wiser than the last, with exactly the
same result. And there again I made him, and many other men, indignant.

e Then I went on to one man after another, realizing that I was arousing indignation
every day, which caused me much pain and anxiety. Still I thought that I must set the god's
command above everything. So I had to go to every man who seemed to possess any
22 knowledge, and investigate the meaning of the oracle. Athenians, I must tell you the truth;
I swear, this was the result of the investigation which I made at the god's command: I found
that the men whose reputation for wisdom stood highest were nearly the most lacking in it,
while others who were looked down on as common people were much more intelligent.
Now I must describe to you the wanderings which I undertook, like Herculean labors, to
b prove the oracle irrefutable. After the politicians, I went to the poets, tragic, dithyrambic,
and others, thinking that there I should find myself manifestly more ignorant than they. So
I took up the poems on which I thought that they had spent most pains, and asked them
what they meant, hoping at the same time to learn something from them. I am ashamed to

*During the totalitarian regime of The Thirty, which remained in power for eight months (404 B.C.), five years before the trial.

tell you the truth, my friends, but I must say it. Almost any one of the bystanders could have
talked about the works of these poets better than the poets themselves. So I soon found that c
it is not by wisdom that the poets create their works, but by a certain instinctive inspiration,
like soothsayers and prophets, who say many fine things, but understand nothing of what
they say. The poets seemed to me to be in a similar situation. And at the same time I perceived that, because of their poetry, they thought that they were the wisest of men in other
matters too, which they were not. So I went away again, thinking that I had the same advantage over the poets that I had over the politicians.

Finally, I went to the artisans, for I knew very well that I possessed no knowledge at
all worth speaking of, and I was sure that I should find that they knew many fine things. d
And in that I was not mistaken. They knew what I did not know, and so far they were wiser
than I. But, Athenians, it seemed to me that the skilled artisans had the same failing as the
poets. Each of them believed himself to be extremely wise in matters of the greatest importance because he was skillful in his own art: and this presumption of theirs obscured their
real wisdom. So I asked myself, on behalf of the oracle, whether I would choose to remain e
as I was, without either their wisdom or their ignorance, or to possess both, as they did. And
I answered to myself and to the oracle that it was better for me to remain as I was.

From this examination, Athenians, has arisen much fierce and bitter indignation,
and as a result a great many prejudices about me. People say that I am "a wise man." For 23
the bystanders always think that I am wise myself in any matter wherein I refute
another. But, gentlemen, I believe that the god is really wise, and that by this oracle he
meant that human wisdom is worth little or nothing. I do not think that he meant that
Socrates was wise. He only made use of my name, and took me as an example, as b
though he would say to men, "He among you is the wisest who, like Socrates, knows
that his wisdom is really worth nothing at all." Therefore I still go about testing and
examining every man whom I think wise, whether he be a citizen or a stranger, as the
god has commanded me. Whenever I find that he is not wise, I point out to him, on the
god's behalf, that he is not wise. I am so busy in this pursuit that I have never had leisure
to take any part worth mentioning in public matters or to look after my private affairs.
I am in great poverty as the result of my service to the god. c

Besides this, the young men who follow me about, who are the sons of wealthy persons and have the most leisure, take pleasure in hearing men cross-examined. They often
imitate me among themselves; then they try their hands at cross-examining other people.
And, I imagine, they find plenty of men who think that they know a great deal when in fact
they know little or nothing. Then the persons who are cross-examined get angry with me
instead of with themselves, and say that Socrates is an abomination and corrupts the
young. When they are asked, "Why, what does he do? What does he teach?" they do not d
know what to say. Not to seem at a loss, they repeat the stock charges against all philosophers, and allege that he investigates things in the air and under the earth, and that he
teaches people to disbelieve in the gods, and to make the worse argument appear the
stronger. For, I suppose, they would not like to confess the truth, which is that they are
shown up as ignorant pretenders to knowledge that they do not possess. So they have been
filling your ears with their bitter prejudices for a long time, for they are ambitious, ener- e
getic, and numerous; and they speak vigorously and persuasively against me. Relying on
this, Meletus, Anytus, and Lycon have attacked me. Meletus is indignant with me on
behalf of the poets, Anytus on behalf of the artisans and politicians, and Lycon on behalf
of the orators. And so, as I said at the beginning, I shall be surprised if I am able, in the 24
short time allowed me for my defense, to remove from your minds this prejudice which
has grown so strong. What I have told you, Athenians, is the truth: I neither conceal nor do

I suppress anything, trivial or important. Yet I know that it is just this outspokenness which
rouses indignation. But that is only a proof that my words are true, and that the prejudice
b against me, and the causes of it, are what I have said. And whether you investigate them
now or hereafter, you will find that they are so.

What I have said must suffice as my defense against the charges of my first
accusers. I will try next to defend myself against Meletus, that "good patriot," as he
calls himself, and my later accusers. Let us assume that they are a new set of accusers,
and read their indictment, as we did in the case of the others. It runs thus: Socrates is
guilty of corrupting the youth, and of believing not in the gods whom the state believes
c in, but in other new divinities. Such is the accusation. Let us examine each point in it
separately. Meletus says that I am guilty of corrupting the youth. But I say, Athenians,
that he is guilty of playing a solemn joke by casually bringing men to trial, and pretending to have a solemn interest in matters to which he has never given a moment's
thought. Now I will try to prove to you that this is so.

d Come here, Meletus. Is it not a fact that you think it very important that the young
should be as good as possible?

Meletus: It is.

Socrates: Come, then, tell the judges who improves them. You care so much,* you must know. You are accusing me, and bringing me to trial, because, as you say, you have discovered that I am the corrupter of the youth. Come now, reveal to the gentlemen who improves them. You see, Meletus, you have nothing to say; you are silent. But don't you think that this is shameful? Is not your silence a conclusive proof of what I say—that you have never cared? Come, tell us, my good man, who makes the young better?

Meletus: The laws.

e Socrates: That, my friend, is not my question. What man improves the young,
who begins by knowing the laws?

Meletus: The judges here, Socrates.

Socrates: What do you mean, Meletus? Can they educate the young and improve them?

Meletus: Certainly.

Socrates: All of them? Or only some of them?

Meletus: All of them.

Socrates: By Hera, that is good news! Such a large supply of benefactors! And
25 do the members of the audience here improve them, or not?

Meletus: They do.

Socrates: And do the councilors?

Meletus: Yes.

Socrates: Well, then, Meletus, do the members of the assembly corrupt the young or do they again all improve them?

Meletus: They, too, improve them.

Socrates: Then all the Athenians, apparently, make the young into good men except me, and I alone corrupt them. Is that your meaning?

Meletus: Certainly, that is my meaning.

Socrates: You have discovered me to be most unfortunate. Now tell me: do
you think that the same holds good in the case of horses? Does one man do them
b harm and everyone else improve them? On the contrary, is it not one man only, or a

*Throughout the following passage, Socrates plays on the etymology of the name "Meletus" as meaning "the man who cares."

very few—namely, those who are skilled with horses—who can improve them, while
the majority of men harm them if they use them and have anything to do with them?
Is it not so, Meletus, both with horses and with every other animal? Of course it is,
whether you and Anytus say yes or no. The young would certainly be very fortunate
if only one man corrupted them, and everyone else did them good. The truth is, c
Meletus, you prove conclusively that you have never thought about the young in
your life. You exhibit your carelessness in not caring for the very matters about
which you are prosecuting me.

Now be so good as to tell us, Meletus, is it better to live among good citizens or
bad ones? Answer, my friend. I am not asking you at all a difficult question. Do not the
bad harm their associates and the good do them good?

MELETUS: Yes.

SOCRATES: Is there anyone who would rather be injured than benefitted by his d
companions? Answer, my good man; you are obliged by the law to answer. Does anyone like to be injured?

MELETUS: Certainly not.

SOCRATES: Well, then, are you prosecuting me for corrupting the young and making them worse, voluntarily or involuntarily?

MELETUS: For doing it voluntarily.

SOCRATES: What, Meletus? Do you mean to say that you, who are so much younger
than I, are yet so much wiser than I that you know that bad citizens always do evil, and that
good citizens do good, to those with whom they come in contact, while I am so extraordi- e
narily ignorant as not to know that, if I make any of my companions evil, he will probably
injure me in some way? And you allege that I do this voluntarily? You will not make me
believe that, nor anyone else either, I should think. Either I do not corrupt the young at all
or, if I do, I do so involuntarily, so that you are lying in either case. And if I corrupt them 26
involuntarily, the law does not call upon you to prosecute me for an error which is involuntary, but to take me aside privately and reprove and educate me. For, of course, I shall cease
from doing wrong involuntarily, as soon as I know that I have been doing wrong. But you
avoided associating with me and educating me; instead you bring me up before the court,
where the law sends persons, not for education, but for punishment.

The truth is, Athenians, as I said, it is quite clear that Meletus has never cared at
all about these matters. However, now tell us, Meletus, how do you say that I corrupt b
the young? Clearly, according to your indictment, by teaching them not to believe in the
gods the state believes in, but other new divinities instead. You mean that I corrupt the
young by that teaching, do you not?

MELETUS: Yes, most certainly I mean that.

SOCRATES: Then in the name of these gods of whom we are speaking, explain c
yourself a little more clearly to me and to these gentlemen here. I cannot understand
what you mean. Do you mean that I teach the young to believe in some gods, but not in
the gods of the state? Do you accuse me of teaching them to believe in strange gods? If
that is your meaning, I myself believe in some gods, and my crime is not that of complete atheism. Or do you mean that I do not believe in the gods at all myself, and that
I teach other people not to believe in them either?

MELETUS: I mean that you do not believe in the gods in any way whatever.

SOCRATES: You amaze me, Meletus! Why do you say that? Do you mean that
I believe neither the sun nor the moon to be gods, like other men? d

MELETUS: I swear he does not, judges. He says that the sun is a stone, and the
moon earth.

SOCRATES: My dear Meletus, do you think that you are prosecuting Anaxagoras?
You must have a very poor opinion of these men, and think them illiterate, if you imagine that they do not know that the works of Anaxagoras of Clazomenae are full of these
doctrines. And so young men learn these things from me, when they can often buy them
e in the theater for a drachma at most, and laugh at Socrates were he to pretend that these
doctrines, which are very peculiar doctrines, too, were his own. But please tell me, do
you really think that I do not believe in the gods at all?

MELETUS: Most certainly I do. You are a complete atheist.

SOCRATES: No one believes that, Meletus, not even you yourself. It seems to me,
Athenians, that Meletus is very insolent and reckless, and that he is prosecuting me simply
out of insolence, recklessness, and youthful bravado. For he seems to be testing me, by ask-
27 ing me a riddle that has no answer. "Will this wise Socrates," he says to himself, "see that
I am joking and contradicting myself? Or shall I deceive him and everyone else who hears
me?" Meletus seems to me to contradict himself in his indictment: it is as if he were to say,
"Socrates is guilty of not believing in the gods, but believes in the gods." This is joking.

Now, my friends, let us see why I think that this is his meaning. You must answer
b me, Meletus, and you, Athenians, must remember the request which I made to you at
the start, and not interrupt me with shouts if I talk in my usual manner.

Is there any man, Meletus, who believes in the existence of things pertaining to
men and not in the existence of men? Make him answer the question, gentlemen, without these interruptions. Is there any man who believes in the existence of horsemanship
and not in the existence of horses? Or in flute playing, and not in flute players? There is
not, my friend. If you will not answer, I will tell both you and the judges. But you must
c answer my next question. Is there any man who believes in the existence of divine
things and not in the existence of divinities?

MELETUS: There is not.

SOCRATES: I am very glad that these gentlemen have managed to extract an
answer from you. Well then, you say that I believe in divine things, whether they be old
or new, and that I teach others to believe in them. At any rate, according to your statement, I believe in divine things. That you have sworn in your indictment. But if I believe
in divine things, I suppose it follows necessarily that I believe in divinities. Is it not so?
It is. I assume that you grant that, as you do not answer. But do we not believe that
d divinities are either gods themselves or the children of the gods? Do you admit that?

MELETUS: I do.

SOCRATES: Then you admit that I believe in divinities. Now, if these divinities are
gods, then, as I say, you are joking and asking a riddle, and asserting that I do not believe in
the gods, and at the same time that I do, since I believe in divinities. But if these divinities
are the illegitimate children of the gods, either by the nymphs or by other mothers, as they
are said to be, then, I ask, what man could believe in the existence of the children of the
e gods, and not in the existence of the gods? That would be as absurd as believing in the existence of the offspring of horses and asses, and not in the existence of horses and asses. You
must have indicted me in this manner, Meletus, either to test me or because you could not
28 find any act of injustice that you could accuse me of with truth. But you will never contrive
to persuade any man with any sense at all that a belief in divine things and things of the
gods does not necessarily involve a belief in divinities, and in the gods.

But in truth, Athenians, I do not think that I need say very much to prove that I have not committed the act of injustice for which Meletus is prosecuting me. What I have said is enough to prove that. But be assured it is certainly true, as I have already told you, that I have aroused much indignation. That is what will cause my condemnation if I am

condemned; not Meletus nor Anytus either, but that prejudice and resentment of the multitude which have been the destruction of many good men before me, and I think will be b
so again. There is no prospect that I shall be the last victim.

Perhaps someone will say: "Are you not ashamed, Socrates, of leading a life
which is very likely now to cause your death?" I should answer him with justice, and
say: "My friend, if you think that a man of any worth at all ought to reckon the chances
of life and death when he acts, or that he ought to think of anything but whether he is
acting justly or unjustly, and as a good or a bad man would act, you are mistaken.
According to you, the demigods who died at Troy would be foolish, and among them c
Achilles, who thought nothing of danger when the alternative was disgrace. For when
his mother—and she was a goddess—addressed him, when he was resolved to slay
Hector, in this fashion, 'My son, if you avenge the death of your comrade Patroclus and
slay Hector, you will die yourself, for fate awaits you next after Hector.' When he heard
this, he scorned danger and death; he feared much more to live a coward and not to d
avenge his friend. 'Let me punish the evildoer and afterwards die,' he said, 'that I may
not remain here by the beaked ships jeered at, encumbering the earth.' "* Do you suppose that he thought of danger or of death? For this, Athenians, I believe to be the truth.
Wherever a man's station is, whether he has chosen it of his own will, or whether he has
been placed at it by his commander, there it is his duty to remain and face the danger
without thinking of death or of any other thing except disgrace.

When the generals whom you chose to command me, Athenians, assigned me my e
station during the battles of Potidaea, Amphipolis, and Delium, I remained where they stationed me and ran the risk of death, like other men. It would be very strange conduct on my
part if I were to desert my station now from fear of death or of any other thing when the god
has commanded me—as I am persuaded that he has done—to spend my life in searching
for wisdom, and in examining myself and others. That would indeed be a very strange 29
thing. Then certainly I might with justice be brought to trial for not believing in the gods,
for I should be disobeying the oracle, and fearing death and thinking myself wise when
I was not wise. For to fear death, my friends, is only to think ourselves wise without really
being wise, for it is to think that we know what we do not know. For no one knows whether
death may not be the greatest good that can happen to man. But men fear it as if they knew
quite well that it was the greatest of evils. And what is this but that shameful ignorance of b
thinking that we know what we do not know? In this matter, too, my friends, perhaps I am
different from the multitude. And if I were to claim to be at all wiser than others, it would
be because, not knowing very much about the other world, I do not think I know. But I do
know very well that it is evil and disgraceful to do an unjust act, and to disobey my superior, whether man or god. I will never do what I know to be evil, and shrink in fear from
what I do not know to be good or evil. Even if you acquit me now, and do not listen to c
Anytus' argument that, if I am to be acquitted, I ought never to have been brought to trial at
all, and that, as it is, you are bound to put me to death because, as he said, if I escape, all
your sons will be utterly corrupted by practicing what Socrates teaches. If you were therefore to say to me, "Socrates, this time we will not listen to Anytus. We will let you go, but
on the condition that you give up this investigation of yours, and philosophy. If you are
found following these pursuits again, you shall die." I say, if you offered to let me go, on
these terms, I should reply: "Athenians, I hold you in the highest regard and affection, but d
I will be persuaded by the god rather than you. As long as I have breath and strength I will
not give up philosophy and exhorting you and declaring the truth to every one of you whom

*Homer, *Iliad*, xviii, 96, 98.

I meet, saying, as I am accustomed, 'My good friend, you are a citizen of Athens, a city
which is very great and very famous for its wisdom and power—are you not ashamed of
e caring so much for the making of money and for fame and prestige, when you neither think
nor care about wisdom and truth and the improvement of your soul?' " If he disputes my
words and says that he does care about these things, I shall not at once release him and go
away: I shall question him and cross-examine him and test him. If I think that he has not
30 attained excellence, though he says that he has, I shall reproach him for undervaluing the
most valuable things, and overvaluing those that are less valuable. This I shall do to everyone whom I meet, young or old, citizen or stranger, but especially to citizens, since they are
more closely related to me. This, you must recognize, the god has commanded me to do.
And I think that no greater good has ever befallen you in the state than my service to the
god. For I spend my whole life in going about and persuading you all to give your first and
b greatest care to the improvement of your souls, and not till you have done that to think of
your bodies or your wealth. And I tell you that wealth does not bring excellence, but that
wealth, and every other good thing which men have, whether in public or in private, comes
from excellence. If then I corrupt the youth by this teaching, these things must be harmful.
But if any man says that I teach anything else, there is nothing in what he says. And therefore, Athenians, I say, whether you are persuaded by Anytus or not, whether you acquit me
c or not, I shall not change my way of life; no, not if I have to die for it many times.

Do not interrupt me, Athenians, with your shouts. Remember the request which
I made to you, and do not interrupt my words. I think that it will profit you to hear them.
I am going to say something more to you, at which you may be inclined to protest, but do
not do that. Be sure that if you put me to death, I who am what I have told you that I am,
you will do yourselves more harm than me. Meletus and Anytus can do me no harm: that
d is impossible, for I am sure it is not allowed that a good man be injured by a worse. He
may indeed kill me, or drive me into exile, or deprive me of my civil rights. Perhaps
Meletus and others think those things great evils. But I do not think so. I think it is a much
greater evil to do what he is doing now, and to try to put a man to death unjustly. And now,
Athenians, I am not arguing in my own defense at all, as you might expect me to do, but
rather in yours in order you may not make a mistake about the gift of the god to you by
e condemning me. For if you put me to death, you will not easily find another who, if I may
use a ludicrous comparison, clings to the state as a sort of gadfly to a horse that is large
and well-bred but rather sluggish because of its size, so that it needs to be aroused. It
31 seems to me that the god has attached me like that to the state, for I am constantly alighting upon you at every point to arouse, persuade, and reproach each of you all day long.
You will not easily find anyone else, my friends, to fill my place; and if you are persuaded
by me, you will spare my life. You are indignant, as drowsy persons are when they are
awakened, and, of course, if you are persuaded by Anytus, you could easily kill me with a
single blow, and then sleep on undisturbed for the rest of your lives, unless the god in his
b care for you sends another to arouse you. And you may easily see that it is the god who
has given me to your city; for it is not human, the way in which I have neglected all my
own interests and allowed my private affairs to be neglected for so many years, while
occupying myself unceasingly in your interests, going to each of you privately, like a
father or an elder brother, trying to persuade him to care for human excellence. There
would have been a reason for it, if I had gained any advantage by this, or if I had been paid
for my exhortations; but you see yourselves that my accusers, though they accuse me of
everything else without shame, have not had the shamelessness to say that I ever either
c exacted or demanded payment. To that they have no witness. And I think that I have sufficient witness to the truth of what I say—my poverty.

Perhaps it may seem strange to you that, though I go about giving this advice privately and meddling in others' affairs, yet I do not venture to come forward in the
assembly and advise the state. You have often heard me speak of my reason for this, and
in many places: it is that I have a certain divine guide, which is what Meletus has cari- d
catured in his indictment. I have had it from childhood. It is a kind of voice which,
whenever I hear it, always turns me back from something which I was going to do, but
never urges me to act. It is this which forbids me to take part in politics. And I think it
does well to forbid me. For, Athenians, it is quite certain that, if I had attempted to take
part in politics, I should have perished at once and long ago without doing any good
either to you or to myself. And do not be indignant with me for telling the truth. There e
is no man who will preserve his life for long, either in Athens or elsewhere, if he firmly
opposes the multitude, and tries to prevent the commission of much injustice and ille-
gality in the state. He who would really fight for justice must do so as a private citizen, 32
not as a political figure, if he is to preserve his life, even for a short time.

I will prove to you that this is so by very strong evidence, not by mere words, but by
what you value more—actions. Listen, then, to what has happened to me, that you may
know that there is no man who could make me consent to commit an unjust act from the
fear of death, but that I would perish at once rather than give way. What I am going to tell
you may be commonplace in the law court; nevertheless, it is true. The only office that
I ever held in the state, Athenians, was that of councilor. When you wished to try the ten b
admirals who did not rescue their men after the battle of Arginusae as a group, which was
illegal, as you all came to think afterwards, the executive committee was composed of
members of the tribe Antiochis, to which I belong.* On that occasion I alone of the committee members opposed your illegal action and gave my vote against you. The orators
were ready to impeach me and arrest me; and you were clamoring and urging them on with
your shouts. But I thought that I ought to face the danger, with law and justice on my side, c
rather than join with you in your unjust proposal, from fear of imprisonment or death. That
was when the state was democratic. When the oligarchy came in, The Thirty sent for me,
with four others, to the council-chamber, and ordered us to bring Leon the Salaminian from
Salamis, that they might put him to death. They were in the habit of frequently giving similar orders to many others, wishing to implicate as many as possible in their crimes. But
then I again proved, not by mere words, but by my actions, that, if I may speak bluntly, I do d
not care a straw for death; but that I do care very much indeed about not doing anything
unjust or impious. That government with all its power did not terrify me into doing anything unjust. When we left the council-chamber, the other four went over to Salamis and
brought Leon across to Athens; I went home. And if the rule of The Thirty had not been
overthrown soon afterwards, I should very likely have been put to death for what I did then. e
Many of you will be my witnesses in this matter.**

*The Council was the administrative body in Athens. Actual administrative functions were performed by an executive committee of the Council, and the members of this committee were recruited from each tribe in turn. The case Socrates is alluding to was that of the admirals who were accused of having failed to rescue the crews of ships that sank during the battle of Arginusae. The six admirals who were actually put on trial were condemned as a group and executed.

**There is evidence that Meletus was one of the four who turned in Leon. Socrates' recalling this earlier lapse from legal procedure is probably also a thrust at Anytus. The Thirty successfully implicated so many Athenians in their crimes that an amnesty was declared, which Anytus strongly favored, in order to enlist wider support for the restored democracy. Thus those who were really implicated could now no longer be prosecuted legally, but Socrates is himself being illegally prosecuted (as he now goes on to suggest) because he was guilty of having associated with such "pupils" as Critias, who was a leader of The Thirty.

Now do you think that I could have remained alive all these years if I had taken part
in public affairs, and had always maintained the cause of justice like a good man, and had
held it a paramount duty, as it is, to do so? Certainly not, Athenians, nor could any other
33 man. But throughout my whole life, both in private and in public, whenever I have had to
take part in public affairs, you will find I have always been the same and have never
yielded unjustly to anyone; no, not to those whom my enemies falsely assert to have been
my pupils. But I was never anyone's teacher. I have never withheld myself from anyone,
b young or old, who was anxious to hear me converse while I was making my investigation;
neither do I converse for payment, and refuse to converse without payment. I am ready to
ask questions of rich and poor alike, and if any man wishes to answer me, and then listen
to what I have to say, he may. And I cannot justly be charged with causing these men to
turn out good or bad, for I never either taught or professed to teach any of them any
knowledge whatever. And if any man asserts that he ever learned or heard anything from
me in private which everyone else did not hear as well as he, be sure that he does not speak
the truth.

Why is it, then, that people delight in spending so much time in my company? You
c have heard why, Athenians. I told you the whole truth when I said that they delight in hearing me examine persons who think that they are wise when they are not wise. It is certainly
very amusing to listen to. And, as I have said, the god has commanded me to examine men,
in oracles and in dreams and in every way in which the divine will was ever declared to
man. This is the truth, Athenians, and if it were not the truth, it would be easily refuted. For
d if it were really the case that I have already corrupted some of the young men, and am now
corrupting others, surely some of them, finding as they grew older that I had given them bad
advice in their youth, would have come forward today to accuse me and take their revenge.
Or if they were unwilling to do so themselves, surely their relatives, their fathers or brothers, or others, would, if I had done them any harm, have remembered it and taken their
e revenge. Certainly I see many of them in court. Here is Crito, of my own district and of my
own age, the father of Critobulus; here is Lysanias of Sphettus, the father of Aeschines; here
is also Antiphon of Cephisus, the father of Epigenes. Then here are others whose brothers
have spent their time in my company—Nicostratus, the son of Theozotides and brother of
Theodotus—and Theodotus is dead, so he at least cannot entreat his brother to be silent;
here is Paralus, the son of Demodocus and the brother of Theages; here is Adeimantus, the
34 son of Ariston, whose brother is Plato here; and Aeantodorus, whose brother is Aristodorus.
And I can name many others to you, some of whom Meletus ought to have called as witnesses in the course of his own speech; but if he forgot to call them then, let him call them
now—I will yield the floor to him—and tell us if he has any such evidence. No, on the contrary, my friends, you will find all these men ready to support me, the corrupter who has
b injured their relatives, as Meletus and Anytus call me. Those of them who have been
already corrupted might perhaps have some reason for supporting me, but what reason can
their relatives have who are grown up, and who are uncorrupted, except the reason of truth
and justice that they know very well that Meletus is lying, and that I am speaking the truth?

Well, my friends, this, and perhaps more like this, is pretty much all I have to offer
in my defense. There may be some one among you who will be indignant when he
c remembers how, even in a less important trial than this, he begged and entreated the
judges, with many tears, to acquit him, and brought forward his children and many of his
friends and relatives in court in order to appeal to your feelings; and then finds that I shall
do none of these things, though I am in what he would think the supreme danger. Perhaps
he will harden himself against me when he notices this; it may make him angry, and he
may cast his vote in anger. If it is so with any of you—I do not suppose that it is, but in
d case it should be so—I think that I should answer him reasonably if I said: "My friend,

I have relatives, too, for, in the words of Homer, I am 'not born of an oak or a rock'* but
of flesh and blood." And so, Athenians, I have relatives, and I have three sons, one of
them nearly grown up, and the other two still children. Yet I will not bring any of them
forward before you and implore you to acquit me. And why will I do none of these
things? It is not from arrogance, Athenians, nor because I lack respect for you—whether e
or not I can face death bravely is another question—but for my own good name, and for
your good name, and for the good name of the whole state. I do not think it right, at my
age and with my reputation, to do anything of that kind. Rightly or wrongly, men have
made up their minds that in some way Socrates is different from the multitude of men.
And it will be shameful if those of you who are thought to excel in wisdom, or in brav-
ery, or in any other excellence, are going to act in this fashion. I have often seen men of
reputation behaving in an extraordinary way at their trial, as if they thought it a terrible
fate to be killed, and as though they expected to live for ever if you did not put them to
death. Such men seem to me to bring shame upon the state, for any stranger would suppose that the best and most eminent Athenians, who are selected by their fellow citizens b
to hold office, and for other honors, are no better than women. Those of you, Athenians,
who have any reputation at all ought not to do these things, and you ought not to allow us
to do them. You should show that you will be much more ready to condemn men who
make the state ridiculous by these pathetic performances than men who remain quiet.

But apart from the question of reputation, my friends, I do not think that it is right
to entreat the judge to acquit us, or to escape condemnation in that way. It is our duty to c
teach and persuade him. He does not sit to give away justice as a favor, but to pronounce
judgment; and he has sworn, not to favor any man whom he would like to favor, but to
judge according to law. And, therefore, we ought not to encourage you in the habit of
breaking your oaths; and you ought not to allow yourselves to fall into this habit, for
then neither you nor we would be acting piously. Therefore, Athenians, do not require
me to do these things, for I believe them to be neither good nor just nor pious; espe- d
cially, do not ask me to do them today when Meletus is prosecuting me for impiety. For
were I to be successful and persuade you by my entreaties to break your oaths, I should
be clearly teaching you to believe that there are no gods, and I should be simply accusing myself by my defense of not believing in them. But, Athenians, that is very far from
the truth. I do believe in the gods as no one of my accusers believes in them; and to you
and to the god I commit my cause to be decided as is best for you and for me.

(He is found guilty by 281 votes to 220.)

I am not indignant at the verdict which you have given, Athenians, for many reasons. I expected that you would find me guilty; and I am not so much surprised at that as e
at the numbers of the votes. I certainly never thought that the majority against me would 36
have been so narrow. But now it seems that if only thirty votes had changed sides,
I should have escaped. So I think that I have escaped Meletus, as it is; and not only have
I escaped him, for it is perfectly clear that if Anytus and Lycon had not come forward to
accuse me, too, he would not have obtained the fifth part of the votes, and would have b
had to pay a fine of a thousand drachmae.

So he proposes death as the penalty. Be it so. And what alternative penalty shall
I propose to you, Athenians?** What I deserve, of course, must I not? What then do
I deserve to pay or to suffer for having determined not to spend my life in ease? I

*Homer, *Odyssey*, xix, 163.

**For certain crimes no penalty was fixed by Athenian law. Having reached a verdict of guilty, the court had still to decide between the alternative penalties proposed by the prosecution and the defense.

neglected the things which most men value, such as wealth, and family interests, and
military commands, and public oratory, and all the civic appointments, and social clubs,
c and political factions, that there are in Athens; for I thought that I was really too honest
a man to preserve my life if I engaged in these affairs. So I did not go where I should
have done no good either to you or to myself. I went, instead, to each one of you privately to do him, as I say, the greatest of benefits, and tried to persuade him not to think
of his affairs until he had thought of himself and tried to make himself as good and wise
as possible, nor to think of the affairs of Athens until he had thought of Athens herself;
and to care for other things in the same manner. Then what do I deserve for such a life?
d Something good, Athenians, if I am really to propose what I deserve; and something
good which it would be suitable for me to receive. Then what is a suitable reward to be
given to a poor benefactor who requires leisure to exhort you? There is no reward,
Athenians, so suitable for him as receiving free meals in the prytaneum. It is a much
more suitable reward for him than for any of you who has won a victory at the Olympic
games with his horse or his chariots. Such a man only makes you seem happy, but I
e make you really happy; he is not in want, and I am. So if I am to propose the penalty
37 which I really deserve, I propose this—free meals in the prytaneum.

Perhaps you think me stubborn and arrogant in what I am saying now, as in what
I said about the entreaties and tears. It is not so, Athenians. It is rather that I am convinced that I never wronged any man voluntarily, though I cannot persuade you of that,
since we have conversed together only a little time. If there were a law at Athens, as
b there is elsewhere, not to finish a trial of life and death in a single day, I think that I
could have persuaded you; but now it is not easy in so short a time to clear myself of
great prejudices. But when I am persuaded that I have never wronged any man, I shall
certainly not wrong myself, or admit that I deserve to suffer any evil, or propose any
evil for myself as a penalty. Why should I? Lest I should suffer the penalty which
Meletus proposes when I say that I do not know whether it is a good or an evil? Shall I
choose instead of it something which I know to be an evil, and propose that as a
c penalty? Shall I propose imprisonment? And why should I pass the rest of my days in
prison, the slave of successive officials? Or shall I propose a fine, with imprisonment
until it is paid? I have told you why I will not do that. I should have to remain in prison,
for I have no money to pay a fine with. Shall I then propose exile? Perhaps you would
agree to that. Life would indeed be very dear to me if I were unreasonable enough to
d expect that strangers would cheerfully tolerate my discussions and arguments when you
who are my fellow citizens cannot endure them, and have found them so irksome and
odious to you that you are seeking now to be relieved of them. No, indeed, Athenians,
that is not likely. A fine life I should lead for an old man if I were to withdraw from
Athens and pass the rest of my days in wandering from city to city, and continually
being expelled. For I know very well that the young men will listen to me wherever I go,
as they do here. If I drive them away, they will persuade their elders to expel me; if I do
e not drive them away, their fathers and other relatives will expel me for their sakes.

Perhaps someone will say, "Why cannot you withdraw from Athens, Socrates, and
hold your peace?" It is the most difficult thing in the world to make you understand why
I cannot do that. If I say that I cannot hold my peace because that would be to disobey the
god, you will think that I am not in earnest and will not believe me. And if I tell you that
38 no greater good can happen to a man than to discuss human excellence every day and the
other matters about which you have heard me arguing and examining myself and others
and that an unexamined life is not worth living, then you will believe me still less. But
that is so, my friends, though it is not easy to persuade you. And, what is more, I am not

Despite refuting his accusers (as recorded in the *Apology*), Socrates was found guilty of impiety toward the gods and of corrupting the youth. He was sentenced to die by drinking the poison hemlock. (©*PHAS*/Getty)

accustomed to think that I deserve anything evil. If I had been rich, I would have proposed as large a fine as I could pay: that would have done me no harm. But I am not rich b
enough to pay a fine unless you are willing to fix it at a sum within my means. Perhaps I
could pay you a mina, so I propose that. Plato here, Athenians, and Crito, and Critobulus,
and Apollodorus bid me propose thirty minae, and they guarantee its payment. So I propose thirty minae. Their security will be sufficient to you for the money. c

(He is condemned to death.)

You have not gained very much time, Athenians, and at the price of the slurs of
those who wish to revile the state. And they will say that you put Socrates, a wise man,
to death. For they will certainly call me wise, whether I am wise or not, when they want
to reproach you. If you had waited for a little while, your wishes would have been fulfilled in the course of nature; for you see that I am an old man, far advanced in years,
and near to death. I am saying this not to all of you, only to those who have voted for my
death. And to them I have something else to say. Perhaps, my friends, you think that I d
have been convicted because I was wanting in the arguments by which I could have persuaded you to acquit me, if I had thought it right to do or to say anything to escape punishment. It is not so. I have been convicted because I was wanting, not in arguments, but
in impudence and shamelessness—because I would not plead before you as you would
have liked to hear me plead, or appeal to you with weeping and wailing, or say and do e

many other things which I maintain are unworthy of me, but which you have been
accustomed to from other men. But when I was defending myself, I thought that I ought
not to do anything unworthy of a free man because of the danger which I ran, and I have
not changed my mind now. I would very much rather defend myself as I did, and die,
39 than as you would have had me do, and live. Both in a lawsuit and in war, there are some
things which neither I nor any other man may do in order to escape from death. In battle, a man often sees that he may at least escape from death by throwing down his arms
and falling on his knees before the pursuer to beg for his life. And there are many other
ways of avoiding death in every danger if a man is willing to say and to do anything.
b But, my friends, I think that it is a much harder thing to escape from wickedness than
from death, for wickedness is swifter than death. And now I, who am old and slow, have
been overtaken by the slower pursuer: and my accusers, who are clever and swift, have
been overtaken by the swifter pursuer—wickedness. And now I shall go away, sentenced by you to death; they will go away, sentenced by truth to wickedness and injustice. And I abide by this award as well as they. Perhaps it was right for these things to be
so. I think that they are fairly balanced.

c And now I wish to prophesy to you, Athenians, who have condemned me. For
I am going to die, and that is the time when men have most prophetic power. And I
prophesy to you who have sentenced me to death that a far more severe punishment
than you have inflicted on me will surely overtake you as soon as I am dead. You have
done this thing, thinking that you will be relieved from having to give an account of
d your lives. But I say that the result will be very different. There will be more men who
will call you to account, whom I have held back, though you did not recognize it. And
they will be harsher toward you than I have been, for they will be younger, and you will
be more indignant with them. For if you think that you will restrain men from reproaching you for not living as you should, by putting them to death, you are very much
mistaken. That way of escape is neither possible nor honorable. It is much more honorable and much easier not to suppress others, but to make yourselves as good as you can.
e This is my parting prophecy to you who have condemned me.

With you who have acquitted me I should like to discuss this thing that has
happened, while the authorities are busy, and before I go to the place where I have to
die. So, remain with me until I go: there is no reason why we should not talk with
40 each other while it is possible. I wish to explain to you, as my friends, the meaning
of what has happened to me. An amazing thing has happened to me, judges—for
I am right in calling you judges.* The prophetic guide has been constantly with me
all through my life till now, opposing me even in trivial matters if I were not going to
act rightly. And now you yourselves see what has happened to me—a thing which
b might be thought, and which is sometimes actually reckoned, the supreme evil. But
the divine guide did not oppose me when I was leaving my house in the morning, nor
when I was coming up here to the court, nor at any point in my speech when I was
going to say anything; though at other times it has often stopped me in the very act
of speaking. But now, in this matter, it has never once opposed me, either in my
words or my actions. I will tell you what I believe to be the reason. This thing that
c has come upon me must be a good; and those of us who think that death is an evil
must needs be mistaken. I have a clear proof that that is so; for my accustomed guide

*The form of address hitherto has always been "Athenians," or "my friends." The "judges" in an Athenian court were simply the members of the jury.

would certainly have opposed me if I had not been going to meet with something
good.

And if we reflect in another way, we shall see that we may well hope that death is
a good. For the state of death is one of two things: either the dead man wholly ceases to
be and loses all consciousness or, as we are told, it is a change and a migration of the
soul to another place. And if death is the absence of all consciousness, and like the sleep
of one whose slumbers are unbroken by any dreams, it will be a wonderful gain. For if d
a man had to select that night in which he slept so soundly that he did not even dream,
and had to compare with it all the other nights and days of his life, and then had to say
how many days and nights in his life he had spent better and more pleasantly than this
night, I think that a private person, nay, even the Great King of Persia himself, would e
find them easy to count, compared with the others. If that is the nature of death, I for
one count it a gain. For then it appears that all time is nothing more than a single night.
But if death is a journey to another place, and what we are told is true—that all who
have died are there—what good could be greater than this, my judges? Would a journey
not be worth taking, at the end of which, in the other world, we should be delivered
from the pretended judges here and should find the true judges who are said to sit in 41
judgment below, such as Minos and Rhadamanthus and Aeacus and Triptolemus, and
the other demigods who were just in their own lives? Or what would you not give to
converse with Orpheus and Musaeus and Hesiod and Homer? I am willing to die many
times if this be true. And for my own part I should find it wonderful to meet there
Palamedes, and Ajax the son of Telamon, and the other men of old who have died b
through an unjust judgment, and to compare my experiences with theirs. That I think
would be no small pleasure. And, above all, I could spend my time in examining those
who are there, as I examine men here, and in finding out which of them is wise, and
which of them thinks himself wise when he is not wise. What would we not give, my
judges, to be able to examine the leader of the great expedition against Troy, or
Odysseus, or Sisyphus, or countless other men and women whom we could name? It c
would be an inexpressible happiness to converse with them and to live with them and to
examine them. Assuredly there they do not put men to death for doing that. For besides
the other ways in which they are happier than we are, they are immortal, at least if what
we are told is true.

And you too, judges, must face death hopefully, and believe this one truth, that no
evil can happen to a good man, either in life or after death. His affairs are not neglected d
by the gods; and what has happened to me today has not happened by chance. I am persuaded that it was better for me to die now, and to be released from trouble; and that was
the reason why the guide never turned me back. And so I am not at all angry with my
accusers or with those who have condemned me to die. Yet it was not with this in mind
that they accused me and condemned me, but meaning to do me an injury. So far I may e
blame them.

Yet I have one request to make of them. When my sons grow up, punish them, my
friends, and harass them in the same way that I have harassed you, if they seem to you
to care for riches or for any other thing more than excellence; and if they think that they
are something when they are really nothing, reproach them, as I have reproached you,
for not caring for what they should, and for thinking that they are something when
really they are nothing. And if you will do this, I myself and my sons will have received 42
justice from you.

But now the time has come, and we must go away—I to die, and you to live.
Which is better is known to the god alone.

CRITO

Characters
Socrates
Crito
Scene—The Prison of Socrates

43 Socrates: Why have you come at this hour, Crito? Is it not still early?

Crito: Yes, very early.

Socrates: About what time is it?

Crito: It is just daybreak.

Socrates: I wonder that the jailer was willing to let you in.

Crito: He knows me now, Socrates; I come here so often, and besides, I have given him a tip.

Socrates: Have you been here long?

Crito: Yes, some time.

b Socrates: Then why did you sit down without speaking? Why did you not wake me at once?

Crito: Indeed, Socrates, I wish that I myself were not so sleepless and sorrowful. But I have been wondering to see how soundly you sleep. And I purposely did not wake you, for I was anxious not to disturb your repose. Often before, all through your life, I have thought that your temperament was a happy one; and I think so more than ever now when I see how easily and calmly you bear the calamity that has come to you.

c Socrates: Nay, Crito, it would be absurd if at my age I were disturbed at having to die.

Crito: Other men as old are overtaken by similar calamities, Socrates; but their age does not save them from being disturbed by their fate.

Socrates: That is so; but tell me why are you here so early? Crito. I am the bearer of sad news, Socrates; not sad, it seems, for you, but for me and for all your friends, both sad and hard to bear; and for none of them, I think, is it as hard to bear as it is for me.

Socrates: What is it? Has the ship come from Delos, at the arrival of which I am
d to die?

Crito: No, it has not actually arrived, but I think that it will be here today, from the news which certain persons have brought from Sunium, who left it there. It is clear from their report that it will be here today; and so, Socrates, tomorrow your life will have to end.

44 Socrates: Well, Crito, may it end well. Be it so, if so the gods will. But I do not think that the ship will be here today,

Crito: Why do you suppose not?

Socrates: I will tell you. I am to die on the day after the ship arrives, am I not?*

Crito: That is what the authorities say.

Socrates: Then I do not think that it will come today, but tomorrow. I am counting on a dream I had a little while ago in the night, so it seems to be fortunate that you did not wake me.

*Criminals could not be put to death while the sacred ship was away on its voyage.

Plato: *Euthyphro,* Apology, Crito, translated by F.J. Church (Pearson/Library of the Liberal Arts, 1987).

Crito: And what was this dream?

Socrates: A fair and beautiful woman, clad in white, seemed to come to me, and call me and say, "O Socrates—On the third day shall you fertile Phthia reach."* b

Crito: What a strange dream, Socrates!

Socrates: But its meaning is clear, at least to me, Crito.

Crito: Yes, too clear, it seems. But, O my good Socrates, I beg you for the last time to listen to me and save yourself. For to me your death will be more than a single disaster; not only shall I lose a friend the like of whom I shall never find again, but many persons who do not know you and me well will think that I might have saved you if I ad been willing to spend money, but that I neglected to do so. And what reputation could be c more disgraceful than the reputation of caring more for money than for one's friends? The public will never believe that we were anxious to save you, but that you yourself refused to escape.

Socrates: But, my dear Crito, why should we care so much about public opinion? Reasonable men, of whose opinion it is worth our while to think, will believe that we acted as we really did.

Crito: But you see, Socrates, that it is necessary to care about public opinion, too. d This very thing that has happened to you proves that the multitude can do a man not the least, but almost the greatest harm, if he is falsely accused to them.

Socrates: I wish that the multitude were able to do a man the greatest harm, Crito, for then they would be able to do him the greatest good, too. That would have been fine. But, as it is, they can do neither. They cannot make a man either wise or foolish: they act wholly at random.

Crito: Well, as you wish. But tell me this, Socrates. You surely are not anxious e about me and your other friends, and afraid lest, if you escape, the informers would say that we stole you away, and get us into trouble, and involve us in a great deal of expense, or perhaps in the loss of all our property, and, it may be, bring some other punishment upon us besides? If you have any fear of that kind, dismiss it. For of course we are 45 bound to run these risks, and still greater risks than these, if necessary, in saving you. So do not, I beg you, refuse to listen to me.

Socrates: I am anxious about that, Crito, and about much besides.

Crito: Then have no fear on that score. There are men who, for no very large sum, are ready to bring you out of prison into safety. And then, you know, these informers are cheaply bought, and there would be no need to spend much upon them. My fortune is at your service, and I think that it is adequate; and if you have any feeling about making use b of my money, there are strangers in Athens whom you know, ready to use theirs; and one of them, Simmias of Thebes, has actually brought enough for this very purpose. And Cebes and many others are ready, too. And therefore, I repeat, do not shrink from saving yourself on that ground. And do not let what you said in the court—that if you went into exile you would not know what to do with yourself—stand in your way; for there are many places for you to go to, where you will be welcomed. If you choose to go to Thessaly, I have friends there who will make much of you and protect you from any c annoyance from the people of Thessaly.

And besides, Socrates, I think that you will be doing what is unjust if you abandon your life when you might preserve it. You are simply playing into your enemies' hands; it is exactly what they wanted—to destroy you. And what is more, to me you seem to be abandoning your children, too. You will leave them to take their chance in

*Homer, *Iliad*, ix, 363.

d life, as far as you are concerned, when you might bring them up and educate them. Most
likely their fate will be the usual fate of children who are left orphans. But you ought
not to bring children into the world unless you mean to take the trouble of bringing
them up and educating them. It seems to me that you are choosing the easy way, and not
the way of a good and brave man, as you ought, when you have been talking all your life
e long of the value that you set upon human excellence. For my part, I feel ashamed both
for you and for us who are your friends. Men will think that the whole thing which has
happened to you—your appearance in court to face trial, when you need not have
appeared at all; the very way in which the trial was conducted; and then last of all this,
the crowning absurdity of the whole affair—is due to our cowardice. It will look as if
46 we had shirked the danger out of miserable cowardice; for we did not save you, and you
did not save yourself, when it was quite possible to do so if we had been good for anything at all. Take care, Socrates, lest these things be not evil only, but also dishonorable
to you and to us. Reflect, then, or rather the time for reflection is past; we must make up
our minds. And there is only one plan possible. Everything must be done tonight. If we
delay any longer, we are lost. Socrates, I implore you not to refuse to listen to me.

b Socrates: My dear Crito, if your anxiety to save me be right, it is most valuable;
but if not, the greater it is the harder it will be to cope with. We must reflect, then,
whether we are to do as you say or not; for I am still what I always have been—a man
who will accept no argument but that which on reflection I find to be truest. I cannot
cast aside my former arguments because this misfortune has come to me. They seem to
c me to be as true as ever they were, and I respect and honor the same ones as I used to.
And if we have no better argument to substitute for them, I certainly shall not agree to
your proposal, not even though the power of the multitude should scare us with fresh
terrors, as children are scared with hobgoblins, and inflict upon us new fines and
imprisonments, and deaths. What is the most appropriate way of examining the question? Shall we go back first to what you say about opinions, and ask if we used to be
d right in thinking that we ought to pay attention to some opinions, and not to others?
Were we right in saying so before I was condemned to die, and has it now become
apparent that we were talking at random and arguing for the sake of argument, and that
it was really nothing but playful nonsense? I am anxious, Crito, to examine our former
argument with your help, and to see whether my present circumstance will appear to me
to have affected its truth in any way or not; and whether we are to set it aside, or to yield
assent to it. Those of us who thought at all seriously always used to say, I think, exactly
e what I said just now, namely, that we ought to respect some of the opinions which men
form, and not others. Tell me, Crito, I beg you, do you not think that they were right?
47 For you in all probability will not have to die tomorrow, and your judgment will not be
biased by that circumstance. Reflect, then, do you not think it reasonable to say that we
should not respect all the opinions of men but only some, nor the opinions of all men
but only of some men? What do you think? Is not this true?

Crito: It is.

Socrates: And we should respect the good opinions, and not the worthless ones?

Crito: Yes.

Socrates: But the good opinions are those of the wise, and the worthless ones
those of the foolish?

Crito: Of course.

Socrates: And what did we say about this? Does a man who is in training, and
b who is serious about it, pay attention to the praise and blame and opinion of all men, or
only of the one man who is a doctor or a trainer?

Crito: He pays attention only to the opinion of the one man.

Socrates: Then he ought to fear the blame and welcome the praise of this one man, not of the multitude?

Crito: Clearly.

Socrates: Then he must act and exercise, and eat and drink in whatever way the one man who is his director, and who understands the matter, tells him; not as others tell him?

Crito: That is so.

Socrates: Good. But if he disobeys this one man, and disregards his opinion and c
his praise, and respects instead what the many say, who understand nothing of the matter, will he not suffer for it?

Crito: Of course he will.

Socrates: And how will he suffer? In what way and in what part of himself?

Crito: Of course in his body. That is disabled.

Socrates: You are right. And, Crito, to be brief, is it not the same in everything? And, therefore, in questions of justice and injustice, and of the base and the honorable, and of good and evil, which we are now examining, ought we to follow the opinion of
the many and fear that, or the opinion of the one man who understands these matters (if d
we can find him), and feel more shame and fear before him than before all other men? For if we do not follow him, we shall corrupt and maim that part of us which, we used to say, is improved by justice and disabled by injustice. Or is this not so?

Crito: No, Socrates, I agree with you.

Socrates: Now, if, by listening to the opinions of those who do not understand,
we disable that part of us which is improved by health and corrupted by disease, is our e
life worth living when it is corrupt? It is the body, is it not?

Crito: Yes.

Socrates: Is life worth living with the body corrupted and crippled?

Crito: No, certainly not.

Socrates: Then is life worth living when that part of us which is maimed by injustice and benefited by justice is corrupt? Or do we consider that part of us, whatever
it is, which has to do with justice and injustice to be of less consequence than our body? 48

Crito: No, certainly not.

Socrates: But more valuable?

Crito: Yes, much more so.

Socrates: Then, my good friend, we must not think so much of what the many will say of us; we must think of what the one man who understands justice and injustice, and of what truth herself will say of us. And so you are mistaken, to begin with, when you invite us to regard the opinion of the multitude concerning the just and the honorable and the good, and their opposites. But, it may be said, the multitude can put us to death?

Crito: Yes, that is evident. That may be said, Socrates. b

Socrates: True. But, my good friend, to me it appears that the conclusion which we have just reached is the same as our conclusion of former times. Now consider whether we still hold to the belief that we should set the highest value, not on living, but on living well?

Crito: Yes, we do.

Socrates: And living well and honorably and justly mean the same thing: do we hold to that or not?

Crito: We do.

Socrates: Then, starting from these premises, we have to consider whether it is just
or not for me to try to escape from prison, without the consent of the Athenians. If we find c

that it is just, we will try; if not, we will give up the idea. I am afraid that considerations of expense, and of reputation, and of bringing up my children, of which you talk, Crito, are only the opinions of the many, who casually put men to death, and who would, if they could, as casually bring them to life again, without a thought. But reason, which is our guide, shows us that we can have nothing to consider but the question which I asked just now—namely, shall we be acting justly if we give money and thanks to the men who are
d to aid me in escaping, and if we ourselves take our respective parts in my escape? Or shall we in truth be acting unjustly if we do all this? And if we find that we should be acting unjustly, then we must not take any account either of death, or of any other evil that may be the consequence of remaining here, where we are, but only of acting unjustly.

CRITO: I think that you are right, Socrates. But what are we to do?

SOCRATES: Let us examine this question together, my friend, and if you can con-
e tradict anything that I say, do so, and I shall be persuaded. But if you cannot, do not go on repeating to me any longer, my dear friend, that I should escape without the consent of the Athenians. I am very anxious to act with your approval and consent. I do not want you to think me mistaken. But now tell me if you agree with the premise from which
49 I start, and try to answer my questions as you think best.

CRITO: I will try.

SOCRATES: Ought we never to act unjustly voluntarily? Or may we act unjustly in some ways, and not in others? Is it the case, as we have often agreed in former times, that it is never either good or honorable to act unjustly? Or have all our former conclusions been overturned in these few days; and did we at our age fail to recognize all
b along, when we were seriously conversing with each other, that we were no better than children? Is not what we used to say most certainly the truth, whether the multitude agrees with us or not? Is not acting unjustly evil and shameful in every case, whether we incur a heavier or a lighter punishment as the consequence? Do we believe that?

CRITO: We do.

SOCRATES: Then we ought never to act unjustly?

CRITO: Certainly not.

SOCRATES: If we ought never to act unjustly at all, ought we to repay injustice with injustice, as the multitude thinks we may?

c CRITO: Clearly not.

SOCRATES: Well, then, Crito, ought we to do evil to anyone?

CRITO: Certainly I think not, Socrates.

SOCRATES: And is it just to repay evil with evil, as the multitude thinks, or unjust?

CRITO: Certainly it is unjust.

SOCRATES: For there is no difference, is there, between doing evil to a man and acting unjustly?

CRITO: True.

SOCRATES: Then we ought not to repay injustice with injustice or to do harm to
d any man, no matter what we may have suffered from him. And in conceding this, Crito, be careful that you do not concede more than you mean. For I know that only a few men hold, or ever will hold, this opinion. And so those who hold it and those who do not have no common ground of argument; they can of necessity only look with contempt on each other's belief. Do you therefore consider very carefully whether or not you agree with me and share my opinion. Are we to start in our inquiry from the premise that it is never right either to act unjustly, or to repay injustice with injustice, or to avenge ourselves on any man who harms us, by harming him in return? Or do you disagree with
e me and dissent from my premise? I myself have believed in it for a long time, and

I believe in it still. But if you differ in any way, explain to me how. If you still hold to
our former opinion, listen to my next point.

Crito: Yes, I hold to it, and I agree with you. Go on.

Socrates: Then, my next point, or rather my next question, is this: Ought a man
to carry out his just agreements, or may he shuffle out of them?

Crito: He ought to carry them out.

Socrates: Then consider. If I escape without the state's consent, shall I be injuring
those whom I ought least to injure, or not? Shall I be abiding by my just agreements or not? 50

Crito: I cannot answer your question, Socrates. I do not understand it.

Socrates: Consider it in this way. Suppose the laws and the commonwealth were to
come and appear to me as I was preparing to run away (if that is the right phrase
to describe my escape) and were to ask, "Tell us, Socrates, what have you in your mind to
do? What do you mean by trying to escape but to destroy us, the laws and the whole state, b
so far as you are able? Do you think that a state can exist and not be overthrown, in which
the decisions of law are of no force, and are disregarded and undermined by private
individuals?" How shall we answer questions like that, Crito? Much might be said, especially by an orator, in defense of the law which makes judicial decisions supreme. Shall I
reply, "But the state has injured me by judging my case unjustly?" Shall we say that? c

Crito: Certainly we will, Socrates.

Socrates: And suppose the laws were to reply, "Was that our agreement? Or was
it that you would abide by whatever judgments the state should pronounce?" And if we
were surprised by their words, perhaps they would say, "Socrates, don't be surprised by
our words, but answer us; you yourself are accustomed to ask questions and to answer
them. What complaint have you against us and the state, that you are trying to destroy d
us? Are we not, first of all, your parents? Through us your father took your mother and
brought you into the world. Tell us, have you any fault to find with those of us that are
the laws of marriage?" "I have none," I should reply. "Or have you any fault to find with
those of us that regulate the raising of the child and the education which you, like
others, received? Did we not do well in telling your father to educate you in music and
athletics?" "You did," I should say. "Well, then, since you were brought into the world e
and raised and educated by us, how, in the first place, can you deny that you are our
child and our slave, as your fathers were before you? And if this be so, do you think that
your rights are on a level with ours? Do you think that you have a right to retaliate if we
should try to do anything to you? You had not the same rights that your father had, or
that your master would have had if you had been a slave. You had no right to retaliate if
they ill-treated you, or to answer them if they scolded you, or to strike them back if they
struck you, or to repay them evil with evil in any way. And do you think that you may 51
retaliate in the case of your country and its laws? If we try to destroy you, because we
think it just, will you in return do all that you can to destroy us, the laws, and your country, and say that in so doing you are acting justly—you, the man who really thinks so
much of excellence? Or are you too wise to see that your country is worthier, more to be
revered, more sacred, and held in higher honor both by the gods and by all men of
understanding, than your father and your mother and all your other ancestors; and that
you ought to reverence it, and to submit to it, and to approach it more humbly when it is b
angry with you than you would approach your father; and either to do whatever it tells
you to do or to persuade it to excuse you; and to obey in silence if it orders you to
endure flogging or imprisonment, or if it sends you to battle to be wounded or to die?
That is just. You must not give way, nor retreat, nor desert your station. In war, and in
the court of justice, and everywhere, you must do whatever your state and your country c

tell you to do, or you must persuade them that their commands are unjust. But it is impious to use violence against your father or your mother; and much more impious to use violence against your country." What answer shall we make, Crito? Shall we say that the laws speak the truth, or not?

CRITO: I think that they do.

SOCRATES: "Then consider, Socrates," perhaps they would say, "if we are right in
saying that by attempting to escape you are attempting an injustice. We brought you
into the world, we raised you, we educated you, we gave you and every other citizen a
d share of all the good things we could. Yet we proclaim that if any man of the Athenians
is dissatisfied with us, he may take his goods and go away wherever he pleases; we give
that privilege to every man who chooses to avail himself of it, so soon as he has reached
manhood, and sees us, the laws, and the administration of our state. No one of us stands
in his way or forbids him to take his goods and go wherever he likes, whether it be to an
Athenian colony or to any foreign country, if he is dissatisfied with us and with the
e state. But we say that every man of you who remains here, seeing how we administer
justice, and how we govern the state in other matters, has agreed, by the very fact of
remaining here, to do whatsoever we tell him. And, we say, he who disobeys us acts
unjustly on three counts: he disobeys us who are his parents, and he disobeys us who
reared him, and he disobeys us after he has agreed to obey us, without persuading us
that we are wrong. Yet we did not tell him sternly to do whatever we told him. We
52 offered him an alternative; we gave him his choice either to obey us or to convince us
that we were wrong; but he does neither.

"These are the charges, Socrates, to which we say that you will expose yourself if
you do what you intend; and you are more exposed to these charges than other
Athenians." And if I were to ask, "Why?" they might retort with justice that I have
bound myself by the agreement with them more than other Athenians. They would say,
b "Socrates, we have very strong evidence that you were satisfied with us and with the
state. You would not have been content to stay at home in it more than other Athenians
unless you had been satisfied with it more than they. You never went away from Athens
to the festivals, nor elsewhere except on military service; you never made other journeys
like other men; you had no desire to see other states or other laws; you were contented
c with us and our state; so strongly did you prefer us, and agree to be governed by us. And
what is more, you had children in this city, you found it so satisfactory. Besides, if you
had wished, you might at your trial have offered to go into exile. At that time you could
have done with the state's consent what you are trying now to do without it. But then
you gloried in being willing to die. You said that you preferred death to exile. And now
you do not honor those words: you do not respect us, the laws, for you are trying to
d destroy us; and you are acting just as a miserable slave would act, trying to run away,
and breaking the contracts and agreement which you made to live as our citizen. First,
therefore, answer this question. Are we right, or are we wrong, in saying that you have
agreed not in mere words, but in your actions, to live under our government?" What are
we to say, Crito? Must we not admit that it is true?

CRITO: We must, Socrates.

SOCRATES: Then they would say, "Are you not breaking your contracts and agree-
e ments with us? And you were not led to make them by force or by fraud. You did not
have to make up your mind in a hurry. You had seventy years in which you might have
gone away if you had been dissatisfied with us, or if the agreement had seemed to you
unjust. But you preferred neither Sparta nor Crete, though you are fond of saying that
they are well governed, nor any other state, either of the Greeks or the Barbarians. You

went away from Athens less than the lame and the blind and the crippled. Clearly you, 53
far more than other Athenians, were satisfied with the state, and also with us who are its
laws; for who would be satisfied with a state which had no laws? And now will you not
abide by your agreement? If you take our advice, you will, Socrates; then you will not
make yourself ridiculous by going away from Athens.

"Reflect now. What good will you do yourself or your friends by thus trans-
gressing and breaking your agreement? It is tolerably certain that they, on their part, b
will at least run the risk of exile, and of losing their civil rights, or of forfeiting their
property. You yourself might go to one of the neighboring states, to Thebes or to
Megara, for instance—for both of them are well governed—but, Socrates, you will
come as an enemy to these governments, and all who care for their city will look
askance at you, and think that you are a subverter of law. You will confirm the judges c
in their opinion, and make it seem that their verdict was a just one. For a man who is
a subverter of law may well be supposed to be a corrupter of the young and thoughtless. Then will you avoid well-governed states and civilized men? Will life be worth
having, if you do? Will you associate with such men, and converse without shame—
about what, Socrates? About the things which you talk of here? Will you tell them
that excellence and justice and institutions and law are the most valuable things that
men can have? And do you not think that that will be a disgraceful thing for Socrates? d
You ought to think so. But you will leave these places; you will go to the friends of
Crito in Thessaly. For there is found the greatest disorder and license, and very likely

Socrates' Prison, near the Acropolis, Athens. The traditional site of the prison where Socrates was held while awaiting execution. (*Forrest E. Baird*)

they will be delighted to hear of the ludicrous way in which you escaped from prison,
dressed up in peasant's clothes, or in some other disguise which people put on when
they are running away, and with your appearance altered. But will no one say how
you, an old man, with probably only a few more years to live, clung so greedily to life
e that you dared to break the highest laws? Perhaps not, if you do not annoy them. But
if you do, Socrates, you will hear much that will make you blush. You will pass your
life as the flatterer and the slave of all men; and what will you be doing but feasting in
Thessaly?* It will be as if you had made a journey to Thessaly for a banquet. And
54 where will be all our old arguments about justice and excellence then? But you wish
to live for the sake of your children? You want to bring them up and educate them?
What? Will you take them with you to Thessaly, and bring them up and educate them
there? Will you make them strangers to their own country, that you may bestow this
benefit of exile on them too? Or supposing that you leave them in Athens, will they be
brought up and educated better if you are alive, though you are not with them? Yes,
your friends will take care of them. Will your friends take care of them if you make a
b journey to Thessaly, and not if you make a journey to Hades? You ought not to think
that, at least if those who call themselves your friends are worth anything at all.

"No, Socrates, be persuaded by us who have reared you. Think neither of children
nor of life, nor of any other thing before justice, so that when you come to the other
world you may be able to make your defense before the rulers who sit in judgment
there. It is clear that neither you nor any of your friends will be happier, or more just, or
more pious in this life, if you do this thing, nor will you be happier after you are dead.
c Now you will go away a victim of the injustice, not of the laws, but of men. But if you
repay evil with evil, and injustice with injustice in this shameful way, and break your
agreements and covenants with us, and injure those whom you should least injure, yourself and your friends and your country and us, and so escape, then we shall be angry
with you while you live, and when you die our brothers, the laws in Hades, will not
receive you kindly; for they will know that on earth you did all that you could to destroy
d us. Listen then to us, and let not Crito persuade you to do as he says."

Be sure, my dear friend Crito, that this is what I seem to hear, as the worshippers
of Cybele seem, in their passion, to hear the music of flutes; and the sound of these
arguments rings so loudly in my ears, that I cannot hear any other arguments. And I feel
sure that if you try to change my mind you will speak in vain. Nevertheless, if you think
that you will succeed, speak.

CRITO: I have nothing more to say, Socrates.

e SOCRATES: Then let it be, Crito, and let us do as I say, since the god is our guide.

*The Athenians disdained the Thessalians as heavy eaters and drinkers.

PHAEDO (selections)

Characters

Phaedo (The Narrator)
Apollodorus
Cebes
Echecrates
Crito
Socrates
Simmias
The Servent of the Eleven
Scene—The Prison of Socrates

[Socrates is speaking] . . . My dear Cebes, if all things in which there is any life were to
die, and when they were dead were to remain in that form and not come to life again,
would not the necessary result be that everything at last would be dead, and nothing
alive? For if living things were generated from other sources than death, and were to 72d
die, the result is inevitable that all things would be consumed by death. Is it not so?

It is indeed, I think, Socrates, said Cebes; I think that what you say is perfectly true.

Yes, Cebes, he said, I think it is certainly so. We are not misled into this conclusion. The dead do come to life again, and the living are generated from them, and the
souls of the dead exist; and with the souls of the good it is well, and with the souls of the e
evil it is evil.

And besides, Socrates, rejoined Cebes, if the doctrine which you are fond of stating, that our learning is only a process of recollection, be true, then I suppose we must
have learned at some former time what we recollect now. And that would be impossible
unless our souls had existed somewhere before they came into this human form. So that 73
is another reason for believing the soul immortal.

But, Cebes, interrupted Simmias, what are the proofs of that? Recall them to me; I am not very clear about them at present.

One argument, answered Cebes, and the strongest of all, is that if you question
men about anything in the right way, they will answer you correctly of themselves. But
they would not have been able to do that unless they had had within themselves knowl- b
edge and right reason. Again, show them such things as geometrical diagrams, and the
proof of the doctrine is complete.

And if that does not convince you, Simmias, said Socrates, look at the matter in another way and see if you agree then. You have doubts, I know, how what is called knowledge can be recollection.

Nay, replied Simmias, I do not doubt. But I want to recollect the argument about recollection. What Cebes undertook to explain has nearly brought your theory back to me and convinced me. But I am nonetheless ready to hear you undertake to explain it.

In this way, he returned. We are agreed, I suppose, that if a man remembers any- c
thing, he must have known it at some previous time.

Certainly, he said.

Plato, *Phaedo* , translated by F.J. Church (Pearson/Library of the Liberal Arts, 1951).

And are we agreed that when knowledge comes in the following way, it is recollection? When a man has seen or heard anything, or has perceived it by some other sense, and then knows not that thing only, but has also in his mind an impression of
d some other thing, of which the knowledge is quite different, are we not right in saying that he remembers the thing of which he has an impression in his mind?

What do you mean?

I mean this. The knowledge of a man is different from the knowledge of a lyre, is it not?

Certainly.

And you know that when lovers see a lyre, or a garment, or anything that their favorites are wont to use, they have this feeling. They know the lyre, and in their mind they receive the image of the youth whose the lyre was. That is recollection. For instance, someone seeing Simmias often is reminded of Cebes; and there are endless examples of the same thing.

Indeed there are, said Simmias.

d Is not that a kind of recollection, he said; and more especially when a man has this feeling with reference to things which the lapse of time and inattention have made him forget?

Yes, certainly, he replied.

Well, he went on, is it possible to recollect a man on seeing the picture of a horse, or the picture of a lyre? Or to recall Simmias on seeing a picture of Cebes?

Certainly.

And it is possible to recollect Simmias himself on seeing a picture of Simmias?

74 No doubt, he said.

Then in all these cases there is recollection caused by similar objects, and also by dissimilar objects?

There is.

But when a man has a recollection caused by similar objects, will he not have a further feeling and consider whether the likeness to that which he recollects is defective in any way or not?

He will, he said.

Now see if this is true, he went on. Do we not believe in the existence of equality—not the equality of pieces of wood or of stones, but something beyond that—equality in the abstract? Shall we say that there is such a thing, or not?

b Yes indeed, said Simmias, most emphatically we will.

And do we know what this abstract equality is?

Certainly, he replied.

Where did we get the knowledge of it? Was it not from seeing the equal pieces of wood, and stones, and the like, which we were speaking of just now? Did we not form from them the idea of abstract equality, which is different from them? Or do you think that it is not different? Consider the question in this way. Do not equal pieces of wood and stones appear to us sometimes equal and sometimes unequal, though in fact they remain the same all the time?

Certainly they do.

c But did absolute equals ever seem to you to be unequal, or abstract equality to be inequality?

No, never, Socrates.

Then equal things, he said, are not the same as abstract equality?

No, certainly not, Socrates.

Yet it was from these equal things, he said, which are different from abstract equality, that you have conceived and got your knowledge of abstract equality?

That is quite true, he replied.

And that whether it is like them or unlike them?

Certainly.

But that makes no difference, he said. As long as the sight of one thing brings d
another thing to your mind, there must be recollection, whether or no the two things
are like.

That is so.

Well then, said he, do the equal pieces of wood, and other similar equal things, of which we have been speaking, affect us at all this way? Do they seem to us to be equal, in the way that abstract equality is equal? Do they come short of being like abstract equality, or not?

Indeed, they come very short of it, he replied.

Are we agreed about this? A man sees something and thinks to himself, "This
thing that I see aims at being like some other thing, but it comes short and cannot be e
like that other thing; it is inferior"; must not the man who thinks that have known at
some previous time that other thing, which he says that it resembles, and to which it is
inferior?

He must.

Well, have we ourselves had the same sort of feeling with reference to equal things, and to abstract equality?

Yes, certainly.

Then we must have had knowledge of equality before we first saw equal things, 73
and perceived that they all strive to be like equality, and all come short of it.

That is so.

And we are agreed also that we have not, nor could we have, obtained the idea of equality except from sight or touch or some other sense; the same is true of all the senses.

Yes, Socrates, for the purposes of the argument that is so.

At any rate, it is by the senses that we must perceive that all sensible objects strive b
to resemble absolute equality, and are inferior to it. Is not that so?

Yes.

Then before we began to see, and to hear, and to use the other senses, we must have received the knowledge of the nature of abstract and real equality; otherwise we could not have compared equal sensible objects with abstract equality, and seen that the former in all cases strive to be like the latter, though they are always inferior to it?

That is the necessary consequence of what we have been saying, Socrates.

Did we not see, and hear, and possess the other senses as soon as we were born?

Yes, certainly.

And we must have received the knowledge of abstract equality before we had c
these senses?

Yes.

Then, it seems, we must have received that knowledge before we were born?

It does.

Now if we received this knowledge before our birth, and were born with it, we
knew, both before and at the moment of our birth, not only the equal, and the greater,
and the less, but also everything of the same kind, did we not? Our present reasoning
does not refer only to equality. It refers just as much to absolute good, and absolute d

beauty, and absolute justice, and absolute holiness; in short, I repeat, to everything which we mark with the name of the real, in the questions and answers of our dialectic. So we must have received our knowledge of all realities before we were born.

That is so.

And we must always be born with this knowledge, and must always retain it throughout life, if we have not each time forgotten it, after having received it. For to know means to receive and retain knowledge, and not to have lost it. Do not we mean by forgetting, the loss of knowledge, Simmias?

e Yes, certainly, Socrates, he said.

But, I suppose, if it be the case that we lost at birth the knowledge which we received before we were born, and then afterward, by using our senses on the objects of sense, recovered the knowledge which we had previously possessed, then what we call learning is the recovering of knowledge which is already ours. And are we not right in calling that recollection?

Certainly.

76 For we have found it possible to perceive a thing by sight, or hearing, or any other sense, and thence to form a notion of some other thing, like or unlike, which had been forgotten, but with which this thing was associated. And therefore, I say, one of two things must be true. Either we are all born with this knowledge and retain it all our life; or, after birth, those whom we say are learning are only recollecting, and our knowledge is recollection.

Yes indeed, that is undoubtedly true, Socrates.

Then which do you choose, Simmias? Are we born with knowledge or do we rec-
b ollect the things of which we have received knowledge before our birth?

I cannot say at present, Socrates.

Well, have you an opinion about this question? Can a man who knows give an account of what he knows, or not? What do you think about that?

Yes, of course he can, Socrates.

And do you think that everyone can give an account of the ideas of which we have been speaking?

I wish I did, indeed, said Simmias, but I am very much afraid that by this time tomorrow there will no longer be any man living able to do so as it should be done.

c Then, Simmias, he said, you do not think that all men know these things?

Certainly not.

Then they recollect what they once learned?

Necessarily.

And when did our souls gain this knowledge? It cannot have been after we were born men.

No, certainly not.

Then it was before?

Yes.

Then, Simmias, our souls existed formerly, apart from our bodies, and possessed intelligence before they came into man's shape.

Unless we receive this knowledge at the moment of birth, Socrates. That time still remains.

d Well, my friend, and at what other time do we lose it? We agreed just now that we are not born with it; do we lose it at the same moment that we gain it, or can you suggest any other time?

I cannot, Socrates. I did not see that I was talking nonsense.

Then, Simmias, he said, is not this the truth? If, as we are forever repeating, beauty,
and good, and the other ideas really exist, and if we refer all the objects of sensible per- e
ception to these ideas which were formerly ours, and which we find to be ours still, and
compare sensible objects with them, then, just as they exist, our souls must have existed
before ever we were born. But if they do not exist, then our reasoning will have been
thrown away. Is it so? If these ideas exist, does it not at once follow that our souls must
have existed before we were born, and if they do not exist, then neither did our souls?

Admirably put, Socrates, said Simmias. I think that the necessity is the same for
the one as for the other. The reasoning has reached a place of safety in the common 77
proof of the existence of our souls before we were born and of the existence of the ideas
of which you spoke. Nothing is so evident to me as that beauty, and good, and the other
ideas which you spoke of just now have a very real existence indeed. Your proof is quite
sufficient for me.

But what of Cebes? said Socrates. I must convince Cebes too.

I think that he is satisfied, said Simmias, though he is the most skeptical of men in argument. But I think that he is perfectly convinced that our souls existed before we were born.

But I do not think myself, Socrates, he continued, that you have proved that the
soul will continue to exist when we are dead. The common fear which Cebes spoke of, b
that she [the soul] may be scattered to the winds at death, and that death may be the end
of her existence, still stands in the way. Assuming that the soul is generated and comes
together from some other elements, and exists before she ever enters the human body,
why should she not come to an end and be destroyed, after she has entered into the
body, when she is released from it?

You are right, Simmias, said Cebes. I think that only half the required proof has c
been given. It has been shown that our souls existed before we were born; but it must
also be shown that our souls will continue to exist after we are dead, no less than that
they existed before we were born, if the proof is to be complete.

That has been shown already, Simmias and Cebes, said Socrates, if you will combine this reasoning with our previous conclusion, that all life is generated from death. d
For if the soul exists in a previous state and if, when she comes into life and is born, she
can only be born from death, and from a state of death, must she not exist after death too,
since she has to be born again? So the point which you speak of has been already proved.

Still I think that you and Simmias would be glad to discuss this question further.
Like children, you are afraid that the wind will really blow the soul away and disperse her
when she leaves the body, especially if a man happens to die in a storm and not in a calm. e

Cebes laughed and said, Try and convince us as if we were afraid, Socrates; or rather, do not think that we are afraid ourselves. Perhaps there is a child within us who has these fears. Let us try and persuade him not to be afraid of death, as if it were a bugbear.

You must charm him every day, until you have charmed him away, said Socrates.

And where shall we find a good charmer, Socrates, he asked, now that you are 78
leaving us?

Hellas is a large country, Cebes, he replied, and good men may doubtless be found in it; and the nations of the Barbarians are many. You must search them all through for such a charmer, sparing neither money nor labor; for there is nothing on which you could spend money more profitably. And you must search for him among yourselves too, for you will hardly find a better charmer than yourselves.

That shall be done, said Cebes. But let us return to the point where we left off, if b
you will.

Yes, I will: why not?

Very good, he replied.

Well, said Socrates, must we not ask ourselves this question? What kind of thing is liable to suffer dispersion, and for what kind of thing have we to fear dispersion? And then we must see whether the soul belongs to that kind or not, and be confident or afraid about our own souls accordingly.

That is true, he answered.

c Now is it not the compound and composite which is naturally liable to be dissolved in the same way in which it was compounded? And is not what is uncompounded alone not liable to dissolution, if anything is not?

I think that that is so, said Cebes.

And what always remains in the same state and unchanging is most likely to be uncompounded, and what is always changing and never the same is most likely to be compounded, I suppose?

Yes, I think so.

Now let us return to what we were speaking of before in the discussion, he said.
d Does the being, which in our dialectic we define as meaning absolute existence, remain
always in exactly the same state, or does it change? Do absolute equality, absolute
beauty, and every other absolute existence, admit of any change at all? Or does absolute
existence in each case, being essentially uniform, remain the same and unchanging, and
never in any case admit of any sort or kind of change whatsoever?

It must remain the same and unchanging, Socrates, said Cebes.

And what of the many beautiful things, such as men, and horses, and garments,
and the like, and of all which bears the names of the ideas, whether equal, or beautiful,
e or anything else? Do they remain the same or is it exactly the opposite with them? In
short, do they never remain the same at all, either in themselves or in their relations?

These things, said Cebes, never remain the same.

79 You can touch them, and see them, and perceive them with the other senses, while
you can grasp the unchanging only by the reasoning of the intellect. These latter are
invisible and not seen. Is it not so?

That is perfectly true, he said.

Let us assume then, he said, if you will, that there are two kinds of existence, the one visible, the other invisible.

Yes, he said.

And the invisible is unchanging, while the visible is always changing.

Yes, he said again.

b Are not we men made up of body and soul?

There is nothing else, he replied.

And which of these kinds of existence should we say that the body is most like, and most akin to?

The visible, he replied; that is quite obvious.

And the soul? Is that visible or invisible?

It is invisible to man, Socrates, he said.

But we mean by visible and invisible, visible and invisible to man; do we not?

Yes; that is what we mean.

Then what do we say of the soul? Is it visible or not visible?

It is not visible.

Then is it invisible?

Yes.

Then the soul is more like the invisible than the body; and the body is like the visible.

That is necessarily so, Socrates. c

Have we not also said that, when the soul employs the body in any inquiry, and makes use of sight, or hearing, or any other sense—for inquiry with the body means inquiry with the senses—she is dragged away by it to the things which never remain the same, and wanders about blindly, and becomes confused and dizzy, like a drunken man, from dealing with things that are ever changing?

Certainly.

But when she investigates any question by herself, she goes away to the pure, and d
eternal, and immortal, and unchangeable, to which she is akin, and so she comes to be ever with it, as soon as she is by herself, and can be so; and then she rests from her wanderings and dwells with it unchangingly, for she is dealing with what is unchanging. And is not this state of the soul called wisdom?

Indeed, Socrates, you speak well and truly, he replied.

Which kind of existence do you think from our former and our present arguments e
that the soul is more like and more akin to?

I think, Socrates, he replied, that after this inquiry the very dullest man would agree that the soul is infinitely more like the unchangeable than the changeable.

And the body?

That is like the changeable.

Consider the matter in yet another way. When the soul and the body are united,
nature ordains the one to be a slave and to be ruled, and the other to be master and to 80
rule. Tell me once again, which do you think is like the divine, and which is like the mortal? Do you not think that the divine naturally rules and has authority, and that the mortal naturally is ruled and is a slave?

I do.

Then which is the soul like?

That is quite plain, Socrates. The soul is like the divine, and the body is like the mortal.

Now tell me, Cebes, is the result of all that we have said that the soul is most like
the divine, and the immortal, and the intelligible, and the uniform, and the indissoluble, b
and the unchangeable; while the body is most like the human, and the mortal, and the unintelligible, and the multiform, and the dissoluble, and the changeable? Have we any other argument to show that this is not so, my dear Cebes?

We have not.

Then if this is so, is it not the nature of the body to be dissolved quickly, and of the soul to be wholly or very nearly indissoluble?

Certainly. c

You observe, he said, that after a man is dead, the visible part of him, his body, which lies in the visible world and which we call the corpse, which is subject to dissolution and decomposition, is not dissolved and decomposed at once? It remains as it was for a considerable time, and even for a long time, if a man dies with his body in good condition and in the vigor of life. And when the body falls in and is embalmed,
like the mummies of Egypt, it remains nearly entire for an immense time. And should it d
decay, yet some parts of it, such as the bones and muscles, may almost be said to be immortal. Is it not so?

Yes.

And shall we believe that the soul, which is invisible, and which goes hence to a place that is like herself, glorious, and pure, and invisible, to Hades, which is rightly

called the unseen world, to dwell with the good and wise God, whither, if it be the will
of God, my soul too must shortly go—shall we believe that the soul, whose nature is so
e glorious, and pure, and invisible, is blown away by the winds and perishes as soon as
she leaves the body, as the world says? Nay, dear Cebes and Simmias, it is not so. I will
tell you what happens to a soul which is pure at her departure, and which in her life has
had no intercourse that she could avoid with the body, and so draws after her, when she
81 dies, no taint of the body, but has shunned it, and gathered herself into herself, for such
has been her constant study—and that only means that she has loved wisdom rightly,
and has truly practiced how to die. Is not this the practice of death?

Yes, certainly.

Does not the soul, then, which is in that state, go away to the invisible that is like herself, and to the divine, and the immortal, and the wise, where she is released from error, and folly, and fear, and fierce passions, and all the other evils that fall to the lot of men, and is happy, and for the rest of time lives in very truth with the gods, as they say that the initiated do? Shall we affirm this, Cebes?

Yes, certainly, said Cebes.

b But if she be defiled and impure when she leaves the body, from being ever with
it, and serving it and loving it, and from being besotted by it and by its desires and pleasures, so that she thinks nothing true but what is bodily and can be touched, and seen,
and eaten, and drunk, and used for men's lusts; if she has learned to hate, and tremble at,
c and fly from what is dark and invisible to the eye, and intelligible and apprehended by
philosophy—do you think that a soul which is in that state will be pure and without
alloy at her departure?

No, indeed, he replied.

She is penetrated, I suppose, by the corporeal, which the unceasing intercourse and company and care of the body has made a part of her nature.

Yes.

And, my dear friend, the corporeal must be burdensome, and heavy, and earthy,
and visible; and it is by this that such a soul is weighed down and dragged back to the
d visible world, because she is afraid of the invisible world of Hades, and haunts, it is
said, the graves and tombs, where shadowy forms of souls have been seen, which are
the phantoms of souls which were impure at their release and still cling to the visible;
which is the reason why they are seen.

That is likely enough, Socrates.

That is likely, certainly, Cebes; and these are not the souls of the good, but of the
evil, which are compelled to wander in such places as a punishment for the wicked lives
that they have lived; and their wanderings continue until, from the desire for the corpo-
e real that clings to them, they are again imprisoned in a body.

And, he continued, they are imprisoned, probably, in the bodies of animals with habits similar to the habits which were theirs in their lifetime.

What do you mean by that, Socrates?

I mean that men who have practiced unbridled gluttony, and wantonness, and drunk-
82 enness probably enter the bodies of asses and suchlike animals. Do you not think so?

Certainly that is very likely.

And those who have chosen injustice, and tyranny, and robbery enter the bodies of wolves, and hawks, and kites. Where else should we say that such souls go?

No doubt, said Cebes, they go into such animals.

In short, it is quite plain, he said, whither each soul goes; each enters an animal with habits like its own.

Certainly, he replied, that is so.

And of these, he said, the happiest, who go to the best place, are those who have
practiced the popular and social virtues which are called temperance and justice, and b
which come from habit and practice, without philosophy or reason.

And why are they the happiest?

Because it is probable that they return into a mild and social nature like their own, such as that of bees, or wasps, or ants; or, it may be, into the bodies of men, and that from them are made worthy citizens.

Very likely.

But none but the philosopher or the lover of knowledge, who is wholly pure when c
he goes hence, is permitted to go to the race of the gods; and therefore, my friends, Simmias and Cebes, the true philosopher is temperate and refrains from all the pleasures of the body, and does not give himself up to them. It is not squandering his substance and poverty that he fears, as the multitude and the lovers of wealth do; nor again does he dread the dishonor and disgrace of wickedness, like the lovers of power and honor. It is not for these reasons that he is temperate.

No, it would be unseemly in him if he were, Socrates, said Cebes.

Indeed it would, he replied, and therefore all those who have any care for their d
souls, and who do not spend their lives in forming and molding their bodies, bid farewell to such persons, and do not walk in their ways, thinking that they know not whither they are going. They themselves turn and follow whithersoever philosophy leads them, for they believe that they ought not to resist philosophy, or its deliverance and purification.

How, Socrates?

I will tell you, he replied. The lovers of knowledge know that when philosophy
receives the soul, she is fast bound in the body, and fastened to it; she is unable to con- e
template what is, by herself, or except through the bars of her prison house, the body;
and she is wallowing in utter ignorance. And philosophy sees that the dreadful thing
about the imprisonment is that it is caused by lust, and that the captive herself is an 83
accomplice in her own captivity. The lovers of knowledge, I repeat, know that philosophy takes the soul when she is in this condition, and gently encourages her, and strives
to release her from her captivity, showing her that the perceptions of the eye, and the
ear, and the other senses are full of deceit, and persuading her to stand aloof from the
senses and to use them only when she must, and exhorting her to rally and gather her- b
self together, and to trust only to herself and to the real existence which she of her own
self apprehends, and to believe that nothing which is subject to change, and which she
perceives by other faculties, has any truth, for such things are visible and sensible, while
what she herself sees is apprehended by reason and invisible. The soul of the true
philosopher thinks that it would be wrong to resist this deliverance from captivity, and
therefore she holds aloof, so far as she can, from pleasure, and desire, and pain, and
fear; for she reckons that when a man has vehement pleasure, or fear, or pain, or desire, c
he suffers from them not merely the evils which might be expected, such as sickness or
some loss arising from the indulgence of his desires; he suffers what is the greatest and
last of evils, and does not take it into account.

What do you mean, Socrates? asked Cebes.

I mean that when the soul of any man feels vehement pleasure or pain, she is forced at the same time to think that the object, whatever it be, of these sensations is the most distinct and truest, when it is not.

* * *

114e . . . A man should be of good cheer about his soul if in his life he has renounced the
pleasures and adornments of the body, because they were nothing to him, and because
he thought that they would do him not good but harm; and if he has instead earnestly
115 pursued the pleasures of learning, and adorned his soul with the adornment of temperance, and justice, and courage, and freedom, and truth, which belongs to her and is her
own, and so awaits his journey to the other world, in readiness to set forth whenever fate
calls him. You, Simmias and Cebes, and the rest will set forth at some future day, each
at his own time. But me now, as a tragic poet would say, fate calls at once; and it is time
for me to betake myself to the bath. I think that I had better bathe before I drink the poison, and not give the women the trouble of washing my dead body.

b When he had finished speaking Crito said, Be it so, Socrates. But have you any
commands for your friends or for me about your children, or about other things? How
shall we serve you best?

Simply by doing what I always tell you, Crito. Take care of your own selves, and
you will serve me and mine and yourselves in all that you do, even though you make no
promises now. But if you are careless of your own selves, and will not follow the path
of life which we have pointed out in our discussions both today and at other times, all
c your promises now, however profuse and earnest they are, will be of no avail.

We will do our best, said Crito. But how shall we bury you?

As you please, he answered; only you must catch me first and not let me escape
you. And then he looked at us with a smile and said, My friends, I cannot convince Crito
that I am the Socrates who has been conversing with you and arranging his arguments
d in order. He thinks that I am the body which he will presently see a corpse, and he asks
how he is to bury me. All the arguments which I have used to prove that I shall not
remain with you after I have drunk the poison, but that I shall go away to the happiness
of the blessed, with which I tried to comfort you and myself, have been thrown away on
him. Do you therefore be my sureties to him, as he was my surety at the trial, but in a
different way. He was surety for me then that I would remain; but you must be my
sureties to him that I shall go away when I am dead, and not remain with you; then he
e will feel my death less; and when he sees my body being burned or buried, he will not
be grieved because he thinks that I am suffering dreadful things; and at my funeral he
will not say that it is Socrates whom he is laying out, or bearing to the grave, or burying.
For, dear Crito, he continued, you must know that to use words wrongly is not only a
fault in itself, it also creates evil in the soul. You must be of good cheer, and say that you
116 are burying my body; and you may bury it as you please and as you think right.

With these words he rose and went into another room to bathe. Crito went with
him and told us to wait. So we waited, talking of the argument and discussing it, and then
again dwelling on the greatness of the calamity which had fallen upon us: it seemed as if
b we were going to lose a father and to be orphans for the rest of our lives. When he had
bathed, and his children had been brought to him—he had two sons quite little, and one
grown up—and the women of his family were come, he spoke with them in Crito's presence, and gave them his last instructions; then he sent the women and children away and
returned to us. By that time it was near the hour of sunset, for he had been a long while
within. When he came back to us from the bath he sat down, but not much was said after
c that. Presently the servant of the Eleven came and stood before him and said, "I know
that I shall not find you unreasonable like other men, Socrates. They are angry with me
and curse me when I bid them drink the poison because the authorities make me do it.
But I have found you all along the noblest and gentlest and best man that has ever come
d here; and now I am sure that you will not be angry with me, but with those who you

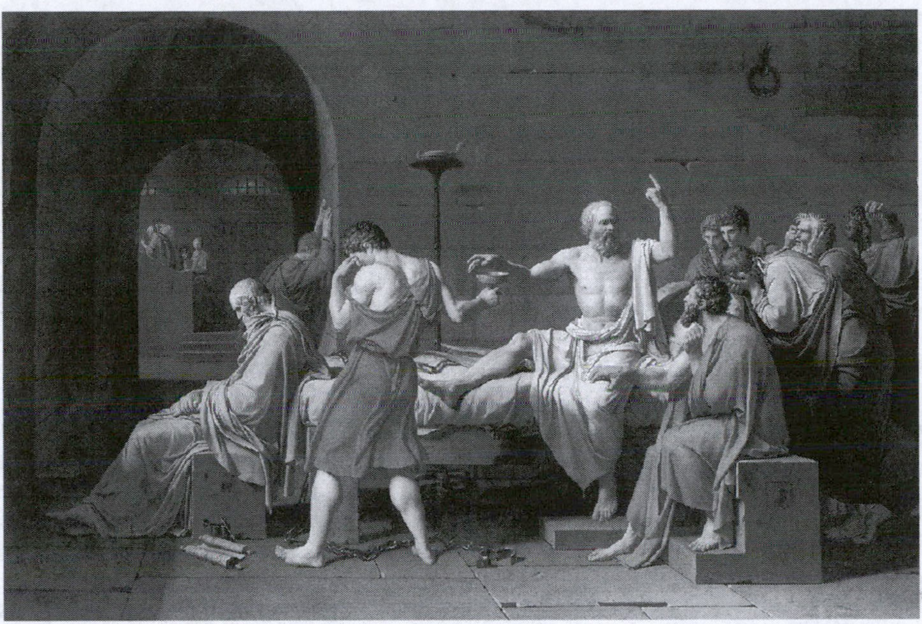

Jacques-Louis David, "The Death of Socrates." (*Image copyright ©The Metropolitan Museum of Art. Image source: Art Resource, NY)*

know are to blame. And so farewell, and try to bear what must be as lightly as you can; you know why I have come." With that he turned away weeping, and went out.

Socrates looked up at him and replied, Farewell, I will do as you say. Then he turned to us and said, How courteous the man is! And the whole time that I have been here, he has constantly come in to see me, and sometimes he has talked to me, and has been the best of men; and now, how generously he weeps for me! Come, Crito, let us obey him; let the poison be brought if it is ready, and if it is not ready, let it be prepared.

Crito replied: But, Socrates, I think that the sun is still upon the hills; it has not e
set. Besides, I know that other men take the poison quite late, and eat and drink heartily, and even enjoy the company of their chosen friends, after the announcement has been made. So do not hurry; there is still time.

Socrates replied: And those whom you speak of, Crito, naturally do so, for they think that they will be gainers by so doing. And I naturally shall not do so, for I think
that I should gain nothing by drinking the poison a little later, but my own contempt for 117
so greedily saving a life which is already spent. So do not refuse to do as I say.

Then Crito made a sign to his slave who was standing by; and the slave went out, and after some delay returned with the man who was to give the poison, carrying it prepared in a cup. When Socrates saw him, he asked, You understand these things, my good man, what have I to do?

You have only to drink this, he replied, and to walk about until your legs feel b
heavy, and then lie down; and it will act of itself.

With that he handed the cup to Socrates, who took it quite cheerfully, Echecrates, without trembling, and without any change of color or of feature, and looked up at the

man with that fixed glance of his, and asked, What say you to making a libation from
this draught? May I, or not?

c We only prepare so much as we think sufficient, Socrates, he answered.

I understand, said Socrates. But I suppose that I may, and must, pray to the gods
that my journey hence may be prosperous. That is my prayer; may it be so. With these
words he put the cup to his lips and drank the poison quite calmly and cheerfully.

Till then most of us had been able to control our grief fairly well; but when we
saw him drinking and then the poison finished, we could do so no longer: my tears came
fast in spite of myself, and I covered my face and wept for myself; it was not for him,
d but at my own misfortune in losing such a friend. Even before that Crito had been
unable to restrain his tears, and had gone away; and Apollodorus, who had never once
ceased weeping the whole time, burst into a loud wail and made us one and all break
down by his sobbing, except Socrates himself.

e What are you doing, my friends? he exclaimed. I sent away the women chiefly in
order that they might not behave in this way; for I have heard that a man should die in
silence. So calm yourselves and bear up.

When we heard that, we were ashamed, and we ceased from weeping. But he
walked about, until he said that his legs were getting heavy, and then he lay down on his
back, as he was told. And the man who gave the poison began to examine his feet and
legs from time to time. Then he pressed his foot hard and asked if there was any feeling
118 in it, and Socrates said, No; and then his legs, and so higher and higher, and showed us
that he was cold and stiff. And Socrates felt himself and said that when it came to his
heart, he should be gone. He was already growing cold about the groin, when he uncovered his face, which had been covered, and spoke for the last time. Crito, he said, I owe
a cock to Asclepius; do not forget to pay it.*

It shall be done, replied Crito. Is there anything else that you wish? He made no answer to this question; but after a short interval there was a movement, and the man uncovered him, and his eyes were fixed. Then Crito closed his mouth and his eyes.

Such was the end, Echecrates, of our friend, a man, I think, who was the wisest and justest, and the best man I have ever known.

*[Asclepius was the Greek god of healing. When one recovered from an illness it was customary to offer a cock as a sacrifice, so Socrates' last words imply that death is a kind of healing. See, for instance 66b ff., 67c.]

REPUBLIC* (in part)

Characters
Socrates
Glaucon
Adeimantus
Cephalus
Polemarchus
Thrasymachus
Cleitophon
Scene—Cephalus' home at Pireus

BOOK I

* * *

[SOCRATES:] And when Thrasymachus many times, even while we were in the 336b
middle of our conversation, was making motions to take over the argument, he was
prevented by those sitting by him, who wanted to hear the argument out. But when
we paused as I said this, he could no longer keep still, but having gathered himself to
spring like a wild animal, he launched himself at us as if to tear us to pieces. Both I
and Polemarchus were quaking in fear, and he, snarling into our midst, said: "What
drivel are you people full of now, Socrates? And why do you act like idiots kowtow- c
ing to each other? But if you truly want to know what's just, don't merely ask and
then, as befits someone with a passion for honor, cross-examine whenever anybody
answers, knowing that it's easier to ask than to answer, but also answer yourself and
tell what you claim the just thing is. And don't give me any of that about how it's the d
needful or the beneficial or the profitable or the gainful or the advantageous, but tell
me clearly and precisely what you mean, since I won't stand for it if you talk in such
empty words."

*The only speaker in the dialogue is Socrates. He begins recounting a conversation he had on the occasion of a foreign religious festival that took place just outside Athens. Between the day and night portions of the festivities, a group of young men latches on to Socrates, who could be expected to provide entertaining talk. Polemarchus takes the group to his house, where they meet his father Cephalus, a very old man preoccupied with making amends before his death for any injustices in his life. Socrates asks him what he understands justice to be and begins to examine the implications of his answer. [We pick up the conversation as Thrasymachus, a well-known sophist, breaks in to the conversation.]

And I was flabbergasted when I heard this, and was afraid as I looked at him, and
it seemed to me that if I had not seen him before he saw me I would have been struck
dumb.* But as it was, just as he was beginning to be driven wild by the argument I
e looked at him first, and so I was able to answer him, and said, trembling a little, "Don't
be rough on us, Thrasymachus. If we're mistaken in any point in the examination of the
argument, I and this fellow here, you can be assured that we're going astray unwillingly.
For don't even imagine, when, if we were looking for gold, we wouldn't be willing to
kowtow to each other in the search and ruin our chances of finding it, that when we're
looking for justice, a thing more valuable than much gold, we'd be so senseless as to
defer to each other and not be as serious as possible about bringing it to light. Don't so
337a much as imagine that, friend. But I imagine we don't have the power to find it. So it's
much more fitting anyway for us to be pitied by you clever people instead of being
roughed up."

And hearing this, he burst out laughing with great scorn and said "Oh Heracles,
this is that routine irony of Socrates. I knew about this, and I kept telling these people
before that you wouldn't be willing to answer, but you'd be ironic and do everything
else but answer if anyone asked you anything."

"That's because you're wise, Thrasymachus," I said, "so you know very well that
b if you asked anyone how much twelve is, and in asking demanded of him in advance,
'don't give me any of that, fellow, about how twelve is two times six or three times four
or six times two or four times three, since I won't stand for such drivel from you,' it was
clear to you, I imagine, that no one could answer someone who interrogated him that
way. But if he said to you, 'Thrasymachus, how do you mean it? That I must give none
of the answers you prohibited in advance? Not even, you strange fellow, if it happens to
c be one of these, but instead I have to say something other than the truth? Or how do you
mean it?' What would you say to him about that?"

"Oh sure," he said, "as if this was like that."

"Nothing prevents it," I said. "But then even if it isn't like it, but appears to be to
someone who is asked such a question, do you imagine he'll any the less answer the
question the way it appears to him, whether we forbid it or not?"

"So what else," he said; "are you going to do the same thing? Are you going to
give any of those answers I banned?" "I wouldn't be surprised," I said, "if it seemed that
way to me when I had examined it."

d "Then what if I show you a different answer about justice," he said, "beyond all
these, better than they are? What penalty would you think you deserve to suffer?"

"What other penalty," I said, "than the one it's fitting for someone who doesn't
have knowledge to suffer? And it's fitting, no doubt, for him to learn from someone who
has knowledge. So I think I too deserve to suffer this penalty."

"You're amusing," he said, "but in addition to learning, pay a penalty in money too."

"Okay, whenever I get any," I said.

"He's got it," said Glaucon. "So as far as money's concerned, Thrasymachus,
speak up, since all of us will chip in for Socrates."

e "I imagine you will," he said, "so Socrates can go on with his usual routine: he
won't answer but when somebody else answers he'll grab hold of his statement and
cross-examine him."

"Most skillful one," I said, "how could anyone give an answer who in the first place
doesn't know and doesn't claim to know, and then too, even if he supposes something

*[A popular superstition, that if a wolf sees you first, you become dumb.]

about these things, would be banned from saying what he believes by no inconsiderable
man? So it's more like it for you to speak, since you do claim to know and to have some- 338a
thing to say. So don't do anything else but gratify me by answering, and don't be grudging
about teaching Glaucon here as well as the others."

And when I'd said these things, Glaucon and the others kept begging him not to
do otherwise. And Thrasymachus was obviously longing to speak in order to be well
thought of, believing that he had an answer of overwhelming beauty. But he made a
pretense of battling eagerly for me to be the one that answered. But making an end of b
this, he gave way, and then said, "This is the wisdom of Socrates; he himself is not
willing to teach, but he goes around learning from others and doesn't even pay them
any gratitude."

"In saying that I learn from others," I said, "you tell the truth, Thrasymachus, but
when you claim that I don't pay for it in full with gratitude, you lie, for I pay all that is
in my power. I have the power only to show appreciation, since I don't have money. And
how eagerly I do this, if anyone seems to me to speak well, you'll know very well right
away when you answer, for I imagine you'll speak well." c

"Then listen," he said. "I assert that what's just is nothing other than what's advantageous to the stronger. So why don't you show appreciation? But you won't be willing to."

"First I need to understand what you mean," I said, "since now I don't yet know.
You claim that what's advantageous to the stronger is just. Now whatever do you mean
by this, Thrasymachus? For I'm sure you're not saying this sort of thing: that if
Polydamas the no-holds-barred wrestler is stronger than we are, and bull's meat is
advantageous to him for his body, this food would also be advantageous, and at the d
same time just, for us who are weaker than he is."

"You're nauseating, Socrates," he said, "and you grab hold of the statement in the way that you can do it the most damage."

"Not at all, most excellent man," I said, "just say more clearly what you mean."

"So you don't know," he said, "that some cities are run tyrannically, some democratically, and some aristocratically?"

"How could I not?"

"And so this prevails in strength in each city, the ruling part?"

"Certainly."

"And each ruling power sets up laws for the advantage of itself, a democracy e
setting up democratic ones, a tyranny tyrannical ones, and the others likewise. And
having set them up, they declare that this, what's advantageous for them, is just for
those who are ruled, and they chastise someone who transgresses it as a lawbreaker
and a person doing injustice. So this, you most skillful one, is what I'm saying, that
the same thing is just in all cities, what's advantageous to the established ruling 339a
power. And this surely prevails in strength, so the conclusion, for someone who reasons correctly, is that the same thing is just everywhere, what's advantageous to the
stronger."

"Now," I said, "I understand what you mean. But whether it's true or not, I'll try
to learn. So you too answer that the advantageous is just, Thrasymachus, even though
you made a prohibition for me that I could not give this answer, though there is added to b
it 'for the stronger.' "

"A small addendum, no doubt," he said.

"It's not clear yet whether it's a big one. But it is clear that whether you're speaking the truth needs to be examined. For since you're saying and I'm agreeing that what's just is something advantageous, but you're making an addition and claiming it to be that of the stronger, while I don't know that, it needs to be examined."

"So examine it," he said.

"That will be done," I said. "Now tell me, do you not claim, though, that it's also just to obey the rulers?"

"I do."

c "And are the rulers in each city infallible, or the sort of people who also make mistakes?"

"By all means," he said, "they're surely the sort of people who also make mistakes."

"So when they try to set up laws, they set up some correctly and certain others incorrectly?"

"I certainly imagine so."

"Then to set them up correctly is to set up laws that are advantageous to themselves, and incorrectly, disadvantageous ones? Or how do you mean it?"

"That's the way."

"But whatever they set up needs to be done by those who are ruled, and this is what is just?"

"How could it be otherwise?"

d "Then according to your statement, not only is it just to do what's advantageous to the stronger, but also to do the opposite, what's disadvantageous."

"What do you mean?" he said.

"What you mean, it seems to me; but let's examine it better. Wasn't it agreed that when the rulers command those who are ruled to do certain things they're sometimes completely mistaken about what's best for themselves, but what the rulers command is just for those who are ruled to do? Wasn't this agreed?"

"I certainly imagine so," he said.

e "Well then," I said, "imagine also that it was agreed by you that doing what's disadvantageous for those who rule and are stronger is just, whenever the rulers unwillingly command things that are bad for themselves, while you claim that for the others to do those things which they commanded is just. So then, most wise Thrasymachus, doesn't it turn out necessarily in exactly this way, that it's just to do the opposite of what you say? For what's disadvantageous to the stronger is without doubt commanded to the weaker to do."

340a "By Zeus, yes, Socrates," said Polemarchus, "most clearly so."

"If you're going to be a witness for him," Cleitophon interjected.

"And what need is there for a witness? Thrasymachus himself agrees that the rulers sometimes command things that are bad for themselves, and that for the others to do these things is just."

"That's because Thrasymachus set it down, Polemarchus, that doing what's ordered by the rulers is just."

"Because he also set it down, Cleitophon, that what's advantageous to the
b stronger is just. And having set down both these things, he agreed next that sometimes the stronger order things that are disadvantageous to themselves for those who are weaker and ruled to do. And from these agreements what's advantageous to the stronger would be no more just than what's disadvantageous."

"But," said Cleitophon, "he meant that the advantage of the stronger is what the stronger believes is advantageous to himself; this is what needs to be done by the weaker, and he set this down as what's just."

"But he didn't say it that way," said Polemarchus.

"It makes no difference, Polemarchus," I said, "but if Thrasymachus says it c
this way now, let's accept it this way from him. And tell me, Thrasymachus, was this what you wanted to say the just is, what seems to the stronger to be the advantage of the stronger, whether it might be advantageous or not? Shall we say you mean it that way?"

"That least of all," he said. "Do you imagine that I call someone who makes a mistake stronger when he's making a mistake?"

"I did imagine that you were saying that," I said, "when you agreed that the rulers
are not infallible but are even completely mistaken about some things." d

"That's because you're a liar who misrepresents things in arguments, Socrates.
To start with, do you call someone who's completely mistaken about sick people a
doctor on account of that very thing he's mistaken about? Or call someone skilled at
arithmetic who makes a mistake in doing arithmetic, at the time when he's making it,
on account of this mistake? I imagine instead that we talk that way in a manner of
speaking, saying that the doctor made a mistake, or the one skilled at arithmetic made
a mistake, or the grammarian. But I assume that each of these, to the extent that this is e
what we address him as, never makes a mistake, so that in precise speech, since you
too are precise in speech, no skilled worker makes a mistake. For it's by being deficient in knowledge that the one who makes a mistake makes it, in respect to which he
is not a skilled worker. So no one who's a skilled worker or wise or a ruler makes a
mistake at the time when he is a ruler, though everyone would say that the doctor
made a mistake or the ruler made a mistake. Take it then that I too was answering you
just now in that sort of way. But the most precise way of speaking is exactly this, that
the one who rules, to the extent that he is a ruler, does not make mistakes, and in not 341a
making a mistake he sets up what is best for himself, and this needs to be done by the
one who is ruled. And so I say the very thing I've been saying from the beginning is
just, to do what's advantageous to the stronger."

"Okay, Thrasymachus," I said. "I seem to you to misrepresent things by lying?"

"Very much so," he said.

"Because you imagine that I asked the question the way I did out of a plot to do you harm in the argument?"

"I know that very well," he said. "And it's not going to do you any good, because
you couldn't do me any harm without it being noticed, and without being unnoticed you b
wouldn't have the power to do violence with the argument."

"I wouldn't even try, blessed one," I said. "But in order that this sort of thing doesn't happen to us again, distinguish the way you mean someone who rules and is stronger, whether it's the one who is so called or the one in precise speech whom you just now mentioned, for whose advantage, since he's stronger, it will be just for the weaker to act."

"The one who's a ruler in the most precise speech," he said. "Do harm to that and
misrepresent it by lies if you have any power to—I ask for no mercy from you—but you
won't be able to." c

"Do you imagine," I said, "that I'm crazy enough to try to shave a lion or misrepresent Thrasymachus by lies?"

"You certainly tried just now," he said, "but you were a zero even at that."

"That's enough of this sort or thing," I said. "But tell me, the doctor in precise speech that you were just now talking about, is he a moneymaker or a healer of the sick? And speak about the one who is a doctor."

"A healer of the sick," he said.

"And what about a helmsman? Is the one who's a helmsman in the correct way a
d ruler of sailors or a sailor?"

"A ruler of sailors."

"I assume there's no need to take into account that he does sail in the ship, and no need for him to be called a sailor, since it's not on account of sailing that he's called a helmsman, but on account of his art and his ruling position among the sailors."

"That's true," he said.

"Then for each of the latter there's something advantageous?"

"Certainly."

"And isn't art by its nature for this," I said, "for seeking and providing what's advantageous in each case?"

"For that," he said.

"Then is there any advantage for each of the arts other than to be as complete as possible?"

e "In what sense are you asking this?"

"In the same sense," I said, "as, if you were to ask me whether it's sufficient for a body to be a body or whether it needs something extra, I'd say 'Absolutely it needs something extra, and it's for that reason that the medical art has now been discovered, because a body is inadequate and isn't sufficient to itself to be the sort of thing it is. So it's for this reason, in order that it might provide the things that are advantageous for the body, that the art was devised.' Would I seem to you to be speaking correctly in saying this," I said, "or not?"

342a "It's correct," he said.

"What then? Is the medical art itself—or any other art—inadequate, and is it the case that it has need of some extra virtue? Just as eyes need sight and ears need hearing and for these reasons there is need of some art applied to them that will consider and provide what's advantageous for these things, is there then in the art itself some inadequacy in it too, and a need for each art to have another art that will consider what's advantageous for it, and for the one that will consider that to have
b another art in turn of that kind, and this is unending? Or will it consider what's advantageous for itself? Or is there no additional need either for it or for any other art to consider what's advantageous for its inadequacy, because there is no inadequacy or mistake present in any art, nor is it appropriate for an art to look out for the advantage of anything other than that with which the art is concerned, but it itself is without defect and without impurity since it is correct as long as each is the whole precise art that it is. Consider it in that precise speech now: is that the way it is, or is it some other way?"

"That way," he said, "as it appears."

c "So then," I said, "the medical art considers what's advantageous not for the medical art but for a body."

"Yes," he said.

"And horsemanship considers what's advantageous not for horsemanship but for horses, and neither does any other art consider what's advantageous for itself, since there's no extra need for that, but for that with which the art is concerned."

"So it appears," he said.

"But surely, Thrasymachus, the arts rule over and have power over that with which they're concerned."

He went along with that too, very grudgingly.

"Then no sort of knowledge considers or commands what's advantageous for the d
stronger, but what's advantageous for what's weaker and ruled by it."

He finally agreed with this too, though he tried to make a fight about it, and when he agreed I said, "So does anything else follow except that no doctor, to the extent he is a doctor, considers or commands what's advantageous for a doctor, but instead for someone who's sick? For it was agreed that the doctor is precisely a ruler of bodies but not a moneymaker. Or was that not agreed?"

He said so.

"Then the helmsman too was agreed to be precisely a ruler of sailors but not a
sailor?" e

"It was agreed."

"Then this sort of helmsman and ruler at any rate will not consider and command what's advantageous for a helmsman, but what's advantageous for the sailor who's ruled."

He said so, grudgingly.

"Therefore, Thrasymachus," I said, "neither will anyone else in any ruling position, to the extent he is a ruler, consider or command what's advantageous for himself, but what's advantageous for whatever is ruled, for which he himself is a skilled workman, and looking toward that, and to what's advantageous and appropriate for that, he both says and does everything that he says and does."

* * *

"You know that people are said to be passionate for honor and money as a 347b
reproach, and it is one?"

"I do," he said.

"So," I said, "that's why good people aren't willing to rule for the sake of either money or honor. They don't want to be called mercenary if they openly get wages for the ruling office, or thieves if they secretly take money from the office themselves. And they don't rule for the sake of honor either, since they aren't passionate for honor. So there needs to be a necessity attached to it for them, and a c
penalty, if they're going to be willing to rule; that's liable to be where it comes from that it's considered shameful to go willingly to rule rather than to await necessity. And the greatest sort of penalty is to be ruled by someone less worthy, if one is not oneself willing to rule. It's on account of fearing this that decent people appear to me to rule, when they do rule, and then they go to rule not as though they were heading
for something good or as though they were going to have any enjoyment in it, but as d
though to something necessary, since they have no one better than or similar to themselves to entrust it to. Because, if a city of good men were to come into being, they'd be liable to have a fight over not ruling just as people do now over ruling, and it would become obvious there that the person who is a true ruler in his being is not of such a nature as to consider what's advantageous for himself rather than for the one ruled. So everyone with any discernment would choose to be benefited by someone else rather than to have the trouble of benefiting someone else. On this
point, then, I by no means go along with Thrasymachus that what's just is what's e
advantageous for the stronger.

* * *

BOOK II

357a Now when I said these things, I imagined I'd be released from discussion, but as
it seems, it was just a prologue. For Glaucon is always most courageous in confronting
everything, and in particular he wouldn't stand for Thrasymachus's giving up, but said
b "Socrates, do you want to seem to have persuaded us or truly persuade us that in every
way it's better to be just than unjust?"

"If it would be up to me," I said, "I'd choose truly."

"Then you're not doing what you want. For tell me, does it seem to you there's a
certain kind of good that we'd take hold of not because we desire its consequences, but
to embrace it itself for its own sake, such as enjoyment and any of the pleasures that are
harmless and from which nothing comes into the succeeding time other than to enjoy
having them?"

c "It seems to me," I said, "that there is such a thing."

"Then what about the kind that we love both itself for its own sake and for the
things that come from it, such as thinking and seeing and being healthy? For presumably we embrace such things for both reasons."

"Yes," I said.

"And do you see a third form of good," he said, "in which there's gymnastic exercise, and being given medical treatment when sick, and giving medical treatment, as
well as the rest of moneymaking activity? Because we'd say these are burdensome, but
d for our benefit, and we wouldn't take hold of them for their own sake, but we do for the
sake of wages and of all the other things that come from them."

"There is also this third kind," I said, "but what about it?"

"In which of these kinds," he said, "do you put justice?"

358a "I imagine in the most beautiful kind," I said, "which must be loved both for itself
and for the things that come from it by someone who's going to be blessedly happy."

"Well it doesn't seem that way to most people," he said, "but to belong to the burdensome kind that ought to be pursued for the sake of the wages and reputation that
come from opinion, but ought to be avoided itself on its own account as being something difficult."

"I know it seems that way," I said, "and a while ago it was condemned by
Thrasymachus as being that sort of thing, while injustice was praised, but, as it seems,
I'm a slow learner."

b "Come then," he said, "and listen to me, if the same things still seem true to you,
because Thrasymachus appears to me to have been charmed by you like a snake, sooner
than he needed to be. But to my way of thinking, no demonstration has taken place yet
about either one, since I desire to hear what each of them is and what power it has itself
by itself when it's present in the soul, and to say goodbye to the wages and the things
that come from them.

"So I'm going to do it this way, if that seems good to you too: I'll revive
c Thrasymachus's argument, and I'll say first what sort of thing people claim justice is
and where they say it comes from, and second that everyone who pursues it pursues it
unwillingly as something necessary but not good, and third that they do it fittingly since
the life of someone who's unjust is much better than that of someone who's just—as
they say, since it doesn't seem that way to me at all, Socrates, though I'm stumped as
d my ears are talked deaf when I listen to Thrasymachus and tens of thousands of other
people, while I haven't yet heard the argument on behalf of justice, that it's better than

injustice, from anyone in the way I want it. I want to hear it itself by itself praised, and I assume that I'd hear this most of all from you.

"That's why I'll strain myself to speak in praise of the unjust life, and as I speak I'll point out to you in what way I want to hear you in turn condemn injustice and praise justice. But see if what I'm saying is to your liking."

"Most of all," I said, "for what would anyone who has any sense enjoy more to talk about and hear about repeatedly?" e

"You're speaking most beautifully," he said. "Listen then to what I said I'd talk about first, what sort of thing justice is and where it comes from. People claim that doing injustice is by its nature good and suffering injustice is bad, but that suffering injustice crosses over farther into bad than doing injustice does into good, so that when people both do injustice to and suffer it from each other and get a taste of both, it seems profitable to the ones who don't have the power to avoid the latter and 359a choose the former to make a contract with each other neither to do injustice nor suffer it. And from then on they begin to set up laws and agreements among themselves and to name what's commanded by the law both lawful and just, and so this is the origin and being of justice, being in the middle between what is best, if one could do injustice and not pay a penalty, and what is worst, if one were powerless to take revenge when suffering injustice. What's just, being at a mean between these two b things, is something to be content with not as something good, but as something honored out of weakness at doing injustice, since someone with the power to do it and who was truly a man would never make a contract with anyone neither to do nor suffer injustice. He'd be insane.

"So, Socrates, it's the nature of justice to be this and of this sort, and these are the sorts of things it comes from by its nature, as the argument goes. The fact that those who pursue it pursue it unwillingly from a lack of power to do injustice, we might perceive most clearly if we were to do something like this in our thinking: by giving to each of c them, the just and the unjust, freedom to do whatever he wants, we could then follow along and see where his desire will lead each one. Then we could catch the just person in the act of going the same route as the unjust one because of greed for more, which is what every nature, by its nature, seeks as good, though it's forcibly pulled aside by law to respect for equality.

"The sort of freedom I'm talking about would be most possible if the sort of power ever came to them that people say came to the ancestor of Gyges the Lydian. d They say he was a shepherd working as a hired servant to the one who then ruled Lydia, when a big storm came up and an earthquake broke open the earth, and there was a chasm in the place where he was pasturing the sheep. Seeing it and marveling, he went down and saw other marvels people tell legends about as well as a bronze horse, hollowed out, that had windows in it, and when he stooped down to look through them he saw a dead body inside that appeared bigger than a human being. And this body had on it nothing else but a gold ring around its finger, which he took e off and went away.

"And when the customary gathering of the shepherds came along, so that they could report each month to the king about his flocks, he too came and had on the ring. Then while he was sitting with the others, he happened to turn the stone setting of the ring around toward himself into the inside of his hand, and when this happened he 360a became invisible to those sitting beside him, and they talked about him as though he'd gone away. He marveled, and running his hand over the ring again he twisted the stone setting outward, and when he had twisted it he became visible. And reflecting on this,

he tried out whether the ring had this power in it, and it turned out that way for him, to
become invisible when he twisted the stone setting in and visible when he twisted it out.
b Perceiving this, he immediately arranged to become one of the messengers attending
the king, and went and seduced the king's wife, and with her attacked and killed the
king and took possession of his reign.

"Now if there were a pair of rings of that sort, and a just person put on one
while an unjust person put on the other, it would seem that there could be no one so
inflexible that he'd stand firm in his justice and have the fortitude to hold back
and not lay a hand on things belonging to others, when he was free to take what he
c wanted from the marketplace, and to go into houses and have sex with anyone
he wanted, and to kill and set loose from chains everyone he wanted, and to do
everything he could when he was the equal of a god among human beings. And in
acting this way, he would do nothing different from the other, but both would go the
same route.

"And surely someone could claim this is a great proof that no one is just willingly, but only when forced to be, on the grounds that it is not for his private good,
d since wherever each one imagines he'll be able to do injustice he does injustice.
Because every man assumes that injustice is much more profitable to him privately
than justice, and the one saying the things involved in this sort of argument will
claim that he's assuming the truth, because if anyone got hold of such freedom and
was never willing to do injustice or lay a hand on things belonging to others, he'd
seem to be utterly miserable to those who observed it, and utterly senseless as well,
though they'd praise him to each other's faces, lying to one another from fear of suffering injustice.

"So that's the way that part goes. But as for the choice itself of the life of the peo-
e ple we're talking about, we'll be able to decide it correctly if we set the most just person
opposite the most unjust; if we don't, we won't be able to. What then is the way of
opposing them? This: we'll take nothing away either from the injustice of the unjust
person or from the justice of the just person, but set out each as complete in his own pursuit. First, then, let the unjust one do as clever workmen do; a top helmsman, for
361a instance, or doctor, distinguishes clearly between what's impossible in his art and
what's possible, and attempts the latter while letting the former go, and if he still slips
up in any way, he's competent to set himself right again. So too, let the unjust person,
attempting his injustices in the correct way, go undetected, if he's going to be surpass-
ingly unjust. Someone who gets caught must be considered a sorry specimen, since the
ultimate injustice is to seem just when one is not.

"So one must grant the completely unjust person the most complete injustice, and
b not take anything away but allow him, while doing the greatest injustices, to secure for
himself the greatest reputation for justice; and if thereafter he slips up in anything, one
must allow him to have the power to set himself right again, and to be competent both
to speak so as to persuade if he's denounced for any of his injustices, and to use force
for everything that needs force, by means of courage and strength as well as a provision
of friends and wealth. And having set him up as this sort, let's stand the just person
beside him in our argument, a man simple and well bred, wishing not to seem but be
good, as Aeschylus puts it.

c "So one must take away the seeming, for if he's going to seem to be just
there'll be honors and presents for him as one seeming that way. Then it would be
unclear whether he would be that way for the sake of what's just or for the sake of
the presents and honors. So he must be stripped bare of everything except justice and

made to be situated in a way opposite to the one before, for while he does nothing
unjust, let him have a reputation for the greatest injustice, in order that he might be
put to the acid test for justice: its not being softened by bad reputation and the things
that come from that. Let him go unchanged until death, seeming to be unjust
throughout life while being just, so that when both people have come to the ultimate d
point, one of justice and the other of injustice, it can be decided which of the pair is
happier."

"Ayayay, Glaucon my friend," I said, "how relentlessly you scrub each of them pure, like a statue, for the decision between the two men."

"As much as is in my power," he said, "and now that the two are that way, there's
nothing difficult any more, as I imagine, about going on through in telling the sort of e
life that's in store for each of them.

"So it must be said, and if in fact it's said too crudely, don't imagine I'm saying it, Socrates, but the people who praise injustice in preference to justice.

"They'll say this: that situated the way he is, the just person will be beaten with
whips, stretched on the rack, bound in chains, have both eyes burned out, and as an end
after suffering every evil he'll be hacked in pieces, and know that one ought to wish not 362a
to be but seem just. And therefore the lines of Aeschylus would be much more correct to
speak about the unjust person, since they'll claim that the one who is unjust in his being,
inasmuch as he's pursuing a thing in contact with truth and not living with a view to
opinion, wishing not to seem but be unjust

> Gathers in the fruit cultivated deep in his heart b
> From the place where wise counsels breed.

In the first place, he rules in his city as one who seems to be just; next, he takes a
wife from wherever he wants, and gives a daughter to whomever he wants; he contracts to go in partnership with whomever he wishes; and besides benefiting from all
these things, he gains by not being squeamish about doing injustice. So when he
goes into competition both in private and in public, he overcomes his enemies and
comes out with more, and since he has more he is rich and does good to his friends c
and damages his enemies. And to the gods he makes sacrifices in an adequate way
and dedicates offerings in a magnificent way, and does much better service to the
gods, and to the human beings it pleases him to, than the just person does, so that in
all likelihood it's more suitable for him, rather than the just person, to be dearer to
the gods.

"In that way, Socrates, they claim that, on the part of both gods and human beings, a better life is provided for the unjust person than for the just."

* * *

[Socrates responds to Glaucon and Adeimantus]: "You've experienced something 368a
godlike if you haven't been persuaded that injustice is better than justice, though you
have the power to speak that way on behalf of it. And you seem to me truly not persuaded, but I gather this from other indications of your disposition, since from your b
arguments I'd distrust you. But to the degree that I trust you more, I'm that much
more stumped as to how I can be of use, and I have no way to help out, since I seem
to myself to be powerless. A sign of this for me is that I imagined what I said to
Thrasymachus demonstrated that justice is better than injustice, but you didn't let

my argument stand. But neither is there any way for me not to help out, since I'm
c afraid that it would be irreverent to be standing by while justice is being defamed
and not help out as long as I'm still breathing and have the power to utter a sound.
So what has the most force is for me to come to its defense in whatever way is in
my power."

Then Glaucon and the others begged me in every way to help out and not give
up the argument, but to track down what each of them is and what the truth is about
the sort of benefit that goes with the two of them. So I said exactly what seemed to
me the case: "The inquiry we're setting ourselves to is no inconsiderable thing, but
d for someone sharp-sighted, as it appears to me. So since we aren't clever," I said,
"the sort of inquiry for us to make about it seems to me exactly like this: if someone
had ordered people who were not very sharp-sighted to read small print from a distance, and then it occurred to someone that maybe the same letters are also somewhere else, both bigger and on something bigger, it would plainly be a godsend,
I assume, to read those first and examine the smaller ones by that means, if they
were exactly the same."

e "Certainly," Adeimantus said, "but Socrates, what have you spotted in the inquiry
about justice that's of that sort?"

"I'll tell you," I said. "There's justice, we claim, of one man, and there's presumably also justice of a whole city?"

"Certainly," he said.

"Isn't a city a bigger thing than one man?"

"It's bigger," he said.

"Then maybe more justice would be present in the bigger thing, and it would be
369a easier to understand it clearly. So if you people want to, we'll inquire first what sort of
thing it is in cities, and then we'll examine it by that means also in each one of the people, examining the likeness of the bigger in the look of the smaller."

"You seem to me to be saying something beautiful," he said.

"Then if we were to look at a city as it comes into being in speech," I said, "would
we see the justice and injustice that belong to it coming into being as well?"

"Probably so," he said.

b "And then, once it has come into being, is there a hope of seeing what we're looking for more readily?"

"Very much so."

"Does it seem good, then, that we should try to accomplish this? Because I imagine it's not a small task, so you people consider it."

"It's been considered," Adeimantus said. "Don't do anything else."

"Okay," I said. "A city, as I imagine, comes into being because it happens that
each of us is not self-sufficient, but needs many things. Or do you imagine a city is
founded from any other origin?"

"None at all," he said.

"So then when one person associates with another for one use, and with another
c for another use, since they need many things, and many people assemble in one
dwelling place as partners and helpers, to this community we give the name city,
don't we?"

"Certainly."

"And they share things one with another, if they give or take shares of anything,
because each supposes it to be better for himself?"

"Certainly."

Ostraka from 428 B.C., found on the north side of the Acropolis. These clay disks were used in ostracism voting. Each eligible male Athenian citizen scratched the name of the man he thought most undesirable. The "candidate" with the most votes was obliged to leave Athens for ten years. Given that "each of us is not self-sufficient" (*Republic* 369b) and all are dependent on the community, this was a severe punishment. (*Leemage/Universal Images Group Universal Images Group/Newscom*)

"Come then," I said, "and let's make a city from the beginning in our speech. And it seems like what will make it will be our need."

"What else could it be?"

"But surely the first and greatest of needs is the provision of food for the sake of d
being and living."

"Absolutely."

"And second is the need for a dwelling place, and third for clothes and such things."

"That's so."

"Well then," I said, "how big a city will be sufficient to provide this much? Is it anything else than one person as a farmer, another a housebuilder, and some other a weaver? Or shall we add to it a leatherworker or someone who attends to something else for the body?"

"Certainly."

"And the city that's most necessary anyway would consist of four or five men." e

"So it appears."

"And then what? Should each one of these put in his own work for them all in
common, with the farmer, say, who is one, providing food for four and spending four
times the time and effort in the provision of food for the others too to share, or paying
no attention to that, make a fourth part of this food for himself alone in a fourth part of 370a
the time and devote one of the other three to providing for a house, another to a cloak,

and the other to shoes, and not have the trouble of sharing things with others but do himself, by himself, the things that are for himself?"

And Adeimantus said, "Probably, Socrates, the first way would be easier than that one."

"And by Zeus, there's nothing strange about that," I said. "For I'm thinking too
b myself, now that you mention it, that in the first place, each of us doesn't grow up to be
entirely like each, but differing in nature, with a different person in practice growing
toward a different sort of work. Or doesn't it seem that way to you?"

"It does to me."

"Then what? Would someone do a more beautiful job who, being one, worked at many arts, or when one person works at one art?"

"When one person works at one art," he said.

"And I assume this too is clear, that if anyone lets the critical moment in any work go by, it's ruined."

"That's clear."

"Because I don't imagine the thing that's being done is willing to wait for the
c leisure of the person who's doing it, but it's necessary for the one doing it to keep on the
track of the thing he's doing, not when the turn comes for a sideline."

"That's necessary."

"So as a result of these things, everything comes about in more quantity, as more beautiful, and with more ease when one person does one thing in accord with his nature and at the right moment, being free from responsibility for everything else."

"Absolutely so."

"So there's need for more than four citizens, Adeimantus, for the provisions we
were talking about, since the farmer himself, as seems likely, won't make his own plow,
d if it's going to be beautifully made, or his pickax, or any of the other tools for farming.
And neither will the housebuilder, and there's need of many things for that, and likewise
with the weaver and the leatherworker."

"That's true."

"So with carpenters and metalworkers and many such particular kinds of craftsmen coming in as partners in our little city, they'll make it a big one."

"Very much so."

"But it still wouldn't be a very big one if we add cattlemen and shepherds to them,
e and other herdsmen, so that the farmers would have oxen for plowing, and the house-
builders along with the farmers could use teams of animals for hauling, and the weavers
and leatherworkers could use hides and wool."

"It wouldn't be a small city either," he said, "when it had all these."

"But still," I said, "even to situate the city itself in the sort of place in which it won't need imported goods is just about impossible."

"It's impossible."

"Therefore there's still a further need for other people too who'll bring it what it needs from another city."

"There'll be a need."

"And if the courier goes empty-handed, carrying nothing those people need from
371a whom ours will get the things for their own use, he'll leave empty-handed, won't he?"

"It seems that way to me."

"Then they'll need to make not only enough things to be suitable for themselves, but also the kinds and quantity of things suitable for those people they need things from."

"They'll need to."

"So our city will need more of the farmers and other craftsmen."

"More indeed."

"And in particular other couriers no doubt, who'll bring in and carry away each kind of thing, and these are commercial traders aren't they?"

"Yes."

"So we'll also need commercial traders."

"Certainly."

"And if the commerce is carried on by sea, there'll be an additional need for many b
other people gathered together who know the work connected with the sea."

"Very many."

"And how about in the city itself? How are they going to share out with each other the things each sort makes by their work? It was for the sake of this that we even went into partnership and founded the city."

"It's obvious," he said: "by selling and buying."

"So a marketplace will arise out of this for us, and a currency as a conventional medium of exchange?"

"Certainly."

"But if, when the farmer or any other workman has brought any of the things he c
produces into the marketplace, he doesn't arrive at the same time as those who need to exchange things with him, is he going to stay unemployed at his craft sitting in the marketplace?"

"Not at all," he said, "but there are people who, seeing this, take this duty on themselves; in rightly managed cities it's pretty much for the people who are weakest in
body and useless for any other work to do. Because there's a need for it, so they stay d
around the marketplace to give money in exchange to those who need to sell something and to exchange in turn for money with all those who need to buy something."

"Therefore," I said, "this useful service makes for the origin of retail tradesmen in the city. Don't we call people retail tradesmen who are set up in the marketplace providing the service of buying and selling, but call those who travel around to cities commercial traders?"

"Certainly."

"And as I imagine, there are still certain other serviceable people, who don't
entirely merit sharing in the partnership for things that involve thinking but have suffi- e
cient strength of body for labors, so since they sell the use of their strength and call this payment wages, they are called, as I imagine, wage laborers, aren't they?"

"Yes."

"And the wage laborers, as seems likely, are the component that fills up the city?"

"It seems that way to me."

"Well then Adeimantus, has our city already grown to be complete?"

"Maybe."

"Then where in it would the justice and the injustice be? And together with which of the things we examined did they come to be present?"

"I have no idea, Socrates," he said, "unless it's somewhere in some usefulness of 372a
these people themselves to each other."

"And maybe you're putting it beautifully," I said. "We need to examine it though and not be shy about it. So first, let's consider what style of life people will lead who've been provided for in this way. Will they do otherwise than produce grain and wine and cloaks and shoes? And when they've built houses, by summer they'll work at most things lightly clad
and barefoot, but in winter adequately clothed and in shoes. And they'll nourish themselves b

by preparing cereal from barley and flour from wheat, baking the latter and shaping the former by hand, and when they've set out fine cakes of barley meal and loaves of wheat bread on some sort of straw or clean leaves, reclining on leafy beds spread smooth with yew and myrtle, they and their children will feast themselves, drinking wine to top it off, while crowned with wreaths and singing hymns to the gods, joining with each other pleasurably,
c and not producing children beyond their means, being cautious about poverty or war."

And Glaucon broke in, saying "It looks like you're making your men have a feast without any delicacies."

"That's true," I said. "As you say, I forgot that they'll have delicacies too, salt obviously, as well as olives and cheese, and they'll boil up the sorts of roots and greens that are
d cooked in country places. And as sweets we'll doubtless set out for them some figs and chickpeas and beans, and at the fire they'll roast myrtle berries and acorns, while sipping wine in moderation. And in this way it's likely that, going through life in peace combined with health and dying in old age, they'll pass on another life of this sort to their offspring."

And he said, "And if you were making provisions for a city of pigs, Socrates, what would you fatten them on besides this?"

"But how should they be provided for, Glaucon?" I said.

"With the very things that are customary," he said. "I assume they'll lie back on
e couches so they won't get uncomfortable, and take their meals from tables, and have exactly those delicacies and sweets that people do now."

"Okay, I understand," I said. "We're examining, it seems, not just how a city comes into being, but a city that lives in luxury. And maybe that's not a bad way to do it, since by examining that kind of city we might quickly spot the way that justice and injustice take root in cities. Now it seems to me though that the true city is the one we've gone over, just as it's a healthy one. But if you want us also to look in turn at an infected
373a city, nothing prevents it. For these things, it seems, aren't sufficient for some people, and neither is this way of life, but couches and tables and the other furnishings will be added, and especially delicacies as well as perfumed ointments and incense and harem girls and pastries, and each of these in every variety. And so it's no longer the necessities we were speaking of at first—houses, cloaks, and shoes—that have to be put in place, but painting and multicolored embroidery have to be set in motion, and gold and ivory and all that sort of thing have to be acquired, don't they?"

"Yes," he said.

b "Isn't there a need then to make the city bigger again? Because that healthy one isn't sufficient any longer, but is already filled with a mass of things and a throng of people, things that are no longer in the cities for the sake of necessity, such as all the hunters as well as the imitators [i.e., artists], many of whom are concerned with shapes and colors, many others with music, and also the poets and their assistants, the reciters,
c actors, dancers, theatrical producers, and craftsmen for all sorts of gear, including makeup for women and everything else. And we'll especially need more providers of services, or doesn't it seem there'll be a need for tutors, wet nurses, nannies, beauticians, barbers, and also delicacy-makers and chefs? Furthermore, there'll be an extra need for pig farmers; this job wasn't present in our earlier city because there was no need for it, but in this one there's the extra need for this too. And there'll be a need for a great multitude of other fattened livestock too, if one is going to eat them. Isn't that so?"

"How could it be otherwise?"

d "Then won't we be much more in need of doctors when people live this way instead of the earlier way?"

"Very much so."

"And doubtless the land that was sufficient then to feed the people will now have gone from sufficient to small. Or how do we put it?"

"That way," he said.

"Then does something have to be cut off by us from our neighbors' land if we're
going to have enough to graze on and plow, and by them in turn from ours if they too give
themselves over to the unlimited acquisition of money, exceeding the limit of necessities?" e

"That's a great necessity, Socrates," he said.

"So what comes after this, Glaucon, is that we go to war? Or how will it be?"

"That way," he said.

"And let's say nothing yet, at any rate," I said, "about whether war accomplishes anything bad or good, but only this much, that we have discovered in its turn the origin of war, in those things out of which most of all cities incur evils both in private and in public, when they do incur them."

"Very much so."

"So, my friend, there's a need for the city to be still bigger, not by a small amount but
by a whole army, which will go out in defense of all their wealth and in defense of the 374a
things we were just now talking about, and do battle with those who come against them."

"Why's that?" he said. "Aren't they themselves sufficient?"

"Not if it was beautifully done," I said, "for you and all of us to be in agreement when we were shaping the city; surely we agreed, if you recall, that one person has no power to do a beautiful job at many arts."

"What you say is true," he said.

"Then what?" I said. "Does the contest involved in war not seem to you to b
require art?"

"Much of it," he said.

"So is there any need to go to more trouble over leatherworking than over warfare?"

"By no means."

"But that's the very reason we prevented the leatherworker from attempting at the
same time to be a farmer or a weaver or a housebuilder, but just be a leatherworker, so that
the work of leathercraft would be done beautifully for us, and in the same way we gave out
one job to one person for each of the others, the job into which each had grown naturally c
and for which he was going to stay at leisure from the other jobs, working at it throughout
life and not letting the critical moments slip by to accomplish it beautifully. But isn't it of
the greatest consequence that the things involved in war be accomplished well? Or are they
so easy that even some farmer is going to be skilled at warfare at the same time, or a
leatherworker or anyone working at any other art whatever, while no one could become
sufficiently skillful at playing checkers or dice who didn't practice that very thing from his
youth but treated it as a sideline? And someone who picks up a shield or any other weapon
or implement of war, on that very day is going to be an adequate combatant in heavy-armor d
fighting or any other sort of battle that's needed in war, when no other implement that's
picked up is going to make anyone a craftsman or fighter or even be usable to someone who
hasn't gotten any knowledge about it or been supplied with adequate training?"

"Those implements would be worth a lot," he said.

"So then," I said, "to the extent that the work of the guardians is the most impor- e
tant, would it also be in need of the most leisure compared to other pursuits, as well as
of the greatest art and care?"

"I certainly imagine so," he said.

"So wouldn't it also need a nature adapted to that very pursuit?"

"How could it not?"

"So it would be our task, likely, if we're going to be capable of it, to pick out which and which sort of natures are adapted to the guarding of the city."

"Ours indeed."

"By Zeus," I said, "it's no light matter we've called down as a curse on ourselves. Still, it's not something to run away from in fear, at least to the extent our power permits."

375a "Certainly not," he said.

"So do you imagine that for guarding" I said, "there's any difference in nature between a pure bred puppy and a well bred young man?"

"What sort of nature are you talking about?"

"For instance, each of the pair, I suppose, needs to be sharp at perceiving things, nimble at pursuing what it perceives, and also strong, if it needs to fight when it catches something."

"There is certainly a need for all these things," he said.

"And to be courageous too, if it's going to fight well."

"How could it be otherwise?"

"But will a horse or a dog or any other animal whatever that's not spirited be likely to
b be courageous? Or haven't you noticed how indomitable and invincible spiritedness is, and how, when it's present, every soul is both fearless and unyielding against everything?"

"I've noticed."

"And surely it's obvious what the guardian needs to be like in the things that belong to his body."

"Yes."

"And particularly in what belongs to the soul, that he has to be spirited."

"That too."

"Then how, Glaucon," I said, "when they're that way in their natures, will they not be fierce toward each other and toward the other citizens?"

"By Zeus," he said, "not easily."

c "But surely they need to be gentle toward their own people but rough on their enemies, and if they aren't, they won't wait for others to destroy them but do it first themselves."

"True," he said.

"So what will we do?" I said. "Where are we going to find a character that's gentle and high-spirited at the same time? For presumably a gentle nature is opposite to a spirited one."

"So it appears."

"But surely if someone lacks either one of these things, he won't become a good guardian. But these things seem like impossibilities, and so it follows that a good
d guardian becomes an impossibility."

"It's liable to be that way," he said.

I too was stumped and was thinking over what had been said before, and I said, "Justly are we stumped, my friend, because we've gotten away from the image we were setting up."

"How do you mean that?"

"We didn't notice that there are natures, after all, of the sort we were imagining there aren't, that have these opposites in them."

"But where?"

"One might see it in other animals too, though not least in the one we set beside the guardian for comparison. Because you know, no doubt, about pure bred dogs,
e that this is their character by nature, to be as gentle as possible with those they're accustomed to and know, but the opposite with those they don't know."

“Certainly I know it.”

“Therefore,” I said, “this is possible, and it’s not against nature for the guardian to be of the sort we’re looking for.”

“It doesn’t seem like it.”

“Well then, does it seem to you that there’s still a further need for this in the one who’ll be fit for guarding, that in addition to being spirited he also needs to be a philosopher by nature?”

“How’s that?” he said. “I don’t get it.” 376a

“You’ll notice this too in dogs,” I said, “which is also worth wondering at in the beast.”

“What sort of thing?”

“That when it sees someone it doesn’t know, it gets angry, even when it hasn’t been treated badly by that person before, while anyone familiar it welcomes eagerly, even when nothing good has ever been done to it by that one. Or haven’t you ever wondered at this?”

“Till this moment,” he said, “I haven’t paid it any mind at all. That they do this, though, is certainly obvious.”

“But surely it shows an appealing attribute of its nature and one that’s philosophic b
in a true sense.”

“In what way?”

“In that it distinguishes a face as friend or enemy,” I said, “by nothing other than the fact that it has learned the one and is ignorant of the other. And indeed, how could it not be a lover of learning when it determines what’s its own and what’s alien to it by means of understanding and ignorance?”

“There’s no way it couldn’t,” he said.

“But surely,” I said, “the love of learning and the love of wisdom are the same thing?”

“They’re the same,” he said.

“Then shall we have the confidence to posit for a human being too, that if he’s
going to be at all gentle to his own people and those known to him, he needs to be by c
nature a lover of wisdom and of learning?”

“Let’s posit it.”

“So someone who’s going to be a beautiful and good guardian of our city will be philosophic, spirited, quick, and strong by nature.”

“Absolutely so,” he said.

“So he’d start out that way. But now in what manner will they be brought up and educated by us? And if we examine it, is there anything that gets us forward toward
catching sight of the thing for the sake of which we’re examining all this, the manner in d
which justice and injustice come into being in a city? The point is that we might not allow enough discussion, or we might go through a long one.”

And Glaucon’s brother said, “For my part, I expect this examination to be one that gets us very far along into that.”

“By Zeus, Adeimantus my friend,” I said, “it’s not to be given up then, even if it happens to be overlong.”

“Not at all.”

“Come then, and just as if they were in a story and we were telling the story and remaining at leisure, let’s educate the men in our speech.”

“We should do just that.”

* * *

BOOK III

* * *

412b “Okay,” I said, “what would be the next thing after that for us to distinguish?
c Wouldn’t it be which of these same people will rule and which will be ruled?”

“Sure.”

“And it’s clear that the older ones should be the rulers and the younger should be ruled?”

“That’s clear.”

“And that it should be the best among them?”

“That too.”

“And aren’t the best farmers the ones most adept at farming?”

“Yes.”

“But since in this case they need to be the best among the guardians, don’t they need to be the most adept at safeguarding the city?”

“Yes.”

“So don’t they need, to start with, to be intelligent at that as well as capable, and also protective of the city?”

d “That’s so.”

“But someone would be most protective of that which he happened to love.”

“Necessarily.”

“And surely someone would love that thing most which he regarded as having the same things advantageous to it as to himself, and believed that when it fared well it followed that he himself fared well, and the other way around when it didn’t.”

“That’s the way it is,” he said.

“Therefore the men who need to be selected from among the rest of the guardians
e are those who appear to us, when we examine the whole course of their lives, as if they
most of all would do wholeheartedly whatever they’d regard as advantageous to the city, and who wouldn’t be willing in any way to do what was not.”

“They’d be suited to it,” he said.

“It seems to me, then, that they need to be observed in all stages of life to see if they’re adept guardians of this way of thinking, and don’t drop it when they’re bewitched or subjected to force, forgetting their opinion that they ought to do what’s best for the city.”

“What do you mean by dropping?” he said.

“I’ll tell you,” I said. “It appears to me that an opinion goes away from one’s
413a thinking either willingly or unwillingly. A false one goes away willingly from someone
who learns differently, but every true one unwillingly.”

“The case of the willing dropping I understand,” he said, “but I need to learn about the unwilling case.”

“What?” I said. “Don’t you too believe human beings are deprived of good things unwillingly but of bad ones willingly? Isn’t it a bad thing to think falsely about the truth and a good thing to think truly? Or doesn’t believing things that are seem to you to be thinking truly?”

“You’re certainly speaking rightly,” he said, “and it does seem to me that people are unwilling to be deprived of the truth.”

b “And don’t they suffer this by being robbed, bewitched, or overpowered?”

"Now I'm not understanding again," he said.

"I guess I'm speaking like a tragedy," I said. "By those who are robbed, I mean people who are persuaded to change their minds and people who forget, because from the latter, time, and from the former, speech takes opinions away without their noticing it. Now presumably you understand?"

"Yes."

"And by those who are overpowered I mean people that some grief or pain causes to change their opinions."

"I understand that too," he said, "and you're speaking rightly."

"And I imagine that you too would claim that people are bewitched who change c
their opinions when they're either entranced by pleasure or in dread of something
frightening."

"Yes," he said, "it's likely that everything that fools people is bewitching."

"Then as I was just saying, one needs to find out which of them are the best
guardians of the way of thinking they have at their sides, that the thing they always need
to do is to do what seems to them to be best for the city. So they need to be observed
right from childhood by people who set tasks for them in which someone would be
most likely to forget such a thing or be fooled out of it; anyone who remembers it and is
hard to fool is to be chosen and anyone who doesn't is to be rejected. Isn't that so?" d

"Yes."

"And laborious jobs, painful sufferings, and competitions also need to be set up for them in which these same things are to be observed."

"That's right," he said.

"Thus a contest needs to be made," I said, "for the third form as well, that of
bewitchment, and it needs to be watched. The same way people check out whether
colts are frightened when they lead them into noisy commotions, the guardians, when
young, need to be taken into some terrifying situations and then quickly shifted into e
pleasant ones, so as to test them much more than gold is tested in a fire. If someone
shows himself hard to bewitch and composed in everything, a good guardian of himself and of the musical style that he learned, keeping himself to a rhythm and harmony
well-suited to all these situations, then he's just the sort of person who'd be most valuable both to himself and to a city. And that one among the children and the youths and
the men who is tested and always comes through unscathed is to be appointed as ruler 414a
of the city as well as guardian, and honors are to be given to him while he's living and
upon his death, when he's allotted the most prized of tombs and other memorials.
Anyone not of that sort is to be rejected. It seems to me, Glaucon," I said, "that the
selection and appointment of rulers and guardians is something like that, described in
outline, not with precision."

"It looks to me too like it would be done some such way," he said.

"Isn't it most correct, then, to call these the guardians in the true sense, complete b
guardians for outside enemies and also for friends inside, so that the latter won't want to
do any harm and the former won't have the power to? The young ones that we've been
calling guardians up to now, isn't it most correct to call auxiliaries and reinforcements
for the decrees of the rulers?"

"It seems that way to me," he said.

"Then could we come up with some contrivance," I said, "from among the lies that
come along in case of need, the ones we were talking about just now, some one noble lie c
told to persuade at best even the rulers themselves, but if not, the rest of the city?"

"What sort of thing?" he said.

"Nothing new," I said, "but something Phoenician* that has come into currency in
many places before now, since the poets assert it and have made people believe; but it
hasn't come into currency in our time and I don't know if it could—it would take a lot
of persuading."

"You seem a lot like someone who's reluctant to speak," he said.

"And I'll seem to you very appropriately reluctant," I said, "when I do speak."

"Speak," he said. "Don't be shy."

d "I'll speak, then. And yet I don't know how I'll get up the nerve or find the words
to tell it. First I'll try my hand at persuading the rulers themselves and the soldiers, and
then also the rest of the city, that, after all, the things we nurtured and educated them on
were like dreams; they seemed to be experiencing all those things that seemed to be
happening around them, but in truth they themselves were at the time under the soil
e inside the earth being molded and cultivated, and their weapons and other gear were
being crafted, and when they were completely formed, the earth, that was their mother,
made them spring up. So now, as if the land they dwell in were a mother and nurse, it's
up to them to deliberate over it, to defend it if anyone were to attack, and to take thought
on behalf of the rest of the citizens as their earthborn siblings."

"It's not without reason," he said, "that you were ashamed for so long to tell the lie."

415a "It was entirely reasonable," I said. "But all the same, listen to the rest of the story
as well. What we'll say in telling them the story is: 'All of you in the city are brothers,
but the god, when he molded those of you who are competent to be rulers, mixed gold
into them at their formation—that's why they're the most honorable—but all the auxiliaries have silver in them, and there's iron and bronze in the farmers and other skilled
b workers. So since you're all kin, for the most part you'll produce children like yourselves, but it's possible for a silver offspring sometimes to be born from a gold parent,
and a gold from a silver, and all the others likewise from one another. So the god exhorts
the rulers first and foremost to be good guardians of their children, of nothing more diligently than that, and to keep watch for nothing so diligently as for what they have inter-
c mixed in their souls. And if a child of theirs is born with bronze or iron mixed in it,
they'll by no means give way to pity, but paying it the honor appropriate to its nature,
they'll drive it out among the craftsmen or farmers, and if in turn any children are born
from those parents with gold or silver mixed in them, they'll honor them and take them
up, some to the guardian group, the others to the auxiliary, because there's an oracle
foretelling that the city will be destroyed when an iron or bronze guardian has guardianship over it.' So do you have any contrivance to get them to believe this story?"

"There's no way," he said, "at least for these people themselves. There might be
d one, though, for their sons and the next generation and the rest of humanity after that."

"But even that," I said, "would get things going well toward their being more protective of the city and of one another, because I understand pretty well what you mean.
And that's that it will carry on the way an oral tradition leads it. But once we've armed
these offspring of the earth, let's bring them forth with their rulers in the lead. And when
they've come, let them look for the most beautifully situated spot in the city to set up a
e military camp, from which they could most effectively restrain the people in the city if

*Cadmus, the legendary founder of the Greek city Thebes, came from Phoenicia (the region roughly the same as modern Lebanon). To found the city he had to kill a dragon. A god told him to plant the dragon's teeth, and the first inhabitants of the city sprang up from those seeds. When Socrates says the story was current in many places, he means there were other local legends of races sprung from the ground they now live on, all originally brothers and sisters whose first mother is the land that feeds them and that they defend and love.

any of them were unwilling to obey the laws, and defend against those outside it if any enemy, like a wolf, were to attack the flock. And when they've set up the camp and offered sacrifices to those whom they ought, let them make places to sleep. Or how should it be?"

"That way," he said.

"The sort of places that would be adequate to give shelter in both winter and summer?"

"Of course," he said, "because you seem to be talking about dwellings."

"Yes," I said, "dwellings for soldiers anyway, but not for moneymakers."

"How do you mean the one differs from the other?" he said. 416a

"I'll try to tell you," I said. "Because it's surely the most dreadful and shameful of all things for a shepherd to raise dogs as auxiliaries for the flock that are of the sort and brought up in such a way that, from intemperance or hunger or some bad habit of another kind, the dogs themselves try to do harm to the sheep, acting like wolves instead of dogs."

"It is dreadful," he said; "how could it be anything else?"

"Then isn't there a need to be on guard in every way so that our auxiliaries won't b
do that sort of thing to the citizens, since they're the stronger, becoming like savage
masters instead of benevolent allies?"

"There's a need to be on guard," he said.

"And wouldn't they have been provided with the most effective safeguard if they've been beautifully educated in their very being?"

"But surely they have been," he said.

And I said, "That's not something that deserves to be asserted with certainty,
Glaucon my friend. What we were saying just now does deserve to be, though, that they c
need to get the right education, whatever it is, if they're going to what's most important
for being tame, both toward themselves and toward those who are guarded by them."

"That's certainly right," he said.

"Now in addition to this education, any sensible person would claim that they
need to be provided with dwellings and other property of that sort, whatever it takes for
them not to be stopped from being the best possible guardians and not to be tempted to d
do harm to the citizens."

"And he'll be claiming something true."

"Then see whether they need to live and be housed in some such way as this,"
I said, "if they're going to be that sort of people. First, no private property that's not
completely necessary is to be possessed by any of them. Next, there's to be no house
or treasure room belonging to any of them except one that everyone who wants to
will enter. Provisions, of all things men need who are moderate and courageous
fighters in war, they're to receive at fixed times from the other citizens as recom- e
pense for guarding them, of such an amount that they have nothing over and nothing
lacking each year. Going regularly to public dining halls, they're to live in common
like soldiers in a camp. About gold and silver, it's to be said to them that they have
the divine sort from gods always in their souls, and have no further need of the
human sort, and that it's not pious to defile their possession of the former by mixing
with it the possession of mortal gold, because many impious deeds have occurred 417a
over the currency most people use, while the sort they have with them is uncorrupted. And for them alone of those in the city, it's not lawful to handle or touch gold
and silver, or even to go under the same roof with them, or wear them as ornaments,
or drink out of silver or gold cups.

"And in this way they'd keep themselves and the city safe. But whenever they possess private land and houses and currency, they'll be heads of households and farm
b owners instead of guardians, and they'll become hostile masters instead of allies of the other citizens, and spend their whole lives hating and being hated, and plotting and being plotted against, fearing those inside the city instead of and much more than the enemies outside it, as they and the rest of the city race onward, already very close to destruction.

"For all these reasons, then," I said, "we'll declare that's the way the guardians need to be provided for in the matter of housing and the rest, and we'll set these things down as laws, won't we?"

"Very much so," said Glaucon.

BOOK IV

* * *

427c "Your city, son of Ariston," I said, "[has] now be founded. So after that, take a
d look around in it yourself, once you've provided a light from somewhere, and call in your brother and Polemarchus and the others, if in any way we might see wherever its justice might be, and its injustice, and what differentiates the pair from each other, and which of the two someone who's going to be happy ought to get hold of, whether he goes unnoticed or not by all gods and human beings."

"You're talking nonsense," said Glaucon. "You took it on yourself to search for it
e because it's irreverent for you not to come to the aid of justice in every way to the limit of your power."

"It's true," I said, "as you remind me, and so it must be done, but you folks need to do your part too."

"Well that's what we'll do," he said.

"Then I hope to find it this way," I said. "I imagine our city, if in fact it's been correctly founded, is completely good."

"Necessarily," he said.

"So it's clear that it's wise and courageous and moderate and just."

"That's clear."

"Then whatever we find in it from among them, the leftover part will be what hasn't
428a been found?"

"Of course."

"Then just as with any other four things, if we were looking for a particular one of them in whatever it was, whenever we recognized that one first that would be good enough for us, but if we recognized the three first, by that very means we would have recognized the thing we're looking for, because it's obvious that it couldn't any longer be anything else than the thing left over."

"You're saying it correctly," he said.

"So for these things too, since they happen to be four, they need to be looked for in the same way?"

"Obviously."

"Well then, the first thing that seems to me to be clearly visible in it is wisdom. b
And there seems to be something strange about it."

"What?" he said.

"The city that we went over seems to me to be wise in its very being. Because it is well-counseled, isn't it?"

"Yes."

"And surely it's clear that this very thing, good counsel, is a certain kind of knowledge, since it's presumably not by ignorance but by knowledge that people counsel well."

"That's clear."

"But many kinds of knowledge of all varieties are surely present in the city."

"How could there not be?"

"Then is it on account of the carpenters' knowledge that the city is called wise and well-counseled?"

"Not at all," he said, "on account of that it's called skilled in carpentry." c

"Then it's not on account of the knowledge that counsels about how wooden equipment would be best that a city is called wise."

"No indeed."

"Well then, is it the knowledge about things made of bronze or anything else of that sort?"

"None whatever of those," he said.

"And it's not the knowledge about growing the fruits of the earth; that makes it skilled in farming."

"It seems that way to me."

"What about it, then?" I said. "Is there any knowledge in the city just now
founded by us, on the part of any of its citizens, by which it counsels not about things in d
the city pertaining to someone in particular, but about itself as a whole, and in what way
it would interact best within itself and with other cities?"

"There certainly is."

"What is it," I said, "and in which of them?"

"It's guardianship," he said, "and it's in those rulers whom we were just now naming complete guardians."

"So on account of this sort of knowledge, what do you call the city?"

"Well-counseled," he said, "and wise in its very being."

"Now do you imagine," I said, "that there will be more metalworkers present in
our city than these true guardians?" e

"A lot more metalworkers," he said.

"And compared also to all the rest who are given names for having any particular kinds of knowledge, wouldn't these guardians be the fewest of them all?"

"By a lot."

"Therefore it's by means of the smallest group and part of itself, the part that
directs and rules, and by the knowledge in it, that a whole city founded in accord with
nature would be wise. And it seems likely that this turns out by nature to be the smallest 429a
class, the one that's appropriately allotted a share of that knowledge which, alone
among the other kinds of knowledge, ought to be called wisdom."

"Very true, just as you say," he said.

"So we've discovered this one of the four—how we did it I don't know—both it and where in the city it's lodged."

"It seems to me at any rate," he said, "to have been discovered well enough."

"But as for courage, it and the part of the city it lies in, and through which the city is called courageous, are surely not very hard to see."

"How so?"

b "Who," I said, "would say a city was cowardly or courageous by looking to anything other than that part of it which defends it and takes the field on its behalf?"

"No one," he said, "would look to anything else."

"Because I don't imagine," I said, "that whether the other people in it are cowards or courageous would be what determines it to be the one sort or the other."

"No."

"Then a city is also courageous by means of a certain part of itself, by its having in it a power such that it will safeguard through everything its opinion about what's
c to be feared, that it's the same things or the sorts of things that the lawgiver passed on to them in their education. Or isn't that what you call courage?"

"I haven't quite understood what you're saying," he said; "just say it again."

"I mean," I said, "that courage is a certain kind of preservation."

"What kind of preservation exactly?"

"Of the opinion instilled by law through education about what things and what sorts of things are to be feared. By preserving it through everything I meant keeping it intact
d when one is in the midst of pains and pleasures and desires and terrors and not dropping it. I'm willing to make an image of what it seems to me to be like if you want me to."

"I want you to."

"You know, don't you," I said, "that dyers, when they want to dye wool so it will be purple, first select, from among the many colors, wool of the single nature belonging to white things, and then prepare it in advance, taking care with no little preparation that
e it will accept the pigment as much as possible, and only so dip it in the dye? And what is dyed in this way becomes impervious to fading, and washing it, whether without soaps or with them, has no power to remove the color from it, but what is not done that way—well, you know what it comes out like, whether one dyes it with other colors or this one without having taken care in advance."

"I know," he said, "that it's washed out and laughable."

"Then understand," I said, "that we too were doing something like that to the extent
430a of our power when we were selecting the soldiers and educating them with music and gymnastic training. Don't imagine that we devised that for any reason other than so they, persuaded by us, would take the laws into themselves like a dye in the most beautiful way possible, so that their opinion about what's to be feared, and about everything else, would become impervious to fading, because they'd had the appropriate nature and upbringing, and the dye couldn't be washed out of them by those soaps that are so formidable at scour-
b ing, either pleasure, which is more powerful at doing that than every sort of lye and alkaline ash, or pain, terror, and desire, more powerful than any other soaps. This sort of power and preservation through everything of a right and lawful opinion about what is and isn't to be feared, I for my part call courage, and I set it down as such unless you say otherwise."

"No," he said, "I don't say anything different, because it seems to me that you're considering the right opinion about these same things that comes about without education, as animal-like or slavish, and not entirely reliable, and that you'd call it something other than courage."

c "Entirely true," I said, "as you say."

"Then I accept this as being courage," he said.

"Yes, do accept it," I said, "but as a citizen's courage, and you'll be accepting it the right way. We'll go over something still more beautiful in connection with it later if you want, because what we've been looking for now is not that but justice. For the inquiry about that, I imagine this is sufficient."

"Yes," he said, "beautifully said."

"So two things are still left," I said, "that it's necessary to catch sight of in the city,
moderation, and the one for the sake of which we're looking for them all, justice." d

"Quite so."

"How, then, might we discover justice so that we won't have to bother any more about moderation?"

"Well," he said, "I don't know and I wouldn't want it to come to light first anyway if we're no longer going to examine moderation. So if you want to gratify me, consider this before that."

"I certainly do want to," I said; "unless I'd be doing an injustice."

"Consider it, then," he said. e

"It's got to be considered," I said, "and as seen from where we are, it looks more like a sort of consonance and harmony than the ones before."

"How?"

"Presumably," I said, "moderation is a certain well-orderedness, and a mastery over certain pleasures and desires, as people say—being stronger than oneself—though in what way they mean that I don't know. And some other things of that sort are said that are like clues to it, aren't they?"

"They most of all," he said.

"But then isn't being stronger than oneself absurd? Because the one who's stronger than himself would presumably also be weaker than himself, and the weaker
stronger, since the same person is referred to in all these terms." 431a

"How could it not be the same one?"

"But it appears to me," I said, "that this phrase intends to say that there's something to do with the soul within a human being himself that has something better and something worse in it, and whenever what's better by nature is master over what's worse, calling this 'being stronger than oneself' at least praises it. But whenever, from a
bad upbringing or some sort of bad company, the better part that's smaller is mastered b
by the larger multitude of the worse part, this as a reproach is blamed and called 'being weaker than oneself,' and the person so disposed is called intemperate."

"That's likely it," he said.

"Then look over toward our new city," I said, "and you'll find one of these things present in it. Because you'll claim that it's justly referred to as stronger than itself, if in fact something in which the better rules over the worse ought to be called moderate and stronger than itself."

"I am looking over at it," he said, "and you're telling the truth."

"And surely one would find a multitude and variety of desires as well as pleasures c
and pains, in children especially, and in women and menial servants, and also in most of the lower sorts of people among those who are called free."

"Very much so."

"But you'll meet with simple and measured desires and pleasures, which are guided by reasoning with intelligence and right opinion, in few people, who are both best in nature and best educated."

"True," he said.

"Then don't you see that these too are present in your city, and that the desires in
most people and those of the lower sorts are mastered there by the desires and intelli- d
gence of the lesser number of more decent people?"

"I do," he said.

"So if one ought to refer to any city as stronger than pleasures and desires, and than itself, that needs to be applied to this one."

"Absolutely so," he said.

"So then isn't it moderate too in all these respects?"

"Very much so," he said.

"And also, if in any city the same opinion is present in both the rulers and the
e ruled about who ought to rule, it would be present in this one. Doesn't that seem so?"

"Emphatically so," he said.

"Then as for being moderate, in which group of citizens will you say it's present when they're in this condition, in the rulers or in the ruled?"

"In both, presumably," he said.

"So do you see," I said, "that we had an appropriate premonition just now that moderation is like a certain harmony?"

"Why's that?"

"Because it's not like courage and wisdom, each of which by its presence in a
432a certain part showed the city to be either wise or courageous. It doesn't act that way, but is in fact stretched through the whole across the scale, showing the weakest, the strongest, and those in between to be singing the same song together, whether you want to rank them in intelligence, or, if you want, in strength, or even by their number or their money or by anything whatever of that sort. So we'd be most correct in claiming that this like-mindedness is moderation, a concord of the naturally worse and better about
b which ought to rule, both in the city and in each one."

"The way it seems to me is completely in accord with that," he said.

"Well then," I said, "three of them have been spotted in our city—at least it seems that way. So what would be the remaining form by which the city would further partake in virtue? For it's clear that this is justice."

"That's clear."

"So now, Glaucon, don't we need to take up positions like hunters in a circle around a patch of woods and concentrate our attention, so that justice doesn't escape
c anywhere, disappear from our sight, and become obscure? Because it's evident that it's in there somewhere. So look and make a spirited effort to catch sight of it, in case you spot it in any way before I do, and you'll show it to me."

"If only I were able to," he said. "Instead, if you treat me as a follower who's capable of seeing what's pointed out to him, you'll be handling me in an entirely sensible way."

"Follow then," I said, "after offering up prayers along with me."

"I'll do that," he said; "just you lead."

"The place sure does look like an inaccessible and shadowy one," I said; "at any rate it's dark and hard to scout through. But still, one needs to go on."

d "Yes, one does need to go on," he said.

And spotting something, I called, "Got it! Got it, Glaucon! We've probably got its trail, and I don't think it's going to get away from us at all."

"You bring good tidings," he said.

"But oh what a slug-like condition we were in," I said.

"In what sort of way?"

"All this time, you blessed fellow, and it seems it's been rolling around in front of our feet from the beginning, and we didn't see it for all that, but were utterly ridiculous;
e the way people holding something in their hands sometimes look for the things they're

holding, we too weren't looking at the thing itself but were gazing off into the distance somewhere, which is probably the very reason it escaped our notice."

"How do you mean?" he said.

"Like this," I said: "it seems to me that although we've been saying it and hearing it all along, we haven't learned from our own selves that we were in a certain way saying it."

"That's a long prologue for someone who's eager to hear," he said.

"Well then, hear whether I mean anything after all," I said. 433a

"Because from the beginning the thing we've set down as what we needed to do all through everything when we were founding the city, this, it seems to me, or else some form of this, is justice. Surely we set down, and said often, if you remember, that each one person needed to pursue one of the tasks that are involved in the city, the one to which his nature would be naturally best adapted."

"We did say that."

"And surely we've heard it said by many others that doing what's properly one's own and not meddling in other people's business is justice, and we've said it often b ourselves."

"We have said that."

"This, then, my friend," I said, "when it comes about in a certain way, is liable to be justice, this doing what's properly one's own. Do you know where I find an indication of this?"

"No, tell me," he said.

"It seems to me," I said, "that the thing that's left over in the city from the ones we've considered—moderation, courage, and wisdom—is what provided all of them with the power to come into being in it and provides their preservation once they've come into being, for as long as it's in it. And in fact we were claiming that justice would c be what was left over from them if we were to find the three."

"And that is necessary," he said.

"And certainly," I said, "if one had to judge which of these would do our city the most good by coming to be present in it, it would be hard to decide whether it's the agreement of opinion of the rulers and ruled, or the preservation of a lawful opinion that arises in the soldiers about what things are and aren't to be feared, or the judgment and guardianship present in the rulers, or whether it's this that does it the most good by d being in it, in a child and a woman and a slave and a free person and a craftsman and a ruler and one who's ruled, the fact that each of them, being one person, did what was properly his own and didn't meddle in other people's business."

"It's hard to decide," he said; "how could it not be?"

"Therefore, it seems that, with a view to a city's virtue, the power that comes from each person's doing what's properly his own in it is a match for its wisdom and moderation and courage."

"Very much so," he said.

"And wouldn't you place justice as a match for these as to a city's virtue?"

"Absolutely so."

"Then consider whether it will seem that way in this respect too: will you assign e the judging of lawsuits in the city to the rulers?"

"Certainly."

"And will they judge them with their sights on anything else besides this, that each party not have another's property or be deprived of his own?"

"No, only on that."

"Because it's the just thing?"

"Yes."

434a "Then in this respect too, having and doing what's properly one's own would be agreed to be justice."

"That's so."

"Now see if the same thing seems so to you that does to me. If a carpenter tries to work at the job of a leatherworker, or a leatherworker at that of a carpenter, or if they trade their tools and honors with each other, or even if the same person tries to do both jobs, and everything else gets traded around, would it seem to you to do the city any great harm?"

"Not very great," he said.

"But I imagine when someone who's a craftsman by nature, or some other sort of
b moneymaker, but proud of his wealth or the multitude of his household or his strength or anything else of the sort, tries to get in among the warrior kind, or one of the warriors into the deliberative and guardian kind when he doesn't merit it, and they trade their tools and honors with each other, or when the same person tries to do all these jobs at the same time, then I imagine it would seem to you too that this change and meddling among them would be the ruin of the city."

"Absolutely so."

"Therefore among the three classes there are, any meddling or changing into one
c another is of the greatest harm to the city, and would most correctly be referred to as the greatest wrongdoing."

"Precisely so."

"And wouldn't you say the greatest wrongdoing toward one's own city is injustice?"

"How could it not be?"

"So this is injustice. And let's say this the other way around; the minding of their own business by the moneymaking, auxiliary, and guardian classes, when each of them does what properly belongs to it in a city, is the opposite of that and would be justice and would show the city to be just?"

"It doesn't seem to be any other way than that to me," he said.

d "Let's not say it in quite so rigid a way yet, but if this form is agreed by us to be present in each one of the people as well and to be justice there, then we'll join in going along with it. What more would there be to say? And if not, then we'll consider something else. But for now let's complete the examination by which we imagined it would be easier to catch sight of what sort of thing justice is in one human being if we tried to see
e it first in some bigger thing that has justice in it. And it seemed to us that a city is just that, and so we founded the best one in our power, knowing well that it would be present in a good one at least. So let's carry over what came to light for us there to one person,
435a and if they're in accord, it will turn out beautifully; but if something different shows up in the single person, we'll go back to the city again and test it. And maybe, by examining them side by side and rubbing them together like sticks, we could make justice flame forth from them, and once it's become evident we could substantiate it for ourselves."

"Then it's down the road you indicate," he said, "and it behooves us to go there too."

"Well then," I said, "does the bigger or smaller thing that someone refers to by the same name happen to be unlike the other one in the respect in which it's called the same, or like it?"

"Like it," he said.

b "Therefore a just man will not differ at all from a just city with respect to the form of justice, but he'll be like it."

"He'll be like it," he said.

"But the city seemed to be just because each of the three classes of natures present in it did what properly belonged to it, while it seemed also to be moderate, courageous, and wise on account of certain other attributes and characteristic activities of these same classes."

"True," he said.

"Therefore, my friend, we'll regard a single person in this way too, as having these same forms in his soul, and as rightly deserving to have the same names applied to c
them as in the city as a result of the same attributes."

"There's every need to," he said.

"It's certainly a light question about the soul we've landed ourselves into now, you strange fellow," I said, "whether it has these three forms in it or not."

"It's not quite such a light one we seem to me to be in," he said. "It's probably because the saying is true, Socrates, that beautiful things are difficult."

"So it appears," I said. "And know for sure, Glaucon, that it's my opinion we'll never get hold of this in a precise way along the sorts of paths we're now taking in our d
arguments, because there's another, longer and more rigorous road that leads to it. Maybe, though, we can get hold of it in a way worthy, at least, of the things that have already been said and considered."

"Isn't that something to be content with?" he said. "For me, at present anyway, it would be good enough."

"Yes, certainly," I said, "that will be quite sufficient for me too."

"Don't get tired, then," he said; "just examine it."

"Well then," I said, "isn't there a great necessity for us to agree that the same forms and states of character are present in each of us as are in the city? Because pre- e
sumably they didn't get there from anywhere else. It would be ridiculous if anyone imagined the spirited character didn't come to be in the cities from particular people who also have this attribute, like those in Thrace and Scythia, and pretty generally in the northern region, or similarly with the love of learning, which one might attribute espe- 436a
cially to the region round about us, or the love of money that one might claim to be not least round about the Phoenicians and those in Egypt."

"Very much so," he said.

"That's just the way it is," I said, "and it's not difficult to recognize."

"Certainly not."

"But this now is difficult: whether we act each way by means of the same thing, or in the different ways by means of different things, of which there are three—whether we learn by means of one of the things in us, become spirited by means of another, and feel desires in turn by means of a third for the pleasures having to do with nourishment b
and procreation and as many things as are closely related to these, or whether we act by means of the whole soul in each of them, once we're aroused. These are the things that will be difficult to determine in a manner worthy of the discussion."

"It seems that way to me too," he said.

"Then let's try to mark out whether they're the same as one another or different, in this way."

"How?"

"It's obvious that the same thing isn't going to put up with doing or undergoing opposite things in the same respect and in relation to the same thing at the same time, so c
presumably if we find that happening in the things in question, we'll know that they're not the same but more than one thing."

"Okay."

"Then consider what I say."

"Say it," he said.

"Does the same thing have the power to stand still and move," I said, "at the same time in the same respect?"

"Not at all."

"Then let's agree about it in a still more precise way, so that we won't be quibbling
as we go on. Because if anyone were to say of a person who was standing still but moving
his hands and his head, that the same person was standing still and moving at the same
d time, I imagine we wouldn't consider that he ought to say it that way, but that some one
thing about the person stands still while another moves. Isn't that so?"

"It's so."

"So if the one who said that were to get still more cute, making the subtle point
that tops stand still as a whole and move at the same time, when they spin around with
the point fixed in the same place, or that anything else going around in a circle on the
same spot does that, we wouldn't accept it, since it's not with respect to the same things
about themselves that such things are in that case staying in place and being carried
e around, but we'd claim that they have in them something straight and something surrounding it, and stand still with respect to the straight part, since they don't tilt in any
direction, but move in a circle with respect to the surrounding part; and when the
straight axis is leaning to the right or the left, or forward or back, at the same time it's
spinning around, then it's not standing still in any way."

"You've got that right," he said.

"Therefore, when such things are said they won't knock us off course at all, any
437a more than they'll persuade us that in any way, the same thing, at the same time, in the
same respect, in relation to the same thing, could ever undergo, be, or do opposite things."

"Not me at any rate," he said.

"Be that as it may," I said, "in order that we won't be forced to waste time going through all the objections of that sort and establishing that they aren't true, let's go forward on the assumption that this is how it is, having agreed that, if these things should ever appear otherwise than that, all our conclusions from it will have been refuted."

"That's what one ought to do," he said.

b "Well then, would you place nodding 'yes' as compared to shaking one's head
'no' among things that are opposite to each other, and having a craving to get something
as compared to rejecting it, and drawing something to oneself as compared to pushing it
away, and everything of that sort? Whether they're things one does actively or experiences passively, there won't be any difference on that account."

"Sure," he said, "they're opposites."

"And what about thirst and hunger and the desires in general," I said, "as well as
wishing and wanting? Wouldn't you place all these things somewhere in those forms
c just mentioned? For example, wouldn't you claim that the soul of someone who desires
either has a craving for what it desires, or draws to itself what it wants to become its
own, or, in turn, to the extent it wishes something to be provided to it, nods its assent to
this to itself as though it had asked some question, stretching out toward its source?"

"I would indeed."

"And what about this? Won't we place not wanting and not wishing and not desiring in with pushing away and banishing from itself and in with all the opposites of the former things?"

"How could we not?"

d "Now these things being so, are we going to claim that there's a form consisting
of desires, and that among these themselves, the most conspicuous ones are what we
call thirst and what we call hunger?"

"We're going to claim that," he said.

"And the one is for drink, the other for food?"

"Yes."

"Now to the extent that it's thirst, would it be a desire in the soul for anything beyond that of which we say it's a desire? For instance, is thirst a thirst for a hot drink or a cold one, or a big or a little one, or in a word, for any particular sort of drink? Or, if
there's any heat present in addition to the thirst, wouldn't that produce an additional e
desire for cold, or if cold is present, a desire for heat? And if by the presence of magnitude the thirst is a big one, that will add a desire for a big drink, or of smallness, for a little one? But being thirsty itself will never turn into a desire for anything other than the very thing it's naturally for, for drink, or being hungry in turn for food?"

"It's like that," he said; "each desire itself is only for the very thing it's naturally for, while the things attached to it are for this or that sort."

"Then let's not be unprepared, and let someone get us confused, on the grounds 438a
that no one desires drink, but decent quality drink, and not food but decent quality food, since everyone, after all, desires good things. So if thirst is a desire, it would be for a decent quality of drink, or of whatever else it's a desire for, and the same way with the other desires."

"Well, maybe there could seem to be something in what he's saying," he said, "when he says that."

"But surely," I said, "with all such things that are related to something, the
ones that are of particular kinds are related to something of a particular kind, as it b
seems to me, while the sorts that are just themselves are related only to something that's just itself."

"I don't understand," he said.

"Don't you understand," I said, "that what's greater is of such a sort as to be greater than something?"

"Certainly."

"Than a lesser thing?"

"Yes."

"And a much greater thing than one that's much less, right?"

"Yes."

"And also a thing that was greater than one that was less, and a thing that's going to be greater than one that's going to be less?"

"Yes, of course," he said.

"And something more numerous is related to something that's fewer, and something twice as many to something that's half as many, and all that sort of thing, and also c
something heavier to something lighter and faster to slower, and in addition, hot things are related to cold things, and isn't everything like that the same way?"

"Very much so."

"And what about the kinds of knowledge? Aren't they the same way? Knowledge just by itself is knowledge of what's learnable just by itself, or of whatever one ought to set down knowledge as being of, while a particular knowledge or a particular sort is of a particular thing or a particular sort of thing. I mean this sort of thing: when a knowledge of constructing houses came into being, didn't it differ from the other kinds of d
knowledge so that it got called housebuilding?"

"Certainly."

"And wasn't that because it's a particular kind of knowledge, and any of the others is a different sort?"

"Yes."

"And wasn't it because it was about a particular sort of thing that it too came to be of a particular sort, and the same way for the other arts and kinds of knowledge?"

"That's the way it is."

"Well then," I said, "if you've understood it now, call that what I meant to say then,
e that with all the things that are such as to be about something, the ones that are only themselves are about things that are only themselves, while the ones that are of particular kinds are about things of particular kinds. And I'm not saying at all that the sorts of things they're about are the same sorts they themselves are, as a result of which the knowledge of what's healthy and sick would be healthy and sickly, and the knowledge of bad and good things would be bad and good; instead, I'm saying that when a knowledge came into being that was not just about the very thing knowledge is about, but about a particular thing, and that was what's healthy and sick, it too as a result came to be of a particular sort. And this made it no longer be called simply knowledge, but, with the particular sort included, medicine."

"I've understood it," he said, "and it does seem that way to me."

439a "So wouldn't you place thirst," I said, "among those things in which to be for something is exactly what they are? Thirst is, of course, for something."

"I would, yes," he said; "it's for drink anyway."

"And isn't a particular sort of thirst for a particular sort of drink, while thirst itself is not for a lot or a little, or for a good or a bad one, or, in a word, for any particular sort, but thirst itself is naturally just for drink itself?"

"Absolutely so."

"Therefore the soul of someone who's thirsty, to the extent he's thirsty, wants
b nothing other than to drink, and stretches out to this, and sets itself in motion toward it."

"Clearly so."

"So if anything ever pulls it back when it's thirsty, it would be some different thing in it from the very thing that's thirsty, and that tows it like an animal toward drinking? Because we claim that the same thing couldn't be doing opposite things in the same part of itself in relation to the same thing at the same time."

"No, it couldn't."

"In the same way, I imagine, one doesn't do well to say about an archer that his
c hands push and pull the bow at the same time, but rather that one hand is the one pushing it and the other the one pulling it."

"Absolutely so," he said.

"Now do we claim that there are some people who sometimes, while they're thirsty, aren't willing to drink?"

"Very much so," he said, "many people and often."

"Well what should one say about them?" I said. "Isn't there something in their soul telling them to drink and something preventing them from it that's different from and mastering what's telling them to?"

"It seems that way to me," he said.

d "And doesn't the thing that prevents such things come about in it, when it does come about, from reasoning? But the things that tug and pull come to it from passions and disorders?"

"It looks that way."

"So not unreasonably will we regard them as being two things and different from each other, referring to that in the soul by which it reasons as its reasoning part, and that by which it feels erotic love, hunger, and thirst, and is stirred with the other desires, as its irrational and desiring part, associated with certain satisfactions and pleasures."

"No, we'd regard them that way quite reasonably," he said.

"So let these two forms be marked off in the soul," I said. "But is the part that has e
to do with spiritedness, and by which we're spirited, a third thing, or would it be of the same nature as one of these two?"

"Maybe the same as one of them," he said, "the desiring part."

"But I once heard something that I believe," I said, "about how Leontius, Aglaion's son, was going up from Piraeus along the outside of the north wall, and noticed dead bodies lying beside the executioner. He desired to see them, but at the same time felt disgust and turned himself away; for a while he struggled and covered his eyes, but then he was 440a
overcome by his desire, and running toward the bodies holding his eyes wide open, he said, 'See for yourselves, since you're possessed! Take your fill of the lovely sight.'"

"I've heard that myself," he said.

"This story certainly indicates," I said, "that anger sometimes makes war against the desires as though it were one thing acting against another."

"It does indicate that," he said.

"And don't we often observe it in many other ways as well," I said, "when desires overpower someone contrary to his reasoning part, that he scolds himself and is aroused b
against the part in him that's overpowering him, and just as if there were a pair of warring factions, the spiritedness of such a person becomes allied with his reason? But as for its making a partnership with the desires to act in defiance when reason has decided what ought not to be done, I don't suppose you'd claim you'd ever noticed such a thing happening in yourself, or, I imagine, in anyone else."

"No, by Zeus!" he said.

"Then what about when someone thinks he's being unjust?" I said. "The more noble he is, won't he be that much less capable of getting angry at being hungry or cold c
or suffering anything else at all of the sort from the person he thinks is doing those things to him justly, and won't he be unwilling, as I'm saying, for his spirit to be aroused against that person?"

"That's true," he said.

"But what about when he regards himself as being treated unjustly? Doesn't the spirit in him seethe and harden and ally itself with what seems just, and submitting to suffering through hunger and cold and all such things, it prevails and doesn't stint its d
noble struggles until it gains its end or meets its death, or else, called back, like a dog by a herdsman, by the reason that stands by it, it becomes calm?"

"It is very much like what you describe," he said. "And certainly in our city we set up the auxiliaries like dogs obedient to the rulers, who were like shepherds of the city."

"You conceive what I want to say beautifully," I said, "especially if you've taken it to heart in this respect in addition to that one."

"In what sort of respect?"

"That it's looking the opposite of the way it did to us just now with the spirited e
part, because then we imagined it was something having to do with desire, but now we're claiming that far from that, it's much more inclined in the faction within the soul to take arms on the side of the reasoning part."

"Absolutely," he said.

"Then is it different from that too, or some form of the reasoning part, so that there aren't three but two forms in the soul, a reasoning one and a desiring one? Or just as, in the city, there were three classes that held it together, moneymaking, auxiliary, 441a
and deliberative, so too in the soul is there this third, spirited part, which is by nature an auxiliary to the reasoning part, unless it's corrupted by a bad upbringing?"

"It's necessarily a third part," he said.

c "Yes," I said, "as long as it comes to light as something differing from the reasoning part, the same way it manifested itself as different from the desiring part."

"But it's not hard to make that evident," he said, "since one could see this even in small children, that they're full of spiritedness right from birth, while some of them
b seem to me never to get any share of reasoning, and most get one at a late time of life."

"Yes, by Zeus," I said, "you put it beautifully. And also in animals one could see that what you're describing is that way. And in addition to these things, what we cited from Homer in some earlier place in the conversation will bear witness to it:

> Striking his chest, he scolded his heart with words.

Here Homer has clearly depicted that which reflects on the better and the worse as one
c thing rebuking another, that which is irrationally spirited."

"You've said it exactly right," he said.

"Well, with a lot of effort we've managed to swim through these waters, and we're tolerably well agreed that the same classes in the city are present in the soul of each one person, and are equal in number."

"They are."

"Isn't it already a necessary consequence, then, that a private person is wise in the same manner and by the same means that a city was wise?"

"How else?"

"And the means by which and manner in which a private person is courageous is
d that by which and in which a city was courageous, and everything else related to virtue is the same way for both?"

"Necessarily."

"So, Glaucon, I imagine we'll claim also that a man is just in the very same manner in which a city too was just."

"This too is entirely necessary."

"But surely we haven't forgotten somewhere along the way that the city was just because each of the three classes that are in it do what properly belongs to them."

"We don't seem to me to have forgotten that," he said.

"Therefore we need to remember also that for each of us, that whoever has each
e of the things within him doing what properly belongs to it will be just himself and be someone who does what properly belongs to him."

"It needs to be remembered very well indeed," he said.

"Then isn't it appropriate for the reasoning part to rule, since it's wise and has forethought on behalf of the whole soul, and for the spirited part to be obedient to it and allied with it?"

"Very much so."

"Then as we were saying, won't a blending of music with gymnastic exercise
442a make them concordant, tightening up the one part and nourishing it with beautiful speeches and things to learn while relaxing the other with soothing stories, taming it with harmony and rhythm?"

"Exactly so," he said.

"So once this pair have been nurtured in this way, and have learned and been educated in the things that truly belong to them, they need to be put in charge of the desiring part, which is certainly the largest part of the soul in each person and by nature the most insatiable for money. This part needs to be watched over so that it doesn't get filled with the so-called pleasures of the body and, when it becomes big
b and strong, not do the things that properly belong to it, but try to enslave and rule over

things that are not of a kind suited to it, so that it turns the whole life of all the parts upside-down."

"Very much so," he said.

"And wouldn't this pair also stand guard on behalf of the whole soul and body against their external enemies in the most beautiful way," I said, "one part deliberating while the other goes to war, following its ruler and accomplishing with its courage the things that have been decided?"

"That's the way it is."

"And I imagine we call each one person courageous on account of this part, when c
the spirited part of him preserves through pains and pleasures what's been passed on to it by speeches as something to be feared or not."

"Rightly so," he said.

"And wise by that little part, the one that ruled in him and passed those things on, and it in turn has knowledge in it of what's advantageous for each part and for the whole consisting of the three of them in common."

"Very much so."

"And what next? Isn't each person moderate by the friendship and concord
among these same things, when the ruling part and the pair that are ruled are of the same d
opinion that the reasoning part ought to rule and aren't in revolt against it?"

"Moderation is certainly nothing other than that," he said, "in a city or a private person."

"But each person will be just on account of the thing we repeat so often, and in that manner."

"That's a big necessity."

"Then what about this?" I said. "Surely it hasn't gotten fuzzy around the edges for us in any way, has it, so it would seem to be some other sort of justice than the one that came to light in the city?"

"It doesn't seem to me it has," he said.

"Well," I said, "we could establish this beyond all doubt, if anything in our soul
still stands unconvinced, by applying the commonplace standards to it." e

"What sort of standards exactly?"

"For example, if we were asked to come to an agreement about that city and the
man who's like that by nature and upbringing, as to whether it seemed such a man
would steal a deposit of gold or silver he'd accepted in trust, do you think anyone would 443a
imagine he'd be more likely to do that than all those not of his sort?"

"No one would," he said.

"And wouldn't temple robberies, frauds, and betrayals, either of friends in private or cities in public capacities, be out of the question for this person?"

"Out of the question."

"And in no way whatever would he be unfaithful to oaths or other agreements."

"How could he?"

"And surely adultery, neglect of parents, and lack of attentiveness to the gods belong more to any other sort of person than to this one."

"Any other sort for sure," he said.

"And isn't the thing responsible for all that the fact that each of the parts within b
him does what properly belongs to it in connection with ruling and being ruled?"

"That and nothing else."

"So are you still looking for justice to be anything other than the power that produces men and cities of that sort?"

"By Zeus," he said, "not I."

"So our dream has come to complete fulfillment; we said we suspected, right
c from when we started founding the city, that by the favor of some god we were liable to
have gotten to an origin and outline of justice."

"Absolutely so."

"And what it was in fact, Glaucon—and this is why it was so helpful—was an image of justice, that it was right for the natural leatherworker to do leatherwork and not do anything else, and for the carpenter to do carpentry, and the same way for the rest."

"So it appears."

"And the truth is, justice was something like that, as it seems, but not anything connected with doing what properly belongs to oneself externally, but with what's on the
d inside, that truly concerns oneself and properly belongs to oneself, not allowing each
thing in him to do what's alien to it, or the classes of things in his soul to meddle with one
another, but setting his own house in order in his very being, he himself ruling over and
bringing order to himself and becoming his own friend and harmonizing three things,
exactly like the three notes marking a musical scale at the low end, the high end, and the
e middle; and if any other things happen to be between them, he binds all of them together
and becomes entirely one out of many, moderate and harmonized. Only when he's in this
condition does he act, if he performs any action having to do with acquiring money, or
taking care of the body, as well as anything of a civic kind or having to do with private
transactions; in all these cases he regards an action that preserves that condition and helps
to complete it as a just and beautiful act, and gives it that name, and regards as wisdom the
444a knowledge that directs that action. Anything that always breaks down that condition, he
regards as an unjust action, and the opinion that directs that, he regards as ignorance."

"You're absolutely telling the truth, Socrates," he said.

"Okay," I said, "if we were to claim that we've discovered the just man and the just city, and exactly what justice is in them, I imagine we wouldn't seem to be telling a total lie."

"By Zeus, certainly not," he said.

"Shall we claim that, then?"

"Let's claim it."

"So be it," I said. "What needs to be examined after this, I imagine, is injustice."

"Clearly."

b "Doesn't it in turn have to be some sort of faction among these three things, a
meddling and butting in and an uprising of a certain part of the soul against the whole,
in order to rule in it when that's not appropriate, because it's of such a kind by nature
that it's only fitting for it to be a slave? I imagine we'll claim something like that, and
that the disorder and going off course of these parts is injustice as well as intemperance,
cowardice, foolishness, and all vice put together."

c "Those are the very things it is," he said.

"Then as for doing unjust things and being unjust," I said, "and in turn doing just things, isn't it by now patently obvious exactly what all these are, if indeed that's so for both injustice and justice?"

"How so?"

"Because," I said, "they don't happen to be any different from what's healthy or diseased; what those are in a body, these are in a soul."

"In what way?" he said.

"Presumably, healthful things produce health and diseased things produce disease."

"Yes."

d "Then is it also the case that doing just things produces justice, while doing unjust
things produces injustice?"

"Necessarily."

"And producing health is settling the things in the body into a condition of mastering and being mastered by one another in accord with nature, while producing disease is settling them into ruling and being ruled one by another contrary to nature."

"That's it."

"Then in turn, as for producing justice," I said, "isn't that settling the things in the soul into a condition of mastering and being mastered by one another in accord with nature, while producing injustice is settling them into ruling and being ruled one by another contrary to nature?"

"Exactly," he said.

"Therefore, it seems likely that virtue would be a certain health, beauty, and good
condition of the soul, while vice would be a disease, deformity, and weakness." e

"That's what they are."

"And don't beautiful practices lead to the acquisition of virtue, and shameful ones to vice?"

"Necessarily."

"So what remains at this point, it seems, is for us to consider next whether it's
profitable to perform just actions, pursue beautiful practices, and be just, whether or not 445a
it goes unnoticed that one is of that sort, or to do injustice and be unjust, so long as one
doesn't pay the penalty or become better by being corrected."

"But Socrates," he said, "the question already appears to me to have become
laughable, whether, when life doesn't seem worth living with the body's nature
corrupted, even with all the foods and drinks and every sort of wealth and political rule,
it will then be worth living with the nature of that very thing by which we live disor- b
dered and corrupted, even if someone does whatever he wants, but not the thing by
which he'll get rid of vice and injustice and acquire justice and virtue, seeing as how it's
become obvious that each of them is of the sort we've gone over."

"It is laughable," I said. "Nevertheless, since we've come this far, far enough to be able to see clearly that this is the way it is, it wouldn't be right to get tired out."

"By Zeus," he said, "getting tired out is the last thing we ought to do."

"Come up to the mark now," I said, "so you too can see how many forms vice has, c
the way it seems to me, at least the ones that are even worth looking at."

"I'm following," he said; "just speak."

"Well," I said, "as though from a lookout spot, since we've climbed up to this point in the discussion, there appears to me to be one look that belongs to virtue and infinitely many to vice, but some four among them that are even worth mentioning."

"How do you mean?" he said.

"There are liable to be as many dispositions of a soul," I said, "as there are dispositions among polities that have looks to them."

"How many, exactly?" d

"Five for polities," I said, "and five for a soul."

"Say which ones," he said.

"I say that one," I said, "would be this type of polity we've been going over, but it could be named in two ways, since if one exceptional man arose among the rulers it would be called kingship, but aristocracy if there were more than one."

"True," he said.

"This, then," I said, "is one form that I'm talking about, since whether one or more
than one man arose, it wouldn't change any of the laws of the city worthy of mention, e
since the upbringing and education they got would be the way we went over."

"Likely not," he said.

BOOK V

449 "Well, I call that kind of city and polity, and that kind of man, good and right, and if this sort are right, the rest are bad and wrong, in the ways the cities are managed and the way the soul's disposition is constituted in private persons, and the badness takes four forms."

"What sorts are they?" he said.

And I was going on to describe them in order, the way it appeared to me they
b change out of one another in each case, but Polemarchus, who was sitting a little way
from Adeimantus, reached out his hand and grabbed him from above by his cloak at the
shoulder, drew him near, stretching himself forward, and was saying something while
stooping toward him, of which we heard nothing but this: "Shall we let it go, then," he
said, "or what shall we do?"

"Not in the least," said Adeimantus, now speaking loudly.

And I said, "What in particular won't you let go?"

"You," he said.

c "Because of what in particular?" I said.

"You seem to us to be taking the lazy way out," he said, "and to be cheating us out of a whole form that belongs to the argument, and not the least important one, to avoid going over it, and you seem to have imagined you'd get away with speaking of it dismissively, saying it's obvious, about women and children, that what belongs to friends will be shared in common."

"And wasn't I right, Adeimantus?" I said.

"Yes," he said, "but this 'right' needs explanation, like the rest of it, about what
d the manner of the sharing would be, since there could be many. So don't pass over
which of them you're talking about, since we've been waiting all this time imagining
you'd make some mention somewhere about the procreation of children, how they'll be
produced and once they're born how they'll be raised, and of this whole sharing of
women and children you're talking about. Because we think it has a big bearing, in fact
a total impact, on whether the polity comes into being in the right way or not. But now,
since you're taking on another polity before you've determined these things sufficiently,
450a it seemed right to us to do what you've heard, to refuse to let you go until you've gone
over all these things just like the rest."

"Me too," said Glaucon; "put me down as a partner in this vote."

"Don't worry," said Thrasymachus, "consider these things as having seemed good to all of us, Socrates."

"Oh what you folks have done by ambushing me," I said. "So much discussion
about the polity you're setting in motion again, as though from the beginning, when
I was rejoicing at having already gotten to the end of it, feeling content if anyone would
b leave these things alone and accept them the way they were stated then. You have no
idea what a big swarm of arguments you've stirred up with the things you're now
demanding; since I saw that at the time I passed it by, fearing it would cause a lot of
trouble."

"What!" said Thrasymachus. "Do you imagine these people have come this far now to fritter away their time looking for gold rather than to listen to arguments?"

"All well and good," I said, "but within measure."

"The measure in hearing such arguments, Socrates," said Glaucon, "for anyone who has any sense, is a whole life. So give up on that as far as we're concerned; just see

that you don't get tired in any way of going all through the way it seems to you about c
the things we're asking, what the sharing of children and women will be among our
guardians, and about the rearing of those who are still young that takes place in the time
between birth and education, which seems to be the most troublesome time. So try to
say in what way it needs to happen."

"It's not easy to go through, you happy fellow," I said, "because it has a lot of
doubtful points, even more than the things we went through before. It could even be
doubted that what's spoken of is possible, and even if it came about as much as it possibly could, there will also be doubts even in that case that this would be the best thing.
That's why there was a certain reluctance to touch on these things, for fear, dear com- d
rade, the argument would seem to be only a prayer."

"Don't be reluctant at all," he said, "since your listeners won't be unfair or disbe-
lieving or ill-disposed."

And I said, "Most excellent fellow, I take it you're saying that to give me
courage?"

"I am," he said.

"Well you're doing exactly the opposite," I said. "If I believed I knew what I was
talking about, your pep talk would have been a beautiful one; to speak when one knows e
the truth, among people who are intelligent and friendly, about things that are of greatest
importance and dear to us, is secure and encouraging, but to make one's arguments at the
same time one is doubtful and searching, which is exactly what I'm doing, is a frighten- 451a
ing and perilous thing. It's not because I'm liable to be laughed at—that's childish—
but from fear that I'll not only tumble away myself from the truth, about things one least
ought to fall down on, but that I'll also be lying in ruins with the friends I've dragged
down with me. So instead I'll fall on my face in obeisance to Adrasteia, Glaucon, for her
favor for what I'm about to say. I hope it's a lesser sin to become an unwilling murderer
of someone than a deceiver about what's beautiful and good and just and lawful. That's a
risk it's better to run among enemies rather than friends, so it's a good thing you gave me
encouragement."

And Glaucon, with a laugh, said, "Okay, Socrates, if we experience anything b
discordant from what you say, we'll release you like someone purified from being a
murderer and cleared as no deceiver of us. Just speak up boldly."

"Well, certainly someone who's released even in that situation is purified," I said,
"as the law says, so it's likely that if it's that way there, it is here too."

"Speak, then," he said, "with that assurance."

"It's necessary to go back again now," I said, "and say what probably should
have been said then in the proper place. And maybe this would be the right way, after c
the male drama has been completely finished, to finish the female drama in turn,
especially since you're calling for it this way. To my way of thinking, for human
beings born and educated in the way we went over, there is no other right way for
them to get and treat children and women than to hasten down that road on which we
first started them. We tried, I presume, in the argument, to set the men up like
guardians of a herd."

"Yes."

"Then let's follow that up by giving them the sort of birth and rearing that closely d
resemble that, and consider whether it suits us or not."

"How?" he said.

"This way. Do we imagine that the females among the guard dogs ought to join
in guarding the things the males guard, and hunt with them and do everything else in

common, or should they stay inside the house as though they were disabled by bearing and nursing the puppies, while the males do the work and have all the tending of the flock?"

"Everything in common," he said, "except that we'd treat the females as weaker and the males as stronger."

e "Is it possible, then," I said, "to use any animal for the same things if you don't give it the same rearing and training?"

"It's not possible."

"So if you're going to make use of women at the same tasks as men, they'll also have to be taught the same things."

"Yes."

452a "Music and gymnastic exercise were given to the men."

"Yes."

"Therefore this pair of arts needs to be made available to the women too, as well as the things connected with war, and they need to be applied in the same manner."

"It's likely, based on what you're saying," he said.

"Probably," I said, "many of the things being talked about now would look absurd if they're done the way they're being described, just because they're contrary to custom."

"Very much so indeed," he said.

"Do you see which of them would be most absurd?" I said. "Isn't it obvious that
b it would be for the women to be exercising naked in the wrestling schools alongside the men, and not just the young ones but also those who're already on the older side, like the old men who're still devoted to exercising in the gyms when they're wrinkled and not a pleasant sight?"

"By Zeus," he said, "that would look absurd, at least the way things are at present."

"But as long as we've got ourselves started talking about it, we shouldn't be afraid, should we, of all the jokes of whatever sort from witty people at the advent such
c a change in both gymnastic exercise and music, and not least about having war 'tools' and 'mounting' horses?"

"You've got that right," he said.

"Instead, since we have started to talk about it, we need to pass right to the tough part of the law, asking these guys not to do what properly belongs to them but to be serious, and to recall that it's not much time since it seemed to the Greeks the way it does now to many of the barbarians, that it's shameful and absurd to look at a naked man, and when
d the people of Crete first introduced gymnasiums, and then the Spartans, the fashionable people of the time took the opportunity to ridicule all that. Don't you imagine they did?"

"I do."

"But since it appeared to those who adopted the practice, I imagine, that it was better to uncover all such things than to hide them, what had been absurd in their eyes was stripped away by what was exposed as best in their reasoning. And this reveals that one who considers anything absurd other than what's bad is empty-headed, as is one who tries to get a laugh by looking at any other sight as laughable than one that's sense-
e less and bad, or who takes seriously any mark of what's beautiful that he's set up other than what's good."

"Absolutely so," he said.

"Well then, isn't this the first thing that needs to be agreed about these things: whether they're possible or not? And shouldn't a chance for disputes be given to anyone

who wants to dispute it, whether it's someone fun-loving or the serious type, as to 453a
whether female human nature is capable of sharing in all the work that belongs to the nature of the male kind, or not in any at all, or in some sorts and not others, and whether in particular this last applies to things connected with war? Wouldn't someone be likely to get to the end of the subject most beautifully by starting off the most beautifully in this way?"

"By far," he said.

"Then do you want us to carry on the dispute ourselves against ourselves, on behalf of the others," I said, "so that the opposing argument won't be under siege undefended?"

"There's no reason not to," he said.

"So let's say, on their behalf, 'Socrates and Glaucon, there's no need for anyone b
else to dispute with you, because you yourselves, at the beginning of the process of settling the city that you founded, agreed that each one person had to do the one thing that properly belonged to him by nature.'"

"Suppose we did agree to that; how could we not?"

"'Well is there any way that a woman isn't completely different from a man in her nature?'"

"How could she not be different?"

"Then isn't it also appropriate to assign each of them different work that's in accord with their nature?"

"Of course."

"So why aren't you mistaken now and contradicting yourselves, when you also c
declare that men and women ought to do the same things, despite having the most diverse natures? Will you be able to make any defense against this, you amazing fellow?'"

"Not very easily, just on the spur of the moment," he said; "but I'll ask you, in fact I am asking you, to be the interpreter of the argument on our side too, whatever it is."

"This is what I was afraid of a long time ago, Glaucon," I said, "as well as many
other things I foresaw, and I was reluctant to touch on the law about the way of having d
and bringing up women and children."

"No, by Zeus," he said, "it seems like it's no easy matter to digest."

"No, it's not," I said. "But it's like this: whether one falls into a little swimming tank or into the middle of the biggest sea, all the same one just swims none the less."

"Quite so."

"Well then, don't we too have to swim and try to save ourselves from the argument, and just hope for some dolphin to pick us up on his back or for some other sort of rescue that's hard to count on?"

"It looks that way," he said.

"Come on then," I said, "let's find a way out somewhere if we can. Because we're e
agreed that a different nature needs to follow a different pursuit, and that a woman and a man are different in nature; but we're claiming now that these different natures need to follow the same pursuits. Are these the things we're accused of?"

"Precisely."

"Oh Glaucon," I said, "what a noble power the debater's art has." 454a

"Why in particular?"

"Because many people even seem to me to fall into it unwillingly," I said, "and imagine they're not being contentious but having a conversation, because they're not able to examine something that's being said by making distinctions according to forms, but pounce on the contradiction in what's been said according to a mere word, subjecting one another to contention and not conversation."

"That is exactly the experience of many people," he said, "but that surely doesn't apply to us in the present circumstance, does it?"

b "It does absolutely," I said. "At any rate, we're running the risk of engaging in debate unintentionally."

"How?"

"We're pouncing, in an altogether bold and contentious manner, on 'the nature that's not the same' as a result of a word, because that's what's required not to have the same pursuits, but we didn't give any consideration whatever to what form of different or same nature we were marking off, and how far it extended, at the time when we delivered up different pursuits to a different nature and the same ones to the same nature."

"No, we didn't consider that," he said.

c "Well, according to that, then," I said, "it seems like we're entitled to ask ourselves whether it's the same nature that belongs to bald people as to longhaired ones, and not the opposite one, and whenever we agree that it's opposite, if bald people do leatherwork, not allow longhaired people to, or if the longhaired ones do, not allow the others."

"That would certainly be ridiculous," he said.

"Well is it ridiculous for any other reason," I said, "than because we weren't reck-
d oning on every sort of same and different nature at the time, but only watching out for that form of otherness and likeness that was relevant to the pursuits themselves? For example, with a male doctor and a female doctor, we meant that it's the soul that has the same nature. Don't you think so?"

"I do."

"But with a male doctor and a male carpenter, it's different?"

"Completely different, I presume."

"So," I said, "if the men's or women's kind is manifestly superior in relation to any art or other pursuit, won't we claim that this needs to be given over to that one of
e the two? But if they apparently differ only in that the female bears the young and the male mounts the female, we'll claim instead that it hasn't yet been demonstrated in any way that a woman differs from a man in respect to what we're talking about, and we'll still believe that our guardians and the women with them ought to pursue the same activities."

"Rightly so," he said.

455a "Now after this, don't we invite the one who says the opposite to teach us this very thing, what art or what pursuit it is, among those involved in the setup of the city, for which the nature of a woman is not the same as but different from that of a man?"

"That's the just thing to do, anyway."

"And perhaps someone else as well might say the very thing you were saying a little while ago, that it's not easy to say anything adequate on the spot, but not hard if someone has been considering it."

"He would say that."

"Then do you want us to ask the person who contradicts this sort of thing to follow
b us, if we somehow show him that no pursuit related to the running of a city is uniquely for a woman?"

"Certainly."

"'Come on then,' we'll say to him, 'answer: is this the way you meant that one person is naturally fitted for something and another isn't, that in it the one learns something

easily, the other with difficulty? And that the one, on the basis of a brief study, would be
apt to discover a lot about what he'd learned, while the other, even when he's gotten a lot
of study and practice, couldn't even hang on to what he'd learned? And for the one, the
aptitudes of his body would adequately serve the purposes of his thinking, while for the c
other it would be the opposite? Are there any other things than these by which you
marked off the one naturally suited for each thing from the one who's not?'"

"No one's going to claim there're any others," he said.

"Then do you know of anything practiced by human beings in which the man's
kind isn't of a condition that surpasses the woman's in all these respects? Or shall we
make a long story out of it, talking about the art of weaving, and tending to things that
are baked or boiled, the activities in which the female kind is held in high repute and for d
which it's most absurd of all for it to be outdone?"

"You're telling the truth," he said, "that the one kind is dominated by the other by far in everything, as one might put it. But many women are certainly better than many men at many things, though on the whole it's the way you say."

"Therefore, my friend, there isn't any pursuit of the people who run a city that
belongs to a woman because she's a woman or to a man because he's a man, but the
kinds of natures are spread around among both kinds of animal alike, and by nature a
woman takes part in all pursuits and a man in them all, but in all of them a woman is e
weaker than a man."

Steps in Cloth-Making. Black-figure lekythos (oil jug) attributed to the potter Amasis (sixth century B.C.). The women on the left are hand spinning thread; those in the center are weaving wool. Given that Greek women generally remained at home fulfilling such domestic occupations, Plato's suggestions in the *Republic* were quite revolutionary. Though he claims that in all pursuits "a woman is weaker than a man," Plato's character, Socrates, concludes, ". . . there isn't any pursuit of the people who run a city that belongs to a woman because she's a woman or to a man because he's a man, but the kinds of natures are spread around among both. . . ." (*Image copyright ©The Metropolitan Museum of Art. Image source: Art Resource, NY*)

"Quite so."

"So are we going to assign all of them to men and none to women?"

"Really, how could we?"

"But we'll claim, I imagine, that there's a woman with an aptitude for the medical art and another without it, and a woman with an aptitude for music and another who's unmusical by nature."

"Of course."

456a "Then isn't there a woman with an aptitude for gymnastic training and warfare, and one who's unwarlike and not fond of gymnastic exercise?"

"I imagine so."

"What else? Is one woman philosophic and another antiphilosophic? Is one spirited and another lacking in spirit?"

"These things are possible too."

"Then it's also possible for there to be a woman with an aptitude as a guardian, and another without one. Wasn't it that sort of nature we also selected as belonging to the men with an aptitude for being guardians?"

"That very sort."

"And therefore the same nature for guardianship of a city belongs to a woman as to a man, except to the extent that one is weaker or stronger."

"So it appears."

b "And so women of that sort need to be selected to live together and guard together with men of that sort, since they're competent and are akin to them in their nature."

"Entirely so."

"And don't the same pursuits need to be assigned to the same natures?"

"The same ones."

"Then we've come back around to what we said before, and we're agreed that it's not contrary to nature for the women among the guardians to be assigned to music and gymnastic training."

"Absolutely so."

c "So we weren't legislating things that are impossible or like prayers, since we set down the law in accord with nature. But it seems instead that it's the things that are done now, contrary to these, that are done contrary to nature."

"So it seems."

"Wasn't our question whether the things we'd be talking about are possible and best?"

"It was indeed."

"And it's been agreed that they're possible?"

"Yes."

"And that they're best is the thing that needs to be agreed to next?"

"Clearly."

"Now as for turning out a woman skilled at guardianship, one education won't
d produce men for us and another one women, will it, especially since it gets the same
nature to work with?"

"No other one."

"Then what's the state of your opinion about this in particular?"

"About what exactly?"

"About assuming in your own estimation that one man is better and another worse. Or do you regard them as all alike?"

"Not at all."

"Then in the city we've been founding, which do you imagine would turn out as better men, the guardians, when they've gotten the education we went over, or the leatherworkers, educated in leathercraft?"

"You're asking a ridiculous question," he said.

"I understand," I said. "What about it then? Compared to the rest of the citizens, aren't these the best men?"

"By far."

"And what about the women? Won't these be the best among the women?" e

"They too, by far," he said.

"And is there anything better for a city than for the best possible women and men to arise in it?"

"There isn't."

"And music and gymnastic training, when they come to their aid in the way we've gone over, bring this about?" 457a

"How could they not?"

"Therefore the ordinance we set down for the city is not only something possible but also the best thing."

"So it is."

"Then the women among the guardians need to take off their clothes, since they're going to be clothed in virtue instead of a cloak, and they need to share in war and the rest of the guardianship connected with the city, and not engage in other activities, but less arduous parts of these same activities need to be given to the women than to the men because of the weakness of their kind. And a man who laughs at naked women engaged in gymnastic exercise for the sake of what's best 'plucks a laugh from b
his wisdom while it's still an unripe fruit,' having no idea, it seems, what he's laughing at or what he's doing. For the most beautiful thing that's being said or will have been said is this: that what's beneficial is beautiful and what's harmful is ugly."

"Absolutely so."

"Then shall we claim that we're escaping from one wave, so to speak, by saying this about the law pertaining to women, so that we don't get completely swamped when we set it down that our male and female guardians must pursue all things in common, c
but that in a way the argument that says that's possible and beneficial is in agreement with itself?"

"And it's certainly no small wave you're escaping," he said.

"But you'll claim it's no big one either," I said, "when you see what comes after this."

"Speak, then, and I'll see," he said.

"A law that goes along with this one," I said, "and with the others that preceded it, is, as I imagine, the following."

"What?"

"That all these women are to be shared among all these men, and none of the d
women is to live together privately with any of the men, and their children are to be shared too; a parent is not to know the offspring that are its own, or a child its parent."

"This is much bigger than the former one," he said, "in respect to doubtfulness about both what's possible and what's beneficial."

"About what's beneficial, anyway," I said, "I don't imagine there'd be any arguing that it's not the greatest good for the women to be shared or for the children to be shared, if possible; but about whether it's possible or not, I imagine there'd be a very great dispute."

"There could very well be dispute about both," he said. e

"You're talking about a unified front among arguments," I said, "and here I was imagining I could run away from one of them, if it seemed to you to be beneficial, and I'd have the one about whether it's possible or not left."

"But you didn't get away with running away," he said, "so give an account of yourself on both counts."

"I'll have to stand trial," I said. "Do me this much of a favor though; let me go
458a about it holiday-style, like dawdlers who're in the habit of feasting on their own thoughts when they're walking by themselves. People like that, you know, before finding out how there can be some thing they desire, put that aside so they won't wear themselves out pondering about what's possible or not, and taking it for granted that the thing they want is already there, they're already arranging the rest and enjoying going
b through the sorts of things they'll do when it happens, and otherwise making a lazy soul even lazier. I've gotten soft myself by now, and on those questions I desire to put them off and consider later how they're possible, but now, taking it for granted that they're possible, if you let me, I'll consider how the rulers will organize them when they happen, and what would be the most advantageous way, for both the city and the guardians, for them to be done. I'll try together with you to consider these things first, and those later, if you give permission."

"I do give permission," he said; "go ahead and consider."

"I imagine, then," I said, "if in fact the rulers are going to be worthy of that
c name, and their auxiliaries by the same token worthy of theirs, the ones will wish to follow orders and the others to give them, while the latter themselves obey the laws on some matters, but imitate the laws on all the other matters that we'll leave up to their judgment."

"That sounds right," he said.

"Then you," I said, "as their lawgiver, once you've selected the women in the same way you also selected the men, will distribute them as far as possible to those with similar natures; and they, since they have their houses and meals in common, and none
d of them possesses any property of that sort privately, will be together, and while they're mingled together in the gyms and in the rest of their upbringing, they'll be led, I imagine, by an inborn necessity, toward mingling with each other sexually. Or do the things I'm talking about not seem necessary to you?"

"Not in the geometrical sense anyway," he said, "but they seem to be necessities of an erotic sort, which are liable to be sharper than the former at persuading and attracting most of the populace."

"Very much so," I said. "But the next thing to consider, Glaucon, is that unregu-
e lated sexual contact with one another, or doing anything else at all of that sort, isn't pious in a city of people favored by destiny, and the rulers aren't going to allow it."

"No, it wouldn't be just," he said.

"So it's clear that the next thing we'll do is make marriages sacred to the greatest extent possible, and it's the most beneficial ones that would be sacred."

"Absolutely so."

459a "So in what way will they be the most beneficial? Tell me this, Glaucon, because I see in your household both hunting dogs and true-bred birds in great numbers. Well, by Zeus, have you paid any attention to their matings and breeding?"

"To what sort of thing?" he said.

"First, among those of the same kind, even though they're true bred, aren't there some that also turn out best?"

"There are."

"Then do you breed from all of them alike, or are you eager to breed as much as possible from the best ones?"

"From the best ones."

"And then what? From the youngest, or from the oldest, or as much as possible from those in their prime?" b

"From those in their prime."

"And if they weren't bred that way, do you expect the race of birds or of dogs would be much worse?"

"I do," he said.

"And what do you suppose about horses," I said, "and the rest of the animals? That it would be any different?"

"That would certainly be strange," he said.

"Ayayay, dear comrade," I said, "how greatly in need we are, then, of top-notch rulers if it's also the same way with the human race." c

"Well it is the same way," he said, "but what does that have to do with the rulers?"

"There'll be a necessity," I said, "for them to use a lot of medicines. Presumably we believe that for bodies that don't need medicines, those of people willing to follow a prescribed way of life, even a rather ordinary doctor is sufficient; but when there's a need to use medicine, we know that a more courageous doctor is needed."

"True, but what point are you making?"

"This one," I said: "our rulers are liable to need to use falsehood and deception in abundance for the benefit of those they rule. And we claimed, of course, that all that sort of thing is useful in the form of medicine." d

"And rightly so," he said.

"Well, it seems like it's not least in the marriages and procreation that this rightness comes into play."

"How so?"

"It follows from the things that have been agreed to," I said, "that as often as possible the best men ought to have sex with the best women, and the worst on the contrary with the worst, and the offspring of the former ought to be reared, but not those of the latter, if the flock is going to be of top quality to the highest degree possible. And all these things ought to happen without the notice of anyone except the rulers themselves, if the guardians' herd is also going to be as free as possible of internal conflict." e

"With the utmost rightness," he said.

"Then don't some sort of festivals and sacrifices need to be set up by law, in which we'll bring together the brides and grooms, and suitable hymns need to be made by our poets for the marriages that take place? We'll make the number of marriages be up to the rulers, in order that they might preserve the same number of men as much as they can, having regard to wars, diseases, and everything of the sort, and in order that, as far as possible, our city might not become either big or little." 460a

"Rightly," he said.

"I imagine some ingenious lotteries need to be made up, so that the ordinary man mentioned before will blame chance and not the rulers for each marriage pairing."

"Very much so," he said.

"And presumably those among the young men who are good in war or anywhere else need to be given special honors and prizes, and among other things a more unrestricted privilege to sleep with the women, so that on this pretext, as great a number of children as possible would also at the same time be begotten by such people." b

"Rightly so."

“And won’t the officials set up for this purpose take over the offspring born on each occasion, male or female officials or both, since, of course, the ruling offices are shared among the women and men?”

“Yes.”

c “So I expect they’ll take those born to the good ones into the fold and turn them over to some sort of nurses who live separately in a certain part of the city; but the offspring of the worse sort of people, and any of the others that might have been born with defects, they’ll hide away in a place not spoken of and not seen, as is fitting.”

“If indeed the race of the guardians is going to be pure,” he said.

“Won’t these officials also be in charge of the feeding, bringing the mothers to the
d fold when they’re swollen with milk, contriving every sort of means so that none of
them will recognize her own child, and providing other women who have milk if they don’t have enough, and see to it that the mothers themselves suckle for a moderate time, but turn over the watchfulness and other work to wet nurses and nurses?”

“You’re describing a great ease of childbearing,” he said, “for the women among the guardians.”

“And it’s appropriate,” I said. “Let’s go on to the next thing we proposed, since we claimed that the offspring ought to be born particularly from those in their prime.”

“True.”

e “Then do you share my opinion that twenty years is the average time of the prime of life for a woman, and thirty for a man?”

“Which of the years?” he said.

“Starting from her twentieth and up to her fortieth, for a woman to bear children for the city,” I said, “and for a man, once he passes his swiftest peak at running, to beget children for the city from then until his fifty-fifth.”

461a “For them both,” he said, “that’s certainly their prime both in body and in intelligence.”

“Then if someone older or younger than that engages in generating offspring into the community, we’ll claim it’s a transgression that’s not pious or just, since it produces for the city a child that, if it escapes notice, will have been brought forth without being born with the sacrifices and prayers that would be offered at every marriage by priestesses, priests, and the whole city together, that from good and beneficial people better
b and more beneficial offspring might always come forth; instead, it will have been born
under cover of darkness in the presence of terrible unrestraint.”

“We’ll rightly make that claim,” he said.

“And the same law applies,” I said, “if any of the men still propagating has sexual contact with any of the women who are of childbearing age when a ruler hasn’t joined him with her; we’ll charge him with bringing a bastard child into the city, unsanctioned and unconsecrated.”

“Quite rightly,” he said.

“But, I imagine, when both the women and the men get beyond the age to repro-
c duce, we’ll no doubt leave them free to have sex with anyone they want, except with a
daughter, a mother, a daughter’s children, a mother’s parent, or the women with a son or his children or with a father or his parent, and all that only after it’s been insisted that they take the most zealous care not to bring forth even a single fetus into the light of day, if one is conceived, and if any is forced on them, to handle it on the understanding that there’s to be no raising of such a child.”

“These things too are reasonably said,” he said; “but how are they going to distinguish their fathers and daughters, and the others you just mentioned, one from another?”

"There's no way," I said. "But from that day on which any of them becomes a d
bridegroom, whatever offspring are born in the tenth month after that, or even the seventh, to all of these he'll apply the name sons to the males and daughters to the females, and they'll call him father, and in the same way he'll call their offspring his grandchildren, and they in turn will call people like him grandfathers and grandmothers, and they'll call those who were born at the same time their mothers and fathers were pro- e
ducing children sisters and brothers, so that, as we were just saying, they won't have sexual contact with one another. But the law will grant brothers and sisters permission to be joined together if the lottery falls out that way and the Pythia* confirms it."

"Quite rightly," he said.

"So, Glaucon, this or something like it is the way of sharing women and children among the guardians of your city. The next thing after this ought to be to have it established out of the argument that this goes along with the rest of the polity and is by far the best way. Or how should we proceed?"

"That way, by Zeus," he said. 462a

"Well then, wouldn't this be a source from which an agreement might come, that we ask ourselves what's the greatest good we can state in the organization of a city, at which the lawgiver ought to aim in setting down the laws, and what's the greatest evil, and then consider on that basis whether the things we were just now going over fit into the footprint of the good while they don't fit into that of the evil?"

"That most of all would be the way," he said.

"Then can we have any greater evil in a city than that which tears it apart and
makes it many instead of one? Or a greater good than that which binds it together and b
makes it one?"

"No we can't."

"And doesn't the sharing of pleasure and pain bind it together, when as much as possible all the citizens feel joy and pain in almost the same way at the coming into being and passing away of the same things?"

"Absolutely so," he said.

"But the private appropriation of such things dissolves it, when some people become overwhelmed with pain and others overcome with joy at the same experiences of the city and of the people in the city?"

"How could it not?" c

"And doesn't that sort of thing come from this, that people in the city don't utter such words as mine and not mine at the same time, and the same with somebody else's?"

"Exactly so."

"So isn't that city governed best in which the most people say this mine and not mine on the same occasion about the same things?"

"Much the best."

"And this is precisely whichever city is in a condition closest to that of a single human being? For instance, whenever a finger of any of us is wounded, presumably the
whole community extending from the body to the soul in a single ordering under the ruler d
within it would be aware of it, and it all would suffer pain as a whole together with the part that's afflicted, and is that the sense in which we mean that a human being has a pain in his finger? And is it the same story for any other part of a human being whatever, both for a part afflicted with pain and for one that's eased by pleasure?"

*The priestess of Apollo at Delphi. Presumably the rulers would know which cases involved actual incest and avoid them, and would take her into their confidence.

"It's the same," he said, "and as for what you're asking, the best constituted city is the one situated closest to such a condition."

"So I imagine that when one of its citizens undergoes anything at all, good or bad,
e such a city most of all will claim the thing that happened to him as its own, and all of it
will share the pleasure or share the pain."

"Necessarily," he said, "if it's one with good laws, anyway."

* * *

473b "It looks like the next thing for us to do is try to search out and demonstrate whatever is now done badly in cities, on account of which they aren't managed this way, and what would be the smallest change by which a city could come into this mode of political association— preferably a change of one thing, or if not that, of two, and if not that, of as few things as possible in number and the smallest in strength."

c "Absolutely so," he said.

"Well with one change," I said, "it seems to me we can show that it could be transformed, though it's not a small or easy one, but it is possible."

"What's that?" he said.

"I'm in for it now," I said, "up against what we likened to the biggest wave. But it's got to be said, even if, literally just like an uproarious wave, it's going to drown me in laughter and humiliation. Consider what I'm about to say."

"Say it," he said.

d "Unless philosophers rule as kings in their cities," I said, "or those now called
kings and supreme rulers genuinely and adequately engage in philosophy, and this combination of political power and philosophy joins together in the same position, while the many natures that are now carried away to one of the two in isolation are forcibly blocked off from that, there is no rest from evils for the cities, dear Glaucon, or, I think, for the human race, and this polity that we've now gone over in speech will never before
e that sprout as far as it can and see the light of the sun. This is what's been putting a
reluctance to speak in me all this time, my seeing that it would be proclaimed to be far beyond belief, because it's hard to see that in no other way would anyone be happy in private, or any city in public."

* * *

BOOK VI

* * *

502c "Then since, by effort, [our discussion of lawgiving has] reached an end, don't the
things that remain after it need to be spoken about: in what manner, by what kinds of
d things learned and pursued, the saviors of the polity will be present among us, and at
what ages each group of them will take up each activity?"

"That surely needs to be spoken about," he said.

"It didn't turn out to be a wise thing in the earlier discussion," I said, "for me to have left out the objectionable matter of possessing women, the propagation of children, and

the instituting of the rulers, even though I knew that the complete truth would be offensive
and a hard thing to bring about, because as it is, the need to go through these things came e
along nonetheless. And while the particular things about women and children are finished,
it's necessary to go into the ones about the rulers as if from the beginning. And we were
saying, if you recall, that they must be seen to be passionately devoted to the city, standing 503a
the test amid pleasures and pains, and being seen not to drop this conviction through
drudgery or terrors or any other vicissitude, or else the person who's incapable is to be
rejected, while the one who comes through untarnished in every way, like gold tested in
the fire, is to be established as a ruler and given honors and prizes both while living and at
his death. Some such things as that were being said when the discussion slipped past them
with its face covered, in fear of setting in motion what's now at hand."

"You're telling the exact truth," he said; "I do recall." b

"I was reluctant, dear friend," I said, "to state what has now been daringly exposed, but now let it be boldly stated: it's imperative to put philosophers in place as guardians in the most precise sense."

"Let it be so stated," he said.

"Then consider it likely that you'll have few of them, since the nature we went through needs to belong to them, but its parts are rarely inclined to grow together in the same place, but in most cases grow as something severed."

"How do you mean?" he said.

"With natures that are good learners, have memories, are intellectually flexible, c
are quick, and have everything else that goes with these things, and are youthfully spirited and lofty in their thinking as well, you know that they aren't willing at the same time to grow up being the sort of natures that want to live with calmness and stability in an orderly way, but instead are the kind that are carried off wherever their quickness happens to take them, and everything stable goes right out of them."

"You're telling the truth," he said.

"But with those natures with stable characters, on the other hand, that are not easily
changeable, those one would treat as more trustworthy and that would be unmoved con- d
fronting terrors in war, wouldn't they be the same way confronting things to be learned also? They're hard to move and slow to learn as though they'd been numbed, and they're full of sleepiness and yawning whenever anything of the sort needs to be worked at."

"That's how they are," he said.

"But we claimed it was necessary to have a good-sized and high-quality share of both, or else not be allowed to take part in the most precise sort of education or in honor or in ruling."

"Rightly," he said.

"And don't you imagine that will be rare?"

"How could it not be?"

"So not only does it need to be tested in the labors, terrors, and pleasures we spoke of
then but also, something we passed over then and speak of now, one needs to give it exercise e
in many kinds of studies to examine whether it will be capable of holding up under the
greatest studies, or whether it will shy away like people who show cowardice in other areas." 504a

"It's certainly appropriate to examine it that way," he said, "but what sort of studies in particular are you saying are the greatest?"

"No doubt you remember," I said, "that we pieced together what justice, moderation, courage, and wisdom each would be by distinguishing three forms that belong to the soul."

"If I didn't remember that," he said, "it would be just for me not to hear the rest."

"And what about what was said by way of preface to that?"

"What was it?"

b "We were saying something to the effect that getting the most beautiful possible look at these things would take another, longer way around, which would make them become evident to someone who traveled that road, though it would be possible to provide illustrations approximating to the things that had already been said earlier, and you folks declared that would be sufficient. And so the things said at that time, as far as precision goes, as it appeared to me, were deficient; as for whether they were satisfactory to you people, that's something you could say."

"To me? In a measured way," he said, "and it looked like they were to the others as well."

c "My friend," I said, "measuredness in such matters that stops short in any respect whatever of what *is* turns out not to measure anything at all, because nothing incomplete is a measure of anything.

"But sometimes it seems to some people that they're well enough off already and don't need to search any further."

"A great many people feel that way a lot," he said, "because of laziness."

"That feeling, anyway," I said, "is one there's the least need for in a guardian of a city and its laws."

"Likely so," he said.

"So, my comrade," I said, "it's necessary for such a person to go around by the
d longer road, and he needs to work as a learner no less hard than at gymnastic training, or else, as we were just saying, he'll never get to the end of the greatest and most relevant study."

"So these aren't the greatest ones," he said, "but there's something still greater than justice and the things we've gone over?"

"Not only is there something greater," I said, "but even for those things themselves, it's necessary not just to look at a sketch, the way we've been doing now, but not to stop short of working them out to their utmost completion. Wouldn't it be ridiculous to make a concentrated effort in every way over other things of little worth, to have
e them be as precise and pure as possible, while not considering the greatest things to be worthy of the greatest precision?"

"Very much so," he said, "and a creditable thought it is, but what you mean by the greatest study, and what it's about—do you imagine," he said, "that anyone's going to let you off without asking you what it is?"

"Not at all," I said. "Just you ask. For all that, you've heard it no few times, but
505a now you're either not thinking of it or else, by latching onto me, you think you'll cause me trouble. But I imagine it's more the latter, since you've often heard that the greatest learnable thing is the look of the good, which just things and everything else need in addition in order to become useful and beneficial. So now you know pretty well that I'm going to say that, and in addition to it that we don't know it well enough. But if we don't know it, and we do know everything else as much as possible without it, you can be sure
b that nothing is any benefit to us, just as there would be none if we possessed something without the good. Or do you imagine it's any use to acquire any possession that's not good? Or to be intelligent about everything else without the good, and have no intelligence where anything beautiful and good is concerned?"

"By Zeus, I don't!" he said.

"And surely you know this too, that to most people, the good seems to be pleasure, and to the more sophisticated ones, intelligence."

"How could I not?"

"And, my friend, that the ones who believe the latter can't specify what sort of
intelligence, but are forced to end up claiming it's about the good."

"It's very ridiculous," he said.

"How could it be otherwise," I said, "if after reproaching us because we don't c
know what's good they turn around and speak to us as though we do know? Because
they claim that it's intelligence about the good as though we for our part understand
what they mean when they pronounce the name of the good."

"That's very true," he said.

"And what about the people who define the good as pleasure? Are they any less
full of inconsistency than the others? Aren't they also forced to admit that there are bad
pleasures?"

"Emphatically so."

"So I guess they turn out to be conceding that the same things that are good are
also bad. Isn't that so?"

"Certainly." d

"Then isn't it clear that the disagreements about it are vast and many?"

"How could it not be clear?"

"And what about this? Isn't it clear that many people would choose the things that
seem to be just and beautiful, and even when they aren't, would still do them, possess them,
and have the seeming, though no one is content to possess what seems good, but people
seek the things that are good, and in that case everyone has contempt for the seeming?"

"Very much so," he said.

"So this is exactly what every soul pursues, for the sake of which it does everything, e
having a sense that it's something but at a loss and unable to get an adequate grasp of what
it is, or even have the reliable sort of trust it has about other things; because of this it misses
out even on any benefit there may have been in the other things. On such a matter, of such
great importance, are we claiming that even the best people in the city, the ones in whose 506a
hands we're going to put everything, have to be in the dark in this way?"

"Not in the least," he said.

"I imagine anyway," I said, "that when there's ignorance of the way in which just
and beautiful things are good, they won't have gotten a guardian for themselves who's
worth much of anything, in someone who's ignorant of that, and I have a premonition
that no one's going to discern them adequately before that."

"You're very good at premonitions," he said.

"Then won't our polity be perfectly ordered if that sort of guardian does watch b
over it, one who knows these things?"

"Necessarily," he said. "But you in particular, Socrates, do you claim the good is
knowledge or pleasure or some other thing besides these?"

"That's a man for you," I said; "you've done a beautiful job of making it plain all
along that the way things seem to others about these things won't be good enough for you."

"But it doesn't seem just to me either, Socrates," he said, "to be able to state the
opinions of others but not one's own, when one has been concerned about these things c
for such a long time."

"Well does it seem to you to be just," I said, "to talk about things one doesn't
know as though one knew them?"

"Not by any means as though one knew them," he said, "but certainly it's just to
be willing to say what one thinks as something one thinks."

"What?" I said, "Haven't you noticed about opinions without knowledge that
they're all ugly? The best of them are blind. Or do people who hold any true opinion

without insight seem to you to be any different from blind people who travel along the right road?"

"No different," he said.

"Then do you want to gaze on ugly things, blind and crooked, when you'll be able to hear bright and beautiful ones from others?"

d "Before Zeus, Socrates," said Glaucon, "you're not going to stand down as if you were at the end. It'll be good enough for us if, the same way you went over what has to do with justice and moderation and the other things, you also go over what has to do with the good."

"For me too, comrade," I said, "and more than good enough. But I'm afraid I won't be capable of it, but I'll make a fool of myself in my eagerness and pay for it in ridicule. But, you blessed fellows, let's leave aside for the time being what the good
e itself is, since it appears to me to be beyond the trajectory of the impulse we've got at present to reach the things that now seem to me to be the case. But I'm willing to speak about what appears to be an offspring of the good and most like it, if that's also congenial to you folks, or if not, to let it go."

"Just speak," he said, "and some other time you'll pay off the balance with a description of the father."

507a "I'd like to have the power to pay it in full and for you folks to receive it, and not just the interest on it as you will now. Give a reception, then, to this dividend and offspring of the good itself. Be on your guard, though, in case I unintentionally deceive you by paying my account with counterfeit interest."

"We'll be on guard according to our power," he said, "so just speak."

"After I've gotten your agreement," I said, "and reminded you of things mentioned in the previous discussion and often spoken of before now elsewhere."

"What sort of things?" he said.

b "We claim that there are many beautiful things," I said, "and many good things, and the same way for each kind, and we distinguish them in speech."

"We do."

"But also a beautiful itself, and a good itself, and the same way with everything we were then taking as many, we go back the other way and take according to a single look of each kind, as though there is only one, and we refer to it as what each kind is."

"That's it."

"And we claim that the former are seen but not thought, while the 'looks' in turn are thought but not seen."

"Completely and totally so."

c "And by which of the things within ourselves do we see the ones that are seen?"

"By sight," he said.

"And perceive the things heard by hearing, and all the perceptible things by the other senses?" I said.

"Of course."

"Well," I said, "have you reflected about the craftsman of the senses, how he was by far the most bountiful in crafting the power of seeing and being seen?"

"Not at all," he said.

"Then look at it this way: for one thing to hear and another to be heard, is there
d any need for another kind of thing in addition to the sense of hearing and a sound, such that, if that third thing isn't present, the first won't hear and the second won't be heard?"

"There's nothing like that," he said.

"And I don't imagine," I said, "that there are many others either, not to say none, that have any additional need for such a thing, or can you name any?"

"Not for my part," he said.

"But don't you realize that the power of sight and being seen does have an additional need?"

"How's that?"

"Presumably you're aware that when sight is present in eyes and the one who has it attempts to use it, and color is present there in things, unless there's also a third kind of thing present, of a nature specifically for this very purpose, sight will see nothing and e
colors will be invisible."

"What's this thing you're speaking of?" he said.

"The one you call light," I said.

"It's true, as you say," he said.

"Then the sense of sight and the power of being seen have been bound together by a bond more precious, by no small look, than that uniting other pairs, unless light is 508a
something to be despised."

"Surely it's far from being despised," he said.

"And which of the divine beings in the heavens can you point out as the ruling power responsible for this, whose light makes our sight see and visible things be seen as beautifully as possible?"

"The same one you and everyone else would," he said, "since it's obvious you're asking about the sun."

"And is it this way that sight is by its nature related to this god?"

"How?"

"The sun is not sight itself, nor is it that in which sight is present, what we call an eye." b

"No indeed."

"But I imagine that's the most sunlike of the sense organs."

"By far."

"And doesn't it acquire the power that it has as an overflow from that which is bestowed by the sun?"

"Very much so."

"So while the sun isn't sight, but is the thing responsible for it, isn't it seen by that very thing?"

"That's how it is," he said.

"Now then," I said, "say that this is what I'm calling the offspring of the good, which the good generated as something analogous to itself; the very thing the good c
itself is in the intelligible realm in relation to insight and the intelligible things, this is in the visible realm in relation to sight and the visible things."

"How so?" he said. "Go into it more for me."

"With eyes," I said, "do you know that when one no longer turns them on those things to whose colors the light of day extends, but on those on which nocturnal lights fall, they grow dim, and appear nearly blind, just as though no pure sight was present in them?"

"Very much so," he said.

"But I imagine that whenever one turns them to the things the sun illumines, they see them clearly, and pure sight is manifestly present in these very same eyes." d

"Certainly."

"In this manner, think of the power of the soul too as being the same way. Whenever it becomes fixed on that which truth and being illumine, it has insight, discerns, and shows itself to have an intellect, but whenever it becomes fixed on something mixed with darkness, something that comes into and passes out of being, it deals in seeming and grows dim, changing its opinions up and down, and is like something that has no intellect."

"It does seem like that."

e "Then say that what endows the things known with truth, and gives that which
knows them its power, is the look of the good. Since it's the cause of knowledge and truth,
think of it as something known, but though both of these, knowing and truth, are so beautiful, by regarding it as something else, still more beautiful than they are, you'll regard it
509a rightly. And as far as knowledge and truth are concerned, just as it's right over there to
consider light and sight sunlike, but isn't right to consider them to be the sun, so too here
it's right to consider both of these as like the good, but not right to regard either of them as
being the good; the condition of the good requires that it be held in still greater honor."

"You're talking about a beauty hard to conceive," he said, "if it endows things with knowledge and truth but is itself beyond these in beauty, because it's sure not pleasure you mean."

"Watch your mouth," I said; "but look into the image of it still more closely."

"In what way?"

b "I imagine you'd claim that the sun not only endows the visible things with their power of being seen, but also with their coming into being, their growth, and their nurture, though it's not itself coming-into-being."

"How could it be?"

"Then claim as well that the things that are known not only get their being-known furnished by the good, but they're also endowed by that source with their very being and their being what they are, even though the good is not being, but something over and above being, beyond it in seniority and surpassing it in power."

c And Glaucon, in a very comical manner, said "By Apollo, that's a stupendous stretcher."

"You're to blame for it," I said, "for forcing me to tell the way things seem to me about it."

"And don't by any means stop," he said, "not if there are any other things for you to go over in the likeness to the sun, in case you're leaving something out anywhere."

"That's for sure," I said; "I'm leaving out scads of things."

"Well don't skip over any little bit," he said.

"I suspect I'll skip over a lot," I said, "but be that as it may, as far as it's possible at present, I won't willingly leave anything out."

"See that you don't," he said.

d "Well then, as we're saying," I said, "think of them as being a pair, one ruling as king over the intelligible race and realm, and the other, for its part, over the visible—note that I'm not saying 'over the heavens,' so I won't seem to you to be playing verbal tricks with the name. But do you grasp these two forms, visible, intelligible?"

"I've got them."

"Then take them as being like a line divided into two unequal segments, one for
the visible class and the other for the intelligible, and cut each segment again in the
same ratio, and you'll get the parts to one another in their relation of clarity and obscu-
510a rity; in the visible section, one segment [*A*] will be for images, and by images I mean
first of all shadows, then semblances formed in water and on all dense, smooth, bright
surfaces, and everything of that sort, if you get the idea."

"I get it."

"Then in the other part [*B*], put what this one is likened to, the animals around us, and every plant, and the whole class of artificial things."

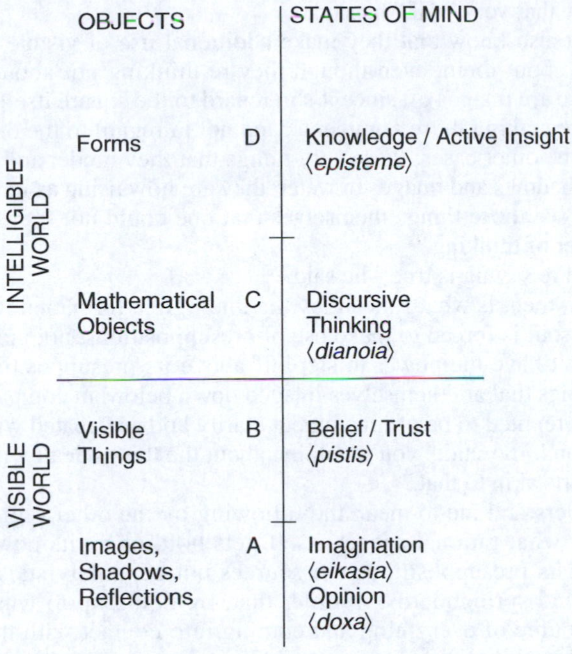

"I'm putting them," he said.

"And would you also be willing to claim," I said, "that it's divided with respect to truth and its lack, such that the copy is to the thing it's copied from as a seeming is to something known?"

"I would," he said, "very much so." b

"Then consider next the way the division of the intelligible part needs to be made."

"What way is that?"

"Such that in one part of it [*C*] a soul takes as images the things that were imitated before, and is forced to inquire based on presuppositions, proceeding not to a beginning but to an end, while in the other part [*D*] it goes from a presupposition to a beginning free of presuppositions, without the images involved in the other part, making its investigation into forms themselves and by means of them."

"I didn't sufficiently understand what you mean by these things," he said.

"Once more, then," I said; "since you'll understand more easily after the fol- c
lowing preface. [*C*] Now I imagine you know that people who concern themselves with matters of geometry and calculation and such things presuppose in accord with each investigation the odd and the even, the geometrical shapes, the three kinds of angles, and other things related to these; treating these as known and making them presuppositions, they don't think it's worth giving any further account of them
either to themselves or to anyone else, as though they were obvious to everyone, but d
starting from these things and going through the subsequent things from that point, they arrive at a conclusion in agreement with that from which they set their inquiry in motion."

"I do know that very well," he said.

"Then you also know that they make additional use of visible forms, and make their arguments about them, even though they're thinking not about these but about those things these are images of, since it's in regard to the square itself, and its diagonal
e itself, that they're making those arguments, and not in regard to the one that they draw, and likewise in the other cases; these very things that they model and draw, which also
511a have their own shadows and images in water, they are now using as images in their turn, in an attempt to see those things themselves that one could not see* in any other way than by the power of thinking."

"What you're saying is true," he said.

"The latter, then, is what I meant by the intelligible form, and it's for the inquiry about it that the soul is forced to make use of presuppositions, not going to the source, because it doesn't have the power to step off above its presuppositions, but using as images those things that are themselves imaged down below, in comparison with which these images are reputed to be of preeminent clarity and are treated with honor."

b "I understand," he said; "you're talking about the things dealt with by geometrical studies and the arts akin to that."

"Then understand me to mean the following by the other segment of the intelligible part [*D*]: what rational speech itself gets hold of by its power of dialectical motion, making its presuppositions not sources but genuinely standing places, like steppingstones and springboards, in order that, by going up to what is presuppositionless at the source of everything and coming into contact with this, by following back again the things that follow from it, rational speech may descend in that way to
c a conclusion, making no more use in any way whatever of anything perceptible, but dealing with forms themselves, arriving at them by going through them, it ends at forms as well."

"I understand," he said, "though not sufficiently, because you seem to me to be talking about a tremendous amount of work; however, I understand that you want to mark off that part of what is and is intelligible that's contemplated by the knowledge that comes from dialectical thinking as being clearer than what's contemplated by what are called arts, which have presuppositions as their starting points. Those who contemplate things by means of the arts are forced to contemplate them by thinking
d and not by sense perception, but since they examine things not by going up to the source but on the basis of presuppositions, they seem to you to have no insight into them, even though, by means of their starting point, they're dealing with things that are intelligible. And you seem to me to be calling the activity of geometers and such people thinking but not insight, on the grounds that thinking is something in between opinion and insight."

"You took it in utterly sufficiently," I said. "Along with me, take it too that for the four segments of the line there are these four kinds of experiences that arise in the soul,
e active insight for the highest and thinking for the second, and assign the names trust to the third and imagination to the last, drawing them up as a proportion and holding that, in the same manner these experiences have their shares of clarity, the things they're directed to have corresponding shares of truth."

"I understand," he said, "and I go along with it and rank them as you say."

*A geometrical line is understood as having no breadth, and a plane figure as having no depth. A drawing in the sand, a shape cut out of some flat material, or even any appearance in our pictorial imaginations must falsify what it images if it is to image it at all.

BOOK VII

"Next," I said, "make an image of our nature as it involves education and the lack 514a
of it, by likening it to a condition such as the following: picture human beings in a cave-
like dwelling underground, having a long pathway open to the light all across the cave.
They're in it from childhood on with their legs and necks in restraints, so that they're b
held in place and look only to the front, restricted by the neck-restraint from twisting
their heads around. For them, the light is from a fire burning up above and a long way
behind them, and between the fire and the prisoners there's an upper road. Picture a little wall built along this road, like the low partitions puppeteers use to screen the humans
who display the puppets above them."

"I see it," he said.

"Then see the humans going along this little wall carrying all sorts of articles that c
jut out over the wall, figurines of men and other animals fashioned out of stone and 515a
wood and materials of all kinds, with some of the people carrying them past making
appropriate sounds and others silent."

"You're describing a bizarre image and bizarre prisoners," he said.

"Like us," I said. "First of all, do you imagine such people would have seen anything of themselves or one another other than the shadows cast by the fire onto the part of the cave right across from them?"

"How could they," he said, "if they were forced to keep their heads immobile b
throughout life?"

"And what would they have seen of the things carried past? Wouldn't that be the same thing?"

"What else?"

"So if they were able to converse with one another, don't you think they'd speak of these very things they see as the beings?"

"Necessarily."

"And what if their prison also had an echo from the side across from them? Any time any of the people carrying things past uttered a sound, do you imagine they'd believe anything other than the passing shadow had made the sound?"

"By Zeus, I don't," he said.

"So in every way," I said, "such people wouldn't consider anything to be the truth c
other than the shadows of artificial things."

"That's a great necessity," he said.

"Then consider," I said, "what their release would be like, and their recovery
from their restraints and their delusion, if things like that were to happen to them by
nature. Whenever one of them would be released, and suddenly required to stand up,
and turn his neck around, and walk, and look up toward the light, he'd suffer pain
from doing all these things, and because of the blazes of light, he wouldn't have the d
power to get a clear sight of the things whose shadows he'd seen before. What do
you imagine he'd say if someone were to tell him that he'd been seeing rubbish then,
but now, somewhat nearer to what is and turned toward the things that have more
being, he was seeing more accurately? And especially if, pointing to each of the
things passing by, one forced him to answer as he asked what they are, don't you
imagine he'd be at a loss and believe the things he'd seen before were truer than the
ones pointed out to him now?"

"Very much so," he said.

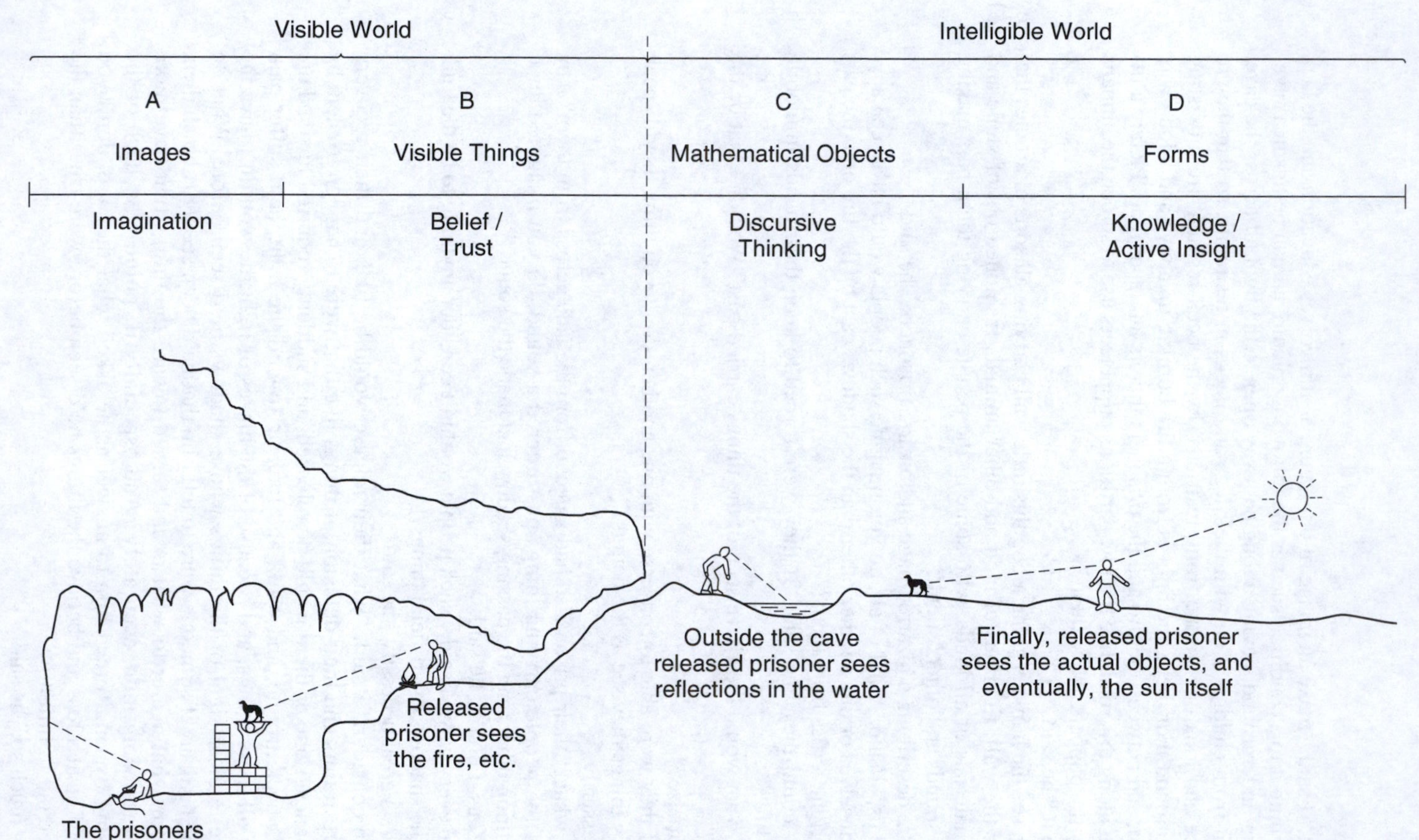

Adapted from N. Jordan, *Western Philosophy: From Antiquity to the Middle Ages* (Pearson, 1987), p. 75.

"And if one forced him to look at the light itself, wouldn't he have pain in his eyes e
and escape by turning back toward those things he was able to make out, and consider them clearer in their very being than the ones pointed out to him?"

"That's how it would be," he said.

"And if one were to drag him away from there by force," I said, "along the rough, steep road up, and didn't let go until he'd dragged him out into the light of the sun,
wouldn't he be feeling pain and anger from being dragged, and when he came into the 516a
light and had his eyes filled with its dazzle, wouldn't he be unable to see even one of the things now said to be the true ones?"

"That's right," he said, "at least not right away."

"So I imagine he'd need to get accustomed to it, if he were going to have sight of the things above. At first, he'd most easily make out the shadows, and after that the images of human beings and other things in water, and only later the things themselves; and turning from those things, he'd gaze on the things in the heavens, and at the heavens themselves, more easily by night, looking at the starlight and moonlight, than by b
day, at the sun and its light."

"How could it be otherwise?"

"Then at last, I imagine, he'd gain sight of the sun, not its appearances in water or in any setting foreign to it, but he'd have the power to see it itself, by itself, in its own realm, and contemplate it the way it is."

"Necessarily," he said.

"And after that, he could now draw the conclusion about it that this is what provides the seasons and the years, and has the governance of all things in the visible c
realm, and is in a certain manner the cause of all those things they'd seen."

"It's clear that he'd come to these conclusions after those experiences," he said.

"And then what? When he recalled his first home and the wisdom there and the people he was imprisoned with then, don't you imagine he'd consider himself happy because of the change and pity the others?"

"Greatly so."

"And if there had been any honors and commendations and prizes for them then from one another for the person who had the sharpest sight of the things passing by and
remembered best all the things that usually passed by before and after them and at the d
same time, and based on those things had greatest ability to predict what was going to come, do you think he'd be longing for those rewards and feel jealousy toward the ones honored by those people and in power among them, or would he feel what Homer depicts, and wish powerfully

To be a bond-servant to another, tilling the soil
For a man without land of his own,

and submit to anything whatever rather than hold those opinions and live that way?"

"The latter, I imagine," he said; "he'd submit to enduring everything rather than e
live in that way."

"Then give this some thought too," I said. "If such a person were to go back down and sit in the same spot, wouldn't he get his eyes filled with darkness by coming suddenly out of the sun?"

"Indeed he would," he said.

"And if he had to compete with those who'd always been imprisoned, at passing
judgments on those shadows, at a time when his sight was dim before his eyes settled 517a

back in, and if this period of adjustment was not very short, wouldn't he make a laugh-
ingstock of himself, and wouldn't it be said about him that after having gone up above
he returned with his eyes ruined, and that it's not worth it even to make the effort to go
up? And as for anyone who attempted to release them and lead them up, if they had the
power in any way to get him into their hands and kill him, wouldn't they kill him?"

"Ferociously," he said.

b "Now this image, dear Glaucon," I said, "needs to be connected as a whole with
what was said before, by likening the realm disclosed by sight to the prison dwelling, and
the light of the fire within it to the power of the sun; and if you take the upward journey
and sight of the things above as the soul's road up into the intelligible region, you won't
miss my intended meaning, since you have a desire to hear about that. No doubt a god
knows whether it happens to be true. What appears true to me appears this way: in the
knowable region, the last thing to be seen, with great effort, is the look of the good, but
c once it's been seen, it has to be concluded that it's the very cause, for all things, of all
things right and beautiful, that it generates light and its source in the visible realm, and is
itself the source that bestows truth and insight in the intelligible realm. Anyone who's
going to act intelligently in private or in public needs to have sight of it."

"I too join in assuming that," he said, "at least in whatever way I'm able to."

"Come, then," I said, "and join in assuming the following as well, and don't be
surprised that those who've come to this point aren't willing to do what belongs to
d human beings, but their souls are eager to spend all their time up above; presumably it's
likely to be that way, if this also stands in accord with the image already described."

"It's certainly likely," he said.

"And what about this? Do you imagine it's anything surprising," I said, "if someone coming from contemplation of divine things to things of a human sort is awkward
and looks extremely ridiculous while his sight is still dim and if, before he's become
sufficiently accustomed to the darkness around him, he's forced, in law courts or anywhere else, to contend over the shadows of the just or the images they're the shadows
of, and to compete about that in whatever way these things are understood by people
e who've never looked upon justice itself?"

"It's not surprising in any way whatsoever," he said.

518a "But if someone had any sense," I said, "he'd remember that two sorts of disturbances occur in the eyes from two causes, when they're removed from light into darkness as well as from darkness into light. If he regarded these same things as occurring
also with the soul, when he saw one that was confused and unable to make anything out,
he wouldn't react with irrational laughter but would consider whether it had come from
b a brighter life and was darkened by its unaccustomed condition, or was coming out of a
greater ignorance into a brighter place and was overwhelmed by the dazzle of a greater
radiance. That way, he'd congratulate the one soul on the happiness of its experience
and life and pity the other, and if he did want to laugh at that one, he'd be less laughable
for laughing at it than someone who laughed at the one coming out of the light above."

"You're speaking in a very balanced way," he said.

"So," I said, "if those things are true, we ought to regard them in the following
way: education is not the sort of thing certain people who claim to be professors of it
c claim that it is. Surely they claim they put knowledge into a soul it wasn't present in, as
though they were putting sight into blind eyes."

"Indeed they do claim that," he said.

"But the current discussion indicates," I said, "that this power is present in the
soul of each person, and the instrument by which each one learns, as if it were an eye

that's not able to turn away from darkness toward the light in any other way than along
with the whole body, needs to be turned around along with the whole soul, away from
what's fleeting, until it becomes able to endure gazing at what is and at the brightest of d
what is, and this, we're claiming, is the good. Isn't that right?"

"Yes."

"Then there would be an art to this very thing," I said, "this turning around, having to do with the way the soul would be most easily and effectively redirected, not an
art of implanting sight in it, but of how to contrive that for someone who has sight, but
doesn't have it turned the right way or looking at what it needs to."

"That seems likely," he said.

"Then the other virtues said to belong to a soul probably tend to be near the things
belonging to the body, since they're not present in the being of the soul before they've
been inculcated by habits and practice, but the virtue involving understanding, more e
than all, attains to being something more divine, as it seems, which never loses its
power, but by the way it's turned becomes either useful and beneficial or useless and 519a
harmful. Or haven't you ever reflected about the people said to be depraved but wise,
how penetrating a gaze their little souls have and how sharply they discern the things
they're turned toward, since they don't have poor sight but force it to serve vice, so that
the more sharply it sees, that much more evil it accomplishes?"

"Very much so," he said.

"But surely," I said, "if, straight from childhood, this tendency of such a nature had
been curtailed by having the edges knocked off that have an affinity with becoming, like b
lead weights that, through eating and the pleasures and greediness involved in such things,
get to be growths on the soul that turn its sight excessively downward, and if, freed from
them, it was turned toward things that are true, this same power of these same people would
have seen them too most sharply, just as it sees the ones it's now turned toward."

"Very likely," he said.

"And what about this?" I said. "Isn't it likely, even necessary from what's been
said before, that those who are uneducated and lacking experience with truth could c
never adequately manage a city, and neither could those who've been allowed to devote
all their time to education—the former because they don't have any one goal in life that
they need to aim at in doing all the things they do in private and in public, and the latter
because they wouldn't willingly engage in action, believing they'd taken up residence
in the Isles of the Blessed while still living?"

"True," he said.

"So our job as founders," I said, "is to require the best natures to get to the study
we were claiming earlier is the greatest thing, to see the good as well as to climb the d
path up to it, and when, having climbed up, they've seen it sufficiently, not to allow
what they're now permitted to do."

"What in particular?"

"To stay there," I said, "and not be willing to come back down among those prisoners or take part beside them in their labors and honors, the more frivolous ones or
even the more serious."

"What?" he said. "Are we going to do them an injustice and make them live worse
when it's possible for them to live better?"

"My friend," I said, "you let it slip back out of your memory that this is no concern e
of the law, for some one class of people in a city to be exceptionally well off, but that it
contrive things so that this arises in the city as a whole, by harmonizing the citizens
through persuasion and compulsion and making them contribute to one another a share of 520a

the benefit with which each sort is capable of improving the community; the law doesn't
produce men of this sort in the city to allow them to turn whichever way each one wants
but so that it may make full use of them for the binding together of the city."

"That's true," he said; "that did slip my mind."

"Then consider, Glaucon," I said, "that we won't be doing any injustice anyway to
the philosophers who arise among us, but we'll be asking just things of them in requiring
b them also to care for the other people and watch over them. We'll tell them that when people of their sort come along in other cities, it's reasonable for them not to share the burdens in those cities, since they spring up spontaneously in each of them against the will of
the polity, and something that grows up on its own, not owing its upbringing to anyone,
has just cause not to be too keen on paying for its support. 'But we've bred you both for
yourselves and for the rest of the city like the rulers and kings in beehives, to be educated
c in a better and more complete way than the others and more capable of taking part in both
ways of life. So it's necessary for each of you in turn to go down into the communal
dwelling and to get used to gazing at dark objects with the others, because when you're
used to it you'll see thousands of times better than the people there, and recognize each
sort of image for what it is and what it's an image of, from having seen the truth about
beautiful and just and good things. And so the city will be governed by you and by us wide
awake, and not in a dream the way most are governed now by people who fight with each
d other over shadows and form factions over ruling, as though that were some great good.
But the truth is surely this: that city in which those who are going to rule are least eager to
rule is necessarily governed best and with the least divisiveness, while the one that gets the
opposite sort of rulers is governed in the opposite way.'"

"Quite so," he said.

"Then do you imagine those who've been brought up will be unpersuaded by us
when they hear these things, and be unwilling to share, each in turn, in the labors of the
city while dwelling among themselves a lot of the time in the pure region?"

e "It's not possible," he said, "because we'll be giving just obligations to people
who are just. More than anything, each of them will go into ruling as something
unavoidable, which is opposite to what those who rule in each city now do."

"That's how it is, my comrade," I said; "if you find a way of life better than ruling
521a for those who are going to rule, there's a possibility for a well-governed city to come
into being for you, because only in it will the rulers be those who are rich in their very
being, not in gold but in that in which someone who's happy needs to be rich: a good
and intelligent life. But if beggars and people hungry for private goods go into public
life imagining that's where they need to go to steal off with the good, there's no possibility, because when ruling becomes something that's fought over, since that sort of war,
being domestic and internal, destroys them and the rest of the city."

"Very true," he said.

b "Well," I said, "do you know of any way of life other than that of true philosophy
that looks down on political offices?"

"No, by Zeus," he said.

"It's necessary, though, for people who aren't in love with ruling to go after it; if
they don't, the rival lovers will do battle."

"Certainly."

"And who else are you going to require to go into guarding the city than the people who are most thoughtful about those things by which a city is governed best, and
who have other honors and a better life than the political sort?"

"None other than they," he said.

ARISTOTLE
384–322 B.C.

Aristotle was born in Stagira, on the border of Macedonia. His mother, Phaestis, was from a family of doctors, and his father, Nicomachus, was the court physician to the king of Macedonia. At seventeen, Aristotle was sent to Athens. There he studied in Plato's Academy for two decades, but, as he later wrote, he loved the truth more than he loved Plato, and so he had no mind to remain a mere disciple. In 347 B.C., after Plato's death, he left Athens and spent the next four years conducting zoological investigations on the islands of Assos and Lesbos.

About 343 B.C., he was called to Macedonia by King Philip to tutor the king's son—the future Alexander the Great. Upon Alexander's ascension to the throne seven years later, Aristotle returned to Athens to set up the Lyceum, a rival to the Academy. Aristotle did much of his teaching walking up and down the colonnades with advanced students. As a result, his school and philosophy came to be called by the Greek word for walking around: <*peripatetikos*>, from which we get our word "peripatetic." Tradition has it that as Alexander the Great moved east, conquering Persia and moving into India, he would send back biological specimens for Aristotle's school. Although most scholars doubt this popular story, it is nevertheless clear that under Alexander's patronage, the Lyceum flourished.

However, the connection to Alexander proved a liability in the end. On Alexander's death in 323 B.C., Athenians went on a rampage against any and all associated with him. Indicted on charges of impiety, Aristotle fled Athens, "lest," as he put it, "the Athenians sin twice against philosophy" (referring, of course, to the unjust trial and death of Socrates). Aristotle died a year later. A popular but again highly questionable story says he drowned investigating marine life.

There is no doubt that after Plato, Aristotle is the most influential philosopher of all time. In the early Middle Ages, his thought was preserved and commented upon by the great Arab philosophers. He dominated later medieval philosophy to such an extent that St. Thomas Aquinas referred to him simply as *philosophus*, the "philosopher." Logic, as taught until about the time of World War II, was essentially Aristotle's logic. His *Poetics* is still a classic of literary criticism, and his dicta on tragedy are widely accepted even today. Criticism of Aristotle's metaphysical and epistemological views has spread ever since Bacon and Descartes inaugurated modern philosophy; but for all that, the problems Aristotle saw, the distinctions he introduced, and the terms he defined are still central in many, if not most, philosophical discussions. His influence and prestige, like Plato's, are international and beyond all schools.

* * *

Aristotle found Plato's theory of Forms unacceptable. Like Plato, he wanted to discover universals, but he did not believe they existed apart from particulars. The form of a chair, for instance, can be thought of apart from the matter out of which the chair is made, but the form does not subsist as a separate invisible entity. The universal of "chairness" exists only in particular chairs—there is no other-worldly "Form of Chairness." Accordingly, Aristotle began his philosophy not with reflection on or dialogue about eternal Forms but with observations of particular objects.

In observing the world, Aristotle saw four "causes" responsible for making an object what it is: the material, formal, efficient, and final. In the case of a chair, for example, the chair's material cause is its wood and cloth, its formal cause is the structure or form given in its plan or blueprint, its efficient cause is the worker who made it, and its final cause is sitting. The material cause, then, is that *out of which* a thing is made, the formal cause is that *into which* a thing is made, the efficient cause is that *by which* a thing is made, and the final cause is that *for which* a thing is made. It is the last of these, the final cause, that Aristotle held to be most important, for it determined the other three. The "goal" or "end" (*telos* in Greek), the final cause, of any given substance is the key to its understanding. This means that all nature is to be understood in terms of final causes or purposes. This is known as a "teleological" explanation of reality.

As Aristotle applied these insights to human beings, he asked what the *telos* of a person could be. By observing what is unique to persons and what they, in fact, do seek, Aristotle came to the conclusion that the highest good or end for humans is *eudaimonia.* While this word is generally translated as "happiness," one must be careful to acknowledge that Aristotle's understanding of "happiness" is rather different from ours. *Eudaimonia* happiness is not a feeling of euphoria—in fact, it is not a feeling at all. It is rather "activity in accordance with virtue." Much of the material from the *Nicomachean Ethics* presented here is devoted both to clarifying the word and to discovering how this kind of "happiness" is to be achieved.

* * *

Aristotle's extant works lack the literary grace of Plato's. Like Plato, Aristotle is said to have written popular dialogues—the "exoteric" writings intended for those who were not students at the Lyceum—but they have not survived. What we have instead are the difficult "esoteric" works: lecture notes for classes at school.

According to some scholars, these are not even Aristotle's notes, but the notes of students collected by editors. In any case, the writings as we have them contain much overlapping, repetition, and apparent contradiction.

Book II of the *Physics*, with which we begin, deals with some of the main questions of physical science. After defining the term "nature," Aristotle discusses change and necessity. And making a distinction between physics and mathematics, he discusses the four causes. Throughout this text, Aristotle displays his teleological understanding of nature—that is, that natural processes operate for an end or purpose.

The *Metaphysics* probably consists of several independent treatises. Book I (*Alpha*) of this collection develops Aristotle's four causes and reviews the history of philosophy to his time. Book XII (*Lambda*) employs many of the concepts previously introduced, such as substance, actuality, and potency, and then moves to Aristotle's theology of the Unmoved Mover. The work concludes with Aristotle's rejection of Platonic Forms as separate, mathematical entities. Apparently Aristotle was responding to Plato's successors, who emphasized the mathematical nature of the Forms.

The first part of the selection presented from Aristotle's *On the Soul (De Anima)* gives a definition of the soul and distinguishes its faculties. The second part discusses the passive and the active mind. As this selection makes clear, Aristotle rejected Plato's view of a soul separate from the body. The selections from *Physics*, *Metaphysics*, and *On the Soul* are all translated by Joe Sachs.

The *Nicomachean Ethics*, is still considered one of the greatest works in ethics. Named for Aristotle's son, Nicomachus, it discusses the nature of the good and of moral and intellectual virtues, as well as investigating specific virtues. The lengthy selection presented here (about one-half of the complete work) reflects this vast range of topics and includes discussions of the subject matter and nature of ethics; of the good for an individual; of moral virtue; of the mean; of the conditions of responsibility for an action; of pride, vanity, humility, and the great-souled man (Aristotle's ideal); of the superiority of loving over being loved; and finally, of human happiness. The translation is Martin Ostwald's.

The marginal page numbers, with their "a" and "b," are those of all scholarly editions—Greek, English, German, French, and others.

* * *

Timothy A. Robinson, *Aristotle in Outline* (Indianapolis, IN: Hackett, 1995) provides an excellent short introduction for the beginning student. W.K.C. Guthrie, *A History of Greek Philosophy, VI: Aristotle: An Encounter* (Cambridge: Cambridge University Press, 1981) and the classic W.D. Ross, *Aristotle* (1923; reprinted in New York: Meridian Books, 1959) are more advanced studies. John Herman Randall, Jr., *Aristotle* (New York: Columbia University Press, 1960); Marjorie Grene, *A Portrait of Aristotle* (Chicago: University of Chicago Press, 1963); J.L. Ackrill, *Aristotle the Philosopher* (Oxford: Oxford University Press, 1981); Jonathan Barnes, *Aristotle* (Oxford: Oxford University Press, 1982); Jonathan Lear, *Aristotle: The Desire to Understand* (Cambridge: Cambridge University Press, 1988); Terence Irwin, *Aristotle's First Principles* (Oxford: Oxford University Press, 1988); Jonathan Barnes, ed., *The Cambridge Companion to Aristotle* (Cambridge: Cambridge University Press, 1995); Kenneth McLeisch, *Aristotle* (London: Routledge, 1999);

and Christopher Shields, *Aristotle* (London: Routledge, 2006) also provide helpful overviews of Aristotle's life and thought. For general collections of essays, see R. Bambrough, ed., *New Essays on Plato and Aristotle* (London: Routledge & Kegan Paul, 1965); J.M.E. Moravcsik, ed., *Aristotle: A Collection of Critical Essays* (New York: Anchor Doubleday, 1967); J. Barnes, M. Schofield, and R. Sorabji, eds., *Articles on Aristotle*, four volumes (London: Duckworth, 1979); Terence Irwin, ed., *Aristotle's Ethics, Aristotle: Substance, Form, and Matter* and *Aristotle: Metaphysics, Epistemology, Natural Philosophy* (all three, Hamden, CT: Garland Publishing, 1995); Cynthia A. Freeland, ed., *Feminist Interpretations of Aristotle* (College Park, PA: Pennsylvania State University Press, 1998); Lloyd P. Gerson, ed., *Aristotle* (London: Routledge, 1999); and George Klosko, ed., *Aristotle* (Burlington, VT: Ashgate, 2007). For help with specific works (besides the *Nicomachean Ethics*), see Lindsay Judson, ed., *Aristotle's* Physics: *A Collection of Essays* (Oxford: Oxford University Press, 1991); Helen S. Lang, *Aristotle's* Physics *and Its Medieval Varieties* (Albany: SUNY Press, 1992); Martha C. Nussbaum and Amelie O. Rorty, eds., *Essays on Aristotle's* De Anima (Oxford: Oxford University Press, 1992); Michael Durrant, ed., *Aristotle's* De Anima *in Focus* (Oxford: Routledge, 1993); Helen S. Lang, *The Order of Nature in Aristotle's* Physics (Cambridge: Cambridge University Press, 1998); Wolfgang-Rainer Mann, *The Discovery of Things: Aristotle's* Categories *and Their Context* (Princeton: Princeton University Press, 2000); C.D.C. Reeve, *Substantial Knowledge: Aristotle's* Metaphysics (Indianapolis, IN: Hackett, 2000); Vasilas Politis, *Routledge Philosophy Guidebook to Aristotle and the* Metaphysics (London: Routledge, 2004); and Ronald Polansky, *Aristotle's* De Anima: *A Critical Commentary* (Cambridge: Cambridge University Press, 2007). The *Nichomachean Ethics* has been such an influential book that many commentaries and essays have been written about it. Among these are H.H. Joachim, *Aristotle: The* Nicomachean Ethics, edited by D.A. Rees (Oxford: Clarendon Press, 1951); W.F.R. Hardie, *Aristotle's Ethical Theory*, 2nd edition (Oxford: Oxford University Press, 1980); Amelie O. Rorty, ed., *Essays on Aristotle's* Ethics (Berkeley: University of California Press, 1980); J.O. Urmson, *Aristotle's* Ethics (Oxford: Basil Blackwell, 1988); Sarah Brodie, *Ethics with Aristotle* (Oxford: Oxford University Press, 1991); Francis Sparshott, *Taking Life Seriously: A Study of the Argument of the* Nichomachean Ethics (Toronto: University of Toronto Press, 1994); Nancy Sherman, ed., *Aristotle's* Ethics: *Critical Essays* (Lanham, MD: Rowman and Littlefield, 1999); Gerard J. Hughes, *Routledge Philosophy Guidebook to Aistotle on Ethics* (NY: Routledge, 2001); Michael Pakaluk, *Aristotle's* Nichomachean Ethics: *An Introduction* (Cambridge: Cambridge University Press, 2005); and Christopher Warne, *Arisototle's* Nichomachean Ethics: *A Reader's Guide* (London: Continuum, 2006). Alasdair C. MacIntyre's pair of books, *After Virtue: A Study in Moral Theory* (Notre Dame, IN: University of Notre Dame Press, 1981) and *Whose Justice? Which Rationality?* (Notre Dame, IN: University of Notre Dame Press, 1988) are interesting examples of recent attempts to apply Aristotle's ethics to contemporary moral problems.

PHYSICS (in part)

BOOK II

1. Of the things that are, some are by nature, others through other causes: by nature are animals and their parts, plants, and the simple bodies, such as earth, fire, air, and water (for these things and such things we say to be by nature), and all of them obviously differ from the things not put together by nature. For each of these has in itself a source of motion and rest, either in place, or by growth and shrinkage, or by alteration; but a bed or a cloak, or any other such kind of thing there is, in the respect in which it has happened upon each designation and to the extent that it is from art, has no innate impulse of change at all. But in the respect in which they happen to be of stone or earth or a mixture of these, they do have such an impulse, and to that extent, since nature is a certain source and cause of being moved and of coming to rest in that to which it belongs primarily, in virtue of itself and not incidentally. (I say not incidentally because someone might himself become a certain cause of health in himself if he is a doctor. Still, it is not in the respect in which he is cured that he has the medical art, but it happens to the same person to be a doctor and be cured, on account of which they are also sometimes separated from each other.) And similarly with each of the other things produced: for none of them has in itself the source of its making, but some in other things and external, such as a house and each of the other products of manual labor, others in themselves but not from themselves, as many as incidentally become causes for themselves.

Nature then is what has been said, and as many things have a nature as have such a source. And every thing that has a nature is an independent thing, since it is something that underlies [and persists through change], and nature is always in an underlying thing. According to nature are both these things and as many things as belong to these in virtue of themselves, as being carried up belongs to fire. For this is not a nature, nor does it have a nature, but it is something by nature and according to nature. What nature is, then, has been said, and what is something by nature and according to nature. *That* nature is, it would be ridiculous to try to show, for it is clear that among the things that are, such things are many. But to show things that are clear by means of things that are unclear is the act of one who cannot distinguish what is known through itself from what is known not through itself. (That it is possible to suffer this is not unclear, for someone blind from birth might reason about colors.) So it is necessary that the speech of such people be about names, while they have insight into nothing.

Now to some it seems that nature or the thinghood* of things by nature is the first thing present in each which is unarranged as far as it itself is concerned; thus the nature of a bed would be wood, and of a statue, bronze. And Antiphon says that a sign of this is that, if someone were to bury a bed, and what rotted had the power to put up a sprout, it would not become a bed but wood, since what belongs to it by accident is the

*<*ousia*>, often translated "substance," means (as our translator puts it) "the way of being that belongs to anything which has attributes but is not an attribute of anything, which is also separate and a *this.* Whatever has being in this way is an independent thing."

arrangement according to convention and art, while the thinghood of it is that which remains continuously even while it is undergoing these things. And if each of *these* things is in the same case in relation to something else (as bronze or gold to water, and bones or wood to earth, and similarly with anything else at all), *that* would be the nature and thinghood of them. On account of which, some say fire, some earth, some air, some water, some say some of these, and some all of these to be the nature of things that are. For whatever from among these anyone supposes to be such, whether one of them or more, this one or this many he declares to be all thinghood, while everything else is an attribute or condition or disposition of these; and whatever is among these he declares to be eternal (since for them there could be no change out of themselves), while the other things come into being and pass away an unlimited number of times.

In one way then, nature is spoken of thus, as the first material underlying each of the things that have in themselves a source of motion and change, but in another way as the form, or the look that is disclosed in speech. For just as art is said of what is according to art or artful, so also nature is said of what is according to nature and natural. We would not yet say anything to be according to art if it is only potentially a bed and does not yet have the look of a bed, nor that it is art, and similarly not in the case of things composed by nature. For what is potentially flesh or bone does not yet have its own 193b nature, until it takes on the look that is disclosed in speech, that by means of which we define when we say what flesh or bone is, and not until then is it by nature. So in this other way, nature would be, of the things having in themselves a source of motion, the form or look, which is not separate other than in speech. (What comes from these, such as a human being, is not nature but by nature.)

And this form or look is nature more than the material is. For each thing is meant when it is fully at work, more than when it *is* potentially. Moreover, a human being comes about from a human being, but not a bed from a bed. On this account, they say that not the shape but the wood is the nature, since if it were to sprout, it would become not a bed but wood. But if, therefore, this is nature, then also the form is nature, for from a human being comes a human being. And still further, the nature spoken of as coming into being is a road into nature. For it is not like the process of medicine, which is meant to be a road not into the medical art but into health, for it is necessary that the medical process be from the medical art and not into it. But not thus is nature related to nature, but the growing thing, insofar as it grows, does proceed from something into something. What then is it that grows? Not the from-which, but the to-which. Therefore nature is the form.

But form and nature are meant in two ways, for deprivation is a sort of form. But whether in the case of a simple coming-into-being there is or is not a deprivation and an opposite, must be looked into later.

2. Now that nature has been marked off in a number of ways, after this one must see how the mathematician differs from one who studies nature (for natural bodies too have surfaces and solids and lengths and points, about which the mathematician inquires), and whether astronomy is different from or part of the study of nature. For if it belongs to the one who studies nature to know what the sun and moon are, but none of the properties that belong to them in themselves, this would be absurd, both in other ways and because those concerned with nature obviously speak about the shape of the moon and sun and especially whether the earth and the cosmos are of spherical shape or not.

The mathematician does busy himself about the things mentioned, but not insofar as each is a limit of a natural body, nor does he examine their properties insofar as they

belong to them because they pertain to natural bodies. On account of this also he separates them. For in his thinking they are separated from motion, and it makes no difference, nor do they become false by being separated. Those who speak of the forms also do this, but without being aware of it, for they separate the natural things, which are less separable than the mathematical ones. This would become clear if one should try to state 194a
the definitions of each of these things, both of themselves and of their properties. For the odd and even, and the straight and the curved, and further, number, line, and figure will be without motion, but no longer so with flesh, bone, or human being, but these are spoken of like a snub-nose and not like the curved. The more natural of the mathematical studies, such as optics, harmonics, and astronomy, also show this, for they in a certain way stand contrariwise to geometry. For geometry inquires about a natural line, but not as natural, but optics about a mathematical line, not as mathematical but as natural.

But since nature is twofold, and is both form and material, we must consider it as though we were inquiring about what snubness is. As a result, such things will be neither without material, nor determined by their material. And in fact, since there are two natures, one might be at an impasse about which of them belongs to the study of nature. Or is it about that which comes from both? But if it is about that which comes from both, it is also about each of the two. Then does it belong to the same study or different ones to know each? If one looks to the ancients, it would seem to be about material (for only a little bit did Empedocles and Democritus touch on form or the what-it-is-to-be of things). But if art imitates nature, and if it belongs to the same knowledge to know the form and the material to some extent (as it is the doctor's job to know health and also bile and phlegm, in which health is, and the housebuilder's to know both the form of a house and its material, that it is bricks and lumber, and in like manner with the rest), it would also be part of the study of nature to pay attention to both natures.

Further, that for the sake of which, or the end, as well as whatever is for the sake of these, belong to the same study. But nature is an end and a that-for-the-sake-of-which. (For of those things of which there is an end, if the motion is continuous, the end is both the last stage and that for the sake of which; which induced the poet to say, absurdly, "He has his death, for the sake of which he was born." For not every last thing professes itself to be an end, but only what is best.) And the arts make even their material, some simply and others working it up, and we make use of everything there is as though it is for our sake (for we are also in some way an end, and "that for the sake of which" is double in meaning, but this is discussed in the writings on philosophy). But the arts which govern and understand the material are two, one of using and one of directing the 194b
making. The art of using is for that very reason somehow directive of the making, but they differ in that the one is attentive to the form, the other, as productive, to the material. For the steersman recognizes and gives orders about what sort of form belongs to the rudder, but someone else about what sort of wood and processes it will come from. In things that come from art, then, we make the material for the sake of the work, but in natural things it is in being from the beginning. Further, material is among the relative things: for a different form, a different material.

To what extent is it necessary for the one who studies nature to know the form or whatness? Is it just as the doctor knows connective tissue or the metal-worker knows bronze, to the extent of knowing what each is for the sake of, even about those things which, while separate in form, are present in material? For both a human being and the sun beget a human being. But what manner of being the separate thing and the whatness have, it is the work of first philosophy to define.

3. These things having been marked out, it is necessary to examine the causes, both what sort there are and how many in number. For since this work is for the sake of knowing, but we think we do not yet know each thing until we have taken hold of the why of it (and to do this is to come upon the first cause), it is clear that we too must do this about both coming into being and passing away and about every natural change, so that, once we know them, we may try to lead back to them each of the things we inquire about.

One way cause is meant, then, is that out of which something comes into being, still being present in it, as bronze of a statue or silver of a bowl, or the kinds of these. In another way it is the form or pattern, and this is the gathering in speech of the what-it-is-for-it-to-be, or again the kinds of this (as of the octave, the two-to-one ratio, or generally number), and the parts that are in its articulation. In yet another it is that from which the first beginning of change or of rest is, as the legislator is a cause, or the father of a child, or generally the maker of what is made, or whatever makes a changing thing change. And in still another way it is meant as the end. This is that for the sake of which, as health is of walking around. Why is he walking around? We say "in order to be healthy," and in so saying think we have completely given the cause. Causes also are as many things as come between the mover of something else and the end, as, of health, fasting or purging or drugs or instruments. For all these are for the sake of the end, but
195a they differ from one another in that some are deeds and others tools.

Bust of Aristotle, first century copy of Greek sculpture, Louvre. Using Aristotle's Four Causes, we would say the *material cause* of this bust is marble (that *out of which* it was made), the *formal cause* is a bust of Aristotle (that *into which* it was made), the *efficient cause* is the sculptor who carved it (that *by which* it was made), and the *final cause* is to honor or memorialize Aristotle (that *for the sake of which* it was made). (©*Print Collector/Getty)*

The causes then are meant in just about this many ways, and it happens, since they are meant in more than one way, that the non-accidental causes of the same thing are also many, as of the statue both the art of sculpture and bronze, not as a consequence of anything else but just as a statue, though they are not causes in the same way, but the one as material and the other as that from which the motion was. And there are also in a certain way causes of one another, as hard work is a cause of good condition and this in turn is a cause of hard work, though again not in the same way, but the one as end and the other as source of motion. Further, the same thing is a cause of opposite things. For the present thing is responsible for this result, and we sometimes blame it, when it is absent, for the opposite result, as the absence of the pilot for the ship's overturning, whose presence was the cause of its keeping safe. But all the causes now being spoken of fall into four most evident ways. For the letters of syllables and the material of processed things and fire (and such things) of bodies and parts of a whole and hypotheses of a conclusion are causes as that out of which, and while the one member of each of these pairs is a cause as what underlies, such as parts, the other is so as the what-it-is-for-it-to-be, a whole or composite or form. But the semen and the doctor and the legislator, and generally the maker, are all causes as that from which the source of change or rest is, but other things are causes as the end or the good of the remaining ones. For that-for-the-sake-of-which means to be the best thing and the end of the other things, and let it make no difference to say the good itself or the apparent good.

The causes then are these and are so many in form, but the ways the causes work are many in number, though even these are fewer if they are brought under headings. For cause is meant in many ways, and of those of the same form, as preceding and following one another. For example, the cause of health is the doctor and also the skilled knower, and of the octave the double and also number, and always comprehensive things in relation to particular ones. Further, there is what is incidental, and the kinds of these, as of the statue, in one way Polycleitus and in another the sculptor, because it is incidental to the sculptor to be Polycleitus. And there are the things comprehensive of the incidental cause, as if a human being were the cause of a statue, or generally, an animal. And also among incidental things, some are more remote and others nearer, as if the pale man or the one with a refined education were said to be the cause of a statue. And all of them, both those meant properly and those incidentally, are meant some as potential and others as at-work, as of building a house, either the builder or the builder building. And similarly to the things that have been said, an account will be given for those things of which the causes are causes, as of this statue or a statue or in general an image, and of this bronze or of bronze or in general of material, and likewise with the incidental things. Further, things tangling these and those together will be said, such as not Polycleitus nor a sculptor but the sculptor Polycleitus.

Nevertheless, all these are six in multitude, but spoken of in a twofold way: there is the particular or the kind, the incidental or the kind of the incidental thing, and these entangled or spoken of simply, and all as either at-work or in potency. And they differ to this extent, that what is at-work and particular is and is not at the same time as that of which it is the cause, as this one healing with this one being cured or this one building with this thing being built, but not always so with what is potential. The house and the housebuilder are not finished off simultaneously.

And it is necessary always to seek out the ultimate cause of each thing, and in just the same way as with the others. (For example, a man builds because he is a builder, but is a builder as a result of the housebuilder's art; this, then, is the prior cause, and thus with everything.) Further, the kinds belong to the kinds and the particulars to the particulars (as a sculptor to a statue, but this sculptor to this statue). Also the potencies belong to the potencies, but what is at work corresponds to what is being worked upon. How many then are the causes and in what way they are causes, let it have been marked out sufficiently for us.

4. Fortune and chance are spoken of among the causes, and many things are said to be and to come about through fortune or through chance. In what way, then, fortune and chance are among these causes, and whether fortune and chance are the same or different, and in general what fortune and chance are, must be examined. For some people are at an impasse even about whether they exist or not. For they say nothing comes about from fortune, but that, for everything whatever that we say comes from chance or fortune, there is some definite cause; for example, of coming by fortune into the marketplace and catching up with someone whom one wanted, but did not expect, to find, the cause is wanting to go to use the marketplace. And similarly with the rest of the things said to be from fortune, there is always something to take as the cause, but not fortune, since if fortune were anything it would seem strange, and truly so; and one might find it impossible to understand why in the world none of the ancient wise men, speaking about the causes of coming-to-be and passing away, demarcated anything about fortune, but as it seems, they too regarded nothing as being from fortune. But this too is to be wondered at. For many things both come about and are from fortune and from chance, which everyone, though not ignorant that it is possible to refer each of them back to some cause of its coming about, which the earlier argument declared to be the abolition of fortune, nevertheless says are from fortune, some of them, though some are not. For this reason they were obliged to make some mention of it in some way. But surely they did not regard fortune to be any of those things such as friendship and strife, or intellect, or fire, or anything else of that sort. It is strange, then, either if they did not acknowledge it to be, or if, supposing it, they left it aside, despite even sometimes making use of it, as Empedocles says that the air is not always separated in the highest place, but however it falls out. Certainly he says in his cosmogony that "it fell out thus as it was flowing at one time, but often otherwise." And most of them say that the parts of animals have come into being from fortune.

There are some who make chance responsible for this cosmos and all worlds. For they say that by chance there came about a vortex and a motion of separating out and settling into this arrangement of the whole. And this itself is in fact mightily worth wondering at. For they are saying that animals and plants neither are nor come to be by fortune, but that either nature or intellect or some other such thing is the cause (for what comes into being from each seed is not whatever falls out, but from this one an olive tree, from that one a human being), but that the heavens and the most divine of visible things have come from chance, and there is in no way such a cause as there is of the animals and plants. But if this is the way things are, this itself is worth bringing one to a stop, and it would have been good for something to have been said about it. In this respect as well as others, what is said is strange, and it is stranger still to say these things when one sees nothing in the heavens happening by chance, but many things falling out by fortune among the things not assigned to fortune, though it would surely seem that the opposite would happen.

There are others to whom it seems that fortune is a cause, but one not disclosed to human understanding, as though it were something divine and more appropriate to miraculous agency. So it is necessary to examine what each is, and whether chance and fortune are the same or different, and how they fall in with the causes that have been marked out.

5. First, then, since we see some things always happening in a certain way, and others for the most part, it is clear that of neither of these is fortune or what comes from fortune said to be the cause, neither of what is out of necessity and always, nor of what is for the most part. But since there are other things besides these that happen, and everyone says that they are from fortune, it is clear that fortune or chance is in some way. For we know that things of this kind are from fortune and that things from fortune are of this kind.

Now of things that happen, some happen for the sake of something and some not (and of the former, some in accordance with choice, some not in accordance with choice, but both are among things for the sake of something), so that it is clear that even among things apart from what is necessary or for the most part, there are some to which it is possible that being for the sake of something belongs. And for the sake of something are as many things as are brought about from thinking or from nature. But whenever such things come about incidentally, we say that they are from fortune. (For just as a thing is something either in virtue of itself or incidentally, so also is it possible to be a cause, as of a house, the cause in virtue of itself is the builder's art, but an incidental one is the pale or educated man; the cause in virtue of itself, then, is definite, but the incidental one indefinite, for to one thing, infinitely many things incidentally belong.) Just as was said, then, whenever this happens among things happening for the sake of something, in that case it is said to be from chance or from fortune. (The difference between these in relation to one another is something that must be distinguished later; for now let this be clearly seen, that both are among the things for the sake of something.) For example, someone gathering contributions would have come for the sake of collecting money, if he had known; but he came not for the sake of this, but it happened to him incidentally to go and to do this. And this was not through frequenting the place for the most part or out of necessity, but the end, the collection, though not belonging to the causes in him, is among choices and things that result from thinking. And in this case he is said to have come by fortune, but if he had chosen to, and for the sake of this, or if he frequented the place always or for the most part, not by fortune. It is clear then that fortune is an incidental cause among things proceeding from choice, which in turn are among those for the sake of something. Whence thinking and fortune concern the same thing, for there is no choice without thinking.

It is necessary, then, that the causes be indefinite from which what arises from fortune comes about. Whence fortune too seems to be indefinite, and obscure to humans, and it is possible for it to seem that nothing comes about from fortune. For all these things are said correctly, reasonably. That is, there are things that come about from fortune: they come about incidentally, and fortune is an incidental cause, but of nothing is it the cause simply. As of a house, the cause is the builder's art, but incidentally a flute-player, also of coming to collect money when one has not come for the sake of this, the multitude of causes is unlimited. One wanted either to see someone, or look for someone, or get away from someone, or see a show. It is even correct to say that fortune is something non-rational, for a reasoned account belongs to what happens either always or for the most part, and fortune is among things that come about outside of these ways. Thus, since causes of this kind are indefinite, fortune too is indefinite. Still, in some situations, one might be at a loss whether the things that happen to occur would become causes of fortune, as of health, the wind or the sun's warmth, but not having had a haircut. For among incidental causes, some are nearer than others.

Whenever something good turns out, fortune is called good, or indifferent when it is something indifferent, but good fortune or ill fortune are only spoken of when these outcomes are of some magnitude. For this reason too, to come within a hairsbreadth of obtaining some great evil or good is to be fortunate or unfortunate, because our thinking picks out what comes out, but seems to hold off what was within a hairsbreadth as nothing. Further, good fortune is unstable, and reasonably, for fortune is unstable, since it is not possible for any of the things from fortune to be always or for the most part. Both, then, are causes, incidental ones as was said, both fortune and chance, among those things which admit of coming into being neither simply nor for the most part, belonging in turn to those which could come about for the sake of something.

6. They differ because chance is more extensive, for everything from fortune is from chance, but not everything from it is from fortune. For fortune and what comes from fortune are present to beings to whom being fortunate, or generally, action, might belong. For this reason also, fortune is necessarily concerned with actions. (A sign is that good fortune seems to be either the same thing as happiness or nearly so, while happiness is a kind of action, namely doing well.) So whatever cannot act cannot do anything as a result of fortune either. And for this reason no inanimate thing nor any animal or small child can do anything as a result of fortune, because they do not have the power to choose in advance. Neither good fortune nor misfortune belongs to them, except metaphorically, as Protarchus says the stones out of which altars are made are fortunate, because they are honored, while their quarry-mates are trampled on. But it belongs even to these things to be affected by fortune, whenever an active being acts on them in some way that results from fortune, but in no other way. Chance, though, belongs to the other animals and to many inanimate things, as we say a horse came along by chance, because he was saved by his coming, though he did not come for the sake of the being saved. Or a tripod fell down by chance, for it stood there in order to be sat upon, but did not fall down in order to be sat upon. So it is clear, among things happening for the sake of something simply, whenever they happen not for the sake of what turned out, of which the cause was external, we then say that they are from chance. And as many of these things that happen by chance are choices, and happen to those having the power of choice, as are from fortune.

A sign of this is the phrase "in vain," which is said whenever what is for the sake of another thing does not come to pass for the sake of that, as, if taking a walk were for the sake of evacuation, but when one had walked this did not happen, we would say that having walked was vain and taking a walk futile, as though this was the "in vain": for something by nature for the sake of another thing, the not being brought to accomplishment of that for the sake of which it was and to which it was naturally disposed, since if someone said he had bathed in vain because the sun was not eclipsed, it would be ridiculous, for this was not for the sake of that. Thus, even from its name, chance [*to automaton*] is that which itself happens in vain [*to auto maten*]. For the stone fell not for the sake of knocking someone out; therefore the stone fell by chance, because it could have fallen by some agency and for the sake of the knocking out.

Chance is separated most of all from what comes from fortune in things that happen by nature. For whenever something happens contrary to nature, we say that it happened not by fortune but by chance. But it is also possible that this is for a different reason, since of the one the cause is outside, of the other inside.

What, then, chance and fortune are has been said, and how they differ from each other. And of the ways of being a cause, both of them are among things from which the source of motion is; for they are always among either things in some way by nature, or causes that come from thinking, but the multitude of them is infinite. But since chance and fortune are causes of things for which either intelligence or nature might have been responsible, whenever something incidentally becomes responsible for these same things, but nothing incidental is prior to things in virtue of themselves, it is clear that neither is the incidental cause prior to what is in virtue of itself. Therefore chance and fortune are subordinate to intelligence and nature, so that if chance is responsible for the heavens as much as possible, it is necessary that intelligence and nature have a prior responsibility, not only for many other things, but also for this whole.

7. That there are causes, and that they are as many in number as we said, is clear, for the why includes so many in number. For the why ultimately leads back either to the what-it-is, among motionless things (as in mathematics, for it ultimately leads back to the definition of straight or commensurable or something else), or to the first source of motion (as, Why did they go to war? Because they were plundered), or something for the sake of which (in order to rule), or, among things that come into being, the material.

That the causes, then, are these and this many, is clear; and since there are four causes, it belongs to the one who studies nature to know about all of them, and he will supply what is due in the way of natural inquiry by tracing back the why to them all: the material, the form, the mover, and that for the sake of which. But often three of them turn back into one, for the what-it-is and that for the sake of which are one, and that whence the motion first is, is the same in form with these; for a human being brings forth a human being, and in general, as many things as, being moved themselves, cause motion, are the same in form with the things moved. (Whatever is not like this does not belong to the study of nature. For it causes motion not by having motion or a source of motion in itself, but being motionless. On which account there are three studies, one about motionless things, one about things moved but indestructible, and one about destructible things.) So they supply what is due by tracing back the why to the material, and to the what-it-is, and to the first mover. About coming into being, they examine the cause mostly in this way: what comes about after what, and what did it do first, or how was it acted upon, and so on always in succession.

The sources which bring about motion naturally are twofold, of which one kind is not natural, for sources of that kind do not have in themselves a source of motion. And of this kind is whatever causes motion without being moved, as does not only what is completely motionless and the first of all beings, but also the what-it-is or form, for it is an end and that for the sake of which. So, since nature is for the sake of something, it is also necessary to know this, and one must supply the why completely: for example, that from this necessarily comes that (from this either simply or for the most part), *and* that if it is going to be, this will be (as from the premises, the conclusion), and that this is what it is for it to be, and because it is better thus, not simply, but in relation to the thinghood of each thing.

8. One must say, first, why nature is among the causes for the sake of something, then, about the necessary, how it holds a place among natural things. For everybody traces things back to this cause, inasmuch as, since the hot and the cold and each thing of this kind are by nature a certain way, these things are and come into being out of necessity. For even if they also speak of another cause, they send it on its way after only so much as touching on it, one on friendship and strife, another on intellect.

Here is an impasse: what prevents nature from doing things not for the sake of anything, nor because they are best, but just as Zeus rains, not in order that the grain might grow, but out of necessity? (For it is necessary that what is taken up be cooled, and that what is cooled, becoming water, come down; when this happens, growing incidentally happens to the grain.) Likewise, if the grain is ruined on the threshing-floor, not for the sake of this did it rain, to spoil it, but this was incidental. So what prevents the parts in something that is by nature from being the same way, say the teeth growing with the front ones sharp out of necessity, suitable for tearing, but the molars flat and useful for grinding the food, although not happening for the sake of this, but just falling together? Likewise with the other parts, to however many being for the sake of something seems to belong, wherever everything happened to come together just as if it had been for the sake of something, these were preserved, having been put together advantageously by chance. Anything that is not like that has perished and still perishes, just as Empedocles says of man-headed offspring of cattle.

The account, then, by means of which one might come to an impasse, is this one or any other that might be of this kind; but it is impossible for things to be this way. For these things and all things that are by nature come about as they do either always or for the most part, but none of the things from fortune or chance do. For it does not seem to be from fortune or by coincidence that it rains often in winter, but it does if this happens in the dog days, nor scorching heat in the dog days, but in winter. If, then, it seems that something is either by coincidence or for the sake of something, and if things by nature cannot be by either coincidence or chance, they would be for the sake of something. But surely such things are all by nature, as even those making these arguments would say. Therefore, there is being-for-the-sake-of-something among things that happen and are by nature.

Further, among all things that are for some end, it is for the sake of this that what precedes it in succession is done. Accordingly, in the way that one performs an action, so also are things by nature, and as things are by nature, so does one perform each action unless something interferes. But one acts for the sake of something, and therefore what is by nature is for the sake of something. For example, if a house were something that came into being by nature, it would come about in just the way that it now does by art, and if the things by nature were to come about not only by nature but also by art, they too would come about in exactly the same way as they do by nature. Therefore each is for the sake of another. And in general, art in some cases completes what nature is unable to finish off, but in others imitates nature. If then, what comes from art is for the sake of something, it is clear that what comes from nature is too, for the series of things from art and from nature are alike, each to each, in the way that the later things are related to the earlier.

This is clear most of all in the other animals, which do nothing by art, inquiry, or deliberation; for which reason some people are completely at a loss whether it is by intelligence or in some other way that spiders, ants, and such things work. But if we move forward little by little in this way, it becomes apparent that even in plants what is brought together comes about in relation to the end, as the leaves for the sake of protection for the fruit. So if both by nature and for the sake of something the swallow makes a nest and the spider a web, and the plants make their leaves for the sake of their fruit, and their roots not upward but downward for the sake of nourishment, it is clear that there is such a cause in things that come into being and are by nature. And since nature is twofold, both material and form, and the latter is an end but the former is for the sake of an end, the form would be the cause for the sake of which.

Now missing the mark happens even among things done according to art (for the grammarian on occasion writes, or the doctor gives out a drug, incorrectly), so it is clear that this is possible also among things done by nature. But if there are some things according to art in which what is done correctly is for the sake of something, but in the ones that miss the mark what is done is for the sake of something that is attempted but missed, it is the same among natural things, and monsters are failures of that for the sake of which they are. Therefore even the cattle-offspring, in their original constitution, if they were not able to come to some limit and end, would have come into being when some originating cause in them was disabled, as might happen now with the seed. Still it is necessary that a seed come into being first, and not straightaway the animals; "first the mixed-natured" was the seed. That for the sake of which is also present in plants, though less articulated. So then did there come about among the plants, like the man-headed offspring of cattle, also olive-headed offspring of grapevines, or not? It would be strange, but it would be necessary, if it also happened among animals.

In general, it would be necessary, among seeds, that whatever chanced come into being, but the one speaking this way abolishes nature and what is by nature. For by nature are as many things as, moved continuously by some source in themselves, reach some end; from each beginning does not come the same end for them all, nor just what chances, but each always reaches the same end unless something interferes. That for the sake of which, and that which is for the sake of this, might also happen by fortune, as we say that a stranger came by fortune and, having paid the ransom, went away, when he acted as though having come for the sake of this, but did not come for the sake of this. And this is incidental (for fortune is among the incidental causes, just as we said before), but whenever this happens always or for the most part, it is neither incidental nor by fortune. But among natural things, things happen always in the same way, unless something interferes.

It is absurd to think that a thing does not happen for the sake of something if we do not see what sets it in motion deliberating. Surely even art does not deliberate. If shipbuilding were present in wood, it would act in the same way as nature does, so if being for the sake of something is present in art, it is also present in nature. This is most clear when someone practices medicine himself on himself; for nature is like that. That, then, nature is a cause, and in this way, for the sake of something, is clear.

---

9. Does what is by necessity belong to things conditionally or simply? For now people suppose that what is by necessity is in the coming into being of things, as if someone were to think that the wall of a house came into being by necessity, because the heavy things are of a nature to be carried downward and the light ones on top, so that the stones and foundations are at the bottom, the earth above on account of its lightness, and at the very top the wood, since it is lightest. But even though it did not come into being without these things, it surely did not do so as a result of them, except as by means of material, but rather for the sake of enclosing and sheltering certain things. And similarly with everything else, in whatever being-for-the-sake-of something is present, each thing is neither without things having necessity in their nature, nor as a result of them other than as material, but for the sake of something. For example, why is a saw thus? In order to do this and for the sake of this. But this which it is for the sake of would be incapable of coming about if it were not made of iron. It is necessary, therefore, that it be of iron if the saw and its work are to be. So the necessary is conditional, unlike the end. For the necessary is in the material, but that for the sake of which is in what is grasped in speech.

The necessary is present both in mathematics and in things that come about by nature, in ways closely resembling one another. For since the straight is a certain way, it is necessary that the triangle be equal to two right angles, but not the former because of the latter, despite the fact that were this not so, neither would the straight be as it is. But in things that come to be for the sake of something, contrariwise, if the end is to be or is, then what precedes it will be or is; and if not, just as there [in mathematics] the first principle will not be so when the conclusion is not, so also here [in nature] with the end and that for the sake of which. For this too is a starting point, not of action but of reasoning (and of reasoning there; for there are no actions). So that if a house is to be, it is necessary that there come into being or be present or in general be these things as material for the sake of something, such as bricks and stones if it is a house. Nevertheless, the end is not present as a result of these, other than as material, nor will it be, just because of them. In general, however, neither the house nor the saw will be if the bricks, in the former case, and the iron in the latter, are not; for neither will the starting points be the case there if the triangle is not two right angles.

It is clear that the necessary in natural things is the so-called material and its motions. And both must be stated as causes by the one who studies nature, but more so that for the sake of which. For this is responsible for the material, but the material is not responsible for the end. And the end is that for the sake of which, and the beginning comes from the definition and that which is grasped in speech; just as in things that come from art, since the house is such, these things must come into being or be present necessarily, and since health is such, *these* things must come into being or be present necessarily—so also if a human being is such, these things, but if these, these others in turn. Perhaps the necessary is even in the definition. For the work of sawing having been defined as a certain kind of dividing, this will not be unless it has teeth of a certain kind, and these will not be of that kind unless they are of iron. For even in the definition there are certain parts, as material of the definition.

METAPHYSICS (in part)

BOOK I

1. All human beings by nature stretch themselves out toward knowing. A sign of this is our love of the senses; for even apart from their use, they are loved on their own account, and above all the rest, the one through the eyes. For not only in order that we might act, but even when we are not going to act at all, we prefer seeing, one might say, as against everything else. And the cause is that, among the senses, this one most of all makes us discover things, and makes evident many differences. By nature, then, the animals come into being having sense perception, though in some of them memory does not emerge out of this, while in others it does. And for this reason, these latter are more intelligent and more able to learn than those that are unable to remember, while as many of them as are not able to hear sounds are intelligent without learning (such as a bee, or any other kind of animal that might be of this sort), but as many do learn as have this

sense in addition to memory. So the other animals live by images and memories, but have a small share of experience, but the human race lives also by art and reasoning. And for human beings, experience arises from memory, since many memories of the 981a
same thing bring to completion a capacity for one experience.

Now experience seems to be almost the same thing as knowledge or art, but for human beings, knowledge and art result from experience, for experience makes art, as Polus says and says rightly, but inexperience makes chance. And art comes into being whenever, out of many conceptions from experience, one universal judgment arises about those that are similar. For to have a judgment that this thing was beneficial to Callias when he was sick with this disease, and to Socrates, and one by one in this way to many people, belongs to experience. But the judgment that it was beneficial to all such people, marked out as being of one kind, when they were sick with this disease, such as to sluggish or irritable people when they were feverish with heat, belongs to art. For the purpose of acting, experience doesn't seem to differ from art at all, and we even see people with experience being more successful than those who have a rational account without experience. (The cause of this is that experience is familiarity with things that are particular, but art with those that are universal, while actions and all becoming are concerned with what is particular. For the doctor does not cure a human being, except incidentally, but Callias or Socrates or any of the others called by such a name, who happens to be a human being. So if someone without experience has the reasoned account and is familiar with the universal, but is ignorant of what is particular within it, he will often go astray in his treatment, since what is treated is particular.)

Nevertheless, we think that knowing and understanding are present in art more than is experience and we take the possessors of arts to be wiser than people with experience, as though in every instance wisdom is more something resulting from and following along with knowing; and this is because the ones know the cause while the others do not. For people with experience know the what, but do not know the why, but the others are acquainted with the why and the cause. For this reason we also think the master craftsmen in each kind of work are more honorable and know more than the manual laborers, and are also wiser, because they know the causes of the 981b
things they do, as though people are wiser not as a result of being skilled at action, but as a result of themselves having the reasoned account and knowing the causes. And in general, a sign of the one who knows and the one who does not is being able to teach, and for this reason we regard the art, more than the experience, to be knowledge, since the ones can, but the others cannot, teach.

Further, we consider none of the senses to be wisdom, even though they are the most authoritative ways of knowing particulars; but they do not pick out the why of anything, such as why fire is hot, but only that it is hot. So it is likely that the one who first discovered any art whatever that was beyond the common perceptions was wondered at by people, not only on account of there being something useful in his discoveries, but as someone wise and distinguished from other people. But once more arts had been discovered, and some of them were directed toward necessities but others toward a way of living, it is likely that such people as were discoverers of the latter kind were always considered wiser, because their knowledge was not directed toward use. Hence when all such arts had been built up, those among the kinds of knowledge directed at neither pleasure nor necessity were discovered, and first in those places where there was leisure. It is for this reason that the mathematical arts were first constructed in the neighborhood of Egypt, for there the tribe of priests was allowed to live in leisure.

Now it has been said in the writings on ethics what the difference is among art, demonstrative knowledge, and the other things of a similar kind, but the purpose for which we are now making this argument is that all people assume that what is called wisdom is concerned with first causes and origins. Therefore, as was said above, the person with experience seems wiser than those who have any perception whatever, the artisan wiser than those with experience, the master craftsman wiser than the manual laborer, and the contemplative arts more so than the productive ones. It is apparent, then, that wisdom is a knowledge concerned with certain sources and causes.

2. Since we are seeking this knowledge, this should be examined: about what sort of causes and what sort of sources wisdom is the knowledge. Now if one takes the accepted opinions we have about the wise man, perhaps from this it will become more clear. We assume first that the wise man knows all things, in the way that it is possible, though he does not have knowledge of them as particulars. Next, we assume that the one who is able to know things that are difficult, and not easy for a human being to know, is wise; for perceiving is common to everyone, for which reason it is an easy thing and nothing wise. Further, we assume the one who has more precision and is more able to teach the causes is wiser concerning each kind of knowledge. And among the kinds of knowledge, we assume the one that is for its own sake and chosen for the sake of knowing more to be wisdom than the one chosen for the sake of results, and that the more ruling one is wisdom more so than the more subordinate one; for the wise man ought not to be commanded but to give orders, and ought not to obey someone else, but the less wise ought to obey him.

We have, then, such and so many accepted opinions about wisdom and those who are wise. Now of these, the knowing of all things must belong to the one who has most of all the universal knowledge, since he knows in a certain way all the things that come under it; and these are just about the most difficult things for human beings to know, those that are most universal, since they are farthest away from the senses. And the most precise of the kinds of knowledge are the ones that are most directed at first things, since those that reason from fewer things are more precise than those that reason from extra ones, as arithmetic is more precise than geometry. But surely the skill that is suited to teach is the one that has more insight into causes, for those people teach who give an account of the causes about each thing. And knowing and understanding for their own sakes belong most to the knowledge of what is most knowable. For the one who chooses what is known through itself would most of all be choosing that which is knowledge most of all, and of this sort is the knowledge of what is most knowable. But what are most knowable are the first things and the causes, for through these and from these the other things are known, but these are not known through what comes under them. And the most ruling of the kinds of knowledge, or the one more ruling than what is subordinate to it, is the one that knows for what purpose each thing must be done; and this is the good of each thing, and in general the best thing in the whole of nature. So from all the things that have been said, the name sought falls to the same kind of knowledge, for it must be a contemplation of the first sources and causes, since also the good, or that for the sake of which, is one of the causes.

That it is not a productive knowledge is clear too from those who first engaged in philosophy. For by way of wondering, people both now and at first began to philosophize, wondering first about the strange things near at hand, then going forward little by little in this way and coming to impasses about greater things, such as about the attributes of the moon and things pertaining to the sun and the stars and the coming into being of the whole. But someone who wonders and is at an impasse considers himself to be ignorant (for which reason the lover of myth is in a certain way philosophic, since a myth is composed of wonders). So if it was by fleeing ignorance that they philosophized, it is clear that by means of knowing they were in pursuit of knowing, and not for the sake of any kind of use. And the following testifies to the same thing: for it was when just about all the necessities were present, as well as things directed toward the greatest ease and recreation, that this kind of understanding began to be sought. It is clear then that we seek it for no other use at all, but just as that human being is free, we say, who has his being for his own sake and not for the sake of someone else, so also do we seek it as being the only one of the kinds of knowledge that is free, since it alone is for its own sake.

For this reason one might justly regard the possession of it as not appropriate to humans. For in many ways human nature is slavish, so that, according to Simonides, "only a god should have this honor," but a man is not worthy of seeking anything but the kind of knowledge that fits him. If indeed the poets have a point and it is the nature of the divine power to be jealous, it would be likely to happen most of all in this case, and all extraordinary people would be ill-fated. But it is not even possible for the divine power to be jealous, but according to the common saying "many lyrics are lies," and one ought not to regard anything else as more honorable than this knowledge. For the most divine is also the most honorable, and this knowledge by itself would be most divine in two ways. For what most of all a god would have is that among the kinds of knowledge that is divine, if in fact any of them were about divine things. But this one alone happens to have both these characteristics; for the divine seems to be among the causes for all things, and to be a certain source, and such knowledge a god alone, or most of all, would have. All kinds of knowledge, then, are more necessary than this one, but none is better.

It is necessary, however, for the possession of it to settle for us in a certain way into the opposite of the strivings with which it began. For everyone begins, as we are saying, from wondering whether things are as they seem, such as the self-moving marvels, or about the reversals of the sun or the incommensurability of the diagonal (for it seems amazing to all those who have not yet seen the cause if anything is not measured by the smallest part). But it is necessary to end in what is opposite and better, as the saying goes, just as in these cases when people understand them; for nothing would be so surprising to a geometer as if the diagonal were to become commensurable. What, then, is the nature of the knowledge being sought, has been said, and what the object is on which the inquiry and the whole pursuit must alight.

3. Since it is clear that one must take hold of a knowledge of the causes that originate things (since that is when we say we know each thing, when we think we know its first cause), while the causes are meant in four ways, of which one is thinghood,* or what it is for something to be (since the why leads back to the ultimate reasoned account, and the first why is a cause and source), another is the material or underlying thing, a third is that from which the source of motion is, and the fourth is the cause opposite to that one, that for the sake of which or the good (since it is the completion of every coming-into-being and motion), which have been sufficiently looked into by us in the writings about nature, still, let us take up also those who came before us into the

*<*ousia*>, often translated "substance," means (as our translator puts it) "the way of being that belongs to anything which has attributes but is not an attribute of anything, which is also separate and a *this*. Whatever has being in this way is an independent thing."

inquiry about beings and philosophized about truth. For it is clear that they too speak of certain sources and causes. So for those who go back over these things, there will be some profit for the present pursuit; for we will either find out some other kind of cause or be more persuaded about the ones we are now speaking of. Of those who first engaged in philosophy, most thought that the only sources of all things were of the species of material; that of which all things are made, out of which they first come into being and into which they are at last destroyed, its thinghood abiding but changing in its attributes, this they claim is the element and origin of things, for which reason nothing ever comes into being or perishes, since this sort of nature is always preserved, just as we would not say either that Socrates simply comes into being when he becomes beautiful or educated in refined pursuits, or that he perishes when he sheds these conditions, since the underlying thing, Socrates himself, persists, so neither does anything else. For there must be some nature, either one or multiple, out of which the other things come into being while that one is preserved. About the number and kind of such sources, however, they do not all say the same thing, but Thales, the founder of this sort of philosophy, says it is water (for which reason too he declared that the earth is on water), getting hold of this opinion perhaps from seeing that the nourishment of all things is fluid, and that heat itself comes about from it and lives by means of it (and that out of which things come into being is the source of them all). So he got hold of this opinion by this means, and because the seeds of all things have a fluid nature, while water is in turn the source of the nature of fluid things.

There are some who think that very ancient thinkers, long before the present age, who gave the first accounts of the gods, had an opinion of this sort about nature. For they made Ocean and Tethys the parents of what comes into being, and made the oath of the gods be by water, called Styx by them; for what is oldest is most honored, and that
984a by which one swears is the most honored thing. But whether this opinion about nature is something archaic and ancient might perhaps be unclear, but Thales at least is said to have spoken in this way about the first cause. (One would not consider Hippo worthy to place among these, on account of his cut-rate thinking.) Anaximenes and Diogenes set down air as more primary than water and as the most originative of the simple bodies, while Hippasus of Metapontium and Heraclitus of Ephesus set down fire, and Empedocles, adding earth as a fourth to those mentioned, sets down the four (for he says these always remain and do not come into being except in abundance or fewness, being combined and separated into or out of one). Anaxagoras of Clazomenae, who was before Empedocles in age but after him in his works, said the sources were infinite; for he said that almost all homogeneous things are just like water or fire in coming into being or perishing only by combination and separation, but otherwise neither come into being nor perish but remain everlasting.

From these things, then, one might suppose that the only cause is the one accounted for in the species of material; but as people went forward in this way, their object of concern itself opened a road for them, and contributed to forcing them to inquire along it. For no matter how much every coming-into-being and destruction is out of some one or more kinds of material, why does this happen and what is its cause? For surely the underlying material itself does not make itself change. I mean, for example, neither wood nor bronze is responsible, respectively, for its own changing, nor does the wood make a bed or the bronze a statue, but something else is responsible for the change. But to inquire after this is to seek that other kind of source, which we would call that from which the origin of motion is. Now some of these who from the very beginning applied themselves to this sort of pursuit and said that the underlying material was one thing, were not at all displeased with their own accounts, but some of those who said it was one, as though defeated by this inquiry, said that the one and the whole of nature were motionless, not only with respect to coming into being and destruction (for this is present from the beginning and everyone agrees to it), but also with respect to every other kind of change, and this is peculiar to them. So of those who said that the whole is one, none happened to catch sight of this sort of cause unless in fact Parmenides did, and he only to the extent that he set down the causes as being not only one but in some way two. But it is possible to say so about those who made things more than one, such as hot and cold, or fire and earth; for they use the nature of fire as having the power to set things in motion, but water and earth and such things as the opposite.

But after these people and sources of this kind, since they were not sufficient to generate the nature of things, again by the truth itself, as we say, people were forced to look for the next kind of source. For that some beings are in a good or beautiful condition, or come into being well or beautifully, it is perhaps not likely that fire or earth or any other such thing is responsible, nor that they would have thought so. Nor, in turn, would it be a good idea to turn over so great a concern to chance or luck. So when someone said an intellect was present, just as in animals, also in nature as the cause of the cosmos and of all order, he looked like a sober man next to people who had been speaking incoherently beforehand. Obviously we know that Anaxagoras reached as far as saying these things, but Hermotimus of Clazomenae is given credit for saying them earlier. Those, then, who took things up in this way set down a source which is at the same time the cause of the beautiful among things and the sort of cause from which motion belongs to things.

4. One might suspect that Hesiod was the first one to seek out such a thing, or someone else who had set down love or desire among the beings as a source, as Parmenides also did; for he, in getting things ready for the coming into being of the whole, says that first "of all the gods, [the all-governing divinity] devised love," while Hesiod says

Chaos came into being as the very first of all things, but then
Broad-breasted earth . . . and also
Love, who shines out from among all the immortals,

as though there needed to be present among beings some sort of cause that would move things and draw them together. Now how I ought to distribute their portions to them about who was first, permit me to postpone judging. But since the opposites of the good things are obviously also present in nature, and there is not only order and beauty but also disorder and ugliness, and more bad and ordinary things than good and beautiful ones, in this way someone else brought in friendship and strife, each as the cause of one of these kinds of thing. For if one were to pursue and get hold of Empedocles' thinking, rather than what he said inarticulately, one would find that friendship was the cause of the good things and strife of the bad. So if one were to claim that Empedocles both says and is the first to say that bad and good are sources, one would perhaps speak rightly, if in fact the cause of all good things is the good itself.

So these people, as we are saying, evidently got this far with two causes out of those we distinguished in the writings about nature, the material and that from which the motion is, but did so dimly and with no clarity, rather in the way non-athletes do in fights; for while dancing around they often land good punches, but they do not do so out

of knowledge, nor do these people seem to know what they are saying. For it is obvious that they use these causes scarcely ever, and only to a tiny extent. For Anaxagoras uses the intellect as a makeshift contrivance for cosmos production, and whenever he comes to an impasse about why something is necessarily a certain way, he drags it in, but in the other cases he assigns as the causes of what happens everything but the intellect; and Empedocles, though he uses his causes more than that, surely does not either use them sufficiently or come up with any consistency with them. Certainly in many places friendship separates things for him, and strife combines things. For whenever the whole is divided by strife into its elements, fire is combined into one, as is each of the other elements; but whenever they come back together into one, the parts must be separated back out of each element. Empedocles was the first who, beyond those before him, brought in this sort of cause by dividing it, making the source of motion not one thing but different and opposite ones, and furthermore, he first spoke of the so-called four elements as the causes in the species of material. (In fact, though, he didn't use them as
985b four, but as though they were only two: fire on one side by itself, and its opposites, earth, air, and water, as one nature on the other side. One may get this by looking carefully at what is in the verses.)

So as we are saying, he claimed that the sources were of this sort and this many. But Leucippus and his colleague Democritus say the elements are the full and the void, of which the one, as what is, is full and solid, while the other, what is not, is void (for which reason they say that being in no sense *is* more than nonbeing, nor body more so than void), and that these are responsible for things as material. And just as those who make the underlying being one, and generate the other things by means of modifications of it, set down the rare and the dense as the sources of the modifications, in the same way these people too say that the differences in the material are responsible for the other things. They, however, say these differences are three: shape, order, and position. For they say that what is differs only by means of "design, grouping, and twist," but of these, design is shape, grouping is order, and twist is position. For A differs from N in shape, AN from NA in order, and Z from N in position. As for motion, from what source or in what way it belongs to things, these people, much like the others, lazily let it go. So about the two causes, as we are saying, the inquiry seems to have gone this far on the part of our predecessors.

* * *

6. After the philosophic speculations that have been mentioned came the careful
987a work of Plato, which in many ways followed the lead of these people, but also had separate features that went beyond the philosophy of the Italians. For having become acquainted from youth at first with Cratylus and the Heracleitean teachings that all sensible things are always in flux and that there is no knowledge of them, he also conceived
987b these things that way later on. And since Socrates exerted himself about ethical matters and not at all about the whole of nature, but in the former sought the universal and was the first to be skilled at thinking about definitions, Plato, when he adopted this, took it up as applying to other things and not to sensible ones, because of this: it was impossible that there be any common definition of any of the perceptible things since they were always changing. So he called this other sort of beings forms, and said the perceptible things were apart from these and all spoken of derivatively from these, for the many things with the same names as the forms were results of participation. He changed only the name participation, for the Pythagoreans said that beings *are* by way of imitation of

the numbers, but Plato by way of participation, having changed the name. What this participation or imitation of the forms might be, however, they were in unison in leaving behind to be sought.

What's more, apart from the sensible things and the forms, he said there were among things mathematical ones, in between, differing from the sensible ones in being everlasting and motionless, and from the forms in that there are any multitude of them alike, while each form itself is only one. And since the forms are the causes of the others, he thought that the elements of the forms were the elements of all beings. As material, then, the great and the small were the sources, and as thinghood, the one, for out of the former, by participation in the one, the forms are composed as numbers. So in saying that the one was an independent thing, and not any other thing said to be one, he spoke in much the same way as the Pythagoreans, and in saying that numbers were the causes of thinghood for other things he spoke exactly as they did; but to have made a dyad in place of the infinite as one thing, and to have made the infinite out of the great and the small, was peculiar to him. It was also peculiar to him to set the numbers apart from the perceptible things, while they had said that the things themselves were numbers, and they did not set the mathematical things between them. Now his having made the one and the numbers be apart from the things we handle, and not the same way the Pythagoreans had said, and his introduction of the forms came about because of his investigation in the realm of definitions (for the earlier thinkers had no part in dialectic), but his having made the other nature a dyad was so that the numbers, outside of the primes, might be gener- 988a
ated out of it in a natural way, as though from some sort of modeling clay.

But surely things happen in the opposite way, for this way is not reasonable. For they make many things out of this material, while the form generates only once, but it is apparent that from one material comes one table, while the person who brings the form to bear, though he is one, makes many tables. And it is similar with the male in relation to the female; for she becomes pregnant by one act of intercourse, while the male is the cause of many pregnancies, and surely these things are images of the origins of things. But Plato made distinctions in this way about the things that are being sought, and it is clear from what has been said that he used only two causes, the one that is responsible for the what-it-is and the one that results from material (for the forms are causes for the other things of what they are, and the one is such a cause for the forms). And it is clear what the underlying material is said to be, over against which the forms are, in the case of perceptible things, and the one, among the forms, that it is the dyad of the great and the small. And further, he referred the cause of what is good and bad respectively to each of the two elements, just as we say certain of the earlier philosophers, such as Empedocles and Anaxagoras, were trying to find a way to do.

* * *

9. As far as the Pythagoreans are concerned, then, let the things now said be left
alone (for it is enough to touch on them this much). But as for those who set up the 990b
forms, first of all, in seeking to understand the causes of the things around us, they brought in other things, equal to these in number, as though someone who wanted to count a smaller number of things thought he couldn't do it, but could count them if he made them more. For the forms are just about equal to, or not fewer than, those things in search of the causes of which they went on from the latter to the former. For over against each particular thing there is something with the same name, and also for the other things besides the beings, to which there belongs a one-over-many, both among

the things around us and among the everlasting things. What's more, of those ways by which we show that there are forms, it is not evident by any of them. For from some of them no necessary conclusion results, while from others there turn out to be forms of those things which we believe do not have them. For as a result of the arguments from the kinds of knowledge, there will be forms of all those things of which there is knowledge, and as a result of the one-over-many there will even be forms of negations, while as a result of the thinking of something that has been destroyed, there will be forms of things that have passed away, since there is an image of these things. On top of this, some of the most precise of the arguments produce forms of relations, which we claim is not a kind in its own right, while other ones imply the third man.*

And in general, the arguments about the forms abolish things which we want there to be, more than we want there to be forms. For it turns out that not the dyad, but number, is primary, and that what is relative is more primary than what *is* in its own right, as well as all those things which certain people who took the opinions about the forms to their logical conclusions showed to be opposed to the original sources of things. What's more, by the assumption by which we say there are forms, there will be forms not only of beings but also of many other things. (For the object of the intellect is one thing not only as concerns beings but also as applied to other things, and there is demonstrative knowledge not only about thinghood but also about other sorts of being, and vast numbers of other such conclusions follow.) But both necessarily and as a result of the opinions about them, if the forms are shared in, there must be forms only of independent things. For things do not share in them incidentally, but must share in each by virtue of that by which it is not attributed to an underlying subject. (I mean, for example, if something partakes of the double, then this also partakes of the everlasting, but incidentally, since it is incidental to the double to be everlasting.) Therefore, the forms will be the thinghood of things, and the same things will signify thinghood there as here. Otherwise, what would the something be that is said to be apart from the things around us, the one-over-many? And if the forms and the things that participate in them have the same form, there would be something common. (For why is *two* one and the same thing as applied both to destructible pairs and to those that are many but everlasting, more so than as applied both to itself and to something?) But if the form is not the same, there would be ambiguity, and it would be just as if someone were to call both Callias and a block of wood "human being" while observing nothing at all common to them.

But most of all, one might be completely at a loss about what in the world the forms contribute to the perceptible things, either to the everlasting ones or to the ones that come into being and perish. For they are not responsible for any motion or change that belongs to them. But they don't assist in any way toward the knowledge of the other things either (for they are not the thinghood of them, since in that case they would be in them), nor toward their being, inasmuch as they are not present in the things that partake of them. In that manner they might perhaps seem to be causes, after the fashion of the white that is mingled in white things, but this argument, which Anaxagoras first, Eudoxus later, and some others made, is truly a pushover (for it is easy to collect many impossibilities related to this opinion). But surely it is not true either that the other things

*["The third man" refers to a problem with Plato's theory of forms. If we say that two things are instances of the same characteristic because they share in a "form," and if the "form" itself has characteristics, then there must be a third thing ("the third man") whose characteristics the original two things and the "form" share. And this third thing, if it also has characteristics, must share with the original two objects and the "form" some fourth thing, and so on, ad infinitum. Plato was aware of this problem, pointing it out himself (but without a solution) in *Parmenides* 132a–133a.]

are made out of the forms in any of the usual ways that is meant. And to say that they are patterns and the other things participate in them is to speak without content and in poetic metaphors. For what is the thing that is at work, looking off toward the forms? And it is possible for anything whatever to be or become like something without being an image of it, so that whether Socrates is or is not, one might become like Socrates, and it is obvious that it would be the same even if Socrates were everlasting. And there would be more than one pattern for the same thing, and so too with the forms; for example, of a human being, there would be animal and at the same time two footed, as well as human being itself. What's more, the forms will be patterns not only of the perceptible things but also of themselves, such as the form *genus,* since it is a genus of forms, and so the same thing would be a pattern and an image. 991b

Further, one would think it was impossible for the thinghood and that of which it is the thinghood to be separate: so how could the forms be the thinghood of things if they are separate? In the *Phaedo* it is put this way: that the forms are responsible for both being and becoming. Yet even if there are forms, still the things that partake of them do not come into being if there is not something that causes motion, and many other things do come into being, such as a house or a ring, of which we say there are no forms. So it is clear that the other things too admit of being and becoming by means of the sort of causes which produce the ones just mentioned.

Again, if the forms are numbers, how would they be causes? Is it because the beings are various numbers, this number human being, that one Socrates, this other one Callias? Why then are those the causes of these? And it will make no difference if the ones are everlasting and the others not. But if it is because the things here are ratios of numbers, as harmony is, it is clear that there is some one thing of which they are ratios. So if this is something, as material, it is apparent that the numbers themselves will also be particular ratios of one thing to another. I mean, for example, if Callias is a ratio among numbers consisting of fire, earth, water, and air, then the form too will be a number consisting of certain other underlying things, and human being itself, whether or not it is a sort of number, will still be a ratio among numbers *of something,* and not a number, nor would it be on this account a certain number. What's more, from many numbers comes one number, but in what way is one form made of forms? But if it is not made of them but of the things that are in a number, as in ten thousand, how does it stand with the units? For if they are homogeneous, many absurdities will follow, and also if they are not homogeneous, either one the same as another or a whole group the same as a whole group; for in what respect will they differ if they are without attributes? For these things are neither reasonable nor in agreement with a thoughtful viewing of the matter.

And on top of this, it is necessary to construct a different kind of number, with which the art of arithmetic is concerned, and all those things that are said by some to be in-between; in what way *are* they and from what sources? Or by what cause are they between the things here and those things? Again, each of the units in the number two comes from some more primary dyad, yet this is impossible. Again, by what cause is a number one thing when it is taken all together? Again, on top of the things that have been said, if the units are to differ, it would behoove one to speak in the same way as those who say there are four, or two, elements. For each of these people speaks of as an element not what is common, such as body, but fire or earth, whether body is something common or not. But as it is, one speaks as though the one were homogeneous, just like fire or water; and if this is so, the numbers will not be independent things. But it is clear that, if there is something that is the one itself, and this is a source, *one* is meant in more than one way, for otherwise it is impossible.

Now when we want to lead things back to their sources, we set down length as being composed of the short and the long, a certain kind of small and large, and surface of the wide and the narrow, and solid of the deep and the shallow. In what way, though, will the surface have a line in it, or the solid have a line or a surface? For the wide and the narrow are different kinds of thing from the deep and the shallow; so just as number is not present in them either, because the many and the few differ from these, it is clear that neither will any other of the higher things be present in the lower. But surely neither is the wide a class of the deep, for then a solid would be a certain kind of surface. And from what source will the points come to be present in them? Plato used to fight against this class of things as a geometrical dogma, but he called the source of the line—and he set this down often—indivisible lines. And yet there must necessarily be some limit of these; so from the argument from which the line is deduced, the point too is deduced.

In general, though we are seeking wisdom about what is responsible for the appearances, we have ignored this (for we say nothing about the cause from which the source of change is), but supposing that we are speaking about the thinghood of them, we say that there are other independent things, but as for how those are the thinghood of these we speak in vain. For "participating," as we said before, is no help. But on that which we see to be a cause in the various kinds of knowledge, for the sake of which every intellect and every nature produces things, and on that sort of cause which we say is one of the sources of things, the forms do not even touch, but philosophy has turned into mathematical things for people now, though they claim that it is for the sake of other
992b things that one ought to study them. But still, one might assume that the underlying being which serves as material is too mathematical, and is something to be attributed to or be a distinction within the being or material, rather than being material; for instance, the great and the small are just the same as what the writers on nature call the rare and the dense, claiming that these are the first distinctions within the underlying material, since they are a certain kind of the more and less. And as for motion, if these are a process of moving, it is clear that the forms would be moved; but if they are not, where does it come from? For then the whole investigation about nature would be abolished.

And what seems to be easy, to show that all things are one, does not happen; for from the premises set out, even if one grants them all, it does not come out that all things are one, but that something is the one itself; and not even this comes out if one will not grant that the universal is a genus, which in some cases is impossible. And there is no explanation of the lengths, surfaces, and solids that are present with the numbers, not of how they are or could be nor of what capacity they have; for it is not possible for them to be forms (since they are not numbers), nor the in-between things (since those are the mathematical ones), nor perishable things, but this seems in turn to be some other fourth kind.

In general, to search for the elements of whatever *is* without distinguishing the many ways this is meant, is to seek what is impossible to find, both for those inquiring in other ways and those inquiring in this way about what sort of elements things are made of. For out of what elements acting is made, or being acted upon, or the straight, is just not there to be grasped, but if of anything, it is of independent things alone that it can possibly be. Therefore to suppose that one is seeking or has the elements of *all* beings is not true. And how could anyone learn the elements of all things? For it is clear that it is not possible for someone to begin by knowing it beforehand. For just as it is possible for the one who is learning to do geometry to know other things in advance, though he does not already know any of the things of which geometry is the knowledge and about which he is going to learn, so it is also with other things, so if there is any knowledge of all things, of the sort that some people say there is, he could not start out already knowing anything.

And yet all learning is by means of things all or some of which are already known, whether it is by means of demonstration or by way of definitions (for it is necessary that one already know and be familiar with those things out of which the definition is made), and likewise with learning through examples. But if it happens to be innate, it is surely a wonder how we fail to notice that we have the most powerful kind of knowledge. Furthermore, in what way will one know what something is made of, and how will it be evident? For this too contains an impasse: for one might dispute in the same way as about some syllables. For some people say that *za* is made of *s, d,* and *a*, while some others say that it is a distinct sound and not made of any familiar ones. What's more, how could someone know those things of which sense perception consists if he did not have the sense capacity? And yet he must, if indeed the elements out of which all things are made are the same, in just the way that composite sounds are made of the elements that belong to them.

* * *

BOOK XII

* * *

6. Now since there are three kinds of thinghood, two of them natural and one motionless, about the latter one must explain that it is necessary for there to be some everlasting motionless independent thing. For independent things are primary among beings, and if they were all destructible, everything would be destructible; but it is impossible for motion either to come into being or to be destroyed (since it always is), and impossible too for time. For if there were no time, there could be no before and after; and motion is continuous in just the way that time is, since time is either the same as or some attribute of motion. But there is no continuous motion other than in place, and among these, other than in a circle.

But surely if there is something capable of moving and producing things, but not at work in any way, there will not be motion; for what has a potency admits of not being at work. Therefore, there is no benefit even if we adopt everlasting independent things, as do those who bring in the forms, unless there is in them some source capable of producing change; moreover, even this is not enough, not even if there is another independent thing besides the forms, since if it is not going to be at work, there will not be motion. What's more, it is not enough even if it will be at work, if the thinghood of it is potency, for there would not be everlasting motion, since what has being in potency admits of not being. Therefore it is necessary that there be a source of such a kind that the thinghood of it is being-at-work.* On top of that, it is necessary that these independent things be without material, for they must be everlasting, if indeed anything else is everlasting. Therefore they are being-at-work.

*<*energeia*>, often translated "actuality." As our translator puts it, "Aristotle's central thought is that all being is being-at-work, and that anything inert would cease to be. The primary sense of the word belongs to activities that are not motions; examples of these are seeing, knowing, and happiness, each understood as an ongoing state that is complete at every instant."

And yet there is an impasse: for it seems that, while everything that is at work is capable of it, not everything that is capable of it is at work, so that the potency would take precedence. But surely if this were so, there would be no beings at all, since it is possible to be capable of being and not yet be. Nevertheless, there is the same impossibility if things are the way those who write about the gods say, who generate all things out of night, or the way of those who write about nature, who say "all things were together." For how will things have been set in motion, if there were not some responsible thing at work? For material itself, at any rate, will not set itself in motion, but a craftsman will cause it to, nor will the menstrual fluid or the earth set themselves in motion, but semen or seeds will cause them to. And this is why some people, such as Leucippus and Plato, bring in an everlasting activity, for they say that there is always motion. But why there is this motion, and what it is, they do not say, nor the cause of its being a certain way or some other way. For nothing moves at random, but always something must be present to it, just as now something moves in a certain way by nature, but in some other way by force or by the action of intelligence or something else. And then, what sort of motion is primary? For this makes so much difference one can hardly conceive it. But surely it is not even possible for Plato to say what he sometimes thinks the source of motion is, which itself sets itself in motion; for the soul is derivative, and on the same level as the heavens, as he says.

Now to suppose that potency takes precedence over being-at-work is in a sense right but in a sense not right (and in what sense has been said); and Anaxagoras testifies that being-at-work takes precedence (since intellect is a being-at-work), as does Empedocles with love and strife, and so do those who say there is always motion, such as Leucippus; therefore there was not chaos or night for an infinite time, but the same things have always been so, either in a cycle or in some other way, if being-at-work takes precedence over potency. So if the same thing is always so in a cycle, it is necessary for something to persist always at work in the same way. But if there is going to be generation and destruction, there must be something else that is always at work in different ways. Therefore it must necessarily be at work in a certain way in virtue of itself, and in another way in virtue of something else, in virtue, that is, of either a different thing or the first one. And it is necessarily in virtue of the first one, since it would in turn be responsible for both itself and that different one. Accordingly it is better that it be the first one, for it was responsible for what is always the same way, while another thing was responsible for what happens in different ways, and obviously both together are responsible for what happens in different ways always. And without doubt motions are this way. Why then must one look for other sources?

7. But since it is possible for it to be this way, and if it is not this way things will come from night and from "all things together" and from not-being, these questions could be resolved; and there is a certain ceaseless motion that is always moving, and it is in a circle (and this is evident not only to reason but in fact), so that the first heaven would be everlasting. Accordingly, there is also something that moves it. And since what is in motion and causes motion is something intermediate, there is also something that causes motion without being in motion, which is everlasting, an independent thing, and a being-at-work. But what is desired and what is thought cause motion in that way: not being in motion, they cause motion. But the primary instances of these are the same things, for what is yearned for is what seems beautiful, while what is wished for primarily is what is beautiful; but we desire something because of the way it seems, rather than its seeming so because we desire it, for the act of thinking is the beginning. But the

power of thinking is set in motion by the action of the thing thought, and what is thought in its own right belongs to an array of affirmative objects of which thinghood is primary, and of this the primary kind is that which is simple and at work. (But what is one and what is simple are not the same, for oneness indicates a measure, but what is simple is itself a certain way.) But surely the beautiful and what is chosen in virtue of itself are also in that same array, and what is primary is always best, or analogous to it. And that-for-the-sake-of-which is possible among motionless things, as the [following] distinction makes evident; for that-for-the-sake-of-which is either *for* something or *belonging to* something, of which the former is and the latter is not present among motionless things. And it causes motion in the manner of something loved, and by means of what is moved moves other things.

Now if something is moved, it admits of being otherwise than it is; and so, even if the primary kind of change of place is a being-at-work, insofar as something is moved, it is in that respect at least capable of being otherwise, with respect to place even if not with respect to thinghood. But since there is something that causes motion while being itself motionless, this does not admit of being otherwise than it is in any respect at all. For among changes, the primary one is change of place, and of this the primary kind is in a circle, but this is what this mover causes. Therefore it is something that has being necessarily, and inasmuch as it is by necessity it is beautiful and in that way a source. For the necessary has this many senses: what is by force because it is contrary to a thing's impulse, that without which something will not be in a good condition, and that which does not admit of being any way other than in a simple condition. On such a source, therefore, the cosmos and nature depend.

And the course of its life is of such a kind as the best we have for a short time. This is because it is always the same way (which for us is impossible), and because its being-at-work is also pleasure (which is what makes being awake, perceiving, and thinking the most pleasant things, while hopes and memories are pleasant on account of these). And the thinking that is just thinking by itself is a thinking of what is best just as itself, and especially so with what is so most of all. But by partaking in what it thinks, the intellect thinks itself, for it becomes what it thinks by touching and contemplating it, so that the intellect and what it thinks are the same thing. For what is receptive of the intelligible and of thinghood is the intellect, and it is at work when it has them; therefore it is the being-at-work rather than the receptivity the intellect has that seems godlike, and its contemplation is pleasantest and best. So if the divine being is always in this good condition that we are sometimes in, that is to be wondered at; and if it is in it to a greater degree than we are, that is to be wondered at still more. And that is the way it is. But life belongs to it too, for the being-at-work of intellect is life, and that being *is* being-at-work, and its being-at-work is in itself the best life and is everlasting. And we say that it is a god who everlastingly lives the best life, so that life and continuous and everlasting duration belong to a god; for this being is god.

And those who assume, as do the Pythagoreans and Speusippus, that what is most beautiful and best is not present in the source of anything, since, while the sources of plants and or animals are responsible for them, what is beautiful and complete is in the effects that come from them, do not think rightly. For the seed comes from other, earlier, complete beings, and what is first is not the seed but the complete being, just as one would say that a human being precedes the germinal fluid, not the one who comes into being from it, but another one from whom the germinal fluid came.

That, then, there is an independent thing that is everlasting, motionless, and separate from perceptible things, is clear from what has been said. And it has also been demonstrated that this independent thing can have no magnitude, but is without parts and indivisible (for it causes motion for an infinite time, while no finite thing has an infinite power, and since every magnitude must be either infinite or finite, it cannot have magnitude, either finite, for the reason given, or infinite, because there is no infinite magnitude at all). But surely it has also been demonstrated that it cannot be affected or altered, since all other motions are derivative from change of place. So it is clear why these things are this way.

8. But whether one must set down one or more than one such independent thing, and how many, must not go unnoticed; but one has to mention, as far as the pronouncements of others are concerned, that about the number of them they have said nothing which can even be stated clearly. For the assumption about the forms contains no particular speculation about it (for those who speak of the forms say the forms are numbers, and about the numbers, sometimes they speak as though about infinitely many, but sometimes as though they had a limit at the number ten, but why the multitude of the numbers is just so much, nothing is said with a serious effort at demonstrative reasoning). But it is necessary for us to argue from the things that have been laid down and distinguished. For the source and the first of beings is not movable either in its own right or incidentally, but sets in motion the primary motion, that is one and everlasting. But since what is in motion must be moved by something, and the first mover must be itself motionless, and an everlasting motion must be caused by an everlasting source of motion and one motion by one mover, while we see in addition to the simple motion of the whole heaven, which we claim the first motionless independent thing causes, other everlasting motions which belong to the planets (for the body that goes in a circle does so everlastingly and without stopping, which is demonstrated in the writings on nature), it is necessary that each of these motions also be caused by something that is itself motionless and an everlasting independent thing. For the nature of the stars is for each to be an everlasting independent thing, while the mover is everlasting and takes precedence over the thing moved, and what takes precedence over an independent thing must be an independent thing. Accordingly, it is clear that there must be that many independent things and that they must have a nature 1073^b such that they are everlasting and motionless in virtue of themselves, and, for the reason stated above, without magnitude.

That, then, there are independent things, and of these a first one and a second, following the same order as the motions of the stars, is evident; but the number of motions is already something one must examine from that kind of mathematical knowledge that is the nearest kin to philosophy, namely from astronomy. For this kind makes its study about perceptible, everlasting thinghood, while the others, such as those concerned with numbers and with geometry, are not about thinghood at all. Now the fact that the motions are greater in number than the things moved is clear to those who have touched on the subject even moderately (since each of the wandering stars is carried along more than one motion); but as for how many these happen to be, we now state what some of the mathematicians say, for the sake of a conception of it, in order that some definite number be grasped in our thinking, and as for what remains, it is necessary to inquire into some things ourselves, while listening to what other inquirers say about others. If something should seem to those who busy themselves with these matters to be contrary to what has just now been said, it is necessary to welcome both accounts, but trust the more precise one.

Eudoxus, then, set it down that the motion of both the sun and the moon is in three spheres, of which the first is that of the fixed stars, the second rotates along a path through the midst of the zodiac, and the third along a path inclined along the width of the zodiac (but with that along which the moon is carried inclined to a greater width than that along which the sun is carried); but he set it down that the motion of each of the wandering stars is in four spheres, of which the first and second are the same as the former ones (for the sphere of the fixed stars is that which moves them all, and the sphere assigned to the place under this and having its motion along a path through the midst of the zodiac is common to them all), while the poles of the third sphere for all of them are in the path through the midst of the zodiac, and the motion of the fourth is along a path inclined to the equator of the third. And he set it down that the poles of the third sphere are peculiar to the different planets, but those for Venus and Mercury are the same. Callippus set down the same arrangement of spheres as did Eudoxus, and gave the same number as he did for Jupiter and Saturn, but for the sun and the moon he thought there were two spheres still to be added if one were going to account for the appearances, and one for each of the remaining planets.

But it is necessary, in order to account for the appearances, if all the spheres are going to be fit together, that there be for each of the planets (less one) other spheres, turn- 1074a
ing backwards and continuously restoring to the same position the first sphere of the star situated next below; for only in that way is it possible for them all to produce the motion of the planets. Since, then, the spheres in which they themselves are carried are eight [for Jupiter and Saturn] and twenty-five [for the sun and moon, Mars, Venus, and Mercury], and of these one, that in which the star situated lowest is carried, does not need to be counter-turned, the spheres to counter-turn those of the first two planets will be six, while the ones to counter-turn those of the four lower ones will be sixteen; so the number of all the carrying spheres plus those that turn backward against them will be fifty-five. But if one were not to add to the moon and the sun the motions which we mentioned, all the spheres will be forty-seven. So let the number of the spheres be so many, so that it is reasonable to assume that the number of independent things which are motionless sources is also that many (for let the number that is necessary be left for more relentless people to say).

But if it is impossible for there to be any motion that is not directed into the motion of a star, and if in addition every nature and every independent thing that is unaffected and has, by virtue of itself, attained its best condition, must be regarded as an end, there could be no other nature besides these, but this is necessarily the number of independent things. For if there were others, they would be movers as final causes of motion; but it is impossible for there to be other motions besides those mentioned. And this is reasonable to assume from the things that are moved. For if what carries something is naturally for the sake of what is carried, and every motion belongs to something that is carried, no motion could be for the sake of itself or for the sake of another motion, but they are for the sake of the stars. For if there were to be a motion for the sake of a motion, the latter too would have to be for the sake of another one; so since this cannot go to infinity, there will be as an end for every motion one of the divine bodies carried through the heaven. And it is clear that there is one heaven. For if there were a plurality of heavens, as there is of human beings, there would be one *kind* of source for each one, but many of them in number. But those things that are many in number contain material (for one and the same articulation belongs to many things, as does the articulation of a human being, but Socrates is one). But what it primarily is for something to be does not contain material, for it is a being-at-work-staying-itself.*

*<*entelecheia*>, often translated "actuality," means (as our translator puts it), "a fusion of the idea of completeness with that of continuity or persistence. Aristotle invents the word by combining <*enteles*> (complete, full-grown) with <*echein*> (to be a certain way by the continuing effort of holding on in that condition."

Therefore the first motionless being that causes motion is one both in articulation and in number; and therefore what is moved always and continuously is also one. Therefore there is only one heaven.

1074b There has been handed down from people of ancient and earliest times a heritage, in the form of myth, to those of later times, that these original beings are gods, and that the divine embraces the whole of nature. The rest of it was presently introduced in mythical guise for the persuasion of the masses and into the laws for use and benefit; for the myths say the gods are of human form or like some of the other animals, and other things that follow along with and approximate these that have been mentioned. If one were to take only the first of these things, separating it out, that they thought the primary independent things were gods, one would regard this as having been said by divine inspiration, and, since it is likely that every kind of art and philosophy has been discovered to the limit of its potential many times, and passed away in turn, one would consider these opinions of those people to have been saved like holy relics up to now. So the opinion of our forefathers that comes from the first ages is clear to us but only to this extent.

9. Now concerning the intellect there are certain impasses, for it seems to be the most divine of the things that are manifest to us, but the way it is if it is to be of that sort contains some things that are hard to digest. For if it thinks nothing, what would be solemn about that? Rather, it would be just like someone sleeping. But if it does think, but something else has power over it, then, since it is not thinking but potency that is the thinghood of it, it could not be the best independent thing, for it is on account of its act of thinking that its place of honor belongs to it. And still, whether the thinghood of it is a power of thinking or an activity of thinking, what does it think? For this is either itself or something else, and if it is something else, either always the same one or different ones. And then does it make any difference, or none, whether its thinking is of what is beautiful or of some random thing? Isn't it even absurd for its thinking to be about some things? Surely it is obvious that it thinks the most divine and honorable things, and does not change, since its change would be for the worse, and such a thing would already be a motion. First, then, if it is not an activity of thinking but a potency, it is reasonable to suppose that the continuation of its thinking would be wearisome; and next, it is clear that something else would then be more honorable than the intellect, namely what it thinks. For thinking and the activity of thinking would belong even to something that thinks the worst thing, and if this is to be avoided (for it can even be more advantageous not to see some things than to see them), then the activity of thinking would not be the best thing. Therefore what it thinks is itself, if it is the most excellent thing, and its thinking is a thinking of thinking.

But knowledge and perception and opinion and step-by-step thinking seem always to be about something else, and about themselves only as something secondary. What's more, if the thinking and the being thought are different, then in virtue of which of them does what is good belong to it? For to be an act of thinking and to be something
1075a thought are not the same. Or is it rather that in some cases the knowledge is the thing it is concerned with, so that in the case of the kinds of knowing that make something, the thinghood without material and what it is for something to be, or in the case of the contemplative kinds of knowing, the articulation, is both the thing the knowledge is concerned with and the activity of thinking it? So since what is thought and what is thinking are not different with as many things as have no material, they will be the same, and the act of thinking will be one with what is thought.

But there is still an impasse left as to whether what is thought is composite, for then the thinking would be changing among the parts of the whole. Or is it the case that everything that has no material is indivisible? So the condition the human intellect, or that of any composite being, is in at some period of time (for it does not have hold of what is good at this or that time, but in some whole stretch of time it has hold of what is best, since that is something other than itself), is the condition the thinking that thinks itself is in over the whole of time.

ON THE SOUL (in part)

BOOK II

1. Let this be our discussion of the things handed on about the soul by those who 412a
came before us. But let us go back again and, as though from the beginning, try to distinguish what the soul is and what articulation of it would be most common to all its instances. One of the most general ways of being we call thinghood;* of this, one sort has being as material, which in its own right is not a *this*, but another sort is the form or look of a thing, directly as a result of which something is called a *this*, and the third sort is what is made out of these. Now the material is a potency, but the form is a being-at-work-staying-itself,** and this in two senses, one in the manner of knowledge, the other in the manner of the act of contemplating.

The things that seem most of all to be independent things are bodies, and of these, the natural ones, for these are the sources of the others. And of natural bodies, some have life while others do not. By life we mean self-nourishing as well as growth and wasting away. So every natural body having a share in life would be an independent thing having thinghood as a composite [of material and form]. And since this is a body, and one of a certain sort, namely having life, the soul could not be a body, since it is not the body that is in an underlying thing, but rather the body has being as an underlying thing and material [for something else]. Therefore it is necessary that the soul have its thinghood as the form of a natural body having life as a potency. But this sort of thinghood is a being-at-work-staying-itself; therefore the soul is the being-at-work-staying-itself of such a body. But this is meant in two ways, the one in the sense that knowledge is a being-at-work-staying-itself, the other in the sense that the act of contemplating is. It is clear, then, that the soul is a being-at-work-staying-itself in the way that knowledge is, for both sleep and waking are in what belongs to the soul, and waking is analogous to the act of contemplating but sleep to holding the capacity for contemplating while not

*<*ousia*>, often translated "substance," means (as our translator puts it) "the way of being that belongs to anything which has attributes but is not an attribute of anything, which is also separate and a *this.* Whatever has being in this way is an independent thing."

**<*entelecheia*>, often translated "actuality," means (as our translator puts it), "a fusion of the idea of completeness with that of continuity or persistence. Aristotle invents the word by combining <*enteles*> (complete, full-grown) with <*echein*> (to be a certain way by the continuing effort of holding on in that condition)."

putting it to work. But in the same person it is knowledge that is first in coming into being; for this reason the soul is a being-at-work-staying-itself of the first kind of a natural body having life as a potency. But such a body is organized [i.e., has parts subordi-
412b nated to the whole as instruments of it]. (And even the parts of plants are organs, though utterly simple ones, as the leaf is a covering for the peel and the peel for the fruit, while the roots are analogous to the mouth, since both take in food.) So if one needs to say what is common to every soul, it would be that it is a being-at-work-staying-itself of the first kind of a natural, organized body. And for this reason it is not necessary to seek out whether the soul and body are one, any more than with wax and the shape molded in it, or generally with the material of each thing and that of which it is the material; for even though *one* and *are* are meant in more than one way, the governing sense of each of them is being-at-work-staying-itself.

So what soul is has been said in general, for it is thinghood as it is unfolded in speech, and this is what such-and-such a body keeps on being in order to be at all. It would be as though some tool, such as an axe, were a natural body, since its being-an-axe would be the thinghood of it, and that would be its soul; for if this were separated from it, it would no longer be an axe, other than ambiguously. But in fact it is an axe, since it is not of this sort of body that the soul is the meaning and the what-it-is-for-it-to-be, but of a certain sort of natural body, one that has a source of motion and rest in itself. But one ought to consider what has been said as applying even to the parts of such a body. For if the eye were an animal, the soul of it would be its sight, since this is the thinghood of an eye as it is disclosed in speech (and the eye is the material of sight); if its sight were left out it would no longer be an eye, except ambiguously, in the same way as a stone eye or a painted one.

Now one should take what applies to the part up to the whole living body, for there is an analogy: as part [of perceiving] is to part [of the body], so is perceiving as a whole to the whole perceptive body as such. And it is not the body that has lost its soul that is in potency to be alive, but the one that has it, and the seed and fruit are in potency to be certain sorts of bodies. So just as the act of cutting is for the axe and the act of see-
413a ing for the eye, so too is the waking condition a being-at-work-staying-itself, but as the power of sight is to the eye and the capacity of the tool to the axe, so is the soul a being-at-work-staying-itself, while the body is what has being in potency. But just as the eyeball and the power of sight are the eye, so here the soul and the body are the living thing. So it is not difficult to see why the soul, or at least certain parts of it, is not separate from the body, if the soul is of such a nature as to be divided, since for some parts of the body, the soul is the being-at-work-staying-itself of those parts themselves. Nevertheless, nothing prevents some parts from being separate, so long as they are not the being-at-work* of any part of the body. But it would be difficult to see [why the soul is not separate from the body] if the soul were the being-at-work of the body in the way that the sailor is of the boat. But let this stand as marking off and sketching out in an outline what concerns the soul.

2. Now since what is clear and more knowable by reason arises out of what is unclear but more obvious, it is necessary to try again to go on in this way about the soul.

*<*energeia*>, often translated "actuality." As our translator puts it, "Aristotle's central thought is that all being is being-at-work, and that anything inert would cease to be. The primary sense of the word belongs to activities that are not motions; examples of these are seeing, knowing, and happiness, each understood as an ongoing state that is complete at every instant."

For the defining statement not only needs to make clear what something is, as most definitions do, but also needs to include and display the cause. As it is, the statements of definitions are like conclusions. For example, what is squaring? The equality of an equilateral rectangle to an oblong rectangle. But this sort of definition is a statement of the conclusion, while one who says that squaring is the finding of a mean proportional states the cause of the thing.

So we say, taking this as a starting point for the inquiry, that what is ensouled is distinguished from what is soulless by living. But living is meant in more than one way, and if any one alone of the following is present in something, we say it is alive: intellect, perception, moving and stopping with respect to place, and the motion that results from nourishment, that is, wasting away as well as growing. And for this reason all plants seem to be alive, since they evidently have in themselves this sort of power and source, through which they have growth and decay in opposite directions, for they do not just grow upward but not downward, but in both directions alike, and in every direction, all of them that are continually nourished and live for the sake of their ends, so long as they are able to get food. The latter capacity can be present in separation from the others, but the others cannot be present in separation from it in mortal beings. This is obvious in the case of plants, since no other potency of soul belongs to them.

Life belongs to living things, then, through this source, but to an animal, first of all, through sense perception; for even those that do not move or change their places, if they have perception, we call animals and do not merely say they are alive. Now of perception, the kind that first belongs to them all is touch, and just as the nutritive power is able to be present separately from touch and all sense perception, so is touch able to be present separately from the other senses. (By the nutritive power, we mean the part of the soul of which the plants have a share; and it is obvious that animals all have the sense of touch.) Through what cause each of these things happens, we will say later. For now, let us say this much only, that the soul is the source of these things that have been mentioned and is defined by them: by nutrition, by sense perception, by thinking things through, and by motion.

Whether each of these is a soul or part of a soul, and if a part, whether in such a way as to be separated only in speech or also in place, is for some of these not difficult to see, but some present an impasse. For just as in the case of plants, some parts obviously live when divided and separated from each other, as though the soul in them is one in each plant in the sense of being-at-work-staying-itself but is in potency more than one, so too we see it happen with other capacities of the soul in the case of insects that have been cut in half; for each of the two parts even has both perception and motion with respect to place, and if it has perception, also imagination and appetite, since where there is perception there is also pain and pleasure, and where these are there is necessarily also desire. But about the intellect, that is, the contemplative faculty, nothing is yet clear, but it seems that it is a distinct class of soul and that it alone admits of being separated from body, as the everlasting from the destructible. As for the remaining parts of the soul, it is clear from what has been said that they cannot be separate, as some people say, though it is obvious that they are distinct in speech. For being perceptive is different from being capable of having opinion, if perceiving is also different from having opinion, and similarly with each of the other parts mentioned. Further, some animals have all these capacities, others some of them, and still others only one (and this makes the difference among animals); why this is so must be considered later. And it turns out much the same with the senses, since some animals have them all, others some of them, and still others the one that is most necessary, touch.

And seeing that the means by which we live and perceive is meant two ways, as is the means by which we know (by which is meant in one sense knowledge but in another the soul, since by means of each of these we say we know something), likewise also we are healthy in one sense by means of health, but in another by means of either some part of the body or the whole of it. Now of these, the knowledge or the health is a form, and a certain look, and an articulation in speech, and a kind of being-at-work of what is receptive, in the one case a being-at-work of what is capable of knowing, in the other a being-at-work of what is capable of being healthy (for it seems that the being-at-work of what is active is present in what is acted on and placed in a certain condition). So since the soul is that by which in the primary sense we live and perceive and think things through, it would be a certain sort of articulation and form, and not an underlying material. For thinghood is meant in three ways, as we said, of which one way is as form, one as material, and one as what is made of both, while of these the material is potency and the form is being-at-work-staying-itself, so since what is ensouled is made of both, it is not the body that is the being-at-work-staying-itself of the soul, but the soul is the being-at-work-staying-itself of some body.

Discus Thrower, by Myron. A Roman copy after a bronze original of ca. 450 B.C. Myron's athlete epitomizes the ideal Olympian goals of godlike perfection and rational beauty. (©*Lanmas/Alamy Stock Photo*)

For this reason, those who think the soul neither has being without a body, nor is any sort of body, get hold of it well, for it is not a body but something that belongs to a body, and this is why it is present in a body and in a body of a certain kind, and those earlier thinkers did not think well who stuck it into a body without also distinguishing which bodies and of what sort, even though there is no evidence that any random thing admits just any random thing within it. And this happens in accord with reason, since the being-at-work-staying-itself of each thing naturally comes to be present in something that *is* it in potency and in the material appropriate to it. That, then, the soul is a certain being-at-work-staying-itself and articulation of that which has the potency to be in that way, is clear from these things.

3. Now of the potencies of the soul, all of those that have been mentioned belong to some living things, as we said, while to others some of them belong, and to still others only one. The potencies we are speaking of are those for nutrition, perception, motion with respect to place, and thinking things through. And in plants the nutritive potency alone is present, while in other living things this is present along with the perceptive. But 414b
if the perceptive potency is present, then so is that of appetite, for appetite consists of desire and spiritedness and wishing, while all animals have at least one of the senses, that of touch, and in that in which sense perception is present there are also pleasure and pain, as well as pleasant and painful sensations, and where these are present so is desire, since this is an appetite for the pleasant. Besides, they have a perception of food, for touch is the sense that perceives food since all animals are nourished by what is dry or moist and warm or cold, of which the sense is touch, though incidentally it is perceptive of other things. For neither sound nor color nor smell contributes anything to nourishment, but the flavor that comes from food is one of the things perceived by touch. Hunger and thirst are desires for, in the former case, what is dry and warm, and in the latter, what is moist and cold, while the flavor is a way of making these pleasant. One must get clear about these things later, but for now let this much be said, that those living things that have touch also have appetite; it is unclear whether they must also have imagination, but this needs to be examined later. And in some living things, in addition to these potencies, there is present also that for motion with respect to place, and in others also the potency for thinking things through as well as intellect, as in human beings and any other living things there might be that are of that sort or more honorable.

So it is clear that there could be a single account of soul in the same way as of geometrical figure; for neither in that case is there any figure aside from the triangle and those that follow in succession, nor in this is there any soul aside from the ones discussed. But even in the case of the figures, there could be a common account which would fit them all, but would be appropriate to none of them in particular, and similarly in the case of the souls that were discussed. Hence it would be ridiculous to inquire after the common account, both in the one case and in the other, which would not be the particular account of any thing there is, nor apply to any proper and indivisible kind, while neglecting an account that is of that sort. (For what applies to the soul is just about the same as what concerns geometrical figures, for always in the one next in succession there is present in potency the previous one, both in figures and in things with souls, as the triangle is in the quadrilateral and the nutritive potency in the perceptive one.) Therefore, for each kind, one needs to inquire what the soul of each is, as for a plant, a human, and a wild animal. And why they are in this sort of succession must be consid- 415a
ered. For without the nutritive potency there is no perceptive potency, while the nutritive is present in separation from the perceptive in plants. Again, without the sense of touch

none of the other senses is present, but touch is present without the others, for many animals have neither sight nor hearing nor a sense of smell. And among animals with the perceptive potency, some have the potency for motion with respect to place while others do not. Last and most rare are reasoning and thinking things through; for in those destructible beings in which reasoning is present, all the other potencies are also present, while reasoning is not present in all animals, but some do not even have imagination, though others live by this alone. But about the contemplative intellect there is a different account. It is clear, then, that the account that deals with each of these potencies is also the most appropriate account of the soul.

* * *

BOOK III

429a 4. About the part of the soul by which the soul knows and understands, whether it is a separate part, or not separate the way a magnitude is but in its meaning, one must consider what distinguishing characteristic it has, and how thinking ever comes about. If thinking works the same way perceiving does, it would either be some way of being acted upon by the intelligible thing, or something else of that sort. Therefore it must be without attributes but receptive of the form and in potency not to be the form but to be such as it is; and it must be similar so that as the power of perception is to the perceptible things, so is the intellect to the intelligible things. Therefore necessarily, since it thinks all things, it is unmixed, just as Anaxagoras says, in order to master them, that is, in order to know them (since anything alien that appeared in it besides what it thinks would hinder it and block its activity); and so intellect has no nature at all other than this, that it is a potency. Therefore the aspect of the soul that is called intellect (and I mean by intellect that by which the soul thinks things through and conceives that something is the case) is not actively any of the things that *are* until it thinks. This is why it is not reasonable that it be mixed with the body, since it would come to be of a certain sort, either cold or warm, and there would be an organ for it, as there is for the perceptive potency, though in fact there is none. And it is well said that the soul is a place of forms, except that this is not the whole soul but the thinking soul, and it is not the forms in its being-at-work-staying-itself, but in potency.

The absence of attributes is not alike in the perceptive and thinking potencies; this is clear in its application to the sense organs and perception. For the sense is
429b unable to perceive anything from an excessive perceptible thing, neither any sound from loud sounds, nor to see or smell anything from strong colors and odors, but when the intellect thinks something exceedingly intelligible it is not less able to think the lesser things but even more able, since the perceptive potency is not present without a body, but the potency to think is separate from body. And when the intellect has come to be each intelligible thing, as the knower is said to do when he is a knower in the active sense (and this happens when he is able to put his knowing to work on his own), the intellect is even then in a sense those objects in potency, but not in the same way it was before it learned and discovered them, and it is then able to think itself.

Now since a magnitude is different from being a magnitude, and water is different from being water (and so too in many other cases, though not in all, since in some cases the two are the same), being flesh is distinguished either by a different potency from the one that distinguishes flesh, or by the same one in a different relation. For flesh is not present without material, but like a snub nose, it is this in that. So it is by the perceptive potency that one distinguishes hot and cold, and the other things of which flesh is a certain ratio, but it is by a different potency that one distinguishes the being-flesh, either separate from the first or else with the two having the relation a bent line has to itself straightened out. Among the things that have being in abstraction, straightness is in its way just like snubness, since it is combined with continuity; but what it is for it to be, if being straight is different from what is straight, is something else—let it be twoness. Therefore one distinguishes it by a different potency, or by one in a different relation. So in general, in whatever way things are separate from their material, so too are the potencies that have to do with intellect separate from one another.

But one might find it an impasse, if the intellect is simple and without attributes and has nothing in common with anything, as Anaxagoras says, how it could think, if thinking is a way of being acted upon (for it seems to be by virtue of something common that is present in both that one thing acts and another is acted upon), and also whether the intellect is itself an intelligible thing. For either there would be intellect in everything else, if it is not by virtue of something else that it is itself intelligible, but what is intelligible is something one in kind, or else there would be something mixed in it, which makes it intelligible like other things. As for a thing's being acted upon in virtue of something common, the distinction was made earlier, that the intellect *is* in a certain way the intelligible things in potency, but is actively none of them before it thinks them; it is in potency in the same way a tablet is, when nothing written is present in it actively—this is exactly what happens with the intellect. And it is itself intelligible in the same way its intelligible objects are, for in the case of things without material what thinks and what is thought are the same thing, for contemplative knowing and what is known in that way are the same thing (and one must consider the reason why this sort of thinking is not always happening); but among things having material, each of them is potentially something intelligible, so that there is no intellect present in them (since intellect is a potency to be such things without their material), but there is present in them something intelligible.

5. But since in all nature one thing is the material for each kind (this is what is in potency all the particular things of that kind), but it is something else that is the causal and productive thing by which all of them are formed, as is the case with an art in relation to its material, it is necessary in the soul too that these distinct aspects be present; the one sort is intellect by becoming all things, the other sort by forming all things, in the way an active condition such as light does, for in a certain way light too makes the colors that are in potency be at work as colors. This sort of intellect is separate, as well as being without attributes and unmixed, since it is by its thinghood a being-at-work, for what acts is always distinguished in stature above what is acted upon, as a governing source is above the material it works on. Knowledge, in its being-at-work, is the same as the thing it knows, and while knowledge in potency comes first in time in any one knower, in the whole of things it does not take precedence even in time. This does not mean that at one time it thinks but at another time it does not think, but when separated it is just exactly what it is, and this alone is deathless and everlasting (though we have no memory, because this sort of intellect is not acted upon, while the sort that is acted upon is destructible), and without this nothing thinks.

NICOMACHEAN ETHICS (in part)

BOOK I

1094a *1. The Good as the Aim of Action:* Every art or applied science and every systematic investigation, and similarly every action and choice, seem to aim at some good; the good, therefore, has been well defined as that at which all things aim.* But it is clear that there is a difference in the ends at which they aim: in some cases the activity is the end, in others the end is some product beyond the activity. In cases where the end lies beyond the action the product is naturally superior to the activity.

Since there are many activities, arts, and sciences, the number of ends is correspondingly large: of medicine the end is health, of shipbuilding a vessel, of strategy, victory, and of household management, wealth. In many instances several such pursuits are grouped together under a single capacity: the art of bridle-making, for example, and everything else pertaining to the equipment of a horse are grouped together under horsemanship; horsemanship in turn, along with every other military action, is grouped together under strategy; and other pursuits are grouped together under other capacities. In all these cases the ends of the master sciences are preferable to the ends of the subordinate sciences, since the latter are pursued for the sake of the former. This is true whether the ends of the actions lie in the activities themselves or, as is the case in the disciplines just mentioned, in something beyond the activities.

2. Politics as the Master Science of the Good: Now, if there exists an end in the realm of action which we desire for its own sake, an end which determines all our other desires; if, in other words, we do not make all our choices for the sake of something else—for in this way the process will go on infinitely so that our desire would be futile and pointless—then obviously this end will be the good, that is, the highest good. Will not the knowledge of this good, consequently, be very important to our lives? Would it not better equip us, like archers who have a target to aim at, to hit the proper mark? If so, we must try to comprehend in outline at least what this good is and to which branch of knowledge or to which capacity it belongs.

This good, one should think, belongs to the most sovereign and most comprehensive master science, and politics** clearly fits this description. For it determines which sciences ought to exist in states, what kind of sciences each group of citizens must learn,
1094b and what degree of proficiency each must attain. We observe further that the most honored capacities, such as strategy, household management, and oratory, are contained in politics. Since this science uses the rest of the sciences, and since, moreover, it legislates

*We do not know who first gave this definition of the good. It is certainly implied in the Platonic dialogues, especially in *Republic,* Book VI; but the most likely candidate for the formulation here is Eudoxus.

***Politike* is the science of the city-state, the *polis,* and its members, not merely in our narrow "political" sense of the word but also in the sense that a civilized human existence is, according to Plato and Aristotle, only possible in the *polis.* Thus *politike* involves not only the science of the state, "politics," but of our concept of "society" as well.

Aristotle, *The Nichomachean Ethics,* translated by Martin Ostwald (Pearson/Library of the Liberal Arts, 1999).

what people are to do and what they are not to do, its end seems to embrace the ends of the other sciences. Thus it follows that the end of politics is the good for man. For even if the good is the same for the individual and the state, the good of the state clearly is the greater and more perfect thing to attain and to safeguard. The attainment of the good for one man alone is, to be sure, a source of satisfaction; yet to secure it for a nation and for states is nobler and more divine. In short, these are the aims of our investigation, which is in a sense an investigation of social and political matters.

3. The Limitations of Ethics and Politics: Our discussion will be adequate if it achieves clarity within the limits of the subject matter. For precision cannot be expected in the treatment of all subjects alike, any more than it can be expected in all manufactured articles. Problems of what is noble and just, which politics examines, present so much variety and irregularity that some people believe that they exist only by convention and not by nature. The problem of the good, too, presents a similar kind of irregularity, because in many cases good things bring harmful results. There are instances of men ruined by wealth, and others by courage. Therefore, in a discussion of such subjects, which has to start from a basis of this kind, we must be satisfied to indicate the truth with a rough and general sketch: when the subject and the basis of a discussion consist of matters that hold good only as a general rule, but not always, the conclusions reached must be of the same order. The various points that are made must be received in the same spirit. For a well-schooled man is one who searches for that degree of precision in each kind of study which the nature of the subject at hand admits: it is obviously just as foolish to accept arguments of probability from a mathematician as to demand strict demonstrations from an orator.

Each man can judge competently the things he knows, and of these he is a good judge. Accordingly, a good judge in each particular field is one who has been trained in it, and a good judge in general, a man who has received an all-round schooling. For that reason, a young man is not equipped to be a student of politics; for he has no experience in the actions which life demands of him, and these actions form the basis and subject matter of the discussion. Moreover, since he follows his emotions, his study will be pointless and unprofitable, for the end of this kind of study is not knowledge but action. Whether he is young in years or immature in character makes no difference; for his deficiency is not a matter of time but of living and of pursuing all his interests under the influence of his emotions. Knowledge brings no benefit to this kind of person, just as it brings none to the morally weak. But those who regulate their desires and actions by a rational principle* will greatly benefit from a knowledge of this subject. So much by way of a preface about the student, the limitations which have to be accepted, and the objective before us.

4. Happiness Is the Good, But Many Views Are Held About It: To resume the discussion: since all knowledge and every choice is directed toward some good, let us discuss what is in our view the aim of politics, i.e., the highest good attainable by action. As far as its name is concerned, most people would probably agree: for both the common run of

*The fundamental meaning of *Logos* is "speech," "statement," in the sense of a coherent and rational arrangement of words; but it can apply to a rational principle underlying many things, and may be translated in different contexts by "rational account," "explanation," "argument," "treatise," or "discussion." In Chapters 7 and 13 below, *Logos* is used in a normative sense, describing the human faculty which comprehends and formulates rational principles and thus guides the conduct of a good and reasonable man.

people and cultivated men call it happiness, and understand by "being happy" the same as "living well" and "doing well." But when it comes to defining what happiness is, they disagree, and the account given by the common run differs from that of the philosophers. The former say it is some clear and obvious good, such as pleasure, wealth, or honor; some say it is one thing and others another, and often the very same person identifies it with different things at different times: when he is sick he thinks it is health, and when he is poor he says it is wealth; and when people are conscious of their own ignorance, they admire those who talk above their heads in accents of greatness. Some thinkers used to believe that there exists over and above these many goods another good, good in itself and by itself, which also is the cause of good in all these things. An examination of all the different opinions would perhaps be a little pointless, and it is sufficient to concentrate on those which are most in evidence or which seem to make some sort of sense.

Nor must we overlook the fact that arguments which proceed from fundamental principles are different from arguments that lead up to them. Plato, too, rightly recognized this as a problem and used to ask whether the discussion was proceeding from or leading up to fundamental principles, just as in a race course there is a difference [1095b] between running from the judges to the far end of the track and running back again.* Now, we must start with the known. But this term has two connotations: "what is known to us" and "what is known" pure and simple. Therefore, we should start perhaps from what is known to us. For that reason, to be a competent student of what is right and just, and of politics generally, one must first have received a proper upbringing in moral conduct. The acceptance of a fact as a fact is the starting point, and if this is sufficiently clear, there will be no further need to ask why it is so. A man with this kind of background has or can easily acquire the foundations from which he must start. But if he neither has nor can acquire them, let him lend an ear to Hesiod's words:

> That man is all-best who himself works out every problem. . . .
> That man, too, is admirable who follows one who speaks well.
> He who cannot see the truth for himself, nor, hearing it from others, store it away in his mind, that man is utterly useless.

5. Various Views on the Highest Good: But to return to the point from which we digressed. It is not unreasonable that men should derive their concept of the good and of happiness from the lives which they lead. The common run of people and the most vulgar identify it with pleasure, and for that reason are satisfied with a life of enjoyment. For the most notable kinds of life are three: the life just mentioned, the political life, and the contemplative life.

The common run of people, as we saw, betray their utter slavishness in their preference for a life suitable to cattle; but their views seem plausible because many people in high places share the feelings of Sardanapallus.** Cultivated and active men, on the other hand, believe the good to be honor, for honor, one might say, is the end of the political life. But this is clearly too superficial an answer: for honor seems to depend on those who confer it rather than on him who receives it, whereas our guess is that the

*A Greek race course was U-shaped with the starting line at the open end, which is also where the judges would have their place. The race was run around a marker set up toward the opposite end of the U, and back again to the starting line.

**Sardanapallus is the Hellenized name of the Assyrian king Ashurbanipal (669–626 B.C.). Many stories about his sensual excesses were current in antiquity.

good is a man's own possession which cannot easily be taken away from him. Furthermore, men seem to pursue honor to assure themselves of their own worth; at any rate, they seek to be honored by sensible men and by those who know them, and they want to be honored on the basis of their virtue or excellence [<aretē>].* Obviously, then, excellence, as far as they are concerned, is better than honor. One might perhaps even go so far as to consider excellence rather than honor as the end of political life. However, even excellence proves to be imperfect as an end: for a man might possibly possess it while asleep or while being inactive all his life, and while, in addition, undergoing the greatest suffering and misfortune. Nobody would call the life of such a man happy, except for the sake of maintaining an argument. But enough of this: the subject has been sufficiently treated in our publications addressed to a wider audience. In the third place there is the contemplative life, which we shall examine later on. As for the money-maker, his life is led under some kind of constraint: clearly, wealth is not the good which we are trying to find, for it is only useful, i.e., it is a means to something else. Hence one might rather regard the aforementioned objects as ends, since they are valued for their own sake. But even they prove not to be the good, though many words have been wasted to show that they are. Accordingly, we may dismiss them.

6. Plato's View of the Good: But perhaps we had better examine the universal good and face the problem of its meaning, although such an inquiry is repugnant, since those who have introduced the doctrine of Forms** are dear to us. But in the interest of truth, one should perhaps think a man, especially if he is a philosopher, had better give up even [theories that once were] his own and in fact must do so. Both are dear to us, but it is our sacred duty to honor truth more highly [than friends].

The proponents of this theory did not make Forms out of those classes within which they recognized an order involving priority and posteriority; for that reason they made no provision, either, for a Form comprising all numbers.*** However, the term "good" is used in the categories of substance, of quality, and of relatedness alike; but a thing-as-such, i.e., a substance, is by nature prior to a relation into which it can enter: relatedness is, as it were, an offshoot or logical accident of substance. Consequently, there cannot be a Form common to the good-as-such and the good as a relation.

Secondly, the term "good" has as many meanings as the word "is": it is used to describe substances, e.g., divinity and intelligence are good; qualities, e.g., the virtues are good; quantities, e.g., the proper amount is good; relatedness, e.g., the useful is good; time, e.g., the right moment is good; place, e.g., a place to live is good; and so forth. It is clear, therefore, that the good cannot be something universal, common to all cases, and single; for if it were, it would not be applicable in all categories but only in one.

**Aretē* denotes the functional excellence of any person, animal, or thing—that quality which enables the possessor to perform his own particular function well. Thus the *aretai* (plural) of man in relation to other men are his qualities which enable him to function well in society. The translation "virtue" often seems too narrow, and accordingly "excellence" and "goodness," or a combination of these, will also be used.

**The reference is of course to Plato's theory of *eide* or *ideai* and especially the Form of the Good, which is Aristotle's chief target here.

***Since for Plato and his followers the Forms are absolute being, in which there is no room for becoming or any kind of development, they do not recognize a Form of a developing series, in which each successive member implies the preceding members of the same series. But, as Aristotle proceeds to show, the term "good" belongs to such a developing series: if we call a certain quality, e.g., blueness, "good," we have to assume first that there is such a thing as blueness; i.e., we have to predicate it in the category of substance before we can predicate it in the category of quality.

Thirdly, since the things which are included under one Form are the subject matter of a single science, there should be a single science dealing with all good things. But in actual fact there are many sciences dealing even with the goods that fall into a single category. To take, for example, the right moment: in war it is the proper concern of strategy, whereas in treating a disease it is part of the study of medicine. Or to take the proper amount: in food it is the subject of medicine; in physical training, of gymnastics.

One might even [go further and] raise the question what exactly they mean by a "thing-as-such"; for the selfsame definition of "man" applies to both "man-as-such" and a particular man. For inasmuch as they refer to "man," there will be no difference between the two; and if this is true, there will be no difference, either, between "good-as-such" and "good," since both are good. Nor indeed will the "good-as-such" be more of a good because it is everlasting: after all, whiteness which lasts for a long time is no whiter than whiteness which lasts only for a day.

The argument of the Pythagoreans on this point seems to be more convincing. They give unity a place in the column of goods; and indeed even Speusippus* seems to follow them. But more about this elsewhere.

An objection might be raised against what we have said on the ground that the [Platonic] doctrine does not refer to every kind of good, and that only things which are pursued and loved for their own sake are called "good" by reference to one single Form. That which produces good or somehow guarantees its permanence, [the Platonists argue,] or that which prevents the opposite of a good from asserting itself is called "good" because it is conducive to the intrinsically good and in a different sense. Now, the term "good" has obviously two different meanings: (1) things which are intrinsically good, and (2) things which are good as being conducive to the intrinsically good. Let us, therefore, separate the intrinsically good things from the useful things and examine whether they are called "good" by reference to a single Form.

What sort of things could be called intrinsically good? Are they the goods that are pursued without regard to additional benefits, such as thought, sight, certain pleasures and honors? For even if we pursue these also for the sake of something else, one would still classify them among things intrinsically good. Or is nothing good except the Form of Good? If that is the case, the Form will be pointless. But if, on the contrary, thought, sight, etc. also belong to the group of intrinsically good things, the same definition of "good" will have to be manifested in all of them, just as, for example, the definition of whiteness is the same in snow and in white paint. But in actual fact, the definitions of "good" as manifested in honor, thought, and pleasure are different and distinct. The good, therefore, is not some element common to all these things as derived from one Form.

What, then, is the meaning of "good" [in these different things]? Surely, it is not that they merely happen to have the same name. Do we call them "good" because they are derived from a single good, or because they all aim at a single good? Or do we rather call them "good" by analogy, e.g., as sight is good in the body, so intelligence is good in the soul, and so other things are good within their respective fields?

But perhaps this subject should be dismissed for the present, because a detailed discussion of it belongs more properly to a different branch of philosophy, [namely, first philosophy]. The same applies to the Form [of the Good]: for, assuming that there is some single good which different things possess in common, or that there exists a good

*Speusippus was Plato's nephew and disciple who succeeded him a head of the Academy from 347–339 B.C.

absolutely in itself and by itself, it evidently is something which cannot be realized in action or attained by man. But the good which we are now seeking must be attainable.

Perhaps one may think that the recognition of an absolute good will be advantageous for the purpose of attaining and realizing in action the goods which can be 1097[a] attained and realized. By treating the absolute good as a pattern, [they might argue,] we shall gain a better knowledge of what things are good for us, and once we know that, we can achieve them. This argument has, no doubt, some plausibility; however, it does not tally with the procedure of the sciences. For while all the sciences aim at some good and seek to fulfill it, they leave the knowledge of the absolute good out of consideration. Yet if this knowledge were such a great help, it would make no sense that all the craftsmen are ignorant of it and do not even attempt to seek it. One might also wonder what benefit a weaver or a carpenter might derive in the practice of his own art from a knowledge of the absolute Good, or in what way a physician who has contemplated the Form of the Good will become more of a physician or a general more of a general. For actually, a physician does not even examine health in this fashion; he examines the health of man, or perhaps better, the health of a particular man, for he practices his medicine on particular cases. So much for this.

7. The Good Is Final and Self-Sufficient; Happiness Is Defined: Let us return again to our investigation into the nature of the good which we are seeking. It is evidently something different in different actions and in each art: it is one thing in medicine, another in strategy, and another again in each of the other arts. What, then, is the good of each? Is it not that for the sake of which everything else is done? That means it is health in the case of medicine, victory in the case of strategy, a house in the case of building, a different thing in the case of different arts, and in all actions and choices it is the end. For it is for the sake of the end that all else is done. Thus, if there is some one end for all that we do, this would be the good attainable by action; if there are several ends, they will be the goods attainable by action.

Our argument has gradually progressed to the same point at which we were before, and we must try to clarify it still further. Since there are evidently several ends, and since we choose some of these—e.g., wealth, flutes, and instruments generally—as a means to something else, it is obvious that not all ends are final. The highest good, on the other hand, must be something final. Thus, if there is only one final end, this will be the good we are seeking; if there are several, it will be the most final and perfect of them. We call that which is pursued as an end in itself more final than an end which is pursued for the sake of something else; and what is never chosen as a means to something else we call more final than that which is chosen both as an end in itself and as a means to something else. What is always chosen as an end in itself and never as a means to something else is called final in an unqualified sense. This description seems to apply to happiness above all else: for we always choose happiness as an end in itself and never 1097[b] for the sake of something else. Honor, pleasure, intelligence, and all virtue we choose partly for themselves—for we would choose each of them even if no further advantage would accrue from them—but we also choose them partly for the sake of happiness, because we assume that it is through them that we will be happy. On the other hand, no one chooses happiness for the sake of honor, pleasure, and the like, nor as a means to anything at all.

We arrive at the same conclusion if we approach the question from the standpoint of self-sufficiency. For the final and perfect good seems to be self-sufficient. However, we define something as self-sufficient not by reference to the "self" alone. We do not mean a man who lives his life in isolation, but a man who also lives with parents, children, a wife, and friends and fellow citizens generally, since man is by nature a social and political being. But some limit must be set to these relationships; for if they are extended to include ancestors, descendants, and friends of friends, they will go on to infinity. However, this point must be reserved for investigation later. For the present we define as "self-sufficient" that which taken by itself makes life something desirable and deficient in nothing. It is happiness, in our opinion, which fits this description. Moreover, happiness is of all things the one most desirable, and it is not counted as one good thing among many others. But if it were counted as one among many others, it is obvious that the addition of even the least of the goods would make it more desirable; for the addition would produce an extra amount of good, and the greater amount of good is always more desirable than the lesser. We see then that happiness is something final and self-sufficient and the end of our actions.

To call happiness the highest good is perhaps a little trite, and a clearer account of what it is, is still required. Perhaps this is best done by first ascertaining the proper function of man. For just as the goodness and performance of a flute player, a sculptor, or any kind of expert, and generally of anyone who fulfills some function or performs some action, are thought to reside in his proper function, so the goodness and performance of man would seem to reside in whatever is his proper function. Is it then possible that while a carpenter and a shoemaker have their own proper functions and spheres of action, man as man has none, but was left by nature a good-for-nothing without a function? Should we not assume that just as the eye, the hand, the foot, and in general each part of the body clearly has its own proper function, so man too has some function over and above the functions of his parts? What can this function possibly be? Simply living? He shares that even with plants, but we are now looking for something peculiar to man. Accordingly, the life of nutrition and growth must be excluded. Next in line there is a life of sense perception. But this, too, man has in common with the horse, the ox, and every animal. There remains then an active life of the rational element. The rational element has two parts: one is rational in that it obeys the rule of reason, the other in that it possesses and conceives rational rules. Since the expression "life of the rational element" also can be used in two senses, we must make it clear that we mean a life determined by the activity, as opposed to the mere possession, of the rational element. For the activity, it seems, has a greater claim to be the function of man.

The proper function of man, then, consists in an activity of the soul in conformity with a rational principle or, at least, not without it. In speaking of the proper function of a given individual we mean that it is the same in kind as the function of an individual who sets high standards for himself: the proper function of a harpist, for example, is the same as the function of a harpist who has set high standards for himself. The same applies to any and every group of individuals: the full attainment of excellence must be added to the mere function. In other words, the function of the harpist is to play the harp; the function of the harpist who has high standards is to play it well. On these assumptions, if we take the proper function of man to be a certain kind of life, and if this kind of life is an activity of the soul and consists in actions performed in conjunction with the rational element, and if a man of high standards is he who performs these actions well and properly, and if a function is well performed when it is performed in accordance with the excellence appropriate to it; we reach the conclusion that the good of man is an activity of the soul in conformity with excellence or virtue, and if there are several virtues, in conformity with the best and most complete.

But we must add "in a complete life." For one swallow does not make a spring, nor does one sunny day; similarly, one day or a short time does not make a man blessed* and happy.

This will suffice as an outline of the good: for perhaps one ought to make a general sketch first and fill in the details afterwards. Once a good outline has been made, anyone, it seems, is capable of developing and completing it in detail, and time is a good inventor or collaborator in such an effort. Advances in the arts, too, have come about in this way, for anyone can fill in gaps. We must also bear in mind what has been said above, namely that one should not require precision in all pursuits alike, but in each field precision varies with the matter under discussion and should be required only to the extent to which it is appropriate to the investigation. A carpenter and a geometrician both want to find a right angle, but they do not want to find it in the same sense: the former wants to find it to the extent to which it is useful for his work, the latter, wanting to see truth, tries to ascertain what it is and what sort of thing it is. We must, likewise, approach other subjects in the same spirit, in order to prevent minor points from assuming a greater importance than the major tasks. Nor should we demand to know a causal explanation in all matters alike; in some instances, e.g., when dealing with fundamental principles, it is sufficient to point out convincingly that such-and-such is in fact the case. The fact here is the primary thing and the fundamental principle. Some fundamental principles can be apprehended by induction, others by sense perception, others again by some sort of habituation,** and others by still other means. We must try to get at each of them in a way naturally appropriate to it, and must be scrupulous in defining it correctly, because it is of great importance for the subsequent course of the discussion. Surely, a good beginning is more than half the whole, and as it comes to light, it sheds light on many problems.

8. Popular Views About Happiness Confirm Our Position: We must examine the fundamental principle with which we are concerned, [happiness,] not only on the basis of the logical conclusion we have reached and on the basis of the elements which make up its definition, but also on the basis of the views commonly expressed about it. For in a true statement, all the facts are in harmony; in a false statement, truth soon introduces a discordant note.

Good things are commonly divided into three classes: (1) external goods, (2) goods of the soul, and (3) goods of the body. Of these, we call the goods pertaining to the soul goods in the highest and fullest sense. But in speaking of "soul," we refer to our soul's actions and activities. Thus, our definition tallies with this opinion which has been current for a long time and to which philosophers subscribe. We are also right in defining the end as consisting of actions and activities; for in this way the end is included among the goods of the soul and not among external goods.

Also the view that a happy man lives well and fares well fits in with our definition: for we have all but defined happiness as a kind of good life and well-being.

Moreover, the characteristics which one looks for in happiness are all included in our definition. For some people think that happiness is virtue, others that it is practical

*The distinction Aristotle seems to observe between *makarios,* "blessed" or "supremely happy," and *eudaimon,* "happy," is that the former describes happiness insofar as it is god-given, while the latter describes happiness as attained by man through his own efforts.

**This, according to Aristotle, is the way in which the fundamental principles of ethics are learned, and for that reason a person must be mature in order to be able to study ethics properly. Aristotle is not trying to persuade his listener of the truth of these principles, but takes it for granted that the listener has learned them at home.

wisdom, others that it is some kind of theoretical wisdom; others again believe it to be all or some of these accompanied by, or not devoid of, pleasure; and some people also include external prosperity in its definition.* Some of these views are expressed by many people and have come down from antiquity, some by a few men of high prestige, and it is not reasonable to assume that both groups are altogether wrong; the presumption is rather that they are right in at least one or even in most respects.

Now, in our definition we are in agreement with those who describe happiness as virtue or as some particular virtue, for our term "activity in conformity with virtue" implies virtue. But it does doubtless make a considerable difference whether we think of the highest good as consisting in the possession or in the practice of virtue, viz., as being a characteristic or an activity. For a characteristic may exist without producing
1099a any good result, as for example, in a man who is asleep or incapacitated in some other respect. An activity, on the other hand, must produce a result: [an active person] will necessarily act and act well. Just as the crown at the Olympic Games is not awarded to the most beautiful and the strongest but to the participants in the contests—for it is among them that the victors are found—so the good and noble things in life are won by those who act rightly.

The life of men active in this sense is also pleasant in itself. For the sensation of pleasure belongs to the soul, and each man derives pleasure from what he is said to love: a lover of horses from horses, a lover of the theater from plays, and in the same way a lover of justice from just acts, and a lover of virtue in general from virtuous acts. In most men, pleasant acts conflict with one another because they are not pleasant by nature, but men who love what is noble derive pleasure from what is naturally pleasant. Actions which conform to virtue are naturally pleasant, and, as a result, such actions are not only pleasant for those who love the noble but also pleasant in themselves. The life of such men has no further need of pleasure as an added attraction, but it contains pleasure within itself. We may even go so far as to state that the man who does not enjoy performing noble actions is not a good man at all. Nobody would call a man just who does not enjoy acting justly, nor generous who does not enjoy generous actions, and so on. If this is true, actions performed in conformity with virtue are in themselves pleasant.

Of course it goes without saying that such actions are good as well as noble, and they are both in the highest degree, if the man of high moral standards displays any right judgment about them at all; and his judgment corresponds to our description. So we see that happiness is at once the best, noblest, and most pleasant thing, and these qualities are not separate, as the inscription at Delos makes out:

> The most just is most noble, but health is the best, and to win what one loves is pleasantest.

For the best activities encompass all these attributes, and it is in these, or in the best one of them, that we maintain happiness consists.

Still, happiness, as we have said, needs external goods as well. For it is impossible or at least not easy to perform noble actions if one lacks the wherewithal. Many

*The view that virtue alone constitutes happiness was espoused by Antisthenes and the Cynics (and later by the Stoics); the doctrine that all virtues are forms of *phronesis* or "practical wisdom" is attributed to Socrates; theoretical wisdom as virtue may perhaps be attributed to Anaxagoras and his doctrine of *Nous;* the view that pleasure must be added to virtue and wisdom is that of Plato; and the ancient commentators on this passage identify Xenocrates, Plato's pupil and later head of the Academy, as regarding external goods as essential for the good life.

actions can only be performed with the help of instruments, as it were: friends, wealth, 1099b and political power. And there are some external goods the absence of which spoils supreme happiness, e.g., good birth, good children, and beauty: for a man who is very ugly in appearance or ill-born or who lives all by himself and has no children cannot be classified as altogether happy; even less happy perhaps is a man whose children and friends are worthless, or one who has lost good children and friends through death. Thus, as we have said, happiness also requires well-being of this kind, and that is the reason why some classify good fortune with happiness, while others link it to virtue.

9. How Happiness Is Acquired: This also explains why there is a problem whether happiness is acquired by learning, by discipline, or by some other kind of training, or whether we attain it by reason of some divine dispensation or even by chance. Now, if there is anything at all which comes to men as a gift from the gods, it is reasonable to suppose that happiness above all else is god-given; and of all things human it is the most likely to be god-given, inasmuch as it is the best. But although this subject is perhaps more appropriate to a different field of study, it is clear that happiness is one of the most divine things, even if it is not god-sent but attained through virtue and some kind of learning or training. For the prize and end of excellence and virtue is the best thing of all, and it is something divine and blessed. Moreover, if happiness depends on excellence, it will be shared by many people; for study and effort will make it accessible to anyone whose capacity for virtue is unimpaired. And if it is better that happiness is acquired in this way rather than by chance, it is reasonable to assume that this is the way in which it is acquired. For, in the realm of nature, things are naturally arranged in the best way possible—and the same is also true of the products of art and of any kind of causation, especially the highest. To leave the greatest and noblest of things to chance would hardly be right.

A solution of this question is also suggested by our earlier definition, according to which the good of man, happiness, is some kind of activity of the soul in conformity with virtue. All the other goods are either necessary prerequisites for happiness, or are by nature co-workers with it and useful instruments for attaining it. Our results also tally with what we said at the outset: for we stated that the end of politics is the best of ends; and the main concern of politics is to engender a certain character in the citizens and to make them good and disposed to perform noble actions.

We are right, then, when we call neither a horse nor an ox nor any other animal happy, for none of them is capable of participating in an activity of this kind. For the 1100a same reason, a child is not happy, either; for, because of his age, he cannot yet perform such actions. When we do call a child happy, we do so by reason of the hopes we have for his future. Happiness, as we have said, requires completeness in virtue as well as a complete lifetime. Many changes and all kinds of contingencies befall a man in the course of his life, and it is possible that the most prosperous man will encounter great misfortune in his old age, as the Trojan legends tell about Priam. When a man has met a fate such as his and has come to a wretched end, no one calls him happy.

10. Can a Man Be Called "Happy" During His Lifetime?: Must we, then, apply the term "happy" to no man at all as long as he is alive? Must we, as Solon would have us do, wait to see his end?* And, on this assumption, is it also true that a man is actually

*This is one of the main points made by Solon, Athenian statesman and poet of the early sixth century B.C., in his conversation with the Lydian king, Croesus.

happy after he is dead? Is this not simply absurd, especially for us who define happiness as a kind of activity? Suppose we do not call a dead man happy, and interpret Solon's words to mean that only when a man is dead can we safely say that he has been happy, since he is now beyond the reach of evil and misfortune—this view, too, is open to objection. For it seems that to some extent good and evil really exist for a dead man, just as they may exist for a man who lives without being conscious of them, for example, honors and disgraces, and generally the successes and failures of his children and descendants. This presents a further problem. A man who has lived happily to his old age and has died as happily as he lived may have many vicissitudes befall his descendants: some of them may be good and may be granted the kind of life which they deserve, and others may not. It is, further, obvious that the descendants may conceivably be removed from their ancestors by various degrees. Under such circumstances, it would be odd if the dead man would share in the vicissitudes of his descendants and be happy at one time and wretched at another. But it would also be odd if the fortunes of their descendants did not affect the ancestors at all, not even for a short time.

But we must return to the problem raised earlier, for through it our present problem perhaps may be solved. If one must look to the end and praise a man not as being happy but as having been happy in the past, is it not paradoxical that at a time when a man actually is happy this attribute, though true, cannot be applied to him? We are
1100b unwilling to call the living happy because changes may befall them and because we believe that happiness has permanence and is not amenable to changes under any circumstances, whereas fortunes revolve many times in one person's lifetime. For obviously, if we are to keep pace with a man's fortune, we shall frequently have to call the same man happy at one time and wretched at another and demonstrate that the happy man is a kind of chameleon, and that the foundations [of his life] are unsure. Or is it quite wrong to make our judgment depend on fortune? Yes, it is wrong, for fortune does not determine whether we fare well or ill, but is, as we said, merely an accessory to human life; activities in conformity with virtue constitute happiness, and the opposite activities constitute its opposite.

The question which we have just discussed further confirms our definition. For no function of man possesses as much stability as do activities in conformity with virtue: these seem to be even more durable than scientific knowledge. And the higher the virtuous activities, the more durable they are, because men who are supremely happy spend their lives in these activities most intensely and most continuously, and this seems to be the reason why such activities cannot be forgotten.

The happy man will have the attribute of permanence which we are discussing, and he will remain happy throughout his life. For he will always or to the highest degree both do and contemplate what is in conformity with virtue; he will bear the vicissitudes of fortune most nobly and with perfect decorum under all circumstances, inasmuch as he is truly good and "four-square beyond reproach."

But fortune brings many things to pass, some great and some small. Minor instances of good and likewise of bad luck obviously do not decisively tip the scales of life, but a number of major successes will make life more perfectly happy; for, in the first place, by their very nature they help to make life attractive, and secondly, they afford the opportunity for noble and good actions. On the other hand, frequent reverses can crush and mar supreme happiness in that they inflict pain and thwart many activities. Still, nobility shines through even in such circumstances, when a man bears many great misfortunes with good grace not because he is insensitive to pain but because he is noble and high-minded.

If, as we said, the activities determine a man's life, no supremely happy man can ever become miserable, for he will never do what is hateful and base. For in our opinion, the man who is truly good and wise will bear with dignity whatever fortune may bring, and will always act as nobly as circumstances permit, just as a good general makes the most strategic use of the troops at his disposal, and a good shoemaker makes the best shoe he can from the leather available, and so on with experts in all other fields. If this is true, a happy man will never become miserable; but even so, supreme happiness will not be his if a fate such as Priam's befalls him. And yet, he will not be fickle and changeable; he will not be dislodged from his happiness easily by any misfortune that comes along, but only by great and numerous disasters such as will make it impossible for him to become happy again in a short time; if he recovers his happiness at all, it will be only after a long period of time, in which he has won great distinctions.

Is there anything to prevent us, then, from defining the happy man as one whose activities are an expression of complete virtue, and who is sufficiently equipped with external goods, not simply at a given moment but to the end of his life? Or should we add that he must die as well as live in the manner which we have defined? For we cannot foresee the future, and happiness, we maintain, is an end which is absolutely final and complete in every respect. If this be granted, we shall define as "supremely happy" those living men who fulfill and continue to fulfill these requirements, but blissful only as human beings. So much for this question.

11. Do the Fortunes of the Living Affect the Dead?: That the fortunes of his descendants and of all those near and dear to him do not affect the happiness of a dead man at all, seems too unfeeling a view and contrary to the prevailing opinions. Many and different in kind are the accidents that can befall us, and some hit home more closely than others. It would, therefore, seem to be a long and endless task to make detailed distinctions, and perhaps a general outline will be sufficient. Just as one's own misfortunes are sometimes momentous and decisive for one's life and sometimes seem comparatively less important, so the misfortunes of our various friends affect us to varying degrees. In each case it makes a considerable difference whether those who are affected by an event are living or dead; much more so than it matters in a tragedy whether the crimes and horrors have been perpetrated before the opening of the play or are part of the plot. This difference, too, must be taken into account and perhaps still more the problem whether the dead participate in any good or evil. These considerations suggest that even if any good or evil reaches them at all, it must be something weak and negligible (either intrinsically or in relation to them), or at least something too small and insignificant to make the unhappy happy or to deprive the happy of their bliss. The good as well as the bad fortunes of their friends seem, then, to have some effect upon the dead, but the nature and magnitude of the effect is such as not to make the happy unhappy or to produce any similar changes.

12. The Praise Accorded to Happiness: Now that we have settled these questions, let us consider whether happiness is to be classified among the things which we praise or rather among those which we honor; for it is clear that it is not a potential [but an actual good].

The grounds on which we bestow praise on anything evidently are its quality and the relation in which it stands to other things. In other words, we praise a just man, a courageous man, and in general any good man, and also his virtue or excellence, on the basis of his actions and achievements; moreover, we praise a strong man, a swift runner, and so forth, because he possesses a certain natural quality and stands in a certain relation to something good and worth while. Our feelings about praising the gods provide a further illustration of this point. For it is ridiculous to refer the gods to our standards; but this is precisely what praising them amounts to, since praise, as we said, entails a reference to something else. But if praise is appropriate only for relative things, it is clear that the best things do not call for praise but for something greater and better, as indeed is generally recognized: for we call the gods "blessed" and "happy" and use these terms also for the most godlike man. The same is true of good things: no one praises happiness in the same sense in which he praises justice, but he exalts its bliss as something better and more nearly divine.

Eudoxus, too, seems to have used the right method for advocating that pleasure is the most excellent, for he took the fact that pleasure, though a good, is not praised as an indication of its superiority to the things that are praised, as god and the good are, for they are the standards to which we refer everything else.

Praise is proper to virtue or excellence, because it is excellence that makes men capable of performing noble deeds. Eulogies, on the other hand, are appropriate for achievements of the body as well as of the mind. However, a detailed analysis of this subject is perhaps rather the business of those who have made a study of eulogies. For our present purposes, we may draw the conclusion from the preceding argument that
1102a happiness is one of the goods that are worthy of honor and are final. This again seems to be due to the fact that it is a starting point or fundamental principle, since for its sake all of us do everything else. And the source and cause of all good things we consider as something worthy of honor and as divine.

13. The Psychological Foundations of the Virtues: Since happiness is a certain activity of the soul in conformity with perfect virtue, we must now examine what virtue or excellence is. For such an inquiry will perhaps better enable us to discover the nature of happiness. Moreover, the man who is truly concerned about politics seems to devote special attention to excellence, since it is his aim to make the citizens good and law-abiding. We have an example of this in the lawgivers of Crete and Sparta and in other great legislators. If an examination of virtue is part of politics, this question clearly fits into the pattern of our original plan.

There can be no doubt that the virtue which we have to study is human virtue. For the good which we have been seeking is a human good and the happiness a human happiness. By human virtue we do not mean the excellence of the body, but that of the soul, and we define happiness as an activity of the soul. If this is true, the student of politics must obviously have some knowledge of the workings of the soul, just as the man who is to heal eyes must know something about the whole body. In fact, knowledge is all the more important for the former, inasmuch as politics is better and more valuable than medicine, and cultivated physicians devote much time and trouble to gain knowledge about the body. Thus, the student of politics must study the soul, but he must do so with his own aim in view, and only to the extent that the objects of his inquiry demand: to go into it in greater detail would perhaps be more laborious than his purposes require.

Some things that are said about the soul in our less technical discussions are adequate enough to be used here, for instance, that the soul consists of two elements, one irrational and one rational. Whether these two elements are separate, like the parts of the body or any other divisible thing, or whether they are only logically separable though in reality indivisible, as convex and concave are in the circumference of a circle, is irrelevant for our present purposes.

Of the irrational element, again, one part seems to be common to all living things and vegetative in nature: I mean that part which is responsible for nurture and growth. We must assume that some such capacity of the soul exists in everything that takes nourishment, in the embryonic stage as well as when the organism is fully developed; 1102b for this makes more sense than to assume the existence of some different capacity at the latter stage. The excellence of this part of the soul is, therefore, shown to be common to all living things and is not exclusively human. This very part and this capacity seem to be most active in sleep. For in sleep the difference between a good man and a bad is least apparent—whence the saying that for half their lives the happy are no better off than the wretched. This is just what we would expect, for sleep is an inactivity of the soul in that it ceases to do things which cause it to be called good or bad. However, to a small extent some bodily movements do penetrate to the soul in sleep, and in this sense the dreams of honest men are better than those of average people. But enough of this subject: we may pass by the nutritive part, since it has no natural share in human excellence or virtue.

In addition to this, there seems to be another integral element of the soul which, though irrational, still does partake of reason in some way. In morally strong and morally weak men we praise the reason that guides them and the rational element of the soul, because it exhorts them to follow the right path and to do what is best. Yet we see in them also another natural strain different from the rational, which fights and resists the guidance of reason. The soul behaves in precisely the same manner as do the paralyzed limbs of the body. When we intend to move the limbs to the right, they turn to the left, and similarly, the impulses of morally weak persons turn in the direction opposite to that in which reason leads them. However, while the aberration of the body is visible, that of the soul is not. But perhaps we must accept it as a fact, nevertheless, that there is something in the soul besides the rational element, which opposes and reacts against it. In what way the two are distinct need not concern us here. But, as we have stated, it too seems to partake of reason; at any rate, in a morally strong man it accepts the leadership of reason, and is perhaps more obedient still in a self-controlled and courageous man, since in him everything is in harmony with the voice of reason.

Thus we see that the irrational element of the soul has two parts: the one is vegetative and has no share in reason at all, the other is the seat of the appetites and of desire in general and partakes of reason insofar as it complies with reason and accepts its leadership; it possesses reason in the sense that we say it is "reasonable" to accept the advice of a father and of friends, not in the sense that we have a "rational" understanding of mathematical propositions. That the irrational element can be persuaded by the rational is shown by the fact that admonition and all manner of rebuke and exhortation are possible. If it is correct to say that the appetitive part, too, has reason, 1103a it follows that the rational element of the soul has two subdivisions: the one possesses reason in the strict sense, contained within itself, and the other possesses reason in the sense that it listens to reason as one would listen to a father.

Virtue, too, is differentiated in line with this division of the soul. We call some virtues "intellectual" and others "moral": theoretical wisdom, understanding, and practical wisdom are intellectual virtues, generosity and self-control moral virtues. In speaking of a man's character, we do not describe him as wise or understanding, but as gentle or self-controlled; but we praise the wise man, too, for his characteristic, and praiseworthy characteristics are what we call virtues.

BOOK II

1. Moral Virtue as the Result of Habits: Virtue, as we have seen, consists of two kinds, intellectual virtue and moral virtue. Intellectual virtue or excellence owes its origin and development chiefly to teaching, and for that reason requires experience and time. Moral virtue, on the other hand, is formed by habit, *ethos,* and its name, *ethike,* is therefore derived, by a slight variation, from *ethos.* This shows, too, that none of the moral virtues is implanted in us by nature, for nothing which exists by nature can be changed by habit. For example, it is impossible for a stone, which has a natural downward movement, to become habituated to moving upward, even if one should try ten thousand times to inculcate the habit by throwing it in the air; nor can fire be made to move downward, nor can the direction of any nature-given tendency be changed by habituation. Thus, the virtues are implanted in us neither by nature nor contrary to nature: we are by nature equipped with the ability to receive them, and habit brings this ability to completion and fulfillment.

Furthermore, of all the qualities with which we are endowed by nature, we are provided with the capacity first, and display the activity afterward. That this is true is shown by the senses: it is not by frequent seeing or frequent hearing that we acquired our senses, but on the contrary we first possess and then use them; we do not acquire them by use. The virtues, on the other hand, we acquire by first having put them into action, and the same is also true of the arts. For the things which we have to learn before we can do them we learn by doing: men become builders by building houses, and harpists by playing the harp. Similarly, we become just by the practice of just actions, self-controlled by exercising self-control, and courageous by performing acts of courage.

This is corroborated by what happens in states. Lawgivers make the citizens good by inculcating [good] habits in them, and this is the aim of every lawgiver; if he does not succeed in doing that, his legislation is a failure. It is in this that a good constitution differs from a bad one.

Moreover, the same causes and the same means that produce any excellence or virtue can also destroy it, and this is also true of every art. It is by playing the harp that men become both good and bad harpists, and correspondingly with builders and all the other craftsmen: a man who builds well will be a good builder, one who builds badly a bad one. For if this were not so, there would be no need for an instructor, but everybody would be born as a good or a bad craftsman. The same holds true of the virtues: in our transactions with other men it is by action that some become just and others unjust, and it is by acting in the face of danger and by developing the habit of feeling fear or confidence that some become brave men and others cowards. The same applies to the appetites and feelings of anger: by reacting in one way or in another to given circumstances some people become self-controlled and gentle, and others self-indulgent and short-tempered. In a word, characteristics develop from corresponding activities. For that reason, we must see to it that our activities are of a certain kind, since any variations in them will be reflected in our characteristics. Hence it is no small matter whether one habit or another is inculcated in us from early childhood; on the contrary, it makes a considerable difference, or, rather, all the difference.

2. Method in the Practical Sciences: The purpose of the present study is not, as it is in other inquiries, the attainment of theoretical knowledge: we are not conducting this inquiry in order to know what virtue is, but in order to become good, else there would be no advantage in studying it. For that reason, it becomes necessary to examine the problem of actions, and to ask how they are to be performed. For, as we have said, the actions determine what kind of characteristics are developed.

That we must act according to right reason is generally conceded and may be assumed as the basis of our discussion. We shall speak about it later and discuss what right reason is and examine its relation to the other virtues. But let us first agree that any discussion on matters of action cannot be more than an outline and is bound to lack 1104a
precision; for as we stated at the outset, one can demand of a discussion only what the subject matter permits, and there are no fixed data in matters concerning action and questions of what is beneficial, any more than there are in matters of health. And if this is true of our general discussion, our treatment of particular problems will be even less precise, since these do not come under the head of any art which can be transmitted by precept, but the agent must consider on each different occasion what the situation demands, just as in medicine and in navigation. But although such is the kind of discussion in which we are engaged, we must do our best.

First of all, it must be observed that the nature of moral qualities is such that they are destroyed by defect and by excess. We see the same thing happen in the case of strength and of health, to illustrate, as we must, the invisible by means of visible examples: excess as well as deficiency of physical exercise destroys our strength, and similarly, too much and too little food and drink destroys our health; the proportionate amount, however, produces, increases, and preserves it. The same applies to self-control, courage, and the other virtues: the man who shuns and fears everything and never stands his ground becomes a coward, whereas a man who knows no fear at all and goes to meet every danger becomes reckless. Similarly, a man who revels in every pleasure and abstains from none becomes self-indulgent, while he who avoids every pleasure like a boor becomes what might be called insensitive. Thus we see that self-control and courage are destroyed by excess and by deficiency and are preserved by the mean.

Not only are the same actions which are responsible for and instrumental in the origin and development of the virtues also the causes and means of their destruction, but they will also be manifested in the active exercise of the virtues. We can see the truth of this in the case of other more visible qualities, e.g., strength. Strength is produced by consuming plenty of food and by enduring much hard work, and it is the strong man who is best able to do these things. The same is also true of the virtues: by abstaining from pleasures we become self-controlled, and once we are self-controlled we are best able to abstain from pleasures. So also with courage: by becoming habituated to despise 1104b
and to endure terrors we become courageous, and once we have become courageous we will best be able to endure terror.

3. Pleasure and Pain as the Test of Virtue: An index to our characteristics is provided by the pleasure or pain which follows upon the tasks we have achieved. A man who abstains from bodily pleasures and enjoys doing so is self-controlled; if he finds abstinence troublesome, he is self-indulgent; a man who endures danger with joy, or at least without pain, is courageous; if he endures it with pain, he is a coward. For moral excellence is concerned with pleasure and pain; it is pleasure that makes us do base actions and pain that prevents us from doing noble actions. For that reason, as Plato says, men must be brought up from childhood to feel pleasure and pain at the proper things; for this is correct education.

Furthermore, since the virtues have to do with actions and emotions, and since pleasure and pain are a consequence of every emotion and of every action, it follows from this point of view, too, that virtue has to do with pleasure and pain. This is further indicated by the fact that punishment is inflicted by means of pain. For punishment is a kind of medical treatment and it is the nature of medical treatments to take effect through the introduction of the opposite of the disease.* Again, as we said just now, every characteristic of the soul shows its true nature in its relation to and its concern with those factors which naturally make it better or worse. But it is through pleasures and pains that men are corrupted, i.e., through pursuing and avoiding pleasures and pains either of the wrong kind or at the wrong time or in the wrong manner, or by going wrong in some other definable respect. For that reason some people define the virtues as states of freedom from emotion and of quietude. However, they make the mistake of using these terms absolutely and without adding such qualifications as "in the right manner," "at the right or wrong time," and so forth. We may, therefore, assume as the basis of our discussion that virtue, being concerned with pleasure and pain in the way we have described, makes us act in the best way in matters revolving pleasure and pain, and that vice does the opposite.

The following considerations may further illustrate that virtue is concerned with pleasure and pain. There are three factors that determine choice and three that determine avoidance: the noble, the beneficial, and the pleasurable, on the one hand, and on the other their opposites: the base, the harmful, and the painful. Now a good man will go right and a bad man will go wrong when any of these, and especially when pleasure is involved. For pleasure is not only common to man and the animals, but also accompanies all objects of choice: in fact, the noble and the beneficial seem pleasant to us. Moreover, a love of pleasure has grown up with all of us from infancy. Therefore, this emotion has come to be ingrained in our lives and is difficult to erase. Even in our actions we use, to a greater or smaller extent, pleasure and pain as a criterion. For this reason, this entire study is necessarily concerned with pleasure and pain; for it is not unimportant for our actions whether we feel joy and pain in the right or the wrong way. Again, it is harder to fight against pleasure than against anger, as Heraclitus says; and both virtue and art are always concerned with what is harder, for success is better when it is hard to achieve. Thus, for this reason also, every study both of virtue and of politics must deal with pleasures and pains, for if a man has the right attitude to them, he will be good; if the wrong attitude, he will be bad.

We have now established that virtue or excellence is concerned with pleasures and pains; that the actions which produce it also develop it and, if differently performed, destroy it; and that it actualizes itself fully in those activities to which it owes its origin.

4. Virtuous Action and Virtue: However, the question may be raised what we mean by saying that men become just by performing just actions and self-controlled by practicing self-control. For if they perform just actions and exercise self-control, they are already just and self-controlled, in the same way as they are literate and musical if they write correctly and practice music.

But is this objection really valid, even as regards the arts? No, for it is possible for a man to write a piece correctly by chance or at the prompting of another: but he will be

*The idea here evidently is that the pleasure of wrongdoing must be cured by applying its opposite, i.e., pain.

literate only if he produces a piece of writing in a literate way, and that means doing it in accordance with the skill of literate composition which he has in himself.

Moreover, the factors involved in the arts and in the virtues are not the same. In the arts, excellence lies in the result itself, so that it is sufficient if it is of a certain kind. But in the case of the virtues an act is not performed justly or with self-control if the act itself is of a certain kind, but only if in addition the agent has certain characteristics as he performs it: first of all, he must know what he is doing; secondly, he must choose to act the way he does, and he must choose it for its own sake; and in the third place, the act must spring from a firm and unchangeable character. With the exception of knowing what one is about, these considerations do not enter into the mastery of the 1105b
arts; for the mastery of the virtues, however, knowledge is of little or no importance, whereas the other two conditions count not for a little but are all-decisive, since repeated acts of justice and self-control result in the possession of these virtues. In other words, acts are called just and self-controlled when they are the kind of acts which a just or self-controlled man would perform; but the just and self-controlled man is not he who performs these acts, but he who also performs them in the way just and self-controlled men do.

Thus our assertion that a man becomes just by performing just acts and self-controlled by performing acts of self-control is correct; without performing them, nobody could even be on the way to becoming good. Yet most men do not perform such acts, but by taking refuge in argument they think that they are engaged in philosophy and that they will become good in this way. In so doing, they act like sick men who listen attentively to what the doctor says, but fail to do any of the things he prescribes. That kind of philosophical activity will not bring health to the soul any more than this sort of treatment will produce a healthy body.

5. Virtue Defined: The Genus: The next point to consider is the definition of virtue or excellence. As there are three kinds of things found in the soul: (1) emotions, (2) capacities, and (3) characteristics, virtue must be one of these. By "emotions" I mean appetite, anger, fear, confidence, envy, joy, affection, hatred, longing, emulation, pity, and in general anything that is followed by pleasure or pain; by "capacities" I mean that by virtue of which we are said to be affected by these emotions, for example, the capacity which enables us to feel anger, pain, or pity; and by "characteristics" I mean the condition, either good or bad, in which we are, in relation to the emotions: for example, our condition in relation to anger is bad, if our anger is too violent or not violent enough, but if it is moderate, our condition is good; and similarly with our condition in relation to the other emotions. Now the virtues and vices cannot be emotions, because we are not called good or bad on the basis of our emotions, but on the basis of our virtues and vices. Also, we are neither praised nor blamed for our emotions: a man does not receive praise for being frightened or angry, nor blame for being angry pure and simple, but for being angry in a certain way. Yet we are praised or blamed for our virtues and vices. Furthermore, no choice is involved when we experience anger or fear, 1106a
while the virtues are some kind of choice or at least involve choice. Moreover, with regard to our emotions we are said to be "moved," but with regard to our virtues and vices we are not said to be "moved" but to be "disposed" in a certain way.

For the same reason, the virtues cannot be capacities, either, for we are neither called good or bad nor praised or blamed simply because we are capable of being affected. Further, our capacities have been given to us by nature, but we do not by nature develop into good or bad men. We have discussed this subject before. Thus, if the virtues are neither emotions nor capacities, the only remaining alternative is that they are characteristics. So much for the genus of virtue.

6. Virtue Defined: The Differentia: It is not sufficient, however, merely to define virtue in general terms as a characteristic: we must also specify what kind of characteristic it is. It must, then, be remarked that every virtue or excellence (1) renders good the thing itself of which it is the excellence, and (2) causes it to perform its function well. For example, the excellence of the eye makes both the eye and its function good, for good sight is due to the excellence of the eye. Likewise, the excellence of a horse makes it both good as a horse and good at running, at carrying its rider, and at facing the enemy. Now, if this is true of all things, the virtue or excellence of man, too, will be a characteristic which makes him a good man, and which causes him to perform his own function well. To some extent we have already stated how this will be true; the rest will become clear if we study what the nature of virtue is.

Of every continuous entity that is divisible into parts it is possible to take the larger, the smaller, or an equal part, and these parts may be larger, smaller, or equal either in relation to the entity itself, or in relation to us. The "equal" part is something median between excess and deficiency. By the median of an entity I understand a point equidistant from both extremes, and this point is one and the same for everybody. By the median relative to us I understand an amount neither too large nor too small, and this is neither one nor the same for everybody. To take an example: if ten is many and two is few, six is taken as the median in relation to the entity, for it exceeds and is exceeded by the same amount, and is thus the median in terms of arithmetical propor-
1106b tion. But the median relative to us cannot be determined in this manner: if ten pounds of food is much for a man to eat and two pounds little, it does not follow that the trainer will prescribe six pounds, for this may in turn be much or little for him to eat; it may be little for Milo* and much for someone who has just begun to take up athletics. The same applies to running and wrestling. Thus we see that an expert in any field avoids excess and deficiency, but seeks the median and chooses it—not the median of the object but the median relative to us.

If this, then, is the way in which every science perfects its work, by looking to the median and by bringing its work up to that point—and this is the reason why it is usually said of a successful piece of work that it is impossible to detract from it or to add to it, the implication being that excess and deficiency destroy success while the mean safeguards it (good craftsmen, we say, look toward this standard in the performance of their work)—and if virtue, like nature, is more precise and better than any art, we must conclude that virtue aims at the median. I am referring to moral virtue: for it is moral virtue that is concerned with emotions and actions, and it is in emotions and actions that excess, deficiency, and the median are found. Thus we can experience fear, confidence, desire, anger, pity, and generally any kind of pleasure and pain either too much or too little, and in either case not properly. But to experience all this at the right time, toward the right objects, toward the right people, for the right reason, and in the right manner—that is the median and the best course, the course that is a mark of virtue.

Similarly, excess, deficiency, and the median can also be found in actions. Now virtue is concerned with emotions and actions; and in emotions and actions excess and deficiency miss the mark, whereas the median is praised and constitutes success. But

*Milo of Croton, said to have lived in the second half of the sixth century B.C., was a wrestler famous for his remarkable strength.

both praise and success are signs of virtue or excellence. Consequently, virtue is a mean in the sense that it aims at the median. This is corroborated by the fact that there are many ways of going wrong, but only one way which is right—for evil belongs to the indeterminate, as the Pythagoreans imagined, but good to the determinate. This, by the way, is also the reason why the one is easy and the other hard: it is easy to miss the target but hard to hit it. Here, then, is an additional proof that excess and deficiency characterize vice, while the mean characterizes virtue: for "bad men have many ways, good men but one."

We may thus conclude that virtue or excellence is a characteristic involving choice, and that it consists in observing the mean relative to us, a mean which is defined by a rational principle, such as a man of practical wisdom would use to determine it. 1107a
It is the mean by reference to two vices: the one of excess and the other of deficiency. It is, moreover, a mean because some vices exceed and others fall short of what is required in emotion and in action, whereas virtue finds and chooses the median. Hence, in respect of its essence and the definition of its essential nature virtue is a mean, but in regard to goodness and excellence it is an extreme.

Not every action nor every emotion admits of a mean. There are some actions and emotions whose very names connote baseness, e.g., spite, shamelessness, envy; and among actions, adultery, theft, and murder. These and similar emotions and actions imply by their very names that they are bad; it is not their excess nor their deficiency which is called bad. It is, therefore, impossible ever to do right in performing them: to perform them is always to do wrong. In cases of this sort, let us say adultery, rightness and wrongness do not depend on committing it with the right woman at the right time and in the right manner, but the mere fact of committing such action at all is to do wrong. It would be just as absurd to suppose that there is a mean, an excess, and a deficiency in

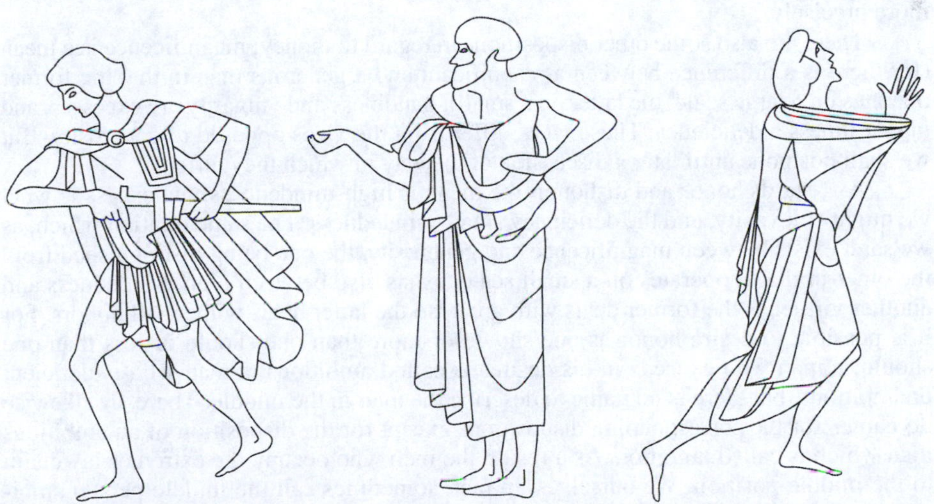

According to Aristotle, virtue or excellence "is the mean by reference to two vices: the one of excess and the other of deficiency." For example, in this drawing the person on the left has an excess of confidence and hence is reckless. The person on the right is deficient in confidence and so is cowardly. In terms of fear, the person on the left has a defect and the person on the right has an excess. In both these cases we should seek to rationally choose the "Golden Mean" of the person in the middle: courage.

an unjust or a cowardly or a self-indulgent act. For if there were, we would have a mean of excess and a mean of deficiency, and an excess of excess and a deficiency of deficiency. Just as there cannot be an excess and a deficiency of self-control and courage—because the intermediate is, in a sense, an extreme—so there cannot be a mean, excess, and deficiency in their respective opposites: their opposites are wrong regardless of how they are performed; for, in general, there is no such thing as the mean of an excess or a deficiency, or the excess and deficiency of a mean.

7. Examples of the Mean in Particular Virtues: However, this general statement is not enough; we must also show that it fits particular instances. For in a discussion of moral actions, although general statements have a wider range of application, statements on particular points have more truth in them: actions are concerned with particulars and our statements must harmonize with them. Let us now take particular virtues and vices from the following table.

In feelings of fear and confidence courage is the mean. As for the excesses, there 1107b is no name that describes a man who exceeds in fearlessness—many virtues and vices have no name; but a man who exceeds in confidence is reckless, and a man who exceeds in fear and is deficient in confidence is cowardly.

In regard to pleasures and pains—not all of them and to a lesser degree in the case of pains—the mean is self-control and the excess self-indulgence. Men deficient in regard to pleasure are not often found, and there is therefore no name for them, but let us call them "insensitive."

In giving and taking money, the mean is generosity, the excess and deficiency are extravagance and stinginess. In these vices excess and deficiency work in opposite ways: an extravagant man exceeds in spending and is deficient in taking, while a stingy man exceeds in taking and is deficient in spending. For our present purposes, we may rest content with an outline and a summary, but we shall later define these qualities more precisely.

There are also some other dispositions in regard to money: magnificence is a mean (for there is a difference between a magnificent and a generous man in that the former operates on a large scale, the latter on a small); gaudiness and vulgarity are excesses, and niggardliness a deficiency. These vices differ from the vices opposed to generosity. But we shall postpone until later a discussion of the way in which they differ.

As regards honor and dishonor, the mean is high-mindedness, the excess is what we might call vanity, and the deficiency small-mindedness. The same relation which, as we said, exists between magnificence and generosity, the one being distinguished from the other in that it operates on a small scale, exists also between high-mindedness and another virtue: as the former deals with great, so the latter deals with small honors. For it is possible to desire honor as one should or more than one should or less than one should: a man who exceeds in his desires is called ambitious, a man who is deficient unambitious, but there is no name to describe the man in the middle. There are likewise no names for the corresponding dispositions except for the disposition of an ambitious man which is called ambition. As a result, the men who occupy the extremes lay claim to the middle position. We ourselves, in fact, sometimes call the middle person ambi- 1108a tious and sometimes unambitious; sometimes we praise an ambitious and at other times an unambitious man. The reason why we do that will be discussed in the sequel; for the present, let us discuss the rest of the virtues and vices along the lines we have indicated.

In regard to anger also there exists an excess, a deficiency, and a mean. Although there really are no names for them, we might call the mean gentleness, since we call a man who occupies the middle position gentle. Of the extremes, let the man who exceeds be called short-tempered and his vice a short temper, and the deficient man apathetic and his vice apathy.

There are, further, three other means which have a certain similarity with one another, but differ nonetheless one from the other. They are all concerned with human relations in speech and action, but they differ in that one of them is concerned with truth in speech and action and the other two with pleasantness: *(a)* pleasantness in amusement and *(b)* pleasantness in all our daily life. We must include these, too, in our discussion, in order to see more clearly that the mean is to be praised in all things and that the extremes are neither praiseworthy nor right, but worthy of blame. Here, too, most of the virtues and vices have no name, but for the sake of clarity and easier comprehension we must try to coin names for them, as we did in earlier instances.

To come to the point; in regard to truth, let us call the man in the middle position truthful and the mean truthfulness. Pretense in the form of exaggeration is boastfulness and its possessor boastful, while pretense in the form of understatement is self-depreciation and its possessor a self-depreciator.

Concerning pleasantness in amusement, the man in the middle position is witty and his disposition wittiness; the excess is called buffoonery and its possessor a buffoon; and the deficient man a kind of boor and the corresponding characteristic boorishness.

As far as the other kind of pleasantness is concerned, pleasantness in our daily life, a man who is as pleasant as he should be is friendly and the mean is friendliness. A man who exceeds is called obsequious if he has no particular purpose in being pleasant, but if he is acting for his own material advantage, he is a flatterer. And a man who is deficient and unpleasant in every respect is a quarrelsome and grouchy kind of person.

A mean can also be found in our emotional experiences and in our emotions. Thus, while a sense of shame is not a virtue, a bashful or modest man is praised. For even in these matters we speak of one kind of person as intermediate and of another as exceeding if he is terror-stricken and abashed at everything. On the other hand, a man who is deficient in shame or has none at all is called shameless, whereas the intermediate man is bashful or modest.

Righteous indignation is the mean between envy and spite, all of these being 1108b
concerned with the pain and pleasure which we feel in regard to the fortunes of our neighbors. The righteously indignant man feels pain when someone prospers undeservedly; an envious man exceeds him in that he is pained when he sees anyone prosper; and a spiteful man is so deficient in feeling pain that he even rejoices [when someone suffers undeservedly].

But we shall have an opportunity to deal with these matters again elsewhere. After that, we shall discuss justice; since it has more than one meaning, we shall distinguish the two kinds of justice and show in what way each is a mean.

8. The Relation between the Mean and Its Extremes: There are, then, three kinds of disposition: two are vices (one marked by excess and one by deficiency), and one, virtue, the mean. Now, each of these dispositions is, in a sense, opposed to both the others: the extremes are opposites to the middle as well as to one another, and the middle is opposed to the extremes. Just as an equal amount is larger in relation to a smaller and smaller in relation to a larger amount, so, in the case both of emotions and of actions, the middle characteristics exceed in relation to the deficiencies and are deficient in relation to the excesses. For example, a brave man seems reckless in relation to a coward, but in relation to a reckless man he seems cowardly. Similarly, a self-controlled man seems self-indulgent in relation to an insensitive man and insensitive in relation to a self-indulgent man, and a generous man extravagant in relation to a stingy man and stingy in relation to an extravagant man. This is the reason why people at the extremes each push the man in the middle over to the other extreme: a coward calls a brave man reckless and a reckless man calls a brave man a coward, and similarly with the other qualities.

However, while these three dispositions are thus opposed to one another, the extremes are more opposed to one another than each is to the median; for they are further apart from one another than each is from the median, just as the large is further removed from the small and the small from the large than either one is from the equal. Moreover, there appears to be a certain similarity between some extremes and their median, e.g., recklessness resembles courage and extravagance generosity; but there is a very great dissimilarity between the extremes. But things that are furthest removed from one another are defined as opposites, and that means that the further things are removed from one another the more opposite they are.

1109a In some cases it is the deficiency and in others the excess that is more opposed to the median. For example, it is not the excess, recklessness, which is more opposed to courage, but the deficiency, cowardice; while in the case of self-control it is not the defect, insensitivity, but the excess, self-indulgence which is more opposite. There are two causes for this. One arises from the nature of the thing itself: when one of the extremes is closer and more similar to the median, we do not treat it but rather the other extreme as the opposite of the median. For instance, since recklessness is believed to be more similar and closer to courage, and cowardice less similar, it is cowardice rather than recklessness which we treat as the opposite of courage. For what is further removed from the middle is regarded as being more opposite. So much for the first cause which arises from the thing itself. The second reason is found in ourselves: the more we are naturally attracted to anything, the more opposed to the median does this thing appear to be. For example, since we are naturally more attracted to pleasure we incline more easily to self-indulgence than to a disciplined kind of life. We describe as more opposed to the mean those things toward which our tendency is stronger; and for that reason the excess, self-indulgence, is more opposed to self-control than is its corresponding deficiency.

9. How to Attain the Mean: Our discussion has sufficiently established (1) that moral virtue is a mean and in what sense it is a mean; (2) that it is a mean between two vices, one of which is marked by excess and the other by deficiency; and (3) that it is a mean in the sense that it aims at the median in the emotions and in actions. That is why it is a hard task to be good; in every case it is a task to find the median: for instance, not everyone can find the middle of a circle, but only a man who has the proper knowledge. Similarly, anyone can get angry—that is easy—or can give away money or spend it; but to do all this to the right person, to the right extent, at the right time, for the right reason, and in the right way is no longer something easy that anyone can do. It is for this reason that good conduct is rare, praiseworthy, and noble.

The first concern of a man who aims at the median should, therefore, be to avoid the extreme which is more opposed to it, as Calypso advises: "Keep clear your ship of yonder spray and surf." For one of the two extremes is more in error than the other, and since it is extremely difficult to hit the mean, we must, as the saying has it, sail in the
1109b second best way and take the lesser evil; and we can best do that in the manner we have described.

Moreover, we must watch the errors which have the greatest attraction for us personally. For the natural inclination of one man differs from that of another, and we each come to recognize our own by observing the pleasure and pain produced in us [by the different extremes]. We must then draw ourselves away in the opposite direction, for by pulling away from error we shall reach the middle, as men do when they straighten warped timber. In every case we must be especially on our guard against pleasure and what is pleasant, for when it comes to pleasure we cannot act as unbiased judges. Our attitude toward pleasure should be the same as that of the Trojan elders was toward Helen, and we should repeat on every occasion the words they addressed to her. For if we dismiss pleasure as they dismissed her, we shall make fewer mistakes.

In summary, then, it is by acting in this way that we shall best be able to hit the median. But this is no doubt difficult, especially when particular cases are concerned. For it is not easy to determine in what manner, with what person, on what occasion, and for how long a time one ought to be angry. There are times when we praise those who are deficient in anger and call them gentle, and other times when we praise violently angry persons and call them manly. However, we do not blame a man for slightly deviating from the course of goodness, whether he strays toward excess or toward deficiency, but we do blame him if his deviation is great and cannot pass unnoticed. It is not easy to determine by a formula at what point and for how great a divergence a man deserves blame; but this difficulty is, after all, true of all objects of sense perception: determinations of this kind depend upon particular circumstances, and the decision rests with our [moral] sense.

This much, at any rate, is clear: that the median characteristic is in all fields the one that deserves praise, and that it is sometimes necessary to incline toward the excess and sometimes toward the deficiency. For it is in this way that we will most easily hit upon the median, which is the point of excellence.

* * *

BOOK IV

* * *

3. High-Mindedness, Pettiness, and Vanity: High-mindedness, as its very name 1123a
suggests, seems to be concerned with great and lofty matters. Let us take the nature of these matters as the first point of our discussion. It makes no difference whether we 1123b
investigate the characteristic or the man who is characterized by it. A man is regarded as high-minded when he thinks he deserves great things and actually deserves them; one who thinks he deserves them but does not is a fool, and no man, insofar as he is virtuous, is either foolish or senseless. This then is the description of a high-minded man. A person who deserves little and thinks he deserves little is not high-minded, but is a man who knows his limitations. For high-mindedness implies greatness, just as beauty implies stature in body: small people may have charm and proportion but not beauty. A man who thinks he deserves great things but does not deserve them is vain, though not everybody who overestimates himself is vain. One who underestimates himself is small-minded regardless of whether his actual worth is great or moderate, or whether it is small and he thinks that it is smaller still. A man of great deserts, it would seem, is most [liable to be small-minded,] for what would he do if his deserts were not as great as they are? Thus, measured by the standard of greatness, the high-minded man is an

extreme, but by the standard of what is right he occupies the median; for his claims correspond to his deserts, whereas the others exceed or fall short.

Accordingly, if a high-minded man thinks he deserves and actually does deserve great things, especially the greatest, there is one matter that will be his major concern. "Deserts" is a relative term that refers to external goods; and as the greatest external good, we may posit that which we pay as a tribute to the gods, for which eminent people strive most, and which is the prize for the noblest achievements. Honor fits that description, for it is the greatest of external goods. Consequently, it is in matters of honor and dishonor that a high-minded man has the right attitude. It is an obvious fact, and need not be argued, that the high-minded are concerned with honor. For they regard themselves as worthy of honor above all else, but of an honor that they deserve. A small-minded man falls short both in view of his own deserts and in relation to the claims of a high-minded person, while a vain man exceeds his own deserts but does not exceed the high-minded.

This means that the high-minded man, inasmuch as he deserves what is greatest, is the best. For the deserts of the better man are always greater, and those of the best man the greatest. It follows that a truly high-minded man must be good. And what is great in each virtue would seem to be the mark of a high-minded person. It would be quite out of character for him to run away in battle with arms swinging or to do wrong to anyone. For what motive does he have to act basely, he to whom nothing is great? If we were to examine [his qualities] one by one, we should see the utter absurdity of thinking of a high-minded man as being anything but good. If he were base, he would not even deserve honor, for honor is the prize of excellence and virtue, and it is reserved
1124a as a tribute to the good. High-mindedness thus is the crown, as it were, of the virtues: it magnifies them and it cannot exist without them. Therefore, it is hard to be truly high-minded and, in fact, impossible without goodness and nobility.

A high-minded man is, then, primarily concerned with honor and dishonor. From great honors and those that good men confer upon him he will derive a moderate amount of pleasure, convinced that he is only getting what is properly his or even less. For no honor can be worthy of perfect virtue. Yet he will accept it, because they have no greater tribute to pay to him. But he will utterly despise honors conferred by ordinary people and on trivial grounds, for that is not what he deserves. Similarly, he will despise dishonor, for no dishonor can be justified in his case. A high-minded man, as we have stated, is concerned primarily with honors. But he will of course also have a moderate attitude toward wealth, power, and every manner of good or bad luck that may befall him. He will not be overjoyed when his luck is good, nor will bad luck be very painful to him. For even toward honor, his attitude is that it is not of the greatest moment. Power and wealth are desirable for the honor they bring; at any rate, those who have them wish to gain honor through them. But a person who attaches little importance even to honor will also attach little importance to power and wealth. As a result, he is regarded as haughty.

Gifts of fortune, it is believed, also contribute to high-mindedness. Men of noble birth, of power, or of wealth are regarded as worthy of honor, since they occupy a superior position, and whatever is superior in goodness is held in greater honor. That is why the gifts of fortune make men more high-minded, for they are honored by some people [for having them]. But in truth it is the good man alone that ought to be honored, though a man who has both excellence and good fortune is regarded as still more worthy of honor. Whoever possesses the goods of fortune without possessing excellence or virtue is not justified in claiming great deserts for himself, nor is it correct to call him high-minded, for neither is possible without perfect virtue. Their good fortune notwithstanding, such people become haughty and arrogant, for without virtue it is not easy to bear the gifts of fortune gracefully. Unable to bear them and considering themselves superior, they look down upon others, while they themselves do whatever they please. They imitate the high-minded man wherever they can, but they are not really like him. Thus, they look down upon others, but they do not act in conformity with excellence. A high-minded person is justified in looking down upon others for he has the right opinion of them, but the common run of people do so without rhyme or reason.

A high-minded man does not take small risks and, since there are only a few things which he honors, he is not even fond of risks. But he will face great risks, and in the midst of them he will not spare his life, aware that life at any cost is not worth having. He is the kind of man who will do good, but who is ashamed to accept a good turn, because the former marks a man as superior, the latter as inferior. Moreover, he will requite good with a greater good, for in this way he will not only repay the original benefactor but put him in his debt at the same time by making him the recipient of an added benefit. The high-minded also seem to remember the good turns they have done, but not those they have received. For the recipient is inferior to the benefactor, whereas a high-minded man wishes to be superior. They listen with pleasure to what good they have done, but with displeasure to what good they have received. That is apparently why Thetis does not mention the good turns she had done to Zeus,* and why the Spartans did not mention theirs to the Athenians, but only the good they had received. It is, further, typical of a high-minded man not to ask for any favors, or only reluctantly, but to offer aid readily. He will show his stature in his relations with men of eminence and fortune, but will be unassuming toward those of moderate means. For to be superior to the former is difficult and dignified, but superiority over the latter is easy. Furthermore, there is nothing ignoble in asserting one's dignity among the great, but to do so among the lower classes is just as crude as to assert one's strength against an invalid. He will not go in for pursuits that the common people value, nor for those in which the first place belongs to others. He is slow to act and procrastinates, except when some great honor or achievement is at stake. His actions are few, but they are great and distinguished. He must be open in hate and open in love, for to hide one's feelings and to care more for the opinion of others than for truth is a sign of timidity. He speaks and acts openly: since he looks down upon others his speech is free and truthful, except when he deliberately depreciates himself in addressing the common run of people. He cannot adjust his life to another, except a friend, for to do so is slavish. That is, [by the way,] why all flatterers are servile and people from the lower classes are flatterers. He is not given to admiration, for nothing is great to him. He bears no grudges, for it is not typical of a high-minded man to have a long memory, especially for wrongs, but rather to overlook them. He is not a gossip, for he will talk neither about himself nor about others, since he is not interested in hearing himself praised or others run down. Nor again is he given to praise; and for the same reason he does not speak evil of others, not even of his enemies, except to scorn them. When he encounters misfortunes that are unavoidable or insignificant, he will not lament and ask for help. That kind of attitude belongs to someone who takes such matters seriously. He is a person who will rather possess beautiful and profitless objects than objects which are profitable and useful, for they mark him more as self-sufficient.

*The reference is to Thetis' intercession with Zeus to help avenge the wrong done her son Achilles by Agamemnon.

Alexander the Great, detail from ancient Roman mosaic of the Battle of Issus. Aristotle tutored the young Alexander and later benefitted from Alexander's patronage. (*Corbis/Bettmann*)

Further, we think of a slow gait as characteristic of a high-minded man, a deep voice, and a deliberate way of speaking. For a man who takes few things seriously is unlikely to be in a hurry, and a person who regards nothing as great is not one to be excitable. But a shrill voice and a swift gait are due to hurry and excitement.

Such, then, is the high-minded man. A man who falls short is small-minded, and one who exceeds is vain. Now here, too, these people are not considered to be bad—for they are not evildoers—but only mistaken. For a small-minded man deprives himself of the good he deserves. What seems to be bad about him is due to the fact that he does not think he deserves good things and that he does not know himself; if he did, he would desire what he deserves, especially since it is good. It is not that such people are regarded as foolish, but rather [that they are looked upon] as retiring. However, a reputation of this sort seems to make them even worse. For while any given kind of man strives to get what he deserves, these people keep aloof even from noble actions and pursuits and from external goods as well, because they consider themselves undeserving.

Vain people, on the other hand, are fools and do not know themselves, and they show it openly. They take in hand honorable enterprises of which they are not worthy, and then they are found out. They deck themselves out with clothes and showy gear and that sort of thing, and wish to publicize what fortune has given them. They talk about their good fortune in the belief that that will bring them honor.

Small-mindedness is more opposed to high-mindedness than vanity is, for it occurs more frequently and is worse. Thus, as we have said, high-mindedness is concerned with high honors.

* * *

BOOK VI

1. Moral and Intellectual Excellence; the Psychological Foundations of Intellectual Excellence: We stated earlier that we must choose the median, and not excess or deficiency, and that the median is what right reason dictates. Let us now analyze this second point.

In all the characteristics we have discussed, as in all others, there is some target on which a rational man keeps his eye as he bends and relaxes his efforts to attain it. There is also a standard that determines the several means which, as we claim, lie between excess and deficiency, and which are fixed by right reason. But this statement, true though it is, lacks clarity. In all other fields of endeavor in which scientific knowledge is possible, it is indeed true to say that we must exert ourselves or relax neither too much nor too little, but to an intermediate extent and as right reason demands. But if this is the only thing a person knows, he will be none the wiser: he will, for example, not know what kind of medicines to apply to his body, if he is merely told to apply whatever medical science prescribes and in a manner in which a medical expert applies them. Accordingly, in discussing the characteristics of the soul, too, it is not enough that the statement we have made be true. We must also have a definition of what right reason is and what standard determines it.

In analyzing the virtues of the soul we said that some are virtues of character and others excellence of thought or understanding. We have now discussed the moral virtues, [i.e., the virtues of character]. In what follows, we will deal with the others, [i.e., the intellectual virtues,] beginning with some prefatory remarks about the soul. We said in our earlier discussion that the soul consists of two parts, one rational and one irrational. We must now make a similar distinction in regard to the rational part. Let it be assumed that there are two rational elements: with one of these we apprehend the realities whose fundamental principles do not admit of being other than they are, and with the other we apprehend things which do admit of being other. For if we grant that knowledge presupposes a certain likeness and kinship of subject and object, there will be a generically different part of the soul naturally corresponding to each of two different kinds of object. Let us call one the scientific and the other the calculative element. Deliberating and calculating are the same thing, and no one deliberates about objects that cannot be other than they are. This means that the calculative constitutes one element of the rational part of the soul. Accordingly, we must now take up the question which is the best characteristic of each element, since that constitutes the excellence or virtue of each. But the virtue of a thing is relative to its proper function.

2. The Two Kinds of Intellectual Excellence and Their Objects: Now, there are three elements in the soul which control action and truth: sense perception, intelligence, and desire. Of these sense perception does not initiate any action. We can see this from the fact that animals have sense perception but have no share in action.* What affirmation and negation are in the realm of thought, pursuit and avoidance are in the realm of desire. Therefore, since moral virtue is a characteristic involving choice, and since choice is a deliberate desire, it follows that, if the choice is to be good, the reasoning must be true and the desire correct; that is, reasoning must affirm what desire pursues. This then is the kind of thought and the kind of truth that is practical and concerned with action. On the other hand, in the kind of thought involved in theoretical knowledge and not in action or production, the good and the bad state are, respectively, truth and falsehood; in fact, the attainment of truth is the function of the intellectual faculty as a whole. But in intellectual activity concerned with action, the good state is truth in harmony with correct desire.

Choice is the starting point of action: it is the source of motion but not the end for the sake of which we act, i.e., the final cause. The starting point of choice, however, is desire and reasoning directed toward some end. That is why there cannot be choice either without intelligence and thought or without some moral characteristic; for good and bad action in human conduct are not possible without thought and character. Now thought alone moves nothing; only thought which is directed to some end and concerned with action can do so. And it is this kind of thought also which initiates production. For whoever produces something produces it for an end. The product he makes is not an end in an unqualified sense, but an end only in a particular relation and of a particular operation. Only the goal of action is an end in the unqualified sense: for the good life is an end, and desire is directed toward this. Therefore, choice is either intelligence motivated by desire or desire operating through thought, and it is as a combination of these two that man is a starting point of action.

(No object of choice belongs to the past: no one chooses to have sacked Troy. For deliberation does not refer to the past but only to the future and to what is possible; and it is not possible that what is past should not have happened. Therefore, Agathon is right when he says:

> One thing alone is denied even to god:
> to make undone the deeds which have been done.**)

As we have seen, truth is the function of both intellectual parts [of the soul]. Therefore, those characteristics which permit each part to be as truthful as possible will be the virtues of the two parts.

3. The Qualities by Which Truth Is Attained: (a) Pure Science or Knowledge: So let us make a fresh beginning and discuss these characteristics once again. Let us take for granted that the faculties by which the soul expresses truth by way of affirmation or denial are five in number: art, science, practical wisdom, theoretical wisdom, and intelligence. Conviction and opinion do not belong here, for they may be false.

What pure science or scientific knowledge is—in the precise sense of the word and not in any of its wider uses based on mere similarity—will become clear in the following. We are all convinced that what we *know* scientifically cannot be otherwise than it is; but of facts which can possibly be other than they are we do not know whether

*Throughout the *Ethics,* Aristotle uses *praxis* ("action") as equivalent to "moral action," "conduct," and assumes animals are not capable of this.

**Agathon was a tragic poet who flourished in the last quarter of the fifth century B.C. Plato's *Symposium* is set in his house.

or not they continue to be true when removed from our observation. Therefore, an object of scientific knowledge exists of necessity, and is, consequently, eternal. For everything that exists of necessity in an unqualified sense is eternal, and what is eternal is ungenerated and imperishable [and hence cannot be otherwise].

Moreover, all scientific knowledge is held to be teachable, and what is scientifically knowable is capable of being learned. All teaching is based on what is already known, as we have stated in the *Analytics;* some teaching proceeds by induction and some by syllogism. Now, induction is the starting point [for knowledge] of the universal as well [as the particular], while syllogism proceeds *from* universals. Consequently, there are starting points or principles from which a syllogism proceeds and which are themselves not arrived at by a syllogism. It is, therefore, induction that attains them. Accordingly, scientific knowledge is a capacity for demonstration and has, in addition, all the other qualities which we have specified in the *Analytics.* When a man believes something in the way there specified, and when the starting points or principles on which his beliefs rest are known to him, then he has scientific knowledge; unless he knows the starting points or principles better than the conclusion, he will have scientific knowledge only incidentally. So much for our definition of scientific knowledge or pure science.

4. (b) Art or Applied Science: Things which admit of being other than they are 1140a
include both things made and things done. Production is different from action—for that point we can rely even on our less technical discussions. Hence, the characteristic of acting rationally is different from the characteristic of producing rationally. It also follows that one does not include the other, for action is not production nor production action. Now, building is an art or applied science, and it is essentially a characteristic or trained ability of rationally producing. In fact, there is no art that is not a characteristic or trained ability of rationally producing, nor is there a characteristic of rationally producing that is not an art. It follows that art is identical with the characteristic of producing under the guidance of true reason. All art is concerned with the realm of coming-to-be, i.e., with contriving and studying how something which is capable both of being and of not being may come into existence, a thing whose starting point or source is in the producer and not in the thing produced. For art is concerned neither with things which exist or come into being by necessity, nor with things produced by nature: these have their source of motion within themselves.

Since production and action are different, it follows that art deals with production and not with action. In a certain sense, fortune and art are concerned with the same things, as Agathon says: "Fortune loves art and art fortune." So, as we have said, art is a characteristic of producing under the guidance of true reason, and lack of art, on the contrary, is a characteristic of producing under the guidance of false reason; and both of them deal with what admits of being other than it is.

5. (c) Practical Wisdom: We may approach the subject of practical wisdom by studying the persons to whom we attribute it. Now, the capacity of deliberating well about what is good and advantageous for oneself is regarded as typical of a man of practical wisdom—not deliberating well about what is good and advantageous in a partial sense, for example, what contributes to health or strength, but what sort of thing contributes to the good life in general. This is shown by the fact that we speak of men as having practical wisdom in a particular respect, i.e., not in an unqualified sense, when they calculate well with respect to some worthwhile end, one that cannot be attained by an applied science or art. It follows that, in general, a man of practical wisdom is he who has the ability to deliberate.

Now no one deliberates about things that cannot be other than they are or about actions that he cannot possibly perform. Since, as we saw, pure science involves demonstration, while things whose starting points or first causes can be other than they are do not admit of demonstration—for such things too and not merely their first causes can all be other than they are—and since it is impossible to deliberate about what exists by necessity, we may conclude that practical wisdom is neither a pure science nor an art. It is not a pure science, because matters of action admit of being other than they are, and it is not an applied science or art, because action and production are generically different.

What remains, then, is that it is a truthful characteristic of acting rationally in matters good and bad for man. For production has an end other than itself, but action does not: good action is itself an end. That is why we think that Pericles* and men like him have practical wisdom. They have the capacity of seeing what is good for themselves and for mankind, and these are, we believe, the qualities of men capable of managing households and states.

This also explains why we call "self-control" *sophrosyne:* it "preserves" our "practical wisdom." What it preserves is the kind of conviction we have described. For the pleasant and the painful do not destroy and pervert every conviction we hold—not, for example, our conviction that a triangle has or does not have the sum of its angles equal to two right angles—but only the convictions we hold concerning how we should act. In matters of action, the principles or initiating motives are the ends at which our actions are aimed. But as soon as a man becomes corrupted by pleasure or pain, the goal no longer appears to him as a motivating principle: he no longer sees that he should choose and act in every case for the sake of and because of this end. For vice tends to destroy the principle or initiating motive of action.

Necessarily, then, practical wisdom is a truthful rational characteristic of acting in matters involving what is good for man. Furthermore, whereas there exists such a thing as excellence in art, it does not exist in practical wisdom.** Also, in art a man who makes a mistake voluntarily is preferable to one who makes it involuntarily; but in practical wisdom, as in every virtue or excellence, such a man is less desirable. Thus it is clear that practical wisdom is an excellence or virtue and not an art. Since there are two parts of the soul that contain a rational element, it must be the virtue of one of them, namely of the part that forms opinions.*** For opinion as well as practical wisdom deals with things that can be other than they are. However, it is not merely a rational characteristic or trained ability. An indication that it is something more may be seen in the fact that a trained ability of that kind can be forgotten, whereas practical wisdom cannot.

6. (d) Intelligence: Since pure science or scientific knowledge is a basic conviction concerning universal and necessary truths, and since everything demonstrable and all pure science begins from fundamental principles (for science proceeds rationally), the fundamental principle or starting point for scientific knowledge cannot itself be the

*The name of Pericles (ca. 495–429 B.C.) is almost synonymous with the Athenian democracy.

**Because practical wisdom is itself a complete virtue or excellence, while the excellence of art depends on the goodness or badness of its product.

***"Opinion" here corresponds to the "calculative element" in Chapter 1: both are defined by reference to contingent facts, those which may be otherwise than they are.

object either of science, of art, or of practical wisdom. For what is known scientifically is demonstrable, whereas art and practical wisdom are concerned with things that can be other than they are. Nor are these fundamental principles the objects of theoretical wisdom: for it is the task of a man of theoretical wisdom to have a demonstration for 1141[a] certain truths.* Now, if scientific knowledge, practical wisdom, theoretical wisdom, and intelligence are the faculties by which we attain truth and by which we are never deceived both in matters which can and in those matters which cannot be other than they are; and if three of these—I am referring to practical wisdom, scientific knowledge, and theoretical wisdom—cannot be the faculty in question, we are left with the conclusion that it is intelligence that apprehends fundamental principles.

7. *(e) Theoretical Wisdom:* We attribute "wisdom" in the arts to the most precise and perfect masters of their skills: we attribute it to Phidias as a sculptor in marble and to Polycletus as a sculptor in bronze. In this sense we signify by "wisdom" nothing but excellence of art or craftsmanship. However, we regard some men as being wise in general, not in any partial sense or in some other particular respect, as Homer says in the *Margites:*

> The gods let him not be a digger or a ploughman nor wise at anything.

It is, therefore, clear, that wisdom must be the most precise and perfect form of knowledge. Consequently, a wise man must not only know what follows from fundamental principles, but he must also have true knowledge of the fundamental principles themselves. Accordingly, theoretical wisdom must comprise both intelligence and scientific knowledge. It is science in its consummation, as it were, the science of the things that are valued most highly.

For it would be strange to regard politics or practical wisdom as the highest kind of knowledge, when in fact man is not the best thing in the universe. Surely, if "healthy" and "good" mean one thing for men and another for fishes, whereas "white" and "straight" always mean the same, "wise" must mean the same for everyone, but "practically wise" will be different. For each particular being ascribes practical wisdom in matters relating to itself to that thing which observes its interests well, and it will entrust itself to that thing. That is the reason why people attribute practical wisdom even to some animals—to all those which display a capacity of forethought in matters relating to their own life.

It is also evident that theoretical wisdom is not the same as politics. If we are to call "theoretical wisdom" the knowledge of what is helpful to us, there will be many kinds of wisdom. There is no single science that deals with what is good for all living things any more than there is a single art of medicine dealing with everything that is, but a different science deals with each particular good. The argument that man is the best of living things makes no difference. There are other things whose nature is much more 1141[b] divine than man's: to take the most visible example only, the constituent parts of the universe.

Our discussion has shown that theoretical wisdom comprises both scientific knowledge and [apprehension by the] intelligence of things which by their nature are valued most highly. That is why it is said that men like Anaxagoras and Thales have

*In other words, the undemonstrable first or fundamental principles cannot be the proper and complete object of theoretical wisdom: as the next chapter shows, they are included within its sphere.

theoretical but not practical wisdom: when we see that they do not know what is advantageous to them, we admit that they know extraordinary, wonderful, difficult, and superhuman things, but call their knowledge useless because the good they are seeking is not human.

Practical wisdom, on the other hand, is concerned with human affairs and with matters about which deliberation is possible. As we have said, the most characteristic function of a man of practical wisdom is to deliberate well: no one deliberates about things that cannot be other than they are, nor about things that are not directed to some end, an end that is a good attainable by action. In an unqualified sense, that man is good at deliberating who, by reasoning, can aim at and hit the best thing attainable to man by action.

Nor does practical wisdom deal only with universals. It must also be familiar with particulars, since it is concerned with action and action has to do with particulars. This explains why some men who have no scientific knowledge are more adept in practical matters, especially if they have experience, than those who do have scientific knowledge. For if a person were to know that light meat is easily digested, and hence wholesome, but did not know what sort of meat is light, he will not produce health, whereas someone who knows that poultry is light and wholesome is more likely to produce health.*

Now, practical wisdom is concerned with action. That means that a person should have both [knowledge of universals and knowledge of particulars] or knowledge of particulars rather [than knowledge of universals]. But here, too, it seems, there is a supreme and comprehensive science involved, [i.e., politics].

8. Practical Wisdom and Politics: Political wisdom and practical wisdom are both the same characteristic, but their essential aspect is not the same. There are two kinds of wisdom concerning the state: the one, which acts as practical wisdom supreme and comprehensive, is the art of legislation; the other, which is practical wisdom as dealing with particular facts, bears the name which, [in everyday speech,] is common to both kinds, politics, and it is concerned with action and deliberation. For a decree, [unlike a law, which lays down general principles,] is a matter for action, inasmuch as it is the last step [in the deliberative process]. That is why only those who make decrees are said to engage in politics, for they alone, like workmen, "do" things.**

It is also commonly held that practical wisdom is primarily concerned with one's own person, i.e., with the individual, and it is this kind that bears the name "practical wisdom," which properly belongs to others as well. The other kinds are called household management, legislation, and politics, the last of which is subdivided into deliberative and judicial.***

Now, knowing what is good for oneself is, to be sure, one kind of knowledge; but
1142a it is very different from the other kinds. A man who knows and concerns himself with

*The point here is that, in practical matters, a man who knows by experience that poultry is wholesome is likely to be more successful than a man who only has the scientific knowledge that light meat is digestible and therefore wholesome, without knowing the particular fact that poultry is light meat.

**I.e., lawgivers and other men who are concerned with political wisdom in the supreme and comprehensive sense are not generally regarded as being engaged in politics. The analogy to workmen represents of course not Aristotle's view, which vigorously distinguishes action from production, but rather reflects a widespread attitude toward politics.

***In Athens, "deliberative" politics referred to matters debated in the Council and the Popular Assembly, and "judicial" politics to matters argued in the lawcourts.

his own interests is regarded as a man of practical wisdom, while men whose concern is politics are looked upon as busybodies. Euripides' words are in this vein:

> How can I be called "wise," who might have filled a common soldier's place, free from all care, sharing an equal lot . . . ? For those who reach too high and are too active. . . .

For people seek their own good and think that this is what they should do. This opinion has given rise to the view that it is such men who have practical wisdom. And yet, surely one's own good cannot exist without household management nor without a political system. Moreover, the problem of how to manage one's own affairs properly needs clarification and remains to be examined.

An indication that what we have said is correct is the following common observation. While young men do indeed become good geometricians and mathematicians and attain theoretical wisdom in such matters, they apparently do not attain practical wisdom. The reason is that practical wisdom is concerned with particulars as well [as with universals], and knowledge of particulars comes from experience. But a young man has no experience, for experience is the product of a long time. In fact, one might also raise the question why it is that a boy may become a mathematician but not a philosopher or a natural scientist. The answer may be that the objects of mathematics are the result of abstraction, whereas the fundamental principles of philosophy and natural science come from experience. Young men can assert philosophical and scientific principles but can have no genuine convictions about them, whereas there is no obscurity about the essential definitions in mathematics.

Moreover, in our deliberations error is possible as regards either the universal principle or the particular fact: we may be unaware either that all heavy water is bad, or that the particular water we are faced with is heavy.

That practical wisdom is not scientific knowledge is [therefore] evident. As we stated, it is concerned with ultimate particulars, since the actions to be performed are ultimate particulars. This means that it is at the opposite pole from intelligence. For the intelligence grasps limiting terms and definitions that cannot be attained by reasoning, while practical wisdom has as its object the ultimate particular fact, of which there is perception but no scientific knowledge. This perception is not the kind with which [each of our five senses apprehends] its proper object, but the kind with which we perceive that in mathematics the triangle is the ultimate figure. For in this direction, too, we shall have to reach a stop. But this [type of mathematical cognition] is more truly perception than practical wisdom, and it is different in kind from the other [type of perception which deals with the objects proper to the various senses].

9. Practical Wisdom and Excellence in Deliberation: There is a difference between investigating and deliberating: to deliberate is to investigate a particular kind of object. We must also try to grasp what excellence in deliberation is: whether it is some sort of scientific knowledge, opinion, shrewd guessing, or something generically different from any of these.

Now, scientific knowledge it is certainly not:* people do not investigate matters they already know. But good deliberation is a kind of deliberation, and when a person 1142b

*Here, as in most of the following paragraph, Aristotle seems to be taking issue with Plato, who had identified the two, e.g., in *Republic,* Book IV, 428b.

deliberates he is engaged in investigating and calculating [things not yet decided]. Nor yet is it shrewd guessing. For shrewd guessing involves no reasoning and proceeds quickly, whereas deliberation takes a long time. As the saying goes, the action which follows deliberation should be quick, but deliberation itself should be slow. Furthermore, quickness of mind is not the same as excellence in deliberation: quickness of mind is a kind of shrewd guessing. Nor again is excellence in deliberation any form of opinion at all. But since a person who deliberates badly makes mistakes, while he who deliberates well deliberates correctly, it clearly follows that excellence in deliberation is some kind of correctness. But it is correctness neither of scientific knowledge nor of opinion. There cannot be correctness of scientific knowledge any more than there can be error of scientific knowledge; and correctness of opinion is truth. Moreover, anything that is an object of opinion is already fixed and determined, while deliberation deals with objects which remain to be determined. Still, excellence in deliberation does involve reasoning, and we are, consequently, left with the alternative that it is correctness of a process of thought; for thinking is not yet an affirmation. For while opinion is no longer a process of investigation but has reached the point of affirmation, a person who deliberates, whether he does so well or badly, is still engaged in investigating and calculating something [not yet determined].

Good deliberation is a kind of correctness of deliberation. We must, therefore, first investigate what deliberation is and with what objects it is concerned. Since the term "correctness" is used in several different senses, it is clear that not every kind of correctness in deliberation [is excellence in deliberation]. For (1) a morally weak or a bad man will, as a result of calculation, attain the goal which he has proposed to himself as the right goal to attain. He will, therefore, have deliberated correctly, but what he will get out of it will be a very bad thing. But the result of good deliberation is generally regarded as a good thing. It is this kind of correctness of deliberation which is good deliberation, a correctness that attains what is good.

But (2) it is also possible to attain something good by a false syllogism, i.e., to arrive at the right action, but to arrive at it by the wrong means when the middle term is false. Accordingly, this process, which makes us attain the right goal but not by the right means, is still not good deliberation.

Moreover, (3) it is possible that one man attains his goal by deliberating for a long time, while another does so quickly. Now, long deliberation, too, is not as such good deliberation: excellence in deliberation is correctness in assessing what is beneficial, i.e., correctness in assessing the goal, the manner, and the time.

Again, (4) it is possible for a person to have deliberated well either in general, in an unqualified sense, or in relation to some particular end. Good deliberation in the unqualified sense of course brings success in relation to what is, in an unqualified sense, the end, [i.e., in relation to the good life]. Excellence in deliberation as directed toward some particular end, however, brings success in the attainment of some particular end.

Thus we may conclude that, since it is a mark of men of practical wisdom to have deliberated well, excellence in deliberation will be correctness in assessing what is conducive to the end, concerning which practical wisdom gives a true conviction.

10. Practical Wisdom and Understanding: Understanding, i.e., excellence in under-
1143a standing, the quality which makes us call certain people "men of understanding" and "men of good understanding," is in general not identical with scientific knowledge or with opinion. For [if it were opinion,] everyone would be a man of understanding, [since everyone forms opinions]. Nor is it one of the particular branches of science, in the sense in which

medicine, for example, is the science of matters pertaining to health, or geometry the science which deals with magnitudes. For understanding is concerned neither with eternal and unchangeable truth nor with anything and everything that comes into being [and passes away again]. It deals with matters concerning which doubt and deliberation are possible. Accordingly, though its sphere is the same as that of practical wisdom, understanding and practical wisdom are not the same. Practical wisdom issues commands: its end is to tell us what we ought to do and what we ought not to do. Understanding, on the other hand, only passes judgment. [There is no difference between understanding and excellence in understanding:] for excellence in understanding is the same as understanding, and men of understanding are men of good understanding.

Thus understanding is neither possession nor acquisition of practical wisdom. Just as learning is called "understanding" when a man makes use of his faculty of knowledge, so [we speak of "understanding"] when it implies the use of one's faculty of opinion in judging statements made by another person about matters which belong to the realm of practical wisdom—and in judging such statements rightly, for *good* understanding means that the judgment is right. It is from this act of learning or understanding [what someone else says] that the term "understanding" as predicated of "men of good understanding" is derived. For we frequently use the words "learning" and "understanding" synonymously.

11. Practical Wisdom and Good Sense: As for what is called "good sense," the quality which makes us say of a person that he has the sense to forgive others, [i.e., sympathetic understanding], and that he has good sense, this is a correct judgment of what is fair or equitable. This is indicated by the fact that we attribute to an equitable man especially sympathetic understanding and that we say that it is fair, in certain cases, to have the sense to forgive. Sympathetic understanding is a correct critical sense or judgment of what is fair; and a correct judgment is a true one.

All these characteristics, as one would expect, tend toward the same goal. We attribute good sense, understanding, practical wisdom, and intelligence to the same persons, and in saying that they have good sense, we imply at the same time that they have a mature intelligence and that they are men of practical wisdom and understanding. For what these capacities [have in common is that they are] all concerned with ultimate particular facts. To say that a person has good judgment in matters of practical wisdom implies that he is understanding and has good sense or that he has sympathetic understanding; for equitable acts are common to all good men in their relation with someone else. Now, all matters of action are in the sphere of the particulars and ultimates. Not only must a man of practical wisdom take cognizance of particulars, but understanding and good sense, too, deal with matters of action, and matters of action are ultimates. As for intelligence, it deals with ultimates at both ends of the scale. It is intelligence, not reasoning, that has as its objects primary terms and definitions as well as ultimate particulars. Intelligence grasps, on the one hand, the unchangeable, primary terms and concepts 1143b for demonstrations; on the other hand, in questions of action, it grasps the ultimate, contingent fact and the minor premise. For it is particular facts that form the starting points or principles for [our knowledge of] the goal of action: universals arise out of particulars. Hence one must have perception of particular facts, and this perception is intelligence.* Intelligence is, therefore, both starting point and end; for demonstrations start with ultimate terms and have ultimate facts as their objects.

*I.e., we can attain the end—happiness—only by discovering the general rules of moral conduct, and these, in turn, rest on the immediate apprehension by intelligence of particular moral facts.

That is why these characteristics are regarded as natural endowments and, although no one is provided with theoretical wisdom by nature, we do think that men have good sense, understanding, and intelligence by nature. An indication of this is that we think of these characteristics as depending on different stages of life, and that at a given stage of life a person acquires intelligence and good sense: the implication is that [human] nature is the cause. Therefore, we ought to pay as much attention to the sayings and opinions, undemonstrated though they are, of wise and experienced older men as we do to demonstrated truths. For experience has given such men an eye with which they can see correctly.*

We have now completed our discussion of what practical and theoretical wisdom are; we have described the sphere in which each operates, and we have shown that each is the excellence of a different part of the soul.

12. The Use of Theoretical and Practical Wisdom: One might raise some questions about the usefulness of these two virtues. Theoretical wisdom, [as we have described it,] will study none of the things that make a man happy, for it is not at all concerned with the sphere of coming-to-be [but only with unchanging realities]. Practical wisdom, on the other hand, *is* concerned with this sphere, but for what purpose do we need it? (1) It is true that practical wisdom deals with what is just, noble, and good for man; and it is doing such things that characterizes a man as good. But our ability to perform such actions is in no way enhanced by knowing them, since the virtues are characteristics, [that is to say, fixed capacities for action, acquired by habit]. The same also applies, after all, to matters of health and well-being (not in the sense of "producing health and well-being" but in the sense of "being healthy and well" as the manifestation of a physical condition or a characteristic): our ability to perform actions [which show that we are healthy and well] is in no way enhanced by a mastery of the science of medicine or of physical training.

(2) But if we are to say that the purpose of practical wisdom is not to *know* what is just, noble, and good, but to *become* just, noble, and good, it would be of no use at all to a man who is already good. Moreover, it is of no use to those who do not have virtue, for it makes no difference whether they have practical wisdom themselves or listen to others who have it. It is quite sufficient to take the same attitude as we take toward health: we want to be healthy, yet we do not study medicine.

(3) In addition, it would seem strange if practical wisdom, though [intrinsically] inferior to theoretical wisdom, should surpass it in authority, because that which produces a thing rules and directs it.

These, then, are the questions we must discuss: so far we have only stated them as problems.

1144a First of all, then, we should insist that both theoretical and practical wisdom are necessarily desirable in themselves, even if neither of them produces anything. For each one of them is the virtue of a different part of the soul.

Secondly, they do in fact produce something: theoretical wisdom produces happiness, not as medicine produces health, but as health itself makes a person healthy. For since theoretical wisdom is one portion of virtue in its entirety, possessing and actualizing it makes a man happy. [For happiness, as we have seen (Book I, 7) consists in the activity of virtue.]

In the third place, a man fulfills his proper function only by way of practical wisdom and moral excellence or virtue: virtue makes us aim at the right target, and

*The "eye given by experience" is of course *nous,* "intelligence."

practical wisdom makes us use the right means. The fourth part of the soul, the nutritive, does not have a virtue [which makes man fulfill his proper function,] since it does not play any role in the decision to act or not to act.

Finally, the argument has to be met that our ability to perform noble and just acts is in no way enhanced by practical wisdom. We have to begin a little further back and take the following as our starting point. It is our contention that people may perform just acts without actually being just men, as in the case of people who do what has been laid down by the laws but do so either involuntarily or through ignorance or for an ulterior motive, and not for the sake of performing just acts. [Such persons are not just men] despite the fact that they act the way they should, and perform all the actions which a morally good man ought to perform. On the other hand, it seems that it is possible for a man to be of such a character that he performs each particular act in such a way as to make him a good man—I mean that his acts are due to choice and are performed for the sake of the acts themselves. Now, it is virtue which makes our choice right. It is not virtue, however, but a different capacity, which determines the steps which, in the nature of the case, must be taken to implement this choice.

We must stop for a moment to make this point clearer. There exists a capacity called "cleverness," which is the power to perform those steps which are conducive to a goal we have set for ourselves and to attain that goal. If the goal is noble, cleverness deserves praise; if the goal is base, cleverness is knavery. That is why men of practical wisdom are often described as "clever" and "knavish." But in fact this capacity [alone] is not practical wisdom, although practical wisdom does not exist without it. Without virtue or excellence, this eye of the soul, [intelligence,] does not acquire the characteristic of practical wisdom: that is what we have just stated and it is obvious. For the syllogisms which express the principles initiating action run: "Since the end, or the highest good, is such-and-such . . ."—whatever it may be; what it really is does not matter for our present argument. But whatever the true end may be, only a good man can judge it correctly. For wickedness distorts and causes us to be completely mistaken about the fundamental principles of action. Hence it is clear that a man cannot have practical wisdom unless he is good.

13. Practical Wisdom and Moral Virtue: Accordingly, we must also re-examine 1144b
virtue or excellence. Virtue offers a close analogy to the relation that exists between practical wisdom and cleverness. Just as these two qualities are not identical but similar, so we find the same relation between natural virtue and virtue in the full sense. It seems that the various kinds of character inhere in all of us, somehow or other, by nature. We tend to be just, capable of self-control, and to show all our other character traits from the time of our birth. Yet we still seek something more, the good in a fuller sense, and the possession of these traits in another way. For it is true that children and beasts are endowed with natural qualities or characteristics, but it is evident that without intelligence these are harmful. This much, to be sure, we do seem to notice: as in the case of a mighty body which, when it moves without vision, comes down with a mighty fall because it cannot see, so it is in the matter under discussion. If a man acts blindly, i.e., using his natural virtue alone, he will fail; but once he acquires intelligence, it makes a great difference in his action. At that point, the natural characteristic will become that virtue in the full sense which it previously resembled.

Consequently, just as there exist two kinds of quality, cleverness and practical wisdom, in that part of us which forms opinions, [i.e., in the calculative element,] so also there are two kinds of quality in the moral part of us, natural virtue and virtue in the full sense. Now virtue in the full sense cannot be attained without practical wisdom.

That is why some people maintain that all the virtues are forms of practical wisdom, and why Socrates' approach to the subject was partly right and partly wrong. He was wrong in believing that all the virtues are forms of wisdom, but right in saying that there is no virtue without wisdom. This is indicated by the fact that all the current definitions of virtue,* after naming the characteristic and its objects, add that it is a characteristic "guided by right reason." Now right reason is that which is determined by practical wisdom. So we see that these thinkers all have some inkling that virtue is a characteristic of this kind, namely, a characteristic guided by practical wisdom.

But we must go a little beyond that. Virtue or excellence is not only a characteristic which is guided by right reason, but also a characteristic which is united with right reason; and right reason in moral matters is practical wisdom.** In other words, while Socrates believed that the virtues *are* rational principles—he said that all of them are forms of knowledge—we, on the other hand, think that they are *united with* a rational principle.

Our discussion, then, has made it clear that it is impossible to be good in the full sense of the word without practical wisdom or to be a man of practical wisdom without moral excellence or virtue. Moreover, in this way we can also refute the dialectical argument which might be used to prove that the virtues exist independently of one another. The same individual, it might be argued, is not equally well-endowed by nature for all the virtues, with the result that at a given point he will have acquired one virtue but not yet another. In the case of the natural virtues this may be true, but it cannot happen in the case of those virtues which entitle a man to be called good in an unqualified sense. For in the latter case, as soon as he possesses this single virtue of practical wisdom, he will also possess all the rest.

It is now clear that we should still need practical wisdom, even if it had no bearing on action, because it is the virtue of a part of our soul. But it is also clear that [it does have an important bearing on action, since] no choice will be right without practical wisdom and virtue. For virtue determines the end, and practical wisdom makes us do what is conducive to the end.

Still, practical wisdom has no authority over theoretical wisdom or the better part of our soul*** any more than the art of medicine has authority over health. [Just as medicine does not use health but makes the provisions to secure it, so] practical wisdom does not use theoretical wisdom but makes the provisions to secure it. It issues commands to attain it, but it does not issue them to wisdom itself. To say the contrary would be like asserting that politics governs the gods, because it issues commands about everything in the state, [including public worship].

BOOK VII

1. Moral Strength and Moral Weakness: Their Relation to Virtue and Vice and Current Beliefs about Them: We have to make a fresh start now by pointing out that the qualities of character to be avoided are three in kind: vice, moral weakness, and brutishness. The oppo-

*The reference is to the doctrines of Plato's successors in the Academy.

**I.e., right reason is not only an external standard of action, but it also lives in us and makes us virtuous.

***That is, the scientific or cognitive part in the soul, the rational element which grasps necessary and permanent truths.

sites of two of these are obvious: one is called virtue or excellence and the other moral strength. The most fitting description of the opposite of brutishness would be to say that it is superhuman virtue, a kind of heroic and divine excellence; just as Homer has Priam say about Hector that he was of surpassing excellence:

> for he did not seem like one who was child of a mortal man, but of god.

Therefore, if, as is said, an excess of virtue can change a man into a god, the characteristic opposed to brutishness must evidently be something of this sort. For just as vice and virtue do not exist in brute beasts, no more can they exist in a god. The quality of gods is something more worthy of honor than [human] virtue or excellence, and the quality of a brute is generically different from [human] vice.

If it is rare to find a man who is divine—as the Spartans, for example, customarily use the attribute "divine man" to express an exceptionally high degree of admiration for a person—it is just as rare that a brute is found among men. It does happen, particularly among barbarians, but in some cases disease and physical disability can make a man brutish. "Brutishness" is also used as a term of opprobrium for those who exceed all other men in vice.

But we must defer until later some mention of this kind of disposition, and vice has already been discussed. We must now discuss moral weakness, softness, and effeminacy, also moral strength and tenacity. We will do so on the assumption that each of these two sets of characteristics is neither identical with virtue or with wickedness nor 1145b
generically different from it, but different species respectively of the covering genera, [namely, qualities to be sought and qualities to be avoided].

The proper procedure will be the one we have followed in our treatment of other subjects: we must present phenomena, [that is, the observed facts of moral life and the current beliefs about them,] and, after first stating the problems inherent in these, we must, if possible, demonstrate the validity of all the beliefs about these matters,* and, if not, the validity of most of them or of the most authoritative. For if the difficulties are resolved and current beliefs are left intact, we shall have proved their validity sufficiently.

Now the current beliefs are as follows: (1) Moral strength and tenacity are qualities of great moral value and deserve praise, while moral weakness and softness are base and deserve blame. (2) A man who is morally strong tends to abide by the results of his calculation, and a morally weak man tends to abandon them. (3) A morally weak man does, on the basis of emotion, what he knows to be base, whereas a morally strong man, knowing that certain appetites are base, refuses to follow them and accepts the guidance of reason. (4) Though a self-controlled man is called morally strong and tenacious, some people affirm and others deny [the converse, namely,] that a morally strong person is self-controlled in every respect; likewise, some people call a self-indulgent person "morally weak" and a morally weak person "self-indulgent" without discriminating between the two, while others say that they are different. (5) Sometimes it is said that a man of practical wisdom cannot possibly be morally weak, and sometimes people who have practical wisdom and who are clever are said to be morally weak. (6) Finally, it is said that moral weakness is shown even in anger and in the pursuit of honor and profit. These, then, are the opinions commonly heard.

*"Matters" here translates the Greek word *pathos,* which we usually render as "emotion" or "affect." Here, however, it is used in a loose and general sense to include the whole class of moral phenomena. In other words, Aristotle does not mean to deny here that the qualities enumerated above are lasting characteristics.

2. Problems in the Current Beliefs About Moral Strength and Moral Weakness: The problems we might raise are these. [As to (3):] how can a man be morally weak in his actions, when his basic assumption is correct [as to what he should do]? Some people claim that it is impossible for him to be morally weak if he has knowledge [of what he ought to do]. Socrates, for example, believed that it would be strange if, when a man possesses knowledge, something else should overpower it and drag it about like a slave. In fact, Socrates was completely opposed to the view [that a man may know what is right but do what is wrong], and did not believe that moral weakness exists. He claimed that no one acts contrary to what is best in the conviction [that what he is doing is bad], but through [ignorance of the fact that it is bad].

Now this theory is plainly at variance with the observed facts, and one ought to investigate the emotion [involved in the acts of a morally weak man]: if it comes about through ignorance, what manner of ignorance is it? For evidently a man who is morally weak in his actions does not think [that he ought to act the way he does] before he is in the grip of emotion.

There are some people* who accept only certain points of Socrates' theory, but reject others. They agree that nothing is better or more powerful than *knowledge,* but they do not agree that no one acts contrary to what he *thought* was the better thing to do. Therefore, they say, a [morally weak person] does not have knowledge but opinion when he is overpowered by pleasures.

However, if it really is opinion and not knowledge, if, in other words, the basic conviction which resists [the emotion] is not strong but weak, as it is when people are in doubt, we can forgive a man for not sticking to his opinions in the face of strong appetites. But we do not forgive wickedness or anything else that deserves blame [as moral weakness does. Hence it must be something stronger than opinion which is overpowered]. But does that mean that it is practical wisdom** which resists [the appetite]? This, after all, is the strongest [kind of conviction]. But that would be absurd: for it would mean that the same man will have practical wisdom and be morally weak at the same time, and there is no one who would assert that it is the mark of a man of practical wisdom to perform voluntarily the basest actions. In addition, it has been shown before that a man of practical wisdom is a man of action he is concerned with ultimate particulars that he possesses the other virtues.

Furthermore, [as regards (4)]: if being a morally strong person involves having strong and base appetites, a self-controlled man will not be morally strong nor a morally strong man self-controlled. It is out of character for a self-controlled person to have excessive or base appetites. Yet a morally strong man certainly must have such appetites: for if the appetites are good, the characteristic which prevents him from following them is bad, and that would mean that moral strength is not always morally good. If, on the other hand, our appetites are weak and not base, there is nothing extraordinary in resisting them, nor is it a great achievement if they are base and weak.

Again, [to take (1) and (2),] if moral strength makes a person abide by any and every opinion, it is a bad thing; for example, if it makes him persist in a false opinion. And if moral weakness makes a man abandon any and every opinion, moral weakness will occasionally be morally good, as, for example, in the case of Neoptolemus in Sophocles' *Philoctetes.* Neoptolemus deserves praise when he does not abide by the

*I.e., Plato's followers in the Academy.

**The point is this: if the kind of conviction a morally weak man has is neither knowledge nor a weak conviction, it must be a strong conviction, and practical wisdom is such a conviction.

resolution which Odysseus had persuaded him to adopt, because it gives him pain to tell a lie.

Further, [concerning (1) and (3),] the sophistic argument presents a problem. The Sophists want to refute their opponents by leading them to conclusions which contradict generally accepted facts. Their purpose is to have success bring them the reputation of being clever, and the syllogism which results only becomes a problem or quandary [for their opponents]. For the mind is in chains when, because it is dissatisfied with the conclusion it has reached, it wishes not to stand still, while on the other hand its inability to resolve the argument makes forward movement impossible. Now, they have one argument which leads to the conclusion that folly combined with moral weakness is virtue. This is the way it runs: [if a man is both foolish and morally weak,] he acts contrary to his conviction because of his moral weakness; but [because of his folly,] his conviction is that good things are bad and that he ought not to do them. Therefore, [acting contrary to his conviction,] he will do what is good and not what is bad.

A further problem [arises from (2) and (4)]. A person who, in his actions, pursues, and prefers what is pleasant, convinced or persuaded [that it is good],* would seem to be better than one who acts the same way not on the basis of calculation, but because of moral weakness. For since he may be persuaded to change his mind, he can be cured more easily. To a morally weak man, on the other hand, applies the proverb, "When water chokes you, what can you wash it down with?" For if he had been persuaded to act the way he does, he would have stopped acting that way when persuaded to change 1146b
his mind. But as it is, though persuaded that he ought to do one thing, he nevertheless does another.

Finally, if everything is the province of moral weakness and moral strength, who would be morally weak in the unqualified sense of the word? No one has every form of moral weakness, but we do say of some people that they are morally weak in an unqualified sense.

These are the sort of problems that arise. Some of the conflicting opinions must be removed and others must be left intact. For the solution of a problem is the discovery [of truth].

3. Some Problems Solved: Moral Weakness and Knowledge: Our first step is, then, to examine (1) whether morally weak people act knowingly or not, and, if knowingly, in what sense. Secondly, (2) we must establish the kind of questions with which a morally weak and a morally strong man are concerned. I mean, are they concerned with all pleasure and pain or only with certain distinct kinds of them? Is a morally strong person the same as a tenacious person or are they different? Similar questions must also be asked about all other matters germane to this study.

The starting point of our investigation is the question *(a)* whether the morally strong man and the morally weak man have their distinguishing features in the situations with which they are concerned or in their manner [of reacting to the situation]. What I mean is this: does a morally weak person owe his character to certain situations to [which he reacts], or to the manner [in which he reacts], or to both? Our second question *(b)* is whether or not moral weakness and moral strength are concerned with all [situations and feelings. The answer to both these questions is that] a man who is morally weak in the unqualified sense is not [so described because of his reaction] to every situation, but only to those situations in which also a self-indulgent man may get

*I.e., a self-indulgent person.

involved. Nor is he morally weak because of the mere fact of his relationship to these situations, [namely, that he yields to temptation]. In that case moral weakness would be the same as self-indulgence. Instead, his moral weakness is defined by the manner [in which he yields]. For a self-indulgent person is led on by his own choice, since he believes that he should always pursue the pleasure of the moment. A morally weak man, on the other hand, does not think he should, but pursues it, nonetheless.

(1) The contention that it is true opinion rather than knowledge which a morally weak man violates in his actions has no bearing on our argument. For some people have no doubts when they hold an opinion, and think they have exact knowledge. Accordingly, if we are going to say that the weakness of their belief is the reason why those who hold opinion will be more liable to act against their conviction than those who have knowledge, we shall find that there is no difference between knowledge and opinion. For some people are no less firmly convinced of what they believe than others are of what they know: Heraclitus is a case in point.* *(a)* But the verb "to know" has two meanings: a man is said to "know" both when he does not use the knowledge he has and when he does use it. Accordingly, when a man does wrong it will make a difference whether he is not exercising the knowledge he has, [viz., that it is wrong to do what he is doing,] or whether he is exercising it. In the latter case, we would be baffled, but not if he acted without exercising his knowledge.

Moreover, *(b)* since there are two kinds of premise,** [namely, universal and particular,] it may well happen that a man knows both [major and minor premise of a practical syllogism] and yet acts against his knowledge, because the [minor] premise which he uses is universal rather than particular. [In that case, he cannot apply his knowledge to his action,] for the actions to be performed are particulars. Also, there are two kinds of universal term to be distinguished: one applies to *(i)* the agent, and the other *(ii)* to the thing. For example, when a person knows that dry food is good for all men, [he may also know] *(i)* that he is a man, or *(ii)* that this kind of food is dry. But whether the particular food before him is of this kind is something of which a morally weak man either does not have the knowledge or does not exercise it. So we see that there will be a tremendous difference between these two ways of knowing. We do not regard it as at all strange that a morally weak person "knows" in the latter sense [with one term nonspecific], but it would be surprising if he "knew" in the other sense, [namely with both terms apprehended as concrete particulars].

There is *(c)* another way besides those we have so far described, in which it is possible for men to have knowledge. When a person has knowledge but does not use it, we see that "having" a characteristic has different meanings. There is a sense in which a person both has and does not have knowledge, for example, when he is asleep, mad, or

*The reference is not to any specific utterance of Heraclitus, but to the tone of intense conviction with which he asserted all his doctrines, some of which Aristotle finds patently false, and hence examples of opinion rather than knowledge.

**What is involved in this paragraph is the practical syllogism. However, a refinement is added here, which requires further explanation. A major premise, Aristotle says, may contain two kinds of universal, e.g., the premise that "dry food is good for all men" makes a universal statement about (*i*) men and (*ii*) about dry food. Accordingly, two kinds of syllogism can be developed from this major premise. The first: "dry food is good for all men"; "I am a man"; therefore, "dry food is good for me" is here neglected by Aristotle, because the agent is obviously always aware of being a person. But the second possible syllogism: "dry food is good for all men"; "this kind of food is dry"; therefore, "this kind of food is good for me," leaves the agent only with the general knowledge that, for example, cereals are good, but the individual will not yet know whether this barley is a cereal. "Knowledge" of this sort will obviously not serve to check a healthy appetite faced with an attractive bowl of porridge.

drunk. But this is precisely the condition of people who are in the grip of the emotions. Fits of passion, sexual appetites, and some other such passions actually cause palpable changes in the body, and in some cases even produce madness. Now it is clear that we must attribute to the morally weak a condition similar to that of men who are asleep, mad, or drunk. That the words they utter spring from knowledge [as to what is good] is no evidence to the contrary. People can repeat geometrical demonstrations and verses of Empedocles even when affected by sleep, madness, and drink; and beginning students can reel off the words they have heard, but they do not yet know the subject. The subject must grow to be part of them, and that takes time. We must, therefore, assume that a man who displays moral weakness repeats the formulae [of moral knowledge] in the same way as an actor speaks his lines.

Further, *(d)* we may also look at the cause [of moral weakness] from the viewpoint of the science of human nature, in the following way. [In the practical syllogism,] one of the premises, the universal, is a current belief, while the other involves particular facts which fall within the domain of sense perception. When two premises are combined into one, [i.e., when the universal rule is realized in a particular case,] the soul is thereupon bound to affirm the conclusion, and if the premises involve action, the soul is bound to perform this act at once. For example, if [the premises are]: "Everything sweet ought to be tasted" and "This thing before me is sweet" ("this thing" perceived as an individual particular object), a man who is able [to taste] and is not prevented is bound to act accordingly at once.

Now, suppose that there is within us one universal opinion forbidding us to taste [things of this kind], and another [universal] opinion which tells us that everything sweet is pleasant, and also [a concrete perception], determining our activity, that the particular thing before us is sweet; and suppose further that the appetite [for pleasure] happens to be present. [The result is that] one opinion tells us to avoid that thing, while appetite, capable as it is of setting in motion each part of our body, drives us to it. [This is the case we have been looking for, the defeat of reason in moral weakness.] Thus it turns out that a morally weak man acts under the influence of some kind of reasoning and opinion, an opinion which is not intrinsically but only incidentally opposed to right reason; for it is not opinion but appetite that is opposed to right reason.* And this explains why animals cannot be morally weak: they do not have conceptions of universals, but have only the power to form mental images and memory of particulars.

How is the [temporary] ignorance of a morally weak person dispelled and how does he regain his [active] knowledge [of what is good]? The explanation is the same as it is for drunkenness and sleep, and it is not peculiar to the affect of moral weakness. To get it we have to go to the students of natural science.

The final premise, consisting as it does in an opinion about an object perceived by the senses, determines our action. When in the grip of emotion, a morally weak man either does not have this premise, or he has it not in the sense of knowing it, but in the sense of uttering it as a drunken man may utter verses of Empedocles. [Because he is not in active possession of this premise,] and because the final [concrete] term of his

*The point is this: there is a kind of reasoning involved in the actions of a morally weak person: such a person starts out with the opinion that everything sweet is pleasant, finds a particular sweet thing, and knows that the thing is pleasant. But this person also has right reason, which warns not to taste everything sweet. However, the appetite for pleasure, taking hold of the opinion that everything sweet is pleasant, transforms this opinion into the action of tasting. What is contrary to right reason (i.e., contrary to the knowledge that not everything sweet should be tasted) is not the person's opinion (that sweet things are pleasant) but rather the person's appetite for pleasure.

reasoning is not a universal and does not seem to be an object of scientific knowledge in the same way that a universal is, [for both these reasons] we seem to be led to the conclusion which Socrates sought to establish. Moral weakness does not occur in the presence of knowledge in the strict sense, and it is sensory knowledge, not science, which is dragged about by emotion.

This completes our discussion of the question whether a morally weak person acts with knowledge or without knowledge, and in what sense it is possible for him to act knowingly.

4. More Problems Solved: The Sphere in Which Moral Weakness Operates: (2) The next point we have to discuss is whether it is possible for a man to be morally weak in the unqualified sense, or whether the moral weakness of all who have it is concerned with particular situations. If the former is the case, we shall have to see with what kind of situations he is concerned.

Now, it is clearly in their attitude to pleasures and pains that men are morally strong and tenacious and morally weak and soft. There are two sources of pleasure: some are necessary, and others are desirable in themselves but admit of excess. The necessary kind are those concerned with the body: I mean sources of pleasure such as food and drink and sexual intercourse, in short, the kind of bodily pleasures which we assigned to the sphere of self-indulgence and self-control.* By sources of pleasure which are not necessary but desirable in themselves, I mean, for example, victory, honor, wealth, and similar good and pleasant things. Now, *(a)* those who violate the right reason that they possess by excessive indulgence in the second type of pleasures, are not called morally weak in the unqualified sense, but only with a qualification: we call them "morally weak in regard to material goods," or profit, or honor, or anger, but not "morally weak" pure and simple. They are different from the morally weak in the unqualified sense and share the same name only by analogy, as
1148a in our example of the man called Man, who won an Olympic victory. In his case there is not much difference between the general definition of man and the definition proper to him alone, and yet there was a difference. [That there is similarly a difference between the two senses of morally weak] is shown by the fact that we blame moral weakness—regardless of whether it is moral weakness in the unqualified sense or moral weakness concerning some particular bodily pleasure—not only as an error, but also as a kind of vice. But we do not blame as vicious those [who are morally weak in matters of material goods, profit, ambition, anger, and so forth].

(b) We now come to those bodily enjoyments which, we say, are the sphere of the self-controlled and the self-indulgent. Here a man who pursues the excesses of things pleasant and avoids excesses of things painful (of hunger, thirst, heat, cold, and of anything we feel by touch or taste), and does so not by choice but against his choice and thinking, is called "morally weak" without the addition of "in regard to such-and-such," e.g., "in regard to feelings of anger," but simply morally weak without qualification. The truth of this is proved by the fact that persons who indulge in bodily pleasures are called "soft," but not persons who indulge in feelings of anger and so forth. For this reason, we class the morally weak man with the self-indulgent, and the morally strong with the self-controlled. But we do not include [in the same category] those who indulge in feelings of anger, because moral weakness and self-indulgence are, in a way, concerned with the same pleasures and pains. That is, they are concerned with the same pleasures

*I.e., the sensual pleasures of taste and touch.

and pains but not in the same way. Self-indulgent men pursue the excess by choice, but the morally weak do not exercise choice.

That is why we are probably more justified in calling a person self-indulgent who shows little or no appetite in pursuing an excess of pleasures and in avoiding moderate pains, than a person who is driven by strong appetite [to pursue pleasure and to avoid pain]. For what would the former do, if, in addition, he had the vigorous appetite of youth and felt strong pain at lacking the objects necessary for his pleasure?

Some appetites and desires are generically noble and worth while—[let us remember] our earlier distinction of pleasant things into those which are by nature desirable, the opposite of these, and those which are intermediate between the two—for example, material goods, profit, victory, and honor. Now, people are not blamed for being affected by all these and similar objects of pleasure and by those of the intermediate kind, nor are they blamed for having an appetite or a liking for them; they are blamed only for the manner in which they do so, if they do so to excess. This, by the way, is why [we do not regard as wicked] all those who, contrary to right reason, are overpowered by something that is noble and good by nature, or who pursue it—those, for example, who devote themselves to the pursuit of honor or to their children and parents more than they should. All these things are good, and those who devote themselves to them are praised. And yet even here there is an element of excess, if, like Niobe, one were to fight against the gods [for the sake of one's children], or if one
showed the same excessively foolish devotion to his father as did Satyros, nicknamed "the 1148b
filial."* So we see that there cannot be any wickedness in this area, because, as we stated, each of these things is in itself naturally desirable. But excess in one's attachment to them is base and must be avoided.

Similarly, there cannot be moral weakness in this area [of things naturally desirable]. Moral weakness is not only something to be avoided, but it is also something that deserves blame. Still, because there is a similarity in the affect, people do call it "moral weakness," but they add "in regard to [such-and-such]," in the same way as they speak of a "bad" doctor or a "bad" actor without meaning to imply that the person is bad in the unqualified sense. So just as in the case of the doctor and the actor [we do not speak of "badness" in the unqualified sense], because their badness is not vice but only something similar to vice by analogy, so it is clear that, in the other case, we must understand by "moral weakness" and "moral strength" only that which operates in the same sphere as self-control and self-indulgence. When we use these terms of anger, we do so only in an analogous sense. Therefore, we add a qualification and say "morally weak in regard to anger," just as we say "morally weak in regard to honor or profit."

5. Moral Weakness and Brutishness: (1) Some things are pleasant by nature, partly *(a)* without qualification, and partly *(b)* pleasant for different classes of animals and humans. Then (2) there are things which are not pleasant by nature, but which come to be pleasant *(a)* through physical disability, *(b)* through habit, or *(c)* through an [innate] depravity of nature. We can observe characteristics corresponding to each of the latter group (2), just as [we did in discussing (1), things pleasant by nature]. I mean (2*c*) characteristics of brutishness, for instance, the female who is said to rip open pregnant women and devour the infants; or what is related about some of the savage tribes

*Niobe boasted that, with her six (or in some versions, seven) sons and an equal number of daughters, she was at least equal to the goddess Leto, who only had two children, the twins Apollo and Artemis. Apollo and Artemis thereupon killed all her children, and Niobe was turned into stone. Who exactly Satyros was, we do not know. Ancient commentators tell us that he committed suicide when his father died, or that he called his father a god.

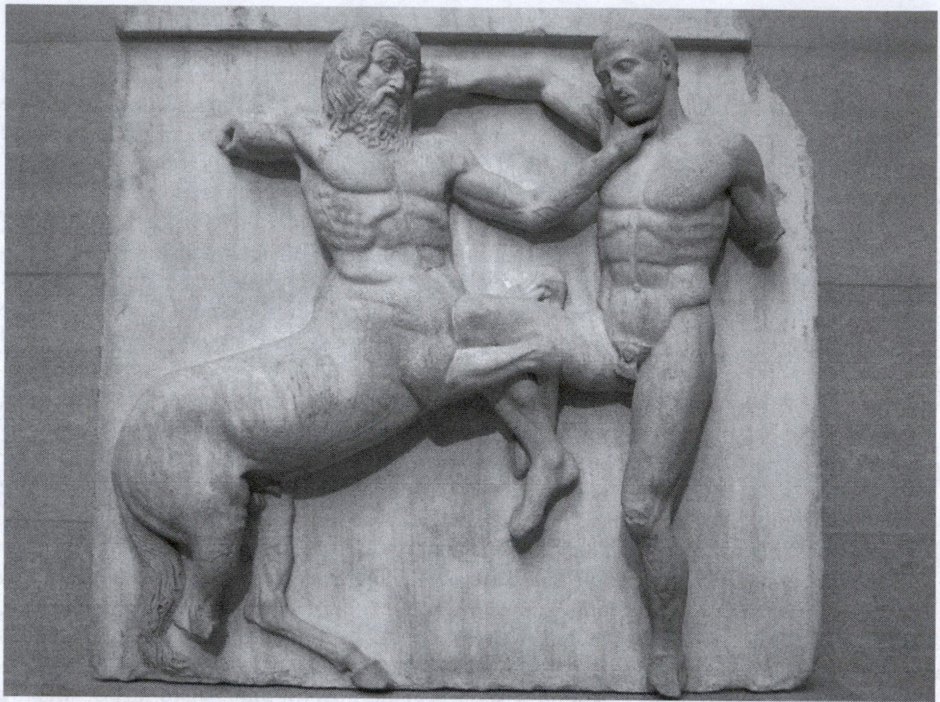

Lapith and Centaur, Metope from Parthenon, 477–438 B.C. According to a Greek myth, the Lapiths invited the Centaurs to the wedding feast of their king, Peirthon, as a gesture of goodwill. Upon seeing the beauty of the Lapiety bride, the Centaurs succumbed to their animal instincts of lust and drunkenness and turned the feast into an abduction attempt and brawl. The Lapith warriors, under the cool wisdom of Apollo, brought a sense of calm to the chaos. The image is a symbolic lesson in its appeal for human reason and order over the lower animal instinct of passion and brutishness—a lesson also taught by Aristotle in the *Nicomachean Ethics.* (© SEF/Art Resource, NY)

near the Black Sea, that they delight in eating raw meat or human flesh, and that some of them lend each other their children for a feast; or the story told about Phalaris.*

These are characteristics of brutishness. Another set of characteristics (2*a*) develops through disease and occasionally through insanity, as, for example, in the case of the man who offered his mother as a sacrifice to the gods and ate of her, or the case of the slave who ate the liver of his fellow slave. Other characteristics are the result of disease or (2*b*) of habit, e.g., plucking out one's hair, gnawing one's fingernails, or even chewing coal or earth, and also sexual relations between males. These practices are, in some cases, due to nature, but in other cases they are the result of habit, when, for example, someone has been sexually abused from childhood.

When nature is responsible, no one would call the persons affected morally weak any more than one would call women morally weak, because they are passive and not

*Phalaris, tyrant of Acragas in the second quarter of the sixth century B.C., was said to have built a hollow brazen bull, in which he roasted his victims alive, presumably to eat them afterwards. There were several other stories current in antiquity about his brutality.

active in sexual intercourse. Nor would we apply the term to persons in a morbid condition as a result of habit. To have one of these characteristics means to be outside the limits of vice, just as brutishness, too, lies outside the limits of vice. To have such characteristics 1149a and to master them or be mastered by them does not constitute moral [strength or] weakness in an unqualified sense but only by analogy, just as a person is not to be called morally weak without qualification when he cannot master his anger, but only morally weak in regard to the emotion involved.

For all excessive folly, cowardice, self-indulgence, and ill-temper is either brutish or morbid. When someone is by nature the kind of person who fears everything, even the rustling of a mouse, his cowardice is brutish, while the man's fear of the weasel was due to disease. In the case of folly, those who are irrational by nature and live only by their senses, as do some distant barbarian tribes, are brutish, whereas those whose irrationality is due to a disease, such as epilepsy, or to insanity, are morbid.

Sometimes it happens that a person merely possesses one of these characteristics without being mastered by it—I mean, for example, if a Phalaris had restrained his appetite so as not to eat the flesh of a child or so as not to indulge in some perverse form of sexual pleasure. But it also happens that a man not only has the characteristic but is mastered by it. Thus, just as the term "wickedness" refers in its unqualified sense to man alone, while in another sense it is qualified by the addition of "brutish" or "morbid," in precisely the same way it is plain that there is a brutish and a morbid kind of moral weakness [i.e., being mastered by brutishness or disease], but in its unqualified sense the term "moral weakness" refers only to human self-indulgence.

It is, accordingly, clear that moral weakness and moral strength operate only in the same sphere as do self-indulgence and self-control, and that the moral weakness which operates in any other sphere is different in kind, and is called "moral weakness" only by extension, not in an unqualified sense.

6. Moral Weakness in Anger: At this point we may observe that moral weakness in anger is less base than moral weakness in regard to the appetites. For (1) in a way, anger seems to listen to reason, but to hear wrong, like hasty servants, who run off before they have heard everything their master tells them, and fail to do what they were ordered, or like dogs, which bark as soon as there is a knock without waiting to see if the visitor is a friend. In the same way, the heat and swiftness of its nature make anger hear but not listen to an order, before rushing off to take revenge. For reason and imagination indicate that an insult or a slight has been received, and anger, drawing the conclusion, as it were, that it must fight against this sort of thing, simply flares up at once. Appetite, on the other hand, is no sooner told by reason and perception that something is pleasant than it rushes off to enjoy it. 1149b Consequently, while anger somehow follows reason, appetite does not. Hence appetite is baser [than anger]. For when a person is morally weak in anger, he is in a sense overcome by reason, but the other is not overcome by reason but by appetite.

Further, (2) it is more excusable to follow one's natural desires, inasmuch as we are also more inclined to pardon such appetites as are common to all men and to the extent that they are common to all. Now anger and ill temper are more natural than are the appetites which make us strive for excess and for what is not necessary. Take the example of the man who was defending himself against the charge of beating his father with the words: "Yes, I did it: my father, too, used to beat his father, and he beat his, and"—pointing to his little boy—"he will beat me when he grows up to be a man. It runs in the family." And the story goes that the man who was being dragged out of the house by his son asked him to stop at the door, on the grounds that he himself had not dragged his father any further than that.

Moreover, (3) the more underhanded a person is, the more unjust he is. Now, a hot-tempered man is not underhanded; nor is anger: it is open. But appetite has the same attribute as Aphrodite, who is called "weaver of guile on Cyprus born," and as her "pattern-pierced zone," of which Homer says: "endearment that steals the heart away even from the thoughtful." Therefore, since moral weakness of this type [which involves the appetite] is more unjust and baser than moral weakness concerning anger, it is this type which constitutes moral weakness in the unqualified sense and is even a kind of vice.*

Again, (4) no one feels pain when insulting another without provocation, whereas everyone who acts in a fit of anger acts with pain. On the contrary, whoever unprovoked insults another, feels pleasure. If, then, acts which justify outbursts of anger are more unjust than others, it follows that moral weakness caused by appetite [is more unjust than moral weakness caused by anger], for anger does not involve unprovoked insult.

It is now clear that moral weakness in regard to the appetites is more disgraceful than moral weakness displayed in anger, and also that moral strength and weakness operate in the sphere of the bodily appetites and pleasures. But we must still grasp the distinctions to be made within bodily appetites and pleasures. For, as we stated at the beginning, some pleasures are human, i.e., natural in kind as well as in degree, while others are brutish, and others again are due to physical disability and disease. It is only with the first group of these, [i.e., the human pleasures,] that self-control and self-indulgence are concerned. For that reason, we do not call beasts either self-controlled or self-indulgent; if we do so, we do it only metaphorically, in cases where a general distinction can be drawn between one class of animals and another on the basis of wantonness, destructiveness, and indiscriminate voracity. [This use is only metaphorical] because beasts are incapable of choice and calculation, but [animals of this type] stand outside the pale of their nature, just as madmen do among humans.

1150a Brutishness is a lesser evil than vice, but it is more horrifying. For [in a beast] the better element cannot be perverted, as it can be in man, since it is lacking. [To compare a brute beast and a brutish man] is like comparing an inanimate with an animate being to see which is more evil. For the depravity of a being which does not possess the source that initiates its own motion is always less destructive [than the depravity of a being that possesses this source], and intelligence is such a source. A similar comparison can be made between injustice [as such] and an unjust man: each is in some sense worse than the other, for a bad man can do ten thousand times as much harm as a beast.

7. Moral Strength and Moral Weakness: Tenacity and Softness: As regards the pleasures, pains, appetites, and aversions that come to us through touch and taste, and which we defined earlier as the sphere of self-indulgence and self-control, it is possible to be the kind of person who is overcome even by those which most people master; but it is also possible to master those by which most people are overcome. Those who are overcome by pleasure or master it are, respectively, morally weak and morally strong; and in the case of pain, they are, respectively, soft and tenacious. The disposition which characterizes the majority of men lies between these two, although they tend more to the inferior characteristics.

Some pleasures are necessary, up to a certain point, and others are not, whereas neither excesses nor deficiencies of pleasure are necessary. The same is also true of

*But it is not vice in the unqualified sense, for that would involve choice.

appetites and pains. From all this it follows that a man is self-indulgent when he pursues excesses of pleasant things, or when he [pursues necessary pleasures] to excess, by choice, for their own sakes, and not for an ulterior result. A man of this kind inevitably feels no regret, and is as a result incorrigible. For a person who feels no regret is incorrigible. A person deficient [in his pursuit of the necessary pleasures] is the opposite [of self-indulgent], and the man who occupies the middle position is self-controlled. In the same way, a man who avoids bodily pain [is self-indulgent], provided he does so by choice and not because he is overcome by them.

A choice is not exercised either by a person who is driven by pleasure, or by a person who is avoiding the pain of [unsatisfied] appetite. There is, accordingly, a difference between indulging by choice and not by choice. Everyone would think worse of a man who would perform some disgraceful act actuated only slightly or not at all by appetite, than of a person who was actuated by a strong appetite. And we would regard as worse a man who feels no anger as he beats another man, than someone who does so in anger. For what would he do, if he were in the grip of emotion when acting? Hence a self-indulgent man is worse than one who is morally weak.

So we see that one of the characteristics described, [viz., the deliberate avoidance of pain,] constitutes rather a kind of softness, while a person possessing the other, [viz., the deliberate pursuit of excessive pleasures,] is self-indulgent.

A morally strong is opposed to a morally weak man, and a tenacious to a soft man. For being tenacious consists in offering resistance, while moral strength consists in mastering. Resistance and mastery are two different things, just as not being defeated differs from winning a victory. Hence, moral strength is more desirable than tenacity. A man who is deficient [in his resistance to pains] which most people withstand successfully is soft and effeminate. For effeminacy is a form of softness. A man of this kind lets his cloak trail, in order to save himself the pain of lifting it up, and plays the invalid without believing himself to be involved in the misery which a true invalid suffers.

The situation is similar in the case of moral strength and moral weakness. If a person is overcome by powerful and excessive pleasures or pains, we are not surprised. In fact, we find it pardonable if he is overcome while offering resistance, as, for example, Theodectes' Philoctetes* does when bitten by the snake, or as Cercyon in Carcinus' *Alope,*** or as people who try to restrain their laughter burst out in one great guffaw, as actually happened to Xenophantus.*** But we are surprised if a man is overcome by and unable to withstand those [pleasures and pains] which most people resist successfully, unless his disposition is congenital or caused by disease, as among the kings of Scythia, for example, in whom softness is congenital,[†] and as softness distinguishes the female from the male.

*Theodectes (ca. 375–334 B.C.) spent most of his life at Athens. He studied under Plato, Isocrates, and Aristotle, and in addition to writing tragedies, won a considerable reputation as an orator. An ancient note on this passage tells us that, in Theodectes' tragedy, Philoctetes, after repressing his pain for a long time, finally bursts out: "Cut off my hand!"

**Carcinus was a fourth-century B.C. Athenian tragic poet. According to an ancient commentator, "Cercyon had a daughter Alope. Upon learning that his daughter Alope had committed adultery, he asked her who had perpetrated the deed, and said: 'If you tell me, I will not be grieved at all.' When Alope told him who the adulterer was, Cercyon was so overcome with grief that he could no longer stand life and renounced living."

***The occasion is not known. Xenophantus is said to have been a musician at the court of Alexander the Great (356–323 B.C.). Seneca tells us that when Xenophantus sang, Alexander was so stirred that he seized his weapons in his hands.

†According to the Hippocratic treatise *On Airs, Waters, and Places* 22, horseback riding caused softness among the Scythian aristocracy.

A man who loves amusement is also commonly regarded as being self-indulgent, but he is actually soft. For amusement is relaxation, inasmuch as it is respite from work, and a lover of amusement is a person who goes in for relaxation to excess.

One kind of moral weakness is impetuosity and another is a lack of strength. People of the latter kind deliberate but do not abide by the results of their deliberation, because they are overcome by emotion, while the impetuous are driven on by emotion, because they do not deliberate. [If they deliberated, they would not be driven on so easily,] for as those who have just been tickled are immune to being tickled again, so some people are not overcome by emotion, whether pleasant or painful, when they feel and see it coming and have roused themselves and their power of reasoning in good time. Keen and excitable persons are the most prone to the impetuous kind of moral weakness. Swiftness prevents the keen and vehemence the excitable from waiting for reason to guide them, since they tend to be led by their imagination.

8. Moral Weakness and Self-Indulgence: A self-indulgent man, as we stated, is one who feels no regret, since he abides by the choice he has made. A morally weak person, on the other hand, always feels regret. Therefore, the formulation of the problem, as we posed it above, does not correspond to the facts: it is a self-indulgent man who cannot be cured, but a morally weak man is curable. For wickedness is like a disease such as dropsy or consumption, while moral weakness resembles epilepsy: the former is chronic, the latter intermittent. All in all, moral weakness and vice are generically different from each other. A vicious man is not aware of his vice, but a morally weak man knows his weakness.

Among the morally weak, those who lose themselves in [emotion, i.e., the impetuous,] are better than those who have a rational principle but do not abide by it, [i.e., those who lack strength]. For they are overcome by a lesser emotion and do not yield without previous deliberation, as the impetuous do. A man who has this kind of moral weakness resembles those who get drunk quickly and on little wine, or on less wine than most people do.

That moral weakness is not a vice [in the strict sense] is now evident, though in a certain sense it is perhaps one. For moral weakness violates choice, whereas vice is in accordance with choice. Nevertheless, they are similar in the actions to which they lead, just as Demodocus said of the Milesians:

> The Milesians are no stupid crew, except that they do what the stupid do.*

Similarly, the morally weak are not unjust, but they will act like unjust men.

A morally weak man is the kind of person who pursues bodily pleasures to excess and contrary to right reason, though he is not persuaded [that he ought to do so]; the self-indulgent, on the other hand, is persuaded to pursue them because he is the kind of man who does so. This means that it is the former who is easily persuaded to change his mind, but the latter is not. For virtue or excellence preserves and wickedness destroys the initiating motive or first cause [of action], and in actions the initiating motive or first cause is the end at which we aim, as the hypotheses are in mathematics. For neither in mathematics nor in moral matters does reasoning teach us the principles or starting points; it is virtue, whether natural or habitual, that inculcates right opinion about the

*Demodocus wrote lampooning epigrams in the sixth century B.C.

principle or first premise. A man who has this right opinion is self-controlled, and his opposite is self-indulgent.

But there exists a kind of person who loses himself under the impact of emotion and violates right reason, a person whom emotion so overpowers that he does not act according to the dictates of right reason, but not sufficiently to make him the kind of man who is persuaded that he must abandon himself completely to the pursuit of such pleasures. This is the morally weak man: he is better than the self-indulgent, and he is not bad in the unqualified sense of the word. For the best thing in him is saved: the principle or premise [as to how he should act]. Opposed to him is another kind of man, who remains steadfast and does not lose himself, at least not under the impact of emotion. These considerations make it clear that moral strength is a characteristic of great moral worth, while moral weakness is bad.

9. Steadfastness in Moral Strength and Moral Weakness: Is a man morally strong when he abides by any and every dictate of reason and choice, or only when he abides by the right choice? And is a man morally weak when he does not abide by every choice and dictate of reason, or only when he fails to abide by the rational dictate which is not false and the choice which is right? This is the problem we stated earlier. Or is it true reason and right choice as such, but any other kind of choice incidentally, to which the one remains steadfast and the other does not? [This seems to be the correct answer,] for if a person chooses and pursues the attainment of *a* by means of *b*, his pursuit and 1151b
choice are for *a* as such but for *b* incidentally. And by "as such" we mean "in the unqualified sense." Therefore, there is a sense in which the one abides by and the other abandons any and every kind of opinion, but in the unqualified sense, only true opinion.

There are those who remain steadfast to their opinion and are called "obstinate." They are hard to convince and are not easily persuaded to change their mind. They bear a certain resemblance to a morally strong person, just as an extravagant man resembles one who is generous, and a reckless man resembles one who is confident. But they are, in fact, different in many respects. The one, the morally strong, will be a person who does not change under the influence of emotion and appetite, but on occasion he will be persuaded [by argument]. Obstinate men, on the other hand, are not easily persuaded by rational argument; but to appetites they are amenable, and in many cases are driven on by pleasures. The various kinds of obstinate people are the opinionated, the ignorant, and the boorish. The opinionated let themselves be influenced by pleasure and pain: they feel the joy of victory, when someone fails to persuade them to change their mind, and they feel pain when their views are overruled, like decrees that are declared null and void. As a result, they bear a greater resemblance to the morally weak than to the morally strong.

Then there are those who do not abide by their decisions for reasons other than moral weakness, as, for example, Neoptolemus in Sophocles' *Philoctetes.* Granted it was under the influence of pleasure that he did not remain steadfast, but it was a noble pleasure: it was noble in his eyes to be truthful, but he was persuaded by Odysseus to tell a lie. For not anybody who acts under the influence of pleasure is self-indulgent, bad, or morally weak, but only those who do so under the influence of a base pleasure.

There is also a type who feels less joy than he should at the things of the body and, therefore, does not abide by the dictates of reason. The median between this type and the morally weak man is the man of moral strength. For a morally weak person does not abide by the dictates of reason, because he feels more joy than he should [in bodily things], but the man under discussion feels less joy than he should. But a morally strong man remains steadfast and does not change on either account. Since moral strength is good, it follows that both characteristics opposed to it are bad, as they in fact turn out to be. But since one of the two opposites is in evidence only in a few people and on few occasions, moral strength is generally regarded as being the only opposite of moral weakness, just as self-control is thought to be opposed only to self-indulgence.

Since many terms are used in an analogical sense, we have come to speak analogically of the "moral strength" of a self-controlled man. [There is a resemblance between the two] since a morally strong man is the kind of person who does nothing contrary to 1152a the dictates of reason under the influence of bodily pleasures, and the same is true of a self-controlled man. But while a morally strong man has base appetites, a self-controlled man does not and is, moreover, a person who finds no pleasure in anything that violates the dictates of reason. A morally strong man, on the other hand, does find pleasure in such things, but he is not driven by them. There is also a similarity between the morally weak and the self-indulgent in that both pursue things pleasant to the body; but they are different in that a self-indulgent man thinks he ought to pursue them, while the morally weak thinks he should not.

10. Moral Weakness and Practical Wisdom: It is not possible for the same person to have practical wisdom and be morally weak at the same time, for it has been shown that a man of practical wisdom is *ipso facto* a man of good character. Moreover, to be a man of practical wisdom, one must not only know [what one ought to do], but he must also be able to act accordingly. But a morally weak man is not able so to act. However, there is no reason why a clever man could not be morally weak. That is why occasionally people are regarded as possessing practical wisdom, but as being morally weak at the same time; it is because cleverness differs from practical wisdom in the way we have described in our first discussion of the subject. They are closely related in that both follow the guidance of reason, but they differ in that [practical wisdom alone] involves moral choice.

Furthermore, a morally weak man does not act like a man who has knowledge and exercises it, but like a man asleep or drunk. Also, even though he acts voluntarily—for he knows in a sense what he is doing and what end he is aiming at—he is not wicked, because his moral choice is good,* and that makes him only half-wicked. He is not unjust, either, for he is no underhanded plotter. [For plotting implies deliberation,] whereas one type of morally weak man does not abide by the results of his deliberation, while the other, the excitable type, does not even deliberate. So we see that a morally weak person is like a state which enacts all the right decrees and has laws of a high moral standard, but does not apply them, a situation which Anaxandrides made fun of: "Thus wills the state, that cares not for its laws."** A wicked man, on the other hand, resembles a state which does apply its laws, but the laws are bad.

In relation to the characteristics possessed by most people, moral weakness and moral strength lie at the extremes. For a morally strong person remains more steadfast and a morally weak person less steadfast than the capacity of most men permits.

The kind of moral weakness displayed by excitable people is more easily cured than the moral weakness of those who deliberate but do not abide by their decisions; and those who are morally weak through habituation are more curable than those who

*I.e., his basic moral purpose is good, even though it is eventually vitiated by appetite.

**Anaxandrides (fl. 382–349 B.C.) migrated from his native Rhodes (or Colophon) to Athens, where he gained fame as a poet of the Middle Comedy.

are morally weak by nature. For it is easier to change habit than to change nature. Even habit is hard to change, precisely because it resembles nature, as Euenus says:

A habit, friend, is of long practice born,
and practice ends in fashioning man's nature.*

We have now completed our definitions of moral strength, moral weakness, tenacity, and softness, and stated how these characteristics are related to one another.

11. Pleasure: Some Current Views: It is the role of a political philosopher to study 1152b
pleasure and pain. For he is the supreme craftsman of the end to which we look when we call one particular thing bad and another good in the unqualified sense. Moreover, an examination of this subject is one of the tasks we must logically undertake, since we established that virtue and vice of character are concerned with pains and pleasures, and most people claim that happiness involves pleasure. That is why the word "blessed" is derived from the word "enjoy."

Now, (1) some people believe that no pleasure is good, either in itself or incidentally, since the good and pleasure are not the same thing.** (2) Others hold that, though some pleasures are good, most of them are bad.*** (3) Then there is a third view, according to which it is impossible for pleasure to be the highest good, even if all pleasures are good.†

[The following arguments are advanced to support (1) the contention that] pleasure is not a good at all: *(a)* All pleasure is a process or coming-to-be leading to the natural state [of the subject] and perceived [by the subject]; but no process is of the same order as its ends, e.g., the building process is not of the same order as a house. Further, *(b)* a self-controlled man avoids pleasures. Again, *(c)* a man of practical wisdom does not pursue the pleasant, but what is free from pain.†† Moreover, *(d)* pleasures are an obstacle to good sense: the greater the joy one feels, e.g., in sexual intercourse, the greater the obstacle; for no one is capable of rational insight while enjoying sexual relations.††† Also, *(e)* there is no art of pleasure; yet every good is the result of an art. Finally, *(f)* children and beasts pursue pleasures, whereas they do not know what is good.

[The arguments for the view (2) that] not all pleasures are good are: *(a)* Some pleasures are disgraceful and cause for reproach; and *(b)* some pleasures are harmful, for there are pleasant things that may cause disease.

[And the argument in favor of (3), the contention that] pleasure is not the highest good, is that it is not an end but a process or coming-to-be. These are roughly the views put forward.

12. The Views Discussed: (1) Is Pleasure a Good Thing?: But the following considerations will show that the arguments we have enumerated do not lead us to the conclusion

*Euenus of Paros was a famous Sophist, who lived in the late fifth century B.C.

**This view seems to have been propounded by Speusippus, Plato's nephew and disciple, who succeeded him as head of the Academy from 347–339 B.C. A similar view had been espoused by Antisthenes (ca. 455–ca. 360 B.C.), the friend of Socrates and precursor of the Cynic School.

***This is probably a reference to the view stated by Plato in *Philebus* 13b.

†No particular proponents of this view can be identified, but they are also discussed in Plato's *Philebus* 53c–55c.

††Arguments (*b*) and (*c*) had probably been used by Speusippus and before him perhaps by Antisthenes.

†††This argument may come from Archytas, a Pythagorean philosopher, mathematician, ruler of Tarentum, and friend of Plato, in the first half of the fourth century B.C.

that (1) pleasure is not a good, or (3) that it is not the highest good. In the first place, [to answer argument (1*a*) and (3),] we use the word "good" in two senses: a thing may be good in the unqualified sense, or "good" for a particular person. Hence the term has also two meanings when applied to natural states and characteristics [of persons], and consequently also when applied to their motions and processes. This means that motions and processes which are generally held to be bad are partly bad without qualification, but not bad for a particular person, and even desirable for him; and partly not even desirable for a particular person except on occasion and for a short time, though they are not desirable in an unqualified sense. Others again are not even pleasures, but only appear to be, for example, all processes accompanied by pain and undergone for remedial purposes, such as the processes to which the sick are subjected.

Secondly, the good has two aspects: it is both an activity and a characteristic. Now, the processes which restore us to our natural characteristic condition are only incidentally pleasant; but the activity which is at work when our appetites [want to see us restored] is the activity of that part of our characteristic condition and natural state which has been left unimpaired. For that matter, there are pleasures which do not involve pain
1153a and appetite (e.g., the activity of studying) and we experience them when there is nothing deficient in our natural state. [That processes of restoration are only incidentally pleasant] is shown by the fact that the pleasant things which give us joy while our natural state is being replenished are not the same as those which give us joy once it has been restored. Once restored, we feel joy at what is pleasant in the unqualified sense, but while the replenishment goes on, we enjoy even its opposite: for instance, we enjoy sharp and bitter things, none of which are pleasant either by nature or in the unqualified sense. Consequently, the pleasures [derived from them, too, are not pleasant either by nature or in the unqualified sense], for the difference that exists between various pleasant things is the same as that which is found between the pleasures derived from them.

In the third place, there is no need to believe that there exists something better than pleasure which is different from it, just as, according to some, the end is better than the process which leads to it. For pleasures are not processes, nor do all pleasures involve processes: they are activities and an end, and they result not from the process of development we undergo, but from the use we make of the powers we have. Nor do all pleasures have an end other than themselves; that is only true of the pleasures of those who are being led to the perfection of their natural states. For that reason, it is not correct, either, to say that pleasure is a process perceived [by the subject]: one should rather call it an "activity of our characteristic condition as determined by our natural state," and instead of "perceived" we should call it "unobstructed." (There are some who believe pleasure to be process on the ground that it is good in the true sense of the word, for they think that activity is process, but it is, as a matter of fact, different.)

The argument (2*b*) that pleasures [are bad, because] some pleasant things may cause disease, is like arguing that wholesome things are bad, because some of them are bad for making money. Both pleasant and wholesome things are bad in the relative senses mentioned, but that does not make them bad in themselves: even studying is occasionally harmful to health.

Also, (1*d*) neither practical wisdom nor any characteristic is obstructed by the pleasure arising from it, but only by alien pleasures extraneous to it. The pleasures arising from study and learning will only intensify study and learning, [but they will never obstruct it].

The argument (1*e*) that no pleasure is the result of an art makes good sense. For art never produces any activity at all: it produces the capacity for the activity.

Nevertheless, the arts of perfume-making as well as of cooking are generally regarded as arts of pleasure.

The arguments (1*b*) that a self-controlled person avoids pleasure, (1*c*) that a man of practical wisdom pursues a life free from pain, and (1*f*) that children and beasts pursue pleasure, are all refuted by the same consideration. We have stated in what sense pleasures are good without qualification and in what sense not all pleasures are good. These last mentioned are the pleasures which beasts and children pursue, while a man of practical wisdom wants to be free from the pain which they imply. They are the pleasures that involve appetite and pain, i.e., the bodily pleasures—for they are of this sort—and their excesses, in terms of which a self-indulgent man is self-indulgent. That is why a self-controlled man avoids these pleasures. But there are pleasures even for the self-controlled.

13. The Views Discussed: (3) Is Pleasure the Highest Good?: To continue: there is general agreement that pain is bad and must be avoided. One kind of pain is bad in the unqualified sense, and another kind is bad, because in some way or other it obstructs us. Now, the opposite of a thing to be avoided—in the sense that it must be avoided and is bad—is good. It follows, therefore, necessarily that pleasure is a good. Speusippus tried to solve the question by saying that, just as the greater is opposed both to the less and to the equal, [so pleasure is opposed both to pain and to the good]. But this solution does not come out correctly: surely, he would not say that pleasure is essentially a species of evil.

But (2*a*) even if some pleasures are bad, it does not mean that the highest good cannot be some sort of pleasure, just as the highest good may be some sort of knowledge, even though some kinds of knowledge are bad. Perhaps we must even draw the necessary conclusion that it is; for since each characteristic has its unobstructed activities, the activity of all characteristics or of one of them—depending on whether the former or the latter constitutes happiness—if unobstructed, must be the most desirable of all. And this activity is pleasure. Therefore, the highest good is some sort of pleasure, despite the fact that most pleasures are bad and, if you like, bad in the unqualified sense of the word. It is for this reason that everyone thinks that the happy life is a pleasant life, and links pleasure with happiness. And it makes good sense this way: for no activity is complete and perfect as long as it is obstructed, and happiness is a complete and perfect thing. This is why a happy man also needs the goods of the body, external goods, and the goods of fortune, in order not to be obstructed by their absence.

But those who assert* that a man is happy even on the rack and even when great misfortunes befall him, provided that he is good, are talking nonsense, whether they know it or not. Since happiness also needs fortune, some people regard good fortune as identical with happiness. But that is not true, for even good fortune, if excessive, can be an obstruction; perhaps we are, in that case, no longer justified in calling it "good fortune," for its definition is determined by its relation to happiness.

Also, the fact that all beasts and all men pursue pleasure is some indication that it is, in a sense, the highest good:

> There is no talk that ever quite dies down,
> if spread by many men. . . .

But since no single nature and no single characteristic condition is, or is regarded, as the best [for all], people do not all pursue the same pleasure, yet all pursue pleasure. Perhaps

*The Cynics are probably meant.

they do not even pursue the pleasure which they think or would say they pursue, but they all pursue the same [thing], pleasure. For everything has by nature something divine about it. But the bodily pleasures have arrogated the name "pleasure" unto themselves as their own private possession, because everyone tends to follow them and participates in them more frequently than in any others. Accordingly, since these are the only pleasures with which they are familiar, people think they are the only ones that exist.

1154a It is also evident that if pleasure, i.e., the activity [of our faculties], is not good, it will be impossible for a happy man to live pleasantly. For to what purpose would he need pleasure, if it were not a good and if it is possible that a happy man's life is one of pain? For if pain is neither good nor bad, pleasure is not, either: so why should he avoid it? Surely, the life of a morally good man is no pleasanter [than that of anyone else], if his activities are not more pleasant.

14. The Views Discussed: (2) Are Most Pleasures Bad?: The subject of the pleasures of the body demands the attention of the proponents of the view that, though some pleasures—for instance, the noble pleasures—are highly desirable, the pleasures of the body—that is, the pleasures which are the concern of the self-indulgent man—are not. If that is true, why then are the pains opposed to them bad? For bad has good as its opposite. Is it that the necessary pleasures are good in the sense in which anything not bad is good? Or are they good up to a certain point? For all characteristics and motions which cannot have an excess of good cannot have an excess of pleasure, either; but those which can have an excess of good can also have an excess of pleasure. Now, excess is possible in the case of the goods of the body, and it is the pursuit of excess, but not the pursuit of necessary pleasures, that makes a man bad. For all men get some kind of enjoyment from good food, wine, and sexual relations, but not everyone enjoys these things in the proper way. The reverse is true of pain: a bad person does not avoid an excess of it, but he avoids it altogether. For the opposite of an excess is pain only for the man who pursues the excess.

It is our task not only to say what is true, but also to state what causes error, since that helps carry conviction. For when we can give a reasoned explanation why something which appears to be true is, in fact, not true, it makes us give greater credence to what is true. Accordingly, we must now explain why the pleasures of the body appear to be more desirable.

The first reason, then, is that pleasure drives out pain. When men experience an excess of pain, they pursue excessive pleasure and bodily pleasure in general, in the belief that it will remedy the pain. These remedial [pleasures] become very intense—and that is the very reason why they are pursued—because they are experienced in contrast with their opposite.

As a matter of fact, these two reasons which we have stated also explain why pleasure is not regarded as having any moral value: some pleasures are the actions that spring from a bad natural state—either congenitally bad, as in the case of a beast, or bad by habit, as in the case of a bad man—while other pleasures are remedial and indicate a deficient natural state, and to be in one's natural state is better than to be moving toward
1154b it. But since the remedial pleasures only arise in the process of reaching the perfected state, they are morally good only incidentally.

The second reason is that the pleasures of the body are pursued because of their intensity by those incapable of enjoying other pleasures. Take, for example, those who induce themselves to be thirsty. There is no objection to this practice, if the pleasures are harmless; but if they are harmful, it is bad. For many people have nothing else to give them joy, and because of their nature, it is painful for them to feel neither [pleasure nor pain]. Actually, animal nature is under a constant strain, as the students of natural science attest when they say that seeing and hearing are painful, but [we do not feel the pain because,] as they assert, we have become accustomed to it. Similarly, whereas the growing process [we go through] in our youth puts us into the same [exhilarated] state as that of a drunken man, and [makes] youth the age of pleasure, excitable natures, on the other hand, always need remedial action: as a result of [the excess of black bile in their] constitutional blend, their bodies are exposed to constant gnawing sensations, and they are always in a state of vehement desire. Now, since pain is driven out by the pleasure opposed to it or by any strong pleasure at all, excitable people become self-indulgent and bad.

Pleasures unattended by pain do not admit of excess. The objects of these pleasures are what is pleasant by nature and not what is incidentally pleasant. By "things incidentally pleasant" I mean those that act as remedies. For since it is through some action of that part of us which has remained sound that a cure is effected, the remedy is regarded as being pleasant. But [pleasant by nature it is not]: pleasant by nature are those things which produce the action of an unimpaired natural state.

There is no single object that continues to be pleasant forever, because our nature is not simple but contains another natural element, which makes us subject to decay. Consequently, whenever one element does something, it runs counter to the nature of the other; and whenever the two elements are in a state of equilibrium, the act performed seems neither painful nor pleasant. If there is a being with a simple nature, the same action will always be the most pleasant to him. That is why the divinity always enjoys one single and simple pleasure: for there is not only an activity of motion but also an activity of immobility, and pleasure consists in rest rather than in motion. But "change in all things is pleasant," as the poet has it, because of some evil in us. For just as a man who changes easily is bad, so also is a nature that needs to change. The reason is that such a nature is not simple and not [entirely] good.

This completes our discussion of moral strength and moral weakness, and of pleasure and pain. We have stated what each of them is and in what sense some of them are good and some bad. It now remains to talk about friendship.

* * *

BOOK X

* * *

6. Happiness and Activity: Now that we have completed our discussion of the 1176[a] virtues, and of the different kinds of friendship and pleasure, it remains to sketch an outline of happiness, since, as we assert, it is the end or goal of human [aspirations]. Our account will be more concise if we recapitulate what we have said so far.

We stated, then, that happiness is not a characteristic; if it were, a person who passes his whole life in sleep, vegetating like a plant, or someone who experiences the greatest misfortunes could possess it. If, then, such a conclusion is unacceptable, we must, in accordance with our earlier discussion, classify happiness as some sort of activ- 1176[b] ity. Now, some activities are necessary and desirable only for the sake of something else, while others are desirable in themselves. Obviously, happiness must be classed as an activity desirable in itself and not for the sake of something else. For happiness lacks nothing and is self-sufficient. Activities desirable in themselves are those from which we seek to derive nothing beyond the actual exercise of the activity. Actions in conformity with virtue evidently constitute such activities; for to perform noble and good deeds is something desirable for its own sake.

Pleasant amusements, too, [are desirable for their own sake]. We do not choose them for the sake of something else, since they lead to harm rather than good when we become neglectful of our bodies and our property. But most of those who are considered happy find an escape in pastimes of this sort, and this is why people who are well versed in such pastimes find favor at the courts of tyrants; they make themselves pleasant by providing what the tyrants are after, and what they want is amusement. Accordingly, such amusements are regarded as being conducive to happiness, because men who are in positions of power devote their leisure to them. But perhaps such persons cannot be [regarded as] evidence. For virtue and intelligence, which are the sources of morally good activities, do not consist in wielding power. Also, if these men, who have never tasted pure and generous pleasure, find an escape in the pleasures of the body, this is no sufficient reason for thinking that such pleasures are in fact more desirable. For children, too, think that what they value is actually the best. It is, therefore, not surprising that as children apparently do not attach value to the same things as do adults, so bad men do not attach value to the same things as do good men. Accordingly, as we have stated repeatedly, what is valuable and pleasant to a morally good man actually is valuable and pleasant. Each individual considers that activity most desirable which corresponds to his own proper characteristic condition, and a morally good man, of course, so considers activity in conformity with virtue.

Consequently, happiness does not consist in amusement. In fact, it would be strange if our end were amusement, and if we were to labor and suffer hardships all our life long merely to amuse ourselves. For, one might say, we choose everything for the sake of something else—except happiness; for happiness is an end. Obviously, it is foolish and all too childish to exert serious efforts and toil for purposes of amusement. Anacharsis* seems to be right when he advises to play in order to be serious; for amusement is a form of rest, and since we cannot work continuously we need rest. Thus rest is not an end, for
1177a we take it for the sake of [further] activity. The happy life is regarded as a life in conformity with virtue. It is a life which involves effort and is not spent in amusement.

Moreover, we say that what is morally good is better than what is ridiculous and brings amusement, and the better the organ or man—whichever may be involved in a particular case—the greater the moral value of the activity. But the activity of the better organ or the better man is in itself superior and more conducive to happiness.

Furthermore, any person at all, even a slave, can enjoy bodily pleasures no less than the best of men. But no one would grant that a slave has a share in happiness any more than that he lives a life of his own. For happiness does not consist in pastimes of this sort, but in activities that conform with virtue, as we have stated earlier.

7. Happiness, Intelligence, and the Contemplative Life: Now, if happiness is activity in conformity with virtue, it is to be expected that it should conform with the highest virtue, and that is the virtue of the best part of us. Whether this is intelligence or something else which, it is thought, by its very nature rules and guides us and which

*Anacharsis, who is said to have lived early in the sixth century B.C., was a Scythian whose travels all over the Greek world brought him a reputation for wisdom. He allegedly met Solon at Athens and was numbered in some ancient traditions among the Seven Wise Men.

gives us our notions of what is noble and divine; whether it is itself divine or the most divine thing in us; it is the activity of this part [when operating] in conformity with the excellence or virtue proper to it that will be complete happiness. That it is an activity concerned with theoretical knowledge or contemplation has already been stated.

This would seem to be consistent with our earlier statements as well as the truth. For this activity is not only the highest—for intelligence is the highest possession we have in us, and the objects which are the concern of intelligence are the highest objects of knowledge—but also the most continuous: we are able to study continuously more easily than to perform any kind of action. Furthermore, we think of pleasure as a necessary ingredient in happiness. Now everyone agrees that of all the activities that conform with virtue activity in conformity with theoretical wisdom is the most pleasant. At any rate, it seems that [the pursuit of wisdom or] philosophy holds pleasures marvelous in purity and certainty, and it is not surprising that time spent in knowledge is more pleasant than time spent in research. Moreover, what is usually called "selfsufficiency" will be found in the highest degree in the activity which is concerned with theoretical knowledge. Like a just man and any other virtuous man, a wise man requires the necessities of life; once these have been adequately provided, a just man still needs people toward whom and in company with whom to act justly, and the same is true of a self-controlled man, a courageous man, and all the rest. But a wise man is able to study even by himself, and the wiser he is the more is he able to do it. Perhaps he could do it better if he had colleagues to work with him, but he still is the most self-sufficient of all. Again, study seems to be the only activity which is loved 1177b
for its own sake. For while we derive a greater or a smaller advantage from practical pursuits beyond the action itself, from study we derive nothing beyond the activity of studying. Also, we regard happiness as depending on leisure; for our purpose in being busy is to have leisure, and we wage war in order to have peace. Now, the practical virtues are activated in political and military pursuits, but the actions involved in these pursuits seem to be unleisurely. This is completely true of military pursuits, since no one chooses to wage war or foments war for the sake of war; he would have to be utterly bloodthirsty if he were to make enemies of his friends simply in order to have battle and slaughter. But the activity of the statesman, too, has no leisure. It attempts to gain advantages beyond political action, advantages such as political power, prestige, or at least happiness for the statesman himself and his fellow citizens, and that is something other than political activity: after all, the very fact that we investigate politics shows that it is not the same [as happiness]. Therefore, if we take as established (1) that political and military actions surpass all other actions that conform with virtue in nobility and grandeur; (2) that they are unleisurely, aim at an end, and are not chosen for their own sake; (3) that the activity of our intelligence, inasmuch as it is an activity concerned with theoretical knowledge, is thought to be of greater value than the others, aims at no end beyond itself, and has a pleasure proper to itself—and pleasure increases activity; and (4) that the qualities of this activity evidently are self-sufficiency, leisure, as much freedom from fatigue as a human being can have, and whatever else falls to the lot of a supremely happy man; it follows that the activity of our intelligence constitutes the complete happiness of man, provided that it encompasses a complete span of life; for nothing connected with happiness must be incomplete.

However, such a life would be more than human. A man who would live it would do so not insofar as he is human, but because there is a divine element within him. This divine element is as far above our composite nature* as its activity is above the active

*Human beings, consisting of soul and body, i.e., of form and matter, are composite beings, whereas the divine, being all intelligence, is not.

exercise of the other, [i.e., practical,] kind of virtue. So if it is true that intelligence is divine in comparison with man, then a life guided by intelligence is divine in comparison with human life. We must not follow those who advise us to have human thoughts, since we are [only] men, and mortal thoughts, as mortals should; on the contrary, we should try to become immortal as far as that is possible and do our utmost to live in 1178a accordance with what is highest in us. For though this is a small portion [of our nature], it far surpasses everything else in power and value. One might even regard it as each man's true self, since it is the controlling and better part. It would, therefore, be strange if a man chose not to live his own life but someone else's.

Moreover, what we stated before will apply here, too: what is by nature proper to each thing will be at once the best and the most pleasant for it. In other words, a life guided by intelligence is the best and most pleasant for man, inasmuch as intelligence, above all else, is man. Consequently, this kind of life is the happiest.

8. The Advantages of the Contemplative Life: A life guided by the other kind of virtue, [the practical,] is happy in a secondary sense, since its active exercise is confined to man. It is in our dealings with one another that we perform just, courageous, and other virtuous acts, when we observe the proper kind of behavior toward each man in private transactions, in meeting his needs, in all manner of actions, and in our emotions, and all of these are, as we see, peculiarly human. Moreover, some moral acts seem to be determined by our bodily condition, and virtue or excellence of character seems in many ways closely related to the emotions. There is also a close mutual connection between practical wisdom and excellence of character, since the fundamental principles of practical wisdom are determined by the virtues of character, while practical wisdom determines the right standard for the moral virtues. The fact that these virtues are also bound up with the emotions indicates that they belong to our composite nature, and the virtues of our composite nature are human virtues; consequently, a life guided by these virtues and the happiness [that goes with it are likewise human]. The happiness of the intelligence, however, is quite separate [from that kind of happiness]. That is all we shall say about it here, for a more detailed treatment lies beyond the scope of our present task.

It also seems that such happiness has little need of external trimmings, or less need than moral virtue has. Even if we grant that both stand in equal need of the necessities of life, and even if the labors of a statesman are more concerned with the needs of our body and things of that sort—in that respect the difference between them may be small—yet, in what they need for the exercise of their activities, their difference will be great. A generous man will need money to perform generous acts, and a just man will need it to meet his obligations. For the mere wish to perform such acts is inscrutable, and even an unjust man can pretend that he wishes to act justly. And a courageous man will need strength if he is to accomplish an act that conforms with his 1178b virtue, and a man of self-control the possibility of indulgence. How else can he or any other virtuous man make manifest his excellence? Also, it is debatable whether the moral purpose or the action is the more decisive element in virtue, since virtue depends on both. It is clear of course that completeness depends on both. But many things are needed for the performance of actions, and the greater and nobler the actions the more is needed. But a man engaged in study has no need of any of these things, at least not for the active exercise of studying; in fact one might even go so far as to say that they are a hindrance to study. But insofar as he is human and lives in the society of his fellow men, he chooses to act as virtue demands, and accordingly, he will need externals for living as a human being.

A further indication that complete happiness consists in some kind of contemplative activity is this. We assume that the gods are in the highest degree blessed and happy. But what kind of actions are we to attribute to them? Acts of justice? Will they not look ridiculous making contracts with one another, returning deposits, and so forth? Perhaps acts of courage—withstanding terror and taking risks, because it is noble to do so? Or generous actions? But to whom will they give? It would be strange to think that they actually have currency or something of the sort. Acts of self-control? What would they be? Surely, it would be in poor taste to praise them for not having bad appetites. If we went through the whole list we would see that a concern with actions is petty and unworthy of the gods. Nevertheless, we all assume that the gods exist and, consequently, that they are active; for surely we do not assume them to be always asleep like Endymion.* Now, if we take away action from a living being, to say nothing of production, what is left except contemplation? Therefore, the activity of the divinity which surpasses all others in bliss must be a contemplative activity, and the human activity which is most closely akin to it is, therefore, most conducive to happiness.

This is further shown by the fact that no other living being has a share in happiness, since they all are completely denied this kind of activity. The gods enjoy a life blessed in its entirety; men enjoy it to the extent that they attain something resembling the divine activity; but none of the other living beings can be happy, because they have no share at all in contemplation or study. So happiness is coextensive with study, and the greater the opportunity for studying, the greater the happiness, not as an incidental effect but as inherent in study; for study is in itself worthy of honor. Consequently, happiness is some kind of study or contemplation.

But we shall also need external well-being, since we are only human. Our nature is not self-sufficient for engaging in study: our body must be healthy and we must have food and generally be cared for. Nevertheless, if it is not possible for a man to be supremely happy without external goods, we must not think that his needs will be great and many in order to be happy; for self-sufficiency and moral action do not consist in an excess [of 1179[a]
possessions]. It is possible to perform noble actions even without being ruler of land and sea; a man's actions can be guided by virtue also if his means are moderate. That this is so can be clearly seen in the fact that private individuals evidently do not act less honorably but even more honorably than powerful rulers. It is enough to have moderate means at one's disposal, for the life of a man whose activity is guided by virtue will be happy.

Solon certainly gave a good description of a happy man, when he said that he is a man moderately supplied with external goods, who had performed what he, Solon, thought were the noblest actions, and who had lived with self-control. For it is possible to do what one should even with moderate possessions. Also Anaxagoras, it seems, did not assume that a happy man had to be rich and powerful. He said that he would not be surprised if a happy man would strike the common run of people as strange, since they judge by externals and perceive nothing but externals. So it seems that our account is in harmony with the opinion of the wise.

Now, though such considerations carry some conviction, in the field of moral action truth is judged by the actual facts of life, for it is in them that the decisive element lies. So we must examine the conclusions we have reached so far by applying them to the actual facts of life: if they are in harmony with the facts we must accept them, and if they clash we must assume that they are mere words.

*Supposedly the most beautiful of men, Endymion was loved by the Moon, who cast him into a perpetual sleep that she might descend and embrace him each night.

A man whose activity is guided by intelligence, who cultivates his intelligence and keeps it in the best condition, seems to be most beloved by the gods. For if the gods have any concern for human affairs—and they seem to have—it is to be expected that they rejoice in what is best and most akin to them, and that is our intelligence; it is also to be expected that they requite with good those who most love and honor intelligence, as being men who care for what is dear to the gods and who act rightly and nobly. That a wise man, more than any other, has all these qualities is perfectly clear. Consequently, he is the most beloved by the gods, and as such he is, presumably, also the happiest. Therefore, we have here a further indication that a wise man attains a higher degree of happiness than anyone.

HELLENISTIC AND ROMAN PHILOSOPHY

Following the death of Alexander the Great in 323 B.C., three of his generals, Ptolemy, Seleucus, and Antigonus, carved up the empire he had created. For the next three centuries the descendants of these three men ruled the eastern Mediterranean world. By 30 B.C., with the Roman Emperor Octavian's defeat of Anthony and Cleopatra and the annexation of Egypt, the period of Greek rule was over. Real power in the area had shifted westward to emerging Rome.

This shift from Greek to Roman authority did not happen without social and political turmoil, and the philosophies that developed during this period reflect that turmoil. The emphasis now was not on complete systems of thought, such as those proposed by Plato and Aristotle. In their place were theories focusing on the practical questions of the good life for individuals. In a world that seemed more and more chaotic and uncontrollable, philosophers began to seek personal salvation more than comprehensive theories. Even the Platonic Academy and the Aristotelian Lyceum, which continued for centuries, moved from the constructive doctrines of their founders to more narrowly defined critical issues.

The roots of the Epicurean school can be traced back to an early Socratic school, the Cyrenaics. The Cyrenaic school was founded by one of Socrates' associates and admirers, Aristippus of Cyrene, from Libya, in northern Africa. The Cyrenaics disparaged speculative philosophy and extolled the pleasure of the moment. But, following Aristippus, they maintained that the purest pleasure derives from self-mastery and the philosophic life. Only philosophy can protect human beings from passion, which inevitably brings suffering. While despising popular opinion, the Cyrenaics did believe that custom, law, and altruism contributed to long-range pleasure. The Cyrenaic philosophy, with its understanding of the good life as enjoyment of stable pleasures, led to the development of the Epicurean school as expressed by Epicurus.

The history of the Stoic school begins with the thought of Socrates' follower Antisthenes. Antisthenes, a rhetorician with an Athenian father and a Phrygian, non-Greek mother, had been a teacher before he met Socrates, who made a profound impression on him. It seems to have been Socrates' character—his self-control and self-sufficiency, his indifference to winter cold, his serenely ironic superiority in every experience, and the opinions of others (see the *Apology*)—that struck Antisthenes with the force of revelation. What he learned from Socrates was neither a metaphysic nor even a philosophic method but, as he put it, "to live with myself." When he disposed of his possessions, keeping only a ragged old coat, Socrates is said to have taunted him: "I see your vanity through the holes of your coat." Antisthenes founded a school whose members acquired the nickname of "Cynics" <*kynikos*>, Greek for "doglike." The Cynics slept on the ground, neglected their clothes, let their beards grow to unusual lengths, and despised the conventions of society, insisting that virtue and happiness consist of self-control and independence. They believed that human dignity was independent of human laws and customs.

Of Antisthenes' Cynic disciples, none was more famous than Diogenes, who went about carrying a lantern in daylight and, when asked why, would reply, "I am looking for an honest man." He made his home in a tub. His eccentric behavior

Laocoön, second century B.C., by Hagesandros, Polydoros, and Athenodoros, all of Rhodes. The Trojan priest Laocoön protested against bringing the Greeks' wooden horse into the city. According to one version of the legend, he was punished for his interference when Apollo sent two serpents to kill him and his sons. The Hellenistic 2nd Roman philosophers sought relief from tortured emotions such as this work depicts. (*Hirmer Fotoarchiv*)

attracted the attention of even Alexander the Great, who, on visiting him, asked whether there was anything at all that he could do to please him. Diogenes replied: "Yes, get out of my sunlight."

Emphasizing self-control and independence, and locating human dignity outside law and convention, the Cynicism of Antisthenes and Diogenes flowed like a tributary into Stoicism. Stoicism, in turn, became the dominant philosophy of the Roman Empire.

A third Hellenistic school of philosophy, Skepticism, also had its roots in Socrates' teachings: specifically, in Socrates' repeated claim that he did not know anything. Based on the work of Pyrrho of Elis (ca. 360–270 B.C.), this movement stressed the contradictory nature of knowledge and advocated suspending judgment and achieving an attitude of detachment.

The last great movement of ancient philosophy was Neoplatonism. The leader of this return to Platonic concepts, Plotinus (A.D. 204–270), did not lack enthusiasm, but he was, nevertheless, more remote from classical Greek attitudes than were the Hellenistic philosophers. He extolled the spirit to the point of saying he was ashamed to have a body; his fervor was entirely mystical, and he longed, to cite his famous words, to attain "the flight of the Alone to the Alone." Thus he perfected the less classical tendencies of Plato's thought, merging those tendencies with Neopythagoreanism and with Oriental notions such as the emanations from the One.

In A.D. 529, Plato's Academy was closed by Emperor Justinian, bringing to an end a millennium of Greek and Roman philosophy.

* * *

For clear, concise introductions to the Hellenistic and Roman philosophers, see Frederick Copleston, "Post-Aristotelian Philosophy," in his *A History of Philosophy: Volume I, Greece & Rome, Part II* (Garden City, NY: Image Books, 1962), and D.W. Hamlyn, "Greek Philosophy after Aristotle," in D.J. O'Connor, ed., *A Critical History of Western Philosophy* (New York: The Free Press, 1964). Eduard Zeller, *The Stoics, Epicureans, and Sceptics,* translated by Oswald J. Reichel (New York: Russell & Russell, 1962); Émile Bréhier, *The Hellenistic and Roman Age,* translated by Wade Baskin (Chicago: University of Chicago Press, 1965); A.A. Long, *Hellenistic Philosophy: Stoics, Epicureans, Sceptics* (New York: Scribners, 1974); R.W. *Sharples, Stoics, Epicureans and Sceptics* (Oxford: Routledge, 1996); John Dillon, *The Middle Platonists, 80 B.C. to A.D. 220* (Ithaca, NY: Cornell University Press, 1996); and Mark Morford, *Roman Philosophers* (London: Routledge, 2002), are all solid histories of the period. A.A. Long and D.N. Sedley, eds., *The Hellenistic Philosophers,* two vols. (Cambridge: Cambridge University Press, 1987) and Keimpe Algra, et al., eds., *The Cambridge History of Hellenistic Philosophy* (Cambridge: Cambridge University Press, 1999) provide source material and discussions, while Jacques Brunschwig, *Papers in Hellenistic Philosophy,* translated by Janet Lloyd (Cambridge: Cambridge University Press, 1994) and Terence Irwin, ed., *Hellenistic Philosophy* (Hamden, CT: Garland Publishing, 1995) give technical expositions of a number of important issues. For an interesting comparative approach to the Hellenistic thinkers, see Martha C. Nussbaum, *The Therapy of Desire: Theory and Practice in Hellenistic Ethics* (Princeton: Princeton University Press, 1994).

EPICURUS
341–270 B.C.

Like Pythagoras, Epicurus was born on the Greek island of Samos. At eighteen he went to Athens for a year, then joined his father in Colophon, the city where Xenophanes had been born. He studied the writings of Democritus and eventually set up his own school on the island of Lesbos. From there he moved to the Hellespont and, finally, to Athens in 307 B.C. As he moved from place to place, many of his students followed him. In Athens he established a community known as the "Garden," where he spent the rest of his life teaching and writing.

Epicurus's community welcomed people of all classes and of both sexes. The school required no fee from students, accepting what each individual was able and willing to pay. Epicurus himself was almost worshiped by his disciples, and members of his group had to swear an oath: "I will be faithful to Epicurus in accordance with whom I have made it my choice to live."* Among the later followers of Epicurus's thought, the Roman poet Lucretius (98–55 B.C.) considered him to be a god. Yet Epicurus was not overbearing or authoritarian. According to all accounts, he was kind and generous, treating his followers as friends, not subordinates. While dying in agony from a urinary obstruction, Epicurus wrote a letter that illustrates his gracious spirit. The extant portion includes these words to his friend Idomeneus: "I have a bulwark against all this pain from the joy in my soul at the memory of our conversations together."**

Epicurus wrote over three hundred volumes, but all that has survived are some fragments, three complete letters, and a short treatise summarizing his views. These surviving works provide an understanding of Epicurus's physics and ethics

*From Introduction To Greek Philosophy by J.V. Luce (C) 1992. Reprinted by kind permission of Thames & Hudson Ltd., London.

**Ibid.

and give some sense of his psychology and theory of knowledge. Epicurus's first letter, *To Herodotus,* explains his atomistic theory. Like Democritus, Epicurus asserts that reality is composed of atoms and the void. But unlike Democritus, whose atomism is deterministic, Epicurus broaches the notion that atoms sometimes inexplicably "swerve." As atoms "fell downward" through the void, some of them swerved from their paths and collided with other atoms, setting off a chain reaction that eventually led to the world as we know it. Epicurus goes on to explore the implications of this theory for perception and knowledge.

The second letter, *To Pythocles*, on astronomy and meteorology, is of questionable origin and adds little to our understanding of Epicurus's thought. But the third letter, *To Menoeceus*, together with the short work *Principle Doctrines* explains his central ethical theory. Epicurus declares that pleasure is the highest good, though some pleasures are unnatural and unnecessary. In contrast to the modern understanding of the word "epicurean," Epicurus opposed exotic meals and profuse consumption. Such indulgences never bring permanent pleasure and frequently lead to its opposite: pain. Instead Epicurus advocates enjoying only the "natural" pleasures—those most likely to lead to contentment and repose. Epicurus's ethical works are reprinted here, complete, in the Russel M. Geer translations.

* * *

The classic secondary work on Epicurus is Cyril Bailey, *The Greek Atomists and Epicurus* (Oxford: Clarendon Press, 1928). Norman Wentworth De Witt, *Epicurus and His Philosophy* (Minneapolis: University of Minnesota Press, 1954), provides an interesting interpretation—one which John M. Rist, *Epicurus: An Introduction* (Cambridge: Cambridge University Press, 1972), contests. A.E. Taylor, *Epicurus* (1911; reprinted New York: Books for Libraries Press, 1969); G.K. Stradach, *The Philosophy of Epicurus* (Evanston, IL: Northwestern University Press, 1963); and Diskin Clay, *Lucretius and Epicurus* (Ithaca, NY: Cornell University Press, 1983), give helpful overviews. A.J. Festugière, *Epicurus and His Gods*, translated by C.W. Chilton (1955; reprinted London: Russell, 1969); James H. Nichols, Jr., *Epicurean Political Philosophy* (Ithaca, NY: Cornell University Press, 1976); and Tim O'Keefe, *Epicurus on Freedom* (Cambridge: Cambridge University Press, 2005), deal with specific topics.

LETTER TO MENOECEUS

I. INTRODUCTION

Epicurus to Menoeceus, greeting.

Let no young man delay the study of philosophy, and let no old man become weary of it; for it is never too early nor too late to care for the well-being of the soul. The man who says that the season for this study has not yet come or is already past is like the man who says it is too early or too late for happiness. Therefore, both the young and the old should study philosophy, the former so that as he grows old he may still retain the happiness of youth in his pleasant memories of the past, the latter so that although he is old he may at the same time be young by virtue of his fearlessness of the future. We must therefore study the means of securing happiness, since if we have it we have everything, but if we lack it we do everything in order to gain it.

II. BASIC TEACHINGS

A. THE GODS

The gods exist; but it is impious to accept the common beliefs about them. They have no concern with men.

Practice and study without ceasing that which I was always teaching you, being assured that these are the first principles of the good life. After accepting god as the immortal and blessed being depicted by popular opinion, do not ascribe to him anything in addition that is alien to immortality or foreign to blessedness, but rather believe about him whatever can uphold his blessed immortality. The gods do indeed exist, for our perception of them is clear; but they are not such as the crowd imagines them to be, for most men do not retain the picture of the gods that they first receive. It is not the man who destroys the gods of popular belief who is impious, but he who describes the gods in the terms accepted by the many. For the opinions of the many about the gods are not perceptions but false suppositions. According to these popular suppositions, the gods send great evils to the wicked, great blessings to the righteous, for they, being always well disposed to their own virtues, approve those who are like themselves, regarding as foreign all that is different.*

B. DEATH

Philosophy, showing that death is the end of all consciousness, relieves us of all fear of death. A life that is happy is better than one that is merely long.

*The ambiguous rendition of the last part of this sentence is intentional. "They" may be the gods, who approve men like themselves, or men, who approve gods.

Epicurus, *Letters, Principal Doctrines, and Vatican Sayings*, translated by Russel M. Geer (Pearson/Library of the Liberal Arts, 1964).

Accustom yourself to the belief that death is of no concern to us, since all good and evil lie in sensation and sensation ends with death. Therefore the true belief that death is nothing to us makes a mortal life happy, not by adding to it an infinite time, but by taking away the desire for immortality. For there is no reason why the man who is thoroughly assured that there is nothing to fear in death should find anything to fear in life. So, too, he is foolish who says that he fears death, not because it will be painful when it comes, but because the anticipation of it is painful; for that which is no burden when it is present gives pain to no purpose when it is anticipated. Death, the most dreaded of evils, is therefore of no concern to us; for while we exist death is not present, and when death is present we no longer exist. It is therefore nothing either to the living or to the dead since it is not present to the living, and the dead no longer are.

But men in general sometimes flee death as the greatest of evils, sometimes long for it as a relief from the evils of life.

The wise man neither renounces life nor fears its end; for living does not offend him, nor does he suppose that not to live is in any way an evil. As he does not choose the food that is most in quantity but that which is most pleasant, so he does not seek the enjoyment of the longest life but of the happiest.

He who advises the young man to live well, the old man to die well, is foolish, not only because life is desirable, but also because the art of living well and the art of dying well are one. Yet much worse is he who says that it is well not to have been born, but once born, be swift to pass through Hades' gates.

If a man says this and really believes it, why does he not depart from life? Certainly the means are at hand for doing so if this really be his firm conviction. If he says it in mockery, he is regarded as a fool among those who do not accept his teaching.

Remember that the future is neither ours nor wholly not ours, so that we may neither count on it as sure to come nor abandon hope of it as certain not to be.

III. The Moral Theory

A. Pleasure as the Motive

The necessary desires are for health of body and peace of mind; if these are satisfied, that is enough for the happy life.

You must consider that of the desires some are natural, some are vain, and of those that are natural, some are necessary, others only natural. Of the necessary desires, some are necessary for happiness, some for the ease of the body, some for life itself. The man who has a perfect knowledge of this will know how to make his every choice or rejection tend toward gaining health of body and peace of mind, since this is the final end of the blessed life. For to gain this end, namely freedom from pain and fear, we do everything. When once this condition is reached, all the storm of the soul is stilled, since the creature need make no move in search of anything that is lacking, nor seek after anything else to make complete the welfare of the soul and the body. For we only feel the lack of pleasure when from its absence we suffer pain; but when we do not suffer pain, we no longer are in need of pleasure. For this reason we say that pleasure is the beginning and the end of the blessed life. We recognize pleasure as the first and natural good; starting from pleasure we accept or reject; and we return to this as we judge every good thing, trusting this feeling of pleasure as our guide.

B. PLEASURES AND PAINS

Pleasure is the greatest good; but some pleasures bring pain, and in choosing, we must consider this.

For the very reason that pleasure is the chief and the natural good, we do not choose every pleasure, but there are times when we pass by pleasures if they are outweighed by the hardships that follow; and many pains we think better than pleasures when a greater pleasure will come to us once we have undergone the long-continued pains. Every pleasure is a good since it has a nature akin to ours; nevertheless, not every pleasure is to be chosen. Just so, every pain is an evil, yet not every pain is of a nature to be avoided on all occasions. By measuring and by looking at advantages and disadvantages, it is proper to decide all these things; for under certain circumstances we treat the good as evil, and again, the evil as good.

C. SELF-SUFFICIENCY

The truly wise man is the one who can be happy with a little.

We regard self-sufficiency as a great good, not so that we may enjoy only a few things, but so that, if we do not have many, we may be satisfied with the few, being firmly persuaded that they take the greatest pleasure in luxury who regard it as least needed, and that everything that is natural is easily provided, while vain pleasures are hard to obtain. Indeed, simple sauces bring a pleasure equal to that of lavish banquets if once the pain due to need is removed; and bread and water give the greatest pleasure when one who is in need consumes them. To be accustomed to simple and plain living is conducive to health and makes a man ready for the necessary tasks of life. It also makes us more ready for the enjoyment of luxury if at intervals we chance to meet with it, and it renders us fearless against fortune.

D. TRUE PLEASURE

The truest happiness does not come from enjoyment of physical pleasures but from a simple life, free from anxiety, with the normal physical needs satisfied.

When we say that pleasure is the end, we do not mean the pleasure of the profligate or that which depends on physical enjoyment—as some think who do not understand our teachings, disagree with them, or give them an evil interpretation—but by pleasure we mean the state wherein the body is free from pain and the mind from anxiety. Neither continual drinking and dancing, nor sexual love, nor the enjoyment of fish and whatever else the luxurious table offers brings about the pleasant life; rather, it is produced by the reason which is sober, which examines the motive for every choice and rejection, and which drives away all those opinions through which the greatest tumult lays hold of the mind.

E. PRUDENCE

Prudence or practical wisdom should be our guide.

Of all this the beginning and the chief good is prudence. For this reason prudence is more precious than philosophy itself. All the other virtues spring from it. It teaches that it is not possible to live pleasantly without at the same time living prudently, nobly, and justly, nor to live prudently, nobly, and justly without living pleasantly; for the virtues have grown up in close union with the pleasant life, and the pleasant life cannot be separated from the virtues.

IV. CONCLUSION

A. PANEGYRIC* ON THE PRUDENT MAN

Whom then do you believe to be superior to the prudent man: he who has reverent opinions about the gods, who is wholly without fear of death, who has discovered what is the highest good in life and understands that the highest point in what is good is easy to reach and hold and that the extreme of evil is limited either in time or in suffering, and who laughs at that which some have set up as the ruler of all things, Necessity? He thinks that the chief power of decision lies within us, although some things come about by necessity, some by chance, and some by our own wills; for he sees that necessity is irresponsible and chance uncertain, but that our actions are subject to no power. It is for this reason that our actions merit praise or blame. It would be better to accept the myth about the gods than to be a slave to the determinism of the physicists; for the myth hints at a hope for grace through honors paid to the gods, but the necessity of determinism is inescapable. Since the prudent man does not, as do many, regard chance as a god for the gods do nothing in disorderly fashion or as an unstable cause of all things, he believes that chance does not give man good and evil to make his life happy or miserable, but that it does provide opportunities for great good or evil. Finally, he thinks it better to meet misfortune while acting with reason than to happen upon good fortune while acting senselessly; for it is better that what has been well-planned in our actions should fail than that what has been ill-planned should gain success by chance.

B. FINAL WORDS TO MENOECEUS

Meditate on these and like precepts, by day and by night, alone or with a like-minded friend. Then never, either awake or asleep, will you be dismayed; but you will live like a god among men; for life amid immortal blessings is in no way like the life of a mere mortal.

*[Formal praise for a festival]

PRINCIPAL DOCTRINES

I. That which is blessed and immortal is not troubled itself, nor does it cause trouble to another. As a result, it is not affected by anger or favor, for these belong to weakness.

II. Death is nothing to us; for what has been dissolved has no sensation, and what has no sensation is nothing to us.

III. The removal of all that causes pain marks the boundary of pleasure. Wherever pleasure is present and as long as it continues, there is neither suffering nor grieving nor both together.

IV. Continuous bodily suffering does not last long. Intense pain is very brief, and even pain that barely outweighs physical pleasure does not last many days. Long illnesses permit physical pleasures that are greater than the pain.

V. It is impossible to live pleasantly without living prudently, well, and justly, and to live prudently, well, and justly without living pleasantly. Even though a man live well and justly, it is not possible for him to live pleasantly if he lacks that from which stems the prudent life.

VI. Any device whatever by which one frees himself from the fear of others is a natural good.

VII. Some, thinking thus to make themselves safe from men, wished to become famous and renowned. They won a natural good if they made their lives secure; but if their lives were not secure, they did not have that for which, following the rule of nature, they first sought.

VIII. No pleasure is evil in itself; but the means by which certain pleasures are gained bring pains many times greater than the pleasures.

IX. If every pleasure were cumulative, and if this were the case both in time and in regard to the whole or the most important parts of our nature, then pleasures would not differ from each other.

X. If the things that produce the pleasures of the dissolute were able to drive away from their minds their fears about what is above them and about death and pain, and to teach them the limit of desires, we would have no reason to find fault with the dissolute; for they would fill themselves with pleasure from every source and would be free from pain and sorrow, which are evil.

XI. If our dread of the phenomena above us, our fear lest death concern us, and our inability to discern the limits of pains and desires were not vexatious to us, we would have no need of the natural sciences.

XII. It is not possible for one to rid himself of his fears about the most important things if he does not understand the nature of the universe but dreads some of the things he has learned in the myths. Therefore, it is not possible to gain unmixed happiness without natural science.

XIII. It is of no avail to prepare security against other men while things above us and beneath the earth and in the whole infinite universe in general are still dreaded.

Epicurus, *Letters, Principal Doctrines, and Vatican Sayings*, translated by Russel M. Geer (Pearson/ Library of the Liberal Arts, 1964).

XIV. When reasonable security from men has been attained, then the security that comes from peace of mind and withdrawal from the crowd is present, sufficient in strength and most unmixed in well-being.

XV. Natural wealth is limited and easily obtained; the wealth defined by vain fancies is always beyond reach.

XVI. Fortune seldom troubles the wise man. Reason has controlled his greatest and most important affairs, controls them throughout his life, and will continue to control them.

XVII. The just man is least disturbed; the unjust man is filled with the greatest turmoil.

XVIII. When once the pain caused by need has been removed, bodily pleasure will not be increased in amount but only varied in quality. The mind attains its utmost pleasure in reflecting on the very things that used to cause the greatest mental fears and on things like them.

XIX. Time that is unlimited and time that is limited afford equal pleasure if one measures pleasure's extent by reason.

XX. The flesh believes that pleasure is limitless and that it requires unlimited time; but the mind, understanding the end and limit of the flesh and ridding itself of fears of the future, secures a complete life and has no longer any need for unlimited time. It does not, however, avoid pleasure; and when circumstances bring on the end of life, it does not depart as if it still lacked any portion of the good life.

XXI. The man who understands the limits of living knows that it is easy to obtain that which removes the pain caused by want and that which perfects the whole life. Therefore, he has no need of things that involve struggle.

XXII. It is necessary to take into account the real purpose of knowledge and all the evidence of that clear perception to which we refer our opinions. If we do not, all will be full of bad judgment and confusion.

XXIII. If you struggle against all your sensations, you will have no standard of comparison by which to measure even the sensations you judge false.

XXIV. If you reject any sensation, and if you fail to distinguish between conjecture based upon that which awaits confirmation and evidence given by the senses, by the feelings, and by the mental examinations of confirmed concepts, you will confuse the other sensations with unfounded conjecture and thus destroy the whole basis for judgment. If among all opinions you accept as equally valid both those that await confirmation and those that have been confirmed, you will not free yourself from error, since you will have preserved all the uncertainty about every judgment of what is true and what is not true.

XXV. If you do not at all times refer each of your actions to the natural end,* but fall short of this and turn aside to something else in choosing and avoiding, your deeds will not agree with your words.

XXVI. Those desires that do not bring pain if they are not satisfied are not necessary; and they are easily thrust aside whenever to satisfy them appears difficult or likely to cause injury.

XXVII. Of the things that wisdom prepares for insuring lifelong happiness, by far the greatest is the possession of friends.

*That is, to pleasure.

XXVIII. The same wisdom that permits us to be confident that no evil is eternal or even of long duration also recognizes that in our limited state the security that can be most perfectly gained is that of friendship.

XXIX. Of the desires, some are natural and necessary; some are natural but not necessary; and others are neither natural nor necessary but arise from empty opinion.

XXX. Among the bodily desires, those rest on empty opinion that are eagerly pursued although if unsatisfied they bring no pain. That they are not got rid of is because of man's empty opinion, not because of their own nature.

XXXI. Natural justice is a compact resulting from expediency by which men seek to prevent one man from injuring others and to protect him from being injured by them.

XXXII. There is no such thing as justice or injustice among those beasts that cannot make agreements not to injure or be injured. This is also true of those tribes that are unable or unwilling to make agreements not to injure or be injured.

XXXIII. There is no such thing as justice in the abstract; it is merely a compact between men in their various relations with each other, in whatever circumstances they may be, that they will neither injure nor be injured.

XXXIV. Injustice is not evil in itself, but only in the fear and apprehension that one will not escape those who have been set up to punish the offense.

XXXV. If a man has secretly violated any of the terms of the mutual compact not to injure or be injured, he cannot feel confident that he will be undetected in the future even if he has escaped ten thousand times in the past; for until his death it will remain uncertain whether he will escape.

XXXVI. In general, justice is the same for all, a thing found useful by men in their relations with each other; but it does not follow that it is the same for all in each individual place and circumstance.

XXXVII. Among the things commonly held just, that which has proved itself useful in men's mutual relationships has the stamp of justice whether or not it be the same for all; if anyone makes a law and it does not prove useful in men's relationships with each other, it is no longer just in its essence. If, however, the law's usefulness in the matter of justice should change and it should meet men's expectations only for a short time, nonetheless during that short time it was just in the eyes of those who look simply at facts and do not confuse themselves with empty words.

XXXVIII. If, although no new circumstances have arisen, those things that were commonly held just in these matters did not in their actual effects correspond with that conception, they were not just. Whenever, as a result of new circumstances, the same things that had been regarded as just were no longer useful, they were just at the time when they were useful for the relations of citizens to each other; but afterwards, when they were no longer useful, they were no longer just.

XXXIX. He who has best controlled his lack of confidence in the face of external forces has, as far as possible, treated these externals as akin to himself or, when that was impossible, at least as not alien. Where he was not able to do even this, he kept to himself and avoided whatever it was best to avoid.

XL. Those who were best able to prepare security for themselves in relation to their neighbors* lived most pleasantly with their neighbors since they had the most perfect assurance; and enjoying the most complete intimacy, they did not lament the death of one who died before his time as if it were an occasion for sorrow.

*That is, those who were most self-sufficient and least dependent upon others

EPICTETUS
ca. A.D. 50–ca. A.D. 130

Epictetus was born a slave in Hierapolis, a small town in Phrygia, Asia Minor (in present-day Turkey). His master was Epaphroditus, a member of Emperor Nero's personal staff in Rome. As was often done at that time, Epaphroditus saw to it that Epictetus had a good education, sending him to study with the Roman Stoic, Rufus. Epictetus gained his freedom sometime after the death of the emperor in A.D. 68 and began to teach philosophy in Rome. In A.D. 89 or 93 Emperor Domitian expelled all philosophers from Rome. Domitian seems to have been especially angry with the Stoics for teaching that sovereignty comes from God and is for the benefit of the people. (Epictetus's reported claim that he had the same regard for the emperor as for his water-pot could not have helped.) Epictetus moved to Nicropolis in Epirus (northwestern Greece), where he established a thriving Stoic school and lived a simple life with few material goods. As an old man, he married so that he could adopt a child who otherwise would have been "exposed," that is, left to die. Those whom he taught described him as a humble, charitable man of great moral and religious devotion.

Epictetus never wrote anything, but one of his admiring students, Arrian, composed eight *Discourses* based on Epictetus's lectures, along with a summary of the great man's thought, the *Handbook* (*Enchiridion*). The *Handbook,* given here complete in the outstanding new Keith Seddon translation, builds on the early Stoa's concept of *Logos.* Since the *Logos* or natural law permeates everything, it provides us with moral intuition, so all persons have the capacity for virtue. But in order to live the moral life, one must apply these intuitions to specific cases. Education is necessary if we are to learn how to properly connect moral insights with life. We must begin by recognizing the fact that we cannot change events that happen to us, but we can change our attitude toward those events. To accomplish this and achieve the good life, we must go through three stages. First, we must order our desires and overcome our fears. Next, we must perform our duties—in whatever role fate has given us. Finally, we must think clearly and judge accurately. Only then will we gain inner tranquility.

Despite Emperor Domitian's condemnation, Stoicism had a special appeal to the Roman mind. The Romans were not much interested in the speculative and theoretical content of Zeno's early Stoa. Instead, in the austere moral emphasis of Epictetus, with his concomitant stress on self-control and superiority to pain, the Romans found an ideal for the wise man, whereas the Stoic description of natural law provided a basis for Roman law. One might say that the pillars of republican Rome tended to be Stoical, even if some Romans had never heard of Stoicism.

* * *

For general introductions to the Stoics, see E. Vernon Arnold, *Roman Stoicism* (1911; reprinted New York: Humanities Press, 1958); L. Edelstein, *The Meaning of Stoicism* (Cambridge, MA: Harvard University Press, 1966); John M. Rist, *Stoic Philosophy* (Cambridge: Cambridge University Press, 1969); F.H. Sandbach, *The Stoics* (New York: Norton, 1975); Margaret E. Reeser, *The Nature of Man in Early Stoic Philosophy* (New York: St. Martin's Press, 1989); and Brad Inwood, ed., *The Cambridge Companion to the Stoics* (Cambridge: Cambridge University Press, 2003). For comparisons between Stoicism and other Hellenistic schools, see R.M. Wenley, *Stoicism and Its Influence* (1924; reprinted New York: Cooper Square, 1963); Edwin R. Bevan, *Stoics and Sceptics* (Oxford: Clarendon Press, 1913); and R.D. Hicks, *Stoic and Epicurean* (1910; reprinted New York: Russell, 1962). For collections of essays consult A.A. Long, ed., *Problems in Stoicism* (London: Athlone Press, 1971); J.M. Rist, ed., *The Stoics* (Berkeley: University of California Press, 1978); A.A. Long, ed., *Stoic Studies* (Cambridge: Cambridge University Press, 1996); and Steven K. Strange and Jack Zupko, eds., *Stoicism: Traditions and Transformations* (Cambridge: Cambridge University Press, 2004).

For volumes specifically on Epictetus, see John Bonforte, *The Philosophy of Epictetus* (New York: Philosophical Library, 1955) and William O. Stephens, *Stoic Ethics: Epictetus and Happiness as Freedom* (London: Continuum, 2007). Iason Xenakis, *Epictetus: Philosopher-Therapist* (The Hague, Netherlands: Martinus Nijhoff, 1969), makes an interesting application of Epictetus; while W.A. Oldfather, *Contributions Towards a Bibliography of Epictetus* (Urbana: University of Illinois Press, 1927; supplement, 1952), furnishes a bibliography. For a study of Epictetus' star pupil, see Philip A. Stadter, *Arrian of Nicomedia* (Chapel Hill: University of North Carolina Press, 1980).

HANDBOOK (ENCHIRIDION)

Chapter 1: [1] On the one hand, there are things that are in our power, whereas other things are not in our power. In our power are opinion, impulse, desire, aversion, and, in a word, whatever is our own doing. Things not in our power include our body, our possessions, our reputations, our status, and, in a word, whatever is not our own doing.

[2] Now, things that are in our power are by nature free, unhindered, unimpeded; but things not in our power are weak, slavish, hindered, and belong to others. [3] Remember, therefore, that whenever you suppose those things that are by nature slavish to be free, or those things that belong to others to be your own, you will be hindered, miserable and distressed, and you will find fault with both gods and men. If, however, you suppose to be yours only what is yours, and what belongs to another to belong to another (as indeed it does), no one will ever compel you, no one will hinder you; you will find fault with no one, reproach no one, nor act against your own will; you will have no enemies and no one will harm you, for no harm can touch you.

[4] Thus, when aiming at such great things remember that securing them requires more than a modest effort: some things you will have to give up altogether, and others you will have to put aside for the time being. If you want such great things but at the same time strive for status and wealth, you may well not even obtain these latter things because you are seeking the former; at any rate, you will certainly fail to secure those former great things which alone bring freedom and happiness.

[5] Straightaway then, train yourself to say to every unpleasant impression, "You are an impression, and by no means what you appear to be." Then examine it and test it by the rules that you have, first (in this way especially) by asking whether it concerns things that are in our power or things that are not in our power: and if it concerns something not in our power, have ready to hand the answer, "This is nothing to me."

Chapter 2: [1] Remember that, on the one hand, desires command you to obtain what you long for and, on the other, aversions command you to avoid what you dislike. Those who fail to gain what they desire are unfortunate, whilst those who fall into what they seek to avoid are miserable. So if you seek to avoid only those things contrary to nature amongst the things that are in your power, you will accordingly fall into nothing to which you are averse; but if you seek to avoid sickness, or death, or poverty, you will be miserable. [2] Therefore, remove altogether your aversion for anything that is not in our power, and transfer it to those things contrary to nature that *are* in our power. For the time being, completely restrain your desires, for if you desire any of those things not in our power you are bound to suffer misfortune. For of those things in our power, which it would be proper to desire, none is yet within your grasp. Use only impulse and repulsion, but use even these lightly, with reservation, and without straining.

Chapter 3: With respect to any of those things you find attractive or useful or have a fondness for, recall to mind what kind of thing it is, beginning with the most trifling. So if you are fond of an earthenware pot, say, "I am fond of an earthenware pot." Then you will not be upset if it gets broken. When you kiss your child or wife, say that you are kissing a human being; then, should they die, you will not be distressed.

Chapter 4: When you are about to undertake some task, remind yourself what sort of business it is. If you are going out to bathe, bring to mind what happens at the baths: there will be those who splash you, those who will jostle you, some will be abusive to you, and others will steal from you. And thus you will undertake the affair more securely if you say to yourself from the start, "I wish to take a bath, but also to keep my moral character in accordance with nature." Do likewise with every undertaking. For thus, if anything should happen that interferes with your bathing, be ready to say, "Oh well, it was not only this that I wanted, but also to keep my moral character in accordance with nature, and I cannot do that if I am irritated by things that happen."

Chapter 5: It is not circumstances themselves that trouble people, but their judgments about those circumstances. For example, death is nothing terrible, for if it were, it would have appeared so to Socrates; but having the opinion that death is terrible, *this* is what is terrible. Therefore, whenever we are hindered or troubled or distressed, let us never blame others, but ourselves, that is, our own judgments. The uneducated person blames others for their failures; those who have just begun to be instructed blame themselves; those whose learning is complete blame neither others nor themselves.

Chapter 6: Do not take pride in any excellence that is not your own. If a horse were to say proudly, "I am beautiful," one could put up with that. But when you say proudly, "I have a beautiful horse," remember that you are boasting about something good that belongs to the horse. What, then, belongs to *you*? The use of impressions. Whenever you are in accordance with nature regarding the way you use impressions, then be proud, for then you will be proud of a good that is your own.

Chapter 7: Just as on a voyage, when the ship has anchored, if you go ashore to get water you may also pick up a shell-fish or a vegetable from the path, but you should keep your thoughts fixed on the ship, and you should look back frequently in case the captain calls, and, if he should call, you must give up all these other things to avoid being bound and thrown on board like a sheep; so in life also, if instead of a vegetable and a shell-fish you are given a wife and a child, nothing will prevent you from taking them—but if the captain calls, give up all these things and run to the ship without even turning to look back. And if you are old, do not even go far from the ship, lest you are missing when the call comes.

Chapter 8: Do not demand that things should happen just as you wish, but wish them to happen just as they do, and all will be well.

Chapter 9: Illness interferes with one's body, but not with one's moral character, unless one so wishes. Lameness interferes with one's leg, but not with one's moral character. Say this to yourself regarding everything that happens to you, for you will find that what happens interferes with something else, but not with you.

Chapter 10: On every occasion when something happens to you, remember to turn to yourself to see what capacity you have for dealing with it. If you are attracted to a beautiful boy or woman, you will find that self-control is the capacity to use for that. If hardship befalls you, you will find endurance; if abuse, you will find patience. Make this your habit and you will not be carried away by impressions.

Chapter 11: Never say of anything, "I have lost it," but rather "I have given it back." Has your child died? It has been given back. Has your wife died? She has been given back. Has your land been taken from you? Well, that too has been given back. "But the one who took it from me is a bad man!" What concern is it of yours by whose hand the Giver asks for its return? For the time that these things are given to you, take care of them as things that belong to another, just as travelers do an inn.

Chapter 12: [1] If you want to make progress, set aside all considerations like these: "If I neglect my affairs, I will have nothing to live on"; "If I do not punish my slave-boy, he will be bad." For it is better to die of hunger, free from distress and fear, than to live perturbed amidst plenty. It is better for your slave-boy to be bad than for you to be wretched. [2] Begin therefore with little things. The olive oil is spilled. The wine is stolen. Say to yourself, "This is the price for peace of mind, and this is the price for being free of troubles. Nothing can be had without paying the price." And when you call your slave-boy, bear in mind that it is quite possible he won't heed you, or even if he does heed you it is quite possible that he won't do the things you tell him to. But he is not in so fine a position that your peace of mind depends upon him.

Chapter 13: If you want to make progress, submit to appearing foolish and stupid with regard to external things. Do not wish to appear knowledgeable about anything and, if others think you amount to something, distrust yourself. For you should know that it is not easy both to keep your moral character in accordance with nature and to keep secure external things, for in attending to one, you will inevitably neglect the other.

Chapter 14: [1] It is foolish to wish that your children and your wife and your friends should live forever, for you are wishing for things to be in your power which are not, and wishing for what belongs to others to be your own. It is foolish in the same way, too, to wish that your slave-boy should never do wrong, for now you want badness not to be badness, but something else. However, if you wish not to fail in what you desire, this you are able to do. Exercise yourself, therefore, in what you *are* able to do. [2] A person's master is the one who has power over that which is wished for or not wished for, so as to secure it or take it away. Therefore, anyone who wishes to be free should neither wish for anything nor avoid anything that depends on others; those who do not observe this rule will of necessity be the slaves of others.

Chapter 15: Remember, you ought to behave in life as you would at a banquet. Something is carried round and comes to you: reach out and take a modest portion. It passes by? Do not stop it. It has not yet arrived? Do not stretch your desire towards it, but wait until it comes to you. So it should be concerning your children, your wife, your status, your wealth, and one day you will be worthy to share a banquet with the gods. If, however, you do not take these things even when they are put before you, but have no regard for them, not only will you share a banquet with the gods, but also rule with them. By acting in this way, Diogenes and Heraclitus, and people like them, were deservedly gods and were deservedly called so.

Chapter 16: When you see someone weeping in grief because their child has gone abroad or because they have lost their property, take care not to be carried away by the impression that these external things involve them in anything bad, but be ready to say immediately, "This person is not distressed by what has happened (for it does not distress anyone else), but by the judgement they make of it." Do not hesitate, however, to sympathise with words, or if it so happens, to weep with them; but take care not to weep inwardly.

Chapter 17: Remember that you are an actor in a play of such a kind as the playwright chooses: short, if he wants it short, long if he wants it long. If he wants you to play the part of a beggar, play even this part well; and so also for the parts of a disabled person, an administrator, or a private individual. For this is your business, to play well the part you are given; but choosing it belongs to another.

Chapter 18: When a raven croaks inauspiciously, do not be carried away by the impression, but straightaway draw a distinction and say to yourself, "This portent signifies nothing with respect to me, but only with regard to my body, my possessions, my reputation, my children or my wife. To me, however, all portents are auspicious, if I wish them so. For however the affair turns out, it is in my power to benefit from it."

Chapter 19: [1] You can be invincible if you never enter a contest in which it is not in your power to win. [2] Beware that, when you see someone honoured before others, enjoying great power, or otherwise highly esteemed, you do not get carried away by the impression and think them happy. For if the essence of good lies in what is in our power, it is wrong to feel envy or jealousy, and you yourself will not wish to be praetor, senator

Theater at Hieropolis, Phrygia, Asia Minor (present-day Turkey). Built during Epictetus's lifetime—in his hometown—this theater had a capacity for more than twelve thousand spectators. All-day festivals of drama on every phase of life from the tragic to the comic were presented here. It is not surprising that Epictetus uses the image of the play and the playwright to make his point. (*Forrest E. Baird*)

or consul, but someone who is free. There is only one way to attain this end, and this is to have no concern for the things that are not in our power.

Chapter 20: Remember that the insult does not come from the person who abuses you or hits you, but from your judgement that such people are insulting you. Therefore, whenever someone provokes you, be aware that it is your own opinion that provokes you. Try, therefore, in the first place, not to be carried away by your impressions, for if you can gain time and delay, you will more easily control yourself.

Chapter 21: Let death and exile, and all other things that seem terrible, appear daily before your eyes, but especially death—and you will never entertain any abject thought, nor long for anything excessively.

Chapter 22: If you set your heart on philosophy, be prepared from the very start to be ridiculed and jeered at by many people who will say, "Suddenly he's come back to us a philosopher!" and "Where do you suppose he got that supercilious look?" Now, for your part, do not show a supercilious look, but hold to the things that seem best to you, as someone who has been assigned to this post by God. And remember that if you persist in your principles, those who at first ridiculed you will later admire you. But if, on the other hand, you are defeated by such people, you will be doubly ridiculed.

Chapter 23: If at any time it should happen that you turn to external things with the aim of pleasing someone, understand that you have ruined your life's plan. Be content, then, in everything, with being a philosopher; and if you wish also to be regarded as such, appear so to yourself, and that will be sufficient.

Chapter 24: [1] Do not be troubled by thoughts such as these: "I will be valued by no one my whole life long, a nobody everywhere!" For if lacking value is something bad (which it is), you cannot be involved in anything bad through other people any more than you can be involved in anything disgraceful. Is it any business of yours, then, to acquire status or to be invited to a banquet? Certainly not! How, then, can this be regarded as lacking value? And how will you be a nobody everywhere, when all you have to be is a somebody concerning those things that are in your power, with respect to which you can be someone of the greatest value?

[2] "But my friends," you say, "will lack support."

What do you mean, "lack support"? Certainly they won't get much cash from you, neither will you make them Roman citizens! Who told you, then, that these things are amongst those that are in our power, and not the business of other people? And who can give to others things they do not have themselves?

[3] "Get some money, then," someone says, "so that we can have some too!"

If I can get it whilst also preserving my self-respect, my trustworthiness, my magnanimity, show me how, and I will get it. But if you ask me to forsake those things that are good and my own, in order that you may acquire those things that are not good, see for yourself how unfair and thoughtless you are. Besides, what would you rather have, money, or a friend who is trustworthy and has self-respect? Therefore help me towards this end, and do not ask me to do anything by which I will lose those very qualities.

[4] "But my country," you say, "as far as it depends on me, will be without my help."

I ask again, what help do you mean? It will not have colonnades and bathhouses on your account. But what does that mean? For neither is it provided with shoes by a smith, nor weapons by a shoemaker: it is enough if everyone properly attends to their own business. But if you were to provide it with another trustworthy citizen who has self-respect, would that not be of use to your country?

"Yes."

Well, then, you also cannot be useless to it.

[5] "What place, then," you ask, "will I have in the community?"

That which you may have whilst also preserving your trustworthiness and self-respect. But if, by wishing to be useful, you throw away these qualities, of what use can you be to your community if you become shameless and untrustworthy?

Chapter 25: [1] Has someone been honoured above you at a banquet, or in a greeting, or in being called in to give advice? If these things are good, you should be pleased for the person who has received them. If, on the other hand, they are bad, do not be upset that you did not receive them yourself. Remember, with respect to acquiring things that are not in our power, you cannot expect an equal share if you do not behave in the same way as other people. [2] How is it possible, if you do not hang around someone's door, accompany them or praise them, to have an equal share with people who do these things? You will be unjust, therefore, and insatiable, if you refuse to pay the price for which these things are sold, but wish instead to obtain them for nothing. [3] For what price are lettuces sold? An obol, let's say. When someone else, then, pays an obol and takes the lettuce, whilst you, not paying it go without, do not imagine that this person has gained an advantage over you. Whereas they have the lettuce, you still have the obol that you did not pay.

[4] So, in the present case, if you have not been invited to someone's banquet, that is because you have not paid them the price for which a banquet is sold. They sell it for praise; they sell it for flattery. Pay the price, then, for which it is sold, if you think this will be to your advantage. But if at the same time you do not want to pay the one, yet wish to receive the other, you are insatiable and foolish.

[5] Do you have nothing, then, in place of the banquet? You have this—you have not had to praise the person you did not want to praise, and you have not had to bear the insolence of their doorkeepers.

Chapter 26: We can understand the will of nature from those things in which we do not differ from one another. For example, when our neighbour's slave has broken a cup, we are immediately ready to say, "Well, such things happen." Understand, then, that when your own cup gets broken you should react in just the same way as when someone else's cup gets broken. Apply the same principle to matters of greater importance. Has someone else's child or wife died? There is no one who would not say, "Such is the way of things." But when someone's own child dies they immediately cry, "Woe is me! How wretched I am!" But we should remember how we feel when we hear of the same thing happening to other people.

Chapter 27: Just as a target is not set up in order to be missed, so neither does the nature of evil exist in the world.

Chapter 28: How angry you would be if someone handed over your body to just any person who happened to meet you! Are you not ashamed, then, when you hand over your mind to just any person you happen to meet, such that when they abuse you, you are upset and troubled?

Chapter 29: [1] In every undertaking, consider what comes first and what comes after, then proceed to the action itself. Otherwise you will begin with a rush of enthusiasm having failed to think through the consequences, only to find that later, when difficulties appear, you will give up in disgrace. [2] Do you want to win at the Olympic Games? So do I, by the gods! For that is a fine achievement. But consider what comes first and what comes after, and only then begin the task. You must be well-disciplined, submit to a diet, abstain from sweet things, follow a training schedule at the set times, in the heat, in the cold—no longer having cold drinks or wine just when you like. In a word, you must hand yourself over to your trainer, just as you would to a doctor. And then, when the contest comes, you may strain your wrist, twist your ankle, swallow lots of sand, sometimes be whipped, and after all that, suffer defeat. [3] Think about all this, and if you still want to, then train for the games, otherwise you will behave like children, who first play at being wrestlers, then at being gladiators, then they blow trumpets, then act in a play. In the same way, you will first be an athlete, then a gladiator, then an orator, then a philosopher, but you will do none of these things wholeheartedly—but like a monkey, you will mimic whatever you see, as first one thing, then another, takes your fancy. All this because you do not undertake anything after properly considering it from all sides, but randomly and half-heartedly. [4] So it is when some people go to see a philosopher and hear someone speak such as Euphrates (and who can speak like him?)—they too want to be philosophers. [5] But first consider what sort of undertaking this is, then examine your own capacities to see if you can bear it. So you want to be a pentathlete or a wrestler? Look at your arms, your thighs, examine your back. Different people are naturally suited to different tasks. [6] Do you think that if you do these things you can still eat in the same way, drink in the same way, give way to anger and irritation, just as you do now? You must go without sleep, endure hardship, live away from home, be looked down on by a slave-boy, be laughed at by those whom you meet, and in everything get the worst of it: in honours, in status, in the law courts, and in every little affair. [7] Consider carefully whether you are willing to pay such a price for peace of mind, freedom and serenity, for if you are not, do not approach philosophy, and do not behave like children, being first a philosopher, next a tax-collector, then an orator, and later a procurator of the Emperor. These things are not compatible. You must be one person, either good or bad. You must cultivate either your ruling principle or external things, seek to improve things inside or things outside. That is, you must play the role either of a philosopher or an uneducated person.

Chapter 30: The actions that are appropriate for us can generally be determined by our relationships. He is your father. This tells you to take care of him, to yield to him in all things, to put up with him when he abuses you or beats you.

"But he is a bad father."

Nature did not provide for you a good father, but a father. Your brother wrongs you? Well then, maintain your relationship to him. Do not think about what he is doing, but about what you will have to do if you want to keep your moral character in accordance with nature. For no one can harm you unless you wish it. You will be harmed only when you think you are harmed. If you get into the habit of looking at the relationships implied by "neighbour," "citizen," "commander," you will discover what is proper to expect from each.

Chapter 31: [1] Know that the most important thing regarding devotion to the gods is to have the right opinions about them—that they exist and administer the universe well and justly—to stand ready to obey them, to submit to everything that happens, and to follow it willingly as something being accomplished by the most perfect intelligence. Do this and you will never blame the gods nor accuse them of neglecting you. [2] But you will not be able to do this unless you remove the notions of good and bad from things that are *not* in our power, and apply them only to those things that *are* in our power. For if you believe that anything not in our power is good or bad, then when you fail to get what you want or get what you do not want, it is inevitable that you will blame and hate those responsible. [3] For every living thing naturally flees and avoids things that appear harmful (and their causes), and pursues and admires things that are beneficial (and their causes). It is impossible, then, for someone who thinks they are being harmed to take delight in what they suppose is causing the harm, just as it is impossible for them to take delight in the harm itself. [4] This is why even a father is reproached by his son when he does not give him a share of those things the son regards as good. Thus, in thinking a king's throne to be something good, Eteocles and Polynices became enemies. This is why the farmer reproaches the gods, and so too the sailor, the merchant, and those who lose their wives and children. For people are devoted to what they find advantageous. Therefore, whoever takes proper care of their desires and aversions, at the same time also cares properly for their devotion. [5] But it is everyone's duty to offer libations, sacrifices and first-fruits according to tradition, with a pure disposition, not slovenly or carelessly, neither too meanly nor beyond our means.

Chapter 32: [1] When you make use of divination, remember that you do not know how events will turn out (this is what you have come to learn from the diviner), but if you really are a philosopher you know before you come what sort of thing it is. For if it is one of the things that are not in our power, then necessarily what will happen will be neither good nor bad. [2] Therefore do not bring desire and aversion to the diviner (for, if you do, you will be fearful of what you may hear), but go with the understanding that everything that happens will be indifferent and of no concern to you, for whatever it may be it is in your power to make good use of it, and in this no one can hinder you. Go with confidence to the gods as your counselors, and afterwards, when some advice has been given, remember from whom you have received it and whose counsel you will be disregarding if you disobey. [3] Approach the diviner in the way Socrates thought appropriate, that is, only in those cases when the whole question turns upon the outcome of events, and when there are no means afforded by reason or any other art for discovering what is going to happen. Therefore, when it is necessary to share a danger with a friend or with your country, do not ask the diviner whether you should share the danger. For even if the diviner should happen to tell you that the omens are unfavourable, that death is foretold, or mutilation to some part of the body, or exile—even at this risk, reason requires you to stand by your friend or share the danger with your country. Pay attention, therefore, to the greater diviner, Pythian Apollo, who threw from the temple the man who did not help his friend when he was being murdered.

Chapter 33: [1] From the outset, establish for yourself a certain character and disposition that you will maintain both when you are by yourself and with other people. [2] For the most part, keep silent, or say only what is required in few words. On rare occasions, when circumstances call for it, we will speak, but not about ordinary things: not about gladiators, nor horse-racing, not about athletes, nor about food and drink (which are the usual topics); and especially do not talk about people, blaming or praising or comparing them. [3] If at all possible, turn the conversation of the company by what you say to more suitable topics; and if you happen to be alone amidst strangers, keep silent. [4] Do not laugh a great deal, nor at many things, nor without restraint. [5] Avoid swearing oaths altogether, if possible; otherwise refuse to do so as far as circumstances allow. [6] Avoid banquets given by strangers and uneducated people. But if there is ever an occasion to join in them, take every care never to slip into the ways of the uneducated; be assured that if your companion is dirty it is inevitable that in their company you will become dirty yourself, even if you happen to start out clean. [7] As to things concerning the body, take only what bare necessity requires with respect to such things as food, drink, clothing, shelter and household slaves: exclude everything that is for outward show or luxury. [8] As for sex, you should stay pure before marriage as far as you can, but if you have to indulge, do only what is lawful. However, do not be angry with those who do indulge, or criticise them, and do not boast of the fact that you do not yourself indulge. [9] If you are told that someone is saying bad things about you, do not defend yourself against what is said, but answer, "Obviously this person is ignorant of my other faults, otherwise they would not have mentioned only these ones." [10] It is not necessary for the most part to go to public games; but if it is ever appropriate for you to go, show that your first concern is for no one other than yourself—that is, wish only to happen what does happen, and wish only those to win who do win, and in this way you will meet with no hindrance. Refrain entirely from shouting or laughing at anyone, or getting greatly excited. And after you have left, do not talk a great deal about what happened (except in so far as it contributes to your own improvement), for doing so would make it clear that you have been impressed by the spectacle. [11] Do not go randomly or thoughtlessly to public readings; but when you do go, maintain your own dignity and equanimity, and guard against offending anyone. [12] When you are about to meet someone, especially someone who enjoys high esteem, ask yourself what Socrates or Zeno would have done in such circumstances, and you will have no difficulty in making proper use of the occasion. [13] When you go to see someone who has great power, propose to yourself that you will not find them at home, that you will be shut out, that the doors will be slammed in your face, that this person will pay no attention to you. And if in spite of all this it is your duty to go, then go, and bear what happens, and never say to yourself, "It wasn't worth the trouble!" For that is the way of the uneducated person, someone who is bewildered by external things. [14] In conversations, avoid talking at great length or excessively about your own affairs and adventures; however pleasant it may be for you to talk about the risks you have run, it is not equally pleasant for other people to hear about your adventures. [15] Avoid also trying to excite laughter, for this is the sort of behaviour that slips easily into vulgarity and at the same time is liable to diminish the respect your neighbours have for you. [16] There is danger also in lapsing into foul language. So whenever anything like this happens, if the opportunity arises, go so far as to rebuke those who behave in this way; otherwise, by keeping silent and blushing and frowning, make it clear that you disapprove of such language.

Chapter 34: When you get an impression of some pleasure, as in the case of other impressions, guard against being carried away by it, but let the matter wait for you, and delay a little. Now consider these two periods of time, that during which you will enjoy the pleasure, and that when the pleasure has passed during which you will regret it and reproach yourself. Next set against these how pleased you will be if you refrain, and how you will commend yourself. When, however, the time comes to act, take care that the attraction, allure and seductiveness of the pleasure do not overcome you, but set against all this the thought of how much better it is to be conscious of having won this victory over it.

Chapter 35: When you do something from a clear judgement that it ought to be done, never try to avoid being seen doing it, even if you expect most people to disapprove. If, however, it would not be right to do it, avoid the deed itself. But if it *is* right, why be afraid of anyone who wrongly disapproves?

Chapter 36: Just as the propositions "It is day" and "It is night" can be used meaningfully in a disjunctive proposition, but make no sense in a conjunctive proposition, so at a banquet, to choose the largest share may make sense with respect to nourishing the body, but makes no sense for maintaining the proper kind of social feeling. Therefore, when you are eating with someone else, bear in mind not merely the value to your body of what is set before you, but also the value of maintaining the proper respect for your host.

Chapter 37: If you undertake a role that is beyond your capacities, you both disgrace yourself in that one and also fail in the role that you might have filled successfully.

Chapter 38: Just as in walking about you take care not to step on a nail or twist your ankle, so also you should take care not to harm your ruling principle. If we guard against this in every action, we will engage in affairs with greater security.

Chapter 39: Everyone's body is the measure for their possessions, as the foot is a measure for the shoe. If then you hold to this principle you will maintain the proper measure, but if you go beyond it, you will inevitably be carried over a cliff. Thus, in the case of the shoe, if you go beyond the foot, first you will get a gilded shoe, then a purple one, and then an embroidered one. For once you have gone beyond the measure, there is no limit.

Chapter 40: Once they reach the age of fourteen years, women are addressed by men as "madam." Accordingly, when they see that there is nothing else but pleasing men with sex, they begin to use cosmetics and dress up, and to place all their hopes in that. It is worth our while, then, to make sure they understand that they are valued for nothing other than their good behaviour and self-respect.

Chapter 41: It is a sign of foolishness to spend a lot of time on things that concern the body, such as exercising a great deal, eating and drinking a lot, defecating and having sex. These are things that should be done in passing. Instead, you should turn your whole attention to the care of your mind.

Chapter 42: When someone treats you badly or says bad things about you, remember that they do or say these things because they think it is appropriate. This is because it is not possible for someone to act on how things appear *to you*, but on how things appear *to them*. Accordingly, if someone holds a false opinion, because *this* is the person who has been deceived, it is *they* who suffer the harm. In the same way, if someone supposes that a true conjunction is false, it is not the conjunction that is harmed, but the person who has been deceived. If you proceed, then, from these principles, you will be gentle with the person who abuses you, saying on all such occasions, "To them, this is how it seemed."

Chapter 43: Every circumstance has two handles. Use one, and it may be carried; but use the other, and it cannot be carried. Therefore, whenever your brother treats you unjustly, do not take hold of the matter by the handle that he has wronged you (for this is the handle by which the matter cannot be carried), but rather by the other handle, that he is your brother, that you were raised up together, and you will take hold of it using the handle by which it may be carried.

Chapter 44: These inferences are invalid: "I am richer than you, therefore I am better than you"; "I am more eloquent than you, therefore I am better than you." But these are better argued: "I am richer than you, therefore my property is greater than yours;" "I am more eloquent than you, therefore my speech is superior to yours." For *you,* of course, are neither property nor speech.

Chapter 45: Does someone bathe hastily? Do not say that they do so badly, but hastily. Does someone drink a great deal of wine? Do not say that they do this badly, but that they drink a great deal. For until you understand their motives, how do you know that what they do is bad? Understand this and you will never receive convincing impressions but assent to quite different ones.

Chapter 46: [1] On no occasion call yourself a philosopher, and do not talk a great deal amongst uneducated people about philosophical principles, but do what follows from those principles. For example, at a banquet do not talk about how people ought to eat, but eat as someone should. Remember how Socrates had so completely eliminated ostentation that people would come to him wanting him to introduce them to philosophers, and he would take them off to other philosophers: so little did he care about being overlooked. [2] And if a discussion about philosophical principles should arise in uneducated people, keep silent for the most part, for there is great danger that you will immediately vomit up what you have not yet digested. And when someone says to you that you know nothing, and you are not offended, then know that you have begun your work. For sheep do not show the shepherd how much they have eaten by vomiting up their fodder, but they digest their food within to produce wool and milk on the outside. So do not display your philosophical principles to uneducated people, but show them the actions that result from the principles when you digest them.

Chapter 47: Once you have adapted your body to plain simple living, do not make a show of it. When you drink water, do not declare on every occasion that you are drinking water. If you want to train yourself to endure hardships, do it by yourself, away from other people. Do not embrace statues, but if you are ever thirsty, take a mouthful of cold water and spit it out without telling anyone.

Chapter 48: [1] The condition and character of the uneducated person is this: they never look for benefit or harm to come from themselves, but from external things. The condition and character of the philosopher is this: they look for every benefit and harm to come from themselves. [2] The signs that someone is making progress are these: they blame no one, they praise no one, they find fault with no one, they accuse no one, they never say anything of themselves as though they amount to something or know anything. When they are impeded or hindered, they blame themselves. If someone praises them, they laugh inwardly at the person who praises them, and if anyone censures them, they make no defence. They go about as if they were sick, cautious not to disturb what is healing before they are fully recovered. [3] They have rid themselves of all desires, and have transferred their aversion to only those things contrary to nature that are in our power. They have no strong preferences in regard to anything. If they appear foolish or ignorant, they do not care. In a word, they keep guard over themselves as though they are their own enemy lying in wait.

Chapter 49: When someone prides themselves on being able to understand and explain Chrysippus, say to yourself, "If Chrysippus had not written obscurely, this person would have nothing on which to pride themselves." But what do I want? To understand nature, and to follow her. Therefore I seek someone who can explain this to me, and when I hear that Chrysippus can do so, I go to him. But I do not understand his writings; so I seek someone who can explain them to me. Now, up to this point there is nothing to be proud of.

When I find someone to explain them, what remains is my putting his principles into practice; this is the only thing to be proud of. But if I am impressed merely by the act of explaining, what else have I accomplished but become a philologist instead of a philosopher, except only that I can explain Chrysippus instead of Homer? No, when someone says to me, "Explain Chrysippus to me," rather than feel proud, I would blush when I am unable to manifest actions that agree and harmonise with Chrysippus' teaching.

Chapter 50: Hold fast to the things herein proposed as if they were laws, as if it would be sacrilegious to transgress them. Pay no attention to what people say about you, for this is no longer yours.

Chapter 51: [1] For how long will you put off demanding of yourself the best, and never to transgress the dictates of reason? You have received the philosophical principles to which you ought to agree, and you have accepted them. What sort of teacher are you waiting for, that you put off improving yourself until they come? You are no longer a child, but a grown adult. If you remain negligent and lazy, always piling up delay upon delay, fixing first one day then another after which you will attend to yourself, you will fail to make progress without even realising, but will continue to live as someone uneducated until you die. [2] From this moment commit yourself to living as an adult, as someone who is making progress, and let everything that appears best to you be a law that you cannot transgress. And if you are presented with anything laborious, or something pleasant, with anything reputable or disreputable, remember that the contest is *now*, that the Olympic Games are *now*, that it is no longer possible to put them off, and that progress is won or lost as the result of just once giving in. [3] This is how Socrates attained perfection, by paying attention to nothing but reason in everything that he encountered. But even if you are not yet Socrates, you should live as someone who wishes to be Socrates.

Chapter 52: [1] The first and most necessary topic in philosophy concerns putting principles to practical use, such as, "We ought not to lie." The second is concerned with demonstrations, such as, "Why is it that we ought not to lie?" And the third is concerned with confirming and articulating the first two: for example, "Why is this a demonstration?" For what is a demonstration, what is entailment, what is contradiction, what is truth, and what is falsehood? [2] Thus the third topic of study is necessary for the second, and the second is necessary for the first. But the most necessary, the one where we ought to rest, is the first. But we do the opposite—we spend our time on the third topic, upon this we expend all our efforts, whilst entirely neglecting the first topic. Thus, whilst at the same time as lying, we are more than ready to explain why it is wrong to lie.

Chapter 53: [1] We must always have these thoughts at hand:

"Lead me, Zeus, and you too, Destiny,
Wherever you have assigned me to go,
and I'll follow without hesitating; but if I am not willing,
because I am bad, I'll follow all the same."
—Cleanthes

[2] "Whosoever properly with necessity complies
we say is wise, and understands things divine."
—Euripides

[3] "Well, Crito, if this pleases the gods, let it happen this way."
—Socrates [*Crito,* 43D]

[4] "Certainly, Anytus and Meletus may put me to death, but they cannot harm me."
—Socrates [*Apology,* 30C]

Pyrrho
ca. 360–ca. 270 B.C.

Sextus Empiricus
A.D. third century

Pyrrho was born in the town of Elis on the Greek Peloponnesus. He joined the expedition of Alexander the Great to India and there met several of the learned magi of the East. Following Alexander's death in 323 B.C., Pyrrho returned to Elis and spent the rest of his life teaching there.

Pyrrho was greatly influenced by the Democritean notion that the world is not as our sense perceptions would lead us to believe. According to Pyrrho, we can know only appearances relative to each person—there is no way we can know things as they really are. This means that any statement we might make about reality can be opposed by an equally valid statement that contradicts it. Given this inability to know which assertion is true, Pyrrho said we should develop an attitude of "suspended judgment" <*epoche*> and thus gradually attain "unperturbedness" or "quietude" <*ataraxia*>. This claimed inability to know came to be called "Skepticism."

Pyrrho left no writings, but his philosophy is well represented by the works of the third-century A.D. author Sextus Empiricus. Little is known about this writer other than that he was apparently a Greek physician, that he was the head of a Skeptical school in some major city, and that he wrote the Outlines of Pyrrhonism. The selection reprinted here, in the R.G. Bury translation, begins by dividing philosophers into three categories: "Dogmatists," who claim to know the truth; those inheritors of Plato's Academy, such as Carneades, who made the opposite dogmatic claim that no truth is possible; and the Pyrrhoist skeptics, who suspend judgment while looking for the truth. Sextus Empiricus goes on to explain the nature of such a suspension of judgment and concludes with a discussion of how this suspension leads to "quietude." In the process of his explication, Sextus avoids self-refutation by explaining that he is not describing what is really true (which would be dogmatism), but only how things *appear* to him to be.

As for its impact, elements of Pyrrhoist skepticism are echoed in Hegel's concept of the dialectic (with the claim that every statement can be contradicted by its opposite) and in Husserl's use of <*epochē*>. Thinkers such as Montaigne, Hume, and Santayana have used skepticism to attack the dogmatic philosophies of their day. While it has rarely been an established school of thought, skepticism has raised questions for all systematic philosophers since the time of Pyrrho.

* * *

For general accounts of Greek skepticism, see Mary Mills Patrick, *The Greek Skeptics* (New York: Columbia University Press, 1929); Charlotte L. Stough, *Greek Skepticism: A Study in Epistemology* (Berkeley: University of California Press, 1969); Leo Groarke, *Greek Scepticism: Anti-Realist Trends in Ancient Thought* (Montreal: McGill-Queen's University Press, 1990); R.J. Hankinson, *The Skeptics* (Oxford: Routledge, 1995); Myles Burnyest and Michael Frede, *The Original Sceptics* (Indianapolis, IN: Hackett, 1996); and a collection of essays, Malcolm Schofield, Myles Burnyeat, and Jonathan Barnes, eds., *Doubt and Dogmatism: Studies in Hellenistic Epistemology* (Oxford: Clarendon Press, 1979). For a study of Pyrrho, see Richard Bett, *Pyrrho, His Antecedents, and His Legacy* (Oxford: Oxford University Press, 2000). For works on Sextus Empiricus, see Mary Mills Patrick, *Sextus Empiricus and Greek Scepticism* (Cambridge: D. Bell, 1899) and Benson Mates, *The Skeptic Way: Sextus Empiricus's Outlines of Pyrrhonism* (Oxford: Oxford University Press, 1995). Edwyn Robert Bevan, *Stoics and Skeptics* (Oxford: Clarendon Press, 1913); Benson Mates, *Stoic Logic* (Berkeley: University of California Press, 1953); and Adrian Kuzminski, *Pyrronism: How the Ancient Greeks Reinvented Buddhism* (Lanham, MD: Lexington Books, 2008) provide more specialized studies.

OUTLINES OF PYRRHONISM (in part)

BOOK I

1. *Of the Main Difference Between Philosophic Systems.* The natural result of any investigation is that the investigators either discover the object of their search or deny that it is discoverable and confess it to be inapprehensible or persist in their search. So, too, with regard to the objects investigated by philosophy, this is probably why some have claimed to have discovered the truth, others have asserted that it cannot be apprehended, while others again go on inquiring. Those who believe they have discovered it are the "Dogmatists," specially so called—Aristotle, for example, and Epicurus

and the Stoics and certain others; Cleitomachus and Carneades and other Academics treat it as inapprehensible; the Sceptics keep on searching. Hence it seems reasonable to hold that the main types of philosophy are three—the Dogmatic, the Academic, and the Sceptic. Of the other systems it will best become others to speak: our task at present is to describe in outline the Sceptic doctrine, first premising that of none of our future statements do we positively affirm that the fact is exactly as we state it, but we simply record each fact, like a chronicler, as it appears to us at the moment.

2. *Of the Arguments of Scepticism.* Of the Sceptic philosophy one argument (or branch of exposition) is called "general," the other "special." In the general argument we set forth the distinctive features of Scepticism, stating its purport and principles, its logical methods, criterion, and end or aim; the "Tropes," also, or "Modes," which lead to suspension of judgment, and in what sense we adopt the Sceptic formulae, and the distinction between Scepticism and the philosophies which stand next to it. In the special argument we state our objections regarding the several divisions of so-called philosophy. Let us, then, deal first with the general argument, beginning our description with the names given to the Sceptic School.

3. *Of the Nomenclature of Scepticism.* The Sceptic School, then, is also called "Zetetic" from its activity in investigation and inquiry, and "Ephectic" or Suspensive from the state of mind produced in the inquirer after his search, and "Aporetic" or Dubitative either from its habit of doubting and seeking, as some say, or from its indecision as regards assent and denial, and "Pyrrhonean" from the fact that Pyrrho appears to us to have applied himself to Scepticism more thoroughly and more conspicuously than his predecessors.

4. *What Scepticism Is.* Scepticism is an ability, or mental attitude, which opposes appearances to judgements in any way whatsoever, with the result that, owing to the equipollence of the objects and reasons thus opposed, we are brought firstly to a state of mental suspense and next to a state of "unperturbedness" or quietude. Now we call it an "ability" not in any subtle sense, but simply in respect of its "being able." By "appearances" we now mean the objects of sense-perception, whence we contrast them with the objects of thought or "judgements." The phrase "in any way whatsoever" can be connected either with the word "ability," to make us take the word "ability," as we said, in its simple sense, or with the phrase "opposing appearances to judgements"; for inasmuch as we oppose these in a variety of ways—appearances to appearances, or judgements to judgements, or *alternando* appearances to judgements,—in order to ensure the inclusion of all these antitheses we employ the phrase "in any way whatsoever." Or, again, we join "in any way whatsoever" to "appearances and judgements" in order that we may not have to inquire how the appearances appear or how the thought-objects are judged, but may take these terms in the simple sense. The phrase "opposed judgements" we do not employ in the sense of negations and affirmations only but simply as equivalent to "conflicting judgements." "Equipollence" we use of equality in respect of probability and improbability, to indicate that no one of the conflicting judgements takes precedence of any other as being more probable. "Suspense" is a state of mental rest owing to which we neither deny nor affirm anything. "Quietude" is an untroubled and tranquil condition of soul. And how quietude enters the soul along with suspension of judgement we shall explain in our chapter [12] "What Is the End of Scepticism."

5. *Of the Sceptic.* In the definition of the Sceptic system there is also implicitly included that of the Pyrrhonean philosopher: he is the man who participates in this "ability."

6. *Of the Principles of Scepticism.* The originating cause of Scepticism is, we say, the hope of attaining quietude. Men of talent, who were perturbed by the contradictions in things and in doubt as to which of the alternatives they ought to accept, were led on to inquire what is true in things and what false, hoping by the settlement of the question to attain quietude. The main basic principle of the Sceptic system is that of opposing to every proposition an equal proposition; for we believe that as a consequence of this we end by ceasing to dogmatize.

7. *Does the Sceptic Dogmatize?* When we say that the Sceptic refrains from dogmatizing we do not use the term "dogma," as some do, in the broader sense of "approval of a thing" (for the Sceptic gives assent to the feelings which are the necessary results of sense-impressions, and he would not, for example, say when feeling hot or cold "I believe that I am not hot or cold"); but we say that "he does not dogmatize" using "dogma" in the sense, which some give it, of "assent to one of the non-evident objects of scientific inquiry"; for the Pyrrhonean philosopher assents to nothing that is non-evident. Moreover, even in the act of enunciating the Sceptic formulae concerning things non-evident—such as the formula "No more (one thing than another)," or the formula "I determine nothing," or any of the others which we shall presently mention,—he does not dogmatize. For whereas the dogmatizer posits the things about which he is said to be dogmatizing as really existent, the Sceptic does not posit these formulae in any absolute sense; for he conceives that, just as the formula "All things are false" asserts the falsity of itself as well as of everything else, as does the formula "Nothing is true," so also the formula "No more" asserts that itself like all the rest, is "No more this than that," and thus cancels itself along with the rest. And of the other formulae we say the same. If then, while the dogmatizer posits the matter of his dogma as substantial truth, the Sceptic enunciates his formulae so that they are virtually canceled by themselves, he should not be said to dogmatize in his enunciation of them. And, most important of all, in his enunciation of these formulae he states what appears to himself and announces his own impression in an undogmatic way, without making any positive assertion regarding the external realities.

8. *Has the Sceptic a Doctrinal Rule?* We follow the same lines in replying to the question "Has the Sceptic a doctrinal rule?" For if one defines a "doctrinal rule" as "adherence to a number of dogmas which are dependent both on one another and on appearances," and defines "dogma" as "assent to a non-evident proposition," then we shall say that he has not a doctrinal rule. But if one defines "doctrinal rule" as "procedure which, in accordance with appearance, follows a certain line of reasoning, that reasoning indicating how it is possible to seem to live rightly (the word 'rightly' being taken, not as referring to virtue only, but in a wider sense) and tending to enable one to suspend judgement," then we say that he has a doctrinal rule. For we follow a line of reasoning which, in accordance with appearances, points us to a life conformable to the customs of our country and its laws and institutions, and to our own instinctive feelings.

9. *Does the Sceptic Deal with Physics?* We make a similar reply also to the question "Should the Sceptic deal with physical problems?" For while, on the one hand, so far as regards making firm and positive assertions about any of the matters dogmatically treated in physical theory, we do not deal with physics; yet, on the other hand, in respect of our mode of opposing to every proposition an equal proposition and of our theory of quietude we do treat of physics. This, too, is the way in which we approach the logical and ethical branches of so-called "philosophy."

10. *Do the Sceptics Abolish Appearances?* Those who say that "the Sceptics abolish appearances," or phenomena, seem to me to be unacquainted with the statements of

our School. For, as we said above, we do not overthrow the affective sense-impressions which induce our assent involuntarily; and these impressions are "the appearances." And when we question whether the underlying object is such as it appears, we grant the fact that it appears, and our doubt does not concern the appearance itself but the account given of the appearance,—and that is a different thing from questioning the appearance itself. For example, honey appears to us to be sweet (and this we grant, for we perceive sweetness through the senses), but whether it is also sweet in its essence is for us a matter of doubt, since this is not an appearance but a judgement regarding the appearance. And even if we do actually argue against the appearances, we do not propound such arguments with the intention of abolishing appearances, but by way of pointing out the rashness of the Dogmatists; for if reason is such a trickster as to all but snatch away the appearances from under our very eyes, surely we should view it with suspicion in the case of things non-evident so as not to display rashness by following it.

11. *Of the Criterion of Scepticism.* That we adhere to appearances is plain from what we say about the Criterion of the Sceptic School. The word "Criterion" is used in two senses: in the one it means "the standard regulating belief in reality or unreality," (and this we shall discuss in our refutation); in the other it denotes the standard of action by conforming to which in the conduct of life we perform some actions and abstain from others; and it is of the latter that we are now speaking. The criterion, then, of the Sceptic School is, we say, the appearance, giving this name to what is virtually the sense-presentation. For since this lies in feeling and involuntary affection, it is not open to question. Consequently, no one, I suppose, disputes that the underlying object has this or that appearance; the point in dispute is whether the object is in reality such as it appears to be.

Adhering, then, to appearances we live in accordance with the normal rules of life, undogmatically, seeing that we cannot remain wholly inactive. And it would seem that this regulation of life is fourfold, and that one part of it lies in the guidance of Nature, another in the constraint of the passions, another in the tradition of laws and customs, another in the instruction of the arts. Nature's guidance is that by which we are naturally capable of sensation and thought; constraint of the passions is that whereby hunger drives us to food and thirst to drink; tradition of customs and laws, that whereby we regard piety in the conduct of life as good, but impiety as evil; instruction of the arts, that whereby we are not inactive in such arts as we adopt. But we make all these statements undogmatically.

12. *What Is the End of Scepticism?* Our next subject will be the End of the Sceptic system. Now an "End" is "that for which all actions or reasonings are undertaken, while it exists for the sake of none"; or, otherwise, "the ultimate object of appetency." We assert still that the Sceptic's End is quietude in respect of matters of opinion and moderate feeling in respect of things unavoidable. For the Sceptic, having set out to philosophize with the object of passing judgement on the sense-impressions and ascertaining which of them are true and which false, so as to attain quietude thereby, found himself involved in contradictions of equal weight, and being unable to decide between them suspended judgement; and as he was thus in suspense there followed, as it happened, the state of quietude in respect of matters of opinion. For the man who opines that anything is by nature good or bad is forever being disquieted: when he is without the things which he deems good he believes himself to be tormented by things naturally bad and he pursues after the things which are, as he thinks, good; which when he has obtained he keeps falling into still more perturbations because of his irrational and immoderate elation, and in his dread of a change of fortune he uses every endeavour to

avoid losing the things which he deems good. On the other hand, the man who determines nothing as to what is naturally good or bad neither shuns nor pursues anything eagerly; and, in consequence, he is unperturbed.

The Sceptic, in fact, had the same experience which is said to have befallen the painter Apelles. Once, they say, when he was painting a horse and wished to represent in the painting the horse's foam, he was so unsuccessful that he gave up the attempt and flung at the picture the sponge on which he used to wipe the paints off his brush, and the mark of the sponge produced the effect of a horse's foam. So, too, the Sceptics were in hopes of gaining quietude by means of a decision regarding the disparity of the objects of sense and of thought, and being unable to effect this they suspended judgement; and they found that quietude, as if by chance, followed upon their suspense, even as a shadow follows its substance. We do not, however, suppose that the Sceptic is wholly untroubled; but we say that he is troubled by things unavoidable; for we grant that he is old at times and thirsty, and suffers various affections of that kind. But even in these cases, whereas ordinary people are afflicted by two circumstances,—namely, by the affections themselves and in no less a degree, by the belief that these conditions are evil by nature,—the Sceptic, by his rejection of the added belief in the natural badness of all these conditions, escapes here too with less discomfort. Hence we say that, while in regard to matters of opinion the Sceptic's End is quietude, in regard to things unavoidable it is "moderate affection." But some notable Sceptics have added the further definition "suspension of judgement in investigations."

13. *Of the General Modes Leading to Suspension of Judgement.* Now that we have been saying that tranquility follows on suspension of judgement, it will be our next task to explain how we arrive at this suspension. Speaking generally, one may say that it is the result of setting things in opposition. We oppose either appearances to appearances or objects of thought to objects of thought or *alternando.* For instance, we oppose appearances when we say "The same tower appears round from a distance, but square from close at hand"; and thoughts to thoughts, when in answer to him who argues the existence of Providence from the order of the heavenly bodies we oppose the fact that often the good fare ill and the bad fare well, and draw from this the inference that Providence does not exist. And thoughts we oppose to appearances, as when Anaxagoras countered the notion that snow is white with the argument, "Snow is frozen water, and water is black; therefore snow also is black." With a different idea we oppose things present sometimes to things present, as in the foregoing examples, and sometimes to things past or future, as, for instance, when someone propounds to us a theory which we are unable to refute, we say to him in reply, "Just as, before the birth of the founder of the School to which you belong, the theory it holds was not as yet apparent as a sound theory, although it was really in existence, so likewise it is possible that the opposite theory to that which you now propound is already really existent, though not yet apparent to us, so that we ought not as yet to yield assent to this theory which at the moment seems to be valid."

Plotinus
ca. A.D. 204–270

Plotinus was the most influential of the Neoplatonists. Born in Lykopolis, Egypt, in A.D. 204, he moved in his late twenties to Alexandria. There he studied with Ammonius Saccas, an unknown figure who was also the teacher of Origen. After eleven years with Ammonius, Plotinus joined an expedition to Persia to gain knowledge of Persian and Indian wisdom. The trek proved unsuccessful, and Plotinus moved on to Rome. There he established a school of philosophy and became friends with the emperor Gallenius. At one point, he sought permission to found a city based on Plato's *Republic,* but the plan came to naught. He stayed in Rome, teaching and writing, until the death of the emperor in A.D. 268. He then moved to the home of a friend where he died in A.D. 270, apparently from leprosy.

Developing Plato's dualistic understanding of reality, Plotinus taught that true reality lies "beyond" the physical world. This "reality beyond reality" has no limits and so cannot be described by words since words invariably have limits. Plotinus, again borrowing from Plato, calls it the "Good" or the "One." The One/Good has no limits and is so supremely rich that it overflows or "emanates" to produce "Intellectual-Principle" or "Divine Mind" ⟨*Nous*⟩. This Intellectual-Principle, in turn, overflows and "Divine-Soul" emanates from it. This process continues as Divine-Soul generates the material world. The lowest level of emanation, at the furthest extreme from the One/Good, is the utter formlessness and unreality of matter.

The goal of philosophy is to awaken individuals to recognize reality beyond the material world. But philosophy alone cannot take a person to the highest reality of the One/Good. Only in a mystical experience can an individual unite with the One/Good. Plotinus himself claimed to have achieved such a union, a "flight of the Alone to the Alone" to cite his famous words, four times during his life. His experiences of nonmaterial reality were so powerful that he said he was ashamed to have a body.

Plotinus' writings were edited by one of his pupils, Porphyry, in the form of six groups of nine "Tractates" (treatises), published as the so-called *Enneads* (from the Greek word for "nine"). The selection given here, in the A.H. Armstrong translation, is Plotinus' "Treatise on Beauty." This tractate explains how the ascent of the soul to the One/Good depends on beauty of soul, a godlike disposition.

Neoplatonism, with its emphasis on the otherworldly and the need for escape from the physical world, was the perfect philosophy for the chaotic final days of the Roman Empire. St. Augustine, in particular, was strongly influenced by Neoplatonic thought. Indeed, if St. Thomas is considered an Aristotelian, St. Augustine may be called a Neoplatonist. Many later thinkers, such as Meister Eckhart, Nicholas Cusanas, John Comenius, Jacob Boehme, G.W.F. Hegel, and Friedrich Schelling, also had their philosophy molded by Neoplatonist doctrines.

* * *

Joseph Katz, *Plotinus' Search for the Good* (New York: King's Crown Press, 1950); Émile Bréhier, *The Philosophy of Plotinus,* translated by Joseph Thomas (Chicago: University of Chicago Press, 1958); and Lloyd P. Gerson, *Plotinus* (Oxford: Routledge, 1994) are good introductions to the study of Plotinus. For more advanced studies, see A.H. Armstrong, *The Architecture of the Intelligible Universe in the Philosophy of Plotinus* (Cambridge: Cambridge University Press, 1940); J.M. Rist, *Plotinus: The Road to Reality* (Cambridge: Cambridge University Press, 1967); Lloyd P. Gerson, ed., *The Cambridge Companion to Plotinus* (Cambridge: Cambridge University Press, 1996); and Margaret R. Miles, *Plotinus on Body and Beauty* (Oxford: Basil Blackwell, 1999). E.R. Dodds, *Select Passages Illustrating Neoplatonism,* translated by E.R. Dodds (New York: Macmillan, 1923), and Dominic J. O'Meara, *Plotinus: An Introduction to the* Enneads (Oxford: Oxford University Press, 1993), provide anthologies of the *Enneads* with discussions of important passages. For discussions of Neoplatonism as a school, see Thomas Whittaker, *The Neo-Platonists* (Cambridge: Cambridge University Press, 1918); Arthur O. Lovejoy's influential book, *The Great Chain of Being* (Cambridge, MA: Harvard University Press, 1936); R.T. Wallis, *Neoplatonism* (London: Duckworth, 1972); and the collection of essays, R. Baine Harris, ed., *The Structure of Being: A Neoplatonic Approach* (Norfolk, VA: International Society for Neoplatonic Studies, 1982).

ENNEADS (in part)

Ennead I, Tractate 6: Beauty

1. Beauty is mostly in sight, but it is to be found too in things we hear, in combinations of words and also in music, and in all music [not only in songs]; for tunes and rhythms are certainly beautiful: and for those who are advancing upwards from sense-perception ways of life and actions and characters and intellectual activities are beautiful, and there is the beauty of virtue. If there is any beauty prior to these, this discussion will reveal it.

Very well then, what is it which makes us imagine that bodies are beautiful and attracts our hearing to sounds because of their beauty? And how are all the things which depend on soul beautiful? Are they all made beautiful by one and the same beauty or is there one beautifulness in bodies and a different one in other things? And what are they, or what is it? Some things, bodies for instance, are not beautiful from the nature of the objects themselves, but by participation, others are beauties themselves, like the nature of virtue. The same bodies appear sometimes beautiful, sometimes not beautiful, so that their being bodies is one thing, their being beautiful another. What is this principle, then, which is present in bodies? We ought to consider this first. What is it that attracts the gaze of those who look at something, and turns and draws them to it and makes them enjoy the sight? If we find this perhaps we can use it as a stepping-stone and get a sight of the rest. Nearly everyone says that it is good proportion of the parts to each other and to the whole, with the addition of good colour, which produces visible beauty, and that with the objects of sight and generally with everything else, being beautiful is being well-proportioned and measured. On this theory nothing single and simple but only a composite thing will have any beauty. It will be the whole which is beautiful, and the parts will not have the property of beauty by themselves, but will contribute to the beauty of the whole. But if the whole is beautiful the parts must be beautiful too; a beautiful whole can certainly not be composed of ugly parts; all the parts must have beauty. For these people, too, beautiful colours, and the light of the sun as well, since they are simple and do not derive their beautifulness from good proportion, will be excluded from beauty. And how do they think gold manages to be beautiful? And what makes lightning in the night and stars beautiful to see? And in sounds in the same way the simple will be banished, though often in a composition which is beautiful as a whole each separate sound is beautiful. And when, though the same good proportion is there all the time, the same face sometimes appears beautiful and sometimes does not, surely we must say that being beautiful is something else over and above good proportion, and good proportion is beautiful because of something else? But if when these people pass on to ways of life and beautiful expressions of thought they allege good proportion as the cause of beauty in these too, what can be meant by good proportion in beautiful ways of life or laws or studies or branches of knowledge? How can speculations be well-proportioned in relation to each other? If it is because they agree, there can be concord and agreement between bad ideas. The statement that "righteousness is a fine sort of silliness" agrees with and is in tune with the saying that "morality is stupidity"; the two fit perfectly. Again, every sort of virtue is a beauty of the soul, a truer beauty than those mentioned before; but how is virtue well-proportioned? Not like magnitudes or a number. We grant that the soul has several parts, but what is the formula for the composition or mixture in the soul of parts or speculations? And what [on this theory], will the beauty of the intellect alone by itself be?

2. So let us go back to the beginning and state what the primary beauty in bodies really is. It is something which we become aware of even at the first glance; the soul speaks of it as if it understood it, recognises and welcomes it and as it were adapts itself to it. But when it encounters the ugly it shrinks back and rejects it and turns away from it and is out of tune and alienated from it. Our explanation of this is that the soul, since it is by nature what it is and is related to the higher kind of reality in the realm of being, when it sees something akin to it or a trace of its kindred reality, is delighted and thrilled and returns to itself and remembers itself and its own possessions. What likeness, then, is there between beautiful things here and There? If there is a likeness, let us agree that they are alike. But how are both the things in that world and the things in this beautiful? We maintain that the things in this world are beautiful by participating in form; for every shapeless thing which is naturally capable of receiving shape and form is ugly and outside the divine formative power as long as it has no share in formative power and form. This is absolute ugliness. But a thing is also ugly when it is not completely dominated by shape and formative power, since its matter has not submitted to be completely shaped according to the form. The form, then, approaches and composes that which is to come into being from many parts into a single ordered whole; it brings it into a completed unity and makes it one by agreement of its parts; for since it is one itself, that which is shaped by it must also be one as far as a thing can be which is composed of many parts. So beauty rests upon the material thing when it has been brought into unity, and gives itself to parts and wholes alike. When it comes upon something that is one and composed of like parts it gives the same gift to the whole; as sometimes art gives beauty to a whole house with its parts, and sometimes nature gives beauty to a single stone. So then the beautiful body comes into being by sharing in a formative power, ⟨*logos*⟩ which comes from the divine forms.

3. The power ordained for the purpose recognises this, and there is nothing more effective for judging its own subject-matter, when the rest of the soul judges along with it; or perhaps the rest of the soul too pronounces the judgment by fitting the beautiful body to the form in itself and using this for judging beauty as we use a ruler for judging straightness. But how does the bodily agree with that which is before body? How does the architect declare the house outside beautiful by fitting it to the form of house within him? The reason is that the house outside, apart from the stones, is the inner form divided by the external mass of matter, without parts but appearing in many parts. When sense-perception, then, sees the form in bodies binding and mastering the nature opposed to it, which is shapeless, and shape riding gloriously upon other shapes, it gathers into one that which appears dispersed and brings it back and takes it in, now without parts, to the soul's interior and presents it to that which is within as something in tune with it and fitting it and dear to it; just as when a good man sees a trace of virtue in the young, which is in tune with his own inner truth, the sight delights him. And the

simple beauty of colour comes about by shape and the mastery of the darkness in matter by the presence of light which is incorporeal and formative power and form. This is why fire itself is more beautiful than all other bodies, because it has the rank of form in relation to the other elements; it is above them in place and is the finest and subtlest of all bodies, being close to the incorporeal. It alone does not admit the others; but the others admit it for it warms them but is not cooled itself; it has colour primarily and all other things take the form of colour from it. So it shines and glitters as if it was a form. The inferior thing which becomes faint and dull by the fire's light, is not beautiful any more, as not participating in the whole form of colour. The melodies in sounds, too, the imperceptible ones which make the perceptible ones, make the soul conscious of beauty in the same way, showing the same thing in another medium. It is proper to sensible melodies to be measured by numbers, not according to any and every sort of formula but one which serves for the production of form so that it may dominate. So much, then, for the beauties in the realm of sense, images and shadows which, so to speak, sally out and come into matter and adorn it and excite us when they appear.

4. But about the beauties beyond, which it is no more the part of sense to see, but the soul sees them and speaks of them without instruments—we must go up to them and contemplate them and leave sense to stay down below. Just as in the case of the beauties of sense it is impossible for those who have not seen them or grasped their beauty—those born blind, for instance,—to speak about them, in the same way only those can speak about the beauty of ways of life who have accepted the beauty of ways of life and kinds of knowledge and everything else of the sort; and people cannot speak about the splendour of virtue who have never even imagined how fair is the face of justice and moral order; "neither the evening nor the morning star are as fair." But there must be those who see this beauty by that with which the soul sees things of this sort, and when they see it they must be delighted and overwhelmed and excited much more than by those beauties we spoke of before, since now it is true beauty they are grasping. These experiences must occur whenever there is contact with any sort of beautiful thing, wonder and a shock of delight and longing and passion and a happy excitement. One can have these experiences by contact with invisible beauties, and souls do have them, practically all, but particularly those who are more passionately in love with the invisible, just as with bodies all see them, but all are not stung as sharply, but some, who are called lovers, are most of all.

5. Then we must ask the lovers of that which is outside sense "What do you feel about beautiful ways of life, as we call them, and beautiful habits and well-ordered characters and in general about virtuous activities and dispositions and the beauty of souls? What do you feel when you see your own inward beauty? How are you stirred to wild exultation, and long to be with yourselves, gathering your selves together away from your bodies?" For this is what true lovers feel. But what is it which makes them feel like this? Not shape or colour or any size, but soul, without colour itself and possessing a moral order without colour and possessing all the other light of the virtues; you feel like this when you see, in yourself or in someone else, greatness of soul, a righteous life, a pure morality, courage with its noble look, and dignity and modesty advancing in a fearless, calm and unperturbed disposition, and the godlike light of intellect shining upon all this. We love and delight in these qualities, but why do we call them beautiful? They exist and appear to us and he who sees them cannot possibly say anything else except that they are what really exists. What does "really exists" mean?

That they exist as beauties. But the argument still requires us to explain why real beings make the soul lovable. What is this kind of glorifying light on all the virtues? Would you like to take the opposites, the uglinesses in soul, and contrast them with the beauties? Perhaps a consideration of what ugliness is and why it appears so will help us to find what we are looking for. Suppose, then, an ugly soul, dissolute and unjust, full of all lusts, and all disturbance, sunk in fears by its cowardice and jealousies by its pettiness, thinking mean and mortal thoughts as far as it thinks at all, altogether distorted, loving impure pleasures, living a life which consists of bodily sensations and finding delight in its ugliness. Shall we not say that its ugliness came to it as a "beauty" brought in from outside, injuring it and making it impure and "mixed with a great deal of evil," with its life and perceptions no longer pure, but by the admixture of evil living a dim life and diluted with a great deal of death, no longer seeing what a soul ought to see, no longer left in peace in itself because it keeps on being dragged out, and down, and to the dark? Impure, I think, and dragged in every direction towards the objects of sense, with a great deal of bodily stuff mixed into it, consorting much with matter and receiving a form other than its own it has changed by a mixture which makes it worse; just as if anyone gets into mud or filth he does not show any more the beauty which he had what is seen is what he wiped off on himself from the mud and filth; his ugliness has come from an addition of alien matter, and his business, if he is to be beautiful again, is to wash and clean himself and so be again what he was before. So we shall be right in saying that the soul becomes ugly by mixture and dilution and inclination towards the body and matter. This is the soul's ugliness, not being pure and unmixed, like gold, but full of earthiness; if anyone takes the earthy stuff away the gold is left, and is beautiful, when it is singled out from other things and is alone by itself. In the same way the soul too, when it is separated from the lusts which it has through the body with which it consorted too much, and freed from its other affections, purged of what it gets from being embodied, when it abides alone has put away all the ugliness which came from the other nature.

6. For, as was said in old times, self-control, and courage and every virtue, is a purification, and so is even wisdom itself. This is why the mysteries are right when they say riddlingly that the man who has not been purified will lie in mud when he goes to Hades, because the impure is fond of mud by reason of its badness; just as pigs, with their unclean bodies, like that sort of thing. For what can true self-control be except not keeping company with bodily pleasures, but avoiding them as impure and belonging to something impure? Courage, too, is not being afraid of death. And death is the separation of body and soul; and a man does not fear this if he welcomes the prospect of being alone. Again, greatness of soul is despising the things here and wisdom is an intellectual activity which turns away from the things below and leads the soul to those above. So the soul when it is purified becomes form and formative power, altogether bodiless and intellectual and entirely belonging to the divine, whence beauty springs and all that is akin to it. Soul, then, when it is raised to the level of intellect increases in beauty. Intellect and the things of intellect are its beauty, its own beauty and not another's, since only then [when it is perfectly conformed to intellect] is it truly soul. For this reason it is right to say that the soul's becoming something good and beautiful is its being made like to God, because from Him come beauty and all else which falls to the lot of real beings. Or rather, beautifulness is reality, and the other kind of thing is the ugly, and this same is the primary evil; so for God the qualities of goodness and beauty are the same, or the realities, the good and the beautiful. So we must follow the same line of enquiry to discover beauty and

The School of Plato, Roman mosaic, n.d. The Platonism of late antiquity (and the Middle Ages) was strongly influenced by Plotinus' development and modification of Plato's thought. (*Scala/Art Resource, NY*)

goodness, and ugliness and evil. And first we must posit beauty which is also the good; from this immediately comes intellect, which is beauty; and soul is given beauty by intellect. Everything else is beautiful by the shaping of soul, the beauties in actions and in ways of life. And soul makes beautiful the bodies which are spoken of as beautiful; for since it is a divine thing and a kind of part of beauty, it makes everything it grasps and masters beautiful, as far as they are capable of participation.

7. So we must ascend again to the good, which every soul desires. Anyone who has seen it knows what I mean when I say that it is beautiful. It is desired as good, and the desire for it is directed to good, and the attainment of it is for those who go up to the

higher world and are converted and strip off what we put on in our descent; (just as for those who go up to the celebrations of sacred rites there are purifications, and strippings off of the clothes they wore before, and going up naked) until, passing in the ascent all that is alien to the God, one sees with one's self alone That alone, simple, single and pure, from which all depends and to which all look and are and live and think for it is the cause of life and mind and being. If anyone sees it, what passion will he feel, what longing in his desire to be united with it, what a shock of delight! The man who has not seen it may desire it as good, but he who has seen it glories in its beauty and is full of wonder and delight, enduring a shock which causes no hurt, loving with true passion and piercing longing; he laughs at all other loves and despises what he thought beautiful before; it is like the experience of those who have met appearances of gods or spirits and do not any more appreciate as they did the beauty of other bodies. "What then are we to think, if anyone contemplates the absolute beauty which exists pure by itself, uncontaminated by flesh or body, not in earth or heaven, that it may keep its purity?" All these other things are external additions and mixtures and not primary, but derived from it. If then one sees That which provides for all and remains by itself and gives to all but receives nothing into itself, if he abides in the contemplation of this kind of beauty and rejoices in being made like it, how can he need any other beauty? For this, since it is beauty most of all, and primary beauty, makes its lovers beautiful and lovable. Here the greatest, the ultimate contest is set before our souls; all our toil and trouble is for this, not to be left without a share in the best of visions. The man who attains this is blessed in seeing that "blessed sight," and he who fails to attain it has failed utterly. A man has not failed if he fails to win beauty of colours or bodies, or power or office or kingship even, but if he fails to win this and only this. For this he should give up the attainment of kingship and of rule over all earth and sea and sky, if only by leaving and overlooking them he can turn to That and see.

8. But how shall we find the way? What method can we devise? How can one see the "inconceivable beauty" which stays within in the holy sanctuary and does not come out where the profane may see it? Let him who can, follow and come within, and leave outside the sight of his eyes and not turn back to the bodily splendours which he saw before. When he sees the beauty in bodies he must not run after them; we must know that they are images, traces, shadows, and hurry away to that which they image. For if a man runs to the image and wants to seize it as if it was the reality (like a beautiful reflection playing on the water, which some story somewhere, I think, said riddlingly a man wanted to catch and sank down into the stream and disappeared) then this man who clings to beautiful bodies and will not let them go, will, like the man in the story, but in soul, not in body, sink down into the dark depths where intellect has no delight, and stay blind in Hades, consorting with shadows there and here. This would be truer advice "Let us fly to our dear country." What then is our way of escape, and how are we to find it? We shall put out to sea, as Odysseus did, from the witch Circe or Calypso—as the poet says (I think with a hidden meaning)—and was not content to stay though he had delights of the eyes and lived among much beauty of sense. Our country from which we came is there, our Father is there. How shall we travel to it, where is our way of escape? We cannot get there on foot; for our feet only carry us everywhere in this world, from one country to another. You must not get ready a carriage, either, or a boat. Let all these things go, and do not look. Shut your eyes, and change to and wake another way of seeing, which everyone has but few use.

9. And what does this inner sight see? When it is just awakened it is not at all able to look at the brilliance before it. So that the soul must be trained, first of all to look at beautiful ways of life then at beautiful works, not those which the arts produce, but the works of men who have a name for goodness: then look at the souls of the people who produce the beautiful works. How then can you see the sort of beauty a good soul has? Go back into yourself and look; and if you do not yet see yourself beautiful, then, just as someone making a statue which has to be beautiful cuts away here and polishes there and makes one part smooth and clears another till he has given his statue a beautiful face, so you too must cut away excess and straighten the crooked and clear the dark and make it bright, and never stop "working on your statue" till the divine glory of virtue shines out on you, till you see "self-mastery enthroned upon its holy seat." If you have become this, and see it, and are at home with yourself in purity, with nothing hindering you from becoming in this way one, with no inward mixture of anything else, but wholly yourself, nothing but true light, not measured by dimensions, or bounded by shape into littleness, or expanded to size by unboundedness, but everywhere unmeasured, because greater than all measure and superior to all quantity; when you see that you have become this, then you have become sight; you can trust yourself then; you have already ascended and need no one to show you; concentrate your gaze and see. This alone is the eye that sees the great beauty. But if anyone comes to the sight bleary-eyed with wickedness, and unpurified, or weak and by his cowardice unable to look at what is very bright, he sees nothing, even if someone shows him what is there and possible to see. For one must come to the sight with a seeing power made akin and like to what is seen. No eye ever saw the sun without becoming sunlike, nor can a soul see beauty without becoming beautiful. You must become first all godlike and all beautiful if you intend to see God and beauty. First the soul will come in its ascent to intellect and there will know the Forms, all beautiful, and will affirm that these, the Ideas, are beauty; for all things are beautiful by these, by the products and essence of intellect. That which is beyond this we call the nature of the Good, which holds beauty as a screen before it. So in a loose and general way of speaking the Good is the primary beauty; but if one distinguishes the intelligibles [from the Good] one will say that the place of the Forms is the intelligible beauty, but the Good is That which is beyond, the "spring and origin" of beauty; or one will place the Good and the primal beauty on the same level. In any case, however, beauty is in the intelligible world.

CHRISTIANITY AND MEDIEVAL PHILOSOPHY

With only a few exceptions, European medieval thought was deeply imbued with Christian faith. As a result, it is not possible to understand medieval philosophy without at least a rudimentary understanding of Christian beliefs as presented in the Bible. Whether or not today's reader accepts the veracity of the claims put forth in these writings, most medievals did believe them, and that belief formed the foundation of their thought.

Beginning as a Jewish sect, Christianity continued to hold a number of beliefs in common with Judaism, including the following bedrock convictions: that the Hebrew Bible (called the "Old Testament" by Christians) is the revealed Word of God; that God is superior to and distinct from the created world; that the world was created by God at a specific point in time and that the world will come to an end; that God is personal and desires a special relationship with the human race; that humans have sinned against God's Law and need God's forgiveness; that God requires righteousness as a means of a right relationship with God and others; and that God would send the Anointed One ("Messiah" in Hebrew, "Christ" in Greek) to set the people of God free.

But while Christians accepted the foundational beliefs of their Jewish ancestors, they differed on one key point: the identity of the Messiah. Whereas the Jews anticipated a spiritual-political figure to save them from the oppression of their enemies, Christians believed the Christ saved his people mainly from the spiritual oppressors of sin and death. Whereas the Jews believed the Messiah would scrupulously follow the Law, favoring and associating only with those who did likewise, the Christ of the Christians seemed to enjoy a remarkable freedom in relation to several of Israel's most venerable institutions—for example, Sabbath observances, the Temple, and ritual purity—while associating with the "lowlifes" of society. In short, whereas the Jewish people were (and still are) awaiting the Messiah, Christians believed (and still believe) Jesus of Nazareth was the Messiah.

Christians held that after his death by crucifixion, Jesus rose from the dead (the Resurrection) and taught his followers for forty days before ascending into heaven. As part of that teaching, Jesus promised that he would return again (the Second Coming ⟨*parousia*⟩) and that in the meantime his followers should spread the Christian faith to all the world.

The basic Christian belief was (and still is) that Jesus is the Son of God who became a human (the Incarnation) to atone for human sin (Redemption). The severed relationship between the Holy God and sinful humanity could be restored only through the sacrifice of one who was consummate righteousness. As the Word (⟨*Logos*⟩) of God made flesh, Jesus was that righteousness, made that sacrifice, and offered that restoration. Through faith, Christians accept this work done on their behalf (Justification) and receive the power of God's spirit to overcome sin and to serve others (Sanctification).

As Christians spread this message throughout the Roman Empire, they encountered resistance and persecution from both Jewish and Roman authorities. Many Jewish leaders objected to the Christian identification of Jesus with God; Roman authorities objected to the Christians' unwillingness to participate in emperor worship. Jews, too, had refused to participate in state religion and had often been persecuted. But Christians posed a unique threat to the Romans because, unlike the Jews, Christians proclaimed a supranational, supraracial, universal Lord—one very much in competition with Caesar. And Christians indefatigably sought converts to their universal Savior. Accordingly, they were persecuted on and off for three centuries.

Despite persecution, Christianity grew steadily in the centuries after Christ. There have been many explanations for that growth. The eighteenth-century historian Edward Gibbon* listed five causes: (1) Christianity's inheritance of the zeal of the Jews; (2) its connection to the philosophical doctrine of the immortality of the soul; (3) its claim of miracles; (4) the virtue of the early Christians; and (5) the organization of the church. Recent historians have pointed to the moral exclusivity of Christians, who demanded deep commitment; the definite and absolute character of Christian belief in an age of uncertainty; and the social dimensions of Christianity, which made it attractive to women, the poor, and the oppressed.**

As Christianity grew, doctrinal disputes inevitably arose. What was true Christianity? The answers tended to reflect deep convictions about two essential issues: the nature of the person and work of Jesus Christ and the relationship between faith and reason. What was the relationship between Jesus and God? Did Jesus have two distinct natures: one divine and one human? Or were they merged into a single unique nature? Moreover, if there is only one God, how could God also be three (Father, Son, and Holy Spirit)? And how could reason resolve issues of faith?

***The Decline and Fall of the Roman Empire,* Chapter XV.

**Of course, Christians have always claimed that none of these reasons is entirely adequate and that the most acceptable explanation for the rise of Christianity is a supernatural one.

The first issue, the nature of Christ, was resolved at the Council of Nicea, convened and presided over by the first Christian emperor, Constantine, in A.D. 325. The Council determined that the Son was exactly the same substance, "consubstantial" ⟨*homoousios*⟩, and not just "of like substance" ⟨*homoiousios*⟩, with God the Father. (The single Greek letter "iota," meant a great deal more than "one iota of difference" to the early church.) By the middle of the first millenium, the "Nicene Creed" was confessed by virtually all Christendom as the orthodox answer to the nature-of-Christ question. The Nicene Creed is still authoritative in Orthodox, Catholic, and Protestant churches.

Even though the Christological question was answered at Nicea, the question of the right relation between faith and reason continued to be argued throughout the medieval period. The early Christians had a simple faith in Jesus as Messiah (if they were Jewish Christians) and as Lord (if they were Gentile Christians), and they believed Jesus had lived, taught, died, and risen for them and all others. But almost immediately, that simple faith encountered sophisticated Hellenistic thought throughout the Roman Empire. How much should Christian faith concede to the competence of philosophic reason? What was the relation between sacred writings (i.e., the Bible) and secular writings (e.g., philosophy)? In Acts 17, the Apostle Paul, the early Christian convert, used reason and quoted pagan poets to help him preach the gospel to Epicurean and Stoic philosophers in Athens. Yet later, in Colossians 2:8, he warned, "See to it that no one takes you captive through philosophy and empty deceit. . . ." Some early Church Fathers, such as Justin Martyr, used philosophy to help interpret Christian faith. Other Church Fathers, such as Tertullian, argued that reason could be inimical to faith: "What has Jerusalem to do with Athens?" he asked.

Some in the early church even claimed to have special esoteric knowledge not available to the rabble either in the sacred Scriptures or secular reason. They were known as "Gnostics," from the Greek word for knowledge ⟨*gnosis*⟩. These Gnostics emphasized the Platonic belief in the soul as good and the body as evil, and they sought to free the soul from the body by extreme ascetic practices. Some of the Gnostics taught that Jesus was not *really* a physical person (since the body is evil) and that the Old Testament God, Yahweh, who had created bodies and matter, was really the devil. Manicheaism, which rivaled Christianity in the third and fourth centuries, and for a time claimed Augustine as one of its believers, was based on Gnostic thought.

For the most part, the early medieval philosophers sought to resolve these theological issues within the broad framework of Platonic thought. Augustine (as either the last classical thinker or the first medieval one), Boethius, Anselm, and Hildegard of Bingen all used Neoplatonic concepts. In the early Middle Ages, most of Aristotle's writings were not available in the West. But in the East, Islamic philosophers, such as Ibn-Sina and Ibn Rushd (or Averroës), and Jewish thinkers, such as Moses Maimonides, read and commented on a wide range of Aristotelian works. These works, along with the Muslim and Jewish commentaries on them, were reintroduced to Western Europe in the late–Middle Ages and became the basis for the monumental work of Thomas Aquinas.

While Thomas lived during a period of relative calm and well-being, the centuries following his death were filled with tumult and upheaval. As a part of the often vicious conflict between church and state, Philip IV of France captured Pope Boniface VIII in 1303 and soon thereafter moved the papal court to Avignon,

France—the so-called Babylonian Captivity of the Church. Beginning in 1347, the bubonic plague, or Black Death, struck Western Europe. Responses to the plague ranged from fanatical anti-intellectual apocalypticism to self-indulgent hedonism. Some even blamed the plague on intellectuals such as Thomas Aquinas, saying they provoked divine wrath by explaining God's ways rationally; others simply counseled, "Let us eat, drink, and be merry, for tomorrow we die." Many turned to superstition or to scapegoating Jews. At the same time, England and France were involved in the Hundred Years' War (1337–1453), which brought enormous casualties. Because of the plague and the war, in the years from 1300 to 1450, the population of Western Europe was reduced by half—perhaps by as much as two-thirds. In 1378, the Great Schism divided the Catholic Church as the Italians reinstituted the papacy in Rome, while a second pope reigned in Avignon. For over thirty years, rival popes condemned and excommunicated one another. In 1409, an attempt to end the schism with a compromise pope led only to a third pope and thus a third claimant to St. Peter's universal chair. Finally, in 1417, the church united around one pope ruling in Rome. But by now the power and prestige of the papacy had been severely diminished, and a hundred years later, in the Protestant Reformation, the Western church split decisively.

The philosophy of this later medieval period is commonly viewed in the light of these social upheavals, and, indeed, there does seem to be some connection. Thomas had harmonized philosophy and theology in a systematic way reflective of the relative peacefulness of the thirteenth century. Just as social stability—particularly in the relationship between church and state—deteriorated in the centuries following Thomas, so also the philosophies that developed during this period tended to separate reason and faith. William of Ockham, for example, held that philosophy and theology were separate realms with separate rules. The Renaissance thinker Pico della Mirandola developed a philosophy essentially excluding faith while using reason to draw from sources both within and outside Christendom. In Pico's philosophy, reason and faith were no longer systematically conjoined: Reason stood supremely alone. Clearly the coherent, rational Christian synthesis of Thomas had unraveled.

But as Frederick Copleston has pointed out, there are other ways of understanding this transition. Instead of seeing late-medieval–early-Renaissance philosophy as destructive to a grand synthesis or as reactive to societal chaos, "one can see . . . philosophy being reborn and growing up under the shadow and care of theology, reaching a more or less adult stage and then tending to go its own way and assert its independence" (*A History of Medieval Philosophy*, p. 314). While acknowledging the disintegration of the peculiarly Thomistic approach to synthesis, this view sees the late-medieval period as a natural development of Western European thought.

* * *

For discussions of the interaction between Christianity and its surrounding culture, see A.H. Armstrong and R.A. Markus, *Christian Faith and Greek Philosophy* (New York: Sheed and Ward, 1960); E.R. Dodds, *Pagan and Christian in an Age of Anxiety* (Cambridge: Cambridge University Press, 1965); Jaroslav Pelikan, *The Christian Tradition: A History of the Development of Doctrine*, five volumes (Chicago: University of Chicago Press, 1971–1989); and R.A. Markus, *Christianity in the Roman World* (London: Thames & Hudson, 1974). For a discussion of Christian beliefs in their historical context, see J.N.D. Kelly, *Early Christian Doctrines*, 5th edition (London: Black, 1978). For basic introductions to traditional Christian beliefs, see John R.W. Stott, *Basic Christianity* (Downers Grove, IL: Inter-Varsity Press, 1971), and Hans Küng, *On Being a Christian*, translated by Edward Quinn (Garden City, NY: Doubleday, 1976).

Étienne Gilson's work, *History of Christian Philosophy in the Middle Ages* (New York: Random House, 1955), is the classic study of this time period, while Maurice De Wulf, *History of Mediaeval Philosophy* (New York: Dover, 1952); Armand A. Maurer, *Medieval Philosophy* (New York: Random House, 1962); Michael Haren, *Medieval Thought: The Western Intellectual Tradition from Antiquity to the Thirteenth Century* (New York: St. Martin's Press, 1985); B.B. Price, *Medieval Thought* (Oxford: Blackwell, 1992); John Marenbon, ed., *Medieval Philosophy* (London: Routledge, 2003); and John Marenbon, *Medieval Philosophy: An Introduction* (London: Routledge, 2006) are also useful. Frederick Copleston's work on medieval philosophy includes several volumes of his multi-volume set, *A History of Philosophy* (1950; reprinted Garden City, NY: Image Doubleday, 1962–1963), as well as the later single volume, *A History of Medieval Philosophy* (New York: Harper & Row, 1972). Hans-Werner Goetz, *Life in the Middle Ages*, translated by Albert Wimmer (Notre Dame, IN: Notre Dame University Press, 1994) provides historical context. For general essays on this period, see Jorge J.E. Garcia and Timothy B. Noone, eds., *A Companion to Philosophy in the Middle Ages* (Oxford: Blackwell, 2003) and A.S. McGrade, ed., *The Cambridge Companion to Medieval Philosophy* (Cambridge: Cambridge University Press, 2003).

For books specifically on the early medieval period, see A.H. Armstrong, ed., *The Cambridge History of Later Greek and Early Medieval Philosophy* (Cambridge: Cambridge University Press, 1967); and John Marenbon, *Early Medieval Philosophy (480–1150): An Introduction* (London: Routledge & Kegan Paul, 1983). For books on the later medieval period, see Ray C. Petry, ed., *Late Medieval Mysticism* (Philadelphia: Westminster Press, 1957); Gordon Leff, *The Dissolution of the Medieval Outlook: An Essay on Intellectual and Spiritual Change in the Fourteenth Century* (New York: New York University Press, 1976); Norman Kretzmann et al., eds., *The Cambridge History of Later Medieval Philosophy: From the Rediscovery of Aristotle to the Disintegration of Scholasticism 1100–1600* (Cambridge: Cambridge University Press, 1982); and John Marenbon, *Later Medieval Philosophy (1150–1350): An Introduction* (London: Routledge & Kegan Paul, 1987).

AUGUSTINE
A.D. 354–430

Aurelius Augustinus, Saint Augustine, was born of a Christian mother and a pagan father in Thagaste, a small town in what is now Algeria, North Africa. In many ways, his family's mixed religious background represented the crumbling Roman Empire. Even though the influence of Christianity had grown since Emperor Constantine's edict of religious toleration in A.D. 313, there were still many rivals to his mother's faith.

As a boy, Augustine showed intellectual promise, and at 17 he was sent to Carthage to study rhetoric. While there, Augustine found philosophy, rejected Christianity, took a mistress (who bore him a son), and began to investigate some of the religions of the time. He turned first to the followers of the prophet Mani—the Manichaeans. Mani was a third-century prophet who called himself "the apostle of God." He developed the ancient Persian teaching of Zoroaster (or Zarathustra), which said that there are two great forces in the world, one good and one evil, and that neither can overcome the other. Living a life of sensual indulgence, Augustine took comfort from the idea that God could no more overcome evil in the universe than Augustine could in his own life.

In 375, Augustine returned to Thagaste to begin teaching rhetoric. When his mother, Monica (later sainted for her perseverance in prayer for her son), discovered that he had become a Manichaean, she expelled him from her house. Finding Thagaste boring, and his mother difficult, Augustine returned to Carthage. Over the next seven years, he grew disenchanted with Manichaeism. In 384, he left Carthage for teaching positions in Rome and finally Milan. In Milan, Augustine encountered the writings of Plotinus and was converted to Neoplatonism. At the same time, he came into contact with a group of Christians led by the Bishop of Milan, Ambrose. Under the influence of this group, Augustine was forced to reconsider his earlier rejection of Christianity, yet he was still unwilling to give up his life of self-gratification. In 386, while sitting in a friend's garden, he heard what he thought was a child's voice saying, "Pick it up and read, pick it up and read." Augustine later recounted what happened:

> I returned to the place where Alypius was sitting, for on leaving it I had put down there the book of the apostle's letters. I snatched it up, opened it and read in silence the passsage on which my eyes first lighted: "Not in dissipation and drunkenness, nor in debauchery and lewdness, nor in arguing and jealousy; but put on the Lord Jesus Christ, and make no provision for the flesh or the gratification of your desires." [Rom. 13:13–14] I had no wish to read further, nor was there need. No sooner had I reached the end of the verse than the light of certainty flooded my heart and all dark shades of doubt fled away.*

The following year, Augustine was baptized and returned to Africa to found a monastic community. Within two years he left the cloister, answering the church's call to priesthood. He served as a priest, and later as bishop, in the African town of Hippo for the rest of his life.

* * *

While at Hippo, Augustine wrote voluminously on a variety of theological and philosophical topics. Many of his works sought to define exactly what was and was not "Christian." His doctrinal works, such as *The Trinity,* established Christian essentials; whereas his polemical works, directed against "heresies" (positions unacceptable to the church), outlined what was not admissible. Augustine fought two major heresies: the Pelagian and the Donatist. The Pelagians held that sin had affected only Adam, that the will is free from sin, and that God's grace is given on the basis of human merit. The Donatists maintained that the sacraments were effective only when administered by a priest in a state of grace. Augustine argued passionately that both heresies put too much emphasis on human ability and not enough on God's grace.

Augustine's most famous work, the *Confessions,* invented the genre of introspective autobiography. The *Confessions* are full of both psychological and spiritual insight and so can be read as either devotional tract or philosophical essay. Books I through IX are Augustine's life story from the perspective of Christian conversion (detailed in our selection from Book VIII). As Augustine reflects on his life, he sees both his sinfulness and his intellectual aimlessness apart from God's grace. He also gives early glimpses of his mature epistemological position that God must illumine the mind in order for an individual to gain wisdom. Following his conversion, Augustine continued to seek understanding—though now firmly founded on faith. Books X to XII illustrate this "faith seeking understanding," as Augustine examines the questions of memory, time, and creation. Our selection from Book XI explores the nature of time and God's relation to it. Augustine argues that God must be "outside" time in an eternal present. This view of God as timelessly eternal was developed by Boethius and is still influential today (see the suggested readings that follow). I am pleased to offer this selection in the outstanding new translation by Maria Boulding.

*Saint Augustine, *Confessions,* Book VIII. See reading on p. 275.

Of Augustine's many other works, *The City of God* is by far the most influential. During the fourth century, Christianity had become the state religion of the Roman Empire; in 410, Rome fell to the Visigoths, and the eternal city was sacked for the first time. Naturally, many considered the sack of Rome a punishment for the betrayal of the old Roman religion. Augustine wrote *The City of God* to answer this charge and in so doing he developed yet another first: the first Western philosophy of history. Rather than a cycle of repeated events, Augustine described history as being linear—from creation to consummation and final judgment. As history moves from beginning to end, we can observe two cities: the City of God, consisting of those who love God; and the City of Man, those who love self rather than God. The first selection, from Book XI, presents Augustine's final argument against the skeptics. Augustine's insistence that he *knows* he exists anticipates Descartes's argument twelve centuries later.

The second selection, from Book XII, explains the origin of evil and of the City of Man. Augustine begins by insisting, against the Manichaeans, that there is no being capable of opposing God: God is all-powerful. But, despite the presence of evil, God is also all-good and everything God created is good. Evil arises when a moral agent (angel or human) wills to love a lesser good (self) rather than the highest good (God). There is no evil "thing" to choose—there is only evil choosing. This leads to the question of what caused the will to choose evilly—a question Augustine says cannot be answered. Both selections have been ably translated by Gerald G. Walsh, Daniel J. Honan, and Grace Monahan.

Augustine's impact has been enormous. Medieval Catholic philosophers, such as Anselm and Thomas Aquinas, as well as Protestant reformers, such as Martin Luther and John Calvin, wanted to be Augustine's heirs. Many contemporary Christian thinkers still appeal to Augustine's ideas, such as his defense of grace and his explanation of evil. But Augustine's influence has not been limited to theologians and philosophers of religion. Ludwig Wittgenstein began his *Philosophical Investigations* by examining Augustine's theory of language, and Bertrand Russell claimed Augustine's theory of time superior even to that of Kant. Echoes of Augustine's understanding of history as the unfolding of divine purpose can be heard in the writings of Hegel, whereas Augustine's idea that some kind of faith must precede fruitful understanding has been adapted by thinkers in such fields as the sociology of knowledge and philosophy of science.

* * *

The best general account of Augustine's philosophy remains Étienne Gilson, *The Christian Philosophy of Saint Augustine,* translated by L.E.M. Lynch (New York: Random House, 1960); Peter Brown, *Augustine of Hippo: A Biography* (Berkeley: University of California Press, 1967), provides an excellent biography. For brief introductions to Augustine's life and thought, see Henry Chadwick's pair of books, *Augustine* and *Augustine: A Very Short Introduction* (Oxford: Oxford University Press, 1986 and 2001). For more extensive discussions of Augustine's thought, see Robert E. Meagher, *An Introduction to Augustine* (New York: New York University Press, 1978); Christopher Kirwan, *Augustine* (London: Routledge, 1989); and Benedict J. Groeschel, *Augustine: Major Writings* (New York: Crossroads, 1995). J.N. Figgis, *The Political Aspects of St. Augustine's* City of God (London: Longmans, Green, 1921); Ronald H. Nash, *The Light of the Mind: St. Augustine's*

Theory of Knowledge (Lexington: University Press of Kentucky, 1969); R.A. Markus, *Saeculum: History and Society in the Theology of St. Augustine* (Cambridge: Cambridge University Press, 1970); Robert J. O'Connell's pair of books, *St. Augustine's* Confessions and *Images of Conversion in St. Augustine's* Confessions (New York: Fordham University Press, 1989 and 1996); Brian Stock, *Augustine the Reader* (Cambridge, MA; Harvard University Press, 1996); and Robert Dyson, *St. Augustine of Hippo: The Christian Transformation of Political Philosophy* (London: Continuum, 2005) deal with the specialized topics indicated by their respective titles. John M. Rist, *Augustine: Ancient Thought Baptized* (Cambridge: Cambridge University Press, 1994) explores the connections between Augustine and Platonic thought. For collections of essays, see M.C. D'Arcy et al., *Saint Augustine* (New York: Meridian, 1957), and R.A. Markus, ed., *Augustine: A Collection of Critical Essays* (Garden City, NY: Anchor, Doubleday, 1972).

CONFESSIONS (in part)

BOOK VIII—CONVERSION

5, 10. . . . It was no iron chain imposed by anyone else that fettered me, but the iron of my own will. The enemy had my power of willing in his clutches, and from it had forged a chain to bind me. The truth is that disordered lust springs from a perverted will; when lust is pandered to, a habit is formed; when habit is not checked, it hardens into compulsion. These were like interlinking rings forming what I have described as a chain, and my harsh servitude used it to keep me under duress.

A new will had begun to emerge in me, the will to worship you disinterestedly and enjoy you, O God, our only sure felicity; but it was not yet capable of surmounting that earlier will strengthened by inveterate custom. And so the two wills fought it out—the old and the new, the one carnal, the other spiritual—and in their struggle tore my soul apart.

* * *

8, 19. Within the house of my spirit the violent conflict raged on, the quarrel with my soul that I had so powerfully provoked in our secret dwelling, my heart, and at the height of it I rushed to Alypius with my mental anguish plain upon my face. "What is happening to us?" I exclaimed. "What does this mean? What did you make of it? The untaught are rising up and taking heaven by Storm, while we with all our dreary teachings are still groveling in this world of flesh and blood! Are we ashamed to follow, just

Saint Augustine, *Confessions*, Book VIII (5, 8–12) and XI (14–28), translated by Maria Boulding (New York: New City Press, 1997).

because they have taken the lead, yet not ashamed of lacking the courage even to follow?" Some such words as these I spoke, and then my frenzy tore me away from him, while he regarded me in silent bewilderment. Unusual, certainly, was my speech, but my brow, cheeks and eyes, my flushed countenance and the cadences of my voice expressed my mind more fully than the words I uttered.

Adjacent to our lodgings was a small garden. We were free to make use of it as well as of the house, for our host, who owned the house, did not live there. The tumult in my breast had swept me away to this place, where no one would interfere with the blazing dispute I had engaged in with myself until it should be resolved. What the outcome would be you knew, not I. All I knew was that I was going mad, but for the sake of my sanity, and dying that I might live, aware of the evil that I was but unaware of the good I was soon to become. So I went out into the garden and Alypius followed at my heels; my privacy was not infringed by his presence, and, in any case, how could he abandon me in that state? We sat down as far as possible from the house. I was groaning in spirit and shaken by violent anger because I could form no resolve to enter into a covenant with you, though in my bones I knew that this was what I ought to do, and everything in me lauded such a course to the skies. It was a journey not to be undertaken by ship or carriage or on foot, nor need it take me even that short distance I had walked from the house to the place where we were sitting; for to travel—and more, to reach journey's end—was nothing else but to want to go there, but to want it valiantly and with all my heart, not to whirl and toss this way and that a will half crippled by the struggle, as part of it rose up to walk while part sank down.

20. While this vacillation was at its most intense many of my bodily gestures were of the kind that people sometimes want to perform but cannot, either because the requisite limbs are missing, or because they are bound and restricted, or paralyzed through illness, or in some other way impeded. If I tore out my hair, battered my forehead, entwined my fingers and clasped them round my knee, I did so because I wanted to. I might have wanted to but found myself unable, if my limbs had not been mobile enough to obey. So then, there were plenty of actions that I performed where willing was not the same thing as being able; yet I was not doing the one thing that was incomparably more desirable to me, the thing that I would be able to do as soon as I willed, because as soon as I willed—why, then, I would be willing it! For in this sole instance the faculty to act and the will to act precisely coincide, and the willing is already the doing. Yet this was not happening. My body was more ready to obey the slightest whim of my soul in the matter of moving my limbs, than the soul was to obey its own command in carrying out this major volition, which was to be accomplished within the will alone.

9, 21. How did this bizarre situation arise, how develop? May your mercy shed light on my inquiry, so that perhaps an answer may be found in the mysterious punishments meted out to humankind, those utterly baffling pains that afflict the children of Adam. How then did this bizarre situation arise, how develop? The mind commands the body and is instantly obeyed; the mind commands itself, and meets with resistance. When the mind orders the hand to move, so smooth is the compliance that command can scarcely be distinguished from execution; yet the mind is mind, while the hand is body. When the mind issues its command that the mind itself should will something (and the mind so commanded is no other than itself), it fails to do so. How did this bizarre situation arise, how develop? As I say, the mind commands itself to will something: it would not be giving the order if it did not want this thing; yet it does not do what it commands.

Evidently, then, it does not want this thing with the whole of itself, and therefore the command does not proceed from an undivided mind. Inasmuch as it issues the command, it does will it, but inasmuch as the command is not carried out, it does not will it. What the will is ordering is that a certain volition should exist, and this volition is not some alien thing, but its very self. Hence it cannot be giving the order with its whole self. It cannot be identical with that thing which it is commanding to come into existence, for if it were whole and entire it would not command itself to be, since it would be already.

This partial willing and partial non-willing is thus not so bizarre, but a sickness of the mind, which cannot rise with its whole self on the wings of truth because it is heavily burdened by habit. There are two wills, then, and neither is the whole: what one has the other lacks.

10, 22. Some there are who on perceiving two wills engaged in deliberation assert that in us there are two natures, one good, the other evil, each with a mind of its own. Let them perish from your presence, O God, as perish all who talk wildly and lead our minds astray. They are evil themselves as long as they hold these opinions, yet these same people will be good if they embrace true opinions and assent to true teaching, and so merit the apostle's commendation, You were darkness once, but now you are light in the Lord. The trouble is that they want to be light not in the Lord but in themselves, with their notion that the soul is by nature divine, and so they have become denser darkness still, because by their appalling arrogance they have moved further away from you, the true Light, who enlighten everyone who comes into the world. I warn these people, Take stock of what you are saying, and let it shame you; but once draw near to him and be illumined, and your faces will not blush with shame.

When I was making up my mind to serve the Lord my God at last, as I had long since purposed, I was the one who wanted to follow that course, and I was the one who wanted not to. I was the only one involved. I neither wanted it wholeheartedly nor turned from it wholeheartedly. I was at odds with myself, and fragmenting myself. This disintegration was occurring without my consent, but what it indicated was not the presence in me of a mind belonging to some alien nature but the punishment undergone by my own. In this sense, and this sense only, it was not I who brought it about, but the sin that dwelt within me as penalty for that other sin committed with greater freedom;* for I was a son of Adam.

23. Moreover, if we were to take the number of conflicting urges to signify the number of natures present in us, we should have to assume that there are not two, but many. If someone is trying to make up his mind whether to go to a Manichean conventicle or to the theater, the Manichees declare, "There you are, there's the evidence for two natures: the good one is dragging him our way, the bad one is pulling him back in the other direction. How else explain this dithering between contradictory wills?" But I regard both as bad, the one that leads him to them and the one that lures him back to the theater. They, on the contrary, think that an inclination toward them can only be good.

But consider this: suppose one of our people is deliberating, and as two desires clash he is undecided whether to go to the theater or to our church, will not our opponents too be undecided what attitude to take? Either they will have to admit that it is

*[That is, by Adam. Augustine uses the comparative to suggest a relative freedom enjoyed by Adam, superior to our own but short of perfect freedom. He was to spell out the distinction later in *Correction and Grace* XII, 33 between *posse non peccare* (the ability not to sin, Adam's privilege), and *non posse peccare* (the perfection of freedom in heaven)].

good will that leads a person to our church, just as good as that which leads to theirs the people who are initiated into their sacred rites and trapped there—and this they are unwilling to admit; or they will conclude that two evil natures and two bad minds are pitted against each other within one person, in which case their habitual assertion of one good and one evil nature will be erroneous; or, finally, they will be brought round to the truth and no longer deny that when a person is deliberating there is but one soul, thrown into turmoil by divergent impulses.

24. When, therefore, they observe two conflicting impulses within one person, let them stop saying that two hostile minds are at war, one good, the other evil, and that these derive from two hostile substances and two hostile principles. For you are true, O God, and so you chide and rebuke them and prove them wrong. The choice may lie between two impulses that are both evil, as when a person is debating whether to murder someone with poison or a dagger; whether to annex this part of another man's property or that, assuming he cannot get both; whether to buy himself pleasure by extravagant spending or hoard his money out of avarice; whether to go to the circus or the theater if both performances are on the same day—and I would even add a third possibility: whether to go and steal from someone else's house while he has the chance, and a fourth as well: whether to commit adultery while he is about it. All these impulses may occur together, at exactly the same time, and all be equally tempting, but they cannot all be acted upon at once. The mind is then rent apart by the plethora of desirable objects as four inclinations, or even more, do battle among themselves; yet the Manichees do not claim that there are as many disparate substances in us as this.

The same holds true for good impulses. I would put these questions to them: Is it good to find delight in a reading from the apostle? To enjoy the serenity of a psalm? To discuss the gospel? To each point they will reply, "Yes, that is good." Where does that leave us? If all these things tug at our will with equal force, and all together at the same time, will not these divergent inclinations put a great strain on the human heart, as we deliberate which to select? All are good, but they compete among themselves until one is chosen, to which the will, hitherto distracted between many options, may move as a united whole. So too when the joys of eternity call us from above, and pleasure in temporal prosperity holds us fast below, our one soul is in no state to embrace either with its entire will. Claimed by truth for the one, to the other clamped by custom, the soul is torn apart in its distress.

11, 25. Such was the sickness in which I agonized, blaming myself more sharply than ever, turning and twisting in my chain as I strove to tear free from it completely, for slender indeed was the bond that still held me. But hold me it did. In my secret heart you stood by me, Lord, redoubling the lashes of fear and shame in the severity of your mercy, lest I give up the struggle and that slender, fragile bond that remained be not broken after all, but thicken again and constrict me more tightly. "Let it be now," I was saying to myself. "Now is the moment, let it be now," and merely by saying this I was moving toward the decision. I would almost achieve it, but then fall just short; yet I did not slip right down to my starting-point, but stood aside to get my breath back. Then I would make a fresh attempt, and now I was almost there, almost there . . . I was touching the goal, grasping it . . . and then I was not there, not touching, not grasping it. I shrank from dying to death and living to life, for ingrained evil was more powerful in me than new-grafted good. The nearer it came, that moment when I would be changed, the more it pierced me with terror. Dismayed, but not quite dislodged, I was left hanging.

26. The frivolity of frivolous aims, the futility of futile pursuits, these things that had been my cronies of long standing, still held me back, plucking softly at my garment

of flesh and murmuring in my ear, "Do you mean to get rid of us? Shall we never be your companions again after that moment . . . never . . . never again? From that time onward so-and-so will be forbidden to you, all your life long." And what was it that they were reminding me of by those words, "so-and-so," O my God, what were they bringing to my mind? May your mercy banish such memories far from me! What foul deeds were they not hinting at, what disgraceful exploits! But now their voices were less than half as loud, for they no longer confronted me directly to argue their case, but muttered behind my back and slyly tweaked me as I walked away, trying to make me look back. Yet they did slow me down, for I could not bring myself to tear free and shake them off and leap across to that place whither I was summoned, while aggressive habit still taunted me: "Do you imagine you will be able to live without these things?"

27. The taunts had begun to sound much less persuasive, however; for a revelation was coming to me from that country toward which I was facing, but into which I trembled to cross. There I beheld the chaste, dignified figure of Continence. Calm and cheerful was her manner, though modest, pure and honorable her charm as she coaxed me to come and hesitate no longer, stretching kindly hands to welcome and embrace me, hands filled with a wealth of heartening examples. A multitude of boys and girls were there, a great concourse of youth and persons of every age, venerable widows and women grown old in their virginity, and in all of them I saw this that this same Continence was by no means sterile, but the fruitful mother of children conceived in joy from you, her Bridegroom. She was smiling at me, but with a challenging smile, as though to say, "Can you not do what these men have done, these women? Could any of them achieve it by their own strength, without the Lord their God? He it was, the Lord their God, who granted me to them. Why try to stand by yourself, only to lose your footing? Cast yourself on him and do not be afraid: he will not step back and let you fall. Cast yourself upon him trustfully; he will support and heal you." And I was bitterly ashamed, because I could still hear the murmurs of those frivolities, and I was still in suspense, still hanging back. Again she appealed to me, as though urging, "Close your ears against those unclean parts of you which belong to the earth and let them be put to death. They tell you titillating tales, but have nothing to do with the law of the Lord your God."

All this argument in my heart raged only between myself and myself. Alypius stood fast at my side, silently awaiting the outcome of my unprecedented agitation.

12, 28. But as this deep meditation dredged all my wretchedness up from the secret profundity of my being and heaped it all together before the eyes of my heart, a huge storm blew up within me and brought on a heavy rain of tears. In order to pour them out unchecked with the sobs that accompanied them I arose and left Alypius, for solitude seemed to me more suitable for the business of weeping. I withdrew far enough to ensure that his presence—even his—would not be burdensome to me. This was my need, and he understood it, for I think I had risen to my feet and blurted out something, my voice already choked with tears. He accordingly remained, in stunned amazement, at the place where we had been sitting. I flung myself down somehow under a fig-tree and gave free rein to the tears that burst from my eyes like rivers, as an acceptable sacrifice to you. Many things I had to say to you, and the gist of them, though not the precise words, was: "O Lord, how long? How long? Will you be angry for ever? Do not remember our age-old sins." For by these I was conscious of being held prisoner. I uttered cries of misery: "Why must I go on saying, 'Tomorrow . . . tomorrow'? Why not now? Why not put an end to my depravity this very hour?"

29. I went on talking like this and weeping in the intense bitterness of my broken heart. Suddenly I heard a voice from a house nearby—perhaps a voice of some boy or girl, I do not know—singing over and over again, "Pick it up and read, pick it up and read." My expression immediately altered and I began to think hard whether children ordinarily repeated a ditty like this in any sort of game, but I could not recall ever having heard it anywhere else. I stemmed the flood of tears and rose to my feet, believing that this could be nothing other than a divine command to open the Book and read the first passage I chanced upon; for I had heard the story of how Antony had been instructed by a gospel text. He happened to arrive while the gospel was being read, and took the words to be addressed to himself when he heard, "Go and sell all you possess and give the money to the poor: you will have treasure in heaven. Then come, follow me" [Matt. 19:21]. So he was promptly converted to you by this plainly divine message. Stung into action, I returned to the place where Alypius was sitting, for on leaving it I had put down there the book of the apostle's letters. I snatched it up, opened it and read in silence the passage on which my eyes first lighted: "Not in dissipation and drunkenness, nor in debauchery and lewdness, nor in arguing and jealousy; but put on the Lord Jesus Christ, and make no provision for the flesh or the gratification of your desires" [Rom. 13:13–14]. I had no wish to read further, nor was there need. No sooner had I reached the end of the verse than the light of certainty flooded my heart and all dark shades of doubt fled away.

30. I closed the book, marking the place with a finger between the leaves or by some other means, and told Alypius what had happened. My face was peaceful now. He in return told me what had been happening to him without my knowledge. He asked to see what I had read: I showed him, but he looked further than my reading had taken me. I did not know what followed, but the next verse was, "Make room for the person who is weak in faith." He referred this text to himself and interpreted it to me. Confirmed by this admonition he associated himself with my decision and good purpose without any upheaval or delay, for it was entirely in harmony with his own moral character, which for a long time now had been far, far better than mine.

We went indoors and told my mother, who was overjoyed. When we related to her how it had happened she was filled with triumphant delight and blessed you, who have power to do more than we ask or understand, for she saw that you had granted her much more in my regard than she had been wont to beg of you in her wretched, tearful groaning. Many years earlier you had shown her a vision of me standing on the rule of faith; and now indeed I stood there, no longer seeking a wife or entertaining any worldly hope, for you had converted me to yourself. In so doing you had also converted her grief into a joy far more abundant than she had desired, and much more tender and chaste than she could ever have looked to find in grandchildren from my flesh.

* * *

Book XI—Time and Eternity

14, 17. There was therefore never any time when you had not made anything, because you made time itself. And no phases of time are coeternal with you, for you abide, and if they likewise were to abide, they would not be time. For what is time? Who could find any quick or easy answer to that? Who could even grasp it in his thought

God in Act of Creation, from a thirteenth-century French Bible. In the *Confessions,* Augustine argues that God created the world *ex nihilo* (out of nothing) and that God is outside of time. (*Corbis-Bettmann*)

clearly enough to put the matter into words? Yet is there anything to which we refer in conversation with more familiarity, any matter of more common experience, than time? And we know perfectly well what we mean when we speak of it, and understand just as well when we hear someone else refer to it. What, then, is time? If no one asks me, I know; if I want to explain it to someone who asks me, I do not know. I can state with confidence, however, that this much I do know: if nothing passed away there would be no past time; if there was nothing still on its way there would be no future time; and if nothing existed, there would be no present time.

Now, what about those two times, past and future: in what sense do they have real being, if the past no longer exists and the future does not exist yet? As for present time, if that were always present and never slipped away into the past, it would not be time at all; it would be eternity. If, therefore, the present's only claim to be called "time" is that it is slipping away into the past, how can we assert that this thing *is,* when its only title to being is that it will soon cease to be? In other words, we cannot really say that time exists, except because it tends to non-being.*

15, 18. Nonetheless we speak of a long time or a short time, and we do so only of time past or time in the future. For example, we call a hundred years ago a long time in

*[This is the heart of the matter for Augustine. He pursues the argument relentlessly throughout the rest of this Book XI, revealing time as something elusive that slips the more swiftly through our fingers the more we try to analyze it or justify our habit of measuring it. The inexorable rush of time toward non-being reveals the fragility of time-bound, time-conditioned creatures, whose only refuge from their native nothingness is the eternity of God.]

the past, and likewise a hundred years hence a long time in the future; but we call—say—ten days ago a short time past, and ten days hence a short time in the future. But on what grounds can something that does not exist be called long or short? The past no longer exists and the future does not exist yet. We ought not, therefore, to say, "That is a long time," but, when speaking of the past, we should say, "That was long," and of the future, "That will be long."

O my Lord, my light, will your truth not deride us humans for speaking so? This long time in the past: was it long when it was already past, or earlier than that, when it was still present? If the latter, yes, then it might have been long, because there was something to be long; but if it was already past it no longer existed, and therefore could not have been long, since it was not in existence at all. We ought not, therefore, to say, "That era in the past was a long one," for we shall not find anything that was long, for since that point at which it became past time it has no longer had any being. Rather, we ought to say, "That era of time was long while present," because while it was present it was long. It had not yet passed away and so passed out of existence, and so there was something there which could be long. But when it passed away it ceased to be long at that very point when it ceased to be at all.

19. Now, human mind, let us consider whether present time can be long, as you seem to think it can, since you have been granted the power to be aware of duration and to measure it. Answer my questions, then. Is the present century a long period of time? Before you say yes, reflect whether a hundred years can be present. If the first of them is running its course, that year is present, but ninety-nine others are future and therefore as yet have no being. If the second year is running its course, one year is already past, another is present, and the remainder are still to come. In the same fashion we may represent any one of the intervening years of the century as present, and always the years that preceded it will be past, and those that follow it future. Evidently, then, a hundred years cannot be present.

Well then, consider whether the one current year at least can be present. If we are in the first month of it, the other months are in the future; if we are in the second, the first month is already past and the rest do not yet exist. Even the current year, then, is not present in its totality, and if it is not present in its totality, the year is not present; for a year consists of twelve months, and while any one of them is current that one is present, but the others are either past or future.

But we must go further, and notice that the current month is not in fact present, because only one day of it is: if we are on the first day, the rest are future; if on the last, the others are past; if on any day in the middle, we shall be midway between past and future days.

20. Look where this leaves us. We saw earlier that present time was the only one of the three that might properly be called long, and now this present time has been pared down to the span of a bare day. But let us take the discussion further, because not even a single day is present all at once. It is made up of night hours and day hours, twenty-four in all. From the standpoint of the first hour all the rest are still future; the last hour looks to all those already past; and any one we pick in between has some before it, others to follow. Even a single hour runs its course through fleeing minutes: whatever portion of it has flown is now past, and what remains is future. If we can conceive of a moment in time which cannot be further divided into even the tiniest of minute particles, that alone can be rightly termed the present; yet even this flies by from the future into the past with such haste that it seems to last no time at all. Even if it has some duration, that too is divisible into past and future; hence the present is reduced to vanishing-point.

What kind of time, then, can be referred to as "a long time"? Future time, perhaps? Then we must not say, "That is a long time," because there is as yet nothing to be long; we will have to say, "That will be long." But when will it be so? If at the point of speaking that period is still in the future, it will not be long, because nothing yet exists to be long; if, however, at the moment when we speak it has begun to exist by emerging from the non-existent future, and so has become present, so that there is something in existence to be long, then this present time proclaims itself incapable of being long for the reasons already discussed.

16, 21. All the same, Lord, we are conscious of intervals of time, and we compare them with each other and pronounce some longer, others shorter. We also calculate by how much this period of time is longer or shorter than that other, and we report that the one is twice or three times as long as the other, or that it is the same length. But when we measure periods of time by our awareness of them, what we measure is passing time. Could anyone measure past periods that no longer exist, or future periods that do not yet exist? Only someone who is bold enough to claim that what has no being can be measured. So then, while time is passing it can be felt and measured, but once past it cannot, because it no longer exists.

17, 22. I am asking questions, Father, not making assertions: rule me, O my God, and shepherd me. For who would make so bold as to tell me that there are not really three tenses or times—past, present and future—as we learned as children and as we in our turn have taught our children, but that there is only present, since the other two do not exist? Or is the truth perhaps that they do exist, but that when a future thing becomes present it emerges from some hiding-place, and then retreats into another hiding-place when it moves from the present into the past? Where, otherwise, did soothsayers see future events, if they do not yet exist? What has no being cannot be seen. Nor would people who tell stories about the past be telling true tales if they had no vision of those past events in their minds; and if the events in question were non-existent they could not be seen. The future and the past must exist, then?

18, 23. Allow me, Lord, to press the question further: O my hope, do not let me lose the thread. If future and past things do exist, I want to know where they are. If this is not yet within my compass, I do know at any rate that, wherever they are, they are not there as future or past, but as present. For if in that place too future things are future, they are not there yet; and if there too past things are past, they are there no longer. Clearly, then, wherever they are and whatever they are, they can only be present. Nonetheless, when a true account is given of past events, what is brought forth from the memory is not the events themselves, which have passed away, but words formed from images of those events which as they happened and went on their way left some kind of traces in the mind through the medium of the senses. This is the case with my childhood, which no longer exists: it belongs to past time which exists no longer, but when I recall it and tell the story I contemplate the image of it which is still in my memory.

Whether something similar occurs in the prediction of future events, in that the seer has a presentiment of images which exist already, I confess, O my God, that I do not know. But this I undoubtedly do know, that we often plan our future actions beforehand, and that the plans in our mind are present to us, though the action we are planning has as yet no being, because it is future. When we set about it, and begin to do what we were planning, then the action will have real being, because then it will be not future but present.

24. However the mysterious presentiment of future events may be explained, only what exists can be seen. But what already exists is not future but present. Therefore

when it is claimed that future events are seen, it is not that these things are seen in themselves, because they have as yet no existence, being still future. It may be, however, that their causes, or signs of them, are seen, because these already exist; hence they are not future but present to the people who discern them, and from them future events may take shape in the mind and can be foretold. These ideas in the mind also exist already, and can be inwardly contemplated by people who predict the future.

Let me take an example from a wealth of such occurrences. I watch the dawn, and I give advance notice that the sun is about to rise. What I am looking at is present; what I foretell is future. Not that the sun is future, of course—no, that exists already, but its rising is future; it has not yet happened, yet unless I could imagine the sunrise in my mind, as I do now while I speak of it, I would be unable to forecast it. The dawn, which I am watching in the sky, is not the sunrise, but only precedes it; and similarly the picture I have in my mind is not the sunrise either. But these two realities are present and open to observation, so that the future event can be announced before its time.

We must conclude, then, that future events have no being as yet, and if they have no being yet they do not exist, and if they do not exist it is absolutely impossible for anyone to see them. But they can be predicted on the basis of other things which are already present and hence can be seen.

19, 25. You are the king of your creation; tell me, then: how do you instruct people's minds about the future? You did so teach the prophets. What method can you adopt for teaching what is future, when to you nothing is future at all? Would it be better to say that you teach what is present but has a bearing on the future? Yes, because what does not exist obviously cannot be taught. This method of yours is far above the reach of my mind; it is too much for me and of myself I cannot see it, but I will see it with your help, when you grant me this gift, O gracious light of my secret eyes.

20, 26. What is now clear and unmistakable is that neither things past nor things future have any existence, and that it is inaccurate to say, "There are three tenses or times: past, present and future," though it might properly be said, "There are three tenses or times: the present of past things, the present of present things, and the present of future things." These are three realities in the mind, but nowhere else as far as I can see, for the present of past things is memory, the present of present things is attention, and the present of future things is expectation. If we are allowed to put it that way, I do see three tenses or times, and admit that they are three. Very well, then, let the phrase pass: "There are three tenses or times: past, present and future," as common usage improperly has it: let people go on saying this. I do not mind, nor will I put up any opposition or offer correction, provided we understand what we are saying, and do not assert that either the future or the past exists now. There are few things, in fact, which we state accurately; far more we express loosely, but what we mean is understood.

21, 27. I said just now* that we measure periods of time as they pass, so as to declare this interval twice as long as that, or this equal to that, and report anything else about segments of time that our measurements have revealed. It follows, then, that we measure these intervals of time as they are passing by, as I remarked, and if anyone asks me, "How do you know that?" I must be allowed to reply, "I know it because we do in fact measure them; but what does not exist we cannot measure, and past and future do not exist." But how can we measure present time, when it has no extension?** We can

*[That is, in XI, 16, 21.]

**[That is, the ideal present is a point, which has position but no magnitude.]

only hope to measure it as it passes by, because once it has passed by there will be no measuring; it will not exist to be measured.

But when it is measured, where does it come from, by what path does it pass, and whither go? Where from, if not from the future? By what path, if not the present? Whither, if not into the past? It comes, then, from what is not yet real, travels through what occupies no space, and is bound for what is no longer real. But what are we trying to measure, if not time that does have some extension? We speak of "half as long," "double the time," "three times as long," "equal in length," and make similar statements about time only in reference to extended time, or duration. Where then is this duration which will give us a chance to measure passing time? In the future, whence it has come to pass us by? But we do not measure what does not yet exist. In the present, perhaps, through which it passes on its way? But where there is no extension we cannot measure. In the past, then, to which it has gone? But we cannot measure what no longer exists.

22, 28. My mind is on fire to solve this most intricate enigma. O Lord, my God, my good Father, through Christ I beg you not to shut against me the door to these truths, so familiar yet so mysterious. Do not slam the door in the face of my desire, nor forbid me entrance to that place where I may watch these things grow luminous as your mercy sheds its light upon them, Lord. To whom should I put my questions about them? And to whom should I confess my stupidity with greater profit than to you, who do not weary of my intense, burning interest in your scriptures? Give me what I love; for I love indeed, and this love you have given me. Give this to me, Father, for you truly know how to give good gifts to your children; give me this gift, for I have only just begun to understand, and the labor is too much for me until you open the door. Through Christ I implore you, in the name of that holy of holies, let no noisy person stand in my way. I too have believed, and so I too speak. This is my hope, for this I live: to contemplate the delight of the Lord. See how old you have made my days; they are slipping away and I know not how.

We speak of one time and another time, of this period of time or that; we ask, "How long did that man speak?" or "How long did he take to do it?" We say, "What a long time it is since I saw so-and-so," and "This syllable has twice the length of that short one." We say these things and listen to them, we are understood and we understand. They are perfectly plain and fully familiar, yet at the same time deeply mysterious, and we still need to discover their meaning.

23, 29. I was once told by a certain learned man that the movements of the sun, moon and stars themselves constitute time. I did not agree with him. Why, in that case, should not the movements of all corporeal things constitute time? Suppose the luminaries of heaven were to halt, but a potter's wheel went on turning, would there not still be time by which we could measure those rotations, and say either that all of them took the same time, or (if the speed of the wheel varied) that some were of longer duration, others shorter? And when we said this, would we too not be speaking within time; and in the words we used, would there not be some long syllables and some short; and why could that be said of them, unless because some of them had taken a longer time to pronounce than others?

Through this small thing, O God, grant our human minds insight into the principles common to small things and great. The stars and the other luminaries in the sky are there to mark our times and days and years. Yes, granted; but as I would not assert that the revolution of that little wooden wheel itself constituted a day, so my learned informant on the other hand had no business to say that its gyrations did not occupy a space of time.

30. I want to know the essence and nature of time, whereby we measure the movement of bodies and say, for instance, that one movement lasts twice as long as another. Now I have a question to ask. Taking the word "day" to apply not only to the period of sunlight on earth—day as opposed to night, that is—but to the sun's whole course from the east and back to the east again, in the sense that we say, "So many days elapsed," meaning to include the nights, and not reckoning the nights as extra time over and above the days; taking it, then, that the movement of the sun in its circular course from the east back to the east completes a day, this is my question: is it the movement itself that constitutes a day? Or the time it takes? Or both? If the movement constitutes a day, then it would still be one day if the sun were to achieve its circuit in an interval of time equivalent to a single hour. If it is the time it takes, there would not be a day if the space between one sunrise and the next were as short as an hour; the sun would have to go round twenty-four times to make up a day. If both were required complete circuit of the sun and the customary duration of this—we could not call it a day if the sun traveled through its whole circuit in the space of an hour, nor could we if the sun stopped and as much time elapsed as it usually takes to run its whole course from morning to morning.

My question now is not, therefore, what is it that we call a day, but what is time itself, the time whereby we would be able to measure the sun's revolution and say that it had been completed in only half the usual time, if the circuit had occupied only that space of time represented by twelve hours? We could compare the two periods in terms of time and say that one was twice the length of the other, and this would still be possible even if the sun sometimes took the single period, and sometimes the double, to circle from the east and back to the east again. Let no one tell me, then, that time is simply the motion of the heavenly bodies. After all, at the prayer of a certain man the sun halted so that he could press home the battle to victory. The sun stood still, but time flowed on its way, and that fight had all the time it needed to be carried through to the finish.

I see, therefore, that time is a kind of strain or tension. But do I really see it? Or only seem to see? You will show me, O Light, O Truth.

24, 31. Are you commanding me to agree with someone who says that time is the motion of a body? You do not so command me. No corporeal object moves except within time: this is what I hear; this is what you tell me. But that a corporeal object's movement is itself time I do not hear; this you do not say. When a body moves, I measure in terms of time how long it is in motion, from the moment when it begins until its motion ceases. If I did not notice when it began, and it continues to move without my seeing when it stops, I cannot measure the time, except perhaps the interval between the moment when I began to watch and that when I ceased to observe it. If my observation is prolonged, I can only say that the process went on for a long time; I cannot say exactly how long, because when we add a definite indication of a length of time we do so by reference to some agreed standard. "This is as long as that," we say; or "This is twice as long as that other," or something similar. If, on the other hand, we have been able to note the position of some corporeal object when it moves (or when parts of it move, if, for example, it is being turned on a lathe), and we have observed its starting-point and its point of arrival, then we are able to state how much time has elapsed while the movement of the object was effected from the one place to the other, or how long it has taken to revolve on its axis.

Therefore if the motion of an object is one thing, and the standard by which we measure its duration another, is it not obvious which of the two has the stronger claim to be called time? Moreover, if the motion is irregular, so that the object is sometimes moving and sometimes stationary, we measure not only its motion but also its static periods in terms of time, and say, "Its stationary periods were equivalent in length to its phases of motion," or "It was stationary for two or three times as long as it was in motion," or whatever else our calculation has ascertained or estimated roughly—more or less, as we customarily say. Clearly, then, time is not the movement of any corporeal object.

25, 32. I confess to you, Lord, that even today I am still ignorant of what time is; but I praise you, Lord, for the fact that I know I am making this avowal within time, and for my realization that within time I am talking about time at such length, and that I know this "length" itself is long only because time has been passing all the while. But how can I know that, when I do not know what time is? Or perhaps I simply do not know how to articulate what I know? Woe is me, for I do not even know what I do not know!

Behold me here before you, O my God; see that I do not lie. As I speak, this is the true state of my heart. You, you alone, will light my lamp, O Lord; O my God, you will illumine my darkness.

26, 33. Am I not making a truthful confession to you when I praise you for my ability to measure time? But this must mean, O my God, that though I can measure it, I do not know what I am measuring! I measure the movement of a body in terms of time, but surely I am by that same calculation measuring time itself? Would it be possible for me to measure a body's motion, to calculate how long it lasts and how long the object takes to travel from here to there, without also measuring the time within which the motion occurs? With what, then, do I measure time itself? Do we measure a longer time by the standard of a shorter, as we use the cubit to measure the span of a cross-beam? That indeed seems to be how we measure the quantity of a long syllable by that of a short syllable, and decide that the former is twice as long. Similarly we measure the length of poems by the length of their lines, and the length of the lines by the length of the feet, and the length of each foot by the length of its syllables, and the length of a long syllable by that of a short syllable. We do not reckon by the number of pages—that would be to impose a spatial, not a temporal standard—but by the pronunciation as voices recite them and die away. We declare, "That is a lengthy poem, for it consists of so many lines; the lines are long, since each is composed of so many feet; the feet are long, since each extends over so many syllables; and a syllable is long, when it is twice the quantity of a short one."

But the mensuration of time by these methods yields no result that is absolute, since it may happen that the sound of a shorter line, spoken with a drawl, actually lasts longer than that of a longer one hurried over. The same holds for the whole poem, a foot, and a syllable.

I have therefore come to the conclusion that time is nothing other than tension: but tension of what, I do not know, and I would be very surprised if it is not tension of consciousness itself. What am I measuring, I beg you to tell me, my God, when I say in imprecise terms, "This is longer than that," or even, precisely, "This is twice that"? That I am measuring time, I know; but I am not measuring future time, because it does not yet exist, not present time, which is a point without extension, nor past time, which exists no more. What, then, am I measuring? Time as it passes by, but not once it has passed? That was what I said earlier.

27, 34. Stick to it, now, my mind, and pay close attention. God is our ally; and he made us, not we ourselves. Mark where truth brightens to the dawn!

Suppose now that a physical voice begins to sound . . . and goes on sounding . . . and is still sounding . . . and now stops. Now there is silence, and that voice is past and is a voice no longer. Before it sounded forth it was a future thing, so it could not be measured because it did not yet exist; neither can it be now, because it exists no more. Perhaps, then, it could be measured while it was sounding forth, because something did then exist that could be measured? But at that time it was not standing still; it was but a fleeting thing that was speeding on its way. Was it therefore any more measurable while sounding than before or after? Only as something transient was it extended over a period of time whereby it might be measured—only as transient, because the present moment has no duration. If it is argued that the sound could, nevertheless, be measured while it lasted, consider this: another voice begins to sound and is still sounding in a continuous, steady tone. Let us measure it, then, while it is sounding, for once it has fallen silent it will be a thing of the past, and nothing measurable will then exist. By all means let us measure it now, and state how long it lasts.

Ah, but it is still sounding, and there is no way of timing it except from its beginning, when the sound originated, to its end, when it ceases. Obviously we measure any interval of time from some inception to some ending. Hence the sound of a voice which has not yet finished cannot be measured in such a way that anyone can say how long or how short it is, nor can it be declared to be of the same length as something else, or half the length, or twice the length, or anything of the kind. But once finished, it will not exist. So by what criteria will it then be subject to measurement?

All the same we do measure periods of time, not periods which as yet have no being, nor those which have ceased to be, nor those which have no duration, nor those which have no terminus. We measure neither future nor past nor present nor passing time. Yet time we do measure.

35. Take the line, *Deus, creator omnium.** This line consists of eight syllables, short and long alternating. The four short ones—the first, third, fifth and seventh—are thus half the length of the four long ones—the second, fourth, sixth and eighth. Each of these latter lasts twice as long as each of the former; I have only to pronounce the line to report that this is the case, insofar as clear sense-perception can verify it. Relying on this unmistakable evidence of my ear I measure each long syllable by the criterion of a short one, and perceive that it is twice the quantity. But the syllables make themselves heard in succession; and if the first is short and the second long, how am I to hold on to the short one, how am I to apply it to the long one as a measuring-rod in order to discover that the long one has twice the quantity, when the long one does not begin to sound until the short one has ceased? Am I to measure the long one while it is present? Impossible, because I cannot measure something unfinished. But its completion is its passing away, so what now exists for me to measure? Where is the short syllable I was going to use as a standard? What has become of the long one I want to measure? Both have made their sound, and flown away, and passed by, and exist no more; yet I do my calculation and confidently assert that insofar as the testimony of my trained ear can be trusted, the short is half the long, the long twice the short; and obviously I am speaking about a space of time. I can only do this because the syllables have passed away and are completed. Evidently, then, what I am measuring is not the syllables themselves, which no longer exist, but something in my memory, something fixed and permanent there.

36. In you, my mind, I measure time. Do not interrupt me by clamoring that time has objective existence, nor hinder yourself with the hurly-burly of your impressions. In you, I say, do I measure time. What I measure is the impression which passing

*[Ambrose's evening hymn: "God, Creator of all."]

phenomena leave in you, which abides after they have passed by: that is what I measure as a present reality, not the things that passed by so that the impression could be formed. The impression itself is what I measure when I measure intervals of time. Hence either time is this impression, or what I measure is not time.

What about when we measure silences, and say that this silent pause lasted as long as that sound? Do we not strain our thought to retain the feeling of a sound's duration, as though it were still audible, so as to be able to estimate the intervals of silence in relation to the whole space of time in question? Without any articulate word or even opening our mouths we go over in our minds poems, their lines, a speech, and we assess their developmental patterns and the time they occupied in relation to one another; and our estimate is no different from what it would have been if we had been reciting them aloud.

Suppose a person wishes to utter a fairly long sound, and has determined beforehand in his own mind how long it is to be. He must have first thought through that period of time in silence and committed the impression of it to memory; then he begins to utter the sound, which continues until it reaches the predetermined end. Or rather, it does not "continue," because the sound is evidently both something already heard and something still to be heard, for the part of it already completed is sound that has been, but the part that remains is sound still to be. Thus it is carried through as our present awareness drags what is future into the past. As the future dwindles the past grows, until the future is used up altogether and the whole thing is past.

28, 37. But how can a future which does not yet exist dwindle or be used up, and how can a past which no longer exists grow? Only because there are three realities in the mind which conducts this operation. The mind expects, and attends, and remembers, so that what it expects passes by way of what it attends to into what it remembers. No one, surely, would deny that the future is as yet non-existent? Yet an expectation of future events does exist in the mind. And would anyone deny that the past has ceased to be? Yet the memory of past events still lives on in the mind. And who would deny that the present has no duration, since it passes in an instant? Yet our attention does endure, and through our attention what is still to be makes its way into the state where it is no more. It is not, therefore, future time which is long, for it does not exist; a long future is simply an expectation of the future which represents it as long. Nor is the past along period of time, because it does not exist at all; a long past is simply a memory of the past which represents it as long.

38. Suppose I have to recite a poem I know by heart. Before I begin, my expectation is directed to the whole poem, but once I have begun, whatever I have plucked away from the domain of expectation and tossed behind me to the past becomes the business of my memory, and the vital energy of what I am doing is in tension between the two of them: it strains toward my memory because of the part I have already recited, and to my expectation on account of the part I still have to speak. But my attention is present all the while, for the future is being channeled through it to become the past. As the poem goes on and on, expectation is curtailed and memory prolonged, until expectation is entirely used up, when the whole completed action has passed into memory.

What is true of the poem as a whole is true equally of its individual stanzas and syllables. The same is true of the whole long performance, in which this poem may be a single item. The same thing happens in the entirety of a person's life, of which all his actions are parts; and the same in the entire sweep of human history, the parts of which are individual human lives.

CITY OF GOD (in part)

BOOK XI

CHAPTER 26

We ourselves can recognize in ourselves an image of God, in the sense of an image of the Trinity. Of course, it is merely an image and, in fact, a very remote one. There is no question of identity nor of co-eternity nor, in one word, of consubstantiality with Him. Nevertheless, it is an image which by nature is nearer to God than anything else in all creation, and one that by transforming grace can be perfected into a still closer resemblance.

For, we are, and we know that we are, and we love to be and to know that we are. And in this trinity of being, knowledge, and love there is not a shadow of illusion to disturb us. For, we do not reach these inner realities with our bodily senses as we do external objects, as, for example, color by seeing, sound by hearing, odor by smelling, flavor by tasting, hard or soft objects by touching. In the case of such sensible things, the best we can do is to form very close and immaterial images which help us to turn them over in our minds, to hold them in our memory, and thus to keep our love for them alive. But, without any illusion of image, fancy, or phantasm, I am certain that I am, that I know that I am, and that I love to be and to know.

In the face of these truths, the quibbles of the skeptics lose their force. If they say; "What if you are mistaken?"—well, if *I* am mistaken, I am. For, if one does not exist, he can by no means be mistaken. Therefore, I am, if I am mistaken. Because, therefore, I am, if I am mistaken, how can I be mistaken that I am, since it is certain that I am, if I am mistaken? And because, if I could be mistaken, I would have to be the one who is mistaken, therefore, I am most certainly not mistaken in knowing that I am. Nor, as a consequence, am I mistaken in knowing that I know. For, just as I know that I am, I also know that I know. And when I love both to be and to know, then I add to the things I know a third and equally important knowledge, the fact that I love.

Nor am I mistaken that I love, since I am not mistaken concerning the objects of my love. For, even though these objects were false, it would still be true that I loved illusions. For, if this were not true, how could I be reproved and prohibited from loving illusions? But, since these objects are true and certain, who can doubt that, when they are loved, the loving of them is also true and certain? Further, just as there is no one who does not wish to be happy, so there is no one who does not wish to exist. For, how can anyone be happy if he does not exist?

* * *

St. Augustine, *City of God,* Books XI, 26 and XII, 1–9 from *Fathers of the Church; Writings of Saint Augustine; Saint Augustine: City of God,* translated by Gerald G. Walsh, Daniel J. Honan, and Grace Monahan (Washington, DC: The Catholic University of America Press, 1952, 1954). Reprinted by permission.

BOOK XII

CHAPTER 1

In the previous book we saw something of the beginning of the two cities, so far as angels are concerned. In the same way, we must now proceed to the creation of men and see the beginning of the cities so far as it concerns the kind of rational creatures who are mortal. First, however, a few remarks about the angels must be made in order to make it as clear as I can how there is no real difficulty or impropriety in speaking of a single society composed of both men and angels; and why, therefore, it is right to say that there are not four cities or societies, namely, two of angels and two of men, but only two, one of them made up of the good—both angels and men—and the other of those who are evil.

There is no reason to doubt that the contrary dispositions which have developed among these good and bad angels are due, not to different natures and origins, for God the Author and Creator of all substances has created them both, but to the dissimilar choices and desires of these angels themselves. Some, remaining faithful to God, the common good of all, have lived in the enjoyment of His eternity, truth, and love, while others, preferring the enjoyment of their own power, as though they were their own good, departed from the higher good and common blessedness for all and turned to goods of their own choosing.

Preferring the pomp of pride to this sublimity of eternity, the craftiness of vanity to the certainty of truth, and the turmoil of dissension to the union of love, they became proud, deceitful, and envious.

Since the happiness of all angels consists in union with God, it follows that their unhappiness must be found in the very contrary, that is, in not adhering to God. To the question: "Why are the good angels happy?" the right answer is: "Because they adhere to God." To the question: "Why are the others unhappy?" the answer is: "Because they do not adhere to God." In fact, there is no other good which can make any rational or intellectual creature happy except God. Not every creature has the potentialities for happiness. Beasts, trees, stones, and such things neither acquire nor have the capacity for this gift. However, every creature which has this capacity receives it, not from itself, since it has been created out of nothing, but from its Creator. To possess Him is to be happy; to lose Him is to be in misery. And, of course, that One whose beatitude depends upon Himself as His own good and not on any other good can never be unhappy since He can never lose Himself.

Thus, there can be no unchangeable good except our one, true, and blessed God. All things which He has made are good because made by Him, but they are subject to change because they were made, not out of Him, but out of nothing. Although they are not supremely good, since God is a greater good than they, these mutable things are, none the less, highly good by reason of their capacity for union with and, therefore, beatitude in the Immutable Good which is so completely their good that, without this good, misery is inevitable.

But it does not follow that other creatures in the universe are better off merely because they are incapable of misery. That would be like saying that other members of the body are better than the eyes because they can never become blind. A sentient nature even in pain is better than a stone that cannot suffer. In the same way, a rational nature even in misery is higher than one which, because it lacks reason or sensation, cannot suffer misery.

This being the case, it is nothing less than a perversion of the nature of the angels if they do not adhere to God. For, remember, their nature is so high in the order of creation that, mutable as it is, it can attain beatitude by adhering to the immutable and supreme Good, which is God, and that, unless it achieves beatitude, this nature fails to satisfy its inmost exigencies, and, finally, that nothing but God can satisfy these needs of the angelic nature.

Now, this perversion, like every imperfection in a nature, harms nature and, therefore, is contrary to the nature. It follows, therefore, that what makes the wicked angels differ from the good ones is not their nature but a perversion or imperfection; and this very blemish is a proof of how highly to be esteemed is the nature itself. Certainly, no blemish in a thing ought to be blamed unless we are praising the thing as a whole, for the whole point of blaming the blemish is that it mars the perfection of something we would like to see praised.

For example, when we say that blindness is a defect of the eyes, we imply that it is the very nature of the eyes to see, and when we say that deafness is a malady of the ears, we are supposing that it is their nature to hear. So, too, when we say that it is a failure in an angel not to attain union with God, we openly proclaim that they were meant by nature to be one with God.

Of course, no one can fully comprehend or properly express the ineffable union of being one with God in His life, in His wisdom, in His joy, and all this without a shadow of death or darkness or disturbance. One thing is certain. The very failure of the bad angels to cling to God—a desertion that damaged their nature like a disease—is itself proof enough that the nature God gave them was good—so good that not to be one with God was for them a disaster.

CHAPTER 2

This explanation just given seemed to me necessary to forestall the objection that the apostate spirits might have received from some principle other than God a nature different from that of the other angels. The malice of this mistake can be more easily and speedily removed the more clearly one grasps what God meant by the words, "I AM WHO AM" (Exod. 3:14), spoken through the medium of an angel at the time when Moses was being sent to the children of Israel.

Since God is supreme being, that is, since He supremely is and, therefore, is immutable, it follows that He gave "being" to all that He created out of nothing; not, however, absolute being. To some things He gave more of being and to others less and, in this way, arranged an order of natures in a hierarchy of being. (This noun, "being," is derived from the verb "to be," just as "wisdom" is from the verb "to be wise." In Latin, *essentia*, "being," is a new word, not used by the ancient writers, recently adopted in order to find an equivalent of the Greek, ⟨*ousía*⟩, of which *essentia* is the exact translation.)

Consequently, no nature—except a non-existent one—can be contrary to the nature which is supreme and which created whatever other natures have being. In other words, nonentity stands in opposition to that which is. Therefore, there is no being opposed to God who is the Supreme Being and Source of all beings without exception.

CHAPTER 3

In Scripture, those who oppose God's rule, not by nature but by sin, are called His enemies. They can do no damage to Him, but only to themselves; their enmity is not a power to harm, but merely an inclination to oppose Him. In any case, God is immutable and completely invulnerable. Hence, the malice by which His so-called enemies oppose God is not a menace to Him, but merely bad for themselves—an evil because what is good in their nature is wounded. It is not their nature, but the wound in their nature, that is opposed to God—as evil is opposed to good.

No one will deny that God is supremely good. Thus, any lack of goodness is opposed to God as evil is opposed to good. At the same time, the nature itself is not less good because the lack of goodness is evil and, therefore, the evil of lacking some goodness is opposed to this good, which is the goodness of the nature. Note that in respect to God the contrast is merely that of evil to good, but in respect to the nature which suffers a lack of something good, the lack is not only evil but also harmful. No evils, of course, can be harmful to God, but only to mutable and corruptible natures—and, even then, the harm done bears witness to the goodness of the natures which suffer, for, unless they were good, they could not suffer the wounds of a lack of goodness.

Just consider the harm done by these wounds—the loss of integrity, of beauty, of health, of virtue, or of any other natural good which can be lost or lessened by sin or sickness. If a nature has nothing of goodness to lose, then there is no harm done by lacking this nothing and, consequently, there is nothing wrong. For, there is no such thing as something wrong that does no harm.

The conclusion is that, although no defect can damage an unchangeable good, no nature can be damaged by a defect unless that nature itself is good—for the simple reason that a defect exists only where harm is done. To put the matter in another way: a defect can never be found in the highest good, nor ever apart from some kind of good.

Thus, good things without defects can sometimes be found; absolutely bad things, never—for even those natures that were vitiated at the outset by an evil will are only evil in so far as they are defective, while they are good in so far as they are natural. And when a vitiated nature is being punished, in addition to the good of being what it is, it is a good for it not to go unpunished, since this is just and whatever is just is certainly good. No one is punished for natural defects, but only for deliberate faults. And even for a vice to develop, by force of habit and overindulgence, into a strong natural defect, the vice must have begun in the will. But here, of course, I am speaking of the vices of that nature which has a mind illumined by an immaterial light in virtue of which it can distinguish what is just from what is unjust.

CHAPTER 4

Of course, in the case of beasts, trees, and other mutable and mortal creatures which lack not merely an intellect, but even sensation or life itself, it would be ridiculous to condemn in them the defects which destroy their corruptible nature. For, it was by the will of the Creator that they received that measure of being whereby their comings and goings and fleeting existences should contribute to that special, if lowly, loveliness of our earthly seasons which chimes with the harmony of the universe. For, there was never any need for the things of earth either to rival those of heaven or to remain uncreated merely because the latter are better.

It is, in fact, the very law of transitory things that, here on earth where such things are at home, some should be born while others die, the weak should give way to the strong and the victims should nourish the life of the victors. If the beauty of this order fails to delight us, it is because we ourselves, by reason of our mortality, are so enmeshed in this

St. Matthew, from the Lindisfarne Gospels, before A.D. 698. (*The British Library/SuperStock, Inc.*)

corner of the cosmos that we fail to perceive the beauty of a total pattern in which the particular parts, which seem ugly to us, blend in so harmonious and beautiful a way. That is why, in those situations where it is beyond our power to understand the providence of God, we are rightly commanded to make an act of faith rather than allow the rashness of human vanity to criticize even a minute detail in the masterpiece of our Creator.

Although these defects in the things of earth are involuntary and unpunishable, yet, like voluntary ones, when properly contemplated, they reveal the excellence in the natures themselves, all of which have God for their Author and Creator. For, in both cases, what we dislike is the lack by defect of something which we like in the nature as a whole. Sometimes, of course, natures themselves are displeasing to men because they happen to be harmful. It is a case of regarding only their utility, not the things themselves, as with the plague of frogs and flies which scourged the pride of the Egyptians. But, with such reasoning, fault could be found even with the sun, since criminals and debtors have sometimes been judicially condemned to solar exposure. It is not by our comfort or inconvenience, but by the nature considered in itself, that glory is given to its Creator. So, even the nature of unquenchable fire is, without doubt, worthy of praise, although it is to serve as a punishment for the damned. Is there anything, in fact, more beautiful than a leaping, luminous flame of fire? Or anything more useful, when it warms us, heals us, cooks our food? Yet, nothing is more painful when it burns us. Thus, the same thing applied in one way is harmful, but when properly used is extremely beneficial. It is all but impossible to enumerate all the good uses to which fire is put throughout the world.

We should pay no attention to those who praise fire for its light but condemn its heat—on the principle that a thing should be judged not by its nature, but by our comfort or inconvenience. They like to see it, but hate to be burnt. What they forget is that the same light which they like is injurious and unsuitable for weak eyes, and that the heat which they hate is, for some animals, the proper condition for a healthy life.

CHAPTER 5

All natures, then, are good simply because they exist and, therefore, have each its own measure of being, its own beauty, even, in a way, its own peace. And when each is in the place assigned by the order of nature, it best preserves the full measure of being that was given to it. Beings not made for eternal life, changing for better or for worse according as they promote the good and improvement of things to which, by the law of the Creator, they serve as means, follow the direction of Divine Providence and tend toward the particular end which forms a part of the general plan for governing the universe. This means that the dissolution which brings mutable and mortal things to their death is not so much a process of annihilation as a progress toward something they were designed to become.

The conclusion from all this is that God is never to be blamed for any defects that offend us, but should ever be praised for all the perfection we see in the natures He has made. For God is Absolute Being and, therefore, all other being that is relative was made by Him. No being that was made from nothing could be on a par with God, nor could it even be at all, were it not made by Him.

CHAPTER 6

It follows that the true cause of the good angels' beatitude lies in their union with Absolute Being. And if we seek the cause of the bad angels' misery, we are right in finding it in this, that they abandoned Him whose Being is absolute and turned to themselves whose being is relative—a sin that can have no better name than pride. "For pride is the beginning of all sin" (Eccli. 10:15). They refused to reserve their strength for Him. They might have had more of being if they had adhered to Him whose Being is supreme, but, by preferring themselves to Him, they preferred what was less in the order of being.

Such was the first defect, the first lack, the first perversion of that nature which, being created, could not be absolute, and yet, being created for beatitude, might have rejoiced in Him who is Absolute Being; but which, having turned from Him, was doomed, not to be nothing but to have so much less of being that it was bound to be wretched.

If one seeks for the efficient cause of their evil will, none is to be found. For, what can make the will bad when it is the will itself which makes an action bad? Thus, an evil will is the efficient cause of a bad action, but there is no efficient cause of an evil will. If there is such a cause, it either has or has not a will. If it has, then that will is either good or bad. If good, one would have to be foolish enough to conclude that a good will makes a bad will. In that case, a good will becomes the cause of sin—which is utterly absurd. On the other hand, if the hypothetical cause of a bad will has itself a bad will, I would have to ask what made this will bad, and, to put an end to the inquiry: What made the first bad will bad? Now, the fact is that there was no first bad will that was made bad by any other bad will—it was made bad by itself. For, if it were preceded by a cause that made it evil, that cause came first. But, if I am told that nothing made the will evil but that it always was so, then I ask whether or not it existed in some nature.

If this evil will existed in no nature, then it did not exist at all. If it existed in some nature, then it vitiated, corrupted, injured that nature and, therefore, deprived it of some good. An evil will could not exist in an evil nature but only in a good one, mutable enough to suffer harm from this deprivation. For, if no harm were done, then there was no deprivation and, consequently, no right to call the will evil. But, if harm was done, it was done by destroying or diminishing what was good. Thus, an evil will could not have existed from all eternity in a nature in which a previously existing good had to be eliminated before the evil will could harm the nature. But, if it did not exist from all eternity, who, then, caused this evil will?

The only remaining suggestion is that the cause of the evil will was something which had no will. My next question is whether this "something" was superior, inferior, or equal to the will. If superior, then it was better. So, then, how can it have had no will and not rather a good will? If equal, the case is the same: for, as long as two wills are equally good, one cannot produce an evil will in the other. The supposition remains, then, that it was an inferior thing without a will which produced the evil will of the angelic nature which first sinned.

But that thing itself, whatever it was, even though it was low to the lowest point of earthliness, was, without doubt good since it was a nature and a being having its own character and species in its own genus and order. How, then, can a good thing be the efficient cause of an evil will? How, I ask, can good be the cause of evil? For, when the will, abandoning what is above it, turns itself to something lower, it becomes evil because the very turning itself and not the thing to which it turns is evil. Therefore, an inferior being does not make the will evil but the will itself, because it is a created will, wickedly and inordinately seeks the inferior being.

Take the case of two men whose physical and mental make-up is exactly the same. They are both attracted by the exterior beauty of the same person. While gazing at this loveliness, the will of one man is moved with an illicit desire; the will of the other remains firm in its purity. Why did the will become evil in one case and not in the other? What produced the evil will in the man in whom it began to be evil? The physical beauty of the person could not have been the cause, since that was seen by both in exactly the same way and yet both wills did not become evil. Was the cause the flesh of one of those who looked? Then why not the flesh of the other, also? Or was the cause the mind of one of them? Again, why not the mind of both? For the supposition is that both are equally constituted in mind and body. Must we say, then, that one was tempted by a secret suggestion of the Devil, as if it were not rather by his own will that he consented to this suggestion or enticement or whatever it was?

If so, then what was it in him that was the cause of his consent, of the evil will to follow the evil suggestion? To settle this difficulty, let us suppose that the two men are tempted equally, that one yields and consents to the temptation, that the other remains as he was before. The obvious conclusion is that one was unwilling, the other willing, to fail in chastity. And what else could be the cause of their attitudes but their own wills, since both men have the same constitution and temperament? The beauty which attracted the eyes of both was the same; the secret suggestion by which both were tempted was the same. However carefully they examine the situation, eager to learn what is was that made one of the two evil, no cause is apparent.

For, suppose we say that the man himself made his will evil. Very well, but what was the man himself before he made his will evil? He was a good nature, created by God, the immutable God.

Take a person who says that the one who consents to the temptation and enticement made his own will evil although previously he had been entirely good. Recall the facts. The one consents, while the other does not, to a sinful desire concerning a beautiful person; the beauty was seen by both equally, and before the temptation both men were absolutely alike in mind and body. Now, the person who talks of a man making his own will evil must ask why the man made his will evil, whether because he is a nature or because he is nature made out of nothing? He will learn that the evil arises not from the fact that the man is a nature, but from the fact that the nature was made out of nothing.

For, if a nature is the cause of an evil will, then we are compelled to say that evil springs from good and that good is the cause of evil—since a bad will comes from a good nature. But how can it come about that a good, though mutable, nature, even before its will is evil, can produce something evil, namely, this evil will itself?

CHAPTER 7

No one, therefore, need seek for an efficient cause of an evil will. Since the "effect" is, in fact, a deficiency, the cause should be called "deficient." The fault of an evil will begins when one falls from Supreme Being to some being which is less than absolute. Trying to discover causes of such deficiencies—causes which, as I have said, are not efficient but deficient—is like trying to see darkness or hear silence. True, we have some knowledge of both darkness and silence: of the former only by the eyes; of the latter only by the ears. Nevertheless, we have no sensation but only the privation of sensation.

So there is no point in anyone trying to learn from me what I know I do not know—unless, perhaps, he wants to know how not to know what, as he ought to know, no one can know. For, things we know, not by sensation, but by the absence of sensation, are known—if the word says or means anything—by some kind of "unknowing," so that they are both known and not known at the same time. For example, when the vision of the eye passes from sensation to sensation, it sees darkness only when it begins not to see. So, too, no other sense but the ear can perceive silence, yet silence can only be heard by not being heard.

So, too, it is only the vision of the mind that discerns the species intellegibilis when it understands intelligible realities. But, when the realities are no longer intelligible, the mind, too, knows by "unknowing." For "who can understand sins?" (Ps. 18:13).

CHAPTER 8

This I know, that the nature of God can never and nowhere be deficient in anything, while things made out of nothing can be deficient. In regard to these latter, the more they have of being and the more good things they do or make—for then they are doing or making something positive—the more their causes are efficient; but in so far as they fail or are defective and, in that sense, "do evil"—if a "defect" can be "done"—then their causes are "deficient." I know, further, that when a will "is made" evil, what happens would not have happened if the will had not wanted it to happen. That is why the punishment which follows is just, since the defection was not necessary but voluntary.

The will does not fall "into sin"; it falls "sinfully." Defects are not mere relations to natures that are evil; they are evil in themselves because, contrary to the order of natures, there is a defection from Being that is supreme to some lesser being.

Thus, greed is not a defect in the gold that is desired but in the man who loves it perversely by falling from justice which he ought to esteem as incomparably superior to gold; nor is lust a defect in bodies which are beautiful and pleasing: it is a sin in the soul of the one who loves corporal pleasures perversely, that is, by abandoning that temperance which joins us in spiritual and unblemishable union with realities far more beautiful and pleasing; nor is boastfulness a blemish in words of praise: it is a failing in the soul of one who is so perversely in love with other peoples' applause that he despises the voice of his own conscience; nor is pride a vice in the one who delegates power, still less a flaw in the power itself: it is a passion in the soul of the one who loves his own power so perversely as to condemn the authority of one who is still more powerful.

In a word, anyone who loves perversely the good of any nature whatsoever and even, perhaps, acquires this good makes himself bad by gaining something good and sad by losing something better.

CHAPTER 9

There is, then, no natural efficient cause of an evil will or, if I may use the word, no essential cause. The reason for this is that it is the evil will itself that starts that evil in mutable spirits, which is nothing but a weakening and worsening of the good in their nature. What "makes" the will evil is, in reality, an "unmaking," a desertion from God. The very defection is deficient—in the sense of having no cause. However, in saying that there is no efficient cause even of a good will, we must beware of believing that the good will of the good angels was uncreated and co-eternal with God. But, if good angels were created, how can we say that their good will was not created? The fact is, it was created; the only question is whether it was created simultaneously with the creation of the angels or whether they first existed without a good will. If simultaneously, then, undoubtedly, it was created by Him who created the angels, so that, as soon as they were created, they adhered to Him who created them by means of that love with which they were created. Thus, the reason why the bad were separated from the society of good angels was that the good persevered in the same good will, whereas the others changed themselves into bad angels by defection from good will. The only thing that "made" their will bad was that they fell away from a will which was good. Nor would they have fallen away, had they not chosen to fall away.

In the hypothesis, however, that the good angels, existing at first without a good will, produced it in themselves without the help of God, they must have made themselves better than what they were when God created them. This is nonsense. For, without a good will, what could they be but evil? Or, if we may not say evil, since their will was not yet evil—for they could hardly fall away from what they had not yet begun to have—at least, they certainly were not good angels—not as good as they were to become when they came to possess a good will.

So much for the hypothesis. Since they could not make themselves better than God made them—for no one can make anything better than God can—then it follows that, without the co-operation of their Creator, they could never have come into possession of that good will which made them better.

Now, it is true that their good will was not only the cause of their turning and adhering to Him, who is Perfect Being, rather than to themselves, whose being was less than perfect, but also the reason why they had more of being than before and could live wisely and happily in union with God. Nevertheless, this merely shows that any will, however good, would have been destitute and destined to remain in hopeless desire, did not He who had created their good nature out of nothing, and had given it a capacity for union with Himself, first awaken in the will a greater longing for this union and then fill the will with some of His very Being in order to make it better.

This raises another issue. For, if the good angels did something themselves to bring about their good will, did they do this with or without a will? If without, then, of course, they were not the agents. If with a will, was it an evil or a good one? If evil, how could it produce a good will? If good, well, then, they had a good will already. And who made this but God Himself who created them with a good will (that is, with the unblemished love by which they could adhere to Him) and who at the same time created their nature and enriched it with grace?

Thus, we are compelled to believe that the holy angels never existed without a good will, that is, without the love of God. But what of those angels who were created good and became evil by their own bad will for which their good nature is not responsible except in so far as there was a deliberate defection from good—for it is never good, but a defection from good, that is the cause of evil? These angels either received less grace of divine love than those who persevered in grace, or, if both were created equally good, then, while the former were falling by bad will, the latter were increasingly aided to reach that plenitude of beatitude which made them certain that they would never fall—a matter which I discussed in the preceding Book.

Thus with our praise to our Creator, we should all proclaim that, not only of holy men, but also of holy angels, it may be said that "the charity of God is poured forth" in them "by the Holy Spirit who has been given" to them (Rom. 5:5). Nor is it the good only of men, but first and foremost that of angels, which is referred to in the words: "It is good for me to adhere to my God" (Ps. 72:28).

And they who share this common good are in a holy communion both with Him to whom they adhere and one with another, and they form a single community, one City of God, which is also His living sacrifice and His living temple.

This ends the discussion of the origin of this City in so far as it concerns the angels. I must now turn to the rise of that part of the City which is made up of mortal men, created by the same God, who will one day be united to the immortal angels and who, at present, are either sojourning on earth or, if dead, are resting in the hidden sanctuaries where the souls of the departed have their abode.

It was from one man, the first whom God created, that the whole human race took its start. This is the faith revealed in Holy Scripture, a faith that has gained marvelous and merited authority throughout the world and among all peoples—as, along with other truths, Scripture itself divinely predicted would be the case.

Boethius
ca. A.D. 480–ca. A.D. 524

Anicius Manlius Severinus Boethius was the son of a Roman high-government official. Possibly educated in Athens or Alexandria, Boethius had a special interest in the writings of Plato and Aristotle. His intention was to translate all their works into Latin and provide full commentary. He hoped to show the essential unity between Plato and Aristotle, but he finished only Aristotle's logical works. In 510, Boethius became consul and first minister to King Theodoric, the Ostrogothic ruler of Italy. Boethius served the next twelve years in government, wrote commentaries on Porphyry and Cicero, and began his work on Plato and Aristotle. Boethius's sons were named consuls in 522, and Boethius was made the important "master of the offices." But within a year, tragedy struck. Boethius was accused of treason, imprisoned, and executed sometime around 524. The specific charges are not known, but religious differences were probably involved. Theodoric followed the teachings of Arius (ca. A.D. 256–336) that Jesus Christ was neither coeternal with God the Father nor of the same substance. Boethius, as a Catholic, accepted the conclusions of the Council of Nicea (A.D. 325), which condemned Arian theology.

While in prison, Boethius wrote his most famous work, *The Consolation of Philosophy*. Written as a dialogue between Boethius and Lady Philosophy, it begins with Boethius protesting innocence and complaining of God's injustice and fortune's caprice. Using arguments rooted in both Stoic and Platonic thought, Philosophy replies that fortune is indeed fickle, but that the highest Good is found not in circumstances but in God. The selection given here, translated by Richard Green, is from the final book of the *Consolation* and examines how God's foreknowledge is compatible with free will. Boethius asks how one could be free to perform an action if God knew *beforehand* what one would do. Using a conception of time similar to Augustine's in Book XI of the *Confessions,* Lady Philosophy explains that God is completely outside time. This means that God "sees all things in his eternal present as you see some things in your temporal present. . . . This divine foreknowledge does not change the nature and properties of things; it simply sees things present before it as they will later turn out to be in what we regard as the future." For example, just as I know what my son is doing now even though his action is free, so God can know what I will do tomorrow though I act freely—because for God tomorrow *is* now.

It may seem odd that a devout Catholic presented his final thoughts in Neoplatonic and Stoic terms, without any specifically Christian references. Yet Boethius's *magnum opus* was a source of great comfort to Christians in the Middle Ages for, as Étienne Gilson points out, "even when he is speaking only as a philosopher, Boethius thinks as a Christian."

* * *

For background work on Boethius, see Howard Rollin Patch, *The Tradition of Boethius: A Study of His Importance in Medieval Culture* (New York: Oxford University Press, 1935) and Helen Marjorie Barrett, *Boethius: Some Aspects of His Times and Work* (Cambridge: Cambridge University Press, 1940). Henry Chadwick, *Boethius: The Consolations of Music, Logic, Theology, and Philosophy* (Oxford: Clarendon Press, 1981) and Edmund Reiss, *Boethius* (Boston: Twayne, 1982) study Boethius's writings, whereas Ralph M. McInerny, *Boethius and Aquinas* (Washington, DC: Catholic University of America Press, 1990) shows his influence on Thomas Aquinas. For collections of essays, see Michael Masi, ed., *Boethius and the Liberal Arts: A Collection of Essays* (Las Vegas, NV: Peter Lang, 1981), and Margaret Gibson, ed., *Boethius, His Life, Thought, and Influence* (Oxford: Blackwell, 1981).

In recent years, there has been renewed interest in the problems posed by Boethius's conception of God's timelessness and foreknowledge. Paul Helm, *Eternal God: A Study of God Without Time* (Oxford: Clarendon Press, 1988), for example, argues in favor of Boethius's position, whereas Richard Swinburne, *The Coherence of Theism* (Oxford: Clarendon Press, 1977) and Stephen T. Davis, *Logic and the Nature of God* (Grand Rapids, MI: Eerdmans, 1983) oppose it. For a summary of positions, see Gregory E. Ganssle, *God & Time: 4 Views* (Downers Grove, IL: InterVarsity Press, 2001). Much of the most interesting work in this area is found only in journals such as the *Journal of Philosophy* and *Faith and Philosophy*.

Boethius in Prison (from the 1385 manuscript of On the Consolation of Philosophy). Boethius was consul and first minister to King Theodoric, the Ostrogothic ruler of Italy. But in 522 Boethius was accused of treason, imprisoned, and executed sometime around 524. The specific charges are not known, but probably involved religious differences between the Catholic Boethius and the Arian Theodoric. *(Public Domain)*

THE CONSOLATION OF PHILOSOPHY (in part)

Book V

Chapter 6: Philosophy Solves the Problem of Providence and Free Will by Distinguishing Between Simple and Conditional Necessity

"Since, as we have shown, whatever is known is known according to the nature of the knower, and not according to its own nature, let us now consider as far as is lawful the nature of the Divine Being, so that we may discover what its knowledge is. The common judgment of all rational creatures holds that God is eternal. Therefore let us consider what eternity is, for this will reveal both the divine nature and the divine knowledge.

"Eternity is the whole, perfect, and simultaneous possession of endless life. The meaning of this can be made clearer by comparison with temporal things. For whatever

Boethius, *The Consolation of Philosophy,* Book V, Chapters (prose) 2, 3, 6, translated by Richard Green (Pearson/Library of the Liberal Arts, 1962).

lives in time lives in the present, proceeding from past to future, and nothing is so constituted in time that it can embrace the whole span of its life at once. It has not yet arrived at tomorrow, and it has already lost yesterday; even the life of this day is lived only in each moving, passing moment. Therefore, whatever is subject to the condition of time, even that which—as Aristotle conceived the world to be—has no beginning and will have no end in a life coextensive with the infinity of time, is such that it cannot rightly be thought eternal. For it does not comprehend and include the whole of infinite life all at once, since it does not embrace the future which is yet to come. Therefore, only that which comprehends and possesses the whole plenitude of endless life together, from which no future thing nor any past thing is absent, can justly be called eternal. Moreover, it is necessary that such a being be in full possession of itself, always present to itself, and hold the infinity of moving time present before itself.

"Therefore, they are wrong who, having heard that Plato held that this world did not have a beginning in time and would never come to an end, suppose that the created world is coeternal with its Creator. For it is one thing to live an endless life, which is what Plato ascribed to the world, and another for the whole of unending life to be embraced all at once as present, which is clearly proper to the divine mind. Nor should God be thought of as older than His creation in extent of time, but rather as prior to it by virtue of the simplicity of His nature. For the infinite motion of temporal things imitates the immediate present of His changeless life and, since it cannot reproduce or equal life, it sinks from immobility to motion and declines from the simplicity of the present into the infinite duration of future and past. And, since it cannot possess the whole fullness of its life at once, it seems to imitate to some extent that which it cannot completely express, and it does this by somehow never ceasing to be. It binds itself to a kind of present in this short and transitory period which, because it has a certain likeness to that abiding, unchanging present, gives everything it touches a semblance of existence. But, since this imitation cannot remain still, it hastens along the infinite road of time, and so it extends by movement the life whose completeness it could not achieve by standing still. Therefore, if we wish to call things by their proper names, we should follow Plato in saying that God indeed is eternal, but the world is perpetual.

"Since, then, every judgment comprehends the subjects presented to it according to its own nature, and since God lives in the eternal present, His knowledge transcends all movement of time and abides in the simplicity of its immediate present. It encompasses the infinite sweep of past and future, and regards all things in its simple comprehension as if they were now taking place. Thus, if you will think about the foreknowledge by which God distinguishes all things, you will rightly consider it to be not a foreknowledge of future events, but knowledge of a never changing present. For this reason, divine knowledge is called providence, rather than prevision, because it resides above all inferior things and looks out on all things from their summit.

"Why then do you imagine that things are necessary which are illuminated by this divine light, since even men do not impose necessity on the things they see? Does your vision impose any necessity upon things which you see present before you?"

"Not at all," I answered.

"Then," Philosophy went on, "if we may aptly compare God's present vision with man's, He sees all things in his eternal present as you see some things in your temporal present. Therefore, this divine foreknowledge does not change the nature and properties of things; it simply sees things present before it as they will later turn out to be in what we regard as the future. His judgment is not confused; with a single intuition of his mind He knows all things that are to come, whether necessarily or not. Just as, when you happen to see simultaneously a man walking on the street and the sun shining in the sky, even though you see both at once, you can distinguish between them and realize that one action is voluntary, the other necessary; so the divine mind, looking down on all things, does not disturb the nature of the things which are present before it but are future with respect to time. Therefore, when God knows that something will happen in the future, and at the same time knows that it will not happen through necessity, this is not opinion but knowledge based on truth.

"If you should reply that whatever God foresees as happening cannot help but happen, and that whatever must happen is bound by necessity—if you pin me down to this word 'necessity'—I grant that you state a solid truth, but one which only a profound theologian can grasp. I would answer that the same future event is necessary with respect to God's knowledge of it, but free and undetermined if considered in its own nature. For there are two kinds of necessity: one is simple, as the necessity by which all men are mortals; the other is conditional, as is the case when, if you know that someone is walking, he must necessarily be walking. For whatever is known, must be as it is known to be; but this condition does not involve that other, simple necessity. It is not caused by the peculiar nature of the person in question, but by an added condition. No necessity forces the man who is voluntarily walking to move forward; but as long as he is walking, he is necessarily moving forward. In the same way, if Providence sees anything as present, that thing must necessarily be, even though it may have no necessity by its nature. But God sees as present those future things which result from free will. Therefore, from the standpoint of divine knowledge these things are necessary because of the condition of their being known by God; but, considered only in themselves, they lose nothing of the absolute freedom of their own natures.

"There is no doubt, then, that all things will happen which God knows will happen; but some of them happen as a result of free will. And, although they happen, they do not, by their existence, lose their proper natures by which, before they happened, they were able not to happen. But, you may ask, what does it mean to say that these events are not necessary, since by reason of the condition of divine knowledge they happen just as if they were necessary? The meaning is the same as in the example I used a while ago of the sun rising and the man walking. At the time they are happening, they must necessarily be happening; but the sun's rising is governed by necessity even before it happens, while the man's walking is not. Similarly, all the things God sees as present will undoubtedly come to pass; but some will happen by the necessity of their natures, others by the power of those who make them happen. Therefore, we quite properly said that these things are necessary if viewed from the standpoint of divine knowledge, but if they are considered in themselves, they are free of the bonds of necessity. In somewhat the same way, whatever is known by the senses is singular in itself, but universal as far as the reason is concerned.

"But, you may say, if I can change my mind about doing something, I can frustrate Providence, since by chance I may change something which Providence foresaw. My answer is this: you can indeed alter what you propose to do, but, because the present truth of Providence sees that you can, and whether or not you will, you cannot frustrate the divine knowledge any more than you can escape the eye of someone who is present and watching you, even though you may, by your free will, vary your actions. You may still wonder, however, whether God's knowledge is changed by your decisions, so that when you wish now one thing, now another, the divine knowledge undergoes corresponding changes. This is not the case. For divine Providence anticipates every future action and converts it to its own present knowledge. It does not change, as you imagine, foreknowing this or that in succession, but in a single instant, without being changed itself, anticipates and grasps your changes. God has this present comprehension and immediate vision of all things not from the outcome of future events, but from the simplicity of his own nature. In this way, the problem you raised a moment ago is settled. You observed that it would be unworthy of God if our future acts were said to be the cause of divine knowledge. Now you see that this power of divine knowledge, comprehending all things as present before it, itself constitutes the measure of all things and is in no way dependent on things that happen later.

"Since this is true, the freedom of the human will remains inviolate, and laws are just since they provide rewards and punishments to human wills which are not controlled by necessity. God looks down from above, knowing all things, and the eternal present of his vision concurs with the future character of our actions, distributing rewards to the good and punishments to the evil. Our hopes and prayers are not directed to God in vain, for if they are just they cannot fail. Therefore, stand firm against vice and cultivate virtue. Lift up your soul to worthy hopes, and offer humble prayers to heaven. If you will face it, the necessity of virtuous action imposed upon you is very great, since all your actions are done in the sight of a Judge who sees all things."

ANSELM (AND GAUNILO)
1033–1109

Saint Anselm was born to a noble family in Aosta, in what is now Italy. Following a youth of travel and learning, Anselm joined the Benedictine monastery in the town of Bec, Normandy (in modern France). He remained in this monastery for the next thirty-three years, the last fifteen as abbot. During this time, he wrote a number of books on theological and philosophical topics. In 1093, Anselm was coerced into leaving the monastery to become Archbishop of Canterbury. Most of his sixteen years in Canterbury were spent skirmishing with the king of England for control of the church (a pattern that continued for five centuries until Henry VIII severed the English church from Rome entirely in 1534). Anselm died in 1109 and was canonized in 1494.

Anselm's thought can be summed up in the Augustinian phrase, "faith seeking understanding." Anselm was a deeply devoted Christian who began his thinking with the assumption that the doctrines of Christianity are true. And this faith drove him to seek understanding, to find rational explanations for the Christian teachings he already believed. His writings reflected this yearning to understand rationally particular problems in faith; he wrote a number of short treatises on such subjects as the Incarnation and the Trinity. He believed that he could demonstrate the truth of these revealed doctrines.

Anselm's most famous work is his attempt to prove the existence of God in the *Proslogion* (or *Discourse*) known now as the "ontological argument" (from Immanuel Kant's description). The ontological argument attempts to show that if one can conceive of "something greater than which we can conceive of nothing," one must also acknowledge that this being exists in reality as well as in the understanding. That is, if God is thought of, then God must exist. Recent scholars have pointed out that there are actually two arguments here: one, in Chapter II, that proves that God exists in reality; and another, in Chapters III to IV, that proves that God's existence is necessary.

Anselm's argument was attacked by a fellow monk named Gaunilo. Anselm's exchange with Gaunilo has been preserved and the key sections are reprinted here, along with selections from *Proslogion,* in the John F. Wippel and Allan B. Wolter translation.

Despite the fact that this argument has fascinated thinkers for more than nine hundred years, a student's first response to this passage is often one of confusion or simple denial: "He can't do that!" The student is not alone in being confused; the history of the argument is full of misrepresentations and misinterpretations. To be sure, careful thinkers such as Hume and Kant have attacked this argument. But it is notoriously difficult to say exactly what is wrong with Anselm's logic, and many purported refutations have actually been refutations of arguments quite different from Anselm's.

In recent years, there has been renewed interest in the argument, with Charles Hartshorne, Norman Malcom, and Alvin Plantinga claiming that it is successful. There has also been a tradition, beginning with the medieval thinker Bonaventure and continuing through Karl Barth in the twentieth century, that claims the *Proslogion*, Chapters II to IV, is not a philosophical argument at all. These theologians are convinced that Anselm is not "proving" anything, that he is simply showing the implications of God's self-revelation.

While the debate continues to rage, one fact is clear: Anselm raised some of the most basic questions in the history of philosophy. Questions about modes of existence, possible beings, necessity and contingency, as well as a range of issues in logic, all emerge in discussions of this provocative passage.

* * *

For a study of the complete *Proslogion*, see M.J. Charlesworth, *St. Anselm's* Proslogion (Oxford: Clarendon Press, 1965). For the rest of Anselm's major works see, Anselm of Canterbury, *The Major Works,* edited by Brian Davies and G.R. Evans, (Oxford: Oxford University Press, 1998). For a study of Anselm's life and times, see R.W. Southern's books *Saint Anselm and His Biographer* (Cambridge: Cambridge University Press, 1963) and *Saint Anselm: A Portrait in a Landscape* (Cambridge: Cambridge University Press, 1990); and William H. Shannon, *Anselm: The Joy of Faith* (New York: Crossroads, 1999). Jasper Hopkins, *A Companion to the Study of St. Anselm* (Minneapolis: University of Minnesota Press, 1972), provides a comprehensive discussion of Anselm and his work. For essays on Anselm's thought, see Brian Davies and Brian Leftow, eds., *The Cambridge Companion to Anselm* (Cambridge: Cambridge University Press, 2005).

For further reading on the ontological argument, the best source is John Hick and Arthur C. McGill, eds., *The Many-Faced Argument* (New York: Macmillan, 1967). Charles Hartshorne, *Anselm's Discovery: A Re-Examination of the Ontological Argument for God's Existence* (LaSalle, IL: Open Court, 1965); Alvin Plantinga, *The Nature of Necessity* (Oxford: Clarendon Press, 1974)—and his "simplified" version of this difficult work, Alvin Plantinga, *God, Freedom, and Evil* (Grand Rapids, MI: Eerdmans, 1977); and Richard Campbell, *From Belief to Understanding* (Canberra: Australian National University Press, 1976), all defend the argument. For theological interpretations, see Karl Barth, *Anselm: Fides Quaren Intellectum,* translated by Ian W. Robinson (London: SCM Press, 1960). (Key chapters from this work are included in Hick and McGill's *The Many-Faced Argument*.)

PROSLOGION [in part]

PREFACE

Some time ago at the pressing invitation of some brethren I did a small work* as a sample of meditation based on faith. The work was written in the person of one seeking to throw light on an area of ignorance by silently reasoning with himself. Reflecting that what I had woven together was really a chain of many arguments, I began to ask myself whether one might not be able to find a single argument, needing no proof beyond itself, which would suffice by itself to link together such conclusions as that God truly exists, that he is the highest good—needing no other but needed for the existence and well-being of all else-and whatever else we believe to be true of the divine being. Diligently and often did I pursue this quest. Sometimes the solution seemed almost at hand; at other times it simply eluded the grasp of my mind. Finally I decided in despair to cease the search for something so impossible to find. But when I tried to put the matter out of mind lest I waste time that might profitably be spent on other matters in such a fruitless quest, it continued to importune me despite my unwillingness and efforts at resistance. And so it was that one day when I was weary of struggling against this obsession the solution I had despaired of finding suddenly appeared amidst the welter of my conflicting thoughts and I eagerly seized the idea I had been so strenuously fending off.

Thinking that, if I put down in writing what I was so happy to find, others too would find pleasure reading it, I did the following little tract which takes up this and some allied matters from the viewpoint of one who tries to bring his mind to contemplate God and seeks to understand what he believes. . . .

CHAPTER 1

. . . It is not your sublimity, O Lord, I seek to penetrate, for my mind is no match for it, but I do desire to understand something of your truth which I believe and love in my heart. For I seek not to understand that I may believe, but I believe that I may understand. For this too I believe: "Unless I believe, I shall not understand!"

CHAPTER 2

O Lord, who grants understanding to faith, make me, so far as is good for me, to understand that you exist, as we believe, and that you are what we believe you to be. Now we believe you to be something greater than which we can conceive of nothing.** Could

*[*Monologion* (i.e., a soliloquy)]

**[This complicated formulation is difficult to understand, yet cannot be easily simplified without losing Anselm's meaning. Throughout this reading I have stayed with Wolter's wording. It might help the student to think of the phrase, "something greater than which we can conceive of nothing," as a single entity. For a discussion of this complicated formulation, see M.J. Charlesworth, *St. Anselm's Proslogion* (Oxford: Oxford University Press, 1965).]

From John F. Wippel and Allan B. Wolter, eds., *Medieval Philosophy: From St. Augustine to Nicholas of Cusa* (New York: The Free Press, 1969).

it be then that there is no such nature, since "the fool says in his heart, 'There is no God'" [Ps. 13:1]? But surely this same fool, when he hears me say this, "something than which we can conceive of nothing greater," understands what he hears and what he understands is in his understanding even if he does not understand it to exist. For it is one thing for something to be in the understanding and quite another to understand that the thing in question exists. When a painter thinks of the work he will make beforehand, he has it in his understanding, but he does not think that what he has yet to make exists. But once he has painted it, he not only has it in his understanding but he understands that what he has made exists. Even the fool then must be convinced that in his understanding at least there is something than which nothing greater can be conceived, for when he hears this, he understands it and whatever is understood is in the understanding. But surely if the thing be such that we cannot conceive of something greater, it does not exist solely in the understanding. For if it were there only, one could also think of it as existing in reality and this is something greater. If the thing than which none greater can be thought were in the mind alone, then this same thing would both be and not be something than which nothing greater can be conceived. But surely this cannot be. Without doubt then there exists both in the understanding and in reality a being greater than which nothing can be conceived.

CHAPTER 3

So truly does such a thing exist that it cannot be thought of as not existing. For we can think of something as existing which cannot be thought of as not existing, and such a thing is greater than what can be thought not to be. Wherefore, if the thing than which none greater can be thought could be conceived of as not existing, then this very thing than which none greater can be thought is not a thing than which none greater can be thought. But this is not possible. Hence, something greater than which nothing can be conceived so truly exists that it cannot be conceived not to be.

O Lord, our God, you are this being. So truly do you exist that you cannot even be thought of as nonexistent. And rightly so, for if some mind could think of something better than you, then the creature would rise above the Creator and would judge him, which is absurd. It is possible indeed to think of anything other than you as nonexistent. Of all beings then you alone have existence in the truest and highest sense, for nothing else so truly is or has existence in so great a measure. Why then does the fool "say in his heart, 'There is no God,'" when it is so evident to a reasoning mind that of all things you exist in a supreme degree? Why indeed save that he is stupid and a fool!

CHAPTER 4

But how did he come to say in his heart what he could not think? Or why was it he could not think what he said in his heart? For after all, to say in one's heart and to think are the same. And if it be true, or rather, since it is true that be thought it because he said it in his heart, and it is also true that he did not say it in his heart because he could not think it, it follows that there is not just one way to think of something or to say it in one's heart. In one sense, we think of something when we think of the word that signifies that something; in another sense, we think of it when we think of the thing itself. In the first sense, then, God can be thought of as not existing, but in the second sense, he cannot be thought of as not existing. For no one who really understands what God is can think that he does not exist, despite the fact that these words may be said in his heart either without any meaning whatsoever or with some peripheral sense. For God is that than which none greater can be thought, and whoever understands this correctly must understand that he so exists that he cannot even be thought of as nonexistent. Hence, he who understands that God exists in this way cannot think of him as nonexistent.

My thanks to you, good Lord, my thanks to you! For now I understand by your light what I once believed by your grace, so that even if I were to refuse to believe that you exist, I should be unable not to understand this to be true.

GAUNILO AND ANSELM: DEBATE

GAUNILO: [5.] Now the proof I am given that such a being exists not only in the understanding but also in reality is this. If such were not the case, then whatever really exists would be greater than this thing already proved to exist in the intellect. Hence the latter will not really be greater than everything else. To this I reply. Should one say that there is in the understanding something which cannot be conceived as actual, I would not deny it is in me in this way. But since this does not guarantee it any real existence, I shall not admit it has such until unquestionable proof be given. Now he who says: "This being which is greater than all exists, because otherwise it would not be greater than all" does not pay sufficient attention to what he is saying. For I would still not admit, indeed I would doubt or deny, that this [thing in the understanding] is greater than any real thing. Neither would I grant it any other existence (if it should be called "existence") than you have when the mind, on the basis of a word one only hears, tries to imagine something it has no knowledge of. But how do you prove to me this has any greater claim to real existence because it is assumed to be greater than all other things? For I deny or doubt that it is in my intellect or thought in any greater measure than are many dubious and uncertain things. For you must first assure me that it really exists somewhere and then, from the fact that it is greater than everything else, it will be clear that it also subsists of itself.

ANSELM: [II.] . . . I have said that if it is only in the understanding, it could be conceived to be also existing in reality, and this is greater. If it is only in the understanding, then one and the same thing is such that one both can and cannot conceive of anything greater. Which follows more logically, I ask: that it exists in the intellect alone, but cannot be thought to exist also in reality, or that it can be thought to exist in reality, and one who

I have followed the procedure of John Hick, *Classical and Contemporary Readings in the Philosophy of Religion* (Englewood Cliffs, NJ: Prentice Hall, 1964) and put the main points of Gaunilo's critique together with Anselm's replies. The numbers before each section refer to the paragraph numbers of Gaunilo's *A Reply to the Foregoing by a Certain Writer on Behalf of the Fool* (in Arabic numbers) and Anselm's *Reply to the Foregoing by the Author of the Book in Question* (in Roman numerals).

thinks this thinks of something greater than if it were only in the intellect? What follows more logically than this: if a being than which none greater is conceivable is only in the understanding, then it is not such that none greater can be conceived? But surely in no intellect will you find a thing with both these properties, viz. "greater than which something is conceivable" and "greater than which nothing is conceivable." Does it not follow then that if "a thing greater than which nothing is conceivable" is in any understanding, then such a thing is not only in the understanding? For if it were, it is "a thing greater than which something is conceivable," which is not consistent.

* * *

GAUNILO: [6.] . . . They say that somewhere in the ocean there is an island, which because of the difficulty, or better, the impossibility of finding what does not exist, some call the lost island. And they say this island is inestimably wealthy, having all kinds of delights and riches in greater abundance even than the fabled "Fortunate Islands." And since it has no possessor or inhabitant, it excels all other inhabited countries in its possessions. Now should someone tell me that there is such an island, I could readily understand what he says, since there is no problem there. But suppose he adds, as though it were already implied: "You can't doubt any more that this island, which is more excellent than any land, really exists somewhere, since you don't doubt that it is in your understanding and that it is more excellent not to be in the understanding only. Hence it is necessary that it really exists, for if it did not, any land which does would excel it and consequently the island which you already understand to be more excellent would not be such." If one were to try to prove to me that this island in truth exists and its existence should no longer be questioned, either I would think he was joking or I would not know whether to consider him or me the greater fool, me for conceding his argument or him for supposing he had established with any certainty such an island's existence without first showing such excellence to be real and its existence indubitable rather than just a figment of my understanding, whose existence is uncertain.

ANSELM: [III.] But you claim our argument is on a par with the following. Someone imagines an island in the ocean which surpasses all lands in its fertility. Because of the difficulty, or rather impossibility, of finding what does not exist, he calls it "Lost Island." He might then say you cannot doubt that it really exists, because anyone can readily understand it from its verbal description. I assert confidently that if anyone finds something for me, besides that "than which none greater is conceivable," which exists either in reality or concept alone to which the logic of my argument can be applied, I will find and give him his "Lost Island," never to be lost again. . . .

GAUNILO: [7.] This then is an answer the fool [in *Proslogion,* Ch. 3] could make to your arguments against him. When he is first assured that this being is so great that its nonexistence is inconceivable, and that this in turn is established for no other reason than that otherwise it would not excel all things, he could counter the same way and say: "When have I admitted there really is any such thing, i.e. something so much greater than everything else that one could prove to me it is so real, it could not even be conceived as unreal?" What we need at the outset is a very firm argument to show there is some superior being, bigger and better than all else that exists, so that we can go on from this to prove all the other attributes such a bigger and better being has to have.

a.

b.

The Romanesque Cathedral
a. Exterior view of the Abbey Church of the Madeleine, Vezelay, France, built in the twelfth century. This church typifies the Romanesque style that flourished from about 1000 to 1200. The rounded arches above the portals are reminiscent of the arches of Roman construction. The thickness of the stone walls, together with the relatively simple facade, gives the structure the impression of solidity and solemnity. (©*Ivan Vdovin/Alamy Stock Photo*)
b. The nave. The rounded interior arches distribute the weight of the roof outward as well as downward, necessitating thick stone walls. As a result, only a few small windows are possible in a Romanesque church—adding to the fortress-like feel of the architecture. (©*Nat Farbman*/The LIFE Picture Collection/Getty Images)

ANSELM: [III.] . . . It now seems obvious that a thing such that none greater can be conceived cannot be thought of as nonexistent since it exists on such firm grounds of truth. For otherwise it would not exist at all. If anyone says he thinks it does not exist, then I declare that when he thinks this he either thinks of something than which a greater is inconceivable, or else he does not think at all. If he does not think, then neither does he think that what he is not thinking of is nonexistent. But if he does think, then he thinks of something which cannot be thought of as not existing. For if it could be conceived as nonexistent, it could be conceived as having a beginning and an end. Now this is impossible. Hence if anyone thinks of it, he thinks of something that cannot even be conceived to be nonexistent. Now whoever conceives it thus doesn't think of it as nonexistent, for if he did he would conceive what can't be conceived. Nonexistence is inconceivable, then, of something greater than which nothing can be conceived.

GAUNILO: [7.] As for the statement that it is inconceivable that the highest thing of all should not exist, it might be better to say its nonexistence or even its possibility of nonexistence is unintelligible. For according to the true meaning of the word, unreal things are not intelligible, but their existence is conceivable in the way that the fool thinks that God does not exist. I most certainly know I exist, but for all that, I know my nonexistence is possible. As for that supreme being which God is, I understand without doubt both his existence and the impossibility of his nonexistence. But whether I can conceive of my nonexistence as long as I most certainly know I exist, I don't know. But if I am able to, why can I not conceive of the nonexistence of whatever else I know with the same certainty? But if I cannot, then such an inability will not be something peculiar to God [i.e., being such that He cannot be thought not to exist.]

ANSELM: [IV.] You claim moreover that when we say this supreme reality cannot be conceived of as nonexistent, it would be perhaps better to say that its nonexistence or even the possibility of its nonexistence is not understandable. But it is better to say it cannot be conceived. For had I said that the reality itself could not be understood not to exist, perhaps you, who insist that according to proper usage what is false cannot be understood, would object that nothing existing could be understood not to exist. For it is false to claim that what exists does not exist. Hence it would not be peculiar to God to be unable to be understood as nonexistent. If any one of the things that most certainly exist can be understood to be nonexistent, however, then other certain things can also be understood to be nonexistent. But this objection cannot be applied to "conceiving," if this is correctly understood. For though none of the things that exist can be understood not to exist, still they can all be conceived as nonexistent, except the greatest. For all—and only—those things can be conceived as nonexistent which have a beginning or end or consist of parts or do not exist in their entirety in any time or place, as I have said. Only that being which cannot be conceived to be nonexistent must be conceived as having no beginning or end or composition of parts but is whole and entire always and everywhere.

Consequently you must realize that you can conceive of yourself as nonexistent, though you most certainly know that you exist. You surprise me when you say you are not sure of this. For we conceive of many things as nonexistent which we know to exist and of many things as existent which we know do not exist. And we conceive them thus not by judging but by imagining them so. We can indeed conceive of something as existent even while we know it does not exist, because we are able to conceive the one at the same time that we know the other. But we cannot conceive nonexistence while knowing existence, because we cannot conceive existence and nonexistence at the same time. If anyone distinguishes between the two senses of the statement in this fashion, then, he will understand that nothing, as long as it is known to be, can be conceived not to be, and that whatever exists, with the exception of a thing such that no greater is conceivable, can be conceived of as nonexistent even when it is known to exist. This inability to be conceived of as nonexistent, then, is peculiar to God, even though there are many objects which cannot be conceived not to be while they are. As for the way in which God can still be said to be conceived as not existing, I believe this has been explained clearly enough in my little book itself.

Hildegard of Bingen
1098–1179

The monasteries and convents were as important to the intellectual life of twelfth-century Europe as were the developing universities. Those religious houses contained both scholars seeking the reconciliation of faith and reason and contemplatives who emphasized the nonrational and mystical elements of Christianity. For example, both the academic Peter Abelard and the mystic St. Bernard of Clairvaux, his adversary, were monks. The cloister was also one of the few places where women could get an education, write, and assume positions of intellectual leadership. Among the leading nuns who wrote during this period was the mystic, Hildegard of Bingen.

Hildegard was born in Bermersheim, near Mainz, Germany. As their tenth and last child, her parents gave her as a "tithe" (literally a "tenth") to the church when she was eight years old. She took the vows of the Order of St. Benedict at around fifteen and spent her next two decades as a devoted Benedictine nun at Disibodenberg. In 1137, Hildegard became the abbess of her convent and soon thereafter began her writing career. Over the next forty-two years, Hildegard not only wrote, she also founded two new convents, worked for social and church reform, and preached throughout the Rhine River basin. Sought out for advice by kings and popes as well as by common people, she wrote numerous letters of counsel and warning. Hildegard was fearlessly direct in these letters, as the opening lines of her letter to Pope Anastasius IV indicate:

> So it is, O man, that you who sit in the chief seat of the Lord, hold him in contempt when you embrace evil, since you do not reject [evil] but kiss it, by silently tolerating

> it in depraved men. . . . Beware, therefore, of wanting to associate yourself with the ways of the pagans, lest you fall.*

In addition to letters, Hildegard's works include an explication of the Rule of St. Benedict (a list of rules used to govern monastic life), commentaries on the Gospels, scientific and medical treatises, poetry, songs, and the earliest known morality play. But Hildegard is best known for her visionary trilogy, *Scivias.*

Perhaps from as early as age three, Hildegard had visions, and she continued to have them throughout her life. As she explained in her preface to the *Scivias,* these visions did not come to her while sleeping or in a trance, "but by God's will [I] beheld them wide awake and clearly, with the mind, eyes, and ears of the inner person." In the passage from this work, reprinted here as translated by Mother Columba Hart and Jane Bishop, Hildegard relates a vision of a fetus receiving a soul. She goes on to discuss the relation between the body and the soul, as well as the interrelations among the various parts of the soul: senses, intellect, will, reason. She ends this interesting discussion with a pictorial analogy that illustrates her visual style.

* * *

For an overview of mysticism, begin with the classic by Evelyn Underhill, *Mysticism: A Study in the Nature and Development of Man's Spiritual Consciousness*, 12th edition (London: Methuen, 1930). W.T. Stace, *Mysticism and Philosophy* (London: Macmillan, 1960); M.D. Knowles, *The Nature of Mysticism* (New York: Hawthorn Books, 1966); Georgia Harkness, *Mysticism: Its Meaning and Message* (Nashville, TN: Abingdon Press, 1973); and S.T. Katz, *Mysticism and Philosophical Analysis* (New York: Oxford University Press, 1978) also give good general introductions. Paul E. Szarmach, *An Introduction to the Medieval Mystics of Europe* (Albany, NY: SUNY Press, 1984) provides sketches of virtually every major medieval mystic.

For a study of Hildegard of Bingen's life and thought, see Sabina Flanagan, *Hildegard of Bingen, 1098–1179: A Visionary Life* (London: Routledge, 1989); and Renate Craine, *Hildegard: Prophet of the Cosmic Christ* (New York: Crossroads, 1997). Surveys with sections on Hildegard include Lina Eckenstein, *Women under Monasticism* (New York: Russell and Russell, 1963); Peter Dronke, *Women Writers of the Middle Ages* (Cambridge: Cambridge University Press, 1984); Margaret Alic, *Hypatia's Heritage: A History of Women in Science from Antiquity through the Nineteenth Century* (Boston: Beacon Press, 1986); and Elisabeth Gössmann, "Hildegard of Bingen" in Mary Ellen Waithe, *A History of Women Philosophers, Volume II: Medieval, Renaissance and Enlightenment Women Philosophers, 500–1600* (Dordrecht, The Netherlands: Kluwer Academic, 1989).

*Hildegard of Bingen, *Mystical Writings,* edited by Fiona Bowie and Oliver Davies, translated by Robert Carver (New York: Crossroads, 1990), p. 134. Portentously, Pope Anastasius IV died soon after this letter was sent.

SCIVIAS (in part)

BOOK I, VISION 4

16: AN INFANT IS VIVIFIED IN THE WOMB AND CONFIRMED BY A SOUL ON LEAVING IT

And you see the image of a woman who has a perfect human form in her womb. This means that after a woman has conceived by human semen, an infant with all its members whole is formed in the secret chamber of her womb. And behold! *By the secret design of the Supernal Creator that form moves with vital motion;* for, by God's secret and hidden command and will, fitly and rightly at the divinely appointed time the infant in the maternal womb receives a spirit, and shows by the movements of its body that it lives, just as the earth opens and brings forth the flowers of its use when the dew falls on it. *So that a fiery globe which has no human lineaments possesses the heart of that form;* that is, the soul, burning with a fire of profound knowledge, which discerns whatever is within the circle of its understanding, and, without the form of human members, since it is not corporeal or transitory like a human body, gives strength to the heart and rules the whole body as its foundation, as the firmament of Heaven contains the lower regions and touches the higher. *And it also touches the person's brain;* for in its powers it knows not only earthly but also heavenly things, since it wisely knows God; *and it spreads itself through all the person's members;* for it gives vitality to the marrow and veins and members of the whole body, as the tree from its root gives sap and greenness to all the branches. *But then this human form, in this way vivified, comes forth from the woman's womb, and changes its color according to the movement the globe makes in that form;* which is to say that after the person has received the vital spirit in the maternal womb and is born and begins his actions, his merits will be according to the works his soul does with the body, for he will put on brightness from the good ones and darkness from the evil ones.

17: HOW THE SOUL SHOWS ITS POWERS ACCORDING TO THE POWERS OF THE BODY

The soul now shows its powers according to the powers of the body, so that in a person's infancy it produces simplicity, in his youth strength, and in adulthood, when all the person's veins are full, it shows its strongest powers in wisdom; as the tree in its first shoots is tender and then shows that it can bear fruit, and finally, in its full utility, bears it. But then in human old age, when the marrow and veins start to incline to weakness, the soul's powers are gentler, as if from a weariness at human knowledge; as when winter approaches the sap of the tree diminishes in the branches and the leaves, and the tree in its old age begins to bend.

Body and Soul, from an early edition of *Scivias.* One of the souls in heaven (represented by the eyes) is entering the fetus in the womb. As Hildegard writes, ". . . at the divinely appointed time the infant in the maternal womb receives a spirit, and shows by the movements of its body that it lives." (*Art from Hildegard of Bingen: Scivias (CWS), Translated by Mother Columba Hart and Jane Bishop; Introduced by Barbara J. Newman. Copyright©1990 by the Abbey of Regina Laudis: Benedictine congregation Regina Laudis of the strict Observance, Inc. Paulist Press, Inc., New York/ Mahwah, NJ. www.paulistpress.com. Used with Permission).*

18: A Person Has Three Paths Within Himself

But a person has within himself three paths. What are they? The soul, the body and the senses; and all human life is led in these. How? The soul vivifies the body and conveys the breath of life to the senses; the body draws the soul to itself and opens the senses; and the senses touch the soul and draw the body. For the soul gives life to the body as fire gives light to darkness, with two principal powers like two arms, intellect and will; the soul has arms not so as to move itself, but so as to show itself in these powers as the sun shows itself by its brilliance. Therefore, O human, who are not just a bundle of marrow, pay attention to scriptural knowledge!

19: On the Intellect

The intellect is joined to the soul like an arm to the body. For as the arm, joined to the hand with its fingers, branches out from the body, so the intellect, working with the other powers of the soul, by which it understands human actions, most certainly proceeds from the soul. For before all the other powers of the soul it understands whatever is in human works, whether good or evil, so that through it, as through a teacher, everything is understood; for it sifts things as wheat is purified of any foreign matter, inquiring whether they are useful or useless, lovable or hateful, pertinent to life or death. Thus, as food without salt is tasteless, the other powers of the soul without intellect are insipid and undiscerning. But the intellect is also to the soul as the shoulder is to the body, the very core of the other powers of the soul; as the bodily shoulder is strong, so it understands the divinity and the humanity in God, which is the joint of the arm, and it has true faith in its work, which is the joint of the hand, with which it chooses among the various works wisely as if with fingers. But it does not work in the same way as the other powers of the soul. What does this mean?

20: On the Will

The will activates the work, and the mind receives it, and the reason produces it. But the intellect understands the work, knowing good and evil, just as the angels, who have intellect, love good and despise evil. And where the heart is in the body, there the intellect is in the soul, exercising its power in that part of the soul as the will does in another part. How? Because the will has great power in the soul. How? The soul stands in a corner of the house, that is, by the prop of the heart, like a man who stands in a corner of his house, so that looking through the whole house he may command all its contents, lifting his right arm to point out what is useful in the house and turning to the East. Thus the soul should do, looking along the streets of the body toward the rising sun. Thus it puts its will, like a right arm, as the support of the veins and marrow and the movement of the whole body; for the will does every work, whether it be good or bad.

21: Analogy of Fire and Bread

For the will is like a fire, baking each deed as if in a furnace. Bread is baked so that people may be nourished by it and be able to live. So too the will is the strength of the whole work, for it starts by kneading it and when it is firm adds the yeast and pounds it severely; and, thus preparing the work in contemplation as if it were bread, it bakes it in perfection by the full action of its ardor, and so makes a greater food for humans in the work they do than in the bread they eat. A person stops eating from time to time, but the work of his will goes on in him till his soul leaves his body. And in whatever differing circumstances the work is performed, whether in infancy, youth, adulthood or bent old age, it always progresses in the will and in the will comes to perfection.

22: How in the Will's Tabernacle All Powers Are Activated and Come Together

But the will has in the human breast a tabernacle, the mind, upon which the intellect and that same will and a sort of force of the soul all breathe in strength. And all these are activated and come together in the same tabernacle. How? If anger arises, gall is produced and brings the anger to its height by filling the tabernacle with smoke. If wicked delight rises up, the flame of lust touches its structure, and so the wantonness that pertains to that sin is elevated and in that tabernacle united with it. But there is another, lovely kind of joy, which is kindled in that tabernacle by the Holy Spirit, and the rejoicing soul receives it faithfully and perfects good works in the desire of Heaven. And there is a kind of sadness that engenders in the tabernacle, out of those humors that surround the gall, the sloth which produces disdain, obduracy and stubbornness in people and depresses the soul, unless the grace of God comes quickly to rescue it.

But since in that tabernacle there occur contrary conditions, it is often disturbed by hatred and other deadly emotions, which kill the soul and try to lay it waste in perdition. But when the will wills, it can move the implements in the tabernacle and in its burning ardor dispose of them, whether they are good or evil. But if these implements please the will, it bakes its food there and offers it to people to enjoy. So in that tabernacle a great throng of good and evil things arises, like an army gathered in some place of assembly; when the commander of an army arrives, if the army pleases him he accepts it, but if it displeases him he orders it to disband. The will does the same. How? If good or evil arises in the breast, the will either carries it out or ignores it.

23: On the Reason

But both in the intellect and in the will reason stands forth as the loud sound of the soul, which makes known every work of God or Man. For sound carries words on high, as the wind lifts the eagle so that it can fly. Thus the soul utters the sound of reason in the hearing and the understanding of humanity, that its powers may be understood and its every work brought to perfection. But the body is the tabernacle and support of all the powers of the soul, since the soul resides in the body and works with the body, and the body with it, whether for good or for evil.

24: On the Senses

It is the senses on which the interior powers of the soul depend, so that these powers are known through them by the fruits of each work. The senses are subject to these powers, since they guide them to the work, but the senses do not impose work on the powers, for they are their shadow and do what pleases them. The exterior human being awakens with senses in the womb of his mother before he is born, but the other powers of the soul still remain in hiding. What is this? The dawn announces the daylight; just so the human senses manifest the reason and all the powers of the soul. And as on the two commandments of God hang all the Law and the prophets, so also on the soul and its powers depend the human senses. What does this mean?

The Law is ordained for human salvation, and the prophets show forth the hidden things of God; so also human senses protect a person from harmful things and lay bare the soul's interior. For the soul emanates the senses. How? It vivifies a person's face and glorifies him with sight, hearing, taste, smell and touch, so that by this touch he becomes watchful in all things. For the senses are the sign of all the powers of the soul, as the body is the vessel of the soul. What does this mean? A person is recognized by his face, sees with his eyes, hears with his ears, opens his mouth to speak, feels with his hands, walks with his feet; and so the senses are to a person as precious stones and as a rich treasure sealed in a vase. But as the treasure within is known when the vase is seen, so also the powers of the soul are inferred by the senses.

25: That the Soul Is the Mistress and the Flesh the Handmaid

The soul is the mistress, the flesh the handmaid. How? The soul rules the body by vivifying it, and the body is ruled by this vivification, for if the soul did not vivify the body it would fall apart and decay. But when a person does an evil deed and the soul knows it, it is as bitter for the soul as poison is for the body when it knowingly takes it. But the soul rejoices in a sweet deed as the body delights in sweet food. And the soul flows through the body like sap through a tree. What does this mean? By the sap, the tree grows green and produces flowers and then fruit. And how is this fruit matured? By the air's tempering. How? The sun warms it, the rain waters it, and thus by the tempering of the air it is perfected. What does this mean? The mercy of God's grace, like the sun, will illumine the person, the breath of the Holy Spirit, like the rain, will water him, and so discernment, like the tempering of the air, will lead him to the perfection of good fruits.

26: Analogy of a Tree to the Soul

The soul in the body is like sap in a tree, and the soul's powers are like the form of the tree. How? The intellect in the soul is like the greenery of the tree's branches and leaves, the will like its flowers, the mind like its bursting firstfruits, the reason like the perfected mature fruit, and the senses like its size and shape. And so a person's body is strengthened and sustained by the soul. Hence, O human, understand what you are in your soul, you who lay aside your good intellect and try to liken yourself to the brutes.

Moses Maimonides
1135–1204

Moses ben Maimon, or Maimonides (referred to by Jewish scholars as "Rambam" for "Rabbi Moses ben Maimon"), was born at 1:00 P.M. on March 30, 1135, and died on December 13, 1204. The fact that we have such precise dates indicates the esteem with which he was held in his lifetime. As a boy in Córdoba, Spain, he was taught the Torah and the Talmud by his father, along with philosophy and science. At age 13, Maimonides and his family were forced to flee Spain after a time of peaceful coexistence between Jews and Muslims came to an end. Following a period of travel, which included a stay in Palestine, Maimonides and his family settled in Cairo, Egypt. There, Maimonides and his brother David became jewel merchants. Within a few years, Maimonides lost both his father and David, the latter killed in a shipwreck in the Indian Ocean during a business trip. Maimonides gave up the jewel business and turned to medicine. His expertise as a doctor eventually led to his appointment as a court physician for the ruler Saladin (the same Saladin who defeated Richard the Lionhearted in the Third Crusade). Maimonides' spiritual insights led to his being named the head of the Egyptian Jewish community. While serving both his religion and the state, he still found time to write extensively. His death in 1204 was mourned by Jews throughout the Mediterranean region, and his remains were taken from Cairo to Tiberias, on the Sea of Galilee, where his tomb is still visited today.

Maimonides' philosophical fame rests squarely on his major work, *The Guide for the Perplexed*. This work was written not for the majority of believers, but for those who knew both Jewish Law and Greek philosophy and were perplexed on how to harmonize the two. Though his religion was different, Maimonides faced questions similar to those of his neighboring Muslims and Christians: how to reconcile faith and reason. In the *Guide,* Maimonides asserts that there can be no conflict between faith and reason. Using Aristotle's philosophy (with some Neoplatonic spin), Maimonides believed he could answer a number of philosophical questions about the nature of God and of God's creation in a way that was consistent with sacred writings. Apparent disagreements between philosophy and theology frequently resulted from either taking figurative passages in Scripture literally or misunderstanding difficult philosophical arguments. Occasionally, philosophy is simply incapable of answering a given question and one must accept "the authority of Prophecy, which can teach things beyond the reach of human speculation." But even in such cases, philosophy can still provide general reasons for believing Scripture. For example, philosophy is inconclusive in determining whether or not the world is eternal. But whichever position we assume, says Maimonides, we can use that assumption to prove that God exists (when using arguments that Maimonides collected).

The selection from the *Guide* given here, in the M. Friedländer translation, presents Maimonides' arguments for God's existence. This passage greatly influenced Thomas Aquinas, and echoes of Maimonides' thought can be heard throughout Thomas's writings.

* * *

For selections from Maimonides' writings, see Jacob Samuel Minkin, *The World of Moses Maimonides, with Selections From His Writings* (New York: T. Yoseloff, 1957); Moses Maimonides, *The Guide for the Perplexed,* translated by Shlomo Pines (Chicago: Chicago University Press, 1963); and Moses Maimonides, *Rambam: Readings in the Philosophy of Moses Maimonides,* translated by Lenn Evan Goodman (New York: Viking Press, 1976).

Among the many general introductions to Maimonides' life and thought, more recent helpful studies include Abraham Joshua Heschel, *Maimonides: A Biography*, translated by Joachim Neugroschel (New York: Farrar, Straus & Giroux, 1982); Oliver Leaman, *Moses Maimonides* (London: Routledge, 1990); and Herbert A. Davidson, *Moses Maimonides* (Oxford: Oxford University Press, 2004). For more specialized studies, see Carol Klein, *The Credo of Maimonides: A Synthesis* (New York: Philosophical Library, 1958); Jehuda Melber, *The Universality of Maimonides* (New York: Jonathan David, 1968); Menachem Marc Kellner, *Dogma in Medieval Jewish Thought: From Maimonides to Abravanel* (Oxford: Oxford University Press, 1986); Raymond L. Weiss, *Maimonides' Ethics* (Chicago: University of Chicago Press, 1991); Howard Kreisel, *Maimonides' Political Thought* (Albany, NY: SUNY Press, 1999); David Hartman, *Maimonides' Torah and Philosophic Quest* (Philadelphia, PA: Jewish Publication Society, 2000); and James Arthur Diamond, *Maimonides and the Hermeneutics of Concealment: Deciphering Scripture and Midrash in* The Guide of the Preplexed (Albany, NY: SUNY Press, 2002). For collections of essays, see Salo Whittmay Baron, ed., *Essays on Maimonides: An Octocennial Volume*(New York: Columbia University Press, 1941); Joseph A. Buijs, ed., Maimonides: *A Collection of Critical Essays* (Notre Dame, IN: University of Notre Dame Press, 1988); Eric L. Ormsby, ed., *Moses Maimonides and His Time* (Washington, DC: Catholic University of America Press, 1989); and Kenneth Seeskin, ed., *The Cambridge Companion to Maimonides* (Cambridge: Cambridge University Press, 2005).

THE GUIDE FOR THE PERPLEXED (in part)

PART II

INTRODUCTION: Twenty-five of the propositions which are employed in the proof for the existence of God, or in the arguments demonstrating that God is neither corporeal nor a force connected with a material being, or that He is One, have been fully established, and their correctness is beyond doubt. Aristotle and the Peripatetics who followed him have proved each of these propositions. There is, however, one proposition which we do not accept—namely, the proposition which affirms the Eternity of the Universe, but we will admit it for the present, because by doing so we shall be enabled clearly to demonstrate our own theory.

PROPOSITION I: The existence of an infinite magnitude is impossible.

PROPOSITION II: The co-existence of an infinite number of finite magnitudes is impossible.

PROPOSITION III: The existence of an infinite number of causes and effects is impossible, even if these were not magnitudes; if, e.g., one Intelligence were the cause of a second, the second the cause of a third, the third the cause of a fourth, and so on, the series could not be continued ad infinitum.

PROPOSITION IV: Four categories are subject to change:—

(a) *Substance*—Changes which affect the substance of a thing are called genesis and destruction.
(b) *Quantity*—Changes in reference to quantity are increase and decrease.
(c) *Quality*—Changes in the qualities of things are transformations.
(d) *Place*—Change of place is called motion.

The term "motion" is properly applied to change of place, but is also used in a general sense of all kinds of changes.

PROPOSITION V: Motion implies change and transition from potentiality to actuality.

PROPOSITION VI: The motion of a thing is either essential or accidental; or it is due to an external force, or to the participation of the thing in the motion of another thing. This latter kind of motion is similar to the accidental one. An instance of essential motion may be found in the translation of a thing from one place to another. The accident of a thing, as, e.g., its black color, is said to move when the thing itself changes its place. The upward motion of a stone, owing to a force applied to it in that direction, is an instance of a motion due to an external force. The motion of a nail in a boat may serve to illustrate motion due to the participation of a thing in the motion of another thing; for when the boat moves, the nail is said to move likewise. The same is the case with everything composed of several parts: when the thing itself moves, every part of it is likewise said to move.

PROPOSITION VII: Things which are changeable are, at the same time, divisible. Hence everything that moves is divisible, and consequently corporeal; but that which is indivisible cannot move, and cannot therefore be corporeal.

PROPOSITION VIII: A thing that moves accidentally must come to rest, because it does not move of its own accord; hence accidental motion cannot continue for ever.

PROPOSITION IX: A corporeal thing that sets another corporeal thing in motion can only effect this by setting itself in motion at the time it causes the other thing to move.

PROPOSITION X: A thing which is said to be contained in a corporeal object must satisfy either of the two following conditions: it either exists through that object, as is the case with accidents, or it is the cause of the existence of that object; such is, e.g., its essential property. In both cases it is a force existing in a corporeal object.

PROPOSITION XI: Among the things which exist through a material object, there are some which participate in the division of that object, and are therefore accidentally divisible, as, e.g., its color, and all other qualities that spread throughout its parts. On the other hand, among the things which form the essential elements of an object, there are some which cannot be divided in any way, as, e.g., the soul and the intellect.

PROPOSITION XII: A force which occupies all parts of a corporeal object is finite, that object itself being finite.

PROPOSITION XIII: None of the several kinds of change can be continuous, except motion from place to place, provided it be circular.

PROPOSITION XIV: Locomotion is in the natural order of the several kinds of motion the first and foremost. For genesis and corruption are preceded by transformation, which, in its turn, is preceded by the approach of the transforming agent to the object which is to be transformed. Also, increase and decrease are impossible without previous genesis and corruption.

PROPOSITION XV: Time is an accident that is related and joined to motion in such a manner that the one is never found without the other. Motion is only possible in time, and the idea of time cannot be conceived otherwise than in connection with motion; things which do not move have no relation to time.

PROPOSITION XVI: Incorporeal bodies can only be numbered when they are forces situated in a body; the several forces must then be counted together with substances or objects in which they exist. Hence purely spiritual beings, which are neither corporeal nor forces situated in corporeal objects, cannot be counted, except when considered as causes and effects.

PROPOSITION XVII: When an object moves, there must be some agent that moves it, from without, as, e.g., in the case of a stone set in motion by the hand; or from within, e.g., when the body of a living being moves. Living beings include in themselves, at the same time, the moving agent and the thing moved; when, therefore, a living being dies, and the moving agent, the soul, has left the body, i.e., the thing moved, the body remains for some time in the same condition as before, and yet cannot move in the manner it has moved previously. The moving agent, when included in the thing moved, is hidden from, and imperceptible to, the senses. This circumstance gave rise to the belief that the body of an animal moves without the aid of a moving agent. When we therefore affirm, concerning a thing in motion, that it is its own moving agent, or, as is generally said, that it moves of its own accord, we mean to say that the force which really sets the body in motion exists in that body itself.

PROPOSITION XVIII: Everything that passes over from a state of potentiality to that of actuality, is caused to do so by some external agent; because if that agent existed in the thing itself, and no obstacle prevented the transition, the thing would never be in a state of potentiality, but always in that of actuality. If, on the other hand, while the thing itself contained that agent, some obstacle existed, and at a certain time that obstacle was removed, the same cause which removed the obstacle would undoubtedly be described as the cause of the transition from potentiality to actuality [and not the force situated within the body]. Note this.

PROPOSITION XIX: A thing which owes its existence to certain causes has in itself merely the possibility of existence; for only if these causes exist, the thing likewise exists. It does not exist if the causes do not exist at all, or if they have ceased to exist, or if there has been a change in the relation which implies the existence of that thing as a necessary consequence of those causes.

PROPOSITION XX: A thing which has in itself the necessity of existence cannot have for its existence any cause whatever.

PROPOSITION XXI: A thing composed of two elements has necessarily their composition as the cause of its present existence. Its existence is therefore not necessitated by its own essence; it depends on the existence of its two component parts and their combination.

PROPOSITION XXII: Material objects are always composed of two elements [at least], and are without exception subject to accidents. The two component elements of all bodies are substance and form. The accidents attributed to material objects are quantity, geometrical form, and position.

PROPOSITION XXIII: Everything that exists potentially, and whose essence includes a certain state of possibility, may at some time be without actual existence.

PROPOSITION XXIV: That which is potentially a certain thing is necessarily material, for the state of possibility is always connected with matter.

PROPOSITION XXV: Each compound substance consists of matter and form, and requires an agent for its existence, viz., a force which sets the substance in motion, and thereby enables it to receive a certain form. The force which thus prepares the substance of a certain individual being, is called the immediate motor. Here the necessity arises of investigating into the properties of motion, the moving agent and the thing moved. But this has already been explained sufficiently; and the opinion of Aristotle may be expressed in the following proposition: Matter does not move of its own accord—an important proposition that led to the investigation of the Prime Motor (the first moving agent).

Of these foregoing twenty-five propositions some may be verified by means of a little reflection and the application of a few propositions capable of proof, or of axioms or theorems of almost the same force, such as have been explained by me. Others require many arguments and propositions, all of which, however, have been established by conclusive proofs partly in the Physics and its commentaries, and partly in the Metaphysics and its commentary. I have already stated that in this work it is not my intention to copy the books of the philosophers or to explain difficult problems, but simply to mention those propositions which are closely connected with our subject, and which we want for our purpose.

To the above propositions one must be added which enunciates that the universe is eternal, and which is held by Aristotle to be true, and even more acceptable than any other theory. For the present we admit it, as a hypothesis, only for the purpose of demonstrating our theory. It is the following proposition:—

PROPOSITION XXVI: Time and motion are eternal, constant, and in actual existence.

In accordance with this proposition, Aristotle is compelled to assume that there exists actually a body with constant motion, viz., the fifth element. He therefore says that the heavens are not subject to genesis or destruction, because motion cannot be generated nor destroyed. He also holds that every motion must necessarily be preceded by another motion, either of the same or of a different kind. The belief that the locomotion of an animal is not preceded by another motion, is not true; for the animal is caused to move, after it had been in rest, by the intention to obtain those very things which bring about that locomotion. A change in its state of health, or some image, or some new idea can produce a desire to seek that which is conducive to its welfare and to avoid that which is contrary. Each of these three causes sets the living being in motion, and each of them is produced by various kinds of motion. Aristotle likewise asserts that everything which is created must, before its actual creation, have existed in potentiâ. By inferences drawn from this assertion he seeks to establish his proposition, viz., the thing that moves is finite, and its path finite; but it repeats the motion in its path an infinite number of times. This can only take place when the motion is circular, as has been stated in Proposition XIII. Hence follows also the existence of an infinite number of things which do not co-exist but follow one after the other.

Aristotle frequently attempts to establish this proposition; but I believe that he did not consider his proofs to be conclusive. It appeared to him to be the most probable and acceptable proposition. His followers, however, and the commentators of his books, contend that it contains not only a probable but a demonstrative proof, and that it has, in fact, been fully established. On the other hand, the Mutakallemim try to prove that the proposition cannot be true, as, according to their opinion, it is impossible to conceive how an infinite number of things could even come into existence successively. They assume this impossibility as an axiom. I, however, think that this proposition is admissible, but neither demonstrative, as the commentators of Aristotle assert, nor, on the other hand, impossible, as the Mutakallemim say. We have no intention to explain here the proofs given by Aristotle, or to show our doubts concerning them, or to set forth our opinions on the creation of the universe. I here simply desire to mention those propositions which we shall require for the proof of the three principles stated above. Having thus quoted and admitted these propositions, I will now proceed to explain what may be inferred from them.

THOMAS AQUINAS
1225–1274

Saint Thomas Aquinas was indisputably the greatest of the medieval philosophers. He was born in his family's castle of Roccasecca near the town of Aquino, about halfway between Rome and Naples. The seventh son of the Count of Aquino, Landolfo, and his wife Teodora, at the age of 5 Thomas was sent to the Benedictine monastery of Monte Casino, where his uncle was the abbot. His parents hoped he would get a good education at the monastery and perhaps one day become abbot of Monte Casino. However, political struggles between the pope and the emperor made the monastery unsafe, and at age 14 Thomas moved to the Imperial University in Naples.

At this university, Thomas came under the influence of the Dominicans, a mendicant, or begging, order of friars. Even though the Dominicans were admired by many for their religious commitment, Thomas's family was appalled when in 1244 he announced his plans to join the order. They considered the Dominicans religious fanatics, virtually a cult, with none of the sophistication, prestige, or power of the long-established Benedictines. At his parents' instigation, Thomas's brothers kidnapped him and held him captive in the family castle. For a year they tried reasoning, shouting, intimidating—even tempting him with a prostitute—but Thomas would not be swayed. He eventually managed to escape and became a Dominican friar.

Thomas went to Paris, where he studied with Albertus Magnus (Albert the Great), an advocate of the newly rediscovered Aristotelian writings, and he even followed his teacher to Cologne to continue his study of Aristotle. As a student, Thomas was so stolid and methodical that many of his peers thought he was dull or downright stupid. Given his deliberate manner and his portly build, his classmates dubbed him "the Dumb Ox." But Albertus saw his potential and turned this cruel epithet into a prophecy, saying, "You call him a Dumb Ox; I tell you the Dumb Ox will bellow so loud his bellowing will fill the world." In 1252, Thomas returned to Paris for graduate studies, eventually receiving the magistrate (doctorate) in theology in 1256.

On concluding his studies, it seemed natural that Thomas would join the faculty of the University of Paris. However, scholars from the mendicant orders were held in suspicion by the regular faculty of the university. Along with the great Franciscan friar Bonaventure, Thomas was not allowed to teach in Paris until the pope himself intervened.

The rest of Thomas's life was spent teaching in France and Italy and writing extensively on philosophical and theological subjects. His complete works in Latin comprise twenty-five volumes. Thomas was also called upon to intervene in several disputes. In addition to defending his Dominican order, he was forced to articulate a middle position between those who rejected Aristotelian philosophy as anti-Christian and those who accepted Aristotle (or, rather, a version of Averroës' interpretation of Aristotle) too uncritically. Throughout his writings, Thomas negotiated a middle path of critical admiration for Aristotle.

Like other Christian thinkers, Thomas was concerned with the relation between reason and faith. Using basically Aristotelian categories, Thomas taught that natural reason could establish some of the truths of religion (such as the existence, unity, and goodness of God), but other truths were accessible only through faith. Contrary to some of the Latin Averroists, Thomas taught that there was no

The Benedictine Monastery of Monte Casino. At the age of 5, St. Thomas Aquinas was sent here to study. His parents hoped that he might someday become abbot of the monastery, but he chose to join the Dominican order instead. (*AP/Wide World Photos*)

conflict between the teachings of philosophy and those of theology. To use a later analogy, Thomas believed that "the book of nature" (i.e., the created world) and the "Book of Scripture" were in perfect harmony.

In December 1273, Thomas suddenly stopped writing, apparently the result of a mystical experience. He reported to a friend that "all I have written seems like straw to me." A few months later, he was called to a church council in Lyon, France. On the way there, his health forced him to stop at Fossanova (south of Rome) where he died on March 7, 1274, at the age of 49.

Three years after his death, several of Thomas's teachings were condemned by the Bishop of Paris. However, the condemnation did not stand long, and in 1323, Saint Thomas Aquinas was canonized. In 1879, Pope Leo XII commended the study of Aquinas's philosophy in an encyclical, *Aeterni Patris*. This papal proclamation did not launch a revival of Thomism, as is often said, but it did lend an enormous prestige to the study of Thomas and his work. The encyclical praises the saint in the highest terms: "As far as man is concerned, reason can now hardly rise higher than she rose, borne up in the flight of Thomas; and Faith can hardly gain more help from reason than those which Thomas gave her." Despite the encouragement of Leo XII and others, not all Catholic philosophers are by any means Thomists; many twentieth-century Catholic thinkers have shown more interest in existentialism and phenomenology. Today Thomas is studied and admired as much by Protestants and non-Christians as he is by Catholics.

* * *

Thomas's most famous work, the *Summa Theologica,* is one of the most comprehensive and systematic works of theology ever written. It has often been likened in its complexity and grandeur to a Gothic cathedral. This monumental classic is divided into four sections that, collectively, include 512 "Questions." Each Question raises a topic or area of investigation and is, in turn, made up of several "Articles" that explore specific concerns. These Articles range from abstract philosophical issues, such as "Whether one can intend two things at the same time," to such minutiae of theology as "Whether one angel can speak to another in such a way that others will not know what he is saying." Each Article is examined in the same manner, beginning with a question, offering an answer that Thomas considers inadequate, then supporting this answer with several "objections." At this point, a quotation or argument that contradicts the position taken thus far is introduced with the words "On the contrary (*sed contra*) . . ." The dramatic tension between two opposing positions is then resolved by the author's concise and straightforward *Respondeo,* or "I answer that . . .," which introduces his own view. In presenting his answer, Thomas tries to avoid directly denying the preceding objections, seeing them instead as limited truths that his *Respondeo* supersedes. Finally, Thomas moves on to answer, one by one, each of the initial objections. (The reader should keep in mind that the *first* things Thomas says about a subject are the *opposite* of the position he will subsequently defend.)

The selections from the *Summa Theologica* given here include readings from Thomas's "Treatise on God" (including his famous "Five Ways" or five arguments for God's existence); "Treatise on Man" (including a discussion of the nature of the soul); "Treatise on Human Acts" (including his definition of happiness); "Treatise on Law" (describing the kinds of law); and "Treatise on War" (describing his arguments for a just war). The translation is that of the Fathers of the English Dominican Province.

* * *

The classic introductions to Thomas Aquinas are F.C. Copleston, *Aquinas* (Baltimore, MD: Penguin Books, 1955), and Étienne Gilson, *The Christian Philosophy of St. Thomas Aquinas* (New York: Random House, 1956). More recent helpful studies include Josef Pieper, *Guide to Thomas Aquinas* (New York: Pantheon, 1962); Ralph McInerny, *St. Thomas Aquinas* (Boston: Twayne, 1977); Anthony Kenny, *Aquinas* (New York: Hill and Wang, 1980); Brian Davies, *The Thought of Thomas Aquinas* (Oxford: Oxford University Press, 1992); Jean-Pierre Torrell, *Saint Thomas Aquinas, Volume I: The Person and His Work* (Washington, DC: Catholic University of America Press, 1996); and Thomas F. O'Meara, *Thomas Aquinas, Theologian* (Notre Dame, IN: Notre Dame University Press, 1997). James A. Weisheipl, *Friar Thomas D'Aquino: His Life, Thought, and Works* (Garden City, NY: Doubleday, 1974) offers a biography. G.K. Chesterton's impressionistic study entitled *St. Thomas Aquinas: The "Dumb Ox"* (1933; reprinted New York: Doubleday Image, 1956) is also a good place to become acquainted with Thomas. For a discussion of recent interpretation of Thomas Aquinas' work, see Fergus Karr, *Aquinas: Conflicting Versions of Thomism* (Oxford: Basil Blackwell, 2000). For collections of general essays, see Anthony Kenny, ed., *Aquinas: A Collection of Critical Essays* (Garden City, NY: Anchor Doubleday, 1969); Norman Kretzmann and Eleonore Stump, eds., *The Cambridge Companion to Aquinas* (Cambridge: Cambridge University Press, 1993); Scott MacDonald and Eleonore Stump, *Aquinas's Moral Theory* (Ithaca, NY: Cornell University Press, 1999); and Brian Davies, ed., *Aquinas's* Summa Theologiae (Lanham, MD: Rowman & Littlefield, 2005).

There are many studies on aspects of Thomas' thought. For example, a sampling of works on the "Five Ways" includes A.G.N. Flew, *God and Philosophy* (London: Hutchinson, 1966); Anthony Kenny, *The Five Ways: St. Thomas Aquinas' Proofs of God's Existence* (London: Routledge & Kegan Paul, 1969); Richard Swinburne, *The Existence of God* (Oxford: Clarendon Press, 1979); and J.L. Mackie, *The Miracle of Theism: Arguments for and against the Existence of God* (Oxford: Clarendon Press, 1982). Other recent studies of particular areas of Thomas' thought include John Milbank and Catherine Pickstock, *Truth in Aquinas* (London: Routledge, 2001); Anthony Kenny, *Aquinas on Being* (Oxford: Oxford University Press, 2002); Robert Pasnau, *Thomas Aquinas on Human Nature: A Philosophical Study of* Summa Theologiae, 1a 75–89 (Cambridge: Cambridge University Press, 2002); and Alex Hall, *Thomas Aquinas & John Duns Scotus: Natural Theology in the High Middle Ages* (London: Continuum, 2007).

SUMMA THEOLOGICA (selections)

FIRST PART

TREATISE ON GOD

QUESTION 2: THE EXISTENCE OF GOD (IN THREE ARTICLES)

Because the chief aim of sacred doctrine is to teach the knowledge of God, not only as He is in Himself, but also as He is the beginning of things and their last end, and especially of rational creatures, as is clear from what has been already said, therefore, in our endeavor to expound this science, we shall treat: (1) Of God; (2) Of the rational creature's advance towards God; (3) Of Christ, Who as man, is our way to God.

In treating of God there will be a threefold division:—

For we shall consider (1) Whatever concerns the Divine Essence; (2) Whatever concerns the distinctions of Persons; (3) Whatever concerns the procession of creatures from Him.

Concerning the Divine Essence, we must consider:—

(1) Whether God exists? (2) The manner of His existence, or, rather, what is *not* the manner of His existence; (3) Whatever concerns His operations—namely, His knowledge, will, power.

Concerning the first, there are three points of inquiry:—

(1) Whether the proposition "God exists" is self-evident? (2) Whether it is demonstrable? (3) Whether God exists?

First Article

WHETHER THE EXISTENCE OF GOD IS SELF-EVIDENT?

We Proceed Thus to the First Article:—

Objection 1. It seems that the existence of God is self-evident. Now those things are said to be self-evident to us the knowledge of which is naturally implanted in us, as we can see in regard to first principles. But as Damascene says (*De Fid. Orth.* i. 1, 3), *the knowledge of God is naturally implanted in all.* Therefore the existence of God is self-evident.

*Obj.*2. Further, those things are said to be self-evident which are known as soon as the terms are known, which the Philosopher (1 *Poster.* iii) says is true of the first principles of demonstration. Thus, when the nature of a whole and of a part is known, it is at once recognized that every whole is greater than its part. But as soon as the signification of the word "God" is understood, it is at once seen that God exists. For by

From St. Thomas Aquinas, *Summa Theologica*, Treatise on God (Part I, Q. 2); Treatise on Man (Part I, Q. 75, a. 2; Q. 76, a. 1); Treatise on Human Acts (Part I–II, Q. 2, a. 8; Q. 3, a. 4, 8; Q. 5, a.5); Treatise on Law (Part I–II, Q. 94, a. 2, 4; Q. 95, a. 1, 2; Q. 96, a. 2); Treatise on War (Part II–II, q. 40, a. 1), translated by the Fathers of the English Dominican Province (New York: Benziger Brothers, 1947). Reprinted by permission.

this word is signified that thing than which nothing greater can be conceived. But that which exists actually and mentally is greater than that which exists only mentally. Therefore, since as soon as the word "God" is understood it exists mentally, it also follows that it exists actually. Therefore the proposition "God exists" is self-evident.

*Obj.*3. Further, the existence of truth is self-evident. For whoever denies the existence of truth grants that truth does not exist: and if truth does not exist, then the proposition "Truth does not exist" is true: and if there is anything true, there must be truth. But God is truth itself: *I am the way, the truth, and the life* (John xiv. 6). Therefore "God exists" is self-evident.

On the contrary, No one can mentally admit the opposite of what is self-evident; as the Philosopher (*Metaph.* iv., lect. vi) states concerning the first principles of demonstration. But the opposite of the proposition "God is" can be mentally admitted: *The fool said in his heart, There is no God* (Ps. liii. 1). Therefore, that God exists is not self-evident.

I answer that, A thing can be self-evident in either of two ways; on the one hand, self-evident in itself, though not to us; on the other, self-evident in itself, and to us. A proposition is self-evident because the predicate is included in the essence of the subject, as "Man is an animal," for animal is contained in the essence of man. If, therefore the essence of the predicate and subject be known to all, the proposition will be self-evident to all; as is clear with regard to the first principles of demonstration, the terms of which are common things that no one is ignorant of, such as being and non-being, whole and part, and such like. If, however, there are some to whom the essence of the predicate and subject is unknown, the proposition will be self-evident in itself, but not to those who do not know the meaning of the predicate and subject of the proposition. Therefore, it happens, as Boethius says (*Hebdom., the title of which is: "Whether all that is, is good"*), "that there are some mental concepts self-evident only to the learned, as that incorporeal substances are not in space." Therefore I say that this proposition, "God exists," of itself is self-evident, for the predicate is the same as the subject; because God is His own existence as will be hereafter shown (Q. 3, A. 4). Now because we do not know the essence of God, the proposition is not self-evident to us; but needs to be demonstrated by things that are more known to us, though less known in their nature—namely, by effects.

Reply Obj. 1. To know that God exists in a general and confused way is implanted in us by nature, inasmuch as God is man's beatitude. For man naturally desires happiness, and what is naturally desired by man must be naturally known to him. This, however, is not to know absolutely that God exists; just as to know that someone is approaching is not the same as to know that Peter is approaching, even though it is Peter who is approaching; for many there are who imagine that man's perfect good which is happiness, consists in riches, and others in pleasures, and others in something else.

Reply Obj. 2. Perhaps not everyone who hears this word "God" understands it to signify something than which nothing greater can be thought, seeing that some have believed God to be a body. Yet, granted that everyone understands that by this word "God" is signified something than which nothing greater can be thought, nevertheless, it does not therefore follow that he understands that what the word signifies exists actually, but only that it exists mentally. Nor can it be argued that it actually exists, unless it be admitted that there actually exists something than which nothing greater can be thought; and this precisely is not admitted by those who hold that God does not exist.

Reply Obj. 3. The existence of truth in general is self-evident but the existence of a Primal Truth is not self-evident to us.

Second Article

WHETHER IT CAN BE DEMONSTRATED THAT GOD EXISTS?

We Proceed Thus to the Second Article:—

Objection 1. It seems that the existence of God cannot be demonstrated. For it is an article of faith that God exists. But what is of faith cannot be demonstrated, because a demonstration produces scientific knowledge; whereas faith is of the unseen (Heb. xi. 1). Therefore it cannot be demonstrated that God exists.

*Obj.*2. Further, the essence is the middle term of demonstration. But we cannot know in what God's essence consists, but solely in what it does not consist; as Damascene says (*De Fid. Orth.* i. 4). Therefore we cannot demonstrate that God exists.

*Obj.*3. Further, if the existence of God were demonstrated, this could only be from His effects. But His effects are not proportionate to Him, since He is infinite and His effects are finite; and between the finite and infinite there is no proportion. Therefore, since a cause cannot be demonstrated by an effect not proportionate to it, it seems that the existence of God cannot be demonstrated.

On the contrary, The Apostle says: *The invisible things of Him are clearly seen, being understood by the things that are made* (Rom. i. 20). But this would not be unless the existence of God could be demonstrated through the things that are made; for the first thing we must know of anything is, whether it exists.

I answer that, Demonstration can be made in two ways: One is through the cause, and is called *a priori,* and this is to argue from what is prior absolutely. The other is through the effect, and is called a demonstration *a posteriori;* this is to argue from what is prior relatively only to us. When an effect is better known to us than its cause, from the effect we proceed to the knowledge of the cause. And from every effect the existence of its proper cause can be demonstrated, so long as its effects are better known to us; because since every effect depends upon its cause, if the effect exists, the cause must pre-exist. Hence the existence of God, in so far as it is not self-evident to us, can be demonstrated from those of His effects which are known to us.

Reply Obj. 1. The existence of God and other like truths about God, which can be known by natural reason, are not articles of faith, but are preambles to the articles; for faith presupposes natural knowledge, even as grace presupposes nature, and perfection supposes something that can be perfected. Nevertheless, there is nothing to prevent a man, who cannot grasp a proof, accepting, as a matter of faith, something which in itself is capable of being scientifically known and demonstrated.

Reply Obj. 2. When the existence of a cause is demonstrated from an effect, this effect takes the place of the definition of the cause in proof of the cause's existence. This is especially the case in regard to God, because, in order to prove the existence of anything, it is necessary to accept as a middle term the meaning of the word, and not its essence, for the question of its essence follows on the question of its existence. Now the names given to God are derived from His effects; consequently, in demonstrating the existence of God from His effects, we may take for the middle term the meaning of the word "God."

Reply Obj. 3. From effects not proportionate to the cause no perfect knowledge of that cause can be obtained. Yet from every effect the existence of the cause can be clearly demonstrated, and so we can demonstrate the existence of God from His effects; though from them we cannot perfectly know God as He is in His essence.

Third Article

WHETHER GOD EXISTS?

We Proceed Thus to the Third Article:—

Objection 1. It seems that God does not exist; because if one of two contraries be infinite, the other would be altogether destroyed. But the word "God" means that He is infinite goodness. If, therefore, God existed, there would be no evil discoverable; but there is evil in the world. Therefore God does not exist.

Obj. 2. Further, it is superfluous to suppose that what can be accounted for by a few principles has been produced by many. But it seems that everything we see in the world can be accounted for by other principles, supposing God did not exist. For all natural things can be reduced to one principle, which is nature; and all voluntary things can be reduced to one principle, which is human reason, or will. Therefore there is no need to suppose God's existence.

On the contrary, It is said in the person of God: *I am Who am* (Exod. iii. 14).

I answer that, The existence of God can be proved in five ways.

The first and more manifest way is the argument from motion. It is certain, and evident to our senses, that in the world some things are in motion. Now whatever is in motion is put in motion by another, for nothing can be in motion except it is in potentiality to that towards which it is in motion; whereas a thing moves inasmuch as it is in act. For motion is nothing else than the reduction of something from potentiality to actuality. But nothing can be reduced from potentiality to actuality, except by something in a state of actuality. Thus that which is actually hot, as fire, makes wood, which is potentially hot, to be actually hot, and thereby moves and changes it. Now it is not possible that the same thing should be at once in actuality and potentiality in the same respect, but only in different respects. For what is actually hot cannot simultaneously be potentially hot; but it is simultaneously potentially cold. It is therefore impossible that in the same respect and in the same way a thing should be both mover and moved, *i.e.,* that it should move itself. Therefore, whatever is in motion must be put in motion by another. If that by which it is put in motion be itself put in motion, then this also must needs be put in motion by another, and that by another again. But this cannot go on to infinity, because then there would be no first mover, and, consequently, no other mover; seeing that subsequent movers move only inasmuch as they are put in motion by the first mover; as the staff moves only because it is put in motion by the hand. Therefore it is necessary to arrive at a first mover, put in motion by no other; and this everyone understands to be God.

The second way is from the nature of the efficient cause. In the world of sense we find there is an order of efficient causes. There is no case known (neither is it, indeed, possible) in which a thing is found to be the efficient cause of itself; for so it would be prior to itself, which is impossible. Now in efficient causes it is not possible to go on to infinity, because in all efficient causes following in order, the first is the cause of the intermediate cause, and the intermediate is the cause of the ultimate cause, whether the intermediate cause be several, or one only. Now to take away the cause is to take away the effect. Therefore if there be no first cause among efficient causes, there will be no ultimate, nor any intermediate cause. But if in efficient causes it is possible to go on to infinity, there will be no first efficient cause, neither will there be an ultimate effect, nor any intermediate efficient causes; all of which is plainly false. Therefore it is necessary to admit a first efficient cause, to which everyone gives the name of God.

The third way is taken from possibility and necessity, and runs thus. We find in nature things that are possible to be and not to be, since they are found to be generated, and to corrupt, and consequently, they are possible to be and not to be. But it is impossible for these always to exist, for that which is possible not to be at some time is not. Therefore, if everything is possible not to be, then at one time there could have been nothing in existence. Now if this were true, even now there would be nothing in existence, because that which does not exist only begins to exist by something already existing. Therefore, if at one time nothing was in existence, it would have been impossible for anything to have begun to exist; and thus even now nothing would be in existence—which is absurd. Therefore, not all beings are merely possible, but there must exist something the existence of which is necessary. But every necessary thing either has its necessity caused by another, or not. Now it is impossible to go on to infinity in necessary things which have their necessity caused by another, as has been already proved in regard to efficient causes. Therefore we cannot but postulate the existence of some being having of itself its own necessity, and not receiving it from another, but rather causing in others their necessity. This all men speak of as God.

The fourth way is taken from the gradation to be found in things. Among beings there are some more and some less good, true, noble, and the like. But "more" and "less" are predicated of different things, according as they resemble in their different ways something which is the maximum, as a thing is said to be hotter according as it more nearly resembles that which is hottest; so that there is something which is truest, something best, something noblest, and, consequently, something which is uttermost being; for those things that are greatest in truth are greatest in being, as it is written in *Metaph.* ii. Now the maximum in any genus is the cause of all in that genus; as fire, which is the maximum of heat, is the cause of all hot things. Therefore there must also be something which is to all beings the cause of their being, goodness, and every other perfection; and this we call God.

The fifth way is taken from the governance of the world. We see that things which lack intelligence, such as natural bodies, act for an end, and this is evident from their acting always, or nearly always, in the same way, so as to obtain the best result. Hence it is plain that not fortuitously, but designedly, do they achieve their end. Now whatever lacks intelligence cannot move towards an end, unless it be directed by some being endowed with knowledge and intelligence; as the arrow is shot to its mark by the archer. Therefore some intelligent being exists by whom all natural things are directed to their end; and this being we call God.

Reply Obj. 1. As Augustine says (*Enchir.* xi): *Since God is the highest good, He would not allow any evil to exist in His works, unless His omnipotence and goodness were such as to bring good even out of evil.* This is part of the infinite goodness of God, that He should allow evil to exist, and out of it produce good.

Reply Obj. 2. Since nature works for a determinate end under the direction of a higher agent, whatever is done by nature must needs be traced back to God, as to its first cause. So also whatever is done voluntarily must also be traced back to some higher cause other than human reason or will, since these can change and fail; for all things that are changeable and capable of defect must be traced back to an immovable and self-necessary first principle, as was shown in the body of the *Article.*

* * *

TREATISE ON MAN

QUESTION 75: OF MAN WHO IS COMPOSED OF A SPIRITUAL AND A CORPOREAL SUBSTANCE: AND IN THE FIRST PLACE CONCERNING WHAT BELONGS TO THE ESSENCE OF THE SOUL

* * *

Second Article

WHETHER THE HUMAN SOUL IS SOMETHING SUBSISTENT?

We Proceed Thus to the Second Article:—

Objection 1. It would seem that the human soul is not something subsistent. For that which subsists is said to be *this particular thing.* Now *this particular thing* is said not of the soul, but of that which is composed of soul and body. Therefore the soul is not something subsistent.

Obj. 2. Further, everything subsistent operates. But the soul does not operate; for, as the Philosopher says (*De Anima* i. 4), *to say that the soul feels or understands is like saying that the soul weaves or builds.* Therefore the soul is not subsistent.

Obj. 3. Further, if the soul were subsistent, it would have some operation apart from the body. But it has no operation apart from the body, not even that of understanding: for the act of understanding does not take place without a phantasm, which cannot exist apart from the body. Therefore the human soul is not something subsistent.

On the contrary, Augustine says (*de Trin.* x. 7): *Whoever understands that the nature of the soul is that of a substance and not that of a body, will see that those who maintain the corporeal nature of the soul, are led astray through associating with the soul those things without which they are unable to think of any nature—i.e., imaginary pictures of the corporal things.* Therefore the nature of the human intellect is not only incorporeal, but it is also a substance, that is, something subsistent.

I answer that, It must necessarily be allowed that the principle of intellectual operation which we call the soul, is a principle both incorporeal and subsistent. For it is clear that by means of the intellect man can have knowledge of all corporeal things. Now whatever knows certain things cannot have any of them in its own nature; because that which is in it naturally would impede the knowledge of anything else. Thus we observe that a sick man's tongue being vitiated by a feverish and bitter humor, is insensible to anything sweet and everything seems bitter to it. Therefore if the intellectual principle contained the nature of a body it would be unable to know all bodies. Now every body has its own determinate nature. Therefore it is impossible for the intellectual principle to be a body. It is likewise impossible for it to understand by means of a bodily organ; since the determinate nature of that organ would impede knowledge of all bodies; as when a certain determinate color is not only in the pupil of the eye, but also in a glass vase, the liquid in the vase seems to be of that same color.

Therefore the intellectual principle which we call the mind or the intellect has the operation *per se* apart from the body. Now only that which subsists can have an operation *per se*. For nothing can operate but what is actual: wherefore a thing operates according as it is; for which reason we do not say that heat imparts heat, but that what is hot gives heat. We must conclude, therefore, that the human soul, which is called the intellect or the mind, is something incorporeal and subsistent.

Reply Obj. 1. *This particular thing* can be taken in two senses. Firstly, for anything subsistent; secondly, for that which subsists, and is complete in a specific nature. The former sense excludes the inherence of an accident or of a material form; the latter excludes also the imperfection of the part, so that a hand can be called *this particular thing* in the first sense, but not in the second. Therefore as the human soul is a part of human nature, it can indeed be called *this particular thing,* in the first sense, as being something subsistent; but not in the second, for in this sense, what is composed of body and soul is said to be *this particular thing.*

Reply Obj. 2. Aristotle wrote those words as expressing not his own opinion, but the opinion of those who said that to understand is to be moved, as is clear from the context. Or we may reply that to operate *per se* belongs to what exists *per se*. But for a thing to exist *per se,* it suffices sometimes that it be not inherent, as an accident or a material form; even though it be part of something. Nevertheless, that is rightly said to subsist *per se,* which is neither inherent in the above sense nor part of anything else. In this sense, the eye or the hand cannot be said to subsist *per se;* nor can it for that reason be said to operate *per se*. Hence the operation of the parts is through each part attributed to the whole. For we say that the man sees with the eye, and feels with the hand and, and not in the same sense as when we say that what is hot gives heat by its heat; for heat, strictly speaking, does not give heat. We may therefore say that the soul understands, as the eye sees; but it is more correct to say that man understands through the soul.

Reply Obj. 3. The body is necessary for intellect, not as its origin of action, but on the part of the object; for the phantasm is to the intellect what color is to the sight. Neither does such a dependence on the body prove the intellect to be non-subsistent; otherwise it would follow that an animal is not subsistent, since it requires external objects of the senses in order to perform its act of perception.

* * *

QUESTION 76: OF THE UNION OF BODY AND SOUL

* * *

First Article

WHETHER THE INTELLECTUAL PRINCIPLE IS UNITED TO THE BODY AS ITS FORM?

We Proceed Thus to the First Article:—

Objection 1. It seems that the intellectual principle is not united to the body as its form. For the Philosopher says (*De Anima* iii. 4) that "the intellect is separate," and that it is not the act of any body. Therefore it is not united to the body as its form.

Obj. 2. Further, every form is determined according to the nature of the matter of which it is the form; otherwise no proportion would be required between matter and form. Therefore if the intellect were united to the body as its form since every body has a determinate nature it would follow that the intellect has a determinate nature; and thus, it would not be capable of knowing all things, as is clear from what has been said (Q. 75, A. 2), which is contrary to the notion of intellect. Therefore the intellect is not united to the body as its form.

Obj. 3. Further, whatever receptive power is an act of a body receives a form materially and individually; for what is received must be received according to the mode of the receiver. But the form of the thing understood is not received into the intellect materially and individually, but rather immaterially and universally; otherwise the intellect would not be capable of the knowledge of immaterial and universal objects, but only of individuals, like the senses. Therefore the intellect is not united to the body as its form.

Obj. 4. Further, power and action have the same subject; for the same subject is what can, and does, act. But the intellectual action is not the action of a body, as appears from above (Q. 75, A. 2). Therefore neither is the intellectual power a power of the body. But virtue or power cannot be more abstract or more simple than the essence from which the virtue or power is derived. Therefore neither is the substance of the intellect the form of a body.

Obj. 5. Further, whatever has *per se* being is not united to the body as its form, because a form is that by which a thing is, so that the very being of a form does not belong to the form by itself. But the intellectual principle has *per se* being and is subsistent, as was said above (Q. 75, A. 2). Therefore it is not united to the body as its form.

Obj. 6. Further, whatever exists in a thing by reason of its nature exists in it always. But to be united to matter belongs to the form by reason of its nature. For form is the act of matter not by any accidental quality, but by its own essence; otherwise matter and form would not make a thing substantially one, but only accidentally one. Therefore a form cannot be without its own proper matter. But the intellectual principle, since it is incorruptible, as was shown above (Q. 75, A. 6), remains separate from the body after the dissolution of the body. Therefore the intellectual principle is not united to the body as its form.

On the contrary, According to the Philosopher (*Metaph.* vii. 2), difference is derived from the form. But the difference which constitutes man is *rational* which is applied to man on account of his intellectual principle. Therefore the intellectual principle is the form of man.

I answer that, We must assert that the intellect which is the principle of intellectual operation is the form of the human body. For that whereby primarily anything acts is a form of the thing to which the act is to be attributed; for instance, that whereby a body is primarily healed is health and that whereby the soul knows primarily is knowledge; hence health is a form of the body, and knowledge is a form of the soul. The reason is because nothing acts except so far as it is in act; hence a thing acts by that whereby it is in act. Now it is clear that the first thing by which the body lives is the soul. And as life appears through various operations in different degrees of living things, that whereby we primarily perform each of all these vital actions is the soul. For the soul is the primary principle of our nourishment, sensation, and local movement; and likewise of our understanding. Therefore this principle by which we primarily understand, whether it be called the intellect or the intellectual soul, is the form of the body. This is the demonstration used by Aristotle (*De Anima* ii. 2).

But if anyone say that the intellectual soul is not the form of the body he must first explain how it is that this action of understanding is the action of this particular man; for each one is conscious that it is himself who understands. Now an action may be attributed to anyone in three ways, as is clear from the Philosopher. "For a thing is said to move or act either by virtue of its whole self, for instance, as a physician heals; or by virtue of a part, as a man sees by his eye; or through an accidental quality, as when we say that something that is white build, because it is accidental to the builder to be white" (*Phys.* v. 1) So when we say that Socrates or Plato understands, it is clear that this is not attributed to him accidentally, since it is ascribed to him as man, which is predicated of him essentially. We must therefore say either that Socrates understands by virtue of his whole self, as Plato maintained, holding that man is an intellectual soul, or that the intellect is a part of Socrates. The first cannot stand, as was shown above (Q. 75, A. 4), for this reason, that it is one and the same man who is conscious both that he understands, and that he senses. But one cannot sense without a body; therefore the body must be some part of man. It remains therefore that the intellect by which Socrates understands is a part of Socrates, so that in some way it is united to the body of Socrates.

The Commentator [Averroës] held that this union is through the intelligible species, as having a double subject: in the possible intellect, and in the phantasms which are in the corporeal organs (*De Anima* iii, Comm. 5). Thus through the intelligible species the possible intellect is linked to the body of this or that particular man. But this link or union does not sufficiently explain the fact that the act of the intellect is the act of Socrates. This can be clearly seen from comparison with the sensitive power, from which Aristotle proceeds to consider things relating to the intellect. For the relation of phantasms to the intellect is like the relation of colours to the sense of sight, as he says in the book on the *Soul* (iii. 7). Therefore, as the species of colours are in the sight, so are the species of phantasms in the possible-intellect. Now it is clear that because the colours, the likenesses of which are in the sight, are on a wall, the action of seeing is not attributed to the wall, for we do not say that the wall sees, but rather that it is seen. Therefore, from the fact that the species of phantasms are in the possible intellect it does not follow that Socrates, in whom are the phantasms, understands, but that he or his phantasms are understood.

Some, however, tried to maintain that the intellect is united to the body as its mover, and hence that the intellect and body form one thing so that the act of the intellect could be attributed to the whole. This is groundless however, for many reasons. First, because the intellect does not move the body except through desire, the movement of which presupposes the operation of the intellect. The reason therefore why Socrates understands is not because he is moved by his intellect, but rather, contrariwise, he is moved by his intellect because he understands. Secondly, because, since Socrates is an individual in a nature of one essence composed of matter and form, if the intellect be not the form, it follows that it must be outside the essence, and then the intellect is to the whole Socrates as a mover to the thing moved. The act of intellect however remains in the agent, and does not pass into something else, as does the action of heating. Therefore the act of understanding cannot be attributed to Socrates for the reason that he is moved by his intellect. Thirdly, because the action of a mover is never attributed to the thing moved, except as to an instrument; as the action of a carpenter to a saw. Therefore if understanding is attributed to Socrates, as the action of what moves him, it follows that it is attributed to him as to an instrument. This is contrary to the teaching of the Philosopher, who holds that understanding is not possible through a corporeal instrument (*De Anima* iii. 4). Fourthly, because, although the action of a part

The Gothic Cathedral

a. The Cathedral of Notre Dame de Chartres, Chartres, France, begun in the 1140s. The word "Gothic" was originally a perjorative term coined by Renaissance thinkers who considered this style to be a barbaric break from classical tradition. The two towers shown here, for example, are not symmetrical. Even though the overall design of the cathedral may not be symmetrical, each of its elements was designed to reflect the harmony and beauty of God's creation. (© *LatitudeStock*/Alamy Stock Photo)

b. Interior, Chartres Cathedral. By using pointed arches, it was possible to make soaring open spaces in the nave (main sanctuary) of the Gothic cathedral. The weight was shifted downward instead of outward. (©PATRICK KOVARIC/Getty)

c. Flying Buttresses at Reims Cathedral, ca. 1230–1235, by Villard De Honnecourt. To leave the interior unencumbered, the remaining outward stresses were often buttressed from outside the building. In some cathedrals exterior buttresses could not be built directly along the outside walls because of side aisles. Instead they were built outside the side aisles and connected to the pillars of the nave by stone ribs. These supporting ribs appear to "fly" over the side aisles. (©*Scala/Art Resource, NY)*

d. The Rose Window, Notre Dame Cathedral, Paris, thirteenth century. By using pointed arches and flying buttresses, the walls of a cathedral did not have to bear the weight of the roof. Instead they could be used as screens for stained glass ornamentation such as this. (©Bridgeman-Giraudon/Art Resource, NY) be attributed to the whole, as the action of the eye is attributed to a man, yet it is never attributed to another part, except perhaps accidentally; for we do not say that the hand sees because the eye sees. Therefore if the intellect and Socrates are united in the above manner, the action of the intellect cannot be attributed to Socrates. If, however, Socrates be a whole composed of a union of the intellect with whatever else belongs to Socrates, while nevertheless the intellect is united to those other things only as a mover, it follows that Socrates is not one absolutely, and consequently neither a being absolutely, for a thing is a being according as it is one.

There remains, therefore, no other explanation than that given by Aristotle (*De Anima* ii. 2)—namely, that this particular man understands because the intellectual principle is his form. Thus from the very operation of the intellect it is made clear that the intellectual principle is united to the body as its form.

The same can be clearly shown from the nature of the human species. For the nature of each thing is shown by its operation. Now the proper operation of man as man is to understand, because he thereby surpasses all other animals. From this, too, Aristotle concludes (*Ethic.* x. 7) that the ultimate happiness of man must consist in this operation as properly belonging to him. Man must therefore derive his species from that which is the principle of this operation. But the species of anything is derived from its form. It follows therefore that the intellectual principle is the proper form of man.

But we must observe that the nobler a form is, the more it rises above corporeal matter, the less it is merged in matter, and the more it excels matter by its power and its operation; hence we find that the form of a mixed body has another operation not caused by its elemental qualities. And the higher we advance in the nobility of forms, the more we find that the power of the form excels the elementary matter; as the vegetative soul excels the form of the metal, and the sensitive soul excels the vegetative soul. Now the human soul is the highest and noblest of forms. Therefore it excels corporeal matter in its power by the fact that it has an operation and a power in which corporeal matter has no share whatever. This power is called the intellect.

It is well to remark that if anyone holds that the soul is composed of matter and form, it would follow that in no way could the soul be the form of the body. For since the form is an act, and matter is only a being in potency, that which is composed of matter and form cannot be the form of another by virtue of itself as a whole. But if it is a form by virtue of some part of itself, then that part which is the form we call the soul, and that of which it is the form we call the first thing animated, as was said above (Q. 75, A. 5).

Reply Obj. 1. As the Philosopher Says (*Phys.* ii. 2), the ultimate natural form to which the consideration of the natural philosopher is directed, namely, the human soul, is indeed separate; yet it exists in matter. He proves this from the fact that "man and the sun generate man from matter." It is separate indeed according to its intellectual power, because the intellectual power does not belong to a corporeal organ, as the power of seeing is the act of the eye; for understanding is an act which cannot be performed by a corporeal organ, like the act of seeing. But it exists in matter so far as the soul itself, to which this power belongs, is the form of the body, and the term of human generation. And so the Philosopher says (*De Anima* ii. 2) that "the intellect is separate" because it is not the power of a corporeal organ.

From this it is clear how to answer the *Second and Third objections.* For, in order that man may be able to understand all things by means of his intellect, and that his intellect may understand all things immaterial and universal, it is sufficient that the intellectual power be not the act of the body.

Reply Obj. 4. The human soul, by reason of its perfection, is not a form merged in matter, or entirely embraced by matter. Therefore there is nothing to prevent one of its powers not being the act of the body, although the soul is essentially the form of the body.

Reply Obj. 5. The soul communicates that being in which it subsists to the corporeal matter, out of which, combined with the intellectual soul, there results unity of being so that the being of the whole composite is also the being of the soul. This is not the case with other nonsubsistent forms. For this reason the human soul retains its own being after the dissolution of the body, though this is not so with other forms.

Reply Obj. 6. To be united to the body pertains to the soul by reason of itself, as it pertains to a light body by reason of itself to be raised up. And as a light body remains light when removed from its proper place, retaining meanwhile an aptitude and an inclination for its proper place, so the human soul retains its proper being when separated from the body, having an aptitude and a natural inclination to be united to the body.

* * *

First Part of the Second Part(I–II)

Treatise on Human Acts

* * *

QUESTION 2: OF THOSE THINGS IN WHICH MAN 'S HAPPINESS CONSISTS

* * *

Eighth Article

Whether Any Created Good Constitutes Man's Happiness?

We Proceed Thus to the Eighth Article:—

Objection 1. It would seem that some created good constitutes man's happiness. For Dionysius says (*Div. Nom.* vii) that Divine wisdom *unites the ends of first things to the beginnings of second things,* from which we may gather that the summit of a lower nature touches the base of the higher nature. But man's highest good is happiness. Since then the angel is above man in the order of nature, as stated in the First Part (Q. 111, A. 1), it seems that man's happiness consists in man somehow reaching the angel.

Obj. 2. Further, the last end of each thing is that which, in relation to it, is perfect: hence the part is for the whole, as for its end. But the universe of creatures which is called the macrocosm, is compared to man who is called the microcosm (*Phys.* viii. 2), as perfect to imperfect. Therefore man's happiness consists in the whole universe of creatures.

Obj. 3. Further, man is made happy by that which lulls his natural desire. But man's natural desire does not reach out to a good surpassing his capacity. Since then man's capacity does not include that good which surpasses the limits of all creation, it seems that man can be made happy by some created good. Consequently some created good constitutes man's happiness.

On the contrary, Augustine says (*De Civ. Dei* xix. 26): *As the soul is the life of the body, so God is man's life of happiness: of Whom it is written: "Happy is that people whose God is the Lord"* (Ps. cxliii. 15).

I answer that, It is impossible for any created good to constitute man's happiness. For happiness is the perfect good, which lulls the appetite altogether; else it would not be the last end, if something yet remained to be desired. Now the object of the will, *i.e.,* of man's appetite, is the universal good; just as the object of the intellect is the universal true. Hence it is evident that naught can lull man's will, save the universal good. This is to be found, not in any creature, but in God alone; because every creature has goodness by participation. Wherefore God alone can satisfy the will of man, according to the words of Ps. cii. 5: *Who satisfieth thy desire with good things.* Therefore God alone constitutes man's happiness.

Reply Obj. 1. The summit of man does indeed touch the base of the angelic nature, by a kind of likeness; but man does not rest there as in his last end, but reaches out to the universal fount itself of good, which is the common object of happiness of all the blessed, as being the infinite and perfect good.

Reply Obj. 2. If a whole be not the last end, but ordained to a further end, then the last end of a part thereof is not the whole itself, but something else. Now the universe of creatures, to which man is compared as part to whole, is not the last end, but is ordained to God, as to its last end. Therefore the last end of man is not the good of the universe, but God himself.

Reply Obj. 3. Created good is not less than that good of which man is capable, as of something intrinsic and inherent to him: but it is less than the good of which he is capable, as of an object, and which is infinite. And the participated good which is in an angel, and in the whole universe, is a finite and restricted good.

* * *

QUESTION 3: WHAT IS HAPPINESS?

* * *

Fourth Article

WHETHER, IF HAPPINESS IS IN THE INTELLECTIVE PART, IT IS AN OPERATION OF THE INTELLECT OR OF THE WILL?

We Proceed Thus to the Fourth Article:—

Objection 1. It would seem that happiness consists in an act of the will. For Augustine says (*De Civ. Dei* xix. 10, 11), that man's happiness consists in peace; wherefore it is written (Ps. cxlvii. 3): *Who hath placed peace in thy end.* But peace pertains to the will. Therefore man's happiness is in the will.

Obj. 2. Further, happiness is the supreme good. But good is the object of the will. Therefore happiness consists in an operation of the will.

Obj. 3. Further, the last end corresponds to the first mover: thus the last end of the whole army is victory, which is the end of the general, who moves all the men. But the first mover in regard to operations is the will: because it moves the other powers, as we shall state further on (Q. 9, AA. 1, 3). Therefore happiness regards the will.

Obj. 4. Further, if happiness be an operation, it must needs be man's most excellent operation. But the love of God, which is an act of the will, is a more excellent operation than knowledge, which is an operation of the intellect, as the Apostle declares (1 Cor. xiii). Therefore it seems that happiness consists in an act of the will.

Obj. 5. Further, Augustine says (*De Trin.* xiii. 5) that *happy is he who has whatever he desires, and desires nothing amiss.* And a little further on (6) he adds: *He is almost happy who desires well, whatever he desires: for good things make a man happy, and such a man already possesses some good—i.e., a good will.* Therefore happiness consists in an act of the will.

On the contrary, Our Lord said (Jo. xvii. 3): *This is eternal life: that they may know Thee, the only true God.* Now eternal life is the last end, as stated above (A. 2 *ad* 1). Therefore man's happiness consists in the knowledge of God, which is an act of the intellect.

I answer that, As stated above (Q. 2, A. 6) two things are needed for happiness: one, which is the essence of happiness: the other, that is, as it were, its proper accident, *i.e.,* the delight connected with it. I say, then, that as to the very essence of happiness, it is impossible for it to consist in an act of the will. For it is evident from what has been said (AA. 1, 2; Q. 2, A. 7) that happiness is the attainment of the last end. But the attainment of the end does not consist in the very act of the will. For the will is directed to the end, both absent, when it desires it; and present, when it is delighted by resting therein. Now it is evident that the desire itself of the end is not the attainment of the end, but is a movement towards the end: while delight comes to the will from the end being present; and not conversely, is a thing made present, by the fact that the will delights in it. Therefore, that the end be present to him who desires it, must be due to something else than an act of the will.

This is evidently the case in regard to sensible ends. For if the acquisition of money were through an act of the will, the covetous man would have it from the very moment that he wished for it. But at that moment it is far from him; and he attains it, by grasping it in his hand, or in some like manner; and then he delights in the money got. And so it is with an intelligible end. For at first we desire to attain an intelligible end; we attain it, through its being made present to us by an act of the intellect; and then the delighted will rests in the end when attained.

So, therefore, the essence of happiness consists in an act of the intellect: but the delight that results from happiness pertains to the will. In this sense Augustine says (*Conf.* x. 23) that happiness is *joy in truth,* because, to wit, joy itself is the consummation of happiness.

Reply Obj. 1. Peace pertains to man's last end, not as though it were the very essence of happiness; but because it is antecedent and consequent thereto: antecedent, in so far as all those things are removed which disturb and hinder man in attaining the last end: consequent, inasmuch as, when man has attained his last end, he remains at peace, his desire being at rest.

Reply Obj. 2. The will's first object is not its act: just as neither is the first object of the sight, vision, but a visible thing. Wherefore, from the very fact that happiness belongs to the will, as the will's first object, it follows that it does not belong to it as its act.

Reply Obj. 3. The intellect apprehends the end before the will does: yet motion towards the end begins in the will. And therefore to the will belongs that which last of all follows the attainment of the end, viz., delight or enjoyment.

Reply Obj. 4. Love ranks above knowledge in moving, but knowledge precedes love in attaining: *for naught is loved save what is known,* as Augustine says (*De Trin.* x. 1). Consequently we first attain an intelligible end by an act of the intellect; just as we first attain a sensible end by an act of sense.

Reply Obj. 5. He who has whatever he desires, is happy, because he has what he desires: and this indeed is by something other than the act of his will. But to desire nothing amiss is needed for happiness, as a necessary disposition thereto. And a good will is reckoned among the good things which make a man happy, forasmuch as it is an inclination of the will: just as a movement is reduced to the genus of its terminus, for instance, *alteration* to the genus *quality.*

Eighth Article

WHETHER MAN'S HAPPINESS CONSISTS IN THE VISION OF THE DIVINE ESSENCE?

We Proceed Thus to the Eighth Article:—

Objection 1. It would seem that man's happiness does not consist in the vision of the Divine Essence. For Dionysius says (*Myst. Theol.* i) that by that which is highest in his intellect, man is united to God as to something altogether unknown. But that which is seen in its essence is not altogether unknown. Therefore the final perfection of the intellect, namely, happiness, does not consist in God being seen in His Essence.

Obj. 2. Further, the higher perfection belongs to the higher nature. But to see His own Essence is the perfection proper to the Divine intellect. Therefore the final perfection of the human intellect does not reach to this, but consists in something less.

On the contrary, It is written (1 Jo. iii. 2): *When He shall appear, we shall be like to Him; and we shall see Him as He is.*

I answer that, Final and perfect happiness can consist in nothing else than the vision of the Divine Essence. To make this clear, two points must be observed. First, that man is not perfectly happy, so long as something remains for him to desire and seek: secondly, that the perfection of any power is determined by the nature of its object. Now the object of the intellect is *what a thing is, i.e.,* the essence of a thing, according to *De Anima* iii. 6. Wherefore the intellect attains perfection, in so far as it knows the essence of a thing. If therefore an intellect know the essence of some effect, whereby it is not possible to know the essence of the cause, *i.e.* to know of the cause *what it is;* that intellect cannot be said to reach that cause simply, although it may be able to gather from the effect the knowledge that the cause is. Consequently, when man knows an effect, and knows that it has a cause, there naturally remains in man the desire to know about that cause, *what it is.* And this desire is one of wonder, and causes inquiry, as is stated in the beginning of the *Metaphysics* (i. 2). For instance, if a man, knowing the eclipse of the sun, consider that it must be due to some cause, and know not what that cause is, he wonders about it, and from wondering proceeds to inquire. Nor does this inquiry cease until he arrive at a knowledge of the essence of the cause.

If therefore the human intellect, knowing the essence of some created effect, knows no more of God than *that He is;* the perfection of that intellect does not yet reach simply the First Cause, but there remains in it the natural desire to seek the cause.

Wherefore it is not yet perfectly happy. Consequently, for perfect happiness the intellect needs to reach the very Essence of the First Cause. And thus it will have its perfection through union with God as with that object, in which alone man's happiness consists, as stated above (AA. 1, 7; Q. 2, A. 8).

Reply Obj. 1. Dionysius speaks of the knowledge of wayfarers journeying towards happiness.

Reply Obj. 2. As stated above (Q. 1, A. 8), the end has a twofold acceptation. First, as to the thing itself which is desired: and in this way, the same thing is the end of the higher and of the lower nature, and indeed of all things, as stated above (*ibid.*). Secondly, as to the attainment of this thing; and thus the end of the higher nature is different from that of the lower, according to their respective habitudes to that thing. So then the happiness of God, Who, in understanding his Essence, comprehends It, is higher than that of a man or angel who sees It indeed, but comprehends It not.

* * *

QUESTION 5: OF THE ATTAINMENT OF HAPPINESS

* * *

Fifth Article

WHETHER MAN CAN ATTAIN HAPPINESS BY HIS NATURAL POWERS?

We Proceed Thus to the Fifth Article:—

Objection 1. It would seem that man can attain Happiness by his natural powers. For nature does not fail in necessary things. But nothing is so necessary to man as that by which he attains the last end. Therefore this is not lacking to human nature. Therefore man can attain Happiness by his natural powers.

Obj. 2. Further, since man is more noble than irrational creatures, it seems that he must be better equipped than they. But irrational creatures can attain their end by their natural powers. Much more therefore can man attain Happiness by his natural powers.

Obj. 3. Further, Happiness is a *perfect operation,* according to the Philosopher (*Ethic.* vii. 13). Now the beginning of a thing belongs to the same principle as the perfecting thereof. Since, therefore, the imperfect operation, which is as the beginning in human operations, is subject to man's natural power, whereby he is master of his own actions; it seems that he can attain to perfect operation, *i.e.,* Happiness, by his natural powers.

On the contrary, Man is naturally the principle of his action, by his intellect and will. But final Happiness prepared for the saints, surpasses the intellect and will of man; for the Apostle says (1 Cor. ii. 9): *Eye hath not seen, nor ear heard, neither hath it entered into the heart of man, what things God hath prepared for them that love Him.* Therefore man cannot attain Happiness by his natural powers.

I answer that, Imperfect happiness that can be had in this life, can be acquired by man by his natural powers, in the same way as virtue, in whose operation it consists: on this point we shall speak further on (Q. 63). But man's perfect Happiness, as stated above (Q. 3, A. 8), consists in the vision of the Divine Essence. Now the vision of God's Essence surpasses the nature not only of man, but also of every creature, as was shown in the First Part (Q. 12, A. 4). For the natural knowledge of every creature is in keeping with the mode of his substance: thus it is said of the intelligence (*De Causis;* Prop. viii.) that *it knows things that are above it, and things that are below it, according to the mode of its substance.* But every knowledge that is according to the mode of created substance, falls short of the vision of the Divine Essence, which infinitely surpasses all created substance. Consequently neither man, nor any creature, can attain final Happiness by his natural powers.

Reply Obj. 1. Just as nature does not fail man in necessaries, although it has not provided him with weapons and clothing, as it provided other animals, because it gave him reason and hands, with which he is able to get these things for himself; so neither did it fail man in things necessary, although it gave him not the wherewithal to attain Happiness: since this it could not do. But it did give him freewill, with which he can turn to God, that He may make him happy. *For what we do by means of our friends, is done, in a sense, by ourselves* (*Ethic.* iii. 3).

Reply Obj. 2. The nature that can attain perfect good, although it needs help from without in order to attain it, is of more noble condition than a nature which cannot attain perfect good, but attains some imperfect good, although it need no help from without in order to attain it, as the Philosopher says (*De Cœlo* ii. 12). Thus he is better disposed to health who can attain perfect health, albeit by means of medicine, than he who can attain but imperfect health, without the help of medicine. And therefore the rational creature, which can attain the perfect good of happiness, but needs the Divine assistance for the purpose, is more perfect than the irrational creature, which is not capable of attaining this good, but attains some imperfect good by its natural powers.

Reply Obj. 3. When imperfect and perfect are of the same species, they can be caused by the same power. But this does not follow of necessity, if they be of different species: for not everything, that can cause the disposition of matter, can produce the final perfection. Now the imperfect operation, which is subject to man's natural power, is not of the same species as that perfect operation which is man's happiness: since operation takes its species from its object. Consequently the argument does not prove.

* * *

TREATISE ON LAW

QUESTION 94: OF THE NATURAL LAW

* * *

Second Article

WHETHER THE NATURAL LAW CONTAINS SEVERAL PRECEPTS, OR ONE ONLY?

We Proceed Thus to the Second Article:—

Objection 1. It would seem that the natural law contains, not several precepts, but one only. For law is a kind of precept, as stated above (Q. 92, A. 2). If therefore there were many precepts of the natural law, it would follow that there are also many natural laws.

Obj. 2. Further, the natural law is consequent to human nature. But human nature, as a whole, is one; though, as to its parts, it is manifold. Therefore, either there is but one precept of the law of nature, on account of the unity of nature as a whole; or there are many, by reason of the number of parts of human nature. The result would be that even things relating to the inclination of the concupiscible faculty belong to the natural law.

Obj. 3. Further, law is something pertaining to reason, as stated above (Q. 90, A. 1). Now reason is but one in man. Therefore there is only one precept of the natural law.

On the contrary, The precepts of the natural law in man stand in relation to practical matters, as the first principles to matters of demonstration. But there are several first indemonstrable principles. Therefore there are also several precepts of the natural law.

I answer that, As stated above (Q. 91, A. 3), the precepts of the natural law are to the practical reason, what the first principles of demonstrations are to the speculative reason; because both are self-evident principles. Now a thing is said to be self-evident in two ways: first, in itself; secondly, in relation to us. Any proposition is said to be self-evident in itself, its predicate is contained in the notion of the subject: although, to one who knows not the definition of the subject, it happens that such a proposition is not self-evident. For instance, this proposition, *Man is a rational being,* is, in its very nature, self-evident, since who says *man,* says *a rational being:* and yet to one who knows not what a man is, this proposition is not self-evident. Hence it is that, as Boethius says (*De Hebdom.*), certain axioms or propositions are universally self-evident to all; and such are those propositions whose terms are known to all, as, *Every whole is greater than its part,* and, *Things equal to one and the same are equal to one another.* But some propositions are self-evident only to the wise, who understand the meaning of the terms of such propositions: thus to one who understands that an angel is not a body, it is self-evident that an angel is not circumscriptively in a place: but this is not evident to the unlearned, for they cannot grasp it.

Now a certain order is to be found in those things that are apprehended universally. For that which, before aught else, falls under apprehension, is *being,* the notion of which is included in all things whatsoever a man apprehends. Wherefore the first indemonstrable principle is that *the same thing cannot be affirmed and denied at the same time,* which is based on the notion of being and not-being: and on this principle all others are based, as is stated in *Metaph.* iv, text. 9. Now as being is the first thing that falls under the apprehension simply, so *good* is the first thing that falls under the apprehension of the practical reason, which is directed to action: since every agent acts for an end under the aspect of good. Consequently the first principle in the practical reason is one founded on the notion of good, viz., that *good is that which all things seek after.* Hence this is the first precept of law, that *good is to be done and pursued, and evil is to be avoided.* All other precepts of the natural law are based upon this: so that whatever the practical reason naturally apprehends as man's good (or evil) belongs to the precepts of the natural law as something to be done or avoided.

Since, however, good has the nature of an end, and evil, the nature of a contrary, hence it is that all those things to which man has a natural inclination, are naturally apprehended by reason as being good, and consequently as objects of pursuit, and their contraries as evil, and objects of avoidance. Wherefore according to the order of natural inclinations, is the order of the precepts of the natural law. Because in man there is first of all an inclination to good in accordance with the nature which he has in common with all substances: inasmuch as every substance seeks the preservation of its own being, according to its nature: and by reason of this inclination, whatever is a means of preserving human life, and of warding off its obstacles, belongs to the natural law.

Secondly, there is in man an inclination to things that pertain to him more specially, according to that nature which he has in common with other animals: and in virtue of this inclination, those things are said to belong to the natural law, *which nature has taught to all animals,* such as sexual intercourse, education of offspring and so forth. Thirdly, there is in man an inclination to good, according to the nature of his reason, which nature is proper to him: thus man has a natural inclination to know the truth about God, and to live in society: and in this respect, whatever pertains to this inclination belongs to the natural law; for instance, to shun ignorance, to avoid offending those among whom one has to live, and other such things regarding the above inclination.

Reply Obj. 1. All these precepts of the law of nature have the character of one natural law, inasmuch as they flow from one first precept.

Reply Obj. 2. All the inclinations of any parts whatsoever of human nature, *e.g.,* of the concupiscible and irascible parts, in so far as they are ruled by reason, belong to the natural law, and are reduced to one first precept, as stated above: so that the precepts of the natural law are many in themselves, but are based on one common foundation.

Reply Obj. 3. Although reason is one in itself, yet it directs all things regarding man; so that whatever can be ruled by reason, is contained under the law of reason.

* * *

Fourth Article

WHETHER THE NATURAL LAW IS THE SAME IN ALL MEN?

We Proceed Thus to the Fourth Article:—

Objection 1. It would seem that the natural law is not the same in all. For it is stated in the Decretals (*Dist.* i) that *the natural law is that which is contained in the Law and the Gospel.* But this is not common to all men; because, as it is written (Rom. x. 16), *all do not obey the gospel.* Therefore the natural law is not the same in all men.

Obj. 2. Further, *Things which are accordingly to the law are said to be just,* as stated in *Ethic.* v. But it is stated in the same book that nothing is so universally just as not to be subject to change in regard to some men. Therefore even the natural law is not the same in all men.

Obj. 3. Further, as stated above (AA. 2, 3), to the natural law belongs everything to which a man is inclined according to his nature. Now different men are naturally inclined to different things; some to the desire of pleasures, others to the desire of honors, and other men to other things. Therefore there is not one natural law for all.

On the contrary, Isidore says (*Etym.* v. 4): *The natural law is common to all nations.*

I answer that, As stated above (AA. 2, 3), to the natural law belongs those things to which a man is inclined naturally: and among these it is proper to man to be inclined to act according to reason. Now the process of reason is from the common to the proper, as stated in *Phys.* i. The speculative reason, however, is differently situated in this matter, from the practical reason. For, since the speculative reason is busied chiefly with necessary things, which cannot be otherwise than they are, its proper conclusions, like the universal principles, contain the truth without fail. The practical reason, on the other hand, is busied with contingent matters, about which human actions are concerned: and consequently, although there is necessity in the general principles, the more we descend to matters of detail, the more frequently we encounter defects. Accordingly then in speculative matters truth is the same in all men, both as to principles and as to conclusions: although the truth is not known to all as regards the conclusions, but only as regards the principles which are called *common notions.* But in matters of action, truth or practical rectitude is not the same for all, as to matters of detail, but only as to the general principles: and where there is the same rectitude in matters of detail, it is not equally known to all.

It is therefore evident that, as regards the general principles whether of speculative or of practical reason, truth or rectitude is the same for all, and is equally known by all. As to the proper conclusions of the speculative reason, the truth is the same for all, but is not equally known to all: thus it is true for all that the three angles of a triangle are together equal to two right angles, although it is not known to all. But as to the proper conclusions of the practical reason, neither is the truth or rectitude the same for all, nor, where it is the same, is it equally known by all. Thus it is right and true for all to act according to reason: and from this principle it follows as a proper conclusion, that goods entrusted to another should be restored to their owner. Now this is true for the majority of cases: but it may happen in a particular case that it would be injurious, and therefore unreasonable, to restore goods held in trust; for instance if they are claimed for the purpose of fighting against one's country. And this principle will be found to fail the more, according as we descend further into detail, e.g., if one were to say that goods held in trust should be restored with such and such a guarantee, or in such and such a way; because the greater the number of conditions added, the greater the number of ways in which the principle may fail, so that it be not right to restore or not to restore.

Consequently we must say that the natural law, as to general principles, is the same for all, both as to rectitude and as to knowledge. But as to certain matters of detail, which are conclusions, as it were, of those general principles, it is the same for all in the majority of cases, both as to rectitude and as to knowledge; and yet in some few cases it may fail, both as to rectitude, by reason of certain obstacles (just as natures subject to generation and corruption fail in some few cases on account of some obstacle), and as to knowledge, since in some the reason is perverted by passion, or evil habit, or an evil disposition of nature; thus formerly, theft, although it is expressly contrary to the natural law, was not considered wrong among the Germans, as Julius Caesar relates (*De Bello Gall.* vi).

Reply Obj. 1. The meaning of the sentence quoted is not that whatever is contained in the Law and the Gospel belongs to the natural law, since they contain many things that are above nature; but that whatever belongs to the natural law is fully contained in them. Wherefore Gratian, after saying that *the natural law is what is contained in the Law and the Gospel,* adds at once, by way of example, *by which everyone is commanded to do to others as he would be done by.*

Reply Obj. 2. The saying of the Philosopher is to be understood of things that are naturally just, not as general principles, but as conclusions drawn from them, having rectitude in the majority of cases, but failing in a few.

Reply Obj. 3. As, in man, reason rules and commands the other powers, so all the natural inclinations belonging to the other powers must needs be directed according to reason. Wherefore it is universally right for all men, that all their inclinations should be directed according to reason.

* * *

QUESTION 95: OF HUMAN LAW

* * *

First Article

WHETHER IT WAS USEFUL FOR LAWS TO BE FRAMED BY MEN?

We Proceed Thus to the First Article:—

Objection 1. It would seem that it was not useful for laws to be framed by men. Because the purpose of every law is that man be made good thereby, as stated above (Q. 92, A. 1). But men are more to be induced to be good willingly by means of admonitions, than against their will, by means of laws. Therefore there was no need to frame laws.

Obj. 2. Further, as the Philosopher says (*Ethic.* v. 4), *men have recourse to a judge as to animate justice.* But animate justice is better than inanimate justice, which is contained in laws. Therefore it would have been better for the execution of justice to be entrusted to the decision of judges, than to frame laws in addition.

Obj. 3. Further, every law is framed for the direction of human actions, as is evident from what has been stated above (Q. 90, AA. 1, 2). But since human actions are about singulars, which are infinite in number, matters pertaining to the direction of human actions cannot be taken into sufficient consideration except by a wise man, who looks into each one of them. Therefore it would have been better for human acts to be directed by the judgment of wise men, than by the framing of laws. Therefore there was no need of human laws.

On the contrary, Isidore says (*Etym.* v. 20): *Laws were made that in fear thereof human audacity might be held in check, that innocence might be safeguarded in the midst of wickedness, and that the dread of punishment might prevent the wicked from doing harm.* But these things are most necessary to mankind. Therefore it was necessary that human laws should be made.

I answer that, As stated above (Q. 63, A. 1; Q. 94, A. 3), man has a natural aptitude for virtue; but the perfection of virtue must be acquired by man by means of some kind of training. Thus we observe that man is helped by industry in his necessities, for instance, in food and clothing. Certain beginnings of these he has from nature, viz., his reason and his hands; but he has not the full complement, as other animals have, to whom nature has given sufficiency of clothing and food. Now it is difficult to see how man could suffice for himself in the matter of this training: since the perfection of virtue consists chiefly in withdrawing man from undue pleasures, to which above all man is inclined, and especially the young, who are more capable of being trained. Consequently a man needs to receive this training from another, whereby to arrive at the perfection of virtue. And as to those young people who are inclined to acts of virtue, by their good natural disposition, or by custom, or rather by the gift of God, paternal training suffices, which is by admonitions. But since some are found to be depraved, and prone to vice, and not easily amenable to words, it was necessary for such to be restrained from evil by force and fear, in order that, at least, they might desist from evildoing, and leave others in peace, and that they themselves, by being habituated in this way, might be brought to do willingly what hitherto they did from fear, and thus become virtuous. Now this kind of training, which compels through fear of punishment, is the discipline of laws. Therefore, in order that man might have peace and virtue, it was necessary for laws to be framed: for, as the Philosopher says (Polit. i. 2), *as man is the most noble of animals if he be perfect in virtue, so is he the lowest of all, if he be severed from law and righteousness;* because man can use his reason to devise means of satisfying his lusts and evil passions, which other animals are unable to do.

Reply Obj. 1. Men who are well disposed are led willingly to virtue by being admonished better than by coercion: but men who are evilly disposed are not led to virtue unless they are compelled.

Reply Obj. 2. As the Philosopher says (*Rhet.* i. 1), *it is better that all things be regulated by law, than left to be decided by judges: and this for three reasons. First, because it is easier to find a few wise men competent to frame right laws, than to find the many who would be necessary to judge aright of each single case.—Secondly, because those who make laws consider long beforehand* what laws to make; whereas judgment on each single case has to be pronounced as soon as it arises: and it is easier for man to see what is right, by taking many instances into consideration, than by considering one solitary fact.—Thirdly, because lawgivers judge in the abstract and of future events; whereas those who sit in judgment judge of things present, towards which they are affected by love, hatred, or some kind of cupidity; wherefore their judgment is perverted.

Since then the animated justice of the judge is not found in every man, and since it can be deflected, therefore it was necessary, whenever possible, for the law to determine how to judge, and for very few matters to be left to the decision of men.

Reply Obj. 3. Certain individual facts which cannot be covered by the law *have necessarily to be committed to judges,* as the Philosopher says in the same passage: for instance, *concerning something that has happened or not happened,* and the like.

Second Article

WHETHER EVERY HUMAN LAW IS DERIVED FROM THE NATURAL LAW?

We Proceed Thus to the Second Article:—

Objection 1. It would seem that not every human law is derived from the natural law. For the Philosopher says (*Ethic.* v. 7) that *the legal just is that which originally was a matter of indifference.* But those things which arise from the natural law are not matters of indifference. Therefore the enactments of human laws are not all derived from the natural law.

Obj. 2. Further, positive law is contrasted with natural law, as stated by Isidore (*Etym.* v. 4) and the Philosopher (*Ethic.* v, *loc. cit.*). But those things which flow as conclusion from the general principles of the natural law belong to the natural law, as stated above (Q. 94, A. 4). Therefore that which is established by human law does not belong to the natural law.

Obj. 3. Further, the law of nature is the same for all; since the Philosopher says (*Ethic.* v. 7) that *the natural just is that which is equally valid everywhere.* If therefore human laws were derived from the natural law, it would follow that they too are the same for all: which is clearly false.

Obj. 4. Further, it is possible to give a reason for things which are derived from the natural law. But *it is not possible to give the reason for all the legal enactments of the lawgivers,* as the jurist says. Therefore not all human laws are derived from the natural law.

On the contrary, Tully says (*Rhetor.* ii): *Things which emanated from nature and were approved by custom, were sanctioned by fear and reverence for the laws.*

I answer that, As Augustine says (*De Lib. Arb.* i. 5), *that which is not just seems to be no law at all: wherefore the force of a law depends on the extent of its justice. Now in human affairs a thing is said to be just, from being right, according to the rule of reason. But the first rule of reason is the law of nature, as is clear from what has been stated* above (Q. 91, A. 2 *ad* 2). Consequently every human law has just so much of the nature of law, as it is derived from the law of nature. But if in any point it deflects from the law of nature, it is no longer a law but a perversion of law.

But it must be noted that something may be derived from the natural law in two ways: first, as a conclusion from premises, secondly, by way of determination of certain generalities. The first way is like to that by which, in sciences, demonstrated conclusions are drawn from the principles: while the second mode is likened to that whereby, in the arts, general forms are particularized as to details: thus the craftsman needs to determine the general form of a house to some particular shape. Some things are therefore derived from the general principles of the natural law, by way of conclusions; *e.g.,* that *one must not kill* may be derived as a conclusion from the principle that one should do harm to no man: while some are derived therefrom by way of determination; *e.g.,* the law of nature has it that the evil-doer should be punished; but that he be punished in this or that way, is a determination of the law of nature.

Accordingly both modes of derivation are found in the human law. But those things which are derived in the first way, are contained in human law not as emanating therefrom exclusively, but have some force from the natural law also. But those things which are derived in the second way, have no other force than that of human law.

Reply Obj. 1. The Philosopher is speaking of those enactments which are by way of determination or specification of the precepts of the natural law.

Reply Obj. 2. This argument avails for those things that are derived from the natural law, by way of conclusions.

Reply Obj. 3. The general principles of the natural law cannot be applied to all men in the same way on account of the great variety of human affairs: and hence arises the diversity of positive laws among various people.

Reply Obj. 4. These words of the Jurist are to be understood as referring to decisions of rulers in determining particular points of the natural law: on which determinations the judgment of expert and prudent men is based as on its principles; in so far, to wit, as they see at once what is the best thing to decide.

Hence the Philosopher says (*Ethic.* vi. 11) that in such matters, *we ought to pay as much attention to the undemonstrated sayings and opinions of persons who surpass us in experience, age and prudence, as to their demonstrations.*

* * *

QUESTION 96: OF THE POWER OF HUMAN LAW

* * *

Second Article

WHETHER IT BELONGS TO THE HUMAN LAW TO REPRESS ALL VICES?

We Proceed Thus to the Second Article:—

Objection 1. It would seem that it belongs to human law to repress all vices. For Isidore says (*Etym.* v. 20) that *laws were made in order that, in fear thereof, man's audacity might be held in check.* But it would not be held in check sufficiently, unless all evils were repressed by law. Therefore human law should repress all evils.

Obj. 2. Further, the intention of the lawgiver is to make the citizens virtuous. But a man cannot be virtuous unless he forbear from all kinds of vice. Therefore it belongs to human law to repress all vices.

Obj. 3. Further, human law is derived from the natural law, as stated above (Q. 95, A. 2). But all vices are contrary to the law of nature. Therefore human law should repress all vices.

On the contrary, We read in *De Lib. Arb.* i. 5: *It seems to me that the law which is written for the governing of the people rightly permits these things, and that Divine providence punishes them.* But Divine providence punishes nothing but vices. Therefore human law rightly allows some vices, by not repressing them.

I answer that, As stated above (Q. 90, AA. I, 2), law is framed as a rule or measure of human acts. Now a measure should be homogeneous with that which it measures, as stated in *Metaph.* x, text. 3, 4, since different things are measured by different measures. Wherefore laws imposed on men should also be in keeping with their condition, for, as Isidore says (*Etym.* v. 21), law should be *possible both according to nature, and according to the customs of the country.* Now possibility or faculty of action is due to an interior habit or disposition: since the same thing is not possible to one who has not a virtuous habit, as is possible to one who has. Thus the same is not possible to a child as to a full-grown man: for which reason the law for children is not the same as for adults, since many things are permitted to children, which in an adult are punished by law or at any rate are open to blame. In like manner many things are permissible to men not perfect in virtue, which would be intolerable in a virtuous man.

Now human law is framed for a number of human beings, the majority of whom are not perfect in virtue. Wherefore human laws do not forbid all vices, from which the virtuous abstain, but only the more grievous vices, from which it is possible for the majority to abstain; and chiefly those that are to the hurt of others, without the prohibition of which human society could not be maintained: thus human law prohibits murder, theft and such like.

Reply Obj. 1. Audacity seems to refer to the assailing of others. Consequently it belongs to those sins chiefly whereby one's neighbor is injured: and these sins are forbidden by human law, as stated.

Reply Obj. 2. The purpose of human law is to lead men to virtue, not suddenly, but gradually. Wherefore it does not lay upon the multitude of imperfect men the burdens of those who are already virtuous, viz., that they should abstain from all evil. Otherwise these imperfect ones, being unable to bear such precepts, would break out into yet greater evils: thus it is written (Prov. xxx. 33): *He that violently bloweth his nose, bringeth out blood;* and (Matth. ix. 17) that if *new wine,* i.e., precepts of a perfect life, *is put into old bottles,* i.e., into imperfect men, *the bottles break, and the wine runneth out,* i.e., the precepts are despised, and those men, from contempt, break out into evils worse still.

Reply Obj. 3. The natural law is a participation in us of the eternal law: while human law falls short of the eternal law. Now Augustine says (*De Lib. Arb.* i. 5): *The law which is framed for the government of states, allows and leaves unpunished many things that are punished by Divine providence. Nor, if this law does not attempt to do everything, is this a reason why it should be blamed for what it does.* Wherefore, too, human law does not prohibit everything that is forbidden by the natural law.

* * *

SECOND PART OF THE SECOND PART(II–II)

* * *

QUESTION 40: OF WAR

* * *

First Article

WHETHER IT IS ALWAYS SINFUL TO WAGE WAR?

We Proceed Thus to the First Article:—

Objection 1. It would seem that it is always sinful to wage war. Because punishment is not inflicted except for sin. Now those who wage war are threatened by Our Lord with punishment, according to Matth. xxvi. 52: *All that take the sword shall perish with the sword.* Therefore all wars are unlawful.

Obj. 2. Further, whatever is contrary to a Divine precept is a sin. But war is contrary to a Divine precept, for it is written (Matth. v. 39): *But I say to you not to resist evil;* and (Rom. xii. 19): *Not revenging yourselves, my dearly beloved, but give place unto wrath.* Therefore war is always sinful.

Obj. 3. Further, nothing, except sin, is contrary to an act of virtue. But war is contrary to peace. Therefore war is always a sin.

Obj. 4. Further, the exercise of a lawful thing is itself lawful, as is evident in scientific exercises. But warlike exercises which take place in tournaments are forbidden by the Church, since those who are slain in these trials are deprived of ecclesiastical burial. Therefore it seems that war is a sin in itself.

On the contrary, Augustine says in a sermon on the son of the centurion [*Ep. ad Marcel.,* cxxxviii.]: *If the Christian Religion forbade war altogether, those who sought salutary advice in the Gospel would rather have been counselled to cast aside their arms, and to give up soldiering altogether. On the contrary, they were told: "Do violence to no man; . . . and be content with your pay."* [Luke iii. 14] *If he commanded them to be content with their pay, he did not forbid soldiering.*

I answer that, In order for a war to be just, three things are necessary. First, the authority of the sovereign by whose command the war is to be waged. For it is not the business of a private individual to declare war, because he can seek for redress of his rights from the tribunal of his superior. Moreover it is not the business of a private individual to summon together the people, which has to be done in wartime. And as the care of the common weal is committed to those who are in authority, it is their business to watch over the common weal of the city, kingdom or province subject to them. And just as it is lawful for them to have recourse to the sword in defending that common weal against internal disturbances, when they punish evil-doers, according to the words of the Apostle

Three Orders of Society, from *L'image du monde,* Franco-Flemish, late-thirteenth century. This detail from an illustated manuscript page shows the hierarchy of medieval society with monk, knight, and peasant. (*By permission of The British Museum* © The British Library Board, Sloane 2435).

(Rom. xiii. 4): *He beareth not the sword in vain: for he is God's minister, an avenger to execute wrath upon him that doth evil;* so too, it is their business to have recourse to the sword of war in defending the common weal against external enemies. Hence it is said to those who are in authority (Ps. lxxxi. 4): *Rescue the poor: and deliver the needy out of the hand of the sinner;* and for this reason Augustine says (*Contra Faust.* xxii. 75): *The natural order conducive to peace among mortals demands that the power to declare and counsel war should be in the hands of those who hold the supreme authority.*

Secondly, a just cause is required, namely that those who are attacked, should be attacked because they deserve it on account of some fault. Wherefore Augustine says (QQ. *in Hept.*, qu. x, *super Jos.*): *A just war is wont to be described as one that avenges wrongs, when a nation or state has to be punished, for refusing to make amends for the wrongs inflicted by its subjects, or to restore what it has seized unjustly.*

Thirdly, it is necessary that the belligerents should have a rightful intention, so that they intend the advancement of good, or the avoidance of evil. Hence Augustine says *De Verb. Dom: True religion looks upon as peaceful those wars that are waged not for motives of aggrandizement or cruelty, but with the object of securing peace, of punishing evil-doers, and of uplifting the good.* For it may happen that the war is declared by the legitimate authority, and for a just cause, and yet be rendered unlawful through a wicked intention. Hence Augustine says (*Contra Faust.* xxii. 74): *The passion for inflicting harm, the cruel thirst for vengeance, an unpacific and relentless spirit, the fever of revolt, the lust of power, and such like things, all these are rightly condemned in war.*

Reply Obj. 1. As Augustine says (*Contra Faust.* xxii. 70): *To take the sword is to arm oneself in order to take the life of anyone, without the command or permission of superior or lawful authority.* On the other hand, to have recourse to the sword (as a private person) by the authority of the sovereign or judge, or (as a public person) through zeal for justice, and by the authority, so to speak, of God, is not to *take the sword,* but to use it as commissioned by another, wherefore it does not deserve punishment. And yet even those who make sinful use of the sword are not always slain with the sword, yet they always perish with their own sword, because, unless they repent, they are punished eternally for their sinful use of the sword.

Reply Obj. 2. Such like precepts, as Augustine observes (*De Serm. Dom. in Monte* i. 19), should always be borne in readiness of mind, so that we be ready to obey them, and, if necessary, to refrain from resistance or self-defense. Nevertheless it is necessary sometimes for a man to act otherwise for the common good, or for the good of those with whom he is fighting. Hence Augustine says (*Ep. ad Marcellin.* cxxxviii): *Those whom we have to punish with a kindly severity, it is necessary to handle in many ways against their will. For when we are stripping a man of the lawlessness of sin, it is good for him to be vanquished, since nothing is more hopeless than the happiness of sinners, whence arises a guilty impunity, and an evil will, like an internal enemy.*

Reply Obj. 3. Those who wage war justly aim at peace, and so they are not opposed to peace, except to the evil peace, which Our Lord *came not to send upon earth* (Matth. x. 34). Hence Augustine says (*Ep. ad Bonif.* clxxxix): *We do not seek peace in order to be at war, but we go to war that we may have peace. Be peaceful, therefore, in warring, so that you may vanquish those whom you war against, and bring them to the prosperity of peace.*

Reply Obj. 4. Manly exercises in warlike feats of arms are not all forbidden, but those which are inordinate and perilous, and end in slaying or plundering. In olden times warlike exercises presented no such danger, and hence they were called *exercises of arms* or bloodless wars, as Jerome states in an epistle.

William of Ockham
ca. 1285–1349

William was born in Ockham, Surrey, near London, between 1280 and 1290. He joined the Franciscan order as a young man. In 1309 or 1310, he went to Oxford, where his studies included the work of Duns Scotus. Despite his success as a student and, later, as a student lecturer, Ockham was denied a license to teach. The chancellor of the university accused him of heresy, even going to the papal court in Avignon, France, in 1323 to press charges. The following year Ockham was summoned to Avignon by Pope John XXII. The affair dragged on for four years. Meanwhile, Ockham kept writing and came into conflict with the pope again when he joined the general of his Franciscan order in advocating apostolic poverty.

In 1328, Ockham was forced to flee Avignon when the pope was prepared to condemn the Franciscan position on poverty. He eventually found refuge in Munich under the protection of Emperor Ludwig of Bavaria, who was angry with the pope for not recognizing his crown. Ockham reportedly told the emperor, "Defend me with your sword, and I will defend you with my pen."

Over the next twenty years, Ockham did indeed defend the emperor, arguing that imperial power flows from God through the people, not through the pope—a position that anticipated later political theories. Following Ludwig's death in 1347, Ockham sought reconciliation with the pope (now Clement VI), and a document of submission was drawn up. We do not know whether Ockham ever signed the document, for he died in 1349, apparently from the plague.

Ockham's philosophy reflects his times: He is much less optimistic than was Thomas Aquinas about the ability of human reason to understand the things of God. Ockham criticized the proofs for God's existence, arguing that theological truth can be known only by revelation, not reason. In so arguing, he separated philosophy from theology and reason from faith more completely than had any of his predecessors.

Ockham is probably best known for his "Law of Parsimony," or "Ockham's Razor." This principle has often been formulated as *entia non sunt multiplicanda praeter necessitatem,* "entities are not to be multiplied beyond necessity," though none of Ockham's known works contains that exact phrase.* Essentially this principle holds that we should always seek the simplest explanation, a principle still used by philosophers and scientists. Ockham was not the first to enunciate this principle: It can be found earlier in the writings of Thomas Aquinas,** Duns Scotus, and even, in embryonic form, in Aristotle.*** But the skill with which Ockham wielded this "razor" ensured its association with his name.

Ockham was especially effective in using his razor on the question of universals. Contrary to the moderate realism dominant in his day, Ockham saw no need to posit universals as real entities beyond individual things. This critique is clear in the selections on universals given here. Following some defining of terms, Ockham argues against the realist position and, with great care, against the position of the "Subtle Doctor," Duns Scotus. Ockham asserts that "in a particular substance there is nothing substantial except the particular form, the particular matter, or the composite of the two"—that is, there is no real universal apart from the particular thing.

* * *

Marilyn McCord Adams's *William Ockham,* two volumes (Notre Dame, IN: University of Notre Dame Press, 1987) is the definitive introduction to Ockham, whereas Meyrick Heath Carré, *Realists and Nominalist*s (London: Oxford University Press, 1946), and Sharon M. Kaye and Robert M. Martin, *On Ockham* (Belmont, CA: Wadsworth, 2001) provide helpful overviews. Specialized studies include E.A. Moody, *The Logic of William of Ockham* (1935; reprinted New York: Russell and Russell, 1965); Damascene Webering, *The Theory of Demonstration According to William Ockham* (St. Bonaventure, NY: Franciscan Institute, 1953); Herman Shapiro, *Motion, Time and Place According to William Ockham* (St. Bonaventure, NY: Franciscan Institute, 1957); Arthur Stephen McGrade, *The Political Thought of William of Ockham: Personal and Institutional Principles* (London: Cambridge University Press, 1974); and Rega Wood, *Ockham on the Virtues* (West Lafayette, IN: Purdue University Press, 1997). For collections of essays, see Philotheus Bohner, ed., *Collected Articles on Ockham* (St. Bonaventure, NY: Franciscan Institute, 1958) and Paul V. Spade, ed., *The Cambridge Companion to Ockham* (Cambridge: Cambridge University Press, 1999).

*Ockham's extant writings do include the phrases *pluralitas non est ponenda sine necessitate*, "plurality is not to be posited without necessity," and *frustra fit per plura quod potest fieri per pauciora,* "what can be explained by the assumption of fewer things is vainly explained by the assumption of more things." Perhaps applying his principle to its own formulation, we should say, "Why use many if few will do?"

**See his *Summa Theologica,* Part I, Q. 2, a. 3, obj. 2—page 334 in this volume.

***See *Posterior Analytics* I.25, 86a33–35 and *Physics* I.4, 188a17–18; VIII.6, 259a8–12.

Plague Victim, from *Das Buch der Cirurgia*, 1497, by Hieronymus Brunschwig. Beginning in 1347 the Bubonic Plague, or "Black Death," struck western Europe. Transmitted by flea bite, the disease was characterized by enormous swelling or "buboes" in the groin or armpits. The patient in this woodcut has a large buboe on his armpit—a sure sign that he will be dead within two or three days. Apparently William of Ockham met such a fate in 1349. (*Library of Congress*)

ON UNIVERSALS (in part)

Summa Logicae, Part I

Chapter 14: On the Universal

It is not enough for the logician to have a merely general knowledge of terms; he needs a deep understanding of the concept of a term. Therefore, after discussing some general divisions among terms we should examine in detail the various headings under these divisions.

First, we should deal with terms of second intention and afterwards with terms of first intention. I have said that "universal," "genus," and "species" are examples of terms of second intention. We must discuss those terms of second intention which are called the five universals, but first we should consider the common term "universal." It is predicated of every universal and is opposed to the notion of a particular.

First, it should be noted that the term "particular" has two senses. In the first sense a particular is that which is one and not many. Those who hold that a universal is a certain quality residing in the mind which is predicable of many (not suppositing for itself, of course, but for the many of which it is predicated) must grant that, in this sense of the word, every universal is a particular. Just as a word, even if convention makes it common, is a particular, the intention of the soul signifying many is numerically one thing a particular; for although it signifies many things it is nonetheless one thing and not many.

In another sense of the word we use "particular" to mean that which is one and not many and which cannot function as a sign of many. Taking "particular" in this sense no universal is a particular, since every universal is capable of signifying many and of being predicated of many. Thus, if we take the term "universal" to mean that which is not one in number, as many do, then, I want to say that nothing is a universal. One could, of course, abuse the expression and say that a population constitutes a single universal because it is not one but many. But that would be puerile.

Therefore, it ought to be said that every universal is one particular thing and that it is not a universal except in its signification, in its signifying many things. This is what Avicenna means to say in his commentary on the fifth book of the *Metaphysics*. He says, "One form in the intellect is related to many things, and in this respect it is a universal; for it is an intention of the intellect which has an invariant relationship to anything you choose." He then continues, "Although this form is a universal in its relationship to individuals, it is a particular in its relationship to the particular soul in which it resides; for it is just one form among many in the intellect." He means to say that a universal is an intention of a particular soul. Insofar as it can be predicated of many things not for itself but for these many, it is said to be a universal; but insofar as it is a particular form actually existing in the intellect, it is said to be a particular. Thus "particular" is predicated of a universal in the first sense but not in the second. In the same way we say that the sun is a universal cause and, nevertheless, that it is really and truly a particular or individual cause. For the sun is said to be a universal cause because it is the cause of many things (i.e., every object that is generable and corruptible), but it is said to be a particular cause because it is one cause and not many. In the same way the intention of the soul is said to be a universal because it is a sign predicable of many things, but it is said to be a particular because it is one thing and not many.

But it should be noted that there are two kinds of universals. Some things are universal by nature; that is, by nature they are signs predicable of many in the same way that the smoke is by nature a sign of fire; weeping, a sign of grief; and laughter, a sign of internal joy. The intention of the soul, of course, is a universal by nature. Thus, no substance outside the soul, nor any accident outside the soul is a universal of this sort. It is of this kind of universal that I shall speak in the following chapters.

Other things are universals by convention. Thus, a spoken word, which is numerically one quality, is a universal; it is a sign conventionally appointed for the signification of many things. Thus, since the word is said to be common, it can be called a universal. But notice it is not by nature, but only by convention, that this label applies.

Chapter 15: That the Universal Is Not a Thing Outside the Mind

But it is not enough just to state one's position; one must defend it by philosophical arguments. Therefore, I shall set forth some arguments for my view, and then corroborate it by an appeal to the authorities.

That no universal is a substance existing outside the mind can be proved in a number of ways:

No universal is a particular substance, numerically one; for if this were the case, then it would follow that Socrates is a universal; for there is no good reason why one substance should be a universal rather than another. Therefore no particular substance is a universal; every substance is numerically one and a particular. For every substance is either one thing and not many or it is many things. Now, if a substance is one thing and not many, then it is numerically one; for that is what we mean by "numerically one." But if, on the other hand, some substance is several things, it is either several particular things or several universal things. If the first alternative is chosen, then it follows that some substance would be several particular substances; and consequently that some substance would be several men. But although the universal would be distinguished from a single particular, it would not be distinguished from several particulars. If, however, some substance were to be several universal entities, I take one of those universal entities and ask, "Is it many things or is it one and not many?" If the second is the case then it follows that the thing is particular. If the first is the case then I ask, "Is it several particular things or several universal things?" Thus, either an infinite regress will follow or it will be granted that no substance is a universal in a way that would be incompatible with its also being a particular. From this it follows that no substance is a universal.

Again, if some universal were to be one substance existing in particular substances, yet distinct from them, it would follow that it could exist without them; for everything that is naturally prior to something else can, by God's power, exist without that thing; but the consequence is absurd.

Again, if the view in question were true, no individual would be able to be created. Something of the individual would pre-exist it, for the whole individual would not take its existence from nothing if the universal which is in it were already in something else. For the same reason it would follow that God could not annihilate an individual substance without destroying the other individuals of the same kind. If He were to annihilate some individual, he would destroy the whole which is essentially that individual and, consequently, He would destroy the universal which is in that thing and in others of the same essence. Consequently, other things of the same essence would not remain, for they could not continue to exist without the universal which constitutes a part of them.

Again, such a universal could not be construed as something completely extrinsic to the essence of an individual; therefore, it would belong to the essence of the individual; and, consequently, an individual would be composed of universals, so that the individual would not be any more a particular than a universal.

Again, it follows that something of the essence of Christ would be miserable and damned, since that common nature really existing in Christ would be damned in the damned individual; for surely that essence is also in Judas. But this is absurd.

Many other arguments could be brought forth, but in the interests of brevity, I shall dispense with them. Instead, I shall corroborate my account by an appeal to authorities.

First, in the seventh book of the *Metaphysics,* Aristotle is treating the question of whether a universal is a substance. He shows that no universal is a substance. Thus, he says, "It is impossible that substance be something that can be predicated universally."

Again, in the tenth book of the *Metaphysics,* he says, "Thus, if, as we argued in the discussions on substance and being, no universal can be a substance, it is not possible that a universal be a substance in the sense of a one over and against the many."

From these remarks it is clear that, in Aristotle's view, although universals can supposit for substances, no universal is a substance.

Again, the Commentator in his forty-fourth comment on the seventh book of the *Metaphysics* says, "In the individual, the only substance is the particular form and matter out of which the individual is composed."

Again, in the forty-fifth comment, he says, "Let us say, therefore, that it is impossible that one of those things we call universals be the substance of anything, although they do express the substances of things."

And, again, in the forty-seventh comment, "It is impossible that they (universals) be parts of substances existing of and by themselves."

Again, in the second comment on the eighth book of the *Metaphysics,* he says, "No universal is either a substance or a genus."

Again, in the sixth comment on the tenth book, he says, "Since universals are not substances, it is clear that the common notion of being is not a substance existing outside the mind."

Using these and many other authorities, the general point emerges: no universal is a substance regardless of the viewpoint from which we consider the matter. Thus, the viewpoint from which we consider the matter is irrelevant to the question of whether something is a substance. Nevertheless, the meaning of a term is relevant to the question of whether the expression "substance" can be predicated of the term. Thus, if the term "dog" in the proposition "The dog is an animal" is used to stand for the barking animal, the proposition is true; but if it is used for the celestial body which goes by that name, the proposition is false. But it is impossible that one and the same thing should be a substance from one viewpoint and not a substance from another.

Therefore, it ought to be granted that no universal is a substance regardless of how it is considered. On the contrary, every universal is an intention of the mind which, on the most probable account, is identical with the act of understanding. Thus, it is said that the act of understanding by which I grasp men is a natural sign of men in the same way that weeping is a natural sign of grief. It is a natural sign such that it can stand for men in mental propositions in the same way that a spoken word can stand for things in spoken propositions.

That the universal is an intention of the soul is clearly expressed by Avicenna in the fifth book of the *Metaphysics,* in which he comments, "I say, therefore, that there are three senses of 'universal.' For we say that something is a universal if (like 'man') it is actually predicated of many things; and we also call an intention a universal if it could be predicated of many." Then follows the remark, "An intention is also called a universal if there is nothing inconceivable in its being predicated of many."

From these remarks it is clear that the universal is an intention of the soul capable of being predicated of many. The claim can be corroborated by argument. For every one agrees that a universal is something predicable of many, but only an intention of the soul or a conventional sign is predicated. No substance is ever predicated of anything. Therefore, only an intention of the soul or a conventional sign is a universal; but I am not here using the term "universal" for conventional signs, but only for signs that are universals by nature. That substance is not capable of functioning as predicate is clear; for if it were, it would follow that a proposition would be composed of particular substances; and, consequently, the subject would be in Rome and the predicate in England which is absurd.

Furthermore, propositions occur only in the mind, in speech, or in writing; therefore, their parts can exist only in the mind, in speech, and in writing. Particular substances, however, cannot themselves exist in the mind, in speech, or in writing. Thus, no proposition can be composed of particular substances. Propositions are, however, composed of universals; therefore, universals cannot conceivably be substances.

CHAPTER 16: AGAINST SCOTUS' ACCOUNT OF THE UNIVERSAL

It may be clear to many that a universal is not a substance outside the mind which exists in, but is distinct from, particulars. Nevertheless, some want to claim that the universal is, in some way, outside the soul and in particulars; and while they do not want to say that a universal is really distinct from particulars, they say that it is formally distinct from particulars. Thus, they say that in Socrates there is human nature which is contracted to Socrates by an individual difference which is not really, but only formally, distinct from that nature. Thus, while there are not two things, one is not formally the other.

I do not find this view tenable:

First, in creatures there can never be any distinction outside the mind unless there are distinct things; if, therefore, there is any distinction between the nature and the difference, it is necessary that they really be distinct things. I prove my premise by the following syllogism: the nature is not formally distinct from itself; this individual difference is formally distinct from this nature; therefore, this individual difference is not this nature.

Again, the same entity is not both common and proper, but in their view the individual difference is proper and the universal is common; therefore, no universal is identical with an individual difference.

Again, opposites cannot be attributed to one and the same created thing, but *common* and *proper* are opposites; therefore, the same thing is not both common and proper. Nevertheless, that conclusion would follow if an individual difference and a common nature were the same thing.

Again, if a common nature were the same thing as an individual difference, there would be as many common natures as there are individual differences; and, consequently, none of those natures would be common, but each would be peculiar to the difference with which it is identical.

Again, whenever one thing is distinct from another it is distinguished from that thing either of and by itself or by something intrinsic to itself. Now, the humanity of Socrates is something different from the humanity of Plato; therefore, they are distinguished of and by themselves and not by differences that are added to them.

Again, according to Aristotle things differing in species also differ in number, but the nature of a man and the nature of a donkey differ in species of and by themselves; therefore, they are numerically distinguished of and by themselves; therefore, each of them is numerically one of and by itself.

Again, that which cannot belong to many cannot be predicated of many; but such a nature, if it really is the same thing as the individual difference, cannot belong to many since it cannot belong to any other particular. Thus, it cannot be predicable of many; but, then, it cannot be a universal.

Again, take an individual difference and the nature which it contracts. Either the difference between these two things is greater or less than the difference between two particulars. It is not greater because they do not differ really; particulars, however, do differ really. But neither is it less because then they would admit of one and the same definition, since two particulars, can admit of the same definition. Consequently, if one of them is, by itself, one in number, the other will also be.

Again, either the nature is the individual difference or it is not. If it is the difference I argue as follows: this individual difference is proper and not common; this individual difference is this nature; therefore this nature is proper and not common, but that is what I set out to prove. Likewise, I argue as follows: the individual difference is not formally distinct from the individual difference; the individual difference is the nature; therefore, the nature is not formally distinct from the individual difference. But if it be said that the individual difference is not the nature, my point has been proved; for it follows that if the individual difference is not the nature, the individual difference is not really the nature; for from the opposite of the consequent follows the opposite of the antecedent. Thus, if it is true that the individual difference really is the nature, then the individual difference is the nature. The inference is valid, for from a determinable taken with its determination (where the determination does not detract from or diminish the determinable) one can infer the determinable taken by itself; but "really" does not express a determination that detracts or diminishes. Therefore, it follows that if the individual difference is really the nature, the individual difference is the nature.

Therefore, one should grant that in created things there is no such thing as a formal distinction. All things which are distinct in creatures are really distinct and, therefore, different things. In regard to creatures modes of argument like the following ought never be denied: this is *A;* this is *B;* therefore, *B* is *A;* and this is not *A;* this is *B;* therefore, *B* is not *A*. Likewise, one ought never deny that, as regards creatures, there are distinct things where contradictory notions hold. The only exception would be the case where contradictory notions hold true because of some syncategorematic element or similar determination, but in the same present case this is not so.

Therefore, we ought to say with the philosophers that in a particular substance there is nothing substantial except the particular form, the particular matter, or the composite of the two. And, therefore, no one ought to think that in Socrates there is a humanity or a human nature which is distinct from Socrates and to which there is added an individual difference which contracts that nature. The only thing in Socrates which can be construed as substantial is this particular matter, this particular form, or the composite of the two. And, therefore, every essence and quiddity and whatever belongs to substance, if it is really outside the soul, is just matter, form, or the composite of these or, following the doctrine of the Peripatetics, a separated and immaterial substance.

Giovanni Pico della Mirandola
1463–1494

In the late 1300s, some Italian thinkers began to talk about a rebirth or "renaissance." They wrote disparagingly of the "Middle" or "Dark Ages," depicting that time as a period of barbarian ignorance from which they had just emerged. They saw themselves as awakening to their classical past and continuing the civilizing work of the ancient Greeks and Romans.

Although few scholars today would accept this self-characterization, there was something different about the late-medieval/early-modern period. Whereas the medievals had access to some classical texts, the Renaissance thinkers had a wide, and often contradictory, variety of ancient Greek and Roman works. Whereas the philosophers of the Middle Ages tended to use ancient materials to reinforce their Christian beliefs, the early-modern thinkers found new uses for these ancient texts. But most important, whereas the Middle Ages tended to be vertically oriented, focusing on God and God's Kingdom, the early-modern period became more and more horizontally oriented, examining the created world and celebrating its most important inhabitants, human beings.

The person who most typifies this use of ancient texts to express the importance and "dignity of man" is Count Giovanni Pico della Mirandola. Pico was born in Mirandola, near Ferrara, northern Italy. The son of a minor Italian prince, his education included a variety of subjects and a diversity of institutions. In 1477, he went to the University of Bologna to study canon (church) law. After two years, he moved to study philosophy at the universities of Ferrara and Padua. Finally in 1482, he concluded his studies by examining Hebrew and Arabic thought while in Florence and Paris.

Pico believed it was possible to reconcile the seeming contradictions among the various systems of thought he had studied. Drawing out what he considered the best in each thinker and system he encountered, he developed a philosophy known as "syncretism." Syncretism holds that all schools of philosophy have some truth and so should be examined and defended; but no system of thought has all the truth, and so one must also expose the errors in each scheme.

Applying his philosophy of syncretism, in 1486 Pico drew up a list of nine hundred true theses (or propositions), using various Greek, Arabic, Hebrew, and Roman thinkers who summarized his views. He invited scholars from all over Europe to come to Rome, where he would defend his positions against all challengers. However, the disputation never occurred. Pope Innocent VIII suspended the debate and appointed a commission to investigate the nine hundred theses. Seven of the propositions were subsequently declared unorthodox and six more held to be dangerous. Pico publicly protested the decision by publishing a defense of his positions. This succeeded only in infuriating the pope. The pope condemned all nine hundred propositions, reportedly commenting, "That young man wants someone to burn him." Pico fled to France but was arrested there by papal envoys. Through the intervention of friends in Italy, Pico was released by the French king. He spent the rest of his short life in Florence under the protection of the powerful Medici family.

The *Oration on the Dignity of Man* was intended as an introductory speech for the proposed debate in Rome. In the selection reprinted here, translated by Charles Glenn Wallis, Pico exhibits his syncretistic willingness to draw from many different sources. Quoting from a wide variety of writings, he argues that God has given all creatures besides humans a unique, fixed nature. They have a certain kind of being that they cannot change. But we as human beings do not have a given being—we alone have the freedom to choose what we will become. Even though we can choose to become animals or "couch potatoes" or angelic philosophers, it is the ability to *choose* that gives us dignity.

* * *

Pico's life was chronicled by his nephew in the difficult-to-find Giovanni Francesco Pico, *Giovanni Pico della Mirandola: His Life by His Nephew Giovanni Francesco Pico,* translated by Sir Thomas More, edited by J.M. Rigg (London: D. Nutt, 1890). For a general overview of Pico, see William G. Craven, *Giovanni Pico della Mirandola, Symbol of His Age: Modern Interpretations of a Renaissance Philosopher* (Geneve: Droz, 1981). For a collection of essays, see M.V. Doughtery, ed., *Pico della Mirandola: New Essays* (Cambridge: Cambridge University Press, 2008).

For collections of primary source readings in Renaissance philosophy, see Ernst Cassirer, Paul O. Kristeller, and John H. Randall, Jr., eds., *The Renaissance Philosophy of Man* (Chicago: University of Chicago Press, 1948), and Arturo B. Fallico and Herman Shapiro, eds., *Renaissance Philosophy,* two volumes (New York: Random House, 1967–1969). For general studies of Renaissance thought, see Ernst Cassirer, *The Individual and Cosmos in Renaissance Philosophy,* translated by Mario Domandi (New York: Harper & Row, 1963); Paul O. Kristeller, *Renaissance Thought and Its Sources* (New York: Columbia University Press, 1979); Charles B. Schmitt, Quentin Skinner, and Eckhard Kessler, eds., *The Cambridge History of Renaissance Philosophy* (Cambridge: Cambridge University Press, 1988); and Brian P. Copenhaver and Charles B. Schmitt, *Renaissance Philosophy,* Vol. 3 of *History of Western Philosophy* (Oxford: Oxford University Press, 1992).

ORATION ON THE DIGNITY OF MAN (in part)

Now the highest Father, God the master-builder, had, by the laws of his secret wisdom, fabricated this house, this world which we see, a very superb temple of divinity. He had adorned the super-celestial region with minds. He had animated the celestial globes with eternal souls; he had filled with a diverse throng of animals the cast-off and residual parts of the lower world. But, with the work finished, the Artisan desired that there be someone to reckon up the reason of such a big work, to love its beauty, and to wonder at its greatness. Accordingly, now that all things had been completed, as Moses and Timaeus testify, He lastly considered creating man. But there was nothing in the archetypes from which He could mold a new sprout, nor anything in His storehouses which He could bestow as a heritage upon a new son, nor was there an empty judiciary seat where this contemplator of the universe could sit. Everything was filled up; all things had been laid out in the highest, the lowest, and the middle orders. But it did not belong to the paternal power to have failed in the final parturition, as though exhausted by childbearing; it did not belong to wisdom, in a case of necessity, to have been tossed back and forth through want of a plan; it did not belong to the lovingkindness which was going to praise divine liberality in others to be forced to condemn itself. Finally, the best of workmen decided that that to which nothing of its very own could be given should be, in composite fashion, whatsoever had belonged individually to each and every thing. Therefore He took up man, a work of indeterminate form; and, placing him at the midpoint of the world, He spoke to him as follows:

"We have given to thee, Adam, no fixed seat, no form of thy very own, no gift peculiarly thine, that thou mayest feel as thine own, have as thine own, possess as thine own the seat, the form, the gifts which thou thyself shalt desire. A limited nature in other creatures is confined within the laws written down by Us. In conformity with thy free judgment, in whose hands I have placed thee, thou art confined by no bounds; and thou wilt fix limits of nature for thyself. I have placed thee at the center of the world, that from there thou mayest more conveniently look around and see whatsoever is in the world. Neither heavenly nor earthly, neither mortal nor immortal have We made thee. Thou, like a judge appointed for being honorable, art the molder and maker of thyself; thou mayest sculpt thyself into whatever shape thou dost prefer. Thou canst grow downward into the lower natures which are brutes. Thou canst again grow upward from thy soul's reason into the higher natures which are divine."

O great liberality of God the Father! O great and wonderful happiness of man! It is given him to have that which he chooses and to be that which he wills. As soon as brutes are born, they bring with them, "from their dam's bag," as Lucilius, says, what they are going to possess. Highest spirits have been, either from the beginning or soon after, that which they are going to be throughout everlasting eternity. At man's birth the Father placed in him every sort of seed and sprouts of every kind of life. The seeds that each man cultivates will grow and bear their fruit in him. If he cultivates vegetable

Pico della Mirandola, *On the Dignity of Man,* translated by Charles Glenn Wallis (Englewood Cliffs, NJ: Prentice Hall, 1985).

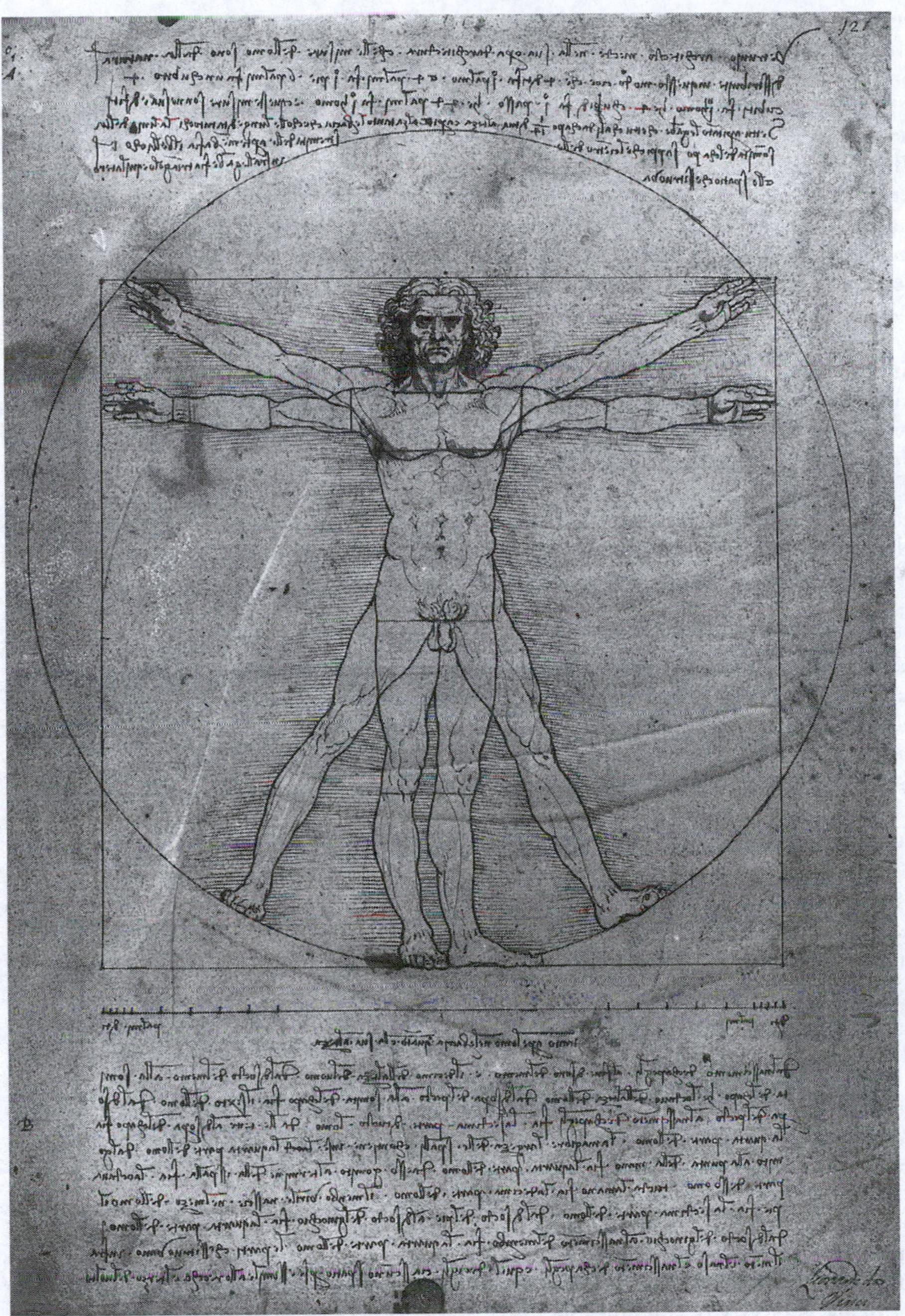

Study of Human Proportions, by Leonardo da Vinci (1452–1519). Like Pico, Leonardo enjoyed the patronage of Lorenzo de Medici; and also like Pico, Leonardo celebrated the "dignity of man" and exuberantly exhibited his own ability. (© *Alinari/Art Resource, NY*)

seeds, he will become a plant. If the seeds of sensation, he will grow into brute. If rational, he will come out a heavenly animal. If intellectual, he will be an angel, and a son of God. And if he is not contented with the lot of any creature but takes himself up into the center of his own unity, then, made one spirit with God and settled in the solitary darkness of the Father, who is above all things, he will stand ahead of all things. Who does not wonder at this chameleon which we are? Or who at all feels more wonder at anything else whatsoever? It was not unfittingly that Asclepius the Athenian said that man was symbolized by Prometheus in the secret rites, by reason of our nature sloughing its skin and transforming itself; hence metamorphoses were popular among the Jews and the Pythagoreans. For the more secret Hebrew theology at one time reshapes holy Enoch into an angel of divinity, whom they call *malach hashechina,* and at other times reshapes other men into other divinities. According to the Pythagoreans, wicked men are deformed into brutes and, if you believe Empedocles, into plants too. And copying them, Mohammed often had it on his lips that he who draws back from divine law becomes a brute. And his saying so was reasonable: for it is not the rind which makes the plant, but a dull and non-sentient nature; not the hide which makes a beast of burden, but a brutal and sensual soul; not the spherical body which makes the heavens, but right reason; and not a separateness from the body but a spiritual intelligence which makes an angel. For example, if you see a man given over to his belly and crawling upon the ground, it is a bush not a man that you see. If you see anyone blinded by the illusions of his empty and Calypso-like imagination, seized by the desire of scratching, and delivered over to the senses, it is a brute not a man that you see. If you come upon a philosopher winnowing out all things by right reason, he is a heavenly not an earthly animal. If you come upon a pure contemplator, ignorant of the body, banished to the innermost places of the mind, he is not an earthly, not a heavenly animal; he more superbly is a divinity clothed with human flesh.

Who is there that does not wonder at man? And it is not unreasonable that in the Mosaic and Christian holy writ man is sometimes denoted by the name "all flesh" and at other times by that of "every creature"; and man fashions, fabricates, transforms himself into the shape of all flesh, into the character of every creature. Accordingly, where Evantes the Persian tells of the Chaldaean theology, he writes that man is not any inborn image of himself, but many images coming in from the outside: hence that saying of the Chaldaeans: *enosh hu shinuy vekamah tevaoth baal chayim,* that is, man is an animal of diverse, multiform, and destructible nature.

But why all this? In order for us to understand that, after having been born in this state so that we may be what we will to be, then, since we are held in honor, we ought to take particular care that no one may say against us that we do not know that we are made similar to brutes and mindless beasts of burden. But rather, as Asaph the prophet says: "Ye are all gods, and sons of the most high," unless by abusing the very indulgent liberality of the Father, we make the free choice, which he gave to us, harmful to ourselves instead of helpful toward salvation. Let a certain holy ambition invade the mind, so that we may not be content with mean things but may aspire to the highest things and strive with all our forces to attain them: for if we will to, we can. Let us spurn earthly things; let us struggle toward the heavenly. Let us put in last place whatever is of the world; and let us fly beyond the chambers of the world to the chamber nearest the most lofty divinity. There, as the sacred mysteries reveal, the seraphim, cherubim, and thrones occupy the first places. Ignorant of how to yield to them and unable to endure the second places, let us compete with the angels in dignity and glory. When we have willed it, we shall be not at all below them.

MODERN PHILOSOPHY

To a large extent, modern philosophy begins with a rejection of tradition. Whereas medieval philosophers such as Thomas Aquinas had taken great pains to incorporate and reconcile ancient writings, early modern philosophers such as René Descartes encouraged their readers to make a clean sweep of the past. Previous thinkers had been deluded by errors in thinking or had relied too heavily on authority. In the modern age, the wisdom of the past was to be discarded as error-prone. As Descartes observed in his *Meditations*,

> Some years ago I was struck by the large number of falsehoods that I had accepted as true in my childhood, and by the highly doubtful nature of the whole edifice that I had subsequently based on them. I realized that it was necessary, once in the course of my life, to demolish everything completely and start again right from the foundations if I wanted to establish anything at all in the sciences that was stable and likely to last.

This quest to establish a stable intellectual foundation on which to build something "likely to last" characterized seventeenth- and eighteenth-century European philosophy. "British Empiricists," such as Thomas Hobbes, John Locke, and David Hume found such a foundation in sensory experience and developed their thought on that basis. On the other hand, the "Continent Rationalists," philosophers such as Descartes, Baruch Spinoza, and Gottfried Leibniz, thought the senses inadequate for such a task. They considered reason superior to experience and sought to establish their philosophies on the basis of more certain principles. The greatest of the modern philosophers, Immanuel Kant, sought to combine these two approaches and in so doing developed a uniquely influential system of philosophy.

Contemporary thinkers in the West are still trying to come to grips with these modern philosophers. For better or for worse, their ideas have influenced virtually all areas of Euro-American civilization. The subtlety and clarity with which these thinkers wrote continues to demand careful study even in this "postmodern" age.

* * *

There are a number of fine introductions to modern philosophy. Among the classics in this area are Étienne Gilson, *Modern Philosophy: Descartes to Kant* (New York: Random House, 1963); the appropriate works from Frederick Copleston, *A History of Philosophy, Volume IV: Descartes to Leibniz; Volume V: Hobbes to Hume;* and *Volume VI: Wolff to Kant* (1950; reprinted New York: Image Doubleday, 1959–1960); and W.T. Jones' books, *Hobbes to Hume*, 2nd edition and *Kant and the Nineteenth Century*, 2nd edition, revised (both New York: Harcourt, Brace & World, 1969 and 1975). More recent general surveys include Roger Scruton, *A Short History of Modern Philosophy: From Descartes to Wittgenstein* (London: Routledge, 1984), Wallace I. Matson, *A New History of Philosophy, Volume II: Modern* (San Diego, CA: Harcourt Brace Jovanovich, 1987); Jeffrey Tlumak, *Classical Modern Philosophy* (London: Routledge, 2006); and Anthony Kenny, *The Rise of Modern Philosophy: A New History of Western Philosophy* (Oxford: Oxford University Press, 2006). The following volumes from the *Routledge History of Philosophy* series include essays on this period: G.H.R. Parkinson, ed., *Volume 4: The Renaissance and Seventeenth Century Rationalism*; Stuart Brown, ed., *Volume 5: British Empiricism and the Enlightenment*; and Robert Solomon and Kathleen Higgins, eds., *Volume 6: The Age of German Idealism* (all London: Routledge, 1993), as does Steven Nadler, ed., *A Companion to Early Modern Philosophy* (London: Routledge, 2002). A sampling of the many specialized books on specific topics from this era includes Louis E. Loeb, *From Descartes to Hume: Continental Metaphysics and the Development of Modern Philosophy* (Ithaca, NY: Cornell University Press, 1981); Robert C. Solomon, *Continental Philosophy Since 1750: The Rise and Fall of the Self* (Oxford: Oxford University Press, 1988); and Iain Hampshire-Monk, *A History of Modern Political Thought* (Oxford: Blackwell, 1992).

René Descartes
1596–1650

René Descartes was born into the family of a minor noble in the town of La Haye in Touraine, France. At age 10, René began a nine-year course of studies at the Royal Jesuit College of La Flèche. There he studied the humanities, theology, and philosophy (which included morals, logic, mathematics, metaphysics, and science). Though he did well in school, he was disillusioned by the uncertainty of his studies and their contradictory conclusions. Like many modern students, he felt overwhelmed by the multitude of opinions he encountered. He later wrote in his *Discourse on Method* that upon completing his course of study, "I found myself embarrassed with so many doubts and errors that it seemed to me that the effort to instruct myself had no effect other than the increasing discovery of my own ignorance."

However, there was one discipline in which he found the certainty he was seeking: mathematics. The truths of mathematics were assured regardless of one's metaphysical or epistemological assumptions: $2 + 2 = 4$ whether one is a Platonist or an Aristotelian; $3 \times 3 = 9$ whether one is a Roman Catholic or a Protestant. Given mathematical certainty, Descartes found it odd that on such a firm basis "no loftier edifice had been reared."

Left a modest inheritance by his father, Descartes spent the rest of his life seeking the certainty not found in college. After receiving a law degree at Poitiers in 1616, he served as a gentleman volunteer in the army of Maurice of Nassau. While soldiering, he began to develop the idea of connecting mathematical certainty with philosophy. In 1619, he had a series of dreams convincing him that the "spirit of truth" was leading him and that he had divine approval for his studies. For the next ten years, while traveling and serving in the army, he developed his ideas. In 1628, he had a debate with Chandoux, a scientist who claimed that science could be founded only on probability. Descartes argued eloquently that knowledge must be based on certainty and that he had a system that provided that basis. Encouraged by others to develop his system, he retired to Holland, where he found a greater degree of intellectual freedom and spent the next twenty years writing and publishing his ideas. His major philosophical works include *Rules for the Direction of the Mind* (written 1628, but not published until 1701), *Discourse on Method* (published in 1637 as a preface to the essays *Geometry*, *Dioptric*, and *Meteors*), and *Meditations on First Philosophy* (1641). Descartes also published seven sets of *Objections to the Meditations* of thinkers such as Hobbes, Arnauld, and Gassendi, accompanied by his *Reply to Objections.* In addition to his work in philosophy, Descartes made major contributions to the fields of optics, anatomy, physiology, and mathematics (especially analytic geometry in which "Cartesian coordinates" are still used).

Descartes chose to write his works in French as well as Latin in order to reach beyond the academics to a wider audience. His writings did, indeed, reach learned people throughout Europe and that fact, unfortunately, led indirectly to his death. In 1649, Queen Christina of Sweden invited Descartes to join a circle of leading thinkers to instruct her in philosophy. Although he initially resisted the invitation, he finally felt compelled to accept. Upon arriving in Sweden, Descartes discovered that Queen Christina had time to see him only at five each morning. Descartes had been used to lying in bed until late in the morning, reflecting and philosophizing. Within a year, the rigorous new schedule, together with Sweden's harsh weather, led to his death.

* * *

Descartes began his philosophy by sweeping away all the "errors of the past." Whereas Bacon turned to empirical observation to escape the "tyranny" of the past, Descartes turned to mathematics, specifically geometry. He began by establishing twenty-one *Rules for the Direction of the Mind*. He would begin by finding knowledge that he could "clearly and evidently intuit, or deduce with certainty." Then he would build from this knowledge deductively, one step at a time. This procedure would parallel the geometrical method of moving with deductive certainty from postulates to axioms. His *Meditations on First Philosophy,* reprinted here (complete) in the outstanding John Cottingham translation, chronicles this process.

The key was to find the knowledge that he could "clearly and evidently intuit" that could serve as his starting point. Although uncertainty and doubt were the enemies, Descartes hit upon the idea of using doubt as a tool or a weapon. Instead of fighting doubt, he would use it to find certainty. He would use doubt as an acid to pour over every "truth" to see if there was anything that would not be dissolved, any "truth" that could not be doubted. Some of his doubts may seem extreme (such as that the earth may not exist or that I may be dreaming all this), but in order to find 100-percent certainty he had to find a starting point with zero-percent doubt.

After subjecting all his knowledge to the acid of doubt, he concluded that there was one thing he could not doubt: that he was doubting. The one fact the acid of doubt could not dissolve was doubt itself. This meant there had to be an "I" who was doing the doubting. Even if he were deceived about everything else, he had to exist in order to be deceived. This led Descartes to his famous statement, *Cogito ergo sum,* meaning "I think, therefore I am" (although these exact words do not appear in the *Meditations*). Here was the "clearly and evidently intuited" knowledge, the starting point, that Descartes had been seeking.

Having established that there is an "I," a self, a starting point, Descartes began to explore the nature of this "I":

> But what then am I? A thing that thinks. What is that? A thing that doubts, understands, affirms, denies, is willing, is unwilling, and also imagines and has sensory perceptions.

Among the ideas of this "thinking thing" called the "I" is the idea of a perfect God. Descartes went on to argue that nothing less than God could have caused the idea of God. He therefore concluded with a second certainty: that God exists.

From here Descartes moved to his third certainty: We have a strong tendency to believe in the existence of a reality beyond our consciousness. If there is no such external world, then we are terribly deceived. But a perfect God would not allow us to be unavoidably deceived, since deceit implies imperfection. Accordingly, we can conclude that we are not misled about those natural beliefs, such as the existence of an external world, so long as they can withstand the scrutiny of reason and are not willfully disregarded.

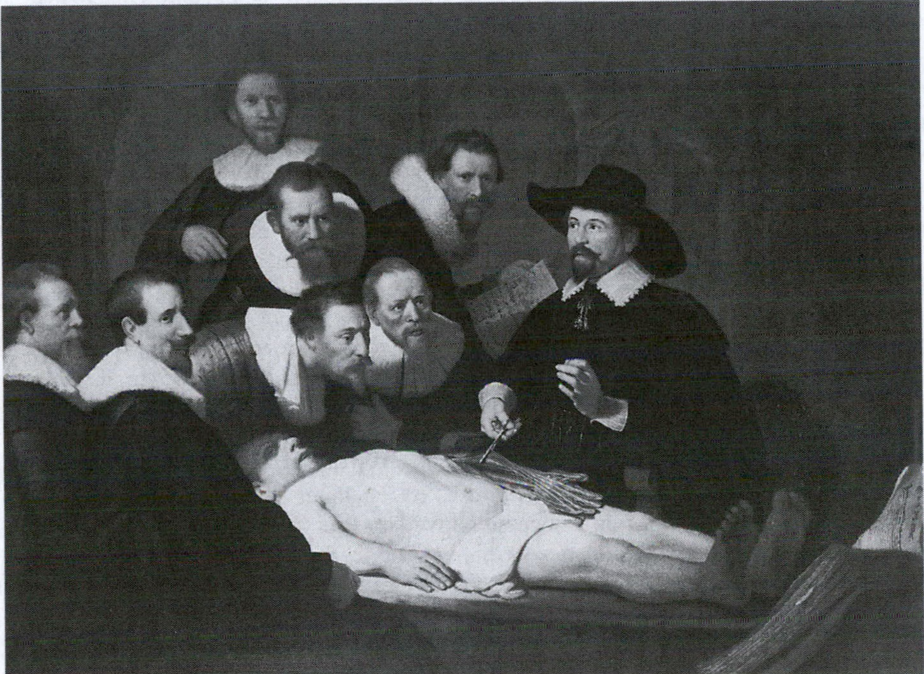

The Anatomy Lesson, 1632, by Rembrandt (1606–1669). Members of the Surgeons and Physicians Guild personify the Age of Observation with their intense scientific inquiry into human anatomy. Descartes was also interested in anatomy, making such important discoveries as that muscles work in opposition to each other. (*©Heritage Image Partnership Ltd/Alamy Stock*)

Descartes had now established a basis for accepting the "obvious" truths he had thrown out earlier by his method of doubt. He had at the same time identified the criterion needed to distinguish the foundational truths upon which his knowledge rested, namely, the criterion that a truth must be "clearly and distinctly perceived." An example of his rationalistic dependence upon such intuitions is his claim that the essential nature of a material object can only be known intuitively, not through sense perceptions.

One final point needs to be noted. The "I" that Descartes found at the end of his methodological doubting was "entirely distinct from the body." This "I" was an immaterial mind, a "spiritual" thing. The body is an "extended, non-thinking thing." As such, it is part of the material world, subject to the same laws of motion as a billiard ball. The "I," or the mind, on the other hand, is not bound by physical laws. This Cartesian distinction leads to a problem about the relationship between body and mind. One of the first to raise the issue was Princess Elizabeth of Bohemia (1618–1680). Her correspondence with Descartes, given here in the Anscombe and Geach translation, addresses questions with which we still struggle today.

* * *

For a concise treatment of Descartes' thought in its historical context, see Alexandre Koyré, "Introduction," in E. Anscombe and P.T. Geach, eds., *René Descartes' Philosophical Writings* (Edinburgh: Nelson, 1954). Among the best of several excellent general studies of Descartes are Anthony Kenny, *Descartes: A Study of His Philosophy* (New York: Random House, 1968); Margaret Dauler Wilson, *Descartes* (Oxford: Routledge, 1983); John Cottingham, *Descartes* (Oxford: Basil Blackwell, 1986); Stephen Gauktoger, *Descartes: An Intellectual Biography* (Oxford: Oxford University Press, 1995); Genevieve Rodis-Lewis, *Descartes: His Life and Thought* (Ithaca, NY: Cornell University Press, 1999); and Desmond Clark, *Descartes: A Biography* (Cambridge: Cambridge University Press, 2006). For the fascinating story of what happened to Descartes' body after his death, see Russell Shorto, *Descartes' Bones: A Skeletal History of the Conflict between Faith and Reason* (New York: Doubleday, 2008). For discussions of Descartes' *Meditations*, see L.J. Beck, *The Metaphysics of Descartes: A Study of the* Meditations (Oxford: Clarendon Press, 1965); Stanley Tweyman, ed., *Rene Descartes'* Meditations on First Philosophy *in Focus* (Oxford: Routledge, 1993); Gary Hatfield, *Routledge Philosophy Guidebook to Descartes'* Meditations (London: Routledge, 2002); Catherine Wilson, *Descartes'* Meditations (Cambridge: Cambridge University Press, 2003); Janet Broughton, *Descartes's Method of Doubt* (Princeton: Princeton University Press, 2003); Richard Francks, *Descartes'* Meditations: *A Reader's Guide* (London: Continuum, 2008); and John Carriero, *Between Two Worlds: A Reading of Descartes's* Meditations (Princeton: Princeton University Press, 2009). S. Woolhouse, *Descartes, Spinoza, Leibniz: The Concept of Substance in Seventeenth-Century Metaphysics* (London: Routledge, 1993) provides a comparative study, whereas John Cottingham, *A Descartes Dictionary* (Oxford: Basil Blackwell, 1993) provides a helpful reference work. For collections of essays on Descartes, see Willis Doney, ed., *Descartes: A Collection of Critical Essays*(Garden City, NY: Doubleday, 1967); Amelie O. Rorty, ed., *Essays on Descartes'* Meditations (Berkeley: University of California Press, 1986);

Georges J.D. Moyal, ed., *René Descartes: Critical Assessments* (London: Routledge, 1991); Vere Chappell, ed., *Essays on Early Modern Philosophers: René Descartes* (Hamden, CT: Garland, 1992); John Cottingham, ed., *The Cambridge Companion to Descartes* (Cambridge: Cambridge University Press, 1992); the multivolume George J.D. Moyal, ed., *René Descartes: Critical Assessments* (Oxford: Routledge, 1992); Stephen Voss, ed., *Essays on the Philosophy and Science of René Descartes* (Oxford: Oxford University Press, 1993); John Cottingham, ed., *Descartes* (Oxford: Oxford University Press, 1998); Tom Sorell, ed., *Descartes* (New York: Ashgate, 1999); and Paul Hoffman, ed., *Essays on Descartes* (Oxford: Oxford University Press, 2009). Gilbert Ryle, *The Concept of Mind* (London: Hutchinson's University Library, 1949) is the classic critique of Descartes' views on body and mind, while Marleen Rozemond, *Descartes' Dualism* (Cambridge, MA: Harvard University Press, 1998); Lilli Alanen, *Descartes's Concept of Mind* (Cambridge, MA: Harvard University Press, 2003); and Desmond Clarke, *Descarte's Theory of Mind* (Oxford: Oxford University Press, 2003) are more recent studies.

MEDITATIONS ON THE FIRST PHILOSOPHY

[Dedicatory letter to the Sorbonne]

To those most learned and distinguished men, the Dean and Doctors of the Sacred Faculty of Theology at Paris, from René Descartes. 1

I have a very good reason for offering this book to you, and I am confident that you will have an equally good reason for giving it your protection once you understand the principle behind my undertaking; so much so, that my best way of commending it to you will be to tell you briefly of the goal which I shall be aiming at in the book.

I have always thought that two topics—namely God and the soul—are prime examples of subjects where demonstrative proofs ought to be given with the aid of philosophy rather than theology. For us who are believers, it is enough to accept on faith that the human soul does not die with the body, and that God exists; but in the case of 2
unbelievers, it seems that there is no religion, and practically no moral virtue, that they can be persuaded to adopt until these two truths are proved to them by natural reason. And since in this life the rewards offered to vice are often greater than the rewards of virtue, few people would prefer what is right to what is expedient if they did not fear God or have the expectation of an after-life. It is of course quite true that we must believe in the existence of God because it is a doctrine of Holy Scripture, and conversely, that we must believe Holy Scripture because it comes from God; for since faith

is the gift of God, he who gives us grace to believe other things can also give us grace to believe that he exists. But this argument cannot be put to unbelievers because they would judge it to be circular. Moreover, I have noticed both that you and all other theologians assert that the existence of God is capable of proof by natural reason, and also that the inference from Holy Scripture is that the knowledge of God is easier to acquire than the knowledge we have of many created things—so easy, indeed, that those who do not acquire it are at fault. This is clear from a passage in the Book of Wisdom, Chapter 13: "Howbeit they are not to be excused; for if their knowledge was so great that they could value this world, why did they not rather find out the Lord thereof?" And in Romans, Chapter I it is said that they are "without excuse." And in the same place, in the passage "that which is known of God is manifest in them," we seem to be told that everything that may be known of God can be demonstrated by reasoning which has no other source but our own mind. Hence I thought it was quite proper for me to inquire how this may be, and how God may be more easily and more certainly known than the things of this world.

3 As regards the soul, many people have considered that it is not easy to discover its nature, and some have even had the audacity to assert that, as far as human reasoning goes, there are persuasive grounds for holding that the soul dies along with the body and that the opposite view is based on faith alone. But in its eighth session the Lateran Council held under Leo X condemned those who take this position,* and expressly enjoined Christian philosophers to refute their arguments and use all their powers to establish the truth; so I have not hesitated to attempt this task as well.

In addition, I know that the only reason why many irreligious people are unwilling to believe that God exists and that the human mind is distinct from the body is the alleged fact that no one has hitherto been able to demonstrate these points. Now I completely disagree with this: I think that when properly understood almost all the arguments that have been put forward on these issues by the great men have the force of demonstrations, and I am convinced that it is scarcely possible to provide any arguments which have not already been produced by someone else. Nevertheless, I think there can be no more useful service to be rendered in philosophy than to conduct a careful search, once and for all, for the best of these arguments, and to set them out so precisely and clearly as to produce for the future a general agreement that they amount to demonstrative proofs. And finally, I was strongly pressed to undertake this task by several people who knew that I had developed a method for resolving certain difficulties in the sciences—not a new method (for nothing is older than the truth), but one which they had seen me use with some success in other areas; and I therefore thought it my duty to make some attempt to apply it to the matter in hand.

4 The present treatise contains everything that I have been able to accomplish in this area. Not that I have attempted to collect here all the different arguments that could be put forward to establish the same results, for this does not seem worthwhile except in cases where no single argument is regarded as sufficiently reliable. What I have done is to take merely the principal and most important arguments and develop them in such a way that I would now venture to put them forward as very certain and evident demonstrations. I will add that these proofs are of such a kind that I reckon they leave no room for the possibility that the human mind will ever discover better ones. The vital importance of the cause and the glory of God, to which the entire

*The Lateran Council of 1513 condemned the Averroist heresy that denied personal immortality.

undertaking is directed, here compel me to speak somewhat more freely about my own achievements than is my custom. But although I regard the proofs as quite certain and evident, I cannot therefore persuade myself that they are suitable to be grasped by everyone. In geometry there are many writings left by Archimedes, Apollonius, Pappus, and others which are accepted by everyone as evident and certain because they contain absolutely nothing that is not very easy to understand when considered on its own, and each step fits in precisely with what has gone before; yet because they are somewhat long, and demand a very attentive reader, it is only comparatively few people who understand them. In the same way, although the proofs I employ here are in my view as certain and evident as the proofs of geometry, if not more so, it will, I fear, be impossible for many people to achieve an adequate perception of them, both because they are rather long and some depend on others, and also, above all, because they require a mind which is completely free from preconceived opinions and which can easily detach itself from involvement with the senses. Moreover, people who have an aptitude for metaphysical studies are certainly not to be found in the world in any greater numbers than those who have an aptitude for geometry. What is more, there is 5
the difference that in geometry everyone has been taught to accept that as a rule no proposition is put forward in a book without there being a conclusive demonstration available; so inexperienced students make the mistake of accepting what is false, in their desire to appear to understand it, more often than they make the mistake of rejecting what is true. In philosophy, by contrast, the belief is that everything can be argued either way; so few people pursue the truth, while the great majority build up their reputation for ingenuity by boldly attacking whatever is most sound.

Hence, whatever the quality of my arguments may be, because they have to do with philosophy I do not expect they will enable me to achieve any very worthwhile results unless you come to my aid by granting me your patronage.* The reputation of your Faculty is so firmly fixed in the minds of all, and the name of the Sorbonne has such authority that, with the exception of the Sacred Councils, no institution carries more weight than yours in matters of faith; while as regards human philosophy, you are thought of as second to none, both for insight and soundness and also for the integrity and wisdom of your pronouncements. Because of this, the results of your careful attention to this book, if you deigned to give it, would be threefold. First, the errors in it would be corrected—for when I remember not only that I am a human being, but above all that I am an ignorant one, I cannot claim it is free of mistakes. Secondly, any passages which are defective, or insufficiently developed or requiring further explanation, would be supplemented, completed and clarified, either by yourselves or by me after you have given me your advice. And lastly, once the arguments in the book proving that God exists and that the mind is distinct from the body have been brought, as I am sure they can be, to such a pitch of clarity that they are fit to be regarded as very exact 6
demonstrations, you may be willing to declare as much, and make a public statement to that effect. If all this were to happen, I do not doubt that all the errors which have ever existed on these subjects would soon be eradicated from the minds of men. In the case of all those who share your intelligence and learning, the truth itself will readily ensure that they subscribe to your opinion. As for the atheists, who are generally posers rather than people of real intelligence or learning, your authority will induce them to lay aside the spirit of contradiction; and, since they know that the arguments are regarded as

*Although the title page of the first edition of the *Meditations* carries the words "with the approval of the learned doctors," Descartes never, in fact, obtained the endorsement from the Sorbonne which he sought.

demonstrations by all who are intellectually gifted, they may even go so far as to defend them, rather than appear not to understand them. And finally, everyone else will confidently go along with so many declarations of assent, and there will be no one left in the world who will dare to call into doubt either the existence of God or the real distinction between the human soul and body. The great advantage that this would bring is something which you, in your singular wisdom, are in a better position to evaluate than anyone; and it would ill become me to spend any more time commending the cause of God and religion to you, who have always been the greatest tower of strength to the Catholic Church.

7 PREFACE TO READER

I briefly touched on the topics of God and the human mind in my *Discourse on the method of rightly conducting reason and seeking the truth in the sciences*, which was published in French in 1637. My purpose there was not to provide a full treatment, but merely to offer a sample, and learn from the views of my readers how I should handle these topics at a later date. The issues seemed to me of such great importance that I considered they ought to be dealt with more than once; and the route which I follow in explaining them is so untrodden and so remote from the normal way, that I thought it would not be helpful to give a full account of it in a book written in French and designed to be read by all and sundry, in case weaker intellects might believe that they ought to set out on the same path.

In the *Discourse* I asked anyone who found anything worth criticizing in what I had written to be kind enough to point it out to me. In the case of my remarks concerning God and the soul, only two objections worth mentioning were put to me, which I shall now briefly answer before embarking on a more precise elucidation of these topics.

8 The first objection is this. From the fact that the human mind, when directed towards itself, does not perceive itself to be anything other than a thinking thing, it does not follow that its nature or essence consists only in its being a thinking thing, where the word "only" excludes everything else that could be said to belong to the nature of the soul. My answer to this objection is that in that passage it was not my intention to make those exclusions in an order corresponding to the actual truth of the matter (which I was not dealing with at that stage) but merely in an order corresponding to my own perception. So the sense of the passage was that I was aware of nothing at all that I knew belonged to my essence, except that I was a thinking thing, or a thing possessing within itself the faculty of thinking. I shall, however, show below how it follows from the fact that I am aware of nothing else belonging to my essence, that nothing else does in fact belong to it.

The second objection is this. From the fact that I have within me an idea of a thing more perfect than myself, it does not follow that the idea itself is more perfect than me, still less that what is represented by the idea exists. My reply is that there is an ambiguity here in the word "idea." "Idea" can be taken materially, as an operation of the intellect, in which case it cannot be said to be more perfect than me. Alternatively, it can be taken objectively, as the thing represented by that operation; and this thing, even if it is not regarded as existing outside the intellect, can still, in virtue of its essence, be more perfect than myself. As to how, from the mere fact that there is within me an idea of something more perfect than me, it follows that this thing really exists, this is something which will be fully explained below.

Apart from these objections, there are two fairly lengthy essays which I have looked at, but these did not attack my reasoning on these matters so much as my conclusions, and employed arguments lifted from the standard sources of the atheists. But arguments of this sort can carry no weight with those who understand my reasoning. 9
Moreover, the judgement of many people is so silly and weak that, once they have accepted a view, they continue to believe it, however false and irrational it may be, in preference to a true and well-grounded refutation which they hear subsequently. So I do not wish to reply to such arguments here, if only to avoid having to state them. I will only make the general point that all the objections commonly tossed around by atheists to attack the existence of God invariably depend either on attributing human feelings to God or on arrogantly supposing our own minds to be so powerful and wise that we can attempt to grasp and set limits to what God can or should perform. So, provided only that we remember that our minds must be regarded as finite, while God is infinite and beyond our comprehension, such objections will not cause us any difficulty.

But now that I have, after a fashion, taken an initial sample of people's opinions, I am again tackling the same questions concerning God and the human mind; and this time I am also going to deal with the foundations of First Philosophy in its entirety. But I do not expect any popular approval, or indeed any wide audience. On the contrary I would not urge anyone to read this book except those who are able and willing to meditate seriously with me, and to withdraw their minds from the senses and from all preconceived opinions. Such readers, as I well know, are few and far between. Those who do not bother to grasp the proper order of my arguments and the connection between them, but merely try to carp at individual sentences, as is the fashion, will not 10
get much benefit from reading this book. They may well find an opportunity to quibble in many places, but it will not be easy for them to produce objections which are telling or worth replying to.

But I certainly do not promise to satisfy my other readers straightaway on all points, and I am not so presumptuous as to believe that I am capable of foreseeing all the difficulties which anyone may find. So first of all, in the *Meditations*, I will set out the very thoughts which have enabled me, in my view, to arrive at a certain and evident knowledge of the truth, so that I can find out whether the same arguments which have convinced me will enable me to convince others. Next, I will reply to the objections of various men of outstanding intellect and scholarship who had these *Meditations* sent to them for scrutiny before they went to press. For the objections they raised were so many and so varied that I would venture to hope that it will be hard for anyone else to think of any point—at least of any importance—which these critics have not touched on. I therefore ask my readers not to pass judgement on the *Meditations* until they have been kind enough to read through all these objections and my replies to them.

SYNOPSIS OF FOLLOWING SIX MEDITATIONS 12

In the First Meditation reasons are provided which give us possible grounds for doubt about all things, especially material things, so long as we have no foundations for the sciences other than those which we have had up till now. Although the usefulness of such extensive doubt is not apparent at first sight, its greatest benefit lies in freeing us from all our preconceived opinions, and providing the easiest route by which the mind may be led away from the senses. The eventual result of this doubt is to make it impossible for us to have any further doubts about what we subsequently discover to be true.

In the Second Meditation, the mind uses its own freedom and supposes the non-existence of all the things about whose existence it can have even the slightest doubt; and in so doing the mind notices that it is impossible that it should not itself exist during this time. This exercise is also of the greatest benefit, since it enables the mind to distinguish without difficulty what belongs to itself, i.e. to an intellectual nature, from what belongs to the body. But since some people may perhaps expect arguments for the immortality of the soul in this section, I think they should be
13 warned here and now that I have tried not to put down anything which I could not precisely demonstrate. Hence the only order which I could follow was that normally employed by geometers, namely to set out all the premisses on which a desired proposition depends, before drawing any conclusions about it. Now the first and most important prerequisite for knowledge of the immortality of the soul is for us to form a concept of the soul which is as clear as possible and is also quite distinct from every concept of body; and that is just what has been done in this section. A further requirement is that we should know that everything that we clearly and distinctly understand is true in a way which corresponds exactly to our understanding of it; but it was not possible to prove this before the Fourth Meditation. In addition we need to have a distinct concept of corporeal nature, and this is developed partly in the Second Meditation itself, and partly in the Fifth and Sixth Meditations. The inference to be drawn from these results is that all the things that we clearly and distinctly conceive of as different substances (as we do in the case of mind and body) are in fact substances which are really distinct one from the other; and this conclusion is drawn in the Sixth Meditation. This conclusion is confirmed in the same Meditation by the fact that we cannot understand a body except as being divisible, while by contrast we cannot understand a mind except as being indivisible. For we cannot conceive of half of a mind, while we can always conceive of half of a body, however small; and this leads us to recognize that the natures of mind and body are not only different, but in some way opposite. But I have not pursued this topic any further in this book, first because these arguments are enough to show that the decay of the body does not imply the destruction of the mind, and are hence enough to give mortals the hope of an afterlife, and secondly because the premisses which lead to the conclusion that the soul is
14 immortal depend on an account of the whole of physics. This is required for two reasons. First, we need to know that absolutely all substances, or things which must be created by God in order to exist, are by their nature incorruptible and cannot ever cease to exist unless they are reduced to nothingness by God's denying his concurrence* to them. Secondly, we need to recognize that body, taken in the general sense, is a substance, so that it too never perishes. But the human body, in so far as it differs from other bodies, is simply made up of a certain configuration of limbs and other accidents** of this sort; whereas the human mind is not made up of any accidents in

*The continuous divine action necessary to maintain things in existence.

**Descartes here uses this scholastic term to refer to those features of a thing which may alter, e.g. the particular size, shape, etc. of a body, or the particular thoughts, desires, etc. of a mind.

this way, but is a pure substance. For even if all the accidents of the mind change, so that it has different objects of the understanding and different desires and sensations, it does not on that account become a different mind; whereas a human body loses its identity merely as a result of a change in the shape of some of its parts. And it follows from this that while the body can very easily perish, the mind* is immortal by its very nature.

In the Third Meditation I have explained quite fully enough, I think, my principal argument for proving the existence of God. But in order to draw my readers' minds away from the senses as far as possible, I was not willing to use any comparison taken from bodily things. So it may be that many obscurities remain; but I hope they will be completely removed later, in my Replies to the Objections. One such problem, among others, is how the idea of a supremely perfect being, which is in us, possesses so much objective reality that it can come only from a cause which is supremely perfect. In the Replies this is illustrated by the comparison of a very perfect machine, the idea of which is in the mind of some engineer. Just as the objective intricacy belonging to the idea must have some cause, namely the scientific knowledge of the engineer, or of someone else who passed the idea on to him, so the idea of God which is in us must have God 15
himself as its cause.

In the Fourth Meditation it is proved that everything that we clearly and distinctly perceive is true, and I also explain what the nature of falsity consists in. These results need to be known both in order to confirm what has gone before and also to make intelligible what is to come later. (But here it should be noted in passing that I do not deal at all with sin, i.e. the error which is committed in pursuing good and evil, but only with the error that occurs in distinguishing truth from falsehood. And there is no discussion of matters pertaining to faith or the conduct of life, but simply of speculative truths which are known solely by means of the natural light.)

In the Fifth Meditation, besides an account of corporeal nature taken in general, there is a new argument demonstrating the existence of God. Again, several difficulties may arise here, but these are resolved later in the Replies to the Objections. Finally I explain the sense in which it is true that the certainty even of geometrical demonstrations depends on the knowledge of God.

Lastly, in the Sixth Meditation, the intellect is distinguished from the imagination; the criteria for this distinction are explained; the mind is proved to be really distinct from the body, but is shown, notwithstanding, to be so closely joined to it that the mind and the body make up a kind of unit; there is a survey of all the errors which commonly come from the senses, and an explanation of how they may be avoided; and, lastly, there is a presentation of all the arguments which enable the existence of material things to be inferred. The great benefit of these arguments is not, in my view, that they prove what they establish—namely that there really is a world, and that human beings have bodies 16
and so on—since no sane person has ever seriously doubted these things. The point is that in considering these arguments we come to realize that they are not as solid or as transparent as the arguments which lead us to knowledge of our own minds and of God, so that the latter are the most certain and evident of all possible objects of knowledge for the human intellect. Indeed, this is the one thing that I set myself to prove in these Meditations. And for that reason I will not now go over the various other issues in the book which are dealt with as they come up.

*". . . or the soul of man, for I make no distinction between them" (added in French version).

First Meditation

What can be called into doubt

Some years ago I was struck by the large number of falsehoods that I had accepted as true in my childhood, and by the highly doubtful nature of the whole edifice that I had subsequently based on them. I realized that it was necessary, once in the course of my life, to demolish everything completely and start again right from the foundations if I wanted to establish anything at all in the sciences that was stable and likely to last. But the task looked an enormous one, and I began to wait until I should reach a mature enough age to ensure that no subsequent time of life would be more suitable for tackling such inquiries. This led me to put the project off for so long that I would now be to blame if by pondering over it any further I wasted the time still left for
18 carrying it out. So today I have expressly rid my mind of all worries and arranged for myself a clear stretch of free time. I am here quite alone, and at last I will devote myself sincerely and without reservation to the general demolition of my opinions.

But to accomplish this, it will not be necessary for me to show that all my opinions are false, which is something I could perhaps never manage. Reason now leads me to think that I should hold back my assent from opinions which are not completely certain and indubitable just as carefully as I do from those which are patently false. So, for the purpose of rejecting all my opinions, it will be enough if I find in each of them at least some reason for doubt. And to do this I will not need to run through them all individually, which would be an endless task. Once the foundations of a building are undermined, anything built on them collapses of its own accord; so I will go straight for the basic principles on which all my former beliefs rested.

Whatever I have up till now accepted as most true I have acquired either from the senses or through the senses. But from time to time I have found that the senses deceive, and it is prudent never to trust completely those who have deceived us even once.

Yet although the senses occasionally deceive us with respect to objects which are very small or in the distance, there are many other beliefs about which doubt is quite impossible, even though they are derived from the senses—for example, that I am here, sitting by the fire, wearing a winter dressing-gown, holding this piece of paper in my hands, and so on Again, how could it be denied that these hands or this whole body are
19 mine? Unless perhaps I were to liken myself to madmen, whose brains are so damaged by the persistent vapours of melancholia that they firmly maintain they are kings when they are paupers, or say they are dressed in purple when they are naked, or that their heads are made of earthenware or that they are pumpkins, or made of glass. But such people are insane and I would be thought equally mad if I took anything from them as: model for myself.

A brilliant piece of reasoning! As if I were not a man who sleeps a night, and regularly has all the same experiences while asleep a madmen do when awake—indeed sometimes even more improbable ones. How often, asleep at night, am I convinced of just such familiar events—that I am here in my dressing-gown, sitting by the fire—when in fact I am lying undressed in bed! Yet at the moment my eyes are certainly wide awake when I look at this piece of paper; I shake my head and it is not asleep; as I stretch out and feel my hand I do so deliberately, and I know what I am doing. All this would not happen with such distinctness to someone asleep. Indeed! As if I did not remember other occasions when I have been tricked by exactly similar thoughts while asleep! As I think about this more carefully, I see plainly that there are never any sure signs by means of which being awake can be distinguished from being asleep. The result is that I begin to feel dazed, and this very feeling only reinforces the notion that I may be asleep.

Suppose then that I am dreaming, and that these particulars—that my eyes are
open, that I am moving my head and stretching out my hands—are not true. Perhaps,
indeed, I do not even have such hands or such a body at all. Nonetheless, it must surely
be admitted that the visions which come in sleep are like paintings, which must have
been fashioned in the likeness of things that are real, and hence that at least these
general kinds of things—eyes, head, hands and the body as a whole—are things which
are not imaginary but are real and exist. For even when painters try to create sirens and
satyrs with the most extraordinary bodies, they cannot give them natures which are new 20
in all respects; they simply jumble up the limbs of different animals. Or if perhaps they
manage to think up something so new that nothing remotely similar has ever been seen
before—something which is therefore completely fictitious and unreal—at least the
colours used in the composition must be real. By similar reasoning, although these
general kinds of things—eyes, head, hands and so on—could be imaginary, it must at
least be admitted that certain other even simpler and more universal things are real.
These are as it were the real colours from which we form all the images of things,
whether true or false, that occur in our thought.

This class appears to include corporeal nature in general, and its extension; the shape of extended things; the quantity, or size and number of these things; the place in which they may exist, the time through which they may endure, and so on.

So a reasonable conclusion from this might be that physics, astronomy, medicine, and all other disciplines which depend on the study of composite things, are doubtful; while arithmetic, geometry and other subjects of this kind, which deal only with the simplest and most general things, regardless of whether they really exist in nature or not, contain something certain and indubitable. For whether I am awake or asleep, two and three added together are five, and a square has no more than four sides. It seems impossible that such transparent truths should incur any suspicion of being false.

And yet firmly rooted in my mind is the long-standing opinion that there is an 21
omnipotent God who made me the kind of creature that I am. How do I know that he has
not brought it about that there is no earth, no sky, no extended thing, no shape, no size,
no place, while at the same time ensuring that all these things appear to me to exist just
as they do now? What is more, since I sometimes believe that others go astray in cases
where they think they have the most perfect knowledge, may I not similarly go wrong
every time I add two and three or count the sides of a square, or in some even simpler
matter, if that is imaginable? But perhaps God would not have allowed me to be
deceived in this way, since he is said to be supremely good. But if it were inconsistent
with his goodness to have created me such that I am deceived all the time, it would seem
equally foreign to his goodness to allow me to be deceived even occasionally; yet this
last assertion cannot be made.

Perhaps there may be some who would prefer to deny the existence of so powerful a God rather than believe that everything else is uncertain. Let us not argue with them, but grant them that everything said about God is a fiction. According to their supposition, then, I have arrived at my present state by fate or chance or a continuous chain of events, or by some other means; yet since deception and error seem to be imperfections, the less powerful they make my original cause, the more likely it is that I am so imperfect as to be deceived all the time. I have no answer to these arguments, but am finally compelled to admit that there is not one of my former beliefs about which a doubt may not properly be raised; and this is not a flippant or ill-considered

22 conclusion, but is based on powerful and well thought-out reasons. So in future I must withhold my assent from these former beliefs just as carefully as I would from obvious falsehoods, if I want to discover any certainty.

But it is not enough merely to have noticed this; I must make an effort to remember it. My habitual opinions keep coming back, and, despite my wishes, they capture my belief, which is as it were bound over to them as a result of long occupation and the law of custom. I shall never get out of the habit of confidently assenting to these opinions, so long as I suppose them to be what in fact they are, namely highly probable opinions—opinions which, despite the fact that they are in a sense doubtful, as has just been shown, it is still much more reasonable to believe than to deny. In view of this, I think it will be a good plan to turn my will in completely the opposite direction and deceive myself, by pretending for a time that these former opinions are utterly false and imaginary. I shall do this until the weight of preconceived opinion is counter-balanced and the distorting influence of habit no longer prevents my judgement from perceiving things correctly. In the meantime, I know that no danger or error will result from my plan, and that I cannot possibly go too far in my distrustful attitude. This is because the task now in hand does not involve action but merely the acquisition of knowledge.

I will suppose therefore that not God, who is supremely good and the source of truth, but rather some malicious demon of the utmost power and cunning has employed all his energies in order to deceive me. I shall think that the sky, the air, the earth, colours, shapes, sounds and all external things are merely the delusions of
23 dreams which he has devised to ensnare my judgement. I shall consider myself as not having hands or eyes, or flesh, or blood or senses, but as falsely believing that I have all these things. I shall stubbornly and firmly persist in this meditation; and, even if it is not in my power to know any truth, I shall at least do what is in my power, that is, resolutely guard against assenting to any falsehoods, so that the deceiver, however powerful and cunning he may be, will be unable to impose on me in the slightest degree. But this is an arduous undertaking, and a kind of laziness brings me back to normal life. I am like a prisoner who is enjoying an imaginary freedom while asleep; as he begins to suspect that he is asleep, he dreads being woken up, and goes along with the pleasant illusion as long as he can. In the same way, I happily slide back into my old opinions and dread being shaken out of them, for fear that my peaceful sleep may be followed by hard labour when I wake, and that I shall have to toil not in the light, but amid the inextricable darkness of the problems I have now raised.

SECOND MEDITATION

The nature of the human mind, and how it is better known than the body

So serious are the doubts into which I have been thrown as a result of yesterday's meditation that I can neither put them out of my mind nor see any way of resolving
24 them. It feels as if I have fallen unexpectedly into a deep whirlpool which tumbles me around so that I can neither stand on the bottom nor swim up to the top. Nevertheless I will make an effort and once more attempt the same path which I started on yesterday. Anything which admits of the slightest doubt I will set aside just as if I had found it to be wholly false; and I will proceed in this way until I recognize something certain, or, if

nothing else, until I at least recognize for certain that there is no certainty. Archimedes used to demand just one firm and immovable point in order to shift the entire earth; so I too can hope for great things if I manage to find just one thing, however slight, that is certain and unshakeable.

I will suppose then, that everything I see is spurious. I will believe that my memory tells me lies, and that none of the things that it reports ever happened. I have no senses. Body, shape, extension, movement and place are chimeras. So what remains true? Perhaps just the one fact that nothing is certain.

Yet apart from everything I have just listed, how do I know that there is not something else which does not allow even the slightest occasion for doubt? Is there not a
God, or whatever I may call him, who puts into me the thoughts I am now having? But
why do I think this, since I myself may perhaps be the author of these thoughts? In that
case am not I, at least, something? But I have just said that I have no senses and no
body. This is the sticking point: what follows from this? Am I not so bound up with a
body and with senses that I cannot exist without them? But I have convinced myself that 25
there is absolutely nothing in the world, no sky, no earth, no minds, no bodies. Does it
now follow that I too do not exist? No: if I convinced myself of something then I certainly existed. But there is a deceiver of supreme power and cunning who is deliberately
and constantly deceiving me. In that case I too undoubtedly exist, if he is deceiving me;
and let him deceive me as much as he can, he will never bring it about that I am nothing
so long as I think that I am something. So after considering everything very thoroughly,
I must finally conclude that this proposition, *I am, I exist,* is necessarily true whenever
it is put forward by me or conceived in my mind.

But I do not yet have a sufficient understanding of what this "I" is, that now necessarily exists. So I must be on my guard against carelessly taking something else to be this "I," and so making a mistake in the very item of knowledge that I maintain is the most certain and evident of all. I will therefore go back and meditate on what I originally believed myself to be, before I embarked on this present train of thought. I will then subtract anything capable of being weakened, even minimally, by the arguments now introduced, so that what is left at the end may be exactly and only what is certain and unshakeable.

What then did I formerly think I was? A man. But what is a man? Shall I say "a
rational animal"? No; for then I should have to inquire what an animal is, what rationality is, and in this way one question would lead me down the slope to other harder ones,
and I do not now have the time to waste on subtleties of this kind. Instead I propose to
concentrate on what came into my thoughts spontaneously and quite naturally when- 26
ever I used to consider what I was. Well, the first thought to come to mind was that I had
a face, hands, arms and the whole mechanical structure of limbs which can be seen in a
corpse, and which I called the body. The next thought was that I was nourished, that
I moved about, and that I engaged in sense-perception and thinking; and these actions
I attributed to the soul. But as to the nature of this soul, either I did not think about this
or else I imagined it to be something tenuous, like a wind or fire or ether, which perme-
ated my more solid parts. As to the body, however, I had no doubts about it, but thought
I knew its nature distinctly. If I had tried to describe the mental conception I had of it,
I would have expressed it as follows: by a body I understand whatever has a determinable shape and a definable location and can occupy a space in such a way as to
exclude any other body; it can be perceived by touch, sight, hearing, taste or smell, and
can be moved in various ways, not by itself but by whatever else comes into contact
with it. For, according to my judgement, the power of self-movement, like the power of

sensation or of thought, was quite foreign to the nature of a body; indeed, it was a source of wonder to me that certain bodies were found to contain faculties of this kind.

But what shall I now say that I am, when I am supposing that there is some supremely powerful and, if it is permissible to say so, malicious deceiver, who is deliberately trying to trick me in every way he can? Can I now assert that I possess even the most insignificant of all the attributes which I have just said belong to the nature of a
27 body? I scrutinize them, think about them, go over them again, but nothing suggests itself; it is tiresome and pointless to go through the list once more. But what about the attributes I assigned to the soul? Nutrition or movement? Since now I do not have a body, these are mere fabrications. Sense-perception? This surely does not occur without a body, and besides, when asleep I have appeared to perceive through the senses many things which I afterwards realized I did not perceive through the senses at all. Thinking? At last I have discovered it—thought; this alone is inseparable from me. I am, I exist—that is certain. But for how long? For as long as I am thinking. For it could be that were I totally to cease from thinking, I should totally cease to exist. At present I am not admitting anything except what is necessarily true. I am, then, in the strict sense only a thing that thinks; that is, I am a mind, or intelligence, or intellect, or reason—words whose meaning I have been ignorant of until now. But for all that I am a thing which is real and which truly exists. But what kind of a thing? As I have just said—a thinking thing.

What else am I? I will use my imagination. I am not that structure of limbs which is called a human body. I am not even some thin vapour which permeates the limbs—a wind, fire, air, breath, or whatever I depict in my imagination; for these are things which I have supposed to be nothing. Let this supposition stand; for all that I am still something. And yet may it not perhaps be the case that these very things which I am supposing to be nothing, because they are unknown to me, are in reality identical with the "I" of which I am aware? I do not know, and for the moment I shall not argue the point, since I can make judgements only about things which are known to me. I know that I exist; the question is, what is this "I" that I know? If the "I" is understood strictly as we have been taking it, then it is quite certain that knowledge of it does not depend
28 on things of whose existence I am as yet unaware; so it cannot depend on any of the things which I invent in my imagination. And this very word "invent" shows me my mistake. It would indeed be a case of fictitious invention if I used my imagination to establish that I was something or other; for imagining is simply contemplating the shape or image of a corporeal thing. Yet now I know for certain both that I exist and at the same time that all such images and, in general, everything relating to the nature of body, could be mere dreams [and chimeras]. Once this point has been grasped, to say "I will use my imagination to get to know more distinctly what I am" would seem to be as silly as saying "I am now awake, and see some truth; but since my vision is not yet clear enough, I will deliberately fall asleep so that my dreams may provide a truer and clearer representation." I thus realize that none of the things that the imagination enables me to grasp is at all relevant to this knowledge of myself which I possess, and that the mind must therefore be most carefully diverted from such things if it is to perceive its own nature as distinctly as possible.

But what then am I? A thing that thinks. What is that? A thing that doubts, understands, affirms, denies, is willing, is unwilling, and also imagines and has sensory perceptions.

This is a considerable list, if everything on it belongs to me. But does it? Is it not one and the same "I" who is now doubting almost everything, who nonetheless understands some things, who affirms that this one thing is true, denies everything else, desires

to know more, is unwilling to be deceived, imagines many things even involuntarily, and 29
is aware of many things which apparently come from the senses? Are not all these things just as true as the fact that I exist, even if I am asleep all the time, and even if he who created me is doing all he can to deceive me? Which of all these activities is distinct from my thinking? Which of them can be said to be separate from myself? The fact that it is I who am doubting and understanding and willing is so evident that I see no way of making it any clearer. But it is also the case that the "I" who imagines is the same "I." For even if, as I have supposed, none of the objects of imagination are real, the power of imagination is something which really exists and is part of my thinking. Lastly, it is also the same "I" who has sensory perceptions, or is aware of bodily things as it were through the senses. For example, I am now seeing light, hearing a noise, feeling heat. But I am asleep, so all this is false. Yet I certainly *seem* to see, to hear, and to be warmed. This cannot be false; what is called "having a sensory perception" is strictly just this, and in this restricted sense of the term it is simply thinking.

From all this I am beginning to have a rather better understanding of what I am. But it still appears—and I cannot stop thinking this—that the corporeal things of which images are formed in my thought, and which the senses investigate, are known with much more distinctness than this puzzling "I" which cannot be pictured in the imagination. And yet it is surely surprising that I should have a more distinct grasp of things which I realize are doubtful, unknown and foreign to me, than I have of that which is true and known—my own self. But I see what it is: my mind enjoys wandering off and will not yet submit to being restrained within the bounds of truth. Very well then; just 30
this once let us give it a completely free rein, so that after a while, when it is time to tighten the reins, it may more readily submit to being curbed.

Let us consider the things which people commonly think they understand most distinctly of all; that is, the bodies which we touch and see. I do not mean bodies in general—for general perceptions are apt to be somewhat more confused—but one particular body. Let us take, for example, this piece of wax. It has just been taken from the honeycomb; it has not yet quite lost the taste of the honey; it retains some of the scent of the flowers from which it was gathered; its colour, shape and size are plain to see; it is hard, cold and can be handled without difficulty; if you rap it with your knuckle it makes a sound. In short, it has everything which appears necessary to enable a body to be known as distinctly as possible. But even as I speak, I put the wax by the fire, and look: the residual taste is eliminated, the smell goes away, the colour changes, the shape is lost, the size increases; it becomes liquid and hot; you can hardly touch it, and if you strike it, it no longer makes a sound. But does the same wax remain? It must be admitted that it does; no one denies it, no one thinks otherwise. So what was it in the wax that I understood with such distinctness? Evidently none of the features which I arrived at by means of the senses; for whatever came under taste, smell, sight, touch or hearing has now altered—yet the wax remains.

Perhaps the answer lies in the thought which now comes to my mind; namely, the wax was not after all the sweetness of the honey, or the fragrance of the flowers, or the whiteness, or the shape, or the sound, but was rather a body which presented itself to me in these various forms a little while ago, but which now exhibits different ones. But what exactly is it that I am now imagining? Let us concentrate, take away everything 31
which does not belong to the wax, and see what is left: merely something extended, flexible and changeable. But what is meant here by "flexible" and "changeable"? Is it what I picture in my imagination: that this piece of wax is capable of changing from a round shape to a square shape, or from a square shape to a triangular shape? Not at all;

for I can grasp that the wax is capable of countless changes of this kind, yet I am unable to run through this immeasurable number of changes in my imagination, from which it follows that it is not the faculty of imagination that gives me my grasp of the wax as flexible and changeable. And what is meant by "extended"? Is the extension of the wax also unknown? For it increases if the wax melts, increases again if it boils, and is greater still if the heat is increased. I would not be making a correct judgement about the nature of wax unless I believed it capable of being extended in many more different ways than I will ever encompass in my imagination. I must therefore admit that the nature of this piece of wax is in no way revealed by my imagination, but is perceived by the mind alone. (I am speaking of this particular piece of wax; the point is even clearer with regard to wax in general.) But what is this wax which is perceived by the mind alone? It is of course the same wax which I see, which I touch, which I picture in my imagination, in short the same wax which I thought it to be from the start. And yet, and here is the point, the perception I have of it is a case not of vision or touch or imagination—nor has it ever been, despite previous appearances—but of purely mental scrutiny; and this can be imperfect and confused, as it was before, or clear and distinct as it is now, depending on how carefully I concentrate on what the wax consists in.

But as I reach this conclusion I am amazed at how [weak and] prone to error my mind is. For although I am thinking about these matters within myself, silently and
32 without speaking, nonetheless the actual words bring me up short, and I am almost tricked by ordinary ways of talking. We say that we see the wax itself, if it is there before us, not that we judge it to be there from its colour or shape; and this might lead me to conclude without more ado that knowledge of the wax comes from what the eye sees, and not from the scrutiny of the mind alone. But then if I look out of the window and see men crossing the square, as I just happen to have done, I normally say that I see the men themselves, just as I say that I see the wax. Yet do I see any more than hats and coats which could conceal automatons? I *judge* that they are men. And so something which I thought I was seeing with my eyes is in fact grasped solely by the faculty of judgement which is in my mind.

However, one who wants to achieve knowledge above the ordinary level should feel ashamed at having taken ordinary ways of talking as a basis for doubt. So let us proceed, and consider on which occasion my perception of the nature of the wax was more perfect and evident. Was it when I first looked at it, and believed I knew it by my external senses, or at least by what they call the "common" sense—that is, the power of imagination? Or is my knowledge more perfect now, after a more careful investigation of the nature of the wax and of the means by which it is known? Any doubt on this issue would clearly be foolish; for what distinctness was there in my earlier perception? Was there anything in it which an animal could not possess? But when I distinguish the wax from its outward forms—take the clothes off, as it were, and consider it naked—then although my judgement may still contain errors, at least my perception now requires a human mind.

33 But what am I to say about this mind, or about myself? (So far, remember, I am not admitting that there is anything else in me except a mind.) What, I ask, is this "I" which seems to perceive the wax so distinctly? Surely my awareness of my own self is not merely much truer and more certain than my awareness of the wax, but also much more distinct and evident. For if I judge that the wax exists from the fact that I see it, clearly this same fact entails much more evidently that I myself also exist. It is possible that what I see is not really the wax; it is possible that I do not even have eyes with which to see anything. But when I see, or think I see (I am not here distinguishing the

two), it is simply not possible that I who am now thinking am not something. By the same token, if I judge that the wax exists from the fact that I touch it, the same result follows, namely that I exist. If I judge that it exists from the fact that I imagine it, or for any other reason, exactly the same thing follows. And the result that I have grasped in the case of the wax may be applied to everything else located outside me. Moreover, if my perception of the wax seemed more distinct after it was established not just by sight or touch but by many other considerations, it must be admitted that I now know myself even more distinctly. This is because every consideration whatsoever which contributes to my perception of the wax, or of any other body, cannot but establish even more effectively the nature of my own mind. But besides this, there is so much else in the mind itself which can serve to make my knowledge of it more distinct, that it scarcely seems worth going through the contributions made by considering bodily things.

I see that without any effort I have now finally got back to where I wanted. I now 34
know that even bodies are not strictly perceived by the senses or the faculty of imagination but by the intellect alone, and that this perception derives not from their being touched or seen but from their being understood; and in view of this I know plainly that I can achieve an easier and more evident perception of my own mind than of anything else. But since the habit of holding on to old opinions cannot be set aside so quickly, I should like to stop here and meditate for some time on this new knowledge I have gained, so as to fix it more deeply in my memory.

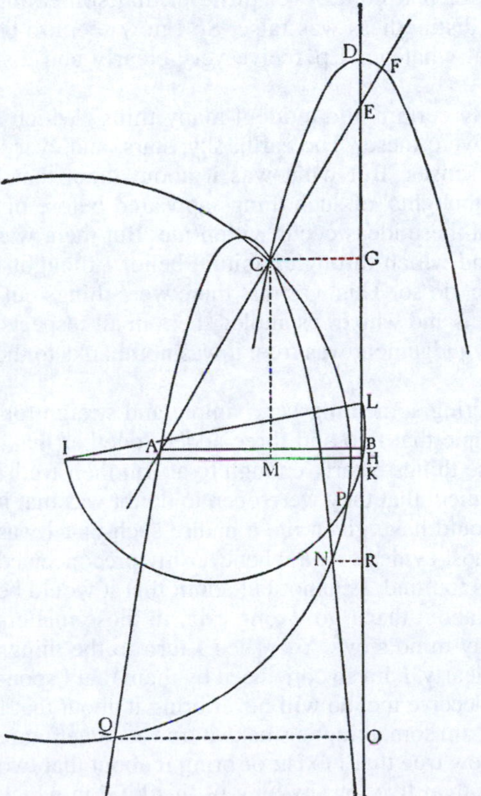

Geometry formula from Descartes' *Geometry* (1637). The X–Y axes in analytic geometry, which Descartes invented, are still called "Cartesian coordinates." (*Library of Congress*)

Third Meditation

The existence of God

I will now shut my eyes, stop my ears, and withdraw all my senses. I will eliminate from my thoughts all images of bodily things, or rather, since this is hardly possible, I will regard all such images as vacuous, false and worthless. I will converse with myself and scrutinize myself more deeply; and in this way I will attempt to achieve, little by little, a more intimate knowledge of myself. I am a thing that thinks: that is, a thing that doubts, affirms, denies, understands a few things, is ignorant of many things, is willing, is unwilling, and also which imagines and has sensory perceptions; for as I have noted before, even though the objects of my sensory experience and imagination may have no existence outside me, nonetheless the modes of thinking which I refer to as
35 cases of sensory perception and imagination, in so far as they are simply modes of thinking, do exist within me—of that I am certain.

In this brief list I have gone through everything I truly know, or at least everything I have so far discovered that I know. Now I will cast around more carefully to see whether there may be other things within me which I have not yet noticed. I am certain that I am a thinking thing. Do I not therefore also know what is required for my being certain about anything? In this first item of knowledge there is simply a clear and distinct perception of what I am asserting; this would not be enough to make me certain of the truth of the matter if it could ever turn out that something which I perceived with such clarity and distinctness was false. So I now seem to be able to lay it down as a general rule that whatever I perceive very clearly and distinctly is true.

Yet I previously accepted as wholly certain and evident many things which I afterwards realized were doubtful. What were these? The earth, sky, stars, and everything else that I apprehended with the senses. But what was it about them that I perceived clearly? Just that the ideas, or thoughts, of such things appeared before my mind. Yet even now I am not denying that these ideas occur within me. But there was something else which I used to assert, and which through habitual belief I thought I perceived clearly, although I did not in fact do so. This was that there were things outside me which were the sources of my ideas and which resembled them in all respects. Here was my mistake; or at any rate, if my judgement was true, it was not thanks to the strength of my perception.

But what about when I was considering something very simple and straightforward
36 in arithmetic or geometry, for example that two and three added together make five, and so on? Did I not see at least these things clearly enough to affirm their truth? Indeed, the only reason for my later judgement that they were open to doubt was that it occurred to me that perhaps some God could have given me a nature such that I was deceived even in matters which seemed most evident. And whenever my preconceived belief in the supreme power of God comes to mind, I cannot but admit that it would be easy for him, if he so desired, to bring it about that I go wrong even in those matters which I think I see utterly clearly with my mind's eye. Yet when I turn to the things themselves which I think I perceive very clearly, I am so convinced by them that I spontaneously declare: let whoever can do so deceive me, he will never bring it about that I am nothing, so long as I continue to think I am something; or make it true at some future time that I have never existed, since it is now true that I exist; or bring it about that two and three added together are more or less than five, or anything of this kind in which

I see a manifest contradiction. And since I have no cause to think that there is a deceiving God, and I do not yet even know for sure whether there is a God at all, any reason for doubt which depends simply on this supposition is a very slight and, so to speak, metaphysical one. But in order to remove even this slight reason for doubt, as soon as the opportunity arises I must examine whether there is a God, and, if there is, whether he can be a deceiver. For if I do not know this, it seems that I can never be quite certain about anything else.

First, however, considerations of order appear to dictate that I now classify my
thoughts into definite kinds, and ask which of them can properly be said to be the bear- 37
ers of truth and falsity. Some of my thoughts are as it were the images of things, and it is only in these cases that the term "idea" is strictly appropriate—for example, when I think of a man, or a chimera, or the sky, or an angel, or God. Other thoughts have various additional forms: thus when I will, or am afraid, or affirm, or deny, there is always a particular thing which I take as the object of my thought, but my thought includes something more than the likeness of that thing. Some thoughts in this category are called volitions or emotions, while others are called judgements.

Now as far as ideas are concerned, provided they are considered solely in themselves and I do not refer them to anything else, they cannot strictly speaking be false; for whether it is a goat or a chimera that I am imagining, it is just as true that I imagine the former as the latter. As for the will and the emotions, here too one need not worry about falsity; for even if the things which I may desire are wicked or even non-existent, that does not make it any less true that I desire them. Thus the only remaining thoughts where I must be on my guard against making a mistake are judgements. And the chief and most common mistake which is to be found here consists in my judging that the ideas which are in me resemble, or conform to, things located outside me. Of course, if I considered just the ideas themselves simply as modes of my thought, without referring them to anything else, they could scarcely give me any material for error.

Among my ideas, some appear to be innate, some to be adventitious,* and others
to have been invented by me. My understanding of what a thing is, what truth is, and 38
what thought is, seems to derive simply from my own nature. But my hearing a noise, as I do now, or seeing the sun, or feeling the fire, comes from things which are located outside me, or so I have hitherto judged. Lastly, sirens, hippogriffs and the like are my own invention. But perhaps all my ideas may be thought of as adventitious, or they may all be innate, or all made up; for as yet I have not clearly perceived their true origin.

But the chief question at this point concerns the ideas which I take to be derived from things existing outside me: what is my reason for thinking that they resemble these things? Nature has apparently taught me to think this. But in addition I know by experience that these ideas do not depend on my will, and hence that they do not depend simply on me. Frequently I notice them even when I do not want to: now, for example, I feel the heat whether I want to or not, and this is why I think that this sensation or idea of heat comes to me from something other than myself, namely the heat of the fire by which I am sitting. And the most obvious judgement for me to make is that the thing in question transmits to me its own likeness rather than something else.

I will now see if these arguments are strong enough. When I say "Nature taught me to think this," all I mean is that a spontaneous impulse leads me to believe it, not that its truth has been revealed to me by some natural light. There is a big difference here. Whatever is revealed to me by the natural light—for example that from the fact that

*". . . foreign to me and coming from outside" (French version).

I am doubting it follows that I exist, and so on—cannot in any way be open to doubt. This is because there cannot be another faculty both as trustworthy as the natural light
39 and also capable of showing me that such things are not true. But as for my natural impulses, I have often judged in the past that they were pushing me in the wrong direction when it was a question of choosing the good, and I do not see why I should place any greater confidence in them in other matters.

Then again, although these ideas do not depend on my will, it does not follow that they must come from things located outside me. Just as the impulses which I was speaking of a moment ago seem opposed to my will even though they are within me, so there may be some other faculty not yet fully known to me, which produces these ideas without any assistance from external things; this is, after all, just how I have always thought ideas are produced in me when I am dreaming.

And finally, even if these ideas did come from things other than myself, it would not follow that they must resemble those things. Indeed, I think I have often discovered a great disparity [between an object and its idea] in many cases. For example, there are two different ideas of the sun which I find within me. One of them, which is acquired as it were from the senses and which is a prime example of an idea which I reckon to come from an external source, makes the sun appear very small. The other idea is based on astronomical reasoning, that is, it is derived from certain notions which are innate in me (or else it is constructed by me in some other way), and this idea shows the sun to be several times larger than the earth. Obviously both these ideas cannot resemble the sun which exists outside me; and reason persuades me that the idea which seems to have emanated most directly from the sun itself has in fact no resemblance to it at all.

40 All these considerations are enough to establish that it is not reliable judgement but merely some blind impulse that has made me believe up till now that there exist things distinct from myself which transmit to me ideas or images of themselves through the sense organs or in some other way.

But it now occurs to me that there is another way of investigating whether some of the things of which I possess ideas exist outside me. In so far as the ideas are [considered] simply [as] modes of thought, there is no recognizable inequality among them: they all appear to come from within me in the same fashion. But in so far as different ideas [are considered as images which] represent different things, it is clear that they differ widely. Undoubtedly, the ideas which represent substances to me amount to something more and, so to speak, contain within themselves more objective reality than the ideas which merely represent modes or accidents. Again, the idea that gives me my understanding of a supreme God, eternal, infinite, [immutable,] omniscient, omnipotent and the creator of all things that exist apart from him, certainly has in it more objective reality than the ideas that represent finite substances.

Now it is manifest by the natural light that there must be at least as much [reality] in the efficient and total cause as in the effect of that cause. For where, I ask, could the effect get its reality from, if not from the cause? And how could the cause give it to the effect unless it possessed it? It follows from this both that something cannot arise from nothing, and also that what is more perfect—that is, contains in itself more reality—
41 cannot arise from what is less perfect. And this is transparently true not only in the case of effects which possess [what the philosophers call] actual or formal reality, but also in the case of ideas, where one is considering only [what they call] objective reality. A stone, for example, which previously did not exist, cannot begin to exist unless it is produced by something which contains, either formally or eminently everything to be found in the stone; similarly, heat cannot be produced in an object which was not

previously hot, except by something of at least the same order [degree or kind] of perfection as heat, and so on. But it is also true that the idea of heat, or of a stone, cannot exist in me unless it is put there by some cause which contains at least as much reality as I conceive to be in the heat or in the stone. For although this cause does not transfer any of its actual or formal reality to my idea, it should not on that account be supposed that it must be less real. The nature of an idea is such that of itself it requires no formal reality except what it derives from my thought, of which it is a mode. But in order for a given idea to contain such and such objective reality, it must surely derive it from some cause which contains at least as much formal reality as there is objective reality in the idea. For if we suppose that an idea contains something which was not in its cause, it must have got this from nothing; yet the mode of being by which a thing exists objectively [or representatively] in the intellect by way of an idea, imperfect though it may be, is certainly not nothing, and so it cannot come from nothing.

And although the reality which I am considering in my ideas is merely objective
reality, I must not on that account suppose that the same reality need not exist formally 42
in the causes of my ideas, but that it is enough for it to be present in them objectively. For just as the objective mode of being belongs to ideas by their very nature, so the formal mode of being belongs to the causes of ideas—or at least the first and most important ones—by *their* very nature. And although one idea may perhaps originate from another, there cannot be an infinite regress here; eventually one must reach a primary idea, the cause of which will be like an archetype which contains formally [and in fact] all the reality [or perfection] which is present only objectively [or representatively] in the idea. So it is clear to me, by the natural light, that the ideas in me are like [pictures, or] images which can easily fall short of the perfection of the things from which they are taken, but which cannot contain anything greater or more perfect.

The longer and more carefully I examine all these points, the more clearly and distinctly I recognize their truth. But what is my conclusion to be? If the objective reality of any of my ideas turns out to be so great that I am sure the same reality does not reside in me, either formally or eminently, and hence that I myself cannot be its cause, it will necessarily follow that I am not alone in the world, but that some other thing which is the cause of this idea also exists. But if no such idea is to be found in me, I shall have no arguments to convince me of the existence of anything apart from myself. For despite a most careful and comprehensive survey, this is the only argument I have so far been able to find.

Among my ideas, apart from the idea which gives me a representation of myself,
which cannot present any difficulty in this context, there are ideas which variously 43
represent God, corporeal and inanimate things, angels, animals and finally other men like myself.

As far as concerns the ideas which represent other men, or animals, or angels, I have no difficulty in understanding that they could be put together from the ideas I have of myself, of corporeal things and of God, even if the world contained no men besides me, no animals and no angels.

As to my ideas of corporeal things, I can see nothing in them which is so great [or excellent] as to make it seem impossible that it originated in myself. For if I scrutinize them thoroughly and examine them one by one, In the way in which I examined the idea of the wax yesterday, I notice that the things which I perceive clearly and distinctly in them are very few in number. The list comprises size, or extension in length, breadth and depth; shape, which is a function of the boundaries of this extension; position, which is a relation between various items possessing shape; and motion, or

change in position; to these may be added substance, duration and number. But as for all the rest, including light and colours, sounds, smells, tastes, heat and cold and the other tactile qualities, I think of these only in a very confused and obscure way, to the extent that I do not even know whether they are true or false, that is, whether the ideas I have of them are ideas of real things or of non-things. For although, as I have noted before, falsity in the strict sense, or formal falsity, can occur only in judgements, there is another kind of falsity, material falsity, which occurs in ideas, when they represent
44 non-things as things. For example, the ideas which I have of heat and cold contain so little clarity and distinctness that they do not enable me to tell whether cold is merely the absence of heat or vice versa, or whether both of them are real qualities, or neither is. And since there can be no ideas which are not as it were of things, if it is true that cold is nothing but the absence of heat, the idea which represents it to me as something real and positive deserves to be called false; and the same goes for other ideas of this kind.

Such ideas obviously do not require me to posit a source distinct from myself. For on the one hand, if they are false, that is, represent non-things, I know by the natural light that they arise from nothing—that is, they are in me only because of a deficiency and lack of perfection in my nature. If on the other hand they are true, then since the reality which they represent is so extremely slight that I cannot even distinguish it from a non-thing, I do not see why they cannot originate from myself.

With regard to the clear and distinct elements in my ideas of corporeal things, it appears that I could have borrowed some of these from my idea of myself, namely substance, duration, number and anything else of this kind. For example, I think that a stone is a substance, or is a thing capable of existing independently, and I also think that I am a substance. Admittedly I conceive of myself as a thing that thinks and is not extended, whereas I conceive of the stone as a thing that is extended and does not think, so that the two conceptions differ enormously; but they seem to agree with respect to the classification "substance." Again, I perceive that I now exist, and remember that I have existed for some time; moreover, I have various thoughts which I can count; it is
45 in these ways that I acquire the ideas of duration and number which I can then transfer to other things. As for all the other elements which make up the ideas of corporeal things, namely extension, shape, position and movement, these are not formally contained in me, since I am nothing but a thinking thing; but since they are merely modes of a substance, and I am a substance, it seems possible that they are contained in me eminently.

So there remains only the idea of God; and I must consider whether there is anything in the idea which could not have originated in myself. By the word "God" I understand a substance that is infinite, [eternal, immutable,] independent, supremely intelligent, supremely powerful, and which created both myself and everything else (if anything else there be) that exists. All these attributes are such that, the more carefully I concentrate on them, the less possible it seems that they could have originated from me alone. So from what has been said it must be concluded that God necessarily exists.

It is true that I have the idea of substance in me in virtue of the fact that I am a substance; but this would not account for my having the idea of an infinite substance, when I am finite, unless this idea proceeded from some substance which really was infinite.

And I must not think that, just as my conceptions of rest and darkness are arrived at by negating movement and light, so my perception of the infinite is arrived at not by means of a true idea but merely by negating the finite. On the contrary, I clearly understand that

there is more reality in an infinite substance than in a finite one, and hence that my perception of the infinite, that is God, is in some way prior to my perception of the finite, that is 46
myself. For how could I understand that I doubted or desired—that is, lacked something—and that I was not wholly perfect, unless there were in me some idea of a more perfect being which enabled me to recognize my own defects by comparison?

Nor can it be said that this idea of God is perhaps materially false and so could have come from nothing, which is what I observed just a moment ago in the case of the ideas of heat and cold, and so on. On the contrary, it is utterly clear and distinct, and contains in itself more objective reality than any other idea; hence there is no idea which is in itself truer or less liable to be suspected of falsehood. This idea of a supremely perfect and infinite being is, I say, true in the highest degree; for although perhaps one may imagine that such a being does not exist, it cannot be supposed that the idea of such a being represents something unreal, as I said with regard to the idea of cold. The idea is, moreover, utterly clear and distinct; for whatever I clearly and distinctly perceive as being real and true, and implying any perfection, is wholly contained in it. It does not matter that I do not grasp the infinite, or that there are countless additional attributes of God which I cannot in any way grasp, and perhaps cannot even reach in my thought; for it is in the nature of the infinite not to be grasped by a finite being like myself. It is enough that I understand the infinite,* and that I judge that all the attributes which I clearly perceive and know to imply some perfection—and perhaps countless others of which I am ignorant—are present in God either formally or eminently. This is enough to make the idea that I have of God the truest and most clear and distinct of all my ideas.

But perhaps I am something greater than I myself understand, and all the perfections which I attribute to God are somehow in me potentially, though not yet emerging or actualized. For I am now experiencing a gradual increase in my knowledge, and I see 47
nothing to prevent its increasing more and more to infinity. Further, I see no reason why I should not be able to use this increased knowledge to acquire all the other perfections of God. And finally, if the potentiality for these perfections is already within me, why should not this be enough to generate the idea of such perfections?

But all this is impossible. First, though it is true that there is a gradual increase in my knowledge, and that I have many potentialities which are not yet actual, this is all quite irrelevant to the idea of God, which contains absolutely nothing that is potential; indeed, this gradual increase in knowledge is itself the surest sign of imperfection. What is more, even if my knowledge always increases more and more, I recognize that it will never actually be infinite, since it will never reach the point where it is not capable of a further increase; God, on the other hand, I take to be actually infinite, so that nothing can be added to his perfection. And finally, I perceive that the objective being of an idea cannot be produced merely by potential being, which strictly speaking is nothing, but only by actual or formal being.

If one concentrates carefully, all this is quite evident by the natural light. But when I relax my concentration, and my mental vision is blinded by the images of things perceived by the senses, it is not so easy for me to remember why the idea of a being more perfect than myself must necessarily proceed from some being which is in reality more perfect. I should therefore like to go further and inquire whether I myself, who 48
have this idea, could exist if no such being existed.

*According to Descartes one can know or understand something without fully grasping it "just as we can touch a mountain but not put our arms around it. To grasp something is to embrace it in one's thought; to know something, it suffices to touch it with one's thought" (letter to Mersenne, 26 May 1630).

From whom, in that case, would I derive my existence? From myself presumably, or from my parents, or from some other beings less perfect than God; for nothing more perfect than God, or even as perfect, can be thought of or imagined.

Yet if I derived my existence from myself, then I should neither doubt nor want, nor lack anything at all; for I should have given myself all the perfections of which I have any idea, and thus I should myself be God. I must not suppose that the items I lack would be more difficult to acquire than those I now have. On the contrary, it is clear that, since I am a thinking thing or substance, it would have been far more difficult for me to emerge out of nothing than merely to acquire knowledge of the many things of which I am ignorant—such knowledge being merely an accident of that substance. And if I had derived my existence from myself, which is a greater achievement, I should certainly not have denied myself the knowledge in question, which is something much easier to acquire, or indeed any of the attributes which I perceive to be contained in the idea of God; for none of them seem any harder to achieve. And if any of them were harder to achieve, they would certainly appear so to me, if I had indeed got all my other attributes from myself, since I should experience a limitation of my power in this respect.

I do not escape the force of these arguments by supposing that I have always existed as I do now, as if it followed from this that there was no need to look for any author of my
49 existence. For a life-span can be divided into countless parts, each completely independent of the others, so that it does not follow from the fact that I existed a little while ago that I must exist now, unless there is some cause which as it were creates me afresh at this moment—that is, which preserves me. For it is quite clear to anyone who attentively considers the nature of time that the same power and action are needed to preserve anything at each individual moment of its duration as would be required to create that thing anew if it were not yet in existence. Hence the distinction between preservation and creation is only a conceptual one, and this is one of the things that are evident by the natural light.

I must therefore now ask myself whether I possess some power enabling me to bring it about that I who now exist will still exist a little while from now. For since I am nothing but a thinking thing—or at least since I am now concerned only and precisely with that part of me which is a thinking thing—if there were such a power in me, I should undoubtedly be aware of it. But I experience no such power, and this very fact makes me recognize most clearly that I depend on some being distinct from myself.

But perhaps this being is not God, and perhaps I was produced either by my parents or by other causes less perfect than God. No; for as I have said before, it is quite clear that there must be at least as much in the cause as in the effect. And therefore whatever kind of cause is eventually proposed, since I am a thinking thing and have within me some idea of God, it must be admitted that what caused me is itself a thinking thing and possesses the idea of all the perfections which I attribute to God. In respect of this cause one may again inquire whether it derives its existence from itself or from another cause. If from itself, then it is clear from what has been said that it is itself
50 God, since if it has the power of existing through its own might, then undoubtedly it also has the power of actually possessing all the perfections of which it has an idea—that is, all the perfections which I conceive to be in God. If, on the other hand, it derives its existence from another cause, then the same question may be repeated concerning this further cause, namely whether it derives its existence from itself or from another cause, until eventually the ultimate cause is reached, and this will be God.

It is clear enough that an infinite regress is impossible here, especially since I am dealing not just with the cause that produced me in the past, but also and most importantly with the cause that preserves me at the present moment.

Nor can it be supposed that several partial causes contributed to my creation, or that I received the idea of one of the perfections which I attribute to God from one cause and the idea of another from another—the supposition here being that all the perfections are to be found somewhere in the universe but not joined together in a single being, God. On the contrary, the unity, the simplicity, or the inseparability of all the attributes of God is one of the most important of the perfections which I understand him to have. And surely the idea of the unity of all his perfections could not have been placed in me by any cause which did not also provide me with the ideas of the other perfections; for no cause could have made me understand the interconnection and inseparability of the perfections without at the same time making me recognize what they were.

Lastly, as regards my parents, even if everything I have ever believed about them is
true, it is certainly not they who preserve me; and in so far as I am a thinking thing, they
did not even make me; they merely placed certain dispositions in the matter which I have
always regarded as containing me, or rather my mind, for that is all I now take myself to 51
be. So there can be no difficulty regarding my parents in this context. Altogether then, it
must be concluded that the mere fact that I exist and have within me an idea of a most
perfect being, that is, God, provides a very clear proof that God indeed exists.

It only remains for me to examine how I received this idea from God. For I did not acquire it from the senses; it has never come to me unexpectedly, as usually happens with the ideas of things that are perceivable by the senses, when these things present themselves to the external sense organs—or seem to do so. And it was not invented by me either; for I am plainly unable either to take away anything from it or to add anything to it. The only remaining alternative is that it is innate in me, just as the idea of myself is innate in me.

And indeed it is no surprise that God, in creating me, should have placed this idea
in me to be, as it were, the mark of the craftsman stamped on his work—not that the
mark need be anything distinct from the work itself. But the mere fact that God created
me is a very strong basis for believing that I am somehow made in his image and likeness, and that I perceive that likeness, which includes the idea of God, by the same faculty which enables me to perceive myself. That is, when I turn my mind's eye upon
myself, I understand that I am a thing which is incomplete and dependent on another
and which aspires without limit to ever greater and better things; but I also understand
at the same time that he on whom I depend has within him all those greater things, not
just indefinitely and potentially but actually and infinitely, and hence that he is God.
The whole force of the argument lies in this: I recognize that it would be impossible for
me to exist with the kind of nature I have—that is, having within me the idea of God— 52
were it not the case that God really existed. By "God" I mean the very being the idea of
whom is within me, that is, the possessor of all the perfections which I cannot grasp, but
can somehow reach in my thought, who is subject to no defects whatsoever. It is clear
enough from this that he cannot be a deceiver, since it is manifest by the natural light
that all fraud and deception depend on some defect.

But before examining this point more carefully and investigating other truths which may be derived from it, I should like to pause here and spend some time in the contemplation of God; to reflect on his attributes, and to gaze with wonder and adoration on the beauty of this immense light, so far as the eye of my darkened intellect can bear it. For just as we believe through faith that the supreme happiness of the next life consists solely in the contemplation of the divine majesty, so experience tells us that this same contemplation, albeit much less perfect, enables us to know the greatest joy of which we are capable in this life.

Fourth Meditation

Truth and falsity

During these past few days I have accustomed myself to leading my mind away from the senses; and I have taken careful note of the fact that there is very little about
53 corporeal things that is truly perceived, whereas much more is known about the human mind, and still more about God. The result is that I now have no difficulty in turning my mind away from imaginable things and towards things which are objects of the intellect alone and are totally separate from matter. And indeed the idea I have of the human mind, in so far as it is a thinking thing, which is not extended in length, breadth or height and has no other bodily characteristics, is much more distinct than the idea of any corporeal thing. And when I consider the fact that I have doubts, or that I am a thing that is incomplete and dependent, then there arises in me a clear and distinct idea of a being who is independent and complete, that is, an idea of God. And from the mere fact that there is such an idea within me, or that I who possess this idea exist, I clearly infer that God also exists, and that every single moment of my entire existence depends on him. So clear is this conclusion that I am confident that the human intellect cannot know anything that is more evident or more certain. And now, from this contemplation of the true God, in whom all the treasures of wisdom and the sciences lie hidden, I think I can see a way forward to the knowledge of other things.

To begin with, I recognize that it is impossible that God should ever deceive me. For in every case of trickery or deception some imperfection is to be found; and although the ability to deceive appears to be an indication of cleverness or power, the will to deceive is undoubtedly evidence of malice or weakness, and so cannot apply to God.

Next, I know by experience that there is in me a faculty of judgement which, like
54 everything else which is in me, I certainly received from God. And since God does not wish to deceive me, he surely did not give me the kind of faculty which would ever enable me to go wrong while using it correctly.

There would be no further doubt on this issue were it not that what I have just said appears to imply that I am incapable of ever going wrong. For if everything that is in me comes from God, and he did not endow me with a faculty for making mistakes, it appears that I can never go wrong. And certainly, so long as I think only of God, and turn my whole attention to him, I can find no cause of error or falsity. But when I turn back to myself, I know by experience that I am prone to countless errors. On looking for the cause of these errors, I find that I possess not only a real and positive idea of God, or a being who is supremely perfect, but also what may be described as a negative idea of nothingness, or of that which is farthest removed from all perfection. I realize that I am, as it were, something intermediate between God and nothingness, or between supreme being and non-being: my nature is such that in so far as I was created by the supreme being, there is nothing in me to enable me to go wrong or lead me astray; but in so far as I participate in nothingness or non-being, that is, in so far as I am not myself the supreme being and am lacking in countless respects, it is no wonder that I make mistakes. I understand, then, that error as such is not something real which depends on God, but merely a defect. Hence my going wrong does not require me to have a faculty specially bestowed on me by God; it simply happens as a result of the fact that the faculty of true judgement which I have from God is in my case not infinite.

But this is still not entirely satisfactory. For error is not a pure negation, but rather 55
a privation or lack of some knowledge which somehow should be in me. And when I concentrate on the nature of God, it seems impossible that he should have placed in me a faculty which is not perfect of its kind, or which lacks some perfection which it ought to have. The more skilled the craftsman the more perfect the work produced by him; if this is so, how can anything produced by the supreme creator of all things not be complete and perfect in all respects? There is, moreover, no doubt that God could have given me a nature such that I was never mistaken; again, there is no doubt that he always wills what is best. Is it then better that I should make mistakes than that I should not do so?

As I reflect on these matters more attentively, it occurs to me first of all that it is no cause for surprise if I do not understand the reasons for some of God's actions; and there is no call to doubt his existence if I happen to find that there are other instances where I do not grasp why or how certain things were made by him. For since I now know that my own nature is very weak and limited, whereas the nature of God is immense, incomprehensible and infinite, I also know without more ado that he is capable of countless things whose causes are beyond my knowledge. And for this reason alone I consider the customary search for final causes to be totally useless in physics; there is considerable rashness in thinking myself capable of investigating the [impenetrable] purposes of God.

It also occurs to me that whenever we are inquiring whether the works of God are perfect, we ought to look at the whole universe, not just at one created thing on its own. For what would perhaps rightly appear very imperfect if it existed on its own is quite
perfect when its function as a part of the universe is considered. It is true that, since my 56
decision to doubt everything, it is so far only myself and God whose existence I have been able to know with certainty; but after considering the immense power of God, I cannot deny that many other things have been made by him, or at least could have been made, and hence that I may have a place in the universal scheme of things.

Next, when I look more closely at myself and inquire into the nature of my errors (for these are the only evidence of some imperfection in me), I notice that they depend on two concurrent causes, namely on the faculty of knowledge which is in me, and on the faculty of choice or freedom of the will; that is, they depend on both the intellect and the will simultaneously. Now all that the intellect does is to enable me to perceive the ideas which are subjects for possible judgements; and when regarded strictly in this light, it turns out to contain no error in the proper sense of that term. For although countless things may exist without there being any corresponding ideas in me, it should not, strictly speaking, be said that I am deprived of these ideas, but merely that I lack them, in a negative sense. This is because I cannot produce any reason to prove that God ought to have given me a greater faculty of knowledge than he did; and no matter how skilled I understand a craftsman to be, this does not make me think he ought to have put into every one of his works all the perfections which he is able to put into some of them. Besides, I cannot complain that the will or freedom of choice which I received from God is not sufficiently extensive or perfect, since I know by experience that it is not
restricted in any way. Indeed, I think it is very noteworthy that there is nothing else in 57
me which is so perfect and so great that the possibility of a further increase in its perfection or greatness is beyond my understanding. If, for example, I consider the faculty of understanding, I immediately recognize that in my case it is extremely slight and very finite, and I at once form the idea of an understanding which is much greater—indeed supremely great and infinite; and from the very fact that I can form an idea of it, I perceive that it belongs to the nature of God. Similarly, if I examine the faculties of

memory or imagination, or any others, I discover that in my case each one of these faculties is weak and limited, while in the case of God it is immeasurable. It is only the will, or freedom of choice, which I experience within me to be so great that the idea of any greater faculty is beyond my grasp; so much so that it is above all in virtue of the will that I understand myself to bear in some way the image and likeness of God. For although God's will is incomparably greater than mine, both in virtue of the knowledge and power that accompany it and make it more firm and efficacious, and also in virtue of its object, in that it ranges over a greater number of items, nevertheless it does not seem any greater than mine when considered as will in the essential and strict sense. This is because the will simply consists in our ability to do or not do something (that is, to affirm or deny, to pursue or avoid); or rather, it consists simply in the fact that when the intellect puts something forward for affirmation or denial or for pursuit or avoidance, our inclinations are such that we do not feel we are determined by any external force. In order to be free, there is no need for me to be inclined both ways; on the
58 contrary, the more I incline in one direction—either because I clearly understand that reasons of truth and goodness point that way, or because of a divinely produced disposition of my inmost thoughts—the freer is my choice. Neither divine grace nor natural knowledge ever diminishes freedom; on the contrary, they increase and strengthen it. But the indifference I feel when there is no reason pushing me in one direction rather than another is the lowest grade of freedom; it is evidence not of any perfection of freedom, but rather of a defect in knowledge or a kind of negation. For if I always saw clearly what was true and good, I should never have to deliberate about the right judgement or choice; in that case, although I should be wholly free, it would be impossible for me ever to be in a state of indifference.

From these considerations I perceive that the power of willing which I received from God is not, when considered in itself, the cause of my mistakes; for it is both extremely ample and also perfect of its kind. Nor is my power of understanding to blame; for since my understanding comes from God, everything that I understand I undoubtedly understand correctly, and any error here is impossible. So what then is the source of my mistakes? It must be simply this: the scope of the will is wider than that of the intellect; but instead of restricting it within the same limits, I extend its use to matters which I do not understand. Since the will is indifferent in such cases, it easily turns aside from what is true and good, and this is the source of my error and sin.

For example, during these past few days I have been asking whether anything in the world exists, and I have realized that from the very fact of my raising this question it follows quite evidently that I exist. I could not but judge that something which I
59 understood so clearly was true; but this was not because I was compelled so to judge by any external force, but because a great light in the intellect was followed by a great inclination in the will, and thus the spontaneity and freedom of my belief was all the greater in proportion to my lack of indifference. But now, besides the knowledge that I exist, in so far as I am a thinking thing, an idea of corporeal nature comes into my mind; and I happen to be in doubt as to whether the thinking nature which is in me, or rather which I am, is distinct from this corporeal nature or identical with it. I am making the further supposition that my intellect has not yet come upon any persuasive reason in favour of one alternative rather than the other. This obviously implies that I am indifferent as to whether I should assert or deny either alternative, or indeed refrain from making any judgement on the matter.

What is more, this indifference does not merely apply to cases where the intellect is wholly ignorant, but extends in general to every case where the intellect does not have sufficiently clear knowledge at the time when the will deliberates. For although probable conjectures may pull me in one direction, the mere knowledge that they are simply conjectures, and not certain and indubitable reasons, is itself quite enough to push my assent the other way. My experience in the last few days confirms this: the mere fact that I found that all my previous beliefs were in some sense open to doubt was enough to turn my absolutely confident belief in their truth into the supposition that they were wholly false.

If, however, I simply refrain from making a judgement in cases where I do not perceive the truth with sufficient clarity and distinctness, then it is clear that I am behaving correctly and avoiding error. But if in such cases I either affirm or deny, then I am not using my free will correctly. If I go for the alternative which is false, then obviously 60
I shall be in error; if I take the other side, then it is by pure chance that I arrive at the truth, and I shall still be at fault since it is clear by the natural light that the perception of the intellect should always precede the determination of the will. In this incorrect use of free will may be found the privation which constitutes the essence of error. The privation, I say, lies in the operation of the will in so far as it proceeds from me, but not in the faculty of will which I received from God, nor even in its operation, in so far as it depends on him.

And I have no cause for complaint on the grounds that the power of understanding or the natural light which God gave me is no greater than it is; for it is in the nature of a finite intellect to lack understanding of many things, and it is in the nature of a created intellect to be finite. Indeed, I have reason to give thanks to him who has never owed me anything for the great bounty that he has shown me, rather than thinking myself deprived or robbed of any gifts he did not bestow.

Nor do I have any cause for complaint on the grounds that God gave me a will which extends more widely than my intellect. For since the will consists simply of one thing which is, as it were, indivisible, it seems that its nature rules out the possibility of anything being taken away from it. And surely, the more widely my will extends, then the greater thanks I owe to him who gave it to me.

Finally, I must not complain that the forming of those acts of will or judgements in which I go wrong happens with God's concurrence. For in so far as these acts depend on God, they are wholly true and good; and my ability to perform them means that there is in a sense more perfection in me than would be the case if I lacked this ability. As for the privation involved—which is all that the essential definition of falsity and wrong 61
consists in—this does not in any way require the concurrence of God, since it is not a thing; indeed, when it is referred to God as its cause, it should be called not a privation but simply a negation. For it is surely no imperfection in God that he has given me the freedom to assent or not to assent in those cases where he did not endow my intellect with a clear and distinct perception; but it is undoubtedly an imperfection in me to misuse that freedom and make judgements about matters which I do not fully understand. I can see, however, that God could easily have brought it about that without losing my freedom, and despite the limitations in my knowledge, I should nonetheless never make a mistake. He could, for example, have endowed my intellect with a clear and distinct perception of everything about which I was ever likely to deliberate; or he could simply have impressed it unforgettably on my memory that I should never make a judgement about anything which I did not clearly and distinctly understand. Had God made me this way, then I can easily understand that, considered as a totality, I would have been more perfect than I am now. But I cannot therefore deny that there may in some way be more perfection in the universe as a whole because some of its parts are not immune from

error, while others are immune, than there would be if all the parts were exactly alike. And I have no right to complain that the role God wished me to undertake in the world is not the principal one or the most perfect of all.

What is more, even if I have no power to avoid error in the first way just mentioned, which requires a clear perception of everything I have to deliberate on, I can
62 avoid error in the second way, which depends merely on my remembering to withhold judgement on any occasion when the truth of the matter is not clear. Admittedly, I am aware of a certain weakness in me, in that I am unable to keep my attention fixed on one and the same item of knowledge at all times; but by attentive and repeated meditation I am nevertheless able to make myself remember it as often as the need arises, and thus get into the habit of avoiding error.

It is here that man's greatest and most important perfection is to be found, and I therefore think that today's meditation, involving an investigation into the cause of error and falsity, has been very profitable. The cause of error must surely be the one I have explained; for if, whenever I have to make a judgement, I restrain my will so that it extends to what the intellect clearly and distinctly reveals, and no further, then it is quite impossible for me to go wrong. This is because every clear and distinct perception is undoubtedly something, and hence cannot come from nothing, but must necessarily have God for its author. Its author, I say, is God, who is supremely perfect, and who cannot be a deceiver on pain of contradiction; hence the perception is undoubtedly true. So today I have learned not only what precautions to take to avoid ever going wrong, but also what to do to arrive at the truth. For I shall unquestionably reach the truth, if only I give sufficient attention to all the things which I perfectly understand, and separate these from all the other cases where my apprehension is more confused and obscure. And this is just what I shall take good care to do from now on.

63 FIFTH MEDITATION

The essence of material things, and the existence of God considered a second time

There are many matters which remain to be investigated concerning the attributes of God and the nature of myself, or my mind; and perhaps I shall take these up at another time. But now that I have seen what to do and what to avoid in order to reach the truth, the most pressing task seems to be to try to escape from the doubts into which I fell a few days ago, and see whether any certainty can be achieved regarding material objects.

But before I inquire whether any such things exist outside me, I must consider the ideas of these things, in so far as they exist in my thought, and see which of them are distinct, and which confused.

Quantity, for example, or "continuous" quantity as the philosophers commonly call it, is something I distinctly imagine. That is, I distinctly imagine the extension of the quantity (or rather of the thing which is quantified) in length, breadth and depth. I also enumerate various parts of the thing, and to these parts I assign various sizes, shapes, positions and local motions; and to the motions I assign various durations.

Not only are all these things very well known and transparent to me when regarded in this general way, but in addition there are countless particular features regarding shape, number, motion, and so on, which I perceive when I give them my attention. And
64 the truth of these matters is so open and so much in harmony with my nature, that on first

discovering them it seems that I am not so much learning something new as remembering what I knew before; or it seems like noticing for the first time things which were long present within me although I had never turned my mental gaze on them before.

But I think the most important consideration at this point is that I find within me countless ideas of things which even though they may not exist anywhere outside me still cannot be called nothing; for although in a sense they can be thought of at will, they are not my invention but have their own true and immutable natures. When, for example, I imagine a triangle, even if perhaps no such figure exists, or has ever existed, anywhere outside my thought, there is still a determinate nature, or essence, or form of the triangle which is immutable and eternal, and not invented by me or dependent on my mind. This is clear from the fact that various properties can be demonstrated of the triangle, for example that its three angles equal two right angles, that its greatest side subtends its greatest angle, and the like; and since these properties are ones which I now clearly recognize whether I want to or not, even if I never thought of them at all when I previously imagined the triangle, it follows that they cannot have been invented by me.

It would be beside the point for me to say that since I have from time to time seen bodies of triangular shape, the idea of the triangle may have come to me from external things by means of the sense organs. For I can think up countless other shapes which there can be no suspicion of my ever having encountered through the senses, and yet I
can demonstrate various properties of these shapes, just as I can with the triangle. All 65
these properties are certainly true, since I am clearly aware of them, and therefore they are something, and not merely nothing; for it is obvious that whatever is true is something; and I have already amply demonstrated that everything of which I am clearly aware is true. And even if I had not demonstrated this, the nature of my mind is such that I cannot but assent to these things, at least so long as I clearly perceive them. I also remember that even before, when I was completely preoccupied with the objects of the senses, I always held that the most certain truths of all were the kind which I recognized clearly in connection with shapes, or numbers or other items relating to arithmetic or geometry, or in general to pure and abstract mathematics.

But if the mere fact that I can produce from my thought the idea of something entails that everything which I clearly and distinctly perceive to belong to that thing really does belong to it, is not this a possible basis for another argument to prove the existence of God? Certainly, the idea of God, or a supremely perfect being, is one which I find within me just as surely as the idea of any shape or number. And my understanding that it belongs to his nature that he always exists is no less clear and distinct than is the case when I prove of any shape or number that some property belongs to its nature. Hence, even if it turned out that not everything on which I have meditated in these past
days is true, I ought still to regard the existence of God as having at least the same level 66
of certainty as I have hitherto attributed to the truths of mathematics.

At first sight, however, this is not transparently clear, but has some appearance of being a sophism. Since I have been accustomed to distinguish between existence and essence in everything else, I find it easy to persuade myself that existence can also be separated from the essence of God, and hence that God can be thought of as not existing. But when I concentrate more carefully, it is quite evident that existence can no more be separated from the essence of God than the fact that its three angles equal two right angles can be separated from the essence of a triangle, or than the idea of a mountain can be separated from the idea of a valley. Hence it is just as much of a contradiction to think of God (that is, a supremely perfect being) lacking existence (that is, lacking a perfection), as it is to think of a mountain without a valley.

However, even granted that I cannot think of God except as existing, just as I cannot think of a mountain without a valley, it certainly does not follow from the fact that I think of a mountain with a valley that there is any mountain in the world; and similarly, it does not seem to follow from the fact that I think of God as existing that he does exist. For my thought does not impose any necessity on things; and just as I may imagine a winged horse even though no horse has wings, so I may be able to attach existence to God even though no God exists.

But there is a sophism concealed here. From the fact that I cannot think of a mountain without a valley, it does not follow that a mountain and valley exist anywhere, but
67 simply that a mountain and a valley, whether they exist or not, are mutually inseparable. But from the fact that I cannot think of God except as existing, it follows that existence is inseparable from God, and hence that he really exists. It is not that my thought makes it so, or imposes any necessity on any thing; on the contrary, it is the necessity of the thing itself, namely the existence of God, which determines my thinking in this respect. For I am not free to think of God without existence (that is, a supremely perfect being without a supreme perfection) as I am free to imagine a horse with or without wings.

And it must not be objected at this point that while it is indeed necessary for me to suppose God exists, once I have made the supposition that he has all perfections (since existence is one of the perfections), nevertheless the original supposition was not necessary. Similarly, the objection would run, it is not necessary for me to think that all quadrilaterals can be inscribed in a circle; but given this supposition, it will be necessary for me to admit that a rhombus can be inscribed in a circle—which is patently false. Now admittedly, it is not necessary that I ever light upon any thought of God; but whenever I do choose to think of the first and supreme being, and bring forth the idea of God from the treasure house of my mind as it were, it is necessary that I attribute all perfections to him, even if I do not at that time enumerate them or attend to them individually. And this necessity plainly guarantees that, when I later realize that existence is a perfection, I am correct in inferring that the first and supreme being exists. In the same way, it is not necessary for me ever to imagine a triangle; but whenever I do wish to consider a rectilinear figure having just three angles, it is necessary
68 that I attribute to it the properties which license the inference that its three angles equal no more than two right angles, even if I do not notice this at the time. By contrast, when I examine what figures can be inscribed in a circle, it is in no way necessary for me to think that this class includes all quadrilaterals. Indeed, I cannot even imagine this, so long as I am willing to admit only what I clearly and distinctly understand. So there is a great difference between this kind of false supposition and the true ideas which are innate in me, of which the first and most important is the idea of God. There are many ways in which I understand that this idea is not something fictitious which is dependent on my thought, but is an image of a true and immutable nature. First of all, there is the fact that, apart from God, there is nothing else of which I am capable of thinking such that existence belongs to its essence. Second, I cannot understand how there could be two or more Gods of this kind; and after supposing that one God exists, I plainly see that it is necessary that he has existed from eternity and will abide for eternity. And finally, I perceive many other attributes of God, none of which I can remove or alter.

But whatever method of proof I use, I am always brought back to the fact that it is only what I clearly and distinctly perceive that completely convinces me. Some of the things I clearly and distinctly perceive are obvious to everyone, while others are discovered only by those who look more closely and investigate more carefully; but once they

have been discovered, the latter are judged to be just as certain as the former. In the case of a right-angled triangle, for example, the fact that the square on the hypotenuse is equal to the square on the other two sides is not so readily apparent as the fact that the 69
hypotenuse subtends the largest angle; but once one has seen it, one believes it just as strongly. But as regards God, if I were not overwhelmed by preconceived opinions, and if the images of things perceived by the senses did not besiege my thought on every side, I would certainly acknowledge him sooner and more easily than anything else. For what is more self-evident than the fact that the supreme being exists, or that God, to whose essence alone existence belongs, exists?

Although it needed close attention for me to perceive this, I am now just as certain of it as I am of everything else which appears most certain. And what is more, I see that the certainty of all other things depends on this, so that without it nothing can ever be perfectly known.

Admittedly my nature is such that so long as I perceive something very clearly and distinctly I cannot but believe it to be true. But my nature is also such that I cannot fix my mental vision continually on the same thing, so as to keep perceiving it clearly; and often the memory of a previously made judgement may come back, when I am no longer attending to the arguments which led me to make it. And so other arguments can now occur to me which might easily undermine my opinion, if I did not possess knowledge of God; and I should thus never have true and certain knowledge about anything, but only shifting and changeable opinions. For example, when I consider the nature of a triangle, it appears most evident to me, steeped as I am in the principles of geometry, that its three angles are equal to two right angles; and so long as I attend to the proof, I cannot but believe this to be true. But as soon as I turn my mind's eye away from the 70
proof, then in spite of still remembering that I perceived it very clearly, I can easily fall into doubt about its truth, if I am without knowledge of God. For I can convince myself that I have a natural disposition to go wrong from time to time in matters which I think I perceive as evidently as can be. This will seem even more likely when I remember that there have been frequent cases where I have regarded things as true and certain, but have later been led by other arguments to judge them to be false.

Now, however, I have perceived that God exists, and at the same time I have understood that everything else depends on him, and that he is no deceiver; and I have drawn the conclusion that everything which I clearly and distinctly perceive is of necessity true. Accordingly, even if I am no longer attending to the arguments which led me to judge that this is true, as long as I remember that I clearly and distinctly perceived it, there are no counter-arguments which can be adduced to make me doubt it, but on the contrary I have true and certain knowledge of it. And I have knowledge not just of this matter, but of all matters which I remember ever having demonstrated, in geometry and so on. For what objections can now be raised? That the way I am made makes me prone to frequent error? But I now know that I am incapable of error in those cases where my understanding is transparently clear. Or can it be objected that I have in the past regarded as true and certain many things which I afterwards recognized to be false? But none of these were things which I clearly and distinctly perceived: I was ignorant of this rule for establishing the truth, and believed these things for other reasons which I later discovered to be less reliable. So what is left to say? Can one raise the objection I put to myself a while ago, that I may be dreaming, or that everything which I am now thinking has as little truth as what comes to the mind of one who is asleep? Yet even this does not 71
change anything. For even though I might be dreaming, if there is anything which is evident to my intellect, then it is wholly true.

Thus I see plainly that the certainty and truth of all knowledge depends uniquely on my knowledge of the true God, to such an extent that I was incapable of perfect knowledge about anything else until I knew him. And now it is possible for me to achieve full and certain knowledge of countless matters, both concerning God himself and other things whose nature is intellectual, and also concerning the whole of that corporeal nature which is the subject-matter of pure mathematics.

Sixth Meditation

The existence of material things, and the real distinction between mind and body

It remains for me to examine whether material things exist. And at least I now know they are capable of existing, in so far as they are the subject-matter of pure mathematics, since I perceive them clearly and distinctly. For there is no doubt that God is capable of creating everything that I am capable of perceiving in this manner; and I have never judged that something could not be made by him except on the grounds that there would be a contradiction in my perceiving it distinctly. The conclusion that material things exist is also suggested by the faculty of imagination, which I am aware of using when I turn my mind to material things. For when I give more attentive consideration to
72 what imagination is, it seems to be nothing else but an application of the cognitive faculty to a body which is intimately present to it, and which therefore exists.

To make this clear, I will first examine the difference between imagination and pure understanding. When I imagine a triangle, for example, I do not merely understand that it is a figure bounded by three lines, but at the same time I also see the three lines with my mind's eye as if they were present before me; and this is what I call imagining. But if I want to think of a chiliagon, although I understand that it is a figure consisting of a thousand sides just as well as I understand the triangle to be a three-sided figure, I do not in the same way imagine the thousand sides or see them as if they were present before me. It is true that since I am in the habit of imagining something whenever I think of a corporeal thing, I may construct in my mind a confused representation of some figure; but it is clear that this is not a chiliagon. For it differs in no way from the representation I should form if I were thinking of a myriagon, or any figure with very many sides. Moreover, such a representation is useless for recognizing the properties which distinguish a chiliagon from other polygons. But suppose I am dealing with a pentagon: I can ofcourse understand the figure of a pentagon, just as I can the figure of a chiliagon, without the help of the imagination; but I can also imagine a pentagon, by applying my mind's eye to its five sides and the area contained within them. And in doing this I notice quite clearly that imagination requires a peculiar effort of mind
73 which is not required for understanding; this additional effort of mind clearly shows the difference between imagination and pure understanding.

Besides this, I consider that this power of imagining which is in me, differing as it does from the power of understanding, is not a necessary constituent of my own essence, that is, of the essence of my mind. For if I lacked it, I should undoubtedly remain the same individual as I now am; from which it seems to follow that it depends on something distinct from myself. And I can easily understand that, if there does exist some body to which the mind is so joined that it can apply itself to contemplate it, as it were, whenever it pleases, then it may possibly be this very body that enables me to imagine corporeal things. So the difference between this mode of thinking and pure understanding may simply be this: when the mind understands, it in some way turns towards itself and inspects one of the ideas which are within it; but when it imagines, it turns towards the body and looks at something in the body which conforms to an idea understood by the mind or perceived by the senses. I can, as I say, easily understand that this is how imagination comes about, if the body exists; and since there is no other equally suitable way of explaining imagination that comes to mind, I can make a probable conjecture that the body exists. But this is only a probability; and despite a careful and comprehensive investigation, I do not yet see how the distinct idea of corporeal nature which I find in my imagination can provide any basis for a necessary inference that some body exists.

But besides that corporeal nature which is the subject-matter of pure mathe- 74
matics, there is much else that I habitually imagine, such as colours, sounds, tastes, pain and so on—though not so distinctly. Now I perceive these things much better by means of the senses, which is how, with the assistance of memory, they appear to have reached the imagination. So in order to deal with them more fully, I must pay equal attention to the senses, and see whether the things which are perceived by means of that mode of thinking which I call "sensory perception" provide me with any sure argument for the existence of corporeal things.

To begin with, I will go back over all the things which I previously took to be perceived by the senses, and reckoned to be true; and I will go over my reasons for thinking this. Next, I will set out my reasons for subsequently calling these things into doubt. And finally I will consider what I should now believe about them.

First of all then, I perceived by my senses that I had a head, hands, feet and other limbs making up the body which I regarded as part of myself, or perhaps even as my whole self. I also perceived by my senses that this body was situated among many other bodies which could affect it in various favourable or unfavourable ways; and I gauged the favourable effects by a sensation of pleasure, and the unfavourable ones by a sensation of pain. In addition to pain and pleasure, I also had sensations within me of hunger, thirst, and other such appetites, and also of physical propensities towards cheerfulness, sadness,
anger and similar emotions. And outside me, besides the extension, shapes and move- 75
ments of bodies, I also had sensations of their hardness and heat, and of the other tactile qualities. In addition, I had sensations of light, colours, smells, tastes and sounds, the variety of which enabled me to distinguish the sky, the earth, the seas, and all other bodies, one from another. Considering the ideas of all these qualities which presented themselves to my thought, although the ideas were, strictly speaking, the only immediate objects of my sensory awareness, it was not unreasonable for me to think that the items which I was perceiving through the senses were things quite distinct from my thought, namely bodies which produced the ideas. For my experience was that these ideas came to me quite without my consent, so that I could not have sensory awareness of any object, even if I wanted to, unless it was present to my sense organs; and I could not avoid having sensory awareness of it when it was present. And since the ideas perceived by the senses were much more lively and vivid and even, in their own way, more distinct than any of those which I deliberately formed through meditating or which I found impressed on my memory, it seemed impossible that they should have come from within me; so the only alternative was that they came from other things. Since the sole source of my knowledge of these things was the ideas themselves, the supposition that the things resembled the ideas was bound to occur to me. In addition, I remembered that the use of my senses had come first, while the use of my reason came only later; and I saw that the ideas which I formed myself were less vivid than those which I perceived with the senses and were, for the most

part, made up of elements of sensory ideas. In this way I easily convinced myself that I
76 had nothing at all in the intellect which I had not previously had in sensation. As for the body which by some special right I called "mine," my belief that this body, more than any other, belonged to me had some justification. For I could never be separated from it, as I could from other bodies; and I felt all my appetites and emotions in, and on account of, this body; and finally, I was aware of pain and pleasurable ticklings in parts of this body, but not in other bodies external to it. But why should that curious sensation of pain give rise to a particular distress of mind; or why should a certain kind of delight follow on a tickling sensation? Again, why should that curious tugging in the stomach which I call hunger tell me that I should eat, or a dryness of the throat tell me to drink, and so on? I was not able to give any explanation of all this, except that nature taught me so. For there is absolutely no connection (at least that I can understand) between the tugging sensation and the decision to take food, or between the sensation of something causing pain and the mental apprehension of distress that arises from that sensation. These and other judgements that I made concerning sensory objects, I was apparently taught to make by nature; for I had already made up my mind that this was how things were, before working out any arguments to prove it.

Later on, however, I had many experiences which gradually undermined all the faith I had had in the senses. Sometimes towers which had looked round from a distance appeared square from close up; and enormous statues standing on their pediments did not seem large when observed from the ground. In these and countless other such cases, I found that the judgements of the external senses were mistaken. And this applied not just to the external senses but to the internal senses as well. For what can
77 be more internal than pain? And yet I had heard that those who had had a leg or an arm amputated sometimes still seemed to feel pain intermittently in the missing part of the body. So even in my own case it was apparently not quite certain that a particular limb was hurting, even if I felt pain in it. To these reasons for doubting, I recently added two very general ones. The first was that every sensory experience I have ever thought I was having while awake I can also think of myself as sometimes having while asleep; and since I do not believe that what I seem to perceive in sleep comes from things located outside me, I did not see why I should be any more inclined to believe this of what I think I perceive while awake. The second reason for doubt was that since I did not know the author of my being (or at least was pretending not to), I saw nothing to rule out the possibility that my natural constitution made me prone to error even in matters which seemed to me most true. As for the reasons for my previous confident belief in the truth of the things perceived by the senses, I had no trouble in refuting them. For since I apparently had natural impulses towards many things which reason told me to avoid, I reckoned that a great deal of confidence should not be placed in what I was taught by nature. And despite the fact that the perceptions of the senses were not dependent on my will, I did not think that I should on that account infer that they proceeded from things distinct from myself, since I might perhaps have a faculty not yet known to me which produced them.

But now, when I am beginning to achieve a better knowledge of myself and the author of my being, although I do not think I should heedlessly accept everything I
78 seem to have acquired from the senses, neither do I think that everything should be called into doubt.

First, I know that everything which I clearly and distinctly understand is capable of being created by God so as to correspond exactly with my understanding of it. Hence the fact that I can clearly and distinctly understand one thing apart from another is enough to make me certain that the two things are distinct, since they are capable of being separated, at least by God. The question of what kind of power is required to bring about such a separation does not affect the judgement that the two things are distinct. Thus, simply by knowing that I exist and seeing at the same time that absolutely nothing else belongs to my nature or essence except that I am a thinking thing, I can infer correctly that my essence consists solely in the fact that I am a thinking thing. It is true that I may have (or, to anticipate, that I certainly have) a body that is very closely joined to me. But nevertheless, on the one hand I have a clear and distinct idea of myself, in so far as I am simply a thinking, non-extended thing; and on the other hand I have a distinct idea of body,* in so far as this is simply an extended, non-thinking thing. And accordingly, it is certain that I am really distinct from my body, and can exist without it.

Besides this, I find in myself faculties for certain special modes of thinking, namely imagination and sensory perception. Now I can clearly and distinctly understand myself as a whole without these faculties; but I cannot, conversely, understand these faculties without me, that is, without an intellectual substance to inhere in. This is because there is an intellectual act included in their essential definition; and hence I perceive that the distinction between them and myself corresponds to the distinction between the modes of a thing and the thing itself. Of course I also recognize that there are other faculties (like those of changing position, of taking on various shapes, and so on) which, like sensory perception and imagination, cannot be understood apart from some substance for them to 79
inhere in, and hence cannot exist without it. But it is clear that these other faculties, if they exist, must be in a corporeal or extended substance and not an intellectual one; for the clear and distinct conception of them includes extension, but does not include any intellectual act whatsoever. Now there is in me a passive faculty of sensory perception, that is, a faculty for receiving and recognizing the ideas of sensible objects; but I could not make use of it unless there was also an active faculty, either in me or in something else, which produced or brought about these ideas. But this faculty cannot be in me, since clearly it presupposes no intellectual act on my part, and the ideas in question are produced without my cooperation and often even against my will. So the only alternative is that it is in another substance distinct from me—a substance which contains either formally or eminently all the reality which exists objectively in the ideas produced by this faculty (as I have just noted). This substance is either a body, that is, a corporeal nature, in which case it will contain formally [and in fact] everything which is to be found objectively [or representatively] in the ideas; or else it is God, or some creature more noble than a body, in which case it will contain eminently whatever is to be found in the ideas. But since God is not a deceiver, it is quite clear that he does not transmit the ideas to me either directly from himself, or indirectly, via some creature which contains the objective reality of the ideas not formally but only eminently. For God has given me no faculty at all for recognizing any such source for these ideas; on the contrary, he has given me a great propensity to believe that they are produced by corporeal things. So I do not see how God could be 80
understood to be anything but a deceiver if the ideas were transmitted from a source other than corporeal things. It follows that corporeal things exist. They may not all exist in a way that exactly corresponds with my sensory grasp of them, for in many cases the grasp of the senses is very obscure and confused. But at least they possess all the properties which I clearly and distinctly understand, that is, all those which, viewed in general terms, are comprised within the subject-matter of pure mathematics.

*The Latin term corpus as used here by Descartes is ambiguous between "body" (i.e. corporeal matter in general) and "the body" (i.e. this particular body of mine). The French version preserves the ambiguity.

What of the other aspects of corporeal things which are either particular (for example that the sun is of such and such a size or shape), or less clearly understood, such as light or sound or pain, and so on? Despite the high degree of doubt and uncertainty involved here, the very fact that God is not a deceiver, and the consequent impossibility of there being any falsity in my opinions which cannot be corrected by some other faculty supplied by God, offers me a sure hope that I can attain the truth even in these matters. Indeed, there is no doubt that everything that I am taught by nature contains some truth. For if nature is considered in its general aspect, then I understand by the term nothing other than God himself, or the ordered system of created things established by God. And by my own nature in particular I understand nothing other than the totality of things bestowed on me by God.

There is nothing that my own nature teaches me more vividly than that I have a body, and that when I feel pain there is something wrong with the body, and that when I am hungry or thirsty the body needs food and drink, and so on. So I should not doubt that there is some truth in this.

81 Nature also teaches me, by these sensations of pain, hunger, thirst and so on, that I am not merely present in my body as a sailor is present in a ship, but that I am very closely joined and, as it were, intermingled with it, so that I and the body form a unit. If this were not so, I, who am nothing but a thinking thing, would not feel pain when the body was hurt, but would perceive the damage purely by the intellect, just as a sailor perceives by sight if anything in his ship is broken. Similarly, when the body needed food or drink, I should have an explicit understanding of the fact, instead of having confused sensations of hunger and thirst. For these sensations of hunger, thirst, pain and so on are nothing but confused modes of thinking which arise from the union and, as it were, intermingling of the mind with the body.

I am also taught by nature that various other bodies exist in the vicinity of my body, and that some of these are to be sought out and others avoided. And from the fact that I perceive by my senses a great variety of colours, sounds, smells and tastes, as well as differences in heat, hardness and the like, I am correct in inferring that the bodies which are the source of these various sensory perceptions possess differences corresponding to them, though perhaps not resembling them. Also, the fact that some of the perceptions are agreeable to me while others are disagreeable makes it quite certain that my body, or rather my whole self, in so far as I am a combination of body and mind, can be affected by the various beneficial or harmful bodies which surround it.

82 There are, however, many other things which I may appear to have been taught by nature, but which in reality I acquired not from nature but from a habit of making ill-considered judgements; and it is therefore quite possible that these are false. Cases in point are the belief that any space in which nothing is occurring to stimulate my senses must be empty; or that the heat in a body is something exactly resembling the idea of heat which is in me; or that when a body is white or green, the selfsame whiteness or greenness which I perceive through my senses is present in the body; or that in a body which is bitter or sweet there is the selfsame taste which I experience, and so on; or, finally, that stars and towers and other distant bodies have the same size and shape which they present to my senses, and other examples of this kind. But to make sure that my perceptions in this matter are sufficiently distinct, I must more accurately define exactly what I mean when I say that I am taught something by nature. In this context I am taking nature to be something more limited than the totality of things bestowed on me by God. For this includes many things that belong to the mind alone—for example my perception that what is done cannot be undone, and all other things that are known by the natural light; but at this stage I am not speaking

of these matters. It also includes much that relates to the body alone, like the tendency to move in a downward direction, and so on; but I am not speaking of these matters either. My sole concern here is with what God has bestowed on me as a combination of mind and body. My nature, then, in this limited sense, does indeed teach me to avoid what induces a feeling of pain and to seek out what induces feelings of pleasure, and so on. But it does not appear to teach us to draw any conclusions from these sensory perceptions about things located outside us without waiting until the intellect has examined the matter. For knowledge of the truth about such things seems to belong to the mind alone, not to the combination of mind and body. Hence, although a star has no greater effect on my eye than the 83
flame of a small light, that does not mean that there is any real or positive inclination in me to believe that the star is no bigger than the light; I have simply made this judgement from childhood onwards without any rational basis. Similarly, although I feel heat when I go near a fire and feel pain when I go too near, there is no convincing argument for supposing that there is something in the fire which resembles the heat, any more than for supposing that there is something which resembles the pain. There is simply reason to suppose that there is something in the fire, whatever it may eventually turn out to be, which produces in us the feelings of heat or pain. And likewise, even though there is nothing in any given space that stimulates the senses, it does not follow that there is no body there. In these cases and many others I see that I have been in the habit of misusing the order of nature. For the proper purpose of the sensory perceptions given me by nature is simply to inform the mind of what is beneficial or harmful for the composite of which the mind is a part; and to this extent they are sufficiently clear and distinct. But I misuse them by treating them as reliable touchstones for immediate judgements about the essential nature of the bodies located outside us; yet this is an area where they provide only very obscure information.

I have already looked in sufficient detail at how, notwithstanding the goodness of God, it may happen that my judgements are false. But a further problem now comes to mind regarding those very things which nature presents to me as objects which I should seek out or avoid, and also regarding the internal sensations, where I seem to have detected errors—e.g. when someone is tricked by the pleasant taste of some food into
eating the poison concealed inside it. Yet in this case, what the man's nature urges him 84
to go for is simply what is responsible for the pleasant taste, and not the poison, which his nature knows nothing about. The only inference that can be drawn from this is that his nature is not omniscient. And this is not surprising, since man is a limited thing, and so it is only fitting that his perfection should be limited.

And yet it is not unusual for us to go wrong even in cases where nature does urge us towards something. Those who are ill, for example, may desire food or drink that will shortly afterwards turn out to be bad for them. Perhaps it may be said that they go wrong because their nature is disordered, but this does not remove the difficulty. A sick man is no less one of God's creatures than a healthy one, and it seems no less a contradiction to suppose that he has received from God a nature which deceives him. Yet a clock constructed with wheels and weights observes all the laws of its nature just as closely when it is badly made and tells the wrong time as when it completely fulfils the wishes of the clockmaker. In the same way, I might consider the body of a man as a kind of machine equipped with and made up of bones, nerves, muscles, veins, blood and skin in such a way that, even if there were no mind in it, it would still perform all the same movements as it now does in those cases where movement is not under the control of the will or, consequently, of the mind. I can easily see that if such a body suffers from dropsy, for example, and is affected by the dryness of the throat which normally produces in the mind the sensation of thirst, the resulting condition of the nerves and other parts will dispose the

body to take a drink, with the result that the disease will be aggravated. Yet this is just as natural as the body's being stimulated by a similar dryness of the throat to take a drink
85 when there is no such illness and the drink is beneficial. Admittedly, when I consider the
purpose of the clock, I may say that it is departing from its nature when it does not tell the right time; and similarly when I consider the mechanism of the human body, I may think that, in relation to the movements which normally occur in it, it too is deviating from its nature if the throat is dry at a time when drinking is not beneficial to its continued health. But I am well aware that "nature" as I have just used it has a very different significance from "nature" in the other sense. As I have just used it, "nature" is simply a label which depends on my thought; it is quite extraneous to the things to which it is applied, and depends simply on my comparison between the idea of a sick man and a badly-made clock, and the idea of a healthy man and a well-made clock. But by "nature" in the other sense I understand something which is really to be found in the things themselves; in this sense, therefore, the term contains something of the truth.

When we say, then, with respect to the body suffering from dropsy, that it has a disordered nature because it has a dry throat and yet does not need drink, the term "nature" is here used merely as an extraneous label. However, with respect to the composite, that is, the mind united with this body, what is involved is not a mere label, but a true error of nature, namely that it is thirsty at a time when drink is going to cause it harm. It thus remains to inquire how it is that the goodness of God does not prevent nature, in this sense, from deceiving us.

The first observation I make at this point is that there is a great difference between the mind and the body, inasmuch as the body is by its very nature always divisible, while
86 the mind is utterly indivisible. For when I consider the mind, or myself in so far as I am
merely a thinking thing, I am unable to distinguish any parts within myself; I understand myself to be something quite single and complete. Although the whole mind seems to be united to the whole body, I recognize that if a foot or arm or any other part of the body is cut off, nothing has thereby been taken away from the mind. As for the faculties of willing, of understanding, of sensory perception and so on, these cannot be termed parts of the mind, since it is one and the same mind that wills, and understands and has sensory perceptions. By contrast, there is no corporeal or extended thing that I can think of which in my thought I cannot easily divide into parts; and this very fact makes me understand that it is divisible. This one argument would be enough to show me that the mind is completely different from the body, even if I did not already know as much from other considerations.

My next observation is that the mind is not immediately affected by all parts of the body, but only by the brain, or perhaps just by one small part of the brain, namely the part which is said to contain the "common" sense. Every time this part of the brain is in a given state, it presents the same signals to the mind, even though the other parts of the body may be in a different condition at the time. This is established by countless observations, which there is no need to review here.

I observe, in addition, that the nature of the body is such that whenever any part of it is moved by another part which is some distance away, it can always be moved in the same fashion by any of the parts which lie in between, even if the more distant part
87 does nothing. For example, in a cord ABCD, if one end D is pulled so that the other
end A moves, the exact same movement could have been brought about if one of the intermediate points B or C had been pulled, and D had not moved at all. In similar fashion, when I feel a pain in my foot, physiology tells me that this happens by means of nerves distributed throughout the foot, and that these nerves are like cords which go from the foot right up to the brain. When the nerves are pulled in the foot, they in turn

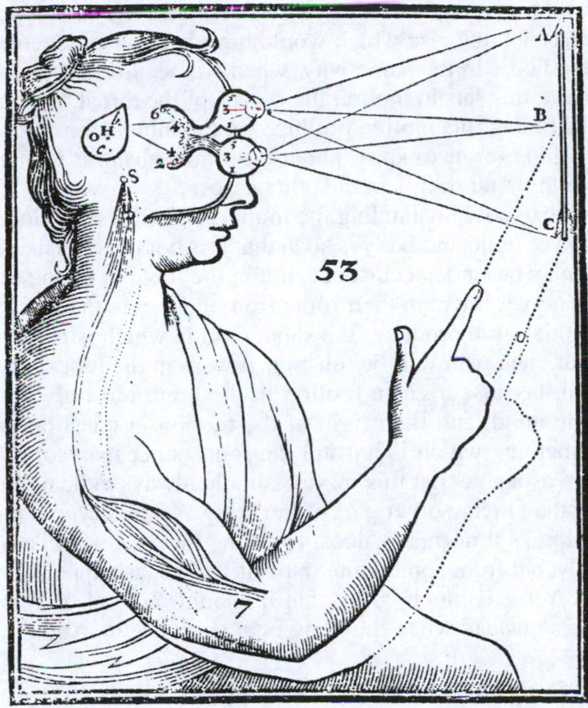

A diagram from Descartes' *Tractatus de Homine* (1677) showing how the pineal gland (shown here at the back of the head) connects sensory images from the eyes to the muscles of the arm. (© Science & Society Picture Library/Getty)

pull on inner parts of the brain to which they are attached, and produce a certain motion in them; and nature has laid it down that this motion should produce in the mind a sensation of pain, as occurring in the foot. But since these nerves, in passing from the foot to the brain, must pass through the calf, the thigh, the lumbar region, the back and the neck, it can happen that, even if it is not the part in the foot but one of the intermediate parts which is being pulled, the same motion will occur in the brain as occurs when the foot is hurt, and so it will necessarily come about that the mind feels the same sensation of pain. And we must suppose the same thing happens with regard to any other sensation.

My final observation is that any given movement occurring in the part of the brain that immediately affects the mind produces just one corresponding sensation; and hence the best system that could be devised is that it should produce the one sensation which, of all possible sensations, is most especially and most frequently conducive to the preservation of the healthy man. And experience shows that the sensations which nature has given us are all of this kind; and so there is absolutely nothing to be found in them
that does not bear witness to the power and goodness of God. For example, when the 88
nerves in the foot are set in motion in a violent and unusual manner, this motion, by way of the spinal cord, reaches the inner parts of the brain, and there gives the mind its signal for having a certain sensation, namely the sensation of a pain as occurring in the foot. This stimulates the mind to do its best to get rid of the cause of the pain, which it takes to be harmful to the foot. It is true that God could have made the nature of man such that this particular motion in the brain indicated something else to the mind; it might, for example, have made the mind aware of the actual motion occurring in the

brain, or in the foot, or in any of the intermediate regions; or it might have indicated something else entirely. But there is nothing else which would have been so conducive to the continued well-being of the body. In the same way, when we need drink, there arises a certain dryness in the throat; this sets in motion the nerves of the throat, which in turn move the inner parts of the brain. This motion produces in the mind a sensation of thirst, because the most useful thing for us to know about the whole business is that we need drink in order to stay healthy. And so it is in the other cases.

It is quite clear from all this that, notwithstanding the immense goodness of God, the nature of man as a combination of mind and body is such that it is bound to mislead him from time to time. For there may be some occurrence, not in the foot but in one of the other areas through which the nerves travel in their route from the foot to the brain, or even in the brain itself; and if this cause produces the same motion which is generally produced by injury to the foot, then pain will be felt as if it were in the foot. This deception of the senses is natural, because a given motion in the brain must always produce the same sensation in the mind; and the origin of the motion in question is much more often going to be something which is hurting the foot, rather than some-
89 thing existing elsewhere. So it is reasonable that this motion should always indicate to the mind a pain in the foot rather than in any other part of the body. Again, dryness of the throat may sometimes arise not, as it normally does, from the fact that a drink is necessary to the health of the body, but from some quite opposite cause, as happens in the case of the man with dropsy. Yet it is much better that it should mislead on this occasion than that it should always mislead when the body is in good health. And the same goes for the other cases.

This consideration is the greatest help to me, not only for noticing all the errors to which my nature is liable, but also for enabling me to correct or avoid them without difficulty. For I know that in matters regarding the well-being of the body, all my senses report the truth much more frequently than not. Also, I can almost always make use of more than one sense to investigate the same thing; and in addition, I can use both my memory, which connects present experiences with preceding ones, and my intellect, which has by now examined all the causes of error. Accordingly, I should not have any further fears about the falsity of what my senses tell me every day; on the contrary, the exaggerated doubts of the last few days should be dismissed as laughable. This applies especially to the principal reason for doubt, namely my inability to distinguish between being asleep and being awake. For I now notice that there is a vast difference between the two, in that dreams are never linked by memory with all the other actions of life as waking experiences are. If, while I am awake, anyone were suddenly to appear to me and then disappear immediately, as happens in sleep, so that I could not see where he had
90 come from or where he had gone to, it would not be unreasonable for me to judge that he was a ghost, or a vision created in my brain, rather than a real man. But when I distinctly see where things come from and where and when they come to me, and when I can connect my perceptions of them with the whole of the rest of my life without a break, then I am quite certain that when I encounter these things I am not asleep but awake. And I ought not to have even the slightest doubt of their reality if, after calling upon all the senses as well as my memory and my intellect in order to check them, I receive no conflicting reports from any of these sources. For from the fact that God is not a deceiver it follows that in cases like these I am completely free from error. But since the pressure of things to be done does not always allow us to stop and make such a meticulous check, it must be admitted that in this human life we are often liable to make mistakes about particular things, and we must acknowledge the weakness of our nature.

CORRESPONDENCE WITH PRINCESS ELIZABETH (selections)

1.a. Princess Elizabeth to Descartes [On the Relation of Soul and Body]

The Hague, 6–16 May 1643.

. . . I beg of you to tell me how the human soul can determine the movement of the animal spirits in the body so as to perform voluntary acts—being as it is merely a conscious (*pensante*) substance. For the determination of movement seems always to come about from the moving body's being propelled—to depend on the kind of impulse it gets from what sets it in motion, or again, on the nature and shape of this latter thing's surface. Now the first two conditions involve contact, and the third involves that the impelling thing has extension; but you utterly exclude extension from your notion of soul, and contact seems to me incompatible with a thing's being immaterial.

I therefore ask you for a more specific definition of the soul than you give in your metaphysics: a definition of its substance, as distinct from its activity, consciousness (*pensée*). Even if we supposed these to be in fact inseparable—a matter hard to prove in regard to children in their mother's womb and severe fainting-fits—to be inseparable as the divine attributes are: nevertheless we may get a more perfect idea of them by considering them apart.

1.b. Descartes to Princess Elizabeth

Egmond, 21 May 1643.

. . . I may truly say that what your Highness is propounding seems to me to be the question people have most right to ask me in view of my published works. For there are two facts about the human soul on which there depends any knowledge we may have as to its nature: first, that it is conscious; secondly, that, being united to a body, it is able to act and suffer along with it. Of the second fact I said almost nothing; my aim was simply to make the first properly understood; for my main object was to prove the distinction of soul and body; and to this end only the first was serviceable, the second might have been prejudicial. But since your Highness sees too clearly for dissimulation to be possible, I will here try to explain how I conceive the union of soul and body and how the soul has the power of moving the body.

My first observation is that there are in us certain primitive notions—the originals, so to say, on the pattern of which we form all other knowledge. These notions are very few in number. First, there are the most general ones, existence, number, duration, etc., which apply to everything we can conceive. As regards body in particular, we have merely the notion of extension and the consequent notions of shape and movement. As

René Descartes, "Correspondence with Princess Elizabeth," from Descartes, *Philosophical Writings*, translated by Elizabeth Anscombe and Peter Thomas Geach (Pearson/Library of the Liberal Arts, 1971).

regards the soul taken by itself, we have merely the notion of consciousness, which comprises the conceptions (*perceptions*) of the intellect and the inclinations of the will. Finally, as regards the soul and body together, we have merely the notion of their union; and on this there depend our notions of the soul's power to move the body, and of the body's power to act on the soul and cause sensations and emotions.

I would also observe that all human knowledge consists just in properly distinguishing these notions and attaching each of them only to the objects that it applies to. If we try to explain some problem by means of a notion that does not apply, we cannot help making mistakes; we are just as wrong if we try to explain one of these notions in terms of another, since, being primitive, each such notion has to be understood in itself. The use of our senses has made us much more familiar with notions of extension, shape, and movement than with others; thus the chief cause of our errors is that ordinarily we try to use these notions to explain matters to which they do not apply; e.g. we try to use our imagination in conceiving the nature of the soul, or to conceive the way the soul moves the body in terms of the way that one body is moved by another body.

In the Meditations that your Highness condescended to read, I tried to bring before the mind the notions that apply to the soul taken by itself, and to distinguish them from those that apply to the body taken by itself. Accordingly, the next thing I have to explain is how we are to form the notions that apply to the union of the soul with the body, as opposed to those that apply to the body taken by itself or the mind taken by itself. . . . These simple notions are to be sought only within the soul, which is naturally endowed with all of them, but does not always adequately distinguish between them, or again, does not always attach them to the right objects.

So I think people have hitherto confused the notions of the soul's power to act within the body and the power one body has to act within another; and they have ascribed both powers not to soul, whose nature was so far unknown, but to various qualities of bodies—gravity, heat, etc. These qualities were imagined to be real, i.e. to have an existence distinct from the existence of bodies; consequently, they were imagined to be substances, although they were called qualities. In order to conceive of them, people have used sometimes notions that we have for the purpose of knowing body, and sometimes those that we have for the purpose of knowing the soul, according as they were ascribing to them a material or an immaterial nature. For example, on the supposition that gravity is a real quality, about which we know no more than its power of moving the body in which it occurs towards the centre of the Earth, we find no difficulty in conceiving how it moves the body or how it is united to it; and we do not think of this as taking place by means of real mutual contact between two surfaces; our inner experience shows (*nous expérimentons*) that that notion is a specific one. Now I hold that we misuse this notion by applying it to gravity (which, as I hope to show in my Physics, is nothing really distinct from body), but that it has been given to us in order that we may conceive of the way that the soul moves the body.

2.a. Princess Elizabeth to Descartes [On the Relation of Soul and Body]

The Hague, 10–20 June 1643.

. . . [I cannot] understand the idea by means of which we are to judge of the way that the soul, unextended and immaterial, moves the body, in terms of the idea you used to have about gravity. You used falsely to ascribe to gravity, under the style of a "quality," the power of carrying bodies towards the centre of the Earth. But I cannot see why this should convince us that a body may be impelled by something immaterial; why we should not rather be confirmed in the view that this is impossible, by the demonstration of a true [view of gravity], opposed [to this], which you promise us in your *Physics;* especially as the idea [that a body may be so impelled] cannot claim the same degree of perfection and representative reality (*réalité objective*) as the idea of God, and may be a figment resulting from ignorance of what really moves bodies towards the centre. Since no material cause was apparent to the senses, people may well have ascribed this to the opposite cause, the immaterial, but I have never been able to conceive *that,* except as a negation of matter, which can have no communication with matter.

And I must confess that I could more readily allow that the soul has matter and extension than that an immaterial being has the capacity of moving a body and being affected by it. If the first, [the soul's moving the body], took place by [the soul's giving] information [to the body], then the [animal] spirits, which carry out the movement, would have to be intelligent; but you do not allow intelligence to anything corporeal. You do indeed show the possibility of the second thing [the body's affecting the soul], in your Metaphysical Meditations; but it is very hard to see how a soul such as you describe, after possessing the power and the habit of correct reasoning, may lose all that because of some vapours [in the brain]; or why the soul is so much governed by the body, when it can subsist separately, and has nothing in common with it. . . .

2.b. Descartes to Princess Elizabeth

Egmond, 28 June 1643.

I am most deeply obliged to your Highness for condescending, after experience of my previous ill success in explaining the problem you were pleased to propound to me, to be patient enough to listen to me once more on the same subject, and to give me an opportunity of making remarks on matters I had passed over. My chief omissions seem to be the following. I began by distinguishing three kinds of primitive ideas or notions, each of which is known in a specific way and not by comparison to another kind; viz. the notion of soul, the notion of body, and the notion of the union between soul and body. I still had to explain the difference between the operations of the soul by means of which we get them, and to show the means of becoming readily familiar with each kind. Further, I had to explain why I used the comparison of gravity. Next, I had to show that even if we try to conceive of the soul as material (which means, properly speaking, to conceive of its union with the body), we cannot help going on to recognise that it is separable from the body. This, I think, is the sum of the task your Highness has set me.

In the first place, then, I discern this great difference between the three kinds of notions: the soul is conceived only by pure intellect; body (i.e. extension, shape, and movement) can likewise be known by pure intellect, but is known much better when intellect is aided by imagination; finally, what belongs to the union of soul and body can be understood only in an obscure way either by pure intellect or even when the intellect is aided by imagination, but is understood very clearly by means of the senses. Consequently, those who never do philosophise and make use only of their senses have no doubt that the soul moves the body and the body acts on the soul; indeed, they consider the two as a single thing, i.e. they conceive of their union; for to conceive of the union between two things is to conceive of them as a single thing. Metaphysical reflections, which exercise the pure intellect, are what make us familiar with the notion of soul; the study of mathematics, which chiefly exercises the imagination in considering figures and movements, accustoms us to form very distinct notions of body; finally, it is just by means of ordinary life and conversation, by abstaining from meditating and from studying things that exercise the imagination, that one learns to conceive the union of soul and body.

I am half afraid that your Highness may think I am not speaking seriously here; but that would be contrary to the respect that I owe to your Highness and will never fail to pay. I can truly say that the chief rule I have always observed in my studies, and the one I think has been most serviceable to me in acquiring some measure of knowledge, has been never to spend more than a few hours a day in thoughts that demand imagination, or more than a few hours a year in thoughts that demand pure intellect; I have given all the rest of my time to the relaxation of my senses and the repose of my mind. I here count among exercises of imagination all serious conversations, and everything that demands attention. This is what made me retire to the country; it is true that in the busiest city in the world I might have as many hours to myself as I now spend in study, but I could not employ them so usefully when my mind was wearied by the attention that the troubles of life demand.

I take the liberty of writing thus to your Highness, to express my sincere admiration of your Highness's ability, among all the business and cares that are never lacking to persons who combine high intelligence and high birth, to find leisure for the meditations that are necessary for proper understanding of the distinction between soul and body. I formed the opinion that it was these meditations, rather than thoughts demanding less attention, that made your Highness find some obscurity in our notion of their union. It seems to me that the human mind is incapable of distinctly conceiving both the distinction between body and soul and their union, at one and the same time; for that requires our conceiving them as a single thing and simultaneously conceiving them as two things, which is self-contradictory. I supposed that your Highness still had very much in mind the arguments proving the distinction of soul and body; and I did not wish to ask you to lay them aside, in order to represent to yourself that notion of their union which everybody always has in himself without doing philosophy—viz. that there is one single person who has at once body and consciousness, so that this consciousness can move the body and be aware of the events that happen to it. Accordingly, I used in my previous letter the simile of gravity and other qualities, which we imagine to be united to bodies as consciousness is united to ours. I did not worry over the fact that this simile is lame, because these qualities are not, as one imagines, realities; for I thought your Highness was already fully convinced that the soul is a substance distinct from the body.

Your Highness, however, makes the remark that it is easier to ascribe matter and extension to the soul than to ascribe to it the power of moving a body and being moved by it without having any matter. Now I would ask your Highness to hold yourself free to ascribe "matter and extension" to the soul; for this is nothing else than to conceive the soul as united to the body. After forming a proper conception of this, and experiencing it in your own case, your Highness will find it easy to reflect that the matter you thus ascribe to your consciousness (*pensée*) is not the consciousness itself; again, the extension of the matter is essentially different from the extension of the consciousness, for the first extension is determined to a certain place, and excludes any other corporeal extension from that place, whereas the second does not. In this way your Highness will assuredly find it easy to come back to a realisation of the distinction between soul and body, in spite of having conceived of them as united.

Finally, I think it is very necessary to have got a good understanding, for once in one's life, of the principles of metaphysics, because it is from these that we have knowledge of God and of our soul. But I also think it would be very harmful to occupy one's intellect often with meditating on them, for it would be the less able to find leisure for the functioning of the imagination and the senses; the best thing is to be content with retaining in memory and in belief the conclusions one has drawn once for all, and to spend the rest of one's time for study in reflections in which the intellect cooperates with the imagination and the senses. . . .

THOMAS HOBBES
1588–1679

Born prematurely when his mother heard of the approach of the Spanish Armada, Thomas Hobbes often quipped that he was born "a twin with fear." Hobbes saw much to fear in his long life. He observed a civil war, the execution of Charles I, and periods of great political and social upheaval. On more than one occasion, he was forced to flee England, and he often feared for his life. It is not surprising, then, that he developed a political philosophy emphasizing fear of death and the need for security.

Hobbes was born in Malmesbury, Whiltshire, England, the son of a disreputable vicar. His father was forced to leave the Whiltshire area after brawling outside his church. Young Thomas was sent to live with a rich uncle. At the age of 14, he went to Oxford University. Like Descartes, he found most of his schooling to be a waste of time. He particularly disliked the Aristotelianism of his college, Magdalen Hall. In 1608, he became the tutor to the son of William Cavendish, Earl of Devonshire. For the rest of his life, Hobbes remained a friend of the Cavendish family and a royalist sympathizer.

Hobbes made several extended visits to the Continent—some voluntary, some a result of running for his life. At home and on the Continent, Hobbes met and conversed with leading thinkers such as Descartes, Galileo, and Bacon. Although he, of course, had differences with them, he nevertheless used each thinker's ideas to refine his own philosophy. From Descartes, he learned to value the geometric method. Descartes used geometry to establish epistemological certainty. Hobbes used geometry to develop a political theory. In opposition to the dominant Aristotelian thesis that rest is the natural state of objects, Galileo had proposed that all bodies are naturally in motion. Hobbes took Galileo's postulate and proceeded to argue that all things in the world, including human beings, are bodies in motion. With Bacon, Hobbes agreed that scientific knowledge was primarily useful for improving the human condition.

In 1628, Hobbes published his first literary work: a translation of *Thucydides*, by which he hoped to use history to enlighten the English people. In Thucydides' *Peloponnesian War,* democratic Athens had been defeated by monarchical Sparta. Hobbes wanted to warn his fellow citizens of the creeping democracy threatening England. Hobbes was convinced that democracy led to chaos and that a strong central government was essential for national stability. In 1640, Hobbes was forced to flee England for Paris when the Long Parliament supplanted the king. In Paris, Hobbes wrote the book for which he is famous, *Leviathan or the Matter, Form, and Power of a Commonwealth, Ecclesiastical and Civil*. The book was published between the execution of Charles I (1649) and the Protectorate of Cromwell (1653), a time ripe for political philosophy.

Cromwell permitted Hobbes to return to England in 1652. Although Hobbes had always been a royalist, his argument for the absolute power of the sovereign was not restricted to kings. Thus Cromwell had no reason to consider Hobbes's doctrine seditious—nor did Charles II, whom Hobbes had tutored in Paris, and who was later restored to the monarchy.

Hobbes's later years were spent writing and arguing for his ideas. Although he continued to have enemies, with the king's friendship he managed to stay out of serious trouble. In his early eighties, Hobbes wrote a history of the period 1640 to 1660, which he called *Behemoth*. When he was 84, Hobbes published his autobiography in Latin verse; at 86, he produced a verse translation of both the *Iliad* and the *Odyssey* (for lack of anything better to do, he commented). He died in 1679 at the age of 91.

* * *

The *Leviathan* is known primarily for its political philosophy, but it touches on a number of other issues including epistemology, metaphysics, ethics, and religion. Hobbes begins with a thoroughgoing version of materialism. Everything in the world, including humans, consists of bodies in motion. Knowledge of the world begins in sensation. Bodies in motion outside of a person cause motion within the person. Memories, imagination, and other "mental" phenomena are the aftershocks of sensations—what Hobbes calls "decaying sense." *Willing* is that "beginning of motion" that leads to action when individuals move and so move other bodies.

Using a mechanistic explanation of "voluntary motions," which he calls "endeavors," Hobbes believes that in human life, self-interest and the desire for power are the basic motive powers. According to Hobbes, each person constantly seeks an advantage over everyone else. Yet since all are born equal, there is no inherent reason why one person should give way to another. The result is what Hobbes calls "a war of every man against every man . . . [in which] the notions of right and wrong, justice and injustice, have no place." In such an environment, life is "solitary, poor, nasty, brutish, and short."

To avoid this natural state of anarchy, individuals must enter into a social contract or covenant with all other individuals to give up their power irrevocably to a sovereign: "This is the generation of that great LEVIATHAN, or rather, to speak more reverently, of that 'mortal god,' to which we owe under the 'immortal God,' our peace and defence." This contract is not binding on the sovereign, as the sovereign is not a party to it. Hence there is no legal limitation on the sovereign's power. The sovereign is the essence of the commonwealth, which can be defined as

> one person, of whose acts a great multitude, by mutual covenants one with another, have made themselves every one the author, to the end he may use the strength and means of them all, as he shall think expedient, for their peace and common defence. . . . And he that carries this person, is called SOVEREIGN, and said to have sovereign power; and every one besides, his SUBJECT.

Hobbes believes this sovereign did not have to be a single person—sovereignty could reside in an individual (a monarchy), a small group (an aristocracy), or in the entire population (a democracy)—though he shows a marked preference for monarchy because of its greater stability and efficiency. What matters to Hobbes above all else is that the sovereign has absolute power in order to keep the peace and to guarantee security. To be sure, an absolute sovereign might abuse power, but the only alternative to this possible abuse, Hobbes claims, is an unthinkable anarchy.

* * *

Hobbes wrote many books over the course of his long life—the standard Oxford edition of his English works includes eleven volumes with another five volumes of his Latin works—but *Leviathan* (1651) is the basis of his fame. The key sections of this work, from Chapters 1–3, 6, 9, 12, 15, 17–18, and 21, are reprinted here. The spelling has been updated and standardized.

For a general introduction to Hobbes's life and thought, see Richard Peters, *Hobbes* (Baltimore, MD: Penguin Books, 1956); Tom Sorell, *Hobbes* (London: Routledge, 1986); A.P. Martinich, *Hobbes: A Biography* (Cambridge: Cambridge University Press, 1999); A.P. Martinich, *Hobbes* (London: Routledge, 2005); and Stephen J. Finn, *Hobbes: A Guide for the Perplexed* (London: Continuum, 2007). For discussions of Hobbes's ethical and political thought as developed in *Leviathan*, see Leo Strauss, *The Political Philosophy of Hobbes* (Chicago: University of Chicago Press, 1952); Howard Warrender, *The Political Philosophy of Hobbes: His Theory of Obligation* (Oxford: Clarendon Press, 1957); David P. Gauthier, *The Logic of* Leviathan: *The Moral and Political Theory of Thomas Hobbes* (Oxford: Clarendon Press, 1969); Michael Oakeshott, *Hobbes on Civil Association* (Berkeley: University of California Press, 1975). More general guides to the *Leviathan* include Glen Newey, *Routledge Philosophy Guidebook to Hobbes and* Leviathan (Abingdon, UK: Routledge, 2002); and L.M.J. Bagby, *Hobbes's* Leviathan: *A Reader's Guide* (London: Continuum, 2007). A.P. Martinich, *A Hobbes Dictionary* (Oxford: Basil Blackwell, 1995) provides a helpful reference work. For collections of essays on Hobbes, see Keith Brown, ed., *Hobbes Studies* (Cambridge, MA: Harvard University Press, 1965); G.A.J. Rogers and Alan Ryan, eds., *Perspectives on Thomas Hobbes* (Oxford: Oxford University Press, 1989); Tom Sorell, ed., *The Cambridge Companion to Hobbes* (Cambridge: Cambridge University Press, 1996); the multi-volume G.A.J. Rogers, ed., *Critical Responses to Hobbes* (Oxford: Routledge, 1997); Patricia Springborg, ed., *The Cambridge Companion to Hobbes's* Leviathan (Cambridge: Cambridge University Press, 2007); and Gabriella Slomp, ed., *Thomas Hobbes* (Burlington, VT: Ashgate, 2008).

LEVIATHAN OR THE MATTER, FORM, AND POWER OF A COMMONWEALTH, ECCLESIASTICAL AND CIVIL (in part)

PART I—OF MAN

CHAPTER 1. OF SENSE

Concerning the thoughts of man, I will consider them first singly, and afterwards in train, or dependence upon one another. Singly, they are every one a "representation" or "appearance" of some quality, or other accident of a body without us, which is commonly called an "object." Which object works on the eyes, ears, and other parts of a man's body, and, by diversity of working, produces diversity of appearances.

The title page of Hobbes's *Leviathan* (1651). The sovereign in the background, whose body is composed of the people, is supreme. He is shown here holding the symbols of both church and state. (*Library of Congress*)

The original of them all is that which we call "sense," for there is no conception in a man's mind which hath not at first, totally or by parts, been begotten upon the organs of sense. The rest are derived from that original.

To know the natural cause of sense is not very necessary to the business now in hand; and I have elsewhere written of the same at large. Nevertheless, to fill each part of my present method I will briefly deliver the same in this place.

The cause of sense is the external body, or object, which presses the organ proper to each sense, either immediately, as in the taste and touch, or mediately, as in seeing, hearing, and smelling; which pressure, by the mediation of the nerves and other strings and membranes of the body continued inwards to the brain and heart, causes there a resistance, or counter-pressure, or endeavor of the heart to deliver itself, which endeavor, because "outward," seems to be some matter without. And this "seeming" or "fancy" is that which men call "sense" and consists, as to the eye, in a "light" or "color figured"; to the ear, in a "sound"; to the nostril, in an "odor"; to the tongue and palate, in a "savor"; and to the rest of the body, in "heat," "cold," "hardness," "softness," and such other qualities as we discern by "feeling." All which qualities, called "sensible" are in the object that causes them but so many several motions of the matter, by which it presses our organs diversely. Neither in us that are pressed are they anything else but divers motions; for motion produces nothing but motion. But their appearance to us is fancy, the same waking that dreaming. And as pressing, rubbing, or striking the eye, makes us fancy a light, and pressing the ear produces a din, so do the bodies also we see or hear produce the same by their strong, though unobserved, action. For if those colors and sounds were in the bodies, or objects that cause them, they could not be severed from them, as by glasses, and in echoes by reflection, we see they are, where we know the thing we see is in one place, the appearance in another. And though at some certain distance the real and very object seem invested with the fancy it begets in us, yet still the object is one thing, the image or fancy is another. So that sense in all cases is nothing else but original fancy, caused, as I have said, by the pressure, that is by the motion, of external things upon our eyes, ears, and other organs thereunto ordained.

But the philosophy schools through all the universities of Christendom, grounded upon certain texts of Aristotle, teach another doctrine, and say, for the cause of "vision," that the thing seen sends forth on every side a "visible species," in English, a "visible show," "apparition," or "aspect," or "a being seen"; the receiving whereof into the eye is "seeing." And for the cause of "hearing," that the thing heard sends forth an "audible species," that is an "audible aspect," or "audible being seen," which entering at the ear makes "hearing." Nay, for the cause of "understanding" also, they say the thing understood sends forth an "intelligible species," that is, an "intelligible being seen," which, coming into the understanding, makes us understand. I say not this as disproving the use of universities; but, because I am to speak hereafter of their office in a commonwealth. I must let you see on all occasions by the way what things would be amended in them, amongst which the frequency of insignificant speech is one.

CHAPTER 2. OF IMAGINATION

That when a thing lies still, unless somewhat else stir it, it will lie still for ever, is a truth that no man doubts of. But that when a thing is in motion, it will eternally be in motion, unless somewhat else stay it, though the reason be the same, namely that nothing can change itself, is not so easily assented to. For men measure not only other men but all other things, by themselves; and, because they find themselves subject after motion to pain and lassitude, think everything else grows weary of motion, and seeks repose of its own accord; little considering whether it be not some other motion wherein that desire of rest they find in themselves consists. From hence it is that the schools say heavy bodies fall downwards out of an appetite to rest, and to conserve their nature in that place which is most proper for them; ascribing appetite and knowledge of what is good for their conservation, which is more than man has, to things inanimate, absurdly.

When a body is once in motion, it moves, unless something else hinder it, eternally; and whatsoever hinders it cannot in an instant, but in time and by degrees, quite extinguish it; and, as we see in the water though the wind cease the waves give not over rolling for a long time after: so also it happens in that motion which is made in the internal parts of a man, then, when he sees, dreams, etc. For, after the object is removed, or the eye shut, we still retain an image of the thing seen, though more obscure than when we see it. And this is it the Latins call "imagination," from the image made in seeing; and apply the same, though improperly, to all the other senses. But the Greeks call it "fancy," which signifies "appearance," and is as proper to one sense as to another. "Imagination," therefore, is nothing but "decaying sense," and is found in men, and many other living creatures, as well sleeping as waking.

The decay of sense in men waking is not the decay of the motion made in sense, but an obscuring of it in such manner as the light of the sun obscures the light of the stars, which stars do no less exercise their virtue, by which they are visible, in the day than in the night. But because amongst many strokes which our eyes, ears, and other organs, receive from external bodies, the predominant only is sensible; therefore, the light of the sun being predominant, we are not affected with the action of the stars. And any object being removed from our eyes, though the impression it made in us remain, yet other objects more present succeeding and working on us, the imagination of the past is obscured and made weak, as the voice of a man is in the noise of the day. From whence it follows that the longer the time is, after the sight or sense of any object, the weaker is the imagination. For the continual change of man's body destroys in time the parts which in sense were moved; so that distance of time, and of place, hath one and the same effect in us. For as at a great distance of place that which we look at appears dim and without distinction of the smaller parts, and as voices grow weak and inarticulate, so also after great distance of time our imagination of the past is weak; and we lose, for example, of cities we have seen many particular streets, and of actions many particular circumstances. This "decaying sense," when we would express the thing itself, I mean "fancy" itself, we call "imagination," as I said before; but when we would express the decay, and signify that the sense is fading, old, and past, it is called "memory." So that imagination and memory are but one thing, which for divers considerations hath divers names.

Much memory, or memory of many things, is called "experience." Again, imagination being only of those things which have been formerly perceived by sense, either all at once or by parts at several times the former, which is the imagining the whole object as it was presented to the sense, is "simple" imagination, as when one imagines a man, or horse, which he hath seen before. The other is "compounded," as when, from the sight of a man at one time, and of a horse at another, we conceive in our mind a Centaur. So when a man compounds the image of his own person with the image of the actions of another man, as when a man images himself a Hercules or an Alexander, which happens often to them that are much taken with reading of romances, it is a compound imagination, and properly but a fiction of the mind. There be also other imaginations that rise in men, though waking, from the great impression made in sense; as, from gazing upon the sun, the impression leaves an image of the sun before our eyes a long time after; and, from being long and vehemently intent upon geometrical figures, a man shall in the dark, though awake, have the images of lines and angles before his eyes; which kind of fancy hath no particular name, as being a thing that doth not commonly fall into men's discourse.

The imaginations of them that sleep are those we call "dreams." And these also, as also all other imaginations, have been before, either totally or by parcels, in the sense. And, because in sense, the brain and nerves, which are the necessary organs of sense, are so benumbed in sleep as not easily to be moved by the action of external objects, there can happen in sleep no imagination, and therefore no dream, but what proceeds from the agitation of the inward parts of man's body; which inward parts, for the connection they have with the brain and other organs, when they be distempered, do keep the same in motion; whereby the imaginations there formerly made, appear as if a man were waking; saving that the organs of sense being now benumbed, so as there is no new object which can master and obscure them with a more vigorous impression, a dream must needs be more clear in this silence of sense than our waking thoughts. And hence it comes to pass that it is a hard matter, and by many thought impossible, to distinguish exactly between sense and dreaming. For my part, when I consider that in dreams I do not often nor constantly think of the same persons, places, objects, and actions, that I do waking, nor remember so long a train of coherent thoughts, dreaming, as at other times, and because waking I often observe the absurdity of dreams, but never dream of the absurdities of my waking thoughts, I am well satisfied, that, being awake, I know I dream not, though when I dream I think myself awake.

And, seeing dreams are caused by the distemper of some of the inward parts of the body, divers distempers must needs cause different dreams. And hence it is that lying cold breeds dreams of fear, and raises the thought and image of some fearful object, the motion from the brain to the inner parts and from the inner parts to the brain being reciprocal; and that, as anger causes heat in some parts of the body when we are awake, so when we sleep the overheating of the same parts causes anger, and raises up in the brain the imagination of an enemy. In the same manner, as natural kindness, when we are awake, causes desire, and desire makes heat in certain other parts of the body; so also too much heat in those parts, while we sleep, raises in the brain an imagination of some kindness shown. In sum, our dreams are the reverse of our waking imaginations, the motion when we are awake beginning at one end, and when we dream at another.

The most difficult discerning of a man's dream from his waking thoughts is, then, when by some accident we observe not that we have slept: which is easy to happen to a man full of fearful thoughts, and whose conscience is much troubled, and that sleeps without the circumstances of going to bed or putting off his clothes, as one that nods in a chair. For he that takes pains, and industriously lays himself to sleep, in case any uncouth and exorbitant fancy come unto him, cannot easily think it other than a dream. We read of Marcus Brutus (one that had his life given him by Julius Cæsar, and was also his favorite, and notwithstanding murdered him) how at Philippi, the night before he gave battle to Augustus Cæsar, he saw a fearful apparition, which is commonly related by historians as a vision; but, considering the circumstances, one may easily judge to have been but a short dream. For, sitting in his tent, pensive and troubled with the horror of his rash act, it was not hard for him, slumbering in the cold, to dream of that which most frightened him; which fear, as by degrees it made him wake, so also it must needs make the apparition by degrees to vanish; and, having no assurance that he slept, he could have no cause to think it a dream or anything but a vision. And this is no very rare accident; for even they that be perfectly awake, if they be timorous and superstitious, possessed with fearful tales, and alone in the dark, are subject to the like fancies, and believe they see spirits and dead men's ghosts walking in churchyards; whereas it is either their fancy only, or else the knavery of such persons as make use of such superstitious fear to pass disguised in the night to places they would not be known to haunt.

From this ignorance of how to distinguish dreams and other strong fancies from vision and sense, did arise the greatest part of the religion of the Gentiles in time past, that worshipped satyrs, fawns, nymphs, and the like; and now-a-days the opinion that rude people have of fairies, ghosts, and goblins, and of the power of witches. For as for witches, I think not that their witchcraft is any real power; but yet that they are justly punished for the false belief they have that they can do such mischief, joined with their purpose to do it if they can; their trade being nearer to a new religion than to a craft or science. And for fairies and walking ghosts, the opinion of them has, I think, been on purpose either taught, or not confuted, to keep in credit the use of exorcism, of crosses, of holy water, and other such inventions of ghostly men. Nevertheless there is no doubt but God can make unnatural apparitions; but that He does it so often as men need to fear such things more than they fear the stay or change of the course of nature, which He also can stay and change, is no point of Christian faith. But evil men, under pretext that God can do anything, are so bold as to say anything when it serves their turn, though they think it untrue; it is the part of a wise man to believe them no farther than right reason makes that which they say appear credible. If this superstitious fear of spirits were taken away, and with it prognostics from dreams, false prophecies, and many other things depending thereon, by which crafty ambitious persons abuse the simple people, men would be much more fitted than they are for civil obedience.

And this ought to be the work of the schools; but they rather nourish such doctrine. For, not knowing what imagination or the senses are, what they receive they teach; some saying that imaginations rise of themselves and have no cause; others that they rise most commonly from the will, and that good thoughts are blown (inspired) into a man by God, and evil thoughts by the devil; or that good thoughts are poured (infused) into a man by God, and evil ones by the devil. Some say the senses receive the species of things, and deliver them to the common sense, and the common sense delivers them over to the fancy, and the fancy to the memory, and the memory to the judgment, like handling of things from one to another, with many words making nothing understood.

The imagination that is raised in man, or any other creature endowed with the faculty of imagining, by words or other voluntary signs, is that we generally call "understanding," and is common to man and beast. For a dog by custom will understand the call or the rating of his master; and so will many other beasts. That understanding which is peculiar to man, is the understanding not only his will, but his conceptions and thoughts, by the sequel and contexture of the names of things into affirmations, negations, and other forms of speech; and of this kind of understanding I shall speak hereafter.

CHAPTER 3. OF THE CONSEQUENCE OR TRAIN OF IMAGINATIONS

By "consequence," or "train," of thoughts I understand that succession of one thought to another which is called, to distinguish it from discourse in words, "mental discourse."

When a man thinks on anything whatever, his next thought after is not altogether so casual as it seems to be. Not every thought to every thought succeeds indifferently.

But as we have no imagination whereof we have not formerly had sense, in whole or in parts, so we have no transition from one imagination to another whereof we never had the like before in our senses. The reason whereof is this. All fancies are motions within us, relics of those made in the sense, and those motions that immediately succeeded one another in the sense continue also together after sense: in so much as the former coming again to take place, and be predominant, the latter followeth, by coherence of the matter moved, in such manner as water upon a plane table is drawn which way any one part of it is guided by the finger. But because in sense to one and the same thing perceived, sometimes one thing sometimes another, succeeds, it comes to pass in time that in the imagining of anything there is no certainty what we shall imagine next: only this is certain, it shall be something that succeeded the same before, at one time or another.

This train of thoughts, or mental discourse, is of two sorts. The first is "unguided," "without design," and inconstant; wherein there is no passionate thought, to govern and direct those that follow, to itself, as the end and scope of some desire or other passion: in which case the thoughts are said to wander, and seem impertinent one to another as in a dream. Such are commonly the thoughts of men that are not only without company but also without care of anything; though even then their thoughts are as busy as at other times, but without harmony; as the sound which a lute out of tune would yield to any man, or in tune to one that could not play. And yet in this wild ranging of the mind a man may oft-times perceive the way of it, and the dependence of one thought upon another. For in a discourse of our present civil war, what could seem more impertinent than to ask, as one did, what was the value of a Roman penny. Yet the coherence to me was manifest enough. For the thought of the war introduced the thought of the delivering up the king to his enemies, the thought of that brought in the thought of the delivering up of Christ; and that again the thought of the thirty pence, which was the price of that treason; and thence easily followed that malicious question; and all this in a moment of time—for thought is quick.

The second is more constant; as being "regulated" by some desire and design. For the impression made by such things as we desire, or fear, is strong and permanent, or, if it cease for a time, of quick return: so strong it is sometimes as to hinder and break our sleep. From desire arises the thought of some means we have seen produce the like of that which we aim at; and from the thought of that, the thought of means to that mean, and so continually till we come to some beginning within our own power. And because the end, by the greatness of the impression, comes often to mind, in case our thoughts begin to wander, they are quickly again reduced into the way: which observed by one of the Seven Wise Men, made him give men this precept, which is now worn out, *Respice finem;* that is to say, in all your actions look often upon what you would have as the thing that directs all your thoughts in the way to attain it.

The train of regulated thoughts is of two kinds; one, when of an effect imagined we seek the causes or means that produce it; and this is common to man and beast. The other is when imagining anything whatsoever we seek all the possible effects that can by it be produced, that is to say, we imagine what we can do with it when we have it. Of which I have not at any time seen any sign but in man only; for this is a curiosity hardly incident to the nature of any living creature that has no other passion but sensual, such as are hunger, thirst, lust, and anger. In sum, the discourse of the mind, when it is governed by design, is nothing but "seeking," or the faculty of invention, which the Latins called sagacitas, and solertia; a hunting out of the causes, of some effect, present or past; or of the effects, of some present or past cause. Sometimes a man seeks what he hath lost; and from that place and time wherein he misses it his mind runs back, from place to place, and time to time, to find where and when he had it, that is to say, to find some certain and limited time and place in which to begin a method of seeking. Again, from thence his thoughts run over the same places and times to find what action or other occasion might make him lose it. This we call "remembrance," or calling to mind: the Latins call it *reminiscentia*, as it were a "re-conning" of our former actions.

Sometimes a man knows a place determinate, within the compass whereof he is to seek; and then his thoughts run over all the parts thereof, in the same manner as one would sweep a room to find a jewel, or as a spaniel ranges the field till he find a scent, or as a man should run over the alphabet to start a rhyme.

Sometimes a man desires to know the event of an action; and then he thinks of some like action past, and the events thereof one after another, supposing like events will follow like actions. As he that foresees what will become of a criminal recons what he has seen follow on the like crime before, having this order of thoughts, the crime, the officer, the prison, the judge, and the gallows. Which kind of thoughts is called "foresight," and "prudence," or "providence," and sometimes "wisdom," though such conjecture, through the difficulty of observing all circumstances, be very fallacious. But this is certain: by how much one man has more experience of things past than another, by so much also he is more prudent, and his expectations the seldomer fail him. The "present" only has a being in nature; things "past" have a being in the memory only, but things "to come" have no being at all, the "future" being but a fiction of the mind, applying the sequels of actions past to the actions that are present; which with most certainty is done by him that has most experience, but not with certainty enough. And though it be called prudence, when the event answers our expectation, yet, in its own nature, it is but presumption. For the foresight of things to come, which is providence, belongs only to him by whose will they are to come. From him only, and supernaturally, proceeds prophecy. The best prophet naturally is the best guesser; and the best guesser he that is most versed and studied in the matters he guesses at, for he hath most "signs" to guess by.

A "sign" is the event antecedent of the consequent; and, contrarily, the consequent of the antecedent, when the like consequences have been observed before; and the oftener they have been observed, the less uncertain is the sign. And therefore he that has most experience in any kind of business has most signs whereby to guess at the future time, and consequently is the most prudent; and so much more prudent than he that is new in that kind of business as not to be equalled by any advantage of natural and extemporary wit; though perhaps many young men think the contrary.

Nevertheless it is not prudence that distinguishes man from beast. There be beasts that at a year old observe more, and pursue that which is for their good more prudently than a child can do at ten.

As prudence is a "presumption" of the "future" contracted from the "experience" of time "past," so there is a presumption of things past taken from other things, not future, but past also. For he that hath seen by what courses and degrees a flourishing state hath first come into civil war, and then to ruin, upon the sight of the ruins of any other state will guess the like war and the like courses have been there also. But this conjecture has the same uncertainty almost with the conjecture of the future, both being grounded only upon experience.

There is no other act of man's mind that I can remember naturally planted in him, so as to need no other thing to the exercise of it but to be born a man, and live with the use of his five senses. Those other faculties of which I shall speak by and by, and which seem proper to man only, are acquired and increased by study and industry, and of most men learned by instruction and discipline; and proceed all from the invention of words and speech. For besides sense, and thoughts, and the train of thoughts, the mind of man has no other motion, though by the help of speech and method the same faculties may be improved to such a height as to distinguish men from all other living creatures.

Whatsoever we imagine is "finite." Therefore there is no idea or conception of any thing we call "infinite." No man can have in his mind an image of infinite magnitude, nor conceive infinite swiftness, infinite time, or infinite force, or infinite power. When we say anything is infinite, we signify only that we are not able to conceive the ends and bounds of the things named; having no conception of the thing, but of our own inability. And therefore the name of God is used, not to make us conceive Him, for He is incomprehensible, and His greatness and power are inconceivable, but that we may honor Him. Also because, whatsoever, as I said before, we conceive, has been perceived first by sense, either all at once or by parts; a man can have no thought representing anything not subject to sense. No man therefore can conceive anything but he must conceive it in some place, and endowed with some determinate magnitude, and which may be divided into parts; nor that anything is all in this place and all in another place at the same time; nor that two or more things can be in one and the same place at once: for none of these things ever have or can be incident to sense, but are absurd speeches, taken upon credit, without any signification at all, from deceived philosophers, and deceived or deceiving schoolmen.

* * *

CHAPTER 6. OF THE INTERIOR BEGINNINGS OF VOLUNTARY MOTIONS; COMMONLY CALLED THE PASSIONS; AND THE SPEECHES BY WHICH THEY ARE EXPRESSED

There be in animals two sorts of "motions" peculiar to them: one called "vital," begun in generation, and continued without interruption through their whole life, such as are the "course" of the "blood," the "pulse," the "breathing," the "concoction, nutrition, excretion," etc., to which motions there needs no help of imagination: the other is "animal motion," otherwise called "voluntary motion," as to "go," to "speak," to "move" any of our limbs in such manner as is first fancied in our minds. That sense is motion in the organs and interior parts of man's body, caused by the action of the things we see, hear, etc.; and that fancy is but the relics of the same motion, remaining after sense, has been already said in the first and second chapters. And, because "going," "speaking," and the like voluntary motions, depend always upon a precedent thought of "whither," "which way," and "what," it is evident that the imagination is the first internal beginning of all voluntary motion. And, although unstudied men do not conceive any motion at all to be there where the thing moved is invisible, or the space it is moved in is, for the shortness of it, insensible, yet that doth not hinder but that such motions are. For, let a space be never so little, that which is moved over a greater space, whereof that little one is part, must first be moved over that. These small beginnings of motion within the body of man before they appear in walking, speaking, striking, and other visible actions, are commonly called "endeavor."

This endeavor, when it is toward something which causes it, is called "appetite," or "desire," the latter being the general name, and the other oftentimes restrained to signify the desire of food, namely "hunger" and "thirst." And, when the endeavor is fromward something, it is generally called "aversion." These words, "appetite" and "aversion," we have from the Latins—and they both of them signify the motions, one of approaching, the other of retiring. So also do the Greek words for the same, which are ⟨*horma*⟩ and ⟨*aphorma*⟩. For Nature itself does often press upon men those truths which afterwards, when they look for somewhat beyond Nature, they stumble at. For the schools find in mere appetite to go, or move, no actual motion at all; but, because some motion they must acknowledge, they call it metaphorical motion, which is but an absurd speech; for though words may be called metaphorical, bodies and motions cannot.

That which men desire they are also said to "love"; and to "hate" those things for which they have aversion. So that desire and love are the same thing, save that by desire we always signify the absence of the object, by love most commonly the presence of the same. So also by aversion we signify the absence, and by hate, the presence of the object.

Of appetites and aversions, some are born with men, as appetite of food, appetite of excretion, and exoneration, which may also and more properly be called aversions from somewhat they feel in their bodies; and some other appetites, not many. The rest, which are appetites of particular things, proceed from experience and trial of their effects upon themselves or other men. For of things we know not at all, or believe not to be, we can have no further desire than to taste and try. But aversion we have for things not only which we know have hurt us, but also that we do not know whether they will hurt us or not.

Those things which we neither desire nor hate we are said to "contemn," "contempt" being nothing else but an immobility or contumacy of the heart in resisting the action of certain things, and proceeding from that the heart is already moved otherwise by other more potent objects, or from want of experience of them.

And, because the constitution of a man's body is in continual mutation, it is impossible that all the same things should always cause in him the same appetites and aversions: much less can all men consent in the desire of almost any one and the same object.

But whatsoever is the object of any man's appetite or desire, that is it which he for his part calls "good"; and the object of his hate and aversion, "evil"; and of his contempt "vile" and "inconsiderable." For these words of good, evil, and contemptible, are ever used with relation to the person that uses them, there being nothing simply and absolutely so; nor any common rule of good and evil, to be taken from the nature of the objects themselves; but from the person of the man, where there is no commonwealth, or, in a commonwealth, from the person that represents it; or from an arbitrator or judge, whom men disagreeing shall by consent set up, and make his sentence the rule thereof.

The Latin tongue has two words whose significations approach to those of good and evil, but are not precisely the same; and those are *pulchrum* and *turpe*. Whereof the former signifies that which by some apparent signs promises good; and the latter that which promises evil. But in our tongue we have not so general names to express them by. But for pulchrum we say in some things "fair," in others, "beautiful," or "handsome," or "gallant," or "honorable," or "comely," or "amiable"; and for *turpe*, "foul," "deformed," "ugly," "base," "nauseous," and the like, as the subject shall require; all which words, in their proper places, signify nothing else but the "mien," or countenance, that promises good and evil. So that of good there be three kinds: good in the promise, that is *pulchrum*; good in effect, as the end desired, which is called *jucundum*, "delightful"; and good as the means which is called *utile*, "profitable"; and as many of evil: for "evil" in promise is that they call *turpe*; evil in effect, and end is molestum, "unpleasant," "troublesome"; and evil in the means, *inutile*, "unprofitable," "hurtful."

As, in sense, that which is really within us is, as I have said before, only motion caused by the action of external objects but in appearance—to the sight, light and color; to the ear, sound; to the nostril, odor, etc.; so, when the action of the same object is continued from the eyes, ears, and other organs to the heart, the real effect there is nothing but motion or endeavor which consists in appetite, or aversion, to or from the object moving. But the appearance, or sense of that motion, is that we either call "delight" or "trouble of mind."

This motion, which is called appetite, and for the appearance of it "delight" and "pleasure," seems to be a corroboration of vital motion, and a help thereunto; and therefore such things as caused delight were not improperly called *jucunda—juvando*, from helping or fortifying; and the contrary *molesta*, "offensive," from hindering and troubling the motion vital.

"Pleasure," therefore, or "delight," is the appearance or sense of good; and "molestation," or "displeasure," the appearance or sense of evil. And consequently all appetite, desire, and love, is accompanied with some delight more or less; and all hatred and aversion with more or less displeasure and offence.

Of pleasures or delights some arise from the sense of an object present; and those may be called "pleasures of sense," the word "sensual," as it is used by those only that condemn them, having no place till there be laws. Of this kind are all onerations and exonerations of the body, as also all that is pleasant in the "sight," "hearing," "smell," "taste," or "touch." Others arise from the expectation that proceeds from foresight of the end or consequence of things, whether those things in the sense please or displease. And these are "pleasures of the mind" of him that draws those consequences, and are generally called "joy." In the like manner, displeasures are some in the sense, and called "pain"; others in the expectation of consequences, and are called "grief."

These simple passions called "appetite," "desire," "love," "aversion," "hate," "joy," and "grief," have their names for divers considerations diversified. As first, when they one succeed another, they are diversely called from the opinion men have of the likelihood of attaining what they desire. Secondly, from the object loved or hated. Thirdly, from the consideration of many of them together. Fourthly, from the alteration or succession itself.

For "appetite" with an opinion of attaining is called "hope."

The same without such opinion, "despair."

"Aversion" with opinion of "hurt" from the object "fear."

The same with hope of avoiding that hurt by resistance, "courage."

Sudden "courage," "anger."

Constant "hope," "confidence" of ourselves.

Constant "despair," "diffidence" of ourselves.

"Anger" for great hurt done to another, when we conceive the same to be done by injury, "indignation."

"Desire" of good to another, "benevolence," "good will," "charity." If to man generally, "good-nature."

"Desire" of riches, "covetousness," a name used always in signification of blame, because men contending for them are displeased with one another attaining them, though the desire in itself be to be blamed, or allowed, according to the means by which those riches are sought.

"Desire" of office, or precedence, "ambition," a name used also in the worse sense, for the reason before mentioned.

"Desire" of things that conduce but a little to our ends, and fear of things that are but of little hindrance, "pusillanimity."

"Contempt" of little helps and hindrances, "magnanimity."

"Magnanimity" in danger of death or wounds, "valor," "fortitude."

"Magnanimity" in the use of riches, "liberality."

"Pusillanimity" in the same, "wretchedness," "miserableness," or "parsimony," as it is liked or disliked.

"Love" of persons for society, "kindness."

"Love" of persons for pleasing the sense only, "natural lust."

"Love" of the same, acquired from rumination, that is imagination of pleasure past, "luxury."

"Love" of one singularly, with desire to be singularly beloved, "the passion of love." The same, with fear that the love is not mutual, "jealousy."

"Desire," by doing hurt to another, to make him condemn some fact of his own, "revengefulness."

"Desire" to know why and how, "curiosity," such as is in no living creature but "man," so that man is distinguished not only by his reason but also by this singular passion from other "animals," in whom the appetite of food, and other pleasures of sense, by predominance take away the care of knowing causes, which is a lust of the mind, that by a perseverance of delight in the continual and indefatigable generation of knowledge exceeds the short vehemence of any carnal pleasure.

"Fear" of power invisible, feigned by the mind or imagined from tales publicly allowed, "religion," not allowed, "superstition." And when the power imagined is truly such as we imagine, "true religion."

"Fear," without the apprehension of why or what, "panic terror," called so from the fables that make Pan the author of them, whereas in truth there is always in him that so fears, first some apprehension of the cause, though the rest run away by example, every one supposing his fellow to know why. And therefore this passion happens to none but in a throng or multitude of people.

"Joy," from apprehension of novelty "admiration," proper to man, because it excites the appetite of knowing the cause.

"Joy," arising from imagination of a man's own power and ability is that exultation of the mind which is called "glorying," which, if grounded upon the experience of his own former actions, is the same as "confidence," but if grounded on the flattery of others or only supposed by himself for delight in the consequences of it, is called "vain-glory," which name is properly given, because a well-grounded "confidence" begets attempt, whereas the supposing of power does not, and is therefore rightly called "vain."

"Grief" from opinion of want of power is called "dejection of mind."

The "vain-glory" which consists in the feigning or supposing of abilities in ourselves which we know are not is most incident to young men, and nourished by the histories or fictions of gallant persons, and is corrected oftentimes by age and employment.

"Sudden glory" is the passion which makes those "grimaces" called "laughter"; and is caused either by some sudden act of their own that pleases them, or by the apprehension of some deformed thing in another by comparison whereof they suddenly applaud themselves. And it is incident most to them that are conscious of the fewest abilities in themselves; who are forced to keep themselves in their own favor by observing the imperfections of other men. And therefore much laughter at the defects of others is a sign of pusillanimity. For of great minds one of the proper works is to help and free others from scorn and compare themselves only with the most able.

On the contrary, "sudden dejection" is the passion that causes "weeping," and is caused by such accidents as suddenly take away some vehement hope or some prop of their power; and they are most subject to it that rely principally on helps external, such as are women and children. Therefore some weep for the loss of friends, others for their unkindness, others for the sudden stop made to their thoughts of revenge by reconciliation. But in all cases, both laughter and weeping, are sudden motions, custom taking them both away. For no man laughs at old jests, or weeps for an old calamity.

"Grief" for the discovery of some defect of ability is "shame," or the passion that discovers itself in "blushing," and consists in the apprehension of something dishonorable; and in young men is a sign of the love of good reputation, and commendable: in old men it is a sign of the same; but, because it comes too late, not commendable.

The "contempt" of good reputation is called "impudence."

"Grief" for the calamity of another is "pity," and arises from the imagination that the like calamity may befall himself; and therefore is called also "compassion," and in the phrase of this present time a "fellow-feeling"; and therefore for calamity arriving from great wickedness the best men have the least pity; and for the same calamity those have least pity that think themselves least obnoxious to the same.

"Contempt," or little sense of the calamity of others, is that which men call "cruelty," proceeding from security of their own fortune. For, that any man should take pleasure in other men's great harms without other end of his own, I do not conceive it possible.

"Grief" for the success of a competitor in wealth, honor, or other good, if it be joined with endeavor to enforce our own abilities to equal or exceed him, is called "emulation"; but joined with endeavor to supplant or hinder a competitor, "envy."

When in the mind of man, appetites and aversions, hopes and fears, concerning one and the same thing, arise alternately, and divers good and evil consequences of the doing or omitting the thing propounded, come successively into our thoughts, so that sometimes we have an appetite to it, sometimes an aversion from it, sometimes hope to be able to do it, sometimes despair or fear to attempt it, the whole sum of desires, aversions, hopes, and fears, continued till the thing be either done or thought impossible, is that we call "deliberation."

Therefore of things past there is no "deliberation," because manifestly impossible to be changed; nor of things known to be impossible, or thought so, because men know, or think, such deliberation vain. But of things impossible which we think possible we may deliberate, not knowing it is in vain. And it is called "deliberation," because it is a putting an end to the "liberty" we had of doing or omitting according to our own appetite or aversion.

This alternate succession of appetites, aversions, hopes, and fears, is no less in other living creatures than in man; and therefore beasts also deliberate.

Every "deliberation" is then said to "end" when that whereof they deliberate is either done or thought impossible because till then we retain the liberty of doing or omitting according to our appetite or aversion.

In "deliberation," the last appetite, or aversion, immediately adhering to the action, or to the omission thereof, is that we call the "will," the act, not the faculty, of "willing." And beasts that have "deliberation" must necessarily also have "will." The definition of the "will" given commonly by the schools, that it is a "rational appetite," is not good. For if it were, then could there be no voluntary act against reason. For a "voluntary act" is that which proceeds from the "will" and no other. But if instead of a rational appetite we shall say an appetite resulting from a precedent deliberation, then the definition is the same that I have given here. Will, therefore, is the last appetite in deliberating. And, though we say in common discourse a man had a will once to do a thing, that nevertheless he forbore to do, yet that is properly but an inclination, which makes no action voluntary; because the action depends not of it, but of the last inclination or appetite. For if the intervenient appetites make any action voluntary, then by the same reason all intervenient aversions should make the same action involuntary; and so one and the same action should be both voluntary and involuntary.

By this it is manifest that not only actions that have their beginning from covetousness, ambition, lust, or other appetites to the thing propounded, but also those that have their beginning from aversion, or fear of those consequences that follow the omission, are "voluntary actions."

The forms of speech by which the passions are expressed are partly the same, and partly different from those by which we express our thoughts. And, first, generally all passions may be expressed "indicatively," as "I love," "I fear," "I joy," "I deliberate," "I will," "I command," but some of them have particular expressions by themselves, which nevertheless are not affirmations, unless it be when they serve to make other inferences besides that of the passion they proceed from. Deliberation is expressed "subjunctively," which is a speech proper to signify suppositions, with their consequences: as, "if this be done, then this will follow," and differs not from the language of reasoning, save that reasoning is in general words—but deliberation for the most part is of particulars. The language of desire, and aversion, is "imperative," as "do this," "forbear that," which when the party is obliged to do, or forbear, is "command"; otherwise "prayer," or else "counsel." The language of vain-glory, of indignation, pity and revengefulness, "optative," but of the desire to know there is a peculiar expression, called "interrogative," as "what is it"? "when shall it"? "how is it done"? and "why so"? Other language of the passions I find none; for cursing, swearing, reviling, and the like, do not signify as speech, but as the actions of a tongue accustomed.

These forms of speech, I say, are expressions, or voluntary significations of our passions—but certain signs they be not, because they may be used arbitrarily, whether they that use them have such passions or not. The best signs of passions present are either in the countenance, motions of the body, actions, and ends, or aims, which we otherwise know the man to have.

And because in deliberation the appetites and aversions are raised by foresight of the good and evil consequences, and sequels of the action whereof we deliberate, the good or evil effect thereof depends on the foresight of a long chain of consequences of which very seldom any man is able to see to the end. But for so far as a man sees, if the good in those consequences be greater than the evil, the whole chain is that which writers call "apparent" or "seeming good." And, contrarily, when the evil exceeds the good, the whole is "apparent" or "seeming evil," so that he who hath by experience, or reason, the greatest and surest prospect of consequences, deliberates best himself, and is able, when he will, to give the best counsel unto others.

"Continual success" in obtaining those things which a man from time to time desires, that is to say continual prospering, is that men call "felicity"; I mean the felicity of this life. For there is no such thing as perpetual tranquility of mind while we live here, because life itself is but motion, and can never be without desire, nor without fear, no more than without sense. What kind of felicity God hath ordained to them that devoutly honor Him a man shall no sooner know than enjoy, being joys that now are as incomprehensible as the word of schoolmen "beatifical vision" is unintelligible.

The form of speech whereby men signify their opinion of the goodness of anything is "praise." That whereby they signify the power and greatness of anything is "magnifying." And that whereby they signify the opinion they have of a man's felicity is by the Greeks called ⟨*makarismos*⟩ for which we have no name in our tongue. And thus much is sufficient for the present purpose, to have been said of the "passions."

* * *

CHAPTER 9. OF THE SEVERAL SUBJECTS OF KNOWLEDGE

There are of "knowledge" two kinds, whereof one is "knowledge of fact," the other "knowledge of the consequence of one affirmation to another." The former is nothing else but sense and memory, and is "absolute knowledge," as when we see a fact doing or remember it done; and this is the knowledge required in a witness. The latter is called "science," and is "conditional," as when we know that "if the figure shown be a circle, then any straight line through the center shall divide it into two equal parts." And this is the knowledge required in a philosopher, that is to say of him that pretends to reasoning.

The register of "knowledge of fact" is called "history," whereof there be two sorts: one called "natural history," which is the history of such facts or effects of Nature as have no dependence on man's "will," such as are the histories of "metals," "plants," "animals," "regions," and the like. The other is "civil history," which is the history of the voluntary actions of men in commonwealths.

The registers of science are such "books," as contain the "demonstrations" of consequences of one affirmation to another, and are commonly called "books of philosophy," whereof the sorts are many, according to the diversity of the matter, and may be divided in such manner as I have divided them in the . . . table [see following page].

* * *

CHAPTER 12. OF RELIGION

Seeing there are no signs nor fruit of "religion" but in man only, there is no cause to doubt but that the seed of "religion" is also only in man—and consists in some peculiar quality or at least in some eminent degree thereof not to be found in other living creatures.

And, first, it is peculiar to the nature of man to be inquisitive into the causes of the events they see, some more, some less; but all men so much as to be curious in the search of the causes of their own good and evil fortune.

Secondly, upon the sight of anything that hath a beginning to think also it had a cause which determined the same to begin, then when it did, rather than sooner or later.

Thirdly, whereas there is no other felicity of beasts but the enjoying of their quotidian food, ease, and lusts, as having little or no foresight of the time to come, for want of observation and memory of the order, consequence, and dependence of the things they see, man observes how one event hath been produced by another, and remembers in them antecedence and consequence; and, when he cannot assure himself of the true causes of things (for the causes of good and evil fortune for the most part are invisible), he supposes causes of them, either such as his own fancy suggests, or trusts the authority of other men, such as he thinks to be his friends and wiser than himself.

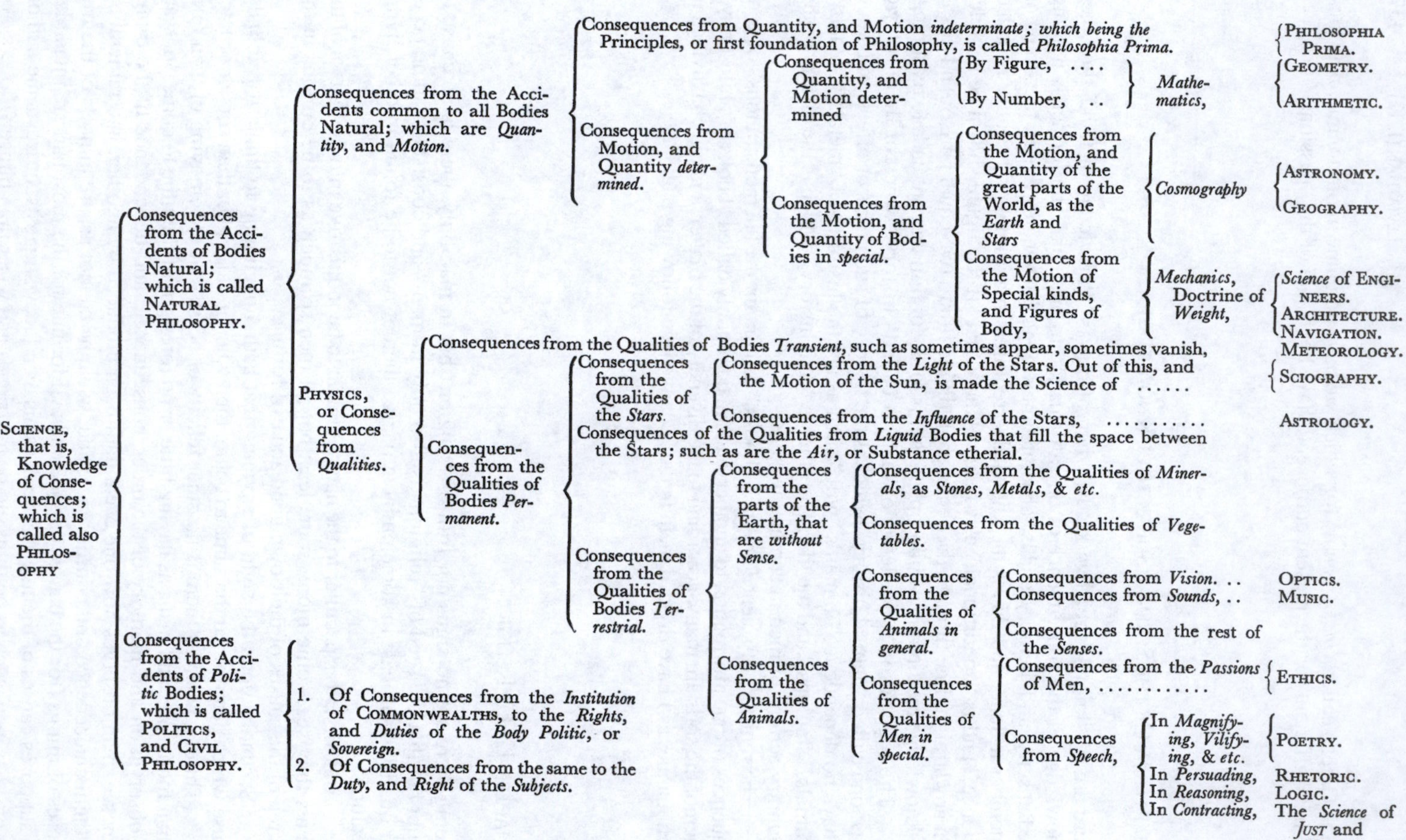
SCIENCE, that is, Knowledge of Consequences; which is called also PHILOSOPHY
Consequences from the Accidents of Bodies Natural; which is called NATURAL PHILOSOPHY.
Consequences from the Accidents common to all Bodies Natural; which are Quantity, and Motion.
Consequences from Quantity, and Motion indeterminate; which being the Principles, or first foundation of Philosophy, is called Philosophia Prima.
PHILOSOPHIA PRIMA.
Consequences from Motion, and Quantity determined.
Consequences from Quantity, and Motion determined
By Figure, ...
By Number, ..
Mathematics,
GEOMETRY.
ARITHMETIC.
Consequences from the Motion, and Quantity of Bodies in special.
Consequences from the Motion, and Quantity of the great parts of the World, as the Earth and Stars
Cosmography
ASTRONOMY.
GEOGRAPHY.
Consequences from the Motion of Special kinds, and Figures of Body,
Mechanics, Doctrine of Weight,
Science of ENGINEERS.
ARCHITECTURE.
NAVIGATION.
PHYSICS, or Consequences from Qualities.
Consequences from the Qualities of Bodies Transient, such as sometimes appear, sometimes vanish,
METEOROLOGY.
Consequences from the Qualities of Bodies Permanent.
Consequences from the Qualities of the Stars.
Consequences from the Light of the Stars. Out of this, and the Motion of the Sun, is made the Science of .....
SCIOGRAPHY.
Consequences from the Influence of the Stars, ...
ASTROLOGY.
Consequences of the Qualities from Liquid Bodies that fill the space between the Stars; such as are the Air, or Substance etherial.
Consequences from the Qualities of Bodies Terrestrial.
Consequences from the parts of the Earth, that are without Sense.
Consequences from the Qualities of Minerals, as Stones, Metals, & etc.
Consequences from the Qualities of Vegetables.
Consequences from the Qualities of Animals.
Consequences from the Qualities of Animals in general.
Consequences from Vision. ..
OPTICS.
Consequences from Sounds, ..
MUSIC.
Consequences from the rest of the Senses.
Consequences from the Qualities of Men in special.
Consequences from the Passions of Men, ...
ETHICS.
Consequences from Speech,
In Magnifying, Vilifying, & etc.
POETRY.
In Persuading,
RHETORIC.
In Reasoning,
LOGIC.
In Contracting,
The Science of JUST and UNJUST
Consequences from the Accidents of Politic Bodies; which is called POLITICS, and CIVIL PHILOSOPHY.
1. Of Consequences from the Institution of COMMONWEALTHS, to the Rights, and Duties of the Body Politic, or Sovereign.
2. Of Consequences from the same to the Duty, and Right of the Subjects.

The two first make anxiety. For, being assured that there be causes of all things that have arrived hitherto or shall arrive hereafter, it is impossible for a man, who continually endeavors to secure himself against the evil he fears and procure the good he desires, not to be in a perpetual solicitude of the time to come; so that every man, especially those that are over-provident, are in a state like to that of Prometheus. For as Prometheus, which interpreted is "the prudent man," was bound to the hill Caucasus, a place of large prospect, where an eagle feeding on his liver devoured in the day as much as was repaired in the night, so that man, which looks too far before him in the care of future time, hath his heart all the day long gnawed on by fear of death, poverty, or other calamity, and has no repose nor pause of his anxiety but in sleep.

This perpetual fear, always accompanying mankind in the ignorance of causes, as it were in the dark, must needs have for object something. And therefore, when there is nothing to be seen, there is nothing to accuse, either of their good or evil fortune, but some "power" or agent "invisible" in which sense perhaps it was that some of the old poets said that the gods were at first created by human fear; which spoken of the gods, that is to say of the many gods of the Gentiles, is very true. But the acknowledging of one God, eternal, infinite, and omnipotent, may more easily be derived, from the desire men have to know the causes of natural bodies and their several virtues and operations, than from the fear of what was to befall them in time to come. For he that from any effect he sees come to pass should reason to the next and immediate cause thereof, and from thence to the cause of that cause, and plunge himself profoundly in the pursuit of causes, shall at last come to this, that there must be, as even the heathen philosophers confessed, one first mover, that is, a first and an eternal cause of all things, which is that which men mean by the name of God, and all this without thought of their fortune; the solicitude whereof both inclines to fear and hinders them from the search of the causes of other things, and thereby gives occasion of feigning of as many gods as there be men that feign them.

* * *

CHAPTER 13. OF THE NATURAL CONDITION OF MANKIND AS CONCERNING THEIR FELICITY AND MISERY

Nature hath made men so equal in the faculties of the body and mind, as that, though there be found one man sometimes manifestly stronger in body or of quicker mind than another, yet when all is reckoned together the difference between man and man is not so considerable as that one man can thereupon claim to himself any benefit to which another may not pretend as well as he. For, as to the strength of body, the weakest has strength enough to kill the strongest, either by secret machination or by confederacy with others that are in the same danger with himself.

And, as to the faculties of the mind, setting aside the arts grounded upon words and especially that skill of proceeding upon general and infallible rules called science, which very few have and but in few things, as being not a native faculty born with us, nor attained, as prudence, while we look after somewhat else, I find yet a greater equality amongst men than that of strength. For prudence is but experience, which equal time equally bestows on all men in those things they equally apply themselves unto. That which may perhaps make such equality incredible is but a vain conceit of one's own wisdom, which almost all men think they have in a greater degree than the vulgar, that is, than all men but themselves, and a few others whom by fame or for concurring with themselves they approve. For such is the nature of men that, howsoever they may acknowledge many others to be more witty or more eloquent or more learned, yet they will hardly believe there be many so wise as themselves, for they see their own wit at hand and other men's at a distance. But this proves rather that men are in that point equal than unequal. For there is not ordinarily a greater sign of the equal distribution of anything than that every man is contented with his share.

From this equality of ability arises equality of hope in the attaining of our ends. And therefore, if any two men desire the same thing which nevertheless they cannot both enjoy, they become enemies—and, in the way to their end, which is principally their own conservation and sometimes their delectation only, endeavor to destroy or subdue one another. And from hence it comes to pass that, where an invader hath no more to fear than another man's single power, if one plant, sow, build, or possess, a convenient seat others may probably be expected to come prepared with forces united to dispossess and deprive him not only of the fruit of his labor but also of his life or liberty. And the invader again is in the like danger of another.

And from this diffidence of one another there is no way for any man to secure himself so reasonable as anticipation, that is, by force or wiles to master the persons of all men he can so long till he see no other power great enough to endanger him; and this is no more than his own conservation requires and is generally allowed. Also, because there be some that, taking pleasure in contemplating their own power in the acts of conquest, which they pursue farther than their security requires, if others, that otherwise would be glad to be at ease within the modest bounds, should not by invasion increase their power, they would not be able for a long time, by standing only on their defence, to subsist. And by consequence, such augmentation of dominion over men being necessary to a man's conservation, it ought to be allowed him.

Again, men have no pleasure, but on the contrary a great deal of grief, in keeping company where there is no power able to overawe them all. For every man looks that his companion should value him at the same rate he sets upon himself, and, upon all signs of contempt or undervaluing, naturally endeavors as far as he dares (which amongst them that have no common power to keep them in quiet, is far enough to make them destroy each other) to extort a greater value from his condemners by damage, and from others by the example.

So that in the nature of man we find three principal causes of quarrel. First, competition; secondly, diffidence; thirdly, glory.

The first makes man invade for gain; the second, for safety; and the third, for reputation. The first use violence, to make themselves masters of other men's persons, wives, children, and cattle; the second, to defend them; the third, for trifles, as a word, a smile, a different opinion, and any other sign of undervalue, either direct in their persons or by reflection in their kindred, their friends, their nation, their profession, or their name.

Hereby it is manifest that, during the time men live without a common power to keep them all in awe, they are in that condition which is called war, and such a war as is of every man against every man. For "war" consists not in battle only or the act of fighting, but in a tract of time wherein the will to contend by battle is sufficiently known, and therefore the notion of "time" is to be considered in the nature of war, as it is in the nature of weather. For as the nature of foul weather lies not in a shower or two of rain but in an inclination thereto of many days together, so the nature of war consists not in actual fighting but in the known disposition thereto during all the time there is no assurance to the contrary. All other time is "peace."

Whatsoever therefore is consequent to a time of war where every man is enemy to every man, the same is consequent to the time wherein men live without other security than what their own strength and their own invention shall furnish them withal. In such condition there is no place for industry, because the fruit thereof is uncertain, and consequently no culture of the earth, no navigation nor use of the commodities that may be imported by sea, no commodious building, no instruments of moving and removing such things as require much force, no knowledge of the face of the earth; no account of time, no arts, no letters, no society, and, which is worst of all, continual fear and danger of violent death, and the life of man solitary, poor, nasty, brutish, and short.

It may seem strange to some man that has not well weighed these things that Nature should thus dissociate and render men apt to invade and destroy one another; and he may therefore, not trusting to this inference made from the passions, desire perhaps to have the same confirmed by experience. Let him therefore consider with himself, when taking a journey, he arms himself and seeks to go well accompanied; when going to sleep, he locks his doors; when even in his house, he locks his chests; and this when he knows there be laws and public officers armed to revenge all injuries shall be done him; what opinion he has of his fellow-subjects, when he rides armed—of his fellow-citizens, when he locks his doors; and of his children and servants, when he locks his chests. Does he not there as much accuse mankind by his actions as I do by my words? But neither of us accuse man's nature in it. The desires and other passions of man are in themselves no sin. No more are the actions that proceed from those passions, till they know a law that forbids them; which, till laws be made, they cannot know, nor can any law be made till they have agreed upon the person that shall make it.

It may peradventure be thought there was never such a time nor condition of war as this; and I believe it was never generally so over all the world, but there are many places where they live so now. For the savage people in many places of America, except the government of small families the concord whereof depends on natural lust, have no government at all, and live at this day in that brutish manner as I said before. Howsoever, it may be perceived what manner of life there would be where there were no common power to fear, by the manner of life which men that have formerly lived under a peaceful government use to degenerate into, in a civil war. But, though there had never been any time wherein particular men were in a condition of war one against another, yet in all times kings and persons of sovereign authority, because of their independence, are in continual jealousies and in the state and posture of gladiators, having their weapons pointing, and their eyes fixed on one another, that is, their forts, garrisons, and guns, upon the frontiers of their kingdoms, and continual spies upon their neighbors: which is a posture of war. But because they uphold thereby the industry of their subjects, there does not follow from it that misery which accompanies the liberty of particular men.

To this war of every man against every man this also is consequent, that nothing can be unjust. The notions of right and wrong, justice and injustice, have there no place. Where there is no common power, there is no law; where no law, no injustice. Force and fraud are in war the two cardinal virtues. Justice and injustice are none of the faculties neither of the body nor mind. If they were, they might be in a man that were alone in the world, as well as his senses and passions. They are qualities that relate to men in society, not in solitude. It is consequent also to the same condition that there be no propriety, no dominion, no "mine" and "thine" distinct, but only that to be every man's that he can get, and for so long as he can keep it. And thus much for the ill condition which man by mere nature is actually placed in, though with a possibility to come out of it, consisting partly in the passions, partly in his reason.

The passions that incline men to peace are fear of death, desire of such things as are necessary to commodious living, and a hope by their industry to obtain them. And reason suggests convenient articles of peace, upon which men may be drawn to agreement. These articles are they which otherwise are called the Laws of Nature, whereof I shall speak more particularly in the two following chapters.

CHAPTER 14. OF THE FIRST AND SECOND NATURAL LAWS, AND OF CONTRACTS

"The right of Nature," which writers commonly call *jus naturale*, is the liberty each man hath to use his own power as he will himself for the preservation of his own nature, that is to say, of his own life; and consequently of doing anything which in his own judgment and reason he shall conceive to be the aptest means thereunto.

By "liberty" is understood, according to the proper signification of the word, the absence of external impediments which impediments may oft take away part of a man's power to do what he would, but cannot hinder him from using the power left him according as his judgment and reason shall dictate to him.

A "law of Nature," *lex naturalis*, is a precept or general rule found out by reason by which a man is forbidden to do that which is destructive of his life or takes away the means of preserving the same, and to omit that by which he thinks it may be best preserved. For, though they that speak of this subject use to confound *jus* and *lex*, "right" and "law," yet they ought to be distinguished; because "right" consists in liberty to do or to forbear, whereas "law" determines and binds to one of them: so that law and right differ as much as obligation and liberty; which in one and the same matter are inconsistent.

And because the condition of man, as hath been declared in the precedent chapter, is a condition of war of every one against every one, in which case every one is governed by his own reason, and there is nothing he can make use of that may not be a help unto him in preserving his life against his enemies, it follows that in such a condition every man has a right to everything, even to one another's body. And therefore, as long as this natural right of every man to everything endures, there can be no security to any man, how strong or wise soever he be, of living out the time which Nature ordinarily allows men to live. And consequently it is a precept or general rule of reason "that every man ought to endeavor peace as far as he has hope of obtaining it, and, when he cannot obtain it, that he may seek and use all helps and advantages of war." The first branch of which rule contains the first and fundamental law of Nature, which is, "to seek peace, and follow it." The second, the sum of the right of Nature, which is, "by all means we can, to defend ourselves."

From this fundamental law of Nature, by which men are commanded to endeavor peace, is derived this second law, "that a man be willing, when others are so too, as farforth as for peace and defence of himself he shall think it necessary, to lay down this right to all things, and be contented with so much liberty against other men as he would allow other men against himself." For as long as every man holds this right of doing anything he likes, so long are all men in the condition of war. But if other men will not lay down their right as well as he, then there is no reason for any one to divest himself of his: for that were to expose himself to prey, which no man is bound to, rather than to dispose himself to peace. This is that law of the Gospel: "whatsoever you require that others should do to you, that do ye to them." And that law of all men, *quod tibi fieri non vis, alteri ne feceris*.

To "lay down" a man's "right" to anything is to "divest" himself of the "liberty," of hindering another of the benefit of his own right to the same. For he that renounces or passes away his right gives not to any other man a right which he had not before, because there is nothing to which every man had not right by Nature; but only stands out of his way that he may enjoy his own original right without hindrance from him, not without hindrance from another. So that the effect which redounds to one man, by another man's defect of right, is but so much diminution of impediments to the use of his own right original.

Right is laid aside either by simply renouncing it, or by transferring it to another. By "simply renouncing" when he cares not to whom the benefit thereof redounds. By "transferring," when he intends the benefit thereof to some certain person or persons. And, when a man hath in either manner abandoned or granted away his right, then is he said to be "obliged" or "bound" not to hinder those to whom such right is granted or abandoned from the benefit of it; and that he "ought," and it is his "duty," not to make void that voluntary act of his own; and that such hindrance is "injustice" and "injury" as being sine jure, the right being before renounced or transferred. So that "injury" or "injustice," in the controversies of the world, is somewhat like to that which in the disputations of scholars is called "absurdity." For, as it is there called an absurdity to contradict what one maintained in the beginning, so in the world it is called injustice and injury voluntarily to undo that from the beginning he had voluntarily done. The way by which a man either simply renounces or transfers his right is a declaration or signification, by some voluntary and sufficient sign or signs, that he doth so renounce or transfer, or hath so renounced or transferred, the same, to him that accepts it. And these signs are either words only or actions only, or, as it happens most often, both words and actions. And the same are the "bonds" by which men are bound and obliged: bonds that have their strength not from their own nature, for nothing is more easily broken than a man's word, but from fear of some evil consequence upon the rupture.

Whensoever a man transfers his right or renounces it, it is either in consideration of some right reciprocally transferred to himself, or for some other good he hopes for thereby. For it is a voluntary act: and of the voluntary acts of every man the object is some good "to himself." And therefore there be some rights which no man can be understood by any words or other signs to have abandoned or transferred. As first a man cannot lay down the right of resisting them that assault him by force to take away his life, because he cannot be understood to aim thereby at any good to himself. The same may be said of wounds, and chains, and imprisonment, both because there is no benefit consequent to such patience, as there is to the patience of suffering another to be wounded or imprisoned, as also because a man cannot tell when he sees men proceed against him by violence whether they intend his death or not. And lastly the motive and end for which this renouncing and transferring of right is introduced is nothing else but the security of a man's person in his life and in the means of so preserving life as not to be weary of it. And therefore if a man by words or other signs seem to despoil himself of the end for which those signs were intended, he is not to be understood as if he meant it or that it was his will, but that he was ignorant of how such words and actions were to be interpreted.

The mutual transferring of right is that which men call "contract."

* * *

CHAPTER 15. OTHER LAWS OF NATURE

From that law of Nature by which we are obliged to transfer to another such rights as, being retained, hinder the peace of mankind, there follows a third, which is this, "that men perform their covenants made"; without which covenants are in vain, and but empty words: and the right of all men to all things remaining, we are still in the condition of war.

And in this law of Nature consists the fountain and original of "justice." For, where no covenant hath preceded, there hath no right been transferred, and every man has right to everything; and consequently, no action can be unjust. But when a covenant is made, then to break it is "unjust"; and the definition of "injustice" is no other than "the not performance of covenant." And whatsoever is not unjust is "just."

But because covenants of mutual trust, where there is a fear of not performance on either part, as hath been said in the former chapter, are invalid, though the original of justice be the making of covenants, yet injustice actually there can be none, till the cause of such fear be taken away, which, while men are in the natural condition of war, cannot be done. Therefore, before the names of just and unjust can have place, there must be some coercive power to compel men equally to the performance of their covenants, by the terror of some punishment greater than the benefit they expect by the breach of their covenant; and to make good that propriety which by mutual contract men acquire in recompense of the universal right they abandon; and such power there is none before the erection of a commonwealth. And this is also to be gathered out of the ordinary definition of justice in the schools; for they say that "justice is the constant will of giving to every man his own." And therefore where there is no "own" there is no propriety, there is no injustice; and where there is no coercive power erected, that is, where there is no commonwealth, there is no propriety, all men having right to all things: therefore, where there is no commonwealth, there nothing is unjust. So that the nature of justice consists in keeping of valid covenants; but the validity of covenants begins not but with the constitution of a civil power sufficient to compel men to keep them; and then it is also that propriety begins.

The fool hath said in his heart there is no such thing as justice, and sometimes also with his tongue, seriously alleging that every man's conservation and contentment, being committed to his own care, there could be no reason why every man might not do what he thought conduced thereunto; and therefore also to make or not make, keep or not keep, covenants was not against reason when it conduced to one's benefit. He does not therein deny that there be covenants, and that they are sometimes broken, sometimes kept, and that such breach of them may be called injustice, and the observance of them justice; but he questions whether injustice taking away the fear of God, for the same fool hath said in his heart there is no God, may not sometimes stand with that reason which dictates to every man his own good; and particularly then when it conduces to such a benefit as shall put a man in a condition to neglect not only the dispraise and revilings, but also the power, of other men. The kingdom of God is gotten by violence; but what if it could be gotten by unjust violence? Were it against reason so to get it, when it is impossible to receive hurt by it? And, if it be not against reason, it is not against justice, or else justice is not to be approved for good. From such reasoning as this, successful wickedness hath obtained the name of virtue, and some that in all other things have disallowed the violation of faith, yet have allowed it when it is for the getting of a kingdom. And the heathen that believed that Saturn was deposed by his son Jupiter believed nevertheless the same Jupiter to be the avenger of injustice somewhat like to a piece of law in Coke's *Commentaries on Littleton*, where he says, if the right heir of the crown be attainted of treason, yet the crown shall descend to him, and *eo instante* the attainder be void; from which instances a man will be very prone to infer that, when the heir apparent of a kingdom shall kill him that is in possession, though his father, you may call it injustice or by what other name you will, yet it can never be against reason seeing all the voluntary actions of men tend to the benefit of themselves; and those actions are most reasonable that conduce most to their ends. This specious reasoning is nevertheless false.

For the question is not of promises mutual, where there is no security of performance on either side, as when there is no civil power erected over the parties promising, for such promises are no covenants, but either where one of the parties has performed already, or where there is a power to make him perform, there is the question whether it be against reason, that is against the benefit of the other to perform or not. And I say it is not against reason. For the manifestation whereof we are to consider, first that when a man doth a thing which notwithstanding anything can be foreseen and reckoned on tends to his own destruction, howsoever some accident which he could not expect, arriving may turn it to his benefit, yet such events do not make it reasonably or wisely done. Secondly, that, in a condition of war, wherein every man to every man, for want of a common power to keep them all in awe, is an enemy, there is no man who can hope by his own strength or wit to defend himself from destruction without the help of confederates; where every one expects the same defence by the confederation that any one else does; and therefore he which declares he thinks it reason to deceive those that help him can in reason expect no other means of safety than what can be had from his own single power. He therefore that breaks his covenant, and consequently declares that he thinks he may with reason do so, cannot be received into any society that unite themselves for peace and defence but by the error of them that receive him; nor, when he is received, be retained in it without seeing the danger of their error; which errors a man cannot reasonably reckon upon as the means of his security; and therefore, if he be left or cast out of society, he perishes; and if he live in society, it is by the errors of other men which he could not foresee nor reckon upon, and consequently against the reason of his preservation; and so, as all men that contribute not to his destruction, forbear him only out of ignorance of what is good for themselves.

As for the instance of gaining the secure and perpetual felicity of heaven by any way, it is frivolous; there being but one way imaginable; and that is not breaking, but keeping of covenant.

And, for the other instance of attaining sovereignty by rebellion, it is manifest that, though the event follow, yet, because it cannot reasonably be expected, but rather the contrary, and because by gaining it so, others are taught to gain the same in like manner, the attempt thereof is against reason. Justice therefore, that is to say keeping of covenant, is a rule of reason by which we are forbidden to do anything destructive to our life; and consequently a law of Nature.

There be some that proceed further, and will not have the law of Nature to be those rules which conduce to the preservation of man's life on earth, but to the attaining of an eternal felicity after death; to which they think the breach of covenant may conduce; and consequently be just and reasonable; such are they that think it a work of merit to kill or depose or rebel against the sovereign power constituted over them by their own consent. But, because there is no natural knowledge of man's estate after death, much less of the reward that is then to be given to breach of faith, but only a belief grounded upon other men's saying that they know it supernaturally, or that they know those that knew them, that knew others, that knew it supernaturally; breach of faith cannot be called a precept of reason or nature.

Others that allow for a law of Nature the keeping of faith do nevertheless make exception of certain persons as heretics and such as use not to perform their covenant to others; and this also is against reason. For if any fault of a man be sufficient to discharge our covenant made, the same ought in reason to have been sufficient to have hindered the making of it.

The names of just and unjust, when they are attributed to men, signify one thing; and when they are attributed to actions, another. When they are attributed to men they signify conformity or inconformity of manners to reason. But, when they are attributed to actions, they signify the conformity or inconformity to reason, not of manners or manner of life but of particular actions. A just man, therefore, is he that takes all the care he can that his actions may be all just, and an unjust man is he that neglects it. And such men are more often in our language styled by the names of righteous and unrighteous than just and unjust, though the meaning be the same. Therefore a righteous man does not lose that title by one or a few unjust actions that proceed from sudden passion or mistake of things or persons; nor does an unrighteous man lose his character for such actions as he does, or forbears to do, for fear, because his will is not framed by the justice but by the apparent benefit of what he is to do. That which gives to human actions the relish of justice is a certain nobleness or gallantness of courage, rarely found, by which a man scorns to be beholden for the contentment of his life to fraud or breach of promise. This justice of the manners is that which is meant where justice is called a virtue, and injustice a vice.

But the justice of actions denominates men not just, "guiltless"; and the injustice of the same, which is also called injury, gives them but the name of "guilty."

Again, the injustice of manners is the disposition or aptitude to do injury, and is injustice before it proceeds to act, and without supposing any individual person injured. But the injustice of an action, that is to say injury, supposes an individual person injured, namely him to whom the covenant was made; and therefore many times the injury is received by one man when the damage redounds to another. As when the master commands his servant to give money to a stranger: if it be not done, the injury is done to the master, whom he had before covenanted to obey; but the damage redounds to the stranger, to whom he had no obligation, and therefore could not injure him. And so also in commonwealths. Private men may remit to one another their debts, but not robberies or other violences whereby they are endamaged, because the detaining of debt is an injury to themselves, but robbery and violence are injuries to the person of the commonwealth.

Whatsoever is done to a man conformable to his own will signified to the doer is no injury to him. For, if he that does it hath not passed away his original right to do what he please by some antecedent covenant, there is no breach of covenant, and therefore no injury done him. And if he have, then his will to have it done being signified is a release of that covenant, and so again there is no injury done him.

Justice of action is by writers divided into "commutative" and "distributive"; and the former they say consists in proportion arithmetical, the latter in proportion geometrical. Commutative, therefore, they place in the equality of value of the things contracted for—and distributive, in the distribution of equal benefit to men of equal merit. As if it were injustice to sell dearer than we buy, or to give more to a man than he merits. The value of all things contracted for is measured by the appetite of the contractors; and therefore the just value is that which they be contented to give. And merit, besides that which is by covenant, where the performance on one part merits the performance of the other part, and falls under justice commutative not distributive, is not due by justice, but is rewarded of grace only. And therefore this distinction, in the sense wherein it uses to be expounded, is not right. To speak properly, commutative justice is the justice of a contractor; that is, a performance of covenant in buying and selling, hiring and letting to hire, lending and borrowing, exchanging, bartering, and other acts of contract.

And distributive justice, the justice of an arbitrator; that is to say, the act of defining what is just. Wherein, being trusted by them that make him arbitrator, if he perform his trust he is said to distribute to every man his own; and this is indeed just distribution, and may be called, though improperly, distributive justice, but more properly equity, which also is a law of Nature, as shall be shown in due place.

As justice depends on antecedent covenant, so does "gratitude" depend on antecedent grace, that is to say, antecedent free gift; and is the fourth law of Nature; which may be conceived in this form, "that a man, which receives benefit from another of mere grace, endeavor that he which gives it have no reasonable cause to repent him of his good will." For no man gives but with intention of good to himself; because gift is voluntary; and of all voluntary acts the object is to every man his own good, of which, if men see they shall be frustrated, there will be no beginning of benevolence, or trust, nor consequently of mutual help, nor of reconciliation of one man to another; and therefore they are to remain still in the condition of "war," which is contrary to the first and fundamental law of Nature, which commands men to "seek peace." The breach of this law is called "ingratitude," and hath the same relation to grace that injustice hath to obligation by covenant.

A fifth law of Nature, is "complaisance," that is to say, "that every man strive to accommodate himself to the rest." For the understanding whereof, we may consider that there is in men's aptness to society, a diversity of nature, rising from their diversity of affections, not unlike to that we see in stones brought together for building of an edifice. For as that stone which by the asperity and irregularity of figure takes more room from others than itself fills, and for the hardness cannot be easily made plain, and thereby hinders the building, is by the builders cast away as unprofitable and troublesome, so also a man that by asperity of nature will strive to retain those things which to himself are superfluous and to others necessary, and for the stubbornness of his passions cannot be corrected, is to be left or cast out of society as cumbersome thereunto. For seeing every man, not only by right but also by necessity of nature, is supposed to endeavor all he can to obtain that which is necessary for his conversation, he that shall oppose himself against it for things superfluous is guilty of the war that thereupon is to follow; and therefore doth that which is contrary to the fundamental law of Nature, which commands "to seek peace." The observers of this law may be called "sociable"— the Latins call them *commodi;* the contrary, "stubborn," "insociable," "froward," "intractable."

A sixth law of Nature is this, "that, upon caution of the future time, a man ought to pardon the offenses past of them that, repenting, desire it." For "pardon" is nothing but granting of peace, which, though granted to them that persevere in their hostility, be not peace but fear; yet not granted to them that give caution of the future time is sign of an aversion to peace, and therefore contrary to the law of Nature.

A seventh is, "that in revenges," that is, retribution of evil for evil, "men look not at the greatness of the evil past but the greatness of the good to follow." Whereby we are forbidden to inflict punishment with any other design than for correction of the offender or direction of others. For this law is consequent to the next before it, that commands pardon, upon security of the future time. Besides, revenge, without respect to the example and profit to come, is a triumph or glorying in the hurt of another tending to no end; for the end is always somewhat to come; and glorying to no end is vain-glory and contrary to reason, and to hurt without reason tends to the introduction of war, which is against the law of Nature, and is commonly by the name of "cruelty."

* * *

PART II—OF COMMONWEALTH

CHAPTER 17. OF THE CAUSES, GENERATION, AND DEFINITION OF A COMMONWEALTH

The final cause, end, or design of men, who naturally love liberty, and dominion over others, in the introduction of that restraint upon themselves, in which we see them live in commonwealths, is the foresight of their own preservation, and of a more contented life thereby; that is to say, of getting themselves out from that miserable condition of war, which is necessarily consequent, as hath been shown in Chapter XIII, to the natural passions of men, when there is no visible power to keep them in awe, and tie them by fear of punishment to the performance of their covenants, and observation of those laws of nature set down in the fourteenth and fifteenth chapters.

For the laws of nature, as "justice," "equity," "modesty," "mercy," and, in sum, "doing to others, as we would be done to," of themselves, without the terror of some power, to cause them to be observed, are contrary to our natural passions, that carry us to partiality, pride, revenge, and the like. And covenants, without the sword, are but words, and of no strength to secure a man at all. Therefore notwithstanding the laws of nature (which every one hath then kept, when he has the will to keep them, when he can do it safely) if there be no power erected, or not great enough for our security; every man will, and may lawfully rely on his own strength and art, for caution against all other men. And in all places, where men have lived by small families, to rob and spoil one another, has been a trade, and so far from being reputed against the law of nature, that the greater spoils they gained, the greater was their honor; and men observed no other laws therein, but the laws of honor; that is, to abstain from cruelty, leaving to men their lives, and instruments of husbandry. And as small families did then; so now do cities and kingdoms which are but greater families, for their own security, enlarge their dominions, upon all pretenses of danger, and fear of invasion, or assistance that may be given to invaders, and endeavor as much as they can, to subdue, or weaken their neighbors, by open force, and secret arts, for want of other caution, justly; and are remembered for it in after ages with honor.

Nor is it the joining together of a small number of men, that gives them this security; because in small numbers, small additions on the one side or the other, make the advantage of strength so great, as is sufficient to carry the victory; and therefore gives encouragement to an invasion. The multitude sufficient to confide in for our security, is not determined by any certain number, but by comparison with the enemy we fear; and is then sufficient, when the odds of the enemy is not of so visible and conspicuous moment, to determine the event of war, as to move him to attempt.

The execution of King Charles I of England, 1649, engraving by Wenceslaus Holler (1607–1677). Hobbes considered this event a horrible example of what happens when the sovereign does not have absolute power. (*Library of Congress*)

And be there never so great a multitude; yet if their actions be directed according to their particular judgments, and particular appetites, they can expect thereby no defence, nor protection, neither against a common enemy, nor against the injuries of one another. For being distracted in opinions concerning the best use and application of their strength, they do not help but hinder one another; and reduce their strength by mutual opposition to nothing: whereby they are easily, not only subdued by a very few that agree together; but also when there is no common enemy, they make war upon each other, for their particular interests. For if we could suppose a great multitude of men to consent in the observation of justice, and other laws of nature, without a common power to keep them all in awe; we might as well suppose all mankind to do the same; and then there neither would be, nor need to be any civil government, or commonwealth at all; because there would be peace without subjection.

Nor is it enough for the security, which men desire should last all the time of their life, that they be governed, and directed by one judgment, for a limited time; as in one battle, or one war. For though they obtain a victory by their unanimous endeavor against a foreign enemy; yet afterwards, when either they have no common enemy, or he that by one part is held for an enemy, is by another part held for a friend, they must needs by the difference of their interests dissolve, and fall again into a war amongst themselves.

It is true that certain living creatures, as bees, and ants, live sociably one with another, which are therefore by Aristotle numbered amongst political creatures; and yet have no other direction, than their particular judgments and appetites; nor speech, whereby one of them can signify to another, what he thinks expedient for the common benefit: and therefore some man may perhaps desire to know, why mankind cannot do the same. To which I answer,

First, that men are continually in competition for honor and dignity, which these creatures are not; and consequently amongst men there arises on that ground, envy and hatred, and finally war; but amongst these not so.

Secondly, that amongst these creatures, the common good differs not from the private; and being by nature inclined to their private, they procure thereby the common benefit. But man, whose joy consists in comparing himself with other men, can relish nothing but what is eminent.

Thirdly, that these creatures, having not, as man, the use of reason, do not see, nor think they see any fault, in the administration of their common business; whereas amongst men, there are very many, that think themselves wiser, and abler to govern the public, better than the rest; and these strive to reform and innovate, one this way, another that way; and thereby bring it into distraction and civil war.

Fourthly, that these creatures, though they have some use of voice, in making known to one another their desires, and other affections; yet they want that art of words, by which some men can represent to others, that which is good, in the likeness of evil; and evil, in the likeness of good; and augment, or diminish the apparent greatness of good and evil; discontenting men, and troubling their peace at their pleasure.

Fifthly, irrational creatures cannot distinguish between "injury," and "damage"; and therefore as long as they be at ease, they are not offended with their fellows: whereas man is then most troublesome, when he is most at ease: for then it is that he loves to shew his wisdom, and control the actions of them that govern the commonwealth.

Lastly, the agreement of these creatures is natural; that of men, is by covenant only, which is artificial: and therefore it is no wonder if there be somewhat else required, besides covenant, to make their agreement constant and lasting; which is a common power, to keep them in awe, and to direct their actions to the common benefit.

The only way to erect such a common power, as may be able to defend them from the invasion of foreigners, and the injuries of one another, and thereby to secure them in such sort, as that by their own industry, and by the fruits of the earth, they may nourish themselves and live contentedly; is, to confer all their power and strength upon one man, or upon one assembly of men, that may reduce all their wills, by plurality of voices, unto one will: which is as much as to say, to appoint one man, or assembly of men, to bear their person; and every one to own, and acknowledge himself to be author of whatsoever he that so bears their person, shall act, or cause to be acted, in those things which concern the common Peace and safety; and therein to submit their wills, every one to his will, and their judgments, to his judgment. This is more than consent, or concord; it is a real unity of them all, in one and the same person, made by covenant of every man with every man, in such manner, as if every man should say to every man, "I authorize and give up my right of governing myself to this man, or to this assembly of men, on this condition, that thou give up thy right to him, and authorize all his actions in like manner." This done, the multitude so united in one person, is called a COMMONWEALTH, in Latin *CIVITAS*. This is the generation of that great LEVIATHAN, or rather, to speak more reverently, of that "mortal god," to which we owe under the "immortal God," our peace and defence. For by this authority, given him by every particular man in the commonwealth, he hath the use of so much power and strength conferred on him, that by terror thereof, he is enabled to form the wills of them all, to peace at home, and mutual aid against their enemies abroad. And in him consists the essence of the commonwealth; which, to define it, "is one person, of whose acts a great multitude, by mutual covenants one with another, have made themselves every one the author, to the end he may use the strength and means of them all, as he shall think expedient, for their peace and common defence."

And he that carries this person, is called SOVEREIGN, and said to have sovereign power; and every one besides, his SUBJECT.

The attaining to this sovereign power, is by two ways. One, by natural force; as when a man makes his children, to submit themselves, and their children to his government, as being able to destroy them if they refuse; or by war subdues his enemies to his will, giving them their lives on that condition. The other, is when men agree amongst themselves, to submit to some man, or assembly of men, voluntarily, on confidence to be protected by him against all others. This latter, may be called a political commonwealth, or commonwealth by "institution"; and the former, a commonwealth by "acquisition." And first, I shall speak of a commonwealth by institution.

CHAPTER 18. OF THE RIGHTS OF SOVEREIGNS BY INSTITUTION

A "commonwealth" is said to be "instituted," when a "multitude" of men do agree, and "covenant, every one, with every one," that to whatsoever "man," or "assembly of men," shall be given by the major part, the "right" to "present" the person of them all, that is to say, to be their "representative"; every one, as well he that "voted for it," as he that "voted against it," shall "authorize" all the actions and judgments, of that man, or assembly of men, in the same manner, as if they were his own, to the end, to live peaceably amongst themselves, and be protected against other men.

From this institution of a commonwealth are derived all the "rights," and faculties of him, or them, on whom the sovereign power is conferred by the consent of the people assembled.

First, because they covenant, it is to be understood, they are not obliged by former covenant to any thing repugnant hereunto. And consequently they that have already instituted a commonwealth, being thereby bound by covenant, to own the actions, and judgments of one, cannot lawfully make a new covenant, amongst themselves, to be obedient to any other, in any thing whatsoever, without his permission. And therefore, they that are subjects to a monarch, cannot without his leave cast off monarchy, and return to the confusion of a disunited multitude; nor transfer their person from him that bears it, to another man, or other assembly of men: for they are bound, every man to every man, to own, and be reputed author of all, that he that already is their sovereign, shall do, and judge fit to be done: so that any one man dissenting, all the rest should break their covenant made to that man, which is injustice: and they have also every man given the sovereignty to him that bears their person; and therefore if they depose him, they take from him that which is his own, and so again it is injustice. Besides, if he that attempts to depose his sovereign, be killed, or punished by him for such attempt, he is author of his own punishment, as being by the institution, author of all his sovereign shall do: and because it is injustice for a man to do any thing, for which he may be punished by his own authority, he is also upon that title, unjust. And whereas some men have pretended for their disobedience to their sovereign, a new covenant, made, not with men, but with God; this also is unjust: for there is no covenant with God, but by mediation of somebody that represents God's person which none doth but God's lieutenant, who hath the sovereignty under God. But this pretence of covenant with God, is so evident a lie, even in the pretenders' own consciences, that it is not only an act of an unjust, but also of a vile, and unmanly disposition.

Secondly, because the right of bearing the person of them all, is given to him they make sovereign, by covenant only of one to another, and not of him to any of them; there can happen no breach of covenant on the part of the sovereign; and consequently none of his subjects, by any pretence of forfeiture, can be freed from his subjection. That he which is made sovereign makes no covenant with his subjects beforehand, is manifest; because either he must make it with the whole multitude, as one party to the covenant; or he must make a several covenant with every man. With the whole, as one party, it is impossible; because as yet they are not one person: and if he make so many several covenants as there be men, those covenants after he hath the sovereignty are void; because what act soever can be pretended by any one of them for breach thereof, is the act both of himself, and of all the rest, because done in the person, and by the right of every one of them in particular. Besides, if any one, or more of them, pretend a breach of the covenant made by the sovereign at his institution; and others, or one other of his subjects, or himself alone, pretend there was no such breach, there is in this case, no judge to decide the controversy; it returns therefore to the sword again; and every man recovers the right of protecting himself by his own strength, contrary to the design they had in the institution. It is therefore in vain to grant sovereignty by way of precedent covenant. The opinion that any monarch receives his power by covenant, that is to say, on condition, proceeds from want of understanding this easy truth, that covenants being but words and breath, have no force to oblige, contain, constrain, or protect any man, but what it has from the public sword; that is, from the untied hands of that man, or assembly of men that hath the sovereignty, and whose actions are avouched by them all, and performed by the strength of them all, in him united. But when an assembly of men is made sovereign; then no man imagines any such covenant to have passed in the institution; for no man is so dull as to say, for example, the people of Rome made a covenant with the Romans, to hold the sovereignty on such or such conditions; which not performed, the Romans might lawfully depose the Roman people. That men see not the reason to be alike in a monarchy, and in a popular government, proceeds from the ambition of some, that are kinder to the government of an assembly, whereof they may hope to participate, than of monarchy, which they despair to enjoy.

Thirdly, because the major part hath by consenting voices declared a sovereign; he that dissented must now consent with the rest—that is, be contented to avow all the actions he shall do, or else justly be destroyed by the rest. For if he voluntarily entered into the congregation of them that were assembled, he sufficiently declared thereby his will, and therefore tacitly covenanted, to stand to what the major part should ordain: and therefore if he refuse to stand thereto, or make protestation against any of their decrees, he does contrary to his covenant, and therefore unjustly. And whether he be of the congregation, or not; and whether his consent be asked, or not, he must either submit to their decrees, or be left in the condition of war he was in before; wherein he might without injustice be destroyed by any man whatsoever.

Fourthly, because every subject is by this institution author of all the actions, and judgments of the sovereign instituted; it follows, that whatsoever he doth, it can be no injury to any of his subjects; nor ought he to be by any of them accused of injustice. For he that doth anything by authority from another, doth therein no injury to him by whose authority he acts: but by this institution of a commonwealth, every particular man is author of all the sovereign doth: and consequently he that complains of injury from his sovereign, complains of that whereof he himself is author, and therefore ought not to accuse any man but himself; no nor himself of injury; because to do injury to one's self, is impossible. It is true that they that have sovereign power may commit iniquity; but not injustice, or injury in the proper signification.

Fifthly, and consequently to that which was said last, no man that hath sovereign power can justly be put to death, or otherwise in any manner by his subject punished. For seeing every subject is author of the actions of his sovereign; he punishes another for the actions committed by himself.

And because the end of this institution, is the peace and defence of them all; and whosoever has right to the end, has right to the means; it belongs of right, to whatsoever man, or assembly that hath the sovereignty, to be judge both of the means of peace and defence, and also of the hindrances, and disturbances of the same; and to do whatsoever he shall think necessary to be done, both beforehand, for the preserving of peace and security, by prevention of discord at home, and hostility from abroad; and, when peace and security are lost, for the recovery of the same. And therefore,

Sixthly, it is annexed to the sovereignty, to be judge of what opinions and doctrines are averse, and what conducing to peace; and consequently, on what occasions, how far, and what men are to be trusted withal, in speaking to multitudes of people; and who shall examine the doctrines of all books before they be published. For the actions of men proceed from their opinions; and in the well-governing of opinions, consists the well-governing of men's actions, in order to their peace, and concord. And though in matter of doctrine, nothing ought to be regarded but the truth; yet this is not repugnant to regulating the same by peace. For doctrine repugnant to peace, can no more be true, than peace and concord can be against the law of nature. It is true, that in a commonwealth, where by the negligence, or unskillfulness of governors, and teachers, false doctrines are by time generally received; the contrary truths may be generally offensive. Yet the most sudden, and rough bustling in of a new truth, that can be, does never break the peace, but only sometimes awake the war. For those men that are so remissly governed, that they dare take up arms to defend, or introduce an opinion, are still in war; and their condition not peace, but only a cessation of arms for fear of one another; and they live, as it were, in the precincts of battle continually. It belongs therefore to him that hath the sovereign power, to be judge, or constitute all judges of opinions and doctrines, as a thing necessary to peace; thereby to prevent discord and civil war.

Seventhly, is annexed to the sovereignty, the whole power of prescribing the rules, whereby every man may know, what goods he may enjoy, and what actions he may do, without being molested by any of his fellow-subjects; and this is it men call "propriety." For before constitution of sovereign power, as hath already been shown, all men had right to all things; which necessarily causes war: and therefore this propriety, being necessary to peace, and depending on sovereign power, is the act of that power, in order to the public peace. These rules of propriety, or *meum* and *tuum*, and of "good," "evil," "lawful," and "unlawful" in the actions of subjects, are the civil laws; that is to say, the laws of each commonwealth in particular; though the name of civil law be now restrained to the ancient civil laws of the city of Rome—which being the head of a great part of the world, her laws at that time were in these parts the civil law.

Eighthly, is annexed to the sovereignty, the right judicature; that is to say, of hearing and deciding all controversies, which may arise concerning law, either civil, or natural; or concerning fact. For without the decision of controversies, there is no protection of one subject, against the injuries of another; the laws concerning *meum* and *tuum* are in vain; and to every man remains, from the natural and necessary appetite of his own conservation, the right of protecting himself by his private strength, which is the condition of war, and contrary to the end for which every commonwealth is instituted.

Ninthly, is annexed to the sovereignty, the right of making war and peace with other nations, and commonwealths; that is to say, of judging when it is for the public good, and how great forces are to be assembled, armed, and paid for that end; and to levy money upon the subjects, to defray the expenses thereof. For the power by which the people are to be defended, consists in their armies; and the strength of an army, in the union of their strength under one command, which command the sovereign instituted, therefore hath; because the command of the "militia," without other institution, makes him that hath it sovereign. And therefore whosoever is made general of an army, he that hath the sovereign power is always generalissimo.

Tenthly, is annexed to the sovereignty, the choosing of all counsellors, ministers, magistrates, and officers, both in peace, and war. For seeing the sovereign is charged with the end, which is the common peace and defence, he is understood to have power to use such means, as he shall think most fit for his discharge.

Eleventhly, to the sovereign is committed the power of rewarding with riches, or honor, and of punishing with corporal or pecuniary punishment, or with ignominy, every subject according to the law he hath formerly made; or if there be no law made, according as he shall judge most to conduce to the encouraging of men to serve the commonwealth, or deterring of them from doing disservice to the same.

Lastly, considering what value men are naturally apt to set upon themselves; what respect they look for from others; and how little they value other men; from whence continually arise amongst them, emulation, quarrels, factions, and at last war, to the destroying of one another, and diminution of their strength against a common enemy; it is necessary that there be laws of honor, and a public rate of the worth of such men as have deserved, or are able to deserve well of the commonwealth; and that there be force in the hands of some or other, to put those laws in execution. But it hath already been shown, that not only the whole "militia," or forces of the commonwealth; but also the judicature of all controversies, is annexed to the sovereignty. To the sovereign therefore it belongs also to give titles of honor; and to appoint what order of place, and dignity, each man shall hold; and what signs of respect, in public or private meetings, they shall give to one another.

These are the rights, which make the essence of sovereignty, and which are the marks, whereby a man may discern in what man, or assembly of men, the sovereign power is placed, and resides. For these are incommunicable, and inseparable. The power to coin money; to dispose of the estate and persons of infant heirs; to have pre-emption in markets; and all other statute prerogatives, may be transferred by the sovereign; and yet the power to protect his subjects be retained. But if he transfer the "militia," he retains the judicature in vain, for want of execution of the laws: or if he grant away the power of raising money; the "militia" is in vain; or if he give away the government of doctrines, men will be frighted into rebellion with the fear of spirits. And so if we consider any one of the said rights, we shall presently see, that the holding of all the rest will produce no effect, in the conservation of peace and justice, the end for which all commonwealths are instituted. And this division is it, whereof it is said, "a kingdom divided in itself cannot stand": for unless this division precede, division into opposite armies can never happen. If there had not first been an opinion received of the greatest part of England, that these powers were divided between the King, and the Lords, and the House of Commons, the people had never been divided and fallen into this civil war; first between those that disagreed in politics; and after between the dissenters about the liberty of religion; which have so instructed men in this point of sovereign right, that there be few now in England that do not see, that these rights are inseparable, and will be so generally acknowledged at the next return of peace; and so continue, till their miseries are forgotten; and no longer, except the vulgar be better taught than they have hitherto been.

And because they are essential and inseparable rights, it follows necessarily, that in whatsoever words any of them seem to be granted away, yet if the sovereign power itself be not in direct terms renounced, and the name of sovereign no more given by the grantees to him that grants them, the grant is void: for when he has granted all he can, if we grant back the sovereignty, all is restored, as inseparably annexed thereunto.

This great authority being indivisible and inseparably annexed to the sovereignty, there is little ground for the opinion of them, that say of sovereign kings, though they be *singulis majores*, of greater power than every one of their subjects, yet they be *universis minores*, of less power than them all together. For if by "all together," they mean not the collective body as one person, then "all together," and "every one," signify the same; and the speech is absurd. But if by "all together," they understand them as one person, which person the sovereign bears, then the power of all together, is the same with the sovereign's power; and so again the speech is absurd: which absurdity they see well enough, when the sovereignty is in an assembly of the people; but in a monarch they see it not; and yet the power of sovereignty is the same in whomsoever it be placed.

And as the power, so also the honor of the sovereign, ought to be greater, than that of any, or all the subjects. For in the sovereignty is the fountain of honor. The dignities of lord, earl, duke, and prince are his creatures. As in the presence of the master, the servants are equal, and without any honor at all; so are the subjects, in the presence of the sovereign. And though they shine some more, some less, when they are out of his sight; yet in his presence, they shine no more than the stars in the presence of the sun.

But a man may here object, that the condition of subjects is very miserable; as being obnoxious to the lusts, and other irregular passions of him, or them that have so unlimited a power in their hands. And commonly they that live under a monarch, think it the fault of monarchy; and they that live under the government of democracy, or other sovereign assembly, attribute all the inconvenience to that form of commonwealth; whereas the power in all forms, if they be perfect enough to protect them, is the same: not considering that the state of man can never be without some incommodity or other; and that the greatest, that in any form of government can possibly happen to the people in general, is scarce sensible in respect of the miseries, and horrible calamities, that accompany a civil war, or that dissolute condition of masterless men, without subjection to laws, and a coercive power to tie their hands from rapine and revenge: nor considering that the greatest pressure of sovereign governors, proceeds not from any delight, or profit they can expect in the damage or weakening of their subjects, in whose vigor, consists their own strength and glory; but in the restiveness of themselves, that unwillingly contributing to their own defence, make it necessary for their governors to draw from them what they can in time of peace, that they may have means on any emergent occasion, or sudden need, to resist, or take advantage on their enemies. For all men are by nature provided of notable multiplying glasses, that is their passions and self-love, through which, every little payment appears a great grievance; but are destitute of those prospective glasses, namely moral and civil science, to see afar off the miseries that hang over them, and cannot without such payments be avoided.

* * *

CHAPTER 21. OF THE LIBERTY OF SUBJECTS

LIBERTY, or FREEDOM, signifies, properly, the absence of opposition; by opposition, I mean external impediments of motion; and may be applied no less to irrational, and inanimate creatures, than to rational. For whatsoever is so tied, or environed, as it cannot move but within a certain space, which space is determined by the opposition of some external body, we say it hath not liberty to go further. And so of all living creatures, whilst they are imprisoned, or restrained, with walls, or chains; and of the water whilst it is kept in by banks, or vessels, that otherwise would spread itself into a larger space, we use to say, they are not at liberty, to move in such manner, as without those external impediments they would. But when the impediment of motion, is in the constitution of the thing itself, we use not to say; it wants the liberty; but the power to move; as when a stone lies still, or a man is fastened to his bed by sickness.

And according to this proper, and generally received meaning of the word, a FREEMAN, is he, that in those things, which by his strength and wit he is able to do, is not hindered to do what he has a will to. But when the words "free," and "liberty," are applied to any thing but "bodies," they are abused; for that which is not subject to motion, is not subject to impediment: and therefore, when it is said, for example, the way is free, no liberty of the way is signified, but of those that walk in it without stop. And when we say a gift is free, there is not meant any liberty of the gift but of the giver, that was not bound by any law or covenant to give it. So when we "speak freely," it is not the liberty of voice, or pronunciation, but of the man, whom no law hath obliged to speak otherwise than he did. Lastly, from the use of the word "free-will," no liberty can be inferred of the will, desire, or inclination, but the liberty of the man; which consists in this, that he finds no stop, in doing what he has the will, desire, or inclination to do.

Fear and liberty are consistent; as when a man throws his goods into the sea for "fear" the ship should sink, he doth it nevertheless very willingly, and may refuse to do it if he will: it is therefore the action of one that was "free"; so a man sometimes pays his debt, only for "fear" of imprisonment, which because nobody hindered him from detaining, was the action of a man at "liberty." And generally all actions which men do in commonwealths, for fear of the law, are actions, which the doers had liberty to omit.

"Liberty," and "necessity" are consistent: as in the water, that hath not only "liberty," but a "necessity" of descending by the channel; so likewise in the actions which men voluntarily do: which, because they proceed from their will, proceed from liberty; and yet, because every act of man's will, and every desire, and inclination proceeds from some cause, and that from another cause, in a continual chain, whose first link is in the hand of God the first of all causes, proceed from "necessity." So that to him that could see the connection of those causes, the necessity of all men's voluntary actions, would appear manifest. And therefore God, that sees, and disposes all things, sees also that the "liberty" of man in doing what he will, is accompanied with the "necessity" of doing that which God will, and no more, nor less. For though men may do many things, which God does not command, nor is therefore author of them; yet they can have no passion, nor appetite to any thing, of which appetite God's will is not the cause. And did not his will assure the "necessity" of man's will, and consequently of all that on man's will depends, the "liberty" of men would be a contradiction, and impediment to the omnipotence and "liberty" of God. And this shall suffice, as to the matter in hand, of that natural "liberty," which only is properly called "liberty."

But as men, for the attaining of peace, and conservation of themselves thereby, have made an artificial man, which we call a commonwealth; so also have they made artificial chains, called "civil laws," which they themselves, by mutual covenants, have fastened at one end, to the lips of that man, or assembly, to whom they have given the sovereign power; and at the other end to their own ears. These bonds, in their own nature but weak, may nevertheless be made to hold, by the danger, though not by the difficulty of breaking them.

In relation to these bonds only it is, that I am to speak now, of the "liberty" of "subjects." For seeing there is no commonwealth in the world, wherein there be rules enough set down, for the regulating of all the actions, and words of men; as being a thing impossible: it follows necessarily, that in all kinds of actions by the laws pretermitted, men have the liberty, of doing what their own reasons shall suggest, for the most profitable to themselves. For if we take liberty in the proper sense, for corporal liberty; that is to say, freedom from chains and prison; it were very absurd for men to clamor as they do, for the liberty they so manifestly enjoy. Again, if we take liberty, for an exemption from laws, it is no less absurd, for men to demand as they do, that liberty, by which all other men may be masters of their lives. And yet, as absurd as it is, this is it they demand; not knowing that the laws are of no power to protect them, without a sword in the hands of a man, or men, to cause those laws to be put in execution. The liberty of a subject, lies therefore only in those things, which in regulating their actions, the sovereign hath pretermitted: such as is the liberty to buy, and sell, and otherwise contract with one another; to choose their own abode, their own diet, their own trade of life, and institute their children as they themselves think fit; and the like.

Nevertheless we are not to understand, that by such liberty, the sovereign power of life and death, is either abolished, or limited. For it has been already shown, that nothing the sovereign representative can do to a subject, on what pretence soever, can properly be called injustice, or injury; because every subject is author of every act the sovereign doth; so that he never wants right to any thing, otherwise, than as he himself is the subject of God, and bound thereby to observe the laws of nature. And therefore it may, and doth often happen in commonwealths, that a subject may be put to death, by the command of the sovereign power; and yet neither do the other wrong: as when Jephtha caused his daughter to be sacrificed: in which, and the like cases, he that so dies, had liberty to do the action, for which he is nevertheless, without injury put to death. And the same holds also in a sovereign prince, that puts to death an innocent subject. . . .

The liberty, whereof there is so frequent and honorable mention, in the histories, and philosophy of the ancient Greeks, and Romans, and in the writings, and discourse of those that from them have received all their learning in the politics, is not the liberty of particular men; but the liberty of the commonwealth: which is the same with that which every man then should have, if there were no civil laws, nor commonwealth at all. And the effects of it also be the same. For as amongst masterless men, there is perpetual war, of every man against his neighbor; no inheritance, to transmit to the son, nor to expect from the father; no propriety of goods, or lands; no security; but a full and absolute liberty in every particular man: so in states, and commonwealths not dependent on one another, every commonwealth, not every man, has an absolute liberty, to do what it shall judge, that is to say, what that man, or assembly that represents it, shall judge most conducing to their benefit. But withal, they live in the condition of a perpetual war, and upon the confines of battle, with their frontiers armed, and cannons planted against their neighbors round about. The Athenians, and Romans were free; that is, free commonwealths: not that any particular men had the liberty to resist their own representative; but that their representative had the liberty to resist, or invade other people.

There is written on the turrets of the city of Lucca in great characters at this day, the word LIBERTAS; yet no man can thence infer, that a particular man has more liberty, or immunity from the service of the commonwealth there, than in Constantinople. Whether a commonwealth be monarchical, or popular, the freedom is still the same.

But it is an easy thing, for men to be deceived, by the specious name of liberty; and for want of judgment to distinguish, mistake that for their private inheritance, and birth-right, which is the right of the public only. And when the same error is confirmed by the authority of men in reputation for their writings on this subject, it is no wonder if it produce sedition, and change of government. . . .

To come now to the particulars of the true liberty of a subject; that is to say, what are the things, which though commanded by the sovereign, he may nevertheless, without injustice, refuse to do; we are to consider, what rights we pass away, when we make a commonwealth; or, which is all one, what liberty we deny ourselves, by owning all the actions, without exception, of the man, or assembly we make our sovereign. For in the act of our "submission," consists both our "obligation," and our "liberty"; which must therefore be inferred by arguments taken from thence; there being no obligation on any man, which arises not from some act of his own; for all men equally, are by nature free. And because such arguments, must either be drawn from the express words, I "authorize all his actions," or from the intention of him that submits himself to his power, which intention is to be understood by the end for which he so submits; the obligation, and liberty of the subject, is to be derived, either from those words, or others equivalent; or else from the end of the institution of sovereignty, namely, the peace of the subjects within themselves, and their defence against a common enemy.

First therefore, seeing sovereignty by institution, is by covenant of every one to every one; and sovereignty by acquisition, by covenants of the vanquished to the victor, or child to the parent; it is manifest, that every subject has liberty in all those things, the right whereof cannot by covenant be transferred. I have shown before in the 14th chapter, that covenants, not to defend a man's own body, are void. Therefore,

If the sovereign command a man, though justly condemned, to kill, wound, or maim himself; or not to resist those that assault him; or to abstain from the use of food, air, medicine, or any other thing, without which he cannot live; yet hath that man the liberty to disobey.

If a man be interrogated by the sovereign, or his authority, concerning a crime done by himself, he is not bound, without assurance of pardon, to confess it; because no man, as I have shown in the same chapter, can be obliged by covenant to accuse himself.

Again, the consent of a subject to sovereign power, is contained in these words, "I authorize, or take upon me, all his actions"; in which there is no restriction at all, of his own former natural liberty: for by allowing him to "kill me," I am not bound to kill myself when he commands me. It is one thing to say, "kill me, or my fellow, if you please"; another thing to say, "I will kill myself, or my fellow." It follows therefore, that No man is bound by the words themselves, either to kill himself, or any other man; and consequently, that the obligation a man may sometimes have, upon the command of the sovereign to execute any dangerous, or dishonorable office, depends not on the words of our submission; but on the intention, which is to be understood by the end thereof. When therefore our refusal to obey, frustrates the end for which the sovereignty was ordained; then there is no liberty to refuse: otherwise there is.

Upon this ground, a man that is commanded as a soldier to fight against the enemy, though his sovereign have right enough to punish his refusal with death, may nevertheless in many cases refuse, without injustice; as when he substitutes a sufficient soldier in his place: for in this case he deserts not the service of the commonwealth. And there is allowance to be made for natural timorousness; not only to women, of whom no such dangerous duty is expected, but also to men of feminine courage. When armies fight, there is on one side, or both, a running away; yet when they do it not out of treachery, but fear, they are not esteemed to do it unjustly, but dishonorably. For the same reason, to avoid battle, is not injustice, but cowardice. But he that enrolls himself a soldier, or takes imprest money, takes away the excuse of a timorous nature; and is obliged, not only to go to the battle, but also not to run from it, without his captain's leave. And when the defence of the commonwealth, requires at once the help of all that are able to bear arms, every one is obliged; because otherwise the institution of the commonwealth, which they have not the purpose, or courage to preserve, was in vain.

To resist the sword of the commonwealth, in defence of another man, guilty, or innocent, no man hath liberty; because such liberty, takes away from the sovereign, the means of protecting us; and is therefore destructive of the very essence of government. But in case a great many men together, have already resisted the sovereign power unjustly, or committed some capital crime, for which every one of them expects death, whether have they not the liberty then to join together, and assist, and defend one another? Certainly they have: for they but defend their lives, which the guilty man may as well do, as the innocent. There was indeed injustice in the first breach of their duty; their bearing of arms subsequent to it, though it be to maintain what they have done, is no new unjust act. And if it be only to defend their persons, it is not unjust at all. But the offer of pardon takes from them, to whom it is offered, the plea of self-defence, and makes their perseverance in assisting, or defending the rest, unlawful.

As for other liberties, they depend on the silence of the law. In cases where the sovereign has prescribed no rule, there the subject hath the liberty to do, or forbear, according to his own discretion. And therefore such liberty is in some places more, and in some less; and in some times more, in other times less, according as they that have the sovereignty shall think most convenient. As for example, there was a time, when in England a man might enter into his own land, and dispossess such as wrongfully possessed it, by force. But in aftertimes, that liberty of forcible entry, was taken away by a statute made, by the king, in parliament. And in some places of the world, men have the liberty of many wives: in other places, such liberty is not allowed.

If a subject have a controversy with his sovereign, of debt, or of right of possession of lands or goods, or concerning any service required at his hands, or concerning any penalty, corporal, or pecuniary, grounded on a precedent law; he hath the same liberty to sue for his right, as if it were against a subject; and before such judges, as are appointed by the sovereign. For seeing the sovereign demands by force of a former law, and not by virtue of his power; he declares thereby, that he requires no more, than shall appear to be due by that law. The suit therefore is not contrary to the will of the sovereign; and consequently the subject hath the liberty to demand the hearing of his cause; and sentence, according to that law. But if he demand, or take any thing by pretence of his power; there lies, in that case, no action of law; for all that is done by him in virtue of his power, is done by the authority of every subject, and consequently he that brings an action against the sovereign, brings it against himself.

If a monarch, or sovereign assembly, grant a liberty to all, or any of his subjects, which grant standing, he is disabled to provide for their safety, the grant is void; unless he directly renounce, or transfer the sovereignty to another. For in that he might openly, if it had been his will, and in plain terms, have renounced, or transferred it, and did not; it is to be understood it was not his will, but that the grant proceeded from ignorance of the repugnancy between such a liberty and the sovereign power; and therefore the sovereignty is still retained; and consequently all those powers, which are necessary to the exercising thereof; such as are the power of war, and peace, of judicature, of appointing officers, and councilors, of levying money, and the rest named in the eighteenth chapter.

The obligation of subjects to the sovereign, is understood to last as long, and no longer, than the power lasts, by which he is able to protect them. For the right men have by nature to protect themselves, when none else can protect them, can by no covenant be relinquished. The sovereignty is the soul of the commonwealth which once departed from the body, the members do no more receive their motion from it. The end of obedience is protection; which, wheresoever a man sees it, either in his own, or in another's sword, nature applies his obedience to it, and his endeavor to maintain it. And though sovereignty, in the intention of them that make it, be immortal; yet is it in its own nature, not only subject to violent death, by foreign war; but also through the ignorance, and passions of men, it hath in it, from the very institution, many seeds of a natural mortality, by intestine discord.

If a subject be taken prisoner in war; or his person, or his means of life be within the guards of the enemy, and hath his life and corporal liberty given him, on condition to be subject to the victor, he hath liberty to accept the condition; and having accepted it, is the subject of him that took him; because he had no other way to preserve himself. The case is the same, if he be detained on the same terms, in a foreign country. But if a man be held in prison, or bonds, or is not trusted with the liberty of his body; he cannot be understood to be bound by covenant to subjection; and therefore may, if he can, make his escape by any means whatsoever.

If a monarch shall relinquish the sovereignty, both for himself, and his heirs; his subjects return to the absolute liberty of nature; because, though nature may declare who are his sons, and who are the nearest of his kin; yet it depends on his own will, as hath been said in the precedent chapter, who shall be his heir. If therefore he will have no heir, there is no sovereignty, nor subjection. The case is the same, if he die without known kindred, and without declaration of his heir. For then there can no heir be known, and consequently no subjection be due.

If the sovereign banish his subject; during the banishment, he is not subject. But he that is sent on a message, or hath leave to travel, is still subject; but it is, by contract between sovereigns, not by virtue of the covenant of subjection. For whosoever enters into another's dominion, is subject to all the laws thereof; unless he have a privilege by the amity of the sovereigns, or by special license.

If a monarch subdued by war, render himself subject to the victor; his subjects are delivered from their former obligation, and become obliged to the victor. But if he be held prisoner, or have not the liberty of his own body; he is not understood to have given away the right of sovereignty; and therefore his subjects are obliged to yield obedience to the magistrates formerly placed, governing not in their own name, but in his. For, his right remaining, the question is only of the administration; that is to say, of the magistrates and officers; which, if he have not means to name, he is supposed to approve those, which he himself had formerly appointed.

BLAISE PASCAL
1623–1662

Blaise Pascal was the middle child of an upper-class magistrate in Clermont-Ferrand, France. His mother died when he was 3 years old, and five years later Pascal's father moved the family to Paris. His father, Etienne, an excellent amateur mathematician, educated young Blaise at home. Etienne first taught Blaise Latin and Greek, deciding to wait on his own love, mathematics, until his son was older. By the age of 12, however, Blaise had figured out many of the principles of Euclidian geometry on his own. His father finally relented and bought Blaise a copy of Euclid, which he devoured. Over the next several years, father and son attended weekly mathematical lectures and were regular guests at important intellectual salons in Paris. In 1638, the family underwent another trauma when Etienne Pascal was forced to flee Paris because of a conflict with the powerful Cardinal Richelieu. However, Blaise Pascal's younger sister, Jacqueline, performed so well in a children's play for the Cardinal that their father was given a pardon and installed as tax commissioner for Rouen.

At Rouen, Blaise Pascal began to concentrate on mathematics. While still a teenager, he wrote his first book (on conic sections in geometry) and developed a plan for a calculating machine to help his father with his tax work. In 1644, he built the first of the machine's several working models—no small feat given the state of metalworking at the time. Pascal's contributions to mathematics and computing machines were so important that a major contemporary programming language is named in his honor. Pascal also experimented on the nature of a vacuum showing that, contrary to Aristotle's belief, "Nature has no abhorrence of a vacuum."

In 1647, Pascal became seriously ill and returned to Paris with his younger sister to recover. Following his father's death in 1651, his sister entered a convent, leaving Pascal alone. Over the next several years, Pascal seemed to drift: he outwardly enjoyed the social life of Paris as a successful mathematician and eligible bachelor, but he was inwardly dissatisfied. Although he had undergone a conversion in 1646 under the influence of the Jansenists, a group of devout Catholics, Pascal still found himself without direction. On the night of November 23, 1654, Pascal had a remarkable second conversion experience, the description of which he sewed inside his coat:

> . . . From about half past ten in the evening until about half past midnight.
> Fire.
> God of Abraham, God of Isaac, God of Jacob, not of philosophers and scholars.
> Certainty, joy, certainty, emotion, sight, joy
> God of Jesus Christ . . . .
> Oblivious to the world and to everything except GOD . . . .
> This is life eternal, that they might know you,
> the only true God, and him whom you sent,
> Jesus Christ
> Jesus Christ
> I have cut myself off from him for ever. I have fled from him, denied
> him, crucified him.
> Let me never be cut off from him.
> He can only be kept by the ways taught in the Gospel.
> Sweet and total renunciation.
> Total submission to Jesus Christ and my director.
> Everlasting joy for one day's tribulation on earth.
> *I will not forget thy word.* Amen.*

Pascal committed himself to living out his faith by doing good works. He wrote a remarkable series of *Provincial Letters* defending the Jansenists against the Jesuits. Pascal also worked on one of the first regularly scheduled public transit services, with profits for the poor; the line became operational shortly before Pascal's death in 1662. But Pascal's most important mature work was his *Apology for the Christian Religion,* the completed portion of which is now known as the *Pensées* (*Thoughts*).

* * *

Collected and published after Pascal's death at age 39, the *Pensées* is considered a French classic—despite its fragmentary character. Touching on numerous areas of religious and philosophical thought, the *Pensées* portray humanity "engulfed in the infinite immensity" of the universe. Unlike Descartes, Pascal claims that reason is insufficient to find certainty. Although the *cogito* ("I think") is indeed one of God's greatest gift to humanity and "all our dignity consists . . . in thought," there is nevertheless something more important than thought and reason: the heart. As Pascal put it, "The heart has its reasons, which reason does not know."

As for knowledge of God, Pascal claims that reason is utterly insufficient for the enterprise. Against Descartes, St. Thomas Aquinas, and others, proofs for God's existence and the Christian truth "are not of such a nature that they can be said to be absolutely convincing." There is always "both evidence and obscurity [enough] to enlighten some and [to] confuse others." Given that one can never *know* if there is a God, how can one *live* one's life? According to Pascal, one can never have true knowledge of *anything* until one has submitted to it—and so there can be no true knowledge of God until one has submitted to God as revealed in Jesus Christ. Is

*"The Memorial," Blaise Pascal, *Pensées and Other Writings,* translated by Honor Levi (Oxford: Oxford University Press, 1995), p. 178.

there, then, no rational basis for making the Christian commitment? In the selection given here, Pascal appeals to the *bon vivants* of Paris by asking them to consider faith as a wager. If you bet your life on God and you turn out to be right, you have gained eternity. If you are wrong and there is no God, what have you lost—except the possibility of "those poisonous pleasures, glory and luxury"? But, if you bet your life against the reality of God, you gain little if correct, but lose eternally if wrong.

Some critics have argued that Pascal's Wager hardly seems like faith at all—that it is a "calculating and self-regarding attitude" and is "profoundly irreligious."* Others have claimed that the wager leads not to Christianity, but to any religion with a great reward for belief and a great penalty for disbelief. Still others argue that the most reasonable choice is to avoid wagering at all until the evidence is clear. (See the suggested readings that follow.) However, to be fair, Pascal never claimed the wager was the *way* to faith or that it provided the *means* for proving Christian truth. His two goals were to show that while being *supra*rational, belief is not *ir*rational and one *must* decide. As Pascal put it,

> Do not then reprove for error those who have made a choice; for you know nothing about it. "No, but I blame them for having made, not this choice, but a choice . . . The true course is not to wager at all."
>
> Yes; but you must wager. It is not optional. You are embarked. Which will you choose then?

* * *

There is little consistency in the numbering of different editions of the *Pensées*. The translation and numbering used here are by W.F. Trotter.

The best general introduction to Pascal remains J.H. Broome, *Pascal* (London: E. Arnold, 1972). Other general studies include Émile Cailliet, *Pascal: The Emergence of Genius,* 2nd edition (New York: Harper, 1961); Morris Bishop, *Pascal: The Life of a Genius* (1936; reprint Westport, CO: Greenwood Press, 1968); Jean Mesnard, *Pascal,* translated by Claude and Marcia Abraham (University, AL: University of Alabama Press, 1969); Alban Krailsheimer, *Pascal,* Past Masters Series (Oxford: Oxford University Press, 1980); Hugh M. Davidson, *Blaise Pascal* (Boston: Twayne, 1983); Ben Rogers, *Pascal* (London: Routledge, 1999); and Nicholas Hammond, ed., *The Cambridge Companion to Pascal* (Cambridge: Cambridge University Press, 2003). More specialized studies include F.T.H. Fletcher, *Pascal and the Mystical Tradition* (Oxford: Basil Blackwell, 1954); Jan Miel, *Pascal and Theology* (Baltimore, MD: Johns Hopkins University Press, 1969); Robert James Nelson, *Pascal: Adversary and Advocate* (Cambridge, MA: Harvard University Press, 1981); Sara E. Melzer, *Discourses of the Fall: A Study of Pascal's* Pensées (Berkeley, CA: University of California Press, 1986); Nicholas Hammond, *Playing with Truth: Language and the Human Condition in Pascal's 'Pensées'* (Oxford: Oxford University Press, 1994); and Charles Sherrard MacKenzie, *Blaise Pascal: Apologist to Skeptics* (Lanham, MD: University Press of America, 2008). For discussions of Pascal's wager, see Nicholas Rescher, *Pascal's Wager: A Study of Practical Reasoning in Philosophical Theology* (Notre Dame, IN: University of Notre Dame Press, 1985) and Jeff Jordan, ed., *Gambling on God: Essays on Pascal's Wager* (Lanham, MD: Rowman & Littlefield, 1994).

*John Hick, *Philosophy of Religion,* 4th ed. (Englewood Cliffs, NJ: Prentice Hall, 1990), p. 59.

PENSÉES (selections)

185. The conduct of God, who disposes all things kindly, is to put religion into the mind by reason, and into the heart by grace. But to will to put it into the mind and heart by force and threats is not to put religion there, but terror. . . .

187. Order.—Men despise religion; they hate it, and fear it is true. To remedy this, we must begin by showing that religion is not contrary to reason; that it is venerable, to inspire respect for it; then we must make it lovable, to make good men hope it is true; finally, we must prove it is true.

194. . . . Let them at least learn what is the religion they attack, before attacking it. If this religion boasted of having a clear view of God, and of possessing it open and unveiled, it would be attacking it to say that we see nothing in the world which shows it with this clearness. But since, on the contrary, it says that men are in darkness and estranged from God, that He has hidden Himself from their knowledge, that this is in fact the name which He gives Himself in the Scriptures, *Deus absconditus* [hidden God]; and finally, if it endeavors equally to establish these two things: that God has set up in the Church visible signs to make Himself known to those who should seek Him sincerely, and that He has nevertheless so disguised them that He will only be perceived by those who seek Him with all their heart; . . .

We do not require great education of the mind to understand that here is no real and lasting satisfaction; that our pleasures are only vanity; that our evils are infinite; and, lastly, that death, which threatens us every moment, must infallibly place us within a few years under the dreadful necessity of being for ever either annihilated or unhappy.

There is nothing more real than this, nothing more terrible. Be we as heroic as we like, that is the end which awaits the noblest life in the world. Let us reflect on this, and then say whether it is not beyond doubt that there is no good in this life but in the hope of another; that we are happy only in proportion as we draw near it; and that, as there are no more woes for those who have complete assurance of eternity, so there is no more happiness for those who have no insight into it.

199. Let us imagine a number of men in chains, and all condemned to death, where some are killed each day in the sight of the others, and those who remain see their own fate in that of their fellows, and wait their turn, looking at each other sorrowfully and without hope. It is an image of the condition of men.

205. When I consider the short duration of my life, swallowed up in the eternity before and after, the little space which I fill, and even can see, engulfed in the infinite immensity of spaces of which I am ignorant, and which know me not, I am frightened, and am astonished at being here rather than there; for there is no reason why here rather than there, why now rather than then. Who has put me here? By whose order and direction have this place and time been allotted to me? . . .

206. The eternal silence of these infinite spaces frightens me.

210. The last act is tragic, however happy all the rest of the play is; at the last a little earth is thrown upon our head, and that is the end for ever.

229. . . . If I saw nothing there which revealed a Divinity, I would come to a negative conclusion; if I saw everywhere the signs of a Creator, I would remain peacefully in

A mechanical calculator invented by Blaise Pascal (1623–1662) with numerals visible in slots above a row of numbered metal wheels. (*Dave King © Dorling Kindersley, Courtesy of The Science Museum, London*)

faith. But, seeing too much to deny and too little to be sure, I am in a state to be pitied; wherefore I have a hundred times wished that if a God maintains nature, she should testify to Him unequivocally, and that, if the signs she gives are deceptive, she should suppress them altogether; that she should say everything or nothing, that I might see which cause I ought to follow. Whereas in my present state, ignorant of what I am or of what I ought to do, I know neither my condition nor my duty. My heart inclines wholly to know where is the true good, in order to follow it; nothing would be too dear to me for eternity.

I envy those whom I see living in the faith with such carelessness, and who make such a bad use of a gift of which it seems to me I would make such a different use.

230. It is incomprehensible that God should exist, and it is incomprehensible that He should not exist; that the soul should be joined to the body, and that we should have no soul; that the world should be created, and that it should not be created, etc., that original sin should be, and that it should not be.

233. [*The Wager*] . . . Let us then examine this point, and say, "God is, or He is not." But to which side shall we incline? Reason can decide nothing here. There is an infinite chaos which separated us. A game is being played at the extremity of this infinite distance where heads or tails will turn up. What will you wager? According to reason, you can do neither the one thing nor the other; according to reason, you can defend neither of the propositions.

Do not then reprove for error those who have made a choice; for you know nothing about it. "No, but I blame them for having made, not this choice, but a choice; for again both he who chooses heads and he who chooses tails are equally at fault, they are both in the wrong. The true course is not to wager at all."

Yes; but you must wager. It is not optional. You are embarked. Which will you choose then? Let us see. Since you must choose, let us see which interests you least. You have two things to lose, the true and the good; and two things to stake, your reason and your will, your knowledge and your happiness; and your nature has two things to shun, error and misery. Your reason is no more shocked in choosing one rather than the other, since you must of necessity choose. This is one point settled. But your happiness? Let us weight the gain and the loss in wagering that God is. Let us estimate these two chances. If you gain, you gain all; if you lose, you lose nothing. Wager, then, without hesitation that

He is.— "That is very fine. Yes, I must wager; but I may perhaps wager too much."—Let us see. Since there is an equal risk of gain and of loss, but if you had only to gain two lives, instead of one, you might still wager. But if there were three lives to gain, you would have to play (since you are under the necessity of playing), and you would be imprudent, when you are forced to play, not chance your life to gain three at a game where there is an equal risk of loss and gain. But there is an eternity of life and happiness. And this being so, if there were an infinity of chances, of which one only would be for you, you would still be right in wagering one to win two, and you would act stupidly, being obliged to play, by refusing to stake one life against three at a game in which out of an infinity of chances there is one for you, if there were an infinity of an infinitely happy life to gain. But there is here an infinity of an infinitely happy life to gain, a chance to gain against a finite number of chances to lose, and what you stake is finite. . . .

And so our proposition is of infinite force, when there is the finite to stake in a game where there are equal risks of gain and of loss, and the infinite to gain. This is demonstrable: and if men are capable of any truths, this is one.

"I confess it, I admit it. But, still, is there no means of seeing the faces of the cards?"—Yes, Scripture and the rest, etc. "Yes, but I have my hands tied and my mouth closed; I am forced to wager, and am not free. I am not released, and am so made that I cannot believe. What, then, would you have me do?"

True. But at least learn your inability to believe, since reason brings you to this, and yet you cannot believe. Endeavour then to convince yourself, not by increase of proofs of God, but by the abatement of your passions. You would like to attain faith, and do not know the way; you would like to cure yourself of unbelief, and ask the remedy for it. Learn of those who have been bound like you, and who now stake all their possessions. These are people who know the way which you would follow, and who are cured of an ill of which you would be cured. Follow the way by which they began; by acting as if they believed, taking the holy water, having masses said, etc. Even this will naturally make you believe, and deaden your acuteness.—"But this is what I am afraid of."—And why? What have you to lose? . . .

The end of this discourse.—Now, what harm will befall you in taking this side? You will be faithful, honest, humble, grateful, generous, a sincere friend, truthful. Certainly you will not have those poisonous pleasures, glory and luxury; but will you not have other? I will tell you that you will thereby gain in this life, and that, at each step you take on this road, you will see so great certainty of gain, so much nothingness in what you risk, that you will at last recognize that you have wagered for something certain and infinite, for which you have given nothing.

"Ah! This discourse transports me, charms me," etc.

If this discourse pleases you and seems impressive, know that it is made by a man who has knelt, both before and after it, in prayer to that Being, infinite and without parts, before whom he lays all he has, for you also to lay before Him all you have for your own good and for His glory, so that strength may be given to lowliness.

240. "I would soon have renounced pleasure," say they, "had I faith."

For my part I tell you, "You would soon have faith, if you renounced pleasure." Now, it is for you to begin. . . .

242. I admire the boldness with which these persons undertake to speak of God. In addressing their argument to infidels, their first chapter is to prove Divinity from the works of nature. I should not be astonished at their enterprise, if they were addressing their argument to the faithful; for it is certain that those who have the living faith in their heart see at once that all existence is none other than the work of the God whom they adore. But for

those in whom this light is extinguished, and in whom we purpose to rekindle it, persons destitute of faith and grace, who, seeking with all their light, whatever they see in nature that can bring them to this knowledge, find only obscurity and darkness; to tell them that they have only to look at the smallest things which surround them, and they will see God openly, to give them, as a complete proof of this great and important matter, the course of the moon and planets, and to claim to have concluded the proof with such an argument, is to give them ground for believing that the proofs of our religion are very weak. And I see by reason and experience that nothing is more calculated to arouse their contempt.

It is not after this manner that Scripture speaks, which has a better knowledge of the things that are of God. It says, on the contrary, that God is a hidden God, and that, since the corruption of nature, He has left men in a darkness from which they can escape only through Jesus Christ, without whom all communion with God is cut off. . . .

253. Two extremes: to exclude reason, to admit reason only.

277. The heart has its reasons, which reason does not know. We feel it in a thousand things. I say that the heart naturally loves the Universal Being, and also itself naturally, according as it gives itself to them; and it hardens itself against one or the other at its will. You have rejected the one, and kept the other at its will. You have rejected the one, and kept the other. Is it by reason that you love yourself?

278. It is the heart which experiences God, and not the reason. This, then, is faith: God felt by the heart, not by the reason.

Faith is a gift of God; do not believe that we said it was a gift of reasoning. Other religions do not say this of their faith. They only give reasoning in order to arrive at it, and yet it does not bring them to it.

280. The knowledge of God is very far from the love of Him.

282. We know truth, not only by the reason, but also by the heart, and it is in this last way that we know first principles; and reason, which has no part in it, tries in vain to impugn them. The skeptics, who have only this for their object, labor to no purpose. We know that we do not dream, and however impossible it is for us to prove it by reason, this inability demonstrates only the weakness of our reason, but not, as they affirm, the uncertainty of all our knowledge. For the knowledge of first principles, as space, time, motion, number, is as sure as any of those which we get from reasoning. And reason must trust these intuitions of the heart, and must base on them every argument. (We have intuitive knowledge of the tri-dimensional nature of space, and of the infinity of number, and reason then shows that there are no two square numbers one of which is double of the other. Principles are intuited, propositions are inferred, all with certainty, though in different ways.) And it is as useless and absurd for reason to demand from the heart proofs of her first principles, before admitting them, as it would be for the heart to demand from reason an intuition of all demonstrated propositions before accepting them.

This inability ought, then, to serve only to humble reason, which would judge all, but not to impugn our certainty, as if only reason were capable of instructing us. Would to God, on the contrary, that we had never need of it, and that we knew everything by instinct and intuition! But nature has refused us this boon. On the contrary, she has given us but very little knowledge of this kind; and all the rest can be acquired only by reasoning.

Therefore, those to whom God has imparted religion by intuition are very fortunate, and justly convinced. But to those who do not have it, we can give it only by reasoning, waiting for God to give them spiritual insight, without which faith is only human, and useless for salvation.

347. Man is but a reed, the most feeble thing in nature; but he is a thinking reed. The entire universe need not arm itself to crush him. A vapor, a drop of water suffices to kill him. But, if the universe were to crush him, man would still be more noble than that which killed him, because he knows that he dies and the advantage which the universe has over him; the universe knows nothing of this.

All our dignity consists, then, in thought. By it we must elevate ourselves, and not by space and time which we cannot fill. Let us endeavour, then, to think well; this is the principle of morality.

365. Thought.—All the dignity of man consists in thought. Thought is therefore by its nature a wonderful and incomparable thing. It must have strange defects to be contemptible. But it has such, so that nothing is more ridiculous. How great it is in its nature! How vile it is in its defects!

But what is this thought? How foolish it is!

409. The greatness of man.—The greatness of man is so evident, that it is even proved by his wretchedness. For what in animals is nature we call in man wretchedness; by which we recognize that, his nature being now like that of animals, he has fallen from a better nature which once was his.

For who is unhappy at not being a king, except a deposed king? Was Paulus Aemilius unhappy at being no longer consul? On the contrary, everybody thought him happy in having been consul, because the office could only be held for a time. But men thought Perseus so unhappy in being no longer king, because the condition of kingship implied his being always king, that they thought it strange that he endured life. Who is unhappy at having only one eye? Probably no man ever ventured to mourn at not having three eyes. But any one is inconsolable at having none.

430. The greatness and the wretchedness of man are so evident that the true religion must necessarily teach us both that there is in man some great source of greatness, and a great source of wretchedness. It must then give us a reason for these astonishing contradictions. . . .

434. . . . Again, no person is certain, apart from faith, whether he is awake or sleeps, seeing that during sleep we believe that we are awake as firmly as we do when we are awake; we believe that we see space, figure, and motion; we are aware of the passage of time, we measure it; and in fact we act as if we were awake. So that half of our life being passed in sleep, we have on our own admission no idea of truth, whatever we may imagine. As all our intuitions are then illusions, who knows whether the other half of our life, in which we think we are awake, is not another sleep a little different from the former, from which we awake when we suppose ourselves asleep? . . .

What then shall man do in this state? Shall he doubt everything? Shall he doubt whether he is awake, whether he is being pinched, or whether he is being burned? Shall he doubt whether he doubts? Shall he doubt whether he exists? We cannot go so far as that; and I lay it down as a fact that there never has been a real complete skeptic. Nature sustains our feeble reason, and prevents it raving to this extent.

Shall he then say, on the contrary, that he certainly possesses truth—he who, when pressed ever so little, can show no title to it, and is forced to let go his hold?

What a chimera then is man! What a novelty! What a monster, what a chaos, what a contradiction, what a prodigy! Judge of all things, imbecile worm of the earth; depositary of truth, a sink of uncertainty and error; the pride and refuse of the universe!

Who will unravel this tangle? Nature confutes the skeptics, and reason confutes the dogmatists. What then will you become, O men! who try to find out by your natural reason what is your true condition? You cannot avoid one of these sects, nor adhere to one of them.

Know then, proud man, what a paradox you are to yourself. Humble yourself, weak reason; be silent, foolish nature; learn that man infinitely transcends man, and learn from your Master your true condition, of which you are ignorant. Hear God. . . .

555. . . . The Christian religion, then, teaches men these two truths; that there is a God whom men can know, and that there is a corruption in their nature which renders them unworthy of Him. It is equally important to men to know both these points; and it is equally dangerous for man to know God without knowing his own wretchedness, and to know his own wretchedness without knowing the Redeemer who can free him from it. The knowledge of only one of these points gives rise either to the pride of philosophers, who have known God, and not their own wretchedness, or to the despair of atheists, who know their own wretchedness, but not the Redeemer.

And, as it is alike necessary to man to know these two points, so is it alike merciful to God to have made us know them. The Christian religion does this; it is in this that it consists.

Let us herein examine the order of the world, and see if all things do not tend to establish these two chief points of this religion: Jesus Christ is the end of all, and the center to which all tends. Whoever knows Him knows the reason of everything.

Those who fall into error err only through failure to see one of these two things. We can then have an excellent knowledge of God without that of our own wretchedness, and of our own wretchedness without that of God. But we cannot know Jesus Christ without knowing at the same time both God and our own wretchedness. . . .

The God of Christians is not a God who is simply the author of mathematical truths, or of the order of the elements; that is the view of heathens and Epicureans. He is not merely a God who exercises His providence over the life and fortunes of men, to bestow on those who worship Him a long and happy life. That was the portion of the Jews. But the God of Abraham, the God of Isaac, and God of Jacob, and God of Christians, is a God of love and of comfort, a God who fills the soul and heart of those whom He possesses, a God who makes them conscious of their inward wretchedness, and His infinite mercy, who unites Himself to their inmost soul, who fills it with humility and joy, with confidence and love, who renders them incapable of any other end than Himself.

All who seek God without Jesus Christ, and who rest in nature, either find no light to satisfy them, or come to form for themselves a means of knowing God and serving Him without a mediator. Thereby they fall either into atheism, or into deism, two things which the Christian religion abhors almost equally. . . . . .

563. The prophecies, the very miracles and proofs of our religion, are not of such a nature that they can be said to be absolutely convincing. But they are also of such a kind that it cannot be said that it is unreasonable to believe them. Thus there is both evidence and obscurity to enlighten some and confuse others. But the evidence is such that it surpasses, or at least equals, the evidence to the contrary; so that it is not reason which can determine men not to follow it, and thus it can only be lust or malice of heart. And by this means there is sufficient evidence to condemn, and insufficient to convince; so that it appears in those who follow it, that it is grace, and not reason, which makes them follow it; and in those who shun it, that it is lust, not reason, which makes them shun it.

Baruch Spinoza
1632–1677

Except for Socrates himself, it would be difficult to find a philosopher who was a more highly regarded person than Benedict (Baruch) Spinoza. Like Socrates, he was not interested in power or wealth. Like Socrates, he was accused of atheism and was hounded for his unorthodox beliefs. Like Socrates, he was interested in philosophy as a way of life, not as a professional discipline.

Spinoza was born in Amsterdam, the son of Jewish refugees who had fled from Portugal to escape persecution. As a young man, he was trained in Jewish tradition under a celebrated Talmudist, Saul Levi Morteira. He later studied with Manasseh ben Israel, the man who persuaded Cromwell to allow Jews to return to England, and with a Dutch physician, Franz van der Ende.

As a Jew, Spinoza was an outsider in Holland—not even entitled to citizenship because of his faith. As an original thinker, Spinoza soon became an outsider within the Jewish community as well. He was accused of heresy by the synagogue of Amsterdam and required to disavow his teachings. Spinoza refused and was officially excommunicated in 1656, when he was 23 years old. (In the twentieth century, the new state of Israel formally revoked the ban.)

With no wish to join any other religious community, Spinoza left Amsterdam and eventually settled in The Hague. He lived very simply, supporting himself by grinding and polishing lenses, a craft he had adopted out of respect for the Jewish tradition, which required scholars to learn a trade.

Spinoza published only two works during his lifetime. His first work was *Principles of Descartes' Philosophy* (1663), which critically examined the presuppositions and structure of Descartes' system. Using what later came to be called "higher criticism," his second book, *Theological-Political Treatise* (1670), subjected Scripture to rational analysis. He concluded that the Bible does not aim at truth but at pious and obedient behavior. Writing soon after the Thirty Years

War (1618–1648), he proposed that religion and truth be separated altogether. This separation, he believed, would be the best safeguard against fanaticism. And pious conduct flourishes best in an atmosphere of free speech.

His *Theological-Political Treatise* attracted a great deal of criticism. It also brought an invitation to the chair of philosophy at the University of Heidelberg, Germany. Although the invitation included a guarantee of academic freedom, Spinoza rejected it out of his passion for freedom to speak and write as he saw fit.

The rigor of his simple life, with the glass dust of his trade, hastened his death from consumption at the age of 44, two years before Hobbes died at 91. Immediately following his death, Spinoza's other works, including *Political Treatise* (which supports individual liberty, religious tolerance, and democracy); *On the Improvement of the Intellect*; and his masterpiece, *Ethics*, were published.

* * *

Whereas Descartes and Hobbes used the geometrical *method*, Spinoza used geometrical *form* as well. The *Ethics* is presented as a geometrical system, developing propositions from axioms and definitions.

In Books I and II of his *Ethics,* reprinted here in the Samuel Shirley translation, Spinoza explores God and the nature and origin of mind. He begins by accepting Descartes' idea that "infinite substance" is completely independent and necessary. But he claims that Descartes had contradicted himself by allowing for "finite substances" as well. Instead, Spinoza claims that there could only be one substance: God. God exists necessarily and as God is the only substance, what we call "Nature" is also God. This also means that whatever happens is necessary (though individuals are often confused and do not understand the connections).

Although God is the only substance, God has infinite attributes. The only two divine attributes we can know are thought (of which minds are modifications) and extension (of which bodies are modifications). To Spinoza, Descartes was wrong to present mind and body as two separate substances (with all the concomitant problems of interaction). Instead, says Spinoza, body and mind are both attributes of the One substance. Thinking substance and extended substance are really the same substance.

In Books III to V of thc *Ethics*, Spinoza argues that we must free ourselves from the tyranny of the passions. The key to this freedom is an understanding of God that allows us to see the necessary, rational structure of reality: "The more this knowledge, that things are necessary, is applied to particular things . . . the greater is the power of the mind over the emotions." The final goal of this knowledge is "blessedness," which consists of intellectual love toward God. This program of overcoming the passions by reason may be difficult, but Spinoza concludes that "all things excellent are as difficult as they are rare" (an apt description of Spinoza's classic).

* * *

For a general introduction to Spinoza's life and thought, see Stuart Hampshire, *Spinoza* (Baltimore, MD: Penguin Books, 1952); Henry E. Allison, *Benedict De Spinoza*, rev. ed. (New Haven, CT: Yale University Press, 1987); Alan Donagan, *Spinoza* (Chicago: University of Chicago Press, 1988); Herman De Dijn, *Spinoza: The Way to Wisdom* (West Lafayette, IN: Purdue University Press, 1996); Roger

Scraton, *Spinoza* (London: Routledge, 1999); Steven Nadler, *Spinoza: A Life* (Cambridge: Cambridge University Press, 1999); and Michael Della Rocca, *Spinoza* (Abingdon, UK: Routledge, 2008). For an interesting study of Spinoza's thought in relation to the other Continental rationalists, see John Cottingham, *The Rationalists* (Oxford: Oxford University Press, 1988). The generally accepted "classic" commentary on the *Ethics* remains Harry Austryn Wolfson, *The Philosophy of Spinoza: Unfolding the Latent Processes of His Reasoning* (1934; reprint New York: Schocken, 1969). For more recent discussions of Spinoza's *Ethics,* see Jonathan Bennett, *A Study of Spinoza's* Ethics (Indianapolis, IN: Hackett, 1984); Edwin Curley, *Behind the Geometrical Method: A Reading of Spinoza's* Ethics (Princeton, NJ: Princeton University Press, 1988); Genevieve Lloyd, *Spinoza and the* Ethics (Oxford: Routledge, 1996); Steven Nadler, *Spinoza's* Ethics: *An Introduction* (Cambridge: Cambridge University Press, 2006); and J. Thomas Cook, *Spinoza's* Ethics: *A Reader's Guide* (London: Continuum, 2007). For collections of essays on Spinoza, see S. Paul Kashap, ed., *Studies in Spinoza* (Berkeley: University of California Press, 1972); Robert W. Shahan and J.I. Biro, eds., *Spinoza: New Perspectives* (Norman, OK: University of Oklahoma Press, 1978); Richard Kennington, ed., *The Philosophy of Baruch Spinoza* (Washington, DC: Catholic University of America Press, 1980); Don Garrett, ed., *The Cambridge Companion to Spinoza* (Cambridge: Cambridge University Press, 1995); and Yirmiahu Yorel and Gideon Segal, eds., *Spinoza* (New York: Ashgate, 2000). Richard Mason, *The God of Spinoza: A Philosophical Study* (Cambridge: Cambridge University Press, 1997) is a study of Spinoza's philosophy of religion while the Jewish character of Spinoza's thought is discussed in Yirmiyahu Yovel's pair of books, *The Marrano of Reason* and *The Adventures of Immanence* (both Princeton, NJ: Princeton University Press, 1991) and Steven Smith, *Spinoza, Liberalism, and the Question of Jewish Identity* (New Haven, CT: Yale University Press, 1997).

ETHICS (in part)

PART I

CONCERNING GOD

Definitions

1. By that which is self-caused I mean that whose essence involves existence; or that whose nature can be conceived only as existing.

2. A thing is said to be finite in its own kind [*in suo genere finita*] when it can be limited by another thing of the same nature. For example, a body is said to be finite

because we can always conceive of another body greater than it. So, too, a thought is limited by another thought. But body is not limited by thought, nor thought by body.

3. By substance I mean that which is in itself and is conceived through itself; that is, that the conception of which does not require the conception of another thing from which it has to be formed.

4. By attribute I mean that which the intellect perceives of substance as constituting its essence.

5. By mode I mean the affections of substance, that is, that which is in something else and is conceived through something else.

6. By God I mean an absolutely infinite being, that is, substance consisting of infinite attributes, each of which expresses eternal and infinite essence.

Explication: I say "absolutely infinite," not "infinite in its kind." For if a thing is only infinite in its kind, one may deny that it has infinite attributes. But if a thing is absolutely infinite, whatever expresses essence and does not involve any negation belongs to its essence.

7. That thing is said to be free [*liber*] which exists solely from the necessity of its own nature, and is determined to action by itself alone. A thing is said to be necessary [*necessarius*] or rather, constrained [*coactus*], if it is determined by another thing to exist and to act in a definite and determinate way.

8. By eternity I mean existence itself insofar as it is conceived as necessarily following solely from the definition of an eternal thing.

Explication: For such existence is conceived as an eternal truth, just as is the essence of the thing, and therefore cannot be explicated through duration or time, even if duration be conceived as without beginning and end.

Axioms

1. All things that are, are either in themselves or in something else.

2. That which cannot be conceived through another thing must be conceived through itself.

3. From a given determinate cause there necessarily follows an effect; on the other hand, if there be no determinate cause, it is impossible that an effect should follow.

4. The knowledge of an effect depends on, and involves, the knowledge of the cause.

5. Things which have nothing in common with each other cannot be understood through each other; that is, the conception of the one does not involve the conception of the other.

6. A true idea must agree with that of which it is the idea [*ideatum*].

7. If a thing can be conceived as not existing, its essence does not involve existence.

PROPOSITION 1: *Substance is by nature prior to its affections.*

Proof: This is evident from Defs. 3 and 5.

PROPOSITION 2: *Two substances having different attributes have nothing in common.*

Proof: This too is evident from Def. 3; for each substance must be in itself and be conceived through itself; that is, the conception of the one does not involve the conception of the other.

PROPOSITION 3: *When things have nothing in common, one cannot be the cause of the other.*

Proof: If things have nothing in common, then (Ax. 5) they cannot be understood through one another, and so (Ax. 4) one cannot be the cause of the other.

PROPOSITION 4: *Two or more distinct things are distinguished from one another either by the difference of the attributes of the substances or by the difference of the affections of the substances.*

Proof: All things that are, are either in themselves or in something else (Ax. 1); that is (Defs. 3 and 5), nothing exists external to the intellect except substances and their affections. Therefore, there can be nothing external to the intellect through which several things can be distinguished from one another except substances or (which is the same thing) (Def. 4) the attributes and the affections of substances.

PROPOSITION 5: *In the universe there cannot be two or more substances of the same nature or attribute.*

Proof: If there were several such distinct substances, they would have to be distinguished from one another either by a difference of attributes or by a difference of affections (Pr. 4). If they are distinguished only by a difference of attributes, then it will be granted that there cannot be more than one substance of the same attribute. But if they are distinguished by a difference of affections, then, since substance is by nature prior to its affections (Pr. 1), disregarding therefore its affections and considering substance in itself, that is (Def. 3 and Ax. 6), considering it truly, it cannot be conceived as distinguishable from another substance. That is (Pr. 4), there cannot be several such substances but only one.

PROPOSITION 6: *One substance cannot be produced by another substance.*

Proof: In the universe there cannot be two substances of the same attribute (Pr. 5), that is (Pr. 2), two substances having something in common. And so (Pr. 3) one cannot be the cause of the other; that is, one cannot be produced by the other.

Corollary: Hence it follows that substance cannot be produced by anything else. For in the universe there exists nothing but substances and their affections, as is evident from Ax. 1 and Defs. 3 and 5. But, by Pr. 6, it cannot be produced by another substance. Therefore, substance cannot be produced by anything else whatsoever.

Another Proof: This can be proved even more readily by the absurdity of the contradictory. For if substance could be produced by something else, the knowledge of substance would have to depend on the knowledge of its cause (Ax. 4), and so (Def. 3) it would not be substance.

PROPOSITION 7: *Existence belongs to the nature of substance.*

Proof: Substance cannot be produced by anything else (Cor. Pr. 6) and is therefore self-caused [*causa sui*]; that is (Def. 1), its essence necessarily involves existence; that is, existence belongs to its nature.

PROPOSITION 8: *Every substance is necessarily infinite.*

Proof: There cannot be more than one substance having the same attribute (Pr. 5), and existence belongs to the nature of substance (Pr. 7). It must therefore exist either as finite or as infinite. But it cannot exist as finite, for (Def. 2) it would have to be limited by another substance of the same nature, and that substance also would have to exist (Pr. 7). And so there would exist two substances of the same attribute, which is absurd (Pr. 5). Therefore, it exists as infinite.

Scholium 1: Since in fact to be finite is in part a negation and to be infinite is the unqualified affirmation of the existence of some nature, it follows from Proposition 7 alone that every substance must be infinite.

Scholium 2: I do not doubt that for those who judge things confusedly and are not accustomed to know things through their primary causes it is difficult to grasp the proof of Proposition 7. Surely, this is because they neither distinguish between the modification of substances and substances themselves, nor do they know how things are produced. And so it comes about that they ascribe to substances a beginning which they see natural things as having; for those who do not know the true causes of things confuse everything. Without any hesitation they imagine trees as well as men talking and stones as well as men being formed from seeds; indeed, any forms whatsoever are imagined to change into any other forms. So too, those who confuse the divine nature with human nature easily ascribe to God human emotions, especially so long as they are ignorant of how the latter are produced in the mind. But if men were to attend to the nature of substance, they would not doubt at all the truth of Proposition 7; indeed, this Proposition would be an axiom to all and would be ranked among universally accepted truisms. For by substance they would understand that which is in itself and is conceived through itself; that is, that the knowledge of which does not require the knowledge of any other thing. By modifications they would understand that which is in another thing, and whose conception is formed from the thing in which they are. Therefore, in the case of nonexistent modifications we can have true ideas of them since their essence is included in something else, with the result that they can be conceived through that something else, although they do not exist in actuality externally to the intellect. However, in the case of substances, because they are conceived only through themselves, their truth external to the intellect is only in themselves. So if someone were to say that he has a clear and distinct—that is, a true—idea of substance and that he nevertheless doubts whether such a substance exists, this would surely be just the same as if he were to declare that he has a true idea but nevertheless suspects that it may be false (as is obvious to anyone who gives his mind to it). Or if anyone asserts that substance is created, he at the same time asserts that a false idea has become true, than which nothing more absurd can be conceived. So it must necessarily be admitted that the existence of substance is as much an eternal truth as is its essence.

From here we can derive in another way that there cannot be but one [substance] of the same nature, and I think it worthwhile to set out the proof here. Now to do this in an orderly fashion I ask you to note:

1. The true definition of each thing involves and expresses nothing beyond the nature of the thing defined. Hence it follows that—

2. No definition involves or expresses a fixed number of individuals, since it expresses nothing but the nature of the thing defined. For example, the definition of a triangle expresses nothing other than simply the nature of a triangle, and not a fixed number of triangles.

3. For each individual existent thing there must necessarily be a definite cause for its existence.

4. The cause for the existence of a thing must either be contained in the very nature and definition of the existent thing (in effect, existence belongs to its nature) or must have its being independently of the thing itself.

From these premises it follows that if a fixed number of individuals exist in Nature, there must necessarily be a cause why those individuals and not more or fewer exist. If, for example, in Nature twenty men were to exist (for the sake of greater clarity I suppose that they exist simultaneously and that no others existed in Nature before them), in order to account for the existence of these twenty men, it will not be enough for us to demonstrate the cause of human nature in general; it will furthermore be necessary to demonstrate the cause why not more or fewer than twenty men exist, since (Note 3) there must necessarily be a cause for the existence of each one. But this cause (Notes 2 and 3) cannot be contained in the nature of man, since the true definition of man does not involve the number twenty. So (Note 4) the cause of the existence of these twenty men, and consequently of each one, must necessarily be external to each one, and therefore we can reach the unqualified conclusion that whenever several individuals of a kind exist, there must necessarily be an external cause for their existence. Now since existence belongs to the nature of substance (as has already been shown in this Scholium) the definition of substance must involve necessary existence, and consequently the existence of substance must be concluded solely from its definition. But the existence of several substances cannot follow from the definition of substance (as I have already shown in Notes 2 and 3). Therefore, from the definition of substance it follows necessarily that there exists only one substance of the same nature, as was proposed.

PROPOSITION 9: *The more reality or being a thing has, the more attributes it has.*

Proof: This is evident from Definition 4.

PROPOSITION 10: *Each attribute of one substance must be conceived through itself.*

Proof: For an attribute is that which intellect perceives of substance as constituting its essence (Def. 4), and so (Def. 3) it must be conceived through itself.

Scholium: From this it is clear that although two attributes be conceived as really distinct, that is, one without the help of the other, still we cannot deduce therefrom that they constitute two entities, or two different substances. For it is in the nature of substance that each of its attributes be conceived through itself, since all the attributes it possesses have always been in it simultaneously, and one could not have been produced by another; but each expresses the reality or being of substance. So it is by no means absurd to ascribe more than one attribute to one substance. Indeed, nothing in Nature is clearer than that each entity must be conceived under some attribute, and the more reality or being it has, the more are its attributes which express necessity, or eternity, and infinity. Consequently, nothing can be clearer than this, too, that an absolutely infinite entity must necessarily be defined (Def. 6) as an entity consisting of infinite attributes, each of which expresses a definite essence, eternal and infinite. Now if anyone asks by what mark can we distinguish between different substances, let him read the following Propositions, which show that in Nature there exists only one substance, absolutely infinite. So this distinguishing mark would be sought in vain.

PROPOSITION 11: *God, or substance consisting of infinite attributes, each of which expresses eternal and infinite essence, necessarily exists.*

Proof: If you deny this, conceive, if you can, that God does not exist. Therefore (Ax. 7), his essence does not involve existence. But this is absurd (Pr. 7). Therefore, God necessarily exists.

Second Proof: For every thing a cause or reason must be assigned either for its existence or for its nonexistence. For example, if a triangle exists, there must be a reason, or cause, for its existence. If it does not exist, there must be a reason or cause which prevents it from existing, or which annuls its existence. Now this reason or cause must either be contained in the nature of the thing or be external to it. For example, the reason why a square circle does not exist is indicated by its very nature, in that it involves a contradiction. On the other hand, the reason for the existence of substance also follows from its nature alone, in that it involves existence (Pr. 7). But the reason for the existence or nonexistence of a circle or a triangle does not follow from their nature, but from the order of universal corporeal Nature. For it is from this latter that it necessarily follows that either the triangle necessarily exists at this moment or that its present existence is impossible. This is self-evident, and therefrom it follows that a thing necessarily exists if there is no reason or cause which prevents its existence. Therefore, if there can be no reason or cause which prevents God from existing or which annuls his existence, we are bound to conclude that he necessarily exists. But if there were such a reason or cause, it would have to be either within God's nature or external to it; that is, it would have to be in another substance of another nature. For if it were of the same nature, by that very fact it would be granted that God exists. But a substance of another nature would have nothing in common with God (Pr. 2), and so could neither posit nor annul his existence. Since, therefore, there cannot be external to God's nature a reason or cause that would annul God's existence, then if indeed he does not exist, the reason or cause must necessarily be in God's nature, which would therefore involve a contradiction. But to affirm this of a Being absolutely infinite and in the highest degree perfect is absurd. Therefore, neither in God nor external to God is there any cause or reason which would annul his existence. Therefore, God necessarily exists.

A Third Proof: To be able to not exist is weakness; on the other hand, to be able to exist is power, as is self-evident. So if what now necessarily exists is nothing but finite entities, then finite entities are more potent than an absolutely infinite Entity— which is absurd. Therefore, either nothing exists, or an absolutely infinite Entity necessarily exists, too. But we do exist, either in ourselves or in something else which necessarily exists (Ax. 1 and Pr. 7). Therefore, an absolutely infinite Entity—that is (Def. 6), God—necessarily exists.

Scholium: In this last proof I decided to prove God's existence a posteriori so that the proof may be more easily perceived, and not because God's existence does not follow a priori from this same basis. For since the ability to exist is power, it follows that the greater the degree of reality that belongs to the nature of a thing, the greater amount of energy it has for existence. So an absolutely infinite Entity or God will have from himself absolutely infinite power to exist, and therefore exists absolutely.

But perhaps many will not readily find this proof convincing because they are used to considering only such things as derive from external causes. Of these things they observe that those which come quickly into being—that is, which readily exist—likewise readily perish, while things which they conceive as more complex they regard as more difficult to bring into being—that is, not so ready to exist. However, to free them from these misconceptions I do not need at this point to show what measure of truth there is in the saying, "Quickly come, quickly go," neither need I raise the question whether or not everything is equally easy in respect of Nature as a whole. It is enough to note simply this, that I am not here speaking of things that come into being through external causes, but only of substances, which (Pr. 6) cannot be produced by any external cause.

For whether they consist of many parts or few, things that are brought about by external causes owe whatever degree of perfection or reality they possess entirely to the power of the external cause, and so their existence has its origin solely in the perfection of the external cause, and not in their own perfection. On the other hand, whatever perfection substance possesses is due to no external cause; therefore its existence, too, must follow solely from its own nature, and is therefore nothing else but its essence. So perfection does not annul a thing's existence: on the contrary, it posits it; whereas imperfection annuls a thing's existence. So there is nothing of which we can be more certain than the existence of an absolutely infinite or perfect Entity; that is, God. For since his essence excludes all imperfection and involves absolute perfection, it thereby removes all reason for doubting his existence and affords the utmost certainty of it. This, I think, must be quite clear to all who give a modicum of attention to the matter.

PROPOSITION 12: *No attribute of substance can be truly conceived from which it would follow that substance can be divided.*

Proof: The parts into which substance thus conceived would be divided will either retain the nature of substance or they will not. In the first case each part will have to be infinite (Pr. 8) and self-caused (Pr. 6) and consist of a different attribute (Pr. 5); and so several substances could be formed from one substance, which is absurd (Pr. 6). Furthermore, the parts would have nothing in common with the whole (Pr. 2), and the whole could exist and be conceived without its parts (Def. 4 and Pr. 10), the absurdity of which none can doubt. But in the latter case in which the parts will not retain the nature of substance—then when the whole substance would have been divided into equal parts it would lose the nature of substance and would cease to be. This is absurd (Pr. 7).

PROPOSITION 13: *Absolutely infinite substance is indivisible.*

Proof: If it were divisible, the parts into which it would be divided will either retain the nature of absolutely infinite substance, or not. In the first case, there would therefore be several substances of the same nature, which is absurd (Pr. 5). In the second case, absolutely infinite substance can cease to be, which is also absurd (Pr. 11).

Corollary: From this it follows that no substance, and consequently no corporeal substance, insofar as it is substance, is divisible.

Scholium: The indivisibility of substance can be more easily understood merely from the fact that the nature of substance can be conceived only as infinite, and that a part of substance can mean only finite substance, which involves an obvious contradiction (Pr. 8).

PROPOSITION 14: *There can be, or be conceived, no other substance but God.*

Proof: Since God is an absolutely infinite being of whom no attribute expressing the essence of substance can be denied (Def. 6), and since he necessarily exists (Pr. 11), if there were any other substance but God, it would have to be explicated through some attribute of God, and so there would exist two substances with the same attribute, which is absurd (Pr. 5). So there can be no substance external to God, and consequently no such substance can be conceived. For if it could be conceived, it would have to be conceived necessarily as existing; but this is absurd (by the first part of this proof). Therefore, no substance can be or be conceived external to God.

Corollary 1: Hence it follows quite clearly that God is one: that is (Def. 6), in the universe there is only one substance, and this is absolutely infinite, as I have already indicated in Scholium Pr. 10.

Corollary 2: It follows that the thing extended and the thing thinking are either attributes of God or (Ax. 1) affections of the attributes of God.

PROPOSITION 15: *Whatever is, is in God, and nothing can be or be conceived without God.*

Proof: Apart from God no substance can be or be conceived (Pr. 14), that is (Def. 3), something which is in itself and is conceived through itself. Now modes (Def. 5) cannot be or be conceived without substance; therefore, they can be only in the divine nature and can be conceived only through the divine nature. But nothing exists except substance and modes (Ax. 1). Therefore, nothing can be or be conceived without God.

Scholium: Some imagine God in the likeness of man, consisting of mind and body, and subject to passions. But it is clear from what has already been proved how far they stray from the true knowledge of God. These I dismiss, for all who have given any consideration to the divine nature deny that God is corporeal. They find convincing proof of this in the fact that by body we understand some quantity having length, breadth, and depth, bounded by a definite shape; and nothing more absurd than this can be attributed to God, a being absolutely infinite.

At the same time, however, by other arguments which they try to prove their point, they show clearly that in their thinking corporeal or extended substance is set completely apart from the divine nature, and they assert that it is created by God. But they have no idea from what divine power it could have been created, which clearly shows that they don't know what they are saying. Now I have clearly proved—at any rate, in my judgment (Cor. Pr. 6 and Sch. 2 Pr. 8)—that no substance can be produced or created by anything else. Furthermore, in Proposition 14 we showed that apart from God no substance can be or be conceived, and hence we deduced that extended substance is one of God's infinite attributes.

However, for a fuller explanation I will refute my opponents' arguments, which all seem to come down to this. Firstly, they think that corporeal substance, insofar as it is substance, is made up of parts, and so they deny that it can be infinite, and consequently that it can pertain to God. This they illustrate with many examples, of which I will take one or two. They say that if corporeal substance is infinite, suppose it to be divided into two parts. Each of these parts will be either finite or infinite. If the former, then the infinite is made up of two finite parts, which is absurd. If the latter, then there is an infinite which is twice as great as another infinite, which is also absurd.

Again, if an infinite length is measured in feet, it will have to consist of an infinite number of feet; and if it is measured in inches, it will consist of an infinite number of inches. So one infinite number will be twelve times greater than another infinite number.

Lastly, if from one point in an infinite quantity two lines, AB and AC, be drawn of fixed and determinate length, and thereafter be produced to infinity, it is clear that the distance between B and C continues to increase and finally changes from a determinate distance to an indeterminate distance.

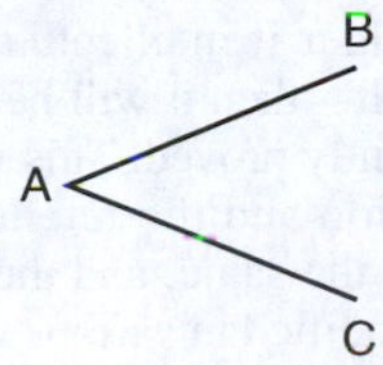

As these absurdities follow, they think, from supposing quantity to be infinite, they conclude that corporeal substance must be finite and consequently cannot pertain to God's essence.

The second argument is also drawn from God's consummate perfection. Since God, they say, is a supremely perfect being, he cannot be that which is acted upon. But corporeal substance, being divisible, can be acted upon. It therefore follows that corporeal substance does not pertain to God's essence.

These are the arguments I find put forward by writers who thereby seek to prove that corporeal substance is unworthy of the divine essence and cannot pertain to it. However, the student who looks carefully into these arguments will find that I have already replied to them, since they are all founded on the same supposition that material substance is composed of parts, and this I have already shown to be absurd (Pr. 12 and Cor. Pr. 13). Again, careful reflection will show that all those alleged absurdities (if indeed they are absurdities, which is not now under discussion) from which they seek to prove that extended substance is finite do not at all follow from the supposition that quantity is infinite, but that infinite quantity is measurable and is made up of finite parts. Therefore, from the resultant absurdities no other conclusion can be reached but that infinite quantity is not measurable and cannot be made up of finite parts. And this is exactly what we have already proved (Pr. 12). So the weapon they aimed at us is in fact turned against themselves. If therefore from this "reductio ad absurdum" argument of theirs they still seek to deduce that extended substance must be finite, they are surely just like one who, having made the supposition that a circle has the properties of a square, deduces therefrom that a circle does not have a center from which all lines drawn to the circumference are equal. For corporeal substance, which can be conceived only as infinite, one, and indivisible (Prs. 8, 5, and 12) they conceive as made up of finite parts, multiplex, and divisible, so as to deduce that it is finite. In the same way others, too, having supposed that a line is composed of points, can find many arguments to prove that a line cannot be infinitely divided. Indeed, it is just as absurd to assert that corporeal substance is composed of bodies or parts as that a body is composed of surfaces, surfaces of lines, and lines of points. This must be admitted by all who know clear reason to be infallible, and particularly those who say that a vacuum cannot exist. For if corporeal substance could be so divided that its parts were distinct in reality, why could one part not be annihilated while the others remain joined together as before? And why should all the parts be so fitted together as to leave no vacuum? Surely, in the case of things which are in reality distinct from one another, one can exist without the other and remain in its original state. Since therefore there is no vacuum in Nature (of which [more] elsewhere) and all its parts must so harmonize that there is no vacuum, it also follows that the parts cannot be distinct in reality; that is, corporeal substance, insofar as it is substance, cannot be divided.

If I am now asked why we have this natural inclination to divide quantity, I reply that we conceive quantity in two ways, to wit, abstractly, or superficially—in other words, as represented in the imagination—or as substance, which we do only through the intellect. If therefore we consider quantity insofar as we represent it in the imagination—and this is what we more frequently and readily do— we find it to be finite, divisible, and made up of parts. But if we consider it intellectually and conceive it insofar as it is substance—and this is very difficult—then it will be found to be infinite, one, and indivisible, as we have already sufficiently proved. This will be quite clear to those who can distinguish between the imagination and the intellect, especially if this point also is stressed, that matter is everywhere the same, and there are no distinct parts in it except insofar as we conceive matter as modified in various ways. Then its parts are distinct, not really but only modally. For example, we conceive water to be divisible and to have separate parts insofar as it is water, but not insofar as it is material substance. In this latter respect it is not capable of separation or division. Furthermore, water, qua water, comes into existence and goes out of existence; but qua substance it does not come into existence nor go out of existence [*corrumpitur*].

I consider that in the above I have also replied to the second argument, since this too is based on the supposition that matter, insofar as it is substance, is divisible and made up of parts. And even though this were not so, I do not know why matter should be unworthy of the divine nature, since (Pr. 14) there can be no substance external to God by which it can be acted upon. All things, I repeat, are in God, and all things that come to pass do so only through the laws of God's infinite nature and follow through the necessity of his essence (as I shall later show). Therefore, by no manner of reasoning can it be said that God is acted upon by anything else or that extended substance is unworthy of the divine nature, even though it be supposed divisible, as long as it is granted to be eternal and infinite.

But enough of this subject for the present.

PROPOSITION 16: *From the necessity of the divine nature there must follow infinite things in infinite ways [*modis*] (that is, everything that can come within the scope of infinite intellect).*

Proof: This proposition should be obvious to everyone who will but consider this point, that from the given definition of any one thing the intellect infers a number of properties which necessarily follow in fact from the definition (that is, from the very essence of the thing), and the more reality the definition of the thing expresses (that is, the more reality the essence of the thing defined involves), the greater the number of its properties. Now since divine nature possesses absolutely infinite attributes (Def. 6), of which each one also expresses infinite essence in its own kind, then there must necessarily follow from the necessity of the divine nature an infinity of things in infinite ways (that is, everything that can come within the scope of the infinite intellect).

Corollary 1: Hence it follows that God is the efficient cause of all things that can come within the scope of the infinite intellect.

Corollary 2: Secondly, it follows that God is the cause through himself, not *per accidens*.

Corollary 3: Thirdly, it follows that God is absolutely the first cause.

PROPOSITION 17: *God acts solely from the laws of his own nature, constrained by none.*

Proof: We have just shown that an infinity of things follow, absolutely, solely from the necessity of divine nature, or—which is the same thing—solely from the laws of that same nature (Pr. 16); and we have proved (Pr. 15) that nothing can be or be conceived without God, but that everything is in God. Therefore, there can be nothing external to God by which he can be determined or constrained to act. Thus, God acts solely from the laws of his own nature and is constrained by none.

Corollary 1: Hence it follows, firstly, that there is no cause, except the perfection of his nature, which either extrinsically or intrinsically moves God to act.

Corollary 2: It follows, secondly, that God alone is a free cause. For God alone exists solely from the necessity of his own nature (Pr. 11 and Cor. 1 Pr. 14) and acts solely from the necessity of his own nature (Pr. 17). So he alone is a free cause (Def. 7).

Scholium: Others take the view that God is a free cause because—so they think—he can bring it about that those things which we have said follow from his nature—that is, which are within his power—should not come about; that is, they should not be produced by him. But this is as much as to say that God can bring it about that it should not follow from the nature of a triangle that its three angles are equal to two right angles, or that from a given cause the effect should not follow, which is absurd.

Furthermore, I shall show later on without the help of this proposition that neither intellect nor will pertain to the nature of God. I know indeed that there are many who think they can prove that intellect in the highest degree and free will belong to the nature of God; for they say they know of nothing more perfect which they may attribute to God than that which is the highest perfection in us. Again, although they conceive of God as having in actuality intellect in the highest degree, they yet do not believe he can bring about the existence of everything which in actuality he understands, for they think they would thereby be nullifying God's power. If, they say, he had created everything that is within his intellect, then he would not have been able to create anything more; and this they regard as inconsistent with God's omnipotence. So they have preferred to regard God as indifferent to everything and as creating nothing but what he has decided, by some absolute exercise of will, to create. However, I think I have shown quite clearly (Pr. 16) that from God's supreme power or infinite nature an infinity of things in infinite ways—that is, everything—has necessarily flowed or is always following from that same necessity, just as from the nature of a triangle it follows from eternity to eternity that its three angles are equal to two right angles. Therefore, God's omnipotence has from eternity been actual and will remain for eternity in the same actuality. In this way, I submit, God's omnipotence is established as being far more perfect. Indeed my opponents—let us speak frankly—seem to be denying God's omnipotence. For they are obliged to admit that God understands an infinite number of creatable things which nevertheless he can never create. If this were not so, that is, if he were to create all the things that he understands, he would exhaust his omnipotence, according to them, and render himself imperfect. Thus, to affirm God as perfect they are reduced to having to affirm at the same time that he cannot bring about everything that is within the bounds of his power. I cannot imagine anything more absurd than this, or more inconsistent with God's omnipotence.

Furthermore, I have something here to say about the intellect and will that is usually attributed to God. If intellect and will do indeed pertain to the eternal essence of God, one must understand in the case of both these attributes something very different from the meaning widely entertained. For the intellect and will that would constitute the essence of God would have to be vastly different from human intellect and will, and would have no point of agreement except the name. They could be no more alike than the celestial constellation of the Dog and the dog that barks. This I will prove as follows. If intellect does pertain to the divine nature, it cannot, like man's intellect, be posterior to (as most thinkers hold) or simultaneous with the objects of understanding, since God is prior in causality to all things (Cor. 1 Pr. 16). On the contrary, the truth and formal essence of things is what it is because it exists as such in the intellect of God as an object of thought. Therefore, God's intellect, insofar as it is conceived as constituting God's essence, is in actual fact the cause of things, in respect both of their essence and their existence. This seems to have been recognized also by those who have asserted that God's intellect, will, and power are one and the same. Since therefore God's intellect is the one and only cause of things, both of their essence and their existence, as we have shown, it must necessarily be different from them both in respect of essence and existence. For that which is caused differs from its cause precisely in what it has from its cause. For example, a man is the cause of the existence of another man, but not of the other's essence; for the essence is an eternal truth. So with regard to their essence the two men can be in full agreement, but they must differ with regard to existence; and for that reason if the existence of the one should cease, the existence of the other would not thereby cease. But if the essence of the one could be destroyed and rendered false, so too would the essence of the other. Therefore, a thing which is the cause of the essence and existence of some effect must differ from that effect both in respect of essence and existence. But God's intellect is the cause of the essence and existence of man's intellect. Therefore, God's intellect, insofar as it is conceived as constituting the divine essence, differs from man's intellect both in respect of essence and existence, and cannot agree with it in any respect other than name—which is what I sought to prove. In the matter of will, the proof is the same, as anyone can readily see.

PROPOSITION 18: *God is the immanent, not the transitive, cause of all things.*

Proof: All things that are, are in God, and must be conceived through God (Pr. 15), and so (Cor. 1 Pr. 16) God is the cause of the things that are in him, which is the first point. Further, there can be no substance external to God (Pr. 14); that is (Def. 3), a thing which is in itself external to God—which is the second point. Therefore, God is the immanent, not the transitive, cause of all things.

PROPOSITION 19: *God [is eternal], that is, all the attributes of God are eternal.*

Proof: God is substance (Def. 6) which necessarily exists (Pr. 11); that is (Pr. 7), a thing to whose nature it pertains to exist, or—and this is the same thing—a thing from whose definition existence follows; and so (Def. 8) God is eternal. Further, by the attributes of God must be understood that which expresses the essence of the Divine substance (Def. 4), that is, that which pertains to substance. It is this, I say, which the attributes themselves must involve. But eternity pertains to the nature of substance (as I have shown in Pr. 7). Therefore, each of the attributes must involve eternity, and so they are all eternal.

Scholium: This proposition is also perfectly clear from the manner in which I proved the existence of God (Pr. 11). From this proof, I repeat, it is obvious that God's existence is, like his essence, an eternal truth. Again, I have also proved God's eternity in another way in Proposition 19 of my *Descartes's Principles of Philosophy,* and there is no need here to go over that ground again.

PROPOSITION 20: *God's existence and his essence are one and the same.*

Proof: God and all his attributes are eternal (Pr. 19); that is, each one of his attributes expresses existence (Def. 8). Therefore, the same attributes of God that explicate his eternal essence (Def. 4) at the same time explicate his eternal existence; that is, that which constitutes the essence of God at the same time constitutes his existence, and so his existence and his essence are one and the same.

Corollary 1: From this it follows, firstly, that God's existence, like his essence, is an eternal truth.

Corollary 2: It follows, secondly, that God is immutable; that is, all the attributes of God are immutable. For if they were to change in respect of existence, they would also have to change in respect of essence (Pr. 10); that is—and this is self-evident—they would have to become false instead of true, which is absurd.

PROPOSITION 21: *All things that follow from the absolute nature of any attribute of God must have existed always, and as infinite; that is, through the said attribute they are eternal and infinite.*

Proof: Suppose this proposition be denied and conceive, if you can, that something in some attribute of God, following from its absolute nature, is finite and has a determinate existence or duration; for example, the idea of God in Thought. Now Thought, being assumed to be an attribute of God, is necessarily infinite by its own nature (Pr. 11). However, insofar as it has the idea of God, it is being supposed as finite. Now (Def. 2) it cannot be conceived as finite unless it is determined through Thought itself. But it cannot be determined through Thought itself insofar as Thought constitutes the idea of God, for it is in that respect that Thought is supposed to be finite. Therefore, it is determined through Thought insofar as Thought does not constitute the idea of God, which Thought must nevertheless necessarily exist (Pr. 11). Therefore, there must be Thought which does not constitute the idea of God, and so the idea of God does not follow necessarily from its nature insofar as it is absolute Thought. (For it is conceived as constituting and as not constituting the idea of God.) This is contrary to our hypothesis. Therefore, if the idea of God in Thought, or anything in some attribute of God (it does not matter what is selected, since the proof is universal), follows from the necessity of the absolute nature of the attribute, it must necessarily be infinite. That was our first point.

Furthermore, that which thus follows from the necessity of the nature of some attribute cannot have a determinate existence, or duration. If this be denied, suppose that there is in some attribute of God a thing following from the necessity of the nature of the attribute, for example, the idea of God in Thought, and suppose that this thing either did not exist at some time, or will cease to exist in the future. Now since Thought is assumed as an attribute of God, it must necessarily exist, and as immutable (Pr. 11 and Cor. 2 Pr. 20). Therefore, outside the bounds of the duration of the idea of God (for this idea is supposed at some time not to have existed, or will at some point cease to exist), Thought will have to exist without the idea of God. But this is contrary to the hypothesis, for it is supposed that when Thought is granted the idea of God necessarily follows. Therefore, the idea of God in Thought, or anything that necessarily follows from the absolute nature of some attribute of God, cannot have a determinate existence, but is eternal through that same attribute. That was our second point. Note that the same holds for anything in an attribute of God which necessarily follows from the absolute nature of God.

PROPOSITION 22: *Whatever follows from some attribute of God, insofar as the attribute is modified by a modification that exists necessarily and as infinite through that same attribute, must also exist both necessarily and as infinite.*

Proof: This proposition is proved in the same way as the preceding one.

PROPOSITION 23: *Every mode which exists necessarily and as infinite must have necessarily followed either from the absolute nature of some attribute of God or from some attribute modified by a modification which exists necessarily and as infinite.*

Proof: A mode is in something else through which it must be conceived (Def. 5); that is (Pr. 15), it is in God alone and can be conceived only through God. Therefore, if a mode is conceived to exist necessarily and to be infinite, both these characteristics must necessarily be inferred or perceived through some attribute of God insofar as that attribute is conceived to express infinity and necessity of existence, or (and by Def. 8 this is the same) eternity; that is (Def. 6 and Pr. 19), insofar as it is considered absolutely. Therefore, a mode which exists necessarily and as infinite must have followed from the absolute nature of some attribute of God, either directly (Pr. 21) or through the mediation of some modification which follows from the absolute nature of the attribute; that is (Pr. 22), which exists necessarily and as infinite.

PROPOSITION 24: *The essence of things produced by God does not involve existence.*

Proof: This is evident from Def. 1. For only that whose nature (considered in itself) involves existence is self-caused and exists solely from the necessity of its own nature.

Corollary: Hence it follows that God is the cause not only of the coming into existence of things but also of their continuing in existence, or, to use a scholastic term, God is the cause of the being of things [*essendi rerum*]. For whether things exist or do not exist, in reflecting on their essence we realize that this essence involves neither existence nor duration. So it is not their essence which can be the cause of either their existence or their duration, but only God, to whose nature alone existence pertains (Cor. 1 Pr. 14).

PROPOSITION 25: *God is the efficient cause not only of the existence of things but also of their essence.*

Proof: If this is denied, then God is not the cause of the essence of things, and so (Ax. 4) the essence of things can be conceived without God. But this is absurd (Pr. 15). Therefore, God is also the cause of the essence of things.

Scholium: This proposition follows more clearly from Pr. 16; for from that proposition it follows that from the given divine nature both the essence and the existence of things must be inferred. In a word, in the same sense that God is said to be self-caused he must also be said to be the cause of all things. This will be even clearer from the following Corollary.

Corollary: Particular things are nothing but affections of the attributes of God, that is, modes wherein the attributes of God find expression in a definite and determinate way. The proof is obvious from Pr. 15 and Def. 5.

PROPOSITION 26: *A thing which has been determined to act in a particular way has necessarily been so determined by God; and a thing which has not been determined by God cannot determine itself to act.*

Proof: That by which things are said to be determined to act in a particular way must necessarily be something positive (as is obvious). So God, from the necessity of his nature, is the efficient cause both of its essence and its existence (Prs. 25 and 16)—which was the first point. From this the second point quite clearly follows as well. For if a thing which has not been determined by God could determine itself, the first part of this proposition would be false, which, as I have shown, is absurd.

PROPOSITION 27: *A thing which has been determined by God to act in a particular way cannot render itself undetermined.*

Proof: This proposition is evident from Axiom 3.

PROPOSITION 28: *Every individual thing, i.e., anything whatever which is finite and has a determinate existence, cannot exist or be determined to act unless it be determined to exist and to act by another cause which is also finite and has a determinate existence, and this cause again cannot exist or be determined to act unless it be determined to exist and to act by another cause which is also finite and has a determinate existence, and so ad infinitum.*

The Synagogue, Amsterdam, n.d., by Rembrandt (1606–1669). Spinoza was a member of the Amsterdam Synagogue until he was excommunicated in 1656. (©*Bridgman-Giraudon/ Art Resource, NY*)

Proof: Whatever is determined to exist and to act has been so determined by God (Pr. 26 and Cor. Pr. 24). But that which is finite and has a determinate existence cannot have been produced by the absolute nature of one of God's attributes, for whatever follows from the absolute nature of one of God's attributes is infinite and eternal (Pr. 21). It must therefore have followed from God or one of his attributes insofar as that is considered as affected by some mode; for nothing exists but substance and its modes (Ax. 1 and Defs. 3 and 5), and modes (Cor. Pr. 25) are nothing but affections of God's attributes. But neither could a finite and determined thing have followed from God or one of his attributes insofar as that is affected by a modification which is eternal and infinite (Pr. 22). Therefore, it must have followed, or been determined to exist and to act, by God or one of his attributes insofar as it was modified by a modification which is finite and has a determinate existence. That was the first point. Then again this cause or this mode (the reasoning is the same as in the first part of this proof) must also have been determined by another cause, which is also finite and has a determinate existence, and again this last (the reasoning is the same) by another, and so ad infinitum.

Scholium: Since some things must have been produced directly by God (those things, in fact, which necessarily follow from his absolute nature) and others through the medium of these primary things (which other things nevertheless cannot be or be conceived without God), it follows, firstly, that God is absolutely the proximate cause of things directly produced by him. I say "absolutely" [*absolute*], and not "within their own kind" [*suo genere*], as some say. For the effects of God can neither be nor be conceived without their cause (Pr. 15 and Cor. Pr. 24). It follows, secondly, that God cannot properly be said to be the remote cause of individual things, unless perchance for the purpose of distinguishing these things from things which he has produced directly, or rather, things which follow from his absolute nature. For by "remote cause" we understand a cause which is in no way conjoined with its effect. But all things that are, are in God, and depend on God in such a way that they can neither be nor be conceived without him.

PROPOSITION 29: *Nothing in nature is contingent, but all things are from the necessity of the divine nature determined to exist and to act in a definite way.*

Proof: Whatever is, is in God (Pr. 15). But God cannot be termed a contingent thing, for (Pr. 11) he exists necessarily, not contingently. Again, the modes of the divine nature have also followed from it necessarily, not contingently (Pr. 16), and that, too, whether insofar as the divine nature is considered absolutely (Pr. 21) or insofar as it is considered as determined to act in a definite way (Pr. 27). Furthermore, God is the cause of these modes not only insofar as they simply exist (Cor. Pr. 26), but also insofar as they are considered as determined to a particular action (Pr. 26). Now if they are not determined by God (Pr. 26), it is an impossibility, not a contingency, that they should determine themselves. On the other hand (Pr. 27), if they are determined by God, it is an impossibility, not a contingency, that they should render themselves undetermined. Therefore, all things are determined from the necessity of the divine nature not only to exist but also to exist and to act in a definite way. Thus, there is no contingency.

Scholium: Before I go any further, I wish to explain at this point what we must understand by *"Natura naturans"* and *"Natura naturata."* I should perhaps say not "explain," but "remind the reader," for I consider that it is already clear from what has gone before that by *"Natura naturans"* we must understand that which is in itself and is conceived through itself; that is, the attributes of substance that express eternal and infinite essence; or (Cor. 1 Pr. 14 and Cor. 2 Pr. 17), God insofar as he is considered a free cause. By *"Natura naturata"* I understand all that follows from the necessity of God's nature, that is, from the necessity of each one of God's attributes; or all the modes of God's attributes insofar as they are considered as things which are in God and can neither be nor be conceived without God.

PROPOSITION 30: *The finite intellect in act or the infinite intellect in act must comprehend the attributes of God and the affections of God, and nothing else.*

Proof: A true idea must agree with its object [*ideatum*] (Ax. 6); that is (as is self-evident), that which is contained in the intellect as an object of thought must necessarily exist in Nature. But in Nature (Cor. 1 Pr. 14) there is but one substance—God—and no other affections (Pr. 15) than those which are in God and that can neither be nor be conceived (Pr. 15) without God. Therefore, the finite intellect in act or the infinite intellect in act must comprehend the attributes of God and the affections of God, and nothing else.

PROPOSITION 31: *The intellect in act, whether it be finite or infinite, as also will, desire, love, etc., must be related to* Natura naturata, *not to* Natura naturans.

Proof: By intellect (as is self-evident) we do not understand absolute thought, but only a definite mode of thinking which differs from other modes such as desire, love, etc., and so (Def. 5) must be conceived through absolute thought—that is (Pr. 15 and Def. 6), an attribute of God which expresses the eternal and infinite essence of thought—in such a way that without this attribute it can neither be nor be conceived; and therefore (Sch. Pr. 29) it must be related to *Natura naturata,* not to *Natura naturans,* just like the other modes of thinking.

Scholium: The reason for my here speaking of the intellect in act is not that I grant there can be any intellect in potentiality, but that, wishing to avoid any confusion, I want to confine myself to what we perceive with the utmost clarity, to wit, the very act of understanding, than which nothing is more clearly apprehended by us. For we can understand nothing that does not lead to a more perfect cognition of the understanding.

PROPOSITION 32: *Will cannot be called a free cause, but only a necessary cause.*

Proof: Will, like intellect, is only a definite mode of thinking, and so (Pr. 28) no single volition can exist or be determined to act unless it is determined by another cause, and this cause again by another, and so ad infinitum. Now if will be supposed infinite, it must also be determined to exist and to act by God, not insofar as he is absolutely infinite substance, but insofar as he possesses an attribute which expresses the infinite and eternal essence of Thought (Pr. 23). Therefore, in whatever way will is conceived, whether finite or infinite, it requires a cause by which it is determined to exist and to act; and so (Def. 7) it cannot be said to be a free cause, but only a necessary or constrained cause.

Corollary 1: Hence it follows, firstly, that God does not act from freedom of will.

Corollary 2: It follows, secondly, that will and intellect bear the same relationship to God's nature as motion-and-rest and, absolutely, as all natural phenomena that must be determined by God (Pr. 29) to exist and to act in a definite way. For will, like all the rest, stands in need of a cause by which it may be determined to exist and to act in a definite manner. And although from a given will or intellect infinite things may follow, God cannot on that account be said to act from freedom of will any more than he can be said to act from freedom of motion-and-rest because of what follows from motion-and-rest (for from this, too, infinite things follow). Therefore, will pertains to God's nature no more than do other natural phenomena. It bears the same relationship to God's nature as does motion-and-rest and everything else that we have shown to follow from the necessity of the divine nature and to be determined by that divine nature to exist and to act in a definite way.

PROPOSITION 33: *Things could not have been produced by God in any other way or in any other order than is the case.*

Proof: All things have necessarily followed from the nature of God (Pr. 16) and have been determined to exist and to act in a definite way from the necessity of God's nature (Pr. 29). Therefore, if things could have been of a different nature or been determined to act in a different way so that the order of Nature would have been different, then God's nature, too, could have been other than it now is, and therefore (Pr. 11) this different nature, too, would have had to exist, and consequently there would have been two or more Gods, which (Cor. 1 Pr. 14) is absurd. Therefore, things could not have been produced by God in any other way or in any other order than is the case.

Scholium 1 Since I have here shown more clearly than the midday sun that in things there is absolutely nothing by virtue of which they can be said to be "contingent," I now wish to explain briefly what we should understand by "contingent"; but I must first deal with "necessary" and "impossible." A thing is termed "necessary" either by reason of its essence or by reason of its cause. For a thing's existence necessarily follows either from its essence and definition or from a given efficient cause. Again, it is for these same reasons that a thing is termed "impossible"—that is, either because its essence or definition involves a contradiction or because there is no external cause determined to bring it into existence. But a thing is termed "contingent" for no other reason than the deficiency of our knowledge. For if we do not know whether the essence of a thing involves a contradiction, or if, knowing full well that its essence does not involve a contradiction, we still cannot make any certain judgment as to its existence because the chain of causes is hidden from us, then that thing cannot appear to us either as necessary or as impossible. So we term it either "contingent" or "possible."

Scholium 2 It clearly follows from the above that things have been brought into being by God with supreme perfection, since they have necessarily followed from a most perfect nature. Nor does this imply any imperfection in God, for it is his perfection that has constrained us to make this affirmation. Indeed, from its contrary it would clearly follow (as I have just shown) that God is not supremely perfect, because if things had been brought into being in a different way by God, we should have to attribute to God another nature different from that which consideration of a most perfect Being has made us attribute to him.

However, I doubt not that many will ridicule this view as absurd and will not give their minds to its examination, and for this reason alone, that they are in the habit of attributing to God another kind of freedom very different from that which we (Def. 7) have assigned to him, that is, an absolute will. Yet I do not doubt that if they were willing to think the matter over and carefully reflect on our chain of proofs they would in the end reject the kind of freedom which they now attribute to God not only as nonsensical but as a serious obstacle to science. It is needless for me here to repeat what was said in the Scholium to Proposition 17. Yet for their sake I shall proceed to show that, even if it were to be granted that will pertains to the essence of God, it would nevertheless follow from his perfection that things could not have been created by God in any other way or in any other order. This will readily be shown if we first consider—as they themselves grant—that on God's decree and will alone does it depend that each thing is what it is.

For otherwise God would not be the cause of all things. Further, there is the fact that all God's decrees have been sanctioned by God from eternity, for otherwise he could be accused of imperfection and inconstancy. But since the eternal does not admit of "when" or "before" or "after," it follows merely from God's perfection that God can never decree otherwise nor ever could have decreed otherwise; in other words, God could not have been prior to his decrees nor can he be without them. "But," they will say, "granted the supposition that God had made a different universe, or that from eternity he had made a different decree concerning Nature and her order, no imperfection in God would follow therefrom." But if they say this, they will be granting at the same time that God can change his decrees. For if God's decrees had been different from what in fact he has decreed regarding Nature and her order—that is, if he had willed and conceived differently concerning Nature—he would necessarily have had a different intellect and a different will from that which he now has. And if it is permissible to attribute to God a different intellect and a different will without any change in his essence and perfection, why should he not now be able to change his decrees concerning created things, and nevertheless remain equally perfect? For his intellect and will regarding created things and their order have the same relation to his essence and perfection, in whatever manner it be conceived.

Then again, all philosophers whom I have read grant that in God there is no intellect in potentiality but only intellect in act. Now since all of them also grant that his intellect and will are not distinct from his essence, it therefore follows from this, too, that if God had

had a different intellect in act and a different will, his essence too would necessarily have been different. Therefore—as I deduced from the beginning—if things had been brought into being by God so as to be different from what they now are, God's intellect and will—that is (as is granted), God's essence—must have been different, which is absurd. Therefore, since things could not have been brought into being by God in any other way or order—and it follows from God's supreme perfection that this is true—surely we can have no sound reason for believing that God did not wish to create all the things that are in his intellect through that very same perfection whereby he understands them.

"But," they will say, "there is in things no perfection or imperfection; that which is in them whereby they are perfect or imperfect, and are called good or bad, depends only on the will of God. Accordingly, if God had so willed it he could have brought it about that that which is now perfection should be utmost imperfection, and vice versa." But what else is this but an open assertion that God, who necessarily understands that which he wills, can by his will bring it about that he should understand things in a way different from the way he understands them—and this, as I have just shown, is utterly absurd. So I can turn their own argument against them, as follows. All things depend on the power of God. For things to be able to be otherwise than as they are, God's will, too, would necessarily have to be different. But God's will cannot be different (as we have just shown most clearly from the consideration of God's perfection). Therefore, neither can things be different.

I admit that this view which subjects everything to some kind of indifferent will of God and asserts that everything depends on his pleasure diverges less from the truth than the view of those who hold that God does everything with the good in mind. For these people seem to posit something external to God that does not depend upon him, to which in acting God looks as if it were a model, or to which he aims, as if it were a fixed target. This is surely to subject God to fate; and no more absurd assertion can be made about God, whom we have shown to be the first and the only free cause of both the essence and the existence of things. So I need not spend any more time in refuting this absurdity.

PROPOSITION 34: *God's power is his very essence.*

Proof: From the sole necessity of God's essence it follows that God is self-caused (Pr. 11) and the cause of all things (Pr. 16 and Cor.). Therefore, God's power, whereby he and all things are and act, is his very essence.

PROPOSITION 35: *Whatever we conceive to be within God's power necessarily exists.*

Proof: Whatever is within God's power must be so comprehended in his essence (Pr. 34) that it follows necessarily from it, and thus necessarily exists.

PROPOSITION 36: *Nothing exists from whose nature an effect does not follow.*

Proof: Whatever exists expresses God's nature or essence in a definite and determinate way (Cor. Pr. 25); that is (Pr. 34), whatever exists expresses God's power, which is the cause of all things, in a definite and determinate way, and so (Pr. 16) some effect must follow from it.

Appendix

I have now explained the nature and properties of God: that he necessarily exists, that he is one alone, that he is and acts solely from the necessity of his own nature, that he is the free cause of all things and how so, that all things are in God and are so dependent on him that they can neither be nor be conceived without him, and lastly, that all things have been predetermined by God, not from his free will or absolute pleasure, but from the absolute nature of God, his infinite power. Furthermore, whenever the opportunity arose I have striven to remove prejudices that might hinder the apprehension of my proofs. But since there still remain a considerable number of prejudices, which have been, and still are, an obstacle—indeed, a very great obstacle—to the acceptance of the concatenation of things in the manner which I have expounded, I have thought it proper at this point to bring these prejudices before the bar of reason.

Now all the prejudices which I intend to mention here turn on this one point, the widespread belief among men that all things in Nature are like themselves in acting with an end in view. Indeed, they hold it as certain that God himself directs everything to a fixed end; for they say that God has made everything for man's sake and has made man so that he should worship God. So this is the first point I shall consider, seeking the reason why most people are victims of this prejudice and why all are so naturally disposed to accept it. Secondly, I shall demonstrate its falsity; and lastly I shall show how it has been the source of misconceptions about good and bad, right and wrong, praise and blame, order and confusion, beauty and ugliness, and the like.

However, it is not appropriate here to demonstrate the origin of these misconceptions from the nature of the human mind. It will suffice at this point if I take as my basis what must be universally admitted, that all men are born ignorant of the causes of things, that they all have a desire to seek their own advantage, a desire of which they are conscious. From this it follows, firstly, that men believe that they are free, precisely because they are conscious of their volitions and desires; yet concerning the causes that have determined them to desire and will they do not think, not even dream about, because they are ignorant of them. Secondly, men act always with an end in view, to wit, the advantage that they seek. Hence it happens that they are always looking only for the final causes of things done, and are satisfied when they find them, having, of course, no reason for further doubt. But if they fail to discover them from some external source, they have no recourse but to turn to themselves, and to reflect on what ends would normally determine them to similar actions, and so they necessarily judge other minds by their own. Further, since they find within themselves and outside themselves a considerable number of means very convenient for the pursuit of their own advantage—as, for instance, eyes for seeing, teeth for chewing, cereals and living creatures for food, the sun for giving light, the sea for breeding fish—the result is that they look on all the things of Nature as means to their own advantage. And realizing that these were found, not produced by them, they come to believe that there is someone else who produced these means for their use. For looking on things as means, they could not believe them to be self-created, but on the analogy of the means which they are accustomed to produce for themselves, they were bound to conclude that there was some governor or governors of Nature, endowed with human freedom, who have attended to all their needs and made everything for their use. And having no information on the subject, they also had to estimate the character of these rulers by their own, and so they asserted that the gods direct everything for man's use so that they may bind men to them and be held in the highest honor by them. So it came about that every individual devised different methods of worshipping God as he thought fit in order that God should love him beyond others and direct the whole of Nature so as to serve his blind cupidity and insatiable greed. Thus it was that this misconception developed into superstition and became deep-rooted in the minds of men, and it was for this reason that every man strove most earnestly to understand and to explain the final causes of all things. But in seeking to show that Nature does nothing in vain—that is, nothing that is not to man's advantage—they seem to have shown only this, that Nature and the gods are as crazy as mankind.

Consider, I pray, what has been the upshot. Among so many of Nature's blessings they were bound to discover quite a number of disasters, such as storms, earthquakes, diseases and so forth, and they maintained that these occurred because the gods were angry at the wrongs done to them by men, or the faults committed in the course of their worship. And although daily experience cried out against this and showed by any number of examples that blessings and disasters befall the godly and the ungodly alike without discrimination, they did not on that account abandon their ingrained prejudice. For they found it easier to regard this fact as one among other mysteries they could not understand and thus maintain their innate condition of ignorance rather than to demolish in its entirety the theory they had constructed and devise a new one. Hence they made it axiomatic that the judgment of the gods is far beyond man's understanding. Indeed, it is for this reason, and this reason only, that truth might have evaded mankind forever had not Mathematics, which is concerned not with ends but only with the essences and properties of figures, revealed to men a different standard of truth. And there are other causes too—there is no need to mention them here—which could have made men aware of these widespread misconceptions and brought them to a true knowledge of things.

I have thus sufficiently dealt with my first point. There is no need to spend time in going on to show that Nature has no fixed goal and that all final causes are but figments of the human imagination. For I think that this is now quite evident, both from the basic causes from which I have traced the origin of this misconception and from Proposition 16 and the Corollaries to Proposition 32, and in addition from the whole set or proofs I have adduced to show that all things in Nature proceed from all eternal necessity and with supreme perfection. But I will make this additional point, that this doctrine of Final Causes turns Nature completely upside down, for it regards as an effect that which is in fact a cause, and vice versa. Again, it makes that which is by nature first to be last; and finally, that which is highest and most perfect is held to be the most imperfect. Omitting the first two points as self-evident, Propositions 21, 22, and 23 make it clear that that effect is most perfect which is directly produced by God, and an effect is the less perfect in proportion to the number of intermediary causes required for its production. But if the things produced directly by God were brought about to enable him to attain an end, then of necessity the last things for the sake of which the earlier things were brought about would excel all others. Again, this doctrine negates God's perfection; for if God acts with an end in view, he must necessarily be seeking something that he lacks. And although theologians and metaphysicians may draw a distinction between a purpose arising from want and an assimilative purpose, they still admit that God has acted in all things for the sake of himself, and not for the sake of the things to be created. For prior to creation they are not able to point to anything but God as a purpose for God's action. Thus they have to admit that God lacked and desired those things for the procurement of which he willed to create the means—as is self-evident.

I must not fail to mention here that the advocates of this doctrine, eager to display their talent in assigning purpose to things, have introduced a new style of argument to prove their doctrine, i.e., a reduction, not to the impossible, but to ignorance, thus revealing the lack of any other argument in its favor. For example, if a stone falls from the roof on somebody's head and kills him, by this method of arguing they will prove that the stone fell in order to kill the man; for if it had not fallen for this purpose by the will of God, how could so many circumstances (and there are often many coinciding circumstances) have chanced to concur? Perhaps you will reply that the event occurred because the wind was blowing and the man was walking that way. But they will persist in asking why the wind blew at that time and why the man was walking that way at that very time. If you again reply that the wind sprang up at that time because on the previous day the sea had begun to toss after a period of calm and that the man had been invited by a friend, they will again persist—for there is no end to questions—"But why did the sea toss, and why was the man invited for that time?" And so they will go on and on asking the causes of causes, until you take refuge in the will of God—that is, the sanctuary of ignorance. Similarly, when they consider the structure of the human body, they are astonished, and being ignorant of the causes of such skillful work they conclude that it is fashioned not by mechanical art but by divine or supernatural art, and is so arranged that no one part shall injure another.

As a result, he who seeks the true causes of miracles and is eager to understand the works of Nature as a scholar, and not just to gape at them like a fool, is universally considered an impious heretic and denounced by those to whom the common people bow down as interpreters of Nature and the gods. For these people know that the dispelling of ignorance would entail the disappearance of that astonishment, which is the one and only support for their argument and for safeguarding their authority. But I will leave this subject and proceed to the third point that I proposed to deal with.

When men become convinced that everything that is created is created on their behalf, they were bound to consider as the most important quality in every individual thing that which was most useful to them, and to regard as of the highest excellence all those things by which they were most benefited. Hence they came to form these abstract notions to explain the natures of things: Good, Bad, Order, Confusion, Hot, Cold, Beauty, Ugliness; and since they believed that they are free, the following abstract notions came into being: Praise, Blame, Right, Wrong. The latter I shall deal with later on after I have treated of human nature; at this point I shall briefly explain the former.

All that conduces to well-being and to the worship of God they call Good, and the contrary, Bad. And since those who do not understand the nature of things, but only imagine things, make no affirmative judgments about things themselves and mistake their imagination for intellect, they are firmly convinced that there is order in things, ignorant as they are of things and of their own nature. For when things are in such arrangement that, being presented to us through our senses, we can readily picture them and thus readily remember them, we say that they are well arranged; if the contrary, we say that they are ill arranged, or confused. And since those things we can readily picture we find pleasing compared with other things, men prefer order to confusion, as though order were something in Nature other than what is relative to our imagination. And they say that God has created all things in an orderly way, without realizing that they are thus attributing human imagination to God—unless perchance they mean that God, out of consideration for the human imagination, arranged all things in the way that men could most easily imagine. And perhaps they will find no obstacle in the fact that there are any number of things that far surpass our imagination, and a considerable number that confuse the imagination because of its weakness.

But I have devoted enough time to this. Other notions, too, are nothing but modes of imagining whereby the imagination is affected in various ways, and yet the ignorant consider them as important attributes of things because they believe—as I have said—that all things were made on their behalf, and they call a thing's nature good or bad, healthy or rotten and corrupt, according to its effect on them. For instance, if the motion communicated to our nervous system by objects presented through our eyes is conducive to our feeling of well-being, the objects which are its cause are said to be beautiful, while the objects which provoke a contrary motion are called ugly. Those things that we sense through the nose are called fragrant or fetid; through the tongue, sweet or bitter, tasty or tasteless; those that we sense by touch are called hard or soft, rough or smooth, and so on. Finally, those that we sense through our ears are said to give forth noise, sound, or harmony, the last of which has driven men to such madness that they used to believe that even God delights in harmony. There are philosophers who have convinced themselves that the motions of the heavens give rise to harmony. All this goes to show that everyone's judgment is a function of the disposition of his brain, or rather, that he mistakes for reality the way his imagination is affected. Hence it is no wonder—as we should note in passing—that we find so many controversies arising among men, resulting finally in skepticism. For although human bodies agree in many respects, there are very many differences, and so one man thinks good what another thinks bad; what to one man is well ordered, to another is confused; what to one is pleasing, to another is displeasing, and so forth. I say no more here because this is not the place to treat at length of this subject, and also because all are well acquainted with it from experience. Everybody knows those sayings: "So many heads, so many opinions," "everyone is wise in his own sight," "brains differ as much as palates," all of which show clearly that men's judgment is a function of the disposition of the brain, and they are guided by imagination rather than intellect. For if men understood things, all that I have put forward would be found, if not attractive, at any rate convincing, as Mathematics attests.

We see therefore that all the notions whereby the common people are wont to explain Nature are merely modes of imagining, and denote not the nature of anything but only the constitution of the imagination. And because these notions have names as if they were the names of entities existing independently of the imagination I call them "entities of imagination" [*entia imaginationis*] rather than "entities of reason" [*entia rationis*]. So all arguments drawn from such notions against me can be easily refuted. For many are wont to argue on the following lines: If everything has followed from the necessity of God's most perfect nature, why does Nature display so many imperfections, such as rottenness to the point of putridity, nauseating ugliness, confusion, evil, sin, and so on? But, as I have just pointed out, they are easily refuted. For the perfection of things should be measured solely from their own nature and power; nor are things more or less perfect to the extent that they please or offend human senses, serve or oppose human interests. As to those who ask why God did not create men in such a way that they should be governed solely by reason, I make only this reply, that he lacked not material for creating all things from the highest to the lowest degree of perfection; or, to speak more accurately, the laws of his nature were so comprehensive as to suffice for the production of everything that can be conceived by an infinite intellect, as I proved in Proposition 16.

These are the misconceptions which I undertook to deal with at this point. Any other misconception of this kind can be corrected by everyone with a little reflection.

PART II

OF THE NATURE AND ORIGIN OF THE MIND

I now pass on to the explication of those things that must necessarily have followed from the essence of God, the eternal and infinite Being; not indeed all of them—for we proved in Proposition 16, Part I that from his essence there must follow infinite things in infinite ways—but only those things that can lead us as it were by the hand to the knowledge of the human mind and its utmost blessedness.

Definitions

1. By "body" I understand a mode that expresses in a definite and determinate way God's essence insofar as he is considered as an extended thing. (See Cor. Pr. 25, I.)

2. I say that there pertains to the essence of a thing that which, when granted, the thing is necessarily posited, and by the annulling of which the thing is necessarily annulled; or that without which the thing can neither be nor be conceived, and, vice versa, that which cannot be or be conceived without the thing.

3. By idea I understand a conception of the Mind which the Mind forms because it is a thinking thing.

Explication: I say "conception" rather than "perception" because the term perception seems to indicate that the Mind is passive to its object whereas conception seems to express an activity of the Mind.

4. By an adequate idea I mean an idea which, insofar as it is considered in itself without relation to its object, has all the properties, that is, intrinsic characteristics, of a true idea [*ideatum*].

Explication: I say "intrinsic" so as to exclude the extrinsic characteristic—to wit the agreement of the idea with that of which it is an idea.

5. Duration is the indefinite continuance of existing.

Explication: I say "indefinite" because it can in no wise be determined through the nature of the existing thing, nor again by the thing's efficient cause which necessarily posits, but does not annul, the existence of the thing.

6. By reality and perfection I mean the same thing.

7. By individual things [*res singulares*] I mean things that are finite and have a determinate existence. If several individual things concur in one act in such a way as to be all together the simultaneous cause of one effect, I consider them all, in that respect, as one individual.

Axioms

1. The essence of man does not involve necessary existence; that is, from the order of Nature it is equally possible that a certain man exists or does not exist.

2. Man thinks.

3. Modes of thinking such as love, desire, or whatever emotions are designated by name, do not occur unless there is in the same individual the idea of the thing loved, desired, etc. But the idea can be without any other mode of thinking.

4. We feel a certain body to be affected in many ways.

5. We do not feel or perceive any individual things except bodies and modes of thinking. [N.B.: For Postulates, see after Proposition 13.]

PROPOSITION 1: *Thought is an attribute of God; i.e., God is a thinking thing.*

Proof: Individual thoughts, or this and that thought, are modes expressing the nature of God in a definite and determinate way (Cor. Pr. 25, I). Therefore, there belongs to God (Def. 5, I) an attribute the conception of which is involved in all individual thoughts, and through which they are conceived. Thought, therefore, is one of God's infinite attributes, expressing the eternal and infinite essence of God (Def. 6, I); that is, God is a thinking thing.

Scholium: This Proposition is also evident from the fact that we can conceive of an infinite thinking being. For the more things a thinking being can think, the more reality or perfection we conceive it to have. Therefore, a being that can think infinite things in infinite ways is by virtue of its thinking necessarily infinite. Since therefore by merely considering Thought we conceive an infinite being, Thought is necessarily one of the infinite attributes of God (Defs. 4 and 6, I), as we set out to prove.

PROPOSITION 2: *Extension is an attribute of God; i.e., God is an extended thing.*

Proof: This Proposition is proved in the same way as the preceding proposition.

PROPOSITION 3: *In God there is necessarily the idea both of his essence and of everything that necessarily follows from his essence.*

Proof: For God can (Pr. l, II) think infinite things in infinite ways, or (what is the same thing, by Pr. 16, I) can form the idea of his own essence and of everything that necessarily follows from it. But all that is in God's power necessarily exists (Pr. 35, I). Therefore, such an idea necessarily exists, and only in God (Pr. 15, I).

Scholium: By God's power the common people understand free will and God's right over all things that are, which things are therefore commonly considered as contingent. They say that God has power to destroy everything and bring it to nothing. Furthermore, they frequently compare God's power with that of kings. But this doctrine we have refuted in Cors. 1 and 2, Pr. 32, I; and in Pr. 16, I, we proved that God acts by the same necessity whereby he understands himself; that is, just as it follows from the necessity of the divine Nature (as is universally agreed) that God understands himself, by that same necessity it also follows that God acts infinitely in infinite ways. Again, we showed in Pr. 34, I that God's power is nothing but God's essence in action, and so it is as impossible for us to conceive that God does not act as that God does not exist. Furthermore if one wished to pursue the matter, I could easily show here that the power that common people assign to God is not only a human power (which shows that they conceive God as a man or like a man) but also involves negation of power. But I am reluctant to hold forth so often on the same subject. I merely request the reader most earnestly to reflect again and again on what we said on this subject in Part I from Proposition 16 to the end. For nobody will rightly apprehend what I am trying to say unless he takes great care not to confuse God's power with a king's human power or right.

PROPOSITION 4: *The idea of God, from which infinite things follow in infinite ways, must be one, and one only.*

Proof: Infinite intellect comprehends nothing but the attributes of God and his affections (Pr. 30, I). But God is one, and one only (Cor. 1, Pr. 14, I). Therefore, the idea of God, from which infinite things follow in infinite ways, must be one, and one only.

PROPOSITION 5: *The formal being1 of ideas recognizes God as its cause only insofar as he is considered as a thinking thing, and not insofar as he is explicated by any other attribute; that is, the ideas both of God's attributes and of individual things recognize as their efficient cause not the things of which they are ideas, that is, the things perceived, but God himself insofar as he is a thinking thing.*

Proof: This is evident from Pr. 3, II. For there our conclusion that God can form the idea of his own essence and of everything that necessarily follows therefrom was inferred solely from God's being a thinking thing, and not from his being the object of his own idea. Therefore, the formal being of ideas recognizes God as its cause insofar as he is a thinking thing. But there is another proof, as follows. The formal being of ideas is a mode of thinking (as is self-evident); that is (Cor. Pr. 25, I), a mode which expresses in a definite manner the nature of God insofar as he is a thinking thing, and so does not involve (Pr. 10, I) the conception of any other attribute of God. Consequently (Ax. 4, I), it is the effect of no other attribute but thought; and so the formal being of ideas recognizes God as its cause only insofar as he is considered as a thinking thing.

PROPOSITION 6: *The modes of any attribute have God for their cause only insofar as he is considered under that attribute, and not insofar as he is considered under any other attribute.*

Proof: Each attribute is conceived through itself independently of any other (Pr. 10, I). Therefore, the modes of any attribute involve the conception of their own attribute, and not that of any other. Therefore, they have God for their cause only insofar as he is considered under the attribute of which they are modes, and not insofar as he is considered under any other attribute (Ax. 4, I).

Corollary: Hence it follows that the formal being of things that are not modes of thinking does not follow from the nature of God by reason of his first having known them; rather, the objects of ideas follow and are inferred from their own attributes in the same way and by the same necessity as we have shown ideas to follow from the attribute of Thought.

PROPOSITION 7: *The order and connection of ideas is the same as the order and connection of things.*

Proof: This is evident from Ax. 4, I; for the idea of what is caused depends on the knowledge of the cause of which it is the effect.

Corollary: Hence it follows that God's power of thinking is on par with his power of acting. That is, whatever follows formally from the infinite nature of God, all this follows from the idea of God as an object of thought in God according to the same order and connection.

Scholium: At this point, before proceeding further, we should recall to mind what I have demonstrated above—that whatever can be perceived by infinite intellect as constituting the essence of substance pertains entirely to the one sole substance. Consequently, thinking substance and extended substance are one and the same substance, comprehended now under this attribute, now under that. So, too, a mode of Extension and the idea of that mode are one and the same thing, expressed in two ways. This truth seems to have been glimpsed by some of the Hebrews, who hold that God, God's intellect, and the things understood by God are one and the same. For example, a circle existing in Nature and the idea of the existing circle—which is also in God—are one and the same thing, explicated through different attributes. And so, whether we conceive Nature under the attribute of Extension or under the attribute of Thought or under any other attribute, we find one and the same order, or one and the same connection of causes—that is, the same things following one another. When I said that God is the cause, e.g., of the idea of a circle only insofar as he is a thinking thing, and of a circle only insofar as he is an extended thing, my reason was simply this, that the formal being of the idea of a circle can be perceived only through another mode of thinking as its proximate cause, and that mode through another, and so ad infinitum, with the result that as long as things are considered as modes of thought, we must explicate the order of the whole of Nature, or the connection of causes, through the attribute of Thought alone; and insofar as things are considered as modes of Extension, again the order of the whole of Nature must be explicated through the attribute of Extension only. The same applies to other attributes. Therefore God, insofar as he consists of infinite attributes, is in fact the cause of things as they are in themselves. For the present, I cannot give a clearer explanation.

PROPOSITION 8: *The ideas of nonexisting individual things or modes must be comprehended in the infinite idea of God in the same way as the formal essences of individual things or modes are contained in the attributes of God.*

Proof: This proposition is obvious from the preceding one, but may be understood more clearly from the preceding Scholium.

Corollary: Hence it follows that as long as individual things do not exist except insofar as they are comprehended in the attributes of God, their being as objects of thought—that is, their ideas—do not exist except insofar as the infinite idea of God exists; and when individual things are said to exist not only insofar as they are comprehended in the attributes of God but also insofar as they are said to have duration, their ideas also will involve the existence through which they are said to have duration.

Scholium: Should anyone want an example for a clearer understanding of this matter, I can think of none at all that would adequately explicate the point with which I am here dealing, for it has no parallel. Still, I shall try to illustrate it as best I can. The nature of a circle is such that the rectangles formed from the segments of its intersecting chords are equal. Hence an infinite number of equal rectangles are contained in a circle, but none of them can be said to exist except insofar as the circle exists, nor again can the idea of any one of these rectangles be said to exist except insofar as it is comprehended in the idea of the circle. Now of this infinite number of intersecting chords let two, E and D, exist.

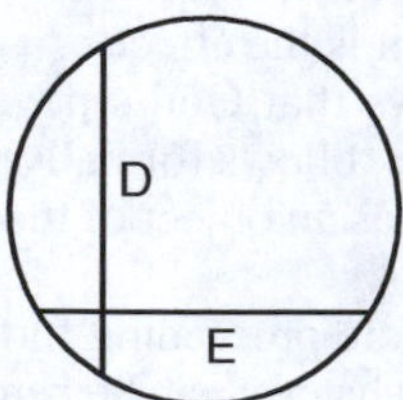

Now indeed their ideas also exist not only insofar as they are merely comprehended in the idea of the circle but also insofar as they involve the existence of those rectangles, with the result that they are distinguished from the other ideas of the other rectangles.

PROPOSITION 9: *The idea of an individual thing existing in actuality has God for its cause not insofar as he is infinite but insofar as he is considered as affected by another idea of a thing existing in actuality, of which God is the cause insofar as he is affected by a third idea, and so ad infinitum.*

Proof: The idea of an individual actually existing thing is an individual mode of thinking distinct from other modes (Cor. and Sch. Pr. 8, II), and so (Pr. 6, II) it has God as its cause only insofar as he is a thinking thing. But not (Pr. 28, I) insofar as he is a thinking thing absolutely, but insofar as he is considered as affected by another definite mode of thinking. And of this latter God is also the cause insofar as he is affected by another definite mode of thinking, and so ad infinitum. But the order and connection of ideas is the same as the order and connection of causes (Pr. 7, II). Therefore, an individual idea is caused by another idea; i.e., God insofar as he is considered as affected by another idea. And this last idea is caused by God, insofar as he is affected by yet another idea, and so ad infinitum.

Corollary: Whatsoever happens in the individual object of any idea, knowledge of it is in God only insofar as he has the idea of that object.

Proof: Whatsoever happens in the object of any idea, the idea of it is in God (Pr. 3, II) not insofar as he is infinite, but insofar as he is considered as affected by another idea of an individual thing (preceding Pr.). But the order and connection of ideas is the same as the order and connection of things (Pr. 7, II). Therefore, the knowledge of what happens in an individual object is in God only insofar as he has the idea of that object.

PROPOSITION 10: *The being of substance does not pertain to the essence of man; i.e., substance does not constitute the form [*forma*] of man.*

Proof: The being of substance involves necessary existence (Pr. 7, I). So if the being of substance pertained to the essence of man, man would necessarily be granted together with the granting of substance (Def. 2, II) and consequently man would necessarily exist, which is absurd (Ax. 1, II). Therefore . . . etc.

Scholium: This Proposition is also proved from Pr. 5, I, which states that there cannot be two substances of the same nature. Now since many men can exist, that which constitutes the form of man is not the being of substance. This Proposition is furthermore evident from the other properties of substance—that substance is by its own nature infinite, immutable, indivisible, etc., as everyone can easily see.

Corollary: Hence it follows that the essence of man is constituted by definite modifications of the attributes of God.

Proof: For the being of substance does not pertain to the essence of man (preceding Pr.), which must therefore be something that is in God, and which can neither be nor be conceived without God; i.e., an affection or mode (Cor. Pr. 25, I) which expresses the nature of God in a definite and determinate way.

Scholium: All must surely admit that nothing can be or be conceived without God. For all are agreed that God is the sole cause of all things, both of their essence and of their existence; that is, God is the cause of things not only in respect of their coming into being [*secundum fieri*], as they say, but also in respect of their being. But at the same time many assert that that without which a thing can neither be nor be conceived pertains to the essence of the thing, and so they believe that either the nature of God pertains to the essence of created things or that created things can either be or be conceived without God; or else, more probably, they hold no consistent opinion. I think that the reason for this is their failure to observe the proper order of philosophical inquiry. For the divine nature, which they should have considered before all else—it being prior both in cognition and in Nature—they have taken to be last in the order of cognition, and the things that are called objects of sense they have taken as prior to everything. Hence it has come about that in considering natural phenomena, they have completely disregarded the divine nature. And when thereafter they turned to the contemplation of the divine nature, they could find no place in their thinking for those fictions on which they had built their natural science, since these fictions were of no avail in attaining knowledge of the divine nature. So it is little wonder that they have contradicted themselves on all sides.

But I pass over these points, for my present purpose is restricted to explaining why I have not said that that without which a thing can neither be nor be perceived pertains to the essence of the thing. My reason is that individual things can neither be nor be conceived without God, and yet God does not pertain to their essence. But I did say that that necessarily constitutes the essence of a thing which, when posited, posits the thing, and by the annulling of which the thing is annulled; i.e., that without which the thing can neither be nor be conceived, and vice versa, that which can neither be nor be conceived without the thing.

PROPOSITION 11: *That which constitutes the actual being of the human mind is basically nothing else but the idea of an individual actually existing thing.*

Proof: The essence of man (Cor. Pr. 10, II) is constituted by definite modes of the attributes of God, to wit (Ax. 2, II), modes of thinking. Of all these modes the idea is prior in nature (Ax. 3, II), and when the idea is granted, the other modes—modes to which the idea is prior by nature—must be in the same individual (Ax. 3, II). And so the idea is that which basically constitutes the being of the human mind. But not the idea of a nonexisting thing; for then (Cor. Pr. 8, II) the idea itself could not be said to exist. Therefore, it is the idea of an actually existing thing. But not the idea of an infinite thing, for an infinite thing (Prs. 21 and 22, I) must always necessarily exist, and this is absurd (Ax. 1, II). Therefore, that which first constitutes the actual being of the human mind is the idea of an individual actually existing thing.

Corollary: Hence it follows that the human mind is part of the infinite intellect of God; and therefore when we say that the human mind perceives this or that, we are saying nothing else but this: that God—not insofar as he is infinite but insofar as he is explicated through the nature of the human mind, that is, insofar as he constitutes the essence of the human mind—has this or that idea. And when we say that God has this or that idea not only insofar as he constitutes the essence of the human mind but also insofar as he has the idea of another thing simultaneously with the human mind, then we are saying that the human mind perceives a thing partially or inadequately.

Scholium: At this point our readers will no doubt find themselves in some difficulty and will think of many things that will give them pause. So I ask them to proceed slowly step by step with me, and to postpone judgment until they have read to the end.

PROPOSITION 12: *Whatever happens in the object of the idea constituting the human mind is bound to be perceived by the human mind; i.e., the idea of that thing will necessarily be in the human mind. That is to say, if the object of the idea constituting the human mind is a body, nothing can happen in that body without its being perceived by the mind.*

Proof: Whatever happens in the object of any idea, knowledge thereof is necessarily in God (Cor. Pr. 9, II) insofar as he is considered as affected by the idea of that object; that is (Pr. 11, II), insofar as he constitutes the mind of something. So whatever happens in the object of the idea constituting the human mind, knowledge thereof is necessarily in God insofar as he constitutes the nature of the human mind; that is (Cor. Pr. 11, II), knowledge of that thing is necessarily in the mind; i.e., the mind perceives it.

Scholium: This Proposition is also obvious, and is more clearly understood from Sch. Pr. 7, II, above.

PROPOSITION 13: *The object of the idea constituting the human mind is the body—i.e., a definite mode of extension actually existing, and nothing else.*

Proof: If the body were not the object of the human mind, the ideas of the affections of the body would not be in God (Cor. Pr. 9, II) insofar as he constitutes our mind, but insofar as he constitutes the mind of another thing; that is (Cor. Pr. 11, II), the ideas of the affections of the body would not be in our mind. But (Ax. 4, II) we do have ideas of the affections of a body. Therefore, the object of the idea constituting the human mind is a body, a body actually existing (Pr. 11, II). Again, if there were another object of the mind apart from the body, since nothing exists from which some effect does not follow (Pr. 36, I), there would necessarily have to be in our mind the idea of some effect of it (Pr. 12, II). But (Ax. 5, II) there is no such idea. Therefore, the object of our mind is an existing body, and nothing else.

Corollary: Hence it follows that man consists of mind and body, and the human body exists according as we sense it.

Scholium: From the above we understand not only that the human Mind is united to the Body but also what is to be understood by the union of Mind and Body. But nobody can understand this union adequately or distinctly unless he first gains adequate knowledge of the nature of our body. For what we have so far demonstrated is of quite general application, and applies to men no more than to other individuals, which are all animate, albeit in different degrees. For there is necessarily in God an idea of each thing whatever, of which idea God is the cause in the same way as he is the cause of the idea of the human body. And so whatever we have asserted of the idea of the human body must necessarily be asserted of the idea of each thing. Yet we cannot deny, too, that ideas differ among themselves as do their objects, and that one is more excellent and contains more reality than another, just as the object of one idea is more excellent than that of another and contains more reality. Therefore, in order to determine the difference between the human mind and others and in what way it surpasses them, we have to know the nature of its object (as we have said), that is, the nature of the human body. Now I cannot here explain this nature, nor is it essential for the points that I intend to demonstrate. But I will make this general assertion, that in proportion as a body is more apt than other bodies to act or be acted upon simultaneously in many ways, so is its mind more apt than other minds to perceive many things simultaneously; and in proportion as the actions of one body depend on itself alone and the less that other bodies concur with it in its actions, the more apt is its mind to understand distinctly. From this we can realize the superiority of one mind over others, and we can furthermore see why we have only a very confused knowledge of our body, and many other facts which I shall deduce from this basis in what follows. Therefore, I have thought it worthwhile to explicate and demonstrate these things more carefully. To this end there must be a brief preface concerning the nature of bodies.

Axiom 1: All bodies are either in motion or at rest.

Axiom 2: Each single body can move at varying speeds.

Lemma 1: *Bodies are distinguished from one another in respect of motion-and-rest, quickness and slowness, and not in respect of substance.*

Proof: The first part of this Lemma I take to be self-evident. As to bodies not being distinguished in respect of substance, this is evident from both Pr. 5 and Pr. 8, Part I, and still more clearly from Sch. Pr. 15, Part I.

Lemma 2: *All bodies agree in certain respects.*

Proof: All bodies agree in this, that they involve the conception of one and the same attribute (Def. 1, II), and also in that they may move at varying speeds, and may be absolutely in motion or absolutely at rest.

Lemma 3: *A body in motion or at rest must have been determined to motion or rest by another body, which likewise has been determined to motion or rest by another body, and that body by another, and so ad infinitum.*

Proof: Bodies are individual things (Def. 1, II) which are distinguished from one another in respect of motion-and-rest (Lemma 1), and so (Pr. 28, I) each body must have been determined to motion or rest by another individual thing, namely, another body (Pr. 6, II), which is also in motion or at rest (Ax. 1). But this body again—by the same reasoning—could not have been in motion or at rest unless it had been determined to motion or rest by another body, and this body again—by the same reasoning—by another body, and so on, ad infinitum.

Corollary: Hence it follows that a body in motion will continue to move until it is determined to rest by another body, and a body at rest continues to be at rest until it is determined to move by another body. This, too, is self-evident; for when I suppose, for example, that a body A is at rest and I give no consideration to other moving bodies, I can assert nothing about body A but that it is at rest. Now if it should thereafter happen that body A is in motion, this surely could not have resulted from the fact that it was at rest; for from that fact nothing else could have followed than that body A should be at rest. If on the other hand A were supposed to be in motion, as long as we consider only A, we can affirm nothing of it but that it is in motion. If it should thereafter happen that A should be at rest, this surely could not have resulted from its previous motion; for from its motion nothing else could have followed but that A was in motion. So this comes about from a thing that was not in A, namely, an external cause by which the moving body A was determined to rest.

Axiom 1: All the ways in which a body is affected by another body follow from the nature of the affected body together with the nature of the body affecting it, so that one and the same body may move in various ways in accordance with the various natures of the bodies causing its motion; and, on the other hand, different bodies may be caused to move in different ways by one and the same body.

Axiom 2: When a moving body collides with a body at rest and is unable to cause it to move, it is reflected so as to continue its motion, and the angle between the line of motion of the reflection and the plane of the body at rest with which it has collided is equal to the angle between the line of incidence of motion and the said plane.

So far we have been discussing the simplest bodies, those which are distinguished from one another solely by motion-and-rest, quickness and slowness. Now let us advance to composite bodies.

Definition: When a number of bodies of the same or different magnitude form close contact with one another through the pressure of other bodies upon them, or if they are moving at the same or different rates of speed so as to preserve an unvarying relation of movement among themselves, these bodies are said to be united with one another and all together to form one body or individual thing, which is distinguished from other things through this union of bodies.

Axiom 3: The degree of difficulty with which the parts of an individual thing or composite body can be made to change their position and consequently the degree of difficulty with which the individual takes on different shapes is proportional to the extent of the surface areas along which they are in close contact. Hence bodies whose parts maintain close contact along large areas of their surfaces I term hard; those whose parts maintain contact along small surface areas I term soft; while those whose parts are in a state of motion among themselves I term liquid.

Lemma 4: *If from a body, or an individual thing composed of a number of bodies, certain bodies are separated, and at the same time a like number of other bodies of the same nature take their place, the individual thing will retain its nature as before, without any change in its form* [forma].

Proof: Bodies are not distinguished in respect of substance (Lemma 1). That which constitutes the form of the individual thing consists in a union of bodies (preceding definition). But this union, by hypothesis, is retained in spite of the continuous change of component bodies. Therefore, the individual thing will retain its own nature as before, both in respect of substance and of mode.

Lemma 5: *If the parts of an individual thing become greater or smaller, but so proportionately that they all preserve the same mutual relation of motion-and-rest as before, the individual thing will likewise retain its own nature as before without any change in its form.*

Proof: The reasoning is the same as in the preceding Lemma.

Lemma 6: *If certain bodies composing an individual thing are made to change the existing direction of their motion, but in such a way that they can continue their motion and keep the same mutual relation as before, the individual thing will likewise preserve its own nature without any change of form.*

Proof: This is evident; for, by hypothesis, the individual thing retains all that we, in defining it, asserted as constituting its form.

Lemma 7: *Furthermore, the individual thing so composed retains its own nature, whether as a whole it is moving or at rest, and in whatever direction it moves, provided that each constituent part retains its own motion and continues to communicate this motion to the other parts.*

Proof: This is evident from its definition, which you will find preceding Lemma 4.

Scholium: We thus see how a composite individual can be affected in many ways and yet preserve its nature. Now previously we have conceived an individual thing composed solely of bodies distinguished from one another only by motion-and-rest and speed of movement; that is, an individual thing composed of the simplest bodies. If we now conceive another individual thing composed of several individual things of different natures, we shall find that this can be affected in many other ways while still preserving its nature. For since each one of its parts is composed of several bodies, each single part can therefore (preceding Lemma), without any change in its nature, move with varying degrees of speed and consequently communicate its own motion to other parts with varying degrees of speed. Now if we go on to conceive a third kind of individual things composed of this second kind, we shall find that it can be affected in many other ways without any change in its form. If we thus continue to infinity, we shall readily conceive the whole of Nature as one individual whose parts—that is, all the constituent bodies—vary in infinite ways without any change in the individual as a whole. If my intention had been to write a full treatise on body, I should have had to expand my explications and demonstrations. But I have already declared a different intention, and the only reason for my dealing with this subject is that I may readily deduce therefrom what I have set out to prove.

Postulates

1. The human body is composed of very many individual parts of different natures, each of which is extremely complex.
2. Of the individual components of the human body, some are liquid, some are soft, and some are hard.
3. The individual components of the human body, and consequently the human body itself, are affected by external bodies in a great many ways.
4. The human body needs for its preservation a great many other bodies, by which, as it were [*quasi*], it is continually regenerated.
5. When a liquid part of the human body is determined by an external body to impinge frequently on another part which is soft, it changes the surface of that part and impresses on it certain traces of the external body acting upon it.
6. The human body can move external bodies and dispose them in a great many ways.

PROPOSITION 14: *The human mind is capable of perceiving a great many things, and this capacity will vary in proportion to the variety of states which its body can assume.*

Proof: The human body (Posts. 3 and 6) is affected by external bodies in a great many ways and is so structured that it can affect external bodies in a great many ways. But the human mind must perceive all that happens in the human body (Pr. 12, II). Therefore, the human mind is capable of perceiving very many things, and . . . etc.

PROPOSITION 15: *The idea which constitutes the formal being of the human mind is not simple, but composed of very many ideas.*

Proof: The idea which constitutes the formal being of the human mind is the idea of the body (Pr. 13, II), which is composed of a great number of very composite individual parts (Postulate 1). But in God there is necessarily the idea of every individual component part (Cor. Pr. 8, II). Therefore (Pr. 7, II), the idea of the human body is composed of these many ideas of the component parts.

PROPOSITION 16: *The idea of any mode wherein the human body is affected by external bodies must involve the nature of the human body together with the nature of the external body.*

Proof: All the modes wherein a body is affected follow from the nature of the body affected together with the nature of the affecting body (Ax. 1 after Cor. Lemma 3). Therefore, the idea of these modes will necessarily involve the nature of both bodies (Ax. 4, I). So the idea of any mode wherein the human body is affected by an external body involves the nature of the human body and the external body.

Corollary 1: Hence it follows that the human mind perceives the nature of very many bodies along with the nature of its own body.

Corollary 2: Secondly, the ideas that we have of external bodies indicate the constitution of our own body more than the nature of external bodies. This I have explained with many examples in Appendix, Part I.

PROPOSITION 17: *If the human body is affected in a way [*modo*] that involves the nature of some external body, the human mind will regard that same external body as actually existing, or as present to itself, until the human body undergoes a further modification which excludes the existence or presence of the said body.*

Proof: This is evident; for as long as the human body is thus affected, so long will the human mind (Pr. 12, II) regard this affection of the body; that is (by the preceding Proposition), so long will it have the idea of a mode existing in actuality, an idea involving the nature of an external body; that is, an idea which does not exclude but posits the existence or presence of the nature of the external body. So the mind (Cor. 1 of the preceding proposition) will regard the external body as actually existing, or as present, until . . . etc.

Corollary: The mind is able to regard as present external bodies by which the human body has been once affected, even if they do not exist and are not present.

Proof: When external bodies so determine the fluid parts of the human body that these frequently impinge on the softer parts, they change the surfaces of these softer parts (Post. 5). Hence it comes about (Ax. 2 after Cor. Lemma 3) that the fluid parts are reflected therefrom in a manner different from what was previously the case; and thereafter, again coming into contact with the said changed surfaces in the course of their own spontaneous motion, they are reflected in the same way as when they were impelled toward those surfaces by external bodies. Consequently, in continuing this reflected motion they affect the human body in the same manner, which manner will again be the object of thought in the mind (Pr. 12, II); that is (Pr. 17, II), the mind will again regard the external body as present. This will be repeated whenever the fluid parts of the human body come into contact with those same surfaces in the course of their own spontaneous motion. Therefore, although the external bodies by which the human body has once been affected may no longer exist, the mind will regard them as present whenever this activity of the body is repeated.

Scholium: So we see how it comes about that we regard as present things which are not so, as often happens. Now it is possible that there are other causes for this fact, but it is enough for me at this point to have indicated one cause through which I can explicate the matter just as if I had demonstrated it through its true cause. Yet I do not think that I am far from the truth, since all the postulates that I have assumed contain scarcely anything inconsistent with experience; and after demonstrating that the human body exists just as we sense it (Cor. Pr. 13, II), we may not doubt experience.

In addition (preceding Cor. and Cor. 2 Pr. 16, II), this gives a clear understanding of the difference between the idea, e.g., of Peter which constitutes the essence of Peter's mind, and on the other hand the idea of Peter which is in another man, say Paul. The former directly explicates the essence of Peter's body, and does not involve existence except as long as Peter exists. The latter indicates the constitution of Paul's body rather than the nature of Peter; and so, while that constitution of Paul's body continues to be, Paul's mind will regard Peter as present to him although Peter may not be in existence. Further, to retain the usual terminology, we will assign the word "images" [*imagines*] to those affections of the human body the ideas of which set forth external bodies as if they were present to us, although they do not represent shapes. And when the mind regards bodies in this way, we shall say that it "imagines" [*imaginari*].

At this point, to begin my analysis of error, I should like you to note that the imaginations of the mind, looked at in themselves, contain no error; i.e., the mind does not err from the fact that it imagines, but only insofar as it is considered to lack the idea which excludes the existence of those things which it imagines to be present to itself. For if the mind, in imagining nonexisting things to be present to it, knew at the same time that those things did not exist in fact, it would surely impute this power of imagining not to the defect but to the strength of its own nature, especially if this faculty of imagining were to depend solely on its own nature; that is (Def. 7, I), if this faculty of imagining were free.

PROPOSITION 18: *If the human body has once been affected by two or more bodies at the same time, when the mind afterward imagines one of them, it will straightway remember the others too.*

Proof: The mind imagines (preceding Cor.) any given body for the following reason, that the human body is affected and conditioned by the impressions of an external body in the same way as it was affected when certain of its parts were acted upon by the external body. But, by hypothesis, the human mind was at that time conditioned in such a way that the mind imagined two bodies at the same time. Therefore, it will now also imagine two bodies at the same time, and the mind, in imagining one of them, will straightway remember the other as well.

Scholium: Hence we clearly understand what memory is. It is simply a linking of ideas involving the nature of things outside the human body, a linking which occurs in the mind parallel to the order and linking of the affections of the human body. I say, firstly, that it is only the linking of those ideas that involve the nature of things outside the human body, not of those ideas that explicate the nature of the said things. For they are in fact (Pr. 16, II) ideas of the affections of the human body which involve the nature both of the human body and of external bodies. Secondly, my purpose in saying that this linking occurs in accordance with the order and linking of the affections of the human body is to distinguish it from the linking of ideas in accordance with the order of the intellect whereby the mind perceives things through their first causes, and which is the same in all men.

Furthermore, from this we clearly understand why the mind, from thinking of one thing, should straightway pass on to thinking of another thing which has no likeness to the first. For example, from thinking of the word "pomum" [apple] a Roman will straightway fall to thinking of the fruit, which has no likeness to that articulated sound nor anything in common with it other than that the man's body has often been affected by them both; that is, the man has often heard the word "pomum" while seeing the fruit. So everyone will pass on from one thought to another according as habit in each case has arranged the images in his body. A soldier, for example, seeing the tracks of a horse in the sand will straightway pass on from thinking of the horse to thinking of the rider, and then thinking of war, and so on. But a peasant, from thinking of a horse, will pass on to thinking of a plough, and of a field, and so on. So every person will pass on from thinking of one thing to thinking of another according as he is in the habit of joining together and linking the images of things in various ways.

PROPOSITION 19: *The human mind has no knowledge of the body, nor does it know it to exist, except through ideas of the affections by which the body is affected.*

Proof: The human mind is the very idea or knowledge of the human body (Pr. 13, II), and this idea is in God (Pr. 9, II) insofar as he is considered as affected by another idea of a particular thing; or, since (Post. 4) the human body needs very many other bodies by which it is continually regenerated, and the order and connection of ideas is the same (Pr. 7, II) as the order and connection of causes, this idea is in God insofar as he is considered as affected by the ideas of numerous particular things. Therefore, God has the idea of the human body, or knows the human body, insofar as he is affected by numerous other ideas, and not insofar as he constitutes the nature of the human mind; that is (Cor. Pr. 11, II), the human mind does not know the human body. But the ideas of the affections of the body are in God insofar as he does constitute the nature of human mind; i.e., the human mind perceives these affections (Pr. 12, II) and consequently perceives the human body (Pr. 16, II), and perceives it as actually existing (Pr. 17, II). Therefore, it is only to that extent that the human mind perceives the human body.

PROPOSITION 20: *There is also in God the idea or knowledge of the human mind, and this follows in God and is related to God in the same way as the idea or knowledge of the human body.*

Proof: Thought is an attribute of God (Pr. 1, II), and so (Pr. 3, II) the idea of both Thought and its affections—and consequently of the human mind as well—must necessarily be in God. Now this idea or knowledge of the mind does not follow in God insofar as he is infinite, but insofar as he is affected by another idea of a particular thing (Pr. 9, II). But the order and connection of ideas is the same as the order and connection of causes (Pr. 7, II). Therefore, the idea or knowledge of the mind follows in God and is related to God in the same way as the idea or knowledge of the body.

PROPOSITION 21: *This idea of the mind is united to the mind in the same way as the mind is united to the body.*

Proof: That the mind is united to the body we have shown from the fact that the body is the object of the mind (Prs. 12 and 13, II), and so by the same reasoning the idea of the mind must be united to its object—that is, to the mind itself—in the same way as the mind is united to the body.

Scholium: This proposition is understood far more clearly from Sch. Pr. 7, II. There we showed that the idea of the body and the body itself—that is (Pr. 13, II), mind and body—are one and the same individual thing, conceived now under the attribute of

Thought and now under the attribute of Extension. Therefore, the idea of the mind and the mind itself are one and the same thing, conceived under one and the same attribute, namely, Thought. The idea of the mind, I repeat, and the mind itself follow in God by the same necessity and from the same power of thought. For in fact the idea of the mind—that is, the idea of an idea—is nothing other than the form [*forma*] of the idea insofar as the idea is considered as a mode of thinking without relation to its object. For as soon as anyone knows something, by that very fact he knows that he knows, and at the same time he knows that he knows that he knows, and so on ad infinitum. But I will deal with this subject later.

PROPOSITION 22: *The human mind perceives not only the affections of the body but also the ideas of these affections.*

Proof: The ideas of ideas of affections follow in God and are related to God in the same way as ideas of affections, which can be proved in the same manner as Pr. 20, II. But the ideas of affections of the body are in the human mind (Pr. 12, II); that is (Cor. Pr. 11, II), in God insofar as he constitutes the essence of the human mind. Therefore, the ideas of these ideas will be in God insofar as he has knowledge or the idea of the human mind; that is (Pr. 21, II), they will be in the human mind itself, which therefore perceives not only the affections of the body but also the ideas of these affections.

PROPOSITION 23: *The mind does not know itself except insofar as it perceives ideas of affections of the body.*

Proof: The idea or knowledge of the mind (Pr. 20, II) follows in God and is related to God in the same way as the idea or knowledge of the body. But since (Pr. 19, II) the human mind does not know the human body—that is (Cor. Pr. 11, II), since the knowledge of the human body is not related to God insofar as he constitutes the nature of the human mind—therefore, neither is knowledge of the mind related to God insofar as he constitutes the essence of the human mind. And so (Cor. Pr. 11, II) the human mind to that extent does not know itself. Again, the ideas of the affections by which the body is affected involve the nature of the human body (Pr. 16, II); that is (Pr. 13, II), they are in agreement [*conveniunt*] with the nature of the mind. Therefore, the knowledge of these ideas will necessarily involve knowledge of the mind. But (preceding Pr.) the knowledge of these ideas is in the human mind. Therefore, the human mind knows itself but only to that extent.

PROPOSITION 24: *The human mind does not involve an adequate knowledge of the component parts of the human body.*

Proof: The component parts of the human body do not pertain to the essence of the body itself save insofar as they preserve an unvarying relation of motion with one another (Def. after Cor. Lemma 3), and not insofar as they can be considered as individual things apart from their relation to the human body. For the parts of the human body (Post. 1) are very composite individual things, whose parts can be separated from the human body (Lemma 4) without impairing in any way its nature and specific reality [*forma*], and can establish a quite different relation of motion with other bodies (Ax. 1 after Lemma 3). Therefore (Pr. 3, II), the idea or knowledge of any component part will be in God, and will be so (Pr. 9, II) insofar as he is considered as affected by another idea of a particular thing, a particular thing which is prior in Nature's order to the part itself (Pr. 7, II). Further, the same holds good of any part of an individual component part of the human body, and so of any component part of the human body there is knowledge in God insofar as he is affected by very many ideas of things, and not insofar as he has the idea only of the human body, that is (Pr. 13, II), the idea that constitutes the nature of the human mind. So (Cor. Pr. 11, II) the human mind does not involve adequate knowledge of the component parts of the human body.

PROPOSITION 25: *The idea of any affection of the human body does not involve an adequate knowledge of an external body.*

Proof: We have shown that the idea of an affection of the human body involves the nature of an external body insofar as the external body determines the human body in some definite way (Pr. 16, II). But insofar as the external body is an individual thing that is not related to the human body, the idea or knowledge of it is in God (Pr. 9, II) insofar as God is considered as affected by the idea of another thing which is (Pr. 7, II) prior in nature to the said external body. Therefore, an adequate knowledge of the external body is not in God insofar as he has the idea of an affection of the human body; i.e., the idea of an affection of the human body does not involve an adequate knowledge of an external body.

PROPOSITION 26: *The human mind does not perceive any external body as actually existing except through the ideas of affections of its own body.*

Proof: If the human body is not affected in any way by an external body, then (Pr 7, II) neither is the idea of the human body—that is (Pr. 13, II), the human mind—affected in any way by the idea of the existence of that body; i.e., it does not in any way perceive the existence of that external body. But insofar as the human body is affected in some way by an external body, to that extent it perceives the external body (Pr. 16, II, with Cor. 1).

Corollary: Insofar as the human mind imagines [*imaginatur*] an external body, to that extent it does not have an adequate knowledge of it.

Proof: When the human mind regards external bodies through the ideas of affections of its own body, we say that it imagines [*imaginatur*] (see Sch. Pr. 17, II), and in no other way can the mind imagine external bodies as actually existing (preceding Pr.). Therefore, insofar as the mind imagines external bodies (Pr. 25, II), it does not have adequate knowledge of them.

PROPOSITION 27: *The idea of any affection of the human body does not involve adequate knowledge of the human body.*

Proof: Any idea whatsoever of any affection of the human body involves the nature of the human body only to the extent that the human body is considered to be affected in some definite way (Pr. 16, II). But insofar as the human body is an individual thing that can be affected in many other ways, the idea . . . etc. (see Proof Pr. 25, II).

PROPOSITION 28: *The ideas of the affections of the human body, insofar as they are related only to the human mind, are not clear and distinct, but confused.*

Proof: The ideas of the affections of the human body involve the nature both of external bodies and of the human body itself (Pr. 16, II), and must involve the nature not only of the human body but also of its parts. For affections are modes in which parts of the human body (Post. 3), and consequently the body as a whole, are affected. But (Prs. 24 and 25, II) an adequate knowledge of external bodies, as also of the component parts of the human body, is not in God insofar as he is considered as affected by the human mind, but insofar as he is considered as affected by other ideas. Therefore, these ideas of affections, insofar as they are related only to the human mind, are like conclusions without premises; that is, as is self-evident, confused ideas.

Scholium: The idea that constitutes the nature of the human mind is likewise shown, when considered solely in itself, not to be clear and distinct, as is also the idea of the human mind and the ideas of affections of the human body insofar as they are related only to the human mind, as everyone can easily see.

PROPOSITION 29: *The idea of the idea of any affection of the human body does not involve adequate knowledge of the human mind.*

Proof: The idea of an affection of the human body (Pr. 27, II) does not involve adequate knowledge of the body itself; in other words, it does not adequately express the nature of the body; that is (Pr. 13, II), it does not adequately agree [*convenit*] with the nature of the mind. So (Ax. 6, I) the idea of this idea does not adequately express the nature of the human mind; i.e., it does not involve an adequate knowledge of it.

Corollary: Hence it follows that whenever the human mind perceives things after the common order of nature, it does not have an adequate knowledge of itself, nor of its body, nor of external bodies, but only a confused and fragmentary knowledge. For the mind does not know itself save insofar as it perceives ideas of the affections of the body (Pr. 23, II). Now it does not perceive its own body (Pr. 19, II) except through ideas of affections of the body, and also it is only through these affections that it perceives external bodies (Pr. 26, II). So insofar as it has these ideas, it has adequate knowledge neither of itself (Pr. 29, II) nor of its own body (Pr. 27, II) nor of external bodies (Pr. 25, II), but only a fragmentary [*mutilatam*] and confused knowledge (Pr. 28, II and Sch.).

Scholium: I say expressly that the mind does not have an adequate knowledge, but only a confused and fragmentary knowledge, of itself, its own body, and external bodies whenever it perceives things from the common order of nature, that is, whenever it is determined externally—namely, by the fortuitous run of circumstance—to regard this or that, and not when it is determined internally, through its regarding several things at the same time, to understand their agreement, their differences, and their opposition. For whenever it is conditioned internally in this or in another way, then it sees things clearly and distinctly, as I shall later show.

PROPOSITION 30: *We can have only a very inadequate knowledge of the duration of our body.*

Proof: The duration of our body does not depend on its essence (Ax. 1, II), nor again on the absolute nature of God (Pr. 21, I), but (Pr. 28, I) it is determined to exist and to act by causes which are also determined by other causes to exist and to act in a definite and determinate way, and these again by other causes, and so ad infinitum. Therefore, the duration of our body depends on the common order of nature and the structure of the universe. Now there is in God adequate knowledge of the structure of the universe insofar as he has ideas of all the things in the universe, and not insofar as he has only the idea of the human body (Cor. Pr. 9, II). Therefore, knowledge of the duration of our body is very inadequate in God insofar as he is considered only to constitute the nature of the human mind. That is (Cor. Pr. 11, II), this knowledge is very inadequate in the human mind.

PROPOSITION 31: *We can have only a very inadequate knowledge of the duration of particular things external to us.*

Proof: Each particular thing, just like the human body, must be determined by another particular thing to exist and to act in a definite and determinate way, and this latter thing again by another, and so on ad infinitum (Pr. 28, I). Now since we have shown in the preceding Proposition that from this common property of particular things we can have only a very inadequate knowledge of the duration of the human body, in the case of the duration of particular things we have to come to the same conclusion: that we can have only a very inadequate knowledge thereof.

Corollary: Hence it follows that all particular things are contingent and perishable. For we can have no adequate knowledge of their duration (preceding Pr.), and that is what is to be understood by contingency and perishability (Sch. 1, Pr. 33, I). For apart from this there is no other kind of contingency (Pr. 29, I).

PROPOSITION 32: *All ideas are true insofar as they are related to God.*

Proof: All ideas, which are in God, agree completely with the objects of which they are ideas (Cor. Pr. 7, II), and so they are all true (Ax. 6, I).

PROPOSITION 33: *There is nothing positive in ideas whereby they can be said to be false.*

Proof: If this be denied, conceive, if possible, a positive mode of thinking which constitutes the form [*forma*] of error or falsity. This mode of thinking cannot be in God (preceding Pr.), but neither can it be or be conceived externally to God (Pr. 15, I). Thus there can be nothing positive in ideas whereby they can be called false.

PROPOSITION 34: *Every idea which in us is absolute, that is, adequate and perfect, is true.*

Proof: When we say that there is in us an adequate and perfect idea, we are saying only this (Cor. Pr. 11, II), that there is adequate and perfect idea in God insofar as he constitutes the essence of our mind. Consequently, we are saying only this, that such an idea is true (Pr. 32, II).

PROPOSITION 35: *Falsity consists in the privation of knowledge which inadequate ideas, that is, fragmentary and confused ideas, involve.*

Proof: There is nothing positive in ideas which constitutes the form [*forma*] of falsity (Pr. 33, II). But falsity cannot consist in absolute privation (for minds, not bodies, are said to err and be deceived), nor again in absolute ignorance, for to be ignorant and to err are different. Therefore, it consists in that privation of knowledge which inadequate knowledge, that is, inadequate and confused ideas, involves.

Scholium: In Sch. Pr. 17, II I explained how error consists in the privation of knowledge, but I will give an example to enlarge on this explanation. Men are deceived in thinking themselves free, a belief that consists only in this, that they are conscious of their actions and ignorant of the causes by which they are determined. Therefore, the idea of their freedom is simply the ignorance of the cause of their actions. As to their saying that human actions depend on the will, these are mere words without any corresponding idea. For none of them knows what the will is and how it moves the body, and those who boast otherwise and make up stories of dwelling places and habitations of the soul provoke either ridicule or disgust.

As another example, when we gaze at the sun, we see it as some two hundred feet distant from us. The error does not consist in simply seeing the sun in this way but in the fact that while we do so we are not aware of the true distance and the cause of our seeing it so. For although we may later become aware that the sun is more than six hundred times the diameter of the earth distant from us, we shall nevertheless continue to see it as close at hand. For it is not our ignorance of its true distance that causes us to see the sun to be so near; it is that the affection of our body involves the essence of the sun only to the extent that the body is affected by it.

PROPOSITION 36: *Inadequate and confused ideas follow by the same necessity as adequate, or clear and distinct, ideas.*

Proof: All ideas are in God (Pr. 15, I), and insofar as they are related to God, they are true (Pr. 32, II) and adequate (Cor. Pr. 7, II). So there are no inadequate or confused ideas except insofar as they are related to the particular mind of someone (see Prs. 24 and 28, II). So all ideas, both adequate and inadequate, follow by the same necessity (Cor. Pr. 6, II).

PROPOSITION 37: *That which is common to all things (see Lemma 2 above) and is equally in the part as in the whole does not constitute the essence of any one particular thing.*

Proof: If this is denied, conceive, if possible, that it does constitute the essence of one particular thing, B. Therefore, it can neither be nor be conceived without B (Def. 2, II). But this is contrary to our hypothesis. Therefore, it does not pertain to B's essence, nor does it constitute the essence of any other particular thing.

PROPOSITION 38: *Those things that are common to all things and are equally in the part as in the whole can be conceived only adequately.*

Proof: Let A be something common to all bodies, and equally in the part of any body as in the whole. I say that A can be conceived only adequately. For its idea (Cor. Pr. 7, II) will necessarily be in God both insofar as he has the idea of the human body and insofar as he has the ideas of affections of the human body, affections which partly involve the natures of both the human body and external bodies (Prs. 16, 25, and 27, II). That is (Prs. 12 and 13, II), this idea will necessarily be adequate in God insofar as he constitutes the human

Interior of a House, ca. 1660, by Pieter De Hooch (1629–1684). This Dutch Baroque painting provides a visual metaphor for the precise geometry of Spinoza's *Ethics.* (*© Alinari/Art Resource, NY*)

mind; that is, insofar as he has the ideas which are in the human mind. Therefore, the mind (Cor. Pr. 11, II) necessarily perceives A adequately, and does so both insofar as it perceives itself and insofar as it perceives its own body or any external body; nor can A be perceived in any other way.

Corollary: Hence it follows that there are certain ideas or notions common to all men. For (by Lemma 2) all bodies agree in certain respects, which must be (preceding Pr.) conceived by all adequately, or clearly and distinctly.

PROPOSITION 39: *Of that which is common and proper to the human body and to any external bodies by which the human body is customarily affected, and which is equally in the part as well as in the whole of any of these bodies, the idea also in the mind will be adequate.*

Proof: Let A be that which is common and proper to the human body and to any external bodies and which is equally in the human body as in those same external bodies, and which is finally equally in the part of any external body as in the whole. There will be in God an adequate idea of A (Cor. Pr. 7, II) both insofar as he has the idea of the human body and insofar as he has ideas of those posited external bodies. Let it now be supposed that the human body is affected by an external body through that which is common to them both, that is, A. The idea of this affection will involve the property A (Pr. 16, II), and so (Cor. Pr. 7, II) the idea of this affection, insofar as it involves the property A, will be adequate in God insofar as he is affected by the idea of the human body; that is (Pr. 13, II), insofar as he constitutes the nature of the human mind. So this idea will also be adequate in the human mind (Cor. Pr. 11, II).

Corollary: Hence it follows that the mind is more capable of perceiving more things adequately in proportion as its body has more things in common with other bodies.

PROPOSITION 40: *Whatever ideas follow in the mind from ideas that are adequate in it are also adequate.*

Proof: This is evident. For when we say that an idea follows in the human mind from ideas that are adequate in it, we are saying no more than that there is in the divine intellect an idea of which God is the cause, not insofar as he is infinite nor insofar as he is affected by ideas of numerous particular things, but only insofar as he constitutes the essence of the human mind.

Scholium 1: I have here set forth the causes of those notions that are called "common," and which are the basis of our reasoning processes. Now certain axioms or notions have other causes which it would be relevant to set forth by this method of ours; for thus we could establish which notions are useful compared with others, and which are of scarcely any value. And again, we could establish which notions are common to all, which ones are clear and distinct only to those not laboring under prejudices [*praejudiciis*] and which ones are ill-founded. Furthermore, this would clarify the origin of those notions called "secondary"—and consequently the axioms which are based on them—as well as other related questions to which I have for some time given thought. But I have decided not to embark on these questions at this point because I have set them aside for another treatise, and also to avoid wearying the reader with too lengthy a discussion of this subject. Nevertheless, to omit nothing that it is essential to know, I shall briefly deal with the question of the origin of the so-called "transcendental terms," such as "entity," "thing," "something" [*ens, res, aliquid*].

These terms originate in the following way. The human body, being limited, is capable of forming simultaneously in itself only a certain number of distinct images.

(I have explained in Sch. Pr. 17, II what an image is.) If this number be exceeded, these images begin to be confused, and if the number of distinct images which the body is capable of forming simultaneously in itself be far exceeded, all the images will be utterly confused with one another. This being so, it is evident from Cor. Pr. 17 and Pr. 18, II that the human mind is able to imagine simultaneously and distinctly as many bodies as there are images that can be formed simultaneously in its body. But when the images in the body are utterly confused, the mind will also imagine all the bodies confusedly without any distinction, and will comprehend them, as it were, under one attribute, namely, that of entity, thing, etc. This conclusion can also be reached from the fact that images are not always equally vivid, and also from other causes analogous to these, which I need not here explicate. For it all comes down to this, that these terms signify ideas confused in the highest degree.

Again, from similar causes have arisen those notions called "universal," such as "man," "horse," "dog," etc.; that is to say, so many images are formed in the human body simultaneously (e.g., of man) that our capacity to imagine them is surpassed, not indeed completely, but to the extent that the mind is unable to imagine the unimportant differences of individuals (such as the complexion and stature of each, and their exact number) and imagines distinctly only their common characteristic insofar as the body is affected by them. For it was by this that the body was affected most repeatedly, by each single individual. The mind expresses this by the word "man," and predicates this word of an infinite number of individuals. For, as we said, it is unable to imagine the determinate number of individuals.

But it should be noted that not all men form these notions in the same way; in the case of each person the notions vary according as that thing varies whereby the body has more frequently been affected, and which the mind more readily imagines or calls to mind. For example, those who have more often regarded with admiration the stature of men will understand by the word "man" an animal of upright stature, while those who are wont to regard a different aspect will form a different common image of man, such as that man is a laughing animal, a featherless biped, or a rational animal. Similarly, with regard to other aspects, each will form universal images according to the conditioning of his body. Therefore, it is not surprising that so many controversies have arisen among philosophers who have sought to explain natural phenomena through merely the images of these phenomena.

Scholium 2: From all that has already been said it is quite clear that we perceive many things and form universal notions:

1. From individual objects presented to us through the senses in a fragmentary [*mutilate*] and confused manner without any intellectual order (see Cor. Pr. 29, II); and therefore I call such perceptions "knowledge from casual experience."

2. From symbols. For example, from having heard or read certain words we call things to mind and we form certain ideas of them similar to those through which we imagine things (Sch. Pr. 18, II).

Both these ways of regarding things I shall in future refer to as "knowledge of the first kind," "opinion," or "imagination."

3. From the fact that we have common notions and adequate ideas of the properties of things (see Cor. Pr. 38 and 39 with its Cor., and Pr. 40, II). I shall refer to this as "reason" and "knowledge of the second kind."

Apart from these two kinds of knowledge there is, as I shall later show, a third kind of knowledge, which I shall refer to as "intuition." This kind of knowledge proceeds from an adequate idea of the formal essence of certain attributes of God to an adequate knowledge of the essence of things. I shall illustrate all these kinds of knowledge by one single example. Three numbers are given; it is required to find a fourth which is related to the third as the second to the first. Tradesmen have no hesitation in multiplying the second by the third and dividing the product by the first, either because they have not yet forgotten the rule they learned without proof from their teachers, or because they have in fact found this correct in the case of very simple numbers, or else from the force of the proof of Proposition 19 of the Seventh Book of Euclid, to wit, the common property of proportionals. But in the case of very simple numbers, none of this is necessary. For example, in the case of the given numbers 1, 2, 3, everybody can see that the fourth proportional is 6, and all the more clearly because we infer in one single intuition the fourth number from the ratio we see the first number bears to the second.

PROPOSITION 41: *Knowledge of the first kind is the only cause of falsity; knowledge of the second and third kind is necessarily true.*

Proof: In the preceding Scholium we asserted that all those ideas which are inadequate and confused belong to the first kind of knowledge; and thus (Pr. 35, II) this knowledge is the only cause of falsity. Further, we asserted that to knowledge of the second and third kind there belong those ideas which are adequate. Therefore (Pr. 34, II), this knowledge is necessarily true.

PROPOSITION 42: *Knowledge of the second and third kind, and not knowledge of the first kind, teaches us to distinguish true from false.*

Proof: This Proposition is self-evident. For he who can distinguish the true from the false must have an adequate idea of the true and the false; that is (Sch. 2 Pr. 40, II), he must know the true and the false by the second or third kind of knowledge.

PROPOSITION 43: *He who has a true idea knows at the same time that he has a true idea, and cannot doubt its truth.*

Proof: A true idea in us is one which is adequate in God insofar as he is explicated through the nature of the human mind (Cor. Pr. 11, II). Let us suppose, then, that there is in God, insofar as he is explicated through the nature of the human mind, an adequate idea, A. The idea of this idea must also necessarily be in God, and is related to God in the same way as the idea A (Pr. 20, II, the proof being of general application). But by our supposition the idea A is related to God insofar as he is explicated through the nature of the human mind. Therefore, the idea of the idea A must be related to God in the same way; that is (Cor. Pr. 11, II), this adequate idea of the idea A will be in the mind which has the adequate idea A. So he who has an adequate idea, that is, he who knows a thing truly (Pr. 34, II), must at the same time have an adequate idea, that is, a true knowledge of his knowledge; that is (as is self-evident), he is bound at the same time to be certain.

Scholium: I have explained in the Scholium to Pr. 21, II what is an idea of an idea; but it should be noted that the preceding proposition is sufficiently self-evident. For nobody who has a true idea is unaware that a true idea involves absolute certainty. To have a true idea means only to know a thing perfectly, that is, to the utmost degree. Indeed, nobody can doubt this, unless he thinks that an idea is some dumb thing like a picture on a tablet, and not a mode of thinking, to wit, the very act of understanding. And who, pray, can know that he understands some thing unless he first understands it? That is, who can know that he is certain of something unless he is first certain of it? Again, what standard of truth can there be that is clearer and more certain than a true idea? Indeed, just as light makes manifest both itself and darkness, so truth is the standard both of itself and falsity.

I think I have thus given an answer to those questions which can be stated as follows: If a true idea is distinguished from a false one only inasmuch as it is said to correspond with that of which it is an idea, then a true idea has no more reality or perfection than a false one (since they are distinguished only by an extrinsic characteristic) and consequently neither is a man who has true ideas superior to one who has only false ideas. Secondly, how do we come to have false ideas? And finally, how can one know for certain that one has ideas which correspond with that of which they are ideas? I have now given an answer, I repeat, to these problems. As regards the difference between a true and a false idea, it is clear from Pr. 35, II that the former is to the latter as being to non-being. The causes of falsity I have quite clearly shown from Propositions 19 to 35 with the latter's Scholium, from which it is likewise obvious what is the difference between a man who has true ideas and one who has only false ideas. As to the last question, how can a man know that he has an idea which corresponds to that of which it is an idea, I have just shown, with abundant clarity, that this arises from the fact that he does have an idea that corresponds to that of which it is an idea; that is, truth is its own standard. Furthermore, the human mind, insofar as it perceives things truly, is part of the infinite intellect of God (Cor. Pr. 11, II), and thus it is as inevitable that the clear and distinct ideas of the mind are true as that God's ideas are true.

PROPOSITION 44: *It is not in the nature of reason to regard things as contingent, but as necessary.*

Proof: It is in the nature of reason to perceive things truly (Pr. 41, II), to wit (Ax. 6, I), as they are in themselves; that is (Pr. 29, I), not as contingent, but as necessary.

Corollary 1: Hence it follows that it solely results from imagination [*imaginatio*] that we regard things, both in respect of the past and of the future, as contingent.

Scholium: I shall explain briefly how this comes about. We have shown above (Pr. 17, II and Cor.) that although things may not exist, the mind nevertheless always imagines them as present unless causes arise which exclude their present existence. Further, we have shown (Pr. 18, II) that if the human body has once been affected by two external bodies at the same time, when the mind later imagines one of them, it will straightway call the other to mind as well; that is, it will regard both as present to it unless other causes arise which exclude their present existence. Furthermore, nobody doubts that time, too, is a product of the imagination, and arises from the fact that we see some bodies move more slowly than others, or more quickly, or with equal speed. Let us therefore suppose that yesterday a boy saw Peter first of all in the morning, Paul at noon, and Simon in the evening, and that today he again sees Peter in the morning. From Pr. 18, II it is clear that as soon as he sees the morning light, forthwith he will imagine the sun as traversing the same tract of sky as on the previous day, that is, he will imagine a whole day, and he will imagine Peter together with morning, Paul with midday, and Simon with evening; that is, he will imagine the existence of Paul and Simon with reference to future time. On the other hand, on seeing Simon in the evening he will refer Paul and Peter to time past by imagining them along with time past. This train of events will be the more consistent the more frequently he sees them in that order. If it should at some time occur that on another evening he sees James instead of Simon, then the following morning he will imagine along with evening now Simon, now James, but not both together.

For we are supposing that he has seen only one of them in the evening, not both at the same time. Therefore, his imagination will waver, and he will imagine, along with a future evening, now one, now the other; that is, he will regard neither of them as going to be there for certain, but both of them contingently. This wavering of the imagination occurs in the same way if the imagination be of things which we regard with relation to past or present time, and consequently we shall imagine things, as related both to present and past or future time, as contingent.

Corollary 2: It is in the nature of reason to perceive things in the light of eternity [*sub quadam specie aeternitatis*].

Proof: It is in the nature of reason to regard things as necessary, not as contingent (previous Pr.). Now it perceives this necessity truly (Pr. 41, II); that is, as it is in itself (Ax. 6, I). But (Pr. 16, I) this necessity is the very necessity of God's eternal nature. Therefore, it is in the nature of reason to regard things in this light of eternity. Furthermore, the basic principles of reason are those notions (Pr. 38, II) which explicate what is common to all things, and do not explicate (Pr. 37, II) the essence of any particular thing, and therefore must be conceived without any relation to time, but in the light of eternity.

PROPOSITION 45: *Every idea of any body or particular thing existing in actuality necessarily involves the eternal and infinite essence of God.*

Proof: The idea of a particular thing actually existing necessarily involves both the essence and the existence of the thing (Cor. Pr. 8, II). But particular things cannot be conceived without God (Pr. 15, I). Now since they have God for their cause (Pr. 6, II) insofar as he is considered under that attribute of which the things themselves are modes, their ideas (Ax. 4, I) must necessarily involve the conception of their attribute; that is (Def. 6, I), the eternal and infinite essence of God.

Scholium: Here by existence I do not mean duration, that is, existence insofar as it is considered in the abstract as a kind of quantity. I am speaking of the very nature of existence, which is attributed to particular things because they follow in infinite numbers in infinite ways from the eternal necessity of God's nature (Pr. 16, I). I am speaking, I repeat, of the very existence of particular things insofar as they are in God. For although each particular thing is determined by another particular thing to exist in a certain manner, the force by which each perseveres in existing follows from the eternal necessity of God's nature. See Cor. Pr. 24, I.

PROPOSITION 46: *The knowledge of the eternal and infinite essence of God which each idea involves is adequate and perfect.*

Proof: The proof of the preceding proposition is universally valid, and whether a thing be considered as a part or a whole, its idea, whether of whole or part, involves the eternal and infinite essence of God (preceding Pr.). Therefore, that which gives knowledge of the eternal and infinite essence of God is common to all things, and equally in the part as in the whole. And so this knowledge will be adequate (Pr. 38, II).

PROPOSITION 47: *The human mind has an adequate knowledge of the eternal and infinite essence of God.*

Proof: The human mind has ideas (Pr. 22, II) from which (Pr. 23, II) it perceives itself, its own body (Pr. 19, II), and external bodies (Cor. 1, Pr. 16 and Pr. 17, II) as actually existing, and so it has an adequate knowledge of the eternal and infinite essence of God (Prs. 45 and 46, II).

Scholium: Hence we see that God's infinite essence and his eternity are known to all. Now since all things are in God and are conceived through God, it follows that from this knowledge we can deduce a great many things so as to know them adequately and thus to form that third kind of knowledge I mentioned in Sch. 2 Pr. 40, II, of the superiority and usefulness of which we shall have occasion to speak in Part V. That men do not have as clear a knowledge of God as they do of common notions arises from the fact that they are unable to imagine God as they do bodies, and that they have connected the word "God" with the images of things which they commonly see; and this they can scarcely avoid, being affected continually by external bodies. Indeed, most errors result solely from the incorrect application of words to things. When somebody says that the lines joining the center of a circle to its circumference are unequal, he surely understands by circle, at least at that time, something different from what mathematicians understand. Likewise, when men make mistakes in arithmetic, they have different figures in mind from those on paper. So if you look only to their minds, they indeed are not mistaken; but they seem to be wrong because we think that they have in mind the figures on the page. If this were not the case, we would not think them to be wrong, just as I did not think that person to be wrong whom I recently heard shouting that his hall had flown into his neighbor's hen, for I could see clearly what he had in mind. Most controversies arise from this, that men do not correctly express what is in their mind, or they misunderstand another's mind. For, in reality, while they are hotly contradicting one another, they are either in agreement or have different things in mind, so that the apparent errors and absurdities of their opponents are not really so.

PROPOSITION 48: *In the mind there is no absolute, or free, will. The mind is determined to this or that volition by a cause, which is likewise determined by another cause, and this again by another, and so ad infinitum.*

Proof: The mind is a definite and determinate mode of thinking (Pr. 11, II), and thus (Cor. 2, Pr. 17, I) it cannot be the free cause of its actions: that is, it cannot possess an absolute faculty of willing and nonwilling. It must be determined to will this or that (Pr. 28, I) by a cause, which likewise is determined by another cause, and this again by another, etc.

Scholium: In the same way it is proved that in the mind there is no absolute faculty of understanding, desiring, loving, etc. Hence it follows that these and similar faculties are either entirely fictitious or nothing more than metaphysical entities or universals which we are wont to form from particulars. So intellect and will bear the same relation to this or that idea, this or that volition, as stoniness to this or that stone, or man to Peter and Paul. As to the reason why men think they are free, we explained that in the Appendix to Part I.

But before proceeding further, it should here be noted that by the will I mean the faculty of affirming and denying, and not desire. I mean, I repeat, the faculty whereby the mind affirms or denies what is true or what is false, not the desire whereby the mind seeks things or shuns them. But now that we have proved that these faculties are universal notions which are not distinct from the particulars from which we form them, we must inquire whether volitions themselves are anything more than ideas of things. We must inquire, I say, whether there is in the mind any other affirmation and denial apart from that which the idea, insofar as it is an idea, involves. On this subject see the following proposition and also Def. 3, II, lest thought becomes confused with pictures. For by ideas I do not mean images such as are formed at the back of the eye—or if you like, in the middle of the brain—but conceptions of thought.

PROPOSITION 49: *There is in the mind no volition, that is, affirmation and negation, except that which an idea, insofar as it is an idea, involves.*

Proof: There is in the mind (preceding Pr.) no absolute faculty of willing and non-willing, but only particular volitions, namely, this or that affirmation, and this or that negation. Let us therefore conceive a particular volition, namely, a mode of thinking whereby the mind affirms that the three angles of a triangle are equal to two right angles. This affirmation involves the conception, or idea, of a triangle; that is, it cannot be conceived without the idea of a triangle. For to say that A must involve the conception of B is the same as to say that A cannot be conceived without B. Again, this affirmation (Ax. 3, II) cannot even be without the idea of a triangle. Therefore, this idea can neither be nor be conceived without the idea of a triangle. Furthermore, this idea of a triangle must involve this same affirmation, namely, that its three angles are equal to two right angles. Therefore, vice versa, this idea of a triangle can neither be nor be conceived without this affirmation, and so (Def. 2, II) this affirmation belongs to the essence of the idea of a triangle, and is nothing more than the essence itself. And what I have said of this volition (for it was arbitrarily selected) must also be said of every volition, namely, that it is nothing but an idea.

Corollary: Will and intellect are one and the same thing.

Proof: Will and intellect are nothing but the particular volitions and ideas (Pr. 48, II and Sch.). But a particular volition and idea are one and the same thing (preceding Pr.). Therefore, will and intellect are one and the same thing.

Scholium: By this means we have removed the cause to which error is commonly attributed. We have previously shown that falsity consists only in the privation that fragmentary and confused ideas involve. Therefore, a false idea, insofar as it is false, does not involve certainty. So when we say that a man acquiesces in what is false and has no doubt thereof, we are not thereby saying that he is certain, but only that he does not doubt, or that he acquiesces in what is false because there is nothing to cause his imagination to waver. On this point see Sch. Pr. 44, II. So however much we suppose a man to adhere to what is false, we shall never say that he is certain. For by certainty we mean something positive (Pr. 43, II and Sch.), not privation of doubt. But by privation of certainty we mean falsity.

But for a fuller explanation of the preceding proposition some things remain to be said. Then, again, there is the further task of replying to objections that may be raised against this doctrine of ours. Finally, to remove every shred of doubt, I have thought it worthwhile to point out certain advantages of this doctrine. I say certain advantages, for the most important of them will be better understood from what we have to say in Part V.

I begin, then, with the first point, and I urge my readers to make a careful distinction between an idea—i.e., a conception of the mind—and the images of things that we imagine. Again, it is essential to distinguish between ideas and the words we use to signify things. For since these three—images, words, and ideas—have been utterly confused by many, or else they fail to distinguish between them through lack of accuracy, or, finally, through lack of caution, our doctrine of the will, which it is essential to know both for theory and for the wise ordering of life, has never entered their minds. For those who think that ideas consist in images formed in us from the contact of external bodies are convinced that those ideas of things whereof we can form no like image are not ideas, but mere fictions fashioned arbitrarily at will. So they look on ideas as dumb pictures on a tablet, and misled by this preconception they fail to see that an idea, insofar as it is an idea, involves affirmation or negation. Again, those who confuse words with idea, or with the affirmation which an idea involves, think that when they affirm or deny something merely by words contrary to what they feel, they are able to will contrary to what they feel. Now one can easily dispel these misconceptions if one attends to the nature of thought, which is quite removed from the concept of extension. Then one will clearly understand that an idea, being a mode of thinking, consists neither in the image of a thing nor in words. For the essence of words and images is constituted solely by corporeal motions far removed from the concept of thought. With these few words of warning, I turn to the aforementioned objections.

The first of these rests on the confident claim that the will extends more widely than the intellect, and therefore is different from it. The reason for their belief that the will extends more widely than the intellect is that they find—so they say—that they do not need a greater faculty of assent, that is, of affirming and denying, than they already possess, in order to assent to an infinite number of other things that we do not perceive, but that we do need an increased faculty of understanding. Therefore, will is distinct from intellect, the latter being finite and the former infinite.

Second, it may be objected against us that experience appears to tell us most indisputably that we are able to suspend judgment so as not to assent to things that we perceive, and this is also confirmed by the fact that nobody is said to be deceived insofar as he perceives something, but only insofar as he assents or dissents. For instance, he who imagines a winged horse does not thereby grant that there is a winged horse; that is, he is not thereby deceived unless at the same time he grants that there is a winged horse. So experience appears to tell us most indisputably that the will, that is, the faculty of assenting, is free, and different from the faculty of understanding.

Third, it may be objected that one affirmation does not seem to contain more reality than another; that is, we do not seem to need greater power in order to affirm that what is true is true than to affirm that what is false is true. On the other hand, we do perceive that one idea has more reality or perfection than another. For some ideas are more perfect than others in proportion as some objects are superior to others. This, again, is a clear indication that there is a difference between will and intellect.

Fourth, it may be objected that if man does not act from freedom of will, what would happen if he should be in a state of equilibrium like Buridan's ass? Will he perish of hunger and thirst? If I were to grant this, I would appear to be thinking of an ass or a statue, not of a man. If I deny it, then the man will be determining himself, and consequently will possess the faculty of going and doing whatever he wants.

Besides these objections there may possibly be others. But since I am not obliged to quash every objection that can be dreamed up, I shall make it my task to reply to these objections only, and as briefly as possible.

To the first objection I reply that, if by the intellect is meant clear and distinct ideas only, I grant that the will extends more widely than the intellect, but I deny that the will extends more widely than perceptions, that is, the faculty of conceiving. Nor indeed do I see why the faculty of willing should be termed infinite any more than the faculty of sensing. For just as by the same faculty of willing we can affirm an infinite number of things (but in succession, for we cannot affirm an infinite number of things simultaneously), so also we can sense or perceive an infinite number of bodies (in succession) by the same faculty of sensing. If my objectors should say that there are an infinite number of things that we cannot sense, I retort that we cannot grasp them by any amount of thought, and consequently by any amount of willing. But, they say, if God wanted to bring it about that we should perceive these too, he would have had to give us a greater faculty of perceiving, but not a greater faculty of willing than he has already given us. This is the same as saying that if God wishes to bring it about that we should understand an infinite number of other entities, he would have to give us a greater intellect than he already has, so as to encompass these same infinite entities, but not a more universal idea of entity. For we have shown that the will is a universal entity, or the idea whereby we explicate all particular volitions; that is, that which is common to all particular volitions. So if they believe that this common or universal idea of volitions is a faculty, it is not at all surprising that they declare this faculty to extend beyond the limits of the intellect to infinity. For the term "universal" is applied equally to one, to many, and to an infinite number of individuals.

To the second objection I reply by denying that we have free power to suspend judgment. For when we say that someone suspends judgment, we are saying only that he sees that he is not adequately perceiving the thing. So suspension of judgment is really a perception, not free will. To understand this more clearly, let us conceive a boy imagining a winged horse and having no other perception. Since this imagining involves the existence of a horse (Cor. Pr. 17, II), and the boy perceives nothing to annul the existence of the horse, he will regard the horse as present and he will not be able to doubt its existence, although he is not certain of it. We experience this quite commonly in dreams, nor do I believe there is anyone who thinks that while dreaming he has free power to suspend judgment regarding the contents of his dream, and of bringing it about that he should not dream what he dreams that he sees. Nevertheless, it does happen that even in dreams we suspend judgment, to wit, when we dream that we are dreaming. Furthermore, I grant that nobody is deceived insofar as he has a perception; that is, I grant that the imaginings of the mind, considered in themselves, involve no error (see Sch. Pr. 17, II). But I deny that a man makes no affirmation insofar as he has a perception. For what else is perceiving a winged horse than affirming wings of a horse? For if the mind should perceive nothing apart from the winged horse, it would regard the horse as present to it, and would have no cause to doubt its existence nor any faculty of dissenting, unless the imagining of the winged horse were to be connected to an idea which annuls the existence of the said horse, or he perceives that the idea which he has of the winged horse is inadequate. Then he will either necessarily deny the existence of the horse or he will necessarily doubt it.

In the above I think I have also answered the third objection by my assertion that the will is a universal term predicated of all ideas and signifying only what is common to all ideas, namely, affirmation, the adequate essence of which, insofar as it is thus conceived as an abstract term, must be in every single idea, and the same in all in this respect only. But not insofar as it is considered as constituting the essence of the idea, for in that respect particular affirmations differ among themselves as much as do ideas. For example, the affirmation which the idea of a circle involves differs from the affirmation which the idea of a triangle involves as much as the idea of a circle differs from the idea of a triangle. Again, I absolutely deny that we need an equal power of thinking to affirm that what is true is true as to affirm that what is false is true. For these two affirmations, if you look to their meaning and not to the words alone, are related to one another as being to nonbeing. For there is nothing in ideas that constitutes the form of falsity (see Pr. 35, II with Sch. and Sch. Pr. 47, II). Therefore, it is important to note here how easily we are deceived when we confuse universals with particulars, and mental constructs [*entia rationis*] and abstract terms with the real.

As to the fourth objection, I readily grant that a man placed in such a state of equilibrium (namely, where he feels nothing else but hunger and thirst and perceives nothing but such-and-such food and drink at equal distances from him) will die of hunger and thirst. If they ask me whether such a man is not to be reckoned an ass rather than a man,

I reply that I do not know, just as I do not know how one should reckon a man who hangs himself, or how one should reckon babies, fools, and madmen.

My final task is to show what practical advantages accrue from knowledge of this doctrine, and this we shall readily gather from the following points:

1. It teaches that we act only by God's will, and that we share in the divine nature, and all the more as our actions become more perfect and as we understand God more and more. Therefore, this doctrine, apart from giving us complete tranquillity of mind, has the further advantage of teaching us wherein lies our greatest happiness or blessedness, namely, in the knowledge of God alone, as a result of which we are induced only to such actions as are urged on us by love and piety. Hence we clearly understand how far astray from the true estimation of virtue are those who, failing to understand that virtue itself and the service of God are happiness itself and utmost freedom, expect God to bestow on them the highest rewards in return for their virtue and meritorious actions as if in return for the basest slavery.

2. It teaches us what attitude we should adopt regarding fortune, or the things that are not in our power, that is, the things that do not follow from our nature; namely, to expect and to endure with patience both faces of fortune. For all things follow from God's eternal decree by the same necessity as it follows from the essence of a triangle that its three angles are equal to two right angles.

3. This doctrine assists us in our social relations, in that it teaches us to hate no one, despise no one, ridicule no one, be angry with no one, envy no one. Then again, it teaches us that each should be content with what he has and should help his neighbor, not from womanish pity, or favor, or superstition, but from the guidance of reason as occasion and circumstance require. This I shall demonstrate in Part IV.

4. Finally, this doctrine is also of no small advantage to the commonwealth, in that it teaches the manner in which citizens should be governed and led; namely, not so as to be slaves, but so as to do freely what is best.

And thus I have completed the task I undertook in this Scholium, and thereby I bring to an end Part II, in which I think I have explained the nature of the human mind and its properties at sufficient length and as clearly as the difficult subject matter permits, and that from my account can be drawn many excellent lessons, most useful and necessary to know.

John Locke
1632–1704

John Locke was born in Wrington, Somerset, the son of a Puritan lawyer. His father fought on the side of the Parliament against Charles I, and Locke himself was a lifelong defender of the parliamentary system.

As a teenager, Locke attended Westminster School, studying classics under the harsh discipline of the time. He later condemned the English educational system for its brutality and one-sided emphasis on the past. In 1652, he entered Christ Church, Oxford, where he received his B.A. in 1656 and an M.A. in 1658. Again, he found his Oxford education obsessed with the past—in particular the Scholasticism of the late Middle Ages. Hence, he sought knowledge in the emerging sciences. In 1659, he was named a Senior Student at Oxford—a position he held until he lost it for political reasons in 1684.

In 1662, Locke met Lord Ashley, the Earl of Shaftesbury. Locke and Shaftesbury became close friends and in 1667 Locke went to live with Shaftesbury as his personal physician, securing his medical degree and license in 1674. Locke also helped Shaftesbury with several projects, including writing a constitution for the colony of Carolina. As a member of Shaftesbury's entourage, Locke traveled extensively and met many of the leading thinkers of his day.

When Shaftesbury became the leader of the parliamentary opposition to the king, Locke's friendship became a liability. Shaftesbury was tried for treason in 1681; although he was acquitted, he fled to Holland where he died in 1683. Without the backing of his powerful patron, Locke also fled to Holland, where he became an advisor to William and Mary of Orange. Following the Glorious Revolution of 1688, which removed Locke's enemy, James II, from the throne, Locke returned home in the company of William and Mary—now king and queen of England.

Following his return to England, Locke published his two most important works, *Essay Concerning Human Understanding* (1690) and *Two Treatises of Government* (1690). Locke spent the rest of his life writing and serving the new government as Commissioner of Appeals and, later, as Commissioner of Trade and Plantations. He died quietly at the home of a friend in 1704.

* * *

Locke begins his first major work, *Essays Concerning Human Understanding*, with several arguments against the Cartesian notion of innate ideas. He claims that the mind is a *tabula rasa*, a blank tablet or "white paper, void of all characters, without any ideas." All ideas come from one source: experience. Experience, in turn, is of two types: sensation or reflection. Sensations are derived from our sensory perceptions of the external world. Reflection, on the other hand, provides ideas by the mind "reflecting on its own operations within itself."

Having explained the *origin* of ideas, Locke then explains the *nature* of ideas. All ideas are either simple or complex. Simple ideas are uncompounded; that is, they cannot be broken down further, such as the ideas of "sweetness" or "redness." Complex ideas are composed of two or more simple ideas, such as the idea of a red, sweet apple. Locke then classifies simple and complex ideas by sources (sensation, reflection, or both).

Having explained the sources of ideas, Locke next asks if the ideas that come from sensation actually resemble the qualities of the external objects that gave rise to them. He answers first by dividing qualities into primary and secondary. Primary qualities are "utterly inseparable" from external objects regardless of their state—such qualities include solidity, extension, figure, motion, rest, and number. On the other hand, secondary qualities are "nothing in the objects themselves, but powers to produce various sensations in us by their primary qualities." These secondary qualities would include such characteristics as colors, sounds, tastes, and the like. So, for example, the primary qualities of an apple (a solid, being extended in space, etc.) have the power to produce the secondary quality of a sweet taste and a red color. This analysis means that the world *as we experience it* is only a representation of the way the world actually is. The blooming, buzzing, colorful world of our experience is not the real world.

Finally, Locke asks what these primary and secondary qualities are qualities *of*. He argues that there must be "some *substratum* wherein [ideas] do subsist, and from which they do result, which therefore we call *substance*." Although we cannot have any idea of substance, nor can we explain the concept, we must posit substance as a "supporter" of qualities—a "something I know not what," Locke said.

Locke spent twenty years preparing his *Essay Concerning Human Uunderstanding* for publication in 1690. The *Essay* went through several editions while Locke was still living, including an abridgment with his consent. The following selection is an abridgment by Walter Kaufmann, which I have modified. This abridgment owes much to John Wynne's (1695) editing and to the modern work of A.S. Pringle-Pattison.

In addition this work, Locke wrote *Two Treatises of Government* (1690), *The Reasonableness of Christianity as Delivered in the Scriptures* (1695), *Vindications of the Reasonableness of Christianity* (1695 and 1697), and several "Letters" concerning toleration.

* * *

The best commentary on Locke's thought in general and on the *Essay* in particular is Richard I. Aaron, *John Locke* (Oxford: Clarendon Press, 1971). Also useful as a general overview are D.J. O'Connor, *John Locke* (Harmondsworth, Middlesex: Penguin Books, 1952); John W. Yolton, *Locke and the Way of Ideas* (Oxford: Clarendon Press, 1968); R.S. Woolhouse, *Locke* (Minneapolis: University of Minnesota Press, 1983); John Dunn, *Locke* (New York: Oxford University Press, 1984)—part of the "Past Masters" series, now reprinted in the combined volume of John Dunn et al., eds., *The British Empiricists* (Oxford: Oxford University Press, 1992); Michael Ayers, *Locke* (Oxford: Routledge, 1994); Nicholas Jolley, *Locke: His Philosophical Thought* (Oxford: Oxford University Press, 1999); and Roger Woolhouse, *Locke: A Biography* (Cambridge: Cambridge University Press, 2007). For help with Locke's *Essay*, see John W. Yolton, *Locke and the Compass of Human Understanding: A Selective Commentary on the "Essay"* (London: Cambridge University Press, 1970); John L. Mackie, *Problems from Locke* (Oxford: Oxford University Press, 1976); Gary Fuller et al, *John Locke:* An Essay Concerning Human Understanding *in Focus* (London: Routledge, 2000); and E.J. Lowe, *Locke* (London: Routledge, 2005); Lex Newman, ed., *The Cambridge Companion to Locke's* Essay Concerning Human Understanding (Cambridge: Cambridge University Press, 2007); and William Uzgalis, *Locke's* Essay Concerning Human Understanding: *A Reader's Guide* (London: Continuum, 2007). Nicholas Wolterstorff, *John Locke and the Ethics of Belief* (Cambridge: Cambridge University Press, 1996) provides guidance to the last section of the *Essay*. For guides to Locke's political thought, see John Dunn, *The Political Thought of John Locke* (Cambridge: Cambridge University Press, 1969); J.W. Gough, *John Locke's Political Philosophy* (Oxford: Clarendon Press, 1973); and Greg Forster, *John Locke's Politics of Moral Consensus* (Cambridge: Cambridge University Press, 2005). John Yolton, *A Locke Dictionary* (Oxford: Basil Blackwell, 1993) provides a useful reference work. For collections of essays on Locke's thought, see C.B. Martin and D.M. Armstrong, eds., *Locke and Berkeley: A Collection of Critical Essays* (Notre Dame, IN: Notre Dame University Press, 1968); John W. Yolton, ed., *John Locke: Problems and Perspectives: A Collection of New Essays* (Cambridge: Cambridge University Press, 1969); Vere Chappell's books, *Essays on Early Modern Philosophers: John Locke—Theory of Knowledge, John Locke—Political Philosophy* (all Hamden, CT: Garland Press, 1992), and *The Cambridge Companion to Locke* (Cambridge: Cambridge University Press, 1994); J.R. Milton, ed., *Locke's Moral, Political and Legal Philosophy* (New York: Ashgate, 1999); and Udo Thiel, ed., *Locke: Epistemology and Metaphysics* (New York: Ashgate, 2001). For an interesting, if unusual, analysis of Locke's political thought, see Leo Strauss, *Natural Right and History* (Chicago: University of Chicago Press, 1952).

AN ESSAY CONCERNING HUMAN UNDERSTANDING (abridged)

INTRODUCTION

1. *An enquiry into the understanding, pleasant and useful.*—Since it is the *understanding* that sets man above the rest of sensible beings, and gives him all the advantage and dominion which he has over them, it is certainly a subject, even for its nobleness, worth our labour to enquire into. The understanding, like the eye, whilst it makes us see and perceive all other things, takes no notice of itself; and it requires art and pains to set it at a distance, and make it its own object. But whatever be the difficulties that lie in the way of this enquiry; whatever it be that keeps us so much in the dark to ourselves; sure I am that all the light we can let in upon our own minds, all the acquaintance we can make with our own understandings, will not only be very pleasant, but bring us great advantage in directing our thoughts in the search of other things.

2. *Design.*—This, therefore, being my purpose, to enquire into the original, certainty, and extent of *human knowledge*, together with the grounds and degrees of *belief, opinion*, and *assent*, I shall not at present meddle with the physical consideration of the mind, or trouble myself to examine wherein its essence consists, or by what motions of our spirits, or alterations of our bodies, we come to have any *sensation* by our organs, or any *ideas* in our understandings; and whether those ideas do, in their formation, any or all of them, depend on matter or no. These are speculations which, however curious and entertaining, I shall decline, as lying out of my way in the design I am now upon. It shall suffice to my present purpose, to consider the discerning faculties of a man as they are employed about the objects which they have to do with: and I shall imagine I have not wholly misemployed myself in the thoughts I shall have on this occasion, if, in this historical, plain method, I can give any account of the ways whereby our understandings come to attain those notions of things we have, and can set down any measures of the certainty of our knowledge, or the grounds of those persuasions which are to be found amongst men, so various, different, and wholly contradictory; and yet asserted somewhere or other with such assurance, and confidence, that he that shall take a view of the opinions of mankind, observe their opposition, and at the same time consider the fondness and devotion wherewith they are embraced, the resolution and eagerness wherewith they are maintained, may perhaps have reason to suspect that either there is no such thing as truth at all, or that mankind hath no sufficient means to attain a certain knowledge of it.

3. *Method.*—It is therefore worth while to search out the bounds between opinion and knowledge, and examine by what measures, in things whereof we have no certain knowledge, we ought to regulate our assent, and moderate our persuasions. In order whereunto, I shall pursue this following method:—

First, I shall enquire into the original of those *ideas*, notions, or whatever else you please to call them, which a man observes, and is conscious to himself he has in his mind; and the ways whereby the understanding comes to be furnished with them.

Secondly, I shall endeavour to show what *knowledge* the understanding hath by those ideas, and the certainty, evidence, and extent of it.

Thirdly, I shall make some enquiry into the nature and grounds of *faith* or *opinion*: whereby I mean that assent which we give to any proposition as true, of whose truth yet we have no certain knowledge. And here we shall have occasion to examine the reasons and degrees of assent.

* * *

8. *What "idea" stands for.*—Thus much I thought necessary to say concerning the occasion of this enquiry into human understanding. But, before I proceed on to what I have thought on this subject, I must here, in the entrance, beg pardon of my reader for the frequent use of the word *idea* which he will find in the following treatise. It being that term which, I think, serves best to stand for whatsoever is the object of the understanding when a man thinks, I have used it to express whatever is meant by *phantasm, notion, species, or whatever it is which the mind can be employed about in thinking*; and I could not avoid frequently using it.

I presume it will be easily granted me, that there are such *ideas* in men's minds; every one is conscious of them in himself, and men's words and actions will satisfy him that they are in others.

Our first enquiry then shall be,—how they come into the mind.

BOOK I. NEITHER PRINCIPLES NOR IDEAS ARE INNATE

CHAPTER 1. NO INNATE PRINCIPLES IN THE MIND

1. *The way shown how we come by any knowledge, sufficient to prove it not innate.*—It is an established opinion amongst some men, that there are in the understanding certain innate principles; some primary notions, ⟨*koinai ennoiai*⟩, characters, as it were stamped upon the mind of man, which the soul receives in its very first being, and brings into the world with it. It would be sufficient to convince unprejudiced readers of the falseness of this supposition, if I should only show (as I hope I shall in the following parts of this discourse) how men, barely by the use of their natural faculties, may attain to all the knowledge they have, without the help of any innate impressions; and may arrive at certainty, without any such original notions or principles. For I imagine any one will easily grant, that it would be impertinent to suppose the ideas of colours innate in a creature to whom God hath given sight, and a power to receive them by the eyes from external objects: and no less unreasonable would it be to attribute several truths to the impressions of nature and innate characters, when we may observe in ourselves faculties fit to attain as easy and certain knowledge of them as if they were originally imprinted on the mind.

But because a man is not permitted without censure to follow his own thoughts in the search of truth, when they lead him ever so little out of the common road, I shall set down the reasons that made me doubt of the truth of that opinion, as an excuse for my mistake, if I be in one; which I leave to be considered by those who, with me, dispose themselves to embrace truth wherever they find it.

2. *General assent the great argument.*—There is nothing more commonly taken for granted, than that there are certain principles, both *speculative* and *practical* (for they speak of both), universally agreed upon by all mankind; which therefore, they argue, must needs be the constant impressions which the souls of men receive in their

first beings and which they bring into the world with them, as necessarily and really as they do any of their inherent faculties.

3. *Universal consent proves nothing innate.*—This argument, drawn from universal consent, has this misfortune in it, that if it were true in matter of fact, that there were certain truths wherein all mankind agreed, it would not prove them innate, if there can be any other way shown, how men may come to that universal agreement in the things they do consent in; which I presume may be done.

4. *"What is, is," and "It is impossible for the same Thing to be and not to be," not universally assented to.*—But, which is worse, this argument of universal consent which is made use of to prove innate principles, seems to me a demonstration that there are none such: because there are none to which all mankind give an universal assent. I shall begin with the speculative, and instance in those magnified principles of demonstration, "Whatsoever is, is," and "It is impossible for the same thing to be and not to be"; which, of all others, I think have the most allowed title to innate. These have so settled a reputation of maxims universally received, that it will no doubt be thought strange if any one should seem to question it. But yet I take liberty to say, that these propositions are so far from having an universal assent, that there are a great part of mankind to whom they are not so much as known.

5. *Not on the mind naturally imprinted, because not known to children, idiots, etc.*—For, first, it is evident, that all children and idiots have not the least apprehension or thought of them. And the want of that is enough to destroy that universal assent, which must needs be the necessary concomitant of all innate truths: it seeming to me near a contradiction to say, that there are truths imprinted on the soul which it perceives or understands not; imprinting, if it signify anything, being nothing else but the making certain truths to be perceived . . . No proposition can be said to be in the mind which it never yet knew, which it was never yet conscious of. For if any one may, then, by the same reason, all propositions that are true, and the mind is *capable* ever of assenting to, may be said to be in the mind, and to be imprinted; since if any one can be said to be in the mind, which it never yet knew, it must be only because it is capable of knowing it; and so the mind is of all truths it ever shall know. Nay, thus truths may be imprinted on the mind which it never did, nor ever shall know: for a man may live long, and die at last in ignorance of many truths which his mind was capable of knowing, and that with certainty. So that if the capacity of knowing be the natural impression contended for, all the truths a man ever comes to know will, by this account, be every one of them innate: and this great point will amount to no more, but only to a very high improper way of speaking. But then, to what end such contest for certain innate maxims? If truths can be imprinted on the understanding without being perceived, I can see no difference there can be between any truths the mind is capable of knowing in respect of their original: they must all be innate, or all adventitious; in vain shall a man go about to distinguish them. He therefore that talks of innate notions in the understanding, cannot (if he intend thereby any distinct sort of truths) mean such truths to be in the understanding as it never perceived, and is yet wholly ignorant of. For if these words "to be in the understanding" have any propriety, they signify to be understood. If therefore these two propositions: "Whatsoever is, is," and, "It is impossible for the same thing to be, and not to be," are by nature imprinted, children cannot be ignorant of them; infants, and all that have souls, must necessarily have them in their understandings, know the truth of them, and assent to it.

* * *

BOOK II. OF IDEAS

CHAPTER 1. OF IDEAS IN GENERAL AND THEIR ORIGINAL

1. *Idea is the object of thinking.*—Every man being conscious to himself that he thinks, and that which his mind is applied about whilst thinking being the ideas that are there, it is past doubt that men have in their minds several ideas, such as are those expressed by the words *whiteness*, *hardness*, *sweetness*, *thinking*, *motion*, *man*, *elephant*, *army*, *drunkenness*, and others. It is in the first place then to be enquired, How he comes by them?

I know it is a received doctrine, that men have native ideas and original characters stamped upon their minds in their very first being. This opinion I have at large examined already; and, I suppose, what I have said in the foregoing Book will be much more easily admitted, when I have shown whence the understanding may get all the ideas it has, and by what ways and degrees they may come into the mind; for which I shall appeal to every one's own observation and experience.

2. *All ideas come from sensation or reflection.*—Let us then suppose the mind to be, as we say, white paper, void of all characters, without any ideas; how comes it to be furnished? Whence comes it by that vast store, which the busy and boundless fancy of man has painted on it with an almost endless variety? Whence has it all the *materials* of reason and knowledge? To this I answer, in one word, from EXPERIENCE; in that all our knowledge is founded, and from that it ultimately derives itself. Our observation, employed either about external sensible objects, or about the internal operations of our minds, perceived and reflected on by ourselves, is that which supplies our understandings with all the materials of thinking. These two are the fountains of knowledge, from whence all the ideas we have or can naturally have, do spring.

3. *The objects of sensation one source of ideas.*—First, our senses, conversant about particular sensible objects, do convey into the mind several distinct perceptions of things, according to those various ways wherein those objects do affect them; and thus we come by those *ideas* we have of *yellow*, *white*, *heat*, *cold*, *soft*, *hard*, *bitter*, *sweet*, and all those which we call sensible qualities; which when I say the senses convey into the mind, I mean, they from external objects convey into the mind what produces there those perceptions. This great source of most of the ideas we have, depending wholly upon our senses, and derived by them to the understanding, I call, SENSATION.

4. *The operations of our minds the other source of them.*—Secondly, the other fountain, from which experience furnishes the understanding with ideas, is the perception of the operations of our mind within us, as it is employed about the ideas it has got; which operations, when the soul comes to reflect on and consider, do furnish the understanding with another set of ideas which could not be had from things without: and such are *perception*, *thinking*, *doubting*, *believing*, *reasoning*, *knowing*, *willing*, and all the different actings of our own minds; which we being conscious of, and observing in ourselves, do from these receive into our understanding as distinct ideas, as we do from bodies affecting our senses. This source of ideas every man has wholly in himself: and though it be not sense, as having nothing to do with external objects, yet it is very like it, and might properly enough be called *internal sense*. But as I call the other SENSATION, so I call this REFLECTION, the ideas it affords being such only as the mind gets by reflecting on its own operations within itself. By Reflection, then, in the following part of this discourse, I would be understood to mean that notice which the mind takes of its own

St. Paul's Cathedral, London, facade, built 1675–1710. Like Locke, Sir Christopher Wren (1632–1723) was interested in science and combining reason and religion. The left turret of the facade he designed for St. Paul's conceals an observatory (opposite the clock in the right turret). (*©Angelo Hornak/Alamy Stock Photo)*

operations, and the manner of them, by reason whereof there come to be ideas of these operations in the understanding. These two, I say, viz., external material things as the objects of SENSATION, and the operations of our own minds within as the objects of REFLECTION are, to me, the only originals from whence all our ideas take their beginnings. The term *operations* here, I use in a large sense, as comprehending not barely the actions of the mind about its ideas, but some sort of passions arising sometimes from them, such as is the satisfaction or uneasiness arising from any thought.

5. *All our ideas are of the one or the other of these.*—The understanding seems to me not to have the least glimmering of any ideas which it doth not receive from one of these two. *External objects* furnish the mind with the ideas of sensible qualities, which are all those different perceptions they produce in us; and *the mind* furnishes the understanding with ideas of its own operations. These, when we have taken a full survey of them, and their several modes, combinations, and relations, we shall find to contain all our whole stock of ideas; and that we have nothing in our minds which did not come in one of these two ways. Let any one examine his own thoughts, and thoroughly search into his understanding, and then let him tell me, whether all the original ideas he has there, are any other than of the objects of his senses, or of the operations of his mind considered as objects of his reflection; and how great a mass of knowledge soever he imagines to be lodged there, he will, upon taking a strict view, see that he has not any idea in his mind but what one of these two have imprinted, though perhaps with infinite variety compounded and enlarged by the understanding, as we shall see hereafter.

6. *Observable in children.*—He that attentively considers the state of a child at his first coming into the world, will have little reason to think him stored with plenty of ideas that are to be the matter of his future knowledge. It is *by degrees* he comes to be

furnished with them: and though the ideas of obvious and familiar qualities themselves before the memory begins to keep a register of time and order, yet it is often so late before some unusual qualities come in the way, that there are few men that cannot recollect the beginning of their acquaintance with them: and if it were worth while, no doubt a child might be so ordered as to have but a very few even of the ordinary ideas till he were grown up to a man. But all that are born into the world being surrounded with bodies that perpetually and diversely affect them, variety of ideas, whether care be taken about it or no, are imprinted on the minds of children. Light and colours are busy and at hand everywhere when the eye is but open; sounds and some tangible qualities fail not to solicit their proper senses, and force an entrance to the mind; but yet I think it will be granted easily, that if a child were kept in a place where he never saw any other but black and white till he were a man, he would have no more ideas of scarlet or green, than he that from his childhood never tasted an oyster or a pineapple has of those particular relishes.

7. *Men are differently furnished with these according to the different objects they converse with.*—Men then come to be furnished with fewer or more simple ideas from without, according as the objects they converse with afford greater or less variety; and from the operations of their minds within, according as they more or less reflect on them. For, though he that contemplates the operations of his mind cannot but have plain and clear ideas of them; yet, unless he turn his thoughts that way, and considers them *attentively*, he will no more have clear and distinct ideas of all the operations of his mind, and all that may be observed therein, than he will have all the particular ideas of any landscape, or of the parts and motions of a clock, who will not turn his eyes to it, and with attention heed all the parts of it. The picture or clock may be so placed, that they may come in his way every day; but yet he will have but a confused idea of all the parts they are made up of, till he applies himself with attention to consider them each in particular.

8. *Ideas of reflection later, because they need attention.*—And hence we see the reason why it is pretty late before most children get ideas of the operations of their own minds; and some have not any very clear or perfect ideas of the greatest part of them all their lives. Because, though they pass there continually, yet, like floating visions, they make not deep impressions enough to leave in the mind clear, distinct, lasting ideas, till the understanding turns inward upon itself, reflects on its own operations, and makes them the object of its own contemplation. Children, when they come first into it, are surrounded with a world of new things, which, by a constant solicitation of their senses, draw the mind constantly to them, forward to take notice of new, and apt to be delighted with the variety of changing objects. Thus the first years are usually employed and diverted in looking abroad. Men's business in them is to acquaint themselves with what is to be found without; and so, growing up in a constant attention to outward sensations, seldom make any considerable reflection on what passes within them till they come to be of riper years; and some scarce ever at all.

9. *The soul begins to have ideas when it begins to perceive.*—To ask, at what time a man has first any ideas, is to ask when he begins to perceive; having ideas, and perception, being the same thing. I know it is an opinion, that the soul always thinks; and that it has the actual perception of ideas in itself constantly, as long as it exists; and that actual thinking is as inseparable from the soul, as actual extension is from the body: which if true, to enquire after the beginning of a man's ideas is the same as to enquire after the beginning of his soul. For by this account, soul and its ideas, as body and its extension, will begin to exist both at the same time.

* * *

CHAPTER 2. OF SIMPLE IDEAS

1. *Uncompounded appearances.*—The better to understand the nature, manner, and extent of our knowledge, one thing is carefully to be observed concerning the ideas we have; and that is, that some of them are *simple*, and some *complex*.

Though the qualities that affect our senses are, in the things themselves, so united and blended that there is no separation, no distance between them; yet it is plain the ideas they produce in the mind enter by the senses simple and unmixed. For though the sight and touch often take in from the same object at the same time different ideas; as a man sees at once motion and colour, the hand feels softness and warmth in the same piece of wax; yet the simple ideas thus united in the same subject are as perfectly distinct as those that come in by different senses. The coldness and hardness which a man feels in a piece of ice being as distinct ideas in the mind as the smell and whiteness of a lily, or as the taste of sugar and smell of a rose: and there is nothing can be plainer to a man than the clear and distinct perception he has of those simple ideas; which, being each in itself uncompounded, contains in it nothing but *one uniform appearance or conception in the mind*, and is not distinguishable into different ideas.

2. *The mind can neither make nor destroy them.*—These simple ideas, the materials of all our knowledge, are suggested and furnished to the mind only by those two ways above mentioned, viz., sensation and reflection. When the understanding is once stored with these simple ideas, it has the power to repeat, compare, and unite them, even to an almost infinite variety, and so can make at pleasure new complex ideas. But it is not in the power of the most exalted wit or enlarged understanding, by any quickness or variety of thought, to *invent* or *frame* one new simple idea in the mind, not taken in by the ways before mentioned; nor can any force of the understanding *destroy* those that are there. The dominion of man in this little world of his own understanding, being much-what the same as it is in the great world of visible things, wherein his power, however managed by art and skill, reaches no farther than to compound and divide the materials that are made to his hand, but can do nothing towards the making the least particle of new matter, or destroying one atom of what is already in being. The same inability will every one find in himself, who shall go about to fashion in his understanding any simple idea not received in by his senses from external objects, or by reflection from the operations of his own mind about them. I would have any one try to fancy any taste which had never affected his palate, or frame the idea of a scent he had never smelt; and when he can do this, I will also conclude, that a blind man hath ideas of colours, and a deaf man true distinct notions of sounds.

3. *Only the qualities that affect the sense are imaginable.*—This is the reason why, though we cannot believe it impossible to God to make a creature with other organs, and more ways to convey into the understanding the notice of corporeal things than those five, as they are usually counted, which he has given to man—yet I think it is *not possible* for any one to imagine any other qualities in bodies, howsoever constituted, whereby they can be taken notice of, besides sounds, tastes, smells, visible and tangible qualities. And had mankind been made with but four senses, the qualities then which are the object of the fifth sense, had been as far from our notice, imagination, and conception, as now any belonging to a sixth, seventh, or eighth sense, can possibly be: which, whether yet some other creatures, in some other parts of this vast and stupendous universe, may not have, will be a great presumption to deny. He that will not set himself proudly at the top of all things, but will consider the immensity of this fabric, and the great variety that is to be found in this little and inconsiderable part of it which he has to do with, may be apt to

think, that in other mansions of it there may be other and different intelligible beings, of whose faculties he has as little knowledge or apprehension, as a worm shut up in one drawer of a cabinet hath of the senses or understanding of a man; such variety and excellency being suitable to the wisdom and power of the Maker. I have here followed the common opinion of man's having but five senses, though perhaps there may be justly counted more, but either supposition serves equally to my present purpose.

CHAPTER 3. OF IDEAS OF ONE SENSE

1. *Division of simple ideas.*—The better to conceive the ideas we receive from sensation, it may not be amiss for us to consider them in reference to the different ways whereby they make their approaches to our minds, and make themselves perceivable by us.

First, then, There are some which come into our minds *by one sense only*.

Secondly. There are others that convey themselves into the mind *by more senses than one*.

Thirdly. Others that are from *reflection only*.

Fourthly. There are some that make themselves way, and are suggested to the mind *by all the ways of sensation and reflection*.

We shall consider them apart under these several heads.

Ideas of one sense. There are some ideas which have admittance only through one sense, which is peculiarly adapted to receive them. Thus light and colours, as white, red, yellow, blue, with their several degrees or shades and mixtures, as green, scarlet, purple, sea-green, and the rest come in only by the eyes; all kinds of noises, sounds, and tones, only by the ears; the several tastes and smells, by the nose and palate. And if these organs, or the nerves which are the conduits to convey them from without to their audience in the brain, the mind's presence-room (as I may so call it), are, any of them, so disordered as not to perform their functions, they have no postern to be admitted by, no other way to bring themselves into view, and be perceived by the understanding.

The most considerable of those belonging to the touch are heat, and cold, and solidity; all the rest, consisting almost wholly in the sensible configuration, as smooth and rough; or else, more or less firm adhesion of the parts, as hard and soft, tough and brittle, are obvious enough.

2. *Few simple ideas have names.*—I think it will be needless to enumerate all the particular simple ideas belonging to each sense. Nor indeed is it possible if we would, there being a great many more of them belonging to most of the senses than we have names for. The variety of smells, which are as many almost, if not more than species of bodies in the world, do most of them want names. Sweet and stinking commonly serve our turn for these ideas, which in effect is little more than to call them pleasing or displeasing; though the smell of a rose and violet, both sweet, are certainly very distinct ideas. Nor are the different tastes that by our palates we receive ideas of, much better provided with names. Sweet, bitter, sour, harsh, and salt, are almost all the epithets we have to denominate that numberless variety of relishes which are to be found distinct, not only in almost every sort of creatures, but in the different parts of the same plant, fruit, or animal. The same may be said of colours and sounds. I shall therefore, in the account of simple ideas I am here giving, content myself to set down only such as are most material to our present purpose, or are in themselves less apt to be taken notice of, though they are very frequently the ingredients of our complex ideas; amongst which, I think, I may well account solidity, which therefore I shall treat of in the next chapter.

CHAPTER 4. OF SOLIDITY

1. *We receive this idea from touch.*—The idea of solidity we receive by our touch; and it arises from the resistance which we find in body to the entrance of any other body into the place it possesses, till it has left it. There is no idea which we receive more constantly from sensation than solidity. Whether we move or rest, in what posture soever we are, we always feel something under us that supports us, and hinders our farther sinking downwards; and the bodies which we daily handle make us perceive that whilst they remain between them, they do, by an insurmountable force, hinder the approach of the parts of our hands that press them. *That which thus hinders the approach of two bodies, when they are moving one towards another, I call solidity.* I will not dispute whether this acceptation of the word solid be nearer to its original signification than that which mathematicians use it in: it suffices that, I think, the common notion of solidity will allow, if not justify, this use of it; but if any one think it better to call it *impenetrability*, he has my consent. Only I have thought the term solidity the more proper to express this idea, not only because of its vulgar use in that sense, but also because it carries something more of positive in it than impenetrability, which is negative, and is, perhaps, more a consequence of solidity than solidity itself. This, of all other, seems the idea most intimately connected with and essential to body, so as nowhere else to be found or imagined, but only in matter; and though our senses take no notice of it, but in masses of matter, of a bulk sufficient to cause a sensation in us; yet the mind, having once got this idea from such grosser sensible bodies, traces it farther, and considers it, as well as figure, in the minutest particle of matter that can exist, and finds it inseparably inherent in body, wherever or however modified.

2. *Solidity fills space.*—This is the idea which belongs to body, whereby we conceive it to fill space. The idea of which filling of space is,—that where we imagine any space taken up by a solid substance, we conceive it so to possess it, that it excludes all other solid substances; and will for ever hinder any other two bodies, that move towards one another in a straight line, from coming to touch one another, unless it removes from between them in a line not parallel to that which they move in. This idea of it, the bodies which we ordinarily handle sufficiently furnish us with.

3. *Distinct from space.*—This resistance, whereby it keeps other bodies out of the space which it possesses, is so great, that no force, how great soever, can surmount it. All the bodies in the world, pressing a drop of water on all sides, will never be able to overcome the resistance which it will make, as soft as it is, to their approaching one another, till it be removed out of their way: whereby our idea of solidity is distinguished both from pure space, which is capable neither of resistance nor motion, and from the ordinary idea of hardness. For a man may conceive two bodies at a distance so as they may approach one another without touching or displacing any solid thing till their superficies come to meet; whereby, I think, we have the clear idea of space without solidity. For (not to go so far as annihilation of any particular body) I ask, whether a man cannot have the idea of the motion of one single body alone, without any other succeeding immediately into its place? I think it is evident he can: the idea of motion in one body no more including the idea of motion in another, than the idea of a square figure in one body includes the idea of a square figure in another. I do not ask, whether bodies do so exist, that the motion of one body cannot really be without the motion of another? To determine this either way is to beg the question for or against a *vacuum*. But my question is, whether one cannot have the *idea* of one body moved, whilst others are at rest?

And I think this no one will deny: if so, then the place it deserted gives us the idea of pure space without solidity, whereinto another body may enter without either resistance or protrusion of anything. When the sucker in a pump is drawn, the space it filled in the tube is certainly the same, whether any other body follows the motion of the sucker or no; nor does it imply a contradiction that upon the motion of one body, another that is only contiguous to it should not follow it. The necessity of such a motion is built only on the supposition, that the world is full, but not on the distinct *ideas* of space and solidity; which are as different as resistance and not resistance, protrusion and not protrusion. And that men have ideas of space without body, their very disputes a vacuum plainly demonstrate as is showed in another place.

4. *From hardness.*—Solidity is hereby also differenced from hardness, in that solidity consists in repletion, and so an utter exclusion of other bodies out of the space it possesses; but hardness, in a firm cohesion of the parts of matter, making up masses of a sensible bulk, so that the whole does not easily change its figure. And, indeed, hard and soft are names that we give to things only in relation to the constitutions of our own bodies; that being generally called hard by us which will put us to pain sooner than change figure by the pressure of any part of our bodies; and that, on the contrary, soft which changes the situation of its parts upon an easy and unpainful touch.

But this difficulty of changing the situation of the sensible parts amongst themselves, or of the figure of the whole, gives no more solidity to the hardest body in the world than to the softest; nor is an adamant one jot more solid than water. For though the two flat sides of two pieces of marble will more easily approach each other, between there is nothing but water or air, than if there be a diamond between them; yet it is not that the parts of the diamond are more solid than those of water, or resist more, but because the parts of water being more easily separable from each other, they will by a side-motion be more easily removed and give way to the approach of the two pieces of marble: but if they could be kept from making place by that side-motion, they would eternally hinder the approach of these two pieces of marble as much as the diamond. The softest body in the world will as invincibly resist the coming together of any two other bodies, if it be not put out of the way, but remain between them, as the hardest that can be found or imagined. He that shall fill a yielding soft body well with air or water will quickly find its resistance: and he that thinks that nothing but bodies that are hard can keep his hands from approaching one another, may be pleased to make a trial with the air enclosed in a football. The experiment I have been told was made at Florence, with a hollow globe of gold filled with water, and exactly closed, farther shows the solidity of so soft a body as water. For the golden globe thus filled being put into a press which was driven by the extreme force of screws, the water made its way through the pores of that very close metal, and finding no room for a nearer approach of its particles within, got to the outside, where it rose like a dew, and so fell in drops before the sides of the globe could be made to yield to the violent compression of the engine that squeezed it.

5. *On solidity depend impulse, resistance, and protrusion.*—By this idea of solidity is the extension of body distinguished from the extension of space. The extension of body being nothing but the cohesion or continuity of solid, separable parts; and the extension of space, the continuity of unsolid, inseparable, and immovable parts. Upon the solidity of bodies also depend their mutual impulse, resistance, and protrusion. Of pure space then, and solidity, there are several (amongst which I confess myself one) who persuade themselves they have clear and distinct ideas; and that they can think on

space without anything in it that resists or is protruded by body. This is the idea of pure space, which they think they have as clear as any idea they can have of the extension of body . . .

6. *What solidity is.*—If any one asks me, *what this solidity is,* I send him to his senses to inform him: let him put a flint or a football between his hands, and then endeavour to join them, and he will know. If he thinks this is not a sufficient explanation of solidity, what it is, and wherein it consists, I promise to tell him what it is, and wherein it consists, when he tells me what thinking is, or wherein it consists; or explains to me what extension or motion is, which perhaps seems much easier. The simple ideas we have are such as experience teaches them to us; but if, beyond that, we endeavour by words to make them clearer in the mind, we shall succeed no better than if we went about to clear up the darkness of a blind man's mind by talking, and to discourse into him the ideas of light and colours. The reason of this I shall show in another place.

Chapter 5. Of Simple Ideas of Divers Senses

Ideas received both by seeing and touching.—The ideas we get by more than one sense are of space or extension, figure, rest and motion: for these make perceivable impressions both on the eyes and touch; and we can receive and convey into our minds the ideas of the extension, figure, motion, and rest of bodies, both by seeing and feeling. But having occasion to speak more at large of these in another place, I here only enumerate them.

Chapter 6. Of Simple Ideas of Reflection

1. *Simple ideas are the operations of the mind about its other ideas.*—The mind, receiving the ideas mentioned in the foregoing chapters from without, when it turns its view inward upon itself, and observes its own actions about those ideas it has, takes from thence other ideas, which are as capable to be the objects of its contemplation as any of those it received from foreign things.

2. *The idea of perception, and idea of willing, we have from reflection.*—The two great and principal actions of the mind, which are most frequently considered, and which are so frequent that every one that pleases may take notice of them in himself, are these two:—*Perception* or *Thinking*, and *Volition* or *Willing*. The power of thinking is called the *Understanding* and the power of volition is called the *Will*; and these two powers of abilities in the mind are denominated *faculties*. Of some of the *modes* of these simple ideas of reflection, such as are *remembrance*, *discerning*, *reasoning*, *judging*, *knowledge*, *faith*, *etc.*, I shall have occasion to speak hereafter.

Chapter 7. Of Simple Ideas of Both Sensation and Reflection

1. *Ideas of pleasure and pain.*—There be other simple ideas which convey themselves into the mind by all the ways of sensation and reflection; viz., *pleasure* or *delight*, and its opposite, *pain* or *uneasiness*; *power*; *existence*; *unity*.

2. *Mix with almost all our other ideas.*—Delight or uneasiness, one or other of them, join themselves to almost all our ideas both of sensation and reflection; and there is scarce any affection of our senses from without, any retired thought of our mind within, which is not able to produce in us pleasure or pain. By pleasure and pain, I would be understood to signify whatsoever delights or molests us; whether it arises from the thoughts of our minds, or anything operating on our bodies. For whether we call it satisfaction, delight, pleasure, happiness, etc., on the one side, or uneasiness, trouble, pain, torment, anguish, misery, etc., on the other, they are still but different degrees of the same thing, and belong to the ideas of pleasure and pain, delight or uneasiness; which are the names I shall most commonly use for those two sorts of ideas.

3. *As motives of our actions.*—The infinite wise Author of our being, . . . to excite us to these actions of thinking and motion that we are capable of, has been pleased to join to several thoughts and several sensations a perception of delight. If this were wholly separated from all our outward sensations and inward thoughts, we should have no reason to prefer one thought or action to another, negligence to attention, or motion to rest. And so we should neither stir our bodies, nor employ our minds, but let our thoughts (if I may so call it) run adrift, without any direction or design; and suffer the ideas of our minds, like unregarded shadows, to make their appearances there as it happened, without attending to them. In which state man, however furnished with the faculties of understanding and will, would be a very idle, unactive creature, and pass his time only in a lazy, lethargic dream . . .

4. *An end and use of pain.*—Pain has the same efficacy and use to set us on work that pleasure has, we being as ready to employ our faculties to avoid that, as to pursue this: only this is worth our consideration, that pain is often produced by the same objects and ideas that produce pleasure in us . . . Thus heat, that is very agreeable to us in one degree, by a little greater increase of it proves no ordinary torment; and the most pleasant of all sensible objects, light itself, if there be too much of it, if increased beyond a due proportion to our eyes, causes a very painful sensation. Which is wisely and favourably so ordered by nature, that when any object does by the vehemency of its operation disorder the instruments of sensation, whose structures cannot but be very nice and delicate, we might by the pain be warned to withdraw before the organ be quite put out of order, and so be unfitted for its proper functions for the future.

* * *

7. *Ideas of existence and unity.*—Existence and unity are two other ideas that are suggested to the understanding by every object without, and every idea within. When ideas are in our minds, we consider them as being actually there, as well as we consider things to be actually without us: which is, that they exist, or have existence. And whatever we can consider as one thing, whether a real being or idea, suggests to the understanding the idea of unity.

8. *Idea of power.*—Power also is another of those ideas which we receive from sensation and reflection. For, observing in ourselves that we do and can think, and that we can at pleasure move several parts of our bodies which were at rest, the effects also that natural bodies are able to produce in one another occurring every moment to our senses, we both these ways get the idea of power.

9. *Idea of succession.*—Besides these there is another idea, which though suggested by our senses yet is more constantly offered us by what passes in our own minds; and that is the idea of succession. For if we look immediately into ourselves, and reflect

on what is observable there, we shall find our ideas always, whilst we are awake or have any thought, passing in train, one going and another coming without intermission.

10. *Simple ideas the materials of all our knowledge.*—These, if they are not all, are at least (as I think) the most considerable of those simple ideas which the mind has, and out of which is made all its other knowledge: all of which it receives only by the two forementioned ways of sensation and reflection.

Nor let any one think these too narrow bounds for the capacious mind of man to expatiate in, which takes its flight farther than the stars, and cannot be confined by the limits of the world. I grant all this, but desire any one to assign any *simple idea* which is not received from one of those inlets before mentioned, or any *complex idea* not made out of those simple ones.

Nor will it be so strange to think these few simple ideas sufficient to employ the quickest thought or largest capacity, and to furnish the materials of all that various knowledge and more various fancies and opinions of all mankind, if we consider how many words may be made out of the various composition of twenty-four letters; or if, going one step farther, we will but reflect on the variety of combinations may be made with barely one of the above-mentioned ideas, viz., number, whose stock is inexhaustible and truly infinite: and what a large and immense field doth extension alone afford the mathematicians?

Chapter 8. Some Further Considerations Concerning Our Simple Ideas of Sensation

* * *

7. *Ideas in the mind, qualities in bodies.*—To discover the nature of our ideas the better, and to discourse of them intelligibly, it will be convenient to distinguish them *as they are ideas or perceptions in our minds, and as they are modifications of matter in the bodies that cause such perceptions in us:* that so we may not think (as perhaps usually is done) that they are exactly the images and resemblances of something inherent in the subject; most of those of sensation being in the mind no more the likeness of something existing without us than the names that stand for them are the likeness of our ideas, which yet upon hearing they are apt to excite in us.

8. *Our ideas and the qualities of bodies.*—Whatsoever the mind perceives *in itself*, or is the immediate object of perception, thought, or understanding, that I call *idea*; and the power to produce any idea in our mind, I call *quality* of the subject wherein that power is. Thus a snowball having the power to produce in us the ideas of white, cold, and round, the powers to produce those ideas in us as they are in the snowball, I call qualities; and as they are sensations or perceptions in our understandings, I call them ideas; which *ideas*, if I speak of them sometimes as in the things themselves, I would be understood to mean those qualities in the objects which produce them in us.

9. *Primary qualities of bodies.*—Qualities thus considered in bodies are, *First*, such as are utterly inseparable from the body, in what estate soever it be; such as, in all the alterations and changes it suffers, all the force can be used upon it, it constantly keeps; and such as sense constantly finds in every particle of matter which has bulk enough to be perceived, and the mind finds inseparable from every particle of matter, though less than to make itself singly be perceived by our senses: v.g., take a grain of wheat, divide it into two parts, each part has still solidity, extension, figure, and mobility;

divide it again, and it retains still the same qualities: and so divide it on, till the parts become insensible; they must retain still each of them all those qualities . . . These I call *original* or *primary qualities* of body, which I think we may observe to produce simple ideas in us, viz., solidity, extension, figure, motion or rest, and number.

10. *Secondary qualities of bodies.*—Secondly, such qualities, which in truth are nothing in the objects themselves, but powers to produce various sensations in us by their primary qualities, i.e., by the bulk, figure, texture, and motion of their insensible parts, as colours, sounds, tastes, etc., these I call *secondary qualities*. To these might be added a third sort, which are allowed to be barely powers, though they are as much real qualities in the subject as those which I, to comply with the common way of speaking, call qualities, but, for distinction, secondary qualities. For the power in fire to produce a new colour or consistence in *wax* or *clay* by its primary qualities, is as much a quality in fire as the power it has to produce in me a new idea or sensation of warmth or burning, which I felt not before, by the same primary qualities, viz., the bulk, texture, and motion of its insensible parts.

11. *How bodies produce ideas in us.*—The next thing to be considered is, how bodies produce ideas in us; and that is manifestly by impulse, the only way which we can conceive bodies operate in.

12. *By motions, external, and in our organism.*—If, then, external objects be not united to our minds when they produce ideas in it, and yet we perceive these original qualities in such of them as singly fall under senses, it is evident that some motion must be thence continued by our nerves or animal spirits, by some parts of our bodies, to the brains or the seat of sensation, there to produce in our minds the particular ideas we have of them. And since the extension, figure, number, and motion of bodies of an observable bigness, may be perceived at a distance by the sight, it is evident some singly imperceptible bodies must come from them to the eyes, and thereby convey to the brain some motion which produces these ideas which we have of them in us.

13. *How secondary qualities produce their ideas.*—After the same manner that the ideas of these original qualities are produced in us, we may conceive that the ideas of *secondary* qualities are also produced, viz., by the operation of insensible particles on our senses . . . The different motions and figures, bulk and number of such particles, affecting the several organs of our senses, produce in us those different sensations which we have from the colours and smells of bodies; v.g., that a violet, by the impulse of such insensible particle, of matter of peculiar figures and bulks, and in different degrees and modifications of their motions, causes the ideas of the blue colour and sweet scent of that flower to be produced in our minds. It being no more impossible to conceive that God should annex such ideas to such motions with which they have no similitude, than that he should annex the idea of pain to the motion of a piece of steel dividing our flesh, with which that idea hath no resemblance.

14. *They depend on the primary qualities.*—What I have said concerning colours and smells may be understood also of tastes and sounds, and other the like sensible qualities; which, whatever reality we by mistake attribute to them, are in truth nothing in the objects themselves, but powers to produce various sensations in us, and depend on those primary qualities, viz., bulk, figure, texture, and motion of parts, as I have said.

15. *Ideas of primary qualities are resemblances; of secondary, not.*—From whence I think it is easy to draw this observation, that the ideas of primary qualities of bodies are resemblances of them, and their patterns do really exist in the bodies themselves; but the ideas produced in us by these secondary qualities have no resemblance of them at all. There is nothing like our ideas existing in the bodies themselves. They are,

in the bodies we denominate from them, only a power to produce those sensations in us: and what is sweet, blue, or warm in idea, is but the certain bulk, figure, and motion of the insensible parts in the bodies themselves, which we call so.

16. *Examples.*—Flame is denominated hot and light; snow, white and cold; and manna, white and sweet, from the ideas they produce in us. Which qualities are commonly thought to be the same in those bodies that those ideas are in us, the one the perfect resemblance of the other, as they are in a mirror; and it would by most men be judged very extravagant, if one should say otherwise. And yet he that will consider that the same fire that at one distance produces in us the sensation of warmth, does at a nearer approach produce in us the far different sensation of pain, ought to bethink himself what reason he has to say, that his idea of warmth which was produced in him by the fire, is *actually in the fire*; and his idea of pain which the same fire produced in him the same way is not in the fire. Why is whiteness and coldness in snow, and pain not, when it produces the one and the other idea in us, and can do neither, but by the bulk, figure, number, and motion of its solid parts?

17. *The ideas of the primary alone really exist.*—The particular bulk, number, figure, and motion of the parts of fire or snow are really in them, whether any one's senses perceive them or no; and therefore they may be called *real* qualities, because they really exist in those bodies. But light, heat, whiteness, or coldness, are no more really in them than sickness or pain is in manna. Take away the sensation of them; let not the eyes see light or colours, nor the ears hear sounds; let the palate not taste, nor the nose smell; and all colours, tastes, odours, and sounds, *as they are such particular ideas*, vanish and cease, and are reduced to their causes, i.e., bulk, figure, and motion of parts.

18. *Secondary exist only as modes of the primary.*—A piece of manna of a sensible bulk is able to produce in us the idea of a round or square figure; and, by being removed from one place to another, the idea of motion. This idea of motion represents it as it really is in the manna moving; a circle or square are the same, whether in idea or existence, in the mind or in the manna; and this, both motion and figure are really in the manna, whether we take notice of them or no: this everybody is ready to agree to. Besides, manna, by the bulk, figure, texture, and motion of its parts, has a power to produce the sensations of sickness, and sometimes of acute pains or gripings, in us. That these ideas of sickness and pain are not in the manna, but effects of its operations on us, and are nowhere when we feel them not: this also every one readily agrees to. And yet men are hardly to be brought to think that sweetness and whiteness are not really in manna, which are but the effects of the operations of manna by the motion, size, and figure of its particles on the eyes and palate: as the pain and sickness caused by manna are confessedly nothing but the effects of its operations on the stomach . . . Why the pain and sickness, ideas that are the effects of manna, should be thought to be nowhere when they are not felt; and yet the sweetness and whiteness, effects of the same manna on other parts of the body, by ways equally as unknown, should be thought to exist in the manna, when they are not seen nor tasted, would need some reason to explain.

19. *Examples.*—Let us consider the red and white colours in porphyry: hinder light but from striking on it, and its colours vanish; it no longer produces any such ideas in us. Upon the return of light, it produces these appearances on us again. Can any one think any real alterations are made in the porphyry by the presence or absence of light, and that those ideas of whiteness and redness are really in porphyry in the light, when it is plain *it has no colour in the dark?* It has indeed such a configuration of particles, both night and day, as are apt, by the rays of light rebounding from some parts of that hard

stone, to produce in us the idea of redness, and from others the idea of whiteness: but whiteness or redness are not in it at any time, but such a texture that hath the power to produce such a sensation in us.

* * *

22. *Excursion into natural philosophy.*—I have, in what just goes before, been engaged in physical enquiries a little farther than perhaps I intended. But it being necessary to make the nature of sensation a little understood, and to make the difference between the *qualities* in bodies and the *ideas* produced by them in the mind to be distinctly conceived, without which it were impossible to discourse intelligibly of them, I hope I shall be pardoned this little excursion into natural philosophy, it being necessary in our present enquiry to distinguish the *primary* and *real* qualities of bodies, which are always in them (viz., solidity, extension, figure, number, and motion or rest, and are sometimes perceived by us, viz., when the bodies they are in are big enough singly to be discerned), from those *secondary* and *imputed* qualities, which are but the powers of several combinations of those primary ones, when they operate without being distinctly discerned: whereby we also may come to know what ideas are, and what are not, resemblances of something really existing in the bodies we denominate from them.

23. *Three sorts of qualities in bodies.*—The qualities then that are in bodies, rightly considered, are of three sorts:

First, the bulk, figure, number, situation, and motion or rest of their solid parts. Those are in them, whether we perceive them or no; and when they are of that size that we can discover them, we have by these an idea of the thing as it is in itself, as is plain in artificial things. These I call *primary qualities*.

Secondly, the power that is in any body, by reason of its insensible primary qualities, to operate after a peculiar manner on any of our senses, and thereby produce in us the different ideas of several colours, sounds, smells, tastes, etc. These are usually called *sensible qualities*.

Thirdly, the power that is in any body, by reason of the particular constitution of its primary qualities, to make such a change in the bulk, figure, texture, and motion of *another body*, as to make it operate on our senses differently from what it did before. Thus the sun has a power to make wax white, and fire, to make lead fluid. These are usually called *powers*.

The first of these, as has been said, I think may be properly called real, original, or primary qualities, because they are in the things themselves, whether they are perceived or no: and upon their different modifications it is that the secondary qualities depend.

The other two are only powers to act differently upon other things, which powers result from the different modifications of those primary qualities.

24. *The first are resemblances; the second thought to be resemblances, but are not; the third neither are, nor are thought so.*—But though these two latter sorts of qualities are powers barely, and nothing but powers, relating to several other bodies, and resulting from the different modifications of the original qualities, yet they are generally otherwise thought of . . . V.g., the idea of heat or light which we receive by our eyes or touch from the sun, are commonly thought real qualities existing in the sun, and something more than mere powers in it. But when we consider the sun in reference to wax, which it melts or blanches, we look upon the whiteness and softness produced in the wax, not as qualities in the sun, but effects produced by powers in it: whereas, if rightly

considered, these qualities of light and warmth, which are perceptions in me when I am warmed or enlightened by the sun, are no otherwise in the sun than the changes made in the wax, when it is blanched or melted, are in the sun. They are all of them equally powers in the sun, depending on its primary qualities . . .

25. *Why the secondary are ordinarily taken for real qualities, and not for bare powers.*—The reason why the one are ordinarily taken for real qualities, and the other only for bare powers, seems to be because the ideas we have of distinct colours, sounds, etc., containing nothing at all in them of bulk, figure, or motion, we are not apt to think them the effects of these primary qualities which appear not to our senses to operate in their production, and with which they have not any apparent congruity, or conceivable connexion. Hence it is that we are so forward to imagine that those ideas are the resemblances of something really existing in the objects themselves . . . But, in the other case, in the operations of bodies changing the qualities one of another, we plainly discover that the quality produced hath commonly no resemblance with anything in the thing producing it; wherefore we look on it as a bare effect of power . . .

* * *

CHAPTER 9. OF PERCEPTION

1. *Perception the first simple idea of reflection.*—PERCEPTION, as it is the first faculty of the mind exercised about our ideas; so it is the first and simplest idea we have from reflection, and is by some called thinking in general. Though thinking, in the propriety of the English tongue, signifies that sort of operation in the mind about its ideas, wherein the mind is active; where it, with some degree of voluntary attention, considers anything. For in bare naked perception, the mind is, for the most part, only passive; and what it perceives, it cannot avoid perceiving.

2. *Reflection alone can give us the idea of what, perception is.*—What perception is, every one will know better by reflecting on what he does himself, when he sees, hears, feels, etc., or thinks, than by any discourse of mine. Whoever reflects on what passes in his own mind cannot miss it. And if he does not reflect, all the words in the world cannot make him have any notion of it.

3. *Arises in sensation only when the mind notices the organic impression.*—This is certain, that whatever alterations are made in the body, if they reach not the mind; whatever impressions are made on the outward parts, if they are not taken notice of within, there is no perception. Fire may burn our bodies with no other effect than it does a billet, unless the motion be continued to the brain, and there the sense of heat, or idea of pain, produced in the mind; wherein consists actual perception.

4. *Impulse on the organ insufficient.*—How often may a man observe in himself, that whilst his mind is intently employed in the contemplation of some objects, and curiously surveying some ideas that are there, it takes no notice of impressions of sounding bodies made upon the organ of hearing, with the same alteration that uses to be for the producing the idea of sound? A sufficient impulse there may be on the organ; but it not reaching the observation of the mind, there follows no perception: and though the motion that uses to produce the idea of sound be made in the ear, yet no sound is heard. Want of sensation, in this case, is not through any defect in the organ, or that the man's ears are less affected than at other times when he does hear: but that which uses to produce the idea, though conveyed in by the usual organ, not being taken notice of in the understanding, and so imprinting no idea in the mind, there follows no sensation.

So that wherever there is sense or perception, there some idea is actually produced, and present in the understanding.

* * *

8. *Sensations often changed by the judgment.*—We are further to consider concerning perception, that the ideas we receive by sensation are often, in grown people, altered by the judgment, without our taking notice of it. When we set before our eyes a round globe of any uniform colour, v.g., gold, alabaster, or jet, it is certain that the idea thereby imprinted on our mind is of a flat circle, variously shadowed, with several degrees of light and brightness coming to our eyes. But we having, by use, been accustomed to perceive what kind of appearance convex bodies are wont to make in us; what alterations are made in the reflections of light by the difference of the sensible figures of bodies;—the judgment presently, by an habitual custom, alters the appearances into their causes. So that from that which is truly variety of shadow or colour, collecting the figure, it makes it pass for a mark of figure, and frames to itself the perception of a convex figure and an uniform colour; when the idea we receive from thence is only a plane variously coloured, as is evident in painting. To which purpose I shall here insert a problem of that very ingenious and studious promoter of real knowledge, the learned and worthy Mr. Molyneux, which he was pleased to send me in a letter some months since; and it is this:—"Suppose a man born blind, and now adult, and taught by his touch to distinguish between a cube and a sphere of the same metal, and nighly of the same bigness, so as to tell, when he felt one and the other, which is the cube, which the sphere. Suppose then the cube and sphere placed on a table, and the blind man be made to see: *quære* whether *by his sight, before he touched them*, he could now distinguish and tell which is the globe, which the cube?" To which the acute and judicious proposer answers, "Not. For, though he has obtained the experience of how a globe, how a cube affects his touch, yet he has not yet obtained the experience, that what affects his touch so or so, must affect his sight so or so; or that a protuberant angle in the cube, that pressed his hand unequally, shall appear to his eye as it does in the cube."—I agree with this thinking gentleman, whom I am proud to call my friend, in his answer to this problem; and am of opinion that the blind man, at first sight, would not be able with certainty to say which was the globe, which the cube, whilst he only saw them; though he could unerringly name them by his touch, and certainly distinguish them by the difference of their figures felt. This I have set down, and leave with my reader, as an occasion for him to consider how much he may be beholden to experience, improvement, and acquired notions, where he thinks he had not the least use of, or help from them. And the rather, because this observing gentleman further adds, that "having, upon the occasion of my book, proposed this to divers very ingenious men, he hardly ever met with one that at first gave the answer to it which he thinks true, till by hearing his reasons they were convinced."

* * *

CHAPTER 12. OF COMPLEX IDEAS

1. *Made by the mind out of simple ones.*—We have hitherto considered those ideas, in the reception whereof the mind is only passive, which are those simple ones received from sensation and reflection before mentioned, whereof the mind cannot

make one to itself, nor have any idea which does not wholly consist of them. [But as the mind is wholly passive in the reception of all its simple ideas, so it exerts several acts of its own, whereby out of its simple ideas, as the materials and foundations of the rest, the other are framed. The acts of the mind wherein it exerts its power over its simple ideas are chiefly these three: (1) Combining several simple ideas into one compound one; and thus all *complex ideas* are made. (2) The second is bringing two ideas, whether simple or complex, together, and setting them by one another, so as to take a view of them at once, without uniting them into one; by which it gets all its *ideas of relations*. (3) The third is separating them from all other ideas that accompany them in their real existence; this is called abstraction: and thus all its *general ideas* are made. This shows man's power and its way of operation to be much the same in the material and intellectual world. For, the materials in both being such as he has no power over, either to make or destroy, all that man can do is either to unite them together, or to set them by one another, or wholly separate them. I shall here begin with the first of these in the consideration of complex ideas, and come to the other two in their due places.] As simple ideas are observed to exist in several combinations united together, so the mind has a power to consider several of them united together as one idea; and that not only as they are united in external objects, but as itself has joined them. Ideas thus made up of several simple ones put together I call *complex*; such as are beauty, gratitude, a man, an army, the universe; which, though complicated of various simple ideas or complex ideas made up of simple ones, yet are, when the mind pleases, considered each by itself as one entire thing, and signified by one name.

2. *Made voluntarily.*—In this faculty of repeating and joining together its ideas, the mind has great power in varying and multiplying the objects of its thoughts infinitely beyond what sensation or reflection furnished it with: but all this still confined to those simple ideas which it received from those two sources, and which are the ultimate materials of all its compositions. For simple ideas are all from things themselves; and of these the mind can have no more nor other than what are suggested to it. It can have no other ideas of sensible qualities than what come from without by the senses, nor any ideas of other kind of operations of a thinking substance than what it finds in itself: but when it has once got these simple ideas, it is not confined barely to observation, and what offers itself from without; it can, by its own power, put together those ideas it has, and make new complex ones which it never received so united.

3. *Complex ideas are either modes, substances, or relations.*—COMPLEX IDEAS, however compounded and decompounded, though their number be infinite, and the variety endless wherewith they fill and entertain the thoughts of men, yet I think they may be all reduced under these three heads: 1. *Modes*. 2. *Substances*. 3. *Relations*.

4. *Ideas of modes.*—First, *Modes* I call such complex ideas which, however compounded, contain not in them the supposition of subsisting by themselves, but are considered as dependences on, or affections of substances; such as are the ideas signified by the words triangle, gratitude, murder, etc. And if in this I use the word mode in somewhat a different sense from its ordinary signification, I beg pardon; it being unavoidable in discourses differing from the ordinary received notions, either to make new words, or to use old words in somewhat a new signification: the latter whereof, in our present case, is perhaps the more tolerable of the two.

5. *Simple and mixed modes of simple ideas.*—Of these modes there are two sorts which deserve distinct consideration. First, there are some which are only variations or different combinations of the same simple idea, without the mixture of any other, as a dozen, or score; which are nothing but the ideas of so many distinct units added

together: and these I call *simple modes*, as being contained within the bounds of one simple idea. Secondly, there are others compounded of simple ideas of several kinds, put together to make one complex one; v.g., beauty, consisting of a certain composition of colour and figure, causing delight in the beholder; theft, which, being the concealed change of the possession of anything, without the consent of the proprietor, contains, as is visible, a combination of several ideas of several kinds: and these I call *mixed modes*.

6. *Ideas of substances, single or collective.*—Secondly, the ideas of *Substances* are such combinations of simple ideas as are taken to represent distinct particular things subsisting by themselves, in which the supposed or confused idea of substance, such as it is, is always the first and chief. Thus, if to substance be joined the simple idea of a certain dull whitish colour, with certain degrees of weight, hardness, ductility, and fusibility, we have the idea of lead; and a combination of the ideas of a certain sort of figure, with the powers of motion, thought, and reasoning, joined to substance, make the ordinary idea of a man. Now of substances also there are two sorts of ideas, one of single substances, as they exist separately, as of a man or a sheep; the other of several of those put together, as an army of men, or flock of sheep; which *collective* ideas of several substances thus put together, are as much each of them one single idea as that of a man or an unit.

7. *Ideas of relation.*—Thirdly, the last sort of complex ideas is that we call Relation, which consists in the consideration and comparing one idea with another. Of these several kinds we shall treat in their order.

8. *The abstrusest ideas we can have are all from two sources.*—If we will trace the progress of our minds, and with attention observe how it repeats, adds together, and unites its simple ideas received from sensation or reflection, it will lead us farther than at first perhaps we should have imagined. And I believe we shall find, if we warily observe the originals of our notions, that *even the most abstruse ideas*, how remote soever they may seem from sense, or from any operation of our own minds, are yet only such as the understanding frames to itself, by repeating and joining together ideas that it had either from objects of sense, or from its own operations about them: so that those even large and abstract ideas are *derived from sensation or reflection*, being no other than what the mind, by the ordinary use of its own faculties, employed about ideas received from objects of sense, or from the operations it observes in itself about them, may and does attain unto. This I shall endeavour to show in the ideas we have of space, time, and infinity, and some few other, that seem the most remote from those originals.

* * *

CHAPTER 21. OF POWER

1. *This idea how got.*—The mind being every day informed, by the senses, of the alteration of those simple ideas it observes in things without; and taking notice how one comes to an end and ceases to be, and another begins to exist which was not before; reflecting also, on what passes within itself, and observing a constant change of its ideas, sometimes by the impression of outward objects on the senses, and sometimes by the determination of its own choice; and concluding from what it has so constantly observed to have been, that the like changes will for the future be made in the same things by like agents, and by the like ways; considers in one thing the possibility of having any of its

simple ideas changed, and in another the possibility of making that change; and so comes by that idea which we call *power*. Thus we say, fire has a power to melt gold, i.e., to destroy the consistency of its insensible parts, and consequently its hardness, and make it fluid; and gold has a power to be melted: that the sun has a power to blanch wax; and wax a power to be blanched by the sun, whereby the yellowness is destroyed, and whiteness made to exist in its room. In which and the like cases, the power we consider is in reference to the change of perceivable ideas. For we cannot observe any alteration to be made in, or operation upon, anything, but by the observable change of its sensible ideas: nor conceive any alteration to be made, but by conceiving a change of some of its ideas.

2. *Power, active and passive.*—Power thus considered is twofold, viz., as able to make, or able to receive, any change: the one may be called *active*, and the other passive, power. Whether matter be not wholly destitute of active power, as its author, God, is truly above all passive power; and whether the intermediate state of created spirits be not that alone which is capable of both active and passive power, may be worth consideration. I shall not now enter into that enquiry: my present business being not to search into the original of power, but how we come by the *idea* of it. But since active powers make so great a part of our complex ideas of natural substances (as we shall see hereafter), yet they being not, perhaps, so truly active powers as our hasty thoughts are apt to represent them, I judge it not amiss, by this intimation, to direct our minds to the consideration of God and spirits, for the clearest idea of *active* power.

3. *Power includes relation.*—I confess power includes in it some kind of relation (a relation to action or change), as indeed, which of our ideas, of what kind soever, when attentively considered, does not? For our ideas of extension, duration, and number, do they not all contain in them a secret relation of the parts? Figure and motion have something relative in them much more visibly: and sensible qualities, as colours and smells, etc., what are they but the powers of different bodies in relation to our perception? And if considered in the things themselves, do they not depend on the bulk, figure, texture, and motion of the parts? All which include some kind of relation in them. Our idea therefore of power, I think, may well have a place amongst other *simple ideas*, and be considered as one of them, being one of those that make a principal ingredient in our complex ideas of substances, as we shall hereafter have occasion to observe.

4. *The clearest idea of active power had from spirit.*—We are abundantly furnished with the idea of passive power, by almost all sorts of sensible things. In most of them we cannot avoid observing their sensible qualities, nay, their very substances, to be in a continual flux: and therefore with reason we look on them as liable still to the same change. Nor have we of *active* power (which is the more proper signification of the word power) fewer instances. Since whatever change is observed, the mind must collect a power somewhere, able to make that change, as well as a possibility in the thing itself to receive it. But yet, if we will consider it attentively, bodies by our senses do not afford us so clear and distinct an idea of active power as we have from reflection on the operations of our minds. For all power relating to action, and there being but two sorts of action whereof we have any idea, viz., thinking and motion, let us consider whence we have the clearest ideas of the powers which produce these actions. (1) Of thinking, body affords us no idea at all: it is only from reflection that we have that. (2) Neither have we from body any idea of the beginning of motion. A body at rest affords us no idea of any active power to move; and when it is set in motion itself, that motion is rather a passion than an action in it. For when the ball

obeys the stroke of a billiard-stick, it is not any action of the ball, but bare passion. Also when by impulse it sets another ball in motion that lay in its way, it only communicates the motion it had received from another, and loses in itself so much as the other received: which gives us but a very obscure idea of an *active* power of moving in body, whilst we observe it only to *transfer*, but not *produce* any motion . . . The idea of the *beginning* of motion we have only from reflection on what passes in ourselves, where we find by experience, that, barely by willing it, barely by a thought of the mind, we can move the parts of our bodies which were before at rest. So that it seems to me, we have, from the observation of the operation of bodies by our senses, but a very imperfect, obscure idea of *active* power, since they afford us not any idea in themselves of the power to begin any action, either motion or thought. But if, from the impulse bodies are observed to make one upon another, any one thinks he has a clear idea of power, it serves as well to my purpose, sensation being one of those ways whereby the mind comes by its ideas: only I thought it worth while to consider here by the way, whether the mind doth not receive its idea of active power clearer from reflection on its own operations, than it doth from any external sensation.

* * *

The Funeral of Phocion, 1648, by Nicholas Poussin (1594–1665). In this classical-style painting, nature is depicted in geometrical terms that imply a sense of permanence. Locke believed that the complex ideas we have about such scenes are built up out of "a great number of the simple ideas conveyed in by the senses." (*The Louvre/Paris/© Photo R.M.N.*)

CHAPTER 23. OF OUR COMPLEX IDEAS OF SUBSTANCES

1. *Ideas of particular substances, how made.*—The mind being, as I have declared, furnished with a great number of the simple ideas conveyed in by the senses, as they are found in exterior things, or by reflection on its own operations, takes notice also, that a certain number of these simple ideas go constantly together; which being presumed to belong to one thing, and words being suited to common apprehensions, and made use of for quick dispatch, are called, so united in one subject, by one name; which, by inadvertency, we are apt afterward to talk of and consider as one simple idea, which indeed is a complication of many ideas together: because, as I have said, not imagining how these simple ideas can subsist by themselves, we accustom ourselves to suppose some *substratum* wherein they do subsist, and from which they do result, which therefore we call *substance*.

2. *Our obscure idea of substance in general.*—So that if any one will examine himself concerning his notion of pure substance in general, he will find he has no other idea of it at all, but only a supposition of he knows not what *support* of such qualities which are capable of producing simple ideas in us; which qualities are commonly called accidents. If any one should be asked, what is the subject wherein colour or weight inheres, he would have nothing to say, but the solid extended parts: and if he were demanded, what is it that that solidity and extension inhere in, he would not be in a much better case than the Indian before mentioned, who saying that the world was supported by a great elephant, was asked, what the elephant rested on; to which his answer was, a great tortoise: but being again pressed to know what gave support to the broad-backed tortoise, replied, *something, he knew not what*. And thus here, as in all other cases where we use words without having clear and distinct ideas, we talk like children; who being questioned what such a thing is which they know not, readily give this satisfactory answer, that it is *something*; which in truth signifies no more, when so used, either by children or men, but that they know not what; and that the thing they pretend to know, and talk of, is what they have no distinct idea of at all, and so are perfectly ignorant of it, and in the dark. The idea, then, we have, to which we give the general name substance, being nothing but the supposed, but unknown, support of those qualities we find existing, which we imagine cannot subsist *sine re substante*, without something to support them, we call that support *substantia*; which, according to the true import of the word, is, in plain English, standing under, or upholding.

3. *Of the sorts of substances.*—An obscure and relative idea of *substance in general* being thus made, we come to have the ideas of *particular sorts of substances*, by collecting *such* combinations of simple ideas as are, by experience and observation of men's senses, taken notice of to exist together, and are therefore supposed to flow from the particular internal constitution or unknown essence of that substance. Thus we come to have the ideas of a man, horse, gold, water, etc., of which substances, whether any one has any other *clear* idea, farther than of certain simple ideas coexisting together, I appeal to every one's own experience. It is the ordinary qualities observable in iron or a diamond, put together, that make the true complex idea of those substances, which a smith or a jeweller commonly knows better than a philosopher; who, whatever *substantial forms* he may talk of, has no other idea of those substances than what is framed by a collection of those simple ideas which are to be found in them. Only we must take notice, that our complex ideas of substances, besides all these simple ideas they are made up of, have always the confused idea of something to which they belong and in which they subsist. And therefore, when we speak of any sort of substance, we

say it is a thing having such or such qualities; as body is a thing that is extended, figured, and capable of motion; a spirit, a thing capable of thinking; and so hardness, friability, and power to draw iron, we say, are qualities to be found in a loadstone. These and the like fashions of speaking intimate that the substance is supposed always *something besides* the extension, figure, solidity, motion, thinking, or other observable ideas, though we know not what it is.

4. *No clear or distinct idea of substance in general.*—Hence, when we talk or think of any particular sort of corporeal substances, as horse, stone, etc., though the idea we have of either of them be but the complication or collection of those several simple ideas of sensible qualities which we use to find united in the thing called horse or stone; yet *because we cannot conceive how they should subsist alone, nor one in another*, we suppose them existing in, and supported by, some common subject; which support we denote by the name substance, though it be certain we have no clear or distinct idea of that thing we suppose a support.

5. *As clear an idea of spiritual substance as of corporeal substance.*—The same happens concerning the operations of the mind, viz., thinking, reasoning, fearing, etc., which we concluding not to subsist of themselves, nor apprehending how they can belong to body, or be produced by it, we are apt to think these the actions of some other *substance*, which we call *spirit*; whereby yet it is evident, that having no other idea or notion of matter, but something wherein those many sensible qualities which affect our senses do subsist; by supposing a substance wherein thinking, knowing, doubting, and a power of moving, etc., do subsist; we have as clear a notion of the substance of spirit as we have of body; the one being supposed to be (without knowing what it is) the *substratum* to those simple ideas we have from without; and the other supposed (with a like ignorance of what it is) to be the *substratum* to those operations which we experiment in ourselves within. It is plain, then, that the idea of *corporeal substance* in matter is as remote from our conceptions and apprehensions as that of *spiritual substance* or spirit; and therefore, from our not having any notion of the substance of spirit, we can no more conclude its nonexistence than we can, for the same reason, deny the existence of body: it being as rational to affirm there is no body, because we have no clear and distinct idea of the substance of matter, as to say there is no spirit, because we have no clear and distinct idea of the substance of a spirit.

6. *Our ideas of particular sorts of substances.*—Whatever therefore be the secret and abstract nature of substance in general, all the ideas we have of particular distinct sorts of substances are nothing but several combinations of simple ideas coexisting in such, though unknown, cause of their union, as makes the whole subsist of itself. It is by such combinations of simple ideas, and nothing else, that we represent particular sorts of substances to ourselves. Such are the ideas we have of their several species in our minds; and such only do we, by their specific names, signify to others, v.g., man, horse, sun, water, iron; upon hearing which words, every one who understands the language frames in his mind a combination of those several simple ideas which he has usually observed or fancied to exist together under that denomination; all which he supposes to rest in, and be, as it were, adherent to, that unknown common subject, which inheres not in anything else. Though in the meantime it be manifest, and every one upon enquiry into his own thoughts will find, that he has no other idea of any substance but what he has barely of those sensible qualities, which he supposes to inhere, with a supposition of such a *substratum*, as gives, as it were, a support to those qualities or simple ideas, which he has observed to exist united together. Thus the idea of the sun, what is it but an aggregate of those several simple ideas, bright, hot, roundish, having a constant regular

motion, at a certain distance from us, and perhaps some other? As he who thinks and discourses of the sun, has been more or less accurate in observing those sensible qualities, ideas, or properties, which are in that thing which he calls the sun.

7. *Their active and passive powers a great part of our complex ideas of substances.*—For he has the perfectest idea of any of the particular sorts of substances who has gathered and put together most of those simple ideas which do exist in it, among which are to be reckoned its active powers and passive capacities; which, though not simple ideas, yet in this respect, for brevity's sake, may conveniently enough be reckoned amongst them; . . . We immediately by our senses perceive in fire its heat and colour; which are, if rightly considered, nothing but powers in it to produce those ideas in us: we also by our senses perceive the colour and brittleness of charcoal, whereby we come by the knowledge of another power in fire, which it has to change the colour and consistency of *wood.* By the former, fire immediately, by the latter, it mediately discovers to us these several powers; which therefore we look upon to be a part of the qualities of fire, and so make them a part of the complex idea of it. For all those powers that we take cognizance of, terminating only in the alteration of some sensible qualities in those subjects on which they operate, and so making them exhibit to us new sensible ideas; therefore it is that I have reckoned these powers amongst the simple ideas which make the complex ones of the sorts of substances; though these powers, considered in themselves, are truly complex ideas . . .

8. *And why.*—Nor are we to wonder that powers make a great part of our complex ideas of substances, since their secondary qualities are those which, in most of them, serve principally to distinguish substances one from another and commonly make a considerable part of the complex idea of the several sorts of them. For our senses failing us in the discovery of the bulk, texture, and figure of the minute parts of bodies, on which their real constitutions and differences depend, we are fain to make use of their secondary qualities as the characteristical notes and marks whereby to frame ideas of them in our minds, and distinguish them one from another. All which secondary qualities, as has been shown, are nothing but bare powers. For the colour and taste of opium are, as well as its soporific or anodyne virtues, mere powers depending on its primary qualities, whereby it is fitted to produce different operations on different parts of our bodies.

9. *Three sorts of ideas make our complex ones of corporeal substances.*—The ideas that make our complex ones of corporeal substances are of these three sorts. First, the ideas of the primary qualities of things which are discovered by our senses, and are in them even when we perceive them not: such are the bulk, figure, number, situation, and motion of the parts of bodies, which are really in them, whether we take notice of them or no. Secondly, the sensible secondary qualities which, depending on these, are nothing but the powers those substances have to produce several ideas in us by our senses; which ideas are not in the things themselves otherwise than as anything is in its cause. Thirdly, the aptness we consider in any substance to give or receive such alterations of primary qualities as that the substance so altered should produce in us different ideas from what it did before; these are called active and passive powers: all which powers, as far as we have any notice or notion of them, terminate only in sensible simple ideas. For whatever alteration a loadstone has the power to make in the minute particles of iron, we should have no notion of any power it had at all to operate on iron, did not its sensible motion discover it; and I doubt not but there are a thousand changes that bodies we daily handle have a power to cause in one another, which we never suspect, because they never appear in sensible effects.

10. *Powers thus make a great part of our complex ideas of particular substances.*—Powers therefore justly make a great part of our complex ideas of substances. He that will examine his complex idea of gold, will find several of its ideas that make it up to be only powers: as the power of being melted, but of not spending itself in the fire, of being dissolved in *aqua regia*, are ideas as necessary to make up our complex idea of gold, as its colour and weight: which, if duly considered, are also nothing but different powers. For to speak truly, yellowness is not actually in gold, but is a power in gold to produce that idea in us by our eyes when placed in a due light: and the heat which we cannot leave out of our idea of the sun, is no more really in the sun than the white colour it introduces into wax . . .

11. *The now secondary qualities of bodies would disappear, if we could discover the primary ones of their minute parts.*—Had we senses acute enough to discern the minute particles of bodies, and the real constitution on which their sensible qualities depend, I doubt not but they would produce quite different ideas in us, and that which is now the yellow colour of gold would then disappear, and instead of it we should see an admirable texture of parts of a certain size and figure. This microscopes plainly discover to us; for what to our naked eyes produces a certain colour is, by thus augmenting the acuteness of our senses, discovered to be quite a different thing; and the thus altering, as it were, the proportion of the bulk of the minute parts of a coloured object to our usual sight, produces different ideas from what it did before. Thus sand, or pounded glass, which is opaque and white to the naked eye, is pellucid in a microscope: . . . blood to the naked eye appears all red; but by a good microscope, wherein its lesser parts appear, shows only some few globules of red, swimming in a pellucid liquor; and how these red globules would appear, if glasses could be found that yet could magnify them one thousand or ten thousand times more, is uncertain.

* * *

37. *Recapitulation.*—And thus we have seen what kind of ideas we have of *substances of all kinds*, wherein they consist, and how we come by them. From whence, I think, it is very evident,

First, That all our ideas of the several *sorts* of substances are nothing but collections of simple ideas, with a supposition of *something* to which they belong, and in which they subsist; though of this supposed something we have no clear distinct idea at all.

Secondly, That all the simple ideas that, thus united in one common *substratum*, make up our complex ideas of several *sorts* of substances, are no other but such as we have received from sensation or reflection . . .

Thirdly, That most of the simple ideas that make up our complex ideas of substances, when truly considered, are only *powers*, however we are apt to take them for positive qualities: v.g., the greatest part of the ideas that make our complex idea of *gold* are yellowness, great weight, ductility, fusibility, and solubility in *aqua regia*, etc., all united together in an unknown *substratum*; all which ideas are nothing else but so many relations to other substances, and are not really in the gold considered barely in itself, though they depend on those real and primary qualities of its internal constitution, whereby it has a fitness differently to operate and be operated on by several other substances.

* * *

CHAPTER 27. OF IDENTITY AND DIVERSITY

1. *Wherein identity consists.*—Another occasion the mind often takes of comparing, is the very being of things, when, considering *anything as existing at any determined time and place*, we compare it with *itself existing at another time*, and thereon form the ideas of *identity* and *diversity*. When we see anything to be in any place in any instant of time, we are sure (be it what it will) that it is that very thing, and not another which at that same time exists in another place, how like and undistinguishable soever it may be in all other respects: and in this consists *identity*, when the ideas it is attributed to vary not at all from what they were that moment wherein we consider their former existence, and to which we compare the present. For we never finding, nor conceiving it possible, that two things of the same kind should exist in the same place at the same time, we rightly conclude, that, whatever exists anywhere at any time, excludes all of the same kind, and is there itself alone. When therefore we demand whether anything be the *same* or no, it refers always to something that existed such a time in such a place, which it was certain, at that instant, was the same with itself, and no other. From whence it follows, that one thing cannot have two beginnings of existence, nor two things one beginning; it being impossible for two things of the same kind to be or exist in the same instant, in the very same place; or one and the same thing in different places. That, therefore, that had one beginning, is the same thing; and that which had a different beginning in time and place from that, is not the same, but diverse. That which has made the difficulty about this relation has been the little care and attention used in having precise notions of the things to which it is attributed.

2. *Identity of substances.*—We have the ideas but of three sorts of substances: 1. *God*. 2. *Finite intelligences*. 3. *Bodies*.

First, *God* is without beginning, eternal, unalterable, and everywhere, and therefore concerning his identity there can be no doubt.

Secondly, *finite spirits* having had each its determinate time and place of beginning to exist, the relation to that time and place will always determine to each of them its identity, as long as it exists.

Thirdly, The same will hold of every *particle of matter*, to which no addition or subtraction of matter being made, it is the same. For, though these three sorts of substances, as we term them, do not exclude one another out of the same place, yet we cannot conceive but that they must necessarily each of them exclude any of the same kind out of the same place: or else the notions and names of identity and diversity would be in vain, and there could be no such distinctions of substances, or anything else one from another. For example: could two bodies be in the same place at the same time; then those two parcels of matter must be one and the same, take them great or little; nay, all bodies must be one and the same. For, by the same reason that two particles of matter may be in one place, all bodies may be in one place: which, when it can be supposed, takes away the distinction of identity and diversity of one and more, and renders it ridiculous. But it being a contradiction that two or more should be one, identity and diversity are relations and ways of comparing well founded, and of use to the understanding.

Identity of modes and relations.—All other things being but modes or relations ultimately terminated in substances, the identity and diversity of each particular existence of them too will be by the same way determined: only as to things whose existence is in succession, such as are the actions of finite beings, v.g., *motion* and *thought*, both which consist in a continued train of succession, concerning *their* diversity there can be no question: because each perishing the moment it begins, they cannot exist in different times, or in different places, as permanent beings can at different times exist in distant places; and therefore no motion or thought, considered as at different times, can be the same, each part thereof having a different beginning of existence.

3. *Principium individuationis.*—From what has been said, it is easy to discover what is so much inquired after, the *principium individuationis*; and that, it is plain, is existence itself; which determines a being of any sort to a particular time and place, incommunicable to two beings of the same kind. This, though it seems easier to conceive in simple substances or modes; yet, when reflected on, is not more difficult in compound ones, if care be taken to what it is applied: v.g., let us suppose an atom, i.e., a continued body under one immutable superficies, existing in a determined time and place; it is evident, that, considered in any instant of its existence, it is in that instant the same with itself. For, being at that instant what it is, and nothing else, it is the same, and so must continue as long as its existence is continued; for so long it will be the same, and no other. In like manner, if two or more atoms be joined together into the same mass, every one of those atoms will be the same, by the foregoing rule: and whilst they exist united together, the mass, consisting of the same atoms, must be the same mass, or the same body, let the parts be ever so differently jumbled. But if one of these atoms be taken away, or one new one added, it is no longer the same mass or the same body. In the state of living creatures, their identity depends not on a mass of the same particles, but on something else. For in them the variation of great parcels of matter alters not the identity: an oak growing from a plant to a great tree, and then lopped, is still the same oak; and a colt grown up to a horse, sometimes fat, sometimes lean, is all the while the same horse: though, in both these cases, there may be a manifest change of the parts; so that truly they are not either of them the same masses of matter, though they be truly one of them the same oak, and the other the same horse. The reason whereof is, that, in these two cases—a *mass of matter* and a *living body*—identity is not applied to the same thing.

4. *Identity of vegetables.*—We must therefore consider wherein an oak differs from a mass of matter, and that seems to me to be in this, that the one is only the cohesion of particles of matter any how united, the other such a disposition of them as constitutes the parts of an oak; and such an organization of those parts as is fit to receive and distribute nourishment, so as to continue and frame the wood, bark, and leaves, etc., of an oak, in which consists the vegetable life. That being then one plant which has such an organization of parts in one coherent body, partaking of one common life, it continues to be the same plant as long as it partakes of the same life, though that life be communicated to new particles of matter vitally united to the living plant, in a like continued organization conformable to that sort of plants. For this organization, being at any one instant in any one collection of matter, is in that particular concrete distinguished from all other, and is that individual life, which existing constantly from that moment both forwards and backwards, in the same continuity of insensibly succeeding parts united to the living body of the plant, it has that identity which makes the same plant, and all the parts of it, parts of the same plant, during all the time that they exist united in that continued organization, which is fit to convey that common life to all the parts so united.

5. *Identity of animals.*—The case is not so much different in brutes but that any one may hence see what makes an animal and continues it the same. Something we have like this in machines, and may serve to illustrate it. For example, what is a watch? It is plain it is nothing but a fit organization or construction of parts to a certain end, which, when a sufficient force is added to it, it is capable to attain. If we would suppose this machine one continued body, all whose organized parts were repaired, increased, or diminished by a constant addition or separation of insensible parts, with one common

life, we should have something very much like the body of an animal; with this difference, That, in an animal the fitness of the organization, and the motion wherein life consists, begin together, the motion coming from within; but in machines the force coming sensibly from without, is often away when the organ is in order, and well fitted to receive it.

6. *The identity of man.*—This also shows wherein the identity of the same *man* consists; viz., in nothing but a participation of the same continued life, by constantly fleeting particles of matter, in succession vitally united to the same organized body. He that shall place the identity of man in anything else, but, like that of other animals, in one fitly organized body, taken in any one instant, and from thence continued, under one organization of life, in several successively fleeting particles of matter united to it, will find it hard to make an embryo, one of years, mad and sober, the *same* man, by any supposition, that will not make it possible for Seth, Ismael, Socrates, Pilate, St. Austin, and Caesar Borgia, to be the same man. For if the identity of *soul alone* makes the same *man*; and there be nothing in the nature of matter why the same individual spirit may not be united to different bodies, it will be possible that those men, living in distant ages, and of different tempers, may have been the same man: which way of speaking must be from a very strange use of the word man, applied to an idea out of which body and shape are excluded. And that way of speaking would agree yet worse with the notions of those philosophers who allow of transmigration, and are of opinion that the souls of men may, for their miscarriages, be detruded into the bodies of beasts, as fit habitations, with organs suited to the satisfaction of their brutal inclinations. But yet I think nobody, could he be sure that the *soul* of Heliogabalus were in one of his hogs, would yet say that hog were a *man* or Heliogabalus.

7. *Idea of identity suited to the idea it is applied to.*—It is not therefore unity of substance that comprehends all sorts of identity, or will determine it in every case; but to conceive and judge of it aright, we must consider what idea the word it is applied to stands for: it being one thing to be the same *substance*, another the same *man*, and a third the same *person*, if *person, man*, and *substance*, are three names standing for three different ideas;—for such as is the idea belonging to that name, such must be the identity; which, if it had been a little more carefully attended to, would possibly have prevented a great deal of that confusion which often occurs about this matter, with no small seeming difficulties, especially concerning personal identity, which therefore we shall in the next place a little consider.

* * *

9. *Personal identity.*—This being premised, to find wherein personal identity consists, we must consider what *person* stands for;—which, I think, is a thinking intelligent being, that has reason and reflection, and can consider itself as itself, the same thinking thing, in different times and places; which it does only by that consciousness which is inseparable from thinking, and, as it seems to me, essential to it: it being impossible for any one to perceive without *perceiving* that he does perceive. When we see, hear, smell, taste, feel, meditate, or will anything, we know that we do so. Thus it is always as to our present sensations and perceptions: and by this every one is to himself that which he calls *self*:—it not being considered, in this case, whether the same self be continued in the same or divers substances. For, since consciousness always accompanies thinking, and it is that which makes every one to be what he calls self, and thereby distinguishes himself from all other thinking things, in this alone consists personal identity, i.e., the

sameness of a rational being: and as far as this consciousness can be extended backwards to any past action or thought, so far reaches the identity of that person; it is the same self now it was then; and it is by the same self with this present one that now reflects on it, that that action was done.

10. *Consciousness makes personal identity.*—But it is further inquired, whether it be the same identical substance. This few would think they had reason to doubt of, if these perceptions, with their consciousness, always remained present in the mind, whereby the same thinking thing would be always consciously present, and, as would be thought, evidently the same to itself. But that which seems to make the difficulty is this, that this consciousness being interrupted always by forgetfulness, there being no moment of our lives wherein we have the whole train of all our past actions before our eyes in one view, but even the best memories losing the sight of one part whilst they are viewing another; and we sometimes, and that the greatest part of our lives, not reflecting on our past selves, being intent on our present thoughts, and in sound sleep having no thoughts at all, or at least none with that consciousness which remarks our waking thoughts,—I say, in all these cases, our consciousness being interrupted, and we losing the sight of our past selves, doubts are raised whether we are the same thinking thing, i.e., the same *substance* or no. Which, however reasonable or unreasonable, concerns not *personal* identity at all. The question being what makes the same person, and not whether it be the same identical substance, which always thinks in the same person, which, in this case, matters not at all: different substances, by the same consciousness (where they do partake in it) being united into one person, as well as different bodies by the same life are united into one animal, whose identity is preserved in that change of substances by the unity of one continued life. For, it being the same consciousness that makes a man be himself to himself, personal identity depends on that only, whether it be annexed solely to one individual substance, or can be continued in a succession of several substances. For as far as any intelligent being *can* repeat the idea of any past action with the same consciousness it had of it at first, and with the same consciousness it has of any present action; so far it is the same personal self. For it is by the consciousness it has of its present thoughts and actions, that it is *self* to *itself* now, and so will be the same self, as far as the same consciousness can extend to actions past or to come; and would be by distance of time, or change of substance, no more two persons, than a man be two men by wearing other clothes today than he did yesterday, with a long or a short sleep between: the same consciousness uniting those distant actions into the same person, whatever substances contributed to their production.

* * *

16. *Consciousness alone unites actions into the same person.*—But though the same immaterial substance or soul does not alone, wherever it be, and in whatsoever state, make the same *man*; yet it is plain, consciousness, as far as ever it can be extended—should it be to ages past—unites existences and actions very remote in time into the same *person*, as well as it does the existences and actions of the immediately preceding moment: so that whatever has the consciousness of present and past actions, is the same person to whom they both belong. Had I the same consciousness that I saw the ark and Noah's flood, as that I saw an overflowing of the Thames last winter, or as that I write now, I could no more doubt that I who write this now, that saw the Thames overflowed last winter, and that viewed the flood at the general deluge, was the same *self*,—place that self in what *substance* you please—than that I who write this am the

same myself now whilst I write (whether I consist of all the same substance, material or immaterial, or no) that I was yesterday. For as to this point of being the same self, it matters not whether this present self be made up of the same or other substances—I being as much concerned, and as justly accountable for any action that was done a thousand years since, appropriated to me now by this self consciousness, as I am for what I did the last moment.

17. *Self depends on consciousness, not on substance.*—Self is that conscious thinking thing,—whatever substance made up of, (whether spiritual or material, simple or compounded, it matters not)—which is sensible or conscious of pleasure and pain, capable of happiness or misery, and so is concerned for itself, as far as that consciousness extends. Thus every one finds that, whilst comprehended under that consciousness, the little finger is as much a part of himself as what is most so. Upon separation of this little finger, should this consciousness go along with the little finger, and leave the rest of the body, it is evident the little finger would be the person, the same person; and self then would have nothing to do with the rest of the body. As in this case it is the consciousness that goes along with the substance, when one part is separate from another, which makes the same person, and constitutes this inseparable self: so it is in reference to substances remote in time. That with which the consciousness of this present thinking thing *can* join itself, makes the same person, and is one self with it, and with nothing else; and so attributes to itself, and owns all the actions of that thing, as its own, as far as that consciousness reaches, and no further; as every one who reflects will perceive.

18. *Persons, not substances, the objects of reward and punishment.*—In this personal identity is founded all the right and justice of reward and punishment; happiness and misery being that for which every one is concerned for *himself*, and not mattering what becomes of any *substance*, not joined to, or affected with that consciousness. For, as it is evident in the instance I gave but now, if the consciousness went along with the little finger when it was cut off, that would be the same self which was concerned for the whole body yesterday, as making part of itself, whose actions then it cannot but admit as its own now. Though, if the same body should still live, and immediately from the separation of the little finger have its own peculiar consciousness, whereof the little finger knew nothing, it would not at all be concerned for it, as a part of itself, or could own any of its actions, or have any of them imputed to him.

19. *Which shows wherein personal identity consists.*—This may show us wherein personal identity consists: not in the identity of substance, but, as I have said, in the identity of consciousness, wherein if Socrates and the present mayor of Queinborough agree, they are the same person: if the same Socrates waking and sleeping do not partake of the same consciousness, Socrates waking and sleeping are not the same person. And to punish Socrates waking for what Socrates sleeping thought, and waking Socrates was never conscious of, would be no more of right, than to punish one twin for what his brother-twin did, whereof he knew nothing, because their outsides were so alike, that they could not be distinguished; for such twins have been seen.

20. *Absolute oblivion separates what is thus forgotten from the person, but not from the man.*—But yet possibly it will still be objected,—Suppose I wholly lose the memory of some parts of my life, beyond a possibility of retrieving them, so that perhaps I shall never be conscious of them again; yet am I not the same person that did those actions, had those thoughts that I once was conscious of, though I have now forgot them? To which I answer, that we must here take notice what the word *I* is applied to; which, in this case, is the *man* only. And the same man being presumed to be the

same person, I is easily here supposed to stand also for the same person. But if it be possible for the same man to have distinct incommunicable consciousness at different times, it is past doubt the same man would at different times make different persons; which, we see, is the sense of mankind in the solemnest declaration of their opinions, human laws not punishing the mad man for the sober man's actions, nor the sober man for what the mad man did,—thereby making them two persons: which is somewhat explained by our way of speaking in English when we say such an one is "not himself," or is "beside himself"; in which phrases it is insinuated, as if those who now, or at least first used them, thought that self was changed; the self-same person was no longer in that man.

* * *

22. *Is not a man drunk and sober the same person?*—Why else is he punished for the fact he commits when drunk, though he be never afterwards conscious of it? Just as much the same person as a man that walks, and does other things in his sleep, is the same person, and is answerable for any mischief he shall do in it. Human laws punish both, with a justice suitable to *their* way of knowledge;—because, in these cases, they cannot distinguish certainly what is real, what counterfeit: and so the ignorance in drunkenness or sleep is not admitted as a plea. For, though punishment be annexed to personality, and personality to consciousness, and the drunkard perhaps be not conscious of what he did, yet human judicatures justly punish him; because the fact is proved against him, but want of consciousness cannot be proved for him. But in the Great Day, wherein the secrets of all hearts shall be laid open, it may be reasonable to think, no one shall be made to answer for what he knows nothing of; but shall receive his doom, his conscience accusing or excusing him.

* * *

25. *Consciousness unites substances, material or spiritual, with the same personality.* — I agree, that more probable opinion is, that this consciousness is annexed to, and the affection of, one individual immaterial substance.

But let men, according to their diverse hypotheses, resolve of that as they please. This every intelligent being, sensible of happiness or misery, must grant—that there is something that is *himself*, that he is concerned for, and would have happy; that this self has existed in a continued duration more than one instant, and therefore it is possible may exist, as it has done, months and years to come, without any certain bounds to be set to its duration; and may be the same self, by the same consciousness continued on for the future. And thus, by this consciousness he finds himself to be the same self which did such and such an action some years since, by which he comes to be happy or miserable now. In all which account of self, the same numerical substance is not considered as making the same self; but the same continued *consciousness*, in which several substances may have been united, and again separated from it, which, whilst they continued in a vital union with that wherein this consciousness then resided, made a part of that same self. Thus any part of our bodies, vitally united to that which is conscious in us, makes a part of ourselves: but upon separation from the vital union by which that consciousness is communicated, that which a moment since was part of ourselves, is now no more so than a part of another man's self is a part of me: and it is not impossible but in a little time may become a real part of another person. And so we have the same numerical substance become a part of two different persons; and the same person preserved under the change of various substances. Could we suppose any spirit wholly stripped of all its memory or consciousness of past actions, as we find our minds always are of a great part of ours, and sometimes of them all; the union or separation of such a spiritual substance would make no variation of personal identity, any more than that of any particle of matter does. Any substance vitally united to the present thinking being is a part of that very same self which now is; anything united to it by a consciousness of former actions, makes also a part of the same self, which is the same both then and now.

* * *

Book III. Of Words

Chapter 2. Of the Signification of Words

1. *Words are sensible signs, necessary for communication of ideas.*—Man, though he have great variety of thoughts, and such from which others as well as himself might receive profit and delight; yet they are all within his own breast, invisible and hidden from others, nor can of themselves be made to appear. The comfort and advantage of society not being to be had without communication of thoughts, it was necessary that man should find out some external sensible signs, whereof those invisible ideas, which his thoughts are made up of, might be made known to others. For this purpose nothing was so fit, either for plenty or quickness, as those articulate sounds, which with so much ease and variety he found himself able to make. Thus we may conceive how words, which were by nature so well adapted to that purpose, came to be made use of by men as the signs of their ideas; not by any natural connexion that there is between particular articulate sounds and certain ideas, for then there would be but one language amongst all men; but by a voluntary imposition, whereby such a word is made arbitrarily the mark of such an idea. The use, then, of words, is to be sensible marks of ideas; and the ideas they stand for are their proper and immediate signification.

* * *

3. *Examples of this.*—This is so necessary in the use of language, that in this respect the knowing and the ignorant, the learned and the unlearned, use the words they speak (with any meaning) all alike. They, in every man's mouth, stand for the ideas he has, and which he would express by them. A child having taken notice of nothing in the metal he hears called *gold*, but the bright shining yellow colour, he applies the word gold only to his own idea of that colour, and nothing else; and therefore calls the same colour in a peacock's tail gold. Another that hath better observed, adds to shining yellow great weight: and then the sound gold, when he uses it, stands for a complex idea of a shining yellow and a very weighty substance. Another adds to those qualities fusibility: and then the word gold signifies to him a body, bright, yellow, fusible, and very heavy. Another adds malleability. Each of these uses equally the word gold, when they

have occasion to express the idea which they have applied it to: but it is evident that each can apply it only to his own idea; nor can he make it stand as a sign of such a complex idea as he has not.

* * *

CHAPTER 3. OF GENERAL TERMS

1. *The greatest part of words are general terms.*—All things that exist being particulars, it may perhaps be thought reasonable that words, which ought to be conformed to things, should be so too,—I mean in their signification: but yet we find quite the contrary. The far greatest part of words that make all languages are general terms: which has not been the effect of neglect or chance, but of reason and necessity.

2. *That every particular thing should have a name for itself is impossible.*—First, It is impossible that every particular thing should have a distinct peculiar name. For, the signification and use of words depending on that connexion which the mind makes between its ideas and the sounds it uses as signs of them, it is necessary, in the application of names to things, that the mind should have distinct ideas of the things, and retain also the particular name that belongs to every one, with its peculiar appropriation to that idea. But it is beyond the power of human capacity to frame and retain distinct ideas of all the particular things we meet with: every bird and beast men saw; every tree and plant that affected the senses, could not find a place in the most capacious understanding. If it be looked on as an instance of a prodigious memory, that some generals have been able to call every soldier in their army by his proper name, we may easily find a reason why men have never attempted to give names to each sheep in their flock, or crow that flies over their heads; much less to call every leaf of plants, or grain of sand that came in their way, by a peculiar name.

3. *And would be useless, if it were possible.*—Secondly, If it were possible, it would yet be useless; because it would not serve to the chief end of language. Men would in vain heap up names of particular things, that would not serve them to communicate their thoughts. Men learn names, and use them in talk with others, only that they may be understood: which is then only done when, by use or consent, the sound I make by the organs of speech, excites in another man's mind who hears it, the idea I apply it to in mine, when I speak it. This cannot be done by names applied to particular things; whereof I alone having the ideas in my mind, the names of them could not be significant or intelligible to another, who was not acquainted with all those very particular things which had fallen under my notice.

4. *A distinct name for every particular thing, not fitted for enlargement of knowledge.*—Thirdly, But yet, granting this also feasible, (which I think is not), yet a distinct name for every particular thing would not be of any great use for the improvement of knowledge: which, though founded in particular things, enlarges itself by general views; to which things reduced into sorts, under general names, are properly subservient. These, with the names belonging to them, come within some compass, and do not multiply every moment, beyond what either the mind can contain, or use requires. And therefore, in these, men have for the most part stopped: but yet not so as to hinder themselves from distinguishing particular things by appropriated names, where convenience demands it. And therefore in their own species, which they have most to do with,

and wherein they have often occasion to mention particular persons, they make use of proper names; and there distinct individuals have distinct denominations.

5. *What things have proper names, and why.*—Besides persons, countries also, cities, rivers, mountains, and other the like distinctions of place have usually found peculiar names, and that for the same reason; they being such as men have often an occasion to mark particularly, and, as it were, set before others in their discourses with them. And I doubt not but, if we had reason to mention particular horses as often as we have to mention particular men, we should have proper names for the one, as familiar as for the other, and Bucephalus would be a word as much in use as Alexander. And therefore we see that, amongst jockeys, horses have their proper names to be known and distinguished by, as commonly as their servants: because, amongst them, there is often occasion to mention this or that particular horse when he is out of sight.

6. *How general words are made.*—The next thing to be considered is,—How general words come to be made. For, since all things that exist are only particulars, how come we by general terms; or where find we those general natures they are supposed to stand for? Words become general by being made the signs of general ideas: and ideas become general, by separating from them the circumstances of time and place, and any other ideas that may determine them to this or that particular existence. By this way of abstraction they are made capable of representing more individuals than one; each of which having in it a conformity to that abstract idea, is (as we call it) of that sort.

7. *Shown by the way we enlarge our complex ideas from infancy.*—But, to deduce this a little more distinctly, it will not perhaps be amiss to trace our notions and names from their beginning, and observe by what degrees we proceed, and by what steps we enlarge our ideas from our first infancy. There is nothing more evident, than that the ideas of the persons children converse with (to instance in them alone) are like the persons themselves, only particular. The ideas of the nurse and the mother are well framed in their minds; and, like pictures of them there, represent only those individuals. The names they first gave to them are confined to these individuals; and the names of *nurse* and *mamma*, the child uses, determine themselves to those persons. Afterwards, when time and a larger acquaintance have made them observe that there are a great many other things in the world, that in some common agreements of shape, and several other qualities, resemble their father and mother, and those persons they have been used to, they frame an idea, which they find those many particulars do partake in; and to that they give, with others, the name *man*, for example. And thus they come to have a general name, and a general idea. Wherein they make nothing new; but only leave out of the complex idea they had of Peter and James, Mary and Jane, that which is peculiar to each, and retain only what is common to them all.

8. *And further enlarge our complex ideas, by still leaving out properties contained in them.*—By the same way that they come by the general name and idea of man, they easily advance to more general names and notions. For, observing that several things that differ from their idea of man, and cannot therefore be comprehended under that name, have yet certain qualities wherein they agree with man, by retaining only those qualities, and uniting them into one idea, they have again another and more general idea; to which having given a name they make a term of a more comprehensive extension: which new idea is made, not by any new addition, but only as before, by

leaving out the shape, and some other properties signified by the name man, and retaining only a body, with life, sense, and spontaneous motion, comprehended under the name animal.

9. *General natures are nothing but abstract end partial ideas of more complex ones.*—That this is the way whereby men first formed general ideas, and general names to them, I think is so evident, that there needs no other proof of it but the considering of a man's self, or others, and the ordinary proceedings of their minds in knowledge. And he that thinks *general natures* or *notions* are anything else but such abstract and partial ideas of more complex ones, taken at first from particular existences, will, I fear, be at a loss where to find them. For let any one effect, and then tell me, wherein does his idea of *man* differ from that of *Peter* and *Paul*, or his idea of horse from that of *Bucephalus*, but in the leaving out something that is peculiar to each individual, and retaining so much of those particular complex ideas of several particular existences as they are found to agree in? Of the complex ideas signified by the names *man* and *horse*, leaving out but those particulars wherein they differ, and retaining only those wherein they agree, and of those making a new distinct complex idea, and giving the name *animal* to it, one has a more general term, that comprehends with man several other creatures. Leave out of the idea of *animal*, sense and spontaneous motion, and the remaining complex idea, made up of the remaining simple ones of body, life, and nourishment, becomes a more general one, under the more comprehensive term, *vivens*. And, not to dwell longer upon this particular, so evident in itself; by the same way the mind proceeds to *body*, *substance*, and at last to *being*, *thing*, and such universal terms, which stand for any of our ideas whatsoever. To conclude: this whole mystery of genera and species, which make such a noise in the schools, and are with justice so little regarded out of them, is nothing else but *abstract ideas*, more or less comprehensive, with names annexed to them. In all which this is constant and unvariable, that every more general term stands for such an idea, and is but a part of any of those contained under it.

10. *Why the genus is ordinarily made use of in definitions.*—This may show us the reason why, in the defining of words, which is nothing but declaring their signification, we make use of the *genus*, or next general word that comprehends it. Which is not out of necessity, but only to save the labour of enumerating the several simple ideas which the next general word or genus stands for; or, perhaps, sometimes the shame of not being able to do it. But though defining by *genus* and *differentia* (I crave leave to use these terms of art, though originally Latin, since they most properly suit those notions they are applied to), I say, though defining by the *genus* be the shortest way, yet I think it may be doubted whether it be the best. This I am sure, it is not the only, and so not absolutely necessary. For, definition being nothing but making another understand by words what idea the term defined stands for, a definition is best made by enumerating those simple ideas that are combined in the signification of the term defined: and, if, instead of such an enumeration, men have accustomed themselves to use the next general term, it has not been out of necessity, or for greater clearness, but for quickness and dispatch sake. For I think that, to one who desired to know what idea the word man stood for; if it should be said, that man was a solid extended substance, having life, sense, spontaneous motion, and the faculty of reasoning, I doubt not but the meaning of the term man would be as well understood, and the idea it stands for be at least as clearly made known, as when it is defined to be a rational animal: which, by the several definitions of *animal*, *vivens*, and *corpus*, resolves itself into those enumerated ideas.

I have, in explaining the term man, followed here the ordinary definition of the schools; which, though perhaps not the most exact, yet serves well enough to my present purpose. And one may, in this instance, see what gave occasion to the rule, that a definition must consist of *genus* and *differentia*; and it suffices to show us the little necessity there is of such a rule, or advantage in the strict observing of it. For, definitions, as has been said, being only the explaining of one word by several others, so that the meaning or idea it stands for may be certainly known; languages are not always so made according to the rules of logic, that every term can have its signification exactly and clearly expressed by two others. Experience sufficiently satisfies us to the contrary; or else those who have made this rule have done ill, that they have given us so few definitions conformable to it. But of definitions more in the next chapter.

11. *General and universal are creatures of the understanding, and belong not to the real existence of things.*—To return to general words: it is plain, by what has been said, that *general* and *universal* belong not to the real existence of things; but are the inventions and creatures of the understanding, made by it for its own use, and concern only signs, whether words or ideas. Words are general, as has been said, when used for signs of general ideas, and so are applicable indifferently to many particular things; and ideas are general when they are set up as the representatives of many particular things: but universality belongs not to things themselves, which are all of them particular in their existence, even those words and ideas which in their signification are general. When therefore we quit particulars, the generals that rest are only creatures of our own making; their general nature being nothing but the capacity they are put into, by the understanding, of signifying or representing many particulars. For the signification they have is nothing but a relation that, by the mind of man, is added to them.

12. *Abstract ideas are the essences of genera and species.*—The next thing therefore to be considered is, What kind of signification it is that general words have. For, as it is evident that they do not signify barely one particular thing; for then they would not be general terms, but proper names, so, on the other side, it is as evident they do not signify a plurality; for *man* and *men* would then signify the same; and the distinction of numbers (as the grammarians call them) would be superfluous and useless. That then which general words signify is a *sort* of things; and each of them does that, by being a sign of an abstract idea in the mind; to which idea, as things existing are found to agree, so they come to be ranked under that name, or, which is all one, be of that sort. Whereby it is evident that the *essences* of the sorts, or, if the Latin word pleases better, *species* of things, are nothing else but these abstract ideas. For the having the essence of any species, being that which makes anything to be of that species; and the conformity to the idea to which the name is annexed being that which gives a right to that name; the having the essence, and the having that conformity, must needs be the same thing: since to be of any species, and to have a right to the name of that species, is all one. As, for example, to be a *man*, or of the *species* man, and to have right to the *name* man, is the same thing. Again, to be a man, or of the species man, and have the *essence* of a man, is the same thing. Now, since nothing can be a man, or have a right to the name man, but what has a conformity to the abstract idea the name man stands for, nor anything be a man, or have a right to the species man, but what has the essence of that species; it follows, that the abstract idea for which the name stands, and the essence of the species, is one and the same. From whence it is easy to observe, that the essences of the sorts of things, and, consequently, the sorting of things, is the workmanship of the understanding that abstracts and makes those general ideas.

13. *They are the workmanship of the understanding, but have their foundation in the similitude of things.*—I would not here be thought to forget, much less to deny, that Nature, in the production of things, makes several of them alike: there is nothing more obvious, especially in the races of animals, and all things propagated by seed. But yet I think we may say, *the sorting of them under names is the workmanship of the understanding, taking occasion, from the similitude it observes amongst them, to make abstract general ideas*, and set them up in the mind, with names annexed to them, as patterns or forms (for, in that sense, the word *form* has a very proper signification) to which as particular things existing are found to agree, so they come to be of that species, have that denomination, or are put into that *classis*. For when we say this is a man, that a horse; this justice, that cruelty; this a watch, that a jack; what do we else but rank things under different specific names, as agreeing to those abstract ideas, of which we have made those names the signs? And what are the essences of those species set out and marked by names, but those abstract ideas in the mind; which are, as it were, the bonds between particular things that exist, and the names they are to be ranked under? And when general names have any connexion with particular beings, these abstract ideas are the medium that unites them: so that the essences of species, as distinguished and denominated by us, neither are nor can be anything but those precise abstract ideas we have in our minds. And therefore the supposed real essences of substances, if different from our abstract ideas, cannot be the essences of the species we rank things into. For two species may be one, as rationally as two different essences be the essence of one species: and I demand what are the alterations [which] may, or may not be made in a *horse* or *lead*, without making either of them to be of another species? In determining the species of things by *our* abstract ideas, this is easy to resolve, but if any one will regulate himself herein by supposed *real* essences, he will, I suppose, be at a loss: and he will never be able to know when anything precisely ceases to be of the species of a *horse* or *lead*.

14. *Each distinct abstract idea is a distinct essence.*—Nor will any one wonder that I say these essences, or abstract ideas (which are the measures of name, and the boundaries of species) are the workmanship of the understanding, who considers that at least the complex ones are often, in several men, different collections of simple ideas; and therefore that is *covetousness* to one man, which is not so to another. Nay, even in substances, where their abstract ideas seem to be taken from the things themselves, they are not constantly the same; no, not in that species which is most familiar to us, and with which we have the most intimate acquaintance: it having been more than once doubted, whether the *fetus* born of a woman were a *man*, even so far as that it hath been debated, whether it were or were not to be nourished and baptized: which could not be, if the abstract idea or essence to which the name man belonged were of nature's making; and were not the uncertain and various collection of simple ideas, which the understanding put together, and then, abstracting it, affixed a name to it. So that, in truth, every distinct abstract idea is a distinct essence; and the names that stand for such distinct ideas are the names of things essentially different. Thus a circle is as essentially different from an oval as a sheep from a goat; and rain is as essentially different from snow as water from earth: that abstract idea which is the essence of one being impossible to be communicated to the other. And thus any two abstract ideas, that in any part vary one from another, with two distinct names annexed to them, constitute two distinct sorts, or, if you please, species, as essentially different as any two of the most remote or opposite in the world.

15. *Several significations of the word "essence."*—But since the essences of things are thought by some (and not without reason) to be wholly unknown, it may not be amiss to consider the several significations of the word essence.

Real essence.—First, Essence may be taken for the very being of anything, whereby it is what it is. And thus the real internal, but generally (in substances) unknown constitution of things, whereon their discoverable qualities depend, may be called their essence. This is the proper original signification of the word, as is evident from the formation of it; *essentia*, in its primary notation, signifying properly, being. And in this sense it is still used, when we speak of the essence of *particular* things, without giving them any name.

Nominal essences.—Secondly, The learning and disputes of the schools having been much busied about *genus* and *species*, the word *essence* has almost lost its primary signification: and, instead of the real constitution of things, has been almost wholly applied to the artificial constitution of *genus* and *species*. It is true, there is ordinarily supposed a real constitution of the sorts of things; and it is past doubt there must be some real constitution, on which any collection of simple ideas co-existing must depend. But, it being evident that things are ranked under names into sorts or species, only as they agree to certain abstract ideas, to which we have annexed those names, the essence of each *genus*, or sort, comes to be nothing but that abstract idea which the general, or sortal (if I may have leave so to call it from sort, as I do general from genus) name stands for. And this we shall find to be that which the word essence imports in its most familiar use.

These two sorts of essences, I suppose, may not unfitly be termed, the one the *real*, the other *nominal essence*.

* * *

Book IV. Of Knowledge and Probability

Chapter 1. Of Knowledge in General

1. *Our knowledge conversant about our ideas only.*—Since the mind, in all its thoughts and reasonings, hath no other immediate object but its own ideas, which it alone does or can contemplate, it is evident that our knowledge is only conversant about them.

2. *Knowledge is the perception of the agreement or disagreement of two ideas.*—*Knowledge* then seems to me to be nothing but the *perception of the connexion and agreement, or disagreement and repugnancy, of any of our ideas*. In this alone it consists. Where this perception is, there is knowledge; and where it is not, there, though we may fancy, guess, or believe, yet we always come short of knowledge. For when we know that white is not black, what do we else but perceive that these two ideas do not agree? When we possess ourselves with the utmost security of the demonstration that the three angles of a triangle are equal to two right ones, what do we more but perceive, that equality to two right ones does necessarily agree to, and is inseparable from, the three angles of a triangle?

3. *This agreement or disagreement may be any of four sorts.*—But to understand a little more distinctly wherein this agreement or disagreement consists, I think we may

reduce it all to these four sorts: (1) *Identity,* or *diversity*. (2) *Relation*. (3) *Coexistence*, or *necessary connexion*. (4) *Real existence*.

4. *Of identity, or diversity in ideas.—First*, As to the first sort of agreement or disagreement, viz., *identity*, or *diversity*. It is the first act of the mind, when it has any sentiments or ideas at all, to perceive its ideas, and, so far as it perceives them, to know each what it is, and thereby also to perceive their difference, and that one is not another. This is so absolutely necessary, that without it there could be no knowledge, no reasoning, no imagination, no distinct thoughts at all. By this the mind clearly and infallibly perceives each idea to agree with itself, and to be what it is; and all distinct ideas to disagree, i.e., the one not to be the other: and this it does without pains, labour, or deduction; but at first view, by its natural power of perception and distinction. And though men of art have reduced this into those general rules, *What is, is*; and, *It is impossible for the same thing to be and not to be*, for ready application in all cases wherein there may be occasion to reflect on it; yet it is certain that the first exercise of this faculty is about particular ideas. A man infallibly knows, as soon as ever he has them in his mind, that the ideas he calls *white* and *round* are the very ideas they are, and that they are not other ideas which he calls *red* or *square*. Nor can any maxim or proposition in the world make him know it clearer or surer than he did before, and without any such general rule. This then is the first agreement or disagreement which the mind perceives in its ideas; which it always perceives at first sight; and if there ever happen any doubt about it, it will always be found to be about the names, and not the ideas themselves, whose identity and diversity will always be perceived as soon and as clearly as the ideas themselves are, nor can it possibly be otherwise.

5. *Of abstract relations between ideas.—Secondly*, The next sort of agreement or disagreement the mind perceives in any of its ideas may, I think, be called *relative*, and is nothing but the perception of the *relation* between any two ideas, of what kind soever, whether substances, modes, or any other. For, since all distinct ideas must eternally be known not to be the same, and so be universally and constantly denied one of another, there could be no room for any positive knowledge at all, if we could not perceive any relation between our ideas, and find out the agreement or disagreement they have one with another, in several ways the mind takes of comparing them.

6. *Of their necessary coexistence in substances.—Thirdly*, The third sort of agreement or disagreement to be found in our ideas, which the perception of the mind is employed about, is *coexistence*, or *non-coexistence* in the *same subject*; and this belongs particularly to substances. Thus when we pronounce concerning gold that it is fixed, our knowledge of this truth amounts to no more but this, that fixedness, or a power to remain in the fire unconsumed, is an idea that always accompanies and is joined with that particular sort of yellowness, weight, fusibility, malleableness, and solubility in aqua regia, which make our complex idea, signified by the word gold.

7. *Of real existence agreeing to any idea.—Fourthly*, The fourth and last sort is that of *actual real existence* agreeing to any idea. Within these four sorts of agreement or disagreement is, I suppose, contained all the knowledge we have or are capable of; for all the enquiries that we can make concerning any of our ideas, all that we know or can affirm concerning any of them, is, that it is or is not the same with some other; that it does or does not always coexist with some other idea in the same subject; that it has this or that relation to some other idea; or that it has a real existence without the mind. Thus, "Blue is not yellow," is of identity. "Two triangles upon equal bases between two parallels are equal," is of relation. "Iron is susceptible of magnetical

impressions," is of coexistence. "God is," is of real existence. Though identity and coexistence are truly nothing but relations, yet they are so peculiar ways of agreement or disagreement of our ideas, that they deserve well to be considered as distinct heads, and not under relation in general: since they are so different grounds of affirmation and negation, as will easily appear to any one who will but reflect on what is said in several places of this Essay. I should now proceed to examine the several degrees of our knowledge, but that it is necessary first to consider the different acceptations of the word knowledge.

8. *Knowledge is either actual or habitual.*—There are several ways wherein the mind is possessed of truth, each of which is called knowledge.

(1) There is *actual knowledge*, which is the present view the mind has of the agreement or disagreement of any of its ideas, or of the relation they have one to another.

(2) A man is said to know any proposition which having been once laid before his thoughts, he evidently perceived the agreement or disagreement of the ideas whereof it consists; and so lodged it in his memory, that whenever that proposition comes again to be reflected on, he, without doubt or hesitation, embraces the right side, assents to and is certain of the truth of it. This, I think, one may call *habitual knowledge* . . . For our finite understandings being able to think clearly and distinctly but on one thing at once, if men had no knowledge of any more than what they actually thought on, they would all be very ignorant; and he that knew most would know but one truth, that being all he was able to think on at one time.

9. *Habitual knowledge is of two degrees.*—Of habitual knowledge there are also, vulgarly speaking, two degrees:—

First, The one of such truths laid up in the memory as, whenever they occur to the mind, it *actually perceives the relation is between those ideas*. And this is in all those truths whereof we have an intuitive knowledge, where the ideas themselves, by an immediate view, discover their agreement or disagreement one with another.

Secondly, The other is of such truths, whereof the mind having been convinced, it retains *the memory of the conviction without the proofs*. Thus a man that remembers certainly that he once perceived the demonstration that the three angles of a triangle are equal to two right ones, is certain that he knows it, because he cannot doubt of the truth of it. In his adherence to a truth where the demonstration by which it was at first known is forgot, though a man may be thought rather to believe his memory than really to know, and this way of entertaining a truth seemed formerly to me like something between opinion and knowledge, a sort of assurance which exceeds bare belief, for that relies on the testimony of another; yet, upon a due examination, I find it comes not short of perfect certainty, and is, in effect, true knowledge. That which is apt to mislead our first thoughts into a mistake in this matter is, that the agreement or disagreement of the ideas in this case is not perceived, as it was at first, by an actual view of all the intermediate ideas whereby the agreement or disagreement of those in the proposition was at first perceived; but by other intermediate ideas, that show the agreement or disagreement of the ideas contained in the proposition whose certainty we remember. For example: in this proposition, that "the three angles of a triangle are equal to two right ones," one who has seen and clearly perceived the demonstration of this truth knows it to be true, when that demonstration is gone out of his mind, so that at present it is not actually in view, and possibly cannot be recollected; but he knows it in a different way from what he did before. The agreement of the two ideas joined in that proposition is perceived; but it is by the intervention of other ideas than those which at first produced that perception. He remembers, i.e., he knows (for remembrance is but the reviving of some past knowledge) that he was once certain of the truth of this proposition, that "the three angles of a triangle are equal to two right ones." The immutability of the same relations between the same immutable things is now the idea that shows him, that if the three angles of a triangle were once equal to two right ones, they will always be equal to two right ones. And hence he comes to be certain, that what was once true in the case is always true; what ideas once agreed will always agree: and consequently, what he once knew to be true he will always know to be true, as long as he can remember that he once knew it. Upon this ground it is that particular demonstrations in mathematics afford general knowledge. If then the perception that the same ideas will eternally have the same habitudes and relations be not a sufficient ground of knowledge, there could be no knowledge of general propositions in mathematics; for no mathematical demonstration would be any other than particular and when a man had demonstrated any proposition concerning one triangle or circle, his knowledge would not reach beyond that particular diagram. If he would extend it farther, he must renew his demonstration in another instance, before he could know it to be true in another like triangle, and so on by which means one could never come to the knowledge of any general propositions. Nobody, I think, can deny that Mr. Newton certainly knows any proposition that he now at any time reads in his book to be true, though he has not in actual view that admirable chain of intermediate ideas whereby he at first discovered it to be true. Such a memory as that, able to retain such a train of particulars, may be well thought beyond the reach of human faculties, when the very discovery, perception, and laying together that wonderful connexion of ideas is found to surpass most readers' comprehension. But yet it is evident the author himself knows the proposition to be true, remembering he once saw the connexion of those ideas, as certainly as he knows such a man wounded another, remembering that he saw him run him through. But because the memory is not always so clear as actual perception, and does in all men more or less decay in length of time, this amongst other differences, is one which shows that *demonstrative* knowledge is much more imperfect than *intuitive*, as we shall see in the following chapter.

CHAPTER 2. OF THE DEGREES OF OUR KNOWLEDGE

1. *Of the degree, or differences in clearness, of our knowledge:* I. *Intuitive*—All our knowledge consisting, as I have said, in the view the mind has of its own ideas, which is the utmost light and greatest certainty we, with our faculties and in our way of knowledge, are capable of, it may not be amiss to consider a little the degrees of its evidence. The different clearness of our knowledge seems to me to lie in the different way of perception the mind has of the agreement or disagreement of any of its ideas. For if we will reflect on our own ways of thinking, we shall find that sometimes the mind perceives the agreement or disagreement of two ideas *immediately by themselves*, without the intervention of any other and this, I think, we may call *intuitive knowledge*. For in this the mind is at no pains of proving or examining, but perceives the truth, as the eye doth light, only by being directed towards it. Thus the mind perceives that *white* is not black, that a *circle* is not a *triangle*, that *three* are more than *two*, and equal to *one and two*. Such kind of truths the mind perceives at the first sight of the ideas together, by bare intuition, without the intervention of any other idea; and this kind of knowledge is

the clearest and most certain that human frailty is capable of. This part of knowledge is irresistible, and like bright sunshine, forces itself immediately to be perceived as soon as ever the mind turns its view that way; and leaves no room for hesitation, doubt, or examination, but the mind is presently filled with the clear light of it. *It is on this intuition that depends all the certainty and evidence of all our knowledge*; which certainty every one finds to be so great, that he cannot imagine, and therefore not require, a greater for a man cannot conceive himself capable of a greater certainty, than to know that any idea in his mind is such as he perceives it to be; and that two ideas wherein he perceives a difference, are different, and not precisely the same. He that demands a greater certainty that this demands he knows not what, and shows only that he has a mind to be a skeptic without being able to be so. Certainty depends so wholly on this intuition, that in the next degree of knowledge, which I call demonstrative, this intuition is necessary in all the connexions of the intermediate ideas, without which we cannot attain knowledge and certainty.

2. II. *Demonstrative.*—The next degree of knowledge is, where the mind perceives the agreement or disagreement of any ideas, but not immediately . . . In this case, when the mind cannot so bring its ideas together as, by their immediate comparison and, as it were, juxtaposition or application one to another, to perceive their agreement or disagreement, it is fain, by the intervention of other ideas (one or more, as it happens), to discover the agreement or disagreement which it searches; and this is that which we call *reasoning*. Thus the mind, being willing to know the agreement or disagreement in bigness between the three angles of a triangle and two right ones, cannot, by an immediate view and comparing them, do it: because the three angles of a triangle cannot be brought at once, and be compared with any other one or two angles; and so of this the mind has no immediate, no intuitive knowledge. In this case the mind is fain to find out some other angles, to which the three angles of a triangle have an equality; and finding those equal to two right ones, comes to know their equality to two right ones.

3. *Demonstration depends on clearly perceived proofs.*—Those intervening ideas which serve to show the agreement of any two others, are called *proofs*; and where the agreement or disagreement is by this means plainly and clearly perceived, it is called *demonstration*, it being *shown* to the understanding, and the mind made to see that it is so. A quickness in the mind to find out these intermediate ideas (that shall discover the agreement or disagreement of any other), and to apply them right, is, I suppose, that which is called *sagacity*.

4. *As certain, but not so easy and ready as intuitive knowledge.*—This knowledge by intervening proofs, though it be certain, yet the evidence of it is not altogether so clear and bright, nor the assent so ready, as in intuitive knowledge. For though in demonstration the mind does at last perceive the agreement or disagreement of the ideas it considers, yet it is not without pains and attention: there must be more than one transient view to find it. A steady application and pursuit is required to this discovery: and there must be a progression by steps and degrees before the mind can in this way arrive at certainty . . .

5. *The demonstrated conclusion not without doubt, precedent to the demonstration.*—Another difference between intuitive and demonstrative knowledge is, that though in the latter all doubt be removed, when by the intervention of the intermediate ideas the agreement or disagreement is perceived; yet before the demonstration there was a doubt; which in intuitive knowledge cannot happen to the mind that has its faculty of perception left to a degree capable of distinct ideas, no more than it can be a doubt to the eye (that can distinctly see white and black), whether this ink and this paper be all of a colour . . .

6. *Not so clear as intuitive knowledge.*—It is true, the perception produced by demonstration is also very clear; yet it is often with a great abatement of that evident lustre and full assurance that always accompany that which I call intuitive; like a face reflected by several mirrors one to another, where, as long as it retains the similitude and agreement with the object, it produces a knowledge; but it is still, in every successive reflection, with a lessening of that perfect clearness and distinctness which is in the first, till at last, after many removes, it has a great mixture of dimness, and is not at first sight so knowable, especially to weak eyes. Thus it is with knowledge made out by a long train of proofs.

7. *Each step in demonstrated knowledge must have intuitive evidence.*—Now, in every step reason makes in demonstrative knowledge, there is an intuitive knowledge of that agreement or disagreement it seeks with the next intermediate idea, which it uses as a proof: for it were not so, that yet would need a proof; since without the perception of such agreement or disagreement there is no knowledge produced . . . This intuitive perception of the agreement or disagreement of the intermediate ideas, in each step and progression of the demonstration, must also be carried exactly in the mind, and a man must be sure that no part is left out: which, because in long deductions, and the use of many proofs, the memory does not always so readily and exactly retain; therefore it comes to pass, that this is more imperfect than intuitive knowledge, and men embrace often falsehood for demonstrations.

8. *Hence the mistake, ex præcognitis et præconcessis.*—The necessity of this intuitive knowledge, in each step of scientifical or demonstrative reasoning, gave occasion, I imagine, to that mistaken axiom, that all reasoning was *ex præcognitis et præconcessis*; which how far it is mistaken, I shall have occasion to show more at large where I come to consider propositions, and particularly those propositions which are called "maxims"; and to show that it is by a mistake that they are supposed to be the foundations of all our knowledge and reasonings.

9. *Demonstration not limited to ideas of mathematical quantity.*—It has been generally taken for granted, that mathematics alone are capable of demonstrative certainty: but to have such an agreement or disagreement as may intuitively be perceived being, as I imagine, not the privilege of the ideas of number, extension, and figure alone, it may possibly be the want of due method and application in us, and not of sufficient evidence in things, that demonstration has been thought to have so little to do in other parts of knowledge, and been scarce so much as aimed at by any but mathematicians . . .

10. *Why it has been thought to be so limited.*—The reason why it has been generally sought for and supposed to be only in those, I imagine, has been not only the general usefulness of those sciences, but because, in comparing their equality or excess, the modes of numbers have every the least difference very clear and perceivable: and though in extension every the least excess is not so perceptible, yet the mind has found out ways to examine and discover demonstratively the just equality of two angles, or extensions, or figures . . .

11. *Modes of qualities not demonstrable like modes of quantity.*—But in other simple ideas, whose modes and differences are made and counted by degrees, and not quantity, we have not so nice and accurate a distinction of their differences as to perceive or find ways to measure their just equality or the least differences. For those other simple ideas, being appearances or sensations produced in us by the size, figure, number, and motion of minute corpuscles singly insensible, their different degrees also depend upon

the variation of some or all of those causes; which since it cannot be observed by us in particles of matter whereof each is too subtle to be perceived, it is impossible for us to have any exact measures of the different degrees of these simple ideas . . .

* * *

13. *The secondary qualities of things not discovered by demonstration.*—Not knowing what number of particles, nor what motion of them, is fit to produce any precise degree of whiteness, we cannot demonstrate the certain equality of any two degrees of whiteness; because we have no certain standard to measure them by, nor means to distinguish every the least real difference; the only help we have being from our senses, which in this point fail us. But where the difference is so great as to produce in the mind clearly distinct ideas, whose differences can be perfectly retained, there these ideas of colours, as we see in different kinds, as blue and red, are as capable of demonstration as ideas of number and extension. What I have here said of whiteness and colours, I think, holds true in all secondary qualities, and their modes.

14. *Sensitive knowledge of the particular existence of finite beings without us.*—These two, viz., intuition and demonstration, are the degrees of our *knowledge*; whatever comes short of one of these, with what assurance soever embraced, is but *faith* or *opinion*, but not knowledge, at least in all general truths. There is, indeed, another perception of the mind employed about *the particular existence of finite beings without us*, which, going beyond bare probability, and yet not reaching perfectly to either of the foregoing degrees of certainty, passes under the name of *knowledge*. There can be nothing more certain, than that the idea we receive from an external object is in our minds; this is intuitive knowledge. But whether there be anything more than barely that idea in our minds, whether we can thence certainly infer the existence of anything without us which corresponds to that idea, is that whereof some men think there may be a question made; because men may have such ideas in their minds when no such thing exists, no such object affects their senses. But yet here, I think, we are provided with an evidence that puts us past doubting; for I ask any one, whether he be not invincibly conscious to himself of a different perception when he looks on the sun by day, and thinks on it by night; when he actually tastes wormwood, or smells a rose, or only thinks on that savour or odour? We as plainly find the difference there is between any idea revived in our minds by our own memory, and actually coming into our minds by our senses, as we do between any two distinct ideas. If any one say, a dream may do the same thing, and all these ideas may be produced in us without any external objects; he may please to dream that I make him this answer: (1) That it is no great matter whether I remove his scruple or no: where all is but dream, reasoning and arguments are of no use, truth and knowledge nothing. (2) That I believe he will allow a very manifest difference between dreaming of being in the fire, and being actually in it. But yet if he be resolved to appear so skeptical as to maintain, that what I call being actually in the fire is nothing but a dream; and that we cannot thereby certainly know that any such thing as fire actually exists without us; I answer, that we certainly finding that pleasure or pain follows upon the application of certain objects to us, whose existence we perceive, or dream that we perceive, by our senses; this certainly is as great as our happiness or misery, beyond which we have no concernment to know or to be. So that, I think, we may add to the two former sorts of knowledge this also, of the existence of particular external objects by that perception and consciousness we have of the actual entrance of ideas from them, and allow these three degrees of knowledge, viz.,

intuitive, *demonstrative*, and *sensitive*: in each of which there are different degrees and ways of evidence and certainty.

* * *

CHAPTER 3. OF THE EXTENT OF HUMAN KNOWLEDGE

1. *Extent of our knowledge.*—KNOWLEDGE, as has been said, lying in the perception of the agreement or disagreement of any of our ideas, it follows from hence that,

It extends no farther than we have ideas.—First, We can have knowledge no farther than we have ideas.

2. *It extends no farther than we can perceive their agreement or disagreement.*—Secondly, That we can have no knowledge farther than we can have perception of that agreement or disagreement: which perception being, (1) Either by *intuition*, or the immediate comparing any two ideas; or, (2) By *reason*, examining the agreement or disagreement of two ideas by the intervention of some others; or (3) By *sensation*, perceiving the existence of particular things; hence it also follows,

3. *Intuitive knowledge extends itself not to all the relations of all our ideas.*—Thirdly, that we cannot have an *intuitive knowledge* that shall extend itself to all our ideas, and all that we would know about them; because we cannot examine and perceive all the relations they have one to another by juxtaposition, or an immediate comparison one with another. Thus having the ideas of an obtuse and an acute angled triangle, both drawn from equal bases, and between parallels, I can by intuitive knowledge perceive the one not to be the other; but cannot that way know whether they be equal or no: because their agreement or disagreement in equality can never be perceived by an immediate comparing them; the difference of figure makes their parts incapable of an exact immediate application; and therefore there is need of some intervening quantities to measure them by, which is demonstration or rational knowledge.

4. *Nor does demonstrative knowledge.*—Fourthly, It follows also, from what is above observed, that our *rational knowledge* cannot reach to the whole extent of our ideas. Because between two different ideas we would examine, we cannot always find such mediums as we can connect one to another with an intuitive knowledge, in all the parts of the deduction; and wherever that fails, we come short of knowledge and demonstration.

5. *Sensitive knowledge narrower than either.*—Fifthly, *Sensitive knowledge*, reaching no farther than the existence of things actually present to our senses, is yet much narrower than either of the former.

* * *

CHAPTER 9. OF OUR THREEFOLD KNOWLEDGE OF EXISTENCE

1. *General propositions that are certain concern not existence.*—Hitherto we have only considered the essences of things; which being only abstract ideas, and thereby removed in our thoughts from particular existence, (that being the proper operation of the mind, in abstraction, to consider an idea under no other existence but what

it has in the understanding,) gives us no knowledge of real existence at all. Where, by the way, we may take notice, that universal propositions of whose truth or falsehood we can have certain knowledge concern not existence: and further, that all particular affirmations or negations that would not be certain if they were made general, are only concerning existence; they declaring only the accidental union or separation of ideas in things existing, which, in their abstract natures, have no known necessary union or repugnancy.

2. *A threefold knowledge of existence.*—But, leaving the nature of propositions, and different ways of predication to be considered more at large in another place, let us proceed now to inquire concerning our knowledge of the *existence of things*, and how we come by it. I say, then, that we have the knowledge of *our own* existence by intuition; of the existence of *God* by demonstration; and of *other things* by sensation.

3. *Our knowledge of our own existence is intuitive.*—As for our own existence, we perceive it so plainly and so certainly, that it neither needs nor is capable of any proof. For nothing can be more evident to us than our own existence. I think, I reason, I feel pleasure and pain: can any of these be more evident to me than my own existence? If I doubt of all other things, that very doubt makes me perceive my own existence, and will not suffer me to doubt of that. For if I know I feel pain, it is evident I have as certain perception of my own existence, as of the existence of the pain I feel: or if I know I doubt, I have as certain perception of the existence of the thing doubting, as of that thought which I *call doubt*. Experience then convinces us, that we have an *intuitive knowledge* of our own existence, and an internal infallible perception that we are. In every act of sensation, reasoning, or thinking, we are conscious to ourselves of our own being; and, in this matter, come not short of the highest degree of certainty.

CHAPTER 10. OF OUR KNOWLEDGE OF THE EXISTENCE OF A GOD

1. *We are capable of knowing certainly that there is a God.*—Though God has given us no innate ideas of himself; though he has stamped no original characters on our minds, wherein we may read his being; yet having furnished us with those faculties our minds are endowed with, he hath not left himself without witness: since we have sense, perception, and reason, and cannot want a clear proof of him, as long as we carry *ourselves* about us. Nor can we justly complain of our ignorance in this great point; since he has so plentifully provided us with the means to discover and know him; so far as is necessary to the end of our being, and the great concernment of our happiness. But, though this be the most obvious truth that reason discovers, and though its evidence be (if I mistake not) equal to mathematical certainty: yet it requires thought and attention; and the mind must apply itself to a regular deduction of it from some part of our intuitive knowledge, or else we shall be as uncertain and ignorant of this as of other propositions, which are in themselves capable of clear demonstration. To show, therefore, that we are capable of *knowing*, i.e., *being certain* that there is a God, and *how we may come by* this certainty, I think we need go no further than *ourselves*, and that undoubted knowledge we have of our own existence.

2. *For man knows that he himself exists.*—I think it is beyond question, that man has a clear idea of his own being; he knows certainly he exists, and that he is something. He that can doubt—whether he be anything or no, I speak not to; no more than I would argue with pure nothing, or endeavour to convince nonentity that it were something. If any one pretends to be so sceptical as to deny his own existence,

(for really to doubt of it is manifestly impossible,) let him for me enjoy his beloved happiness of being nothing, until hunger or some other pain convince him of the contrary. This, then, I think I may take for a truth, which every one's certain knowledge assures him of, beyond the liberty of doubting, viz., that he is something that actually exists.

3. *He knows also that nothing cannot produce a being; therefore something must have existed from eternity.*—In the next place, man knows, by an intuitive certainty, that bare *nothing can no more produce any real being, than it can be equal to two right angles*. If a man knows not that nonentity, or the absence of all being, cannot be equal to two right angles, it is impossible he should know any demonstration in Euclid. If, therefore, we know there is some real being, and that nonentity cannot produce any real being, it is an evident demonstration, that *from eternity there has been something*; since what was not from eternity had a beginning; and what had a beginning must be produced by something else.

4. *And that eternal Being must be most powerful.*—Next, it is evident, that what had its being and beginning from another, must also have all that which is in and belongs to its being from another too. All the powers it has must be owing to and received from the same source. This eternal source, then, of all being must also be the source and original of all power; and so *this eternal Being must be also the most powerful*.

5. *And most knowing.*—Again, a man finds in *himself* perception and knowledge. We have then got one step further; and we are certain now that there is not only some being, but some knowing, intelligent being in the world. There was a time, then, when there was no knowing being and when knowledge began to be; or else there has been also a *knowing being from eternity*. If it be said, there was a time when no being had any knowledge, when that eternal being was void of all understanding; I reply, that then it was impossible there should ever have been any knowledge: it being as impossible that things wholly void of knowledge, and operating blindly, and without any perception, should produce a knowing being, as it is impossible that a triangle should make itself three angles bigger than two right ones. For it is as repugnant to the idea of senseless matter, that it should put into itself sense, perception, and knowledge, as it is repugnant to the idea of a triangle, that it should put into itself greater angles than two right ones.

6. *And therefore God.*—Thus, from the consideration of ourselves, and what we infallibly find in our own constitutions, our reason leads us to the knowledge of this certain and evident truth,—*That there is an eternal, most powerful, and most knowing Being*; which whether any one will please to call God, it matters not. The thing is evident, and from this idea duly considered, will easily be deduced all those other attributes, which we ought to ascribe to this eternal Being. If, nevertheless, any one should be found so senselessly arrogant, as to suppose man alone knowing and wise, but yet the product of mere ignorance and chance; and that all the rest of the universe acted only by that blind haphazard; I shall leave with him that very rational and emphatical rebuke of Tully, to be considered at his leisure: "What can be more sillily arrogant and misbecoming, than for a man to think that he has a mind and understanding in him, but yet in all the universe beside there is no such thing? Or that those things, which with the utmost stretch of his reason he can scarce comprehend, should be moved and managed without any reason at all?" . . .

From what has been said, it is plain to me we have a more certain knowledge of the existence of a God, than of anything our senses have not immediately discovered to us. Nay, I presume I may say, that we more certainly know that there is a God, than that there is anything else without us. When I say we *know*, I mean there is such a knowledge within our reach which we cannot miss, if we will but apply our minds to that, as we do to several other inquiries.

* * *

CHAPTER 11. OF OUR KNOWLEDGE OF THE EXISTENCE OF OTHER THINGS

1. *Knowledge of the existence of other finite beings is to be had only by actual sensation.*—The knowledge of our own being we have by intuition. The existence of a God, reason clearly makes known to us, as has been shown.

The knowledge of the existence of *any other thing* we can have only by sensation: for there being no necessary connexion of real existence with any idea a man hath in his memory; nor of any other existence but that of God with the existence of any particular man: no particular man can know the existence of any other being, but only when, by actual operating upon him, it makes itself perceived by him. For, the having the idea of anything in our mind, no more proves the existence of that thing, than the picture of a man evidences his being in the world, or the visions of a dream make thereby a true history.

2. *Instance: whiteness of this paper.*—It is therefore the *actual receiving* of ideas from without that gives us notice of the existence of other things, and makes us know, that something doth exist at that time without us, which causes that idea in us; though perhaps we neither know nor consider how it does it. For it takes not from the certainty of our senses, and the ideas we receive by them, that we know not the manner wherein they are produced: v.g., whilst I write this, I have, by the paper affecting my eyes, that idea produced in my mind, which, whatever object causes, I call *white*; by which I know that that quality or accident (i.e., whose appearance before my eyes always causes that idea) doth really exist, and hath a being without me. And of this, the greatest assurance I can possibly have, and to which my faculties can attain, is the testimony of my eyes, which are the proper and sole judges of this thing; whose testimony I have reason to rely on as so certain, that I can no more doubt, whilst I write this, that I see white and black, and that something really exists that causes that sensation in me, than that I write or move my hand; which is a certainty as great as human nature is capable of, concerning the existence of anything, but a man's self alone, and of God.

3. *This notice by our senses, though not so certain as demonstration, yet may be called knowledge, and proves the existence of things without us.*—The notice we have by our senses of the existing of things without us, though it be not altogether so certain as our intuitive knowledge, or the deductions of our reason employed about the clear abstract ideas of our own minds; yet it is an assurance that deserves the name of *knowledge*. If we persuade ourselves that our faculties act and inform us right concerning the existence of those objects that affect them, it cannot pass for an ill-grounded confidence: for I think nobody can, in earnest, be so sceptical as to be uncertain of the existence of those things which he sees and feels. At least, he that can doubt so far, (whatever he may have with his own thoughts,) will never have any controversy with

me; since he can never be sure I say anything contrary to his own opinion. As to myself, I think God has given me assurance enough of the existence of things without me: since, by their different application, I can produce in myself both pleasure and pain, which is one great concernment of my present state. This is certain: the confidence that our faculties do not herein deceive us, is the greatest assurance we are capable of concerning the existence of material beings. For we cannot act anything but by our faculties; nor talk of knowledge itself, but by the help of those faculties which are fitted to apprehend even what knowledge is.

But besides the assurance we have from our senses themselves, that they do not err in the information they give us of the existence of things without us, when they are affected by them, we are further confirmed in this assurance by other concurrent reasons:—

4. I. *Confirmed by concurrent reasons:—First, because we cannot have ideas of sensation but by the inlet of the senses.*—It is plain those perceptions are produced in us by exterior causes affecting our senses: because those that want the organs of any sense, never can have the ideas belonging to that sense produced in their minds. This is too evident to be doubted: and therefore we cannot but be assured that they come in by the organs of that sense, and no other way. The organs themselves, it is plain, do not produce them: for then the eyes of a man in the dark would produce colours, and his nose smell roses in the winter: but we see nobody gets the relish of a pineapple, till he goes to the Indies, where it is, and tastes it.

5. II. *Secondly, Because we find that an idea from actual sensation, and another from memory, are very distinct perceptions.*—Because sometimes I find that *I cannot avoid the having those ideas produced in my mind*. For though, when my eyes are shut, or windows fast, I can at pleasure recall to my mind the ideas of light, or the sun, which former sensations had lodged in my memory; so I can at pleasure lay by *that* idea, and take into my view that of the smell of a rose, or taste of sugar. But, if I turn my eyes at noon towards the sun, I cannot avoid the ideas which the light or sun then produces in me. So that there is a manifest difference between the ideas laid up in my memory, (over which, if they were there only, I should have constantly the same power to dispose of them, and lay them by at pleasure,) and those which force themselves upon me, and I cannot avoid having. And therefore it must needs be some exterior cause, and the brisk acting of some objects without me, whose efficacy I cannot resist, that produces those ideas in my mind, whether I will or no. Besides, there is nobody who doth not perceive the difference in himself between contemplating the sun, as he hath the idea of it in his memory, and actually looking upon it: of which two, his perception is so distinct, that few of his ideas are more distinguishable one from another. And therefore he hath certain knowledge that they are not *both* memory, or the actions of his mind, and fancies only within him; but that actual seeing hath a cause without.

6. III. *Thirdly, because pleasure or pain, which accompanies actual sensation, accompanies not the returning of those ideas without the external objects*—Add to this, that many of those ideas are *produced in us with pain*, which afterwards we remember without the least offence. Thus, the pain of heat or cold, when the idea of it is revived in our minds, gives us no disturbance; which, when felt, was very troublesome; and is again, when actually repeated: which is occasioned by the disorder the external object causes in our bodies when applied to them: and we remember the pains of hunger, thirst, or the headache, without any pain at all; which would either never disturb us, or else constantly do it, as often as we thought of it, were there nothing more but ideas

floating in our minds, and appearances entertaining our fancies, without the real existence of things affecting us from abroad. The same may be said of *pleasure*, accompanying several actual sensations. And though mathematical demonstration depends not upon sense, yet the examining them by diagrams gives great credit to the evidence of our sight, and seems to give it a certainty approaching to that of demonstration itself. For, it would be very strange, that a man should allow it for an undeniable truth, that two angles of a figure, which he measures by lines and angles of a diagram, should be bigger one than the other, and yet doubt of the existence of those lines and angles, which by looking on he makes use of to measure that by.

7. IV. *Fourthly, because our senses assist one Another's testimony of the existence of outward things, and enable us to predict.*—Our senses in many cases *bear witness to the truth of each other's report*, concerning the existence of sensible things without us. He that sees a fire, may, if he doubt whether it be anything more than a bare fancy, *feel* it too; and be convinced, by putting his hand in it. Which certainly could never be put into such exquisite pain by a bare idea or phantom, unless that the pain be a fancy too: which yet he cannot, when the burn is well, by raising the idea of it, bring upon himself again.

Thus I see, whilst I write this, I can change the appearance of the paper; and by designing the letters, tell *beforehand* what new idea it shall exhibit the very next moment, by barely drawing my pen over it: which will neither appear (let me fancy as much as I will) if my hands stand still; or though I move my pen, if my eyes be shut: nor, when those characters are once made on the paper, can I choose afterwards but see them as they are; that is, have the ideas of such letters as I have made. Whence it is manifest, that they are not barely the sport and play of my own imagination, when I find that the characters that were made at the pleasure of my own thoughts, do not obey them; nor yet cease to be, whenever I shall fancy it, but continue to affect my senses constantly and regularly, according to the figures I made them. To which if we will add, that the sight of those shall, from another man, draw such sounds as I beforehand design they shall stand for, there will be little reason left to doubt that those words I write do really exist without me, when they cause a long series of regular sounds to affect my ears, which could not be the effect of my imagination, nor could my memory retain them in that order.

8. *This certainty is as great as our condition needs.*—But yet, if after all this any one will be so sceptical as to distrust his senses, and to affirm that all we see and hear, feel and taste, think and do, during our whole being, is but the series and deluding appearances of a long dream, whereof there is no reality; and therefore will question the existence of all things, or our knowledge of anything: I must desire him to consider, that, if all be a dream, then he doth but dream that he makes the question, and so it is not much matter that a waking man should answer him. But yet, if he pleases, he may dream that I make him this answer, That the certainty of things existing in *rerum natura* when we have the testimony of our senses for it is not only as great as our frame can attain to, but as our condition needs. For, our faculties being suited not to the full extent of being, nor to a perfect, clear, comprehensive knowledge of things free from all doubt and scruple; but to the preservation of us, in whom they are; and accommodated to the use of life: they serve to our purpose well enough, if they will but give us certain notice of those things, which are convenient or inconvenient to us. For he that sees a candle burning, and hath experimented the force of its flame by putting his finger in it, will little doubt that this is something existing without him, which does him harm, and puts him to great pain: which is assurance enough, when no man requires

greater certainty to govern his actions by than what is as certain as his actions themselves. And if our dreamer pleases to try whether the glowing heat of a glass furnace be barely a wandering imagination in a drowsy man's fancy, by putting his hand into it, he may perhaps be wakened into a certainty greater than he could wish, that it is something more than bare imagination. So that this evidence is as great as we can desire, being as certain to us as our pleasure or pain, i.e., happiness or misery; beyond which we have no concernment, either of knowing or being. Such an assurance of the existence of things without us is sufficient to direct us in the attaining the good and avoiding the evil which is caused by them, which is the important concernment we have of being made acquainted with them.

9. *But reaches no further than actual sensation.*—In fine, then, when our senses do actually convey into our understandings any idea, we cannot but be satisfied that there doth something *at that time* really exist without us, which doth affect our senses, and by them give notice of itself to our apprehensive faculties, and actually produce that idea which we then perceive: and we cannot so far distrust their testimony, as to doubt that such *collections* of simple ideas as we have observed by our senses to be united together, do really exist together. But this knowledge extends as far as the present testimony of our senses, employed about particular objects that do then affect them, and no further. For if I saw such a collection of simple ideas as is wont to be called *man*, existing together one minute since, and am now alone, I cannot be certain that the same man exists now, since there is no *necessary connexion* of his existence a minute since with his existence now: by a thousand ways he may cease to be, since I had the testimony of my senses for his existence. And if I cannot be certain that the man I saw last today is now in being, I can less be certain that he is so who hath been longer removed from my senses, and I have not seen since yesterday, or since the last year: and much less can I be certain of the existence of men that I never saw. And, therefore, though it be highly probable that millions of men do now exist, yet, whilst I am alone, writing this, I have not that certainty of it which we strictly call knowledge; though the great likelihood of it puts me past doubt, and it be reasonable for me to do several things upon the confidence that there are men (and men also of my acquaintance, with whom I have to do) now in the world: but this is but probability, not knowledge.

10. *Folly to expect demonstration in everything.*—Whereby yet we may observe how foolish and vain a thing it is for a man of a narrow knowledge, who having reason given him to judge of the different evidence and probability of things, and to be swayed accordingly; how vain, I say, it is to expect demonstration and certainty in things not capable of it—and refuse assent to very rational propositions, and act contrary to very plain and clear truths, because they cannot be made out so evident, as to surmount every the least (I will not say reason, but) pretence of doubting. He that, in the ordinary affairs of life, would admit of nothing but direct plain demonstration would be sure of nothing in this world but of perishing quickly. The wholesomeness of his meat or drink would not give him reason to venture on it: and I would fain know what it is he could do upon such grounds as are capable of no doubt, no objection.

Gottfried Leibniz
1646–1716

Gottfried Wilhelm Von Leibniz was born and raised in academe. His father was a professor of moral philosophy at the University of Leipzig, and his mother was the daughter of a law professor at the same institution. His advance was prodigious: At 15, he began his study of the history of philosophy at the university; at 17, after defending his thesis, he proceeded to the University of Jena where he studied mathematics and law; at 18, he published his treatise on law; and at 20, he was ready to present himself as a candidate for the doctor of law degree, but he was declared too young. So he moved to the University of Altdorf, where he not only received his doctoral degree but was offered a professorship. He declined this invitation and settled into a position with Johann Philipp von Schönborn, elector of Mainz.

While in the service of the Mainz court, he lived for a time in Paris, where he made the acquaintance of leading thinkers of his day, such as the physicist Christian Huygens and the philosophers Antoine Arnauld and Nicolas Malebranche. As part of his mission in Paris, Leibniz prepared a plan for invading Egypt for Louis XIV (hoping to deflect Louis from military action in Europe). Though Louis never acted on the plan, many scholars believe that Napoleon used the scheme 120 years later.

In addition to diplomatic initiatives, Leibniz worked extensively on mathematics while he was in Paris. He invented a calculating machine that could add, subtract, multiply, divide, and extract square roots. When he demonstrated his machine in London, he was made a member of the Royal Society (1673). He also discovered differential and integral calculus—though years later there was an unpleasant dispute over whether Leibniz or Newton should get the credit for it. Did one of these great men steal the idea from the other? The Royal Society officially belittled Leibniz's achievement (quite unjustly according to the verdict of subsequent scholarship). It has been said that the dispute "redounded to the discredit of all concerned." It may be best to credit both men with the discovery. It is interesting that Leibniz's notation proved the more convenient and is the system currently used.

In 1676, Leibniz went into the service of the Duke of Brunswick in Hanover, where he remained the rest of his life. He traveled extensively and met notable people such as Spinoza and the chemist Robert Boyle. In 1700, he was elected a foreign member of the French Academy. In the same year, by his inspiration, the *Akademie der Wissenschaften* was founded in Berlin and he was elected its first president. He was a close friend of Sophie Charlotte, the wife of the Elector of Brandenburg (subsequently the first king of Prussia). The only large systematic philosophic work he published, *Theodicy* (1710), grew out of his discussions with Sophie Charlotte.

Despite his accomplishments, Leibniz was not well liked. As Bertrand Russell later commented, "Leibniz was one of the supreme intellects of all time, but he was not admirable." Leibniz's death in 1716 was ignored not only by the Royal Society in London but also by the *Akademie* in Berlin and by the court at Hanover. His secretary is said to have been his only mourner, and an eyewitness reports in his memoirs that Leibniz "was buried more like a robber than what he really was, the ornament of his country."

Leibniz Stamp, 1980. Leibniz's death in 1716 was ignored by virtually everyone and, as one eyewitness said, he "was buried more like a robber than what he really was, the ornament of his country." The neglect of Leibniz in his lifetime has given way to great admiration for the scope and originality of his thought. (*Deutsche Bundespost*)

At his death, he left an enormous number of unpublished letters and manuscripts. One major work was published in 1765: his detailed critique of Locke's *Essay,* entitled *Nouveaux essais sur L'entendement humain*. Leibniz had completed the book in 1704 but withheld it from publication when Locke died the same year. The book greatly stimulated Immanuel Kant, particularly his *Critique of Pure Reason*. In the twentieth century, thinkers such as Bertrand Russell and Ernst Cassirer have focused attention on Leibniz's work in logic. The neglect of Leibniz in his lifetime has given way to the current great admiration for the scope and originality of his thought.

* * *

Leibniz's philosophy begins by rejecting the notion that extension is a substance (as Descartes claimed) or an attribute of substance (as Spinoza thought). Instead of understanding nature as a collection of discrete extended entities, such as atoms, Leibniz says that the basic substance is a "Monad," or a unit of psychic force. Such Monads are without parts (i.e., simple) and have no interaction with one another. As Leibniz puts it, they have "no windows through which anything may come in or go out." Each Monad has within itself an internal principle of "appetition" that causes it to change. Although there is no causal interaction between Monads, they may *appear* to influence one another. This connection is merely a reflection of the "pre-established harmony" by which God created each of the Monads to "mirror" the others. A Monad's entire past and present are contained within it so that whatever it does, it does so by necessity. If we could know the entire past of a given Monad, we could predict its entire future.

Monads all differ qualitatively and occupy different points of view. This means that each Monad "mirrors" the world in a slightly different way and with different levels of clarity. Rocks and dirt are made of colonies of "low-level" Monads that have only dull and confused perceptions as they mirror the world. It might seem odd to talk about rocks as having perceptions at all, but according to Leibniz, every Monad has some sort of psychic life: Each Monad has an "internal state [by which it] represent[s] external things." Those Monads whose perceptions are "more distinct and are accompanied by memory" are on a higher level. The dominant Monad of an animal, for example, has distinct perceptions and memory of those perceptions: "If you show a stick to a dog, for instance, it remembers the pain caused by it and howls or runs away." This dominant Monad Leibniz calls a "soul" to distinguish it from lower level or "naked" Monads. Human beings are Monad aggregates of yet a higher degree. Whereas human bodies are colonies of lower Monads, the dominant Monad in a person is a "spirit," because it is capable of performing "reflective acts." Spirits are also capable of knowing the universe and of entering into a relationship with the chief Monad, God.

Leibniz's metaphysics seems to exclude the possibility of freedom. If each Monad has its entire future within it, and if it thus unfolds that future by necessity, how can we, as colonies of a dominant "spirit" Monad and lower "body" Monads, be free? Leibniz's answer to this question turns on his definition of "freedom." To be "free," claims Leibniz, does not mean "liberty of indifference." Instead we are "free" in that our actions flow from our wills and there is no logical contradiction in our willing other than we do. As Leibniz put it, "there is always a prevailing reason which prompts the will to its choice, and for the maintenance of freedom for the will it suffices that this reason should incline without necessitating." Of course, he also claims that our wills are created by God and that God foreknows what we will will ourselves to do. But the action of our wills is not necessary in the sense that willing something else involves a logical contradiction; hence, our wills can be said to be "free."

* * *

Leibniz never wrote a *magnum opus* that clearly defined his position on philosophical issues. *The Discourse on Metaphysics* (1686), reprinted here (complete) in the Martin and Brown translation, gives his early ideas on metaphysics. The *Monadology* (1714), also reprinted here (complete) in the Paul Schrecker and Anne Martin Schrecker translation, presents his mature position on metaphysics.

For general introductions to Leibniz's philosophy, see Nicholas Rescher, *The Philosophy of Leibniz* (Englewood Cliffs, NJ: Prentice Hall, 1967); C.D. Broad, *Leibniz: An Introduction*, edited by C. Lewy (Cambridge: Cambridge University Press, 1975); Stuart Brown, *Leibniz* (Minneapolis: University of Minnesota Press, 1984); Robert Merrihew Adams, *Leibniz: Determinist, Theist, Idealist* (Oxford: Oxford University Press, 1994); Donald Rutherford, *Leibniz and the Rational Order of Nature* (Cambridge: Cambridge University Press, 1997); Nicholas Jolley, *Leibniz* (London: Routledge, 2005); Lloyd Strickland, *Leibniz Reinterpreted* (London: Continuum, 2006); Franklin Perkins, *Leibniz; A Guide for the Perplexed* (London: Continuum, 2007); and Maria Rosa Antognazza, *Leibniz: An Intellectual Biography* (Cambridge: Cambridge University Press, 2009). For a discussion of the logic and metaphysics of Leibniz, Bertrand Russell, *A Critical Exposition of the Philosophy of Leibniz* (London: George Allen & Unwin, 1900), is still a valuable source. For more recent treatments of these issues, see Hidé Ishiguro, *Leibniz's Philosophy of Logic and Language* (Ithaca, NY: Cornell University Press, 1972); Benson Mates, *The Philosophy of Leibniz: Metaphysics and Language* (Oxford: Oxford University Press, 1986); Reginald Osburn Savage, *Real Alternatives: Leibniz's Metaphysics of Choice* (Norwell, MA: Kluwer, 1998); Christia Mercer, *Leibniz's Metaphysics: Its Origins and Development* (Cambridge: Cambridge University Press, 1999) and Daniel Garber, *Leibniz: Body, Substance, Monad* (Oxford: Oxford University Press, 2009). For a commentaries on *The Monadology*, see Herbert Wildon Carr, *The Monadology of Leibniz* (Los Angeles: University of Southern California Press, 1930) and Anthony Savile, *Routledge Philosophy Guidebook to Leibniz and the* Monadology (London: Routledge, 2000). For collections of essays, see Harry G. Frankfurt, ed., *Leibniz: A Collection of Critical Essays* (Garden City, NY: Doubleday, 1972); R.S. Woolhouse, ed., *Leibniz: Metaphysics and Philosophy of Science* (Oxford: Oxford University Press, 1981); Michael Hooker, *Leibniz: Critical and Interpretive Essays* (Minneapolis: University of Minnesota Press, 1984); Vere Chappell, ed., *Essays on Early Modern Philosophers: Gottfried Wilhelm Leibniz* (Hamden, CT: Garland Press, 1992); Nicholas Jolley, ed., *The Cambridge Companion to Leibniz* (Cambridge: Cambridge University Press, 1995); Catherine Wilson, ed., *Leibniz* (New York: Ashgate, 2000); and Donald Rutherford and J.A. Cover, eds., *Leibniz: Nature and Freedom* (Oxford: Oxford University Press, 2005).

DISCOURSE ON METAPHYSICS

1. On the Divine Perfection: God Does Everything in the Most Desirable Way

The most commonly accepted notion of God we have, and the one most full of meaning, is well enough expressed in these terms: God is an absolutely perfect being. Not enough thought, however, is given to its consequences. If we are to make progress, it is relevant to note that in nature there are several entirely different perfections, that God possesses them all together, and that each belongs to Him to the highest degree.

We also need to understand what a perfection is. A sure enough mark of one is that forms or natures not admitting of an ultimate degree are not perfections, as for example the nature of numbers or of shape. For the greatest of all numbers (or rather the number of all numbers), and the greatest of all shapes imply contradictions while omniscience and omnipotence involve no impossibility. Consequently, power and knowledge are perfections, and to the extent that they belong to God, they have no limits.

Hence it follows that since God possesses supreme and infinite wisdom, He acts in the most perfect manner, not only in the metaphysical sense, but also morally speaking. From our point of view we can express ourselves thus: the more we are enlightened and informed about the works of God, the more we shall be disposed to find that they are excellent and satisfactory in every way we could hope.

2. Against Those Who Maintain that There Is No Goodness in the Works of God, or that the Rules of Goodness and Beauty Are Arbitrary

Thus I am far removed from the opinion of those who maintain that there are no rules of goodness or perfection in the nature of things or in the ideas God has of them, and that the works of God are good only for the formal reason that God made them. For if that were so, since God knew He was their author, He had only to look at them after making them to find them good, in accordance with the testimony of Holy Scripture. But Scripture seems to have made use of this anthropomorphic way of speaking only to make us realise that we recognise the excellence of God's works by considering them by themselves, even when we disregard the purely extrinsic denomination that refers them to their cause. This is all the more true in that it is by considering the works that we can discover the Worker, so that the works must carry His marks in themselves. I confess that the contrary opinion seems to me extremely dangerous, and very close to

Gottfried Leibniz, Discourse on Metaphysics and Related Writings, edited and translated with an introduction, notes and glossary by R. Niall D. Martin and Stuart Brown, Manchester University Press, 1988. [The translation used comes from our edition in which we attempted to help scholars understand the document and the thinking behind it by including additions and deletions to highlight Leibniz ś evolving thought, and to show other relevant documents from the same period for a like purpose. We would encourage users of this edition particulary interested in Leibniz to consult our edition and its scholarly apparatus.]

[Leibniz made minor additions, deletions, and/or changes to virtually every paragraph of this work. I have chosen to reproduce Leibniz's text minus all material deleted by Leibniz.]

the way the Spinozists think of goodness and harmony. Their opinion is that the beauty of the universe and the goodness we attribute to the works of God are no more than the chimeras of men who conceive God according to their own way of thinking. Also, if we say that things are good by no rule of goodness beyond the will of God alone, we thoughtlessly destroy, I feel, all the love and glory of God. For why praise Him for what He had done if He would be equally praiseworthy for doing the opposite? Where will His justice and His wisdom be, if all that remains of Him is some kind of a despotic power, if His will takes the place of reason, and if, by the very definition of tyranny, what pleases the Almighty is *ipso facto* just? Besides, it seems that every act of willing presupposes some reason for willing, and that reason is naturally prior to will. That is why I still find altogether strange the expression of Descartes who says that even the eternal truths of metaphysics and geometry, and consequently also the rules of goodness, justice and perfection are no more than the effects of God's will. It seems to me, rather, that they are no more than the consequences of His understanding, which certainly does not depend on His will, any more His essence does.

3. AGAINST THOSE WHO THINK GOD COULD HAVE DONE BETTER

Neither can I approve the opinion of some scholastics who maintain boldly that what God has done is not absolutely perfect, and that He could have done much better. For it seems to me that the consequences of this opinion are altogether contrary to the glory of God. "Just as the lesser evil contains a proportion of good, so the lesser good contains a proportion of evil." To act with less perfection than one could have done is to act imperfectly. To show that an architect could have done better is to find fault with his work. It also runs counter to the assurance of the goodness of God's works in Holy Scripture. For, since perfections decrease to infinity, however God did his work, it would always be good in comparison with the less perfect, if that were enough. But a thing is not very praiseworthy if it is only so in that way. I also think that a very large number of passages favouring my opinion could be found in the divine Scriptures and the holy Fathers, with scarcely any favouring that of those new scholastics a view unknown, in my opinion, to the whole of antiquity. It is based on our insufficient knowledge of the general harmony of the universe and of the hidden reasons for God's conduct which lead us to the rash judgement that many things could have been done better. Besides, these moderns insist on some subtleties that are not very sound, for they imagine that nothing is so perfect but that there is something that is more perfect, which is a mistake. There is an infinity of regular figures, but one is the most perfect, namely the circle. If a triangle had to be made and there was no further specification of the kind of triangle, God would assuredly make an equilateral triangle because, absolutely speaking, that is the most perfect.

They also think that in this way they are providing for the liberty of God, as if it were not the highest liberty to act in accordance with sovereign reason. For, apart from its apparent impossibility, the belief that God acts in some matter without any reason for His act of will is hardly consistent with His glory. Suppose, for example, that God chooses between A and B, and that He takes A without any reason for preferring it to B; I say that that action of God would at the least not be praiseworthy. For every praise must be based on some reason and here *ex hypothesi* there is none. On the contrary, I hold that God does nothing for which He does not merit being glorified.

4. Loving God Demands Complete Satisfaction with and Acquiescence in what He Does, but We Do Not, on that Account, Have to be Quietists

The general recognition of this great truth—that God always acts in the most perfect and desirable manner possible—is to my mind the basis of the love we owe to God concerning all things. For he who loves seeks his satisfaction in the happiness or perfection of the loved one and his actions. "True friendship is to want the same and to reject the same." And I think that it is difficult to love God well when not disposed to will what He wills, if changing that were in our power. Indeed those who are not satisfied with what He does seem to me like discontented subjects of a king or of a republic whose intentions are little different from those of rebels.

Hence, in accordance with these principles, I hold that to act in conformity with the love of God it is not enough to be patient under duress. We must be truly satisfied with all that happens to us in consequence of His will. I mean this acquiescence to apply to the past. As far as the future is concerned, we must not be quietists nor wait ridiculously with arms folded for what God will do, in accordance with the sophism the Ancients called ⟨*logon aegon*⟩ lazy reason. On the contrary, we must act in accordance with the presumptive will of God, as far as we can judge it, trying with all our ability to contribute to the general good, especially to the adornment and perfection of what concerns us or is near us, or, so to speak, within our range. For when the outcome shows that God may perhaps not want our good will to have its effect for the present, it does not follow that He does not want us to do what we have done. On the contrary, since He is the best of all masters, He never asks for more than the right intentions, and it is for Him to know the hour and the place for bringing good plans to fruition.

5. What Are the Rules of Perfection of God's Conduct; and that the Simplicity of Means Is Balanced by the Richness of Effects

Hence it is enough to have this confidence in God, that He does everything for the best and that nothing can harm those who love him. But to know in detail the reasons that could have moved Him to choose this order of the universe, to allow sins, or to dispense His saving grace in a particular way, is beyond the power of a finite mind, particularly of a finite mind that has not yet attained enjoyment of the sight of God.

Nevertheless, some general remarks can be made on the conduct of Providence in the government of things. Thus it can be said that whatever encloses more reality in less volume is more perfect, that he who acts perfectly is like an excellent geometer who knows how to find the best constructions for a problem; like a good architect who arranges his site and the funds intended for the building in the most advantageous manner, so as to leave nothing that jars or lacks the beauty of which it is capable; like a good householder who uses his property so that nothing is left uncultivated or barren; like a skilled engineer who achieves his result by the least complicated way that could be chosen; like an experienced author who includes as much reality as he is able in the least space. Now the most perfect of all beings, occupying the least volume, in other words, those which hinder the least, are minds, and their perfections are the virtues. That is why we must not doubt that the happiness of minds is the principal objective of God and that He pursues it as much as the general harmony allows. More will be said of this presently.

As for the simplicity of God's ways, that applies properly in respect of means whereas the variety, richness or abundance applies to aims or effects. The one has to be in balance with the other, like the expenses of a building with the size and beauty expected of it. It is true that nothing costs God anything, much less than it costs a philosopher to make hypotheses for the construction of his imaginary world, since God has only to make decrees to bring a real world to birth; but in relation to wisdom, in so far as they are mutually independent, decrees or hypotheses take the place of expenditure, for reason demands that we avoid a multiplicity of hypotheses or principles; in almost the same way the simplest system is always preferred in astronomy.

6. God Does Nothing Out of Order and It Is Not Even Possible to Imagine Events that Are Not Regular

The decisions or actions of God are commonly divided into ordinary and extraordinary. But it is well to bear in mind that God does nothing out of order. So, whatever passes for extraordinary is only so in relation to some particular order established among creatures. For, in relation to the universal order, everything conforms to it. So true is this, that not only does nothing happen in the world that is absolutely irregular, but such a thing cannot even be imagined. Suppose, for example, that someone puts a number of points on paper completely at random like those who practise the ridiculous art of geomancy, then I say that it is possible to find a geometric line whose notion is constant and uniform according to some rule, so that this line passes through all these points and does so in the same order as they were made by the hand.

And if someone were to draw in one movement a line that was sometimes straight, sometimes circular, and sometimes of some other kind, it is possible to find a notion, a rule, or an equation common to all the points in that line and in virtue of which these same changes had to occur. For example there is no face whose contour is not part of a geometric line and cannot be drawn all in one movement by some rule-governed motion. But when a rule is very complicated, what conforms to it is taken to be irregular.

Thus it can be said that however God might have created the world, it would always have been regular and within some general order. But God chose that world that is the most perfect, i.e. the one that is simultaneously the simplest in hypotheses and richest in phenomena, just as a geometric line might be if its construction was easy but its properties most admirable and extensive. I make use of these comparisons to sketch some kind of imperfect resemblance to the divine wisdom and to say something that could at least raise our minds to conceive in some way what cannot be adequately expressed. But by this I do not claim to explain the great mystery on which the whole universe depends.

7. Miracles Conform to the General Order Although They Are Contrary to Subaltern Norms. What God Wishes or Permits by a General or Particular Will

Now, since nothing can take place that is not within the order, it can be said that miracles are just as much within the order as natural operations, are so called because they conform to certain subaltern norms we call the nature of things. For it can be said that this "nature" is no more than a custom of God from which He can exempt Himself in virtue of a stronger reason than the one that moved Him to make use of these norms.

As for the general and particular wills, depending on how we take the matter, it can be said that God does everything in accordance with His most general will, the one in conformity with the most perfect order He chose. But it can also be said that He has particular wills, which are exceptions to the subaltern norms mentioned above; for the most general of the laws of God, by means of which He regulates the whole universe, are without exception.

It can also be said that God wills everything that is an object of His particular will. But as for the objects of His general will, such as the actions of other creatures, particularly of those that are rational, and with which, (i.e. the *actions*) God wishes to concur, we must draw a distinction: if the action is good in itself, it can be said that God wills it and sometimes commands it, even when it does not happen; but if it is evil in itself, and only becomes good by accident, it has to be said that God permits it and not that He wills it, though He concurs in it through the laws of nature established by Him, and because he is able to draw from it greater good. This comes about because the sequence of things, particularly punishment and recompense, corrects its evil nature, and compensates for the evil with interest, so that in the end there is more perfection in all that follows than if none of the evil had happened.

8. In Order to Distinguish the Actions of God From Those of Creatures, an Explanation Is Given of the Notion of an Individual Substance

It is rather difficult to distinguish the actions of God from those of creatures as well as the actions and passions of these same creatures. For there are those who think that God does everything, while others imagine that He does no more than conserve the force He has given to creatures. What follows will show how far either of these can be said. Now since, properly speaking, actions belong to individual substances ("actions belong to supposita"), it will be necessary to explain just what such a substance is.

It seems to me that when several predications are attributed to the same subject and this subject is not attributed to any other, this subject is called an individual substance. But that is not enough and such an explanation is merely nominal, so we need to consider what it is to be truly attributed to a particular subject.

Now it is acknowledged that all true predication has some basis in the nature of things, and when a proposition is not an identity, that is, when the predicate is not expressly included in the subject, it must be so included virtually. That is what the Philosophers call *inesse*, when they say that the predicate is in the subject. Thus the subject term must always include that of the predicate, so that whoever understood the notion of the subject perfectly would also judge that the predicate belongs to it.

That being so, we can say that the nature of an individual substance or complete being is to have such a complete notion as to include and entail all the predicates of the subject that notion is attributed to. In contrast, an accident is a being whose notion does not include all that can be attributed to the subject it is attributed to. Thus* the quality of being king that belongs to Alexander the Great, taken in abstraction from the subject, is

*The first edition of the text used the following example: "Thus the circular figure of the ring of Gyges, does not contain everything that makes up the individual notion of this ring. Whereas God sees in it at the same time the foundation and cause for all the predicates that can truly be applied to it, such as that it would be swallowed by a fish and nevertheless returned to its master. I speak here as if this ring were a substance."

not sufficiently determinate for one individual, and does not include the other qualities of the same subject, nor everything that the notion of this prince includes, whereas God who sees the individual notion or *haecceity*** of Alexander sees in it at the same time the foundation and reason for all the predicates that can truly be ascribed to him, such as that he would defeat Darius and Porus even to the point of knowing *a priori* (and not by experience) whether he died naturally or by poison, something we can only know historically. Also, when we consider well the connection of things, we can say that there is in the soul of Alexander for all time traces of everything that happened to him, and marks of everything that will happen to him, and even traces of everything happening in the universe, though to recognise them all belongs to God alone.

9. Each Unique Substance Expresses the Whole Universe in Its Own Way, and Included in Its Notion Are All the Events that Happen to It With all their Circumstances, and the Whole Sequence of External Things

Among several paradoxical conclusions following from this, is that it is not true that two substances are completely alike, differing only numerically, and what St Thomas has to say on this point about angels and intelligences ("in these cases every individual is a lowest species") is true of all substances provided that the specific difference is taken in the way geometers take it in relation to their figures. Likewise, if bodies are substances, their natures cannot possibly consist solely in size, figure and motion: something else is needed. Likewise, a substance can begin only by creation and perish only by annihilation; a substance cannot be divided into two, nor can two substances become one, and so the number of substances does not naturally increase or diminish, though they are frequently transformed.

Moreover every substance is as it were an entire world and a mirror of God, or rather of the whole universe, expressing it in its own way, somewhat as the same town is variously represented according to the different positions of an observer. It can even be said that every substance bears in some way the mark of the infinite wisdom and omnipotence of God, imitating Him as far as it is capable. For it expresses, if only confusedly, all that happens in the universe, past, present and future, and this has some resemblance to an infinite perception or knowledge. And since all other substances in turn express it and are accommodated to it, it can be said to extend its power over all the others in imitation of the omnipotence of the Creator.

10. There is Some Soundness to the Belief in Substantial Forms, but These Make no Difference to the Phenomena, and Should Not Be Used to Explain Particular Effects

It seems that the ancients in distinguishing an *ens per se* from an *ens per accidens* and in introducing substantial forms, as well as the many able people who were accustomed to profound meditations and who taught theology and philosophy centuries ago, many

**Literally "thisness," an allusion to the theory of what makes something an individual substance produced by Duns Scotus and in which Leibniz had taken an interest when writing a student dissertation. Every individual has its own *haecceity*, according to Duns Scotus, though (like Leibniz) he believed it was only known to God.

of them praiseworthy for their sanctity, had some knowledge of what we have just said. This is what led them to introduce and uphold the substantial forms so much in disfavour today. But they are neither so far from the truth nor as ridiculous as the common run of our modern philosophers imagine.

I agree that the knowledge of forms is of no use in the details of physics and should not be used for explaining the particulars of phenomena. That is where our scholastics went wrong, and with them the physicians of the past who followed their example, in thinking to account for the properties of bodies by mentioning forms and qualities without taking the trouble to examine their manner of operation. It is as if we were to content ourselves with saying that a clock has the horodictic [time-telling] quality deriving from its form without considering what that consists in. That indeed might be enough for whoever buys the clock, provided he left its maintenance to someone else.

But this shortcoming and misuse of forms should not make us reject something whose knowledge is so necessary in metaphysics that without it, I hold, the first principles cannot be well understood, nor the mind sufficiently raised to the knowledge of incorporeal natures and the wonders of God.

Nevertheless, a geometer has no need to trouble his mind with the famous labyrinth of the composition of the continuum, and neither has any moral philosopher, and still less any legal expert or politician, any need to trouble himself with the great difficulties involved in reconciling the freedom of the will with the providence of God. For the geometer can complete all his demonstrations and the politician conclude all his deliberations without entering into these discussions, important as they are in philosophy and theology. In the same way, a physicist can account for experiments, sometimes by means of simpler experiments carried out before, and sometimes by means of geometrical and mechanical demonstrations, without the need of forms and other general considerations belonging to another sphere. If he employs the extraordinary concurrence of God, or some soul, *arché* or other thing of that nature, he is wandering as far off course as he who tries to introduce the nature of destiny and our liberty into a deliberation about an important practical matter. Men often make this mistake without thinking when they trouble their minds by considering fate, and sometimes they are even diverted from some good resolution or necessary care as a result.

11. The Meditations of the Theologians and Philosophers Called "Scholastics" Are Not to Be Despised Entirely

I know that in claiming in some way to rehabilitate the old philosophy and restore the all but banished substantial forms to which not enough justice has been done to life, I am proposing a big paradox. But I only do this on the supposition that it is possible to speak of bodies as substances. But perhaps I shall not be lightly condemned if it is known that I have long meditated on modern philosophy, and spent much time on physical experiments and geometrical demonstrations, and that I was long persuaded of the vanity of such beings. But I was eventually obliged to take them up again against my will and as if by force. It was as a result of carrying out my own researches that I was made to recognise that our moderns do not do full justice to St. Thomas and other great men of those times, and that the opinions of scholastic philosophers and theologians are much more sound than is imagined, as long as they are used appropriately and in their place. I am even convinced that if some exact and reflecting mind took the trouble to clarify and digest their thoughts in the manner of analytical geometry, he would find a treasure store of very important truths which could be demonstrated completely.

12. Notions Defined by Extension Involve Something Imaginary and Cannot Constitute the Essence of Bodies

But, to take up again the thread of our considerations, I believe that any one who meditates on the nature of substance as I have explained it above will find that either bodies are not substances in strict metaphysical rigour (the view indeed of the Platonists), or that the whole nature of body does not consist solely in extension, i.e. in size, shape and motion. On the contrary, something related to souls which is commonly called a "substantial form" has necessarily to be recognised in them, though that makes no more difference to the phenomena than the souls of animals, if they have any. It can even be demonstrated that the notions of size, shape and motion are not so distinct as is imagined and that they involve something imaginary and relative to our perceptions, just as colour, heat and other similar qualities also do, (to an even greater extent)—we may doubt that these are truly in the nature of external things. That is why qualities of these kinds could not constitute any substance. And if there were no other principle of identity in body than the one just considered, no body would ever last more than a moment.

Nevertheless, souls and substantial forms of other bodies are very different from intelligent souls, who alone know what they do, and which not only do not naturally perish but even for ever retain the basis of the knowledge of what they are. This makes them liable to punishment and reward, and makes them citizens of the republic of the universe whose monarch is God. It also follows that all other creatures ought to serve them, something we shall discuss more fully presently.

13. Since the Individual Notion of Every Person Includes Once for All Everything that Will Ever Happen to Him, in It Are to Be Seen the *A Priori* Proofs of Each Event, or Rather Why One Happened Rather than the Other. But Although These Truths Are Assured, They Do Not Cease to Be Contingent, Since They Are Based on the Free Will of God or of Creatures. There Are Always Reasons for Their Choices but These Incline Without Necessitating

But a great difficulty can arise from the foundations laid above, and before proceeding further, we must try to deal with it. We said that the notion of an individual substance includes once for all everything that can ever happen to it, and that by considering this notion, we can see in it everything that can truly be stated about it, just as we can see in the nature of the circle all the properties that can be derived from it. But from that it seems that all events will become fatally necessary that the difference between necessary and contingent truths will be destroyed, that all the fate of the Stoics will take the place of liberty, there will no longer be any room for human liberty, and absolute fate will reign over all our actions as well as over all other events in the world. My reply is: we must distinguish between what is certain and what is necessary. Everyone agrees that future contingents are assured since God foresees them, but it is not for all that admitted that they are necessary. But (it will be said) if some conclusion can be infallibly deduced from a definition or notion, it will be necessary. Now in fact we do maintain that everything that is to happen to a person is already included virtually in his nature or notion, just as the properties of a circle are included in its definition. So the difficulty remains. In order to give a sound answer, I claim that connection or derivation is of two kinds: one is absolutely necessary (its contrary implies a contradiction) and occurs with eternal truths like those of geometry; the other is necessary only *ex hypothesi*, by accident, so to speak, but in itself it is contingent, since its contrary does not imply a contradiction. This connection is based, not on the absolutely pure ideas and God's bare understanding alone, but also on His free decrees and the connection of the universe.

Let us take an example. Since Peter will deny our Lord, that action is included in his notion, for we are supposing it to be in the nature of such a perfect notion to include everything, so that the predicate should be included in it, *ut possit inesse subjecto*. We could say that it is not in virtue of this notion or idea or nature that he must sin, since that only applies to him because God knows everything. But, it will be insisted, his nature or form corresponds to his notion. I reply that it is indeed true and since God imposed this personality on him he must henceforth conform to it. I could reply with the objection of future contingents, for these have as yet no reality outside the understanding and the will, and since God gave them this form in advance, they will have to conform to it all the same.

But I prefer to deal with difficulties than make excuses for them with examples of some other similar difficulties, and what I am going to say will help clarify both. Thus it is here that we must apply the distinction between the kinds of connection. I say that what happens in accordance with these prior conditions is assured, but that it is not necessary; and if he did the opposite, he would be doing nothing impossible in itself though it would be *ex hypothesi* impossible that this should happen. For if someone were capable of completing the whole of the demonstration by virtue of which he proved the connection between the subject Peter and the predicate (namely, his denial), he would show that this fact had its basis in his notion or nature, and that it was reasonable and consequently assured that it should come about; but he would not show that it was necessary in itself, nor that its contrary implied a contradiction. In almost the same way, it is reasonable and assured that God will always do the best, although what is less perfect involves no contradiction in itself.

For it would be found that this demonstration of this predicate of Peter is not as absolute as those of numbers and geometry, but that it supposes the sequence of things freely chosen by God and founded on the first free decree of God, which always leads him to do what is most perfect, as well as on the decree God made (in consequence of the first) concerning human nature, which is that man will always (although freely) do what seems best. Now every truth founded on decrees of this kind is contingent, although certain, since those decrees make no difference to the possibility of things and, as I have already said, although God assuredly always chooses the best, that does not prevent what is less perfect remaining possible in itself, though it does not happen. It is not its impossibility but its imperfection that causes it to be rejected. Nothing is necessary if its contrary is possible.

Hence, we are in a position to meet such difficulties, great as they may appear to be (and indeed they are no less pressing for all others who have ever dealt with this matter), provided it is fully realised that contingent propositions have reasons for being that way rather than otherwise, or (what comes to the same thing) that there are *a priori* proofs of their truth which make them certain and show that the subject-predicate connection in these propositions has its basis in the nature of each. But these are not necessary demonstrations, since these reasons are only based on the principle of the contingency or of the existence of things, i.e. on what is or seems to be the best of several equally possible things; whereas necessary truths are founded on the principle of contradiction and on the possibility or impossibility of the essences themselves, without regard to the free will of God or of creatures.

14. God Produces Different Substances According to the Different Views He Has of the Universe. The Distinctive Nature of Each Substance Ensures, by the (Mediation) of God, that what Happens to Each Corresponds to what Happens to All the Others, Without Them Acting Directly on Each Other

Having after a fashion come to know what the nature of created substances consists in, we must try to explain their mutual dependence and their actions and passions. Now, in the first place, it is altogether obvious that created substances depend on God who conserves them—and even continually produces them by a kind of emanation, as we do our thoughts. For as God, so to speak, turns on all its sides and in all ways the general system of phenomena which He finds it good to produce to manifest His glory, and as He looks at all the faces of the world in all possible ways—because there is no relation that escapes His omniscience—the result of each view of the universe as if seen from a particular place is a substance expressing the universe in conformity with that view, if God finds it good to make His thought effective and produce this substance. And since the view of God is always true, our perceptions are so too; it is those of our judgements that derive from us that deceive us.

Now we have said above, and it follows from what we have just said, that each substance is like a world on its own, independent of everything else apart from God. Hence all our phenomena, that is, all that can ever happen to us, are consequences of our natures and, since we are free substances, of our wills. Since these phenomena preserve a particular order conforming to our nature or, so to speak, the world within us, so that we are able (to make observations useful for regulating our conduct which are justified by the favourable outcome of future phenomena) and to judge the future by the past without error, this enables us to say that these phenomena are true, without worrying whether they are outside us or whether others perceive them as well. Nevertheless, it is very true that the perceptions or qualities of all substances correspond with each other, so that each, carefully following the particular reasons or laws it has observed, fits in with the other in doing the same, just as when several people agree with each other to be at a particular place at a prearranged day, they can in fact do so if they wish. Now although all express the same phenomena, it does not follow from this that their expressions should be perfectly similar: it is enough that they are proportionate to each other. In the same way several spectators think they have seen the same thing and indeed agree with each other, although each sees and speaks according to his point of view.

Now it is God from whom all substances emanate continually and He sees the universe, not only as they see it, but quite differently from them all as well. He is the only cause of this correspondence between their phenomena, and He alone makes what is peculiar to one public to all, otherwise there would be no connection between them.

Hence it can be said in a manner of speaking and in a sense that is good, though remote from ordinary usage that a particular substance never acts on another particular substance and is not acted upon by another either. This follows if we remember that what happens to each is only a consequence of its idea or complete notion alone, since that idea already includes all the predicates or events, and expresses the whole universe. Indeed, nothing can happen to us but thoughts and perceptions, and all our thoughts and our future perceptions are no more than consequences, albeit contingent, of our previous thoughts and perceptions. Hence, if I were capable of considering distinctly everything happening or appearing to me at the present time, I would be able to see therein everything that would ever happen or appear to me. This would not fail, but would happen in any case, if everything outside me were destroyed and only God and myself remained. But as we attribute to other things, as if to causes acting on us, what we perceive in some way in other things, we have to consider the basis of this judgement, and what truth there is in it.

It is above all agreed that if we desire some phenomenon to happen at a certain time and it occurs in the ordinary course of things, we say that we acted and that we were the cause of it, as when I want to, as we say, "move my hand." Also, when it seems to me that by my will something happens to what I call another substance (and that this is the way it would happen as I judge from frequent observation) although it was not willed by it, I judge that this substance is acted upon. I admit this of myself when something happens to me in accordance with the will of another substance. Also, when we will something to happen, and something else follows from it that we did not want, we still say that we did it, provided that we understood how it followed. There are also some phenomena of extension that we attribute to ourselves more particularly and which have their basis *a parte rei* in what is called our body. As everything of importance happening to it (i.e. all the notable changes appearing to us in it) make themselves strongly felt in it, ordinarily at least, we attribute all the passions to this body to ourselves. We do so with very good reason, for even if we did not perceive them at the time, we do not fail to become well aware of the consequences, just as if we had been transported from one place to another while asleep. We also attribute to ourselves the actions of this body, as when we run, hit or fall, and when our body, continuing the motion once begun, has some effect. But I do not attribute to myself what happens to other bodies, because I realise that great changes can happen that I cannot perceive, unless my body is exposed to them in a way I conceive appropriate to that assumption.

So it is quite clear that although all the bodies of the universe belong to us in some way and harmonise with ours, we do not attribute to ourselves what happens to them. For when my body is pushed, I say that I myself have been pushed, but if someone else is pushed, I do not say that I have been pushed, even though I may perceive it and some passion in me may arise from it, since I measure where I am by the place my body is in. And this language is highly reasonable because it is appropriate for clear expression in everyday practice. As for the mind, it can be said briefly that our acts of will and judgements or reasonings are actions while our perceptions or sensations are passions. As for the body, we say that a change that happens to it is an action when it follows from a previous change, but otherwise it is a passion.

In general, to give our terms a meaning that reconciles metaphysics with practice, it can be said that when several powers are affected by the same change the one that passes to a higher degree of perfection or continues in the same acts, while the one that immediately becomes more limited thereby, so that its expressions become more confused, is acted upon.

15. The Action of One Finite Substance on Another Consists Solely in the Increase in the Degree of Its Expression Together With the Diminution of that of the Other, in so Far as God Has Made Them Conform to Each Other

But without getting involved in a long discussion, it is enough for the present to reconcile the language of metaphysics with that of practice by noting that we attribute to ourselves our more clear and distinct perceptions and that we can in general attribute to a substance its more clear and distinct expression and, with reason, the phenomena we express more perfectly, while we attribute to other substances what each best expresses. Thus a substance of infinite extension, in so far as it expresses everything, becomes limited by its more or less perfect manner of expression. Thus in this way it is possible to conceive that substances mutually hinder or limit each other and, consequently, in this sense, to say that they act on each other and, so to speak, are obliged to conform to each other. For it can happen that a change which increases the expression of the one diminishes that of the other. Now, the virtue of a particular substance is to express well the glory of God, and it is there that it is least limited, and everything that exerts its virtue or power, that is when it acts, changes for the better and is extended in so far as it acts. Thus when a change affects several substances (since indeed every change touches all of them), I think that it can be said that the one that thereby passes to a higher degree of perfection or to a more perfect expression exerts its power and acts, while the other one that passes to a lesser degree shows its weakness and is acted upon. So I hold that every action of a substance possessing perception implies some pleasure and every passion some pain, and vice versa. This notwithstanding that it can easily happen that a present advantage is destroyed in what follows. Hence it follows that it is possible to sin by acting or exerting one's power and finding pleasure therein.

16. The Extraordinary Concurrence of God Is Included in the Expression of our Essence Because It Applies to Everything, but It Transcends the Powers of Our Nature of Distinct Expression (Which Is Finite and Follows Particular Subaltern Norms)

All that remains for the present is to explain how it is sometimes possible for God to have influence on men or other substances through an extraordinary or miraculous concurrence, since it seems that everything that has to happen to them is natural in so far as it is a consequence of their substance. But what we said above about miracles in the universe must be remembered: they always conform to the universal laws of the general order, even though these transcend the subordinate norms. And, to the extent that every person or substance is like a little world expressing the great one, it can even be said that this extraordinary concurrence of God is included in the general order of the universe in so far as that is expressed by the nature of this person, but it does not cease to be miraculous and to be beyond the norms. That is why, if everything it expresses is included in our nature, nothing is supernatural with respect to it, for it extends to everything, since an effect always expresses its cause and God is the true cause of substances. But since what our nature expresses more perfectly particularly belongs to it, that is what its power consists in—and since, as I have just explained, it is limited, there are many things that surpass the powers of our natures, and even those of every limited nature. Consequently, to speak more clearly, I say that miracles and the extraordinary acts of God's concurrence have the particular character that they could not be foreseen by the reasoning of any created mind, however enlightened it might be, since the comprehension of the general order surpasses them all, while everything called natural depends on the less general norms creatures can understand. Hence, in order to say nothing of these norms or laws of nature that might cause offence, it would be good to link particular ways of speaking with particular thoughts: whatever includes everything we express could then be called our essence or idea, and since it expresses our union with God, it has no limits and nothing exceeds it. But what is limited in us could be called our nature or power, and in this respect what exceeds the natures of all created substances is supernatural.

17. Example of a Subaltern Norm or Law of Nature; In Which It Is Shown that God Always Preserves the Same Force, but not the Same Quantity of Motion . . . Against the Cartesians and Some Others

I have often mentioned subaltern maxims or laws of nature already, and it would be good to give an example. Our new philosophers commonly make use of that famous rule advanced by Descartes that God always preserves the same quantity of motion in the world. It seems highly plausible indeed, and in the past I held it to be indubitable. But I have since come to recognise wherein lay its error. It is that Descartes and many other able mathematicians thought that the quantity of motion (i.e. the speed times the size of the mobile) was the same thing as the force, or at least expressed it perfectly, or geometrically speaking, that the forces are in compound proportion of the speeds and the bodies. Now it is obvious indeed that the same force should always be preserved in the universe. So, when we attend to the phenomena with care, we see clearly that mechanical perpetual motion does not occur, because then the force of a machine, which is continually being slightly diminished by friction, and must consequently soon cease, would be replaced and so would increase of itself without any new impulsion from outside. We also note that the force of a body is diminished solely to the extent that it gives some of it to neighbouring bodies or to its own parts in so far as these have independent motions.

Thus they thought that what can be said of force could also be said of quantity of motion. But, to show the difference, I suppose that a body falling from a particular height acquires the force needed to climb up again, if its direction of travel should take it that way, unless there are hindrances. For example, a pendulum would rise right back again to the height it had fallen from if the resistance of the air and other small obstacles did not somehow diminish the force acquired.

I *suppose* also that as much force is needed to raise a body A of one pound a height CD of four fathoms as to raise a body B of four pounds a height EF of one fathom. All this is accepted by our new philosophers.

Hence, it is manifest that body (A), after falling from the height CD has acquired as much force precisely as body (B) after falling from the height EF. For when body (B) has arrived at F and has the force to climb back to E (by the first supposition), it has in consequence the force to carry a body of four pounds, that is its own body, to the height EF of one fathom, and similarly, when body (A) has reached D and has the force to climb back to C, it has the force to carry a body of one pound, that is its own body, to

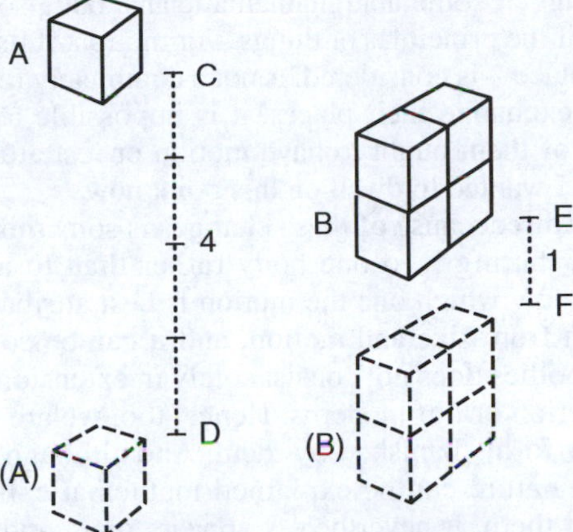

the height CD of four fathoms. Hence (by the second supposition), the forces of the two bodies are equal.

Now let us see whether the quantity of motion is also the same in both cases: but it is here that there will be surprise at finding a very great difference. For it has been demonstrated by Galileo that the speed acquired in the fall CD is twice that acquired in the fall EF, though the height is quadruple. If then, we multiply the body (A), in the proportion 1, by the speed, in the proportion 2, the product or quantity of motion will be as 2, and if on the other hand, we multiply the body (B), which is as 4, by its speed, which is as 1, then the product or quantity of motion will be as 4. Hence the quantity of motion of body (A) at point D is half the quantity of motion of body (B) at point F, though their forces are equal. Hence there is a great difference between the quantity of motion and the force, as was to be proved.

From this it is seen that the force must be measured by the quantity of the effect it can produce, e.g. by the height to which a heavy body of a particular size and kind can be raised, something very different from the speed that can be given it, and that to give it twice the speed more than twice the force is needed.

Nothing is simpler than this proof. Descartes only fell into error here because he trusted too much in his thoughts before they had matured enough with a confidence based on the happy success of some of his thoughts and on his experience of the penetration of his mind, which rendered him rather too rash in the end. But I am astonished that his followers have not recognised this error since, and I fear that little by little they begin to imitate the Peripatetics they so make fun of, and that like them they grow accustomed to consulting the books of their master rather than reason and nature.

18. Importance of the Distinction Between Force and Quantity of Motion Inter Alia in Deciding that We Must Have Recourse to Metaphysical Considerations Distinct from Extension to Explain the Nature of Bodies

This consideration of the distinction of force from quantity of motion is important enough, not only in physics and mechanics in the discovery of the true laws of nature and rules of motions, and even in the correction of several practical errors that have slipped into the writings of some able mathematicians, but also in metaphysics, in the better understanding of the principles of things. For motion, if its precise formal content only—i.e. change of place—is considered, is not a completely real thing, and when several bodies mutually exchange their places, it is impossible to determine from these changes alone which of them ought to have motion or rest attributed to it, as I could show geometrically if I wanted to dwell on this point now.

But the force or direct cause of these changes is something more real, and there is some basis for attributing it to one body rather than to another, and it is only thereby that we can know which one the motion is best attributed to. Now, this force is something different from size and motion, and it can be concluded from this that what is conceived in bodies does not consist solely in extension and its modifications, contrary to the conviction of our moderns. Hence, too, we are obliged to re-establish some of the beings or forms banished by them. And although all the particular phenomena of corporeal nature can be explained mathematically or mechanically by those who understand them, it nevertheless appears more and more that the general principles of corporeal mechanical nature itself are metaphysical rather than geometrical, belonging to forms or indivisible natures functioning as causes of the matter or extension rather than to corporeal or extended mass—a reflection capable of reconciling the mechanical philosophy of the moderns with the circumspection of some intelligent well-intentioned people who fear quite reasonably that we are moving too far from immaterial beings to the disadvantage of piety.

19. Usefulness of Final Causes in Physics

As I do not like to judge people's intentions, or only do so favourably if I can, I am not accusing our new philosophers of impiety when they claim to banish final causes in physics. Nevertheless I am obliged to admit that I do not recognise their usual intelligence and prudence therein and that the consequences of this opinion seem dangerous to me, particularly when it is connected with that refuted by me at the beginning of this discourse, which seems to lead to their removal altogether, as if God never had any aim, whether good or active, or as if the good were not the object of His will. . . . For my part, I hold on the contrary that it is just there that we have to seek the principle of all existences and even of the laws of nature, since God always intends what is best and most perfect.

I am happy to admit that we are liable to error when we want to determine the aims and counsels of God, but that is only when we try to restrict them to a particular plan, in the belief that He has only one single thing in view, whereas in fact He considers everything at once. Thus, when we think that God made the world for us alone, we are greatly mistaken, although it is true that He made it in its totality for us and that there is nothing in the world that does not affect us and does not also conform to His concerns for us, in accordance with the above principles. Thus, when we see some good effect or perfection happening or resulting from the works of God, we can certainly say that God intended it, for He does nothing by chance and unlike us does not sometimes fail to do well. That is why, far from being in an error here, akin to that of the overly political who attribute excessive refinement to the designs of princes, or to that of commentators who search for too much erudition in their authors, we cannot attribute too many reflections to this infinite Wisdom, and there is no matter in which there is less danger of error as long as we only affirm and avoid negative propositions here that limit the plans of God.

Everyone who sees the admirable structure of animals is led to recognise the wisdom of the Author of things, and I advise those with any feeling of piety or even of true Philosophy to avoid the expression of some would-be tough minds who say that we see because we happen to have eyes, without noting that the eyes were made to see. If we are seriously involved in these opinions that assign everything to the necessity of matter or to a particular chance (although both must seem ridiculous to those who understand what we have explained above), we will inevitably fail to recognise an intelligent Author of nature. For it is ridiculous to introduce a Sovereign Intelligence as the Ordainer of things and not use His wisdom to account for phenomena. As if, in accounting for the conquest of a great prince in capturing an important position, a historian tried to say that it was because the particles of the gunpowder liberated by lighting the fuse escaped at a speed capable of pushing a hard heavy body against the walls of the position, while the branches of the particles composing the copper of the cannon were sufficiently intertwined not to be separated by this speed, instead of showing how the foresight of the victor caused him to choose the appropriate time and means, and how his power overcame all the obstacles.

20. Remarkable Passage of Socrates in Plato Against Excessively Materialistic Philosophers. M

This point reminds me of a fine passage of Socrates in Plato's *Phaedo*. In marvellous agreement with my thoughts on this point, it seems to be written expressly against our excessively materialistic philosophers. So this account made me want to translate it, and though it is rather long, perhaps this sample will give one of us the occasion to share many other fine sound thoughts from the writings of the great man.

"One day," he said, "I heard someone read a book of Anaxagoras, where there were these words 'that an Intelligent Being was the cause of all things, and that He arranged and adorned them.' I was extremely pleased with that, for I thought that if the world was the result of an Intelligence, everything would have been made in the most perfect way possible. That is why I thought that he who wanted to explain why things came to be, perished or subsisted had to search for what suited the perfection of each. Thus man would only have to consider in himself or in some other thing, what was best or most perfect, alone. For he who knew the most perfect would easily decide thereby what was imperfect, since there is only one true knowledge of both.

"In view of all this, I rejoiced to have found a master able to teach the reason of things: whether, for example, the earth was round or flat, and why it was best that way rather than otherwise. . . . Moreover, I expected that when he said that the earth was or was not at the centre of the universe, he would explain to me why that was the most suitable. And when he said the same of the sun, the moon, the stars and their motions. . . . And finally, after showing what was suitable to each thing individually, he would show me what was best in general.

"Full of this hope, I took and skimmed through the books of Anaxagoras with great eagerness, but I was far from my expectation, for I was surprised to see that he made no use of this governing Intelligence, set out in advance, that he spoke no more of the adornment and the perfection of things, and introduced some rather implausible ethereal matters.

"In this he was rather like the man who said that Socrates did things intelligently, but when he came to explaining in particular the causes of his actions, thereupon said that he was sitting here because he had a body composed of bone, flesh and nerves, that the bones were solid, but had gaps and joints, that the nerves could be tensed or relaxed, and that was why the body was flexible and I was sitting. Or if he wanted to explain the present speech, he had recourse to the air, to vocal and aural organs and like things, while forgetting the true causes, that is that the Athenians thought it better to condemn than to acquit me, and I for my part thought it better to sit here than to take flight. For, by my faith, these nerves and these bones would long since be with the Boeotians and the Megarans, if I had not found it more just and more honest for me to suffer the penalty the fatherland wants to impose on me than live elsewhere a wanderer in exile. That is why it is unreasonable to call these bones and nerves and their motions causes.

"It is true that whoever said that I could not do all this without bones and nerves would be right, but the true cause is something else . . . and that is no more than a condition without which the cause could not be the cause. . . .

"People who say no more than, for example, that the motions of the bodies surrounding the earth support the earth where it is, forget that the divine power arranges everything in the finest way, and do not understand that it is the good and the beautiful that join, form and preserve the world. . . ." Thus far Socrates, for the things about ideas or forms that follow in Plato are not less excellent but a bit more difficult.

21. If the Rules of Mechanics Depended on Geometry Alone Without Metaphysics, the Phenomena Would Be Quite Different

Now, since the wisdom of God has always been recognised in the details of the mechanical structures of particular bodies, it is very necessary that it should also be shown in the general set-up of the world and the constitution of the laws of nature. This is so true that the counsels of this Wisdom are observed in the laws of motion in general. For if there were nothing else to bodies but an extended mass and nothing to motion but change of place, and if everything had to and could be deduced from these definitions alone by geometrical necessity, it would follow, as I have shown elsewhere, that the least body would give the same speed as its own to the largest resting body it met without losing any of its own, and many other rules of this sort would have to be accepted, such as are altogether contrary to the construction of a system. But the decree of the divine wisdom to preserve always the same total force and direction has provided for this.

I even find that many natural effects can be demonstrated doubly, i.e. through the efficient cause and separately through the final cause as well, by using for example the decree of God to produce His effect by the simplest and most determinate ways, as I have shown elsewhere in my account of the rules of catoptrics and dioptrics, and I shall say more of it below.

22. Reconciliation of the Two Ways by Final and Efficient Causes in Defence of Both Those Who Explain Nature Mechanically and Those Who Have Recourse to Incorporeal Natures

It is good to note this point to reconcile those who hope to explain mechanically the formation of the first tissues of an animal and the complete machine of its parts with those who account for the same structure by final causes. Both are good and both can be useful, not only for admiring the artifice of the great Workman, but also in discovering something useful in physics and medicine. Authors who follow these different routes should not be hard on each other.

For I see that those who concentrate on explaining the beauty of divine Anatomy laugh at others who imagine that an apparently fortuitous motion of particular fluids can make such a beautiful variety of members, and call such people rash and profane, while on the other hand the latter call the former simple and superstitious like the ancients who took it that the physicists were impious when they held that it was not Jupiter that thundered but some matter in the clouds. The best thing would be to unite both considerations, for, to use a vulgar comparison, the skill of a workman is recognised and praised not only by showing what designs he had when he made the parts of his machine, but also by explaining the tools he used to make each part, particularly when these tools are simple and ingeniously contrived. *God is skilful enough an artisan* to produce a machine a thousand times still more ingenious than that of our body if that were possible, using only a few simple enough fluids expressly formed so that only the ordinary laws of nature are needed to sort them out as necessary to produce such an admirable effect, but it is also true that this would not happen if God were not the Author of nature.

I find, nevertheless, that the way of efficient causes is while indeed more profound and in one way more direct and *a priori*, on the other hand rather difficult when we get down to details and I think that our Philosophers are most often still rather far from that. In contrast, the way of final causes is easier and is moreover often helpful in guessing important and useful truths that would have been a long time in the searching by the former more physical route, and of this Anatomy can furnish important examples. I also hold that Snell, the first discoverer of the rules of refraction, would have taken a long time to find them if he had tried to find out first how light was formed. But he seems to have followed the method the ancients used in catoptrics, that of final causes in fact. For, in the search for the easiest way of conducting a ray from one given point to another by reflection at a given plane (supposing that this is nature's design), they discovered the equality of the angles of incidence and reflection, as can be seen in a little treatise of Heliodorus of Larissa and elsewhere. That is what in my opinion Snell, and after him (though without knowing anything about him) Fermat, applied more ingeniously to refraction. For when in the same media the rays observe the same proportion of sines which is also that of the resistances of the media, it turns out to be the easiest, or at least the most determinate way of passing from a given point in one medium to a given point in the other. The demonstration Descartes tried to give of this same theorem by the way of efficient causes is far from being as good. At least there are grounds for suspecting that he would never have found it that way if he had not heard something of Snell's discovery in Holland.

23. Returning to Immaterial Substances; the Explanation of How God Acts on the Understanding of Minds and of Whether We Always Have an Idea of What We Think

I have found it relevant to insist somewhat on these considerations concerning final causes, incorporeal natures and an Intelligent Cause in relation to bodies, to make known their use even in physics and mathematics. On the one hand, this is to purge the mechanical philosophy of the profanity imputed to it. On the other hand it is to raise the minds of our philosophers from mere material considerations to more noble meditations. It is now time to return from bodies to immaterial natures, to minds in particular, and to say something of the ways God uses to illumine them and act on them, for we must not doubt that here too there are laws of nature, a point I could discuss more fully elsewhere. For now, it is enough to touch a little on ideas, on whether we see all things in God, and on how God is our light.

Now, it is relevant to note that several errors are occasioned by the misuse of ideas. For when we reason on something we imagine we have an idea of it, and on that foundation some recent authors have built a demonstration of God that is, rigorously speaking, very imperfect. For, they say, I must have an idea of God or of a perfect being, since I am thinking of Him, and it is impossible to think without an idea. Now the idea of this Being includes all the perfections and existence is one of these, so that consequently He exists. But as we often think of impossible chimerae, such as the ultimate degree of speed or the greatest number or the meeting of the conchoid [a plane curve in geometry] with its base or rule, this reasoning is not enough. Hence in this sense a person can say he has true or false ideas according as the thing in question is possible or not, and it is only when we are assured of its possibility that we can boast of having an idea of the thing. Thus the above argument proves at least that God necessarily exists if He is possible. This is indeed an excellent privilege of the divine nature: to need only its possibility or essence to exist in fact, just what is called an *Ens a se*.

24. JUST WHAT IS CLEAR OR OBSCURE, DISTINCT OR CONFUSED, ADEQUATE AND INTUITIVE OR SUPPOSITIVE KNOWLEDGE, AND WHAT ARE NOMINAL, REAL, CAUSAL AND ESSENTIAL DEFINITIONS

The better to understand the nature of ideas, we have to touch a little on the varieties of knowledge. When I know only through experience that something is possible, because everything that exists is possible, my knowledge is confused. It is in this way that we know bodies and their qualities. But when I can prove *a priori* that something is possible, this knowledge is distinct. When I can recognise one thing among others without being able to say in what its *differentiae* or properties consist, my knowledge is confused. Thus it is that we sometimes know *clearly* without being in any doubt at all whether a poem or picture is well or badly made, because there is an I don't know what that satisfies or shocks us. But only when I can explain the marks available to me is my knowledge called *distinct*. Such is the knowledge of the assayer who discerns the true and the false by particular tests or marks comprising the definition of gold.

But there are degrees of distinct knowledge, for the notions that enter the definition would ordinarily themselves need definition and are only confusedly known. But when every thing that enters a definition or distinct item of knowledge is distinctly known right back to the primitive notions, I call this knowledge *adequate*, and when my mind understands all the primitive ingredients of a notion all at once and distinctly, then it has an intuitive knowledge of it, something very rare since most human knowledge is confused or even *suppositive*.

It is also good to distinguish nominal definitions from real ones. I refer to a nominal definition when it is still possible to doubt that the notion defined is possible. Thus, for example, when I say that an endless screw is a solid line whose parts are congruent or can coincide with each other, whoever did not otherwise know what an endless screw was could doubt the possibility of such a line, though indeed it was a reciprocal property of an endless screw, since the other lines whose parts are congruent are planar (the circumference of the circle and the straight line only), that is they can be drawn *in a plane*. This shows that every reciprocal property can be used in a nominal definition, whereas when the property makes known the possibility of the thing, it makes the definition real. As long as we have a mere nominal definition, we could never be sure of the consequences drawn from it, for if it concealed some contradiction or impossibility, contrary conclusions could be drawn from it. That is why truths do not depend on names and are not arbitrary as held by some new philosophers.

25. IN WHAT CASE OUR KNOWLEDGE IS JOINED TO THE CONTEMPLATION OF THE IDEA

Now it is obvious that we have no idea of a notion when it is impossible. And when our knowledge is merely *suppositive*, when we have the idea we do not contemplate it, for such a notion is known only in the same way as those that are occultly impossible, and if it is possible it is not learned by that method of knowing. For example, when I think of a thousand, or of chiliagon [a group of one thousand things], I often do so without contemplating the idea, as when I say that a thousand is ten times a hundred without putting myself to the trouble of thinking what ten and a hundred are. That is because I *suppose* I know it and see no need for the present to pause to conceive it. Thus it can easily happen, as indeed it does often enough, that I am in error with respect to a notion I suppose or believe I understand, although in truth it is impossible, or at least incompatible with the others I join it to. Whether or not I am in error, this suppositive way of conceiving remains the same. Hence, it is only when our knowledge of confused things is *clear* or our knowledge of distinct things intuitive, that we contemplate the complete idea of them.

26. WE HAVE ALL IDEAS IN US; PLATO'S NOTION OF REMINISCENCE

If we are to conceive properly what an idea is, we must avoid an ambiguity. For there are some who take the idea to be the form or way of distinguishing our thoughts. On this view we have the idea in our minds only to the extent that we think of it, and whenever we think of it again, we have ideas of the same thing different from though similar to the previous ones. But it seems that others take the idea to be an immediate object of thought, or some permanent form remaining when we do not contemplate it. Indeed, there is always in our souls the capacity to conceive any nature or form whatever, when the opportunity of thinking of it presents itself. I think that this capacity of our souls, to the extent that it expresses some nature, form or essence, is properly speaking the idea of the thing, in us and always in us, whether we think of it or not. For our soul expresses God and the universe, and all essences as well as all existences.

This follows from my principles, for nothing enters our minds naturally from outside, and it is a bad habit of ours to think as if our souls received some messenger—species or had gates and windows. We have all the forms in our minds, for all time even, because the mind always expresses all its future thoughts, and already thinks confusedly everything it will ever think distinctly. Nothing could be taught us whose idea was not already present in our minds as the matter from which this thought was formed.

That is what Plato understood so well when he put forward his doctrine of reminiscence, which is very sound provided we take it the right way and purge it of the error of pre-existence, and do not imagine that the soul has to have once known and distinctly thought what it is now learning and thinking. He also confirmed his opinion by a beautiful experiment. He introduced a little boy in his dialogue called *Meno* whom he led insensibly into the most difficult geometrical truths concerning incommensurables, without teaching him anything, merely putting relevant questions in order. This shows that our souls have virtual knowledge of everything. They need only attention to know the truths, and consequently have at least the truths on which these truths depend. It can even be said, if the latter are taken for the relations of ideas, that they already possess these truths.

27. In what Sense Our Souls May Be Compared to Empty Tablets, and How Our Notions Come from the Senses

Aristotle preferred to compare our souls to tablets that were still bare with space for writing on, and he claimed that nothing was in our understanding that did not come from the senses. As is the way with Aristotle, this is more in conformity with popular notions, whereas Plato goes deeper. Nevertheless, such everyday expressions or practical sayings are liable to pass into common usage, almost as with the followers of Copernicus who continue to say that the sun rises and sets. I often find, even, that a good sense can be given to them in accordance with which there is nothing wrong with them. Just as I have already remarked on the way it is possible to say truly that particular substances act on each other, in this same sense it can be said that we receive some knowledge from outside by the ministry of the senses, because some external things contain, or more particularly express, the reasons determining our souls to particular thoughts. But when we are concerned with the accuracy of metaphysical truths, it is important to recognise the extent and independence of our souls. This goes infinitely further than is vulgarly supposed, although in the ordinary course of life only what is more certainly perceived and belongs to us in a particular way is attributed to it, since there is no purpose in going further.

Nevertheless, it would be good to choose special terms for both senses to avoid ambiguity. Hence, expressions in our souls, whether conceived or not, can be called ideas, while those we conceive or form can be called *notions* or *concepts*. But however we take it, it is always false to say that all our notions come from the senses called external, since the one I have of myself, and of my thoughts, and consequently of being, substance, action, identity and many others, comes from internal experience.

28. God Alone Is the Immediate Object of Our Perceptions Existing Outside Us, for He Alone Is Our Light

Now, in the rigour of metaphysical truth, there is no external cause acting on us but God alone, and He alone communicates himself to us directly in virtue of our continual dependence. It follows from this that there is no other external object touching our souls and exciting our perceptions directly. So it is only in virtue of the continual action of God on us that we have in our souls the ideas of everything, i.e. because every effect expresses its cause and hence the essence of our souls is a particular expression, imitation, or image of the essence, thought and will of God and of all the ideas included in Him. Hence, it can be said that God alone is our immediate object outside us, and that it is in Him that we see all things. For example, when we see the sun and the stars, it is God who gave us them and preserves their ideas in us, and in fact determines us to think of them at the time at which our senses are disposed in a particular way, through His ordinary concurrence and in accordance with the laws established by Him. God is the sun and light of souls, "the light enlightening every man born into the world." It is not just today that people are of this opinion. After Holy Scripture and the Fathers—always more for Plato than for Aristotle—I recall noticing once that in the time of the Scholastics some believed that God was the light of the soul and, in their way of speaking, "the active intellect of the rational soul." The Averroists gave this a bad meaning, but others such as, I think, William of St. Amour, doctor of the Sorbonne, and several mystical theologians, took it in a manner worthy of God and capable of raising the soul to the knowledge of its good.

29. Nevertheless We Think Directly by Our Own Ideas and Not by Those of God

Nevertheless I am not of the opinion of some able philosophers who seem to maintain that our very ideas are in God, and not at all in us. In my opinion, this comes about because they have still not pondered enough what we have just explained concerning substances, nor the entire extent and independence of our souls (which means that they include everything happening to them and express the essence of God, and with Him all possible and actual beings, like an effect its cause). Also, it is inconceivable that I should think by means of the thoughts of someone else. It is very necessary that an effect should express its cause and it is also very necessary that the soul should be actually affected in a particular way when it thinks of something and that it should have in advance, not only the passive power of being affected in this way, something already determined, but also an active power, in virtue of which there has always been in its nature the marks of the future production of that thought and dispositions to produce it when the time came. All this already includes the idea contained in that thought.

30. How God Inclines Without Necessitating; We Have No Right to Complain, and We Must Not Ask Why Judas Sins Since this Free Action Is Included in His Notion, Only Why Judas the Sinner Is Admitted to Existence in Preference to Other Possible Persons. The Origin of Evil Comes From this, the Original Imperfection Before Sin, and the Degrees of Grace

Concerning the action of God on the human will, there are many rather difficult questions that would take time to pursue here. Nevertheless, in outline, this is what can be said. When God concurs in our actions, He ordinarily does no more than follow the laws of nature He has established, i.e. He preserves and continually produces our nature, so that the thoughts spontaneously and naturally or freely happen to us in the order carried by the notion of our individual substance, within which they could have been foreseen from all eternity. Moreover, in virtue of the decree that the will should always tend towards the apparent good, and so express or imitate God's will in certain particular respects in respect of which this apparent good always has something of the true, He determines our will to choose what seems the best without nonetheless necessitating it. For, absolutely speaking, in so far as it may be opposed to necessity, our will is indifferent and has the power to do otherwise or to suspend its action altogether, since both are and remain possible.

Hence it falls to the soul to take precautions against the appearances taking it by surprise by means of a firm resolve to reflect and to refuse to act or judge on particular occasions without thorough deliberation. Nevertheless it is true and even certain from all eternity that a particular soul will not use this power on one such occasion. But who could do anything about it or do other than complain about himself? For all complaints after the fact are unjust when they would have been unjust before. Now would this soul, shortly before sinning, be in the right to complain of God, who has not determined him to flee from the sin as if He had determined him to sin? Since God's determinations in these matters are unforeseeable, how does he know himself to be determined to sin, unless in fact he is already actually sinning? It is only a matter of not willing, and God could propose no easier or juster condition. Moreover, any judge stops only to consider how far a man's will is bad without searching for the reasons disposing him to have a bad will. But perhaps it is certain from all eternity that I will sin? Answer yourself: perhaps not. Do not think about what you cannot know and cannot enlighten you, but act in accordance with the duty you know.

But, someone else will ask, whence comes it that that man will certainly do this sin? The answer is easy: otherwise he would not be that man. For God sees for all time that there will be a certain Judas whose notion, or idea God has of him, contains this future free action. Hence the only question that remains is why such a Judas, the traitor, who is merely a possible in the idea of God actually exists. But to that question there is no answer to be expected here below, unless that in general we must say that since God thought it good for him to exist, despite the sin he foresaw this evil must be repaid with interest in the universe, that God will obtain a greater good from it; and that in all He will find this sequence of things including the existence of this sinner the most perfect of all the other possible ones. But to explain in all cases the admirable economy of this choice is not possible while we are travellers in this vale of tears in this world. It is enough to know without understanding it. It is time here to recognise "the height of the riches," the width and depth of the divine wisdom, without seeking a detail involving these infinite considerations.

Nevertheless, it is clear that God is not the cause of evil. For not only did original sin take hold of the soul after the loss of innocence but before then there was a limitation or original imperfection common to the natures of all creatures making them capable of sin or liable to fail. Thus there is no more difficulty with regard to the supralapsarians* than with the others. In my opinion, it is to this that the opinion of St. Augustine and other authors that the root of evil is in nothingness should be reduced, i.e. in the privation or the limitation of creatures that God graciously remedies by giving them the degree of perfection it pleases Him to give. Whether ordinary or extraordinary, this grace of God has its degrees and measures, always in itself efficacious in producing a proportionate effect. Moreover it is always sufficient, not only to guarantee us against sin, but to produce salvation, if the man joins himself to it with his will, though it is not always sufficient to surmount human inclinations, otherwise it would depend on nothing more,

*Calvinists who believe that election to heaven or hell was a part of God's original plan.

and that is reserved to the absolutely efficacious grace alone that is always victorious whether by itself or by the congruity of circumstances.

31. The Foreknowledge of Merit, the Dispensing of Grace, the Motives of Election, the Middle Knowledge, the Absolute Decree; that Everything Reduces to the Reason Why God Chose a Particular Possible Person for Existence, Whose Notion Includes that Particular Sequence of Graces and Free Actions, so that All the Difficulties Are Removed at Once

In the end, the graces of God are graces pure and simple over which creatures have no claim. However, just as when we are giving an account of the action of God in dispensing these graces it is not enough to have recourse to His fore-sight, whether absolute or conditional, of the future actions of men, so we must not imagine absolute decrees with no reasonable motive. As regards God's fore-sight of faith and good works, it is very true that God has elected only those whose faith and charity He foresaw, "those He foreknew He would give faith to," but the same question returns: why God will give the grace of faith and good works to some rather than to others. As for this middle knowledge of God's, the fore-sight, not of good works, but of their matter and predisposition, or of what the man would contribute from his side (since it is true that there is diversity on the human side wherever there is on the side of grace, and since indeed, although man needs to be excited towards the good and converted, it is very necessary that he should also play his part here after the fact) some people think that it could be said that since God sees what man would do without grace or extraordinary assistance, or at least what he will have on his side apart from grace, He could resolve to give grace to those whose natural disposition was the best or at any rate the least imperfect or least evil. But if that was the case, it could be said that these natural dispositions, in so far as they are good, are still the effect of an act of grace, even if an ordinary one, since God has advantaged some more than others. And since He well knows that these natural advantages He gives will provide the motive for grace or extraordinary assistance, does it not follow from the doctrine that truly everything in the end reduces to His mercy?

Hence, I believe (since we do not know how much or how God takes account of natural dispositions in dispensing grace) that the most accurate and certain thing to say is, as already noted and in conformity with our principles, that among the possible beings there should be the person of Peter or John whose notion or idea contains the whole sequence of ordinary and extraordinary graces and all the other events along with their circumstances, and that it pleased God to choose him from among an infinity of other equally possible persons for actual existence. After that it seems that there is no more to ask and that all the difficulties disappear.

For, considering this single great question, why it pleased God to choose one from so many other possible persons, we would have to be unreasonable indeed not to be satisfied with the general reasons given, for which the detail is beyond our reach. So, we should not have recourse to an absolute decree, which is unreasonable since there is no reason for it, or to reasons that do not succeed in resolving the difficulty. Instead the best will be to say with St. Paul that there are certain grand reasons for this unknown to mortals and founded in the general order whose aim is the greatest perfection of the universe, and that God has observed these. It is to this that the motives of the glory of God and the manifestation of His justice reduce, as well as His mercy and His perfections generally, and finally that immense depth of His riches Paul's soul was enchanted with.

32. Usefulness of These Principles in Matters of Piety and Religion

For the rest, it seems that the thoughts we have just explained, particularly the grand principle of the perfection of the operations of God and the notion of the substance including all the events with all their circumstances, far from harming religion, serve to confirm it, removing very great difficulties, inflaming souls with a divine love and raising minds to the knowledge of incorporeal substances to a much greater extent than the hypotheses we have seen up to now. For it is clear that just as thoughts depend on our substance, all other substances depend on God, that God is all in all, and that He is intimately united with all creatures (though to the extent of their perfection), and that He alone determines them externally by His influence. And if to act is to determine directly, it can be said in this sense, in the language of metaphysics, that God operates on me and is alone able to do me good or ill, while other substances are nothing but occasional causes, for the reason that as God considers all of them, He distributes His acts of goodness and obliges them to conform to each other. Also, God alone makes the connection and communication of substances, and it is by Him that phenomena of any given substance meet and fit with those of the others, and consequently that there is reality in our perceptions. But in practice action is attributed to particular occasional causes in the sense explained above, because it is not always necessary to mention the universal cause in particular cases.

It is seen also that every substance has a perfect spontaneity (which in intelligent substances becomes liberty): that everything that happens to it is a consequence of its ideas or being, and that it is determined by nothing but God alone. That is why a person of noble mind whose sanctity is greatly revered used to say that the soul must often think as if there were only God and it in the world.

Now nothing makes immortality more completely comprehensible than this independence and extent of the soul. It protects it absolutely from all external things, since it alone constitutes the whole world and, with God, suffices to itself. It is also impossible for it to perish other than by annihilation, and impossible for the world (of which it is a living and perpetual expression) to destroy itself. Hence, it is not possible for the changes in that extended mass called our body to do anything to our soul, or for the disappearance of that body to destroy what is indivisible.

33. Explanation of the Union of Soul and Body Something Once Thought Inexplicable or Miraculous, and the Origin of Confused Perceptions

Also clear is the unexpected solution of that great mystery of the union of soul and body, i.e. how it happens that the actions and passions of the one are accompanied by the actions and passions, or rather appropriate phenomena, of the other. For there is no way of conceiving any influence of the one on the other, and it is unreasonable simply to have recourse to the extraordinary operation of the universal cause in something ordinary and particular. But here is the true reason. We have said that everything happening to the soul and to every substance is a consequence of its notion. Hence the very idea or essence of the soul makes all its appearances or perceptions arise spontaneously out of its own nature, and just so, that they answer of themselves to what happens in the whole universe, though particularly in the body assigned to it, because in a way and for a time, it is in accordance with the relation of other bodies to its own that the soul expresses the state of the universe. This shows yet again how our bodies belong to us without nevertheless being attached to our essences. I believe that persons able to meditate will see advantage in our principles in just this, that it is easy to see in what exactly the connection between soul and body—apparently inexplicable by any other means—consists.

It can also be seen that the perceptions of our senses, even when they are clear, must necessarily contain some confused sensations. For as all the bodies in the universe are in sympathy, ours receive the impressions of all the others. Although our senses relate to everything, it is not possible for our souls to attend to all individually, and that is why our confused sensations are the result of a variety, altogether infinite, of perceptions. It is almost like the confused murmur heard by those approaching the shores of the sea that arises from the accumulation of the reverberations of innumerable waves. Now if of several perceptions (not coming together to become a single one) none stands out above the others, and if they make almost equally strong impressions, or are equally capable of determining the attention of the soul, it can only register them confusedly.

34. The Excellence of Minds Compared with Other Substances or Substantial Forms. The Immortality Called for Implies Memory

One thing I do not propose to decide is whether in metaphysical rigour bodies are substances or are no more than *true* phenomena like the rainbow, nor consequently whether there are substances, souls or substantial forms that are not intelligent. But if we suppose that bodies like man that constitute unities in themselves are substances and have substantial forms, we are obliged to admit that these souls and substantial forms could no more entirely perish than atoms if there are any or ultimate particles of matter can, in the opinion of other philosophers. For though it may become quite different, no substance perishes. Although more imperfectly than minds, they too express the whole universe. But the principal difference is that they do not know what they are nor what they are doing. Consequently, since they have no power of reflection, they are unable to discover necessary and universal truths. It is also for want of reflection on themselves that they have no moral qualities, so that, when we consider how a caterpillar changes into a butterfly through almost a thousand transformations, it comes to the same for morals and practice as saying that they perish, as can indeed be said physically (as we say of bodies that they perish by corruption). But the intelligent soul that knows what it is, and is capable of pronouncing this me which says so much, not only remains the same metaphysically to a greater extent than the others, but it also remains morally the same and constitutes the same personality. For it is the memory and knowledge of this me that makes it liable to punishment and reward. Also, the immortality called for both in morality and religion does not consist merely in that perpetual subsistence proper to all substances. For without the memory of what has been, there would be nothing desirable about it. Let us suppose that some poor wretch suddenly became King of China, but only on condition that he forgot what he had been, as if he had just been reborn: does that not come to the same in practice, or in the effects that could be registered, as if he had to be annihilated and a King of China created at the same instant and at the same place? Something this individual has no reason to desire.

35. THE EXCELLENCE OF MINDS. GOD CONSIDERS THEM IN PREFERENCE TO OTHER CREATURES. MINDS EXPRESS GOD RATHER THAN THE WORLD, BUT OTHER SUBSTANCES EXPRESS THE WORLD RATHER THAN GOD

But to show by natural reasons that God always will preserve not only our substance but also our personality, that is memory and knowledge of what we are although distinct knowledge of that may sometimes be suspended when asleep or unconscious, morality must be joined to Metaphysics. That is, God has not only to be considered as the principle and cause of all substances and all beings, but also as the chief of all persons or intelligent substances and the absolute monarch of the most perfect city or republic, like that of the universe composed of all minds together, since God himself is the most accomplished of all Minds as well as the greatest of all Beings. For assuredly, minds are either the only substances existing in the world if bodies are no more than true phenomena, or else they are at least the most perfect ones. And since the whole nature, end, virtue and function of substances is merely to express God and the universe, as has been sufficiently explained, there are no grounds for doubting that substances expressing Him in the knowledge of what they are doing, and capable of knowing great truths regarding God and the universe, express Him incomparably better than those natures that are either animal and incapable of knowing truths, or altogether destitute of sense and knowledge; and the difference between intelligent substances and those that are not is as great as that between the mirror and he who sees.

And since God Himself is the greatest and wisest of minds, it is easy to conclude that beings with whom He can so to speak enter into conversation or even into fellowship, communicating His thoughts and intentions individually, so that they can know and love their Benefactor, must concern Him infinitely more than all other beings, able only to pass for the tools of minds, just as we can see wise persons taking infinitely more account of a man than of some other thing, however precious that may be. It seems that the greatest satisfaction an otherwise contented soul can have is to see himself loved by others although in respect of God there is this difference that His glory and our worship can add nothing to His satisfaction, since the knowledge of creatures is no more than a consequence of His sovereign and perfect happiness and very far from contributing to the latter or being part of the cause thereof. Nevertheless, what is good and reasonable in finite minds is supremely so in Him and just as we would praise a king who preferred to preserve the life of a man before the most precious and rare of animals, we should not doubt that the most enlightened and just of all Monarchs is of the same opinion.

36. GOD IS THE MONARCH OF THAT MOST PERFECT REPUBLIC THAT CONSISTS OF ALL MINDS, AND THE HAPPINESS OF THIS CITY OF GOD IS HIS PRINCIPAL DESIGN

In fact, minds are the most perfectible of all substances and their perfections have this characteristic that they hinder each other the least, or rather that they assist each other, for only the most virtuous can be the most perfect friends. Hence it manifestly follows that God who always looks to the greatest perfection in general, will have the most care of minds, and will give them, not only generally but to each individually, the greatest perfection the universal harmony can permit.

It can even be said that God, in so far as He is a mind, is the origin of existent things—if there were no will to choose best there would be no reason for one possible thing to exist in preference to others. Hence God's quality of being Himself a mind precedes all other considerations He may have with respect to creatures. Minds only are made in His image, and it is as if they are of His race and children of His house, since they alone can serve Him freely and act consciously in imitation of the divine nature. One mind is worth an entire world, since it does not only express it, but knows it, and governs itself there in the manner of God. So much so that it seems that while every substance expresses the whole universe, other substances express the world rather than God while minds express God rather than the world. And this natural nobility of minds, which brings them as near to the divine as is possible for mere creatures, means that God receives from them infinitely more glory than from other beings, or rather other beings merely give minds matter for glorifying Him.

That is why this moral quality of God that makes Him the Lord and Monarch of Minds, affects Him so to speak personally in a quite special manner. It is in this that He becomes human and is willing to allow human ways of speaking about Him, and enters into fellowship with us like a Prince with his subjects. This consideration is so dear to Him that the happy and flourishing state of His empire, that consists in the greatest possible happiness of the inhabitants, becomes the supreme subaltern law of His conduct. For happiness is to persons what perfection is to beings, and if the first principle of existence of the physical world is the decree giving it the greatest possible perfection, the first principle of existence of the moral world or City of God, the most noble part of the universe, must be to spread as much happiness as possible in it.

Hence it must not be doubted that God so ordained (not only that minds could live forever, which is inevitable, but also that they should conserve forever their moral nature) so that this city should lose no person just as the world loses no substance. And consequently, they will always know what they are, otherwise they would not be liable to reward or punishment, which however is the essence of any republic, above all of one that is the most perfect, in which nothing can be neglected.

Finally, since God is at once the most just and the most good-natured of monarchs, and asks only for good will, provided that it is sincere and serious, His subjects could not hope for better conditions: to make them perfectly happy, He wants only that they love Him.

37. Jesus Christ Has Revealed to Men the Mystery and Admirable Laws of the Kingdom of Heaven and the Greatness of the Supreme Happiness God Prepares for Those Who Love Him

The ancient philosophers had very little knowledge of these important truths. Jesus Christ alone expressed them divinely well and in such a clear and familiar way, that the most crude minds came to understand them. So His gospel changed the entire face of human affairs. He brought us knowledge of the Kingdom of Heaven or this perfect republic of minds that merits the title "City of God" whose admirable laws he revealed to us, and he alone shows us how much God loves us; the exactness with which He has provided for all that concerns us; that since He cares for sparrows, He will not neglect the reasonable creatures who are infinitely more dear to Him; that all the hairs in our heads are counted; that heaven and earth will pass away before the Word of God and everything belonging to the pattern of our salvation is changed; God has more concern with the least of intelligent souls than with the whole machine of the world; that we must not fear those who can destroy the body but are unable to harm souls, since God alone can make them happy or unhappy; that the just are in His hand protected from all the revolutions of the universe, since nothing can act on them but God alone; that none of our actions is forgotten; that everything is taken into account, right down to unguarded words, and a spoonful of water well used; and finally that all things must result in the greatest good for those that are good; that the just are like suns and that neither our senses nor our minds have ever tasted anything approaching the happiness God prepares for those who love Him.

THE MONADOLOGY

1. The object of this discourse, the *monad*, is nothing else than a simple substance, which enters into the composites; *simple* meaning, which has no parts.

2. And there must be simple substances, since there are composites; for the composite is nothing else than an accumulation or aggregate of the simples.

3. But where there are no parts, neither extension, nor figure, nor divisibility is possible. Thus, these monads are the veritable atoms of nature, and, in one word, the elements of all things.

4. Hence no dissolution is to be feared for them, and a simple substance cannot perish naturally in any conceivable manner.

5. For the same reason, no simple substance can come into being naturally, since it cannot be formed by composition.

6. Thus it may be maintained that monads cannot begin or end otherwise than instantaneously, that is, they can begin only by creation, and end only by annihilation; while what is complete begins and ends through and in its parts.

7. It is impossible also to explain how a monad can be altered, that is, internally changed, by any other creature. For there is nothing in it which might be transposed, nor can there be conceived in it any internal movement which could be excited, directed, or diminished. In composites this is possible, since the parts can interchange place. The monads have no windows through which anything could come in or go out.

8. Nevertheless, the monads must have some qualities, otherwise they would not even be beings. And if the simple substances did not differ through their qualities, there would be no means at all of perceiving any change in things. For what is in the composites can come only from the ingredient simples. So the monads, if they were without qualities, would be indistinguishable the one from the other, since they do not differ in quantity either. The plenum being presupposed, no space, consequently, could ever receive through movement anything but the equivalent of what has been in it, and one state of things would be indiscernible from another.

9. Each monad must even be different from every other. For in nature there are never two beings which are perfectly like one another, and between which it would not be possible to find an internal difference, that is, a difference founded on an intrinsic denomination.

10. I take it also for granted that all created beings, consequently the created monads as well, are subject to change, and that this change is even continual in each one.

Gottfried Wilhelm Von Leibniz, *Monadology and Other Philosophical Essays,* translated by Paul Schrecker and Anne Martin Schrecker (Pearson/Library of the Liberal Arts, 1965).

11. In consequence of what has been said, the natural changes of the monads must result from an *internal principle*, since no external cause could influence their interior.

12. But besides the principle of change, there must be a *particular trait of what is changing*, which produces, so to speak, the specification and variety of the simple substances.

13. This particular must comprehend a multiplicity in the unity, that is, in the simple. For since all natural change proceeds by degrees, something changes and something remains. Consequently, there must be in the simple substance a plurality of affections and relations, though it has no parts.

14. The passing state which comprehends and represents a multiplicity in the unity or simple substance is nothing but what is called *perception*; it must be clearly distinguished from apperception or consciousness, as will become clear later on. On this point the Cartesian doctrine has been very defective, since it has entirely neglected those perceptions which are not apperceived; the same failure to distinguish has made the Cartesians believe that only spirits are monads, and that there are neither animal souls nor other entelechies. Therefore, they, like the unlearned, have confused a long swoon with death, strictly speaking, and yielded to the scholastic prejudice that there are entirely separated souls. The same error has even confirmed unsound minds in the opinion that souls are mortal.

15. The action of the internal principle which produces change, that is, the passage from one perception to another, may be called *appetition*. It is true that appetition may not always entirely attain the whole perception toward which it tends, but it always obtains something and arrives at new perceptions.

16. We ourselves experience a multiplicity in the simple substance, when we observe that the least thought which we apperceive in ourselves comprehends a variety in its object. Thus, all those who recognize that the soul is a simple substance must recognize this multiplicity in the monad. Pierre Bayle should not have found a difficulty in this theory, as he indeed did in the article "Rorarius" of his *Dictionary.*

17. Moreover, it must be avowed that *perception* and what depends upon it *cannot possibly be explained by mechanical reasons*, that is, by figure and movement. Suppose that there be a machine, the structure of which produces thinking, feeling, and perceiving; imagine this machine enlarged but preserving the same proportions, so that you could enter it as if it were a mill. This being supposed, you might visit its inside; but what would you observe there? Nothing but parts which push and move each other, and never anything that could explain perception. This explanation must therefore be sought in the simple substance, not in the composite, that is, in the machine. However, there is nothing else to be found in the simple substance but perceptions and their changes. In this alone can consist all the *internal actions* of simple substances.

18. The name *entelechies* would fit all the simple substances or created monads. For they have in themselves a certain perfection *[echousi to enteles]*, and they are endowed with a selfsufficiency *[autarkeia]* which makes them the sources of their own actions and, so to speak, incorporeal automata.

19. If we want to call *soul* all that has perception and appetition, in the general sense explained above, we might give the name soul to all simple substances or created monads. But since sensation is something more than a simple perception, I agree that the general name monad or entelechy may suffice for those simple substances which have nothing but perception and appetition; the name souls may then be reserved for those having perception that is more distinct and is accompanied by memory.

20. Indeed, we experience in ourselves a state in which we remember nothing and have no distinct perception at all, e.g., when we faint or are overcome by a deep and

dreamless sleep. In this state the soul is not noticeably different from a simple monad. However, since this state does not last, the soul being able to pull itself out of it, the soul is more than a simple monad.

21. Besides, it does not follow at all that in such a state the simple substance entirely lacks perception. For the reasons propounded a while ago, this lack is not possible; for the monad cannot perish, nor can it subsist without some affection, which is nothing but its perception. But when there is a great multitude of minute perceptions lacking distinctness, one becomes dizzy: for example, when you turn around several consecutive times, you get a vertigo which may make you faint and leave you without any distinct perception. Death may throw animals into such a state for a time.

22. The present state of a simple substance is the natural result of its precedent state, so much so that the present is pregnant with the future.

23. Therefore, since on awakening from such a swoon, you apperceive your perceptions, it follows that you must have had some perceptions immediately before, though you did not apperceive them. For a perception cannot come naturally except from another perception, just as movement cannot come naturally except from another movement.

24. Hence it is evident that if in our perceptions there were nothing distinct nor anything, so to speak, in relief and of a more marked taste, we would always be in a swoon. And that is the state of the mere naked monads.

25. We see indeed that nature has given distinct perceptions to the animals, for care has been taken to provide them with organs which collect several light rays or several air waves, to unite them and thereby give them greater effect. Something similar occurs in scent, taste, and touch, and perhaps in many other senses unknown to us. I shall explain soon how what occurs in the soul represents what occurs in the sense organs.

26. Memory provides the souls with a sort of *consistency* which imitates reason but has to be distinguished from it. For we see that animals, perceiving something which impresses them and of which they have previously had a resembling perception, are brought by the representation of their memory to expect what has been associated with this perception in the past and are moved to feelings similar to those they had then. If you show a stick to a dog, for instance, it remembers the pain caused by it and howls or runs away.

27. The vividness of the imagination which strikes and moves animals comes from either the strength or the frequency of preceding perceptions. For often one strong impression produces at once the effect of a long *habit* or of many reiterated impressions of minor strength.

28. Men act like animals in so far as the succession of their perceptions is brought about by the principle of memory. In this they resemble medical empiricists whose practice is not backed by theory. In fact, we are mere empiricists in three quarters of all our actions. If you expect, for instance, that the sun will rise tomorrow because up to now it has always happened, you act as an empiricist. The astronomer alone judges by reason.

29. Knowledge of necessary and eternal truths, however, distinguishes us from mere animals and grants us *reason* and the sciences, elevating us to the knowledge of ourselves and of God. This possession is what is called our reasonable soul or *spirit*.

30. By this knowledge of necessary truths and by the abstractions made possible through them, we also are raised to *acts of reflection* which enable us to think of the socalled *self* and to consider this or that to be in us. Thinking thus about ourselves, we think of being, substance, the simple and the composite, the immaterial, and even of God, conceiving what is limited in us as without limit in him. These acts of reflection furnish the principal objects of our reasoning.

31. Our reasoning is founded on two great principles: The first is the principle of *contradiction*, by virtue of which we consider as false what implies a contradiction and as true what is the opposite of the contradictory or false.

32. The second is the principle of *sufficient reason*, by virtue of which we hold that no fact can be true or existing and no statement truthful without a sufficient reason for its being so and not different; albeit these reasons most frequently must remain unknown to us.

33. There are also two kinds of *truths*: those of *reason*, which are necessary and of which the opposite is impossible, and those of *fact*, which are contingent and of which the opposite is possible. When a truth is necessary, the reasons for it can be found through analysis, that is, by resolving it into simpler ideas and truths until one comes to primitives.

34. Thus the mathematicians, using the analytical method, reduce the speculative theorems and the practical canons to *definitions*, *axioms*, and *postulates*.

35. In the end, there are simple ideas of which no definition can be given. Moreover, there are axioms and postulates, in short, *primitive principles*, which cannot be demonstrated and do not need demonstration. They are *identical propositions*, the opposite of which contains an express contradiction.

36. A *sufficient reason*, however, must also exist for *contingent truths* or *truths of fact*, that is, for the series of things comprehended in the universe of creatures. Here the resolution into particular reasons could be continued without limit; for the variety of natural things is immense, and bodies are infinitely divided. There is an infinity of figures and movements, past and present, which contribute to the efficient cause of my presently writing this. And there is an infinity of minute inclinations and dispositions of my soul, which contribute to the final cause of my writing.

37. Now, all of this detail implies previous or more particular contingents, each of which again stands in need of a similar analysis to be accounted for, so that nothing is gained by such an analysis. The sufficient or ultimate reason must therefore exist outside the succession or series of contingent particulars, infinite though this series may be.

38. Consequently, the ultimate reason of all things must subsist in a necessary substance, in which all particular changes may exist only virtually as in its source: this substance is what we call *God*.

39. Now, this substance is the sufficient reason for all this particular existence which is, moreover, interconnected throughout. Hence, there is but one God, and this God suffices.

40. This Supreme Substance is unique, universal, and necessary. There is nothing existing apart from it which would be independent of it, and the existence of this being is a simple consequence of its possibility. It follows that this substance does not admit of any limitation and must contain as much reality as is possible.

41. God, therefore, is absolutely perfect, *perfection* meaning the quantity of positive reality. In things which have limits, that is, in finite things, this perfection has to be strictly interpreted, namely as the quantity of positive reality within their given limits. But where there are no limits, namely in God, perfection is absolutely infinite.

42. It follows that creatures owe their perfections to the divine influence, but their imperfections to their proper nature, which is incapable of being without limits. For it is in this that they are distinguished from God. The created things' *original imperfection* manifests itself through the *natural inertia* of all bodies.

43. Moreover, it is true that in God is the source not only of all existence, but also of all essence endowed with reality, that is, the source of what is real in the possibles. For the divine understanding is the region of the eternal truths and of the ideas on which

they depend, and without him there would not be anything real in the possibles; that is, without him there would not only be nothing existing, but even nothing possible.

44. Indeed, if there is to be any reality in the essences or possibles, that is, in the necessary truths, this reality must be founded on the existence of the necessary being whose essence implies its existence, that is, to which it suffices to be possible in order to be actual.

45. Thus God alone (or the necessary being) has the privilege of existing necessarily, provided only he be possible. Now, since nothing can hinder the possibility of the substance which contains no limits, no negation, and hence no contradiction, this provides a sufficient reason for the knowledge *a priori* of God's existence. Besides, we have proved it by the reality of the eternal truths. In addition, we also have proved this existence *a posteriori* by the existence of contingent beings. For the sufficient and ultimate reason of these can lie only in the necessary being which has in itself the reason of its existence.

46. It must not be imagined, however, as certain authors have imagined, that since the eternal truths depend upon God, they are arbitrary and depend upon his will. Descartes seems to have thought so, and after him Poiret. This is true only of the contingent truths which are based on the principle of fitness, that is, the choice of the best possible; while the necessary truths depend only on his understanding, of which they are the internal object.

47. Thus God is the only primitive unit or the only original simple substance, of which all the created or derivative monads are the products, born, so to speak, every moment by continual fulgurations from the divinity, and limited by the capacities of creatures, to which limitation is essential.

48. In God there are his *power* which is the source of everything, his *knowledge* which contains the particulars of the ideas, and finally his *will* which is the source of change or production and acts according to the principle of the best possible. Corresponding to these divine attributes, there is in the created monads the subject or basis, namely, the faculty of perception and the faculty of appetition. In God, however, these attributes are absolutely infinite and perfect, whereas in the created monads or *entelechies* (Hermolaus Barbarus translated this word into Latin by *perfectihabies*) these attributes are only likenesses, possessed by the monads in proportion to their perfections.

49. Creatures are said to act outwardly in so far as they have perfection, and to *suffer* from other creatures in so far as they are imperfect. Thus *activity* has to be attributed to the monad in so far as it has distinct perceptions, and passivity in so far as it has confused perceptions.

50. One creature is more perfect than another, in so far as there is found in the former a reason to account *a priori* for what is happening in the latter; this is why one says that the former acts upon the latter.

51. But in the simple substances this influence of one monad upon the other is but *ideal* and can take effect only through the intervention of God; in the ideas of God, indeed, any monad reasonably requires that in his ruling of all others, God, from the beginning, take that monad into consideration. For since no created monad can exercise a physical influence upon the interior of any other, this is the only means by which the one can depend upon the other.

52. By this means actions and passions among creatures are mutual. For when God compares two simple substances, he finds in either one reasons which oblige him to adjust the other to it. What appears as active in certain respects, consequently appears as passive from another point of view: it appears as *active* in so far as what is distinctly known in one monad serves to account for what happens in another; it appears as passive in so far as the reason for what happens in it is to be found in what is distinctly known in another.

53. Now, since in the divine ideas there is an infinity of possible universes of which only one can exist, the choice made by God must have a sufficient reason which determines him to the one rather than to another.

54. This reason can be found only in fitness, that is, in the degree of perfection contained in these worlds. For each possible has a right to claim existence in proportion to the perfection it involves. Thus nothing is entirely arbitrary.

55. This is the cause for the existence of the best, which is disclosed to him by his wisdom, determines his choice by his goodness, and is produced by his power.

56. This *connection* of all created things with every single one of them and their adaptation to every single one, as well as the connection and adaptation of every single thing to all others, has the result that every single substance stands in relations which express all the others. Whence every single substance is a perpetual living mirror of the universe.

57. Just as the same city regarded from different sides offers quite different aspects, and thus appears multiplied *by the perspective*, so it also happens that the infinite multitude of simple substances creates the appearance of as many different universes. Yet they are but perspectives of a single universe, varied according to the *points of view*, which differ in each monad.

58. This is the means of obtaining the greatest possible variety, together with the greatest possible order; in other words, it is the means of obtaining as much perfection as possible.

59. Only by this hypothesis (which I dare to call demonstrated) can the greatness of God be exalted as it ought to be. Pierre Bayle has recognized this when he objected to the hypothesis in the article "Rorarius" of his *Dictionary*. In that passage he was inclined to believe that I attributed to God too much, and even more than is possible. But he was unable to adduce any reason why this universal harmony, due to which every substance exactly expresses all the others through the relations it has with them, should be impossible.

60. In what I have just stated, there can also be discerned reasons *a priori* why things could not be different. For God, legislating the whole, has considered every part and particularly every monad. And since the nature of every monad is representative, there is nothing which could limit it to representing only a part of all things. It is true, however, that this representation is but confused concerning the particulars of the whole universe and can be distinct concerning only a small part of all things, namely those which are either the nearest or the largest in respect to each of the monads. For otherwise every monad would be a deity. It is not in the objects of their knowledge, but in the modes of this knowledge that the monads are limited. All of them have a confused knowledge of the infinite, that is, of the whole; but they are limited and distinguished by the degrees of distinct perception.

61. The composite substances are in this respect symbols of the simples. For since all is a plenum, all matter is connected and all movement in the plenum produces some effect on the distant bodies, in proportion to the distance. Hence every body is affected not only by those with which it is in contact, and thus feels in some way everything that happens to them; but through them it also feels those that touch the ones with which it is in immediate contact. Hence it follows that this communication extends over any distance whatever. Consequently, every body experiences everything that goes on in the universe, so much so that he who sees everything might read in any body what is happening anywhere, and even what has happened or will happen. He would be able to observe in the present what is remote in both time and space: [*sumpnoia panta*], as Hippocrates stated. A soul, however, can read in itself only what is distinctly represented in it; it is unable to unfold all at once all its folds; for these go on into infinity.

62. Thus, every created monad represents the whole universe; nevertheless, it represents more distinctly the body which is particularly attached to it and of which it is the entelechy. And since this body expresses the whole universe through the interconnection of all the matter in the plenum, the soul, too, represents the whole universe by representing this body which in a particular manner belongs to it.

63. The body belonging to a monad which is its entelechy or its soul constitutes, together with this entelechy, what may be called a *living unit*, and together with this soul what may be called an *animal*. This body of a living being or of an animal is always an organism. For since every monad is, in its way, a mirror of the universe, and since the universe is ruled in a perfect order, there must also be an order in the representing, that is, in the perceptions of the soul, and consequently in the body. The representation of the universe in the body evinces this order.

64. Thus every body of a living being is a sort of divine machine or natural automaton, which infinitely surpasses all artificial automata. For a machine made by human art is not a machine in all its parts. The cog on a brass wheel, for instance, has parts or fragments which for us are no longer artificial things, and are no longer proper to the machine with respect to the purpose for which the wheel was designed. The machines of nature (namely, the living bodies) are, on the contrary, machines even in their smallest parts without any limit. Herein lies the difference between nature and art, that is, between divine and human art.

65. The author of nature, indeed, has been able to practice this divine and infinitely marvellous art because any portion of matter is not only infinitely divisible, as the ancients recognized, but also actually subdivided *ad infinitum*: every part having parts each of which has its own particular movement. For otherwise it would be impossible for every portion of matter to express the whole universe.

66. Hence it can be seen that in the smallest portion of matter there is a world of creatures, living beings, animals, entelechies, and souls.

67. Thus every portion of matter can be conceived as a garden full of plants or as a pond full of fish. But every branch of the plant, every limb of the animal, every drop of its humors, is again such a garden or such a pond.

68. And though the soil and the air in the intervals between the plants of the garden is not a plant, nor the water between the fishes a fish, yet these intervals contain again plants or fishes. But these living beings most frequently are so minute that they remain imperceptible to us.

69. Thus there is nothing uncultured, sterile or dead in the universe, no chaos, no disorder, though this may be what appears. It would be about the same with a pond seen from a distance: you would perceive a confused movement, a squirming of fishes, if I may say so, without discerning the single fish.

70. Hence it becomes clear that every living body has a dominant entelechy which in an animal is its soul. But the limbs of this living body are full of other living beings, plants or animals, each of which again has its entelechy or its dominant soul.

71. But you must not imagine—like some authors who have misinterpreted my thought—that each soul has a mass or portion of matter forever belonging or attached to it and that, consequently, it owns other living, though inferior, beings forever destined to serve it. For all bodies are, like rivers, in a perpetual flux; small parts enter and leave them continually.

72. Thus the soul changes its body bit by bit, and by degrees, so that it never is deprived all at once of all its organs; in animals there is frequently metamorphosis. Never, however, is there metempsychosis nor transmigration of souls. Nor are there any totally separate *souls*, nor *genii* without body. God alone is entirely bodiless.

73. This also proves that, strictly speaking, there never is either complete generation or perfect death, which would consist in the separation of the soul. What we call *generation* consists in developments and growths, just as what we call *death* consists in involutions and diminutions.

74. Philosophers formerly have been very perplexed concerning the origin of forms, entelechies, or souls. Today, however, it has been discovered through precise observations made on plants, insects, and animals that the organized bodies of nature are never produced out of a chaos or putrefaction, but always out of seeds, in which doubtless there has been some *preformation*. Hence it has been concluded, not only that the organized body was already in the seed before conception, but also that there was a soul in this body, and, in short, the animal itself. Through the conception, furthermore, the animal has only been disposed to a great transformation, namely to become an animal of a different species. Something similar can even be observed outside generation, as, for instance, when worms become flies, or caterpillars butterflies.

75. Those animals among which some are elevated by means of the conception to the grade of larger animals, may be called *spermatic*; while those among them which remain within their species, that is, the majority, are born, multiply, and are destroyed like the large animals. Only a small number of elect pass on to a greater stage.

76. This, so far, has been but half the truth. Therefore I have concluded that if it be true that the animal never begins naturally, it will not end naturally either, and that consequently there will be, strictly speaking, neither generation nor entire destruction, that is, death. These arguments made a posteriori and drawn from experience agree perfectly with my principles deduced *a priori* a while ago.

77. Thus it may be said that not only the soul (mirror of an indestructible universe) is indestructible, but also that the animal itself is indestructible, albeit its machine often partly perishes, and casts off or takes on organic accretions.

78. These principles have enabled me to propose a natural explanation for the union or conformity of the soul and the organized body. The soul follows its own laws, and so does the body. They meet by virtue of the *pre-established harmony* prevailing among all substances, since they all are representations of one and the same universe.

79. The souls act according to the laws of final causes, through appetitions, ends, and means. The bodies act according to the laws of efficient causes, that is, of motion. And the two realms, that of efficient causes and that of final causes, are in mutual harmony.

80. Descartes has recognized that souls cannot impart force to bodies, because there is always the same quantity of force in matter. He believed, however, that the soul was able to change the directions of bodies. For at his time it was unknown yet that there is a law of nature according to which the total direction of matter is equally conserved. If he had been aware of this, he would have hit upon my system of preestablished harmony.

81. This system maintains that bodies act as though there were no souls (assuming the impossible); and that souls act as though there were no bodies; and that both act as though the one influenced the other.

82. As to *spirits* or reasonable souls, I find that essentially all the living beings and animals have the same nature, as I have said before, namely that the animal and the soul begin with the world and end no more than the world. Nevertheless, the reasonable souls have this in particular, that their little spermatic animals have only ordinary or sensitive souls, as long as they remain undeveloped. As soon, however, as those who, so to speak, are elected attain human nature through an actual conception, their sensitive souls are promoted to the rank of human nature and to the prerogative of spirits.

83. Among other differences existing between ordinary souls and spirits, some of which I have already pointed out, there is also this one, that souls in general are living mirrors or images of the created universe, while the spirits are in addition the images of the Deity itself or of the author of nature himself. They are capable of knowing the system of the universe and of imitating some of it by architectonic specimens, each spirit being like a small deity in his field.

84. This is the reason why the spirits are capable of entering a kind of society with God, and why with respect to them he is not only as an inventor is to his machine (this being the relation of God to the other creatures), but also as a prince to his subjects and even as a father to his children.

85. Hence it may easily be concluded that the assemblage of all the spirits must compose the City of God, that is, the most perfect city possible, under the most perfect monarch possible.

86. This City of God, this truly universal monarchy, is a moral world within the natural world; it is among the works of God the most exalted and the most divine. In it consists veritably the glory of God: for he would be without glory unless his greatness and goodness were recognized and admired by the spirits. Properly speaking, his goodness is directed toward this divine City, while his wisdom and power manifest themselves everywhere.

87. We have established above the perfect harmony between two natural realms, that of efficient causes and the other of final causes. To this we must add here still another harmony, namely, between the physical realm of nature and the moral realm of grace, that is, between God considered as the architect of the machine of the universe, and God considered as the monarch of the divine city of the spirits.

88. This harmony has the result that events lead to grace through the very processes of nature, and that our globe, for instance, must be destroyed and repaired through natural processes at the moments when the government of the spirits so demands, to chastise some and to reward others.

89. One may add that God as the architect satisfies in all respects God as the legislator. Thus sin must entail punishment according to the order of nature and as the very result of the mechanical structure of the universe; and, analogously, good actions will attract their rewards through machinelike corporeal processes. Of course, these results cannot be and ought not always to be obtained as an immediate consequence.

90. Finally, under this perfect government, no good action will remain without its reward, no evil action without its punishment. All events in this city conspire to the advantage of the good people, that is, of those who are not discontented in this great State; who, once they have fulfilled their duties, trust in providence and duly love and imitate the author of all good; who enjoy the contemplation of his perfections as required by the nature of the true *pure love*, which consists in taking pleasure in the felicity of the beloved. This pure love makes the wise and virtuous people work at everything that seems conformable to the divine will, presumed or antecedent, and yet renders them contented with any event that God actually brings about through his secret, consequent, and decisive will. They realize that, could we only understand sufficiently the order of the universe, we should find that this order surpasses all the wishes of the wisest and that it is impossible to improve it; that it is the best not only for the whole in general, but also for ourselves in particular. For ourselves, that is, provided we are duly attached to the author of all things, not only as to the architect and efficient cause of our being, but also as to the master and to the final cause who ought to provide the sole goal of our will and who alone can give us happiness.

George Berkeley
1685–1753

George Berkeley was born near Kilkenny, Ireland, and, although an Anglican of English descent, he emphatically considered himself to be Irish. He studied at Kilkenny College and in 1700 went on to Trinity College, Dublin. There he read Descartes, Newton, and Locke. In 1707, he became a Fellow of the College and was ordained in the Anglican church. The next six years were to be the most philosophically productive in his life. In 1709, he published his *New Theory of Vision,* and in the following year his most important philosophic work, *A Treatise Concerning the Principles of Human Knowledge*. In 1711, he wrote *Discourse on Passive Obedience*. Two years later, he published a more popular exposition of the doctrine of his *Principles* in the form of *Three Dialogues Between Hylas and Philonous*.

For the next eleven years, Berkeley traveled widely, visiting with many of the great thinkers of his day. He became Dean of Derry in 1724, though most of his energy at this time seems to have been given to the founding of a college in the Bermudas. With promises of financial support, he sailed for Rhode Island in 1728 to establish farms for supplying his future college with food. Berkeley spent two and a half years in Rhode Island with his new wife and friends, waiting for the 20,000 pounds the government had promised. When the funds never arrived, he finally gave up and returned to London.

In 1733, he published *Alciphron*, or *The Minute Philosopher*, against the freethinkers (agnostics), and in the following year *The Analyst*, a criticism of Newton. That same year, he was made Bishop of Cloyne. For the next eighteen years, he energetically served his remote, poor diocese. Among the works he wrote during this period are *The Querist* (1737), which used questions to propose public works and education as remedies to the crushing poverty he observed, and *Siris* (1744), an unusual work dealing with the medicinal value of tar water. In 1751, he lost his eldest son, and the next year he moved to Oxford, where another son was beginning his studies. On January 14, 1753, Berkeley died suddenly; he was buried at Christ Church, Oxford.

* * *

Like Locke before him, Berkeley accepted the empiricist doctrine that all we can know are ideas and that ideas come from perception or reflection. But Berkeley saw a problem in Locke's assertion of an external world of material "substances" giving rise to perceptions. If all we can know are ideas, how can we know there is a world "out there" giving rise to our ideas? Locke had said that the primary qualities of an "external object" (such as extension and solidity) are "utterly inseparable" from the objects themselves, whereas this is not the case with secondary qualities (such as color, taste, etc.). But again, asked Berkeley, how can Locke know this? He cannot get "outside himself" to see which of his perceptions are actually a part of objects "out there." Berkeley concluded that Locke's philosophy will lead to skepticism, whereby we must admit that we cannot really know anything about the world "out there."

To avoid this skepticism, Berkeley made the radical claim that there is no "out there," or, more precisely, there is no *matter*. Berkeley's position, which is called "idealism," can be summed up in his famous phrase "*esse* is *percipi*": to be is to be perceived. What we call "bodies," or physical objects, are simply stable collections of perceptions to which we give names such as "apples," "trees," and so on. These collections of perceptions have no existence apart from a perceiving mind. The answer to the famous conundrum "If a tree falls in the forest and no one hears it, does it make a sound?" is that if no one is perceiving it, it not only does not make a sound, the tree does not even exist!

Does this mean that trees go out of existence when no one is left in the forest to perceive them and that they come back into existence when someone enters the forest to perceive them again? It would seem that Berkeley must accept this odd conclusion were it not for one important point: God never leaves the forest, and God is *always* perceiving the trees. By always holding all collections of perceptions in the divine mind, God ensures their continued existence and the perceived regularity in what we call "nature." This point has been classically formulated in the following limericks:

There was a young man who said, "God,
Must think it exceedingly odd
If he finds that this tree
Continues to be
When there's no one about in the Quad."

REPLY:
"Dear Sir: Your astonishment's odd:
I am always about in the Quad.
And that's why the tree
Continues to be,
Since observed by, Yours faithfully, God."

Berkeley saw his philosophy as a common-sense attack on the metaphysical excesses of medieval Scholastics, Continental Rationalists, and even fellow empiricists such as Hobbes and Locke. Although Berkeley understood his philosophy to be common sense, his readers drew different conclusions. One prominent physician of his day claimed Berkeley was insane. The great Dr. Samuel Johnson dismissed Berkeley's ideas with his famous "I refute Berkeley *thus*" and then he kicked a rock. Of course, this did not refute Berkeley at all. It only proved Johnson had not understood Berkeley's point. Berkeley did not claim the nonexistence of stones or that kicking a stone will not produce sensation. He claimed the rock did not exist apart from the perception of its solidity or the perception of pain when struck, and so on. An oft-repeated epitaph summarizes the general reaction to Berkeley: "His arguments produce no conviction, though they cannot be refuted."

* * *

In our reading, *Three Dialogues between Hylas and Philonous* (1713), given here complete, Philonous represents Berkeley's position while Hylas is his adversary. (The name "Hylas" is a derivative of the Greek word for "matter"—against which Berkeley argues.)

For general introductions to Berkeley, see G.J. Warnock, *Berkeley* (Harmondsworth, Middlesex: Penguin Books, 1953); Harry M. Bracken, *Berkeley* (New York: St. Martin's Press, 1974); J.O. Urmson, *Berkeley* (Oxford: Oxford University Press, 1982)—part of the Past Masters series, now reprinted in the combined volume John Dunn et al., eds., *The British Empiricists* (Oxford: Oxford University Press, 1992); David Berman, *George Berkeley: Idealism and the Man* (Oxford: Oxford University Press, 1994); David Berman, *Berkeley* (London: Routledge, 1999); George S. Pappas, *Berkeley's Thought* (Ithaca, NY: Cornell University Press, 2000); Anthony Savile, *Routledge Philosophy Guidebook to Berkeley and the* Principles of Human Knowledge (London: Routledge, 2001); and David Berman, *Berkeley and Irish Philosophy* (London: Continuum, 2005). For a discussion of our reading, see Aaron Garrett, *Berkeley's* Three Dialogues: *A Reader's Guide* (London: Continuum, 2008).For interesting but difficult discussions of Berkeley's arguments, see George Pitcher, *Berkeley* (London: Routledge, 1977) or Kenneth Winkler, *Berkeley: An Interpretation* (Oxford: Oxford University Press, 1989). For collections of essays, see Gale W. Engle and Gabriele Taylor, eds., *Berkeley's* Principles of Human Knowledge (Belmont, CA: Wadsworth, 1968); Colin M. Turbayne, ed., *Berkeley: Critical and Interpretive Essays* (Minneapolis: University of Minnesota Press, 1982); John Foster and Howard Robinson, eds., *Essays on Berkeley: A Tercentennial Celebration* (Oxford: Oxford University Press, 1985); D.M. Armstrong and C.B. Martin, *Berkeley: A Collection of Critical Essays* (Hamden, CT: Garland, 1992)—a reprint of the second half of*Locke and Berkeley: A Collection of Critical Essays* (Garden City, NY: Doubleday, 1968); and Kenneth P. Winkler, ed., *The Cambridge Companion to Berkeley* (Cambridge: Cambridge University Press, 2006).

THREE DIALOGUES BETWEEN HYLAS AND PHILONOUS, IN OPPOSITION TO SCEPTICS AND ATHEISTS

THE FIRST DIALOGUE

PHILONOUS: Good morrow, HYLAS: I did not expect to find you abroad so early.

HYLAS: It is indeed something unusual; but my thoughts were so taken up with a subject I was discoursing of last night, that finding I could not sleep, I resolved to rise and take a turn in the garden.

PHILONOUS: It happened well, to let you see what innocent and agreeable pleasures you lose every morning. Can there be a pleasanter time of the day, or a more delightful season of the year? That purple sky, those wild but sweet notes of birds, the fragrant bloom upon the trees and flowers, the gentle influence of the rising sun, these

Fruits and Dishes on the Table, by Jan Davids de Heem (1606–1683). The underlying theme of *Vanitas* in Dutch still life presents a dual message in the arrangement of fine and rare objects. On the one hand, the objects represent the joy of possessions and the good life, yet the half-eaten pie and the peeled fruit cause reflection on the brevity of human existence and the fleeting nature of material objects. Berkeley takes this a step further by denying material substance and claiming that such objects do not exist apart from a perceiving mind. (*©Bridgeman-Giraudon/Art Resource, NY*)

and a thousand nameless beauties of nature inspire the soul with secret transports; its faculties too being at this time fresh and lively, are fit for those meditations, which the solitude of a garden and tranquillity of the morning naturally dispose us to. But I am afraid I interrupt your thoughts: for you seemed very intent on something.

HYLAS: It is true, I was, and shall be obliged to you if you will permit me to go on in the same vein; not that I would by any means deprive myself of your company, for my thoughts always flow more easily in conversation with a friend, than when I am alone: but my request is, that you would suffer me to impart my reflexions to you.

PHILONOUS: With all my heart, it is what I should have requested myself if you had not prevented me.

HYLAS: I was considering the odd fate of those men who have in all ages, through an affectation of being distinguished from the vulgar, or some unaccountable turn of thought, pretended either to believe nothing at all, or to believe the most extravagant things in the world. This however might be borne, if their paradoxes and scepticism did not draw after them some consequences of general disadvantage to mankind. But the mischief lies here; that when men of less leisure see them who are supposed to have spent their whole time in the pursuits of knowledge professing an entire ignorance of all things, or advancing such notions as are repugnant to plain and commonly received principles, they will be tempted to entertain suspicions concerning the most important truths, which they had hitherto held sacred and unquestionable.

PHILONOUS: I entirely agree with you, as to the ill tendency of the affected doubts of some philosophers, and fantastical conceits of others. I am even so far gone of late in this way of thinking, that I have quitted several of the sublime notions I had got in their schools for vulgar opinions. And I give it you on my word; since this revolt from metaphysical notions to the plain dictates of nature and common sense, I find my understanding strangely enlightened, so that I can now easily comprehend a great many things which before were all mystery and riddle.

HYLAS: I am glad to find there was nothing in the accounts I heard of you.

PHILONOUS: Pray, what were those?

HYLAS: You were represented, in last night's conversation, as one who maintained the most extravagant opinion that ever entered into the mind of man, to wit, that there is no such thing as *material substance* in the world.

PHILONOUS: That there is no such thing as what philosophers call *material substance,* I am seriously persuaded: but, if I were made to see anything absurd or sceptical in this, I should then have the same reason to renounce this that I imagine I have now to reject the contrary opinion.

HYLAS: What! Can anything be more fantastical, more repugnant to common sense, or a more manifest piece of scepticism, than to believe there is no such thing as *matter?*

PHILONOUS: Softly, good Hylas. What if it should prove that you, who hold there is, are, by virtue of that opinion, a greater *sceptic,* and maintain more paradoxes and repugnances to common sense, than I who believe no such thing?

HYLAS: You may as soon persuade me, the part is greater than the whole, as that, in order to avoid absurdity and scepticism, I should ever be obliged to give up my opinion in this point

PHILONOUS: Well then, are you content to admit that opinion for true, which upon examination shall appear most agreeable to common sense, and remote from scepticism?

HYLAS: With all my heart. Since you are for raising disputes about the plainest things in nature, I am content for once to hear what you have to say.

PHILONOUS: Pray, Hylas, what do you mean by a *sceptic?*

HYLAS: I mean what all men mean—one that doubts of everything.

PHILONOUS: He then who entertains no doubts concerning some particular point, with regard to that point cannot be thought a *sceptic*.

HYLAS: I agree with you.

PHILONOUS: Whether does doubting consist in embracing the affirmative or negative side of a question?

HYLAS: In neither; for whoever understands English cannot but know that doubting signifies a suspense between both.

PHILONOUS: He then that denies any point, can no more be said to doubt of it, than he who affirms it with the same degree of assurance.

HYLAS: True.

PHILONOUS: And, consequently, for such his denial is no more to be esteemed a *sceptic* than the other.

HYLAS: I acknowledge it.

PHILONOUS: How comes it to pass then, Hylas, that you pronounce me a *sceptic,* because I deny what you affirm, to wit the existence of matter? Since, for aught you can tell I am as peremptory in my denial, as you in your affirmation.

HYLAS: Hold, Philonous, I have been a little out in my definition; but every false step a man makes in discourse is not to be insisted on. I said indeed that a sceptic was one who doubted of everything; but I should have added, or who denies the reality and truth of things.

PHILONOUS: What things? Do you mean the principles and theorems of sciences? But these you know are universal intellectual notions, and consequently independent of matter. The denial therefore of this does not imply the denying them.

HYLAS: I grant it. But are there no other things? What think you of distrusting the senses, of denying the real existence of sensible things, or pretending to know nothing of them. Is not this sufficient to denominate a man a *sceptic?*

PHILONOUS: Shall we therefore examine which of us it is that denies the reality of sensible things, or professes the greatest ignorance of them; since, if I take you rightly, he is to be esteemed the greatest *sceptic?*

HYLAS: That is what I desire.

PHILONOUS: What mean you by Sensible Things?

HYLAS: Those things which are perceived by the senses. Can you imagine that I mean anything else?

PHILONOUS: Pardon me, Hylas, if I am desirous clearly to apprehend your notions, since this may much shorten our inquiry. Suffer me then to ask you this farther question. Are those things only perceived by the senses which are perceived immediately? Or, may those things properly be said to be *sensible* which are perceived mediately, or not without the intervention of others?

HYLAS: I do not sufficiently understand you.

PHILONOUS: In reading a book, what I immediately perceive are the letters; but mediately, or by means of these, are suggested to my mind the notions of God, virtue, truth, &c. Now, that the letters are truly sensible things, or perceived by sense, there is no doubt: but I would know whether you take the things suggested by them to be so too.

HYLAS: No, certainly: it were absurd to think *God* or *virtue* sensible things; though they may be signified and suggested to the mind by sensible marks, with which they have an arbitrary connexion.

PHILONOUS: It seems then, that by *sensible things* you mean those only which can be perceived immediately by sense?

HYLAS: Right.

PHILONOUS: Does it not follow from this, that though I see one part of the sky red, and another blue, and that my reason does thence evidently conclude there must be some cause of that diversity of colours, yet that cause cannot be said to be a sensible thing, or perceived by the sense of seeing?

HYLAS: It does.

PHILONOUS: In like manner, though I hear variety of sounds, yet I cannot be said to hear the causes of those sounds?

HYLAS: You cannot.

PHILONOUS: And when by my touch I perceive a thing to be hot and heavy, I cannot say, with any truth or propriety, that I feel the cause of its heat or weight?

HYLAS: To prevent any more questions of this kind, I tell you once for all, that by *sensible things* I mean those only which are perceived by sense; and that in truth the senses perceive nothing which they do not perceive immediately: for they make no inferences. The deducing therefore of causes or occasions from effects and appearances, which alone are perceived by sense, entirely relates to reason.

PHILONOUS: This point then is agreed between us—That *sensible things are those only which are immediately perceived by sense.* You will farther inform me, whether we immediately perceive by sight anything beside light, and colours, and figures; or by hearing, anything but sounds; by the palate, anything beside tastes; by the smell, beside odours; or by the touch, more than tangible qualities.

HYLAS: We do not.

PHILONOUS: It seems, therefore, that if you take away all sensible qualities, there remains nothing sensible?

HYLAS: I grant it.

PHILONOUS: Sensible things therefore are nothing else but so many sensible qualities, or combinations of sensible qualities?

HYLAS: Nothing else.

PHILONOUS: Heat then is a sensible thing?

HYLAS: Certainly.

PHILONOUS: Does the reality of sensible things consist in being perceived? Or, is it something distinct from their being perceived, and that bears no relation to the mind?

HYLAS: To *exist* is one thing, and to be *perceived* is another.

PHILONOUS: I speak with regard to sensible things only. And of these I ask, whether by their real existence you mean a subsistence exterior to the mind, and distinct from their being perceived?

HYLAS: I mean a real absolute being, distinct from, and without any relation to, their being perceived.

PHILONOUS: Heat therefore, if it be allowed a real being, must exist without the mind?

HYLAS: It must.

PHILONOUS: Tell me, Hylas, is this real existence equally compatible to all degrees of heat, which we perceive; or is there any reason why we should attribute it to some, and deny it to others? And if there be, pray let me know that reason.

HYLAS: Whatever degree of heat we perceive by sense, we may be sure the same exists in the object that occasions it.

PHILONOUS: What! The greatest as well as the least?

HYLAS: I tell you, the reason is plainly the same in respect of both. They are both perceived by sense; nay, the greater degree of heat is more sensibly perceived, and consequently, if there is any difference, we are more certain of its real existence than we can be of the reality of a lesser degree.

PHILONOUS: But is not the most vehement and intense degree of heat a very great pain?

HYLAS: No one can deny it.

PHILONOUS: And is any unperceiving thing capable of pain or pleasure?

HYLAS: No, certainly.

PHILONOUS: Is your material substance a senseless being, or a being endowed with sense and perception?

HYLAS: It is senseless without doubt.

PHILONOUS: It cannot therefore be the subject of pain?

HYLAS: By no means.

PHILONOUS: Nor consequently of the greatest heat perceived by sense, since you acknowledge this to be no small pain?

HYLAS: I grant it.

PHILONOUS: What shall we say then of your external object; is it a material substance, or no?

HYLAS: It is a material substance with the sensible qualities inhering in it.

PHILONOUS: How then can a great heat exist in it, since you own it cannot in a material substance? I desire you would clear this point.

HYLAS: Hold, Philonous, I fear I was out in yielding intense heat to be a pain. It should seem rather, that pain is something distinct from heat, and the consequence or effect of it.

PHILONOUS: Upon putting your hand near the fire, do you perceive one simple uniform sensation, or two distinct sensations?

HYLAS: But one simple sensation.

PHILONOUS: Is not the heat immediately perceived?

HYLAS: It is.

PHILONOUS: And the pain?

HYLAS: True.

PHILONOUS: Seeing therefore they are both immediately perceived at the same time, and the fire affects you only with one simple or uncompounded idea, it follows that this same simple idea is both the intense heat immediately perceived, and the pain; and, consequently, that the intense heat immediately perceived is nothing distinct from a particular sort of pain.

HYLAS: It seems so.

PHILONOUS: Again, try in your thoughts, Hylas, if you can conceive a vehement sensation to be without pain or pleasure.

HYLAS: I cannot.

PHILONOUS: Or can you frame to yourself an idea of sensible pain or pleasure in general, abstracted from every particular idea of heat, cold, tastes, smells etc.?

HYLAS: I do not find that I can.

PHILONOUS: Does it not therefore follow, that sensible pain is nothing distinct from those sensations or ideas, in an intense degree?

HYLAS: It is undeniable; and, to speak the truth, I begin to suspect a very great heat cannot exist but in a mind perceiving it.

PHILONOUS: What! Are you then in that *sceptical* state of suspense, between affirming and denying?

HYLAS: I think I may be positive in the point. A very violent and painful heat cannot exist without the mind.

PHILONOUS: It hath not therefore, according to you, any real being?

HYLAS: I own it.

PHILONOUS: Is it therefore certain, that there is no body in nature really hot?

HYLAS: I have not denied there is any real heat in bodies. I only say, there is no such thing as an intense real heat.

PHILONOUS: But, did you not say before that all degrees of heat were equally real; or, if there was any difference, that the greater were more undoubtedly real than the lesser?

HYLAS: True: but it was because I did not then consider the ground there is for distinguishing between them, which I now plainly see. And it is this: because intense heat is nothing else but a particular kind of painful sensation; and pain cannot exist but in a perceiving being; it follows that no intense heat can really exist in an unperceiving corporeal substance. But this is no reason why we should deny heat in an inferior degree to exist in such a substance.

PHILONOUS: But how shall we be able to discern those degrees of heat which exist only in the mind from those which exist without it?

HYLAS: That is no difficult matter. You know the least pain cannot exist unperceived; whatever, therefore, degree of heat is a pain exists only in the mind. But, as for all other degrees of heat, nothing obliges us to think the same of them.

PHILONOUS: I think you granted before that no unperceiving being was capable of pleasure, any more than of pain.

HYLAS: I did.

PHILONOUS: And is not warmth, or a more gentle degree of heat than what causes uneasiness, a pleasure?

HYLAS: What then?

PHILONOUS: Consequently, it cannot exist without the mind in an unperceiving substance, or body.

HYLAS: So it seems.

PHILONOUS: Since, therefore, as well those degrees of heat that are not painful, as those that are, can exist only in a thinking substance; may we not conclude that external bodies are absolutely incapable of any degree of heat whatsoever?

HYLAS: On second thoughts, I do not think it so evident that warmth is a pleasure as that a great degree of heat is a pain.

PHILONOUS: I do not pretend that warmth is as great a pleasure as heat is a pain. But, if you grant it to be even a small pleasure, it serves to make good my conclusion.

HYLAS: I could rather call it an *indolence*. It seems to be nothing more than a privation of both pain and pleasure. And that such a quality or state as this may agree to an unthinking substance, I hope you will not deny.

PHILONOUS: If you are resolved to maintain that warmth, or a gentle degree of heat, is no pleasure, I know not how to convince you otherwise than by appealing to your own sense. But what think you of cold?

HYLAS: The same that I do of heat. An intense degree of cold is a pain; for to feel a very great cold, is to perceive a great uneasiness: it cannot therefore exist without the mind; but a lesser degree of cold may, as well as a lesser degree of heat.

PHILONOUS: Those bodies, therefore, upon whose application to our own, we perceive a moderate degree of heat, must be concluded to have a moderate degree of heat or warmth in them—and those, upon whose application we feel a like degree of cold, must be thought to have cold in them.

HYLAS: They must.

PHILONOUS: Can any doctrine be true that necessarily leads a man into an absurdity?

HYLAS: Without doubt it cannot.

PHILONOUS: Is it not an absurdity to think that the same thing should be at the same time both cold and warm?

HYLAS: It is.

PHILONOUS: Suppose now one of your hands hot, and the other cold, and that they are both at once put into the same vessel of water, in an intermediate state; will not the water seem cold to one hand, and warm to the other?

HYLAS: It will.

PHILONOUS: Ought we not therefore, by your principles, to conclude it is really both cold and warm at the same time, that is, according to your own concession, to believe an absurdity?

HYLAS: I confess it seems so.

PHILONOUS: Consequently, the principles themselves are false, since you have granted that no true principle leads to an absurdity.

HYLAS: But, after all, can anything be more absurd than to say, *there is no heat in the fire?*

PHILONOUS: To make the point still clearer; tell me whether, in two cases exactly alike, we ought not to make the same judgment?

HYLAS: We ought.

PHILONOUS: When a pin pricks your finger, does it not rend and divide the fibres of your flesh?

HYLAS: It does.

PHILONOUS: And when a coal burns your finger, does it any more?

HYLAS: It does not.

PHILONOUS: Since, therefore, you neither judge the sensation itself occasioned by the pin, nor anything like it to be in the pin; you should not, conformably to what you have now granted, judge the sensation occasioned by the fire, or anything like it, to be in the fire.

HYLAS: Well, since it must be so, I am content to yield this point, and acknowledge that heat and cold are only sensations existing in our minds. But there still remain qualities enough to secure the reality of external things.

PHILONOUS: But what will you say, Hylas, if it shall appear that the case is the same with regard to all other sensible qualities, and that they can no more be supposed to exist without the mind, than heat and cold?

HYLAS: Then indeed you will have done something to the purpose; but that is what I despair of seeing proved.

PHILONOUS: Let us examine them in order. What think you of tastes—do they exist without the mind, or no?

HYLAS: Can any man in his senses doubt whether sugar is sweet, or wormwood bitter?

PHILONOUS: Inform me, Hylas. Is a sweet taste a particular kind of pleasure or pleasant sensation, or is it not?

HYLAS: It is.

PHILONOUS: And is not bitterness some kind of uneasiness or pain?

HYLAS: I grant it.

PHILONOUS: If therefore sugar and wormwood are unthinking corporeal substances existing without the mind, how can sweetness and bitterness, that is, pleasure and pain, agree to them?

HYLAS: Hold, Philonous, I now see what it was deluded me all this time. You asked whether heat and cold, sweetness and bitterness, were not particular sorts of pleasure and pain; to which I answered simply, that they were. Whereas I should have thus distinguished:—those qualities, as perceived by us, are pleasures or pains; but not as existing in the external objects. We must not therefore conclude absolutely, that there is no heat in the fire, or sweetness in the sugar, but only that heat or sweetness, as perceived by us, are not in the fire or sugar. What say you to this?

PHILONOUS: I say it is nothing to the purpose. Our discourse proceeded altogether concerning sensible things, which you defined to be, the things we *immediately perceive by our senses.* Whatever other qualities, therefore, you speak of as distinct from these, I know nothing of them, neither do they at all belong to the point in dispute. You may, indeed, pretend to have discovered certain qualities which you do not perceive, and assert those insensible qualities exist in fire and sugar. But what use can be made of this to your present purpose, I am at a loss to conceive. Tell me then once more, do you acknowledge that heat and cold, sweetness and bitterness (meaning those qualities which are perceived by the senses), do not exist without the mind?

HYLAS: I see it is to no purpose to hold out, so I give up the cause as to those mentioned qualities. Though I profess it sounds oddly, to say that sugar is not sweet.

PHILONOUS: But, for your farther satisfaction, take this along with you: that which at other times seems sweet, shall, to a distempered palate, appear bitter. And, nothing can be plainer than that divers persons perceive different tastes in the same food; since that which one man delights in, another abhors. And how could this be, if the taste was something really inherent in the food?

HYLAS: I acknowledge I know not how.

PHILONOUS: In the next place, *odours* are to be considered. And, with regard to these, I would fain know whether what hath been said of tastes does not exactly agree to them? Are they not so many pleasing or displeasing sensations?

HYLAS: They are.

PHILONOUS: Can you then conceive it possible that they should exist in an unperceiving thing?

HYLAS: I cannot.

PHILONOUS: Or, can you imagine that filth and ordure affect those brute animals that feed on them out of choice, with the same smells which we perceive in them?

HYLAS: By no means.

PHILONOUS: May we not therefore conclude of smells, as of the other forementioned qualities, that they cannot exist in any but a perceiving substance or mind?

HYLAS: I think so.

PHILONOUS: Then as to *sounds,* what must we think of them: are they accidents really inherent in external bodies, or not?

HYLAS: That they inhere not in the sonorous bodies is plain from hence: because a bell struck in the exhausted receiver of an air- pump sends forth no sound. The air, therefore, must be thought the subject of sound.

PHILONOUS: What reason is there for that, Hylas?

HYLAS: Because, when any motion is raised in the air, we perceive a sound greater or lesser, according to the air's motion; but without some motion in the air, we never hear any sound at all.

PHILONOUS: And granting that we never hear a sound but when some motion is produced in the air, yet I do not see how you can infer from thence, that the sound itself is in the air.

HYLAS: It is this very motion in the external air that produces in the mind the sensation of *sound.* For, striking on the drum of the ear, it causes a vibration, which by the auditory nerves being communicated to the brain, the soul is thereupon affected with the sensation called *sound.*

PHILONOUS: What! Is sound then a sensation?

HYLAS: I tell you, as perceived by us, it is a particular sensation in the mind.

PHILONOUS: And can any sensation exist without the mind?

HYLAS: No, certainly.

PHILONOUS: How then can sound, being a sensation, exist in the air, if by the *air* you mean a senseless substance existing without the mind?

HYLAS: You must distinguish, Philonous, between sound as it is perceived by us, and as it is in itself; or (which is the same thing) between the sound we immediately perceive, and that which exists without us. The former, indeed, is a particular kind of sensation, but the latter is merely a vibrative or undulatory motion in the air.

PHILONOUS: I thought I had already obviated that distinction, by the answer I gave when you were applying it in a like case before. But, to say no more of that, are you sure then that sound is really nothing but motion?

HYLAS: I am.

PHILONOUS: Whatever therefore agrees to real sound, may with truth be attributed to motion?

HYLAS: It may.

PHILONOUS: It is then good sense to speak of *motion* as of a thing that is *loud, sweet, acute,* or *grave.*

HYLAS: I see you are resolved not to understand me. Is it not evident those accidents or modes belong only to sensible sound, or *sound* in the common acceptation of the word, but not to *sound* in the real and philosophic sense; which, as I just now told you, is nothing but a certain motion of the air?

PHILONOUS: It seems then there are two sorts of sound—the one vulgar, or that which is heard, the other philosophical and real?

HYLAS: Even so.

PHILONOUS: And the latter consists in motion?

HYLAS: I told you so before.

PHILONOUS: Tell me, Hylas, to which of the senses, think you, the idea of motion belongs? To the hearing?

HYLAS: No, certainly; but to the sight and touch.

PHILONOUS: It should follow then, that, according to you, real sounds may possibly be *seen* or *felt,* but never *heard.*

HYLAS: Look you, Philonous, you may, if you please, make a jest of my opinion, but that will not alter the truth of things. I own, indeed, the inferences you draw me into sound something oddly, but common language, you know, is framed by, and for the use of the vulgar: we must not therefore wonder if expressions adapted to exact philosophic notions seem uncouth and out of the way.

PHILONOUS: Is it come to that? I assure you, I imagine myself to have gained no small point, since you make so light of departing from common phrases and opinions; it being a main part of our inquiry, to examine whose notions are widest of the common road, and most repugnant to the general sense of the world. But, can you think it no more than a philosophical paradox, to say that *real sounds are never heard,* and that the idea of them is obtained by some other sense? And is there nothing in this contrary to nature and the truth of things?

HYLAS: To deal ingenuously, I do not like it. And, after the concessions already made, I had as well grant that sounds too have no real being without the mind.

PHILONOUS: And I hope you will make no difficulty to acknowledge the same of colours.

HYLAS: Pardon me: the case of colours is very different. Can anything be plainer than that we see them on the objects?

PHILONOUS: The objects you speak of are I suppose, corporeal substances existing without the mind?

HYLAS: They are.

PHILONOUS: And have true and real colours inhering in them?

HYLAS: Each visible object hath that colour which we see in it.

PHILONOUS: How! Is there anything visible but what we perceive by sight?

HYLAS: There is not.

PHILONOUS: And, do we perceive anything by sense which we do not perceive immediately?

HYLAS: How often must I be obliged to repeat the same thing? I tell you, we do not.

PHILONOUS: Have patience, good Hylas; and tell me once more, whether there is anything immediately perceived by the senses, except sensible qualities. I know you asserted there was not; but I would now be informed, whether you still persist in the same opinion.

HYLAS: I do.

PHILONOUS: Pray, is your corporeal substance either a sensible quality, or made up of sensible qualities?

HYLAS: What a question that is! Who ever thought it was?

PHILONOUS: My reason for asking was, because in saying, *each visible object hath that colour which we see in it,* you make visible objects to be corporeal substances; which implies either that corporeal substances are sensible qualities, or else that there is something besides sensible qualities perceived by sight: but, as this point was formerly agreed between us, and is still maintained by you, it is a clear consequence, that your corporeal substance is nothing distinct from sensible qualities.

HYLAS: You may draw as many absurd consequences as you please, and endeavour to perplex the plainest things; but you shall never persuade me out of my senses. I clearly understand my own meaning.

PHILONOUS: I wish you would make me understand it too. But, since you are unwilling to have your notion of corporeal substance examined, I shall urge that point no farther. Only be pleased to let me know, whether the same colours which we see exist in external bodies, or some other.

HYLAS: The very same.

PHILONOUS: What! Are then the beautiful red and purple we see on yonder clouds really in them? Or do you imagine, they have in themselves any other form than that of a dark mist or vapour?

HYLAS: I must own, Philonous, those colours are not really in the clouds as they seem to be at this distance. They are only apparent colours.

PHILONOUS: *Apparent* call you them? How shall we distinguish these apparent colours from real?

HYLAS: Very easily. Those are to be thought apparent which, appearing only at a distance, vanish upon a nearer approach.

PHILONOUS: And those, I suppose, are to be thought real which are discovered by the most near and exact survey.

HYLAS: Right.

PHILONOUS: Is the nearest and exactest survey made by the help of a microscope, or by the naked eye?

HYLAS: By a microscope, doubtless.

PHILONOUS: But a microscope often discovers colours in an object different from those perceived by the unassisted sight. And, in case we had microscopes magnifying to any assigned degree, it is certain that no object whatsoever, viewed through them, would appear in the same colour which it exhibits to the naked eye.

HYLAS: And what will you conclude from all this? You cannot argue that there are really and naturally no colours on objects: because by artificial managements they may be altered, or made to vanish.

PHILONOUS: I think it may evidently be concluded from your own concessions, that all the colours we see with our naked eyes are only apparent as those on the clouds, since they vanish upon a more close and accurate inspection which is afforded us by a microscope. Then, as to what you say by way of prevention: I ask you whether the real and natural state of an object is better discovered by a very sharp and piercing sight, or by one which is less sharp?

HYLAS: By the former without doubt.

PHILONOUS: Is it not plain from *Dioptrics* that microscopes make the sight more penetrating, and represent objects as they would appear to the eye in case it were naturally endowed with a most exquisite sharpness?

HYLAS: It is.

PHILONOUS: Consequently the microscopical representation is to be thought that which best sets forth the real nature of the thing, or what it is in itself. The colours, therefore, by it perceived are more genuine and real than those perceived otherwise.

HYLAS: I confess there is something in what you say.

PHILONOUS: Besides, it is not only possible but manifest, that there actually are animals whose eyes are by nature framed to perceive those things which by reason of their minuteness escape our sight. What think you of those inconceivably small animals perceived by glasses? Must we suppose they are all stark blind? Or, in case they see, can it be imagined their sight hath not the same use in preserving their bodies from injuries, which appears in that of all other animals? And if it hath, is it not evident they must see particles less than their own bodies; which will present them with a far different view in each object from that which strikes our senses? Even our own eyes do not always represent objects to us after the same manner. In the jaundice every one knows that all things seem yellow. Is it not therefore highly probable those animals in whose eyes we discern a very different texture from that of ours, and whose bodies abound with different humors, do not see the same colours in every object that we do? From all which, should it not seem to follow that all colours are equally apparent, and that none of those which we perceive are really inherent in any outward object?

HYLAS: It should.

PHILONOUS: The point will be past all doubt, if you consider that, in case colours were real properties or affections inherent in external bodies, they could admit of no alteration without some change wrought in the very bodies themselves: but, is it not evident from what hath been said that, upon the use of microscopes, upon a change happening in the humors of the eye, or a variation of distance, without any manner of real alteration in the thing itself, the colours of any object are either changed, or totally disappear? Nay, all other circumstances remaining the same, change but the situation of some objects, and they shall present different colours to the eye. The same thing happens upon viewing an object in various degrees of light. And what is more known than that the same bodies appear differently colored by candle-light from what they do in the open day? Add to these the experiment of a prism which, separating the heterogeneous rays of light, alters the colour of any object, and will cause the whitest to appear of a deep blue or red to the naked eye. And now tell me whether you are still of opinion that every body hath its true real colour inhering in it; and, if you think it hath, I would fain know farther from you, what certain distance and position of the object, what peculiar texture and formation of the eye, what degree or kind of light is necessary for ascertaining that true colour, and distinguishing it from apparent ones.

HYLAS: I own myself entirely satisfied, that they are all equally apparent, and that there is no such thing as colour really inhering in external bodies, but that it is altogether in the light. And what confirms me in this opinion is, that in proportion to the light colours are still more or less vivid; and if there be no light, then are there no colours perceived. Besides, allowing there are colours on external objects, yet, how is it possible for us to perceive them? For no external body affects the mind, unless it acts first on our organs of sense. But the only action of bodies is motion; and motion cannot be communicated otherwise than by impulse. A distant object therefore cannot act on the eye, nor consequently make itself or its properties perceivable to the soul. Whence it plainly follows that it is immediately some contiguous substance, which, operating on the eye, occasions a perception of colours: and such is light.

PHILONOUS: How! Is light then a substance?

HYLAS: I tell you, Philonous, external light is nothing but a thin fluid substance, whose minute particles being agitated with a brisk motion, and in various manners reflected from the different surfaces of outward objects to the eyes, communicate different motions to the optic nerves; which, being propagated to the brain, cause therein various impressions; and these are attended with the sensations of red, blue, yellow, &c.

PHILONOUS: It seems then the light does no more than shake the optic nerves.

HYLAS: Nothing else.

PHILONOUS: And consequent to each particular motion of the nerves, the mind is affected with a sensation, which is some particular colour.

HYLAS: Right.

PHILONOUS: And these sensations have no existence without the mind.

HYLAS: They have not.

PHILONOUS: How then do you affirm that colours are in the light; since by light you understand a corporeal substance external to the mind?

HYLAS: Light and colours, as immediately perceived by us, I grant cannot exist without the mind. But in themselves they are only the motions and configurations of certain insensible particles of matter.

PHILONOUS: Colours then, in the vulgar sense, or taken for the immediate objects of sight, cannot agree to any but a perceiving substance.

HYLAS: That is what I say.

PHILONOUS: Well then, since you give up the point as to those sensible qualities which are alone thought colours by all mankind beside, you may hold what you please with regard to those invisible ones of the philosophers. It is not my business to dispute about them; only I would advise you to bethink yourself, whether, considering the inquiry we are upon, it be prudent for you to affirm—*the red and blue which we see are not real colours, but certain unknown motions and figures which no man ever did or can see are truly so.* Are not these shocking notions, and are not they subject to as many ridiculous inferences, as those you were obliged to renounce before in the case of sounds?

HYLAS: I frankly own, Philonous, that it is in vain to stand out any longer. Colours, sounds, tastes, in a word all those termed *secondary qualities,* have certainly no existence without the mind. But by this acknowledgment I must not be supposed to derogate anything from the reality of matter, or external objects; seeing it is no more than several philosophers maintain, who nevertheless are the farthest imaginable from denying matter. For the clearer understanding of this, you must know sensible qualities are by philosophers divided into *primary* and *secondary.* The former are extension, figure, solidity, gravity, motion, and rest; and these they hold exist really in bodies. The latter are those above enumerated; or, briefly, all sensible qualities beside the primary; which they assert are only so many sensations or ideas existing nowhere but in the mind. But all this, I doubt not, you are apprised of. For my part, I have been a long time sensible there was such an opinion current among philosophers, but was never thoroughly convinced of its truth until now.

PHILONOUS: You are still then of opinion that extension and figures are inherent in external unthinking substances?

HYLAS: I am.

PHILONOUS: But what if the same arguments which are brought against secondary qualities will hold good against these also?

HYLAS: Why then I shall be obliged to think, they too exist only in the mind.

PHILONOUS: Is it your opinion the very figure and extension which you perceive by sense exist in the outward object or material substance?

HYLAS: It is.

PHILONOUS: Have all other animals as good grounds to think the same of the figure and extension which they see and feel?

HYLAS: Without doubt, if they have any thought at all.

PHILONOUS: Answer me, Hylas. Think you the senses were bestowed upon all animals for their preservation and well-being in life? Or were they given to men alone for this end?

HYLAS: I make no question but they have the same use in all other animals.

PHILONOUS: If so, is it not necessary they should be enabled by them to perceive their own limbs, and those bodies which are capable of harming them?

HYLAS: Certainly.

PHILONOUS: A mite therefore must be supposed to see his own foot, and things equal or even less than it, as bodies of some considerable dimension, though at the same time they appear to you scarce discernible, or at best as so many visible points?

HYLAS: I cannot deny it.

PHILONOUS: And to creatures less than the mite they will seem yet larger?

HYLAS: They will.

PHILONOUS: Insomuch that what you can hardly discern will to another extremely minute animal appear as some huge mountain?

HYLAS: All this I grant.

PHILONOUS: Can one and the same thing be at the same time in itself of different dimensions?

HYLAS: That were absurd to imagine.

PHILONOUS: But, from what you have laid down it follows that both the extension by you perceived, and that perceived by the mite itself, as likewise all those perceived by lesser animals, are each of them the true extension of the mite's foot; that is to say, by your own principles you are led into an absurdity.

HYLAS: There seems to be some difficulty in the point.

PHILONOUS: Again, have you not acknowledged that no real inherent property of any object can be changed without some change in the thing itself?

HYLAS: I have.

PHILONOUS: But, as we approach to or recede from an object, the visible extension varies, being at one distance ten or a hundred times greater than another. Does it not therefore follow from hence likewise that it is not really inherent in the object?

HYLAS: I own I am at a loss what to think.

PHILONOUS: Your judgment will soon be determined, if you will venture to think as freely concerning this quality as you have done concerning the rest. Was it not admitted as a good argument, that neither heat nor cold was in the water, because it seemed warm to one hand and cold to the other?

HYLAS: It was.

PHILONOUS: Is it not the very same reasoning to conclude, there is no extension or figure in an object, because to one eye it shall seem little, smooth, and round, when at the same time it appears to the other, great, uneven, and regular?

HYLAS: The very same. But does this latter fact ever happen?

PHILONOUS: You may at any time make the experiment, by looking with one eye bare, and with the other through a microscope.

HYLAS: I know not how to maintain it; and yet I am loath to give up *extension,* I see so many odd consequences following upon such a concession.

PHILONOUS: Odd, say you? After the concessions already made, I hope you will stick at nothing for its oddness. But, on the other hand, should it not seem very odd, if the general reasoning which includes all other sensible qualities did not also include extension? If it be allowed that no idea, nor anything like an idea, can exist in an unperceiving substance, then surely it follows that no figure, or mode of extension, which we can either perceive, or imagine, or have any idea of, can be really inherent in matter; not to mention the peculiar difficulty there must be in conceiving a material substance, prior to and distinct from extension to be the *substratum* of extension. Be the sensible quality what it will—figure, or sound, or colour, it seems alike impossible it should subsist in that which does not perceive it.

HYLAS: I give up the point for the present, reserving still a right to retract my opinion, in case I shall hereafter discover any false step in my progress to it.

PHILONOUS: That is a right you cannot be denied. Figures and extension being dispatched, we proceed next to *motion.* Can a real motion in any external body be at the same time very swift and very slow?

HYLAS: It cannot.

PHILONOUS: Is not the motion of a body swift in a reciprocal proportion to the time it takes up in describing any given space? Thus a body that describes a mile in an hour moves three times faster than it would in case it described only a mile in three hours.

HYLAS: I agree with you.

PHILONOUS: And is not time measured by the succession of ideas in our minds?

HYLAS: It is.

PHILONOUS: And is it not possible ideas should succeed one another twice as fast in your mind as they do in mine, or in that of some spirit of another kind?

HYLAS: I own it.

PHILONOUS: Consequently the same body may to another seem to perform its motion over any space in half the time that it does to you. And the same reasoning will hold as to any other proportion: that is to say, according to your principles (since the motions perceived are both really in the object) it is possible one and the same body shall be really moved the same way at once, both very swift and very slow. How is this consistent either with common sense, or with what you just now granted?

HYLAS: I have nothing to say to it.

PHILONOUS: Then as for *solidity;* either you do not mean any sensible quality by that word, and so it is beside our inquiry: or if you do, it must be either hardness or resistance. But both the one and the other are plainly relative to our senses: it being evident that what seems hard to one animal may appear soft to another, who hath greater force and firmness of limbs. Nor is it less plain that the resistance I feel is not in the body.

HYLAS: I own the very sensation of resistance, which is all you immediately perceive, is not in the *body;* but the cause of that sensation is.

PHILONOUS: But the causes of our sensations are not things immediately perceived, and therefore are not sensible. This point I thought had been already determined.

HYLAS: I own it was; but you will pardon me if I seem a little embarrassed: I know not how to quit my old notions.

PHILONOUS: To help you out, do but consider that if extension be once acknowledged to have no existence without the mind, the same must necessarily be granted of motion, solidity, and gravity; since they all evidently suppose extension. It is therefore superfluous to inquire particularly concerning each of them. In denying extension, you have denied them all to have any real existence.

HYLAS: I wonder, Philonous, if what you say be true, why those philosophers who deny the secondary qualities any real existence should yet attribute it to the primary. If there is no difference between them, how can this be accounted for?

PHILONOUS: It is not my business to account for every opinion of the philosophers. But, among other reasons which may be assigned for this, it seems probable that pleasure and pain being rather annexed to the former than the latter may be one. Heat and cold, tastes and smells, have something more vividly pleasing or disagreeable than the ideas of extension, figure, and motion affect us with. And, it being too visibly absurd to hold that pain or pleasure can be in an unperceiving substance, men are more easily weaned from believing the external existence of the secondary than the primary qualities. You will be satisfied there is something in this, if you recollect the difference you made between an intense and more moderate degree of heat; allowing the one a real existence, while you denied it to the other. But, after all, there is no rational ground for that distinction; for, surely an indifferent sensation is as truly a *sensation* as one more pleasing or painful; and consequently should not any more than they be supposed to exist in an unthinking subject.

HYLAS: It is just come into my head, Philonous, that I have somewhere heard of a distinction between absolute and sensible extension. Now, though it be acknowledged that *great* and *small,* consisting merely in the relation which other extended beings have to the parts of our own bodies, do not really inhere in the substances themselves; yet nothing obliges us to hold the same with regard to *absolute extension,* which is something abstracted from *great* and *small,* from this or that particular magnitude or figure. So likewise as to motion; *swift* and *slow* are altogether relative to the succession of ideas in our own minds. But, it does not follow, because those modifications of motion exist not without the mind, that therefore absolute motion abstracted from them does not.

PHILONOUS: Pray what is it that distinguishes one motion, or one part of extension, from another? Is it not something sensible, as some degree of swiftness or slowness, some certain magnitude or figure peculiar to each?

HYLAS: I think so.

PHILONOUS: These qualities, therefore, stripped of all sensible properties, are without all specific and numerical differences, as the schools call them.

HYLAS: They are.

PHILONOUS: That is to say, they are extension in general, and motion in general.

HYLAS: Let it be so.

PHILONOUS: But it is a universally received maxim that *Everything which exists is particular.* How then can motion in general, or extension in general, exist in any corporeal substance?

HYLAS: I will take time to solve your difficulty.

PHILONOUS: But I think the point may be speedily decided. Without doubt you can tell whether you are able to frame this or that idea. Now I am content to put our dispute on this issue. If you can frame in your thoughts a distinct abstract idea of motion or extension, divested of all those sensible modes, as swift and slow, great and small, round and square, and the like, which are acknowledged to exist only in the mind, I will then yield the point you contend for. But if you cannot, it will be unreasonable on your side to insist any longer upon what you have no notion of.

HYLAS: To confess ingenuously, I cannot.

PHILONOUS: Can you even separate the ideas of extension and motion from the ideas of all those qualities which they who make the distinction term *secondary?*

HYLAS: What! Is it not an easy matter to consider extension and motion by themselves, abstracted from all other sensible qualities? Pray how do the mathematicians treat of them?

PHILONOUS: I acknowledge, Hylas, it is not difficult to form general propositions and reasonings about those qualities, without mentioning any other; and, in this sense, to consider or treat of them abstractedly. But, how does it follow that, because I can pronounce the word *motion* by itself, I can form the idea of it in my mind exclusive of body? Or, because theorems may be made of extension and figures, without any mention of *great* or *small,* or any other sensible mode or quality, that therefore it is possible such an abstract idea of extension, without any particular size or figure, or sensible quality, should be distinctly formed, and apprehended by the mind? Mathematicians treat of quantity, without regarding what other sensible qualities it is attended with, as being altogether indifferent to their demonstrations. But, when laying aside the words, they contemplate the bare ideas, I believe you will find, they are not the pure abstracted ideas of extension.

HYLAS: But what say you to *pure intellect?* May not abstracted ideas be framed by that faculty?

PHILONOUS: Since I cannot frame abstract ideas at all, it is plain I cannot frame them by the help of *pure intellect;* whatsoever faculty you understand by those words. Besides, not to inquire into the nature of pure intellect and its spiritual objects, as *virtue, reason, God,* or the like, thus much seems manifest—that sensible things are only to be perceived by sense, or represented by the imagination. Figures, therefore, and extension, being originally perceived by sense, do not belong to pure intellect: but, for your farther satisfaction, try if you can frame the idea of any figure, abstracted from all particularities of size, or even from other sensible qualities.

HYLAS: Let me think a little—I do not find that I can.

PHILONOUS: And can you think it possible that should really exist in nature which implies a repugnancy in its conception?

HYLAS: By no means.

PHILONOUS: Since therefore it is impossible even for the mind to disunite the ideas of extension and motion from all other sensible qualities, does it not follow, that where the one exist there necessarily the other exist likewise?

HYLAS: It should seem so.

PHILONOUS: Consequently, the very same arguments which you admitted as conclusive against the secondary qualities are, without any farther application of force, against the primary too. Besides, if you will trust your senses, is it not plain all sensible qualities coexist, or to them appear as being in the same place? Do they ever represent a motion, or figure, as being divested of all other visible and tangible qualities?

HYLAS: You need say no more on this head. I am free to own, if there be no secret error or oversight in our proceedings hitherto, that all sensible qualities are alike to be denied existence without the mind. But, my fear is that I have been too liberal in my former concessions, or overlooked some fallacy or other. In short, I did not take time to think.

PHILONOUS: For that matter, Hylas, you may take what time you please in reviewing the progress of our inquiry. You are at liberty to recover any slips you might have made, or offer whatever you have omitted which makes for your first opinion.

HYLAS: One great oversight I take to be this—that I did not sufficiently distinguish the *object* from the *sensation.* Now though this latter may not exist without the mind, yet it will not thence follow that the former cannot.

PHILONOUS: What object do you mean? The object of the senses?

HYLAS: The same.

PHILONOUS: It is then immediately perceived?

HYLAS: Right.

PHILONOUS: Make me to understand the difference between what is immediately perceived and a sensation.

HYLAS: The sensation I take to be an act of the mind perceiving; besides which, there is something perceived, and this I call the *object.* For example, there is red and yellow on that tulip. But then the act of perceiving those colours is in me only, and not in the tulip.

PHILONOUS: What tulip do you speak of? Is it that which you see?

HYLAS: The same.

PHILONOUS: And what do you see beside colour, figure, and extension?

HYLAS: Nothing.

PHILONOUS: What you would say then is that the red and yellow are coexistent with the extension; is it not?

HYLAS: That is not all; I would say they have a real existence without the mind, in some unthinking substance.

PHILONOUS: That the colours are really in the tulip which I see is manifest. Neither can it be denied that this tulip may exist independent of your mind or mine; but, that any immediate object of the senses—that is, any idea, or combination of ideas—should exist in an unthinking substance, or exterior to all minds, is in itself an evident contradiction. Nor can I imagine how this follows from what you said just now, to wit, that the red and yellow were on the tulip *you saw,* since you do not pretend to see that unthinking substance.

HYLAS: You have an artful way, Philonous, of diverting our inquiry from the subject.

PHILONOUS: I see you have no mind to be pressed that way. To return then to your distinction between *sensation* and *object;* if I take you right, you distinguish in every perception two things, the one an action of the mind, the other not.

HYLAS: True.

PHILONOUS: And this action cannot exist in, or belong to, any unthinking thing; but, whatever beside is implied in a perception may?

HYLAS: That is my meaning.

PHILONOUS: So that if there was a perception without any act of the mind, it were possible such a perception should exist in an unthinking substance?

HYLAS: I grant it. But it is impossible there should be such a perception.

PHILONOUS: When is the mind said to be active?

HYLAS: When it produces, puts an end to, or changes, anything.

PHILONOUS: Can the mind produce, discontinue, or change anything, but by an act of the will?

HYLAS: It cannot.

PHILONOUS: The mind therefore is to be accounted active in its perceptions so far forth as volition is included in them?

HYLAS: It is.

PHILONOUS: In plucking this flower I am *active;* because I do it by the motion of my hand, which was consequent upon my *volition;* so likewise in applying it to my nose. But is either of these smelling?

HYLAS: No.

PHILONOUS: I act too in drawing the air through my nose; because my breathing so rather than otherwise is the effect of my volition. But neither can this be called *smelling:* for, if it were, I should smell every time I breathed in that manner?

HYLAS: True.

PHILONOUS: Smelling then is somewhat consequent to all this?

HYLAS: It is.

PHILONOUS: But I do not find my will concerned any farther. Whatever more there is—as that I perceive such a particular smell, or any smell at all—this is independent of my will, and therein I am altogether passive. Do you find it otherwise with you, Hylas?

HYLAS: No, the very same.

PHILONOUS: Then, as to seeing, is it not in your power to open your eyes, or keep them shut; to turn them this or that way?

HYLAS: Without doubt.

PHILONOUS: But does it in like manner depend on your will that in looking on this flower you perceive *white* rather any other colour? Or, directing your open eyes towards yonder part of the heaven, can you avoid seeing the sun? Or is light or darkness the effect of your volition?

HYLAS: No, certainly.

PHILONOUS: You are then in these respects altogether passive?

HYLAS: I am.

PHILONOUS: Tell me now, whether *seeing* consists in perceiving light and colours, or in opening and turning the eyes?

HYLAS: Without doubt, in the former.

PHILONOUS: Since therefore you are in the very perception of light and colours altogether passive, what is become of that action you were speaking of as an ingredient in every sensation? And, does it not follow from your own concessions, that the perception of light and colours, including no action in it, may exist in an unperceiving substance? And is not this a plain contradiction?

HYLAS: I know not what to think of it.

PHILONOUS: Besides, since you distinguish the *active* and *passive* in every perception, you must do it in that of pain. But how is it possible that pain, be it as little active as you please, should exist in an unperceiving substance? In short, do but consider the point, and then confess ingenuously, whether light and colours, tastes, sounds, &c. are not all equally passions or sensations in the soul. You may indeed call them *external objects,* and give them in words what subsistence you please. But, examine your own thoughts, and then tell me whether it be not as I say?

HYLAS: I acknowledge, Philonous, that, upon a fair observation of what passes in my mind I can discover nothing else but that I am a thinking being, affected with variety of sensations; neither is it possible to conceive how a sensation should exist in an unperceiving substance.—But then, on the other hand, when I look on sensible things in a different view, considering them as so many modes and qualities, I find it necessary to suppose a *material* substratum, without which they cannot be conceived to exist.

PHILONOUS: *Material substratum* call you it? Pray, by which of your senses came you acquainted with that being?

HYLAS: It is not itself sensible; its modes and qualities only being perceived by the senses.

PHILONOUS: I presume then it was by reflexion and reason you obtained the idea of it?

HYLAS: I do not pretend to any proper positive idea of it. However, I conclude it exists, because qualities cannot be conceived to exist without a support.

PHILONOUS: It seems then you have only a relative notion of it, or that you conceive it not otherwise than by conceiving the relation it bears to sensible qualities?

HYLAS: Right.

PHILONOUS: Be pleased therefore to let me know wherein that relation consists.

HYLAS: Is it not sufficiently expressed in the term *substratum,* or *substance?*

PHILONOUS: If so, the word *substratum* should import that it is spread under the sensible qualities or accidents?

HYLAS: True.

PHILONOUS: And consequently under extension?

HYLAS: I own it.

PHILONOUS: It is therefore somewhat in its own nature entirely distinct from extension?

HYLAS: I tell you, extension is only a mode, and matter is something that supports modes. And is it not evident the thing supported is different from the thing supporting?

PHILONOUS: So that something distinct from, and exclusive of, extension is supposed to be the substratum of extension?

HYLAS: Just so.

PHILONOUS: Answer me, Hylas. Can a thing be spread without extension? or is not the idea of extension necessarily included in *spreading?*

HYLAS: It is.

PHILONOUS: Whatsoever therefore you suppose spread under anything must have in itself an extension distinct from the extension of that thing under which it is spread?

HYLAS: It must.

PHILONOUS: Consequently, every corporeal substance, being the *substratum* of extension, must have in itself another extension, by which it is qualified to be a *substratum:* and so on to infinity. And I ask whether this be not absurd in itself, and repugnant to what you granted just now, to wit, that the *substratum* was something distinct from and exclusive of extension?

HYLAS: Aye but, Philonous, you take me wrong. I do not mean that matter is *spread* in a gross literal sense under extension. The word *substratum* is used only to express in general the same thing with *substance.*

PHILONOUS: Well then, let us examine the relation implied in the term *substance.* Is it not that it stands under accidents?

HYLAS: The very same.

PHILONOUS: But, that one thing may stand under or support another, must it not be extended?

HYLAS: It must.

PHILONOUS: Is not therefore this supposition liable to the same absurdity with the former?

HYLAS: You still take things in a strict literal sense. That is not fair, Philonous.

PHILONOUS: I am not for imposing any sense on your words: you are at liberty to explain them as you please. Only, I beseech you, make me understand something by them. You tell me matter supports or stands under accidents. How! is it as your legs support your body?

HYLAS: No; that is the literal sense.

PHILONOUS: Pray let me know any sense, literal or not literal, that you understand it in.—How long must I wait for an answer, Hylas?

HYLAS: I declare I know not what to say. I once thought I understood well enough what was meant by matter's supporting accidents. But now, the more I think on it the less can I comprehend it: in short I find that I know nothing of it.

PHILONOUS: It seems then you have no idea at all, neither relative nor positive, of matter; you know neither what it is in itself, nor what relation it bears to accidents?

HYLAS: I acknowledge it.

PHILONOUS: And yet you asserted that you could not conceive how qualities or accidents should really exist, without conceiving at the same time a material support of them?

HYLAS: I did.

PHILONOUS: That is to say, when you conceive the real existence of qualities, you do withal conceive something which you cannot conceive?

HYLAS: It was wrong, I own. But still I fear there is some fallacy or other. Pray what think you of this? It is just come into my head that the ground of all our mistake lies in your treating of each quality by itself. Now, I grant that each quality cannot singly subsist without the mind. Colour cannot without extension, neither can figure without some other sensible quality. But, as the several qualities united or blended together form entire sensible things, nothing hinders why such things may not be supposed to exist without the mind.

PHILONOUS: Either, Hylas, you are jesting, or have a very bad memory. Though indeed we went through all the qualities by name one after another, yet my arguments or rather your concessions, nowhere tended to prove that the secondary qualities did not subsist each alone by itself; but, that they were not *at all* without the mind. Indeed, in treating of figure and motion we concluded they could not exist without the mind, because it was impossible even in thought to separate them from all secondary qualities, so as to conceive them existing by themselves. But then this was not the only argument made use of upon that occasion. But (to pass by all that hath been hitherto said, and reckon it for nothing, if you will have it so) I am content to put the whole upon this issue. If you can conceive it possible for any mixture or combination of qualities, or any sensible object whatever, to exist without the mind, then I will grant it actually to be so.

HYLAS: If it comes to that the point will soon be decided. What more easy than to conceive a tree or house existing by itself, independent of, and unperceived by, any mind whatsoever? I do at this present time conceive them existing after that manner.

PHILONOUS: How say you, Hylas, can you see a thing which is at the same time unseen?

HYLAS: No, that were a contradiction.

PHILONOUS: Is it not as great a contradiction to talk of *conceiving* a thing which is *unconceived?*

HYLAS: It is.

PHILONOUS: The tree or house therefore which you think of is conceived by you?

HYLAS: How should it be otherwise?

PHILONOUS: And what is conceived is surely in the mind?

HYLAS: Without question, that which is conceived is in the mind.

PHILONOUS: How then came you to say, you conceived a house or tree existing independent and out of all minds whatsoever?

HYLAS: That was I own an oversight; but stay, let me consider what led me into it.— It is a pleasant mistake enough. As I was thinking of a tree in a solitary place, where no one was present to see it, methought that was to conceive a tree as existing unperceived or unthought of; not considering that I myself conceived it all the while. But now I plainly see that all I can do is to frame ideas in my own mind. I may indeed conceive in my own thoughts the idea of a tree, or a house, or a mountain, but that is all. And this is far from proving that I can conceive them *existing out of the minds of all spirits.*

PHILONOUS: You acknowledge then that you cannot possibly conceive how any one corporeal sensible thing should exist otherwise than in the mind?

HYLAS: I do.

PHILONOUS: And yet you will earnestly contend for the truth of that which you cannot so much as conceive?

HYLAS I profess I know not what to think, but still there are some scruples remain with me. Is it not certain I *see* things at a distance? Do we not perceive the stars and moon, for example, to be a great way off? Is not this, say, manifest to the senses?

PHILONOUS: Do you not in a dream too perceive those or the like objects?

HYLAS: I do.

PHILONOUS: And have they not then the same appearance of being distant?

HYLAS: They have.

PHILONOUS: But you do not thence conclude the apparitions in a dream to be without the mind?

HYLAS: By no means.

PHILONOUS: You ought not therefore to conclude that sensible objects are without the mind, from their appearance, or manner wherein they are perceived.

HYLAS: I acknowledge it. But does not my sense deceive me in those cases?

PHILONOUS: By no means. The idea or thing which you immediately perceive, neither sense nor reason informs you that it actually exists without the mind. By sense you only know that you are affected with such certain sensations of light and colours, etc. And these you will not say are without the mind.

HYLAS: True: but, beside all that, do you not think the sight suggests something of *outness* or *distance?*

PHILONOUS: Upon approaching a distant object, do the visible size and figure change perpetually, or do they appear the same at all distances?

HYLAS: They are in a continual change.

PHILONOUS: Sight therefore does not suggest, or any way inform you, that the visible object you immediately perceive exists at a distance, or will be perceived when you advance farther onward; there being a continued series of visible objects succeeding each other during the whole time of your approach.

HYLAS: It does not; but still I know, upon seeing an object, what object I shall perceive after having passed over a certain distance: no matter whether it be exactly the same or no: there is still something of distance suggested in the case.

PHILONOUS: Good Hylas, do but reflect a little on the point, and then tell me whether there be any more in it than this: from the ideas you actually perceive by sight, you have by experience learned to collect what other ideas you will (according to the standing order of nature) be affected with, after such a certain succession of time and motion.

HYLAS: Upon the whole, I take it to be nothing else.

PHILONOUS: Now, is it not plain that if we suppose a man born blind was on a sudden made to see, he could at first have no experience of what may be suggested by sight?

HYLAS: It is.

PHILONOUS: He would not then, according to you, have any notion of distance annexed to the things he saw; but would take them for a new set of sensations, existing only in his mind?

HYLAS: It is undeniable.

PHILONOUS: But, to make it still more plain: is not *distance* a line turned endwise to the eye?

HYLAS: It is.

PHILONOUS: And can a line so situated be perceived by sight?

HYLAS: It cannot.

PHILONOUS: Does it not therefore follow that distance is not properly and immediately perceived by sight?

HYLAS: It should seem so.

PHILONOUS: Again, is it your opinion that colours are at a distance?

HYLAS: It must be acknowledged they are only in the mind.

PHILONOUS: But do not colours appear to the eye as coexisting in the same place with extension and figures?

HYLAS: They do.

PHILONOUS: How can you then conclude from sight that figures exist without, when you acknowledge colours do not; the sensible appearance being the very same with regard to both?

HYLAS: I know not what to answer.

PHILONOUS: But, allowing that distance was truly and immediately perceived by the mind, yet it would not thence follow it existed out of the mind. For, whatever is immediately perceived is an idea: and can any *idea* exist out of the mind?

HYLAS: To suppose that were absurd: but, inform me, Philonous, can we perceive or know nothing beside our ideas?

PHILONOUS: As for the rational deducing of causes from effects, that is beside our inquiry. And, by the senses you can best tell whether you perceive anything which is not immediately perceived. And I ask you, whether the things immediately perceived are other than your own sensations or ideas? You have indeed more than once, in the course of this conversation, declared yourself on those points; but you seem, by this last question, to have departed from what you then thought.

HYLAS: To speak the truth, Philonous, I think there are two kinds of objects:—the one perceived immediately, which are likewise called *ideas;* the other are real things or external objects, perceived by the mediation of ideas, which are their images and representations. Now, I own ideas do not exist without the mind; but the latter sort of objects do. I am sorry I did not think of this distinction sooner; it would probably have cut short your discourse.

PHILONOUS: Are those external objects perceived by sense or by some other faculty?

HYLAS: They are perceived by sense.

PHILONOUS: How! Is there any thing perceived by sense which is not immediately perceived?

HYLAS: Yes, Philonous, in some sort there is. For example when I look on a picture or statue of Julius Caesar, I may be said after a manner to perceive him (though not immediately) by my senses.

PHILONOUS: It seems then you will have our ideas, which alone are immediately perceived, to be pictures of external things: and that these also are perceived by sense, inasmuch as they have a conformity or resemblance to our ideas?

HYLAS: That is my meaning.

PHILONOUS: And, in the same way that Julius Caesar, in himself invisible, is nevertheless perceived by sight; real things, in themselves imperceptible, are perceived by sense.

HYLAS: In the very same.

PHILONOUS: Tell me, Hylas, when you behold the picture of Julius Caesar, do you see with your eyes any more than some colours and figures, with a certain symmetry and composition of the whole?

HYLAS: Nothing else.

PHILONOUS: And would not a man who had never known anything of Julius Caesar see as much?

HYLAS: He would.

PHILONOUS: Consequently he hath his sight, and the use of it, in as perfect a degree as you?

HYLAS: I agree with you.

PHILONOUS: Whence comes it then that your thoughts are directed to the Roman emperor, and his are not? This cannot proceed from the sensations or ideas of sense by you then perceived; since you acknowledge you have no advantage over him in that respect. It should seem therefore to proceed from reason and memory: should it not?

HYLAS: It should.

PHILONOUS: Consequently, it will not follow from that instance that anything is perceived by sense which is not immediately perceived. Though I grant we may, in one acceptation, be said to perceive sensible things mediately by sense: that is, when, from a frequently perceived connexion, the immediate perception of ideas by one sense suggests to the mind others, perhaps belonging to another sense, which are wont to be connected with them. For instance, when I hear a coach drive along the streets, immediately I perceive only the sound; but, from the experience I have had that such a sound is connected with a coach, I am said to hear the coach. It is nevertheless evident that, in truth and strictness, nothing can be *heard* but *sound;* and the coach is not then properly perceived by sense, but suggested from experience. So likewise when we are said to see a red-hot bar of iron; the solidity and heat of the iron are not the objects of sight, but suggested to the imagination by the colour and figure which are properly perceived by that sense. In short, those things alone are actually and strictly perceived by any sense, which would have been perceived in case that same sense had then been first conferred on us. As for other things, it is plain they are only suggested to the mind by experience, grounded on former perceptions. But, to return to your comparison of Caesar's picture, it is plain, if you keep to that, you must hold the real things, or archetypes of our ideas, are not perceived by sense, but by some internal faculty of the soul, as reason or memory. I would therefore fain know what arguments you can draw from reason for the existence of what you call real *things* or *material objects*. Or, whether you remember to have seen them formerly as they are in themselves; or, if you have heard or read of any one that did.

HYLAS: I see, Philonous, you are disposed to raillery; but that will never convince me.

PHILONOUS: My aim is only to learn from you the way to come at the knowledge of *material beings*. Whatever we perceive is perceived immediately or mediately: by sense, or by reason and reflexion. But, as you have excluded sense, pray show me what reason you have to believe their existence; or what *medium* you can possibly make use of to prove it, either to mine or your own understanding.

HYLAS: To deal ingenuously, Philonous, now I consider the point, I do not find I can give you any good reason for it. But, thus much seems pretty plain, that it is at least possible such things may really exist. And, as long as there is no absurdity in supposing them, I am resolved to believe as I did, till you bring good reasons to the contrary.

PHILONOUS: What! Is it come to this, that you only believe the existence of material objects, and that your belief is founded barely on the possibility of its being true? Then you will have me bring reasons against it: though another would think it reasonable the proof should lie on him who holds the affirmative. And, after all, this very point which you are now resolved to maintain, without any reason, is in effect what you have more than once during this discourse seen good reason to give up. But, to pass over all this; if I understand you rightly, you say our ideas do not exist without the mind, but that they are copies, images, or representations, of certain originals that do?

HYLAS: You take me right.

PHILONOUS: They are then like external things?

HYLAS: They are.

PHILONOUS: Have those things a stable and permanent nature, independent of our senses; or are they in a perpetual change, upon our producing any motions in our bodies—suspending, exerting, or altering, our faculties or organs of sense?

HYLAS: Real things, it is plain, have a fixed and real nature, which remains the same notwithstanding any change in our senses, or in the posture and motion of our bodies; which indeed may affect the ideas in our minds, but it were absurd to think they had the same effect on things existing without the mind.

PHILONOUS: How then is it possible that things perpetually fleeting and variable as our ideas should be copies or images of anything fixed and constant? Or, in other words, since all sensible qualities, as size, figure, colour, &c., that is, our ideas, are continually changing, upon every alteration in the distance, medium, or instruments of sensation; how can any determinate material objects be properly represented or painted forth by several distinct things, each of which is so different from and unlike the rest? Or, if you say it resembles some one only of our ideas, how shall we be able to distinguish the true copy from all the false ones?

HYLAS: I profess, Philonous, I am at a loss. I know not what to say to this.

PHILONOUS: But neither is this all. Which are material objects in themselves—perceptible or imperceptible?

HYLAS: Properly and immediately nothing can be perceived but ideas. All material things, therefore, are in themselves insensible, and to be perceived only by our ideas.

PHILONOUS: Ideas then are sensible, and their archetypes or originals insensible?

HYLAS: Right.

PHILONOUS: But how can that which is sensible be like that which is insensible? Can a real thing, in itself *invisible*, be like a *colour;* or a real thing, which is not *audible*, be like a *sound?* In a word, can anything be like a sensation or idea, but another sensation or idea?

HYLAS: I must own, I think not.

PHILONOUS: Is it possible there should be any doubt on the point? Do you not perfectly know your own ideas?

HYLAS: I know them perfectly; since what I do not perceive or know can be no part of my idea.

PHILONOUS: Consider, therefore, and examine them, and then tell me if there be anything in them which can exist without the mind: or if you can conceive anything like them existing without the mind.

HYLAS: Upon inquiry, I find it is impossible for me to conceive or understand how anything but an idea can be like an idea. And it is most evident that *no idea can exist without the mind.*

PHILONOUS: You are therefore, by your principles, forced to deny the reality of sensible things; since you made it to consist in an absolute existence exterior to the mind. That is to say, you are a downright *sceptic.* So I have gained my point, which was to show your principles led to scepticism.

HYLAS: For the present I am, if not entirely convinced, at least silenced.

PHILONOUS: I would fain know what more you would require in order to a perfect conviction. Have you not had the liberty of explaining yourself all manner of ways? Were any little slips in discourse laid hold and insisted on? Or were you not allowed to retract or reinforce anything you had offered, as best served your purpose? Hath not everything you could say been heard and examined with all the fairness imaginable? In a word, have you not in every point been convinced out of your own mouth? And, if you can at present discover any flaw in any of your former concessions, or think of any remaining subterfuge, any new distinction, colour, or comment whatsoever, why do you not produce it?

HYLAS: A little patience, Philonous. I am at present so amazed to see myself ensnared, and as it were imprisoned in the labyrinths you have drawn me into, that on the sudden it cannot be expected I should find my way out. You must give me time to look about me and recollect myself.

PHILONOUS: Hark; is not this the college bell?

HYLAS: It rings for prayers.

PHILONOUS: We will go in then, if you please, and meet here again tomorrow morning. In the meantime, you may employ your thoughts on this morning's discourse, and try if you can find any fallacy in it, or invent any new means to extricate yourself.

HYLAS: Agreed.

THE SECOND DIALOGUE

HYLAS: I beg your pardon, Philonous, for not meeting you sooner. All this morning my head was so filled with our late conversation that I had not leisure to think of the time of the day, or indeed of anything else.

PHILONOUS: I am glad you were so intent upon it, in hopes if there were any mistakes in your concessions, or fallacies in my reasonings from them, you will now discover them to me.

HYLAS: I assure you I have done nothing ever since I saw you but search after mistakes and fallacies, and, with that view, have minutely examined the whole series of yesterday's discourse: but all in vain, for the notions it led me into, upon review, appear still more clear and evident; and, the more I consider them, the more irresistibly do they force my assent.

PHILONOUS: And is not this, think you, a sign that they are genuine, that they proceed from nature, and are conformable to right reason? Truth and beauty are in this alike, that the strictest survey sets them both off to advantage; while the false lustre of error and disguise cannot endure being reviewed, or too nearly inspected.

HYLAS: I own there is a great deal in what you say. Nor can any one be more entirely satisfied of the truth of those odd consequences, so long as I have in view the reasonings that lead to them. But, when these are out of my thoughts, there seems, on the other hand, something so satisfactory, so natural and intelligible, in the modern way of explaining things that, I profess, I know not how to reject it.

PHILONOUS: I know not what way you mean.

HYLAS: I mean the way of accounting for our sensations or ideas.

PHILONOUS: How is that?

HYLAS: It is supposed the soul makes her residence in some part of the brain, from which the nerves take their rise, and are thence extended to all parts of the body; and that outward objects, by the different impressions they make on the organs of sense, communicate certain vibrative motions to the nerves; and these being filled with spirits propagate them to the brain or seat of the soul, which, according to the various impressions or traces thereby made in the brain, is variously affected with ideas.

PHILONOUS: And call you this an explication of the manner whereby we are affected with ideas?

HYLAS: Why not, Philonous? Have you anything to object against it?

PHILONOUS: I would first know whether I rightly understand your hypothesis. You make certain traces in the brain to be the causes or occasions of our ideas. Pray tell me whether by the brain you mean any sensible thing.

HYLAS: What else think you I could mean?

PHILONOUS: Sensible things are all immediately perceivable; and those things which are immediately perceivable are ideas; and these exist only in the mind. Thus much you have, if I mistake not, long since agreed to.

HYLAS: I do not deny it.

PHILONOUS: The brain therefore you speak of, being a sensible thing, exists only in the mind. Now, I would fain know whether you think it reasonable to suppose that one idea or thing existing in the mind occasions all other ideas. And, if you think so, pray how do you account for the origin of that primary idea or brain itself?

HYLAS: I do not explain the origin of our ideas by that brain which is perceivable to sense—this being itself only a combination of sensible ideas—but by another which I imagine.

PHILONOUS: But are not things imagined as truly *in the mind as* things perceived?

HYLAS: I must confess they are.

PHILONOUS: It comes therefore, to the same thing; and you have been all this while accounting for ideas by certain motions or impressions of the brain; that is, by some alterations in an idea, whether sensible or imaginable it matters not.

HYLAS: I begin to suspect my hypothesis.

PHILONOUS: Besides spirits, all that we know or conceive are our own ideas. When, therefore, you say all ideas are occasioned by impressions in the brain, do you conceive this brain or no? If you do, then you talk of ideas imprinted in an idea causing that same idea, which is absurd. If you do not conceive it, you talk unintelligibly, instead of forming a reasonable hypothesis.

HYLAS: I now clearly see it was a mere dream. There is nothing in it.

PHILONOUS: You need not be much concerned at it; for after all, this way of explaining things, as you called it, could never have satisfied any reasonable man. What connexion is there between a motion in the nerves, and the sensations of sound or colour in the mind? Or how is it possible these should be the effect of that?

HYLAS: But I could never think it had so little in it as now it seems to have.

PHILONOUS: Well then, are you at length satisfied that no sensible things have a real existence; and that you are in truth an arrant *sceptic?*

HYLAS: It is too plain to be denied.

PHILONOUS: Look! Are not the fields covered with a delightful verdure? Is there not something in the woods and groves, in the rivers and clear springs, that soothes, that delights, that transports the soul? At the prospect of the wide and deep ocean, or some huge mountain whose top is lost in the clouds, or of an old gloomy forest, are not our minds filled with a pleasing horror? Even in rocks and deserts is there not an agreeable wildness? How sincere a pleasure is it to behold the natural beauties of the earth! To preserve and renew our relish for them, is not the veil of night alternately drawn over her face, and does she not change her dress with the seasons? How aptly are the elements disposed! What variety and use in the meanest productions of nature! What delicacy, what beauty, what contrivance, in animal and vegetable bodies! How exquisitely are all things suited, as well to their particular ends, as to constitute opposite parts of the whole! And, while they mutually aid and support, do they not also set off and illustrate each other? Raise now your thoughts from this ball of earth to all those glorious luminaries that adorn the high arch of heaven. The motion and situation of the planets, are they not admirable for use and order? Were those (miscalled *erratic*) globes once known to stray, in their repeated journeys through the pathless void? Do they not measure areas round the sun ever proportioned to the times? So fixed, so immutable are the laws by which the unseen author of nature actuates the universe. How vivid and radiant is the lustre of the fixed stars! How magnificent and rich that negligent profusion with which they appear to be scattered throughout the whole azure vault! Yet, if you take the telescope, it brings into your sight a new host of stars that escape the naked eye. Here they seem contiguous and minute, but to a nearer view immense orbs of light at various distances, far sunk in the abyss of space. Now you must call imagination to your aid. The feeble narrow sense cannot descry innumerable worlds revolving round the central fires and in those worlds the energy of an all- perfect mind displayed in endless forms. But, neither sense nor imagination are big enough to comprehend the boundless extent, with all its glittering furniture. Though the labouring mind exert and strain each power to its utmost reach, there still stands out ungrasped a surplusage immeasurable. Yet all the vast bodies that compose this mighty frame, how distant and remote soever, are by some secret mechanism, some divine art and force, linked in a mutual dependence and intercourse with each other; even with this earth, which was almost slipt from my thoughts and lost in the crowd of worlds. Is not the whole system immense, beautiful, glorious beyond expression and beyond thought! What treatment, then, do those philosophers deserve, who would deprive these noble and delightful scenes of all reality? How should those principles be entertained that lead us to think all the visible beauty of the creation a false imaginary glare? To be plain, can you expect this scepticism of yours will not be thought extravagantly absurd by all men of sense?

HYLAS: Other men may think as they please; but for your part you have nothing to reproach me with. My comfort is, you are as much a *sceptic* as I am.

PHILONOUS: There, Hylas, I must beg leave to differ from you.

HYLAS: What! Have you all along agreed to the premises, and do you now deny the conclusion, and leave me to maintain those paradoxes by myself which you led me into? This surely is not fair.

PHILONOUS: I deny that I agreed with you in those notions that led to scepticism. You indeed said the *reality* of sensible things consisted in an *absolute existence* out of the minds of spirits, or distinct from their being perceived. And pursuant to this notion of reality, you are obliged to deny sensible things any real existence: that is, according to your own definition, you profess yourself a *sceptic*. But I neither said nor thought the reality of sensible things was to be defined after that manner. To me it is evident for the reasons you allow of, that sensible things cannot exist otherwise than in a mind or spirit. Whence I conclude, not that they have no real existence, but that, seeing they depend not on my thought, and have an existence distinct from being perceived by me, *there must be some other mind wherein they exist.* As sure, therefore, as the sensible world really exists, so sure is there an infinite omnipresent spirit who contains and supports it.

HYLAS: What! This is no more than I and all Christians hold; nay, and all others too who believe there is a God, and that he knows and comprehends all things.

PHILONOUS: Aye, but here lies the difference. Men commonly believe that all things are known or perceived by God, because they believe the being of a God; whereas I, on the other side, immediately and necessarily conclude the being of a God, because all sensible things must be perceived by him.

HYLAS: But, so long as we all believe the same thing, what matter is it how we come by that belief?

PHILONOUS: But neither do we agree in the same opinion. For philosophers, though they acknowledge all corporeal beings to be perceived by God, yet they attribute to them an absolute subsistence distinct from their being perceived by any mind whatever; which I do not. Besides, is there no difference between saying, *There is a God, therefore he perceives all things;* and saying, *Sensible things do really exist; and, if they really exist, they are necessarily perceived by an infinite mind: therefore there is an infinite mind or God?* This furnishes you with a direct and immediate demonstration, from a most evident principle, of the *being of a God.* Divines and philosophers had proved beyond all controversy, from the beauty and usefulness of the several parts of the creation, that it was the workmanship of God. But that—setting aside all help of astronomy and natural philosophy, all contemplation of the contrivance, order, and adjustment of things—an infinite mind should be necessarily inferred from the bare *existence* of the sensible world, is an advantage to them only who have made this easy reflexion: that the sensible world is that which we perceive by our several senses; and that nothing is perceived by the senses beside ideas; and that no idea or archetype of an idea can exist otherwise than in a mind. You may now, without any laborious search into the sciences, without any subtlety of reason, or tedious length of discourse, oppose and baffle the most strenuous advocate for Atheism. Those miserable refuges, whether in an eternal succession of unthinking causes and effects, or in a fortuitous concourse of atoms; those wild imaginations of Vanini, Hobbes, and Spinoza: in a word, the whole system of Atheism, is it not entirely overthrown, by this single reflexion on the repugnancy included in supposing the whole, or any part, even the most rude and shapeless, of the visible world, to exist without a mind? Let any one of those abettors of impiety but look into his own thoughts, and there try if he can conceive how so much as a rock, a desert, a chaos, or confused jumble of atoms; how anything at all, either sensible or imaginable, can exist independent of a mind, and he need go no farther to be convinced of his folly. Can anything be fairer than to put a dispute on such an issue, and leave it to a man himself to see if he can conceive, even in thought, what he holds to be true in fact, and from a notional to allow it a real existence?

HYLAS: It cannot be denied there is something highly serviceable to religion in what you advance. But do you not think it looks very like a notion entertained by some eminent moderns, of *seeing all things in God?*

PHILONOUS: I would gladly know that opinion: pray explain it to me.

HYLAS: They conceive that the soul, being immaterial, is incapable of being united with material things, so as to perceive them in themselves; but that she perceives them by her union with the substance of God, which, being spiritual, is therefore purely intelligible, or capable of being the immediate object of a spirit's thought. Besides the divine essence contains in it perfections correspondent to each created being; and which are, for that reason, proper to exhibit or represent them to the mind.

PHILONOUS: I do not understand how our ideas, which are things altogether passive and inert, can be the essence, or any part (or like any part) of the essence or substance of God, who is an impassive, indivisible, pure, active being. Many more difficulties and objections there are which occur at first view against this hypothesis; but I shall only add that it is liable to all the absurdities of the common hypothesis, in making a created world exist otherwise than in the mind of a spirit. Besides all which it hath this peculiar to itself; that it makes that material world serve to no purpose. And, if it pass for a good argument against other hypotheses in the sciences, that they suppose nature, or the divine wisdom, to make something in vain, or do that by tedious roundabout methods which might have been performed in a much more easy and compendious way, what shall we think of that hypothesis which supposes the whole world made in vain?

HYLAS: But what say you? Are not you too of opinion that we see all things in God? If I mistake not, what you advance comes near it.

PHILONOUS: Few men think; yet all have opinions. Hence men's opinions are superficial and confused. It is nothing strange that tenets which in themselves are ever so different, should nevertheless be confounded with each other, by those who do not consider them attentively. I shall not therefore be surprised if some men imagine that I run into the enthusiasm of Malebranche; though in truth I am very remote from it. He builds on the most abstract general ideas, which I entirely disclaim. He asserts an absolute external world, which I deny. He maintains that we are deceived by our senses, and know not the real natures or the true forms and figures of extended beings; of all which I hold the direct contrary. So that upon the whole there are no principles more fundamentally opposite than his and mine. It must be owned that I entirely agree with what the holy Scripture says, "That in God we live and move and have our being" [Acts 17:28]. But that we see things in His essence, after the manner above set forth, I am far from believing. Take here in brief my meaning:—It is evident that the things I perceive are my own ideas, and that no idea can exist unless it be in a mind: nor is it less plain that these ideas or things by me perceived, either themselves or their archetypes, exist independently of my mind, since I know myself not to be their author, it being out of my power to determine at pleasure what particular ideas I shall be affected with upon opening my eyes or ears: they must therefore exist in some other mind, whose will it is they should be exhibited to me. The things, I say, immediately perceived are ideas or sensations, call them which you will. But how can any idea or sensation exist in, or be produced by, anything but a mind or spirit? This indeed is inconceivable. And to assert that which is inconceivable is to talk nonsense: is it not?

HYLAS: Without doubt.

PHILONOUS: But, on the other hand, it is very conceivable that they should exist in and be produced by a spirit; since this is no more than I daily experience in myself, inasmuch as I perceive numberless ideas; and, by an act of my will, can form a great variety of them, and raise them up in my imagination: though, it must be confessed, these creatures of the fancy are not altogether so distinct, so strong, vivid, and permanent, as those perceived by my senses—which latter are called *real things.* From all which I conclude, *there is a mind which affects me every moment with all the sensible impressions I perceive.* And, from the variety, order, and manner of these, I conclude the author of them to be *wise, powerful, and good, beyond comprehension.* Mark it well; I do not say, I see things by perceiving that which represents them in the intelligible substance of God. This I do not understand; but I say, the things by me perceived are known by the understanding, and produced by the will of an infinite spirit. And is not all this most plain and evident? Is there any more in it than what a little observation in our own minds, and that which passes in them, not only enables us to conceive, but also obliges us to acknowledge.

HYLAS: I think I understand you very clearly; and own the proof you give of a deity seems no less evident than it is surprising. But, allowing that God is the supreme and universal cause of all things, yet, may there not be still a third nature besides spirits and ideas? May we not admit a subordinate and limited cause of our ideas? In a word, may there not for all that be *matter?*

PHILONOUS: How often must I inculcate the same thing? You allow the things immediately perceived by sense to exist nowhere without the mind; but there is nothing perceived by sense which is not perceived immediately: therefore there is nothing sensible that exists without the mind. The matter, therefore, which you still insist on is something intelligible, I suppose; something that may be discovered by reason, and not by sense.

HYLAS: You are in the right.

PHILONOUS: Pray let me know what reasoning your belief of matter is grounded on; and what this matter is, in your present sense of it.

HYLAS: I find myself affected with various ideas, whereof I know I am not the cause; neither are they the cause of themselves, or of one another, or capable of subsisting by themselves, as being altogether inactive, fleeting, dependent beings. They have therefore some cause distinct from me and them: of which I pretend to know no more than that it is *the cause of my ideas.* And this thing, whatever it be, I call matter.

PHILONOUS: Tell me, Hylas, hath every one a liberty to change the current proper signification attached to a common name in any language? For example, suppose a traveler should tell you that in a certain country men pass unhurt through the fire; and, upon explaining himself, you found he meant by the word *fire* that which others call *water.* Or, if he should assert that there are trees that walk upon two legs, meaning men by the term *trees.* Would you think this reasonable?

HYLAS: No; I should think it very absurd. Common custom is the standard of propriety in language. And for any man to affect speaking improperly is to pervert the use of speech, and can never serve to a better purpose than to protract and multiply disputes where there is no difference in opinion.

PHILONOUS: And does not *matter,* in the common current acceptation of the word, signify an extended, solid, moveable, unthinking, inactive substance?

HYLAS: It does.

PHILONOUS: And, has it not been made evident that no such substance can possibly exist? And, though it should be allowed to exist, yet how can that which is *inactive* be a cause; or that which is *unthinking* be a *cause of thought?* You may, indeed, if you please, annex to the word *matter* a contrary meaning to what is vulgarly received; and tell me you understand by it, an unextended, thinking, active being, which is the cause of our ideas. But what else is this than to play with words, and run into that very fault you just now condemned with so much reason? I do by no means find fault with your reasoning, in that you collect a cause from the *phenomena:* but I deny that the cause deducible by reason can properly be termed matter.

HYLAS: There is indeed something in what you say. But I am afraid you do not thoroughly comprehend my meaning. I would by no means be thought to deny that God, or an infinite spirit, is the supreme cause of all things. All I contend for is, that, subordinate to the supreme agent, there is a cause of a limited and inferior nature, which concurs in the production of our ideas, not by any act of will, or spiritual efficiency, but by that kind of action which belongs to matter, *viz.* motion.

PHILONOUS: I find you are at every turn relapsing into your old exploded conceit, of a moveable, and consequently an extended, substance, existing without the mind. What! Have you already forgotten you were convinced; or are you willing I should repeat what has been said on that head? In truth this is not fair dealing in you, still to suppose the being of that which you have so often acknowledged to have no being. But, not to insist farther on what has been so largely handled, I ask whether all your ideas are not perfectly passive and inert, including nothing of action in them.

HYLAS: They are.

PHILONOUS: And are sensible qualities anything else but ideas?

HYLAS: How often have I acknowledged that they are not.

PHILONOUS: But is not motion a sensible quality?

HYLAS: It is.

PHILONOUS: Consequently it is no action?

HYLAS: I agree with you. And indeed it is very plain that when I stir my finger, it remains passive; but my will which produced the motion is active.

PHILONOUS: Now, I desire to know, in the first place, whether motion being allowed to be no action, you can conceive any action besides volition: and, in the second place, whether to say something and conceive nothing be not to talk nonsense: and, lastly, whether, having considered the premises, you do not perceive that to suppose any efficient or active cause of our ideas, other than *spirit,* is highly absurd and unreasonable?

HYLAS: I give up the point entirely. But, though matter may not be a cause, yet what hinders its being an *instrument,* subservient to the supreme agent in the production of our ideas?

PHILONOUS: An instrument say you; pray what may be the figure, springs, wheels, and motions, of that instrument?

HYLAS: Those I pretend to determine nothing of, both the substance and its qualities being entirely unknown to me.

PHILONOUS: What? You are then of opinion it is made up of unknown parts, that it hath unknown motions, and an unknown shape?

HYLAS: I do not believe that it hath any figure or motion at all, being already convinced, that no sensible qualities can exist in an unperceiving substance.

PHILONOUS: But what notion is it possible to frame of an instrument void of all sensible qualities, even extension itself?

HYLAS: I do not pretend to have any notion of it.

PHILONOUS: And what reason have you to think this unknown, this inconceivable somewhat does exist? Is it that you imagine God cannot act as well without it; or that you find by experience the use of some such thing, when you form ideas in your own mind?

HYLAS: You are always teasing me for reasons of my belief. Pray what reasons have you not to believe it?

PHILONOUS: It is to me a sufficient reason not to believe the existence of anything, if I see no reason for believing it. But, not to insist on reasons for believing, you will not so much as let me know what it is you would have me believe; since you say you have no manner of notion of it. After all, let me entreat you to consider whether it be like a philosopher, or even like a man of common sense, to pretend to believe you know not what, and you know not why.

HYLAS: Hold, Philonous. When I tell you matter is an *instrument,* I do not mean altogether nothing. It is true I know not the particular kind of instrument; but, however, I have some notion of *instrument in general,* which I apply to it.

PHILONOUS: But what if it should prove that there is something, even in the most general notion of *instrument,* as taken in a distinct sense from *cause,* which makes the use of it inconsistent with the divine attributes?

HYLAS: Make that appear and I shall give up the point.

PHILONOUS: What mean you by the general nature or notion of instrument?

HYLAS: That which is common to all particular instruments composes the general notion.

PHILONOUS: Is it not common to all instruments, that they are applied to the doing those things only which cannot be performed by the mere act of our wills? Thus, for instance, I never use an instrument to move my finger, because it is done by a volition. But I should use one if I were to remove part of a rock, or tear up a tree by the roots. Are you of the same mind? Or, can you show any example where an instrument is made use of in producing an effect immediately depending on the will of the agent?

HYLAS: I own I cannot.

PHILONOUS: How therefore can you suppose that an all-perfect spirit, on whose will all things have an absolute and immediate dependence, should need an instrument in his operations, or, not needing it, make use of it? Thus it seems to me that you are obliged to own the use of a lifeless inactive instrument to be incompatible with the infinite perfection of God; that is, by your own confession, to give up the point.

HYLAS: It does not readily occur what I can answer you.

PHILONOUS: But, methinks you should be ready to own the truth, when it has been fairly proved to you. We indeed, who are beings of finite powers, are forced to make use of instruments. And the use of an instrument shows the agent to be limited by rules of another's prescription, and that he cannot obtain his end but in such a way, and by such conditions. Whence it seems a clear consequence, that the supreme unlimited agent uses no tool or instrument at all. The will of an omnipotent spirit is no sooner exerted than executed, without the application of means; which, if they are employed by inferior agents, it is not upon account of any real efficacy that is in them, or necessary aptitude to produce any effect, but merely in compliance with the laws of nature, or those conditions prescribed to them by the first cause, who is himself above all limitation or prescription whatsoever.

Trinity College, Dublin, Ireland. Beginning in 1700, Berkeley attended Trinity College. After becoming a Fellow of the College in 1707, he was a tutor and Greek lecturer. Today, one of the libraries on campus is named after him. (© *2008, Pilise Gábor*)

HYLAS: I will no longer maintain that matter is an instrument. However, I would not be understood to give up its existence neither; since, notwithstanding what hath been said, it may still be an *occasion.*

PHILONOUS: How many shapes is your matter to take? Or, how often must it be proved not to exist, before you are content to part with it? But, to say no more of this (though by all the laws of disputation I may justly blame you for so frequently changing the signification of the principal term)—I would fain know what you mean by affirming that matter is an occasion, having already denied it to be a cause. And, when you have shown in what sense you understand *occasion,* pray, in the next place be pleased to show me what reason induces you to believe there is such an occasion of our ideas?

HYLAS: As to the first point: by *occasion* I mean an inactive unthinking being, at the presence whereof God excites ideas in our minds.

PHILONOUS: And what may be the nature of that inactive unthinking being?

HYLAS: I know nothing of its nature.

PHILONOUS: Proceed then to the second point, and assign some reason why we should allow an existence to this inactive, unthinking, unknown thing.

HYLAS: When we see ideas produced in our minds, after an orderly and constant manner, it is natural to think they have some fixed and regular occasions, at the presence of which they are excited.

PHILONOUS: You acknowledge then God alone to be the cause of our ideas, and that he causes them at the presence of those occasions.

HYLAS: That is my opinion.

PHILONOUS: Those things which you say are present to God, without doubt he perceives.

HYLAS: Certainly; otherwise they could not be to him an occasion of acting.

PHILONOUS: Not to insist now on your making sense of this hypothesis, or answering all the puzzling questions and difficulties it is liable to: I only ask whether the order and regularity observable in the series of our ideas, or the course of nature, be not sufficiently accounted for by the wisdom and power of God; and whether it does not derogate from those attributes, to suppose he is influenced, directed, or put in mind, when and what he is to act, by an unthinking substance? And, lastly, whether, in case I granted all you contend for, it would make anything to your purpose; it not being easy to conceive how the external or absolute existence of an unthinking substance, distinct from its being perceived, can be inferred from my allowing that there are certain things perceived by the mind of God, which are to him the occasion of producing ideas in us?

HYLAS: I am perfectly at a loss what to think, this notion of occasion seeming now altogether as groundless as the rest.

PHILONOUS: Do you not at length perceive that in all these different acceptations of *matter,* you have been only supposing you know not what, for no manner of reason, and to no kind of use?

HYLAS: I freely own myself less fond of my notions since they have been so accurately examined. But still, methinks, I have some confused perception that there is such a thing as *matter.*

PHILONOUS: Either you perceive the being of matter immediately or mediately. If immediately, pray inform me by which of the senses you perceive it. If mediately, let me know by what reasoning it is inferred from those things which you perceive immediately. So much for the perception. Then for the matter itself, I ask whether it is object, *substratum,* cause, instrument, or occasion? You have already pleaded for each of these, shifting your notions, and making matter to appear sometimes in one shape, then in another. And what you have offered hath been disapproved and rejected by yourself. If you have anything new to advance I would gladly bear it.

HYLAS: I think I have already offered all I had to say on those heads. I am at a loss what more to urge.

PHILONOUS: And yet you are loath to part with your old prejudice. But, to make you quit it more easily, I desire that, beside what has been hitherto suggested, you will farther consider whether, upon supposition that matter exists, you can possibly conceive how you should be affected by it. Or, supposing it did not exist, whether it be not evident you might for all that be affected with the same ideas you now are, and consequently have the very same reasons to believe its existence that you now can have.

HYLAS: I acknowledge it is possible we might perceive all things just as we do now, though there was no matter in the world; neither can I conceive, if there be matter, how it should produce any idea in our minds. And, I do farther grant you have entirely satisfied me that it is impossible there should be such a thing as matter in any of the foregoing acceptations. But still I cannot help supposing that there is *matter* in some sense or other. What that is I do not indeed pretend to determine.

PHILONOUS: I do not expect you should define exactly the nature of that unknown being. Only be pleased to tell me whether it is a substance; and if so, whether you can suppose a substance without accidents; or, in case you suppose it to have accidents or qualities, I desire you will let me know what those qualities are, at least what is meant by matter's supporting them?

HYLAS: We have already argued on those points. I have no more to say to them. But, to prevent any farther questions, let me tell you I at present understand by *matter* neither substance nor accident, thinking nor extended being, neither cause, instrument, nor occasion, but something entirely unknown, distinct from all these.

PHILONOUS: It seems then you include in your present notion of matter nothing but the general abstract idea of *entity.*

HYLAS: Nothing else; save only that I superadd to this general idea the negation of all those particular things, qualities, or ideas, that I perceive, imagine, or in anywise apprehend.

PHILONOUS: Pray where do you suppose this unknown matter to exist?

HYLAS: Oh Philonous! Now you think you have entangled me, for, if I say it exists in place, then you will infer that it exists in the mind, since it is agreed that place or extension exists only in the mind. But I am not ashamed to own my ignorance. I know not where it exists; only I am sure it exists not in place. There is a negative answer for you. And you must expect no other to all the questions you put for the future about matter.

PHILONOUS: Since you will not tell me where it exists, be pleased to inform me after what manner you suppose it to exist, or what you mean by its *existence?*

HYLAS: It neither thinks nor acts, neither perceives nor is perceived.

PHILONOUS: But what is there positive in your abstracted notion of its existence?

HYLAS: Upon a nice observation, I do not find I have any positive notion or meaning at all. I tell you again, I am not ashamed to own my ignorance. I know not what is meant by its *existence,* or how it exists.

PHILONOUS: Continue, good Hylas, to act the same ingenuous part, and tell me sincerely whether you can frame a distinct idea of Entity in general, prescinded from and exclusive of all thinking and corporeal beings, all particular things whatsoever.

HYLAS: Hold, let me think a little—I profess, Philonous I do not find that I can. At first glance, methought I had some dilute and airy notion of pure entity in abstract; but, upon closer attention, it hath quite vanished out of sight. The more I think on it, the more am I confirmed in my prudent resolution of giving none but negative answers, and not pretending to the least degree of any positive knowledge or conception of matter, its *where,* its *how,* its *entity,* or anything belonging to it.

PHILONOUS: When, therefore, you speak of the existence of matter, you have not any notion in your mind?

HYLAS: None at all.

PHILONOUS: Pray tell me if the case stands not thus: At first, from a belief of material substance, you would have it that the immediate objects existed without the mind; then that they are archetypes; then causes; next instruments; then occasions: lastly *something in general,* which being interpreted proves *nothing.* So matter comes to nothing. What think you, Hylas, is not this a fair summary of your whole proceeding?

HYLAS: Be that as it will, yet I still insist upon it, that our not being able to conceive a thing is no argument against its existence.

PHILONOUS: That from a cause, effect, operation, sign, or other circumstance, there may reasonably be inferred the existence of a thing not immediately perceived; and that it were absurd for any man to argue against the existence of that thing, from his having no direct and positive notion of it, I freely own. But, where there is nothing of all this; where neither reason nor revelation induces us to believe the existence of a thing; where we have not even a relative notion of it; where an abstraction is made from perceiving and being perceived, from spirit and idea: lastly, where there is not so much as the most inadequate or faint idea pretended to—I will not indeed thence conclude against the reality of any notion, or existence of anything; but my inference shall be, that you mean nothing at all; that you employ words to no manner of purpose, without any design or signification whatsoever. And I leave it to you to consider how mere jargon should be treated.

HYLAS: To deal frankly with you, Philonous, your arguments seem in themselves unanswerable; but they have not so great an effect on me as to produce that entire conviction, that hearty acquiescence, which attends demonstration. I find myself relapsing into an obscure surmise of I know not what, *matter*.

PHILONOUS: But, are you not sensible, Hylas, that two things must concur to take away all scruple, and work a plenary assent in the mind? Let a visible object be set in never so clear a light, yet, if there is any imperfection in the sight, or if the eye is not directed towards it, it will not be distinctly seen. And though a demonstration be never so well grounded and fairly proposed, yet, if there is withal a stain of prejudice, or a wrong bias on the understanding, can it be expected on a sudden to perceive clearly, and adhere firmly to the truth? No; there is need of time and pains: the attention must be awakened and detained by a frequent repetition of the same thing placed oft in the same, oft in different lights. I have said it already, and find I must still repeat and inculcate, that it is an unaccountable licence you take, in pretending to maintain you know not what, for you know not what reason, to you know not what purpose. Can this be paralleled in any art or science, any sect or profession of men? Or is there anything so barefacedly groundless and unreasonable to be met with even in the lowest of common conversation? But, perhaps you will still say, matter may exist; though at the same time you neither know what is meant by *matter,* or by its *existence.* This indeed is surprising, and the more so because it is altogether voluntary, you not being led to it by any one reason; for I challenge you to show me that thing in nature which needs matter to explain or account for it.

HYLAS: The reality of things cannot be maintained without supposing the existence of matter. And is not this, think you, a good reason why I should be earnest in its defence?

PHILONOUS: The reality of things! What things, sensible or intelligible?

HYLAS: Sensible things.

PHILONOUS: My glove for example?

HYLAS: That, or any other thing perceived by the senses.

PHILONOUS: But to fix on some particular thing. Is it not a sufficient evidence to me of the existence of this *glove,* that I see it, and feel it, and wear it? Or, if this will not do, how is it possible I should be assured of the reality of this thing, which I actually see in this place, by supposing that some unknown thing, which I never did or can see, exists after an unknown manner, in an unknown place, or in no place at all? How can the supposed reality of that which is intangible be a proof that anything tangible really exists? Or, of that which is invisible, that any visible thing, or, in general of anything which is imperceptible, that a perceptible exists? Do but explain this and I shall think nothing too hard for you.

HYLAS: Upon the whole, I am content to own the existence of matter is highly improbable, but the direct and absolute impossibility of it does not appear to me.

PHILONOUS: But granting matter to be possible, yet, upon that account merely, it can have no more claim to existence than a golden mountain, or a centaur.

HYLAS: I acknowledge it; but still you do not deny it is possible; and that which is possible, for aught you know, may actually exist.

PHILONOUS: I deny it to be possible; and have, if I mistake not, evidently proved, from your own concessions, that it is not. In the common sense of the word *matter,* is there any more implied than an extended, solid, figured, movable substance, existing without the mind? And have not you acknowledged, over and over, that you have seen evident reason for denying the possibility of such a substance?

HYLAS: True, but that is only one sense of the term matter.

PHILONOUS: But is it not the only proper genuine received sense? And, if matter, in such a sense, be proved impossible, may it not be thought with good grounds absolutely impossible? Else how could anything be proved impossible? Or, indeed, how could there be any proof at all one way or other, to a man who takes the liberty to unsettle and change the common signification of words?

HYLAS: I thought philosophers might be allowed to speak more accurately than the vulgar, and were not always confined to the common acceptation of a term.

PHILONOUS: But this now mentioned is the common received sense among philosophers themselves. But, not to insist on that, have you not been allowed to take matter in what sense you pleased? And have you not used this privilege in the utmost extent; sometimes entirely changing, at others leaving out, or putting into the definition of it whatever, for the present, best served your design, contrary to all the known rules of reason and logic? And hath not this shifting, unfair method of yours spun out our dispute to an unnecessary length; matter having been particularly examined, and by your own confession refuted in each of those senses? And can any more be required to prove the absolute impossibility of a thing, than the proving it impossible in every particular sense that either you or any one else understands it in?

HYLAS: But I am not so thoroughly satisfied that you have proved the impossibility of matter, in the last most obscure abstracted and indefinite sense.

PHILONOUS: When is a thing shown to be impossible?

HYLAS: When a repugnancy is demonstrated between the ideas comprehended in its definition

PHILONOUS: But where there are no ideas, there no repugnancy can be demonstrated between ideas?

HYLAS: I agree with you.

PHILONOUS: Now, in that which you call the obscure indefinite sense of the word matter, it is plain, by your own confession, there was included no idea at all, no sense except an unknown sense; which is the same thing as none. You are not, therefore, to expect I should prove a repugnancy between ideas, where there are no ideas; or the impossibility of matter taken in an *unknown* sense, that is, no sense at all. My business was only to show you meant *nothing;* and this you were brought to own. So that, in all your various senses, you have been showed either to mean nothing at all, or, if anything, an absurdity. And if this be not sufficient to prove the impossibility of a thing, I desire you will let me know what is.

HYLAS: I acknowledge you have proved that matter is impossible; nor do I see what more can be said in defence of it. But, at the same time that I give up this, I suspect all my other notions. For surely none could be more seemingly evident than this once was: and yet it now seems as false and absurd as ever it did true before. But I think we have discussed the point sufficiently for the present. The remaining part of the day I would willingly spend in running over in my thoughts the several heads of this morning's conversation, and tomorrow shall be glad to meet you here again about the same time.

PHILONOUS: I will not fail to attend you.

THE THIRD DIALOGUE

PHILONOUS: Tell me, Hylas, what are the fruits of yesterday's meditation? Has it confirmed you in the same mind you were in at parting? or have you since seen cause to change your opinion?

HYLAS: Truly my opinion is that all our opinions are alike vain and uncertain. What we approve today, we condemn tomorrow. We keep a stir about knowledge, and spend our lives in the pursuit of it, when, alas! we know nothing all the while: nor do I think it possible for us ever to know anything in this life. Our faculties are too narrow and too few. Nature certainly never intended us for speculation.

PHILONOUS: What! Say you we can know nothing, Hylas?

HYLAS: There is not that single thing in the world whereof we can know the real nature, or what it is in itself.

PHILONOUS: Will you tell me I do not really know what fire or water is?

HYLAS: You may indeed know that fire appears hot, and water fluid; but this is no more than knowing what sensations are produced in your own mind, upon the application of fire and water to your organs of sense. Their internal constitution, their true and real nature, you are utterly in the dark as to *that.*

PHILONOUS: Do I not know this to be a real stone that I stand on, and that which I see before my eyes to be a real tree?

HYLAS: Know? No, it is impossible you or any man alive should know it. All you know is, that you have such a certain idea or appearance in your own mind. But what is this to the real tree or stone? I tell you that colour, figure, and hardness, which you perceive, are not the real natures of those things, or in the least like them. The same may be said of all other real things, or corporeal substances, which compose the world. They have none of them anything of themselves, like those sensible qualities by us perceived. We should not therefore pretend to affirm or know anything of them, as they are in their own nature.

PHILONOUS: But surely, Hylas, I can distinguish gold, for example, from iron: and how could this be, if I knew not what either truly was?

HYLAS: Believe me, Philonous, you can only distinguish between your own ideas. That yellowness, that weight, and other sensible qualities, think you they are really in the gold? They are only relative to the senses, and have no absolute existence in nature. And in pretending to distinguish the species of real things, by the appearances in your mind, you may perhaps act as wisely as he that should conclude two men were of a different species, because their clothes were not of the same colour.

PHILONOUS: It seems, then, we are altogether put off with the appearances of things, and those false ones too. The very meat I eat, and the cloth I wear, have nothing in them like what I see and feel.

HYLAS: Even so.

PHILONOUS: But is it not strange the whole world should be thus imposed on, and so foolish as to believe their senses? And yet I know not how it is, but men eat, and drink, and sleep, and perform all the offices of life, as comfortably and conveniently as if they really knew the things they are conversant about.

HYLAS: They do so: but you know ordinary practice does not require a nicety of speculative knowledge. Hence the vulgar retain their mistakes, and for all that make a shift to bustle through the affairs of life. But philosophers know better things.

PHILONOUS: You mean, they know that they *know nothing.*

HYLAS: That is the very top and perfection of human knowledge.

PHILONOUS: But are you all this while in earnest, Hylas; and are you seriously persuaded that you know nothing real in the world? Suppose you are going to write, would you not call for pen, ink, and paper, like another man; and do you not know what it is you call for?

HYLAS: How often must I tell you, that I know not the real nature of any one thing in the universe? I may indeed upon occasion make use of pen, ink, and paper. But what any one of them is in its own true nature, I declare positively I know not. And the same is true with regard to every other corporeal thing. And, what is more, we are not only ignorant of the true and real nature of things, but even of their existence. It cannot be denied that we perceive such certain appearances or ideas; but it cannot be concluded from thence that bodies really exist. Nay, now I think on it, I must, agreeably to my former concessions, farther declare that it is impossible any real corporeal thing should exist in nature.

PHILONOUS: You amaze me. Was ever anything more wild and extravagant than the notions you now maintain: and is it not evident you are led into all these extravagances by the belief of *material substance?* This makes you dream of those unknown natures in everything. It is this occasions your distinguishing between the reality and sensible appearances of things. It is to this you are indebted for being ignorant of what everybody else knows perfectly well. Nor is this all: you are not only ignorant of the true nature of everything, but you know not whether anything really exists, or whether there are any true natures at all; forasmuch as you attribute to your material beings an absolute or external existence, wherein you suppose their reality consists. And, as you are forced in the end to acknowledge such an existence means either a direct repugnancy, or nothing at all, it follows that you are obliged to pull down your own hypothesis of material substance, and positively to deny the real existence of any part of the universe. And so you are plunged into the deepest and most deplorable *scepticism* that ever man was. Tell me, Hylas, is it not as I say?

HYLAS: I agree with you. *Material substance* was no more than an hypothesis; and a false and groundless one too. I will no longer spend my breath in defence of it. But whatever hypothesis you advance, or whatsoever scheme of things you introduce in its stead, I doubt not it will appear every whit as false: let me but be allowed to question you upon it. That is, suffer me to serve you in your own kind, and I warrant it shall conduct you through as many perplexities and contradictions, to the very same state of scepticism that I myself am in at present.

PHILONOUS: I assure you, Hylas, I do not pretend to frame any hypothesis at all. I am of a vulgar cast, simple enough to believe my senses, and leave things as I find them. To be plain, it is my opinion that the real things are those very things I see, and feel, and perceive by my senses. These I know; and, finding they answer all the necessities and purposes of life, have no reason to be solicitous about any other unknown beings. A piece of sensible bread, for instance, would stay my stomach better than ten thousand times as much of that insensible, unintelligible, real bread you speak of. It is likewise my opinion that colours and other sensible qualities are on the objects. I cannot for my life help thinking that snow is white, and fire hot. You indeed, who by *snow* and *fire* mean certain external, unperceived, unperceiving substances, are in the right to deny whiteness or heat to be affections inherent in them. But I, who understand by those words the things I see and feel, am obliged to think like other folks. And, as I am no sceptic with regard to the nature of things, so neither am I as to their existence. That a thing should be really perceived by my senses, and at the same time not really exist, is to me a plain contradiction; since I cannot prescind or abstract, even in thought, the existence of a sensible thing from its being perceived. Wood, stones, fire, water, flesh, iron, and the like things, which I name and discourse of, are things that I know. And I should not have known them but that I perceived them by my senses; and things perceived by the senses are immediately perceived; and things immediately perceived are ideas; and ideas cannot exist without the mind, their existence therefore consists in being perceived; when, therefore, they are actually perceived there can be no doubt of their existence. Away then with all that scepticism, all those ridiculous philosophical doubts. What a jest is it for a philosopher to question the existence of sensible things, till he hath it proved to him from the veracity of God; or to pretend our knowledge in this point falls short of intuition or demonstration! I might as well doubt of my own being, as of the being of those things I actually see and feel.

HYLAS: Not so fast, PHILONOUS: you say you cannot conceive how sensible things should exist without the mind. Do you not?

PHILONOUS: I do.

HYLAS: Supposing you were annihilated, cannot you conceive it possible that things perceivable by sense may still exist?

PHILONOUS: I can, but then it must be in another mind. When I deny sensible things an existence out of the mind, I do not mean my mind in particular, but all minds. Now, it is plain they have an existence exterior to my mind, since I find them by experience to be independent of it. There is therefore some other mind wherein they exist, during the intervals between the times of my perceiving them: as likewise they did before my birth, and would do after my supposed annihilation. And, as the same is true with regard to all other finite created spirits, it necessarily follows there is an *omnipresent eternal mind,* which knows and comprehends all things, and exhibits them to our view in such a manner, and according to such rules, as he himself hath ordained, and are by us termed the *laws of nature.*

HYLAS: Answer me, Philonous. Are all our ideas perfectly inert beings? Or have they any agency included in them?

PHILONOUS: They are altogether passive and inert.

HYLAS: And is not God an agent, a being purely active?

PHILONOUS: I acknowledge it.

HYLAS: No idea therefore can be like unto, or represent the nature of God?

PHILONOUS: It cannot.

HYLAS: Since therefore you have no idea of the mind of God, how can you conceive it possible that things should exist in His mind? Or, if you can conceive the mind of God, without having an idea of it, why may not I be allowed to conceive the existence of matter, notwithstanding I have no idea of it?

PHILONOUS: As to your first question: I own I have properly no idea, either of God or any other spirit; for these being active, cannot be represented by things perfectly inert, as our ideas are. I do nevertheless know that I, who am a spirit or thinking substance, exist as certainly as I know my ideas exist. Farther, I know what I mean by the terms *I* and *myself;* and I know this immediately or intuitively, though I do not perceive it as I perceive a triangle, a colour, or a sound. The mind, spirit, or soul is that indivisible unextended thing which thinks, acts, and perceives. I say *indivisible,* because *unextended;* and unextended, because extended, figured, movable things are ideas; and that which perceives ideas, which thinks and wills, is plainly itself no idea, nor like an idea. Ideas are things inactive, and perceived. And spirits a sort of beings altogether different from them. I do not therefore say my soul is an idea, or like an idea. However, taking the word *idea* in a large sense, my soul may be said to furnish me with an idea, that is, an image or likeness of God—though indeed extremely inadequate. For, all the notion I have of God is obtained by reflecting on my own soul, heightening its powers, and removing its imperfections. I have, therefore, though not an inactive idea, yet in *myself* some sort of an active thinking image of the Deity. And, though I perceive him not by sense, yet I have a notion of him, or know him by reflexion and reasoning. My own mind and my own ideas I have an immediate knowledge of; and, by the help of these, do mediately apprehend the possibility of the existence of other spirits and ideas. Farther, from my own being, and from the dependency I find in myself and my ideas, I do, by an act of reason, necessarily infer the existence of a God, and of all created things in the mind of God. So much for your first question. For the second: I suppose by this time you can answer it yourself. For you neither perceive matter objectively, as you do an inactive being or idea; nor know it, as you do yourself, by a reflex act, neither do you mediately apprehend it by similitude of the one or the other; nor yet collect it by reasoning from that which you know immediately. All which makes the case of *matter* widely different from that of the *Deity*.

HYLAS: You say your own soul supplies you with some sort of an idea or image of God. But, at the same time, you acknowledge you have, properly speaking, no idea of your own soul. You even affirm that spirits are a sort of beings altogether different from ideas. Consequently that no idea can be like a spirit. We have therefore no idea of any spirit. You admit nevertheless that there is spiritual substance, although you have no idea of it; while you deny there can be such a thing as material substance, because you have no notion or idea of it. Is this fair dealing? To act consistently, you must either admit matter or reject spirit. What say you to this?

PHILONOUS: I say, in the first place, that I do not deny the existence of material substance, merely because I have no notion of it, but because the notion of it is inconsistent; or, in other words, because it is repugnant that there should be a notion of it. Many things, for aught I know, may exist, whereof neither I nor any other man hath or can have any idea or notion whatsoever. But then those things must be possible, that is, nothing inconsistent must be included in their definition. I say, secondly, that, although we believe things to exist which we do not perceive, yet we may not believe that any particular thing exists, without some reason for such belief: but I have no reason for believing the existence of matter. I have no immediate intuition thereof: neither can I immediately from my sensations, ideas, notions, actions, or passions, infer an unthinking, unperceiving, inactive substance—either by probable deduction, or necessary consequence. Whereas the being of my Self, that is, my own soul, mind, or thinking principle, I evidently know by reflexion. You will forgive me if I repeat the same things in answer to the same objections. In the very notion or definition of *material substance,* there is included a manifest repugnance and inconsistency. But this cannot be said of the notion of spirit. That ideas should exist in what does not perceive or be produced by what does not act, is repugnant. But, it is no repugnancy to say that a perceiving thing should be the subject of ideas, or an active thing the cause of them. It is granted we have neither an immediate evidence nor a demonstrative knowledge of the existence of other finite spirits; but it will not thence follow that such spirits are on a foot with material substances: if to suppose the one be inconsistent, and it be not inconsistent to suppose the other; if the one can be inferred by no argument, and there is a probability for the other; if we see signs and effects indicating distinct finite agents like ourselves, and see no sign or symptom whatever that leads to a rational belief of matter. I say, lastly, that I have a notion of spirit, though I have not, strictly speaking, an idea of it. I do not perceive it as an idea, or by means of an idea, but know it by reflexion.

HYLAS: Notwithstanding all you have said, to me it seems that, according to your own way of thinking, and in consequence of your own principles, it should follow that you are only a system of floating ideas, without any substance to support them. Words are not to be used without a meaning. And, as there is no more meaning in *spiritual substance* than in *material substance,* the one is to be exploded as well as the other.

PHILONOUS: How often must I repeat, that I know or am conscious of my own being; and that *I myself* am not my ideas, but somewhat else, a thinking, active principle that perceives, knows, wills, and operates about ideas I know that I, one and the same self, perceive both colours and sounds: that a colour cannot perceive a sound, nor a sound a colour: that I am therefore one individual principle, distinct from colour and sound, and, for the same reason, from all other sensible things and inert ideas. But, I am not in like manner conscious either of the existence or essence of matter. On the contrary, I know that nothing inconsistent can exist, and that the existence of matter implies an inconsistency. Farther, I know what I mean when I affirm that there is a spiritual substance or support of ideas, that is, that a spirit knows and perceives ideas. But, I do not know what is meant when it is said that an unperceiving substance hath inherent in it and supports either ideas or the archetypes of ideas. There is therefore upon the whole no parity of case between spirit and matter.

HYLAS: I own myself satisfied in this point. But, do you in earnest think the real existence of sensible things consists in their being actually perceived? If so; how comes it that all mankind distinguish between them? Ask the first man you meet, and he shall tell you, *to be perceived* is one thing, and *to exist* is another.

PHILONOUS: I am content, Hylas, to appeal to the common sense of the world for the truth of my notion. Ask the gardener why he thinks yonder cherry-tree exists in the garden, and he shall tell you, because he sees and feels it; in a word, because he perceives it by his senses. Ask him why he thinks an orange-tree not to be there, and he shall tell you, because he does not perceive it. What he perceives by sense, that he terms a real being, and says it *is* or *exists;* but, that which is not perceivable, the same, he says, has no being.

HYLAS: Yes, Philonous, I grant the existence of a sensible thing consists in being perceivable, but not in being actually perceived.

PHILONOUS: And what is perceivable but an idea? And can an idea exist without being actually perceived? These are points long since agreed between us.

HYLAS: But, be your opinion never so true, yet surely you will not deny it is shocking, and contrary to the common sense of men. Ask the fellow whether yonder tree hath an existence out of his mind: what answer think you he would make?

PHILONOUS: The same that I should myself, to wit, that it does exist out of his mind. But then to a Christian it cannot surely be shocking to say, the real tree, existing without his mind, is truly known and comprehended by (that is *exists in*) the infinite mind of God. Probably he may not at first glance be aware of the direct and immediate proof there is of this; inasmuch as the very being of a tree, or any other sensible thing, implies a mind wherein it is. But the point itself he cannot deny. The question between the materialists and me is not, whether things have a real existence out of the mind of this or that person, but whether they have an absolute existence, distinct from being perceived by God, and exterior to all minds. This indeed some heathens and philosophers have affirmed, but whoever entertains notions of the Deity suitable to the Holy Scriptures will be of another opinion.

HYLAS: But, according to your notions, what difference is there between real things, and chimeras formed by the imagination, or the visions of a dream—since they are all equally in the mind?

PHILONOUS: The ideas formed by the imagination are faint and indistinct; they have, besides, an entire dependence on the will. But the ideas perceived by sense, that is, real things, are more vivid and clear; and, being imprinted on the mind by a spirit distinct from us, have not the like dependence on our will. There is therefore no danger of confounding these with the foregoing; and there is as little of confounding them with the visions of a dream, which are dim, irregular, and confused. And, though they should happen to be never so lively and natural, yet, by their not being connected, and of a piece with the preceding and subsequent transactions of our lives, they might easily be distinguished from realities. In short, by whatever method you distinguish *things* from *chimeras* on your scheme, the same, it is evident, will hold also upon mine. For, it must be, I presume, by some perceived difference; and I am not for depriving you of any one thing that you perceive.

HYLAS: But still, Philonous, you hold, there is nothing in the world but spirits and ideas. And this, you must needs acknowledge, sounds very oddly.

PHILONOUS: I own the word *idea,* not being commonly used for *thing,* sounds something out of the way. My reason for using it was, because a necessary relation to the mind is understood to be implied by that term; and it is now commonly used by philosophers to denote the immediate objects of the understanding. But, however oddly the proposition may sound in words, yet it includes nothing so very strange or shocking in its sense, which in effect amounts to no more than this, to wit, that there are only things perceiving, and things perceived; or that every unthinking being is necessarily, and from the very nature of its existence, perceived by some mind; if not by a finite created mind, yet certainly by the infinite mind of God, in whom "we live, and move, and have our being." Is this as strange as to say, the sensible qualities are not on the objects: or that we cannot be sure of the existence of things, or know any thing of their real natures—though we both see and feel them, and perceive them by all our senses?

HYLAS: And, in consequence of this, must we not think there are no such things as physical or corporeal causes; but that a spirit is the immediate cause of all the phenomena in nature? Can there be anything more extravagant than this?

PHILONOUS: Yes, it is infinitely more extravagant to say—a thing which is inert operates on the mind, and which is unperceiving is the cause of our perceptions, without any regard either to consistency, or the old known axiom: *Nothing can give to another that which it hath not itself.* Besides, that which to you, I know not for what reason, seems so extravagant is no more than the Holy Scriptures assert in a hundred places. In them God is represented as the sole and immediate author of all those effects which some heathens and philosophers are wont to ascribe to nature, matter, fate, or the like unthinking principle. This is so much the constant language of Scripture that it were needless to confirm it by citations.

HYLAS: You are not aware Philonous, that in making God the immediate author of all the motions in nature, you make him the author of murder, sacrilege, adultery, and the like heinous sins.

PHILONOUS: In answer to that, I observe, first, that the imputation of guilt is the same, whether a person commits an action with or without an instrument. In case therefore you suppose God to act by the mediation of an instrument or occasion, called *matter,* you as truly make him the author of sin as I, who think him the immediate agent in all those operations vulgarly ascribed to nature. I farther observe that sin or moral turpitude does not consist in the outward physical action or motion, but in the internal deviation of the will from the laws of reason and religion. This is plain, in that the killing an enemy in a battle, or putting a criminal legally to death, is not thought sinful; though the outward act be the very same with that in the case of murder. Since therefore, sin does not consist in the physical action, the making God an immediate cause of all such actions is not making him the author of sin. Lastly, I have nowhere said that God is the only agent who produces all the motions in bodies. It is true I have denied there are any other agents besides spirits, but this is very consistent with allowing to thinking rational beings, in the production of motions, the use of limited powers, ultimately indeed derived from God, but immediately under the direction of their own wills which is sufficient to entitle them to all the guilt of their actions.

HYLAS: But the denying matter, Philonous, or corporeal substance; there is the point. You can never persuade me that this is not repugnant to the universal sense of mankind. Were our dispute to be determined by most voices, I am confident you would give up the point, without gathering the votes.

PHILONOUS: I wish both our opinions were fairly stated and submitted to the judgment of men who had plain common sense, without the prejudices of a learned education. Let me be represented as one who trusts his senses, who thinks he knows the things he sees and feels, and entertains no doubts of their existence, and you fairly set forth with all your doubts, your paradoxes, and your scepticism about you, and I shall willingly acquiesce in the determination of any indifferent person. That there is no substance wherein ideas can exist beside spirit is to me evident. And that the objects immediately perceived are ideas, is on all hands agreed. And that sensible qualities are objects immediately perceived no one can deny. It is therefore evident there can be no *substratum* of those qualities but spirit; in which they exist, not by way of mode or property, but as a thing perceived in that which perceives it. I deny therefore that there is any unthinking *substratum* of the objects of sense, and in that acceptation that there is any material substance. But if by *material substance* is meant only sensible body—that which is seen and felt (and the unphilosophical part of the world, I dare say, mean no more)—then I am more certain of matter's existence than you or any other philosopher pretend to be. If there be anything which makes the generality of mankind averse from the notions I espouse: it is a misapprehension that I deny the reality of sensible things. But, as it is you who are guilty of that, and not I, it follows that in truth their aversion is against your notions and not mine. I do therefore assert that I am as certain as of my own being, that there are bodies or corporeal substances (meaning the things I perceive by my senses); and that, granting this, the bulk of mankind will take no thought about, nor think themselves at all concerned in the fate of those unknown natures, and philosophical quiddities, which some men are so fond of.

HYLAS: What say you to this? Since, according to you, men judge of the reality of things by their senses, how can a man be mistaken in thinking the moon a plain lucid surface, about a foot in diameter; or a square tower, seen at a distance, round; or an oar, with one end in the water, crooked?

PHILONOUS: He is not mistaken with regard to the ideas he actually perceives, but in the inference he makes from his present perceptions. Thus, in the case of the oar, what he immediately perceives by sight is certainly crooked; and so far he is in the right. But if he thence conclude that upon taking the oar out of the water he shall perceive the same crookedness; or that it would affect his touch as crooked things are wont to do: in that he is mistaken. In like manner, if he shall conclude from what he perceives in one station, that, in case he advances towards the moon or tower, he should still be affected with the like ideas, he is mistaken. But his mistake lies not in what he perceives immediately, and at present, (it being a manifest contradiction to suppose he should err in respect of that) but in the wrong judgment he makes concerning the ideas he apprehends to be connected with those immediately perceived: or, concerning the ideas that, from what he perceives at present, he imagines would be perceived in other circumstances. The case is the same with regard to the Copernican system. We do not here perceive any motion of the earth: but it were erroneous thence to conclude, that, in case we were placed at as great a distance from that as we are now from the other planets, we should not then perceive its motion.

HYLAS: I understand you; and must needs own you say things plausible enough. But, give me leave to put you in mind of one thing. Pray, Philonous, were you not formerly as positive that matter existed, as you are now that it does not?

PHILONOUS: I was. But here lies the difference. Before, my positiveness was founded, without examination, upon prejudice; but now, after inquiry, upon evidence.

HYLAS: After all, it seems our dispute is rather about words than things. We agree in the thing, but differ in the name. That we are affected with ideas from without is evident, and it is no less evident that there must be (I will not say archetypes, but) Powers without the mind, corresponding to those ideas. And, as these Powers cannot subsist by themselves, there is some subject of them necessarily to be admitted; which I call *matter,* and you call *spirit.* This is all the difference.

PHILONOUS: Pray, Hylas, is that powerful being, or subject of powers, extended?

HYLAS: It hath not extension; but it hath the power to raise in you the idea of extension.

PHILONOUS: It is therefore itself unextended?

HYLAS: I grant it.

PHILONOUS: Is it not also active?

HYLAS: Without doubt. Otherwise, how could we attribute powers to it?

PHILONOUS: Now let me ask you two questions: *First,* whether it be agreeable to the usage either of philosophers or others to give the name *matter* to an unextended active being? And, *secondly,* whether it be not ridiculously absurd to misapply names contrary to the common use of language?

HYLAS: Well then, let it not be called matter, since you will have it so, but some *third nature* distinct from matter and spirit. For what reason is there why you should call it spirit? Does not the notion of spirit imply that it is thinking, as well as active and unextended?

PHILONOUS: My reason is this: because I have a mind to have some notion of meaning in what I say: but I have no notion of any action distinct from volition, neither can I conceive volition to be anywhere but in a spirit: therefore, when I speak of an active being, I am obliged to mean a spirit. Beside, what can be plainer than that a thing which hath no ideas in itself cannot impart them to me, and, if it hath ideas, surely it must be a spirit. To make you comprehend the point still more clearly if it be possible, I assert as well as you that, since we are affected from without, we must allow powers to be without, in a being distinct from ourselves. So far we are agreed. But then we differ as to the kind of this powerful being. I will have it to be spirit, you matter, or I know not what (I may add too, you know not what) third nature. Thus, I prove it to be spirit. From the effects I see produced, I conclude there are actions; and, because actions, volitions; and, because there are volitions, there must be a will. Again, the things I perceive must have an existence, they or their archetypes, out of my mind: but, being ideas, neither they nor their archetypes can exist otherwise than in an understanding, there is therefore an understanding. But will and understanding constitute in the strictest sense a mind or spirit. The powerful cause, therefore, of my ideas is in strict propriety of speech a *spirit.*

HYLAS: And now I warrant you think you have made the point very clear, little suspecting that what you advance leads directly to a contradiction. Is it not an absurdity to imagine any imperfection in God?

PHILONOUS: Without a doubt.

HYLAS: To suffer pain is an imperfection?

PHILONOUS: It is.

HYLAS: Are we not sometimes affected with pain and uneasiness by some other being?

PHILONOUS: We are.

HYLAS: And have you not said that being is a spirit, and is not that spirit God?

PHILONOUS: I grant it.

HYLAS: But you have asserted that whatever ideas we perceive from without are in the mind which affects us. The ideas, therefore, of pain and uneasiness are in God; or, in other words, God suffers pain: that is to say, there is an imperfection in the divine nature: which, you acknowledged, was absurd. So you are caught in a plain contradiction.

PHILONOUS: That God knows or understands all things, and that he knows, among other things, what pain is, even every sort of painful sensation, and what it is for His creatures to suffer pain, I make no question. But, that God, though he knows and sometimes causes painful sensations in us, can himself suffer pain, I positively deny. We, who are limited and dependent spirits, are liable to impressions of sense, the effects of an external agent, which, being produced against our wills, are sometimes painful and uneasy. But God, whom no external being can affect, who perceives nothing by sense as we do; whose will is absolute and independent, causing all things, and liable to be thwarted or resisted by nothing: it is evident, such a being as this can suffer nothing, nor be affected with any painful sensation, or indeed any sensation at all. We are chained to a body: that is to say, our perceptions are connected with corporeal motions. By the law of our nature, we are affected upon every alteration in the nervous parts of our sensible body; which sensible body, rightly considered, is nothing but a complexion of such qualities or ideas as have no existence distinct from being perceived by a mind. So that this connexion of sensations with corporeal motions means no more than a correspondence in the order of nature, between two sets of ideas, or things immediately perceivable. But God is a pure spirit, disengaged from all such sympathy, or natural ties. No corporeal motions are attended with the sensations of pain or pleasure in His mind. To know everything knowable, is certainly a perfection; but to endure or suffer, or feel anything by sense, is an imperfection. The former, I say, agrees to God, but not the latter. God knows, or hath ideas; but His ideas are not conveyed to him by sense, as ours are. Your not distinguishing, where there is so manifest a difference, makes you fancy you see an absurdity where there is none.

HYLAS: But, all this while you have not considered that the quantity of matter has been demonstrated to be proportioned to the gravity of bodies. And what can withstand demonstration?

PHILONOUS: Let me see how you demonstrate that point.

HYLAS: I lay it down for a principle, that the moments or quantities of motion in bodies are in a direct compounded reason of the velocities and quantities of matter contained in them. Hence, where the velocities are equal, it follows the moments are directly as the quantity of matter in each. But it is found by experience that all bodies (bating the small inequalities, arising from the resistance of the air) descend with an equal velocity; the motion therefore of descending bodies, and consequently their gravity, which is the cause or principle of that motion, is proportional to the quantity of matter; which was to be demonstrated.

PHILONOUS: You lay it down as a self-evident principle that the quantity of motion in any body is proportional to the velocity and *matter* taken together: and this is made use of to prove a proposition from whence the existence of *matter* is inferred. Pray is not this arguing in a circle?

HYLAS: In the premise I only mean that the motion is proportional to the velocity, jointly with the extension and solidity.

PHILONOUS: But, allowing this to be true, yet it will not thence follow that gravity is proportional to *matter,* in your philosophic sense of the word, except you take it for granted that unknown *substratum,* or whatever else you call it, is proportional to those sensible qualities; which to suppose is plainly begging the question. That there is magnitude and solidity, or resistance, perceived by sense, I readily grant, as likewise, that gravity may be proportional to those qualities I will not dispute. But that either these qualities as perceived by us, or the powers producing them, do exist in a *material substratum;* this is what I deny, and you indeed affirm, but, notwithstanding your demonstration, have not yet proved.

HYLAS: I shall insist no longer on that point. Do you think, however, you shall persuade me the natural philosophers have been dreaming all this while? Pray what becomes of all their hypotheses and explications of the *phenomena,* which suppose the existence of matter?

PHILONOUS: What mean you, Hylas, by the *phenomena?*

HYLAS: I mean the appearances which I perceive by my senses.

PHILONOUS: And the appearances perceived by sense, are they not ideas?

HYLAS: I have told you so a hundred times.

PHILONOUS: Therefore, to explain the phenomena, is, to show how we come to be affected with ideas, in that manner and order wherein they are imprinted on our senses. Is it not?

HYLAS: It is.

PHILONOUS: Now, if you can prove that any philosopher has explained the production of any one idea in our minds by the help of *matter,* I shall for ever acquiesce, and look on all that hath been said against it as nothing; but, if you cannot, it is vain to urge the explication of *phenomena.* That a being endowed with knowledge and will should produce or exhibit ideas is easily understood. But that a being which is utterly destitute of these faculties should be able to produce ideas, or in any sort to affect an intelligence, this I can never understand. This I say, though we had some positive conception of matter, though we knew its qualities, and could comprehend its existence, would yet be so far from explaining things, that it is itself the most inexplicable thing in the world. And yet, for all this, it will not follow that philosophers have been doing nothing; for, by observing and reasoning upon the connexion of ideas, they discover the laws and methods of nature, which is a part of knowledge both useful and entertaining.

HYLAS: After all, can it be supposed God would deceive all mankind? Do you imagine he would have induced the whole world to believe the being of matter, if there was no such thing?

PHILONOUS: That every epidemical opinion, arising from prejudice, or passion, or thoughtlessness, may be imputed to God, as the author of it, I believe you will not affirm. Whatsoever opinion we father on him, it must be either because he has discovered it to us by supernatural revelation; or because it is so evident to our natural faculties, which were framed and given us by God, that it is impossible we should withhold our assent from it. But where is the revelation? Or where is the evidence that extorts the belief of matter? Nay, how does it appear, that matter, taken for something distinct from what we perceive by our senses, is thought to exist by all mankind; or indeed, by any except a few philosophers, who do not know what they would be at? Your question supposes these points are clear; and, when you have cleared them, I shall think myself obliged to give you another answer. In the meantime, let it suffice. That I tell you, I do not suppose God has deceived mankind at all.

HYLAS: But the novelty, Philonous, the novelty! There lies the danger. New notions should always be discountenanced; they unsettle men's minds, and nobody knows where they will end.

PHILONOUS: Why the rejecting a notion that has no foundation, either in sense, or in reason, or in divine authority, should be thought to unsettle the belief of such opinions as are grounded on all or any of these, I cannot imagine. That innovations in government and religion are dangerous, and ought to be discountenanced, I freely own. But is there the like reason why they should be discouraged in philosophy? The making anything known which was unknown before is an innovation in knowledge: and, if all such innovations had been forbidden, men would have made a notable progress in the arts and sciences. But it is none of my business to plead for novelties and paradoxes. That the qualities we perceive are not on the objects: that we must not believe our senses: that we know nothing of the real nature of things, and can never be assured even of their existence: that real colours and sounds are nothing but certain unknown figures and motions: that motions are in themselves neither swift nor slow: that there are in bodies absolute extensions, without any particular magnitude or figure: that a thing stupid, thoughtless, and inactive, operates on a spirit: that the least particle of a body contains innumerable extended parts:—these are the novelties, these are the strange notions which shock the genuine uncorrupted judgment of all mankind; and being once admitted, embarrass the mind with endless doubts and difficulties. And it is against these and the like innovations I endeavour to vindicate common sense. It is true, in doing this, I may perhaps be obliged to use some *ambages,* and ways of speech not common. But, if my notions are once thoroughly understood, that which is most singular in them will, in effect, be found to amount to no more than this:—that it is absolutely impossible, and a plain contradiction, to suppose any unthinking being should exist without being perceived by a mind. And, if this notion be singular, it is a shame it should be so, at this time of day, and in a Christian country.

HYLAS: As for the difficulties other opinions may be liable to, those are out of the question. It is your business to defend your own opinion. Can anything be plainer than that you are for changing all things into ideas? You, I say, who are not ashamed to charge me with *scepticism.* This is so plain, there is no denying it.

PHILONOUS: You mistake me. I am not for changing things into ideas, but rather ideas into things; since those immediate objects of perception, which, according to you, are only appearances of things, I take to be the real things themselves.

HYLAS: Things! You may pretend what you please; but it is certain you leave us nothing but the empty forms of things, the outside only which strikes the senses.

PHILONOUS: What you call the empty forms and outside of things seem to me the very things themselves. Nor are they empty or incomplete, otherwise than upon your supposition—that matter is an essential part of all corporeal things. We both, therefore, agree in this, that we perceive only sensible forms: but herein we differ—you will have them to be empty appearances, I real beings. In short, you do not trust your senses, I do.

HYLAS: You say you believe your senses; and seem to applaud yourself that in this you agree with the vulgar. According to you, therefore, the true nature of a thing is discovered by the senses. If so, whence comes that disagreement? Why is not the same figure, and other sensible qualities, perceived all manner of ways? And why should we use a microscope the better to discover the true nature of a body, if it were discoverable to the naked eye?

PHILONOUS: Strictly speaking, Hylas, we do not see the same object that we feel; neither is the same object perceived by the microscope which was by the naked eye. But, in case every variation was thought sufficient to constitute a new kind of individual, the endless number of confusion of names would render language impracticable. Therefore, to avoid this, as well as other inconveniences which are obvious upon a little thought, men combine together several ideas, apprehended by divers senses, or by the same sense at different times, or in different circumstances, but observed, however, to have some connexion in nature, either with respect to co-existence or succession; all which they refer to one name, and consider as one thing. Hence it follows that when I examine, by my other senses, a thing I have seen, it is not in order to understand better the same object which I had perceived by sight, the object of one sense not being perceived by the other senses. And, when I look through a microscope, it is not that I may perceive more clearly what I perceived already with my bare eyes; the object perceived by the glass being quite different from the former. But, in both cases, my aim is only to know what ideas are connected together; and the more a man knows of the connexion of ideas, the more he is said to know of the nature of things. What, therefore, if our ideas are variable; what if our senses are not in all circumstances affected with the same appearances. It will not thence follow they are not to be trusted; or that they are inconsistent either with themselves or anything else: except it be with your preconceived notion of (I know not what) one single, unchanged, unperceivable, real nature, marked by each name. Which prejudice seems to have taken its rise from not rightly understanding the common language of men, speaking of several distinct ideas as united into one thing by the mind. And, indeed, there is cause to suspect several erroneous conceits of the philosophers are owing to the same original: while they began to build their schemes not so much on notions as on words, which were framed by the vulgar, merely for conveniency and dispatch in the common actions of life, without any regard to speculation.

HYLAS: Methinks I apprehend your meaning.

PHILONOUS: It is your opinion the ideas we perceive by our senses are not real things, but images or copies of them. Our knowledge, therefore, is no farther real than as our ideas are the true representations of those originals. But, as these supposed originals are in themselves unknown, it is impossible to know how far our ideas resemble them; or whether they resemble them at all. We cannot, therefore, be sure we have any real knowledge. Farther, as our ideas are perpetually varied, without any change in the supposed real things, it necessarily follows they cannot all be true copies of them: or, if some are and others are not, it is impossible to distinguish the former from the latter. And this plunges us yet deeper in uncertainty. Again, when we consider the point, we cannot conceive how any idea, or anything like an idea, should have an absolute existence out of a mind: nor consequently, according to you, how there should be any real thing in nature. The result of all which is that we are thrown into the most hopeless and abandoned *scepticism.* Now, give me leave to ask you, *first,* whether your referring ideas to certain absolutely existing unperceived substances, as their originals, be not the source of all this *scepticism? Secondly,* whether you are informed, either by sense or reason, of the existence of those unknown originals? And, in case you are not, whether it be not absurd to suppose them? *Thirdly,* whether, upon inquiry, you find there is anything distinctly conceived or meant by the *absolute or external existence of unperceiving substances? Lastly,* whether, the premises considered, it be not the wisest way to follow nature, trust your senses, and, laying aside all anxious thought about unknown natures or substances, admit with the vulgar those for real things which are perceived by the senses?

HYLAS: For the present, I have no inclination to the answering part. I would much rather see how you can get over what follows. Pray are not the objects perceived by the senses of one, likewise perceivable to others present? If there were a hundred more here, they would all see the garden, the trees, and flowers, as I see them. But they are not in the same manner affected with the ideas I frame in my imagination. Does not this make a difference between the former sort of objects and the latter?

PHILONOUS: I grant it does. Nor have I ever denied a difference between the objects of sense and those of imagination. But what would you infer from thence? You cannot say that sensible objects exist unperceived, because they are perceived by many.

HYLAS: I own I can make nothing of that objection: but it hath led me into another. Is it not your opinion that by our senses we perceive only the ideas existing in our minds?

PHILONOUS: It is.

HYLAS: But the same idea which is in my mind cannot be in yours, or in any other mind. Does it not therefore follow, from your principles, that no two can see the same thing? And is not this highly absurd?

PHILONOUS: If the term *same* be taken in the vulgar acceptation, it is certain (and not at all repugnant to the principles I maintain) that different persons may perceive the same thing; or the same thing or idea exist in different minds. Words are of arbitrary imposition, and since men are used to apply the word *same* where no distinction or variety is perceived, and I do not pretend to alter their perceptions, it follows that, as men have said before, *several saw the same thing,* so they may, upon like occasions, still continue to use the same phrase, without any deviation either from propriety of language, or the truth of things. But, if the term *same* be used in the acceptation of philosophers, who pretend to an abstracted notion of identity, then, according to their sundry definitions of this notion (for it is not yet agreed wherein that philosophic identity consists), it may or may not be possible for divers persons to perceive the same thing. But whether philosophers shall think fit to call a thing the *same* or no, is, I conceive, of small importance. Let us suppose several men together, all endued with the same faculties, and consequently affected in like sort by their senses, and who had yet never known the use of language; they would, without question, agree in their perceptions. Though perhaps, when they came to the use of speech, some regarding the uniformness of what was perceived, might call it the *same* thing: others, especially regarding the diversity of persons who perceived, might choose the denomination of *different* things. But who sees not that all the dispute is about a word? To wit, whether what is perceived by different persons may yet have the term *same* applied to it? Or, suppose a house, whose walls or outward shell remaining unaltered, the chambers are all pulled down, and new ones built in their place; and that you should call this the *same,* and I should say it was not the *same* house:—would we not, for all this, perfectly agree in our thoughts of the house, considered in itself? And would not all the difference consist in a sound? If you should say, We differed in our notions; for that you superadded to your idea of the house the simple abstracted idea of identity, whereas I did not; I would tell you, I know not what you mean by the *abstracted idea of identity;* and should desire you to look into your own thoughts, and be sure you understood yourself.—Why so silent, Hylas? Are you not yet satisfied men may dispute about identity and diversity, without any real difference in their thoughts and opinions, abstracted from names? Take this farther reflexion with you—that whether matter be allowed to exist or no, the case is exactly the same as to the point in hand. For the materialists themselves acknowledge what we immediately perceive by our senses to be our own ideas. Your difficulty, therefore, that no two see the same thing, makes equally against the materialists and me.

HYLAS: But they suppose an external archetype, to which referring their several ideas they may truly be said to perceive the same thing.

PHILONOUS: And (not to mention your having discarded those archetypes) so may you suppose an external archetype on my principles; *external,* I mean, to your own mind: though indeed it must be supposed to exist in that mind which comprehends all things; but then, this serves all the ends of identity, as well as if it existed out of a mind. And I am sure you yourself will not say it is less intelligible.

HYLAS: You have indeed clearly satisfied me—either that there is no difficulty at bottom in this point; or, if there be, that it makes equally against both opinions.

PHILONOUS: But that which makes equally against two contradictory opinions can be a proof against neither.

HYLAS: I acknowledge it. But, after all, Philonous, when I consider the substance of what you advance against *scepticism,* it amounts to no more than this:—We are sure that we really see, hear, feel; in a word, that we are affected with sensible impressions.

PHILONOUS: And how are we concerned any farther? I see this *cherry,* I feel it, I taste it: and I am sure *nothing* cannot be seen, or felt, or tasted: it is therefore *real.* Take away the sensations of softness, moisture, redness, tartness, and you take away the *cherry,* since it is not a being distinct from sensations. A *cherry,* I say, is nothing but a congeries of sensible impressions, or ideas perceived by various senses: which ideas are united into one thing (or have one name given them) by the mind, because they are observed to attend each other. Thus, when the palate is affected with such a particular taste, the sight is affected with a red colour, the touch with roundness, softness, &c. Hence, when I see, and feel, and taste, in such sundry certain manners, I am sure the *cherry* exists, or is real; its reality being in my opinion nothing abstracted from those sensations. But if by the word *cherry* you mean an unknown nature, distinct from all those sensible qualities, and by its existence something distinct from its being perceived; then, indeed, I own, neither you nor I, nor any one else, can be sure it exists.

HYLAS: But, what would you say, Philonous, if I should bring the very same reasons against the existence of sensible things in a mind, which you have offered against their existing in a material *substratum?*

PHILONOUS: When I see your reasons, you shall hear what I have to say to them.

HYLAS: Is the mind extended or unextended?

PHILONOUS: Unextended, without doubt.

HYLAS: Do you say the things you perceive are in your mind?

PHILONOUS: They are.

HYLAS: Again, have I not heard you speak of sensible impressions?

PHILONOUS: I believe you may.

HYLAS: Explain to me now, O Philonous! how it is possible there should be room for all those trees and houses to exist in your mind. Can extended things be contained in that which is unextended? Or, are we to imagine impressions made on a thing void of all solidity? You cannot say objects are in your mind, as books in your study: or that things are imprinted on it, as the figure of a seal upon wax. In what sense, therefore, are we to understand those expressions? Explain me this if you can: and I shall then be able to answer all those queries you formerly put to me about my *substratum.*

PHILONOUS: Look you, Hylas, when I speak of objects as existing in the mind, or imprinted on the senses, I would not be understood in the gross literal sense, as when bodies are said to exist in a place, or a seal to make an impression upon wax. My meaning is only that the mind comprehends or perceives them; and that it is affected from without, or by some being distinct from itself. This is my explication of your difficulty; and how it can serve to make your tenet of an unperceiving material substratum intelligible, I would fain know.

HYLAS: Nay, if that be all, I confess I do not see what use can be made of it. But are you not guilty of some abuse of language in this?

PHILONOUS: None at all. It is no more than common custom, which you know is the rule of language, hath authorised: nothing being more usual, than for philosophers to speak of the immediate objects of the understanding as things existing in the mind. Nor is there anything in this but what is conformable to the general analogy of language; most part of the mental operations being signified by words borrowed from sensible things; as is plain in the terms *comprehend, reflect, discourse,* etc., which, being applied to the mind, must not be taken in their gross, original sense.

HYLAS: You have, I own, satisfied me in this point. But there still remains one great difficulty, which I know not how you will get over. And, indeed, it is of such importance that if you could solve all others, without being able to find a solution for this, you must never expect to make me a proselyte to your principles.

PHILONOUS: Let me know this mighty difficulty.

HYLAS: The Scripture account of the creation is what appears to me utterly irreconcilable with your notions. Moses tells us of a creation: a creation of what? Of ideas? No, certainly, but of things, of real things, solid corporeal substances. Bring your principles to agree with this, and I shall perhaps agree with you.

PHILONOUS: Moses mentions the sun, moon, and stars, earth and sea, plants and animals. That all these do really exist, and were in the beginning created by God, I make no question. If by *ideas* you mean fictions and fancies of the mind, then these are no ideas. If by *ideas* you mean immediate objects of the understanding, or sensible things, which cannot exist unperceived, or out of a mind, then these things are ideas. But whether you do or do not call them *ideas,* it matters little. The difference is only about a name. And, whether that name be retained or rejected, the sense, the truth, and reality of things continues the same. In common talk, the objects of our senses are not termed *ideas,* but *things.* Call them so still: provided you do not attribute to them any absolute external existence, and I shall never quarrel with you for a word. The creation, therefore, I allow to have been a creation of things, of *real* things. Neither is this in the least inconsistent with my principles, as is evident from what I have now said; and would have been evident to you without this, if you had not forgotten what had been so often said before. But as for solid corporeal substances, I desire you to show where Moses makes any mention of them; and, if they should be mentioned by him, or any other inspired writer, it would still be incumbent on you to show those words were not taken in the vulgar acceptation, for things falling under our senses, but in the philosophic acceptation, for matter, or an unknown quiddity, with an absolute existence. When you have proved these points, then (and not till then) may you bring the authority of Moses into our dispute.

HYLAS: It is in vain to dispute about a point so clear. I am content to refer it to your own conscience. Are you not satisfied there is some peculiar repugnancy between the Mosaic account of the creation and your notions?

PHILONOUS: If all possible sense which can be put on the first chapter of Genesis may be conceived as consistently with my principles as any other, then it has no peculiar repugnancy with them. But there is no sense you may not as well conceive, believing as

I do. Since, besides spirits, all you conceive are ideas; and the existence of these I do not deny. Neither do you pretend they exist without the mind.

HYLAS: Pray let me see any sense you can understand it in.

PHILONOUS: Why, I imagine that if I had been present at the creation, I should have seen things produced into being—that is become perceptible—in the order prescribed by the sacred historian. I never before believed the Mosaic account of the creation, and now find no alteration in my manner of believing it. When things are said to begin or end their existence, we do not mean this with regard to God, but His creatures. All objects are eternally known by God, or, which is the same thing, have an eternal existence in His mind: but when things, before imperceptible to creatures, are, by a decree of God, perceptible to them, then are they said to begin a relative existence, with respect to created minds. Upon reading therefore the Mosaic account of the creation, I understand that the several parts of the world became gradually perceivable to finite spirits, endowed with proper faculties; so that, whoever such were present, they were in truth perceived by them. This is the literal obvious sense suggested to me by the words of the Holy Scripture: in which is included no mention, or no thought, either of *substratum,* instrument, occasion, or absolute existence. And, upon inquiry, I doubt not it will be found that most plain honest men, who believe the creation, never think of those things any more than I. What metaphysical sense you may understand it in, you only can tell.

HYLAS: But, Philonous, you do not seem to be aware that you allow created things, in the beginning, only a relative, and consequently hypothetical being: that is to say, upon supposition there were men to perceive them; without which they have no actuality of absolute existence, wherein creation might terminate. Is it not, therefore, according to you, plainly impossible the creation of any inanimate creatures should precede that of man? And is not this directly contrary to the Mosaic account?

PHILONOUS: In answer to that, I say, *first,* created beings might begin to exist in the mind of other created intelligences, beside men. You will not therefore be able to prove any contradiction between Moses and my notions, unless you first show there was no other order of finite created spirits in being, before man. I say farther, in case we conceive the creation, as we should at this time, a parcel of plants or vegetables of all sorts produced, by an invisible Power, in a desert where nobody was present—that this way of explaining or conceiving it is consistent with my principles, since they deprive you of nothing, either sensible or imaginable; that it exactly suits with the common, natural, and undebauched notions of mankind; that it manifests the dependence of all things on God; and consequently hath all the good effect or influence, which it is possible that important article of our faith should have in making men humble, thankful, and resigned to their great creator. I say, moreover, that, in this naked conception of things, divested of words, there will not be found any notion of what you call the *actuality of absolute existence.* You may indeed raise a dust with those terms, and so lengthen our dispute to no purpose. But I entreat you calmly to look into your own thoughts, and then tell me if they are not a useless and unintelligible jargon.

HYLAS: I own I have no very clear notion annexed to them. But what say you to this? Do you not make the existence of sensible things consist in their being in a mind? And were not all things eternally in the mind of God? Did they not therefore exist from all eternity, according to you? And how could that which was eternal be created in time? Can anything be clearer or better connected than this?

PHILONOUS: And are not you too of opinion, that God knew all things from eternity?

HYLAS: I am.

PHILONOUS: Consequently they always had a being in the divine intellect.

HYLAS: This I acknowledge.

PHILONOUS: By your own confession, therefore, nothing is new, or begins to be, in respect of the mind of God. So we are agreed in that point.

HYLAS: What shall we make then of the creation?

PHILONOUS: May we not understand it to have been entirely in respect of finite spirits; so that things, with regard to us, may properly be said to begin their existence, or be created, when God decreed they should become perceptible to intelligent creatures, in that order and manner which he then established, and we now call the laws of nature? You may call this a *relative,* or *hypothetical existence* if you please. But, so long as it supplies us with the most natural, obvious, and literal sense of the Mosaic history of the creation; so long as it answers all the religious ends of that great article; in a word, so long as you can assign no other sense or meaning in its stead; why should we reject this? Is it to comply with a ridiculous sceptical humour of making everything nonsense and unintelligible? I am sure you cannot say it is for the glory of God. For, allowing it to be a thing possible and conceivable that the corporeal world should have an absolute existence extrinsical to the mind of God, as well as to the minds of all created spirits; yet how could this set forth either the immensity or omniscience of the Deity, or the necessary and immediate dependence of all things on him? Nay, would it not rather seem to derogate from those attributes?

HYLAS: Well, but as to this decree of God's, for making things perceptible, what say you, Philonous? Is it not plain, God did either execute that decree from all eternity or at some certain time began to will what he had not actually willed before, but only designed to will? If the former, then there could be no creation, or beginning of existence, in finite things. If the latter, then we must acknowledge something new to befall the Deity; which implies a sort of change: and all change argues imperfection.

PHILONOUS: Pray consider what you are doing. Is it not evident this objection concludes equally against a creation in any sense; nay, against every other act of the Deity, discoverable by the light of nature? None of which can we conceive, otherwise than as performed in time, and having a beginning. God is a being of transcendent and unlimited perfections: His nature, therefore, is incomprehensible to finite spirits. It is not, therefore, to be expected that any man, whether *materialist* or *immaterialist,* should have exactly just notions of the Deity, His attributes, and ways of operation. If then you would infer anything against me, your difficulty must not be drawn from the inadequateness of our conceptions of the divine nature, which is unavoidable on any scheme; but from the denial of matter, of which there is not one word, directly or indirectly, in what you have now objected.

HYLAS: I must acknowledge the difficulties you are concerned to clear are such only as arise from the non-existence of matter, and are peculiar to that notion. So far you are in the right. But I cannot by any means bring myself to think there is no such peculiar repugnancy between the creation and your opinion; though indeed where to fix it, I do not distinctly know.

PHILONOUS: What would you have? Do I not acknowledge a twofold state of things—the one ectypal or natural, the other archetypal and eternal? The former was created in time; the latter existed from everlasting in the mind of God. Is not this agreeable to the common notions of divines? or, is any more than this necessary in order to conceive the creation? But you suspect some peculiar repugnancy, though you know not where it lies. To take away all possibility of scruple in the case, do but consider this one point. Either you are not able to conceive the creation on any hypothesis whatsoever; and, if so, there is no ground for dislike or complaint against any particular opinion on that score: or you are able to conceive it; and, if so, why not on my principles, since thereby nothing conceivable is taken away? You have all along been allowed the full scope of sense, imagination, and reason. Whatever, therefore, you could before apprehend, either immediately or mediately by your senses, or by ratiocination from your senses; whatever you could perceive, imagine, or understand, remains still with you. If, therefore, the notion you have of the creation by other principles be intelligible, you have it still upon mine; if it be not intelligible, I conceive it to be no notion at all; and so there is no loss of it. And indeed it seems to me very plain that the supposition of matter, that is a thing perfectly unknown and inconceivable, cannot serve to make us conceive anything. And, I hope it need not be proved to you that if the existence of matter does not make the creation conceivable, the creation's being without it inconceivable can be no objection against its non-existence.

HYLAS: I confess, Philonous, you have almost satisfied me in this point of the creation.

PHILONOUS: I would fain know why you are not quite satisfied. You tell me indeed of a repugnancy between the Mosaic history and immaterialism: but you know not where it lies. Is this reasonable, Hylas? Can you expect I should solve a difficulty without knowing what it is? But, to pass by all that, would not a man think you were assured there is no repugnancy between the received notions of materialists and the inspired writings?

HYLAS: And so I am.

PHILONOUS: Ought the historical part of Scripture to be understood in a plain obvious sense, or in a sense which is metaphysical and out of the way?

HYLAS: In the plain sense, doubtless.

PHILONOUS: When Moses speaks of herbs, earth, water, &c. as having been created by God; think you not the sensible things commonly signified by those words are suggested to every unphilosophical reader?

HYLAS: I cannot help thinking so.

PHILONOUS: And are not all ideas, or things perceived by sense, to be denied a real existence by the doctrine of the materialist?

HYLAS: This I have already acknowledged.

PHILONOUS: The creation, therefore, according to them, was not the creation of things sensible, which have only a relative being, but of certain unknown natures, which have an absolute being, wherein creation might terminate?

HYLAS: True.

PHILONOUS: Is it not therefore evident the assertors of matter destroy the plain obvious sense of Moses, with which their notions are utterly inconsistent; and instead of it obtrude on us I know not what; something equally unintelligible to themselves and me?

HYLAS: I cannot contradict you.

PHILONOUS: Moses tells us of a creation. A creation of what? of unknown quiddities, of occasions, or *substratum?* No, certainly; but of things obvious to the senses. You must first reconcile this with your notions, if you expect I should be reconciled to them.

HYLAS: I see you can assault me with my own weapons.

PHILONOUS: Then as to *absolute existence;* was there ever known a more jejune notion than that? Something it is so abstracted and unintelligible that you have frankly owned you could not conceive it, much less explain anything by it. But allowing matter to exist, and the notion of absolute existence to be clear as light; yet, was this ever known to make the creation more credible? Nay, hath it not furnished the atheists and infidels of all ages with the most plausible arguments against a creation? That a corporeal substance, which hath an absolute existence without the minds of spirits, should be produced out of nothing, by the mere will of a spirit, hath been looked upon as a thing so contrary to all reason, so impossible and absurd, that not only the most celebrated among the ancients, but even divers modern and Christian philosophers have thought matter co-eternal with the Deity. Lay these things together, and then judge you whether materialism disposes men to believe the creation of things.

HYLAS: I own, Philonous, I think it does not. This of the *creation* is the last objection I can think of; and I must needs own it hath been sufficiently answered as well as the rest. Nothing now remains to be overcome but a sort of unaccountable backwardness that I find in myself towards your notions.

PHILONOUS: When a man is swayed, he knows not why, to one side of the question, can this, think you, be anything else but the effect of prejudice, which never fails to attend old and rooted notions? And indeed in this respect I cannot deny the belief of matter to have very much the advantage over the contrary opinion, with men of a learned education.

HYLAS: I confess it seems to be as you say.

PHILONOUS: As a balance, therefore, to this weight of prejudice, let us throw into the scale the great advantages that arise from the belief of immaterialism, both in regard to religion and human learning. The being of a God, and incorruptibility of the soul, those great articles of religion, are they not proved with the clearest and most immediate evidence? When I say the being of a *God,* I do not mean an obscure general cause of things, whereof we have no conception, but *God,* in the strict and proper sense of the word. A being whose spirituality, omnipresence, providence, omniscience, infinite power and goodness, are as conspicuous as the existence of sensible things, of which (nothwithstanding the fallacious pretences and affected scruples of *sceptics*) there is no more reason to doubt than of our own being. Then, with relation to human sciences. In natural philosophy, what intricacies, what obscurities, what contradictions hath the belief of matter led men into! To say nothing of the numberless disputes about its extent, continuity, homogeneity, gravity, divisibility, &c.—do they not pretend to explain all things by bodies operating on bodies, according to the laws of motion? And yet, are they able to comprehend how one body should move another? Nay, admitting there was no difficulty in reconciling the notion of an inert being with a cause, or in conceiving how an accident might pass from one body to another; yet, by all their strained thoughts and extravagant suppositions, have they been able to reach the mechanical production of any one animal or vegetable body? Can they account, by the laws of motion, for sounds, tastes, smells, or colours; or for the regular course of things? Have they accounted, by physical principles, for the aptitude and contrivance even of the most inconsiderable parts of the universe? But, laying aside matter and corporeal causes, and admitting only the efficiency of an all-perfect mind, are not all the effects of nature easy and intelligible? If the *phenomena* are nothing else but *ideas;* God is a *spirit,* but matter an unintelligent, unperceiving being. If they demonstrate an unlimited power in their cause; God is active and omnipotent, but matter an inert mass. If the order regularity, and usefulness of them can never be sufficiently admired; God is infinitely wise and provident, but matter destitute of all contrivance and design. These surely are great advantages in *physics.* Not to mention that the apprehension of a distant Deity naturally disposes men to a negligence in their *moral* actions; which they would be more cautious of, in case they thought him immediately present, and acting on their minds, without the interposition of matter, or unthinking second causes. Then in *metaphysics:* what difficulties concerning entity in abstract, substantial forms, hylarchic principles, plastic natures, substance and accident, principle of individuation, possibility of matter's thinking, origin of ideas, the manner how two independent substances so widely different as *spirit* and *matter,* should mutually operate on each other? What difficulties, I say, and endless disquisitions, concerning these and innumerable other the like points, do we escape, by supposing only spirits and ideas? Even the *mathematics* themselves, if we take away the absolute existence of extended things, become much more clear and easy; the most shocking paradoxes and intricate speculations in those sciences depending on the infinite divisibility of finite extension; which depends on that supposition. But what need is there to insist on the particular sciences? Is not that opposition to all science whatsoever, that frenzy of the ancient and modern *sceptics,* built on the same foundation? Or can you produce so much as one argument against the reality of corporeal things, or in behalf of that avowed utter ignorance of their natures, which does not suppose their reality to consist in an external absolute existence? Upon this supposition, indeed, the objections from the change of colours in a pigeon's neck, or the appearance of the broken oar in the water, must be allowed to have weight. But these and the like objections vanish, if we do not maintain the being of absolute external originals, but place the reality of things in ideas, fleeting indeed, and changeable; however, not changed at random, but according to the fixed order of nature. For, herein consists that constancy and truth of things which secures all the concerns of life, and distinguishes that which is *real* from the irregular visions of the fancy.

HYLAS: I agree to all you have now said, and must own that nothing can incline me to embrace your opinion more than the advantages I see it is attended with. I am by nature lazy; and this would be a mighty abridgment in knowledge. What doubts, what hypotheses, what labyrinths of amusement, what fields of disputation, what an ocean of false learning, may be avoided by that single notion of *immaterialism!*

PHILONOUS: After all, is there anything farther remaining to be done? You may remember you promised to embrace that opinion which upon examination should appear most agreeable to common sense and remote from *scepticism.* This, by your own confession, is that which denies matter, or the absolute existence of corporeal things. Nor is this all; the same notion has been proved several ways, viewed in different lights, pursued in its consequences, and all objections against it cleared. Can there be a greater evidence of its truth? Or is it possible it should have all the marks of a true opinion and yet be false?

HYLAS: I own myself entirely satisfied for the present in all respects. But, what security can I have that I shall still continue the same full assent to your opinion, and that no unthought-of objection or difficulty will occur hereafter?

PHILONOUS: Pray, Hylas, do you in other cases, when a point is once evidently proved, withhold your consent on account of objections or difficulties it may be liable to? Are the difficulties that attend the doctrine of incommensurable quantities, of the angle of contact, of the asymptotes to curves, or the like, sufficient to make you hold out against mathematical demonstration? Or will you disbelieve the Providence of God, because there may be some particular things which you know not how to reconcile with it? If there are difficulties attending *immaterialism,* there are at the same time direct and evident proofs of it. But for the existence of matter there is not one proof, and far more numerous and insurmountable objections lie against it. But where are those mighty difficulties you insist on? Alas! you know not where or what they are; something which may possibly occur hereafter. If this be a sufficient pretence for withholding your full assent, you should never yield it to any proposition, how free soever from exceptions, how clearly and solidly soever demonstrated.

HYLAS: You have satisfied me, Philonous.

PHILONOUS: But, to arm you against all future objections, do but consider: That which bears equally hard on two contradictory opinions can be proof against neither. Whenever, therefore, any difficulty occurs, try if you can find a solution for it on the hypothesis of the *materialists*. Be not deceived by words; but sound your own thoughts. And in case you cannot conceive it easier by the help of *materialism*, it is plain it can be no objection against *immaterialism*. Had you proceeded all along by this rule, you would probably have spared yourself abundance of trouble in objecting; since of all your difficulties I challenge you to show one that is explained by matter: nay, which is not more unintelligible with than without that supposition; and consequently makes rather *against* than *for* it. You should consider, in each particular, whether the difficulty arises from the *non-existence of matter*. If it does not, you might as well argue from the infinite divisibility of extension against the divine prescience, as from such a difficulty against *immaterialism*. And yet, upon recollection, I believe you will find this to have been often, if not always, the case. You should likewise take heed not to argue on a *petitio principii*. One is apt to say, the unknown substances ought to be esteemed real things, rather than the ideas in our minds: and who can tell but the unthinking external substance may concur, as a cause or instrument, in the productions of our ideas? But is not this proceeding on a supposition that there are such external substances? And to suppose this is it not begging the question? But, above all things, you should beware of imposing on yourself by that vulgar sophism which is called *ignoratio elenchi*. You talked often as if you thought I maintained the non-existence of Sensible Things. Whereas in truth no one can be more thoroughly assured of their existence than I am. And it is you who doubt; I should have said, positively deny it. Everything that is seen, felt, heard, or any way perceived by the senses, is, on the principles I embrace, a real being; but not on yours. Remember, the matter you contend for is an unknown somewhat (if indeed it may be termed *somewhat*), which is quite stripped of all sensible qualities, and can neither be perceived by sense, nor apprehended by the mind. Remember I say, that it is not any object which is hard or soft, hot or cold, blue or white, round or square, &c. For all these things I affirm do exist. Though indeed I deny they have an existence distinct from being perceived; or that they exist out of all minds whatsoever. Think on these points; let them be attentively considered and still kept in view. Otherwise you will not comprehend the state of the question; without which your objections will always be wide of the mark, and, instead of mine, may possibly be directed (as more than once they have been) against your own notions.

HYLAS: I must needs own, Philonous, nothing seems to have kept me from agreeing with you more than this same *mistaking the question*. In denying matter, at first glimpse I am tempted to imagine you deny the things we see and feel: but, upon reflexion, find there is no ground for it. What think you, therefore, of retaining the name *matter*, and applying it to sensible things? This may be done without any change in your sentiments: and, believe me, it would be a means of reconciling them to some persons who may be more shocked at an innovation in words than in opinion.

PHILONOUS: With all my heart: retain the word *matter*, and apply it to the objects of sense, if you please; provided you do not attribute to them any subsistence distinct from their being perceived. I shall never quarrel with you for an expression. *Matter*, or *material substance*, are terms introduced by philosophers; and, as used by them, imply a sort of independency, or a subsistence distinct from being perceived by a mind: but are never used by common people; or, if ever, it is to signify the immediate objects of sense. One would think, therefore, so long as the names of all particular things, with the terms *sensible, substance, body, stuff,* and the like, are retained, the word *matter* should be never missed in common talk. And in philosophical discourses it seems the best way to leave it quite out: since there is not, perhaps, any one thing that hath more favoured and strengthened the depraved bent of the mind towards Atheism than the use of that general confused term.

HYLAS: Well but, Philonous, since I am content to give up the notion of an unthinking substance exterior to the mind, I think you ought not to deny me the privilege of using the word *matter* as I please, and annexing it to a collection of sensible qualities subsisting only in the mind. I freely own there is no other substance, in a strict sense, than *spirit.* But I have been so long accustomed to the term *matter* that I know not how to part with it: to say, there is no matter in the world, is still shocking to me. Whereas to say, there is no *matter,* if by that term be meant an unthinking substance existing without the mind; but if by matter is meant some sensible thing, whose existence consists in being perceived, then there is matter: this distinction gives it quite another turn; and men will come into your notions with small difficulty, when they are proposed in that manner. For, after all, the controversy about *matter* in the strict acceptation of it, lies altogether between you and the philosophers: whose principles, I acknowledge, are not near so natural, or so agreeable to the common sense of mankind, and Holy Scripture, as yours. There is nothing we either desire or shun but as it makes, or is apprehended to make, some part of our happiness or misery. But what has happiness or misery, joy or grief, pleasure or pain, to do with absolute existence; or with unknown entities, abstracted from all relation to us? It is evident, things regard us only as they are pleasing or displeasing: and they can please or displease only so far forth as they are perceived. Farther, therefore, we are not concerned, and thus far you leave things as you found them. Yet still there is something new in this doctrine. It is plain, I do not now think with the philosophers; nor yet altogether with the vulgar. I would know how the case stands in that respect; precisely, what you have added to, or altered in my former notions.

PHILONOUS: I do not pretend to be a setter-up of new notions. My endeavours tend only to unite, and place in a clearer light, that truth which was before shared between the vulgar and the philosophers:—the former being of opinion, that *those things they immediately perceive are the real things;* and the latter, that *the things immediately perceived are ideas, which exist only in the mind.* Which two notions put together, do, in effect, constitute the substance of what I advance.

HYLAS: I have been a long time distrusting my senses: methought I saw things by a dim light and through false glasses. Now the glasses are removed and a new light breaks in upon my understanding. I am clearly convinced that I see things in their native forms, and am no longer in pain about their *unknown natures* or *absolute existence.* This is the state I find myself in at present; though, indeed, the course that brought me to it I do not yet thoroughly comprehend. You set out upon the same principles that Academics, Cartesians, and the like sects usually do; and for a long time it looked as if you were advancing their philosophical *scepticism:* but, in the end, your conclusions are directly opposite to theirs.

PHILONOUS: You see, Hylas, the water of yonder fountain, how it is forced upwards, in a round column, to a certain height; at which it breaks, and falls back into the basin from whence it rose: its ascent, as well as descent, proceeding from the same uniform law or principle of *gravitation.* Just so, the same principles which, at first view, lead to *scepticism,* pursued to a certain point, bring men back to common sense.

David Hume
1711–1776

David Hume was born in Edinburgh, Scotland, in 1711. His father, a lawyer, died before David was 2 years old. He was raised by his mother, a deeply religious woman, on a pleasant, but modest, family estate at Ninewells, near Berwick in southern Scotland. Young David was very religious as a boy, often making lists of his sins so that he could seek forgiveness. But shortly after beginning his studies at the University of Edinburgh, at age 12, he seems to have lost his faith.

Although the family was not poor, there was not enough wealth to provide a comfortable life of study for David, the youngest child. His family decided, therefore, that Hume should follow his father into law. This was not to be, however, for as Hume later wrote, "I found an unsurmountable aversion to everything but the pursuit of philosophy and general learning."

In 1729, when he was only 18, Hume had a breakthrough, discovering what he called "a new Science of Thought." He gave up all pretense of becoming a lawyer and applied his energies to his new insight. To conserve his limited finances, he moved to a small town in France, La Flèche, where Descartes had studied. There he completed his first work, *A Treatise of Human Nature, Being an Attempt to Introduce the Experimental Method of Reasoning into Moral Subjects*, published in 1739 and 1740. Hume hoped this work would give him his "love of literary fame"—while putting him in a more comfortable financial situation. But, as he later said, the work "fell dead-born from the press, without reaching such distinction as even to excite a murmur among the zealots."

For the next thirteen years, Hume held a variety of positions, including tutor to a mad marquess and secretary to a general. During this time, he wrote and published his *Essays, Moral and Political* (1741–1742). The success of this work led him to rewrite Book I of his earlier *Treatise*, this time titled as *An Enquiry Concerning Human Understanding* (1748). He added chapters on miracles, free will, and the argument from design, which he had left out of the earlier work, and he omitted many of his psychological speculations. This book enjoyed some success, though its antireligious nature may have contributed to Hume's rejected applications for two different chairs of philosophy. In 1751, he also recast Book III of the earlier *Treatise*, under the title *Enquiry Concerning the Principles of Morals*.

Hume was appointed Librarian to the Faculty of Advocates in Edinburgh in 1752. In this post, he wrote a multivolume history of England. He also managed to infuriate the library curators with his selections, and in 1757 he was forced to resign when he refused to remove books the curators considered obscene. In the same year, he published *Four Dissertations*, including "The Natural History of Religion," "Of the Passions" (a truncated version of Book II of the *Treatise*), "Of Tragedy," and "Of the Standard of Taste." By now, Hume's works had become well known on the Continent, and when he returned to France in 1763 as part of the British ambassador's staff, he was lionized by French intellectual society. Hume was a favorite at French soirées: Sociable and witty, he was called "le bon David" by his French friends.

When Hume returned to England in 1766, he found that his works had finally brought him the literary fame at home that he had so long desired. In 1767, he took another government post, but two years later he resigned and retired to Edinburgh. There he spent his last years quietly, until his death, probably from cancer, in 1776. His *Dialogues Concerning Natural Religion*, written in the 1750s, was published posthumously in 1779.

* * *

Hume's philosophy, as developed in the *Enquiry*, begins with a rejection of the "abstruse speculations" and "superstitions" of contemporary thought. With Locke, Hume agrees that there are no such things as innate ideas; all knowledge comes through sensory experience. Yet as he worked out the implications of these convictions, he came to conclusions quite different from those of his predecessor.

According to Hume, all the perceptions of the mind may be divided into "impressions" and "ideas." Using an empirical distinction, Hume believes impressions to be "more lively" than ideas. These impressions and ideas are then divided into simple and complex, impressions of sensation and impressions of reflection, and so on. The source of impressions cannot be known empirically, so Hume does not address this question. Simple ideas, on the other hand, must come from impressions. In fact, for an idea to have any meaning whatever, it must be derived from an impression or from a combination of impressions. If I have the idea of a gold mountain, for instance, it is because I have previously had impressions that gave rise to the ideas of "gold" and "mountain" that I am now associating. Using this empirical criterion of meaning, it becomes clear that ideas such as "substance," "God," or even "the self" are without a clear meaning. So according to Hume, Locke's idea of an eternal world of "substances" and Berkeley's idea of an all-perceiving God are without meaning.

Hume then considers the association between ideas and argues that there are "only three principles of connexion among ideas, namely, *Resemblance*, *Contiguity* in time or place, and *Cause* or *Effect*." These associations of ideas are really nothing more than habit or "custom" and so do not necessarily reflect the "real world." Take causality, for example. One could imagine Pavlov's dogs hearing the bell, getting the food, hearing the bell, getting the food, hearing the bell . . . and after a period of time concluding, "bells cause food." But there is obviously no necessary relation between cause and effect in this case. There is no logical reason why the bell might not sound and yet no food appears. Hume argues that all supposed instances of cause and effect are of this kind. We get so used to seeing two events joined that we conclude that one caused the other. Thus, according to Hume, Locke's claim that the "external world" causes sensations and the Thomistic First-Cause argument for God's existence are without empirical foundation. It also means that the "laws of nature" are founded only on past experience and that we have no *a priori* evidence that tomorrow will be the same as today.

The remainder of the *Enquiry* develops the implications of Hume's radical empiricism and deals with the skepticism arising from it. He acknowledges that his own practice does not always reflect his philosophical position. Hume recognizes that despite his causal skepticism, it would not be wise to "throw himself out at the window." As he wrote early on in this work, we must "be modest in our pretensions; and even to discover the difficulty ourselves before it is objected to us. By this means, we may make a kind of merit of our very ignorance."

Philosophers differ in their appraisals of Hume's two greatest works, the *Treatise* and its reworking, the *Enquiry*. Many consider the *Enquiry* more mature; others think the *Treatise* more brilliant. Hume himself said that the *Enquiry*, not the *Treatise*, contained his "philosophical sentiments and principles." The *Enquiry* is reprinted here complete.

* * *

For a comprehensive biography of Hume, including interesting material from his letters, see Ernest Campbell Mossner, *The Life of David Hume* (Oxford: Clarendon Press, 1954, 1980). The classic studies of Hume's thought are Charles William Hendel, *Studies in the Philosophy of David Hume* (Princeton, NJ: Princeton University Press, 1925); and, especially, Norman Kemp Smith, *The Philosophy of David Hume* (London: Macmillan, 1941). Short, clear overviews of his thought include A.J. Ayer, *Hume* (New York: Oxford University Press, 1981)—part of the "Past Masters" series, now reprinted in a combined volume, John Dunn et al., eds., *The British Empiricists* (Oxford: Oxford University Press, 1992), and Anthony Quinton, *Hume* (London: Routledge, 1999). Barry Stroud, *Hume* (Oxford: Routledge, 1981); Terence Penelhum, *David Hume: An Introduction to His Philosophical System* (West Lafayette, IN: Purdue University Press, 1995); Don Garrett, *Hume* (London: Routledge, 2006); and Angela M. Coventry, *Hume: A Guide for the Perplexed* (London: Continuum, 2007) are also useful. For studies in specific areas of Hume's thought, see Tom L. Beauchamp, *Hume and the Problem of Causation* (New York: Oxford University Press, 1981); Robert J. Fogelin, *Hume's Skepticism in the* Treatise of Human Nature (London: Routledge, 1985); David Pears, *Hume's System* (Oxford: Oxford University Press, 1991), George Dicker, *Hume's Epistemology and Metaphysics* (London: Routledge, 1998); H.O. Mounce, *Hume's Naturalism* (London: Routledge, 1999); Harold Noonan, *Routledge Philosophy Guidebook to Hume on Knowledge* (London: Routledge, 1999); A.E. Pitson, *Hume's Philosophy of the Self* (London: Routledge, 2002); Angela M. Coventry, *Hume's Theory of Causation* (London: Continuum, 2006); and Alan Bailey and Dan O'Brien, *Hume's* Enquiry Concerning Human

Understanding: *A Reader's Guide* (London: Continuum, 2006) for epistemology and philosophy of mind; Jonathan Harrison, *Hume's Moral Epistemology* (Oxford: Clarendon Press, 1976), J.L. Mackie, *Hume's Moral Theory* (London: Routledge & Kegan Paul, 1980); and James Baillie, *Routledge Philosophy Guidebook to Hume on Morality* (London: Routledge, 2000) for ethics; and Antony Flew, *Hume's Philosophy of Belief* (London: Routledge & Kegan Paul; New York: Humanities Press, 1961); J.C.A. Gaskin, *Hume's Philosophy of Religion* (New York: Barnes & Noble, 1978); Keith E. Yandell, *Hume's "Inexplicable Mystery": His Views on Religion* (Philadelphia: Temple University Press, 1990); Stanley Tweyman, ed., *David Hume—*Dialogues Concerning Natural Religion *in Focus* (Oxford: Routledge, 1991); David Johnson, *Hume, Holism, and Miracles* (Ithaca, NY: Cornell University Press, 1999); John Earman, *Hume's Abject Failure: The Argument Against Miracles* (Oxford: Oxford University Press, 2000); and David O'Connor, *Routledge Philosophy Guidebook to Hume on Religion* (London: Routledge, 2001) for philosophy of religion. For collections of essays, see David Pears, ed., *David Hume: A Symposium* (London: St. Martin's Press, 1963); A. Sesonke and N. Fleming, eds., *Human Understanding: Studies in the Philosophy of David Hume* (Belmont, CA: Wadsworth, 1965); Vere Chappell, ed., *Hume: A Collection of Critical Essays* (Notre Dame, IN: Notre Dame University Press, 1968); Stanley Tweyman, ed., *David Hume: Critical Assessments,* six volumes (London: Routledge, 1996); and David W.D. Owen, ed., *Hume: General Philosophy* (New York: Ashgate, 2000).

AN ENQUIRY CONCERNING HUMAN UNDERSTANDING

SECTION I. OF THE DIFFERENT SPECIES OF PHILOSOPHY

Moral philosophy, or the science of human nature, may be treated after two different manners; each of which has its peculiar merit, and may contribute to the entertainment, instruction, and reformation of mankind. The one considers man chiefly as born for action; and as influenced in his measures by taste and sentiment; pursuing one object, and avoiding another, according to the value which these objects seem to possess, and according to the light in which they present themselves. As virtue, of all objects, is allowed to be the most valuable, this species of philosophers paint her in the most amiable colours; borrowing all helps from poetry and eloquence, and treating their subject in an easy and obvious manner, and such as is best fitted to please the imagination, and engage the affections. They select the most striking observations and instances from common life; place opposite characters in a proper contrast; and alluring us into the paths of virtue by the views of glory and happiness, direct our steps in these paths by the soundest precepts and most illustrious examples. They make us *feel* the difference between vice and virtue; they excite and regulate our sentiments; and so they can but bend our hearts to the love of probity and true honour, they think, that they have fully attained the end of all their labours.

The other species of philosophers consider man in the light of a reasonable rather than an active being, and endeavour to form his understanding more than cultivate his manners. They regard human nature as a subject of speculation; and with a narrow scrutiny examine it, in order to find those principles, which regulate our understanding, excite our sentiments, and make us to approve or blame any particular object, action, or behaviour. They think it a reproach to all literature, that philosophy should not yet have fixed, beyond controversy, the foundation of morals, reasoning, and criticism; and should for ever talk of truth and falsehood, vice and virtue, beauty and deformity, without being able to determine the source of these distinctions. While they attempt this arduous task, they are deterred by no difficulties; but proceeding from particular instances to general principles, they still push on their enquiries to principles more general, and rest not satisfied till they arrive at those original principles, by which, in every science, all human curiosity must be bounded. Though their speculations seem abstract, and even unintelligible to common readers, they aim at the approbation of the learned and the wise; and think themselves sufficiently compensated for the labour of their whole lives, if they can discover some hidden truths, which may contribute to the instruction of posterity.

It is certain that the easy and obvious philosophy will always, with the generality of mankind, have the preference above the accurate and abstruse; and by many will be recommended, not only as more agreeable, but more useful than the other. It enters more into common life; moulds the heart and affections; and, by touching those principles which actuate men, reforms their conduct, and brings them nearer to that model of perfection which it describes. On the contrary, the abstruse philosophy, being founded on a turn of mind, which cannot enter into business and action, vanishes when the philosopher leaves the shade, and comes into open day; nor can its principles easily retain any influence over our conduct and behaviour. The feelings of our heart, the agitation of our passions, the vehemence of our affections, dissipate all its conclusions, and reduce the profound philosopher to a mere plebeian.

This also must be confessed, that the most durable, as well as justest fame, has been acquired by the easy philosophy, and that abstract reasoners seem hitherto to have enjoyed only a momentary reputation, from the caprice or ignorance of their own age, but have not been able to support their renown with more equitable posterity. It is easy for a profound philosopher to commit a mistake in his subtile reasonings; and one mistake is the necessary parent of another, while he pushes on his consequences, and is not deterred from embracing any conclusion, by its unusual appearance, or its contradiction to popular opinion. But a philosopher, who purposes only to represent the common sense of mankind in more beautiful and more engaging colours, if by accident he falls into error, goes not farther; but renewing his appeal to common sense, and the natural sentiments of the mind, returns into the right path, and secures himself from any dangerous illusions. The fame of Cicero flourishes at present; but that of Aristotle is utterly decayed. La Bruyere passes the seas, and still maintains his reputation: But the glory of Malebranche is confined to his own nation, and to his own age. And Addison, perhaps, will be read with pleasure, when Locke shall be entirely forgotten.

The mere philosopher is a character, which is commonly but little acceptable in the world, as being supposed to contribute nothing either to the advantage or pleasure of society; while he lives remote from communication with mankind, and is wrapped up in principles and notions equally remote from their comprehension. On the other hand, the mere ignorant is still more despised; nor is any thing deemed a surer sign of an illiberal genius in an age and nation where the sciences flourish, than to be entirely destitute of all relish for those noble entertainments. The most perfect character is supposed to lie between those extremes; retaining an equal ability and taste for books, company, and business; preserving in conversation that discernment and delicacy which arise from polite letters; and in business, that probity and accuracy which are the natural result of a just philosophy. In order to diffuse and cultivate so accomplished a character, nothing can be more useful than compositions of the easy style and manner, which draw not too much from life, require no deep application or retreat to be comprehended, and send back the student among mankind full of noble sentiments and wise precepts, applicable to every exigence of human life. By means of such compositions, virtue becomes amiable, science agreeable, company instructive, and retirement entertaining.

Man is a reasonable being; and as such, receives from science his proper food and nourishment: But so narrow are the bounds of human understanding, that little satisfaction can be hoped for in this particular, either from the extent or security of his acquisitions. Man is a sociable, no less than a reasonable being: But neither can he always enjoy company agreeable and amusing, or preserve the proper relish for them. Man is also an active being; and from that disposition, as well as from the various necessities of human life, must submit to business and occupation: But the mind requires some relaxation, and cannot always support its bent to care and industry. It seems, then, that nature has pointed out a mixed kind of life as most suitable to the human race, and secretly admonished them to allow none of these biases to draw too much, so as to incapacitate them for other occupations and entertainments. Indulge your passion for science, says she, but let your science be human, and such as may have a direct reference to action and society. Abstruse thought and profound researches I prohibit, and will severely punish, by the pensive melancholy which they introduce, by the endless uncertainty in which they involve you, and by the cold reception which your pretended discoveries shall meet with, when communicated. Be a philosopher; but, amidst all your philosophy, be still a man.

Were the generality of mankind contented to prefer the easy philosophy to the abstract and profound, without throwing any blame or contempt on the latter, it might not be improper, perhaps, to comply with this general opinion, and allow every man to enjoy, without opposition, his own taste and sentiment. But as the matter is often carried farther, even to the absolute rejecting of all profound reasonings, or what is commonly called *metaphysics*, we shall now proceed to consider what can reasonably be pleaded in their behalf.

We may begin with observing, that one considerable advantage, which results from the accurate and abstract philosophy, is, its subserviency to the easy and humane, which, without the former, can never attain a sufficient degree of exactness in its sentiments, precepts, or reasonings. All polite letters are nothing but pictures of human life in various attitudes and situations; and inspire us with different sentiments, of praise or blame, admiration or ridicule, according to the qualities of the object, which they set before us. An artist must be better qualified to succeed in this undertaking, who, besides a delicate taste and a quick apprehension, possesses an accurate knowledge of the internal fabric, the operations of the understanding, the workings of the passions, and the various species of sentiment which discriminate vice and virtue. How painful soever this inward search or enquiry may appear, it becomes, in some measure, requisite to those, who would describe with success the obvious and outward appearances of life and manners. The anatomist presents to the eye the most hideous and disagreeable objects; but his science is useful to the painter in delineating even a Venus or an Helen. While the latter employs all the richest colours of his art, and gives his figures the most

An Experiment on a Bird in the Air Pump, ca. 1767–1768, by Joseph Wright of Derby (1734–1797). The artist is showing the interplay between rational analysis and human emotion, between reason and feeling. The scientist in the center is demonstrating that a bird cannot fly in a vacuum. In doing so he is also killing the bird—a fact not lost on the little girls to the right. (*Tate Gallery, London/© National Gallery, London*)

graceful and engaging airs; he must still carry his attention to the inward structure of the human body, the position of the muscles, the fabric of the bones, and the use and figure of every part or organ. Accuracy is, in every case, advantageous to beauty and just reasoning to delicate sentiment. In vain would we exalt the one by depreciating the other.

Besides, we may observe, in every art or profession, even those which most concern life or action, that a spirit of accuracy, however acquired, carries all of them nearer their perfection, and renders them more subservient to the interests of society. And though a philosopher may live remote from business, the genius of philosophy, if carefully cultivated by several, must gradually diffuse itself throughout the whole society, and bestow a similar correctness on every art and calling. The politician will acquire greater foresight and subtlety, in the subdividing and balancing of power; the lawyer more method and finer principles in his reasonings; and the general more regularity in his discipline, and more caution in his plans and operations. The stability of modern governments above the ancient, and the accuracy of modern philosophy, have improved, and probably will still improve, by similar gradations.

Were there no advantage to be reaped from these studies, beyond the gratification of an innocent curiosity, yet ought not even this to be despised; as being one accession to those few safe and harmless pleasures, which are bestowed on the human race. The sweetest and most inoffensive path of life leads through the avenues of science and learning; and whoever can either remove any obstructions in this way, or open up any new prospect, ought so far to be esteemed a benefactor to mankind. And though these researches may appear painful and fatiguing, it is with some minds as with some bodies, which being endowed with vigorous and florid health, require severe exercise, and reap a pleasure from what, to the generality of mankind, may seem burdensome and laborious. Obscurity, indeed, is painful to the mind as well as to the eye; but to bring light from obscurity, by whatever labour, must needs be delightful and rejoicing.

But this obscurity in the profound and abstract philosophy, is objected to, not only as painful and fatiguing, but as the inevitable source of uncertainty and error. Here indeed lies the justest and most plausible objection against a considerable part of metaphysics, that they are not properly a science; but arise either from the fruitless efforts of human vanity, which would penetrate into subjects utterly inaccessible to the understanding, or from the craft of popular superstitions, which, being unable to defend themselves on fair ground, raise these entangling brambles to cover and protect their weakness. Chased from the open country, these robbers fly into the forest, and lie in wait to break in upon every unguarded avenue of the mind, and overwhelm it with religious fears and prejudices. The stoutest antagonist, if he remit his watch a moment, is oppressed. And many, through cowardice and folly, open the gates to the enemies, and willingly receive them with reverence and submission, as their legal sovereigns.

But is this a sufficient reason, why philosophers should desist from such researches, and leave superstition still in possession of her retreat? Is it not proper to draw an opposite conclusion, and perceive the necessity of carrying the war into the most secret recesses of the enemy? In vain do we hope, that men, from frequent disappointment, will at last abandon such airy sciences, and discover the proper province of human reason. For, besides, that many persons find too sensible an interest in perpetually recalling such topics; besides this, I say, the motive of blind despair can never reasonably have place in the sciences; since, however unsuccessful former attempts may have proved, there is still room to hope, that the industry, good fortune, or improved sagacity of succeeding generations may reach discoveries unknown to former ages. Each adventurous genius will leap at the arduous prize, and find himself stimulated, rather than discouraged, by the failures of his predecessors; while he hopes that the glory of achieving so hard an adventure is reserved for him alone. The only method of freeing learning, at once, from these abstruse questions, is to enquire seriously into the nature of human understanding, and show, from an exact analysis of its powers and capacity, that it is by no means fitted for such remote and abstruse subjects. We must submit to this fatigue, in order to live at ease ever after: And must cultivate true metaphysics with some care, in order to destroy the false and adulterate. Indolence, which, to some persons, affords a safeguard against this deceitful philosophy, is, with others, overbalanced by curiosity; and despair, which, at some moments, prevails, may give place afterwards to sanguine hopes and expectations. Accurate and just reasoning is the only catholic remedy, fitted for all persons and all dispositions; and is alone able to subvert that abstruse philosophy and metaphysical jargon, which, being mixed up with popular superstition, renders it in a manner impenetrable to careless reasoners, and gives it the air of science and wisdom.

Besides this advantage of rejecting, after deliberate enquiry, the most uncertain and disagreeable part of learning, there are many positive advantages, which result from an accurate scrutiny into the powers and faculties of human nature. It is remarkable concerning the operations of the mind, that, though most intimately present to us, yet, whenever they become the object of reflection, they seem involved in obscurity; nor can the eye readily find those lines and boundaries, which discriminate and distinguish them. The objects are too fine to remain long in the same aspect or situation; and must be apprehended in an instant, by a superior penetration, derived from nature, and improved by habit and reflection. It becomes, therefore, no inconsiderable part of science barely to know the different operations of the mind, to separate them from each other, to class them under their proper heads, and to correct all that seeming disorder, in which they lie involved, when made the object of reflection and enquiry. This talk of ordering and distinguishing, which has no merit, when performed with regard to external bodies, the objects of our senses, rises in its value, when directed towards the operations of the mind, in proportion to the difficulty and labour, which we meet with in performing it. And if we can go no farther than this mental geography, or delineation of the distinct parts and powers of the mind, it is at least a satisfaction to go so far; and the more obvious this science may appear (and it is by no means obvious) the more contemptible still must the ignorance of it be esteemed, in all pretenders to learning and philosophy.

Nor can there remain any suspicion, that this science is uncertain and chimerical; unless we should entertain such a scepticism as is entirely subversive of all speculation, and even action. It cannot be doubted, that the mind is endowed with several powers and faculties, that these powers are distinct from each other, that what is really distinct to the immediate perception may be distinguished by reflection; and consequently, that there is a truth and falsehood in all propositions on this subject, and a truth and falsehood, which lie not beyond the compass of human understanding. There are many obvious distinctions of this kind, such as those between the will and understanding, the imagination and passions, which fall within the comprehension of every human creature; and the finer and more philosophical distinctions are no less real and certain, though more difficult to be comprehended. Some instances, especially late ones, of success in these enquiries, may give us a juster notion of the certainty and solidity of this branch of learning. And shall we esteem it worthy the labour of a philosopher to give us a true system of the planets, and adjust the position and order of those remote bodies; while we affect to overlook those, who, with so much success, delineate the parts of the mind, in which we are so intimately concerned?

But may we not hope, that philosophy, if cultivated with care, and encouraged by the attention of the public, may carry its researches still farther, and discover, at least in some degree, the secret springs and principles, by which the human mind is actuated in its operations? Astronomers had long contented themselves with proving, from the phenomena, the true motions, order, and magnitude of the heavenly bodies: Till a philosopher, at last, arose, who seems, from the happiest reasoning, to have also determined the laws and forces, by which the revolutions of the planets are governed and directed. The like has been performed with regard to other parts of nature. And there is no reason to despair of equal success in our enquiries concerning the mental powers and economy, if prosecuted with equal capacity and caution. It is probable, that one operation and principle of the mind depends on another; which, again, may be resolved into one more general and universal: And how far these researches may possibly be carried, it will be difficult for us, before, or even after, a careful trial, exactly to determine. This is certain, that attempts of this kind are every day made even by those who philosophize the most negligently: And nothing can be more requisite than to enter upon the enterprize with thorough care and attention; that, if it lie within the compass of human understanding, it may at last be happily achieved; if not, it may, however, be rejected with some confidence and security. This last conclusion, surely, is not desirable; nor ought it to be embraced too rashly. For how much must we diminish from the beauty and value of this species of philosophy, upon such a supposition? Moralists have hitherto been accustomed, when they considered the vast multitude and diversity of those actions that excite our approbation or dislike, to search for some common principle, on which this variety of sentiments might depend. And though they have sometimes carried the matter too far, by their passion for some one general principle; it must, however, be confessed, that they are excusable in expecting to find some general principles, into which all the vices and virtues were justly to be resolved. The like has been the endeavour of critics, logicians, and even politicians: Nor have their attempts been wholly unsuccessful; though perhaps longer time, greater accuracy, and more ardent application may bring these sciences still nearer their perfection. To throw up at once all pretensions of this kind may justly be deemed more rash, precipitate, and dogmatical, than even the boldest and most affirmative philosophy, that has ever attempted to impose its crude dictates and principles on mankind.

What though these reasonings concerning human nature seem abstract, and of difficult comprehension? This affords no presumption of their falsehood. On the contrary, it seems impossible, that what has hitherto escaped so many wise and profound philosophers can be very obvious and easy. And whatever pains these researches may cost us, we may think ourselves sufficiently rewarded, not only in point of profit but of pleasure, if, by that means, we can make any addition to our stock of knowledge, in subjects of such unspeakable importance.

But as, after all, the abstractedness of these speculations is no recommendation, but rather a disadvantage to them, and as this difficulty may perhaps be surmounted by care and art, and the avoiding of all unnecessary detail, we have, in the following enquiry, attempted to throw some light upon subjects, from which uncertainty has hitherto deterred the wise, and obscurity the ignorant. Happy, if we can unite the boundaries of the different species of philosophy, by reconciling profound enquiry with clearness, and truth with novelty! And still more happy, if reasoning in this easy manner, we can undermine the foundations of an abstruse philosophy, which seems to have hitherto served only as a shelter to superstition, and a cover to absurdity and error!

SECTION II. OF THE ORIGIN OF IDEAS

Every one will readily allow, that there is a considerable difference between the perceptions of the mind, when a man feels the pain of excessive heat, or the pleasure of moderate warmth, and when he afterwards recalls to his memory this sensation, or anticipates it by his imagination. These faculties may mimic or copy the perceptions of the senses; but they never can entirely reach the force and vivacity of the original sentiment. The utmost we say of them, even when they operate with greatest vigour, is, that they represent their object in so lively a manner, that we could almost say we feel or see it: But, except the mind be disordered by disease or madness, they never can arrive at such a pitch of vivacity, as to render these perceptions altogether undistinguishable. All the colours of poetry, however splendid, can never paint natural objects in such a manner as to make the description be taken for a real landscape. The most lively thought is still inferior to the dullest sensation.

We may observe a like distinction to run through all the other perceptions of the mind. A man in a fit of anger, is actuated in a very different manner from one who only thinks of that emotion. If you tell me, that any person is in love, I easily understand your meaning, and form a just conception of his situation; but never can mistake that conception for the real disorders and agitations of the passion. When we reflect on our past sentiments and affections, our thought is a faithful mirror, and copies its objects truly; but the colours which it employs are faint and dull, in comparison of those in which our original perceptions were clothed. It requires no nice discernment or metaphysical head to mark the distinction between them.

Here therefore we may divide all the perceptions of the mind into two classes or species, which are distinguished by their different degrees of force and vivacity. The less forcible and lively are commonly denominated *Thoughts* or *Ideas*. The other species want a name in our language, and in most others; I suppose, because it was not requisite for any, but philosophical purposes, to rank them under a general term or appellation. Let us, therefore, use a little freedom, and call them *Impressions*; employing that word in a sense somewhat different from the usual. By the term impression, then, I mean all our more lively perceptions, when we hear, or see, or feel, or love, or hate, or desire, or will. And *impressions* are distinguished from ideas which are the less lively perceptions, of which we are conscious, when we reflect on any of those sensations or movements above mentioned.

Nothing, at first view, may seem more unbounded than the thought of man, which not only escapes all human power and authority, but is not even restrained within the limits of nature and reality. To form monsters, and join incongruous shapes and appearances, costs the imagination no more trouble than to conceive the most natural and familiar objects. And while the body is confined to one planet, along which it creeps with pain and difficulty; the thought can in an instant transport us into the most distant regions of the universe; or even beyond the universe, into the unbounded chaos, where nature is supposed to lie in total confusion. What never was seen, or heard of, may yet be conceived; nor is any thing beyond the power of thought, except what implies an absolute contradiction.

But though our thought seems to possess this unbounded liberty, we shall find, upon a nearer examination, that it is really confined within very narrow limits, and that all this creative power of the mind amounts to no more than the faculty of compounding, transposing, augmenting, or diminishing the materials afforded us by the senses and experience. When we think of a golden mountain, we only join two consistent ideas, *gold* and *mountain*, with which we were formerly acquainted. A virtuous horse we can conceive; because, from our own feeling, we can conceive virtue; and this we may unite to the figure and shape of a horse, which is an animal familiar to us. In short, all the materials of thinking are derived either from our outward or inward sentiment: the mixture and composition of these belongs alone to the mind and will. Or, to express myself in philosophical language, all our ideas or more feeble perceptions are copies of our impressions or more lively ones.

To prove this, the two following arguments will, I hope, be sufficient. First, when we analyze our thoughts or ideas, however compounded or sublime, we always find that they resolve themselves into such simple ideas as were copied from a precedent feeling or sentiment. Even those ideas, which, at first view, seem the most wide of this origin, are found, upon a nearer scrutiny, to be derived from it. The idea of God, as meaning an infinitely intelligent, wise, and good Being, arises from reflecting on the operations of our own mind, and augmenting, without limit, those qualities of goodness and wisdom. We may prosecute this enquiry to what length we please; where we shall always find, that every idea which we examine is copied from a similar impression. Those who would assert that this position is not universally true nor without exception, have only one, and that an easy method of refuting it; by producing that idea, which, in their opinion, is not derived from this source. It will then be incumbent on us, if we would maintain our doctrine, to produce the impression, or lively perception, which corresponds to it.

Secondly. If it happens, from a defect of the organ, that a man is not susceptible of any species of sensation, we always find that he is as little susceptible of the correspondent ideas. A blind man can form no notion of colours; a deaf man of sounds. Restore either of them that sense in which he is deficient; by opening this new inlet for his sensations, you also open an inlet for the ideas; and he finds no difficulty in conceiving these objects. The case is the same, if the object, proper for exciting any sensation, has never been applied to the organ. A Laplander or Negro has no notion of the relish of wine. And though there are few or no instances of a like deficiency in the mind, where a person has never felt or is wholly incapable of a sentiment or passion that belongs to his species; yet we find the same observation to take place in a less degree. A man of mild manners can form no idea of inveterate revenge or cruelty; nor can a selfish heart easily conceive the heights of friendship and generosity. It is readily allowed, that other beings may possess many senses of which we can have no conception, because the ideas of them have never been introduced to us in the only manner by which an idea can have access to the mind, to wit, by the actual feeling and sensation.

There is, however, one contradictory phenomenon, which may prove that it is not absolutely impossible for ideas to arise, independent of their correspondent impressions. I believe it will readily be allowed, that the several distinct ideas of colour, which enter by the eye, or those of sound, which are conveyed by the ear, are really different from each other; though, at the same time, resembling. Now if this be true of different colours, it must be no less so of the different shades of the same colour; and each shade produces a distinct idea, independent of the rest. For if this should be denied, it is possible, by the continual gradation of shades, to run a colour insensibly into what is most remote from it; and if you will not allow any of the means to be different, you cannot, without absurdity, deny the extremes to be the same. Suppose, therefore, a person to have enjoyed his sight for thirty years, and to have become perfectly acquainted with colours of all kinds except one particular shade of blue, for instance, which it never has been his fortune to meet with. Let all the different shades of that colour, except that single one, be placed before him, descending gradually from the deepest to lightest; it is plain that he will perceive a blank, where that shade is wanting, and will be sensible that there is a greater distance in that place between the contiguous colours than in any other. Now I ask, whether it be possible for him, from his own imagination, to supply this deficiency, and raise up to himself the idea of that particular shade, though it had never been conveyed to him by his senses? I believe there are few but will be of opinion that he can: and this may serve as a proof that the simple ideas are not always, in every instance, derived from the correspondent impressions; though this instance is so singular, that it is scarcely worth our observing, and does not merit that for it alone we should alter our general maxim.

Here, therefore, is a proposition, which not only seems, in itself, simple and intelligible; but, if a proper use were made of it, might render every dispute equally intelligible, and banish all that jargon, which has so long taken possession of metaphysical reasonings, and drawn disgrace upon them. All ideas, especially abstract ones, are naturally faint and obscure: the mind has but a slender hold of them: they are apt to be confounded with other resembling ideas; and when we have often employed any term, though without a distinct meaning, we are apt to imagine it has a determinate idea annexed to it. On the contrary, all impressions, that is, all sensations, either outward or inward, are strong and vivid: the limits between them are more exactly determined: nor is it easy to fall into any error or mistake with regard to them. When we entertain, therefore, any suspicion that a philosophical term is employed without any meaning or idea (as is but too frequent), we need but enquire, *from what impressions is that supposed idea derived*? And if it be impossible to assign any, this will serve to confirm our suspicion.* By bringing ideas into so clear a light we may reasonably hope to remove all dispute, which may arise, concerning their nature and reality.

SECTION III. OF THE ASSOCIATION OF IDEAS

It is evident that there is a principle of connexion between the different thoughts or ideas of the mind, and that, in their appearance to the memory or imagination, they introduce each other with a certain degree of method and regularity. In our more serious thinking or discourse this is so observable that any particular thought, which breaks in upon the regular tract or chain of ideas, is immediately remarked and rejected. And even in our wildest and most wandering reveries, nay in our very dreams, we shall find, if we reflect, that the imagination ran not altogether at adventures, but that there was still a connexion upheld among the different ideas, which succeeded each other. Were the loosest and freest conversation to be transcribed, there would immediately be observed something which connected it in all its transitions. Or where this is wanting, the person who broke the thread of discourse might still inform you, that there had secretly revolved in his mind a succession of thought, which had gradually led him from the subject of conversation. Among different languages, even where we cannot suspect the least connexion or communication, it is found, that the words, expressive of ideas, the most compounded, do yet nearly correspond to each other: a certain proof that the simple ideas, comprehended in the compound ones, were bound together by some universal principle, which had an equal influence on all mankind.

Though it be too obvious to escape observation, that different ideas are connected together; I do not find that any philosopher has attempted to enumerate or class all the principles of association; a subject, however, that seems worthy of curiosity. To me, there appear to be only three principles of connexion among ideas, namely, *Resemblance*, *Contiguity* in time or place, and *Cause* or *Effect*.

*It is probable that no more was meant by those, who denied innate ideas, than that all ideas were copies of our impressions; though it must be confessed, that the terms, which they employed, were not chosen with such caution, nor so exactly defined, as to prevent all mistakes about their doctrine. For what is meant by *innate*? If innate be equivalent to natural, then all the perceptions and ideas of the mind must be allowed to be innate or natural, in whatever sense we take the latter word, whether in opposition to what is uncommon, artificial, or miraculous. If by innate be meant, contemporary to our birth, the dispute seems to be frivolous; nor is it worth while to enquire at what time thinking begins, whether before, at, or after our birth. Again, the word idea, seems to be commonly taken in a very loose sense, by LOCKE and others; as standing for any of our perceptions, our sensations and passions, as well as thoughts. Now in this sense, I should desire to know, what can be meant by asserting, that self-love, or resentment of injuries, or the passion between the sexes is not innate?

But admitting these terms, *impressions* and *ideas*, in the sense above explained, and understanding by *innate*, what is original or copied from no precedent perception, then may we assert that all our impressions are innate and our ideas not innate.

To be ingenuous, I must own it to be my opinion, that LOCKE was betrayed into this question by the schoolmen, who, making use of undefined terms, draw out their disputes to a tedious length, without ever touching the point in question. A like ambiguity and circumlocution seem to run through that philosopher's reasonings on this as well as most other subjects.

That these principles serve to connect ideas will not, I believe, be much doubted. A picture naturally leads our thoughts to the original:* the mention of one apartment in a building naturally introduces an enquiry or discourse concerning the others:** and if we think of a wound, we can scarcely forbear reflecting on the pain which follows it.*** But that this enumeration is complete, and that there are no other principles of association except these, may be difficult to prove to the satisfaction of the reader, or even to a man's own satisfaction. All we can do, in such cases, is to run over several instances, and examine carefully the principle which binds the different thoughts to each other, never stopping till we render the principle as general as possible.† The more instances we examine, and the more care we employ, the more assurance shall we acquire, that the enumeration, which we form from the whole, is complete and entire.

SECTION IV. SCEPTICAL DOUBTS CONCERNING THE OPERATIONS OF THE UNDERSTANDING

PART I

All the objects of human reason or enquiry may naturally be divided into two kinds, to wit, *Relations of Ideas*, and *Matters of Fact*. Of the first kind are the sciences of Geometry, Algebra, and Arithmetic; and in short, every affirmation which is either intuitively or demonstratively certain. *That the square of the hypothenuse is equal to the squares of the two sides*, is a proposition which expresses a relation between these figures. *That three times five is equal to the half of thirty*, expresses a relation between these numbers. Propositions of this kind are discoverable by the mere operation of thought, without dependence on what is anywhere existent in the universe. Though there never were a circle or triangle in nature, the truths demonstrated by Euclid would for ever retain their certainty and evidence.

Matters of fact, which are the second objects of human reason, are not ascertained in the same manner; nor is our evidence of their truth however great, of a like nature with the foregoing. The contrary of every matter of fact is still possible; because it can never imply a contradiction, and is conceived by the mind with the same facility and distinctness, as if ever so conformable to reality. *That the sun will not rise tomorrow* is no less intelligible a proposition, and implies no more contradiction than the affirmation, *that it will rise*. We should in vain, therefore, attempt to demonstrate its falsehood. Were it demonstratively false, it would imply a contradiction, and could never be distinctly conceived by the mind.

It may, therefore, be a subject worthy of curiosity, to enquire what is the nature of that evidence which assures us of any real existence and matter of fact, beyond the present testimony of our senses, or the records of our memory. This part of philosophy, it is

*Resemblance.

**Contiguity.

***Cause and effect.

†For instance, Contrast or Contrariety is also a connexion among Ideas but it may, perhaps, be considered as a mixture of *Causation* and *Resemblance*. Where two objects are contrary, the one destroys the other; that is, the cause of its annihilation, and the idea of the annihilation of an object implies the idea of its former existence.

observable, has been little cultivated, either by the ancients or moderns; and therefore our doubts and errors, in the prosecution of so important an enquiry, may be the more excusable; while we march through such difficult paths without any guide or direction. They may even prove useful, by exciting curiosity, and destroying that implicit faith and security, which is the bane of all reasoning and free enquiry. The discovery of defects in the common philosophy, if any such there be, will not, I presume, be a discouragement, but rather an incitement, as is usual, to attempt something more full and satisfactory than has yet been proposed to the public.

All reasonings concerning matter of fact seem to be founded on the relation of *Cause* and *Effect*. By means of that relation alone we can go beyond the evidence of our memory and senses. If you were to ask a man, why he believes any matter of fact, which is absent; for instance, that his friend is in the country, or in France; he would give you a reason; and this reason would be some other fact; as a letter received from him, or the knowledge of his former resolutions and promises. A man finding a watch or any other machine in a desert island, would conclude that there had once been men in that island. All our reasonings concerning fact are of the same nature. And here it is constantly supposed that there is a connexion between the present fact and that which is inferred from it. Were there nothing to bind them together, the inference would be entirely precarious. The hearing of an articulate voice and rational discourse in the dark assures us of the presence of some person: Why? because these are the effects of the human make and fabric, and closely connected with it. If we anatomize all the other reasonings of this nature, we shall find that they are founded on the relation of cause and effect, and that this relation is either near or remote, direct or collateral. Heat and light are collateral effects of fire, and the one effect may justly be inferred from the other.

If we would satisfy ourselves, therefore, concerning the nature of that evidence, which assures us of matters of fact, we must enquire how we arrive at the knowledge of cause and effect.

I shall venture to affirm, as a general proposition, which admits of no exception, that the knowledge of this relation is not, in any instance, attained by reasonings *a priori;* but arises entirely from experience, when we find that any particular objects are constantly conjoined with each other. Let an object be presented to a man of ever so strong natural reason and abilities; if that object be entirely new to him, he will not be able, by the most accurate examination of its sensible qualities, to discover any of its causes or effects. Adam, though his rational faculties be supposed, at the very first, entirely perfect, could not have inferred from the fluidity and transparency of water that it would suffocate him, or from the light and warmth of fire that it would consume him. No object ever discovers, by the qualities which appear to the senses, either the causes which produced it, or the effects which will arise from it; nor can our reason, unassisted by experience, ever draw any inference concerning real existence and matter of fact.

This proposition, *that causes and effects are discoverable, not by reason but by experience*, will readily be admitted with regard to such objects, as we remember to have once been altogether unknown to us; since we must be conscious of the utter inability, which we then lay under, of foretelling what would arise from them. Present two smooth pieces of marble to a man who has no tincture of natural philosophy; he will never discover that they will adhere together in such a manner as to require great force to separate them in a direct line, while they make so small a resistance to a lateral pressure. Such events, as bear little analogy to the common course of nature, are also readily confessed to be known only by experience; nor does any man imagine that the explosion of gunpowder, or the attraction of a loadstone, could ever be discovered by arguments *a priori.* In like manner, when an effect is supposed to depend upon an intricate machinery or secret structure of parts, we make no difficulty in attributing all our knowledge of it to experience. Who will assert that he can give the ultimate reason, why milk or bread is proper nourishment for a man, not for a lion or a tiger?

But the same truth may not appear, at first sight, to have the same evidence with regard to events, which have become familiar to us from our first appearance in the world, which bear a close analogy to the whole course of nature, and which are supposed to depend on the simple qualities of objects, without any secret structure of parts. We are apt to imagine that we could discover these effects by the mere operation of our reason, without experience. We fancy, that were we brought on a sudden into this world, we could at first have inferred that one Billiard-ball would communicate motion to another upon impulse; and that we needed not to have waited for the event, in order to pronounce with certainty concerning it. Such is the influence of custom, that, where it is strongest, it not only covers our natural ignorance, but even conceals itself, and seems not to take place, merely because it is found in the highest degree.

But to convince us that all the laws of nature, and all the operations of bodies without exception, are known only by experience, the following reflections may, perhaps, suffice. Were any object presented to us, and were we required to pronounce concerning the effect, which will result from it, without consulting past observation; after what manner, I beseech you, must the mind proceed in this operation? It must invent or imagine some event, which it ascribes to the object as its effect; and it is plain that this invention must be entirely arbitrary. The mind can never possibly find the effect in the supposed cause, by the most accurate scrutiny and examination. For the effect is totally different from the cause, and consequently can never be discovered in it. Motion in the second Billiard-ball is a quite distinct event from motion in the first: nor is there anything in the one to suggest the smallest hint of the other. A stone or piece of metal raised into the air, and left without any support, immediately falls: but to consider the matter *a priori*, is there anything we discover in this situation which can beget the idea of a downward, rather than an upward, or any other motion, in the stone or metal?

And as the first imagination or invention of a particular effect, in all natural operations, is arbitrary, where we consult not experience; so must we also esteem the supposed tie or connexion between the cause and effect, which binds them together, and renders it impossible that any other effect could result from the operation of that cause. When I see, for instance, a Billiard-ball moving in a straight line towards another; even suppose motion in the second ball should by accident be suggested to me, as the result of their contact or impulse; may I not conceive, that a hundred different events might as well follow from that cause? May not both these balls remain at absolute rest? May not the first ball return in a straight line, or leap off from the second in any line or direction? All these suppositions are consistent and conceivable. Why then should we give the preference to one, which is no more consistent or conceivable than the rest? All our reasonings *a priori* will never be able to show us any foundation for this preference.

In a word, then, every effect is a distinct event from its cause. It could not, therefore, be discovered in the cause, and the first invention or conception of it, *a priori*, must be entirely arbitrary. And even after it is suggested, the conjunction of it with the cause must appear equally arbitrary; since there are always many other effects, which, to reason, must seem fully as consistent and natural. In vain, therefore, should we pretend to determine any single event, or infer any cause or effect, without the assistance of observation and experience.

Hence we may discover the reason why no philosopher, who is rational and modest, has ever pretended to assign the ultimate cause of any natural operation, or to show distinctly the action of that power, which produces any single effect in the universe. It is confessed, that the utmost effort of human reason is to reduce the principles, productive of natural phenomena, to a greater simplicity, and to resolve the many particular effects into a few general causes, by means of reasonings from analogy, experience, and observation. But as to the causes of these general causes, we should in vain attempt their discovery; nor shall we ever be able to satisfy ourselves, by any particular explication of them. These ultimate springs and principles are totally shut up from human curiosity and enquiry. Elasticity, gravity, cohesion of parts, communication of motion by impulse; these are probably the ultimate causes and principles which we ever discover in nature; and we may esteem ourselves sufficiently happy, if, by accurate inquiry and reasoning, we can trace up the particular phenomena to, or near to, these general principles. The most perfect philosophy of the natural kind only staves off our ignorance a little longer: as perhaps the most perfect philosophy of the moral or metaphysical kind serves only to discover larger portions of it. Thus the observation of human blindness and weakness is the result of all philosophy, and meets us at every turn, in spite of our endeavours to elude or avoid it.

Nor is geometry, when taken into the assistance of natural philosophy, ever able to remedy this defect, or lead us into the knowledge of ultimate causes, by all that accuracy of reasoning for which it is so justly celebrated. Every part of mixed mathematics proceeds upon the supposition that certain laws are established by nature in her operations; and abstract reasonings are employed, either to assist experience in the discovery of these laws, or to determine their influence in particular instances, where it depends upon any precise degree of distance and quantity. Thus, it is a law of motion, discovered by experience, that the movement or force of any body in motion is in the compound ratio or proportion of its solid contents and its velocity; and consequently, that a small force may remove the greatest obstacle or raise the greatest weight, if, by any contrivance or machinery, we can increase the velocity of that force, so as to make it an overmatch for its antagonist. Geometry assists us in the application of this law, by giving us the just dimensions of all the parts and figures which can enter into any species of machines; but still the discovery of the law itself is owing merely to experience, and all the abstract reasonings in the world could never lead us one step towards the knowledge of it. When we reason *a priori*, and consider merely any object or cause, as it appears to the mind, independent of all observation, it never could suggest to us the notion of any distinct object, such as its effect; much less, show us the inseparable and inviolable connexion between them. A man must be very sagacious who could discover by reasoning that crystal is the effect of heat, and ice of cold, without being previously acquainted with the operation of these qualities.

PART II

But we have not yet attained any tolerable satisfaction with regard to the question first proposed. Each solution still gives rise to a new question as difficult as the foregoing, and leads us on to farther enquiries. When it is asked, *What is the nature of all our reasonings concerning matter of fact?* the proper answer seems to be, that they are founded on the relation of cause and effect. When again it is asked, *What is the foundation of all our reasonings and conclusions concerning that relation?* it may be replied in one word, Experience. But if we still carry on our sifting humour, and ask,

What is the foundation of all conclusions from experience? this implies a new question, which may be of more difficult solution and explication. Philosophers, that give themselves airs of superior wisdom and sufficiency, have a hard task when they encounter persons of inquisitive dispositions, who push them from every corner to which they retreat, and who are sure at last to bring them to some dangerous dilemma. The best expedient to prevent this confusion, is to be modest in our pretensions; and even to discover the difficulty ourselves before it is objected to us. By this means, we may make a kind of merit of our very ignorance.

I shall content myself, in this section, with an easy task, and shall pretend only to give a negative answer to the question here proposed. I say then, that, even after we have experience of the operations of cause and effect, our conclusions from that experience are not founded on reasoning, or any process of the understanding. This answer we must endeavour both to explain and to defend.

It must certainly be allowed, that nature has kept us at a great distance from all her secrets, and has afforded us only the knowledge of a few superficial qualities of objects; while she conceals from us those powers and principles on which the influence of those objects entirely depends. Our senses inform us of the colour, weight, and consistence of bread; but neither sense nor reason can ever inform us of those qualities which fit it for the nourishment and support of a human body. Sight or feeling conveys an idea of the actual motion of bodies; but as to that wonderful force or power, which would carry on a moving body for ever in a continued change of place, and which bodies never lose but by communicating it to others; of this we cannot form the most distant conception. But notwithstanding this ignorance of natural powers* and principles, we always presume, when we see like sensible qualities, that they have like secret powers, and expect that effects, similar to those which we have experienced, will follow from them. If a body of like colour and consistence with that bread, which we have formerly eat, be presented to us, we make no scruple of repeating the experiment, and foresee, with certainty, like nourishment and support. Now this is a process of the mind or thought, of which I would willingly know the foundation. It is allowed on all hands that there is no known connexion between the sensible qualities and the secret powers; and consequently, that the mind is not led to form such a conclusion concerning their constant and regular conjunction, by anything which it knows of their nature. As to past Experience, it can be allowed to give direct and certain information of those precise objects only, and that precise period of time, which fell under its cognizance: but why this experience should be extended to future times, and to other objects, which, for aught we know, may be only in appearance similar; this is the main question on which I would insist. The bread, which I formerly eat, nourished me; that is, a body of such sensible qualities was, at that time, endued with such secret powers: but does it follow, that other bread must also nourish me at another time, and that like sensible qualities must always be attended with like secret powers? The consequence seems nowise necessary. At least, it must be acknowledged that there is here a consequence drawn by the mind; that there is a certain step taken; a process of thought, and an inference, which wants to be explained. These two propositions are far from being the same, *I have found that such an object has always been attended with such an effect, and I foresee, that other objects, which are, in appearance, similar, will be attended with similar effects*. I shall allow, if you please, that the one proposition may justly be inferred from the other; I know, in fact, that it

*The word, Power, is here used in a loose and popular sense. The most accurate explication of it would give additional evidence to this argument. See Sec. 7.

always is inferred. But if you insist that the inference is made by a chain of reasoning, I desire you to produce that reasoning. The connexion between these propositions is not intuitive. There is required a medium, which may enable the mind to draw such an inference, if indeed it be drawn by reasoning and argument. What that medium is, I must confess, passes my comprehension; and it is incumbent on those to produce it, who assert that it really exists, and is the origin of all our conclusions concerning matter of fact.

This negative argument must certainly, in process of time, become altogether convincing, if many penetrating and able philosophers shall turn their enquiries this way and no one be ever able to discover any connecting proposition or intermediate step, which supports the understanding in this conclusion. But as the question is yet new, every reader may not trust so far to his own penetration, as to conclude, because an argument escapes his enquiry, that therefore it does not really exist. For this reason it may be requisite to venture upon a more difficult task; and enumerating all the branches of human knowledge, endeavour to show that none of them can afford such an argument.

All reasonings may be divided into two kinds, namely, demonstrative reasoning, or that concerning relations of ideas, and moral reasoning, or that concerning matter of fact and existence. That there are no demonstrative arguments in the case seems evident; since it implies no contradiction that the course of nature may change, and that an object, seemingly like those which we have experienced, may be attended with different or contrary effects. May I not clearly and distinctly conceive that a body, falling from the clouds, and which, in all other respects, resembles snow, has yet the taste of salt or feeling of fire? Is there any more intelligible proposition than to affirm, that all the trees will flourish in December and January, and decay in May and June? Now whatever is intelligible, and can be distinctly conceived, implies no contradiction, and can never be proved false by any demonstrative argument or abstract reasoning *a priori*.

If we be, therefore, engaged by arguments to put trust in past experience, and make it the standard of our future judgement, these arguments must be probable only, or such as regard matter of fact and real existence, according to the division above mentioned. But that there is no argument of this kind, must appear, if our explication of that species of reasoning be admitted as solid and satisfactory. We have said that all arguments concerning existence are founded on the relation of cause and effect; that our knowledge of that relation is derived entirely from experience; and that all our experimental conclusions proceed upon the supposition that the future will be conformable to the past. To endeavour, therefore, the proof of this last supposition by probable arguments, or arguments regarding existence, must be evidently going in a circle, and taking that for granted, which is the very point in question.

In reality, all arguments from experience are founded on the similarity which we discover among natural objects, and by which we are induced to expect effects similar to those which we have found to follow from such objects. And though none but a fool or madman will ever pretend to dispute the authority of experience, or to reject that great guide of human life, it may surely be allowed a philosopher to have so much curiosity at least as to examine the principle of human nature, which gives this mighty authority to experience, and makes us draw advantage from that similarity which nature has placed among different objects. From causes which appear similar we expect similar effects. This is the sum of all our experimental conclusions. Now it seems evident that, if this conclusion were formed by reason, it would be as perfect at first, and upon one instance, as after ever so long a course of experience. But the case is far otherwise. Nothing so like as eggs; yet no one, on account of this appearing similarity, expects the same taste and relish in all of them. It is only after a long course of uniform experiments in any kind, that we attain a firm reliance and security with regard to a particular event. Now where is that process of reasoning which, from one instance, draws a conclusion, so different from that which it infers from a hundred instances that are nowise different from that single one? This question I propose as much for the sake of information, as with an intention of raising difficulties. I cannot find, I cannot imagine any such reasoning. But I keep my mind still open to instruction, if any one will vouchsafe to bestow it on me.

Should it be said that, from a number of uniform experiments, we *infer* a connexion between the sensible qualities and the secret powers; this, I must confess, seems the same difficulty, couched in different terms. The question still recurs, on what process of argument this *inference* is founded? Where is the medium, the interposing ideas, which join propositions so very wide of each other? It is confessed that the colour, consistence, and other sensible qualities of bread appear not, of themselves, to have any connexion with the secret powers of nourishment and support. For otherwise we could infer these secret powers from the first appearance of these sensible qualities, without the aid of experience; contrary to the sentiment of all philosophers, and contrary to plain matter of fact. Here, then, is our natural state of ignorance with regard to the powers and influence of all objects. How is this remedied by experience? It only shows us a number of uniform effects, resulting from certain objects, and teaches us that those particular objects, at that particular time, were endowed with such powers and forces. When a new object, endowed with similar sensible qualities, is produced, we expect similar powers and forces, and look for a like effect. From a body of like colour and consistence with bread we expect like nourishment and support. But this surely is a step or progress of the mind, which wants to be explained. When a man says, *I have found, in all past instances, such sensible qualities conjoined with such secret powers*: And when he says, *Similar sensible qualities will always be conjoined with similar secret powers*, he is not guilty of a tautology, nor are these propositions in any respect the same. You say that the one proposition is an inference from the other. But you must confess that the inference is not intuitive; neither is it demonstrative: Of what nature is it, then? To say it is experimental, is begging the question. For all inferences from experience suppose, as their foundation, that the future will resemble the past, and that similar powers will be conjoined with similar sensible qualities. If there be any suspicion that the course of nature may change, and that the past may be no rule for the future, all experience becomes useless, and can give rise to no inference or conclusion. It is impossible, therefore, that any arguments from experience can prove this resemblance of the past to the future: since all these arguments are founded on the supposition of that resemblance. Let the course of things be allowed hitherto ever so regular; that alone, without some new argument or inference, proves not that, for the future, it will continue so. In vain do you pretend to have learned the nature of bodies from your past experience. Their secret nature, and consequently all their effects and influence, may change, without any change in their sensible qualities. This happens sometimes, and with regard to some objects: Why may it not happen always, and with regard to all objects? What logic, what process of argument secures you against this supposition? My practice, you say, refutes my doubts. But you mistake the purport of my question. As an agent, I am quite satisfied in the point; but as a philosopher, who has some share of curiosity, I will not say scepticism, I want to learn the foundation of this inference. No reading, no enquiry has yet been able to remove my difficulty, or give me satisfaction in a matter of such importance. Can I do better than propose the difficulty to the public, even though, perhaps, I have small hopes of obtaining a solution? We shall, at least, by this means, be sensible of our ignorance, if we do not augment our knowledge.

I must confess that a man is guilty of unpardonable arrogance who concludes, because an argument has escaped his own investigation, that therefore it does not really exist. I must also confess that, though all the learned, for several ages, should have employed themselves in fruitless search upon any subject, it may still, perhaps, be rash to conclude positively that the subject must, therefore, pass all human comprehension. Even though we examine all the sources of our knowledge, and conclude them unfit for such a subject, there may still remain a suspicion, that the enumeration is not complete, or the examination not accurate. But with regard to the present subject, there are some considerations which seem to remove all this accusation of arrogance or suspicion of mistake.

It is certain that the most ignorant and stupid peasants—nay infants, nay even brute beasts—improve by experience, and learn the qualities of natural objects, by observing the effects which result from them. When a child has felt the sensation of pain from touching the flame of a candle, he will be careful not to put his hand near any candle; but will expect a similar effect from a cause which is similar in its sensible qualities and appearance. If you assert, therefore, that the understanding of the child is led into this conclusion by any process of argument or ratiocination, I may justly require you to produce that argument; nor have you any pretense to refuse so equitable a demand. You cannot say that the argument is abstruse, and may possibly escape your enquiry; since you confess that it is obvious to the capacity of a mere infant. If you hesitate, therefore, a moment, or if, after reflection, you produce any intricate or profound argument, you, in a manner, give up the question, and confess that it is not reasoning which engages us to suppose the past resembling the future, and to expect similar effects from causes which are, to appearance, similar. This is the proposition which I intended to enforce in the present section. If I be right, I pretend not to have made any mighty discovery. And if I be wrong, I must acknowledge myself to be indeed a very backward scholar; since I cannot now discover an argument which, it seems, was perfectly familiar to me long before I was out of my cradle.

SECTION V. SCEPTICAL SOLUTION OF THESE DOUBTS

PART I

The passion for philosophy, like that for religion, seems liable to this inconvenience, that, though it aims at the correction of our manners, and extirpation of our vices, it may only serve, by imprudent management, to foster a predominant inclination, and push the mind, with more determined resolution, towards that side which already *draws* too much, by the bias and propensity of the natural temper. It is certain that, while we aspire to the magnanimous firmness of the philosophic sage, and endeavour to confine our pleasures altogether within our own minds, we may, at last, render our philosophy like that of Epictetus, and other *Stoics*, only a more refined system of selfishness, and reason ourselves out of all virtue as well as social enjoyment. While we study with attention the vanity of human life, and turn all our thoughts towards the empty and transitory nature of riches and honours, we are, perhaps, all the while flattering our natural indolence, which, hating the bustle of the world, and drudgery of business, seeks a pretence of reason to give itself a full and uncontrolled indulgence. There is, however, one species of philosophy which seems little liable to this inconvenience, and that because it strikes in with no disorderly passion of the human mind, nor can mingle itself with any natural affection or propensity; and that is the Academic or Sceptical philosophy. The academics always talk of doubt and suspense of judgement, of danger in hasty determinations, of confining to very narrow bounds the enquiries of the understanding, and of renouncing all speculations which lie not within the limits of common life and practice. Nothing, therefore, can be more contrary than such a philosophy to the supine indolence of the mind, its rash arrogance, its lofty pretensions, and its superstitious credulity. Every passion is mortified by it, except the love of truth; and that passion never is, nor can be, carried to too high a degree. It is surprising, therefore, that this philosophy, which, in almost every instance, must be harmless and innocent, should be the subject of so much groundless reproach and obloquy. But, perhaps, the very circumstance which renders it so innocent is what chiefly exposes it to the public hatred and resentment. By flattering no irregular passion, it gains few partizans: By opposing so many vices and follies, it raises to itself abundance of enemies, who stigmatize it as libertine, profane, and irreligious.

Nor need we fear that this philosophy, while it endeavours to limit our enquiries to common life, should ever undermine the reasonings of common life, and carry its doubts so far as to destroy all action, as well as speculation. Nature will always maintain her rights, and prevail in the end over any abstract reasoning whatsoever. Though we should conclude, for instance, as in the foregoing section, that, in all reasonings from experience, there is a step taken by the mind which is not supported by any argument or process of the understanding; there is no danger that these reasonings, on which almost all knowledge depends, will ever be affected by such a discovery. If the mind be not engaged by argument to make this step, it must be induced by some other principle of equal weight and authority; and that principle will preserve its influence as long as human nature remains the same. What that principle is may well be worth the pains of enquiry.

Suppose a person, though endowed with the strongest faculties of reason and reflection, to be brought on a sudden into this world; he would, indeed, immediately observe a continual succession of objects, and one event following another; but he would not be able to discover anything farther. He would not, at first, by any reasoning, be able to reach the idea of cause and effect; since the particular powers, by which all natural operations are performed, never appear to the senses; nor is it reasonable to conclude, merely because one event, in one instance, precedes another, that therefore the one is the cause, the other the effect. Their conjunction may be arbitrary and casual. There may be no reason to infer the existence of one from the appearance of the other. And in a word, such a person, without more experience, could never employ his conjecture or reasoning concerning any matter of fact, or be assured of anything beyond what was immediately present to his memory and senses.

Suppose, again, that he has acquired more experience, and has lived so long in the world as to have observed familiar objects or events to be constantly conjoined together; what is the consequence of this experience? He immediately infers the existence of one object from the appearance of the other. Yet he has not, by all his experience, acquired any idea or knowledge of the secret power by which the one object produces the other; nor is it, by any process of reasoning, he is engaged to draw this inference. But still he finds himself determined to draw it: And though he should be convinced that his understanding has no part in the operation, he would nevertheless continue in the same course of thinking. There is some other principle which determines him to form such a conclusion.

This principle is Custom or Habit. For wherever the repetition of any particular act or operation produces a propensity to renew the same act or operation, without being impelled by any reasoning or process of the understanding, we always say, that this propensity is the effect of *Custom*. By employing that word, we pretend not to have given the ultimate reason of such a propensity. We only point out a principle of human nature, which is universally acknowledged, and which is well known by its effects. Perhaps we can push our enquiries no farther, or pretend to give the cause of this cause; but must rest contented with it as the ultimate principle, which we can assign, of all our conclusions from experience. It is sufficient satisfaction, that we can go so far, without repining at the narrowness of our faculties because they will carry us no farther. And it is certain we here advance a very intelligible proposition at least, if not a true one, when we assert that, after the constant conjunction of two objects—heat and flame, for instance, weight and solidity—we are determined by custom alone to expect the one from the appearance of the other. This hypothesis seems even the only one which explains the difficulty, why we draw, from a thousand instances, an inference which we are not able to draw from one instance, that is, in no respect, different from them. Reason is incapable of any such variation. The conclusions which it draws from considering one circle are the same which it would form upon surveying all the circles in the universe. But no man, having seen only one body move after being impelled by another, could infer that every other body will move after a like impulse. All inferences from experience, therefore, are effects of custom, not of reasoning.*

*Nothing is more useful than for writers, even, on *moral*, *political*, or *physical* subjects to distinguish between *reason* and *experience*, and to suppose, that these species of argumentation are entirely different from each other. The former are taken for the mere result of our intellectual faculties, which, by considering *a priori* the nature of things, and examining the effects that must follow from their operation, establish particular principles of science and philosophy. The latter are supposed to be derived entirely from sense and observation, by which we learn what has actually resulted from the operation of particular objects, and are thence able to infer, what will, for the future, result from them. Thus, for instance, the limitations and restraints of civil government, and a legal constitution, may be defended, either from *reason*, which reflecting on the great frailty and corruption of human nature, teaches, that no man can safely be trusted with unlimited authority; or from *experience* and history which inform us of the enormous abuses, that ambition, in every age and country, has been found to make of so imprudent a confidence.

The same distribution between reason and experience is maintained in all our deliberations concerning the conduct of life; while the experienced statesman, general, physician, or merchant is trusted and followed; and the unpractised novice, with whatever natural talents endowed, neglected and despised. Though it be allowed, that reason may form very plausible conjectures with regard to the consequences of such a particular conduct in such the assistance of experience, which is alone able to give stability and certainty to the maxims, derived from study and reflection.

But notwithstanding that this distinction be thus universally received, both in the active speculative scenes of life, I shall not scruple to pronounce, that it is, at bottom, erroneous, at least, superficial.

If we examine those arguments, which, in any of the sciences above mentioned, are supposed to be the mere effects of reasoning and reflection, they will be found to terminate at last, in some general principle or conclusion, for which we can assign no reason but observation and experience. The only difference between them and those maxims, which are vulgarly esteemed the result of pure experience, is, that the former cannot be established without some process of thought, and some reflection on what we have observed, in order to distinguish its circumstances, and trace its consequences: Whereas in the latter, the experienced event is exactly and fully familiar to that which we infer as the result of any particular situation. The history of a Tiberius or a Nero makes us dread a like tyranny, were our monarchs freed from the restraints of laws and

Custom, then, is the great guide of human life. It is that principle alone which renders our experience useful to us, and makes us expect, for the future, a similar train of events with those which have appeared in the past. Without the influence of custom, we should be entirely ignorant of every matter of fact beyond what is immediately present to the memory and senses. We should never know to adjust means to ends, or to employ our natural powers in the production of any effect. There would be an end at once of all action, as well as of the chief part of speculation.

But here it may be proper to remark, that though our conclusions from experience carry us beyond our memory and senses, and assure us of matters of fact which happened in the most distant places and most remote ages, yet some fact must always be present to the senses or memory, from which we may first proceed in drawing these conclusions. A man, who should find in a desert country the remains of pompous buildings, would conclude that the country had, in ancient times, been cultivated by civilized inhabitants; but did nothing of this nature occur to him, he could never form such an inference. We learn the events of former ages from history; but then we must peruse the volumes in which this instruction is contained, and thence carry up our inferences from one testimony to another, till we arrive at the eyewitnesses and spectators of these distant events. In a word, if we proceed not upon some fact, present to the memory or senses, our reasonings would be merely hypothetical; and however the particular links might be connected with each other, the whole chain of inferences would have nothing to support it, nor could we ever, by its means, arrive at the knowledge of any real existence. If I ask why you believe any particular matter of fact, which you relate, you must tell me some reason; and this reason will be some other fact, connected with it. But as you cannot proceed after this manner, *in infinitum*, you must at last terminate in some fact, which is present to your memory or senses; or must allow that your belief is entirely without foundation.

What, then, is the conclusion of the whole matter? A simple one; though, it must be confessed, pretty remote from the common theories of philosophy. All belief of matter of fact or real existence is derived merely from some object, present to the memory or senses, and a customary conjunction between that and some other object. Or in other words; having found in many instances, that any two kinds of objects—flame and heat, snow and cold—have always been conjoined together; if flame or snow be presented anew to the senses, the mind is carried by custom to expect heat or cold, and to *believe* that such a quality does exist, and will discover itself upon a nearer approach. This belief is the necessary result of placing the mind in such circumstances. It is an operation of the soul, when we are so situated, as unavoidable as to feel the passion of love, when we

---

senates. But the observation of any fraud or cruelty in private life is sufficient, with the aid of a little thought, to give us the same apprehension; while it serves as an instance of the general corruption of human nature, and shows us the danger which we must incur by reposing an entire confidence in mankind. In both cases, it is experience which is ultimately the foundation of our inference and conclusion.

There is no man so young and experienced, as not to have formed, from observation, many general and just maxims concerning human affairs and the conduct of life; but it must be confessed, that, when a man comes to put these in practice, he will be extremely liable to error, till time and farther experience both enlarge these maxims, and teach him their proper use and application. In every situation or incident, there are many particular and seemingly minute circumstances, which the man of greatest talent is, at first, apt to overlook, though on them the justness of his conclusions, and consequently the prudence of his conduct, entirely depend. Not to mention, that, to a young beginner, the general observations and maxims occur not always on the proper occasions, nor can be immediately applied with due calmness and distinction. The truth is, an unexperienced reasoner could be no reasoner at all, were he absolutely unexperienced; and when we assign that character to any one, we mean it only in a comparative sense, and suppose him possessed of experience, in a smaller and more imperfect degree.

receive benefits; or hatred, when we meet with injuries. All these operations are a species of natural instincts, which no reasoning or process of the thought and understanding is able either to produce or to prevent.

At this point, it would be very allowable for us to stop our philosophical researches. In most questions we can never make a single step farther; and in all questions we must terminate here at last, after our most restless and curious enquiries. But still our curiosity will be pardonable, perhaps commendable, if it carry us on to still farther researches, and make us examine more accurately the nature of this belief, and of the *customary conjunction*, whence it is derived. By this means we may meet with some explications and analogies that will give satisfaction; at least to such as love the abstract sciences, and can be entertained with speculations, which, however accurate, may still retain a degree of doubt and uncertainty. As to readers of a different taste; the remaining part of this section is not calculated for them, and the following enquiries may well be understood, though it be neglected.

PART II

Nothing is more free than the imagination of man; and though it cannot exceed that original stock of ideas furnished by the internal and external senses, it has unlimited power of mixing, compounding, separating, and dividing these ideas, in all the varieties of fiction and vision. It can feign a train of events, with all the appearance of reality, ascribe to them a particular time and place, conceive them as existent, and paint them out to itself with every circumstance, that belongs to any historical fact, which it believes with the greatest certainty. Wherein, therefore, consists the difference between such a *fiction* and *belief?* It lies not merely in any peculiar idea, which is annexed to such a conception as commands our assent, and which is wanting to every known fiction. For as the mind has authority over all its ideas, it could voluntarily annex this particular idea to any fiction, and consequently be able to believe whatever it pleases; contrary to what we find by daily experience. We can, in our conception, join the head of a man to the body of a horse; but it is not in our power to believe that such an animal has ever really existed.

It follows, therefore, that the difference between fiction and belief lies in some sentiment or feeling, which is annexed to the latter, not to the former, and which depends not on the will, nor can be commanded at pleasure. It must be excited by nature, like all other sentiments; and must arise from the particular situation, in which the mind is placed at any particular juncture. Whenever any object is presented to the memory or senses, it immediately, by the force of custom, carries the imagination to conceive that object, which is usually conjoined to it; and this conception is attended with a feeling or sentiment, different from the loose reveries of the fancy. In this consists the whole nature of belief. For as there is no matter of fact which we believe so firmly that we cannot conceive the contrary, there would be no difference between the conception assented to and that which is rejected, were it not for some sentiment which distinguishes the one from the other. If I see a Billiard-ball moving towards another, on a smooth table, I can easily conceive it to stop upon contact. This conception implies no contradiction; but still it feels very differently from that conception by which I represent to myself the impulse and the communication of motion from one ball to another.

Were we to attempt a *definition* of this sentiment, we should, perhaps, find it a very difficult, if not an impossible task; in the same manner as if we should endeavour to define the feeling of cold or passion of anger, to a creature who never had any experience of these sentiments. Belief is the true and proper name of this feeling; and no one is ever at a loss to know the meaning of that term; because every man is every moment conscious of the sentiment represented by it. It may not, however, be improper to attempt a *description* of this sentiment; in hopes we may, by that means, arrive at some analogies, which may afford a more perfect explication of it. I say, then, that belief is nothing but a more vivid, lively, forcible, firm, steady conception of an object, than what the imagination alone is ever able to attain. This variety of terms, which may seem so unphilosophical, is intended only to express that act of the mind, which renders realities, or what is taken for such, more present to us than fictions, causes them to weigh more in the thought, and gives them a superior influence on the passions and imagination. Provided we agree about the thing, it is needless to dispute about the terms. The imagination has the command over all its ideas, and can join and mix and vary them, in all the ways possible. It may conceive fictitious objects with all the circumstances of place and time. It may set them, in a manner, before our eyes, in their true colours, just as they might have existed. But as it is impossible that this faculty of imagination can ever, of itself, reach belief, it is evident that belief consists not in the peculiar nature or order of ideas, but in the *manner* of their conception, and in their *feeling* to the mind. I confess, that it is impossible perfectly to explain this feeling or manner of conception. We may make use of words which express something near it. But its true and proper name, as we observed before, is *belief;* which is a term that every one sufficiently understands in common life. And in philosophy, we can go no farther than assert, that *belief* is something felt by the mind, which distinguishes the ideas of the judgement from the fictions of the imagination. It gives them more weight and influence; makes them appear of greater importance; enforces them in the mind; and renders them the governing principle of our actions. I hear at present, for instance, a person's voice, with whom I am acquainted; and the sound comes as from the next room. This impression of my senses immediately conveys my thought to the person, together with all the surrounding objects. I paint them out to myself as existing at present, with the same qualities and relations, of which I formerly knew them possessed. These ideas take faster hold of my mind than ideas of an enchanted castle. They are very different to the feeling, and have a much greater influence of every kind, either to give pleasure or pain, joy or sorrow.

Let us, then, take in the whole compass of this doctrine, and allow, that the sentiment of belief is nothing but a conception more intense and steady than what attends the mere fictions of the imagination, and that this manner of conception arises from a customary conjunction of the object with something present to the memory or senses: I believe that it will not be difficult, upon these suppositions, to find other operations of the mind analogous to it, and to trace up these phenomena to principles still more general.

We have already observed that nature has established connexions among particular ideas, and that no sooner one idea occurs to our thoughts than it introduces its correlative, and carries our attention towards it, by a gentle and insensible movement. These principles of connexion or association we have reduced to three, namely, *Resemblance*, *Contiguity* and *Causation;* which are the only bonds that unite our thoughts together, and beget that regular train of reflection or discourse, which, in a greater or less degree, takes place among mankind. Now here arises a question, on which the solution of the present difficulty will depend. Does it happen, in all these relations, that, when one of the objects is presented to the senses or memory the mind is not only carried to the conception of the correlative, but reaches a steadier and stronger conception of it than what otherwise it would have been able to attain? This seems to be the case with that belief which arises from the relation of cause and effect. And if the case be the same with the other relations or principles of associations, this may be established as a general law, which takes place in all the operations of the mind.

We may, therefore, observe, as the first experiment to our present purpose, that, upon the appearance of the picture of an absent friend, our idea of him is evidently enlivened by the *resemblance*, and that every passion, which that idea occasions, whether of joy or sorrow, acquires new force and vigour. In producing this effect, there concur both a relation and a present impression. Where the picture bears him no resemblance, at least was not intended for him, it never so much as conveys our thought to him: And where it is absent, as well as the person, though the mind may pass from the thought of the one to that of the other, it feels its idea to be rather weakened than enlivened by that transition. We take a pleasure in viewing the picture of a friend, when it is set before us; but when it is removed, rather choose to consider him directly than by reflection in an image, which is equally distant and obscure.

The ceremonies of the Roman Catholic religion may be considered as instances of the same nature. The devotees of that superstition usually plead in excuse for the mummeries, with which they were upbraided, that they feel the good effect of those external motions, and postures, and actions, in enlivening their devotion and quickening their fervour, which otherwise would decay, if directed entirely to distant and immaterial objects. We shadow out the objects of our faith, say they, in sensible types and images, and render them more present to us by the immediate presence of these types, than it is possible for us to do merely by an intellectual view and contemplation. Sensible objects have always a greater influence on the fancy than any other; and this influence they readily convey to those ideas to which they are related, and which they resemble. I shall only infer from these practices, and reasoning, that the effect of resemblance in enlivening the ideas is very common; and as in every case a resemblance and a present impression must concur, we are abundantly supplied with experiments to prove the reality of the foregoing principle.

We may add force to these experiments by others of a different kind, in considering the effects of *contiguity* as well as of *resemblance*. It is certain that distance diminishes the force of every idea, and that, upon our approach to any object; though it does not discover itself to our senses; it operates upon the mind with an influence, which imitates an immediate impression. The thinking on any object readily transports the mind to what is contiguous; but it is only the actual presence of an object, that transports it with a superior vivacity. When I am a few miles from home, whatever relates to it touches me more nearly than when I am two hundred leagues distant; though even at that distance the reflecting on any thing in the neighbourhood of my friends or family naturally produces an idea of them. But as in this latter case, both the objects of the mind are ideas; notwithstanding there is an easy transition between them; that transition alone is not able to give a superior vivacity to any of the ideas, for want of some immediate impression.* No one can doubt but causation has the same influence as the other two relations of resemblance and contiguity. Superstitious people are fond of the relics

*"Should I call it our nature or some error that leads us to feel more deeply moved upon seeing places where memorable men are said to have spent much time than we feel when hearing of their deeds or reading their writings? Thus I feel deeply moved now. For Plato comes to my mind, who is said to have been the first philosopher to have made a practice of holding discussions here; and his little garden nearby not only stirs memories but makes me all but see him in the flesh. Here is Speusippus, here Xenocrates, here his student Polemo; it was his seat that we see before us. Even looking at our senate building—that of Hostilius, not the new building which looks smaller to me since it was made larger—made me think of Scipio, Cato, Laelius, and above all my grandfather. Such power of stirring recollection resides in places: no wonder that the training of the memory is based on them." Cicero, *De Finibus*, Book V. [Hume's footnote is in Latin, translation by W.K.]

of saints and holy men, for the same reason, that they seek after types or images, in order to enliven their devotion, and give them a more intimate and strong conception of those exemplary lives, which they desire to imitate. Now it is evident, that one of the best relics, which a devotee could procure, would be the handywork of a saint; and if his clothes and furniture are ever to be considered in this light, it is because they were once at his disposal, and were moved and affected by him; in which respect they are to be considered as imperfect effects, and as connected with him by a shorter chain of consequences than any of those, by which we learn the reality of his existence.

Suppose, that the son of a friend, who had been long dead or absent, were presented to us; it is evident, that this object would instantly revive its correlative idea, and recall to our thoughts all past intimacies and familiarities, in more lively colours than they would otherwise have appeared to us. This is another phenomenon, which seems to prove the principle above mentioned.

We may observe, that, in these phenomena, the belief of the correlative object is always presupposed; without which the relation could have no effect. The influence of the picture supposes, that we *believe* our friend to have once existed. Contiguity to home can never excite our ideas of home, unless we *believe* that it really exists. Now I assert, that this belief, where it reaches beyond the memory or senses, is of a similar nature, and arises from similar causes, with the transition of thought and vivacity of conception here explained. When I throw a piece of dry wood into a fire, my mind is immediately carried to conceive, that it augments, not extinguishes the flame. This transition of thought from the cause to the effect proceeds not from reason. It derives its origin altogether from custom and experience. And as it first begins from an object, present to the senses, it renders the idea or conception of flame more strong and lively than any loose, floating reverie of the imagination. That idea arises immediately. The thought moves instantly towards it, and conveys to it all that force of conception, which is derived from the impression present to the senses. When a sword is levelled at my breast, does not the idea of wound and pain strike me more strongly, than when a glass of wine is presented to me, even though by accident this idea should occur after the appearance of the latter object? But what is there in this whole matter to cause such a strong conception, except only a present object and a customary transition to the idea of another object, which we have been accustomed to conjoin with the former? This is the whole operation of the mind, in all our conclusions concerning matter of fact and existence; and it is a satisfaction to find some analogies, by which it may be explained. The transition from a present object does in all cases give strength and solidity to the related idea.

Here, then, is a kind of pre-established harmony between the course of nature and the succession of our ideas; and though the powers and forces, by which the former is governed, be wholly unknown to us; yet our thoughts and conceptions have still, we find, gone on in the same train with the other work of nature. Custom is that principle, by which this correspondence has been effected; so necessary to the subsistence of our species, and the regulation of our conduct, in every circumstance and occurrence of human life. Had not the presence of an object, instantly excited the idea of those objects, commonly conjoined with it, all our knowledge must have been limited to the narrow sphere of our memory and senses; and we should never have been able to adjust means to ends, or employ our natural powers, either to the producing of good, or avoiding of evil. Those, who delight in the discovery and contemplation of *final causes*, have here ample subject to employ their wonder and admiration.

I shall add, for a further confirmation of the foregoing theory, that, as this operation of the mind, by which we infer like effects from like causes, and *vice versa*, is so essential

The North-East View of Edinburgh Castle, 1675, by John Slezer (1650?–1714). David Hume was born and raised in Edinburgh and, apart from his time in France, spent most of his adult life there. (*National Library of Scotland*)

to the subsistence of all human creatures, it is not probable, that it could be trusted to the fallacious deductions of our reason, which is slow in its operations; appears not, in any degree, during the first years of infancy; and at best is, in every age and period of human life, extremely liable to error and mistake. It is more conformable to the ordinary wisdom of nature to secure so necessary an act of the mind, by some instinct or mechanical tendency, which may be infallible in its operations, may discover itself at the first appearance of life and thought, and may be independent of all the laboured deductions of the understanding. As nature has taught us the use of our limbs, without giving us the knowledge of the muscles and nerves, by which they are actuated; so has she implanted in us an instinct, which carries forward the thought in a correspondent course to that which she has established among external objects; though we are ignorant of those powers and forces, on which this regular course and succession of objects totally depends.

SECTION VI. OF PROBABILITY*

Though there be no such thing as *Chance* in the world; our ignorance of the real cause of any event has the same influence on the understanding, and begets a like species of belief or opinion.

There is certainly a probability, which arises from a superiority of chances on any side; and according as this superiority increases, and surpasses the opposite chances,

*Mr. Locke divides all arguments into demonstrative and probable. In this view, we must say, that it is only probable all men must die, or that the sun will rise tomorrow. But to conform our language more to common use, we ought to divide arguments into *demonstrations*, *proofs*, and *probabilities*. By proofs meaning such arguments from experience as leave no room for doubt or opposition.

the probability receives a proportionable increase, and begets still a higher degree of belief or assent to that side, in which we discover the superiority. If a dye were marked with one figure or number of spots on four sides, and with another figure or number of spots on the two remaining sides, it would be more probable, that the former would turn up than the latter; though, if it had a thousand sides marked in the same manner, and only one side different, the probability would be much higher, and our belief or expectation of the event more steady and secure. This process of the thought or reasoning may seem trivial and obvious; but to those who consider it more narrowly, it may, perhaps, afford matter for curious speculation.

It seems evident, that, when the mind looks forward to discover the event, which may result from the throw of such a dye, it considers the turning up of each particular side as alike probable; and this is the very nature of chance, to render all the particular events, comprehended in it, entirely equal. But finding a greater number of sides concur in the one event than in the other, the mind is carried more frequently to that event, and meets it oftener, in revolving the various possibilities or chances, on which the ultimate result depends. This concurrence of several views in one particular event begets immediately, by an inexplicable contrivance of nature, the sentiment of belief, and gives that event the advantage over its antagonist, which is supported by a smaller number of views, and recurs less frequently to the mind. If we allow, that belief is nothing but a firmer and stronger conception of an object than what attends the mere fictions of the imagination, this operation may, perhaps, in some measure, be accounted for. The concurrence of these several views or glimpses imprints the idea more strongly on the imagination; gives it superior force and vigour; renders its influence on the passions and affections more sensible; and in a word, begets that reliance or security, which constitutes the nature of belief and opinion.

The case is the same with the probability of causes, as with that of chance. There are some causes, which are entirely uniform and constant in producing a particular effect; and no instance has ever yet been found of any failure or irregularity in their operation. Fire has always burned, and water suffocated every human creature: The production of motion by impulse and gravity is an universal law, which has hitherto admitted of no exception. But there are other causes which have been found more irregular and uncertain; nor has rhubarb always proved a purge, or opium a soporific to every one, who has taken these medicines. It is true, when any cause fails of producing its usual effect, philosophers ascribe not this to any irregularity in nature; but suppose, that some secret causes, in the particular structure of parts, have prevented the operation. Our reasonings, however, and conclusions concerning the event are the same as if this principle had no place. Being determined by custom to transfer the past to the future, in all our inferences; where the past has been entirely regular and uniform, we expect the event with the greatest assurance, and leave no room for any contrary supposition. But where different effects have been found to follow from causes, which are to *appearance* exactly similar, all these various effects must occur to the mind in transferring the past to the future, and enter into our consideration, when we determine the probability of the event. Though we give the preference to that which has been found most usual, and believe that this effect will exist, we must not overlook the other effects, but must assign to each of them a particular weight and authority, in proportion as we have found it to be more or less frequent. It is more probable, in almost every country of Europe, that there will be frost sometime in January, than that the weather will continue open throughout the whole month; though this probability varies according to the different climates, and approaches to a certainty in the more northern kingdoms. Here then it seems evident, that, when we transfer the past to the future, in order to determine the effect, which will result from any cause, we transfer all the different events, in the same proportion as they have appeared in the past, and conceive one to have existed a hundred times, for instance, another ten times, and another once. As a great number of views do here concur in one event, they fortify and confirm it to the imagination, beget that sentiment which we call *belief*, and give its object the preference above the contrary event, which is not supported by an equal number of experiments, and recurs not so frequently to the thought in transferring the past to the future. Let any one try to account for this operation of the mind upon any of the received systems of philosophy, and he will be sensible of the difficulty. For my part, I shall think it sufficient, if the present hints excite the curiosity of philosophers, and make them sensible how defective all common theories are in treating of such curious and such sublime subjects.

SECTION VII. OF THE IDEA OF NECESSARY CONNEXION

PART I

The great advantage of the mathematical sciences above the moral consists in this, that the ideas of the former, being sensible, are always clear and determinate, the smallest distinction between them is immediately perceptible, and the same terms are still expressive of the same ideas, without ambiguity or variation. An oval is never mistaken for a circle, nor an hyperbola for an ellipsis. The isosceles and scalenum are distinguished by boundaries more exact than vice and virtue, right and wrong. If any term be defined in geometry, the mind readily, of itself, substitutes, on all occasions, the definition for the term defined: Or even when no definition is employed, the object itself may be presented to the senses, and by that means be steadily and clearly apprehended. But the finer sentiments of the mind, the operations of the understanding, the various agitations of the passions, though really in themselves distinct, easily escape us, when surveyed by reflection; nor is it in our power to recall the original object, as often as we have occasion to contemplate it. Ambiguity, by this means, is gradually introduced into our reasonings: Similar objects are readily taken to be the same: And the conclusion becomes at last very wide of the premises.

One may safely, however, affirm, that, if we consider these sciences in a proper light, their advantages and disadvantages nearly compensate each other, and reduce both of them to a state of equality. If the mind, with greater facility, retains the ideas of geometry clear and determinate, it must carry on a much longer and more intricate chain of reasoning, and compare ideas much wider of each other, in order to reach the abstruser truths of that science. And if moral ideas are apt, without extreme care, to fall into obscurity and confusion, the inferences are always much shorter in these disquisitions, and the intermediate steps, which lead to the conclusion, much fewer than in the sciences which treat of quantity and number. In reality, there is scarcely a proposition in Euclid so simple, as not to consist of more parts, than are to be found in any moral reasoning which runs not into chimera and conceit. Where we trace the principles of the human mind through a few steps, we may be very well satisfied with our progress; considering how soon nature throws a bar to all our enquiries concerning causes, and reduces us to an acknowledgment of our ignorance. The chief obstacle, therefore, to our improvement in the moral or metaphysical sciences is the obscurity of the ideas, and ambiguity of the terms. The principal difficulty in the mathematics is the length of inferences and compass of thought, requisite to the forming of any conclusion. And, perhaps, our progress in natural philosophy is chiefly retarded by the want of proper experiments and phenomena, which are often discovered by chance, and cannot always be found, when requisite, even by the most diligent and prudent enquiry. As moral philosophy seems hitherto to have received less improvement than either geometry or physics, we may conclude, that, if there be any difference in this respect among these sciences, the difficulties, which obstruct the progress of the former, require superior care and capacity to be surmounted.

There are no ideas, which occur in metaphysics, more obscure and uncertain, than those of *power, force, energy* or *necessary connexion,* of which it is every moment necessary for us to treat in all our disquisitions. We shall, therefore, endeavour, in this section, to fix, if possible, the precise meaning of these terms, and thereby remove some part of that obscurity, which is so much complained of in this species of philosophy.

It seems a proposition, which will not admit of much dispute, that all our ideas are nothing but copies of our impressions, or, in other words, that it is impossible for us to *think* of any thing, which we have not antecedently *felt*, either by our external or internal senses. I have endeavoured* to explain and prove this proposition, and have expressed my hopes, that, by a proper application of it, men may reach a greater clearness and precision in philosophical reasonings, than what they have hitherto been able to attain. Complex ideas may, perhaps, be well known by definition, which is nothing but an enumeration of those parts or simple ideas, that compose them. But when we have pushed up definitions to the most simple ideas, and find still some ambiguity and obscurity; what resource are we then possessed of? By what invention can we throw light upon these ideas, and render them altogether precise and determinate to our intellectual view? Produce the impressions or original sentiments, from which the ideas are copied. These impressions are all strong and sensible. They admit not of ambiguity. They are not only placed in a full light themselves, but may throw light on their correspondent ideas, which lie in obscurity. And by this means, we may, perhaps, attain a new microscope or species of optics, by which, in the moral sciences, the most minute, and most simple ideas may be so enlarged as to fall readily under our apprehension, and be equally known with the grossest and most sensible ideas, that can be the object of our enquiry.

To be fully acquainted, therefore, with the idea of power or necessary connexion, let us examine its impression; and in order to find the impression with greater certainty, let us search for it in all the sources, from which it may possibly be derived.

When we look about us towards external objects, and consider the operation of causes, we are never able, in a single instance, to discover any power or necessary connexion; and quality, which binds the effect to the cause, and renders the one an infallible consequence of the other. We only find, that the one does actually, in fact, follow the other. The impulse of one Billiard-ball is attended with motion in the second. This is the whole that appears to the *outward senses*. The mind feels no sentiment or *inward* impression from this succession of objects: Consequently there is not, in any single, particular instance of cause and effect, any thing which can suggest the idea of power or necessary connexion.

From the first appearance of an object, we never can conjecture what effect will result from it. But were the power or energy of any cause discoverable by the mind, we could foresee the effect, even without experience; and might, at first, pronounce with certainty concerning it, by mere dint of thought and reasoning.

In reality, there is no part of matter, that does ever, by its sensible qualities, discover any power or energy, or give us ground to imagine, that it could produce any thing, or be followed by any other object, which we could denominate its effect. Solidity, extension,

*Section II.

motion; these qualities are all complete in themselves, and never point out any other event which may result from them. The scenes of the universe are continually shifting, and one object follows another in an uninterrupted succession; but the power of force, which actuates the whole machine, is entirely concealed from us, and never discovers itself in any of the sensible qualities of body. We know, that, in fact, heat is a constant attendant of flame; but what is the connexion between them, we have no room so much as to conjecture or imagine. It is impossible, therefore, that the idea of power can be derived from the contemplation of bodies, in single instances of their operation; because no bodies ever discover any power, which can be the original of this idea.*

Since, therefore, external objects as they appear to the senses, give us no idea of power or necessary connexion, by their operation in particular instances, let us see, whether this idea be derived from reflection on the operations of our own minds, and be copied from any internal impression. It may be said, that we are every moment conscious of internal power; while we feel, that, by the simple command of our will, we can move the organs of our body, or direct the faculties of our mind. An act of volition produces motion in our limbs, or raises a new idea in our imagination. This influence of the will we know by consciousness. Hence we acquire the idea of power or energy; and are certain, that we ourselves and all other intelligent beings are possessed of power. This idea, then, is an idea of reflection, since it arises from reflecting on the operations of our own mind, and on the command which is exercised by will, both over the organs of the body and faculties of the soul.

We shall proceed to examine this pretension; and first with regard to the influence of volition over the organs of the body. This influence, we may observe, is a fact, which, like all other natural events, can be known only by experience, and can never be foreseen from any apparent energy or power in the cause, which connects it with the effect, and renders the one an infallible consequence of the other. The motion of our body follows upon the command of our will. Of this we are every moment conscious. But the means, by which this is effected; the energy, by which the will performs so extraordinary an operation; of this we are so far from being immediately conscious, that it must for ever escape our most diligent enquiry.

For *first;* is there any principle in all nature more mysterious than the union of soul with body; by which a supposed spiritual substance acquires such an influence over a material one, that the most refined thought is able to actuate the grossest matter? Were we empowered, by a secret wish, to remove mountains, or control the planets in their orbit; this extensive authority would not be more extraordinary, nor more beyond our comprehension. But if by consciousness we perceived any power or energy in the will, we must know this power; we must know its connexion with the effect; we must know the secret union of soul and body, and the nature of both these substances; by which the one is able to operate, in so many instances, upon the other.

Secondly, We are not able to move all the organs of the body with a like authority; though we cannot assign any reason besides experience, for so remarkable a difference between one and the other. Why has the will an influence over the tongue and fingers, not over the heart and liver? This question would never embarrass us, were we conscious of a power in the former case, not in the latter. We should then perceive, independent of experience, why the authority of will over the organs of the body is circumscribed within such particular limits. Being in that case fully acquainted with the power or force, by

*Mr. Locke, in his chapter of power, says, that, finding from experience, that there are several new productions in matter, and concluding that there must somewhere be a power capable of producing them, we arrive at last by this reasoning at the idea of power. But no reasoning can ever give us a new, original, simple idea; as this philosopher himself confesses. This, therefore, can never be the origin of that idea.

which it operates, we should also know, why its influence reaches precisely to such boundaries, and no farther.

A man, suddenly struck with palsy in the leg or arm, or who had newly lost those members, frequently endeavours, at first to move them, and employ them in their usual offices. Here he is as much conscious of power to command such limbs, as a man in perfect health is conscious of power to actuate any member which remains in its natural state and condition. But consciousness never deceives. Consequently, neither in the one case nor in the other, are we ever conscious of any power. We learn the influence of our will from experience alone. And experience only teaches us, how one event constantly follows another; without instructing us in the secret connexion, which binds them together, and renders them inseparable.

Thirdly, We learn from anatomy, that the immediate object of power in voluntary motion, is not the member itself which is moved, but certain muscles, and nerves, and animal spirits, and, perhaps, something still more minute and more unknown, through which the motion is successfully propagated, ere it reach the member itself whose motion is the immediate object of volition. Can there be a more certain proof that the power, by which this whole operation is performed, so far from being directly and fully known by an inward sentiment or consciousness, is, to the last degree, mysterious and unintelligible? Here the mind wills a certain event: Immediately another event, unknown to ourselves, and totally different from the one intended, is produced: This event produces another, equally unknown: Till at last, through a long succession, the desired event is produced. But if the original power were felt, it must be known: Were it known, its effect also must be known; since all power is relative to its effect. And *vice versa,* if the effect be not known, the power cannot be known nor felt. How indeed can we be conscious of a power to move our limbs, when we have no such power; but only that to move certain animal spirits, which, though they produce at last the motion of our limbs, yet operate in such a manner as is wholly beyond our comprehension?

We may, therefore, conclude from the whole, I hope, without any temerity, though with assurance; that our idea of power is not copied from any sentiment or consciousness of power within ourselves, when we give rise to animal motion, or apply our limbs, to their proper use and office. That their motion follows the command of the will is a matter of common experience, like other natural events: But the power or energy by which this is effected, like that in other natural events, is unknown and inconceivable.*

Shall we then assert, that we are conscious of a power or energy in our own minds, when, by an act or command of our will, we raise up a new idea, fix the mind to the contemplation of it, turn it on all sides, and at last dismiss it for some other idea, when we think that we have surveyed it with sufficient accuracy? I believe the same arguments will prove, that even this command of the will gives us no real idea of force or energy.

*It may be pretended, that the resistance which we meet with in bodies, obliging us frequently to exert our force, and call up all our power, this gives us the idea of force and power. It is this nisus, or strong endeavour, of which we are conscious, that is the original impression from which this idea is copied. But, *first,* we attribute power to a vast number of objects, where we never can suppose this resistance or exertion of force to take place, to the Supreme Being, who never meets with any resistance; to the mind in its command over its ideas and limbs, in common thinking and motion, where the effect follows immediately upon the will, without any exertion or summoning up of force, to inanimate matter, which is not capable of this sentiment. *Secondly,* This sentiment of an endeavour to overcome resistance has no known connexion with any event: What follows it we know by experience; but could not know it *a priori*. It must, however, be confessed that the animal nisus, which we experience though it can afford no accurate precise idea of power, enters very much into that vulgar, inaccurate idea, which is formed of it.

First, It must be allowed, that, when we know a power, we know that very circumstance is the cause, by which it is enabled to produce the effect: For these are supposed to be synonymous. We must, therefore, know both the cause and effect, and the relation between them. But do we pretend to be acquainted with the nature of the human soul and the nature of an idea, or the aptitude of the one to produce the other? This is a real creation; a production of something out of nothing: Which implies a power so great, that it may seem, at first sight, beyond the reach of any being, less than infinite. At least it must be owned, that such a power is not felt, nor known, nor even conceivable by the mind. We only feel the event, namely, the existence of an idea, consequent to a command of the will: But the manner, in which this operation is performed, the power by which it is produced, is entirely beyond our comprehension.

Secondly, The command of the mind over itself is limited, as well as its command over the body; and these limits are not known by reason, or any acquaintance with the nature of cause and effect, but only by experience and observation, as in all other natural events and in the operation of external objects. Our authority over our sentiments and passions is much weaker than that over our ideas; and even the latter authority is circumscribed within very narrow boundaries, or show why the power is deficient in one case, not in another.

Thirdly, This self-command is very different at different times. A man in health possesses more of it than one languishing with sickness. We are more master of our thoughts in the morning than in the evening: Fasting, than after a full meal. Can we give any reason for these variations, except experience? Where then is the power, of which we pretend to be conscious? Is there not here, either in a spiritual or material substance, or both, some secret mechanism or structure of parts, upon which the effect depends, and which, being entirely unknown to us, renders the power or energy of the will equally unknown and incomprehensible?

Volition is surely an act of the mind, with which we are sufficiently acquainted. Reflect upon it. Consider it on all sides. Do you find anything in it like this creative power, by which it raises from nothing a new idea, and with a kind of *Fiat*, imitates the omnipotence of its Maker, if I may be allowed so to speak, who called forth into existence all the various scenes of nature? So far from being conscious of this energy in the will, it requires as certain experience as that of which we are possessed, to convince us that such extraordinary effects do ever result from a simple act of volition.

The generality of mankind never find any difficulty in accounting for the more common and familiar operations of nature—such as the descent of heavy bodies, the growth of plants, the generation of animals, or the nourishment of bodies by food: But suppose that, in all these cases, they perceive the very force or energy of the cause, by which it is connected with its effect, and is for ever infallible in its operation. They acquire, by long habit, such a turn of mind, that, upon the appearance of the cause, they immediately expect with assurance its usual attendant, and hardly conceive it possible that any other event could result from it. It is only on the discovery of extraordinary phenomena, such as earthquakes, pestilence, and prodigies of any kind, that they find themselves at a loss to assign a proper cause, and to explain the manner in which the effect is produced by it. It is usual for men, in such difficulties, to have recourse to some invisible intelligent principle as the Immediate cause of that event which surprises them, and which, they think, cannot be accounted for from the common powers of nature. But philosophers, who carry their scrutiny a little farther, immediately perceive that, even in the most familiar events, the energy of the cause is as unintelligible as in the most unusual, and that we only learn by experience the frequent *Conjunction* of objects, without being ever able to comprehend anything like *Connexion* between them. Here, then, many philosophers think themselves obliged by reason to have recourse, on all occasions, to the same principle, which the vulgar never appeal to but in cases that appear miraculous and supernatural. They acknowledge mind and intelligence to be, not only the ultimate and original cause of all things, but the immediate and sole cause of every event which appears in nature. They pretend that those objects which are commonly denominated *causes,* are in reality nothing but *occasions;* and that the true and direct principle of every effect is not any power or force in nature, but a volition of the Supreme Being, who wills that such particular objects should for ever be conjoined with each other. Instead of saying that one Billiard-ball moves another by a force which it has derived from the author of nature, it is the Deity himself, they say, who, by a particular volition, moves the second ball, being determined to this operation by the impulse of the first ball, in consequence of those general laws which he has laid down to himself in the government of the universe. But philosophers advancing still in their inquiries, discover that, as we are totally ignorant of the power on which depends the mutual operation of bodies, we are no less ignorant of that power on which depends the operation of mind on body, or of body on mind; nor are we able, either from our sense or consciousness, to assign the ultimate principle in one case more than in the other. The same ignorance, therefore, reduces them to the same conclusion. They assert that the Deity is the immediate cause of the union between soul and body; and that they are not the organs of sense, which, being agitated by external objects, produce sensations in the mind; but that it is a particular volition of our omnipotent Maker, which excites such a sensation, in consequence of such a motion in the organ. In like manner, it is not any energy in the will that produces local motion in our members: It is God himself, who is pleased to second our will, in itself important, and to command that motion which we erroneously attribute to our own power and efficacy. Nor do philosophers stop at this conclusion. They sometimes extend the same inference to the mind itself, in its internal operations. Our mental vision or conception of ideas is nothing but a revelation made to us by our Maker. When we voluntarily turn our thoughts to any object, and raise up its image in the fancy, it is not the will which creates that idea: It is the universal Creator, who discovers it to the mind, and renders it present to us.

Thus, according to these philosophers, every thing is full of God. Not content with the principle, that nothing exists but by his will, that nothing possesses any power but by his concession: They rob nature, and all created beings, of every power, in order to render their dependence on the Deity still more sensible and immediate. They consider not that, by this theory, they diminish, instead of magnifying, the grandeur of those attributes, which they affect so much to celebrate. It argues surely more power in the Deity to delegate a certain degree of power to inferior creatures, than to produce every thing by his own immediate volition. It argues more wisdom to contrive at first the fabric of the world with such perfect foresight that, of itself, and by its proper operation, it may serve all the purposes of providence, than if the great Creator were obliged every moment to adjust its parts, and animate by his breath all the wheels of that stupendous machine.

But if we would have a more philosophical confutation of this theory, perhaps the two following reflections may suffice.

First, It seems to me that this theory of the universal energy and operation of the Supreme Being is too bold ever to carry conviction with it to a man, sufficiently apprized of the weakness of human reason, and the narrow limits to which it is confined in all its operations. Though the chain of arguments which conduct to it were ever so logical, there must arise a strong suspicion, if not an absolute assurance, that it has carried us quite beyond the reach of our faculties, when it leads to conclusions so extraordinary, and so remote from common life and experience. We are got into fairy land, long ere we have reached the last steps of our theory; and *there* we have no reason to trust our common methods of argument, or to think that our usual analogies and probabilities have any authority. Our line is too short to fathom such immense abysses. And however we may flatter ourselves that we are guided, in every step which we take, by a kind of verisimilitude and experience, we may be assured that this fancied experience has no authority when we thus apply it to subjects that lie entirely out of the sphere of experience. But on this we shall have occasion to touch afterwards.*

Secondly, I cannot perceive any force in the arguments on which this theory is founded. We are ignorant, it is true, of the manner in which bodies operate on each other: Their force or energy is entirely incomprehensible: But are we not equally ignorant of the manner of force by which a mind, even the supreme mind, operates either on itself or on body? Whence, I beseech you, do we acquire any idea of it? We have no sentiment or consciousness of this power in ourselves. We have no idea of the Supreme Being but what we learn from reflection on our own faculties. Were our ignorance, therefore, a good reason for rejecting any thing, we should be led into that principle of denying all energy in the Supreme Being as much as in the grossest matter. We surely comprehend as little the operations of one as of the other. Is it more difficult to conceive that motion may arise from impulse than that it may arise from volition? All we know is our profound ignorance in both cases.**

PART II

But to hasten to a conclusion of this argument, which is already drawn out to too great a length: We have sought in vain for an idea of power or necessary connexion in all the sources from which we could suppose it to be derived. It appears that, in single instances of the operation of bodies, we never can, by our utmost scrutiny, discover any thing but one event following another, without being able to comprehend any force or power by which the cause operates, or any connexion between it and its supposed effect. The same difficulty occurs in contemplating the operations of mind on body—where we observe the motion of the latter to follow upon the volition of the former, but are not able to observe or conceive the tie which binds together the motion and volition, or the energy by which the mind produces this effect. The authority of the will over its own faculties and ideas is not a whit more comprehensible: So that, upon the whole, there appears not, throughout all nature, any one instance of connexion which is conceivable by us. All events seem entirely loose and separate. One event follows another; but we never can observe any tie between them. They seem *conjoined,* but never connected. And as we can have no idea of any thing which never appeared to our outward

*Section XII.

**I need not examine at length the *vis inertiae* [force of inertia] which is so much talked of in the new philosophy, and which is ascribed to matter. We find by experience, that a body at rest or in motion continues for ever in its present state, till put from it by some new cause; and that a body impelled takes as much motion from the impelling body as it acquires itself. These are facts. When we call this a *vis inertiae,* we only mark these facts, without pretending to have any idea of the inert power; in the same manner as, when we talk of gravity, we mean certain effects without comprehending that active power. It was never the meaning of SIR ISAAC NEWTON to rob second causes of all forces of energy though some of his followers have endeavoured to establish that theory upon his authority. On the contrary, that great philosopher had recourse to an etherial active fluid to explain his universal attraction; though he was so cautious and modest as to allow that it was a mere hypothesis, not to be insisted on, without more experiments. I must confess, that there is something in the fate of opinions a little extraordinary. DESCARTES insinuated that doctrine of the universal and sole efficacy of the Deity, without insisting on it. MALEBRANCHE and other CARTESIANS made it the foundation of all their philosophy. It had, however, no authority in England. LOCKE, CLARKE, and CUDWORTH, never so much as take notice of it, but suppose all along, that matter has a real, though subordinate and derived power. By what means has it become so prevalent among our modern metaphysicians?

sense or inward sentiment, the necessary conclusion *seems* to be that we have no idea of connexion or power at all, and that these words are absolutely without any meaning, when employed either in philosophical reasonings or common life.

But there still remains one method of avoiding this conclusion, and one source which we have not yet examined. When any natural object or event is presented, it is impossible for us, by any sagacity or penetration, to discover, or even conjecture, without experience, what event will result from it, or to carry our foresight beyond that object which is immediately present to the memory and senses. Even after one instance or experiment where we have observed a particular event to follow upon another, we are not entitled to form a general rule, or foretell what will happen in like cases; it being justly esteemed an unpardonable temerity to judge of the whole course of nature from one single experiment, however accurate or certain. But when one particular species of event has always, in all instances, been conjoined with another, we make no longer any scruple of foretelling one upon the appearance of the other, and of employing that reasoning which can alone assure us of any matter of fact or existence. We then call the one object, *Cause*; the other, *Effect*. We suppose that there is some connexion between them; some power in the one, by which it infallibly produces the other, and operates with the greatest certainty and strongest necessity.

It appears, then, that this idea of a necessary connexion among events arises from a number of similar instances which occur of the constant conjunction of these events; nor can that idea ever be suggested by any one of these instances, surveyed in all possible lights and positions. But there is nothing in a number of instances, different from every single instance, which is supposed to be exactly similar; except only, that after a repetition of similar instances, the mind is carried by habit, upon the appearance of one event, to expect its usual attendant, and to believe that it will exist. This connexion, therefore, which we *feel* in the mind, this customary transition of the imagination from one object to its usual attendant, is the sentiment or impression from which we form the idea of power or necessary connexion. Nothing farther is in the case. Contemplate the subject on all sides; you will never find any other origin of that idea. This is the sole difference between one instance, from which we can never receive the idea of connexion, and a number of similar instances, by which it is suggested. The first time a man saw the communication of motion by impulse, as by the shock of two Billiard-balls, he could not pronounce that the one event was *connected*: but only that it was *conjoined* with the other. After he has observed several instances of this nature, he then pronounces them to be *connected*. What alteration has happened to give rise to this new idea of connexion? Nothing but that he now *feels* these events to be *connected* in his imagination, and can readily foretell the existence of one from the appearance of the other. When we say, therefore, that one object is connected with another, we mean only that they have acquired a connexion in our thought, and give rise to this inference, by which they become proofs of each other's existence: A conclusion which is somewhat extraordinary, but which seems founded on sufficient evidence. Nor will its evidence be weakened by any general diffidence of the understanding, or sceptical suspicion concerning every conclusion which is new and extraordinary. No conclusions can be more agreeable to scepticism than such as make discoveries concerning the weakness and narrow limits of human reason and capacity.

And what stronger instance can be produced of the surprising ignorance and weakness of the understanding than the present? For surely, if there be any relation among objects which it imports to us to know perfectly, it is that of cause and effect. On this are founded all our reasonings concerning matter of fact or existence. By means of it alone we attain any assurance concerning objects which are removed from the present testimony of our memory and senses. The only immediate utility of all sciences, is to teach us, how to control and regulate future events by their causes. Our thoughts and enquiries are, therefore, every moment, employed about this relation: Yet so imperfect are the ideas which we form concerning it, that it is impossible to give any just definition of cause, except what is drawn from something extraneous and foreign to it. Similar objects are always conjoined with similar. Of this we have experience. Suitably to this experience, therefore, we may define a cause to be *an object, followed by another, and where all the objects similar to the first are followed by objects similar to the second. Or in other words where, if the first object had not been, the second never had existed.* The appearance of a cause always conveys the mind, by a customary transition, to the idea of the effect. Of this also we have experience. We may, therefore, suitably to this experience, form another definition of cause, and call it, *an object followed by another and whose appearance always conveys the thought to that other*. But though both these definitions be drawn from circumstances foreign to the cause, we cannot remedy this inconvenience, or attain any more perfect definition, which may point out that circumstance in the cause, which gives it a connexion with its effect. We have no idea of this connexion, nor even any distinct notion what it is we desire to know, when we endeavour at a conception of it. We say, for instance, that the vibration of this string is the cause of this particular sound. But what do we mean by that affirmation? We either mean *that this vibration is followed by this sound, and that all similar vibrations have been followed by similar sounds*: Or, that this vibration is followed by this sound, and that upon the appearance of one the mind anticipates the senses, and forms immediately an idea of the other. We may consider the relation of cause and effect in either of these two lights; but beyond these, we have no idea of it.*

To recapitulate, therefore, the reasonings of this section: Every idea is copied from some preceding impression or sentiment; and where we cannot find any impression, we may be certain that there is no idea. In all single instances of the operation of bodies or minds, there is nothing that produces any impression, nor consequently can suggest any idea of power or necessary connexion. But when many uniform instances appear, and the same object is always followed by the same event; we then begin to entertain the notion of cause and connexion. We then *feel* a new sentiment or impression, to wit, a customary connexion in the thought or imagination between one object and its usual attendant; and this sentiment is the original of that idea which we seek for. For as this idea arises from a number of similar instances, and not from any single instance, it must arise from that circumstance, in which the number of instances differ from every individual instance. But this customary connexion or transition of the

*According to these explanations and definitions, the idea of *power* is relative as much as that of cause; and both have a reference to an effect, or some other event constantly conjoined with the former. When we consider the *unknown* circumstance of an object, by which the degree of quantity of its effect is fixed and determined, we call that its power: And accordingly, it is allowed by all philosophers, that the effect is the measure of the power. But if they had any idea of power, as it is in itself, why could not they measure it in itself? The dispute whether the force of a body in motion be as its velocity, or the square of its velocity; this dispute, I say, need not be decided by comparing its effects in equal or unequal times; but by a direct mensuration and comparison.

As to the frequent use of the words, Force, Power, Energy, etc., which every where occur in common conversation, as well as in philosophy; that is no proof, that we are acquainted, in any instance, with the connecting principle between cause and effect or can account ultimately for the production of one thing to another. These words, as commonly used, have very loose meanings annexed to them; and their ideas in motion without the sentiment of a *nisus* or endeavour; and every animal has a sentiment or feeling from the stroke or blow of an external object, that is in motion. These sensations, which are merely animal, and from which we can *a priori* draw no inference, we are apt to transfer to inanimate objects, and to suppose, that they have some such feelings, whenever they transfer or receive motion. With regard to energies, which are exerted, without our annexing to them any idea of communicated motion, we consider only the constant experienced conjunction of the events; and as we *feel* a customary connexion between the ideas, we transfer that feeling to the objects; as nothing is more usual than to apply to external bodies every internal sensation which they occasion.

imagination is the only circumstance in which they differ. In every other particular they are alike. The first instance which we saw of motion communicated by the shock of two Billiard-balls (to return to this obvious illustration) is exactly similar to any instance that may, at present, occur to us; except only, that we could not, at first, *infer* one event from the other; which we are enabled to do at present, after so long a course of uniform experience. I know not whether the reader will readily apprehend this reasoning. I am afraid that, should I multiply words about it, or throw it into a greater variety of lights, it would only become more obscure and intricate. In all abstract reasonings there is one point of view which, if we can happily hit, we shall go farther towards illustrating the subject than by all the eloquence in the world. This point of view we should endeavour to reach, and reserve the flowers of rhetoric for subjects which are more adapted to them.

SECTION VIII. OF LIBERTY AND NECESSITY

PART I

It might reasonably be expected in questions which have been canvassed and disputed with great eagerness, since the first origin of science and philosophy, that the meaning of all the terms, at least, should have been agreed upon among the disputants; and our enquiries, in the course of two thousand years, been able to pass from words to the true and real subject of the controversy. For how easy may it seem to give exact definitions of the terms employed in reasoning, and make these definitions, not the mere sound of words, the object of future scrutiny and examination? But if we consider the matter more narrowly, we shall be apt to draw a quite opposite conclusion. From this circumstance alone, that a controversy has been long kept on foot, and remains still undecided, we may presume that there is some ambiguity in the expression, and that the disputants affix different ideas to the terms employed in the controversy. For as the faculties of the mind are supposed to be naturally alike in every individual; otherwise nothing could be more fruitless than to reason or dispute together; it were impossible, if men affix the same ideas to their terms, that they could so long form different opinions of the same subject; especially when they communicate their views, and each party turn themselves on all sides, in search of arguments which may give them the victory over their antagonists. It is true, if men attempt the discussion of questions which lie entirely beyond the reach of human capacity, such as those concerning the origin of worlds, or the economy of the intellectual system or region of spirits, they may long beat the air in their fruitless contests, and never arrive at any determinate conclusion. But if the question regard any subject of common life and experience, nothing, one would think, could preserve the dispute so long undecided but some ambiguous expressions, which keep the antagonists still at a distance, and hinder them from grappling with each other.

This has been the case in the long disputed question concerning liberty and necessity; and to so remarkable a degree that, if I be not much mistaken, we shall find, that all mankind, both learned and ignorant, have always been of the same opinion with regard to this subject, and that a few intelligible definitions would immediately have put an end to the whole controversy. I own that this dispute has been so much canvassed on all hands, and has led philosophers into such a labyrinth of obscure sophistry, that it is no wonder, if a sensible reader indulge his ease so far as to turn a deaf ear to the proposal of such a question, from which he can expect neither instruction nor entertainment. But the state of the argument here proposed may, perhaps, serve to renew his attention; as it has more novelty, promises at least some decision of the controversy, and will not much disturb his ease by any intricate or obscure reasoning.

I hope, therefore, to make it appear that all men have ever agreed in the doctrine both of necessity and of liberty, according to any reasonable sense, which can be put on these terms; and that the whole controversy has hitherto turned merely upon words. We shall begin with examining the doctrine of necessity.

It is universally allowed that matter, in all its operations, is actuated by a necessary force, and that every natural effect is so precisely determined by the energy of its cause that no other effect, in such particular circumstances, could possibly have resulted from it. The degree and direction of every motion is, by the laws of nature, prescribed with such exactness that a living creature may as soon arise from the shock of two bodies as motion in any other degree or direction than what is actually produced by it. Would we, therefore, form a just and precise idea of *necessity* we must consider whence that idea arises when we apply it to the operation of bodies.

It seems evident that, if all the scenes of nature were continually shifted in such a manner that no two events bore any resemblance to each other, but every object was entirely new, without any similitude to whatever had been seen before, we should never, in that case, have attained the least idea of necessity, or of a connexion among these objects. We might say, upon such a supposition, that one object or event has followed another; not that one was produced by the other. The relation of cause and effect must be utterly unknown to mankind. Inference and reasoning concerning the operations of nature would, from that moment, be at an end; and the memory and senses remain the only canals, by which the knowledge of any real existence could possibly have access to the mind. Our idea, therefore, of necessity and causation arises entirely from the uniformity observable in the operations of nature, where similar objects are constantly conjoined together, and the mind is determined by custom to infer the one from the appearance of the other. These two circumstances form the whole of that necessity, which we ascribe to matter. Beyond the constant conjunction of similar objects, and the consequent *inference* from one to the other, we have no notion of any necessity or connexion.

If it appear, therefore, that all mankind have ever allowed, without any doubt or hesitation, that these two circumstances take place in the voluntary actions of men, and in the operations of mind; it must follow, that all mankind have ever agreed in the doctrine of necessity, and that they have hitherto disputed, merely for not understanding each other.

As to the first circumstance, the constant and regular conjunction of similar events, we may possibly satisfy ourselves by the following considerations. It is universally acknowledged that there is a great uniformity among the actions of men, in all nations and ages, and that human nature remains still the same, in its principles and operations. The same motives always produce the same actions: The same events follow from the same causes. Ambition, avarice, self-love, vanity, friendship, generosity, public spirit: these passions, mixed in various degrees, and distributed through society, have been, from the beginning of the world, and still are, the source of all the actions and enterprises, which have ever been observed among mankind. Would you know the sentiments, inclinations, and course of life of the Greeks and Romans? Study well the temper and actions of the French and English: You cannot be much mistaken in transferring to the former *most* of the observations which you have made with regard to the latter. Mankind are so much the same, in all times and places, that history informs us of nothing new or strange in this particular. Its chief use is only to discover the constant and universal principles of human nature, by showing men in all varieties of circumstances and situations, and furnishing us with materials from which we may form our observations and become acquainted with the regular springs of human action and behaviour. These records of wars, intrigues, factions, and revolutions, are so many collections of experiments, by which the politician or moral philosopher fixes the principles of his science, in the same manner as the physician or natural philosopher becomes acquainted with the nature of plants, minerals, and other external objects, by the experiments which he forms concerning them. Nor are the earth, water, and other elements, examined by Aristotle, and Hippocrates, more like to those which at present lie under our observation than the men described by Polybius and Tacitus are to those who now govern the world.

Should a traveller, returning from a far country, bring us an account of men, wholly different from any with whom we were ever acquainted; men, who were entirely divested of avarice, ambition, or revenge; who knew no pleasure but friendship, generosity, and public spirit; we should immediately, from these circumstances, detect the falsehood, and prove him a liar, with the same certainty as if he had stuffed his narration with stories of centaurs and dragons, miracles and prodigies. And if we would explode any forgery in history, we cannot make use of a more convincing argument, than to prove, that the actions ascribed to any person are directly contrary to the course of nature, and that no human motives, in such circumstances, could ever induce him to such a conduct. The veracity of Quintus Curtius is as much to be suspected, when he describes the supernatural courage of Alexander, by which he was hurried on singly to attack multitudes, as when he describes his supernatural force and activity, by which he was able to resist them. So readily and universally do we acknowledge a uniformity in human motives and actions as well as in the operations of body.

Hence likewise the benefit of that experience, acquired by long life and a variety of business and company, in order to instruct us in the principles of human nature, and regulate our future conduct, as well as speculation. By means of this guide, we mount up to the knowledge of men's inclinations and motives, from their actions, expressions, and even gestures; and again descend to the interpretation of their actions from our knowledge of their motives and inclinations. The general observations treasured up by a course of experience, give us the clue of human nature, and teach us to unravel all its intricacies. Pretexts and appearances no longer deceive us. Public declarations pass for the specious colouring of a cause. And though virtue and honour be allowed their proper weight and authority, that perfect disinterestedness, so often pretended to, is never expected in multitudes and parties; seldom in their leaders; and scarcely even in individuals of any rank or station. But were there no uniformity in human actions, and were every experiment which we could form of this kind irregular and anomalous, it were impossible to collect any general observations concerning mankind; and no experience, however accurately digested by reflection, would ever serve to any purpose. Why is the aged husbandman more skilful in his calling than the young beginner but because there is a certain uniformity in the operation of the sun, rain, and earth towards the production of vegetables; and experience teaches the old practitioner the rules by which this operation is governed and directed.

We must not, however, expect that this uniformity of human actions should be carried to such a length as that all men, in the same circumstances, will always act precisely in the same manner, without making any allowance for the diversity of characters, prejudices, and opinions. Such a uniformity in every particular, is found in no part of nature. On the contrary, from observing the variety of conduct in different men, we are enabled to form a greater variety of maxims, which still suppose a degree of uniformity and regularity.

Are the manners of men different in different ages and countries? We learn thence the great force of custom and education, which mould the human mind from its infancy and form it into a fixed and established character. Is the behaviour and conduct of the one sex very unlike that of the other? Is it thence we become acquainted with the different characters which nature has impressed upon the sexes, and which she preserves with constancy and regularity? Are the actions of the same person much diversified in the different periods of his life, from infancy to old age? This affords room for many general observations concerning the gradual change of our sentiments and inclinations, and the different maxims which prevail in the different ages of human creatures. Even the characters, which are peculiar to each individual, have a uniformity in their influence; otherwise our acquaintance with the persons and our observation of their conduct could never teach us their dispositions, or serve to direct our behaviour with regard to them.

I grant it possible to find some actions, which seem to have no regular connexion with any known motives, and are exceptions to all the measures of conduct which have ever been established for the government of men. But if we would willingly know what judgement should be formed of such irregular and extraordinary actions, we may consider the sentiments commonly entertained with regard to those irregular events which appear in the course of nature, and the operations of external objects. All causes are not conjoined to their usual effects with like uniformity. An artificer, who handles only dead matter, may be disappointed of his aim, as well as the politician, who directs the conduct of sensible and intelligent agents.

The vulgar, who take things according to their first appearance, attribute the uncertainty of events to such an uncertainty in the causes as makes the latter often fail of their usual influence; though they meet with no impediment in their operation. But philosophers, observing that, almost in every part of nature, there is contained a vast variety of springs and principles, which are hid, by reason of their minuteness or remoteness, find, that it is at least possible the contrariety of events may not proceed from any contingency in the cause, but from the secret operation of contrary causes. This possibility is converted into certainty by farther observation, when they remark that, upon an exact scrutiny, a contrariety of effects always betrays a contrariety of causes, and proceeds from their mutual opposition. A peasant can give no better reason for the stopping of any clock or watch than to say that it does not commonly go right: But an artist easily perceives that the same force in the spring or pendulum has always the same influence on the wheels; but fails of its usual effect, perhaps by reason of a grain of dust, which puts a stop to the whole movement. From the observation of several parallel instances, philosophers form a maxim that the connexion between all causes and effects is equally necessary, and that its seeming uncertainty in some instances proceeds from the secret opposition of contrary causes.

Thus, for instance, in the human body, when the usual symptoms of health or sickness disappoint our expectation; when medicines operate not with their wonted powers; when irregular events follow from any particular cause; the philosopher and physician are not surprised at the matter, nor are ever tempted to deny, in general, the necessity and uniformity of those principles by which the animal economy is conducted. They know that a human body is a mighty complicated machine: That many secret powers lurk in it, which are altogether beyond our comprehension: That to us it must often appear very uncertain in its operations: And that therefore the irregular events, which outwardly discover themselves, can be no proof that the laws of nature are not observed with the greatest regularity in its internal operations and government.

The philosopher, if he be consistent, must apply the same reasoning to the actions and volitions of intelligent agents. The most irregular and unexpected resolutions of men may frequently be accounted for by those who know every particular circumstance of their character and situation. A person of an obliging disposition gives a peevish answer: But he has the toothache, or has not dined. A stupid fellow discovers an uncommon alacrity in his carriage: But he has met with a sudden piece of good fortune. Or even when an action, as sometimes happens, cannot be particularly accounted for, either by the person himself or by others; we know, in general, that the characters of men are, to a certain degree, inconstant and irregular. This is, in a manner, the constant character of human nature; though it be applicable, in a more particular manner, to some persons who have no fixed rule for their conduct, but proceed in a continued course of caprice and inconstancy. The internal principles and motives may operate in a uniform manner, notwithstanding these seeming irregularities; in the same manner as the winds, rain, clouds, and other variations of the weather are supposed to be governed by steady principles; though not easily discoverable by human sagacity and enquiry.

Thus it appears, not only that the conjunction between motives and voluntary actions is as regular and uniform as that between the cause and effect in any part of nature; but also that this regular conjunction has been universally acknowledged among mankind, and has never been the subject of dispute, either in philosophy or common life. Now, as it is from past experience that we draw all inferences concerning the future, and as we conclude that objects will always be conjoined together which we find to have always been conjoined; it may seem superfluous to prove that this experienced uniformity in human actions is a source whence we draw *inferences* concerning them. But in order to throw the argument into a greater variety of lights we shall also insist, though briefly, on this latter topic.

The mutual dependence of men is so great in all societies that scarce any human action is entirely complete in itself, or is performed without some reference to the actions of others, which are requisite to make it answer fully the intention of the agent. The poorest artificer, who labours alone, expects at least the protection of the magistrate, to ensure him the enjoyment of the fruits of his labour. He also expects that, when he carries his goods to market, and offers them at a reasonable price, he shall find purchasers, and shall be able, by the money he acquires, to engage others to supply him with those commodities which are requisite for his subsistence. In proportion as men extend their dealings, and render their intercourse with others more complicated, they always comprehend, in their schemes of life, a greater variety of voluntary actions, which they expect, from the proper motives, to co-operate with their own. In all these conclusions they take their measures from past experience, in the same manner as in their reasonings concerning external objects; and firmly believe that men, as well as all the elements, are to continue, in their operations, the same that they have ever found them. A manufacturer reckons upon the labour of his servants for the execution of any work as much as upon the tools which he employs, and would be equally surprised were his expectations disappointed. In short, this experimental inference and reasoning concerning the actions of others enters so much into human life, that no man, while awake, is ever a moment without employing it. Have we not reason, therefore, to affirm that all mankind have always agreed in the doctrine of necessity according to the foregoing definition and explication of it?

Nor have philosophers ever entertained a different opinion from the people in this particular. For, not to mention that almost every action of their life supposes that opinion, there are even few of the speculative parts of learning to which it is not essential. What would become of *history*, had we not a dependence on the veracity of the historian according to the experience which we have had of mankind? How could *politics* be a science, if laws and forms of government had not a uniform influence upon society? Where would be the foundation of *morals*, if particular characters had no certain or determinate power to produce particular sentiments, and if these sentiments had no constant operation on actions? And with what pretence could we employ our *criticism* upon any poet or polite author, if we could not pronounce the conduct and sentiments of his actors either natural or unnatural to such characters, and in such circumstances? It seems almost impossible, therefore, to engage either in science or action of any kind without acknowledging the doctrine of necessity, and this *inference* from motive to voluntary actions, from characters to conduct.

And indeed, when we consider how aptly *natural* and *moral* evidence link together, and form only one chain of argument, we shall make no scruple to allow that they are of the same nature, and derived from the same principles. A prisoner who has neither money nor interest, discovers the impossibility of his escape, as well when he considers the obstinacy of the gaoler, as the walls and bars with which he is surrounded; and, in all attempts for his freedom, chooses rather to work upon the stone and iron of the one, than upon the inflexible nature of the other. The same prisoner, when conducted to the scaffold, foresees his death as certainly from the constancy and fidelity of his guards, as from the operation of the axe or wheel. His mind runs along a certain train of ideas: The refusal of the soldiers to consent to his escape; the action of the executioner; the separation of the head and body; bleeding, convulsive motions, and death. Here is a connected chain of natural causes and voluntary actions; but the mind feels no difference between them in passing from one link to another: Nor is less certain of the future event than if it were connected with the objects present to the memory or senses, by a train of causes, cemented together by what we are pleased to call a *physical* necessity. The same experienced union has the same effect on the mind, whether the united objects be motives, volition, and actions; or figure and motion. We may change the name of things; but their nature and their operation on the understanding never change.

Were a man, whom I know to be honest and opulent, and with whom I live in intimate friendship, to come into my house, where I am surrounded with my servants, I rest assured that he is not to stab me before he leaves it in order to rob me of my silver standish; and I no more suspect this event than the falling of the house itself, which is new, and solidly built and founded.—*But he may have been seized with a sudden and unknown frenzy.*—So may a sudden earthquake arise, and shake and tumble my house about my ears. I shall therefore change the suppositions. I shall say that I know with certainty that he is not to put his hand into the fire and hold it there till it be consumed: And this event I think I can foretell with the same assurance, as that, if he throw himself out at the window, and meet with no obstruction, he will not remain a moment suspended in the air. No suspicion of an unknown frenzy can give the least possibility to the former event, which is so contrary to all the known principles of human nature. A man who at noon leaves his purse full of gold on the pavement at Charing-Cross, may as well expect that it will fly away like a feather, as that he will find it untouched an hour after. Above one half of human reasonings contain inferences of a similar nature, attended with more or less degrees of certainty proportioned to our experience of the usual conduct of mankind in such particular situations.

I have frequently considered, what could possibly be the reason why all mankind, though they have ever, without hesitation, acknowledged the doctrine of necessity in their whole practice and reasoning, have yet not discovered such a reluctance to acknowledge it in words, and have rather shown a propensity, in all ages, to profess the contrary opinion. The matter, I think, may be accounted for after the following manner. If we examine the operations of body, and the production of effects from their causes, we shall find that all our faculties can never carry us farther in our knowledge of this relation than barely to observe that particular objects are *constantly conjoined* together, and that the mind is carried, by a *customary transition*, from the appearance of one to the belief of the other. But though this conclusion concerning human ignorance be the result of the strictest scrutiny of this subject, men still entertain a strong propensity to believe that they penetrate farther into the powers of nature, and perceive something like a necessary connexion between the cause and the effect. When again they turn their reflections towards the operations of their own minds, and *feel* no such connexion of the motive and the action; they are thence apt to suppose, that there is a difference between the effects which result from material force, and those which arise from thought and intelligence. But being once convinced that we know nothing farther of causation of any kind than merely the *constant conjunction* of objects, and the consequent *inference* of the mind from one to another, and finding that these two circumstances are universally allowed to have place in voluntary actions; we may be more easily led to own the same necessity common to all causes. And though this reasoning may contradict the systems of many philosophers, in ascribing necessity to the determinations of the will, we shall find, upon reflection, that they dissent from it in words only, not in their real sentiment. Necessity, according to the sense in which it is here taken, has never yet been rejected, nor can ever, I think, be rejected by any philosopher. It may only, perhaps, be pretended that the mind can perceive, in the operations of matter, some farther connexion between the cause and effect; and connexion that has no place in voluntary actions of intelligent beings. Now whether it be so or not, can only appear upon examination; and it is incumbent on these philosophers to make good their assertion, by defining or describing that necessity, and pointing it out to us in the operations of material causes.

It would seem, indeed, that men begin at the wrong end of this question concerning liberty and necessity, when they enter upon it by examining the faculties of the soul, the influence of the understanding, and the operations of the will. Let them first discuss a more simple question, namely, the operations of body and of brute unintelligent matter; and try whether they can there form any idea of causation and necessity, except that of a constant conjunction of objects, and subsequent inference of the mind from one to another. If these circumstances form, in reality, the whole of that necessity, which we conceive in matter, and if these circumstances be also universally acknowledged to take place in the operations of the mind, the dispute is at an end; at least, must be owned to be thenceforth merely verbal. But as long as we will rashly suppose, that we have some farther idea of necessity and causation in the operations of external objects; at the same time, that we can find nothing farther in the voluntary actions of the mind; there is no possibility of bringing the question to any determinate issue, while we proceed upon so erroneous a supposition. The only method of undeceiving us is to mount up higher; to examine the narrow extent of science when applied to material causes; and to convince ourselves that all we know of them is the constant conjunction and inference above mentioned. We may, perhaps, find that it is with difficulty we are induced to fix such narrow limits to human understanding: But we can afterwards find no difficulty when we come to apply this doctrine to the actions of the will. For as it is evident that these have a regular conjunction with motives and circumstances and characters, and as we always draw inferences from one to the other, we must be obliged to acknowledge in words that necessity, which we have already avowed, in every deliberation of our lives, and in every step of our conduct and behaviour.*

But to proceed in this reconciling project with regard to the question of liberty and necessity; the most contentious question of metaphysics, the most contentious science; it will not require many words to prove, that all mankind have ever agreed in the doctrine of liberty as well as in that of necessity, and that the whole dispute, in this respect also, has been hitherto merely verbal. For what is meant by liberty, when applied to voluntary actions? We cannot surely mean that actions have so little connexion with motives, inclinations, and circumstances, that one does not follow with a certain degree of uniformity from the other, and that one affords no inference by which we can conclude the existence of the other. For these are plain and acknowledged matters of fact. By liberty, then, we can only mean *a power of acting or not acting, according to the determinations of the will;* that is, if we choose to remain at rest, we may; if we choose to move, we also may. Now this hypothetical liberty is universally allowed to belong to every one who is not a prisoner and in chains. Here, then, is no subject of dispute.

Whatever definition we may give of liberty, we should be careful to observe two requisite circumstances; *first*, that it be consistent with plain matter of fact; *secondly*, that it be consistent with itself. If we observe these circumstances, and render our definition intelligible, I am persuaded that all mankind will be found of one opinion with regard to it.

It is universally allowed that nothing exists without a cause of its existence, and that chance, when strictly examined, is a mere negative word, and means not any real power which has anywhere a being in nature. But it is pretended that some causes are necessary, some not necessary. Here then is the advantage of definitions. Let any one *define* a cause, without comprehending, as a part of the definition, a *necessary connexion* with its effect; and let him show distinctly the origin of the idea, expressed by the definition; and I shall readily give up the whole controversy. But if the foregoing explication

*The prevalence of the doctrine of liberty may be accounted for, from another cause viz. a false sensation or seeming experience which we have, or may have, of liberty or indifference, in many of our actions. The necessity of any action, whether of matter or of mind, is not, properly speaking, a quality in the agent, but in any thinking or intelligent being, who may consider the action; and it consists chiefly in the determination of his thoughts to infer the existence of that action from some preceding objects; as liberty, when opposed to necessity, is nothing but the want of that determination, and a certain looseness or indifference, which we feel, in passing or not passing, from the idea of one object to that of any succeeding one. Now we may observe, that, though, in *reflecting* on human actions, we seldom feel such a looseness, or indifference, but are commonly able to infer them with considerable certainty from their motives, and from the dispositions of the agent; yet it frequently happens, that, in *performing* the actions themselves, we are sensible of something like it: And as all resembling objects are readily taken for each other, this has been employed as a demonstrative and even intuitive proof of human liberty. We feel, that our actions are subject to our will, on most occasions; and imagine we feel, that the will itself is subject to nothing, because, when by a denial of it we are provoked to try, we feel, that it moves easily every way, and produces an image of itself (or a *Velleïty*, as it is called in the schools) even on that side, on which it did not settle. This image, or faint motion, we persuade ourselves, could, at that time, have been completed into the thing itself; because, should that be denied, we find, upon a second trial, that, at present it can. We consider not that the fantastical desire of showing liberty, is here the motive of our actions. And it seems certain, that, however, we may imagine we feel a liberty within ourselves, a spectator can commonly infer our actions from our motives and character, and even where he cannot, he concludes in general, that he might, were he perfectly acquainted with every circumstance of our situation and temper, and the most secret springs of our complexion and disposition. Now this is the very essence of necessity, according to the foregoing doctrine.

of the matter be received, this must be absolutely impracticable. Had not objects a regular conjunction with each other, we should never have entertained any notion of cause and effect; and this regular conjunction produces that inference of the understanding, which is the only connexion, that we can have any comprehension of. Whoever attempts a definition of cause, exclusive of these circumstances, will be obliged either to employ unintelligible terms or such as are synonymous to the term which he endeavours to define.* And if the definition above mentioned be admitted; liberty, when opposed to necessity, not to constraint, is the same thing with chance; which is universally allowed to have no existence.

PART II

There is no method of reasoning more common, and yet none more blameable, than, in philosophical disputes, to endeavour the refutation of any hypothesis, by a pretence of its dangerous consequences to religion and morality. When any opinion leads to absurdities, it is certainly false; but it is not certain that an opinion is false, because it is of dangerous consequence. Such topics, therefore, ought entirely to be forborne; as serving nothing to the discovery of truth, but only to make the person of an antagonist odious. This I observe in general, without pretending to draw any advantage from it. I frankly submit to an examination of this kind, and shall venture to affirm that the doctrines, both of necessity and of liberty, as above explained, are not only consistent with morality, but are absolutely essential to its support.

Necessity may be defined two ways, conformably to the two definitions of *cause,* of which it makes an essential part. It consists either in the constant conjunction of like objects, or in the inference of the understanding from one object to another. Now necessity, in both these senses, (which, indeed, are at bottom the same) has universally, though tacitly, in the schools, in the pulpit, and in common life, been allowed to belong to the will of man; and no one has ever pretended to deny that we can draw inferences concerning human actions, and that those inferences are founded on the experienced union of like actions, with like motives, inclinations, and circumstances. The only particular in which any one can differ, is, that either, perhaps, he will refuse to give the name of necessity to this property of human actions: But as long as the meaning is understood, I hope the word can do no harm: Or that he will maintain it possible to discover something farther in the operations of matter. But this, it must be acknowledged, can be of no consequence to morality or religion, whatever it may be to natural philosophy or metaphysics. We may here be mistaken in asserting that there is no idea of any other necessity or connexion in the actions of body: But surely we ascribe nothing to the actions of the mind, but what everyone does, and must readily allow of. We change no circumstance in the received orthodox system with regard to the will, but only in that with regard to material objects and causes. Nothing, therefore, can be more innocent, at least, than this doctrine.

All laws being founded on rewards and punishments, it is supposed as a fundamental principle, that these motives have a regular and uniform influence on the mind, and both

*Thus, if a cause be defined, *that which produces any thing;* it is easy to observe, that *producing* is synonymous to *causing*. In like manner, if a cause be defined, *that by which any thing exists;* this is liable to the same objection. For what is meant by these words, *by which?* Had it been said, that a cause is *that* after which *any thing constantly exists;* we should have understood the terms. For this is, indeed, all we know of the matter. And this constancy forms the very essence of necessity, nor have we any other idea of it.

produce the good and prevent the evil actions. We may give to this influence what name we please; but, as it is usually conjoined with the action, it must be esteemed a *cause,* and be looked upon as an instance of that necessity, which we would here establish.

The only proper object of hatred or vengeance is a person or creature, endowed with thought and consciousness; and when any criminal or injurious actions excite that passion, it is only by their relation to the person, or connexion with him. Actions are, by their very nature, temporary and perishing; and where they proceed not from some cause in the character and disposition of the person who performed them, they can neither redound to his honour, if good; nor infamy, if evil. The actions themselves may be blameable; they may be contrary to all the rules of morality and religion: But the person is not answerable for them; and as they proceeded from nothing in him that is durable and constant, and leave nothing of that nature behind them, it is impossible he can, upon their account, become the object of punishment or vengeance. According to the principle, therefore, which denies necessity, and consequently causes, a man is as pure and untainted, after having committed the most horrid crime, as at the first moment of his birth, nor is his character anywise concerned in his actions, since they are not derived from it, and the wickedness of the one can never be used as a proof of the depravity of the other.

Men are not blamed for such actions as they perform ignorantly and casually, whatever may be the consequences. Why? but because the principles of these actions are only momentary, and terminate in them alone. Men are less blamed for such actions as they perform hastily and unpremeditately than for such as proceed from deliberation. For what reason? but because a hasty temper, though a constant cause or principle in the mind, operates only by intervals, and infects not the whole character. Again, repentance wipes off every crime, if attended with a reformation of life and manners. How is this to be accounted for? but by asserting that actions render a person criminal merely as they are proofs of criminal principles in the mind; and when, by an alteration of these principles, they cease to be just proofs, they likewise cease to be criminal. But, except upon the doctrine of necessity, they never were just proofs, and consequently never were criminal.

It will be equally easy to prove, and from the same arguments, that *liberty,* according to that definition above mentioned, in which all men agree, is also essential to morality, and that no human actions, where it is wanting, are susceptible of any moral qualities, or can be the objects either of approbation or dislike. For as actions are objects of our moral sentiment, so far only as they are indications of the internal character, passions, and affections; it is impossible that they can give rise either to praise or blame, where they proceed not from these principles, but are derived altogether from external violence.

I pretend not to have obviated or removed all objections to this theory, with regard to necessity and liberty. I can foresee other objections, derived from topics which have not here been treated of. It may be said, for instance, that, if voluntary actions be subjected to the same laws of necessity with the operations of matter, there is a continued chain of necessary causes, pre-ordained and pre-determined, reaching from the original cause of all to every single volition of every human creature. No contingency anywhere in the universe; no indifference; no liberty. While we act, we are, at the same time, acted upon. The ultimate Author of all our volitions is the Creator of the world, who first bestowed motion on this immense machine, and placed all beings in that particular position, whence every subsequent event, by an inevitable necessity, must result. Human actions, therefore, either can have no moral turpitude at all, as proceeding from so good a cause; or if they have any turpitude, they must involve our Creator in the same guilt, while he is acknowledged to be their ultimate cause and author. For as a man, who fired a mine, is answerable for all the consequences whether the train he employed be long or short; so wherever a continued chain of necessary causes is fixed, that Being, either finite or infinite, who produces the first, is likewise the author of all the rest, and must both bear the blame and acquire the praise which belong to them. Our clear and unalterable ideas of morality establish this rule, upon unquestionable reasons, when we examine the consequences of any human action; and these reasons must still have greater force when applied to the volitions and intentions of a Being infinitely wise and powerful. Ignorance or impotence may be pleaded for so limited a creature as man; but those imperfections have no place in our Creator. He foresaw, he ordained, he intended all those actions of men, which we so rashly pronounce criminal. And we must therefore conclude, either that they are not criminal, or that the Deity, not man, is accountable for them. But as either of these positions is absurd and impious, it follows, that the doctrine from which they are deduced cannot possibly be true, as being liable to all the same objections. An absurd consequence, if necessary, proves the original doctrine to be absurd in the same manner as criminal actions render criminal the original cause, if the connexion between them be necessary and inevitable.

This objection consists of two parts, which we shall examine separately; *First*, that, if human actions can be traced up, by a necessary chain, to the Deity, they can never be criminal; on account of the infinite perfection of that Being from whom they are derived, and who can intend nothing but what is altogether good and laudable. Or, *Secondly*, if they be criminal, we must retract the attribute of perfection, which we ascribe to the Deity, and must acknowledge him to be the ultimate author of guilt and moral turpitude in all his creatures.

The answer to the first objection seems obvious and convincing. There are many philosophers who, after an exact scrutiny of all the phenomena of nature, conclude, that the WHOLE, considered as one system is, in every period of its existence, ordered with perfect benevolence; and that the utmost possible happiness will, in the end, result to all created beings, without any mixture of positive or absolute ill or misery. Every physical ill, say they, makes an essential part of this benevolent system, and could not possibly be removed, even by the Deity himself, considered as a wise agent, without giving entrance to greater ill, or excluding greater good, which will result from it. From this theory, some philosophers, and the ancient *Stoics* among the rest, derived a topic of consolation under all afflictions, while they taught their pupils that those ills under which they laboured were, in reality, goods to the universe; and that to an enlarged view, which could comprehend the whole system of nature, every event became an object of joy and exultation. But though this topic be specious and sublime, it was soon found in practice weak and ineffectual. You would surely more irritate than appease a man lying under the racking pains of the gout by preaching up to him the rectitude of those general laws, which produced the malignant humours in his body, and led them through the proper canals, to the sinews and nerves, where they now excite such acute torments. These enlarged views may, for a moment, please the imagination of a speculative man, who is placed in ease and security; but neither can they dwell with constancy on his mind, even though undisturbed by the emotions of pain or passion; much less can they maintain their ground when attacked by such powerful antagonists. The affections take a narrower and more natural survey of their object; and by an economy, more suitable to the infirmity of human minds, regard alone the beings around us, and are actuated by such events as appear good or ill to the private system.

The case is the same with *moral* as with *physical* ill. It cannot reasonably be supposed, that those remote considerations, which are found of so little efficacy with regard to one, will have a more powerful influence with regard to the other. The mind of man is so formed by nature that, upon the appearance of certain characters, dispositions, and actions, it immediately feels the sentiment of approbation or blame; nor are there any emotions more essential to its frame and constitution. The characters which engage our approbation are chiefly such as contribute to the peace and security of human society; as the characters which excite blame are chiefly such as tend to public detriment and disturbance: Whence it may reasonably be presumed, that the moral sentiments arise, either mediately or immediately, from a reflection of these opposite interests. What though philosophical meditations establish a different opinion or conjecture; that everything is right with regard to the WHOLE, and that the qualities, which disturb society, are, in the main, as beneficial, and are as suitable to the primary intention of nature as those which more directly promote its happiness and welfare? Are such remote and uncertain speculations able to counterbalance the sentiments which arise from the natural and immediate view of the objects? A man who is robbed of a considerable sum; does he find his vexation for the loss anywise diminished by these sublime reflections? Why then should his moral resentment against the crime be supposed incompatible with them? Or why should not the acknowledgment of a real distinction between vice and virtue be reconcileable to all speculative systems of philosophy, as well as that of a real distinction between personal beauty and deformity? Both these distinctions are founded in the natural sentiments of the human mind: And these sentiments are not to be controlled or altered by any philosophical theory or speculation whatsoever.

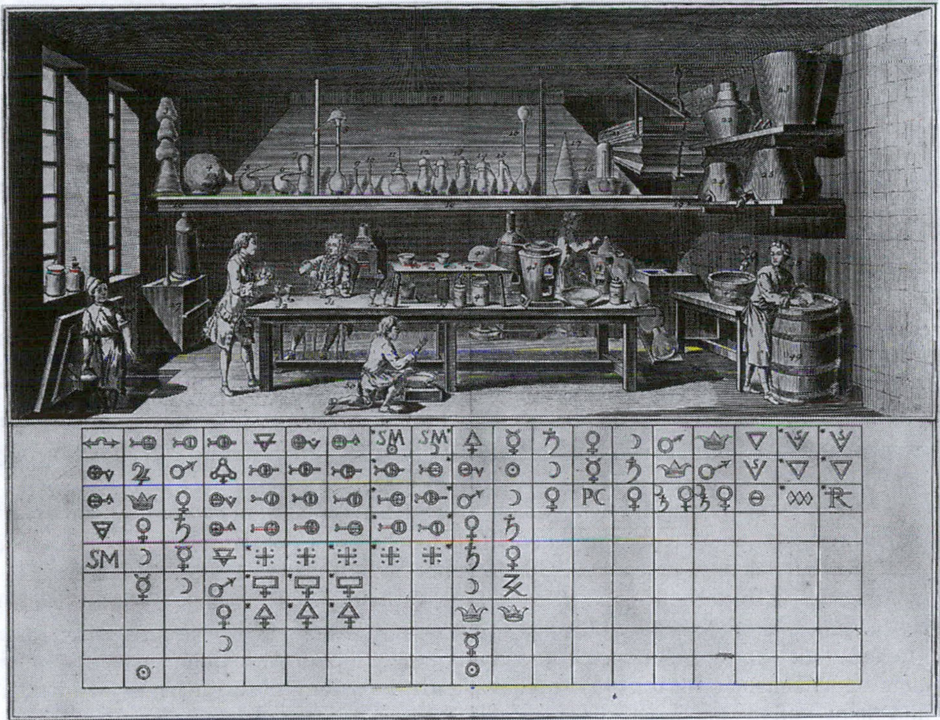

A chemist's laboratory from Denis Diderot's *Encyclopedia* (1751–1772) illustrates the state of empirical science during Hume's lifetime. The symbols below are an early periodic table of elements. (© *DeAgostini/Getty Images*)

The *second* objection admits not of so easy and satisfactory an answer; nor is it possible to explain distinctly, how the Deity can be the mediate cause of all the actions of men, without being the author of sin and moral turpitude. These are mysteries, which mere natural and unassisted reason is very unfit to handle; and whatever system she embraces, she must find herself involved in inextricable difficulties, and even contradictions, at every step which she takes with regard to such subjects. To reconcile the indifference and contingency of human actions with prescience; or to defend absolute decrees, and yet free the Deity from being the author of sin, has been found hitherto to exceed all the power of philosophy. Happy, if she be thence sensible of her temerity, when she pries into these sublime mysteries; and leaving a scene so full of obscurities and perplexities, return, with suitable modesty, to her true and proper province, the examination of common life; where she will find difficulties enough to employ her enquiries, without launching into so boundless an ocean of doubt, uncertainty, and contradiction!

SECTION IX. OF THE REASON OF ANIMALS

All our reasonings concerning matter of fact are founded on a species of Analogy, which leads us to expect from any cause the same events, which we have observed to result from similar causes. Where the causes are entirely similar, the analogy is perfect, and the inference, drawn from it, is regarded as certain and conclusive: nor does any man ever entertain a doubt, when he sees a piece of iron, that it will have weight and cohesion of parts; as in all other instances, which have ever fallen under his observation. But where the objects have not so exact a similarity, the analogy is less perfect, and the inference is less conclusive; though still it has some force, in proportion to the degree of similarity and resemblance. The anatomical observations, formed upon one animal, are, by this species of reasoning, extended to all animals; and it is certain, that when the circulation of the blood for instance, is clearly proved to have place in one creature, as a frog, or fish, it forms a strong presumption, that the same principle has place in all. These analogical observations may be carried farther, even to this science, of which we are now treating; and any theory, by which we explain the operations of the understanding, or the origin and connexion of the passions in man, will acquire additional authority, if we find, that the same theory is requisite to explain the same phenomena in all other animals. We shall make trial of this, with regard to the hypothesis, by which we have, in the foregoing discourse, endeavoured to account for all experimental reasonings; and it is hoped, that this new point of view will serve to confirm all our former observations.

First, It seems evident, that animals as well as men learn many things from experience, and infer, that the same events will always follow from the same causes. By this principle they become acquainted with the more obvious properties of external objects, and gradually, from their birth, treasure up a knowledge of the nature of fire, water, earth, stones, heights, depths, etc., and of the effects which result from their operation. The ignorance and inexperience of the young are here plainly distinguishable from the cunning and sagacity of the old, who have learned, by long observation, to avoid what hurt them, and to pursue what gave ease or pleasure. A horse, that has been accustomed to the field, becomes acquainted with the proper height which he can leap, and will never attempt what exceeds his force and ability. An old greyhound will trust the more fatiguing part of the chase to the younger, and will place himself so as to meet the hare in her doubles; nor are the conjectures, which he forms on this occasion, founded in any thing but his observation and experience.

This is still more evident from the effects of discipline and education on animals, who, by the proper application of rewards and punishments, may be taught any course of action, and most contrary to their natural instincts and propensities. Is it not experience, which renders a dog apprehensive of pain, when you menace him, or lift up the whip to beat him? Is it not even experience, which makes him answer to his name, and infer, from such an arbitrary sound, that you mean him rather than any of his fellows, and intend to call him, when you pronounce it in a certain manner, and with a certain tone and accent?

In all these cases, we may observe, that the animal infers some fact beyond what immediately strikes his senses; and that this inference is altogether founded on past experience, while the creature expects from the present object the same consequences, which it has always found in its observation to result from similar objects.

Secondly, It is impossible, that this inference of the animal can be founded on any process of argument or reasoning, by which he concludes, that like events must follow like objects, and that the course of nature will always be regular in its operations. For if there be in reality any arguments of this nature, they surely lie too abstruse for the observation of such imperfect understandings; since it may well employ the utmost care and attention of a philosophic genius to discover and observe them. Animals, therefore, are not guided in these inferences by reasoning: Neither are children: Neither are the generality of mankind, in their ordinary actions and conclusions: Neither are philosophers themselves, who, in all the active parts of life, are, in the main, the same with the vulgar, and are governed by the same maxims. Nature must have provided some other principle, of more ready, and more general use and application; nor can an operation of such immense consequence in life, as that of inferring effects from causes, be trusted to the uncertain process of reasoning and argumentation. Were this doubtful with regard to men, it seems to admit of no question with regard to the brute creation; and the conclusion being once firmly established in the one, we have a strong presumption, from all the rules of analogy, that it ought to be universally admitted, without any exception or reserve. It is custom alone, which engages animals, from every object, that strikes their senses, to infer its usual attendant, and carries their imagination, from the appearance of the one, to conceive the other, in that particular manner, which we denominate *belief*. No other explication can be given of this operation, in all the higher, as well as lower classes of sensitive beings, which fall under our notice and observation.*

But though animals learn many parts of their knowledge from observation, there are also many parts of it, which they derive from the original hand of nature; which much exceed the share of capacity they possess on ordinary occasions; and in which they improve, little or nothing, by the longest practice and experience. These we denominate Instincts, and are so apt to admire as something very extraordinary, and inexplicable by all the disquisitions of human understanding. But our wonder will, perhaps, cease or diminish, when we consider, that the experimental reasoning itself,

*Since all reasonings concerning facts or causes is derived merely from custom, it may be asked how it happens, that men so much surpass animals in reasoning, and one man so much surpasses another? Has not the same custom the same influence on all?

We shall here endeavour briefly to explain the great difference in human understandings: After which the reason of the difference between men and animals will easily be comprehended.

which we possess in common with beasts, and on which the whole conduct of life depends, is nothing but a species of instinct or mechanical power, that acts in us unknown to ourselves; and in its chief operations, is not directed by any such relations or comparisons of ideas, as are the proper objects of our intellectual faculties. Though the instinct be different, yet still it is an instinct, which teaches a man to avoid the fire; as much as that, which teaches a bird, with such exactness, the art of incubation, and the whole economy and order of its nursery.

SECTION X. OF MIRACLES*

PART I

There is, in Dr. Tillotson's writings, an argument against the *real presence*, which is as concise, and elegant, and strong as any argument can possibly be supposed against a doctrine, so little worthy of a serious refutation. It is acknowledged on all hands, says that learned prelate, that the authority, either of the scripture or of tradition, is founded merely in the testimony of the apostles, who were eye-witnesses to those miracles of our Saviour, by which he proved his divine mission. Our evidence, then, for the truth of the *Christian* religion is less than the evidence for the truth of our senses; because, even in the first authors of our religion, it was no greater; and it is evident it must diminish in passing from them to their disciples; nor can any one rest such confidence in their testimony, as in the immediate object of his senses. But a weaker evidence can never destroy a stronger; and therefore, were the doctrine of the real presence ever so clearly revealed in scripture, it were directly contrary to the rules of just reasoning to give our assent to it. It contradicts sense, though both the scripture and tradition, on which it is supposed to be built, carry not such evidence with them as sense, when they are considered

*1. When we have lived any time, and have been accustomed to the uniformity of nature we acquire a general habit, by which we always transfer the known to the unknown, and conceive the latter to resemble the former. By means of this general habitual principle, we regard even one experiment as the foundation of reasoning, and expect a similar event with some degree of certainty, where the experiment has been made accurately, and free from all foreign circumstances. It is therefore considered as a matter of great importance to observe the consequences of things; and as one man may very much surpass another in attention and memory and observation, this will make a very great difference in their reasoning.

2. Where there is a complication of causes to produce any effect, one mind may be much larger than another, and better able to comprehend the whole system of objects, and to infer justly their consequences.

3. One man is able to carry on a chain of consequences to a greater length than another.

4. Few men can think long without running into a confusion of ideas, and mistaking one for another; and there are various degrees of this infirmity.

5. The circumstance, on which the effect depends, is frequently involved in other circumstances, which are foreign and extrinsic. The separation of it often requires great attention, accuracy, and subtilty.

6. The forming of general maxims from particular observation is a very nice operation; and nothing is more usual, from haste or narrowness of mind which sees not on all sides than to commit mistakes in this particular.

7. When we reason from analogies, the man, who has the greater experience of the greater promptitude of suggesting analogies, will be the better reasoner.

8. Biases from prejudice, education, passion, party, etc., hang more upon one mind than another.

9. After we have acquired a confidence in human testimony, books and conversation enlarge much more the sphere of one man's experience and thought than those of another.

It would be easy to discover many other circumstances that make a difference in the understandings of men.

merely as external evidences, and are not brought home to every one's breast, by the immediate operation of the Holy Spirit.

Nothing is so convenient as a decisive argument of this kind, which must at least *silence* the most arrogant bigotry and superstition, and free us from their impertinent solicitations. I flatter myself, that I have discovered an argument of a like nature, which, if just, will, with the wise and learned, be an everlasting check to all kinds of superstitious delusion, and consequently, will be useful as long as the world endures; for so long, I presume, will the accounts of miracles and prodigies be found in all history, sacred and profane.

Though experience be our only guide in reasoning concerning matters of fact; it must be acknowledged, that this guide is not altogether infallible, but in some cases is apt to lead us into errors. One, who in our climate, should expect better weather in any week of June than in one of December, would reason justly, and conformably to experience; but it is certain, that he may happen, in the event, to find himself mistaken. However, we may observe, that, in such a case, he would have no cause to complain of experience; because it commonly informs us beforehand of the uncertainty, by that contrariety of events, which we may learn from a diligent observation. All effects follow not with like certainty from their supposed causes. Some events are found, in all countries and all ages, to have been constantly conjoined together: Others are found to have been more variable, and sometimes to disappoint our expectations; so that, in our reasonings concerning matter of fact, there are all imaginable degrees of assurance, from the highest certainty to the lowest species of moral evidence.

A wise man, therefore, proportions his belief to the evidence. In such conclusions as are founded on an infallible experience, he expects the event with the last degree of assurance, and regards his past experience as a full *proof* of the future existence of that event. In other cases, he proceeds with more caution: He weighs the opposite experiments: He considers which side is supported by the greater number of experiments: to that side he inclines, with doubt and hesitation; and when at last he fixes his judgement, the evidence exceeds not what we properly call *probability*. All probability, then, supposes an opposition of experiments and observations, where the one side is found to overbalance the other, and to produce a degree of evidence, proportioned to the superiority. A hundred instances or experiments on one side, and fifty on another, afford a doubtful expectation of any event; though a hundred uniform experiments, with only one that is contradictory, reasonably begets a pretty strong degree of assurance. In all cases, we must balance the opposite experiments, where they are opposite, and deduct the smaller number from the greater, in order to know the exact force of the superior evidence.

To apply these principles to a particular instance; we may observe, that there is no species of reasoning more common, more useful, and even necessary to human life, than that which is derived from the testimony of men, and the reports of eye-witnesses and spectators. This species of reasoning, perhaps, one may deny to be founded on the relation of cause and effect. I shall not dispute about a word. It will be sufficient to observe that our assurance in any argument of this kind is derived from no other principle than our observation of the veracity of human testimony, and of the usual conformity of facts to the reports of witnesses. It being a general maxim, that no objects have any discoverable connexion together, and that all the inferences, which we can draw from one to another, are founded merely on our experience of their constant and regular conjunction; it is evident, that we ought not to make an exception to this maxim in favour of human testimony, whose connexion with any event seems, in itself, as little necessary as any other. Were not the memory tenacious to a certain degree; had not men commonly an inclination to truth and a principle of probity, were they not sensible to shame, when detected in a falsehood: Were not these, I say, discovered by *experience* to be qualities, inherent in human nature, we should never repose the least confidence in human testimony. A man delirious, or noted for falsehood and villainy, has no manner of authority with us.

And as the evidence, derived from witnesses and human testimony, is founded on past experience, so it varies with the experience, and is regarded either as *proof* or a *probability*, according as the conjunction between any particular kind of report and any kind of object has been found to be constant or variable. There are a number of circumstances to be taken into consideration in all judgements of this kind; and the ultimate standard, by which we determine all disputes, that may arise concerning them, is always derived from experience and observation. Where this experience is not entirely uniform on any side, it is attended with an unavoidable contrariety in our judgements, and with the same opposition and mutual destruction of argument as in every other kind of evidence. We frequently hesitate concerning the reports of others. We balance the opposite circumstances, which cause any doubt or uncertainty; and when we discover a superiority on one side, we incline to it; but still with a diminution of assurance, in proportion to the force of its antagonist.

This contrariety of evidence, in the present case, may be derived from several different causes; from the opposition of contrary testimony; from the character or number of the witnesses; from the manner of their delivering their testimony; or from the union of all these circumstances. We entertain a suspicion concerning any matter of fact, when the witnesses contradict each other; when they are but few, or of a doubtful character; when they have an interest in what they affirm; when they deliver their testimony with hesitation, or on the contrary, with too violent asseverations. There are many other particulars of the same kind, which may diminish or destroy the force of any argument, derived from human testimony.

Suppose, for instance, that the fact, which the testimony endeavours to establish, partakes of the extraordinary and the marvellous; in that case, the evidence, resulting from the testimony, admits of a diminution, greater or less, in proportion as the fact is more or less unusual. The reason why we place any credit in witnesses and historians, is not derived from any *connexion*, which we perceive *a priori*, between testimony and reality, but because we are accustomed to find a conformity between them. But when the fact attested is such a one as has seldom fallen under our observation, here is a contest of two opposite experiences; of which the one destroys the other, as far as its force goes, and the superior can only operate on the mind by the force, which remains. The very same principle of experience, which gives us a certain degree of assurance in the testimony of witnesses, gives us also, in this case, another degree of assurance against the fact, which they endeavour to establish; from which contradiction there necessarily arises a counterpoise, and mutual destruction of belief and authority.

I should not believe such a story were it told me by Cato, was a proverbial saying in Rome, even during the lifetime of that philosophical patriot.* The incredibility of a fact, it was allowed, might invalidate so great an authority.

The Indian prince, who refused to believe the first relations concerning the effects of frost, reasoned justly; and it naturally required very strong testimony to engage his assent to facts, that arose from a state of nature, with which he was unacquainted, and which bore so

*Plutarch, *Marcus Cato* [*The Life of Cato*].

little analogy to those events, of which he had had constant and uniform experience. Though they were not contrary to his experience, they were not conformable to it.*

But in order to increase the probability against the testimony of witnesses, let us suppose, that the fact, which they affirm, instead of being only marvellous, is really miraculous; and suppose also, that the testimony considered apart and in itself, amounts to an entire proof; in that case, there is proof against proof, of which the strongest must prevail, but still with a diminution of its force, in proportion to that of its antagonist.

A miracle is a violation of the laws of nature; and as a firm and unalterable experience has established these laws, the proof against a miracle, from the very nature of the fact, is as entire as any argument from experience can possibly be imagined. Why is it more than probable, that all men must die; that lead cannot, of itself, remain suspended in the air; that fire consumes wood, and is extinguished by water; unless it be, that these events are found agreeable to the laws of nature, and there is required a violation of these laws, or in other words, a miracle to prevent them? Nothing is esteemed a miracle, if it ever happen in the common course of nature. It is no miracle that a man, seemingly in good health, should die on a sudden: because such a kind of death, though more unusual than any other, has yet been frequently observed to happen. But it is a miracle, that a dead man should come to life; because that has never been observed in any age or country. There must, therefore, be a uniform experience against every miraculous event, otherwise the event would not merit that appellation. And as a uniform experience amounts to a proof, there is here a direct and full *proof*, from the nature of the fact, against the existence of any miracle; nor can such a proof be destroyed, or the miracle rendered credible, but by an opposite proof, which is superior.**

The plain consequence is (and it is a general maxim worthy of our attention), "That no testimony is sufficient to establish a miracle, unless the testimony be of such a kind, that its falsehood would be more miraculous, than the fact, which it endeavours

*No Indian, it is evident, could have experienced that water did not freeze in cold climates. This is placing nature in a situation quite unknown to him; and it is impossible for him to tell *a priori* what will result from it. It is making a new experiment, the consequence of which is always uncertain. One may sometimes conjecture from analogy what will follow; but still this is but conjecture. And it must be confessed, that, in the present case of freezing, the event follows contrary to the rules of analogy, and is such as a rational Indian would not look for. The operations of cold upon water are not gradual according to the degrees of cold; but whenever it comes to the freezing point, the water passes in a moment, from the utmost liquidity to perfect hardness. Such an event, therefore, may be denominated *extraordinary*, and requires a pretty strong testimony, to render it credible to people in a warm climate: But still it is not *miraculous*, nor contrary to uniform experience of the course of nature in cases where all the circumstances are the same. The inhabitants of Sumatra have always seen water fluid in their own climate, and the freezing of their rivers ought to be deemed a prodigy: But they never saw water in Muscovy during the winter, and therefore they cannot reasonably be positive what would there be the consequence.

**Sometimes an event may not, *in itself*, seem to be contrary to the laws of nature, and yet, if it were real, it might, by reason of some circumstances, be denominated a miracle, because, *in fact*, it is contrary to these laws. Thus if a person, claiming a divine authority, should command a sick person to be well, a healthful man to fall down dead, the clouds to pour rain, the winds to blow, in short, should order many natural events, which immediately follow upon his command; these might justly be esteemed miracles, because they are really, in this case, contrary to the laws of nature. For if any suspicion remain, that the event and command concurred by accident, there is no miracle and no transgression of the laws of nature. If this suspicion be removed, there is evidently a miracle, and a transgression of these laws; because nothing can be more contrary to nature than that the voice or command of a man should have such an influence. A miracle may be accurately defined, *a transgression of a law of nature by a particular volition of the Deity, or by the interposition of some invisible agent*. A miracle may either be discovered by men or not. This alters not its nature and essence. The raising of a house or ship into the air is a visible miracle. The raising of a feather, when the wind wants ever so little of a force requisite for that purpose, is as real a miracle, though not so sensible with regard to us.

to establish; and even in that case there is a mutual destruction of arguments, and the superior only gives us an assurance suitable to that degree of force, which remains, after deducting the inferior." When anyone tells me, that he saw a dead man restored to life, I immediately consider with myself, whether it be more probable, that this person should either deceive or be deceived, or that the fact, which he relates, should really have happened. I weigh the one miracle against the other; and according to the superiority, which I discover, I pronounce my decision, and always reject the greater miracle. If the falsehood of his testimony would be more miraculous, than the event which he relates; then, and not till then, can he pretend to command my belief or opinion.

PART II

In the foregoing reasoning we have supposed, that the testimony, upon which a miracle is founded, may possibly amount to an entire proof, and that the falsehood of that testimony would be a real prodigy: But it is easy to shew, that we have been a great deal too liberal in our concession, and that there never was a miraculous event established on so full an evidence.

For *first*, there is not to be found, in all history, any miracle attested by a sufficient number of men, of such unquestioned good-sense, education, and learning, as to secure us against all delusion in themselves; of such undoubted integrity, as to place them beyond all suspicion of any design to deceive others; of such credit and reputation in the eyes of mankind, as to have a great deal to lose in case of their being detected in any falsehood; and at the same time, attesting facts performed in such a public manner and in so celebrated a part of the world, as to render the detection unavoidable: All which circumstances are requisite to give us a full assurance in the testimony of men.

Secondly, We may observe in human nature a principle which, if strictly examined, will be found to diminish extremely the assurance, which we might, from human testimony, have, in any kind of prodigy. The maxim, by which we commonly conduct ourselves in our reasonings, is, that the objects, of which we have no experience, resemble those, of which we have; that what we have found to be most usual is always most probable; and that where there is an opposition of arguments, we ought to give the preference to such as are founded on the greatest number of past observations. But though, in proceeding by this rule, we readily reject any fact which is unusual and incredible in an ordinary degree; yet in advancing farther, the mind observes not always the same rule; but when anything is affirmed utterly absurd and miraculous, it rather the more readily admits of such a fact, upon account of that very circumstance, which ought to destroy all its authority. The passion of *surprise* and *wonder*, arising from miracles, being an agreeable emotion, gives a sensible tendency towards the belief of those events, from which it is derived. And this goes so far, that even those who cannot enjoy this pleasure immediately, nor can believe those miraculous events, of which they are informed, yet love to partake of the satisfaction at second-hand or by rebound, and place a pride and delight in exciting the admiration of others.

With what greediness are the miraculous accounts of travellers received, their descriptions of sea and land monsters, their relations of wonderful adventures, strange men, and uncouth manners? But if the spirit of religion join itself to the love of wonder, there is an end of common sense; and human testimony, in these circumstances, loses all pretensions to authority. A religionist may be an enthusiast, and imagine he sees what has no reality: he may know his narrative to be false, and yet persevere in it, with the best intentions in the world, for the sake of promoting so holy a cause: or even where this delusion has no place, vanity, excited by so strong a temptation, operates on him more powerfully than on the rest of mankind in any other circumstances; and self-interest with equal force. His auditors may not have, and commonly have not, sufficient judgement to canvass his evidence: what judgement they have, they renounce by principle, in these sublime and mysterious subjects: or if they were ever so willing to employ it, passion and a heated imagination disturb the regularity of its operations. Their credulity increases his impudence: and his impudence overpowers their credulity.

Eloquence, when at its highest pitch, leaves little room for reason or reflection; but addressing itself entirely to the fancy or the affections, captivates the willing hearers, and subdues their understanding. Happily, this pitch it seldom attains. But what a Tully or a Demosthenes could scarcely effect over a Roman or Athenian audience, every *Capuchin*, every itinerant or stationary teacher can perform over the generality of mankind, and in a higher degree, by touching such gross and vulgar passions.

The many instances of forged miracles, and prophecies, and supernatural events, which, in all ages, have either been detected by contrary evidence, or which detect themselves by their absurdity, prove sufficiently the strong propensity of mankind to the extraordinary and the marvellous, and ought reasonably to beget a suspicion against all relations of this kind. This is our natural way of thinking, even with regard to the most common and most credible events. For instance: There is no kind of report which rises so easily, and spreads so quickly, especially in country places and provincial towns, as those concerning marriages; insomuch that two young persons of equal condition never see each other twice, but the whole neighbourhood immediately join them together. The pleasure of telling a piece of news so interesting, of propagating it, and of being the first reporters of it, spreads the intelligence. And this is so well known, that no man of sense gives attention to these reports, till he find them confirmed by some greater evidence. Do not the same passions, and others still stronger, incline the generality of mankind to believe and report, with the greatest vehemence and assurance, all religious miracles?

Thirdly, It forms a strong presumption against all supernatural and miraculous relations, that they are observed chiefly to abound among ignorant and barbarous nations; or if a civilized people has ever given admission to any of them, that people will be found to have received them from ignorant and barbarous ancestors, who transmitted them with that inviolable sanction and authority, which always attend received opinions. When we peruse the first histories of all nations, we are apt to imagine ourselves transported into some new world; where the whole frame of nature is disjointed, and every element performs its operations in a different manner, from what it does at present. Battles, revolutions, pestilence, famine and death, are never the effect of those natural causes, which we experience. Prodigies, omens, oracles, judgements, quite obscure the few natural events, that are intermingled with them. But as the former grow thinner every page, in proportion as we advance nearer the enlightened ages, we soon learn, that there is nothing mysterious or super-natural in the case, but that all proceeds from the usual propensity of mankind towards the marvellous, and that, though this inclination may at intervals receive a check from sense and learning, it can never be thoroughly extirpated from human nature.

It is strange, a judicious reader is apt to say, upon the perusal of these wonderful historians, *that such prodigious events never happen in our days*. But it is nothing strange, I hope, that men should lie in all ages. You must surely have seen instances enough of that frailty. You have yourself heard many such marvellous relations started, which, being treated with scorn by all the wise and judicious, have at last been abandoned even by the vulgar. Be assured, that those renowned lies, which have spread and flourished to such a monstrous height, arose from like beginnings; but being sown in a more proper soil, shot up at last into prodigies almost equal to those which they relate.

It was a wise policy in that false prophet, Alexander, who though now forgotten, was once so famous, to lay the first scene of his impostures in Paphlagonia, where, as Lucian tells us, the people were extremely ignorant and stupid, and ready to swallow even the grossest delusion. People at a distance, who are weak enough to think the matter at all worth enquiry, have no opportunity of receiving better information. The stories come magnified to them by a hundred circumstances. Fools are industrious in propagating the imposture; while the wise and learned are contented, in general, to deride its absurdity, without informing themselves of the particular facts, by which it may be distinctly refuted. And thus the impostor above mentioned was enabled to proceed, from his ignorant Paphlagonians, to the enlisting of votaries, even among the Grecian philosophers, and men of the most eminent rank and distinction in Rome: nay, could engage the attention of that sage emperor Marcus Aurelius; so far as to make him trust the success of a military expedition to his delusive prophecies.

The advantages are so great, of starting an imposture among an ignorant people, that, even though the delusion should be too gross to impose on the generality of them (*which, though seldom, is sometimes the case*) it has a much better chance for succeeding in remote countries, than if the first scene had been laid in a city renowned for arts and knowledge. The most ignorant and barbarous of these barbarians carry the report abroad. None of their countrymen have a large correspondence, or sufficient credit and authority to contradict and beat down the delusion. Men's inclination to the marvellous has full opportunity to display itself. And thus a story, which is universally exploded in the place where it was first started, shall pass for certain at a thousand miles distance. But had Alexander fixed his residence at Athens, the philosophers of that renowned mart of learning had immediately spread, throughout the whole Roman empire, their sense of the matter; which, being supported by so great authority, and displayed by all the force of reason and eloquence, had entirely opened the eyes of mankind. It is true; Lucian, passing by chance through Paphlagonia, had an opportunity of performing this good office. But, though much to be wished, it does not always happen, that every Alexander meets with a Lucian, ready to expose and detect his impostures.

I may add as a *fourth* reason, which diminishes the authority of prodigies, that there is no testimony for any, even those which have not been expressly detected, that is not opposed by an infinite number of witnesses; so that not only the miracle destroys the credit of testimony, but the testimony destroys itself. To make this the better understood, let us consider, that, in matters of religion, whatever is different is contrary; and that it is impossible the religions of ancient Rome, of Turkey, of Siam, and of China should, all of them, be established on any solid foundation. Every miracle, therefore, pretended to have been wrought in any of these religions (and all of them abound in miracles), as its direct scope is to establish the particular system to which it is attributed; so has it the same force, though more indirectly, to overthrow every other system. In destroying a rival system, it likewise destroys the credit of those miracles, on which that system was established; so that all the prodigies of different religions are to be regarded as contrary facts, and the evidences of these prodigies, whether weak or strong, as opposite to each other. According to this method of reasoning, when we believe any miracle of Mahomet or his successors, we have for our warrant the testimony of a few barbarous Arabians: And on the other hand, we are to regard the authority of Titus Livius, Plutarch, Tacitus, and, in short, of all the authors and witnesses, Grecian, Chinese, and Roman Catholic, who have related any miracle in their particular religion; I say, we are to regard their testimony in the same light as if they had mentioned that Mahometan miracle, and had in express terms contradicted it, with the same certainty as they have for the miracle they relate. This argument may appear over subtile and refined; but is not in reality different from the reasoning of a judge, who supposes, that the credit of two witnesses, maintaining a crime against any one, is destroyed by the testimony of two others, who affirm him to have been two hundred leagues distant, at the same instant when the crime is said to have been committed.

One of the best attested miracles in all profane history, is that which Tacitus reports of Vespasian, who cured a blind man in Alexandria, by means of his spittle, and a lame man by the mere touch of his foot; in obedience to a vision of the god Serapis, who had enjoined them to have recourse to the Emperor, for these miraculous cures. The story may be seen in that fine historian;* where every circumstance seems to add weight to the testimony, and might be displayed at large with all the force of argument and eloquence, if any one were now concerned to enforce the evidence of that exploded and idolatrous superstition. The gravity, solidity, age, and probity of so great an emperor, who, through the whole course of his life, conversed in a familiar manner with his friends and courtiers, and never affected those extraordinary airs of divinity assumed by Alexander and Demetrius. The historian, a contemporary writer, noted for candour and veracity, and withal, the greatest and most penetrating genius, perhaps, of all antiquity; and so free from any tendency to credulity, that he even lies under the contrary imputation, of atheism and profaneness: The persons, from whose authority he related the miracle, of established character for judgement and veracity, as we may well presume; eye-witnesses of the fact, and confirming their testimony, after the Flavian family was despoiled of the empire, and could no longer give any reward, as the price of a lie. *Utrumque, qui interfuere, nunc quoque memorant, postquam nullum mendacio pretium.*** To which if we add the public nature of the facts, as related, it will appear, that no evidence can well be supposed stronger for so gross and so palpable a falsehood.

There is also a memorable story related by Cardinal de Retz, which may well deserve our consideration. When that intriguing politician fled into Spain, to avoid the persecution of his enemies, he passed through Saragossa, the capital of Arragon, where he was shown, in the cathedral, a man, who had served seven years as a doorkeeper, and was well known to every body in town, that had ever paid his devotions at that church. He had been seen, for so long a time, wanting a leg; but recovered that limb by the rubbing of holy oil upon the stump; and the cardinal assures us that he saw him with two legs. This miracle was vouched by all the canons of the church; and the whole company in town were appealed to for a confirmation of the fact; whom the cardinal found, by their zealous devotion, to be thorough believers of the miracle. Here the relater was also contemporary to the supposed prodigy, of an incredulous and libertine character, as well as of great genius; the miracle of so *singular* a nature as could scarcely admit of a counterfeit, and the witnesses very numerous, and all of them, in a manner, spectators of the fact, to which they gave their testimony. And what adds mightily to the force of the evidence, and may double our surprise on this occasion, is, that the cardinal himself, who relates the story, seems not to give any credit to it, and consequently cannot be suspected of any concurrence in the holy fraud. He considered justly, that it was not requisite, in order to reject a fact of this nature, to be able accurately to disprove the testimony, and to trace its falsehood, through all the circumstances of knavery and credulity which produced it. He knew, that, as this was commonly altogether impossible at any small distance of time and place; so was it extremely difficult, even where one

*Histories, iv. 81. Suetonius gives nearly the same account, *Lives of the Caesars* (Vespasian).

**[Those who were present recount both even now that a lie is no longer rewarded.]

was immediately present, by reason of the bigotry, ignorance, cunning, and roguery of a great part of mankind. He therefore concluded, like a just reasoner, that such an evidence carried falsehood upon the very face of it, and that a miracle, supported by any human testimony, was more properly a subject of derision than of argument.

There surely never was a greater number of miracles ascribed to one person, than those, which were lately said to have been wrought in France upon the tomb of Abbe Paris, the famous Jansenist, with whose sanctity the people were so long deluded. The curing of the sick, giving hearing to the deaf, and sight to the blind, were every where talked of as the usual effects of that holy sepulchre. But what is more extraordinary; many of the miracles were immediately proved upon the spot, before judges of unquestioned integrity, attested by witnesses of credit and distinction, in a learned age, and on the most eminent theatre that is now in the world. Nor is this all: a relation of them was published and dispersed everywhere; nor were the *Jesuits*, though a learned body, supported by the civil magistrate, and determined enemies to those opinions, in whose favour the miracles were said to have been wrought, ever able distinctly to refute or detect them. Where shall we find such a number of circumstances, agreeing to the corroboration of one fact? And what have we to oppose to such a cloud of witnesses, but the absolute impossibility or miraculous nature of the events, which they relate? And this surely, in the eyes of all reasonable people, will alone be regarded as a sufficient refutation.

Is the consequence just, because some human testimony has the utmost force and authority in some cases, when it relates the battle of Philippi or Pharsalia for instance; that therefore all kinds of testimony must, in all cases, have equal force and authority? Suppose that the Caesarean and Pompeian factions had, each of them, claimed the victory in these battles, and that the historians of each party had uniformly ascribed the advantage to their own side; how could mankind, at this distance, have been able to determine between them? The contrariety is equally strong between the miracles related by Herodotus or Plutarch, and those delivered by Mariana, Bede, or any monkish historian.

The wise lend a very academic faith to every report which favours the passion of the reporter; whether it magnifies his country, his family, or himself, or in any other way strikes in with his natural inclinations and propensities. But what greater temptation than to appear a missionary, a prophet, an ambassador from heaven? Who would not encounter many dangers and difficulties, in order to attain so sublime a character? Or if, by the help of vanity and a heated imagination, a man has first made a convert of himself, and entered seriously into the delusion; who ever scruples to make use of pious frauds, in support of so holy and meritorious a cause?

The smallest spark may here kindle into the greatest flame; because the materials are always prepared for it. The *avidum genus auricularum*,* the gazing populace, receive greedily, without examination, whatever soothes superstition, and promotes wonder.

How many stories of this nature have, in all ages, been detected and exploded in their infancy? How many more have been celebrated for a time, and have afterwards sunk into neglect and oblivion? Where such reports, therefore, fly about, the solution of the phenomenon is obvious; and we judge in conformity to regular experience and observation, when we account for it by the known and natural principles of credulity and delusion. And shall we, rather than have a recourse to so natural a solution, allow of a miraculous violation of the most established laws of nature?

*[a genus hungry for gossip] Lucretius, *De Rerum Natura,* iv.

I need not mention the difficulty of detecting, a falsehood in any private or even public history, at the place, where it is said to happen; much more when the scene is removed to ever so small a distance. Even a court of judicature, with all the authority, accuracy, and judgement, which they can employ, find themselves often at a loss to distinguish between truth and falsehood in the most recent actions. But the matter never comes to any issue, if trusted to the common method of altercations and debate and flying rumours; especially when men's passions have taken part on either side.

In the infancy of new religions, the wise and learned commonly esteem the matter too inconsiderable to deserve their attention or regard. And when afterwards they would willingly detect the cheat, in order to undeceive the deluded multitude, the season is now past, and the records and witnesses, which might clear up the matter, have perished beyond recovery.

No means of detection remain, but those which must be drawn from the very testimony itself of the reporters: and these, though always sufficient with the judicious and knowing, are commonly too fine to fall under the comprehension of the vulgar.

Upon the whole, then, it appears, that no testimony for any kind of miracle has ever amounted to a probability, much less to a proof; and that, even supposing it amounted to a proof, it would be opposed by another proof; derived from the very nature of the fact, which it would endeavour to establish. It is experience only, which gives authority to human testimony; and it is the same experience, which assures us of the laws of nature. When, therefore, these two kinds of experience are contrary, we have nothing to do but subtract the one from the other, and embrace an opinion, either on one side or the other, with that assurance which arises from the remainder. But according to the principle here explained, this substraction, with regard to all popular religions, amounts to an entire annihilation; and therefore we may establish it as a maxim, that no human testimony can have such force as to prove a miracle, and make it a just foundation for any such system of religion.

I beg the limitations here made may be remarked, when I say, that a miracle can never be proved, so as to be the foundation of a system of religion. For I own, that otherwise, there may possibly be miracles, or violations of the usual course of nature, of such a kind as to admit of proof from human testimony; though, perhaps, it will be impossible to find any such in all the records of history. Thus, suppose, all authors, in all languages, agree, that, from the first of January 1600, there was a total darkness over the whole earth for eight days: suppose that the tradition of this extraordinary event is still strong and lively among the people: that all travellers, who return from foreign countries, bring us accounts of the same tradition, without the least variation or contradiction: it is evident, that our present philosophers, instead of doubting the fact, ought to receive it as certain, and ought to search for the causes whence it might be derived. The decay, corruption, and dissolution of nature, is an event rendered probable by so many analogies, that any phenomenon, which seems to have a tendency towards that catastrophe, comes within the reach of human testimony, if that testimony be very extensive and uniform.

But suppose, that all the historians who treat of England, should agree, that, on the first of January 1600, Queen Elizabeth died; that both before and after her death she was seen by her physicians and the whole court, as is usual with persons of her rank; that her successor was acknowledged and proclaimed by the parliament; and that, after being interred a month, she again appeared, resumed the throne, and governed England for three years: I must confess that I should be surprised at the concurrence of so many odd circumstances, but should not have the least inclination to believe so miraculous an event. I should not doubt of her pretended death, and of those other public circumstances that followed it: I should only assert it to have been pretended, and that it neither was, nor possibly could be real. You would in vain object to me the difficulty, and almost impossibility of deceiving the world in an affair of such consequence; the wisdom and solid judgement of that renowned queen; with the little or no advantage which she could reap from so poor an artifice: All this might astonish me; but I would still reply, that the knavery and folly of men are such common phenomena, that I should rather believe the most extraordinary events to arise from their concurrence, then admit of so signal a violation of the laws of nature.

But should this miracle be ascribed to any new system of religion; men, in all ages, have been so much imposed on by ridiculous stories of that kind, that this very circumstance would be a full proof of a cheat, and sufficient, with all men of sense, not only to make them reject the fact, but even reject it without farther examination. Though the Being to whom the miracle is ascribed, be, in this case, Almighty, it does not, upon that account, become a whit more probable; since it is impossible for us to know the attributes or actions of such a Being, otherwise than from the experience which we have of his productions, in the usual course of nature. This still reduces us to past observation, and obliges us to compare the instances of the violation of truth in the testimony of men, with those of the violation of the laws of nature by miracles, in order to judge which of them is most likely and probable. As the violations of truth are more common in the testimony concerning religious miracles, than in that concerning any other matter of fact; this must diminish very much the authority of the former testimony, and make us form a general resolution, never to lend any attention to it, with whatever specious pretence it may be covered.

Lord Bacon seems to have embraced the same principles of reasoning. "We ought," says he, "to make a collection or particular history of all monsters and prodigious births or productions, and in a word of every thing new, rare, and extraordinary in nature. But this must be done with the most severe scrutiny, lest we depart from truth. Above all, every relation must be considered as suspicious, which depends in any degree upon religion, as the prodigies of Livy: And no less so, every thing that is to be found in the writers of natural magic or alchemy, or such authors, who seem, all of them, to have an unconquerable appetite for falsehood and fable.*

I am the better pleased with the method of reasoning here delivered, as I think it may serve to confound those dangerous friends or disguised enemies to the *Christian Religion*, who have undertaken to defend it by the principles of human reason. Our most holy religion is founded on *Faith*, not on reason; and it is a sure method of exposing it to put it to such a trial as it is, by no means, fitted to endure. To make this more evident, let us examine those miracles, related in scripture; and not to lose ourselves in too wide a field, let us confine ourselves to such as we find in the *Pentateuch*, which we shall examine, according to the principles of these pretended Christians, not as the word or testimony of God himself, but as the production of a mere human writer and historian. Here then we are first to consider a book, presented to us by a barbarous and ignorant people, written in an age when they were still more barbarous, and in all probability long after the facts which it relates, corroborated by no concurring testimony, and resembling those fabulous accounts, which every nation gives of its origin. Upon reading this book, we find it full of prodigies and miracles. It gives an account of a state of the world and of human nature entirely different from the present: Of our fall from that state: Of the age of man, extended to near a thousand years: Of the destruction of the world by a deluge: Of the arbitrary choice of one

**Novum Organum*, II, aphorism 29.

people, as the favourites of heaven; and that people the countrymen of the author: Of their deliverance from bondage by prodigies the most astonishing imaginable: I desire any one to lay his hand upon his heart, and after a serious consideration declare, whether he thinks that the falsehood of such a book, supported by such a testimony, would be more extraordinary and miraculous than all the miracles it relates; which is, however, necessary to make it be received, according to the measures of probability above established.

What we have said of miracles may be applied, without any variation, to prophecies; and indeed, all prophecies are real miracles, and as such only, can be admitted as proofs of any revelation. If it did not exceed the capacity of human nature to foretell future events, it would be absurd to employ any prophecy as an argument for a divine mission or authority from heaven. So that, upon the whole, we may conclude, that the *Christian Religion* not only was at first attended with miracles, but even at this day cannot be believed by any reasonable person without one. Mere reason is insufficient to convince us of its veracity: And whoever is moved by *Faith* to assent to it, is conscious of a continued miracle in his own person, which subverts all the principles of his understanding, and gives him a determination to believe what is most contrary to custom and experience.

SECTION XI. OF A PARTICULAR PROVIDENCE AND OF A FUTURE STATE

I was lately engaged in conversation with a friend who loves sceptical paradoxes; where, though he advanced many principles, of which I can by no means approve, yet as they seem to be curious, and to bear some relation to the chain of reasoning carried on throughout this enquiry, I shall here copy them from my memory as accurately as I can, in order to submit them to the judgement of the reader.

Our conversation began with my admiring the singular good fortune of philosophy, which, as it requires entire liberty above all other privileges, and chiefly flourishes from the free opposition of sentiments and argumentation, received its first birth in an age and country of freedom and toleration, and was never cramped, even in its most extravagant principles, by any creeds, confessions, or penal statutes. For, except the banishment of Protagoras, and the death of Socrates, which last event proceeded partly from other motives, there are scarcely any instances to be met with, in ancient history, of this bigoted jealousy, with which the present age is so much infested. Epicurus lived at Athens to an advanced age, in peace and tranquillity: Epicureans were even admitted to receive the sacerdotal character, and to officiate at the altar, in the most sacred rites of the established religion: And the public encouragement of pensions and salaries was afforded equally, by the wisest of all the Roman emperors, to the professors of every sect of philosophy. How requisite such kind of treatment was to philosophy, in her early youth, will easily be conceived, if we reflect, that, even at present, when she may be supposed more hardy and robust, she bears with much difficulty the inclemency of the seasons, and those harsh winds of calumny and persecution, which blow upon her.

You admire, says my friend, as the singular good fortune of philosophy, what seems to result from the natural course of things, and to be unavoidable in every age and nation. This pertinacious bigotry, of which you complain, as so fatal to philosophy, is really her offspring, who, after allying with superstition, separates himself entirely from the interest of his parent, and becomes her most inveterate enemy and persecutor.

Speculative dogmas of religion, the present occasions of such furious dispute, could not possibly be conceived or admitted in the early ages of the world; when mankind, being wholly illiterate, formed an idea of religion more suitable to their weak apprehension, and composed their sacred tenets of such tales chiefly as were the objects of traditional belief, more than of argument or disputation. After the first alarm, therefore, was over, which arose from the new paradoxes and principles of the philosophers; these teachers seem ever after, during the ages of antiquity, to have lived in great harmony with the established superstition, and to have made a fair partition of mankind between them; the former claiming all the learned and wise, the latter possessing all the vulgar and illiterate.

It seems then, say I, that you leave politics entirely out of the question, and never suppose, that a wise magistrate can justly be jealous of certain tenets of philosophy, such as those of Epicurus, which, denying a divine existence, and consequently a providence and a future state, seem to loosen, in a great measure, the ties of morality, and may be supposed, for that reason, pernicious to the peace of civil society.

I know, replied he, that in fact these persecutions never, in any age, proceeded from calm reason, or from experience of the pernicious consequences of philosophy; but arose entirely from passion and prejudice. But what if I should advance farther, and assert, that if Epicurus had been accused before the people, by any of the *sycophants* or informers of those days, he could easily have defended his cause, and proved his principles of philosophy to be as salutary as those of his adversaries, who endeavoured, with such zeal, to expose him to the public hatred and jealousy?

I wish, said I, you would try your eloquence upon so extraordinary a topic, and make a speech for Epicurus, which might satisfy, not the mob of Athens, if you will allow that ancient and polite city to have contained any mob, but the more philosophical part of his audience, such as might be supposed capable of comprehending his arguments.

The matter would not be difficult, upon such conditions, replied he: And if you please, I shall suppose myself Epicurus for a moment, and make you stand for the Athenian people, and shall deliver you such an harangue as will fill all the urn with white beans, and leave not a black one to gratify the malice of my adversaries.

Very well: Pray proceed upon these suppositions.

I come hither, O ye Athenians, to justify in your assembly what I maintained in my school, and I find myself impeached by furious antagonists, instead of reasoning with calm and dispassionate enquirers. Your deliberations, which of right should be directed to questions of public good, and the interest of the commonwealth, are diverted to the disquisitions of speculative philosophy; and these magnificent, but perhaps fruitless enquiries, take place of your more familiar but more useful occupations. But so far as in me lies, I will prevent this abuse. We shall not here dispute concerning the origin and government of worlds. We shall only enquire how far such questions concern the public interest. And if I can persuade you, that they are entirely indifferent to the peace of society and security of government, I hope that you will presently send us back to our schools, there to examine, at leisure, the question the most sublime, but at the same time, the most speculative of all philosophy.

The religious philosophers, not satisfied with the tradition of your forefathers, and doctrine of your priests (in which I willingly acquiesce), indulge a rash curiosity, in trying how far they can establish religion upon the principles of reason; and they thereby excite, instead of satisfying, the doubts, which naturally arise from a diligent and scrutinous enquiry. They paint, in the most magnificent colours, the order, beauty, and wise arrangement of the universe; and then ask, if such a glorious display of intelligence could proceed from the fortuitous concourse of atoms, or if chance could produce what the greatest genius can never sufficiently admire. I shall not examine the justness of this argument. I shall allow it to be as solid as my antagonists and accusers can desire. It is sufficient, if I can prove, from this very reasoning, that the question is entirely speculative, and that, when, in my philosophical disquisitions, I deny a providence and a future state, I undermine not the foundations of society, but advance principles, which they themselves, upon their own topics, if they argue consistently, must allow to be solid and satisfactory.

You then, who are my accusers, have acknowledged, that the chief or sole argument for a divine existence (which I never questioned) is derived from the order of nature; where there appear such marks of intelligence and design, that you think it extravagant to assign for its cause, either chance, or the blind and unguided force of matter. You allow, that this is an argument drawn from effects to causes. From the order of the work, you infer, that there must have been project and forethought in the workman. If you cannot make out this point, you allow, that your conclusion fails; and you pretend not to establish the conclusion in a greater latitude than the phenomena of nature will justify. These are your concessions. I desire you to mark the consequences.

When we infer any particular cause from an effect, we must proportion the one to the other, and can never be allowed to ascribe to the cause any qualities, but what are exactly sufficient to produce the effect. A body of ten ounces raised in any scale may serve as a proof, that the counterbalancing weight exceeds ten ounces; but can never afford a reason that it exceeds a hundred. If the cause, assigned for any effect, be not sufficient to produce it, we must either reject that cause, or add to it such qualities as will give it a just proportion to the effect. But if we ascribe to it further qualities, or affirm it capable of producing other effects, we can only indulge the licence of conjecture, and arbitrarily suppose the existence of qualities and energies, without reason or authority.

The same rule holds, whether the cause assigned be brute unconscious matter, or a rational intelligent being. If the cause be known only by the effect, we never ought to ascribe to it any qualities, beyond what are precisely requisite to produce the effect: Nor can we, by any rules of just reasoning, return back from the cause, and infer other effects from it, beyond those by which alone it is known to us. No one, merely from the sight of one of Zeuxis's pictures, could know, that he was also a statuary or architect, and was an artist no less skilful in stone and marble than in colours. The talents and taste, displayed in the particular work before us; these we may safely conclude the workmen to be possessed of. The cause must be proportioned to the effect; and if we exactly and precisely proportion it, we shall never find in it any qualities, that point farther, or afford an inference concerning any other design or performance. Such qualities must be somewhat beyond what is merely requisite for producing the effect, which we examine.

Allowing, therefore, the gods to be the authors of the existence or order of the universe; it follows, that they possess that precise degree of power, intelligence, and benevolence, which appears in their workmanship; but nothing farther can ever be proved, except we call in the assistance of exaggeration and flattery to supply the defects of argument and reasoning. So far as the traces of any attributes, at present, appear, so far may we conclude these attributes to exist. The supposition of farther attributes is mere hypothesis; much more the supposition, that, in distant regions of space or periods of time, there has been, or will be, a more magnificent display of these attributes, and a scheme of administration more suitable to such imaginary virtues. We can never be allowed to mount up from the universe, the effect, to Jupiter, the cause; and then descend downwards, to infer any new effect from that cause; as if the present effects alone were not entirely worthy of the glorious attributes, which we ascribe to that deity. The knowledge of the cause being derived solely from the effect, they must be exactly adjusted to each other; and the one can never refer to anything farther, or be the foundation of any new inference and conclusion.

You find certain phenomena in nature. You seek a cause or author. You imagine that you have found him. You afterwards become so enamoured of this offspring of your brain, that you imagine it impossible, but he must produce something greater and more perfect than the present scene of things, which is so full of ill and disorder. You forget, that this superlative intelligence and benevolence are entirely imaginary, or, at least, without any foundation in reason; and that you have no ground to ascribe to him any qualities, but what you see he has actually exerted and displayed in his productions. Let your gods, therefore, O philosophers, be suited to the present appearances of nature: and presume not to alter these appearances by arbitrary suppositions, in order to suit them to the attributes, which you so fondly ascribe to your deities.

When priests and poets, supported by your authority, O Athenians, talk of a golden or silver age, which preceded the present state of vice and misery, I hear them with attention and with reverence. But when philosophers, who pretend to neglect authority, and to cultivate reason, hold the same discourse, I pay them not, I own, the same obsequious submission and pious deference. I ask, who carried them into the celestial regions, who admitted them into the councils of the gods, who opened to them the book of fate, that they thus rashly affirm, that their deities have executed, or will execute, any purpose beyond what has actually appeared? If they tell me, that they have mounted on the steps or by the gradual ascent of reason, and by drawing inferences from effects to causes, I still insist, that they have aided the ascent of reason by the wings of imagination; otherwise they could not thus change their manner of inference, and argue from causes to effects; presuming, that a more perfect production than the present world would be more suitable to such perfect beings as the gods, and forgetting that they have no reason to ascribe to these celestial beings any perfection or any attribute, but what can be found in the present world.

Hence all the fruitless industry to account for the ill appearance of nature, and save the honour of the gods; while we must acknowledge the reality of that evil and disorder, with which the world so much abounds. The obstinate and intractable qualities of matter, we are told, or the observance of general laws, or some such reason, is the sole cause, which controlled the power and benevolence of Jupiter, and obliged him to create mankind and every sensible creature so imperfect and so unhappy. These attributes then, are, it seems, beforehand, taken for granted, in their greatest latitude. And upon that supposition, I own that such conjectures may, perhaps, be admitted as plausible solutions of the ill phenomena. But still I ask, Why take these attributes for granted, or why ascribe to the cause any qualities but what actually appear in the effect? Why torture your brain to justify the course of nature upon suppositions, which, for aught you know, may be entirely imaginary, and of which there are to be found no traces in the course of nature?

The religious hypothesis, therefore, must be considered only as a particular method of accounting for the visible phenomena of the universe: but no just reasoner will ever presume to infer from it any single fact, and alter or add to the phenomena, in any single particular. If you think, that the appearances of things prove such causes, it is allowable for you to draw an inference concerning the existence of these causes. In such complicated and sublime subjects, every one should be indulged in the liberty of conjecture and argument. But here you ought to rest. If you come backward, and arguing from your inferred causes, conclude, that any other fact has existed, or will exist, in the course of nature, which may serve as a fuller display of particular attributes; I must admonish you, that you have departed from the method of reasoning, attached to the present subject, and have certainly added something to the attributes of the cause, beyond what appears in the effect; otherwise you could never, with tolerable sense or propriety, add anything to the effect, in order to render it more worthy of the cause.

Where, then, is the odiousness of that doctrine, which I teach in my school, or rather, which I examine in my gardens? Or what do you find in this whole question, wherein the security of good morals, or the peace and order of society, is in the least concerned?

I deny a providence, you say, and supreme governor of the world, who guides the course of events, and punishes the vicious with infamy and disappointment, and rewards the virtuous with honour and success, in all their undertakings. But surely, I deny not the course itself of events, which lies open to every one's inquiry and examination. I acknowledge, that, in the present order of things, virtue is attended with more peace of mind than vice, and meets with a more favour able reception from the world. I am sensible, that, according to the past experience of mankind, friendship is the chief joy of human life, and moderation the only source of tranquillity and happiness. I never balance between the virtuous and the vicious course of life; but am sensible, that, to a well-disposed mind, every advantage is on the side of the former. And what can you say more, allowing all your suppositions and reasonings? You tell me, indeed, that this disposition of things proceeds from intelligence and design. But whatever it proceeds from, the disposition itself, on which depends our happiness or misery, and consequently our conduct and deportment in life is still the same. It is still open for me, as well as you, to regulate my behaviour, by my experience of past events. And if you affirm, that, while a divine providence is allowed, and a supreme distributive justice in the universe, I ought to expect some more particular reward of the good, and punishment of the bad, beyond the ordinary course of events; I here find the same fallacy, which I have before endeavoured to detect. You persist in imagining, that, if we grant that divine existence, for which you so earnestly contend, you may safely infer consequences from it, and add something to the experienced order of nature, by arguing from the attributes which you ascribe to your gods. You seem not to remember, that all your reasonings on this subject can only be drawn from effects to causes; and that every argument, deducted from causes to effects, must of necessity be a gross sophism; since it is impossible for you to know anything of the cause, but what you have antecedently, not inferred, but discovered to the full, in the effect.

But what must a philosopher think of those vain reasoners, who, instead of regarding the present scene of things as the sole object of their contemplation, so far reverse the whole course of nature, as to render this life merely a passage to something farther; a porch, which leads to a greater, and vastly different building; a prologue, which serves only to introduce the piece, and give it more grace and propriety? Whence, do you think, can such philosophers derive their idea of the gods? From their own conceit and imagination surely. For if they derived it from the present phenomena, it would never point to anything farther, but must be exactly adjusted to them. That the divinity may *possibly* be endowed with attributes, which we have never seen exerted, may be governed by principles of action, which we cannot discover to be satisfied: all this will freely be allowed. But still this is mere *possibility* and hypothesis. We never can have reason to *infer* any attributes, or any principles of action in him, but so far as we know them to have been exerted and satisfied.

Are there *any marks of a distributive justice in the world?* If you answer in the affirmative, I conclude, that, since justice here exerts itself, it is satisfied. If you reply in the negative, I conclude, that you have then no reason to ascribe justice, in our sense of it, to the gods. If you hold a medium between affirmation and negation, by saying, that the justice of the gods, at present, exerts itself in part, but not in its full extent; I answer, that you have no reason to give it any particular extent, but only so far as you see it, *at present,* exert itself.

Thus I bring the dispute, O Athenians, to a short issue with my antagonists. The course of nature lies open to my contemplation as well as to theirs. The experienced train of events is the great standard, by which we all regulate our conduct. Nothing else can be appealed to in the field, or in the senate. Nothing else ought ever to be heard of in the schools, or in the closet. In vain would our limited understanding break through those boundaries, which are too narrow for our fond imagination. While we argue from the course of nature, and infer a particular intelligent cause, which first bestowed, and still preserves order in the universe, we embrace a principle, which is both uncertain and useless. It is uncertain; because the subject lies entirely beyond the reach of human experience. It is useless; because our knowledge of this cause being derived entirely from the course of nature, we can never, according to the rules of just reasoning, return back from the cause with any new inference, or making additions to the common and experienced course of nature, establish any new principles of conduct and behaviour.

I observe (said I, finding he had finished his harangue) that you neglect not the artifice of the demagogues of old; and as you were pleased to make me stand for the people, you insinuate yourself into my favour by embracing those principles, to which, you know, I have always expressed a particular attachment. But allowing you to make experience (as indeed I think you ought) the only standard of our judgement concerning this, and all other questions of fact; I doubt not but, from the very same experience, to which you appeal, it may be possible to refute this reasoning, which you have put into the mouth of Epicurus. If you saw, for instance, a half-finished building, surrounded with heaps of brick and stone and mortar, and all the instruments of masonry; could you not *infer* from the effect, that it was a work of design and contrivance? And could you not return again, from this inferred cause, to infer new additions to the effect, and conclude, that the building would soon be finished, and receive all the further improvements, which art could bestow upon it? If you saw upon the sea-shore the print of one human foot, you would conclude, that a man had passed that way, and that he had also left the traces of the other foot, though effaced by the rolling of the sands or inundation of the waters. Why then do you refuse to admit the same method of reasoning with regard to the order of nature? Consider the world and the present life only as an imperfect building, from which you can infer a superior intelligence; and arguing from that superior intelligence, which can leave nothing imperfect; why may you not infer a more finished scheme or plan, which will receive its completion in some distant point of space or time? Are not these methods of reasoning exactly similar? And under what pretence can you embrace the one, while you reject the other?

The infinite difference of the subjects, replied he, is a sufficient foundation for this difference in my conclusions. In works of *human* art and contrivance, it is allowable to advance from the effect to the cause, and returning back from the cause, to form new inferences concerning the effect, and examine the alterations, which it has probably undergone, or may still undergo. But what is the foundation of this method of reasoning? Plainly this: that man is a being, whom we know by experience, whose motives and designs we are acquainted with, and whose projects and inclinations have a certain connexion and coherence, according to the laws which nature has established for the government of such a creature. When, therefore, we find, that any work has proceeded from the skill and industry of man; as we are otherwise acquainted with the nature of the animal, we can draw a hundred inferences concerning what may be expected from him; and these inferences will all be founded in experience and observation. But did we know man only from the single work or production which we examine, it were impossible for us to argue in this manner; because our knowledge of all the qualities, which we ascribe to him, being in that case derived from the production, it is impossible they could point to anything further, or be the foundation of any new inference. The print of a foot in the sand can only prove, when considered alone, that there was some figure adapted to it, by which it was produced: but the print of a human foot proves likewise, from our other experience, that there was probably another foot, which also left its impression, though effaced by time or other accidents. Here we mount from the effect to the cause; and descending again from the cause, infer alterations in the effect; but this is not a continuation of the same simple chain of reasoning. We comprehend in this case a hundred other experiences and observations, concerning the *usual* figure and members of that species of animal, without which this method of argument must be considered as fallacious and sophistical.

The case is not the same with our reasonings from the works of nature. The Deity is known to us only by his productions, and is a single being in the universe, not comprehended under any species or genus, from whose experienced attributes or qualities, we can, by analogy, infer any attribute or quality in him. As the universe shows wisdom and goodness, we infer wisdom and goodness. As it shows a particular degree of these perfections, we infer a particular degree of them, precisely adapted to the effect which we examine. But further attributes or further degrees of the same attributes, we can never be authorized to infer or suppose, by any rules of just reasoning. Now, without some such license of supposition, it is impossible for us to argue from the cause, or infer any alteration in the effect, beyond what has immediately fallen under our observation. Greater good produced by this Being must still prove a greater degree of goodness: a more impartial distribution of rewards and punishments must proceed from a greater regard to justice and equity. Every supposed addition to the works of nature makes an addition to the attributes of the Author of nature; and consequently, being entirely unsupported by any reason or argument, can never be admitted but as mere conjecture and hypothesis.*

The great source of our mistake in this subject, and of the unbounded licence of conjecture, which we indulge, is, that we tacitly consider ourselves, as in the place of the Supreme Being, and conclude, that he will, on every occasion, observe the same conduct, which we ourselves, in his situation, would have embraced as reasonable and eligible. But, besides that the ordinary course of nature may convince us, that almost everything is regulated by principles and maxims very different from ours; besides, this, I say, it must evidently appear contrary to all rules of analogy to reason, from the intentions and projects of men, to those of a Being so different, and so much superior. In human nature, there is a certain experienced coherence of designs and inclinations; so that when, from

*In general, it may, I think, be established as a maxim, that where any cause is known only by its particular effects, it must be impossible to infer any new effects from that cause; since the qualities, which are requisite to produce these new effects along with the former, must either be different, or superior, or of more extensive operation, than those which simply produced the effect, whence alone the cause is supposed to be known to us. We can never, therefore, have any reason to suppose the existence of these qualities. To say, that the new effects proceed only from a continuation of the same energy, which is already known from the first effects, will not remove the difficulty. For even granting this to be the case (which can seldom be supposed), the very continuation and exertion of a like energy (for it is impossible it can be absolutely the same), I say, this exertion of a like energy, in a different period of space and time, is a very arbitrary supposition, and what there cannot possibly be any traces of in the effects, from which all our knowledge of the cause is originally derived. Let the *inferred* cause be exactly proportioned (as it should be) to the known effect; and it is impossible that it can possess any qualities, from which new or different effects can be *inferred*.

any fact, we have discovered one intention of any man, it may often be reasonable, from experience, to infer another, and draw a long chain of conclusions concerning his past or future conduct. But this method of reasoning can never have place with regard to a Being, so remote and incomprehensible, who bears much less analogy to any other being in the universe than the sun to a waxen taper, and who discovers himself only by some faint traces or outlines, beyond which we have no authority to ascribe to him any attribute or perfection. What we imagine to be a superior perfection, may really be a defect. Or were it ever so much a perfection, the ascribing of it to the Supreme Being, where it appears not to have been really exerted, to the full, in his works, savours more of flattery and panegyric, than of just reasoning and sound philosophy. All the philosophy, therefore, in the world, and all the religion, which is nothing but a species of philosophy, will never be able to carry us beyond the usual course of experience, or give us measures of conduct and behaviour different from those which are furnished by reflections on common life. No new fact can ever be inferred from the religious hypothesis; no event foreseen or foretold: no reward or punishment expected or dreaded, beyond what is already known by practice and observation. So that my apology for Epicurus will still appear solid and satisfactory; nor have the political interests of society any connexion with the philosophical disputes concerning metaphysics and religion.

There is still one circumstance, replied I, which you seem to have overlooked. Though I should allow your premises, I must deny your conclusion. You conclude, that religious doctrines and reasonings *can* have no influence on life, because they *ought* to have no influence; never considering, that men reason not in the same manner you do, but draw many consequences from the belief of a divine Existence, and suppose that the Deity will inflict punishments on vice, and bestow rewards on virtue, beyond what appear in the ordinary course of nature. Whether this reasoning of theirs be just or not, is no matter. Its influence on their life and conduct must still be the same. And, those, who attempt to disabuse them of such prejudices, may, for aught I know, be good reasoners, but I cannot allow them to be good citizens and politicians; since they free men from one restraint upon their passions, and make the infringement of the laws of society, in one respect, more easy and secure.

After all, I may, perhaps, agree to your general conclusion in favour of liberty, though upon different premises from those, on which you endeavour to found it. I think, that the state ought to tolerate every principle of philosophy; nor is there an instance, that any government has suffered in its political interests by such indulgence. There is no enthusiasm among philosophers; their doctrines are not very alluring to the people; and no restraint can be put upon their reasonings, but what must be of dangerous consequences to the sciences, and even to the state, by paving the way for persecution and oppression in points, where the generality of mankind are more deeply interested and concerned.

But there occurs to me (continued I) with regard to your main topic, a difficulty, which I shall just propose to you without insisting on it; lest it lead into reasonings of too nice and delicate a nature. In a word, I much doubt whether it be possible for a cause to be known only by its effect (as you have all along supposed) or to be of so singular and particular a nature as to have no parallel and no similarity with any other cause or object, that has ever fallen under our observation. It is only when two *species* of objects are found to be constantly conjoined, that we can infer the one from the other; and were an effect presented, which was entirely singular, and could not be comprehended under any known species, I do not see, that we could form any conjecture or inference at all concerning its cause. If experience and observation and analogy be, indeed, the only guides which we can reasonably follow in inferences of this nature; both the effect and cause must bear a similarity and resemblance to other effects and causes, which we know, and which we have found, in many instances, to be conjoined with each other. I leave it to your own reflection to pursue the consequences of this principle. I shall just observe, that, as the antagonists of Epicurus always suppose the universe, an effect quite singular and unparalleled, to be the proof of a Deity, a cause no less singular and unparalleled; your reasonings, upon that supposition, seem, at least, to merit our attention. There is, I own, some difficulty, how we can ever return from the cause to the effect, and, reasoning from our ideas of the former, infer any alteration on the latter, or any addition to it.

SECTION XII. OF THE ACADEMICAL OR SCEPTICAL PHILOSOPHY

PART I

There is not a greater number of philosophical reasonings, displayed upon any subject, than those, which prove the existence of a Deity, and refute the fallacies of *Atheists;* and yet the most religious philosophers still dispute whether any man can be so blinded as to be a speculative atheist. How shall we reconcile these contradictions? The knightserrant, who wandered about to clear the world of dragons and giants, never entertained the least doubt with regard to the existence of these monsters.

The *Sceptic* is another enemy of religion, who naturally provokes the indignation of all divines and graver philosophers; though it is certain, that no man ever met with any such absurd creature, or conversed with a man, who had no opinion or principle concerning any subject, either of action or speculation. This begets a very natural question; What is meant by a sceptic? And how far is it possible to push these philosophical principles of doubt and uncertainty?

There is a species of scepticism, *antecedent* to all study and philosophy, which is much inculcated by Des Cartes and others, as a sovereign preservative against error and precipitate judgement. It recommends an universal doubt, not only of all our former opinions and principles, but also of our very faculties; of whose veracity, say they, we must assure ourselves, by a chain of reasoning, deduced from some original principle, which cannot possibly be fallacious or deceitful. But neither is there any such original principle, which has a prerogative above others, that are self-evident and convincing: or if there were, could we advance a step beyond it, but by the use of those very faculties, of which we are supposed to be already diffident. The Cartesian doubt, therefore, were it ever possible to be attained by any human creature (as it plainly is not) would be entirely incurable; and no reasoning could ever bring us to a state of assurance and conviction upon any subject.

It must, however, be confessed, that this species of scepticism, when more moderate, may be understood in a very reasonable sense, and is a necessary preparative to the study of philosophy, by preserving a proper impartiality in our judgements, and weaning our mind from all those prejudices, which we may have imbibed from education or rash opinion. To begin with clear and self-evident principles, to advance by timorous and sure steps, to review frequently our conclusions, and examine accurately all their consequences; though by these means we shall make both a slow and a short progress in our systems; are the only methods, by which we can ever hope to reach truth, and attain a proper stability and certainty in our determinations.

There is another species of scepticism, *consequent* to science and enquiry, when men are supposed to have discovered either the absolute fallaciousness of their mental faculties, or their unfitness to reach any fixed determination in all those curious subjects of speculation, about which they are commonly employed. Even our very senses are brought into dispute, by a certain species of philosophers; and the maxims of common life are subjected to the same doubt as the most profound principles or conclusions of metaphysics and theology. As these paradoxical tenets (if they may be called tenets) are to be met with in some philosophers, and the refutation of them in several, they naturally excite our curiosity, and make us enquire into the arguments, on which they may be founded.

I need not insist upon the more trite topics, employed by the sceptics in all ages, against the evidence of *sense;* such as those which are derived from the imperfection and fallaciousness of our organs, on numberless occasions; the crooked appearance of an oar in water; the various aspects of objects, according to their different distances; the double images which arise from the pressing one eye; with many other appearances of a like nature. These sceptical topics, indeed, are only sufficient to prove, that the senses alone are not implicitly to be depended on; but that we must correct their evidence by reason, and by considerations, derived from the nature of the medium, the distance of the object, and the disposition of the organ, in order to render them, without their sphere, the proper *criteria* of truth and falsehood. There are other more profound arguments against the senses, which admit not of so easy a solution.

It seems evident, that men are carried, by a natural instinct or prepossession, to repose faith in their senses; and that, without any reasoning, or even almost before the use of reason, we always suppose an external universe, which depends not on our perception, but would exist, though we and every sensible creature were absent or annihilated. Even the animal creations are governed by a like opinion, and preserve this belief of external objects, in all their thoughts, designs, and actions.

It seems also evident, that, when men follow this blind and powerful instinct of nature, they always suppose the very images, presented by the senses, to be the external objects, and never entertain any suspicion, that the one are nothing but representations of the other. This very table, which we see white, and which we feel hard, is believed to exist, independent of our perception, and to be something external to our mind, which perceives it. Our presence bestows not being on it: our absence does not annihilate it. It preserves its existence uniform and entire, independent of the situation of intelligent beings, who perceive or contemplate it.

But this universal and primary opinion of all men is soon destroyed by the slightest philosophy, which teaches us, that nothing can ever be present to the mind but an image or perception, and that the senses are only the inlets, through which these images are conveyed, without being able to produce any immediate intercourse between the mind and the object. The table, which we see, seems to diminish, as we remove farther from it: but the real table, which exists independent of us, suffers no alteration: it was, therefore, nothing but its image, which was present to the mind. These are the obvious dictates of reason; and no man, who reflects, ever doubted, that the existences, which we consider, when we say, *this house* and *that tree,* are nothing but perceptions in the mind, and fleeting copies or representations of other existences, which remain uniform and independent.

So far, then, are we necessitated by reasoning to contradict or depart from the primary instincts of nature, and to embrace a new system with regard to the evidence of our senses. But here philosophy finds herself extremely embarrassed, when she would justify this new system, and obviate the cavils and objections of the sceptics. She can no longer plead the infallible and irresistible instinct of nature: for that led us to a quite different system, which is acknowledged fallible and even erroneous. And to justify this pretended philosophical system, by a chain of clear and convincing argument, or even any appearance of argument, exceeds the power of all human capacity.

By what argument can it be proved, that the perceptions of the mind must be caused by external objects, entirely different from them, though resembling them (if that be possible) and could not arise either from the energy of the mind itself, or from the suggestion of some invisible and unknown spirit, or from some other cause still more unknown to us? It is acknowledged, that, in fact, many of these perceptions arise not from anything external, as in dreams, madness, and other diseases. And nothing can be more inexplicable than the manner, in which body should so operate upon mind as ever to convey an image of itself to a substance, supposed of so different, and even contrary a nature.

It is a question of fact, whether the perceptions of the senses be produced by external objects, resembling them: how shall this question be determined? By experience surely; as all other questions of a like nature. But here experience is, and must be entirely silent. The mind has never anything present to it but the perceptions, and cannot possibly reach any experience of their connexion with objects. The supposition of such a connexion is, therefore, without any foundation in reasoning.

To have recourse to the veracity of the Supreme Being, in order to prove the veracity of our senses, is surely making a very unexpected circuit. If his veracity were at all concerned in this matter, our senses would be entirely infallible; because it is not possible that he can ever deceive. Not to mention, that, if the external world be once called in question, we shall be at a loss to find arguments, by which we may prove the existence of that Being or any of his attributes.

This is a topic, therefore, in which the profounder and more philosophical sceptics will always triumph, when they endeavour to introduce an universal doubt into all subjects of human knowledge and enquiry. Do you follow the instincts and propensities of nature, may they say, in assenting to the veracity of sense? But these lead you to believe that the very perception or sensible image is the external object. Do you disclaim this principle, in order to embrace a more rational opinion, that the perceptions are only representations of something external? You here depart from your natural propensities and more obvious sentiments; and yet are not able to satisfy your reason, which can never find any convincing argument from experience to prove, that the perceptions are connected with any external objects.

There is another sceptical topic of a like nature, derived from the most profound philosophy, which might merit our attention, were it requisite to dive so deep, in order to discover arguments and reasonings, which can so little serve to any serious purpose. It is universally allowed by modern enquirers, that all the sensible qualities of objects, such as hard, soft, hot, cold, white, black, etc. are merely secondary, and exist not in the objects themselves, but are perceptions of the mind, without any external archetype or model, which they represent. If this be allowed, with regard to secondary qualities, it must also follow, with regard to the supposed primary qualities of extension and solidity; nor can the latter be any more entitled to that denomination than the former. The idea of extension is entirely acquired from the senses of sight and feeling; and if all the qualities, perceived by the senses, be in the mind, not in the object, the same conclusion must reach the idea of extension, which is wholly dependent on the sensible ideas or the ideas of secondary qualities. Nothing can save us from this conclusion, but the asserting, that the ideas of those primary qualities are attained by *Abstraction,* an opinion, which, if we examine it accurately, we shall find to be unintelligible, and even absurd. An extension, that is neither tangible nor visible, cannot possibly be conceived: and a tangible or visible extension, which is neither hard nor soft, black or white, is equally beyond the reach of human conception. Let any man try to conceive a triangle in general, which is neither *Isosceles* nor *Scalenum,* nor has any particular length or proportion of sides; and he will soon perceive the absurdity of all the scholastic notions with regard to abstraction and general ideas.*

Thus the first philosophical objection to the evidence of sense or to the opinion of external existence consists in this, that such an opinion, if rested on natural instinct, is contrary to reason, and if referred to reason, is contrary to natural instinct, and at the same time carries no rational evidence with it, to convince an impartial enquirer. The second objection goes farther, and represents this opinion as contrary to reason: at least, if it be a principle of reason, that all sensible qualities are in the mind, not in the object. Bereave matter of all its intelligible qualities, both primary and secondary, you in a manner annihilate it, and leave only a certain unknown, inexplicable *something,* as the cause of our perceptions; a notion so imperfect, that no sceptic will think it worth while to contend against it.

PART II

It may seem a very extravagant attempt of the sceptics to *destroy* reason by argument and ratiocination; yet is this the grand scope of all their enquiries and disputes. They endeavour to find objections, both to our abstract reasonings, and to those which regard matter of fact and existence.

The chief objection against all *abstract* reasonings is derived from the ideas of space and time; ideas, which, in common life and to a careless view, are very clear and intelligible, but when they pass through the scrutiny of the profound sciences (and they are the chief object of these sciences) afford principles, which seem full of absurdity and contradiction. No priestly *dogmas,* invented on purpose to tame and subdue the rebellious reason of mankind, ever shocked common sense more than the doctrine of the infinite divisibility of extension, with its consequences; as they are pompously displayed by all geometricians and metaphysicians, with a kind of triumph and exultation. A real quantity, infinitely less than any finite quantity, containing quantities infinitely less than itself, and so on *in infinitum;* this is an edifice so bold and prodigious, that it is too weighty for any pretended demonstration to support, because it shocks the clearest and most natural principles of human reason.** But what renders the matter more

*This argument is drawn from Dr. Berkeley; and indeed most of the writings of that very ingenious author form the best lessons of scepticism, which are to be found either among the ancient or modern philosophers. Bayle not excepted. He professes, however, in his title-page (and undoubtedly with great truth) to have composed his book against the sceptics as well as against the atheists and freethinkers. But that all his arguments, though otherwise intended, are, in reality, merely sceptical, appears from this, that *they admit of no answer and produce no conviction*. Their only effect is to cause that momentary amazement and irresolution and confusion, which is the result of scepticism.

**Whatever disputes there may be about mathematical points, we must allow that there are physical points; that is, parts of extension which cannot be divided or lessened, either by the eye or imagination. These images, then, which are present to the fancy or senses, are absolutely indivisible, and consequently must be allowed by mathematicians to be infinitely less than any real part of extension; and yet nothing appears more certain to reason, than that an infinite number of them composes an infinite extension. How much more an infinite number of those infinitely small parts of extension, which are still supposed infinitely divisible. It seems to extraordinary, is, that these seemingly absurd opinions are supported by a chain of reasoning, the clearest and most natural; nor is it possible for us to allow the premises without admitting the consequences. Nothing can be more convincing and satisfactory than all the conclusions concerning the properties of circles and triangles; and yet, when these are once received, how can we deny, that the angle of contact between a circle and its tangent is infinitely less than any rectilineal angle, that as you may increase the diameter of the circle *in infinitum,* this angle of contact becomes still less, even *in infinitum,* and that the angle of contact between other curves and their tangents may be infinitely less than those between any circle and its tangent, and so on, *in infinitum?* The demonstration of these principles seems as unexceptionable as that which proves the three angles of a triangle to be equal to two right ones, though the latter opinion be natural and easy, and the former big with contradiction and absurdity. Reason here seems to be thrown into a kind of amazement and suspense, which, without the suggestions of any sceptic, gives her a diffidence of herself, and of the ground on which she treads. She sees a full light, which illuminates certain places; but that light borders upon the most profound darkness. And between these she is so dazzled and confounded, that she scarcely can pronounce with certainty and assurance concerning any one object.

The absurdity of these bold determinations of the abstract sciences seems to become, if possible, still more palpable with regard to time than extension. An infinite number of real parts of time, passing in succession, and exhausted one after another, appears so evident a contradiction, that no man, one should think, whose judgment is not corrupted, instead of being improved, by the sciences, would ever be able to admit of it.

Yet still reason must remain restless, and unquiet, even with regard to that scepticism, to which she is driven by these seeming absurdities and contradictions. How any clear, distinct idea can contain circumstances, contradictory to itself, or to any other clear, distinct idea, is absolutely incomprehensible; and is, perhaps, as absurd as any proposition, which can be formed. So that nothing can be more sceptical, or more full of doubt and hesitation, than this scepticism itself, which arises from some of the paradoxical conclusions of geometry or the science of quantity.*

---

me not impossible to avoid these absurdities and contradictions, if it be admitted, that there is no such thing as abstract or general ideas, properly speaking; but that all general ideas are, in reality, particular ones, attached to a general term, which recalls, upon occasion, other particular ones that resemble, in certain circumstances, the idea, present to the mind. Thus when the term Horse is pronounced, we immediately figure to ourselves the idea of a black or a white animal, of a particular size or figure: But as that term is also usually applied to animals of other colours, figures and sizes these ideas, though not actually present to the imagination, are easily recalled, and our reasoning and conclusion proceed in the same way, as if they were actually present. If this be admitted (as seems reasonable) it follows that all the ideas of quantity, upon which mathematicians reason, are nothing but particular, and such as are suggested by the senses and imagination, and consequently, cannot be infinitely divisible. It is sufficient to have dropped this hint at present, without prosecuting it any farther. It certainly concerns all lovers of science not to expose themselves to the ridicule and contempt of the ignorant by their conclusions; and this seems the readiest solution of these difficulties.

*It seems to me not impossible to avoid these absurdities and contradictions, if it be admitted, that there is no such thing as abstract or general ideas, properly speaking; but that all general ideas are, in reality, particular ones, attached to a general term, which recalls, upon occasion, other particular ones that resemble, in certain circumstances, the idea, present to the mind. Thus when the term Horse is pronounced, we immediately figure to ourselves the idea of a black or a white animal, of a particular size or figure: But as that term is also usually applied to animals of other colours, figures and sizes these ideas, though not actually present to the imagination, are easily recalled, and our reasoning and conclusion proceed in the same way, as if they were actually present. If this be admitted (as seems reasonable) it follows that all the ideas of quantity, upon which mathematicians reason, are nothing but particular, and such as are suggested

The sceptical objections to *moral* evidence, or to the reasonings concerning matter of fact, are either *popular* or *philosophical*. The popular objections are derived from the natural weakness of human understanding; the contradictory opinions, which have been entertained in different ages and nations; the variations of our judgement in sickness and health, youth and old age, prosperity and adversity; the perpetual contradiction of each particular man's opinions and sentiments; with many other topics of that kind. It is needless to insist farther on this head. These objections are but weak. For as, in common life, we reason every moment concerning fact and existence, and cannot possibly subsist, without continually employing this species of argument, any popular objections, derived from thence, must be insufficient to destroy that evidence. The great subverter of *Pyrrhonism* or the excessive principles of scepticism is action, and employment, and the occupations of common life. These principles may flourish and triumph in the schools; where it is, indeed, difficult, if not impossible, to refute them. But as soon as they leave the shade, and by the presence of the real objects, which actuate our passions and sentiments, are put in opposition to the more powerful principles of our nature, they vanish like smoke, and leave the most determined sceptic in the same condition as other mortals.

The sceptic, therefore, had better keep within his proper sphere, and display those *philosophical* objections, which arise from more profound researches. Here he seems to have ample matter of triumph; while he justly insists, that all our evidence for any matter of fact, which lies beyond the testimony of sense or memory, is derived entirely from the relation of cause and effect; that we have no other idea of this relation than that of two objects, which have been frequently *conjoined* together; that we have no argument to convince us, that objects, which have, in our experience, been frequently conjoined, will likewise, in other instances, be conjoined in the same manner; and that nothing leads us to this inference but custom or a certain instinct of our nature; which it is indeed difficult to resist, but which, like other instincts, may be fallacious and deceitful. While the sceptic insists upon these topics, he shows his force, or rather, indeed, his own and our weakness; and seems, for the time at least, to destroy all assurance and conviction. These arguments might be displayed at greater length, if any durable good or benefit to society could ever be expected to result from them.

For here is the chief and most confounding objection to *excessive* scepticism, that no durable good can ever result from it; while it remains in its full force and vigour. We need only ask a sceptic, *What his meaning is? And what he proposes by all these curious researches?* He is immediately at a loss, and knows not what to answer. A Copernican or Ptolemaic, who supports each his different system of astronomy, may hope to produce a conviction, which will remain constant and durable, with his audience. A Stoic or Epicurean displays principles, which may not be durable, but which have an effect on conduct and behaviour. But a Pyrrhonian cannot expect, that his philosophy will have any constant influence on the mind: or if it had, that its influence would be beneficial to society. On the contrary, he must acknowledge, if he will acknowledge anything, that all human life must perish, were his principles universally and steadily to prevail. All discourse, all action would immediately cease; and men remain in a total lethargy, till the necessities of nature, unsatisfied, put an end to their miserable existence. It is true; so fatal an event is very little to be dreaded. Nature is always too strong for principle. And though a Pyrrhonian may throw himself or others into a momentary amazement and confusion by

---

by the senses and imagination, and consequently, cannot be infinitely divisible. It is sufficient to have dropped this hint at present, without prosecuting it any farther. It certainly concerns all lovers of science not to expose themselves to the ridicule and contempt of the ignorant by their conclusions; and this seems the readiest solution of these difficulties.

his profound reasonings; the first and most trivial event in life will put to flight all his doubts and scruples, and leave him the same, in every point of action and speculation, with the philosophers of every other sect, or with those who never concerned themselves in any philosophical researches. When he awakes from his dream, he will be the first to join in the laugh against himself, and to confess, that all his objections are mere amusement, and can have no other tendency than to show the whimsical condition of mankind, who must act and reason and believe; though they are not able, by their most diligent enquiry, to satisfy themselves concerning the foundation of these operations, or to remove the objections, which may be raised against them.

PART III

There is, indeed, a more *mitigated* scepticism or *academical* philosophy, which may be both durable and useful, and which may, in part, be the result of this Pyrrhonism, or excessive scepticism, when its undistinguished doubts are, in some measure, corrected by common sense and reflection. The greater part of mankind are naturally apt to be affirmative and dogmatical in their opinions; and while they see objects only on one side, and have no idea of any counterpoising argument, they throw themselves precipitately into the principles, to which they are inclined; nor have they any indulgence for those who entertain opposite sentiments. To hesitate or balance perplexes their understanding, checks their passion, and suspends their action. They are, therefore, impatient till they escape from a state, which to them is so uneasy: and they think, that they could never remove themselves far enough from it, by the violence of their affirmations and obstinacy of their belief. But could such dogmatical reasoners become sensible of the strange infirmities of human understanding, even in its most perfect state, and when most accurate and cautious in its determination; such a reflection would naturally inspire them with more modesty and reserve, and diminish their fond opinion of themselves, and their prejudice against antagonists. The illiterate may reflect on the disposition of the learned, who, amidst all the advantages of study and reflection, are commonly still diffident in their determinations: and if any of the learned be inclined, from their natural temper, to haughtiness and obstinacy, a small tincture of Pyrrhonism might abate their pride, by showing them, that the few advantages, which they may have attained over their fellows, are but inconsiderable, if compared with the universal perplexity and confusion, which is inherent in human nature. In general, there is a degree of doubt, and caution, and modesty, which, in all kinds of scrutiny and decision, ought for ever to accompany a just reasoner.

Another species of *mitigated* scepticism which may be of advantage to man-kind, and which may be the natural result of the Pyrrhonian doubts and scruples, is the limitation of our enquiries to such subjects as are best adapted to the narrow capacity of human understanding. The *imagination* of man is naturally sublime, delighted with whatever is remote and extraordinary, and running, without control, into the most distant parts of space and time in order to avoid the objects, which custom has rendered too familiar to it. A correct *judgement* observes a contrary method, and avoiding all distant and high enquiries, confines itself to common life, and to such subjects as fall under daily practice and experience; leaving the more sublime topics to the embellishment of poets and orators, or to the arts of priests and politicians. To bring us to so salutary a determination, nothing can be more serviceable, than to be once thoroughly convinced of the force of the Pyrrhonian doubt, and of the impossibility, that anything, but the strong power of natural instinct, could free us from it. Those who have a propensity to philosophy, will still continue their researches; because they reflect, that, besides the immediate pleasure, attending such an occupation, philosophical decisions are nothing but the reflections of common life, methodized and corrected. But they will never be tempted to go beyond common life, so long as they consider the imperfection of those faculties which they employ, their narrow reach, and their inaccurate operations. While we cannot give a satisfactory reason, why we believe, after a thousand experiments, that a stone will fall, or fire burn; can we ever satisfy ourselves concerning any determination, which we may form, with regard to the origin of worlds, and the situation of nature, from, and to eternity?

This narrow limitation, indeed, of our enquiries, is, in every respect, so reasonable, that it suffices to make the slightest examination into the natural powers of the human mind and to compare them with their objects, in order to recommend it to us. We shall then find what are the proper subjects of science and enquiry.

It seems to me, that the only objects of the abstract science or of demonstration are quantity and number, and that all attempts to extend this more perfect species of knowledge beyond these bounds are mere sophistry and illusion. As the component parts of quantity and number are entirely similar, their relations become intricate and involved; and nothing can be more curious, as well as useful, than to trace, by a variety of mediums their equality or inequality, through their different appearances. But as all other ideas are clearly distinct and different from each other, we can never advance farther, by our utmost scrutiny, than to observe this diversity, and, by an obvious reflection, pronounce one thing not to be another. Or if there be any difficulty in these decisions, it proceeds entirely from the undeterminate meaning of words, which is corrected by juster definitions. That *the square of the hypothenuse is equal to the square of the other two sides,* cannot be known,

Ninewells, the Hume family estate, near Berwick in southern Scotland. David Hume lived here until age twelve when he went to the University of Edinburgh. *(Culver Pictures, Inc.)*

let the terms be ever so exactly defined, without a train of reasoning and enquiry. But to convince us of this proposition, *that where there is no property, there can be no injustice,* it is only necessary to define the terms, and explain injustice to be a violation of property. This proposition is, indeed, nothing but a more imperfect definition. It is the same case with all those pretended syllogistical reasonings, which may be found in every other branch of learning, except the sciences of quantity and number and these may safely, I think, be pronounced the only proper objects of knowledge and demonstration.

All other enquiries of men regard only matter of fact and existence; and these are evidently incapable of demonstration. Whatever *is* may *not be.* No negation of a fact can involve a contradiction. The non-existence of any being, without exception, is as clear and distinct an idea as its existence. The proposition, which affirms it not to be, however false, is no less conceivable and intelligible, than that which affirms it to be. The case is different with the sciences, properly so called. Every proposition, which is not true, is there confused and unintelligible. That the cube root of 64 is equal to the half of 10, is a false proposition, and can never be distinctly conceived. But that Caesar, or the angel Gabriel, or any being never existed, may be a false proposition, but still is perfectly conceivable, and implies no contradiction.

The existence, therefore, of any being can only be proved by arguments from its cause or its effect; and these arguments are founded entirely on experience. If we reason *a priori,* anything may appear able to produce anything. The falling of a pebble may, for aught we know, extinguish the sun; or the wish of a man control the planets in their orbits. It is only experience, which teaches us the nature and bounds of cause and effect, and enables us to infer the existence of one object from that of another.* Such is the foundation of moral reasoning, which forms the greater part of human knowledge, and is the source of all human action and behaviour.

Moral reasonings are either concerning particular or general facts. All deliberations in life regard the former; as also all disquisitions in history, chronology, geography, and astronomy.

The sciences, which treat of general facts, are politics, natural philosophy, physic, chemistry, etc. where the qualities, causes and effects of a whole species of objects are enquired into.

Divinity or Theology, as it proves the existence of a Deity, and the immortality of souls, is composed partly of reasonings concerning particular, partly concerning general facts. It has a foundation in *reason,* so far as it is supported by experience. But its best and most solid foundation is *faith* and divine revelation.

Morals and criticism are not so properly objects of the understanding as of taste and sentiment. Beauty, whether moral or natural, is felt, more properly than perceived. Or if we reason concerning it, and endeavour to fix its standard, we regard a new fact, to wit, the general tastes of mankind, or some such fact, which may be the object of reasoning and enquiry.

When we run over libraries, persuaded of these principles, what havoc must we make? If we take in our hand any volume; of divinity or school metaphysics, for instance; let us ask, *Does it contain any abstract reasoning concerning quantity or number?* No. *Does it contain any experimental reasoning concerning matter of fact and existence?* No. Commit it then to the flames: for it can contain nothing but sophistry and illusion.

*That impious maxim of the ancient philosophy, Ex nihilo, nihil fit [From nothing, nothing issues], by which the creation of matter was excluded, ceases to be a maxim according to this philosophy. Not only the will of the supreme Being may create matter; but, for aught we know a priori, the will of any other being might create it, of any other cause, that the most whimsical imagination can assign.

Jean-Jacques Rousseau 1712–1778

Jean-Jacques Rousseau was born in 1712 in the independent city-state of Geneva. His mother, Suzanne Bernard, was a member of the city's elite, while his father, Isaac Rousseau, was a working-class watchmaker. Within a week of his birth, his mother died and with her death young Jean-Jacques and his father lost their place in high society.

The Rousseaus' position fell even further when Isaac was exiled from Geneva for challenging a superior to a duel. Jean-Jacques was taken from his father and became a ward of his mother's brother, sent with his cousin to live outside the walls of Geneva. As he reached the age to take on a career, Rousseau was apprenticed to a low-class engraver. The situation was so intolerable that Rousseau fled to Italy and eventually ended up in the household of the Baroness de Warens, a slightly disreputable but generous women. Under the protection of the baroness, Rousseau was able to develop his intellectual gifts.

At the age of 27, Rousseau left Italy for France where he developed friendships with the leading philosophers of the French Enlightenment such as Diderot and Voltaire. The next ten years were spent working as a secretary in Italy and France and writing articles for Diderot's *Encyclopedia*—the premiere work of the Enlightenment. Rousseau might well have continued working in a similar vein had he not had what he later called his "illumination." While walking to Vincennes to visit Diderot, Rousseau saw a notice of an essay competition on the question "Has the revival of the arts and sciences done more to corrupt or to purify morals?" Contrary to the prevailing belief of the time—and the dominant view of his *Encyclopedia* colleagues—Rousseau realized in a flash that far from saving humankind, the arts and sciences were bringing ruin. The more sophisticated and learned society became, the less happy, less virtuous, and more corrupt the people became. In fact, the rationalism of his age was destroying the spontaneous feelings that liberate the individual. Moreover, the arts and sciences neither rise from nor lead to morality. As Rousseau put it,

> Astronomy was born of superstition, eloquence of ambition, hatred, falsehood, and flattery; geometry of avarice; physics of an idle curiosity; and moral philosophy, like all the rest, of human pride. Thus the arts and sciences owe their birth to our vices.*

Rousseau not only won the prize, but the publication of his essay, *Discourse on the Sciences and Arts* (1750), brought him instant fame. Applying his genius next to music, Rousseau wrote the opera *Le Devin de Village* (1752), a work that glorified the Italian themes of melody and simplicity in its stories of ordinary people (in contrast to the French operatic tradition of sophisticated and complex music with stories of kings and gods). Returning to Geneva, Rousseau worked out the implications of his prize essay in his *Discourse on the Origin of Inequality* (1755), which explained the loss of the "state of nature." Contrary to Thomas Hobbes, Rousseau claimed that virtually all unpleasantries in life are the result of society and that in a true state of nature humans are, as Hobbes claimed, solitary, but they are also happy, free, and good. In his novel *The New Heloise* (1761), Rousseau fictionalized the value of simple life. In *Emile* (1762), he applied his insights to education, appealing for the protection of the unspoiled child from the grind of traditional education. *The Social Contract* (1762) most clearly and forcefully laid out Rousseau's political ideals and became one of the most influential books of all time.

Rousseau's advocacy of the simple, natural life and the importance of emotion over reason was an important contribution to the early Romantic movement. But it also led to a break with his Enlightenment friends. (For example, after receiving a copy of *Discourse on the Origin of Inequality,* Voltaire wrote Rousseau to thank him for "your new book against the human race.") Furthermore, Rousseau's often implicit—and occasionally explicit—condemnation of government authorities eventually led to a warrant for his arrest. Unwelcome in France and Geneva, Rousseau took refuge in England with David Hume. However, by now Rousseau was becoming paranoid. He began to accuse Hume of conspiring with his enemies. The quarrel was publicized and Rousseau's reputation suffered. He eventually returned to France, but the authorities—as well as the public—were no longer very interested in him. He spent his last years wandering France before dying obscure and penniless in 1778. His *Confessions* began to be published posthumously in 1782.

* * *

Whereas Rousseau's *Discourse on the Origin of Inequality* gives a description of how the freedom and happiness of the state of nature were lost, his magnum opus, *The Social Contract,* offers a prescription for human reclamation. Rousseau begins *The Social Contract* with the bold assertion, "Man was born free, and everywhere he is in chains." But Rousseau does not think the answer lies in a kind

*Jean-Jacques Rousseau, *Discourse on the Sciences and the Arts* in *Rousseau: Selections,* edited by Maurice Cranston (New York: Macmillan, 1988), p. 52.

of anarchy. The "fundamental problem" as Rousseau sees it, is to find an association that both defends the "person and property of every associate" and yet still allows for freedom.

The solution, claims Rousseau, is to be found in the social contract. But such a contract is not a Hobbesian exchange of rights for peace. As Rousseau points out, in our selection (translated by Maurice Cranston), tranquility is not really the goal: "Men live tranquilly also in dungeons; is that enough to make them contented there?" Instead of submitting to some tyrant in exchange for peace, Rousseau saw the social contract as an agreement among free individuals to give up their rights to the "general will." Such an agreement creates a sovereign, but not the sovereignty of a king. Instead, the sovereign is the expression of the general will, which alone is sacred and absolute.

But such an understanding of the social contract does not make Rousseau a democrat. In the first place, the general will is not necessarily the will of the majority. A few farsighted individuals may understand the general will better than the majority. Furthermore, what is to be done if a given individual does not properly understand the general will, or if that individual's own will is in conflict with the general will? According to Rousseau, "whoever refuses to obey the general will shall be constrained to do so by the whole body." In short, that person "shall be forced to be free."

It is not difficult to see how both the glories and horrors of the French Revolution found resources in Rousseau's work. The early revolutionary call to move past the divine right of kings to liberty, fraternity, and equality has its intellectual roots in *The Social Contract.* So too does the bloody suppression of dissent in the later years of the Terror as Robespierre and others claimed to be promoting the general will while they "forced [the people] to be free."

* * *

The best general introduction to Rousseau is still Ronald Grimsley, *The Philosophy of Rousseau* (London: Oxford University Press, 1973). Other general studies include Harald Høffding, *Jean Jacques Rousseau and His Philosophy,* translated by William Richards and Leo E. Saidla (New Haven, CT: Yale University Press, 1930); Charles William Hendel, *Jean-Jacques Rousseau, Moralist* (Indianapolis, IN: Bobbs Merrill, 1934); Nicholas Dent *Rousseau* (London: Routledge, 2005); and Matthew Simpson, *Rousseau: A Guide for the Perplexed* (London: Continuum, 2007). Irving Babbitt, *Rousseau and Romanticism* (Boston: Houghton Mifflin, 1919) is the classic work on Rousseau's historical context while N.J.H. Dent, *Rousseau: An Introduction to His Psychological, Social and Political Theory* (Oxford: Basil Blackwell, 1988) is a more recent study. For biographies, see Frederick Charles Green, *Jean-Jacques Rousseau: A Critical Study of His Life and Writings* (Cambridge: Cambridge University Press, 1955); Jean Guéhenno, *Jean-Jacques Rousseau,* translated by John and Doreen Weightman (London: Routledge and Keegan Paul, 1966); and J. H. Huizinga, *Rousseau: The Self-Made Saint* (New York: Grossman, 1976).

For general studies of Rousseau's political philosophy, see John C. Hall, *Rousseau: An Introduction to His Political Philosophy* (Cambridge, MA: Schenkman 1973); Merle L. Perkins, *Jean-Jacques Rousseau on the Individual and Society* (Lexington, KY: University Press of Kentucky, 1974); Ramon M.

Lemos, *Rousseau's Political Philosophy: An Exposition and Interpretation* (Athens, GA: University of Georgia Press, 1977); and James Miller, *Rousseau and Democracy* (New Haven, CT: Yale University Press, 1984). Lester G. Crocker, *Rousseau's* Social Contract: *An Interpretive Essay* (Cleveland, OH: Case Western Reserve University Press, 1968); Hilail Gildin, *Rousseau's* Social Contract: *The Design of the Argument* (Chicago: University of Chicago Press, 1983); and Christopher Bertram, *Rousseau and the* Social Contract (London: Routledge, 2003) focus specifically on our selection, while N.J.H. Dent, *The Rousseau Dictionary* (Oxford: Blackwell, 1992) provides a useful resource. Recent collections of essays include Patrick Riley, ed., *The Cambridge Companion to Rousseau* (Cambridge: Cambridge University Press, 2001); Lynda Lange, ed., *Feminist Interpretations of Jean-Jacques Rousseau* (College Park, PA: Penn State University Press, 2002); and Timothy O'Hagan, ed., *Jean-Jacques Rousseau* (Burlington, VT: Ashgate, 2007).

THE SOCIAL CONTRACT (in part)

INTRODUCTORY NOTE

I wish to enquire whether, taking men as they are and laws as they can be made, it is possible to establish some just and certain rule of administration in civil affairs. In this investigation I shall always strive to reconcile what right permits with what interest prescribes, so that justice and utility may not be severed.

BOOK ONE

1. *The subject of Book One.* Man was born free, and everywhere he is in chains. Many a one believes himself the master of others, and yet he is a greater slave than they. How has this change come about? I do not know. What can render it legitimate? I believe that I can settle this question.

If I considered only force and the results that proceed from it, I should say that so long as a people is compelled to obey and does obey, it does well; but that, so soon as it can shake off the yoke and does shake it off, it does better; for, if men recover their freedom by virtue of the same right by which it was taken away, either they are justified in resuming it, or there was no justification for depriving them of it. But the social order is a sacred right which serves as a foundation for all others. This right, however, does not come from nature. It is therefore based on conventions. The question is to know what these conventions are. Before coming to that, I must establish what I have just laid down.

Jean-Jacques Rousseau, "The Social Contract" from *Rousseau: Selections,* edited by Maurice Cranston (New York: Macmillam, 1988).

2. *The first societies.* The earliest of all societies, and the only natural one, is the family; yet children remain attached to their father only so long as they have need of him for their own preservation. As soon as this need ceases, the natural bond is dissolved. The children being freed from the obedience which they owed to their father, and the father from the cares which he owed to his children, become equally independent. If they remain united, it is no longer naturally but voluntarily; and the family itself is kept together only by convention.

This common liberty is a consequence of man's nature. His first law is to attend to his own preservation, his first cares are those which he owes to himself; and as soon as he comes to years of discretion, being sole judge of the means adapted for his own preservation, he becomes his own master.

The family is, then, if you will, the primitive model of political societies; the chief is the analogue of the father, while the people represent the children; and all, being born free and equal, alienate their liberty only for their own advantage. The whole difference is that, in the family, the father's love for his children repays him for the care that he bestows upon them; while, in the State, the pleasure of ruling makes up for the chief's lack of love for his people.

Grotius denies that all human authority is established for the benefit of the governed, and he cites slavery as an instance. His invariable mode of reasoning is to establish right by fact.* A juster method might be employed, but none more favorable to tyrants.

It is doubtful, then, according to Grotius, whether the human race belongs to a hundred men, or whether these hundred men belong to the human race; and he appears throughout his book to incline to the former opinion, which is also that of Hobbes. In this way we have mankind divided like herds of cattle, each of which has a master, who looks after it in order to devour it.

Just as a herdsman is superior in nature to his herd, so chiefs, who are the herdsmen of men, are superior in nature to their people. Thus, according to Philo's account, the Emperor Caligula reasoned, inferring truly enough from this analogy that kings are gods, or that men are brutes.

The reasoning of Caligula is tantamount to that of Hobbes and Grotius. Aristotle, before them all, had likewise said that men are not naturally equal, but that some are born for slavery and others for dominion.

Aristotle was right, but he mistook the effect for the cause. Every man born in slavery is born for slavery; nothing is more certain. Slaves lose everything in their bonds, even the desire to escape from them; they love their servitude as the companions of Ulysses loved their brutishness.** If, then, there are slaves by nature, it is because there have been slaves contrary to nature. The first slaves were made such by force; their cowardice kept them in bondage.

I have said nothing about King Adam nor about Emperor Noah, the father of three great monarchs who shared the universe, like the children of Saturn with whom they are supposed to be identical. I hope that my moderation will give satisfaction; for, as I am a direct descendant of one of these princes, and perhaps of the eldest branch, how do I know whether, by examination of titles, I might not find myself the lawful

*"Learned researches in public law are often nothing but the history of ancient abuses; and to devote much labor to studying them is misplaced pertinacity" (*Treatise on the Interests of France in relation to her Neighbours,* by the Marquis d'Argenson). That is exactly what Grotius did.

**See a small treatise by Plutarch entitled *That Brutes employ Reason.*

king of the human race? Be that as it may, it cannot be denied that Adam was sovereign of the world, as Robinson was of his island, so long as he was its sole inhabitant; and it was an agreeable feature of that empire that the monarch, secure on his throne, had nothing to fear from rebellions, or wars, or conspirators.

3. *The rights of the strongest.* The strongest man is never strong enough to be always master, unless he transforms his power into right, and obedience into duty. Hence the right of the strongest—a right apparently assumed in irony, and really established in principle. But will this phrase never be explained to us? Force is a physical power; I do not see what morality can result from its effects. To yield to force is an act of necessity, not of will; it is at most an act of prudence. In what sense can it be a duty?

Let us assume for a moment this pretended right. I say that nothing results from it but inexplicable nonsense; for if force constitutes right, the effect changes with the cause, and any force which overcomes the first succeeds to its rights. As soon as men can disobey with impunity, they may do so legitimately; and since the strongest is always in the right, the only thing is to act in such a way that one may be the strongest. But what sort of a right is it that perishes when force ceases? If it is necessary to obey by compulsion, there is no need to obey from duty; and if men are no longer forced to obey, obligation is at an end. We see, then, that this word right adds nothing to force; it here means nothing at all.

Obey the powers that be. If that means, Yield to force, the precept is good but superfluous; I reply that it will never be violated. All power comes from God, I admit; but every disease comes from him too; does it follow that we are prohibited from calling in a physician? If a brigand should surprise me in the recesses of a wood, am I bound not only to give up my purse when forced, but am I also morally bound to do so when I might conceal it? For, in effect, the pistol which he holds is a superior force.

Let us agree, then, that might does not make right, and that we are bound to obey none but lawful authorities. Thus my original question ever recurs.

4. *Slavery.* Since no man has any natural authority over his fellow-men, and since force is not the source of right, conventions remain as the basis of all lawful authority among men.

If an individual, says Grotius, can alienate his liberty and become the slave of a master, why should not a whole people be able to alienate theirs, and become subject to a king? In this there are many equivocal terms requiring explanation; but let us confine ourselves to the word alienate. To alienate is to give or sell. Now, a man who becomes another's slave does not give himself, he sells himself at the very least for his subsistence. But why does a nation sell itself? So far from a king supplying his subjects with their subsistence, he draws his from them; and, according to Rabelais, a king does not live on a little. Do subjects, then, give up their persons on condition that their property also shall be taken? I do not see what is left for them to keep.

It will be said that the despot secures to his subjects civil peace. Be it so; but what do they gain by that, if the wars which his ambition brings upon them, together with his insatiable greed and the vexations of his administration, harass them more than their own dissensions would? What do they gain by it If this tranquillity is itself one of their miseries? Men live tranquilly also in dungeons; is that enough to make them contented there? The Greeks confined in the cave of the Cyclops lived peacefully until their turn came to be devoured.

To say that a man gives himself for nothing is to say what is absurd and inconceivable; such an act is illegitimate and invalid, for the simple reason that he who performs it is not in his right mind. To say the same thing of a whole nation is to suppose a nation of fools; and madness does not confer rights.

Even if each person could alienate himself, he could not alienate his children; they are born free men; their liberty belongs to them, and no one has a right to dispose of it except themselves. Before they have come to years of discretion, the father can, in their name, stipulate conditions for their preservation and welfare, but not surrender them irrevocably and unconditionally; for such a gift is contrary to the ends of nature, and exceeds the rights of paternity. In order, then, that an arbitrary government might be legitimate, it would be necessary that the people in each generation should have the option of accepting or rejecting it; but in that case such a government would no longer be arbitrary.

To renounce one's liberty is to renounce one's quality as a man, the rights and also the duties of humanity. For him who renounces everything there is no possible compensation. Such a renunciation is incompatible with man's nature, for to take away all freedom from his will is to take away all morality from his actions. In short, a convention which stipulates absolute authority on the one side and unlimited obedience on the other is vain and contradictory. Is it not clear that we are under no obligations whatsoever towards a man from whom we have a right to demand everything? And does not this single condition, without equivalent, without exchange, involve the nullity of the act? For what right would my slave have against me, since all that he has belongs to me? His rights being mine, this right of me against myself is a meaningless phrase.

Grotius and others derive from war another origin for the pretended right of slavery. The victor having, according to them, the right of slaying the vanquished, the latter may purchase his life at the cost of his freedom; an agreement so much the more legitimate that it turns to the advantage of both.

But it is manifest that this pretended right of slaying the vanquished in no way results from the state of war. Men are not naturally enemies, if only for the reason that, living in their primitive independence, they have no mutual relations sufficiently durable to constitute a state of peace or a state of war. It is the relation of things and not of men which constitutes war; and since the state of war cannot arise from simple personal relations, but only from real relations, private war—war between man and man—cannot exist either in the state Of nature, where there is no settled ownership, or in the social state, where everything is under the authority of the laws.

Private combats, duels, and encounters are acts which do not constitute a state of war; and with regard to the private wars authorized by the Establishments of Louis IX, King of France, and suspended by the Peace of God, they were abuses of the feudal government, an absurd system if ever there was one, contrary both to the principles of natural right and to all sound government.

War, then, is not a relation between man and man, but a relation between State and State, in which individuals are enemies only by accident, not as men, nor even as citizens,* but as soldiers; not as members of the fatherland, but as its defenders. In

*The Romans, who understood and respected the rights of war better than any nation in the world, carried their scruples so far in this respect that no citizen was allowed to serve as a volunteer without enlisting expressly against the enemy, and by name against a certain enemy. A legion in which Cato the Younger made his first campaign under Popilius having been re-formed, Cato the Elder wrote to Popilius that, if he consented to his son's continuing to serve under him, it was necessary that he should take a new military oath, because, the first being annulled, he could no longer bear arms against the enemy (Cicero, *De Officiis* I., 11). And Cato also wrote to his son to abstain from appearing in battle until he had taken this new oath. I know that it will be possible to urge against me the siege of Clusium and other particular cases; but I cite laws and customs (Livy, V. 35–37). No nation has transgressed its laws less frequently than the Romans, and no nation has had laws so admirable.

short, each State can have as enemies only other States and not individual men, inasmuch as it is impossible to fix any true relation between things of different kinds.

This principle is also conformable to the established maxims of all ages and to the invariable practice of all civilized nations. Declarations of war are not so much warnings to the powers as to their subjects. The foreigner, whether king, or nation, or private person, that robs, slays, or detains subjects without declaring war against the government, is not an enemy, but a brigand. Even in open war, a just prince, while he rightly takes possession of all that belongs to the State in an enemy's country, respects the person and property of individuals; he respects the rights on which his own are based. The aim of war being the destruction of the hostile State, we have a right to slay its defenders so long as they have arms in their hands; but as soon as they lay them down and surrender, ceasing to be enemies or instruments of the enemy, they become again simply men, and no one has any further right over their lives. Sometimes it is possible to destroy the State without killing a single one of its members; but war confers no right except what is necessary to its end. These are not the principles of Grotius; they are not based on the authority of poets, but are derived from the nature of things, and are founded on reason.

With regard to the right of conquest, it has no other foundation than the law of the strongest. If war does not confer on the victor the right of slaying the vanquished, this right, which he does not possess, cannot be the foundation of a right to enslave them. If we have a right to slay an enemy only when it is impossible to enslave him, the right to enslave him is not derived from the right to kill him; it is, therefore, an iniquitous bargain to make him purchase his life, over which the victor has no right, at the cost of his liberty. In establishing the right of life and death upon the right of slavery, and the right of slavery upon the right of life and death, is it not manifest that one falls into a vicious circle?

Even if we grant this terrible right of killing everybody, I say that a slave made in war, or a conquered nation, is under no obligation at all to a master, except to obey him so far as compelled. In taking an equivalent for his life the victor has conferred no favor on the slave; instead of killing him unprofitably, he has destroyed him for his own advantage. Far, then, from having acquired over him any authority in addition to that of force, the state of war subsists between them as before, their relation even is the effect of it; and the exercise of the rights of war supposes that there is no treaty of peace. They have made a convention. Be it so; but this convention, far from terminating the state of war, supposes its continuance.

Thus, in whatever way we regard things, the right of slavery is invalid, not only because it is illegitimate, but because it is absurd and meaningless. These terms, *slavery* and *right,* are contradictory and mutually exclusive. Whether addressed by a man to a man, or by a man to a nation, such a speech as this will always be equally foolish: "I make an agreement with you wholly at your expense and wholly for my benefit, and I shall observe it as long as I please, while you also shall observe it as long as I please."

5. *That it is always necessary to go back to a first contract.* If I should concede all that I have so far refuted, those who favor despotism would be no farther advanced. There will always be a great difference between subduing a multitude and ruling a society. When isolated men, however numerous they may be, are subjected one after another to a single person, this seems to me only a case of master and slaves, not of a nation and its chief; they form, if you will, an aggregation, but not an association, for they have neither public property nor a body politic. Such a man, had he enslaved half the world, is never anything but an individual; his interest, separated from that of the rest, is never anything but a

private interest. If he dies, his empire after him is left disconnected and disunited, as an oak dissolves and becomes a heap of ashes after the fire has consumed it.

A nation, says Grotius, can give itself to a king. According to Grotius, then, a nation is a nation before it gives itself to a king. This gift itself is a civil act, and presupposes a public resolution. Consequently, before examining the act by which a nation elects a king, it would be proper to examine the act by which a nation becomes a nation; for this act, being necessarily anterior to the other, is the real foundation of the society.

In fact, if there were no anterior contract, where, unless the election were unanimous, would be the obligation upon the minority to submit to the decision of the majority? And whence do the hundred who desire a master derive the right to vote on behalf of ten who do not desire one? The law of the plurality of votes is itself established by convention, and presupposes unanimity once at least.

6. *The social contract.* I assume that men have reached a point at which the obstacles that endanger their preservation in the state of nature overcome, by their resistance, the forces which each individual can exert with a view to maintaining himself in that state. Then this primitive condition can no longer subsist, and the human race would perish unless it changed its mode of existence.

Now, as men cannot create any new forces, but only combine and direct those that exist, they have no other means of self-preservation than to form by aggregation a sum of forces which may overcome the resistance, to put them in action by a single motive power, and to make them work in concert.

This sum of forces can be produced only by the combination of many; but the strength and freedom of each man being the chief instruments of his preservation, how can he pledge them without injuring himself, and without neglecting the cares which he owes to himself? This difficulty, applied to my subject, may be expressed in these terms: "To find a form of association which may defend and protect with the whole force of the community the person and property of every associate, and by means of which each, coalescing with all, may nevertheless obey only himself, and remain as free as before." Such is the fundamental problem of which the social contract furnishes the solution.

The clauses of this contract are so determined by the nature of the act that the slightest modification would render them vain and ineffectual; so that, although they have never perhaps been formally enunciated, they are everywhere the same, everywhere tacitly admitted and recognized, until, the social pact being violated, each man regains his original rights and recovers his natural liberty, whilst losing the conventional liberty for which he renounced it.

These clauses, rightly understood, are reducible to one only, viz. the total alienation to the whole community of each associate with all his rights; for, in the first place, since each gives himself up entirely, the conditions are equal for all; and, the conditions being equal for all, no one has any interest in making them burdensome to others.

Further, the alienation being made without reserve, the union is as perfect as it can be, and an individual associate can no longer claim anything; for, if any rights were left to individuals, since there would be no common superior who could judge between them and the public, each, being on some point his own judge, would soon claim to be so on all; the state of nature would still subsist, and the association would necessarily become tyrannical or useless.

In short, each giving himself to all, gives himself to nobody; and as there is not one associate over whom we do not acquire the same rights which we concede to him over ourselves, we gain the equivalent of all that we lose, and more power to preserve what we have.

If, then, we set aside what is not of the essence of the social contract, we shall find that it is reducible to the following terms: "Each of us puts in common his person and his whole power under the supreme direction of the general will; and in return we receive every member as an indivisible part of the whole."

Forthwith, instead of the individual personalities of all the contracting parties, this act of association produces a moral and collective body, which is composed of as many members as the assembly has voices, and which receives from this same act its unity, its common self (*moi*), its life, and its will. This public person, which is thus formed by the union of all the individual members, formerly took the name of city, and now takes that of *republic* or *body politic,* which is called by its members State when it is passive, *sovereign* when it is active, *power* when it is compared to similar bodies. With regard to the associates, they take collectively the name of *people,* and are called individually, *citizens,* as participating in the sovereign power, and *subjects,* as subjected to the laws of the State. But these terms are often confused and are mistaken one for another; it is sufficient to know how to distinguish them when they are used with complete precision.

7. *The sovereign.* We see from this formula that the act of association contains a reciprocal engagement between the public and individuals, and that every individual, contracting so to speak with himself, is engaged in a double relation, viz. as a member of the sovereign towards individuals, and as a member of the State towards the sovereign. But we cannot apply here the maxim of civil law that no one is bound by engagements made with himself; for there is a great difference between being bound to oneself and to a whole of which one forms part.

We must further observe that the public resolution which can bind all subjects to the sovereign in consequence of the two different relations under which each of them is regarded cannot, for a contrary reason, bind the sovereign to itself, and that accordingly it is contrary to the nature of the body politic for the sovereign to impose on itself a law which it cannot transgress. As it can only be considered under one and the same relation, it is in the position of an individual contracting with himself; whence we see that there is not, nor can be, any kind of fundamental law binding upon the body of the people, not even the social contract. This does not imply that such a body cannot perfectly well enter into engagements with others in what does not derogate from this contract; for, with regard to foreigners, it becomes a simple being, an individual.

But the body politic or sovereign, deriving its existence only from the sanctity of the contract, can never bind itself, even to others, in anything that derogates from the original act, such as alienation of some portion of itself, or submission to another sovereign. To violate the act by which it exists would be to annihilate itself, and what is nothing produces nothing.

So soon as the multitude is thus united in one body, it is impossible to injure one of the members without attacking the body, still less to injure the body without the members feeling the effects. Thus duty and interest alike oblige the two contracting parties to give mutual assistance; and the men themselves should seek to combine in this twofold relationship all the advantages which are attendant on it.

Now, the sovereign, being formed only of the individuals that compose it, neither has nor can have any interest contrary to theirs; consequently the sovereign power needs no guarantee towards its subjects, because it is impossible that the body should wish to injure all its members; and we shall see hereafter that it can injure no one as an individual. The sovereign, for the simple reason that it is so, is always everything that it ought to be.

But this is not the case as regards the relation of subjects to the sovereign, which, notwithstanding the common interest, would have no security for the performance of their engagements, unless it found means to ensure their fidelity.

Indeed, every individual may, as a man, have a particular will contrary to, or divergent from, the general will which he has as a citizen; his private interest may prompt him quite differently from the common interest; his absolute and naturally independent existence may make him regard what he owes to the common cause as a gratuitous contribution, the loss of which will be less harmful to others than the payment of it will be burdensome to him; and, regarding the moral person that constitutes the State as an imaginary being because it is not a man, he would be willing to enjoy the rights of a citizen without being willing to fulfill the duties of a subject. The progress of such injustice would bring about the ruin of the body politic.

In order, then, that the social pact may not be a vain formulary, it tacitly includes this engagement, which can alone give force to the others—that whoever refuses to obey the general will shall be constrained to do so by the whole body; which means nothing else than that he shall be forced to be free; for such is the condition which, uniting every citizen to his native land, guarantees him from all personal dependence, a condition that ensures the control and working of the political machine, and alone renders legitimate civil engagements, which, without it, would be absurd and tyrannical, and subject to the most enormous abuses.

8. *The civil state.* The passage from the state of nature to the civil state produces in man a very remarkable change, by substituting in his conduct justice for instinct, and by giving his actions the moral quality that they previously lacked. It is only when the voice of duty succeeds physical impulse, and law succeeds appetite, that man, who till then had regarded only himself, sees that he is obliged to act on other principles, and to consult his reason before listening to his inclinations. Although, in this state, he is deprived of many advantages that he derives from nature, he acquires equally great ones in return; his faculties are exercised and developed; his ideas are expanded; his feelings are ennobled; his whole soul is exalted to such a degree that, if the abuses of this new condition did not often degrade him below that from which he has emerged, he ought to bless without ceasing the happy moment that released him from it for ever, and transformed him from a stupid and ignorant animal into an intelligent being and a man.

Let us reduce this whole balance to terms easy to compare. What man loses by the social contract is his natural liberty and an unlimited right to anything which tempts him and which he is able to attain; what he gains is civil liberty and property in all that he possesses. In order that we may not be mistaken about these compensations, we must clearly distinguish natural liberty, which is limited only by the powers of the individual, from civil liberty, which is limited by the general will; and possession, which is nothing but the result of force or the right of first occupancy, from property, which can be based only on a positive title.

Besides the preceding, we might add to the acquisitions of the civil state moral freedom, which alone renders man truly master of himself; for the impulse of mere appetite is slavery, while obedience to a self-prescribed law is liberty. But I have already said too much on this head, and the philosophical meaning of the term *liberty* does not belong to my present subject.

9. *The real domain.* Every member of the community at the moment of its formation gives himself up to it, just as he actually is, himself and all his powers, of which the

property that he possesses forms part. By this act, possession does not change its nature when it changes hands, and become property in those of the sovereign; but, as the powers of the State (*cité*) are incomparably greater than those of an individual, public possession is also, in fact, more secure and more irrevocable, without being more legitimate, at least in respect of foreigners; for the State, with regard to its members, is owner of all their property by the social contract, which, in the State, serves as the basis of all rights; but with regard to other powers, it is owner only by the right of first occupancy which it derives from individuals.

The right of first occupancy, although more real than that of the strongest, becomes a true right only after the establishment of that of property. Every man has by nature a right to all that is necessary to him; but the positive act which makes him a proprietor of certain property excludes him from all the residue. His portion having been allotted, he ought to confine himself to it, and he has no further right to the undivided property. That is why the right of first occupancy, so weak in the state of nature, is respected by every member of a State. In this right men regard not so much what belongs to others as what does not belong to themselves.

In order to legalize the right of first occupancy over any domain whatsoever, the following conditions are, in general, necessary; first, the land must not yet be inhabited by any one; secondly, a man must occupy only the area required for his subsistence; thirdly, he must take possession of it, not by an empty ceremony, but by labor and cultivation, the only mark of ownership which, in default of legal title, ought to be respected by others.

Indeed, if we accord the right of first occupancy to necessity and labor, do we not extend it as far as it can go? Is it impossible to assign limits to this right? Will the mere setting foot on common ground be sufficient to give an immediate claim to the ownership of it? Will the power of driving away other men from it for a moment suffice to deprive them for ever of the right of returning to it? How can a man or a people take possession of an immense territory and rob the whole human race of it except by a punishable usurpation, since other men are deprived of the place of residence and the sustenance which nature gives to them in common? When Nuñez Balboa on the seashore took possession of the Pacific Ocean and of the whole of South America in the name of the crown of Castille, was this sufficient to dispossess all the inhabitants, and exclude from it all the princes in the world? On this supposition, such ceremonies might have been multiplied vainly enough; and the Catholic king in his cabinet might, by a single stroke, have taken possession of the whole world, only cutting off afterwards from his empire what was previously occupied by other princes.

We perceive how the lands of individuals, united and contiguous, become public territory, and how the right of sovereignty, extending itself from the subjects to the land which they occupy, becomes at once real and personal; which places the possessors in greater dependence, and makes their own powers a guarantee for their fidelity—an advantage which ancient monarchs do not appear to have clearly perceived, for, calling themselves only kings of the Persians or Scythians or Macedonians, they seem to have regarded themselves as chiefs of men rather than as owners of countries. Monarchs of today call themselves more cleverly kings of France, Spain, England, etc.; in thus holding the land they are quite sure of holding its inhabitants.

The peculiarity of this alienation is that the community, in receiving the property of individuals, so far from robbing them of it, only assures them lawful possession, and changes usurpation into true right, enjoyment into ownership. Also, the possessors; being considered as depositaries of the public property, and their rights being respected by all the members of the State, as well as maintained by all its power against foreigners, they have, as it were, by a transfer advantageous to the public and still more to themselves, acquired all that they have given up—a paradox which is easily explained by distinguishing between the rights which the sovereign and the proprietor have over the same property, as we shall see hereafter.

It may also happen that men begin to unite before they possess anything, and that afterwards occupying territory sufficient for all, they enjoy it in common or share it among themselves, either equally or in proportions fixed by the sovereign. In whatever way this acquisition is made, the right which every individual has over his property is always subordinate to the right which the community has over all; otherwise there would be no stability in the social union, and no real force in the exercise of sovereignty.

I shall close this chapter and this book with a remark which ought to serve as a basis for the whole social system; it is that instead of destroying natural equality, the fundamental pact, on the contrary, substitutes a moral and lawful equality for the physical inequality which nature imposed upon men, so that, although unequal in strength or intellect, they all become equal by convention and legal right.*

*Under bad governments this equality is only apparent and illusory; it serves only to keep the poor in their misery and the rich in their usurpations. In fact, laws are always useful to those who possess and injurious to those that have nothing; whence it follows that the social state is advantageous to men only so far as they all have something, and none of them has too much.

IMMANUEL KANT
1724–1804

Whereas most modern philosophers (such as Descartes, Berkeley, and Hume) arrived at their basic philosophical positions early in life, Immanuel Kant did not work out his views until well into middle age. Whereas the earlier thinkers wrote major works when still young, Kant's important pieces were written between the ages of 57 and 67. Whereas the others' works were written for a broad general audience and are relatively accessible to educated readers, Kant wrote in an academic style that is notoriously difficult to follow. Whereas most of the earlier philosophers traveled widely, Kant never left the provincial city in which he was born. Unlike his predecessors, who held many different positions and practiced philosophy on the side, Kant earned his living as a professor of philosophy. Yet Kant is the most important and influential of all modern philosophers.

Kant was born, raised, lived, and died in the town of Königsberg in East Prussia. His parents were lower middle-class, hard-working, simple folk. They belonged to the Lutheran Pietist movement, which cultivated high moral standards and personal devotion to God in Christ. Like Hume, who had a similar religious upbringing (Calvinist Presbyterian), Kant was later critical of his background. But unlike Hume, he remained a deeply religious man.

Through the intervention of his mother's favorite preacher, who was also a professor at the University of Königsberg, young Immanuel gained admittance to a local high school. There he received a solid Pietist education and a firm grounding in the classics. At 16, Kant was admitted to the university, where he planned to study the classics. But under the influence of a strong teacher, Martin Knutzen, Kant moved into philosophy and was attracted to the comprehensive scholasticism of Christian Wolff (1679–1754), who had developed Leibniz's philosophy into a rationalistic system.

Following his university studies, Kant worked as a private tutor to wealthy families. By 1755, he was back in the university, where he was employed as an unsalaried lecturer for the next fifteen years. (Given the difficulty of his writing, it is worth noting that his lectures were very popular.) His early lectures focused on the external world, dealing with issues in physics and physical geography. He published an important early work, *Universal History of Nature and Theory of the Heavens* (1755), which explained the structure of the universe in terms of Newtonian physics, without reference to God. During this period, Kant's focus began to shift to the inner world of the mind and the nature of morality. At this time, he also encountered the writings of Hume, which challenged the rationalism he had imbibed from Wolff. He later said that Hume "interrupted my dogmatic slumber, and gave my investigations in the field of speculative philosophy quite a new direction."

In 1770, Kant was given what he had long desired—the chair of logic and metaphysics at the University of Königsberg. In his inaugural address, *Dissertation on the Form and Principles of Sensible and Intelligible Worlds,* Kant declared his intention to reconstruct philosophy. Over the next ten years, he carefully and quietly thought through all his ideas. Finally he wrote his major work, *Critique of Pure Reason*. He wrote it, as he later told a friend, "within four or five months, with the utmost attention to the contents, but with less concern for the presentation or for making things easy for the reader." Unfortunately, when the book appeared, his indifference to readers left most people lost. In 1783, he restated his main points in a work "for the benefit of teachers," the *Prolegomena to Any Future Metaphysics,* and in 1787 he rewrote the *Critique* itself.

Kant's first major work on ethics, *Foundations of the Metaphysics of Morals,* was published in 1785. A further development of his moral views, *Critique of Practical Reason,* appeared in 1788. In 1790, Kant published his third and last critique, the *Critique of Judgment,* which deals with aesthetic judgments and the question of purpose in nature. Kant's other important works include *Metaphysical Foundations of Natural Science* (1786), *Religion Within the Limits of Reason Alone* (1793), *Toward Eternal Peace* (1795), and *Foundations of the Metaphysics of Morals* (1797).

Whereas Kant's writings revolutionized the philosophical world, his personal life was quiet, almost boring. With one minor exception late in life, he was never involved in any scandals or controversies. He never traveled more than a few miles outside Königsberg. A lifelong bachelor, he is said to have awakened and gone to bed at exactly the same time each day. His daily walks were reportedly so regular that people could set their clocks by his approach. A rather frail man, he so carefully guarded his health that he lived a long, productive life. Yet he was also a delightful conversationalist and host, and he had many friends and admirers. At his death in 1804, he was the best-known philosopher in Germany, read, if not understood, throughout Europe.

* * *

Responding to the skeptical empiricism of Hume, Kant argued that the mind is not simply a repository of impressions and ideas but it is actively involved in knowing the objects it experiences. Prior to Kant, most thinkers believed that the mind, in knowing, conformed to objects: that the ideas of the mind took on the "shape" of the world outside the mind. Kant argued instead that objects conform to the mind: that how one experiences the world is a result of the way the mind operates. Knowledge is a result of human understanding applied to sense experience.

Space and time are two ways the mind operates. They are not "objects" in the world, derived from sense experience; rather, they are the precondition for our having sense-experience at all: They are the *a priori* (meaning "known independently of sense perceptions," "indubitable") foundations of sensibility. Space and time must be presupposed in order to have experience at all.

Kant goes on to consider the *a priori* foundations of human understanding. He argues that there must be categories of the mind, such as causality and substance, that unify our perceptions. These categories are not found in sense experience; they are innate structures of the mind and the necessary conditions for having any knowledge at all. Without these categories, the world of experience would be utterly chaotic and unknowable.

Of course, this knowledge is only a knowledge of things as we experience them in the "phenomenal world." The way things really are, apart from our experience of them, the "noumenal world" of the "things-in-themselves," is not available to us by pure reason. This, according to Kant, means that we cannot have knowledge of God, the world, or even the substantial self. But rather than letting this end in Humean skepticism, Kant suggests that these three "ideas of reason" (God, world, self) stimulate and unify knowledge. They point beyond themselves to possibilities in the noumenal world that pure reason cannot reach. As long as we do not think that we have real knowledge of their objects, these three ideas of reason serve a useful purpose.

Turning to moral theory, Kant develops a "deontological," or "duty-based," theory of morality. An action is good not because it produces consequences such as pleasure or happiness, but because it is done out of duty by a good will. To establish what a person's duty is, Kant develops the "categorical imperative." In the *Foundations of the Metaphysics of Morals,* Kant discusses several versions of this imperative, the most important of which is this: "Act only on that maxim whereby you can at the same time will that it should become a universal law." The short essay, "On a Supposed Right to Lie From Altruistic Motives," shows some of the implications of Kant's deontological moral theory.

Although Kant is best known for his work in epistemology and ethics, he wrote on many topics. His earlier essay "Idea for a Universal History with Cosmopolitan Intent" (1784) is an example of Kant at his nontechnical best. Here the Königsberg recluse shows himself as a brilliant citizen of the world when he introduces the idea of a League of Nations:

> By means of wars and the high tension of never relaxed armaments for these wars, and by means of the distress which every nation must thus suffer, even during times of peace, [Nature] drives man at first to imperfect attempts, but finally, after many devastations and disturbances and even exhaustion of all powers, she drives toward a situation which reason might have anticipated without so many sad experiences: Men leave the lawless state of savages and enter a League of Nations. Thus every state, including the smallest, can find a guarantee for its security and its rights, not in its own power or in its own views of what is just, but in this great League of Nations.

* * *

Kant's condensation of the *Critique*, the *Prolegomena to Any Future Metaphysics*, his *Foundations of the Metaphysics of Morals,* and the essay, "On a Supposed Right to Lie From Altruistic Motives," are all given here (complete) in the Lewis White Beck translations. The marginal page numbers are those of all scholarly editions.

Among the many available books on Kant, Stephen Körner, *Kant* (Baltimore, MD: Penguin Books, 1955) is almost universally accepted as the best introduction. John Kemp, *The Philosophy of Kant* (Oxford: Oxford University Press, 1968); Ralph C.S. Walker, *Kant: The Arguments of the Philosophers* (London: Routledge & Kegan Paul, 1978); C.D. Broad, *Kant: An Introduction* (Cambridge: Cambridge University Press, 1978); Ernst Cassirer, *Kant's Life and Thought*, translated by James Haden (New Haven, CT: Yale University Press, 1982); Ermanno Bencivenga, *Kant's Copernican Revolution* (Oxford: Oxford University Press, 1987); Otfried Höffe, *Immanuel Kant*, translated by Marshall Farrier (Albany, NY: SUNY Press, 1994); Ralph Walker, *Kant* (London: Routledge, 1999); Manfred Kuehn, *Kant: A Biography* (Cambridge: Cambridge University Press, 2001); Allen W. Wood, *Kant* (Oxford: Blackwell, 2005); Paul Guyer, *Kant* (Abbington, UK: Routledge, 2006); and T.K. Seung, *Kant: A Guide for the Perplexed* (London: Continuum, 2007) are also helpful. Justus Hartnack, *Kant's Theory of Knowledge* (Indianapolis, IN: Hackett, 2001); Georges Dicker, *Kant's Theory of Knowledge: An Analytical Introduction* (Oxford: Oxford University Press, 2004); and Wayne Waxman, *Kant and the Empiricists: Understanding Understanding* (Oxford: Oxford University Press, 2005) provide help with Kant's epistemology. For works on Kant's moral theory, see W.D. Ross, *Kant's Ethical Theory: A Commentary on the* Grundlegung zur Metaphysik der Sitten [Foundations of the Metaphysics of Morals] (Oxford: Clarendon Press, 1954); H.J. Paton, *The Categorical Imperative* (London: 1947; reprinted, New York: Harper & Row, 1967); Roger Sullivan, *An Introduction to Kant's Ethics* (Cambridge: Cambridge University Press, 1994); Marcia W. Baron, *Kantian Ethics Almost Without Apology* (Ithaca, NY: Cornell University Press, 1999); Allen W. Wood, *Kant's Ethical Thought* (Cambridge: Cambridge University Press, 1999); Paul Guyer, *Kant's* Groundwork for the Metaphysics of Morals: *A Reader's Guide* (London: Continuum, 2007); and Jens Timmermann, *Kant's* Groundwork of the Metaphysics of Morals: *A Commentary* (Cambridge: Cambridge University Press, 2007). Howard Caygill, *A Kant Dictionary* (Oxford: Basil Blackwell, 1995) provides a useful reference work. For collections of essays, see Lewis White Beck, ed., *Studies in the Philosophy of Kant* (Indianapolis, IN: Bobbs-Merrill, 1965); R.P. Wolff, ed., *Kant* (Garden City, NY: Doubleday, 1967); Ralph C.S. Walker, ed., *Kant on Pure Reason* (Oxford: Oxford University Press, 1982); Beryl Logan, ed., *Immanuel Kant's* Prolegomena to Any Future Metaphysics *in Focus* (Oxford: Routledge, 1996); Robin May Schott, ed., *Feminist Interpretations of Kant* (College Park, PA: Pennsylvania State University Press, 1997); Heiner Klemme, ed., *Immanuel Kant,* 2 volumes (New York: Ashgate, 1999); Paul Guyer, ed., *The Cambridge Companion to Kant and Modern Philosophy* (Cambridge: Cambridge University Press, 2006); and Daniel Garber and Beatrice Longuenesse, eds., *Kant and the Early Moderns* (Princeton: Princeton University Press, 2008).

PROLEGOMENA TO ANY FUTURE METAPHYSICS

INTRODUCTION

These *Prolegomena* are for the use, not of mere learners, but of future teachers, and 255
even the latter should not expect that they will be serviceable for the systematic exposition of a ready-made science, but merely for the discovery of the science itself.

There are scholarly men to whom the history of philosophy (both ancient and modern) is philosophy itself; for these the present *Prolegomena* are not written. They must wait till those who endeavor to draw from the fountain of reason itself have completed their work; it will then be the turn of these scholars to inform the world of what has been done. Unfortunately, nothing can be said which, in their opinion, has not been said before, and truly the same prophecy applies to all future time; for since the human reason has for many centuries speculated upon innumerable objects in various ways, it is hardly to be expected that we should not be able to discover analogies for every new idea among the old sayings of past ages.

My purpose is to persuade all those who think metaphysics worth studying that it is absolutely necessary to pause a moment and, regarding all that has been done as though undone, to propose first the preliminary question, "Whether such a thing as metaphysics be even possible at all?"

If it be science, how is it that it cannot, like other sciences, obtain universal and
lasting recognition? If not, how can it maintain its pretensions and keep the human mind 256
in suspense with hopes never ceasing, yet never fulfilled? Whether then we demonstrate our knowledge or our ignorance in this field, we must come once for all to a definite conclusion respecting the nature of this so-called science, which cannot possibly remain on its present footing. It seems almost ridiculous, while every other science is continually advancing, that in this, which pretends to be wisdom incarnate, for whose oracle everyone inquires, we should constantly move round the same spot, without gaining a single step. And so its votaries having melted away, we do not find men confident of their ability to shine in other sciences venturing their reputation here, where everybody, however ignorant in other matters, presumes to deliver a final verdict, because in this domain there is actually as yet no standard weight and measure to distinguish sound knowledge from shallow talk.

After all it is nothing extraordinary in the elaboration of a science that, when men begin to wonder how far it has advanced, the question should at last occur whether and how such a science is possible at all. Human reason so delights building that it has several times built up a tower and then razed it to see how the foundation was laid. It is never too late to become reasonable and wise; but if the knowledge comes late, there is always more difficulty in starting a reform.

The question whether a science be possible presupposes a doubt as to its actuality. But such a doubt offends the men whose whole fortune consists of this supposed

Immanuel Kant, *Prolegomena to Any Future Metaphysics,* a revision of the Paul Carus translation with an introduction by Lewis White Black (Pearson/Library of the Liberal Arts, 1950).

jewel; hence he who raises the doubt must expect opposition from all sides. Some, in the proud consciousness of their possessions, which are ancient and therefore considered legitimate, will take their metaphysical compendia in their hands and look down on him with contempt; others, who never see anything except it be identical with what they have elsewhere seen before, will not understand him, and everything will remain for a time as if nothing had happened to excite the concern or the hope for an impending change.

Nevertheless, I venture to predict that the independent reader of these *Prolegomena*
257 will not only doubt his previous science, but ultimately be fully persuaded that it cannot exist unless the demands here stated on which its possibility depends be satisfied; and, as this has never been done, that there is, as yet, no such thing as metaphysics. But as it can never cease to be in demand*—since the interest of common sense are so intimately interwoven with it—he must confess that a radical reform, or rather a new birth of the science, after a new plan, is unavoidable, however men may struggle against it for a while.

Since the *Essays* of Locke and Leibniz, or rather since the origin of metaphysics so far as we know its history, nothing has ever happened which could have been more decisive to its fate than the attack made upon it by David Hume. He threw no light on this species of knowledge, but he certainly struck a spark by which light might have been kindled had it caught some inflammable substance and had its smouldering fire been carefully nursed and developed.

Hume started chiefly from a single but important concept in metaphysics, namely, that of the connection of cause and effect (including its derivatives force and action, and so on). He challenged reason, which pretends to have given birth to this concept of herself, to answer him by what right she thinks anything could be so constituted that if that thing be posited, something else also must necessarily be posited; for this is the meaning of the concept of cause. He demonstrated irrefutably that it was perfectly impossible for reason to think *a priori* and by means of concepts such a combination, for it implies necessity. We cannot at all see why, in consequence of the existence of one thing, another must necessarily exist or how the concept of such a combination can arise *a priori.* Hence he inferred that reason was altogether deluded with reference to this concept, which she erroneously considered as one of her own children, whereas in reality it was nothing but a bastard of imagination,
258 impregnated by experience, which subsumed certain representations under the law of association and mistook a subjective necessity (habit) for an objective necessity arising from insight. Hence he inferred that reason had no power to think such combinations, even in general, because her concepts would then be purely fictitious and all her pretended *a priori* cognitions nothing but common experiences marked with a

*Says Horace:
Rusticus expectat, dum defluat amnis, at ille
Labitur et labetur in omne volubilis aevum.

["A rustic fellow waiteth on the shore
For the river to flow away,
But the river flows, and flows on as before,
And it flows forever and aye."]

Epistle I, 2, 42f.

false stamp. In plain language, this means that there is not and cannot be any such thing as metaphysics at all.*

However hasty and mistaken Hume's inference may appear, it was at least founded upon investigation, and this investigation deserved the concentrated attention of the brighter spirits of his day as well as determined efforts on their part to discover, if possible, a happier solution of the problem in the sense proposed by him, all of which would have speedily resulted in a complete reform of the science.

But Hume suffered the usual misfortune of metaphysicians, of not being understood. It is positively painful to see how utterly his opponents, Reid, Oswald, Beattie, and lastly Priestley, missed the point of the problem; for while they were ever taking for granted that which he doubted, and demonstrating with zeal and often with impudence that which he never thought of doubting, they so misconstrued his valuable suggestion that everything remained in its old condition, as if nothing had happened. The question was not whether the concept of cause was right, useful, and even indispensable for our knowledge of nature, for this Hume had never doubted; but whether that concept could be thought by reason *a pri-*
ori, and consequently whether it possessed an inner truth, independent of all experience, 259
implying a perhaps more extended use not restricted merely to objects of experience. This was Hume's problem. It was solely a question concerning the *origin,* not concerning the *indispensable* need of using the concept. Were the former decided, the conditions of the use and the sphere of its valid application would have been determined as a matter of course.

But to satisfy the conditions of the problem, the opponents of the great thinker should have penetrated very deeply into the nature of reason, so far as it is concerned with pure thinking—a task which did not suit them. They found a more convenient method of being defiant without any insight, namely, the appeal to *common sense.* It is indeed a great gift of God to possess right or (as they now call it) plain common sense. But this common sense must be shown in action by well-considered and reasonable thoughts and words, not by appealing to it as an oracle when no rational justification for one's position can be advanced. To appeal to common sense when insight and science fail, and no sooner—this is one of the subtile discoveries of modern times, by means of which the most superficial ranter can safely enter the lists with the most thorough thinker and hold his own. But as long as a particle of insight remains, no one would think of having recourse to this subterfuge. Seen clearly, it is but an appeal to the opinion of the multitude, of whose applause the philosopher is ashamed, while the popular charlatan glories and boasts in it. I should think that Hume might fairly have laid as much claim to common sense as Beattie and, in addition, to a critical reason (such as the latter did not possess), which keeps common sense in check and prevents it from speculating, or, if speculations are under discussion, restrains the desire to decide because it cannot satisfy itself concerning its own premises. By this means alone can common sense remain sound. Chisels and hammers may suffice to work a piece of wood, but for etching we require an etcher's needle. Thus common sense and speculative understanding are each serviceable, but each in its own way: the former in judgments which apply

*Nevertheless Hume called this destructive science metaphysics and attached to it great value. "Metaphysics and morals," he declares, "are the most considerable branches of science. Mathematics and natural philosophy are not half so valuable" ["Of the Rise and Progress of the Arts and Sciences," *Essays Moral, Political, and Literary,* XIV (edited by Green and Grose, I, 187)]. But the acute man merely regarded the negative use arising from the moderation of extravagant claims of speculative reason, and the complete settlement of the many endless and troublesome controversies that mislead mankind. He overlooked the positive injury that results if reason be deprived of its most important prospects, which can alone supply to the will the highest aim for all its endeavors.

immediately to experience; the latter when we judge universally from mere concepts, as
260 in metaphysics, where that which calls itself, in spite of the inappropriateness of the
name, sound common sense, has no right to judge at all.

I openly confess my recollection* of David Hume was the very thing which many years ago first interrupted my dogmatic slumber and gave my investigations in the field of speculative philosophy a quite new direction. I was far from following him in the conclusions at which he arrived by regarding, not the whole of his problem, but a part, which by itself can give us no information. If we start from a well-founded, but undeveloped, thought which another has bequeathed to us, we may well hope by continued reflection to advance farther than the acute man to whom we owe the first spark of light.

I therefore first tried whether Hume's objection could not be put into a general form, and soon found that the concept of the connection of cause and effect was by no means the only concept by which the understanding thinks the connection of things *a priori,* but rather that metaphysics consists altogether of such concepts. I sought to ascertain their number; and when I had satisfactorily succeeded in this by starting from a single principle, I proceeded to the deduction of these concepts, which I was now certain were not derived from experience, as Hume had attempted to derive them, but sprang from the pure understanding. This deduction (which seemed impossible to my acute predecessor, which had never even occurred to anyone else, though no one had hesitated to use the concepts without investigating the basis of their objective validity) was the most difficult task which ever could have been undertaken in the service of metaphysics; and the worst was that metaphysics, such as it is, could not assist me in the least because this deduction alone can render metaphysics possible. But as soon as I had
succeeded in solving Hume's problem, not merely in a particular case, but with respect
261 to the whole faculty of pure reason, I could proceed safely, though slowly, to determine
the whole sphere of pure reason completely and from universal principles, in its boundaries as well as in its contents. This was required for metaphysics in order to construct its system according to a safe plan.

But I fear that the execution of Hume's problem in its widest extent (namely, my *Critique of Pure Reason*) will fare as the problem itself fared when first proposed. It will be misjudged because it is misunderstood, and misunderstood because men choose to skim through the book and not to think through it—a disagreeable task, because the work is dry, obscure, opposed to all ordinary notions, and moreover long-winded. I confess, however, I did not expect to hear from philosophers complaints of want of popularity, entertainment, and facility when the existence of highly prized and indispensable knowledge is at stake, which cannot be established otherwise than by the strictest rules of a scholastic precision. Popularity may follow, but is inadmissible at the beginning. Yet as regards a certain obscurity, arising partly from the diffuseness of the plan, owing to which the principal points of the investigation are easily lost sight of, the complaint is just, and I intend to remove it by the present *Prolegomena.*

The first-mentioned work, which discusses the pure faculty of reason in its whole compass and bounds, will remain the foundation, to which the *Prolegomena,* as a preliminary exercise, refer; for critique as a science must first be established as complete and perfect before we can think of letting metaphysics appear on the scene or even have the most distant hope of attaining it.

*[*Erinnerung.* Kant had probably read Hume before 1760, but only much later (1772?) did he begin to follow "a new direction" under Hume's influence—L.W.B.]

We have been long accustomed to seeing antiquated knowledge produced as new by taking it out of its former context and fitting it into a systematic garment of any fancy pattern with new titles. Most readers will set out by expecting nothing else from the *Critique;* but these *Prolegomena* may persuade him that it is a perfectly new science, of which no one 262
has ever even thought, the very idea of which was unknown, and for which nothing hitherto accomplished can be of the smallest use, except it be the suggestion of Hume's doubts. Yet even he did not suspect such a formal science, but ran his ship ashore, for safety's sake, landing on scepticism, there to let it lie and rot; whereas my object is rather to give it a pilot, who, by means of safe principles of navigation drawn from a knowledge of the globe, and provided with a complete chart and compass, may steer the ship safely whither he listeth.

If in a new science which is wholly isolated and unique in its kind, we started with the prejudice that we can judge of things by means of alleged knowledge previously acquired—though this is precisely what has first to be called in question—we should only fancy we saw everywhere what we had already known, because the expressions have a similar sound. But everything would appear utterly metamorphosed, senseless, and unintelligible, because we should have as a foundation our own thoughts, made by long habit a second nature, instead of the author's. But the long-windedness of the work, so far as it depends on the subject and not on the exposition, its consequent unavoidable dryness and its scholastic precision, are qualities which can only benefit the science, though they may discredit the book.

Few writers are gifted with the subtlety and, at the same time, with the grace of David Hume, or with the depth, as well as the elegance, of Moses Mendelssohn. Yet I flatter myself I might have made my own exposition popular had my object been merely to sketch out a plan and leave its completion to others, instead of having my heart in the welfare of the science to which I had devoted myself so long; in truth, it required no little constancy, and even self-denial, to postpone the sweets of an immediate success to the prospect of a slower, but more lasting, reputation.

Making plans is often the occupation of an opulent and boastful mind, which thus obtains the reputation of a creative genius by demanding what it cannot itself supply, by censuring what it cannot improve, and by proposing what it knows not where to find. And 263
yet something more should belong to a sound plan of a general critique of pure reason than mere conjectures if this plan is to be other than the usual declamations of pious aspirations. But pure reason is a sphere so separate and self-contained that we cannot touch a part without affecting all the rest. We can do nothing without first determining the position of each part and its relation to the rest; for, as our judgment within this sphere cannot be corrected by anything without, the validity and use of every part depends upon the relation in which it stands to all the rest within the domain of reason. As in the structure of an organized body, the end of each member can only be deduced from the full conception of the whole. It may, then, be said of such a critique that it is never trustworthy except it be perfectly complete, down to the most minute elements of pure reason. In the sphere of this faculty you can determine and define either everything or nothing.

But although a mere sketch preceding the *Critique of Pure Reason* would be unintelligible, unreliable, and useless, it is all the more useful as a sequel. It enables us to grasp the whole, to examine in detail the chief points of importance in the science, and to improve in many respects our exposition, as compared with the first execution of the work.

With that work complete, I offer here a sketch based on an *analytical* method, while the *Critique* itself had to be executed in the *synthetical* style, in order that the science may present all its articulations, as the structure of a peculiar cognitive faculty, in their natural combination. But should any reader find this sketch, which I publish as the *Prolegomena*

to Any Future Metaphysics, still obscure, let him consider that not everyone is bound to study metaphysics; that many minds will succeed very well in the exact and even in deep sciences more closely allied to the empirical, while they cannot succeed in investigations
264 dealing exclusively with abstract concepts. In such cases men should apply their talents to other subjects. But he who undertakes to judge or, still more, to construct a system of metaphysics must satisfy the demands here made, either by adopting my solution or by thoroughly refuting it and substituting another. To evade it is impossible.

In conclusion, let it be remembered that this much abused obscurity (frequently serving as a mere pretext under which people hide their own indolence or dullness) has its uses, since all who in other sciences observe a judicious silence speak authoritatively in metaphysics and make bold decisions, because their ignorance is not here contrasted with the knowledge of others. Yet it does contrast with sound critical principles, which we may therefore commend in the words of Virgil:

*Ignavum, fucos, pecus a praesepibus arcent.**

265 PROLEGOMENA

PREAMBLE ON THE PECULIARITIES OF ALL METAPHYSICAL KNOWLEDGE

§ I. Of the Sources of Metaphysics

If it becomes desirable to organize any knowledge as science, it will be necessary first to determine accurately those peculiar features which no other science has in common with it, constituting its peculiarity; otherwise the boundaries of all sciences become confused, and none of them can be treated thoroughly according to its nature.

The peculiar characteristic of a science may consist of a simple difference of object, or of the sources of knowledge, or of the kind of knowledge, or perhaps of all three conjointly. On these, therefore, depends the idea of a possible science and its territory.

First, as concerns the sources of metaphysical knowledge, its very concept implies that they cannot be empirical. Its principles (including not only its maxims but its basic notions) must never be derived from experience. It must not be physical but metaphysical knowledge, namely, knowledge lying beyond experience. It can therefore
266 have for its basis neither external experience, which is the source of physics proper, nor internal, which is the basis of empirical psychology. It is therefore *a priori* knowledge, coming from pure understanding and pure reason.

But so far metaphysics would not be distinguishable from pure mathematics; it must therefore be called *pure philosophical* knowledge; and for the meaning of this term I refer to the *Critique of the Pure Reason,*** where the distinction between these two employments of reason is sufficiently explained. So far concerning the sources of metaphysical knowledge.

*["They defend the hives against drones, those indolent creatures"—*Georgics* IV 168.]
***Critique of Pure Reason,* "Methodology," Ch. I, Sec. 2.

§ 2. *Concerning the Kind of Knowledge Which Can Alone Be Called Metaphysical*

a. *On the Distinction between Analytical and Synthetical Judgments in General.*—The peculiarity of its sources demands that metaphysical knowledge must consist of nothing but *a priori* judgments. But whatever be their origin or their logical form, there is a distinction in judgments, as to their content, according to which they are either merely *explicative,* adding nothing to the content of knowledge, or *expansive,* increasing the given knowledge. The former may be called *analytical,* the latter *synthetical,* judgments.

Analytical judgments express nothing in the predicate but what has been already actually thought in the concept of the subject, though not so distinctly or with the same (full) consciousness. When I say: "All bodies are extended," I have not amplified in the least my concept of body, but have only analyzed it, as extension was really thought to belong to that concept before the judgment was made, though it was not expressed. This judgment is therefore analytical. On the contrary, this judgment, "All bodies have weight," contains in its predicate something not actually thought in the universal con- 267
cept of body; it amplifies my knowledge by adding something to my concept, and must therefore be called synthetical.

b. *The Common Principle of All Analytical Judgments Is the Law of Contradiction.*—All analytical judgments depend wholly on the law of contradiction, and are in their nature *a priori* cognitions, whether the concepts that supply them with matter be empirical or not. For the predicate of an affirmative analytical judgment is already contained in the concept of the subject, of which it cannot be denied without contradiction. In the same way its opposite is necessarily denied of the subject in an analytical, but negative, judgment, by the same law of contradiction. Such is the nature of the judgments: "All bodies are extended," and "No bodies are unextended (that is, simple)."

For this very reason all analytical judgments are *a priori* even when the concepts are empirical, as, for example, "Gold is a yellow metal"; for to know this I require no experience beyond my concept of gold as a yellow metal. It is, in fact, the very concept, and I need only analyze it without looking beyond it.

c. *Synthetical Judgments Require a Different Principle from the Law of Contradiction.*—There are synthetical *a posteriori* judgments of empirical origin; but there are also others which are certain *a priori,* and which spring from pure understanding and reason. Yet they both agree in this, that they cannot possibly spring from the principle of analysis, namely, the law of contradiction, alone. They require a quite different principle from which they may be deduced, subject, of course, always to the law of contradiction, which must never be violated, even though everything cannot be deduced from it. I shall first classify synthetical judgments.

1. *Judgments of Experience* are always synthetical. For it would be absurd to base an analytical judgment on experience, as our concept suffices for the purpose without 268
requiring any testimony from experience. That body is extended is a judgment established *a priori,* and not an empirical judgment. For before appealing to experience, we already have all the conditions of the judgment in the concept, from which we have but to elicit the predicate according to the law of contradiction, and thereby to become conscious of the necessity of the judgment, which experience could not in the least teach us.

2. *Mathematical Judgments* are all synthetical. This fact seems hitherto to  have altogether escaped the observation of those who have analyzed human reason: it even seems directly opposed to all their conjectures, though it is incontestably certain and most important in its consequences. For as it was found that the conclusions

of mathematicians all proceed according to the law of contradiction (as is demanded by all apodictic certainty), men persuaded themselves that the fundamental principles were known from the same law. This was a great mistake, for a synthetical proposition can indeed be established by the law of contradiction, but only by presupposing another synthetical proposition from which it follows, but never by that law alone.

First of all, we must observe that all strictly mathematical judgments are *a priori,* and not empirical, because they carry with them necessity, which cannot be obtained from experience. But if this be not conceded to me, very good; I shall confine my assertion to *pure mathematics,* the very notion of which implies that it contains pure *a priori* and not empirical knowledge.

It must at first be thought that the proposition 7 + 5 = 12 is a mere analytical judgment, following from the concept of the sum of seven and five, according to the law of contradiction. But on closer examination it appears that the concept of the sum of 7 + 5 contains merely their union in a single number, without its being at all thought what the
269 particular number is that unites them. The concept of twelve is by no means thought by merely thinking of the combination of seven and five; and, analyze this possible sum as we may, we shall not discover twelve in the concept. We must go beyond these concepts, by calling to our aid some intuition which corresponds to one of the concepts—that is, either our five fingers or five points (as Segner has it in his *Arithmetic*)—and we must add successively the units of the five given in the intuition to the concept of seven. Hence our concept is really amplified by the proposition 7 + 5 = 12, and we add to the first concept a second concept not thought in it. Arithmetical judgments are therefore synthetical, and the more plainly according as we take larger numbers; for in such cases it is clear that, however closely we analyze our concepts without calling intuition to our aid, we can never find the sum by such mere dissection.

Just as little is any principle of geometry analytical. That a straight line is the shortest path between two points is a synthetical proposition. For my concept of straight contains nothing of quantity, but only a quality. The concept "shortest" is therefore altogether additional and cannot be obtained by any analysis of the concept "straight line." Here, too, intuition must come to aid us. It alone makes the synthesis possible. What usually makes us believe that the predicate of such apodictic judgments is already contained in our concept, and that the judgment is therefore analytical, is the duplicity of the expression. We must think a certain predicate as attached to a given concept, and necessity indeed belongs to the concepts. But the question is not what we must join in thought *to* the given concept, but what we actually think together with and in it, though obscurely; and so it appears that the predicate belongs to this concept necessarily indeed, yet not directly but indirectly by means of an intuition which must be present.

Some other principles, assumed by geometers, are indeed actually analytical, and depend on the law of contradiction; but they only serve, as identical propositions, as a method of concatenation, and not as principles—for example $a = a$, the whole is equal to itself, or $a + b > a$, the whole is greater than its part. And yet even these, though they are recognized as valid from mere concepts, are admitted in mathematics only because
272 they can be represented in some intuition.

The essential and distinguishing feature of pure mathematical knowledge among all other *a priori* knowledge is that it cannot at all proceed from concepts, but only by means of the construction of concepts.* As therefore in its propositions it must proceed beyond the concept to that which its corresponding intuition contains, these

***Critique of Pure Reason,** "Methodology," Ch. I, Sec. 1.

propositions neither can, nor ought to, arise analytically, by dissection of the concept, but are all synthetical.

I cannot refrain from pointing out the disadvantage resulting to philosophy from the neglect of this easy and apparently insignificant observation. Hume being prompted to cast his eye over the whole field of *a priori* cognitions in which human understanding claims such mighty possessions (a calling he felt worthy of a philosopher) heedlessly severed from it a whole, and indeed its most valuable, province, namely, pure mathematics; for he imagined its nature or, so to speak, the state constitution of this empire depended on totally different principles, namely, on the law of contradiction alone; and although he did not divide judgments in this manner formally and universally as I have done here, what he said was equivalent to this: that mathematics contains only analytical, but metaphysics synthetical, *a priori* propositions. In this, however, he was greatly mistaken, and the mistake had a decidedly injurious effect upon his whole conception. But for this, he would have extended his question concerning the origin of our synthetical judgments far beyond the metaphysical concept of causality and included in it the possibility of mathematics *a priori* also, for this
latter he must have assumed to be equally synthetical. And then he could not have 273
based his metaphysical propositions on mere experience without subjecting the axioms of mathematics equally to experience, a thing which he was far too acute to do. The good company into which metaphysics would thus have been brought would have saved it from the danger of a contemptuous ill-treatment, for the thrust intended for it must have reached mathematics, which was not and could not have been Hume's intention. Thus that acute man would have been led into considerations which must needs be similar to those that now occupy us, but which would have gained inestimably by his inimitably elegant style.

3. *Metaphysical Judgments,* properly so called, are all synthetical. We must distinguish judgments pertaining to metaphysics from metaphysical judgments properly so called. Many of the former are analytical, but they only afford the means for metaphysical judgments, which are the whole end of the science and which are always synthetical. For if there be concepts pertaining to metaphysics (as, for example, that of substance), the judgments springing from simple analysis of them also pertain to metaphysics, as, for example, substance is that which only exists as subject, etc.; and by means of several such analytical judgments we seek to approach the definition of the concepts. But as the analysis of a pure concept of the understanding (the kind of concept pertaining to metaphysics) does not proceed in any different manner from the dissection of any other, even empirical, concepts, not belonging to metaphysics (such as, air is an elastic fluid, the elasticity of which is not destroyed by any known degree of cold), it follows that the concept indeed, but not the analytical judgment, is properly metaphysical. This science has something peculiar in the production of its *a priori* cognitions, which must therefore be distinguished from the features it has in common with other rational knowledge. Thus the judgment that all the substance in things is permanent is a synthetical and properly metaphysical judgment.

If the *a priori* concepts which constitute the materials and tools of metaphysics have first been collected according to fixed principles, then their analysis will be of great value; it might be taught as a particular part (as a *philosophia definitiva*), containing nothing but analytical judgments pertaining to metaphysics, and could be
treated separately from the synthetical which constitute metaphysics proper. For 274
indeed these analyses are not of much value except in metaphysics, that is, as regards

the synthetical judgments which are to be generated by these previously analyzed concepts.

The conclusion drawn in this section then is that metaphysics is properly concerned with synthetical propositions *a priori,* and these alone constitute its end, for which it indeed requires various dissections of its concepts, namely, analytical judgments, but wherein the procedure is not different from that in every other kind of knowledge, in which we merely seek to render our concepts distinct by analysis. But the generation of *a priori* knowledge by intuition as well as by concepts, in fine, of synthetical propositions *a priori,* especially in philosophical knowledge, constitutes the essential subject of metaphysics.

270 *§ 3. A Remark on the General Division of Judgment into Analytical and Synthetical*

This division is indispensable, as concerns the critique of human understanding, and therefore deserves to be called classical in such critical investigation, though otherwise it is of little use. But this is the reason why dogmatic philosophers, who always seek the sources of metaphysical judgments in metaphysics itself, and not apart from it in the pure laws of reason generally, altogether neglected this apparently obvious distinction. Thus the celebrated Wolff and his acute follower Baumgarten came to seek the proof of the principle of sufficient reason, which is clearly synthetical, in the principle of contradiction. In Locke's *Essay,* however, I find an indication of my division. For in the fourth book (Chapter III, § 9, seq.), having discussed the various connections of representations in judgments, and their sources, one of which he makes "identity or contradiction" (analytical judgments) and another the coexistence of ideas in a subject (synthetical judgments), he confesses (§ 10) that our (*a priori*) knowledge of the latter is very narrow and almost nothing. But in his remarks on this species of knowledge, there is so little of what is definite and reduced to rules that we cannot wonder if no one, not even Hume, was led to make investigations concerning this sort of proposition. For such general and yet definite principles are not easily learned from other men, who have had them only obscurely in their minds. One must hit on them first by one's own reflection; then one finds them elsewhere, where one could not possibly have found them at first because the authors themselves did not know that such an idea lay at the basis of their observations. Men who never think independently have nevertheless the acuteness to discover everything, after it has been once shown them, in what was said long since, though no one was ever able to see it there before.

271 *§ 4. The General Question of the Prolegomena: Is Metaphysics at All Possible?*

Were a metaphysics which could maintain its place as a science really in existence, could we say: "Here is metaphysics; learn it and it will convince you irresistibly and irrevocably of its truth"? This question would then be useless, and there would only remain that other question (which would rather be a test of our acuteness than a proof of the existence of the thing itself): "How is the science possible, and how does reason come to attain it?" But human reason has not been so fortunate in this case. There is no single book to which you can point as you do to Euclid, and say: "This is metaphysics; here you may find the noblest objects of this science, the knowledge of a highest being and of a future existence, proved from principles of pure reason." We can be shown indeed many propositions, demonstrably certain and never questioned; but these are all analytical, and rather concern the materials and the scaffolding for metaphysics than the extension of knowledge, which is our proper object in studying it (§ 2). Even supposing you produce synthetical judgments (such as the law of sufficient reason, which you have never proved, as you ought to, from pure reason *a priori,* though we gladly concede its truth), you lapse, when you try to employ them for your principal purpose, into such doubtful assertions that in all ages one metaphysics has contradicted another, either in its assertions or their proofs, and thus has itself destroyed its own claim to lasting assent. Nay, the very attempts to set up such a science are the main cause of the early appearance of skepticism, a mental attitude in which reason treats itself with such violence that it could never have arisen save from complete despair of ever satisfying its most important aspirations. For long before men began to inquire into nature methodically, they consulted abstract reason, which had to some extent been exercised by means of ordinary experience; for reason is ever present, while laws of nature must usually be discovered with labor. So metaphysics floated to the surface, like foam, which dissolved the moment it was scooped off. But immediately there appeared a new supply on the surface, to be ever eagerly gathered up by some; while others, instead of seeking in the depths the cause of the phenomenon, thought they showed their wisdom by ridiculing the idle labor of their neighbors.

Weary therefore of dogmatism, which teaches us nothing, and of skepticism, which 274
does not even promise us anything—even the quiet state of a contented ignorance—disquieted by the importance of knowledge so much needed, and rendered suspicious by long experience of all knowledge which we believe we possess or which offers itself in the name of pure reason, there remains but one critical question on the answer to which our future procedure depends, namely, "Is metaphysics at all possible?" But this question must be answered, not by sceptical objections to the asseverations of some actual system of metaphysics (for we do not as yet admit such a thing to exist), but from the conception, as yet only problematical, of a science of this sort.

In the *Critique of Pure Reason* I have treated this question synthetically, by making inquiries into pure reason itself and endeavoring in this source to determine the elements as well as the laws of its pure use according to principles. The task is difficult and requires a resolute reader to penetrate by degrees into a system based on no data except reason itself, and which therefore seeks, without resting upon any fact, to unfold knowledge from its original germs. The *Prolegomena,* however, are designed for preparatory exercises; they are intended to point out what we have to do in order to make a science actual if it is possible, rather than to propound it. The
Prolegomena must therefore rest upon something already known as trustworthy, 275
from which we can set out with confidence and ascend to sources as yet unknown, the discovery of which will not only explain to us what we knew but exhibit a sphere of many cognitions which all spring from the same sources. The method of prolegomena, especially of those designed as a preparation for future metaphysics, is consequently analytical.

But it happens, fortunately, that though we cannot assume metaphysics to be an actual science, we can say with confidence that there is actually given certain pure *a priori* synthetical cognitions, pure mathematics and pure physics; for both contain propositions which are unanimously recognized, partly apodictically certain by mere reason, partly by general consent arising from experience and yet as independent of experience. We have therefore at least some uncontested synthetical knowledge *a priori* and need not ask *whether* it be possible, for it is actual, but *how* it is possible, in order that we may deduce from the principle which makes the given knowledge possible the possibility of all the rest.

§ 5. The General Problem: How Is Knowledge from Pure Reason Possible?

276 We have already learned the significant distinction between analytical and synthetical judgments. The possibility of analytical propositions was easily comprehended, being entirely founded on the law of contradiction. The possibility of synthetical *a posteriori* judgments, of those which are gathered from experience, also requires no particular explanations, for experience is nothing but a continued synthesis of perceptions. There remain therefore only synthetical propositions *a priori,* of which the possibility must be sought or investigated, because they must depend upon other principles than the law of contradiction.

But here we need not first establish the possibility of such propositions so as to ask whether they are possible. For there are enough of them which indeed are of undoubted certainty; and, as our present method is analytical, we shall start from the fact that such synthetical but purely rational knowledge actually exists; but we must now inquire into the ground of this possibility and ask *how* such knowledge is possible, in order that we may, from the principles of its possibility, be enabled to determine the conditions of its use, its sphere and its limits. The real problem upon which all depends, when expressed with scholastic precision, is therefore: "How are synthetic propositions *a priori* possible?"

For the sake of popular understanding I have above expressed this problem somewhat differently, as an inquiry into purely rational knowledge, which I could do for once without detriment to the desired insight, because, as we have only to do here with metaphysics and its sources, the reader will, I hope, after the foregoing reminders, keep in mind that when we speak of knowing by pure reason we do not mean analytical but synthetical knowledge.*

Metaphysics stands or falls with the solution of this problem; its very existence
277 depends upon it. Let anyone make metaphysical assertions with ever so much plausibility, let him overwhelm us with conclusions; but if he has not previously proved able to answer this question satisfactorily, I have a right to say: This is all vain, baseless philosophy and false wisdom. You speak through pure reason and claim, as it were, to create cognitions *a priori* not only by dissecting given concepts, but also by asserting connections which do not rest upon the law of contradiction, and which you claim to conceive quite independently of all experience; how do you arrive at this, and how will you justify

*It is unavoidable that, as knowledge advances, certain expressions which have become classical after having been used since the infancy of science will be found inadequate and unsuitable, and a newer and more appropriate application of the terms will give rise to confusion. [This is the case with the term "analytical."] The analytical method, so far as it is opposed to the synthetical, is very different from one that consists of analytical propositions; it signifies only that we start from what is sought, as if it were given, and ascend to the only conditions under which it is possible. In this method we often use nothing but synthetical propositions, as in mathematical analysis, and it were better to term it the *regressive* method, in contradistinction to the *synthetic* or *progressive.* A principal part of logic too is distinguished by the name of analytic, which here signifies the logic of truth in contrast to dialectic, without considering whether the cognitions belonging to it are analytical or synthetical.

such pretensions? An appeal to the consent of the common sense of mankind cannot be allowed, for that is a witness whose authority depends merely upon rumor. Says Horace:

*Quodcunque ostendis mihi sic, incredulus odi.**

The answer to this question is as indispensable as it is difficult; and although the principal reason that it was not sought long ago is that the possibility of the question never occurred to anybody, there is yet another reason, namely, that a satisfactory answer to this one question requires a much more persistent, profound, and painstaking reflection than the most diffuse work on metaphysics, which on its first appearance promised immortal fame to its author. And every intelligent reader, when he carefully reflects what this problem requires, must at first be struck with its difficulty, and would regard it as insoluble and even impossible did there not actually exist pure synthetical cognitions *a priori*. This actually happened to David Hume, though he did not conceive the question in its entire universality as is done here and as must be done if the answer is to be decisive for all metaphysics. For how is it possible, says that acute man, that when a concept is given me I can go beyond it and connect with it another which is not contained in it, in such a manner as if the latter *necessarily* belonged to the former? Nothing but experience can furnish us with such connections (thus he concluded from the difficulty which he took to be impossibility), and all that vaunted necessity or, what is the same thing, knowledge assumed to be *a priori* is nothing but a long habit of accepting something as true, and hence of mistaking subjective necessity for objective.

Should my reader complain of the difficulty and the trouble which I shall occa- 278
sion him in the solution of this problem, he is at liberty to solve it himself in an easier way. Perhaps he will then feel under obligation to the person who has undertaken for him a labor of so profound research and will rather feel some surprise at the facility with which, considering the nature of the subject, the solution has been attained. Yet it has cost years of work to solve the problem in its whole universality (using the term in the mathematical sense, namely, for that which is sufficient for all cases), and finally to exhibit it in the analytical form, as the reader will find it here.

All metaphysicians are therefore solemnly and legally suspended from their occupations till they shall have adequately answered the question, "How are synthetic cognitions *a priori* possible?" For the answer contains the only credentials which they must show when they have anything to offer us in the name of pure reason. But if they do not possess these credentials, they can expect nothing else of reasonable people, who have been deceived so often, than to be dismissed without further inquiry.

If they, on the other hand, desire to carry on their business, not as a science, but as an art of wholesome persuasion suitable to the common sense of man, this calling cannot in justice be denied them. They will then speak the modest language of a rational belief; they will grant that they are not allowed even to conjecture, far less to know, anything which lies beyond the bounds of all possible experience, but only to assume (not for speculative use, which they must abandon, but for practical use only) the existence of something possible and even indispensable for the guidance of the understanding and of the will in life. In this manner alone can they be called useful and wise men, and the more

*["To all that which thou provest me thus, I refuse to give credence, and hate"—*Epistle* II, 3, 188.]

so as they renounce the title of metaphysicians. For the latter profess to be speculative philosophers; and since, when judgments *a priori* are under discussion, poor probabili-
279 ties cannot be admitted (for what is declared to be known *a priori* is thereby announced as necessary), such men cannot be permitted to play with conjectures, but their assertion must be either science or nothing at all.

It may be said that the entire transcendental philosophy, which necessarily precedes all metaphysics, is nothing but the complete solution of the problem here propounded, in systematic order and completeness, and hence we have hitherto never had any transcendental philosophy. For what goes by its name is properly a part of metaphysics, whereas the former science is intended only to constitute the possibility of the latter and must therefore precede all metaphysics. And it is not surprising that when a whole science, deprived of all help from other sciences and consequently in itself quite new, is required to answer a single question satisfactorily, we should find the answer troublesome and difficult, nay, even shrouded in obscurity.

As we now proceed to this solution according to the analytical method, in which we assume that such cognitions from pure reason actually exist, we can only appeal to two sciences of theoretical knowledge (which alone is under consideration here), namely, pure mathematics and pure natural science. For these alone can exhibit to us objects in intuition, and consequently (if there should occur in them a cognition *a priori*) can show the truth or conformity of the cognition to the object *in concreto,* that is, its actuality, from which we could proceed to the ground of its possibility by the analytical method. This facilitates our work greatly for here universal considerations are not only applied to facts, but even start from them, while in a synthetic procedure they must strictly be derived *in abstracto* from concepts.

But in order to rise from these actual and, at the same time, well-grounded pure cognitions *a priori* to a possible knowledge of the kind as we are seeking, namely, to metaphysics as a science, we must comprehend that which occasions it—I mean the mere natural, though in spite of its truth still suspect, cognition *a priori* which lies at the basis of that science, the elaboration of which without any critical investigation of its possibility is commonly called metaphysics. In a word, we must
280 comprehend the natural conditions of such a science as a part of our inquiry, and thus the transcendental problem will be gradually answered by a division into four questions:

1. How is pure mathematics possible?
2. How is pure natural science possible?
3. How is metaphysics in general possible?
4. How is metaphysics as a science possible?

It may be seen that the solution of these problems, though chiefly designed to exhibit the essential matter of the *Critique,* has yet something peculiar, which for itself alone deserves attention. This is the search for the sources of given sciences in reason itself, so that its faculty of knowing something *a priori* may by its own deeds be investigated and measured. By this procedure these sciences gain, if not with regard to their contents, yet as to their proper use; and while they throw light on the higher question concerning their common origin, they give, at the same time, an occasion better to explain their own nature.

FIRST PART OF THE MAIN TRANSCENDENTAL PROBLEM

HOW IS PURE MATHEMATICS POSSIBLE?

§ 6. Here is a great and established branch of knowledge, encompassing even now a wonderfully large domain and promising an unlimited extension in the future, yet carrying with it thoroughly apodictic certainty, that is, absolute necessity, and therefore resting upon no empirical grounds. Consequently it is a pure product of reason; and, moreover, it is thoroughly synthetical. [Hence the question arises:] "How then is it possible for human reason to produce such knowledge entirely *a priori?*"

Does not this faculty [which produces mathematics], as it neither is nor can be based upon experience, presuppose some ground of knowledge *a priori,* which lies deeply hidden but which might reveal itself by these its effects if their first beginnings were but diligently ferreted out?

§ 7. But we find that all mathematical cognition has this peculiarity: it must first 281
exhibit its concept in intuition and indeed *a priori;* therefore in an intuition which is not empirical but pure. Without this mathematics cannot take a single step; hence its judgments are always *intuitive;* whereas philosophy must be satisfied with *discursive* judgments from mere concepts, and though it may illustrate its doctrines through an intuition, can never derive them from it. This observation on the nature of mathematics gives us a clue to the first and highest condition of its possibility, which is that some pure intuition must form its basis, in which all its concepts can be exhibited or constructed, *in concreto* and yet *a priori.* If we can uncover this pure intuition and its possibility, we may thence easily explain how synthetical propositions *a priori* are possible in pure mathematics, and consequently how this science itself is possible. For just as empirical intuition [namely, sense-perception] enables us without difficulty to enlarge the concept which we frame of an object of intuition by new predicates which intuition itself presents synthetically in experience, so also pure intuition does likewise, only with this difference, that in the latter case the synthetical judgment is *a priori* certain and apodictic, in the former only *a posteriori* and empirically certain; because this latter contains only that which occurs in contingent empirical intuition, but the former that which must necessarily be discovered in pure intuition. Here intuition, being an intuition *a priori,* is inseparably joined with the concept *prior to all experience* or particular perception.

§ 8. But with this step our perplexity seems rather to increase than to lessen. For the question now is, "How is it possible to intuit anything *a priori?*" An intuition is
such a representation as would immediately depend upon the presence of the object. 282
Hence it seems impossible to intuit spontaneously *a priori,* because intuition would in that event have to take place without either a former or a present object to refer to, and in consequence could not be intuition. Concepts indeed are such that we can easily form some of them *a priori,* namely, such as contain nothing but the thought of an object in general; and we need not find ourselves in an immediate relation to the object. Take, for instance, the concepts of quantity, of cause, etc. But even these require, in order to be meaningful and significant, a certain concrete use—that is, an application to some intuition by which an object of them is given us. But how can the intuition of the object precede the object itself?

§ 9. If our intuition were of such a nature as to represent things as they are in themselves, there would not be any intuition *a priori,* but intuition would be always empirical. For I can only know what is contained in the object in itself if it is present and given to me. It is indeed even then incomprehensible how the intuition of a present thing should make me know this thing as it is in itself, as its properties cannot migrate into my faculty of representation. But even granting this possibility, an intuition of that sort would not take place *a priori,* that is, before the object were presented to me; for without this latter fact no ground of a relation between my representation and the object can be imagined, unless it depend upon a direct implantation.

Therefore in one way only can my intuition anticipate the actuality of the object, and be a cognition *a priori,* namely: *if my intuition contains nothing but the form of sensibility, antedating in my mind all the actual impressions through which I am affected by objects.*

For that objects of sense can only be intuited according to this form of sensibility I can know *a priori.* Hence it follows that propositions which concern this form of sensuous intuition only are possible and valid for objects of the senses; as also, conversely, that intuitions which are possible *a priori* can never concern any other things than objects of our senses.

283 § 10. Accordingly, it is only the form of sensuous intuition by which we can intuit things *a priori,* but by which we can know objects only as they *appear* to us (to our senses), not as they are in themselves; and this assumption is absolutely necessary if synthetical propositions *a priori* be granted as possible or if, in case they actually occur, their possibility is to be comprehended and determined beforehand.

Now, the intuitions which pure mathematics lays at the foundation of all its cognitions and judgments which appear at once apodictic and necessary are space and time. For mathematics must first present all its concepts in intuition, and pure mathematics in pure intuition; that is, it must construct them. If it proceeded in any other way, it would be impossible to take a single step; for mathematics proceeds, not analytically by dissection of concepts, but synthetically, and if pure intuition be wanting there is nothing in which the matter for synthetical judgments *a priori* can be given. Geometry is based upon the pure intuition of space. Arithmetic achieves its concept of number by the successive addition of units in time, and pure mechanics cannot attain its concepts of motion without employing the representation of time. Both representations, however, are only intuitions; for if we omit from the empirical intuitions of bodies and their alterations (motion) everything empirical, that is, belonging to sensation, space and time still remain, which are therefore pure intuitions that lie *a priori* at the basis of the empirical. Hence they can never be omitted; but at the same time, by their being pure intuitions *a priori,* they prove that they are mere forms of our sensibility, which must precede all empirical intuition, that is, perception of actual objects, and conformably to which objects can be known *a priori,* but only as they appear to us.

§ 11. The problem of the present section is therefore solved. Pure mathematics, as synthetical cognition *a priori,* is possible only by referring to no other objects than those
284 of the senses. At the basis of their empirical intuition lies a pure intuition (of space and of time) which is *a priori,* because the latter intuition is nothing but the mere form of sensibility, which precedes the actual appearance of the objects, since in fact it makes them possible. Yet this faculty of intuiting *a priori* affects not the matter of the phenomenon (that is, the sensation in it, for this constitutes that which is empirical), but its form, namely, space and time. Should any man venture to doubt that these are determinations adhering not to things in themselves, but to their relation to our sensibility, I should be glad to know how he can find it possible to know *a priori* how their intuition will be characterized before we have any acquaintance with them and before they are presented to us. Such, however, is the case with space and time. But this is quite comprehensible as soon as both count for nothing more than formal conditions of our sensibility, while the

objects count merely as phenomena; for then the form of the phenomenon, that is, pure intuition, can by all means be represented as proceeding from ourselves, that is, *a priori.*

§ 12. In order to add something by way of illustration and confirmation, we need only watch the ordinary and unavoidable procedure of geometers. All proofs of the complete congruence of two given figures (where the one can in every respect be substituted for the other) come ultimately to this, that they may be made to coincide, which is evidently nothing else than a synthetical proposition resting upon immediate intuition; and this intuition must be pure or given *a priori,* otherwise the proposition could not rank as apodictically certain, but would have empirical certainty only. In that case, it could only be said that it is always found to be so and holds good only as far as our perception reaches. That everywhere space (which [in its entirety] is itself no longer the boundary of another space) has three dimensions and that space cannot in any way have more is based on the proposition that not more than three lines can intersect at right angles in one point; 285
but this proposition cannot by any means be shown from concepts, but rests immediately on intuition, and indeed on pure and *a priori* intuition because it is apodictically certain. That we can require a line to be drawn to infinity (*in indefinitum*) or that a series of changes (for example, spaces traversed by motion) shall be infinitely continued presupposes a representation of space and time, which can only attach to intuition—namely, so far as it in itself is bounded by nothing—for from concepts it could never be inferred. Consequently, the basis of mathematics actually is pure intuitions, which make its synthetical and apodictically valid propositions possible. Hence our transcendental deduction of the notions of space and of time explains at the same time the possibility of pure mathematics. Without such a deduction and the assumption "that everything which can be given to our senses (to the external senses in space, to the internal one in time) is intuited by us as it appears to us, not as it is in itself," the truth of pure mathematics may be granted, but its existence could by no means be understood.

§ 13. Those who cannot yet rid themselves of the notion that space and time are actual qualities inherent in things in themselves may exercise their acumen on the following paradox. When they have in vain attempted its solution and are free from prejudices at least for a few moments, they will suspect that the degradation of space and time to mere forms of our sensuous intuition may perhaps be well founded.

If two things are quite equal in all respects as much as can be ascertained by all means possible, quantitatively and qualitatively, it must follow that the one can in all cases and under all circumstances replace the other, and this substitution would not occasion the least perceptible difference. This in fact is true of plane figures in geometry; but some spherical figures exhibit, notwithstanding a complete internal agreement, such a difference in their external relation that the one figure cannot possibly be put in the place of the other. For instance, two spherical triangles on opposite hemispheres, which have an arc of the equator as their common base, may be quite equal, both as regards sides and angles, so that nothing is to be found in either, if it be described for itself alone and com- 286
pleted, that would not equally be applicable to both; and yet the one cannot be put in the place of the other (that is, upon the opposite hemisphere). Here, then, is an internal difference between the two triangles, which difference our understanding cannot describe as internal and which only manifests itself by external relations in space. But I shall adduce examples, taken from common life, that are more obvious still.

What can be more similar in every respect and in every part more alike to my hand and to my ear than their images in a mirror? And yet I cannot put such a hand as is seen in the glass in the place of its original; for if this is a right hand, that in the glass is a left one, and the image or reflection of the right ear is a left one, which never can take the place of the other. There are in this case no internal differences which our understanding could determine by thinking alone. Yet the differences are internal as the senses teach, for, notwithstanding their complete equality and similarity, the left hand cannot be enclosed in the same bounds as the right one (they are not congruent); the glove of one hand cannot be used for the other. What is the solution? These objects are not representations of things as they are in themselves and as some mere* understanding would know them, but sensuous intuitions, that is, appearances whose possibility rests upon the relation of certain things unknown in themselves to something else, namely, to our sensibility. Space is the form of the external intuition of this sensibility, and the internal determination of every space is possible only by the determination of its external relation to the whole of space, of which it is a part (in other words, by its relation to the outer sense). That is to say, the part is possible only through the whole, which is never the case with things in themselves, as objects of the mere understanding, but which may well be the case with mere appearances. Hence the difference between similar and equal things which are not congruent (for instance, two symmetric helices) cannot be made intelligible by any concept, but only by the relation to the right and the left hands which immediately refers to intuition.

287 REMARK I

Pure mathematics, and especially pure geometry, can have objective reality only on condition that they refer merely to objects of sense. But in regard to the latter the principle holds good that our sense representation is not a representation of things in themselves, but of the way in which they appear to us. Hence it follows that the propositions of geometry are not the results of a mere creation of our poetic imagination, and that therefore they cannot be referred with assurance to actual objects; but rather that they are necessarily valid of space, and consequently of all that may be found in space, because space is nothing else than the form of all external appearances, and it is this form alone in which objects of sense can be given to us. Sensibility, the form of which is the basis of geometry, is that upon which the possibility of external appearance depends. Therefore these appearances can never contain anything but what geometry prescribes to them.

It would be quite otherwise if the senses were so constituted as to represent objects as they are in themselves. For then it would not by any means follow from the representation of space, which, with all its properties, serves to the geometer as an *a priori* foundation, that this foundation and everything which is thence inferred must be so in nature. The space of the geometer would be considered a mere fiction, and it would not be credited with objective validity because we cannot see how things must of necessity agree with an image of them which we make spontaneously and previous to our acquaintance with them. But if this image, or rather this formal intuition, is the essential property of our sensibility by means of which alone objects are given to us, and if this sensibility represents not things in themselves but their appearances, then we shall easily comprehend, and at the same time indisputably prove, that all external objects of our world of sense must necessarily coincide in the most rigorous way with the propositions of geometry; because sensibility, by means of its form of external intuition, namely, by space, with which the geometer is occupied, makes those objects possible as mere appearances.

*[In German, *pure.* The clause is meant ironically.—L.W.B.]

University of Königsberg (from an old postcard). Immanuel Kant attended and later taught at the University. These University buildings were destroyed in 1944 by an air raid—only the Cathedral in the background survived.

It will always remain a remarkable phenomenon in the history of philosophy that there was a time when even mathematicians who at the same time were philosophers began to doubt, not of the accuracy of their geometrical propositions so far as they 288
concerned space, but of their objective validity and the applicability of this concept itself, and of all its corollaries, to nature. They showed much concern whether a line in nature might not consist of physical points, and consequently that true space in the object might consist of simple parts, while the space which the geometer has in his mind cannot be such. They did not recognize that this thought space renders possible the physical space, that is, the extension of matter itself; that this pure space is not at all a quality of things in themselves, but a form of our sensuous faculty of representation; and that all objects in space are mere appearances, that is, not things in themselves but representations of our sensuous intuition. But such is the case, for the space of the geometer is exactly the form of sensuous intuition which we find *a priori* in us, and contains the ground of the possibility of all external appearances (according to their form); and the latter must necessarily and most rigorously agree with the propositions of the geometer, which he draws, not from any fictitious concept, but from the subjective basis of all external appearances which is sensibility itself. In this and no other way can geometry be made secure as to the undoubted objective reality of its propositions against all the intrigues of a shallow metaphysics, which is surprised at them [the geometrical propositions] because it has not traced them to the sources of their concepts.

Remark II

Whatever is given us as object must be given us in intuition. All our intuition, however, takes place by means of the senses only; the understanding intuits nothing but only reflects. And as we have just shown that the senses never and in no manner enable us to know things in themselves, but only their appearances, which are mere representations of the sensibility, we conclude that "all bodies, together with the space in which they are, must be considered nothing but mere representations in us, and exist nowhere but in our thoughts." Is not this manifest idealism?

Idealism consists in the assertion that there are none but thinking beings, all other things which we think are perceived in intuition, being nothing but representations in the thinking beings, to which no object external to them in fact corresponds. I, on the contrary, 289 say that things as objects of our senses existing outside us are given, but we know nothing of what they may be in themselves, knowing only their appearances, that is, the representations which they cause in us by affecting our senses. Consequently I grant by all means that there are bodies without us, that is, things which, though quite unknown to us as to what they are in themselves, we yet know by the representations which their influence on our sensibility procures us. These representations we call "bodies," a term signifying merely the appearance of the thing which is unknown to us, but not therefore less actual. Can this be termed idealism? It is the very contrary.

Long before Locke's time, but assuredly since him, it has been generally assumed and granted without detriment to the actual existence of external things that many of their predicates may be said to belong, not to the things in themselves, but to their appearances, and to have no proper existence outside our representation. Heat, color, and taste, for instance, are of this kind. Now, if I go farther and, for weighty reasons, rank as mere appearances the remaining qualities of bodies also, which are called primary—such as extension, place, and, in general, space, with all that which belongs to it (impenetrability or materiality, shape, etc.)—no one in the least can adduce the reason of its being inadmissible. As little as the man who admits colors not to be properties of the object in itself, but only as modifications of the sense of sight, should on that account be called an idealist, so little can my thesis be named idealistic merely because I find that more, nay, *all the properties which constitute the intuition of a body belong merely to its appearance.*

The existence of the thing that appears is thereby not destroyed, as in genuine idealism, but it is only shown that we cannot possibly know it by the senses as it is in itself.

I should be glad to know what my assertions must be in order to avoid all idealism. Undoubtedly, I should say that the representation of space is not only perfectly conformable to the relation which our sensibility has to objects—that I have said—but that it is quite similar to the object—an assertion in which I can find as little meaning as if I said that the sensation of red has a similarity to the property of cinnabar which excites this sensation in me.

Remark III

Hence we may at once dismiss an easily foreseen but futile objection, "that by admitting the ideality of space and of time the whole sensible world would be turned into mere sham." After all philosophical insight into the nature of sensuous cognition was spoiled by making the sensibility merely a confused mode of representation, according to which we still know things as they are, but without being able to reduce everything in this our representation to a clear consciousness, I proved that sensibility consists, not in this logical distinction of clearness and obscurity, but in the genetic one of the origin of knowledge itself. For sensuous perception represents things not at all as they are, but only the mode in which they affect our senses; and consequently by sensuous perception appearances only, and not things themselves, are given to the understanding for reflection. After this necessary correction an objection rises from an unpardonable and almost intentional misconception, as if my doctrine turned all the things of the world of sense into mere illusion.

When an appearance is given us, we are still quite free as to how we should judge the matter. The appearance depends upon the senses, but the judgment upon the understanding; and the only question is whether in the determination of the object there is truth

or not. But the difference between truth and dreaming is not ascertained by the nature of
the representations which are referred to objects (for they are the same in both cases), but
by their connection according to those rules which determine the coherence of the representations in the concept of an object, and by ascertaining whether they can subsist 291
together in experience or not. And it is not the fault of the appearances if our cognition
takes illusion for truth, that is, if the intuition, by which an object is given us, is considered
a concept of the thing or even of its existence which the understanding can only think. The
senses represent to us the course of the planets as now progressive, now retrogressive; and
herein is neither falsehood nor truth, because as long as we hold this to be nothing but
appearance we do not judge of the objective character of their motion. But as a false judgment may easily arise when the understanding is not on its guard against this subjective
mode of representation being considered objective, we say they appear to move backward; it is not the senses however which must be charged with the illusion, but the understanding, whose province alone it is to make an objective judgment from appearances.

Thus, even if we did not at all reflect on the origin of our representations, whenever
we connect our intuitions of sense (whatever they may contain) in space and in time,
according to the rules of the coherence of all knowledge in experience, illusion or truth will
arise according as we are negligent or careful. It is merely a question of the use of sensuous
representations in the understanding, and not of their origin. In the same way, if I consider
all the representations of the senses, together with their form, space and time, to be nothing
but appearances, and space and time to be a mere form of the sensibility, which is not to be
met with in objects out of it, and if I make use of these representations in reference to possible experience only, there is nothing in my regarding them as appearances that can lead
astray or cause illusion. For all that they can correctly cohere according to rules of truth in
experience. Thus all the propositions of geometry hold good of space as well as of all the
objects of the senses, consequently, of all possible experience, whether I consider space as
a mere form of the sensibility or as something cleaving to the things themselves. In the
former case, however, I comprehend how I can know *a priori* these propositions concerning all the objects of external intuition. Otherwise, everything else as regards all possible
experience remains just as if I had not departed from the common view.

But if I venture to go beyond all possible experience with my concepts of space
and time, which I cannot refrain from doing if I proclaim them characters inherent in
things in themselves (for what should prevent me from letting them hold good of the
same things, even though my senses might be different, and unsuited to them?), then a 292
grave error may arise owing to an illusion, in which I proclaim to be universally valid
what is merely a subjective condition of the intuition of things and certain only for all
objects of senses—namely, for all possible experience; I would refer this condition to
things in themselves, and not limit it to conditions of experience.

My doctrine of the ideality of space and of time, therefore, far from reducing the
whole sensible world to mere illusion, is the only means of securing the application of one
of the most important kinds of knowledge (that which mathematics propounds *a priori*) to
actual objects and of preventing its being regarded as mere illusion. For without this observation it would be quite impossible to make out whether the intuitions of space and time,
which we borrow from no experience and which yet lie in our representation *a priori,* are
not mere phantasms of our brain to which objects do not correspond, at least not adequately; and, consequently, whether we have been able to show its unquestionable validity
with regard to all the objects of the sensible world just because they are mere appearances.

Secondly, though these my principles make appearances of the representations
of the senses, they are so far from turning the truth of experience into mere illusion

that they are rather the only means of preventing the transcendental illusion, by which metaphysics has hitherto been deceived and led to the childish endeavor of catching at bubbles, because appearances, which are mere representations, were taken for things in themselves. Here originated the remarkable occurrence of the antinomy of reason which I shall mention later and which is solved by the single observation that appearance, as long as it is employed in experience, produces truth; but the moment it transgresses the bounds of experience, and consequently becomes transcendent, produces nothing but illusion.

Inasmuch, therefore, as I leave to things as we obtain them by the senses their
293 actuality and only limit our sensuous intuition of these things to this: that it represents in no respect, not even in the pure intuitions of space and of time, anything more than mere appearance of those things, but never their constitution in themselves, this is not a sweeping illusion invented for nature by me. My protestation, too, against all charges of idealism is so valid and clear as even to seem superfluous, were there not incompetent judges who, while they would have an old name for every deviation from their perverse though common opinion and never judge of the spirit of philosophic nomenclature, but cling to the letter only, are ready to put their own conceits in the place of well-defined notions, and thereby deform and distort them. I have myself given this my theory the name of transcendental idealism, but that cannot authorize anyone to confound it either with the empirical idealism of Descartes (indeed, his was only an insoluble problem, owing to which he thought everyone at liberty to deny the existence of the corporeal world because it could never be proved satisfactorily), or with the mystical and visionary idealism of Berkeley, against which and other similar phantasms our *Critique* contains the proper antidote. My idealism concerns not the existence of things (the doubting of which, however, constitutes idealism in the ordinary sense), since it never came into my head to doubt it, but it concerns the sensuous representation of things to which space and time especially belong. Of these [namely, space and time], consequently of all appearances in general, I have only shown that they are neither things (but mere modes of representation) nor determinations belonging to things in themselves. But the word "transcendental," which with me never means a reference of our knowledge to things, but only to the cognitive faculty, was meant to obviate this misconception. Yet rather than give further occasion to it by this word, I now retract it and desire this idealism of mine to be called "critical." But if it be really an objectionable idealism to convert actual things (not appearances) into mere representations, by what name shall we call him who conversely changes mere representations to things? It may,
294 I think, be called "dreaming idealism," in contradistinction to the former, which may be called "visionary," both of which are to be refuted by my transcendental or, better, *critical* idealism.

SECOND PART OF THE MAIN TRANSCENDENTAL PROBLEM

HOW IS PURE SCIENCE OF NATURE POSSIBLE?

§ 14. Nature is the existence of things, so far as it is determined according to universal laws. Should nature signify the existence of things in themselves, we could never know it either *a priori* or *a posteriori.* Not *a priori,* for how can we know what belongs to things in themselves, since this never can be done by the dissection of our concepts (in analytical propositions)? For I do not want to know what is contained in my concept of a thing (for that belongs to its logical essence), but what in the actuality of the thing is superadded to my concept and by which the thing itself is determined in its existence apart from the concept. My understanding and the conditions on which alone it can connect the determination of things in their existence do not prescribe any rule to things [in] themselves; these do not conform to my understanding, but it would have to conform itself to them; they would therefore have to be first given me in order to gather these determinations from them, wherefore they would not be known *a priori.*

But knowledge of the nature of things in themselves *a posteriori* would be equally impossible. For, if experience is to teach us laws to which the existence of things is subject, these laws, if they have reference to things in themselves, would have to hold them of necessity even outside our experience. But experience teaches us what exists and how it exists, but never that it must necessarily exist so and not otherwise. Experience therefore can never teach us the nature of things in themselves.

§ 15. We nevertheless actually possess a pure science of nature in which are
propounded, *a priori* and with all the necessity requisite to apodictical propositions, 295
laws to which nature is subject. I need only call to witness that propaedeutic of natural science which, under the title of the universal science of nature, precedes all physics (which is founded upon empirical principles). In it we have mathematics applied to appearances, and also merely discursive principles (or those derived from concepts), which constitute the philosophical part of the pure knowledge of nature. But there are several things in it which are not quite pure and independent of empirical sources, such as the concept of *motion,* that of *impenetrability* (upon which the empirical concept of matter rests), that of *inertia,* and many others, which prevent its being called a perfectly pure science of nature. Besides, it only refers to objects of the outer sense, and therefore does not give an example of a universal science of nature, in the strict sense, for such a science must bring nature in general, whether it regards the object of the outer or that of the inner sense (the object of physics as well as psychology), under universal laws. But among the principles of this universal physics there are a few which actually have the required universality; for instance, the propositions that "substance is permanent," that "every event is determined by a cause according to constant laws," etc. These are actually universal laws of nature, which hold completely *a priori.* There is then in fact a pure science of nature, and the question arises, *How is it possible?*

§ 16. The word *nature* assumes yet another meaning which defines the object, whereas in the former sense it only denotes the conformity to law of the determinations of the existence of things generally. If we consider it *materialiter,* "nature is the complex of all the objects of experience." And with this only are we now concerned, for anyhow things which can never be objects of experience, if they had to be known as to their nature, would oblige us to have recourse to concepts whose meaning could never be given *in concreto* (by any example of possible experience). Consequently we would have to form for ourselves a list of concepts of their nature, the reality whereof could never be determined. That is, we could never learn whether they actually referred to objects or were mere
creations of thought. The knowledge of what cannot be an object of experience would be 296
hyperphysical, and with things hyperphysical we are here not concerned, but only with the knowledge of nature, the actuality of which can be confirmed by experience, though this knowledge is possible *a priori* and precedes all experience.

§ 17. The formal aspect of nature in this narrower sense is therefore the conformity to law of all the objects of experience and, so far as it is known *a priori,* their *necessary* conformity. But it has just been shown that the laws of nature can never be known *a priori* in objects so far as they are considered, not in reference to possible experience, but as things in themselves. And our inquiry here extends, not to things in themselves (the properties of which we pass by), but to things as objects of possible experience, and the complex of these is what we here properly designate as nature. And now I ask, when the possibility of knowledge of nature *a priori* is in question, whether it is better to arrange the problem thus: "How can we know *a priori* that things as objects of experience necessarily conform to law?" or thus: "How is it possible to know *a priori* the necessary conformity to law of experience itself as regards all its objects generally?"

Closely considered, the solution of the problem represented in either way amounts, with regard to the pure knowledge of nature (which is the point of the question at issue), entirely to the same thing. For the subjective laws, under which alone an empirical knowledge of things is possible, hold good of these things as objects of possible experience (not as things in themselves, which are not considered here). It is all the same whether I say: "A judgment of perception can never rank as experience without the law that, whenever an event is observed, it is always referred to some antecedent, which it follows according to a universal rule," or: "Everything of which experience teaches that it happens must have a cause."

297 It is, however, more suitable to choose the first formula. For we can *a priori* and prior to all given objects have a knowledge of those conditions on which alone experience of them is possible, but never of the laws to which things may in themselves be subject, without reference to possible experience. We cannot, therefore, study the nature of things *a priori* otherwise than by investigating the conditions and the universal (though subjective) laws, under which alone such a cognition as experience (as to mere form) is possible, and we determine accordingly the possibility of things as objects of experience. For if I should choose the second formula and seek the *a priori* conditions under which nature as an object of experience is possible, I might easily fall into error and fancy that I was speaking of nature as a thing in itself, and then move round in endless circles, in a vain search for laws concerning things of which nothing is given me.

Accordingly, we shall here be concerned with experience only and the universal conditions of its possibility, which are given *a priori.* Thence we shall define nature as the whole object of all possible experience. I think it will be understood that I here do not mean the rules of the observation of a nature that is already given, for these already presuppose experience. Thus I do not mean how (through experience) we can study the laws of nature, for these would not then be laws *a priori* and would yield us no pure science of nature; but [I mean to ask] how the conditions *a priori* of the possibility of experience are at the same time the sources from which all universal laws of nature must be derived.

§ 18. In the first place we must state that, while all judgments of experience are empirical (that is, have their ground in immediate sense-perception), all empirical judgments are not judgments of experience; but, besides the empirical, and in general besides what is given to the sensuous intuition, special concepts must yet be superadded—concepts which have their origin wholly *a priori* in the pure understanding, and under which every perception must be first of all subsumed and then by their means changed into experience.

298 Empirical judgments, so far as they have objective validity, are *judgments of experience,* but those which are only subjectively valid I name mere *judgments of perception.* The latter require no pure concept of the understanding, but only the logical connection of perception in a thinking subject. But the former always require, besides the representation of the sensuous intuition, special *concepts originally begotten in the understanding,* which make possible the objective validity of the judgment of experience.

All our judgments are at first merely judgments of perception; they hold good only for us (that is, for our subject), and we do not till afterward give them a new reference (to an object) and desire that they shall always hold good for us and in the same way for everybody else; for when a judgment agrees with an object, all judgments concerning the same object must likewise agree among themselves, and thus the objective validity of the judgment of experience signifies nothing else than its necessary universal validity. And conversely when we have ground for considering a judgment as necessarily having universal validity (which never depends upon perception, but upon the pure concept of the understanding under which the perception is subsumed), we must consider that it is objective also—that is, that it expresses not merely a reference of our perception to a subject, but a characteristic of the object. For there would be no reason for the judgments of other men necessarily agreeing with mine if it were not the unity of the object to which they all refer and with which they accord; hence they must all agree with one another.

§ 19. Therefore objective validity and necessary universality (for everybody) are equivalent terms, and though we do not know the object in itself, yet when we consider a judgment as universal, and hence necessary, we thereby understand it to have objective validity. By this judgment we know the object (though it remains unknown as it is in itself) by the universal and necessary connection of the given perceptions. As this is the case with all objects of sense, judgments of experience take their objective validity,
not from the immediate knowledge of the object (which is impossible), but from the 299
condition of universal validity of empirical judgments, which, as already said, never rests upon empirical or, in short, sensuous conditions, but upon a pure concept of the understanding. The object in itself always remains unknown; but when by the concept of the understanding the connection of the representations of the object, which it gives to our sensibility, is determined as universally valid, the object is determined by this relation, and the judgment is objective.

To illustrate the matter: when we say, "The room is warm, sugar sweet, and wormwood bitter,"* we have only subjectively valid judgments. I do not at all expect that I or any other person shall always find it as I now do; each of these sentences only expresses a relation of two sensations to the same subject, that is, myself, and that only in my present state of perception; consequently they are not valid of the object. Such are judgments of perception. Judgments of experience are of quite a different nature. What experience teaches me under certain circumstances, it must always teach me and everybody; and its validity is not limited to the subject nor to its state at a particular time. Hence I pronounce all such judgments objectively valid. For instance, when I say the air is elastic, this judgment is as yet a judgment of perception only; I do nothing but refer two of my sensations to each other. But if I would have it called a judgment of experience, I require this connection to stand under a condition which makes it universally valid. I desire therefore that I and everybody else should always connect necessarily the same perceptions under the same circumstances.

§ 20. We must consequently analyze experience in general in order to see what is 300
contained in this product of the senses and of the understanding, and how the judgment of experience itself is possible. The foundation is the intuition of which I become conscious, that is, perception (*perceptio*), which pertains merely to the senses. But in

*I freely grant that these examples do not represent such judgments of perception as ever could become judgments of experience, even though a concept of the understanding were superadded, because they refer merely to feeling, which everybody knows to be merely subjective and which of course can never be attributed to the object, and consequently never become objective. I only wished to give here an example of a judgment that is merely subjectively valid, containing no ground for necessary universal validity and thereby for a relation to the object. An example of the judgments of perception which become judgments of experience by superadded concepts of the understanding will be given in the next note.

the next place, there is judging (which belongs only to the understanding). But this judging may be twofold: first, I may merely compare perceptions and connect them in a consciousness of my particular state; or, secondly, I may connect them in consciousness in general. The former judgment is merely a judgment of perception, and hence is of subjective validity only; it is merely a connection of perceptions in my mental state, without reference to the object. Hence it does not, as is commonly imagined, suffice for experience that perceptions are compared and connected in consciousness through judgment; thence arises no universal validity and necessity by virtue of which alone consciousness can be objectively valid, that is, can be called experience.

Quite another judgment therefore is required before perception can become experience. The given intuition must be subsumed under a concept which determines the form of judging in general relatively to the intuition, connects empirical consciousness of intuition in consciousness in general, and thereby procures universal validity for empirical judgments. A concept of this nature is a pure *a priori* concept of the understanding, which does nothing but determine for an intuition the general way in which it can be used for judgments. Let the concept be that of cause; then it determines the intuition which is subsumed under it, for example, that of air, relative to judging in general—namely, the concept of air in respect to its expansion serves in the relation of antecedent to consequent in a hypothetical judgment. The concept of cause accordingly is a pure concept of the understanding, which is totally disparate from all possible perception and only serves to determine the representation subsumed under it, with respect to judging in general, and so to make a universally valid judgment possible.

301 Before, therefore, a judgment of perception can become a judgment of experience, it is requisite that the perception should be subsumed under some such concept of the understanding; for instance, air belongs under the concept of cause, which determines our judgment about it in respect to its expansion as hypothetical.* Thereby the expansion of the air is represented, not as merely belonging to the perception of the air in my present state or in several states of mine, or in the perceptual state of others, but as belonging to it necessarily. The judgment, "Air is elastic," becomes universally valid and a judgment of experience only because certain judgments precede it which subsume the intuition of air under the concept of cause and effect; and they thereby determine the perceptions, not merely with respect to one another in me, but with respect to the form of judging in general (which is here hypothetical), and in this way they render the empirical judgment universally valid.

If all our synthetical judgments are analyzed so far as they are objectively valid, it will be found that they never consist of mere intuitions connected only (as is commonly believed) by comparison into a judgment; but that they would be impossible were not a pure concept of the understanding superadded to the concepts abstracted from intuition, under which concept these latter are subsumed and in this manner only combined into an objectively valid judgment. Even the judgments of pure mathematics in their simplest axioms are not exempt from this condition. The principle, "A straight line is the shortest distance between two points," presupposes that the line is subsumed under the concept of magnitude, which certainly is no mere intuition, but has its seat in the

*As an easier example, we may take the following: "When the sun shines on the stone, it grows warm." This judgment, however often I and others may have perceived it, is a mere judgment of perception and contains no necessity; perceptions are only usually conjoined in this manner. But if I say, "The sun warms the stone," I add to the perception a concept of the understanding, namely, that of cause, which necessarily connects with the concept of sunshine that of heat, and the synthetical judgment becomes of necessity universally valid, namely, objective, and is converted from a perception into experience.

understanding alone and serves to determine the intuition (of the line) with regard to the judgments which may be made about it, in respect to their quantity, that is, to plurality (as *judicia plurativa*).* For under them it is understood that in a given intuition there is 302
contained a plurality of homogeneous parts.

LOGICAL TABLE OF JUDGMENTS

1	2
As to Quantity	*As to Quality*
Universal	Affirmative
Particular	Negative
Singular	Infinite

3	4	303
As to Relation	*As to Modality*	
Categorical	Problematic	
Hypothetical	Assertoric	
Disjunctive	Apodeictic	

TRANSCENDENTAL TABLE OF THE CONCEPTS OF THE UNDERSTANDING

1	2
As to Quantity	*As to Quality*
Unity (Measure)	Reality
Plurality (Magnitude)	Negation
Totality (Whole)	Limitation

3	4
As to Relation	*As to Modality*
Substance	Possibility
Cause	Existence
Community	Necessity

PURE PHYSICAL TABLE OF THE UNIVERSAL PRINCIPLES OF THE SCIENCE OF NATURE

1	2
Axioms of Intuition	Anticipations of Perception

3	4
Analogies of Experience	Postulates of Empirical Thinking Generally

*This name seems preferable to the term *particularia,* which is used for these judgments in logic. For the latter implies the idea that they are not universal. But when I start from unity (in singular judgments) and so proceed to totality, I must not [even indirectly and negatively] imply any reference to totality. I think plurality merely without totality, and not the exception from totality. This is necessary if logical distinctions are to form the basis of the pure concepts of the understanding. However, logical usage need not be changed.

§ 21. To prove, then, the possibility of experience so far as it rests upon pure concepts of the understanding *a priori,* we must first represent what belongs to judging in general and the various functions of the understanding in a complete table. For the pure concepts of the understanding must run parallel to these functions, as such concepts are nothing more than concepts of intuitions in general, so far as these are determined by one or other of these functions of judging, in themselves, that is, necessarily and universally. Hereby also the *a priori* principles of the possibility of all experience, as objectively valid empirical knowledge, will be precisely determined. For they are nothing but propositions which subsume all perception (under certain universal conditions of intuition) under those pure concepts of the understanding.

304 § 21a. In order to comprise the whole matter in one idea, it is first necessary to remind the reader that we are discussing, not the origin of experience, but that which lies in experience. The former pertains to empirical psychology and would even then never be adequately explained without the latter, which belongs to the critique of knowledge, and particularly of the understanding.

Experience consists of intuitions, which belong to the sensibility, and of judgments, which are entirely a work of the understanding. But the judgments which the understanding forms solely from sensuous intuitions are far from being judgments of experience. For in the one case the judgment connects only the perceptions as they are given in sensuous intuition, while in the other the judgments must express what experience in general and not what the mere perception (which possesses only subjective validity) contains. The judgment of experience must therefore add to the sensuous intuition and its logical connection in a judgment (after it has been rendered universal by comparison) something that determines the synthetical judgment as necessary and therefore as universally valid. This can be nothing else than that concept which represents the intuition as determined in itself with regard to one form of judgment rather than another, namely, a concept of that synthetical unity of intuitions which can only be represented by a given logical function of judgments.

§ 22. The sum of the matter is this: the business of the senses is to intuit, that of the understanding is to think. But thinking is uniting representations in one consciousness. This union originates either merely relative to the subject and is accidental and subjective, or takes place absolutely and is necessary or objective. The union of representations in one consciousness is judgment. Thinking, therefore, is the same as judging or referring representations to judgments in general. Hence judgments are
305 either merely subjective, when representations are referred to a consciousness in one subject only and united in it, or objective, when they are united in consciousness in general, that is, necessarily. The logical functions of all judgments are but various modes of uniting representations in consciousness. But if they serve for concepts, they are concepts of the necessary union of representations in [any] consciousness, and so are principles of objectively valid judgments. This union in consciousness is either analytical, by identity, or synthetical, by the combination and addition of various representations one to another. Experience consists in the synthetical connection of phenomena (perceptions) in consciousness, so far as this connection is necessary. Hence the pure concepts of the understanding are those under which all perceptions must be subsumed ere they can serve for judgments of experience, in

which the synthetical unity of the perceptions is represented as necessary and universally valid.*

§ 23. Judgments, when considered merely as the condition of the union of given representations in a consciousness, are rules. These rules, so far as they represent the union as necessary, are rules *a priori,* and, insofar as they cannot be deduced from higher rules, are principles. But in regard to the possibility of all experience, merely in relation to the form of thinking in it, no conditions of judgments of experience are higher than those which bring the appearances, according to the various form of their intuition, under pure concepts of the understanding, which render the empirical judgment objectively 306
valid. These are therefore the *a priori* principles of possible experience.

The principles of possible experience are then at the same time universal laws of nature, which can be known *a priori.* And thus the problem of our second question, "How is the pure science of nature possible?" is solved. For the system which is required for the form of a science is to be met with in perfection here, because, beyond the above-mentioned formal conditions of all judgments in general (and hence of all rules in general) offered in logic, no others are possible, and these constitute a logical system. The concepts grounded thereupon, which contain the *a priori* conditions of all synthetical and necessary judgments, accordingly constitute a transcendental system. Finally the principles, by means of which all phenomena are subsumed under these concepts, constitute a physical system, that is, a system of nature, which precedes all empirical knowledge of nature, and makes it possible. It may in strictness be denominated the universal and pure science of nature.

§ 24. The first of the physical principles subsumes all phenomena, as intuitions in space and time, under the concept of quantity, and is thus a principle of the application of mathematics to experience. The second one subsumes the strictly empirical element, namely, sensation, which denotes the real in intuitions, not indeed directly under the concept of quantity, because sensation is not an intuition that *contains* either space or time, though it places the respective object corresponding to it in both. But still there is between reality (sense-representation) and the zero, or total void of intuition in time, a difference which has a quantity. For between every given degree of light and of darkness, between every degree of heat and of absolute cold, between every degree of weight and of absolute lightness, between every degree of occupancy space and of totally void space, 307
diminishing degrees can be conceived, in the same manner as between consciousness and total unconsciousness (psychological darkness) ever-diminishing degrees obtain. Hence there is no perception that can prove an absolute absence; for instance, no psychological darkness that cannot be considered as consciousness which is only outbalanced by a stronger consciousness. This occurs in all cases of sensation, and so the understanding can anticipate even sensations, which constitute the peculiar quality of empirical representations

*But how does the proposition that judgments of experience contain necessity in the synthesis of perceptions agree with my statement so often before inculcated that experience as cognition *a posteriori* can afford contingent judgments only? When I say that experience teaches me something, I mean only the perception that lies in experience—for example, that heat always follows the shining of the sun on a stone; consequently the proposition of experience is always so far accidental. That this heat necessarily follows the shining of the sun is contained indeed in the judgment of experience (by means of the concept of cause), yet is a fact not learned by experience; for conversely, experience is first of all generated by this addition of the concept of the understanding (of cause) to perception. How perception attains this addition may be seen by referring in the *Critique* itself to the [first] section of the "Transcendental Faculty of Judgment."

(appearances), by means of the principle that they all have degree (and consequently that what is real in all appearance has degree). Here is the second application of mathematics (*mathesis intensorum*) to the science of nature.

§ 25. Anent the relation of appearances merely with a view to their existence, the determination of the relation is not mathematical but dynamical, and can never be objectively valid, consequently never fit for experience, if it does not come under *a priori* principles by which the empirical knowledge relative to appearances first becomes possible. Hence appearances must be subsumed under the concept of substance, which as a concept of a thing is the foundation of all determination of existence; or, secondly—so far as a succession is found among appearances, that is, an event—under the concept of an effect with reference to cause; or lastly—so far as coexistence is to be known objectively, that is, by a judgment of experience—under the concept of community (action and reaction). Thus *a priori* principles form the basis of objectively valid, though empirical, judgments—that is, of the possibility of experience so far as it must connect objects as existing in nature. These principles are the real laws of nature, which may be termed "dynamical."

Finally knowledge of the agreement and connection, not only of appearances among themselves in experience, but of their relation to experience in general, belongs to the judgments of experience. This relation contains either their agreement with the
308 formal conditions, which the understanding recognizes, or their coherence with the materials of the senses and of perception, or combines both into one concept. Consequently, their relation to experience in general entails possibility, actuality, and necessity, according to universal laws of nature. This would constitute the physical doctrine of method for distinguishing truth from hypotheses and for determining the limits of certainty of the latter.

§ 26. The third table of principles drawn by the critical method from the nature of the understanding itself shows an inherent perfection, which raises it far above every other table which has hitherto, though in vain, been tried or may yet be tried by analyzing the objects themselves dogmatically. It exhibits all synthetical *a priori* principles completely and according to one principle, namely, the faculty of judging in general, constituting the essence of experience as regards the understanding; so that we can be certain that there are no more such principles. This affords a satisfaction which can never be attained by the dogmatic method. Yet this is not all; there is a still greater merit in it.

We must carefully bear in mind the premise which shows the possibility of this cognition *a priori* and, at the same time, limits all such principles to a condition which must never be lost sight of if we desire it not to be misunderstood and extended in use beyond the original sense which the understanding attaches to it. This limit is that they contain nothing but the conditions of possible experience in general so far as it is subjected to laws *a priori.* Consequently, I do not say that things *in themselves* possess a magnitude; that their reality possesses a degree, their existence a connection of accidents in a substance, etc. This nobody can prove, because such a synthetical connection from mere concepts, without any reference to sensuous intuition on the one side or connection of it in a possible experience on the other, is absolutely impossible. The essential limitation of the concepts in these principles then is that all things *as objects of experience only* stand necessarily *a priori* under the aforementioned conditions.

Hence there follows, secondly, a specifically peculiar mode of proof of these principles; they are not directly referred to appearances and to their relation, but to the
309 possibility of experience, of which appearances constitute the matter only, not the form. Thus they are referred to objectively and universally valid synthetical propositions, in

which we distinguish judgments of experience from those of perception. This takes place because appearances, as mere intuitions *occupying a part of space and time,* come under the concept of quantity, which synthetically unites their multiplicity *a priori* according to rules. Again, insofar as the perception contains, besides intuition, sensation, and between the latter and nothing (that is, the total disappearance of sensation), there is an ever-decreasing transition, it is apparent that the real within appearances must have a degree, so far as it (namely, the sensation) *does not itself occupy any part of space or of time.** Still the transition to this real from empty time or empty space is possible only in time. Consequently, although sensation, as the quality of empirical intuition specifically differentiating it from other sensations, can never be known *a priori,* yet it can, in a possible experience in general, as quantity of perception be intensively distinguished from every other similar perception. Hence the application of mathematics to nature, as regards the sensuous intuition by which nature is given to us, thus becomes possible and definite.

Above all, the reader must pay attention to the mode of proof of the principles which occur under the title of "analogies of experience." For these do not refer to the genesis of intuitions, as do the principles of applying mathematics to natural science in general, but to the connection of their existence in an experience; and this can be nothing 310
but the determination of their existence in time according to necessary laws, under which alone the connection is objectively valid and thus becomes experience. The proof, therefore, does not turn on the synthetical unity in the connection of things in themselves, but merely of perceptions; and of these, not in regard to their matter, but to the determination of time and of the relation of their existence in it according to universal laws. If the empirical determination in relative time is indeed to be objectively valid (that is, to be experience), these universal laws must contain the necessary determination of existence in time generally (namely, according to a rule of the understanding *a priori*).

As these are prolegomena I cannot here further descant on the subject, but my reader (who has probably been long accustomed to consider experience a mere empirical synthesis of perceptions, and hence has not considered that it goes much beyond them since it imparts to empirical judgments universal validity, and for that purpose requires a pure and *a priori* unity of the understanding) is recommended to pay special attention to this distinction of experience from a mere aggregate of perceptions and to judge the mode of proof from this point of view.

§ 27. Now we are prepared to remove Hume's doubt. He justly maintains that we cannot comprehend by reason the possibility of causality, that is, of the reference of the existence of one thing to the existence of another which is necessitated by the former. I add that we comprehend just as little the concept of subsistence, that is, the necessity that at the foundation of the existence of things there lies a subject which cannot itself be a predicate of any other thing; nay, we cannot even form a notion of the possibility of such a thing (though we can point out examples of its use in experience). The very same incomprehensibility affects the community of things, as we cannot comprehend how from the

*Heat and light are in a small space just as large, as to degree, as in a large one; in like manner the internal representations, pain, consciousness generally, whether they last a short or a long time, need not vary as to the degree. Hence the quantity is here in a point and in a moment just as great as in any space or time, however great. Degrees are quantities not in intuition, but in mere sensation (or the quantity of the content [*Grundes*] of an intuition). Hence they can only be estimated quantitatively by the relation of 1 to 0, namely, by their capability of decreasing by infinite intermediate degrees to disappearance, or of increasing from naught through infinite gradations to a determinate sensation in a certain time. *Quantitas qualitatis est gradus.* "The quantity of quality is degree."

state of one thing an inference to the state of quite another thing beyond it, and *vice versa,*
311 can be drawn, and how substances which have each their own separate existence should depend upon one another necessarily. But I am very far from holding these concepts to be derived merely from experience, and the necessity represented in them to be imaginary and a mere illusion produced in us by long habit. On the contrary, I have amply shown that they and the principles derived from them are firmly established *a priori* before all experience and have their undoubted objective value, though only with regard to experience.

§ 28. Although I have no notion of such a connection of things in themselves, how they can either exist as substances, or act as causes, or stand in community with others (as parts of a real whole), and I can just as little conceive such properties in appearances as such (because those concepts contain nothing that lies in the appearances, but only what the understanding alone must think), we have yet a concept of such a connection of representations in our understanding and in judgments generally. This concept is: that representations appear, in one sort of judgments, as subject in relation to predicates; in another, as ground in relation to consequent; and, in a third, as parts which constitute together a total possible cognition. Furthermore, we know *a priori* that without considering the representation of an object as determined in one or the other of these respects, we can have no valid knowledge of the object; and, if we should occupy ourselves about the object in itself, there is not a single possible attribute by which I could know that it is determined under any of these aspects, that is, under the concept either of substance, or of cause, or (in relation to other substances) of community, for I have no concept of the possibility of such a connection of existence. But the question is not how things in themselves but how the empirical knowledge of things is determined, as regards the above aspects of judgments in general; that is, how things, as objects of experience, can and must be subsumed under these concepts of the understanding. And then it is clear that I completely comprehend, not only the possibility, but also the necessity, of subsuming all appearances under these concepts—that is, of using them for principles of the possibility of experience.

312 § 29. In order to test Hume's problematical concept (his *crux metaphysicorum*), the concept of cause, we are first given *a priori,* by means of logic, the form of a conditional judgment in general; that is, we have one cognition given as antecedent and another as consequent. But it is possible that in perception we may meet with a rule of relation which runs thus: that a certain appearance is constantly followed by another (though not conversely); and this is a case for me to use the hypothetical judgment and, for instance, to say if the sun shines long enough upon a body it grows warm. Here there is indeed as yet no necessity of connection or concept of cause. But I proceed and say that, if this proposition, which is merely a subjective connection of perceptions, is to be a proposition of experience, it must be seen as necessary and universally valid. Such a proposition would be that the sun is by its light the cause of heat. The empirical rule is now considered as a law, and as valid, not merely of appearances but valid of them for the purposes of a possible experience which requires universal and therefore necessarily valid rules. I therefore easily comprehend the concept of cause, as a concept necessarily belonging to the mere form of experience, and its possibility as a synthetical union of perceptions in consciousness in general; but I do not at all comprehend the possibility of a thing in general as a cause, because the concept of cause denotes a condition not at all belonging to things, but to experience. For experience can be nothing but objectively valid knowledge of appearances and of their succession, only so far as the earlier can be conjoined with the later according to the rule of hypothetical judgments.

§ 30. Hence if even the pure concepts of the understanding are thought to go beyond objects of experience to things in themselves (*noumena*), they have no meaning whatever.

They serve, as it were, only to decipher appearances, that we may be able to read them as experience. The principles which arise from their reference to the sensible world only serve our understanding for empirical use. Beyond this they are arbitrary combinations 313
without objective reality, and we can neither know their possibility *a priori* nor verify—or even render intelligible by any example—their reference to objects; because examples can only be borrowed from some possible experience, and consequently the objects of these concepts can be found nowhere but in a possible experience.

This complete (though to its originator unexpected) solution of Hume's problem rescues for the pure concepts of the understanding their *a priori* origin and for the universal laws of nature their validity as laws of the understanding, yet in such a way as to limit their use to experience, because their possibility depends solely on the reference of the understanding to experience, but with a completely reversed mode of connection which never occurred to Hume—they do not derive from experience, but experience derives from them.

This is, therefore, the result of all our foregoing inquiries: "All synthetical principles *a priori* are nothing more than principles of possible experience" and can never be referred to things in themselves, but to appearances as objects of experience. And hence pure mathematics as well as a pure science of nature can never be referred to anything more than mere appearances, and can only represent either that which makes experience in general possible, or else that which, as it is derived from these principles, must always be capable of being represented in some possible experience.

§ 31. And thus we have at last something definite upon which to depend in all metaphysical enterprises, which have hitherto, boldly enough but always blindly, attempted everything without discrimination. That the aim of their exertions should be so near struck neither the dogmatic thinkers nor those who, confident in their supposed sound common sense, started with concepts and principles of pure reason (which were legitimate and natural, but destined for mere empirical use) in quest of insights to which they neither 314
knew nor could know any definite bounds, because they had never reflected nor were able to reflect on the nature or even on the possibility of such a pure understanding.

Many a naturalist of pure reason (by which I mean the man who believes he can decide in matters of metaphysics without any science) may pretend that he, long ago, by the prophetic spirit of his sound sense, not only suspected but knew and comprehended what is here propounded with so much ado, or, if he likes, with prolix and pedantic pomp: "that with all our reason we can never reach beyond the field of experience." But when he is questioned about his rational principles individually, he must grant that there are many of them which he has not taken from experience and which are therefore independent of it and valid *a priori.* How then and on what grounds will he restrain both himself and the dogmatist, who makes use of these concepts and principles beyond all possible experience because they are recognized to be independent of it? And even he, this adept in sound sense, in spite of all his assumed and cheaply acquired wisdom, is not exempt from wandering inadvertently beyond objects of experience into the field of chimeras. He is often deeply enough involved in them; though, in announcing everything as mere probability, rational conjecture, or analogy, he gives by his popular language a color to his groundless pretensions.

§ 32. Since the oldest days of philosophy, inquirers into pure reason have conceived, besides the things of sense, or appearances (*phenomena*), which make up the sensible world, certain beings of the understanding (*noumena*), which should constitute an intelligible world. And as appearance and illusion were by those men identified (a thing which we may well excuse in an undeveloped epoch), actuality was only conceded to the beings of the understanding.

And we indeed, rightly considering objects of sense as mere appearances, con-
315 fess thereby that they are based upon a thing in itself, though we know not this thing as it is in itself but only know its appearances, namely, the way in which our senses are affected by this unknown something. The understanding, therefore, by assuming appearances, grants the existence of things in themselves also; and to this extent we may say that the representation of such things as are the basis of appearances, consequently of mere beings of the understanding, is not only admissible but unavoidable.

Our critical deduction by no means excludes things of that sort (*noumena*), but rather limits the principles of the Aesthetic* to this, that they shall not extend to all things—as everything would then be turned into mere appearance—but that they shall hold good only of objects of possible experience. Hereby, then, beings of the understanding are granted, but with the inculcation of this rule which admits of no exception: that we neither know nor can know anything at all definite of these pure beings of the understanding, because our pure concepts of the understanding as well as our pure intuitions extend to nothing but objects of possible experience, consequently to mere things of sense; and as soon as we leave this sphere, these concepts retain no meaning whatever.

§ 33. There is indeed something seductive in our pure concepts of the understanding which tempts us to a transcendent use—a use which transcends all possible experience. Not only are our concepts of substance, of power, of action, of reality, and others, quite independent of experience, containing nothing of sense appearance, and so apparently applicable to things in themselves (*noumena*), but, what strengthens this conjecture, they contain a necessity of determination in themselves, which experience never attains. The concept of cause implies a rule according to which one state follows another necessarily; but experience can only show us that one state of things often or, at most, commonly follows another, and therefore affords neither strict universality nor necessity.

Hence the concepts of the understanding seem to have a deeper meaning and import than can be exhausted by their merely empirical use, and so the understanding
316 inadvertently adds for itself to the house of experience a much more extensive wing, which it fills with nothing but beings of thought, without ever observing that it has transgressed with its otherwise legitimate concepts the bounds of their use.

§ 34. Two important and even indispensable, though very dry, investigations therefore became indispensable in the *Critique of Pure Reason* [namely, the chapters "The Schematism of the Pure Concepts of the Understanding" and "On the Ground of the Distinction of All Objects as Phenomena and Noumena."] In the former it is shown that the senses furnish, not the pure concepts of the understanding *in concreto,* but only the schema for their use, and that the object conformable to it occurs only in experience (as the product of the understanding from materials of the sensibility). In the latter it is shown that, although our pure concepts of the understanding and our principles are independent of experience, and despite the apparently greater sphere of their use, still nothing whatever can be thought by them beyond the field of experience, because they can do nothing but merely determine the logical form of the judgment relatively to given intuitions. But as there is no intuition at all beyond the field of the sensibility, these pure concepts, as they cannot possibly be exhibited *in concreto,* are void of all meaning; consequently all these *noumena,* together with their

*[That is, the first part of the *Critique of Pure Reason,* establishing space and time as pure intuitions.—L.W.B.]

complex, the intelligible world,* are nothing but representation of a problem, of which the object in itself is possible but the solution, from the nature of our understanding, totally impossible. For our understanding is not a faculty of intuition, but of the connection of given intuitions in one experience. Experience must therefore contain all the objects for our concepts; but beyond it no concepts have any significance, 317
as there is no intuition that might offer them a foundation.

§ 35. The imagination may perhaps be forgiven for occasional vagaries and for not keeping carefully within the limits of experience, since it gains life and vigor by such flights and since it is always easier to moderate its boldness than to stimulate its languor. But the understanding which ought to *think* can never be forgiven for indulging in vagaries; for we depend upon it alone for assistance to set bounds, when necessary, to the vagaries of the imagination.

But the understanding begins its aberrations very innocently and modestly. It first brings to light the elementary cognitions which inhere in it prior to all experience, but which yet must always have their application in experience. It gradually drops these limits—and what is there to prevent it, as it has quite freely derived its principles from itself? It then proceeds first to newly imagined powers in nature, then to beings outside nature—in short, to a world for whose construction the materials cannot be wanting, because fertile fiction furnishes them abundantly, and though not confirmed it is never refuted by experience. This is the reason that young thinkers are so partial to metaphysics constructed in a truly dogmatic manner, and often sacrifice to it their time and their talents, which might be otherwise better employed.

But there is no use in trying to moderate these fruitless endeavors of pure reason by all manner of cautions as to the difficulties of solving questions so occult, by complaints of the limits of our reason, and by degrading our assertions into mere conjectures. For if their impossibility is not distinctly shown, and reason's knowledge of itself does not become a true science, in which the field of its right use is distinguished, so to say, with geometrical certainty from that of its worthless and idle use, these fruitless efforts will never be wholly abandoned.

§ 36. How is nature itself possible? This question—the highest point that tran- 318
scendental philosophy can ever reach, and to which, as its boundary and completion, it must proceed—really contains two questions.

First: How is nature in the material sense, that is, as to intuition, or considered as the totality of appearances, possible; how are space, time, and that which fills both—the object of sensation—possible generally? The answer is: By means of the constitution of our sensibility, according to which it is in its own way affected by objects which are in themselves unknown to it and totally distinct from those appearances. This answer is given in the *Critique* itself in the "Transcendental Aesthetic," and in these *Prolegomena* by the solution of the first general problem.

Secondly: How is nature possible in the formal sense, as the totality of the rules under which all appearances must come in order to be thought as connected in experience? The answer must be this: It is only possible by means of the constitution of our understanding, according to which all the above representations of the sensibility are necessarily referred to

*We speak of the "intelligible world," not (as the usual expression is) "intellectual world." For cognitions are intellectual through the understanding and refer to our world of sense also; but objects, in so far as they can be represented merely by the understanding, and to which none of our sensible intuitions can refer, are termed "intelligible." But as some possible intuition must correspond to every object, we would have to assume an understanding that intuits things immediately; but of such we have not the least notion, nor have we any notion of the *beings of the understanding* to which it should be applied.

a consciousness, and by which the peculiar way in which we think (namely, by rules) and hence experience also are possible, but must be clearly distinguished from an insight into the objects in themselves. This answer is given in the *Critique* itself in the "Transcendental Logic" and in these *Prolegomena,* in the course of the solution of the second main problem.

But how this peculiar property of our sensibility itself is possible, or that of our understanding and of the apperception which is necessarily its basis and that of all thinking, cannot be further analyzed or answered, because it is of them that we are in need for all our answers and for all our thinking about objects.

There are many laws of nature which we can know only by means of experience; but conformity to law in the connection of appearances, that is, in nature in general, we cannot
319 discover by any experience, because experience itself requires laws which are *a priori* at the basis of its possibility.

The possibility of experience in general is therefore at the same time the universal law of nature, and the principles of experience are the very laws of nature. For we know nature only as the totality of appearances, that is, of representations in us; and hence we can only derive the laws of their connection from the principles of their connection in us, that is, from the conditions of their necessary union in one consciousness which constitutes the possibility of experience.

Even the main proposition expounded throughout this section—that universal laws of nature can be known *a priori*—leads naturally to the proposition that the highest legislation of nature must lie in ourselves, that is, in our understanding; and that we must not seek the universal laws of nature in nature by means of experience, but conversely must seek nature, as to its universal conformity to law, in the conditions of the possibility of experience which lie in our sensibility and in our understanding. For how were it otherwise possible to know *a priori* these laws, as they are not rules of analytical knowledge but truly synthetical extensions of it?

Such a necessary agreement of the principles of possible experience with the laws of the possibility of nature can only proceed from one of two causes: either these laws are drawn from nature by means of experience, or conversely nature is derived from the laws of the possibility of experience in general and is quite the same as the mere universal conformity to law of the latter. The former is self-contradictory, for the universal laws of nature can and must be known *a priori* (that is, independently of all experience) and be the foundation of all empirical use of the understanding; the latter alternative therefore alone remains.*

320 But we must distinguish the empirical laws of nature, which always presuppose particular perceptions, from the pure or universal laws of nature, which, without being based on particular perceptions, contain merely the conditions of their necessary union in experience. In relation to the latter, nature and possible experience are quite the same; and as the conformity to law in the latter depends upon the necessary connection of appearances in experience (without which we cannot know any object whatever in the sensible world), consequently upon the original laws of the understanding, it seems at first strange, but is not the less certain, to say: *The understanding does not derive its laws* (a priori) *from, but prescribes them to, nature.*

§ 37. We shall illustrate this seemingly bold proposition by an example, which will show that laws which we discover in objects of sensuous intuition (especially when

*Crusius alone thought of a compromise: that a spirit, who can neither err nor deceive, implanted these laws in us originally. But since false principles often intrude themselves, as indeed the very system of this man shows in not a few instances, we are involved in difficulties as to the use of such a principle in the absence of sure criteria to distinguish the genuine origin from the spurious, since we never can know certainly what the spirit of truth or the father of lies may have instilled into us.

these laws are known as necessary) are commonly held by us to be such as have been placed there by the understanding, in spite of their being similar in all points to the laws of nature which we ascribe to experience.

§ 38. If we consider the properties of the circle, by which this figure combines in itself so many arbitrary determinations of space in a universal rule, we cannot avoid attributing a constitution to this geometrical thing. Two straight lines, for example, which intersect each other and the circle, howsoever they may be drawn, are always divided so that the rectangle constructed with the segments of the one is equal to that constructed with the segments of the other. The question now is: Does this law lie in the circle or in the 321
understanding? That is, does this figure, independently of the understanding, contain in itself the ground of the law; or does the understanding, having constructed according to its concepts (of the equality of the radii) the figure itself, introduce into it this law of the chords intersecting in geometrical proportion? When we follow the proofs of this law, we soon perceive that it can only be derived from the condition on which the understanding founds the construction of this figure, namely, the concept of the equality of the radii. But if we enlarge this concept to pursue further the unity of various properties of geometrical figures under common laws and consider the circle as a conic section, which of course is subject to the same fundamental conditions of construction as other conic sections, we shall find that all the chords which intersect within the ellipse, parabola, and hyperbola always intersect so that the rectangles of their segments are not indeed equal but always bear a constant ratio to one another. If we proceed still farther to the fundamental teachings of physical astronomy, we find a physical law of reciprocal attraction applicable to all material nature, the rule of which is that it decreases inversely as the square of the distance from each attracting point, that is, as the spherical surfaces increase over which this force spreads, which law seems to be necessarily inherent in the very nature of things, and hence is usually propounded as knowable *a priori.* Simple as the sources of this law are, merely resting upon the relation of spherical surfaces of different radii, its consequences are so valuable with regard to the variety and simplicity of their agreement that not only are all possible orbits of the celestial bodies conic sections, but such a relation of these orbits to one another results that no other law of attraction than that of the inverse square of the distance can be imagined as fit for a cosmical system.

Here accordingly is nature, which rests upon laws that the understanding knows *a priori,* and chiefly from the universal principles of the determination of space. Now I ask: Do the laws of nature lie in space, and does the understanding learn them by merely endeavoring to find out the enormous wealth of meaning that lies in space; or do they inhere in the understanding and in the way in which it determines space according to the conditions of the synthetical unity in which its concepts are all centered?

Space is something so uniform and as to all particular properties so indeterminate that we should certainly not seek a store of laws of nature in it. Whereas that which determines space to assume the form of a circle, or the figures of a cone and a sphere, is 322
the understanding, so far as it contains the ground of the unity of their constructions.

The mere universal form of intuition, called space, must therefore be the substratum of all intuitions determinable to particular objects; and in it, of course, the condition of the possibility and of the variety of these intuitions lies. But the unity of the objects is entirely determined by the understanding and on conditions which lie in its own nature; and thus the understanding is the origin of the universal order of nature, in that it comprehends all appearances under its own laws and thereby produces, in an *a priori* manner, experience (as to its form), by means of which whatever is to be known only by experience is necessarily subjected to its laws. For we are not concerned with the nature of things in themselves, which is independent of the conditions both of our sensibility and our understanding, but with nature as an object of possible experience; and in this case the understanding, since it makes experience possible, thereby insists that the sensuous world is either not an object of experience at all or that it is nature [namely, the existence of things determined according to universal laws].

APPENDIX TO THE PURE SCIENCE OF NATURE

§ 39. *Of the System of the Categories*. There can be nothing more desirable to a philosopher than to be able to derive the scattered multiplicity of the concepts or principles which had occurred to him in concrete use from a principle *a priori,* and to unite everything in this way in one cognition. He formerly only believed that those things which remained after a certain abstraction, and seemed by comparison among one another to constitute a particular kind of cognitions, were completely collected; but this was only an *aggregate.* Now he knows that just so many, neither more nor less, can constitute the kind of cognition, and perceives the necessity of his division. This constitutes comprehension; and only then has he attained a *system.*

To search in our common knowledge for the concepts which do not rest upon particular experience and yet occur in all knowledge from experience, of which they as
323 it were constitute the mere form of connection, presupposes neither greater reflection nor deeper insight than to detect in a language the rules of the actual use of words generally and thus to collect elements for a grammar (in fact both researches are very nearly related), even though we are not able to give a reason why each language has just this and no other formal constitution, and still less why any precise number of such formal determinations in general, neither more nor less, can be found in it.

Aristotle collected ten pure elementary concepts under the name of *categories.** To these, which are also called "predicaments," he found himself obliged afterward to add five post-predicaments,** some of which however (*prius, simul,* and *motus*) are contained in the former; but this rhapsody must be considered (and commended) as a mere hint for future inquirers, not as an idea developed according to rule; and hence it has, in the present more advanced state of philosophy, been rejected as quite useless.

After long reflection on the pure elements of human knowledge (those which contain nothing empirical), I at last succeeded in distinguishing with certainty and in separating the pure elementary notions of the sensibility (space and time) from those of the understanding. Thus the seventh, eighth, and ninth categories had to be excluded from the old list. And the others were of no service to me because there was no principle on which the understanding could be exhaustively investigated, and all the functions, whence its pure concepts arise, determined exhaustively and precisely.

But in order to discover such a principle, I looked about for an act of the understanding which comprises all the rest and is distinguished only by various modifications or phases, in reducing the multiplicity of representation to the unity of thinking in general. I found this act of the understanding to consist in judging. Here, then, the labors of the logicians were ready at hand, though not yet quite free from defects; and with this help I was enabled to exhibit a complete table of the pure functions of the

*1. *Substantia.* 2. *Qualitas.* 3. *Quantitas.* 4. *Relatio.* 5. *Actio.* 6. *Passio.* 7. *Quando.* 8. *Ubi.* 9. *Situs.* 10. *Habitus.*

***Oppositum. Prius. Simul. Motus. Habere.*

understanding, which are however undetermined with respect to any object. I finally 324 referred these functions of judging to objects in general, or rather to the condition of determining judgments as objectively valid; and so there arose the pure concepts of the understanding, concerning which I could make certain that these, and this exact number only, constitute our whole knowledge of things by pure understanding. I was justified in calling them by their old name "categories," while I reserved for myself the liberty of adding, under the title of "predicables," a complete list of all the concepts deducible from them by combinations, whether among themselves, or with the pure form of the appearance, that is, space or time, or with its matter, so far as it is not yet empirically determined (namely, the object of sensation in general), as soon as a system of transcendental philosophy should be completed, with the construction of which I was engaged in the *Critique of Pure Reason* itself.

Now the essential point in this system of categories, which distinguishes it from the old rhapsody which proceeded without any principle and for which alone it deserves to be considered as philosophy, consists in this: that, by means of it, the true significance of the pure concepts of the understanding and the condition of their use could be precisely determined. For here it became obvious that they are themselves nothing but logical functions, and as such do not produce the least concept of an object, but require sensuous intuition as a basis. These concepts, therefore, only serve to determine empirical judgments (which are otherwise undetermined and indifferent as regards all functions of judging) with respect to the functions of judging, thereby procuring them universal validity and, by means of them, making judgments of experience in general possible.

Such an insight into the nature of the categories, which limits them at the same time to use merely in experience, never occurred either to their first author or to any of his successors; but without this insight (which immediately depends upon their derivation or deduction), they are quite useless and only a miserable list of names, without explanation or rule for their use. Had the ancients ever conceived such a notion, doubtless the whole study of pure rational knowledge, which under the name of metaphysics has for centuries spoiled many a sound mind, would have reached us 325 in quite another shape and would have enlightened the human understanding, instead of actually exhausting it in obscure and vain speculations and rendering it unfit for true science.

This system of categories makes all treatment of every object of pure reason itself systematic, and affords a direction or clue how and through what points of inquiry every metaphysical consideration must proceed in order to be complete; for it exhausts all the possible functions of the understanding, among which every concept must be classed. In like manner the table of principles has been formulated, the completeness of which we can only vouch for by the system of the categories. Even in the division of the concepts,* which must go beyond the physical application of the understanding, it is always the very same clue, which, as it must always be determined *a priori* by the same fixed points of the human understanding, always forms a closed circle. There is no doubt that the object of a pure concept, either of the understanding or of reason, so far as it is to be estimated philosophically and on *a priori* principles, can in this way be completely known. I could not therefore omit to make use of this clue with regard to one of the most abstract ontological divisions, namely, the various distinctions of the

*Cf. the tables in the *Critique of Pure Reason* in the chapters on "The Paralogisms of Pure Reason" and the "System of Cosmological Ideas."

concepts of something and of nothing, and to construct accordingly* a systematic and necessary table of their divisions.**

326 And this system, like every other true one founded on a universal principle, shows its inestimable value in that it excludes all foreign concepts which might otherwise intrude among the pure concepts of the understanding, and determines the place of every cognition. Those concepts, which under the name of "concepts of reflection" have been likewise arranged in a table according to the clue of the categories, intrude into ontology without any privilege or just claim to be among the pure concepts of the understanding. The latter are concepts of connection, and thereby of the objects themselves, whereas the former are only concepts of mere comparison of concepts already given, and hence are of quite another nature and use. By my systematic division*** they are saved from this confusion. But the value of the special table of the categories will be still more obvious when we separate—as we are about to do—the table of the transcendental concepts of reason from the concepts of the understanding. As the transcendental concepts of reason are of an entirely different nature and origin, the table of them must have quite another form than the table of categories. This so necessary separation has never yet been made in any system of metaphysics, where, as a rule, these Ideas of reason are all mixed up with the concepts of the understanding, as if they were children of the same family—a confusion which was unavoidable in the absence of a definite system of categories.

327 THIRD PART OF THE MAIN TRANSCENDENTAL PROBLEM

HOW IS METAPHYSICS IN GENERAL POSSIBLE?

§ 40. Pure mathematics and pure science of nature had, for their own safety and certainty, no need for such a deduction as we have made of both. For the former rests upon its own evidence, and the latter (though sprung from pure sources of the understanding) upon experience and its thorough confirmation. The pure science of nature cannot altogether refuse and dispense with the testimony of experience; because with all its certainty it can never, as philosophy, rival mathematics. Both sciences, therefore, stood in need of this inquiry, not for themselves, but for the sake of another science: metaphysics.

*In the chapter on "The Amphiboly of the Concepts of Reflection," in the *Critique of Pure Reason.*

**On the table of the categories many neat observations may be made, for instance: (1) that the third arises from the first and the second, joined in one concept; (2) that in those of quantity and of quality there is merely a progress from unity to totality or from something to nothing (for this purpose the categories of quality must stand thus: reality, limitation, total negation), without *correlata* or *opposita,* whereas those of relation and of modality have them; (3) that, as in logic categorical judgments are the basis of all others, so the category of substance is the basis of all concepts of actual things; (4) that, as modality in the judgment is not a particular predicate, so by the modal concepts a determination is not superadded to things, etc. Such observations are of great use. If we enumerate all the predicables, which we can find pretty completely in any good ontology (for example, Baumgarten's), and arrange them in classes under the categories, in which operation we must not neglect to add as complete a dissection of all these concepts as possible, there will then arise a merely analytical part of metaphysics which does not contain a single synthetical proposition, which might precede the second (the synthetical) and would, by its precision and completeness, be not only useful but, in virtue of its system, be even to some extent elegant.

***See *Critique of Pure Reason,* "The Amphiboly of the Concepts of Reflection."

Metaphysics has to do not only with concepts of nature, which always find their application in experience, but also with pure rational concepts, which never can be given in any possible experience whatever. Consequently it deals with concepts whose objective reality (namely, that they are not mere chimeras) and with assertions whose truth or falsity cannot be discovered or confirmed by any experience. This part of metaphysics, however, is precisely what constitutes its essential end, to which the rest is only a means, and thus this science is in need of such a deduction for its own sake. The third question now proposed relates therefore as it were to the root and peculiarity of metaphysics, that is, the occupation of reason merely with itself and the supposed knowledge of objects arising immediately from this brooding over its own concepts, without requiring, or indeed being able to reach that knowledge through, experience.*

Without solving this problem, reason can never satisfy itself. The empirical use to which reason limits the pure understanding does not fully satisfy the proper calling of 328
reason. Every single experience is only a part of the whole sphere of its domain, but the absolute totality of all possible experience is itself not experience. Yet it is a necessary problem for reason, the mere representation of which requires concepts quite different from the pure concepts of the understanding, whose use is only *immanent,* or refers to experience, so far as it can be given. Whereas the concepts of reason aim at the completeness, that is, the collective unity of all possible experience, and thereby transcend every given experience. Thus they become *transcendent.*

As the understanding stands in need of categories for experience, reason contains in itself the source of Ideas, by which I mean necessary concepts whose object *cannot* be given in any experience. The latter are inherent in the nature of reason, as the former are in that of the understanding. While the former carry with them an illusion likely to mislead, the illusion of the latter is inevitable, though it certainly can be kept from misleading us.

Since all illusion consists in holding the subjective ground of our judgments to be objective, a self-knowledge of pure reason in its transcendent (presumptuous) use is the sole preservative from the aberrations into which reason falls when it mistakes its calling and transcendently refers to the object that which concerns only its own subject and its guidance in all immanent use.

§ 41. The distinction of Ideas—that is, of pure concepts of reason—from categories, or pure concepts of the understanding, as cognitions of a quite distinct species, origin, and use, is so important a point in founding a science which is to contain the system of all these *a priori* cognitions that, without this distinction, metaphysics is 329
absolutely impossible or is at best a random, bungling attempt to build a castle in the air without a knowledge of the materials or of their fitness for this or any purpose. Had the *Critique of Pure Reason* done nothing but first point out this distinction, it would thereby have contributed more to clear up our conception of, and to guide our inquiry in, the field of metaphysics than all the vain efforts which had hitherto been made to satisfy the transcendent problems of pure reason, but which had never surmised that we were in quite another field than that of the understanding, and hence classed concepts of the understanding and those of reason together as if they were of the same kind.

§ 42. All pure cognitions of the understanding have this feature that their concepts present themselves in experience, and their principles can be confirmed by it; whereas

*If we can say that a science is actual, at least in the idea of all men, as soon as it appears that the problems which lead to it are proposed to everybody by the nature of human reason, and that therefore many (though faulty) endeavors are unavoidably made in its behalf, then we are bound to say that metaphysics is subjectively (and indeed necessarily) actual, and therefore, we justly ask, how is it (objectively) possible.

the transcendent cognitions of reason cannot either, as Ideas, appear in experience or, as propositions, ever be confirmed or refuted by it. Hence whatever errors may slip in unawares can only be discovered by pure reason itself—a discovery of much difficulty, because this very reason naturally becomes dialectical by means of its Ideas; and this unavoidable illusion cannot be limited by any objective and dogmatic researches into things, but only by a subjective investigation of reason itself as a source of ideas.

§ 43. In the *Critique of Pure Reason* it was always my greatest care to endeavor, not only carefully to distinguish the several species of knowledge, but to derive concepts belonging to each one of them from their common source. I did this in order that, by knowing whence they originated, I might determine their use with safety and also have the unanticipated but invaluable advantage of knowing, according to principles, the completeness of my enumeration, classification, and specification of concepts *a priori.*
330 Without this, metaphysics is mere rhapsody, in which no one knows whether he has enough or whether and where something is still wanting. We can indeed have this advantage only in pure philosophy, but of this philosophy it constitutes the very essence.

As I had found the origin of the categories in the four logical forms of all the judgments of the understanding, it was quite natural to seek the origin of the Ideas in the three forms of syllogisms. For as soon as these pure concepts of reason (the transcendental Ideas) are given, they could hardly, except they be held innate, be found anywhere else than in the same activity of reason, which, so far as it regards mere form, constitutes the logical element of syllogisms; but, so far as it represents judgments of the understanding as determined *a priori* with respect to one or another form, constitutes transcendental concepts of pure reason.

The formal distinction of syllogisms renders necessary their division into categorical, hypothetical, and disjunctive. The concepts of reason founded on them contain therefore, first, the Idea of the complete subject (the substantial); secondly, the Idea of the complete series of conditions; thirdly, the determination of all concepts in the Idea of a complete complex of that which is possible.* The first idea is psychological, the second cosmological, the third theological; and, as all three give occasion to dialectic, yet each in its own way, the division of the whole dialectic of pure reason into its paralogism, its antinomy, and its Ideal was arranged accordingly. Through this deduction we may feel assured that all the claims of pure reason are completely represented and that none can be wanting, because the faculty of reason itself, whence they all take their origin, is thereby completely surveyed.

331 § 44. In these general considerations it is also remarkable that the Ideas of reason, unlike the categories, are of no service to the use of our understanding in experience, but quite dispensable, and become even an impediment to the maxims of a rational knowledge of nature. Yet in another aspect still to be determined they are necessary. Whether the soul is or is not a simple substance is of no consequence to us in the explanation of its phenomena. For we cannot render the concept of a simple being sensuous and thus concretely intelligible by any possible experience. The concept is therefore

*In disjunctive judgments, we consider all possibility as divided in respect to a particular concept. By the ontological principle of the universal determination of a thing in general, I understand the principle that either the one or the other of all possible contradictory predicates must be assigned to any object. This is, at the same time, the principle of all disjunctive judgments, constituting the foundation of a complete whole of possibility, and in it the possibility of every object in general is considered as determined. This may serve as a slight explanation of the above propositions: that the activity of reason in disjunctive syllogisms is formally the same as that by which it fashions the idea of a complete whole of all reality, containing in itself that which is positive in all pairs of contradictory predicates.

quite void as regards all hoped-for insight into the cause of appearances and cannot at all serve as a principle of the explanation of that which inner or outer experience supplies. Similarly, the cosmological Ideas of the beginning of the world or of its eternity (*a parte ante*) cannot be of any service to us for the explanation of any event in the world itself. And finally we must, according to a right maxim of the philosophy of nature, refrain from explaining the design of nature as drawn from the will of a Supreme Being, because this would not be natural philosophy but a confession that we have come to the end of it. The use of these Ideas, therefore, is quite different from that of those categories by which (and by the principles built upon which) experience itself first becomes possible. But our laborious Analytic of the understanding would be superfluous if we had nothing else in view than the mere knowledge of nature as it can be given in experience; for reason does its work, both in mathematics and in the science of nature, quite safely and well without any of this subtle deduction. Therefore our critical examination of the understanding combines with the Ideas of pure reason for a purpose which lies beyond the empirical use of the understanding; but such an extended use of the understanding we have above declared to be totally inadmissible and without any object or meaning. Yet there must be a harmony between the nature of reason and that of the understanding, and the former must contribute to the perfection of the latter and cannot possibly upset it.

The solution of this question is as follows: Pure reason does not in its Ideas 332
point to particular objects which lie beyond the field of experience, but only requires completeness of the use of the understanding in the system of experience. But this completeness can be a completeness of principles only, not of intuitions and of objects. In order, however, to represent the Ideas definitely, reason conceives them after the fashion of the knowledge of an object. This knowledge is, as far as these rules are concerned, completely determined; but the object is only an Idea [invented for the purpose of] bringing the knowledge of the understanding as near as possible to the completeness indicated by that Idea.

PREFATORY REMARK TO THE DIALECTIC OF PURE REASON

§ 45. We have shown in §§ 33 and 34 that the purity of the categories from all admixture of sensuous restrictions may mislead reason into extending their use beyond all experience to things in themselves; for though these categories themselves find no intuition which can give them meaning or sense *in concreto,* they, as mere logical functions, can represent a thing in general, but not give by themselves alone a determinate concept of anything. Such hyperbolical objects are distinguished by the appellation of *noumena,* or pure beings of the understanding (or better, beings of thought)—such as, for example, "substance"—but conceived without permanence in time, or "cause," but not acting in time, etc. Here predicates that only serve to make the conformity-to-law of experience possible are applied to these concepts, and yet they are deprived of all the conditions of intuition on which alone experience is possible, and so these concepts lose all significance.

There is no danger, however, of the understanding spontaneously making an excursion so very wantonly beyond its own bounds into the field of the mere beings of thought unless it is impelled by foreign laws. But when reason, which cannot be fully

satisfied with any empirical use of the rules of the understanding, as being always conditioned, requires a completion of this chain of conditions, then the understanding is forced out of its sphere. And then it partly represents objects of experience in a series so
333 extended that no experience can grasp it; partly even (with a view to complete the series) it seeks entirely beyond it *noumena,* to which it can attach that chain; and so, having at last escaped from the conditions of experience, it makes its stand as it were final. These are then the transcendental Ideas, which, in accord with the true but hidden ends of the natural destiny of our reason, aim, not at extravagant concepts, but at an unbounded extension of their empirical use, yet seduce the understanding by an unavoidable illusion to a transcendent use, which, though deceitful, cannot be restrained within the bounds of experience by any resolution, but only by scientific instruction and with much difficulty.

I. THE PSYCHOLOGICAL IDEAS*

§ 46. People have long since observed that in all substances the subject proper, that which remains after all the accidents (as predicates) are abstracted, consequently the *substantial,* remains unknown, and various complaints have been made concerning these limits to our knowledge. But it will be well to consider that the human understanding is not to be blamed for its inability to know the substance of things—that is, to determine it by itself—but rather for demanding definitely to know substance, which is a mere Idea, as though it were a given object. Pure reason requires us to seek for every predicate of a thing its own subject, and for this subject, which is itself necessarily nothing but a predicate, its subject, and so on indefinitely (or as far as we can reach). But hence it follows that we must not hold anything at which we can arrive to be an ultimate subject, and that substance itself never can be thought by our understanding, however deep we may penetrate, even if all nature were unveiled to us. For the specific nature of our understanding consists in thinking everything discursively, that is, by
334 concepts, and so by mere predicates, to which, therefore, the absolute subject must always be wanting. Hence all the real properties by which we know bodies are mere accidents—not excepting even impenetrability, which we can only represent to ourselves as the effect of a power of which the subject is unknown to us.

Now we appear to have this substance in the consciousness of ourselves (in the thinking subject), and indeed in an immediate intuition; for all the predicates of an internal sense refer to the *ego,* as a subject, and I cannot conceive myself as the predicate of any other subject. Hence completeness in the reference of the given concepts as predicates to a subject—not merely an Idea, but an object—that is, the absolute subject itself, seems to be given in experience. But this expectation is disappointed. For the ego is not a concept,** but only the indication of the object of the inner sense, so far as we know it by no further predicate. Consequently it cannot indeed be itself a predicate of any other thing; but just as little can it be a definite concept of an absolute subject, but is, as in all other cases, only the reference of the inner phenomena to their unknown subject. Yet this idea (which serves very well as a regulative principle totally to destroy

*See *Critique of Pure Reason,* "The Paralogisms of Pure Reason."

**Were the representation of the apperception (the Ego) a concept, by which anything whatever could be thought, it could be used as a predicate of other things or contain predicates in itself. But it is nothing more than the feeling of an existence without the least concept and is only the representation of that to which all thinking stands in relation (*relatione accidentis*).

all materialistic explanations of the internal phenomena of the soul) occasions by a very natural misunderstanding a very specious argument, which infers its nature from this supposed knowledge of the substance of our thinking being. This is specious so far as the knowledge of it falls quite without the complex of experience.

§ 47. But though we may call this thinking self (the soul) "substance," as being the ultimate subject of thinking which cannot be further represented as the predicate of another thing, it remains quite empty and without significance if permanence—the quality which renders the concept of substances in experience fruitful—cannot be proved of it.

But permanence can never be proved of the concept of a substance as a thing in 335
itself, but for the purposes of experience only. This is sufficiently shown by the first Analogy of Experience,* and whoever will not yield to this proof may try for himself whether he can succeed in proving, from the concept of a subject which does not exist itself as the predicate of another thing, that its existence is absolutely permanent and that it cannot either in itself or by any natural cause originate or be annihilated. These synthetical *a priori* propositions can never be proved in themselves, but only in reference to things as objects of possible experience.

§ 48. If, therefore, from the concept of the soul as a substance we would infer its permanence, this can hold good as regards possible experience only, not of the soul as a thing in itself and beyond all possible experience. Life is the subjective condition of all our possible experience; consequently we can only infer the permanence of the soul in life, for the death of a man is the end of all experience which concerns the soul as an object of experience, except the contrary be proved—which is the very question in hand. The permanence of the soul can therefore only be proved (and no one cares to do that) during the life of man, but not, as we desire to do, after death. The reason for this is that the concept of substance, so far as it is to be considered necessarily combined with the concept of permanence, can be so combined only according to the principles of possible experience, and therefore for the purposes of experience only.**

§ 49. That there is something real outside us which not only corresponds but must 336
correspond to our outer perceptions can likewise be proved to be, not a connection of things in themselves, but for the sake of experience. This means that there is something empirical, that is, some appearance in space without us, that admits of a satisfactory proof; for we have nothing to do with other objects than those which belong to possible experience, because objects which cannot be given us in any experience are nothing for us. Empirically outside me is that which is intuited in space; and space, together with all

*In the *Critique of Pure Reason.*

**It is indeed very remarkable how carelessly metaphysicians have always passed over the principle of the permanence of substances without ever attempting a proof of it; doubtless because they found themselves abandoned by all proofs as soon as they began to deal with the concept of substance. Common sense, which felt distinctly that without this presupposition no union of perceptions in experience is possible, supplied the want by a postulate. From experience itself it never could derive such a principle, partly because material things (substances) cannot be so traced in all their alterations and dissolutions that the matter can always be found undiminished, partly because the principle contains *necessity,* which is always the sign of an *a priori* principle. People then boldly applied this postulate to the concept of soul as a *substance,* and concluded a necessary continuance of the soul after the death of man (especially as the simplicity of this substance, which is inferred from the indivisibility of consciousness, secured it from destruction by dissolution). Had they found the genuine source of this principle—a discovery which requires deeper researches than they were ever inclined to make—they would have seen that the law of the permanence of substances arises for the purposes of experience only, and hence can hold good of things so far as they are to be known and conjoined with others in experience, but never independently of all possible experience, and consequently cannot hold good of the soul after death.

the appearances it contains, belongs to the representations whose connection, according to laws of experience, proves their objective truth, just as the connection of the appearances of the inner sense proves the actuality of my soul (as an object of the inner sense). By means of outer experience I am conscious of the actuality of bodies as external appearances in space, in the same manner as by means of the inner experience I am conscious of the existence of my soul in time; but this soul is known only as an object of the inner sense by appearances that constitute an inner state and of which the being in itself, which forms the basis of these appearances, is unknown. Cartesian idealism therefore does nothing but distinguish outer experience from a dream and the confor-
337 mity to law (as a criterion of its truth) of the former from the irregularity and false illusion of the latter. In both it presupposes space and time as conditions of the existence of objects, and it only inquires whether the objects of the outer senses which we, when awake, put in space, are as actually to be found in it as the object of the internal sense, the soul, is in time; that is, whether experience carries with it sure criteria to distinguish it from imagination. This doubt, however, may easily be disposed of, and we always do so in common life by investigating the connection of appearances in both space and time according to universal laws of experience, and we cannot doubt, when the representation of external things throughout agrees therewith that they constitute truthful experience. Material idealism, in which appearances are considered as such only according to their connection in experience may accordingly be very easily refuted; and it is just as sure an experience that bodies exist outside us (in space) as that I myself exist according to the representation of the inner sense (in time), for the concept "outside us" only signifies existence in space. However, as the Ego in the proposition "I am" means not only the object of inner intuition (in time) but the subject of consciousness, just as body means not only outer intuition (in space) but the thing in itself which is the basis of this appearance, then the question whether bodies (as appearances of the outer sense) exist as bodies in nature apart from my thoughts may without any hesitation be denied. But the question whether I myself as an appearance of the inner sense (the soul according to empirical psychology) exist apart from my faculty of representation in time is an exactly similar one and must likewise be answered in the negative. And in this manner everything, when it is reduced to its true meaning, is decided and certain. The formal (which I have also called "transcendental") actually abolishes the material, or Cartesian, idealism. For if space be nothing but a form of my sensibility, it is as a representation in me just as actual as I myself am, and nothing but the empirical truth of the appearances in it remains for consideration. But if this is not the case, if space and the appearances in it are something existing outside us, then all the criteria of experience besides our perception can never prove the actuality of these objects outside us.

338 II. THE COSMOLOGICAL IDEAS*

§ 50. This product of pure reason in its transcendent use is its most remarkable phenomenon. It serves as a very powerful agent to rouse philosophy from its dogmatic slumber and to stimulate it to the arduous task of undertaking a critical examination of reason itself.

I term this Idea cosmological because it always takes its object only in the sensible world and does not need any other world than one whose object is given to sense; consequently it remains in this respect in its native home, does not become transcendent, and is therefore so far not an Idea; whereas to conceive the soul as a simple

*Cf. *Critique of Pure Reason,* "The Antinomy of Pure Reason."

substance, on the contrary, means to conceive such an object (the simple) as cannot be presented to the senses. Yet, in spite of this, the cosmological idea extends the connection of the conditioned with its condition (whether this is mathematical or dynamical) so far that experience never can keep up with it. It is therefore with regard to this point always an Idea, whose object never can be adequately given in any experience.

§ 51. In the first place, the use of a system of categories becomes here so obvious and unmistakable that, even if there were not several other proofs of it, this alone would sufficiently prove it indispensable in the system of pure reason. There are only four such transcendent Ideas, as many as there are classes of categories; in each of which, however, they refer only to the absolute completeness of the series of the conditions for a given conditioned. In accordance with these cosmological Ideas, there are only four kinds of dialectical assertions of pure reason, which, being dialectical, prove that to each of them, on equally specious principles of pure reason, a contradictory assertion stands opposed. As all the metaphysical art of the most subtle distinction cannot prevent this opposition, it 339
compels the philosopher to recur to the first sources of pure reason itself. This antinomy, not arbitrarily invented but founded in the nature of human reason, and hence unavoidable and never ceasing, contains the following four theses together with their antitheses:

1

Thesis

The world has, as to time and space, a beginning (limit).

Antithesis

The world is, as to time and space, infinite.

2

Thesis

Everything in the world consists of [elements that are] simple.

Antithesis

There is nothing simple, but everything is composite.

3

Thesis

There are in the world causes through freedom.

Antithesis

There is no freedom, but all is nature.

4

Thesis

In the series of the world-causes there is some necessary being.

Antithesis

There is nothing necessary in the world, but in this series all is contingent.

§ 52*a.* Here is the most singular phenomenon of human reason, no other instance of which can be shown in any other use of reason. If we, as is commonly done, represent to ourselves the appearances of the sensible world as things in themselves, if we assume the principles of their combination as principles universally valid of things in themselves and not merely of experience, as is usually, nay, without our *Critique* unavoidably, done, there arises an unexpected conflict which never can be removed in the common dogmatic way; because the thesis, as well as the antithesis, can be shown by equally clear, evident, and irresistible proofs—for I pledge myself as to the correctness of all these proofs—and reason therefore perceives that it is divided against itself, a state at which the skeptic rejoices, but which must make the critical philosopher pause and feel ill at ease.

340 § 52*b.* We may blunder in various ways in metaphysics without any fear of being detected in falsehood. If we but avoid self-contradiction, which in synthetical though purely fictitious propositions is quite possible, then whenever the concepts which we connect are mere Ideas that cannot be given (with respect to their whole content) in experience, we cannot be refuted by experience. For how can we make out by experience whether the world is from eternity or had a beginning, whether matter is infinitely divisible or consists of simple parts? Such concepts cannot be given in any experience, however extensive, and consequently the falsehood either of the affirmative or the negative proposition cannot be discovered by this touchstone.

The only possible way in which reason could have revealed unintentionally its secret dialectic, falsely announced as its dogmatics, would be when it were made to ground an assertion upon a universally admitted principle and to deduce the exact contrary with the greatest accuracy of inference from another which is equally granted. This is actually here the case with regard to four natural Ideas of reason, whence four assertions on the one side and as many counterassertions on the other arise, each consistently following from universally acknowledged principles. Thus they reveal, by the use of these principles, the dialectical illusion of pure reason, which would otherwise forever remain concealed.

This is therefore a decisive experiment, which must necessarily expose any error
341 lying hidden in the assumptions of reason.* Contradictory propositions cannot both be false, except the concept on which each is founded is self-contradictory; for example, the propositions, "A square circle is round," and "A square circle is not round," are both false. For, as to the former, it is false that the circle is round because it is quadrangular; and it is likewise false that it is not round, that is, angular, because it is a circle. For the logical criterion of the impossibility of a concept consists in this that, if we presuppose it, two contradictory propositions both become false; consequently, as no middle between them is conceivable, nothing at all is thought by that concept.

§ 52*c.* The first two antinomies, which I call mathematical because they are concerned with the addition or division of the homogeneous, are founded on such a contradictory concept; and hence I explain how it happens that both the thesis and antithesis of the two are false.

When I speak of objects in time and in space, it is not of things in themselves, of which I know nothing, but of things in appearance, that is, of experience, as the particular way of knowing objects which is afforded to man. I must not say of what I think in time or in space, that in itself, and independent of these my thoughts, it exists in space and in time, for in that case I should contradict myself; because space and time, together
342 with the appearances in them, are nothing existing in themselves and outside of my representations, but are themselves only modes of representation, and it is palpably contradictory to say that a mere mode of representation exists without our representation.

*I therefore would be pleased to have the critical reader to devote to this antinomy of pure reason his chief attention, because nature itself seems to have established it with a view to stagger reason in its daring pretensions and to force it to self-examination. For every proof which I have given of both thesis and antithesis I undertake to be responsible, and thereby to show the certainty of the inevitable antinomy of reason. When the reader is brought by this curious phenomenon to fall back upon the proof of the presumption upon which it rests, he will feel himself obliged to investigate the ultimate foundation of all knowledge by pure reason with me more thoroughly.

Objects of the senses therefore exist only in experience, whereas to give them a self-subsisting existence apart from experience or before it is merely to represent to ourselves that experience actually exists apart from experience or before it.

Now if I inquire into the magnitude of the world, as to space and time, it is equally impossible, as regards all my concepts, to declare it infinite or to declare it finite. For neither assertion can be contained in experience, because experience either of an infinite space or of an infinite elapsed time, or again, of the boundary of the world by a void space or by an antecedent void time, is impossible; these are mere Ideas. The magnitude of the world, decided either way, would therefore have to exist in the world itself apart from all experience. But this contradicts the concept of a world of sense, which is merely a complex of the appearances whose existence and connection occur only in our representations, that is, in experience; since this latter is not an object in itself but a mere mode of representation. Hence it follows that, as the concept of an absolutely existing world of sense is self-contradictory, the solution of the problem concerning its magnitude, whether attempted affirmatively or negatively, is always false.

The same holds of the second antinomy, which relates to the division of appearances. For these are mere representations; and the parts exist merely in their representation, consequently in the division—that is, in a possible experience in which they are given—and the division reaches only as far as the possible experience reaches. To assume that an appearance, for example, that of body, contains in itself before all experience all the parts which any possible experience can ever reach is to impute to a mere appearance, which can exist only in experience, an existence previous to experience. In other words, it would mean that mere representations exist before they can be found in our faculty of representation. Such an assertion is self-contradictory, as also every solution of our misunderstood problem, whether we maintain that bodies in themselves consist of an infinite number of parts or of a finite number of simple parts.

§ 53. In the first (the mathematical) class of antinomies the falsehood of the 343
presupposition consists in representing in one concept something self-contradictory as if it were compatible (that is, an appearance as a thing in itself). But, as to the second (the dynamical) class of antinomies, the falsehood of the presupposition consists in representing as contradictory what is compatible; so that while in the former case the opposed assertions were both false, in this case, on the other hand, where they are opposed to one another by mere misunderstanding, they may both be true.

Any mathematical connection necessarily presupposes homogeneity of what is connected (in the concept of magnitude), while the dynamical one by no means requires this. When we have to deal with extended magnitudes all the parts must be homogeneous with one another and with the whole, whereas in the connection of cause and effect homogeneity may indeed likewise be found but is not necessary; for the concept of causality (by means of which something is posited through something else quite different from it) does not in the least require it.

If the objects of the world of sense are taken for things in themselves and the above laws of nature for laws of things in themselves, the contradiction would be unavoidable. So also, if the subject of freedom were, like other objects, represented as mere appearance, the contradiction would be just as unavoidable; for the same predicate would at once be affirmed and denied of the same kind of object in the same sense. But if natural necessity is referred merely to appearances and freedom merely to things in themselves, no contradiction arises if we at the same time assume or admit both kinds of causality, however difficult or impossible it may be to make the latter kind conceivable.

In appearance every effect is an event, or something that happens in time; it must, according to the universal law of nature, be preceded by a determination of the causal

act of its cause—this determination being a state of the cause—which it follows according to a constant law. But this determination of the cause to a causal act must likewise be something that takes place or happens; the cause must have begun to act, otherwise
344 no succession between it and the effect could be conceived. Otherwise the effect, as well as the causal act of the cause, would have always existed. Therefore the determination of the cause to act must also have originated among appearances and must consequently, like its effect, be an event, which must again have its cause, and so on; hence natural necessity must be the condition on which efficient causes are determined. Whereas if freedom is to be a property of certain causes of appearances, it must, as regards these, which are events, be a faculty of starting them spontaneously. That is, it would not require that the causal act of the cause should itself begin [in time], and hence it would not require any other ground to determine its start. But then the cause, as to its causal act, could not rank under time-determinations of its state; that is, it could not be an appearance, but would have to be considered a thing in itself, while only its effects would be appearances.* If without contradiction we can think of the beings of understanding as exercising such an influence on appearances, then natural necessity will attach to all connections of cause and effect in the sensuous world; though, on the other hand, freedom can be granted to the cause which is itself not an appearance (but the foundation of appearance). Nature and freedom therefore can without contradiction be attributed to the very same thing, but in different relations—on one side as an appearance, on the other as a thing in itself.

We have in us a faculty which not only stands in connection with its subjective
345 determining grounds [motives] which are the natural causes of its actions and is so far the faculty of a being that itself belongs to appearances, but is also related to objective grounds which are only Ideas so far as they can determine this faculty. This connection is expressed by the word *ought.* This faculty is called "reason," and, so far as we consider a being (man) entirely according to this objectively determinable reason, he cannot be considered as a being of sense; this property is a property of a thing in itself, a property whose possibility we cannot comprehend. I mean we cannot comprehend how the *ought* should determine (even if it never has actually determined) its activity and could become the cause of actions whose effect is an appearance in the sensible world. Yet the causality of reason would be freedom with regard to the effects in the sensuous world, so far as we can consider *objective grounds,* which are themselves Ideas, as their determinants. For its action in that case would not depend upon subjective conditions, consequently not upon those of time, and of course not upon the law of nature which serves to determine them, because grounds of reason give the rule universally to actions, according to principles, without influence of the circumstances of either time or place.

*The Idea of freedom occurs only in the relation of the intellectual, as cause, to the appearance, as effect. Hence we cannot attribute freedom to matter in regard to the incessant action by which it fills its space, though this action takes place from an internal principle. We can likewise find no notion of freedom suitable to purely rational beings, for instance, to God, so far as his action is immanent. For his action, though independent of external determining causes, is determined in his eternal reason, that is, in the divine *nature.* It is only if *something is to start* by an action, and so the effect occurs in the sequence of time, or in the world of sense (for example, the beginning of the world), that we can put the question whether the causal act of the cause must in its turn have been started or whether the cause can originate an effect without its causal act itself beginning. In the former case, the concept of this activity is a concept of natural necessity; in the latter, that of freedom. From this the reader will see that as I explained freedom to be the faculty of starting an event spontaneously, I have exactly hit the concept which is the problem of metaphysics.

What I adduce here is merely meant as an example to make the thing intelligible and does not necessarily belong to our problem, which must be decided from mere concepts independently of the properties which we meet in the actual world.

Now I may say without contradiction that all the actions of rational beings, so far as they are appearances (met with in any experience), are subject to the necessity of nature, but the very same actions, as regards merely the rational subject and its faculty of acting according to mere reason, are free. For what is required for the necessity of nature? Nothing more than the determinability of every event in the world of sense according to constant laws, that is, a reference to cause in the [world of] appearance; in this process the thing in itself at its foundation and its causality remain unknown. But, I say, the law of nature remains, whether the rational being is the cause of the effects in the sensuous world from reason—that is, through freedom—or whether it does not determine them on grounds of reason. For if the former is the case, the action is performed according to maxims, the
effect of which as appearance is always conformable to constant laws; if the latter is the 346
case, and the action not performed on principles of reason, it is subjected to the empirical laws of the sensibility, and in both cases the effects are connected according to constant laws; more than this we do not require or know concerning natural necessity. But in the former case reason is the cause of these laws of nature, and therefore free; in the latter, the effects follow according to mere natural laws of sensibility, because reason does not influence it. But reason itself is not determined on that account by the sensibility (which is impossible) and is therefore free in this case too. Freedom is therefore no hindrance to natural law in appearances; neither does this law abrogate the freedom of the practical use of reason, which is connected with things in themselves, as determining grounds.

Thus practical freedom, namely, the freedom in which reason possesses causality according to objectively determining grounds, is rescued; and yet natural necessity is not in the least curtailed with regard to the very same effects, as appearances. The same remarks will serve to explain what we had to say concerning transcendental freedom and its compatibility with natural necessity in the same subject, but not taken in the same context. For, as to this, every beginning of the action of a being from objective causes regarded as determining grounds is always a *first beginning,* though the same action is in the series of appearances only a *subordinate beginning,* which must be preceded by a state of the cause which determines it and is itself determined in the same manner by another immediately preceding. Thus we are able, in rational beings, or in beings generally so far as their causality is determined in them as things in themselves, to think of a faculty of beginning from themselves a series of states without falling into contradiction with the laws of nature. For the relation of the action to objective grounds of reason is not a time relation; in this case that which determines the causality does not precede in time the action, because such determining grounds represent, not a reference to objects of sense, for example, to causes in the appearances, but to determining causes as things in themselves, which do not fall under conditions of time. And in this way the action, with regard to the causality of reason, can be considered as a first beginning, while in respect to the series of appearances as merely a subordinate beginning. We may
therefore without contradiction consider it in the former aspect as free, but in the latter 347
(as it is merely appearance) as subject to natural necessity.

As to the fourth antinomy, it is solved in the same way as the conflict of reason with itself in the third. For, provided the cause *in* the appearance is distinguished from the cause *of* the appearances (so far as it can be thought as a thing in itself), both propositions are perfectly reconcilable: the one, that there is nowhere in the sensuous world a cause (according to similar laws of causality) whose existence is absolutely necessary; the other, that this world is nevertheless connected with a necessary being as its cause (but of another kind and according to another law). The incompatibility of these propositions rests entirely upon the mistake of extending what is valid merely of appearances to things in themselves and in confusing both in one concept.

§ 54. This, then, is the exposition, and this the solution of the whole antinomy in which reason finds itself involved in the application of its principles to the sensible world. The former alone (the mere exposition) would be a considerable service in the cause of our knowledge of human reason, even though the solution might fail fully to satisfy the reader, who has here to combat a natural illusion which has been but recently exposed to him and which he had hitherto always regarded as genuine. For one result at least is unavoidable. As it is quite impossible to prevent this conflict of reason with itself—so long as the objects of the sensible world are taken for things in themselves and not for mere appearances, which they are in fact—the reader is thereby compelled to examine over again the deduction of all our *a priori* knowledge and the proof which I have given of my deduction in order to come to a decision on the question. This is all I require at present; for when in this occupation he shall have thought himself deep enough into the nature of pure reason, those concepts by which alone the solution of the
348 conflict of reason is possible will become sufficiently familiar to him. Without this preparation, I cannot expect an unreserved assent even from the most attentive reader.

III. THE THEOLOGICAL IDEA*

§ 55. The third transcendental Idea, which affords matter for the most important but (if pursued only speculatively) transcendent and thereby dialectical use of reason, is the Ideal of pure reason. Reason in this case does not, as with the psychological and the cosmological Ideas, begin from experience and err by exaggerating its grounds in striving to attain, if possible, the absolute completeness of their series. Rather, it totally breaks with experience and from mere concepts of what constitutes the absolute completeness of a thing in general; and thus, by means of the Idea of a most perfect primal Being, it proceeds to determine the possibility and therefore the actuality of all other things. And so the mere presupposition of a Being conceived, not in the series of experience yet for the purposes of experience, for the sake of comprehending its connection, order, and unity—in a word, the Idea—is more easily distinguished from the concept of the understanding here than in the former cases. Hence we can easily expose the dialectical illusion which arises from our making the subjective conditions of our thinking objective conditions of objects themselves, and from making an hypothesis necessary for the satisfaction of our reason into a dogma. As the observations of the *Critique* on the pretensions of transcendental theology are intelligible, clear, and decisive, I have nothing more to add on the subject.

General Remark on the Transcendental Ideas

§ 56. The objects which are given us by experience are in many respects
349 incomprehensible, and many questions to which the law of nature leads us when carried beyond a certain point (though still quite conformably to the laws of nature) admit of no answer. An example is the question: Why do material things attract one another? But if we entirely quit nature or, in pursuing its combinations, exceed all possible experience, and so enter the realm of mere Ideas, we cannot then say that the object is incomprehensible and

*Cf. *Critique of Pure Reason,* "The Transcendental Ideal."

that the nature of things proposes to us insoluble problems. For we are not then concerned with nature or even with given objects, but with mere concepts which have their origin solely in our reason, and with mere beings of thought; and all the problems that arise from our concepts of them must be solved, because of course reason can and must give a full account of its own procedure.* As the psychological, cosmological, and theological Ideas are nothing but pure concepts of reason which cannot be given in any experience, the questions which reason asks us about them are put to us, not by the objects, but by mere maxims of our reason for the sake of its own satisfaction. They must all be capable of satisfactory answers, which are given by showing that they are principles which bring our use of the understanding into thorough agreement, completeness, and synthetical unity, and that they thus hold good of experience only, but of experience as a whole.

Although an absolute whole of experience is impossible, the Idea of a whole of knowledge according to principles must impart to our knowledge a peculiar kind of unity, that of a system, without which it is nothing but piecework and cannot be used for 350
proving the existence of a highest purpose (which can only be the general system of all purposes). I do not here refer only to the practical, but also to the highest purpose of the speculative use of reason.

The transcendental Ideas therefore express the peculiar vocation of reason as a principle of systematic unity in the use of the understanding. Yet if we assume this unity of the mode of knowledge to pertain to the object of knowledge, if we regard that which is merely *regulative* to be *constitutive,* and if we persuade ourselves that we can by means of these Ideas widen our knowledge transcendently or far beyond all possible experience, while it only serves to render experience within itself as nearly complete as possible, that is, to limit its progress by nothing that cannot belong to experience—if we do this, I say—we suffer from a mere misunderstanding in our estimate of the proper role of our reason and of its principles, and a dialectic arises which both confuses the empirical use of reason and sets reason at variance with itself.

CONCLUSION

ON THE DETERMINATION OF THE BOUNDS OF PURE REASON

§ 57. Having adduced the clearest arguments, it would be absurd for us to hope that we can know more of any object than belongs to the possible experience of it or lay claim to the least knowledge of anything not assumed to be an object of possible experience which would determine it according to the constitution it has in itself. For how could we

*Herr Platner, in his *Aphorismen,* acutely says (§§ 728, 729), "If reason be a criterion, no concept which is incomprehensible to human reason can be possible. Incomprehensibility has place in what is actual only. Here incomprehensibility arises from the insufficiency of the acquired ideas." It sounds paradoxical, but is otherwise not strange to say that in nature there is much that is incomprehensible (for example, the faculty of reproduction); but if we mount still higher and go even beyond nature, everything again becomes comprehensible. For we then quit entirely the objects which can be given us and occupy ourselves merely about Ideas, in which occupation we can easily comprehend the law that reason prescribes by them to the understanding for its use in experience, because the law is the reason's own production.

A drawing from Andreas Cellarius' *Harmonia Macrocosmica* (1661) with some of the greatest names of astronomy and cosmology, including (from left to right): Tycho Brahe (1546–1601), Ptolemy (fl. A.D. 130), St. Augustine (A.D. 354–430), Nicholas Copernicus (1473–1543), Galileo Galilei (with pointer) (1564–1642), and Andreas Cellarius (seated at right). (*Library of Congress*)

determine anything in this way, since time, space, and all the concepts of the understanding, and still more all the concepts formed by empirical intuition (perception) in the sensible world, have and can have no other use than to make experience possible? And if this condition is omitted from the pure concepts of the understanding, they do not determine any object and have no meaning whatever.

But it would be, on the other hand, a still greater absurdity if we conceded no
351 things in themselves or set up our experience as the only possible mode of knowing things, our intuition of them in space and in time for the only possible intuition and our discursive understanding for the archetype of every possible understanding; for this would be to wish to have the principles of the possibility of experience considered universal conditions of things in themselves.

Our principles, which limit the use of reason to possible experience, might in this way become transcendent and the limits of our reason be set up as limits of the possibility of things in themselves (as Hume's *Dialogues* may illustrate) if a careful critique did not guard the bounds of our reason with respect to its empirical use and set a limit to its pretensions. Skepticism originally arose from metaphysics and its anarchic dialectic. At first it might, merely to favor the empirical use of reason, announce everything that transcends this use as worthless and deceitful; but by and by, when it was perceived that the very same principles that are used in experience insensibly and apparently with the same right led still further than experience extends, then men began to doubt even the principles of experience. But here there is no danger, for common sense will doubtless always assert its rights. A certain confusion, however, arose in science, which cannot determine how far reason is to be trusted, and why only so far and no farther; and this confusion can only be cleared up and all future relapses obviated by a formal determination, on principle, of the boundary of the use of our reason.

We cannot indeed, beyond all possible experience, form a definite concept of what things in themselves may be. Yet we are not at liberty to abstain entirely from inquiring into them; for experience never satisfies reason fully but, in answering questions, refers us further and further back and leaves us dissatisfied with regard to their complete solution. This anyone may gather from the dialectic of pure reason, which therefore has its good subjective grounds. Having acquired, as regards the nature of our soul, a clear conception of the subject, and having come to the conviction that its manifestations cannot be explained materialistically, who can refrain from asking what the 352
soul really is and, if no concept of experience suffices for the purpose, from accounting for it by a concept of reason (that of a simple immaterial being), though we cannot by any means prove its objective reality? Who can satisfy himself with mere empirical knowledge in all the cosmological questions of the duration and of the magnitude of the world, of freedom or of natural necessity, since every answer given on principles of experience begets a fresh question, which likewise requires its answer and thereby clearly shows the insufficiency of all physical modes of explanation to satisfy reason? Finally, who does not see in the thoroughgoing contingency and dependence of all his thoughts and assumptions on mere principles of experience the impossibility of stopping there? And who does not feel himself compelled, notwithstanding all interdictions against losing himself in transcendent Ideas, to seek rest and contentment, beyond all the concepts which he can vindicate by experience, in the concept of a Being the possibility of the Idea of which cannot be conceived but at the same time cannot be refuted, because it relates to a mere being of the understanding and without it reason must needs remain forever dissatisfied?

Bounds (in extended beings) always presuppose a space existing outside a certain definite place and inclosing it; limits do not require this, but are mere negations which affect a quantity so far as it is not absolutely complete. But our reason, as it were, sees in its surroundings a space for knowledge of things in themselves, though we can never have definite concepts of them and are limited to appearances only.

As long as the knowledge of reason is homogeneous, definite bounds to it are inconceivable. In mathematics and in natural philosophy, human reason admits of limits but not of bounds, namely, it admits that something indeed lies without it, at which it can never arrive, but not that it will at any point find completion in its internal progress. The enlarging of our views in mathematics and the possibility of new discoveries are infinite; and the same is the case with the discovery of new properties of nature, of new powers and laws, by continued experience and its rational combination. But limits 353
cannot be mistaken here, for mathematics refers to appearances only, and what cannot be an object of sensuous intuition, such as the concepts of metaphysics and of morals, lies entirely without its sphere; it can never lead to them, but neither does it require

them. There is, therefore, not a continual progress and approximation towards these sciences, and there is not, as it were, any point or line of contact. Natural science will never reveal to us the internal constitution of things, which, though not appearance, yet can serve as the ultimate ground for explaining appearances. Nor does that science require this for its physical explanations. Nay, even if such grounds should be offered from other sources (for instance, the influence of immaterial beings), they must be rejected and not used in the progress of its explanations. For these explanations must only be grounded upon that which as an object of sense can belong to experience, and be brought into connection with our actual perceptions and empirical laws.

But metaphysics leads us towards bounds in the dialectical attempts of pure reason (not undertaken arbitrarily or wantonly, but stimulated thereto by the nature of reason itself). And the transcendental Ideas, as they do not admit of evasion but are never capable of realization, serve to point out to us actually not only the bounds of the pure use of reason, but also the way to determine them. Such is the end and the use of this natural predisposition of our reason, which has brought forth metaphysics as its favorite child, whose generation, like every other in the world, is not to be ascribed to blind chance but to an original germ, wisely organized for great ends. For metaphysics, in its fundamental features, perhaps more than any other science, is placed in us by nature itself and cannot be considered the production of an arbitrary choice or a casual enlargement in the progress of experience from which it is quite disparate.

Reason through all its concepts and laws of the understanding which are sufficient to it for empirical use, that is, within the sensible world, finds in it no satisfaction, because ever-recurring questions deprive us of all hope of their complete solution. The transcendental Ideas which have that completion in view are such
354 problems of reason. But it sees clearly that the sensuous world cannot contain this completion; neither, consequently, can all the concepts which serve merely for understanding the world of sense, for example, space and time, and what we have adduced under the name of pure concepts of the understanding. The sensuous world is nothing but a chain of appearances connected according to universal laws; it has therefore no subsistence by itself; it is not the thing in itself, and consequently must point to that which contains the basis of this appearance, to beings which cannot be known merely as appearances, but as things in themselves. In the knowledge of them alone can reason hope to satisfy its desire for completeness in proceeding from the conditioned to its conditions.

We have above (§§ 33 and 34) indicated the limits of reason with regard to all knowledge of mere beings of thought. Now, since the transcendental Ideas have made it necessary to approach them and thus have led us, as it were, to the spot where the occupied space (namely, experience) touches the void (that of which we can know nothing, namely, *noumena*), we can determine the bounds of pure reason. For in all bounds there is something positive (for example, a surface is the boundary of corporeal space, and is therefore itself a space; a line is a space, which is the boundary of the surface, a point the boundary of the line, but yet always a place in space), but limits contain mere negations. The limits pointed out in those paragraphs are not enough after we have discovered that beyond them there still lies something (though we can never know what it is in itself). For the question now is, What is the attitude of our reason in this connection of what we know with what we do not, and never shall, know? This is an actual connection of a known thing with one quite unknown (and which will always remain so), and though what is unknown should not become in the least more known—which we cannot even hope—yet the concept of this connection must be definite and capable of being rendered distinct.

We must therefore think an immaterial being, a world of understanding, and a Supreme Being (all mere *noumena*), because in them only, as things in themselves, reason finds that completion and satisfaction which it can never hope for in the deriva- 355 tion of appearances from their homogeneous grounds, and because these actually have reference to something distinct from them (and totally heterogeneous), as appearances always presuppose an object in itself and therefore suggest its existence whether we can know more of it or not.

But as we can never know these beings of understanding as they are in themselves, that is, as definite, yet must assume them as regards the sensible world and connect them with it by reason, we are at least able to think this connection by means of such concepts as express their relation to the world of sense. If we represent to ourselves a being of the understanding by nothing but pure concepts of the understanding, we then indeed represent nothing definite to ourselves, and consequently our concept has no significance; but if we think of it by properties borrowed from the sensuous world, it is no longer a being of understanding, but is conceived phenomenally and belongs to the sensible world. Let us take an instance from the notion of the Supreme Being.

The deistic conception is a quite pure concept of reason, but represents only a thing containing all reality, without being able to determine any one reality [in it]; because for that purpose an example must be taken from the world of sense, in which case I should have an object of sense only, not something quite heterogeneous which can never be an object of sense. Suppose I attribute to the Supreme Being understanding, for instance; I have no concept of an understanding other than my own, one that must receive its intuitions by the senses and which is occupied in bringing them under rules of the unity of consciousness. Then the elements of my concept would always lie in the appearance; I should, however, by the insufficiency of the appearance have to go beyond them to the concept of a being which neither depends upon appearances nor is bound up with them as conditions of its determination. But if I separate understanding from sensibility to obtain a pure understanding, then nothing remains but the mere form of thinking without intuition, by which form alone I can know nothing definite and consequently no object. For that purpose I should finally have to conceive another understanding, such as would intuit its objects but of which I have not the least concept, because the human understanding is discursive and can know only by means of general concepts. And the very same difficulties arise if we attribute a will to the Supreme 356 Being, for I have this concept only by drawing it from my inner experience, and therefore from my dependence for satisfaction upon objects whose existence I require; and so the concept rests upon sensibility, which is absolutely incompatible with the pure concept of the Supreme Being.

Hume's objections to deism are weak, and affect only the proofs and not the deistic assertion itself. But as regards theism, which depends on a stricter determination of the concept of the Supreme Being, which in deism is merely transcendent, they are very strong and, as this concept is formed, in certain (in fact in all common) cases irrefutable. Hume always insists that by the mere concept of an original being to which we apply only ontological predicates (eternity, omnipresence, omnipotence) we think nothing definite, and that properties which could yield a concept *in concreto* would have to be superadded. He further insists that it is not enough to say it is cause, but we must explain the nature of its causality, for example, that it is that of an understanding and of a will. He then begins his attacks on the essential point itself, that is, theism, as he had previously directed his battery only against the proofs of deism, an attack which is not very dangerous to it in its consequences. All his dangerous arguments refer to anthropomorphism, which he holds to be inseparable from theism and to make it contradictory in itself; but if the former be abandoned, the latter must vanish with it and nothing remain but deism, of which nothing can come, which is of no value and which cannot serve as any foundation to religion or morals. If this anthropomorphism were really unavoidable, no proofs whatever of the existence of a Supreme Being, even were they all granted, could determine for us the concept of this Being without involving us in contradictions.

If we connect with the command to avoid all transcendent judgments of pure reason the command (which apparently conflicts with it) to proceed to concepts that lie beyond the field of its immanent (empirical) use, we discover that both can subsist
357 together, but only at the boundary of all permitted use of reason. For this boundary belongs to the field of experience as well as to that of the beings of thought, and we are thereby taught how these so remarkable Ideas serve merely for marking the bounds of human reason. On the one hand, they give warning not boundlessly to extend knowledge of experience, as if nothing but world remained for us to know, and yet, on the other hand, not to transgress the bounds of experience and to think of judging about things beyond them as things in themselves.

But we stop at this boundary if we limit our judgment merely to the relation which the world may have to a Being whose very concept lies beyond all the knowledge which we can attain within the world. For we then do not attribute to the Supreme Being any of the properties in themselves by which we represent objects of experience, and thereby avoid *dogmatic* anthropomorphism; but we attribute them to the relation of this Being to the world and allow ourselves a *symbolical* anthropomorphism, which in fact concerns language only and not the object itself.

If I say that we are compelled to consider the world *as if* it were the work of a Supreme Understanding and Will, I really say nothing more than that a watch, a ship, a regiment, bears the same relation to the watchmaker, the shipbuilder, the commanding officer as the world of sense (or whatever constitutes the substratum of this complex of appearances) does to the unknown, which I do not hereby know as it is in itself but as it is for me, that is, in relation to the world of which I am a part.

§ 58. Such a cognition is one of analogy and does not signify (as is commonly understood) an imperfect similarity of two things, but a perfect similarity of relations
358 between two quite dissimilar things.* By means of this analogy, however, there remains a concept of the Supreme Being sufficiently determined *for us,* though we have left out everything that could determine it absolutely or *in itself;* for we determine it as regards the world and hence as regards ourselves, and more do we not require. The attacks which Hume makes upon those who would determine this concept absolutely, by taking the materials for so doing from themselves and the world, do not affect us; and he cannot object to us that we have nothing left if we give up the objective anthropomorphism of the concept of the Supreme Being.

*There is, for example, an analogy between the juridical relation of human actions and the mechanical relation of moving forces. I never can do anything to another man without giving him a right to do the same to me on the same conditions; just as no mass can act with its moving forces on another mass without thereby occasioning the other to react equally against it. Here right and moving force are quite dissimilar things, but in their relation there is complete similarity. By means of such an analogy, I can obtain a notion of the relation of things which absolutely are unknown to me. For instance, as the promotion of the welfare of children (= a) is to the love of parents (= b), so the welfare of the human species (= c) is to that unknown character in God (= x), which we call love; not as if it had the least similarity to any human inclination, but because we can suppose its relation to the world to be similar to that which things of the world bear one another. But the concept of relation in this case is a mere category, namely, the concept of cause, which has nothing to do with sensibility.

For let us assume at the outset (as Hume in his *Dialogues* makes Philo grant Cleanthes), as a necessary hypothesis, the deistic concept of the First Being, in which this Being is thought by the mere ontological predicates of substance, of cause, and so on. This must be done because reason, actuated in the sensible world by mere conditions which are themselves always conditional, cannot otherwise have any satisfaction; and it therefore can be done without falling into anthropomorphism (which transfers predicates from the world of sense to a Being quite distinct from the world) because those predicates are mere categories which, though they do not give a determinate concept of that Being, yet give a concept not limited to any conditions of sensibility. Thus nothing can prevent our predicating of this Being a causality through reason with regard to the world, and thus passing to theism, without being obliged to attribute to this Being itself this kind 359
of reason, as a property inherent in it. For as to the former, the only possible way of prosecuting the use of reason (as regards all possible experience in complete harmony with itself) in the world of sense to the highest point is to assume a supreme reason as a cause of all the connections in the world. Such a principle must be quite advantageous to reason and can hurt it nowhere in its application to nature. As to the latter, reason is thereby not transferred as a property to the First Being in itself, but only to its relation to the world of sense, and so anthropomorphism is entirely avoided. For nothing is considered here but the cause of the form of reason which is perceived everywhere in the world, and reason is indeed attributed to the Supreme Being so far as it contains the ground of this form of reason in the world, but according to analogy only—that is, so far as this expression shows merely the relation which the Supreme Cause, unknown to us, has to the world in order to determine everything in it conformably to reason in the highest degree. We are thereby kept from using reason as an attribute for the purpose of conceiving God, but not from conceiving the world in such a manner as is necessary to have the greatest possible use of reason within it according to principle. We thereby acknowledge that the Supreme Being is quite inscrutable and even unthinkable in any definite way as to what it is in itself. We are thereby kept, on the one hand, from making a transcendent use of the concepts which we have of reason as an efficient cause (by means of the will), in order to determine the Divine Nature by properties which are only borrowed from human nature, and from losing ourselves in gross and extravagant notions; and, on the other hand, from deluging the contemplation of the world with hyperphysical modes of explanation according to our notions of human reason which we transfer to God, and so from losing for this contemplation its proper rôle, according to which it should be a rational study of mere nature and not a presumptuous derivation of its appearances from a Supreme Reason. The expression suited to our feeble notions is: we conceive the world *as if* it came, in its existence and internal plan, from a Supreme Reason. By this, on the one hand, we know the constitution which belongs to the world itself without pretending to determine the nature of its cause in itself; and, on the other hand, we transfer the ground of this constitution (of the form of reason in the world) upon the *relation* of the Supreme 360
Cause to the world, without finding the world sufficient by itself for that purpose.*

Thus the difficulties which seem to oppose theism disappear by combining with Hume's principle, "not to carry the use of reason dogmatically beyond the field of all

*I may say that the causality of the Supreme Cause holds the same place with regard to the world that human reason does with regard to its works of art. Here the nature of the Supreme Cause itself remains unknown to me; I only compare its effects (the order of the world), which I know, and their conformity to reason to the effects of human reason, which I also know; and hence I term the former "reason," without attributing to it on that account what I understand in man by this term, or attaching to it anything else known to me as its property.

possible experience," this other principle, which he quite overlooked, "not to consider the field of experience as one which bounds itself in the eyes of our reason." The *Critique of Pure Reason* here points out the true mean between dogmatism, which Hume combats, and skepticism, which he would substitute for it—a mean which is not like others that we find advisable to determine for ourselves, as it were mechanically (by adopting something from one side and something from the other), and by which nobody is taught a better way, but such a one as can be precisely determined on principles.

§ 59. At the beginning of this note I made use of the metaphor of a boundary, in order to establish the limits of reason in regard to its suitable use. The world of sense contains merely appearances, which are not things in themselves; but the understanding, because it recognizes that the objects of experience are mere appearances, must assume that there are things in themselves, namely, *noumena.* In our reason both are comprehended, and the question is, How does reason proceed to set boundaries to the understanding as regards both these fields? Experience, which contains all that belongs to the sensible world, does not bound itself; it only proceeds in every case from the conditioned to some other equally conditioned object. That which bounds it must lie
361 quite without it, and this is the field of the pure beings of the understanding. But this field, so far as the *determination* of the nature of these beings is concerned, is an empty space for us; and apart from dogmatically defined concepts, we cannot pass beyond the field of possible experience. But as a boundary itself is something positive, which belongs to that which lies within as well as to the space that lies without the given content, it is still an actual positive cognition which reason only acquires by enlarging itself to this boundary, yet without attempting to pass it because it there finds itself in the presence of an empty space in which it can conceive forms of things, but not things themselves. But the setting of a boundary to the field of the understanding by something which is otherwise unknown to it is still a cognition which belongs to reason even at this point, and by which it is neither confined within the sensible nor strays beyond it, but only limits itself, as befits the knowledge of a boundary, to the relation between that which lies beyond it and that which is contained within it.

Natural theology is such a concept at the boundary of human reason, being constrained to look beyond this boundary to the Idea of a Supreme Being (and, for practical purposes, to that of an intelligible world also), not in order to determine anything relatively to this pure being of the understanding, and thus to determine something that lies beyond the world of sense, but in order to guide the use of reason within it according to principles of the greatest possible (theoretical as well as practical) unity. For this purpose, it makes use of the reference of the world of sense to an independent reason as the cause of all its connections. Thereby it does not just *invent* a being, but, as beyond the sensible world there must be something that can be thought only by the pure understanding, it determines that something in this particular way, though only of course by analogy.

And thus there remains our original proposition, which is the *résumé* of the whole *Critique:* "Reason by all its *a priori* principles never teaches us anything more than objects of possible experience, and even of these nothing more than can be known in experience." But this limitation does not prevent reason from leading us to the objective boundary of experience, namely, to the relation to something which is not itself an
362 object of experience but is the ground of all experience. Reason does not, however, teach us anything concerning the thing in itself; it only instructs us as regards its own complete and highest use in the field of possible experience. But this is all that can be reasonably desired in the present case, and with it we have cause to be satisfied.

§ 60. Thus we have fully exhibited metaphysics, in its subjective possibility, as it is actually given in the natural predisposition of human reason and in that which constitutes the essential end of its pursuit. Though we have found that this merely natural use of such a predisposition of our reason, if no discipline arising only from a scientific critique bridles and sets limits to it, involves it in transcendent and specious inferences and really conflicting dialectical inferences, and this fallacious metaphysics is not only unnecessary as regards the promotion of our knowledge of nature but even disadvantageous to it, there yet remains a problem worthy of investigation, which is to find out the natural ends intended by this disposition to transcendent concepts in our nature, because everything that lies in nature must be originally intended for some useful purpose.

Such an inquiry is of a doubtful nature, and I acknowledge that what I can say about it is conjecture only, like every speculation about the ultimate ends of nature. Such conjecture may be allowed me here, for the question does not concern the objective validity of metaphysical judgments but our natural predisposition to them, and therefore does not belong to the system of metaphysics but to anthropology.

When I compare all the transcendental Ideas, the totality of which constitutes the proper problem of natural pure reason, compelling it to quit the mere contemplation of nature, to transcend all possible experience, and in this endeavor to produce the thing (be it knowledge or fiction) called metaphysics, I think I perceive that the aim of this natural tendency is to free our concepts from the fetters of experience and from the limits of the mere contemplation of nature so far as at least to open to us a field containing mere objects for the pure understanding which no sensibility can reach, not indeed for the purpose of speculatively occupying ourselves with them (for there we can find no ground to stand on), but 363
in order that practical principles [may be assumed as at least possible]; for practical principles, unless they find scope for their necessary expectation and hope, could not expand to the universality which reason unavoidably requires from a moral point of view.

So I find that the psychological Idea (however little it may reveal to me the nature of the human soul, which is elevated above all concepts of experience), shows the insufficiency of these concepts plainly enough and thereby deters me from materialism, a psychological concept which is unfit for any explanation of nature and which moreover confines reason in practical respects. The cosmological Ideas, by the obvious insufficiency of all possible knowledge of nature to satisfy reason in its legitimate inquiry, serve in the same manner to keep us from naturalism, which asserts nature to be sufficient for itself. Finally, all natural necessity in the sensible world is conditional, as it always presupposes the dependence of things upon others, and unconditional necessity must be sought only in the unity of a cause different from the world of sense. But as the causality of this cause, in its turn, were it merely nature, could never render the existence of the contingent (as its consequent) comprehensible, reason frees itself by means of the theological Idea from fatalism (both as a blind natural necessity in the coherence of nature itself, without a first principle, and as a blind causality of this principle itself) and leads to the concept of a cause possessing freedom or of a Supreme Intelligence. Thus the transcendental Ideas serve, if not to instruct us positively, at least to destroy the narrowing assertions of materialism, of naturalism, and of fatalism, and thus to afford scope for the moral Ideas beyond the field of speculation. These considerations, I should think, explain in some measure the natural predisposition of which I spoke.

The practical value, which a merely speculative science may have, lies without the bounds of this science, and can therefore be considered as a scholium merely, and like all scholia does not form part of the science itself. This application, however, surely lies within the bounds of philosophy, especially of philosophy drawn from the pure sources

of reason, where its speculative use in metaphysics must necessarily be at one with its practical use in morals. Hence the unavoidable dialectic of pure reason, considered in
364 metaphysics as a natural tendency, deserves to be explained not as a mere illusion, which is to be removed, but also, if possible, as a natural provision as regards its end, though this task, a work of supererogation, cannot justly be assigned to metaphysics proper.

The solutions of these questions which are treated in the *Critique** should be considered a second scholium, which, however, has a greater affinity with the subject of metaphysics. For there certain rational principles are expounded which determine *a priori* the order of nature or rather of the understanding, which seeks nature's laws through experience. They seem to be constitutive and legislative with regard to experience, though they spring from pure reason, which cannot be considered, like the understanding, as a principle of possible experience. Now whether or not this harmony rests upon the fact that, just as nature does not inhere in appearances or in their source (the sensibility) itself, but only in the relation of the latter to the understanding, a thorough unity in applying the understanding to bring about an entirety of all possible experience (in a system) can only belong to the understanding when in relation to reason, with the consequence that experience is in this way mediately subordinate to the legislation of reason—this question may be discussed by those who desire to trace the nature of reason even beyond its use in metaphysics, into the general principles, which will make a history of nature in general systematic. I have presented this task as important, but not attempted its solution in the book itself.**

365 And thus I conclude the analytical solution of the main question which I had proposed: "How is metaphysics in general possible?" by ascending from the data of its actual use, as shown in its consequences, to the grounds of its possibility.

SOLUTION OF THE GENERAL QUESTION OF THE *PROLEGOMENA*

How Is Metaphysics Possible as Science?

Metaphysics, as a natural disposition of reason, is actual; but if considered by itself alone (as the analytical solution of the third principal question showed), dialectical and illusory. If we think of taking principles from it, and in using them follow the natural, but on that account not less false, illusion, we can never produce science, but only a vain dialectical art, in which one school may outdo another but none can ever acquire a just and lasting approbation.

In order that as a science metaphysics may be entitled to claim, not mere fallacious plausibility, but insight and conviction, a critique of reason itself must exhibit the whole stock of *a priori* concepts, their division according to their various sources (sensibility, understanding, and reason), together with a complete table of them, the analysis of all these concepts, with all their consequences, and especially the possibility of synthetical knowledge *a priori* by means of a deduction of these concepts, the principles and the bounds of their application, all in a complete system. Critique, therefore, and critique

**Critique of Pure Reason,* "Regulative Use of the Ideas of Pure Reason."

**Throughout in the *Critique* I never lost sight of the plan not to neglect anything, were it ever so recondite, that could render the inquiry into the nature of pure reason complete. Everybody may afterward carry his research as far as he pleases, when he has been merely shown what yet remains to be done. This can reasonably be expected of him who has made it his business to survey the whole field, in order to consign it to others for future cultivation and allotment. And to this branch both the scholia belong, which will hardly recommend themselves because of their dryness to amateurs, and hence are added here for connoisseurs only.

alone contains in itself the whole well-proved and well-tested plan, and even all the means, required to establish metaphysics as a science; by other ways and means it is impossible. The question here, therefore, is not so much how this performance is possible as how to set it going and to induce men of clear heads to quit their hitherto perverted and fruitless cultivation for one that will not deceive, and how such a union for the common end may best be directed.

This much is certain, that whoever has once tasted critique will be ever after 366
disgusted with all dogmatic twaddle which he formerly had to put up with because his reason had to have something and could find nothing better for its support.

Critique stands in the same relation to the common metaphysics of the schools as chemistry does to alchemy, or as astronomy to the astrology of the fortune teller. I pledge myself that nobody who has thought through and grasped the principles of critique, even in these *Prolegomena* only, will ever return to that old and sophistical pseudo-science; but will rather with a certain delight look forward to metaphysics, which is now indeed in his power, requiring no more preparatory discoveries and affording permanent satisfaction to reason at last. For here is an advantage upon which, of all possible sciences, metaphysics alone can with certainty reckon: that it can be brought to such completion and fixity as to be in need of no further change or be subject to any augmentation by new discoveries; because here reason has the sources of its knowledge in itself, not in objects and their observation, by which its stock of knowledge could be further increased. When, therefore, it has exhibited the fundamental laws of its faculty completely and so definitely as to avoid all misunderstanding, there remains nothing further which pure reason could know *a priori;* nay, there is no ground even to raise further questions. The sure prospect of knowledge so definite and so compact has a peculiar charm, even though we should set aside all its advantages, of which I shall hereafter speak.

All false art, all vain wisdom, lasts its time but finally destroys itself, and its highest culture is also the epoch of its decay. That this time is come for metaphysics appears from the state into which it has fallen among all learned nations, despite all the zeal with which other sciences of every kind are prosecuted. The old arrangement of our university studies still preserves its shadow. Now and then an academy of science tempts men by offering prizes to write some essay on it, but it is no longer numbered among the rigorous sciences; and let anyone judge for himself how a sophisticated man, if he were called a great metaphysician, would receive the compliment, which may be well meant but is scarcely envied by anybody.

Yet, though the period of the downfall of all dogmatic metaphysics has undoubt- 367
edly arrived, we are yet far from being able to say that the period of its regeneration is come by means of a thorough and complete critique of reason. All transitions from a tendency to its contrary pass through the stage of indifference, and this moment is the most dangerous for an author but, in my opinion, the most favorable for the science. For when party spirit has died out by a total dissolution of former connections, minds are in the best state to listen to several proposals for an organization according to a new plan.

When I say that I hope these *Prolegomena* will excite investigation in the field of critique and afford a new and promising object to sustain the general spirit of philosophy, which seems on its speculative side to want sustenance, I can imagine beforehand that everyone whom the thorny paths of my *Critique* have tired and put out of humor will ask me upon what I found this hope. My answer is: upon the irresistible law of necessity.

That the human mind will ever give up metaphysical researches is as little to be expected as that we, to avoid inhaling impure air, should prefer to give up breathing altogether. There will, therefore, always be metaphysics in the world; nay, everyone, especially every reflective man, will have it and, for want of a recognized standard, will shape it for himself after his own pattern. What has hitherto been called metaphysics cannot satisfy any critical mind, but to forego it entirely is impossible; therefore a *Critique of Pure Reason* itself must now be attempted or, if one exists, investigated and brought to the full test, because there is no other means of supplying this pressing want which is something more than mere thirst for knowledge.

Ever since I have come to know critique, whenever I finish reading a book of metaphysical contents which, by the preciseness of its notions, by variety, order, and an
368 easy style, was not only entertaining but also helpful, I cannot help asking, "Has this author indeed advanced metaphysics a single step?" The learned men whose works have been useful to me in other respects and always contributed to the culture of my mental powers will, I hope, forgive me for saying that I have never been able to find either their essays or my own less important ones (though self-love may recommend them to me) to have advanced the science of metaphysics in the least.

There is a very obvious reason for this: metaphysics did not then exist as a science, nor can it be gathered piecemeal; but its germ must be fully preformed in critique. But, in order to prevent all misconception, we must remember what has been already said—that, by the analytical treatment of our concepts, the understanding gains indeed a great deal; but the science of metaphysics is thereby not in the least advanced, because these dissections of concepts are nothing but the materials from which the intention is to carpenter our science. Let the concepts of substance and of accident be ever so well dissected and determined; all this is very well as a preparation for some future use. But if we cannot prove that in all which exists the substance endures and only the accidents vary, our science is not the least advanced by all our analyses.

Metaphysics has hitherto never been able to prove *a priori* either this proposition or that of sufficient reason, still less any more complex theorem such as belongs to psychology or cosmology, or indeed any synthetical proposition. By all its analyzing, therefore, nothing is affected, nothing obtained or forwarded; and the science, after all this bustle and noise, still remains as it was in the days of Aristotle, though there were far better preparations for it than of old if only the clue to synthetical cognitions had been discovered.

If anyone thinks himself offended, he is at liberty to refute my charge by producing a single synthetical proposition belonging to metaphysics which he would prove dogmatically *a priori;* for until he has actually performed this feat I shall not grant that he has truly advanced the science, even if this proposition should be sufficiently confirmed by common experience. No demand can be more moderate or more equitable
369 and, in the (inevitably certain) event of its nonperformance, no assertion more just than that hitherto metaphysics has never existed as a science.

But there are two things which, in case the challenge be accepted, I must deprecate: first, trifling about probability and conjecture, which are suited as little to metaphysics as to geometry; and secondly, a decision by means of the magic wand of socalled common sense, which does not convince everyone but accommodates itself to personal peculiarities.

For as to the former, nothing can be more absurd than in metaphysics, a philosophy from pure reason, to think of grounding our judgments upon probability and conjecture. Everything that is to be known *a priori* is thereby announced as apodictically certain, and must therefore be proved in this way. We might as well think of grounding geometry or arithmetic upon conjectures. As to the calculus of probabilities in the latter, it does not contain probable but perfectly certain judgments concerning the degree of the possibility of certain cases under given uniform conditions, which, in the sum of all possible cases, must infallibly happen according to the rule, though the rule is not sufficiently definite with respect to every single instance. Conjectures (by means of induction and of analogy) can be suffered in an empirical science of nature only, yet even there at least the possibility of what we assume must be quite certain.

The appeal to common sense is even more absurd—if anything more absurd can be imagined—when it is a question of concept and principles claimed as valid, not in so far as they hold with regard to experience, but beyond the conditions of experience. For what is common sense? It is normal good sense, so far it judges right. But what is normal good sense? It is the faculty of the knowledge and use of rules *in concreto,* as distinguished from the speculative understanding, which is a faculty of knowing rules *in abstracto.* Common sense can hardly understand the rule that every event is determined by means of its cause and can never comprehend it in its generality. It therefore demands an example from experience; and when it hears that this rule means nothing but what it always thought when a pane was broken or a kitchen utensil missing, it then 370
understands the principle and grants it. Common sense, therefore, is only of use so far as it can see its rules (though they actually are *a priori*) confirmed by experience; consequently to comprehend them *a priori,* or independently of experience, belongs to the speculative understanding and lies quite beyond the horizon of common sense. But the province of metaphysics is entirely confined to the latter kind of knowledge, and it is certainly a bad sign of common sense to appeal to it as a witness, for it cannot here form any opinion whatever, and men look down upon it with contempt until they are in straits and can find in their speculation neither advice nor help.

It is a common subterfuge of those false friends of common sense (who occasionally prize it highly, but usually despise it) to say that there must surely be at all events some propositions which are immediately certain and of which there is no occasion to give any proof, or even any account at all, because we otherwise could never stop inquiring into the grounds of our judgments. But if we except the principle of contradiction, which is not sufficient to show the truth of synthetical judgments, they can never adduce, in proof of this privilege, anything else indubitable which they can immediately ascribe to common sense, except mathematical propositions, such as twice two make four, between two points there is but one straight line, etc. But these judgments are radically different from those of metaphysics. For in mathematics I can by thinking itself construct whatever I represent to myself as possible by a concept: I add to the first two the other two, one by one, and myself make the number four, or I draw in thought from one point to another all manner of lines, equal as well as unequal; yet I can draw one only which is like itself in all its parts. But I cannot, by all my power of thinking, extract from the concept of a thing the concept of something else whose existence is necessarily connected with the former; for this I must call in experience. And though my understanding furnishes me *a priori* (yet only in reference to possible experience) with the concept of such a connection (that is causation), I cannot exhibit it, like the concepts of mathematics, by intuiting it *a priori,* and so show its possibility *a priori.* This concept, together with the principles of its application, always 371
requires, if it shall hold *a priori*—as is requisite in metaphysics—a justification and deduction of its possibility, because we cannot otherwise know how far it holds good and whether it can be used in experience only or beyond it also.

Therefore in metaphysics, as a speculative science of pure reason, we can never appeal to common sense, but may do so only when we are forced to surrender it and to renounce all pure speculative knowledge which must always be theoretical cognition, and thereby under some circumstances to forego metaphysics itself and its instruction for the sake of adopting a rational faith which alone may be possible for us, sufficient to our wants, and perhaps even more salutary than knowledge itself. For in this case the state of affairs is quite altered. Metaphysics must be science, not only as a whole, but in all its parts; otherwise it is nothing at all; because, as speculation of pure reason, it finds a hold only on common convictions. Beyond its field, however, probability and common sense may be used justly and with advantage, but on quite special principles, the importance of which always depends on their reference to practical life.

This is what I hold myself justified in requiring for the possibility of metaphysics as a science.

APPENDIX

ON WHAT CAN BE DONE TO MAKE METAPHYSICS AS A SCIENCE ACTUAL

Since all the ways heretofore taken have failed to attain the goal, and since without a preceding critique of pure reason it is not likely ever to be attained, the present attempt has a right to an accurate and careful examination, unless it be thought more advisable
372 to give up all pretensions to metaphysics, to which, if men but would consistently adhere to their purpose, no objection can be made.

If we take the course of things as it is, not as it ought to be, there are two sorts of judgments: (1) one a judgment which precedes investigation (in our case one in which the reader from his own metaphysics pronounces judgment on the *Critique of Pure Reason,* which was intended to discuss the very possibility of metaphysics); (2) the other a judgment subsequent to investigation. In the latter, the reader is enabled to ignore for a while the consequences of the critical researches that may be repugnant to his formerly adopted metaphysics, and first examines the grounds whence those consequences are derived. If what common metaphysics propounds were demonstrably certain, as is the case with the theorems of geometry, the former way of judging would hold good. For if the consequences of certain principles are repugnant to established truths, these principles are false and without further inquiry to be repudiated. But if metaphysics does not possess a stock of indisputably certain (synthetical) propositions, and should it even be the case that there are a number of them, which, though among the most plausible, are by their consequences in mutual conflict, and if no sure criterion of the truth of peculiarly metaphysical (synthetical) propositions is to be met with in it, then the former way of judging is not admissible, but the investigation of the principles of the *Critique* must precede all judgments as to its value.

A SPECIMEN OF A JUDGMENT OF THE CRITIQUE PRIOR TO ITS EXAMINATION

Such a judgment is to be found in the *Göttingische gelehrte Anzeigen,* in the supplement to the third part, of January 19, 1782, pages 40 *et seq.*

When an author who is familiar with the subject of his work and endeavors to present his independent reflections in its elaboration falls into the hands of a reviewer who, in his turn, is keen enough to discern the points on which the worth or worthlessness of the book rests, who does not cling to words but goes to the heart of the subject, sifting and testing the principles which the author takes as his point of departure, the severity of the
373 judgment may indeed displease the author, but the public does not care, as it gains thereby. And the author himself may be contented, as an opportunity of correcting or explaining his positions is afforded to him at an early date by the examination of a competent judge,

in such a manner that if he believes himself fundamentally right, he can remove in time any stumbling block that might hurt the success of his work.

I find myself, with my reviewer, in quite another position. He seems not to see at all the real matter of the investigation with which (successfully or unsuccessfully) I have been occupied. It is either impatience at thinking out a lengthy work, or vexation at a threatened reform of a science in which he believed he had brought everything to perfection long ago, or, what I am reluctant to suspect, real narrow-mindedness that prevents him from ever carrying his thoughts beyond his school metaphysics. In short, he passes impatiently in review a long series of propositions, of which, without knowing their premises, one can understand nothing, intersperses here and there his censure, the reason of which the reader understands just as little as the propositions against which it is directed; and hence [his report] can neither serve the public nor damage me in the judgment of experts. I should, for these reasons, have passed over this judgment altogether, were it not that it may afford me occasion for some explanations which may in some cases save the readers of these *Prolegomena* from a misconception.

In order to take a position from which my reviewer could most easily set the whole work in a most unfavorable light, without venturing to trouble himself with any special investigation, he begins and ends by saying: "This work is a system of transcendental (or, as he translates it, of higher*) idealism."

A glance at this line soon showed me the sort of criticism that I had to expect, much 374
as though the reviewer were one who had never seen or heard of geometry, having found a Euclid and coming upon various figures in turning over its leaves, were to say, on being asked his opinion of it: "The work is a textbook of drawing; the author introduces a peculiar terminology, in order to give dark, incomprehensible directions, which in the end teach nothing more than what everyone can effect by a fair natural accuracy of eye, etc."

Let us see, in the meantime, what sort of an idealism it is that goes through my whole work, although it does not by a long way constitute the soul of the system.

The dictum of all genuine idealists, from the Eleatic school to Bishop Berkeley, is contained in this formula: "All knowledge through the senses and experience is nothing but sheer illusion, and only in the ideas of the pure understanding and reason is there truth."

The principle that throughout dominates and determines my idealism, is on the contrary: "All knowledge of things merely from pure understanding or pure reason is nothing but sheer illusion, and only in experience is there truth."

But this is directly contrary to idealism proper. How came I then to use this expression for quite an opposite purpose, and how came my reviewer to see it everywhere?

The solution of this difficulty rests on something that could have been very easily understood from the general bearing of the work if the reader had only desired to understand it. Space and time, together with all that they contain, are not things in themselves or their qualities, but belong merely to the appearances of the things in themselves. Up to this point I am one in confession with the above idealists. But these, and among them more particularly Berkeley, regarded space as a mere empirical representation that, like

*By no means "higher." High towers and metaphysically great men resembling them, round both of which there is commonly much wind, are not for me. My place is the fruitful bathos of experience; and the word "transcendental," the meaning of which is so often explained by me but not once grasped by my reviewer (so carelessly has he regarded everything), does not signify something passing beyond all experience but something that indeed precedes it *a priori,* but that is intended simply to make knowledge of experience possible. If these conceptions overstep experience, their employment is termed "transcendent," which must be distinguished from the immanent use, that is, use restricted to experience. All misunderstandings of this kind have been sufficiently guarded against in the work itself, but my reviewer found his advantage in misunderstanding me.

375 the appearances it contains, is, together with its determinations, known to us only by means of experience or perception. I, on the contrary, prove in the first place that space (and also time, which Berkeley did not consider) and all its *a priori* determinations can be known by us, because, no less than time, it inheres in us as a pure form of our sensibility before all perception or experience and makes all intuition of the form, and therefore all appearances, possible. It follows from this that, as truth rests on universal and necessary laws as its criteria, experience, according to Berkeley, can have no criteria of truth because its phenomena* (according to him) have nothing *a priori* at their foundation, whence it follows that experience is nothing but sheer illusion; whereas with us, space and time (in conjunction with the pure concept of the understanding) prescribe their law to all possible experience *a priori* and, at the same time, afford the certain criterion for distinguishing truth from illusion therein.

My so-called (properly critical) idealism is of quite a special character, in that it subverts the ordinary idealism and in that only through it all *a priori* knowledge, even that of geometry, receives objective reality, which, without my demonstrated ideality of space and time, could not be maintained by the most zealous realists. This being the state of the case, I could wish, in order to avoid all misunderstanding, to have named this conception of mine otherwise, but to alter it altogether is probably impossible. It may be permitted me however, in future, as has been above intimated, to term it "formal" or, better still, "critical" idealism, to distinguish it from the dogmatic idealism of Berkeley and from the skeptical idealism of Descartes.

Beyond this, I find nothing remarkable in the judgment of my book. The reviewer
376 makes sweeping criticisms, a mode prudently chosen, since it does not betray one's own knowledge or ignorance; a single thorough criticism in detail, had it touched the main question, as is only fair, would have exposed either my error or my reviewer's measure of insight into this species of research. It was, moreover, not a badly conceived plan, in order at once to take from readers (who are accustomed to form their conceptions of books from newspaper reports) the desire to read the book itself, to pour out in one breath a number of passages in succession which, torn from their connection with their premises and explanations, must necessarily sound senseless, especially considering how antipathetic they are to all school-metaphysics; to exhaust the reader's patience *ad nauseam,* and then, having made me acquainted with the lucid proposition that persistent illusion is truth, to conclude with the crude paternal moralization: to what end, then, the quarrel with accepted language; to what end, and whence, the idealistic distinction? A judgment which seeks all that is characteristic of my book, first supposed to be metaphysically heterodox, in a mere innovation of the nomenclature proves clearly that my would-be judge has understood nothing of the subject and, in addition, has not understood himself.**

*Idealism proper always has a mystical tendency, and can have no other, but mine is solely designed for the purpose of comprehending the possibility of our *a priori* knowledge of objects of experience, which is a problem never hitherto solved or even suggested. In this way all mystical idealism falls to the ground, for (as may be seen in Plato) it inferred from our cognitions *a priori* (even from those of geometry) another intuition different from that of the senses (namely, an intellectual intuition), because it never occurred to anyone that the senses themselves might intuit *a priori.*

**The reviewer often fights with his own shadow. When I oppose the truth of experience to dream, he never thinks that I am here speaking simply of the well-known *somnio objective sumto* of the Wolffian philosophy, which is merely formal, and with which the distinction between sleeping and waking is in no way concerned—a distinction which can indeed have no place in a transcendental philosophy. For the rest, he calls my deduction of the categories and table of the principles of the understanding "common well-known axioms of logic and ontology, expressed in an idealistic manner." The reader need only consult these *Prolegomena* upon this point to convince himself that a more miserable and historically incorrect judgment could hardly be made.

My reviewer speaks like a man who is conscious of important and superior insight which he keeps hidden, for I am aware of nothing recent with respect to metaphysics that could justify his tone. But he should not withhold his discoveries from the world, for there are doubtless many who, like myself, have not been able to find in all the fine things that have for long past been written in this department anything that has advanced the science by so much as a finger's breadth; we find indeed the giving a new 377
point to definitions, the supplying of lame proofs with new crutches, the adding to the crazy-quilt of metaphysics fresh patches or changing its pattern. But all this is not what the world requires. The world is tired of metaphysical assertions; it wants [to know] the possibility of this science, the sources from which certainty therein can be derived, and certain criteria by which it may distinguish the dialectical illusion of pure reason from truth. To this the critic seems to possess a key, otherwise he would never have spoken out in such a high tone.

But I am inclined to suspect that no such requirement of the science has ever entered his thoughts, for in that case he would have directed his judgment to this point, and even a mistaken attempt in such an important matter would have won his respect. If that be the case, we are once more good friends. He may penetrate as deeply as he likes into his metaphysics, without any one hindering him; only as concerns that which lies outside metaphysics, its sources, which are to be found in reason, he cannot form a judgment. That my suspicion is not without foundation is proved by the fact that he does not mention a word about the possibility of synthetic knowledge *a priori,* the special problem upon the solution of which the fate of metaphysics wholly rests and upon which my *Critique* (as well as the present *Prolegomena*) entirely hinges. The idealism he encountered and which he hung upon was only taken up in the doctrine as the sole means of solving the above problem (although it received its confirmation on other grounds), and hence he must have shown either that the above problem does not possess the importance I attribute to it (even in these *Prolegomena*) or that, by my conception of appearances, it is either not solved at all or can be better solved in another way; but I do not find a word of this in the criticism. The reviewer, then, understands nothing of my work and possibly also nothing of the spirit and essential nature of metaphysics itself; and it is not, what I would rather assume, the hurry of a reviewer to finish his review, incensed at the labor of plodding through so many obstacles, that threw an unfavorable shadow over the work lying before him and made its fundamental features unrecognizable.

There is a good deal to be done before a learned journal, it matters not with what 378
care its writers may be selected, can maintain its otherwise well-merited reputation in the field of metaphysics as elsewhere. Other sciences and branches of knowledge have their standard. Mathematics has it in itself, history and theology in profane or sacred books, natural science and the art of medicine in mathematics and experience, jurisprudence in law books, and even matters of taste in the examples of the ancients. But for the judgment of the thing called metaphysics, the standard has yet to be found. I have made an attempt to determine it, as well as its use. What is to be done, then, until it be found when works of this kind have to be judged of? If they are of a dogmatic character, one may do what one likes; no one will play the master over others here for long before someone else appears to deal with him in the same manner. If, however, they are critical in character, not indeed with reference to other works but to reason itself, so that the standard of judgment cannot be assumed but has first of all to be sought for, then, though objection and blame may indeed be permitted, yet a certain degree of leniency is indispensable, since the need is common to us all and the lack of the necessary insight makes the high-handed attitude of judge unwarranted.

In order, however, to connect my defense with the interest of the philosophical commonwealth, I propose a test, which must be decisive as to the mode whereby all metaphysical investigations may be directed to their common purpose. This is nothing more than what mathematicians have done in establishing the advantage of their methods by competition. I challenge my critic to demonstrate, as is only just, on *a priori* grounds, in his own way, any single really metaphysical proposition asserted by him. Being metaphysical, it must be synthetical and known *a priori* from concepts, but it may also be any one of the most indispensable propositions, as, for instance, the principle of the persistence of substance or of the necessary determination of events in the world by their causes. If he cannot do this (silence however is confession), he must admit that, since metaphysics without apodictic certainty of propositions of this kind is nothing at all, its
379 possibility or impossibility must before all things be established in a critique of pure reason. Thus he is bound either to confess that my principles in the *Critique* are correct, or he must prove their invalidity. But as I can already foresee that, confidently as he has hitherto relied on the certainty of his principles, when it comes to a strict test he will not find a single one in the whole range of metaphysics he can boldly bring forward, I will concede to him an advantageous condition, which can only be expected in such a competition, and will relieve him of the *onus probandi* by laying it on myself.

He finds in these *Prolegomena* and in my *Critique** eight propositions, of which one in each pair contradicts the other, but each of which necessarily belongs to metaphysics, by which it must either be accepted or rejected (although there is not one that has not in its time been assumed by some philosopher). Now he has the liberty of selecting any one of these eight propositions at his pleasure and accepting it without any proof, of which I shall make him a present, but only one (for waste of time will be just as little serviceable to him as to me), and then of attacking my proof of the opposite proposition. If I can save this one and at the same time show that, according to principles which every dogmatic metaphysics must necessarily recognize, the opposite of the proposition adopted by him can be just as clearly proved, it is thereby established that metaphysics has an hereditary failing not to be explained, much less set aside, until we ascend to its birthplace, pure reason itself. And thus my *Critique* must either be accepted or a better one take its place; at least it must be studied, which is the only thing I now require. If, on the other hand, I cannot save my demonstration, then a synthetic proposition *a priori* from dogmatic principles is to be reckoned to the score of my opponent, and I shall deem my impeachment of ordinary metaphysics unjust and pledge myself to recognize his stricture on my *Critique* as justified (although this would not be the consequence by a long way). To this end it would be necessary, it seems to me, that he should step out of his incognito. Otherwise I do not see how it could be avoided that,
380 instead of dealing with one, I should be honored or besieged by several challenges coming from anonymous and unqualified opponents.

PROPOSALS AS TO AN INVESTIGATION OF THE "CRITIQUE" UPON WHICH A JUDGMENT MAY FOLLOW

I feel obliged to the learned public even for the silence with which it for a long time honored my *Critique,* for this proves at least a postponement of judgment and some supposition that, in a work leaving all beaten tracks and striking out on a new path, in

*[The reference is to the theses and antitheses of the antinomies.—L.W.B.]

which one cannot at once perhaps so easily find one's way, something may perchance lie from which an important but at present dead branch of human knowledge may derive new life and productiveness. Hence may have originated a solicitude for the as yet tender shoot, lest it be destroyed by a hasty judgment. A specimen of a judgment, delayed for the above reasons, is now before my eye in the *Gothaische gelehrte Zeitung,* the thoroughness of which—disregarding my praise, which might be suspicious—every reader will himself perceive from the clear and unperverted presentation of a fragment of one of the first principles of my work.

Since an extensive structure cannot be judged of as a whole from a hurried glance, I suggest that it be tested piece by piece from the ground up, and in this, the present *Prolegomena* may fitly be used as a general outline with which the work itself may occasionally be compared. This notion, if it were founded on nothing more than my conceit of importance, such as vanity commonly attributes to all of one's own productions, would be immodest and would deserve to be repudiated with indignation. But now the interests of speculative philosophy have arrived at the point of total extinction, while human reason hangs upon them with inextinguishable affection; and only after having been ceaselessly deceived, does it vainly attempt to change this into indifference.

In our thinking age, it is not to be supposed but that many deserving men would use any good opportunity of working for the common interest of the more and more
enlightened reason, if there were only some hope of attaining the goal. Mathematics, 381
natural science, laws, arts, even morality, etc., do not completely fill the soul; there is always a space left over reserved for pure and speculative reason, the emptiness of which prompts us to seek in vagaries, buffooneries, and mysticism for what seems to be employment and entertainment, but what actually is mere pastime undertaken in order to deaden the troublesome voice of reason, which, in accordance with its nature, requires something that can satisfy it and does not merely subserve other ends or the interests of our inclinations. A consideration, therefore, which is concerned only with reason as it exists for it itself has, as I may reasonably suppose, a great fascination for everyone who has attempted thus to extend his conceptions, and I may even say a greater fascination than any other theoretical branch of knowledge, for which he would not willingly exchange it because here all other branches of knowledge and even purposes must meet and unite themselves in a whole.

I offer, therefore, these *Prolegomena* as a sketch and textbook for this investigation, and not the work itself. Although I am even now perfectly satisfied with the latter as far as contents, order, and mode of presentation, and the care that I have expended in weighing and testing every sentence before writing it down are concerned (for it has taken me years to satisfy myself fully, not only as regards the whole, but in some cases even as to the sources of one particular proposition); yet I am not quite satisfied with my exposition in some sections of the Doctrine of Elements,* as for instance in the deduction of the concepts of the understanding or in the chapter on the paralogisms of pure reason, because a certain diffuseness takes away from their clearness, and in place of them what is here said in the *Prolegomena* respecting these sections may be made the basis of the test.**

It is the boast of the Germans that, where steady and continuous industry are requisite, they can carry things farther than other nations. If this opinion be well founded, an

*[The first part of the *Critique of Pure Reason,* the other being the Methodology.—L.W.B.]

**[These sections were almost completely rewritten in the second edition of the *Critique* (1787), though the new deduction of the categories does not follow the argument of the *Prolegomena.*—L.W.B.]

opportunity, a task, presents itself the successful issue of which we can scarcely doubt and in which all thinking men can equally take part, though they have hitherto been unsuccessful in accomplishing it and in thus confirming the above good opinion. This is chiefly because the science in question is of so peculiar a kind that it can all at once be brought to
382 completion and to that enduring state beyond which it can never be developed, in the least degree enlarged by later discoveries, or changed if we leave out of account adornment by greater clearness in some places or additional uses. This is an advantage no other science has or can have, because there is none so fully isolated and independent of others and so exclusively concerned with the faculty of cognition pure and simple. And the present moment seems not to be unfavorable to my expectation, for just now, in Germany, no one seems to know wherewith to occupy himself, apart from the so-called useful sciences, so as to pursue not mere play but a business possessing an enduring purpose.

To discover how the endeavors of the learned may be united in such a purpose I must leave to others. In the meantime, it is not my intention to persuade anyone merely to follow my propositions or even to flatter me with the hope that he will do so; but attacks, repetitions, limitations, or confirmation, completion, and extension, as the case may be, should be appended. If the matter be but investigated from its foundation, it cannot fail that a system, albeit not my own, shall be erected that shall be a possession for future generations for which they may have reason to be grateful.

It would lead us too far here to show what kind of metaphysics may be expected when the principles of criticism have been perfected and how, though the old false feathers have been pulled out, it need by no means appear poor and reduced to an insignificant figure but may be in other respects richly and respectably adorned. But other and great uses which would result from such a reform strike one immediately. The ordinary metaphysics had its uses, in that it sought out the elementary concepts of the pure understanding in order to make them clear through analysis and definite through definitions. In this way it was a training for reason, in whatever direction it might be turned. But this was all the good it did. The service was subsequently effaced when it favored conceit by venturesome assertions, sophistry by subtle distinctions and adornment, and shallowness by the ease with which it decided the most difficult problems by
383 means of a little school wisdom, which is only the more seductive the more it has the choice, on the one hand, of taking something from the language of science and, on the other, from that of popular discourse—thus being everything to everybody but in reality nothing at all. By criticism, however, a standard is given to our judgment whereby knowledge may be with certainty distinguished from pseudo-science and firmly founded, being brought into full operation in metaphysics—a mode of thought extending by degrees its beneficial influence over every other use of reason, at once infusing into it the true philosophical spirit. But the service that metaphysics performs also for theology, by making it independent of the judgment of dogmatic speculation and thereby assuring it completely against the attacks of all such opponents, is certainly not to be valued lightly. For ordinary metaphysics, although it promised theology much advantage, could not keep this promise, and by summoning speculative dogmatics to its assistance did nothing but arm enemies against itself. Mysticism, which can prosper in a rationalistic age only when it hides itself behind a system of school metaphysics, under the protection of which it may venture to rave with a semblance of rationality, is driven from theology, its last hiding place, by critical philosophy. Last, but not least, it cannot be otherwise than important to a teacher of metaphysics to be able to say with universal assent that what he expounds is *science,* and that by it genuine services will be rendered to the commonweal.

FOUNDATIONS OF THE METAPHYSICS OF MORALS

PREFACE 387

Ancient Greek philosophy was divided into three sciences: physics, ethics, and logic. This division conforms perfectly to the nature of the subject, and one need improve on it perhaps only by supplying its principle in order both to insure its exhaustiveness and to define correctly the necessary subdivisions.

All rational knowledge is either material, and concerns some object, or formal, and is occupied only with the form of understanding and reason itself and with the universal rules of thinking, without regard to distinctions among objects. Formal philosophy is called logic. Material philosophy, however, which has to do with definite objects and the laws to which they are subject, is divided into two parts. This is because these laws are either laws of nature or laws of freedom. The science of the former is called physics, and that of the latter ethics. The former is also called theory of nature and the latter theory of morals.

Logic can have no empirical part—a part in which universal and necessary laws of thinking would rest upon grounds taken from experience. For in that case it would not be logic (i.e., a canon for understanding or reason which is valid for all thinking and which must be demonstrated). Natural and moral philosophy, on the other hand, can each have its empirical part. The former must do so, for it must determine the laws of nature as an object of experience, and the latter must do so because it must determine the human will
so far as it is affected by nature. The laws of the former are laws according to which every- 388
thing happens; those of the latter are laws according to which everything ought to happen, but allow for conditions under which what ought to happen often does not.

All philosophy, so far as it is based on experience, may be called empirical; but, so far as it presents its doctrines solely on the basis of *a priori* principles, it may be called pure philosophy. Pure philosophy, when formal only, is logic; when limited to definite objects of the understanding, it is metaphysics.

In this way there arises the idea of a two-fold metaphysics—a metaphysics of nature and a metaphysics of morals. Physics, therefore, will have an empirical part and also a rational part, and ethics likewise. In ethics, however, the empirical part may be called more specifically practical anthropology; the rational part, morals proper.

All crafts, handiworks, and arts have gained by the division of labor, for when one person does not do everything but each limits himself to a particular job which is distinguished from all the others by the treatment it requires, he can do it with greater perfection and more facility. Where work is not thus differentiated and divided, where everyone is a jack-of-all-trades, the crafts remain at a primitive level. It might be worth considering whether pure philosophy in each of its parts does not require a man particularly devoted to it, and whether it would not be better for the learned profession as a whole to warn those who are in the habit of catering to the taste of the public by mixing up the empirical with the rational in all sorts of proportions which they themselves do

Immanuel Kant, *Foundations of the Metaphysics of Morals,* 2nd ed., translated by Lewis White Beck (Pearson/Library of the Liberal Arts, 1989).

not know—a warning to those who call themselves independent thinkers and who give the name of speculator to those who apply themselves exclusively to the rational part of philosophy. This warning would be that they should not, at one and the same time, carry on two employments which differ widely in the treatment they require, and for each of which perhaps a special talent is required, since the combination of these talents in one person produces only bunglers. I only ask whether the nature of the science does not require that a careful separation of the empirical from the rational part be made, with a metaphysics of nature put before real (empirical) physics and a metaphysics of morals before practical anthropology. Each branch of metaphysics must be carefully purified of
389 everything empirical so that we can know how much pure reason can accomplish in each case and from what sources it creates its *a priori* teaching, whether the latter inquiry be conducted by all moralists (whose name is legion) or only by some who feel a calling to it.

Since my purpose here is directed to moral philosophy, I narrow my proposed question to this: Is it not of the utmost necessity to construct a pure moral philosophy which is completely freed from everything which may be only empirical and thus belong to anthropology? That there must be such a philosophy is self-evident from the common idea of duty and moral laws. Everyone must admit that a law, if it is to hold morally (i.e., as a ground of obligation), must imply absolute necessity; he must admit that the command: Thou shalt not lie, does not apply to men only as if other rational beings had no need to observe it. The same is true for all other moral laws properly so called. He must concede that the ground of obligation here must not be sought in the nature of man or in the circumstances in which he is placed but *a priori* solely in the concepts of pure reason, and that every precept which rests on principles of mere experience, even a precept which is in certain respects universal, so far as it leans in the least on empirical grounds (perhaps only in regard to the motive involved) may be called a practical rule but never a moral law.

Thus not only are moral laws together with their principles essentially different from all practical knowledge in which there is anything empirical, but all moral philosophy rests solely on its pure part. Applied to man, it borrows nothing from knowledge of him (anthropology) but gives man, as a rational being, *a priori* laws. No doubt these laws require a power of judgment sharpened by experience partly in order to decide in which cases they apply and partly to procure for them access to man's will and to provide an impetus to their practice. For man is affected by so many inclinations that, though he is capable of the Idea of a practical pure reason, he is not so easily able to make it concretely effective in the conduct of his life.

390 A metaphysics of morals is therefore indispensable, not merely because of motives to speculation on the source of the *a priori* practical principles which lie in our reason, but also because morals themselves remain subject to all kinds of corruption so long as the guide and supreme norm for their correct estimation is lacking. For it is not sufficient to that which should be morally good that it conform to the law; it must be done for the sake of the law. Otherwise its conformity is merely contingent and spurious because, though the unmoral ground may indeed now and then produce lawful actions, more often it brings forth unlawful ones. But the moral law can be found in its purity and genuineness (which is the central concern in the practical) nowhere else than in a pure philosophy; therefore metaphysics must lead the way, and without it there can be no moral philosophy. Philosophy which mixes pure principles with empirical ones does not deserve the name, for what distinguishes philosophy from common sense knowledge is its treatment in separate sciences of what is confusedly apprehended in such

knowledge. Much less does it deserve the name of moral philosophy, since by this confusion it spoils the purity of morals themselves, and works contrary to its own end.

It should not be thought that what is here required is already present in the celebrated Wolff's propaedeutic to his moral philosophy (i.e., in what he calls *Universal Practical Philosophy*) and that it is not an entirely new field which is to be opened. Precisely because his work was to be universal practical philosophy, it contained no will of any particular kind, such as one determined without any empirical motives by *a priori* principles; in a word, it had nothing which could be called a pure will, since it considered only volition in general with all the actions and conditions which pertain to it in this general sense. Thus his propaedeutic differs from a metaphysic of morals in the same way that general logic is distinguished from transcendental philosophy, the former expounding the actions and rules of thinking in general, and the latter presenting the actions and rules of pure thinking (thinking by which objects are known completely *a priori*). For the metaphysics of morals is meant to investigate the Idea and principles of a possible pure will and not the actions and conditions of human 391
volition as such, which for the most part are drawn from psychology.

That universal practical philosophy discussed (though improperly) laws and duty is no objection to my assertion. For the authors of this science remain even here true to their idea of it. They do not distinguish the motives which are presented completely *a priori* by reason alone and which are thus moral in the proper sense of the world, from empirical motives which the understanding raises to universal concepts by comparing experiences. Rather, they consider motives without regard to the difference in their source but only with reference to their larger or smaller number (as they are considered to be all of the same kind); they thus formulate their concept of obligation, which is anything but moral, but which is all that can be desired in a philosophy which does not decide whether the origin of all possible practical concepts is *a priori* or *a posteriori*.

As a preliminary to a *Metaphysics of Morals* which I intend to publish someday, I issue these *Foundations*. There is, to be sure, no other foundation for such a metaphysics than a critical examination of pure practical reason, just as there is no other foundation for metaphysics than the already published critical examination of pure speculative reason. But, in the first place, a critical examination of pure practical reason is not of such extreme importance as that of the speculative reason, because human reason, even in the commonest mind, can easily be brought to a high degree of correctness and completeness in moral matters while, on the other hand, in its theoretical but pure use it is wholly dialectical. In the second place, I require of a critical examination of pure practical reason, if it is to be complete, that its unity with the speculative be subject to presentation under a common principle, because in the final analysis there can be but one and the same reason which must be different only in application. But I could not bring this to such a completeness without bringing in observations of an altogether different kind and without thereby confusing the reader. For these reasons I have employed the title, *Foundations of the Metaphysics of Morals,* instead of *Critique of Pure Practical Reason.*

Because, in the third place, a *Metaphysics of Morals,* in spite of its forbidding title, is capable of a high degree of popular adaptation to common understanding, I find it useful to separate this preliminary work of laying the foundation, in order not to have to introduce unavoidable subtleties into the latter, more comprehensible work. 392

The present foundations, however, are nothing more than the search for and establishment of the supreme principle of morality. This constitutes a task altogether complete in design and one which should be kept separate from all other moral inquiry. My conclusions concerning this important question, which has not yet been discussed nearly enough, would, of course, be clarified by application of the principle to the whole system of morality, and it would receive much confirmation by the adequacy which it would everywhere show. But I must forego this advantage which would be, in the final analysis, more personally gratifying than commonly useful, because ease of use and apparent adequacy of a principle are not any sure proof of correctness, but rather awaken a certain partiality which prevents a rigorous investigation and evaluation of it for itself without regard to consequences.

I have adopted in this writing the method which is, I think, most suitable if one wishes to proceed analytically from common knowledge to the determination of its supreme principle, and then synthetically from the examination of this principle and its sources back to common knowledge where it finds its application. The division is therefore as follows:

1. First Section. Transition from Common Sense Knowledge of Morals to the Philosophical
2. Second Section. Transition from Popular Moral Philosophy to the Metaphysics of Morals
3. Third Section. Final Step from the Metaphysics of Morals to the Critical Examination of Pure Practical Reason

393 FIRST SECTION

TRANSITION FROM COMMON SENSE* KNOWLEDGE OF MORALS TO THE PHILOSOPHICAL

Nothing in the world—indeed nothing even beyond the world—can possibly be conceived which could be called good without qualification except a GOOD WILL. Intelligence, wit, judgment, and other talents of the mind however they may be named, or courage, resoluteness, and perseverence as qualities of temperament, are doubtless in many respects good and desirable; but they can become extremely bad and harmful if the will, which is to make use of these gifts of nature and which in its special constitution is called character, is not good. It is the same with gifts of fortune. Power, riches, honor, even health, general well-being and the contentment with one's condition which is called happiness make for pride and even arrogance if there is not a good will to correct their influence on the mind and on its principle of action, so as to make it generally fitting to its entire end. It need hardly be mentioned that the sight of a being adorned with no feature of a pure and good will yet enjoying lasting good fortune can never give pleasure to an impartial rational observer. Thus the good will seems to constitute the indispensable condition even of worthiness to be happy.

*[*gemeine Vernunfterkenntnis* ("common rational knowledge") is one of several expressions Kant uses which may sometimes best be translated as "common sense." Kant is very strict in his censure of those who appeal to common sense as an arbiter in philosophical disputes, yet he accepts it as a starting point, especially in ethics, where he says that the man of common sense has at least as much chance to be right as the philosopher. In this title "common sense" is not being used as a technical term; it just means "what everyone knows" about morality.]

Some qualities seem to be conducive to this good will and can facilitate its action, 394
but in spite of that they have no intrinsic unconditional worth. They rather presuppose a good will, which limits the high esteem which one otherwise rightly has for them and prevents their being held to be absolutely good. Moderation in emotions and passions, self-control, and calm deliberation not only are good in many respects but seem even to constitute part of the inner worth of the person. But however unconditionally they were esteemed by the ancients, they are far from being good without qualification, for without the principles of a good will they can become extremely bad, and the coolness of a villain makes him not only far more dangerous but also more directly abominable in our eyes than he would have seemed without it.

The good will is not good because of what it effects or accomplishes or because of its competence to achieve some intended end; it is good only because of its willing (i.e., it is good in itself). And, regarded for itself, it is to be esteemed as incomparably higher than anything which could be brought about by it in favor of any inclination or even of the sum total of all inclinations. Even if it should happen that, by a particularly unfortunate fate or by the niggardly provision of a step-motherly nature, this will should be wholly lacking in power to accomplish its purpose, and if even the greatest effort should not avail it to achieve anything of its end, and if there remained only the good will—not as a mere wish, but as the summoning of all the means in our power—it would sparkle like a jewel all by itself, as something that had its full worth in itself. Usefulness or fruitlessness can neither diminish nor augment this worth. Its usefulness would be only its setting, as it were, so as to enable us to handle it more conveniently in commerce or to attract the attention of those who are not yet connoisseurs, but not to recommend it to those who are experts or to determine its worth.

But there is something so strange in this idea of the absolute worth of the will alone, in which no account is taken of any use, that, notwithstanding the agreement even of common sense, the suspicion must arise that perhaps only high-flown fancy is its hidden basis,
and that we may have misunderstood the purpose of nature in appointing reason as the 395
ruler of our will. We shall therefore examine this idea from this point of view.

In the natural constitution of an organized being (i.e., one suitably adapted to life), we assume as an axiom that no organ will be found for any purpose which is not the fittest and best adapted to that purpose. Now if its preservation, its welfare, in a word its happiness, were the real end of nature in a being having reason and will, then nature would have hit upon a very poor arrangement in appointing the reason of the creature to be the executor of this purpose. For all the actions which the creature has to perform with this intention of nature, and the entire rule of his conduct, would be dictated much more exactly by instinct, and the end would be far more certainly attained by instinct than it ever could be by reason. And if, over and above this, reason should have been granted to the favored creature, it would have served only to let him contemplate the happy constitution of his nature, to admire it, to rejoice in it, and to be grateful for it to its beneficent cause. But reason would not have been given in order that the being should subject his faculty of desire to that weak and delusive guidance and to meddle with the purpose of nature. In a word, nature would have taken care that reason did not break forth into practical use nor have the presumption, with its weak insight, to think out for itself the plan of happiness and the means of attaining it. Nature would have taken over the choice not only of ends but also of the means, and with wise foresight she would have entrusted both to instinct alone.

And, in fact, we find that the more a cultivated reason deliberately devotes itself to the enjoyment of life and happiness, the more the man falls short of true contentment.

From this fact there arises in many persons, if only they are candid enough to admit it, a certain degree of misology, hatred of reason. This is particularly the case with those who are most experienced in its use. After counting all the advantages which they draw—I will not say from the invention of the arts of common luxury—from the sciences (which in the end seem to them to be also a luxury of the understanding), they nevertheless find
396 that they have actually brought more trouble on their shoulders instead of gaining in happiness; they finally envy, rather than despise, the common run of men who are better guided by merely natural instinct and who do not permit their reason much influence on their conduct. And we must at least admit that a morose attitude or ingratitude to the goodness with which the world is governed is by no means found always among those who temper or refute the boasting eulogies which are given of the advantages of happiness and contentment with which reason is supposed to supply us. Rather, their judgment is based on the Idea of another and far more worthy purpose of their existence for which, instead of happiness, their reason is properly intended; this purpose, therefore, being the supreme condition to which the private purposes of men must, for the most part, defer.

Since reason is not competent to guide the will safely with regard to its objects and the satisfaction of all our needs (which it in part multiplies), to this end an innate instinct would have led with far more certainty. But reason is given to us as a practical faculty (i.e., one which is meant to have an influence on the will). As nature has elsewhere distributed capacities suitable to the functions they are to perform, reason's proper function must be to produce a will good in itself and not one good merely as a means, since for the former, reason is absolutely essential. This will need not be the sole and complete good, yet it must be the condition of all others, even of the desire for happiness. In this case it is entirely compatible with the wisdom of nature that the cultivation of reason, which is required for the former unconditional purpose, at least in this life restricts in many ways—indeed, can reduce to nothing—the achievement of the latter unconditional purpose, happiness. For one perceives that nature here does not proceed unsuitably to its purpose, because reason, which recognizes its highest practical vocation in the establishment of a good will, is capable of a contentment of its own kind (i.e., one that springs from the attainment of a purpose determined by reason), even though this injures the ends of inclination.

397 We have, then, to develop the concept of a will which is to be esteemed as good in itself without regard to anything else. It dwells already in the natural and sound understanding and does not need so much to be taught as only to be brought to light. In the estimation of the total worth of our actions it always takes first place and is the condition of everything else. In order to show this, we shall take the concept of duty. It contains the concept of a good will, though with certain subjective restrictions and hindrances, but these are far from concealing it and making it unrecognizable, for they rather bring it out by contrast and make it shine forth all the more brightly.

I here omit all actions which are recognized as opposed to duty, even though they may be useful in one respect or another, for with these the question does not arise as to whether they may be done from duty, since they conflict with it. I also pass over actions which are really in accord with duty and to which one has no direct inclination, rather doing them because impelled to do so by another inclination. For it is easily decided whether an action in accord with duty is done from duty or for some selfish purpose. It is far more difficult to note this difference when the action is in accord with duty and, in addition, the subject has a direct inclination to do it. For example, it is in accord with duty that a dealer should not overcharge an inexperienced customer, and wherever there is much trade the prudent merchant does not do so, but has a fixed price for everyone so that a child may buy from him as cheaply as any other. Thus the customer is honestly served, but this is far from sufficient to warrant the belief that the merchant has behaved in this way from duty and principles of honesty. His own advantage required this behavior, but it cannot be assumed that over and above that he had a direct inclination to his customers and that, out of love, as it were, he gave none an advantage in price over another. The action was done neither from duty nor from direct inclination but only for a selfish purpose.

On the other hand, it is a duty to preserve one's life, and moreover everyone has a direct inclination to do so. But for that reason, the often anxious care which most men take of it has no intrinsic worth, and the maxim of doing so has no moral import. They 398
preserve their lives according to duty, but not from duty. But if adversities and hopeless sorrow completely take away the relish for life; if an unfortunate man, strong in soul, is indignant rather than despondent or dejected over his fate and wishes for death, and yet preserves his life without loving it and from neither inclination nor fear but from duty—then his maxim has moral merit.

To be kind where one can is a duty, and there are, moreover, many persons so sympathetically constituted that without any motive of vanity or selfishness they find an inner satisfaction in spreading joy and rejoice in the contentment of others which they have made possible. But I say that, however dutiful and however amiable it may be, that kind of action has no true moral worth. It is on a level with [actions done from] other inclinations, such as the inclination to honor, which, if fortunately directed to what in fact accords with duty and is generally useful and thus honorable, deserve praise and encouragement, but no esteem. For the maxim lacks the moral import of an action done not from inclination but from duty. But assume that the mind of that friend to mankind was clouded by a sorrow of his own which extinguished all sympathy with the lot of others, and though he still had the power to benefit others in distress their need left him untouched because he was preoccupied with his own. Now suppose him to tear himself, unsolicited by inclination, out of his dead insensibility and to do this action only from duty and without any inclination—then for the first time his action has genuine moral worth. Furthermore, if nature has put little sympathy into the heart of a man, and if he, though an honest man, is by temperament cold and indifferent to the sufferings of others perhaps because he is provided with special gifts of patience and fortitude and expects and even requires that others should have them too—and such a man would certainly not be the meanest product of nature—would not he find in himself a source from which to give himself a far higher worth than he could have got by having a good-natured temperament? This is unquestionably true even though nature did not make him philanthropic, for it is just here that the worth of character is brought out, which is morally the 399
incomparably highest of all: he is beneficent not from inclination, but from duty.

To secure one's own happiness is at least indirectly a duty, for discontent with one's condition under pressure from many cares and amid unsatisfied wants could easily become a great temptation to transgress against duties. But, without any view to duty, all men have the strongest and deepest inclination to happiness, because in this Idea all inclinations are summed up. But the precept of happiness is often so formulated that it definitely thwarts some inclinations, and men can make no definite and certain concept of the sum of satisfaction of all inclinations, which goes under the name of happiness. It is not to be wondered at, therefore, that a single inclination, definite as to what it promises and as to the time at which it can be satisfied, can outweigh a fluctuating idea and that, for example, a man with the gout can choose to enjoy what he likes and to suffer what he may, because according to his calculations at least on this occasion he has not sacrificed the enjoyment of the present moment to a perhaps groundless expectation of a happiness supposed to lie in health. But even in this case if the universal inclination to happiness did not determine his will, and if health were not at least for him a necessary factor in these calculations, there would still remain, as in all other cases, a law that he ought to promote his happiness not from inclination but from duty. Only from this law could his conduct have true moral worth.

It is in this way, undoubtedly, that we should understand those passages of Scripture which command us to love our neighbor and even our enemy, for love as an inclination cannot be commanded. But beneficence from duty, even when no inclination impels it and even when it is opposed by a natural and unconquerable aversion, is practical love, not pathological* love; it resides in the will and not in the propensities of feeling, in principles of action and not in tender sympathy; and it alone can be commanded.

[Thus the first proposition of morality is that to have genuine moral worth, an action must be done from duty.] The second proposition is: An action done from duty does not have its moral worth in the purpose which is to be achieved through it but in the maxim
400 whereby it is determined. Its moral value, therefore, does not depend upon the realization of the object of the action but merely on the principle of the volition by which the action is done irrespective of the objects of the faculty of desire. From the preceding discussion it is clear that the purposes we may have for our actions and their effects as ends and incentives of the will cannot give the actions any unconditional and moral worth. Wherein, then, can this worth lie, if it is not in the will in its relation to its hoped-for effect? It can lie nowhere else than in the principle of the will irrespective of the ends which can be realized by such action. For the will stands, as it were, at the crossroads halfway between its *a priori* principle which is formal and its posteriori incentive which is material. Since it must be determined by something, if it is done from duty it must be determined by the formal principle of volition as such, since every material principle has been withdrawn from it.

The third principle, as a consequence of the two preceding, I would express as follows: Duty is the necessity to do an action from respect for law. I can certainly have an inclination to an object as an effect of the proposed action, but I can never have respect for it precisely because it is a mere effect and not an activity of a will. Similarly, I can have no respect for any inclination whatsoever, whether my own or that of another; in the former case I can at most approve of it and in the latter I can even love it (i.e., see it as favorable to my own advantage). But that which is connected with my will merely as ground and not as consequence, that which does not serve my inclination but overpowers it or at least excludes it from being considered in making a choice—in a word, law itself—can be an object of respect and thus a command. Now as an act from duty wholly excludes the influence of inclination and therewith every object of the will, nothing remains which can determine the will objectively except law and subjectively except pure respect for this practical law. This subjective element is the maxim** that
401 I should follow such a law even if it thwarts all my inclinations.

Thus the moral worth of an action does not lie in the effect which is expected from it or in any principle of action which has to borrow its motive from this expected effect. For all these effects (agreeableness of my own condition, indeed even the promotion of the happiness of others) could be brought about through other causes and would not require the will of a rational being, while the highest and unconditional good can be found only in such a will. Therefore the preeminent good can consist only in the

*[Here as elsewhere Kant uses the word pathological to describe motives and actions arising from feeling or bodily impulses, with no suggestion of abnormality or disease.]

**A maxim is the subjective principle of volition. The objective principle (i.e., that which would serve all rational beings also subjectively as a practical principle if reason had full power over the faculty of desire) is the practical law.

conception of law in itself (which can be present only in a rational being) so far as this conception and not the hoped-for effect is the determining ground of the will. This preeminent good, which we call moral, is already present in the person who acts according to this conception, and we do not have to look for it first in the result.*

But what kind of law can that be, the conception of which must determine the will 402
without reference to the expected result? Under this condition alone can the will be called absolutely good without qualification. Since I have robbed the will of all impulses which could come to it from obedience to any law, nothing remains to serve as a principle of the will except universal conformity to law as such. That is, I ought never to act in such a way that I could not also will that my maxim should be a universal law. Strict conformity to law as such (without assuming any particular law applicable to certain actions) serves as the principle of the will, and it must serve as such a principle if duty is not to be a vain delusion and chimerical concept. The common sense of mankind (*gemeine Menschenvernunft*) in its practical judgments is in perfect agreement with this and has this principle constantly in view.

Let the question, for example, be: May I, when in distress, make a promise with the intention not to keep it? I easily distinguish the two meanings which the question can have, viz., whether it is prudent to make a false promise, or whether it conforms to duty. The former can undoubtedly be often the case, though I do see clearly that it is not sufficient merely to escape from the present difficulty by this expedient, but that I must consider whether inconveniences much greater than the present one may not later spring from this lie. Even with all my supposed cunning, the consequences cannot be so easily foreseen. Loss of credit might be far more disadvantageous than the misfortune I am now seeking to avoid, and it is hard to tell whether it might not be more prudent to act according to a universal maxim and to make it a habit not to promise anything without intending to fulfill it. But it is soon clear to me that such a maxim is based only on an apprehensive concern with consequences.

To be truthful from duty, however, is an entirely different thing from being truthful out of fear of untoward consequences, for in the former case the concept of the action itself contains a law for me, while in the latter I must first look about to see what results for me may be connected with it. To deviate from the principle of duty is certainly bad, but
to be unfaithful to my maxim of prudence can sometimes be very advantageous to me, 403
though it is certainly safer to abide by it. The shortest but most infallible way to find the answer to the question as to whether a deceitful promise is consistent with duty is to ask

*It might be objected that I seek to take refuge in an obscure feeling behind the word "respect," instead of clearly resolving the question with a concept of reason. But though respect is a feeling, it is not one received through any [outer] influence but is self-wrought by a rational concept; thus it differs specifically from all feelings of the former kind which may be referred to inclination or fear. What I recognize directly as a law for myself I recognize with respect, which means merely the consciousness of the submission of my will to a law without the intervention of other influences on my mind. The direct determination of the will by law and the consciousness of this determination is respect; thus respect can be regarded as the effect of the law on the subject and not as the cause of the law. Respect is properly the conception of a worth which thwarts my self-love. Thus it is regarded as an object neither of inclination nor of fear, though it has something analogous to both. The only object of respect is law, and indeed only the law which we impose on ourselves and yet recognize as necessary in itself. As a law we are subject to it without consulting self-love; as imposed on us by ourselves, it is a consequence of our will. In the former respect it is analogous to fear and in the latter to inclination. All respect for a person is only respect for the law (of righteousness, etc.) of which the person provides an example. Because we see the improvement of our talents as a duty, we think of a person of talent as the example of a law, as it were (the law that we should by practice become like him in his talents), and that constitutes our respect. All so-called moral interest consists solely in respect for the law.

myself: Would I be content that my maxim of extricating myself from difficulty by a false promise should hold as a universal law for myself as well as for others? And could I say to myself that everyone may make a false promise when he is in a difficulty from which he otherwise cannot escape? Immediately I see that I could will the lie but not a universal law to lie. For with such a law there would be no promises at all, inasmuch as it would be futile to make a pretense of my intention in regard to future actions to those who would not believe this pretense or—if they overhastily did so—would pay me back in my own coin. Thus my maxim would necessarily destroy itself as soon as it was made a universal law.

I do not, therefore, need any penetrating acuteness to discern what I have to do in order that my volition may be morally good. Inexperienced in the course of the world, incapable of being prepared for all its contingencies, I only ask myself: Can I will that my maxim become a universal law? If not, it must be rejected, not because of any disadvantage accruing to myself or even to others, but because it cannot enter as a principle into a possible enactment of universal law, and reason extorts from me an immediate respect for such legislation. I do not as yet discern on what it is grounded (this is a question the philosopher may investigate), but I at least understand that it is an estimation of a worth which far outweighs all the worth of whatever is recommended by the inclinations, and that the necessity that I act from pure respect for the practical law constitutes my duty. To duty every other motive must give place, because duty is the condition of a will good in itself, whose worth transcends everything.

Thus within the moral knowledge of ordinary human reason (*gemeine Menschenvernunft*) we have attained its principle. To be sure, ordinary human reason does not think this principle abstractly in such a universal form, but it always has the principle in view and uses it as the standard for its judgments. It would be easy to show how ordinary human
404 reason, with this compass, knows well how to distinguish what is good, what is bad, and what is consistent or inconsistent with duty. Without in the least teaching common reason anything new, we need only to draw its attention to its own principle (in the manner of Socrates), thus showing that neither science nor philosophy is needed in order to know what one has to do in order to be honest and good, and even wise and virtuous. We might have conjectured beforehand that the knowledge of what everyone is obliged to do and thus also to know would be within the reach of everyone, even of the most ordinary man. Here we cannot but admire the great advantages which the practical faculty of judgment has over the theoretical in ordinary human understanding. In the theoretical, if ordinary reason ventures to go beyond the laws of experience and perceptions of the senses, it falls into sheer inconceivabilities and selfcontradictions, or at least into a chaos of uncertainty, obscurity, and instability. In the practical, on the other hand, the power of judgment first shows itself to advantage when common understanding excludes all sensuous incentives from practical laws. It then even becomes subtle, quibbling with its own conscience or with other claims to what should be called right, or wishing to determine accurately, for its own instruction, the worth of certain actions. But the most remarkable thing about ordinary human understanding in its practical concern is that it may have as much hope as any philosopher of hitting the mark. In fact, it is almost more certain to do so that the philosopher, for while he has no principle which common understanding lacks, his judgment is easily confused by a mass of irrelevant considerations so that it easily turns aside from the correct way. Would it not, therefore, be wiser in moral matters to acquiesce in ordinary reasonable judgment and at most to call in philosophy in order to make the system of morals more complete and comprehensible and its rules more convenient for use (especially in disputation), than to steer the ordinary understanding from its happy simplicity in practical matters and to lead it through philosophy into a new path of inquiry and instruction?

Innocence is indeed a glorious thing, but it is very sad that it cannot well maintain 405
itself, being easily led astray. For this reason, even wisdom—which consists more in acting than in knowing—needs science, not so as to learn from it but to secure admission and permanence to its precepts. Man feels in himself a powerful counterpoise against all commands of duty which reason presents to him as so deserving of respect. This counterpoise is his needs and inclinations, the complete satisfaction of which he sums up under the name of happiness. Now reason issues inexorable commands without promising anything to the inclinations. It disregards, as it were, and holds in contempt those claims which are so impetuous and yet so plausible, and which refuse to be suppressed by any command. From this a natural dialectic arises, i.e., a propensity to argue against the stern laws of duty and their validity, or at least to place their purity and strictness in doubt and, where possible, to make them more accordant with our wishes and inclinations. This is equivalent to corrupting them in their very foundations and destroying their dignity—a thing which even ordinary practical reason cannot finally call good.

In this way ordinary human reason is impelled to go outside its sphere and to take a step into the field of practical philosophy. But it is forced to do so not by any speculative need, which never occurs to it so long as it is satisfied to remain merely healthy reason; rather, it is impelled on practical grounds to obtain information and clear instruction respecting the source of its principle and the correct definition of this principle in its opposition to the maxims based on need and inclination. It seeks this information in order to escape from the perplexity of opposing claims and to avoid the danger of losing all genuine moral principles through the equivocation in which it is easily involved. Thus when ordinary practical reason cultivates itself, a dialectic surreptitiously ensues which forces it to seek aid in philosophy, just as the same thing happens in the theoretical use of reason. Ordinary practical reason, like theoretical reason, will find rest only in a complete critical examination of our reason.

SECOND SECTION 406

TRANSITION FROM POPULAR MORAL PHILOSOPHY TO THE METAPHYSICS OF MORALS

Although we have derived our earlier concept of duty from the ordinary use of our practical reason, it is by no means to be inferred that we have treated it as an empirical concept. On the contrary, if we attend to our experience of the way men act, we meet frequent and, as we must confess, justified complaints that we cannot cite a single sure example of the disposition to act from pure duty. There are also justified complaints that, though much may be done that accords with what duty commands, it is nevertheless always doubtful whether it is done from duty and thus whether it has moral worth. There have always been philosophers who for this reason have absolutely denied the reality of this disposition in human actions, attributing everything to more or less refined self-love. They have done so without questioning the correctness of the concept of morality. Rather they spoke with sincere regret of the frailty and corruption of human nature, which is noble enough to take as its precept an Idea so worthy of respect but which at the same time is too weak to follow it, employing reason, which should give laws for human nature, only to provide for the interest of the inclinations either singly or, at best, in their greatest possible harmony with one another.

407 It is, in fact, absolutely impossible by experience to discern with complete certainty a single case in which the maxim of an action, however much it might conform to duty, rested solely on moral grounds and on the conception of one's duty. It sometimes happens that in the most searching self-examination we can find nothing except the moral ground of duty which could have been powerful enough to move us to this or that good action and to such great sacrifice. But from this we cannot by any means conclude with certainty that a secret impulse of self-love, falsely appearing as the Idea of duty, was not actually the true determining cause of the will. For we like to flatter ourselves with a pretended nobler motive, while in fact even the strictest examination can never lead us entirely behind the secret incentives, for when moral worth is in question it is not a matter of actions which one sees but of their inner principles which one does not see.

Moreover, one cannot better serve the wishes of those who ridicule all morality as a mere phantom of human imagination overreaching itself through self-conceit than by conceding that the concepts of duty must be derived only from experience (for they are ready, from indolence, to believe that this is true of all other concepts too). For, by this concession, a sure triumph is prepared for them. Out of love for humanity I am willing to admit that most of our actions are in accord with duty; but if we look more closely at our thoughts and aspirations, we come everywhere upon the dear self, which is always turning up, and it is this instead of the stern command of duty (which would often require self-denial) which supports our plans. One need not be an enemy of virtue, but only a cool observer who does not confuse even the liveliest aspiration for the good with its actuality, to be sometimes doubtful whether true virtue can really be found anywhere in the world. This is especially true as one's years increase and the power of judgment is made wiser by experience and more acute in observation. This being so, nothing can secure us against the
408 complete abandonment of our ideas of duty and preserve in us a well-founded respect for its law except the conviction that, even if there never were actions springing from such pure sources, our concern is not whether this or that was done, but that reason of itself and independently of all appearances commanded what ought to be done. Our concern is with actions of which perhaps the world has never had an example, with actions whose feasibility might be seriously doubted by those who base everything on experience, and yet with actions inexorably commanded by reason. For example, pure sincerity in friendship can be demanded of every man, and this demand is not in the least diminished if a sincere friend has never existed, because this duty, as duty in general, prior to all experience lies in the Idea of reason which determines the will on *a priori* grounds.

No experience, it is clear, can give occasion for inferring the possibility of such apodictic laws. This is especially clear when we add that, unless we wish to deny all truth to the concept of morality and renounce its application to any possible object, we cannot refuse to admit that the law is of such broad significance that it holds not merely for men but for all rational beings as such; we must grant that it must be valid with absolute necessity, and not merely under contingent conditions and with exceptions. For with what right could we bring into unlimited respect something that might be valid only under contingent human conditions? And how could laws of the determination of our will be held to be laws of the determination of the will of any rational being whatever and of ourselves in so far as we are rational beings, if they were merely empirical and did not have their origin completely *a priori* in pure, but practical, reason?

Nor could one given poorer counsel to morality than to attempt to derive it from examples. For each example of morality which is exhibited must itself have been previously judged according to principles of morality to see whether it was worthy to serve as an original example or model. By no means could it authoritatively furnish the concept of

morality. Even the Holy One of the Gospel must be compared with our ideal of moral perfection before He is recognized as such; even He says of Himself, "Why call ye Me 409
(Whom you see) good? None is good (the archetype of the good) except God only (Whom you do not see)." But whence do we have the concept of God as the highest good? Solely from the Idea of moral perfection which reason formulates *a priori* and which it inseparably connects with the concept of a free will. Imitation has no place in moral matters, and examples serve only for encouragement. That is, they put beyond question the possibility of performing what the law commands, and they make visible that which the practical rule expresses more generally. But they can never justify our guiding ourselves by examples and our setting aside their true original, which lies in reason.

If there is thus no genuine supreme principle of morality which does not rest on pure reason alone independent of all possible experience, I do not believe it is necessary even to ask whether it is well to exhibit these concepts generally (in abstracto), which, together with the principles belonging to them, are established *a priori*. At any rate, the question need not be asked if knowledge of them is to be distinguished from ordinary knowledge and called philosophical. But in our times this question may be necessary. For if we collected votes as to whether pure rational knowledge separated from all experience (i.e., a metaphysics of morals) or popular practical philosophy is to be preferred, it is easily guessed on which side the majority would stand.

This condescension to popular notions is certainly very commendable once the ascent to the principles of pure reason has been satisfactorily accomplished. That would mean the prior establishment of the doctrine of morals on metaphysics and then, when it is established, procuring a hearing for it through popularization. But it is extremely absurd to want to achieve popular appeal in the first investigation, where everything depends on the correctness of the fundamental principles. Not only can this procedure never make claim to that rarest merit of true philosophical popularity, since there is really no art in being generally comprehensible if one thereby renounces all basic insight; but it produces a disgusting jumble of patched-up observations and half-reasoned principles. Shallow pates enjoy this, for it is very useful in everyday chitchat, while the more sensible feel confused and dissatisfied and avert their eyes without being able to help themselves. But philosophers, who see through this delusion, get little hearing when they call people away 410
from this would-be popularity so that they may have genuine popular appeal once they have gained a definite understanding.

One need only look at the essays on morality favored by popular taste. One will sometimes meet with the particular vocation of human nature (but occasionally with the Idea of a rational nature in general), sometimes perfection and sometimes happiness, here moral feeling, there fear of God, a little of this and a little of that in a marvelous mixture. It never occurs to the authors, however, to ask whether the principles of morality are, after all, to be sought anywhere in knowledge of human nature (which we can derive only from experience). And if this is not the case, if the principles are *a priori*, free from everything empirical, and found exclusively in pure rational concepts and not at all in any other place, they never ask whether they should undertake this investigation as a separate inquiry (i.e., as pure practical philosophy) or (if one may use a name so decried) a metaphysics* of morals. They never think of dealing with it alone and bringing it by

*If one wishes, the pure philosophy (metaphysics) of morals can be distinguished from the applied (i.e., applied to human nature), just as pure mathematics and pure logic are distinguished from applied mathematics and applied logic. By this designation one is immediately reminded that moral principles are not founded on the peculiarities of human nature but must stand of themselves *a priori*, and that from such principles practical rules for every rational nature, and accordingly for man, must be derivable.

itself to completeness and of requiring the public, which desires popularization, to await the outcome of this undertaking.

But a completely isolated metaphysics of morals, mixed with no anthropology, no theology, no physics or hyperphysics, and even less with occult qualities (which might be called hypophysical), is not only an indispensable substrate of all theoretically sound and definite knowledge of duties; it is also a desideratum of the highest importance to the actual fulfillment of its precepts. For the thought of duty and of the moral law generally, with no admixture of empirical inducements, has an influence on the human heart so
411 much more powerful than all other incentives* which may be derived from the empirical field that reason, in the consciousness of its dignity, despises them and gradually becomes master over them. It has this influence only through reason alone, which thereby first realizes that it can of itself be practical. A mixed theory of morals which is put together from incentives of feelings and inclinations and from rational concepts must, on the other hand, make the mind vacillate between motives which cannot be brought together under any principle and which can lead only accidentally to the good, and frequently lead to the bad.

From what has been said it is clear that all moral concepts have their seat and origin entirely *a priori* in reason. This is just as much the case in the most ordinary reason as in the reason which is speculative to the highest degree. It is obvious that they can be abstracted from no empirical and hence merely contingent cognitions. In the purity of origin lies their worthiness to serve us as supreme practical principles, and to the extent that something empirical is added to them, just this much is subtracted from their genuine influence and from the unqualified worth of actions. Furthermore, it is evident that it is not only of the greatest necessity from a theoretical point of view when it is a question of speculation but also of the utmost practical importance to derive the concepts and laws of morals from pure reason and to present them pure and unmixed, and to determine the scope of this entire practical but pure rational knowledge (the entire faculty of pure prac-
412 tical reason) without making the principles depend upon the particular nature of human reason, as speculative philosophy may permit and even find necessary. But since moral laws should hold for every rational being as such, the principles must be derived from the universal concept of a rational being in general. In this manner all morals, which need anthropology for their application to men, must be completely developed first as pure philosophy (i.e., metaphysics), independently of anthropology (a thing feasibly done in such distinct fields of knowledge). For we know well that if we are not in possession of such a metaphysics, it is not merely futile [to try to] define accurately for the purposes of speculative judgment the moral element of duty in all actions which accord with duty, but impossible to base morals on legitimate principles for even ordinary practical use, especially in moral instruction; and it is only in this manner that pure moral dispositions can be produced and engrafted on men's minds for the purpose of the highest good in the world.

*I have a letter from the late excellent Sulzer in which he asks me why the theories of virtue accomplish so little even though they contain so much that is convincing to reason. My answer was delayed in order that I might make it complete. The answer is only that the teachers themselves have not completely clarified their concepts, and when they wish to make up for this by hunting in every quarter for motives to the morally good so as to make their physic right strong, they spoil it. For the commonest observation shows that if we imagine an act of honesty performed with a steadfast soul and sundered from all view to any advantage in this or another world and even under the greatest temptations of need or allurement, it far surpasses and eclipses any similar action which was affected in the least by any foreign incentive; it elevates the soul and arouses the wish to be able to act in this way. Even moderately young children feel this impression, and one should never represent duties to them in any other way.

In this study we do not advance merely from the common moral judgment (which here is very worthy of respect) to the philosophical, as this has already been done; but we advance by natural stages from popular philosophy (which goes no farther than it can grope by means of examples) to metaphysics (which is not held back by anything empirical and which, as it must measure out the entire scope of rational knowledge of this kind, reaches even Ideas, where examples fail us). In order to make this advance, we must follow and clearly present the practical faculty of reason from its universal rules of determination to the point where the concept of duty arises from it.

Everything in nature works according to laws. Only a rational being has the capacity of acting according to the *conception* of laws (i.e., according to principles). This capacity is the will. Since reason is required for the derivation of actions from laws, will is nothing less than practical reason. If reason infallibly determines the will, the actions which such a being recognizes as objectively necessary are also subjectively necessary. That is, the will is a faculty of choosing only that which reason, independently of inclination, recognizes as practically necessary (i.e., as good). But if reason of itself does not sufficiently determine the will, and if the will is subjugated to subjective conditions (certain incentives) which do not always agree with the objective conditions—in a word,
if the will is not of itself in complete accord with reason (which is the actual case with 413
men), then the actions which are recognized as objectively necessary are subjectively contingent, and the determination of such a will according to objective laws is a constraint. That is, the relation of objective laws to a will which is not completely good is conceived as the determination of the will of a rational being by principles of reason to which this will is not by its nature necessarily obedient.

The conception of an objective principle, so far as it constrains a will, is a command (of reason), and the formula of this command is called an *imperative*.

All imperatives are expressed by an "ought" and thereby indicate the relation of an objective law of reason to a will which is not in its subjective constitution necessarily determined by this law. This relation is that of constraint. Imperatives say that it would be good to do or to refrain from doing something, but they say it to a will which does not always do something simply because the thing is presented to it as good to do. Practical good is what determines the will by means of the conception of reason and hence not by subjective causes but objectively, on grounds which are valid for every rational being as such. It is distinguished from the pleasant, as that which has an influence on the will only by means of a sensation from purely subjective causes, which hold for the senses only of this or that person and not as a principle of reason which holds for everyone.*

A perfectly good will, therefore, would be equally subject to objective laws of the 414
good, but it could not be conceived as constrained by them to accord with them, because

*The dependence of the faculty of desire on sensations is called inclination, and inclination always indicates a need. The dependence of a contingently determinable will on principles of reason, however, is called interest. An interest is present only in a dependent will which is not of itself always in accord with reason; in the divine will we cannot conceive of an interest. But even the human will can take an interest in something without thereby acting from interest. The former means the practical interest in the action; the latter, the pathological interest in the object of the action. The former indicates only the dependence of the will on principles of reason in themselves, while the latter indicates dependence on the principles of reason for the purpose of inclination, since reason gives only the practical rule by which the needs of inclination are to be aided. In the former case the action interests me, and in the latter the object of the action (so far as it is pleasant for me) interests me. In the First Section we have seen that, in the case of an action done from duty, no regard must be given to the interest in the object, but merely to the action itself and its principle in reason (i.e., the law).

it can be determined to act by its own subjective constitution only through the conception of the good. Thus no imperatives hold for the divine will or, more generally, for a holy will. The "ought" here is out of place, for the volition of itself is necessarily in unison with the law. Therefore imperatives are only formulas expressing the relation of objective laws of volition in general to the subjective imperfection of the will of this or that rational being, for example, the human will.

All imperatives command either *hypothetically* or *categorically*. The former present the practical necessity of a possible action as a means to achieving something else which one desires (or which one may possibly desire). The categorical imperative would be one which presented an action as of itself objectively necessary, without regard to any other end.

Since every practical law presents a possible action as good and thus as necessary for a subject practically determinable by reason, all imperatives are formulas of the determination of action which is necessary by the principle of a will which is in any way good. If the action is good only as a means to something else, the imperative is hypothetical; but if it is thought of as good in itself, and hence as necessary in a will which of itself conforms to reason as the principle of this will, the imperative is categorical.

The imperative thus says what action possible for me would be good, and it presents the practical rule in relation to a will which does not forthwith perform an action simply because it is good, in part because the subject does not always know that the action is good, and in part (when he does know it) because his maxims can still be opposed to the objective principles of a practical reason.

415 The hypothetical imperative, therefore, says only that the action is good to some purpose, possible or actual. In the former case, it is a problematical, in the latter an assertorical, practical principle. The categorical imperative, which declares the action to be of itself objectively necessary without making any reference to any end in view (i.e., without having any other purpose), holds as an apodictical practical principle.

We can think of what is possible only through the powers of some rational being as a possible end in view of any will. As a consequence, the principles of action thought of as necessary to attain a possible end in view which can be achieved by them, are in reality infinitely numerous. All sciences have some practical part consisting of problems which presuppose some purpose as well as imperatives directing how it can be reached. These imperatives can therefore be called, generally, imperatives of skill. Whether the purpose is reasonable and good is not in question at all, for the questions concerns only what must be done in order to attain it. The precepts to be followed by a physician in order to cure his patient and by a poisoner to bring about certain death are of equal value in so far as each does that which will perfectly accomplish his purpose. Since in early youth we do not know what purposes we may have in the course of our life, parents seek to let their children learn a great many things and provide for skill in the use of means to all sorts of ends which they might choose, among which they cannot determine whether any one of them will become their child's actual purpose, though it may be that someday he may have it as his actual purpose. And this anxiety is so great that they commonly neglect to form and correct their children's judgment on the worth of the things which they may make their ends.

There is one end, however, which we may presuppose as actual in all rational beings so far as imperatives apply to them, that is, so far as they are dependent beings. There is one purpose which they not only can have but which we can presuppose that they all *do* have by a necessity of nature. This purpose is happiness. The hypothetical imperative which represents the practical necessity of an action as means to the promotion of happiness is an assertorical imperative. We may not expound it as necessary to a

Immanuel Kant and Luncheon Guests, 1893, by E. Doestling. While Kant led a simple, routine-filled life, he was known as a delightful conversationalist and host who had many friends and admirers. (©*ullstein bild/Getty*)

merely uncertain and merely possible purpose, but as necessary to a purpose which we 416
can *a priori* and with assurance assume for everyone because it belongs to his essence. Skill in the choice of means to one's own highest well-being can be called prudence* in the narrowest sense. Thus the imperative which refers to the choice of means to one's own happiness (i.e., the precept of prudence) is still only hypothetical, and the action is not commanded absolutely but commanded only as a means to another end in view.

*The word "prudence" may be taken in two senses, and it may bear the names of prudence with reference to things of the world and private prudence. The former sense means the skill of a man in having an influence on others so as to use them for his own purposes. The latter is the ability to unite all these purposes to his own lasting advantage. The worth of the first is finally reduced to the latter, and of one who is prudent in the former sense but not in the latter we might better say that he is clever and cunning yet, on the whole, imprudent.

Finally, there is one imperative which directly commands certain conduct without making its condition some purpose to be reached by it. This imperative is categorical. It concerns not the material of the action and its intended result, but the form and principle from which it originates. What is essentially good in it consists in the mental disposition, the result being what it may. This imperative may be called the imperative of morality.

Volition according to these three principles is plainly distinguished by the dissimilarity in the constraints by which they subject the will. In order to clarify this dissimilarity, I believe that they are most suitably named if one says that they are either rules of skill, counsels of prudence, or commands (laws) of morality, respectively. For law alone implies the concept of an unconditional and objective and hence universally valid necessity, and commands are laws which must be obeyed even against inclination. Counsels do indeed involve necessity, but a necessity that can hold only under a subjectively contingent condition (i.e., whether this or that man counts this or that as part of his happiness). The categorical imperative, on the other hand, is restricted by no condition. As absolutely, though practically, necessary it can be called a command in the strict sense. We could also
417 call the first imperatives technical (belonging to art), the second *pragmatic** (belonging to well-being), and the third moral (belonging to free conduct as such, i.e., to morals).

The question now arises: How are all these imperatives possible? This question does not require an answer as to how the action which the imperative commands can be performed, but only an answer as to how the constraint of the will, which the imperative expresses in setting the problem, can be conceived. How an imperative of skill is possible requires no particular discussion. Whoever wills the end, so far as reason has decisive influence on his action, wills also the indispensably necessary steps to it that he can take. This proposition, in what concerns the will, is analytical; for, in the willing of an object as an effect, my causality, as an acting cause of this effect shown in my use of the means to it, is already thought, and the imperative derives the concept of actions necessary to this purpose from the concept of willing this purpose. Synthetical propositions undoubtedly are necessary for determining the means to a proposed end, but they do not concern the ground, the act of the will, but only the way to achieve the object. Mathematics teaches, by synthetical propositions only, that in order to bisect a line according to an infallible principle, I must make two intersecting arcs from each of its extremities; but if I know the proposed result can be obtained only by such an action, then it is an analytical proposition that, if I fully will the effect, I must also will the action necessary to produce it. For it is one and the same thing to conceive of something as an effect which is in a certain way possible through me, and to conceive of myself as acting in this way.

If it were only easy to give a definite concept of happiness, the imperatives of pru-
418 dence would perfectly correspond to those of skill and would likewise be analytical. For it could then be said in this case as well as in the former that whoever wills the end wills also (necessarily according to reason) the only means to it which are in his power. But it is a misfortune that the concept of happiness is so indefinite that, although each person wishes to attain it, he can never definitely and self-consistently state what it is that he really wishes and wills. The reason for this is that all elements which belong to the concept of happiness are empirical (i.e., they must be taken from experience), while for the Idea of happiness an absolute whole, a maximum, of well-being is needed in my present

*It seems to me that the proper meaning of the word "pragmatic" could be most accurately defined in this way. For sanctions which properly flow not from the law of states as necessary statutes but from provision for the general welfare are called pragmatic. A history is pragmatically composed when it teaches prudence (i.e., instructs the world how it could provide for its interest better than, or at least as well as, has been done in the past).

and in every future condition. Now it is impossible for even a most clear-sighted and most capable but finite being to form here a definite concept of that which he really wills. If he wills riches, how much anxiety, envy, and intrigues might he not thereby draw upon his shoulders! If he wills much knowledge and vision, perhaps it might become only an eye that much sharper to show him as more dreadful the evils which are now hidden from him and which are yet unavoidable; or it might be to burden his desires—which already sufficiently engage him—with even more needs! If he wills long life, who guarantees that it will not be long misery! If he wills at least health, how often has not the discomfort of his body restrained him from excesses into which perfect health would have led him? In short, he is not capable, on any principle and with complete certainty, of ascertaining what would make him truly happy; omniscience would be needed for this. He cannot, therefore, act according to definite principles so as to be happy, but only according to empirical counsels (e.g., those of diet, economy, courtesy, restraint, etc.) which are shown by experience best to promote well-being on the average. Hence the imperatives of prudence cannot, in the strict sense, command (i.e., present actions objectively as practically necessary); thus they are to be taken as counsels (*consilia*) rather than as commands (*praecepta*) of reason, and the task of determining infallibly and universally what action will promote the happiness of a rational being is completely unsolvable. 419
There can be no imperative which would, in the strict sense, command us to do what makes for happiness, because happiness is an ideal not of reason but of imagination, depending only on empirical grounds which one would expect in vain to determine an action through which the totality of consequences—which in fact is infinite—could be achieved. Assuming that the means to happiness could be infallibly stated, this imperative of prudence would be an analytically practical proposition for it differs from the imperative of skill only in that its purpose is given, while in the imperative of skill it is merely a possible purpose. Since both, however, command the means to that which one presupposes as a willed purpose, the imperative which commands the willing of the means to him who wills the end is in both cases analytical. There is, consequently, no difficulty in seeing the possibility of such an imperative.

To see how the imperative of morality is possible, then, is without doubt the only question needing an answer. It is not hypothetical, and thus the objectively conceived necessity cannot be supported by any presupposed purpose, as was the case with the hypothetical imperatives. But it must not be overlooked that it cannot be shown by any example (i.e., it cannot be empirically shown) that there is such an imperative. Rather, it is to be suspected that all imperatives which appear to be categorical are tacitly hypothetical. For instance, when it is said, "Thou shalt not make a false promise," we assume that the necessity of this prohibition is not a mere counsel for the sake of escaping some other evil, so that it would read: "Thou shalt not make a false promise, lest, if it comes to light, thou ruinest thy credit." [In so doing] we assume that an action of this kind must be regarded as in itself bad and that the imperative prohibiting it is categorical, but we cannot show with certainty by any example that the will is here determined by the law alone without any other incentives, although it appears to be so. For it is always possible that secretly fear of disgrace, and perhaps also obscure apprehension of other dangers, may have had an influence on the will. Who can prove by experience the nonexistence of a cause when experience shows us only that we do not perceive the cause? In such a case the so-called moral imperative, which as such appears to be categorical and unconditional, would be actually only a pragmatic precept which makes us attentive to our own advantage and teaches us to consider it.

Thus we shall have to investigate purely *a priori* the possibility of a categorical imperative, for we do not have the advantage that experience would show us the reality
420 of this imperative so that the [demonstration of its] possibility would be necessary only for its explanation, and not for its establishment. In the meantime, this much at least may be seen: the categorical imperative alone can be taken as a practical law, while all other imperatives may be called principles of the will but not laws. This is because what is necessary merely for the attainment of some chosen end can be regarded as itself contingent and we get rid of the precept once we give up the end in view, whereas the unconditional command leaves the will no freedom to choose the opposite. Thus it alone implies the necessity which we require of a law.

Secondly, in the case of the categorical imperative or law of morality, the cause of the difficulty in discerning its possibility is very weighty. This imperative is an *a priori* synthetical practical proposition* and since to discern the possibility of propositions of this sort is so difficult in theoretical knowledge it may well be gathered that it will be no less difficult in practical knowledge.

In attacking this problem, we will first inquire whether the mere concept of a categorical imperative does not also furnish the formula containing the proposition which alone can be a categorical imperative. For even when we know the formula of the imperative, to learn how such an absolute command is possible will require difficult and special labors which we shall postpone to the last Section.

If I think of a hypothetical imperative as such, I do not know what it will contain until the condition is stated [under which it is an imperative]. But if I think of a categorical imperative, I know immediately what it will contain. For since the imperative
421 contains, besides the law, only the necessity of the maxim** of acting in accordance with the law, while the law contains no condition to which it is restricted, nothing remains except the universality of law as such to which the maxim of the action should conform; and this conformity alone is what is represented as necessary by the imperative.

There is, therefore, only one categorical imperative. It is: Act only according to that maxim by which you can at the same time will that it should become a universal law.

Now if all imperatives of duty can be derived from this one imperative as a principle, we can at least show what we understand by the concept of duty and what it means, even though it remain undecided whether that which is called duty is an empty concept or not.

The universality of law according to which effects are produced constitutes what is properly called nature in the most general sense (as to form) (i.e., the existence of things so far as it is determined by universal laws). [By analogy], then, the universal imperative of duty can be expressed as follows: Act as though the maxim of your action were by your will to become a universal law of nature.

*I connect *a priori*, and hence necessarily, the action with the will without supposing as a condition that there is any inclination [to the action] (though I do so only objectively, i.e., under the Idea of a reason which would have complete power over all subjective motives). This is, therefore, a practical proposition which does not analytically derive the willing of an action from some other volition already presupposed (for we do not have such a perfect will); it rather connects it directly with the concept of the will of a rational being as something which is not contained within it.

**A maxim is the subjective principle of acting and must be distinguished from the objective principle (i.e., the practical law). The former contains the practical rule which reason determines according to the conditions of the subject (often his ignorance or inclinations) and is thus the principle according to which the subject acts. The law, on the other hand, is the objective principle valid for every rational being, and the principle by which it ought to act, i.e., an imperative.

We shall now enumerate some duties, adopting the usual division of them into duties to ourselves and to others and into perfect and imperfect duties.*

1. A man who is reduced to despair by a series of evils feels a weariness with life 422
but is still in possession of his reason sufficiently to ask whether it would not be contrary to his duty to himself to take his own life. Now he asks whether the maxim of his action could become a universal law of nature. His maxim, however is: For love of myself, I make it my principle to shorten my life when by a longer duration it threatens more evil than satisfaction. But it is questionable whether this principle of self-love could become a universal law of nature. One immediately sees a contradiction in a system of nature whose law would be to destroy life by the feeling whose special office is to impel the improvement of life. In this case it would not exist as nature; hence that maxim cannot obtain as a law of nature, and thus it wholly contradicts the supreme principle of all duty.

2. Another man finds himself forced by need to borrow money. He well knows that he will not be able to repay it, but he also sees that nothing will be lent him if he does not firmly promise to repay it at a certain time. He desires to make such a promise, but he has enough conscience to ask himself whether it is not improper and opposed to duty to relieve his distress in such a way. Now, assuming he does decide to do so, the maxim of his action would be as follows: When I believe myself to be in need of money, I will borrow money and promise to repay it, although I know I shall never be able to do so. Now this principle of self-love or of his own benefit may very well be compatible with his whole future welfare, but the question is whether it is right. He changes the pretension of self-love into a universal law and then puts the question: How would it be if my maxim became a universal law? He immediately sees that it could never hold as a universal law of nature and be consistent with itself; rather it must necessarily contradict itself. For the universality of a law which says that anyone who believes himself to be in need could promise what he pleased with the intention of not fulfilling it would make the promise itself and the end to be accomplished by it impossible; no one would believe what was promised to him but would only laugh at any such assertion as vain pretense.

3. A third finds in himself a talent which could, by means of some cultivation,
make him in many respects a useful man. But he finds himself in comfortable circum- 423
stances and prefers indulgence in pleasure to troubling himself with broadening and improving his fortunate natural gifts. Now, however, let him ask whether his maxim of neglecting his gifts, besides agreeing with his propensity to idle amusement, agrees also with what is called duty. He sees that a system of nature could indeed exist in accordance with such a law, even though man (like the inhabitants of the South Sea Islands) should let his talents rust and resolve to devote his life merely to idleness, indulgence, and propagation—in a word, to pleasure. But he cannot possibly will that this should become a universal law of nature or that it should be implanted in us by a natural instinct. For, as a rational being, he necessarily wills that all his faculties should be developed, inasmuch as they are given him and serve him for all sorts of purposes.

4. A fourth man, for whom things are going well, sees that others (whom he could help) have to struggle with great hardships, and he asks, "What concern of mine is it? Let each one be as happy as heaven wills, or as he can make himself; I will not take anything

*It must be noted here that I reserve the division of duties for a future *Metaphysics of Morals* and that the division here stands as only an arbitrary one (chosen in order to arrange my examples). For the rest, by a perfect duty I here understand a duty which permits no exception in the interest of inclination; thus I have not merely outer but also inner perfect duties. This runs contrary to the usage adopted in the schools, but I am not disposed to defend it here because it is all one to my purpose whether this is conceded or not.

from him or even envy him; but to his welfare or to his assistance in time of need I have no desire to contribute." If such a way of thinking were a universal law of nature, certainly the human race could exist, and without doubt even better than in a state where everyone talks of sympathy and good will or even exerts himself occasionally to practice them while, on the other hand, he cheats when he can and betrays or otherwise violates the right of man. Now although it is possible that a universal law of nature according to that maxim could exist, it is nevertheless impossible to will that such a principle should hold everywhere as a law of nature. For a will which resolved this would conflict with itself, since instances can often arise in which he would need the love and sympathy of others, and in which he would have robbed himself, by such a law of nature springing from his own will, of all hope of the aid he desires.

424 The foregoing are a few of the many actual duties, or at least of duties we hold to be actual, whose derivation from the one stated principle is clear. We must be able to will that a maxim of our action become a universal law; this is the canon of the moral estimation of our action generally. Some actions are of such a nature that their maxim cannot even be *thought* as a universal law of nature without contradiction, far from it being possible that one could will that it should be such. In others this internal impossibility is not found, though it is still impossible to *will* that that maxim should be raised to the universality of a law of nature, because such a will would contradict itself. We easily see that a maxim of the first kind conflicts with stricter or narrower (imprescriptable) duty, that of the latter with broader (meritorious) duty. Thus all duties, so far as the kind of obligation (not the object of their action) is concerned, have been completely exhibited by these examples in their dependence upon the same principle.

When we observe ourselves in any transgression of a duty, we find that we do not actually will that our maxim should become a universal law. That is impossible for us; rather, the contrary of this maxim should remain as a law generally, and we only take the liberty of making an exception to it for ourselves or for the sake of our inclination, and for this one occasion. Consequently, if we weighed everything from one and the same standpoint, namely, reason, we would come upon a contradiction in our own will, viz., that a certain principle is objectively necessary as a universal law and yet subjectively does not hold universally but rather admits exceptions. However, since we regard our action at one time from the point of view of a will wholly conformable to reason and then from that of a will affected by inclinations, there is actually no contradiction, but rather an opposition of inclination to the precept of reason (*antagonismus*). In this the universality of the principle (*universalitas*) is changed into mere generality (*generalitas*), whereby the practical principle of reason meets the maxim halfway. Although this cannot be justified in our own impartial judgment, it does show that we actually acknowledge the validity of the categorical imperative and allow ourselves (with all respect to it) only a few exceptions which seem to us to be unimportant and forced upon us.

425 We have thus at least established that if duty is a concept which is to have significance and actual law-giving authority for our actions, it can be expressed only in categorical imperatives and not at all in hypothetical ones. For every application of it we have also clearly exhibited the content of the categorical imperative which must contain the principle of all duty (if there is such). This is itself very much. But we are not yet advanced far enough to prove *a priori* that that kind of imperative really exists, that there is a practical law which of itself commands absolutely and without any incentives, and that obedience to this law is duty.

With a view to attaining this, it is extremely important to remember that we must not let ourselves think that the reality of this principle can be derived from the particular constitution of human nature. For duty is practical unconditional necessity of action; it must, therefore, hold for all rational beings (to which alone an imperative can apply), and only for that reason can it be a law for all human wills. Whatever is derived from the particular natural situation of man as such, or from certain feelings and propensities, or even from a particular tendency of the human reason which might not hold necessarily for the will of every rational being (if such a tendency is possible), can give a maxim valid for us but not a law; that is, it can give a subjective principle by which we might act if only we have the propensity and inclination, but not an objective principle by which we would be directed to act even if all our propensity, inclination, and natural tendency were opposed to it. This is so far the case that the sublimity and intrinsic worth of the command is the better shown in a duty the fewer subjective causes there are for it and the more they are against it; the latter do not weaken the constraint of the law or diminish its validity.

Here we see philosophy brought to what is, in fact, a precarious position, which should be made fast even though it is supported by nothing in either heaven or earth. Here philosophy must show its purity, as the absolute sustainer of its laws, and not as the herald of laws which an implanted sense or who knows what tutelary nature whispers to it. Those may be better than nothing at all, but they can never afford fundamental principles, which reason alone dictates. These fundamental principles must originate entirely 426
a priori and thereby obtain their commanding authority; they can expect nothing from the inclination of men but everything from the supremacy of the law and due respect for it. Otherwise they condemn man to self-contempt and inner abhorrence.

Thus everything empirical is not only wholly unworthy to be an ingredient in the principle of morality but is even highly prejudicial to the purity of moral practices themselves. For, in morals, the proper and inestimable worth of an absolutely good will consists precisely in the freedom of the principle of action from all influences from contingent grounds which only experience can furnish. We cannot too much or too often warn against the lax or even base manner of thought which seeks its principles among empirical motives and laws, for human reason in its weariness is glad to rest on this pillow. In a dream of sweet illusions (in which it embraces not Juno but a cloud), it substitutes for morality a bastard patched up from limbs of very different parentage, which looks like anything one wishes to see in it, but not like virtue to anyone who has ever beheld her in her true form.*

The question then is: Is it a necessary law for all rational beings that they should always judge their actions by such maxims as they themselves could will to serve as universal laws? If there is such a law, it must be connected wholly *a priori* with the concept of the will of a rational being as such. But in order to discover this connection, we must, however reluctantly, take a step into metaphysics, although in a region of it different from speculative philosophy, namely into the metaphysics of morals. In a practical philosophy it is not a question of assuming grounds for what happens but of 427
assuming laws of what ought to happen even though it may never happen (that is to say, we assume objective practical laws). Hence in practical philosophy we need not inquire into the reasons why something pleases or displeases, how the pleasure of mere feeling differs from taste, and whether this is distinct from a general satisfaction of reason. Nor need we ask on what the feeling of pleasure or displeasure rests, how desires and inclinations arise, and how, finally, maxims arise from desires and inclination under the

*To behold virtue in her proper form is nothing else than to exhibit morality stripped of all admixture of sensuous things and of every spurious adornment of reward or self-love. How much she then eclipses everything which appears charming to the senses can easily be seen by everyone with the least effort of his reason, if it be not spoiled for all abstraction.

co-operation of reason. For all these matters belong to empirical psychology, which would be the second part of physics if we consider it as philosophy of nature so far as it rests on empirical laws. But here it is a question of objectively practical laws and thus of the relation of a will to itself so far as it determines itself only by reason, for everything which has a relation to the empirical automatically falls away, because if reason of itself alone determines conduct, it must necessarily do so *a priori*. The possibility of reason's thus determining conduct must now be investigated.

The will is thought of as a faculty of determining itself to action in accordance with the conception of certain laws. Such a faculty can be found only in rational beings. That which serves the will as the objective ground of its self-determination is a purpose, and if it is given by reason alone it must hold alike for all rational beings. On the other hand, that which contains the ground of the possibility of the action, whose result is an end, is called the means. The subjective ground of desire is the incentive (Triebfeder) while the objective ground of volition is the motive (Bewegungsgrund). Thus arises the distinction between subjective purposes, which rest on incentives, and objective purposes, which depend on motives valid for every rational being. Practical principles are formal when they disregard all subjective purposes; they are material when they have subjective purposes and thus certain incentives as their basis. The purposes that a rational being holds before himself by choice as consequences of his action are material purposes and are without exception only relative, for only their relation to a particularly constituted faculty of desire in the subject gives them their worth. And this worth cannot afford any universal
428 principles for all rational beings or any principles valid and necessary for every volition. That is, they cannot give rise to any practical laws. All these relative purposes, therefore, are grounds for hypothetical imperatives only.

But suppose that there were something the existence of which in itself had absolute worth, something which, as an end in itself, could be a ground of definite laws. In it and only in it could lie the ground of a possible categorical imperative (i.e., of a practical law).

Now, I say, man and, in general, every rational being exists as an end in himself and not merely as a means to be arbitrarily used by this or that will. In all his actions, whether they are directed toward himself or toward other rational beings, he must always be regarded at the same time as an end. All objects of inclination have only conditional worth, for if the inclinations and needs founded on them did not exist, their object would be worthless. The inclinations themselves as the sources of needs, however, are so lacking in absolute worth that the universal wish of every rational being must be indeed to free himself completely from them. Therefore, the worth of any objects to be obtained by our actions is at times conditional. Beings whose existence does not depend on our will but on nature, if they are not rational beings, have only relative worth as means, and are therefore called "things"; rational beings, on the other hand, are designated "persons" because their nature indicates that they are ends in themselves (i.e., things which may not be used merely as means). Such a being is thus an object of respect, and as such restricts all [arbitrary] choice. Such beings are not merely subjective ends whose existence as a result of our action has a worth for us, but are objective ends (i.e., beings whose existence is an end in itself). Such an end is one in the place of which no other end, to which these beings should serve merely as means, can be put. Without them, nothing of absolute worth could be found, and if all worth is conditional and thus contingent, no supreme practical principle for reason could be found anywhere.

Thus if there is to be a supreme practical principle and a categorical imperative for the human will, it must be one that forms an objective principle of the will from the conception of that which is necessarily an end for everyone because it is an end in itself. Hence this objective principle can serve as a universal law. The ground of this principle is: rational nature exists as an end in itself. Man necessarily thinks of his own existence 429
in this way, and thus far it is a subjective principle of human actions. Also every other rational being thinks of his existence on the same rational ground which holds also for myself;* thus it is at the same time an objective principle from which, as a supreme practical ground, it must be possible to derive all laws of the will. The practical imperative, therefore, is the following: Act so that you treat humanity, whether in your own person or in that of another, always as an end and never as a means only. Let us now see whether this can be achieved. To return to our previous examples:

First, according to the concept of necessary duty to oneself, he who contemplates suicide will ask himself whether his action can be consistent with the idea of humanity as an end in itself. If in order to escape from burdensome circumstances he destroys himself, he uses a person merely as a means to maintain a tolerable condition up to the end of life. Man, however, is not a thing, and thus not something to be used merely as a means; he must always be regarded in all his actions as an end in himself. Therefore I cannot dispose of man in my own person so as to mutilate, corrupt, or kill him. (It belongs to ethics proper to define more accurately this basic principle so as to avoid all misunderstanding, e.g., as to amputating limbs in order to preserve myself, or to exposing my life to danger in order to save it; I must therefore omit them here.)

Second, as concerns necessary or obligatory duties to others, he who intends a deceitful promise to others sees immediately that he intends to use another man merely as a means, without the latter at the same time containing the end in himself. For he whom I want to use for my own purposes by means of such a promise cannot possibly assent to 430
my mode of acting against him and thus share in the purpose of this action. This conflict with the principle of other men is even clearer if we cite examples of attacks on their freedom and property, for then it is clear that he who violates the rights of men intends to make use of the person of others merely as means, without considering that, as rational beings, they must always be esteemed at the same time as ends (i.e., only as beings who must be able to embody in themselves the purpose of the very same action).**

Third, with regard to contingent (meritorious) duty to oneself, it is not sufficient that the action not conflict with humanity in our person as an end in itself; it must also harmonize with it. In humanity there are capacities for greater perfection which belong to the purpose of nature with respect to humanity in our own person, and to neglect these might perhaps be consistent with the preservation of humanity as an end in itself, but not with the furtherance of that end.

Fourth, with regard to meritorious duty to others, the natural purpose that all men have is their own happiness. Humanity might indeed exist if no one contributed to the happiness of others, provided he did not intentionally detract from it, but this harmony

*Here I present this proposition as a postulate, but in the last Section grounds for it will be found.

**Let it not be thought that the banal "what you do not wish to be done to you . . ." could here serve as guide or principle, for it is only derived from the principle and is restricted by various limitations. It cannot be a universal law, because it contains the ground neither of duties to one's self nor of the benevolent duties to others (for many a man would gladly consent that others should not benefit him, provided only that he might be excused from showing benevolence to them). Nor does it contain the ground of obligatory duties to another, for the criminal would argue on this ground against the judge who sentences him. And so on.

with humanity as an end in itself is only negative, not positive, if everyone does not also endeavor, as far as he can, to further the purposes of others. For the ends of any person, who is an end in himself, must as far as possible be also my ends, if that conception of an end in itself is to have its full effect on me.

431 This principle of humanity, and in general of every rational creature an end in itself, is the supreme limiting condition on the freedom of action of each man. It is not borrowed from experience, first, because of its universality, since it applies to all rational beings generally, and experience does not suffice to determine anything about them; and secondly, because in experience humanity is not thought of (subjectively) as the purpose of men (i.e., as an object which we of ourselves really make our purpose). Rather it is thought of as the objective end which ought to constitute the supreme limiting condition of all subjective ends whatever they may be. Thus this principle must arise from pure reason. Objectively the ground of all practical legislation lies (according to the first principle) in the rule and form of universality, which makes it capable of being a law (at least a natural law); subjectively it lies in the end. But the subject of all ends is every rational being as an end in itself (by the second principle); from this there follows the third practical principle of the will as the supreme condition of its harmony with universal practical reason, viz, the Idea of the will of every rational being as making universal law.

By this principle all maxims are rejected which are not consistent with the will's giving universal law. The will is not only subject to the law, but subject in such a way that it must be conceived also as itself prescribing the law, of which reason can hold itself to be the author; it is on this ground alone that the will is regarded as subject to the law.

By the very fact that the imperatives are thought of as categorical, either way of conceiving them—as imperatives demanding the lawfulness of actions, resembling the lawfulness of the natural order; or as imperatives of the universal prerogative of the purposes of rational beings as such—excludes from their sovereign authority all admixture of any interest as an incentive to obedience. But we have been assuming the imperatives to be categorical, for that was necessary if we wished to explain the concept of duty; that there are practical propositions which command categorically could not of itself be proved independently, just as little as it can be proved anywhere in this section. One thing, however could have been done: to indicate in the imperative itself, by some determination inherent in it, that in willing from duty the renunciation of all interest is the specific mark of the categorical imperative, distinguishing it from the hypothetical. And this is now done in the third formulation of the principle, viz., in the Idea of the will of every rational being as a will giving universal law. A will which is subject to laws can be bound to them by an interest, but a will giving the supreme law cannot possibly depend upon any interest, for such a dependent will would itself need still another law which
432 would restrict the interest of its self-love to the condition that its [maxim] should be valid as a universal law.

Thus the principle of every human will as a will giving universal law in all its maxims* is very well adapted to being a categorical imperative, provided it is otherwise correct. Because of the Idea of giving universal law, it is based on no interest; and thus of all possible imperatives, it alone can be unconditional. Or, better, converting the proposition: if there is a categorical imperative (a law for the will of every rational being), it can command only that everything be done from the maxim of its will as one which could have as its object only itself considered as giving universal law. For only in

*I may be excused from citing examples to elucidate this principle, for those that have already illustrated the categorical imperative and its formula can here serve the same purpose.

this case are the practical principle and the imperative which the will obeys unconditional, because the will can have no interest as its foundation.

If now we look back upon all previous attempts which have ever been undertaken to discover the principle of morality, it is not to be wondered at that they all had to fail. Man was seen to be bound to laws by his duty, but it was not seen that he is subject to his own, but still universal, legislation, and that he is bound to act only in accordance with his own will, which is, however, designed by nature to be a will giving universal law. For if one thought of him as only subject to a law (whatever it may be), this necessarily implied some interest as a stimulus or compulsion to obedience because the law 433
did not arise from his will. Rather, his will had to be constrained by something else to act in a certain way. By this strictly necessary consequence, however, all the labor of finding a supreme ground for duty was irrevocably lost, and one never arrived at duty but only at the necessity of acting from a certain interest. This might be his own interest or that of another, but in either case the imperative always had to be conditional, and could not at all serve as a moral command. The moral principle I will call the principle of *autonomy* of the will in contrast to all other principles which I accordingly count under *heteronomy*.

The concept of any rational being as a being that must regard itself as giving universal law through all the maxims of its will, so that it may judge itself and its actions from this standpoint, leads to a very fruitful concept, namely that of a *realm of ends*.

By *realm* I understand the systematic union of different rational beings through common laws. Because laws determine which ends have universal validity, if we abstract from personal differences of rational beings, and thus from all content of their private purposes, we can think of a whole of all ends in systematic connection, a whole of rational beings as ends in themselves as well as a whole of particular purposes which each may set for himself. This is a realm of ends, which is possible on the principles stated above. For all rational beings stand under the law that each of them should treat himself and all others never merely as means, but in every case at the same time as an end in himself. Thus there arises a systematic union of rational beings through common objective laws. This is a realm which may be called a realm of ends (certainly only an ideal) because what these laws have in view is just the relation of these beings to each other as ends and means.

A rational being belongs to the realm of ends as a member when he gives univer- 434
sal laws in it while also himself subject to these laws. He belongs to it as sovereign when, as legislating, he is subject to the will of no other. The rational being must regard himself always as legislative in a realm of ends possible through the freedom of the will whether he belongs to it as member or as sovereign. He cannot maintain his position as sovereign merely through the maxims of his will, but only when he is a completely independent being without need and with unlimited power adequate to his will.

Morality, therefore, consists in the relation of every action to the legislation through which alone a realm of ends is possible. This legislation must be found in every rational being. It must be able to arise from his will, whose principle then is to do no action according to any maxim which would be inconsistent with its being a universal law, and thus to act only so that the will through its maxims could regard itself at the same time as giving universal law. If the maxims do not by their nature already necessarily conform to this objective principle of rational beings as giving universal law, the necessity of acting according to that principle is called practical constraint, which is to say: duty. Duty pertains not to the sovereign of the realm of ends, but rather to each member and to each in the same degree.

The practical necessity of acting according to this principle (duty) does not rest at all on feelings, impulses, and inclinations; it rests solely on the relation of rational beings to one another, in which the will of a rational being must always be regarded as legislative, for otherwise it could not be thought of as an end in itself. Reason, therefore, relates every maxim of the will as giving universal laws to every other will and also to every action towards itself; it does not do so for the sake of any other practical motive or future advantage but rather from the Idea of the dignity of a rational being who obeys no law except one which he himself also gives.

In the realm of ends everything has either a *price* or a *dignity*. Whatever has a price can be replaced by something else as its equivalent; on the other hand, whatever is above all price and therefore admits of no equivalent, has dignity.

That which is related to general human inclinations and needs has a *market price*.
435 That which, without presupposing any need, accords with a certain taste (i.e., with pleasure in the purposeless play of our faculties) has a *fancy price*. But that which constitutes the condition under which alone something can be an end in itself does not have mere relative worth (price) but an intrinsic worth (*dignity*).

Morality is the condition under which alone a rational being can be an end in himself, because only through it is it possible to be a lawgiving member in the realm of ends. Thus morality, and humanity so far as it is capable of morality, alone have dignity. Skill and diligence in work have a market value; wit, lively imagination, and humor have a fancy price; but fidelity in promises and benevolence on principle (not benevolence from instinct) have intrinsic worth. Nature and likewise art contain nothing which could make up for their lack, for their worth consists not in the effects which flow from them nor in any advantage and utility which they procure; it consists only in mental dispositions, maxims of the will, which are ready to reveal themselves in this manner through actions even though success does not favor them. These actions need no recommendation from my subjective disposition or taste in order that they may be looked upon with immediate favor and satisfaction, nor do they have need of any direct propensity or feeling directed to them. They exhibit the will which performs them as the object of an immediate respect, since nothing but reason is required in order to impose them upon the will. The will is not to be cajoled into them, for this, in the case of duties, would be a contradiction. This esteem lets the worth of such a turn of mind be recognized as dignity and puts it infinitely beyond any price; with things of price it cannot in the least be brought into any competition or comparison without, as it were, violating its holiness.

And what is it that justifies the morally good disposition or virtue in making such lofty claims? It is nothing less that the participation it affords the rational being in giving universal laws. He is thus fitted to be a member in a possible realm of ends, to which his own nature already destined him. For, as an end in himself, he is destined to be a lawgiver in the realm of ends, free from all laws of nature and obedient only to those laws which he himself gives. Accordingly, his maxims can belong to a univer-
436 sal legislation to which he is at the same time subject. A thing has no worth other than that determined for it by the law. The lawgiving which determines all worth must therefore have a dignity (i.e., an unconditional and incomparable worth). For the esteem which a rational being must have for it, only the word "respect" is suitable. Autonomy is thus the basis of the dignity of both human nature and every rational nature.

The three aforementioned ways of presenting the principle of morality are fundamentally only so many formulas of the very same law, and each of them unites the others in itself. There is, nevertheless, a difference between them, but the difference is more subjectively than objectively practical, for the difference is intended to bring an Idea of reason closer to intuition (by means of a certain analogy) and thus nearer to feeling. All maxims have:

1. A form, which consists in universality, and in this respect the formula of the moral imperative requires that maxims be chosen as though they should hold as universal laws of nature.
2. A material (i.e., an end), and in this respect the formula says that the rational being, as by its nature an end and thus as an end in itself, must serve in every maxim as the condition restricting all merely relative and arbitrary ends.
3. A complete determination of all maxims by the formula that all maxims which stem from autonomous legislation ought to harmonize with a possible realm of ends as with a realm of nature.*

There is a progression here like that through the categories of the unity of the form of the will (its universality), the plurality of material (the objects, ends), to the all-comprehensiveness or totality of the system of ends. But it is better in moral valuation to follow the rigorous method and to make the universal formula of the categorical 437 imperative the basis: Act according to the maxim which can at the same time make itself a universal law. But if one wishes to gain a hearing for the moral law, it is very useful to bring one and the same action under the three stated principles and thus, so far as possible, bring it nearer to intuition.

We can now end where we started, with the concept of an unconditionally good will. That will is absolutely good which cannot be bad, and thus it is a will whose maxim, when made universal law, can never conflict with itself. Thus this principle is also its supreme law: Always act according to that maxim whose universality as law you can at the same time will. This is the only condition under which a will can never come into conflict with itself, and such an imperative is categorical. Because the validity of the will as a universal law for possible actions has an analogy with the universal connection of the existence of things under universal laws, which is the formal element of nature in general, the categorical imperative can be expressed also as follows: Act on those maxims which can at the same time have themselves as universal laws of nature as their object. Such, then, is the formula of an absolutely good will.

Rational nature is distinguished from others in that it proposes an end to itself. This end would be the material of every good will. Since, however, in the Idea of an absolutely good will without the limiting condition that this or that end be achieved, we must abstract from every end to be actually effected (as any particular end would make each will only relatively good), we must conceive the end here not as one to be brought about, but as a self-existent end, and thus merely negatively, as that which must never be acted against and which consequently must never be valued merely as a means but in every volition also as an end. Now this end can never be other than the subject of all possible ends themselves, because this is at the same time the subject of a possible will which is absolutely good, for the latter cannot without contradiction be made secondary to any other object. The principle: Act with reference to every rational being (whether yourself or another) so 438 that in your maxim it is an end in itself, is thus basically identical with the principle: Act by a maxim which involves its own universal validity for every rational being.

*Teleology considers nature as a realm of ends; morals regards a possible realm of ends as a realm of nature. In the former the realm of ends is a theoretical Idea for the explanation of what actually is. In the latter it is a practical Idea for bringing about that which does not exist but which can become actual through our conduct and for making it conform with this Idea.

That in the use of means to any end I should restrict my maxim to the condition of its universal validity as a law for every subject is tantamount to saying that the subject of ends (i.e., the rational being itself) must be made the basis of all maxims of actions and thus be treated never as a mere means but as the supreme limiting condition in the use of all means (i.e., as at the same time an end).

It follows incontestably that every rational being must be able to regard himself as an end in himself with reference to all laws to which he may be subject whatever they may be, and thus see himself as giving universal laws. For it is just the fitness of his maxims to universal legislation that indicates that he is an end in himself. It also follows that his dignity (his prerogative) over all merely natural beings entails that he must take his maxims from the point of view that regards himself, and hence also every other rational being, as legislative. Rational beings are, on this account, called persons. In this way, a world of rational beings (*mundus intelligibilis*) is possible as a realm of ends, because of the legislation belonging to all persons as members. Consequently every rational being must act as if by his maxims he were at all times a legislative member of the universal realm of ends. The formal principle of these maxims is: So act as if your maxims should serve at the same time as universal law (for all rational beings).

A realm of ends is thus possible only by analogy with a realm of nature. The former is possible only by maxims (i.e., self-imposed rules), while the latter is possible by laws of efficient causes of things externally necessitated. Regardless of this difference, by analogy we call the natural whole a realm of nature so far as it is related to rational beings as its end; we do so even though the natural whole is looked upon as a machine. Such a realm of ends would actually be realized through maxims whose rule is prescribed to all rational beings by the categorical imperative, if they were universally obeyed. But a rational being, though he scrupulously follow this maxim, cannot for that reason expect every other rational being to be true to it, nor can he expect the realm of nature and its orderly design to harmonize with him as a fitting member of a realm of ends which is possible through himself. That is, he cannot count on its favoring his
439 expectation of happiness. Still the law: Act according to the maxim of a member of a merely potential realm of ends who gives universal law, remains in full force because it commands categorically. And just in this lies the paradox that simply the dignity of humanity as rational nature without any end or advantage to be gained by it, and thus respect for a mere Idea, should serve as the inflexible precept of the will. [There is the further paradox that] the sublimity of the maxims and the worthiness of every rational subject to be a law-giving member in the realm of ends consist precisely in the independence of his maxims from all such incentives. Otherwise he would have to be viewed as subject to only the natural law of his needs. Although the realm of nature as well as that of ends would be thought of as united under a sovereign, so that the latter would no longer remain a mere Idea but would receive true reality, the realm of ends would undoubtedly gain a strong urge in its favor though its intrinsic worth would not be augmented. Regardless of this, even the one and only absolute legislator would still have to be conceived as judging the worth of rational beings only by the disinterested conduct which they prescribe to themselves merely from the Idea. The essence of things is not changed by their external relations, and without reference to these relations a man must be judged only by what constitutes his absolute worth, and this is true whoever his judge may be, even if it be the Supreme Being. Morality is thus the relation of actions to the autonomy of the will (i.e., to the possible giving of universal law by the maxims of the will). The action which can be compatible with the autonomy of the will is permitted; that which does not agree with it is prohibited. The will whose maxims

are necessarily in harmony with the laws of autonomy is a holy will or an absolutely good will. The dependence of a will not absolutely good on the principle of autonomy (moral constraint) is *obligation*. Hence obligation cannot be predicated of a holy will. The objective necessity of an action from obligation is called *duty*.

From what has just been said, it can easily be explained how it happens that,
although in the concept of duty we think of subjection to law, we do nevertheless at the
same time ascribe a certain sublimity and dignity to the person who fulfills all his 440
duties. For though there is no sublimity in him in so far as he is subject to the moral law, yet he is sublime in so far as he is the giver of the law and subject to it for this reason only. We have also shown above how neither fear of nor inclination to the law is the incentive which can give moral worth to action; only respect for it can do so. Our own will, so far as it would act only under the condition of a universal legislation rendered possible by its maxims—this will ideally possible for us—is the proper object of respect, and the dignity of humanity consists just in its capacity to give universal laws under the condition that it is itself subject to this same legislation.

The Autonomy of the Will as the Supreme Principle of Morality

Autonomy of the will is that property of it by which it is a law to itself independent of any property of the objects of its volition. Hence the principle of autonomy is: Never choose except in such a way that the maxims of the choice are comprehended as universal law in the same volition. That this practical rule is an imperative, that is, that the will of every rational being is necessarily bound to it as a condition, cannot be proved by a mere analysis of the concepts occurring in it, because it is a synthetical proposition. To prove it, we would have to go beyond the knowledge of objects to a critical examination of the subject (i.e., to a critique of pure practical reason), for this synthetical proposition which commands apodictically must be susceptible of being known *a priori*. This matter, however, does not belong in the present section. But that the principle of autonomy, which is now in question, is the sole principle of morals can be readily shown by mere analysis of the concepts of morality; for by this analysis we find that its principle must be a categorical imperative and that the imperative commands neither more nor less than this very autonomy.

The Heteronomy of the Will as the Source of All Spurious Principles of Morality 441

If the will seeks the law which is to determine it elsewhere than in the fitness of its maxims to be given as universal law, and if thus it goes outside and seeks the law in the property of any of its objects, heteronomy always results. For then the will does not give itself the law, but the object through its relation to the will gives the law to it. This relation, whether it rests on inclination or on conceptions of reason, admits of only hypothetical imperatives: I should do something for the reason that I will something else. The moral (categorical) imperative, on the other hand, says that I should act in this or that way even though I have not willed anything else. For example, the former says that I should not lie if I wish to keep my good name. The latter says that I should not lie even though it would not cause me the least injury. The latter, therefore, must disregard every object to such an extent that it has absolutely no influence on the will; it must so disregard it that practical reason (will) may not just minister to any interest not its own but rather show its commanding authority as the supreme legislation. Thus, for instance, I should seek to further the happiness of others, not as though its realization were of consequence to me (because of a direct inclination or some satisfaction related to it indirectly through reason); I should do so solely because the maxim which excludes it from my duty cannot be comprehended as a universal law in one and the same volition.

Classification of All Possible Principles of Morality Following from the Assumed Principle of Heteronomy

Here as everywhere in the pure use of reason so long as a critical examination of it is lacking, human reason tries all possible wrong ways before it succeeds in finding the one true way.

All principles which can be taken from this point of view are either empirical or
442 rational. The former, drawn from the principles of happiness, are based on physical or moral feeling; the latter, drawn from the principle of perfection, are based either on the rational concept of perfection as a possible result or on the concept of an independent perfection (the will of God) as the determining ground of the will.

Empirical principles are not at all suited to serve as the basis of moral laws. For if the basis of the universality by which they should be valid for all rational beings without distinction (the unconditional practical necessity which is thereby imposed upon them) is derived from a particular tendency of human nature or the accidental circumstance in which it is found, that universality is lost. But the principle of one's own happiness is the most objectionable of the empirical principles. This is not merely because it is false and because experience contradicts the supposition that well-being is always proportional to good conduct, nor yet because this principle contributes nothing to the establishment of morality inasmuch as it is a very different thing to make a man happy from making him good, and to make him prudent and farsighted for his own advantage is far from making him virtuous. Rather, it is because this principle supports morality with incentives which undermine it and destroy all its sublimity, for it puts the motives to virtue and those to vice in the same class, teaching us only to make a better calculation while obliterating the specific difference between them. On the other hand, there is the alleged special sense,* the moral feeling. The appeal to it is superficial, since those who cannot think expect help from feeling, even with respect to that which concerns universal laws; they do so even though feelings naturally differ so infinitely in degree that they are incapable of furnishing a uniform standard of the good and bad, and also in spite of the fact that one cannot validly judge for others by means of one's own feeling. Nevertheless, the moral feeling is nearer to morality and its dignity, inasmuch as it pays
443 virtue the honor of ascribing the satisfaction and esteem for her directly to morality, and does not, as it were, say to her face that it is not her beauty but only our advantage which attaches us to her.

Among the rational principles of morality, there is the ontological concept of perfection. It is empty, indefinite, and consequently useless for finding in the immeasurable field of possible reality the greatest possible sum which is suitable to us; and, in specifically distinguishing the reality which is here in question from all other reality, it inevitably tends to move in a circle and cannot avoid tacitly presupposing the morality which it ought to explain. Nevertheless, it is better than the theological concept, which derives morality from a most perfect divine will. It is better

*I count the principle of moral feeling under that of happiness, because every empirical interest promises to contribute to our well-being by the agreeableness that a thing affords, either directly and without a view to future advantage or with a view to it. We must likewise, with Hutcheson, count the principle of sympathy with the happiness of others under the moral sense which he assumed.

not merely because we cannot intuit the perfection of the divine will, having rather to derive it only from our own concepts of which morality itself is foremost, but also because if we do not so derive it (and to do so would involve a most flagrant circle in explanation), the only remaining concept of the divine will is made up of the attributes of desire for glory and dominion combined with the awful conceptions of might and vengeance, and any system of ethics based on them would be directly opposed to morality.

But if I had to choose between the concept of the moral sense and that of perfection in general (neither of which at any rate weakens morality, though neither is capable of serving as its foundation), I would decide for the latter, because it preserves the indefinite Idea of a will good in itself free from corruption until it can be more narrowly defined. It at least withdraws the decision on the question from the realm of sensibility and brings it to the court of pure reason, although it does not even there decide the question.

For the rest, I think I may be excused from a lengthy refutation of all these doctrines. It is so easy, and presumably so well understood even by those whose office requires them to decide for one of these theories (since their students would not tolerate suspension of judgment), that such a refutation would be superfluous. What interests us more, however, is to know that all these principles set up nothing other than heteronomy of the will as the first ground of morality, and thus they necessarily miss their goal.

In every case in which the object of the will must be assumed as prescribing the 444
rule which is to determine the will, the rule is nothing else than heteronomy. The imperative in this case is conditional, stating that if or because one wills such and such an object, one ought to act thus or so. Therefore the imperative can never command morally, that is, categorically. The object may determine the will by means of inclination, as in the principle of one's own happiness, or by means of reason directed to objects of our possible volition in general, as in the principle of perfection; but the will in these cases never determines itself directly by the conception of the action itself but only by the incentive which the foreseen result of the action incites in the will—that is: I ought to do something because I will something else. And here still another law must be assumed in me as the basis for this imperative; it would be a law by which I would necessarily will that other thing; but this law would in its turn require an imperative to restrict this maxim. Since the conception of a result to be obtained by one's own powers incites in the will an impulse which depends upon the natural characteristic of the subject, either of his sensibility (inclination and taste) or understanding and reason; and since these faculties according to the particular constitution of their nature find satisfaction in exercising themselves on the result of the voluntary action, it follows that it would really be nature which would give the law [to the action]. This law, as a law of nature, would have to be known and proved by experience, and as in itself contingent it would be unfit to be an apodictical practical rule such as the moral rule must be. Such a law always represents heteronomy of the will: the will does not give itself the law, but an external impulse gives the law to the will according to nature of the subject which is susceptible to receive it.

The absolutely good will, the principle of which must be a categorical imperative, is thus undetermined with reference to any object. It contains only the form of volition in general, and this form is autonomy. That is, the capability of the maxims of every good will to make themselves universal laws is itself the sole law which the will of every rational being imposes on himself, and it does not need to support this by any incentive or interest.

How such a synthetical practical *a priori* proposition is possible and why it is necessary is a problem whose solution does not lie within the boundaries of the metaphysics of morals. Moreover, we have not here affirmed its truth, and even less
445 professed to command a proof of it. We showed only through the development of the generally received concept of morals that autonomy of the will is unavoidably connected with it, or rather that it is its foundation. Whoever, therefore, holds morality to be something real and not a chimerical idea without truth must also concede its principle which has been derived here. Consequently, this section, like the first, was merely analytical. To prove that morality is not a mere phantom of the mind—and if the categorical imperative, and with it the autonomy of the will, is true and absolutely necessary as an *a priori* proposition, it follows that it is no phantom—requires that a synthetical use of pure practical reason be possible. But we must not venture on this use without first making a critical examination of this faculty of reason. In the last section we shall give the principal features of such an examination that will be sufficient for our purpose.

446 THIRD SECTION

TRANSITION FROM THE METAPHYSICS OF MORALS TO THE CRITICAL EXAMINATION OF PURE PRACTICAL REASON

The Concept of Freedom Is the Key to the Explanation of the Autonomy of the Will

As will is a kind of causality of living beings so far as they are rational, freedom would be that property of this causality by which it can be effective independent of foreign causes determining it, just as natural necessity is the property of the causality of all irrational beings by which they are determined to activity by the influence of foreign causes.

The preceding definition of freedom is negative and therefore affords no insight into its essence. But a positive concept of freedom flows from it which is so much the richer and more fruitful. Since the concept of a causality entails that of laws according to which something (i.e., the effect) must be established through something else which we call cause, it follows that freedom is by no means lawless even though it is not a property of the will according to laws of nature. Rather, it must be a causality of a peculiar kind according to immutable laws. Otherwise a free will would be an absurdity.
447 Natural necessity is, as we have seen, a heteronomy of efficient causes, for every effect is possible only according to the law that something else determines the efficient cause to its causality. What else, then, can the freedom of the will be but autonomy (i.e., the property of the will to be law to itself)? The proposition that the will is a law to itself in all its actions, however, only expresses the principle that we should act according to no other maxim than that which can also have itself as a universal law for its object. And this is just the formula of the categorical imperative and the principle of morality. Therefore a free will and a will under moral laws are identical.

Thus if freedom of the will is presupposed, morality together with its principle follows from it by the mere analysis of its concepts. But the principle: An absolutely good will is one whose maxim can always include itself as a universal law, is nevertheless a synthetical proposition. It is synthetical because by analysis of the concept of an absolutely good will that property of the maxim cannot be found in it. Such synthetical propositions, however, are made possible only by the fact that the two cognitions are connected with each other through their union with a third in which both are to be found. The positive concept of freedom furnishes this third cognition, which cannot be, as in the case of physical causes, the sensible world of nature, in the concept of which we find conjoined the concepts of something as cause in relation to something else as effect. We cannot yet show directly what this third cognition is to which freedom directs us and of which we have an *a priori* Idea, nor can we yet explain the deduction of the concept of freedom from pure practical reason, and therewith the possibility of a categorical imperative. For this, some further preparation is needed.

Freedom Must be Presupposed as the Property of the Will of All Rational Beings

It is not enough to ascribe freedom to our will, on whatever grounds, if we do not also have sufficient grounds for attributing it to all rational beings. For since morality serves as a law for us only as rational beings, it must hold for all rational beings, and since it must be derived exclusively from the property of freedom, freedom as a property of the will of all rational beings must be demonstrated. And it does not suffice to prove it from certain alleged experiences of human nature (which is indeed impossible, as it can 448
be proved only *a priori*), but we must prove it as belonging universally to the activity of rational beings endowed with a will. Now I say that every being which cannot act otherwise than under the Idea of freedom is thereby really free in a practical respect. That is to say, all laws which are inseparably bound with freedom hold for it just as if its wills were proved free in itself by theoretical philosophy.* Now I affirm that we must necessarily grant that every rational being who has a will also has the Idea of freedom and that it acts only under this Idea. For in such a being we think of a reason which is practical (i.e., a reason which has causality with respect to its object). Now we cannot conceive of a reason which, in making its judgments, consciously responds to a bidding from the outside, for then the subject would attribute the determination of its power of judgment not to reason but to an impulse. Reason must regard itself as the author of its principles, independently of alien influences; consequently as practical reason or as the will of a rational being it must regard itself as free. That is to say, the will of a rational being can be a will of its own only under the Idea of freedom, and therefore from a practical point of view such a will must be ascribed to all rational beings.

Of the Interest Attaching to the Ideas of Morality

We have finally reduced the definite concept of morality to the Idea of freedom, but we could not prove freedom to be actual in ourselves and in human nature. We saw 449
only that we must presuppose it if we would think of a being as rational and conscious of its causality with respect to actions, that is, as endowed with a will; and so we find that on the very same grounds we must ascribe to each being endowed with reason and will the property of determining itself to action under the Idea of its freedom.

*I propose this argument as sufficient to our purpose: Freedom as an Idea is posited by all rational beings as the basis for their actions. I do so in order to avoid having to prove freedom also in its theoretical aspect. For even if the latter is left unproved, the laws which would obligate a being who was really free would hold for a being who cannot act except under the Idea of his own freedom. Thus we escape the onus which has been pressed on theory.

From presupposing this Idea [of freedom] there followed also the consciousness of a law of action: that the subjective principles of actions (i.e., maxims) must in every instance be so chosen that they can hold also as objective (i.e., universal) principles, and can thus serve as principles for our giving universal laws. But why should I, as a rational being, and why should all other beings endowed with reason, subject ourselves to this law? I will admit that no interest impels me to do so, for that would then give no categorical imperative. But I must nevertheless take an interest in it and see how it comes about, for this *ought* is properly a *would* that is valid for every rational being provided reason were practical for it without hindrance [i.e., exclusively determined its action]. For beings who, like ourselves, are affected by the senses as incentives different from reason, and who do not always do that which reason by itself alone would have done, that necessity of action is expressed as only an *ought*. The subjective necessity is thus distinguished from the objective.

It therefore seems that we have only presupposed the moral law, the principle of the autonomy of the will in the Idea of freedom, as if we could not prove its reality and objective necessity by itself. Even if that were so, we would still have gained something because we would at least have defined the genuine principle more accurately than had been done before; but with regard to its validity and the practical necessity of subjection to it, we would not have advanced a single step, for we could give no satisfactory answer to anyone who asked us why the universal validity of our maxim as a law had to be the restricting condition of our action. We could not tell on what is based the worth which we ascribe to actions of this kind—a worth so great that there can be no higher
450 interest—nor could we tell how it happens that man believes that it is only through this that he feels his own personal worth, in contrast to which the worth of a pleasant or unpleasant state is to be regarded as nothing.

We do find sometimes that we can take an interest in a personal quality which involves no [personal] interest in any [external] condition, provided only that the [possession of] this quality makes us fit to participate in the [desired] condition in case reason were to effect the allotment of this condition. That is, being worthy of happiness, even without the motive of partaking in happiness, can interest of itself. But this judgment is in fact only the effect of the importance already ascribed to moral laws (if by the Idea of freedom we detach ourselves from every empirical interest). But that we ought so to detach ourselves from every empirical interest, to regard ourselves as free in acting and yet as subject to certain laws, in order to find a worth wholly in our person which would compensate for the loss of everything which could make our situation desirable—how this is possible and hence on what grounds the moral law obligates us still cannot be seen in this way.

We must openly confess that there is a kind of circle here from which it seems that there is no escape. We assume that we are free in the order of efficient causes so that we can conceive of ourselves as subject to moral laws in the order of ends. And then we think of ourselves subject to these laws because we have ascribed freedom of the will to ourselves. This is circular because freedom and self-legislation of the will are both autonomy and thus are reciprocal concepts, and for that reason one of them cannot be used to explain the other and to furnish a ground for it. At most they can be used for the logical purpose of bringing apparently different conceptions of the same object under a single concept (as we reduce different fractions of the same value to the lowest common terms).

One recourse, however, remains open to us, namely, to inquire whether we do not assume a different standpoint when we think of ourselves as causes *a priori* efficient through freedom from that which we occupy when we conceive of ourselves in the light of our actions as effects which we see before our eyes.

The following remark requires no subtle reflection, and we may suppose that even the commonest understanding can make it, though it does so, after its fashion, by an obscure discernment of judgment which it calls feeling: all conceptions, like those of the 451
senses, which come to us without our choice enable us to know objects only as they affect us, while what they are in themselves remains unknown to us; therefore, as regards this kind of conception, even with the closest attention and clearness which understanding may ever bring to them we can attain only a knowledge of appearances and never a knowledge of things as they are in themselves. When this distinction is once made (perhaps merely because of a difference noticed between conceptions which are given to us from somewhere else and to which we are passive, and those which we produce from ourselves only and in which we show our own activity), it follows of itself that we must admit and assume behind the appearances something else which is not appearance, i.e., things as they are in themselves, although we must admit that we cannot approach them more closely and can never know what they are in themselves, since they can never be known by us except as they affect us. This must furnish a distinction, though a crude one, between a world of sense and a world of understanding. The former, by differences in our sensible faculties, can be very different to various observers, while the latter, which is its foundation, remains always the same. A man may not presume to know even himself as he really is by knowing himself through inner sensation. For since he does not, as it were, produce himself or derive his concept of himself *a priori* but only empirically, it is natural that he obtain his knowledge of himself through inner sense and consequently only through the appearance of his nature and the way in which his consciousness is affected. But beyond the characteristic of his own subject which is compounded of these mere appearances, he necessarily assumes something else as its basis, namely, his ego as it is in itself. Thus in respect to mere perception and receptivity to sensations he must count himself as belonging to the world of sense; but in respect to that which may be pure activity in himself (i.e., in respect to that which reaches consciousness directly and not by affecting the senses) he must reckon himself as belonging to the intellectual world. But he has no further knowledge of that world.

To such a conclusion the thinking man must come with respect to all things which may present themselves to him. Presumably it is to be met with in the commonest understanding which, as is well known, is very much inclined to expect behind the 452
objects of the senses something else invisible and acting of itself. But common understanding soon spoils it by trying to make the invisible again sensible (i.e., to make it an object of intuition). Thus the common understanding becomes not in the least wiser.

Now man really finds in himself a faculty by which he distinguishes himself from all other things, even from himself so far as he is affected by objects. This faculty is reason. As a pure, spontaneous activity it is elevated even above understanding. For though the latter is also a spontaneous activity and does not, like sense, which is passive, merely contain representations which arise only when one is affected by things, it cannot produce by its activity any other concepts than those which serve to bring the sensible representations under rules and thereby to unite them in one consciousness. Without this use of sensibility it would think nothing at all; on the other hand, reason shows such a pure spontaneity in the case of Ideas that it far transcends anything that sensibility can give to consciousness, and shows its chief occupation in distinguishing the world of sense from the world of understanding, thereby prescribing limits to the understanding itself.

For this reason a rational being must regard itself qua intelligence (and not from the side of his lower faculties) as belonging to the world of understanding and not to that of the senses. Thus it has two standpoints from which it can consider itself and recognize the laws [governing] the employment of its powers and all its actions: first, as belonging to the world of sense, under the laws of nature (heteronomy), and, second, as belonging to the intelligible world under laws which, independent of nature, are not empirical but founded on reason alone.

As a rational being and thus as belonging to the intelligible world, man cannot think of the causality of his own will except under the Idea of freedom, for independence from the determining causes of the world of sense (an independence which reason must always ascribe to itself) is freedom. The concept of autonomy is inseparably connected with the Idea of freedom, and with the former there is inseparably bound
453 the universal principle of morality, which is the ground in Idea of all actions of rational beings, just as natural law is the ground of all appearances.

We have now removed the suspicion which we raised that there might be a hidden circle in our reasoning from freedom to autonomy and from the latter to the moral law. This suspicion was that we laid down the Idea of freedom for the sake of the moral law in order later to derive the law from freedom, and that we were thus unable to give any basis for the law, presenting it only as a *petitio principii* [begging the question] which well-disposed minds might gladly allow us, but which we could never advance as a demonstrable proposition. But we now see that, if we think of ourselves as free, we transport ourselves into the intelligible world as members of it and know the autonomy of the will together with its consequence, morality; whereas if we think of ourselves as obligated, we consider ourselves as belonging both to the world of sense and at the same time to the intelligible world.

How Is a Categorical Imperative Possible?

The rational being counts himself, *qua* intelligence, as belonging to the intelligible world, and only as an efficient cause belonging to it does he call his causality will. On the other side, however, he is conscious of himself as a part of the world of sense in which his actions are found as mere appearances of that causality. But we do not discern how they are possible on the basis of that causality which we do not know; rather, those actions must be regarded as determined by other appearances, namely, desires and inclinations belonging to the world of sense. As a member of the intelligible world only, all my actions would completely accord with the principle of the autonomy of the pure will, and as a part only of the world of sense would they have to be assumed to conform wholly to the natural law of desires and inclinations and thus to the heteronomy of nature. (The former actions would rest on the supreme principle of morality, and the latter on that of happiness.) But since the intelligible world contains the ground of the world of sense and hence of its laws, the intelligible world is (and must be conceived as) directly legislative for my will, which belongs wholly to the intelligible world. Therefore I recognize myself *qua* intelligence as subject to the law of the world of understanding and to the autonomy of the will. That is, I recognize myself as subject to the law of reason which contains in the Idea of freedom the law of the intelligible world, while at the
454 same time I must acknowledge that I am a being which belongs to the world of sense. Therefore I must regard the laws of the intelligible world as imperatives for me, and actions in accord with this principle as duties.

Thus categorical imperatives are possible because the Idea of freedom makes me a member of an intelligible world. Consequently, if I were a member of that world only, all my actions *would* always be in accordance with the autonomy of the will. But since I intuit myself at the same time as a member of the world of sense, my actions *ought* to conform to it, and this categorical "ought" presents a synthetic *a priori* proposition, since besides my will affected by my sensuous desires there is added the Idea of exactly the same will as pure, practical of itself, and belonging to the intelligible world, which according to reason contains the supreme condition of the sensuously affected will. It is similar to the manner in which concepts of the understanding, which of themselves mean nothing but lawful form in general, are added to the intuitions of the sensible world, thus rendering possible *a priori* synthetic propositions on which all knowledge of a system of nature rests.

The practical use of ordinary human reason confirms the correctness of this deduction. When we present examples of honesty of purpose, of steadfastness in following good maxims, and of sympathy and general benevolence even with great sacrifices of advantage and comfort, there is no man, not even the most malicious villain (provided he is otherwise accustomed to using his reason), who does not wish that he also might have these qualities, but because of his inclinations and impulses cannot bring this about, yet at the same time wishes to be free from such inclinations which are burdensome even to him. He thus proves that with a will free from all impulses of sensibility, he in thought transfers himself into an order of things altogether different from that of his desires in the field of sensibility. He cannot expect to obtain by that wish any gratification of desires or any state which would satisfy his actual or even imagined inclinations, for the Idea itself, which elicits this wish from him, would lose its preeminence if he had any such expectation. He imagines himself to be this better person when he transfers himself to the standpoint of a member of the intelligible 455
world to which he is involuntarily impelled by the Idea of freedom (i.e., of independence from the determining causes in the world of sense); and from this standpoint he is conscious of a good will, which on his own confession constitutes the law for his bad will as a member of the world of sense. He acknowledges the authority of the law even while he transgresses it. The moral "ought" is therefore his own volition as a member of the intelligible world, and it is conceived by him as an "ought" only insofar as he regards himself at the same time as a member of the world of sense.

On the Extreme Boundary of All Practical Philosophy

In respect to their will, all men think of themselves as free. Hence arise all judgments of acts as being such as ought to have been done, although they were not done. But this freedom is not an empirical concept and cannot be such, for it continues to hold even though experience shows the contrary of the demands which are necessarily conceived to be consequences of the supposition of freedom. On the other hand it is equally necessary that everything that happens should be inexorably determined by natural laws, and this natural necessity is likewise no empirical concept because it implies the concept of necessity and thus of *a priori* knowledge. But this concept of a system of nature is confirmed by experience, and it is inevitably presupposed if experience, which is knowledge of the objects of the sense interconnected by universal laws, is to be possible. Therefore freedom is only an Idea of reason whose objective reality in itself is doubtful, while nature is a concept of the understanding which shows and must necessarily show its reality by examples of experience.

There now arises a dialectic of reason, since the freedom ascribed to the will seems to stand in contradiction to natural necessity. At this parting of the ways reason in its speculative aspect finds the path of natural necessity more well-beaten and usable than that of freedom, but in its practical aspect the path of freedom is the only one on which it 456 is possible to make use of reason in our conduct. Hence it is as impossible for the subtlest philosophy as for the commonest reasoning to argue freedom away. Philosophy must therefore assume that no true contradiction will be found between freedom and natural necessity in the same human actions, for it cannot give up the concept of nature any more than that of freedom.

Hence if we should never be able to conceive how freedom is possible, at least this apparent contradiction must be convincingly eradicated. For if even the thought of freedom contradicted itself or nature, it would have to be surrendered in competition with natural necessity.

But it would be impossible to escape this contradiction if the subject, who seems to himself to be free, thought of himself in the same sense or in the same relationship when he calls himself free as when he assumes that in the same action he is subject to natural law. Therefore it is an inescapable task of speculative philosophy to show at least that its illusion of contradiction rests on the fact that we [do not] think of man in a different sense and relationship when we call him free from that in which we consider him as part of nature and subject to its laws. It must show not only that they can very well coexist but also that they must be thought of as necessarily united in one and the same subject; for otherwise no ground could be given as to why we should burden reason with an Idea which, though it may without contradiction be united with another that is sufficiently established, nevertheless involves us in a perplexity which sorely embarrasses reason in its theoretical use. This duty is imposed only on theoretical philosophy, so that it may clear the way for practical philosophy. Thus the philosopher has no choice as to whether he will remove the apparent contradiction or leave it untouched, for in the latter case the theory of it would be unoccupied land, into the possession of which the fatalist could rightly enter and drive all morality from its alleged property as occupying it without title.

Yet we cannot say here that we have reached the boundary of practical philosophy. For the settlement of the controversy does not belong to practical philosophy, as the latter
457 only demands from theoretical reason that it put an end to the discord in which it entangles itself in theoretical questions, so that practical reason may have rest and security from outward attacks which could dispute it the ground on which it desires to erect its edifice.

The title to freedom of the will claimed by ordinary reason is based on the consciousness and the conceded presupposition of the independence of reason from merely subjectively determining causes which together constitute what belongs only to sensation and is included under the general name of sensibility. Man, who in this way regards himself as intelligence, puts himself in a different order of things and in a relationship to determining grounds of an altogether different kind when he thinks of himself as intelligence with a will and thus as endowed with causality, compared with that other order of things and that other set of determining grounds which become relevant when he perceives himself as a phenomenon in the world of sense (as he really is also) and submits his causality to external determination according to natural laws. Now he soon realizes that both can subsist together—indeed, that they must. For there is not the least contradiction between a thing in appearance (as belonging to the world of sense) being subject to certain laws from which, as a thing or being regarded as it is in itself, it is independent. That he must think of himself in this twofold manner rests, with regard to the first, on the consciousness of himself as an object affected through the senses, and, with regard to what is required by the second, on the consciousness of himself as intelligence (i.e., as independent of sensible impressions in the use of reason), and thus as belonging to the intelligible world.

This is why man claims to possess a will which does not make him accountable for what belongs only to his desires and inclinations, but thinks of actions which can be done only by disregarding all his desires and sensuous attractions as possible and indeed as necessary for him. The causality of these actions lies in him as an intelligence and in effects and actions in accordance with principles of an intelligible world, of which he knows only that reason alone, and indeed pure reason independent of sensibility, gives the law in it. Moreover, since it is only as intelligence that he is his proper self (as man he is only appearance of himself), he knows that those laws apply to him directly and categorically, so that that to which inclinations and impulses and hence the entire nature of the world of sense incite him cannot
in the least impair the laws of his volition as an intelligence. He does not even hold 458
himself responsible for these inclinations and impulses or attribute them to his proper self (i.e., his will), though he does impute to his will the indulgence which he may grant to them when he permits them to influence his maxims to the detriment of the rational laws of his will.

When practical reason thinks itself into an intelligible world, it does in no way transcend its boundaries. It would do so, however, if it tried to intuit or feel itself into it. The intelligible world is only a negative thought with respect to the world of sense, which does not give reason any laws for determining the will. It is positive only in the single point that freedom as negative determination is at the same time connected with a positive power and even a causality of reason. This causality we call a will to act so that the principle of actions will accord with the essential characteristic of a rational cause (i.e., with the condition of universal validity of a maxim as law). But if it were to borrow an object of the will (i.e., a motive) from the intelligible world, it would overstep its boundaries and pretend to be acquainted with something of which it knows nothing. The concept of a world of understanding is therefore only a standpoint from which reason sees itself forced to take outside appearances, in order to think of itself as practical. If the influences of sensibility were determining for man, this would not be possible; but it is necessary unless he is to be denied the consciousness of himself as an intelligence, and thus as a rational and rationally active cause (i.e., a cause acting in freedom). This thought certainly implies the Idea of an order and legislation different from that of natural mechanism, which applies to the world of sense; and it makes necessary the concept of an intelligible world, the whole of rational beings as things regarded as they are in themselves. But it does not give us the least occasion to think of it otherwise than according to its formal condition only (i.e., the universality of the maxim of the will as law and thus the autonomy of the will), which alone is consistent with freedom. All laws, on the other hand, which are directed to an object make for heteronomy, which belongs only to natural laws and which can apply only to the world of sense.

But reason would overstep its bounds if it undertook to explain how pure reason 459
can be practical, which is the same problem as explaining how freedom is possible.

We can explain nothing but what we can reduce to laws whose object can be given in some possible experience. But freedom is only an Idea, the objective reality which can in no way be shown to accord with natural laws or to be in any possible experience. Since no example in accordance with any analogy can support it, it can never be comprehended or even imagined. It holds only as the necessary presupposition of reason in a being who believes himself conscious of a will (i.e., of a faculty different from the mere faculty of desire, or a faculty of determining himself to act as an intelligence and thus according to laws of reason independently of natural instincts. But where determination according to natural laws comes to an end, there too all explanation ceases, and nothing remains but defense (i.e., refutation of the objections from those who pretend to have seen more deeply into the essence of things and who boldly declare freedom to be impossible). We can show them only that the supposed contradiction they have discovered lies nowhere else than in their necessarily regarding man [only] as appearance in order to make natural law valid with respect to human actions, and now when we require them to think of man *qua* intelligence as a thing regarded as it is in itself, they still persist in considering him as appearance [only]. Obviously, then, the detachment of his causality (his will) from all natural laws of the world of sense in one and the same subject is a contradiction, but this disappears when they reconsider and confess, as is reasonable, that behind the appearances things regarded as they are in themselves must stand as their hidden ground, and that we cannot expect the laws of the activity of these grounds to be the same as those under which their appearances stand.

460 The subjective impossibility of explaining the freedom of the will is the same as the impossibility of discovering and explaining an interest* which man can take in moral laws. Nevertheless, he does actually take an interest in them, and the foundation of this interest in us we will call the moral feeling. This moral feeling has been erroneously construed by some as the standard for our moral judgment, whereas it must be regarded rather as the subjective effect which the law has upon the will to which reason alone gives objective grounds.

In order to will an action which reason alone prescribes to the sensuously affected rational being as the action which he ought to will, there is certainly required a power of will to instill a feeling of pleasure of satisfaction in the fulfilment of duty, and hence there must be a causality of reason to determine sensibility in accordance with its own principles. But it is wholly impossible to discern, i.e., to make *a priori* conceivable, how a mere thought containing nothing sensuous is able to produce a sensation of pleasure or displeasure. For that is a particular kind of causality of which, as of all causality, we cannot determine anything *a priori* but must consult experience only. But since experience can exemplify the relation of cause to effect only as subsisting between two objects of experience, while here pure reason by mere Ideas (which furnish no object for experience) is to be the cause of an effect which does lie within experience, an explanation of how and why the universality of the maxim as law (and hence morality) interests us is completely impossible for us men. Only this much is certain: that it is valid for us not because it interests us (for that is heteronomy and
461 dependence of practical reason on sensibility, i.e., on a basic feeling; and thus it could never be morally legislating); but that it interests us because it is valid for us as men, inasmuch as it has arisen from our will as intelligence and hence from our proper self; but what belongs to mere appearance is necessarily subordinated to the character of the thing regarded as it is in itself.

*Interest is that by which reason becomes practical (i.e., a cause determining the will). We therefore say only of a rational being that he takes an interest in something; irrational creatures feel only sensuous impulses. A direct interest in the action is taken by reason only if the universal validity of its maxim is a sufficient determining ground of the will. Only such an interest is pure. But if reason can determine the will only by means of another object of desire or under the presupposition of a particular feeling of the subject, reason takes merely an indirect interest in the action, and since reason for itself alone without experience can discover neither objects of the will nor a particular feeling which lies at its root, that indirect interest would be only empirical and not a pure interest of reason. The logical interest of reason in advancing its insights is never direct but rather presupposes purposes for which they are to be used.

Thus the question *How is a categorical imperative possible?* can be answered to this extent: We can cite the only presupposition under which it is possible. This is the Idea of freedom, and we can have insight into the necessity of this presupposition which is sufficient to the practical use of reason (i.e., to the conviction of the validity of this imperative and hence also of the moral law). But how this presupposition itself is possible can never be discerned by any human reason. However, on the presupposition of freedom of the will as an intelligence, its autonomy as the formal condition under which alone it can be determined is a necessary consequence. To presuppose the freedom of the will is not only quite possible, as speculative philosophy itself can prove, for it does not involve itself in a contradiction with the principle of natural necessity in the interconnection of appearances in the world of sense. But it is also unconditionally necessary that a rational being conscious of its causality through reason, and thus conscious of a will different from desires, should practically presuppose freedom (i.e., presuppose it in the Idea as the fundamental condition of all his voluntary acts). Yet how pure reason, without any other incentives whencesoever derived, can by itself be practical (i.e., how the simple principle of the universal validity of its maxims as laws—which would certainly be the form of a pure practical reason—without any material (object) of the will in which we might in advance take some interest), and can itself furnish an incentive and produce an interest which would be called purely moral; or, in other words, *how pure reason can be practical*—to explain this, all human reason is wholly incompetent, and all the pain and work of seeking an explanation of it are wasted.

It is just the same as if I sought to find out how freedom itself as the causality of a will is possible, for in so doing I would leave the philosophical basis of explanation 462
behind, and I have no other. Certainly I could revel in the intelligible world, the world of intelligences, which still remains to me; but although I have a well-founded Idea of it, still I do not have the least knowledge of it, nor can I ever attain knowledge of it by all the exertions of my natural faculty of reason. This intelligible world signifies only a something which remains when I have excluded from the determining grounds of my will everything belonging to the world of sense, in order to isolate the principle of motives from the field of sensibility. I do so by limiting it and showing that it does not contain absolutely everything in itself but that outside it there is still more; but this more I do not know. After banishing all material (i.e., knowledge of objects) from pure reason which formulates this ideal, there remain to me only the form, the practical law of the universal validity of maxims, and, in accordance with this, reason in relation to a pure intelligible world as a possible efficient cause determining the will. Any incentive must here be totally absent unless this Idea of an intelligible world or that in which reason directly takes an interest be the incentive. But to make this conceivable is precisely the problem we cannot solve.

Here, then, is the outermost boundary of all moral inquiry. To define it is very important, both in order that reason may not seek around, on the one hand, in the world of sense, in a way harmful to morals, for the supreme motive and for a comprehensible but empirical interest; and so that it will not, on the other hand, impotently flap its wings in the space (for it, an empty space) of transcendent concepts which we call the intelligible world, without being able to move from its starting point and so losing itself amid phantoms. Furthermore, the Idea of a pure intelligible world as a whole of all intelligences to which we ourselves belong as rational beings (though on the other side we are at the same time members of the world of sense) is always a useful and permissible Idea for the purpose of a rational faith. This is so even though all knowledge terminates at its boundary, for the glorious ideal of a

universal realm of ends regarded as they are in themselves (rational beings) can awaken in
463 us a lively interest in the moral law. To that realm we can belong as members only when we scrupulously conduct ourselves by maxims of freedom as if they were laws of nature.

Concluding Remark

The speculative use of reason with respect to nature leads to the absolute necessity of some supreme cause of the world. The practical use of reason with respect to freedom leads also to an absolute necessity, but to the necessity only of laws of actions of a rational being as such. Now it is an essential principle of all use of reason to push its knowledge to an awareness of its necessity, for otherwise it would not be rational knowledge. But it is also an equally essential restriction of this very same reason that it cannot discern the necessity of what is or of what occurs or of what ought to be done unless a condition under which it is or occurs or ought to be done is presupposed. In this way, however, the satisfaction of reason is only postponed further and further by the unceasing search for the condition. Reason, therefore, restlessly seeking the unconditionally necessary, sees itself compelled to assume it though it has no means by which to make it comprehensible; it is happy enough if it can discover only the concept which is compatible with this presupposition. It is, therefore, no objection to our deduction of the supreme principle of morality, but a reproach that we must make to human reason generally, that it cannot render comprehensible the absolute necessity of an unconditional practical law (such as the categorical imperative must be). Reason cannot be blamed for being unwilling to explain it by a condition (i.e., by making some interest its basis), for then the law would cease to be moral and would no longer be the supreme law of freedom. And so we do not indeed comprehend the unconditional practical necessity of the moral imperative; yet we do comprehend its incomprehensibility, which is all that can fairly be demanded of a philosophy which in its principles strives to reach the boundary of human reason.

ON A SUPPOSED RIGHT TO LIE FROM ALTRUISTIC MOTIVES

In the journal *France* for 1797, Part VI, No. 1, page 123, in an article entitled "On Political Reactions" by Benjamin Constant,* there appears the following passage:

> The moral principle, "It is a duty to tell the truth," would make any society impossible if it were taken singly and unconditional!" We have proof of this in the very direct consequences which a German philosopher has drawn from this principle. This philosopher goes so far as to assert that it would be a crime to lie to a murderer who asked whether our friend who is pursued by him had taken refuge in our house.

*Henri Benjamin Constant de Rebecque (1767–1830), the French writer, statesman, and orator.

Critique of Pratical Reason and Other Writings in Moral Philosophy, translated by Lewis White Beck (Chicago: University of Chicago Press, 1949). Reprinted by permission.

The French philosopher refutes this principle in the following manner:

> It is a duty to tell the truth. The concept of duty is inseparable from the concept of right. A duty is that which in one being corresponds to the rights of another. Where there are no rights, there are no duties. To tell the truth is thus a duty; but it is a duty only in respect to one who has a right to the truth. But no one has a right to a truth which injures others.

The <proton pseudos> ["first lie"] in this argument lies in the sentence: "To tell the truth is a duty, but it is a duty only toward one who has a right to the truth."

It must first be noted that the expression, "to have a right to truth" is without meaning. One must rather say, "Man has a right to his own truthfulness," i.e., to the subjective truth in his own person. For to have objectively a right to truth would mean that it is a question of one's will (as in questions of what belongs to individuals generally) whether a given sentence is to be true or false. This would certainly produce an extraordinary logic.

Now the first question is: Does a man, in cases where he cannot avoid answering "Yes" or "No," have a right to be untruthful? The second question is: Is he not in fact bound to tell an untruth, when he is unjustly compelled to make a statement, in order to protect himself or another from a threatened misdeed?

Truthfulness in statements which cannot be avoided is the formal duty of an individual to everyone,* however great may be the disadvantage accruing to himself or to another. If, by telling an untruth, I do not wrong him who unjustly compels me to make a statement, nevertheless by this falsification, which must be called a lie (though not in a legal sense), I commit a wrong against duty generally in a most essential point. That is, so far as in me lies I cause that declarations should in general find no credence, and hence that all rights based on contracts should be void and lose their force, and this is a wrong done to mankind generally.

Thus the definition of a lie as merely an intentional untruthful declaration to another person does not require the additional condition that it must harm another, as jurists think proper in their definition (*mendacium est falsiloquium in praeiudiciun alterius*).** For a lie always harms another; if not some other particular man, still it harms mankind generally, for it vitiates the source of law itself.

This benevolent lie, however, can become punishable under civil law through an accident, and that which escapes liability to punishment only by accident can also be condemned as wrong even by external laws. For instance, if by telling a lie you have prevented murder, you have made yourself legally responsible for all the consequences; but if you have held rigorously to the truth, public justice can lay no hand on you, whatever the unforeseen consequences may be. After you have honestly answered the murderer's question as to whether his intended victim is at home, it may be that he has slipped out so that he does not come in the way of the murderer, and thus that the murder may not be committed. But if you had lied and said he was not at home when he had really gone out without your knowing it, and if the murderer had then met him as he went away and murdered him, you might justly be accused as the cause of his death. For if you had told the truth as far as you knew it, perhaps the murderer might

*I should not like to sharpen this principle to the point of saying, "Untruthfulness is a violation of duty to one's self." This principle belongs to ethics, but here we are concerned with a legal duty. [Ethics as a] theory of virtue sees in this transgression only worthlessness, which is the reproach the liar draws upon himself.

**A lie is something spoken deceitfully in prejudgement of another."

have been apprehended by the neighbors while he searched the house and thus the deed might have been prevented. Therefore, whoever tells a lie, however well intentioned he might be, must answer for the consequences, however unforseeable they were, and pay the penalty for them even in a civil tribunal. This is because truthfulness is a duty which must be regarded as the ground of all duties based on contract, and the laws of these duties would be rendered uncertain and useless if even the least exception to them were admitted.

To be truthful (honest) in all declarations, therefore, is a sacred and absolutely commanding decree of reason, limited by no expediency.

Mr. Constant makes a thoughtful and correct remark on decrying principles so strict that they are alleged to lose themselves in such impracticable ideas that they are to be rejected. He says, "In every case where a principle which has been proved to be true appears to be inapplicable, the reason is that we do not know the middle principle which contains the means of its application." He adduces the doctrine of equality as the first link of the social chain, saying:

> No man can be bound by any laws except those to the formulation of which he has contributed. In a very limited society this principle can be applied directly and needs no mediating principle in order to become a common principle. But in a society consisting of very many persons, another principle must be added to this one we have stated. This mediating principle is: the individuals can participate in the formulation of laws either in their own person or through their representatives. Whoever wished to apply the former principle to a large society without making use of the mediating principle would invariably bring about the destruction of the society. But this circumstance, which would only show the ignorance or the incompetence of the legislator, proves nothing against the principle.

He concludes that "a principle acknowledged to be true must never be abandoned, however obviously danger seems to be involved in it." (And yet the good man himself abandoned the unconditional principle of truthfulness on account of the danger which it involved for society. He did so because he could find no mediating principle which could serve to prevent this danger; and, in fact, there is no principle to be interpolated here.)

If we wish to preserve the names of the persons as they have been cited here, the "French philosopher" confuses the action by which someone does harm to another in telling the truth when he cannot avoid making a statement, with the action whereby he does the other a wrong. It was only an accident that the truth of the statement harmed the occupant of the house; it was not a free act (in a juristic sense). For to demand of another that he should lie to one's own advantage would be a claim opposed to all lawfulness. Each man has not only a right but even the strict duty to be truthful in statements he cannot avoid making, whether they harm himself or others. In so doing, he does not do harm to him who suffers as a consequence; accident causes this harm. For one is not at all free to choose in such a case, since truthfulness (if he must speak) is an unconditional duty.

The "German philosopher" will not take as one of his principles the proposition: "To tell the truth is a duty, but only to him who has a right to the truth." He will not do so, first, because of the ambiguous formulation of this proposition, for truth is not a possession the right to which can be granted to one and denied to another. But he will not do so chiefly because the duty of truthfulness (which is the only thing in question here) makes no distinction between persons to whom one has this duty and to whom one can exempt himself from this duty; rather, it is an unconditional duty which holds in all circumstances.

Now in order to proceed from a metaphysics of law (which abstracts from all empirical conditions) to a principle of politics (which applies these concepts to cases met with in experience), and by means of this to achieve the solution of a problem of politics in accord with the universal principle of law, the philosopher will enunciate three notions. The first is an axiom, i.e., an apodictically certain proposition which springs directly from the definition of external law (the harmony of the freedom of each with the freedom of all others according to a universal law). The second is a postulate of external public law (the will of all united according to the principle of equality, without which no one would have any freedom). Third, there is the problem of how it is to be arranged that, in a society however large, harmony may be maintained in accordance with principles of freedom and equality (namely, by means of a representative system). The latter will then become a principle of politics, the organization and establishment of which will entail decrees drawn from the practical knowledge of men, which will have in view only the mechanism of the administration of justice and how this may be suitably carried out. Law must never be accommodated to politics but politics always accommodated to law.

The author says, "A principle recognized as true (I add, recognized as an *a priori* and hence apodictic principle) must never be abandoned, however obviously danger seems to be involved in it." But one must only understand the danger not as a danger of accidentally doing a harm but only as a danger of doing a wrong. This would happen if I made the duty of being truthful, which is unconditional and the supreme juridical condition in testimony, into a conditional duty subordinate to other considerations. Although in telling a certain lie I do not actually do anyone a wrong, I formally but not materially violate the principle of right with respect to all unavoidably necessary utterances. And this is much worse than to do injustice to any particular person, because such a deed against an individual does not always presuppose the existence of a principle in the subject which produces such an act.

If one is asked whether he intends to speak truthfully in a statement that he is about to make and does not receive the question with indignation at the suspicion it expressed that he might be a liar, but rather asks permissions to consider possible exceptions, that person is already potentially a liar. That is because he shows that he does not acknowledge truthfulness as an intrinsic duty but makes reservations with respect to a rule which does not permit any exception, inasmuch as any exception would directly contradict itself.

All practical principles of right must contain rigorous truth, and the so-called "mediating principles" can contain only the more accurate definition of their application to actual cases (according to rules of policy), but they can never contain exceptions from the former. Such exceptions would nullify their universality, and that is precisely the reason that they are called principles.

Mary Wollstonecraft
1759–1797

Mary Wollstonecraft's life is the fascinating story of a nonconformist seeking her way in an English society that had no place for her. She was born in London, the second of seven children, to an abusive, alcoholic father and a submissive, victimized mother. While still a child, Wollstonecraft had to take a great deal of responsibility for her family. She frequently intervened—even taking blows in the protection of her mother.

As a young woman, Wollstonecraft showed remarkable intellectual ability, despite the fact that she was largely self-taught. Following a period as a grade-school teacher, and at the urging of close friends, she took up writing. She published her first work, *Thoughts on the Education of Daughters,* in 1786. Over the next six years, Wollstonecraft worked extensively as a writer, book reviewer, and translator for the London publishing house of Joseph Johnson. Among the works published in this period were her *Original Stories* (1788), her autobiographical novel *Mary* (1788), and her response to Edmund Burke's *Reflections on the Revolution in France, A Vindication of the Rights of Man* (1790; revised 1791). The work for which Wollstonecraft is best known is *A Vindication of the Rights of Woman,* published in 1792.

Beginning in 1793, Wollstonecraft was involved in a series of scandals. She conceived a child out of wedlock, was mentioned in a treason trial, married twice, and twice attempted suicide. In this tumultuous period, she also managed to publish her *Historical and Moral View of the Origin and Progress of the French Revolution* (1794). In 1797, she died from complications following the birth of her second daughter. This second child, also named Mary, went on to fame as the author of the classic horror novel *Frankenstein* (1818), and as the wife of the poet Percy Bysshe Shelley.

* * *

In *A Vindication of the Rights of Woman,* Wollstonecraft argues that women's voices have been silenced because women are denied educational opportunities. Since reason is the key characteristic of human beings, *anyone* denied the possibility of developing reason, male or female, will seem inferior. If women were more "rationally educated, they could take a more comprehensive view of things" and participate more fully in philosophy.

In the selection that follows, Wollstonecraft acknowledges that the women in her society were intellectually inferior. But the reason for this inferiority had nothing to do with "sexual character." Rather they were "inferior" because they had been taught to focus all attention on becoming docile beauties attractive to men.

Although in many ways Wollstonecraft is an Enlightenment thinker (who died at age 38 before the turn of the century), her concerns were echoed by others in the nineteenth century. For example, in *On the Subjection of Women,* John Stuart Mill argued that women's subordination to men is "one of the chief hindrances to human improvement." Wollstonecraft's ideas stand as a challenge to the nineteenth century: How can women be a part of the "Age of Progress"?

* * *

Wollstonecraft's fascinating life has been chronicled by many writers, beginning with her second husband. William Godwin, in *Memoirs of the Author of a* Vindication of the Rights of Woman (London, 1798; reprinted, New York: Greenburg, 1927). Among more recent biographies are Ralph M. Wardle, *Mary Wollstonecraft: A Critical Biography* (Lincoln: University of Nebraska Press, 1951); Eleanor Flexner, *Mary Wollstonecraft: A Biography* (New York: Coward, McCann & Geoghegan, 1972); Claire Tomlin, *The Life and Death of Mary Wollstonecraft* (New York: Harcourt, Brace, Jovanovich, 1974); Jean Detre, *A Most Extraordinary Pair: Mary Wollstonecraft and William Godwin* (Garden City, NY: Doubleday, 1975); Janet M. Todd, *Mary Wollstonecraft: A Revolutionary Life* (New York: Columbia University Press, 2001); and Lyndall Gordon, *Mary Wollstonecraft* (New York: Little, Brown, 2005). For a discussion of the relationship between Wollstonecraft's life and her thought, see Margaret George, *One Woman's "Situation": A Study of Mary Wollstonecraft* (Urbana: University of Illinois Press, 1970). For a brief overview of Wollstonecraft's philosophy, see Kate Lindemann, "Mary Wollstonecraft" in Mary Ellen Waithe, *A History of Women Philosophers, Volume III: Modern Women Philosophers, 1600–1900* (Dordrecht, The Netherlands: Kluwer Academic, 1991), pp. 153–70. For books examining Wollstonecraft's contributions to feminist theory, see Jennifer Lorch, *Mary Wollstonecraft: The Making of a Radical Feminist* (New York: St. Martin's Press, 1990); Gary Kelly, *Revolutionary Feminism: The Mind and Career of Mary Wollstonecraft* (Houndmills, England: Macmillan, 1992); Maria J. Falco, ed., *Feminist Interpretations of Mary Wollstonecraft* (College Park, PA: Pennsylvania State University Press, 1996); and Barbara Taylor, *Mary Wollstonecraft and the Feminist Imagination* (Cambridge: Cambridge University Press, 2003). For her political theory, see Virginia Sapiro, *A Vindication of Political Virtue: The Political Theory of Mary Wollstonecraft* (Chicago: University of Chicago Press, 1992). Finally, Mary Wollstonecraft, *A Vindication of the Rights of Woman: An Authoritative Text, Backgrounds, The Wollstonecraft Debate, Criticism,* 2nd edition, ed. by Carol H. Poston (New York: W.W. Norton, 1988); and Claudia L. Johnson, ed., *The Cambridge Companion to Mary Wollstonecraft* (Cambridge: Cambridge University Press, 2002) contain helpful essays.

A VINDICATION OF THE RIGHTS OF WOMAN (in part)

CHAPTER 6

THE EFFECT WHICH AN EARLY ASSOCIATION OF IDEAS HAS UPON THE CHARACTER

Educated in [an] enervating style . . . and not having a chance, from their subordinate state in society, to recover their lost ground, is it surprising that women every where appear a defect in nature? Is it surprising, when we consider what a determinate effect an early association of ideas has on the character, that they neglect their understandings, and turn all their attention to their persons?

The great advantages which naturally result from storing the mind with knowledge, are obvious from the following consideration. The association of our ideas is either habitual or instantaneous; and the latter mode seems rather to depend on the original temperature of the mind than on the will. When the ideas, and matters of fact, are once taken in, they lie by for use, till some fortuitous circumstance make the information dart into the mind with illustrative force, that has been received at very different periods of our lives. Like the lightning's flash are many recollections; one idea assimilating and explaining another, with astonishing rapidity. I do not now allude to that quick perception of truth, which is so intuitive that it baffles research, and makes us at a loss to determine whether it is reminiscence or ratiocination, lost sight of in its celerity, that opens the dark cloud. Over those instantaneous associations we have little power; for when the mind is once enlarged by excursive flights, or profound reflection, the raw materials will, in some degree, arrange themselves. The understanding, it is true, may keep us from going out of drawing when we group our thoughts, or transcribe from the imagination the warm sketches of fancy; but the animal spirits, the individual character, give the colouring. Over this subtile electric fluid,* how little power do we possess, and over it how little power can reason obtain! These fine intractable spirits appear to be the essence of genius, and beaming in its eagle eye, produce in the most eminent degree the happy energy of associating thoughts that surprise, delight, and instruct. These are the glowing minds that concentrate pictures

*I have sometimes, when inclined to laugh at materialists, asked whether, as the most powerful effects in nature are apparently produced by fluids, the magnetic, &c. the passions might not be fine volatile fluids that embraced humanity, keeping the more refractory elementary parts together—or whether they were simply a liquid fire that pervaded the more sluggish materials giving them life and heat?

for their fellow-creatures; forcing them to view with interest the objects reflected from the impassioned imagination, which they passed over in nature.

I must be allowed to explain myself. The generality of people cannot see or feel poetically, they want fancy, and therefore fly from solitude in search of sensible objects; but when an author lends them his eyes they can see as he saw, and be amused by images they could not select, though lying before them.

Education thus only supplies the man of genius with knowledge to give variety and contrast to his associations; but there is an habitual association of ideas, that grows "with our growth," which has a great effect on the moral character of mankind; and by which a turn is given to the mind that commonly remains throughout life. So ductile is the understanding, and yet so stubborn, that the associations which depend on adventitious circumstances, during the period that the body takes to arrive at maturity, can seldom be disentangled by reason. One idea calls up another, its old associate, and memory, faithful to the first impressions, particularly when the intellectual powers are not employed to cool our sensations, retraces them with mechanical exactness.

This habitual slavery, to first impressions, has a more baneful effect on the female than the male character, because business and other dry employments of the understanding, tend to deaden the feelings and break associations that do violence to reason. But females, who are made women of when they are mere children, and brought back to childhood when they ought to leave the gocart for ever, have not sufficient strength of mind to efface the superinductions of art that have smothered nature.

Everything that they see or hear serves to fix impressions, call forth emotions, and associate ideas, that give a sexual character to the mind. False notions of beauty and delicacy stop the growth of their limbs and produce a sickly soreness, rather than delicacy of organs; and thus weakened by being employed in unfolding instead of examining the first associations, forced on them by every surrounding object, how can they attain the vigour necessary to enable them to throw off their factitious character?—where find strength to recur to reason and rise superiour to a system of oppression, that blasts the fair promises of spring? This cruel association of ideas, which everything conspires to twist into all their habits of thinking, or, to speak with more precision, of feeling, receives new force when they begin to act a little for themselves; for they then perceive that it is only through their address to excite emotions in men, that pleasure and power are to be obtained. Besides, all the books professedly written for their instruction, which make the first impression on their minds, all inculcate the same opinions. Educated then in worse than Egyptian bondage, it is unreasonable, as well as cruel, to upbraid them with faults that can scarcely be avoided, unless a degree of native vigour be supposed, that falls to the lot of very few amongst mankind.

For instance, the severest sarcasms have been levelled against the sex, and they have been ridiculed for repeating "a set of phrases learnt by rote," when nothing could be more natural, considering the education they receive, and that their "highest praise is to obey, unargued"—the will of man. If they are not allowed to have reason sufficient to govern their own conduct—why, all they learn—must be learned by rote! And when all their ingenuity is called forth to adjust their dress, "a passion for a scarlet coat," is so natural, that it never surprised me; and, allowing Pope's summary of their character to be just, "that every woman is at heart a rake," why should they be bitterly censured for seeking a congenial mind, and preferring a rake to a man of sense?

Rakes know how to work on their sensibility, whilst the modest merit of reasonable men has, of course, less effect on their feelings, and they cannot reach the heart by the way of the understanding, because they have few sentiments in common.

The Orgy from *The Rake's Progress, Tavern Scene,* Plate III, 1735, by William Hogarth (1697–1764) depicts the lifetyle of the eighteenth-century English upper classes—and a view of women that Wollstonecraft sought to change. Etching and engraving. (©By Courtesy of the Trustees of Sir John Soane's Museum)

It seems a little absurd to expect women to be more reasonable than men in their *likings,* and still to deny them the uncontrolled use of reason. When do men *fall-in-love* with sense? When do they, with their superior powers and advantages, turn from the person to the mind? And how can they then expect women, who are only taught to observe behaviour, and acquire manners rather than morals, to despise what they have been all their lives labouring to attain? Where are they suddenly to find judgment enough to weigh patiently the sense of an awkward virtuous man, when his manners, of which they are made critical judges, are rebuffing, and his conversation cold and dull, because it does not consist of pretty repartees, or well turned compliments? In order to admire or esteem any thing for a continuance, we must, at least, have our curiosity excited by knowing, in some degree, what we admire; for we are unable to estimate the value of qualities and virtues above our comprehension. Such a respect, when it is felt, may be very sublime; and the confused consciousness of humility may render the dependent creature an interesting object, in some points of view; but human love must have grosser ingredients; and the person very naturally will come in for its share—and, an ample share it mostly has!

Love is, in a great degree, an arbitrary passion, and will reign, like some other stalking mischiefs, by its own authority, without deigning to reason; and it may also be easily distinguished from esteem, the foundation of friendship, because it is often excited by evanescent beauties and graces, though to give an energy to the sentiment, something more solid must deepen their impression and set the imagination to work, to make the most fair—the first good.

Common passions are excited by common qualities.—Men look for beauty and the simper of good-humoured docility: women are captivated by easy manners; a gentleman-like man seldom fails to please them, and their thirsty ears eagerly drink the insinuating nothings of politeness, whilst they turn from the unintelligible sounds of the charmer—reason, charm he never so wisely. With respect to superficial accomplishments, the rake certainly has the advantage; and of these females can form an opinion, for it is their own ground. Rendered gay and giddy by the whole tenor of their lives, the very aspect of wisdom, or the severe graces of virtue, must have a lugubrious appearance to them; and produce a kind of restraint from which they and love, sportive child, naturally revolt. Without taste, excepting of the lighter kind, for taste is the offspring of judgment, how can they discover that true beauty and grace must arise from the play of the mind? and how can they be expected to relish in a lover what they do not, or very imperfectly, possess themselves? The sympathy that unites hearts, and invites to confidence, in them is so very faint, that it cannot take fire, and thus mount to passion. No, I repeat it, the love cherished by such minds, must have grosser fuel!

The inference is obvious; till women are led to exercise their understandings, they should not be satirized for their attachment to rakes; nor even for being rakes at heart, when it appears to be the inevitable consequence of their education. They who live to please—must find their happiness, in pleasure! It is a trite, yet true remark, that we never do any thing well, unless we love it for its own sake.

Supposing, however, for a moment, that women were, in some future revolution of time, to become, what I sincerely wish them to be, even love would acquire more serious dignity, and be purified in its own fires; and virtue giving true delicacy to their affections, they would turn with disgust from a rake. Reasoning then, as well as feeling, the only province of woman, at present, they might easily guard against exteriour graces, and quickly learn to despise the sensibility that had been excited and hackneyed in the ways of women, whose trade was vice; and allurements, wanton airs. They would recollect that the flame, one must use appropriated expressions, which they wished to light up, had been exhausted by lust, and that the sated appetite losing all relish for pure and simple pleasures, could only be roused by licentious arts or variety. What satisfaction could a woman of delicacy promise herself in a union with such a man, when the very artlessness of her affection might appear insipid? Thus does Dryden describe the situation.

> Where love is duty, on the female side,
> On theirs mere sensual gust, and sought with surly pride.

But one grand truth women have yet to learn, though much it imports them to act accordingly. In the choice of a husband, they should not be led astray by the qualities of a lover—for a lover the husband, even supposing him to be wise and virtuous, cannot long remain.

Were women more rationally educated, could they take a more comprehensive view of things, they would be contented to love but once in their lives; and after marriage calmly let passion subside into friendship—into that tender intimacy, which is the best refuge from care; yet is built on such pure, still affections, that idle jealousies would not be allowed to disturb the discharge of the sober duties of life, nor to engross the thoughts that ought to be otherwise employed. This is a state in which many men live; but few, very few women. And the difference may easily be accounted for, without recurring to a sexual character. Men, for whom we are told women were made, have too much occupied the thoughts of women; and this association has so entangled love with all their motives of action; and, to harp a little on an old string, having been solely employed either to prepare themselves to excite love, or actually putting their lessons in practice, they cannot live without love. But, when a sense of duty, or fear of shame, obliges them to restrain this pampered desire of pleasing beyond certain lengths, too far for delicacy, it is true, though far from criminality, they obstinately determine to love, I speak of the passion, their husbands to the end of the chapter—and then acting the part which they foolishly exacted from their lovers, they became abject wooers, and fond slaves.

Men of wit and fancy are often rakes; and fancy is the food of love. Such men will inspire passion. Half the sex, in its present infantile state, would pine for a Lovelace; a man so witty, so graceful, and so valiant: and can they *deserve* blame for acting according to principles so constantly inculcated? They want a lover, and protector; and, behold him kneeling before them—bravely prostrate to beauty! The virtues of a husband are thus thrown by love into the background, and gay hopes, or lively emotions, banish reflection till the day of reckoning comes; and come it surely will, to turn the sprightly lover into a surly suspicious tyrant, who contemptuously insults the very weakness he fostered. Or, supposing the rake reformed, he cannot quickly get rid of old habits. When a man of abilities is first carried away by his passions, it is necessary that sentiment and taste varnish the enormities of vice, and give a zest to brutal indulgences; but when the gloss of novelty is worn off, and pleasure palls upon the sense, lasciviousness becomes barefaced, and enjoyment only the desperate effort of weakness flying from reflection as from a legion of devils. Oh! virtue thou are not an empty name! All that life can give—thou givest!

If much comfort cannot be expected from the friendship of a reformed rake of superior abilities, what is the consequence when he lacks sense, as well as principles? Verily misery, in its most hideous shape. When the habits of weak people are consolidated by time, a reformation is barely possible; and actually makes the beings miserable who have not sufficient mind to be amused by innocent pleasure; like the tradesman who retires from the hurry of business, nature presents to them only a universal blank; and the restless thoughts prey on the damped spirits.* Their reformation, as well as his retirement, actually makes them wretched because it deprives them of all employment, by quenching the hopes and fears that set in motion their sluggish mind.

If such is the force of habit; if such is the bondage of folly, how carefully ought we to guard the mind from storing up vicious associations; and equally careful should we be to cultivate the understanding, to save the poor wight from the weak dependent state of even harmless ignorance. For it is the right use of reason alone which makes us independent of everything—excepting the unclouded Reason—"Whose service is perfect freedom."

*I have frequently seen this exemplified in women, whose beauty could no longer be repaired. They have retired from the noisy scenes of dissipation; but, unless they become methodists, the solitude of the select society of their family connexions or acquaintances, has presented only a fearful void; consequently, nervous complaints and all the vapourish train of idleness, rendered them quite as useless, and far more unhappy, than when they joined the giddy throng.

NINETEENTH-CENTURY PHILOSOPHY

The nineteenth century has often been described as the Age of Progress. The scientific discoveries of the seventeenth and eighteenth centuries led to numerous technological advances in Europe and America. These advances, in turn, made possible the Industrial Revolution and the incredible outpouring of goods it produced. Millions of people left the hard life of the farm, moving to cities and working in factories. In England, for example, in 1800 only 21 percent of the population lived in cities with a population of more than ten thousand. By 1890, city-dwellers had become 62 percent of the population. Life in the city seemed full of promise, and the good life seemed within reach of all.

The early nineteenth-century philosophies of Hegel and Mill epitomized this optimism about the future. Hegel claimed that "Idea" (or "Spirit" or "Mind") was guiding all of history. Contradictions in thought and practice would be overcome as history progressed. For his part, Mill wrote in his major work, *Utilitarianism,* of the "progress of science [that] holds out a promise for the future." Mill argued that free individuals representing the "wisdom of society" could overcome the social problems of the nineteenth century.

Yet by the middle of the century, doubts began to emerge among some thinkers. Kierkegaard questioned the optimistic assumptions of Hegel and expressed skepticism about the inevitability of progress. More fundamentally, Kierkegaard claimed that Hegel's entire system was flawed, because it assumed an objectivity that is unavailable and a finality that does not exist within history. For his part, Marx noted the effect of the Industrial Revolution on the factory worker and called for a change in the social and economic order. Marx also raised questions about Hegel, focusing his attack on Hegel's concept of "Idea."

Toward the end of the century, Nietzsche added his voice to those of the skeptics about nineteenth-century progress. Nietzsche decried the lack of passion brought on by the comforts of the Industrial Revolution. He called on thinking persons to recognize that there are no standards, that "God is dead," and he wished them to assert their "will to power" in overcoming the comfortable mediocrity of his age.

Though Nietzsche died in 1900, the nineteenth century really did not come to an end, in terms of ideas, until 1914. In that year, all the impressive technology that had been developed over the previous century was brought to bear in World War I with the goal of killing people. A system of alliances that had been established in the mid-nineteenth century on the basis of rational, pragmatic considerations ensured that virtually the entire world was involved in the struggle. By the time the war ended, the nineteenth-century optimistic assumption of progress had died.

* * *

There are a number of general introductions to nineteenth-century philosophy. Among the classics in this area are Étienne Gilson, *Recent Philosophy: Hegel to the Present* (New York: Random House, 1966); the appropriate works from Frederick Copleston's series, *A History of Philosophy: Volume VII, Fichte to Nietzsche; Volume VIII, Bentham to Russell;* and *Volume IX, Maine de Biran to Sartre* (New York: Image Doubleday, 1963, 1966, 1974); and from Emile Brehier's series, *The History of Philosophy: Volume 6, The Nineteenth Century: Period of Systems, 1800–1850; Volume 7, Contemporary Philosophy, Since 1850,* translated by Joseph Thomas (Chicago: University of Chicago Press, 1969); Karl Löwith, *From Hegel to Nietzsche: The Revolution in Nineteenth-Century Thought,* translated by David E. Green (1964; reprinted New York: Columbia University Press, 1991); and W.T. Jones, *Kant and the Nineteenth Century,* 2nd edition, revised (New York: Harcourt, Brace & World, 1975). More recent general surveys include Roger Scruton, *A Short History of Modern Philosophy: From Descartes to Wittgenstein* (London: Routledge, 1984); Wallace I. Matson, *A New History of Philosophy: Volume II, Modern* (San Diego, CA: Harcourt Brace Jovanovich, 1987); and C.L. Ten, ed., *Routledge History of Philosophy, Volume 7: The Nineteenth Century* (London: Routledge, 1994). The following is a sampling of the many books on specific topics from this era: William Barrett, *Irrational Man* (New York: Doubleday, 1958); David Knight, *The Age of Science: The Scientific World-View in the Nineteenth Century* (Oxford: Blackwell, 1986); Robert C. Solomon, *Hegel to Existentialism* (Oxford: Oxford University Press, 1987); David Jasper and T.R. Wright, eds., *The Critical Spirit and the Will to Believe: Essays in Nineteenth-Century Literature and Religion* (London: Macmillan, 1989); Mary Ellen Waithe, *A History of Women Philosophers: Volume III, Modern Women Philosophers, 1600–1900* (Dordrecht, Netherlands: Kluwer Academic, 1991); and Mark Francis and John Morrow, *A History of English Political Thought in the Nineteenth Century* (London: Duckworth, 1994).

G.W.F. Hegel
1770–1831

Georg Wilhelm Friedrich Hegel was born in Stuttgart, in southern Germany. Hegel and his father, a minor government official; his mother, a loving hausfrau (housewife); and his sister and brother were all close, affectionate, and loving. It is easy to see why Hegel would later describe the family as the "immediate Ethical Substance." Following grade school in Stuttgart, at age 18, Hegel won a scholarship to Tübingen University, where he studied theology. While there, he met and befriended the poet Johann Christian Friedrich Hölderlin and the philosopher Friedrich Wilhelm Joseph Schelling. The work Hegel submitted to his professors at the university gave no indication of the brilliant philosophical career that was to follow. In fact, his diploma from the university recorded that his knowledge of theology was fair, but his knowledge of philosophy was inadequate. Nevertheless, Hegel was already beginning to write insightful essays, not for classroom assignments, but to clarify his own thoughts.

After graduating from the university in 1793, Hegel spent seven years as a tutor for wealthy families in Bern and Frankfurt. During this time he continued to write essays—mostly on religious topics—that indicated he had moved far away from orthodox Christianity. For example, one early essay compared Jesus and Socrates, and Socrates' ethical teaching was seen as superior.

Following his father's death in 1799, Hegel inherited a modest sum of money, quit tutoring, and joined his friend Schelling at the University of Jena. There, Hegel became a *Privatdozent* (an unsalaried lecturer) and co-edited a philosophic journal with Schelling. While at Jena, Hegel wrote his first great work, *The Phenomenology of Spirit* (1807), which laid out the major themes of his philosophy. This work included a critique of Schelling's ideas, which ended the friendship. Before this important work could be published, Napoleon's war with Prussia closed the University of Jena, and so Hegel, whose inheritance had now been exhausted, was forced to find other employment.

After a stint as a newspaper editor, Hegel served eight years in Nürnberg as the rector of a *Gymnasium* (high school). There he published his second major work, *Science of Logic* (1812–1816). He also met and married a young woman from a distinguished family who was half his age, and they had two sons. In 1816, Hegel accepted a chair of philosophy at the University of Heidelberg. He continued his practice of producing a major book at each place he worked by publishing the *Encyclopedia of the Philosophical Sciences in Outline* in 1817. In 1818, Hegel moved to his final institution, the University of Berlin. There he published his *Philosophy of Right* (1821)—and became famous throughout Europe. He remained in Berlin until his death from cholera in 1831.

Following his death, a group of his friends published an eighteen-volume collection of his works, including his early essays and his lectures on aesthetics, the history of philosophy, the philosophy of history (portions of which are reprinted here), and the philosophy of religion.

* * *

Like all philosophers of his age, Hegel was greatly influenced by Kant. Kant had managed to synthesize two previously disparate realities—the rational world of ideas (emphasized by rationalists) with the phenomenal world of perception (emphasized by empiricists). But in so doing, Kant separated the noumenal world of "things-in-themselves" from the phenomenal world of experience and declared the noumenal world unknowable. In a sense, he had reconciled two competing epistemologies—Continental Rationalism and British Empiricism—at the expense of abandoning metaphysics. Hegel sought to go one step further than Kant and effect a complete synthesis that would not only draw together competing epistemologies but would also show the connection between epistemology and metaphysics. The key to this synthesis is the recognition that consciousness is the ultimate reality, or, to use his famous phrase, "What is real is rational—what is rational is real." That is, metaphysical reality (the real) *is* Idea or Spirit or Mind (that which knows). The resulting philosophy is called "Absolute Idealism" because all things that exist are essentially related to absolute Idea or Spirit or Mind.

According to Hegel, traditional rationalism (what he calls *raisonnement*) tends to classify all experience formally into abstract, lifeless universals. Taken to its logical extreme, rationalists end up with the abstraction "Being": "But this mere Being, as it is mere abstraction, is therefore the absolutely negative: which, in a similarly immediate aspect, is just NOTHING." By abstracting away the concreteness or particularity of actual experience, one is left with Being which is Nothing. The short article "Who Thinks Abstractly?" (1807–1808?), reprinted here in Walter Kaufmann's translation, clearly conveys Hegel's contempt for the process of abstraction.

Whereas Being and Nothing are both identical and yet contradictory, according to Hegel, "the truth of Being and Nothing is . . . the unity of the two: and this unity is BECOMING." The unity of Becoming does not obliterate Being and Nothing but holds both in tension in a higher truth. The two parts of the contradiction, together with that which unites or overcomes them, make up a triad. This method of overcoming contradictions by moving to a higher level of truth is known as the "dialectic." Hegel proposed to develop a complete dialectical system of reality based on the three foundational triads of "Being—Nothing—Becoming," "Being—Essence—Notion," and "Idea—Nature—Mind." Though he developed several proposals for this system, Hegel never completed any of them.

Although Hegel never developed a complete system, he did use the dialectical method to explain consciousness. In the section entitled "Relations of Master and Servant" from *The Phenomenology of Spirit* (1807), reprinted here in the J.L.H. Thomas translation, Hegel explains one stage in the dialectical development of consciousness. He begins by pointing out that only by acknowledging an "other" is self-consciousness possible. But if there is an other, then the original self-consciousness feels threatened and asserts its freedom by trying to dominate that other and force acknowledgment of its dominance. The ensuing struggle results in a master who dominates and a servant who is dominated. The master then forces the servant to produce material goods for the enjoyment of the master.

But at this point, the master now depends upon the servant he has dominated. In the first place, his self-consciousness as master is subject to his recognition as master by the servant. But more important, while the master has been consuming or destroying what the servant makes, the servant has been learning to create—to bend nature to his will—and so has established his own self-consciousness in relation to what he has created. Furthermore, the labor of the servant has a permanent quality, whereas the master's consumption again depends on the servant's production. So by dominating the servant, the master is dominated.

The solution to this contradiction is to acknowledge that neither master nor servant is free and that freedom is not possible in relationships of domination. The next stage in the dialectic is for the mind to seek freedom within itself.

Hegel's ideas have been both lauded and attacked. His insights on the master-servant relationship made a powerful impression on Marx and Nietzsche. Indeed, Hegel's understanding of dialectical development became a central feature of Marx's thought—though Marx rejected the notion of Absolute Spirit. Phenomenology developed Hegel's insights about the different types of consciousness. The sociology of knowledge developed his notions about the connection between consciousness and the culture of a particular epoch. Chief among Hegel's critics was Kierkegaard, who objected strenuously to the devaluing of the individual, questioned the implicit optimism of the dialectic, and mocked the incompleteness of Hegel's "System." Perhaps Hegel's greatest legacy was not any specific idea, but the vision of a complete historical development of thought.

* * *

For a selection of primary source readings for Hegel, see *Hegel, The Essential Writings,* edited by Frederick G. Weiss (New York: Harper & Row, 1974). Many secondary books about Hegel are difficult for beginning students. Two accessible classics are W.T. Stace, *The Philosophy of Hegel* (1924; reprinted New York: Dover, 1955) and G.R.G. Mure, *An Introduction to Hegel* (Oxford: Clarendon Press, 1940). Recent helpful studies include J.N. Findlay, *Hegel: A Re-examination* (New York: Macmillan, 1958); Walter Kaufmann, *Hegel: Reinterpretation, Texts and Commentary* (Garden City, NY: Doubleday, 1965); Peter Singer, *Hegel* (Oxford: Oxford University Press, 1983); Raymond Plant, *Hegel* (London: Routledge, 1999); Terry Pinkard, *Hegel: A Biography* (Cambridge: Cambridge University Press, 2001); Frederick Beiser, *Hegel* (London: Routledge, 2005); David James, *Hegel: A Guide for the Perplexed* (London: Continuum, 2007); and Allen Speight, *The Philosophy of Hegel* (Montreal: McGill–Queen's University Press, 2008). Charles

Taylor's massive *Hegel* (Cambridge: Cambridge University Press, 1975) can be consulted for particular topics. For specialized topics, see Ivan Soll, *An Introduction to Hegel's Metaphysics* (Chicago: University of Chicago Press, 1969); Walter Kaufmann, ed., *Hegel's Political Philosophy* (New York: Atherton Press, 1970); Quentin Lauer, *Hegel's Idea of Philosophy* (New York: Fordham University Press, 1971); Quentin Lauer, *A Reading of Hegel's "Phenomenology of Spirit"* (New York: Fordham University Press, 1976); Robert C. Solomon, *From Hegel to Existentialism* (New York: Oxford University Press, 1987); Merold Westphal, *History and Truth in Hegel's "Phenomenology"* (Atlantic Highlands, NJ: Humanities Press, 1990); H.S. Harris, *Hegel: Phenomenology and System* (Cambridge, MA: Hackett, 1995); John Russon, *The Self and Its Body in Hegel's* Phenomenology of Spirit (Toronto: University of Toronto Press, 1997); Joseph McCarney, *Routledge Philosophy Guidebook to Hegel on History* (London: Routledge, 2000); Robert Stern, *Routledge Philosophy Guidebook to Hegel and the* Phenomenology of Spirit (London: Routledge, 2002); and Howard Kainz, *Hegel's* Phenomenology of Spirit: *Not Missing the Trees for the Forest* (Lanham, MD: Lexington Books, 2008). Karl Marx, *Critique of Hegel's "Philosophy of Right,"* edited by Joseph O'Malley (Cambridge: Cambridge University Press, 1970) is both a critical review of Hegel's work and a major work in its own right. Michael Inwood, *A Hegel Dictionary* (Oxford: Basil Blackwell, 1992) provides a useful reference work. General collections of critical essays include W.E. Steinkraus, ed., *New Studies in Hegel's Philosophy* (New York: Holt, Rinehart & Winston, 1971); Alasdair MacIntyre, ed., *Hegel: A Collection of Critical Essays* (Notre Dame, IN: University of Notre Dame Press, 1972); Michael Inwood, ed., *Hegel* (Oxford: Oxford University Press, 1985); Frederick C. Beiser, ed., *The Cambridge Companion to Hegel* (Cambridge: Cambridge University Press, 1993); the multi-volume Robert Stern, ed., *G.W.F. Hegel: Critical Assessments* (London: Routledge, 1993); Patricia Jagentowicz Mills, ed., *Feminist Interpretations of Hegel* (College Park, PA: Pennsylvania State University Press, 1996); and Michael Baur and John Russon, eds., *Hegel and the Tradition* (Toronto: University of Toronto Press, 1998).

PHENOMENOLOGY OF SPIRIT

Independence and Dependence of Self-Consciousness: Relations of Master and Servant

Self-consciousness is *in* and *for itself* in and through being in and for itself for another self-consciousness; that is, it is only as something acknowledged, or recognized. The concept of this unity of self-consciousness in its duplication, of the infinitude realising itself in self-consciousness, is a many-sided and many-sensed complex, so that the

Hegel, *Phenomenology of Spirit* (B, IV, A: "Independence and Dependence of Self-Consciousness: Relations of Master and Servant"). Translated by J.L.H. Thomas. Reprinted from *Hegel: Selections,* edited by M.J. Inwood, *The Great Philosophers* series, Paul Edwards, general editor (New York: Macmillan, 1989).

moments of this complex must both be held carefully apart, and at the same time taken and understood in this differentiation as not distinct, or always also in their opposed sense. The double-sensedness of what is distinguished lies in the essence of self-consciousness, of being infinite, or boundless, that is, immediately the contrary of the determination in which it is established. The laying-apart of the concept of this spiritual unity in its duplication presents to us the movement of *acknowledging.*

There is for self-consciousness another self-consciousness; it has come *outside itself.* This has a twofold significance: *first,* self-consciousness has lost itself, for it finds itself as *another* being; *second,* it has thereby done away with the other, for it does not see the other either as the essential being, but *it itself* in the *other.*

Self-consciousness must do away with this *otherness it* has; this is the doing away with of the first double-sense, and hence itself a second double-sense: *first,* it must set out to do away with *the other* independent being in order thereby to become certain of *itself* as the essential being; *second,* in so doing it sets out to do away with *itself,* for this other being is itself.

This double-sensed doing away with its double-sensed otherness is equally a double-sensed return *into itself;* for, *first,* through doing away it gets itself back, for it becomes once more equal to itself through doing away with *its* otherness; *second,* however, it no less gives back the other self-consciousness to the latter again, for it had itself in the other, it does away with this being *it* has in the other, thus letting the other go free again.

This movement of self-consciousness in its relation to another self-consciousness has been presented in this way now, as *the doing of the one;* but this doing of the one has itself the two-fold significance of being as much *its doing* as *the doing of the other;* for the other is no less independent, shut up within itself, and there is nothing in it that is not owing to itself. The first self-consciousness does not have the object before it as the latter to begin with is merely for desire, but an independent object existing for itself, over which therefore it has of itself no power, unless the object does with itself what self-consciousness does with it. The movement is thus in all respects the double movement of both self-consciousnesses. Each sees the *other one* do the same as it does; each does itself what it demands of the other, and so does what it does only inasmuch as the other does the same; a one-sided doing would be unavailing, because what it is intended should occur can come about only through both.

The doing is therefore double-sensed not only inasmuch as it is a doing as much *to itself* as *to the other,* but also inasmuch as it is undividedly as much the *doing of the one* as *of the other.*

In this movement we see the process repeat itself which presented itself as the play of forces, but in consciousness. What in the earlier process was for us, is here for the extremes themselves. The centre is self-consciousness, which puts itself apart into the extremes; and each extreme is this exchanging of its determination and absolute going over into the opposed extreme. But though, as consciousness, it does indeed come *out of itself,* yet it is in its being-out-of-itself at the same time held back within itself, is *for itself,* and its "outside-itself" is *for it.* It is for consciousness that it immediately *is* and *is not* another consciousness; and, equally, that this other is only for itself in doing away with itself as something being for itself, and only in the being-for-itself of the other is for itself. Each is to the other the centre through which each brings into relation and connects itself with itself, and each is to itself and to the other an immediate entity existing for itself, which at the same time is thus for itself only through this relating, or mediation. They *acknowledge* one another as *mutually acknowledging one other.*

This pure concept of acknowledgement, the duplication of self-consciousness in its unity, will now be studied in the way in which its process appears for self-consciousness. This process will first present the facet of the *inequality* of the two, or the coming out of the centre into the extremes, which, being extremes, are opposed to one another, the one acknowledged only, the other acknowledging only.

Self-consciousness is to begin with simple being-for-itself, equal-with-itself through the exclusion of everything *other from itself;* its essence and absolute object is to it "*I*"; and it is in this *immediacy,* or in this *being* of its being-for-itself, an *individual.* Whatever else there is for it, is as an inessential object, one marked with the character of the negative. But the other is also a self-consciousness: an individual comes on opposite an individual. Thus *immediately* coming on, they are for each other in the way of common objects: *independent* forms, consciousnesses immersed in the *existence* of *life*—for it is as life that the existent object has here determined itself—which have not yet carried out *for each other* the movement of absolute abstraction, of expunging all immediate existence and of being merely the purely negative existence of consciousness equal-with-itself, or which have not yet presented themselves to each other as pure *being-for-self,* that is, as *self*-consciousness. Each is indeed certain of itself, but not of the other, and consequently each's own certainty of itself has as yet no truth; for its truth could only be that its own being-for-itself had presented itself to it as an independent object or, what amounts to the same thing, that the object had presented itself as this pure certainty of itself. This, however, on the concept of acknowledgement is not possible, save that as the other does for the one, so the one does for the other, each with itself through its own activity, and again through the activity of the other, carrying out this pure abstraction of being-for-itself.

The *presentation* of oneself as the pure abstraction of self-consciousness, however, consists in showing oneself to be the pure negation of one's objective way of being, that is, in showing oneself not to be attached to a particular *concrete existence,* nor to the universal individuality of concrete existence in general, nor even to life. This presentation is a *double* doing: doing of the other, and doing through oneself. Inasmuch as it is the doing *of the other,* each then is set upon the death of the other. But in this there is present also the second doing, *the doing through oneself;* for the former contains within itself the staking of one's own life. The relation of the two self-consciousnesses is hence determined in such a way that through the combat for life and death they *prove* themselves and each other.—They must enter this combat, for they must raise the certainty of themselves, *of being for themselves,* to truth in the other and in themselves. And it is solely through the staking of life that freedom arises, that it is confirmed to self-consciousness that it is not *being,* not the *immediate* way in which it comes on, not its being immersed in the expanse of life which is its essence—but that there is nothing present in it which is not for it a vanishing moment, that it is just pure *being-for-itself.* The individual that has not risked life can indeed be acknowledged as a *person;* but it has not attained the truth of this state of acknowledgement as that of an independent self-consciousness. Likewise, each must as much aim at the death of the other as it stakes its own life; for the other means no more to it than it itself does; the individual's essence presents itself to it as another, it is outside itself, it must do away with its being-outside-itself; the other is a consciousness engaged and existing in manifold ways; it must view its otherness as pure being-for-self, or as absolute negation.

This proving through death does away, however, with the truth that was to result from it, just as much as it thereby also does away with the certainty of oneself altogether; for just as life was the *natural* position of consciousness, independence without absolute negativity, so death is the *natural* negation of consciousness, negation without independence, which therefore remains without the required sense of acknowledgement. Through death the certainty has indeed arisen that both risked their life and despised it in themselves and in the other; though not for those who underwent this combat. They do away with their consciousness set in this alien essentiality that is natural concrete existence, or they do away with themselves, and are done away with as the *extremes* which would be for themselves. There thereby vanishes, however, from the play of exchange the essential moment of setting oneself apart into extremes of opposed determinations; and the centre collapses into a dead unity, which is set apart into dead, merely existent, not opposed, extremes; and the two do not mutually give back and receive back themselves from each other through consciousness, but let each other free merely indifferently, as things. Their deed is abstract negation, not the negation of consciousness, which *does away* in such a manner that it *puts by* and *preserves* what is done away, and consequently survives its being-done-away.

In this experience self-consciousness comes to realise that life is as essential to it as pure self-consciousness is. In immediate self-consciousness the simple "I" is the absolute object, which however, for us or in itself, is absolute mediation and has existent independence as an essential moment. The dissolution of that simple unity is the result of the first experience; through it there is established a pure self-consciousness, and a consciousness which is not purely for itself, but is for another consciousness, that is, is as *existent,* or is consciousness in the form of *thinghood.* Both moments are essential;—but as they are to begin with unequal and opposed, and their reflexion into unity is not yet a reality, they are as two opposed forms of consciousness: one, the independent consciousness, to which being-for-self is the essence; the other, the dependent consciousness, to which life or being for another is the essence: the former is the *master,* the latter the *servant.*

The master is the consciousness existing *for itself,* though no longer merely the concept of the latter, but a consciousness existing for itself which is in mediate relation with itself through *another* consciousness, namely through one to whose essence it pertains to be synthesised with independent *being* or thinghood in general. The master relates himself to both these moments, to a *thing* as such, the object of desire, and to the consciousness to whom thinghood is what is essential; and since he (a), *qua* concept of self-consciousness, is immediate relation of *being-for-himself,* but (b) now is also as mediation, or as a being-for-self which is for itself only through another, so he relates himself (a) immediately to both and (b) mediately to each through the other. The master relates himself *to the servant mediately through independent being;* for it is precisely to this that the servant is kept; it is his chain, from which in the combat he could not abstract, and consequently showed himself to be dependent, to have his independence in thinghood. The master, however, is the power over the being in question, for he showed in the combat that it meant merely something negative to him; since he is the power over this being, while this being is the power over the other, the master thus has in this conjunction the other under himself. Likewise the master relates himself *mediately through the servant to the thing,* the servant relates himself, *qua* self-consciousness as such, to the thing negatively also, and does away with it; but the thing is at the same time independent for him, and hence he cannot through his negating dispose of it so far as to destroy it, or he *works* it merely. The master on the other hand *gains* through this mediation the *immediate* relation as the pure negation of the thing, or the *enjoyment;* where desire did not succeed, he succeeds, namely in disposing of the thing and in satisfying himself in the enjoyment of it. Desire did not succeed in this on account of the independence of the thing; the master, however, who has interposed the servant between the thing and himself, thereby connects himself only with the nonindependence of the thing, and enjoys it in its purity; the facet of independence, on the other hand, he leaves to the servant, who works it.

In these two moments the master has his acknowledgement, or recognition, by another consciousness granted him; for the other consciousness establishes itself in these moments as something inessential, first, in the working of the thing, second, in the dependence upon a particular existence; in both it cannot achieve mastery over being and attain absolute negation. There is therefore present here the following moment of recognition, that the other consciousness does away with itself as being-foritself, and so itself does what the other does to it. Likewise the other moment is present, that this doing of the second consciousness is the first's own doing for what the servant does is really the doing of the master; to the latter, solely being-for-himself is the essence; he is the pure negative power to which the thing is nothing, and hence the pure essential doing in this situation; while the servant is not a pure doing, but an inessential one. But for true recognition there is lacking the moment that what the master does to the other he also does to himself, and what the servant does to himself he also does to the other. Thus there has arisen a one-sided and unequal recognizing.

The inessential consciousness is here for the master the object which constitutes the *truth* of the certainty of oneself. But it is evident that this object does not match its concept, and that there where the master has fulfilled himself, he has instead had something quite other than an independent consciousness come to be. It is not such a consciousness that is for him, but a dependent one rather; he is consequently not certain of *being-for-himself* as the truth, and his truth is rather the inessential consciousness, and the inessential doing of the latter.

The *truth* of independent consciousness is accordingly the servile or *subject consciousness.* The latter admittedly appears at first *outside* itself, and not as the truth of self-consciousness. But just as masterhood or dominion, showed that its essence is the converse of what it itself would be, so too, as we shall see, subjection will in its fulfillment turn rather into the contrary of what it is immediately; it will, *qua* consciousness *driven back* into itself, go into itself and turn about to true independence.

We have seen only what subjection is in the context of dominion. But the former is self-consciousness, and accordingly we shall now see what it is in and for itself. First of all, for subjection the master is the essence; hence the *independent consciousness existing for itself* is to subjection *the truth,* which however *for subjection* is not yet *in subjection.* But it has this truth of pure negativity and of *being-for-itself in the event in itself;* for subjection has *experienced* this essence within itself. This consciousness was, namely, not afraid for this or that, or for this instant or that, but for its whole being; for it has felt the fear of death, the absolute lord, or master. In this fear it has been internally broken up, it has been thoroughly shaken in itself, and everything fixed has trembled within it. This pure universal movement, the absolute becoming fluid of all that is permanent, is however the simple essence of self-consciousness, absolute negativity, *pure being-for-itself,* which is consequently *in* this consciousness. This moment of pure being-for-itself is also *for it,* for in the master it has it as its *object.* It is further not merely this universal dissolution *in general,* but in serving it *actually* brings it about; in serving it does away in all *particular* moments with its dependency on natural existence, and works that existence off.

But the feeling of absolute power, in general and in the particulars of service, is only the dissolution *in itself,* and although "the fear of the Lord is the beginning of wisdom," consciousness in this fear is *for its self,* not *being-for-itself.* Through work, however, it comes to itself. In the moment which corresponds to desire in the consciousness of the master, the facet of the inessential relation to the thing seemed to have fallen to the consciousness that serves, inasmuch as in this relation the thing retains its independence. Desire has reserved to itself the pure negating of the object and thereby the unmixed feeling-of-self. This satisfaction is on that account, however, itself just a vanishing, for it lacks the facet of the *object,* or *permanency.* Work by contrast is *contained* desire, *arrested* vanishing, or work *improves.* The negative relation to the object turns into the *form* of the object and into something *enduring,* precisely because to the worker the object has independence. This *negative* centre, or the *activity* that forms, or fashions, is at the same time *the particularity,* or the pure being-for-self of consciousness, which now in work steps out of consciousness into the element of permanency; the consciousness that works therefore attains as a consequence a view of independent being *as itself.*

The fashioning has not only this positive significance, however, that in it the consciousness that serves has itself as pure *being-for-itself* become something *existent;* but also a negative significance as against its first moment, the fear. For, in the improving of the thing, the consciousness which serves has its own negativity, its being-for-itself, become object only by doing away with the opposed existent *form.* But this objective, *negative* thing is precisely the alien being before which it trembled. Now, however, it destroys this alien negative thing, sets *itself* as something negative into the element of permanency, and thereby comes to be *for itself,* something *existing-for-itself.* In the master it has being-for-self as *an other,* or as merely *for it;* in the fear being-for-self is *in the consciousness itself that serves;* in the improving being-for-self comes to be for the consciousness that serves as *its own,* and the latter becomes conscious that it itself is in and for itself. Through being *set outside,* the form does not become to the consciousness that serves something other than the consciousness itself; for it is precisely the form that is its pure being-for-itself, which thereby to consciousness becomes the truth. Through this refinding of itself by itself, then, the consciousness that serves becomes a mind or *sense of its own,* and in the very work in which it seemed to be only *another's sense.*—For this reflexion both moments, that of fear and service in general, as well as that of improving, are necessary, and at the same time both in a general way. Without the discipline of service and obedience, fear remains at the formal stage, and does not spread itself upon the known reality of concrete existence. Without the improving, fear remains inward and silent, and consciousness does not become for itself. If consciousness fashions, or forms, without the initial absolute fear, it is merely a vain sense of self; for its form or negativity is not negativity *in itself,* and its fashioning cannot therefore give it the consciousness of itself as the essence. If it has not endured absolute fear, but only some anxiety, then it has the negative essence remain something external, its substance has not been infected through and through by the negative essence. Inasmuch as not all aspects of its natural consciousness have become insecure, it still *in itself* belongs to some particular existence; its self-sense is *self-will,* a freedom which as yet remains within subjection. No more than it can have the pure form become essence, no more is the form, regarded as something spread over individual things, a universal cultivating, an absolute concept, but is instead a dexterity which has power over merely some things, not over universal power and the whole objective realm of being.

LECTURES ON THE HISTORY OF PHILOSOPHY (in part)

THE FINAL RESULT

The present standpoint of philosophy is that the Idea is known in its necessity; the sides of its diremption, nature and spirit, are each recognized as representing the totality of the Idea, and not only as being in themselves identical, but as producing this one identity from themselves; and thus the identity is recognized as necessary. Nature, and the spiritual world, history, are the two actualities; what exists as actual nature is an image of divine reason; the forms of self-conscious reason are also forms of nature. The ultimate aim and concern of philosophy is to reconcile thought or the concept with actuality. It is easy to adopt subordinate standpoints, to find satisfaction in modes of intuition and of feeling. But the deeper the spirit goes within itself, the stronger the opposition, the more abundant the wealth without; depth is to be measured by the greatness of the need with which spirit seeks to find itself in what lies outside of itself. We saw the thought which apprehends itself emerge; it strove to make itself concrete within itself. Its first activity is formal; Aristotle was the first to say that *nous* is the thinking of thinking. The result is the thought which is at home with itself, and at the same time embraces the universe, and transforms it into an intelligent world. In conceptualisation the spiritual and the natural universe interpenetrate as one harmonious universe, which flees from itself into itself, and in its aspects develops the absolute into a totality, to become thereby conscious of itself in its unity, in thought. Philosophy is thus the true theodicy, as contrasted with art and religion and the feelings which these call up—a reconciliation of spirit, of the spirit which has apprehended itself in its freedom and in the riches of its actuality.

To this point the world-spirit has come, and each stage has its own form in the true system of philosophy; nothing is lost, all principles are preserved, since philosophy in its final aspect is the totality of forms. This concrete Idea is the result of the strivings of spirit during almost twenty-five centuries of earnest work to become objective to itself, to know itself:

> *Tantae molis erat, se ipsam cognoscere mentem.*

All this time was required to produce the philosophy of our day; so tardily and slowly did the world-spirit work to reach this goal. What we pass in rapid review when we recall it, stretched itself out in actuality to this great length of time. For in this period, the concept of spirit, invested with its entire concrete development, external subsistence, wealth, strives to bring spirit to perfection, to make progress itself and to emerge from spirit. It goes ever on and on, because spirit is progress alone. Spirit often seems to have forgotten and lost itself, but inwardly opposed to itself, it is inwardly working ever forward (as Hamlet says of the ghost of his father, "Well said, old mole! canst work i' the ground so fast?"), until grown strong in itself it bursts asunder the crust of earth which divided it from

From the Second (1840) Edition of *Lectures on the History of Philosophy,* translated by E.S. Haldane and F.H. Simson (1892–1896), with revisions by M.J. Inwood. Reprinted from *Hegel: Selections,* edited by M.J. Inwood, *The Great Philosophers,* series, Paul Edwards, general ed. (New York: Macmillan, 1989).

the sun, its concept, so that the earth crumbles away. At such a time, when the encircling crust, like a soulless decaying tenement, crumbles away, and spirit displays itself arrayed in new youth, the seven league boots are put on. This work of the spirit to know itself, this activity to find itself, is the life of the spirit and the spirit itself. Its result is the concept which it takes up of itself; the history of philosophy is a revelation of what has been the aim of spirit in its history; it is therefore the world's history in its innermost signification. This work of the human spirit in inner thinking is parallel with all the stages of actuality. No philosophy oversteps its own time. The importance of the determinations of thought is another matter, which does not belong to the history of philosophy. These concepts are the simplest revelation of the world spirit: in their more concrete form they are history.

We must, therefore, firstly, not esteem lightly what spirit has won, and won now. Older philosophy is to be reverenced as necessary, and as a link in this sacred chain, but all the same only a link. The present is the highest stage. Secondly, all the various philosophies are no mere fashions or the like; they are neither chance products nor the blaze of a fire of straw, nor casual eruptions here and there, but a spiritual, rational, forward advance; they are of necessity one philosophy in its development, the revelation of God, as He knows Himself to be. Where several philosophies appear at the same time, they are different sides which make up one totality forming their basis; and on account of their one-sidedness we see the refutation of the one by the other. Thirdly, we do not find here feeble little efforts to establish or to criticize this or that particular point; each philosophy sets up a *principle* of its own, and this must be recognized.

If we glance at the main epochs in the whole history of philosophy, and grasp the necessary succession of stages in the leading moments, each of which expresses a determinate Idea, we find that after the Oriental whirl of subjectivity, which attains to no understanding and therefore to no subsistence, the light of thought dawned among the Greeks.

1. The philosophy of the ancients had the absolute Idea as its thought; and the realization or reality of it consisted in comprehending the existing present world, and regarding it as it is in and for itself. This philosophy did not start from the Idea itself, but from the objective as something given, and transformed it into the Idea: the being of Parmenides.

2. Abstract thought, *nous,* became known to itself as universal essence, not as subjective thinking: the universal of Plato.

3. In Aristotle the concept emerges, free and unconstrained, as conceptual thinking, permeating and spiritualizing all the formations of the universe.

4. The concept as subject, its becoming for itself, its inwardness, abstract separation, is represented by the Stoics, Epicureans and Sceptics: not the free concrete form, but universality abstract and in itself formal.

5. The thought of totality, the intelligible world, is the concrete Idea as we have seen it in the Neo-Platonists. This principle is ideality in general in all reality, the Idea as totality, but not the Idea which knows itself: this is not reached until the principle of subjectivity, individuality, found a place in it, and God as spirit became actual to Himself in self-consciousness.

6. But it is the work of modern times to grasp this Idea as spirit, as the Idea that knows itself. In order to proceed from the knowing Idea to the self-knowing, we must have the infinite opposition, the Idea must have come to the consciousness of its bifurcation. As spirit had the thought of objective essence, philosophy thus perfected the intellectuality of the world, and produced this spiritual world as an object existing beyond present actuality, like a nature—the first creation of spirit. The work of the spirit now consisted in bringing this Beyond back to actuality and into self-consciousness. This is accomplished by self-consciousness thinking itself, and recognizing the absolute essence to be the self-consciousness that thinks itself. With Descartes pure thought directed itself

on that bifurcation. Self-consciousness, first, thinks of itself as consciousness; therein is contained all objective actuality and the positive, intuitive connexion of its actuality with the other. With Spinoza thought and being are opposed and yet identical; he has the intuition of substance, but the knowledge of substance in his case is external. We have here the principle of reconciliation taking its rise from thought as such, in order to sublimate the subjectivity of thought: this is the ease in Leibniz's monad, which possesses the power of representation.

7. Secondly, self-consciousness thinks of itself as being self-consciousness; in being self-conscious it is for itself, but still for itself it has a negative connexion with another. This is infinite subjectivity, which appears at one time as the critique of thought in Kant, and at another time, in Fichte, as the impulse towards the concrete. Absolutely pure, infinite form is expressed as self-consciousness, the ego.

8. This is a light that breaks forth on spiritual substance, and shows absolute content and absolute form to be identical; substance is in itself identical with knowledge. Self-consciousness thus, thirdly, recognizes its positive connexion as its negative, and its negative as its positive,—or it recognizes these opposite activities as the same, i.e. it recognizes pure thought or being as self-equality, and this again as bifurcation. This is intellectual intuition; but it is requisite in order that it be in truth intellectual, that we hear of, but absolute knowledge. This intuition which does not cognize itself is taken as starting-point as if it were absolutely presupposed; it has in itself intuition only as immediate knowledge, not as self-knowledge: or it knows nothing, and what it intuits it does not really know,—for, at its best, it consists of beautiful thoughts, but not knowledge.

But intellectual intuition is known, since firstly, in spite of the separation of each of the opposed sides from the other, all external reality is known as internal. If it is known according to its essence, as it is, it shows itself as not existing of itself, but as essentially consisting in the movement of transition. This Heraclitean or sceptical principle, that nothing is at rest, must be demonstrated of each individual thing; and thus in this consciousness—that the essence of each thing lies in determinacy, in the opposite of itself—there appears the comprehended unity with its opposite. Similarly this unity is, secondly, to be cognized even in its essence; its essence as this identity is likewise to pass over into its opposite, or to realize itself, to become something different; and thus the opposition in it is brought about by itself. Again, it may be said of the opposition, thirdly, that it is not in the absolute; this absolute is the essence, the eternal, etc. This is however itself an abstraction in which the absolute is apprehended in a one-sided manner only and the opposition is only ideal; but in fact it is form, as the essential moment of the movement of the absolute. This absolute is not at rest, and that opposition is not the unresting concept; for the Idea, unresting though it is, is yet at rest and satisfied in itself. Pure thought has advanced to the opposition of the subjective and objective; the true reconciliation of the opposition is the perception that this opposition, when pushed to its absolute extreme, resolves itself; as Schelling says, the opposites are in themselves identical—and not only in themselves, but eternal life consists in the very process of eternally producing the opposition and eternally reconciling it. To know opposition in unity, and unity in opposition—this is absolute knowledge; and science is the knowledge of this unity in its whole development by means of itself.

This is now the need of the time in general and of philosophy. A new epoch has arisen in the world. It would appear as if the world-spirit had at last succeeded in stripping off from itself all alien objective being, and apprehending itself at last as absolute spirit, in developing from itself what for it is objective, and keeping it in its power, yet remaining at rest. The strife of the finite self-consciousness with the absolute self-consciousness, which seemed to the former to lie outside itself, now ceases. Finite self consciousness has ceased to be finite; and in this way absolute self-consciousness has, on the other hand, acquired the actuality which it lacked before. This is the whole history of the world in general up to the present, and the history of philosophy in particular, which only depicts this strife. Now it seems to have reached its goal, when this absolute self-consciousness, which it had the work of representing, has ceased to be alien, and when spirit is thus actualized as spirit. For it becomes such only by knowing itself to be absolute spirit, and this it knows in science. Spirit produces itself as nature, as the state; nature is its unconscious work, in which it appears to itself something different, not spirit; but in the deeds and life of history, as also of art, it brings itself to pass with consciousness; it knows very various modes of its actuality, yet they are only modes. In science alone it knows itself as absolute spirit; and this knowledge, or spirit, is its only true existence. This then is the standpoint of the present day, and the series of spiritual forms is with it for now concluded.

At this point I bring this history of philosophy to a close. It has been my desire that you should learn from it that the history of philosophy is not a blind collection of brainwaves, nor a fortuitous progression. I have rather sought to show the necessary development of the successive philosophies from one another, so that the one of necessity presupposes the preceding. The general result of the history of philosophy is this: (1) at all times there has been only one philosophy, the contemporary differences of which constitute the necessary aspects of the one principle; (2) the succession of philosophic systems is not due to chance, but the necessary succession of stages in the development of this science; (3) the final philosophy of a period is the result of this development, and is truth in the highest form which the self-consciousness of spirit affords of itself. The latest philosophy contains therefore those which went before; it embraces in itself all the stages; it is the product and result of those that preceded it. We can now be Platonists no longer. We must rise above the pettinesses of individual opinions, thoughts, objections, and difficulties; and also above our own vanity, as if our own thoughts were of particular value. For to apprehend the inward substantial spirit is the standpoint of the individual; within the whole, individuals are like blind men, driven forward by the inner spirit. Our standpoint now is accordingly the knowledge of this Idea as spirit, as absolute spirit, which in this way opposes another spirit, the finite, the principle of which is to know absolute spirit, so that absolute spirit is for it. I have tried to develop and bring before your thoughts this series of spiritual forms of philosophy in its progress, and to indicate the connection between them. This series is the true kingdom of spirits, the only kingdom of spirits that there is—it is a series which is not a multiplicity, nor does it even remain a series or succession, but in the very process of coming to knowledge of itself it is transformed into the moments of the one spirit, of the one self-present spirit. This long procession of spirits is formed by the individual pulses which beat in its life; they are the organism of our substance, an absolutely necessary progression, which expresses nothing less than the nature of spirit itself, and which lives in us all. We have to give ear to its urgency—when the mole within forces its way on—and we have to give it actuality. It is my desire that this history of philosophy should contain for you a summons to grasp the spirit of the time, which is in us by nature, and—each in his own place—consciously to bring it from its natural condition, from its lifeless seclusion, into the light of day.

I have to express my thanks to you for the attention with which you have listened to me while I have been making this attempt; it is also due to you that my efforts have met with so great a measure of success. And it has been a source of pleasure to myself to have been associated with you in this spiritual community; I ought not to speak of it as if it were a thing of the past, for I hope that a spiritual bond has been knit between us which will prove permanent. I bid you a most hearty farewell.

JOHN STUART MILL
1806–1873

John Stuart Mill was born in London, the eldest of James and Harriet Burrow Mill's nine children. His father, a well-known philosopher and follower of Jeremy Bentham, educated young John at home. Beginning with Greek at age 3 and Latin at age 8, the younger Mill had read six of Plato's dialogues by the age of 10. John spent most of the day in the study with his father, who was writing a history of India. Each morning, they would go on a walk and James would quiz his son on what he had learned the previous day. During these walks, James would often discourse on various topics and then expect his son to prepare a summary of his points for the following day. Given the severity of this schooling—and the fact that his father showed no "signs of feeling"—it is not surprising that John later concluded, "I never was a boy."

The publication of the elder Mill's work on India in 1818 resulted in his receiving a government post as an Assistant Examiner at the East India House. Five years later, James managed to arrange a similar position for his 17-year-old son. John worked for the East India House for the next thirty-four years, eventually becoming chief of his department. In his early years as a clerk, John was, like his father, a disciple of Bentham's utilitarianism. John established the Utilitarian Society, contributed articles to the *Westminster Review,* and was active in the London Debating Society. He was developing a reputation as a polemicist for the "philosophic radicals"—those who sought social changes along the lines of Bentham's theories.

But in 1826, at age 20, Mill suffered a breakdown and went through a period of severe depression. He discovered to his horror that even if all the social changes he advocated were enacted and all the ideas he was taught about happiness were proven correct, it would not make *him* happy. As he later wrote in his *Autobiography,* "All my happiness was to have been found in the continual pursuit of this end. The end had ceased to charm, and how could there ever again be any interest in the means? I seemed to have nothing left to live for." He eventually came to the conclusion that his rigorous intellectual training had weakened his ability to feel emotion. Reading such writers as Wordsworth and Coleridge, he began to teach himself to feel as his father had taught him to think. During this period, he encountered divergent philosophies, such as those of socialist philosopher Claude-Henry Saint-Simon and positivist thinker Auguste Comte, and he began to see some of the inadequacies of the strict quantificational method of Bentham.

In 1831, Mill was introduced to Harriet Taylor, the wife of a successful merchant. They quickly developed a strong friendship and collaborated on a number of works, including *Principles of Political Economy, On Liberty,* and *The Subjection of Women*. Mill attributed to Taylor a number of his most important ideas, including his liberal feminism, and claimed that next to his father, she was the chief intellectual influence on his life. He even claimed she was the inspiration for his major epistemological work, *A System of Logic* (1843). Following her husband's death in 1849, they were finally married in 1851.

John and Harriet Mill moved to Avignon, France, in 1858, with neither of them in good health. Shortly after arriving, Harriet Taylor Mill died, and her daughter came to take care of her stepfather. Over the next seven years, Mill published *On Liberty* (1859), *Utilitarianism* (1861), *Considerations on Representative Government* (1861), *Auguste Comte and Positivism* (1865), and *The Subjection of Women* (written 1861, published 1869). In 1865, Mill was surprised by an offer to run for Parliament. Without campaigning he was elected and spent two years working on behalf of women's suffrage, Irish land reform, and the rights of blacks in Jamaica. Returning once again to the south of France, he wrote his *Autobiography* just before dying in 1873.

* * *

Although Mill wrote on a variety of topics and his work on induction is still used today, he is best known for his modification of Bentham's utilitarianism and his defense of individual liberty. Bentham had taught that ethics should be grounded on maximizing pleasure and minimizing pain, rather than on abstractions such as Kant's "duty" or conscience. Accordingly, Bentham developed a "hedonistic calculus," a mathematical method of determining which actions would most likely provide a greater quantity of pleasure over pain and hence yield happiness. Whereas this system might seem egoistic and individualistic, Bentham claimed that it would be to each individual person's advantage to seek the "greatest happiness of the greatest number."

In his *Utilitarianism,* given here (complete), Mill accepts Bentham's quantitative hedonism and argues that happiness, or pleasure, is the one thing that all people seek. But whereas Bentham's system merely measured quantities of pleasure and pain, Mill maintains that the *quality* of a given pleasure or pain has to be considered as well. Even though a pig might gain a great *quantity* of pleasure from wallowing in the mud, it would be a very low *quality* pleasure; and "It is better to be a human being dissatisfied than a pig satisfied; better to be Socrates dissatisfied than a fool satisfied." According to Mill, the person best able to make a qualitative determination between rival pleasures is the one who has experienced both. Presumably anyone who has both wallowed in the mud *and* studied philosophy would prefer the difficult but fulfilling pleasures of the latter.

Mill's contemporary critics pointed out that there seemed to be discrepancies between the philosophy of *Utilitarianism* and that of Mill's other works that advocated individual freedom. For example, following the greatest happiness principle of *Utilitarianism,* wouldn't it make sense for society to increase general happiness by intruding on an individual's liberty? Mill countered this objection by arguing that on balance, *laissez-faire* individualism will ultimately benefit society, that the diversity of individual choices is more conducive to general happiness than any socially imposed standard.

More recent critics have questioned Mill's distinction between private and public—for example, what you choose to do to yourself in the privacy of your home may cost the public money if you end up in a tax-supported hospital. Feminist critics have pointed out the potential oppression of the private/public distinction, questioned the possibility of "perfect equality" if paternalistic structures continue, and assailed Mill's "equal opportunity until marriage" doctrine. But there is no question that as a reforming impulse, Mill's beliefs—about the rights of the individual, the rights of women and minorities, freedom from societal intrusion into personal affairs, and utility rather than tradition—have had an enormous influence.

* * *

There are several good overviews of Mill's life and thought, including R.P. Anschutz, *The Philosophy of John Stuart Mill* (Oxford: Oxford University Press, 1953); Karl Britton, *John Stuart Mill* (1953; reprinted New York: Dover, 1969); Alan Ryan, *J.S. Mill* (London: Routledge & Kegan Paul, 1974); William Thomas, *Mill* (Oxford: Oxford University Press, 1985); and Nicholas Capaldi, *John Stuart Mill: A Biography* (Cambridge: Cambridge University Press, 2004). F.A. Hayek, *John Stuart Mill and Harriet Taylor* (Chicago: University of Chicago Press, 1951) presents a study of Mill's relationship with Harriet Taylor. For a critical evaluation of his work, see H.J. McCloskey, *John Stuart Mill: A Critical Study* (London: Macmillan, 1971). Guides to specific works of Mill include John Gray and G.W. Smith, eds., *J.S. Mill's "On Liberty" in Focus* (London: Routledge, 1991); Roger Crisp, *Routledge Philosophy Guidebook to Mill's* Utilitarianism (London: Routledge, 1997); and Henry R. West, *Mill's* Utilitarianism: *A Reader's Guide* (London: Continuum, 2007). For more specialized studies, see Dennis F. Thompson, *John Stuart Mill and Representative Government* (Princeton, NJ: Princeton University Press, 1976); Gertrude Himmelfarb, *On Liberty and Liberalism: The Case of John Stuart Mill* (New York: Knopf, 1974); Andrew Pyle's pair of books, *Liberty: Contemporary Responses to John Stuart Mill* and The Subjection of Women:*Contemporary Responses to John Stuart Mill* (both Bristol, UK: Thoemmes Press, 1994 and 1995); Joseph Hamburger, *John Stuart Mill on Liberty and Control* (Princeton, NJ: Princeton University Press, 1999); Colin Heydt, *Rethinking Mill's Ethics* (London: Continuum, 2006); and John R. Fitzpatrick, *John Stuart Mill's Political Philosophy* (London: Continuum, 2006). For collections of essays, see J.B. Schneewind, ed., *Mill: A Collection of Critical Essays* (Garden City, NY: Anchor Doubleday, 1968), J.M. Smith and E. Sosa, eds., *Mill's* Utilitarianism

(Belmont, CA: Wadsworth, 1969); John Skorupski, ed., *The Cambridge Companion to Mill* (Cambridge: Cambridge University Press, 1997) and G.W. Smith, ed., *John Stuart Mill's Social and Political Thought: Critical Assessments;* four volumes (London: Routledge, 1998).

UTILITARIANISM

CHAPTER 1: GENERAL REMARKS

There are few circumstances among those which make up the present condition of human knowledge, more unlike what might have been expected, or more significant of the backward state in which speculation on the most important subjects still lingers, than the little progress which has been made in the decision of the controversy respecting the criterion of right and wrong. From the dawn of philosophy, the question concerning the *summum bonum,* or, what is the same thing, concerning the foundation of morality, has been accounted the main problem in speculative thought, has occupied the most gifted intellects, and divided them into sects and schools, carrying on a vigorous warfare against one another. And after more than two thousand years the same discussions continue, philosophers are still ranged under the same contending banners, and neither thinkers nor mankind at large seem nearer to being unanimous on the subject, than when the youth Socrates listened to the old Protagoras, and asserted (if Plato's dialogue be grounded on a real conversation) the theory of utilitarianism against the popular morality of the so-called sophist.

It is true that similar confusion and uncertainty, and in some cases similar discordance, exist respecting the first principles of all the sciences, not excepting that which is deemed the most certain of them, mathematics; without much impairing, generally indeed without impairing at all, the trustworthiness of the conclusions of those sciences. An apparent anomaly, the explanation of which is, that the detailed doctrines of a science are not usually deduced from, nor depend for their evidence upon, what are called its first principles. Were it not so, there would be no science more precarious, or whose conclusions were more insufficiently made out, than algebra; which derives none of its certainty from what are commonly taught to learners as its elements, since these, as laid down by some of its most eminent teachers, are as full of fictions as English law, and of mysteries as theology. The truths which are ultimately accepted as the first principles of a science, are really the last results of metaphysical analysis, practised on the elementary notions with which the science is conversant; and their relation to the science is not that of foundations to an edifice, but of roots to a tree, which may perform their office equally well though they be never dug down to and exposed to light. But though in science the particular truths precede the general theory, the contrary might be expected to be the case with a practical art, such as morals or legislation. All action is for the sake of some end, and rules of action, it seems natural to suppose, must take their whole character and colour from the end to which they are subservient. When we engage in a pursuit, a clear and precise conception of what we are pursuing would seem to be the first thing we need, instead of the last we are to look forward to. A test of right and wrong must be the means, one would think, of ascertaining what is right or wrong, and not a consequence of having already ascertained it.

The difficulty is not avoided by having recourse to the popular theory of a natural faculty, a sense or instinct, informing us of right and wrong. For—besides that the existence of such a moral instinct is itself one of the matters in dispute—those believers in it who have any pretensions to philosophy, have been obliged to abandon the idea that it discerns what is right or wrong in the particular case in hand, as our other senses discern the sight or sound actually present. Our moral faculty, according to all those of its interpreters who are entitled to the name of thinkers, supplies us only with the general principles of moral judgments; it is a branch of our reason, not of our sensitive faculty; and must be looked to for the abstract doctrines of morality, not for perception of it in the concrete. The intuitive, no less than what may be termed the inductive, school of ethics, insists on the necessity of general laws. They both agree that the morality of an individual action is not a question of direct perception, but of the application of a law to an individual case. They recognise also, to a great extent, the same moral laws; but differ as to their evidence, and the source from which they derive their authority. According to the one opinion, the principles of morals are evident *a priori,* requiring nothing to command assent, except that the meaning of the terms be understood. According to the other doctrine, right and wrong, as well as truth and falsehood, are questions of observation and experience. But both hold equally that morality must be deduced from principles; and the intuitive school affirm as strongly as the inductive, that there is a science of morals. Yet they seldom attempt to make out a list of the *a priori* principles which are to serve as the premises of the science; still more rarely do they make any effort to reduce those various principles to one first principle, or common ground of obligation. They either assume the ordinary precepts of morals as of *a priori* authority, or they lay down as the common groundwork of those maxims, some generality much less obviously authoritative than the maxims themselves, and which has never succeeded in gaining popular acceptance. Yet to support their pretensions there ought either to be some one fundamental principle or law, at the root of all morality, or if there be several, there should be a determinate order of precedence among them; and the one principle, or the rule for deciding between the various principles when they conflict, ought to be self-evident.

To inquire how far the bad effects of this deficiency have been mitigated in practice, or to what extent the moral beliefs of mankind have been vitiated or made uncertain by the absence of any distinct recognition of an ultimate standard, would imply a complete survey and criticism of past and present ethical doctrine. It would, however, be easy to show that whatever steadiness or consistency these moral beliefs have attained, has been mainly due to the tacit influence of a standard not recognised. Although the non-existence of an acknowledged first principle has made ethics not so much a guide as a consecration of men's actual sentiments, still, as men's sentiments, both of favour and of aversion, are greatly influenced by what they suppose to be the effects of things upon their happiness, the principle of utility, or as Bentham latterly called it, the Greatest Happiness Principle, has had a large share in forming the moral doctrines even of those who most scornfully reject its authority. Nor is there any school of thought which refuses to admit that the influence of actions on happiness is a most material and even predominant consideration in many of the details of morals, however unwilling to acknowledge it as the fundamental principle of morality, and the source of moral obligation. I might go much further, and say that to all those *a priori* moralists who deem it necessary to argue at all, utilitarian arguments are indispensable. It is not my present purpose to criticise these thinkers; but I cannot help referring, for illustration, to a systematic treatise by one of the most illustrious of them, the *Metaphysics of Ethics* by Kant. This remarkable man, whose system of thought will long remain one of the landmarks in the history of philosophical speculation, does, in the treatise in question, lay down a universal first principle as the origin and ground of moral obligation; it is this:—"So act, that the rule on which thou actest would admit of being adopted as a law by all rational beings." But when he begins to deduce from this precept any of the actual duties of morality, he fails, almost grotesquely, to show that there would be any contradiction, any logical (not to say physical) impossibility, in the adoption by all rational beings of the most outrageously immoral rules of conduct. All he shows is that the *consequences* of their universal adoption would be such as no one would choose to incur.

On the present occasion, I shall, without further discussion of the other theories, attempt to contribute something towards the understanding and appreciation of the Utilitarian or Happiness theory, and towards such proof as it is susceptible of. It is evident that this cannot be proof in the ordinary and popular meaning of the term. Questions of ultimate ends are not amenable to direct proof. Whatever can be proved to be good, must be so by being shown to be a means to something admitted to be good without proof. The medical art is proved to be good by its conducing to health; but how is it possible to prove that health is good? The art of music is good, for the reason, among others, that it produces pleasure; but what proof is it possible to give that pleasure is good? If, then, it is asserted that there is a comprehensive formula, including all things which are in themselves good, and that whatever else is good, is not so as an end, but as a mean, the formula may be accepted or rejected, but is not a subject of what is commonly understood by proof. We are not, however, to infer that its acceptance or rejection must depend on blind impulse, or arbitrary choice. There is a larger meaning of the word proof, in which this question is as amenable to it as any other of the disputed questions of philosophy. The subject is within the cognisance of the rational faculty; and neither does that faculty deal with it solely in the way of intuition. Considerations may be presented capable of determining the intellect either to give or withhold its assent to the doctrine; and this is equivalent to proof.

We shall examine presently of what nature are these considerations; in what manner they apply to the case, and what rational grounds, therefore, can be given for accepting or rejecting the utilitarian formula. But it is a preliminary condition of rational acceptance or rejection, that the formula should be correctly understood. I believe that the very imperfect notion ordinarily formed of its meaning, is the chief obstacle which impedes its reception; and that could it be cleared, even from only the grosser misconceptions, the question would be greatly simplified, and a large proportion of its difficulties removed. Before, therefore, I attempt to enter into the philosophical grounds which can be given for assenting to the utilitarian standard, I shall offer some illustrations of the doctrine itself; with the view of showing more clearly what it is, distinguishing it from what it is not, and disposing of such of the practical objections to it as either originate in, or are closely connected with, mistaken interpretations of its meaning. Having thus prepared the ground, I shall afterwards endeavour to throw such light as I can upon the question, considered as one of philosophical theory.

CHAPTER 2: WHAT UTILITARIANISM IS

A passing remark is all that needs be given to the ignorant blunder of supposing that those who stand up for utility as the test of right and wrong, use the term in that restricted and merely colloquial sense in which utility is opposed to pleasure. An apology is due to the philosophical opponents of utilitarianism, for even the momentary appearance of confounding them with any one capable of so absurd a misconception; which is the more extraordinary, inasmuch as the contrary accusation, of referring everything to pleasure, and that too in its grossest form, is another of the common charges against utilitarianism: and, as has been pointedly remarked by an able writer, the same sort of persons, and often the very same persons, denounce the theory "as impracticably dry when the word 'utility' precedes the word 'pleasure,' and as too practicably voluptuous when the word 'pleasure' precedes the word 'utility.'" Those who know anything about the matter are aware that every writer, from Epicurus to Bentham, who maintained the theory of utility, meant by it, not something to be contradistinguished from pleasure, but pleasure itself, together with exemption from pain; and instead of opposing the useful to the agreeable or the ornamental, have always declared that the useful means these, among other things. Yet the common herd, including the herd of writers, not only in newspapers and periodicals, but in books of weight and pretension, are perpetually falling into this shallow mistake. Having caught up the word Utilitarian, while knowing nothing whatever about it but its sound, they habitually express by it the rejection, or the neglect, of pleasure in some of its forms; of beauty, of ornament, or of amusement. Nor is the term thus ignorantly misapplied solely in disparagement, but occasionally in compliment; as though it implied superiority to frivolity and the mere pleasures of the moment. And this perverted use is the only one in which the word is popularly known, and the one from which the new generation are acquiring their sole notion of its meaning. Those who introduced the word, but who had for many years discontinued it as a distinctive appellation, may well feel themselves called upon to resume it, if by doing so they can hope to contribute anything towards rescuing it from this utter degradation.*

The creed which accepts as the foundation of morals Utility or the Greatest Happiness Principle holds that actions are right in proportion as they tend to promote happiness, wrong as they tend to produce the reverse of happiness. By happiness is intended pleasure, and the absence of pain; by unhappiness, pain, and the privation of pleasure. To give a clear view of the moral standard set up by the theory, much more requires to be said; in particular, what things it includes in the ideas of pain and pleasure; and to what extent this is left an open question. But these supplementary explanations do not affect the theory of life on which this theory of morality is grounded—namely, that pleasure, and freedom from pain, are the only things desirable as ends; and that all desirable things (which are as numerous in the utilitarian as in any other scheme) are desirable either for the pleasure inherent in themselves, or as means to the promotion of pleasure and the prevention of pain.

Now, such a theory of life excites in many minds, and among them in some of the most estimable in feeling and purpose, inveterate dislike. To suppose that life has (as they express it) no higher end than pleasure—no better and nobler object of desire and pursuit—they designate as utterly mean and grovelling; as a doctrine worthy only of swine, to whom the followers of Epicurus were, at a very early period, contemptuously

*The author of this essay has reason for believing himself to be the first person who brought the word "utilitarian" into use. He did not Invent it, but adopted It from a passing expression in Mr. Galt's *Annals of the Parish*. After using it as a designation for several years, he and others abandoned it from a growing dislike to anything resembling a badge or watchword of sectarian distinction. But as a name for one single opinion, not a set of opinions—to denote the recognition of utility as a standard not any particular way of applying it—the term supplies a want in the language, and offers, in many cases, a convenient mode of avoiding tiresome circumlocution.

likened; and modern holders of the doctrine are occasionally made the subject of equally polite comparisons by its German, French, and English assailants.

When thus attacked, the Epicureans have always answered, that it is not they; but their accusers, who represent human nature in a degrading light; since the accusation supposes human beings to be capable of no pleasures except those of which swine are capable. If this supposition were true, the charge could not be gainsaid, but would then be no longer an imputation; for if the sources of pleasure were precisely the same to human beings and to swine, the rule of life which is good enough for the one would be good enough for the other. The comparison of the Epicurean life to that of beasts is felt as degrading, precisely because a beast's pleasures do not satisfy a human being's conceptions of happiness. Human beings have faculties more elevated than the animal appetites, and when once made conscious of them, do not regard anything as happiness which does not include their gratification. I do not, indeed, consider the Epicureans to have been by any means faultless in drawing out their scheme of consequences from the utilitarian principle. To do this in any sufficient manner, many Stoic, as well as Christian elements require to be included. But there is no known Epicurean theory of life which does not assign to the pleasures of the intellect, of the feelings and imagination, and of the moral sentiments, a much higher value as pleasures than to those of mere sensation. It must be admitted, however, that utilitarian writers in general have placed the superiority of mental over bodily pleasures chiefly in the greater permanency, safety, uncostliness, etc., of the former—that is, in their circumstantial advantages rather than in their intrinsic nature. And on all these points utilitarians have fully proved their case; but they might have taken the other, and, as it may be called, higher ground, with entire consistency. It is quite compatible with the principle of utility to recognise the fact, that some kinds of pleasure are more desirable and more valuable than others. It would be absurd that while, in estimating all other things, quality is considered as well as quantity, the estimation of pleasures should be supposed to depend on quantity alone.

If I am asked, what I mean by difference of quality in pleasures, or what makes one pleasure more valuable than another, merely as a pleasure, except its being greater in amount, there is but one possible answer. Of two pleasures, if there be one to which all or almost all who have experience of both give a decided preference, irrespective of any feeling of moral obligation to prefer it, that is the more desirable pleasure. If one of the two is, by those who are competently acquainted with both, placed so far above the other that they prefer it, even though knowing it to be attended with a greater amount of discontent, and would not resign it for any quantity of the other pleasure which their nature is capable of, we are justified in ascribing to the preferred enjoyment a superiority in quality, so far outweighing quantity as to render it, in comparison, of small account.

Now it is an unquestionable fact that those who are equally acquainted with, and equally capable of appreciating and enjoying, both, do give almost marked preference to the manner of existence which employs their higher faculties. Few human creatures would consent to be changed into any of the lower animals, for a promise of the fullest allowance of a beast's pleasures; no intelligent human being would consent to be a fool, no instructed person would be an ignoramus, no person of feeling and conscience would be selfish and base, even though they should be persuaded that the fool, the dunce, or the rascal is better satisfied with his lot than they are with theirs. They would not resign what they possess more than he for the most complete satisfaction of all the desires which they have in common with him. If they ever fancy they would, it is only in cases of unhappiness so extreme, that to escape from it they would exchange their lot for almost any other, however undesirable in their own eyes. A being of higher faculties requires more to make him happy, is capable probably of more acute suffering, and certainly accessible to it at more points, than one of an inferior type; but in spite of these liabilities, he can never really wish to sink into what he feels to be a lower grade of existence. We may give what explanation we please of this unwillingness; we may attribute it to pride, a name which is given indiscriminately to some of the most and to some of the least estimable feelings of which mankind are capable: we may refer it to the love of liberty and personal independence, an appeal to which was with the Stoics one of the most effective means for the inculcation of it; to the love of power, or to the love of excitement, both of which do really enter into and contribute to it: but its most appropriate appellation is a sense of dignity, which all human beings possess in one form or other, and in some, though by no means in exact, proportion to their higher faculties, and which is so essential a part of the happiness of those in whom it is strong, that nothing which conflicts with it could be, otherwise than momentarily, an object of desire to them. Whoever supposes that this preference takes place at a sacrifice of happiness—that the superior being, in anything like equal circumstances, is not happier than the inferior—confounds the two very different ideas, of happiness, and content. It is indisputable that the being whose capacities of enjoyment are low, has the greatest chance of having them fully satisfied; and a highly endowed being will always feel that any happiness which he can look for, as the world is constituted, is imperfect. But he can learn to bear its imperfections, if they are at all bearable; and they will not make him envy the being who is indeed unconscious of the imperfections, but only because he feels not at all the good which those imperfections qualify. It is better to be a human being dissatisfied than a pig satisfied; better to be Socrates dissatisfied than a fool satisfied. And if the fool, or the pig, are of a different opinion, it is because they only know their own side of the question. The other party to the comparison knows both sides.

It may be objected, that many who are capable of the higher pleasures, occasionally, under the influence of temptation, postpone them to the lower. But this is quite compatible with a full appreciation of the intrinsic superiority of the higher. Men often, from infirmity of character, make their election for the nearer good, though they know it to be the less valuable; and this no less when the choice is between two bodily pleasures, than when it is between bodily and mental. They pursue sensual indulgences to the injury of health, though perfectly aware that health is the greater good. It may be further objected, that many who begin with youthful enthusiasm for everything noble, as they advance in years sink into indolence and selfishness. But I do not believe that those who undergo this very common change, voluntarily choose the lower description of pleasures in preference to the higher. I believe that before they devote themselves exclusively to the one, they have already become incapable of the other. Capacity for the nobler feelings is in most natures a very tender plant, easily killed, not only by hostile influences, but by mere want of sustenance; and in the majority of young persons it speedily dies away if the occupations to which their position in life has devoted them, and the society into which it has thrown them, are not favourable to keeping that higher capacity in exercise. Men lose their high aspirations as they lose their intellectual tastes, because they have not time or opportunity for indulging them; and they addict themselves to inferior pleasures, not because they deliberately prefer them, but because they are either the only ones to which they have access, or the only ones which they are any longer capable of enjoying. It may be questioned whether any one who has remained equally susceptible to both classes of pleasures, ever knowingly and calmly preferred the lower; though many, in all ages, have broken down in an ineffectual attempt to combine both.

From this verdict of the only competent judges, I apprehend there can be no appeal. On a question which is the best worth having of two pleasures, or which of two modes of existence is the most grateful to the feelings, apart from its moral attributes and from its consequences, the judgment of those who are qualified by knowledge of both, or, if they differ, that of the majority among them, must be admitted as final. And there needs be the less hesitation to accept this judgment respecting the quality of pleasures, since there is no other tribunal to be referred to even on the question of quantity. What means are there of determining which is the acutest of two pains, or the intensest of two pleasurable sensations, except the general suffrage of those who are familiar with both? Neither pains nor pleasures are homogeneous, and pain is always heterogeneous with pleasure. What is there to decide whether a particular pleasure is worth purchasing at the cost of a particular pain, except the feelings and judgment of the experienced? When, therefore, those feelings and judgment declare the pleasures derived from the higher faculties to be preferable in kind, apart from the question of intensity, to those of which the animal nature, disjoined from the higher faculties, is suspectible, they are entitled on this subject to the same regard.

I have dwelt on this point, as being a necessary part of a perfectly just conception of Utility or Happiness, considered as the directive rule of human conduct. But it is by no means an indispensable condition to the acceptance of the utilitarian standard; for that standard is not the agent's own greatest happiness, but the greatest amount of happiness altogether; and if it may possibly be doubted whether a noble character is always the happier for its nobleness, there can be no doubt that it makes other people happier, and that the world in general is immensely a gainer by it. Utilitarianism, therefore, could only attain its end by the general cultivation of nobleness of character, even if each individual were only benefited by the nobleness of others, and his own, so far as happiness is concerned, were a sheer deduction from the benefit. But the bare enunciation of such an absurdity as this last, renders refutation superfluous.

According to the Greatest Happiness Principle, as above explained, the ultimate end, with reference to and for the sake of which all other things are desirable (whether we are considering our own good or that of other people), is an existence exempt as far as possible from pain, and as rich as possible in enjoyments, both in point of quantity and quality; the test of quality, and the rule for measuring it against quantity, being the preference felt by those who in their opportunities of experience, to which must be added their habits of self-consciousness and self-observation, are best furnished with the means of comparison. This, being, according to the utilitarian opinion, the end of human action, is necessarily also the standard of morality; which may accordingly be defined "the rules and precepts for human conduct" by the observance of which an existence such as has been described might be, to the greatest extent possible, secured to all mankind; and not to them only, but, so far as the nature of things admits, to the whole sentient creation.

Against this doctrine, however, arises another class of objectors, who say that happiness, in any form, cannot be the rational purpose of human life and action; because, in the first place, it is unattainable: and they contemptuously ask, what right hast thou to be happy? a question which Mr. Carlyle clenches by the addition, What right, a short time ago, hadst thou even to be? Next, they say, that men can do without happiness; that all noble human beings have felt this, and could not have become noble but by learning the lesson of Entsagen, or renunciation; which lesson, thoroughly learnt and submitted to, they affirm to be the beginning and necessary condition of all virtue.

The first of these objections would go to the root of the matter were it well founded; for if no happiness is to be had at all by human beings, the attainment of it cannot be the end of morality, or of any rational conduct. Though, even in that case, something might still be said for the utilitarian theory; since utility includes not solely the pursuit of happiness, but the prevention or mitigation of unhappiness; and if the former aim be chimerical, there will be all the greater scope and more imperative need for the latter, so long at least as mankind think fit to live, and do not take refuge in the simultaneous act of suicide recommended under certain conditions by Novalis.* When, however, it is thus positively asserted to be impossible that human life should be happy, the assertion, if not something like a verbal quibble, is at least an exaggeration. If by happiness be meant a continuity of highly pleasurable excitement, it is evident enough that this is impossible. A state of exalted pleasure lasts only moments, or in some cases, and with some intermissions, hours or days, and is the occasional brilliant flash of enjoyment, not its permanent and steady flame. Of this the philosophers who have taught that happiness is the end of life were as fully aware as those who taunt them. The happiness which they meant was not a life of rapture; but moments of such, in an existence made up of few and transitory pains, many and various pleasures, with a decided predominance of the active over the passive, and having as the foundation of the whole, not to expect more from life than it is capable of bestowing. A life thus composed, to those who have been fortunate enough to obtain it, has always appeared worthy of the name of happiness. And such an existence is even now the lot of many, during some considerable portion of their lives. The present wretched education, and wretched social arrangements, are the only real hindrance to its being attainable by almost all.

The objectors perhaps may doubt whether human beings, if taught to consider happiness as the end of life, would be satisfied with such a moderate share of it. But great numbers of mankind have been satisfied with much less. The main constituents of a satisfied life appear to be two, either of which by itself is often found sufficient for the purpose: tranquillity, and excitement. With much tranquillity, many find that they can be content with very little pleasure: with much excitement, many can reconcile themselves to a considerable quantity of pain. There is assuredly no inherent impossibility in enabling even the mass of mankind to unite both; since the two are so far from being incompatible that they are in natural alliance, the prolongation of either being a preparation for, and exciting a wish for, the other. It is only those in whom indolence amounts to a vice, that do not desire excitement after an interval of repose: it is only those in whom the need of excitement is a disease, that feel the tranquillity which follows excitement dull and insipid, instead of pleasurable in direct proportion to the excitement which preceded it. When people who are tolerably fortunate in their outward lot do not find in life sufficient enjoyment to make it valuable to them, the cause generally is, caring for nobody but themselves. To those who have neither public nor private affections, the excitements of life are much curtailed, and in any case dwindle in value as the time approaches when all selfish interests must be terminated by death: while those who leave after them objects of personal affection, and especially those who have also cultivated a fellow-feeling with the collective interests of mankind, retain as lively an interest in life on the eve of death as in the vigour of youth and health. Next to selfishness, the principal cause which makes life unsatisfactory is want of mental cultivation. A cultivated mind—I do not mean that of a philosopher, but any mind to which the fountains of knowledge have been opened, and which has been taught, in any tolerable degree, to exercise its faculties—finds sources of inexhaustible interest in all that surrounds it; in the objects of nature, the achievements of art, the

*[The German poet Friedrich Leopold Freiherr von Hardenberg (1772–1801).]

imaginations of poetry, the incidents of history, the ways of mankind, past and present, and their prospects in the future. It is possible, indeed, to become indifferent to all this, and that too without having exhausted a thousandth part of it; but only when one has had from the beginning no moral or human interest in these things, and has sought in them only the gratification of curiosity.

Now there is absolutely no reason in the nature of things why an amount of mental culture sufficient to give an intelligent interest in these objects of contemplation, should not be the inheritance of every one born in a civilised country. As little is there an inherent necessity that any human being should be a selfish egotist, devoid of every feeling or care but those which centre in his own miserable individuality. Something far superior to this is sufficiently common even now, to give ample earnest of what the human species may be made. Genuine private affections, and a sincere interest in the public good, are possible, though in unequal degrees, to every rightly brought up human being. In a world in which there is so much to interest, so much to enjoy, and so much also to correct and improve, every one who has this moderate amount of moral and intellectual requisites is capable of an existence which may be called enviable; and unless such a person, through bad laws, or subjection to the will of others, is denied the liberty to use the sources of happiness within his reach, he will not fail to find this enviable existence, if he escape the positive evils of life, the great sources of physical and mental suffering—such as indigence, disease, and the unkindness, worthlessness, or premature loss of objects of affection. The main stress of the problem lies, therefore, in the contest with these calamities, from which it is a rare good fortune entirely to escape; which, as things now are, cannot be obviated, and often cannot be in any material degree mitigated. Yet no one whose opinion deserves a moment's consideration can doubt that most of the great positive evils of the world are in themselves removable, and will, if human affairs continue to improve, be in the end reduced within narrow limits. Poverty, in any sense implying suffering, may be completely extinguished by the wisdom of society, combined with the good sense and providence of individuals. Even that most intractable of enemies, disease, may be indefinitely reduced in dimensions by good physical and moral education, and proper control of noxious influences; while the progress of science holds out a promise for the future of still more direct conquests over this detestable foe. And every advance in that direction relieves us from some, not only of the chances which cut short our own lives, but, what concerns us still more, which deprive us of those in whom our happiness is wrapt up. As for vicissitudes of fortune, and other disappointments connected with worldly circumstances, these are principally the effect either of gross imprudence, of ill-regulated desires, or of bad or imperfect social institutions. All the grand sources, in short, of human suffering are in a great degree, many of them almost entirely, conquerable by human care and effort; and though their removal is grievously slow—though a long succession of generations will perish in the breach before the conquest is completed, and this world becomes all that, if will and knowledge were not wanting, it might easily be made—yet every mind sufficiently intelligent and generous to bear a part, however small and unconspicuous, in the endeavour, will draw a noble enjoyment from the contest itself, which he would not for any bribe in the form of selfish indulgence consent to be without.

And this leads to the true estimation of what is said by the objectors concerning the possibility, and the obligation, of learning to do without happiness. Unquestionably it is possible to do without happiness; it is done involuntarily by nineteen-twentieths of mankind, even in those parts of our present world which are least deep in barbarism;

Crystal Palace, London, 1851, designed by Joseph Paxton (1801–1865). Built for the Works of Industry of All Nations exhibit, the building covered nineteen acres and enclosed over thirty million cubic feet. *(CORBIS)*

and it often has to be done voluntarily by the hero or the martyr, for the sake of something which he prizes more than his individual happiness. But this something, what is it, unless the happiness of others, or some of the requisites of happiness? It is noble to be capable of resigning entirely one's own portion of happiness, or chances of it: but, after all, this self-sacrifice must be for some end; it is not its own end; and if we are told that its end is not happiness, but virtue, which is better than happiness, I ask, would the sacrifice be made if the hero or martyr did not believe that it would earn for others immunity from similar sacrifices? Would it be made if he thought that his renunciation of happiness for himself would produce no fruit for any of his fellow creatures, but to make their lot like his, and place them also in the condition of persons who have renounced happiness? All honour to those who can abnegate for themselves the personal enjoyment of life, when by such renunciation they contribute worthily to increase the amount of happiness in the world; but he who does it, or professes to do it, for any other purpose, is no more deserving of admiration than the ascetic mounted on his pillar. He may be an inspiriting proof of what men *can* do, but assuredly not an example of what they *should*.

Though it is only in a very imperfect state of the world's arrangements that any one can best serve the happiness of others by the absolute sacrifice of his own, yet so long as the world is in that imperfect state, I fully acknowledge that the readiness to make such a sacrifice is the highest virtue which can be found in man. I will add, that in this condition of the world, paradoxical as the assertion may be, the conscious ability to do without happiness gives the best prospect of realising such happiness as is attainable. For nothing except that consciousness can raise a person above the chances of life, by making him feel that, let fate and fortune do their worst, they have not power to subdue

Interior, Crystal Palace. The palace was a shrine to science, industrialization, and progress. This architectural marvel represented in concrete form Mill's optimism when he spoke of the "wisdom of society" and the "progress of science [which] holds out a promise for the future." *(Victoria and Albert Museum, London/ V&A Picture Library)*

him: which, once felt, frees him from excess of anxiety concerning the evils of life, and enables him, like many a Stoic in the worst times of the Roman Empire, to cultivate in tranquillity the sources of satisfaction accessible to him, without concerning himself about the uncertainty of their duration, any more than about their inevitable end.

Meanwhile, let utilitarians never cease to claim the morality of self devotion as a possession which belongs by as good a right to them, as either to the Stoic or to the Transcendentalist. The utilitarian morality does recognise in human beings the power of sacrificing their own greatest good for the good of others. It only refuses to admit that the sacrifice is itself a good. A sacrifice which does not increase, or tend to increase, the sum total of happiness, it considers as wasted. The only self-renunciation which it applauds, is devotion to the happiness, or to some of the means of happiness, of others; either of mankind collectively, or of individuals within the limits imposed by the collective interests of mankind.

I must again repeat, what the assailants of utilitarianism seldom have the justice to acknowledge, that the happiness which forms the utilitarian standard of what is right in conduct, is not the agent's own happiness, but that of all concerned. As between his own happiness and that of others, utilitarianism requires him to be as strictly impartial as a disinterested and benevolent spectator. In the golden rule of Jesus of Nazareth, we read the complete spirit of the ethics of utility. "To do as you would be done by," and "to love your neighbour as yourself," constitute the ideal perfection of utilitarian morality. As the means of making the nearest approach to this ideal, utility would enjoin, first, that laws and social arrangements should place the happiness, or (as speaking practically it may be called) the interest, of every individual, as nearly as possible in harmony with the interest of the whole; and secondly, that education and opinion, which have so vast a power over human character, should so use that power as to establish in the mind of every individual an indissoluble association between his own happiness and the good of the whole; especially between his own happiness and the practice of such modes of conduct, negative and positive, as regard for the universal happiness prescribes; so that not only he may be unable to conceive the possibility of happiness to himself, consistently with conduct opposed to the general good, but also that a direct impulse to promote the general good may be in every individual one of the habitual motives of action, and the sentiments connected therewith may fill a large and prominent place in every human being's sentient existence. If the impugners of the utilitarian morality represented it to their own minds in this its true character, I know not what recommendation possessed by any other morality they could possibly affirm to be wanting to it; what more beautiful or more exalted developments of human nature any other ethical system can be supposed to foster, or what springs of action, not accessible to the utilitarian, such systems rely on for giving effect to their mandates.

The objectors to utilitarianism cannot always be charged with representing it in a discreditable light. On the contrary, those among them who entertain anything like a just idea of its disinterested character, sometimes find fault with its standard as being too high for humanity. They say it is exacting too much to require that people shall always act from the inducement of promoting the general interests of society. But this is to mistake the very meaning of a standard of morals, and confound the rule of action with the motive of it. It is the business of ethics to tell us what are our duties, or by what test we may know them; but no system of ethics requires that the sole motive of all we do shall be a feeling of duty; on the contrary, ninety-nine hundredths of all our actions are done from other motives, and rightly so done, if the rule of duty does not condemn them. It is the more unjust to utilitarianism that this particular misapprehension should be made a ground of objection to it, inasmuch as utilitarian moralists have gone beyond almost all others in affirming that the motive has nothing to do with the morality of the action, though much with the worth of the agent. He who saves a fellow creature from drowning does what is morally right, whether his motive be duty, or the hope of being paid for his trouble; he who betrays the friend that trusts him, is guilty of a crime, even if his object be to serve another friend to whom he is under greater obligations. But to speak only of actions done from the motive of duty, and in direct obedience to principle: it is a misapprehension of the utilitarian mode of thought, to conceive it as implying that people should fix their minds upon so wide a generality as the world, or society at large. The great majority of good actions are intended not for the benefit of the world, but for that of individuals, of which the good of the world is made up; and the thoughts of the most virtuous man need not on these occasions travel beyond the particular persons concerned, except so far as is necessary to assure himself that in benefiting them he is not violating the rights, that is, the legitimate and authorised expectations, of any one else. The multiplication of happiness is, according to the utilitarian ethics, the object of virtue: the occasions on which any person (except one in a thousand) has it in his power to do this on an extended scale, in other words to be a public benefactor, are but exceptional; and on these occasions alone is he called on to consider public utility; in every other case, private utility, the interest or happiness of some few persons, is all he has to attend to. Those alone the influence of whose actions extends to society in general, need concern themselves habitually about so large an object. In the case of abstinences indeed—of things which people forbear to do from moral considerations, though the consequences in the particular case might be beneficial—it would be unworthy of an intelligent agent not to be consciously aware that the action is of a class which, if practised generally, would be generally injurious, and that this is the ground of the obligation to abstain from it. The amount of regard for the public interest implied in this recognition, is no greater than is demanded by every system of morals, for they all enjoin to abstain from whatever is manifestly pernicious to society.

The same considerations dispose of another reproach against the doctrine of utility, founded on a still grosser misconception of the purpose of a standard of morality, and of the very meaning of the words "right" and "wrong." It is often affirmed that utilitarianism renders men cold and unsympathising; that it chills their moral feelings towards individuals; that it makes them regard only the dry and hard consideration of the consequences of actions, not taking into their moral estimate the qualities from which those actions emanate. If the assertion means that they do not allow their judgment respecting the rightness or wrongness of an action to be influenced by their opinion of the qualities of the person who does it, this is a complaint not against utilitarianism, but against having any standard of morality at all; for certainly no known ethical standard decides an action to be good or bad because it is done by a good or a bad man, still less because done by an amiable, a brave, or a benevolent man, or the contrary. These considerations are relevant, not to the estimation of actions, but of persons; and there is nothing in the utilitarian theory inconsistent with the fact that there are other things which interest us in persons besides the rightness and wrongness of their actions. The Stoics, indeed, with the paradoxical misuse of language which was part of their system, and by which they strove to raise themselves above all concern about anything but virtue, were fond of saying that he who has that has everything; that he, and only he, is rich, is beautiful, is a king. But no claim of this description is made for the virtuous man by the utilitarian doctrine. Utilitarians are quite aware that there are other desirable possessions and qualities besides virtue, and are perfectly willing to allow to all of them their full worth. They are also aware that a right action does not necessarily indicate a virtuous character, and that actions which are blamable, often proceed from qualities entitled to praise. When this is apparent in any particular case, it modifies their estimation, not certainly of the act, but of the agent. I grant that they are, notwithstanding, of opinion, that in the long run the best proof of a good character is good actions; and resolutely refuse to consider any mental disposition as good, of which the predominant tendency is to produce bad conduct. This makes them unpopular with many people; but it is an unpopularity which they must share with every one who regards the distinction between right and wrong in a serious light; and the reproach is not one which a conscientious utilitarian need be anxious to repel.

If no more be meant by the objection than that many utilitarians look on the morality of actions, as measured by the utilitarian standard, with too exclusive a regard, and do not lay sufficient stress upon the other beauties of character which go towards making a human being lovable or admirable, this may be admitted. Utilitarians who have cultivated their moral feelings, but not their sympathies nor their artistic perceptions, do fall into this mistake; and so do all other moralists under the same conditions. What can be said in excuse for other moralists is equally available for them, namely, that, if there is to be any error, it is better that it should be on that side. As a matter of fact, we may affirm that among utilitarians as among adherents of other systems, there is every imaginable degree of rigidity and of laxity in the application of their standard: some are even puritanically rigorous, while others are as indulgent as can possibly be desired by sinner or by sentimentalist. But on the whole, a doctrine which brings prominently forward the interest that mankind have in the repression and prevention of conduct which violates the moral law, is likely to be inferior to no other in turning the sanctions of opinion again such violations. It is true, the question, "What does violate the moral law?" is one on which those who recognise different standards of morality are likely now and then to differ. But difference of opinion on moral questions was not first introduced into the world by utilitarianism, while that doctrine does supply, if not always an easy, at all events a tangible and intelligible mode of deciding such differences.

It may not be superfluous to notice a few more of the common misapprehensions of utilitarian ethics, even those which are so obvious and gross that it might appear impossible for any person of candour and intelligence to fall into them; since persons, even of considerable mental endowments, often give themselves so little trouble to understand the bearings of any opinion against which they entertain a prejudice, and men are in general so little conscious of this voluntary ignorance as a defect, that the vulgarest misunderstandings of ethical doctrines are continually met with in the deliberate writings of persons of the greatest pretensions both to high principle and to philosophy. We not uncommonly hear the doctrine of utility inveighed against as a godless doctrine. If it be necessary to say anything at all against so mere an assumption, we may say that the question depends upon what idea we have formed of the moral character of the Deity. If it be a true belief that God desires, above all things, the happiness of his creatures, and that this was his purpose in their creation, utility is not only not a godless doctrine, but more profoundly religious than any other. If it be meant that utilitarianism does not recognise the revealed will of God as the supreme law of morals, I answer, that a utilitarian who believes in the perfect goodness and wisdom of God, necessarily believes that whatever God has thought fit to reveal on the subject of morals, must fulfil the requirements of utility in a supreme degree. But others besides utilitarians have been of opinion that the Christian revelation was intended, and is fitted, to inform the hearts and minds of mankind with a spirit which should enable them to find for themselves what is right, and incline them to do it when found, rather than to tell them, except in a very general way, what it is; and that we need a doctrine of ethics, carefully followed out, to *interpret* to us the will of God. Whether this opinion is correct or not, it is superfluous here to discuss; since whatever aid religion, either natural or revealed, can afford to ethical investigation, is as open to the utilitarian moralist as to any other. He can use it as the testimony of God to the usefulness or hurtfulness of any given course of action, by as good a right as others can use it for the indication of a transcendental law, having no connection with usefulness or with happiness.

Again, Utility is often summarily stigmatised as an immoral doctrine by giving it the name of "expediency," and taking advantage of the popular use of that term to contrast it with Principle. But the Expedient, in the sense in which it is opposed to the Right, generally means that which is expedient for the particular interest of the agent himself; as when a minister sacrifices the interests of his country to keep himself in place. When it means anything better than this, it means that which is expedient for some immediate object, some temporary purpose, but which violates a rule whose observance is expedient in a much higher degree. The Expedient, in this sense, instead of being the same thing with the useful, is a branch of the hurtful. Thus, it would often be expedient, for the purpose of getting over some momentary embarrassment, or attaining some object immediately useful to ourselves or others, to tell a lie. But inasmuch as the cultivation in ourselves of a sensitive feeling on the subject of veracity, is one of the most useful, and the enfeeblement of that feeling one of the most hurtful, things to which our conduct can be instrumental; and inasmuch as any, even unintentional, deviation from truth, does that much towards weakening the trustworthiness of human assertion, which is not only the principal support of all present social well-being, but the insufficiency of which does more than any one thing that can be named to keep back civilisation, virtue, everything on which human happiness on the largest scale depends; we feel that the violation, for a present advantage, of a rule of such transcendant expediency, is not expedient, and that he who, for the sake of a convenience to himself or to some other individual, does what depends on him to deprive mankind of the good, and inflict upon them the evil, involved in the greater or less reliance which they can place in each other's word, acts the part of one of their worst enemies. Yet that even this rule, sacred as it is, admits of possible exceptions, is acknowledged by all moralists; the chief of which is when the withholding of some fact (as of information from a malefactor, or of bad news from a person dangerously ill) would save an individual (especially an individual other than oneself) from great and unmerited evil, and when the withholding can only be effected by denial. But in order that the exception may not extend itself beyond the need, and may have the least possible effect in weakening reliance on veracity, it ought to be recognised, and, if possible, its limits defined; and if the principle of utility is good for anything, it must be good for weighing these conflicting utilities against one another, and marking out the region within which one or the other preponderates.

Again, defenders of utility often find themselves called upon to reply to such objections as this—that there is not time, previous to action, for calculating and weighing the effects of any line of conduct on the general happiness. This is exactly as if any one were to say that it is impossible to guide our conduct by Christianity, because there is not time, on every occasion on which anything has to be done, to read through the Old and New Testaments. The answer to the objection is, that there has been ample time, namely, the whole past duration of the human species. During all that time, mankind have been learning by experience the tendencies of actions; on which experience all the prudence, as well as all the morality of life, are dependent. People talk as if the commencement of this course of experience had hitherto been put off, and as if, at the moment when some man feels tempted to meddle with the property or life of another, he had to begin considering for the first time whether murder and theft are injurious to human happiness. Even then I do not think that he would find the question very puzzling; but, at all events, the matter is now done to his hand. It is truly a whimsical supposition that, if mankind were agreed in considering utility to be the test of morality, they would remain without any agreement as to what is useful, and would take no measures for having their notions on the subject taught to the young, and enforced by law and opinion. There is no difficulty in proving any ethical standard whatever to work ill, if we suppose universal idiocy to be conjoined with it; but on any hypothesis short of that, mankind must by this time have acquired positive beliefs as to the effects of some actions on their happiness; and the beliefs which have thus come down are the rules of morality for the multitude, and for the philosopher until he has succeeded in finding better. That philosophers might easily do this, even now, on many subjects; that the received code of ethics is by no means of divine right; and that mankind have still much to learn as to the effects of actions on the general happiness, I admit, or rather, earnestly maintain. The corollaries from the principle of utility, like the precepts of every practical art, admit of indefinite improvement, and, in a progressive state of the human mind, their improvement is perpetually going on. But to consider the rules of morality as improvable, is one thing; to pass over the intermediate generalisations entirely, and endeavour to test each individual action directly by the first principle, is another. It is a strange notion that the acknowledgment of a first principle is inconsistent with the admission of secondary ones. To inform a traveller respecting the place of his ultimate destination, is not to forbid the use of landmarks and direction-posts on the way. The proposition that happiness is the end and aim of morality, does not mean that no road ought to be laid down to that goal, or that persons going thither should not be advised to take one direction rather than another. Men really ought to leave off talking a kind of nonsense on this subject, which they would neither talk nor listen to on other matters of practical concernment. Nobody argues that the art of navigation is not founded on astronomy, because sailors cannot wait to calculate the *Nautical Almanac.* Being rational creatures, they go to sea with it ready calculated; and all rational creatures go out upon the sea of life with their minds made up on the common questions of right and wrong, as well as on many of the far more difficult questions of wise and foolish. And this, as long as foresight is a human quality, it is to be presumed they will continue to do. Whatever we adopt as the fundamental principle of morality, we require subordinate principles to apply it by; the impossibility of doing without them, being common to all systems, can afford no argument against any one in particular; but gravely to argue as if no such secondary principles could be had, and as if mankind had remained till no, and always must remain, without drawing any general conclusions from the experience of human life, is as high a pitch, I think, as absurdity has ever reached in philosophical controversy.

The remainder of the stock arguments against utilitarianism mostly consist in laying to its charge the common infirmities of human nature, and the general difficulties which embarrass conscientious persons in shaping their course through life. We are told that a utilitarian will be apt to make his own particular case an exception to moral rules, and, when under temptation, will see a utility in the breach of a rule, greater than he will see in its observance. But is utility the only creed which is able to furnish us with excuses for evil doing, and means of cheating our own conscience? They are afforded in abundance by all doctrines which recognise as a fact in morals the existence of conflicting considerations; which all doctrines do, that have been believed by sane persons. It is not the fault of any creed, but of the complicated nature of human affairs, that rules of conduct cannot be so framed as to require no exceptions, and that hardly any kind of action can safely be laid down as either always obligatory or always condemnable. There is no ethical creed which does not temper the rigidity of its laws, by giving a certain latitude, under the moral responsibility of the agent, for accommodation to peculiarities of circumstances; and under every creed, at the opening thus made, self-deception and dishonest casuistry get in. There exists no moral system under which there do not arise unequivocal cases of conflicting obligation. These are the real difficulties, the knotty points both in the theory of ethics, and in the conscientious guidance of personal conduct. They are overcome practically, with greater or with less success, according to the intellect and virtue of the individual; but it can hardly be pretended that any one will be the less qualified for dealing with them, from possessing an ultimate standard to which conflicting rights and duties can be referred. If utility is the ultimate source of moral obligations, utility may be invoked to decide between them when their demands are incompatible. Though the application of the standard may be difficult, it is better than none at all: while in other systems, the moral laws all claiming independent authority, there is no common umpire entitled to interfere between them; their claims to precedence one over another rest on little better than sophistry, and unless determined, as they generally are, by the unacknowledged influence of considerations of utility, afford a free scope for the action of personal desires and partialities. We must remember that only in these cases of conflict between secondary principles is it requisite that first principles should be appealed to. There is no case of moral obligation in which some secondary principle is not involved; and if only one, there can seldom be any real doubt which one it is, in the mind of any person by whom the principle itself is recognised.

CHAPTER 3: OF THE ULTIMATE SANCTION OF THE PRINCIPLE OF UTILITY

The question is often asked, and properly so, in regard to any supposed moral standard—What is its sanction? what are the motives to obey it? or more specifically, what is the source of its obligation? whence does it derive its binding force? It is a necessary part of moral philosophy to provide the answer to this question; which, though frequently assuming the shape of an objection to the utilitarian morality, as if it had some special applicability to that above others, really arises in regard to all standards. It arises, in fact, whenever a person is called on to *adopt* a standard, or refer morality to any basis on which he has not been accustomed to rest it. For the customary morality, that which education and opinion have consecrated, is the only one which presents itself to the mind with the feeling of being *in itself* obligatory; and when a person is asked to believe that this morality *derives* its obligation from some general principle round which custom has not thrown the same halo, the assertion is to him a paradox; the supposed corollaries seem to have a more binding force than the original theorem; the superstructure seems to stand better without, than with, what is represented as its foundation. He says to himself, I feel that I am bound not to rob or murder, betray or deceive; but why am I bound to promote the general happiness? If my own happiness lies in something else, why may I not give that the preference?

If the view adopted by the utilitarian philosophy of the nature of the moral sense be correct, this difficulty will always present itself, until the influences which form moral character have taken the same hold of the principle which they have taken of some of the consequences—until, by the improvement of education, the feeling of unity with our fellow-creatures shall be (what it cannot be denied that Christ intended it to be) as deeply rooted in our character, and to our own consciousness as completely a part of our nature, as the horror of crime is in an ordinarily well brought up young person. In the meantime, however, the difficulty has no peculiar application to the doctrine of utility, but is inherent in every attempt to analyse morality and reduce it to principles; which, unless the principle is already in men's minds invested with as much sacredness as any of its applications, always seems to divest them of a part of their sanctity.

The principle of utility either has, or there is no reason why it might not have, all the sanctions which belong to any other system of morals. Those sanctions are either external or internal. Of the external sanctions it is not necessary to speak at any length. They are, the hope of favour and the fear of displeasure, from our fellow-creatures or from the Ruler of the Universe, along with whatever we may have of sympathy or affection for them, or of love and awe of Him, inclining us to do his will independently of selfish consequences. There is evidently no reason why all these motives for observance should not attach themselves to the utilitarian morality, as completely and as powerfully as to any other. Indeed, those of them which refer to our fellow-creatures are sure to do so, in proportion to the amount of general intelligence; for whether there be any other ground of moral obligation than the general happiness or not, men do desire happiness;

and however imperfect may be their own practice, they desire and commend all conduct in others towards themselves, by which they think their happiness is promoted. With regard to the religious motive, if men believe, as most profess to do, in the goodness of God, those who think that conduciveness to the general happiness is the essence, or even only the criterion of good, must necessarily believe that it is also that which God approves. The whole force therefore of external reward and punishment, whether physical or moral, and whether proceeding from God or from our fellow men, together with all that the capacities of human nature admit of disinterested devotion to either, become available to enforce the utilitarian morality, in proportion as that morality is recognised; and the more powerfully, the more the appliances of education and general cultivation are bent to the purpose.

So far as to external sanctions. The internal sanction of duty, whatever our standard of duty may be, is one and the same—a feeling in our own mind; a pain, more or less intense, attendant on violation of duty, which in properly cultivated moral natures rises, in the more serious cases, into shrinking from it as an impossibility. This feeling, when disinterested, and connecting itself with the pure idea of duty, and not with some particular form of it, or with any of the merely accessory circumstances, is the essence of Conscience; though in that complex phenomenon as it actually exists, the simple fact is in general all encrusted over with collateral associations, derived from sympathy, from love, and still more from fear; from all the forms of religious feeling; from the recollections of childhood and of all our past life; from self-esteem, desire of the esteem of others, and occasionally even self-abasement. This extreme complication is, I apprehend, the origin of the sort of mystical character which, by a tendency of the human mind of which there are many other examples, is apt to be attributed to the idea of moral obligation, and which leads people to believe that the idea cannot possibly attach itself to any other objects than those which, by a supposed mysterious law, are found in our present experience to excite it. Its binding force, however, consists in the existence of a mass of feeling which must be broken through in order to do what violates our standard of right, and which, if we do nevertheless violate that standard, will probably have to be encountered afterwards in the form of remorse. Whatever theory we have of the nature or origin of conscience, this is what essentially constitutes it.

The ultimate sanction, therefore, of all morality (external motives apart) being a subjective feeling in our own minds, I see nothing embarrassing to those whose standard is utility, in the question, "What is the sanction of that particular standard?" We may answer, the same as of all other moral standards—the conscientious feelings of mankind. Undoubtedly this sanction has no binding efficacy on those who do not possess the feelings it appeals to; but neither will these persons be more obedient to any other moral principle than to the utilitarian one. On them morality of any kind has no hold but through the external sanctions. Meanwhile the feelings exist, a fact in human nature, the reality of which, and the great power with which they are capable of acting on those in whom they have been duly cultivated, are proved by experience. No reason has ever been shown why they may not be cultivated to as great intensity in connection with the utilitarian, as with any other rule of morals.

There is, I am aware, a disposition to believe that a person who sees in moral obligation a transcendental fact, an objective reality belonging to the province of "things in themselves," is likely to be more obedient to it than one who believes it to be entirely subjective, having its seat in human consciousness only. But whatever a person's opinion may be on this point of Ontology, the force he is really urged by is his own subjective feeling, and is exactly measured by its strength. No one's belief that duty is an objective reality is stronger than the belief that God is so; yet the belief in God, apart from the expectation of actual reward and punishment, only operates on conduct through, and in proportion to, the subjective religious feeling. The sanction, so far as it is disinterested, is always in the mind itself; and the notion therefore of the transcendental moralists must be, that this sanction will not exist *in* the mind unless it is believed to have its root out of the mind; and that if a person is able to say to himself, "This which is restraining me, and which is called my conscience, is only a feeling in my own mind," he may possibly draw the conclusion that when the feeling ceases the obligation ceases, and that if he find the feeling inconvenient, he may disregard it, and endeavour to get rid of it. But is this danger confined to the utilitarian morality? Does the belief that moral obligation has its seat outside the mind make the feeling of it too strong to be got rid of? The fact is so far otherwise, that all moralists admit and lament the ease with which, in the generality of minds, conscience can be silenced or stifled. The question, "Need I obey my conscience?" is quite as often put to themselves by persons who never heard of the principle of utility, as by its adherents. Those whose conscientious feelings are so weak as to allow of their asking this question, if they answer it affirmatively, will not do so because they believe in the transcendental theory, but because of the external sanctions.

It is not necessary, for the present purpose, to decide whether the feeling of duty is innate or implanted. Assuming it to be innate, it is an open question to what objects it naturally attaches itself; for the philosophic supporters of that theory are now agreed that the intuitive perception is of principles of morality and not of the details. If there be anything innate in the matter, I see no reason why the feeling which is innate should not be that of regard to the pleasures and pains of others. If there is any principle of morals which is intuitively obligatory, I should say it must be that. If so, the intuitive ethics would coincide with the utilitarian, and there would be no further quarrel between them. Even as it is, the intuitive moralists, though they believe that there are other intuitive moral obligations, do already believe this to be one; for they unanimously hold that a large *portion* of morality turns upon the consideration due to the interests of our fellow-creatures. Therefore, if the belief in the transcendental origin of moral obligation gives any additional efficacy to the internal sanction, it appears to me that the utilitarian principle has already the benefit of it.

On the other hand, if, as is my own belief, the moral feelings are not innate, but acquired, they are not for that reason the less natural. It is natural to man to speak, to reason, to build cities, to cultivate the ground, though these are acquired faculties. The moral feelings are not indeed a part of our nature, in the sense of being in any perceptible degree present in all of us; but this, unhappily, is a fact admitted by those who believe the most strenuously in their transcendental origin. Like the other acquired capacities above referred to, the moral faculty, if not a part of our nature, is a natural outgrowth from it; capable, like them, in a certain small degree, of springing up spontaneously; and susceptible of being brought by cultivation to a high degree of development. Unhappily it is also susceptible, by a sufficient use of the external sanctions and of the force of early impressions, of being cultivated in almost any direction: so that there is hardly anything so absurd or so mischievous that it may not, by means of these influences, be made to act on the human mind with all the authority of conscience. To doubt that the same potency might be given by the same means to the principle of utility, even if it had no foundation in human nature, would be flying in the face of all experience.

But moral associations which are wholly of artificial creation, when intellectual culture goes on, yield by degrees to the dissolving force of analysis: and if the feeling of duty, when associated with utility, would appear equally arbitrary; if there were no leading department of our nature, no powerful class of sentiments, with which that association would harmonise, which would make us feel it congenial, and incline us not only to foster it in others (for which we have abundant interested motives), but also to cherish it in ourselves; if there were not, in short, a natural basis of sentiment for utilitarian morality, it might well happen that this association also, even after it had been implanted by education, might be analysed away.

But there *is* this basis of powerful natural sentiment; and this it is which, when once the general happiness is recognised as the ethical standard, will constitute the strength of the utilitarian morality. This firm foundation is that of the social feelings of mankind; the desire to be in unity with our fellow creatures, which is already a powerful principle in human nature, and happily one of those which tend to become stronger, even without express inculcation, from the influences of advancing civilisation. The social state is at once so natural, so necessary, and so habitual to man, that, except in some unusual circumstances or by an effort of voluntary abstraction, he never conceives himself otherwise than as a member of a body; and this association is riveted more and more, as mankind are further removed from the state of savage independence. Any condition, therefore, which is essential to a state of society, becomes more and more an inseparable part of every person's conception of the state of things which he is born into, and which is the destiny of a human being. Now, society between human beings, except in the relation of master and slave, is manifestly impossible on any other footing than that the interests of all are to be consulted. Society between equals can only exist on the understanding that the interests of all are to be regarded equally. And since in all states of civilisation, every person, except an absolute monarch, has equals, every one is obliged to live on these terms with somebody; and in every age some advance is made towards a state in which it will be impossible to live permanently on other terms with anybody. In this way people grow up unable to conceive as possible to them a state of total disregard of other people's interests. They are under a necessity of conceiving themselves as at least abstaining from all the grosser injuries, and (if only for their own protection) living in a state of constant protest against them. They are also familiar with the fact of cooperating with others and proposing to themselves a collective, not an individual interest as the aim (at least for the time being) of their actions. So long as they are cooperating, their ends are identified with those of others; there is at least a temporary feeling that the interests of others are their own interests. Not only does all strengthening of social ties, and all healthy growth of society, give to each individual a stronger personal interest in practically consulting the welfare of others; it also leads him to identify his *feelings* more and more with their good, or at least with an even greater degree of practical consideration for it. He comes, as though instinctively, to be conscious of himself as a being who *of course* pays regard to others. The good of others becomes to him a thing naturally and necessarily to be attended to, like any of the physical conditions of our existence. Now, whatever amount of this feeling a person has, he is urged by the strongest motives both of interest and of sympathy to demonstrate it, and to the utmost of his power encourage it in others; and even if he has none of it himself, he is as greatly interested as any one else that others should have it. Consequently the smallest germs of the feeling are laid hold of and nourished by the contagion of sympathy and the influences of education; and a complete web of corroborative association is woven round it, by the powerful agency of the external sanctions. This mode of conceiving ourselves and human life, as civilisation goes on, is felt to be more and more natural. Every step in political improvement renders it more so, by removing the sources of opposition of interest, and levelling those inequalities of legal privilege between individuals or classes, owing to which there are large portions of mankind whose happiness it is still practicable to disregard. In an improving state of the human mind, the influences are constantly on the increase, which tend to generate in each individual a feeling of unity with all the rest; which, if perfect, would make him never think of, or desire, any beneficial condition for himself, in the benefits of which they are not included. If we now suppose this feeling of unity to be taught as a religion, and the whole force of education, of institutions, and of opinion, directed, as it once was in the case of religion, to make every person grow up from infancy surrounded on all sides both by the profession and the practice of it, I think that no one, who can realise this conception, will feel any misgiving about the sufficiency of the ultimate sanction for the Happiness morality. To any ethical student who finds the realisation difficult, I recommend, as a means of facilitating it, the second of M. Comte's two principal works, the *Traité de Politique Positive*. I entertain the strongest objections to the system of politics and morals set forth in that treatise; but I think it has superabundantly shown the possibility of giving to the service of humanity, even without the aid of belief in a Providence, both the psychological power and the social efficacy of a religion; making it take hold of human life, and colour all thought, feeling, and action, in a manner of which the greatest ascendancy ever exercised by any religion may be but a type and foretaste; and of which the danger is, not that it should be insufficient, but that it should be so excessive as to interfere unduly with human freedom and individuality.

Neither is it necessary to the feeling which constitutes the binding force of the utilitarian morality on those who recognise it, to wait for those social influences which would make its obligation felt by mankind at large. In the comparatively early state of human advancement in which we now live, a person cannot indeed feel that entireness of sympathy with all others, which would make any real discordance in the general direction of their conduct in life impossible; but already a person in whom the social feeling is at all developed, cannot bring himself to think of the rest of his fellow-creatures as struggling rivals with him for the means of happiness, whom he must desire to see defeated in their object in order that he may succeed in his. The deeply rooted conception which every individual even now has of himself as a social being, tends to make him feel it one of his natural wants that there should be harmony between his feelings and aims and those of his fellow-creatures. If differences of opinion and of mental culture make it impossible for him to share many of their actual feelings—perhaps make him denounce and defy those feelings—he still needs to be conscious that his real aim and theirs do not conflict; that he is not opposing himself to what they really wish for, namely their own good, but is, on the contrary, promoting it. This feeling in most individuals is much inferior in strength to their selfish feelings, and is often wanting altogether. But to those who have it, it possesses all the characters of a natural feeling. It does not present itself to their minds as a superstition of education, or a law despotically imposed by the power of society, but as an attribute which it would not be well for them to be without. This conviction is the ultimate sanction of the greatest happiness morality. This it is which makes any mind, of well-developed feelings, work with, and not against, the outward motives to care for others, afforded by what I have called the external sanctions; and when those sanctions are wanting, or act in an opposite direction, constitutes in itself a powerful internal binding force, in proportion to the sensitiveness and thoughtfulness of the character; since few but those whose mind is a moral blank, could bear to lay out their course of life on the plan of paying no regard to others except so far as their own private interest compels.

CHAPTER 4: OF WHAT SORT OF PROOF THE PRINCIPLE OF UTILITY IS SUSCEPTIBLE

It has already been remarked, that questions of ultimate ends do not admit of proof, in the ordinary acceptation of the term. To be incapable of proof by reasoning is common to all first principles; to the first premises of our knowledge, as well as to those of our conduct. But the former, being matters of fact, may be the subject of a direct appeal to the faculties which judge of fact—namely, our senses, and our internal consciousness. Can an appeal be made to the same faculties on questions of practical ends? Or by what other faculty is cognisance taken of them?

Questions about ends are, in other words, questions what things are desirable. The utilitarian doctrine is, that happiness is desirable, and the only thing desirable, as an end; all other things being only desirable as means to that end. What ought to be required of this doctrine—what conditions is it requisite that the doctrine should fulfil—to make good its claim to be believed?

The only proof capable of being given that an object is visible, is that people actually see it. The only proof that a sound is audible, is that people hear it: and so of the other sources of our experience. In like manner, I apprehend, the sole evidence it is possible to produce that anything is desirable, is that people do actually desire it. If the end which the utilitarian doctrine proposes to itself were not, in theory and in practice, acknowledged to be an end, nothing could ever convince any person that it was so. No reason can be given why the general happiness is desirable, except that each person, so far as he believes it to be attainable, desires his own happiness. This, however, being a fact, we have not only all the proof which the case admits of, but all which it is possible to require, that happiness is a good: that each person's happiness is a good to that person, and the general happiness, therefore, a good to the aggregate of all persons. Happiness has made out its title as one of the ends of conduct, and consequently one of the criteria of morality.

But it has not, by this alone, proved itself to be the sole criterion. To do that, it would seem, by the same rule, necessary to show, not only that people desire happiness, but that they never desire anything else. Now it is palpable that they do desire things which, in common language, are decidedly distinguished from happiness. They desire, for example, virtue, and the absence of vice, no less really than pleasure and the absence of pain. The desire of virtue is not as universal, but it is as authentic a fact, as the desire of happiness. And hence the opponents of the utilitarian standard deem that they have a right to infer that there are other ends of human action besides happiness, and that happiness is not the standard of approbation and disapprobation.

But does the utilitarian doctrine deny that people desire virtue, or maintain that virtue is not a thing to be desired? The very reverse. It maintains not only that virtue is to be desired, but that it is to be desired disinterestedly, for itself. Whatever may be the opinion of utilitarian moralists as to the original conditions by which virtue is made virtue; however they may believe (as they do) that actions and dispositions are only virtuous because they promote another end than virtue; yet this being granted, and it having been decided, from considerations of this description, what is virtuous, they not only place virtue at the very head of the things which are good as means to the ultimate end, but they also recognise as a psychological fact the possibility of its being, to the individual, a good in itself, without looking to any end beyond it; and hold, that the mind is not in a right state, not in a state conformable to Utility, not in the state most conducive to the general happiness, unless it does love virtue in this manner—as a thing desirable in itself, even although, in the individual instance, it should not produce those other desirable consequences which it tends to produce, and on account of which it is held to be virtue. This opinion is not, in the smallest degree, a departure from the Happiness principle. The ingredients of happiness are very various, and each of them is desirable in itself, and not merely when considered as swelling an aggregate. The principle of utility does not mean that any given pleasure, as music, for instance, or any given exemption from pain, as for example health, is to be looked upon as means to a collective something termed happiness, and to be desired on that account. They are desired and desirable in and for themselves; besides being means, they are a part of the end. Virtue, according to the utilitarian doctrine, is not naturally and originally part of the end, but it is capable of becoming so; and in those who love it disinterestedly it has become so, and is desired and cherished, not as a means to happiness, but as a part of their happiness.

To illustrate this farther, we may remember that virtue is not the only thing, originally a means, and which if it were not a means to anything else, would be and remain indifferent, but which by association with what it is a means to, comes to be desired for itself, and that too with the utmost intensity. What, for example, shall we say of the love of money? There is nothing originally more desirable about money than about any heap of glittering pebbles. Its worth is solely that of the things which it will buy; the desires for other things than itself, which it is a means of gratifying. Yet the love of money is not only one of the strongest moving forces of human life, but money is, in many cases, desired in and for itself; the desire to possess it is often stronger than the desire to use it, and goes on increasing when all the desires which point to ends beyond it, to be compassed by it, are falling off. It may, then, be said truly, that money is desired not for the sake of an end, but as part of the end. From being a means to happiness, it has come to be itself a principal ingredient of the individual's conception of happiness. The same may be said of the majority of the great objects of human life—power, for example, or fame; except that to each of these there is a certain amount of immediate pleasure annexed, which has at least the semblance of being naturally inherent in them; a thing which cannot be said of money. Still, however, the strongest natural attraction, both of power and of fame, is the immense aid they give to the attainment of our other wishes; and it is the strong association thus generated between them and all our objects of desire, which gives to the direct desire of them the intensity it often assumes, so as in some characters to surpass in strength all other desires. In these cases the means have become a part of the end, and a more important part of it than any of the things which they are means to. What was once desired as an instrument for the attainment of happiness, has come to be desired for its own sake. In being desired for its own sake it is, however, desired as *part* of happiness. The person is made, or thinks he would be made, happy by its mere possession; and is made unhappy by failure to obtain it. The desire of it is not a different thing from the desire of happiness, any more than the love of music, or the desire of health. They are included in happiness. They are some of the elements of which the desire of happiness is made up. Happiness is not an abstract idea, but a concrete whole; and these are some of its parts. And the utilitarian standard sanctions and approves their being so. Life would be a poor thing, very ill provided with sources of happiness, if there were not this provision of nature, by which things originally indifferent, but conducive to, or otherwise associated with, the satisfaction of our primitive desires, become in themselves sources of pleasure more valuable than the primitive pleasures, both in permanency, in the space of human existence that they are capable of covering, and even in intensity.

Virtue, according to the utilitarian conception, is a good of this description. There was no original desire of it, or motive to it, save its conduciveness to pleasure, and especially to protection from pain. But through the association thus formed, it may be felt a good in itself, and desired as such with as great intensity as any other good; and with this difference between it and the love of money, of power, or of fame, that all of these may, and often do, render the individual noxious to the other members of the society to which he belongs, whereas there is nothing which makes him so much a blessing to them as the cultivation of the disinterested love of virtue. And consequently, the utilitarian standard, while it tolerates and approves those other acquired desires, up to the point beyond which they would be more injurious to the general happiness than promotive of it, enjoins and requires the cultivation of the love of virtue up to the greatest strength possible, as being above all things important to the general happiness.

It results from the preceding considerations, that there is in reality nothing desired except happiness. Whatever is desired otherwise than as a means to some end beyond itself, and ultimately to happiness, is desired as itself a part of happiness, and is not desired for itself until it has become so. Those who desire virtue for its own sake, desire it either because the consciousness of it is a pleasure, or because the consciousness of being without it is a pain, or for both reasons united; as in truth the pleasure and pain seldom exist separately, but almost always together, the same person feeling pleasure in the degree of virtue attained, and pain in not having attained more. If one of these gave him no pleasure, and the other no pain, he would not love or desire virtue, or would desire it only for the other benefits which it might produce to himself or to persons whom he cared for.

We have now, then, an answer to the question, of what sort of proof the principle of utility is susceptible. If the opinion which I have now stated is psychologically true—if human nature is so constituted as to desire nothing which is not either a part of happiness or a means of happiness—we can have no other proof, and we require no other, that these are the only things desirable. If so, happiness is the sole end of human action, and the promotion of it the test by which to judge of all human conduct; from whence it necessarily follows that it must be the criterion of morality, since a part is included in the whole.

And now to decide whether this is really so; whether mankind do desire nothing for itself but that which is a pleasure to them, or of which the absence is a pain; we have evidently arrived at a question of fact and experience, dependent, like all similar questions, upon evidence. It can only be determined by practised self-consciousness and self-observation, assisted by observation of others. I believe that these sources of evidence, impartially consulted, will declare that desiring a thing and finding it pleasant, aversion to it and thinking of it as painful, are phenomena entirely inseparable, or rather two parts of the same phenomenon—in strictness of language, two different modes of naming the same psychological fact: that to think of an object as desirable (unless for the sake of its consequences), and to think of it as pleasant, are one and the same thing; and that to desire anything, except in proportion as the idea of it is pleasant, is a physical and metaphysical impossibility.

So obvious does this appear to me, that I expect it will hardly be disputed: and the objection made will be, not that desire can possibly be directed to anything ultimately except pleasure and exemption from pain, but that the will is a different thing from desire; that a person of confirmed virtue, or any other person whose purposes are fixed, carries out his purposes without any thought of the pleasure he has in contemplating them, or expects to derive from their fulfilment; and persists in acting on them, even though these pleasures are much diminished, by changes in his character or decay of his passive sensibilities, or are out weighed by the pains which the pursuit of the purposes may bring upon him. All this I fully admit, and have stated it elsewhere, as positively and emphatically as any one. Will, the active phenomenon, is a different thing from desire, the state of passive sensibility, and though originally an offshoot from it, may in time take root and detach itself from the parent stock; so much so, that in the case of an habitual purpose, instead of willing the thing because we desire it, we often desire it only because we will it. This, however, is but an instance of that familiar fact, the power of habit, and is no wise confined to the case of virtuous actions. Many indifferent things, which men originally did from a motive of some sort, they continue to do from habit. Sometimes this is done unconsciously, the consciousness coming only after the action: at other times with conscious volition, but volition which has become habitual, and is put in operation by the force of habit, in opposition perhaps to the deliberate preference, as often happens with those who have contracted habits of vicious or hurtful indulgence. Third and last comes the case in which the habitual act of will in the individual instance is not in contradiction to the general intention prevailing at other times, but in fulfilment of it; as in the case of the person of confirmed virtue, and of all who pursue deliberately and consistently any determinate end. The distinction between will and desire thus understood is an authentic and highly important psychological fact; but the fact consists solely in this—that will, like all other parts of our constitution, is amenable to habit, and that we may will from habit what we no longer desire for itself, or desire only because we will it. It is not the less true that will, in the beginning, is entirely produced by desire; including in that term the repelling influence of pain as well as the attractive one of pleasure. Let us take into consideration, no longer the person who has a confirmed will to do right, but him in whom that virtuous will is still feeble, conquerable by temptation, and not to be fully relied on; by what means can it be strengthened? How can the will to be virtuous, where it does not exist in sufficient force, be implanted or awakened? Only by making the person *desire* virtue—by making him think of it in a pleasurable light, or of its absence in a painful one. It is by associating the doing right with pleasure, or the doing wrong with pain, or by eliciting and impressing and bringing home to the person's experience the pleasure naturally involved in the one or the pain in the other, that it is possible to call forth that will to be virtuous, which, when confirmed, acts without any thought of either pleasure or pain. Will is the child of desire, and passes out of the dominion of its parent only to come under that of habit. That which is the result of habit affords no presumption of being intrinsically good; and there would be no reason for wishing that the purpose of virtue should become independent of pleasure and pain, were it not that the influence of the pleasurable and painful associations which prompt to virtue is not sufficiently to be depended on for unerring constancy of action until it has acquired the support of habit. Both in feeling and in conduct, habit is the only thing which imparts certainty; and it is because of the importance to others of being able to rely absolutely on one's feelings and conduct, and to oneself of being able to rely on one's own, that the will to do right ought to be cultivated into this habitual independence. In other words, this state of the will is a means to good, not intrinsically a good; and does not contradict the doctrine that nothing is a good to human beings but in so far as it is either itself pleasurable, or a means of attaining pleasure or averting pain.

But if this doctrine be true, the principle of utility is proved. Whether it is so or not, must now be left to the consideration of the thoughtful reader.

Chapter 5: On the Connection Between Justice and Utility

In all ages of speculation, one of the strongest obstacles to the reception of the doctrine that Utility or Happiness is the criterion of right and wrong, has been drawn from the idea of Justice. The powerful sentiment, and apparently clear perception, which that word recalls with a rapidity and certainty resembling an instinct, have seemed to the majority of thinkers to point to an inherent quality in things; to show that the Just must have an existence in Nature as something absolute, generically distinct from every variety of the Expedient, and, in idea, opposed to it, though (as is commonly acknowledged) never, in the long run, disjoined from it in fact.

In the case of this, as of our other moral sentiments, there is no necessary connection between the question of its origin, and that of its binding force. That a feeling is bestowed on us by Nature, does not necessarily legitimate all its promptings. The feeling of justice might be a peculiar instinct, and might yet require, like our other instincts, to be controlled and enlightened by a higher reason. If we have intellectual instincts, leading us to judge in a particular way, as well as animal instincts that prompt us to act in a particular way, there is no necessity that the former should be more infallible in their sphere than the latter in theirs: it may as well happen that wrong judgments are occasionally suggested by those, as wrong actions by these. But though it is one thing to believe that we have natural feelings of justice, and another to acknowledge them as an ultimate criterion of conduct, these two opinions are very closely connected in point of fact. Mankind are always predisposed to believe that any subjective feeling, not otherwise accounted for, is a revelation of some objective reality. Our present object is to determine whether the reality, to which the feeling of justice corresponds, is one which needs any such special revelation; whether the justice or injustice of an action is a thing intrinsically peculiar, and distinct from all its other qualities, or only a combination of certain of those qualities, presented under a peculiar aspect. For the purpose of this inquiry it is practically important to consider whether the feeling itself, of justice and injustice, is *sui generis* like our sensations of colour and taste, or a derivative feeling, formed by a combination of others. And this it is the more essential to examine, as people are in general willing enough to allow, that objectively the dictates of Justice coincide with a part of the field of General Expediency; but inasmuch as the subjective mental feeling of Justice is different from that which commonly attaches to simple expediency, and, except in the extreme cases of the latter, is far more imperative in its demands, people find it difficult to see, in Justice, only a particular kind or branch of general utility, and think that its superior binding force requires a totally different origin.

To throw light upon this question, it is necessary to attempt to ascertain what is the distinguishing character of justice, or of injustice: what is the quality, or whether there is any quality, attributed in common to all modes of conduct designated as unjust (for justice, like many other moral attributes, is best defined by its opposite), and distinguishing them from such modes of conduct as are disapproved, but without having that particular epithet of disapprobation applied to them. If in everything which men are accustomed to characterise as just or unjust, some one common attribute or collection of attributes is always present, we may judge whether this particular attribute or combination of attributes would be capable of gathering round it a sentiment of that peculiar character and intensity by virtue of the general laws of our emotional constitution, or whether the sentiment is inexplicable, and requires to be regarded as a special provision of Nature. If we find the former to be the case, we shall, in resolving this question, have resolved also the main problem: if the latter, we shall have to seek for some other mode of investigating it.

To find the common attributes of a variety of objects, it is necessary to begin by surveying the objects themselves in the concrete. Let us therefore advert successively to the various modes of action, and arrangements of human affairs, which are classed, by universal or widely spread opinion, as Just or as Unjust. The things well known to excite the sentiments associated with those names are of a very multifarious character. I shall pass them rapidly in review, without studying any particular arrangement.

In the first place, it is mostly considered unjust to deprive any one of his personal liberty, his property, or any other thing which belongs to him by law. Here, therefore, is one instance of the application of the terms "just" and "unjust" in a perfectly definite sense, namely, that it is just to respect, unjust to violate, the *legal rights* of any one. But this judgment admits of several exceptions, arising from the other forms in which the notions of justice and injustice present themselves. For example, the person who suffers the deprivation may (as the phrase is) have *forfeited* the rights which he is so deprived of: a case to which we shall return presently. But also—

Secondly; the legal rights of which he is deprived, may be rights which *ought* not to have belonged to him; in other words, the law which confers on him these rights, may be a bad law. When it is so, or when (which is the same thing for our purpose) it is supposed to be so, opinions will differ as to the justice or injustice of infringing it. Some maintain that no law, however bad, ought to be disobeyed by an individual citizen; that his opposition to it, if shown at all, should only be shown in endeavouring to get it altered by competent authority. This opinion (which condemns many of the most illustrious benefactors of mankind, and would often protect pernicious institutions against the only weapons which, in the state of things existing at the time, have any chance of succeeding against them) is defended, by those who hold it, on grounds of expediency; principally on that of the importance, to the common interest of mankind, of maintaining inviolate the sentiment of submission to law. Other persons, again, hold the directly contrary opinion, that any law, judged to be bad, may blamelessly be disobeyed, even though it be not judged to be unjust, but only inexpedient; while others would confine the licence of disobedience to the case of unjust laws: but again, some say, that all laws which are inexpedient are unjust; since every law imposes some restriction on the natural liberty of mankind, which restriction is an injustice, unless legitimated by tending to their good. Among these diversities of opinion, it seems to be universally admitted that there may be unjust laws, and that law, consequently, is not the ultimate criterion of justice, but may give to one person a benefit, or impose on another an evil, which justice condemns. When, however, a law is thought to be unjust, it seems always to be regarded as being so in the same way in which a breach of law is unjust, namely, by infringing somebody's right; which, as it cannot in this case be a legal right, receives a different appellation, and is called a moral right. We may say, therefore, that a second case of injustice consists in taking or withholding from any person that to which he has a *moral right*.

Thirdly, it is universally considered just that each person should obtain that (whether good or evil) which he *deserves* and unjust that he should obtain a good, or be made to undergo an evil, which he does not deserve. This is, perhaps, the clearest and most emphatic form in which the idea of justice is conceived by the general mind. As it involves the notion of desert, the question arises, what constitutes desert? Speaking in a general way, a person is understood to deserve good if he does right, evil if he does wrong; and in a more particular sense, to deserve good from those to whom he does or has done good, and evil from those to whom he does or has done evil. The precept of returning good for evil has never been regarded as a case of the fulfilment of justice, but as one in which the claims of justice are waived, in obedience to other considerations.

Fourthly, it is confessedly unjust to *break faith* with any one: to violate an engagement, either express or implied, or disappoint expectations raised by our own conduct, at least if we have raised those expectations knowingly and voluntarily. Like the other obligations of justice already spoken of, this one is not regarded as absolute, but as capable of being overruled by a stronger obligation of justice on the other side; or by such conduct on the part of the person concerned as is deemed to absolve us from our obligation to him, and to constitute a *forfeiture* of the benefit which he has been led to expect.

Fifthly, it is, by universal admission, inconsistent with justice to be *partial*—to show favour or preference to one person over another, in matters to which favour and preference do not properly apply. Impartiality, however, does not seem to be regarded as a duty in itself, but rather as instrumental to some other duty; for it is admitted that favour and preference are not always censurable, and indeed the cases in which they are condemned are rather the exception than the rule. A person would be more likely to be blamed than applauded for giving his family or friends no superiority in good offices over strangers, when he could do so without violating any other duty; and no one thinks it unjust to seek one person in preference to another as a friend, connection, or companion. Impartiality where rights are concerned is of course obligatory, but this is involved in the more general obligation of giving to every one his right. A tribunal, for example, must be impartial, because it is bound to award, without regard to any other consideration, a disputed object to the one of two parties who has the right to it. There are other cases in which impartiality means, being solely influenced by desert; as with those who, in the capacity of judges, preceptors, or parents, administer reward and punishment as such. There are cases, again, in which it means, being solely influenced by consideration for the public interest; as in making a selection among candidates for a government employment. Impartiality, in short, as an obligation of justice, may be said to mean, being exclusively influenced by the considerations which it is supposed ought to influence the particular case in hand; and resisting the solicitation of any motives which prompt to conduct different from what those considerations would dictate.

Nearly allied to the idea of impartiality is that of *equality,* which often enters as a component part both into the conception of justice and into the practice of it, and, in the eyes of many persons, constitutes its essence. But in this, still more than in any other case, the notion of justice varies in different persons, and always conforms in its variations to their notion of utility. Each person maintains that equality is the dictate of justice, except where he thinks that expediency requires inequality. The justice of giving equal protection to the rights of all, is maintained by those who support the most outrageous inequality in the rights themselves. Even in slave countries it is theoretically admitted that the rights of the slave, such as they are, ought to be as sacred as those of the master; and that a tribunal which fails to enforce them with equal strictness is wanting in justice; while, at the same time, institutions which leave to the slave scarcely any rights to enforce, are not deemed unjust, because they are not deemed inexpedient. Those who think that utility requires distinctions of rank, do not consider it unjust that riches and social privileges should be unequally dispensed; but those who think this inequality inexpedient, think it unjust also. Whoever thinks that government is necessary, sees no injustice in as much inequality as is constituted by giving to the magistrate powers not granted to other people. Even among those who hold levelling doctrines, there are as many questions of justice as there are differences of opinion about expediency. Some Communists consider it unjust that the produce of the labour of the community should be shared on any other principle than that of exact equality; others think it just that those should receive most whose wants are greatest; while others hold that those who work harder, or who produce more, or whose services are more valuable to the community, may justly claim a larger quota in the division of the produce. And the sense of natural justice may be plausibly appealed to in behalf of every one of these opinions.

Among so many diverse applications of the term "justice," which yet is not regarded as ambiguous, it is a matter of some difficulty to seize the mental link which holds them together, and on which the moral sentiment adhering to the term essentially depends. Perhaps, in this embarrassment, some help may be derived from the history of the word, as indicated by its etymology.

In most, if not in all, languages, the etymology of the word which corresponds to "just" points distinctly to an origin connected with the ordinances of law. *Justum* is a form of *jussum,* that which has been ordered. ⟨*Dikaion*⟩ comes directly from ⟨*dike*⟩, a suit at law. *Recht,* from which came *right* and *righteous,* is synonymous with law. The courts of justice, the administration of justice, are the courts and the administration of law. *La justice,* in French, is the established term for judicature. I am not committing the fallacy imputed with some show of truth to Horne Tooke,* of assuming that a word must still continue to mean what it originally meant. Etymology is slight evidence of what the idea now signified is, but the very best evidence of how it sprang up. There can, I think, be no doubt that the *idée mère,* the primitive element, in the formation of the notion of justice, was conformity to law. It constituted the entire idea among the Hebrews, up to the birth of Christianity; as might be expected in the case of a people whose laws attempted to embrace all subjects on which precepts were required, and who believed those laws to be a direct emanation from the Supreme Being. But other nations, and in particular the Greeks and Romans, who knew that their laws had been made originally, and still continued to be made, by men, were not afraid to admit that those men might make bad laws; might do, by law, the same things, and from the same motives, which if done by individuals without the sanction of law, would be called unjust. And hence the sentiment of injustice came to be attached, not to all violations of law, but only to violations of such laws as *ought* to exist, including such as ought to exist, but do not; and to laws themselves, if supposed to be contrary to what ought to be law. In this manner the idea of law and of its injunctions was still predominant in the notion of justice, even when the laws actually in force ceased to be accepted as the standard of it.

It is true that mankind consider the idea of justice and its obligations as applicable to many things which neither are, nor is it desired that they should be, regulated by law. Nobody desires that laws should interfere with the whole detail of private life; yet every one allows that in all daily conduct a person may and does show himself to be either just or unjust. But even here, the idea of the breach of what ought to be law, still lingers in a modified shape. It would always give us pleasure, and chime in with our feelings of fitness, that acts which we deem unjust should be punished, though we do not always think it expedient that this should be done by the tribunals. We forego that gratification on account of incidental inconveniences. We should be glad to see just conduct enforced and injustice repressed, even in the minutest details, if we were not, with reason, afraid of trusting the magistrate with so unlimited an amount of power over individuals. When

*[John Tooke (1736–1812), a radical writer and close friend of Bentham.]

we think that a person is bound in justice to do a thing, it is an ordinary form of language to say, that he ought to be compelled to do it. We should be gratified to see the obligation enforced by anybody who had the power. If we see that its enforcement by law would be inexpedient, we lament the impossibility, we consider the impunity given to injustice as an evil, and strive to make amends for it by bringing a strong expression of our own and the public disapprobation to bear upon the offender. Thus the idea of legal constraint is still the generating idea of the notion of justice, though undergoing several transformations before that notion, as it exists in an advanced state of society, becomes complete.

The above is, I think, a true account, as far as it goes, of the origin and progressive growth of the idea of justice. But we must observe, that it contains, as yet, nothing to distinguish that obligation from moral obligation in general. For the truth is, that the idea of penal sanction, which is the essence of law, enters not only into the conception of injustice, but into that of any kind of wrong. We do not call anything wrong, unless we mean to imply that a person ought to be punished in some way or other for doing it; if not by law, by the opinion of his fellow-creatures; if not by opinion, by the reproaches of his own conscience. This seems the real turning point of the distinction between morality and simple expediency. It is a part of the notion of Duty in every one of its forms, that a person may rightfully be compelled to fulfil it. Duty is a thing which may be *exacted* from a person, as one exacts a debt. Unless we think that it may be exacted from him, we do not call it his duty. Reasons of prudence, or the interest of other people, may militate against actually exacting it; but the person himself, it is clearly understood, would not be entitled to complain. There are other things, on the contrary, which we wish that people should do, which we like or admire them for doing, perhaps dislike or despise them for not doing, but yet admit that they are not bound to do; it is not a case of moral obligation; we do not blame them, that is, we do not think that they are proper objects of punishment. How we come by these ideas of deserving and not deserving punishment, will appear, perhaps, in the sequel; but I think there is no doubt that this distinction lies at the bottom of the notions of right and wrong; that we call any conduct wrong, or employ, instead, some other term of dislike or disparagement, according as we think that the person ought, or ought not, to be punished for it; and we say, it would be right to do so and so, or merely that it would be desirable or laudable, according as we would wish to see the person whom it concerns, compelled, or only persuaded and exhorted, to act in that manner.*

This, therefore, being the characteristic difference which marks off, not justice, but morality in general, from the remaining provinces of Expediency and Worthiness; the character is still to be sought which distinguishes justice from other branches of morality. Now it is known that ethical writers divide moral duties into two classes, denoted by the ill-chosen expressions, duties of perfect and of imperfect obligation; the latter being those in which, though the act is obligatory, the particular occasions of performing it are left to our choice; as in the case of charity or beneficence, which we are indeed bound to practise, but not towards any definite person, nor at any prescribed time. In the more precise language of philosophic jurists, duties of perfect obligation are those duties in virtue of which a correlative *right* resides in some person or persons; duties of imperfect obligation are those moral obligations which do not give birth to any

*I see this point enforced and illustrated by Professor Bain, in an admirable chapter (entitled "The Ethical Emotions, or the Moral Sense"), of the second of the two treatises composing his elaborate and profound work on the Mind.

right. I think it will be found that this distinction exactly coincides with that which exists between justice and the other obligations of morality. In our survey of the various popular acceptations of justice, the term appeared generally to involve the idea of a personal right—a claim on the part of one or more individuals, like that which the law gives when it confers a proprietary or other legal right. Whether the injustice consists in depriving a person of a possession, or in breaking faith with him, or in treating him worse than he deserves, or worse than other people who have no greater claims, in each case the supposition implies two things—a wrong done, and some assignable person who is wronged. Injustice may also be done by treating a person better than others; but the wrong in this case is to his competitors, who are also assignable persons. It seems to me that this feature in the case—a right in some person, correlative to the moral obligation—constitutes the specific difference between justice, and generosity or beneficence. Justice implies something which it is not only right to do, and wrong not to do, but which some individual person can claim from us as his moral right. No one has a moral right to our generosity or beneficence, because we are not morally bound to practise those virtues towards any given individual. And it will be found with respect to this as to every correct definition, that the instances which seem to conflict with it are those which most confirm it. For if a moralist attempts, as some have done, to make out that mankind generally, though not any given individual, have a right to all the good we can do them, he at once, by that thesis, includes generosity and beneficence within the category of justice. He is obliged to say, that our utmost exertions are due to our fellow-creatures, thus assimilating them to a debt; or that nothing less can be a sufficient return for what society does for us, thus classing the case as one of gratitude; both of which are acknowledged cases of justice. Wherever there is a right, the case is one of justice, and not of the virtue of beneficence: and whoever does not place the distinction between justice and morality in general, where we have now placed it, will be found to make no distinction between them at all, but to merge all morality in justice.

Having thus endeavoured to determine the distinctive elements which enter into the composition of the idea of justice, we are ready to enter on the inquiry, whether the feeling, which accompanies the idea, is attached to it by a special dispensation of nature, or whether it could have grown up, by any known laws, out of the idea itself; and in particular, whether it can have originated in considerations of general expediency.

I conceive that the sentiment itself does not arise from anything which would commonly, or correctly, be termed an idea of expediency; but that though the sentiment does not, whatever is moral in it does.

We have seen that the two essential ingredients in the sentiment of justice are, the desire to punish a person who has done harm and the knowledge or belief that there is some definite individual or individuals to whom harm has been done.

Now it appears to me, that the desire to punish a person who has done harm to some individual is a spontaneous outgrowth from two sentiments, both in the highest degree natural, and which either are or resemble instincts; the impulse of self-defence, and the feeling of sympathy.

It is natural to resent, and to repel or retaliate, any harm done or attempted against ourselves, or against those with whom we sympathise. The origin of this sentiment it is not necessary here to discuss. Whether it be an instinct or a result of intelligence, it is, we know, common to all animal nature; for every animal tries to hurt those who have hurt, or who it thinks are about to hurt, itself or its young. Human beings, on this point, only differ from other animals in two particulars. First, in being capable of sympathising, not solely with their offspring, or, like some of the more noble animals, with some superior animal who is kind to them, but with all human, and even with all sentient, beings. Secondly, in having a more developed intelligence, which gives a wider range to the whole of their sentiments, whether self-regarding or sympathetic. By virtue of his superior intelligence, even apart from his superior range of sympathy, a human being is capable of apprehending a community of interest between himself and the human society of which he forms a part, such that any conduct which threatens the security of the society generally, is threatening to his own, and calls forth his instinct (if instinct it be) of self-defence. The same superiority of intelligence, joined to the power of sympathising with human beings generally, enables him to attach himself to the collective idea of his tribe, his country, or mankind, in such a manner that any act hurtful to them, raises his instinct of sympathy, and urges him to resistance.

The sentiment of justice, in that one of its elements which consists of the desire to punish, is thus, I conceive, the natural feeling of retaliation or vengeance, rendered by intellect and sympathy applicable to those injuries, that is, to those hurts, which wound us through, or in common with, society at large. This sentiment, in itself, has nothing moral in it; what is moral is, the exclusive subordination of it to the social sympathies, so as to wait on and obey their call. For the natural feeling would make us resent indiscriminately whatever any one does that is disagreeable to us; but when moralised by the social feeling, it only acts in the directions conformable to the general good: just persons resenting a hurt to society, though not otherwise a hurt to themselves, and not resenting a hurt to themselves, however painful, unless it be of the kind which society has a common interest with them in the repression of.

It is no objection against this doctrine to say, that when we feel our sentiment of justice outraged, we are not thinking of society at large, or of any collective interest, but only of the individual case. It is common enough certainly, though the reverse of commendable, to feel resentment merely because we have suffered pain; but a person whose resentment is really a moral feeling, that is, who considers whether an act is blamable before he allows himself to resent it—such a person, though he may not say expressly to himself that he is standing up for the interest of society, certainly does feel that he is asserting a rule which is for the benefit of others as well as for his own. If he is not feeling this—if he is regarding the act solely as it affects him individually—he is not consciously just; he is not concerning himself about the justice of his actions. This is admitted even by anti-utilitarian moralists. When Kant (as before remarked) propounds as the fundamental principle of morals, "So act, that thy rule of conduct might be adopted as a law by all rational beings," he virtually acknowledges that the interest of mankind collectively, or at least of mankind indiscriminately, must be in the mind of the agent when conscientiously deciding on the morality of the act. Otherwise he uses words without a meaning: for, that a rule even of utter selfishness could not *possibly* be adopted by all rational beings—that there is any insuperable obstacle in the nature of things to its adoption—cannot be even plausibly maintained. To give any meaning to Kant's principle, the sense put upon it must be, that we ought to shape our conduct by a rule which all rational beings might adopt *with benefit to their collective interest*.

To recapitulate: the idea of justice supposes two things—a rule of conduct, and a sentiment which sanctions the rule. The first must be supposed common to all mankind, and intended for their good. The other (the sentiment) is a desire that punishment may be suffered by those who infringe the rule. There is involved, in addition, the conception of some definite person who suffers by the infringement; whose rights (to use the expression appropriated to the case) are violated by it. And the sentiment of justice appears to me to be, the animal desire to repel or retaliate a hurt or damage to oneself, or to those with whom one sympathises, widened so as to include all persons, by the human capacity of enlarged sympathy, and the human conception of intelligent self-interest. From the latter elements, the feeling derives its morality; from the former, its peculiar impressiveness, and energy of self-assertion.

I have, throughout, treated the idea of a *right* residing in the injured person, and violated by the injury, not as a separate element in the composition of the idea and sentiment, but as one of the forms in which the other two elements clothe themselves. These elements are, a hurt to some assignable person or persons on the one hand, and a demand for punishment on the other. An examination of our own minds, I think, will show, that these two things include all that we mean when we speak of violation of a right. When we call anything a person's right, we mean that he has a valid claim on society to protect him in the possession of it, either by the force of law, or by that of education and opinion. If he has what we consider a sufficient claim, on whatever account, to have something guaranteed to him by society, we say that he has a right to it. If we desire to prove that anything does not belong to him by right, we think this done as soon as it is admitted that society ought not to take measures for securing it to him, but should leave him to chance, or to his own exertions. Thus, a person is said to have a right to what he can earn in fair professional competition; because society ought not to allow any other person to hinder him from endeavouring to earn in that manner as much as he can. But he has not a right to three hundred a year, though he may happen to be earning it; because society is not called on to provide that he shall earn that sum. On the contrary, if he owns ten thousand pounds three percent stock, he *has* a right to three hundred a year because society has come under an obligation to provide him with an income of that amount.

To have a right, then, is, I conceive, to have something which society ought to defend me in the possession of. If the objector goes on to ask, why it ought? I can give him no other reason than general utility. If that expression does not seem to convey a sufficient feeling of the strength of the obligation, nor to account for the peculiar energy of the feeling, it is because there goes to the composition of the sentiment, not a rational only, but also an animal element, the thirst for retaliation; and this thirst derives its intensity, as well as its moral justification, from the extraordinarily important and impressive kind of utility which is concerned. The interest involved is that of security, to every one's feelings the most vital of all interests. All other earthly benefits are needed by one person, not needed by another; and many of them can, if necessary, be cheerfully foregone, or replaced by something else; but security no human being can possibly do without; on it we depend for all our immunity from evil, and for the whole value of all and every good, beyond the passing moment; since nothing but the gratification of the instant could be of any worth to us, if we could be deprived of anything the next instant by whoever was momentarily stronger than ourselves. Now this most indispensable of all necessaries, after physical nutriment, cannot be had, unless the machinery for providing it is kept unintermittedly in active play. Our notion, therefore, of the claim we have on our fellowcreatures to join in making safe for us the very groundwork of our existence, gathers feelings around it so much more intense than those concerned in any of the more common cases of utility, that the difference in degree (as is often the case in psychology) becomes a real difference in kind. The claim assumes that character of absoluteness, that apparent infinity, and incommensurability with all other considerations, which constitute the distinction between the feeling of right and wrong and that of ordinary expediency and inexpediency. The feelings concerned are so powerful, and we count so positively on finding a responsive feeling in others (all being alike interested), that *ought* and *should* grow into *must*, and recognised indispensability becomes a moral necessity, analogous to physical, and often not inferior to it in binding force.

If the preceding analysis, or something resembling it, be not the correct account of the notion of justice; if justice be totally independent of utility, and be a standard per se, which the mind can recognise by simple introspection of itself; it is hard to understand why that internal oracle is so ambiguous, and why so many things appear either just or unjust, according to the light in which they are regarded.

We are continually informed that Utility is an uncertain standard, which every different person interprets differently, and that there is no safety but in the immutable, ineffaceable, and unmistakable dictates of Justice, which carry their evidence in themselves, and are independent of the fluctuations of opinion. One would suppose from this that on questions of justice there could be no controversy; that if we take that for our rule, its application to any given case could leave us in as little doubt as a mathematical demonstration. So far is this from being the fact, that there is as much difference of opinion, and as much discussion, about what is just, as about what is useful to society. Not only have different nations and individuals different notions of justice, but in the mind of one and the same individual, justice is not some one rule, principle, or maxim, but many, which do not always coincide in their dictates, and in choosing between which, he is guided either by some extraneous standard, or by his own personal predilections.

For instance, there are some who say, that it is unjust to punish any one for the sake of example to others; that punishment is just, only when intended for the good of the sufferer himself. Others maintain the extreme reverse, contending that to punish persons who have attained years of discretion, for their own benefit, is despotism and injustice, since if the matter at issue is solely their own good, no one has a right to control their own judgment of it; but that they may justly be punished to prevent evil to others, this being the exercise of the legitimate right of self-defence. Mr. Owen,* again, affirms that it is unjust to punish at all; for the criminal did not make his own character; his education, and the circumstances which surrounded him, have made him a criminal, and for these he is not responsible. All these opinions are extremely plausible; and so long as the question is argued as one of justice simply, without going down to the principles which lie under justice and are the source of its authority, I am unable to see how any of these reasoners can be refuted. For in truth every one of the three builds upon rules of justice confessedly true. The first appeals to the acknowledged injustice of singling out an individual, and making him a sacrifice, without his consent, for other people's benefit. The second relies on the acknowledged justice of self-defence, and the admitted injustice of forcing one person to conform to another's notions of what constitutes his good. The Owenite invokes the admitted principle, that it is unjust to punish any one for what he cannot help. Each is triumphant so long as he is not compelled to take into consideration any other maxims of justice than the one he has selected; but as soon as their several maxims are brought face to face, each disputant seems to have exactly as much to say for himself as the others. No one of them can carry out his own notion of justice without trampling upon another equally binding. These are difficulties; they have always been felt to be such; and many devices have been invented to turn rather than to overcome them. As a refuge from the last of the three, men imagined what they called the freedom of the will; fancying that they could not justify punishing a man whose will is in a thoroughly hateful state, unless it be supposed to have come into that state through no influence of anterior circumstances. To escape from the other difficulties, a favourite contrivance has been the fiction of a contract, whereby at some unknown period all the members of society engaged to obey the laws, and consented to be

*[Robert Owen (1771–1858), a British reformer who argued for environmental determinism.]

punished for any disobedience to them; thereby giving to their legislators the right, which it is assumed they would not otherwise have had, of punishing them, either for their own good or for that of society. This happy thought was considered to get rid of the whole difficulty, and to legitimate the infliction of punishment, in virtue of another received maxim of justice, *volenti non fit injuria;* that is not unjust which is done with the consent of the person who is supposed to be hurt by it. I need hardly remark, that even if the consent were not a mere fiction, this maxim is not superior in authority to the others which it is brought in to supersede. It is, on the contrary, an instructive specimen of the loose and irregular manner in which supposed principles of justice grow up. This particular one evidently came into use as a help to the coarse exigencies of courts of law, which are sometimes obliged to be content with very uncertain presumptions, on account of the greater evils which would often arise from any attempt on their part to cut finer. But even courts of law are not able to adhere consistently to the maxim, for they allow voluntary engagements to be set aside on the ground of fraud, and sometimes on that of mere mistake or misinformation.

Again, when the legitimacy of inflicting punishment is admitted, how many conflicting conceptions of justice come to light in discussing the proper apportionment of punishments to offences. No rule on the subject recommends itself so strongly to the primitive and spontaneous sentiment of justice, as the *lex talionis,* an eye for an eye and a tooth for a tooth. Though this principle of the Jewish and of the Mohammedan law has been generally abandoned in Europe as a practical maxim, there is, I suspect, in most minds, a secret hankering after it; and when retribution accidentally falls on an offender in that precise shape, the general feeling of satisfaction evinced bears witness how natural is the sentiment to which this repayment in kind is acceptable. With many, the test of justice in penal infliction is that the punishment should be proportioned to the offence; meaning that it should be exactly measured by the moral guilt of the culprit (whatever be their standard for measuring moral guilt): the consideration, what amount of punishment is necessary to deter from the offence, having nothing to do with the question of justice, in their estimation: while there are others to whom that consideration is all in all; who maintain that it is not just, at least for man, to inflict on a fellow-creature, whatever may be his offences, any amount of suffering beyond the least that will suffice to prevent him from repeating, and others from imitating, his misconduct.

To take another example from a subject already once referred to. In a co-operative industrial association, is it just or not that talent or skill should give a title to superior remuneration? On the negative side of the question it is argued, that whoever does the best he can, deserves equally well, and ought not in justice to be put in a position of inferiority for no fault of his own; that superior abilities have already advantages more than enough, in the admiration they excite, the personal influence they command, and the internal sources of satisfaction attending them, without adding to these a superior share of the world's goods; and that society is bound in justice rather to make compensation to the less favoured, for this unmerited inequality of advantages, than to aggravate it. On the contrary side it is contended, that society receives more from the more efficient labourer; that his services being more useful, society owes him a larger return for them; that a greater share of the joint result is actually his work, and not to allow his claim to it is a kind of robbery; that if he is only to receive as much as others, he can only be justly required to produce as much, and to give a smaller amount of time and exertion, proportioned to his superior efficiency. Who shall decide between these appeals to conflicting principles of justice? Justice has in this case two sides to it, which it is impossible to bring into harmony, and the two disputants have chosen opposite sides; the one looks to what it is just that the individual should receive, the other to what it is just that the community should give. Each, from his own point of view, is unanswerable; and any choice between them, on grounds of justice, must be perfectly arbitrary. Social utility alone can decide the preference.

How many, again, and how irreconcilable, are the standards of justice to which reference is made in discussing the repartition of taxation. One opinion is, that payment to the State should be in numerical proportion to pecuniary means. Others think that justice dictates what they term graduated taxation; taking a higher percentage from those who have more to spare. In point of natural justice a strong case might be made for disregarding means altogether, and taking the same absolute sum (whenever it could be got) from every one: as the subscribers to a mess, or to a club, all pay the same sum for the same privileges, whether they can all equally afford it or not. Since the protection (it might be said) of law and government is afforded to, and is equally required by all, there is no injustice in making all buy it at the same price. It is reckoned justice, not injustice, that a dealer should charge to all customers the same price for the same article, not a price varying according to their means of payment. This doctrine, as applied to taxation, finds no advocates, because it conflicts so strongly with man's feelings of humanity and of social expediency; but the principle of justice which it invokes is as true and as binding as those which can be appealed to against it. Accordingly it exerts a tacit influence on the line of defence employed for other modes of assessing taxation. People feel obliged to argue that the State does more for the rich than for the poor, as a justification for its taking more from them: though this is in reality not true, for the rich would be far better able to protect themselves, in the absence of law or government, than the poor, and indeed would probably be successful in converting the poor into their slaves. Others, again, so far defer to the same conception of justice, as to maintain that all should pay an equal capitation tax for the protection of their persons (these being of equal value to all), and an unequal tax for the protection of their property, which is unequal. To this others reply, that the all of one man is as valuable to him as the all of another. From these confusions there is no other mode of extrication than the utilitarian.

Is, then, the difference between the Just and the Expedient a merely imaginary distinction? Have mankind been under a delusion in thinking that justice is a more sacred thing than policy, and that the latter ought only to be listened to after the former has been satisfied? By no means. The exposition we have given of the nature and origin of the sentiment, recognises a real distinction; and no one of those who profess the most sublime contempt for the consequences of actions as an element in their morality, attaches more importance to the distinction than I do. While I dispute the pretensions of any theory which sets up an imaginary standard of justice not grounded on utility, I account the justice which is grounded on utility to be the chief part, and incomparably the most sacred and binding part, of all morality. Justice is a name for certain classes of moral rules, which concern the essentials of human well-being more nearly, and are therefore of more absolute obligation, than any other rules for the guidance of life; and the notion which we have found to be of the essence of the idea of justice, that of a right residing in an individual, implies and testifies to this more binding obligation.

The moral rules which forbid mankind to hurt one another (in which we must never forget to include wrongful interference with each other's freedom) are more vital to human well-being than any maxims, however important, which only point out the best mode of managing some department of human affairs. They have also the peculiarity, that they are the main element in determining the whole of the social feelings of mankind. It is their observance which alone preserves peace among human beings: if obedience to them were not the rule, and disobedience the exception, every one would see in every one else an enemy, against whom he must be perpetually guarding himself. What is hardly less important, these are the precepts which mankind have the strongest and the most direct inducements for impressing upon one another. By merely giving to each other prudential instruction or exhortation, they may gain, or think they gain, nothing: in inculcating on each other the duty of positive beneficence they have an unmistakable interest, but far less in degree: a person may possibly not need the benefits of others; but he always needs that they should not do him hurt. Thus the moralities which protect every individual from being harmed by others, either directly or by being hindered in his freedom of pursuing his own good, are at once those which he himself has most at heart, and those which he has the strongest interest in publishing and enforcing by word and deed. It is by a person's observance of these that his fitness to exist as one of the fellowship of human beings is tested and decided; for on that depends his being a nuisance or not to those with whom he is in contact. Now it is these moralities primarily which compose the obligations of justice. The most marked cases of injustice, and those which give the tone to the feeling of repugnance which characterises the sentiment, are acts of wrongful aggression, or wrongful exercise of power over some one; the next are those which consist in wrongfully withholding from him something which is his due; in both cases, inflicting on him a positive hurt, either in the form of direct suffering, or of the privation of some good which he had reasonable ground, either of a physical or of a social kind, for counting upon.

The same powerful motives which command the observance of these primary moralities, enjoin the punishment of those who violate them; and as the impulses of self-defence, of defence of others, and of vengeance, are all called forth against such persons, retribution, or evil for evil, becomes closely connected with the sentiment of justice, and is universally included in the idea. Good for good is also one of the dictates of justice; and this, though its social utility is evident, and though it carries with it a natural human feeling, has not at first sight that obvious connection with hurt or injury, which, existing in the most elementary cases of just and un-just, is the source of the characteristic intensity of the sentiment. But the connection, though less obvious, is not less real. He who accepts benefits, and denies a return of them when needed, inflicts a real hurt, by disappointing one of the most natural and reasonable of expectations, and one which he must at least tacitly have encouraged, otherwise the benefits would seldom have been conferred. The important rank, among human evils and wrongs, of the disappointment of expectation, is shown in the fact that it constitutes the principal criminality of two such highly immoral acts as a breach of friendship and a breach of promise. Few hurts which human beings can sustain are greater, and none wound more, than when that on which they habitually and with full assurance relied, fails them in the hour of need; and few wrongs are greater than this mere withholding of good; none excite more resentment, either in the person suffering, or in a sympathising spectator. The principle, therefore, of giving to each what they deserve, that is, good for good as well as evil for evil, is not only included within the idea of Justice as we have defined it, but is a proper object of that intensity of sentiment, which places the Just, in human estimation, above the simply Expedient.

Most of the maxims of justice current in the world, and commonly appealed to in its transactions, are simply instrumental to carrying into effect the principles of justice which we have now spoken of. That a person is only responsible for what he has done voluntarily, or could voluntarily have avoided; that it is unjust to condemn any person unheard; that the punishment ought to be proportioned to the offence, and the like, are maxims intended to prevent the just principle of evil for evil from being perverted to the infliction of evil without that justification. The greater part of these common maxims have come into use from the practice of courts of justice, which have been naturally led to a more complete recognition and elaboration than was likely to suggest itself to others, of the rules necessary to enable them to fulfil their double function, of inflicting punishment when due, and of awarding to each person his right.

That first of judicial virtues, impartiality, is an obligation of justice, partly for the reason last mentioned; as being a necessary condition of the fulfilment of the other obligations of justice. But this is not the only source of the exalted rank, among human obligations, of those maxims of equality and impartiality, which, both in popular estimation and in that of the most enlightened, are included among the precepts of justice. In one point of view, they may be considered as corollaries from the principles already laid down. If it is a duty to do to each according to his deserts, returning good for good as well as repressing evil by evil, it necessarily follows that we should treat all equally well (when no higher duty forbids) who have deserved equally well of *us,* and that society should treat all equally well who have deserved equally well of *it,* that is, who have deserved equally well absolutely. This is the highest abstract standard of social and distributive justice; towards which all institutions, and the efforts of all virtuous citizens, should be made in the utmost possible degree to converge. But this great moral duty rests upon a still deeper foundation, being a direct emanation from the first principle of morals, and not a mere logical corollary from secondary or derivative doctrines. It is involved in the very meaning of Utility, or the Greatest Happiness Principle. That principle is a mere form of words without rational signification, unless one person's happiness, supposed equal in degree (with the proper allowance made for kind), is counted for exactly as much as another's. Those conditions being supplied, Bentham's dictum, "everybody to count for one, nobody for more than one," might be written under the principle of utility as an explanatory commentary.* The equal claim of everybody to

*This implication, in the first principle of the utilitarian scheme, of perfect impartiality between persons, is regarded by Mr. Herbert Spencer (in his *Social Statics*) as a disproof of the pretensions of utility to be a sufficient guide to right, since (he says) the principle of utility presupposes the anterior principle that everybody has an equal right to happiness. It may be more correctly described as supposing that equal amounts of happiness are equally desirable whether felt by the same or by different persons. This, however, is not a pre-supposition; not a premise needful to support the principle of utility, but the very principle itself; for what is the principle of utility, if it be not that "happiness" and "desirable" are synonymous terms? If there Is any anterior principle Implied, it can be no other than this, that the truths of arithmetic are applicable to the valuation of happiness, as of all other measurable quantities.

(Mr. Herbert Spencer in a private communication on the subject of the preceding note, objects to being considered an opponent of utilitarianism, and states that he regards happiness as the ultimate end of morality; but deems that end only partially attainable by empirical generalisations from the observed results of conduct, and completely attainable only by deducing, from the laws of life and the conditions of existence, what kinds of action necessarily tend to produce happiness, and what kinds to produce unhappiness. With the exception of the word "necessarily," I have no dissent to express from this doctrine; and (omitting that word) I am not aware that any modern advocate of utilitarianism is of a different opinion. Bentham, certainly, to whom in the *Social Statics* Mr. Spencer particularly referred, is, least of all writers, chargeable with unwillingness to deduce the effect of actions on happiness from the laws of human nature and the universal conditions of human life. The common charge against him is of relying too exclusively upon such deductions, and declining altogether to be bound by the generalisations from specific experience which Mr. Spencer thinks that utilitarians generally confine themselves to. My own opinion (and, as I collect, Mr. Spencer's) is, that in ethics, as in all other branches of scientific study, the consilience of the results of both these processes, each corroborating and verifying the other, is requisite to give to any general proposition the kind and degree of evidence which constitutes scientific proof.)

happiness in the estimation of the moralist and of the legislator, involves an equal claim to all the means of happiness, except in so far as the inevitable conditions of human life, and the general interest, in which that of every individual is included, set limits to the maxim; and those limits ought to be strictly construed. As every other maxim of justice, so this is by no means applied or held applicable universally; on the contrary, as I have already remarked, it bends to every person's ideas of social expediency. But in whatever case it is deemed applicable at all, it is held to be the dictate of justice. All persons are deemed to have a *right* to equality of treatment, except when some recognised social expediency requires the reverse. And hence all social inequalities which have ceased to be considered expedient, assume the character not of simple inexpediency, but of injustice, and appear so tyrannical, that people are apt to wonder how they ever could have been tolerated; forgetful that they themselves perhaps tolerate other inequalities under an equally mistaken notion of expediency, the correction of which would make that which they approve seem quite as monstrous as what they have at last learnt to condemn. The entire history of social improvement has been a series of transitions, by which one custom or institution after another, from being a supposed primary necessity of social existence, has passed into the rank of a universally stigmatised injustice and tyranny. So it has been with the distinctions of slaves and freemen, nobles and serfs, patricians and plebeians; and so it will be, and in part already is, with the aristocracies of colour, race, and sex.

It appears from what has been said, that justice is a name for certain moral requirements, which, regarded collectively, stand higher in the scale of social utility, and are therefore of more paramount obligation, than any others; though particular cases may occur in which some other social duty is so important, as to overrule any one of the general maxims of justice. Thus, to save a life, it may not only be allowable, but a duty, to steal, or take by force, the necessary food or medicine, or to kidnap, and compel to officiate, the only qualified medical practitioner. In such cases, as we do not call anything justice which is not a virtue, we usually say, not that justice must give way to some other moral principle, but that what is just in ordinary cases is, by reason of that other principle, not just in the particular case. By this useful accommodation of language, the character of indefeasibility attributed to justice is kept up, and we are saved from the necessity of maintaining that there can be laudable injustice.

The considerations which have now been adduced resolve, I conceive, the only real difficulty in the utilitarian theory of morals. It has always been evident that all cases of justice are also cases of expediency: the difference is in the peculiar sentiment which attaches to the former, as contradistinguished from the latter. If this characteristic sentiment has been sufficiently accounted for; if there is no necessity to assume for it any peculiarity of origin; if it is simply the natural feeling of resentment, moralised by being made coextensive with the demands of social good; and if this feeling not only does but ought to exist in all the classes of cases to which the idea of justice corresponds; that idea no longer presents itself as a stumbling-block to the utilitarian ethics. Justice remains the appropriate name for certain social utilities which are vastly more important, and therefore more absolute and imperative, than any others are as a class (though not more so than others may be in particular cases); and which, therefore, ought to be, as well as naturally are, guarded by a sentiment not only different in degree, but also in kind; distinguished from the milder feeling which attaches to the mere idea of promoting human pleasure or convenience, at once by the more definite nature of its commands, and by the sterner character of its sanctions.

SØREN KIERKEGAARD
1813–1855

Søren Aabye Kierkegaard was born in Copenhagen, Denmark, the youngest child of middle-aged parents. His father, Michael, had been an impoverished serf in a bleak area of northern Denmark. While still a boy, Michael had cursed God for the dreariness of his life and from that point on considered himself and his descendants to be under God's condemnation. The external events of Michael's life gave little indication of such a curse, however, as he worked his way to great wealth as a merchant in Copenhagen. Following the death of his first wife, and before the period of mourning was over, Michael was forced to marry his first wife's maid, Anne Lund, and five months later she bore the first of their five children.

Michael was already 56 and retired from business when Søren was born in 1813. Like James Mill, Michael educated Søren at home and also put his son through rigorous intellectual endeavors. But unlike his predecessor, Michael also communicated to his son a strong religious sentiment and deep, though perhaps warped, emotional feelings. Michael often took Søren on "trips of fantasy" while conversing in the family library.

In 1830, at his father's urging, Kierkegaard entered the University of Copenhagen to study theology. While there, he encountered the work of Hegel and reacted strongly against it. Kierkegaard objected to the implicit optimism and the "swallowing up" of contradictions in Hegel's dialectic. But more important, Kierkegaard claimed that even though Hegel's "System" was an impressive philosophical *tour de force,* it did not relate to the lived existence of the individual—it did not give any guidance as to what a person should *do.* A famous entry from Kierkegaard's journal at this time is worth quoting at length:

What I really lack is to be clear in my mind *what I am to do,* not what I am to know, except in so far as a certain understanding must precede every action. The thing is to understand myself, to see what God really wishes *me* to do; the thing is to find a truth which is true *for me*, to find *the idea for which I can live and die*. What would be the use of discovering so-called objective truth, of working through all the systems of philosophy and of being able, if required, to review them all and show up the inconsistencies within each system;—what good would it do me to be able to develop a theory of the state and combine all the details into a single whole, and so construct a world in which I did not live, but only held up to the view of others;—what good would it do me to be able to explain the meaning of Christianity if it had *no* deeper significance *for me and for my life;*—what good would it do me if truth stood before me, cold and naked, not caring whether I recognised her or not, and producing in me a shudder of fear rather than a trusting devotion? I certainly do not deny that I still recognise an *imperative of understanding* and that through it one can work upon men, *but it must be taken up into*my life, and that is what I now recognise as the most important thing.*

Kierkegaard did not find the answer for "what to do" in his studies in theology and soon began living what he would later call an "aesthetic" life as a rich merchant's son. He spent large sums of money on food, drink, and clothing. He frequented parties and appeared to be having a great time. But hedonistic indulgence did not really give an answer for "what to do" either, and he plunged into despair. Another entry from his journals makes this clear:

I have just returned from a party of which I was the life and soul; wit poured from my lips, everyone laughed and admired me—but I went away—and the dash should be as long as the earth's orbit ——————————————————————————————————————

and wanted to shoot myself.**

On his son's 25th birthday, May 15, 1838, Michael revealed to Søren his own sexual sins as well as his understanding of God's condemnation of their family. Four days later, Søren Kierkegaard underwent a religious conversion and was reconciled to his father, who died shortly afterward. Kierkegaard now had an answer for "what to do"—he would live as a penitent seeking to "become a Christian." Kierkegaard finished his theological studies, prepared to become a Lutheran pastor, and became engaged to marry 17-year-old Regine Olsen.

But by 1841, Kierkegaard realized that he could never live the life of a Lutheran pastor and devoted husband. He came to believe that the Danish Lutheran church had made religion a matter of intellectual assent to certain objective truths and no longer deserved to be called "Christian." For the rest of his life, Kierkegaard opposed institutional Christianity. The decision to break his engagement to Regine Olsen was a torturous one, but one he believed he had to make. He decided that a "divine veto" had been cast against this marriage, that his role as penitent was incompatible with that of husband.

*Søren Kierkegaard, *The Journals of Søren Kierkegaard,* edited and translated by Alexander Dru (London: Oxford University Press, 1938), p. 15 [entry from August 1, 1835].

***Ibid*., p. 27 [entry from early spring, 1836].

Kierkegaard spent the rest of his short life as a writer, publishing a number of books including *Either/Or* (1843), *Fear and Trembling* (1843), *Philosophical Fragments* (1844), *Stages on Life's Way* (1845), *Concluding Unscientific Postscript* (1846), *The Sickness unto Death* (1849), *Training in Christianity* (1850), and *The Attack upon "Christendom"* (1854–1855). All but the last of these works were written under various pseudonyms, and virtually all of them included attacks on the prevailing Hegelian philosophy of his time. In 1855, while returning from the bank with the last of his considerable inheritance, Kierkegaard collapsed on the street and died soon thereafter.

* * *

Kierkegaard's biography is reflected in his philosophical quest to establish what it means to be an individual. In works such as *Either/Or, Stages on Life's Way,* and *Fear and Trembling,* he describes a process of self-actualization through three stages in life: the aesthetic, the ethical, and the religious. At the aesthetic stage, an individual's life centers on either hedonistic pleasure or abstract philosophical speculation. The hedonist lives for the immediate pleasures of the moment without concern for the future. The abstract intellectual (Hegel being the prime example) lives in a theoretical world removed from concrete existence. The hedonist reduces existence to immediate pleasure, whereas the abstract speculator reduces existence to thought; but in both cases, the aesthete has avoided the either/or decisions of real life, and authentic selfhood has not been achieved. The result, says Kierkegaard, is a life of boredom—and the pointless pursuit of diversions to alleviate such boredom. This was the life Kierkegaard himself lived in his early years at the university.

Those who move beyond the aesthetic to the ethical level choose to accept moral standards and attempt to do their duty. By choosing decisively and accepting responsibility for that choice, an individual's life becomes centralized and unified. For example, the seducing man operates on the aesthetic level where every woman he meets is merely a general source of momentary pleasure. He has no past, no future, only the present desire for fulfillment. He is not really a complete person because he is living life as a series of disconnected "nows." On the other hand, the man who has chosen to fulfill the duties of a faithful husband operates on the ethical level. He has a memory of the past and a hope for the future based on his commitments, which give an integrated wholeness to his present.

But even though universal moral standards can become personal when chosen by an individual, the ethical stage is not sufficient to bring a person to complete self-actualization. The ethical stage leads to a point at which one realizes that one cannot entirely fulfill the moral law, that one is sinful in the presence of God. Only in the religious stage, where one "leaps" to passionate commitment to God, is one totally free from meaninglessness and dread. In the religious stage, a person must be willing to give up everything—even abstract ethical universals—to God. In the selection reprinted here from *Fear and Trembling,* in the Howard and Edna Hong translation, Kierkegaard illustrates this movement from the ethical to the religious stage by contrasting the stories of Agamemnon and Abraham. Although both were called upon by a divinity to sacrifice a child, Agamemnon's sacrifice would serve a higher ethical purpose whereas Abraham's would not. In fact, Abraham was in the odd position of being *tempted* to do the ethical: to not murder/sacrifice Isaac.

Yet Abraham had faith in God, rather than Agamemnon's resignation to the gods, and continued to believe that God would return his son to him. Abraham performed a "teleological [i.e., considering the end or goal] suspension of the ethical," giving up what was most dear to him, and by virtue of the absurd, God gave it all back. It is interesting to note that Kierkegaard wrote this work right after he had given up to God what was most dear to him: Regine Olsen. Apparently believing that God would give her back to him, Kierkegaard was shocked when she became engaged to another man.

In the selection from *Concluding Unscientific Postscript,* reprinted here in the Howard and Edna Hong translation, Kierkegaard argues that whereas a logical system is possible, an existential system is not. Hegel's entire systematic enterprise is misguided because it assumes a finality that lived existence never has. When it comes to the important issues of life, such as knowledge of God, no system, no set of objective truths will give any real guidance. According to Kierkegaard, only subjective truth, "An objective uncertainty, held fast through appropriation with the most passionate inwardness," can be the truth for an existing person. Whereas one can never have objective certainty that God exists, one can make it true in one's own life by committing oneself completely and living as if it were true.

Written in Danish and presenting a pessimistic view of objective reason that was out of touch with the spirit of his time, it is not surprising that Kierkegaard's works were ignored for decades. The horror of World War I, together with the work done by Martin Heidegger in philosophy and Karl Barth in theology, brought Kierkegaard's pessimistic assessment of objectivism to prominence. Today Kierkegaard is acknowledged as the "father of existentialism" and is studied widely.

* * *

For representative collections of Kierkegaard's writings, see *A Kierkegaard Anthology,* edited by Robert Bretall (New York: Modern Library, 1936) and Walter A. Kaufmann, ed., *Existentialism from Dostoevsky to Sartre* (New York: Meridian Books, 1956). For biographies of Kierkegaard, see Walter Lowrie, *Kierkegaard* (Oxford: Oxford University Press, 1938) for comprehensive coverage, or Walter Lowrie, *A Short Life of Kierkegaard* (Princeton, NJ: Princeton University Press, 1942) for a more succinct study; Bruce H. Kirmmse, ed., *Encounters with Kierkegaard,* (Princeton, NJ: Princeton University Press, 1996) for descriptions of Kierkegaard by his contemporaries; Alastair Hannay, *Kierkegaard: A Biography* (Cambridge: Cambridge University Press, 2001); and Joakim Garff, *Søren Kierkegaard: A Biography,* translated by Bruce H. Kirmmse (Princeton, NJ: Princeton University Press, 2005) for recent studies. There are a number of general overviews of Kierkegaard's thought, including H. Diem, *Kierkegaard: An Introduction,* translated by David Green (Richmond, VA: John Knox Press, 1966); Josiah Thompson, *Kierkegaard* (New York: Knopf, 1973); Alastair Hannay, *Kierkegaard* (London: Routledge & Kegan Paul, 1982); Diogenes Allen, *Three Outsiders: Pascal, Kierkegaard, Simone Weil* (Cambridge, MA: Cowley, 1983); Patrick Gardiner, *Kierkegaard* (Oxford: Oxford University Press, 1988); George Pattison, *The Philosophy of Kierkegaard* (Montreal: McGill–Queen's University Press, 2005); and Clare Carlisle, *Kierkegaard: A Guide for the Perplexed* (London: Continuum, 2007). For studies of specific aspects of Kierkegaard's thought, see Louis K. Dupre, *Kierkegaard as Theologian* (New York: Sheed and Ward, 1964);

Niels Thulstrup, *Kierkegaard's Relation to Hegel,* translated by George L. Stengren (Princeton, NJ: Princeton University Press, 1980); John W. Elrod, *Kierkegaard and Christendom* (Princeton, NJ: Princeton University Press, 1981); C. Stephen Evans, *Kierkegaard's "Fragments" and "Postscript": The Religious Philosophy of Johannes Climacus* (Atlantic Highlands, NJ: Humanities Press, 1983); Merold Westphal, *Kierkegaard's Critique of Reason and Society* (Macon, GA: Mercer University Press, 1987); C. Stephen Evans, *Passionate Reason: Making Sense of Kierkegaard's* Philosophical Fragments (Bloomington: Indiana University Press, 1992); Louis Pojman, *Kierkegaard's Philosophy of Religion* (New York: University Press of America, 1999); John Lipitt, *Kierkegaard and* Fear and Trembling (London: Routledge, 2003); Michael Theunissen, *Kierkegaard's Concept of Despair,* translated by Barbara Harshav and Helmut Illbruck (Princeton: Princeton University Press, 2005); and David A. Roberts, *Kierkegaard's Analysis of Radical Evil* (London: Continuum, 2006). For collections of essays, see H.A. Johnson and N. Thulstrup, eds., *A Kierkegaard Critique* (Chicago: Henry Regnery, 1967); Jerry H. Gill, ed., *Essays on Kierkegaard* (Minneapolis, MN: Burgess, 1969); Josiah Thompson, ed., *Kierkegaard: A Collection of Critical Essays* (Garden City, NY: Anchor Books, 1972); Harold Bloom, ed., *Søren Kierkegaard* (New York: Chelsea House, 1989); Célline Léon and Sylvia Walsh, eds., *Feminist Interpretations of Søren Kierkegaard* (College Park, PA: Pennsylvania State University Press, 1997); Alistair Hannay and Gordon Marino, eds., *The Cambridge Companion to Kierkegaard* (Cambridge: Cambridge University Press, 1997); and Jonathan Rée and Jane Chamberlain, eds., *Kierkegaard: A Critical Reader* (Oxford: Basil Blackwell, 1997).

FEAR AND TREMBLING (in part)

IS THERE A TELEOLOGICAL SUSPENSION OF THE ETHICAL?

The ethical as such is the universal, and as the universal it applies to everyone, which from another angle means that it applies at all times. It rests immanent in itself, has nothing outside itself that is its ⟨*telos*⟩ [end, purpose] but is itself the ⟨*telos*⟩ for everything outside itself, and when the ethical has absorbed this into itself, it goes not further. The single individual, sensately and psychically qualified in immediacy, is the individual who has his ⟨*telos*⟩ in the universal, and it is his ethical task continually to express himself in this, to annul his singularity in order to become the universal. As soon as the single individual asserts himself in his singularity before the universal, he sins, and only by acknowledging this can he be reconciled again with the universal. Every time the single

Søren Kierkegaard, *Fear and Trembling,*"Teleological Suspension of the Ethical," edited and translated by Howard V. Hong and Edna H. Hong (Princeton: Princeton University Press).

individual, after having entered the universal, feels an impulse to assert himself as the single individual, he is in a spiritual trial [*Anfægtelse*], from which he can work himself only by repentantly surrendering as the single individual in the universal. If this is the highest that can be said of man and his existence, then the ethical is of the same nature as a person's eternal salvation, which is his ⟨*telos*⟩ forevermore and at all times, since it would be a contradiction for this to be capable of being surrendered (that is, teleologically suspended), because as soon as this is suspended it is relinquished, whereas that which is suspended is not relinquished but is preserved in the higher, which is its ⟨*telos*⟩.

If this is the case, then Hegel is right in "The Good and Conscience," where he qualifies man only as the individual and considers this qualification as a "moral form of evil" (see especially *The Philosophy of Right*), which must be annulled [*ophævet*] in the teleology of the moral in such a way that the single individual who remains in that stage either sins or is immersed in spiritual trial. But Hegel is wrong in speaking about faith; he is wrong in not protesting loudly and clearly against Abraham's enjoying honor and glory as a father of faith when he ought to be sent back to a lower court and shown up as a murderer.

Faith is namely this paradox that the single individual is higher than the universal—yet, please note, in such a way that the movement repeats itself, so that after having been in the universal he as the single individual isolates himself as higher than the universal. If this is not faith, then Abraham is lost, then faith has never existed in the world precisely because it has always existed. For if the ethical—that is, social morality—is the highest and if there is in a person no residual incommensurability in some way such that this incommensurability is not evil (i.e., the single individual, who is to be expressed in the universal), then no categories are needed other than what Greek philosophy had or what can be deduced from them by consistent thought. Hegel should not have concealed this, for, after all, he had studied Greek philosophy.

People who are profoundly lacking in learning and are given to clichés are frequently heard to say that a light shines over the Christian world, whereas a darkness enshrouds paganism. This kind of talk has always struck me as strange, inasmuch as every more thorough thinker, every more earnest artist still regenerates himself in the eternal youth of the Greeks. The explanation for such a statement is that one does not know what one should say but only that one must say something. It is quite right to say that paganism did not have faith, but if something is supposed to have been said thereby, then one must have a clearer understanding of what faith is, for otherwise one falls into such clichés. It is easy to explain all existence, faith along with it, without having a conception of what faith is, and the one who counts on being admired for such an explanation is not such a bad calculator, for it is as Boileau says: *Un sot trouve toujours un plus sot, qui l'admire* [One fool always finds a bigger fool, who admires him].

Faith is precisely the paradox that the single individual as the single individual is higher than the universal, is justified before it, not as inferior to it but as superior—yet in such a way, please note, that it is the single individual who, after being subordinate as the single individual to the universal, now by means of the universal becomes the single individual who as the single individual is superior, that the single individual as the single individual stands in an absolute relation to the absolute. This position cannot be mediated, for all mediation takes place only by virtue of the universal; it is and remains for all eternity a paradox, impervious to thought. And yet faith is this paradox, or else (and I ask the reader to bear these consequences *in mente* [in mind] even though it would be too prolix for me to write them all down) or else faith has never existed simply because it has always existed, or else Abraham is lost.

Wanderer Above the Mist. 1817–1818. by Caspar David Friendrich (1774–1840). "Faith is precisely the paradox that the single individual as the single individual is higher than the universal. . . . This position cannot be mediated . . . it is and remains for all eternity a paradox, impervious to thought." Kierkegaard, *Fear and Trembling*. (*©Foto Marburg/Art Resource, NY*)

It is certainly true that the single individual can easily confuse this paradox with spiritual trial [*Anfægtelse*], but it ought not to be concealed for that reason. It is certainly true that many persons may be so constituted that they are repulsed by it, but faith ought not therefore to be made into something else to enable one to have it, but one ought rather to admit to not having it, while those who have faith ought to be prepared to set forth some characteristics whereby the paradox can be distinguished from a spiritual trial.

The story of Abraham contains just such a teleological suspension of the ethical. There is no dearth of keen minds and careful scholars who have found analogies to it. What their wisdom amounts to is the beautiful proposition that basically everything is the same. If one looks more closely, I doubt very much that anyone in the whole wide world will find one single analogy, except for a later one, which proves nothing if it is certain that Abraham represents faith and that it is manifested normatively in him, whose life not only is the most paradoxical that can be thought but is also so paradoxical that it simply cannot be thought. He acts by virtue of the absurd, for it is precisely the absurd that he as the single individual is higher than the universal. This paradox cannot be mediated, for as soon as Abraham begins to do so, he has to confess that he was in a spiritual trial, and if that is the case, he will never sacrifice Isaac, or if he did sacrifice Isaac, then in repentance he must come back to the universal. He gets Isaac back again by virtue of the absurd. Therefore, Abraham is at no time a tragic hero but is something entirely different, either a murderer or a man of faith. Abraham does not have the middle term that saves the tragic hero. This is why I can understand a tragic hero but cannot understand Abraham, even though in a certain demented sense I admire him more than all others.

In ethical terms, Abraham's relation to Isaac is quite simply this: the father shall love the son more than himself. But within its own confines the ethical has various gradations. We shall see whether this story contains any higher expression for the ethical that can ethically explain his behavior, can ethically justify his suspending the ethical obligation to the son, but without moving beyond the teleology of the ethical.

When an enterprise of concern to a whole nation is impeded, when such a project is halted by divine displeasure, when the angry deity sends a dead calm that mocks every effort, when the soothsayer carries out his sad task and announces that the deity demands a young girl as sacrifice—then the father must heroically bring this sacrifice. He must nobly conceal his agony, even though he could wish he were "the lowly man who dares to weep" and not the king who must behave in a kingly manner. Although the lonely agony penetrates his breast and there are only three persons in the whole nation who know his agony, soon the whole nation will be initiated into his agony and also into his deed, that for the welfare of all he will sacrifice her, his daughter, this lovely young girl. O bosom! O fair cheeks, flaxen hair (v. 687). And the daughter's tears will agitate him, and the father will turn away his face, but the hero must raise the knife. And when the news of it reaches the father's house, the beautiful Greek maidens will blush with enthusiasm, and if the daughter was engaged, her betrothed will not be angry but will be proud to share in the father's deed, for the girl belonged more tenderly to him than to the father.

When the valiant judge who in the hour of need saved Israel binds God and himself in one breath by the same promise, he will heroically transform the young maiden's jubilation, the beloved daughter's joy to sorrow, and all Israel will sorrow with her over her virginal youth. But every freeborn man will understand, every resolute woman will admire Jephthah, and every virgin in Israel will wish to behave as his daughter did, because what good would it be for Jephthah to win the victory by means of a promise if he did not keep it—would not the victory be taken away from the people again?

When a son forgets his duty, when the state entrusts the sword of judgment to the father, when the laws demand punishment from the father's hand, then the father must heroically forget that the guilty one is his son, he must nobly hide his agony, but no one in the nation, not even the son, will fail to admire the father, and every time the Roman laws are interpreted, it will be remembered that many interpreted them more learnedly but no one more magnificently than Brutus.

But if Agamemnon, while a favorable wind was taking the fleet under full sail to its destination, had dispatched that messenger who fetched Iphigenia to be sacrificed; if Jephthah, without being bound by any promise that decided the fate of the nation, had said to his daughter: Grieve now for two months over your brief youth, and then I will sacrifice you; if Brutus had had a righteous son and yet had summoned the lictors to put him to death—who would have understood them? If, on being asked why they did this, these three men had answered: It is an ordeal in which we are being tried [*forsøges*]—would they have been better understood?

When in the crucial moment Agamemnon, Jephthah, and Brutus heroically have overcome the agony, heroically have lost the beloved, and have only to complete the task externally, there will never be a noble soul in the world without tears of compassion for their agony, of admiration for their deed. But if in the crucial moment these three men were to append to the heroic courage with which they bore the agony the little phrase: But it will not happen anyway—who then would understand them? If they went on to explain: This we believe by virtue of the absurd—who would understand them any better, for who would not readily understand that it was absurd, but who would understand that one could then believe it?

The difference between the tragic hero and Abraham is very obvious. The tragic hero is still within the ethical. He allows an expression of the ethical to have its ⟨*telos*⟩ in a higher expression of the ethical; he scales down the ethical relation between father and son or daughter and father to a feeling that has its dialectic in its relation to the idea of moral conduct. Here there can be no question of a teleological suspension of the ethical itself.

Abraham's situation is different. By his act he transgressed the ethical altogether and had a higher ⟨*telos*⟩ outside it, in relation to which he suspended it. For I certainly would like to know how Abraham's act can be related to the universal, whether any point of contact between what Abraham did and the universal can be found other than that Abraham transgressed it. It is not to save a nation, not to uphold the idea of the state that Abraham does it; it is not to appease the angry gods. If it were a matter of the deity's being angry, then he was, after all, angry only with Abraham, and Abraham's act is totally unrelated to the universal, is a purely private endeavor. Therefore, while the tragic hero is great because of his moral virtue, Abraham is great because of a purely personal virtue. There is no higher expression for the ethical in Abraham's life than that the father shall love the son. The ethical in the sense of the moral is entirely beside the point. Insofar as the universal was present, it was cryptically in Isaac, hidden, so to speak, in Isaac's loins, and must cry out with Isaac's mouth: Do not do this, you are destroying everything.

Why, then, does Abraham do it? For God's sake and—the two are wholly identical—for his own sake. He does it for God's sake because God demands this proof of his faith; he does it for his own sake so that he can prove it. The unity of the two is altogether correctly expressed in the word already used to describe this relationship. It is an ordeal, a temptation. A temptation—but what does that mean? As a rule, what tempts a person is something that will hold him back from doing his duty, but here the temptation is the ethical itself, which would hold him back from doing God's will. But what is duty? Duty is simply the expression for God's will.

Here the necessity of a new category for the understanding of Abraham becomes apparent. Paganism does not know such a relationship to the divine. The tragic hero does not enter into any private relationship to the divine, but the ethical is the divine, and thus the paradox therein can be mediated in the universal.

Abraham cannot be mediated; in other words, he cannot speak. As soon as I speak, I express the universal, and if I do not do so, no one can understand me. As soon as Abraham wants to express himself in the universal, he must declare that his situation is a spiritual trial [*Anfægtelse*], for he has no higher expression of the universal that ranks above the universal he violates.

Therefore, although Abraham arouses my admiration, he also appalls me. The person who denies himself and sacrifices himself because of duty gives up the finite in order to grasp the infinite and is adequately assured; the tragic hero gives up the certain for the even more certain, and the observer's eye views him with confidence. But the person who gives up the universal in order to grasp something even higher that is not the universal—what does he do? Is it possible that this can be anything other than a spiritual trial? And if it is possible, but the individual makes a mistake, what salvation is there for him? He suffers all the agony of the tragic hero, he shatters his joy in the world, he renounces everything, and perhaps at the same time he barricades himself from the sublime joy that was so precious to him that he would buy it at any price. The observer cannot understand him at all; neither can his eye rest upon him with confidence. Perhaps the believer's intention cannot be carried out at all, because it is inconceivable. Or if it could be done but the individual has misunderstood the deity—what salvation would there be for him? The tragic hero needs and demands tears, and where is the envious eye so arid that it could not weep with Agamemnon, but where is the soul so gone astray that it has the audacity to weep for Abraham? The tragic hero finishes his task at a specific moment in time, but as time passes he does what is no less significant: he visits the person encompassed by sorrow, who cannot breathe because of his anguished sighs, whose thoughts oppress him, heavy with tears. He appears to him, breaks the witchcraft of sorrow, loosens the bonds, evokes the tears, and the suffering one forgets his own sufferings in those of the tragic hero. One cannot weep over Abraham. One approaches him with a *horror religiosus,* as Israel approached Mount Sinai. What if he himself is distraught, what if he had made a mistake, this lonely man who climbs Mount Moriah, whose peak towers sky-high over the flatlands of Aulis, what if he is not a sleepwalker safely crossing the abyss while the one standing at the foot of the mountain looks up, shakes with anxiety, and then in his deference and horror does not even dare to call to him?—Thanks, once again thanks, to a man who, to a person overwhelmed by life's sorrows and left behind naked, reaches out the words, the leafage of language by which he can conceal his misery. Thanks to you, great Shakespeare, you who can say everything, everything, everything just as it is—and yet, why did you never articulate this torment? Did you perhaps reserve it for yourself, like the beloved's name that one cannot bear to have the world utter, for with his little secret that he cannot divulge the poet buys this power of the word to tell everybody else's dark secrets. A poet is not an apostle; he drives out devils only by the power of the devil.

But if the ethical is teleologically suspended in this manner, how does the single individual in whom it is suspended exist? He exists as the single individual in contrast to the universal. Does he sin, then, for from the point of view of the idea, this is the form of sin. Thus, even though the child does not sin, because it is not conscious of its existence as such, its existence, from the point of view of the idea, is nevertheless sin, and the ethical makes its claim upon it at all times. If it is denied that this form can be repeated in such a way that it is not sin, then judgment has fallen upon Abraham. How did Abraham exist? He had faith. This is the paradox by which he remains at the apex, the paradox that he cannot explain to anyone else, for the paradox is that he as the single individual places himself in an absolute relation to the absolute. Is he justified? Again, his justification is the paradoxical, for if he is, then he is justified not by virtue of being something universal but by virtue of being the single individual.

How does the single individual reassure himself that he is legitimate? It is a simple matter to level all existence to the idea of the state or the idea of a society. If this is done, it is also simple to mediate, for one never comes to the paradox that the single individual as the single individual is higher than the universal, something I can also express symbolically in a statement by Pythagoras to the effect that the odd number is more perfect than the even number. If occasionally there is any response at all these days with regard to the paradox, it is likely to be: One judges it by the result. Aware that he is a paradox who cannot be understood, a hero who has become a ⟨*skandalon*⟩ [offense] to his age will shout confidently to his contemporaries: The result will indeed prove that I was justified. This cry is rarely heard in our age, inasmuch as it does not produce heroes—this is its defect—and it likewise has the advantage that it produces few caricatures. When in our age we hear these words: It will be judged by the result—then we know at once with whom we have the honor of speaking. Those who talk this way are a numerous type whom I shall designate under the common name of assistant professors. With security in life, they live in their thoughts: they have a *permanent* position and a *secure* future in a well-organized state. They have hundreds, yes, even thousands of years between them and the earthquakes of existence; they are not afraid that such things can be repeated, for then what would the police and the newspapers say? Their life task is to judge the great men, judge them according to the result. Such behavior toward greatness betrays a strange mixture of arrogance and wretchedness—arrogance because they feel called to pass judgment, wretchedness because they feel that their lives are in no way allied with the lives of the great. Anyone with even a smattering *erectioris ingenii* [of nobility of nature] never becomes an utterly cold and clammy worm, and when he approaches greatness, he is never devoid of the thought that since the creation of the world it has been customary for the result to come last and that if one is truly going to learn something from greatness one must be particularly aware of the beginning. If the one who is to act wants to judge himself by the result, he will never begin. Although the result may give joy to the entire world, it cannot help the hero, for he would not know the result until the whole thing was over, and he would not become a hero by that but by making a beginning.

Moreover, in its dialectic the result (insofar as it is finitude's response to the infinite question) is altogether incongruous with the hero's existence. Or should Abraham's receiving Isaac by a *marvel* be able to prove that Abraham was justified in relating himself as the single individual to the universal? If Abraham actually had sacrificed Isaac, would he therefore have been less justified?

But we are curious about the result, just as we are curious about the way a book turns out. We do not want to know anything about the anxiety, the distress, the paradox. We carry on an esthetic flirtation with the result. It arrives just as unexpectedly but also just as effortlessly as a prize in a lottery, and when we have heard the result, we have built ourselves up. And yet no manacled robber of churches is so despicable a criminal as the one who plunders holiness in this way, and not even Judas, who sold his Lord for thirty pieces of silver, is more contemptible than someone who peddles greatness in this way.

It is against my very being to speak inhumanly about greatness, to make it a dim and nebulous far-distant shape or to let it be great but devoid of the emergence of the humanness without which it ceases to be great, for it is not what happens to me that makes me great but what I do, and certainly there is no one who believes that someone became great by winning the big lottery prize. A person might have been born in lowly circumstances, but I would still require him not to be so inhuman toward himself that he could imagine the king's castle only at a distance and ambiguously dream of its greatness, and destroy it at the same time he elevates it because he elevated it so basely. I require him to be man enough to tread confidently and with dignity there as well. He must not be so inhuman that he insolently violates everything by barging right off the street into the king's hall—he loses more thereby than the king. On the contrary, he should find a joy in observing every bidding of propriety with a happy and confident enthusiasm, which is precisely what makes him a free spirit. This is merely a metaphor, for that distinction is only a very imperfect expression of the distance of spirit. I require every person not to think so inhumanly of himself that he does not dare to enter those palaces where the memory of the chosen ones lives or even those where they themselves live. He is not to enter rudely and foist his affinity upon them. He is to be happy for every time he bows before them, but he is to be confident, free of spirit, and always more than a charwoman, for if he wants to be no more than that, he will never get in. And the very thing that is going to help him is the anxiety and distress in which the great were tried, for otherwise, if he has any backbone, they will only arouse his righteous envy. And anything that can be great only at a distance, that someone wants to make great with empty and hollow phrases—is destroyed by that very person.

Who was as great in the world as that favored woman, the mother of God, the Virgin Mary? And yet how do we speak of her? That she was the favored one among women does not make her great, and if it would not be so very odd for those who listen to be able to think just as inhumanly as those who speak, then every young girl might ask: Why am I not so favored? And if I had nothing else to say, I certainly would not dismiss such a question as stupid, because, viewed abstractly, vis-à-vis a favor, every person is just as entitled to it as the other. We leave out the distress, the anxiety, the paradox. My thoughts are as pure as anybody's, and he who can think this way surely has pure thoughts, and, if not, he can expect something horrible, for anyone who has once experienced these images cannot get rid of them again, and if he sins against them, they take a terrible revenge in a silent rage, which is more terrifying than the stridency of ten ravenous critics. To be sure, Mary bore the child wondrously, but she nevertheless did it "after the manner of women," and such a time is one of anxiety, distress, and paradox. The angel was indeed a ministering spirit, but he was not a meddlesome spirit who went to the other young maidens in Israel and said: Do not scorn Mary, the extraordinary is happening to her. The angel went only to Mary, and no one could understand her. Has any woman been as infringed upon as was Mary, and is it not true here also that the one whom God blesses he curses in the same breath? This is the spirit's view of Mary, and she is by no means—it is revolting to me to say it but even more so that people have inanely and unctuously made her out to be thus—she is by no means a lady idling in her finery and playing with a divine child. When, despite this, she said: Behold, I am the handmaid of the Lord—then she is great, and I believe it should not be difficult to explain why she became the mother of God. She needs worldly admiration as little as Abraham needs tears, for she was no heroine and he was no hero, but both of them became greater than these, not by being exempted in any way from the distress and the agony and the paradox, but became greater by means of these.

It is great when the poet in presenting his tragic hero for public admiration dares to say: Weep for him, for he deserves it. It is great to deserve the tears of those who deserve to shed tears. It is great that the poet dares to keep the crowd under restraint, dares to discipline men to examine themselves individually to see if they are worthy to weep for the hero, for the slop water of the snivellers is a debasement of the sacred.—But even greater than all this is the knight of faith's daring to say to the noble one who wants to weep for him: Do not weep for me, but weep for yourself.

We are touched, we look back to those beautiful times. Sweet sentimental longing leads us to the goal of our desire, to see Christ walking about in the promised land. We forget the anxiety, the distress, the paradox. Was it such a simple matter not to make a mistake? Was it not terrifying that this man walking around among the others was God? Was it not terrifying to sit down to eat with him? Was it such an easy matter to become an apostle? But the result, the eighteen centuries—that helps, that contributes to this mean deception whereby we deceive ourselves and others. I do not feel brave enough to wish to be contemporary with events like that, but I do not for that reason severely condemn those who made a mistake, nor do I depreciate those who saw what was right.

But I come back to Abraham. During the time before the result, either Abraham was a murderer every minute or we stand before a paradox that is higher than all mediations.

The story of Abraham contains, then, a teleological suspension of the ethical. As the single individual he became higher than the universal. This is the paradox, which cannot be mediated. How he entered into it is just as inexplicable as how he remains in it. If this is not Abraham's situation, then Abraham is not even a tragic hero but a murderer. It is thoughtless to want to go on calling him the father of faith, to speak of it to men who have an interest only in words. A person can become a tragic hero through his own strength—but not the knight of faith. When a person walks what is in one sense the hard road of the tragic hero, there are many who can give him advice, but he who walks the narrow road of faith has no one to advise him—no one understands him. Faith is a marvel, and yet no human being is excluded from it; for that which unites all human life is passion, and faith is a passion.

CONCLUDING UNSCIENTIFIC POSTSCRIPT (in part)

Section II, Chapter 2: Subjective Truth, Inwardness; Truth Is Subjectivity

* * *

*When the question about truth is asked objectively, truth is reflected upon objectively as an object to which the knower relates himself. What is reflected upon is not the relation but that what he relates himself to is the truth, the true. If only that to which he relates himself is the truth, the true, then the subject is in the truth. When the question about truth is asked subjectively, the individual's relation is reflected upon subjectively. If only the how of this relation is in truth, the individual is in truth, even if he in this way were to relate himself to untruth.**

*The reader will note that what is being discussed here is essential truth, or the truth that is related essentially to existence, and that it is specifically in order to clarify it as inwardness or as subjectivity that the contrast is pointed out.

Søren Kierkegaard, *Concluding Unscientific Postscript,* Section II, Chapter 2, "Subjective Truth, Inwardness; Truth is Subjectivity," edited and translated by Howard V. Hong and Edna H. Hong (Princeton: Princeton University Press).

Let us take the knowledge of God as an example. Objectively, what is reflected upon is that this is the true God; subjectively, that the individual relates himself to a something in *such a way* that his relation is in truth a God-relation. Now, on which side is the truth? Alas, must we not at this point resort to mediation and say: It is on neither side; it is in the mediation? Superbly stated, if only someone could say how an existing person goes about being in mediation, because to be in mediation is to be finished; to exist is to become. An existing person cannot be in two places at the same time, cannot be subject-object. When he is closest to being in two places at the same time, he is in passion; but passion is only momentary, and passion is the highest pitch of subjectivity.

The existing person who chooses the objective way now enters upon all approximating deliberation intended to bring forth God objectively, which is not achieved in all eternity, because God is a subject and hence only for subjectivity in inwardness. The existing person who chooses the subjective way instantly comprehends the whole dialectical difficulty because he must use some time, perhaps a long time, to find God objectively. He comprehends this dialectical difficulty in all its pain, because he must resort to God at that very moment, because every moment in which he does not have God is wasted.* At that very moment he has God, not by virtue of any objective deliberation but by virtue of the infinite passion of inwardness. The objective person is not bothered by dialectical difficulties such as what it means to put a whole research period into finding God, since it is indeed possible that the researcher would die tomorrow, and if he goes on living, he cannot very well regard God as something to be taken along at his convenience, since God is something one takes along a *tout prix* [at any price], which, in passion's understanding, is the true relationship of inwardness with God.

It is at this point, dialectically so very difficult, that the road swings off for the person who knows what it means to think dialectically and, existing, to think dialectically, which is quite different from sitting as a fantastical being at a desk and writing about something one has never done oneself, quite different from writing *de omnibus dubitandum* and then as an existing person being just as credulous as the most sensate human being. It is here that the road swings off, and the change is this: whereas objective knowledge goes along leisurely on the long road of approximation, itself not actuated by passion, to subjective knowledge every delay is a deadly peril and the decision so infinitely important that it is immediately urgent, as if the opportunity had already passed by unused.

Now, if the problem is to calculate where there is more truth (and, as stated, simultaneously to be on both sides equally is not granted to an existing person but is only a beatifying delusion for a deluded *I–I*), whether on the side of the person who only objectively seeks the true God and the approximating truth of the God-idea or on the side of the person who is infinitely concerned that he in truth relate himself to God with the infinite passion of need—then there can be no doubt about the answer for anyone who is not totally botched by scholarship and science. If someone who lives in the midst of Christianity enters, with knowledge of the true idea of God, the house of God, the house of the true God, and prays, but prays in untruth, and if someone lives in an idolatrous land but prays with all the passion of infinity, although his eyes are resting upon the image of an idol—where, then, is there more truth? The one prays in truth to

*In this way God is indeed a postulate, but not in the loose sense in which it is ordinarily taken. Instead, it becomes clear that this is the only way an existing person enters into a relationship with God: when the dialectical contradiction brings passion to despair and assists him in grasping God with "the category of despair" (faith), so that the postulate, far from being the arbitrary, is in fact *necessary* defense [*Nødværge*], self defense; in this way God is not a postulate, but the existing person's postulating of God is—a necessity [*Nødvendighed*].

God although he is worshiping an idol; the other prays in untruth to the true God and is therefore in truth worshiping an idol.

If someone objectively inquires into immortality, and someone else stakes the passion of the infinite on the uncertainty—where, then, is there more truth, and who has more certainty? The one has once and for all entered upon an approximation that never ends, because the certainty of immortality is rooted in subjectivity; the other is immortal and therefore struggles by contending with the uncertainty.

Let us consider Socrates. These days everyone is dabbling in a few proofs or demonstrations—one has many, another fewer. But Socrates! He poses the question objectively, problematically: if there is an immortality. So, compared with one of the modern thinkers with the three demonstrations, was he a doubter? Not at all. He stakes his whole life on this "if"; he dares to die, and with the passion of the infinite he has so ordered his whole life that it might be acceptable—if there is an immortality. Is there any better demonstration for the immortality of the soul? But those who have the three demonstrations do not order their lives accordingly. If there is an immortality, it must be nauseated by their way of living—is there any better counter-demonstration to the three demonstrations? The "fragment" of uncertainty helped Socrates, because he himself helped with the passion of infinity. The three demonstrations are of no benefit whatever to those others, because they are and remain slugs and, failing to demonstrate anything else, have demonstrated it by their three demonstrations.

In the same way a girl has perhaps possessed all the sweetness of being in love through a weak hope of being loved by the beloved, because she herself staked everything on this weak hope; on the other hand, many a wedded matron, who more than once has submitted to the strongest expression of erotic love, has certainly had demonstrations and yet, strangely enough, has not possessed *quod erat demonstrandum* [that which was to be demonstrated]. The Socratic ignorance was thus the expression, firmly maintained with all the passion of inwardness, of the relation of the eternal truth to an existing person, and therefore it must remain for him a paradox as long as he exists. Yet it is possible that in the Socratic ignorance there was more truth in Socrates than in the objective truth of the entire system that flirts with the demands of the times and adapts itself to assistant professors.

Objectively the emphasis is on what is said; subjectively the emphasis is on how it is said. This distinction applies even esthetically and is specifically expressed when we say that in the mouth of this or that person something that is truth can become untruth. Particular attention should be paid to this distinction in our day, for if one were to express in a single sentence the difference between ancient times and our time, one would no doubt have to say: In ancient times there were only a few individuals who knew the truth; now everyone knows it, but inwardness has an inverse relation to it. Viewed esthetically, the contradiction that emerges when truth becomes untruth in this and that person's mouth is best interpreted comically. Ethically-religiously, the emphasis is again on: *how*. But this is not to be understood as manner, modulation of voice, oral delivery, etc., but it is to be understood as the relation of the existing person, in his very existence, to what is said. Objectively, the question is only about categories of thought; subjectively, about inwardness. At its maximum, this "how" is the passion of the infinite, and the passion of the infinite is the very truth. But the passion of the infinite is precisely subjectivity, and thus subjectivity is truth. From the objective point of view, there is no infinite decision, and thus it is objectively correct that the distinction between good and evil is canceled, along with the principle of contradiction, and thereby also the infinite distinction between truth and falsehood. Only in subjectivity is there decision, whereas wanting to become objective is untruth. The passion of the infinite, not its content, is the deciding factor, for its content is precisely itself. In this way the subjective "how" and subjectivity are the truth.

But precisely because the subject is existing, the "how" that is subjectively emphasized is dialectical also with regard to time. In the moment of the decision of passion, where the road swings off from objective knowledge, it looks as if the infinite decision were thereby finished. But at the same moment, the existing person is in the temporal realm, and the subjective "how" is transformed into a striving that is motivated and repeatedly refreshed by the decisive passion of the infinite, but it is nevertheless a striving.

When subjectivity is truth, the definition of truth must also contain in itself an expression of the antithesis to objectivity, a memento of that fork in the road, and this expression will at the same time indicate the resilience of the inwardness. Here is such a definition of truth: *An objective uncertainty, held fast through appropriation with the most passionate inwardness, is the truth,* the highest truth there is for an existing person. At the point where the road swings off (and where that is cannot be stated objectively, since it is precisely subjectivity), objective knowledge is suspended. Objectively he then has only uncertainty, but this is precisely what intensifies the infinite passion of inwardness, and truth is precisely the daring venture of choosing the objective uncertainty with the passion of the infinite. I observe nature in order to find God, and I do indeed see omnipotence and wisdom, but I also see much that troubles and disturbs. The *summa summarum* [sum total] of this is an objective uncertainty, but the inwardness is so very great, precisely because it grasps this objective uncertainty with all the passion of the infinite. In a mathematical proposition, for example, the objectivity is given, but therefore its truth is also an indifferent truth.

But the definition of truth stated above is a paraphrasing of faith. Without risk, no faith. Faith is the contradiction between the infinite passion of inwardness and the objective uncertainty. If I am able to apprehend God objectively, I do not have faith; but because I cannot do this, I must have faith. If I want to keep myself in faith, I must continually see to it that I hold fast the objective uncertainty, see to it that in the objective uncertainty I am "out on 70,000 fathoms of water" and still have faith.

The thesis that subjectivity, inwardness, is truth contains the Socratic wisdom, the undying merit of which is to have paid attention to the essential meaning of existing, of the knower's being an existing person. That is why, in his ignorance, Socrates was in the truth in the highest sense within paganism. To comprehend this, that the misfortune of speculative thought is simply that it forgets again and again that the knower is an existing person, can already be rather difficult in our objective age. "But to go beyond Socrates when one has not even comprehended the Socratic—that, at least, is not Socratic." See "The Moral" in *Fragments*.

Just as in *Fragments,* let us from this point try a category of thought that actually does go beyond. Whether it is true or false is of no concern to me, since I am only imaginatively constructing, but this much is required, that it be clear that the Socratic is presupposed in it, so that I at least do not end up behind Socrates again.

When subjectivity, inwardness, is truth, then truth, objectively defined, is a paradox; and that truth is objectively a paradox shows precisely that subjectivity is truth, since the objectivity does indeed thrust away, and the objectivity's repulsion, or the expression for the objectivity's repulsion, is the resilience and dynamometer of inwardness. The paradox is the objective uncertainty that is the expression for the passion of inwardness that is truth. So much for the Socratic. The eternal, essential truth, that is, the truth that is related essentially to the existing person by pertaining essentially to what it means to exist (viewed Socratically, all other knowledge is accidental, its degree and scope indifferent), is a paradox. Nevertheless the eternal, essential truth is itself not at all a paradox, but it is a paradox by being related to an existing person. Socratic ignorance is an expression of the objective uncertainty; the inwardness of the existing person is truth. In anticipation of what will be discussed later, the following comment is made here: Socratic ignorance is an analogue to the category of the absurd, except that there is even less objective certainty in the repulsion exerted by the absurd, since there is only the certainty that it is absurd, and for that very reason there is infinitely greater resilience in the inwardness. The Socratic inwardness in existing is an analogue to faith, except that the inwardness of faith, corresponding not to the repulsion exerted by ignorance but to the repulsion exerted by the absurd, is infinitely deeper.

Viewed Socratically, the eternal essential truth is not at all paradoxical in itself, but only by being related to an existing person. This is expressed in another Socratic thesis: that all knowing is a recollecting. This thesis is an intimation of the beginning of speculative thought, but for that very reason Socrates did not pursue it; essentially it became Platonic. This is where the road swings off, and Socrates essentially emphasizes existing, whereas Plato, forgetting this, loses himself in speculative thought. Socrates' infinite merit is precisely that of being an *existing* thinker, not a speculative thinker who forgets what it means to exist. To Socrates, therefore, the thesis that all knowing is a recollecting has, at the moment of parting and as a continually annulled possibility of speculating, a double significance: (1) that the knower is essentially *integer* [uncorrupted] and that for him there is no other dubiousness with regard to knowledge of the eternal truth than this, that he exists, a dubiousness so essential and decisive to him that it signifies that existing, the inward deepening in and through existing, is truth; (2) that existence in temporality has no decisive significance, because there is continually the possibility of taking oneself back into eternity by recollecting, even though this possibility is continually annulled because the inward deepening in existing fills up time.*

*This may be the proper place to elucidate a dubiousness in the design of *Fragments,* a dubiousness that was due to my not wanting immediately to make the matter as dialectically difficult as it is, because in our day terminologies and the like are so muddled that it is almost impossible to safeguard oneself against confusion. In order, if possible, to elucidate properly the difference between the Socratic (which was supposed to be the philosophical, the pagan philosophical position) and the category of imaginatively constructed thought, which actually goes beyond the Socratic, I carried the Socratic back to the thesis that all knowing is a recollecting. It is commonly accepted as such, and only for the person who with a very special interest devotes himself to the Socratic, always returning to the sources, only for him will it be important to distinguish between Socrates and Plato on this point. The thesis certainly belongs to both of them, but Socrates continually parts with it because he wants to exist. By holding Socrates to the thesis that all knowing is recollecting, one turns him into a speculative philosopher instead of what he was, an existing thinker who understood existing as the essential. The thesis that all knowing is recollecting belongs to speculative thought, and recollecting is immanence, and from the point of view of speculation and the eternal there is no paradox. The difficulty, however, is that no human being is speculation, but the speculating person is an existing human being, subject to the claims of existence. To forget this is no merit, but to hold this fast is indeed a merit and that is precisely what Socrates did. To emphasize existence, which contains within it the qualification of inwardness, is the Socratic, whereas the Platonic is to purse recollection and immanence. Basically Socrates is thereby beyond all speculation, because he does not have a fantastical beginning where the speculating person changes clothes and then goes on and on and speculates, forgetting the most important thing, to exist. But precisely because Socrates is in this way beyond speculative thought, he acquires, when rightly depicted, a certain analogous likeness to what the imaginary construction set forth as that which truly goes beyond the Socratic: the truth as paradox is an analog to the paradox *sensu eminetiori* [in the more eminent sense]; the passion of inwardness in existing is then an analog to faith *sensu eminentiori*. That the difference is infinite nevertheless, that the designations in *Fragments* of that which truly goes beyond the Socratic are unchanged,

The great merit of the Socratic was precisely to emphasize that the knower is an existing person and that to exist is the essential. To go beyond Socrates by failing to understand this is nothing but a mediocre merit. This we must keep *in mente* [in mind] and then see whether the formula cannot be changed in such a way that one actually does go beyond the Socratic.

So, then, subjectivity, inwardness, is truth. Is there a *more inward* expression for it? Yes, if the discussion about "Subjectivity, inwardness, is truth" begins in this way: "Subjectivity is untruth." But let us not be in a hurry. Speculative thought also says that subjectivity is untruth but says it in the very opposite direction, namely, that objectivity is truth. Speculative thought defines subjectivity negatively in the direction of objectivity. The other definition, however, puts barriers in its own way at the very moment it wants to begin, which makes the inwardness so much more inward. Viewed Socratically, subjectivity is untruth if it refuses to comprehend that subjectivity is truth but wants, for example, to be objective. Here, on the other hand, in wanting to begin to become truth by becoming subjective, subjectivity is in the predicament of being untruth. Thus the work goes backward, that is, backward in inwardness. The way is so far from being in the direction of the objective that the beginning only lies even deeper in subjectivity.

But the subject cannot be untruth eternally or be presupposed to have been untruth eternally; he must have become that in time or he becomes that in time. The Socratic paradox consisted in this, that the eternal truth was related to an existing person. But now existence has accentuated the existing person a second time; a change so essential has taken place in him that he in no way can take himself back into eternity by Socratically recollecting. To do this is to speculate; to be able to do this but, by grasping the inward deepening in existence, to annul the possibility of doing it is the Socratic. But now the difficulty is that what accompanied Socrates as an annulled possibility has become an impossibility. If speculating was already of dubious merit in connection with the Socratic, it is now only confusion.

The paradox emerges when the eternal truth and existing are placed together, but each time existing is accentuated, the paradox becomes clearer and clearer. Viewed Socratically, the knower was an existing person, but now the existing person is accentuated in such a way that existence has made an essential change in him.

Let us now call the individual's untruth *sin*. Viewed eternally, he cannot be in sin or be presupposed to have been eternally in sin. Therefore, by coming into existence (for the beginning was that subjectivity is untruth), he becomes a sinner. He is not born as a sinner in the sense that he is presupposed to be a sinner before he is born, but he is born in sin and as a sinner. Indeed, we could call this *hereditary sin*. But if existence has in this way obtained power over him, he is prevented from taking himself back into eternity through recollection. If it is already paradoxical that the eternal truth is related to an existing person, now it is absolutely paradoxical that it is related to such an existing person. But the more difficult it is made for him, recollecting, to

---

I can easily show, but I was afraid to make complications by promptly using what seem to be the same designations, at least the same words, about the different things when the imaginary construction was to be presented as different from these. Now, I think there would be no objection to speaking of the paradox in connection with Socrates and faith, since it is quite correct to do so, provided that it is understood correctly. Besides, the ancient Greeks also use the word ⟨*pistis*⟩ [Faith], although by no means in the sense of the imaginary construction, and use it so as to make possible some very illuminating observations bearing upon its dissimilarity to faith *sensu eminentiori,* especially with reference to one of Aristotle's works where the term is employed.

take himself out of existence, the more inward his existing can become in existence; and when it is made impossible for him, when he is lodged in existence in such a way that the back door of recollection is forever closed, then the inwardness becomes the deepest. But let us never forget that the Socratic merit was precisely to emphasize that the knower is existing, because the more difficult the matter becomes, the more one is tempted to rush along the easy road of speculative thought, away from terrors and decisions, to fame, honor, a life of ease, etc. If even Socrates comprehended the dubiousness of taking himself speculatively out of existence back into eternity, when there was no dubiousness for the existing person except that he existed and, of course, that existing was the essential—now it is impossible. He must go forward; to go backward is impossible.

Subjectivity is truth. The paradox came into existence through the relating of the eternal, essential truth to the existing person. Let us now go further; let us assume that the eternal, essential truth is itself the paradox. How does the paradox emerge? By placing the eternal, essential truth together with existing. Consequently, if we place it together in the truth itself, the truth becomes a paradox. The eternal truth has come into existence in time. That is the paradox. If the subject just mentioned was prevented by sin from taking himself back into eternity, now he is not to concern himself with this, because now the eternal, essential truth is not behind him but has come in front of him by existing itself or by having existed, so that if the individual, existing, does not lay hold of the truth in existence, he will never have it.

Existence can never be accentuated more sharply than it has been here. The fraud of speculative thought in wanting to recollect itself out of existence has been made impossible. This is the only point to be comprehended here, and every speculation that insists on being speculation shows *eo ipso* [precisely thereby] that it has not comprehended this. The individual can thrust all this away and resort to speculation, but to accept it and then want to cancel it through speculation is impossible, because it is specifically designed to prevent speculation.

When the eternal truth relates itself to an existing person, it becomes the paradox. Through the objective uncertainty and ignorance, the paradox thrusts away in the inwardness of the existing person. But since the paradox is not in itself the paradox, it does not thrust away intensely enough, for without risk, no faith; the more risk, the more faith; the more objective reliability, the less inwardness (since inwardness is subjectivity); the less objective reliability, the deeper is the possible inwardness. When the paradox itself is the paradox, it thrusts away by virtue of the absurd, and the corresponding passion of inwardness is faith.

But subjectivity, inwardness, is truth; if not, we have forgotten the Socratic merit. But when the retreat out of existence into eternity by way of recollection has been made impossible, then, with the truth facing one as the paradox, in the anxiety of sin and its pain, with the tremendous risk of objectivity, there is no stronger expression for inwardness than—to have faith. But without risk, no faith, not even the Socratic faith, to say nothing of the kind we are discussing here.

When Socrates believed that God is, he held fast the objective uncertainty with the entire passion of inwardness, and faith is precisely in this contradiction, in this risk. Now it is otherwise. Instead of the objective uncertainty, there is here the certainty that, viewed objectively, it is the absurd, and this absurdity, held fast in the passion of inwardness, is faith. Compared with the earnestness of the absurd, the Socratic ignorance is like a witty jest, and compared with the strenuousness of faith, the Socratic existential inwardness resembles Greek nonchalance.

What, then, is the absurd? The absurd is that the eternal truth has come into existence in time, that God has come into existence, has been born, has grown up, etc., has come into existence exactly as an individual human being, indistinguishable from any other human being, inasmuch as all immediate recognizability is pre-Socratic paganism and from the Jewish point of view is idolatry. Every qualification of that which actually goes beyond the Socratic must essentially have a mark of standing in relation to the god's having come into existence, because faith, *sensu strictissimo* [in the strictest sense], as explicated in *Fragments,* refers to coming into existence. When Socrates believed that God is [*er til*], he no doubt perceived that where the road swings off there is a road of objective approximation, for example, the observation of nature, world history, etc. His merit was precisely to shun this road, where the quantifying siren song spellbinds and tricks the existing person. In relation to the absurd, the objective approximation resembles the comedy *Misforstaaelse paa Misforstaaelse* [Misunderstanding upon Misunderstanding], which ordinarily is played by assistant professors and speculative thinkers.

It is by way of the objective repulsion that the absurd is the dynamometer of faith in inwardness. So, then, there is a man who wants to have faith; well, let the comedy begin. He wants to have faith, but he wants to assure himself with the aid of objective deliberation and approximation. What happens? With the aid of approximation, the absurd becomes something else; it becomes probable, it becomes more probable, it may become to a high-degree and exceedingly probable. Now he is all set to believe it, and he dares to say of himself that he does not believe as shoemakers and tailors and simple folk do, but only after long deliberation. Now he is all set to believe it, but, lo and behold, now it has indeed become impossible to believe it. The almost probable, the probable, the to-a-high-degree and exceedingly probable—that he can almost know, or as good as know, to a higher degree and exceedingly almost *know*—but *believe* it, that cannot be done, for the absurd is precisely the object of faith and only that can be believed.

Or there is a man who says he has faith, but now he wants to make his faith clear to himself; he wants to understand himself in his faith. Now the comedy begins again. The object of faith becomes almost probable, it becomes as good as probable, it becomes probable, it becomes to a high degree and exceedingly probable. He has finished; he dares to say of himself that he does not believe as shoemakers and tailors or other simple folk do but that he has also understood himself in his believing. What wondrous understanding! On the contrary, he has learned to know something different about faith than he believed and has learned to know that he no longer has faith, since he almost knows, as good as knows, to a high degree and exceedingly almost knows.

Inasmuch as the absurd contains the element of coming into existence, the road of approximation will also be that which confuses the absurd fact of coming into existence, which is the object of faith, with a simple historical fact, and then seeks historical certainty for that which is absurd precisely because it contains the contradiction that something that can become historical only in direct opposition to all human understanding has become historical. This contradiction is the absurd, which can only be believed. If a historical certainty is obtained, one obtains merely the certainty that what is certain is not what is the point in question. A witness can testify that he has believed it and then testify that, far from being a historical certainty, it is in direct opposition to his understanding, but such a witness repels in the same sense as the absurd repels, and a witness who does not repel in this way is *eo ipso* a deceiver or a man who is talking about something altogether different; and such a witness can be of no help except in obtaining certainty about something altogether different. One hundred thousand individual witnesses, who by the special nature of their testimony (that they have believed the absurd) remain individual witnesses, do not become something else en masse so that the absurd becomes less absurd. Why? Because one hundred thousand people individually have believed that it was absurd? Quite the contrary, those one hundred thousand witnesses repel exactly as the absurd does.

But I do not need to develop this further here. In *Fragments* (especially where the difference between the follower at first hand and the follower at second hand is annulled) and in Part One of this book, I have with sufficient care shown that all approximation is futile, since the point is rather to do away with introductory observations, reliabilities, demonstrations from effects, and the whole mob of pawnbrokers and guarantors, in order to get the absurd clear—so that one can believe if one will—I merely say that this must be extremely strenuous.

If speculative thought wants to become involved in this and, as always, say: From the point of view of the eternal, the divine, the theocentric, there is no paradox—I shall not be able to decide whether the speculative thinker is right, because I am only a poor existing human being who neither eternally nor divinely nor theocentrically is able to observe the eternal but must be content with existing. This much, however, is certain, that with speculative thought everything goes backward, back past the Socratic, which at least comprehended that for an existing person existing is the essential; and much less has speculative thought taken the time to comprehend what it means to be *situated* in existence the way the existing person is in the imaginary construction.

The difference between the Socratic position and the position that goes beyond the Socratic is clear enough and is essentially the same as in *Fragments,* for in the latter nothing has changed, and in the former the matter has only been made somewhat more difficult, but nevertheless not more difficult than it is. It has also become somewhat more difficult because, whereas in *Fragments* I set forth the thought-category of the paradox only in an imaginary construction, here I have also latently made an attempt to make clear the necessity of the paradox, and even though the attempt is somewhat weak, it is still something different from speculatively canceling the paradox.

Christianity has itself proclaimed itself to be the eternal, essential truth that has come into existence in time; it has proclaimed itself as *the paradox* and has required the inwardness of faith with regard to what is an offense to the Jews, foolishness to the Greeks—and an absurdity to the understanding. It cannot be expressed more strongly that subjectivity is truth and that objectivity only thrusts away, precisely by virtue of the absurd, and it seems strange that Christianity should have come into the world in order to be explained, alas, as if it were itself puzzled about itself and therefore came into the world to seek out the wise man, the speculative thinker, who can aid with the explanation. It cannot be expressed more inwardly that subjectivity is truth than when subjectivity is at first untruth, and yet subjectivity is truth.

Karl Marx
1818–1883

It is hard to think of a more influential—or more controversial—nineteenth-century thinker than Karl Marx. Not content simply to develop a theory, Marx sought fundamental change in social, economic, and political structures. As he put it, "The philosophers have only *interpreted* the world in various ways; the point is, to *change it*."

Marx was the third of nine children born to Heinrich and Henrietta Marx in the Rhineland town of Trier. His parents were of Jewish ancestry but had converted to Protestant Christianity to protect Heinrich's job as a government lawyer. In 1835, Karl went to the University of Bonn to study law. Hardly the model student, he spent much of his time drinking or writing love letters to his childhood sweetheart and then fiancée, Jenny von Westphalen. At his father's insistence, Marx transferred to the University of Berlin and began to focus on his studies. While there, he abandoned his legal training and began preparing for an academic career as a philosophy professor. He wrote a dissertation contrasting Democritus and Epicurus that was accepted by the University of Jena, and in 1841 Marx received his doctorate in philosophy.

But the leftist politics Marx had adopted while in Berlin made it impossible for him to obtain a university post, so in 1842 he took a position as editor of the *Rheinische Zeitung (Rhenish Gazette)*, a liberal middle-class newspaper in Cologne. Marx was a successful editor—too successful for the government censors who suppressed the paper after an article by Marx on the poverty of the Mosel winemakers. Marx moved to Paris where he became co-editor of the new journal, the *Deutsch-Französische Jahrbücher (German-French Annals)*. With his future seeming secure, Marx finally felt free to marry Jenny in 1843. But the *Jahrbücher* closed almost immediately and once again he was unemployed. Fortunately, at about the same time, Marx received a sizable settlement from the shareholders of the *Rheinishe Zeitung,* and he and his new bride were able to live comfortably. Freed from his editing duties, Marx wrote extensively on economic and political matters. He also met the man who was to be his lifelong friend, collaborator, and financial backer: Friedrich Engels (1820–1895). Engels came from a family of wealthy textile industrialists and was, himself, the manager of his family's Manchester, England, branch. Together Marx and Engels produced *The Holy Family* (1845), Marx's first published book, which criticized a number of their fellow leftists.

While pursuing his writing projects, Marx was politically active among German communists living in Paris—activity that led to his expulsion from France in 1845. Living for a time in Brussels, Marx produced *The German Ideology* (1846) and *The Poverty of Philosophy* (1847) while continuing his political involvement. In 1847, he attended the congress of the newly formed Communist League in London. He and Engels were commissioned to produce an easy-to-read pamphlet outlining the league's doctrines. The result was the immensely influential *Manifesto of the Communist Party* (1848).

Following another attempt at editing an opposition newspaper in Cologne—and another expulsion by the government—Marx eventually settled in London. The next two decades were a time of poverty and hardship for the Marx family due as much to financial mismanagement as to lack of income. (Marx reflected often on the irony of his extensive work on capital when he had so little talent for managing it personally.) Marx received some income as a correspondent for the *New York Tribune;* but for the rest of his life, his primary source of income was Engels's gifts. In London, Marx became a fixture in the reading room of the British Museum, where he pored over government records, histories, and the writings of other economists, gathering data to document his thought. There he wrote *Critique of Political Economy* (1859) and began his *magnum opus, Das Kapital* (*Capital;* 1867). He also continued his political involvement, becoming the leader of the International Working Men's Association. He worked with the International until factional strife, particularly conflict with the anarchist Mikhail Aleksandrovich Bakunin (1814–1876), led Marx to dismantle the organization in 1872.

It wasn't until Marx's final years that he managed to gain some financial stability and to live the life of a bourgeois Victorian gentleman. But these years also brought tragedy and hardship of a different kind. Marx developed boils over his entire body and used creosote, opium, and arsenic, among other remedies, in a futile attempt to effect a cure. His beloved Jenny died in 1881 and his eldest daughter two years later. Shortly thereafter, Marx himself developed bronchitis and also died in 1883.

* * *

While a student in Berlin, Marx was influenced by Hegelian philosophy. Hegel had understood *history* as a progressive actualization of the Absolute, but he was somewhat ambiguous about the future. One group of followers, the Old Hegelians, argued in a reactionary way that this progressive actualization was now complete and that Christianity was the Absolute Religion, Hegelianism the Absolute Philosophy, and Prussia the Absolute State. Another group, the Young Hegelians, led by Bruno Bauer (1809–1882), argued that the dialectical movement of history was continuing. To move to the next stage in this historical dialectic, they sought to expose the contradictions of the existing order.

Although Marx accepted Hegel's dialectical understanding of history, he became convinced that Hegel's philosophy (and that of the Young Hegelians) devalued humanity by its emphasis on the Absolute. Marx then drew on the materialism espoused in Ludwig Feuerbach's work, *The Essence of Christianity* (1841). Feuerbach had argued that Hegel's philosophy was nothing more than rationalized religion, asserting that humans were merely the "self-alienation," or loss of identity, of God. Instead, Feuerbach advocated an atheistic materialism that claimed that "God" was simply the self-alienation of humans. That is, all the divine characteristics were nothing more than idealized human characteristics objectified and projected onto an imagined deity.

Marx used Feuerbach's work to present his criticism of Hegel. Marx expressed appreciation for Hegel's dialectical understanding of the "self-creation of man as a process" and pointed out that Hegel conceives of "objective man" as the result of "his own labor." But Hegel understood labor as being "abstract mental" labor, not the natural, embodied interaction with real objects that concerned Marx. On the other hand, although he appreciated Feuerbach's materialism, Marx held that his predecessor did not tie his criticism to historical development. "As far as Feuerbach is a materialist he does not deal with history, and as far as he considers history he is not a materialist," wrote Marx. Synthesizing the historical development of Hegel and the materialism of Feuerbach, Marx's theory has often been called "dialectical materialism" (though Marx himself did not use that term).

Marx also adapted Feuerbach's concept of alienation, applying it to political, social, and economic interactions. In the section on "Alienated Labor" from the *Economic and Philosophic Manuscripts of 1844* (given here in the Loyd D. Easton and Kurt H. Guddat translation), Marx explains how a capitalist system results in alienation for the worker. The worker's labor is alien to the worker because it belongs to the capitalist. In return for the worker's labor, the capitalist pays the worker a wage—a wage that competition keeps at a subsistence level. Yet the worker must continue to labor in order to survive. This means the worker is now self-alienated since the life activity, the essence of the worker, becomes "only a means for his existence." But alienation is not limited to individuals. Because they have different interests, workers, as an economic class, are alienated from those who own the means of production. This, in turn, gives rise to class struggle because the interests of one class are always in opposition to the interests of other economic classes. Only by having communal ownership of the means of production, that is, by abolishing private property, will such conflict be overcome. Only then will those who work control both the process and the product of their labor. The selection from *Manifesto of the Communist Party,* co-authored by Friedrich Engels and given here in the Samuel Moore translation, calls on the workers of the world to bring about such a revolutionary change in the modes of production.

Throughout his analysis of the human situation, Marx continually returned to these material forces of production, distribution, exchange, and consumption. In the preface to *A Contribution to the Critique of Political Economy,* reprinted here in the N.I. Stone translation, Marx explains how the real foundations of society are the productive forces and the relations of production. His brief overview of these forces serves as a helpful introduction to his method and program.

Marx's thought, particularly his economic theory, has faced harsh criticism since he first formulated his ideas. One recurring criticism is that Marx's theory fails to acknowledge basic human nature. Marx's nemesis within the International, Mikhail Bakunin, was one of the first to raise this objection in his book *Statehood and Anarchy.* Our final selection from Marx presents a portion of Bakunin's criticism, along with Marx's response.

* * *

Isaiah Berlin's *Karl Marx: His Life and Environment* (1963; reprinted Oxford: Oxford University Press, 1996) is still considered by many to be the best general introduction to Marx's life and philosophy, whereas more recent studies include David McLellan, *Karl Marx: His Life and Thought* (New York: Harper & Row, 1973); David McLellan, *Karl Marx* (New York: Penguin Books, 1975); Peter Singer, *Marx* (Oxford: Oxford University Press, 1980); Allen W. Wood, *Karl Marx* (London: Routledge & Kegan Paul, 1981); Jon Elster, *An Introduction to Karl Marx* (Cambridge: Cambridge University Press, 1986); and Terry Eagleton, *Marx* (London: Routledge, 1999). The following are samples of the many more recent studies in particular areas of Marx's thought: Nicholas Lash, *A Matter of Hope: A Theologian's Reflections on the Thought of Karl Marx* (Notre Dame, IN: University of Notre Dame Press, 1982); Nancy Sue Love, *Marx, Nietzsche, and Modernity* (New York: Columbia University Press, 1986); Harold Mah, *The End of Philosophy, The Origin of "Ideology": Karl Marx and the Crisis of the Young Hegelians* (Berkeley: University of California Press, 1987); Robert Meister, *Political Identity: Thinking Through Marx* (Cambridge, MA: Basil Blackwell, 1990); and G.A. Cohen, *Karl Marx's Theory of History: A Defense* (Princeton, NJ: Princeton University Press, 2000). For the complete text of Bakunin's criticism, see *Bakunin on Anarchy: Selected Works by the Activist-Founder of World Anarchism,* edited and translated by Sam Dolgoff (New York: Knopf, 1972). For collections of critical essays, see Tom Bottomore, ed., *Modern Interpretations of Marx* (Oxford: Basil Blackwell, 1981); David McLellan, ed., *Marx: The First Hundred Years* (New York: St. Martin's Press, 1983); Terence Ball and James Farr, eds., *After Marx* (Cambridge: Cambridge University Press, 1984); Terrell Carver, ed., *The Cambridge Companion to Marx* (Cambridge: Cambridge University Press, 1991); and Scott Meikle, ed., *Marx* (New York: Ashgate, 2001).

ECONOMIC AND PHILOSOPHIC MANUSCRIPTS OF 1844 (in part)

ALIENATED LABOR

We have proceeded from the presuppositions of political economy. We have accepted its language and its laws. We presupposed private property, the separation of labor, capital and land, hence of wages, profit of capital and rent, likewise the division of labor, competition, the concept of exchange value, etc. From political economy itself, in its own words, we have shown that the worker sinks to the level of a commodity, the most

Karl Marx, "Economic and Philosophic Manuscripts (1844)," translated by Lloyd D. Easton and KJurt H. Guddat, from Allen W. Wood, ed., *Marx: Selections* (New York: Macmillan, 1988).

miserable commodity; that the misery of the worker is inversely proportional to the power and volume of his production; that the necessary result of competition is the accumulation of capital in a few hands and thus the revival of monopoly in a more frightful form; and finally that the distinction between capitalist and landowner, between agricultural laborer and industrial worker, disappears and the whole society must divide into the two classes of *proprietors* and *propertyless* workers.

Political economy proceeds from the fact of private property. It does not explain private property. It grasps the actual, *material* process of private property in abstract and general formulae which it then takes as *laws.* It does not *comprehend* these laws, that is, does not prove them as proceeding from the nature of private property. Political economy does not disclose the reason for the division between capital and labor, between capital and land. When, for example, the relation of wages to profits is determined, the ultimate basis is taken to be the interest of the capitalists; that is, political economy assumes what it should develop. Similarly, competition is referred to at every point and explained from external circumstances. Political economy teaches us nothing about the extent to which these external, apparently accidental circumstances are simply the expression of a necessary development. We have seen how political economy regards exchange itself as an accidental fact. The only wheels which political economy puts in motion are *greed* and the *war among the greedy, competition.*

Just because political economy does not grasp the interconnections within the movement, the doctrine of competition could stand opposed to the doctrine of monopoly, the doctrine of freedom of craft to that of the guild, the doctrine of the division of landed property to that of the great estate. Competition, freedom of craft, and division of landed property were developed and conceived only as accidental, deliberate, forced consequences of monopoly, the guild, and feudal property, rather than necessary, inevitable, natural consequences.

We now have to grasp the essential connection among private property, greed, division of labor, capital and landownership, and the connection of exchange with competition, of value with the devaluation of men, of monopoly with competition, etc., and of this whole alienation with the *money*-system.

Let us not put ourselves in a fictitious primordial state like a political economist trying to clarify things. Such a primordial state clarifies nothing. It merely pushes the issue into a gray, misty distance. It acknowledges as a fact or event what it should deduce, namely, the necessary relation between two things for example, between division of labor and exchange. In such a manner theology explains the origin of evil by the fall of man. That is, it asserts as a fact in the form of history what it should explain.

We proceed from a *present* fact of political economy.

The worker becomes poorer the more wealth he produces, the more his production increases in power and extent. The worker becomes a cheaper commodity the more commodities he produces. The *increase in value* of the world of things is directly proportional to the *decrease in value* of the human world. Labor not only produces commodities. It also produces itself and the worker as a *commodity,* and indeed in the same proportion as it produces commodities in general.

This fact simply indicates that the object which labor produces, its product, stands opposed to it as an *alien thing,* as a *power independent* of the producer. The product of labor is labor embodied and made objective in a thing. It is the *objectification* of labor. The realization of labor is its objectification. In the viewpoint of political economy this realization of labor appears as the *diminution* of the worker, the objectification as the *loss of and subservience to the object,* and the appropriation as *alienation [Entfremdung],* as externalization *[Entäusserung].*

So much does the realization of labor appear as diminution that the worker is diminished to the point of starvation. So much does objectification appear as loss of the object that the worker is robbed of the most essential objects not only of life but also of work. Indeed, work itself becomes a thing of which he can take possession only with the greatest effort and with the most unpredictable interruptions. So much does the appropriation of the object appear as alienation that the more objects the worker produces, the fewer he can own and the more he falls under the domination of his product, of capital.

All these consequences follow from the fact that the worker is related to the *product of his labor* as to an *alien* object. For it is clear according to this premise: The more the worker exerts himself, the more powerful becomes the alien objective world which he fashions against himself, the poorer he and his inner world become, the less there is that belongs to him. It is the same in religion. The more man attributes to God, the less he retains in himself. The worker puts his life into the object; then it no longer belongs to him but to the object. The greater this activity, the poorer is the worker. What the product of his work is, he is not. The greater this product is, the smaller he is himself. The *externalization* of the worker in his product means not only that his work becomes an object, an *external* existence, but also that it exists *outside him* independently, alien, an autonomous power, opposed to him. The life he has given to the object confronts him as hostile and alien.

Let us now consider more closely the *objectification,* the worker's production and with it the *alienation* and *loss* of the object, his product.

The worker can make nothing without *nature,* without the *sensuous external world.* It is the material wherein his labor realizes itself, wherein it is active, out of which and by means of which it produces.

But as nature furnishes to labor the *means of life* in the sense that labor cannot *live* without objects upon which labor is exercised, nature also furnishes the *means of life* in the narrower sense, namely, the means of physical subsistence of the worker himself.

The more the worker *appropriates* the external world and sensuous nature through his labor, the more he deprives himself of the *means of life* in two respects: first, that the sensuous external world gradually ceases to be an object belonging to his labor, a *means of life* of his work; secondly, that it gradually ceases to be a *means of life* in the immediate sense, a means of physical subsistence of the worker.

In these two respects, therefore, the worker becomes a slave to his objects; first, in that he receives an *object of labor,* that is, he receives *labor,* and secondly that he receives the *means of subsistence.* The first enables him to exist as a *worker* and the second as a *physical subject.* The terminus of this slavery is that he can only maintain himself as a *physical subject* so far as he is a *worker,* and only as a *physical subject* is he a worker.

(The alienation of the worker in his object is expressed according to the laws of political economy as follows: the more the worker produces, the less he has to consume; the more values he creates the more worthless and unworthy he becomes; the better shaped his product, the more misshapen is he; the more civilized his product, the more barbaric is the worker; the more powerful the work, the more powerless becomes the worker; the more intelligence the work has, the more witless is the worker and the more he becomes a slave of nature.)

Political economy conceals the alienation in the nature of labor by ignoring the direct relationship between the worker (labor) *and production.* To be sure, labor produces marvels for the wealthy but it produces deprivation for the worker. It produces palaces, but hovels for the worker. It produces beauty, but mutilation for the worker. It displaces labor through machines, but it throws some workers back into barbarous labor and turns others into machines. It produces intelligence, but for the worker it produces imbecility and cretinism.

The direct relationship of labor to its products is the relationship of the worker to the objects of his production. The relationship of the rich to the objects of production and to production itself is only a *consequence* of this first relationship and confirms it. Later we shall observe the latter aspect.

Thus, when we ask, What is the essential relationship of labor? we ask about the relationship of the worker to production.

Up to now we have considered the alienation, the externalization of the *worker* only from one side: his *relationship to the products of his labor.* But alienation is shown not only in the result but also in the *process of production,* in the *producing activity* itself. How could the worker stand in an alien relationship to the product of his activity if he did not alienate himself from himself in the very act of production? After all, the product is only the résumé of activity, of production. If the product of work is externalization, production itself must be active externalization, externalization of activity, activity of externalization. Only alienation—and externalization in the activity of labor itself—is summarized in the alienation of the object of labor.

What constitutes the externalization of labor?

First is the fact that labor is *external* to the laborer—that is, it is not part of his nature—and that the worker does not affirm himself in his work but denies himself, feels miserable and unhappy, develops no free physical and mental energy but mortifies

Child factory labor, 1908, North Carolina. Young children were often used in textile mills because of their agility and dexterity. According to Marx, factory workers such as this child are alienated or cut off from (1) the products they produce, (2) their own work activities, (3) themselves, and (4) each other. (*Lewis W. Hine/Courtesy George Eastman House, International Museum of Photography.*)

his flesh and ruins his mind. The worker, therefore feels at ease only outside work, and during work he is outside himself. He is at home when he is not working and when he is working he is not at home. His work, therefore, is not voluntary, but coerced, *forced labor.* It is not the satisfaction of a need but only a *means* to satisfy other needs. Its alien character is obvious from the fact that as soon as no physical or other pressure exists, labor is avoided like the plague. External labor, labor in which man is externalized, is labor of self-sacrifice, of penance. Finally, the external nature of work for the worker appears in the fact that it is not his own but another person's, that in work he does not belong to himself but to someone else. In religion the spontaneity of human imagination, the spontaneity of the human brain and heart, acts independently of the individual as an alien, divine or devilish activity. Similarly, the activity of the worker is not his own spontaneous activity. It belongs to another. It is the loss of his own self.

The result, therefore, is that man (the worker) feels that he is acting freely only in his animal functions—eating, drinking, and procreating, or at most in his shelter and finery—while in his human functions he feels only like an animal. The animalistic becomes the human and the human the animalistic.

To be sure, eating, drinking, and procreation are genuine human functions. In abstraction, however, and separated from the remaining sphere of human activities and turned into final and sole ends, they are animal functions.

We have considered labor, the act of alienation of practical human activity, in two aspects: (1) the relationship of the worker to the *product of labor* as an alien object dominating him. This relationship is at the same time the relationship to the sensuous external world, to natural objects as an alien world hostile to him; (2) the relationship of labor to the *act of production* in *labor.* This relationship is that of the worker to his own activity as alien and not belonging to him, activity as passivity, power as weakness, procreation as emasculation, the worker's own physical and spiritual energy, his personal life—for what else is life but activity—as an activity turned against him, independent of him, and not belonging to him. *Self-alienation,* as against the alienation of the *object,* stated above.

We have now to derive a third aspect of *alienated labor* from the two previous ones.

Man is a species-being *[Gattungswesen]* not only in that he practically and theoretically makes his own species as well as that of other things his object, but also—and this is only another expression for the same thing—in that as present and living species he considers himself to be a *universal* and consequently free being.

The life of the species in man as in animals is physical in that man, (like the animal) lives by inorganic nature. And as man is more universal than the animal, the realm of inorganic nature by which he lives is more universal. As plants, animals, minerals, air, light, etc., in theory form a part of human consciousness, partly as objects of natural science, partly as objects of art—his spiritual inorganic nature or spiritual means of life which he first must prepare for enjoyment and assimilation—so they also form in practice a part of human life and human activity. Man lives physically only by these products of nature; they may appear in the form of food, heat, clothing, housing, etc. The universality of man appears in practice in the universality which makes the whole of nature his inorganic body: (1) as a direct means of life, and (2) as the matter, object, and instrument of his life activity. Nature is the *inorganic body* of man, that is, nature insofar as it is not the human body. Man *lives* by nature. This means that nature is his *body* with which he must remain in perpetual process in order not to die. That the physical and spiritual life of man is tied up with nature is another way of saying that nature is linked to itself, for man is a part of nature.

In alienating (1) nature from man, and (2) man from himself, his own active function, his life activity, alienated labor also alienates the *species* from him; it makes *species-life* the means of individual life. In the first place it alienates *species-life* and the individual life, and secondly it turns the latter in its abstraction into the purpose of the former, also in its abstract and alienated form.

For labor, *life activity,* and *productive life* appear to man at first only as a *means* to satisfy a need, the need to maintain physical existence. Productive life, however, is species-life. It is life begetting life. In the mode of life activity lies the entire character of a species, its species-character; and free conscious activity is the species-character of man. Life itself appears only as a *means of life.*

The animal is immediately one with its life activity, not distinct from it. The animal is *its life activity.* Man makes his life activity itself into an object of will and consciousness. He has conscious life activity. It is not a determination with which he immediately identifies. Conscious life activity distinguishes man immediately from the life activity of the animal. Only thereby is he a species-being. Or rather, he is only a conscious being—that is, his own life is an object for him—since he is a species-being. Only on that account is his activity free activity. Alienated labor reverses the relationship in that man; since he is a conscious being, makes his life activity, his *essence,*only a means for his existence.

The practical creation of an *objective world,* the *treatment* of inorganic nature, is proof that man is a conscious species-being, that is, a being which is related to its species as to its own essence or is related to itself as a species-being. To be sure animals also produce. They build themselves nests, dwelling places, like the bees, beavers, ants, etc. But the animal produces only what is immediately necessary for itself or its young. It produces in a one-sided way while man produces universally. The animal produces under the domination of immediate physical need while man produces free of physical need and only genuinely so in freedom from such need. The animal only produces itself while man reproduces the whole of nature. The animal's product belongs immediately to its physical body while man is free when he confronts his product. The animal builds only according to the standard and need of the species to which it belongs while man knows how to produce according to the standard of any species and at all times knows how to apply an intrinsic standard to the object. Thus man creates also according to the laws of beauty.

In the treatment of the objective world, therefore, man proves himself to be genuinely a *species-being.* This production is his active species-life. Through it nature appears as *his* work and his actuality. The object of labor is thus the *objectification of man's species-life:* he produces himself not only intellectually, as in consciousness, but also actively in a real sense and sees himself in a world he made. In taking from man the object of his production, alienated labor takes from his *species-life,* his actual and objective existence as a species. It changes his superiority to the animal to inferiority, since he is deprived of nature, his inorganic body.

By degrading free spontaneous activity to the level of a means, alienated labor makes the species-life of man a means of his physical existence.

The consciousness which man has from his species is altered through alienation, so that species-life becomes a means for him.

(3) Alienated labor hence turns the *species-existence of man,* and also nature as his mental species-capacity, into an existence *alien* to him, into the *means* of his *individual existence.* It alienates his spiritual nature, his *human essence,* from his own body and likewise from nature outside him.

(4) A direct consequence of man's alienation from the product of his work, from his life activity, and from his species-existence, is the *alienation of man* from *man.* When man confronts himself, he confronts *other* men. What holds true of man's relationship to his work, to the product of his work, and to himself, also holds true of man's relationship to other men, to their labor, and the object of their labor.

In general, the statement that man is alienated from his species-existence means that one man is alienated from another just as each man is alienated from human nature.

The alienation of man, the relation of man to himself, is realized and expressed in the relation between man and other men.

Thus in the relation of alienated labor every man sees the others according to the standard and the relation in which he finds himself as a worker.

We began with an economic fact, the alienation of the worker and his product. We have given expression to the concept of this fact: *alienated, externalized* labor. We have analyzed this concept and have thus analyzed merely a fact of political economy.

Let us now see further how the concept of alienated, externalized labor must express and represent itself in actuality.

If the product of labor is alien to me, confronts me as an alien power, to whom then does it belong?

If my own activity does not belong to me, if it is an alien and forced activity, to whom then does it belong?

To a being *other* than myself.

Who is this being?

Gods? To be sure, in early times the main production, for example, the building of temples in Egypt, India, and Mexico, appears to be in the service of the gods, just as the product belongs to the gods. But gods alone were never workmasters. The same is true of *nature.* And what a contradiction it would be if the more man subjugates nature through his work and the more the miracles of gods are rendered superfluous by the marvels of industry, man should renounce his joy in producing and the enjoyment of his product for love of these powers.

The *alien* being who owns labor and the product of labor, whom labor serves and whom the product of labor satisfies can only be *man* himself.

That the product of labor does not belong to the worker and an alien power confronts him is possible only because this product belongs to *a man other than the worker.* If his activity is torment for him, it must be the pleasure and the lifeenjoyment for another. Not gods, not nature, but only man himself can be this alien power over man.

Let us consider the statement previously made, that the relationship of man to himself is *objective* and *actual* to him only through his relationship to other men. If man is related to the product of his labor, to his objectified labor, as to an *alien,* hostile, powerful object independent of him, he is so related that another alien, hostile, powerful man independent of him is the lord of this object. If he is unfree in relation to his own activity, he is related to it as bonded activity, activity under the domination, coercion, and yoke of another man.

Every self-alienation of man, from himself and from nature, appears in the relationship which he postulates between other men and himself and nature. Thus religious self-alienation appears necessarily in the relation of laity to priest, or also to a mediator, since we are here now concerned with the spiritual world. In the practical real world self-alienation can appear only in the practical real relationships to other men. The means whereby the alienation proceeds is a *practical* means. Through alienated labor man thus not only produces his relationship to the object and to the act of production as an alien man at enmity with him. He also creates the relation in which other men stand to his production and product, and the relation in which he stands to these other men. just as he begets his own production as loss of his reality, as his punishment; just as he begets his own product, as a loss, a product not belonging to him, so he begets the domination of the nonproducer over production and over product. As he alienates his own activity from himself, he confers upon the stranger an activity which is not his own.

Up to this point, we have investigated the relationship only from the side of the worker and will later investigate it also from the side of the non-worker.

Thus through *alienated externalized* labor does the worker create the relation to this work of man alienated to labor and standing outside it. The relation of the worker to labor produces the relation of the capitalist to labor, or whatever one wishes to call the lord of labor. *Private property* is thus product, result, and necessary consequence of *externalized labor,* of the external relation of the worker to nature and to himself.

Private property thus is derived, through analysis, from the concept of *externalized labor,* that is, *externalized man,* alienated labor, alienated life, and *alienated* man.

We have obtained the concept of *externalized labor (externalized life)* from political economy as a result of the *movement of private property.* But the analysis of this idea shows that though private property appears to be the ground and cause of externalized labor, it is rather a consequence of externalized labor, just as gods are *originally* not the cause but the effect of an aberration of the human mind. Later this relationship reverses.

Only at the final culmination of the development of private property does this, its secret, reappear—namely, that on the one hand it is the *product* of externalized labor and that secondly it is the *means* through which labor externalizes itself, the *realization of this externalization.*

This development throws light on several conflicts hitherto unresolved.

(1) Political economy proceeds from labor as the very soul of production and yet gives labor nothing, private property everything. From this contradiction Proudhon decided in favor of labor and against private property. We perceive, however, that this apparent contradiction is the contradiction of *alienated labor* with itself and that political economy has only formulated the laws of alienated labor.

Therefore we also perceive that *wages* and *private property* are identical: for when the product, the object of labor, pays for the labor itself, wages are only a necessary consequence of the alienation of labor. In wages labor appears not as an end in itself but as the servant of wages. We shall develop this later and now only draw some conclusions.

An enforced *raising of wages* (disregarding all other difficulties, including that this anomaly could only be maintained forcibly) would therefore be nothing but a *better slave-salary* and would not achieve either for the worker or for labor human significance and dignity.

Even the *equality of wages,* as advanced by Proudhon, would only convert the relation of the contemporary worker to his work into the relation of all men to labor.* Society would then be conceived as an abstract capitalist.

Wages are a direct result of alienated labor, and alienated labor is the direct cause of private property. The downfall of one is necessarily the downfall of the other.

(2) From the relation of alienated labor to private property it follows further that the emancipation of society from private property, etc., from servitude, is expressed in its *political* form as the *emancipation of workers,* not as though it is only a question of their emancipation but because in their emancipation is contained universal human emancipation. It is contained in their emancipation because the whole of human servitude is involved in the relation of worker to production, and all relations of servitude are only modifications and consequences of the worker's relation to production.

As we have found the concept of *private property* through *analysis* from the concept of *alienated, externalized labor,* so we can develop all the *categories* of political

*[Pierre-Joseph Proudhon (1809–1865), French socialist writer and precursor of anarchism, author of *What Is Property?* (1841).]

economy with the aid of these two factors, and we shall again find in each category—for example, barter, competition, capital, money—only a *particular* and *developed expression* of these primary foundations.

Before considering this configuration, however, let us try to solve two problems.

(1) To determine the general *nature of private property* as a result of alienated labor in its relation to *truly human* and *social property.*

(2) We have taken the *alienation of labor* and its *externalization* as a fact and analyzed this fact. How, we ask now, does it happen that *man externalizes* his *labor,* alienates it? How is this alienation rooted in the nature of human development? We have already achieved much in resolving the problem by *transforming* the question concerning the *origin of private property* into the question concerning the relationship of *externalized labor* to evolution of humanity. In talking about *private property* one believes he is dealing with something external to man. Talking of labor, one is immediately dealing with man himself. This new formulation of the problem already contains its solution.

On (1) *The general nature of private property and its relation to truly human property.*

We have resolved alienated labor into two parts which mutually determine each other or rather are only different expressions of one and the same relationship. *Appropriation* appears as *alienation,* as *externalization; externalization* as *appropriation; alienation* as the true *naturalization.*

We considered the one side, *externalized* labor, in relation to the *worker* himself, that is, the *relation of externalized labor to itself.* We have found the *property relation of the non-worker* to the *worker* and *labor* to be the product, the necessary result, of this relationship. *Private property* as the material, summarized expression of externalized labor embraces both relationships—the *relationship of worker to labor, the product of his work, and the non-worker,* and the relationship of the *non-worker to the worker* and *the product of his labor.*

As we have seen that in relation to the worker who *appropriates* nature through his labor the appropriation appears as alienation—self-activity as activity for another and of another, living as the sacrifice of life, production of the object as loss of it to an alien power, an *alien* man—we now consider the relationship of this *alien* man to the worker, to labor and its object.

It should be noted first that everything which appears with the worker as an *activity of externalization* and an *activity of alienation* appears with the non-worker as a *condition of externalization,* a *condition of alienation.*

Secondly, that the *actual, practical attitude* of the worker in production and to his product (as a condition of mind) appears as a *theoretical* attitude in the non-worker confronting him.

Thirdly, the non-worker does everything against the worker which the worker does against himself, but he does not do against his own self what he does against the worker.*

Let us consider more closely these three relationships.

[Here the manuscript breaks off, unfinished.]

*[This paragraph is an allusion to Hegel's famous discussion of the "master and servant" in *Phenomenology of Spirit.* "Solely being-for-himself is the [master's] essence; he is the pure negative power to which the thing is nothing, and hence the pure essential doing in this situation; while the servant is not a pure doing, but an inessential one. But for true recognition there is lacking the moment that what the master does to the other he also does to himself, and what the servant does to himself he also does to the other." (See page 914.)]

MANIFESTO OF THE COMMUNIST PARTY (in part)

A spectre is haunting Europe—the spectre of Communism. All the powers of old Europe have entered into a holy alliance to exorcise this spectre: Pope and Czar, Metternich and Guizot, French Radicals and German police spies.

Where is the party in opposition that has not been decried as communistic by its opponents in power? Where the opposition that has not hurled back the branding reproach of Communism against the more advanced opposition parties, as well as against its reactionary adversaries?

Two things result from this fact:

I. Communism is already acknowledged by all European powers to be itself a power.
II. It is high time that Communists should openly, in the face of the whole world, publish their views, their aims, their tendencies, and meet this nursery tale of the spectre of Communism with a manifesto of the party itself.

To this end, Communists of various nationalities have assembled in London and sketched the following manifesto, to be published in the English, French, German, Italian, Flemish, and Danish languages.

CHAPTER I: BOURGEOIS AND PROLETARIANS*

The History of all hitherto existing society** is the history of class struggles.

Freeman and slave, patrician and plebeian, lord and serf, guild-master*** and journeyman, in a word, oppressor and oppressed stood in constant opposition to one another, carried on an uninterrupted, now hidden, now open fight, a fight that each time ended either in a revolutionary reconstitution of society at large, or in the common ruin of the contending classes.

In the earlier epochs of history we find almost everywhere a complicated arrangement of society into various orders, a manifold gradation of social rank. In ancient Rome we have patricians, knights, plebeians, slaves; in the Middle Ages, feudal lords, vassals, guild-masters, journeymen, apprentices, serfs; in almost all of these classes, again, subordinate gradations.

*By *bourgeoisie* is meant the class of modern capitalists, owners of the means of social production, and employers of wage labor; by *proletariat,* the class of modern wage laborers who, having no means of production of their own, are reduced to selling their labor power in order to live.

**That is, all *written* history. In 1837, the pre-history of society, the social organization existing previous to recorded history, was all but unknown. Since then Haxthausen discovered common ownership of land in Russia; Maurer proved it to be the social foundation from which all Teutonic races started in history, and, by and by, village communities were found to be, or to have been, the primitive form of society everywhere from India to Ireland. The inner organization of this primitive communistic society was laid bare, in its typical form, by Morgan's crowning discovery of the true nature of the *gens* and its relation to the *tribe.* With the dissolution of these primeval communities society begins to be differentiated into separate and finally antagonistic classes. I have attempted to retrace this process of dissolution in *The Origin of the Family, Private Property and the State.*

***[Guild-master, that is, a full member of a guild, a master within, not a head of a guild.]

The modern bourgeois society that has sprouted from the ruins of feudal society has not done away with class antagonisms. It has but established new classes, new conditions of oppression, new forms of struggle in place of the old ones.

Our epoch, the epoch of the bourgeoisie, possesses, however, this distinctive feature: it has simplified the class antagonisms. Society as a whole is more and more splitting up into two great hostile camps, into two great classes directly facing each other—bourgeoisie and proletariat.

From the serfs of the Middle Ages sprang the chartered burghers of the earliest towns. From these burgesses the first elements of the bourgeoisie were developed.

The discovery of America, the rounding of the Cape, opened up fresh ground for the rising bourgeoisie. The East Indian and Chinese markets, the colonization of America, trade with the colonies, the increase in the means of exchange and in commodities generally, gave to commerce, to navigation, to industry, an impulse never before known, and thereby, to the revolutionary element in the tottering feudal society, a rapid development.

The feudal system of industry, in which industrial production was monopolized by closed guilds, now no longer sufficed for the growing wants of the new markets. The manufacturing system took its place. The guild-masters were pushed aside by the manufacturing middle class; division of labor between the different corporate guilds vanished in the face of division of labor in each single workshop.

Meantime the markets kept ever growing, the demand ever rising. Even manufacture no longer sufficed. Thereupon, steam and machinery revolutionized industrial production. The place of manufacture was taken by the giant, modern industry, the place of the industrial middle class, by industrial millionaires—the leaders of whole industrial armies, the modern bourgeois.

Modern industry has established the world market, for which the discovery of America paved the way. This market has given an immense development to commerce, to navigation, to communication by land. This development has, in its turn, reacted on the extension of industry; and in proportion as industry, commerce, navigation, railways extended, in the same proportion the bourgeoisie developed, increased its capital, and pushed into the background every class handed down from the Middle Ages.

We see, therefore, how the modern bourgeoisie is itself the product of a long course of development, of a series of revolutions in the modes of production and of exchange.

Each step in the development of the bourgeoisie was accompanied by a corresponding political advance of that class. An oppressed class under the sway of the feudal nobility, it became an armed and self-governing association in the medieval commune:* here independent urban republic (as in Italy and Germany); there, taxable "third estate" of the monarchy (as in France); afterwards, in the period of manufacture proper, serving either the semi-feudal or the absolute monarchy as a counterpoise against the nobility, and, in fact, cornerstone of the great monarchies in general. The bourgeoisie has at last, since the establishment of modern industry and of the world market, conquered for itself, in the modern representative state, exclusive political sway. The executive of the modern state is but a committee for managing the common affairs of the whole bourgeoisie.

The bourgeoisie has played a most revolutionary role in history.

*"Commune" was the name taken in France by the nascent towns even before they had conquered from their feudal lords and masters local self-government and political rights as the "Third Estate." Generally speaking, for the economic development of the bourgeoisie, England is here taken as the typical country; for its political development, France.

The bourgeoisie, wherever it has got the upper hand, has put an end to all feudal, patriarchal, idyllic relations. It has pitilessly torn asunder the motley feudal ties that bound man to his "natural superiors," and has left no other bond between man and man than naked self-interest, than callous "cash payment." It has drowned the most heavenly ecstasies of religious fervor, of chivalrous enthusiasm, of philistine sentimentalism, in the icy water of egotistical calculation. It has resolved personal worth into exchange value, and in place of the numberless indefeasible chartered freedoms has set up that single, unconscionable freedom—Free Trade. In one word, for exploitation, veiled by religious and political illusions, it has substituted naked, shameless, direct, brutal exploitation.

The bourgeoisie has stripped of its halo every occupation hitherto honored and looked up to with reverent awe. It has converted the physician, the lawyer, the priest, the poet, the man of science, into its paid wage laborers.

The bourgeoisie has torn away from the family its sentimental veil, and has reduced the family relation to a mere money relation.

The bourgeoisie has disclosed how it came to pass that the brutal display of vigor in the Middle Ages which reactionaries so much admire found its fitting complement in the most slothful indolence. It has been the first to show what man's activity can bring about. It has accomplished wonders far surpassing Egyptian pyramids, Roman aqueducts, and Gothic cathedrals; it has conducted expeditions that put in the shade all former migrations of nations and crusades.

The bourgeoisie cannot exist without constantly revolutionizing the instruments of production, and thereby the relations of production, and with them the whole relations of society. Conservation of the old modes of production in unaltered form was, on the contrary, the first condition of existence for all earlier industrial classes. Constant revolutionizing of production, uninterrupted disturbance of all social conditions, everlasting uncertainty and agitation distinguish the bourgeois epoch from all earlier ones. All fixed, fast-frozen relations with their train of ancient and venerable prejudices and opinions are swept away; all new-formed ones become antiquated before they can ossify. All that is solid melts in air, all that is holy is profaned, and man is at last compelled to face with sober senses his real conditions of life and his relations with his kind.

The need of a constantly expanding market for its products chases the bourgeoisie over the whole surface of the globe. It must nestle everywhere, settle everywhere, establish connections everywhere.

The bourgeoisie has through its exploitation of the world market given a cosmopolitan character to production and consumption in every country. To the great chagrin of reactionaries it has drawn from under the feet of industry the national ground on which it stood. All old-established national industries have been destroyed or are daily being destroyed. They are dislodged by new industries whose introduction becomes a life and death question for all civilized nations; by industries that no longer work up indigenous raw material, but raw material drawn from the remotest zones; industries whose products are consumed, not only at home, but in every quarter of the globe. In place of the old wants, satisfied by the production of the country, we find new wants, requiring for their satisfaction the products of distant lands and climes. In place of the old local and national seclusion and self-sufficiency we have intercourse in every direction, universal inter-dependence of nations. And as in material, so also in intellectual production. The intellectual creations of individual nations become common property. National one-sidedness and narrow-mindedness become more and more impossible, and from the numerous national and local literatures there arises a world literature.

The bourgeoisie, by the rapid improvement of all instruments of production, by the immensely facilitated means of communication, draws all nations, even the most barbarian, into civilization. The cheap prices of its commodities are the heavy artillery with which it batters down all Chinese walls, with which it forces the barbarians' intensely obstinate hatred of foreigners to capitulate. It compels all nations, on pain of extinction, to adopt the bourgeois mode of production; it compels them to introduce what it calls civilization into their midst, i.e., to become bourgeois themselves. In a word, it creates a world after its own image.

The bourgeoisie has subjected the country to the rule of the towns. It has created enormous cities, has greatly increased the urban population as compared with the rural, and has thus rescued a considerable part of the population from the idiocy of rural life. Just as it has made the country dependent on the towns, so it has made barbarian and semi-barbarian countries dependent on the civilized ones, nations of peasants on nations of bourgeois, the East on the West.

More and more the bourgeoisie keeps doing away with the scattered state of the population, of the means of production, and of property. It has agglomerated population, centralized means of production, and has concentrated property in a few hands. The necessary consequence of this was political centralization. Independent, or but loosely connected provinces, with separate interests, laws, governments and systems of taxation, became lumped together into one nation, with one government, one code of laws, one national class interest, one frontier and one customs tariff.

The bourgeoisie during its rule of scarce one hundred years has created more massive and more colossal productive forces than have all preceding generations together. Subjection of nature's forces to man, machinery, application of chemistry to industry and agriculture, steam-navigation, railways, electric telegraphs, clearing of whole continents for cultivation, canalization of rivers, whole populations conjured out of the ground—what earlier century had even a presentiment that such productive forces slumbered in the lap of social labor?

We see, then, that the means of production and of exchange which served as the foundation for the growth of the bourgeoisie were generated in feudal society. At a certain stage in the development of these means of production and of exchange, the conditions under which feudal society produced and exchanged, the feudal organization of agriculture and manufacturing industry, in a word, the feudal relations of property became no longer compatible with the already developed productive forces; they became so many fetters. They had to be burst asunder; they were burst asunder.

Into their place stepped free competition, accompanied by a social and political constitution adapted to it, and by the economic and political sway of the bourgeois class.

A similar movement is going on before our own eyes. Modern bourgeois society with its relations of production, of exchange and of property, a society that has conjured up such gigantic means of production and of exchange, is like the sorcerer who is no longer able to control the powers of the nether world whom he has called up by his spells. For many a decade past the history of industry and commerce is but the history of the revolt of modern productive forces against modern conditions of production, against the property relations that are the conditions for the existence of the bourgeoisie and of its rule. It is enough to mention the commercial crises that by their periodical return put the existence of the entire bourgeois society on trial, each time more threateningly. In these crises a great part not only of the existing products, but also of the previously created productive forces, are periodically destroyed. In these crises there breaks out an epidemic that, in all earlier epochs, would have seemed an absurdity—the epidemic of over-production. Society suddenly finds itself put back into a state of momentary barbarism; it appears as if a famine, a universal war of devastation had cut off the supply of every means of subsistence; industry and commerce seem to be destroyed. And why? Because there is too much civilization, too much means of subsistence, too much industry, too much commerce. The productive forces at the disposal of society no longer tend to further the development of the conditions of bourgeois property; on the contrary, they have become too powerful for these conditions, by which they are fettered, and no sooner do they overcome these fetters than they bring disorder into the whole of bourgeois society, endanger the existence of bourgeois property. The conditions of bourgeois society are too narrow to comprise the wealth created by them. And how does the bourgeoisie get over these crises? On the one hand by enforced destruction of a mass of productive forces; on the other, by the conquest of new markets and by the more thorough exploitation of the old ones. That is to say, by paving the way for more extensive and more destructive crises, and by diminishing the means whereby crises are prevented.

The weapons with which the bourgeoisie felled feudalism to the ground are now turned against the bourgeoisie itself.

But not only has the bourgeoisie forged the weapons that bring death to itself; it has also called into existence the men who are to wield those weapons—the modern working class, the proletarians.

In proportion as the bourgeoisie, i.e., capital, is developed, in the same proportion is the proletariat, the modern working class, developed—a class of laborers, who live only so long as they find work, and who find work only so long as their labor increases capital. These laborers, who must sell themselves piecemeal, are a commodity like every other article of commerce, and are consequently exposed to all the vicissitudes of competition, to all the fluctuations of the market.

Owing to the extensive use of machinery and to division of labor, the work of the proletarians has lost all individual character, and, consequently all charm for the workman. He becomes an appendage of the machine, and it is only the most simple, most monotonous, and most easily acquired knack that is required of him. Hence, the cost of production of a workman is restricted almost entirely to the means of subsistence that he requires for his maintenance and for the propagation of his race. But the price of a commodity, and therefore also of labor, is equal to its cost of production. In proportion, therefore, as the repulsiveness of the work increases, the wage decreases. Nay more, in proportion the burden of toil also increases, whether by prolongation of the working hours, by increase of the work exacted in a given time, or by increased speed of the machinery, etc.

Modern industry has converted the little workshop of the patriarchal master into the great factory of the industrial capitalist. Masses of laborers, crowded into the factory, are organized like soldiers. As privates of the industrial army they are placed under the command of a perfect hierarchy of officers and sergeants. Not only are they slaves of the bourgeois class and of the bourgeois state; they are daily and hourly enslaved by the machine, by the overseer, and, above all, by the individual bourgeois manufacturer himself. The more openly this despotism proclaims gain to be its end and aim, the more petty, the more hateful, and the more embittering it is.

The less the skill and exertion of strength implied in manual labor—in other words, the more modern industry develops—the more is the labor of men superseded by that of women. Differences of age and sex have no longer any distinctive social validity for the working class. All are instruments of labor, more or less expensive to use, according to their age and sex.

No sooner has the laborer received his wages in cash, for the moment escaping exploitation by the manufacturer, than he is set upon by the other portions of the bourgeoisie—the landlord, the shopkeeper, the pawnbroker, etc.

The lower strata of the middle class—the small tradespeople, shopkeepers, and retired tradesmen generally, the handicraftsmen and peasants—all these sink gradually into the proletariat, partly because their diminutive capital does not suffice for the scale on which modern industry is carried on and is swamped in the competition with the large capitalists, partly because their specialized skill is rendered worthless by new methods of production. Thus the proletariat is recruited from all classes of the population.

The proletariat goes through various stages of development. With its birth begins its struggle with the bourgeoisie. At first the contest is carried on by individual laborers, then by the workpeople of a factory, then by the operatives of one trade, in one locality, against the individual bourgeois who directly exploits them. They direct their attacks not against the bourgeois conditions of production, but against the instruments of production themselves; they destroy imported wares that compete with their labor, they smash machinery to pieces, they set factories ablaze, they seek to restore by force the vanished status of the workman of the Middle Ages.

At this stage the laborers still form an incoherent mass scattered over the whole country, and broken up by their mutual competition. If anywhere they unite to form more compact bodies, this is not yet the consequence of their own active union, but of the union of the bourgeoisie, which class, in order to attain its own political ends, is compelled to set the whole proletariat in motion, and is, moreover, still able to do so for a time. At this stage, therefore, the proletarians do not fight their enemies, but the enemies of their enemies, the remnants of absolute monarchy, the landowners, the non-industrial bourgeois, the petty bourgeoisie. Thus the whole historical movement is concentrated in the hands of the bourgeoisie; every victory so obtained is a victory for the bourgeoisie.

But with the development of industry the proletariat not only increases in number; it becomes concentrated in greater masses, its strength grows, and it feels that strength more. The various interests and conditions of life within the ranks of the proletariat are more and more equalized, in proportion as machinery obliterates all distinctions of labor and nearly everywhere reduces wages to the same low level. The growing competition among the bourgeois and the resulting commercial crises make the wages of the workers ever more fluctuating. The unceasing improvement of machinery, ever more rapidly developing, makes their livelihood more and more precarious; the collisions between individual workmen and individual bourgeois take more and more the character of collisions between two classes. Thereupon the workers begin to form combinations (trade unions) against the bourgeoisie; they club together in order to keep up the rate of wages; they found permanent associations in order to make provision beforehand for these occasional revolts. Here and there the contest breaks out into riots.

Now and then the workers are victorious, but only for a time. The real fruit of their battles lies not in the immediate result but in the ever expanding union of the workers. This union is furthered by the improved means of communication which are created by modern industry, and which place the workers of different localities in contact with one another. It was just this contact that was needed to centralize the numerous local struggles, all of the same character, into one national struggle between classes. But every class struggle is a political struggle. And that union, which the burghers of the Middle Ages, with their miserable highways, required centuries to attain, the modern proletarians, thanks to railways achieve in a few years.

This organization of the proletarians into a class, and consequently into a political party, is continually being upset again by the competition between the workers themselves. But it ever rises up again, stronger, firmer, mightier. It compels legislative recognition of particular interests of the workers by taking advantage of the divisions among the bourgeoisie itself. Thus the Ten Hour bill in England was carried.

Altogether, collisions between the classes of the old society further the course of development of the proletariat in many ways. The bourgeoisie finds itself involved in a constant battle—at first with the aristocracy; later on, with those portions of the bourgeoisie itself whose interests have become antagonistic to the progress of industry; at all times with the bourgeoisie of foreign countries. In all these battles it sees itself compelled to appeal to the proletariat, to ask for its help, and thus to drag it into the political arena. The bourgeoisie itself, therefore, supplies the proletariat with its own elements of political and general education; in other words, it furnishes the proletariat with weapons for fighting the bourgeoisie.

Further, as we have already seen, entire sections of the ruling classes are, by the advance of industry, precipitated into the proletariat, or are at least threatened in their conditions of existence. These also supply the proletariat with fresh elements of enlightenment and progress.

Finally, in times when the class struggle nears the decisive hour, the process of dissolution going on within the ruling class, in fact within the whole range of old society, assumes such a violent, glaring character that a small section of the ruling class cuts itself adrift and joins the revolutionary class, the class that holds the future in its hands. Just as, therefore, at an earlier period a section of the nobility went over to the bourgeoisie, so now a portion of the bourgeoisie goes over to the proletariat, and in particular, a portion of the bourgeois ideologists who have raised themselves to the level of comprehending theoretically the historical movement as a whole.

Of all the classes that stand face to face with the bourgeoisie today, the proletariat alone is a really revolutionary class. The other classes decay and finally disappear in the face of modern industry; the proletariat is its special and essential product.

The lower middle class, the small manufacturer, the shopkeeper, the artisan, the peasant—all these fight against the bourgeoisie, to save from extinction their existence as fractions of the middle class. They are, therefore, not revolutionary but conservative. Nay more, they are reactionary, for they try to roll back the wheel of history. If by chance they are revolutionary they are so only in view of their impending transfer into the proletariat; they thus defend not their present but their future interests; they desert their own standpoint to adopt that of the proletariat.

The "dangerous class," the social scum *(Lumpenproletariat),* that passively rotting mass thrown off by the lowest layers of old society, may here and there be swept into the movement by a proletarian revolution; its conditions of life, however, prepare it far more for the part of a bribed tool of reactionary intrigue.

The social conditions of the old society no longer exist for the proletariat. The proletarian is without property; his relation to his wife and children has no longer anything in common with bourgeois family relations; modern industrial labor, modern subjection to capital, the same in England as in France, in America as in Germany, has stripped him of every trace of national character. Law, morality, religion are to him so many bourgeois prejudices, behind which lurk in ambush just as many bourgeois interests.

All the preceding classes that got the upper hand sought to fortify their already acquired status by subjecting society at large to their conditions of appropriation. The proletarians cannot become masters of the productive forces of society except by abolishing their own previous mode of appropriation, and thereby also every other previous mode of appropriation. They have nothing of their own to secure and to fortify; their mission is to destroy all previous securities for, and insurances of, individual property.

All previous historical movements were movements of minorities, or in the interest of minorities. The proletarian movement is the self-conscious, independent movement of the immense majority, in the interest of the immense majority. The proletariat, the lowest stratum of our present society, cannot stir, cannot raise itself up, without the whole superincumbent strata of official society being sprung into the air.

Though not in substance, yet in form, the struggle of the proletariat with the bourgeoisie is at first a national struggle. The proletariat of each country must, of course, first of all settle matters with its own bourgeoisie.

In depicting the most general phases of the development of the proletariat we traced the more or less veiled civil war raging within existing society, up to the point where that war breaks out into open revolution, and where the violent overthrow of the bourgeoisie lays the foundation for the sway of the proletariat.

Hitherto, every form of society has been based, as we have already seen, on the antagonism of oppressing and oppressed classes. But in order to oppress a class certain conditions must be assured to it under which it can, at least, continue its slavish existence. The serf, in the period of serfdom, raised himself to membership in the commune, just as the petty bourgeois, under the yoke of feudal absolutism, managed to develop into a bourgeois. The modern laborer, on the contrary, instead of rising with the progress of industry, sinks deeper and deeper below the conditions of existence of his own class. He becomes a pauper, and pauperism develops more rapidly than population and wealth. And here it becomes evident that the bourgeoisie is unfit any longer to be the ruling class in society and to impose its conditions of existence upon society as an overriding law. It is unfit to rule because it is incompetent to assure an existence to its slave within his slavery, because it cannot help letting him sink into such a state that it has to feed him, instead of being fed by him. Society can no longer live under this bourgeoisie, in other words, its existence is no longer compatible with society.

The essential condition for the existence and sway of the bourgeois class is the formation and augmentation of capital; the condition for capital is wage labor. Wage labor rests exclusively on competition between the laborers. The advance of industry, whose involuntary promoter is the bourgeoisie, replaces the isolation of the laborers, due to competition, by their revolutionary combination, due to association. The development of modern industry, therefore, cuts from under its feet the very foundation on which the bourgeoisie produces and appropriates products. What the bourgeoisie, therefore, produces above all are its own grave-diggers. Its fall and the victory of the proletariat are equally inevitable.

* * *

[The specific measures called for by the Communist Party] will, of course, be different in different countries.

Nevertheless, in the most advanced countries the following will be pretty generally applicable:

1. Abolition of property in land and application of all rents of land to public purposes.
2. A heavy progressive or graduated income tax.
3. Abolition of all right of inheritance.
4. Confiscation of the property of all emigrants and rebels.

5. Centralization of credit in the hands of the state by means of a national bank with state capital and an exclusive monopoly.
6. Centralization of the means of communication and transport in the hands of the state.
7. Extension of factories and instruments of production owned by the state; the bringing into cultivation of waste lands, and the improvement of the soil generally in accordance with a common plan.
8. Equal obligation of all to work. Establishment of industrial armies, especially for agriculture.
9. Combination of agriculture with manufacturing industries; gradual abolition of the distinction between town and country by a more equable distribution of the population over the country.
10. Free education for all children in public schools. Abolition of child factory labor in its present form. Combination of education with industrial production, etc.

* * *

The Communists disdain to conceal their views and aims. They openly declare that their ends can be attained only by the forcible overthrow of all existing social conditions. Let the ruling classes tremble at a Communist revolution. The proletarians have nothing to lose but their chains. They have a world to win.

Workingmen of all countries, unite!

"Capital and Labour," cartoon from *Punch* magazine, 1843. The cartoon shows the suffering of the workers and their families that makes possible the bourgeois capitalists' high life. It was in response to conditions such as this that Marx and Engels wrote in *The Communist Manifesto* (1848), "The proletarians have nothing to lose but their chains. They have a world to win. Workingmen of all countries, unite!" (©*Iberfoto/Iberfoto*)

A CONTRIBUTION TO THE CRITIQUE OF POLITICAL ECONOMY (in part)

AUTHOR'S PREFACE

In the social production which men carry on they enter into definite relations that are indispensable and independent of their will; these relations of production correspond to a definite stage of development of their material powers of production. The sum total of these relations of production constitutes the economic structure of society—the real foundation, on which rise legal and political superstructures and to which correspond definite forms of social consciousness. The mode of production in material life determines the general character of the social, political and spiritual processes of life. It is not the consciousness of men that determines their existence, but, on the contrary, their social existence determines their consciousness. At a certain stage of their development, the material forces of production in society come in conflict with the existing relations of production, or—what is but a legal expression for the same thing—with the property relations within which they had been at work before. From forms of development of the forces of production these relations turn into their fetters. Then comes the period of social revolution. With the change of the economic foundation the entire immense superstructure is more or less rapidly transformed. In considering such transformations the distinction should always be made between the material transformation of the economic conditions of production which can be determined with the precision of natural science, and the legal, political, religious, aesthetic or philosophic—in short ideological forms in which men become conscious of this conflict and fight it out. Just as our opinion of an individual is not based on what he thinks of himself, so can we not judge of such a period of transformation by its own consciousness; on the contrary, this consciousness must rather be explained from the contradictions of material life, from the existing conflict between the social forces of production and the relations of production. No social order ever disappears before all the productive forces, for which there is room in it, have been developed; and new higher relations of production never appear before the material conditions of their existence have matured in the womb of the old society. Therefore, mankind always takes up only such problems as it can solve; since, looking at the matter more closely, we will always find that the problem itself arises only when the material conditions necessary for its solution already exist or are at least in the process of formation. In broad outlines we can designate the Asiatic, the ancient, the feudal, and the modern bourgeois methods of production as so many epochs in the progress of the economic formation of society. The bourgeois relations of production are the last antagonistic form of the social process of production—antagonistic not in the sense of individual antagonism, but of one arising from conditions surrounding the life of individuals in society; at the same time the productive forces developing in the womb of bourgeois society create the material conditions for the solution of that antagonism. This social formation constitutes, therefore, the closing chapter of the prehistoric stage of human society.

NOTES ON BAKUNIN'S *STATEHOOD AND ANARCHY*

BAKUNIN: "Where there is a state, there is inevitably domination and consequently there is also slavery; domination without slavery, open or masked, is unthinkable—that is why we are enemies of the state.

What does it mean to talk of the proletariat 'raised to the level of the ruling estate'"?

MARX: It means that the proletariat, instead of fighting in individual instances against the economically privileged classes, has gained sufficient strength and organization to use general means of coercion in its struggle against them; but it can only make use of such economic means as abolish its own character as wage laborer and hence as a class; when its victory is complete, its rule too is therefore at an end, since its class character will have disappeared.

BAKUNIN: "Will perhaps the entire proletariat stand at the head of the government?"

MARX: In a TRADES UNION, for example, does the entire union form its executive committee? Will all division of labor in the factory come to an end as well as the various functions arising from it? And with Bakunin's constitution "from below," will everyone be "at the top?" If so, there will be no one "at the bottom." Will all the members of the community at the same time administer the common interests of the "region?" If so, there will be no distinction between community and "region."

BAKUNIN: "There are about 40 million Germans. Does this mean that all 40 million will be members of the government?"

MARX: CERTAINLY! For the system starts with the self-government of the communities.

BAKUNIN: "The entire people will rule, and no one will be ruled."

MARX: When a person rules himself, he does not do so according to this principle; for he is only himself and not another.

BAKUNIN: "Then there will be no government, no state, but if there is a state, there will be both rulers and slaves."

MARX: That just means when class rule has disappeared there [will] be no state in the present political sense.

BAKUNIN: "The dilemma in the theory of the Marxists is easily resolved. By people's government they . . . understand the government of the people by means of a small number of representatives chosen (elected) by the people."

MARX: Asine! This is democratic twaddle, political claptrap! Elections—a political form found in the tiniest Russian commune and in the artel. The character of an election does not depend on this name but on the economic foundation, the economic interrelations of the voters, and as soon as the functions have ceased to be political, 1) government functions no longer exist; 2) the distribution of general functions has become a routine matter which entails no domination; 3) elections lose their present political character.

BAKUNIN: "The universal suffrage of the whole people"—

MARX: Such a thing as the whole people, in the present meaning of the word, is an illusion—

BAKUNIN: "To elect its representatives and "rulers of state"—that is the last word of the Marxists and also of the democratic school—is a lie which conceals the despotism of the *ruling minority,* a lie that is all the more dangerous as it appears as the expression of the so-called will of the people."

MARX: With collective ownership the so-called will of the people disappears and makes way for the genuine will of the cooperative.

BAKUNIN: "So the result is the control of the vast majority of the people by a privileged minority. But this minority, the Marxists say,"

MARX: Where?

BAKUNIN: "will consist of workers. Yes, quite possibly of former workers, but, as soon as they have become the representatives or rulers of the people, *they cease to be workers*"—

MARX: No more than a factory owner today ceases to be a capitalist when he becomes a municipal councilor—

BAKUNIN: "And will gaze down upon the whole world of the common workers from the eminence of "statehood"; they will no longer represent the people, but only themselves and their "claims" to govern the people. Anyone who can doubt this knows nothing of human nature"

MARX: If Mr. Bakunin were familiar even with the position of a manager in a workers' co-operative factory, all his fantasies about domination would go to the devil. He should have asked himself: what forms could management functions assume within such a workers' state, if he wants to call it that?

Charles Sanders Peirce
1839–1914

Charles Sanders Peirce (pronounced "Purse") was born in Cambridge, Massachusetts, to Benjamin and Sarah Hunt Mills Peirce. His father was a noted mathematician and professor of astronomy and mathematics at Harvard. Like John Stuart Mill and Søren Kierkegaard, Charles Peirce received his most significant schooling from his father. From an early age, his father taught him mathematics and science, encouraging Peirce in his youthful laboratory experiments. Though Peirce did graduate from both Cambridge High School and Harvard, he did not distinguish himself academically at either institution and had trouble adapting socially. During his college years, he spent much of his time with his father, discussing the elder Peirce's mathematical studies. Following graduation from Harvard in 1859, Peirce studied chemistry at the Lawrence Scientific School. There he met and then married his first wife, Harriet Melusina Fay. In addition to this change in his social life, Peirce's academic performance improved, and in 1863 he graduated from Lawrence *summa cum laude*.

While Peirce was still in school, his father arranged a job for him with the United States Coast and Geodetic Survey. Peirce worked for this agency over the next thirty years but nevertheless found time for a number of other pursuits. He worked as an astronomer at Harvard, continued to perform scientific experiments, read and wrote extensively in philosophy, and lectured on logic at Johns Hopkins University. Peirce also helped form the Metaphysical Club, an informal gathering of friends to discuss philosophical matters. The club included such well-known thinkers as William James and Oliver Wendell Holmes. Though esteemed by his fellow philosophers, Peirce's difficult personality and reputation for "loose living" kept him from a professorship. Peirce's "inability to exercise the proper moral self-control" (James's description) eventually led to a divorce from Harriet Fay in 1883. The following year Peirce married a French woman named Juliette Froisy.

In 1891, Peirce received a small legacy, retired from his job with the U.S. Coast and Geodetic Survey, and moved to Milford, Pennsylvania, where he lived a reclusive life while writing on philosophical themes. His works received virtually no recognition during his lifetime, and on his death his second wife sold all his papers to Harvard for $500.

* * *

Peirce has been called a "philosopher's philosopher." His writings are often difficult for beginning students, partly because of the technical way in which he expresses his ideas. In addition, he developed four more-or-less complete systems, abandoning each in favor of the next. Despite his esoteric and variegated writing, in 1877 and 1878 Peirce published a pair of essays for a general audience in *Popular Science Monthly.* These became his most important works.

The first of these essays, "The Fixation of Belief," is given here (complete). This essay develops Peirce's famous theory of pragmatism. Peirce begins with a brief history of knowledge, concluding that all inquiry begins with doubt. In order to lead to belief, this doubt must be "real and living," the actual state in which we find ourselves. This state of doubt causes us to "struggle to attain a state of belief," which we then try to "fix" in some way.

Peirce explains four methods of moving from doubt to belief: (1) tenacity, accepting one alternative to the doubt and rejecting all possible criticism of it; (2) authority, submitting to the state's or the church's tenaciously held beliefs; (3) the *a priori* method, relying on the inclination to believe; and (4) science. Peirce argues for the scientific method because "it is the only one of the four methods which presents any distinction of a right and a wrong way."

Peirce has been called the father of pragmatism, and his work clearly influenced William James and John Dewey. Apart from the pragmatists, echoes of Peirce's writing can be heard in the verification criterion of meaning of the logical positivists and in the mandate of the later Wittgenstein that "the meaning is the use." Since the publication of his collected essays in the middle of the century, there has been renewed interest in Peirce's thought.

* * *

For general works on pragmatism (which include sections on Peirce and which place his thought in a wider context), see Edward C. Moore, *American Pragmatism: Peirce, James and Dewey* (New York: Columbia University Press, 1961); H.S. Thayer, "Pragmatism," in D.J. O'Connor, ed., *A Critical History of Western Philosophy* (New York: The Free Press, 1964); Amelie O. Rorty, ed., *Pragmatic Philosophy* (New York: Anchor Doubleday, 1966); Frederick Copleston, *A History of Philosophy,* Vol. VIII (Garden City, NY: Anchor Doubleday, 1967); A.J. Ayer, *The Origins of Pragmatism: Studies in the Philosophy of Charles Sanders Peirce and William James* (San Francisco: Freeman, Cooper, 1968); H.S. Thayer, *Meaning and Action: A Critical History of Pragmatism* (Indianapolis, IN: Bobbs-Merrill, 1968); Charles Moore, *The Pragmatic Movement in America* (New York: George Braziller, 1970); Israel Scheffler, *Four Pragmatists: A Critical Introduction to Peirce, James, Mead, and Dewey* (New York: Humanities Press, 1974); John E. Smith, *Purpose and Thought: The Meaning of Pragmatism* (New Haven, CT: Yale University Press,

1978); and Richard Rorty, *The Consequences of Pragmatism* (Minneapolis: University of Minnesota Press, 1982).

All of Peirce's works have been collected in the eight-volume set, *Collected Papers of Charles Sanders Peirce,* edited by Charles Hartshorne and Paul Weiss (Cambridge, MA: Harvard University Press, 1931–1935, 1958)—Volumes I, V, and VI contain the most important philosophical material. For a biography of Peirce, see Joseph Brent, *Charles Sanders Peirce: A Life* (Bloomington: Indiana University Press, 1993). The most comprehensive study of Peirce is James Feibleman, *An Introduction to Peirce's Philosophy* (New York: Harper & Brothers, 1946), whereas Manley Thompson, *The Pragmatic Philosophy of C.S. Peirce* (Chicago: University of Chicago Press, 1953); W.B. Gallie, *Peirce and Pragmatism* (New York: Dover, 1966); Robert F. Almeder, *The Philosophy of Charles S. Peirce: A Critical Introduction* (Totowa, NJ: Rowman and Littlefield, 1980); and Christopher Hookway, *Peirce* (New York: Routledge, 1985) provide helpful introductions. For collections of essays, see Philip P. Wiener and Frederic H. Young, eds., *Studies in the Philosophy of Charles Sanders Peirce* (Cambridge, MA: Harvard University Press, 1952); Edward C. Moore and Richard S. Robin, eds., *Studies in the Philosophy of Charles Sanders Peirce,* Second Series (Amherst: University of Massachusetts Press, 1964); and Richard J. Bernstein, ed., *Perspectives on Peirce* (New Haven, CT: Yale University Press, 1965).

THE FIXATION OF BELIEF

Few persons care to study logic, because everybody conceives himself to be proficient enough in the art of reasoning already. But I observe that this satisfaction is limited to one's own ratiocination, and does not extend to that of other men.

We come to the full possession of our power of drawing inferences, the last of all our faculties; for it is not so much a natural gift as a long and difficult art. The history of its practice would make a grand subject for a book. The medieval schoolman, following the Romans, made logic the earliest of a boy's studies after grammar, as being very easy. So it was as they understood it. Its fundamental principle, according to them, was, that all knowledge rests either on authority or reason; but that whatever is deduced by reason depends ultimately on a premiss derived from authority. Accordingly, as soon as a boy was perfect in the syllogistic procedure, his intellectual kit of tools was held to be complete.

To Roger Bacon, that remarkable mind who in the middle of the thirteenth century was almost a scientific man, the schoolmen's conception of reasoning appeared only an obstacle to truth. He saw that experience alone teaches anything—a proposition which to us seems easy to understand, because a distinct conception of experience has been handed down to us from former generations; which to him likewise seemed perfectly clear, because its difficulties had not yet unfolded themselves. Of all kinds of experience, the best, he thought, was interior illumination, which teaches many things about Nature which the external senses could never discover, such as the transubstantiation of bread.

Four centuries later, the more celebrated Bacon, in the first book of his *Novum Organum,* gave his clear account of experience as something which must be open to verification and reexamination. But, superior as Lord Bacon's conception is to earlier notions, a modern reader who is not in awe of his grandiloquence is chiefly struck by the inadequacy of his view of scientific procedure. That we have only to make some crude experiments, to draw up briefs of the results in certain blank forms, to go through these by rule, checking off everything disproved and setting down the alternatives, and that thus in a few years physical science would be finished up—what an idea! "He wrote on science like a Lord Chancellor," indeed, as Harvey, a genuine man of science said.

The early scientists, Copernicus, Tycho Brahe, Kepler, Galileo, Harvey, and Gilbert, had methods more like those of their modern brethren. Kepler undertook to draw a curve through the places of Mars, and to state the times occupied by the planet in describing the different parts of the curve; but perhaps his greatest service to science was in impressing on men's minds that this was the thing to be done if they wished to improve astronomy; that they were not to content themselves with inquiring whether one system of epicycles was better than another but that they were to sit down to the figures and find out what the curve, in truth, was. He accomplished this by his incomparable energy and courage, blundering along in the most inconceivable way (to us), from one irrational hypothesis to another, until, after trying twenty-two of these, he fell, by the mere exhaustion of his invention, upon the orbit which a mind well furnished with the weapons of modern logic would have tried almost at the outset.

In the same way, every work of science great enough to be well remembered for a few generations affords some exemplification of the defective state of the art of reasoning of the time when it was written; and each chief step in science has been a lesson in logic. It was so when Lavoisier and his contemporaries took up the study of Chemistry. The old chemist's maxim had been, "*Lege, lege, lege, labora, ora, et relege.*" Lavoisier's method was not to read and pray, but to dream that some long and complicated chemical process would have a certain effect, to put it into practice with dull patience, after its inevitable failure, to dream that with some modification it would have another result, and to end by publishing the last dream as a fact: his way was to carry his mind into his laboratory, and literally to make of his alembics and cucurbits instruments of thought, giving a new conception of reasoning as something which was to be done with one's eyes open, in manipulating real things instead of words and fancies.

The Darwinian controversy is, in large part, a question of logic. Mr. Darwin proposed to apply the statistical method to biology. The same thing has been done in a widely different branch of science, the theory of gases. Though unable to say what the movements of any particular molecule of gas would be on a certain hypothesis regarding the constitution of this class of bodies, Clausius and Maxwell were yet able, eight years before the publication of Darwin's immortal work, by the application of the doctrine of probabilities, to predict that in the long run such and such a proportion of the molecules would, under given circumstances, acquire such and such velocities; that there would take place, every second, such and such a number of collisions, etc.; and from these propositions were able to deduce certain properties of gases, especially in regard to their heat-relations. In like manner, Darwin, while unable to say what the operation of variation and natural selection in any individual case will be, demonstrates that in the long run they will, or would, adapt animals to their circumstances. Whether or not existing animal forms are due to such action, or what position the theory ought to take, forms the subject of a discussion in which questions of fact and questions of logic are curiously interlaced.

The object of reasoning is to find out, from the consideration of what we already know, something else which we do not know. Consequently, reasoning is good if it be such as to give a true conclusion from true premisses, and not otherwise. Thus, the question of validity is purely one of fact and not of thinking. A being the facts stated in the premisses and B being that concluded, the question is, whether these facts are really so related that if A were B would generally be. If so, the inference is valid; if not, not. It is not in the least the question whether, when the premisses are accepted by the mind, we feel an impulse to accept the conclusion also. It is true that we do generally reason correctly by nature. But that is an accident; the true conclusion would remain true if we had no impulse to accept it; and the false one would remain false, though we could not resist the tendency to believe in it.

We are, doubtless, in the main logical animals, but we are not perfectly so. Most of us, for example, are naturally more sanguine and hopeful than logic would justify. We seem to be so constituted that in the absence of any facts to go upon we are happy and self-satisfied; so that the effect of experience is continually to contract our hopes and aspirations. Yet a lifetime of the application of this corrective does not usually eradicate our sanguine disposition. Where hope is unchecked by any experience, it is likely that our optimism is extravagant. Logicality in regard to practical matters (if this be understood, not in the old sense, but as consisting in a wise union of security with fruitfulness of reasoning) is the most useful quality an animal can possess, and might, therefore, result from the action of natural selection; but outside of these it is probably of more advantage to the animal to have his mind filled with pleasing and encouraging visions, independently of their truth; and thus, upon unpractical subjects, natural selection might occasion a fallacious tendency of thought.

That which determines us, from given premisses, to draw one inference rather than another, is some habit of mind, whether it be constitutional or acquired. The habit is good or otherwise, according as it produces true conclusions from true premisses or not; and an inference is regarded as valid or not, without reference to the truth or falsity of its conclusion specially, but according as the habit which determines it is such as to produce true conclusions in general or not. The particular habit of mind which governs this or that inference may be formulated in a proposition whose truth depends on the validity of the inferences which the habit determines; and such a formula is called a *guiding principle* of inference. Suppose, for example, that we observe that a rotating disk of copper quickly comes to rest when placed between the poles of a magnet, and we infer that this will happen with every disk of copper. The guiding principle is, that what is true of one piece of copper is true of another. Such a guiding principle with regard to copper would be much safer than with regard to many other substances—brass, for example.

A book might be written to signalize all the most important of these guiding principles of reasoning. It would probably be we must confess, of no service to a person whose thought is directed wholly to practical subjects, and whose activity moves along thoroughly-beaten paths. The problems that present themselves to such a mind are matters of routine which he has learned once for all to handle in learning his business. But let a man venture into an unfamiliar field, or where his results are not continually checked by experience, and all history shows that the most masculine intellect will goal, or even carry him entirely astray. He is like a ship in the open sea, with no one on board who understands the rules of navigation. And in such a case some general study of the guiding principles of reasoning would be sure to be found useful.

The subject could hardly be treated, however, without being first limited; since almost any fact may serve as a guiding principle. But it so happens that there exists a division among facts, such that in one class are all those which are absolutely essential as guiding principles, while in the others are all which have any other interest as objects of research. This division is between those which are necessarily taken for granted in asking why a certain conclusion is thought to follow from certain premisses, and those which are not implied in such a question. A moment's thought will show that a variety of facts are already assumed when the logical question is first asked. It is implied, for instance, that there are such states of mind as doubt and belief—that a passage from one to the other is possible, the object of thought remaining the same, and that this transition is subject to some rules by which all minds are alike bound. As these are facts which we must already know before we can have any clear conception of reasoning at all, it cannot be supposed to be any longer of much interest to inquire into their truth or falsity. On the other hand, it is easy to believe that those rules of reasoning which are deduced from the very idea of the process are the ones which are the most essential; and, indeed, that so long as it conforms to these it will, at least, not lead to false conclusions from true premisses. In point of fact, the importance of what may be deduced from the assumptions involved in the logical question turns out to be greater than might be supposed, and this for reasons which it is difficult to exhibit at the outset. The only one which I shall here mention is, that conceptions which are really products of logical reflection, without being readily seen to be so, mingle with our ordinary thoughts, and are frequently the causes of great confusion. This is the case, for example, with the conception of quality. A quality, as such, is never an object of observation. We can see that a thing is blue or green, but the quality of being blue and the quality of being green are not things which we see; they are products of logical reflections. The truth is, that common-sense, or thought as it first emerges above the level of the narrowly practical, is deeply imbued with that bad logical quality to which the epithet *metaphysical* is commonly applied; and nothing can clear it up but a severe course of logic.

We generally know when we wish to ask a question and when we wish to pronounce a judgment, for there is a dissimilarity between the sensation of doubting and that of believing.

But this is not all which distinguishes doubt from belief. There is a practical difference. Our beliefs guide our desires and shape our actions. The Assassins, or followers of the Old Man of the Mountain, used to rush into death at his least command, because they believed that obedience to him would insure everlasting felicity. Had they doubted this, they would not have acted as they did. So it is with every belief, according to its degree. The feeling of believing is a more or less sure indication of there being established in our nature some habit which will determine our actions. Doubt never has such an effect.

Nor must we overlook a third point of difference. Doubt is an uneasy and dissatisfied state from which we struggle to free ourselves and pass into the state of belief; while the latter is a calm and satisfactory state which we do not wish to avoid, or to change to a belief in anything else. On the contrary, we cling tenaciously, not merely to believing, but to believing just what we do believe.

Thus, both doubt and belief have positive effects upon us, though very different ones. Belief does not make us act at once, but puts us into such a condition that we shall behave in some certain way, when the occasion arises. Doubt has not the least such active effect, but stimulates us to inquiry until it is destroyed. This reminds us of the irritation of a nerve and the reflex action produced thereby; while for the analogue of belief, in the nervous system, we must look to what are called nervous associations—for example, to that habit of the nerves in consequence of which the smell of a peach will make the mouth water.

The irritation of doubt causes a struggle to attain a state of belief. I shall term this struggle *Inquiry,* though it must be admitted that this is sometimes not a very apt designation.

The irritation of doubt is the only immediate motive for the struggle to attain belief. It is certainly best for us that our beliefs should be such as may truly guide our actions so as to satisfy our desires; and this reflection will make us reject every belief which does not seem to have been so formed as to insure this result. But it will only do so by creating a doubt in the place of that belief. With the doubt, therefore, the struggle begins, and with the cessation of doubt it ends. Hence, the sole object of inquiry is the settlement of opinion. We may fancy that this is not enough for us, and that we seek, not merely an opinion, but a true opinion. But put this fancy to the test, and it proves groundless; for as soon as a firm belief is reached we are entirely satisfied, whether the belief be true or false. And it is clear that nothing out of the sphere of our knowledge can be our object, for nothing which does not affect the mind can be the motive for mental effort. The most that can be maintained is, that we seek for a belief that we shall *think* to be true. But we think each one of our beliefs to be true, and, indeed, it is mere tautology to say so.

That the settlement of opinion is the sole end of inquiry is a very important proposition. It sweeps away, at once, various vague and erroneous conceptions of proof. A few of these may be noticed here.

1. Some philosophers have imagined that to start an inquiry it was only necessary to utter a question whether orally or by setting it down upon paper, and have even recommended us to begin our studies with questioning everything! But the mere putting of a proposition into the interrogative form does not stimulate the mind to any struggle after belief. There must be a real and living doubt, and without this all discussion is idle.

2. It is a very common idea that a demonstration must rest on some ultimate and absolutely indubitable propositions. These, according to one school, are first principles of a general nature; according to another, are first sensations. But, in point of fact, an inquiry, to have that completely satisfactory result called demonstration, has only to start with propositions perfectly free from all actual doubt. If the premisses are not in fact doubted at all, they cannot be more satisfactory than they are.

3. Some people seem to love to argue a point after all the world is fully convinced of it. But no further advance can be made. When doubt ceases, mental action on the subject comes to an end; and, if it did go on, it would be without a purpose.

If the settlement of opinion is the sole object of inquiry, and if belief is of the nature of a habit, why should we not attain the desired end, by taking as answer to a question any we may fancy, and constantly reiterating it to ourselves, dwelling on all which may conduce to that belief, and learning to turn with contempt and hatred from anything that might disturb it? This simple and direct method is really pursued by many men. I remember once being entreated not to read a certain newspaper lest it might change my opinion upon free-trade. "Lest I might be entrapped by its fallacies and misstatements," was the form of expression. "You are not," my friend said, "a special student of political economy. You might, therefore, easily be deceived by fallacious arguments upon the subject. You might, then, if you read this paper, be led to believe in protection. But you admit that free-trade is the true doctrine; and you do not wish to believe what is not true." I have often known this system to be delib-erately adopted. Still oftener, the instinctive dislike of an undecided state of mind, exaggerated into a vague dread of doubt, makes men cling spasmodically to the views they already take. The man feels that, if he only holds to his belief without wavering, it will be entirely satisfactory. Nor can it be denied that a steady and immovable faith yields great peace of mind. It may, indeed, give rise to inconveniences, as if a man should resolutely continue to believe that fire would not burn him, or that he would the man who adopts this method will not allow that its inconveniences are greater than its advantages. He will say, "I hold steadfastly to the truth, and the truth is always wholesome." And in many cases it may very well be that the pleasure he derives from his calm faith overbalances any inconveniences resulting from its deceptive character. Thus, if it be true that death is annihilation, then the man who believes that he will certainly go straight to heaven when he dies, provided he has fulfilled certain simple observances in this life, has a cheap pleasure which will not be followed by the least disappointment. A similar consideration seems to have weight with many persons in religious topics, for we frequently hear it said, "Oh, I could not believe so-and-so, because I should be wretched if I did." When an ostrich buries its head in the sand as danger approaches, it very likely takes the happiest course. It hides the danger, and then calmly says there is no danger; and, if it feels perfectly sure there is none, why should it raise its head to see? A man may go through life, systematically keeping out of view all that might cause a change in his opinions, and if he only succeeds—basing his method, as he does, on two fundamental psychological laws—I do not see what can be said against his doing so. It would be an egotistical impertinence to object that his procedure is irrational, for that only amounts to saying that his method of settling belief is not ours. He does not propose to himself to be rational, and, indeed, will often talk with scorn of man's weak and illusive reason. So let him think as he pleases.

But this method of fixing belief, which may be called the method of tenacity, will be unable to hold its ground in practice. The social impulse is against it. The man who adopts it will find that other men think differently from him, and it will be apt to occur to him, in some saner moment, that their opinions are quite as good as his own, and this will shake his confidence in his belief. This conception, that another man's thought or sentiment may be equivalent to one's own, is a distinctly new step, and a highly important one. It arises from an impulse too strong in man to be suppressed without danger of destroying the human species. Unless we make ourselves hermits we shall necessarily influence each other's opinions; so that the problem becomes how to fix belief, not in the individual merely, but in the community.

Let the will of the state act, then? instead of that of the individual. Let an institution be created which shall have for its object to keep correct doctrines before the attention of the people, to reiterate them perpetually, and to teach them to the young; having at the same time power to prevent contrary doctrines from being taught, advocated, or expressed. Let all possible causes of a change of mind be removed from men's apprehensions. Let them be kept ignorant, lest they should learn of some reason to think otherwise than they do. Let their passions be enlisted, so that they may regard private and unusual opinions with hatred and horror. Then, let all men who reject the established belief be terrified into silence. Let the people turn out and tar-and-feather such men, or let inquisitions be made into the manner of thinking of suspected persons, and when they are found guilty of forbidden beliefs, let them be subjected to some signal punishment. When complete agreement could not otherwise be reached, a general massacre of all who have not thought in a certain way has proved a very effective means of settling opinion in a country. If the power to do this be wanting, let a list of opinions be drawn up, to which no man of the least independence of thought can assent, and let the faithful be required to accept all these propositions, in order to segregate them as radically as possible from the influence of the rest of the world.

This method has, from the earliest times, been one of the chief means of upholding correct theological and political doctrines, and of preserving their universal or catholic character. In Rome, especially, it has been practised from the days of Numa Pompilius to those of Pius Nonus. This is the most perfect example in history; but wherever there is a priesthood—and no religion has been without one—this method has been more or less made use of. Wherever there is an aristocracy, or a guild, or any association of a class of men whose interests depend, or are supposed to depend, on certain propositions, there will be inevitably found some traces of this natural product of social feeling. Cruelties always accompany this system; and when it is consistently carried out, they become atrocities of the most horrible kind in the eyes of any rational man. Nor should this occasion surprise, for the officer of a society does not feel justified in surrendering the interests of that society for the sake of mercy, as he might his own private interests. It is natural, therefore, that sympathy and fellowship should thus produce a most ruthless power.

In judging this method of fixing belief, which may be called the method of authority, we must, in the first place, allow its immeasurable mental and moral superiority to the method of tenacity. Its success is proportionately greater; and, in fact, it has over and over again worked the most majestic results. The mere structures of stone which it has caused to be put together—in Siam, for example, in Egypt, and in Europe—have many of them a sublimity hardly more than rivaled by the greatest works of Nature. And, except the geological epochs, there are no periods of time so vast as those which are measured by some of these organized faiths. If we scrutinize the matter closely, we shall find that there has not been one of their creeds which has remained always the same; yet the change is so slow as to be imperceptible during one person's life, so that individual belief remains sensibly fixed. For the mass of mankind, then, there is perhaps no better method than this. If it is their highest impulse to be intellectual slaves, then slaves they ought to remain.

But no institution can undertake to regulate opinions upon every subject. Only the most important ones can be attended to, and on the rest men's minds must be left to the action of natural causes. This imperfection will be no source of weakness so long as men are in such a state of culture that one opinion does not influence another—that is, so long as they cannot put two and two together. But in the most priest ridden states some individuals will be found who are raised above that condition. These men possess a wider sort of social feeling; they see that men in other countries and in other ages have held to very different doctrines from those which they themselves have been brought up to believe; and they cannot help seeing that it is the mere accident of their having been taught as they have, and of their having been surrounded with the manners and associations they have, that has caused them to believe as they do and not far differently. Nor can their candour resist the reflection that there is no reason to rate their own views at a higher value than those of other nations and other centuries; thus giving rise to doubts in their minds.

They will further perceive that such doubts as these must exist in their minds with reference to every belief which seems to be determined by the caprice either of themselves or of those who originated the popular opinions. The willful adherence to a belief, and the arbitrary forcing of it upon others, must, therefore, both be given up. A different new method of settling opinions must be adopted, that shall not only produce an impulse to believe, but shall also decide what proposition it is which is to be believed. Let the action of natural preferences be unimpeded, then, and under their influence let men, conversing together and regarding matters in different lights, gradually develop beliefs in harmony with natural causes. This method resembles that by which conceptions of art have been brought to maturity. The most perfect example of it is to be found in the history of metaphysical philosophy. Systems of this sort have not usually rested upon any observed facts, at least not in any great degree. They have been chiefly adopted because their fundamental propositions seemed "agreeable to reason." This is an apt expression; it does not mean that which agrees with experience, but that which we find ourselves inclined to believe. Plato, for example, finds it agreeable to reason that the distances of the celestial spheres from one another should be proportional to the different lengths of strings which produce harmonious chords. Many philosophers have been led to their main conclusions by considerations like this; but this is the lowest and least developed form which the method takes, for it is clear that another man might find Kepler's theory, that the celestial spheres are proportional to the inscribed and circumscribed spheres of the different regular solids, more agreeable to *his* reason. But the shock of opinions will soon lead men to rest on preferences of a far more universal nature. Take, for example, the doctrine that man only acts selfishly—that is, from the consideration that acting in one way will afford him more pleasure than acting in another. This rests on no fact in the world, but it has had a wide acceptance as being the only reasonable theory.

This method is far more intellectual and respectable from the point of view of reason than either of the others which we have noticed. Indeed, as long as no better method can be applied, it ought to be followed, since it is then the expression of instinct which must be the ultimate cause of belief in all cases. But its failure has been the most manifest. It makes of inquiry something similar to the development of taste; but taste, unfortunately, is always more or less a matter of fashion, and accordingly metaphysicians have never come to any fixed agreement, but the pendulum has swung backward and forward between a more material and a more spiritual philosophy, from the earliest times to the latest. And so from this, which has been called the *a priori* method, we are driven, in Lord Bacon's phrase, to a true induction. We have examined this *a priori* method as something which promised to deliver our opinions from their accidental and capricious element. But development, while it is a process which eliminates the effect of some casual circumstances, only magnifies that of others. This method, therefore, does not differ in a very essential way from that of authority. The government may not have lifted its finger to influence my convictions; I may have been left outwardly quite free to choose, we will say, between monogamy and polygamy, and, appealing to my conscience only, I may have concluded that the latter practice is in itself licentious. But when I come to see that the chief obstacle to the spread of Christianity among a people of as high culture as the Hindoos has been a conviction of the immorality of our way of treating women, I cannot help seeing that, though governments do not interfere, sentiments in their development will be very greatly determined by accidental causes. Now, there are some people, among whom I must suppose that my reader is to be found, who, when they see that any belief of theirs is determined by any circumstance extraneous to the facts, will from that moment not merely admit in words that that belief is doubtful, but will experience a real doubt of it, so that it ceases in some degree at least to be a belief.

To satisfy our doubts, therefore, it is necessary that a method should be found by which our beliefs may be determined by nothing human, but by some external permanency—by something upon which our thinking has no effect. Some mystics imagine that they have such a method in a private inspiration from on high. But that is only a form of the method of tenacity, in which the conception of truth as something public is not yet developed. Our external permanency would not be external, in our sense, if it was restricted in its influence to one individual. It must be something which affects, or might affect, every man. And, though these affections are necessarily as various as are individual conditions, yet the method must be such that the ultimate conclusion of every man shall be the same. Such is the method of science. Its fundamental hypothesis, restated in more familiar language, is this: There are Real things, whose characters are entirely independent of our opinions about them; those Reals affect our senses according to regular laws, and, though our sensations are as different as our relations to the objects, yet, by taking advantage of the laws of perception, we can ascertain by reasoning how things really and truly are; and any man, if he have sufficient experience and he reason enough about it, will be led to the one True conclusion. The new conception here involved is that of Reality. It may be asked how I know that there are any Reals. If this hypothesis is the sole support of my method of inquiry, my method of inquiry must not be used to support my hypothesis. The reply is this: 1. If investigation cannot be regarded as proving that there are Real things, it at least does not lead to a contrary conclusion; but the method and the conception on which it is based remain ever in harmony. No doubts of the method, therefore, necessarily arise from its practice, as is the case with all the others. 2. The feeling which gives rise to any method of fixing belief is a dissatisfaction at two repugnant propositions. But here already is a vague concession that there is some *one* thing which a proposition should represent. Nobody, therefore, can really doubt that there are Reals, for, if he did, doubt would not be a source of dissatisfaction. The hypothesis, therefore, is one which every mind admits. So that the social impulse does not cause men to doubt it. 3. Everybody uses the scientific method about a great many things, and only ceases to use it when he does not know how to apply it. 4. Experience of the method has not led us to doubt it, but, on the contrary, scientific investigation has had the most wonderful triumphs in the way of settling opinion. These afford the explanation of my not doubting the method or the hypothesis which it supposes; and not having any doubt, nor believing that anybody else whom I could influence has, it would be the merest babble for me to say more about it. If there be anybody with a living doubt upon the subject, let him consider it.

To describe the method of scientific investigation is the object of this series of papers. At present I have only room to notice some points of contrast between it and other methods of fixing belief.

This is the only one of the four methods which presents any distinction of a right and a wrong way. If I adopt the method of tenacity, and shut myself out from all influences, whatever I think necessary to doing this, is necessary according to that method. So with the method of authority: the state may try to put down heresy by means which, from a scientific point of view, seem very ill-calculated to accomplish its purposes; wrongly. So with the *a priori* method. The very essence of it is to think as one is inclined to think. All metaphysicians will be sure to do that, however they may be inclined to judge each other to be perversely wrong. The Hegelian system recognizes every natural tendency of thought as logical, although it be certain to be abolished by counter-tendencies. Hegel thinks there is a regular system in the succession of these tendencies, in consequence of which, after drifting one way and the other for a long time, opinion will at last go right. And it is true that metaphysicians do get the right ideas at last; Hegel's system of Nature represents tolerably the science of his day; and one may be sure that whatever scientific investigation shall have put out of doubt will presently receive *a priori* demonstration on the part of the metaphysicians. But with the scientific method the case is different. I may start with known and observed facts to proceed to the unknown; and yet the rules which I follow in doing so may not be such as investigation would approve. The test of whether I am truly following the method is not an immediate appeal to my feelings and purposes, but, on the contrary, itself involves the application of the method. Hence it is that bad reasoning as well as good reasoning is possible; and this fact is the foundation of the practical side of logic.

It is not to be supposed that the first three methods of settling opinion present no advantage whatever over the scientific method. On the contrary, each has some peculiar convenience of its own. The *a priori* method is distinguished for its comfortable conclusions. It is the nature of the process to adopt whatever belief we are inclined to, and there are certain flatteries to the vanity of man which we all believe by nature, until we are awakened from our pleasing dream by rough facts. The method of authority will always govern the mass of mankind; and those who wield the various forms of organized force in the state will never be convinced that dangerous reasoning ought not to be suppressed in some way. If liberty of speech is to be untrammeled from the grosser forms of constraint, then uniformity of opinion will be secured by a moral terrorism to which the respectability of society will give its thorough approval. Following the method of authority is the path of peace. Certain non-conformities are permitted; certain others (considered unsafe) are forbidden. These are different in different countries and in different ages; but, wherever you are, let it be known that you seriously hold a tabooed belief, and you may be perfectly sure of being treated with a cruelty less brutal but more refined than hunting you like a wolf. Thus, the greatest intellectual benefactors of mankind have never dared, and dare not now, to utter the whole of their thought; and thus a shade of *prima facie* doubt is cast upon every proposition which is considered essential to the security of society. Singularly enough, the persecution does not all come from without; but a man torments himself and is oftentimes most distressed at finding himself believing propositions which he has been brought up to regard with aversion. The peaceful and sympathetic man will, therefore, find it hard to resist the temptation to submit his opinions to authority. But most of all I admire the method of tenacity for its strength, simplicity, and directness. Men who pursue it are distinguished for their decision of character, which becomes very easy with such a mental rule. They do not waste time in trying to make up their minds what they want, but, fastening like lightning upon whatever alternative comes first, they hold to it to the end, whatever happens, without an instant's irresolution. This is one of the splendid qualities which generally accompany brilliant, unlasting success. It is impossible not to envy the man who can dismiss reason, although we know how it must turn out at last.

Such are the advantages which the other methods of settling opinion have over scientific investigation. A man should consider well of them; and then he should consider that, after all, he wishes his opinions to coincide with the fact, and that there is no reason why the results of those three first methods should do so. To bring about this effect is the prerogative of the method of science. Upon such considerations he has to make his choice—a choice which is far more than the adoption of any intellectual opinion, which is one of the ruling decisions of his life, to which, when once made, he is bound to adhere. The force of habit will sometimes cause a man to hold on to old beliefs, after he is in a condition to see that they have no sound basis. But reflection upon the state of the case will overcome these habits, and he ought to allow reflection its full weight. People sometimes shrink from doing this, having an idea that beliefs are wholesome which they cannot help feeling rest on nothing. But let such persons suppose an analogous though different case from their own. Let them ask themselves what they would say to a reformed Mussulman who should hesitate to give up his old notions in regard to the relations of the sexes; or to a reformed Catholic who should still shrink from reading the Bible. Would they not say that these persons ought to consider the matter fully, and clearly understand the new doctrine, and then ought to embrace it, in its entirety? But, above all, let it be considered that what is more wholesome than any particular belief is integrity of belief, and that to avoid looking into the support of any belief from a fear that it may turn out rotten is quite as immoral as it is disadvantageous. The person who confesses that there is such a thing as truth, which is distinguished from falsehood simply by this, that if acted on it should, on full consideration, carry us to the point we aim at and not astray, and then, though convinced of this, dares not know the truth and seeks to avoid it, is in a sorry state of mind indeed.

Yes, the other methods do have their merits: a clear logical conscience does cost something—just as any virtue, just as all that we cherish, costs us dear. But we should not desire it to be otherwise. The genius of a man's logical method should be loved and reverenced as his bride, whom he has chosen from all the world. He need not contemn the others; on the contrary, he may honor them deeply, and in doing so he only honors her the more. But she is the one that he has chosen, and he knows that he was right in making that choice. And having made it, he will work and fight for her, and will not complain that there are blows to take, hoping that there may be as many and as hard to give, and will strive to be the worthy knight and champion of her from the blaze of whose splendors he draws his inspiration and his courage.

WILLIAM JAMES
1842–1910

William James was born into one of the leading families of New York City. His grandfather, a strict Calvinist and also named William, was an Irish immigrant who had amassed a fortune in real estate. His father, Henry, rejected the grandfather's religion and became an unorthodox mystic. His mother, Mary, was also a child of wealth, and his brother, Henry Jr., became a famous novelist. The life of the James family was one of creative anarchy. Their dinner table was animated with lively debate in which the children were expected to hold their own with guests such as Ralph Waldo Emerson, Washington Irving, and Oliver Wendell Holmes. To encourage intellectual freedom, and to avoid the rigidity of his own joyless upbringing, Henry Sr. put his children into as many different schools as possible. The family moved often, restlessly wandering back and forth across the Atlantic, alighting temporarily in London, Paris, New York, Geneva, Newport, Bonn, and Albany.

William James reflected his family's wanderlust in his academic pursuits. He studied art for a time before joining an expedition to the Amazon basin as an apprentice naturalist. He then traveled to Germany to study physiology, before returning to the United States to complete a degree in medicine at Harvard Medical School in 1869. In 1872, James was appointed to teach physiology and anatomy at Harvard. His intellectual roving and his unwillingness to be bound by the usual academic disciplines continued when he moved in 1875 to psychology and later to philosophy. He subsequently marveled at his audacity:

> I originally studied medicine in order to be a physiologist, but I drifted into psychology and philosophy from a sort of fatality. I never had any philosophic instruction and the first lecture on psychology I ever heard was the first one I ever gave.

In 1878, James married Alice Howe Gibbens, and they had five children. Although James had experienced ill health as a young man (including smallpox contracted in Brazil), his strength seemed to improve following marriage.

In 1890, William James published his first major work, *The Principles of Psychology*. A two-volume work, *Principles* was one of the first attempts to treat psychology as a legitimate, experimental science, and it quickly became the standard work in the field. James did intense philosophical research over the next seventeen years and published his results: *The Will to Believe and Other Essays* (1897), *Varieties of Religious Experience* (1902), and *Pragmatism* (1907). During this period, he continued to teach at Harvard and to lecture throughout the United States and Europe. Resigning from Harvard in 1907, James gave a series of lectures published as *A Pluralistic Universe* (1909) and *The Meaning of Truth* (1909). James died in 1910, and his last complete work, *Essays in Radical Empiricism,* was published posthumously.

At the time of his death, James was considered the embodiment of American philosophy. All accounts indicate that in addition to his large intellect and breadth of learning, James was a generous, open-minded, and sociable person. One historian of philosophy went so far as to describe him as "one of the sweetest men who ever lived."

* * *

In his most famous work, the series of lectures published as *Pragmatism,* James develops pragmatism as "a method of settling metaphysical disputes that otherwise might be interminable." As a theory of meaning, pragmatism asks what practical effects a belief has, whether that belief is tough- or tender-minded. To discover what a belief *means* is to find what difference such a belief makes "in concrete fact and in conduct consequent upon that fact, imposed on somebody, somehow, somewhere, and somewhen." The proper goal of philosophy is to discover "what definite difference it will make to you and me, at definite instants of our life, if this world-formula or that world-formula be the true one."

But James went further than Peirce and claims that pragmatism provides a theory of *truth* as well as of meaning. Peirce had continued to hold a traditional correspondence theory of truth: An assertion was true if it corresponded with a fact. Instead, James says that an idea *becomes* true if it allows the individual to gain "satisfactory relations with other parts of our experience." These relations are not fixed—they are dynamic, just as our experience is dynamic.

Critics have pointed out that James's theory of pragmatism could be used to make any belief true—provided it produced beneficial results. As H.S. Thayer pointed out, "Standards of veracity thus go slack on the very occasions in which, ordinarily, they need the tightest rein, where passion and personal interests are most in play."* This fact, along with a number of other objections, led Peirce to change the name of *his* philosophy to "pragmaticism," to distinguish it from James's thought. For his part, James claimed that he was only presenting a way of discovering truth, not redefining it.

* * *

*H.S. Thayer, "Pragmatism," in D.J. O'Connor, ed., *A Critical History of Western Philosophy* (New York: The Free Press, 1964), p. 451.

For general works on pragmatism, see the introduction to Peirce (page 1008). For biographies of James, see Gay Wilson Allen, *William James: A Biography* (New York: Viking Press, 1967); Jacques Barzun, *A Stroll with William James* (New York: Harper & Row, 1983); and Daniel W. Bjork, *William James: The Center of His Vision* (New York: Columbia University Press, 1988). The standard study of James's thought is Ralph Barton Perry, *The Thought and Character of William James,* 2 vols. (Boston: Little, Brown, 1935). Other general introductions to his thought include Ellen Kappy Suckiel, *The Pragmatic Philosophy of William James* (Notre Dame, IN: University of Notre Dame Press, 1982); Graham Bird, *William James* (London: Routledge & Kegan Paul, 1986); and Gerald E. Myers, *William James: His Life and Thought* (New Haven, CT: Yale University Press, 1986). Collections of essays include Doris Olin, ed., *William James Pragmatism in Focus* (London: Routledge, 1992); Ruth Anna Putnam, ed., *The Cambridge Companion to William James* (Cambridge: Cambridge University Press, 1997); and Phil Oliver, ed., *William James's "Spring of Delight": The Return to Life* (Nashville, TN: Vanderbilt University Press, 2000).

PRAGMATISM (in part)

LECTURE II: WHAT PRAGMATISM MEANS

Some years ago, being with a camping party in the mountains, I returned from a solitary ramble to find every one engaged in a ferocious metaphysical dispute. The *corpus* of the dispute was a squirrel—a live squirrel supposed to be clinging to one side of a tree-trunk; while over against the tree's opposite side a human being was imagined to stand. This human witness tries to get sight of the squirrel by moving rapidly round the tree, but no matter how fast he goes, the squirrel moves as fast in the opposite direction, and always keeps the tree between himself and the man, so that never a glimpse of him is caught. The resultant metaphysical problem now is this: *Does the man go round the squirrel or not?* He goes round the tree, sure enough, and the squirrel is on the tree; but does he go round the squirrel? In the unlimited leisure of the wilderness, discussion had been worn threadbare. Everyone had taken sides, and was obstinate; and the numbers on both sides were even. Each side, when I appeared therefore appealed to me to make it a majority. Mindful of the scholastic adage that whenever you meet a contradiction you must make a distinction, I immediately sought and found one, as follows: "Which party is right," I said, "depends on what you *practically mean* by 'going round' the squirrel. If you mean passing from the north of him to the east, then to the south, then to the west, and then to the north of him again, obviously the man does go round him, for he occupies these successive positions. But if on the contrary you mean being first in front of him, then on the right of him, then behind him, then on his left, and finally in front again, it is quite as obvious that the man fails to go round him, for by the compensating movements the squirrel makes, he keeps his belly turned towards the man all the time, and his back turned away. Make the distinction, and there is no occasion for any

Guaranty Building, Buffalo, New York, 1895, designed by Louis Sullivan (1856–1924). Sullivan's building epitomizes the pragmatic approach to architecture summarized in his famous dictum, "form follows function." Both the exterior and interior designs complement the purpose for which this building was constructed. (© *Frederic Lewis/Getty*)

farther dispute. You are both right and both wrong according as you conceive the verb 'to go round' in one practical fashion or the other."

Although one or two of the hotter disputants called my speech a shuffling evasion, saying they wanted no quibbling or scholastic hair-splitting, but meant just plain honest English "round," the majority seemed to think that the distinction had assuaged the dispute.

I tell this trivial anecdote because it is a peculiarly simple example of what I wish now to speak of as *the pragmatic method.* The pragmatic method is primarily a method of settling metaphysical disputes that otherwise might be interminable. Is the world one or many?—fated or free?—material or spiritual?—here are notions either of which may or may not hold good of the world; and disputes over such notions are unending. The pragmatic method in such cases is to try to interpret each notion by tracing its respective practical consequences. What difference would it practically make to any one if this notion rather than that notion were true? If no practical difference whatever can be traced, then the alternatives mean practically the same thing, and all dispute is idle. Whenever a dispute is serious, we ought to be able to show some practical difference that must follow from one side or the other's being right.

A glance at the history of the idea will show you still better what pragmatism means. The term is derived from the same Greek word *pragma,* meaning action, from which our words "practice" and "practical" come. It was first introduced into philosophy by Mr. Charles Peirce in 1878. In an article entitled "How to Make Our Ideas Clear," in the "Popular Science Monthly" for January of that year. Mr. Peirce, after pointing out that our beliefs are really rules for action, said that, to develop a thought's meaning, we need only determine what conduct it is fitted to produce: that conduct is for us its sole significance. And the tangible fact at the root of all our thought-distinctions, however subtle, is that there is no one of them so fine as to consist in anything but a possible difference of practice. To attain perfect clearness in our thoughts of an object, then, we need only consider what conceivable effects of a practical kind the object may involve—what sensations we are to expect from it, and what reactions we must prepare. Our conception of these effects, whether immediate or remote, is then for us the whole of our conception of the object, so far as that conception has positive significance at all.

This is the principle of Peirce, the principle of pragmatism. It lay entirely unnoticed by any one for twenty years, until I, in an address before Professor Howison's philosophical union at the University of California, brought it forward again and made a special application of it to religion. By that date (1898) the times seemed ripe for its reception. The word "pragmatism" spread, and at present it fairly spots the pages of the philosophic journals. On all hands we find the "pragmatic movement" spoken of, sometimes with respect, sometimes with contumely, seldom with clear understanding. It is evident that the term applies itself conveniently to a number of tendencies that hitherto have lacked a collective name, and that it has "come to stay."

To take in the importance of Peirce's principle, one must get accustomed to applying it to concrete cases. I found a few years ago that Ostwald, the illustrious Leipzig chemist, had been making perfectly distinct use of the principle of pragmatism in his lectures on the philosophy of science, though he had not called it by that name.

"All realities influence our practice," he wrote me, "and that influence is their meaning for us. I am accustomed to put questions to my classes in this way: In what respects would the world be different if this alternative or that were true? If I can find nothing that would become different, then the alternative has no sense."

That is, the rival views mean practically the same thing, and meaning, other than practical, there is for us none. Ostwald in a published lecture gives this example of what he means. Chemists have long wrangled over the inner constitution of certain bodies called "tautomerous." Their properties seemed equally consistent with the notion that an instable hydrogen atom oscillates inside of them, or that they are instable mixtures of two bodies. Controversy raged, but never was decided. "It would never have begun," says Ostwald, "if the combatants had asked themselves what particular experimental fact could have been made different by one or the other view being correct. For it would then have appeared that no difference of fact could possibly ensue; and the quarrel was as unreal as if, theorizing in primitive times about the raising of dough by yeast, one party should have invoked a 'brownie,' while another insisted on an 'elf' as the true cause of the phenomenon."*

It is astonishing to see how many philosophical disputes collapse into insignificance the moment you subject them to this simple test of tracing a concrete consequence. There can *be* no difference anywhere that doesn't *make* a difference elsewhere—no difference in abstract truth that doesn't express itself in a difference in concrete fact and in conduct consequent upon that fact, imposed on somebody, somehow, somewhere, and somewhen. The whole function of philosophy ought to be to find out what definite difference it will make to you and me, at definite instants of our life, if this world-formula or that world-formula be the true one.

There is absolutely nothing new in the pragmatic method. Socrates was an adept at it. Aristotle used it methodically. Locke, Berkeley, and Hume made momentous contributions to truth by its means. Shadworth Hodgson keeps insisting that realities are only what they are "known as." But these forerunners of pragmatism used it in fragments: they were preluders only. Not until in our time has it generalized itself, become conscious of a universal mission, pretended to a conquering destiny. I believe in that destiny, and I hope I may end by inspiring you with my belief.

Pragmatism represents a perfectly familiar attitude in philosophy, the empiricist attitude, but it represents it, as it seems to me, both in a more radical and in a less objectionable form than it has ever yet assumed. A pragmatist turns his back resolutely and once for all upon a lot of inveterate habits dear to professional philosophers. He turns away from abstraction and insufficiency, from verbal solutions, from bad *a priori* reasons, from fixed principles, closed systems, and pretended absolutes and origins. He turns towards concreteness and adequacy, towards facts, towards action and towards power. That means the empiricist temper regnant and the rationalist temper sincerely given up. It means the open air and possibilities of nature, as against dogma, artificiality, and the pretence of finality in truth.

At the same time it does not stand for any special results. It is a method only. But the general triumph of that method would mean an enormous change in what I called in my last lecture the "temperament" of philosophy. Teachers of the ultra-rationalistic type would be frozen out, much as the courtier type is frozen out in republics, as the ultramontane type of priest is frozen out in protestant lands. Science and metaphysics would come much nearer together, would in fact work absolutely hand in hand.

*"Theorie und Praxis," *Zeitsch. Des Oesterreichischen Ingenieur u. Architecten-Vereines*, 1905, Nr. 4 u. 6. I find a still more radical pragmatism than Ostwald's in an address by Professor W.S. Franklin: "I think that the sickliest notion of physics, even if a student gets it, is that it is 'the science of masses, molecules, and the ether.' And I think that the healthiest notion, even if a student does not wholly get it, is that physics is the science of the ways of taking hold of bodies and pushing them!" (*Science,* January 2, 1903).

Metaphysics has usually followed a very primitive kind of quest. You know how men have always hankered after unlawful magic, and you know what a great part in magic *words* have always played. If you have his name, or the formula of incantation that binds him, you can control the spirit, genie, afrite, or whatever the power may be. Solomon knew the names of all the spirits, and having their names, he held them subject to his will. So the universe has always appeared to the natural mind as a kind of enigma, of which the key must be sought in the shape of some illuminating or power-bringing word or name. That word names the universe's *principle,* and to possess it is after a fashion to possess the universe itself. "God," "Matter," "Reason," "the Absolute," "Energy," are so many solving names. You can rest when you have them. You are at the end of your metaphysical quest.

But if you follow the pragmatic method, you cannot look on any such word as closing your quest. You must bring out of each word its practical cash-value, set it at work within the stream of your experience. It appears less as a solution, then, than as a program for more work, and more particularly as an indication of the ways in which existing realities may be *changed.*

Theories thus become instruments, not answers to enigmas, in which we can rest. We don't lie back upon them, we move forward, and, on occasion, make nature over again by their aid. Pragmatism unstiffens all our theories, limbers them up and sets each one at work. Being nothing essentially new, it harmonizes with many ancient philosophic tendencies. It agrees with nominalism for instance, in always appealing to particulars; with utilitarianism in emphasizing practical aspects; with positivism in its disdain for verbal solutions, useless questions and metaphysical abstractions.

All these, you see, are *anti-intellectualist* tendencies. Against rationalism as a pretension and a method pragmatism is fully armed and militant. But, at the outset, at least, it stands for no particular results. It has no dogmas, and no doctrines save its method. As the young Italian pragmatist Papini has well said, it lies in the midst of our theories, like a corridor in a hotel. Innumerable chambers open out of it. In one you may find a man writing an atheistic volume; in the next some one on his knees praying for faith and strength; in a third a chemist investigating a body's properties. In a fourth a system of idealistic metaphysics is being excogitated; in a fifth the impossibility of metaphysics is being shown. But they all own the corridor, and all must pass through it if they want a practicable way of getting into or out of their respective rooms.

No particular results then, so far, but only an attitude of orientation, is what the pragmatic method means. *The attitude of looking away from first things, principles, "categories," supposed necessities; and of looking towards last things, fruits, consequences, facts.*

So much for the pragmatic method! You may say that I have been praising it rather than explaining it to you, but I shall presently explain it abundantly enough by showing how it works on some familiar problems. Meanwhile the word pragmatism has come to be used in a still wider sense, as meaning also a certain *theory of truth.* I mean to give a whole lecture to the statement of that theory, after first paving the way, so I can be very brief now. But brevity is hard to follow, so I ask for your redoubled attention for a quarter of an hour. If much remains obscure, I hope to make it clearer in the later lectures.

One of the most successfully cultivated branches of philosophy in our time is what is called inductive logic, the study of the conditions under which our sciences have evolved. Writers on this subject have begun to show a singular unanimity as to what the laws of nature and elements of fact mean, when formulated by mathematicians, physicists and chemists. When the first mathematical, logical, and natural uniformities, the first *laws,* were discovered, men were so carried away by the clearness, beauty and simplification that resulted, that they believed themselves to have deciphered authentically the eternal thoughts of the Almighty. His mind also thundered and reverberated in syllogisms. He also thought in conic sections, squares and roots and ratios, and geometrized like Euclid. He made Kepler's laws for the planets to follow; he made velocity increase proportionally to the time in falling bodies; he made the law of the sines for light to obey when refracted; he established the classes, orders, families and genera of plants and animals, and fixed the distances between them. He thought the archetypes of all things, and devised their variations; and when we rediscover any one of these his wondrous institutions, we seize his mind in its very literal intention.

But as the sciences have developed farther, the notion has gained ground that most, perhaps all, of our laws are only approximations. The laws themselves, moreover, have grown so numerous that there is no counting them; and so many rival formulations are proposed in all the branches of science that investigators have become accustomed to the notion that no theory is absolutely a transcript of reality, but that any one of them may from some point of view be useful. Their great use is to summarize old facts and to lead to new ones. They are only a man-made language, a conceptual shorthand, as some one calls them, in which we write our reports of nature; and languages, as is well known, tolerate much choice of expression and many dialects.

Thus human arbitrariness has driven divine necessity from scientific logic. If I mention the names of Sigwart, Mach, Ostwald, Pearson, Milhaud, Poincare, Duhem, Ruyssen, those of you who are students will easily identify the tendency I speak of, and will think of additional names.

Riding now on the front of this wave of scientific logic Messrs. Schiller and Dewey appear with their pragmatistic account of what truth everywhere signifies. Everywhere, these teachers say, "truth" in our ideas and beliefs means the same thing that it means in science. It means, they say, nothing but this, *that ideas (which themselves are but parts of our experience) become true just in so far as they help us to get into satisfactory relation with other parts of our experience,* to summarize them and get about among them by conceptual short-cuts instead of following the interminable succession of particular phenomena. Any idea upon which we can ride, so to speak; any idea that will carry us prosperously from any one part of our experience to any other part, linking things satisfactorily, working securely, simplifying, saving labor; is true for just so much, true in so far forth, true *instrumentally.* This is the "instrumental" view of truth taught so successfully at Chicago, the view that truth in our ideas means their power to "work," promulgated so brilliantly at Oxford.

Messrs. Dewey, Schiller and their allies, in reaching this general conception of all truth, have only followed the example of geologists, biologists and philologists. In the establishment of these other sciences, the successful stroke was always to take some simple process actually observable in operation—as denudation by weather, say, or variation from parental type, or change of dialect by incorporation of new words and pronunciations—and then to generalize it, making it apply to all times, and produce great results by summating its effects through the ages.

The observable process which Schiller and Dewey particularly singled out for generalization is the familiar one by which any individual settles into *new opinions.* The process here is always the same. The individual has a stock of old opinions already, but he meets a new experience that puts them to a strain. Somebody contradicts them; or in a reflective moment he discovers that they contradict each other; or he hears of facts with which they are incompatible; or desires arise in him which they cease to satisfy.

The result is an inward trouble to which his mind till then had been a stranger, and from which he seeks to escape by modifying his previous mass of opinions. He saves as much of it as he can, for in this matter of belief we are all extreme conservatives. So he tries to change first this opinion, and then that (for they resist change very variously), until at last some new idea comes up which he can graft upon the ancient stock with a minimum of disturbance of the latter, some idea that mediates between the stock and the new experience and runs them into one another most felicitously and expediently.

This new idea is then adopted as the true one. It preserves the older stock of truths with a minimum of modification, stretching them just enough to make them admit the novelty, but conceiving that in ways as familiar as the case leaves possible. An *outrée* [exaggerated] explanation, violating all our preconceptions, would never pass for a true account of a novelty. We should scratch round industriously till we found something less excentric. The most violent revolutions in an individual's beliefs leave most of his old order standing. Time and space, cause and effect, nature and history, and one's own biography remain untouched. New truth is always a go-between, a smoother-over of transitions. It marries old opinion to new fact so as ever to show a minimum of jolt, a maximum of continuity. We hold a theory true just in proportion to its success in solving this "problem of maxima and minima." But success in solving this problem is eminently a matter of approximation. We say this theory solves it on the whole more satisfactorily than that theory; but that means more satisfactorily to ourselves, and individuals will emphasize their points of satisfaction differently. To a certain degree, therefore, everything here is plastic.

The point I now urge you to observe particularly is the part played by the older truths. Failure to take account of it is the source of much of the unjust criticism levelled against pragmatism. Their influence is absolutely controlling. Loyalty to them is the first principle—in most cases it is the only principle; for by far the most usual way of handling phenomena so novel that they would make for a serious rearrangement of our preconception is to ignore them altogether, or to abuse those who bear witness for them.

You doubtless wish examples of this process of truth's growth, and the only trouble is their superabundance. The simplest case of new truth is of course the mere numerical addition of new kinds of facts, or of new single facts of old kinds, to our experience—an addition that involves no alteration in the old beliefs. Day follows day, and its contents are simply added. The new contents themselves are not true, they simply *come* and *are.* Truth is *what we say about them,* and when we say that they have come, truth is satisfied by the plain additive formula.

But often the day's contents oblige a rearrangement. If I should now utter piercing shrieks and act like a maniac on this platform, it would make many of you revise your ideas as to the probable worth of my philosophy. "Radium" came the other day as part of the day's content, and seemed for a moment to contradict our ideas of the whole order of nature, that order having come to be identified with what is called the conservation of energy. The mere sight of radium paying heat away indefinitely out of its own pocket seemed to violate that conservation. What to think? If the radiations from it were nothing but an escape of unsuspected "potential" energy, pre-existent inside of the atoms, the principle of conservation would be saved. The discovery of "helium" as the radiation's outcome, opened a way to this belief. So Ramsay's view is generally held to be true, because, although it extends our old ideas of energy, it causes a minimum of alteration in their nature.

I need not multiply instances. A new opinion counts as "true" just in proportion as it gratifies the individual's desire to assimilate the novel in his experience to his beliefs in stock. It must both lean on old truth and grasp new fact; and its success (as I said a moment ago) in doing this, is a matter for the individual's appreciation. When old truth grows, then, by new truth's addition, it is for subjective reasons. We are in the process and obey the reasons. That new idea is truest which performs most felicitously its function of satisfying our double urgency. It makes itself true, gets itself classed as true, by the way it works; grafting itself then upon the ancient body of truth, which thus grows much as a tree grows by the activity of a new layer of cambium.

Now Dewey and Schiller proceed to generalize this observation and to apply it to the most ancient parts of truth. They also once were plastic. They also were called true for human reasons. They also mediated between still earlier truths and what in those days were novel observations. Purely objective truth, truth in whose establishment the function of giving human satisfaction in marrying previous parts of experience with newer parts played no role whatever, is nowhere to be found. The reasons why we call things true is the reason why they are true, for "to be true" means only to perform this marriage-function.

The trail of the human serpent is thus over everything. Truth independent; truth that we *find* merely; truth no longer malleable to human need; truth incorrigible, in a word; such truth exists indeed superabundantly—or is supposed to exist by rationalistically minded thinkers; but then it means only the dead heart of the living tree, and its being there means only that truth also has its paleontology, and its "prescription," and may grow stiff with years of veteran service and petrified in men's regard by sheer antiquity. But how plastic even the oldest truths nevertheless really are has been vividly shown in our day by the transformation of logical and mathematical ideas, a transformation which seems even to be invading physics. The ancient formulas are reinterpreted as special expressions of much wider principles, principles that our ancestors never got a glimpse of in their present shape and formulation.

Mr. Schiller still gives to all this view of truth the name of "Humanism," but, for this doctrine too, the name of pragmatism seems fairly to be in the ascendant, so I will treat it under the name of pragmatism in these lectures.

Such then would be the scope of pragmatism—first, a method; and second, a genetic theory of what is meant by truth. And these two things must be our future topics.

What I have said of the theory of truth will, I am sure, have appeared obscure and unsatisfactory to most of you by reason of its brevity. I shall make amends for that hereafter. In a lecture on "common sense" I shall try to show what I mean by truths grown petrified by antiquity. In another lecture I shall expatiate on the idea that our thoughts become true in proportion as they successfully exert their go between function. In a third I shall show how hard it is to discriminate subjective from objective factors in Truth's development. You may not follow me wholly in these lectures; and if you do, you may not wholly agree with me. But you will, I know, regard me at least as serious, and treat my effort with respectful consideration.

You will probably be surprised to learn, then, that Messrs. Schiller's and Dewey's theories have suffered a hailstorm of contempt and ridicule. All rationalism has risen against them. In influential quarters Mr. Schiller, in particular, has been treated like an impudent schoolboy who deserves a spanking. I should not mention this, but for the fact that it throws so much sidelight upon that rationalistic temper to which I have opposed the temper of pragmatism. Pragmatism is uncomfortable away from facts. Rationalism is comfortable only in the presence of abstractions. This pragmatist talk about truths in the plural, about their utility and satisfactoriness, about the success with which they "work," etc., suggests to the typical intellectualist mind a sort of coarse lame second-rate makeshift article of truth. Such truths are not real truth. Such tests are merely subjective. As against this, objective truth must be something non-utilitarian, haughty, refined, remote, august, exalted. It must be an absolute correspondence of our thoughts with an equally absolute reality. It must be what we ought to think unconditionally. The conditioned ways in which we do think are so much irrelevance and matter for psychology. Down with psychology, up with logic, in all this question!

See the exquisite contrast of the types of mind! The pragmatist clings to facts and concreteness, observes truth at its work in particular cases, and generalizes. Truth, for him, becomes a class-name for all sorts of definite working-values in experience. For the rationalist it remains a pure abstraction, to the bare name of which we must defer. When the pragmatist undertakes to show in detail just why we must defer, the rationalist is unable to recognize the concretes from which his own abstraction is taken. He accuses us of *denying* truth; whereas we have only sought to trace exactly why people follow it and always ought to follow it. Your typical ultra-abstractionist fairly shudders at concreteness: other things equal, he positively prefers the pale and spectral. If the two universes were offered, he would always choose the skinny outline rather than the rich thicket of reality. It is so much purer, clearer, nobler.

I hope that as these lectures go on, the concreteness and closeness to facts of the pragmatism which they advocate may be what approves itself to you as its most satisfactory peculiarity. It only follows here the example of the sister-sciences, interpreting the unobserved by the observed. It brings old and new harmoniously together. It converts the absolutely empty notion of a static relation of "correspondence" (what that may mean we must ask later) between our minds and reality, into that of a rich and active commerce (that any one may follow in detail and understand) between particular thoughts of ours, and the great universe of other experiences in which they play their parts and have their uses.

But enough of this at present? The justification of what I say must be postponed. I wish now to add a word in further explanation of the claim I made at our last meeting, that pragmatism may be a happy harmonizer of empiricist ways of thinking with the more religious demands of human beings.

Men who are strongly of the fact-loving temperament, you may remember me to have said, are liable to be kept at a distance by the small sympathy with facts which that philosophy from the present-day fashion of idealism offers them. It is far too intellectualistic. Old fashioned theism was bad enough, with its notion of God as an exalted monarch, made up of a lot of unintelligible or preposterous "attributes"; but, so long as it held strongly by the argument from design, it kept some touch with concrete realities. Since, however, Darwinism has once for all displaced design from the minds of the "scientific," theism has lost that foothold; and some kind of an immanent or pantheistic deity working in things rather than above them is, if any, the kind recommended to our contemporary imagination. Aspirants to a philosophic religion turn, as a rule, more hopefully nowadays towards idealistic pantheism than towards the older dualistic theism, in spite of the fact that the latter still counts able defenders.

But, as I said in my first lecture, the brand of pantheism offered is hard for them to assimilate if they are lovers of facts, or empirically minded. It is the absolutistic brand, spurning the dust and reared upon pure logic. It keeps no connexion whatever with concreteness. Affirming the Absolute Mind, which is its substitute for God, to be the rational presupposition of all particulars of fact, whatever they may be, it remains supremely indifferent to what the particular facts in our world actually are. Be they what they may, the Absolute will father them. Like the sick lion in Esop's fable, all footprints lead into his den, but *nulla vestigia retrorsum* [no footprints were left]. You cannot redescend into the world of particulars by the Absolute's aid, or deduce any necessary consequences of detail important for your life from your idea of his nature. He gives you indeed the assurance that all is well with *Him,* and for his eternal way of thinking; but thereupon he leaves you to be finitely saved by your own temporal devices.

Far be it from me to deny the majesty of this conception, or its capacity to yield religious comfort to a most respectable class of minds. But from the human point of view, no one can pretend that it doesn't suffer from the faults of remoteness and abstractness. It is eminently a product of what I have ventured to call the rationalistic temper. It disdains empiricism's needs. It substitutes a pallid outline for the real world's richness. It is dapper, it is noble in the bad sense, in the sense in which to be noble is to be inapt for humble service. In this real world of sweat and dirt, it seems to me that when a view of things is "noble," that ought to count as a presumption against its truth, and as a philosophic disqualification. The prince of darkness may be a gentleman, as we are told he is, but whatever the God of earth and heaven is, he can surely be no gentleman. His menial services are needed in the dust of our human trials, even more than his dignity is needed in the empyrean.

Now pragmatism, devoted though she be to facts, has no such materialistic bias as ordinary empiricism labors under. Moreover, she has no objection whatever to the realizing of abstractions, so long as you get about among particulars with their aid and they actually carry you somewhere. Interested in no conclusions but those which our minds and our experiences work out together, she has no a priori prejudices against theology. *If theological ideas prove to have a value for concrete life, they will be true, for pragmatism, in the sense of being good for so much. For how much more they are true, will depend entirely on their relations to the other truths that also have to be acknowledged.*

What I said just now about the Absolute, of transcendental idealism, is a case in point. First, I called it majestic and said it yielded religious comfort to a class of minds, and then I accused it of remoteness and sterility. But so far as it affords such comfort, it surely is not sterile; it has that amount of value; it performs a concrete function. As a good pragmatist, I myself ought to call the Absolute true "in so far forth," then; and I unhesitatingly now do so.

But what does *true in so far forth* mean in this case? To answer, we need only apply the pragmatic method. What do believers in the Absolute mean by saying that their belief affords them comfort? They mean that since, in the Absolute finite evil is "overruled" already, we may, therefore, whenever we wish, treat the temporal as if it were potentially the eternal, be sure that we can trust its outcome, and, without sin, dismiss our fear and drop the worry of our finite responsibility. In short, they mean that we have a right ever and anon to take a moral holiday, to let the world wag in its own way, feeling that its issues are in better hands than ours and are none of our business.

The universe is a system of which the individual members may relax their anxieties occasionally, in which the don't-care mood is also right for men, and moral holidays in order,—that, if I mistake not, is part, at least, of what the Absolute is "known-as," that is the great difference in our particular experiences which his being true makes, for us, that is his cash-value when he is pragmatically interpreted. Farther than that the ordinary lay-reader in philosophy who thinks favorably of absolute idealism does not venture to sharpen his conceptions. He can use the Absolute for so much, and so much is very precious. He is pained at hearing you speak incredulously of the Absolute, therefore, and disregards your criticisms because they deal with aspects of the conception that he fails to follow.

If the Absolute means this, and means no more than this, who can possibly deny the truth of it? To deny it would be to insist that men should never relax, and that holidays are never in order.

I am well aware how odd it must seem to some of you to hear me say that an idea is "true" so long as to believe it is profitable to our lives. That it is good, for as much as it profits, you will gladly admit. If what we do by its aid is good, you will allow the idea itself to be good in so far forth, for we are the better for possessing it. But is it not a strange misuse of the word "truth," you will say, to call ideas also "true" for this reason?

To answer this difficulty fully is impossible at this stage of my account. You touch here upon the very central point of Messrs. Schiller's, Dewey's and my own doctrine of truth, which I can not discuss with detail until my sixth lecture. Let me now say only this, that truth is *one species of good,* and not, as is usually supposed, a category distinct from good, and co-ordinate with it. *The true is the name of whatever proves itself to be good in the way of belief, and good, too, for definite, assignable reasons.* Surely you must admit this, that if there were *no* good for life in true ideas, or if the knowledge of them were positively disadvantageous and false ideas the only useful ones, then the current notion that truth is divine and precious, and its pursuit a duty, could never have grown up or become a dogma. In a world like that, our duty would be to *shun* truth, rather. But in this world, just as certain foods are not only agreeable to our taste, but good for our teeth, our stomach, and our tissues; so certain ideas are not only agreeable to think about, or agreeable as supporting other ideas that we are fond of, but they are also helpful in life's practical struggles. If there be any life that it is really better we should lead, and if there be any idea which, if believed in, would help us to lead that life, then it would be really *better for us* to believe in that idea, *unless, indeed, belief in it incidentally clashed with other greater vital benefits.*

"What would be better for us to believe!" This sounds very like a definition of truth. It comes very near to saying "what we *ought* to believe": and in *that* definition none of you would find any oddity. Ought we ever not to believe what it is *better for us* to believe? And can we then keep the notion of what is better for us, and what is true for us, permanently apart?

Pragmatism says no, and I fully agree with her. Probably you also agree, so far as the abstract statement goes, but with a suspicion that if we practically did believe everything that made for good in our own personal lives, we should be found indulging all kinds of fancies about this world's affairs, and all kinds of sentimental superstitions about a world hereafter. Your suspicion here is undoubtedly well founded, and it is evident that something happens when you pass from the abstract to the concrete that complicates the situation.

I said just now that what is better for us to believe is true *unless the belief incidentally clashes with some other vital benefit.* Now in real life what vital benefits is any particular belief of ours most liable to clash with? What indeed except the vital benefits yielded by *other beliefs* when these prove incompatible with the first ones? In other words, the greatest enemy of any one of our truths may be the rest of our truths. Truths have once for all this desperate instinct of self-preservation and of desire to extinguish whatever contradicts them. My belief in the Absolute, based on the good it does me, must run the gauntlet of all my other beliefs. Grant that it may be true in giving me a moral holiday. Nevertheless, as I conceive it,—and let me speak now confidentially, as it were, and merely in my own private person,—it clashes with other truths of mine whose benefits I hate to give up on its account. It happens to be associated with a kind of logic of which I am the enemy, I find that it entangles me in metaphysical paradoxes that are inacceptable, etc., etc. But as I have enough trouble in life already without adding the trouble of carrying these intellectual inconsistencies, I personally just give up the Absolute. I just *take* my moral holidays; or else as a professional philosopher, I try to justify them by some other principle.

If I could restrict my notion of the Absolute to its bare holiday-giving value, it wouldn't clash with my other truths. But we can not easily thus restrict our hypotheses. They carry supernumerary features, and these it is that clash so. My disbelief in the Absolute means then disbelief in those other supernumerary features, for I fully believe in the legitimacy of taking moral holidays.

You see by this what I meant when I called pragmatism a mediator and reconciler and said, borrowing the word from Papini, that she "unstiffens" our theories. She has in fact no prejudices whatever, no obstructive dogmas, no rigid canons of what shall count as proof. She is completely genial. She will entertain any hypothesis, she will consider any evidence. It follows that in the religious field she is at a great advantage both over positivistic empiricism, with its anti-theological bias, and over religious rationalism, with its exclusive interest in the remote, the noble, the simple, and the abstract in the way of conception.

In short, she widens the field of search for God. Rationalism sticks to logic and the empyrean. Empiricism sticks to the external senses. Pragmatism is willing to take anything, to follow either logic or the senses and to count the humblest and most personal experiences. She will count mystical experiences if they have practical consequences. She will take a God who lives in the very dirt of private fact—if that should seem a likely place to find him.

Her only test of probable truth is what works best in the way of leading us, what fits every part of life best and combines with the collectivity of experience's demands, nothing being omitted. If theological ideas should do this, if the notion of God, in particular, should prove to do it, how could pragmatism possibly deny God's existence? She could see no meaning in treating as "not true" a notion that was pragmatically so successful. What other kind of truth could there be, for her, than all this agreement with concrete reality?

In my last lecture I shall return again to the relations of pragmatism with religion. But you see already how democratic she is. Her manners are as various and flexible, her resources as rich and endless, and her conclusions as friendly as those of mother nature.

Friedrich Nietzsche
1844–1900

Friedrich Wilhelm Nietzsche was born in Röcken, Prussia, in 1844. He was named in honor of the Prussian king, Friedrich Wilhelm IV, whose birthday, October 15, he shared. Nietzsche's father, Ludwig Nietzsche, was a Lutheran minister and his mother, Franziska Oehler Nietzsche, was the daughter of a Lutheran minister. When Nietzsche was only 5 years old, his father died from what was called "softening of the brain," after a year of mental instability. The rest of Nietzsche's childhood was spent in a household of women, including his widowed mother, his sister, his anxiety-prone paternal grandmother, and two maiden aunts.

Following grade school, Nietzsche attended a famous boarding school at Pforta, where he did outstanding work. However, while there, Nietzsche suffered migraine headaches, which continued to afflict him until he experienced a mental breakdown in 1889. The medicine he took to relieve the headaches upset his stomach and left him nauseous. For much of his adult life, he alternated between the extremes of headaches and nausea with only short periods of health in between.

In 1864, he enrolled at the University of Bonn to study theology and classical philology (linguistics), but he left within a year. By this time, he had given up whatever religious faith he had and was no longer interested in theology. He then moved to the University of Leipzig to continue his studies in philology. His professor at Leipzig, Friedrich Ritschl, was so impressed with Nietzsche's work that he published some of his papers and later recommended him for a chair of classical philology at the University of Basel. In 1869, at the unusual age of only 24, Nietzsche was given the chair as an associate professor. He had produced neither a doctoral dissertation nor the additional book normally required of an associate professor, but Leipzig immediately awarded him a doctorate without examination or thesis, and within a year he was promoted to full professor at Basel.

In 1872, Nietzsche published his first book, *The Birth of Tragedy*, which included a laudatory section on Richard Wagner's music. Over the next four years, Nietzsche wrote four meditations (published collectively in English as *Thoughts Out of Season*), the last of which was another tribute to Wagner. During this period, Nietzsche and Wagner were close friends; and Nietzsche often visited Wagner's villa on Lake Lucerne. But by 1878, they had broken relations over Wagner's nationalism and anti-Semitism.

Nietzsche's health began to deteriorate, and he was forced to resign from the university in 1879. Over the next ten years, Nietzsche traveled and devoted all his remaining energy to writing, publishing books such as *The Gay Science* (1882), *Thus Spoke Zarathustra* (1883–1885), *Beyond Good and Evil* (1886), *On the Genealogy of Morality* (1887), and his final denunciation of his former friend *The Case of Wagner* (1888).

By the end of 1888, Nietzsche showed signs of oncoming madness, and in January 1889 he collapsed in the street in Turin, Italy, while hugging the neck of a horse. For the next eleven years until his death in 1900, he lived in the care of his mother and sister. Works that he had written in 1888, including *The Will to Power, Twilight of the Idols, The Anti-Christ,* and his outrageous autobiography *Ecco Homo* (which includes chapter headings such as "Why I Am So Clever"), were published after distorted editing by his sister. Only in the twentieth century have unedited versions of these works become available.

The cause of Nietzsche's insanity has been vigorously debated. Critics have held that his ideas caused it and claim to have found evidence of insanity in many of his writings. His sister romanticized that he went mad because Germany spurned him. More likely explanations are that he contracted syphilis during a rare sexual escapade while a young man or that he simply inherited a brain disease from his father.

* * *

Nietzsche's style of writing in epigrams, aphorisms, stories, poetry, and essays virtually defies an editor to systematically summarize his thought. Nevertheless, even though Nietzsche never sought to build a system, there are recurring, interwoven themes represented by the selections given here.

In *The Birth of Tragedy,* translated by Francis Golffing, Nietzsche presents a distinction between Apollonian and Dionysian tendencies in art. The Apollonian tendency (named for the Greek god of the sun, Apollo) represents the harmony and restraint exemplified by Greek sculpture and architecture. The Dionysian tendency (named for the Greek god of wine and revelry, Dionysos) represents wild abandonment as exemplified by the drunken sexual frenzies of the Dionysian cult festivals or the music of Beethoven's Ninth Symphony. Greek tragedy arises as a synthesis of Apollonian form and Dionysian urges. But Greek tragedy is in turn superseded by Greek rationalism as exemplified by Socrates: the theoretical man who optimistically sees knowledge as the panacea to the problems of life. What is needed now, Nietzsche argues, is a new synthesis of these Dionysian and Apollonian tendencies by an "artistic" Socrates. Such a Socratic figure would be a creative genius who would honestly face the harshness of life without losing a clear rational analytic perspective.

In order to face life honestly and clearly, the creative genius must begin by proclaiming the death of God. With the death of God, slave morality—and all values dependent on some external lawgiver—collapses and the individual is free to create self-defined values. By the "death of God," Nietzsche does not mean that there once was a diety who got old and passed away, nor that people no longer should live holy lives. Rather, Nietzsche claims that all *absolutes* have collapsed, and there is no transcendent basis in any area—whether religion, philosophy, science, or politics—for making meaning out of life. The brief selection here from *The Gay Science,* translated by Walter Kaufmann, is one of several passages in which Nietzsche announces the death of God.

In our selection from *Twilight of the Idols,* also translated by Kaufmann, Nietzsche examines how philosophers have tried to find something transcendent, something permanent. Beginning with the Pre-Socratic thinker Parmenides, philosophers have been unwilling to accept the actual transitory world of "becoming." Instead they have denigrated this world, labeling it "apparent," and have in its place invented an immutable world of "being." But, as Nietzsche explains, "Any distinction between a 'true' and an 'apparent' world—whether in the Christian manner or in the manner of Kant . . . is only a suggestion of decadence, a symptom of the *decline of life.*"

The genius who can embrace "becoming," who acknowledges the death of all external values, could become an *Übermensch* ("overman" or "superman"). Such an overman would be a this-world antithesis to God and would affirm life without any resentment. The overman would be to humans as humans are to apes. But, most important, the overman would be one who acknowledges and celebrates the *will to power.*

According to Nietzsche, all human behavior can be understood in terms of the will to power and every relationship between persons is a power relationship. In master morality, the hero asserts the will to power by taking direct action. In slave morality, as explicated in our final selection from Kaufmann's translation of *The Anti-Christ,* the will to power is perverted into resentment in order to gain the imaginary powers of revenge and pity.

But the will to power can also be expressed *within* the person. That is, more than gaining power over others, the will to power can lead to power over the self. The overman will be the one who uses power in this way to "overcome his animal nature, organize the chaos of his passions, sublimate his impulses, and give style to his character,"* becoming completely free and self-created.

Ironically, despite his distaste for anti-Semitism and his emphasis on the *self-* overcoming aspects of the will to power, Nietzsche was hailed as a hero by the Nazis. They used his emphases on the master morality and the will to power as a justification for their atrocities. Nietzsche's sister, Elisabeth, married a German anti-Semite and in her old age eagerly received Adolph Hitler at the Nietzsche Archives. However, despite its unfortunate association with the Nazis, Nietzsche's thought has continued to be influential, as his insights have been developed by existentialists, phenomenologists, psychoanalysts, post-structuralists, and deconstructionists, as well as poets and novelists.

* * *

*Walter Kaufmann, *Nietzsche: Philosopher, Psychologist, Antichrist* (Princeton: Princeton University Press, 1950), p. 316.

A representative sampling of Neitzsche's thought can be found in *The Portable Nietzsche,* edited by Walter A. Kaufmann (New York: Viking Press, 1968). The best general introduction to Nietzsche's thought remains Walter A. Kaufmann, *Nietzsche: Philosopher, Psychologist, Antichrist* (Princeton: Princeton University Press, 1968). Recent overviews include Graham Parke, *Composing the Soul* (Chicago: University of Chicago Press, 1994); John Richardson, *Nietzsche's System* (Oxford: Oxford University Press, 1995); Michael Tanner, *Nietzsche* (Oxford: Oxford University Press, 1995); Ronald Hayman, *Nietzsche* (London: Routledge, 1999); Brian Leiter, *Routledge Philosophy Guidebook to Nietzsche on Morality* (London: Routledge, 2002); Robert C. Solomon, *Living with Nietzsche: What the Great "Immoralist" Has to Teach Us* (Oxford: Oxford University Press, 2003); and R. Kevin Hill, *Nietzsche: A Guide for the Perplexed* (London: Continuum, 2007). Ivo Frenzel, *Friedrich Nietzsche: An Illustrated Biography,* translated by Joachim Neugroschel (New York: Pegasus, 1967); and Sander L. Gilman, ed., *Conversations with Nietzsche: A Life in the Words of His Contemporaries,* translated by David J. Parent (New York: Oxford University Press, 1987), provide general biographies, whereas H.F. Peters, *Zarathustra's Sister: The Case of Elisabeth and Friedrich Nietzsche* (New York: Crown, 1977), presents a fascinating history of the expropriation of Nietzsche's thought in the service of German anti-Semitism. Jacob Golomb and Robert S. Wistrich, eds., *Nietzsche, Godfather of Fascism?: On the Uses and Abuses of a Philosophy* (Princeton: Princeton University Press, 2002) present essays on the same topic. Walter A. Kaufmann, *Nietzsche, Heidegger, and Buber* (New York: McGraw-Hill, 1980); Allan Megill, *Prophets of Extremity: Nietzsche, Heidegger, Foucault, Derrida* (Berkeley: University of California Press, 1985); and Paul S. Miklowitz, *Metaphysics to Metafictions: Hegel, Nietzsche, and the End of Philosophy* (Albany, NY: SUNY Press, 1999) show the connections between Nietzsche and other important thinkers, whereas Ishay Landa, *The Overman in the Marketplace: Nietzschean Heroism in Popular Culture* (Lanham, MD: Lexington Books, 2009) shows how Nietzsche's ideas have played out in popular culture. For collections of critical essays, see Robert C. Solomon, ed., *Nietzsche: A Collection of Critical Essays* (Garden City, NY: Anchor Doubleday, 1973); Harold Bloom, ed., *Friedrich Nietzsche* (New York: Chelsea House, 1987); Richard Schacht, ed., *Nietzsche, Genealogy, Morality: Essays on Nietzsche's* On the Genealogy of Morals (Berkeley: University of California Press, 1994); Peter Sedgwick, ed., *Nietzsche: A Critical Reader* (Oxford: Basil Blackwell, 1995); Bernd Magnus and Kathleen Higgins, *The Cambridge Companion to Nietzsche* (Cambridge: Cambridge University Press, 1996); Kelly Oliver and Marilyn Pearsall, eds., *Feminist Interpretations of Nietzsche* (College Park, PA: Pennsylvania State University Press, 1998); Daniel W. Conway, Nietzsche: Critical Assessments, four volumes (London: Routledge, 1998); Richard White, ed., *Nietzsche* (New York: Ashgate, 2001); Ken Gemes and Simon May, eds., *Nietzsche on Freedom and Autonomy* (Oxford: Oxford University Press, 2009); and Tracy Strong, ed., *Friedrich Nietzsche* (Burlington, VT: Ashgate, 2009). Finally, Robert C. Solomon and Kathleen M. Higgins, eds., *Reading Nietzsche* (New York: Oxford University Press, 1988) provide helpful introductory essays on several of Nietzsche's works, while Daniel W. Conway, *Nietzsche's Dangerous Game: Philosophy in the* Twilight of the Idols (Cambridge: Cambridge University Press, 1997) focuses on Nietzsche's later work.

THE BIRTH OF TRAGEDY (in part)

I. Much will have been gained for esthetics once we have succeeded in apprehending directly—rather than merely *ascertaining*— that art owes its continuous evolution to the Apollonian-Dionysiac duality, even as the propagation of the species depends on the duality of the sexes, their constant conflicts and periodic acts of reconciliation. I have borrowed my adjectives from the Greeks, who developed their mystical doctrines of art through plausible *embodiments,* not through purely conceptual means. It is by those two art-sponsoring deities, Apollo and Dionysos, that we are made to recognize the tremendous split, as regards both origins and objectives, between the plastic, Apollonian arts and the non-visual art of music inspired by Dionysos. The two creative tendencies developed alongside one another, usually in fierce opposition, each by its taunts forcing the other to more energetic production, both perpetuating in a discordant concord that agon which the term art but feebly denominates: until at last, by the thaumaturgy of an Hellenic act of will, the pair accepted the yoke of marriage and, in this condition, begot Attic tragedy, which exhibits the salient features of both parents.

To reach a closer understanding of both these tendencies, let us begin by viewing them as the separate art realms of *dream* and *intoxication,* two physiological phenomena standing toward one another in much the same relationship as the Apollonian and Dionysiac. It was in a dream, according to Lucretius, that the marvelous gods and goddesses first presented themselves to the minds of men. That great sculptor, Phidias, beheld in a dream the entrancing bodies of more-than-human beings, and likewise, if anyone had asked the Greek poets about the mystery of poetic creation, they too would have referred him to dreams and instructed him much as Hans Sachs instructs us in *Die Meistersinger:*

My friend, it is the poet's work
Dreams to interpret and to mark.
Believe me that man's true conceit
In a dream becomes complete:
All poetry we ever read
Is but true dreams interpreted.

The fair illusion of the dream sphere, in the production of which every man proves himself an accomplished artist, is a precondition not only of all plastic art, but even, as we shall see presently, of a wide range of poetry. Here we enjoy an immediate apprehension of form, all shapes speak to us directly, nothing seems indifferent or redundant. Despite the high intensity with which these dream realities exist for us, we still have a residual sensation that they are illusions; at least such has been my experience—and the frequency, not to say normality, of the experience is borne out in many passages of the poets. Men of philosophical disposition are known for their constant premonition that our everyday reality, too, is an illusion, hiding another, totally different kind of reality. It was Schopenhauer who considered the ability to view at certain times all men and things as mere phantoms or dream images to be the true mark of philosophic talent. The person who is responsive to the stimuli of art behaves toward the reality of dream much the way the philosopher behaves toward the reality of existence: he observes exactly and enjoys his observations, for it is by these images that he interprets life, by these processes that he rehearses it. Nor is it by pleasant images only that such plausible connections are made: the whole divine comedy of life, including its somber aspects, its sudden balkings, impish accidents, anxious expectations, moves past him, not quite like a shadow play—for it is he himself, after all, who lives and suffers through these scenes—yet never without giving a fleeting sense of illusion; and I imagine that many persons have reassured themselves amidst the perils of dream by calling out, "It is a dream! I want it to go on." I have even heard of people spinning out the causality of one and the same dream over three or more successive nights. All these facts clearly bear witness that our innermost being, the common substratum of humanity, experiences dreams with deep delight and a sense of real necessity. This deep and happy sense of the necessity of dream experiences was expressed by the Greeks in the image of Apollo. Apollo is at once the god of all plastic powers and the soothsaying god. He who is etymologically the "lucent" one, the god of light, reigns also over the fair illusion of our inner world of fantasy. The perfection of these conditions in contrast to our imperfectly understood waking reality, as well as our profound awareness of nature's healing powers during the interval of sleep and dream, furnishes a symbolic analogue to the soothsaying faculty and quite generally to the arts, which make life possible and worth living. But the image of Apollo must incorporate that thin line which the dream image may not cross, under penalty of becoming pathological, of imposing itself on us as crass reality: a discreet limitation, a freedom from all extravagant urges, the sapient tranquillity of the plastic god. His eye must be sunlike, in keeping with his origin. Even at those moments when he is angry and ill-tempered there lies upon him the consecration of fair illusion. In an eccentric way one might say of Apollo what Schopenhauer says, in the first part of *The World as Will and Idea,* of man caught in the veil of Maya: "Even as on an immense, raging sea, assailed by huge wave crests, a man sits in a little rowboat trusting his frail craft, so, amidst the furious torments of this world, the individual sits tranquilly, supported by the *principium individuationis* and relying on it." One might say that the unshakable confidence in that principle has received its most magnificent expression in Apollo, and that Apollo himself may be regarded as the marvelous divine image of the *principium individuationis,* whose looks and gestures radiate the full delight, wisdom, and beauty of "illusion."

In the same context Schopenhauer has described for us the tremendous awe which seizes man when he suddenly begins to doubt the cognitive modes of experience, in other words, when in a given instance the law of causation seems to suspend itself. If we add to this awe the glorious transport which arises in man, even from the very depths of nature, at the shattering of the *principium individuationis,* then we are in a position to apprehend the essence of Dionysiac rapture, whose closest analogy is furnished by physical intoxication. Dionysiac stirrings arise either through the influence of those narcotic potions of which all primitive races speak in their hymns, or through the powerful approach of spring, which penetrates with joy the whole frame of nature. So stirred, the individual forgets himself completely. It is the Same Dionysiac power which in medieval Germany drove ever increasing crowds of people singing and dancing from place to place; we recognize in these St. John's and St. Vitus' dancers the bacchic choruses of the Greeks, who had their precursors in Asia Minor and as far back as Babylon and the orgiastic Sacaea. There are people who, either from lack of experience or out of sheer stupidity, turn away from such phenomena, and, strong in the sense of their own sanity, label them either mockingly or pityingly "endemic diseases." These benighted souls have no idea how cadaverous and ghostly their "sanity" appears as the intense throng of Dionysiac revelers sweeps past them.

Not only does the bond between man and man come to be forged once more by the magic of the Dionysiac rite, but nature itself, long alienated or subjugated, rises again to celebrate the reconciliation with her prodigal son, man. The earth offers its gifts voluntarily, and the savage beasts of mountain and desert approach in peace. The chariot of Dionysos is bedecked with flowers and garlands; panthers and tigers stride beneath his yoke. If one were to convert Beethoven's "Paean to Joy" into a painting, and refuse to curb the imagination when that multitude prostrates itself reverently in the dust, one might form some apprehension of Dionysiac ritual. Now the slave emerges as a freeman; all the rigid, hostile walls which either necessity or despotism has erected between men are shattered. Now that the gospel of universal harmony is sounded, each individual becomes not only reconciled to his fellow but actually at one with him—as though the veil of Maya had been torn apart and there remained only shreds floating before the vision of mystical Oneness. Man now expresses himself through song and dance as the member of a higher community; he has forgotten how to walk, how to speak, and is on the brink of taking wing as he dances. Each of his gestures betokens enchantment; through him sounds a supernatural power, the same power which makes the animals speak and the earth render up milk and honey. He feels himself to be godlike and strides with the same elation and ecstasy as the gods he has seen in his dreams. No longer the *artist,* he has himself become a *work of art: the productive power of the whole universe is now manifest in his transport, to the glorious satisfaction of the primordial One. The finest clay, the most precious marble—man—is here kneaded and hewn, and the chisel blows of the Dionysiac world artist* are accompanied by the cry of the Eleusinian mystagogues: "Do you fall on your knees, multitudes, do you divine your creator?"

II. So far we have examined the Apollonian and Dionysiac states as the product of formative forces arising directly from nature without the mediation of the human artist. At this stage artistic urges are satisfied directly, on the one hand through the imagery of dreams, whose perfection is quite independent of the intellectual rank, the artistic development of the individual; on the other hand, through an ecstatic reality which once again takes no account of the individual and may even destroy him, or else redeem him through a mystical experience of the collective. In relation to these immediate creative conditions of nature every artist must appear as "imitator," either as the Apollonian dream artist or the Dionysiac ecstatic artist, or, finally (as in Greek tragedy, for example) as dream and ecstatic artist in one. We might picture to ourselves how the last of these, in a state of Dionysiac intoxication and mystical self-abrogation, wandering apart from the reveling throng, sinks upon the ground, and how there is then revealed to him his own condition—complete oneness with the essence of the universe—in a dream similitude.

Having set down these general premises and distinctions, we now turn to the Greeks in order to realize to what degree the formative forces of nature were developed in them. Such an inquiry will enable us to assess properly the relation of the Greek artist to his prototypes or, to use Aristotle's expression, his "imitation of nature." Of the dreams the Greeks dreamed it is not possible to speak with any certainty, despite the extant dream literature and the large number of dream anecdotes. But considering the incredible accuracy of their eyes, their keen and unabashed delight in colors, one can hardly be wrong in assuming that their dreams too showed a strict consequence of lines and contours, hues and groupings, a progression of scenes similar to their best

Starry Night, 1889, by Vincent van Gogh (1853–1890). It is hard not to think of the paintings of Nietzsche's contemporary Vincent van Gogh when reading Nietzsche's words: "If one were to convert Beethoven's 'Paean to Joy' into a painting, and refuse to curb the imagination when that multitude prostrates itself reverently in the dust, one might form some apprehension of Dionysiac ritual." (*© The Museum of Modern Art, NY./Scale, Florence. Acquired through the Lillie P. Bliss Bequest*)

bas-reliefs. The perfection of these dream scenes might almost tempt us to consider the dreaming Greek as a Homer and Homer as a dreaming Greek; which would be as though the modern man were to compare himself in his dreaming to Shakespeare.

Yet there is another point about which we do not have to conjecture at all: I mean the profound gap separating the Dionysiac Greeks from the Dionysiac barbarians. Throughout the range of ancient civilization (leaving the newer civilizations out of account for the moment) we find evidence of Dionysiac celebrations which stand to the Greek type in much the same relation as the bearded satyr, whose name and attributes are derived from the he-goat, stands to the god Dionysos. The central concern of such celebrations was, almost universally, a complete sexual promiscuity overriding every form of established tribal law; all the savage urges of the mind were unleashed on those occasions until they reached that paroxysm of lust and cruelty which has always struck me as the "witches' cauldron" *par excellence.* It would appear that the Greeks were for a while quite immune from these feverish excesses which must have reached them by every known land or sea route. What kept Greece safe was the proud, imposing image of Apollo, who in holding up the head of the Gorgon to those brutal and grotesque

Dionysiac forces subdued them. Doric art has immortalized Apollo's majestic rejection of all license. But resistance became difficult, even impossible, as soon as similar urges began to break forth from the deep substratum of Hellenism itself. Soon the function of the Delphic god developed into something quite different and much more limited: all he could hope to accomplish now was to wrest the destructive weapon, by a timely gesture of pacification, from his opponent's hand. That act of pacification represents the most important event in the history of Greek ritual; every department of life now shows symptoms of a revolutionary change. The two great antagonists have been reconciled. Each feels obliged henceforth to keep to his bounds, each will honor the other by the bestowal of periodic gifts, while the cleavage remains fundamentally the same. And yet, if we examine what happened to the Dionysiac powers under the pressure of that treaty we notice a great difference: in the place of the Babylonian Sacaea, with their throwback of men to the condition of apes and tigers, we now see entirely new rites celebrated: rites of universal redemption, of glorious transfiguration. Only now has it become possible to speak of nature's celebrating an aesthetic triumph; only now has the abrogation of the *principium individuationis* become an aesthetic event. That terrible witches' brew concocted of lust and cruelty has lost all power under the new conditions. Yet the peculiar blending of emotions in the heart of the Dionysiac reveler—his ambiguity if you will—seems still to hark back (as the medicinal drug harks back to the deadly poison) to the days when the infliction of pain was experienced as joy while a sense of supreme triumph elicited cries of anguish from the heart. For now in every exuberant joy there is heard an undertone of terror, or else a wistful lament over an irrecoverable loss. It is as though in these Greek festivals a sentimental trait of nature were coming to the fore, as though nature were bemoaning the fact of her fragmentation, her decomposition into separate individuals. The chants and gestures of these revelers, so ambiguous in their motivation, represented an absolute *novum* in the world of the Homeric Greeks; their Dionysiac music, in especial, spread abroad terror and a deep shudder. It is true: music had long been familiar to the Greeks as an Apollonian art, as a regular beat like that of waves lapping the shore, a plastic rhythm expressly developed for the portrayal of Apollonian conditions. Apollo's music was a Doric architecture of sound—of barely hinted sounds such as are proper to the cithara. Those very elements which characterize Dionysiac music and, after it, music quite generally: the heart-shaking power of tone, the uniform stream of melody, the incomparable resources of harmony—all those elements had been carefully kept at a distance as being inconsonant with the Apollonian norm. In the Dionysiac dithyramb man is incited to strain his symbolic faculties to the utmost; something quite unheard of is now clamoring to be heard: the desire to tear asunder the veil of Maya, to sink back into the original oneness of nature; the desire to express the very essence of nature symbolically. Thus an entirely new set of symbols springs into being. First all the symbols pertaining to physical features: mouth, face, the spoken word, the dance movement which coordinates the limbs and bends them to its rhythm. Then suddenly all the rest of the symbolic forces—music and rhythm as such, dynamics, harmony—assert themselves with great energy. In order to comprehend this total emancipation of all the symbolic powers one must have reached the same measure of inner freedom those powers themselves were making manifest; which is to say that the votary of Dionysos could not be understood except by his own kind. It is not difficult to imagine the awed surprise with which the Apollonian Greek must have looked on him. And that surprise would be further increased as the latter realized, with a shudder, that all this was not so alien to him after all, that his Apollonian consciousness was but a thin veil hiding from him the whole Dionysiac realm.

III. In order to comprehend this we must take down the elaborate edifice of Apollonian culture stone by stone until we discover its foundations. At first the eye is struck by the marvelous shapes of the Olympian gods who stand upon its pediments, and whose exploits, in shining bas-relief, adorn its friezes. The fact that among them we find Apollo as one god among many, making no claim to a privileged position, should not mislead us. The same drive that found its most complete representation in Apollo generated the whole Olympian world, and in this sense we may consider Apollo the father of that world. But what was the radical need out of which that illustrious society of Olympian beings sprang?

Whoever approaches the Olympians with a different religion in his heart, seeking moral elevation, sanctity, spirituality, loving-kindness, will presently be forced to turn away from them in ill-humored disappointment. Nothing in these deities reminds us of asceticism, high intellect, or duty: we are confronted by luxuriant, triumphant *existence,* which deifies the good and the bad indifferently. And the beholder may find himself dismayed in the presence of such overflowing life and ask himself what potion these heady people must have drunk in order to behold, in whatever direction they looked, Helen laughing back at them, the beguiling image of their own existence. But we shall call out to this beholder, who has already turned his back: Don't go! Listen first to what the Greeks themselves have to say of this life, which spreads itself before you with such puzzling serenity. An old legend has it that King Midas hunted a long time in the woods for the wise Silenus, companion of Dionysos, without being able to catch him. When he had finally caught him the king asked him what he considered man's greatest good. The daemon remained sullen and uncommunicative until finally, forced by the king, he broke into a shrill laugh and spoke: "Ephemeral wretch, begotten by accident and toil, why do you force me to tell you what it would be your greatest boon not to hear? What would be best for you is quite beyond your reach: not to have been born, not to be, to be *nothing.* But the second best is to die soon."

What is the relation of the Olympian gods to this popular wisdom? It is that of the entranced vision of the martyr to his torment.

Now the Olympian magic mountain opens itself before us, showing us its very roots. The Greeks were keenly aware of the terrors and horrors of existence; in order to be able to live at all they had to place before them the shining fantasy of the Olympians. Their tremendous distrust of the titanic forces of nature: *Moira,* mercilessly enthroned beyond the knowable world; the vulture which fed upon the great philanthropist Prometheus; the terrible lot drawn by wise Oedipus; the curse on the house of Atreus which brought Orestes to the murder of his mother: that whole Panic philosophy, in short, with its mythic examples, by which the gloomy Etruscans perished, the Greeks conquered—or at least hid from view—again and again by means of this artificial Olympus. In order to live at all the Greeks had to construct these deities. The Apollonian need for beauty had to develop the Olympian hierarchy of joy by slow degrees from the original titanic hierarchy of terror, as roses are seen to break from a thorny thicket. How else could life have been borne by a race so hypersensitive, so emotionally intense, so equipped for suffering? The same drive which called art into being as a completion and consummation of existence, and as a guarantee of further existence, gave rise also to that Olympian realm which acted as a transfiguring mirror to the Hellenic will. The gods justified human life by living it themselves—the only satisfactory theodicy ever invented. To exist in the clear sunlight of such deities was now felt to be the highest good, and the only real grief suffered by Homeric man was inspired by the thought of leaving that sunlight, especially when the departure seemed imminent. Now it became possible to stand the wisdom of Silenus on its head and proclaim that it was the worst evil for man to die soon, and second worst for him to die at all. Such laments as arise now arise over short-lived Achilles, over the generations ephemeral as leaves, the decline of the heroic age. It is not unbecoming to even the greatest hero to yearn for an afterlife, though it be as a day laborer. So impetuously, during the Apollonian phase, does man's will desire to remain on earth, so identified does he become with existence, that even his lament turns to a song of praise.

It should have become apparent by now that the harmony with nature which we late-comers regard with such nostalgia, and for which Schiller has coined the cant term naive, is by no means a simple and inevitable condition to be found at the gateway to every culture, a kind of paradise. Such a belief could have been endorsed only by a period for which Rousseau's Emile was an artist and Homer just such an artist nurtured in the bosom of nature. Whenever we encounter "naïveté" in art, we are face to face with the ripest fruit of Apollonian culture—which must always triumph first over titans, kill monsters, and overcome the somber contemplation of actuality, the intense susceptibility to suffering, by means of illusions strenuously and zestfully entertained. But how rare are the instances of true naïveté, of that complete identification with the beauty of appearance! It is this achievement which makes Homer so magnificent—Homer, who, as a single individual, stood to Apollonian popular culture in the same relation as the individual dream artist to the oneiric capacity of a race and of nature generally. The naïveté of Homer must be viewed as a complete victory of Apollonian illusion. Nature often uses illusions of this sort in order to accomplish its secret purposes. The true goal is covered over by a phantasm. We stretch out our hands to the latter, while nature, aided by our deception, attains the former. In the case of the Greeks it was the will wishing to behold itself in the work of art, in the transcendence of genius; but in order so to behold itself its creatures had first to view themselves as glorious, to transpose themselves to a higher sphere, without having that sphere of pure contemplation either challenge them or upbraid them with insufficiency. It was in that sphere of beauty that the Greeks saw the Olympians as their mirror images; it was by means of that aesthetic mirror that the Greek will opposed suffering and the somber wisdom of suffering which always accompanies artisic talent. As a monument to its victory stands Homer, the naive artist.

THE GAY SCIENCE (selections)

108. *New struggles.*—After Buddha was dead, his shadow was still shown for centuries in a cave—a tremendous, gruesome shadow. God is dead; but given the way of men, there may still be caves for thousands of years in which his shadow will be shown.—And we—we still have to vanquish his shadow, too.

124. *In the horizon of the infinite.*—We have left the land and have embarked. We have burned our bridges behind us—indeed, we have gone farther and destroyed the land behind us. Now, little ship, look out! Beside you is the ocean: to be sure, it does not always roar, and at times it lies spread out like silk and gold and reveries of graciousness.

But hours will come when you will realize that it is infinite and that there is nothing more awesome than infinity. Oh, the poor bird that felt free and now strikes the walls of this cage! Woe, when you feel homesick for the land as if it had offered more *freedom*—and there is no longer any "land."

125. *The madman.*— Have you not heard of that madman who lit a lantern in the bright morning hours, ran to the market place, and cried incessantly: "I seek God! I seek God!"—As many of those who did not believe in God were standing around just then, he provoked much laughter. Has he got lost? asked one. Did he lose his way like a child? asked another. Or is he hiding? Is he afraid of us? Has he gone on a voyage? emigrated?—Thus they yelled and laughed.

The madman jumped into their midst and pierced them with his eyes. "Whither is God?" he cried; "I will tell you. *We have killed him*—you and I. All of us are his murderers. But how did we do this? How could we drink up the sea? Who gave us the sponge to wipe away the entire horizon? What were we doing when we unchained this earth from its sun? Whither is it moving now? Whither are we moving? Away from all suns? Are we not plunging continually? Backward, sideward, forward, in all directions? Is there still any up or down? Are we not straying as through an infinite nothing? Do we not feel the breath of empty space? Has it not become colder? Is not night continually closing in on us? Do we not need to light lanterns in the morning? Do we hear nothing as yet of the noise of the gravediggers who are burying God? Do we smell nothing as yet of the divine decomposition? Gods, too, decompose. God is dead. God remains dead. And we have killed him.

"How shall we comfort ourselves, the murderers of all murderers? What was holiest and mightiest of all that the world has yet owned has bled to death under our knives: who will wipe this blood off us? What water is there for us to clean ourselves? What festivals of atonement, what sacred games shalt we have to invent? Is not the greatness of this deed too great for us? Must we ourselves not become gods simply to appear worthy of it? There has never been a greater deed: and whoever is born after us—for the sake of this deed he will belong to a higher history than all history hitherto."

Here the madman fell silent and looked again at his listeners; and they, too, were silent and stared at him in astonishment. At last he threw his lantern on the ground, and it broke into pieces and went out. "I have come too early," he said then; "my time is not yet. This tremendous event is still on its way, still wandering; it has not yet reached the ears of men. Lightning and thunder require time; the light of the stars requires time; deeds, though done, still require time to be seen and heard. This deed is still more distant from them than the most distant *stars—and yet they have done it themselves*."

It has been related further that on the same day the madman forced his way into several churches and there struck up his *requiem aeternam deo*. Led out and called to account, he is said always to have replied nothing but: "What after all are these churches now if they are not the tombs and sepulchers of God?"

TWILIGHT OF THE IDOLS (selections)

THE PROBLEM OF SOCRATES

[1] Concerning life, the wisest men of all ages have judged alike: *it is no good.* Always and everywhere one has heard the same sound from their mouths—a sound full of doubt, full of melancholy, full of weariness of life, full of resistance to life. Even Socrates said, as He died; "To live—that means to be sick a long time: I owe Asclepius the Savior a rooster." Even Socrates was tired of it. What does that evidence? What does it evince? Formerly one would have said (—oh, it has been said, and loud enough, and especially by our pessimists): "At least something of all this must be true! The consensus of the sages evidences the truth." Shall we still talk like that today? *May* we? "At least something must be *sick* here," *we* retort. These wisest men of all ages—they should first be scrutinized closely. Were they all perhaps shaky on their legs? late? tottery? decadents? Could it be that wisdom appears on earth as a raven, inspired by a little whiff of carrion?

[2] This irreverent thought that the great sages are *types of decline* first occurred to me precisely in a case where it is most strongly opposed by both scholarly and unscholarly prejudice: I recognized Socrates and Plato to be symptoms of degeneration, tools of the Greek dissolution, pseudo-Greek, anti-Greek (*Birth of Tragedy*, 1872). The consensus of the sages—I comprehended this ever more clearly—proves least of all that they were right in what they agreed on: it shows rather that they themselves, these wisest men, agreed in some *physiological* respect, and hence adopted the same negative attitude to life—*had to* adopt it. Judgments, judgments of value, concerning life, for it or against it, can, in the end, never be true: they have value only as symptoms, they are worthy of consideration only as symptoms; in themselves such judgments are stupidities. One must by all means stretch out one's fingers and make the attempt to grasp this amazing finesse, *that the value of life cannot be estimated.* Not by the living, for they are an interested party, even a bone of contention, and not judges; not by the dead, for a different reason. For a philosopher to see a problem in the value of life is thus an objection to him, a question mark concerning his wisdom, an un-wisdom. Indeed? All these great wise men—they were not only decadents but not wise at all? But I return to the problem of Socrates.

[3] In origin, Socrates belonged to the lowest class: Socrates was plebs. We know, we can still see for ourselves, how ugly he was. But ugliness, in itself an objection, is among the Greeks almost a refutation. Was Socrates a Greek at all? Ugliness is often enough the expression of a development that has been crossed, *thwarted* by crossing. Or it appears as declining development. The anthropologists among the criminologists tell us that the typical criminal is ugly: *monstrum in fronte, monstrum in animo.* But the criminal is a decadent. Was Socrates a typical criminal? At least that would not be contradicted by the famous judgment of the physiognomist which sounded so offensive to the friends of Socrates. A foreigner who knew about faces once passed through Athens and told Socrates to his face that he *was a monstrum*—that he harbored in himself all the bad vices and appetites. And Socrates merely answered: "You know me, sir!"

[4] Socrates' decadence is suggested not only by the admitted wantonness and anarchy of his instincts, but also by the hypertrophy of the logical faculty and that *sarcasm of the rachitic* which distinguishes him. Nor should we forget those auditory hallucinations which, as "the *daimonion* of Socrates," have been interpreted religiously. Everything in him is exaggerated, *buffo,* a caricature, everything is at the same time concealed, ulterior, subterranean. I seek to comprehend what idiosyncrasy begot that Socratic equation of reason, virtue, and happiness: that most bizarre of all equations, which. moreover, is opposed to all the instincts of the earlier Greeks.

[5] With Socrates, Greek taste changes in favor of dialectics. What really happened there? Above all, a *noble* taste is thus vanquished; with dialectics the plebs come to the top. Before Socrates, dialectic manners were repudiated in good society: they were considered bad manners, they were compromising. The young were warned against them. Furthermore, all such presentations of one's reasons were distrusted. Honest things, like honest men, do not carry their reasons in their hands like that. It is indecent to show all five fingers. What must first be proved is worth little. Wherever authority still forms part of good bearing, where one does not give reasons but commands, the dialectician is a kind of buffoon: one laughs at him, one does not take him seriously. Socrates was the buffoon who *got himself taken seriously:* what really happened there?

[6] One chooses dialectic only when one has no other means. One knows that one arouses mistrust with it, that it is not very persuasive. Nothing is easier to erase than a dialectical effect: the experience of every meeting at which there are speeches proves this. It can only be *self-defense* for those who no longer have other weapons. One must have to *enforce* one's right: until one reaches that point, one makes no use of it. The Jews were dialecticians for that reason; Reynard the Fox was one—and Socrates too?

[7] Is the irony of Socrates an expression of revolt? Of plebeian *ressentiment?* Does he, as one oppressed, enjoy his own ferocity in the knife-thrusts of his syllogisms? Does he *avenge* himself on the noble people whom he fascinates? As a dialectician, one holds a merciless tool in one's hand; one can become a tyrant by means of it; one compromises those one conquers. The dialectician leaves it to his opponent to prove that he is no idiot: be makes one furious and helpless at the same time. The dialectician renders the intellect of his opponent powerless. Indeed? Is dialectic only, a form of *revenge* in Socrates?

[8] I have given to understand how it was that Socrates could repel: it is therefore all the more necessary to explain his fascination. That he discovered a new kind of *agon* ["contest"], that he became its first fencing master for the noble circles of Athens, is one point. He fascinated by appealing to the agonistic impulse of the Greeks-he introduced a variation into the wrestling match between young men and youths. Socrates was also a great *erotic.*

[9] But Socrates guessed even more. He saw *through* his noble Athenians; he comprehended that his own case, his idiosyncrasy, was no longer exceptional. The same kind of degeneration was quietly developing everywhere: old Athens was coming to an end. And Socrates understood that all the world *needed* him—his means, his cure, his personal artifice of self-preservation. Everywhere the instincts were in anarchy; everywhere one was within five paces of excess: *monstrum in animo* was the general danger. "The impulses want to play the tyrant; one must invent a *counter-tyrant* who is stronger." When the physiognomist had revealed to Socrates who he was—a cave of bad appetites—the great master of irony let slip another word which is the key to Ms character. "This is true," he said, "but I mastered them all." *How* did Socrates become master over *himself?* His case was, at bottom, merely the extreme case only the most striking instance of what was then beginning to be a universal distress: no one was any longer master over himself, the instincts turned *against* each other. He fascinated, being this

extreme case; his awe-inspiring ugliness proclaimed him as such to all who could see; he fascinated, of course, even more as an answer, a solution, an apparent *cure* of this case.

[10] When one finds it necessary to turn *reason* into a tyrant, as Socrates did, the danger cannot be slight that something else will play the tyrant. Rationality was then hit upon as the savior; neither Socrates nor his "patients" had any choice about being rational: it was *de rigeur,* it was their last resort. The fanaticism with which all Greek reflection throws itself upon rationality betrays a desperate situation; there was danger, there was but one choice: either to perish or—to be *absurdly rational.* The moralism of the Greek philosophers from Plato on is pathologically conditioned; so is their esteem of dialectics. Reason-virtue-happiness, that means merely that one must imitate Socrates and counter the dark appetites with a permanent daylight—the daylight of reason. One must be clever, clear, bright at any price: any concession to the instincts, to the unconscious, leads *downward.*

[11] I have given to understand how it was that Socrates fascinated he seemed to be a physician, a savior. Is it necessary to go on to demonstrate the error in his faith in "rationality at any price"? It is a self-deception on the part of philosophers and moralists if they believe that they are extricating themselves from decadence when they merely wage war against it. Extrication lies beyond their strength: what they choose as a means, as salvation, is itself but another expression of decadence; they change its expression, but they do not get rid of decadence itself. Socrates was a misunderstanding; *the whole improvement—morality, including the Christian, was a misunderstanding.* The most blinding daylight; rationality at any price; life, bright, cold, cautious, conscious, without instinct, in opposition to the instincts—all this too was a mere disease, another disease, and by no means a return to "virtue," to "health," to happiness. To *have* to fight the instincts—that is the formula of decadence: as long as life *is ascending,* happiness equals instinct.

[12] Did he himself still comprehend this, this most brilliant of all self-outwitters? Was this what he said to himself in the end, in the *wisdom* of his courage to die? Socrates *wanted* to die: not Athens, but he himself chose the hemlock; he forced Athens to sentence him. "Socrates is no physician," he said softly to himself; "here death alone is the physician. Socrates himself has merely been sick a long time."

"REASON" IN PHILOSOPHY

[1] You ask me which of the philosophers' traits are really idiosyncrasies? For example, their lack of historical sense, their hatred of the very idea of becoming, their Egypticism. They think that they show their *respect* for a subject when they de-historicize it, *sub specie aeterni*— when they turn it into a mummy. All that philosophers have handled for thousands of years have been concept-mummies; nothing real escaped their grasp alive. When these honorable idolators of concepts worship something, they kill it and stuff it; they threaten the life of everything they worship. Death, change, old age, as well as procreation and growth, are to their minds objections—even refutations. Whatever has being does not become; whatever becomes does not have being. Now they all believe, desperately even, in what has being. But since they never grasp it, they seek for reasons why it is kept from them. "There must be mere appearance, there must be some deception which prevents us from perceiving that which has being: where is the deceiver?"

"We have found him," they cry ecstatically; "it is the senses! These senses, which are so immoral in other ways too, deceive us concerning the *true* world. Moral: let us free ourselves from the deception of the senses, from becoming, from history, from lies; history is nothing but faith in the senses, faith in lies. Moral: let us say No to all who have faith in the senses, to all the rest of mankind; they are all 'mob.' Let us be philosophers! Let us be mummies! Let us represent monotono-theism by adopting the expression of a gravedigger! And above all, away with the body, this wretched *idée fixe* of the senses, disfigured by all the fallacies of logic, refuted, even impossible, although it is impudent enough to behave as if it were real!"

[2] With the highest respect, I except the name of *Heraclitus.* When the rest of the philosophic folk rejected the testimony of the senses because they showed multiplicity and change, he rejected their testimony because they showed things as if they had permanence and unity. Heraclitus too did the senses an injustice. They lie neither in the way the Eleatics believed, nor as he believed—they do not lie at all. What we *make* of their testimony, that alone introduces lies; for example, the lie of unity, the lie of thinghood, of substance, of permanence. "Reason" is the cause of our falsification of the testimony of the senses. Insofar as the senses show becoming, passing away, and change, they do not lie. But Heraclitus will remain eternally right with his assertion that being is an empty fiction. The "apparent" world is the only one: the "true" world is merely added by a lie.

[3] And what magnificent instruments of observation we possess in our senses! This nose, for example, of which no philosopher has yet spoken with reverence and gratitude, is actually the most delicate instrument so far at our disposal: it is able to detect minimal differences of motion which even a spectroscope cannot detect. Today we possess science precisely to the extent to which we have decided to *accept* the testimony of the senses—to the extent to which we sharpen them further, arm them, and have learned to think them through. The rest is miscarriage and not-yet-science-in other words, metaphysics, theology, psychology, epistemology—or formal science, a doctrine of signs, such as logic and that applied logic which is called mathematics. In them reality is not encountered at all, not even as a problem—no more than the question of the value of such a sign-convention as logic.

[4] The other idiosyncrasy of the philosophers is no less dangerous; it consists in confusing the last and the first. They place that which comes at the end—unfortunately! for it ought not to come at all!—namely, the "highest concepts," which means the most general, the emptiest concepts, the last smoke of evaporating reality, in the beginning, *as* the beginning. This again is nothing but their way of showing reverence: the higher *may* not grow out of the lower, may not have grown at all. Moral: whatever is of the first rank must be *causa sui* [self-caused]. Origin out of something else is considered an objection, a questioning of value. All the highest values are of the first rank; all the highest concepts, that which has being, the unconditional, the good, the true, the perfect—all these cannot have become and must therefore be *causa sui.* All these, moreover, cannot be unlike each other or in contradiction to each other. Thus they arrive at their stupendous concept, "God." That which is last, thinnest, and emptiest is put first, as *the* cause, as *ens realissimum* [the most real being]. Why did mankind have to take seriously the brain afflictions of sick web-spinners? They have paid dearly for it!

[5] At long last, let us contrast the very different manner in which we conceive the problem of error and appearance. (I say "we" for politeness' sake.) Formerly, alteration, change, any becoming at all, were taken as proof of mere appearance, as an indication that there must be something which led us astray. Today, conversely, precisely insofar as

the prejudice of reason forces us to posit unity, identity, permanence, substance, cause, thinghood, being, we see ourselves somehow caught in error, compelled into error. So certain are we, on the basis of rigorous examination, that this is where the error lies.

It is no different in this case than with the movement of the sun: there our eye is the constant advocate of error, here it is our language. In its origin language belongs in the age of the most rudimentary form of psychology. We enter a realm of crude fetishism when we summon before consciousness the basic presuppositions of the metaphysics of language, in plain talk, the presuppositions of reason. Everywhere it sees a doer and doing; it believes in will as *the* cause; it believes in the ego, in the ego as being, in the ego as substance, and it projects this faith in the ego-substance upon all things—only thereby does it first *create* the concept of "thing." Everywhere "being" is projected by thought, pushed underneath, as the cause; the concept of being follows, and is a derivative of, the concept of ego. In the beginning there is that great calamity of an error that the will is something which is effective, that will is a capacity. Today we know that it is only a word.

Very much later, in a world which was in a thousand ways more enlightened, philosophers, to their great surprise, became aware of the sureness, the subjective certainty, in our handling of the categories of reason: they concluded that these categories could not be derived from anything empirical—for everything empirical plainly contradicted them. Whence, then, were they derived?

And in India, as in Greece, the same mistake was made: "We must once have been at home in a higher world (instead of a very much lower one, which would have been the truth); we must have been divine, for we have reason!" Indeed, nothing has yet possessed a more naive power of persuasion than the error concerning being, as it has been formulated by the Eleatics, for example. After all, every word we say and every sentence speak in its favor. Even the opponents of the Eleatics still succumbed to the seduction of their concept of being: Democritus, among others, when he invented his atom. "Reason" in language—oh, what an old deceptive female she is! I am afraid we are not rid of God because we still have faith in grammar.

[6] It will be appreciated if I condense so essential and so new an insight into four theses. In that way I facilitate comprehension; in that way I provoke contradiction.

First proposition. The reasons for which "this" world has been characterized as "apparent" are the very reasons which indicate its reality; any other kind of reality is absolutely indemonstrable.

Second proposition. The criteria which have been bestowed on the "true being" of things are the criteria of not-being, of *naught;* the "true world" has been constructed out of contradiction to the actual world: indeed an apparent world, insofar as it is merely a moral-optical illusion.

Third proposition. To invent fables about a world "other" than this one has no meaning at all, unless an instinct of slander, detraction, and suspicion against life has gained the upper hand in us: in that case, we avenge ourselves against life with a phantasmagoria of "another," a "better" life.

Fourth proposition. Any distinction between a "true" and an "apparent" world—whether in the Christian manner or in the manner of Kant (in the end, an underhanded Christian)—is only a suggestion of decadence, a symptom of the *decline of life.* That the artist esteems appearance higher than reality is no objection to this proposition. For "appearance" in this case means reality *once more,* only by way of selection, reinforcement, and correction. The tragic artist is no pessimist: he is precisely the one who says Yes to everything questionable, even to the terrible—he is *Dionysian.*

HOW THE "TRUE WORLD" FINALLY BECAME A FABLE

THE HISTORY OF AN ERROR

1. The true world—attainable for the sage, the pious, the virtuous man; he lives in it, *he is it.*

(The oldest form of the idea, relatively sensible, simple, and persuasive. A circumlocution for the sentence, "I, Plato, *am* the truth.")

2. The true world—unattainable for now, but promised for the sage, the pious, the virtuous man ("for the sinner who repents")

(Progress of the idea: it becomes more subtle, insidious, incomprehensible—*it becomes female,* it becomes Christian.)

3. The true world—unattainable, indemonstrable, unpromisable; but the very thought of it—a consolation, an obligation, an imperative.

(At bottom, the old sun, but seen through mist and skepticism. The idea has become elusive, pale, Nordic, Königsbergian [i.e., Kantian].)

4. The true world—unattainable? At any rate, unattained. And being unattained, also *unknown.* Consequently, not *consoling,* redeeming, or obligating: how could something unknown obligate us?

(Gray morning. The first yawn of reason. The cockcrow of positivism.)

5. The "true" world—an idea which is no longer good for anything, not even obligating—an idea which has become useless and superfluous—*consequently,* a refuted idea: let us abolish it!

(Bright day; breakfast; return of *bon sens* and cheerfulness; Plato's embarrassed blush; pandemonium of all free spirits.)

6. The true world—we have abolished. What world has remained? The apparent one perhaps? But no! *With the true world we have also abolished the apparent one.*

(Noon; moment of the briefest shadow; end of the longest error; high point of humanity; INCIPIT ZARATHUSTRA.)

MORALITY AS ANTI-NATURE

[1] All passions have a phase when they are merely disastrous, when they drag down their victim with the weight of stupidity—and a later, very much later phase when they wed the spirit, when they "spiritualize" themselves. Formerly, in view of the element of stupidity in passion, war was declared on passion itself, its destruction was plotted; all the old moral monsters are agreed on this: *il faut tuer les passions* [one must kill the passions]. The most famous formula for this is to be found in the New Testament, in that Sermon on the Mount, where, incidentally, things are by no means looked at from a height. There it is said, for example, with particular reference to sexuality: "If thy eye offend thee, pluck it out." Fortunately, no Christian acts in accordance with this precept. *Destroying* the passions and cravings, merely as a preventive measure against their stupidity and the unpleasant consequences of this stupidity—today this itself strikes us as merely another acute form of stupidity. We no longer admire dentists who "pluck out" teeth so that they will not hurt any more.

To be fair, it should be admitted, however, that on the ground out of which Christianity grew, the concept of the "*spiritualization* of passion" could never have been formed. After all the first church, as is well known, fought against the "intelligent" in favor of the "poor in spirit." How could one expect from it an intelligent war against passion? The church fights passion with excision in every sense: its practice, its "cure," is *castratism.* It never asks: "How can one spiritualize, beautify, deify a craving?" It has at all times laid the stress of discipline on extirpation (of sensuality, of pride, of the lust to rule, of avarice, of vengefulness). But an attack on the roots of passion means an attack on the roots of life: the practice of the church *is hostile to life.*

[2] The same means in the fight against a craving—castration, extirpation—is instinctively chosen by those who are too weak-willed, too degenerate, to be able to impose moderation on themselves; by those who are so constituted that they require *La Trappe* [The Trappist Order] to use a figure of speech, or (without any figure of speech) some kind of definitive declaration of hostility, a *cleft* between themselves and the passion. Radical means are indispensable only for the degenerate; the weakness of the will—or, to speak more definitely, the inability not to respond to a stimulus—is itself merely another form of degeneration. The radical hostility, the deadly hostility against sensuality, is always a symptom to reflect on: it entitles us to suppositions concerning the total state of one who is excessive in this manner.

This hostility, this hatred, by the way, reaches its climax only when such types lack even the firmness for this radical cure, for this renunciation of their "devil." One should survey the whole history of the priests and philosophers, including the artists: the most poisonous things against the senses have been said not by the impotent, nor by ascetics, but by the impossible ascetics, by those who really were in dire need of being ascetics.

[3] The spiritualization of sensuality is called *love:* it represents a great triumph over Christianity. Another triumph is our spiritualization of *hostility.* It consists in a profound appreciation of the value of having enemies: in short, it means acting and thinking in the opposite way from that which has been the rule. The church always wanted the destruction of its enemies; we, we immoralists and Antichristians, find our advantage in this, that the church exists. In the political realm too, hostility has now become more spiritual—much more sensible, much more thoughtful, much more *considerate.* Almost every party understands how it is in the interest of its own self-preservation that the opposition should not lose all strength; the same is true of power politics. A new creation in particular—the new *Reich,* for example—needs enemies more than friends: in opposition alone does it *feel* itself necessary, in opposition alone does it *become* necessary.

Our attitude to the "internal enemy" is no different: here too we have spiritualized hostility; here too we have come to appreciate its value. The price of fruitfulness is to be rich in internal opposition; one remains young only as long as the soul does not stretch itself and desire peace. Nothing has become more alien to us than that desideratum of former times, "peace of soul," the *Christian* desideratum; there is nothing we envy less than the moralistic cow and the fat happiness of the good conscience. One has renounced the *great* life when one renounces war.

In many cases, to be sure, "peace of soul" is merely a misunderstanding—something else, which lacks only a more honest name. Without further ado or prejudice, a few examples. "Peace of soul" can be, for one, the gentle radiation of a rich animality into the moral (or religious) sphere. Or the beginning of weariness, the first shadow of evening, of any kind of evening. Or a sign that the air is humid, that south winds are approaching. Or unrecognized gratitude for a good digestion (sometimes called "love of man"). Or the attainment of calm by a convalescent who feels a new relish in all things and waits. Or the state which follows a thorough satisfaction of our dominant passion, the well-being of a rare repletion. Or the senile weakness of our will, our cravings, our vices. Or laziness, persuaded by vanity to give itself moral airs. Or the emergence of certainty, even a dreadful certainty, after long tension and torture by uncertainty. Or the expression of maturity and mastery in the midst of doing, creating, working, and willing—calm breathing, *attained* "freedom of the will." *Twilight of the Idols*— who knows? perhaps also only a kind of "peace of soul."

[4] I reduce a principle to a formula. Every naturalism in morality—that is, every healthy morality—is dominated by an instinct of life; some commandment of life is fulfilled by a determinate canon of "shalt" and "shalt not"; some inhibition and hostile element on the path of life is thus removed. *Anti-natural* morality—that is, almost every morality which has so far been taught, revered, and preached—turns, conversely, *against* the instincts of life: it is *condemnation* of these instincts, now secret, now outspoken and impudent. When it says, "God looks at the heart," it says No to both the lowest and the highest desires of life, and posits God as the *enemy* of *life*. The saint in whom God delights is the ideal eunuch. Life has come to an end where the "kingdom of God" begins.

[5] Once one has comprehended the outrage of such a revolt against life as has become almost sacrosanct in Christian morality, one has, fortunately, also comprehended something else: the futility, apparentness, absurdity, and *mendaciousness* of such a revolt. A condemnation of life by the living remains in the end a mere symptom of a certain kind of life: the question whether it is justified or unjustified is not even raised thereby. One would require a position *outside* of life, and yet have to know it as well as one, as many, as all who have lived it, in order to be permitted even to touch the problem of the *value* of life: reasons enough to comprehend that this problem is for us an unapproachable problem. When we speak of values, we speak with the inspiration, with the way of looking at things, which is part of life: life itself forces us to posit values; life itself values through us when we posit values. From this it follows that even that anti-natural morality which conceives of God as the counter-concept and condemnation of life is only a value judgment of life—but of what life? of what kind of life? I have already given the answer: of declining, weakened, weary, condemned life. Morality, as it has so far been understood—as it has in the end been formulated once more by Schopenhauer, as "negation of the will to life"—is; the very *instinct of decadence,* which makes an imperative of itself. It says: *"Perish!"* It is a condemnation pronounced by the condemned.

[6] Let us finally consider how naive it is altogether to say: "Man *ought* to be such and such!" Reality shows us an enchanting wealth of types, the abundance of a lavish play and change of forms—and some wretched loafer of a moralist comments: "No! Man ought to be different." He even knows what man should be like, this wretched bigot and prig: he paints himself on the wall and comments, *"Ecce homo!"* But even when the moralist addresses himself only to the single human being and says to him, "You ought to be such and such!" he does not cease to make himself ridiculous. The single human being is a piece of *fatum* from the front and from the rear, one law more, one necessity more for all that is yet to come and to be. To say to him, "Change yourself!" is to demand that everything be changed, even retroactively. And indeed there have been consistent moralists who wanted man to be different, that is, virtuous—they wanted him remade in their own image as a prig: to that end, they *negated* the world! No small madness! No modest kind of immodesty!

Morality, insofar as it *condemns* for its own sake, and not out of regard for the concerns, considerations, and contrivances of life, is a specific error with which one ought to have no pity—an *idiosyncrasy of degenerates* which has caused immeasurable harm.

We others, we immoralists, have, conversely, made room in our hearts for every kind of understanding, comprehending, and *approving*. We do not easily negate; we make it a point of honor to be *affirmers*. More and more, our eyes have opened to that economy which needs and knows how to utilize all that the holy witlessness of the priest, of the *diseased* reason in the priest, rejects—that economy in the law of life which finds an advantage even in the disgusting species of the prigs, the priests, the virtuous. *What* advantage? But we ourselves, we immoralists, are the answer.

THE FOUR GREAT ERRORS

[1] *The error of confusing cause and effect.* There is no more dangerous error than that of mistaking the effect for the cause. I call it the real corruption of reason. Yet this error belongs among the most ancient and recent habits of mankind. It is even hallowed among us and goes by the name of "religion" or "morality." Every single sentence which religion and morality formulate contains it; priests and legislators of moral codes are the originators of this corruption of reason.

I give an example. Everybody knows the book of the famous Cornaro in which he recommends his slender diet as a recipe for a long and happy life—a virtuous one too. Few books have been read so much; even now thousands of copies are sold in England every year. I do not doubt that scarcely any book (except the Bible, as is meet) has done as much harm, has *shortened* as many lives, as this well-intentioned *curiosum.* The reason: the mistaking of the effect for the cause. The worthy Italian thought his diet was the *cause* of his long life, whereas the precondition for a long life, the extraordinary slowness of his metabolism, the consumption of so little, was the cause of his slender diet. He was not free to eat little *or* much; his frugality was not a matter of "free will": he became sick when he ate more. But whoever is no carp not only does well to eat properly, but needs to. A scholar in our time, with his rapid consumption of nervous energy, would simply destroy himself with Cornaro's diet. *Crede experto* ["Believe him who has tried!"]

[2] The most general formula on which every religion and morality is founded is: "Do this and that, refrain from this and that—then you will be happy! Otherwise . . ." Every morality, every religion, is this imperative; I call it the great original sin of reason, the *immortal unreason.* In my mouth, this formula is changed into its opposite—first example of my "revaluation of all values": a well-turned-out human being, a "happy one," *must* perform certain actions and shrinks instinctively from other actions; he carries the order, which he represents physiologically, into his relations with other human beings and things. In a formula: his virtue is the *effect* of his happiness. A long life, many descendants—this is not the wages of virtue; rather virtue itself is that slowing down of the metabolism which leads, among other things, also to a long life, many descendants—in short, to *Cornarism.*

The church and morality say: "A generation, a people, are destroyed by license and luxury." My *recovered* reason says: when a people approaches destruction, when it degenerates physiologically, then license and luxury *follow* from this (namely, the craving for ever stronger and more frequent stimulation, as every exhausted nature knows it). This young man turns pale early and wilts; his friends say; that is due to this or that disease. I say: that he became diseased, that he did not resist the disease, was already the effect of art impoverished life or hereditary exhaustion. The newspaper reader says: this party destroys itself by making such a mistake. My *higher* politics says: a party which makes such mistakes has reached its end; it has lost its sureness of instinct. Every mistake in every sense is the effect of the degeneration of instinct, of the disintegration of the will: one could almost define what is bad in this way. All that is good is instinct—and hence easy, necessary, free. Laboriousness is an objection; the god is typically different from the hero. (In my language light feet are the first attribute of divinity.)

[3] *The error of a false causality.* People have believed at all times that they knew what a cause is; but whence did we take our knowledge—or more precisely, our faith that we had such knowledge? From the realm of the famous "inner facts," of which not a single one has so far proved to be factual. We believed ourselves to be causal in the act of willing: we thought that here at least we caught causality in the act. Nor did one doubt that all the antecedents of an act, its causes, were to be sought in consciousness and would be found there once sought—as "motives": else one would not have been free and responsible for it. Finally, who would have denied that a thought is caused? that the ego causes the thought?

Of these three "inward facts" which seem to guarantee causality, the first and most persuasive is that of the will as cause. The conception of a consciousness ("spirit") as a cause, and later also that of the ego as cause (the "subject"), are only afterbirths: first the causality of the will was firmly accepted as given, as *empirical.*

Meanwhile we have thought better of it. Today we no longer believe a word of all this. The "inner world" is full of phantoms and will-o'-the-wisps: the will is one of them. The will no longer moves anything, hence does not explain anything either—it merely accompanies vents; it can also be absent. The so-called *motive:* another error. Merely a surface phenomenon of consciousness, something alongside the deed that is more likely to cover up the antecedents of the deeds than to represent them. And as for the *ego!* That has become a fable, a fiction, a play on words: it has altogether ceased to think, feel, or will!

What follows from this? There are no mental causes at all. The whole of the allegedly empirical evidence for that has gone to the devil. That is what follows! And what a fine abuse we had perpetrated with this "empirical, evidence"; we *created* the world on this basis as a world of causes, a world of will, a world of spirits. The most ancient and enduring psychology was at work here and did not do anything else: all that happened was considered a doing, all doing the effect of a will; the world became to it a multiplicity of doers; a doer (a "subject") was slipped under all that happened. It was out of himself that man projected his three "inner facts"—that in which he believed most firmly, the will, the spirit, the ego. He even took the concept of being from, the concept of the ego; he posited "things" as "being," in his image, in accordance with his concept of the ego as a cause. Small wonder that later he always found in things only that *which he had put into them.* The thing itself, to say it once more, the concept of thing is a mere reflex of the faith in the ego as cause. And even your atom, my dear mechanists and physicists—how much error, how much rudimentary psychology is still residual in your atom! Not to mention the "thing-in-itself," the *horrendum pudendum* of the metaphysicians! The error of the spirit as cause mistaken for reality! And made the very measure of reality! And called God!

[4] *The error of Imaginary causes.* To begin with dreams: *ex post facto,* a cause is slipped under a particular sensation (for example, one following a far-off cannon shot)—often a whole little novel in which the dreamer turns up as the protagonist. The sensation endures meanwhile in a kind of resonance: it waits, as it were, until the causal instinct permits it to step into the foreground now no longer as a chance occurrence, but as "meaning." The cannon shot appears in a *causal* mode, in an apparent reversal of time. What is really later, the motivation, is experienced first—often with a hundred details which pass like lightning—and the shot *follows.* What has happened? The representations which were *produced* by a certain state have been misunderstood as its causes.

In fact, we do the same thing when awake. Most of our general feeling—every kind of inhibition, pressure, tension, and explosion in the play and counterplay of our organs, and particularly the state of the *nervus sympathicus*—excite our causal instinct: we want to have a reason for feeling this way or that—for feeling bad or for feeling good. We are never satisfied merely to state the fact that we feel this way or that; we admit this fact only—become conscious of it only—when we have furnished some kind of motivation. Memory, which swings into action in such cases, unknown to us, brings up earlier states of the same kind, together with the causal interpretations associated with them—not their real causes. The faith, to be sure, that such representations, such accompanying conscious processes, are the causes, is also brought forth by memory. Thus originates a habitual acceptance of a particular causal interpretation, which, as a matter of fact, inhibits any investigation into the real cause—even precludes it.

[5] *The psychological explanation of this.* To derive something unknown from something familiar relieves, comforts, and satisfies, besides giving a feeling of power. With the unknown, one is confronted with danger, discomfort, and care; the first instinct is to abolish these painful states. First principle: any explanation is better than none. Since at bottom it is merely a matter of wishing to be rid of oppressive representations, one is not too particular about the means of getting rid of them: the first representation that explains the unknown as familiar feels so good that one "considers it true." The proof of pleasure ("of strength") as a criterion of truth.

The causal instinct is thus conditional upon, and excited by, the feeling of fear. The "why?" shall, if at all possible, not give the cause for its own sake so much as for a *particular kind of cause*—a cause that is comforting, liberating, and relieving. That it is something already familiar, experienced, and inscribed in the memory, which is posited as a cause, that is the first consequence of this need. That which is new and strange and has not been experienced before, is excluded as a cause. Thus one searches not only for some kind of explanation to serve as a cause, but for a particularly selected and preferred kind of explanation—that which has most quickly and most frequently abolished the feeling of the strange, new, and hitherto unexperienced: the *most habitual* explanations. Consequence: one kind of positing of causes predominates more and more, is concentrated into a system, and finally emerges as *dominant,* that is, as simply precluding other causes and explanations. The banker immediately thinks of "business," the Christian of "sin," and the girl of her love.

[6] *The whole realm of morality and religion belongs under this concept of imaginary causes.* The "explanation" of *disagreeable* general feelings. They are produced by beings that are hostile to us (evil spirits: the most famous case—the misunderstanding of the hysterical as witches). They are produced by acts which cannot be approved (the feeling of "sin," of "sinfulness," is slipped under a physiological discomfort; one always finds reasons for being dissatisfied with oneself). They are produced as punishments, as payment for something we should not have done, for what we should not have *been* (impudently generalized by Schopenhauer into a principle in which morality appears as what it really is—as the very poisoner and slanderer of life: "Every great pain, whether physical or spiritual, declares what we deserve; for it could not come to us if we did not deserve it. (*World as Will and Representation* II, 666). They are produced as effects of ill-considered actions that turn out badly. (Here the affects, the senses, are posited as causes, as "guilty"; and physiological calamities are interpreted with the help of other calamities as "deserved.")

The "explanation" of *agreeable* general feelings. They are produced by trust in God. They are produced by the consciousness of good deeds (the so-called "good conscience"—a physiological state which at times looks so much like good digestion that it is hard to tell them apart). They are produced by the successful termination of some enterprise (a naïve fallacy: the successful termination of some enterprise does not by any means give a hypochondriac or a Pascal agreeable general feelings). They are produced by faith, charity, and hope—the Christian virtues.

In truth, all these supposed explanations are resultant states and, as it were, translations of pleasurable or unpleasurable feelings into a false dialect: one is in a state of hope *because* the basic physiological feeling is once again strong and rich; one trusts in God *because* the feeling of fullness and strength gives a sense of rest. Morality and religion belong altogether to the *psychology of error:* in every single case, cause and effect are confused; or truth is confused with the effects of *believing* something to be true; or a state of consciousness is confused with its causes.

[7] *The error of free will.* Today we no longer have any pity for the concept of "free will": we know only too well what it really is—the foulest of all theologians' artifices, aimed at making mankind "responsible" in their sense, that is, *dependent upon them.* Here I simply supply the psychology of all "making responsible."

Wherever responsibilities are sought, it is usually the instinct of wanting to judge and punish which is at work. Becoming has been deprived of its innocence when any being-such-and-such is traced back to will, to purposes, to acts of responsibility: the doctrine of the will has been invented essentially for the purpose of punishment, that is, because one wanted to impute guilt. The entire old psychology, the psychology of will, was conditioned by the fact that its originators, the priests at the head of ancient communities, wanted to create for themselves the right to punish—or wanted to create this right for God. Men were considered "free" so that they might be judged and punished—so that they might become *guilty:* consequently, every act had to be considered as willed, and the origin of every act had to be considered as lying within the consciousness (and thus the most fundamental counterfeit in *psychologicis* was made the principle of psychology itself).

Today, as we have entered into the reverse movement and we immoralists are trying with all our strength to take the concept of guilt and the concept of punishment out of the world again, and to cleanse psychology, history, nature, and social institutions and sanctions of them, there is in our eyes no more radical opposition than that of the theologians, who continue with the concept of a "moral world-order" to infect the innocence of becoming by means of "punishment" and "guilt." Christianity is a metaphysics of the hangman.

[8] What alone can be *our* doctrine? That no one *gives* man his qualities—neither God, nor society, nor his parents and ancestors, nor he himself. (The nonsense of the last idea was taught as "intelligible freedom" by Kant—perhaps by Plato already.) No one is responsible for man's being there at all, for his being such-and-such, or for his being in these circumstances or in this environment. The fatality of his essence is not to be disentangled from the fatality of all that has been and will be. Man is not the effect of some special purpose, of a will, and end; nor is he the object of an attempt to attain an "ideal of humanity" or an "ideal of happiness" or an "ideal of morality." It is absurd to wish to devolve one's essence on some end or other. We have invented the concept of "end": in reality there is no end.

One is necessary, one is a piece of fatefulness, one belongs to the whole, one is in the whole; there is nothing which could judge, measure, compare, or sentence our being, for that would mean judging, measuring, comparing, or sentencing the whole. But there nothing besides the whole. That nobody is held responsible any longer, that the mode of being may not be traced back to a *causa prima,* that the world does not form a unity either as a sensorium or as "spirit"— alone is the great liberation; with this alone is the innocence of becoming restored. The concept of "God" was until now the greatest objection to existence. We deny God, we deny the responsibility in God: only thereby do we redeem the world.

THE ANTI-CHRIST (selections)

FIRST BOOK: ATTEMPT AT A CRITIQUE OF CHRISTIANITY

* * *

2. What is good? Everything that heightens the feeling of power in man, the will to power, power itself.

What is bad? Everything that is born of weakness.

What is happiness? The feeling that power is *growing,* that resistance is overcome.

Not contentedness but more power; not peace but war; not virtue but fitness (Renaissance virtue, *virtù,* virtue that is moraline*-free).

The weak and the failures shall perish: first principle of our love of man. And they shall even be given every possible assistance.

*The coinage of a man who neither smoked nor drank coffee.

What is more harmful than any vice? Active pity for all the failures and all the weak: Christianity.

3. The problem I thus pose is not what shall succeed mankind in the sequence of living beings (man is an *end*), but what type of man shall be *bred,* shall be *willed,* for being higher in value, worthier of life, more certain of a future.

Even in the past this higher type has appeared often—but as a fortunate accident, as an exception, never as something *willed.* In fact, this has been the type most dreaded—almost *the* dreadful—and from dread the opposite type was willed, bred, and *attained:* the domestic animal, the herd animal, the sick human animal—the Christian.

4. Mankind does *not* represent a development toward something better or stronger or higher in the sense accepted today. "Progress" is merely a modern idea, that is, a false idea. The European of today is vastly inferior in value to the European of the Renaissance: further development is altogether *not* according to any necessity in the direction of elevation, enhancement, or strength.

In another sense, success in individual cases is constantly encountered in the most widely different places and cultures: here we really do find a *higher type,* which is, in relation to mankind as a whole, a kind of overman. Such fortunate accidents of great success have always been possible and will perhaps always be possible. And even whole families, tribes, or peoples may occasionally represent such a *bull's-eye.*

5. Christianity should not be beautified and embellished: it has waged deadly war against this higher type of man; it has placed all the basic instincts of this type under the ban; and out of these instincts it has distilled evil and the Evil One: the strong man as the typically reprehensible man, the "reprobate." Christianity has sided with all that is weak and base, with all failures; it has made an ideal of whatever *contradicts* the instinct of the strong life to preserve itself; it has corrupted the reason even of those strongest in spirit by teaching men to consider the supreme values of the spirit as something sinful, as something that leads into error—as temptations. The most pitiful example: the corruption of Pascal, who believed in the corruption of his reason through original sin when it had in fact been corrupted only by his Christianity.

6. It is a painful, horrible spectacle that has dawned on me: I have drawn back the curtain from the *corruption* of man. In my mouth, this word is at least free from one suspicion: that it might involve a moral accusation of man. It is meant—let me emphasize this once more—*moraline-free.* So much so that I experience this corruption most strongly precisely where men have so far aspired most deliberately to "virtue" and "godliness." I understand corruption, as you will guess, in the sense of decadence: it is my contention that all the values in which mankind now sums up its supreme desiderata are *decadence-values.*

I call an animal, a species, or an individual corrupt when it loses its instincts, when it chooses, when it prefers, what is disadvantageous for it. A history of "lofty sentiments," of the "ideals of mankind"—and it is possible that I shall have to write it—would almost explain too *why* man is so corrupt. Life itself is to my mind the instinct for growth, for durability, for an accumulation of forces, for *power:* where the will to power is lacking there is decline. It is my contention that all the supreme values of mankind *lack* this will—that the values which are symptomatic of decline, *nihilistic* values, are lording it under the holiest name.

7. Christianity is called the religion of *pity.* Pity stands opposed to the tonic emotions which heighten our vitality: it has a depressing effect. We are deprived of strength when we feel pity. That loss of strength which suffering as such inflicts on life is still

further increased and multiplied by pity. Pity makes suffering contagious. Under certain circumstances, it may engender a total loss of life and vitality out of all proportion to the magnitude of the cause (as in the case of the death of the Nazarene). That is the first consideration, but there is a more important one.

Suppose we measure pity by the value of the reactions it usually produces; then its perilous nature appears in an even brighter light. Quite in general, pity crosses the law of development, which is the law of *selection.* It preserves what is ripe for destruction; it defends those who have been disinherited and condemned by life; and by the abundance of the failures of all kinds which it keeps alive, it gives life itself a gloomy and questionable aspect.

Some have dared to call pity a virtue (in every *noble* ethic it is considered a weakness); and as if this were not enough, it has been made *the* virtue, the basis and source of all virtues. To be sure—one should always keep this in mind—this was done by a philosophy that was nihilistic and had inscribed the *negation of life* upon its shield. Schopenhauer was consistent enough: pity negates life and renders it *more deserving of negation.*

Pity is the *practice* of nihilism. To repeat: this depressive and contagious instinct crosses those instincts which aim at the preservation of life and at the enhancement of its value. It multiplies misery and conserves all that is miserable, and is thus a prime instrument of the advancement of decadence: pity persuades men to *nothingness!* Of course, one does not say "nothingness" but "beyond" or "God," or "*true* life," or Nirvana, salvation, blessedness.

This innocent rhetoric from the realm of the religious-moral idiosyncrasy appears much less innocent as soon as we realize which tendency it is that here shrouds itself in sublime words: *hostility against life.* Schopenhauer was hostile to life; therefore pity became a virtue for him.

Aristotle, as is well known, considered pity a pathological and dangerous condition, which one would be well advised to attack now and then with a purge: he understood tragedy as a purge. From the standpoint of the instinct of life, a remedy certainly seems necessary for such a pathological and dangerous accumulation of pity as it is represented by the case of Schopenhauer (and unfortunately by our entire literary and artistic decadence from St. Petersburg to Paris, from Tolstoy to Wagner)—to puncture it and make it *burst.*

In our whole unhealthy modernity there is nothing more unhealthy than Christian pity. To be physicians *here,* to be inexorable here, to wield the scalpel *here*— that is *our* part, that is *our* love of man, that is how we are philosophers, we *Hyperboreans.*

* * *

62. With this I am at the end and I pronounce my judgment. I *condemn* Christianity. I raise against the Christian church the most terrible of all accusations that any accuser ever uttered. It is to me the highest of all conceivable corruptions. It has had the will to the last corruption that is even possible. The Christian church has left nothing untouched by its corruption; it has turned every value into an un-value, every truth into a lie, every integrity into a vileness of the soul. Let anyone dare to speak to me of its "humanitarian" blessings! To *abolish* any distress ran counter to its deepest advantages: it lived on distress, it *created* distress to eternalize *itself.*

The worm of sin, for example: with this distress the church first enriched mankind. The "equality of souls before God," this falsehood, this *pretext* for the rancor of all the base-minded, this explosive of a concept which eventually became revolution, modern idea, and the principle of decline of the whole order of society—is *Christian* dynamite. "Humanitarian" blessings of Christianity! To breed out of *humanitas* a self-contradiction, an art of self-violation, a will to lie at any price, a repugnance, a contempt for all good and honest instincts! Those are some of the blessings of Christianity!

Parasitism as the *only* practice of the church; with its ideal of anemia, of "holiness," draining all blood, all love, all hope for life; the beyond as the will to negate every reality; the cross as the mark of recognition for the most subterranean conspiracy that ever existed—against health, beauty, whatever has turned out well, courage, spirit, *graciousness* of the soul, *against life itself.*

This eternal indictment of Christianity I will write on all walls, wherever there are walls—I have letters to make even the blind see.

I call Christianity the one great curse, the one great innermost corruption, the one great instinct of revenge, for which no means is poisonous, stealthy, subterranean, *small* enough—I call it the one immortal blemish of mankind.

And time is reckoned from the *dies nefastus* with which this calamity began—after the *first* day of Christianity! *Why not rather after its last day? After today?* Revaluation of all values!

TWENTIETH-CENTURY PHILOSOPHY

by Hans Bynagle

The major twentieth-century philosophical traditions are notoriously difficult to characterize in a nutshell. Generalizations, especially, are perilous and apt to be misleading. Fortunately, one can begin to sketch a philosophical map, albeit a *very* rough one, in terms that are largely geographical. One of the major lines that can be drawn on our map divides the philosophical tradition that dominates most of the European continent, known accordingly as Continental philosophy, from the dominant philosophical tradition of England, the United States, and some other countries subject to strong British or American influence (such as Canada and Australia) known as Anglo-American philosophy.

I can offer here only the most rudimentary characterizations of a few of the main strands of Continental philosophy beginning with Phenomenology. Founded around the turn of the twentieth century by Edmund Husserl, and developed by Martin Heidegger, Phenomenology is essentially a philosophical method, one that focuses on careful inspection and description of phenomena or appearances, defined as any object of conscious experience, that is, that which we are conscious *of*. The inspection and description are supposed to be effected without any presuppositions, and that includes any presuppositions as to whether such objects of consciousness are "real" or correspond to something "external," or as to what their causes or consequences may be. It is believed that by this method the essential structures of experience and its objects can be uncovered. The sorts of experiences

Adapted from Hans Bynagle, "A Map of Twentieth-Century Philosophy," *Philosophy: A Guide to the Reference Literature,* 2nd edition (Littleton, CO: Libraries Unlimited, 1997). Reprinted by permission of the author.

and phenomena that Phenomenologists have sought to describe are highly varied, including, for instance, time consciousness; mathematics and logic; perception; experience of the social world; our experience of our own bodies; and moral, aesthetic, and religious experience.

Existentialism, unlike Phenomenology, is not primarily a philosophical method. Neither is it exactly a set of doctrines (at least not any *one* set) but more an outlook or attitude supported by diverse doctrines centered on certain common themes. These themes include the human condition, or the relation of the individual to the world; the human response to that condition (described often in strongly affective and preponderantly negative terms such as "despair," "dread," "anxiety," "guilt," "bad faith," "nausea"); being, especially the difference between the being of persons (which is "existence") and the being of other kinds of things; human freedom; the significance (and unavoidability) of choice and decision in the absence of certainty; and the concreteness and subjectivity of life as lived, over against abstractions and false objectifications.

Existentialism is often thought to be antireligious (and is, in some of its versions), but there has in fact been a strong current of Christian Existentialism, beginning with the figure often credited with originating Existentialism, the nineteenth-century Danish philosopher Kierkegaard. Existentialism's relationship to Phenomenology is a matter of some controversy, but at least one can say that many of the later Existentialist thinkers, Sartre among them, have employed Phenomenological methods to arrive at or support their specific variations on Existential themes. Although Existentialism has been on the wane since the 1960s, it has enjoyed exceptional prominence, even popularity, for a philosophical movement, in part because of its literary expressions by writers such as Sartre, Camus, de Beauvoir, and Marcel.

Structuralism is an interdisciplinary movement united by the principle that social and cultural phenomena, including belief systems and every kind of discourse (literary, political, scientific, etc.), are best understood by analogy with language, itself best understood as a structure of relations among its component parts. Just as in language the crucial determinant of meaning (according to the early structural linguist Ferdinand de Saussure) is neither individual words nor their reference to things outside language but their interrelationships within the linguistic structure, so the crucial element in all social and cultural phenomena is the underlying structure that determines the functions of the various parts. A good deal of Structuralist analysis has been concerned with a kind of unmasking, that is, with revealing political, social, or psychological phenomena as (allegedly) not what they seem or what participants believe them to be but as determined by structures often concealed from view.

This unmasking impulse persists with the group of thinkers sometimes designated Post-Structuralists, who both rejected certain presuppositions of Structuralism and added their own more radical ideas about the fundamental role of language in constructing all human perceptions and conceptions of reality. A particular form of this unmasking tendency is Deconstruction, introduced in the work of Jacques Derrida, who is generally counted among Post-Structuralists. Any attempt to define Deconstruction must labor in the shadow of Derrida's apparent rejection in advance of all such attempts. Nonetheless, it has seemed fair to many interpreters to characterize it as a form of textual criticism or interpretation whose aim is to unmask and overcome hidden "privileging" that occurs in texts of all kinds. This privileging, for example the privileging of reason, the masculine, the sacred, the literal, or the objective, and so on, entails the exclusion, suppression, or marginalization of their opposites—passion, the feminine, the profane, the metaphorical, the subjective, and so on—while at the same time it must presuppose these opposites to sustain or even to make sense of the privileged concept. In this way, it is maintained, texts regularly undermine their own assumptions. As a reading technique uncovering alleged hidden agendas behind the ostensible meaning of a text, Deconstruction takes the further step of denying that the text has a definite meaning. This has become a key thesis for the currents of literary theorizing and criticism that followed in Derrida's wake.

* * *

Turning to the other dominant twentieth-century philosophical tradition, it is not uncommon to equate Anglo-American philosophy with what is called Analytic or Analytical philosophy. But the term is also used in a broader sense to encompass other movements that have flourished chiefly on British and American soil, for instance, Pragmatism, Naturalism, and Process Philosophy. There is much to be said for the wider meaning, which avoids the suggestion that philosophy in England and America is more monolithic than it really is. The equation of Anglo-American with Analytic is also unfortunate from another point of view, in that Analytic philosophy has become the dominant mode of philosophizing in some other areas as well, notably the Scandinavian countries, to say nothing of the inroads it has made in areas where other approaches still dominate the field (the other side of the blurring and bridging of the Continental/Anglo-American boundary), for example, in Germany. However, given all those qualifications and others, there is no question that Analytic philosophy is the most important philosophical current within the Anglo-American sphere. It is also the one most often contrasted with (and actively opposed to) the Continental movements described earlier.

What Analytic philosophy *is* is not so easy to say. I believe it is possible to distinguish at least three variants, though they probably represent points on a spectrum rather than discrete alternatives. In the widest and loosest sense, Analytic philosophy is hardly more than a philosophical style, one that takes extreme care with the meanings of words (sometimes with precise definitions of terms and consistency in their use, sometimes with the nuances of ordinary language) that tends to present arguments in meticulous step-by-step fashion (often endeavoring to leave nothing implicit), and that pays close, sometimes minute, attention to logical relations (often using logical symbolism or specialized logical terminology to render such relations transparent). In a narrower sense, "Analytic philosophy" designates a philosophical outlook that holds that the primary task or even (in its more extreme version) the only proper task of philosophy—the primary or proper method for attacking philosophical problems—is analysis of one sort or another: of meanings, of concepts, of logical relations, or all of these. We can call this the methodological version. Finally, one may occasionally encounter the term "Analytic philosophy" in contexts in which it is reserved for one or more specific doctrines regarding the outcome of correct philosophical analysis. Even though the Analytic tradition (in either of the two wider senses) owes a great deal to certain specific doctrinal versions—and to major figures who propounded them, such as Bertrand Russell, Ludwig Wittgenstein, and the Logical Positivists—it would be incorrect to say that Analytic philosophy is the dominant orientation among British and American philosophers if one has in mind this narrower meaning. In fact, it is not clear that this is true under any but the widest meaning distinguished earlier.

Common to those who subscribe to the Analytic approach, whether in the broadest sense or a narrower one, is the conviction that to some significant degree, philosophical problems, puzzles, and errors are rooted in language and can be solved or avoided, as the case may be, by a sound understanding of language and careful attention to its workings. (Willard Van Orman Quine, for example, exhibits this strategy in his careful examination of the analytic-synthetic distinction.) This method has tended to focus much attention on language and on its close relative, logic, as objects of study for their own sake. (The relationship between language and logic is itself a question subjected to considerable inquiry and debate.) Detractors are apt to point to this concern—they might say this obsession—with language and logic as one aspect of the trivialization of philosophy with which they charge the Analytic movement. Many who are generally loyal or sympathetic to Analytic philosophy may agree that it tended to draw philosophy away from "deep" questions. In any case, the past two to three decades have seen, on the one hand, increased self-searching as to the limitations of the Analytic approach, and on the other, more efforts to apply it to deeper questions—about the meaning of life, for instance, or the nature of the moral life—in a way that takes them seriously.

* * *

For secondary works on twentieth-century philosophy, consult the appropriate works from Frederick Copleston's series *A History of Philosophy, Volumes VIII: Bentham to Russell* and *Volume IX: Maine de Brian to Sartre* (New York: Image Doubleday, 1966 and 1974) and Dermont Moran, ed., *The Routledge Companion to Twentieth-Century Philosophy* (Abingdon, UK: Routledge, 2008). For histories and discussions of specific movements in twentieth-century Western philosophy, see Michael Corrado, *The Analytic Tradition in Philosophy: Background and Issues* (Chicago: American Library Association, 1975); Robert C. Solomon, *From Hegel to Existentialism* (Oxford: Oxford University Press, 1987); Richard Kearney, ed., *Twentieth-Century Continental Philosophy* (London: Routledge, 1994); Giovanna Borradori, *The American Philosopher,* translated by Rosanna Crocitto (Chicago: University of Chicago Press, 1994); D.S. Clarke, *Philosophy's Second Revolution: Early and Recent Analytic Philosophy* (La Salle, IL: Open Court, 1997); Simon Critchley and William Schroeder, eds., *A Companion to Continental Philosophy* (Oxford: Basil Blackwell, 1997); Robert D'Amico, *Contemporary Continental Philosophy* (Boulder, CO: Westview Press, 1998); Robert C. Solomon and David Sherman, ed., *Blackwell Guide to Continental Philosophy* (Oxford: Blackwell, 2003); and Richard Kearney, ed., *Continental Philosophy in the 20th Century* (London: Routledge, 2003). Robert Audi, ed., *The Cambridge Dictionary of Philosophy* (Cambridge: Cambridge University Press, 1995); Stuart Brown et al., *Biographical Dictionary of Twentieth-Century Philosophers* (London: Routledge, 1996); and Hans Bynagle, *Philosophy: A Guide to the Reference Literature,* 2nd edition (Littleton, CO: Libraries Unlimited, 1997) provide helpful reference works.

EDMUND HUSSERL
1859–1938

Edmund Husserl was born in Prostējov (Prossnitz), Moravia, in what is now the Czech Republic; at that time, it was part of the Austrian Empire. After attending elementary school in Prostējov, Husserl went to *gymnasia* (high schools) in Vienna and Olmütz before enrolling at the University of Leipzig in 1876. For two years, he studied mathematics, physics, and astronomy, attending philosophy lectures only in his spare time. In 1878, he transferred to the Friedrich-Wilhelm University of Berlin, where he continued his study of mathematics (under the renowned Karl Weierstrass) as well as his hobby of philosophy. After three years, he moved to the University of Vienna, where he received a Ph.D. in mathematics in 1883.

Husserl was offered a teaching position in mathematics at Berlin, but he decided to remain in Vienna so that he could continue studying philosophy. He worked with the philosophical psychologist Franz Brentano (1838–1917) during the next two years. Following Brentano's advice, Husserl then moved to the University of Halle, where he published his first book, *Philosophy of Arithmetic* (1891). In 1901, he moved to the University of Göttingen, where he spent the next sixteen years and published a number of important works, including *Ideas: General Introduction to Pure Phenomenology* (1913). His last post was at the University of Freiburg, where he taught until his retirement in 1928. Among his Freiburg associates was Martin Heidegger. Following retirement, Husserl wrote voluminously—though little was published during his lifetime. Toward the end of his life, the Nazis barred him from formal academic activities because of his Jewish ancestry.

After his death in 1938, the Husserl Archive was established in Louvain, Belgium. The Archive has preserved, transcribed, and, over the decades, published

Husserl's shorthand notes as the *Husserliana series.* The Archive has also hosted congresses on, and published essays in, phenomenology.

* * *

Franz Brentano, Husserl's teacher, criticized British empiricism for its tendency to present consciousness in terms of ideas or representations. Brentano argued that the key constituent of mental states is intentionality—thought's correlation rather than its immobile state. In order to have consciousness, one must be conscious of something. One cannot just think, one must think *about* something; one cannot just desire, one must have desire *for* something; one cannot just be aware, one must be aware *of* something. In each case, the "something" is the "intentional object" of consciousness. Contrary to Kant, Brentano held that consciousness does not *construct* these objects; it only *points to* them.

The end of the nineteenth century brought two quite different responses to Brentano. The Analytic tradition, which tended to dominate English-speaking philosophy, focused almost exclusively on objects of consciousness, ignoring consciousness itself. The Phenomenological tradition, dominant on the European continent, examined the nature of consciousness itself.

Husserl is the acknowledged founder of this Phenomenological response. Like Descartes, Husserl considered consciousness the main topic for philosophy. In examining the form of this consciousness, Husserl discovered what he called "the natural standpoint":

> I am aware of a world, spread out in space endlessly, and in time becoming and become, without end. I am aware of it, that means, first of all, I discover it immediately, intuitively, I experience it. Through sight, touch, hearing, etc., . . . corporeal things somehow spatially distributed are *for me simply there,* . . . "present," whether or not I pay them special attention by busying myself with them, considering, thinking, feeling, willing.*

This is the world as it is actually lived by an individual. Although we can develop "worlds" of arithmetic or science by our knowledge of things from a particular standpoint, the natural standpoint—the world as actually lived by individuals—is always prior to, and conditioning of, any particular knowledge possible.

Yet according to Husserl, it is possible to get behind this natural standpoint to identify an invariant intentional structure. Husserl developed a method of "bracketing," which he called *<epochē>* (from the Greek word for noncommitment or suspended judgment). For example, I may look with pleasure at a blossoming apple tree. From the natural standpoint, I can see that the tree exists outside of me in space and time and that I am enjoying my psychical state of pleasure. From this standpoint, moreover, there is an assumed relation between me and the apple tree. But Descartes had shown that this perception could be mistaken—I could be hallucinating. As a result, my knowledge of the tree is uncertain. But I can suspend my judgments about the tree and perform an *<epochē>*. This "bracketing" moves me from a natural to a phenomenological standpoint, from which I now recognize "a

*Edmund Husserl, *Ideas: General Introduction to Pure Phenomenology,* translated by W.R. Boyce Gibson (Atlantic Highlands, NJ: Humanities Press, 1931), Section 2, Chapter 1, ¶27. (Emphasis in original.)

nexus of exotic experiences of perception and pleasure valuation." Of this nexus of intending tree-experiences I *am* certain. By no longer referring to objective existence, by applying the phenomenological <*epochē*> instead, I have arrived at the pure datum of intending experience.

In the latter part of *Ideas* and in several other works, Husserl developed this method further, showing how to use the newly acquired phenomenological data. For example, in examining the experience of time, Husserl found that "lived time" is not the time of clocks and calendars but is always experienced as now. Similarly, in the experience of "lived space," one always finds oneself *here,* and everything else at different degrees of *there.* In his article on "Phenomenology" for the *Encyclopædia Brittanica,* given here (complete), Husserl explained that it is possible to apply the phenomenological method not only to the *objects* of consciousness but to consciousness itself. When we perform such an <*epochē*> on consciousness, we discover an invariant structure: the transcendental ego. "The 'I' and the 'we,' which we apprehend, presuppose the hidden 'I' and 'we' to whom they are 'present.'"

Husserl's thought continues to be influential. Martin Heidegger used the phenomenological method to develop his ontology, and Jean-Paul Sartre used the method to develop his own "existential" interpretation of consciousness. Maurice Merleau-Ponty refined and further applied the phenomenological method. Husserl has lived on through his followers.

* * *

For works on phenomenology in general, see Herbert Speigelberg, *The Phenomenological Movement,* two volumes (The Hague, The Netherlands: Martinus Nijhoff, 1960); Joseph J. Kockelmans, ed., *Phenomenology* (Garden City, NY: Anchor Doubleday, 1967); and Christopher Macann, *Four Phenomenological Philosophers: Husserl, Heidegger, Sartre, Merleau-Ponty* (London: Routledge, 1993). For a clear and concise comparison of phenomenology and the analytic tradition, see W.T. Jones, *The Twentieth Century to Wittgenstein and Sartre,* 2nd edition (New York: Harcourt Brace Jovanovich, 1975), Chapters 7 and 8.

Marvin Farber, *The Foundations of Phenomenology* (Albany, NY: SUNY Press, 1943) provides a standard study of Husserl's thought, whereas Joseph J. Kockelmans, *A First Introduction to Husserl's Phenomenology* (Pittsburgh, PA: Duquesne University Press, 1967); David Bell, *Husserl* (New York: Routledge, 1990); Rudolf Bernet, Iso Kern, and Eduard Marbach, *An Introduction to Husserlian Phenomenology* (Evanston, IL: Northwestern University Press, 1993); David Woodruff Smith, *Husserl* (Abingdon, UK: Routledge, 2006); and Matheson Russell, *Husserl: A Guide for the Perplexed* (London: Continuum, 2006) provide more recent introductions. Paul Ricoeur, *Husserl: An Analysis of His* Phenomenology, translated by Edward G. Ballard and Lester E. Embree (Evanston, IL: Northwestern University Press, 1967), and Hans-Georg Gadamer, *Philosophical Hermeneutics,* translated by David E. Linge (Berkeley: University of California Press, 1976) have written studies of Husserl as well as important works of philosophy themselves. Among the many studies of particular areas of Husserl's thought, see David Carr, *Phenomenology and the Problem of History: A Study of Husserl's Transcendental Philosophy* (Evanston, IL: Northwestern University Press, 1974); James M. Edie, *Edmund Husserl's* Phenomenology: *A Critical Commentary* (Bloomington: Indiana University Press, 1987); and Kenneth Liberman, *Husserl's Criticism of Reason: With*

Ethnomethodolocial Specifications (Lanham, MD: Lexington Books, 2007). For collections of essays, see R.O. Elveton, ed., *The Phenomenology of Husserl* (Chicago: Quadrangle Books, 1970); Frederick Elliston and Peter McCormick, eds., *Husserl: Expositions and Appraisals* (Notre Dame, IN: University of Notre Dame Press, 1977)—especially David Carr's article, "Husserl's Problematic Concept of the Life-World"; Robert Sokolowski, ed., *Edmund Husserl and the Phenomenological Tradition* (Washington, DC: Catholic University of America Press, 1988); Barry Smith and David Woodruff Smith, eds., *The Cambridge Companion to Husserl* (Cambridge: Cambridge University Press, 1995); and the *Husserl Studies,* an ongoing journal published by Kluwer Academic Publishers, Hingham, MA.

PHENOMENOLOGY

Phenomenology denotes a new, descriptive, philosophical method, which, since the concluding years of the last century, has established (1) an *a priori* psychological discipline, able to provide the only secure basis on which a strong empirical psychology can be built, and (2) a universal philosophy, which can supply an organum for the methodical revision of all the sciences.

I. PHENOMENOLOGICAL PSYCHOLOGY

Present-day psychology, as the science of the "psychical" in its concrete connection with spatio-temporal reality, regards as its material whatever is present in the world as "egoistic"; i.e., "living," perceiving, thinking, willing, etc., actual, potential and habitual. And as the psychical is known as a certain stratum of existence, proper to men and beasts, psychology may be considered as a branch of anthropology and zoology. But animal nature is a part of physical reality, and that which is concerned with physical reality is natural science. Is it, then, possible to separate the psychical cleanly enough from the physical to establish a pure psychology parallel to natural science? That a purely psychological investigation is practicable within limits is shown by our obligation to it for our fundamental conceptions of the psychical, and most of those of the psycho-physical.

But before determining the question of an unlimited psychology, we must be sure of the characteristics of psychological experience and the psychical data it provides. We turn naturally to our immediate experiences. But we cannot discover the psychical in any experience, except by a "reflection," or perversion of the ordinary attitude. We are accustomed to concentrate upon the matters, thoughts, and values of the moment, and not upon the psychical "act of experience" in which these are apprehended. This "act" is revealed by a "reflection"; and a reflection can be practised on every experience.

Instead of the matters themselves, the values, goals, utilities, etc., we regard the subjective experiences in which these "appear." These "appearances" are phenomena, whose nature is to be a "consciousness-of" their object, real or unreal as it be. Common language catches this sense of "relativity," saying, I was thinking *of* something, I was frightened *of* something, etc. Phenomenological psychology takes its name from the "phenomena," with the psychological aspect of which it is concerned: and the word "intentional" has been borrowed from the scholastic to denote the essential "reference" character of the phenomena. All consciousness is "intentional."

In unreflective consciousness we are "directed" upon objects, we "intend" them, and reflection reveals this to be an immanent process characteristic of all experience, though infinitely varied in form. To be conscious of something is no empty having of that something in consciousness. Each phenomenon has its own intentional structure, which analysis shows to be an ever-widening system of individually intentional and intentionally related components. The perception of a cube, for example, reveals a multiple and synthesized intention: a continuous variety in the "appearance" of the cube, according to differences in the points of view from which it is seen, and corresponding differences in "perspective," and all the difference between the "front side" actually seen at the moment and the "backside" which is not seen, and which remains, therefore, relatively "indeterminate," and yet is supposed equally to be existent. Observation of this "stream" of "appearance-aspects" and of the manner of their synthesis, shows that every phase and interval is already in itself a "consciousness-of" something, yet in such a way that with the constant entry of new phases the total consciousness, at any moment, lacks not synthetic unity, and is, in fact, a consciousness of one and the same object. The intentional structure of the train of a perception must conform to a certain type, if any physical object is to be perceived as there! And if the same object be intuited in other modes, if it be imagined, or remembered, or copied, all its intentional forms recur, though modified in character from what they were in the perception, to correspond to their new modes. The same is true of every kind of psychical experience. Judgment, valuation, pursuit, these also are no empty experiences having in consciousness of judgments, values, goals and means, but are likewise experiences compounded of an intentional stream, each conforming to its own fast type.

Phenomenological psychology's comprehensive task is the systematic examination of the types and forms of intentional experience, and the reduction of their structures to the prime intentions, learning thus what is the nature of the psychical, and comprehending the being of the soul.

The validity of these investigations will obviously extend beyond the particularity of the psychologist's own soul. For psychical life may be revealed to us not only in self-consciousness but equally in our consciousness of other selves, and this latter source of experience offers us more than a reduplication of what we find in our self-consciousness, for it establishes the differences between "own" and "other" which we experience, and presents us with the characteristics of the "social-life." And hence the further task accrues to psychology of revealing the intentions of which the "social life" consists.

PHENOMENOLOGICAL-PSYCHOLOGICAL AND EIDETIC REDUCTIONS

The Phenomenological psychology must examine the self's experience of itself and its derivative experience of other selves and of society, but whether, in so doing, it can be free of all psycho-physical admixture, is not yet clear. Can one reach a really pure

Nude Descending a Staircase, Number 2, 1912, by Marcel Duchamp (1887–1968). Duchamp's shattered and reassembled nude figure descending the staircase in robotic rhythm purposely challenges the viewer to derive a personal interpretation of the image—to move beyond the natural standpoint with its judgments concerning spacio-temporal existence. (© Succession Marcel Duchamp/ADAGP, Paris and DACS, London 2016)

self-experience and purely psychical data? This difficulty, even since Brentano's discovery of intentionality, as the fundamental character of the psychical, has blinded psychologists to the possibilities of phenomenological psychology. The psychologist finds his self-consciousness mixed everywhere with "external" experience, and non-psychical realities. For what is experienced as external belongs not to the intentional "internal," though our experience of it belongs there as an experience of the external. The phenomenologist, who will only notice phenomena, and know purely his own "life," must practice an <*epochē*>. He must inhibit every ordinary objective "position," and partake in no judgement concerning the objective world. The experience itself will remain what it was, an experience of this house, of this body, of this world in general, in its particular mode. For one cannot describe any intentional experience, even though it be "illusory," a self-contradicting judgment and the like, without describing what in the experience is, as such, the object of consciousness.

Our comprehensive <*epochē*> puts, as we say, the world between brackets, excludes the world which is simply there! from the subject's field, presenting in its stead the so-and-so-experienced-perceived-remembered-judged-thought-valued-etc., world, as such, the "bracketed" world. Not the world or any part of it appears, but the "sense" of the world. To enjoy phenomenological experience we must retreat from the objects posited in the natural attitude to the multiple modes of their "appearance," to the "bracketed" objects.

The phenomenological reduction to phenomena, to the purely psychical, advances by two steps: (1) systematic and radical <*epochē*> of every objectifying "position" in an experience, practised both upon the regard of particular objects and upon the entire attitude of mind, and (2) expert recognition, comprehension and description of the manifold "appearances" of what are no longer "objects" but "unities" of "sense." So that the phenomenological description will comprise two parts, description of the "noetic" (<*neo*>) or "experiencing" and description of the "noematic" (<*noema*>) or the "experienced." Phenomenological experience, is the only experience which may properly be called "internal" and there is no limit to its practice. And as a similar "bracketing" of objective, and description of what then "appears" (<"*noema*" in "*noesis*">), can be performed upon the "life" of another self which we represent to ourselves, the "reductive" method can be extended from one's own self-experience to one's experience of other selves. And, further, that society, which we experience in a common consciousness, may be reduced not only to the intentional fields of the individual consciousness, but also by the means of an inter-subjective reduction, to that which unites these, namely the phenomenological unity of the social life. Thus enlarged, the psychological concept of internal experience reaches its full extent.

But it takes more than the unity of a manifold "intentional life," with its inseparable complement of "sense-unities," to make a "soul." For from the individual life that "ego-subject" cannot be disjoined, which persists as an identical ego or "pole," to the particular intentions, and the "habits" growing out of these. Thus the "inter-subjective," phenomenologically reduced and concretely apprehended, is seen to be a "society" of "persons," who share a conscious life.

Phenomenological psychology can be purged of every empirical and psychophysical element, but, being so purged, it cannot deal with "matters of fact." Any closed field may be considered as regards its "essence," its <*eidos*>, and we may disregard the factual side of our phenomena, and use them as "examples" merely. We shall ignore individual souls and societies, to learn their *a priori,* their "possible" forms. Our thesis will be "theoretical," observing the invariable through variation, disclosing a typical realm of *a priori.* There will be no psychical existence whose "style" we shall not know. Psychological phenomenology must rest upon eidetic phenomenology.

The phenomenology of the perception of bodies, for example, will not be an account of actually occurring perceptions, or those which may be expected to occur, but of that invariable "structure," apart from which no perception of a body, single or prolonged, can be conceived. The phenomenological reduction reveals the phenomena of actual internal experience; the eidetic reduction, the essential forms constraining psychical existence.

Men now demand that empirical psychology shall conform to the exactness required by modern natural science. Natural science, which was once a vague, inductive empiric, owes its modern character to the *a priori* system of forms, nature as it is "conceivable," which its separate disciplines, pure geometry, laws of motion, time, etc., have contributed. The methods of natural science and psychology are quite distinct, but the latter, like the former, can only reach "exactness" by a rationalization of the "essential."

The psycho-physical has an *a priori* which must be learned by any complete psychology, this *a priori* is not phenomenological, for it depends no less upon the essence of physical, or more particularly organic nature.

II. Transcendental Phenomenology

Transcendental philosophy may be said to have originated in Descartes, and phenomenological psychology in Locke, Berkeley and Hume, although the latter did not grow up primarily as a method or discipline to serve psychology, but to contribute to the solution of the transcendental problematic which Descartes had posed. The theme propounded in the *Meditations* was still dominant in a philosophy which it had initiated. All reality, so it ran, and the whole of the world which we perceive as existent, may be said to exist only as the content of our own representations, judged in our judgments, or, at best, proved by our own knowing. There lay impulse enough to rouse all the legitimate and illegitimate problems of transcendence, which we know. Descartes' "Doubting" first disclosed "transcendental subjectivity," and his "Ego Cogito" was its first conceptual handling. But the Cartesian transcendental "Mens" became the "Human Mind," which Locke undertook to explore; and Locke's exploration turned into a psychology of the internal experience. And since Locke thought his psychology could embrace the transcendental problems, in whose interest he had begun his work, he became the founder of a false psychologistical philosophy which has persisted because men have not analysed their concept of "subjective" into its twofold significance. Once the transcendental problem is fairly stated, the ambiguity of the sense of the "subjective" becomes apparent, and establishes the phenomenological psychology to deal with its one meaning, and the transcendental phenomenology with its other.

Phenomenological psychology has been given the priority in this article, partly because it forms a convenient stepping-stone to the philosophy and partly because it is nearer to the common attitude than is the transcendental. Psychology, both in its eiditic and empirical disciplines, is a "positive" science, promoted in the "natural attitude" with the world before it for the ground of all its themes, while transcendental experience is difficult to realize because it is "supreme" and entirely "unworldly." Phenomenological psychology, although comparatively new, and completely new as far as it uses intentional analysis, can be approached from the gates of any of the positive sciences: and, being once reached, demands only a reemployment, in a more stringent mode, of its formal mechanism of reduction and analysis, to disclose the transcendental phenomena.

But it is not to be doubted that transcendental phenomenology could be developed independently of all psychology. The discovery of the double relativity of consciousness suggests the practice of both reductions. The psychological reduction does not reach beyond the psychical in animal realities, for psychology subserves real existence, and even its eidetic is confined to the possibilities of real worlds. But the transcendental problem will include the entire world and all its sciences, to "doubt" the whole. The world "originates" in us, as Descartes led men to recognize and within us acquires its habitual influence. The general significance of the world, and the definite sense of its particulars, is something of which we are conscious within our perceiving, representing, thinking, valuing life, and therefore something "constituted" in some subjective genesis.

The world and its property, "in and for itself," exists as it exists, whether I, or we, happen, or not, to be conscious of it. But let once this general world, make its "appearance" in consciousness as "the" world. It is thenceforth related to the subjective, and all its existence and the manner of it, assumes a new dimension, becoming "incompletely intelligible," "questionable." Here, then, is the transcendental problem; this "making its appearance," this "being for us" of the world, which can only gain its significance "subjectively," what is it? We may call the world "internal" because it is related to consciousness, but how can this quite "general" world, whose "immanent" being is as shadowy as the consciousness wherein it "exists," contrive to appear before us in a variety of "particular" aspects, which experience assures us are the aspects of an independent, self-existent world? The problem also touches every "ideal" world, the world of pure number, for example, and the world of "truths in themselves." And no existence, or manner of existence, is less wholly intelligible than ourselves. Each by himself, and in society, we, in whose consciousness the world is valid, being men, belong ourselves to the world. Must we, then, refer ourselves to ourselves to gain a worldly sense, a worldly being? Are we both psychologically to be called men, subjects of a psychical life, and yet be transcendental to ourselves and the whole world, being subjects of a transcendental world-constituting life? Psychical subjectivity, the "I" and "we" of everyday intent, may be experienced as it is in itself under the phenomenological-psychological reduction, and being eidetically treated, may establish a phenomenological psychology. But the transcendental subjectivity, which for want of language we can only call again, "I myself," "we ourselves," cannot be found under the attitude of psychological or natural science, being no part at all of the objective world, but that subjective conscious life itself, wherein the world and all its content is made for "us," for "me." We that are, indeed, men, spiritual and bodily, existing in the world, are, therefore, "appearances" unto ourselves, parcel of what "we" have constituted, pieces of the significance "we" have made. The "I" and "we," which we apprehend, presuppose a hidden "I" and "we" to whom they are "present."

To this transcendental subjectivity transcendental experience gives us direct approach. As the psychical experience was purified, so is the transcendental, by a reduction. The transcendental reduction may be regarded as a certain further purification of the psychological interest. The universal is carried to a further stage. Henceforth the "bracketing" includes not the world only but its "souls" as well. The psychologist reduces the ordinarily valid world to a subjectivity of "souls," which are a part of the world which they inhabit. The transcendental phenomenologist reduces the already psychologically purified to the transcendental, that most general, subjectivity, which makes the world and its "souls," and confirms them.

I no longer survey my perception experiences, imagination-experiences, the psychological data which my psychological experience reveals: I learn to survey transcendental experience. I am no longer interested in my own existence. I am interested in the pure intentional life, wherein my psychically real experiences have occurred. This step raises the transcendental problem (the transcendental being defined as the quality of that which is consciousness) to its true level. We have to recognize that relativity to consciousness is not only an actual quality of our world, but, from eidetic necessity, the quality of every conceivable world. We may, in a free fancy, vary our actual world, and transmute it to any other which we can imagine, but we are obliged with the world to vary ourselves also, and ourselves we cannot vary except within the limits prescribed to us by the nature of subjectivity. Change worlds as we may, each must ever be a world such as we could experience, prove upon the evidence of our theories and inhabit with our practice. The transcendental problem is eidetic. My psychological experiences, perceptions, imaginations and the like remain in form and content what they were, but I see them as "structures" now, for I am face to face at last with the ultimate structure of consciousness.

It is obvious that, like every other intelligible problem, the transcendental problem derives the means of its solution from an existence-stratum, which it presupposes and sets beyond the reach of its enquiry. This realm is no other than the bare subjectivity of consciousness in general, while the realm of its investigation remains not less than every sphere which can be called "objective," which considered in its totality, and at its root, is the conscious life. No one, then, can justly propose to solve the transcendental problem by psychology either empirical or eidetic-phenomenological, without *petitio principii* [begging the question], for psychology's "subjectivity" and "consciousness" are not that subjectivity and consciousness, which our philosophy will investigate. The transcendental reduction has supplanted the psychological reduction. In the place of the psychological "I" and "we," the transcendental "I" and "we" are comprehended in the concreteness of transcendental consciousness. But though the transcendental "I" is not my psychological "I," it must not be considered as if it were a second "I," for it is no more separated from my psychological "I" in the conventional sense of separation, than it is joined to it in the conventional sense of being joined.

Transcendental self-experience may, at any moment, merely by a change of attitude, be turned back into psychological self-experience. Passing, thus, from the one to the other attitude, we notice a certain "identity" about the ego. What I saw under the psychological reflection as "my" objectification, I see under the transcendental reflection as self-objectifying, or, as we may also say, as objectified by the transcendental "I." We have only to recognize that what makes the psychological and transcendental spheres of experience parallel is an "identity" in their significance, and that what differentiates them is merely a change of attitude, to realize that the psychological and transcendental phenomenologies will also be parallel. Under the more stringent <*epochē*> the psychological subjectivity is transformed into the transcendental subjectivity, and the psychological inter-subjectivity into the transcendental inter-subjectivity. It is this last which is the concrete, ultimate ground, whence all that transcends consciousness, including all that is real in the world, derives the sense of its existence. For all objective existence is essentially "relative," and owes its nature to a unity of intention, which being established according to transcendental laws, produces consciousness with its habit of belief and its conviction.

PHENOMENOLOGY, THE UNIVERSAL SCIENCE

Thus, as phenomenology is developed, the Leibnitzian foreshadowing of a universal ontology, the unification of all conceivable *a priori* sciences, is improved, and realized upon the new and non-dogmatic basis of phenomenological method. For phenomenology as the science of all concrete phenomena proper to subjectivity and intersubjectivity, is *eo ipso* an *a priori* science of all possible existence and existences. Phenomenology is universal in its scope, because there is no *a priori* which does not depend upon its intentional constitution, and derive from this its power of engendering habits in the consciousness that knows it, so that the establishment of any *a priori* must reveal the subjective process by which it is established.

Once the *a priori* disciplines, such as the mathematical sciences, are incorporated within phenomenology, they cannot thereafter be beset by "paradoxes" or disputes concerning principles: and those sciences which have become *a priori* independently of phenomenology, can only hope to set their methods and premises beyond criticism, by founding themselves upon it. For their very claim to be positive, dogmatic sciences bears witness to their dependency, as branches, merely, of that universal, eidetic ontology, which is phenomenology.

The endless task, this exposition of the universum of the *a priori,* by referring all objectives to their transcendental "origin," may be considered as one function in the construction of a universal science of fact, where every department, including the positive, will be settled on its *a priori.* So that our last division of the complete phenomenology is thus: eidetic phenomenology, or the universal ontology, for a first philosophy; and second philosophy as the science of the transcendental intersubjectivity or universum of fact.

Thus the antique conception of philosophy as the universal science, philosophy in the Platonic, philosophy in the Cartesian, sense, that shall embrace all knowledge, is once more justly restored. All rational problems, and all those problems, which for one reason or another, have come to be known as "philosophical," have their place within phenomenology, finding from the ultimate source of transcendental experience or eidetic intuition, their proper form and the means of their solution. Phenomenology itself learns its proper function of transcendental human "living" from an entire relationship to "self." It can intuite life's absolute norms and learn life's original teleological structure. Phenomenology is not less than man's whole occupation with himself in the service of the universal reason. Revealing life's norms, he does in fact, set free a stream of new consciousness intent upon the infinite idea of entire humanity, humanity in fact and truth.

Metaphysical, teleological, ethical problems, and problems of the history of philosophy, the problem of judgment, all significant problems in general, and the transcendental bonds uniting them, lie within phenomenology's capability.

Phenomenological philosophy is but developing the mainsprings of old Greek philosophy, and the supreme motive of Descartes. These have not died. They split into rationalism and empiricism. They stretch over Kant and German idealism, and reach the present, confused day. They must be reassumed, subjected to methodical and concrete treatment. They can inspire a science without bounds.

Phenomenology demands of phenomenalists that they shall forgo particular closed systems of philosophy, and share decisive work with others toward persistent philosophy.

W.E.B. Du Bois
1868–1963

William Edward Burghardt Du Bois was born and raised in Great Barrington, Massachusetts. His mother, Mary Burghardt, was descended from a West African slave. His father, Alfred Du Bois, came from a long line of French Huguenots (Protestants). As W.E.B. Du Bois himself later put it, he was born "with a flood of Negro blood, a strain of French, a bit of Dutch, but thank God! no Anglo-Saxon."

The town of Great Barrington had a small African American population and a rather informal color line. The only people explicitly oppressed on the basis of race were Irish immigrants. But, as Du Bois explains in our reading, there was also a deeper, more implicit, kind of racism. Du Bois came to see himself as part of a "problem": the "problem of the Negro." He understood that he was different from others in school and that he was "shut out from their world by a vast veil."

Du Bois's initial response was to excel at whatever he did, to make himself exhibit A in putting the lie to racial inferiority. While still in high school, Du Bois became a correspondent for the *New York Globe,* a black newspaper. He excelled academically and, following graduation, several local churches collected money to send him to college. In 1885, Du Bois enrolled at Fisk University, an all-black school in Nashville, Tennessee.

Following graduation from Fisk, Du Bois received a Harvard scholarship for a second bachelor's degree in philosophy. Studying with William James and George Santayana, Du Bois developed a Hegelian philosophy that made sense of the black experience. Du Bois went on to receive an M.A. at Harvard in 1892.

Following travel in Europe, Du Bois taught Greek and Latin at Wilberforce University, a black institution in Xenia, Ohio. At the same time, he completed his doctorate in sociology, becoming the first African American to receive a Ph.D. from Harvard. His dissertation, *The Suppression of the African Slave Trade to the*

United States of America, 1638–1870 (1896), was published as the first in the Harvard Historical Studies Series.

In 1896, Du Bois married Nina Gomer, and together they had two children. That same year, Du Bois accepted a position at the University of Pennsylvania. He was commissioned to produce the first systematic study of blacks, *The Philadelphia Negro,* which was published in 1899. Interviewing more than five thousand people for this study, Du Bois came to the conclusion that hard work, persistence, and patience in seeking reforms were the keys to improving the lot of African Americans in Philadelphia.

Following the study's completion, Du Bois was called to Atlanta University, where he taught for the next thirteen years. In Atlanta, Du Bois's social and political philosophies changed radically. The political climate in the late 1800s grew increasingly antagonistic toward blacks as the remnants of Reconstruction disappeared and *Plessey* v. *Ferguson* (1896) legalized "separate but equal" segregation. Du Bois himself suffered numerous indignities as he traveled in the South. He was especially repelled by the lynching of a black farm laborer in 1899 and by the anti-black Atlanta riots of 1906.

During this period, Du Bois challenged Booker T. Washington, president of Tuskegee Institute and African American leader. Washington advocated that his people accept a posture of submissiveness and modest aspiration, claiming, "It is at the bottom of life we must begin and not at the top."* In his earlier days, Du Bois might have agreed, but he was no longer willing to wait patiently at the bottom. Instead, Du Bois argued that blacks must assert themselves, particularly the "Talented Tenth" in the African American community, who would "be leaders of thought and missionaries of culture among their people."**

At Atlanta University, Du Bois began putting his ideas into political action. He was the secretary of the first Pan-African Conference in 1900 and helped organize the First Universal Races Congress in 1911 (both in London). In 1905, he was a founder of the Niagara Movement, which led in 1910 to the founding of the National Association for the Advancement of Colored People (NAACP). During this period, Du Bois made a number of sociological studies of blacks in the South. He also published his most famous book, *The Souls of Black Folks: Essays and Sketches* (1903).

With the founding of the NAACP in 1910, Du Bois left teaching to become editor of the organization's monthly organ, *The Crisis.* Du Bois's move from social scientist to political activist was now complete. For the next twenty-four years, Du Bois wrote, edited, organized, and labored tirelessly for racial equality.

In 1926, Du Bois accepted an invitation to the Soviet Union and returned full of praise for the new "Socialist Republic." He was now convinced that African Americans could find liberation in socialism. As his views moved further and further left, his relations with the NAACP were strained. Du Bois now regarded the NAACP's ideal of integration as not only unattainable but as even undesirable. When he publicly supported "nondiscriminatory segregation," he was forced to resign his position with the NAACP. He returned to teaching at Atlanta University, where he remained until retiring in 1943.

*Quoted in Julius Lester, ed., *The Seventh Son: The Thought and Writings of W.E.B. Du Bois,* two volumes (New York: Random House, 1971), vol. 1, p. 42.

***Ibid.*, p. 44.

Du Bois spent a busy "retirement" in political activism. For four years, he returned to the NAACP as director of the department of special research. Among his many other activities in retirement, he was a consultant to the founding of the United Nations, co-chair of the Fifth Pan-African Congress, vice-chair of the Council of African Affairs, and chair of the Peace Information Center. At the age of 87, he even ran for senator of New York on the Progressive Party ticket.

In the late 1940s and early 1950s, Du Bois became even more enthusiastic about the USSR and the People's Republic of China. In 1951, as the Cold War warmed up, Du Bois was indicted as an "unregistered agent" of the Soviet Union. Though acquitted of all charges, Du Bois was embittered with life in the United States, and for the rest of the 1950s he traveled extensively in Eastern Europe and China. In 1959, Du Bois received the Lenin Peace Prize, and in 1961 he officially joined the Communist Party of the United States. Du Bois left the United States for good in 1961, becoming a citizen of the African state of Ghana. There he died at the age of 95. Following a state funeral led by Ghana's president Kwame Nkrumah, Du Bois was buried in Accra, Ghana.

* * *

To understand Du Bois's philosophy, one must begin with the Hegelianism that runs through his work. Hegel had argued that the "the study of world history . . . represents the rationally necessary course of the World Spirit."* All human history is a dialectical process whereby the World Spirit becomes conscious of itself as free. Whenever a thesis of freedom is asserted, it is opposed by an antithesis. These are then both overcome by a synthesis that incorporates the best of both. In particular, Hegel held that the World Spirit that is coming to a consciousness of freedom is always the spirit of specific world-historical *peoples,* not individuals. Hegel traced the development of this World Spirit through six historical peoples: Chinese, Indians, Egyptians, Greeks, Romans, and Germans.

Du Bois accepted Hegelian history and applied it to the experience of African Americans. In our reading from *The Souls of Black Folks,* Du Bois refers to Hegel's six historical peoples and adds,

> The Negro is a sort of seventh son, born with a veil, and gifted with second-sight in this American world,—a world which yields him no true self-consciousness, but only lets him see himself through the revelation of the other world.

According to Du Bois, "Black folk's" consciousness of freedom is newer and richer than that of any previous world-historical people because of slavery. As one writer explains,

> Out of slavery and out of the later striving of black folk for whiteness in an oppressive white world came a rising sense of black soul. Thus it was that white thesis bred black antithesis, which took the best of white culture and moved it upward toward a new synthesis.**

*Hegel, *Reason in History: A General Introduction to the Philosophy of History,* see Forrest E. Baird and Walter Kaufmann, *Nineteenth-Century Philosophy* (New York: Prentice Hall, 2000), p. 54.

**Joel Williamson, *The Crucible of Race* (New York: Oxford University Press, 1984), p. 405.

While using Hegelian notions, Du Bois noticed something unique about the self-consciousness of black folk. As a "problem," as an "other," black folk develop a kind of "double-consciousness." Black folk have the "sense of always looking at one's self through the eyes of others." This "twoness," this consciousness of "two souls, two thoughts, two unreconciled strivings; two warring ideals in one dark body," means that black folk must uniquely struggle to find true self-consciousness and self-identity.

Although in some ways Du Bois is more activist than philosopher, his thought has been enormously influential. His identification of a "black soul" provided a theoretical base for African American studies. His identification of a unique black culture gave blacks both dignity and an alternative to the assimilationist tendencies of integrationists. His discovery of double-consciousness and his notion of the "other" anticipated some recent debates in Continental philosophy.

* * *

A good place to begin studying Du Bois is Julius Lester, ed., *The Seventh Son: The Thought and Writings of W.E.B. Du Bois,* two volumes (New York: Random House, 1971). For biographies of Du Bois, see Jack B. Moore, *W.E.B. Du Bois* (Boston: Twayne, 1981); and Du Bois's own autobiographies, *Dusk of Dawn* (New York: Harcourt, Brace, 1940) and *The Autobiography of W.E.B. Du Bois,* edited by Herbert Aptheker (New York: International, 1968). Studies of Du Bois's social and political involvements include Francis L. Broderick, *W.E.B. Du Bois: Negro Leader in a Time of Crisis* (Stanford, CA: Stanford University Press, 1959); Cary D. Wintz, *African-American Political Thought, 1890–1930: Washington, Du Bois, Garvey, and Randolph* (Armonk, NY: Sharpe, 1996); Charles F. Peterson, *DuBois, Fanon, Cabral: The Margins of Elite Anti-Colonial Leadership* (Lanham, MD: Lexington Books, 2007); and Reiland Rabaka's books, *W.E.B. Du Bois and the Problems of the Twenty-First Century: An Essay on Africana Critical Theory*; and *Du Bois's Dialectics: Black Radical Politics and the Reconstruction of Critical Social Theory* (both Lanham, MD: Lexington Books, 2007 and 2008). For a more philosophical treatment of Du Bois, see Joel Williamson, *The Crucible of Race* (New York: Oxford University Press, 1984) and Bernard W. Bell, Emily R. Grosholz, and James B. Stewart, eds., *W.E.B. Du Bois on Race and Culture: Critiques and Extrapolations* (London: Routledge, 1996).

THE SOULS OF BLACK FOLKS (in part)

CHAPTER 1: OF OUR SPIRITUAL STRIVINGS

O water, voice of my heart, crying in the sand,
  All night long crying with a mournful cry,
As I lie and listen, and cannot understand
    The voice of my heart in my side or the voice of the sea,

O water, crying for rest, is it I, is it I?
All night long the water is crying to me.

Unresting water, there shall never be rest
Till the last moon droop and the last tide fail,
And the fire of the end begin to burn in the west;
And the heart shall be weary and wonder and cry like the sea,
All life long crying without avail,
As the water all night long is crying to me.

—*Arthur Symons*

Between me and the other world there is ever an unasked question: unasked by some through feelings of delicacy; by others through the difficulty of rightly framing it. All, nevertheless, flutter round it. They approach me in a half-hesitant sort of way, eye me curiously or compassionately, and then, instead of saying directly, How does it feel to be a problem? they say, I know an excellent colored man in my town; or, I fought at Mechanicsville; or, Do not these Southern outrages make your blood boil? At these I smile, or am interested, or reduce the boiling to a simmer, as the occasion may require. To the real question, How does it feel to be a problem? I answer seldom a word.

And yet, being a problem is a strange experience,—peculiar even for one who has never been anything else, save perhaps in babyhood and in Europe. It is in the early days of rollicking boyhood that the revelation first bursts upon one, all in a day, as it were.

W.E.B. Du Bois (on the left) and his high school graduating class, Great Barrington, Massachusetts, 1884. (*W.E.B. Du Bois Library*)

I remember well when the shadow swept across me. I was a little thing, away up in the hills of New England, where the dark Housatonic winds between Hoosac and Taghkanic to the sea. In a wee wooden schoolhouse, something put it into the boys' and girls' heads to buy gorgeous visiting-cards—ten cents a package—and exchange. The exchange was merry, till one girl, a tall newcomer, refused my card,—refused it peremptorily, with a glance. Then it dawned upon me with a certain suddenness that I was different from the others; or like, mayhap, in heart and life and longing, but shut out from their world by a vast veil. I had thereafter no desire to tear down that veil, to creep through; I held all beyond it in common contempt, and lived above it in a region of blue sky and great wandering shadows. That sky was bluest when I could beat my mates at examination-time, or beat them at a foot-race, or even beat their stringy heads. Alas, with the years all this fine contempt began to fade; for the worlds I longed for, and all their dazzling opportunities, were theirs, not mine. But they should not keep these prizes, I said; some, all, I would wrest from them. Just how I would do it I could never decide: by reading law, by healing the sick, by telling the wonderful tales that swam in my head,—some way. With other black boys the strife was not so fiercely sunny: their youth shrunk into tasteless sycophancy, or into silent hatred of the pale world about them and mocking distrust of everything white; or wasted itself in a bitter cry, Why did God make me an outcast and a stranger in mine own house? The shades of the prison-house closed round about us all: walls strait and stubborn to the whitest, but relentlessly narrow, tall, and unscalable to sons of night who must plod darkly on in resignation, or beat unavailing palms against the stone, or steadily, half hopelessly, watch the streak of blue above.

After the Egyptian and Indian, the Greek and Roman, the Teuton and Mongolian, the Negro is a sort of seventh son, born with a veil, and gifted with second-sight in this American world,—a world which yields him no true self-consciousness, but only lets him see himself through the revelation of the other world. It is a peculiar sensation, this double-consciousness, this sense of always looking at one's self through the eyes of others, of measuring one's soul by the tape of a world that looks on in amused contempt and pity. One ever feels his twoness,—an American, a Negro; two souls, two thoughts, two unreconciled strivings; two warring ideals in one dark body, whose dogged strength alone keeps it from being torn asunder.

The history of the American Negro is the history of this strife,—this longing to attain self-conscious manhood, to merge his double self into a better and truer self. In this merging he wishes neither of the older selves to be lost. He would not Africanize America, for America has too much to teach the world and Africa. He would not bleach his Negro soul in a flood of white Americanism, for he knows that Negro blood has a message for the world. He simply wishes to make it possible for a man to be both a Negro and an American, without being cursed and spit upon by his fellows, without having the doors of Opportunity closed roughly in his face.

This, then, is the end of his striving: to be a co-worker in the kingdom of culture, to escape both death and isolation, to husband and use his best powers and his latent genius. These powers of body and mind have in the past been strangely wasted, dispersed, or forgotten. The shadow of a mighty Negro past flits through the tale of Ethiopia the Shadowy and of Egypt the Sphinx. Throughout history, the powers of single black men flash here and there like falling stars, and die sometimes before the world has rightly gauged their brightness. Here in America, in the few days since Emancipation, the black man's turning hither and thither in hesitant and doubtful striving has often made his very strength to lose effectiveness, to seem like absence of power, like weakness. And yet it is not weakness,—it is the contradiction of double aims. The double-aimed struggle of the black artisan—on the one hand to escape white contempt for a nation of mere hewers of wood and drawers of water, and on the other hand to plough and nail and dig for a poverty-stricken horde—could only result in making him a poor craftsman, for he had but half a heart in either cause. By the poverty and ignorance of his people, the Negro minister or doctor was tempted toward quackery and demagogy; and by the criticism of the other world, toward ideals that made him ashamed of his lowly tasks. The would-be black savant was confronted by the paradox that the knowledge his people needed was a twice-told tale to his white neighbors, while the knowledge which would teach the white world was Greek to his own flesh and blood. The innate love of harmony and beauty that set the ruder souls of his people a-dancing and a-singing raised but confusion and doubt in the soul of the black artist; for the beauty revealed to him was the soul-beauty of a race which his larger audience despised, and he could not articulate the message of another people. This waste of double aims, this seeking to satisfy two unreconciled ideals, has wrought sad havoc with the courage and faith and deeds of ten thousand thousand people,—has sent them often wooing false gods and invoking false means of salvation, and at times has even seemed about to make them ashamed of themselves.

Away back in the days of bondage they thought to see in one divine event the end of all doubt and disappointment; few men ever worshipped Freedom with half such unquestioning faith as did the American Negro for two centuries. To him, so far as he thought and dreamed, slavery was indeed the sum of all villainies, the cause of all sorrow, the root of all prejudice; Emancipation was the key to a promised land of sweeter beauty than ever stretched before the eyes of wearied Israelites, In song and exhortation swelled one refrain—Liberty; in his tears and curses the God he implored had Freedom in his right hand. At last it came,—suddenly, fearfully, like a dream. With one wild carnival of blood and passion came the message in his own plaintive cadences:—

"Shout, O children!
Shout, you're free!
For God has bought your liberty!"

Years have passed away since then,—ten, twenty, forty; forty years of national life, forty years of renewal and development, and yet the swarthy spectre sits in its accustomed seat at the Nation's feast. In vain do we cry to this our vastest social problem:—

"Take any shape but that, and my firm nerves
Shall never tremble!"

The Nation has not yet found peace from its sins; the freedman has not yet found in freedom his promised land. Whatever of good may have come in these years of change, the shadow of a deep disappointment rests upon the Negro people,—a disappointment all the more bitter because the unattained ideal was unbounded save by the simple ignorance of a lowly people.

The first decade was merely a prolongation of the vain search for freedom, the boon that seemed ever barely to elude their grasp,—like a tantalizing will-o'-the-wisp, maddening and misleading the headless host. The holocaust of war, the terrors of the Ku Klux Klan, the lies of carpet-baggers, the disorganization of industry, and the contradictory advice of friends and foes, left the bewildered serf with no new watchword beyond the old cry for freedom. As the time flew, however, he began to grasp a new idea. The ideal of liberty demanded for its attainment powerful means, and these the Fifteenth Amendment gave him. The ballot, which before he had looked upon as a visible sign of freedom, he now regarded as the chief means of gaining and perfecting the liberty with which war had partially endowed him. And why not? Had not votes made war and emancipated millions? Had not votes enfranchised the freedmen? Was anything impossible to a power that had done all this? A million black men started with renewed zeal to vote themselves into the kingdom. So the decade flew away, the revolution of 1876 came, and left the half-free serf weary, wondering, but still inspired. Slowly but steadily, in the following years, a new vision began gradually to replace the dream of political power,—a powerful movement, the rise of another ideal to guide the unguided, another pillar of fire by night after a clouded day. It was the ideal of "book-learning"; the curiosity, born of compulsory ignorance, to know and test the power of the cabalistic letters of the white man, the longing to know. Here at last seemed to have been discovered the mountain path to Canaan; longer than the highway of Emancipation and law, steep and rugged, but straight, leading to heights high enough to overlook life.

Up the new path the advance guard toiled, slowly, heavily, doggedly; only those who have watched and guided the faltering feet, the misty minds, the dull understandings, of the dark pupils of these schools know how faithfully, how piteously, this people strove to learn. It was weary work. The cold statistician wrote down the inches of progress here and there, noted also where here and there a foot had slipped or some one had fallen. To the tired climbers, the horizon was ever dark, the mists were often cold, the Canaan was always dim and far away. If, however, the vistas disclosed as yet no goal, no resting-place, little but flattery and criticism, the journey at least gave leisure for reflection and self-examination; it changed the child of Emancipation to the youth with dawning self-consciousness, self-realization, self-respect. In those sombre forests of his striving his own soul rose before him, and he saw himself,—darkly as through a veil; and yet he saw in himself some faint revelation of his power, of his mission. He began to have a dim feeling that, to attain his place in the world, he must be himself, and not another. For the first time he sought to analyze the burden he bore upon his back, that dead-weight of social degradation partially masked behind a halfnamed Negro problem. He felt his poverty; without a cent, without a home, without land, tools, or savings, he had entered into competition with rich, landed, skilled neighbors. To be a poor man is hard, but to be a poor race in a land of dollars is the very bottom of hardships. He felt the weight of his ignorance,—not simply of letters, but of life, of business, of the humanities; the accumulated sloth and shirking and awkwardness of decades and centuries shackled his hands and feet. Nor was his burden all poverty and ignorance. The red stain of bastardy, which two centuries of systematic legal defilement of Negro women had stamped upon his race, meant not only the loss of ancient African chastity, but also the hereditary weight of a mass of corruption from white adulterers, threatening almost the obliteration of the Negro home.

A people thus handicapped ought not to be asked to race with the world, but rather allowed to give all its time and thought to its own social problems. But alas! while sociologists gleefully count his bastards and his prostitutes, the very soul of the toiling, sweating black man is darkened by the shadow of a vast despair. Men call the shadow prejudice, and learnedly explain it as the natural defence of culture against barbarism, learning against ignorance, purity against crime, the "higher" against the "lower" races. To which the Negro cries Amen! and swears that to so much of this strange prejudice as is founded on just homage to civilization, culture, righteousness, and progress, he humbly bows and meekly does obeisance. But before that nameless prejudice that leaps beyond all this he stands helpless, dismayed, and well-nigh speechless; before that personal disrespect and mockery, the ridicule and systematic humiliation, the distortion of fact and wanton license of fancy, the cynical ignoring of the better and the boisterous welcoming of the worse, the all-pervading desire to inculcate disdain for everything black, from Toussaint to the devil,—before this there rises a sickening despair that would disarm and discourage any nation save that black host to whom "discouragement" is an unwritten word.

But the facing of so vast a prejudice could not but bring the inevitable self-questioning, self-disparagement, and lowering of ideals which ever accompany repression and breed in an atmosphere of contempt and hate. Whisperings and portents came borne upon the four winds: Lo! we are diseased and dying, cried the dark hosts; we cannot write, our voting is vain; what need of education, since we must always cook and serve? And the Nation echoed and enforced this self-criticism, saying: Be content to be servants, and nothing more; what need of higher culture for half-men? Away with the black man's ballot, by force or fraud,—and behold the suicide of a race! Nevertheless, out of the evil came something of good,—the more careful adjustment of education to real life, the clearer perception of the Negroes' social responsibilities, and the sobering realization of the meaning of progress.

So dawned the time of *Sturm und Drang:* storm and stress to-day rocks our little boat on the mad waters of the world-sea; there is within and without the sound of conflict, the burning of body and rending of soul; inspiration strives with doubt, and faith with vain questionings. The bright ideals of the past,—physical freedom, political power, the training of brains and the training of hands,—all these in turn have waxed and waned, until even the last grows dim and overcast. Are they all wrong,—all false? No, not that, but each alone was over-simple and incomplete,—the dreams of a credulous race-childhood, or the fond imaginings of the other world which does not know and does not want to know our power. To be really true, all these ideals must be melted and welded into one. The training of the schools we need to-day more than ever,—the training of deft hands, quick eyes and ears, and above all the broader, deeper, higher culture of gifted minds and pure hearts. The power of the ballot we need in sheer self-defence,—else what shall save us from a second slavery? Freedom, too, the long-sought, we still seek,—the freedom of life and limb, the freedom to work and think, the freedom to love and aspire. Work, culture, liberty,—all these we need, not singly but together, not successively but together, each growing and aiding each, and all striving toward that vaster ideal that swims before the Negro people, the ideal of human brotherhood, gained through the unifying ideal of Race; the ideal of fostering and developing the traits and talents of the Negro, not in opposition to or contempt for other races, but rather in large conformity to the greater ideals of the American Republic, in order that some day on American soil two world-races may give each to each those characteristics both so sadly lack. We the darker ones come even now not altogether empty-handed: there are to-day no truer exponents of the pure human spirit of the Declaration of Independence than the American Negroes; there is no true American music but the wild sweet melodies of the Negro slave; the American fairy tales and folk-lore are Indian and African; and, all in all, we black men seem the sole oasis of simple faith and reverence in a dusty desert of dollars and smartness. Will America be poorer if she replace her brutal dyspeptic blundering with lighthearted but determined Negro humility? or her coarse and cruel wit with loving jovial good-humor? or her vulgar music with the soul of the Sorrow Songs?

Merely a concrete test of the underlying principles of the great republic is the Negro Problem, and the spiritual striving of the freedmen's sons is the travail of souls whose burden is almost beyond the measure of their strength, but who bear it in the name of an historic race, in the name of this the land of their fathers' fathers, and in the name of human opportunity.

BERTRAND RUSSELL
1872–1970

Bertrand Arthur William Russell was born into a prestigious family in Trelleck, Wales. His parents, Lord and Lady Amberley, were close friends with John Stuart Mill, and Russell's grandfather, Lord John Russell, had been prime minister to Queen Victoria. Both of Russell's parents died by the time he was 3, and so, with his brother, he was sent to live with his grandparents, Lord and Lady Russell. When his grandfather died a few years later, his grandmother took responsibility for his education. Unlike most privileged English boys, Russell did not attend a boarding school—Lady Russell did not approve of them. Instead, she arranged for a series of Swiss and German governesses, followed by English tutors, to educate her grandsons. Although Russell thus enjoyed virtually every privilege, he later reported that his adolescent life seemed so bleak that he would have committed suicide had he not been "restrained by the desire to know more mathematics."

In 1890, Russell entered Cambridge University, where he was finally able to study his beloved mathematics on his own. His years at the university were the happiest of his life. He quickly established himself as one of the brightest students, and he formed several close friendships, including a lifelong one with G.E. Moore (1873–1958). Following graduation, Russell served briefly with the British ambassador to France before moving to Berlin to study economics and political theory. In 1895, Russell was elected a fellow of Trinity College, Cambridge, and worked extensively on the foundations of mathematics. He published *Principles of Mathematics* (1903) and, together with Alfred North Whitehead, the epoch-making *Principia Mathematica* (1910–1913). During this time, Russell also made the first of three unsuccessful runs for Parliament.

Russell was appointed lecturer in philosophy at Cambridge in 1910—a position he held until 1916, when he was dismissed for his opposition to the continued fighting of World War I. He also spent six months in jail for alleging that U.S. troops were used for strikebreaking in America. He was reinstated in his Cambridge position in 1919 but soon resigned and never again assumed permanent teaching duties. During his years as a lecturer, Russell also produced some of his most important works of philosophy and logic, including *The Problems of Philosophy* (1912), *Our Knowledge of the External World* (1914), and *Introduction to Mathematical Philosophy* (written while in prison and published in 1919).

In his post-teaching period, Russell wrote and lectured widely—often taking controversial positions on social and political issues. For example, he alienated many of his socialist friends when, after a visit to the Soviet Union in 1920, he published his observations in *The Theory and Practice of Bolshevism:*

> [Russia is] one vast prison in which the jailors were cruel bigots. When I found my friends applauding these men as liberators and regarding the regime that they were creating as a paradise, I wondered . . . whether it was my friends or I that were mad.

His book *Marriage and Morals* (1929) caused a stir by minimizing the seriousness of extramarital affairs and by advocating informal trial marriages. His works on religion, *What I Believe* (1925), *Religion and Science* (1935), and *Why I Am Not a Christian* (1957), made Russell's atheism explicit. Russell also tried his hand at practical social reform. With his second wife Dora, he started a school in 1927 to implement the educational theories of his books *On Education: Especially Early Childhood* (1926) and *Education and the Social Order* (1932).

In 1938, Russell accepted a visiting professorship at the University of Chicago and later at the University of California at Los Angeles. He declined a permanent offer from UCLA in order to accept an invitation from the College of the City of New York; however, before he could begin teaching a judge ruled him unfit, claiming, among other things, that Russell's appointment would constitute "a chair of indecency." Russell mocked the decision on the title page of his *An Inquiry into Meaning and Truth,* published the next year, by listing his many honors and then adding "Judicially pronounced unworthy to be Professor of Philosophy at the College of the City of New York (1940)." To that long list of honors, he would be able to add the Nobel Prize for literature in 1950.

In his later years, Russell continued to write on a variety of topics—and to get into trouble with authorities. At age 89, he served another jail sentence—this time for his part in a nuclear-disarmament rally in London. By the time of his death in 1970, Russell was acknowledged as the leading British philosopher of the century.

* * *

It is difficult to summarize Russell's thought, partly because he developed and abandoned several philosophical theories during his long lifetime. Philosopher C.D. Broad once commented, "As we all know, Mr. Russell produces a different system of philosophy every few years." Even though the specifics of Russell's philosophic enterprise evolved, reflecting his fertile and inventive mind, at least two basic assumptions remained within his mature philosophy.

First, Russell believed philosophy should be scientific and analytical. As he wrote in "Logical Atomism" (1924):

> Although . . . comprehensive construction is part of the business of philosophy, I do not believe it is the most important part. The most important part, to my mind, consists in criticizing and clarifying notions which are apt to be regarded as fundamental and accepted uncritically. As instances I might mention: mind, matter, consciousness, knowledge, experience, causality, will, time. I believe all these notions to be inexact and approximate, essentially infected with vagueness, incapable of forming part of any exact science.

Second, in "criticizing and clarifying notions," Russell was committed to the principle of parsimony known as "Ockham's Razor" (after the medieval thinker, William of Ockham, see p. 358). Ockham's injunction asserted that "entities are not to be multiplied beyond necessity," meaning one should always seek the simplest explanation. Russell's version of this principle, articulated in several of his works, states that "Whenever possible, substitute constructions out of known entities for inferences to unknown entities."

In the selection from *The Problems of Philosophy* reprinted here, Russell wields this razor in an analysis of the common objects of our sensory perception and our language about such objects. Russell points out that sense-data are the only "known entities" actually given in experience:

> What the senses *immediately* tell us is not the truth about the object as it is apart from us, but only the truth about certain sense-data which, so far as we can see, depend upon the relations between us and the object. (Emphasis in original.)

Rather than inferring some "unknown entity" (such as "being" or "substance") as the cause of our sense-data, we can consider a given object to be the class or collection of all sense-data we normally associate with that object. Our knowledge of physical objects is not direct but is gained by "acquaintance" with the sense-data that make up the appearance of an object.

The language used to make propositions about such objects also depends on acquaintance. To use language in a meaningful manner, "the meaning we attach to our words must be something with which we are acquainted" either in terms of a thing or a description. Using Russell's example, a statement about Julius Caesar can be meaningful even though we have no acquaintance with the "thing" (i.e., we have not met Caesar) because we do have in mind some description of Caesar.

Although this selection includes some of Russell's major themes and gives some sense of his style, his contributions to philosophy go beyond what has been included. His work in mathematics and logic changed both of those disciplines; his theory of logical atomism represented an important step in the philosophy of language; his theories of descriptions and of types helped clear up a number of logical puzzles; and in addition there are his writings on education, sociology, politics, and religion. In short, Russell touched on virtually all areas of human existence, and even those who differ with his conclusions cannot help but be impressed with the breadth and depth of his thought.

* * *

For biographical information, see Ronald William Clark, *The Life of Bertrand Russell* (New York: Knopf, 1976); Katharine Tait, *My Father, Bertrand Russell* (Bristol, UK: Thoemmes, 1996); or Russell's autobiography, *The Autobiography of Bertrand Russell* (Boston: Little, Brown, 1967). A.J. Ayer, *Russell and Moore:*

The Analytic Heritage (Cambridge, MA: Harvard University Press, 1971) puts Russell's thought in the context of analytic philosophy, whereas J. Watling, *Bertrand Russell* (New York: British Book Center, 1971); A.J. Ayer, *Bertrand Russell* (Chicago: University of Chicago Press, 1988); John Slater, *Bertrand Russell* (Bristol, Gloucester: Thoemmes, 1994); and Ray Monk, *Russell* (London: Routledge, 1999) provide general introductions. Studies on specific areas of Russell's thought include Lillian Woodworth Aiken, *Bertrand Russell's Philosophy of Morals* (New York: Humanities Press, 1963); Robert J. Clack, *Bertrand Russell's Philosophy of Language* (The Hague, The Netherlands: Martinus Nijhoff, 1969); Elizabeth R. Eames, *Bertrand Russell's Theory of Knowledge* (New York: George Braziller, 1969); Michael K. Potter, *Bertrand Russell's Ethics* (London: Continuum, 2006); and Sajahan Miah, *Russell's Theory of Perception* (London: Continuum, 2006). For collections of essays, see Paul A. Schilpp, ed., *The Philosophy of Bertrand Russell* (New York: Tudor, 1951)—part of the Library of Living Philosophers; Ralph Schoenman, ed., *Bertrand Russell: Philosopher of the Century* (Boston: Little, Brown, 1967); E.D. Klernke, ed., *Essays on Bertrand Russell* (Urbana: University of Illinois Press, 1970); D.F. Pears, ed., *Bertrand Russell* (Garden City, NY: Anchor Doubleday, 1972); A.D. Irvine and G.A. Wedeking, eds., *Russell and Analytic Philosophy* (Toronto: University of Toronto Press, 1993); Ray Monk and Anthony Palmer, eds., *Bertrand Russell and the Origins of Analytical Philosophy* (Bristol, UK: Thoemmes, 1996); and Nicholas Griffin, ed., *The Cambridge Companion to Bertrand Russell* (Cambridge: Cambridge University Press, 2003).

THE PROBLEMS OF PHILOSOPHY (selections)

CHAPTER 1: APPEARANCE AND REALITY

Is there any knowledge in the world which is so certain that no reasonable man could doubt it? This question, which at first sight might not seem difficult, is really one of the most difficult that can be asked. When we have realized the obstacles in the way of a straightforward and confident answer, we shall be well launched on the study of philosophy—for philosophy is merely the attempt to answer such ultimate questions, not carelessly and dogmatically, as we do in ordinary life and even in the sciences, but critically, after exploring all that makes such questions puzzling, and after realizing all the vagueness and confusion that underlie our ordinary ideas.

In daily life, we assume as certain many things which, on a closer scrutiny, are found to be so full of apparent contradictions that only a great amount of thought enables us to know what it is that we really may believe. In the search for certainty, it is natural to begin with our present experiences, and in some sense, no doubt, knowledge is to be derived from them. But any statement as to what it is that our immediate experiences make us know is very likely to be wrong. It seems to me that I am now sitting in a chair, at a table of a certain shape, on which I see sheets of paper with writing or print. By turning my head I see out of the window buildings and clouds and the sun. I believe that the sun is about ninety-three million miles from the earth; that it is a hot globe many times bigger than the earth; that, owing to the earth's rotation, it rises every morning, and will continue to do so for an indefinite time in the future. I believe that, if any other normal person comes into my room, he will see the same chairs and tables and books and papers as I see, and that the table which I see is the same as the table which I feel pressing against my arm. All this seems to be so evident as to be hardly worth stating, except in answer to a man who doubts whether I know anything. Yet all this may be reasonably doubted, and all of it requires much careful discussion before we can be sure that we have stated it in a form that is wholly true.

To make our difficulties plain, let us concentrate attention on the table. To the eye it is oblong, brown, and shiny, to the touch it is smooth and cool and hard; when I tap it, it gives out a wooden sound. Any one else who sees and feels and hears the table will agree with this description, so that it might seem as if no difficulty would arise; but as soon as we try to be more precise our troubles begin. Although I believe that the table is "really" of the same colour all over, the parts that reflect the light look much brighter than the other parts, and some parts look white because of reflected light. I know that, if I move, the parts that reflect the light will be different, so that the apparent distribution of colours on the table will change. It follows that if several people are looking at the table at the same moment, no two of them will see exactly the same distribution of colours, because no two can see it from exactly the same point of view, and any change in the point of view makes some change in the way the light is reflected.

For most practical purposes these differences are unimportant, but to the painter they are all-important: the painter has to unlearn the habit of thinking that things seem to have the colour which common sense says they "really" have, and to learn the habit of seeing things as they appear. Here we have already the beginning of one of the distinctions that cause most trouble in philosophy—the distinction between "appearance" and "reality," between what things seem to be and what they are. The painter wants to know what things seem to be, the practical man and the philosopher want to know what they are; but the philosopher's wish to know this is stronger than the practical man's, and is more troubled by knowledge as to the difficulties of answering the question.

To return to the table. It is evident from what we have found, that there is no colour which preeminently appears to be *the* colour of the table, or even of any one particular part of the table—it appears to be of different colours from different points of view, and there is no reason for regarding some of these as more really its colour than others. And we know that even from a given point of view the colour will seem different by artificial light, or to a colour-blind man, or to a man wearing blue spectacles, while in the dark there will be no colour at all, though to touch and hearing the table will be unchanged. This colour is not something which is inherent in the table, but something depending upon the table and the spectator and the way the light falls on the table. When, in ordinary life, we speak of *the* colour of the table, we only mean the sort of colour which it will seem to have to a normal spectator from an ordinary point of view under usual conditions of light. But the other colours which appear under other conditions have just as good a right to be considered real; and therefore, to avoid favouritism, we are compelled to deny that, in itself, the table has any one particular colour.

The same thing applies to the texture. With the naked eye one can see the grain, but otherwise the table looks smooth and even. If we looked at it through a microscope, we should see roughnesses and hills and valleys, and all sorts of differences that are imperceptible to the naked eye. Which of these is the "real" table? We are naturally tempted to say that what we see through the microscope is more real, but that in turn would be changed by a still more powerful microscope. If, then, we cannot trust what we see with the naked eye, why should we trust what we see through a microscope? Thus, again, the confidence in our senses with which we began deserts us.

The *shape* of the table is no better. We are all in the habit of judging as to the "real" shapes of things, and we do this so unreflectingly that we come to think we actually see the real shapes. But, in fact, as we all have to learn if we try to draw, a given thing looks different in shape from every different point of view. If our table is "really" rectangular, it will look, from almost all points of view, as if it had two acute angles and two obtuse angles. If opposite sides are parallel, they will look as if they converged to a point away from the spectator; if they are of equal length, they will look as if the nearer side were longer. All these things are not commonly noticed in looking at a table, because experience has taught us to construct the "real" shape from the apparent shape, and the "real" shape is what interests us as practical men. But the "real" shape is not what we see, it is something inferred from what we see. And what we see is constantly changing in shape as we move about the room; so that here again the senses seem not to give us the truth about the table itself, but only about the appearance of the table.

Similar difficulties arise when we consider the sense of touch. It is true that the table always gives us a sensation of hardness, and we feel that it resists pressure. But the sensation we obtain depends upon how hard we press the table and also upon what part of the body we press with; thus the various sensations due to various pressures or various parts of the body cannot be supposed to reveal *directly* any definite property of the table, but at most to be *signs* of some property which perhaps *causes* all the sensations, but is not actually apparent in any of them. And the same applies still more obviously to the sounds which can be elicited by rapping the table.

Thus it becomes evident that the real table, if there is one, is not the same as what we immediately experience by sight or touch or hearing. The real table, if there is one, is not *immediately* known to us all, but must be an inference from what is immediately known. Hence, two very difficult questions at once arise; namely, (1) Is there a real table at all? (2) If so, what sort of object can it be?

It will help us in considering these questions to have a few simple terms of which the meaning is definite and clear. Let us give the name of "sense-data" to the things that are immediately known in sensation: such things as colours, sounds, smells, hardnesses, roughnesses, and so on. We shall give the name "sensation" to the experience of being immediately aware of these things. Thus, whenever we see a colour, we have a sensation of the colour, but the colour itself is a sense-datum, not a sensation. The colour is that *of* which we are immediately aware, and the awareness itself is the sensation. It is plain that if we are to know anything about the table, it must be by means of the sense-data—brown colour, oblong shape, smoothness, etc.—which we associate with the table; but, for the reasons which have been given, we cannot say that the table *is* the sense-data, or even that the sense-data are directly properties of the table. Thus a problem arises as to the relation of the sense-data to the real table, supposing there is such a thing.

The real table, if it exists, we will call a "physical object." Thus we have to consider the relation of sense-data to physical objects. The collection of all physical objects is called "matter." Thus our two questions may be re-stated as follows: (1) Is there any such thing as matter? (2) If so, what is its nature?

The philosopher who first brought prominently forward the reasons for regarding the immediate objects of our senses as not existing independently of us was Bishop Berkeley (1685–1753). His *Three Dialogues between Hylas and Philonous, in Opposition to Sceptics and Atheists,* undertake to prove that there is no such thing as matter at all, and that the world consists of nothing but minds and their ideas. Hylas has hitherto believed in matter, but he is no match for Philonous, who mercilessly drives him into contradictions and paradoxes, and makes his own denial of matter seem, in the end, as if it were almost common sense. The arguments employed are of very different value: some are important and sound, others are confused or quibbling. But Berkeley retains the merit of having shown that the existence of matter is capable of being denied without absurdity, and that if there are any things that exist independently of us they cannot be the immediate objects of our sensations.

There are two different questions involved when we ask whether matter exists, and it is important to keep them clear. We commonly mean by "matter" something which is opposed to "mind," something which we think of as occupying space and as radically incapable of any sort of thought or consciousness. It is chiefly in this sense that Berkeley denies matter; that is to say, he does not deny that the sense-data which we commonly take as signs of the existence of the table are really signs of the existence *of* something independent of us, but he does deny that this something is, non-mental, that it is neither mind nor ideas entertained by some mind. He admits that there must be something which continues to exist when we go out of the room or shut our eyes, and that what we call seeing the table does really give us reason for believing in something which persists even when we are not seeing it. But he thinks that this something cannot be radically different in nature from what we see, and cannot be independent of seeing altogether, though it must be independent of *our* seeing. He is thus led to regard the "real" table as an idea in the mind of God. Such an idea has the required permanence and independence of ourselves, without being—as matter would otherwise be—something quite unknowable, in the sense that we can only infer it, and can never be directly and immediately aware of it.

Other philosophers since Berkeley have also held that, although the table does not depend for its existence upon being seen by me, it does depend upon being seen (or otherwise apprehended in sensation) by *some* mind—not necessarily the mind of God, but more often the whole collective mind of the universe. This they hold, as Berkeley does, chiefly because they think there can be nothing real—or at any rate nothing known to be real—except minds and their thoughts and feelings. We might state the argument by which they support their view in some such way as this: "Whatever can be thought of is an idea in the mind of the person thinking of it; therefore nothing can be thought of except ideas in minds; therefore anything else is inconceivable, and what is inconceivable cannot exist."

Such an argument, in my opinion, is fallacious; and of course those who advance it do not put it so shortly or so crudely. But whether valid or not, the argument has been very widely advanced in one form or another; and very many philosophers, perhaps a majority, have held that there is nothing real except minds and their ideas. Such philosophers are called "idealists." When they come to explaining matter, they either say, like Berkeley, that matter is really nothing but a collection of ideas, or they say, like Leibniz (1646–1716), that what appears as matter is really a collection of more or less rudimentary minds.

But these philosophers, though they deny matter as opposed to mind, nevertheless, in another sense, admit matter. It will be remembered that we asked two questions; namely, (1) Is there a real table at all? (2) If so, what sort of object can it be? Now both Berkeley and Leibniz admit that there is a real table, but Berkeley says it is certain ideas in the mind of God, and Leibniz says it is a colony of souls. Thus both of them answer our first question in the affirmative, and only diverge from the views of ordinary mortals in their answer to our second question. In fact, almost all philosophers seem to be agreed that there is a real table: they almost all agree that, however much our sense-data—colour, shape, smoothness, etc.—may depend upon us, yet their occurrence is a sign of something existing independently of us, something differing, perhaps, completely from our sense-data, and yet to be regarded as causing those sense-data whenever we are in a suitable relation to the real table.

Now obviously this point in which the philosophers are agreed—the view that there *is* a real table, whatever its nature may be—is vitally important, and it will be worth while to consider what reasons there are for accepting this view before we go on to the further question as to the nature of the real table. Our next chapter, therefore, will be concerned with the reasons for supposing that there is a real table at all.

Before we go farther it will be well to consider for a moment what it is that we have discovered so far. It has appeared that, if we take any common object of the sort that is supposed to be known by the senses, what the senses *immediately* tell us is not the truth about the object as it is apart from us, but only the truth about certain sense-data which, so far as we can see, depend upon the relations between us and the object. Thus what we directly see and feel is merely "appearance," which we believe to be a sign of some "reality" behind. But if the reality is not what appears, have we any means of knowing whether there is any reality at all? And if so, have we any means of finding out what it is like?

Such questions are bewildering, and it is difficult to know that even the strangest hypotheses may not be true. Thus our familiar table, which has roused but the slightest thoughts in us hitherto, has become a problem full of surprising possibilities. The one thing we know about it is that it is not what it seems. Beyond this modest result, so far, we have the most complete liberty of conjecture. Leibniz tells us it is a community of souls; Berkeley tells us it is an idea in the mind of God; sober science, scarcely less wonderful, tells us it is a vast collection of electric charges in violent motion.

Among these surprising possibilities, doubt suggests that perhaps there is no table at all. Philosophy, if it cannot *answer* so many questions as we could wish, has at least the power of *asking* questions which increase the interest of the world, and show the strangeness and wonder lying just below the surface even in the commonest things of daily life.

* * *

CHAPTER 15: THE VALUE OF PHILOSOPHY

Having now come to the end of our brief and very incomplete review of the problems of philosophy, it will be well to consider, in conclusion, what is the value of philosophy and why it ought to be studied. It is the more necessary to consider this question, in view of the fact that many men, under the influence of science or of practical affairs, are inclined to doubt whether philosophy is anything better than innocent but useless trifling, hair-splitting distinctions, and controversies on matters concerning which knowledge is impossible.

This view of philosophy appears to result, partly from a wrong conception of the ends of life, partly from a wrong conception of the kind of goods which philosophy strives to achieve. Physical science, through the medium of inventions, is useful to innumerable people who are wholly ignorant of it; thus the study of physical science is to be recommended, not only, or primarily, because of the effect on the student, but rather because of the effect on mankind in general. Thus utility does not belong to philosophy. If the study of philosophy has any value at all for others than students of philosophy, it must be only indirectly, through its effects upon the lives of those who study it. It is in these effects, therefore, if anywhere, that the value of philosophy must be primarily sought.

But further, if we are not to fail in our endeavour to determine the value of philosophy, we must first free our minds from the prejudices of what are wrongly called "practical" men. The "practical" man, as this word is often used, is one who recognizes only material needs, who realizes that men must have food for the body, but is oblivious of the necessity of providing food for the mind. If all men were well off, if poverty and disease had been reduced to their lowest possible point, there would still remain much to be done to produce a valuable society; and even in the existing world the goods of the mind are at least as important as the goods of the body. It is exclusively among the goods of the mind that the value of philosophy is to be found; and only those who are not indifferent to these goods can be persuaded that the study of philosophy is not a waste of time.

Philosophy, like all other studies, aims primarily at knowledge. The knowledge it aims at is the kind of knowledge which gives unity and system to the body of sciences, and the kind which results from a critical examination of the grounds of our convictions, prejudices, and beliefs. But it cannot be maintained that philosophy has had any very great measure of success in its attempts to provide definite answers to its questions. If you ask a mathematician, a mineralogist, a historian, or any other man of learning, what definite body of truths has been ascertained by his science, his answer will last as long as you are willing to listen. But if you put the same question to a philosopher, he will, if he is candid, have to confess that his study has not achieved positive results such as have been achieved by other sciences. It is true that this is partly accounted for by the fact that, as soon as definite knowledge concerning any subject becomes possible, this subject ceases to be called philosophy, and now becomes a separate science. The whole study of the heavens, which now belongs to astronomy, was once included in philosophy; Newton's great work was called "the mathematical principles of natural philosophy." Similarly, the study of the human mind, which was a part of philosophy, has now been separated from philosophy and has become the science of psychology. Thus, to a great extent, the uncertainty of philosophy is more apparent than real: those questions which are already capable of definite answers are placed in the sciences, while those only to which, at present, no definite answer can be given, remain to form the residue which is called philosophy.

This is, however, only a part of the truth concerning the uncertainty of philosophy. There are many questions—and among them those that are of the profoundest interest to our spiritual life—which, so far as we can see, must remain insoluble to the human intellect unless its powers become of quite a different order from what they are now. Has the universe any unity of plan or purpose, or is it a fortuitous concourse of atoms? Is consciousness a permanent part of the universe, giving hope of indefinite growth in wisdom, or is it a transitory accident on a small planet on which life must ultimately become impossible? Are good and evil of importance to the universe or only to man? Such questions are asked by philosophy, and variously answered by various philosophers. But it would seem that, whether answers be otherwise discoverable or not, the answers suggested by philosophy are none of them demonstrably true. Yet, however slight may be the hope of discovering an answer, it is part of the business of philosophy to continue the consideration of such questions, to make us aware of their importance, to examine all the approaches to them, and to keep alive that speculative interest in the universe which is apt to be killed by confining ourselves to definitely ascertainable knowledge.

Many philosophers, it is true, have held that philosophy could establish the truth of certain answers to such fundamental questions. They have supposed that what is of most importance in religious beliefs could be proved by strict demonstration to be true. In order to judge of such attempts, it is necessary to take a survey of human knowledge, and to form an opinion as to its methods and its limitations. On such a subject it would be unwise to pronounce dogmatically; but if the investigations of our previous chapters have not led us astray, we shall be compelled to renounce the hope of finding philosophical proofs of religious beliefs. We cannot, therefore, include as part of the value of philosophy any definite set of answers to such questions. Hence, once more, the value of philosophy must not depend upon any supposed body of definitely ascertainable knowledge to be acquired by those who study it.

The value of philosophy is, in fact, to be sought largely in its very uncertainty. The man who has not tincture of philosophy goes through life imprisoned in the prejudices derived from common sense, from the habitual beliefs of his age or his nation, and from convictions which have grown up in his mind without the co-operation or consent of his deliberate reason. To such a man the world tends to become definite, finite, obvious; common objects rouse no questions, and unfamiliar possibilities are contemptuously rejected. As soon as we begin to philosophize, on the contrary, we find, as we saw in our opening chapters, that even the most everyday things lead to problems to which only very incomplete answers can be given. Philosophy, though unable to tell us with certainty what is the true answer to the doubts which it raises, is able to suggest many possibilities which enlarge our thoughts and free them from the tyranny of custom. Thus, while diminishing our feeling of certainty as to what things are, it greatly increases our knowledge as to what they may be; it removes the somewhat arrogant dogmatism of those who have never travelled into the region of liberating doubt, and it keeps alive our sense of wonder by showing familiar things in an unfamiliar aspect.

Apart from its utility in showing unsuspected possibilities, philosophy has a value—perhaps its chief value—through the greatness of the objects which it contemplates, and the freedom from narrow and personal aims resulting from this contemplation. The life of the instinctive man is shut up within the circle of his private interests: family and friends may be included, but the outer world is not regarded except as it may help or hinder what comes within the circle of instinctive wishes. In such a life there is something feverish and confined, in comparison with which the philosophic life is calm and free. The private world of instinctive interests is a small one, set in the midst of a great and powerful world which must, sooner or later, lay our private world in ruins. Unless we can so enlarge our interests as to include the whole outer world, we remain like a garrison in a beleaguered fortress, knowing that the enemy prevents escape and that ultimate surrender is inevitable. In such a life there is no peace, but a constant strife between the insistence of desire and the powerlessness of will. In one way or another, if our life is to be great and free, we must escape this prison and this strife.

One way of escape is by philosophic contemplation. Philosophic contemplation does not, in its widest survey, divide the universe into two hostile camps—friends and foes, helpful and hostile, good and bad—it views the whole impartially. Philosophic contemplation, when it is unalloyed, does not aim at proving that the rest of the universe is akin to man. All acquisition of knowledge is an enlargement of the Self, but this enlargement is best attained when it is not directly sought. It is obtained when the desire for knowledge is alone operative, by a study which does not wish in advance that its objects should have this or that character, but adapts the Self to the characters which it finds in its objects. This enlargement of Self is not obtained when, taking the Self as it is, we try to show that the world is so similar to this Self that knowledge of it is possible without any admission of what seems alien. The desire to prove this is a form of self-assertion and, like all self-assertion, it is an obstacle to the growth of Self which it desires, and of which the Self knows that it is capable. Self-assertion, in philosophic speculation as elsewhere, views the world as a means to its own ends; thus it makes the world of less account than Self, and the Self sets bounds to the greatness of its goods. In contemplation, on the contrary, we start from the not-Self, and through its greatness the boundaries of Self are enlarged; through the infinity of the universe the mind which contemplates it achieves some share in infinity.

For this reason greatness of soul is not fostered by those philosophies which assimilate the universe to Man. Knowledge is a form of union of Self and not-Self; like all union, it is impaired by dominion, and therefore by any attempt to force the universe into conformity with what we find in ourselves. There is a widespread philosophical tendency towards the view which tells us that Man is the measure of all things, that truth is man-made, that space and time and the world of universals are properties of the mind, and that, if there be anything not created by the mind, it is unknowable and of no account for us. This view, if our previous discussions were correct, is untrue; but in addition to being untrue, it has the effect of robbing philosophic contemplation of all that gives it value, since it fetters contemplation to Self. What it calls knowledge is not a union with the not-Self, but a set of prejudices, habits, and desires, making an impenetrable veil between us and the world beyond. The man who finds pleasure in such a theory of knowledge is like the man who never leaves the domestic circle for fear his word might not be law.

The true philosophic contemplation, on the contrary, finds its satisfaction in every enlargement of the not-Self, in everything that magnifies the objects contemplated, and thereby the subject contemplating. Everything, in contemplation, that is personal or private, everything that depends upon habit, self-interest, or desire, distorts the object, and hence impairs the union which the intellect seeks. By thus making a barrier between subject and object, such personal and private things become a prison to the intellect. The free intellect will see as God might see, without a *here* and *now,* without hopes and fears, without the trammels of customary beliefs and traditional prejudices, calmly, dispassionately, in the sole and exclusive desire of knowledge—knowledge as impersonal, as purely contemplative, as it is possible for man to attain. Hence also the free intellect will value more the abstract and universal knowledge into which the accidents of private history do not enter, than the knowledge brought by the senses, and dependent, as such knowledge must be, upon an exclusive and personal point of view and a body whose sense-organs distort as much as they reveal.

The mind which has become accustomed to the freedom and impartiality of philosophic contemplation will preserve something of the same freedom and impartiality in the world of action and emotion. It will view its purposes and desires as parts of the whole, with the absence of insistence that results from seeing them as infinitesimal fragments in a world of which all the rest is unaffected by any one man's deeds. The impartiality which, in contemplation, is the unalloyed desire for truth, is the very same quality of mind which, in action, is justice, and in emotion is that universal love which can be given to all, and not only to those who are judged useful or admirable. Thus contemplation enlarges not only the objects of our thoughts, but also the objects of our actions and our affections: it makes us citizens of the universe, not only of one walled city at war with all the rest. In this citizenship of the universe consists man's true freedom, and his liberation from the thraldom of narrow hopes and fears.

Thus, to sum up our discussion of the value of philosophy; philosophy is to be studied, not for the sake of any definite answers to its questions, since no definite answers can, as a rule, be known to be true, but rather for the sake of the questions themselves; because these questions enlarge our conception of what is possible, enrich our intellectual imagination and diminish the dogmatic assurance which closes the mind against speculation; but above all because, through the greatness of the universe which philosophy contemplates, the mind also is rendered great, and becomes capable of that union with the universe which constitutes its highest good.

Martin Heidegger
1889–1976

Martin Heidegger was born and died in the small German town of Messkirch in the Black Forest region of Baden-Württemberg. His father was the caretaker of the local Catholic church. Heidegger was reared as a Catholic and attended local secondary schools, where he was particularly interested in the ancient Greeks and the classics; this classical heritage remained the bedrock of his intellectual life. As a teenager in a Jesuit seminary, he was captivated by Franz Brentano's work on Aristotle's understanding of "Being." He made the study of Being his life's work and never wavered from that goal.

After a brief period as a Jesuit novice, Heidegger studied philosophy at the University of Freiburg. Excused from World War I for health reasons, he finished his studies in 1916 with a thesis on the medieval thinker John Duns Scotus. For the next seven years, he taught at the university, the last three years as the assistant to Edmund Husserl. During this period of time, Heidegger apprenticed himself to Husserl's phenomenological method, using it on his own special study of Being. In 1923, Heidegger moved to the University of Marburg where, in 1927, he published *Being and Time,* which proved to be his *magnum opus*. This work was dedicated to his teacher and friend Husserl. When Husserl retired in 1928, Heidegger assumed Husserl's chair of philosophy at the University of Freiburg.

What followed is one of the most controversial episodes in recent philosophy. When the Nazis came to power in 1933, the rector of the University of Freiburg was ousted and Heidegger was elected to replace him. In the course of his inaugural lecture as rector, Heidegger made the following remarks:

> "Academic Freedom," celebrated so often, is banished from the German university; . . . this freedom was not genuine because it was only negative. . . . The

> concept of freedom [for] the German student is now brought back to its truth. From this truth the bond and service of the German student will unfold in [the] future.*

Later that same year Heidegger wrote in the student newspaper:

> Doctrine and "ideas" shall no longer govern your existence. The Führer himself, and only he, is the current and future reality of Germany, and his word is your law. Learn to know ever more deeply within you: "From now on every matter demands determination and every action demands responsibility."
>
> Heil Hitler!
>
> MARTIN HEIDEGGER**

Critics claim that Heidegger had always been sympathetic to the Nazi cause and that he apparently disowned his teacher Husserl (who was Jewish). As late as 1953, Heidegger affirmed the "inner truth and greatness" of the Nazi movement. He once said that philosophy could be done properly only in either the German or the Greek language and that among the moderns, the Germans alone, as a people placed by history between the barbarians of America to the west and Russia to the east, could save Western thought.

Heidegger's supporters point to his refusal to endorse the firing of two anti-Nazi deans, which led to his resignation as rector within a year. Furthermore, say some, it is unfair to judge Heidegger's early support for the Nazis from a post–World War II point of view. Heidegger in 1933 could not be expected to know the unspeakable horrors of 1939 to 1945. Finally, supporters ask philosophers especially to avoid the *argumentum ad hominem:* Even if Heidegger were partially compromised, that is not sufficient reason to dismiss a whole body of thought.

Whatever the truth in this debate, Allied occupation powers considered the evidence of Nazi collaboration sufficient to bar Heidegger from teaching between 1945 and 1951. Hence, after the war, Heidegger spent much of his time in his simple hut at Todtnauberg in the Black Forest. He retired permanently from teaching in 1959. Late in life, he visited Greece and France but lived his final years largely in quiet seclusion.

* * *

In his major work, *Being and Time* (*Sein und Zeit*), Heidegger announced the interest that would dominate his writings throughout his life: "The question of the meaning of Being." According to Heidegger, the Pre-Socratics had understood Being, but subsequent Western thinkers had forgotten Being itself by focusing too intently on individual beings. As a result, contemporary metaphysics no longer recalled the seminal question of Being.

In order to gain some understanding of Being, Heidegger suggests we examine the one being with which we are intimately acquainted: the human being. The

**Die Selbstbehauptung der Deutschen Universitätt (The Self-Affirmation of the German University, 1933)* as quoted in Walter Kaufmann, *Discovering the Mind, Volume II: Nietzsche, Heidegger, and Buber* (New York: McGraw-Hill, 1980), p. 221.

***Freiburger Studentenzeitung*, November 3, 1933, p. 1, quoted in Martin Heidegger, *German Existentialism,* translated with an introduction by Dagobert D. Runes (New York: Philosophical Library, 1965), pp. 27–28.

Troops at the 1934 Nuremberg Rally. The lives of an entire generation of philosophers were directly influenced by Hitler's rise to power in 1934. Husserl died as an outcast because of his Jewish ancestry; Heidegger was an early Nazi sympathizer (though there is a great deal of debate about his later feelings toward and involvement with the party); Sartre was a German prisoner-of-war and together with Merleau-Ponty was later a member of the resistance; Wittgenstein volunteered as a hospital orderly in England; and Quine, Austin, and Davidson served in the Allied war effort. (©*CORBIS*)

phenomenological method (Husserl), which "unconceals" the data of experience by allowing these data to "show themselves," provides the way to such an examination. Using this method to examine the self, one discovers one's self as a "being-in-the-world" or *Dasein* ("being-there").

Dasein is different from other realities. First, "in its very Being, that Being is an issue for it"; that is, *Dasein* is aware of Being. Second, the kind of Being of which *Dasein* is aware is called "existence." Human existence is not to be grasped the way one understands the existence of rocks or planets, but in the special ways of anticipation of, and decision for, possibilities. As the self confronts its choices, it especially recognizes that with death, "being-in-the-world" eventually becomes "no-longer-being-there." This awareness of *Dasein* as "being-toward-death" is filled with *Angst* (dread). Borrowing Kierkegaard's analysis of dread, Heidegger says that the self can try to avoid this *Angst* by losing the "I" in the "they"—that is, by ignoring its individuality and becoming part of the crowd. But a "they" existence is "inauthentic" and removed from Being. Instead, authentic being—"being-toward-death"—can reveal to *Dasein* a "freedom" that releases it from the "Illusions of the 'they'" and allows it to embrace Angst.

In our selection from *An Introduction to Metaphysics* (1953), given here in the outstanding Gregory Fried and Richard Polt translation, Heidegger puts the question of Being in stark terms: "Why is there anything at all, rather than nothing?" This might seem an odd question to us, but it is odd (asserts Heidegger) only because we have lost our original amazement in the very presence of Being itself. Following a lengthy discussion of this issue, Heidegger asks the further question, "How is it with being?" Not well at all, he concludes. Heidegger argues that modern "technological frenzy" has led us to the brink of disaster because it induces the awful forgetfulness of Being. But Heidegger does not end with pessimism. It is possible, he concludes,

> to *repeat and retrieve* the inception of our historical-spiritual Dasein, in order to transform it into the other inception. . . . The point is to restore the historical Dasein of human beings . . . back to the power of Being that is to be opened up originally.

Heidegger has had more than his share of critics. Analytic philosophers have particularly criticized his use of language. One such philosopher concluded that "Heidegger's account of human life, where it is not vacuous, is transparently false."* However, despite the criticisms of his life and thought, Heidegger has profoundly affected philosophy—especially in the field he originated: philosophical hermeneutics. Further, his insights have been developed in psychoanalysis and literary theory and in phenomenology and theology, and they continue to shape contemporary views.

* * *

For a biography of Heidegger, see Rudiger Safranski, *Martin Heidegger: Between Good and Evil,* translated by Ewald Osers (Cambridge, MA: Harvard University Press, 1999). General introductions to Heidegger's thought include Marjorie Grene, *Martin Heidegger* (New York: Hillary House, 1957); W.J. Richardson, *Heidegger: Through Phenomenology to Thought* (New York: Humanities Press, 1963); J.A. Kockelman, *Heidegger: A First Introduction to His Philosophy,* translated by T. Schrynemakers (Pittsburgh, PA: Duquesne University Press, 1965); J.L. Mehta, *Martin Heidegger: The Way and the Vision* (Honolulu: University Press of Hawaii, 1976); George Steiner, *Martin Heidegger* (New York: Viking Press, 1978); Michael Inwood, *Heidegger* (Oxford: Oxford University Press, 1997); Herman Philipse, *Heidegger's Philosophy of Being: A Critical Interpretation* (Princeton: Princeton University Press, 1999); Richard Polt, *Heidegger: An Introduction* (Ithaca, NY: Cornell University Press, 1999); Jonathan Ree, *Heidegger* (London: Routledge, 1999); George Pattison, *Routledge Philosophy Guidebook to the Later Heidegger* (London: Routledge, 2000); Daniel O. Dahlstrom, *Heidegger's Concept of Truth* (Cambridge: Cambridge University Press, 2001); and Adam Sharr, *Heidegger's Hut* (Cambridge, MA: MIT Press, 2006). For criticism of Heidegger's thought, see Walter Kaufmann, *Discovering the Mind, Volume II: Nietzsche, Heidegger, and Buber* (New York: McGraw-Hill, 1980); Hans-Georg Gadamer, *Heidegger's Ways,* translated by John W. Stanley (Albany, NY: SUNY Press, 1994); Joanna Hodge, *Heidegger and Ethics* (Oxford: Routledge, 1995); and S.J. McGrath,

*Alasdair MacIntyre, "Existentialism," in D.J. O'Connor, *A Critical History of Western Philosophy* (New York: The Free Press, 1964), p. 518.

Heidegger: A (Very) Critical Introduction (Grand Rapids, MI: Eerdmans, 2008). For a guide to our reading, see Richard Polt and Gregory Fried, eds., *A Companion to Heidegger's* Introduction to Metaphysics (New Haven, CT: Yale University Press, 2001). Michael Inwood, *A Heidegger Dictionary* (Oxford: Blackwell, 1999) provides a useful reference tool. For comparative studies, see Arne Naess, *Four Modern Philosophers: Carnap, Wittgenstein, Heidegger, Sartre,* translated by Alastair Hannay (Chicago: University of Chicago Press, 1968); Timothy J. Stapleton, *Husserl and Heidegger* (Albany, NY: SUNY Press, 1983); Allan Megill, *Prophets of Extremity: Nietzsche, Heidegger, Foucault, Derrida* (Berkeley: University of California Press, 1985); and Ron L. Cooper, *Heidegger and Whitehead: A Phenomenological Examination into the Intelligibility of Experience* (Athens: Ohio University Press, 1993). Collections of essays include Thomas Sheehan, ed., *Heidegger: The Man and the Thinker* (Chicago: Precedent, 1981); Hubert L. Dreyfus and Harrison Hall, eds., *Heidegger: A Critical Reader* (Oxford: Basil Blackwell, 1992); John Sallis, ed., *Reading Heidegger* (Bloomington: Indiana University Press, 1993); Charles Guignon, ed., *The Cambridge Companion to Heidegger* (Cambridge: Cambridge University Press, 1993); the multivolume Christopher Macann, ed., *Martin Heidegger: Critical Assessments* (Oxford: Routledge, 1993); and Nancy J. Holland and Patricia Huntington, *Feminist Interpretations of Martin Heidegger* (College Park, PA: Pennsylvania State University Press, 2001). For advanced studies on Heidegger, see titles in the series "Northwestern University Studies in Phenomenology & Existential Philosophy."

Finally, out of the large number of books on the controversy surrounding Heidegger's Nazi ties, one may consult Victor Farías, *Heidegger and Nazism,* edited by Joseph Margolis and Tom Rockmore (Philadelphia: Temple University Press, 1989); Joseph Margolis and Tom Rockmore, eds., *The Heidegger Case* (Philadelphia: Temple University Press, 1992); Tom Rockmore, *On Heidegger's Nazism and Philosophy* (Berkeley: University of California Press, 1992); Heinrich Wiegrand Petzet, *Encounters and Dialogues with Martin Heidegger 1929–1976,* translated by Parvis Emad and Kenneth Malz (Chicago: University of Chicago Press, 1993); Richard Wolin, ed., *The Heidegger Controversy* (Cambridge, MA: MIT Press, 1993); Leslie Paul Thiele, *Timely Meditations: Martin Heidegger and Postmodern Politics* (Princeton, NJ: Princeton University Press, 1995); Berel Lang, *Heidegger's Silence* (Ithaca, NY: Cornell University Press, 1996); Julian Young, *Heidegger, Philosophy, and Nazism* (Cambridge: Cambridge University Press, 1997); and Emmanuel Faye, *Heidegger: The Introduction of Nazism into Philosophy in Light of the Unpublished Seminars of 1933–1935* (New Haven, CT: Yale University Press, 2009).

INTRODUCTION TO METAPHYSICS (in part)

CHAPTER ONE: THE FUNDAMENTAL QUESTION OF METAPHYSICS*

Why are there beings at all instead of nothing? That is the question. Presumably it is no arbitrary question. "Why are there beings at all instead of nothing?"—this is obviously the first of all questions. Of course, it is not the first question in the chronological sense. Individuals as well as peoples ask many questions in the course of their historical passage through time. They explore, investigate, and test many sorts of things before they run into the question "Why are there beings at all instead of nothing?" Many never run into this question at all, if running into the question means not only hearing and reading the interrogative sentence as uttered, but asking the question, that is, taking a stand on it, posing it, compelling oneself into the state of this questioning.

And yet, we are each touched once, maybe even now and then, by the concealed power of this question, without properly grasping what is happening to us. In great despair, for example, when all weight tends to dwindle away from things and the sense of things grows dark, the question looms. Perhaps it strikes only once, like the muffled tolling of a bell that resounds into Dasein and gradually fades away The question is there in heartfelt joy, for then all things are transformed and surround us as if for the first time, as if it were easier to grasp that they were not, rather than that they are, and are as they are. The question is there in a spell of boredom, when we are equally distant from despair and joy, but when the stubborn ordinariness of beings lays open a wasteland in which it makes no difference to us whether beings are or are not—and then, in a distinctive form, the question resonates once again: Why are there beings at all instead of nothing?

A. The why-question as the first of all questions
B. Philosophy as the asking of the why-question
  1. The untimeliness of philosophy
  2. Two misinterpretations of philosophy
    a. Philosophy as a foundation for culture
    b. Philosophy as providing a picture of the world
  3. Philosophy as extra-ordinary questioning about the extra-ordinary
C. *Phusis:* the fundamental Greek word for beings as such
  1. *Phusis* as the emerging, abiding sway
  2. The later narrowing of the meaning of *phusis*
D. The meaning of "introduction to metaphysics"
  1. Metaphysics as questioning beyond beings as such
  2. The difference between the question of beings as such and the question of Being
  3. Introduction to metaphysics as leading into the asking of the fundamental question
E. Unfolding the why-question by means of the question of Nothing
  1. The seeming superfluity of the phrase "instead of nothing"
  2. The connection between the question of Nothing and the question of Being
  3. The superiority of philosophy and poetry over logic and science

*Outline of *Introduction to Metaphysics,* Chapter One: "The Fundamental Question of Metaphysics"

Martin Heidegger, *An Introduction to Metaphysics,* translated by Gregory Fried and Richard Polt (New Haven, CT: Yale University Press, 2000). Reprinted by permission.

4. An example of poetic talk of Nothing: Knut Hamsun
5. The wavering of beings between Being and the possibility of not-Being

F. The prior question: How does it stand with Being?
1. The mysteriousness of Being
2. Nietzsche: Being as a vapor
3. Our destroyed relation to Being and the decline of the West
a. The geopolitical situation of the Germans as the metaphysical people
b. The failure of traditional ontology to explain the emptiness of Being
c. Philosophical questioning as essentially historical
d. The darkening of the world and the misinterpretation of spirit
e. The genuine essence of spirit: the empowering of the powers of beings
f. Our destroyed relation to Being and our misrelation to language

But whether this question is asked explicitly, or whether it merely passes through our Dasein like a fleeting gust of wind, unrecognized as a question, whether it becomes more oppressive or is thrust away by us again and suppressed under some pretext, it certainly is never the first question that we ask.

But it is the first question in another sense—namely, in rank. This can be clarified in three ways. The question "Why are there beings at all instead of nothing?" is first in rank for us as the broadest, as the deepest, and finally as the most originary question.

The question is the broadest in scope. It comes to a halt at no being of any kind whatsoever. The question embraces all that is, and that means not only what is now present at hand in the broadest sense, but also what has previously been and what will be in the future. The domain of this question is limited only by what simply is not and never is: by Nothing. All that is not Nothing comes into the question, and in the end even Nothing itself—not, as it were, because it is something, a being, for after all we are talking about it, but because it "is" Nothing. The scope of our question is so broad that we can never exceed it. We are not interrogating this being or that being, nor all beings, each in turn; instead, we are asking from the start about the whole of what is, or as we say for reasons to be discussed later: beings as a whole and as such.

Just as it is the broadest question, the question is also the deepest: Why are there beings at all . . . ? Why—that is, what is the ground? From what ground do beings come? On what ground do beings stand? To what ground do beings go?* The question does not ask this or that about beings—what they are in each case, here and there, how they are put together, how they can be changed, what they can be used for, and so on. The questioning seeks the ground for what is, insofar as it is in being. To seek the ground: this means to get to the bottom <*ergründen*>. What is put into question comes into relation with a ground. But because we are questioning, it remains an open question whether the ground is a truly grounding, foundation-effecting, originary ground; whether the ground refuses to provide a foundation, and so is an abyss; or whether the ground is neither one nor the other, but merely offers the perhaps necessary illusion of a foundation and is thus an unground. However this may be, the question seeks a decision with respect to the ground that grounds the fact that what is, is in being as the being that it is. This why-question does not seek causes for beings, causes of the same kind and on the same level as beings themselves. This why-question does not just skim the surface, but presses into the domains that he "at the ground," even pressing into the ultimate, to the limit; the question is turned away from all surface and shallowness, striving for depth; as the broadest, it is at the same time the deepest of the deep questions.

Finally, as the broadest and deepest question, it is also the most originary. What do we mean by that? If we consider our question in the whole breadth of what it puts

**Zu Grunde gehen* (literally "go to the ground") is an idiom meaning "to be ruined."

into question, beings as such and as a whole, then it strikes us right away that in the question, we keep ourselves completely removed from every particular, individual being as precisely this or that being. We do mean beings as a whole, but without any particular preference. Still, it is remarkable that one being always keeps coming to the fore in this questioning: the human beings who pose this question. And yet the question should not be about some particular, individual being Given the unrestricted range of the question, every being counts as much as any other. Some elephant in some jungle in India is in being just as much as some chemical oxidation process on the planet Mars, and whatever else you please.

Thus if we properly pursue the question "Why are there beings at all, instead of nothing?" in its sense as a question, we must avoid emphasizing any particular, individual being, not even focusing on the human being For what is this being, after all! Let us consider the Earth within the dark immensity of space in the universe. We can compare it to a tiny grain of sand; more than a kilometer of emptiness extends between it and the next gram of its size; on the surface of this tiny grain of sand lives a stupefied swarm of supposedly clever animals, crawling all over each other, who for a brief moment have invented knowledge [cf. Nietzsche, "On Truth and Lie in the Extramoral Sense," 1873, published posthumously]. And what is a human lifespan amid millions of years? Barely a move of the second hand, a breath. Within beings as a whole there is no justification to be found for emphasizing precisely *this* being that is called the human being and among which we ourselves happen to belong.

But if beings as a whole are ever brought into our question, then the questioning does come into a distinctive relation with them—distinctive because it is unique—and beings do come into a distinctive relation with this questioning. For through this questioning, beings as a whole are first opened up *as such* and with regards to their possible ground, and they are kept open in the questioning. The asking of this question is not, in relation to beings as such and as a whole, some arbitrary occurrence amid beings, such as the falling of raindrops. The why-question challenges beings as a whole, so to speak, outstrips them, though never completely. But this is precisely how the questioning gains its distinction. What is asked in this question rebounds upon the questioning itself, for the questioning challenges beings as a whole but does not after all wrest itself free from them. Why the Why? What is the ground of this why question itself, a question that presumes to establish the ground of beings as a whole? Is this Why, too, just asking about the ground as a foreground, so that it is still always a *being* that is sought as what does the grounding? Is this "first" question not the first in rank after all, as measured by the intrinsic rank of the question of Being and its transformations?

To be sure—whether the question "Why are there beings at all instead of nothing?" is posed or not makes no difference whatsoever to beings themselves. The planets move in their orbits without this question. The vigor of life flows through plant and animal without this question.

But *if* this question is posed, and provided that it is actually carried out, then this questioning necessarily recoils back from what is asked and what is interrogated, back upon itself. Therefore this questioning in itself is not some arbitrary process but rather a distinctive occurrence that we call a *happening.*

This question and all the questions immediately rooted in it, in which this one question unfolds—this why-question cannot be compared to any other. It runs up against the search for its own Why. The question "Why the Why?" looks externally and at first like a frivolous repetition of the same interrogative, which can go on forever; it looks like an eccentric and empty rumination about insubstantial meanings of words. Certainly, that is how it looks. The only question is whether we are willing to fall victim to this cheap look of things and thus take the whole matter as settled, or whether we are capable of experiencing a provocative happening in this recoil of the why-question back upon itself.

But if we do not let ourselves be deceived by the look of things, it will become clear that this why-question, as a question about beings as such and as a whole, immediately leads us away from mere toying with words, provided that we still possess enough force of spirit to make the question truly recoil into its own Why; for the recoil does not, after all, produce itself on its own. Then we discover that this distinctive why-question has its ground in a leap by which human beings leap away from all the previous safety of their Dasein, be it genuine or presumed. The asking of this question happens only in the leap and as the leap, and otherwise not at all. Later, we will clarify what we mean here by "leap." Our questioning is not yet the leap; for that, it must first be transformed; it still stands, unknowing, in the face of beings. For now, let this comment suffice: the leap <*Sprung*> of this questioning attains its own ground by leaping, performs it in leaping <*erspringt, springend erwirkt*>. According to the genuine meaning of the word, we call such a leap that attains itself as ground by leaping an originary leap <*Ursprung*>: an attaining-the-ground-by-leaping. Because the question "Why are there beings at all instead of nothing?" attains the ground for all genuine questioning by leaping and is thus an originary. leap, we must recognize it as the most originary <*ursprünglich*> of questions.

As the broadest and deepest question, it is the most originary, and conversely.

In this threefold sense the question is the first in rank, first in rank in the order of questioning within that domain which this first question definitively opens up and grounds, giving it its measure. Our question is the question of all true questions—that is, of those that pose themselves to themselves—and it is necessarily asked, knowingly or not, along with every question. No questioning, and consequently no single scientific "problem" either, understands it self if it does not grasp the question of all questions, that is, if it does not ask it. We want to be clear about this from the start: it can never be determined objectively whether anyone is asking—whether we are actually asking this question, that is, whether we are leaping, or whether we are just mouthing the words. The question loses its rank at once in the sphere of a human-historical Dasein to whom *questioning* as an originary power remains foreign.

For example, anyone for whom the Bible is divine revelation and truth already has the answer to the question "Why are there beings at all instead of nothing?" before it is even asked: beings, with the exception of God Himself, are created by Him. God Himself "is" as the uncreated Creator. One who holds on to such faith as a basis can, perhaps, emulate and participate in the asking of our question in a certain way, but he cannot authentically question without giving himself up as a believer, with all the consequences of this step. He can act only "as if"—On the other hand, if such faith does not continually expose itself to the possibility of unfaith, it is not faith but a convenience. It becomes an agreement with oneself to adhere in the future to a doctrine as something that has somehow been handed down. This is neither having faith nor questioning, but indifference—which can then, perhaps even with keen interest, busy itself with everything, with faith as well as with questioning.

Now by referring to safety in faith as a special way of standing in the truth, we are not saying that citing the words of the Bible, "In the beginning God created heaven and earth, etc." represents an answer to our question. Quite aside from whether this sentence of the Bible is true or untrue for faith, it can represent no answer at all to our question, because it has no relation to this question. It has no relation to it, because it simply cannot come into such a relation. What is really asked in our question is, for faith, foolishness.

Philosophy consists in such foolishness. A "Christian philosophy" is a round square and a misunderstanding. To be sure, one can thoughtfully question and work through the world of Christian experience—that is, the world of faith. That is then theology. Only ages that really no longer believe in the true greatness of the task of theology arrive at the pernicious opinion that, through a supposed refurbishment with the help of philosophy, a theology can be gained or even replaced, and can be made more palatable to the need of the age. Philosophy, for originally Christian faith, is foolishness. Philosophizing means asking: "Why are there beings at all. instead of nothing?" Actually asking this means venturing to exhaust, to question thoroughly, the inexhaustible wealth of this question, by unveiling what it demands that we question. Whenever such a venture occurs, there is philosophy.

If we now wanted to talk about philosophy, giving a report, in order to say what it is in more detail, this beginning would be fruitless. But whoever engages in philosophy must know a few things. They can be stated briefly.

All essential questioning in philosophy necessarily remains untimely, and this is because philosophy either projects far beyond its own time or else binds its time back to this times earlier and *inceptive* past. Philosophizing always remains a kind of knowing that not only does not allow itself to be made timely but, on the contrary, imposes its measure on the times.*

Philosophy is essentially untimely because it is one of those few things whose fate it remains never to be able to find a direct resonance in their own time, and never to be permitted to find such a resonance. Whenever this seemingly does take place, whenever a philosophy becomes fashion, either there is no actual philosophy or else philosophy is misinterpreted and, according to some intentions alien to it, misused for the needs of the day.

Philosophy, then, is not a kind of knowledge which one could acquire directly, like vocational and technical expertise, and which, like economic and professional knowledge in general, one could apply directly and evaluate according to its usefulness in each case.

But what is useless can nevertheless be a power—a power in the rightful sense. That which has no direct resonance <*Widerklang*> in everydayness can stand in innermost harmony <*Einklang*> with the authentic happening in the history of a people. It can even be its prelude <*Vorlang*>. What is untimely will have its own times. This holds for philosophy. Therefore we cannot determine what the task of philosophy in itself and in general is, and what must accordingly be demanded of philosophy. Every stage and every inception of its unfolding carries within it its own law One can only say what philosophy cannot be and what it cannot achieve.

A question has been posed: "Why are there beings at all instead of nothing?"— We have claimed that this question is the first. We have explained in what sense it is meant as the first.

Thus we have not yet asked this question; right away we turned aside into a discussion of it. This procedure is necessary, for the asking of this question cannot be compared with customary concerns. There is no gradual transition from the customary by which the question could slowly become more familiar. This is why it must be posed in advance, proposed <*vorgestellt*>, as it were. On the other hand, in this pro-posal of and talk about the question, we must not defer, or even forget, the questioning.

We therefore conclude the preliminary remarks with this session discussions.

Every essential form of spirit is open to ambiguity. The more this form resists comparison with others, the more it is misinterpreted.

Philosophy is one of the few autonomous creative possibilities, and occasional necessities, of human-historical Dasein. The current misinterpretations of philosophy,

*[Heidegger puns on *zeitgemäβ* ("timely"), meaning literally "in measure with the times."]

which all have something to them despite their misunderstandings, are innumerable. Here we will mention only two, which are important for clarifying the situation of philosophy today and in the future.

One misinterpretation consists in demanding too much of the essence of philosophy. The other involves a distortion of the sense of what philosophy can achieve.

Roughly speaking, philosophy always aims at the first and last grounds of beings, and it does so in such a way that human beings themselves, with respect to their way of Being, are emphatically interpreted and given an aim. This readily gives the impression that philosophy can and must provide a foundation for the current and future historical Dasein of a people in every age, a foundation for building culture. But such expectations and requirements demand too much of the capability and essence of philosophy. Usually, this excessive demand takes the form of finding fault with philosophy One says, for example, that because metaphysics did not contribute to preparing the revolution, it must be rejected. That is just as clever as saying that because one cannot fly with a carpenter's bench, it should be thrown away Philosophy can never *directly* supply the forces and create the mechanisms and opportunities that bring about a historical state of affairs, if only because philosophy is always the direct concern of the few. Which few? The ones who transform creatively, who unsettle things. It spreads only indirectly, on back roads that can never be charted in advance, and then finally—sometime, when it has long since been forgotten as originary philosophy—it sinks away in the form of one of Dasein's truisms.

Against this first misinterpretation, what philosophy can and must be according to its essence, is this: a thoughtful opening of the avenues and vistas of a knowing that establishes measure and rank, a knowing in which and from which a people conceives its Dasein in the historical-spiritual world and brings it to fulfillment—that knowing which ignites and threatens and compels all questioning and appraising.

The second misinterpretation that we mention is a distortion of the sense of what philosophy can achieve. Granted that philosophy is unable to lay the foundation of a culture, one says, philosophy nevertheless makes it easier to build up culture. According to this distortion, philosophy orders the whole of beings into overviews and systems, and readies a world picture for our use—a map of the world, as it were—a picture of the various possible things and domains of things, thereby granting us a universal and uniform orientation. Or, more specifically, philosophy relieves the sciences of their labor by meditating on the presuppositions of the sciences, their basic concepts and propositions. One expects philosophy to promote, and even to accelerate, the practical and technical business of culture by alleviating it, making it easier.

But—according to its essence, philosophy never makes things easier, but only more difficult. And it does so not just incidentally, not just because its manner of communication seems strange or even deranged to everyday understanding. The burdening of historical Dasein, and thereby at bottom of Being itself, is rather the genuine sense of what philosophy can achieve. Burdening gives back to things, to beings, their weight (Being). And why? Because burdening is one of the essential and fundamental conditions for the arising of everything great, among which we include above all else the fate of a historical people and its works. But fate is there only where a true knowing about things rules over Dasein. And the avenues and views of such a knowing are opened up by philosophy.

The misinterpretations by which philosophy remains constantly besieged are mainly promoted by what people like us do, that is, by professors of philosophy. Their customary, and also legitimate and even useful business is to transmit a certain educationally appropriate acquaintance with philosophy as it has presented itself so far. This then looks as though it itself were philosophy, whereas at most it is scholarship about philosophy.

When we mention and correct both of these misinterpretations, we cannot intend that you should now come at one stroke into a clear relation with philosophy. But you should become mindful and be on your guard, precisely when the most familiar judgments, and even supposedly genuine experiences, unexpectedly assail you. This often happens in a way that seems entirely innocuous and is quickly convincing. One believes that one has had the experience oneself, and readily hears it confirmed: "nothing comes" of philosophy; "you can't do anything with it." These two turns of phrase, which are especially current among teachers and researchers in the sciences, express observations that have their indisputable correctness. When one attempts to prove that, to the contrary, something does after all "come of philosophy, one merely intensifies and secures the prevailing misinterpretation, which consists in the prejudice that one can evaluate philosophy according to everyday standards that one would otherwise employ to judge the utility of bicycles or the effectiveness of mineral baths."

It is entirely correct and completely in order to say, "You cant do anything with philosophy." The only mistake is to believe that with this, the judgment concerning philosophy is at an end. For a little epilogue arises in the form of a counterquestion: even if we can't do anything with it, may not philosophy in the end do something *with us,* provided that we engage ourselves with it? Let that suffice for us as an explication of what philosophy is not.

At the outset we spoke of a question: "Why are there beings at all instead of nothing?" We asserted that to ask this question is to philosophize. Whenever we set out in the direction of this question, thinking and gazing ahead, then right away we forgo any sojourn in any of the usual regions of beings. We pass over and surpass what belongs to the order of the day. We ask beyond the usual, beyond the ordinary that is ordered in the everyday. Nietzsche once said (VIII, 269): "A philosopher: that is a human being who constantly experiences, sees, hears, suspects, hopes, dreams extraordinary things. . . ."*

Philosophizing is questioning about the extra-ordinary. Yet as we merely intimated at first, this questioning recoils upon itself, and thus not only what is asked about is extraordinary, but also the questioning itself. This means that this questioning does not lie along our way, so that one day we stumble into it blindly or even by mistake. Nor does it stand in the familiar order of the everyday, so that we could be compelled to it on the ground of some requirements or even regulations. Nor does this questioning he in the sphere of urgent concern and the satisfaction of dominant needs. The questioning itself is out-of-order. It is completely voluntary, fully and especially based on the mysterious ground of freedom, on what we have called the leap. The same Nietzsche says: "Philosophy . . . means living voluntarily amid ice and mountain ranges" (XV, 2).** Philosophizing, we can now say, is extra-ordinary questioning about the extra-ordinary.

In the age of the first and definitive unfolding of Western philosophy among the Greeks, when questioning about beings as such and as a whole received its true inception, beings were called *phusis.* This fundamental Greek word for beings is usually translated as "nature." We use the Latin translation *natura,* which really means "to be born," "birth." But with this Latin translation, the originary content of the Greek word *phusis* is already thrust aside, the authentic philosophical naming force of the Greek word is destroyed. This is true not only of the Latin translation of *this* word but of all other translations of Greek philosophical language into Roman. This translation of

*[*Beyond Good and Evil,* §292. Heidegger's references to Nietzsche cite the edition of his works published in Leipzig by C. G. Naumann, 1899–1905.]

**§ 3 of the preface to *Ecce Homo.*

Greek into Roman was not an arbitrary and innocuous process but was the first stage in the isolation and alienation of the originary essence of Greek philosophy. The Roman translation then became definitive for Christianity and the Christian Middle Ages. The Middle Ages translated themselves into modem philosophy, which moves within the conceptual world of the Middle Ages and then creates those familiar representations and conceptual terms that are used even today to understand the inception of Western philosophy. This inception is taken as something left behind long ago and supposedly overcome.

But now we leap over this whole process of deformation and decline, and we seek to win back intact the naming force of language and words; for words and language are not just shells into which things are packed for spoken and written intercourse. In the word, in language, things first come to be and are. For this reason, too, the misuse of language in mere idle talk, in slogans and phrases destroys our genuine relation to things. Now what does the word *phusis* say? It says what emerges from itself (for example, the emergence, the blossoming, of a rose), the unfolding that opens itself up, the coming-into-appearance in such unfolding, and holding itself and persisting in appearance—in short, the emerging-abiding sway. According to the dictionary, *phuein* means to grow to make grow.* But what does growing mean? Does it just mean to increase by acquiring bulk, to become more numerous and bigger?

Phusis as emergence can be experienced everywhere: for example, in celestial processes (the rising of the sun), in the surging of the sea, in the growth of plants, in the coming forth of animals and human beings from the womb. But *phusis,* the emerging sway, is not synonymous with these processes, which we still today count as part of "nature." This emerging and standing-out-in-itself-from-itself may not be taken as just one process among others that we observe in beings. *Phusis* is Being itself, by virtue of which beings first become and remain observable.

It was not in natural processes that the Greeks first experienced what *phusis* is, but the other way around: on the basis of a fundamental experience of Being in poetry and thought, what they had to call *phusis* disclosed itself to them. Only on the basis of this disclosure could they then take a look at nature in the narrower sense. Thus *phusis* originally means both heaven and earth, both the stone and the plant, both the annual and the human, and human history as the work of humans and gods; and finally and first of all, it means the gods who themselves stand under destiny. *Phusis* means the emerging sway, and the enduring over which it thoroughly holds sway. This emerging, abiding sway includes both "becoming" as well as "Being" in the narrower sense of fixed continuity. *Phusis* is the event of *standing forth,* arising from the concealed and thus enabling the concealed to take its stand for the first time.**

But if one understands *phusis,* as one usually does, not in the originary sense of the emerging and abiding sway but in its later and present meaning, as nature, and if one also posits the motions of material things, of atoms and electrons—what modem physics investigates as *phusis*—as the fundamental manifestation of nature, then the inceptive philosophy of the Greeks turns into a philosophy of nature, a representation of all things according to which they are really of a material nature. Then the inception of Greek philosophy, in accordance with our everyday understanding of an inception, gives the impression of being, as we say once again in Latin, primitive. Thus the Greeks become in principle a better kind of Hottentot, in comparison to whom modem science

*The noun *phusis* corresponds to the verb *phuein.*

**[Heidegger is playing on the etymological connection between *Entstehen* (genesis, growth) and *Stand* (a stand, state, situation, condition).]

has progressed infinitely far. Disregarding all the particular absurdities involved in conceiving of the inception of Western philosophy as primitive, it must be said that this interpretation forgets that what is at issue is philosophy—one of the few great things of humanity. But whatever is great can only begin great. In fact, its inception is always what is greatest. Only the small begins small—the small, whose dubious greatness consists in diminishing everything; what is small is the inception of decline, which can then also become great in the sense of the enormity of total annihilation.

The great begins great, sustains itself only through the free recurrence of greatness, and if it is great, also comes to an end in greatness. So it is with the philosophy of the Greeks. It came to an end in greatness with Aristotle. Only the everyday understanding and the small man imagine that the great must endure forever, a duration which he then goes on to equate with the eternal.

What is, as such and as a whole, the Greeks call *phusis.* Let it be mentioned just in passing that already within Greek philosophy, a narrowing of the word set in right away, although its originary meaning did not disappear from the experience, the knowledge, and the attitude of Greek philosophy. An echo of knowledge about the originary meaning still survives in Aristotle, when he speaks of the grounds of beings as such (cf. *Metaphysics* Γ, I, 1003a27).*

But this narrowing of *phusis* in the direction of the "physical" did not happen in the way that we picture it today. We oppose to the physical the "psychical" the mind or soul, what is ensouled, what is alive. But all this, for the Greeks, continues even later to belong to phusis. As a counterphenomenon there arose what the Greeks call *thesis,* positing, ordinance, or *nomos,* law, rule in the sense of mores. But this is not what is moral but instead what concerns mores, that which rests on the commitment of freedom and the assignment of tradition; it is that which concerns a free comportment and attitude, the shaping of the historical Being of humanity, *ēthos,* which under the influence of morality was then degraded to the ethical.

Phusis gets narrowed down by contrast with *technē*—which means neither art nor technology but a kind of *knowledge,* the knowing disposal over the free planning and arranging and controlling of arrangements (cf. Plato's *Phaedrus*).** *Technē* is generating, building, as a knowing producing. (It would require a special study to clarify what is essentially the same in *phusis* and *technē.*) But for all that, the counterconcept to the physical is the historical, a domain of beings that is also understood by the Greeks in the originally broader sense of *phusis.* This, however, does not have the least to do with a naturalistic interpretation of history. Beings, as such and as a whole, are *phusis*—that is, they have as their essence and character the emerging-abiding sway. This is then experienced, above all, in what tends to impose itself on us most immediately in a certain way, and which is later denoted *by phusis* in the narrower sense: *ta phusei onta, ta phusika,* what naturally is. When one asks about *phusis* in general, that is, what beings as such are, then it is above all *ta phusei onta* that provide the foothold, although in such a way that from the start, the questioning is not allowed to dwell on this or that domain of nature—inanimate bodies, plants, animals—but must go on beyond *ta phusika.*

In Greek, "away over something," "over beyond," is *meta.* Philosophical questioning about beings as such is *meta ta phusika;* it questions on beyond beings, it is metaphysics.

*["Now since we are seeking the principles and the highest causes [or grounds], it is clear that these must belong to some *phusis* in virtue of itself. If, then, those who were seeking the elements of beings were also seeking these principles, these elements too must be elements of being, not accidentally, but as being. Accordingly, it is of being as being that we, too, must find the first causes"—*Metaphysics* Γ, I, 1003a26-32.]

***Phaedrus* 260d-274b is devoted to determining how rhetoric can become a proper *technē* and what is required in general of a proper *technē.*

At this point we do not need to trace the history of the genesis and meaning of this term in detail.

The question we have identified as first in rank—"Why are there beings at all instead of nothing?"—is thus the fundamental question of metaphysics. Metaphysics stands as the name for the center and core that determines all philosophy.

[For this introduction, we have intentionally presented all this in a cursory and thus basically ambiguous way. According to our explanation of *phusis,* this word means the Being of beings. If one is asking *peri phuseōs,* about the Being of beings, then the discussion of *phusis,* "physics" in the ancient sense, is in itself already beyond *ta phusika,* on beyond beings, and is concerned with Being. "Physics" determines the essence and the history of metaphysics from the inception onward. Even in the doctrine of Being as *actus purus* (Thomas Aquinas), as absolute concept (Hegel), as eternal recurrence of the same will to power (Nietzsche), metaphysics steadfastly remains "physics."

The question about Being as such, however, has a different essence and a different provenance.

To be sure, within the purview of metaphysics, and if one continues to think in its manner, one can regard the question about Being as such merely as a mechanical repetition of the question about beings as such. The question about Being as such is then just another transcendental question, albeit one of a higher order. This misconstrual of the question about Being as such, blocks the way to unfolding it in a manner befitting the matter.

However, this misconstrual is all too easy, especially because *Being and Time* spoke of a "transcendental horizon." But the "transcendental" meant there does not pertain to subjective consciousness; instead, it is determined by the existential-ecstatic temporality of Being-here. Nevertheless, the question about Being as such is misconstrued as coinciding with the question about beings as such; this misconstrual thrusts itself upon us above all because the essential provenance of the question about beings as such, and with it the essence of metaphysics, lies in obscurity. This drags into indeterminacy all questioning that concerns Being in any way.

The "introduction to metaphysics" attempted here keeps in view this confused condition of the "question of Being."

According to the usual interpretation, the "question of Being" means asking about beings as such (metaphysics). But if we think along the lines of *Being and Time,* the "question of Being" means asking about Being as such. This meaning of the expression is also appropriate both in terms of the matter at stake and in terms of language; for the "question of Being" in the sense of the metaphysical question about beings as such precisely does *not ask* thematically about Being. Being remains forgotten.

But this talk of the "oblivion of Being" is just as ambiguous as the expression "question of Being." One protests quite rightfully that metaphysics does indeed ask about the Being of beings, and that therefore it is manifest foolishness to charge metaphysics with an oblivion of Being.

But if we think the question of Being in the sense of the question about Being as such, then it becomes clear to everyone who accompanies us in thinking that it is precisely Being *as such* that remains concealed, remains in oblivion—and so decisively that the oblivion of Being, an oblivion that itself falls into oblivion, is the unrecognized yet enduring impulse for metaphysical questioning.

If one chooses the designation "metaphysics" for the treatment of the "question of Being" in an indefinite sense, then the title of this lecture course remains ambiguous. For at first it seems as though the questioning held itself within the purview of beings as such, whereas already with the first sentence it strives to depart this zone in order to bring another domain into view with its questions. The title of the course is thus *deliberately* ambiguous.

The fundamental question of the lecture course is of a different kind than the guiding question of metaphysics. Taking *Being and Time* as its point of departure, the lecture course asks about the "*disclosedness of Being*" (*Being and Time,* pp. 21f. and 37f.). Disclosedness means: the openedness of what the oblivion of Being closes off and conceals. Through this questioning, too, fight first falls on the *essence* of metaphysics, which was also concealed up to now.]

"Introduction to metaphysics" accordingly means: leading into the asking of the fundamental question.* But questions, and above all fundamental questions, do not simply occur like stones and water. Questions are not given like shoes, clothes, or books. Questions *are* as they are actually asked, and this is the only way in which they are. Thus the leading into the asking of the fundamental question is not a passage over to something that lies or stands around somewhere; instead, this leading-to must first awaken and create the questioning. Leading is a questioning going-ahead, a questioningahead. This is a leadership that essentially has no following. Whenever one finds pretensions to a following, in a school of philosophy, for example, questioning is misunderstood. There can be such schools only in the sphere of scientific or professional labor. In such a sphere, everything has its distinct hierarchical order. Such labor also belongs, and even necessarily belongs, to philosophy and has today been lost. But the best professional ability will never replace the authentic strength of seeing and questioning and saying.

"Why are there beings at all instead of nothing?" That is the question. To pronounce the interrogative sentence, even in a questioning tone, is not yet to question. We can already see this in the fact that even if we repeat the interrogative sentence several times over and over, this does not necessarily make the questioning attitude any livelier; on the contrary, reciting the sentence repeatedly may well blunt the questioning.

Although the interrogative sentence thus is not the question and is not questioning, neither should it be taken as a mere linguistic form of communication, as if the sentence were only a statement "about" a question. If I say to you, "Why are there beings at all instead of nothing?" then the intent of my asking and saying is not to communicate to you that a process of questioning is now going on inside me. Certainly the spoken interrogative sentence can also be taken this way, but then one is precisely not hearing the questioning. The questioning does not result in any shared questioning and self-questioning. It awakens nothing in the way of a questioning attitude, or even a questioning disposition. For this consists in a *willing*-to-know. Willing this is not just wishing and trying. Whoever wishes to know also seems to question; but he does not get beyond saying the question, he stops short precisely where the question begins. Questioning is willing-to-know. Whoever wills, whoever lays his whole Dasein into a will, is resolute. Resoluteness delays nothing, does not shirk, but acts from the moment and without fail. Open resoluteness is no mere resolution to act; it is the decisive inception. of action that readies ahead of and through all action. To will is to be resolute. [The essence of willing is traced back here to open resoluteness. But the essence of open resoluteness <*Ent-schlossenheit*> lies in the de-concealment <*Ent-borgenheit*> of human Dasein for the clearing of Being and by no means in an accumulation of energy for "activity." Cf. *Being and Time* §44 and §60. But the relation to Being is letting. That all

*[Throughout this passage, Heidegger plays on the connection between *Einführung,* "introduction," and *führen,* "to lead." Etymologically, *Einführung* means "leading into," as do the Latin roots of the English "introduction."]

willing should be grounded in letting strikes the understanding as strange. See the lecture "On the Essence of Truth," 1930.]

But to know means to be able to stand in the truth. Truth is the openness of beings. To know is accordingly to be able to stand in the openness of beings, to stand up to it. Merely to have information, however wide-ranging it may be, is not to know. Even if this information is focused on what is practically most important through courses of study and examination requirements, it is not knowledge. Even if this information, cut back to the most compelling needs, is "close to life," its possession is not knowledge. One who carries such information around with him and has added a few practical tricks to it will still be at a loss and will necessarily bungle in the face of real reality, which is always different from what the philistine understands by closeness to life and closeness to reality. Why? Because he has no knowledge, since to know means *to be able to learn.*

Of course, everyday understanding believes that one has knowledge when one needs to learn nothing more, because one has finished learning. No. The only one who knows is the one who understands that he must always learn again, and who above all, on the basis of this understanding, has brought himself to the point where he continually *can learn.* This is far harder than possessing information.

Being able to learn presupposes being able to question. Questioning is the willing-to-know that we discussed earlier: the open resoluteness to be able to stand in the openness of beings. Because we are concerned with asking the question that is first in rank, clearly the willing as well as the knowing are of a very special *kind.* All the less will the *interrogative sentence* exhaustively reproduce the question, even if it is genuinely said in a questioning way and heard in a partnership of questioning. The question that does indeed resonate in the interrogative sentence, but nevertheless remains closed off and enveloped there, must first be developed. In this way the questioning attitude must clarify and secure itself, establish itself through exercise.

Our next task consists in *unfolding* the question "Why are there beings at an instead of nothing?" In what direction can we unfold it? To begin with, the question is accessible in the interrogative sentence. The sentence takes a stab, as it were, at the question. Hence its linguistic formulation must be correspondingly broad and loose. Let us consider our interrogative sentence in this respect. "Why are there beings at all instead of nothing?" The sentence contains a break. "Why are there beings at all?" With this, the question really has been posed. The posing of the question includes: 1) the definite indication of what is put *into* question, what is *interrogated;* 2) the indication of that with regards to which what is interrogated is interrogated—what is asked about. For what is interrogated is indicated unequivocally: namely, beings. What is asked about, what is *asked,* is the Why—that is, the ground. What follows in the interrogative sentence—"instead of nothing?"—is an embellishing flourish; it is just an appendix that inserts itself, as if on its own, for the sake of an initially loose and introductory way of speaking, as an additional turn of phrase that says nothing more about what is interrogated and what is asked about. In fact, the question is far more unequivocal and decisive *without* the appended turn of phrase, which just comes from the superfluity of imprecise talk. "Why are there beings at all?" But the addition "instead of nothing?" is invalidated not just because we are striving for a precise formulation of the question, but even more because it says nothing at all. For what more are we supposed to ask about Nothing? Nothing is simply nothing. Questioning has nothing more to seek here. Above all, by bringing up Nothing we do not gain the slightest thing for the knowledge of beings.

Whoever talks about Nothing does not know what he is doing. In speaking about Nothing, he makes it into a something. By speaking this way, he speaks against what he means. He contradicts himself. But self-contradictory speech is an offense against the fundamental rule of speech (*logos*), against "logic." Talking about Nothing is illogical. Whoever talks and thinks illogically is an unscientific person. Now whoever goes so far as to talk about Nothing within philosophy, which after all is the home of logic, deserves all the more to be accused of offending against the fundamental rule of all thinking. Such talk about Nothing consists in utterly senseless propositions. Moreover, whoever takes Nothing seriously takes the side of nullity. He obviously promotes the spirit of negation and serves disintegration. Talking about Nothing is not only completely contrary to thought, but it undermines all culture and all faith. Whatever both disregards the fundamental law of thinking and also destroys faith and the will to construct is pure nihilism.

Given such considerations, we will do well to strike from our interrogative sentence the superfluous turn of phrase "instead of nothing?" and restrict the sentence to the simple and precise form: "Why are there beings at all?"

Nothing would stand in the way of this, if . . . if in the formulation of our question, if in the asking of this question altogether, we had as much license as it may have seemed up to now. But in asking the question we stand within a tradition. For philosophy has constantly and always asked about the ground of beings. With this question it had its inception, in this question it will find its end, provided that it comes to an end in greatness and not in a powerless decline. The question about what is not and about Nothing has gone side by side with the question of what is, since its inception. But it does not do so superficially, as an accompanying phenomenon; instead, the question about Nothing takes shape in accordance with the breadth, depth, and originality with which the question about beings is asked on each occasion, and conversely. The manner of asking about Nothing can serve as a gauge and a criterion for the manner of asking about beings.

If we think about this, then the interrogative sentence pronounced at the start, "Why are there beings at all *instead* of nothing?" appears far more suitable to express the question about beings than the abbreviated version after all. Our introduction of talk about Nothing here is not a careless and overly enthusiastic manner of speaking, nor our own invention, but merely strict respect for the originary tradition regarding the sense of the fundamental question.

Still, this talk of Nothing remains contrary to thought in general, and leads to disintegration in particular. But what if both the concern for the proper respect for the fundamental rules of thinking as well as the fear of nihilism, which would both like to advise against talk of Nothing, rested on a misunderstanding? This is in fact the case. Of course, the misunderstanding that is being played out here is not accidental. Its ground is a lack of understanding that has long ruled the question about beings. But this lack of understanding stems from an *oblivion of Being* that is getting increasingly rigid.

For it cannot be decided so readily whether logic and its fandamental rules can provide any measure for the question about beings as such. It could be the other way around, that the whole logic that we know and that we treat like a gift from heaven is grounded in a very definite answer to the question about beings, and that consequently any thinking that simply follows the laws of thought of established logic is intrinsically incapable of even beginning to understand the question about beings, much less of actually unfolding it and leading it toward an answer. In truth, it is only an illusion of rigor and scientificity when one appeals to the principle of contradiction, and to logic in general, in order to prove that all thinking and talk about Nothing is contradictory and therefore senseless. "Logic" is then taken as a tribunal, secure for all eternity, and it goes without saying that no rational human being will call into doubt its authority as the first and last court of appeal. Whoever speaks against logic is suspected, implicitly or explicitly, of arbitrariness. This mere suspicion already counts as an argument and an objection, and one takes oneself to be exempted from further, authentic reflection.

One cannot, in fact, talk about and deal with Nothing as if it were a thing, such as the rain out there, or a mountain, or any object at all; Nothing remains in principle inaccessible to all science. Whoever truly wants to talk of Nothing must necessarily become unscientific. But this is a great misfortune only if one believes that scientific thinking alone is the authentic, rigorous thinking, that it alone can and must be made the measure even of philosophical thinking. But the reverse is the case. All scientific thinking is just a derivative and rigidified form of philosophical thinking Philosophy never arises from or through science. Philosophy can never belong to the same order as the sciences. It belongs to a higher order, and not just "logically," as it were, or in a table of the system of sciences. Philosophy stands in a completely different domain and rank of spiritual Dasein. Only poetry is of the same order as philosophical thinking, although thinking and poetry are not identical. Talking about Nothing remains forever an abomination and an absurdity for science. But aside from the philosopher, the poet can also talk about Nothing—and not because the procedure of poetry, in the opinion of everyday understanding, is less rigorous, but because, in comparison to all mere science, an essential superiority of the spirit holds sway in poetry (only genuine and great poetry is meant). Because of this superiority, the poet always speaks as if beings were expressed and addressed for the first time. In the poetry of the poet and in the thinking of the thinker, there is always so much worldspace to spare that each and every dung—a tree, a mountain, a house, the call of a bird—completely loses its indifference and familiarity.

True talk of Nothing always remains unfamiliar. It does not allow itself to be made common. It dissolves, to be sure, if one places it in the cheap acid of a merely logical cleverness. This is why we cannot begin to speak about Nothing immediately, as we can in describing a picture, for example. But the possibility of such speech about Nothing can be indicated. Consider a passage from one of the latest works of the poet Knut Hamsun, *The Road Leads On,* 1934 translation, p. 464. The work belongs together with *The Wayfarer* and *August.* The Road Leads On* depicts the last years and the end of this man August, who embodies the uprooted, universal knowhow of today's humanity; but in the form of a Dasein that cannot lose its ties to the unfamiliar, because in its despairing powerlessness it remains genuine and superior. In his last days, this August is alone in the high mountains. The poet says: "He sits here between his ears and hears true emptiness. Quite amusing, a fancy. On the ocean (earlier, August often went to sea) something stirred (at least), and there, there was a sound, something audible, a water chorus. Here—nothing meets nothing and is not there, there is not even a hole. One can only shake ones head in resignation."

So there is, after all, something peculiar about Nothing. Thus we want to take up our interrogative sentence again and question through it, and see whether this "instead of nothing?" simply represents a turn of phrase that says nothing and is arbitrarily appended, or whether even in the preliminary expression of the question it has an essential sense.

To this end, let us stick at first to the abbreviated, apparently simpler and supposedly more rigorous question: "Why are there beings at all?" If we ask in this way, we start out from beings. They *are.* They are given to us, they are in front of us and can thus be found before us at any time, and are also known to us within certain domains. Now the beings given to us in this way are immediately interrogated as to their ground. The questioning advances directly toward a ground. Such a method just broadens and enlarges, as it were, a procedure that is practiced every day. Somewhere in the vineyard,

*[Heidegger refers to these novels by the titles of their German translations.]

for example, an infestation turns up, something indisputably present at hand. One asks: where does this come from, where and what is its ground? Similarly, as a whole, beings are present at hand. One asks: where and what is the ground? This kind of questioning is represented in the simple formula: Why are there beings? Where and what is their ground? Tacitly one is asking after another, higher being. But here the question does not pertain at all to beings as a whole and as such.

But now if we ask the question in the form of our initial interrogative sentence—"Why are there beings at all instead of nothing?"—then the addition prevents us, in our questioning, from beginning directly with beings as unquestionably given, and having hardly began, already moving on to the ground we are seeking, which is also in being. Instead, these beings are held out in a questioning manner into the possibility of not-Being. In this way, the Why gains a completely different power and urgency of questioning. Why are beings torn from the possibility of not-Being? Why do they not fall back into it constantly with no further ado? Beings are now no longer what just happens to be present at hand; they begin to waver, regardless of whether we know beings with all certainty, regardless of whether we grasp them in their full scope or not. From now on, beings as such waver, insofar as we put them into question. The oscillation of this wavering reaches out into the most extreme and sharpest counterpossibility of beings, into not-Being and Nothing. The search for the Why now transforms itself accordingly. It does not just try to provide a present-at-hand ground for explaining what is present at hand—instead, we are now searching for a ground that is supposed to ground the dominance of beings as an overcoming of Nothing. The ground in question is now questioned as the ground of the decision for beings over against Nothing—more precisely, as the ground for the wavering of the beings that sustain us and unbind us, half in being, half not in being, which is also why we cannot wholly belong to any thing, not even to ourselves; yet Dasein is in each case mine.

[The qualification "in each case mine" signifies: Dasein is thrown to me so that my self may be Dasein. But Dasein means: care of the Being of beings as such that is ecstatically disclosed in care, not only of human Being. Dasein is "in each case mine"; this means neither that it is posited by me nor that it is confined to an isolated ego. Dasein is *itself* by virtue of its essential *relation* to Being in general. This is what the oft- repeated sentence in *Being and Time* means: the understanding of Being belongs to Dasein.]

Thus it is already becoming clearer that this "instead of nothing?" is no superfluous addition to the real question. Instead, this tam of phrase is an essential component of the whole interrogative sentence, which as a whole expresses a completely different question from what is meant by the question: Why are there beings? With our question we establish ourselves among beings in such a way that they forfeit their self-evidence as beings. Insofar *as beings* come to waver within the broadest and harshest possibility of oscillation—the "either beings—or nothing"—the questioning itself loses every secure foothold. Our Dasein, too, as it questions, comes into suspense, and nevertheless maintains itself, by itself, in this suspense.

But beings are not changed by our questioning. They remain what they are and as they are. After all, our questioning is just a psychospiritual process in us that, however it may play itself out, cannot concern beings themselves. Certainly, beings remain as they are revealed to us. And yet beings are not able to shrug off what is worthy of questioning: they, as what they are and how they are, could also *not* be. By no means do we experience this possibility as something that is just added on by our own thought, but beings themselves declare this possibility, they declare themselves as beings in this possibility. Our questioning just opens up the domain so that beings can break open in such questionworthiness.

What we know about how such questioning happens is all too little and all too crude. In this questioning, we seem to belong completely to ourselves. Yet it is *this* questioning that pushes us into the open, provided that it itself, as a questioning, transforms itself (as does every genuine questioning), and casts a new space over and through everything.

It is simply a matter of not being seduced by overhasty theories, but instead experiencing things as they are in whatever may be nearest. This piece of chalk here is an extended, relatively stable, definitely formed, grayish-white thing, and, furthermore, a thing for writing. As certainly as it belongs precisely to this thing to he here, the capacity not to be here and not to be so big also belongs to it. The possibility of being drawn along the blackboard and used up is not something that we merely add onto the dung with our thought. The chalk itself, as this being, is in this possibility; otherwise it would not be chalk as a writing implement. Every being, in turn, has this Possible in it, in a different way in each case. This Possible belongs to the chalk. It itself has in itself a definite appropriateness for a definite use. Of course, when we look for this Possible in the chalk, we are accustomed and inclined to say that we do not see it and do not grasp it. But that is a prejudice. The elimination of this prejudice is part of the unfolding of our question. For now, this question should just open up beings, in their wavering between not Being and Being Insofar as beings stand up against the extreme possibility of not Being, they themselves stand in Being, and yet they have never thereby overtaken and overcome the possibility of not-Being.

Suddenly we are speaking here about the not-Being and Being of beings, without saying how what we call Being is related to beings themselves. Are they the same? The being and its Being? The distinction! What, for example, is the being <*das Seiende*> in this piece of chalk? Already this question is ambiguous, because the word "being" can be understood in two ways, as can the Greek *to on.* On the one hand, being means what at any time is in being, in particular this grayish-white, light, breakable mass, formed in such and such a way. On the other hand, "being" means that which, as it were, "makes" this be a being instead of nonbeing <*nichtseiend*>,that which makes up the Being in the being, if it is a being. In accordance with this twofold meaning of the word "being," the Greek *to on* often designates the second meaning, that is, not the being itself, *what* is in being, but rather "the in-being," beingness, to be in being, Being. In contrast, the first meaning of "being" names the things them selves that are in being, either individually or as a whole, but always with reference to these things and not to their beingness, *ousia.**

The first meaning of *to on* designates *ta onta* (*entia*), the second means *to einai* (*esse*). We have catalogued what the being is in the piece of chalk. We were able to find this out relatively easily We could also easily see that the chalk can also not be, that this chalk ultimately need not be here and need not be at all. But then, as distinguished from that which can stand in Being or fall back into not-Being, as distinguished from the being—what is Being? Is it the same as the being? We ask this once again. But we did not include Being in our earlier catalogue of attributes—we listed only material mass, grayish-white, light, formed in such and such a manner, breakable. Now where is Being situated? It must after all belong to the chalk, for this chalk itself *is.*

*[The Greek noun *ousia* is formed from the present participle of the verb *einai* (to be). Normally meaning "goods, possessions," it is developed by Plato and Aristotle into a central philosophical concept, and is usually translated as "essence" or "substance." Heidegger's *Seiendheit* (beingness) corresponds directly to the grammatical structure of *ousia.*]

We encounter beings everywhere; they surround us, carry and control us, enchant and fulfill us, elevate and disappoint us, but where in all this is the Being of beings, and what does it consist in? One could answer: this distinction between beings and their Being may at times have some linguistic importance, perhaps even some meaning; one can make this distinction in mere thought, that is, in re-presentation and opinion, without this distinction's corresponding to anything that is. But even this distinction made only in thought is questionable; for it remains *unclear* what we are supposed to think under the name "Being." Meanwhile, it is enough to be familiar with beings and to secure mastery over them. Distinguishing Being on top of this is artificial and leads to nothing.

We have already made some remarks about this popular question of what comes of such distinctions. Let us now simply reflect on our enterprise. We ask, "Why are there beings at all instead of nothing?" And in this question we apparently restrict ourselves only to beings and avoid empty brooding about Being. But what are we really asking? Why beings as such are. We are asking about the ground for the fact that beings *are,* and are what they *are,* and that there is not nothing instead. We are asking at bottom about Being. But how? We are asking about the Being of beings. We are interrogating beings in regards to their Being.

But if we persevere in the questioning, we are really already asking *ahead,* about Being in regard to its ground, even if this question does not develop and it remains undecided whether Being itself is not already in itself a ground and ground enough. If we pose this question about Being as the first question in rank, then should we do so without knowing how it stands with Being and how Being stands in its distinction from beings? How are we even supposed to inquire into the ground for the Being of beings, let alone be able to find it out, if we have not adequately conceived, understood and grasped Being itself? This enterprise would be just as hopeless as if someone wanted to explain the cause and ground of a fire and declared that he need not bother with the course of the fire or the investigation of its scene.

So it turns out that the question "Why are there beings at all instead of nothing?" forces us to the prior question: "*How does it stand with Being?*"

We are now asking about something that we hardly grasp, something that is now no more than the sound of a word for us and that puts us in danger of falling victim to the mere idolization of words in our further questioning. So it is all the more necessary for us to get clear from the outset about how it stands for us at present with Being and with our understanding of Being. Here it is important above all to impress on our experience again and again the fact that we are not able to lay hold of the *Being* of beings directly and expressly, neither by way of beings, nor in beings—nor anywhere else at all.

A few examples should help. Over there, on the other side of the street, stands the high school building. A being. We can scour every side of the building from the outside, roam through the inside from basement to attic, and note everything that can be found there: hallways, stairs, classrooms, and their furnishings. Everywhere we find beings, and in a very definite order. Where now is the Being of this high school? It *is,* after all. The building *is.* The Being of this being belongs to it if anything does, and nevertheless we do not find this Being within the being.

Moreover, Being does not consist in our observing beings. The building stands there even if we do not observe it. We can come across it only because it already is. In addition, the Being of this building does not at all seem to be identical for everybody. For us, as observers or passers-by, it is not what it is for the students who sit inside, not just because they see it only from the inside but because for them this building really is what it is and how it is. One can, as it were, smell the Being of such buildings, and often after decades one still has the scent in ones nose. The scent provides the Being of this being much more directly and truly than it could be communicated by any description or inspection. On the other hand, the subsistence of the building does not depend on this scent that is hovering around somewhere.

How does it stand with Being? Can we see Being? We see beings—the chalk here. But do we see Being as we see color and fight and dark? Or do we hear, smell, taste, or touch Being? We hear the motorcycle roaring along the street. We hear the grouse flying off through the mountain forest in its gliding flight. Yet really we are only hearing the noise of the motor's rattling, the noise that the grouse causes. Furthermore, it is hard and unusual for us to describe the pure noise, because it is precisely not what we generally hear. We always hear more [than the mere noise]. We hear the flying bird, although strictly speaking we have to say: a grouse is nothing we can hear, it is not a tone that could be registered on a scale. And so it is with the other senses. We touch velvet, silk; we see them without further ado as such and such a being, and the one is in being distinctly from the other Where does Being he and in what does it consist?

Yet we must look around us still more thoroughly and contemplate the narrower and wider sphere within which we dwell, daily and hourly, knowing and unknowing, a sphere that constantly shifts its boundaries and suddenly is broken through.

A heavy thunderstorm gathering in the mountains "is," or—it makes no difference here—"was" in the night. What does its Being consist in?

A distant mountain range under a vast sky—such a thing "is." What does its Being consist in? When and to whom does it reveal itself? To the hiker who enjoys the landscape, or to the peasant who makes his daily living from it and in it, or to the meteorologist who has to give a weather report? Who among them lays hold of Being? All and none. Or do these people only lay hold of particular aspects of the mountain range under the vast sky, not the mountain range itself as it "is," not what its real Being consists in? Who can lay hold of this? Or is it nonsensical, against the sense of Being in the first place, to ask about what is in itself, behind those aspects? Does Being lie in the aspects?

The portal of an early Romanesque church is a being. How and to whom does Being reveal itself? To the art historian who visits and photographs it on an excursion, or to the abbot who passes through the portal with his monks for a religious celebration, or to the children who play in its shadow on a summer's day? How does it stand with the Being of this being?

A state—it *is*. What does its Being consist in? In the fact that the state police arrest a suspect, or that in a ministry of the Reich so and so many typewriters clatter away and record the dictation of state secretaries and ministers? Or "is" the state in the discussion between the Führer and the English foreign minister? The state *is*. But where is Being situated? Is it located anywhere at all?

A painting by Van Gogh: a pair of sturdy peasant shoes, nothing else. The picture really represents nothing. Yet you are alone at once with what *is* there, as if you yourself were heading homeward from the field on a late autumn evening, tired, with your hoe, as the last potato fires smolder out. What is in being here? The canvas? The brushstrokes? The patches of color?

In everything we have mentioned, what is the Being of beings? Really, how is it that we can ran around in the world and stand around with our stupid pretensions and our so-called cleverness?

Everything we have mentioned is, after all, and nevertheless—if we want to lay hold of Being it is always as if we were reaching into a void. The Being that we are asking about is almost like Nothing, and yet we are always trying to arm and guard ourselves against the presumption of saying that all beings are *not*.

But Being remains undiscoverable, almost like Nothing, or in the end *entirely* so. The word "Being" is then finally just an empty word. It means nothing actual, tangible, real. Its meaning is an unreal vapor. So in the end Nietzsche is entirely right when he calls the "highest concepts" such as Being "the final wisp of evaporating reality" (*Twilight of the Idols* VIII, 78). Who would want to chase after such a vapor, the term for which is just the name for a huge error! "In fact, nothing up to now has been more naively persuasive than the error of Being . . ." (VIII, 80).

"Being"—a vapor and an error? What Nietzsche says here about Being is no casual remark, jotted down during the frenzy of labor in preparation for his authentic and never completed work. Instead, it is his guiding conception of Being since the earliest days of his philosophical labor. It supports and determines his philosophy from the ground up. But this philosophy remains, even now, well guarded against all the clumsy and trifling importunities of the horde of scribblers that is becoming ever more numerous around him today. It seems that his work hardly has the worst of this misuse behind it. In speaking of Nietzsche here, we want nothing to do with all this—nor with a blind hero worship. The task is much too decisive and, at the same time, too sober for such worship. It consists first and foremost in fully unfolding that which was realized through Nietzsche by means of a truly engaged attack on him. Being—a vapor, an error! If this is so, then the only possible conclusion is that we should also give up the question, "Why are there beings as such and as a whole instead of nothing?" For what is the point of the question anymore, if what it puts into question is just a vapor and an error?

Does Nietzsche speak the truth? Or is he himself only the final victim of a long-standing errancy and neglect, but *as* this victim the unrecognized witness to a new necessity?

Is it Being's fault that Being is so confused, and is it the fault of the word that it remains so empty, or is it our fault, because in all our bustling and chasing after beings, we have nevertheless fallen out of Being? What if the fault is not our own, we of today, nor that of our immediate or most distant forebears, but rather is based in a happening that runs through Western history from the inception onward, a happening that the eyes of all historians will never reach, but which nevertheless happens—formerly, today, and in the future? What if it were possible that human beings, that peoples in their greatest machinations and exploits, have a relation to beings but have long since fallen out of Being, without knowing it, and what if this were the innermost and most powerful ground of their decline? [Cf. *Being and Time,* §38, especially pp. 179f.]

These are not questions that we pose here casually, nor do we pose them on account of some predisposition or worldview. Instead, they are questions to which we are forced by that prior question, which springs necessarily from the main question: "How does it stand with Being?"—a sober question perhaps, but certainly a very useless question, too. And yet a *question, the question:* "Is 'Being' a mere word and its meaning a vapor, or is it the spiritual fate of the West?"

This Europe, in its unholy blindness always on the point of cutting its own throat, lies today in the great pincers between Russia on the one side and America on the other Russia and America, seen metaphysically, are both the same: the same hopeless frenzy of unchained technology and of the rootless organization of the average man. When the farthest corner of the globe has been conquered technologically and can be exploited economically; when any incident you like, in any place you like, at any time you like, becomes accessible as fast as you like; when you can simultaneously "experience" an assassination attempt against a king in France and a symphony concert in Tokyo; when time is nothing but speed, instantaneity, and simultaneity, and time as history has vanished from all Dasein of all peoples; when a boxer counts as the great man of a people; when the tallies of millions at mass meetings are a triumph; then, yes then, there still looms like a specter over all this uproar the question: what for?—where to?—and what then?

The spiritual decline of the earth has progressed so far that peoples are in danger of losing their last spiritual strength, the strength that makes it possible even to see the decline [which is meant in relation to the fate of "Being"] and to appraise it as such. This simple observation has nothing to do with cultural pessimism—nor with any optimism either, of course; for the darkening of the world, the flight of the gods, the destruction of the earth, the reduction of human beings to a mass, the hatred and mistrust of everything creative and free has already reached such proportions throughout the whole earth that such childish categories as pessimism and optimism have long become laughable.

We lie in the pincers. Our people, as standing in the center, suffers the most intense pressure—our people, the people richest in neighbors and hence the most endangered people, and for all that, the metaphysical people. We are sure of this vocation; but this people will gain a fate from its vocation only when it creates *in itself* a resonance, a possibility of resonance for this vocation, and grasps its tradition creatively. All this implies that this people, as a historical people, must transpose itself—and with it the history of the West—from the center of their future happening into the originary realm of the powers of Being. Precisely if the great decision regarding Europe is not to go down the path of annihilation—precisely then can this decision come about only through the development of new, historically *spiritual* forces from the center.

To ask: how does it stand with Being?—this means nothing less than to repeat and retrieve <*wiederholen*> the inception of our historical-spiritual Dasein, in order to transform it into the other inception. Such a thing is possible. It is in fact the definitive form of history, because it has its onset in a happening that grounds history. But an inception is not repeated when one shrinks back to it as something that once was, something that by now is familiar and is simply to be imitated, but rather when the inception is begun again *more originally,* and with all the strangeness, darkness, insecurity that a genuine inception brings with it. Repetition as we understand it is anything but the ameliorating continuation of what has been, by means of what has been.

The question "How does it stand with Being?" is included as a prior question in our guiding question: "Why are there beings at all instead of nothing?" If we now set out to pursue what stands in question in the prior question, namely Being, then Nietzsche's saying at once proves to be completely true after all. For if we look closely, what more is "Being" to us than a mere locution, an indeterminate meaning, intangible as a vapor? Nietzsche's judgment, of course, is meant in a purely dismissive sense. For him, "Being" is a deception that never should have happened. "Being"—indeterminate evanescent as a vapor? It is in fact so. But we don't want to evade this fact. To the contrary, we must try to get clear about its factuality in order to survey its fall scope.

Through our questioning, we are entering a landscape; to be in this landscape is the fundamental prerequisite for restoring rootedness to historical Dasein. We will have to ask why this fact, the fact that "Being" remains a vaporous word for us, stands out precisely today; we will have to ask whether and why it has persisted for a long time. We should learn to know that this fact is not as innocuous as it seems at first sight. For ultimately what matters is not that the word "Being" remains just a noise for us and its meaning just a vapor, but that we have fallen out of what this word is saying, and for now cannot find our way back; it is on *these* grounds and on no others that the word "Being" no longer applies to anything, that everything, if we merely want to take hold of it, dissolves like a shred of cloud in the sun. Because this is so, we ask about Being. And we ask because we know that truths have never yet fallen into a peoples lap. The fact that even now one still cannot understand this question, and does not want to understand it, even if it is asked in a still *more* originary way, takes from this question none of its inevitability.

Of course, one can show oneself to be very clever and superior, and once again trot out the well-known reflection: "Being" is simply the most universal concept. Its range extends to any and every thing, even to Nothing, which, as something thought and said, "is" also something. So there is, in the strict sense of the word, nothing above and beyond the range of this most universal concept "Being" in terms of which it could be further defined. One must be satisfied with this highest generality The concept of Being is an ultimate. And it also corresponds to a law of logic that says: the more comprehensive a concept is in its scope—and what could be more comprehensive than the concept "Being"?—the more indeterminate and empty is its content.

For every normally thinking human being—and we all want to be normal—such trains of thought are immediately and entirely convincing. But now the question is whether the assessment of Being as the most universal concept reaches the essence of Being, or whether it so misinterprets Being from the start that questioning becomes hopeless. The question is whether Being can count only as the most universal concept that unavoidably presents itself in all particular concepts or whether Being has a completely different essence, and thus is anything but the object of an "ontology," if one takes this word in its established meaning.

The term "ontology" was first coined in the seventeenth century. It designates the development of the traditional doctrine of beings into a philosophical discipline and a branch of the philosophical system. But the traditional doctrine is the academic analysis and ordering of what for Plato and Aristotle, and again for Kant, was a question, though to be sure a question that was no longer originary. The word "ontology" is still used this way even today. Under this tide, philosophy busies itself with the composition and exposition of a branch within its system. But one can also take the word "ontology" "in the broadest sense," "without reference to ontological directions and tendencies" (cf. *Being and Time,* 1927, p. 11 top). In this case "ontology" means the effort to put Being into words, and to do so by passing through the question of how it stands with Being [not just with beings as such]. But because until now this question has found neither an accord nor even a resonance, but instead it is explicitly rejected by the various circles of academic philosophical scholarship, which pursues an "ontology" in the traditional sense, it may be good in the future to forgo the use of the terms "ontology" and "ontological." Two modes of questioning which, as is only now becoming clearer, are worlds apart should not bear the same name.

We *ask* the question—How does it stand with Being? What is the meaning of Being?—*not* in order to compose an ontology in the traditional style, much less to reckon up critically the mistakes of earlier attempts at ontology. We are concerned with something completely different. The point is to restore the historical Dasein of human beings—and this also always means our own most future Dasein, in the whole of the history that is allotted to us—back to the power of Being that is to be opened up originally; all this, to be sure, only within the limits of philosophy's capability.

From the fundamental question of metaphysics, "Why are there beings at all instead of nothing?" we have extracted the *prior question* <*Vorfrage*>: How does it stand with Being? The relation between these questions needs to be elucidated, for it is in a class of its own. Usually, a preliminary question <*Vorfrage*> is settled in advance and outside the main question, although with a view to it. But philosophical questions are in principle never settled as if some day one could set them aside. Here the preliminary question does not stand outside the fundamental question at all but is, as it were, the hearth-fire that glows in the asking of the fundamental question, the hearth at the heart of all questioning. That is to say: when we first ask the fundamental question, everything depends on our taking up the decisive fundamental position in asking its *prior question,* and winning and securing the bearing that is essential here. This is why we brought the question about Being into connection with the fate of Europe, where the fate of the earth is being decided, while for Europe itself our historical Dasein proves to be the center.

The question ran:

Is Being a mere word and its meaning a vapor, or does what is named with the word "Being" hold within it the spiritual fate of the West?

To many ears the question may sound forced and exaggerated. For if pressed, one could indeed imagine that discussing the question of Being might ultimately, at a very great remove and in a very indirect manner, have some relation to the decisive historical question of the earth, but by no means in such a way that from out of the history of the earth's spirit, the fundamental position and bearing of our questioning could directly be determined. And yet there is such a connection. Because our aim is to get the asking of the prior question going, we now must show how, and to what extent, the asking of this prior question moves directly, and from the ground up, along with the decisive historical question. To demonstrate this, it is necessary at first to anticipate an essential insight in the form of an assertion.

We assert that the asking of this prior question, and thereby the asking of the fundamental question of metaphysics, is a historical questioning through and through. But does not metaphysics, and philosophy in general, thereby become a historical science? After all, historical science investigates the temporal, while philosophy, in contrast, investigates the supratemporal. Philosophy is historical only insofar as it, like every work of the spirit, realizes itself in the course of time. But in this sense, the designation of metaphysical questioning as historical cannot characterize metaphysics but can only propose something obvious. Thus either the assertion says nothing and is superfluous, or it is impossible, because it mixes up fundamentally different kinds of science: philosophy and the science of history.

In reply to this it must be said:

1. Metaphysics and philosophy are not science at all, and furthermore, the fact that their questioning is at bottom historical cannot make them so.

2. For its part, the science of history does not at all determine, as science, the originary relation to history; instead, it always already presupposes such a relation. This is why the science of history can either deform the relation to history—a relation that is itself always historical—misinterpret it and reduce it to mere antiquarian expertise, or else prepare essential domains of vision for the already grounded relation to history and let history be experienced in its bindingness. A historical relation of our historical Dasein to history can become an object of knowledge and a developed state of knowledge; but it need not. Besides, not all relations to history can be scientifically objectified and become scientific, and in fact it is precisely the essential relations that cannot. The

science of history can never institute the historical relation to history It can only illuminate a relation once it is instituted, ground it informatively, which to be sure is an essential necessity for the historical Dasein of a knowing people, and thus neither merely an "advantage" nor a "disadvantage."* It is only in philosophy—*in distinction from every science*—that essential relations to beings always take shape; and therefore this relation can, indeed must, be an originally historical one for us today.

But in order to understand our assertion that the "metaphysical" asking of the prior question is historical through and through, one must consider one thing above all: in this assertion, history is not equivalent to what is past; for this is precisely what is no longer happening.** But much less is history what is merely contemporary, which also never happens, but always just "passes" makes its entrance and goes by. History as happening is determined from the future, takes over what has been, and acts and endures its way through the *present.* It is precisely the present that vanishes in the happening.

Our asking of the fundamental metaphysical question is historical because it opens up the happening of human Dasein in its essential relations—that is, its relations to beings as such and as a whole—opens it up to possibilities not yet asked about, futures to come <*Zukünften*>, and thereby also binds it back to its inception that has been, and thus sharpens and burdens it in its present. In this questioning, our Dasein is summoned to its history in the full sense of the word and is called to make a decision in it—and this is not a derivative, useful application of this questioning in terms of morality and worldviews. Instead, the fundamental position and bearing of the questioning is in itself historical, stands and holds itself in the happening, and questions on the ground of this happening and for this happening.

But we still lack the essential insight into how far this asking of the question of Being, an asking which is in itself historical, intrinsically belongs to the world history of the earth. We said: on the earth, all over it, a darkening of the world is happening. The essential happenings in this darkening are: the flight of the gods, the destruction of the earth, the reduction of human beings to a mass, the preeminence of the mediocre.

What does "world" mean, when we speak of the darkening of the world? World is always *spiritual* world. The animal has no world <*Welt*>, nor any environment <*Umwelt*>. The darkening of the world contains within itself a *disempowering of the spirit,* its dissolution, diminution, suppression, and misinterpretation. We will try to elucidate this disempowering of the spirit in one respect, namely, the misinterpretation of the spirit. We said: Europe lies in the pincers between Russia and America, which are metaphysically the same, namely in regard to their world-character and their relation to the spirit. The situation of Europe is all the more dire because the disempowering of the spirit comes from Europe itself and—though prepared by earlier factors—is determined at last by its own spiritual situation in the first half of the nineteenth century. Among us at that time something happened that is all too readily and swiftly characterized as the "collapse of German idealism." This formula is like a shield behind which the already dawning spiritlessness, the dissolution of spiritual powers, the deflection of all originary questioning about grounds and the bonding to such grounds, are hidden and obscured. For it was not German idealism that collapsed, but it was the age that was no

*[With the terms "antiquarian," "advantage," and "disadvantage" Heidegger alludes to Nietzsche's "On the Advantage and Disadvantage of History for Life." Cf. *Being and Time,* §76. In the winter semester of 1938–1939 Heidegger gave a lecture course on this essay by Nietzsche.]

**[Throughout this passage and elsewhere, Heidegger plays on *Geschichte* and *geschehen* ("history" and "happen").]

longer strong enough to stand up to the greatness, breadth, and originality of that spiritual world—that is, truly to realize it, which always means something other than merely applying propositions and insights. Dasein began to slide into a world that lacked that depth from which the essential always comes and returns to human beings, thereby forcing them to superiority and allowing them to act on the basis of rank. AD things sank to the same level, to a surface resembling a blind mirror that no longer mirrors, that casts nothing back. The prevailing dimension became that of extension and number. *To be able*—this no longer means to spend and to lavish, thanks to lofty overabundance and the mastery of energies; instead, it means only practicing a routine in which anyone can be trained, always combined with a certain amount of sweat and display. In America and Russia, then, this all intensified until it turned into the measureless so-on-and-so-forth of the ever-identical and the indifferent, until finally this quantitative temper became a quality of its own. By now in those countries the predominance of a cross-section of the indifferent is no longer something inconsequential and merely barren but is the onslaught of that which aggressively destroys all rank and all that is world spiritual, and portrays these as a lie. This is the onslaught of what we call the demonic [in the sense of the destructively evil]. There are many omens of the arising of this demonism, in unison with the growing perplexity and uncertainty of Europe against it and within itself One such omen is the disempowering of the spirit in the sense of its misinterpretation—a happening in the middle of which we still stand today. Let us briefly describe four aspects of this misinterpretation of the spirit.

1. One decisive aspect is the reinterpretation of the spirit as *intelligence,* and this as mere astuteness in the examination, calculation and observation of given things, their possible modification, and their additional elaboration. This astuteness is a matter of mere talent and practice and mass distribution. This astuteness is itself subject to the possibility of organization, none of which ever applies to the spirit. The whole phenomenon of literati and aesthetes is just a late consequence and mutation of the spirit falsified as intelligence. *Mere* ingenuity is the semblance of spirit and veils its absence.

2. Spirit, thus falsified as intelligence, is thereby reduced to the role of a tool in the service of something else, a tool whose handling can be taught and learned. Whether this service of intelligence now relates to the regulation and mastery of the material relations of production (as in Marxism) or in general to the clever ordering and clarification of everything that lies before us and is already posited (as in positivism), or whether it fulfills itself in organizing and directing the vital resources and race of a people—be this as it may, the spirit as intelligence becomes the powerless superstructure to something else, which, because it is spiritless or even hostile to spirit, counts as authentic reality. If one understands spirit as intelligence, as Marxism in its most extreme form has done, then it is completely correct to say in response that the spirit—that is, intelligence, in the ordering of the effective energies of human Dasein—must always be subordinated to healthy bodily fitness and to character. But this ordering becomes untrue as soon as one grasps the essence of spirit in its truth. For all true energy and beauty of the body, all sureness and boldness of the sword, but also all genuineness and ingenuity of the understanding, are grounded in the spirit, and they rise or fall only according to the current power or powerlessness of the spirit. Spirit is what sustains and rules, the first and the last, not a merely indispensable third element.

3. As soon as this instrumental misinterpretation of the spirit sets in, the powers of spiritual happening—poetry and fine arts, statescraft and religion—shift to a sphere where they can be *consciously* cultivated and planned. At the same time, they get

divided up into regions. The spiritual world becomes culture, and in the creation and conservation of culture the individual seeks to fulfill himself. These regions become fields of a free endeavor that sets its own standards for itself, according to the meaning of "standards" that it can still attain. These standards of validity for production and use are called values. Cultural values secure meaning for themselves in the whole of a culture only by restricting themselves to their self-validity: poetry for poetry's sake, art for art's sake, science for sciences sake.

In respect to science, which concerns us especially here in the university, the situation of the last few decades, a situation which remains unchanged today despite some cleansing, is easy to see. Although two seemingly different conceptions of science are now seemingly struggling against each other—science as technical and practical professional knowledge and science as a cultural value in itself—nevertheless *both* are moving along *the same* decadent path of a misinterpretation and disempowering of the spirit. They are distinct only in that the technical and practical conception of science as specialized science may still lay claim to the merit of open and clear consistency within today's situation, whereas the reactionary interpretation of science as a cultural value, which is now again appearing, tries to hide the powerlessness of the spirit through an unconscious mendacity. The confusion of spiritlessness can even go so far that the practical, technical explanation of science confesses itself at the same time to be science as cultural value, so that both understand each other very well in the same dearth of spirit. One may wish to call the arrangement of the amalgam of the specialized sciences for purposes of teaching and research a university, but this is now just a name and no longer an originally unifying spiritual power that imposes duties. What I said here in my inaugural address in 1929 about the German university still applies today: "The regions of science he far asunder. Their ways of handling their subject matters are fundamentally different. This disintegrated multiplicity of disciplines is still meaningfully maintained today only through the technical organization of universities and faculties and through the practical aims of the disciplines. Yet the rootedness of the sciences in their essential ground has atrophied" (*What Is Metaphysics,* 1929, p. 8). In all its areas, science today is a technical, practical matter of gaining information and communicating it. No awakening of the spirit at all can proceed from it as science. Science itself needs such an awakening.

4. The last misinterpretation of the spirit rests on the formerly mentioned falsifications that represent the spirit as intelligence, this intelligence as a tool serviceable for goals, and this tool, together with what can be produced, as the realm of culture. The spirit as intelligence in the service of goals and the spirit as culture finally become showpieces and spectacles that one takes into account along with many others, that one publicly trots out and exhibits as proof that one does *not* want to deny culture in favor of barbarism. Russian Communism, after an initially purely negative attitude, went directly over to such propagandistic tactics.

Against these multiple misinterpretations of the spirit, we determine the essence of the spirit briefly in this way (I choose the formulation from my *Rectoral Address,* because there everything is succinctly brought together in accordance with the occasion): "Spirit is neither empty acuity, nor the noncommittal play of wit, nor the understanding's boundless pursuit of analysis, nor even world reason, but rather spirit is originally attuned, knowing resolution to the essence of Being" (*Rectoral Address,* p. 13). Spirit is the empowering of the powers of beings as such and as a whole. Where spirit rules, beings as such always and in each case come more into being <*wird . . . seinder*>. Asking about beings as such and as a whole, asking the question of Being, is then one of the essential fundamental conditions for awakening the spirit, and thus for an originary world of historical Dasein, and thus for subduing the danger of the darkening of the world, and thus for taking over the historical mission of our people, the people of the center of the West. Only in these broad strokes can we make plain here to what extent asking the question of Being is in itself historical through and through, and that accordingly our question, whether Being is to remain a mere vapor for us or whether it is to become the fate of the West, is anything but an exaggeration and a figure of speech.

But if our question about Being has this essential character of decision, then we must above all proceed in full seriousness with the *fact* that gives the question its immediate necessity: the fact that Being is in fact almost nothing more than a word now, and its meaning is an evanescent vapor. We do not just stand before this fact as something alien and other, which we may simply ascertain as an occurrence in its Being-present-at-hand. The fact is such that we stand within it. It is a state of our Dasein, though certainly not in the sense of a property that we could simply exhibit psychologically, "State" here means our whole constitution, the way in which we ourselves are constituted in relation to Being. This is not a matter of psychology; instead, it concerns our history in an essential respect. If we call it a "fact" that Being for us is a mere word and a vapor, this is a very provisional formulation. With it, we are for once simply establishing and coming to grips with something that has still not been thought through at all, something that we still have no place for, even if it seems as if it were an occurrence among us, we human beings, "in" us, as one likes to say.

One would like to treat the particular fact that Being for us is now just an empty word and an evanescent vapor as a case of the more general fact that many words—indeed, the essential words—are in the same situation, that language in general is used up and abused, that language is an indispensable but masterless, arbitrarily applicable means of communication, as indifferent as a means of public transportation, such as a streetcar, which everyone gets on and off. Thus everyone talks and writes unhindered and above all *unendangered* in language. That is certainly correct. Moreover, only a very few are still in a position to think through in its full scope this misrelation and unrelation of today's Dasein to language.

But the emptiness of the word "Being," the complete withering of its naming force, is not just a particular case of the general abuse of language—instead, the destroyed relation to Being as such is the real ground for our whole misrelation to language.

The organizations for the purification of language and for defense against its progressive mutilation deserve respect. Nevertheless, through such institutions one finally demonstrates only more clearly that one no longer knows what language is all about. Because the fate of language is grounded in the particular *relation* of a people to *Being,* the question about *Being* will be most intimately intertwined with the question about *language* for us. It is more than a superficial accident that now, as we make a start in laying out the above mentioned fact of the vaporization of Being in all its scope, we find ourselves forced to proceed from linguistic considerations.

Ludwig Wittgenstein
1889–1951

Ludwig Wittgenstein was born into one of Vienna's leading families. His father, Karl, was a wealthy steel industrialist and his mother, Leopoldine, a concert pianist. Johannes Brahms, Gustaf Mahler, and Pablo Casals were frequent houseguests of the Wittgensteins. Educated at home by tutors, Wittgenstein showed great promise in mathematics and engineering. According to one report, he built a working sewing machine from matchsticks at age 10.

Wittgenstein remained home until age 15, when he enrolled at the *Linz Realschule,* where he studied engineering for two years before transferring to Berlin. In 1908, Wittgenstein enrolled at the University of Manchester, England, for studies in aerodynamics. While designing a propeller, Wittgenstein developed an interest in mathematics, which led him to Cambridge. There, from 1912 to 1913, he studied with Bertrand Russell. Russell later recalled one of his first encounters with Wittgenstein:

> At the end of his first term at Cambridge he came to me and said, "Will you please tell me whether I am a complete idiot or not?" I replied, "My dear fellow, I don't know. Why are you asking me?" He said, "Because if I am a complete idiot, I shall become an aeronaut; but, if not, I shall become a philosopher." I told him to write me something during the vacation on some philosophical subject and I would then tell him whether he was a complete idiot or not. At the beginning of the following term he brought me the fulfillment of this suggestion. After reading only one sentence, I said to him, "No, you must not become an aeronaut."*

*Bertrand Russell, *Portraits from Memory* (London: George Allen & Unwin, 1957), pp. 26–27.

Wittgenstein immersed himself in philosophical studies, filling notebooks with ideas. When World War I began in 1914, he enlisted as a machine-gunner in the Austrian army. While in the army, he continued his philosophical work, writing a short treatise in 1918 based on his notebooks. That same year, he was captured by the Italian army. In captivity, he managed to send a copy of this treatise to Russell, who considered it a work of genius and arranged for its publication as the *Tractatus Logico-Philosophicus* (1921). This was the only philosophical book Wittgenstein published during his lifetime.

Wittgenstein believed his *Tractatus* gave the definitive answer to all philosophical problems. Following the war, therefore, he left philosophy completely. After a course at a teacher's training college, he spent the next six years as a schoolteacher in remote Austrian villages. But teaching did not suit his temperament, and he was desperately unhappy. He resigned in 1926 and worked as a monastery gardener before moving back to Vienna to design a house for his sister. While in Vienna, Wittgenstein began talking philosophy again with Moritz Schlick, professor of philosophy at the University of Vienna, and with other professors who admired his *Tractatus.*

Philosophically revived, Wittgenstein returned to Cambridge in 1929, and, after submitting his now famous *Tractatus* as a doctoral dissertation, he became a research fellow of Trinity College. Again, Wittgenstein filled notebooks with philosophical reflections and prepared them for publication. But, with the exception of one paper, Wittgenstein never saw any of his new ideas in print; he always considered his newest thoughts incomplete or not yet adequately formulated.

For the rest of his life, Wittgenstein continued his association with Cambridge—though he never felt completely comfortable with academic life. On several occasions, he left the university, sometimes living in isolation in his hut in Norway. In 1939, he was appointed professor of philosophy at Cambridge, succeeding G.E. Moore. But before he could take the chair, World War II began, and he volunteered as a hospital orderly in London. He returned to Cambridge following the war, but he found his job so dreadful that he resigned after two years. Living alone in Ireland, he completed his second major work, *Philosophical Investigations,* though again he could not bring himself to publish it. (It appeared posthumously in 1953.)

During a visit to the United States in 1949, his health began to deteriorate. On his return to Cambridge, doctors discovered prostate cancer, and he died eighteen months later, in 1951. Since his death, his literary executors have published more than a dozen books of uncompleted manuscripts, notes, lectures, and letters.

* * *

Throughout his adult life, Wittgenstein was interested in philosophy as an activity rather than as a set of theories. He believed that the goal of philosophy is to remove or "dissolve" problems, and the primary means for doing this is analysis of language. According to Wittgenstein, most philosophical problems can be traced to a misuse of language. In one of his early notebooks he wrote:

> Philosophy gives no pictures of reality and can neither confirm nor confute scientific investigations. Philosophy teaches us the logical form of propositions: that is its fundamental task.*

*Ludwig Wittgenstein, *Notebooks 1914–1916* (Oxford: John Wiley & Sons, 1981).

Thirty-five years later, he still maintained this philosophical position: "Philosophy is a battle against the bewitchment of our intelligence by means of language."*

But despite this theme, Wittgenstein developed two different ways to understand language. The early Wittgenstein created a "picture theory of meaning" that held that language consists of statements or propositions that picture the world. Just as a picture has something in common with that which it pictures, so language has a logical form in common with the world it pictures. This logical form is usually obscured by ordinary language, so the philosopher's job is to clear up ordinary language by crafting a language that more perfectly pictures the world. This perfected language will have to exclude many propositions (such as those in ethics, metaphysics, or religion), consigning them to silence. Our selection from the *Tractatus,* translated by D.F. Pears and B.F. McGuiness, presents this early theory.

Wittgenstein's early theory was adopted and modified by Moritz Schlick and his "Vienna Circle." This group developed a philosophy that came to be called "logical positivism." Like Wittgenstein, they worked on an ideal language, free from the ambiguities of ordinary discourse, that would clearly exhibit its logical form. They also held that such a language would exclude the propositions of ethics, metaphysics, and religion.

The early Wittgenstein, and the logical positivism that adapted many of his ideas, profoundly impacted the philosophy of the mid-twentieth century. But Wittgenstein himself moved to a different understanding of language: a "language game" theory. This theory found the earlier picture theory too narrow; a perfected language is neither possible nor desirable. As he explains in our selection from the *Investigations,* given here in the G.E.M. Anscombe translation, there are many kinds of meaningful sentences that share certain characteristics, but not others. Just as there is no one characteristic common to all games, so there is no one theory to explain all language uses. The proper way to understand a sentence is not to break it down into its constituent parts and analyze its logical form. Instead, we should examine the "forms of life" out of which the sentence arises, to see what "game" it is playing. "The meaning of a word," Wittgenstein wrote, "is its use in the language."

The later Wittgenstein was not interested in creating a perfect language. He sought rather to expose the underlying assumptions of language and the forms of life out of which our sentences arise. By understanding language in terms of the social environment that gives it birth, the later Wittgenstein encouraged a sociological understanding of language. Accordingly, Wittgenstein argued against the idea of a private language—a language apart from communal interactions.

The influence of Wittgenstein's early work peaked in the 1950s. But his later understanding of philosophy and his lifelong conception of philosophy as activity are still influential, particularly in the English-speaking world. For example, feminist philosophers have used Wittgenstein's insights to show how patriarchal language both influences and is influenced by social structures, and theologians have tried to understand the language of sacred texts by exploring their historical contexts. Wittgenstein's belief that the aim of philosophy is to dissolve problems—"To shew the fly the way out of the fly-bottle"—has continued to impress, or, as critics would say, to depress, philosophy.

* * *

*Ludwig Wittgenstein, *Philosophical Investigations* (New York: Macmillan, 1958), no. 109, p. 47.

Among the many general introductions to Wittgenstein's life and thought, Anthony Kenney, *Wittgenstein* (Cambridge, MA: Harvard University Press, 1973) still provides one of the best. Also helpful are George Pitcher, *The Philosophy of Wittgenstein* (Englewood Cliffs, NJ: Prentice Hall, 1964); David Pears, *Ludwig Wittgenstein* (New York: Viking Press, 1970); A.J. Ayer, *Wittgenstein* (Chicago: University of Chicago Press, 1985); P.M.S. Hacker, *Wittgenstein's Place in Twentieth-Century Analytic Philosophy* (Oxford: Basil Blackwell, 1996); P.M.S. Hacker, *Wittgenstein* (London: Routledge, 1999); and Mark Addis, *Wittgenstein: A Guide for the Perplexed* (London: Continuum, 2006). Norman Malcolm, *Ludwig Wittgenstein: A Memoir* (London: Oxford University Press, 1958); K.T. Fann, ed., *Wittgenstein: The Man and His Philosophy* (New York: Delta, 1967); and O.K. Bouwsma, *Wittgenstein: Conversations, 1949–1951* (Indianapolis, IN: Hackett, 1986) all provide personal memoirs, whereas Allan Janik and Stephen Toulmin, *Wittgenstein's Vienna* (New York: Simon & Schuster, 1973) and Ray Monk, *Ludwig Wittgenstein: The Duty of Genius* (New York: Penguin Books, 1992) give biographies. For guides to Wittgenstein's two major works, see G.E.M. Anscombe, *An Introduction to Wittgenstein's "Tractatus"* (London: Hillary House, 1959); H.O. Mounce, *Wittgenstein's "Tractatus"* (Chicago: University of Chicago Press, 1981); Eli Friedlander, *Signs of Sense: Reading Wittgenstein:* Tractatus (Cambridge, MA: Harvard University Press, 2000); Ian Proops, *Logic and Language in Wittgenstein's* Tractatus (New York: Garland, 2000); Alfred Nordmann, *Wittgenstein's* Tractatus: *An Introduction* (Cambridge: Cambridge University Press, 2005); Roger M. White, *Wittgenstein's* Tractatus Logico-Philosophicus: *A Reader's Guide* (London: Continuum, 2007); Garth Hallett, *A Companion to Wittgenstein's "Philosophical Investigations"* (Ithaca, NY: Cornell University Press, 1977); Marie McGinn, *Routledge Philosophy Guidebook to Wittgenstein and the* Philosophical Investigations (Oxford: Routledge, 1997); William H. Brenner, *Wittgenstein's* Philosophical Investigations (Albany, NY: SUNY Press, 1999); Andrew Lugg, *Wittgenstein's* Investigations 1–132: *A Guide and Interpretation* (London: Routledge, 2000); and David G. Stern, *Wittgenstein's* Philosophical Investigations: *An Introduction* (Cambridge: Cambridge University Press, 2004). Hans-Johann Glock, *A Wittgenstein Dictionary* (Oxford: Basil Blackwell, 1995) provides a useful reference work. Collections of essays include Irving Copi, ed., *Essays on Wittgenstein's "Tractatus"* (New York: Macmillan, 1966); George Pitcher, ed., *Wittgenstein's "Investigations"* (Garden City, NY: Anchor Doubleday, 1966); Peter A. French, Theodore E. Uehling, Jr., and Howard K. Wettstein, eds., *The Wittgenstein Legacy* (Notre Dame, IN: University of Notre Dame Press, 1992); Robert L. Arrington and Johann Glock, eds., *Wittgenstein and Quine* (Oxford: Routledge, 1996); Hans Sluga and David G. Stern, eds., *The Cambridge Companion to Wittgenstein* (Cambridge: Cambridge University Press, 1996); Alice Crary and Rupert Read, eds., *The New Wittgenstein* (London: Routledge, 2000); Robert L. Arrington and Mark Addis, eds., *Wittegenstein and Philosophy of Religion* (London: Routledge, 2001); Naomi Scheman and Peg O'Connor, eds., *Feminist Interpretations of Ludwig Wittgenstein Heidegger* (College Park, PA: Pennsylvania State University Press, 2002); and Meredith Williams, ed., *Wittgenstein's* Philosophical Investigations: *Critical Essays* (Lanham, MD: Rowman & Littlefield, 2006).

TRACTATUS LOGICO-PHILOSOPHICUS (in part)

PREFACE

Perhaps this book will be understood only by someone who has himself already had the thoughts that are expressed in it—or at least similar thoughts.—So it is not a textbook.—Its purpose would be achieved if it gave pleasure to one person who read and understood it.

The book deals with the problems of philosophy, and shows, I believe, that the reason why these problems are posed is that the logic of our language is misunderstood. The whole sense of the book might be summed up in the following words: what can be said at all can be said clearly, and what we cannot talk about we must consign to silence.

Thus the aim of the book is to set a limit to thought, or rather—not to thought, but to the expression of thoughts: for in order to be able to set a limit to thought, we should have to find both sides of the limit thinkable (i.e. we should have to be able to think what cannot be thought).

It will therefore only be in language that the limit can be set, and what lies on the other side of the limit will simply be nonsense.

I do not wish to judge how far my efforts coincide with those of other philosophers. Indeed, what I have written here makes no claim to novelty in detail, and the reason why I give no sources is that it is a matter of indifference to me whether the thoughts that I have had have been anticipated by someone else.

I will only mention that I am indebted to Frege's great works and to the writings of my friend Mr. Bertrand Russell for much of the stimulation of my thoughts.

If this work has any value, it consists in two things: the first is that thoughts are expressed in it, and on this score the better the thoughts are expressed—the more the nail has been hit on the head—the greater will be its value.—Here I am conscious of having fallen a long way short of what is possible. Simply because my powers are too slight for the accomplishment of the task.—May others come and do it better.

On the other hand the *truth* of the thoughts that are here set forth seems to me unassailable and definitive. I therefore believe myself to have found, on all essential points, the final solution of the problems. And if I am not mistaken in this belief, then the second thing in which the value of this work consists is that it shows how little is achieved when these problems are solved.

TRACTATUS LOGICO-PHILOSOPHICUS

1* The world is all that is the case.

1.1 The world is the totality of facts, not of things.

*[The decimal numbers assigned to the individual propositions indicate the logical importance of the propositions, the stress laid on them in my exposition. The propositions *n*.1, *n*.2, *n*.3, etc. are comments on proposition no. *n;* the propositions *n.m*1, *n.m*2, etc. are comments on proposition no. *n.m;* and so on.]

Ludwig Wittgenstein, *Tractatus Logico-Philosophicus,* Translated by D.F. Pears and B.F. McGuiness (London: Routledge & Kegan Paul PLC, 1972). Reprinted by permission of Routledge & Kegan Paul.

1.11 The world is determined by the facts, and by their being *all* the facts.

1.12 For the totality of facts determines what is the case, and also whatever is not the case.

1.13 The facts in logical space are the world.

1.2 The world divides into facts.

1.21 Each item can be the case or not the case while everything else remains the same.

2 What is the case—a fact—is the existence of states of affairs.

2.01 A state of affairs (a state of things) is a combination of objects (things).

2.011 It is essential to things that they should be possible constituents of states of affairs.

2.012 In logic nothing is accidental: if a thing *can* occur in a state of affairs, the possibility of the state of affairs must be written into the thing itself.

2.0121 It would seem to be a sort of accident, if it turned out that a situation would fit a thing that could already exist entirely on its own.

If things can occur in states of affairs, this possibility must be in them from the beginning.

(Nothing in the province of logic can be merely possible. Logic deals with every possibility and all possibilities are its facts.)

Just as we are quite unable to imagine spatial objects outside space or temporal objects outside time, so too there is *no* object that we can imagine excluded from the possibility of combining with others.

If I can imagine objects combined in states of affairs, I cannot imagine them excluded from the *possibility* of such combinations.

2.0122 Things are independent in so far as they can occur in all *possible* situations, but this form of independence is a form of connexion with states of affairs, a form of dependence. (It is impossible for words to appear in two different roles: by themselves, and in propositions.)

2.0123 If I know an object I also know all its possible occurrences in states of affairs.

(Every one of these possibilities must be part of the nature of the object.)

A new possibility cannot be discovered later.

2.01231 If I am to know an object, though I need not know its external properties, I must know all its internal properties.

2.0124 If all objects are given, then at the same time all *possible* states of affairs are also given.

2.013 Each thing is, as it were, in a space of possible states of affairs. This space I can imagine empty, but I cannot imagine the thing without the space.

2.0131 A spatial object must be situated in infinite space. (A spatial point is an argument-place.)

A speck in the visual field, though it need not be red, must have some colour: it is, so to speak, surrounded by colour-space. Tones must have some pitch, objects of the sense of touch *some* degree of hardness, and so on.

2.014 Objects contain the possibility of all situations.

2.0141 The possibility of its occurring in states of affairs is the form of an object.

2.02 Objects are simple.

2.0201 Every statement about complexes can be resolved into a statement about their constituents and into the propositions that describe the complexes completely.

2.021 Objects make up the substance of the world. That is why they cannot be composite.

2.0211 If the world had no substance, then whether a proposition had sense would depend on whether another proposition was true.

2.0212 In that case we could not sketch out any picture of the world (true or false).

2.022 It is obvious that an imagined world, however different it may be from the real one, must have *something*—a form—in common with it.

2.023 Objects are just what constitute this unalterable form.

2.0231 The substance of the world *can* only determine a form, and not any material properties. For it is only by means of propositions that material properties are represented—only by the configuration of objects that they are produced.

2.0232 In a manner of speaking, objects are colourless.

2.0233 If two objects have the same logical form, the only distinction between them, apart from their external properties, is that they are different.

2.02331 Either a thing has properties that nothing else has, in which case we can immediately use a description to distinguish it from the others and refer to it; or, on the other hand, there are several things that have the whole set of their properties in common, in which case it is quite impossible to indicate one of them.

For if there is nothing to distinguish a thing, I cannot distinguish it, since if I do it will be distinguished after all.

2.024 Substance is what subsists independently of what is the case.

2.025 It is form and content.

2.0251 Space, time, and colour (being coloured) are forms of objects.

2.026 There must be objects, if the world is to have an unalterable form.

2.027 Objects, the unalterable, and the subsistent are one and the same.

2.0271 Objects are what is unalterable and subsistent; their configuration is what is changing and unstable.

2.0272 The configuration of objects produces states of affairs.

2.03 In a state of affairs objects fit into one another like the links of a chain.

2.031 In a state of affairs objects stand in a determinate relation to one another.

2.032 The determinate way in which objects are connected in a state of affairs is the structure of the state of affairs.

2.033 Its form is the possibility of its structure.

2.034 The structure of a fact consists of the structures of states of affairs.

2.04 The totality of existing states of affairs is the world.

2.05 The totality of existing states of affairs also determines which states of affairs do not exist.

2.06 The existence and non-existence of states of affairs is reality.

(We also call the existence of states of affairs a positive fact, and their non-existence a negative fact.)

2.061 States of affairs are independent of one another.

2.062 From the existence or non-existence of one state of affairs it is impossible to infer the existence or non-existence of another.

2.063 The sum-total of reality is the world.

2.1 We picture facts to ourselves.

2.11 A picture presents a situation in logical space, the existence and non-existence of states of affairs.

2.12 A picture is a model of reality.

2.13 In a picture objects have the elements of the picture corresponding to them.

2.131 In a picture the elements of the picture are the representatives of objects.

Composition in Yellow, Red, Blue and Black, 1921, by Piet Mondrian (1872–1944). The painter/draftsman Mondrian constructed nonobjective paintings with mathematical precision. The clarity of form and structure, together with the lack of any ornamentation, provides a visual metaphor for the precision and austerity of Wittgenstein's *Tractatus*. (*Giraudon/Art Resource, NY*)

2.14 What constitutes a picture is that its elements are related to one another in a determinate way.

2.141 A picture is a fact.

2.15 The fact that the elements of a picture are related to one another in a determinate way represents that things are related to one another in the same way.

Let us call this connexion of its elements the structure of the picture, and let us call the possibility of this structure the pictorial form of the picture.

2.151 Pictorial form is the possibility that things are related to one another in the same way as the elements of the picture.

2.1511 *That* is how a picture is attached to reality; it reaches right out to it.

2.1512 It is laid against reality like a ruler.

2.15121 Only the end-points of the graduating lines actually *touch* the object that is to be measured.

2.1513 So a picture, conceived in this way, also includes the pictorial relationship, which makes it into a picture.

2.1514 The pictorial relationship consists of the correlations of the picture's elements with things.

2.1515 These correlations are, as it were, the feelers of the picture's elements, with which the picture touches reality.

2.16 If a fact is to be a picture, it must have something in common with what it depicts.

2.161 There must be something identical in a picture and what it depicts, to enable the one to be a picture of the other at all.

2.17 What a picture must have in common with reality, in order to be able to depict it—correctly or incorrectly—in the way it does, is its pictorial form.

2.171 A picture can depict any reality whose form it has.

A spatial picture can depict anything spatial, a coloured one anything coloured, etc.

2.172 A picture cannot, however, depict its pictorial form: it displays it.

2.173 A picture represents its subject from a position outside it. (Its standpoint is its representational form.) That is why a picture represents its subject correctly or incorrectly.

2.174 A picture cannot, however, place itself outside its representational form.

2.18 What any picture, of whatever form, must have in common with reality, in order to be able to depict it—correctly or incorrectly—in any way at all, is logical form, i.e. the form of reality.

2.181 A picture whose pictorial form is logical form is called a logical picture.

2.182 Every picture is *at the same time* a logical one. (On the other hand, not every picture is, for example, a spatial one.)

2.19 Logical pictures can depict the world.

2.2 A picture has logico-pictorial form in common with what it depicts.

2.201 A picture depicts reality by representing a possibility of existence and non-existence of states of affairs.

2.202 A picture represents a possible situation in logical space.

2.203 A picture contains the possibility of the situation that it represents.

2.21 A picture agrees with reality or fails to agree; it is correct or incorrect, true or false.

2.22 What a picture represents it represents independently of its truth or falsity, by means of its pictorial form.

2.221 What a picture represents is its sense.

2.222 The agreement or disagreement of its sense with reality constitutes its truth or falsity.

2.223 In order to tell whether a picture is true or false we must compare it with reality.

2.224 It is impossible to tell from the picture alone whether it is true or false.

2.225 There are no pictures that are true *a priori*.

3 A logical picture of facts is a thought.

3.001 "A state of affairs is thinkable"—this means that we can picture it to ourselves.

3.01 The totality of true thoughts is a picture of the world.

3.02 A thought contains the possibility of the situation of which it is the thought. What is thinkable is possible too.

3.03 Thought can never be of anything illogical, since, if it were, we should have to think illogically.

3.031 It used to be said that God could create anything except what would be contrary to the laws of logic.—The reason being that we could not say what an "illogical" world would look like.

3.032 It is as impossible to represent in language anything that "contradicts logic" as it is in geometry to represent by its co-ordinates a figure that contradicts the laws of space, or to give the co-ordinates of a point that does not exist.

3.0321 Though a state of affairs that would contravene the laws of physics can be represented by us spatially, one that would contravene the laws of geometry cannot.

3.04 If a thought were correct , it would be a thought whose possibility ensured its truth.

3.05 *A priori* knowledge that a thought was true would be possible only if its truth were recognizable from the thought itself (without anything to compare it with).

3.1 In a proposition a thought finds an expression that can be perceived by the senses.

3.11 We use the perceptible sign of a proposition (spoken or written, etc.) as a projection of a possible situation.

The method of projection is to think out the sense of the proposition.

3.12 I call the sign with which we express a thought a propositional sign.—And a proposition is a propositional sign in its projective relation to the world.

3.13 A proposition includes all that the projection includes, but not what is projected.

Therefore, though what is projected is not itself included, its possibility is.

A proposition does not actually contain its sense, but does contain the possibility of expressing it.

("The content of a proposition" means the content of a proposition that has sense.)

A proposition contains the form, but not the content, of its sense.

3.14 What constitutes a propositional sign is that in it its elements (the words) stand in a determinate relation to one another.

A propositional sign is a fact.

3.141 A proposition is not a medley of words.—(Just as a theme in music is not a medley of notes.)

A proposition is articulated.

3.142 Only facts can express a sense, a set of names cannot.

3.143 Although a propositional sign is a fact, this is obscured by the usual form of expression in writing or print.

For in a printed proposition, for example, no essential difference is apparent between a propositional sign and a word.

(That is what made it possible for Frege to call a proposition a composite name.)

3.1431 The essence of a propositional sign is very clearly seen if we imagine one composed of spatial objects (such as tables, chairs, and books) instead of written signs.

Then the spatial arrangement of these things will express the sense of the proposition.

4 A thought is a proposition with a sense.

4.06 A proposition can be true or false only in virtue of being a picture of reality.

4.1 Propositions represent the existence and and non-existence of states of affairs.

5 A proposition is a truth-function of elementary propositions. (An elementary proposition is a truth-function of itself).

5.6 *The limits of my language* mean the limits of my world.

6.4 All propositions are of equal value.

6.41 The sense of the world must lie outside the world. In the world everything is as it is, and everything happens as it does happen: in it no value exists—and if it did, it would have no value.

If there is any value that does have value, it must lie outside the whole sphere of what happens and is the case. For all that happens and is the case is accidental.

What makes it non-accidental cannot lie *within* the world, since if it did it would itself be accidental.

It must lie outside the world.

6.42 And so it is impossible for there to be propositions of ethics.

Propositions can express nothing of what is higher.

6.421 It is clear that ethics cannot be put into words. Ethics is transcendental.

(Ethics and aesthetics are one and the same.)

6.422 When an ethical law of the form, "Thou shalt . . . ," is laid down, one's first thought is, "And what if I do not do it?" It is clear, however, that ethics has nothing to do with punishment and reward in the usual sense of the terms. So our question about the consequences of an action must be unimportant.—At least those consequences should not be events. For there must be something right about the question we posed. There must indeed be some kind of ethical reward and ethical punishment, but they must reside in the action itself.

(And it is also clear that the reward must be something pleasant and the punishment something unpleasant.)

6.423 It is impossible to speak about the will in so far as it is the subject of ethical attributes.

And the will as a phenomenon is of interest only to psychology.

6.43 If good or bad acts of will do alter the world, it can only be the limits of the world that they alter, not the facts, not what can be expressed by means of language.

In short their effect must be that it becomes an altogether different world. It must, so to speak, wax and wane as a whole.

The world of the happy man is a different one from that of the unhappy man.

6.431 So too at death the world does not alter, but comes to an end.

6.4311 Death is not an event in life: we do not live to experience death.

If we take eternity to mean not infinite temporal duration but timelessness, then eternal life belongs to those who live in the present.

Our life has no end in just the way in which our visual field has no limits.

6.4312 Not only is there no guarantee of the temporal immortality of the human soul, that is to say of its eternal survival after death; but, in any case, this assumption completely fails to accomplish the purpose for which it has always been intended. Or is some riddle solved by my surviving for ever? Is not this eternal life itself as much of a riddle as our present life? The solution of the riddle of life in space and time lies *outside* space and time.

(It is certainly not the solution of any problems of natural science that is required.)

6.432 *How* things are in the world is a matter of complete indifference for what is higher. God does not reveal himself *in* the world.

6.4321 The facts all contribute only to setting the problem, not to its solution.

6.44 It is not *how* things are in the world that is mystical, but *that* it exists.

6.45 To view the world *sub specie aeterni* is to view it as a whole—a limited whole.

Feeling the world as a limited whole—it is this that is mystical.

6.5 When the answer cannot be put into words, neither can the question be put into words.

The riddle does not exist.

If a question can be framed at all, it is also *possible* to answer it.

6.51 Scepticism is *not* irrefutable, but obviously nonsensical, when it tries to raise doubts where no questions can be asked.

For doubt can exist only where a question exists, a question only where an answer exists, and an answer only where something *can be said.*

6.52 We feel that even when *all possible* scientific questions have been answered, the problems of life remain completely untouched. Of course there are then no questions left, and this itself is the answer.

6.521 The solution of the problem of life is seen in the vanishing of the problem.

(Is not this the reason why those who have found after a long period of doubt that the sense of life became clear to them have then been unable to say what constituted that sense?)

6.522 There are, indeed, things that cannot be put into words. They *make themselves manifest.* They are what is mystical.

6.53 The correct method in philosophy would really be the following: to say nothing except what can be said, i.e. propositions of natural science—i.e. something that has nothing to do with philosophy—and then, whenever someone else wanted to say something metaphysical, to demonstrate to him that he had failed to give a meaning to certain signs in his propositions. Although it would not be satisfying to the other person—he would not have the feeling that we were teaching him philosophy—*this* method would be the only strictly correct one.

6.54 My propositions serve as elucidations in the following way: anyone who understands me eventually recognizes them as nonsensical, when he has used them—as steps—to climb up beyond them. (He must, so to speak, throw away the ladder after he has climbed up it.)

He must transcend these propositions, and then he will see the world aright.

7 What we cannot speak about we must consign to silence.

PHILOSOPHICAL INVESTIGATIONS (in part)

1. "When they (my elders) named some object, and accordingly moved towards something, I saw this and I grasped that the thing was called by the sound they uttered when they meant to point it out. Their intention was shewn by their bodily movements, as it were the natural language of all peoples: the expression of the face, the play of the eyes, the movement of other parts of the body, and the tone of voice which expresses our state of mind in seeking, having, rejecting, or avoiding something. Thus, as I heard words repeatedly used in their proper places in various sentences, I gradually learnt to understand what objects they signifed; and after I had trained my mouth to form these signs, I used them to express my own desires" (Augustine, *Confessions,* I. 8).

These words, it seems to me, give us a particular picture of the essence of human language. It is this: the individual words in language name objects—sentences are combinations of such names. In this picture of language we find the roots of the following idea: Every word has a meaning. This meaning is correlated with the word. It is the object for which the word stands.

Augustine does not speak of there being any difference between kinds of word. If you describe the learning of language in this way you are, I believe, thinking primarily of nouns like "table," "chair," "bread," and of people's names, and only secondarily of the names of certain actions and properties; and of the remaining kinds of word as something that will take care of itself.

Now think of the following use of language: I send someone shopping. I give him a slip marked "five red apples." He takes the slip to the shopkeeper, who opens the drawer marked "apples"; then he looks up the word "red" in a table and finds a colour

Reprinted with permission of Blackwell Publisher from Ludwig Wittgenstein: *Philosophical Investigations,* 3rd edition, 1–47, 65–71, 241, 257–258, 305, 309, translated by G.E.M. Anscombe.

sample opposite it; then he says the series of cardinal numbers—I assume that he knows them by heart—up to the word "five" and for each number he takes an apple of the same colour as the sample out of the drawer. It is in this and similar ways that one operates with words. "But how does he know where and how he is to look up the word 'red' and what he is to do with the word 'five'?" Well, I assume that he acts as I have described. Explanations come to an end somewhere.—But what is the meaning of the word "five"?—No such thing was in question here, only how the word "five" is used.

2. That philosophical concept of meaning has its place in a primitive idea of the way language functions. But one can also say that it is the idea of a language more primitive than ours.

Let us imagine a language for which the description given by Augustine is right. The language is meant to serve for communication between a builder A and an assistant B. A is building with building-stones: there are blocks, pillars, slabs and beams. B has to pass the stones, and that in the order in which A needs them. For this purpose they use a language consisting of the words "block," "pillar," "slab," "beam." A calls them out;—B brings the stone which he has learnt to bring at such-and-such a call—Conceive this as a complete primitive language.

3. Augustine, we might say, does describe a system of communication; only not everything that we call language is this system. And one has to say this in many cases where the question arises "Is this an appropriate description or not?" The answer is: "Yes, it is appropriate, but only for this narrowly circumscribed region, not for the whole of what you were claiming to describe."

It is as if someone were to say: "A game consists in moving objects about on a surface according to certain rules . . ."—and we replied: You seem to be thinking of board games, but there are others. You can make your definition correct by expressly restricting it to those games.

4. Imagine a script in which the letters were used to stand for sounds, and also as signs of emphasis and punctuation. (A script can be conceived as a language for describing sound-patterns.) Now imagine someone interpreting that script as if there were simply a correspondence of letters to sounds and as if the letters had not also completely different functions. Augustine's conception of language is like such an oversimple conception of the script.

5. If we look at the example in ¶1, we may perhaps get an inkling how much this general notion of the meaning of a word surrounds the working of language with a haze which makes clear vision impossible. It disperses the fog to study the phenomena of language in primitive kinds of application in which one can command a clear view of the aim and functioning of the words.

A child uses such primitive forms of language when it learns to talk. Here the teaching of language is not explanation, but training.

6. We could imagine that the language of ¶2 was the *whole* language of A and B; even the whole language of a tribe. The children are brought up to perform *these* actions, to use these words as they do so, and to react in *this* way to the words of others.

An important part of the training will consist in the teacher's pointing to the objects, directing the child's attention to them, and at the same time uttering a word; for instance, the word "slab" as he points to that shape. (I do not want to call this "ostensive definition," because the child cannot as yet ask what the name is. I will call it "ostensive teaching of words." I say that it will form an important part of the training, because it is so with human beings; not because it could not be imagined otherwise.) This ostensive teaching of words can be said to establish an association between the word and the thing. But what does this mean? Well, it may mean various things; but one very likely thinks first of all that a picture of the object comes before the child's mind when it hears the word. But now, if this does happen—is it the purpose of the word?—Yes, it *may* be the purpose.—I can imagine such a use of words (of series of sounds). (Uttering a word is like striking a note on the keyboard of the imagination.) But in the language of ¶2 it is *not* the purpose of the words to evoke images. (It may, of course, be discovered that that helps to attain the actual purpose.)

But if the ostensive teaching has this effect,—am I to say that it effects an understanding of the word? Don't you understand the call "Slab!" if you act upon it in such-and-such a way?—Doubtless the ostensive teaching helped to bring this about; but only together with a particular training. With different training the same ostensive teaching of these words would have effected a quite different understanding.

"I set the brake up by connecting up rod and lever."—Yes, given the whole of the rest of the mechanism. Only in conjunction with that is it a brake-lever, and separated from its support it is not even a lever; it may be anything, or nothing.

7. In the practice of the use of language (2) one party calls out the words, the other acts on them. In instruction in the language the following process will occur: the learner *names* the objects; that is, he utters the word when the teacher points to the stone.—And there will be this still simpler exercise: the pupil repeats the words after the teacher—both of these being processes resembling language.

We can also think of the whole process of using words in (2) as one of those games by means of which children learn their native language. I will call these games "language-games" and will sometimes speak of a primitive language as a language-game.

And the processes of naming the stones and of repeating words after someone might also be called language-games. Think of much of the use of words in games like ring-a-ring-a-roses.

I shall also call the whole, consisting of language and the actions into which it is woven, the "language-game."

8. Let us now look at an expansion of language (2). Besides the four words "block," "pillar," etc., let it contain a series of words used as the shopkeeper in (I) used the numerals (it can be the series of letters of the alphabet); further, let there be two words, which may as well be "there" and "this" (because this roughly indicates their purpose), that are used in connexion with a pointing gesture; and finally a number of colour samples. A gives an order like: "d—slab—there." At the same time he shews the assistant a colour sample, and when he says "there" he points to a place on the building site. From the stock of slabs B takes one for each letter of the alphabet up to "d," of the same colour as the sample, and brings them to the place indicated by A.—On other occasions A gives the order "this—there." At "this" he points to a building stone. And so on.

9. When a child learns this language, it has to learn the series of 'numerals' a, b, c, . . . by heart. And it has to learn their use.—Will this training include ostensive teaching of the words?—Well, people will, for example, point to slabs and count: "a, b, c slabs."—Something more like the ostensive teaching of the words "block," "pillar," etc. would be the ostensive teaching of numerals that serve not to count but to refer to groups of objects that can be taken in at a glance. Children do learn the use of the first five or six cardinal numerals in this way.

Are "there" and "this" also taught ostensively?—Imagine how one might perhaps teach their use. One will point to places and things—but in this case the pointing occurs in the *use* of the words too and not merely in learning the use.—

10. Now what do the words of this language *signify?*—What is supposed to shew what they signify, if not the kind of use they have? And we have already described that. So we are asking for the expression "This word signifies this" to be made a part of the description. In other words the description ought to take the form: "The word . . . signifies . . ."

Of course, one can reduce the description of the use of the word "slab" to the statement that this word signifies this object. This will be done when, for example, it is merely a matter of removing the mistaken idea that the word "slab" refers to the shape of building-stone that we in fact call a "block"— but the kind of '*referring*' this is, that is to say the use of these words for the rest, is already known.

Equally one can say that the signs "a," "b," etc. signify numbers; when for example this removes the mistaken idea that "a," "b," "c," play the part actually played in language by "block," "slab," "pillar." And one can also say that "c" means this number and not that one; when for example this serves to explain that the letters are to be used in the order a, b, c, d, etc. and not in the order a, b, d, c.

But assimilating the descriptions of the uses of words in this way cannot make the uses themselves any more like one another. For, as we see, they are absolutely unlike.

11. Think of the tools in a toolbox: there is a hammer, pliers, a saw, a screw-driver, a rule, a glue-pot, glue, nails and screws.—The functions of words are as diverse as the functions of these objects. (And in both cases there are similarities.)

Of course, what confuses us is the uniform appearance of words when we hear them spoken or meet them in script and print. For their *application* is not presented to us so clearly. Especially when we are doing philosophy!

12. It is like looking into the cabin of a locomotive. We see handles all looking more or less alike. (Naturally, since they are all supposed to be handled.) But one is the handle of a crank which can be moved continuously (it regulates the opening of a valve); another is the handle of a switch, which has only two effective positions, it is either off or on; a third is the handle of a brake-lever, the harder one pulls on it, the harder it brakes; a fourth, the handle of a pump: it has an effect only so long as it is moved to and fro.

13. When we say: "Every word in language signifies something" we have so far said *nothing whatever;* unless we have explained exactly what distinction we wish to make. (It might be, of course, that we wanted to distinguish the words of language [8] from words 'without meaning' such as occur in Lewis Carroll's poems, or words like "Lilliburlero" in songs.)

14. Imagine someone's saying: "*All* tools serve to modify something. Thus the hammer modifies the position of the nail, the saw the shape of the board, and so on."— And what is modified by the rule, the glue-pot, the nails?—"Our knowledge of a thing's length, the temperature of the glue, and the solidity of the box." Would anything be gained by this assimilation of expressions?—

15. The word "to signify" is perhaps used in the most straightforward way when the object signified is marked with the sign. Suppose that the tools A uses in building bear certain marks. When A shews his assistant such a mark, he brings the tool that has that mark on it.

It is in this and more or less similar ways that a name means and is given to a thing.—It will often prove useful in philosophy to say to ourselves: naming something is like attaching a label to a thing.

16. What about the colour samples that A shews to B: are they part of the *language?* Well, it is as you please. They do not belong among the words; yet when I say to someone: "Pronounce the word 'the'," you will count the second "the" as part

of the sentence. Yet it has a role just like that of a colour-sample in language-game (8); that is, it is a sample of what the other is meant to say.

It is most natural, and causes least confusion, to reckon the samples among the instruments of the language.

(Remark on the reflexive pronoun "*this* sentence.")

17. It will be possible to say: In language (8) we have different kinds *of word.* For the functions of the word "slab" and the word "block" are more alike than those of "slab" and "d." But how we group words into kinds will depend on the aim of the classification,—and on our own inclination.

Think of the different points of view from which one can classify tools or chessmen.

18. Do not be troubled by the fact that languages (2) and (8) consist only of orders. If you want to say that this shews them to be incomplete, ask yourself whether our language is complete;—whether it was so before the symbolism of chemistry and the notation of the infinitesimal calculus were incorporated in it; for these are, so to speak, suburbs of our language. (And how many houses or streets does it take before a town begins to be a town?) Our language can be seen as an ancient city: a maze of little streets and squares, of old and new houses, and of houses with additions from various periods; and this surrounded by a multitude of new boroughs with straight regular streets and uniform houses.

19. It is easy to imagine a language consisting only of orders and reports in battle.—Or a language consisting only of questions and expressions for answering yes and no. And innumerable others.—And to imagine a language means to imagine a form of life.

But what about this: is the call "Slab!" in example (2) a sentence or a word?—If a word, surely it has not the same meaning as the like-sounding word of our ordinary language, for in ¶2 it is a call. But if a sentence, it is surely not the elliptical sentence: "Slab!" of our language. As far as the first question goes you can call "Slab!" a word and also a sentence; perhaps it could be appropriately called a 'degenerate sentence' (as one speaks of a degenerate hyperbola); in fact it is our 'elliptical' sentence.—But that is surely only a shortened form of the sentence "Bring me a slab," and there is no such sentence in example (2).—But why should I not on the contrary have called the sentence "Bring me a slab" a *lengthening* of the sentence "Slab!"?—Because if you shout "Slab!" you really mean: "Bring me a slab."—But how do you do this: how do you mean that while you say "Slab!"? Do you say the unshortened sentence to yourself? And why should I translate the call "Slab!" into a different expression in order to say what someone means by it? And if they mean the same thing—why should I not say: "When he says 'Slab!' he means 'Slab!' "? Again, if you can mean "Bring me the slab," why should you not be able to mean "Slab!"? But when I call "Slab!" then what I want is, *that he should bring me a slab!*—Certainly, but does 'wanting this' consist in thinking in some form or other a different sentence from the one you utter?—

20. But now it looks as if when someone says "Bring me a slab" he could mean this expression as *one* long word corresponding to the single word "Slab!" Then can one mean it sometimes as one word and sometimes as four? And how does one usually mean it? I think we shall be inclined to say: we mean the sentence as four words when we use it in contrast with other sentences such as "*Hand* me a slab," "Bring *him* a slab," "Bring *two* slabs," etc.; that is, in contrast with sentences containing the separate words of our command in other combinations.—But what does using one sentence in contrast with others consist in? Do the others, perhaps, hover before one's mind? *All* of them? And *while* one is saying the one sentence, or before, or afterwards?—No. Even if such an explanation rather tempts us, we need only think for a moment of what actually happens in order to see that we are going astray here. We say that we use the command in

contrast with other sentences because *our language* contains the possibility of those other sentences. Someone who did not understand our language, a foreigner, who had fairly often heard someone giving the order: "Bring me a slab!" might believe that this whole series of sounds was one word corresponding perhaps to the word for "building-stone" in his language. If he himself had then given this order perhaps he would have pronounced it differently, and we should say: he pronounces it so oddly because he takes it for a *single* word.—But then, is there not also something different going on in him when he pronounces it,—something corresponding to the fact that he conceives the sentence as a single word?—Either the same thing may go on in him, or something different. For what goes on in you when you give such an order? Are you conscious of its consisting of four words *while* you are uttering it? Of course you have a mastery of this language—which contains those other sentences as well—but is this having a mastery something that *happens* while you are uttering the sentence?—And I have admitted that the foreigner will probably pronounce a sentence differently if he conceives it differently; but what we call his wrong conception *need* not lie in anything that accompanies the utterance of the command.

The sentence is 'elliptical,' not because it leaves out something that we think when we utter it, but because it is shortened—in comparison with a particular paradigm of our grammar.—Of course one might object here: "You grant that the shortened and the unshortened sentence have the same sense.—What is this sense, then? Isn't there a verbal expression for this sense?" But doesn't the fact that sentences have the same sense consist in their having the same *use?*—(In Russian one says "stone red" instead of "the stone is red"; do they feel the copula to be missing in the sense, or attach it in *thought?*)

21. Imagine a language-game in which A asks and B reports the number of slabs or blocks in a pile, or the colours and shapes of the building-stones that are stacked in such-and-such a place.—Such a report might run: "Five slabs." Now what is the difference between the report or statement "Five slabs" and the order "Five slabs!"?—Well, it is the part which uttering these words plays in the language-game. No doubt the tone of voice and the look with which they are uttered, and much else besides, will also be different. But we could also imagine the tone's being the same—for an order and a report can be spoken in a *variety* of tones of voice and with various expressions of face—the difference being only in the application. (Of course, we might use the words "statement" and "command" to stand for grammatical forms of sentence and intonations; we do in fact call "Isn't the weather glorious to-day?" a question, although it is used as a statement.) We could imagine a language in which *all* statements had the form and tone of rhetorical questions; or every command the form of the question "Would you like to . . .?" Perhaps it will then be said: "What he says has the form of a question but is really a command,"—that is, has the function of a command in the technique of using the language. (Similarly one says "You will do this" not as a prophecy but as a command. What makes it the one or the other?)

22. Frege's idea that every assertion contains an assumption, which is the thing that is asserted, really rests on the possibility found in our language of writing every statement in the form: "It is asserted that such-and-such is the case."—But "that such-and-such is the case" is not a sentence in our language—so far it is not a *move* in the language-game. And if I write, not "It is asserted that . . . . ," but "It is asserted: such-and-such is the case," the words "It is asserted" simply become superfluous.

We might very well also write every statement in the form of a question followed by a "Yes"; for instance: "Is it raining? Yes!" Would this shew that every statement contained a question?

Of course we have the right to use an assertion sign in contrast with a question-mark, for example, or if we want to distinguish an assertion from a fiction or a supposition. It is only a mistake if one thinks that the assertion consists of two actions, entertaining and asserting (assigning the truth-value, or something of the kind), and that in performing these actions we follow the propositional sign roughly as we sing from the musical score. Reading the written sentence loud or soft is indeed comparable with singing from a musical score, but '*meaning*' (thinking) the sentence that is read is not.

Frege's assertion sign marks the *beginning of the sentence.* Thus its function is like that of the full-stop. It distinguishes the whole period from a clause *within* the period. If I hear someone say "it's raining" but do not know whether I have heard the beginning and end of the period, so far this sentence does not serve to tell me anything.

23. But how many kinds of sentences are there? Say assertion, question, and command?—There are *countless* kinds: countless different kinds of use of what we call "symbols," "words," "sentences." And this multiplicity is not something fixed, given once for all; but new types of language, new language-games, as we may say, come into existence, and others become obsolete and get forgotten. (We can get a *rough picture* of this from the changes in mathematics.)

Here the term "language-*game*" is meant to bring into prominence the fact that the *speaking* of language is part of an activity, or of a form of life.

Review the multiplicity of language-games in the following examples, and in others:

Giving orders, and obeying them—
Describing the appearance of an object, or giving its measurements—
Constructing an object from a description (a drawing)—
Reporting an event—
Speculating about an event—
Forming and testing a hypothesis—
Presenting the results of an experiment in tables and diagrams—
Making up a story; and reading it—
Play-acting—
Singing catches—
Guessing riddles—
Making a joke; telling it—
Solving a problem in practical arithmetic—
Translating from one language into another—
Asking, thanking, cursing, greeting, praying.

Imagine a picture representing a boxer in a particular stance. Now, this picture can be used to tell someone how he should stand, should hold himself; or how he should not hold himself; or how a particular man did stand in such-and-such a place; and so on. One might (using the language of chemistry) call this picture a proposition-radical. This will be how Frege thought of the "assumption." [Note added by Wittgenstein.]

—It is interesting to compare the multiplicity of the tools in language and of the ways they are used, the multiplicity of kinds of word and sentence, with what logicians have said about the structure of language. (Including the author of the *Tractatus Logico-Philosophicus.*)

24. If you do not keep the multiplicity of language-games in view you will perhaps be inclined to ask questions like: "What is a question?"—Is it the statement that I do not know such-and-such, or the statement that I wish the other person would tell me . . .? Or is it the description of my mental state of uncertainty?—And is the cry "Help!" such a description?

Think how many different kinds of thing are called "description": description of a body's position by means of its co-ordinates; description of a facial expression; description of a sensation of touch; of a mood.

Of course it is possible to substitute the form of statement or description for the usual form of question: "I want to know whether . . ." or "I am in doubt whether . . ."—but this does not bring the different language-games any closer together.

The significance of such possibilities of transformation, for example of turning all statements into sentences beginning "I think" or "I believe" (and thus, as it were, into descriptions of my inner life) will become clearer in another place. (Solipsism.)

25. It is sometimes said that animals do not talk because they lack the mental capacity. And this means: "they do not think, and that is why they do not talk." But—they simply do not talk. Or to put it better: they do not use language—if we except the most primitive forms of language.—Commanding, questioning, recounting, chatting, are as much a part of our natural history as walking, eating, drinking, playing.

26. One thinks that learning language consists in giving names to objects. Viz., to human beings, to shapes, to colours, to pains, to moods, to numbers, etc. To repeat—naming is something like attaching a label to a thing. One can say that this is preparatory to the use of a word. But *what* is it a preparation *for?*

27. "We name things and then we can talk about them: can refer to them in talk."—As if what we did next were given with the mere act of naming. As if there were only one thing called "talking about a thing." Whereas in fact we do the most various things with our sentences. Think of exclamations alone, with their completely different functions.

Water!
Away!
Ow!
Help!
Fine!
No!

Are you inclined still to call these words "names of objects"?

In languages (2) and (8) there was no such thing as asking something's name. This, with its correlate, ostensive definition, is, we might say, a language-game on its own. That is really to say: we are brought up, trained, to ask: "What is that called?"—upon which the name is given. And there is also a language-game of inventing a name for something, and hence of saying, "This is . . . ." and then using the new name. (Thus, for example, children give names to their dolls and then talk about them and to them. Think in this connexion how singular is the use of a person's name to *call* him!)

28. Now one can ostensively define a proper name, the name of a colour, the name of a material, a numeral, the name of a point of the compass and so on. The definition of the number two, "That is called 'two'"—pointing to two nuts—is perfectly exact.—But how can two be defined like that? The person one gives the definition to doesn't know what one wants to call "two"; he will suppose that "two" is the name given to *this* group

of nuts!—He *may* suppose this; but perhaps he does not. He might make the opposite mistake; when I want to assign a name to this group of nuts, he might understand it as a numeral. And he might equally well take the name of a person, of which I give an ostensive definition, as that of a colour, of a race, or even of a point of the compass. That is to say: an ostensive definition can be variously interpreted in *every* case.

29. Perhaps you say: two can only be ostensively defined in *this* way: "This *number* is called 'two.' " For the word "number" here shews what place in language, in grammar, we assign to the word. But this means that the word "number" must be explained before the ostensive definition can be understood.—The word "number" in the definition does indeed shew this place; does shew the post at which we station the word. And we can prevent misunderstandings by saying: "This *colour* is called so-and-so," "This *length* is called so-and-so," and so on. That is to say: misunderstandings are sometimes averted in this way. But is there only *one* way of taking the word "colour" or "length"?—Well, they just need defining.—Defining, then, by means of other words! And what about the last definition in this chain? (Do not say: "There isn't a 'last' definition." That is just as if you chose to say: "There isn't a last house in this road; one can always build an additional one.")

Whether the word "number" is necessary in the ostensive definition depends on whether without it the other person takes the definition otherwise than I wish. And that will depend on the circumstances under which it is given, and on the person I give it to.

And how he 'takes' the definition is seen in the use that he makes of the word defined.

30. So one might say: the ostensive definition explains the use—the meaning—of the word when the overall role of the word in language is clear. Thus if I know that someone means to explain a colour-word to me the ostensive definition "That is called 'sepia' " will help me to understand the word.—And you can say this, so long as you do not forget that all sorts of problems attach to the words "to know" or "to be clear."

One has already to know (or be able to do) something in order to be capable of asking a thing's name. But what does one have to know?

Could one define the word "red" by pointing to something that was *not red?* That would be as if one were supposed to explain the word "*modest*" to someone whose English was weak, and one pointed to an arrogant man and said "That man is *not* modest." That it is ambiguous is no argument against such a method of definition. Any definition can be misunderstood.

But it might well be asked: are we still to call this "definition"?—For, of course, even if it has the same practical consequences, the same *effect* on the learner, it plays a different part in the calculus from what we ordinarily call "ostensive definition" of the word "red." [Note added by Wittgenstein.]

---

31. When one shews someone the king in chess and says: "This is the king," this does not tell him the use of this piece—unless he already knows the rules of the game up to this last point: the shape of the king. You could imagine his having learnt the rules of the game without ever having been shewn an actual piece. The shape of the chessman corresponds here to the sound or shape of a word.

One can also imagine someone's having learnt the game without ever learning or formulating rules. He might have learnt quite simple board-games first, by watching, and have progressed to more and more complicated ones. He too might be given the explanation "This is the king,"—if, for instance, he were being shewn chessmen of a shape he was not used to. This explanation again only tells him the use of the piece because, as we might say, the place for it was already prepared. Or even: we shall only say that it tells him the use, if the place is already prepared. And in this case it is so, not because the person to whom we give the explanation already knows rules, but because in another sense he is already master of a game.

Consider this further case: I am explaining chess to someone; and I begin by pointing to a chessman and saying: "This is the king; it can move like this, . . . and so on."—In this case we shall say: the words "This is the king" (or "This is called the 'king'") are a definition only if the learner already 'knows what a piece in a game is.' That is, if he has already played other games, or has watched other people playing 'and understood'—*and similar things.* Further, only under these conditions will he be able to ask relevantly in the course of learning the game: "What do you call this?"—that is, this piece in a game.

We may say: only someone who already knows how to do something with it can significantly ask a name.

And we can imagine the person who is asked replying: "Settle the name yourself"—and now the one who asked would have to manage everything for himself.

32. Someone coming into a strange country will sometimes learn the language of the inhabitants from ostensive definitions that they give him; and he will often have to guess the meaning of these definitions; and will guess sometimes right, sometimes wrong.

And now, I think, we can say: Augustine describes the learning of human language as if the child came into a strange country and did not understand the language of the country; that is, as if it already had a language, only not this one. Or again: as if the child could already *think,* only not yet speak. And "think" would here mean something like "talk to itself."

33. Suppose, however, someone were to object: "It is not true that you must already be master of a language in order to understand an ostensive definition: all you need—of course I—is to know or guess what the person giving the explanation is pointing to. That is, whether for example to the shape of the object, or to its colour, or to its number, and so on." And what does 'pointing to the shape,' 'pointing to the colour' consist in? Point to a piece of paper.—And now point to its shape—now to its colour—now to its number (that sounds queer).—How did you do it?—You will say that you 'meant' a different thing each time you pointed. And if I ask how that is done, you will say you concentrated your attention on the colour, the shape, etc. But I ask again: how is *that* done?

Suppose someone points to a vase and says "Look at that marvelous blue—the shape isn't the point."—Or: "Look at the marvelous shape—the colour doesn't matter." Without doubt you will do something *different* when you act upon these two invitations. But do you always do the *same* thing when you direct your attention to the colour? Imagine various different cases. To indicate a few:

"Is this blue the same as the blue over there? Do you see any difference?"—

You are mixing paint and you say "It's hard to get the blue of this sky."

"It's turning fine, you can already see blue sky again."

"Look what different effects these two blues have."

"Do you see the blue book over there? Bring it here."

"This blue signal-light means. . . ."

"What's this blue called?—Is it 'indigo'?"

You sometimes attend to the colour by putting your hand up to keep the outline from view; or by not looking at the outline of the thing; sometimes by staring at the object and trying to remember where you saw that colour before.

You attend to the shape, sometimes by tracing it, sometimes by screwing up your eyes so as not to see the colour clearly, and in many other ways. I want to say: This is the sort of thing that happens while one 'directs one's attention to this or that.' But it isn't these things by themselves that make us say someone is attending to the shape, the colour, and so on. Just as a move in chess doesn't consist simply in moving a piece in such-and-such a way on the board—nor yet in one's thoughts and feelings as one makes the move: but in the circumstances that we call "playing a game of chess," "solving a chess problem," and so on.

34. But suppose someone said: "I always do the same thing when I attend to the shape: my eye follows the outline and I feel. . . ." And suppose this person to give someone else the ostensive definition "That is called a 'circle,'" pointing to a circular object and having all these experiences cannot his hearer still interpret the definition differently, even though he sees the other's eyes following the outline, and even though he feels what the other feels? That is to say: this 'interpretation' may also consist in how he now makes use of the word; in what he points to, for example, when told: "Point to a circle."—For neither the expression "to intend the definition in such-and-such a way" nor the expression "to interpret the definition in such-and-such a way" stands for a process which accompanies the giving and hearing of the definition.

35. There are, of course, what can be called "characteristic experiences" of pointing to (e.g.) the shape. For example, following the outline with one's finger or with one's eyes as one points.—But *this* does not happen in all cases in which I 'mean the shape,' and no more does any other one characteristic process occur in all these cases.—Besides, even if something of the sort did recur in all cases, it would still depend on the circumstances—that is, on what happened before and after the pointing—whether we should say "He pointed to the shape and not to the colour."

For the words "to point to the shape," "to mean the shape," and so on, are not used in the same way as *these:* "to point to this book (not to that one)," "to point to the chair, not to the table," and so on.—Only think how differently we *learn* the use of the words "to point to this thing," "to point to that thing," and on the other hand "to point to the colour, not the shape," "to mean the colour," and so on.

To repeat: in certain cases, especially when one points 'to the shape' or 'to the number' there are characteristic experiences and ways of pointing—'characteristic' because they recur often (not always) when shape or number are 'meant.' But do you also know of an experience characteristic of pointing to a piece in a game *as a piece in a game?* All the same one can say: "I mean that this *piece* is called the 'king,' not this particular bit of wood I am pointing to." (Recognizing, wishing, remembering, etc.)

36. And we do here what we do in a host of similar cases: because we cannot specify any *one* bodily action which we call pointing to the shape (as opposed, for example, to the colour), we say that a *spiritual* [mental, intellectual] activity corresponds to these words.

Where our language suggests a body and there is none: there, we should like to say, is a *spirit.*

37. What is the relation between name and thing named?—Well, what is it? Look at language-game (2) or at another one: there you can see the sort of thing this relation consists in. This relation may also consist, among many other things, in the fact that hearing the name calls before our mind the picture of what is named; and it also consists, among other things, in the name's being written on the thing named or being pronounced when that thing is pointed at.

38. But what, for example, is the word "this" the name of in language-game (8) or the word "that" in the ostensive definition "that is called. . . ."?—If you do not want to produce confusion you will do best not to call these words names at all.—Yet, strange to say, the word "this" has been called the only *genuine* name; so that anything else we call a name was one only in an inexact, approximate sense.

This queer conception springs from a tendency to sublime the logic of our language—as one might put it. The proper answer to it is: we call very different things "names"; the word "name" is used to characterize many different kinds of use of a word, related to one another in many different ways;—but the kind of use that "this" has is not among them.

What is it to mean the words "*That* is blue" at one time as a statement about the object one is pointing to—at another as an explanation of the word "blue"? Well, in the second case one really means "That is called 'blue.'"—Then can one at one time mean the word "is" as "is called" and the word "blue" as "'blue,'" and another time mean "is" really as "is"?

It is also possible for someone to get an explanation of the words out of what was intended as a piece of information. [Marginal note: Here lurks a crucial superstition.]

Can I say "bububu" and mean "If it doesn't rain I shall go for a walk"?—It is only in a language that I can mean something by something. This shews clearly that the grammar of "to mean" is not like that of the expression "to imagine" and the like. [Note added by Wittgenstein.]

It is quite true that, in giving an ostensive definition for instance, we often point to the object named and say the name. And similarly, in giving an ostensive definition for instance, we say the word "this" while pointing to a thing. And also the word "this" and a name often occupy the same position in a sentence. But it is precisely characteristic of a name that it is defined by means of the demonstrative expression "That is N" (or "That is called 'N'"). But do we also give the definitions: "That is called 'this,'" or "This is called 'this'"?

This is connected with the conception of naming as, so to speak, an occult process. Naming appears as a *queer* connexion of a word with an object.—And you really get such a queer connexion when the philosopher tries to bring out *the* relation between name and thing by staring at an object in front of him and repeating a name or even the word "this" innumerable times. For philosophical problems arise when language *goes on holiday.* And *here* we may indeed fancy naming to be some remarkable act of mind, as it were a baptism of an object. And we can also say the word "this" *to* the object, as it were *address* the object as "this"—a queer use of this word, which doubtless only occurs in doing philosophy.

39. But why does it occur to one to want to make precisely this word into a name, when it evidently is *not* a name?—That is just the reason. For one is tempted to make an objection against what is ordinarily called a name. It can be put like this: *a name ought really to signify a simple.* And for this one might perhaps give the following reasons: The word "Excalibur," say, is a proper name in the ordinary sense. The sword Excalibur consists of parts combined in a particular way. If they are combined differently Excalibur does not exist. But it is clear that the sentence "Excalibur has a sharp blade" makes sense whether Excalibur is still whole or is broken up. But if "Excalibur" is the name of an object, this object no longer exists when Excalibur is broken in pieces; and as no object would then correspond to the name it would have no meaning. But then the

sentence "Excalibur has a sharp blade" would contain a word that had no meaning, and hence the sentence would be nonsense. But it does make sense; so there must always be something corresponding to the words of which it consists. So the word "Excalibur" must disappear when the sense is analysed and its place be taken by words which name simples. It will be reasonable to call these words the real names.

40. Let us first discuss *this* point of the argument: that a word has no meaning if nothing corresponds to it.—It is important to note that the word "meaning" is being used illicitly if it is used to signify the thing that 'corresponds' to the word. That is to confound the meaning of a name with the *bearer* of the name. When Mr. N. N. dies one says that the bearer of the name dies, not that the meaning dies. And it would be nonsensical to say that, for if the name ceased to have meaning it would make no sense to say "Mr. N. N. is dead."

41. In §15 we introduced proper names into language (8). Now suppose that the tool with the name "N" is broken. Not knowing this, A gives B the sign "N." Has this sign meaning now or not?—What is B to do when he is given it?—We have not settled anything about this. One might ask: what *will* he do? Well, perhaps he will stand there at a loss, or shew A the pieces. Here one *might* say: "N" has become meaningless; and this expression would mean that the sign "N" no longer had a use in our language-game (unless we gave it a new one). "N" might also become meaningless because, for whatever reason, the tool was given another name and the sign "N" no longer used in the language-game.—But we could also imagine a convention whereby B has to shake his head in reply if A gives him the sign belonging to a tool that is broken.—In this way the command "N" might be said to be given a place in the language-game even when the tool no longer exists, and the sign "N" to have meaning even when its bearer ceases to exist.

42. But has for instance a name which has *never* been used for a tool also got a meaning in that game? Let us assume that "X" is such a sign and that A gives this sign to B—well, even such signs could be given a place in the language-game, and B might have, say, to answer them too with a shake of the head. (One could imagine this as a sort of joke between them.)

43. For a *large* class of cases—though not for all—in which we employ the word "meaning" it can be defined thus: the meaning of a word is its use in the language.

And the *meaning* of a name is sometimes explained by pointing to its *bearer.*

44. We said that the sentence "Excalibur has a sharp blade" made sense even when Excalibur was broken in pieces. Now this is so because in this language-game a name is also used in the absence of its bearer. But we can imagine a language-game with names (that is, with signs which we should certainly include among names) in which they are used only in the presence of the bearer; and so could always be replaced by a demonstrative pronoun and the gesture of pointing.

45. The demonstrative "this" can never be without a bearer. It might be said: "so long as there is a *this,* the word 'this' has a meaning too, whether *this* is simple or complex." But that does not make the word into a name. On the contrary: for a name is not used with, but only explained by means of, the gesture of pointing.

46. What lies behind the idea that names really signify simples?—

Socrates says in the *Theaetetus:* "If I make no mistake, I have heard some people say this: there is no definition of the primary elements—so to speak—out of which we and everything else are composed; for everything that exists in its own right can only be *named,* no other determination is possible, neither that it *is* nor that it *is not.* . . . But what exists in its own right has to be . . . named without any other determination. In consequence it is impossible to give an account of any primary element; for it, nothing is possible but the bare name; its name is all it has. But just as what consists of these primary elements is itself complex, so the names of the elements become descriptive language by being compounded together. For the essence of speech is the composition of names."

Both Russell's 'individuals' and my 'objects' (*Tractatus Logico-Philosophicus*) were such primary elements.

47. But what are the simple constituent parts of which reality is composed?—What are the simple constituent parts of a chair?—The bits of wood of which it is made? Or the molecules, or the atoms?—"Simple" means: not composite. And here the point is: in what sense 'composite'? It makes no sense at all to speak absolutely of the 'simple parts of a chair.'

Again: Does my visual image of this tree, of this chair, consist of parts? And what are its simple component parts? Multi-colouredness is one kind of complexity; another is, for example, that of a broken outline composed of straight bits. And a curve can be said to be composed of an ascending and a descending segment.

If I tell someone without any further explanation: "What I see before me now is composite," he will have the right to ask: "What do you mean by 'composite'? For there are all sorts of things that that can mean!"—The question "Is what you see composite?" makes good sense if it is already established what kind of complexity—that is, which particular use of the word—is in question. If it had been laid down that the visual image of a tree was to be called "composite" if one saw not just a single trunk, but also branches, then the question "Is the visual image of this tree simple or composite?" and the question "What are its simple component parts?" would have a clear sense—a clear use. And of course the answer to the second question is not "The branches" (that would be an answer to the *grammatical* question: "What are here called 'simple component parts'?") but rather a description of the individual branches.

But isn't a chessboard, for instance, obviously, and absolutely, composite?—You are probably thinking of the composition out of thirty-two white and thirty-two black squares. But could we not also say, for instance, that it was composed of the colours black and white and the schema of squares? And if there are quite different ways of looking at it, do you still want to say that the chessboard is absolutely 'composite'?—Asking "Is this object composite?" *outside* a particular language-game is like what a boy once did, who had to say whether the verbs in certain sentences were in the active or passive voice, and who racked his brains over the question whether the verb "to sleep" meant something active or passive.

We use the word "composite" (and therefore the word "simple") in an enormous number of different and differently related ways. (Is the colour of a square on a chessboard simple, or does it consist of pure white and pure yellow? And is white simple, or does it consist of the colours of the rainbow?—Is this length of 2 cm. simple, or does it consist of two parts, each 1 cm. long? But why not of one bit 3 cm. long, and one bit 1 cm. long measured in the opposite direction?)

To the *philosophical* question: "Is the visual image of this tree composite, and what are its component parts?" the correct answer is: "That depends on what you understand by 'composite'." (And that is of course not an answer but a rejection of the question.)

* * *

65. Here we come up against the great question that lies behind all these considerations.—For someone might object against me: "You take the easy way out! You talk about all sorts of language-games, but have nowhere said what the essence of a language-game, and hence of language, is: what is common to all these activities, and

what makes them into language or parts of language. So you let yourself off the very part of the investigation that once gave you yourself most headache, the part about the *general form of propositions* and of language."

And this is true.—Instead of producing something common to all that we call language, I am saying that these phenomena have no one thing in common which makes us use the same word for all,—but that they are *related* to one another in many different ways. And it is because of this relationship, or these relationships, that we call them all "language." I will try to explain this.

66. Consider for example the proceedings that we call "games." I mean board-games, card-games, ball-games, Olympic games, and so on. What is common to them all?—Don't say: "There *must* be something common, or they would not be called 'games' "—but *look* and *see* whether there is anything common to all.—For if you look at them you will not see something that is common to *all,* but similarities, relationships, and a whole series of them at that. To repeat: don't think, but look!—Look for example at board-games, with their multifarious relationships. Now pass to card-games; here you find many correspondences with the first group, but many common features drop out, and others appear. When we pass next to ball-games, much that is common is retained, but much is lost.—Are they all 'amusing'? Compare chess with noughts and crosses. Or is there always winning and losing, or competition between players? Think of patience. In ball-games there is winning and losing; but when a child throws his ball at the wall and catches it again, this feature has disappeared. Look at the parts played by skill and luck; and at the difference between skill in chess and skill in tennis. Think now of games like ring-a-ring-a-roses; here is the element of amusement, but how many other characteristic features have disappeared! And we can go through the many, many other groups of games in the same way; can see how similarities crop up and disappear.

And the result of this examination is: we see a complicated network of similarities overlapping and criss-crossing: sometimes overall similarities, sometimes similarities of detail.

67. I can think of no better expression to characterize these similarities than "family resemblances"; for the various resemblances between members of a family: build, features, colour of eyes, gait, temperament, etc., etc. overlap and criss-cross in the same way.—And I shall say: "games" form a family.

And for instance the kinds of number form a family in the same way. Why do we call something a "number"? Well, perhaps because it has a—dircct—relationship with several things that have hitherto been called number; and this can be said to give it an indirect relationship to other things we call the same name. And we extend our concept of number as in spinning a thread we twist fibre on fibre. And the strength of the thread does not reside in the fact that some one fibre runs through its whole length, but in the overlapping of many fibres.

But if someone wished to say: "There is something common to all these constructions—namely the disjunction of all their common properties"—I should reply: Now you are only playing with words. One might as well say: "Something runs through the whole thread—namely the continuous overlapping of those fibres."

68. "All right: the concept of number is defined for you as the logical sum of these individual interrelated concepts: cardinal numbers, rational numbers, real numbers, etc.; and in the same way the concept of a game as the logical sum of a corresponding set of sub-concepts."—It need not be so. For I *can* give the concept 'number' rigid limits in this way, that is, use the word "number" for a rigidly limited concept, but I can also use it so that the extension of the concept is *not* closed by a frontier. And this is how we do use the

word "game." For how is the concept of a game bounded? What still counts as a game and what no longer does? Can you give the boundary? No. You can *draw* one; for none has so far been drawn. (But that never troubled you before when you used the word "game.")

"But then the use of the word is unregulated, the 'game' we play with it is unregulated."—It is not everywhere circumscribed by rules; but no more are there any rules for how high one throws the ball in tennis, or how hard; yet tennis is a game for all that and has rules too.

69. How should we explain to someone what a game is? I imagine that we should describe *games* to him, and we might add: "This *and similar things* are called 'games'." And do we know any more about it ourselves? Is it only other people whom we cannot tell exactly what a game is?—But this is not ignorance. We do not know the boundaries because none have been drawn. To repeat, we can draw a boundary—for a special purpose. Does it take that to make the concept usable? Not at all! (Except for that special purpose.) No more than it took the definition: 1 pace = 75 cm to make the measure of length 'one pace' usable. And if you want to say "But still, before that it wasn't an exact measure," then I reply: very well, it was an inexact one.—Though you still owe me a definition of exactness.

70. "But if the concept 'game' is uncircumscribed like that, you don't really know what you mean by a 'game'."—When I give the description: "The ground was quite covered with plants"—do you want to say I don't know what I am talking about until I can give a definition of a plant?

My meaning would be explained by, say, a drawing and the words "The ground looked roughly like this." Perhaps I even say "it looked *exactly* like this."—Then were just *this* grass and *these* leaves there, arranged just like this? No, that is not what it means. And I should not accept any picture as exact in *this* sense.

Someone says to me: "Shew the children a game." I teach them gaming with dice, and the other says "I didn't mean that sort of game." Must the exclusion of the game with dice have come before his mind when he gave me the order? [Note added by Wittgenstein.]

---

71. One might say that the concept 'game' is a concept with blurred edges.—"But is a blurred concept a concept at all?"—Is an indistinct photograph a picture of a person at all? Is it even always an advantage to replace an indistinct picture by a sharp one? Isn't the indistinct one often exactly what we need?

Frege compares a concept to an area and says that an area with vague boundaries cannot be called an area at all. This presumably means that we cannot do anything with it.—But is it senseless to say: "Stand roughly there"? Suppose that I were standing with someone in a city square and said that. As I say it I do not draw any kind of boundary, but perhaps point with my hand—as if I were indicating a particular *spot.* And this is just how one might explain to someone what a game is. One gives examples and intends them to be taken in a particular way.—I do not, however, mean by this that he is supposed to see in those examples that common thing which I—for some reason—was unable to express; but that he is now to *employ* those examples in a particular way. Here giving examples is not an *indirect* means of explaining—in default of a better. For any general definition can be misunderstood too. The point is that *this* is how we play the game. (I mean the language-game with the word "game.")

* * *

241. "So you are saying that human agreement decides what is true and what is false?"—It is what human beings say that is true and false; and they agree in the *language* they use. That is not agreement in opinions but in form of life.

* * *

257. "What would it be like if human beings shewed no outward signs of pain (did not groan, grimace, etc.)? Then it would be impossible to teach a child the use of the word 'tooth-ache'."—Well, let's assume the child is a genius and itself invents a name for the sensation!—But then, of course, he couldn't make himself understood when he used the word.—So does he understand the name, without being able to explain its meaning to anyone?—But what does it mean to say that he has 'named his pain'?—How has he done this naming of pain?! And whatever he did, what was its purpose?—When one says "He gave a name to his sensation" one forgets that a great deal of stage-setting in the language is presupposed if the mere act of naming is to make sense. And when we speak of someone's having given a name to pain, what is presupposed is the existence of the grammar of the word "pain"; it shews the post where the new word is stationed.

258. Let us imagine the following case. I want to keep a diary about the recurrence of a certain sensation. To this end I associate it with the sign "S" and write this sign in a calendar for every day on which I have the sensation. I will remark first of all that a definition of the sign cannot be formulated.—But still I can give myself a kind of ostensive definition.—How? Can I point to the sensation? Not in the ordinary sense. But I speak, or write the sign down, and at the same time I concentrate my attention on the sensation—and so, as it were, point to it inwardly.—But what is this ceremony for? for that is all it seems to be! A definition surely serves to establish the meaning of a sign.—Well, that is done precisely by the concentrating of my attention; for in this way I impress on myself the connexion between the sign and the sensation.—But "I impress it on myself" can only mean: this process brings it about that I remember the connexion *right* in the future. But in the present case I have no criterion of correctness. One would like to say: whatever is going to seem right to me is right. And that only means that here we can't talk about 'right.'

* * *

305. "But you surely cannot deny that, for example, in remembering, an inner process takes place."—What gives the impression that we want to deny anything? When one says "Still, an inner process does take place here"—one wants to go on: "After all, you *see* it." And it is this inner process that one means by the word "remembering."—The impression that we wanted to deny something arises from our setting our faces against the picture of the 'inner process.' What we deny is that the picture of the inner process gives us the correct idea of the use of the word "to remember." We say that this picture with its ramifications stands in the way of our seeing the use of the word as it is.

* * *

309. What is your aim in philosophy?—To shew the fly the way out of the flybottle.

JEAN-PAUL SARTRE
1905–1980

In addition to being one of the leading philosophers of the twentieth century, Jean-Paul Sartre was also an essayist, novelist, playwright, and editor. His name has become synonymous with existentialism, a movement that exploded beyond the boundaries of the academy to enter virtually every area of Western culture. Sartre himself became as famous as the philosophy he taught, and at his death in 1980, almost 50,000 people accompanied his casket to Paris's Montparnasse Cemetery.

Jean-Paul-Charles-Aymard Sartre was born in Paris in 1905, the only child of naval officer Jean-Baptiste Sartre and his wife Anne-Marie Schweitzer Sartre. Barely a year after his birth, his father died. Jean-Paul and his mother moved in with her parents. Sartre's maternal grandfather, a German-language teacher, had a study filled with books; this room fascinated the young Sartre. He taught himself to read, and by the age of 8 he had read French classics such as *Madame Bovary.* While still a boy, his devotion to books overwhelmed all other devotions—including that to religion. From about the age of 12, Sartre said that he was a confirmed atheist. He did exceptionally well in his studies, exhibiting a clear independence of mind. One of his teachers noted on his report card: "Excellent student: mind already lively, good at discussing questions, but needs to depend a little less on himself."

In 1924, Sartre enrolled at the prestigious École Normale Supérieure. Over the next four years, he studied for the *agrégation* in philosophy (the highest degree except for the doctorate in the French system), but surprisingly he failed the written examination on his first attempt. He retook the examination a year later and placed first.

The person who took second in that 1929 examination was his study partner, Simone de Beauvoir. That same year, Sartre suggested to her that they take

Guernica, 1937, by Pablo Picasso (1881–1973). In 1937 the city of Guernica was destroyed by German bombers simply for the purpose of testing their new weapons. Sartre's friend Picasso created this painting to memorialize the innocent sacrifice of the Spanish people. This representation of broken, fragmented pieces of humanity wrung by pain and anxiety capture well the reality of death and violence. Sartre insisted that to live fully one must squarely face such suffering. (© *Succession Picasso/DACS, London 2015.*)

"a two-year lease" on each other. Though neither believed in the bourgeois institution of marriage, and each had a variety of lovers, the two remained "companions" for life.

Over the next ten years, Sartre served briefly in the army, studied in Berlin, taught at a number of lycées, and began writing. Among his early publications were the philosophical novel *Nausea* (1938) and the collection of short stories *The Wall* (1939).

In 1939, Sartre was called up for active duty by the French army. Within the year, he was captured by the Germans. Released a few months later, he seemed to return to a quiet life of teaching and writing. But Sartre was secretly a member of the French resistance. He was never involved in the armed resistance but worked with the intellectual resistance group Socialism and Liberty. Even during the war, Sartre continued his writing, and in 1943 he published his most important philosophical text, *Being and Nothingness.* Three years later, *Existentialism Is a Humanism,* his most widely read philosophical work, was published.

After the war, Sartre retired from teaching and, with Maurice Merleau-Ponty and de Beauvoir, founded the influential journal *Les Temps modernes.* He was awarded the Nobel Prize for literature in 1964 but refused to accept it. Together with de Beauvoir, he spent the rest of his life writing and promoting revolutionary political causes. Frequently joining students or union workers in demonstrations, Sartre even served as president of the International War Crimes Tribunal, which condemned U.S. intervention in Vietnam. He was attracted to Marxist thought—though he frequently criticized the French Communist Party for its inadequacies. The discrepancies between the determinism of Marxist theory and Sartre's existentialist emphasis on radical freedom have been the subject of many books. (See the suggested readings.)

Throughout his life, Sartre preferred the pleasures of the café over the joys of the hearth. For years, he and de Beauvoir were fixtures at La Coupole, a restaurant on the Left Bank of Paris frequented by artists. But eventually his health deteriorated, exacerbated by his frequent use of amphetamines, and he was forced to retire to his apartment. After an agonizingly slow decline, Sartre died in 1980.

* * *

Like Heidegger before him, Sartre was fascinated with "being." According to Sartre, there are two categories of being: "being-in-itself" (*étre en-soi*) and "being-for-itself" (*étre pour-soi*). *Being-in-itself* is complete in itself, "solid," fixed, and totally given: "Uncreated, without reason for being, without connection with any other being, being-in-itself is superfluous for all eternity." Like Parmenides' One, being-in-itself simply is. This is the being of rocks and trees. This being-in-itself has no sufficient reason for being, no purpose or meaning—it is "absurd."

Being-for-itself, on the other hand, is incomplete and fluid and without a determined structure. Being-for-itself is the being of human consciousness that at every moment is freely choosing its future. This consciousness arises by virtue of its power of negation, based on freedom: "[Consciousness] constitutes itself in its own flesh as the nihilation of a possibility which another human reality projects as its possibility. For that reason it must arise in the world as a Not." Individual consciousness constitutes itself by freely rejecting all roles that others try to force upon it. It is precisely in the act of saying "No" to all attempts to make me into a being-in-itself that I create myself as a being-for-itself.

In creating myself, I do not choose what I will become on the basis of preexisting values. There are no eternal values, no givens for me to use. Dostoevsky's character Ivan Karamazov had claimed, "If there is no God, all things are lawful." Sartre agreed and added that since there was no God, all things are, indeed, lawful. In fact, there is no possible justification for any choice I might make, since justification implies an appeal to given values. I am free to choose my values without any external justification.

Although this freedom is complete, it is not absolute. In the first place, as a free being, I encounter other free beings. My world is interrupted when the "other" gives me "the look." By looking at me, the other objectifies me, makes me a part of his or her world, part of his or her freedom: "Thus being-seen constitutes me as a being without defenses for a freedom which is not my freedom." But I can regain my freedom by looking back and by an act of will transforming the other into an object for me. (This world of people-objects led Sartre to exclaim, "Hell is other people.")

Second, I must acknowledge the "facticity" found in existence. I cannot change the fact that this tree is in front of me or that I cannot walk through it. But even here my freedom still prevails. I freely create the *meaning* of this tree as an object to climb or as a source of lumber or as a thing to be preserved or as a biological specimen. In creating these meanings, I create the world in which I live.

In *Existentialism Is a Humanism,* translated here by Bernard Frechtman, Sartre expands on this freedom while defending the basic ideas of existentialism. He begins by discussing human artifacts, such as a book or a paper-cutter. An object such as a paper-cutter begins as an essence, that is, as an "ensemble of both the production routines and the properties which enable it to be both produced and defined." One conceives of a paper-cutter (essentially) and how to make it and only then does one construct it. The essence of a paper-cutter precedes its existence. According to Sartre, theists believe that God does the same with human beings. First God conceives of humans and then creates them. But Sartre says that there is no God, and hence no preexisting human essence: "There is no human nature, since there is no God to conceive it." Instead, "Man is nothing else but what he makes of himself." For humans, existence precedes essence.

When one realizes the implications of this atheism and the primacy of freedom, one is brought to anguish and forlornness. But Sartre strongly denied that this state necessarily led to despair. Even though all my actions are indeed ultimately futile because of my eventual death, and existence is in fact absurd, I can still choose my actions and so give my life meaning. As Sartre concluded, "In this sense existentialism is optimistic, a doctrine of action."

* * *

There are many studies of existentialism; see especially Gabriel Marcel, *The Philosophy of Existentialism,* translated by Manya Harari (New York: Citadel Press, 1956); Hazel E. Barnes, *An Existentialist Ethic* (Chicago: University of Chicago Press, 1967); and William Barrett's two books, *Irrational Man* (Garden City, NY: Doubleday, 1962) and *What Is Existentialism?* (New York: Grove Press, 1964); and Steven Earnshaw, *Existentialism: A Guide for the Perplexed* (London: Continuum, 2007). For primary source materials, see Walter Kaufmann, ed., *Existentialism from Dostoevsky to Sartre* (New York: Viking Press, 1956) and Charles Guignon and Derk Pereboom, *Existentialism: Basic Texts* (Indianapolis, IN: Hackett, 1994).

For biographies of Sartre, see Annie Cohen-Solal, *Sartre: A Life,* translated by Anna Cancogni (New York: Pantheon Books, 1987); John Gerassi, *Jean-Paul Sartre: Hated Conscience of His Century* (Chicago: University of Chicago Press, 1989); and Simone de Beauvoir's recounting of Sartre's final days, *Adieux: A Farewell to Sartre* (New York: Pantheon, 1984). For general introductions to Sartre's thought, see Mary Warnock, *The Philosophy of Sartre* (London: Hutchinson, 1965); Anthony Manser, *Sartre: A Philosophic Study* (London: Athlone Press, 1966); Arthur C. Danto, *Jean-Paul Sartre* (New York: Viking Press, 1975); Peter Caws, *Sartre* (London: Routledge & Kegan Paul, 1979); and Gary Cox, *Sartre: A Guide for the Perplexed* (London: Continuum, 2006). Iris Murdoch, *Sartre: Romantic Rationalist* (New Haven, CT: Yale University Press, 1959) explores the philosophical ideas in Sartre's novels. For collections of essays, see Edith Kern, ed., *Sartre: A Collection of Critical Essays* (Englewood Cliffs, NJ: Prentice Hall, 1962); Mary Warnock, ed., *Sartre* (Garden City, NY: Anchor Doubleday, 1971); Hugh J. Silverman and Frederick A. Elliston, eds., *Jean-Paul Sartre: Contemporary Approaches to His Philosophy* (Pittsburgh, PA: Duquesne University Press, 1980); Paul A. Schilpp, ed., *The Philosophy of Jean-Paul Sartre* (La Salle, IL: Open Court, 1981); Christina Howells, ed., *The Cambridge Companion to Sartre* (Cambridge: Cambridge University Press, 1992); and the multi-volume William L. McBride, *Sartre and Existentialism* (Hamden, CT: Garland, 1997).

EXISTENTIALISM IS A HUMANISM

I should like on this occasion to defend existentialism against some charges which have been brought against it.

First, it has been charged with inviting people to remain in a kind of desperate quietism because, since no solutions are possible, we should have to consider action in this world as quite impossible. We should then end up in a philosophy of contemplation; and since contemplation is a luxury, we come in the end to a bourgeois philosophy. The communists in particular have made these charges.

On the other hand, we have been charged with dwelling on human degradation, with pointing up everywhere the sordid, shady, and slimy, and neglecting the gracious and beautiful, the bright side of human nature; for example, according to Mlle. Mercier, a Catholic critic, with forgetting the smile of the child. Both sides charge us with having ignored human solidarity, with considering man as an isolated being. The communists say that the main reason for this is that we take pure subjectivity, *the Cartesian I think,* as our starting point; in other words, the moment in which man becomes fully aware of what it means to him to be an isolated being; as a result, we are unable to return to a state of solidarity with the men who are not ourselves, a state which we can never reach in the *cogito.*

From the Christian standpoint, we are charged with denying the reality and seriousness of human undertakings, since, if we reject God's commandments and the eternal verities, there no longer remains anything but pure caprice, with everyone permitted to do as he pleases and incapable, from his own point of view, of condemning the points of view and acts of others.

I shall try today to answer these different charges. Many people are going to be surprised at what is said here about humanism. We shall try to see in what sense it is to be understood. In any case, what can be said from the very beginning is that by existentialism we mean a doctrine which makes human life possible and, in addition, declares that every truth and every action implies a human setting and a human subjectivity.

As is generally known, the basic charge against us is that we put the emphasis on the dark side of human life. Someone recently told me of a lady who, when she let slip a vulgar word in a moment of irritation, excused herself by saying, "I guess I'm becoming an existentialist." Consequently, existentialism is regarded as something ugly; that is why we are said to be naturalists; and if we are, it is rather surprising that in this day and age we cause so much more alarm and scandal than does naturalism, properly so called. The kind of person who can take in his stride such a novel as Zola's The Earth is disgusted as soon as he starts reading an existentialist novel; the kind of person who is resigned to the wisdom of the ages—which is pretty sad—finds us even sadder. Yet, what can be more disillusioning than saying "true charity begins at home" or "a scoundrel will always return evil for good"?

We know the commonplace remarks made when this subject comes up, remarks which always add up to the same thing: we shouldn't struggle against the powers-that-be; we shouldn't resist authority; we shouldn't try to rise above our station; any action which doesn't conform to authority is romantic; any effort not based on past experience is doomed to failure; experience shows that man's bent is always toward trouble, that there

Jean-Paul Sartre, *Existentialism Is a Humanism,* translated by Bernard Frechtman (New York: Philosophical Library, 1947). Reprinted by permission.

must be a strong hand to hold him in check, if not, there will be anarchy. There are still people who go on mumbling these melancholy old saws, the people who say, "It's only human!" whenever a more or less repugnant act is pointed out to them, the people who glut themselves on *chansons réalistes;* these are the people who accuse existentialism of being too gloomy, and to such an extent that I wonder whether they are complaining about it, not for its pessimism, but much rather its optimism. Can it be that what really scares them in the doctrine I shall try to present here is that it leaves to man a possibility of choice? To answer this question, we must re-examine it on a strictly philosophical plane. What is meant by the term *existentialism?*

Most people who use the word would be rather embarrassed if they had to explain it, since, now that the word is all the rage, even the work of a musician or painter is being called existentialist. A gossip columnist in *Clartés* signs himself *The Existentialist,* so that by this time the word has been so stretched and has taken on so broad a meaning, that it no longer means anything at all. It seems that for want of an avant-garde doctrine analogous to surrealism, the kind of people who are eager for scandal and flurry turn to this philosophy which in other respects does not at all serve their purposes in this sphere.

Actually, it is the least scandalous, the most austere of doctrines. It is intended strictly for specialists and philosophers. Yet it can be defined easily. What complicates matters is that there are two kinds of existentialist; first, those who are Christian, among whom I would include Jaspers and Gabriel Marcel, both Catholic; and on the other hand the atheistic existentialists, among whom I class Heidegger, and then the French existentialists and myself. What they have in common is that they think that existence precedes essence, or, if you prefer, that subjectivity must be the starting point.

Just what does that mean? Let us consider some object that is manufactured, for example, a book or a paper-cutter: here is an object which has been made by an artisan whose inspiration came from a concept. He referred to the concept of what a paper-cutter is and likewise to a known method of production, which is part of the concept, something which is, by and large, a routine. Thus, the paper-cutter is at once an object produced in a certain way and, on the other hand, one having a specific use; and one cannot postulate a man who produces a paper-cutter but does not know what it is used for. Therefore, let us say that, for the paper-cutter, essence—that is, the ensemble of both the production routines and the properties which enable it to be both produced and defined—precedes existence. Thus, the presence of the paper-cutter or book in front of me is determined. Therefore, we have here a technical view of the world whereby it can be said that production precedes existence.

When we conceive God as the Creator, He is generally thought of as a superior sort of artisan. Whatever doctrine we may be considering, whether one like that of Descartes or that of Leibnitz, we always grant that will more or less follows understanding or, at the very least, accompanies it, and that when God creates He knows exactly what He is creating. Thus, the concept of man in the mind of God is comparable to the concept of paper-cutter in the mind of the manufacturer, and, following certain techniques and a conception, God produces man, just as the artisan, following a definition and a technique, makes a paper-cutter. Thus, the individual man is the realization of a certain concept in the divine intelligence.

In the eighteenth century, the atheism of the *philosophes* discarded the idea of God, but not so much for the notion that essence precedes existence. To a certain extent, this idea is found everywhere; we find it in Diderot, in Voltaire, and even in Kant. Man has a human nature; this human nature, which is the concept of the human, is found in all men, which means that each man is a particular example of a universal concept, man. In

Kant, the result of this universality is that the wild-man, the natural man, as well as the bourgeois, are circumscribed by the same definition and have the same basic qualities. Thus, here too the essence of man precedes the historical existence that we find in nature.

Atheistic existentialism, which I represent, is more coherent. It states that if God does not exist, there is at least one being in whom existence precedes essence, a being who exists before he can be defined by any concept, and that this being is man, or, as Heidegger says, human reality. What is meant here by saying that existence precedes essence? It means that, first of all, man exists, turns up, appears on the scene, and, only afterwards, defines himself. If man, as the existentialist conceives him, is indefinable, it is because at first he is nothing. Only afterward will he be something, and he himself will have made what he will be. Thus, there is no human nature, since there is no God to conceive it. Not only is man what he conceives himself to be, but he is also only what he wills himself to be after this thrust toward existence.

Man is nothing else but what he makes of himself. Such is the first principle of existentialism. It is also what is called subjectivity, the name we are labeled with when charges are brought against us. But what do we mean by this, if not that man has a greater dignity than a stone or table? For we mean that man first exists, that is, that man first of all is the being who hurls himself toward a future and who is conscious of imagining himself as being in the future. Man is at the start a plan which is aware of itself, rather than a patch of moss, a piece of garbage, or a cauliflower; nothing exists prior to this plan; there is nothing in heaven; man will be what he will have planned to be. Not what he will want to be. Because by the word "will" we generally mean a conscious decision, which is subsequent to what we have already made of ourselves. I may want to belong to a political party, write a book, get married; but all that is only a manifestation of an earlier, more spontaneous choice that is called "will." But if existence really does precede essence, man is responsible for what he is. Thus, existentialism's first move is to make every man aware of what he is and to make the full responsibility of his existence rest on him. And when we say that a man is responsible for himself, we do not only mean that he is responsible for his own individuality, but that he is responsible for all men.

The word subjectivism has two meanings, and our opponents play on the two. Subjectivism means, on the one hand, that an individual chooses and makes himself; and, on the other, that it is impossible for man to transcend human subjectivity. The second of these is the essential meaning of existentialism. When we say that man chooses his own self, we mean that every one of us does likewise; but we also mean by that that in making this choice he also chooses all men. In fact, in creating the man that we want to be, there is not a single one of our acts which does not at the same time create an image of man as we think he ought to be. To choose to be this or that is to affirm at the same time the value of what we choose, because we can never choose evil. We always choose the good, and nothing can be good for us without being good for all.

If, on the other hand, existence precedes essence, and if we grant that we exist and fashion our image at one and the same time, the image is valid for everybody and for our whole age. Thus, our responsibility is much greater than we might have supposed, because it involves all mankind. If I am a workingman and choose to join a Christian trade-union rather than be a communist, and if by being a member I want to show that the best thing for man is resignation, that the kingdom of man is not of this world, I am not only involving my own case—I want to be resigned for everyone. As a result, my action has involved all humanity. To take a more individual matter, if I want to marry, to have children; even if this marriage depends solely on my own circumstances or passion or wish, I am involving all humanity in monogamy and not merely myself. Therefore,

I am responsible for myself and for everyone else. I am creating a certain image of man of my own choosing. In choosing myself, I choose man.

This helps us understand what the actual content is of such rather grandiloquent words as anguish, forlornness, despair. As you will see, it's all quite simple.

First, what is meant by anguish? The existentialists say at once that man is in anguish. What that means is this: the man who involves himself and who realizes that he is not only the person he chooses to be, but also a law-maker who is, at the same time, choosing all mankind as well as himself, can not help escape the feeling of his total and deep responsibility. Of course, there are many people who are not anxious; but we claim that they are hiding their anxiety, that they are fleeing from it. Certainly, many people believe that when they do something, they themselves are the only ones involved, and when someone says to them, "What if everyone acted that way?" they shrug their shoulders and answer, "Everyone doesn't act that way." But really, one should always ask himself, "What would happen if everybody looked at things that way?" There is no escaping this disturbing thought except by a kind of double-dealing. A man who lies and makes excuses for himself by saying "not everybody does that," is someone with an uneasy conscience, because the act of lying implies that a universal value is conferred upon the lie.

Anguish is evident even when it conceals itself. This is the anguish that Kierkegaard called the anguish of Abraham. You know the story: an angel has ordered Abraham to sacrifice his son; if it really were an angel who has come and said, "You are Abraham, you shall sacrifice your son," everything would be all right. But everyone might first wonder, "Is it really an angel, and am I really Abraham? What proof do I have?"

There was a mad woman who had hallucinations; someone used to speak to her on the telephone and give her orders. Her doctor asked her, "Who is it who talks to you?" She answered, "He says it's God." What proof did she really have that it was God? If an angel comes to me, what proof is there that it's an angel? And if I hear voices, what proof is there that they come from heaven and not from hell, or from the subconscious, or a pathological condition? What proves that they are addressed to me? What proof is there that I have been appointed to impose my choice and my conception of man on humanity? I'll never find any proof or sign to convince me of that. If a voice addresses me, it is always for me to decide that this is the angel's voice; if I consider that such an act is a good one, it is I who will choose to say that it is good rather than bad.

Now, I'm not being singled out as an Abraham, and yet at every moment I'm obliged to perform exemplary acts. For every man, everything happens as if all mankind had its eyes fixed on him and were guiding itself by what he does. And every man ought to say to himself, "Am I really the kind of man who has the right to act in such a way that humanity might guide itself by my actions?" And if he does not say that to himself, he is masking his anguish.

There is no question here of the kind of anguish which would lead to quietism, to inaction. It is a matter of a simple sort of anguish that anybody who has had responsibilities is familiar with. For example, when a military officer takes the responsibility for an attack and sends a number of men to death, he chooses to do so, and in the main he alone makes the choice. Doubtless, orders come from above, but they are too broad; he interprets them, and on this interpretation depend the lives of ten or fourteen or twenty men. In making a decision he can not help having a certain anguish. All leaders know this anguish. That doesn't keep them from acting; on the contrary, it is the very condition of their action. For it implies that they envisage a number of possibilities, and when they choose one, they realize that it has value only because it is chosen. We shall see that this kind of anguish, which is the kind that existentialism describes, is explained, in addition, by a direct responsibility to the other men whom it involves. It is not a curtain separating us from action, but is part of action itself.

When we speak of forlornness, a term Heidegger was fond of, we mean only that God does not exist and that we have to face all the consequences of this. The existentialist is strongly opposed to a certain kind of secular ethics which would like to abolish God with the least possible expense. About 1880, some French teachers tried to set up a secular ethic which went something like this: God is a useless and costly hypothesis; we are discarding it; but, meanwhile, in order for there to be an ethics, a society, a civilization, it is essential that certain values be taken seriously and that they be considered as having an *a priori* existence. It must be obligatory, *a priori,* to be honest, not to lie, not to beat your wife, to have children, etc., etc. So we're going to try a little device which will make it possible to show that values exist all the same, inscribed in a heaven of ideas, though otherwise God does not exist. In other words—and this, I believe, is the tendency of everything called reformism in France—nothing will be changed if God does not exist. We shall find ourselves with the same norms of honesty, progress, and humanism, and we shall have made of God an outdated hypothesis which will peacefully die off by itself.

The existentialist, on the contrary, thinks it very distressing that God does not exist, because all possibility of finding values in a heaven of ideas disappears along with Him; there can no longer be an *a priori* Good, since there is no infinite and perfect consciousness to think it. Nowhere is it written that the Good exists, that we must be honest, that we must not lie; because the fact is we are on a plane where there are only men. Dostoevski said, "If God didn't exist, everything would be possible." That is the very starting point of existentialism. Indeed, everything is permissible if God does not exist, and as a result man is forlorn, because neither within him nor without does he find anything to cling to. He can't start making excuses for himself.

If existence really does precede essence, there is no explaining things away by reference to a fixed and given human nature. In other words, there is not determinism, man is free, man is freedom. On the other hand, if God does not exist, we find no values or commands to turn to which legitimize our conduct. So, in the bright realm of values, we have no excuse behind us, nor justification before us. We are alone, with no excuses.

That is the idea I shall try to convey when I say that man is condemned to be free. Condemned, because he did not create himself, yet, in other respects is free; because, once thrown into the world, he is responsible for everything he does. The existentialist does not believe in the power of passion. He will never agree that a sweeping passion is a ravaging torrent which fatally leads a man to certain acts and is therefore an excuse. He thinks that man is responsible for his passion.

The existentialist does not think man is going to help himself by finding in the world some omen by which to orient himself. Because he thinks that man will interpret the omen to suit himself. Therefore, he thinks that man, with no support and no aid, is condemned every moment to invent man. Ponge, in a very fine article, has said, "Man is the future of man." That's exactly it. But if it is taken to mean that this future is recorded in heaven, that God sees it, then it is false, because it would really no longer be a future. If it is taken to mean that, whatever a man may be, there is a future to be forged, a virgin future before him, then this remark is sound. But then we are forlorn.

To give you an example which will enable you to understand forlornness better, I shall cite the case of one of my students who came to see me under the following circumstances: his father was on bad terms with his mother, and, moreover, was inclined to be a collaborationist; his older brother had been killed in the German offensive of

1940, and the young man, with somewhat immature but generous feelings, wanted to avenge him. His mother lived alone with him, very much upset by the half-treason of her husband and the death of her older son; the boy was her only consolation.

The boy was faced with the choice of leaving for England and joining the Free French Forces—that is, leaving his mother behind—or remaining with his mother and helping her to carry on. He was fully aware that the woman lived only for him and that his going-off—and perhaps his death—would plunge her into despair. He was also aware that every act that he did for his mother's sake was a sure thing, in the sense that it was helping her to carry on, whereas every effort he made toward going off and fighting was an uncertain move which might run aground and prove completely useless; for example, on his way to England he might, while passing through Spain, be detained indefinitely in a Spanish camp; he might reach England or Elgiers and be stuck in an office at a desk job. As a result, he was faced with two very different kinds of action: one, concrete, immediate, but concerning only one individual; the other concerned an incomparably vaster group, a national collectivity, but for that very reason was dubious, and might be interrupted en route. And, at the same time, he was wavering between two kinds of ethics. On the one hand, an ethics of sympathy, of personal devotion; on the other, a broader ethics, but one whose efficacy was more dubious. He had to choose between the two.

Who could help him choose? Christian doctrine? No. Christian doctrine says, "Be charitable, love your neighbor, take the more rugged path, etc., etc." But which is the more rugged path? Whom should he love as a brother? The fighting man or his mother? Which does the greater good, the vague act of fighting in a group, or the concrete one of helping a particular human being to go on living? Who can decide *a priori*? Nobody. No book of ethics can tell him. The Kantian ethics says, "Never treat any person as a means, but as an end." Very well, if I stay with my mother, I'll treat her as an end and not as a means; but by virtue of this very fact, I'm running the risk of treating the people around me who are fighting, as means; and, conversely, if I go to join those who are fighting, I'll be treating them as an end, and, by doing that, I run the risk of treating my mother as a means.

If values are vague, and if they are always too broad for the concrete and specific case that we are considering, the only thing left for us is to trust our instincts. That's what this young man tried to do; and when I saw him, he said, "In the end, feeling is what counts. I ought to choose whichever pushes me in one direction. If I feel that I love my mother enough to sacrifice everything else for her—my desire for vengeance, for action, for adventure—then I'll stay with her. If, on the contrary, I feel that my love for my mother isn't enough, I'll leave."

But how is the value of a feeling determined? What gives his feeling for his mother value? Precisely the fact that he remained with her. I may say that I like so-and-so well enough to sacrifice a certain amount of money for him, but I may say so only if I've done it. I may say "I love my mother well enough to remain with her" if I have remained with her. The only way to determine the value of this affection is, precisely, to perform an act which confirms and defines it. But, since I require this affection to justify my act, I find myself caught in a vicious circle.

On the other hand, Gide has well said that a mock feeling and a true feeling are almost indistinguishable; to decide that I love my mother and will remain with her, or to remain with her by putting on an act, amount somewhat to the same thing. In other words, the feeling is formed by the acts one performs; so, I can not refer to it in order to act upon it. Which means that I can neither seek within myself the true condition which will impel me to act, nor apply to a system of ethics for concepts which will permit me to act. You will say, "At least, he did go to a teacher for advice." But if you seek advice from a priest, for example, you have chosen this priest; you already knew, more or less, just about what advice he was going to give you. In other words, choosing your adviser is involving yourself. The proof of this is that if you are a Christian, you will say, "Consult a priest." But some priests are collaborating, some are just marking time, some are resisting. Which to choose? If the young man chooses a priest who is resisting or collaborating, he has already decided on the kind of advice he's going to get. Therefore, in coming to see me he knew the answer I was going to give him, and I had only one answer to give: "You're free, choose, that is, invent." No general ethics can show you what is to be done; there are no omens in the world. The Catholics will reply, "But there are." Granted—but, in any case, I myself choose the meaning they have.

When I was a prisoner, I knew a rather remarkable young man who was a Jesuit. He had entered the Jesuit order in the following way: he had a number of very bad breaks; in childhood, his father died, leaving him in poverty, and he was a scholarship student at a religious institution where he was constantly made to feel that he was being kept out of charity; then, he failed to get any of the honors and distinctions that children like; later on, at about eighteen, he bungled a love affair; finally, at twenty-two, he failed in military training, a childish enough matter, but it was the last straw.

This young fellow might well have felt that he had botched everything. It was a sign of something, but of what? He might have taken refuge in bitterness or despair. But he very wisely looked upon all this as a sign that he was not made for secular triumphs, and that only the triumphs of religion, holiness, and faith were open to him. He saw the hand of God in all this, and so he entered the order. Who can help seeing that he alone decided what the sign meant?

Some other interpretation might have been drawn from this series of setbacks; for example, that he might have done better to turn carpenter or revolutionist. Therefore, he is fully responsible for the interpretation. Forlornness implies that we ourselves choose our being. Forlornness and anguish go together.

As for despair, the term has a very simple meaning. It means that we shall confine ourselves to reckoning only with what depends upon our will, or on the ensemble of probabilities which make our action possible. When we want something, we always have to reckon with probabilities. I may be counting on the arrival of a friend. The friend is coming by rail or street-car; this supposes that the train will arrive on schedule, or that the street-car will not jump the track. I am left in the realm of possibility; but possibilities are to be reckoned with only to the point where my action comports with the ensemble of these possibilities, and no further. The moment the possibilities I am considering are not rigorously involved by my action, I ought to disengage myself from them, because no God, no scheme, can adapt the world and its possibilities to my will. When Descartes said, "Conquer yourself rather than the world," he meant essentially the same thing.

The Marxists to whom I have spoken reply, "You can rely on the support of others in your action, which obviously has certain limits because you're not going to live forever. That means: rely on both what others are doing elsewhere to help you, in China, in Russia, and what they will do later on, after your death, to carry on the action and lead it to its fulfillment, which will be the revolution. You even *have* to rely upon that, otherwise you're immoral." I reply at once that I will always rely on fellow-fighters insofar as these comrades are involved with me in a common struggle, in the unity of a party or a group in which I can more or less make my weight felt; that is, one whose ranks I am in as a fighter and whose movements I am aware of at every moment. In such a situation, relying on the unity and will of the party is exactly like counting on the fact that the train will arrive on time, or that the car won't jump the track. But, given that man is free and that there is no human nature for me to depend on, I can not count on men whom I do not know by relying on human goodness or man's concern for the good of society. I don't know what will become of the Russian revolution; I may make an example of it to the extent that at the present time it is apparent that the proletariat plays a part in Russia that it plays in no other nation. But I can't swear that this will inevitably lead to a triumph of the proletariat. I've got to limit myself to what I see.

Given that men are free and that tomorrow they will freely decide what man will be, I can not be sure that, after my death, fellow-fighters will carry on my work to bring it to its maximum perfection. Tomorrow, after my death, some men may decide to set up Fascism, and the others may be cowardly and muddled enough to let them do it. Fascism will then be the human reality, so much the worse for us.

Actually, things will be as man will have decided they are to be. Does that mean that I should abandon myself to quietism? No. First, I should involve myself; then, act on the old saw, "Nothing ventured, nothing gained." Nor does it mean that I shouldn't belong to a party, but rather that I shall have no illusions and shall do what I can. For example, suppose I ask myself, "Will socialization, as such, ever come about?" I know nothing about it. All I know is that I'm going to do everything in my power to bring it about. Beyond that, I can't count on anything. Quietism is the attitude of people who say, "Let others do what I can't do." The doctrine I am presenting is the very opposite of quietism, since it declares, "There is no reality except in action." Moreover, it goes further, since it adds, "Man is nothing else than his plan; he exists only to the extent that he fulfills himself; he is therefore nothing else than the ensemble of his acts, nothing else than his life."

According to this, we can understand why our doctrine horrifies certain people. Because often the only way they can bear their wretchedness is to think, "Circumstances have been against me. What I've been and done doesn't show my true worth. To be sure, I've had no great love, no great friendship, but that's because I haven't met a man or woman who was worthy. The books I've written haven't been very good because I haven't had the proper leisure. I haven't had children to devote myself to because I didn't find a man with whom I could have spent my life. So there remains within me, unused and quite viable, a host of propensities, inclinations, possibilities, that one wouldn't guess from the mere series of things I've done."

Now, for the existentialist there is really no love other than one which manifests itself in a person's being in love. There is no genius other than one which is expressed in works of art; the genius of Proust is the sum of Proust's works; the genius of Racine is his series of tragedies. Outside of that, there is nothing. Why say that Racine could have written another tragedy, when he didn't write it? A man is involved in life, leaves his impress on it, and outside of that there is nothing. To be sure, this may seem a harsh thought to someone whose life hasn't been a success. But, on the other hand, it prompts people to understand that reality alone is what counts, that dreams, expectations, and hopes warrant no more than to define a man as a disappointed dream, as miscarried hopes, as vain expectations. In other words, to define him negatively and not positively. However, when we say, "You are nothing else than your life," that does not imply that the artist will be judged solely on the basis of his works of art; a thousand other things will contribute toward summing him up. What we mean is that a man is nothing else than a series of undertakings, that he is the sum, the organization, the ensemble of the relationships which make up these undertakings.

When all is said and done, what we are accused of, at bottom, is not our pessimism, but an optimistic toughness. If people throw up to us our works of fiction in which we write about people who are soft, weak, cowardly, and sometimes even downright bad, it's not because these people are soft, weak, cowardly, or bad; because if we were to say, as Zola did, that they are that way because of heredity, the workings of environment, society, because of biological or psychological determinism, people would be reassured. They would say, "Well, that's what we're like, no one can do anything about it." But when the existentialist writes about a coward, he says that this coward is responsible for his cowardice. He's not like that because he has a cowardly heart or lung or brain; he's not like that on account of his physiological makeup; but he's like that because he has made himself a coward by his acts. There's no such thing as a cowardly constitution; there are nervous constitutions; there is poor blood, as the common people say, or strong constitutions. But the man whose blood is poor is not a coward on that account, for what makes cowardice is the act of renouncing or yielding. A constitution is not an act; the coward is defined on the basis of the acts he performs. People feel, in a vague sort of way, that this coward we're talking about is guilty of being a coward, and the thought frightens them. What people would like is that a coward or a hero be born that way.

One of the complaints most frequently made about *The Ways of Freedom** can be summed up as follows: "After all, these people are so spineless, how are you going to make heroes out of them?" This objection almost makes me laugh, for it assumes that people are born heroes. That's what people really want to think. If you're born cowardly, you may set your mind perfectly at rest; there's nothing you can do about it; you'll be cowardly all your life, whatever you may do. If you're born a hero, you may set your mind just as much at rest; you'll be a hero all your life; you'll drink like a hero and eat like a hero. What the existentialist says is that the coward makes himself cowardly, that the hero makes himself heroic. There's always a possibility for the coward not to be cowardly any more and for the hero to stop being heroic. What counts is total involvement; some one particular action or set of circumstances is not total involvement.

Thus, I think we have answered a number of the charges concerning existentialism. You see that it can not be taken for a philosophy of quietism, since it defines man in terms of action; nor for a pessimistic description of man—there is no doctrine more optimistic, since man's destiny is within himself; nor for an attempt to discourage man from acting, since it tells him that the only hope is in his acting and that action is the only thing that enables a man to live. Consequently, we are dealing here with an ethic of action and involvement.

Nevertheless, on the basis of a few notions like these, we are still charged with immuring man in his private subjectivity. There again we're very much misunderstood. Subjectivity of the individual is indeed our point of departure, and this for strictly philosophic reasons. Not because we are bourgeois, but because we want a doctrine based on truth and not a lot of fine theories, full of hope but with no real basis. There can be no other truth to take off from than this*: I think; therefore I exist.* There we have the absolute truth of consciousness becoming aware of itself. Every theory which takes man out of the moment in which he becomes aware of himself is, at its very beginning, a theory which confounds truth, for outside the Cartesian *cogito,* all views are only probable, and a doctrine of probability which is not bound to a truth dissolves into thin air. In order to describe the probable, you must have a firm hold on the true. Therefore, before there can be any truth whatsoever, there must be an absolute truth; and this one is simple and easily arrived at; it's on everyone's doorstep; it's a matter of grasping it directly.

*[*Les Chennus de la Liberté,* A trilogy of novels of which two—*L'Age de Raison (The Age of Reason)* and *Le Sursis (The Reprieve)*—had been published at the time of this article.]

Secondly, this theory is the only one which gives man dignity, the only one which does not reduce him to an object. The effect of all materialism is to treat all men, including the one philosophizing, as objects, that is, as an ensemble of determined reactions in no way distinguished from the ensemble of qualities and phenomena which constitute a table or a chair or a stone. We definitely wish to establish the human realm as an ensemble of values distinct from the material realm. But the subjectivity that we have thus arrived at, and which we have claimed to be truth, is not a strictly individual subjectivity, for we have demonstrated that one discovers in the *cogito* not only himself, but others as well.

The philosophies of Descartes and Kant to the contrary, through the *I think* we reach our own self in the presence of others, and the others are just as real to us as our own self. Thus, the man who becomes aware of himself through the *cogito* also perceives all others, and he perceives them as the condition of his own existence. He realizes that he can not be anything (in the sense that we say that someone is witty or nasty or jealous) unless others recognize it as such. In order to get any truth about myself, I must have contact with another person. The other is indispensable to my own existence, as well as to my knowledge about myself. This being so, in discovering my inner being I discover the other person at the same time, like a freedom placed in front of me which thinks and wills only for or against me. Hence, let us at once announce the discovery of a world which we shall call intersubjectivity; this is the world in which man decides what he is and what others are.

Besides, if it is impossible to find in every man some universal essence which would be human nature, yet there does exist a universal human condition. It's not by chance that today's thinkers speak more readily of man's condition than of his nature. By condition they mean, more or less definitely, the *a priori* limits which outline man's fundamental situation in the universe. Historical situations vary; a man may be born a slave in a pagan society or a feudal lord or a proletarian. What does not vary is the necessity for him to exist in the world, to be at work there, to be there in the midst of other people, and to be mortal there. The limits are neither subjective nor objective, or, rather, they have an objective and a subjective side. Objective because they are to be found everywhere and are recognizable everywhere; subjective because they are lived and are nothing if man does not live them, that is, freely determine his existence with reference to them. And though the configurations may differ, at least none of them are completely strange to me, because they all appear as attempts either to pass beyond these limits or recede from them or deny them or adapt to them. Consequently, every configuration, however individual it may be, has a universal value.

Every configuration, even the Chinese, the Indian, or the Negro, can be understood by a Westerner. "Can be understood" means that by virtue of a situation that he can imagine, a European of 1945 can, in like manner, push himself to his limits and reconstitute within himself the configuration of the Chinese, the Indian, or the African. Every configuration has universality in the sense that every configuration can be understood by every man. This does not at all mean that this configuration defines man forever, but that it can be met with again. There is always a way to understand the idiot, the child, the savage, the foreigner, provided one has the necessary information.

In this sense we may say that there is a universality of man; but it is not given, it is perpetually being made. I build the universal in choosing myself; I build it in understanding the configuration of every other man, whatever age he might have lived in. This absoluteness of choice does not do away with the relativeness of each epoch. At heart, what existentialism shows is the connection between the absolute character of free involvement, by virtue of which every man realizes himself in realizing a type of mankind, an involvement always comprehensible in any age whatsoever and by any person whosoever, and the relativeness of the cultural ensemble which may result from such a choice; it must be stressed that the relativity of Cartesianism and the absolute character of Cartesian involvement go together. In this sense, you may, if you like, say that each of us performs an absolute act in breathing, eating, sleeping, or behaving in any way whatever. There is no difference between being free, like a configuration, like an existence which chooses its essence, and being absolute. There is no difference between being an absolute temporarily localized, that is, localized in history, and being universally comprehensible.

This does not entirely settle the objection to subjectivism. In fact, the objection still takes several forms. First, there is the following: we are told, "So you're able to do anything, no matter what!" This is expressed in various ways. First we are accused of anarchy; then they say, "You're unable to pass judgment on others, because there's no reason to prefer one configuration to another"; finally they tell us, "Everything is arbitrary in this choosing of yours. You take something from one pocket and pretend you're putting it into the other."

These three objections aren't very serious. Take the first objection. "You're able to do anything, no matter what" is not to the point. In one sense choice is possible, but what is not possible is not to choose. I can always choose, but I ought to know that if I do not choose, I am still choosing. Though this may seem purely formal, it is highly important for keeping fantasy and caprice within bounds. If it is true that in facing a situation, for example, one in which, as a person capable of having sexual relations, of having children, I am obliged to choose an attitude, and if I in any way assume responsibility for a choice which, in involving myself, also involves all mankind, this has nothing to do with caprice, even if no *a priori* value determines my choice.

If anybody thinks that he recognizes here Gide's theory of the arbitrary act, he fails to see the enormous difference between this doctrine and Gide's. Gide does not know what a situation is. He acts out of pure caprice. For us, on the contrary, man is in an organized situation in which he himself is involved. Through his choice, he involves all mankind, and he can not avoid making a choice: either he will remain chaste, or he will marry without having children, or he will marry and have children; anyhow, whatever he may do, it is impossible for him not to take full responsibility for the way he handles this problem. Doubtless, he chooses without referring to preestablished values, but it is unfair to accuse him of caprice. Instead, let us say that moral choice is to be compared to the making of a work of art. And before going any further, let it be said at once that we are not dealing here with an aesthetic ethics, because our opponents are so dishonest that they even accuse us of that. The example I've chosen is a comparison only.

Having said that, may I ask whether anyone has ever accused an artist who has painted a picture of not having drawn his inspiration from rules set up *a priori?* Has anyone ever asked, "What painting ought he to make?" It is clearly understood that there is no definite painting to be made, that the artist is engaged in the making of his painting, and that the painting to be made is precisely the painting he will have made. It is clearly understood that there are no *a priori* aesthetic values, but that there are values which appear subsequently in the coherence of the painting, in the correspondence between what the artist intended and the result. Nobody can tell what the painting of tomorrow will be like. Painting can be judged only after it has once been made. What connection does that have with ethics? We are in the same creative situation. We never say that a work of art is arbitrary. When we speak of a canvas of Picasso, we never say that it is arbitrary; we understand quite well that he was making himself what he is at the very time he was painting, that the ensemble of his work is embodied in his life.

The same holds on the ethical plane. What art and ethics have in common is that we have creation and invention in both cases. We can not decide *a priori* what there is to be done. I think that I pointed that out quite sufficiently when I mentioned the case of the student who came to see me, and who might have applied to all the ethical systems, Kantian or otherwise, without getting any sort of guidance. He was obliged to devise his law himself. Never let it be said by us that this man—who, taking affection, individual action, and kindheartedness toward a specific person as his ethical first principle, chooses to remain with his mother, or who, preferring to make a sacrifice, chooses to go to England—has made an arbitrary choice. Man makes himself. He isn't ready made at the start. In choosing his ethics, he makes himself, and force of circumstances is such that he can not abstain from choosing one. We define man only in relationship to involvement. It is therefore absurd to charge us with arbitrariness of choice.

In the second place, it is said that we are unable to pass judgment on others. In a way this is true, and in another way, false. It is true in this sense, that, whenever a man sanely and sincerely involves himself and chooses his configuration, it is impossible for him to prefer another configuration, regardless of what his own may be in other respects. It is true in this sense, that we do not believe in progress. Progress is betterment. Man is always the same. The situation confronting him varies. Choice always remains a choice in a situation. The problem has not changed since the time one could choose between those for and those against slavery, for example, at the time of the Civil War, and the present time, when one can side with the Maquis Resistance Party, or with the Communists.

But, nevertheless, one can still pass judgment, for, as I have said, one makes a choice in relationship to others. First, one can judge (and this is perhaps not a judgment of value, but a logical judgment) that certain choices are based on error and others on truth. If we have defined man's situation as a free choice, with no excuses and no recourse, every man who takes refuge behind the excuse of his passions, every man who sets up a determinism, is a dishonest man.

The objection may be raised, "But why mayn't he choose himself dishonestly?" I reply that I am not obliged to pass moral judgment on him, but that I do define his dishonesty as an error. One can not help considering the truth of the matter. Dishonesty is obviously a falsehood because it belies the complete freedom of involvement. On the same grounds, I maintain that there is also dishonesty if I choose to state that certain values exist prior to me; it is self-contradictory for me to want them and at the same state that they are imposed on me. Suppose someone says to me, "What if I want to be dishonest?" I'll answer, "There's no reason for you not to be, but I'm saying that that's what you are, and that the strictly coherent attitude is that of honesty."

Besides, I can bring moral judgment to bear. When I declare that freedom in every concrete circumstance can have no other aim than to want itself, if man has once become aware that in his forlornness he imposes values, he can no longer want but one thing, and that is freedom, as the basis of all values. That doesn't mean that he wants it in the abstract. It means simply that the ultimate meaning of the acts of honest men is the quest for freedom as such. A man who belongs to a communist or revolutionary union wants concrete goals; these goals imply an abstract desire for freedom; but this freedom is wanted in something concrete. We want freedom for freedom's sake and in every particular circumstance. And in wanting freedom we discover that it depends entirely on the freedom of others, and that the freedom of others depends on ours. Of course, freedom as the definition of man does not depend on others, but as soon as there is involvement, I am obliged to want others to have freedom at the same time that I want my own freedom. I can take freedom as my goal only if I take that of others as a goal as well. Consequently, when, in all honesty, I've recognized that man is a being in whom existence precedes essence, that he is a free being who, in various circumstances, can want only his freedom, I have at the same time recognized that I can want only the freedom of others.

Therefore, in the name of this will for freedom, which freedom itself implies, I may pass judgment on those who seek to hide from themselves the complete arbitrariness and the complete freedom of their existence. Those who hide their complete freedom from themselves out of a spirit of seriousness or by means of deterministic excuses, I shall call cowards; those who try to show that their existence was necessary, when it is the very contingency of man's appearance on earth, I shall call stinkers. But cowards or stinkers can be judged only from a strictly unbiased point of view.

Therefore though the content of ethics is variable, a certain form of it is universal. Kant says that freedom desires both itself and the freedom of others. Granted. But he believes that the formal and the universal are enough to constitute an ethics. We, on the other hand, think that principles which are too abstract run aground in trying to decide action. Once again, take the case of the student. In the name of what, in the name of what great moral maxim do you think he could have decided, in perfect peace of mind, to abandon his mother or to stay with her? There is no way of judging. The content is always concrete and thereby unforeseeable; there is always the element of invention. The one thing that counts is knowing whether the inventing that has been done has been done in the name of freedom.

For example, let us look at the following two cases. You will see to what extent they correspond, yet differ. Take *The Mill on the Floss.* We find a certain young girl, Maggie Tulliver, who is an embodiment of the value of passion and who is aware of it. She is in love with a young man, Stephen, who is engaged to an insignificant young girl. This Maggie Tulliver, instead of heedlessly preferring her own happiness, chooses, in the name of human solidarity, to sacrifice herself and give up the man she loves. On the other hand, Sanseverina, in *The Charterhouse of Parma,* believing that passion is man's true value, would say that a great love deserves sacrifices; that it is to be preferred to the banality of the conjugal love that would tie Stephen to the young ninny he had to marry. She would choose to sacrifice the girl and fulfill her happiness; and, as Stendhal shows, she is even ready to sacrifice herself for the sake of passion, if this life demands it. Here we are in the presence of two strictly opposed moralities. I claim that they are much the same thing; in both cases what has been set up as the goal is freedom.

You can imagine two highly similar attitudes: one girl prefers to renounce her love out of resignation; another prefers to disregard the prior attachment of the man she loves out of sexual desire. On the surface these two actions resemble those we've just described. However, they are completely different. Sanseverina's attitude is much nearer that of Maggie Tulliver, one of heedless rapacity.

Thus, you see that the second charge is true and, at the same time, false. One may choose anything if it is on the grounds of free involvement.

The third objection is the following: "You take something from one pocket and put it into the other. That is, fundamentally, values aren't serious, since you choose them." My answer to this is that I'm quite vexed that that's the way it is; but if I've discarded God the Father, there has to be someone to invent values. You've got to take things as they are. Moreover, to say that we invent values means nothing else but this: life has no meaning *a priori.* Before you come alive, life is nothing; it's up to you to give it a meaning, and value is nothing else but the meaning that you choose. In that way, you see, there is a possibility of creating a human community.

I've been reproached for asking whether existentialism is humanistic. It's been said, "But you said in *Nausea* that the humanists were all wrong. You made fun of a certain kind of humanist. Why come back to it now?" Actually, the word humanism has two very different meanings. By humanism one can mean a theory which takes man as an end and as a higher value. Humanism in this sense can be found in Cocteau's tale *Around the World in Eighty Hours* when a character, because he is flying over some mountains in an airplane, declares, "Man is simply amazing." That means that I, who did not build the airplanes, shall personally benefit from these particular inventions, and that I, as man, shall personally consider myself responsible for, and honored by, acts of a few particular men. This would imply that we ascribe a value to man on the basis of the highest deeds of certain men. This humanism is absurd, because only the dog or the horse would be able to make such an overall judgment about man, which they are careful not to do, at least to my knowledge.

But it can not be granted that a man may make a judgment about man. Existentialism spares him from any such judgment. The existentialist will never consider man as an end because he is always in the making. Nor should we believe that there is a mankind to which we might set up a cult in the manner of Auguste Comte. The cult of mankind ends in the self-enclosed humanism of Comte, and, let it be said, of fascism. This kind of humanism we can do without.

But there is another meaning of humanism. Fundamentally it is this: man is constantly outside of himself; in projecting himself, in losing himself outside of himself, he makes for man's existing; and, on the other hand, it is by pursuing transcendent goals that he is able to exist; man, being this state of passing-beyond, and seizing upon things only as they bear upon this passing-beyond, is at the heart, at the center of this passing-beyond. There is no universe other than a human universe, the universe of human subjectivity. This connection between transcendency, as a constituent element of man—not in the sense that God is transcendent, but in the sense of passing beyond—and subjectivity, in the sense that man is not closed in on himself but is always present in a human universe, is what we call existentialism humanism. Humanism, because we remind man that there is no law-maker other than himself, and that in his forlornness he will decide by himself; because we point out that man will fulfill himself as man, not in turning toward himself, but in seeking outside of himself a goal which is just this liberation, just this particular fulfillment.

From these few reflections it is evident that nothing is more unjust than the objections that have been raised against us. Existentialism is nothing else than an attempt to draw all the consequences of a coherent atheistic position. It isn't trying to plunge man into despair at all. But if one calls every attitude of unbelief despair, like the Christians, then the word is not being used in its original sense. Existentialism isn't so atheistic that it wears itself out showing that God doesn't exist. Rather, it declares that even if God did exist, that would change nothing. There you've got our point of view. Not that we believe that God exists, but we think that the problem of His existence is not the issue. In this sense existentialism is optimistic, a doctrine of action, and it is plain dishonesty for Christians to make no distinction between their own despair and ours and then to call us despairing.

Simone de Beauvoir
1908–1986

Simone Lucie Ernestine Marie Bertrand de Beauvoir was the elder of two daughters born to attorney Georges Bertrand de Beauvoir and Françoise Brasseur de Beauvoir. The noble-sounding "de" in their name indicated some family prestige, but they were only comfortable, not wealthy. Apart from a five-year period during adulthood, de Beauvoir spent her entire life in the Montparnasse district of Paris. Her mother was a devout Catholic, and as a young girl de Beauvoir regularly attended church and went to confession. She studied in a Catholic school and considered God her personal companion. However, by adolescence she had given up her faith. She later recounted that this loss of belief was both freeing and terrifying: "Alone: for the first time I understood the terrible significance of that word. Alone: without a witness, without anyone to speak to, without refuge."

After the World War I, de Beauvoir's father suffered financial setbacks. He was forced to tell his daughters he could not provide them a dowry and concluded, "My dears, you'll never marry; you'll have to work for your livings." De Beauvoir decided to pursue a career as a philosophy teacher. She was drawn to philosophy because

> It went straight to essentials. . . . I had always wanted to know *everything;* philosophy would allow me to satisfy this desire, for it aimed at total reality.*

She enrolled at the Institut Sainte-Marie in 1925 and studied there for the next four years, simultaneously hearing lectures at the Institut Catholique and the Sorbonne.

*Simone de Beauvoir, *Memoirs of a Dutiful Daughter* (New York: Harper & Row, 1959), p. 158.

In 1929, de Beauvoir met Jean-Paul Sartre and studied with him for the *agrégation* in philosophy (which he had failed the previous year). After both passed the examination with high honors, she agreed to a "two-year lease" relationship with Sartre. During this period, she was an assistant at a lycée in Paris. In 1931, de Beauvoir accepted a full-time position at a lycée in Marseille and a year later moved to nearby Rouen. Though Sartre took a similar position at a lycée in Le Havre, on the opposite side of the country, their relationship continued. In fact, their "two-year lease" became a lifelong companionship, though they never married and were free to have "contingent" relationships.

By 1936, de Beauvoir was back in her beloved Montparnasse, Paris. For the next eight years, she taught at various lycées in Paris until the involvement of a student in her unusual lifestyle led to charges of corrupting a minor, and she was suspended. Though reinstated, she resigned in 1944 and supported herself for the rest of her life by her writings. Her first novel, *She Came to Stay*, was published that year to critical acclaim and financial success. She was heralded (with Albert Camus and Sartre) as one of the leaders of the new existentialist movement. The following year, with Maurice Merleau-Ponty and Sartre, she founded the influential journal *Les Temps modernes* and served as an editor and contributor to the magazine.

In her later years, de Beauvoir became increasingly involved in political issues. With Sartre, she visited Cuba, attended the International War Crimes Tribunal on U.S. War Crimes in Vietnam, and joined the student demonstrations at the Sorbonne. On her own, she worked vigorously for feminist issues such as legalized abortion and care for unmarried mothers. While leading the involved life of a left-wing political activist, de Beauvoir published a total of five novels, two collections of stories, and a play. She also published five volumes of memoirs, giving a picture of France in the twentieth century and of her relationship to Sartre. But de Beauvoir is best known for her philosophical works, especially the groundbreaking feminist text *The Second Sex* (1949).

* * *

The Second Sex is actually two separate volumes united around the question, "What is woman?" The first section, entitled "Facts and Myths," explores biology, psychology, sociology, history, myth, and literature to explain the answers given to this basic question. The second section, "Woman's Life Today," focuses on women's various roles and explores ways to move beyond these roles.

In the introduction to the work, reprinted here in the H.M. Parshley translation, de Beauvoir presents the basic categories that will guide her exploration of what it means to be woman. According to de Beauvoir, woman is the "second sex" because she is defined by man. Borrowing terminology from Sartre, she claims, "He is the Subject, he is the Absolute—she is the Other." Man sets himself up as the standard, the "One"—the definition of what it is to be human—so that immediately woman becomes the "Other." As the "Other," woman is relegated to existence as "*en-soi*": a being-in-itself, an object. Woman is not able to exist as "*pour-soi*," a being-for-itself. She cannot choose her existence because her role is already defined for her as the "Other."

De Beauvoir goes on to ask why women allow this to happen: "Why is it that women do not dispute male sovereignty?" After all, throughout history other groups have been treated as the "Other" and have redefined themselves. Why not women? Later in the book, de Beauvoir speculates that a woman's identity as the "Other" derives in part from her body—especially her reproductive capacity. But in our selection, she points outs that women have always (with rare exceptions) been subordinated to men, "and hence their dependency is not the result of a historical event or a social change—it was not something that *occurred*." Women have accepted their role as the "Other" because otherness "lacks the contingent or incidental nature of historical facts." Women have no past, no history of their own. They are not grouped together as women, they have no solidarity of employment since as a rule they work dispersed among men. In short, they do not have the "concrete means for organizing themselves into a unit which can stand face to face with the correlative unit."

The goal of *The Second Sex* is to move beyond analysis to a "concrete means" for organizing women. According to de Beauvoir, there must be two changes in order to accomplish this goal: (1) Women need to act as authentic subjects choosing their own histories and (2) society must be changed to make this possible. The first of these needed changes reflects de Beauvoir's existentialism, the second her Marxism.

Whereas traditionalists condemned the entire work, feminist critics raised questions about some of de Beauvoir's specific analyses. Many contemporary feminists claim that she did not go to the roots of patriarchy and its pervasive infection of even our language. Other feminists question her existentialist or Marxist assumptions (and her apparent hostility to the female body). But most feminists salute de Beauvoir for calling attention to feminist issues. As one writer put it, *The Second Sex* is for feminists "the base-line from which other works either explicitly . . . or implicitly . . . take off."

* * *

There are several biographies of de Beauvoir, including Axel Madsen, *Hearts and Minds: The Common Journey of Simone de Beauvoir and Jean-Paul Sartre* (New York: Morrow, 1977); the thorough Deirdre Bair, *Simone de Beauvoir: A Biography* (New York: Summit Books, 1990); Ursula Tidd, *Simone de Beauvoir: Gender and Testimony* (Cambridge: Cambridge University Press, 1999); Hazel Rowley, *Tête-à-Tête: Simone de Beauvoir and Jean-Paul Sartre* (New York: HarperCollins, 2005); and her own autobiography, Simone De Beauvoir, *Memoirs of a Dutiful Daughter*, translated by James Kirkup (New York: HarperCollins, 2005). General studies of her writings include Terry Keefe, *Simone de Beauvoir: A Study of Her Writings* (Totowa, NJ: Barnes & Noble, 1983); Judith Okely, *Simone de Beauvoir: A Re-reading* (London: Virago Press, 1986); Renee Winegarten, *Simone de Beauvoir: A Critical View* (New York: St. Martin's Press, 1988); Catharine Savage Brosman, *Simone de Beauvoir Revisited* (Boston: Twayne, 1991); Margaret Crosland, *Simone de Beauvoir: The Woman and Her Work* (London: Heinemann, 1992); and Clandia Card, ed., *The Cambridge Companion to Simone de Beauvoir* (Cambridge: Cambridge University Press, 2003). For material on her feminist theories specifically, see Jean Leighton, *Simone de Beauvoir on Woman* (Rutherford, NJ: Fairleigh Dickinson University Press, 1975); Mary Evans, *Simone de Beauvoir: A Feminist Mandarin* (London: Tavistock, 1985); Rosemarie Tong, *Feminist Thought: A Comprehensive*

Introduction (Boulder, CO: Westview Press, 1989); Toril Moi, *Feminist Theory & Simone de Beauvoir* (Oxford: Blackwell, 1990); Margaret A. Simons, ed., *Feminist Interpretations of Simone de Beauvoir* (College Park, PA: Pennsylvania State University Press, 1995); Debra B. Bergoffen, *The Philosophy of Simone de Beauvoir: Gendered Phenomenologies, Erotic Generosities* (Albany, NY: SUNY Press, 1996); Margaret A. Simons, *Beauvoir and* The Second Sex:*Feminism, Race, and the Origins of Existentialism* (Lanham, MD: Rowman and Littlefield, 2000); and Penelope Deutscher, *The Philosophy of Simone de Beauvoir: Ambiguity, Conversion, Resistance* (Cambridge: Cambridge University Press, 2008). Alice Schwarzer, *After "The Second Sex": Conversations with Simone de Beauvoir* (New York: Pantheon Books, 1984), gives de Beauvoir's reflections on her classic, whereas Donald L. Hatcher, *Understanding "The Second Sex"* (New York: Peter Lang, 1984) and Nancy Bauer, *Simone de Beauvoir, Philosophy, and Feminism* (NY: Columbia University Press, 2001) provide philosophical appraisals of that work.

THE SECOND SEX (in part)

INTRODUCTION

For a long time I have hesitated to write a book on woman. The subject is irritating, especially to women; and it is not new. Enough ink has been spilled in the quarreling over feminism, now practically over, and perhaps we should say no more about it. It is still talked about, however, for the voluminous nonsense uttered during the last century seems to have done little to illuminate the problem. After all, is there a problem? And if so, what is it? Are there women, really? Most assuredly the theory of the eternal feminine still has its adherents who will whisper in your ear: "Even in Russia women still are *women*"; and other erudite persons—sometimes the very same—say with a sigh: "Woman is losing her way, woman is lost." One wonders if women still exist, if they will always exist, whether or not it is desirable that they should, what place they occupy in this world, what their place should be. "What has become of women?" was asked recently in an ephemeral magazine.

But first we must ask: what is a woman? "*Tota mulier in utero*," says one, "woman is a womb." But in speaking of certain women, connoisseurs declare that they are not women, although they are equipped with a uterus like the rest. All agree in recognizing the fact that females exist in the human species; today as always they make up about one half of humanity. And yet we are told that femininity is in danger; we are exhorted to be women, remain women, become women. It would appear, then, that every female human being is not necessarily a woman; to be so considered she must share in that mysterious and threatened reality known as femininity. Is this attribute something secreted by the ovaries? Or is it a Platonic essence, a product of the philosophic imagination? Is a rustling petticoat enough to bring it down to earth? Although some women try zealously to incarnate this essence, it is hardly patentable. It is frequently described in vague and dazzling terms that seem to have been borrowed from the vocabulary of the seers, and indeed in the times of St. Thomas it was considered an essence as certainly defined as the somniferous virtue of the poppy.

But conceptualism has lost ground. The biological and social sciences no longer admit the existence of unchangeably fixed entities that determine given characteristics, such as those ascribed to woman, the Jew, or the Negro. Science regards any characteristic as a reaction dependent in part upon a *situation*. If today femininity no longer exists, then it never existed. But does the word *woman*, then, have no specific content? This is stoutly affirmed by those who hold to the philosophy of the enlightenment, of rationalism, of nominalism; women, to them, are merely the human beings arbitrarily designated by the word woman. Many American women particularly are prepared to think that there is no longer any place for woman as su ch; if a backward individual still takes herself for a woman, her friends advise her to be psychoanalyzed and thus get rid of this obsession. In regard to a work, *Modern Woman: The Lost Sex*, which in other respects has its irritating features, Dorothy Parker has written: "I cannot be just to books which treat of woman as woman. . . . My idea is that all of us, men as well as women, should be regarded as human beings." But nominalism is a rather inadequate doctrine, and the antifemininists have had no trouble in showing that women simply *are not* men. Surely woman is, like man, a human being; but such a declaration is abstract. The fact is that every concrete human being is always a singular, separate individual. To decline to accept such notions as the eternal feminine, the black soul, the Jewish character, is not to deny that Jews, Negroes, women exist today—this denial does not represent a liberation for those concerned, but rather a flight from reality. Some years ago a well-known woman writer refused to permit her portrait to appear in a series of photographs especially devoted to women writers; she wished to be counted among the men. But in order to gain this privilege she made use of her husband's influence! Women who assert that they are men lay claim none the less to masculine consideration and respect. I recall also a young Trotskyite standing on a platform at a boisterous meeting and getting ready to use her fists, in spite of her evident fragility. She was denying her feminine weakness; but it was for love of a militant male whose equal she wished to be. The attitude of defiance of many American women proves that they are haunted by a sense of their femininity. In truth, to go for a walk with one's eyes open is enough to demonstrate that humanity is divided into two classes of individuals whose clothes, faces, bodies, smiles, gaits, interests, and occupations are manifestly different. Perhaps these differences are superficial, perhaps they are destined to disappear. What is certain is that right now they do most obviously exist.

If her functioning as a female is not enough to define woman, if we decline also to explain her through "the eternal feminine," and if nevertheless we admit, provisionally, that women do exist, then we must face the question: what is a woman?

To state the question is, to me, to suggest, at once, a preliminary answer. The fact that I ask it is in itself significant. A man would never get the notion of writing a book on the peculiar situation of the human male. But if I wish to define myself, I must first of all say: "I am a woman"; on this truth must be based all further discussion. A man never begins by presenting himself as an individual of a certain sex; it goes without saying that he is a man. The terms *masculine* and *feminine* are used symmetrically only as a matter of form, as on legal papers. In actuality the relation of the two sexes is not quite like that of two electrical poles, for man represents both the positive and the neutral, as is indicated by the common use of man to designate human beings in general; whereas woman represents only the negative, defined by limiting criteria, without reciprocity. In the midst of an abstract discussion it is vexing to hear a man say: "You think thus and so because you are a woman"; but I know that my only defense is to reply: "I think thus and so because it is true," thereby removing my subjective self from the argument. It would be out of the question to reply: "And you think the contrary because you are a man," for it is understood that the fact of being a man is no peculiarity. A man is in the right in being a man; it is the woman who is in the wrong. It amounts to this: just as for the ancients there was an absolute vertical with reference to which the oblique was defined, so there is an absolute human type, the masculine. Woman has ovaries, a uterus; these peculiarities imprison her in her subjectivity, circumscribe her within the limits of her own nature. It is often said that she thinks with her glands. Man superbly ignores the fact that his anatomy also includes glands, such as the testicles, and that they secrete hormones. He thinks of his body as a direct and normal connection with the world, which he believes he apprehends objectively, whereas he regards the body of woman as a hindrance, a prison, weighed down by everything peculiar to it. "The female is a female by virtue of a certain *lack* of qualities," said Aristotle; "we should regard the female nature as afflicted with a natural defectiveness." And St. Thomas for his part pronounced woman to be an "imperfect man," an "incidental" being. This is symbolized in Genesis where Eve is depicted as made from what Bossuet called "a supernumerary bone" of Adam.

Thus humanity is male and man defines woman not in herself but as relative to him; she is not regarded as an autonomous being. Michelet writes: "Woman, the relative being. . . ." And Benda is most positive in his *Rapport d'Uriel: "The body of man makes sense in itself quite apart from that of woman, whereas the latter seems wanting in significance by itself. . . . Man can think of himself without woman. She cannot think of herself without man." And she is simply what man decrees;* thus she is called "the sex," by which is meant that she appears essentially to the male as a sexual being. For him she is sex—absolute sex, no less. She is defined and differentiated with reference to man and not he with reference to her; she is the incidental, the inessential as opposed to the essential. He is the Subject, he is the Absolute—she is the Other.*

The category of the Other is as primordial as consciousness itself. In the most primitive societies, in the most ancient mythologies, one finds the expression of a duality—that of the Self and the Other. This duality was not originally attached to the division of the sexes; it was not dependent upon any empirical facts. It is revealed in such works as that of Granet on Chinese thought and those of Dumezil on the East Indies and Rome. The feminine element was at first no more involved in such pairs as

*L. Lévinas expresses this idea most explicitly in his essay *Temps et l'Autre*. "Is there not a case in which otherness, alterity *[altérité]*, unquestionably marks the nature of a being, as its essence, an instance of otherness not consisting purely and simply in the opposition of two species of the same genus? I think that the feminine represents the contrary in its absolute sense, this contrariness being in no wise affected by any relation between it and its correlative and thus remaining absolutely other. Sex is not a certain specific difference . . . no more is the sexual difference a mere contradiction. . . . Nor does this difference lie in the duality of two complementary terms, for two complementary terms imply a pre-existing whole. . . . Otherness reaches its full flowering in the feminine, a term of the same rank as consciousness but of opposite meaning."

I suppose that Lévinas does not forget that woman, too, is aware of her own consciousness, or ego. But it is striking that he deliberately takes a man's point of view, disregarding the reciprocity of subject and object. When he writes that woman is mystery, he implies that she is mystery for man. Thus his description, which is intended to be objective, is in fact an assertion of masculine privilege.

Varuna-Mitra, Uranus-Zeus, Sun-Moon, and Day-Night than it was in the contrasts between Good and Evil, lucky and unlucky auspices, right and left, God and Lucifer. Otherness is a fundamental category of human thought.

Thus it is that no group ever sets itself up as the One without at once setting up the Other over against itself. If three travelers chance to occupy the same compartment, that is enough to make vaguely hostile "others" out of all the rest of the passengers on the train. In small-town eyes all persons not belonging to the village are "strangers" and suspect; to the native of a country all who inhabit other countries are "foreigners"; Jews are "different" for the anti-Semite, Negroes are "inferior" for American racists, aborigines are "natives" for colonists, proletarians are the "lower class" for the privileged.

Lévi-Strauss, at the end of a profound work on the various forms of primitive societies, reaches the following conclusion: "Passage from the state of Nature to the state of Culture is marked by man's ability to view biological relations as a series of contrasts; duality, alternation, opposition, and symmetry, whether under definite or vague forms, constitute not so much phenomena to be explained as fundamental and immediately given data of social reality." These phenomena would be incomprehensible if in fact human society were simply a *Mitsein* or fellowship based on solidarity and friendliness. Things become clear, on the contrary, if, following Hegel, we find in consciousness itself a fundamental hostility toward every other consciousness; the subject can be posed only in being opposed—he sets himself up as the essential, as opposed to the other, the inessential, the object.

But the other consciousness, the other ego, sets up a reciprocal claim. The native traveling abroad is shocked to find himself in turn regarded as a "stranger" by the natives of neighboring countries. As a matter of fact, wars, festivals, trading, treaties, and contests among tribes, nations, and classes tend to deprive the concept *Other* of its absolute sense and to make manifest its relativity; willy-nilly, individuals and groups are forced to realize the reciprocity of their relations. How is it, then, that this reciprocity has not been recognized between the sexes, that one of the contrasting terms is set up as the sole essential, denying any relativity in regard to its correlative and defining the latter as pure otherness? Why is it that women do not dispute male sovereignty? No subject will readily volunteer to become the object, the inessential; it is not the Other who, in defining himself as the Other, establishes the One. The Other is posed as such by the One in defining himself as the One. But if the Other is not to regain the status of being the One, he must be submissive enough to accept this alien point of view. Whence comes this submission in the case of woman?

There are, to be sure, other cases in which a certain category has been able to dominate another completely for a time. Very often this privilege depends upon inequality of numbers—the majority imposes its rule upon the minority or persecutes it. But women are not a minority, like the American Negroes or the Jews; there are as many women as men on earth. Again, the two groups concerned have often been originally independent; they may have been formerly unaware of each other's existence, or perhaps they recognized each other's autonomy. But a historical event has resulted in the subjugation of the weaker by the stronger. The scattering of the Jews, the introduction of slavery into America, the conquests of imperialism are examples in point. In these cases the oppressed retained at least the memory of former days; they possessed in common a past, a tradition, sometimes a religion or a culture.

The parallel drawn by Bebel between women and the proletariat is valid in that neither ever formed a minority or a separate collective unit of mankind. And instead of a single historical event it is in both cases a historical development that explains their status as a class and accounts for the membership of *particular individuals* in that class.

But proletarians have not always existed, whereas there have always been women. They are women in virtue of their anatomy and physiology. Throughout history they have always been subordinated to men, and hence their dependency is not the result of a historical event or a social change—it was not something that *occurred*. The reason why otherness in this case seems to be an absolute is in part that it lacks the contingent or incidental nature of historical facts. A condition brought about at a certain time can be abolished at some other time, as the Negroes of Haiti and others have proved; but it might seem that a natural condition is beyond the possibility of change. In truth, however, the nature of things is no more immutably given, once for all, than is historical reality. If woman seems to be the inessential which never becomes the essential, it is because she herself fails to bring about this change. Proletarians say "We"; Negroes also. Regarding themselves as subjects, they transform the bourgeois, the whites, into "others." But women do not say "We," except at some congress of feminists or similar formal demonstration; men say "women," and women use the same word in referring to themselves. They do not authentically assume a subjective attitude. The proletarians have accomplished the revolution in Russia, the Negroes in Haiti, the Indo-Chinese are battling for it in Indo-China; but the women's effort has never been anything more than a symbolic agitation. They have gained only what men have been willing to grant; they have taken nothing, they have only received.

The reason for this is that women lack concrete means for organizing themselves into a unit which can stand face to face with the correlative unit. They have no past, no history, no religion of their own; and they have no such solidarity of work and interest as that of the proletariat. They are not even promiscuously herded together in the way that creates community feeling among the American Negroes, the ghetto Jews, the workers of Saint-Denis, or the factory hands of Renault. They live dispersed among the males, attached through residence, housework, economic condition, and social standing to certain men—fathers or husbands—more firmly than they are to other women. If they belong to the bourgeoisie, they feel solidarity with men of that class, not with proletarian women; if they are white, their allegiance is to white men, not to Negro women. The proletariat can propose to massacre the ruling class, and a sufficiently fanatical Jew or Negro might dream of getting sole possession of the atomic bomb and making humanity wholly Jewish or black; but woman cannot even dream of exterminating the males. The bond that unites her to her oppressors is not comparable to any other. The division of the sexes is a biological fact, not an event in human history. Male and female stand opposed within a primordial *Mitsein*, and woman has not broken it. The couple is a fundamental unity with its two halves riveted together, and the cleavage of society along the line of sex is impossible. Here is to be found the basic trait of woman: she is the Other in a totality of which the two components are necessary to one another.

One could suppose that this reciprocity might have facilitated the liberation of woman. When Hercules sat at the feet of Omphale and helped with her spinning, his desire for her held him captive; but why did she fail to gain a lasting power? To revenge herself on Jason, Medea killed their children; and this grim legend would seem to suggest that she might have obtained a formidable influence over him through his love for his offspring. In *Lysistrata* Aristophanes gaily depicts a band of women who joined forces to gain social ends through the sexual needs of their men; but this is only a play. In the legend of the Sabine women, the latter soon abandoned their plan of remaining sterile to punish their ravishers. In truth woman has not been socially emancipated through man's need—sexual desire and the desire for offspring—which makes the male dependent for satisfaction upon the female.

Migrant Mother, 1936, by Dorothea Lange (1895–1965). This powerful photograph of a migrant mother in central California reveals both anxiety and strength. (*Copyright The Dorothea Lange Collection, The Oakland Museum of California, City of Oakland. Gift of Paul S. Taylor.*)

Master and slave, also, are united by a reciprocal need, in this case economic, which does not liberate the slave. In the relation of master to slave the master does not make a point of the need that he has for the other; he has in his grasp the power of satisfying this need through his own action; whereas the slave, in his dependent condition, his hope and fear, is quite conscious of the need he has for his master. Even if the need is at bottom equally urgent for both, it always works in favor of the oppressor and against the oppressed. That is why the liberation of the working class, for example, has been slow.

Now, woman has always been man's dependent, if not his slave; the two sexes have never shared the world in equality. And even today woman is heavily handicapped, though her situation is beginning to change. Almost nowhere is her legal status the same as man's, and frequently it is much to her disadvantage. Even when her rights are legally recognized in the abstract, long-standing custom prevents their full expression in the mores. In the economic sphere men and women can almost be said to make up two castes; other things being equal, the former hold the better jobs, get higher wages, and have more opportunity for success than their new competitors. In industry and politics men have a great many more positions and they monopolize the most important posts. In addition to all this, they enjoy a traditional prestige that the education of children tends in every way to support, for the present enshrines the past—and in the past all history has been made by men. At the present time, when women are beginning to take part in the affairs of the world, it is still a world that belongs to men—they have no doubt of it at all and women have scarcely any. To decline to be the Other, to refuse to be a party to the deal—this would be for women to renounce all the advantages conferred upon them by their alliance with the superior caste. Man-the-sovereign will provide woman-the-liege with material protection and will undertake the moral justification of her existence; thus she can evade at once both economic risk and the metaphysical risk of a liberty in which ends and aims must be contrived without assistance. Indeed, along with the ethical urge of each individual to affirm his subjective existence, there is also the temptation to forgo liberty and become a thing. This is an inauspicious road, for he who takes it—passive, lost, ruined—becomes henceforth the creature of another's will, frustrated in his transcendence and deprived of every value. But it is an easy road; on it one avoids the strain involved in undertaking an authentic existence. When man makes of woman the *Other*, he may, then, expect her to manifest deep-seated tendencies toward complicity. Thus, woman may fail to lay claim to the status of subject because she lacks definite resources, because she feels the necessary bond that ties her to man regardless of reciprocity, and because she is often very well pleased with her role as the *Other*.

But it will be asked at once: how did all this begin? It is easy to see that the duality of the sexes, like any duality, gives rise to conflict. And doubtless the winner will assume the status of absolute. But why should man have won from the start? It seems possible that women could have won the victory; or that the outcome of the conflict might never have been decided. How is it that this world has always belonged to the men and that things have begun to change only recently? Is this change a good thing? Will it bring about an equal sharing of the world between men and women?

These questions are not new, and they have often been answered. But the very fact that woman *is the Other* tends to cast suspicion upon all the justifications that men have ever been able to provide for it. These have all too evidently been dictated by men's interest. A little-known feminist of the seventeenth century, Poulain de la Barre, put it this way: "All that has been written about women by men should be suspect, for the men are at once judge and party to the lawsuit." Everywhere, at all times, the males have displayed their satisfaction in feeling that they are the lords of creation. "Blessed be God . . . that He did not make me a woman," say the Jews in their morning prayers, while their wives pray on a note of resignation: "Blessed be the Lord, who created me according to His will." The first among the blessings for which Plato thanked the gods was that he had been created free, not enslaved; the second, a man, not a woman. But the males could not enjoy this privilege fully unless they believed it to be founded on the absolute and the eternal; they sought to make the fact of their supremacy into a right. "Being men, those who have made and compiled the laws have favored their own sex, and jurists have elevated these laws into principles," to quote Poulain de la Barre once more.

Legislators, priests, philosophers, writers, and scientists have striven to show that the subordinate position of woman is willed in heaven and advantageous on earth. The religions invented by men reflect this wish for domination. In the legends of Eve and Pandora men have taken up arms against women. They have made use of philosophy and theology, as the quotations from Aristotle and St. Thomas have shown. Since ancient times satirists and moralists have delighted in showing up the weaknesses of women. We are familiar with the savage indictments hurled against women throughout French literature. Montherlant, for example, follows the tradition of Jean de Meung, though with less gusto. This hostility may at times be well founded, often it is gratuitous; but in truth it more or less successfully conceals a desire for self-justification. As Montaigne says, "It is easier to accuse one sex than to excuse the other." Sometimes what is going on is clear enough. For instance, the Roman law limiting the rights of woman cited "the imbecility, the instability of the sex" just when the weakening of family ties seemed to threaten the interests of male heirs. And in the effort to keep the married woman under guardianship, appeal was made in the sixteenth century to the authority of St. Augustine, who declared that "woman is a creature neither decisive nor constant," at a time when the single woman was thought capable of managing her property. Montaigne understood clearly how arbitrary and unjust was woman's appointed lot: "Women are not in the wrong when they decline to accept the rules laid down for them, since the men make these rules without consulting them. No wonder intrigue and strife abound." But he did not go so far as to champion their cause.

It was only later, in the eighteenth century, that genuinely democratic men began to view the matter objectively. Diderot, among others, strove to show that woman is, like man, a human being. Later John Stuart Mill came fervently to her defense. But these philosophers displayed unusual impartiality. In the nineteenth century the feminist quarrel became again a quarrel of partisans. One of the consequences of the industrial revolution was the entrance of women into productive labor, and it was just here that the claims of the feminists emerged from the realm of theory and acquired an economic basis, while their opponents became the more aggressive. Although landed property lost power to some extent, the bourgeoisie clung to the old morality that found the guarantee of private property in the solidity of the family. Woman was ordered back into the home the more harshly as her emancipation became a real menace. Even within the working class the men endeavored to restrain woman's liberation, because they began to see the women as dangerous competitors—the more so because they were accustomed to work for lower wages.

In proving woman's inferiority, the antifeminists then began to draw not only upon religion, philosophy, and theology, as before, but also upon science—biology, experimental psychology, etc. At most they were willing to grant "equality in difference" to the *other* sex. That profitable formula is most significant; it is precisely like the "equal but separate" formula of the Jim Crow laws aimed at the North American Negroes. As is well known, this socalled equalitarian segregation has resulted only in the most extreme discrimination. The similarity just noted is in no way due to chance, for whether it is a race, a caste, a class, or a sex that is reduced to a position of inferiority, the methods of justification are the same. "The eternal feminine" corresponds to "the black soul" and to "the Jewish character." True, the Jewish problem is on the whole very different from the other two—to the anti-Semite the Jew is not so much an inferior as he is an enemy for whom there is to be granted no place on earth, for whom annihilation is the fate desired. But there are deep similarities between the situation of woman and that of the Negro. Both are being emancipated today from a like paternalism, and the former master class wishes to "keep them in their place"— that is, the place chosen for them. In both cases the former masters lavish more or less sincere eulogies, either on the virtues of "the good Negro" with his dormant, childish, merry soul—the submissive Negro—or on the merits of the woman who is "truly feminine"— that is, frivolous, infantile, irresponsible—the submissive woman. In both cases the dominant class bases its argument on a state of affairs that it has itself created. As George Bernard Shaw puts it, in substance, "The American white relegates the black to the rank of shoeshine boy; and he concludes from this that the black is good for nothing but shining shoes." This vicious circle is met with in all analogous circumstances; when an individual (or a group of individuals) is kept in a situation of inferiority, the fact is that he is inferior. But the significance of the verb *to be* must be rightly understood here; it is in bad faith to give it a static value when it really has the dynamic Hegelian sense of "to have become." Yes, women on the whole *are* today inferior to men; that is, their situation affords them fewer possibilities. The question is: should that state of affairs continue?

Many men hope that it will continue; not all have given up the battle. The conservative bourgeoisie still see in the emancipation of women a menace to their morality and their interests. Some men dread feminine competition. Recently a male student wrote in the *Hebdo-Latin*: "Every woman student who goes into medicine or law robs us of a job." He never questioned his rights in this world. And economic interests are not the only ones concerned. One of the benefits that oppression confers upon the oppressors is that the most humble among them is made to *feel* superior; thus, a "poor white" in the South can console himself with the thought that he is not a "dirty nigger"— and the more prosperous whites cleverly exploit this pride.

Similarly, the most mediocre of males feels himself a demigod as compared with women. It was much easier for M. de Montherlant to think himself a hero when he faced women (and women chosen for his purpose) than when he was obliged to act the man among men—something many women have done better than he, for that matter. And in September 1948, in one of his articles in the *Figaro littéraire*, Claude Mauriac—whose great originality is admired by all—could write regarding woman: "We listen on a tone *[sic!]* of polite indifference . . . to the most brilliant among them, well knowing that her wit reflects more or less luminously ideas that come from *us*." Evidently the speaker referred to is not reflecting the ideas of Mauriac himself, for no one knows of his having any. It may be that she reflects ideas originating with men, but then, even among men there are those who have been known to appropriate ideas not their own; and one can well ask whether Claude Mauriac might not find more interesting a conversation reflecting Descartes, Marx, or Gide rather than himself. What is really remarkable is that by using the questionable we he identifies himself with St. Paul, Hegel, Lenin, and Nietzsche, and from the lofty eminence of their grandeur looks down disdainfully upon the bevy of women who make bold to converse with him on a footing of equality. In truth, I know of more than one woman who would refuse to suffer with patience Mauriac's "tone of polite indifference."

I have lingered on this example because the masculine attitude is here displayed with disarming ingenuousness. But men profit in many more subtle ways from the otherness, the alterity of woman. Here is miraculous balm for those afflicted with an inferiority complex, and indeed no one is more arrogant toward women, more aggressive or scornful, than the man who is anxious about his virility. Those who are not fearridden in the presence of their fellow men are much more disposed to recognize a fellow creature in woman; but even to these the myth of Woman, the Other, is precious for many reasons.* They cannot be blamed for not cheerfully relinquishing all the benefits they derive from the myth, for they realize what they would lose in relinquishing woman as they fancy her to be, while they fail to realize what they have to gain from the woman of tomorrow. Refusal to pose oneself as the Subject, unique and absolute, requires great self-denial. Furthermore, the vast majority of men make no such claim explicitly. They do not *postulate* woman as inferior, for today they are too thoroughly imbued with the ideal of democracy not to recognize all human beings as equals.

In the bosom of the family, woman seems in the eyes of childhood and youth to be clothed in the same social dignity as the adult males. Later on, the young man, desiring and loving, experiences the resistance, the independence of the woman desired and loved; in marriage, he respects woman as wife and mother, and in the concrete events of conjugal life she stands there before him as a free being. He can therefore feel that social subordination as between the sexes no longer exists and that on the whole, in spite of differences, woman is an equal. As, however, he observes some points of inferiority—the most important being unfitness for the professions—he attributes these to natural causes. When he is in a co-operative and benevolent relation with woman, his theme is the principle of abstract equality, and he does not base his attitude upon such inequality as may exist. But when he is in conflict with her, the situation is reversed: his theme will be the existing inequality, and he will even take it as justification for denying abstract equality.**

So it is that many men will affirm as if in good faith that women *are* the equals of man and that they have nothing to clamor for, while *at the same* time they will say that women can never be the equals of man and that their demands are in vain. It is, in point of fact, a difficult matter for man to realize the extreme importance of social discriminations which seem outwardly insignificant but which produce in woman moral and intellectual effects so profound that they appear to spring from her original nature. The most sympathetic of men never fully comprehend woman's concrete situation. And there is no reason to put much trust in the men when they rush to the defense of privileges whose full extent they can hardly measure. We shall not, then, permit ourselves to be intimidated by the number and violence of the attacks launched against women, nor to be entrapped by the self-seeking eulogies bestowed on the "true woman," nor to profit by the enthusiasm for woman's destiny manifested by men who would not for the world have any part of it.

We should consider the arguments of the feminists with no less suspicion, however, for very often their controversial aim deprives them of all real value. If the "woman question" seems trivial, it is because masculine arrogance has made of it a

*A significant article on this theme by Michel Carrouges appeared in No. 292 of the *Cahiers du Sud*. He writes indignantly: "Would that there were no woman-myth at all but only a cohort of cooks, matrons, prostitutes, and bluestockings serving functions of pleasure or usefulness!" That is to say, in his view woman has no existence in and for herself; he thinks only of her *function* in the male world. Her reason for existence lies in man. But then, in fact, her poetic "function" as a myth might be more valued than any other. The real problem is precisely to find out why woman should be defined with relation to man.

**For example, a man will say that he considers his wife in no wise degraded because she has no gainful occupation. The profession of housewife is just as lofty, and so on. But when the first quarrel comes, he will exclaim: "Why, you couldn't make your living without me!"

"quarrel"; and when quarreling one no longer reasons well. People have tirelessly sought to prove that woman is superior, inferior, or equal to man. Some say that, having been created after Adam, she is evidently a secondary being; others say on the contrary that Adam was only a rough draft and that God succeeded in producing the human being in perfection when He created Eve. Woman's brain is smaller; yes, but it is relatively larger. Christ was made a man; yes, but perhaps for his greater humility. Each argument at once suggests its opposite, and both are often fallacious. If we are to gain understanding, we must get out of these ruts; we must discard the vague notions of superiority, inferiority, equality which have hitherto corrupted every discussion of the subject and start afresh.

Very well, but just how shall we pose the question? And, to begin with, who are we to propound it at all? Man is at once judge and party to the case; but so is woman. What we need is an angel—neither man nor woman—but where shall we find one? Still, the angel would be poorly qualified to speak, for an angel is ignorant of all the basic facts involved in the problem. With a hermaphrodite we should be no better off, for here the situation is most peculiar; the hermaphrodite is not really the combination of a whole man and a whole woman, but consists of parts of each and thus is neither. It looks to me as if there are, after all, certain women who are best qualified to elucidate the situation of woman. Let us not be misled by the sophism that because Epimenides was a Cretan he was necessarily a liar; it is not a mysterious essence that compels men and women to act in good or in bad faith; it is their situation that inclines them more or less toward the search for truth. Many of today's women, fortunate in the restoration of all the privileges pertaining to the estate of the human being, can afford the luxury of impartiality—we even recognize its necessity. We are no longer like our partisan elders; by and large we have won the game. In recent debates on the status of women the United Nations has persistently maintained that the equality of the sexes is now becoming a reality, and already some of us have never had to sense in our femininity an inconvenience or an obstacle. Many problems appear to us to be more pressing than those which concern us in particular, and this detachment even allows us to hope that our attitude will be objective. Still, we know the feminine world more intimately than do the men because we have our roots in it, we grasp more immediately than do men what it means to a human being to be feminine; and we are more concerned with such knowledge. I have said that there are more pressing problems, but this does not prevent us from seeing some importance in asking how the fact of being women will affect our lives. What opportunities precisely have been given us and what withheld? What fate awaits our younger sisters, and what directions should they take? It is significant that books by women on women are in general animated in our day less by a wish to demand our rights than by an effort toward clarity and understanding. As we emerge from an era of excessive controversy, this book is offered as one attempt among others to confirm that statement.

But it is doubtless impossible to approach any human problem with a mind free from bias. The way in which questions are put, the points of view assumed, presuppose a relativity of interest; all characteristics imply values, and every objective description, so called, implies an ethical background. Rather than attempt to conceal principles more or less definitely implied, it is better to state them openly at the beginning. This will make it unnecessary to specify on every page in just what sense one uses such words as *superior, inferior, better, worse, progress, reaction*, and the like. If we survey some of the works on woman, we note that one of the points of view most frequently adopted is that of the public good, the general interest; and one always means by this the benefit of society as one wishes it to be maintained or established. For our part, we hold that the only public good is that which assures the private good of the citizens; we shall pass judgment on institutions according to their effectiveness in giving concrete opportunities to individuals. But we do not confuse the idea of private interest with that of happiness, although that is another common point of view. Are not women of the harem more happy than women voters? Is not the housekeeper happier than the working-woman? It is not too clear just what the word *happy* really means and still less what true values it may mask. There is no possibility of measuring the happiness of others, and it is always easy to describe as happy the situation in which one wishes to place them.

In particular those who are condemned to stagnation are often pronounced happy on the pretext that happiness consists in being at rest. This notion we reject, for our perspective is that of existentialist ethics. Every subject plays his part as such specifically through exploits or projects that serve as a mode of transcendence; he achieves liberty only through a continual reaching out toward other liberties. There is no justification for present existence other than its expansion into an indefinitely open future. Every time transcendence falls back into immanence, stagnation, there is a degradation of existence into the "*en-soi*"—the brutish life of subjection to given conditions—and of liberty into constraint and contingence. This downfall represents a moral fault if the subject consents to it; if it is inflicted upon him, it spells frustration and oppression. In both cases it is an absolute evil. Every individual concerned to justify his existence feels that his existence involves an undefined need to transcend himself, to engage in freely chosen projects.

Now, what peculiarly signalizes the situation of woman is that she—a free and autonomous being like all human creatures—nevertheless finds herself living in a world where men compel her to assume the status of the Other. They propose to stabilize her as object and to doom her to immanence since her transcendence is to be overshadowed and forever transcended by another ego (*conscience*) which is essential and sovereign. The drama of woman lies in this conflict between the fundamental aspirations of every subject (ego)— who always regards the self as the essential—and the compulsions of a situation in which she is the inessential. How can a human being in woman's situation attain fulfillment? What roads are open to her? Which are blocked? How can independence be recovered in a state of dependency? What circumstances limit woman's liberty and how can they be overcome? These are the fundamental questions on which I would fain throw some light. This means that I am interested in the fortunes of the individual as defined not in terms of happiness but in terms of liberty.

Quite evidently this problem would be without significance if we were to believe that woman's destiny is inevitably determined by physiological, psychological, or economic forces. Hence I shall discuss first of all the light in which woman is viewed by biology, psychoanalysis, and historical materialism. Next I shall try to show exactly how the concept of the "truly feminine" has been fashioned—why woman has been defined as the Other—and what have been the consequences from man's point of view. Then from woman's point of view I shall describe the world in which women must live; and thus we shall be able to envisage the difficulties in their way as, endeavoring to make their escape from the sphere hitherto assigned them, they aspire to full membership in the human race.

Willard Van Orman Quine
1908–2000

Willard Van Orman Quine was the youngest of the sons born to Robert Quine and Harriet Van Orman Quine of Akron, Ohio. His mother was a schoolteacher and his father a worker in heavy industry. As a child, Quine developed a lifelong fascination with travel and maps. On summer vacations, he would draw careful maps of nearby lakes and sell copies to local cabin owners. The young Quine also excelled in mathematics and languages. In 1926, he enrolled at Oberlin College, where he majored in mathematics and studied philosophy. His research led him to mathematical philosophy, logic, and the philosophy of Bertrand Russell. In Russell, he found a kindred spirit—they shared a logical approach to philosophical problems and a religious skepticism.

Quine went to Harvard University for graduate studies in 1930. He married his college sweetheart, buried himself in studies with such noted philosophers as C.I. Lewis and Alfred North Whitehead, finished his course work, passed preliminary examinations, and received his master's degree—all in a year. The following year, he completed a 290-page dissertation on logic and received his Ph.D. degree at age 23. *A System of Logistic* (1934), a revision of this dissertation, became the first of his fifteen published books.

The year Quine received his doctorate, he was also awarded Harvard's Sheldon Traveling Fellowship. He took the title of the fellowship seriously, and in one year he and his wife visited twenty-seven countries. Quine met several members of the Vienna Circle and studied logic in Warsaw with the great Polish logicians Alfred Tarski, Stanisław Leśniewski, and Jan Łukasiewicz. At the end of the year, he was elected into Harvard's Society of Fellows, which gave him, among other emoluments, three years' pay and no duties. Among his five colleagues as junior fellows was the promising young psychologist B.F. Skinner.

Quine taught at Harvard until 1942. During World War II, his skill in languages and his gift for logic were put to use translating and analyzing decoded messages from German submarines. In 1946, Quine returned to Harvard and teaching. Except for sabbaticals and visiting professorships (and traveling in more than 100 countries), Quine remained a professor at Harvard until his retirement in 1978. He spent the next twenty-two years writing and travelling until his death in 2000.

* * *

In his autobiography, Quine explains that he has always despised conceptual constraints and has "been at pains to blur the boundaries between natural science, mathematics, and philosophy." Nowhere is this impatience with divisions more apparent than in Quine's critique of the analytic-synthetic distinction.

Ever since Hume first distinguished between "relations of ideas" and "matters of fact," philosophers have divided all propositions into two categories: analytic and synthetic. Yet in his famous paper "Two Dogmas of Empiricism," reprinted here (complete), Quine argues on the basis of various tests of meaning, synonymity, definition, and semantics that such a division has never been clearly made and that there is no compelling reason for believing such a separation can be made.

For example, the foundational propositions of logic and mathematics have been held to be true by convention independent of any matters of fact. Thus, the proposition (1) "No unmarried man is married" is true regardless of the various interpretations of "man" and "married." But there are also semantic propositions, such as (2) "No bachelor is married," which are claimed to be equally analytic. As Quine points out, it is common to believe that this latter (supposed) analytic proposition can be made into a truth of logic by "putting synonyms for synonyms; thus (2) can be turned into (1) by putting 'unmarried man' for its synonym 'bachelor'." But what is our criterion of synonymity and how is it any more clear than our criterion of "analyticity"? We could say that propositions (1) and (2) are synonymous if the term "bachelor" in (2) is *defined* as "unmarried man." But what is the basis for such a definition? Does analyticity depend on the empirical observations of a lexicographer or the authority of a dictionary? We could say that these propositions are synonymous if proposition (2) is "necessarily true." However, this would be begging the question; to say a proposition is "necessary" is to say it is analytic. Quine concludes that analyticity as a clearly distinguished notion is "an unempirical dogma of empiricists, a metaphysical article of faith."

Having critiqued the analytic-synthetic distinction, Quine next turns his attention to another empirical dogma: the verification theory of meaning and the reductionism that it presupposes. According to this theory of meaning, the meaning of any statement is the "method of empirically confirming or inferring it." But such a theory implies that each meaningful statement can be reduced to an equivalent statement that contains only references to immediate experience. Logical positivists such as A.J. Ayer sought to develop such a reductionistic language. But according to Quine, Ayer and the others are relying on the nonexistent analytic-synthetic distinction to separate the "linguistic components" from the "factual components" in any individual statement. Furthermore, *no* statement, taken by itself, could be confirmed or discredited by sensory experience because there could always be a further experience that would overturn the original statement.

Quine concludes:

> The totality of our so-called knowledge or beliefs, from the most casual matters of geography and history to the profoundest laws of atomic physics or even of pure mathematics and logic, is a man-made fabric which impinges on experience only along the edges.

Individual experiences "along the edges" may be dismissed as errors or hallucinations if they disturb more central beliefs. But even our core beliefs of mathematics and logic are subject to possible revision. There is no final truth nor even a clear distinction between the truths of logic and the truths of experience, that is, between analytic and synthetic.

* * *

Alex Orenstein, *Willard Van Orman Quine* (Boston: Twayne, 1977); Gary Kemp, *Quine: A Guide for the Perplexed* (London: Continuum, 2006); and Peter Hylton, *Quine* (Abingdon, UK: Routledge, 2007) provide good places to begin further study, whereas Roger F. Gibson, *The Philosophy of W.V. Quine: An Expository Essay* (Tampa: University Presses of Florida, 1982); George D. Romanas, *Quine and Analytic Philosophy* (Cambridge: MIT Press, 1983); Ilham Dilman, *Quine on Ontology, Necessity, and Experience: A Philosophical Critique* (Albany, NY: SUNY Press, 1984); and Christopher Hookway, *Quine: Language, Experience, and Reality* (Stanford, CA: Stanford University Press, 1988) have written critical investigations. For information on Quine's life, see his autobiography, *The Time of My Life: An Autobiography* (Cambridge: MIT Press, 1985). For collections of essays, see Donald Davidson and Jaakko Hintikka, eds., *Words and Objections: Essays on the Work of W.V. Quine* (Dordrecht, The Netherlands: D. Reidel, 1969); Robert W. Shahan and Chris Swoyer, eds., *Essays on the Philosophy of W.V. Quine* (Norman: University of Oklahoma Press, 1979); Robert Barrett and Roger Gibson, eds., *Perspectives on Quine* (Oxford: Basil Blackwell, 1993); Paolo Leonardi and Marlo Santambrogio, eds., *On Quine: New Essays* (Cambridge: Cambridge University Press, 1994); Robert L. Arrington and Johann Glock, eds., *Wittgenstein and Quine* (Oxford: Routledge, 1996); Lynn Hankinson Nelson and Jack Nelson, eds., *Feminist Interpretations of W.V. Quine* (College Park, PA: Pennsylvania State University Press, 2003); Roger F. Gibson, Jr., ed., *The Cambridge Companion to Quine* (Cambridge: Cambridge University Press, 2004); and, especially, Lewis Edwin Hahn and Paul Arthur Schilpp, eds., *The Philosophy of W.V. Quine* (La Salle, IL: Open Court, 1986), another volume in the Library of Living Philosophers Series, which includes Quine's responses to critics and a short version of his autobiography.

TWO DOGMAS OF EMPIRICISM

Modern empiricism has been conditioned in large part by two dogmas. One is a belief in some fundamental cleavage between truths which are *analytic,* or grounded in meanings independently of matters of fact, and truths which are *synthetic,* or grounded in fact. The other dogma is *reductionism:* the belief that each meaningful statement is equivalent to some logical construct upon terms which refer to immediate experience. Both dogmas, I shall argue, are ill-founded. One effect of abandoning them is, as we shall see, a blurring of the supposed boundary between speculative metaphysics and natural science. Another effect is a shift toward pragmatism.

1. Background for Analyticity

Kant's cleavage between analytic and synthetic truths was foreshadowed in Hume's distinction between relations of ideas and matters of fact, and in Leibniz's distinction between truths of reason and truths of fact. Leibniz spoke of the truths of reason as true in all possible worlds. Picturesqueness aside, this is to say that the truths of reason are those which could not possibly be false. In the same vein we hear analytic statements defined as statements whose denials are self-contradictory. But this definition has small explanatory value; for the notion of self-contradictoriness, in the quite broad sense needed for this definition of analyticity, stands in exactly the same need of clarification as does the notion of analyticity itself. The two notions are the two sides of a single dubious coin.

Kant conceived of an analytic statement as one that attributes to its subject no more than is already conceptually contained in the subject. This formulation has two shortcomings: it limits itself to statements of subject-predicate form, and it appeals to a notion of containment which is left at a metaphorical level. But Kant's intent, evident more from the use he makes of the notion of analyticity than from his definition of it, can be restated thus: a statement is analytic when it is true by virtue of meanings and independently of fact. Pursuing this line, let us examine the concept of *meaning* which is presupposed.

Meaning, let us remember, is not to be identified with naming. Frege's example of 'Evening Star' and 'Morning Star,' and Russell's of 'Scott' and 'the author of *Waverley,*' illustrate that terms can name the same thing but differ in meaning. The distinction between meaning and naming is no less important at the level of abstract terms. The terms '9' and 'the number of the planets' name one and the same abstract entity but presumably must be regarded as unlike in meaning; for astronomical observation was needed, and not mere reflection on meanings, to determine the sameness of the entity in question.

The above examples consist of singular terms, concrete and abstract. With general terms, or predicates, the situation is somewhat different but parallel. Whereas a singular term purports to name an entity, abstract or concrete, a general term does not; but a general term is *true of* an entity, or of each of many, or of none. The class of all entities of which a general term is true is called the *extension* of the term. Now paralleling the contrast between the meaning of a singular term and the entity named, we must distinguish equally between the meaning of a general term and its extension. The general terms 'creature with a heart' and 'creature with kidneys,' for example, are perhaps alike in extension but unlike in meaning.

Confusion of meaning with extension, in the case of general terms, is less common than confusion of meaning with naming in the case of singular terms. It is indeed a commonplace in philosophy to oppose intension (or meaning) to extension, or, in a variant vocabulary, connotation to denotation.

The Aristotelian notion of essence was the forerunner, no doubt, of the modern notion of intension or meaning. For Aristotle it was essential in men to be rational, accidental to be two-legged. But there is an important difference between this attitude and the doctrine of meaning. From the latter point of view it may indeed be conceded (if only for the sake of argument) that rationality is involved in the meaning of the word 'man' while two-leggedness is not; but two-leggedness may at the same time be viewed as involved in the meaning of 'biped' while rationality is not. Thus from the point of view of the doctrine of meaning it makes no sense to say of the actual individual, who is at once a man and a biped, that his rationality is essential and his two-leggedness accidental or vice versa. Things had essences for Aristotle, but only linguistic forms have meanings. Meaning is what essence becomes when it is divorced from the object of reference and wedded to the word.

For the theory of meaning a conspicuous question is the nature of its objects: what sort of things are meanings? A felt need for meant entities may derive from an earlier failure to appreciate that meaning and reference are distinct. Once the theory of meaning is sharply separated from the theory of reference, it is a short step to recognizing as the primary business of the theory of meaning simply the synonymy of linguistic forms and the analyticity of statements; meanings themselves, as obscure intermediary entities, may well be abandoned.

The problem of analyticity then confronts us anew. Statements which are analytic by general philosophical acclaim are not, indeed, far to seek. They fall into two classes. Those of the first class, which may be called *logically true*, are typified by:

(1) No unmarried man is married.

The relevant feature of this example is that it not merely is true as it stands, but remains true under any and all reinterpretations of 'man' and 'married.' If we suppose a prior inventory of *logical* particles, comprising 'no,' 'un-,' 'not,' 'if,' 'then,' 'and,' etc., then in general a logical truth is a statement which is true and remains true under all reinterpretations of its components other than the logical particles.

But there is also a second class of analytic statements, typified by:

(2) No bachelor is married.

The characteristic of such a statement is that it can be turned into a logical truth by putting synonyms for synonyms; thus (2) can be turned into (1) by putting 'unmarried man' for its synonym 'bachelor.' We still lack a proper characterization of this second class of analytic statements, and therewith of analyticity generally, inasmuch as we have had in the above description to lean on a notion of "synonymy" which is no less in need of clarification than analyticity itself.

In recent years Carnap has tended to explain analyticity by appeal to what he calls state-descriptions. A state-description is any exhaustive assignment of truth values to the atomic, or noncompound, statements of the language. All other statements of the language are, Carnap assumes, built up of their component clauses by means of the familiar logical devices, in such a way that the truth value of any complex statement is fixed for each state-description by specifiable logical laws. A statement is then explained as analytic when it comes out true under every state description. This account is an adaptation of Leibniz's "true in all possible worlds." But note that this version of analyticity serves its purpose only if the atomic statements of the language are, unlike 'John is a bachelor' and 'John is married,' mutually independent. Otherwise there would be a state-description which assigned truth to 'John is a bachelor' and to 'John is married,' and consequently 'No bachelors are married' would turn out synthetic rather than analytic under the proposed criterion. Thus the criterion of analyticity in terms of state-descriptions serves only for languages devoid of extralogical synonym-pairs, such as 'bachelor' and 'unmarried man'—synonym-pairs of the type which give rise to the "second class" of analytic statements. The criterion in terms of state-descriptions is a reconstruction at best of logical truth, not of analyticity.

I do not mean to suggest that Carnap is under any illusions on this point. His simplified model language with its state-descriptions is aimed primarily not at the general problem of analyticity but at another purpose, the clarification of probability and induction. Our problem, however, is analyticity; and here the major difficulty lies not in the first class of analytic statements, the logical truths, but rather in the second class, which depends on the notion of synonymy.

2. DEFINITION

There are those who find it soothing to say that the analytic statements of the second class reduce to those of the first class, the logical truths, by *definition;* 'bachelor,' for example, is *defined* as 'unmarried man.' But how do we find that 'bachelor' is defined as 'unmarried man'? Who defined it thus, and when? Are we to appeal to the nearest dictionary, and accept the lexicographer's formulation as law? Clearly this would be to put the cart before the horse. The lexicographer is an empirical scientist, whose business is the recording of antecedent facts; and if he glosses 'bachelor' as 'unmarried man' it is because of his belief that there is a relation of synonymy between those forms, implicit in general or preferred usage prior to his own work. The notion of synonymy presupposed here has still to be clarified, presumably in terms relating to linguistic behavior. Certainly the "definition" which is the lexicographer's report of an observed synonymy cannot be taken as the ground of the synonymy.

Definition is not, indeed, an activity exclusively of philologists. Philosophers and scientists frequently have occasion to "define" a recondite term by paraphrasing it into terms of a more familiar vocabulary. But ordinarily such a definition, like the philologist's, is pure lexicography, affirming a relation of synonymy antecedent to the exposition in hand.

Just what it means to affirm synonymy, just what the interconnections may be which are necessary and sufficient in order that two linguistic forms be properly describable as synonymous, is far from clear; but, whatever these interconnections may be, ordinarily they are grounded in usage. Definitions reporting selected instances of synonymy come then as reports upon usage.

There is also, however, a variant type of definitional activity which does not limit itself to the reporting of preexisting synonymies. I have in mind what Carnap calls *explication*—an activity to which philosophers are given, and scientists also in their more philosophical moments. In explication the purpose is not merely to paraphrase the definiendum into an outright synonym, but actually to improve upon the definiendum by refining or supplementing its meaning. But even explication, though not merely reporting a preexisting synonymy between definiendum and definiens, does rest nevertheless on *other* preexisting synonymies. The matter may be viewed as follows. Any word worth explicating has some contexts which, as wholes, are clear and precise enough to be useful; and the purpose of explication is to preserve the usage of these favored contexts while sharpening the usage of other contexts. In order that a given definition be suitable for purposes of explication, therefore, what is required is not that the definiendum in its antecedent usage be synonymous with the definiens, but just that each of these favored contexts of the definiendum, taken as a whole in its antecedent usage, be synonymous with the corresponding context of the definiens.

Two alternative definientia may be equally appropriate for the purposes of a given task of explication and yet not be synonymous with each other; for they may serve interchangeably within the favored contexts but diverge elsewhere. By cleaving to one of these definientia rather than the other, a definition of explicative kind generates, by fiat, a relation of synonymy between definiendum and definiens which did not hold before. But such a definition still owes its explicative function, as seen, to preexisting synonymies.

There does, however, remain still an extreme sort of definition which does not hark back to prior synonymies at all: namely, the explicitly conventional introduction of novel notations for purposes of sheer abbreviation. Here the definiendum becomes synonymous with the definiens simply because it has been created expressly for the purpose of being synonymous with the definiens. Here we have a really transparent case of synonymy created by definition; would that all species of synonymy were as intelligible. For the rest, definition rests on synonymy rather than explaining it.

The word 'definition' has come to have a dangerously reassuring sound, owing no doubt to its frequent occurrence in logical and mathematical writings. We shall do well to digress now into a brief appraisal of the role of definition in formal work.

In logical and mathematical systems either of two mutually antagonistic types of economy may be striven for, and each has its peculiar practical utility. On the one hand we may seek economy of practical expression—ease and brevity in the statement of multifarious relations. This sort of economy calls usually for distinctive concise notations for a wealth of concepts. Second, however, and oppositely, we may seek economy in grammar and vocabulary; we may try to find a minimum of basic concepts such that, once a distinctive notation has been appropriated to each of them, it becomes possible to express any desired further concept by mere combination and iteration of our basic notations. This second sort of economy is impractical in one way, since a poverty in basic idioms tends to a necessary lengthening of discourse. But it is practical in another way: it greatly simplifies theoretical discourse *about* the language, through minimizing the terms and the forms of construction wherein the language consists.

Both sorts of economy, though prima facie incompatible, are valuable in their separate ways. The custom has consequently arisen of combining both sorts of economy by forging in effect two languages, the one a part of the other. The inclusive language, though redundant in grammar and vocabulary, is economical in message lengths, while the part, called primitive notation, is economical in grammar and vocabulary. Whole and part are correlated by rules of translation whereby each idiom not in primitive notation is equated to some complex built up of primitive notation. These rules of translation are the so-called *definitions* which appear in formalized systems. They are best viewed not as adjuncts to one language but as correlations between two languages, the one a part of the other.

But these correlations are not arbitrary. They are supposed to show how the primitive notations can accomplish all purposes, save brevity and convenience, of the redundant language. Hence the definiendum and its definiens may be expected, in each case, to be related in one or another of the three ways lately noted. The definiens may be a faithful paraphrase of the definiendum into the narrower notation, preserving a direct synonymy* as of antecedent usage; or the definiens may, in the spirit of explication, improve upon the antecedent usage of the definiendum; or finally, the definiendum may be a newly created notation, newly endowed with meaning here and now.

In formal and informal work alike, thus, we find that definition—except in the extreme case of the explicitly conventional introduction of new notations—hinges on prior relations of synonymy. Recognizing then that the notion of definition does not hold the key to synonymy and analyticity, let us look further into synonymy and say no more of definition.

3. INTERCHANGEABILITY

A natural suggestion, deserving close examination, is that the synonymy of two linguistic forms consists simply in their interchangeability in all contexts without change of truth value—interchangeability, in Leibniz's phrase, *salva veritate.* Note that synonyms so conceived need not even be free from vagueness, as long as the vaguenesses match.

But it is not quite true that the synonyms 'bachelor' and 'unmarried man' are everywhere interchangeable *salva veritate.* Truths which become false under substitution of 'unmarried man' for 'bachelor' are easily constructed with the help of 'bachelor of arts' or 'bachelor's buttons'; also with the help of quotation, thus:

'Bachelor' has less than ten letters.

Such counterinstances can, however, perhaps be set aside by treating the phrases 'bachelor of arts' and 'bachelor's buttons' and the quotation "bachelor" each as a single indivisible word and then stipulating that the interchangeability *salva veritate* which is to be the touchstone of synonymy is not supposed to apply to fragmentary occurrences inside of a word. This account of synonymy, supposing it acceptable on other counts, has indeed the drawback of appealing to a prior conception of "word" which can be counted

*According to an important variant sense of 'definition,' the relation preserved may be the weaker relation of mere agreement in reference. . . . But definition in this sense is better ignored in the present connection, being irrelevant to the question of synonymy.

on to present difficulties of formulation in its turn. Nevertheless some progress might be claimed in having reduced the problem of synonymy to a problem of wordhood. Let us pursue this line a bit, taking "word" for granted.

The question remains whether interchangeability *salva veritate* (apart from occurrences within words) is a strong enough condition for synonymy, or whether, on the contrary, some heteronymous expressions might be thus interchangeable. Now let us be clear that we are not concerned here with synonymy in the sense of complete identity in psychological associations or poetic quality; indeed no two expressions are synonymous in such a sense. We are concerned only with what may be called *cognitive* synonymy. Just what this is cannot be said without successfully finishing the present study; but we know something about it from the need which arose for it in connection with analyticity in ¶1. The sort of synonymy needed there was merely such that any analytic statement could be turned into a logical truth by putting synonyms for synonyms. Turning the tables and assuming analyticity, indeed, we could explain cognitive synonymy of terms as follows (keeping to the familiar example): to say that 'bachelor' and 'unmarried man' are cognitively synonymous is to say no more nor less than that the statement:

(3) All and only bachelors are unmarried men $$$ is analytic.*

What we need is an account of cognitive synonymy not presupposing analyticity—if we are to explain analyticity conversely with help of cognitive synonymy as undertaken in ¶1. And indeed such an independent account of cognitive synonymy is at present up for consideration, namely, interchangeability *salva veritate* everywhere except within words. The question before us, to resume the thread at last, is whether such interchangeability is a sufficient condition for cognitive synonymy. We can quickly assure ourselves that it is, by examples of the following sort. The statement:

(4) Necessarily all and only bachelors are bachelors

is evidently true, even supposing 'necessarily' so narrowly construed as to be truly applicable only to analytic statements. Then, if 'bachelor' and 'unmarried man' are interchangeable *salva veritate,* the result:

(5) Necessarily all and only bachelors are unmarried men

of putting 'unmarried man' for an occurrence of 'bachelor' in (4) must, like (4), be true. But to say that (5) is true is to say that (3) is analytic, and hence that 'bachelor' and 'unmarried man' are cognitively synonymous.

Let us see what there is about the above argument that gives it its air of hocus-pocus. The condition of interchangeability *salva veritate* varies in its force with variations in the richness of the language at hand. The above argument supposes we are working with a language rich enough to contain the adverb 'necessarily,' this adverb being so construed as to yield truth when and only when applied to an analytic statement. But can we condone a language which contains such an adverb? Does the adverb

*This is cognitive synonymy in a primary, broad sense. Carnap and Lewis have suggested how, once this notion is at hand, a narrower sense of cognitive synonymy which is preferable for some purposes can in turn be derived. But this special ramification of concept-building lies aside from the present purposes and must not be confused with the broad sort of cognitive synonymy here concerned.

really make sense? To suppose that it does is to suppose that we have already made satisfactory sense of 'analytic.' Then what are we so hard at work on right now?

Our argument is not flatly circular, but something like it. It has the form, figuratively speaking, of a closed curve in space.

Interchangeability *salva veritate* is meaningless until relativized to a language whose extent is specified in relevant respects. Suppose now we consider a language containing just the following materials. There is an indefinitely large stock of one-place predicates (for example, '*F*' where '*Fx*' means that *x* is a man) and many-place predicates (for example, '*G*' where '*Gxy*' means that *x* loves *y*), mostly having to do with extralogical subject matter. The rest of the language is logical. The atomic sentences consist each of a predicate followed by one or more variables '*x*,' '*y*,' etc.; and the complex sentences are built up of the atomic ones by truth functions ('not,' 'and,' 'or,' etc.) and quantification. In effect such a language enjoys the benefits also of descriptions and indeed singular terms generally, these being contextually definable in known ways. Even abstract singular terms naming classes, classes of classes, etc., are contextually definable in case the assumed stock of predicates includes the two-place predicate of class membership. Such a language can be adequate to classical mathematics and indeed to scientific discourse generally, except in so far as the latter involves debatable devices such as contrary-to-fact conditionals or modal adverbs like 'necessarily.' Now a language of this type is extensional, in this sense: any two predicates which agree extensionally (that is, are true of the same objects) are interchangeable *salva veritate.*

In an extensional language, therefore, interchangeability *salva veritate* is no assurance of cognitive synonymy of the desired type. That 'bachelor' and 'unmarried man' are interchangeable *salva veritate* in an extensional language assures us of no more than that (3) is true. There is no assurance here that the extensional agreement of 'bachelor' and 'unmarried man' rests on meaning rather than merely on accidental matters of fact, as does the extensional agreement of 'creature with a heart' and 'creature with kidneys.'

For most purposes extensional agreement is the nearest approximation to synonymy we need care about. But the fact remains that extensional agreement falls far short of cognitive synonymy of the type required for explaining analyticity in the manner of ¶1. The type of cognitive synonymy required there is such as to equate the synonymy of 'bachelor' and 'unmarried man' with the analyticity of (3), not merely with the truth of (3).

So we must recognize that interchangeability *salva veritate,* if construed in relation to an extensional language, is not a sufficient condition of cognitive synonymy in the sense needed for deriving analyticity in the manner of ¶1. If a language contains an intensional adverb 'necessarily' in the sense lately noted, or other particles to the same effect, then interchangeability *salva veritate* in such a language does afford a sufficient condition of cognitive synonymy; but such a language is intelligible only in so far as the notion of analyticity is already understood in advance.

The effort to explain cognitive synonymy first, for the sake of deriving analyticity from it afterward as in ¶1, is perhaps the wrong approach. Instead we might try explaining analyticity somehow without appeal to cognitive synonymy. Afterward we could doubtless derive cognitive synonymy from analyticity satisfactorily enough if desired. We have seen that cognitive synonymy of 'bachelor' and 'unmarried man' can be explained as analyticity of (3). The same explanation works for any pair of one-place predicates, of course, and it can be extended in obvious fashion to many-place predicates. Other syntactical categories can also be accommodated in fairly parallel fashion. Singular terms may be said to be cognitively synonymous when the statement of identity formed by putting '=' between them is analytic. Statements may be said simply to be cognitively synonymous when their biconditional (the result of joining them by 'if and only if') is analytic.* If we care to lump all categories into a single formulation, at the expense of assuming again the notion of "word" which was appealed to early in this section, we can describe any two linguistic forms as cognitively synonymous when the two forms are interchangeable (apart from occurrences within "words") *salva* (no longer *veritate* but) *analyticitate.* Certain technical questions arise, indeed, over cases of ambiguity or homonymy; let us not pause for them, however, for we are already digressing. Let us rather turn our backs on the problem of synonymy and address ourselves anew to that of analyticity.

4. SEMANTICAL RULES

Analyticity at first seemed most naturally definable by appeal to a realm of meanings. On refinement, the appeal to meanings gave way to an appeal to synonymy or definition. But definition turned out to be a will-o'-the-wisp, and synonymy turned out to be best understood only by dint of a prior appeal to analyticity itself. So we are back at the problem of analyticity.

I do not know whether the statement 'Everything green is extended' is analytic. Now does my indecision over this example really betray an incomplete understanding, an incomplete grasp of the "meanings," of 'green' and 'extended'? I think not. The trouble is not with 'green' or 'extended,' but with 'analytic.'

It is often hinted that the difficulty in separating analytic statements from synthetic ones in ordinary language is due to the vagueness of ordinary language and that the distinction is clear when we have a precise artificial language with explicit "semantical rules." This, however, as I shall now attempt to show, is a confusion.

The notion of analyticity about which we are worrying is a purported relation between statements and languages: a statement *S* is said to be *analytic* for a language *L*, and the problem is to make sense of this relation generally, that is, for variable '*S*' and '*L*.' The gravity of this problem is not perceptibly less for artificial languages than for natural ones. The problem of making sense of the idiom '*S* is analytic for *L*,' with variable '*S*' and '*L*,' retains its stubbornness even if we limit the range of the variable '*L*' to artificial languages. Let me now try to make this point evident.

For artificial languages and semantical rules we look naturally to the writings of Carnap. His semantical rules take various forms, and to make my point I shall have to distinguish certain of the forms. Let us suppose, to begin with, an artificial language L_0 whose semantical rules have the form explicitly of a specification, by recursion or otherwise, of all the analytic statements of L_0. The rules tell us that such and such statements, and only those, are the analytic statements of L_0. Now here the difficulty is simply that the rules contain the word 'analytic,' which we do not understand! We understand what expressions the rules attribute analyticity to, but we do not understand what the rules attribute to those expressions. In short, before we can understand a rule which begins 'A statement *S* is analytic for language L_0 if and only if . . . ,' we must understand the general relative term 'analytic for'; we must understand '*S* is analytic for *L*' where '*S*' and '*L*' are variables.

*The 'if and only if' itself is intended in the true functional sense.

Alternatively we may, indeed, view the so-called rule as a conventional definition of a new simple symbol 'analytic-for-L_0,' which might better be written untendentiously as '*K*' so as not to seem to throw light on the interesting word 'analytic.' Obviously any number of classes *K, M, N,* etc. of statements of L_0 can be specified for various purposes or for no purpose; what does it mean to say that *K,* as against *M, N,* etc., is the class of the "analytic" statements of L_0?

By saying what statements are analytic for L_0 we explain 'analytic-for-L_0' but not 'analytic,' not 'analytic for.' We do not begin to explain the idiom '*S* is analytic for *L*' with variable '*S*' and '*L*,' even if we are content to limit the range of '*L*' to the realm of artificial languages.

Actually we do know enough about the intended significance of 'analytic' to know that analytic statements are supposed to be true. Let us then turn to a second form of semantical rule, which says not that such and such statements are analytic but simply that such and such statements are included among the truths. Such a rule is not subject to the criticism of containing the un-understood word 'analytic'; and we may grant for the sake of argument that there is no difficulty over the broader term 'true.' A semantical rule of this second type, a rule of truth, is not supposed to specify all the truths of the language; it merely stipulates, recursively or otherwise, a certain multitude of statements which, along with others unspecified, are to count as true. Such a rule may be conceded to be quite clear. Derivatively, afterward, analyticity can be demarcated thus: a statement is analytic if it is (not merely true but) true according to the semantical rule.

Still there is really no progress. Instead of appealing to an unexplained word 'analytic,' we are now appealing to an unexplained phrase 'semantical rule.' Not every true statement which says that the statements of some class are true can count as a semantical rule—otherwise *all* truths would be "analytic" in the sense of being true according to semantical rules. Semantical rules are distinguishable, apparently, only by the fact of appearing on a page under the heading 'Semantical Rules'; and this heading is itself then meaningless.

We can say indeed that a statement is *analytic-for-*L_0 if and only if it is true according to such and such specifically appended "semantical rules," but then we find ourselves back at essentially the same case which was originally discussed: '*S* is *analytic-for-*L_0 if and only if . . . .' Once we seek to explain '*S* is analytic for *L*' generally for variable '*L*' (even allowing limitation of '*L*' to artificial languages), the explanation 'true according to the semantical rules of *L*' is unavailing; for the relative term 'semantical rule of' is as much in need of clarification, at least, as 'analytic for.'

It may be instructive to compare the notion of semantical rule with that of postulate. Relative to a given set of postulates, it is easy to say what a postulate is: it is a member of the set. Relative to a given set of semantical rules, it is equally easy to say what a semantical rule is. But given simply a notation, mathematical or otherwise, and indeed as thoroughly understood a notation as you please in point of the translations or truth conditions of its statements, who can say which of its true statements rank as postulates? Obviously the question is meaningless—as meaningless as asking which points in Ohio are starting points. Any finite (or effectively specifiable infinite) selection of statements (preferably true ones, perhaps) is as much a set of postulates as any other. The word 'postulate' is significant only relative to an act of inquiry; we apply the word to a set of statements just in so far as we happen, for the year or the moment, to be thinking of those statements in relation to the statements which can be reached from them by some set of transformations to which we have seen fit to direct our attention. Now the notion of semantical rule is as sensible and meaningful as that of postulate, if conceived in a similarly relative spirit—relative, this time, to one or another particular enterprise of schooling unconversant persons in sufficient conditions for truth of statements of some natural or artificial language *L*. But from this point of view no one signalization of a subclass of the truths of *L* is intrinsically more a semantical rule than another; and, if 'analytic' means 'true by semantical rules,' no one truth of *L* is analytic to the exclusion of another.

It might conceivably be protested that an artificial language *L* (unlike a natural one) is a language in the ordinary sense *plus* a set of explicit semantical rules—the whole constituting, let us say, an ordered pair; and that the semantical rules of *L* then are specifiable simply as the second component of the pair *L*. But, by the same token and more simply, we might construe an artificial language *L* outright as an ordered pair whose second component is the class of its analytic statements; and then the analytic statements of *L* become specifiable simply as the statements in the second component of *L*. Or better still, we might just stop tugging at our bootstraps altogether.

Not all the explanations of analyticity known to Carnap and his readers have been covered explicitly in the above considerations, but the extension to other forms is not hard to see. Just one additional factor should be mentioned which sometimes enters: sometimes the semantical rules are in effect rules of translation into ordinary language, in which case the analytic statements of the artificial language are in effect recognized as such from the analyticity of their specified translations in ordinary language. Here certainly there can be no thought of an illumination of the problem of analyticity from the side of the artificial language.

From the point of view of the problem of analyticity the notion of an artificial language with semantical rules is a *feu follet par excellence*. Semantical rules determining the analytic statements of an artificial language are of interest only in so far as we already understand the notion of analyticity; they are of no help in gaining this understanding.

Appeal to hypothetical languages of an artificially simple kind could conceivably be useful in clarifying analyticity, if the mental or behavioral or cultural factors relevant to analyticity—whatever they may be—were somehow sketched into the simplified model. But a model which takes analyticity merely as an irreducible character is unlikely to throw light on the problem of explicating analyticity.

It is obvious that truth in general depends on both language and extralinguistic fact. The statement 'Brutus killed Caesar' would be false if the world had been different in certain ways, but it would also be false if the word 'killed' happened rather to have the sense of 'begat.' Thus one is tempted to suppose in general that the truth of a statement is somehow analyzable into a linguistic component and a factual component. Given this supposition, it next seems reasonable that in some statements the factual component should be null; and these are the analytic statements. But, for all its a priori reasonableness, a boundary between analytic and synthetic statements simply has not been drawn. That there is such a distinction to be drawn at all is an unempirical dogma of empiricists, a metaphysical article of faith.

5. THE VERIFICATION THEORY AND REDUCTIONISM

In the course of these somber reflections we have taken a dim view first of the notion of meaning, then of the notion of cognitive synonymy, and finally of the notion of analyticity. But what, it may be asked, of the verification theory of meaning? This phrase has established itself so firmly as a catchword of empiricism that we should be very unscientific indeed not to look beneath it for a possible key to the problem of meaning and the associated problems.

The verification theory of meaning, which has been conspicuous in the literature from Peirce onward, is that the meaning of a statement is the method of empirically confirming or infirming it. An analytic statement is that limiting case which is confirmed no matter what.

As urged in ¶1, we can as well pass over the question of meanings as entities and move straight to sameness of meaning, or synonymy. Then what the verification theory says is that statements are synonymous if and only if they are alike in point of method of empirical confirmation or infirmation.

This is an account of cognitive synonymy not of linguistic forms generally, but of statements.* However, from the concept of synonymy of statements we could derive the concept of synonymy for other linguistic forms, by considerations somewhat similar to those at the end of ¶3. Assuming the notion of "word," indeed, we could explain any two forms as synonymous when the putting of the one form for an occurrence of the other in any statement (apart from occurrences within "words") yields a synonymous statement. Finally, given the concept of synonymy thus for linguistic forms generally, we could define analyticity in terms of synonymy and logical truth as in ¶1. For that matter, we could define analyticity more simply in terms of just synonymy of statements together with logical truth; it is not necessary to appeal to synonymy of linguistic forms other than statements. For a statement may be described as analytic simply when it is synonymous with a logically true statement.

So, if the verification theory can be accepted as an adequate account of statement synonymy, the notion of analyticity is saved after all. However, let us reflect. Statement synonymy is said to be likeness of method of empirical confirmation or infirmation. Just what are these methods which are to be compared for likeness? What, in other words, is the nature of the relation between a statement and the experiences which contribute to or detract from its confirmation?

The most naive view of the relation is that it is one of direct report. This is *radical reductionism.* Every meaningful statement is held to be translatable into a statement (true or false) about immediate experience. Radical reductionism, in one form or another, well antedates the verification theory of meaning explicitly so called. Thus Locke and Hume held that every idea must either originate directly in sense experience or else be compounded of ideas thus originating; and taking a hint from Tooke we might rephrase this doctrine in semantical jargon by saying that a term, to be significant at all, must be either a name of a sense datum or a compound of such names or an abbreviation of such a compound. So stated, the doctrine remains ambiguous as between sense data as sensory events and sense data as sensory qualities; and it remains vague as to the admissible ways of compounding. Moreover, the doctrine is unnecessarily and intolerably restrictive in the term-by-term critique which it imposes. More reasonably, and without yet exceeding the limits of what I have called radical reductionism, we may take full statements as our significant units—thus demanding that our statements as wholes be translatable into sense-datum language, but not that they be translatable term by term.

This emendation would unquestionably have been welcome to Locke and Hume and Tooke, but historically it had to await an important reorientation in semantics—the

*The doctrine can indeed be formulated with terms rather than statements as the units. Thus Lewis describes the meaning of a term as "*a criterion in mind,* by reference to which one is able to apply or refuse to apply the expression in question in the case of presented, or imagined, things or situations."

reorientation whereby the primary vehicle of meaning came to be seen no longer in the term but in the statement. This reorientation, seen in Bentham and Frege, underlies Russell's concept of incomplete symbols defined in use; also it is implicit in the verification theory of meaning, since the objects of verification are statements.

Radical reductionism, conceived now with statements as units, set itself the task of specifying a sense-datum language and showing how to translate the rest of significant discourse, statement by statement, into it. Carnap embarked on this project in the *Aufbau.*

The language which Carnap adopted as his starting point was not a sense-datum language in the narrowest conceivable sense, for it included also the notations of logic, up through higher set theory. In effect it included the whole language of pure mathematics. The ontology implicit in it (that is, the range of values of its variables) embraced not only sensory events but classes, classes of classes, and so on. Empiricists there are who would boggle at such prodigality. Carnap's starting point is very parsimonious, however, in its extralogical or sensory part. In a series of constructions in which he exploits the resources of modern logic with much ingenuity, Carnap succeeds in defining a wide array of important additional sensory concepts which, but for his constructions, one would not have dreamed were definable on so slender a basis. He was the first empiricist who, not content with asserting the reducibility of science to terms of immediate experience, took serious steps toward carrying out the reduction.

If Carnap's starting point is satisfactory, still his constructions were, as he himself stressed, only a fragment of the full program. The construction of even the simplest statements about the physical world was left in a sketchy state. Carnap's suggestions on this subject were, despite their sketchiness, very suggestive. He explained spatio-temporal point-instants as quadruples of real numbers and envisaged assignment of sense qualities to point-instants according to certain canons. Roughly summarized, the plan was that qualities should be assigned to point-instants in such a way as to achieve the laziest world compatible with our experience. The principle of least action was to be our guide in constructing a world from experience.

Carnap did not seem to recognize, however, that his treatment of physical objects fell short of reduction not merely through sketchiness, but in principle. Statements of the form 'Quality *q* is at point-instant *x;y;z;t*' were, according to his canons, to be apportioned truth values in such a way as to maximize and minimize certain over-all features, and with growth of experience the truth values were to be progressively revised in the same spirit. I think this is a good schematization (deliberately oversimplified, to be sure) of what science really does; but it provides no indication, not even the sketchiest, of how a statement of the form 'Quality *q* is at *x;y;z;t*' could ever be translated into Carnap's initial language of sense data and logic. The connective 'is at' remains an added undefined connective; the canons counsel us in its use but not in its elimination.

Carnap seems to have appreciated this point afterward; for in his later writings he abandoned all notion of the translatability of statements about the physical world into statements about immediate experience. Reductionism in its radical form has long since ceased to figure in Carnap's philosophy.

But the dogma of reductionism has, in a subtler and more tenuous form, continued to influence the thought of empiricists. The notion lingers that to each statement, or each synthetic statement, there is associated a unique range of possible sensory events such that the occurrence of any of them would add to the likelihood of truth of the statement, and that there is associated also another unique range of possible sensory events whose occurrence would detract from that likelihood. This notion is of course implicit in the verification theory of meaning.

The dogma of reductionism survives in the supposition that each statement, taken in isolation from its fellows, can admit of confirmation or infirmation at all. My countersuggestion, issuing essentially from Carnap's doctrine of the physical world in the *Aufbau,* is that our statements about the external world face the tribunal of sense experience not individually but only as a corporate body.

The dogma of reductionism, even in its attenuated form, is intimately connected with the other dogma—that there is a cleavage between the analytic and the synthetic. We have found ourselves led, indeed, from the latter problem to the former through the verification theory of meaning. More directly, the one dogma clearly supports the other in this way: as long as it is taken to be significant in general to speak of the confirmation and infirmation of a statement, it seems significant to speak also of a limiting kind of statement which is vacuously confirmed, *ipso facto,* come what may; and such a statement is analytic.

The two dogmas are, indeed, at root identical. We lately reflected that in general the truth of statements does obviously depend both upon language and upon extralinguistic fact; and we noted that this obvious circumstance carries in its train, not logically but all too naturally, a feeling that the truth of a statement is somehow analyzable into a linguistic component and a factual component. The factual component must, if we are empiricists, boil down to a range of confirmatory experiences. In the extreme case where the linguistic component is all that matters, a true statement is analytic. But I hope we are now impressed with how stubbornly the distinction between analytic and synthetic has resisted any straightforward drawing. I am impressed also, apart from prefabricated examples of black and white balls in an urn, with how baffling the problem has always been of arriving at any explicit theory of the empirical confirmation of a synthetic statement. My present suggestion is that it is nonsense, and the root of much nonsense, to speak of a linguistic component and a factual component in the truth of any individual statement. Taken collectively, science has its double dependence upon language and experience; but this duality is not significantly traceable into the statements of science taken one by one.

The idea of defining a symbol in use was, as remarked, an advance over the impossible term-by-term empiricism of Locke and Hume. The statement, rather than the term, came with Bentham to be recognized as the unit accountable to an empiricist critique. But what I am now urging is that even in taking the statement as unit we have drawn our grid too finely. The unit of empirical significance is the whole of science.

6. EMPIRICISM WITHOUT THE DOGMAS

The totality of our so-called knowledge or beliefs, from the most casual matters of geography and history to the profoundest laws of atomic physics or even of pure mathematics and logic, is a man-made fabric which impinges on experience only along the edges. Or, to change the figure, total science is like a field of force whose boundary conditions are experience. A conflict with experience at the periphery occasions readjustments in the interior of the field. Truth values have to be redistributed over some of our statements. Reevaluation of some statements entails reevaluation of others, because of their logical interconnections—the logical laws being in turn simply certain further statements of the system, certain further elements of the field. Having reevaluated one statement we must reevaluate some others, which may be statements logically connected with the first or may be the statements of logical connections themselves. But the total field is so underdetermined by its boundary conditions, experience, that there is much latitude of choice as to what statements to reevaluate in the light of any single contrary experience. No particular experiences are linked with any particular statements in the interior of the field, except indirectly through considerations of equilibrium affecting the field as a whole.

If this view is right, it is misleading to speak of the empirical content of an individual statement—especially if it is a statement at all remote from the experiential periphery of the field. Furthermore it becomes folly to seek a boundary between synthetic statements, which hold contingently on experience, and analytic statements, which hold come what may. Any statement can be held true come what may, if we make drastic enough adjustments elsewhere in the system. Even a statement very close to the periphery can be held true in the face of recalcitrant experience by pleading hallucination or by amending certain statements of the kind called logical laws. Conversely, by the same token, no statement is immune to revision. Revision even of the logical law of the excluded middle has been proposed as a means of simplifying quantum mechanics; and what difference is there in principle between such a shift and the shift whereby Kepler superseded Ptolemy, or Einstein Newton, or Darwin Aristotle?

For vividness I have been speaking in terms of varying distances from a sensory periphery. Let me try now to clarify this notion without metaphor. Certain statements, though *about* physical objects and not sense experience, seem peculiarly germane to sense experience—and in a selective way: some statements to some experiences, others to others. Such statements, especially germane to particular experiences, I picture as near the periphery. But in this relation of "germaneness" I envisage nothing more than a loose association reflecting the relative likelihood, in practice, of our choosing one statement rather than another for revision in the event of recalcitrant experience. For example, we can imagine recalcitrant experiences to which we would surely be inclined to accommodate our system by reevaluating just the statement that there are brick houses on Elm Street, together with related statements on the same topic. We can imagine other recalcitrant experiences to which we would be inclined to accommodate our system by reevaluating just the statement that there are no centaurs, along with kindred statements. A recalcitrant experience can, I have urged, be accommodated by any of various alternative reevaluations in various alternative quarters of the total system; but, in the cases which we are now imagining, our natural tendency to disturb the total system as little as possible would lead us to focus our revisions upon these specific statements concerning brick houses or centaurs. These statements are felt, therefore, to have a sharper empirical reference than highly theoretical statements of physics or logic or ontology. The latter statements may be thought of as relatively centrally located within the total network, meaning merely that little preferential connection with any particular sense data obtrudes itself.

As an empiricist I continue to think of the conceptual scheme of science as a tool, ultimately, for predicting future experience in the light of past experience. Physical objects are conceptually imported into the situation as convenient intermediaries—not by definition in terms of experience, but simply as irreducible posits comparable, epistemologically, to the gods of Homer. For my part I do, qua lay physicist, believe in physical objects and not in Homer's gods; and I consider it a scientific error to believe otherwise. But in point of epistemological footing the physical objects and the gods differ only in degree and not in kind. Both sorts of entities enter our conception only as cultural posits. The myth of physical objects is epistemologically superior to most in that it has proved more efficacious than other myths as a device for working a manageable structure into the flux of experience.

Positing does not stop with macroscopic physical objects. Objects at the atomic level are posited to make the laws of macroscopic objects, and ultimately the laws of experience, simpler and more manageable; and we need not expect or demand full definition of atomic and subatomic entities in terms of macroscopic ones, any more than definition of macroscopic things in terms of sense data. Science is a continuation of common sense, and it continues the common-sense expedient of swelling ontology to simplify theory.

Physical objects, small and large, are not the only posits. Forces are another example; and indeed we are told nowadays that the boundary between energy and matter is obsolete. Moreover, the abstract entities which are the substance of mathematics—ultimately classes and classes of classes and so on up—are another posit in the same spirit. Epistemologically these are myths on the same footing with physical objects and gods, neither better nor worse except for differences in the degree to which they expedite our dealings with sense experiences.

The over-all algebra of rational and irrational numbers is underdetermined by the algebra of rational numbers, but is smoother and more convenient; and it includes the algebra of rational numbers as a jagged or gerrymandered part. Total science, mathematical and natural and human, is similarly but more extremely underdetermined by experience. The edge of the system must be kept squared with experience; the rest, with all its elaborate myths or fictions, has as its objective the simplicity of laws.

Ontological questions, under this view, are on a par with questions of natural science. Consider the question whether to countenance classes as entities. This, as I have argued elsewhere, is the question whether to quantify with respect to variables which take classes as values. Now Carnap has maintained that this is a question not of matters of fact but of choosing a convenient language form, a convenient conceptual scheme or framework for science. With this I agree, but only on the proviso that the same be conceded regarding scientific hypotheses generally. Carnap has recognized that he is able to preserve a double standard for ontological questions and scientific hypotheses only by assuming an absolute distinction between the analytic and the synthetic; and I need not say again that this is a distinction which I reject.

The issue over there being classes seems more a question of convenient conceptual scheme; the issue over there being centaurs, or brick houses on Elm Street, seems more a question of fact. But I have been urging that this difference is only one of degree, and that it turns upon our vaguely pragmatic inclination to adjust one strand of the fabric of science rather than another in accommodating some particular recalcitrant experience. Conservatism figures in such choices, and so does the quest for simplicity.

Carnap, Lewis, and others take a pragmatic stand on the question of choosing between language forms, scientific frameworks; but their pragmatism leaves off at the imagined boundary between the analytic and the synthetic. In repudiating such a boundary I espouse a more thorough pragmatism. Each man is given a scientific heritage plus a continuing barrage of sensory stimulation; and the considerations which guide him in warping his scientific heritage to fit his continuing sensory promptings are, where rational, pragmatic.

Jacques Derrida
1930–2004

In the spirit of his celebrated dictum that "there is nothing outside the text," Jacques Derrida long resisted the publication of information about his life. For seventeen years (1962–1979), he even refused to have a personal photograph accompany his texts. However, his fame as the founder of what came to be called "deconstruction" led him to provide biographical "scraps."

Born in 1930 near Algiers, Jacques Derrida as a Jew was forced to leave school in 1942 until the Free French repealed Vichy racial laws. At 19, he moved to Paris to prepare for the École Normale Supérieure, where he subsequently studied and taught philosophy. Though his first published work (1962)—about Husserl's essay on geometry—won a philosophical prize, Derrida was not widely known until 1966. At a conference on France's new structuralism at Johns Hopkins University, Derrida gave a paper—"Structure, Sign, and Play in the Discourse of the Human Sciences"—that daringly exposed contradictions in the thought of structuralism's leading figure, Lévi-Strauss. Derrida's critique became one of the important building blocks in what came to be called "poststructuralism."

The following year, Derrida continued his critique, publishing no less than three books showing how structuralist positions refuted their own theses. The books—*Of Grammatology, Writing and Difference,* and *Speech and Phenomena* (as the titles were translated)—created a storm of philosophical debate in France. In these works, Derrida showed how his critique went beyond structuralism and attacked the enterprise of philosophy itself. "Deconstruction," as Derrida's approach in these works was now called, claimed that the very nature of a written text—of every traditional text and not just the structuralist's—undermines itself. To "deconstruct" a text, then, is to dismantle inherent hierarchical systems of thought, to seek out unregarded details, to find the "margins" of the text, where there are new possibilities of interpretation.

In 1972, Derrida published three additional works, translated as *Dissemination, Margins of Philosophy,* and *Positions,* which continued to influence poststructuralism in the 1970s. As Derrida's fame grew, he accepted a visiting professorship first at Yale University, and then at the University of California in Irvine. In the 1980s, Derrida gave himself to political causes such as the abolition of apartheid. He also became actively interested in architecture, which he regarded as the last bastion of metaphysics. He helped architect Peter Eisenman design a garden in Paris that explores the relationship between center and periphery. Born on the periphery of colonial France, on the margin of Algiers, as a marginalized Jew, Derrida constantly examined the philosophical relation between margin and center (and often employed language that is only marginally understandable). All for a purpose.

* * *

Derrida believes that Western philosophy is built upon a "Metaphysics of Presence": upon, that is to say, the idea that there is an origin of knowledge from which "truth" can be made present. Philosophy has always seen itself as the arbiter of reason, the discipline that adjudicates what is and is not. Forms of writing other than philosophical discourse, such as poetic or literary writing, have been judged inferior, and removed from the truth. In *Of Grammatology,* Derrida calls this positing of a center that can situate certainty *logocentrism.* Philosophy thinks it can talk about "meaning" through a language unsullied by the imprecision of metaphors. *Au Contraire!* As Derrida argues in our selection, translated by Gayatri Chakravorty Spivak, philosophical discourse is not privileged in any way, and any attempt to explain what "meaning" *means* will self-destruct. Put more precisely, the signifiers of language systems cannot refer to a transcendental *signified* originating in the mind of the speaker because the "signified" is itself created by the conventional, and hence arbitrary, signifiers of language. Signifiers therefore merely refer to other signifiers (e.g., words refer only to other words). The "meaning" is always deferred and Presence is never actually present. Signifiers attain significance only in their differences from each other (the signifier "cat" is neither "cap" nor "car") or in what they define themselves against ("to be asleep" is understood in contrast to "to be awake").

To highlight the ambiguities of language, Derrida coined the word *différance* In French, this word sounds no different from the French word *differénce,* which comes from the verb *différer,* meaning both "to differ" and "to defer." Whereas the definition of *differénce* reminds us that signifiers defer meaning as they differ both from their referents and from each other, the written word *différance* calls attention in a striking way to the limitations of the spoken word. The spoken word can establish no aural distinction between *differénce* and *différance.* Derrida thus questions the traditional privileging of speech over writing, which goes back at least as far as Plato. For example, in the *Phaedrus,* Plato had placed writing as one step further removed than speaking from Ideal Form. Derrida shows, however, that even as Plato sought to place speech closer to the source of meaning, he could not keep writing out of his system. At one point in the *Phaedrus,* Plato states that speech "is *written* in the soul of the listener" (emphasis added).

This is just one example of how Derrida repeatedly exposes the repressed figures of speech in even the most systematic of thinkers. According to Derrida, all systems of thought contain "traces" of that which they define themselves against. Thus, whereas many philosophers have thought literature merely sugar-coated philosophy, Derrida has reversed this hierarchy to say that the discourse of philosophy is merely literary medicine—an assumption that is hard for many to swallow. For Derrida, all writing is reduced (or elevated) to the same level, with no privileging of one genre as more "meaning-ful" than another. This may explain why deconstruction—with its close reading of texts to unearth language working against itself—made its greatest impact in literature, rather than in philosophy.

But what about Derrida's writings themselves—do they not represent a conceptual order, an attempt to communicate "meaning"? Derrida goes to great pains to avoid the systemization of his own thought, constantly inventing new terms to destabilize his readers' sense that they understand his "philosophy." In the meantime, although he works to expose the failures of language to make present meaning, he acknowledges that, since language is all we have, he must situate himself inside a system even as he is breaking it apart. He signals this paradox, or *aporia,* of language by borrowing a technique from Heidegger, who simultaneously included and deleted the word Being in his works by placing an *X* over it: Being. Derrida crosses out certain metaphysically loaded words, putting them "under erasure." He asserts the inadequacy of a signifier like nature to have a definitive meaning, while also acknowledging that thought cannot operate without the term. Derrida demonstrates that his own writing—like everyone else's—is not innocent, that it cannot become a coherent theoretical system corresponding to reality. Derrida has therefore been called a nihilist. His defenders, however, call this accusation inaccurate. Derrida never denies the existence of an Absolute; he only asserts the impossibility of putting the Absolute into words.

* * *

For general overviews of Derrida, see Christopher Norris, *Derrida* (Cambridge, MA: Harvard University Press, 1987); Christopher Johnson, *Derrida* (London: Routledge, 1999); James K.A. Smith, *Jacques Derrida: Live Theory* (London: Continuum, 2005); Jason Powell, *Jacques Derrida: A Biography* (London: Continuum, 2006); Barry Stocker, *Derrida on Deconstruction* (London: Routledge, 2006); Julian Wolfreys, *Derrida: A Guide for the Perplexed* (London: Continuum, 2007); Leslie Hill, *The Cambridge Introduction to Jacques Derrida* (Cambridge: Cambridge University Press, 2007); and Mark Dooley and Liam Kavanagh, *The Philosophy of Derrida* (Montreal: McGill-Queen's University Press, 2007). For a recent biography, see Jason Powell, *Jacques Derrida: A Biography* (London: Continuum, 2007). Allan Megill, *Prophets of Extremity: Nietzsche, Heidegger, Foucault, Derrida* (Berkeley: University of California Press, 1985); Diane P. Michelfelder and Richard E. Palmer, eds., *Dialogue and Deconstruction: The Gadamer-Derrida Encounter* (Albany, NY: SUNY Press, 1989); Roy Boyne, *Foucault and Derrida: The Other Side of Reason* (London: Unwin Hyman, 1990); Simon Critchley, *The Ethics of Deconstruction: Derrida & Levinas* (Oxford: Basil Blackwell, 1992); and John McCumber, *Philosophy and Freedom: Derrida, Rorty, Habermas, Foucault* (Indianapolis: Indiana University Press, 2000) provide comparative studies. John D. Caputo, *The Prayers and Tears of Jacques Derrida: Religion without Religion* (Bloomington: Indiana University Press, 1997); and Sean Gaston, *The Impossible Mourning of Jacques Derrida*

(London: Continuum, 2006) are more recent specialized studies. Gary A. Olson and Irene Gale, eds., *(Inter)view: Cross-Disciplinary Perspectives on Rhetoric and Literacy* (Carbondale: Southern Illinois University Press, 1991); Jacques Derrida, *Points. . . : Interview 1974–1994,* edited by Elisabeth Weber (Stanford, CA: Stanford University Press, 1995); John Caputo, ed., *Deconstruction in a Nutshell: A Conversation with Jacques Derrida* (New York: Fordham University Press, 1997); and Jacques Derrida, *Positions: Revised Edition,* translated and annotated by Alan Bass (London: Continuum, 2004) include discussions with Derrida. For a feminist reading of Derrida, see Ellen K. Feder, Mary C. Rawlinson, and Emily Zakin, eds., *Derrida and Feminism* (Oxford: Routledge, 1997). General collections of critical essays include John Sallis, ed., *Deconstruction and Philosophy: The Texts of Jacques Derrida* (Chicago: University of Chicago Press, 1987); David Wood, ed., *Derrida: A Critical Reader* (Oxford: Basil Blackwell, 1992); Harold Coward and Toby Foshay, eds., *Derrida and Negative Theology* (Albany, NY: SUNY Press, 1992); Gary B. Madison, ed., *Working through Derrida* (Evanston, IL: Northwestern University Press, 1993); and Jack Reynolds and Jon Roffe, eds., *Understanding Derrida* (London: Continuum, 2004). Finally, in Geoffrey Bennington and Jacques Derrida, *Jacques Derrida* (Chicago: University of Chicago Press, 1993), the top two-thirds of each page give Bennington's comment on Derrida's thought, whereas Derrida himself writes "in the margin" along the bottom of each page.

OF GRAMMATOLOGY (in part)

CHAPTER 1: THE WRITTEN BEING/THE BEING WRITTEN

The reassuring evidence within which Western tradition had to organize itself and must continue to live would therefore be as follows: the order of the signified is never contemporary, is at best the subtly discrepant inverse or parallel—discrepant by the time of a breath—from the order of the signifier. And the sign must be the unity of a heterogeneity, since the signified (sense or thing, noeme or reality) is not in itself a signifier, a *trace:* in any case is not constituted in its sense by its relationship with a possible trace. The formal essence of the signified is *presence,* and the privilege of its proximity to the logos as *phonè* is the privilege of presence. This is the inevitable response as soon as one asks: "what is the sign?," that is to say, when one submits the sign to the question of essence, to the "ti esti." The "formal essence" of the sign can only be determined in terms of presence. One cannot get around that response, except by challenging the very form of the question and beginning to think that the sign ~~is~~ that ill-named ~~thing~~, the only one, that escapes the instituting question of philosophy: "what is . . . ?*

*I attempt to develop this theme elsewhere (*Speech and Phenomena*).

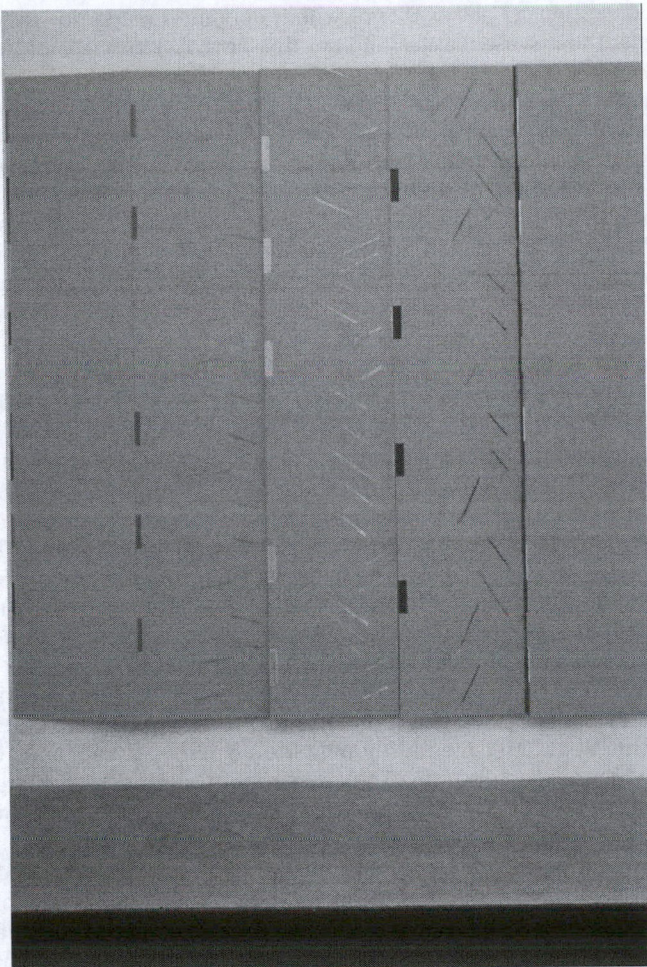

Open Warfare, 1991, by Jeremy Gilbert-Rolfe. Derrida holds that the limits or frame of a given piece defines an inside and an outside but also "permits, and even encourages, a complicated movement or passage across it both from inside-out and outside-in" (from David Carroll, *Paraesthetics: Foucault, Lyotard, Derrida* (New York: Methuen, 1987), p. 136). Gilbert-Rolfe's painting exemplifies this deferral of meaning as its pattern suggests a continuation beyond itself. *(95 x 95 oil on linen, Jeremy Gilbert-Rolfe)*

Radicalizing the concepts of *interpretation, perspective, evaluation, difference,* and all the "empiricist" or nonphilosophical motifs that have constantly tormented philosophy throughout the history of the West, and besides, have had nothing but the inevitable weakness of being produced in the field of philosophy, Nietzsche, far from remaining simply (with Hegel and as Heidegger wished) *within* metaphysics, contributed a great deal to the liberation of the signifier from its dependence or derivation with respect to the logos and the related concept of truth or the primary signified in whatever sense that is understood. Reading, and therefore writing, the text were for Nietzsche "originary"* operations (I put that word within quotation marks for reasons to appear later) with regard to a sense that they do not first have to transcribe or discover, which would not therefore be a truth signified in the original element and presence of the logos, as *topos noetos*, divine understanding, or the structure of a priori necessity. To save Nietzsche from a reading of the Heideggerian type, it seems that we must above all not attempt to restore or make explicit a less naive "ontology," composed of profound ontological intuitions acceding to some originary truth, an entire fundamentality hidden under the appearance of an empiricist or metaphysical text. The virulence of Nietzschean thought could not be more completely misunderstood. On the contrary, one must *accentuate* the "naiveté" of a breakthrough which cannot attempt a step outside of metaphysics, which cannot *criticize* metaphysics radically without still utilizing in a certain way, in a certain type or a certain style of *text*, propositions that, read within the philosophic corpus, that is to say according to Nietzsche ill-read or unread, have always been and will always be "naivetés," incoherent signs of an absolute appurtenance. Therefore, rather than protect Nietzsche from the Heideggerian reading, we should perhaps offer him up to it completely, underwriting that interpretation without reserve; in a *certain way* and up to the point where, the content of the Nietzschean discourse being almost lost for the question of being, its form regains its absolute strangeness, where his text finally invokes a different type of reading, more faithful to his type of writing: Nietzsche has *written what* he has written. He has written that writing—and first of all his own—is not originarily subordinate to the logos and to truth. And that this subordination has *come into being* during an epoch whose meaning we must deconstruct. Now in this direction (but only in this direction, for read otherwise, the Nietzschean demolition remains dogmatic and, like all reversals, a captive of that metaphysical edifice which it professes to overthrow. On that point and in that *order of reading*, the conclusions of Heidegger and Fink are irrefutable), Heideggerian thought would reinstate rather than destroy the instance of the logos and of the truth of being as primum signatum:" the "transcendental" signified ("transcendental" in a certain sense, as in the Middle Ages the transcendental—*ens, unum, verum, bonum***—was said to be the "primum cognitum") implied by all categories or all determined significations, by all lexicons and all syntax, and therefore by all linguistic signifiers, though not to be identified simply with any one of those signifiers, allowing itself to be precomprehended through each of them, remaining irreducible to all the epochal determinations that it nonetheless makes possible, thus opening the history of the logos, yet itself being only through the logos; that is, *being nothing* before the logos and outside of it. The logos *of* being, "Thought obeying the Voice of Being,"*** is the first and the last resource of the sign, of the difference between *signans* and *signatum*. There has to be a transcendental signified for the difference between signifier and

*This does not, by simple inversion, mean that the signifier is fundamental or primary. The "primacy" or "priority" of the signifier would be an expression untenable and absurd to formulate illogically within the very logic that it would legitimately destroy. The signifier will never by rights precede the signified, in which case it would no longer be a signifier and the "signifying" signifier would no longer have a possible signified. The thought that is announced in this impossible formula without being successfully contained therein should therefore be stated in another way; it will clearly be impossible to do so without putting the very idea of the sign into suspicion, the "sign-of" which will always remain attached to what is here put in question. At the limit therefore, that thought would destroy the entire conceptuality organized around the concept of the sign (signifier and signified, expression and content, and so on).

**[In Latin, respectively: being, unity, truth, goodness.]

***Postface to *Was ist Metaphysik?* (Frankfurt am Main, 1960), p. 46. [*What is Metaphysics?,* trans. David Krell in *Basic Writings* (New York: Harper & Row, 1977).] The insistence of the voice also dominates the analysis of *Gewissen* [conscience] in *Sein und Zeit* (pp. 267 f.).

signified to be somewhere absolute and irreducible. It is not by chance that the thought of being, as the thought of this transcendental signified, is manifested above all in the voice: in a language of words. The voice is *heard* (understood)—that undoubtedly is what is called conscience—closest to the self as the absolute effacement of the signifier: pure auto-affection that necessarily has the form of time and which does not borrow from outside of itself, in the world or in "reality," any accessory signifier, any substance of expression foreign to its own spontaneity. It is the unique experience of the signified producing itself spontaneously, from within the self, and nevertheless, as signified concept, in the element of ideality or universality. The unworldly character of this substance of expression is constitutive of this ideality. This experience of the effacement of the signifier in the voice is not merely one illusion among many—since it is the condition of the very idea of truth—but I shall elsewhere show in what it does delude itself. This illusion is the history of truth and it cannot be dissipated so quickly. Within the closure of this experience, the word [*mot*] is lived as the elementary and undecomposable unity of the signified and the voice, of the concept and a transparent substance of expression. This experience is considered in its greatest purity—and at the same time in the condition of its possibility—as the experience of "being." The word "being," or at any rate the words designating the sense of being in different languages, is, with some others, an "originary word" ("*Urwort*"),* the transcendental word assuring the possibility of being-word to all other words. As such, it is precomprehended in all language and—this is the opening of *Being and Time*—only this precomprehension would permit the opening of the question of the sense of being in general, beyond all regional ontologies and all metaphysics: a question that broaches philosophy (for example, in the *Sophist***) and lets itself be taken over by philosophy, a question that Heidegger repeats by submitting the history of metaphysics to it. Heidegger reminds us constantly that the sense of being is neither the word "being" nor the concept of being. But as that sense is nothing outside of language and the language of words, it is tied, if not to a particular word or to a particular system of language (concesso non dato), at least to the possibility of the word in general. And to the possibility of its irreducible simplicity. One could thus think that it remains only to choose between two possibilities. (1) Does a modern linguistics, a science of signification breaking the unity of the word and breaking with its alleged irreducibility, still have anything to do with "language?" Heidegger would probably doubt it. (2) Conversely, is not all that is profoundly meditated as the thought or the question of being enclosed within an old linguistics of the word which one practices here unknowingly? Unknowingly because such a lingiustics, whether spontaneous or systematic, has always had to share the presuppositions of metaphysics. The two operate on the same grounds.

It goes without saying that the alternatives cannot be so simple.

On the one hand, if modern linguistics remains completely enclosed within a classical conceptuality, if especially it naively uses the word *being* and all that it presupposes, that which, within this linguistics, deconstructs the unity of the word in general can no longer, according to the model of the Heideggerian question, as it functions powerfully from the very opening of *Being and Time,* be circumscribed as ontic science or regional ontology. In as much as the question of being unites indisolubly with the precomprehension of the *word being,* without being reduced to it, the linguistics that works for the deconstruction of the constituted unity of that word has only, in

*Cf. *Das Wesen der Sprache,* and *Das Wort,* in *Unterwegs zur Sprache* (Pfüllingen, 1959). ["The Nature of Language" and "words" in *On the Way to Language,* trans. Peter Hertz (New York: Harper & Row, 1971).]

**[A dialogue of Plato's.]

fact or in principle, to have the question of being posed in order to define its field and the order of its dependence.

Not only is its field no longer simply ontic, but the limits of ontology that correspond to it no longer have anything regional about them. And can what I say here of linguistics, or at least of a certain work that may be undertaken within it and thanks to it, not be said of all research *in as much as and to the strict extent that* it would finally deconstitute the founding concept-words of ontology, of being in its privilege? Outside of linguistics, it is in psychoanalytic research that this breakthrough seems at present to have the greatest likelihood of being expanded.

Within the strictly limited space of this breakthrough, these "sciences" are no longer *dominated* by the questions of a transcendental phenomenology or a fundamental ontology. One may perhaps say, following the order of questions inaugurated by *Being and Time* and radicalizing the questions of Husserlian phenomenology, that this breakthrough does not belong to science itself, that what thus seems to be produced within an ontic field or within a regional ontology, does not belong to them by rights and leads back to the question of being itself.

Because it is indeed the *question* of being that Heidegger asks metaphysics. And with it the question of truth, of sense, of the logos. The incessant meditation upon that question does not restore confidence. On the contrary, it dislodges the confidence at its own depth, which, being a matter of the meaning of being, is more difficult than is often believed. In examining the state just before all determinations of being, destroying the securities of onto-theology, such a meditation contributes, quite as much as the most contemporary linguistics, to the dislocation of the unity of the sense of being, that is, in the last instance, the unity of the word.

It is thus that, after evoking the "voice of being," Heidegger recalls that it is silent, mute, insonorous, wordless, originarily *a-phonic* (*die Gewahr der lautlosen Stimme verborgener Quellen* . . .).* The voice of the sources is not heard. A rupture between the originary meaning of being and the word, between meaning and the voice, between "the voice of being" and the "*phonè,*" between "the call of being," and articulated sound; such a rupture, which at once confirms a fundamental metaphor, and renders it suspect by accentuating its metaphoric discrepancy, translates the ambiguity of the Heideggerian situation with respect to the metaphysics of presence and logocentrism. It is at once contained within it and transgresses it. But it is impossible to separate the two. The very movement of transgression sometimes holds it back short of the limit. In opposition to what we suggested above, it must be remembered that, for Heidegger, the sense of being is never simply and rigorously a "signified." It is not by chance that that word is not used; that means that being escapes the movement of the sign, a proposition that can equally well be understood as a repetition of the classical tradition and as a caution with respect to a technical or metaphysical theory of signification. On the other hand, the sense of being is literally neither "primary," nor "fundamental," nor "transcendental," whether understood in the scholastic, Kantian, or Husserlian sense. The restoration of being as "transcending" the categories of the entity, the opening of the fundamental ontology, are nothing but necessary yet provisional moments. From *The Introduction to Metaphysics* onward, Heidegger renounces the project of and the word ontology.** The necessary, originary, and irreducible dissimulation of the meaning of being, its occultation within the very blossoming forth of presence, that

*[The testimony of the soundless voice of hidden origins. . . .]

**[Martin Heidegger, *Einführung in die Metaphysik* (Tübingen, 1953) translated as *An Introduction to* [Me]*taphysics.* See above in this volume.]

retreat without which there would be no history of being which was completely *history* and history of *being,* Heidegger's insistence on noting that being is produced as history only through the logos, and is nothing outside of it, the difference between being and the entity—all this clearly indicates that fundamentally nothing escapes the movement of the signifier and that, in the last instance, the difference between signified and signifier *is nothing.* This proposition of transgression, not yet integrated into a careful discourse, runs the risk of formulating regression itself. One must therefore *go by way of* the question of being as it is directed by Heidegger and by him alone, at and beyond onto-theology, in order to reach the rigorous thought of that strange nondifference and in order to determine it correctly. Heidegger occasionally reminds us that "being," as it is fixed in its general syntactic and lexicological forms within linguistics and Western philosophy, is not a primary and absolutely irreducible signified, that it is still rooted in a system of languages and an historically determined "significance," although strangely privileged as the virtue of disclosure and dissimulation; particularly when he invites us to meditate on the "privilege" of the "third person singular of the present indicative" and the "infinitive." Western metaphysics, as the limitation of the sense of being within the field of presence, is produced as the domination of a linguistic form.* To question the origin of that domination does not amount to hypostatizing a transcendental signified, but to a questioning of what constitutes our history and what produced transcendentality itself. Heidegger brings it up also when in *Zur Seinsfrage,* for the same reason, he lets the word "being" be read only if it is crossed out *(kreuzweise Durchstreichung).* That mark of deletion is not, however, a "merely negative symbol" (p. 31). That deletion is the final writing of an epoch. Under its strokes the presence of a transcendental signified is effaced while still remaining legible. Is effaced while still remaining legible, is destroyed while making visible the very idea of the sign. In as much as it de-limits onto-theology, the metaphysics of presence and logocentrism, this last writing is also the first writing.

To come to recognize, not within but on the horizon of the Heideggerian paths, and yet in them, that the sense of being is not a transcendental or trans-epochal signified (even if it was always dissimulated within the epoch) but already, in a truly *unheard of* sense, a determined signifying trace, is to affirm that within the decisive concept of ontico-ontological difference, *all is not to be thought at one go;* entity and being, ontic and ontological, "ontico-ontological," are, in an original style, *derivative* with regard to difference; and with respect to what I shall later call *differance,* an economic concept designating the production of differing/deferring. The ontico-ontological difference and its ground (*Grund*) in the "transcendence of Dasein" (*Vomn Wesen des Grundes,* p. 16) are not absolutely originary. Difference by itself would be more "originary," but one would no longer be able to call it

**Introduction a la metaphysique,* tr. fr. p. 103 [*Introduction* p. 92]. "All this points in the direction of what we encountered when we characterized the Greek experience and interpretation of being. If we retain the usual interpretation of being, the word 'being' takes its meaning from the unity and determinateness of the horizon which guided our understanding. In short: we understand the verbal substantive 'Sein' through the infinitive, which in turn is related to the 'is' and its diversity that we have described. The definite and particular verb form 'is,' the *third person singular of the present indicative,* has here a pre-eminent rank. We understand 'being' not in regard to the 'thou art,' 'you are,' 'I am,' or 'they would be,' though all of these, just as much as 'is,' represent verbal inflections of 'to be.' . . . And involuntarily, almost as though nothing else were possible, we explain the infinitive 'to be' to ourselves through the 'is.'

"Accordingly, 'being' has the meaning indicated above, recalling the Greek view of the essence of being, hence a determinateness which has not just dropped on us accidentally from somewhere but has dominated our historical being-there since antiquity. At one stroke our search for the definition of the meaning of the word 'being' becomes explicitly what it is, namely a reflection on the source of our hidden history." I should, of course, cite the entire analysis that concludes with these words.

"origin" or "ground," those notions belonging essentially to the history of onto-theology, to the system functioning as the effacing of difference. It can, however, be thought of in the closest proximity to itself only on one condition: that one begins by determining it as the ontico-ontological difference before erasing that determination. The necessity of passing through that erased determination, the necessity of that *trick of writing* is irreducible. An unemphatic and difficult thought that, through much unperceived meditation, must carry the entire burden of our question, a question that I shall provisionally call *historical.* It is with its help that I shall later be able to attempt to relate difference and writing.

The hesitation of these thoughts (here Nietzsche's and Heidegger's) is not an "incoherence": it is a trembling proper to all post-Hegelian attempts and to this passage between two epochs. The movements of deconstruction do not destroy structures from the outside. They are not possible and effective, nor can they take accurate aim, except by inhabiting those structures. Inhabiting them *in a certain way,* because one always inhabits, and all the more when one does not suspect it. Operating necessarily from the inside, borrowing all the strategic and economic resources of subversion from the old structure, borrowing them structurally, that is to say without being able to isolate their elements and atoms, the enterprise of deconstruction always in a certain way falls prey to its own work. This is what the person who has begun the same work in another area of the same habitation does not fail to point out with zeal. No exercise is more widespread today and one should be able to formalize its rules.

Hegel was already caught up in this game. *On the one hand,* he undoubtedly *summed up* the entire philosophy of the logos. He determined ontology as absolute logic; he assembled all the delimitations of philosophy as presence; he assigned to presence the eschatology of parousia, of the self-proximity of infinite subjectivity. And for the same reason he had to debase or subordinate writing. When he criticizes the Leibnizian characteristic, the formalism of the understanding, and mathematical symbolism, he makes the same gesture: denouncing the being-outside-of-itself of the logos in the sensible or the intellectual abstraction. Writing is that forgetting of the self, that exteriorization, the contrary of the interiorizing memory, of the *Erinnerung* [remembering] that opens the history of the spirit. It is this that the *Phaedrus* said: writing is at once mnemotechnique and the power of forgetting. Naturally, the Hegelian critique of writing stops at the alphabet. As phonetic writing, the alphabet is at the same time more servile, more contemptible, more secondary ("alphabetic writing expresses *sounds* which are themselves signs. It consists therefore of the signs of signs") but it is also the best writing, the mind's writing; its effacement before the voice, that in it which respects the ideal interiority of phonic signifiers, all that by which it sublimates space and sight, all that makes of it the writing of history, the writing, that is, of the infinite spirit relating to itself in its discourse and its culture:

> It follows that to learn to read and write an alphabetic writing should be regarded as a means to infinite culture (*unendliches Bildungsmittel*) that is not enough appreciated; because thus the mind, distancing itself from the concrete sense-perceptible, directs its attention on the more formal moment, the sonorous word and its abstract elements, and contributes essentially to the founding and purifying of the ground of interiority within the subject.

In that sense it is the *Aufhebung* of other writings, particularly of hieroglyphic script and of the Leibnizian characteristic that had been criticized previously through one and the same gesture. (*Aufhebung* is, more or less implicitly, the dominant concept of nearly all histories of writing, even today. It is *the* concept of history and of teleology.) In fact, Hegel continues: "Acquired habit later also suppresses the specificity of alphabetic writing, which consists in seeming to be, in the interest of sight, a detour through hearing to arrive at representations, and makes it into a hieroglyphic script for us, such that in using it, we do not need to have present to our consciousness the mediation of sounds."

It is on this condition that Hegel subscribes to the Leibnizian praise of nonphonetic writing. It can be produced by deaf mutes, Leibniz had said. Hegel:

> Beside the fact that, by the practice which transforms this alphabetic script into hieroglyphics, the aptitude for abstraction acquired through such an exercise *is conserved,* the reading of hieroglyphs is for itself a deaf reading and a mute writing (*ein taubes Lesen und ein stummes Schreiben*). What is audible or temporal, visible or spatial, has each its proper basis and in the first place they are of equal value; but in alphabetic script there is only one basis and that following a specific relation, namely, that the visible language is related only as a sign to the audible language; intelligence expresses itself immediately and unconditionally through speech. (ibid.)

What writing itself, in its nonphonetic moment, betrays, is life. It menaces at once the breath, the spirit, and history as the spirit's relationship with itself. It is their end, their finitude, their paralysis. Cutting breath short, sterilizing or immobilizing spiritual creation in the repetition of the letter, in the commentary or the *exegesis,* confined in a narrow space, reserved for a minority, it is the principle of death and of difference in the becoming of being. It is to speech what China is to Europe: "It is only to the exegeticism* of Chinese spiritual culture that their hieroglyphic writing is suited. This type of writing is, besides, the part reserved for a very small section of a people, the section that possesses the exclusive domain of spiritual culture. . . . A hieroglyphic script would require a philosophy as exegetical as Chinese culture generally is" (ibid.).

If the nonphonetic moment menaces the history and the life of the spirit as self-presence in the breath, it is because it menaces substantiality, that other metaphysical name of presence and of *ousia.*** First in the form of the substantive. Nonphonetic writing breaks the noun apart. It describes relations and not appellations. The noun and the word, those unities of breath and concept, are effaced within pure writing. In that regard, Leibniz is as disturbing as the Chinese in Europe: "This situation, the analytic notation of representations in hieroglyphic script, which seduced Leibniz to the point of wrongly preferring this script to the alphabetic, rather contradicts the fundamental exigency of language in general, namely the noun. . . . All difference in analysis would produce another formation of the written substantive."

The horizon of absolute knowledge is the effacement of writing in the logos, the retrieval of the trace in parousia, the reappropriation of difference, the accomplishment of what I have elsewhere called* the *metaphysics of the proper.****

Yet, all that Hegel thought within this horizon, all, that is, except eschatology, may be reread as a meditation on writing. Hegel is *also* the thinker of irreducible difference. He rehabilitated thought as the *memory productive* of signs. And he reintroduced, as I shall try to show elsewhere, the essential necessity of the written trace in a philosophical—that is to say Socratic—discourse that had always believed it possible to do without it; the last philosopher of the book and the first thinker of writing.

**dem Statarischen,* an old German word that one has hitherto been tempted to translate as "immobile" or "static" (see [Jean] Gibelin, [tr. *Lecons sur la philosophie de la religion* (Paris, 1959)], pp. 255-7.

**Ousia is "being" in Greek.

***La parole soufflee," *L'ecriture et la difference*. [*Writing and Difference*, trans. Alan Bass (Chicago: University of Chicago, 1978).]

ανάγκη δὴ στῆναι.
One must stop somewhere.

Aristotle, *Metaphysics*. 1070a4